# THE ENCYCLOPEDIA
# AMERICANA
## INTERNATIONAL EDITION

COMPLETE IN THIRTY VOLUMES
FIRST PUBLISHED IN 1829

GROLIER

A division of Scholastic Inc.
Danbury, Connecticut

**Library of Congress Cataloging-in-Publication Data**
Main entry under title:

The Encyclopedia Americana.—International ed.
    p.     cm.
"First published in 1829."
Includes bibliographical references and index.
ISBN 0-7172-0135-X (set: alk. paper)
1. Encyclopedias and dictionaries. I. Grolier Educational.
AE5.E333          2002                    2001040255
031-dc21

Printed and Manufactured in the U.S.A.

SUMERIAN stone head, about 2200 B.C., of Gudea, ruler of Lagash, an early center of Mesopotamian civilization.

METROPOLITAN MUSEUM OF ART. FLETCHER FUND. 1949

LATE MESOPOTAMIAN statue of Assyrian King Ashurnasirpal II.

EGYPTIAN statuette of Queen Hatshepsut, of about 1480 B.C.

BRITISH MUSEUM

METROPOLITAN MUSEUM OF ART

# CIVILIZATION

**CIVILIZATION,** siv-ə-lə-zā′shən. The term "civilization" is widely used by historians, anthropologists, and other workers in the social sciences, but it has no single, fixed meaning. Any discussion of the concept must begin with the question of definition.

### PROBLEMS OF DEFINITION

Three distinct meanings of the term "civilization" are in common use. Sometimes it refers to the state of being civilized, that is, to the possession of good manners and self-control, as in the phrase "a thoroughly civilized man." This was the original meaning of the term when it was introduced, first into French, during the 18th century by writers like Voltaire.

From this meaning, writers of the 19th century expanded the term "civilization" to mean the growth through time of knowledge and skills that encouraged or allowed men to attain "civilized" behavior. Lewis Henry Morgan, for example, put his central thesis into the title of his book: *Ancient Society, or Researches in the Lines of Human Progress from Savagery Through Barbarism to Civilization* (1877). Karl Marx accepted Morgan's thesis, and many Marxists today defend it as the only correct picture of the human past.

The third meaning of "civilization" came into English usage from German. Johann Gottfried von Herder and other writers of the 18th century took great pains to rescue the German language and style of thought from the borrowed finery of French. In so doing, they stressed the uniqueness of their own nation and the differences of its culture from that of any other folk. By generalizing this idea, civilization of course becomes plural. A writer ought to speak, not of the progress of civilization in general (as the French did), but of the rise and fall of separate German, Roman, Hebrew, Chinese, or Egyptian civilizations.

In the 20th century the anthropological concept of culture as the sum of learned (as distinct from instinctive) behavior fitted into and reinforced this way of using the term "civilization." Robert Redfield, for example, viewed civilizations as the learned behavior of men who belonged to unusually changeable and complex societies. He therefore contrasted civilization to the "culture" acquired by members of simpler, more stable "folk" societies. A different distinction was made by Oswald Spengler, who used the word *Kultur* to refer to the spiritual state of youthful, organic, and still-growing societies, and reserved the term "civilization" to describe older, more rigid, and decaying communities. But Spengler's terminology involved such a conflict with the 19th century

1

equation of civilization with the highest stage of human progress that it never gained much currency in English.

**Civilization as a Stage in Man's Development.** Writers who use "civilization" in the second sense, as meaning a general stage in human development, have to decide what marks civilized societies off from those that do not deserve the name. Morgan's theory was soon discredited by the fact that pastoralism, which he equated with barbarism, does not seem to have antedated agriculture, as he believed had been the case. Moreover, simple Neolithic villages were certainly based on agriculture, and by Morgan's theory therefore should count as civilized. But to regard them as such ran counter to the generally accepted connotations of the term.

By the end of the 19th century, therefore, archaeologists commonly equated the dawn of civilization with the appearance of metal tools in their excavations. Others preferred to date it from the invention of writing and the transition from prehistory to history. Still others argued that the combination of metallurgy, writing, and large-scale building was the hallmark of civilization.

In the 1930's, V. Gordon Childe tried to relieve the prevailing confusion by connecting civilization with what he called the "urban revolution." According to this idea, civilization came into existence not once but many times, whenever men gathered into cities and began to specialize. Occupational specialization, Childe argued, led to the rapid improvement of skills, and the invention of new and better tools. The result was a rather sudden elaboration of the material, intellectual, and artistic aspects of culture to a level of complexity and refinement that deserved to be called "civilized."

Childe's idea still holds the field among archaeologists, although there are more speculative thinkers who have begun to suggest that civilization ought to be viewed overall as a middle stage in human experience. This stage, in their opinion, is framed at the start by the invention of agriculture (echoing Morgan) and at the end by the Industrial Revolution (echoing Marx), which has begun to push mankind willy-nilly into a postcivilizational age. Such writers, among whom Kenneth Boulding may be mentioned as an example, emphasize the break between the stage of "civilization"—when the majority of men were farmers and remained for the most part excluded from the refinements of civilized life—and the (presumed) stage of postcivilization, when mass communications will make it impractical to maintain cultural barriers between social classes or between different regions of the earth.

**Civilization as a National or Regional Style of Life.** Historians who prefer to think of civilization in the plural face equally tricky problems in deciding what they mean by "a" civilization. Is there, for example, an American civilization different from the civilization of Europe? Or does the United States share in something called "Western civilization," along with most European nations and the regions of European settlement overseas? If there is an American civilization, as most historians of the United States believe, what makes it different from English or from Canadian civilization—if, indeed, there is such a thing as Canadian civilization? No agreement on these issues exists, and each writer, if he wishes to avoid misunderstanding, must be careful to define his terms.

The problem is complicated by the fact that through time a civilization (whatever it is) changes and tends to move around in space. Characteristically, in the early stages of a civilization's history boundaries may be relatively easy to draw. In the 5th century B. C., for example, Herodotus had no trouble knowing who were Greeks and who were barbarians. Everybody knew. The distinctions of language, manners, and institutions were self-evident, and were not in the least affected by the fact that some Greeks fought on the Persian side at the time of Xerxes' invasion. By 323 B. C., however, when Alexander the Great died, it was not at all clear whether the Macedonian upper class ought to count as Greek or not. Four and a half centuries later, in the time of the Emperor Hadrian, educated Romans, Syrians, Jews, Egyptians, and many more all spoke Greek and shared Greek ideas and values in some degree, but only a few felt Greek all the way through. Four hundred years later still, in the time of the Emperor Justinian, the definition of who was and who was not a Greek had become easier, for the limit of language and culture had drawn in again and come closer to the original Greek homeland. But the critical question becomes instead whether or not the Greeks of Justinian's age shared in the same civilization Herodotus had known so unambiguously some thousand years before. In fact, most historians prefer to use a new term, "Byzantine," to mark off the civilization of Justinian's empire from all that had gone before.

Custom alone answers such questions; and custom, in these as in other matters, is not always clear and constant. Aside from the conventions of an inherited vocabulary, the only real guide historians have for assigning spatial and temporal limits to "civilizations" is a vague, intuitive sense of social style. Art and literature provide a kind of litmus paper in any such determination, for it appears to be true that changes in these aspects of human activity correspond to (one is tempted to say reflect) changes in society as a whole, and do so in a remarkably sensitive way that can be observed with minimal ambiguity by men of later times. Reliance upon art and literature as indicators of civilizational affinities and divergences has the additional attraction of holding the meaning of the term closer to its original 18th century use, and maintaining a connection between the idea of civilization and enjoyment of the "higher" or "finer" things of human life.

This accords well with current English and French usage, although social scientists in the United States often prefer quantitative, objective criteria to arty, literary, value-loaded subjective determinations. But efforts to find any sort of quantitative basis for measurement of civilization or of civilizations have been notably unsuccessful. On the other hand, subjective definitions that equate a particular civilization with a single dominant state of mind, value system, or some sort of master institution or idea seem equally unsuccessful. Such definitions prove too narrow to take account of the diverse phenomena of the historical record.

From so much imprecision what, then, emerges? It is possible to agree that the term "civilization" should apply only to societies that are more massive and complex than most, and enjoy a more extensive mastery over the natural and human environment than other, weaker, "primitive" societies do. From these characteristics it follows that civilizations must be relatively few as compared to the thousands of societies known to anthropologists. But absolutely no agreement as to how many civilizations there are and have been emerges from this fact. Yet in spite of—or perhaps because of—the ambiguities built into the term, it has entered into wider and wider use of late, aided, in the United States, by the invention, dating from the 1920's, of high school and college courses on Western civilization, American civilization, world civilization, and the like.

### EARLY CIVILIZATIONS

**Mesopotamia.** Scholars nearly all agree that the earliest civilization of which we have knowledge arose among the Sumerians in Mesopotamia. The archaeological record, uncovered in the 1920's and 1930's, shows that a dozen or more places near the mouths of the Tigris and Euphrates rivers saw ordinary large villages grow into walled cities between about 3500 and 3000 B. C. In each location the principal building was a temple of mud brick, raised high above the flat plain. Later, royal palaces and massive city walls rivaled the temple structures in size. In addition, writing began, metallurgy developed, irrigation spread, and sailing vessels, wheeled vehicles, stone sculpture, accurate measurement of time and space, and many other new technologies appeared among the Sumerians during the same 500-year period. The resulting superiority to simpler, older societies seems to justify the epithet "civilized," indicating a breakthrough to a new level of human achievement.

How or why this breakthrough occurred is a matter of debate. On the strength of deductions from the records of one single temple, several scholars arrived at the conclusion that priests had been the organizers of ancient Sumerian society. According to this theory, by persuading ordinary farmers to give part of their harvest to the god, the priests of the god's temple were able to get hold of large quantities of grain and other food. They used this wealth to support experts whose job was to serve the god and keep him well pleased with his people, thus assuring a good harvest each year. But when specialists could be freed to serve their divine master on a full-time basis by making beautiful things for his use and enjoyment, they quickly developed the special skills that produced such a radical change in the buildings and other remains found by archaeologists.

However, Soviet and other scholars have begun to challenge this view of the origins of civilization, arguing instead that Sumerian civilization was based on conquest. According to this theory, overlords compelled farmers to pay part of their harvest as rents or taxes, and then used the wealth they had collected to maintain specialists. Support of the temple, in such a view, was only a part, perhaps a small part, of the use to which Sumerian rulers put the agricultural surplus they were able to collect.

Available records are so scanty, and their interpretation is so uncertain, that no one can really tell which of these two conceivable paths to civilization was in fact followed. However it happened, at the heart of the process was a radical differentiation between the majority, who plowed and reaped and performed all the drudgery of the fields, and the privileged minority, who ate what others had produced and used their free

time to develop the various kinds of specialized activity that characterize civilized society.

**Egypt and the Indus Valley.** Civilizations similar to the Sumerian in structure but completely different in style arose in the Nile and Indus valleys not long afterward. Unmistakable evidence of trade connections between Sumer and early Egypt have been discovered, and circumstantial evidence suggests that the Indus peoples, too, may have traded with Sumer at the time when their civilization first took shape. Archaeological finds do not, however, prove such connections before a time when the Indus cities and civilization had developed fully.

**Borrowing and Invention.** The relationships between the civilization of ancient Sumer and that of Egypt and the Indus can only be inferred from the material traces that survive. Borrowing occurred, but the borrowers changed what they had borrowed, sometimes very greatly, so that within a short period of time the original indebtedness of one to the other was no longer apparent. This pattern of mimicry and subsequent invention is best illustrated by architecture. For a short time, the Egyptians took over the Sumerian idea of building large structures with bricks. But when they shifted to stone, they promptly changed their methods of construction and architectural styles to suit the different building material.

This history, which happens to be particularly well-preserved, is probably indicative of the usual relationship between men of different civilizations or distinct styles of life. One people will borrow some unfamiliar skill or knowledge from another when they can understand what they see and believe it to be better than anything they already have themselves. But all such borrowings have to be fitted into the prevailing cultural and physical environment. In other words, only those things that could be made to fit in with what was already known and revered could find lasting lodgment in the borrowers' world. Yet only things that were different, and thus initially at odds with the established ways of doing things, could seem worth borrowing. We may speculate that the resultant tensions between innovation and routine stimulated the persistent invention and new creation that characterize civilized societies.

Whatever the ultimate driving wheels of civilized history may be, we can safely assume that the skills and ideas, as well as the wealth and beauty, attained by the early civilizations of Sumer, Egypt, and the Indus deeply impressed strangers who came into contact with those ancient cities, temples, and palaces. So far as they could, strangers no doubt wished to acquire for themselves the goods of civilization; but for a long time this was only possible in river floodplains. Here crops were more abundant because of the natural fertility of the soil. Annual floods deposited fresh silt, and made it possible to harvest wheat or barley year after year from the same fields. Perhaps most important of all, the concerted labor needed to construct and maintain irrigation works required unusual social discipline and centralization of control. Without large-scale organized common effort, which had to be planned and managed by someone, irrigation would break down and crops fail. See also AGRICULTURE, HISTORY OF.

Beginning not long before 2000 B. C., however, civilized societies began to grow up on rainwatered land. Trade and war seem to have combined to produce this new breakthrough. Traders from the floodplains had to travel afar to get timber, ores, and (in the case of Mesopotamia) building stone. By offering luxury products from civilized workshops to local chieftains, it was often possible to persuade them to put their followers to work preparing the things the merchants needed. As the scale of such operations increased, local magnates took increasing control over the labor of the community. As his income grew, a chief could then afford to keep skilled artisans in his own household. Specialization could thus begin, with the usual consequences. War and conquest worked along parallel lines, for a conquering stranger could compel his subjects to work for him or pay over goods and service on such a scale as to permit him, too, to create a big household of specialists.

**Satellite Civilizations.** There was, however, a difference. These new centers of civilization arose among people who kept in contact with the older, more fully developed civilizations of the river valleys. Hence when an artisan set out to make something grander or more beautiful than ever before, he had models (either at hand or in his mind's eye) of the splendors produced by skills already familiar in the distant cities of the floodplain. The result, therefore, was likely to be a hybrid, part new creation and part imperfect copy of established civilized styles. We may call the result a satellite civilization, combining local peculiarities with the ambition to attain fuller and fuller participation in the metropolitan civilization at the center of the whole evolution.

By 1800 B. C., Mesopotamia had come to be almost entirely ringed by satellite civilizations of this sort: Elamites, Hurrians, Hittites, Syrians, Canaanites, and others. Still farther away, in the steppe regions of western Asia generally and on the Iranian plateau in particular, horse-raising nomads had also learned something about the riches and charms of civilization as developed in the Middle East. When these barbarians found out how to put civilized artisan skills to use in making war chariots, they became irresistible on the battlefield. As a result, tribes and coalitions of tribes, speaking Indo-European as well as other languages, overran Mesopotamia and Egypt and regions in between not long after 1800 B. C.

Other charioteers invaded the Yellow River valley about 1500 B. C., and established the earliest Chinese civilization there. Aryan charioteers invaded India at about the same time and, after destroying the Indus cities, laid the basis for the rise of later forms of Indian civilization. In the European west, Mycenaean Greeks, whose ancestors, like those of the Aryans, had come from the steppe, destroyed the civilization of Minoan Crete (or helped to do so) about 1400 B. C. and laid the groundwork for the rise of Greek civilization.

Interaction between Mesopotamia and its ring of satellite civilizations on the one hand and the warlike barbarians of the steppe on the other thus played a central role in the early history of the world's civilization. Egypt's impact on neighboring peoples is less well known. Deserts and swamps isolated Egypt quite effectively through much of its long history. But Egyptian civilization had some part in starting the Cretans on their way to the high artistic achievements of Minoan civilization. In Subsaharan Africa it seems likely that the traditional attributes of kingship borrowed a good deal from the divine prerogatives of Egypt's Pharaoh.

As to India, information is even scantier. Modern scholars cannot read the script of the Indus civilization. Little writing survives, so decipherment is not very likely. Archaeological study has not yet advanced far enough to make up for the lack of written materials. All the same, it would be surprising if the skills that allowed men to construct great cities in the Indus Valley did not affect the lives of neighboring peoples— and the lives of neighbors' neighbors—in something like the way we know Mesopotamia affected its neighbors.

## GROWTH AND SPREAD OF CIVILIZATION

Looking at the world as a whole, the history of civilized societies is a history of expansion. There were setbacks and withdrawals. Sometimes regions that had once been civilized became barbarous again for a period of several centuries. The most familiar example is from the history of western Europe. Part of Europe shared in the civilization of the Roman Empire, but then suffered repeated barbarian invasions, with the result that city life and many aspects of classical civilization disappeared entirely. Yet civilized life returned, and when it did took deeper and stronger root than before.

Nevertheless, cases of backsliding to barbarism are exceptional. For the most part, the power of civilized ways to attract strangers and persuade them to try to acquire at least some of the skills and habits of civilized men has prevailed. As this process inched its way through time, all sorts of amalgamations between civilized and local barbarous ways came into existence. Halfway houses, such as that long occupied by the Tibetans, who took much of their religion from India and the rest of their higher culture mainly from China, became possible. With the passage of each century, therefore, frontiers between separate civilizations became more difficult to draw, and zones of transition and mixture became increasingly important.

**Importance of Trade in Eurasia.** By about 100 B. C. the expansion of civilizations in Eurasia had advanced far enough to create a slender belt of civilized territory that ran all the way across the area. Organized caravan trade—policed and taxed by the Chinese, Kushan, Parthian, and Roman empires—extended all the way from the valley of the Yellow River to the east coast of the Mediterranean. Goods, religious ideas, and diseases moved to and fro along these routes more freely than ever before. At nearly the same time, ocean trade between the Red Sea coast and southern India, and between southern India and China, also increased in magnitude and regularity.

All the civilizations of the Old World, together with a fringe of barbarian lands lying both north and south of the civilized belt, thus began to interact with one another more intimately than had been possible in earlier ages. It was in this social landscape that both Christianity and Mahayana Buddhism were born and flourished. The migration and transmutation of art styles across the entire civilized world is another well-known example of the way these contacts altered the Eurasian cultural scene.

**The New World.** In the New World the development of civilization lagged behind Old World achievements. The shift from small farming villages to cities and civilizations seems to have gone much more slowly among the Amerindians than it did in the ancient Middle East.

Evidence for the cultivation of corn dates back surprisingly far if recent radiocarbon dating can be trusted. But the rise of cult centers comparable to the earliest Sumerian cities does not seem to have taken place before the Christian era.

In the Mayan regions of Guatemala and Yucatán, the highest development of stone carving, calendrical calculations, and monumental construction in stone came between 600 and 1000 A. D. Elsewhere dating is uncertain, but the "classical" period in both the Mexican plateau and Peru probably was nearly contemporaneous with the flowering of the Mayan civilization. The level of technical mastery over the environment attained by these peoples of the New World was roughly equivalent to that attained by the ancient Mesopotamians and Egyptians some 4,000 years earlier. It is not surprising, therefore, that the Spaniards found it easy to overthrow the Amerindian civilizations when they burst in upon them in the 16th century.

**Decline of the Han and Roman Empires.** Let us therefore return our attention to the Old World and pick up the chronological thread where we dropped it, about the beginning of the Christian era. The next major landmark in the history of the Old World's civilizations was the simultaneous disruption of the Han empire in China and of the Roman Empire around the Mediterranean. As a result, after about 200 A. D. the organized trade routes that had connected these great states functioned only sporadically. Interchanges among the peoples of Eurasia became correspondingly less intense. Still, the expansion of civilization did not stop. New offshoots sprang up in Ireland, West Africa, Ethiopia, Southeast Asia, and Indonesia. In addition the steppe peoples, from Mongolia to southern Russia, entered into much closer relations with the civilized communities that lay to the south of them. Even in the cold northern forest zone of Europe, within a few centuries deep-rooted civilizations began to thrive. Orthodox Russia grew in the east and Latin Christendom in the west. Japan became civilized at roughly the same time, thus extending the radius of Chinese or Far Eastern styles of civilization northward in much the same way as was happening in Europe.

By 1250 the Old World was again brought together as in the days of the Roman and Han empires. This time it was the Mongol conquests, inaugurated by Genghis Khan and extending from China to Russia and including most of the Middle East and central Asia, that led to the establishment of caravan routes and a speedy pony express that spanned all of Asia. Extended contact was reestablished between China and the rest of the civilized world. Some important exchanges of skill resulted. In particular, Europe and the Muslim world acquired gunpowder, printing, and the compass from the Chinese. Without these, Europe's later overseas expansion could scarcely have taken place.

**Trade and Sea Power.** The breakup of the Mongol empire after 1365 interrupted land communication. Before long, however, European seamen opened up the oceans of the world to their ships. In no more than 30 years, between 1492 (Columbus) and 1522 (Magellan), they established a new sea link between the civilizations of all the earth. Instead of being at one remote extremity of the civilized world, Europe found itself the focus and center of the new oceanic sea routes, in a position to pick and choose from everything the rest of the world had to offer.

The Amerindian civilizations of the New World proved too weak to survive Spanish conquest on anything more than an elementary village level. Yet for several centuries the major Asian civilizations were affected by the appearance of European ships along the shores of Asia only as a healthy man might be by an encounter with a swarm of midges. Still, when ships sailed to and fro unceasingly, interaction among the various peoples of the world took on a heightened pace. American food crops—corn, potatoes, and sweet potatoes in particular—had an important impact in Africa and in parts of Europe and Asia long before other consequences of the opening of the oceans to European navigation affected the lives of Old World peoples very deeply.

**End of the Isolation of China.** The next great landmark in the development of civilization was the loss of the political and military independence of the steppe peoples. For more than two thousand years the Mongols and other peoples had acted as a buffer separating China from the rest of the civilized world of Eurasia. But by 1650 efficient firearms made it possible for civilized infantry to defeat cavalry armed with bows and arrows. The consequence was a speedy advance of the Chinese and Russian frontiers into the steppe lands of Eurasia, so that within a century the two great empires shared a common border that ran from the Pacific coast thousands of miles across the Asian steppes. Westward from central Asia, the Russian border ran along the frontiers of Muslim lands as far as the Black Sea. By 1774 there was no longer any no-man's-land remaining on the Asian continent, except for some patches of jungle in the southeast and the barren tundra of the far north.

Deliberate Chinese policy kept the rest of the civilized world at arm's length until 1842. But when European and American strength had begun to be reinforced by the Industrial Revolution, the Chinese suddenly discovered that they could not keep the Westerners out any longer. Superior weapons and cheap machine-made goods reinforced Western trade and diplomacy. Beginning in 1842, therefore, China had to submit to the "unequal treaties" with the European powers and the United States. The ideas and knowledge that supported Western practical accomplishments proved no less overwhelming once Chinese minds opened themselves to foreign learning.

**Increasing Interaction.** Simultaneously, and within a single decade (1850–1860), Japanese, Hindus, and Muslims also suffered irreparable breakdowns of the traditional ordering of their respective societies. The deep penetration of Africa by European missionaries, traders, and conquerors began in those same extraordinary years. This, then, represents still another major landmark in the history of the world's civilizations. Ever since, the entire world has been caught up in an ever closer network of interacting parts. A worldwide cosmopolitanism seems a likely upshot, though sudden destruction through cataclysmic nuclear explosion is also now a possibility.

## IS THERE A CYCLE OF CIVILIZATION?

The prospect that men may end up by blowing themselves to bits has given fresh impetus to ancient speculations about the possibility of future decline of civilization. The idea that human affairs pass through a natural cycle of growth followed by inevitable decay is very old. Plato, for example, argued that political constitutions passed from monarchy to aristocracy to democracy and back again to monarchy, which, however, lacking customary limits, would be harshly tyrannical. Variations upon this theme became a commonplace of political wisdom among the ancients, and the idea revived in western Europe with the Renaissance.

The Muslim historian Ibn Khaldun developed a different sort of cyclical theory. He detected in history a pattern of conquest from the desert followed by corruption of the rulers as a result of luxury. After three generations, corruption prepared the way for fresh conquest from the desert, to begin the cycle afresh. In more recent centuries, Vico, Herder, Hegel, Karl Lamprecht, and many other European thinkers tried in different ways to combine Judeo-Christian views of time and history as progress in a straight line with the classical notion of historical cycles. On the whole, even those who thought cyclic ups and downs were inevitable accepted optimistic overall estimates of human progress until World Wars I and II. These catastrophes gave the idea of an impending decline and fall a wide hold on popular attention. Oswald Spengler in Germany after World War I and Arnold J. Toynbee in Britain after World War II gained wide audiences for theories of history that seemed to imply an inevitable future decline of Western civilization.

Yet most historians and social scientists are not persuaded by the arguments from analogy upon which both Spengler and Toynbee rely. The limits of the possible remain for all mankind a profound enigma. Who can say what the relationship between human wills and the processes that remain beyond human control or even comprehension really is? That there are some regularities and recurrent patterns in human affairs seems self-evident. But this does not prove that the course of human history as a whole is caught and imprisoned within some sort of necessary and inescapable cycle. After all, the discovery of predictable patterns would change the conditions within which men make decisions, and knowing (or believing they knew) the consequences of their acts, men might change their behavior and thus alter the supposed cycle of history.

For the present and foreseeable future, our knowledge of the nature of human society falls far short of permitting accurate or fully credible predictions. The future remains inscrutable. If there is an inevitable pattern to the future, we simply do not know what it is. We must therefore act in ignorance and as though we were free. Like all our predecessors, we have the task and opportunity of modifying mankind's future each day with every task we perform.

WILLIAM H. MCNEILL
*The University of Chicago*

**Bibliography**

Kroeber, A. L., *A Roster of Civilizations and Culture* (1962; reprint, Greenwood Press 1985).
McNeil, William H., *The Rise of the West* (Univ. of Chicago Press 1963).
Rogers, Perry M., *Aspects of Western Civilization: Problems and Sources in History*, 2 vols. (Prentice-Hall 1988).
Wallbank, T. Walter, and others, *Civilization Past and Present*, 6th ed. (Scott 1987).
Whitehouse, Ruth, and Wilkins, John, *The Making of Civilization: History Discovered Through Archaeology* (Knopf 1986).
Winks, Robin W., and others, *A History of Civilization*, 7th ed. (Prentice-Hall 1988).

**CIVITAVECCHIA,** chē-vē-tä-vek′kyä, is a town and commune in Italy, situated on the Tyrrhenian Sea, 39 miles (63 km) northwest of Rome. It is the chief port of Rome and of the industrial center of Terni, in Umbria. It is also an important fishing center. There are a cement factory and chemical and metal industries in the town.

Civitavecchia was known first in ancient times as *Centum Cellae* and later as *Trajani Portus* (Trajan's Port), because of the artificial harbor that was built there at the order of the Emperor Trajan in 106 A.D. The outstanding architectural feature of the city is the fort, which was begun in 1508 by Bramante and completed by Michelangelo. Giovanni Bernini designed the town's 17th-century naval arsenal. Population: 50,856 (1991 census).

**CLACKMANNAN,** klak-man′ən, a district in Scotland's Central region. A county until 1975, the district is composed of the former county of Clackmannan and a portion of the former county of Perth. Clackmannan is in the central industrial belt of the country. Its southern boundary, on the upper waters of the Firth of Forth, is about 25 miles (40 km) northeast of Glasgow. Alloa is the largest town and administrative center. In the village of Clackmannan are Clach Mannan, or "Stone of Mannan," sacred to the spirit of an ancient local deity; the 16th-century Tolbooth; and the 16th-century Mercat (market) Cross. The district's main industries are agriculture, brewing, mining, and the manufacture of glass, paper, and woolens. Population: 47,209 (1991 census).

CHARLES W. BLACK, *Mitchell Library, Glasgow*

**CLAFLIN,** klaf′lin, **Victoria Woodhull** (1838–1927), American feminist and adventuress. Beautiful, quick-witted, and magnetic, she was widely influential, despite her eccentricities. Victoria Claflin was born in Homer, Ohio, on Sept. 23, 1838. Encouraged by her spiritualist mother, she and her younger sister, Tennessee, began to see visions and hold seances. For many years they traveled as healers and clairvoyants. Victoria was married three times: to Canning Woodhull (1853–1864), Col. James Blood (1866–1876), and John B. Martin (1883–1897); the first two marriages ended in divorce.

In New York City in 1868 the financier Cornelius Vanderbilt, who was interested in spiritualism, established Victoria and Tennessee as stockbrokers, thereby creating a sensation on Wall Street. Two years later the sisters began publishing a reformist journal, *Woodhull and Claflin's Weekly*. On Nov. 2, 1872, the journal charged that the Rev. Henry Ward Beecher had seduced one of his parishioners. Victoria justified her exposure of Beecher by asserting that affections were natural and should not be veiled by hypocrisy.

In 1871, Victoria startled feminists by presenting to the judiciary committee of the U.S. House of Representatives a memorial claiming that women already had the right to vote. In 1872 she formed the Equal Rights party, which nominated her for the U.S. presidency that year.

After 1877, Victoria lived mainly in England. In 1901 she settled down at her country estate near Tewkesbury, Gloucestershire, where she died on June 9, 1927.

KEITH E. MELDER
*Smithsonian Institution*

**CLAIBORNE,** klā'bərn, **William** (1587?–?1677), American colonial official. He was born in Westmoreland county, England, and was appointed surveyor of Virginia in 1621. Five years later he became secretary of state of the colony, serving until 1637 and again from 1652 to 1660.

Under a commission obtained from Charles I, Claiborne settled the Isle of Kent in Chesapeake Bay in 1631. The following year Lord Baltimore received a royal grant of the bay region and claimed the island. A controversy extending to armed conflict followed. In 1637, while Claiborne was in England, agents of Baltimore seized the island, and Baltimore's claim later was confirmed by the crown.

During the English Civil War, Claiborne supported Parliament. In 1651 he was appointed to a commission to bring Virginia to accept Parliamentary supremacy, and he seized control of Maryland for Parliament. However, the restoration of Charles II in 1660 brought a reversal of Claiborne's fortunes, and he never regained title to the isle.

GEORGE D. LANGDON, JR., *Vassar College*

**CLAIBORNE,** klā'bərn, **William C. C.** (1775–1817), American public official. A native of Sussex county, Va., Claiborne moved early in his career to Tennessee, where he established a legal practice and entered politics. He represented Tennessee in Congress (1797–1801) and was governor of the Mississippi Territory (1801–1803). In 1803 he was appointed governor of Orleans Territory, part of the Louisiana Purchase. Creole resentment at coming under American rule ran high, but Claiborne's honesty, pleasant disposition, and later marriages into Creole families alleviated the hostilities. When Louisiana became a state he was elected governor, serving from 1812 to 1816. In 1817, Claiborne was elected to the U. S. Senate, but he died in New Orleans on November 23, before taking office.

ARTHUR SHAFFER, *University of Missouri*

**CLAIR,** klâr, **René** (1898–1981), French film director, who is regarded as the master of French screen comedy between World Wars I and II. He was born René Chomette, in Paris on Nov. 11, 1898. After trying journalism, film acting, and editing, he turned to film directing with *Paris qui dort* (1923), a science fiction fantasy, and *Entr'acte* (1924), an avant-garde short presented as part of a staged ballet. He then made longer fanciful films, including two widely acclaimed Labiche farces, *Un Chapeau de paille d'Italie* (1927) and *Les Deux Timides* (1928).

The transition to sound made possible fuller expression of Clair's originality. Adding music and sound effects to his stylized visual rhythm, he blended these elements into a universal language that made dialogue almost superfluous, as in *Sous les toits de Paris* (1930), which deals with scenes of Parisian life; *Le Million* (1931), which portrays the adventures of a youth who won a lottery but lost the ticket; and *À Nous la liberté* (1931), which was inspired by Charlie Chaplin, and in turn inspired Chaplin's *Modern Times*.

Among the best of Clair's subsequent films are *The Ghost Goes West* (1935; made in England), *La Beauté du diable* (1949), and *Fêtes galantes* (1965). In 1960 he became the first filmmaker elected to the French Academy. He died in Paris on March 15, 1981.

EDWIN JAHIEL, *University of Illinois*

**CLAIRAUT,** kle-rō', **Alexis Claude** (1713–1765), French astronomer, geodesist, and mathematician who wrote the earliest treatise on curves in 3-dimensional space. His other chief works were on the shape of the earth, the orbits of comets, and the theory of lunar motion.

Clairaut was born in Paris on May 13, 1713. At the age of 12 he read a paper to the Académie des Sciences in Paris that laid the foundations for his classic treatise on skew curves, *Recherches sur les courbes à double courbure* (1731), completed when he was 16. Through special dispensation, the age requirement was waived, and Clairaut was elected to the Académie in 1731. In 1736 he accompanied Maupertuis to Lapland to measure there the length of a degree along the meridian. This expedition confirmed the Newtonian view that the earth is flattened at the poles, a result justified theoretically by Clairaut in his *Théorie de la figure de la terre* (1743).

One of Clairaut's most important works was *Tables de la lune* (1745), for which he was awarded the prize of the St. Petersburg academy. But his unfortunate suggestion that the law of gravitation failed to account for the moon's motion was attacked by the encyclopedist d'Alembert, who became his chief rival and critic. When Clairaut announced that Halley's comet would reappear about the middle of April 1759, give or take a month, d'Alembert questioned the calculations. Clairaut's methods, published in *Théorie du mouvement des comètes* (1760), were vindicated when the comet reached perihelion in mid-March 1759.

Clairaut died in Paris on May 17, 1765. Of his 19 brothers and sisters, one had exhibited comparable mathematical precocity. Now known only as "Clairaut le Cadet," this younger brother, at the age of 15, published *Traité de quadratures circulaires et hyperboliques*. In 1732, at the age of 16, he died of smallpox.

CARL B. BOYER
*Brooklyn College*

**CLAIRTON,** klâr'tən, an industrial city in southwestern Pennsylvania, is in Allegheny county, 12 miles (19 km) southeast of Pittsburgh. The United States Steel Corporation's Clairton works, one of the largest coke and coal chemical plants in the world, extends 4½ miles (7 km) along the Monongahela River. Many varieties of chemical products are made by these facilities. Ferromanganese is produced in blast furnaces and various steel products are made in its structural mills.

Clairton was settled about 1770. It became a borough in 1903 and a city in 1922. Government of the city is by a mayor and city council. Population: 8,491.

**CLAIRVAUX,** kler-vō', was a celebrated Cistercian abbey in northeast France. The site is on the River Aube, 40 miles (64 km) from Troyes. The abbey was founded in 1115 by St. Bernard, who was abbot until his death in 1153. Clairvaux became the center of the Cistercian order, with nearly 700 residents and an important library. While he was abbot, St. Bernard founded 68 monasteries, and through these many more claimed descent from Clairvaux. The abbey's greatness declined in the 15th and 16th centuries, but it remained an important Cistercian institution until the French Revolution, when the buildings and land were sold. Most of the surviving structures date from the 18th century.

**CLAIRVOYANCE,** klâr-voi′əns, is that subclass of extrasensory perception (ESP) in which an individual perceives an object or event by some means other than the usual senses. The typical laboratory test of clairvoyance is card guessing. Cards are well shuffled and repeatedly cut, or are arranged according to a random number list, so that their order cannot be inferred. The cards (or other "target" items) are concealed from both subject and experimenter, and the subject guesses their order. Where guesses correspond to targets so markedly that the results cannot sensibly be attributed to chance, and when such clues to the correct order as sensory cues, inferences, and the like are excluded, clairvoyance is said to be demonstrated.

A famous example of clairvoyance outside the laboratory was reported by the Swedish philosopher Emanuel Swedenborg. While at Göteborg he described a great fire raging in Stockholm, about 300 miles (483 km) distant. He reported when and where it stopped. Any such unusual report may, of course, be taken as an example of coincidence.

Although it was formerly believed that few persons were clairvoyant, modern research indicates that clairvoyant ability of a very faint, intermittent sort is widespread. The cumulative score from hundreds of test records may be so high that it cannot be explained by chance, although no single score was high enough to be outstanding.

An interesting finding is that experimental subjects with negative attitudes tend to score below chance, while subjects with good morale and affirmative, outgoing attitudes typically score higher. Schoolchildren who dislike their teacher often do badly at a clairvoyant "guessing game," and adults who are resentful or bored tend to have low scores. Where personality tests indicate a person is withdrawn, his clairvoyance scores are likely to be low, as if he were unconsciously withdrawing from the clairvoyant targets. Such low scores, if they are consistent and predictable, are as meaningful as high ones. (A person who never wins in an honest game of chance would be as extraordinary from the scientific point of view as a person who always wins.) Modern research in clairvoyance therefore ordinarily contrasts two conditions or two types of subjects and predicts that one set of scores will be higher. The difference between the two sets of scores shows whether or not clairvoyance can be said to have occurred.

High scores tend to be associated with relaxed interest and good motivation; low scores with excessive pressure and tension, or low morale. (Perhaps the classical crystal ball helped to induce an appropriate mood: relaxation combined with eagerness.) However, since clairvoyant ability is faint and variable, short series of clairvoyant guesses are undependable. Any particular success or failure therefore may be attributed to coincidence.

The physical mechanism of clairvoyance is unknown. Partly for this reason, partly because some self-proclaimed professional "clairvoyants" are frauds, and partly because of their not having read current research on the subject, many scientists consider that the evidence for clairvoyance remains inconclusive.

See also PARAPSYCHOLOGY.

GERTRUDE SCHMEIDLER, *The City College
of The City University of New York*

**CLAM,** a bivalve mollusk belonging to several marine or freshwater families of the class Pelecypoda. Although all of the 20,000 kinds of clams throughout the world are edible, only about 50 are sufficiently large, tasty, and abundant to be fished commercially.

**Species.** The most abundantly obtained clam in the United States is the eastern surf clam, *Spisula solidissima.* It ranges from Maine to South Carolina and is found from the intertidal zone to a depth of about 100 feet (31 meters). Its smooth, tan-colored, oval shell may reach a length of 7 inches (18 cm).

The hard-shell, or quahog, clam is popular in North America either raw on the half shell or minced in hot chowders. Small quahogs, usually served raw on the half-shell, are called cherrystones. The quahog clam is a heart-shaped clam that lives in the shallow waters of estuaries from southern Massachusetts to Texas. The northern form is *Mercenaria mercenaria;* the southern subspecies is *M. mercenaria campechiensis.*

The soft-shell, or steamer, clam, *Mya arenaria,* has a relatively thin, fragile shell and a long, tubular sheath around its siphon. It lives along the Atlantic coast of North America, usually buried in the sandy mud to a depth of about 8 inches (20 cm).

Along the Pacific coast a number of sand-dwelling, shallow-water clams are used as food. The pismo clam of California, *Tivela stultorum,* and the Washington clam, *Saxidomus,* are abundant at certain seasons. The large geoduck, *Panopea,* of the Pacific Northwest, resembles the eastern *Mya,* but may weigh 5 pounds (2.3 kg).

The largest known living bivalve is the giant clam, *Tridacna gigas,* of the tropical Indo-Pacific area. Its two shell valves may weigh as much as 500 pounds (227 kg) and have a length of 50 inches (127 cm). This clam lives on reefs or in shallow lagoons on sand, with the hinge lying on the bottom and the gaping open end facing up. The swollen, wavy mantle edge resembles a green and blue snake. The giant clam feeds on colonies of marine algae, which it permits to grow under the epidermis of its mantle. The clams are very slow in closing their valves, and there are no authentic cases of persons being trapped by them.

There are several hundred species of freshwater clams, or river mussels, belonging to the family Unionidae. The thick shell is pearly within and the outside is covered with a varnishlike, green to blackish periostracum, or horny coating. The meat is edible but not very palatable. The largest and more colorful species come from the Mississippi River and its tributaries.

**Feeding.** Both marine and freshwater clams are vegetarians. They take food-laden water in through an inhalant siphon (a tube-shaped extension of the mantle) and pass it over the gills. Mucus strands in the gills entangle the microscopic plant particles and carry them to the small, toothless mouth where flaplike palps push the food into the esophagus. An exhalant siphon expels used water and wastes.

**Locomotion.** Clams move mainly by using their single, tongue-shaped foot, which is maneuvered through the sand. The tip of the foot, when swollen by an influx of lymph and blood, serves as an anchor by which the clam pulls itself forward. The tip is then deflated, and the thin foot is thrust forward to repeat the operation. Clams with short siphons usually move about a great deal

## ANATOMY OF A CLAM

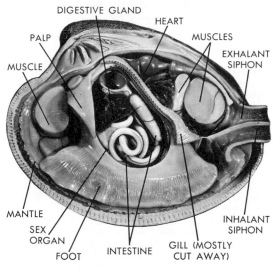

DIGESTIVE GLAND

HEART

PALP

MUSCLES

MUSCLE

EXHALANT SIPHON

MANTLE

SEX ORGAN

FOOT

INTESTINE

GILL (MOSTLY CUT AWAY)

INHALANT SIPHON

AMERICAN MUSEUM OF NATURAL HISTORY

ROBERT HERMES, FROM NATIONAL AUDUBON SOCIETY

A BURROWING CLAM (*right*), the coquina, with its two siphons exposed. The coquina is found on sandy beaches along the southern Atlantic coast of the United States, and it is widely collected for making soup.

and keep within an inch (2.5 cm) of the surface. Clams with long siphons usually remain buried deeply in one place most of their lives.

**Life History.** Clams reproduce sexually. In most species the sexes are separate, but some species are hermaphroditic (one individual contains both male and female sex organs). Fertilized eggs of freshwater clams develop within the adult's gills into small larvae called glochidia. These larvae are expelled into the water; to develop further, they must live as parasites. With small hooks they clamp onto the gills of a fish and suck its blood for several weeks. When their shells become too heavy, the young clams drop to the bottom and begin the normal life of a clam. Many marine clams have a free-swimming larval stage, called the veliger; other clams brood their young inside the mantle cavity.

Clams reach maturity in 1 to 3 years and may live for as long as 20 years. The rings in the shell are not necessarily annual but indicate periods of slow growth in extra cold weather or drought conditions. See also MOLLUSCA.

R. TUCKER ABBOTT
*Academy of Natural Sciences of Philadelphia*

**CLAM WORM** is a common name for several annelid worm species found in or near the low-tide line of the North American seacoast. About 15 inches (38 cm) long, the clam worm's body is composed of about 200 united chambers called somites. The three somites at the front of the body form a head, which normally bears sensory tentacles and palps. The head also bears two pairs of light-sensitive organs. The mouth houses a pair of chitinous jaws used in the capture of prey.

Except for these three, each somite in the clam worm's body has fleshy lobes known as parapodia, which bear numerous bristlelike structures called setae. In addition, the parapodia have a large network of blood vessels. These networks carry out respiration by absorbing oxygen from the water and exchanging it for carbon dioxide. The parapodia, moving in unison, also are used to propel the animal through the water.

**Natural History.** Clam worms often inhabit submerged burrows lined with mucus secreted by the worms' bodies. Occasionally they may be found hiding under rocks, where they await prey. They are quite active during the night hours, when they move out of their burrows in search of food, such as larvae, small animals, and algae.

Reproduction is sexual, and the sexes are separate; however, the reproductive organs are not permanent. The eggs are fertilized externally, and the zygote develops into a free-swimming trochophore larva, which later is transformed into the adult worm.

Clam worms belong to the class Polychaeta in the phylum Annelida; the genus is *Nereis*.

DAVID A. OTTO
*Stephens College, Columbia, Mo.*

**CLAN** refers to several types of groups that claim descent from a common ancestor. The word "clan" comes from the Gaelic *clann*, meaning "offspring" or "descendants."

**Scottish Clans.** The Scottish clan comprised a group of people who traced descent from a common ancestor and considered all members of the clan to be kin. The head of the senior line was chief of the whole clan, and branches of more closely related families within the clan were led by the head of the senior line within the branch. Fellow clansmen fought together and had war cries that were frequently shared by related clans or those that at some time had been allied against a common enemy.

The clan tartan is comparatively recent. In the 18th century the tartans of each locality were similar enough in pattern and color to differentiate them from tartans of other localities. By 1892 there were clan tartans. One of the Macpherson tartans was attributed to the wife of the great-grandfather of the then chief of the Macphersons. The modern clan tartans appear to represent chiefly tartans adopted in the 19th century as nostalgic clan symbols by Scotsmen who had become scattered all over the world.

Scottish clan genealogies normally trace descent through the father's line; that is, they are patrilineal. But on occasion an ancestress appears as a link in genealogy. For example, the Campbell clan takes its name from the Anglo-Norman Gillespie Campbell, who married Eva, heiress of the O'Duins. The clan consisted of the kin of the O'Duins, and in the clan genealogy Eva O'Duin figures prominently. Her son gave the name "Campbell" to the clan.

A clan had an established territory, and the feelings of kinship and common residence were closely associated. The Campbells expanded into the territory of several smaller clans. Since most of these disappeared from the records, one must infer that the clans whose territories were taken over by the Campbells became Campbells.

The clan type of structure, in which people are organized in genealogical kin units which are also political and territorial units, survived longer in Scotland than in most parts of Europe, but early records show that the tribal Latin *gens* and Germanic *sibb* were like the Scottish clan. In tribal Central and Southwest Asia, this type of genealogical kin group is still found.

**The American Indian "Clan."** American anthropologists working with Indian tribes use the term "clan" in a somewhat different meaning. Here it refers to a group that believes itself descended from a common ancestor but is not concerned with genealogies or degree of relationship. An individual always belongs to the clan of his father, if it is patrilineal, or of his mother, if it is matrilineal. He must always marry outside his clan. The American Indian clan is neither a territorial nor a political unit.

ELIZABETH E. BACON
*Anthropologist*

**CLANRICARDE,** klan-rik'ərd, an Irish landowning family. The name Clan-of ricarde belonged to the de Burgh family, which dominated the province of Connaught and influenced Irish political life for many centuries. The de Burghs went to Ireland in the first wave of the Anglo-Norman conquest in the late 1160's, and they acquired vast estates in the west. The Clanricarde men were proud and aggressive feudal magnates who fought continuously for their own survival and aggrandizement, and they helped to hold Ireland subservient to the English crown.

RICHARD DE BURGH (died 1243), to whom King John granted all the lands in Connaught in 1222, led part of the royal army against the Irish leader Aedh of Connaught in 1230. By combining intrigue with force, Richard succeeded in pacifying much of western Ireland.

RICHARD DE BURGH, 2D EARL OF ULSTER, 4TH EARL OF CONNAUGHT (1259?–1326), carried on a long war against native Irish rulers, and in 1286 he deposed Brian O'Neill as head of all the Irish septs, or ruling families.

ULICK DE BURGH, 5TH EARL AND 1ST MARQUESS OF CLANRICARDE (1604–1657), sat in the Parliament of 1639–1640 and was one of the commissioners who presented the grievances of the rebellious Irish leaders to the king in 1642–1643. Appointed lord deputy of Ireland under the authority of Charles II in 1650, Ulick tried to keep the country loyal to the crown, but his anxiety to preserve both his English and Irish estates forced him in 1652 to withdraw to England.

HUBERT GEORGE DE BURGH CANNING, 2D MARQUESS OF CLANRICARDE (1832–1916), struggled against the forces of both Irish nationalism and the British government in defense of his Irish estates. After prolonged agitation and costly litigation he was forced to sell all of his estates except the demesne under the Land Act of 1909 for £238,211. The marquessate became extinct at his death.

L. PERRY CURTIS, JR.
*University of California at Berkeley*

**CLANTON,** klan'tən, a town located in central Alabama, the seat of Chilton county, situated 38 miles (60 km) northwest of Montgomery. The town is a fruit-growing center, specializing in peaches. Some other industries include lumber and cotton mills and processing plants for meat and for animal feeds. Clanton was incorporated in 1887. Population: 7,800.

**CLAPHAM,** klap'əm, **Sir John Harold** (1873–1946), English historian. He was born at Broughton, near Manchester, on Sept. 13, 1873. He graduated in 1895 from Cambridge University with first class honors in history. He was successively fellow, dean, tutor, and vice provost at King's College, Cambridge, and then pursued his academic career as a lecturer and professor of historical and economic subjects at Cambridge, Leeds, and London universities. His best quality was the ability to reduce large masses of detail to systematic form. No other historian has so exhaustively treated the 19th century economics of Britain. His most important publication was *An Economic History of Modern Britain* (3 vols., 1926–1938). He was knighted in 1943. He died on March 29, 1946, while traveling by train from London to Cambridge.

**CLAPP, Margaret** (1910–1974), American educator and author. She was born in East Orange, New Jersey, on April 11, 1910. She graduated from Wellesley College and received her Ph.D. at Columbia University. After teaching at Columbia and at Brooklyn College she was president of Wellesley from 1949 to 1966, when she became president of Lady Doak College in India. From 1968 to 1971 she was chief cultural officer of the U.S. Information Service in India. She died in Tyringham, Massachusetts, on May 3, 1974.

In 1947 Miss Clapp published a biography, *Forgotten First Citizen: John Bigelow*, which was an extension of her Columbia doctoral dissertation. This book won the Pulitzer Prize for biography in 1948. She was also a coeditor of *The Greater City* (1948) and the editor of *The Modern University* (1950).

**CLAPP, Verner Warren** (1901–1972), American librarian. He was born in Johannesburg, South Africa, on June 3, 1901, and attended Trinity College, Hartford, Conn., and Harvard University (1922–1923). In 1923 he began his long career at the Library of Congress, Washington, D. C., where he was chief assistant librarian from 1947 to 1956. In 1956 he became president of the Council on Library Resources, Inc. Clapp also served as librarian for the San Francisco United Nations (UN) Conference (1945), adviser to the delegates of the United Nations Educational, Scientific, and Cultural Organization (UNESCO) in London (1946), chairman of the U. S. Library Mission to Japan (1947–1948), and consultant to the UN Secretariat (1948). He died in Alexandria, Va., on June 15, 1972.

**CLAPPERTON, Hugh** (1788–1827), Scottish explorer, who traveled in central Africa. He was born in Annan, Scotland. In 1820 he met Dr. Walter Oudney, who was appointed British consul in Bornu, now in northeastern Nigeria. In 1822, Clapperton and Maj. Dixon Denham accompanied Oudney across the Sahara to Kuka, the capital of Bornu. While Denham explored around Lake Chad, Clapperton and Oudney went westward toward the Niger River. Oudney died in 1824, and Clapperton proceeded alone to Kano and Sokoto, where Sultan Bello prevented him from continuing on to the Niger River. Clapperton returned to England with Denham in 1825 and assisted him in preparing a book on their travels. It was published as *Narrative of Travels and Discoveries in Northern and Central Africa in the years 1822, 1823, and 1824* (1826).

Promoted to the rank of commander in 1825, Clapperton almost immediately headed a second expedition to Africa, accompanied by Richard Lander. The two men started for the interior from Badagry on the west coast on Dec. 7, 1825. After crossing Yorubaland and the Niger River, they reached Kano and later Sokoto. Sultan Bello of Sokoto would not allow them to visit either Timbuktu or Bornu. Clapperton died in a small village near Sokoto on April 13, 1827.

HARRY R. RUDIN, *Yale University*

**CLAQUE,** klak, a group of persons organized, usually for pay, to applaud or occasionally to show disapproval at a public performance. Various claquers, directed by the *chef du claque,* may specialize in laughter or tears or simply in clapping for encores. The claque existed in the theaters and law courts of ancient Greece and Rome, where the Emperor Nero hired some 5,000 people to applaud his dramatic appearances. Claques were used by individuals from the 16th century in France and became a business in the early 19th century with the organization of the *Assurance des succès dramatiques,* which provided claques for Paris theaters. Claques were also much used in Italy, less so in Germany, England, and the United States.

**CLARE,** klâr, **Saint** (1194–1253), Italian cofounder of the Poor Clares. She was born into a noble family in Assisi, Italy, in 1194. Profoundly impressed by the spirituality of St. Francis of Assisi, she received the religious habit from him at the Portiuncula chapel March, 1212. That year she founded with St. Francis the Poor Clares, or Second Order of Franciscans, especially dedicated to the Franciscan ideal of apostolic poverty and to a contemplative life of prayer. She remained at the order's original monastery at San Damiano, near Assisi, serving as abbess from 1215 until her death there on Aug. 11, 1253. She was bedridden for the last 30 years of her life. Her mother, Blessed Ortolana, and her sisters Beatrice and St. Agnes of Assisi also joined the Poor Ladies (the order's original name) which spread throughout Europe during her lifetime. The Primitive Rule, composed by Clare about 1247, was modeled on the Franciscan rule of 1223. It received papal approval two days before her death. She was canonized in 1255, and her remains have reposed in the church of St. Clare in Assisi since its construction in 1260. Her feast day is celebrated on August 12.

JOHN F. BRODERICK, S. J.
*Weston College, Mass.*

**CLARE, de,** klâr, the name of one of the most powerful baronial houses in medieval England. The Clares were descended from Godfrey, Count of Brionne, an illegitimate son of Richard the Fearless (942–996), 3d Duke of Normandy. Godfrey's son, Count Gilbert, was the father of Richard (died 1090), who accompanied William the Conqueror on his invasion of England in 1066. For his services, Richard received great estates, including his principal seat, Clare in Suffolk, whence his descendants took their family name. The de Clares also had a large property at Tonbridge in Kent, and so Richard's son Gilbert (died 1115), who had his castle there, was often styled "of Tonbridge." Gilbert, who rebelled against William II but under Henry I enjoyed royal favor, made large conquests in South Wales. From Gilbert's elder son, Richard (died 1136), descended the earls of Clare, Hertford, and Gloucester. His younger son, Gilbert (died 1148), founded the earldom of Pembroke.

**Earldoms of Hertford and Gloucester.** Richard de Clare (died 1136) first bore the feudal baronial title of Hertford. He was succeeded by his son Gilbert, 2d Earl of Hertford (died 1151), a rebel against King Stephen. Gilbert was succeeded by his brother Roger (the Good), who died in 1173. Roger's son and successor, Richard (died 1218), the 4th Earl, was appointed one of the barons to enforce the Magna Carta (as was also his son Gilbert). By Richard's marriage to Amicia (2d daughter and co-heir of William, Earl of Gloucester), this same son Gilbert (died 1230) became 6th Earl of Gloucester, besides 5th Earl of Hertford. Gilbert's wife was a daughter of William Marshall (1145–1219), Earl of Pembroke (husband of the Earl of Pembroke's heiress, who finally became her father's heir).

Through all these developments the de Clares had become the kingdom's most powerful subjects. The 6th Earl of Hertford and 7th Earl of Gloucester, Richard (died 1262), was sent as ambassador to France (1259) to renounce England's claims to Normandy. The next was Gilbert (died 1295), surnamed the Red, 7th Earl of Hertford and 8th Earl of Gloucester. At first he took the baronial side against the crown, but he was later reconciled, marrying Edward I's daughter Joan in 1290. The male line ended when his son Gilbert (1291–1314) was killed at Bannockburn, leaving no issue. The Clare barony then passed to Gilbert's three sisters, and to the crown by the youngest sister's marriage in 1360 to Lionel, son of Edward III (hence the royal dukedom of Clarence).

**Earldom of Pembroke.** Gilbert Strongbow (died 1148) became the 1st Earl of Pembroke in 1138. His son was the famous Richard Strongbow (1130–1176) who in 1172 led the Anglo-Norman invasion of Ireland. (From him, County Clare took its name.) With Richard Strongbow, the powerful line ended. His vast holdings passed to his only daughter, Isabel, wife of William Marshall (1145–1219), Earl of Pembroke.

L. G. PINE
*Former Editor of "Burke's Peerage"*

**CLARE,** klâr, **John** (1793–1864), English poet of the romantic school, who was especially concerned with nature. Clare was born at Helpston, Northamptonshire, on July 13, 1793, and he spent much of his life doing farm work in the area. His *Poems Descriptive of Rural Life and Scenery* (1820) made the "peasant poet," as he was called, a popular celebrity; later volumes, including *The Village Minstrel* (1821), *The Shepherd's Calendar* (1827), and *The Rural Muse* (1835), were much less successful. Ill, poor, and increasingly subject to delusions and fits of despondency, Clare was declared insane in 1841 and confined to an asylum at Northampton, where he died on May 20, 1864.

Clare's verse combined close observation of nature with a sympathetic appreciation of the world. At times, as in the opening lines of *Secret Love*, he achieved an intensity comparable to that of William Blake, and in the lyric *I Am* Clare demonstrated a keen and original self-awareness.

THOMAS J. ASSAD
*Tulane University*

**CLARE,** klàr, in western Ireland, a maritime county in the province of Munster, is bounded on the east and south by the River Shannon and its estuary, and on the west by the Atlantic Ocean. It has many beautiful beaches, notably at Lahinch and Kilkee; the cliffs of Moher rise steeply several hundred feet from the Atlantic, and the Burren area is famous for its flora. Potatoes and oats are the main tillage crops; cattle, sheep, and pigs are raised.

Shannon Airport is a major stop for transatlantic passenger planes. There are many industries in an adjoining industrial estate. Ennis, the county capital, has some light industries—flour milling, jute carpets, and textiles.

Killaloe was the seat of the Dál gCais, whose 10th century king, Brian Boru, became King of Ireland. Clare returned Daniel O'Connell to the House of Commons in 1828 to fight the causes of Roman Catholic Emancipation and of the repeal of the Act of Union with England. Population: 90,918 (1991 census).

THOMAS FITZGERALD
*Department of Education, Dublin*

**CLAREMONT,** a city located in southwestern California, in Los Angeles county, situated at the foot of the San Gabriel Mountains, 27 miles (43 km) east of Los Angeles, of which it is a residential suburb. The city packs and ships fruits that are raised on nearby citrus farms. Claremont is an educational center and the seat of the Claremont Colleges.

Incorporated in 1907, Claremont is governed by a city manager. Population: 33,998.

**CLAREMONT,** a city in western New Hampshire, in Sullivan county, on the Sugar River, 45 miles (72 km) west of Concord. The river drops 300 feet (90 meters) in the city, providing abundant waterpower. Claremont is in a farming region and has considerable tourist trade. Manufactured products include mining and mill machinery, woolens, shoes, and paper.

Claremont was settled in 1762 and incorporated as a town in 1764. It annexed part of Unity in 1828. It was incorporated as a city in 1948. Government is by council and manager. Population: 13,151.

**CLAREMONT COLLEGES,** six associated private institutions (five colleges and a graduate school) with adjoining campuses in Claremont, Calif., that share many facilities and academic programs. Of the coeducational colleges, Claremont McKenna College (incorporated 1946)

offers a liberal arts program in economics and government; Harvey Mudd (1955) specializes in science and engineering; and Pomona College (1887) and Pitzer College (1963) offer degrees in liberal arts. Scripps College (1926) is a liberal arts college for women. The Claremont Graduate School (1925) is limited to graduate studies in the liberal arts and is also a graduate-level teachers college. The six institutions are coordinated through the Claremont University Center.

**CLAREMORE,** a city located in northeastern Oklahoma, the seat of Rogers county, 25 miles (40 km) northeast of Tulsa. The city is a health resort, with mineral springs. There are deposits of natural gas, oil, and coal in the area. Claremore was the home of the humorist Will Rogers, who is buried there.

Claremore was settled in the late 19th century. It was incorporated as a town in 1896 and as a city in 1908. Population: 15,873.

**CLARENCE, Dukes of.** The title "Duke of Clarence" has always been borne by a member of the British royal family, usually with misfortune. None of the five creations of the dukedom of Clarence survived the death of the first duke.

The dukedom of Clarence was first created in 1362 by Edward III for the benefit of his third son, Lionel Plantagenet (1338–1368). In 1352, Lionel had married Elizabeth, daughter and heiress of William de Burgh, Earl of Ulster, the heir of the great family of Clare (hence the title of Clarence; see CLARE, DE), Earls of Hertford and Gloucester. Elizabeth died in 1363. Their only child, Philippa, was married at the age of 6 to Edmund Mortimer, 3d Earl of March, a member of the house of York, and from them the Yorkist kings Edward IV and Richard III were descended.

In 1368, Lionel married Violante, daughter of Galeazzo Visconti, lord of Milan. A magnificent wedding was held in Milan, and the feasts attending it lasted for five months until the robust bridegroom became suddenly ill at Alba and died, on Oct. 17, 1368. There were no children, and the first dukedom of Clarence became extinct.

In 1411, Thomas Plantagenet (1388–1421), the second son of Henry IV, was created Duke of Clarence. He had married Margaret, the widow of John Beaufort, Earl of Somerset, and daughter of Thomas Holland, Earl of Kent. Thomas commanded the English fleet when he was 17. After his older brother ascended the throne as Henry V, Thomas engaged in Henry's wars in France. He was mortally wounded at the battle of Baugé in Anjou on March 21, 1421. He left no legitimate issue and his title became extinct.

The third creation of a dukedom of Clarence was for the benefit of George Plantagenet (1449–1478), the brother of Edward IV. George was created duke at the time of Edward's accession in 1461. In 1469, George married Lady Isabel Neville, daughter and coheiress of Richard Neville, Earl of Warwick, the "Kingmaker" and "the last of the barons." Warwick had deserted the cause of King Edward, who had usurped the throne from Henry VI, and after the marriage George joined Warwick in opposition in France. But the "false, fleeting perjured Clarence" of Shakespeare's *Richard III* changed sides too often in the Wars of the Roses. He betrayed Warwick in 1471, caused his death, and seized his estates, but Edward ultimately imprisoned him in the Tower, where he was found dead on Feb. 17 (or 18), 1478. The traditional account is that, being allowed to choose the manner of his death, he elected to be drowned in a butt of wine.

Clarence left two children, but because his dukedom was attainted, it did not pass to either. His son, Edward, who bore the title Earl of Warwick, spent nearly all his life in prison. He was executed in 1499 at the age of 24 by order of Henry VII. He was the last male Plantagenet. His sister, Margaret, Countess of Salisbury, was executed on Tower Hill in 1541, on a trumped-up charge of treason.

The fourth creation of a dukedom of Clarence was in 1789, when Prince William Henry (1765–1837), third son of George III, was made Duke of Clarence and St. Andrews and Earl of Munster. He succeeded to the throne as William IV in 1830. In 1818 he married Princess Adelaide, eldest daughter of George, Duke of Saxe-Meiningen, by whom he had two daughters who died in infancy.

Prince Albert Victor Christian Edward (1864–1892), eldest son of the Prince of Wales, later Edward VII, was created Duke of Clarence and Avondale and Earl of Athlone in 1890. He died unmarried in 1892, and the title became extinct for a fifth time.

L. G. PINE
*Former Editor of "Burke's Peerage"*

**CLARENCE RIVER,** a coastal stream in Australia, flowing through New South Wales. It rises in the McPherson Range, near the Queensland border, and flows southeast and northeast for 245 miles (394 km) to the Pacific Ocean.

**CLARENCE STRAIT,** in Australia, lies between Bathurst and Melville islands on the north and the mainland of Northern Territory on the south. About 90 miles (145 km) long, Clarence Strait links Van Diemen Gulf with the Timor Sea.

**CLARENDON, Earls of.** See HYDE, EDWARD (1st Earl); HYDE, EDWARD (3d Earl); HYDE, HENRY (2d Earl); VILLIERS–*George William Frederick Villiers* (4th Earl).

**CLARENDON, Constitutions of,** klar'ən-dən, legislation formulated in England in 1164 to regulate the relations between church and state. The constitutions provide the first example after the Norman Conquest of a strongly contested legislative act in England. The principle that ecclesiastical causes should be heard in ecclesiastical courts had been accepted by William the Conqueror. In developing its canon law, however, the church inevitably sought to enlarge its jurisdiction, and Henry II, in order to preserve royal authority and public order, set down in writing a reasoned and reasonable statement of customs obtaining under Henry I and earlier.

The document comprised 16 chapters. Six of the chapters were rulings on church authority that were already clearly established by custom. Four chapters defined the boundaries between secular and ecclesiastical jurisdiction and established, among other things, that the royal courts were to decide disputes over advowsons (the rights of patrons to endow benefices), over property alleged to be held by the church in free alms (without an obligation of feudal services), and over debts. Although the church courts retained jurisdiction over clerics charged with crimes, royal courts had jurisdiction in sentencing. The other six chapters limited papal authority in certain matters in which royal prerogative controlled ecclesiastical practice in England.

After lengthy debate the constitutions were accepted by the barons and the prelates. They were ratified on Jan. 30, 1164, and enforced in the royal courts as the law of the land. But Archbishop Thomas Becket soon repudiated his agreement, and the many questions involved were telescoped into the single issue whether clerics found guilty of common law crimes should be subjected only to degradation and penance in a church court or handed over to a secular court for further and more severe punishment. Becket fled into exile in November 1164 in open defiance of the constitutions and was not allowed to return until July 1170. His murder the following Christmas caused the embarrassed King to amend the constitutions. The Compromise of Avranches (in Normandy) in 1172 granted complete freedom of appeals to Rome, but with the all-important reservation that the crown's authority be not diminished thereby. An agreement in 1176 gave ecclesiastical courts exclusive jurisdiction over "criminous" clerks, but this concession was later whittled down. Otherwise the substance of the constitutions was unchanged, the king maintained his ground at all main points, and church and state continued their pragmatic cooperation.

GEORGE OSBORNE SAYLES, *Joint-Author of "Law and Legislation in Mediaeval England"*

**CLARENDON CODE,** klar'ən-dən, the name given to the repressive measures enacted by the English Parliament in a wave of Royalist reaction after the restoration of King Charles II in 1660. These acts reestablished and protected the Anglican Church and laid disabilities upon dissenters. The code consisted of a number of statutes, commonly but perhaps erroneously thought to represent the ecclesiastical policy of Edward Hyde (1609–1674), 1st Earl of Clarendon and the king's chief minister.

Four measures are generally reckoned as the most important parts of the Clarendon Code. (1) The Corporation Act of 1661 required magistrates and other civic officials to abjure any oath they might have taken to the Solemn League and Covenant under the Commonwealth, and to receive Communion in the Church of England before taking office. (2) The Act of Uniformity of 1662 established the use of the Book of Common Prayer, required the assent of the clergy thereto, and prohibited any person not episcopally ordained from ministering in the Church of England. (3) The Conventicle Act of 1664 imposed penalties upon persons attending religious services other than those according to the liturgy of the Church of England. (4) The Five Mile Act of 1665 forbade clergymen who had refused subscription to the Act of Uniformity to reside within five miles of a corporate town, parliamentary borough, or a parish from which they had been ejected. The act also imposed on nonconformist ministers an oath that they would seek no alteration to the established order of church and state.

POWEL MILLS DAWLEY
*The General Theological Seminary, New York*

**CLARET,** klar′ət, is a name for the red wines of Bordeaux, France. It is derived from *clairet*, the term the French used for the light, young, pinkish wines they drank in the Middle Ages. To satisfy the reviving taste for younger wines, a kind of *clairet* is being made today—the rosé wine of Bordeaux. Generally, however, claret means the mature red Bordeaux wines (see BORDEAUX WINES). The term is sometimes loosely applied to the dry red wines produced in other countries.

The true clarets, grown in the districts of Médoc, St.-Émilion, Graves, and Pomerol, are aged from 5 to 25 years or more. The great vintages, like those of 1961 or 1959, take longest to mature. Vintages of lesser years will be ready to drink sooner and will provide a better bottle—at 5 years of age—than greater vintages that have not yet reached their prime.

ALEXIS LICHINE, *Author of "Encyclopedia of Wines & Spirits"*

**CLARINET,** klar-ə-net′, a woodwind instrument, one of a family that also includes the flute, oboe, and bassoon. The name is derived from the Italian *clarinetto* ("little clear one").

In principle the clarinet is a hollow tube, with holes along it to control the pitch—much like a toy whistle. This tube is traditionally made of ebony, although many fine modern clarinets have plastic bodies. The holes along the tube may be covered by padded keys, or uncovered until stopped by the player's fingers.

The sound is made by a reed attached to a mouthpiece at one end of the tube. This reed is a thin, flat slip of cane, cut from a bamboo-like plant. When the player blows through the mouthpiece, the reed vibrates, and the vibrations are amplified by the tube into a mellow tone.

Although the B-flat clarinet is the most familiar, there are more than half a dozen other clarinets in current use. The B-flat clarinet is about two feet long. The smallest and rarest member of the family is the foot-long *sopranino*. Somewhat larger than the sopranino are the E-flat and D clarinets often used in symphony orchestras. Clarinets bigger than the B-flat are the alto, common in bands; the bass, which sounds an octave below the B-flats; and, finally, the great contrabasses, which sound some two octaves lower, stand four feet in height, and are often used in concert bands as a harmonic foundation.

The clarinet was invented in the late 17th century, probably by a German flute maker named Johann Denner (1655–1707). Denner's first clarinet had no keys. The player made melodies by covering or uncovering the holes directly with his fingers and thumb. Since he could cover no more than nine holes at a time while supporting the instrument with one thumb, the player's range, accuracy, and speed were limited. Through the years, other inventors added ingenious key mechanisms that helped the player

cover more than the original nine holes. Today the clarinetist still must use only nine fingers, yet he can control over 20 holes with them and produce more than 40 different tones.

The clarinet's distinctive sound quickly made it a favorite among composers. Vivaldi and Handel were scoring for the clarinet a generation after it was invented. Later, Mozart gave it a regular place in the symphony orchestra, and he also composed some glorious solo music for it.

BENNY GOODMAN, *Clarinetist*

**CLARISSA,** klə-ris′ə, is an epistolary novel by the English author Samuel Richardson. Originally published in seven volumes in 1747–1748, *Clarissa. Or, the History of a Young Lady* is usually considered Richardson's masterpiece.

The book is set in 18th century England. Clarissa, the daughter of a country squire, is attracted to Robert Lovelace, a dashing young nobleman of whom her family disapproves. When she refuses to marry Mr. Solmes, the homely, elderly suitor whom her parents have selected, they keep her a virtual prisoner in the house. In desperation, she places herself under the protection of Lovelace and flees with him. However, he treats her shamefully, ultimately drugging and raping her when she steadily resists his advances. Although he offers to marry her, Clarissa is unable and unwilling to live after her terrible experiences and dies of a broken heart. Lovelace is killed in a duel with her cousin.

The book is remarkable for its penetrating psychological study of character and its sensitive exploration of motivation. In *Clarissa*, Richardson treated the themes of sex, love, and marriage within the framework of 18th century social conventions. To modern readers, the book's most interesting aspect is its study of sexual attraction. Here, however, the emotion is disoriented by sadistic impulses, and sexuality becomes the very agent of destruction, not only of love, but of life itself. Clarissa's physical death, now unbelievable, but in harmony with the social and moral conventions of her time, was, in fact, preceded by her emotional "death," a concept that modern readers readily understand.

Richardson's epistolary style, although somewhat archaic, offers an effective medium of self-disclosure for Clarissa and Lovelace. Their letters become both revelation and mask, since the characters simultaneously confess and dissemble as they write.

The novel was an instant success throughout western Europe. It directly influenced many of Richardson's immediate successors and even such 19th century novelists as Jane Austen and the Brontës. In later years, Richardson's curious sensitivity and undeniable dramatic and stylistic powers continued to fascinate writers, from George Meredith to Virginia Woolf and E. M. Forster.

JOHN W. LOOFBOUROW, *Boston College*

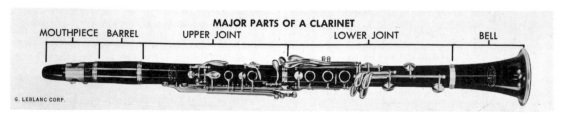

**MAJOR PARTS OF A CLARINET**

MOUTHPIECE    BARREL    UPPER JOINT    LOWER JOINT    BELL

G. LEBLANC CORP.

**CLARK, Abraham** (1726–1794), American political leader, who signed the Declaration of Independence. He was called "Congress Abraham" for his participation in provincial and national congresses. Clark was born in Elizabethtown, N. J., on Feb. 15, 1726. A surveyor, he became known as the "poor man's counselor" because of his arbitration of land disputes. He served in the New Jersey provincial congress (1775), the state legislature (1784–1787), the Continental Congress (1776–1783), and the U. S. Congress (1791–1794). He also was a delegate to the Annapolis Convention of 1786, but ill health prevented his attending the 1787 convention. He died in Rahway, N. J., on Sept. 5, 1794.

**CLARK, Alvan** (1804–1887), American lens maker, who founded with his sons, George Basset Clark (1827–1891) and Alvan Graham Clark (1832–1897), the most famous optical company of the 19th century. Alvan Clark was born in Ashfield, Mass., on March 8, 1804. A portrait painter and engraver by trade, Clark reached middle age before developing the interest in optics that eventually led him to fame. Since he was qualified by neither training nor experience to pursue his special interest, he closed his studio and set about mastering the art of lens grinding. In 1846 he opened the firm of Alvan Clark & Sons in Cambridge, Mass., and started the production of achromatic telescope lenses in the United States. Alvan Clark died in Cambridge on Aug. 19, 1887.

Many years were required in the building of a reputation competitive with those of the established European technicians, and it was only after the sale of several lenses in England in the late 1850's that the firm found itself on a sound financial basis. By 1862, Clark completed an 18½-inch lens, the world's largest to that date. The significance of the achievement became apparent even before the lens was pressed into actual service, when trial observations by Alvan Graham Clark revealed the first sight of the celebrated companion star of Sirius, the existence of which had been postulated a generation earlier by Bessel to account for peculiarities in the proper motion of Sirius. Young Clark's discovery won for him the Lalande Medal of the French Academy of Sciences and brought to prominence the first example of the remarkable stars known to 20th-century astronomy as white dwarfs. The success of the 18½-inch lens brought contracts which resulted in the installation of Clark refractors in observatories all over the country. It also inspired a long series of successful experiments with lenses of ever-larger size.

In 1871, a 26-inch instrument was placed in the U. S. Naval Observatory, where, in 1877, Asaph Hall discovered Phobos and Deimos, two small satellites of Mars. A 30-inch telescope for the Pulkovo Observatory in Russia and a 36-inch one for Lick Observatory in California followed in 1884 and 1888, respectively. A 40-inch instrument was completed in 1897 for the Yerkes Observatory in Wisconsin.

VICTOR E. THOREN, *Indiana University*

**CLARK, Barrett Harper** (1890–1953), American writer-editor, notably in the field of drama. He was born in Toronto, Canada, on Aug. 26, 1890, and was educated at the universities of Chicago and Paris. Clark was an actor and assistant stage manager with the actress Minnie Maddern Fiske and taught drama at Chautauqua, N. Y. He later became literary editor of the Samuel French publishing house for drama (1918–1936) and executive director of the Dramatists' Play Service (from 1936).

Under the pseudonym "Harold Harper," Clark wrote many books on drama, including *Eugene O'Neill* (1926; rev. ed 1947) and *Intimate Portraits* (1951). He edited the *World's Best Plays* in 58 volumes (1915–1926) and *World Drama* (1932), as well as anthologies of short stories and short novels. Clark died at Briarcliff Manor, N. Y. on Aug. 26, 1953.

**CLARK, "Champ"** (1850–1921), American lawyer and public official, who was speaker of the House of Representatives (1911–1919). James Beauchamp Clark was born on March 7, 1850, near Lawrenceburg, Ky. He attended the University of Kentucky and then Bethany College (W. Va.), graduating in 1873. Admitted to the bar in 1875, he settled in Bowling Green, Mo. He became active in local Democratic politics and served in the Missouri legislature (1889–1891). He was elected to Congress in 1892, defeated in 1894, but again elected in 1896 and regularly reelected until 1920.

Gaining prominence as a debater, he became Democratic minority leader in 1907. His outstanding achievement was his role in forging the Democratic-insurgent Republican alliance that broke Speaker Joseph E. Cannon's ironfisted control over the House. After the Democrats won a majority of the House in 1910, Clark was elected speaker. In 1912 he sought the Democratic presidential nomination. Although he led in the early balloting at the national convention, the nomination went to Woodrow Wilson.

Clark was on the whole a loyal supporter of the new President, although he opposed the draft even after the United States entered World War I. He did not play a leading role in the Wilson administration, in part because the revolt against Cannon had weakened the speaker's position. After the Republicans won a House majority in 1918, Clark again served as minority leader. He was defeated for reelection in 1920, and died in Washington on March 2, 1921, before the end of his term. Clark recorded his reminiscences in *My Quarter Century of American Politics* (1920).

Joel Bennett (Champ) Clark (1890–1954), his son, served in the U. S. Senate from 1933 to 1945 as a Democrat from Missouri.

JOHN BRAEMAN, *University of Nebraska*

**CLARK, Charles Edgar** (1843–1922), American naval officer, who commanded the battleship *Oregon* in the Spanish-American War. He was born in Bradford, Vt., on Aug. 10, 1843. After graduating from the U. S. Naval Academy, he served in the Civil War.

At the outbreak of the Spanish-American War, Clark was a captain commanding the *Oregon*, which was in port at San Francisco. This new, powerful warship was ordered to join the Atlantic Fleet off Cuba. Clark left San Francisco on March 19, traversed the Strait of Magellan, and reached Key West, Fla., on May 26. The *Oregon* took part in the destruction of the Spanish squadron off Santiago de Cuba on July 3. Clark was promoted rear admiral in 1902 and retired in 1905. He died in Long Beach, Calif., on Oct. 1, 1922.

Joe Clark, Progressive Conservative party leader, held office briefly as Canada's prime minister in 1979–1980.

**CLARK, Charles Joseph (Joe)** (1939–     ), Canadian political leader who held office as the nation's youngest prime minister for nine months in 1979–1980.

Clark was born in High River, Alberta, on June 5, 1939, the son of a newspaper publisher. He received a B.A. degree in history (1960) and an M.A. in political science (1973) from the University of Alberta, where he also lectured in political science in 1965–1967. After working for a short time as a journalist, he entered politics as private secretary to W. C. J. Kirby, the Progressive Conservative party (PCP) leader for Alberta. Two terms as national president of the PCP Student Federation followed in the early 1960s. Clark also served as an aide to several political leaders, including R. L. Stanfield, the national PCP leader, in 1967–1970.

In October 1972 Clark was elected to the House of Commons, representing the Rocky Mountain constituency. Reelected in 1974, he chaired a number of party committees and was elected the Progressive Conservatives' national leader in February 1976.

In the campaign of 1979 Clark stressed the need for greater initiative on the part of private enterprise and recommended changing several of Canada's public corporations to private companies. He also stood for reduced inflation and increased employment, the use of tax reductions and other devices to stimulate private business, and increased efforts to conserve energy and find new fuel reserves that would meet all of Canada's energy needs in a decade. In the election of May 22, 1979, the PCP won 136 of the 282 seats in the House of Commons. On June 4 Clark succeeded Pierre Trudeau as prime minister.

In the ensuing months the public became dissatisfied with some of Clark's policies, notably his request for higher excise taxes on gasoline, and

in December 1979 his government fell. The Liberals were returned to power from 1980 until 1984 when Brian Mulroney, who had replaced Clark in 1983 as head of the PCP, became prime minister. Clark became external affairs minister in Mulroney's government in September 1984 and accepted the post of constitutional affairs minister in April 1991. Several months after announcing his retirement from politics in 1993, he became a special representative to UN Secretary-General Boutros Boutros-Ghali for Cyprus.

**CLARK, Dutch** (1906–1978), American football player who was an outstanding college and professional quarterback. Earl Harry Clark was born in Fowler, Colo., on Oct. 11, 1906. As a single-wing quarterback at little Colorado College, he received national acclaim as a sophomore when named to the Associated Press All-America team in 1928. He averaged 10 yards per carry in college, scoring in all but one game.

In 1931 he began his professional career with the Portsmouth Spartans (later the Detroit Lions). An All-League quarterback six times between 1931 and 1937, he led the league in scoring in 1935 (55 points) and 1936 (73 points). As playing coach of the Lions (1937–1938), he compiled a 14–8 won-lost record in two seasons. From 1939 to 1942 he coached the Cleveland (later Los Angeles) Rams. Clark was a charter member of the Professional Football Hall of Fame. He died in Canon City, Colo., on Aug. 5, 1978.

MICHAEL QUINN, *"Sports Illustrated"*

**CLARK, Francis Edward** (1851–1927), American clergyman. He was born in Aylmer, Quebec, Canada, on Sept. 12, 1851, and graduated from Dartmouth College and from Andover Theological Seminary. He was pastor of the Congregationalist Williston Church in Portland, Maine, when, in 1881, he organized the Young People's Society of Christian Endeavor to strengthen spiritual life and to promote Christian activities. He left his position as pastor of the Phillips Church in South Boston, Mass., in 1887 to devote himself to Christian Endeavor, which became an international society. He died in Newton, Mass., on May 26, 1927.

**CLARK, George Rogers** (1752–1818), American frontiersman and military leader who won important victories against the British and their Native American allies in the Illinois country during the American Revolution. He was born near Charlottesville, Va., on Nov. 19, 1752. In his youth he studied surveying, and in 1772 he became a surveyor and frontiersman in the Ohio valley. In 1774 he acted as a scout in Lord Dunmore's campaign to protect Kentucky settlements.

When he was 23, Clark led colonists in Transylvania (comprising Kentucky and much of Tennessee) in a revolt against the proprietors—Judge Richard Henderson and other prominent North Carolinians. He charged that Transylvania had been purchased illegally from the Cherokee, that the owners assessed exorbitant quitrents, and that they secured the best lands for themselves. He successfully petitioned Virginia (which claimed the Kentucky region) to make Kentucky a county of Virginia and to protect it.

**Northwest Campaign.** At the outbreak of the American Revolution, Native Americans, who had been incited by British headquarters at Detroit, intensified their raids against Kentucky settlements.

Recognizing that if Kentucky were captured its central location would make every part of the frontier vulnerable, Clark secured Virginia's approval for an offensive against the Illinois country in January 1778. This region, east of the Mississippi River and under British rule, contained a few villages of French settlers. With the support of these inhabitants, Clark in the summer of 1778 took Kaskaskia and Cahokia (now in Illinois) and Vincennes (in Indiana).

After Clark returned to quarters at Kaskaskia, Lt. Gen. Henry Hamilton, the British commander at Detroit, captured unprotected Vincennes in December 1778. Clark responded in February 1779 by leading about 130 men across flooded bottomlands in freezing weather—without artillery, cavalry, or needed supplies—and retook the village. He planned to march against Detroit, but still failing to obtain supplies, he retired in the summer of 1779 to Fort Nelson, at the Falls of the Ohio at Louisville, Ky.

Earlier historians believed it was Clark's military victories that helped the United States acquire the Northwest Territory in the peace negotiations ending the American Revolution in 1783. However, modern research reveals such claims were disallowed because Clark had retired to Fort Nelson before the war's end.

**Later Years.** After the Revolution, Clark was a member of the board of commissioners allotting lands in the Illinois grant that Virginia made to his soldiers. In 1786 he led an expedition against marauding Wabash tribes, but it failed when most of his men mutinied. Then James Wilkinson, a former general in the Continental Army, who was jealous of Clark's position, charged him with illegally raising troops, seizing property, and failing in his campaign because of drunkenness. Congress accepted the charge, and at the age of 35, Clark was shorn of his commission and discredited. Wilkinson got his commission, and Clark was left practically penniless.

Beginning in 1788, Clark made several vain attempts to recoup his fortunes—by planning a colony in Louisiana and later one on the Mississippi, and lastly by leading a French force to take Louisiana. The U. S. government thwarted all these plans. Clark died at Locust Valley, near Louisville, on Feb. 13, 1818. In 1928 the government appropriated $1 million for a memorial to him at Vincennes.

JOHN A. CARUSO, *West Virginia University*

**CLARK, James** (1936–1968), British auto racer, who was the first driver to win both the world road racing championship and the Indianapolis 500, the top American race, in the same year (1965). His Grand Prix triumph came on consecutive victories in the first six races in which he competed. With the Indianapolis victory he became the first non-American driver to triumph there since Dario Resta of Italy in 1916 and the first to win in a car with a rear-engine design (Lotus-Ford V-8).

Clark was born on a farm in Kelso, Scotland, on March 4, 1936. He won his first track race in 1958, taking the Scottish championship. He earned the Grand Prix honors the first time in 1963 at the age of 26, the youngest to take that title, by winning a record number of seven races. By 1968 he surpassed by one Juan Fangio's mark of 24 Grand Prix wins. Clark was killed in a race at Hockenheim, Germany, on April 7, 1968.

BILL BRADDOCK, *New York "Times"*

Gen. George Rogers Clark

**CLARK, Joe,** Canadian public official. See CLARK, CHARLES JOSEPH.

**CLARK, John Bates** (1847–1938), American economist, who was the American leader of marginal economic theory. This theory, together with the theories of Alfred Marshall, dominated U. S. economic thought from the 1900's to the 1930's. Clark was born in Providence, R. I., on Jan. 26, 1847, and was educated at Brown University, Amherst College, and Heidelberg and Zürich universities. He taught at Carleton, Smith, and Amherst colleges before serving as professor of political economy at Columbia University from 1895 to 1923.

Clark's major contribution was the marginal productivity theory of wages. It justified the capitalistic system of functional distribution of income. He explained wage income as controlled by supply and demand, primarily by employers' demand for labor as dictated by the contribution of labor to the value of production. Wages, he held, were determined precisely by the difference in production created by adding one more laborer. The employer could not pay more without loss; he could not pay less because of competition and because he would not get the maximum gain.

Clark assumed natural order, constructive competition, primacy of economic motivation, and harmony of interest. His major work was *The Distribution of Wealth* (1899). He died in New York City on March 21, 1938.

SHERMAN E. GUNDERSON
*Wisconsin State University, Oshkosh*

**CLARK, Kenneth Bancroft** (1914–    ), American educator and civil rights leader, whose work helped bring about the Supreme Court's 1954 ruling against public school segregation. Clark was born in the Panama Canal Zone on July 24, 1914, and moved to New York five years later. He graduated from Howard University and received his Ph. D. in psychology from Columbia University in 1940.

Two years later Clark joined the psychology department of City College, New York. In 1946 he and his wife founded what became the Northside Center for Child Development. In 1950 he issued a report on school segregation, stating that this practice hindered the development of all students, whether Negro or white. This report was cited by the U. S. Supreme Court in the 1954 ruling that segregation in the public schools is unconstitutional.

For a time Clark headed Harlem Youth Opportunities Unlimited (HARYOU), a program to help Harlem dropouts. He received the Spingarn Medal in 1961. Clark was Distinguished University Professor at City College (1970–1975). His books include *Dark Ghetto* (1965) and *The Pathos of Power* (1974).

**CLARK, Sir Kenneth MacKenzie** (1903–1983), English art historian, an expert on the art of the Italian Renaissance and author of several of the most influential modern studies of art. He was born in London on July 13, 1903. After graduating from Trinity College, Oxford, he worked for two years with Bernard Berenson in Italy. He served successively as keeper of fine art at the Ashmolean Museum, Oxford (1931–1933); director of the National Gallery, London (1934–1945); and Slade professor of fine arts, Oxford (1946–1950). As chairman of the Arts Council of Great Britain (1953–1960) and of the Independent Television Authority (1954–1957), he exerted considerable influence on contemporary English art. He conducted two memorable TV series: *Civilisation* (1969) and *Romantic vs Classic Art* (1973).

His best-known work is *The Nude: A Study in Ideal Form* (1956). He also wrote *Leonardo da Vinci* (2d ed., 1952), *Piero della Francesca* (1951), *Looking at Pictures* (1960), *Rembrandt and the Italian Renaissance* (1966), *The Drawings of Botticelli for Dante's Divine Comedy* (1976), and his two-volume autobiography, *Another Part of the Wood* (1974) and *The Other Half* (1977). He died in Hythe, England, on May 21, 1983.

WILLIAM GERDTS
*University of Maryland*

**CLARK, Mark Wayne** (1896–1984), American general, who commanded Allied armies in Italy in World War II and United Nations forces during the Korean War in 1952–1953. Clark was born in Madison Barracks, New York, on May 1, 1896, the son of an Army colonel. He graduated from the U. S. Military Academy in April 1917. In 1918 he went as an infantry officer to France, where he was wounded in action by shrapnel in the Vosges Mountains sector. In the peacetime Army, Clark had varied assignments, including an instructorship at the War College. When World War II erupted in Europe in 1939, he was still a major, but by May 1942 he had been made a major general and became chief of staff of Army Ground Forces. Two months later he was in England, commanding United States ground forces in Europe.

Gen. Dwight D. Eisenhower, only slightly his senior, was impressed by Clark's abilities and selected him to plan the November 1942 invasion of North Africa. Clark made a secret preinvasion trip by submarine to North Africa to confer with pro-Allied French officers, narrowly evading capture, and later carried out delicate negotiations that secured French cooperation. He became Eisenhower's deputy commander in North Africa.

Eisenhower chose Clark to lead the Fifth Army's invasion of Italy in 1943. Clark's men landed at Salerno, near Naples, where furious German counterattacks almost drove them back into the Mediterranean. Clark came under heavy criticism, but not from senior Allied officers who knew that no man could have accomplished more at less cost. Clark's Fifth Army fought its way up the rugged western half of the Italian peninsula against unrelenting German resistance at the Volturno and Rapido rivers and at Monte Cassino. They captured Rome and drove northward. Germany's surrender in early May 1945 came as Clark was poised to drive into Austria and just after he had been made a four-star general.

From 1945 to 1947, as high commissioner and commander of U. S. forces in Austria, Clark's diplomatic skill was tested repeatedly by Soviet provocations. He used his diplomatic talents again in 1952–1953 as United Nations commander during the skirmishing and long-drawn truce talks that finally ended the Korean War. He retired three months later and then turned to writing about his war experiences in *Calculated Risk* (1950) and *From the Danube to the Yalu* (1954). From 1954 until 1966 he was president of The Citadel, a military college in Charleston, S.C. He died in Charleston on April 17, 1984.

CURT ANDERS
*Author of "Fighting Generals"*

**CLARK, Ramsey** (1927–    ), American lawyer. He was born in Dallas, Texas, on Dec. 18, 1927, the son of Supreme Court justice Tom Clark. Ramsey Clark was educated at the Universities of Texas and Chicago. He held positions in the Justice Department from 1961 to 1967 and served as U. S. attorney general from 1967 to 1969.

Clark was a strong supporter of civil rights. As attorney general he opposed the death penalty, criticized "police violence," and refused to use wiretaps except in cases involving national security. Conservatives complained that he was "soft" on crime, and in 1968 Richard Nixon repeatedly promised "a new attorney general" if he won the presidential election. After leaving public office, Clark visited North Vietnam to investigate U.S. bombing of civilian targets.

Clark taught at Howard University (1969–1972) and Brooklyn Law School (1973–1981) and practiced law in New York City. In 1974 he was the unsuccessful Democratic candidate for the U.S. Senate from New York. In 1980, in the midst of the Iranian hostage crisis, he headed a delegation of private U.S. citizens to a conference in Teheran. In 1982, Clark made a fact-finding tour of Nicaragua, again as a private citizen.

**CLARK, Tom C.** (1899–1977), American public official, who was associate justice of the U. S. Supreme Court from 1949 to 1967. He was a member of the court that unanimously declared public school segregation unconstitutional in 1954, and he subsequently wrote the court's opinions upholding the constitutionality of provisions of the Civil Rights Act of 1964 that required desegregation of public accommodations.

Born in Dallas, Texas, on Sept. 23, 1899, Clark earned bachelor's and law degrees (1921 and 1922) at the University of Texas. Until 1937 he practiced law in Dallas, and from 1927 to 1933 he also served as civil district attorney for Dallas county. In 1937 he joined the U. S. Department of Justice as an attorney and in succeeding years headed the department's antitrust division and its criminal division. In 1945 he was named U. S. attorney general by President Harry S Truman, who four years later appointed him to the U. S. Supreme Court. Clark remained on the court until 1967, when he retired to avoid possible conflict of interest when his son, Ramsey Clark, became U. S. attorney general. He died in New York City on June 13, 1977.

On the bench, Justice Clark tended more than some of his colleagues to uphold the government's position in cases ranging from antitrust to internal security and criminal procedure. Yet he wrote several important majority opinions upholding individual rights. Among these were *Burstyn* v. *Wilson* (1952), in which the court first held that motion pictures are a constitutionally protected form of expression, and *Mapp* v. *Ohio* (1961), which required the exclusion of unconstitutionally seized evidence from state criminal trials. His final opinion for the court severely limited state use of eavesdropping devices.

LAWRENCE G. WALLACE
*Duke University*

**CLARK, Walter Van Tilburg** (1909–1971), American writer, best known for his novel *The Ox-Bow Incident* (1940). He was born in East Orland, Me., on Aug. 3, 1909. He graduated from the University of Nevada in 1931 and took an M. A. there and a Ph. D. at Colgate.

Clark's first published works were volumes of poetry in 1930 and 1932. His first novel, *The Ox-Bow Incident,* is an incisive study of mob violence. His second, *The City of Trembling Leaves* (1945), was less successful, but *The Track of the Cat* (1949), his third novel, is a tautly written account of the hunting of a marauding mountain lion. Both *The Ox-Bow Incident* and *The Track of the Cat* were made into films.

Clark was writer-in-residence at the University of Nevada from 1962 until his death, in Reno, on Nov. 11, 1971.

**CLARK, Wilfrid E. Le Gros** (1895–1971), British physical anthropologist. Clark was born at Hemel Hempstead, England, on June 5, 1895. He received his medical education at St. Thomas's Hospital and served as a captain in the Royal Artillery Medical Corps and later as principal medical officer of Sarawak, in Borneo. In 1923 he became a reader in anatomy at the University of London and was professor of anatomy at Oxford University from 1934 to 1962.

A major portion of Clark's work was in the field of evolution, tracing the development of the primates from tree shrews to monkeys, anthropoid apes, and prehistoric and modern man. He was one of the scientists who, in 1953, determined that the Piltdown Man was a hoax.

Clark was named a fellow of the Royal Society, the Royal College of Surgeons and of the Royal Anthropological Institute, and he was knighted in 1955.

**CLARK, William** (1770–1838), American explorer and Indian agent, best known for his participation in the Lewis and Clark Expedition. He was born in Caroline county, Va., on Aug. 1, 1770. Like his older brother, George Rogers Clark, he fought Indians on the frontier—first as a young militiaman and later as an officer in the 4th Sub-Legion of the Army. In 1796 he left the army and returned to his home near Louisville, Ky., where he remained until chosen by Meriweather Lewis to share the leadership of an overland expedition to the Pacific.

Lewis and Clark and their exploring party left St. Louis to ascend the Missouri River in the spring of 1804, instructed by President Thomas Jefferson to make a thorough study of the newly purchased Louisiana Territory. After wintering with the Mandan Indians in what is now North Dakota, they proceeded west the following spring. When they crossed the Rocky Mountains and descended the Columbia River to its mouth, in the fall of 1805, they became the first white men to cross the western part of the North American continent south of Canada.

The geopolitical importance of their journey, when foreign interests were still contending for portions of the continent, and the large amount of data collected when U. S. citizens were eager for information on the West, gave a special prominence to the expedition. One of Clark's special assignments on the journey was to serve as mapmaker. For several years his manuscript papers were the most authentic source of information on the topography of western America.

After the expedition Clark became superintendent of Indian affairs for the Louisiana Territory, serving also as a brigadier general of militia. During the War of 1812 he was largely responsible for keeping the Indians quiescent in the Upper Mississippi Valley. He was governor of Missouri Territory from 1813 until Missouri achieved statehood in 1821, then again held the post of superintendent of Indian affairs until his death in St. Louis on Sept. 1, 1838.

Although the Lewis and Clark Expedition was the single most important event in Clark's career, his total lifetime contribution as a mediator between white man and Indian was perhaps equally important to a nation moving west. See also LEWIS AND CLARK EXPEDITION.

DONALD JACKSON
*University of Illinois*

**CLARK, William Andrews** (1839–1925), American financier, art collector, and senator, who was one of the great owners and developers of copper-mining properties. He was born in Connellsville, Pa., on Jan. 8, 1839. After his family moved to Iowa, he divided his activities between work on the farm and teaching. In 1862 he went to Colorado and began to work in the gold mines. With $1,500 capital saved from his wages, he became a provisioner to the mining camps of the Montana Territory. Clark also carried the U.S. mail from Montana to the West Coast.

Clark became an important figure in Montana mining and banking. He organized or bought into many mining companies, including the great Elm-Orlu mine, one the world's largest copper and zinc sources, and the rich Verde mine of Arizona, which yielded an estimated 4,000 tons (about 3,600 metric tons) of copper per month. Clark's Montana projects, which he usually controlled exclusively, grew to include banks, mines, timberlands, mills, refineries, electric utilities, water systems, street railways, and newspapers.

His political activities soon made him a key figure in Montana Democratic circles. As chairman of the first two constitutional conventions, he was a leader in bringing statehood to Montana in 1889. His ambition to become one of the state's first senators was thwarted by the determined opposition within his party led by Marcus Daly, also a copper tycoon. Eventually Clark succeeded in obtaining a U.S. senatorial seat for the term of 1901–1907 through election by the Montana legislature.

For many years Clark gathered a large collection of paintings and other art objects, which he established in his New York City mansion. He gave this collection in his will to the Metropolitan Museum of Art on condition that the museum keep it as a separate group. When the museum refused to meet this condition, the collection was placed in Washington, D.C.'s Corcoran Gallery.

A man of contradictions, Clark was coldly practical in political and financial matters yet still a person of refined and fastidious tastes. He died in New York City on March 2, 1925.

COURTNEY ROBERT HALL
*Queens College, City University of New York*

## CLARK ART INSTITUTE,

a museum in Williamstown, Mass. Founded in 1950, the museum was incorporated as the Sterling and Francine Clark Art Institute in 1953 and opened to the public in 1955. To the original neoclassical-style building were added a separate service building (1964) and a red granite wing (1973), which houses five galleries, an auditorium, offices, and a library that serves the public and the Williams College Graduate Program in the History of Art, administered jointly with the Clark.

The institute has an outstanding collection of French impressionist paintings, including works by Renoir, Monet, Pissarro, Degas, and Sisley. Earlier paintings include Ugolino da Siena's seven-part altarpiece, Piero della Francesca's *Virgin and Child Enthroned with Four Angels* (c. 1460–1470), and Jean-Honoré Fragonard's *The Warrior* (c. 1769). A small but significant American collection includes works by Winslow Homer, John Singer Sargent, Frederic Remington, and Mary Cassatt.

Among other holdings are one of the finest collections of English domestic silver in the United States and a fine collection of drawings, with examples by Dürer, Rubens, Watteau, Fragonard, and Degas.

## CLARK UNIVERSITY,

a private, nonsectarian, coeducational institution of higher education in Worcester, Mass. It was founded as a graduate school for men in 1887 from an endowment provided by American philanthropist Jonas Gilman Clark to make graduate training in the sciences available in New England at low cost. Clark College, an undergraduate school for men, was established in 1902; a coordinate women's college opened in 1942. Graduate schools in geography (1921) and business administration (1941) were added to widen the university's sphere of interest.

A number of federally sponsored research projects, particularly in science, are carried out at the university. A cooperative doctorate in biomedical science is offered with Worcester Polytechnic Institute. The university has two special institutes, the George Perkins Marsh Institute, devoted to the study of global environmental changes; and the Jacob Hiatt Center for Urban Education, a collaboration of private donors, public schools, and higher education, designed to serve as a national model for public school reform.

## CLARKE, Arthur Charles

(1917–     ), English writer best known for his science fiction, which is distinguished for its scientific plausibility. Clarke was born in Minehead, Somerset, England, on Dec. 16, 1917. He joined the Royal Air Force in 1941 and was placed in charge of the first ground control approach radar unit. In 1945, in a magazine article, he proposed a synchronous communications satellite, a concept not realized until 1967. After World War II, Clarke earned a bachelor's degree from the University of London. In 1949, while a graduate student there in mathematics and astronomy, he was named assistant editor of the journal *Science Abstracts*. A year later he became a full-time writer. *The Sands of Mars*, his first novel, appeared in 1951. He produced numerous works of fiction and nonfiction, some with collaborators and some under the pseudonyms E. G. O'Brien and Charles Willis. In the 1980s he hosted two science fiction television series.

Clarke's best-known novel is probably *2001: A Space Odyssey* (1968), written with Stanley Kubrick as they developed their script for the movie of the same name, itself inspired by Clarke's story "The Sentinel." Sequels were published in 1982 (filmed in 1984) and 1988. *Childhood's End* (1953) and *Rendezvous with Rama* (1973) are among Clarke's other important works.

## CLARKE, Charles Cowden

(1787–1877), English writer and Shakespearean scholar. He was born in Enfield, Middlesex, England, on Dec. 15, 1787. Through John Keats, a pupil at Clarke's father's school, he met Shelley, the Lambs, William Hazlitt, Leigh Hunt, and Vincent Novello. Clarke was a bookseller and publisher in London for a brief time and then joined Novello's son Alfred in music publishing. In 1828 Clarke married Alfred's sister Mary.

Clarke wrote many articles on art and literature and lectured widely on Shakespeare and other literary figures. He and his wife, who compiled the *Complete Concordance to Shakespeare* (1844–1845), collaborated on an annotated edition of Shakespeare with a glossary and chronological table (1864), to which they added a biography (1869). The book was republished as *Cassell's Illustrated Shakespeare* (1886). Their *Shakespeare Key* appeared in 1879, after Clarke's death, in Genoa, Italy, on Mar. 13, 1877.

## CLARKE, James Freeman

(1810–1888), American Unitarian clergyman. He was born in Hanover, N.H., on April 4, 1810, and graduated from Harvard College in 1829. In 1833 he graduated from Harvard Divinity School and received his ordination. Clarke was minister of a Unitarian church in Louisville, Ky., from 1833 to 1840. In 1841 he organized the Church of the Disciples in Boston, which he served continuously (except for a period of ill health in the 1850s) until his death, in Boston, on June 8, 1888.

Clarke was a charter member of the Transcendental Club. He was a member of the Board of Overseers of Harvard and a lecturer on religions at the Harvard Divinity School. A theologian with reformed Calvinistic tendencies, he wrote prolifically. His most important work was *Ten Great Religions* (2 vols., 1871, 1883). Clarke supported movements against slavery and for temperance and woman suffrage.

JAMES H. SMYLIE*
*Union Theological Seminary, Richmond, Va.*

**CLARKE, Jeremiah** (c. 1673–1707), English composer and organist. He began his career as a boy chorister under John Blow at the Chapel Royal (St. James's, London). He was organist of Winchester College from 1692 to 1695 and then of St. Paul's Cathedral. In 1703, Clarke succeeded Blow as master of the choristers of St. Paul's, and in 1704 he was appointed joint organist of the Chapel Royal. On Dec. 1, 1707, Clarke committed suicide, in London, probably as the consequence of a disappointment in love.

The best-known of Clarke's compositions is the famous Trumpet Voluntary in D Major (also called *The Prince of Denmark's March*), which for many years was wrongly ascribed to Henry Purcell. Clarke also composed church services and anthems, choral works, instrumental music, and secular songs and dialogues for a dozen little-known plays. His church music, reminiscent of Purcell's, is transitional between the styles of the Restoration and the early 18th century.

**CLARKE, John** (1609–1676), American Baptist clergyman. He was born in Westrope, England, on Oct. 8, 1609. He arrived in Boston in 1637 just in time to assume a role of leadership among those whom the General Court had branded Antinomians. Clarke left Massachusetts to settle in Rhode Island in 1638. In 1644 he helped to found Newport and became the pastor of the second Baptist church in America.

On a secret visit to a dying friend in Lynn in 1651, Clarke was arrested by Massachusetts authorities, charged with unauthorized preaching, disrespect in an assembly of worship, and denying the lawfulness of the baptism of infants. He was sentenced to be fined or whipped but escaped whipping when friends paid his fine.

In 1651, Clarke accompanied Roger Williams to England to protect the interests of Rhode Island. Williams was forced to return to America before obtaining full confirmation of Rhode Island's charter, but Clarke remained in England and obtained a royal charter from Charles II.

In 1664, Clarke returned to Rhode Island, where he continued to serve as a minister. He served as deputy governor of the colony, helped to codify laws, and contributed to securing liberty of conscience in religious matters. He died at Newport on April 28, 1676.

JAMES H. SMYLIE
*Union Theological Seminary, Richmond, Va.*

**CLARKE, John Hessin** (1857–1945), American judge, who as a justice of the Supreme Court often concurred in dissent with Justices Oliver Wendell Holmes and Louis D. Brandeis. Clarke joined Holmes and Brandeis in dissenting opinions in social welfare and civil liberties cases, such as those invalidating child labor laws, and cases upholding sedition convictions of radicals and pacifists in World War I.

Clarke was born in Lisbon, Ohio, on Sept. 18, 1857. After graduating from Western Reserve University in 1877, he practiced law until 1914, when President Wilson appointed him to the district court for northern Ohio. In 1916 he was elevated to the Supreme Court, reportedly on the advice of Brandeis, to succeed Justice Charles Evans Hughes. Harassed by the hostility of Justice James McReynolds and grieved by his sister's death, Clarke resigned in 1922. He died in San Diego on March 22, 1945.

LEO PFEFFER, *Author, "This Honorable Court"*

**CLARKE, Marcus Andrew Hislop** (1846–1881), Australian author, whose best-known work is *For the Term of His Natural Life* (1870), a powerfully realistic novel of life in a Tasmanian penal colony. Clarke was born in London on April 24, 1846. He emigrated to Australia in 1863, shortly after his father's death. In 1865 he began writing sketches for the *Australian Magazine*, and in 1867 he joined the staff of the Melbourne *Argus*. His first novel, *Long Odds*, was published in 1868. From 1870 until his death Clarke was employed by the Melbourne Public Library. His other works include the novel *'Twixt Shadow and Shine* (1875). Clarke died in Melbourne on Aug. 2, 1881.

**CLARKE, Samuel** (1675–1729), English philosopher and theologian. He was born in Norwich on Oct. 11, 1675. Clarke was a disciple of Sir Isaac Newton, but he became a distinguished philosopher in his own right and one of the most learned clergymen of his age. His Boyle Lectures delivered at Oxford in 1705 and 1706 and printed under the title *The Being and Attributes of God, the Obligations of Natural Religion, and the Truth and Certainty of the Christian Revelation* won him immediate fame. In 1706 he was made a chaplain to Queen Anne. On Newton's death in 1727 he declined an offer to succeed him as master of the mint. Clarke died in London on May 17, 1729.

Clarke's theological writings aroused controversy, for orthodox churchmen thought him little better than the Deists, while the latter were offended by his criticism of Anthony Collins' *Discourse of the Grounds and Reasons of the Christian Religion*. Clarke's *Scripture Doctrine of the Trinity*, published in 1712, brought upon him an accusation of Arianism and stirred Daniel Waterland, the most prominent theologian of the times, to reply in *A Vindication of Christ's Divinity*. Clarke was obliged to affirm his orthodoxy to avoid censure by the Convocation of the Church of England.

POWEL MILLS DAWLEY
*The General Theological Seminary, New York*

**CLARKSBURG** is an industrial city in north-central West Virginia, 92 miles (148 km) northeast of Charleston, on the West Fork of the Monongahela River. It is the seat of Harrison county. The city is a trade and distribution point for an area rich in coal, gas, and oil and is a manufacturing center. A major industry is the manufacture of glass products, including plate and window glass, containers, mirrors, marbles, and novelties. Other products are carbon electrodes, electric motors, oil well machinery, processed zinc, tile, cement, caskets, and evaporated milk. Clarksburg is the seat of a U. S. veterans hospital. It was the birthplace of Thomas Jonathan (Stonewall) Jackson, the Confederate general.

Clarksburg, named for the explorer George Rogers Clark, was settled in 1765. It was originally part of the state of Virginia and was incorporated as a town by the general assembly of Virginia in 1795. It was a Union supply base in the Civil War. Clarksburg was incorporated in 1897 when the first mayor was elected. It adopted a council-manager government in 1921. Population: 16,743.

CLINTON F. ISRAEL
*Clarksburg Public Library*

**CLARKSDALE,** klärks′dāl, a city located in northwestern Mississippi, 135 miles (217 km) northwest of Jackson. The seat of Coahoma county, Clarksdale is situated in the rich cotton lands of the Mississippi Valley, and is an important cotton-processing and shipping center. Leading manufactures are farm machinery, conveyor systems, engine heaters, innertubes, furniture, and cottonseed, dairy, and bakery products. The city is governed by a mayor and commissioners. Population: 20,645.

**CLARKSON,** klärk′sən, **Thomas** (1760–1846), English antislavery agitator, whose role in the early stages of the British abolitionist movement was second only to that of William Wilberforce. Clarkson's work in researching and propagandizing the evils of the slave trade was both an indication and a cause of the growth of a humanitarian spirit in Britain.

Clarkson was born at Wisbeach, England, on March 28, 1760. After graduating from Cambridge in 1783, he entered an essay competition with an impressive indictment of the slave trade, took first prize, and found his life's work. Although Wilberforce became the principal spokesman of the antislavery forces in Parliament in the 1790's, Clarkson was the indispensable source of the data and propaganda that awakened an indifferent public. His research, carried on at a cost to himself of impoverishment and severe illness, contributed substantially to Britain's abolition of the slave trade in 1807 and of slavery itself in 1833. By the time the second of these measures was passed, Clarkson was old and tired, and the major initiative was provided by Henry Brougham, lord chancellor in the Whig government. However, Clarkson lived to see his life's work crowned with success. He died at Ipswich on Sept. 26, 1846.

JOHN W. OSBORNE, *Rutgers University*

**CLARKSTON,** klärks′tən, a city in southeastern Washington, in Asotin county. It is situated on the Snake River, opposite Lewiston, Idaho. The economy of Clarkston centers on farming, fruit growing, and timber operations. The city was founded in 1896 and was chartered in 1902. It has a mayor-council form of government. Population: 7,337.

**CLARKSVILLE,** klärks′vil, a town in southeastern Indiana, in Clark county, 102 miles (164 km) south of Indianapolis. It is across the Ohio River from Louisville, Ky. Clarksville is a commercial center. Grains and dairy cattle are raised nearby. The community was founded in 1784 by George Rogers Clark, American frontier leader. Government is by mayor and council. Population: 21,400.

**CLARKSVILLE,** klärks′vil, a city in northern Tennessee, the seat of Montgomery county. It is situated on the Cumberland and Red rivers, 40 miles (64 km) northwest of Nashville. Clarksville is a leading marketing center for dark tobacco. Its manufactures include snuff, cigars, cheese, rubber, flour, heating and air-conditioning units, garments, and footwear. It is the home of Austin Peay State University, a coeducational institution, founded in 1929. Fort Campbell, a permanent military installation, is 8 miles (13 km) from Clarksville. The city was founded in 1784 and is named for the explorer George Rogers Clark. Population: 103,455.

**CLASS,** klas. In all but the smallest and most undifferentiated human societies, there has always existed what modern social scientists call a "class system," a differentiation among men according to such categories as wealth, position, and power. At least in some rough sense, men have always been aware of differences between rich and poor, the mighty and the lowly, the lord and the peasant, and grievances over these differences have often been a cause of popular rebellion, as in the French and the Bolshevik revolutions and in minority-group agitation for equal rights. But in the modern world, under the impulse to be egalitarian, men are more cognizant of class systems than ever before, and much attention has been given to the scientific analysis of this subject.

**Development of Class Theory.** Karl Marx was the first great figure in the development of social science theory about class. Marx located the cause of class differences in the social structure itself, specifically in what he called "the relations of production" of any given society. Classes were determined according to who owned the means of production (employers) and who operated the means of production (workers).

This "economic" view of the class system was improved upon by the German sociologist Max Weber. He proposed a threefold model for analyzing class systems: *class,* representing a man's ability to gain profit on the market; *status,* representing the extent to which a man is highly evaluated and honored; and *power,* representing the degree of his influence over the actions of others. Unlike Marx, Weber proposed these types of "class" as somewhat independent of one another, although interacting.

More recently, American sociologists like Talcott Parsons have developed Weber's concept of status, stressing the importance of the evaluation of occupational roles as one basis for all class systems. The currently emerging theory of class—or social stratification, to use the modern term—is a clarification and extension of Weber's construction. This theory holds that men in every society are evaluated by their fellow men on a number of different structural bases. For example, they are evaluated in terms of the functional significance of their jobs (what is now called occupational prestige), in terms of their power to control others for both common and individual goals, in terms of their membership in some family or ethnic body (leading to much of what we now study as race and ethnic prejudice), in terms of their religious and ritual purity (particularly emphasized in the Hindu caste system), and in terms of their knowledge or education. All these and other types of evaluation, or class dimensions, are viewed according to the Weberian concept as somewhat independent, mutually interacting, and each as important in principle as every other.

**Modern Analytical Techniques and Conclusions.** Social scientists have improved our knowledge of both the dimensions and the structure of class stratification systems. It was formerly thought that all such systems were pyramidal in shape, with a few people on top in elite positions, a larger number in the middle, and the vast majority at the bottom. It is now seen that some stratification systems, particularly those in modern, highly differentiated societies, have increasingly larger proportions in the middle-ranking positions, while the elite group still remains a relatively stable proportion, and the proportion of those in lower-ranking positions is greatly decreasing.

Better measurement techniques have aided our understanding of class systems. Differences of power, for example, are more clearly established by two new measurement techniques. In the reputational technique, expert participants in a social system report their opinions on who holds how much power in that system. In the decisional technique, social scientists study the actual power decisions made on particular issues in particular social systems. The impressive findings of a recent number of extensive and intensive occupational research studies indicate that there is a great consensus on occupational prestige rankings both within a given society and between societies of strikingly different social type. For example, studies of about 30 developed and underdeveloped societies around the world have shown that jobs like those of military leaders are everywhere evaluated at much the same level, as are jobs like those of doctor, small shopkeeper, or small farmer. Moreover, as a result of more objective and precise techniques, there is now a better understanding of how to use "style of life" —the things that people possess or do that become symbols of their class position—as a measure of different dimensions of class.

**Class Mobility.** Social mobility, or the movement of an individual into a class position higher or lower than the one he or his father had, has also been the subject of much recent study. It is now seen that there is always some mobility in all societies, even in so relatively closed a society as the caste system of India. It also appears that there was a great deal more mobility in the estate type of societies, as in early modern Europe or the Chinese empire, than used to be recognized. Indeed, some scholars have gone so far as to suggest that there was as much mobility in those societies as there is today. Most scholars, however, feel that the greatest amount of mobility is to be found in modern societies. Most movement is, moreover, of small degree—a few levels up or down. There is, however, a small amount of mobility of a very large degree, all the way from bottom to top or vice versa. Even if such mobility is possible for only about 5% to 10% of the members of a society, as research indicates, the fact that this mobility exists is still very significant in its effects on that society.

It is evident that as modern societies become more structurally differentiated and more egalitarian or universalistic in their values, they are becoming more diamond-shaped in their stratification systems, and are permitting more mobility up and down. Utopian equality has not been achieved and cannot be, and there are new strains on societies, families, and individuals resulting from the new emphasis on equality and achievement. But in comparison with earlier systems, the new stratification systems are, on the whole, better understood and probably also more congenial to those who live in them. See also CASTE.

BERNARD BARBER
*Barnard College, Columbia University*

**Further Reading:** Barber, Bernard, *Social Stratification* (Harcourt 1957); Barber, Bernard and Elinor G., eds., *European Social Class* (Macmillan 1965); Collier, Jane F., *Marriage and Inequality in Classless Societies* (Stanford Univ. Press 1988); Keith, Nelson W. and Novella Z., eds., *New Perspectives on Social Class and Socio-Economic Development in the Periphery* (Greenwood Press 1988).

**CLASSICAL ARCHAEOLOGY.** See AEGEAN CIVILIZATION; GREECE—9. *Archaeology;* ITALY—7. *History;* ROME.

**CLASSICAL EDUCATION** is the study of the Greek and Latin languages and Greek and Roman literature. These subjects were part of the curriculum of Roman schools. During the Middle Ages the study of the Latin language continued, though Greek grammar and literature in both languages were neglected. In the Renaissance, interest in Greek and Latin revived, and study of the classics became a tradition of German and later English education. This tradition was carried to the American colonies and became established in the grammar schools and colleges there. The early entrance requirements of Harvard, for example, specified that a student be "able to read Tully [Cicero] or such like classical Latin author *ex tempore,* and make and speak true Latin in verse and prose, and decline perfectly the paradigms of nouns and verbs in the Greek tongue."

Classical studies began to lose their dominant position in the 18th and 19th centuries as vocational preparation and the study of the sciences gained importance.

**CLASSICAL LITERATURE.** See GREECE—11. *Literature;* LATIN—3. *Ancient Latin Literature.*

**CLASSICAL MYTHOLOGY.** See GREECE—14. *Religion and Mythology;* ROME, ANCIENT—*Religion.*

**CLASSICISM** is adherence to the qualities customarily associated with the literature, art, architecture, and thought of ancient Greece and Rome. It involves excellence, permanence, and values based on the Greek concept of life. This concept emphasized order and clarity of thought; dignity and serenity of spirit; simplicity, balance, and proportion of structure; and the union of subject with appropriate form. At the core of classicism are esteem for objectivity, rationality, and moderation, and distrust of subjectivity, emotion, and excess. But because classicism rests on imitation and the acceptance of objective standards, it may lack spontaneity and meaning and degenerate into excessive traditionalism and empty formalism.

The word "classicism" derives from the Latin *classicus,* a term used in Roman law to distinguish the highest category of taxpayers. In the 2d century A. D. the phrase *scriptor classicus* described writers who addressed the "fit though few," as opposed to the common reader. Thus "classicism" and the related terms "classic" and "classical" came to connote demonstrable superiority. "Classical" and especially "classic" may be applied to an object or period of excellence in any civilization.

"Classicism" also has the more limited meaning of the scholarly study of the history and culture of ancient Greece and Rome. In a still more restricted sense it may refer to a Greek or Roman expression used in later writing.

**Periods of Classicism.** Attempts to emulate Greek and Roman standards have characterized various eras of European culture. The Romans themselves copied the Greeks, and in the early Middle Ages Charlemagne tried to imitate the Romans. The Renaissance, beginning in the 14th century, was characterized by a widespread classical revival. The works of Greek and Latin authors were ranked above those of medieval writers and were referred to as "classics." The classicism or, more commonly, the neoclassicism of the 17th and 18th centuries was marked by a strict imitation of Greek and Roman models. Neoclassicism gradually faded with the rise of 19th century romanticism but was revived in the 20th century as part of the cultural diversity of the time.

**Basic Critical Documents.** Three critical documents are essential to an understanding of classicism. Aristotle's *Poetics* places a high premium on form, imitation, and regularity in all areas of art. Horace's *Ars poetica* emphasizes propriety, craftsmanship, polish, conscious balance, and decorum (particularly the relationship of the subject to its form or medium) in literature. Boileau's *L'art poétique* (1674), codified the principles of Aristotle and Horace into a set of rigorous literary rules and a theory of forms or genres defining epic, tragedy, comedy, ode, eclogue, elegy, satire, and fable.

**Literature.** The classical revival in literature was led by 14th and 15th century Renaissance Italian humanists, such as Petrarch, who collected classical manuscripts, and the Platonist scholar Ficino, who translated and interpreted Greek philosophy. English humanists, such as Ben Jonson, Francis Bacon, Dryden, and Pope, wrote in a classical style, as did the 17th century French playwrights Molière, Corneille, and Racine. Later, classicism deeply influenced the 18th century German dramatists Goethe and Schiller.

In the late 17th century, however, war raged between the "ancients" and the "moderns," a conflict that was continued in the 18th century by Friedrich von Schlegel, who defended classicism as an attempt to express the infinite in finite forms, and Mme. de Staël, who rejected classicism as sterile, rule-bound, and restrictive. Gradually, the more emotional, subjective romantic movement triumphed over classicism in the 19th century, but in the 20th century a reaction against romanticism by such writers as Remy de Gourmont, Ezra Pound, and T. S. Eliot resulted in a partial return to themes and attitudes of classical writers.

**Art and Architecture.** Renaissance classicism in art and architecture originated in 13th century Italy with such men as the painter Giotto and the sculptor N. Pisano, who broke away from Gothic symbolism to study the human form in the classic tradition. Classicism was further expressed in the paintings of Mantegna, P. della Francesca, and Raphael, and in the sculpture of Michelangelo. The buildings of Brunelleschi, who sought the ancient principles behind architectural design, and the detailed architectural drawings of Palladio also had a deep influence.

In the 17th century, neoclassicism swept Europe, guided by the theories of Boileau. The movement received added momentum and a scientific basis in the 18th century with the excavations of ancient sites such as Pompeii and Herculaneum, and with the writings of the German scholar J. J. Winckelmann, who saw in Greek art and architecture the perfect expression of form. Neoclassicism culminated in the Empire style of Napoleon, who tried to recreate his own "Roman Empire."

The neoclassical spirit in art was reflected in the sculpture of Canova, and in the paintings of Poussin, who set the academic style, of David,

the court painter of Louis XVI and Napoleon, and of Ingres, opponent of the romantic painter Delacroix. Neoclassical architecture was dominated by the palace of Versailles, built partly by Louis Le Vau, and by the great English houses and churches of Inigo Jones, Christopher Wren, and the Adam brothers. Many American public buildings and antebellum mansions copied first Roman and then Greek styles. Outstanding examples are the Virginia state capitol, designed by Jefferson, and the Bank of Pennsylvania by B. H. Latrobe. In the 20th century, art and architecture regained some of the classic sense of form through the late paintings of Cézanne, cubism, and the work of such architects as Mies van der Rohe.

**Music.** In music, the term "classical" is loosely applied to all compositions that are not "popular." More precisely, it refers to music composed in certain genres that have established criteria of form, such as symphonies, concerti, sonatas, fugues, and suites. In the strictest sense, it refers to the music composed between 1750 and 1820, and particularly to the "masterworks" of Haydn, Mozart, Beethoven, and Schubert. This music is characterized by objectivity, emotional restraint, simplicity, and consciously balanced form. In the 20th century a neoclassical movement in music developed as a reaction to romanticism and an alternate to atonalism. Old forms were revived and there was a tendency toward an objective style. Leaders of the movement were Prokofiev—notably his *Classical Symphony* (1916–1917)—Stravinsky, and Bartók.

C. Hugh Holman
*Coauthor of "A Handbook to Literature"*

**Further Reading:** Reinhold, Meyer, *Classica Americana* (Wayne State Univ. Press 1984); Weisinger, K. D., *The Classical Facade* (Penn. State Univ. Press 1988).

**CLASSIFICATION.** See Animal; Plant—6. *Kinds of Plants.*

**CLASTIC ROCKS,** klas'tik, are sedimentary rocks made up of detritus—that is, particles or fragments derived from older rocks. The detritus is hardened into rock by the pressure of overlying deposits and by the action of a cementing material such as calcite or silica. Conglomerate, breccia, sandstone, mudstone, and shale are clastic rocks. Nonclastic sedimentary rocks have a crystalline structure and are formed by the depositing of precipitates carried in solution.

**CLATHRATE,** klath'rāt, a type of inclusion compound in which one component (the "guest") is completely enclosed within the crystalline lattice structure of the other component (the "host"). The name is derived from the Latin word *clathratus,* meaning enclosed or protected by a grating or cage; it was proposed in 1948 by the British chemist H. M. Powell, who performed much of the fundamental work on the structure of clathrates.

The usual laws of chemical stoichiometry are not applicable in the formation of clathrates because the two components do not react chemically with each other. Clathration does not result from formation of chemical bonds; at most, the interaction between guest and host is a weak one involving van de Waals' forces or dipole attractions. In keeping with their complex nature, clathrates possess some properties of the host molecule, some of the guest molecule and some resulting from mutual effects of the two.

The primary factor determining clathrate formation is a spatial and geometric one. The guest molecule must not be so large that it cannot be accommodated in, nor so small that it can escape from, the enclosure formed by the crystalline framework of host molecules. In addition to possessing the proper shape, the guest must also be properly oriented at the moment the host molecules are crystallizing, or it will fail to be trapped within the cage, and empty holes will result.

The host molecules are linked together in such a manner that an open, rather than a close-packed, structure results. The guest molecules cannot escape from their positions in the lattice unless the strong forces holding the surrounding molecules together are overcome. Thus the presence of a volatile guest component in a clathrate cannot be detected by odor because none of its molecules can escape. However, the guest may be released by simple means such as heating, dissolving, or sometimes by merely grinding the clathrate, which is always a single-phased crystalline solid.

In 1849 the German chemist Friedrich Wöhler prepared the first clathrate compound, by the reaction of hydrogen sulfide (guest) with hydroquinone (host). Other investigators later found that hydroquinone formed similar compounds with certain volatile molecules such as sulfur dioxide, hydrogen cyanide, and hydrogen chloride, and with argon, krypton, and xenon, which are inert gases and rarely form chemical compounds. The hydroquinone clathrate compounds contain one molecule of the guest for each three host molecules.

Next in importance to the hydroquinone clathrates are the "gas hydrates," in which water is the host and the guests are gases or volatile liquids. These hydrates, which are crystals with low melting points, can be divided into two groups: those with small guest molecules, such as chlorine, hydrogen sulfide, or methane, have 6 guest molecules to 46 host molecules; and those in which the guest components are slightly larger molecules, such as methyl iodide, chloroform, or propane, contain 17 host molecules for each guest molecule. In both hydroquinone and gas hydrate clathrates the host molecules are linked together through hydrogen bonding. Clathrates may be formed with many other substances as hosts.

Clathrates are generally prepared by a relatively simple process—slow crystallization from a solution of the components. In cases where the guest component is a gas, high pressures and low temperatures may be required to maintain the maximum ratio of guest to host molecules.

Since clathrate formation requires a highly selective fitting together of guest and host, it has been used, particularly in the petroleum industry, to carry out separations, purifications, identifications, and analyses that are difficult to accomplish by other means. For example, benzene has been purified from its major contaminant, thiophene, by using the method of selective clathration.

GEORGE B. KAUFFMAN
*California State College at Fresno*

**CLAUBERG,** klou'berkh, **Johann** (1622–1665), German philosopher of the Cartesian school. He was born in Solingen, Westphalia, on Feb. 24, 1622. During his studies at Groningen, Paris, Saumur, and Leiden, he was gradually converted from Aristotelianism to the new philosophy of Descartes. From 1649 to 1651 he was professor of theology and philosophy at the Calvinist university at Herborn, Nassau. From 1651 he taught philosophy at the Calvinist gymnasium in Duisburg; when the school became a university in 1655, he was made its rector. He died in Duisburg on Jan. 31, 1665.

In *Defensio cartesiana* (1652) and *Initiatio philosophi* (1655), Clauberg defended the Cartesian philosophy against attacks by Aristotelians. In *Ontosophia nova, quae vulgo metaphysica* (1660) he discarded Aristotle's empirical theory of knowledge for Descartes' theory based on initial doubt and intuition.

**CLAUDE,** klōd, **Georges** (1870–1960), French engineer, who is best known for his work on the technology of gases. Claude was born in Paris on September 24, 1870. He studied under Arsène d'Arsonval and became interested in the work of his teacher on the technology of gases. In 1896 he discovered the relative safety of handling acetylene in acetone solution. Independently of the German engineer Carl von Linde, Claude devised a method for making liquid air, which he also used as a coolant to separate hydrogen from illuminating gas. This hydrogen was needed in the synthesis of ammonia, for which he demonstrated the advantage of using pressures of 1,000 atmospheres instead of the usual 200 atmospheres.

Claude's discovery that an electric discharge in an inert gas produces light marked the beginning of neon lighting and made Claude a wealthy man. It was quite different with his attempts to drive turbines by using the difference in temperature between surface and deep ocean waters, which proved a costly failure.

In 1945 he was convicted of collaborating with the enemy during the German occupation of France and imprisoned, but he was released in 1949 on petition of his many friends. He continued his scientific work in retirement until his death at St.-Cloud on May 23, 1960.

EDUARD FARBER
*Editor of "Great Chemists"*

**CLAUDE LORRAIN,** klōd lô-raN' (1600–1682), French painter, whose idealized landscapes of the Roman countryside have a grandeur, harmony, and beauty inspired by Greek mythology and antique bucolic poetry. His serenely balanced compositions are magnificently suffused in an all-pervading light. The tiny mythical or Biblical figures that appear in his paintings in no way compromise his real subject, which is the landscape.

**Life.** Claude Lorrain, or Le Lorrain, was born Claude Gellée (Gelée) in Chamagne, in the French part of Lorraine, for which he was named. He was said to be a poorly educated, simple man. By 1620 he had moved to Rome, where he lived for most of his life. His principal master was Agostino Tassi, a painter of landscapes. About 1635, Claude passed quite suddenly from relative obscurity to celebrity, with such patrons as Pope Urban VIII and King Philip IV of Spain, and by 1634 he had become so famous that his works were being forged. From that period on, he kept the *Liber veritatis*, six books of detailed drawings of his completed works that are

CLAUDE LORRAIN:
*The Embarkation of
the Queen of Sheba*
(painted in 1648).

still used to verify the authenticity of his work. Claude died in Rome on Nov. 21, 1682.

**Style.** Claude's style owes relatively little to his masters and much to the classicist and realist reforms of mannerism that were then taking place in Rome. The clarity and monumentality of his compositions derive largely from the classical landscapes of Annibale Carracci and Domenichino, and his lighting owes much to the German Adam Elsheimer, who applied the realistic, dramatic light (chiaroscuro) of Caravaggio to landscape. Claude preferred three basic kinds of scenes—mountains and valleys, harbor views, and coastal scenes combining sea and land. His style evolved from an early period in the 1630's, in which he used solid forms, strong colors, and a powerful, raking light; through a middle period, beginning about 1640, of severely balanced landscapes (especially notable in this time are the harbor scenes seen against sunrise or sunset); to the style of his late maturity and old age—spectacular views that are shown in a reverberant light.

**Works.** Among Claude's best-known masterpieces are *The Mill* (1631; Boston Museum of Fine Arts); *Harbor in Mist: The Embarkation of Ulysses* (1646; Louvre, Paris); *Pastoral Landscape* (1647; Metropolitan Museum of Art, New York City); *Seaport: The Embarkation of the Queen of Sheba* (1648) and *Landscape: Hagar and the Angel* (1668; both in the National Gallery, London); and *The Rest on the Flight into Egypt* (1661; Hermitage, Leningrad).

Claude's work lacks the intellectual character and the severe ordering of the paintings of his friend, the great French classicist Nicolas Poussin. It has, nevertheless, an immediately appealing, poetic quality as contrasted with the stoical power behind Poussin's work. Claude's paintings were among the most popular models used by landscape painters until the middle of the 19th century.

GUY WALTON
*New York University*

**CLAUDEL,** klō-del', **Paul** (1868–1955), French dramatist, poet, essayist, and diplomat, who ranks among the outstanding men of letters of the 20th century and among the most eminent contemporary Catholic authors. All his literary work was inspired by his vision of the world as a harmonious concert celebrating God. The splendid imagery and impassioned rhetoric of his cosmic lyricism raise his work far above the timid poetry and realistic, worldly, and often joyless theater of his day. Claudel, the impassioned poet, was also a master of lucid prose in his prolific correspondence and in essays on literature, music, religion, and foreign countries.

**Early Years.** Claudel was born Aug. 6, 1868, in Villeneuve-sur-Fère in the province of Champagne. His father was a minor official of peasant descent, and Claudel himself always retained a solid earthy attitude. He made a brilliant record at the Lycée Louis-le-Grand in Paris, and all his life he remained close to the Greek and Latin classics. As a manifestation of his ardent, rebellious temperament, which he instinctively sought to discipline, Claudel revolted in his late teens against the petty, irreligious lives of Parisian intellectuals. In 1886, after reading the poems of the spiritually troubled Rimbaud, he attended a Christmas mass at Notre Dame, during which he felt himself invaded by a divine illumination. This was followed by four years of inner struggle that culminated in his conversion from a nonpracticing to a devout Catholic.

**Middle Years.** Claudel spent his professional life in the foreign service. In 1893 he was a consul in the United States, and in 1895 he was sent to China, where he remained 14 years. Despite his duties, he began to write. He revealed his romantic anguish in *Tête d'or* (1889), a tense, declamatory drama on a dying conqueror in a mythical land, who discovers pity and humility. *L'échange* (1901), about a rich, crude American and a poor, melancholy Frenchman who exchange wives, although logically strained, contains realistic moments and lofty poetic soliloquies.

In the early years of the 20th century Claudel composed his greatest works. Philosophical essays, such as *Art poétique* (1907), explained the world and poetical inspiration from a deeply Catholic point of view. *Connaissance de l'est* (1900; rev. ed. 1907), probably the finest short prose poems in French, was inspired by Claudel's insight into the scenery and people of China. His mystical lyricism is at its height in *Cinq grandes odes* (1910) and *Cette heure qui est entre le printemps et l'été* (1913; republished in 1931 as *La cantate à trois voix*). Written in "verset" (unrhymed lines regulated by natural breathing rather than formal meter), a form invented by Claudel under the inspiration of Rimbaud, these books resemble Biblical writing.

*Partage de midi* (1906; rev. ed. 1948), Claudel's masterpiece, is the most splendid French love tragedy since Racine. Set on an ocean liner and in China, it presents the conflict between love of man and love of God, a theme that dominated much of Claudel's work. The play reflects his personal experience of love for a married woman followed by harrying remorse and despair leading eventually to repentance and his own marriage. Another of Claudel's most important dramas, *L'annonce faite à Marie* (1912), laid in the late Middle Ages, develops the mystical theme of the self-sacrifice of Violaine to her sister's greed.

**Later Years.** From 1911 to 1921, Claudel held diplomatic posts in Prague, Frankfurt, Hamburg, and Rome and was minister in Rio de Janeiro and Copenhagen. Then he served as ambassador in Tokyo (1921–1927), Washington (1927–1933), and Brussels (1933–1935). In Tokyo he wrote his later masterpiece, *Le soulier de satin* (1929; rev. 1944), a long, elaborate drama of a 16th century Spanish conquistador who loves a married woman but finally renounces her and turns to God. Only after the play was triumphantly staged (1943) by Jean-Louis Barrault was the poet elected to the French Academy, in 1946. Claudel died in Paris on Feb. 23, 1955, and was honored with a national funeral.

HENRI PEYRE
*Yale University*

**CLAUDIAN,** klô'dē-ən, (370?–?404 A.D.), was a Latin poet, who is often called the last poet of classical Rome. Claudius Claudianus was probably born in Alexandria. By 395 he had left the city for the imperial court at Milan and Rome. There, in spite of the fact that his first language was Greek, his Latin poems in praise of the Roman general and minister Stilicho and of Honorius, the Emperor in the West, soon earned him a government post and a statue in his honor in the Forum of Trajan.

While most political poetry of the day was stiff and unbelievable, Claudian's poems were full of ardor and provide a valuable historical guide to the politics of the time, dealing with such matters as Stilicho's rivals and Honorius' marriage to Stilicho's daughter. Claudian spent nine years writing the 10,000 verses of his best work, *The Rape of Proserpine*, an epic that expresses his interest as a pagan in the pre-Christian religion of Rome.

**CLAUDINE,** klō-dēn', is the heroine of four largely autobiographical novels by the French author Colette (q.v.). They are *Claudine à l'école* (1900), *Claudine à Paris* (1901), *Claudine en ménage* (1902), and *Claudine s'en va* (1903). The Claudine books were written at the request of Colette's husband, an impecunious music critic and novelist, who published them under his pen name, Willy. A great success, the novels convey a sympathetic understanding of a charming, spontaneous, slightly silly girl and young woman.

**CLAUDIUS,** klô'dé-əs, was the name of members of the *gens Claudia*, one of the most illustrious and successful families in the entire history of Rome. Eminent statesmen, thoughtful reformers, victorious generals, and men of letters, as well as Roman emperors, traced their ancestry back to the founder of this *gens*.

According to a doubtful tradition, Attius Clausus came to Rome from the Sabine town of Regillus. In Rome he came to be known as Appius Claudius. He brought with him many clients, and he was given land in the state and patrician status. He was also personally enrolled in the Senate. This was the beginning of the *gens Claudia*.

The most famous member of the family in the early period was Appius Claudius the Decemvir, who led the 10-man commission that drew up the code of laws known as the Twelve Tables (451–450 B.C.). Supposedly the Decemvir aimed at establishing a tyranny and either was killed or committed suicide as a result of his failure. Much of the ancient tradition is hostile to the Claudii, who are often pictured as highly reactionary conservatives, the guardians of patrician privilege. However, this interpretation does not fit the program of the Claudii; the Decemvir's codification of the law was a popular measure helpful to the masses.

Perhaps the first individual to emerge clearly out of early Roman history was Appius Claudius, the censor of 312 B.C. He was called Caecus, meaning "blind," because he was said to have been struck blind for his opposition to the plebeians. However, his measures as censor were popular and included the start of construction on the Appian Way (Via Appia), the building of aqueducts, and the introduction of the lowborn into the Senate. Appius, long revered, was as an old man carried into the Senate where he delivered a speech against making peace with Pyrrhus of Epirus, the first speech recorded in Roman history.

Appius Claudius Caudex was the first to lead Roman troops beyond the Italian peninsula, when he commanded an expedition to Sicily at the beginning of the First Punic War (264 B.C.), and Appius Claudius Pulcher was instrumental in the political program of the reformers Tiberius and Gaius Gracchus. Quintus Claudius Quadrigarius was a Roman historian of the time of Sulla.

The emperors Tiberius (reigned 14–37 A.D.), Caligula (reigned 37–41), and Claudius (reigned 41–54) could all claim Claudian ancestry.

RICHARD E. MITCHELL, *University of Illinois*

**CLAUDIUS I,** klô'dē-əs (10 B.C.–54 A.D.), Roman emperor. His official full name as emperor was Tiberius Claudius Nero Germanicus. He was born at Lugdunum (modern Lyon, France), on Aug. 1, 10 B.C., the son of Drusus (the brother of Emperor Tiberius) and Antonia Minor. After the assassination of Caligula in 41 A.D., one of the members of the Praetorian Guard found Claudius hiding behind a curtain in the palace and hauled him off to be proclaimed emperor.

Throughout most of his life up to that time,

Claudius, who was the brother of Germanicus and Caligula's uncle, had been kept from public view by the imperial family. He suffered from a number of physical disabilities, including partial paralysis, stammering, slobbering, and limping. The emperors Augustus and Tiberius tried to conceal him, but Caligula allowed him to hold the consulship in 37 A.D. Because of his confinement, he was able to devote himself to study and became a remarkably learned man. He was particularly interested in history, biography, antiquities, and linguistics. He was the author of histories, now lost, of the Etruscans, the Carthaginians, and the reign of Augustus.

Claudius' reign was marred by the actions of his wives Messalina and Agrippina and by his hostile relations with the senatorial aristocracy. But he accomplished much that was good. He built an administrative bureaucracy around his freedmen, including bureaus for petitions, finance, legal decisions, correspondence, and records. Although the senators resented the influence of the freedmen, this reform did result in greater administrative efficiency.

In the field of foreign affairs, Mauretania and Thrace were added to the empire, and the kingdom of Herod Agrippa was incorporated as a province after Herod's death in 44 A.D. Above all, Britain was conquered and became a province. Claudius was generous in granting Latin rights or citizenship in the provinces. He constructed aqueducts in Rome and in the provinces, built many roads, and constructed a great new harbor at Ostia at the mouth of the Tiber.

But his wives and freedmen created many problems for him in Rome itself. Messalina was executed only after she publicly married another man in hope of making him emperor in Claudius' place. Her successor, Agrippina, successfully schemed to secure the throne for Nero, her son by a previous marriage, despite the fact that Claudius had a son of his own, Britannicus. Claudius eventually adopted Nero and permitted him to marry his daughter Octavia.

Because of senatorial discontent, there were a number of conspiracies against Claudius' life during his reign. According to ancient sources, Claudius executed many senators and equestrians. When he died, he was deified by the Senate, but this was a formality and the attitude of the senatorial aristocracy was one of contempt.

Claudius died in Rome on Oct. 13, 54 A.D. at the hands of his wife Agrippina. When she heard that he wanted to disinherit Nero in favor of Britannicus, she served him a dinner of poisoned mushrooms. He was succeeded by Nero.

ARTHER FERRILL
*University of Washington*

**CLAUSE,** a term in grammar denoting a single construction containing a subject and a predicate. In this basic sense a clause is the same thing as a "simple sentence" and is subject to the same difficulty of precise definition.

Some grammarians use the term "clause" for word groups containing some form of the verb other than one required for a predicate, and speak of "infinitive clauses," "participial clauses," and "gerund clauses," but the more general practice is to call these phrases. Since the idea of the clause is most useful for describing sentences that contain more than one clause, some grammarians use the term only in that context.

As parts of a sentence, clauses have the char-

acter either of a *main clause* (also called independent clause, head clause, coordinate clause, or principal clause) or of a *subordinate clause* (also called dependent clause, subclause, or included clause). A main clause is the essential matrix or leading utterance of the sentence and is not an expansion of any smaller grammatical unit (such as an adjective, noun, or adverb). A subordinate clause either expands a smaller unit, is the equivalent of a smaller unit, or both. Examples of subordinate clauses are:

> He likes the boat *that I bought yesterday.*
> He understood *what had been done.*
> *When she saw the mouse,* she jumped.

Unlike a main clause, a subordinate clause can often be replaced by, or serves the function of, a word or phrase identifiable as a certain part of speech. In the first example above, the subordinate clause is the equivalent of an adjective modifying "boat"; in the second example, the subordinate clause can be replaced by a noun or a noun phrase; in the third example, it can be replaced by an adverb. For this reason, subordinate clauses can be classified according to function as *adjectival, adverbial,* or *nominal (noun).* Such classification underscores their dependency upon the main clause.

Structural grammarians have contributed largely to understanding clauses by describing the patterns of intonation (that is, of accent, pitch, and pause) that mark clause boundaries in spoken language. The transformational grammarians have demonstrated how a finite number of independent clause patterns (kernel sentences) are involved in generating the infinite number of sentences than can be formed and understood.

ROBERT L. CHAPMAN
*Drew University*

**CLAUSEN,** klou'sən, **Jens Christian** (1891–1969) Danish-American botanist, who clarified relationships between and within species of higher plants. In particular, he studied the interaction of heredity and environment. His work influenced many of the concepts underlying plant classification and breeding.

In the early 1920's Clausen demonstrated varying degrees of genetic relationship between species and races of wild pansies (*Viola*), and thus helped to classify them. Meanwhile, Göte Turesson, a Swedish botanist, showed that wide-ranging species are normally composed of distinct ecological races, and H. M. Hall in California studied the differences between altitudinal forms of the same or closely related species.

Clausen joined the Hall group in 1931 and confirmed Turesson's findings. He and his collaborators also showed that ecologic races differ widely in their capacity to survive in different climates, and that they vary in the degree to which they can be modified. These modifications are temporary and reversible and are limited in degree by heredity. He concluded that racial characteristics, including fitness for survival, are inherited through systems of partially linked genes. This provides for the evolution of new races and species through natural selection.

Clausen was born in North Eskilstrup, Denmark on March 11, 1891, and educated in Denmark. He was on the staff of the Carnegie Institution of Washington, Stanford, Calif., from 1931 to 1956. He died on Nov. 22, 1969.

WILLIAM M. HIESEY
*Carnegie Institution*

**CLAUSEWITZ,** klou′sə-vits, **Karl von** (1780–1831), Prussian general, who is considered the most original and influential writer on the subject of war. He was born in Burg, near Magdeburg, Germany, on June 1, 1780. His father was a retired Prussian officer. Clausewitz joined the army at 12, went to war at 13, and was commissioned at 15. In 1801 he entered the War Academy in Berlin. There he came under the influence of the great military reformer Gerhard von Scharnhorst, who materially aided his career. In 1806, Clausewitz participated in the war against Napoleon and was briefly a war prisoner. In 1810 he was attached as major to the Prussian general staff and was made military tutor to the Prussian Crown Prince. He also wrote frequently on military subjects and lectured at the War Academy.

When Prussia concluded an alliance with Napoleon in 1812, Clausewitz, in protest, joined the Russians against Napoleon. While in Russia, he was instrumental in bringing Prussia back into the anti-French coalition. Clausewitz participated in the wars of liberation against Napoleon. Despite his proven military ability, he held only staff positions. After several years of garrison duty, he was promoted to major general in 1818 and appointed director of the War Academy, where he served until 1830. He returned to field duty as chief of staff in a Prussian army of observation on the Polish border. While there he caught cholera, and he died at Breslau (now Wrocław, Poland) on Nov. 16, 1831.

**Writings.** While Clausewitz had a distinguished military career, he is best known for his writings. Most of these, including his famous book *On War* (1833), were published after his death. Most of his work was devoted to systematizing the revolutionary changes in warfare that had occurred during his lifetime. He gave added depth to his works by careful study of many campaigns.

Clausewitz was more than a military historian, however. In an effort to discover the general principles governing all warfare, he evolved a philosophy of war that is as meaningful today as it was when he wrote it. To Clausewitz, war is "an act of violence intended to force our opponent to do our will." He evolved the concept of absolute, unlimited war, in which victory depends on total annihilation of the enemy. In such a war, material strength and military skill are important; but equally important are psychological and moral factors. War is not an end in itself, moreover. It is, in one of Clausewitz' best-known definitions, "a mere continuation of policy by other means." Military leadership, in other words, must submit to political leadership.

The influence of Clausewitz' ideas on war has been widespread and lasting, particularly in his native Germany, where military and political leaders have often misunderstood or misused his theories. His basic book *On War* has been translated into every major language and has influenced the service manuals of most armies. Even the atomic revolution in warfare only enhanced interest in Clausewitz—new German editions of *On War* continue to be published. His lectures on "small war" were first printed in 1966 in the collection, *Schriften, Aufsätze, Studien, Briefe.* They have much to say to students of modern guerrilla warfare.

HANS W. GATZKE, *Yale University*
*Editor-Translator of*
*Clausewitz' "Principles of War"*

Karl von Clausewitz

**CLAUSIUS,** klou′zē-o͝os, **Rudolf Julius Emmanuel** (1822–1888), German theoretical physicist. He was born in Köslin, Pomerania (now in Poland), on Jan. 2, 1822. After studying at several German universities, he graduated from the University of Halle in 1848. He was appointed professor at the Imperial School of Artillery and Engineering in Berlin shortly afterward, and later he held professorships at Zürich, Würzburg, and Bonn. He died in Bonn on Aug. 24, 1888.

**Thermodynamics and Kinetic Theory.** Clausius is best known for having made, in 1850, one of the first unambiguous statements of the two laws of thermodynamics. In 1824, Sadi Carnot had stated the principle that perpetual motion is impossible and, using the caloric theory of heat, had deduced certain relations that had been verified experimentally. However, James Joule had subsequently shown that the caloric theory was incorrect and thus threw doubt on all of Carnot's work. Clausius was the first to recognize that two independent principles were involved; instead of the single "law of heat" (the conservation of caloric) there were two laws, the equivalence of heat and energy (first law) and the impossibility of heat passing spontaneously from a colder to a warmer body (second law). It required great confidence to take the logical step of replacing the single law by two, of daring to say that nature was not as simple as had been thought.

Clausius reworked the older calculations, deducing the correct form of the relation between the vapor pressure and latent heat of any substance, a relation known as the Clausius-Clapeyron equation. In 1865 he defined a new quantity, entropy, since proved one of the most important of physics. It is now known that the entropy of substances is a measure of the disorder of randomness of their molecular movements or arrangements. Clausius eventually stated the laws of thermodynamics in this way: the energy of the universe is a constant while its entropy always increases.

Before about 1850 the great majority of scientists believed that atoms or molecules in gases were essentially static, arranged in a crystalline lattice but repelling one another because of the presence of the caloric. This static repulsion was thought to produce the pressure of the gas. When the caloric theory had to be abandoned, the theory of gases also had to be revised. The first steps were taken by Joule who adapted an unpopular theory that the molecules of a gas were in rapid motion in straight lines, moving at about the speed of sound, hitting the walls of the containing vessel and rebounding. These impacts produced the pressure. This dynamic theory was communicated to the German chemist A. Krönig and then to Clausius. Clausius refined many of the details, proposing that molecules were spinning on their own axes, an assumption that allowed him to calculate specific heats, although this particular suggestion ran into difficulties that remained unresolved till the advent of quantum theory.

It was not easy for this new kinetic theory to explain why gases diffused through one another much more slowly than the calculated speed of the molecules themselves. In 1858, however, Clausius saw that any molecule would only travel a short distance (the "free path") before it collided with another molecule and was deflected. Thus, a molecule might travel backward almost as often as forward, diffusing slowly. He worked out the distribution law for the free paths, the relation of the mean free path to the then unknown size of the molecules and to the diffusion coefficient. In 1865, J. Loschmidt was able to use Clausius' equations to interpret measurements of diffusion coefficients of several gases, together with crude estimates of the densities of the solids or liquids that they might condense to (though they had not yet been liquefied), and in this way made the first reliable estimates of the sizes of molecules.

Clausius also enunciated the virial theorem relating the average kinetic energy of a molecule to the forces acting on it. Later, van der Waals used this theorem to work out his equation of state for imperfect gases.

**Electrolytes and Dielectrics.** The molecular motions in electrolytes—solutions of salts that conduct electricity—were also reinterpreted by Clausius. Previously, it had been assumed that the molecules of salt existed as units inside the solution, and only when current was flowing were the molecules torn apart into positive and negative ions. Clausius realized that this was wrong, for the solution would then conduct electricity only if the potential difference exceeded a certain minimum threshold value, whereas solutions always obey Ohm's law. He proposed instead that the molecules were broken into parts that continually exchanged with one another, even when no current was passing. This is very close to our modern ideas of electrolytes, though the theory did not find favor for some years.

Clausius also worked out a theory of solid dielectrics, based on a simple model of atoms as polarizable spheres embedded in an insulating medium. The relation between molecular polarizability and the dielectric constant is called the Clausius-Mossotti equation.

E. MENDOZA
*University College of North Wales*

**Further Reading:** Day, W. A., *A Commentary on Thermodynamics* (Springer-Verlag 1987).

**CLAUSSEN,** klou'sən, **Sophus Niels Christen** (1865–1931), Danish writer. He was born in Helletoft, on the island of Langeland, on Sept. 12, 1865, the son of a peasant who served for 30 years in the Folketing (Parliament). Claussen received a classical education in Copenhagen, later traveled in Italy, and lived for many years in France.

One of the greatest of modern Danish lyric poets, Claussen was deeply influenced by the French symbolists, especially Baudelaire and Verlaine. His poetry, published in his *Samlede Værker* (1910; *Collected Works*) and in several later volumes, is distinguished by its musicality, romantic imagery, and elegant form. It expresses a pagan and sensual joy in life and in nature. Claussen also wrote short stories dealing with provincial town life, books recording his impressions of Paris and Italy, translations of Shelley, Heine, and Baudelaire, and philosophical essays. He died in Gentofte, near Copenhagen, on April 11, 1931.

**CLAUSTROPHOBIA,** klô-strə-fō'bē'ə, is a morbid fear of small, confined, closed spaces. In the early part of the 20th century, physicians and psychologists favored technical names for numerous fears or phobias, but the more recent trend has been to drop the technical jargon and simply to state what is the object of the individual's fear. A phobia is a morbid, recurring fear that appears to be unwarranted by actual circumstances. Whereas formerly the style was to speak of "acrophobia," the same condition is now called "phobia of high places." Phobia about crossing water was formerly called by the technical term "gephyrophobia." One of the few terms that has survived is claustrophobia.

The individual suffering from claustrophobia becomes very tense and anxious whenever he is in a small room or any small, confined, closed space. He often experiences tightness in the chest, rapid pulse, and sudden weakness of the limbs, and there is a risk of fainting. The most common characteristic is that the individual feels the morbid fear even when he recognizes that it is unwarranted, that objectively there is no true cause for alarm. The individual recognizes that the symptoms arise from his own feelings and not from factors in his current environment. He is aware that factors within him trigger off fear whenever he is placed in very confined quarters. Accordingly, he feels helpless to avoid the reaction when he finds himself in some small enclosed space. His defense against the symptoms is to avoid small enclosed places.

According to generally accepted interpretations of claustrophobia, his fear of cramped spaces is a defense against a more general and diffuse fear. In the typical case, the patient has suffered some anxiety-provoking experience that he has later repressed. When the original experience or conflict is uncovered and revealed to the patient he often feels better able to tolerate the symptoms, although they will not disappear immediately. Sigmund Freud in his famous analysis of Hans (1909), a five-year old boy who had a phobia of horses, demonstrated that the phobia was a case of displacing fear to a less terrifying and more avoidable object. Little Hans was morbidly afraid of his father. Through play, he associated the father with horses and by displacement shifted his fear from his father to horses.

AUSTIN E. GRIGG, *University of Richmond*

**CLAVERACK,** kla'vər-ak, a town in southeastern New York, in Columbia county, 30 miles (48 km) south of Albany and 5 miles (8 km) east of the Hudson River. It is a residential community in a farming area that grows fruit and sweet corn.

Claverack is noted for its many fine colonial buildings, including the Van Rensselaer Manor House (1712), the Dutch Reformed Church (1767), and the Old Hudson County Courthouse, where in 1804 Alexander Hamilton argued a case in favor of freedom of the press.

Claverack was settled by Dutch immigrants in 1660. Organized as a town in 1778, it was the seat of Columbia county from 1786 until 1806, when it was superseded by Hudson. Government is by town meeting. Population: 6,401.

**CLAVICHORD,** klav'ə-kôrd, a small, rectangular keyboard instrument that was in use chiefly from the 16th to the 18th century. It was particularly popular in Germany, where it was valued both as an instrument in its own right and as a practice instrument for organists. It existed as early as the 14th century and perhaps even earlier. Its ancestor was the ancient Greek monochord, a one-stringed instrument on which a variety of pitches could be sounded with the aid of a movable bridge.

The clavichord's strings run parallel to the keyboard. When a key is pressed, a small metal blade, or tangent, rises and strikes the string and remains in contact with it as long as the player's finger stays on the key. The portion of the string to the left of the tangent is automatically stopped, so that a single string yields a variety of pitches, depending on the point at which it is struck. In early clavichords, a relatively small number of strings accounted for a large number of notes. However, as the range of the clavichord increased from a little more than three octaves to five octaves, more and more strings were added and devoted to single notes.

Two characteristic features of the clavichord that recommended it to early players were its sweet tone (notwithstanding its small sound) and its capacity for producing vibrato when properly struck.

One of the instrument's greatest exponents was C. P. E. Bach, who published numerous sets of sonatas and fantasias for the clavichord. His *Essay on the True Art of Playing the Keyboard*

(1753) was the greatest (and last) of clavichord instruction books. The instrument's delicate nature caused it eventually to succumb in popularity to the more robust piano, but it has enjoyed a modest revival in the 20th century.

SHIRLEY FLEMING
*Editor of "Musical America"*

**CLAVICLE.** See COLLARBONE.

**CLAW,** a hard, curved appendage at the tip of a toe or leg. In lobsters and scorpions, the claws, or chelae, are formed by the pairing of the last leg joint with a thumblike extension from the joint above. In spiders and insects, the claws are projections arising from the surface of the last leg joint. Most amphibians are clawless, but some have claws composed of thick, horny, elongated caps of epidermis at the tips of the toes.

The *true claw*, which is composed of a horny upper plate (the unguis) and a somewhat softer lower plate (the subunguis), is found only in reptiles, birds, and mammals. The claws of mammals like the cat are similar to those of reptiles and birds except that the subunguis is reduced in size and in its coverage of the toe.

A *nail*, such as that of man, consists of a broad, flat unguis and covers only the upper surface of the digit. The subunguis is reduced to a tiny ridge between the nail tip and the finger. A *hoof*, like that of a horse, is a broad claw completely covering the end of the toe. The subunguis is extensively developed and forms a pad on the bottom of the foot.

**CLAWSON,** klô'sən, is a city in southeastern Michigan, in Oakland county. It is 14 miles (22 km) north of Detroit, of which it is a suburb. Although the city is primarily a residential center, it manufactures automobile parts, tools, and dies. There is some diversified farming in the vicinity.

The area surrounding Clawson was settled as early as 1833. Clawson was incorporated as a village in 1920 and as a city in 1940. It has a council-manager form of government. Population: 12,732.

**CLAXTON,** klaks'-tən, **Philander Priestley** (1862–1957), American educator. He was U. S. commissioner of education from 1911 to 1921, a period of marked expansion of the activities of the Bureau of Education (later renamed office of Education).

Claxton was born in Bedford county, Tenn., on Sept. 28, 1862. He was educated at the University of Tennessee, at Johns Hopkins, and in Germany. After serving as superintendent of schools in North Carolina, in 1896 he became professor of pedagogy and director of the practice and observation school at the North Carolina State Normal and Industrial College. From 1902 to 1911 he was professor of secondary education at the University of Tennessee, and in 1906 he was made inspector of high schools.

After leaving the U. S. Bureau of Education, Claxton was superintendent of schools in Tulsa, Okla., from 1923 to 1929. From 1930 until his retirement in 1946 he was president of the Austin Peay Normal School in Clarksville, Tenn. Claxton also served as editor of the *North Carolina Journal of Education* and the *Atlantic Educational Journal*. He died on Jan. 12, 1957, in Knoxville, Tenn.

THE CLAVICHORD, forerunner of the piano, was a popular instrument from the 16th to 18th century.

Cassius Marcellus Clay, the son of a slaveholder, was the publisher of a militantly abolitionist newspaper.

**CLAY, Cassius Marcellus** (1810–1903), American abolitionist and diplomat. An early and firm believer in black emancipation, he supported Abraham Lincoln, who later appointed him U.S. minister to Russia. The son of a slaveholder, Clay was born at White Hall, the family estate in Madison county, Ky., on Oct. 19, 1810. A graduate of Yale in 1832, he was elected in 1835 as a Whig to the Kentucky legislature, serving until 1841. There he attracted attention for his emancipationist views. He denounced the scheme of Texas annexation as a plot to extend slavery, and in 1844 he campaigned for the Whig presidential candidate, his distant cousin Henry Clay.

On June 3, 1845, in Lexington, Ky., Cassius Clay began publication of the *True American,* an abolitionist weekly, but a mob seized the press on August 18. Although threatened with assassination, Clay revived the paper in Cincinnati, Ohio, and later published it as the *Examiner,* in Louisville, Ky. A volunteer in the Mexican War, he was captured early in 1847. In the 1848 election he campaigned for Zachary Taylor, and in 1851 he ran unsuccessfully for the governorship of Kentucky. He became a Republican in the 1850's. Expecting to be named Lincoln's secretary of state, he settled for the Russian post, which he filled in 1861 and 1862 and again from 1863 to 1869. He was instrumental in retaining Russian friendship for the Union, and he assisted in the purchase of the Alaskan territory. He was a violent, volatile man, and in his last years he barricaded himself at White Hall, where he died on July 21, 1903.

DAVID L. SMILEY
*Wake Forest University*

**CLAY, Cassius Marcellus, Jr.,** American boxer who became a Black Muslim and changed his name to Muhammad Ali. See ALI, MUHAMMAD.

**CLAY, Henry** (1777–1852), American statesman, whose masterly compromises on sectional issues helped pacify and preserve the nation during the troubled decades preceding the Civil War. In a long career in public service, he was a Kentucky legislator, a congressman and speaker of the House, secretary of state, and several times a senator, but the office of president of the United States eluded him.

Although he was one of the leading statesmen of his period, Clay had great faults as well as great virtues. Impetuous by nature, on occasion rash in action, he was sometimes selfish and arrogant as a Whig party leader. Abraham Lincoln and William H. Seward later agreed that his selfishness had been detrimental to the Whigs.

But Clay's defects were outweighed by other qualities and by important accomplishments. Dashing, magnetic, a marvelous orator in an age that esteemed oratory, he was a charismatic leader who numbered his devoted followers by the tens of thousands.

Clay's championship of Latin American freedom strengthened the prestige of the United States in that part of the world and laid the foundations for Pan-Americanism. As a Whig leader, he played an important role in establishing the two-party system that was so essential to the country's political stability. A gradualist, believing that change should come slowly, and a genius in the art of compromise, he did much to hold the Union together in the four decades before the Civil War. And his devotion to tariffs and internal improvements furnished a basis for the domestic program that kept the Republican party in power in the years after the war and encouraged the nation's economic growth.

**Early Life.** Henry Clay was born in Hanover county, Va. on April 12, 1777, the seventh of nine children. His father, John Clay, was a former Baptist minister turned farmer. His mother, Elizabeth Hudson Clay, was an industrious, kindly woman, endowed with great charm. The family was middle class and fairly well-to-do.

Clay grew up on the family farm in the stirring times of the American Revolution. Hanover county led Virginia in raising troops for the patriot army. Patrick Henry's oratory resounded throughout the countryside. Lt. Col. Banastre Tarleton's dragoons raided the family homestead. It was only natural that the gangling, towheaded boy, in the decade after the Revolution, should be filled with patriotic fervor. He was frequently to be found in the barn or in the cornfield diligently practicing the art of public speaking.

John Clay died in 1781, and 10 years later Elizabeth Clay married Capt. Henry Watkins and moved to Richmond. In 1792 the couple moved to Kentucky, but Henry remained in Richmond as a deputy clerk in the high court of chancery. There he acted as amanuensis to Chancellor George Wythe, who advised him to study law. Clay read law under the direction of Wythe and Attorney General Robert Brooke and, after a brief period of preparation, was admitted to the bar in 1797.

The young man was introduced to Richmond society and blossomed there. Six-foot-one, blond, with a large mouth, gray eyes, a ready smile, a quick wit, and an alert though not profound intelligence, he quickly acquired self-assurance. However, he looked beyond Richmond for a place to hang out his shingle. Kentucky, where land suits were many, was a paradise for lawyers, and Clay made his way there in the winter of 1797–

1798, settling in Lexington, then a town of some 1,600 inhabitants.

Clay found the early West congenial. He established a flourishing law practice, made friends who shared his political views, and on April 11, 1799, married Lucretia Hart, youngest daughter of Col. Thomas Hart, a wealthy merchant and land speculator. By 1805, Clay had acquired considerable property, as his profession brought him into close contact with the landed proprietors and the nascent industrial interests of the growing West.

**Rise in Politics.** A Jeffersonian-Republican by conviction and education, Clay took an interest in politics almost from his arrival in Kentucky. He urged democratization of the state's constitution and a gradual emancipation of slaves. Outspoken on national issues, too, he opposed the Allien and Sedition Acts, championed the Kentucky Resolutions, and campaigned for his party in 1800. In 1803 he was elected to the state legislature, where he sponsored internal improvements and defended a banking venture upon which his friends and relatives had embarked. In 1806, as counsel for Aaron Burr, he obtained that adventurer's exoneration by a grand jury in Frankfort, Ky., which refused to indict Burr on a charge of fomenting an expedition against Mexico. The defense of Burr on this occasion did Clay's reputation no harm, for Burr was then well thought of in Kentucky and Clay had undertaken the case only upon Burr's most solemn pledge of innocence. Clay never forgave Burr for his duplicity. (This early hearing is not to be confused with Burr's trial for treason and acquittal in Richmond, Va., in August 1807, in which Clay took no part.) In 1806, Clay went to the U.S. Senate to fill an unexpired term. His constituents sent him to the Kentucky legislature in 1807, where he was elected speaker of the House of Representatives.

A duel with a Federalist opponent, Humphrey Marshall, in which Clay was slightly wounded, added to his popularity. He was easily reelected to the legislature in 1809 and was chosen by that body to fill another unexpired term in the U.S. Senate, commencing in February 1810. There he stood for protection and declared himself an ardent expansionist. He opposed the recharter of the Bank of the United States in 1811, a stand that was popular with the speculators and state banking interests of Kentucky. On returning home, he was elected to Congress, and when that body convened on Nov. 4, 1811, he was chosen speaker of the House.

As speaker, Clay increased the power of the office and strengthened his own political position. In doing so, he played a prominent part in inciting the War of 1812. One of the Indian-hating, land-hungry "War Hawks," Clay appointed expansionists to important committee posts and by his speeches fomented the rising war fever. He sought vigorous prosecution of the war with Britain and at its close was one of the five American members of the peace commission that concluded a *status quo ante bellum* peace, the Treaty of Ghent. He returned home by way of England, where he helped to conclude a commercial treaty. When Congress reconvened in December 1815, he was reelected speaker.

**"American System."** Ambitious, impetuous, and eloquent, Clay proceeded in the years following the War of 1812 to develop what became known as his "American System." Domestic im-

THE GRANGER COLLECTION

HENRY CLAY in later life, from a daguerreotype portrait by the American photographer Mathew Brady.

provements at national expense, a protective tariff, a national bank, and finally cooperation with the South American patriots to enhance the U.S. position of leadership in the Western Hemisphere constituted the essence of his plan. Its development, he believed, would bring the United States "to that height to which God and nature had destined it."

This program was carried out in part. The national bank was reinstated, and the protective tariff became law in 1816. But Clay's plans for internal improvements at national expense were thwarted by the constitutional scruples of Presidents James Madison and James Monroe, and his demand for early recognition of the South American republics was countered by John C. Calhoun and John Quincy Adams, influential members of Monroe's cabinet. Furthermore, Clay earned Andrew Jackson's enmity by bitterly censuring him for his conduct in the Florida expedition of 1818, and he sorely tried Monroe's patience by a policy of carping criticism, which arose out of disappointment at not having been made secretary of state in 1817. These shortcomings and limitations were more than offset, however, by his brilliant handling of the Missouri Compromise (q.v.), which earned him the title of the "Great Pacificator."

During the 1820's, Clay became more and more closely identified with the nation's economic upper class. His Kentucky estate, Ashland, and other property gave him a tax assessment of over $72,000 in 1831. His views on financial matters during the panic of 1819 classed him with the creditor, antirelief interests. His legal practice identified him closely with the privileged classes. All this boded ill for his political ambition.

**The President Maker.** Clay sought the presidency in 1824, as did Andrew Jackson, John Quincy Adams, and William Harris Crawford, another member of Monroe's cabinet. Clay had the great disadvantage of running against another contestant from the West, Jackson. The latter emerged from the contest with more electoral votes than anyone else, but since no candidate had a majority the election was to be decided in the House of Representatives. Clay, who had run fourth, was no longer a candidate, but he was speaker of the House, and his influence, cast for Adams, was decisive. Adams thereupon made Clay secretary of state, and Jackson and his friends promptly raised the cry of "Bargain and Sale."

Before the election in the House, Adams and Clay in private conversations had disclosed to one another a fundamental harmony of views on public questions. There probably was a general understanding that Clay was to receive some kind of recognition for his support. That the "bargain" went further than this is doubtful, but the charge of "Bargain and Sale" persisted. Clay never ceased his efforts to demonstrate the purity of his motives in the 1824 election, and in 1826 he fought a bloodless duel with Sen. John Randolph of Virginia over the issue.

As secretary of state, Clay sought to broaden U. S. trade and extend American influence in the Western Hemisphere through participation in the Panama Congress of 1826. But the American delegates to Panama, who had to await confirmation from a reluctant Senate, arrived too late, and the role of the United States was ineffectual.

The political opposition to Clay's Pan-American policy was evidence of the crystallization of parties that took place during Adams' administration. Adams and Clay led the National Republicans, who summoned all believers in protection and internal improvements to join their ranks. The opposition, led by Jackson, Calhoun, and Crawford, was a heterogeneous collection of men and principles; but it could claim with some reason that the Clay-Adams party had inherited the mantle of conservative Federalism and that its own standard was the emblem of a revitalized Jeffersonianism which would cater to small farmers, workingmen, and the debtor class. "Democracy" was its battle cry and General Jackson, the hero of New Orleans, its candidate.

**Conservative Leader.** In 1828, Adams went down to defeat before Jackson, and the latter's uneasy coalition took over. Clay was despondent, but his ardent imagination soon began picturing his own elevation to the presidency in 1832. He denounced Jackson's use of the spoils of office and the veto power, and he championed internal improvements and protection. He returned to the Senate in 1831 and that same year was nominated for the presidency by the National Republicans. Jackson was renominated by what was coming to be known as the Democratic party.

Clay's bid for election was based partly upon the assumption that the West was as eager for internal improvements as it was for cheap lands, and that the South would accept protection if it were labeled "incidental." He was wrong on both counts. A further error was his decision to apply for a recharter for the Bank of the United States (q.v.). The bank was unpopular, and the bill for its recharter was promptly vetoed by Jackson in a ringing appeal to class hatred and sectional jealousy. The electorate responded with emphasis in 1832, Clay receiving 49 electoral votes to Jackson's 219.

Defeat did not quench Clay's ardor for public service. He was the guiding spirit in the passage of the Compromise Tariff of 1833, which put an end both to South Carolina's nullification of the tariffs of 1828 and 1832 and to Jackson's threats to use force against that state. The Compromise of 1833 added to Clay's reputation as a compromiser of sectional issues. See NULLIFICATION.

During Jackson's second term the Whig party, an amorphous combination of elements predominantly conservative in tone and nationalistic in outlook, came into being as the successor to the National Republicans. Clay was its logical leader, and from his position in the Senate he strove to marshal the Whig forces in generally fruitless attacks upon Jackson's fiscal policies. The Kentuckian was anxious to obtain renomination for the presidency in 1836, but the Whigs chose instead to follow the futile strategy of running several regional candidates against Martin Van Buren, Jackson's choice as his successor.

Reelected to the Senate in 1837, Clay once more led the assault upon Democratic measures, especially against Van Buren's independent treasury bill and against a proposed democratization of the government's land policy. The first effort wholly and the second partly failed, but they placed Clay more firmly than ever on the side of the vested interests.

In regard to the growing problem of slavery, Clay also displayed his conservatism. Despite a genuine moral repugnance to slavery, as a Kentucky slaveholder he was himself involved in the "peculiar institution." He had always espoused colonization of the Negroes, a harmless, because impractical, remedy for slavery. He hated abolitionism, believing it to be a force that was dividing the sections and leading toward civil war. While upholding the right of petition, he declared that abolitionist petitions should be rejected. He took a moderate position on the proposed annexation of Texas in the late 1830's. In these ways he tried to forestall the controversy over slavery and at the same time retain his popularity in both North and South.

Clay had hoped to be Van Buren's opponent in 1840, but Thurlow Weed, Whig boss of New York state, and other northern Whig politicians wanted a new candidate. To Clay's disappointment, the choice of the Whigs fell upon Gen. William Henry Harrison. The convention then chose John Tyler of Virginia, a supposed admirer of Clay and popular with the southern Whigs, as the vice presidential candidate. Clay supported this ticket, though laying down a program for action which showed his conviction that the leadership of the party still belonged to him.

Dissension among the Whigs followed Harrison's death on April 4, 1841. Tyler was an antibank, anti-internal improvements, low-tariff Southerner who had no desire to promote the American System or to allow Clay to usurp his prerogatives as the presidential leader of the Whig party. The Kentuckian was determined that he should lead and Tyler should follow. Under the circumstances, it was inevitable that Clay's program of a national bank, a higher tariff, and the distribution of land sales to the states should meet a cold reception at the White House. Tyler vetoed two bank bills sponsored by Clay, and a bitter intraparty conflict developed. Out of this Clay emerged as the leader of the Whigs. He resigned from the Senate early in 1842 to chart his course for 1844.

There was no significant challenge to Clay's nomination for the presidency in 1844, but a successful campaign was by no means assured. The question of the annexation of Texas was assuming great importance. In his famous

"Raleigh letter" of April 27, 1844, Clay came out against annexation "at the present time"; a similar letter by Van Buren (collusion has always been suspected but never proved) appeared on the same day. The intent of the letters was to prevent Texas from becoming a campaign issue, but Van Buren's letter cost him the Democratic nomination, which went to expansionist James K. Polk.

Clay was nominated on May 1, and the Whigs conducted a spirited campaign. Texas was the issue. The Democrats declared that Clay was opposed to annexation, and under the weight of this charge his Southern support began slipping away. Clay sought to explain his stand in the so-called Alabama letters, but in the North these letters produced a fatal drift of antislavery men from the Whig ranks. Polk was elected, and Clay gloomily retired to Ashland. There he remained, deeply disturbed by the growth of the sectional conflict over slavery and by the Mexican War, of which he thoroughly disapproved and in which his son, Henry Clay, Jr., was killed.

Clay wanted the Whig nomination again in 1848, but influential leaders in the party, both North and South, stood opposed. Gen. Zachary Taylor, of Mexican War fame, was nominated by the Whigs in June 1848. Resentful, Clay bowed to the will of the convention, but throughout Taylor's successful campaign he remained in retirement at Ashland.

**Compromise of 1850.** Clay returned to the Senate in 1849 to serve again in a time of crisis and division. The cession of California and the Southwest by Mexico at the end of the Mexican War had greatly heightened tension over slavery. Northern opinion demanded the exclusion of slavery from the new territories, and in the South a secessionist movement of formidable proportions developed. Clay believed that if the Union were to be saved, a great effort at compromise must be made. He formulated his plans, obtained Daniel Webster's promise of support, and at the close of January 1850 began his campaign.

In a series of resolutions, Clay discussed the principal questions agitating the country. His most important proposals were the admission of California as a free state, a more rigid fugitive slave law, and provision that the new territories south of 36°30′ should be organized without restriction as to slavery. During the spring and summer of 1850 he fought strenuously for this compromise. His plan, known as the Compromise of 1850, became law after Clay had gone to Newport, R. I., for a rest. Its immediate passage owed much to Stephen A. Douglas and the Democrats in Congress; but to Clay must go the credit for its conception and for arousing public opinion favorable to the measure. See COMPROMISE OF 1850.

**Illness and Death.** Clay was not to live much longer after the passage of the compromise. He spent the summer of 1851 at Ashland, where he made his will, providing for the disposition of his estate and the freeing of his slaves. Though dying of tuberculosis, he returned to Washington that fall and answered to the first Senate roll call. Thereafter he was closely confined to his room in the National Hotel, where he died on the morning of June 29, 1852.

**Place in History.** Clay was a conservative, and his appeal was essentially to the upper middle class. He sought by his American System to link East and West together under his leadership without alienating the South, but opposing sectional interests stood in his way. The protective tariff could not be made into an advantageous issue for a national party. The West preferred cheap lands to a general distribution of land revenues. The South had no more liking for internal improvements than for raising tariff rates.

Clay failed to achieve the presidency because of his mistakes of judgment and the machinations of professional politicians such as Thurlow Weed. But his services to his country in foreign affairs and in effecting compromises at times of national crisis—especially the Compromise of 1850, which history considers his crowning achievement—give him high rank among American statesmen.

GLYNDON G. VAN DEUSEN
*University of Rochester*

**Bibliography**

Colton, Calvin, *The Life and Times of Henry Clay*, 2 vols. (Garland 1975).

Curry, W. H., *Sun Rising on the West: The Saga of Henry Clay and Elizabeth Smith* (Crosby County 1979).

Eaton, Clement, *Henry Clay and the Art of American Politics* (Scott, Foresman 1962).

Peterson, Merrill D., *The Great Triumvirate: Webster, Clay and Calhoun* (Oxford 1987).

Schurz, Carl, *Henry Clay*, 2 vols. (1899; reprint, Chelsea House 1981).

Van Deusen, Glyndon G., *The Life of Henry Clay* (1937; reprint, Greenwood Press 1979).

Van Deusen, G. G., *The Jacksonian Era* (Harper 1959).

**CLAY, Lucius DuBignon** (1897–1978), American general, who directed the airlift that broke the Soviet blockade of the western sector of Berlin in 1948–1949. Born in Marietta, Ga., on April 23, 1897, Clay graduated from the U. S. Military Academy in 1918 and later taught engineering there. He was rivers-and-harbors officer for the Army Engineers and under Gen. Douglas MacArthur was engineering adviser to the Philippine government. Clay engineered the building of the Red River dam in Texas and in 1940 directed the Defense Airports Program, constructing 197 new airports and improving 277.

During World War II, Clay supervised Army procurement. His superior administrative ability was shown when he cleared the logistics bottleneck in Cherbourg in November 1944 and then, as deputy director of the Office of War Mobilization, expedited delivery of supplies to the front.

Clay was deputy (1945–1947), then military governor (1947–1949) of the U. S. zone in West Germany. He became a 4-star general in 1947. He earned a reputation as a stern, autocratic, and efficient governor, but his correspondence reveals sensitivity and warmth. He awakened Americans to Europe's need for a rehabilitated Germany. He personally ordered new elections and influenced greatly the decisions to form the Bonn government and to break the Soviet blockade of the sectors of Berlin occupied by the Western Allies. He supervised the airlift that delivered 1½ million tons of food and fuel to Berlin in a year by a constant shuttle of cargo planes. His book *Decision in Germany* (1950) is the definitive account of the U. S. occupation.

In 1950, Clay became chief executive of Continental Can Co., tripled its sales, and made it the largest U. S. packager. He was also finance chairman of the Republican party and helped Gen. Dwight D. Eisenhower to become president. Living in New York City, he did notable public service for both the federal and city governments. He died in Chatham, Mass., on April 17, 1978.

JOHN GIMBEL
*Author of "A German Community Under American Occupation"*

**CLAY** is a material of widespread occurrence. It is found on the earth's surface as a weathering product of rocks, in stratiform deposits that lie near the surface or at greater depths, and in massive distribution associated with mineral deposits. Sedimentary accumulations of clay occur on the floors of lakes and oceans, in certain glacial deposits, in desert basins and river deltas, in great windblown deposits called *loess,* and in a number of minor forms.

The term "clay" has different shades of meaning. Thus, in a nontechnical sense, common clay is a soft earthy material of very fine particle size—finer than sands or silts—that is derived from the earth's surface. In this use of the word there is little consideration of the material's mineral content or physical properties. Engineers look upon clay as a generally unsubstantial material in comparison with rock. When clay must be used to support foundations it is carefully examined (in advance of construction) for its load characteristics, plasticity, and water content, to determine its stability.

In a mineralogical sense, however, clay is defined as a rock composed of an aggregate of minute flaky or rodlike minerals. The atoms in the clay minerals are usually arranged in layer-like lattice structures, but sometimes in chain-like structures. For the most part the minerals are hydrous aluminum silicates, but different species may contain other elements, such as sodium, potassium, calcium, magnesium, and ferrous or ferric iron. The proportions of water, aluminum, and silicon within a species may also differ.

Commercially usable clays are important primarily because of their plasticity; that is, the wet clays can be molded into a shape that is retained when the clay is hardened by drying or baking. Depending upon the clay materials involved, clay is used as a filler to provide such properties as added firmness, strength, or moldability to a number of products such as plastics, rubber, paper, and paint. The general chemical inertness of clay is important in many applications, as are the low abrasiveness and the resistance to high temperatures of some clay minerals.

### KINDS OF CLAYS

The mineral constituents of clay may be considered in terms of four groups: kaolin, montmorillonite, hydromica, and palygorskite groups. Occasionally one of the minerals of these groups may occur in large, almost pure masses. More frequently, however, clays consist of mixtures of one or more clay minerals with grains of impurities such as quartz or feldspar.

**Kaolin Group.** The term "kaolin" derives from Kaoling, the name of a high ridge in Kiangsi, China, where clay was mined centuries ago. The term was long used for china clay and is now the name of an important clay mineral group. The kaolin group includes three minerals that have essentially the same chemical composition ($Al_2O_3 \cdot 2SiO_2 \cdot 2H_2O$) but that differ in crystallization: kaolinite, dickite, and nacrite. Anauxite ($Al_2O_3 \cdot 3SiO_2 \cdot 2H_2O$), another kaolin mineral, is similar in crystallization to kaolinite but contains more silica.

Halloysite and allophane are other members of the kaolin group. Halloysite, when freshly mined from an underground source, has the composition $Al_2O_3 \cdot 2SiO_2 \cdot 4H_2O$; it may exhibit a luster similar to that of glazed porcelain. On exposure to the atmosphere halloysite loses water and tends to crack and shrink. Allophane is a hydrous aluminum silicate that varies somewhat in composition and is essentially amorphous.

Several members of the kaolin group—dickite, kaolinite, and anauxite—exhibit 6-sided plate-like crystals when viewed by an electron microscope at a magnification of 12,000 times or greater. Halloysite crystals exhibit unusual hollow tubes with such a microscope, whereas nacrite is observed to form irregular flakes; allophane may be structureless or may exhibit small spherical pellets.

**Montmorillonite Group.** At least six clay minerals are recognized as members of the montmorillonite group. This group derives its name from a clay found in the excavation for a building in Montmorillon, France, in 1847. The chemical formula for montmorillonite clays has been given as $OH_{12}Al_4Si_6O_{16} \cdot nH_2O$, but the mineral may also occur in either sodium, magnesium, or calcium-bearing varieties; its physical properties may differ according to which ions are present. Other members of the montmorillonite group are sauconite (zinc-bearing), vermiculite (high in magnesium), nontronite (iron-bearing), and saponite and hectorite (magnesium-bearing).

In general, the members of the group exhibit flakelike forms under the electron microscope. Under the ordinary microscope thin sections of montmorillonite (which is frequently derived from volcanic ash) may show the remaining outlines of glass fragments of volcanic origin. Montmorillonite is also highly hydrous. Sodium montmorillonite, in particular, forms a colloidal gel that may change to a fluid if subjected to a sudden jar; it regains its gel character on standing. This behavior, described as *thixotrophy,* explains the tendency of large masses of such clay to generate landslides after water saturation following heavy rains.

**Hydromica Group.** Hydrous micas are among the most common of clay minerals, particularly in sedimentary formations. At the same time they are chemically the most complex and the most subject to mixture with other layer-lattice minerals, particularly montmorillonite and chlorite (see CHLORITE GROUP). It is believed that actual lattice interlayering of two such minerals may occur. In many instances the members of the hydromica group are described in general terms as the clay mineral *illite.* While this designation lacks precision, it avoids fine discrimination between different group members recognized as polymorphs (different crystalline varieties of the same chemical substance).

**Palygorskite Group.** A series of hydrous magnesium silicates has been designated as the palygorskite group. The principal mineral in the group is attapulgite, found in large stratified deposits in Georgia and Florida. Sepiolite, best known for the meerschaum variety found in Turkey and elsewhere and used in the manufacture of pipes, is also a member of the group. These minerals are considered to have chainlike atomic arrangements, unlike the layer lattices of other groups. Under the electron microscope attapulgite appears in minute rods, while sepiolite forms elongate tubes.

**Clay Minerals in Soil.** Few soils may be found in which clay minerals fail to form prominent constituents. In general, the clay minerals ordinarily reported in soils are illite, vermiculite, montmorillonite, halloysite, attapulgite, and kaolinite; it is also possible to find montmorillonite, chlorite, or vermiculite interlayered with illite. A great deal of the importance of a soil for agricultural purposes may depend upon this clay mineral content. Its value depends upon a number of other factors as well, such as its moisture, chemical constituents, porosity, organic materials, and even the microbiological organisms it contains. However, clay minerals form admirable hosts for these different factors.

## APPLICATIONS

**Ceramics.** One of the best-known applications of clay, and the one of greatest historical significance, is in the manufacture of such articles as pottery, chinaware, and various types of porcelain. When water is added to clay in proper amounts, the clay may be molded or turned on a potter's wheel to produce the desired form. The form is dried gradually to increase its strength; it is then fired at temperatures of about 2000° F (approximately 1100° C). A permanent, tightly bonded porcelain object results.

Kaolinite of high purity and suitable particle size is mined in the southeastern United States, in Cornwall, England, in Czechoslovakia, and elsewhere for use in high-grade ceramic ware. For other ceramic items such as brick, sanitary ware, tile, and heat-resistant refractory materials, the requirements of purity may not, at times, be as exacting. The clay mixtures used for porcelain and dinnerware contain kaolinite, *ball clay* (a darker, fine-grained clay), ground quartz, and feldspar, and should turn white after firing.

Refractory brick for furnace linings and other high-temperature applications may consist largely of kaolinite, frequently mixed with chromite, magnesite, or other natural materials. High-alumina mixtures may consist of bauxite mixed with some kaolinite. A particularly compact and fine-grained kaolinite known as *flint clay* is often used in refractories.

**Paper Industry.** Another major application of kaolinite is in the paper industry, where it may be used either as a filler or for coating paper. In this application the clay's purity is highly important, and particle size must be carefully controlled. Attapulgite has also been used in the preparation of special types of paper.

**Molding Sands.** The metallurgical industry employs clay mixed with sand to form molds that are used in casting molten metal. The molding material may be a natural sand-containing clay or a synthetically prepared mixture of quartz and clay. Water is added to the material in order to make it plastic and to add strength to the mixture. Sodium montmorillonite from Wyoming is one of the most effective clay materials used in molding sand. Other montmorillonite clays may also be employed; or molding sands may be bonded by plastic clays composed largely of kaolinite with small amounts of illite. The clays used in molding sands are mined on all the continents.

**Drilling Muds.** One of the most important applications of clay involves the drilling of oil wells. The wells almost universally are drilled with a rotary bit at the end of a long pipe or drill stem. Fluids forced through the drill stem emerge at the bottom of the drill hole through openings in the bit. These fluids, which contain clay in suspension, are referred to as drilling mud. They rise to the surface in the space between the stem and the wall of the hole. The rising motion carries rock cuttings torn loose by the drill bit to the top of the hole, where they are discharged.

Clay minerals such as attapulgite, sodium montmorillonite, and calcium montmorillonite are particularly useful in increasing the viscosity of a drilling fluid. They are much more effective than the local clays ordinarily encountered in near-surface formations. Large quantities of these clays are mined in Wyoming (montmorillonite) and in Florida and Georgia (attapulgite) and are shipped to areas of active drilling.

**Petroleum Refining.** Clays are important constituents of catalysts for refining petroleum and are used in the separation of gasoline, gas, and coke. Montmorillonite, kaolinite, and halloysite are the principal minerals involved. The precise procedures employed in the manufacture of catalysts are not ordinarily revealed by the manufacturers, in view of the highly competitive nature of the industry. In general, however, montmorillonite is acid treated, washed, and roasted, whereas kaolinite and halloysite are treated less drastically. Heavy oil, which is in the vapor state during the cracking process, is in contact with the catalyst for only 6 to 20 seconds. Action occurs under atmospheric pressure at about 800° to 930° F (425°–500° C). The products of the catalytic reaction may be methane and propane (5%), butane (10%), gasoline (45%), and unchanged feed material (40%); gasoline produced in this way is said to have superior qualities.

## CLAY MOBILITY IN LANDSLIDES

In many areas in Scandinavia, flat-lying strata contain mobile clays of marine-glacial origin. Generally referred to as "quick clays," they were originally deposited in coastal areas and subsequently uplifted. (The clays may also be of freshwater origin and associated with peat bogs, where organic matter makes the clays susceptible to movement.) They usually contain illite and chlorite, occasionally with small amounts of other clay minerals, and are quite fine; about 40% to 50% of the particles of such clays measure less than 2 microns in diameter.

After salt (a common electrolyte) has been leached from a marine clay bed, the bed becomes susceptible to movement. When sliding is imminent, the water content of the bed is high; it may make up more than half the weight of the clay. Such clays are in a sensitive condition and may change from solid to liquid when subjected to a sudden shock; may even change spontaneously. When the change occurs the clay beds flow rapidly to the lowest levels prevailing in the neighborhood, and masses of overlying sandstone or gravel may be carried along. Thus at Surte, Sweden, in 1950, a slide occurred in which 30 multifamily houses were rafted along by the movement, some houses as far as 450 feet (about 135 meters) in a few minutes. The slide also disrupted a paved highway and moved a double-track railroad. The flowage took place on a slope much of which measured less than one degree.

Quick clay slides are known to occur in the St. Lawrence Valley, in western Canada, and in Alaska. At the time of the Alaskan earthquake of March 27, 1964, clay slides initiated at Turnagain Heights, near Anchorage, destroyed 75 houses. The clay minerals involved were largely illite and chlorite.

Thin seams of clay that lie between more substantial rock masses have been responsible for earth movements in many landslide areas. The seams ordinarily are hard and compact, but at times of heavy moisture content (often following winter rains) the clays may become saturated with water and provide a lubricating action that causes overlying rock masses to slip along their surfaces. Such slides are particularly frequent along the Pacific Coast of the United States.

PAUL F. KERR
*Columbia University*

**Bibliography**

Bennett, R., and Hulbert, M. H., *Clay Microstructure* (Intl. Human Resources Development Corp. 1986).

Brownell, W. E., *Structural Clay Products* (Springer-Verlag 1976).

Cairns-Smith, A. G., and Hartman, H., eds., *Clay Minerals and the Origin of Life* (Cambridge 1987).

Velde, B., *Clay Minerals: A Physico-Chemical Explanation of Their Occurrence* (Elsevier Pub. Co. 1985).

Wilson, M. J., ed., *A Handbook of Determinative Methods in Clay Mineralogy* (Routledge 1986).

**CLAY IRONSTONE** is an ore of iron. It consists of the mineral *siderite* (a carbonate of iron), mixed with clay materials, and is found in deposits among sedimentary rocks. Clay ironstone is important as an ore in Britain and Austria. In the United States, it is abundant in Pennsylvania and Ohio, but it is not mined there extensively. See also SIDERITE.

**CLAYMONT,** an unincorporated community in northeastern Delaware, in New Castle county, on the Delaware River. It is 7 miles (11 km) northeast of Wilmington. Claymont is a suburban and industrial center manufacturing ice cream, frozen desserts, and machinery. Population: 9,220.

**CLAYTON, Augustin S.** (1783–1839), American judge and congressman, who was known for his firm stand favoring states' rights. He was born in Fredericksburg, Va., on Nov. 27, 1783, but grew up in Georgia and graduated from the University of Georgia in 1804. After practicing law and serving in the state legislature, he was elected judge of the western superior circuit court, serving from 1819 to 1825 and from 1828 to 1831.

The most famous case he tried concerned the Cherokee Indians, who claimed to be a sovereign state, not subject to Georgia's jurisdiction. When gold was discovered on Indian lands in 1829, the state instituted license and oath of allegiance requirements for white men entering the area. In 1831 a missionary named Worcester and others challenged the Georgia law; Clayton sentenced them each to four years in prison, but was overruled by the U. S. Supreme Court on Worcester's appeal. Judge Clayton was defeated for reelection in 1831, but won a seat in Congress where he served until 1835. He opposed the tariff and the U. S. Bank and supported nullification (q.v.). He died on June 21, 1839.

GERALD M. CAPERS
*Newcomb College, Tulane University*

**CLAYTON, Henry De Lamar** (1857–1929), American jurist and legislator, who was largely responsible for drafting the amendment to the Sherman Antitrust Act that bears his name. Clayton was born in Barbour county, Ala., on Feb. 10, 1857. A graduate of the University of Alabama (1877), he practiced law in Clayton and then in Eufaula, Ala., and in 1893 was appointed U. S. district attorney for the middle district of Alabama. From 1897 to 1914, he served in the U. S. House of Representatives. He was a strong supporter of William Jennings Bryan, and served as chairman of the 1908 Democratic National Convention and of the House caucus in the 60th Congress (1907–1909). As chairman of the House judiciary committee, he played a major role in drafting the Clayton Antitrust Act (q.v.) in 1914. After retiring from the House, he served as a U. S. district judge in Alabama. He died in Montgomery on Dec. 21, 1929.

**CLAYTON, Henry Helm** (1861–1946), American meteorologist, who was one of the pioneers in U. S. weather forecasting. Clayton was born in Murfreesboro, Tenn., on March 12, 1861. In 1886 he joined the staff of the Blue Hill Meteorological Observatory, Harvard University, and began his studies of clouds, which provided the first detailed information on the atmospheric circulation over America. He was involved in the first use of kites to lift recording instruments (1894), and his analyses of the data obtained resulted in new discoveries about the stratification and structure of the atmosphere.

Clayton demonstrated at Blue Hill the superiority of forecasts made locally over those made at a distant central office, and he was an early exponent of forecasting by means of cycles. In Argentina, where he was chief of the forecast service (1913–1922), he experimented with forecasting based upon variations in solar energy. He continued his studies of the relation of solar changes to world weather in cooperation with the Smithsonian Institution and later as a private weather forecaster and consultant. He died in Norwood, Mass., on Oct. 26, 1946.

LEROY E. PAGE
*Wayne State University*

**CLAYTON, John Middleton** (1796–1856), American political leader. As a U. S. senator and as secretary of state under President Zachary Taylor, he generally followed the Whig policies of compromise and cautious expansion. He is remembered for negotiating the Clayton-Bulwer Treaty (q.v.).

Clayton was born in Dagsborough, Del., on July 24, 1796, and was graduated from Yale in 1815. Admitted to the Delaware bar in 1819, he became known for his skill as a cross-examiner. From 1829 to 1836 he served in the U. S. Senate, where, though a staunch Whig, he supported President Andrew Jackson with regard to nullification (q.v.). From 1837 to 1839 he was chief justice of Delaware. He then retired to his scientific farm near New Castle. Returned to the Senate in 1845, he was instrumental in drafting the Clayton Compromise (q.v.) of 1848, concerning slavery in the Western territories, which failed to pass.

In 1848, Clayton supported Gen. Zachary Taylor, the Whig candidate for president, and in 1849 he became secretary of state in the latter's cabinet. The Whigs favored compromise with Britain over British intrusions in Central America, and Clayton initiated negotiations that resulted in the Clayton-Bulwer Treaty of 1850, providing for joint control of any canal that might be built there. The Democrats contended that the treaty was a concession to Britain, but the Senate ratified it. Clayton returned to the Senate in 1853 to defend his work and served there until his death in Dover, Del., on Nov. 9, 1856.

GERALD M. CAPERS
*Newcomb College, Tulane University*

**CLAYTON, Joshua** (1744–1798), American physician and political leader, who was the first governor of the state of Delaware. Born in Cecil county, Md., on Dec. 20, 1744, he attended the Pennsylvania Academy from 1757 to 1762. He then practiced medicine until 1776, when he was elected second major of a battalion recruited from Bohemia Manor, Del. George Washington later commissioned him a colonel in the Continental Army. During the Revolution, Clayton discovered a substance, made from the barks of local trees instead of the unobtainable Peruvian bark, for treating infections.

In 1785, Clayton was elected to the Delaware assembly, and in 1789 he was elected president of Delaware. After the adoption of a new state constitution in 1792, he became governor, serving until 1796. He was elected to the U. S. Senate in January 1798, but the following summer he contracted yellow fever while working to control an epidemic in Philadelphia. He returned to his home in Bohemia Manor, Del., where he died on Aug. 11, 1798.

**CLAYTON, Powell** (1833–1914), American public official. He was born on Aug. 7, 1833, in Bethel, Pa. He migrated to Kansas and became city engineer of Leavenworth in 1859. After service as a Union officer in the Civil War, he acquired a plantation in Arkansas. With the launching of the congressional plan of Reconstruction, he assumed leadership in framing a new government in Arkansas and became the Republican carpetbag governor of the state (1868). Clayton, the undisputed boss of his party and the state's dominant political figure, relied on martial law and Negro militia to suppress Ku-Klux Klan activity and earned the enmity of conservative Democrats.

Clayton represented Arkansas in the U. S. Senate from 1871 to 1877 and then became active in railroad promotion in the state. From 1897 to 1905 he was U. S. ambassador to Mexico. He lived in retirement in Washington, D. C., where he died on Aug. 25, 1914.

WILLIAM E. DERBY
*State University College, Geneseo, N. Y.*

**CLAYTON,** a city in eastern Missouri, situated near the Mississippi River, just west of St. Louis, of which it is a residential suburb. It is the seat and principal commercial center of St. Louis county. The Clayton area was settled in 1820. The city was founded in 1876 and incorporated in 1913. It has a council-manager form of government. Population: 12,825.

**CLAYTON ANTITRUST ACT,** in American history, legislation enacted on Oct. 15, 1914, and named for its chief promoter, former Rep. Henry De Lamar Clayton (q.v.). It attempted to strengthen and to supplement the Sherman Antitrust Act of 1890. It reflected the mood of the period, as Woodrow Wilson and the Democratic party had based much of the 1912 presidential campaign on the principle that "private monopoly" was "indefensible and intolerable."

The act forbade a corporation to purchase stock in a competitive firm, outlawed contracts based on the condition that the purchaser would do no business with the seller's competitors, and made interlocking stockholdings and directorates illegal. It also made corporate officials individually responsible for corporate antitrust violations.

In response to the demands of organized labor, the Clayton Act recognized the right of labor to strike and to picket, exempted unions from antitrust prosecution (traditionally courts had considered them illegal combinations restraining trade), and placed restrictions on the court's power to grant injunctions in labor disputes. Qualifying phrases accompanying the provisions and unsympathetic court interpretations, however, weakened the act in practice and made the labor clauses of no real value.

See also ANTITRUST LAWS.

KEITH W. OLSON
*University of Maryland*

**CLAYTON-BULWER TREATY,** signed by the United States and Britain in April 1850, providing for joint control of any canal or railroad that either country might construct in the isthmus between North and South America. It was negotiated by the U. S. secretary of state, John Middleton Clayton, and the British minister to the United States, Sir Henry Bulwer. One of the most controversial and, in the United States, most unpopular of numerous Anglo-American agreements, it was superseded by the Hay-Pauncefote Treaty of 1901, which gave to the United States exclusive rights to a canal.

Like the Webster-Ashburton Treaty of 1842, the Clayton-Bulwer pact was in line with a consistent Whig policy of compromise and peace with Britain, in contrast to the Democrats' more aggressive stand on expansion in the Western Hemisphere, with its inherent risk of war. By the late 1840's the weak republics of northern Latin America had come under the influence of Britain, then the world's leading maritime and commercial power. Emissaries of President James K. Polk, a Democrat, applying the Monroe Doctrine (q.v.), had signed several agreements with Central American countries in an effort to check British progress in the area, but the succeeding Whig administration of President Zachary Taylor chose to ignore them. Secretary Clayton informed the British minister that he did not hold to Monroe's no-further-colonization edict, opening the way to negotiations.

The Clayton-Bulwer Treaty neutralized the entire Central American area, each country forswearing any exclusive fortifications or colonization and guaranteeing equal commercial rights to the citizens of the other. However, after the signing but before the exchange of ratifications, Bulwer specifically excepted Belize, in what was called British Honduras, and its "dependencies"— meaning the Bay Islands, which Britain made into a crown colony in 1852. Translating the diplomatic jargon to suit their purpose, the British refused to give up any existing protectorate and merely affirmed that they would not use such possessions for domination of a future canal. After consulting with Senate leaders, Clayton concurred, and the Senate ratified the treaty on July 4, 1850.

The Democrats, who pressed for further expansion in the Caribbean, made capital of Whig truckling to Britain. In retrospect it appeared that Clayton conceded more than was necessary, but at the time the United States was in no position to risk war with England. The treaty yielded no vital interest; in fact, it got Britain, then the world's greatest power, to share control of the strategic isthmus.

GERALD M. CAPERS
*Newcomb College, Tulane University*

**CLAYTON COMPROMISE,** a plan for organizing the Oregon and southwest territories with the hope of appeasing both proslavery and antislavery factions. It was drawn up by a Senate committee headed by John Middleton Clayton in 1848. Its provisions included the exclusion of slavery from Oregon, the prohibition of territorial legislation on slavery by California and New Mexico, and the right of slavery cases tried in territorial courts to be appealed in the U. S. Supreme Court. Although passed by the Senate, it was tabled in the House.

**CLAYTONIA,** klā-tō′nē-ə, a genus of perennial plants with fleshy leaves and clusters of small white or pink flowers. Claytonias, sometimes called *spring beauties* or mayflowers, belong to the purslane family (Portulacaceae). The most important species is *Claytonia virginica*, a wild flower widely distributed throughout moist wooded areas of eastern North America. It grows less than a foot (30 cm) tall and bears two narrow leaves about 5 inches (15 cm) long. The dainty white or pink flowers are ¾ of an inch (20 mm) across and appear in April. The stem grows from a small underground tuber.

A similar species, *C. rosea*, is native to Colorado, Utah, and Wyoming. It grows 4 inches (10 cm) tall and bears leaves 2 inches (5 cm) long. Its rosy pink flowers appear in May. *C. caroliniana* is a similar plant, but its leaves are broader, and its flowers are smaller.

DONALD WYMAN
*Arnold Arboretum, Harvard University*

**CLAZOMENAE,** klə-zom′ə-nē, was an ancient city in northern Ionia (now western Turkey). It was located on the south shore of the Gulf of Smyrna, 20 miles (32 km) west of Smyrna (now İzmir). In its early period a member of the Ionian Confederacy, Clazomenae was originally situated on the mainland, near modern Urla. At the beginning of the 5th century B. C. the inhabitants moved the city to an offshore island because of fear of the Persians. In the 4th century B. C. a causeway was built to link the island to the shore; its course can still be traced.

Clazomenae founded a colony at Abdera (now Avdira) in Thrace (about 654 B. C.) and helped found a Greek trading center at Naucratis in Egypt. In the 5th century Clazomenae was in the Athenian League, but revolted in 412. In 386 the city came under Persian rule.

Clazomenae was hampered economically by lack of a hinterland, and from the 3d century B. C. onward its seaborne trade was harmed by competition with refounded Smyrna. It was the birthplace of the philosopher Anaxagoras (about 500 B. C.). In the later 6th century B. C. the most successful black-figure pottery in Ionia was produced by Clazomenae, and also a distinctive type of painted terra-cotta sarcophagi. Excavations at Clazomenae were begun in 1921 but were abruptly broken off, and the excavated material was lost. Remains of harbor works and a theater are still visible.

D. J. BLACKMAN
*Bristol University, England*

**CLEANING FLUID.** See DRY CLEANING.

**CLEANTHES,** klē-an′thēz (c.330–c.231 B. C.), was a Greek philosopher, who succeeded his teacher, Zeno, the founder of Stoicism, as the leader of the Stoic school. In early life Cleanthes had been a boxer, and he used his considerable strength for manual labor at night to earn enough to attend Zeno's lectures during the day. Accused of being an ass, he remarked, "Then perhaps I am the very one to take over Zeno's burden." At the close of his life he abstained from food so that he would not live longer than his master had.

Cleanthes was most interested in theology. He discussed such topics as the origins of religion, fate and free will, proof of God's existence, and the parallel between the microcosm (man) and the macrocosm (the universe). He believed that in music human beings come nearest to an intuition of the divine. Aside from isolated fragments, his only extant work is the 39-line *Hymn to Zeus*, which is one of the finest expressions of Stoic pantheism.

RICHMOND Y. HATHORN
*Author of "Tragedy, Myth, and Mystery"*

**CLEAR AIR TURBULENCE,** regions of turbulent air occurring in the stratosphere or upper troposphere in the absence of clouds. CAT tends to occur where there are marked changes in wind direction or in air temperature and velocity (either horizontally or vertically), but such changes do not necessarily indicate the presence of CAT. Two types of atmospheric phenomena may induce the formation of turbulence under these conditions: a jet stream, especially near the juncture of two branches of the stream; and atmospheric waves that extend into the stratosphere in the lee of mountains.

CAT is dangerous to high-altitude aircraft because it is invisible and there are no instruments with which to measure it. It may produce severe structural oscillations that, even if not directly destructive, cause uncontrollable flight maneuvers resulting in catastrophe for the craft.

GORDON H. STROM
*New York University*

**CLEAR ISLAND** is in the Atlantic Ocean off the southern coast of Ireland, 11 miles (18 km) southwest of Skibbereen, County Cork. It is about 3 miles (5 km) long and 1 mile (1½ km) wide and has ruins of a 15th century castle. Cape Clear, at its southern tip, is the most southerly part of Ireland except for Fastnet Rock, 3½ miles (5½ km) to the southwest. The lighthouse on Fastnet Rock is a well-known landmark.

**CLEAR LAKE,** the largest body of fresh water wholly within California, is a popular recreation area offering excellent fishing. Located in Lake county, 80 miles (130 km) north of San Francisco, it is about 20 miles (32 km) long and varies in width from 1 to 10 miles (1½ to 16 km). Mountains around the lake rise to a height of some 4,000 feet (1,200 meters). Clear Lake State Park and Lakeport, the county seat, are situated on its western shore.

**CLEAR LAKE,** a city in northern Iowa, in Cerro Gordo county. It is situated on the northeastern shore of Clear Lake, approximately 100 miles (160 km) north of Des Moines. Clear Lake is a popular summer resort. Its industries include the manufacture of bakery goods and concrete products. The site was first settled during the 1850s, and Clear Lake was incorporated as a city in 1871. Government is by mayor and council. Population: 8,161.

**CLEARCHUS,** klē-är′kəs (c. 450 B. C.–401 B. C.), Spartan general. During the latter part of the Peloponnesian War he was active in the Spartan campaigns in the Hellespont (battles of Cyzicus, 410, and Arginusae, 406). He served as governor of Byzantium but was ousted by the people for his tyrannous rule. After the war he was nevertheless sent back to settle political disputes and to defend the city from Thracian attacks. However, when he ignored the recall which overtook him before his arrival, he was condemned to death and took refuge with Cyrus the Younger of Persia. In the latter's attempt to wrest the Persian throne from his brother, Artaxerxes II, Clearchus commanded the Greek mercenaries at the Battle of Cunaxa (401) in which Cyrus was killed. After the war, during truce negotiations with the Persian satrap Tissaphernes, Clearchus was treacherously seized, sent to Artaxerxes, and beheaded.

**CLEARFIELD,** a borough in central Pennsylvania, the seat of Clearfield county, approximately 90 miles (144 km) northwest of Harrisburg. It is a coal- and clay-producing center. It also manufactures leather goods, school supplies, stainless steel products, electronics equipment, and sportswear. The community was founded on the site of an old Indian town and is named for nearby Clearfield Creek. It was laid out in 1805 and incorporated in 1840. The borough is governed by a mayor and council. Population: 6,631.

**CLEARFIELD,** a city in northern Utah, in Davis county 26 miles (42 km) north of Salt Lake City and 6 miles (10 km) east of the Great Salt Lake. It is a trade center in an irrigated area that raises sugar beets and other crops. The city has fruit and vegetable canneries. Hill Air Force Base is 2 miles (3 km) to the northeast. Incorporated in 1922, Clearfield is governed by a city manager. Population: 25,974.

**CLEARINGHOUSE.** See BANKS AND BANKING— 7. *Clearinghouse Activities.*

**CLEARWATER,** a coastal city in west central Florida, the seat of Pinellas county, 20 miles (32 km) west of Tampa. It is situated on Clearwater Bay, a lagoon separated from the Gulf of Mexico by Clearwater Beach Island, a sandy key accessible from the city by a 2-mile (3-km) causeway. Clearwater is a year-round resort and a center for the canning, packing, and shipping of citrus fruits grown in the area. Fish canneries, electronics manufacture, and the making of preserves are other industries. The city was originally the site of Fort Harrison which was established here in 1841. In 1891, it was incorporated as Clearwater. Government is by manager and council. Population: 108,787.

**CLEARWING MOTH,** the common name for a large, widely distributed family of small day-flying moths. Because of their long slender legs, partially transparent (scaleless) narrow wings, and often colorfully banded abdomens, these moths resemble many kinds of wasps and hornets. This mimicry is further emphasized by the moths' general behavior.

Most clearwing moths have a wingspan of 1 to 2 inches (2.5 to 5 cm). The hindwings of nearly all species are mostly transparent, while the scaliness of the forewings sometimes varies according to sex. The female's forewings are usually more heavily covered with scales.

The larvae of all species bore into the roots, stems, or trunks of trees and shrubs and sometimes into herbaceous (nonwoody) plants as well. The larvae are uniformly yellowish-white and usually range in length from about 1 to 2½ inches (2.5 to 6.3 cm). Pupation normally occurs underground inside a cocoon made of silk and soil particles.

Clearwings make up the family Aegeriidae of the order Lepidoptera. The larvae of one species, *Sanninoidea exitiosa,* are a major pest of peach trees.

DON DAVIS, *Smithsonian Institution*

**CLEAVELAND,** klĕv′lənd, **Moses** (1754–1806), American soldier and land speculator, who founded the city of Cleveland. He was born in Canterbury, Conn., on Jan. 29, 1754. After graduation from Yale University (1777), he began to practice law. Two years later he was appointed captain of a company of sappers and miners in George Washington's army. After the Revolution he joined the Connecticut militia and rose to the rank of brigadier general in 1796. He was a member of the state legislature (from 1787) and of the state convention that ratified the federal Constitution (1788).

Under the Articles of Confederation, Connecticut received 3.8 million acres (1.5 million hectares) of land in present-day Ohio, most of which was sold in 1795 for $1.2 million to the Connecticut Land Company, of which Cleaveland was a director. Cleaveland led the initial exploring party to "New Connecticut," which arrived at the Conneaut Creek of Lake Erie on July 4, 1796. Further searches led to the founding of a new city on the Cuyahoga River to be known as Cleaveland (later Cleveland). Moses Cleaveland never returned to the West, but he remained active in Connecticut public life until his death in Canterbury on Nov. 16, 1806.

**CLEAVELANDITE,** klĕv′lənd-īt, is a sodium-aluminum silicate mineral named for the American mineralogist Parker Cleaveland. Cleavelandite is a form of albite (a feldspar mineral) that occurs in white crystalline blades or plates. Albite is relatively rare, but occurrences in the form known as cleavelandite are fairly common in the United States; particularly fine crystals are found in Maine, Massachusetts, Connecticut, and Virginia. See also FELDSPAR.

**CLEAVER, Eldridge.** See under BLACK PANTHERS.

**CLEAVERS,** a tall, leafy species of bedstraw that grows as a weed throughout North America. See BEDSTRAW.

**CLEBSCH,** kläpsh, **Rudolf Friedrich Alfred** (1833–1872), German mathematician, who is noted for studies on the singularities of curves and surfaces. He was born in Königsberg, East Prussia (now Kaliningrad, USSR), on Jan. 19, 1833, and received his doctorate in mathematics and physics at the university there in 1854. He taught analytical mechanics at the Polytechnic Institute at Karlsruhe for five years and was professor of mathematics at the University of Göttingen in 1868. He died in Göttingen on Nov. 7, 1872, of diphtheria.

Nineteenth century mathematicians generally fell into two groups: those working in the theory of functions, number theory, and mathematical physics; and those specializing in algebra and analytic geometry. Clebsch at first belonged to the first group, publishing a memoir on elasticity in 1862 and a treatise on Abelian functions in 1866. Thereafter he belonged with the second group, and in his hands the concept of "deficiency," known earlier to Abel and Riemann, became a key tool in the classification of curves.

CARL B. BOYER, *Brooklyn College*

**CLEBURNE,** klĕ′bərn, **Patrick Ronayne** (1828–1864), American Confederate general, who is often called "the Stonewall Jackson of the West." He was born in County Cork, Ireland, on March 17, 1828, of Protestant parents. After briefly attending Trinity College, Dublin, he enlisted in the British Army. In 1849 he went to America and settled in Helena, Ark.

When Arkansas seceded, Cleburne was appointed a colonel in the Confederate Army. In March 1862 he was promoted to brigadier general. His outstanding leadership at the battles of Shiloh, Richmond, Ky., and Perryville brought him promotion to major general in December. Cleburne's Division became the most celebrated command in the Army of Tennessee. It fought superbly at Murfreesboro (Stone River), at Chickamauga, and at Missionary Ridge, where it held its position against superior numbers and then checked the Union pursuit. His proposal to enlist and free the slaves may, however, have prevented his further promotion. Cleburne served gallantly in the Atlanta campaign. He met his death at the head of his troops in the great charge at Franklin, Tenn., on Nov. 30, 1864.

JOSEPH B. MITCHELL
*Author of "Decisive Battles of the Civil War"*

**CLEBURNE,** klĕ′bərn, a city in northern Texas, the seat of Johnson county, 27 miles (43 km) south of Fort Worth. It is the trading and shipping center for a region of diversified farming, dairying, and livestock production. Cleburne's industries include railroad shops, a steel foundry, and the manufacture of sheet metal products, furniture, textiles, garments, fiberglass, trailers, air conditioners, and electronic appliances. Government is by city manager. Population: 26,005.

**CLEF,** klef, a symbol at the beginning of the musical staff to indicate the pitch of the notes. The term is French, meaning "key". There are three clef signs in common use. Two of them are fixed clefs: the G, or treble, clef, indicates that the note on the second line from the bottom of the staff is G above middle C; and the F, or bass, clef,

Treble      Bass      Alto      Tenor

indicates that the fourth line from the bottom is F below middle C. The third clef sign moves; it is called the C clef because its position indicates the location of middle C. There are two commonly used C clefs: the alto clef, which indicates that the third line of the staff is middle C; and the tenor clef, which indicates that the fourth line of the staff is middle C.

**CLEFT PALATE,** kleft pal′ət, a fissure, or opening, in the roof of the mouth, allowing direct communication between the nasal and oral cavities. A cleft palate is a congenital deformity, occurring before birth. It is usually associated with a cleft lip, or harelip, a fissure through the upper lip.

Cleft palates range in severity from a small separation of the uvula (the small fleshy mass of tissue that hangs down from the palate at the back of the mouth) to a complete separation of both the soft (muscular) and hard (bony) portions of the palate. In severe cases, the cleft extends through the gum tissue in the region of one of the upper canines, or eyeteeth, and is continuous with a cleft in the upper lip. In some cases, there are two clefts, one on either side of the palate's midline. In these cases, the central portion of the upper lip and gum are entirely separate from the rest of the lip and gum tissue, and hang from the nose by a projection of the nasal septum.

**Cause.** A cleft palate occurs when the right and left sides of the palate do not fuse together. Normally, this fusion takes place during the 7th to 12th week of embryonic life. Although it is not known exactly why this fusion may fail to occur, it is known that the tendency to develop a cleft palate seems to run in certain families (as a recessive genetic trait of variable penetrance). However, the deformity may occur so infrequently that many families are not aware of other cases that may have occurred among their relatives.

In some laboratory animals a cleft palate can be produced artificially through X-rays, vitamin deficiencies, or the administration of certain drugs, such as cortisone. In human beings, environmental factors do not seem to play an important role. It is estimated that a cleft palate occurs in about one out of every 750 to 1,700 live births.

**Care and Treatment.** Because a baby born with a cleft palate cannot develop suction in its mouth, it has difficulty feeding, and milk that is taken into the mouth tends to escape through the nose rather than be swallowed. To overcome this problem, the baby is usually placed in an upright position and fed by placing the formula on the back portion of the tongue with a special bulb syringe. Swallowing, which is a reflex action, then follows naturally. At the age of 3 or 4 months, feeding can be shifted to a cup and spoon. Sometimes, a special cleft palate nipple is used instead of a cup and spoon.

When the child is from 12 to 14 months old, before he has started to develop speech habits by putting words together to form sentences, the cleft palate is repaired surgically. If the condition is not repaired, the child will have a serious speech defect, characterized by poor articulation and a nasal voice quality.

**Surgical Repair.** In the surgical repair of a cleft palate, an incision is made around the back of the upper gum, just inside the inner gum margin. This incision allows the palatal halves to be freed as flaps that can be sutured together, closing the cleft without tension from the surrounding tissues. Some surgeons lengthen the palate by incising two V-shaped flaps, with the point of each flap pointing toward the front of the mouth. The flaps are then folded toward each other and sutured together, with the sewn incision forming a Y.

During surgery, care is taken to preserve the greater palatine artery, vein, and nerve as they emerge from the opening in the palate bone (the greater palatine foramen). The tensor palatine muscle, which forms part of the soft palate, is relaxed by an inward fracture of the bony process about which it swings. The muscle fibers are handled very gently in order to preserve the normal muscular action that is so important for proper speech.

The final step in the operation consists of sewing together the three layers of the palate—the membrane lining the base of the nasal cavity, the muscle of the soft palate, and the membrane lining the roof of the mouth. Catgut is used for suturing because it is absorbable and the stitches do not have to be removed. Also the sutures retain their tensile strength long enough for satisfactory healing. Usually the incisions heal within 8 days.

After the operation, until the time the wound is healed, the child is fed clear liquids by cup. Arm splints are applied to the child's arms to prevent him from bending his elbows and possibly disturbing the wound with his fingers or with a toy.

**Speech Therapy.** When learning to speak, the child with a repaired cleft palate oftens requires special help, from either his parents or a professional speech therapist. The child's parents can help mold his speech patterns by correcting his pronunciation of the sounds "k," "s," and "t." He may also need help pronouncing the sounds "ch," "sh," and "th." In addition, it is important that the child learn to speak by directing the flow of air through his mouth, rather than through his nose. The technique can be practiced by blowing feathers or ping pong balls off a table. Blowing through horns, whistles, or other simple musical instruments is also helpful. In later years, regular participation in a school band or orchestra, playing one of the brass or woodwind instruments, seems to help prevent nasal speech.

In the great majority of cases where children are helped by their parents in this fashion, good speech will be achieved. In about one out of every four patients, however, the help of a professional speech therapist is required. Some children, who may still fail to develop good speech, should be considered for a second operation, such as a palate lengthening and/or a pharyngeal flap construction, in which the elongated palate is sewn to a flap raised from the rear of the pharynx wall.

**Dental Care.** Children whose cleft palate has involved the gum tissue often must be treated by an orthodontist, a dentist who specializes in correcting and preventing irregularities in the position of the teeth. These children frequently suffer malocclusions due to the inward shifting of the bones holding the upper teeth. Fortunately, this malocclusion, known as cross bite, can be corrected through orthodontic techniques.

DONALD W. MacCOLLUM, M. D.
*Harvard University Medical School*

### Bibliography

Clifford, Edward, *The Cleft Palate Experience: New Perspectives on Management* (C. C. Thomas 1987).
Dronamraju, Krishna R., *Cleft Lip and Palate: Aspects of Reproductive Biology* (C. C. Thomas 1986).
McWilliams, Betty J., and Shelton, Ralph, *Cleft Palate Speech* (Mosby 1984).
Starr, Philip, and others, *Cleft Lip and or Palate: Behavioral Effects from Infancy to Adulthood* (C. C. Thomas 1983).

**CLEISTHENES,** klīs'thə-nēz (6th century B. C.), Athenian statesman, who is generally considered the founder of the Athenian democracy. He was the son of Megacles, of the aristocratic Alcmeonid family, and Agariste, daughter of Cleisthenes, tyrant of Sicyon, a city near Corinth. Cleisthenes of Sicyon had offered his daughter to the winner of a yearlong competition among suitors invited from all Greece; she was won by Megacles.

The Alcmeonidae alternately cooperated and quarreled with the Athenian tyrant Peisistratus, and Cleisthenes was probably in exile when Peisistratus died in 528. But Cleisthenes was reconciled with the new tyrant, Hippias, and became archon in 525. Another period of exile followed, probably after the murder of Hippias' brother Hipparchus in 514. The Alcmeonidae then used their influence at Delphi, where they had played a major role in the rebuilding of the temple, to have the oracle persuade the Spartans to depose Hippias. King Cleomenes of Sparta did so in 510, and Cleisthenes returned to Athens to compete for leadership in the new oligarchic government. When his rival Isagoras was elected archon in 508, Cleisthenes turned for support to the common people, who feared the loss of their citizenship and political privileges granted them under Solon and Peisistratus. Isagoras appealed to Cleomenes for aid, and Cleisthenes withdrew from Athens; but the people rose and ejected the Spartans and Isagoras. Cleisthenes then returned and set up a democratic constitution. This may have taken several years, but ancient sources mention nothing of him thereafter.

**The Reforms of Cleisthenes.** Cleisthenes' reforms changed the basis of Athenian citizenship and the nature of the tribes, which were the political and military divisions of the people. Previously, citizenship had depended upon birth into one of the phratries (brotherhoods), which were subdivisions of the four tribes. Cleisthenes made the basis for citizenship geographical by dividing Attica into more than 150 demes; those living within the boundaries of a deme were put on its roll, and henceforth deme-rolls were the basic citizenship lists. Cleisthenes formed 10 tribes, each composed of groups of demes from the city, the coast, and the interior. The artificial nature of these tribes was meant to break up old regional loyalties and to put city residents in all tribes.

In the democracy the ultimate power lay in the *ecclesia,* the assembly of all adult males, which passed laws and elected officials. To deliberate beforehand and prepare business for this unwieldy group, Cleisthenes instituted the Council of Five Hundred. (See also BOULE.) It was composed of 50 men chosen by lot every year from each of the 10 tribes, and thus in theory representative of the whole citizen body, although in fact it could not be so until a system of payment for holding public office was introduced. Each group of 50 served in turn for one tenth of the year as a standing committee of the council; known as *prytaneis,* they ran the day-to-day business of government and presided over assembly and council meetings. Cleisthenes' system prevailed at Athens for centuries with only a few short interruptions, and became a model for other Greek democracies. Cleisthenes may also have introduced ostracism, although this was not used until 487.

DONALD W. BRADEEN
*University of Cincinnati*

**CLELAND,** klel'ənd, **John** (1709–1789), English author, who is best known for his allegedly pornographic novel *Fanny Hill, or the Memoirs of a Woman of Pleasure* (1750). This novel became the subject of considerable controversy when it was republished in the United States in 1963. In 1965 a Massachusetts court held that it was obscene, but the ruling was reversed by the U. S. Supreme Court in 1965.

Cleland, who was probably a son of Alexander Pope's friend William Cleland, passed his first 40 years in penury and obscurity. After the publication of *Fanny Hill* and *The Memoirs of a Coxcomb* (1751), which is probably his best work, he was awarded an annual government pension of £100 and was able to turn his talents from easily salable licentious writing to a career in journalism. His later work includes plays, philological and other essays, and two novels. Cleland died in London on Jan. 23, 1789.

**CLEMATIS,** klem'ət-əs, a genus of ornamental twining vines with opposite leaves and often large showy blossoms. There are more than 230 different species of clematis and many more varieties. They are widely distributed throughout temperate regions of the Northern Hemisphere.

In some species, such as the virgin's bower (*Clematis virginiana*) and the popular and fragrant sweet autumn clematis (*C. paniculata*), the blossoms are small and white. In some hybrids, such as *C. jackmanii*, the blossoms may be 6 inches (15 cm) in diameter and range in color from white to purple. In all species, however, the true flowers are very small and inconspicuous but are surrounded by 4 large colorful bracts that are popularly mistaken to be petals. Clematis species all require an alkaline soil. They are propagated by cuttings and seeds.

DONALD WYMAN
*The Arnold Arboretum, Harvard University*

JOHN J. SMITH

CLEMATIS: (*Above l.*) Virgin's bower (*C. virginiana*); (*above r.*) large-flowering hybrid; (*below*) *C. paniculata.*

**CLEMENCEAU,** klā-män-sō′, **Georges** (1841–1929), French premier and World War I leader. He was born Georges Eugène Benjamin Clemenceau, on Sept. 28, 1841, at Mouilleron-en-Pareds, in the Vendée, into a family with vigorous republican traditions. Clemenceau studied medicine but maintained at the same time broad philosophical, literary, and political interests. In 1865, after visiting London, he spent three years in the United States, reporting on post–Civil War conditions for French newspapers and also teaching French at a girls' school in Connecticut. He married one of his students, Mary Plummer, but the marriage lasted only seven years.

**Mayor of Montmartre.** Clemenceau was caught up in the turbulent political events that followed the defeat of France by Germany in 1871. After the overthrow of Napoleon III, he became mayor of the Montmartre district of Paris and was elected a deputy to the new National Assembly, where he voted against preliminary peace proposals.

It was in his own Montmartre district that the popular insurrection known as the Commune broke out on March 18, 1871. The Radicals and republicans in Paris, embittered by a four-month siege, suspected that the new President of France, Auguste Thiers, and the Assembly meeting at Versailles would restore some form of monarchy and sign a humiliating peace treaty with Germany. When the government troops from Versailles tried to regain control of cannon in Montmartre that belonged to the Paris national guard, a crowd prevented the seizure. Despite Clemenceau's attempt at intervention, two generals were shot by the mob. The revolutionary government lasted until the end of May, when the troops from Versailles entered the city and took vengeance on the Communards.

Clemenceau, who was opposed to popular violence but sympathetic to the people of Paris, had tried to avert civil war and had consequently found himself unpopular with both sides. After the suppression of the Commune he was tried for not having prevented the execution of the generals, but was cleared. In the aftermath of the trial, he fought the first of his many duels; he became renowned for his skill with sword and pistol.

**Politics.** Returning to medical practice, especially among the poor, Clemenceau also served on the Paris municipal council. Elected to the Chamber of Deputies in 1876, he quickly became the leader of the Radicals. Spokesmen for the lower middle classes and the "little man," the Radicals found themselves increasingly opposed to the vacillating moderates who seemed bent on opposing social legislation indefinitely.

In the years from 1876 to 1893, Clemenceau established a reputation as a fiery critic and sharp-tongued opponent of the moderate and conservative republicans. He was instrumental in the overthrow of many of their ministries, earning in the process his nickname, "the Tiger."

Clemenceau was in the center of all political crises of these years. In the Boulanger episode of 1886–1889 he first supported Gen. Georges Boulanger as a leader who might effectively rally the country to avenge the French defeat in the Franco-Prussian War of 1870–1871. However, when the general revealed his dictatorial and antiparliamentary views, Clemenceau turned against him. In 1887, in a scandal involving the sale of decorations and honors by Daniel Wilson, son-in-law of Jules Grévy, the President of France,

Clemenceau was instrumental in forcing the resignation of President Grévy. In 1892 he himself received a political setback in the Panama Canal scandal. He had had personal and financial relations with Cornelius Hertz, one of the financiers responsible for the Panama Canal speculation in which many leading deputies were implicated. Although full details of Clemenceau's relations with Hertz were never revealed, his enemies exploited the connection, accusing him also of having been in the pay of the English. He lost his seat in the 1893 elections.

Discouraged and without funds, Clemenceau turned to journalism. As a journalist he played a leading role in the Dreyfus affair, in which Alfred Dreyfus, a French army officer, was found guilty of high treason. The case, with its overtones of anti-Semitism and conspiracy in high places, had profound repercussions in the years that followed. Clemenceau became convinced of Dreyfus' innocence and threw himself into the campaign to vindicate the condemned captain. It was Clemenceau who in 1899 published in his newspaper, *l'Aurore*, Émile Zola's sensational letter accusing the French general staff of suppressing the true facts of the Dreyfus case, and it was Clemenceau who gave the letter its famous title, "J'accuse."

In 1902, Clemenceau was elected to the Senate. An ardent champion of the left bloc—a coalition of moderates, radical republicans, and socialists who were determined to weaken the influence of the church, the army, and the monarchists after the Dreyfus affair—he actively supported the anticlerical policies of the Radicals.

In 1906, Clemenceau became minister of the interior in the cabinet of Ferdinand Sarrien and had to face serious labor troubles. Although he was prolabor and opposed to the use of the army in the suppression of strikes, once in office he used the military to uphold law and order. His actions led to a break with the socialists and a rupture of the left bloc, climaxed by a famous debate with the Socialist leader Jean Jaurès.

**Premier of France.** In October 1906, at the age of 65, Clemenceau became premier. During his premiership, which lasted until July 1909, he continued the anticlerical policies of his Radical predecessors. In foreign affairs he cemented relations with England and Russia and helped form the Triple Entente. Although he had earlier opposed imperialism, he now pressed plans to advance French interests in Morocco and to oppose Germany's colonial ambitions. Clemenceau became increasingly preoccupied with the German challenge to France. After his fall from office in 1909, he returned to the Senate, and pressed for the buildup of French armed strength.

**World War I.** With the outbreak of World War I in 1914, Clemenceau called for total mobilization and in his influential newspaper editorials criticized the government as inefficient. As the fighting dragged on, he attacked all manifestations of war-weariness. At one of the darker moments of the war, in November 1917, President Raymond Poincaré called upon Clemenceau to form a government, despite his concern over "the Tiger's" egotistical and domineering personality. At the age of 76, Clemenceau, now at the climax of his career, became premier and war minister.

Clemenceau infused the government and nation with a new energy and vitality, advancing only one slogan in domestic and foreign policy: *"Je fais la guerre!"* ("I wage war!"). Even op-

GEORGES CLEMENCEAU, in retirement after serving twice as premier of France, visits New York City in 1922.

ponents who resented his dictatorial methods admired his strength and determination. He brought Louis Malvy, the former minister of the interior, to trial and instituted charges against the Radical leader Joseph Caillaux for attempting secret peace negotiations. He made frequent visits to the military front and was responsible for the unification of the Allied military command.

**Peace Negotiations.** When the war ended with the Allies victorious, Clemenceau played a key role in the Paris peace negotiations, countering the idealism of President Woodrow Wilson of the United States and the temporizing tendencies of Lloyd George, the British Prime Minister, with a determination to defend French security by weakening Germany. Nevertheless, Clemenceau did not go as far as many of the nationalists in the National Assembly wished. He was accused of bartering away French national interests.

In 1920, Clemenceau fell from power and, as an additional blow, was defeated in the election for the presidency of the republic.

**Retirement.** In his retirement Clemenceau traveled, visited the United States on a speaking tour, and wrote philosophical works and reminiscences. He published a monograph on Claude Monet in 1926, and in 1927 published a discursive philosophical tract, *Au soir de la pensée* (*In the Evening of My Thought*). He was writing a volume of reflections on the war and postwar years when he died in Paris, on Nov. 24, 1929.

Clemenceau was always a solitary and independent figure in politics, an ardent patriot and republican, and a champion of the rights of parliament and of the individual citizen. As a political leader, he was able, with his indomitable will, to mobilize his country and its government at a time of supreme crisis.

JOEL COLTON, *Duke University*

**Further Reading:** Hansen, W. P., and Haney, J., eds., *Clemenceau* (Chelsea House 1987); Jackson, J., *Clemenceau and the Third Republic* (1946; reprint, Hyperion Press 1985).

**CLEMENS, Samuel.** See TWAIN, MARK.

**CLEMENT I,** klem'ənt, **Saint,** was pope from about 92 to 101. He was a Roman whom some have identified with the Clement that St. Paul mentions in the Epistle to the Philippians (4:3), but modern scholars have disproved this theory. Others identified him with Titus Flavius Clemens, a kinsman of the Flavian emperors, but this has also been rejected. It may well be, however, that Clement was connected with the imperial household as the son of a freedman. St. Clement was a martyr, but there are no authentic details of his death. His feast day is November 23.

An interesting story comes down from a 4th or 5th century *Acts of the Martyrs*, which reports that Clement was exiled to the Chersonese peninsula in the Black Sea area. There he was tossed into the sea with an anchor around his neck, and the sea immediately rolled back to reveal his body in a marble shrine. St. Cyril, the Apostle to the Slavs, found some bones with an anchor. Hailed as the relics of Clement, these were eventually placed in the basilica of San Clemente in Rome.

Although many writings have been attributed to Clement, only the famous Epistle to the Corinthians can be cited as his. This letter, written sometime in the last decade of the 1st century, rebukes the factiousness of the Corinthian Christians and urges them to repentance and peace.

JOSEPH S. BRUSHER, S. J.
*Santa Clara University, Calif.*

**CLEMENT II,** klem'ənt (died 1047), was pope from 1046 to 1047. His name was Suidger, and he was born of a noble Saxon family. He became a canon of Halberstadt in 1032 and later was chaplain at the imperial court. Emperor Henry III was so impressed by Suidger that he named him bishop of Bamberg in 1040. When the emperor succeeded in expelling both the antipope Sylvester III and Pope Gregory VI from the papacy at the Synod of Sutri, he named Suidger the new pope. Although he was reluctant to accept the burdens of the papacy, Suidger finally acceded to the emperor's wishes and was enthroned as Clement II on Dec. 5, 1046.

After he crowned Henry and his wife Agnes, Clement initiated reform measures. He condemned simony and kept in close touch with the fiery reformer, St. Peter Damien. Clement died near Pesaro, less than a year after his accession, on Oct. 9, 1047. He was buried in Bamberg where, in 1943, his tomb was opened and his vestments were found to be in good condition.

JOSEPH S. BRUSHER, S. J.
*University of Santa Clara, Calif.*

**CLEMENT III,** klem'ənt (died 1191), was pope from 1187 to 1191. He was born Paolo Scolari, in Rome. He was serving as cardinal bishop of Palestrina when he was elected pope at Pisa on Dec. 19, 1187. With unusual diplomatic skill he negotiated a treaty with the Roman Senate in 1188, ending a long conflict and bringing recognition of the pontiff as temporal lord of Rome. He sought to reconcile the warring princes of Germany, England, and France by uniting them against the forces of Muslim Sultan Saladin in the Third Crusade. Also under Clement, the church in Scotland was made directly dependent upon Rome, and papal protection was given to Jews and other persecuted people. He died on March 27, 1191.

WILLIAM O'LEARY, S. J., *Fordham University*

**CLEMENT III,** klem'ənt, was antipope from 1080 to 1098. Born Wibert of Ravenna, he served as imperial chancellor in Italy, supporting the emperor's candidate Cadato as antipope in 1061. He became reconciled with Pope Alexander II and was made archbishop of Ravenna. With the Cenio family and Cardinal Ugo Candido, he supported Emperor Henry IV against Pope Gregory VII in the Investiture struggle and was elected antipope at Bressanone on June 25, 1080. He took possession of Rome as Clement III and, supported by the Italian imperial party, remained in power until the Pierleoni family deposed him in 1098. He died on Sept. 8, 1100.

FRANCIS X. MURPHY, C. SS. R.
*Academia Alfonsiana, Rome*

**CLEMENT IV,** klem'ənt (died 1268), pope from 1265 to 1268. He was born Guy le Gros Foulques, at St. Gilles, France. He studied law at the University of Paris and won appointment as legal adviser to King Louis IX. Following his wife's death in 1247, Clement began clerical studies and after ordination became successively bishop of Le Puy, archbishop of Narbonne, cardinal legate to England, and diplomatic adviser in Paris. In 1265 he was elected pope and he summoned Charles of Anjou to protect the Holy See against Hohenstaufen military advances from the north. Charles secured the Papal States and established the Angevin dynasty in Italy. Clement also opposed nepotism. He died at Viterbo, Italy, on Nov. 29, 1268.

EDWARD J. CRIPPS, S. J.
*Loyola Seminary, Shrub Oak, N. Y.*

**CLEMENT V,** klem'ənt (c. 1260–1314), was pope from 1305 to 1314. He was born Bertrand de Got, in the Bordelais, France, and studied canon law at Orleans and Bologna. In 1295 he became bishop of Comminges and in 1299 archbishop of Bordeaux. He was elected pope at Perugia on June 5, 1305. A compromise candidate, he had been favored by Philip IV of France against the supporters of the deceased Pope Boniface VIII, in whose death the king was implicated. Crowned as Clement V in Lyon on Nov. 14, he remained in France thereafter for multiple reasons: Rome was fraught with political intrigue due to the papal war with Venice over the city of Ferrara; Tuscany had splintered into warring factions; Emperor Henry VII was demanding his coronation at Rome; and the French papal agents had been unfavorably received in Italy.

Clement's failure to return to Rome set an unfortunate precedent for his successors and began the so-called Babylonian Captivity. It also caused him to become increasingly influenced by Philip IV, who almost immediately pressed him for a trial of Boniface VIII. Philip, whose emissaries were accused of assaulting Boniface at Anagni, wanted his name cleared of involvement in this scandal. In 1311 the court conditionally absolved Nogaret, the king's emissary, and relieved Philip of responsibility for the crime. At the same time, Clement managed to salvage Boniface's memory. Although Clement disapproved of the king's use of blackmail and mass arrests in his campaign against the Knights Templars, he acceded to Philip and the Council of Vienne by suppressing the order (1312).

Clement dealt more successfully with other sovereigns: he proclaimed the absolute right of the Holy See over the Empire in the decree

*Pastoralis cura,* and in the *Multorum querela* attempted to set up controls for the Inquisition of which he disapproved. In 1307, Clement established the University of Perugia, where he created a chair of Asian languages. Despite his authoritarian attempt to centralize the papal government, his emissaries met with strong opposition from the European sovereigns when they attempted to collect taxes or grant benefices. Accused of failing to curb heresy by the Inquisitors and of nepotism by Dante, Clement, who apparently suffered from cancer, seems to have been more guilty of lassitude. He died at Roquemaure, Comtat Venaissin, on April 20, 1314.

FRANCIS X. MURPHY, C. SS. R.
*Academia Alfonsiana, Rome*

**CLEMENT VI,** klem'ənt (c. 1291–1352), was pope from 1342 to 1352. He was born Pierre Roger in what is now the department to Corrèze, France. He became a Benedictine monk and took a degree in theology before serving successively as bishop of Arras, archbishop of Sens, and archbishop of Rouen. Named cardinal in 1338, he succeeded Benedict XII as pope in 1342.

Political turmoil in Italy, and particularly the insurrection of Cola di Rienzi, caused Clement to remain in Avignon rather than return to Rome. He succeeded in bringing peace between the church and the Holy Roman Empire by deposing Louis IV of Bavaria and arranging the election of Charles IV of Luxembourg as emperor in 1347.

The most controversial aspect of Clement's reign was his position on benefices, or revenue-producing properties of the church. In an attempt to centralize church government, Clement decreed that the papacy alone had final rights in granting ecclesiastical benefices. The bishops as well as secular powers objected strongly to this measure, and in 1345, King Edward III seized all the benefices held in England by foreigners. In 1347, Philip VI did the same in France, making an exception for cardinals and members of the papal family and curia. The pope's policy on benefices, combined with his activities as a generous patron of the arts, resulted in the papal treasury being nearly exhausted at the end of his pontificate.

Clement was reproached by many political enemies and by the Spiritual Franciscans, whom he opposed. However, although he was extravagant and his court was ostentatious, his personal life was exemplary and his courage and charity were an inspiration during the plague of the Black Death that occurred during his reign.

FRANCIS X. MURPHY, C. SS. R.
*Academia Alfonsiana, Rome*

**CLEMENT VII,** klem'ənt (1478–1534), was pope from 1523 to 1534. He was born Giulio de' Medici, in Florence, Italy, on May 26, 1478, the illegitimate son of Giuliano de'Medici. After his father was killed in the notorious Pazzi conspiracy, he was raised by his grandfather, Lorenzo the Magnificent. He entered the church and rose to great power during the reign of his cousin, Leo X. He was elected to succeed Adrian IV in 1523.

A moral and cultivated man, Clement VII was nevertheless incapable of dealing with the problems of his reign. Emperor Charles V of Germany and Francis I of France were struggling for supremacy over Europe. When the Pope's efforts to mediate between them failed, he allied himself with France. Charles retaliated: his army of mercenaries mercilessly sacked Rome in 1527 and virtually imprisoned Clement in the castle of Sant'Angelo. After peace was achieved, Clement crowned Charles as Holy Roman Emperor in Bologna in 1530.

At the same time Henry VIII of England was demanding that his marriage to Catherine of Aragon be annulled. The Pope procrastinated so long that Henry revolted from the Roman church and set himself up as head of the Church of England in 1534. Clement was equally unsuccessful in quelling the strong Lutheran movement or in accomplishing any major reforms of the church. He died in Rome on Sept. 25, 1534.

JOSEPH S. BRUSHER, S. J.
*University of Santa Clara, Calif.*

**CLEMENT VII,** klem'ənt, (1342–1394), antipope from 1378 to 1394. He was born in Geneva and was known as Robert of Geneva. He served as bishop of Thérouanne and then of Cambrai before being made a cardinal by Pope Gregory XI in 1371. Following the election of Pope Urban VI in 1378, a group of cardinals revolted against the new pontiff and, later in the same year, chose Robert of Geneva to be Clement VII. The election of the two popes was the beginning of the Great Western Schism, which created great confusion throughout Christendom.

Clement tried to take Rome, but when he failed in this effort, he withdrew to Avignon. France, Scotland, the Spanish kingdoms, and part of Italy supported Clement, as did several saints. Although some efforts were made to reconcile the two factions, the schism was still in effect when Clement died at Avignon on Sept. 16, 1394.

JOSEPH S. BRUSHER, S. J.
*University of Santa Clara, Calif.*

**CLEMENT VIII,** klem'ənt (1536–1605), pope from 1592 to 1605. He was born Ippolito Aldobrandini, in Fano, Italy, on Feb. 24, 1536. He studied law, became a cardinal in 1585, and was elected pope in 1592. By absolving King Henry IV and forming closer ties with France, he ended Spanish domination in Rome. Clement promoted a treaty that terminated fighting between France and Spain in 1598, and he reincorporated Ferrara into the Papal States. He also mediated in the controversy between the Jesuits and Dominicans over the nature of grace. A new edition of the Vulgate was issued under Clement. He died in Rome on March 5, 1605.

ROBERT MUNSCH, S. J.
*Loyola Seminary, Shrub Oak, N. Y.*

**CLEMENT VIII,** klem'ənt, antipope from 1424 to 1429. He was born Aegidius Muñoz and was the successor to antipope Benedict XIII who, during the Great Western Schism, had reigned at Avignon as a rival to the Roman papacy. Benedict, although deposed at the Council of Constance, refused to abdicate and acknowledge Pope Martin V of Rome. Instead, Benedict created his own cardinals and insisted that after his death they should elect a successor. They elected Muñoz. King Alfonso of Aragon, who was hostile to Pope Martin, had Muñoz crowned Clement VIII. Later when Alfonso was reconciled with Pope Martin, Clement resigned.

JOSEPH S. BRUSHER, S. J.
*University of Santa Clara, Calif.*

**CLEMENT IX,** klem′ənt (1600–1669), was pope from 1667 to 1669. He was born Giulio Rospigliosi in Pistoia, Italy, on Jan. 28, 1600. He served as nuncio to Spain, governor of Rome, and papal secretary of state prior to becoming pope. Clement was successful in persuading four Jansenist bishops in France to submit to the Holy See, thus concluding years of unfruitful negotiations and ending the Jansenist controversy for 30 years. After mediating a dispute between France and Spain, he sought help in defending Crete from the Turks, but the island fell shortly before his death in Rome on Dec. 9, 1669.

RAYMOND SWEITZER, S. J.
*Loyola Seminary, Shrub Oak, N. Y.*

**CLEMENT X,** klem′ənt (1590–1676), was pope from 1670 to 1676. He was born Emilio Altieri, in Rome, on July 13, 1590. He entered the ecclesiastical state and served in various diplomatic and pastoral functions under several popes. Despite his claims of unworthiness and old age, he was elected pope after a long conclave as a compromise choice. During his reign he backed Poland against the Turkish invasion and supported John Sobieski's claim to the Polish throne. He opposed Louis XIV's policy of extending the rights of royalty and promoted peace among European states. He died in Rome on July 22, 1676.

JOSEPH PARKES, S. J.
*Loyola Seminary, Shrub Oak, N. Y.*

**CLEMENT XI,** klem′ənt (1649–1721), was pope from 1700 to 1721. He was born Gian Francesco Albani, in Urbino, Italy, on July 22, 1649. He was educated by the Jesuits and became a scholar of some note in Rome, translating a number of Greek works into Latin. He entered the papal service and rose to be an influential figure in the service of four successive popes. He was made a cardinal by Innocent XII.

The conclave of 1700 was disturbed by a number of political questions, and Albani, who was a reluctant candidate for the papacy, was elected in a compromise move. As pope, Clement strove to maintain a delicate neutral position during the War of the Spanish Succession. In this conflict, Louis XIV of France and the Austrian dynasty both offered claimants to the throne vacated by Charles II.

The controversial theories of Jansenism (q.v.) were revived during Clement's reign under a new leader, the French theologian Pasquier Quesnel. The pope condemned the Jansenists in two documents, *Vineam Domini* in 1705 and *Unigenitus* in 1713. He also made an unsuccessful attempt to win over Peter the Great of Russia from Russian orthodoxy to Roman Catholicism.

On the issue of foreign missions, Clement disapproved of the Chinese and Malabar rites, which were attempts at integrating Christianity with Oriental culture. He did, however, show great zeal for the foreign missions by fostering seminaries to train future missionaries. Clement XI died in Rome on March 19, 1721.

JOSEPH S. BRUSHER, S. J.
*University of Santa Clara, Calif.*

**CLEMENT XII,** klem′ənt (1652–1740), was pope from 1730 to 1740. He was born Lorenzo Corsini, in Florence, Italy, on April 7, 1652. He studied at the Roman College and the University of Pisa. After entering the ecclesiastical state he successfully fulfilled important church posts, which led to the papacy. Although he became blind in 1732 and was often in ill health, he vigorously supported missionary training colleges, condemned freemasonry, and took action against the Jansenists. Clement allowed the papacy to lose its feudal rights in the duchies of Parma and Piacenza, but he made significant agreements with Spain and Portugal. He died in Rome on Feb. 6, 1740.

JAMES HAGGERTY, S. J.
*Loyola Seminary, Shrub Oak, N. Y.*

**CLEMENT XIII,** klem′ənt (1693–1769), was pope from 1758 to 1769. He was born Carlo della Torre Rezzonico, in Venice, on March 7, 1693. After training for diplomacy, he was ordained a priest in 1716 and steadily rose in the papal service. He was made a cardinal by Clement XII in 1737, and in 1743 he succeeded to the see of Padua. He proved to be a zealous bishop, and on the death of Benedict XIV he was elected pope, taking the name Clement XIII.

Clement's pontificate was disturbed by fierce attacks on the Jesuits, particularly by members of the Enlightenment movement in France. The Society of Jesus was suppressed in Portugal in 1759, in France in 1764, and in Spain in 1767. Clement protested these measures, but in vain. He saw dangers to the church in the teachings of the French *philosophes,* and during his pontificate, the Holy Office condemned works by the French authors Diderot and Helvétius. Clement's compassion was demonstrated by the aid he provided the people of Rome during a time of drought and famine. He died Feb. 2, 1769.

JOSEPH S. BRUSHER, S. J.
*University of Santa Clara, Calif.*

**CLEMENT XIV,** klem′ənt (1705–1774), was pope from 1769 to 1774. He was born Giovanni Ganganelli at Sant'Arcangelo, Italy, on Oct. 31, 1705. After studying with the Jesuits and Piarists, Giovanni entered the order of Friars Minor Conventual and took the name Lorenzo. Highly thought of in his order, he was made a consultor of the Holy Office by Benedict XIII and was named a cardinal by Clement XIII in 1759.

The conclave held in 1769 to elect a successor to Clement XIII was conducted in an atmosphere of confusion. The Bourbon ambassadors in particular were striving at all costs to elect a pope acceptable to the monarchs of France, Spain, and Naples. Ganganelli was chosen and took the name Clement XIV.

The Bourbon ambassadors, particularly José Moniño of Spain, had an animosity against the Jesuit order. Clement, although he had shown signs of attachment to his old teachers, the Jesuits, gave in to Bourbon political pressure and issued the brief *Dominus ac Redemptor,* in which he suppressed the Society of Jesus.

Although Clement adopted a policy of appeasement toward Catholic monarchs, he was not free from their political interference. He did manage, however, to restore several territories to Roman control. The restored areas included Avignon and Venaissin in France, and Benevento and Pontecorvo in Italy.

Clement also had the satisfaction of effecting a reunion of a group of Nestorians with Rome before his death on Sept. 22, 1774. Rumors that he died of poisoning proved to be unfounded.

JOSEPH S. BRUSHER, S. J.
*University of Santa Clara, Calif.*

**CLÉMENT, René,** klā-mäɴ′ (1913–1996), French filmmaker who was noted for his technical excellence, especially in terms of sets. However, his detached attitude in his films caused him to be criticized as a director in search of a personality.

Clément was born in Bordeaux, France, on March 18, 1913. He studied architecture and made films as an amateur before becoming a professional cameraman and director of short documentaries. His first full-length film, *La Bataille du rail* (1945; *The Battle of the Rails*), about the French Resistance, is in a semidocumentary style, and his second, *Les Maudits* (1947; *The Damned*), is a wartime melodrama strong in technique.

Two of Clément's best works are *Jeux interdits* (1952; *Forbidden Games*), an antiwar story that looks at World War II through the eyes of children (it won an Oscar for best foreign film), and *Gervaise* (1956), based on Émile Zola's tragic novel about a struggling Paris laundrywoman. His other feature films include the epic *Paris brûle-t-il?* (1965; *Is Paris Burning?*), about the 1944 liberation of the French capital; the thrillers *Plein Soleil* (1959; *Purple Noon*) and *Le Passager de la pluie* (1970; *Rider on the Rain*); and the disappointing *La Baby-Sitter* (1975), his final film. He died in southern France on March 17, 1996.

EDWIN JAHIEL*, *University of Illinois*

**CLEMENT OF ALEXANDRIA,** klem′ənt (150?–?215), 3d-century Father of the Church and, with Origen, the principal exponent of the Alexandrian school of theology. The little that is known about his life is deduced from his own works and those of the historians Eusebius of Caesarea and Photius.

He was born Titus Flavius Clemens about 150, evidently in Athens rather than Alexandria. His parents were cultured pagans, probably of substantial means. He received his early education in Athens, where he developed a fondness for Hellenic philosophy and literature, and thereafter he traveled widely. According to Eusebius, on arriving in Alexandria as a new convert to Christianity, Clement studied under Pantaenus, head of the catechetical school there, and succeeded his teacher as head of this school, probably about 200. Eusebius also maintained that Origen was one of Clement's pupils, although this is disputed. Clement was probably ordained a priest during this time. Most of his writings are thought to date from this period in Alexandria. During the persecutions of Septimius Severus, around 202–203, Clement was forced to flee. Nothing certain is known of the remaining years of his life. A letter to the church at Antioch from Alexander, then bishop of Jerusalem, is taken to indicate that Clement died sometime before 215.

Four complete works of Clement are extant. *Protrepticus*, or *Exhortation to the Greeks*, is aimed at the conversion of Alexandria's pagan intellectuals to Christianity. The three-volume *Paedagogus* ("Instructor") is addressed to new converts and outlines an ethical and moral way of life, emphasizing the educational role of the Scriptures. As is indicated by its title, the *Stromata* ("Miscellanies," from the Greek word for carpet bags used to stored miscellaneous blankets and bedding) belongs to a literary genre, prevalent in Clement's time, in which a variety of questions were discussed without any logical plan. The eight books of the *Stromata* deal basically with the relation of Christianity to secular learning, particularly to Greek philosophy. The last extant work is a homily on Mark 10:17–31, addressed to the well-to-do of Alexandria and entitled *Quis dives salvetur?* ("Who Is the Rich Man That Is Saved?").

GEORGE A. MALONEY, S.J., *Fordham University*

**CLEMENT OF ROME.** See CLEMENT I.

**CLEMENTE, Roberto,** klə-men′tē (1934–1972), Puerto Rican baseball player and national hero. He was born in Carolina, a San Juan suburb, on Aug. 18, 1934. After starring in a Puerto Rican league, he was signed by Brooklyn. After a year with Montreal, a Brooklyn "farm," he was drafted by the Pittsburgh Pirates, for whom he played in the outfield from 1955 to 1972.

Clemente excelled at bat, as a base runner, and on defense. He led the National League in batting four times, had a lifetime average of .317, and was named the league's most valuable player in 1966. He led the Pirates to world titles in 1960 and in 1971, when he batted .414 and was voted the most valuable player in the World Series. A double on Sept. 30, 1972, was Clemente's 3,000th and last major league hit. On Dec. 31, 1972, he and four other men carrying supplies to earthquake victims in Nicaragua died when their plane fell into the sea off San Juan. He was elected to the baseball Hall of Fame in 1973.

**CLEMENTI, Muzio,** klä-men′tē (1752–1832), Italian composer, pianist, teacher, and publisher who was described at his death as "the father of pianoforte playing." In the late 18th century he helped develop a specifically pianoforte style that was distinct from that of the harpsichord and clavichord. His best sonatas are enduring contributions to piano literature, and his method of playing influenced later pianists.

Clementi was born in Rome on Jan. 23, 1752. When he was 14, his musical precocity attracted the interest of the Englishman Peter Beckford, under whose patronage Clementi made England his home in 1766. While on a recital tour of Europe in 1781, Clementi put to the test his piano technique—which exploited in particular the percussive qualities of the instrument's sound production—in a historic contest with Mozart in Vienna. Critical opinion was divided at the time, but Clementi later avowed that Mozart's more graceful and limpid style induced him to modify his own.

Following a broad tour of Europe (1802–1810), Clementi abandoned solo performing and devoted himself more fully to a successful music-publishing and piano-manufacturing business he had founded in 1798 with John Longman. He continued to compose, teach, and conduct. He died at his country house near Evesham on March 10, 1832, and was buried in Westminster Abbey.

Clementi's 60-some piano sonatas are the most enduring part of his work. The best of them combine clarity, purity, and conciseness with a passionate intensity suggestive of Beethoven, whose piano style he influenced, and whose major English publisher he became.

GERALD ABRAHAM
*Author of "A Hundred Years of Music"*

**Bibliography:** Plantinga, Leon, *Clementi, His Life and Music* (1976; reprint, Da Capo 1985).

**CLEMSON UNIVERSITY,** klem′sən, a state-controlled coeducational university and land-grant college in Clemson, S.C. It was established in 1889 as

Clemson Agricultural College, on property bequeathed by Thomas G. Clemson, noted U.S. mining engineer and agronomist and the son-in-law of John C. Calhoun. Clemson opened in 1893 and was designated a university in 1964. It has schools of arts and sciences, agriculture, architecture, commerce and industry, education, engineering, forest and recreation resources, and nursing. The graduate school has been functioning since 1945. A postgraduate program in telephone communications is sponsored by the Southern Bell telephone system. A graduate program in nutrition operates in cooperation with Winthrop College. Special research at Clemson centers on water resources, air pollution, food supplements, chemistry, and the biological sciences. Notable library collections include the personal papers of public officials John C. Calhoun and James F. Byrnes and of Sen. Strom Thurmond.

**CLEOBULUS,** klē-ō-bū′ləs, a Greek ruler, poet, and riddlemaker of the 6th century B.C. Ranked among the seven sages of Greece, who were statesmen and reputed authors of maxims in the 7th and 6th centuries B.C., he is credited with the maxim "Moderation is the chief good." According to Diogenes Laërtius, who wrote about Cleobulus's life in the 3d century A.D., Cleobulus, the strong, handsome son of Evagorus, was tyrant of Lindus on the island of Rhodes. He offered Solon of Athens refuge from the tyrant Pisistratus. Cleobulus wrote many lyric poems, perhaps over 3,000 lines, and many riddles, which he may have been the first to put into verse.

**CLEOME,** klē-ō′mē, any of a large group of mostly tropical plants, one of which, the spider flower, is sometimes grown as a garden plant. This species, known botanically as *Cleome spinosa*, is a strong-smelling annual with many rosy-purple or white flowers composed of 4 irregular clawed petals. It ranges in height from 3 to 4 feet (90–120 cm). Its down-covered leaves are mostly compound, consisting of 5 to 7 leaflets; near the top of the stem, the leaves are entire. The flowers of the spider flower are 2 to 3 inches (50–75 mm) long, and each ripens into a long narrow pod borne on a slender stalk.

Cleome.

JOHN J. SMITH

Another species, *C. lutea* (sometimes *C. serrulata*), is native to western North America. It grows about 5 feet (1½ meters) tall and bears clusters of bright orange-yellow flowers.

Cleomes are classified as the genus *Cleome* in the caper family (Capparidaceae).

DONALD WYMAN
*Arnold Arboretum, Harvard University*

**CLEOMENES,** klē-om′ə-nēz, the name of three kings of the Agiad family in ancient Sparta.

CLEOMENES I reigned approximately from 519 to 488 B.C. The chronology and details of his life are uncertain. Herodotus's account is anecdotal and derived from unfriendly sources. Cleomenes was a strong king who tried to extend Sparta's influence outside the Peloponnesus. In 510 he deposed Hippias, tyrant of Athens, and set up a pro-Spartan government there. When his friend the archon Isagoras appealed for help against the faction led by Cleisthenes in 508, Cleomenes went to Athens with a small force, only to be ignominiously expelled. The next year he gathered a large army to restore Isagoras, but the attempt failed because of the opposition of Cleomenes' coruler in Sparta, King Demaratus, and the defection of the Corinthians and other allies of Sparta. A later attempt to restore Hippias was also stopped by the Corinthians. Cleomenes then turned his attention to the Peloponnesus and crushed Argos, probably in 494. Although he had refused help to Samos about 515 and to Miletus in 499 against the Persians in Asia Minor, he aligned Sparta with Athens to resist the Persians when they threatened Greece in 491. Cleomenes punished Sparta's ally Aegina for submitting to Persia and in this was again opposed by Demaratus. By corrupting the Delphic oracle, he then had his colleague deposed on a false charge of illegitimacy. Cleomenes' trickery was soon exposed, and he was exiled. According to Herodotus, he became insane and committed suicide.

CLEOMENES II reigned from 360 to either 334 or 309 B.C. He was so overshadowed by his corulers, Archidamus III and Agis III, that the only information in ancient sources on his reign is in the form of conflicting statements about its length.

CLEOMENES III reigned from 235 to 222 B.C. A capable ruler, he was ambitious to restore Sparta's ancient glory. His wife, the widow of the murdered reformer Agis IV, influenced him in the direction of radical social change. Cleomenes began a program of expansion in 229 by annexing the large Arcadian cities of Mantinea, Tegea, and Orchomenus. Then for two years he fought a successful war against the Achaean League. In 227 he established himself as absolute ruler in Sparta by ejecting the ephors, or magistrates, and abolishing their office. Having thus increased his power, he turned again to external affairs, and by 224 he had captured Argos and was besieging Corinth. In desperation the Achaean League appealed for help to its former enemy, King Antigonus of Macedon, who, in return for control of the fortress of Acrocorinth, went to relieve Corinth. Argos then revolted, leaving Cleomenes on the defensive. He captured Megalopolis in 223 but was decisively defeated by Antigonus at Sellasia in 222. Cleomenes then fled to Egypt, whose king, Ptolemy III Euergetes, had befriended him. On Ptolemy's death Cleomenes was imprisoned, but he escaped and tried to start a revolt in Alexandria. When this failed in 219, Cleomenes committed suicide.

DONALD W. BRADEEN, *University of Cincinnati*

**CLEON,** klē'on (died 422 B.C.), Athenian politician and general. The son of a wealthy tanner, he was the first member of the commercial classes to attain prominence in Athenian politics. Cleon participated in the political attacks of 430 B.C. against Pericles and against Pericles' defensive strategy in the Peloponnesian War with Sparta. After Pericles' death in 429, Cleon eventually emerged as "leader of the people." The historian Thucydides described him as "the most violent of the citizens and by far the most persuasive among the common people" when Cleon convinced the Athenians in 427 to punish the revolt of Mytilene on Lesbos by killing all the men and selling the women and children into slavery. This cruel verdict was reversed at a second assembly, also described by Thucydides, who attributes to Cleon a speech in which he reveals himself as a cold and calculating imperialist and as a demagogue introducing class hatred into internal politics.

In 425, when Athens had forced Sparta to discuss peace by seizing Pylos in Messenia, Cleon convinced the people to continue the war by making excessive demands for the return of territories lost 40 years earlier. Shortly thereafter he publicly accused the Athenian generals of incompetence for failing to capture the Spartans whom they had besieged on the island of Sphacteria, near Pylos. When the general Nicias challenged Cleon to take command and do better, Cleon rashly promised to kill or bring back alive the Spartans within 20 days. He fulfilled this promise, attacking according to a plan conceived by the general Demosthenes. Cleon's return with 292 prisoners raised his prestige even higher.

**Cleon and Brasidas.** In the next year Cleon was responsible for trebling the tribute paid by the subject states of Athens' empire. His attempt to recapture mainland areas earlier lost by Athens was checked at Megara and led to an Athenian defeat at Delium in Boeotia. After the Spartan general Brasidas had won over from Athens several important cities in Thrace, there was a truce in 423 to discuss peace. Peace was not concluded, however, because of the opposition of both Cleon and Brasidas. When the Thracian town of Scione revolted against Athens in 423, Cleon had a decree passed ordering that the men be killed and the women and children enslaved. Upon the expiration of the truce in 422, he led an army to Thrace, where he captured Torone. Shortly thereafter he was defeated and killed by Brasidas at Amphipolis. Since Brasidas also died there, the chief supporters of war were removed, and the Peace of Nicias was signed in 421.

**Evaluation.** Cleon was viciously lampooned by the comic poet Aristophanes, whose charges of dishonesty were probably wildly exaggerated. Yet Cleon invited attack, especially when contrasted with his more aristocratic predecessors and rivals, because of his crudity, demagogy, and vanity. He was also portrayed unsympathetically by Thucydides, perhaps partly because he was responsible for the historian's exile, but mostly because of what Cleon stood for: war and expansion when an honorable peace was possible, harshness in dealing with the subject states, and the introduction of class rivalry and suspicion into Athenian politics. These three factors were to lead to Athens' losing the war, its empire, and, at least temporarily, its democracy.

DONALD W. BRADEEN
*University of Cincinnati*

CLEOPATRA, shown in a contemporary Egyptian relief.

**CLEOPATRA,** klē-ə-pa'trə, was the throne name of a number of Macedonian queens of ancient Egypt, the most famous of whom was Cleopatra VII Philopator (69–30 B.C.). Although she ruled in Alexandria, she was part Macedonian, part Greek and Iranian. In the history of Egypt, Cleopatra is of small importance; she was merely the last of the degenerating Ptolemaic line, which had become accustomed to governing with the aim of exacting as much revenue as possible without causing revolt. Her fame comes from the West: as mistress and wife of Mark Antony she played a decisive role in the course of Roman, and hence subsequent European, history.

**Cleopatra and Caesar.** In 51 B.C., in accordance with the will of their father Ptolemy XII Auletes, Cleopatra and her young brother Ptolemy XIII ascended the throne as joint rulers of Egypt. From the first, the young queen showed a strong will to power, and she struggled with her brother and his supporters for complete control of Egypt. At first unsuccessful, she was exiled from Alexandria (in 49 B.C.). While she was preparing an army to regain her throne, Julius Caesar arrived in Egypt to settle the succession and attempt to gain Egypt's wealth for Rome. Cleopatra returned to the capital in secret and secured Caesar's support; hence, after Caesar had won the Battle of Alexandria (47 B.C.) and Ptolemy XIII had died, she found her position secure. Tradition forced her to take her youngest brother, Ptolemy XIV, as her husband and cosovereign, but Cleopatra was now the effective ruler of Egypt. During several months of rest for the Roman army, she showed Caesar every pleasure and luxury, including a journey up the Nile. It appears that she now began to plan for wider power—as first lady of the Roman world.

Cleopatra's position was consolidated when (in 46 B.C.) she bore Caesar a son, who was called Ptolemy Caesar or Caesarion. Soon afterward she went to Rome, where she was received with honor, although Caesar greatly offended his countrymen by dedicating a golden statue of her in the temple of Venus Genetrix. Provided with a residence on Caesar's property beyond the Tiber, Cleopatra remained in Rome until a month after his assassination in March 44 B.C., when she fled to Alexandria. Ptolemy XIV died, presumably poisoned by her order, and she placed her son with her on the throne as Ptolemy XV Philopator Philometor. (She had made him acceptable at birth to rule in Egypt by having him recognized by the priests of Hermonthis as a son of the god Amon.)

**Cleopatra and Antony.** After the Battle of Philippi (42 B.C.), Mark Antony (a member of the ruling triumvirate with Octavian and Lepidus) called Cleopatra and other Eastern rulers to Tarsus to render account to him. Cleopatra now saw her second great opportunity for world power and fame. In a carefully staged encounter, she used all her wealth, charm, and wit to excite the interest of this passionate man. Not only was she acquitted of a charge of assisting Cassius (one of Caesar's assassins) against the triumvirate, but she soon had Antony granting her every request, even to ordering the murder of her young sister Arsinoë (a barely possible contender for the Egyptian throne), who had taken asylum in the temple at Ephesus. A few months later she received him as her paramour in Alexandria. There during the winter of 41–40 B.C. she made herself indispensable to him as mistress of ceremonies, companion, and confidante.

After a long separation, Antony sent for Cleopatra in the autumn of 37 B.C. to join him in Antioch. There they were married, although Antony was already wedded to Octavian's sister, Octavia, and a polygamous marriage could not be recognized under Roman law. Antony acknowledged as his the twins Cleopatra had borne, Alexander Helios and Cleopatra Selene. In addition, he gave her a considerable part of the territories of central Syria, the island of Cyprus, much of the Phoenician coast, properties in Judaea, and the land east of the Dead Sea in the Nabataean kingdom. Together they planned his next campaign against Parthia. Then, pregnant with Ptolemy Philadelphus, Cleopatra returned to Egypt, but her hold on Antony continued to grow. She led him to insult Octavia, who had been forbearing and staunch in her support of her faithless husband. She outraged Roman pride by persuading him to celebrate a triumph in Alexandria and allow her participation in it (34 B.C.). The honors and favors Antony heaped upon Cleopatra and her children and his acquiescence in Oriental modes of behavior led to scandalous gossip and charges (some true, some false) that progressively alienated his officers and his supporters in Rome until he lost his reputation and was stripped of his powers.

Eventually Cleopatra accompanied Antony everywhere—even in the field—becoming his most trusted counselor. It was against Cleopatra that Octavian finally declared war in 32 B.C. When the two commanders met at Actium in 31 B.C. to decide who should rule the Roman world, it was Cleopatra's plan of battle that Antony used. And when most of his fleet defected, it was in her ships that he fled. Instead of following him to Alexandria, his army surrendered.

Antony's spirit was broken, and it soon became clear to Cleopatra that her dreams of power could no longer be achieved through him. Nor could they be achieved by an Egyptian war against Octavian. Both Antony and Cleopatra unsuccessfully attempted to negotiate with Octavian, who eventually took Pelusium and then Alexandria. According to tradition, Cleopatra provoked Antony's suicide by allowing him to believe she had killed herself. After his death she attempted once more to treat with Octavian for the rights of her children. When she was satisfied that she could obtain nothing, she killed herself. However, she was foiled in a plan to immolate herself and all her family treasure, which she had collected in a mausoleum where she then barricaded herself with two trusted companions. Legend has it that she was detained in conversation at the entrance while a Roman soldier forced a high rear window. From then on she was a prisoner; and almost certainly Octavian acquiesced to her suicide (30 B.C.). This was probably accomplished through the bite of a cobra smuggled to her in a basket of figs. She was buried beside Antony in accordance with a last request. Cleopatra's death brought the 300-year old Ptolemaic dynasty to an end, and Egypt became a Roman province.

**Literature.** Cleopatra has profoundly stirred the imaginations of writers and scholars. This queen —vital, tireless, subtly intelligent, ruthlessly ambitious, ensnarer of two great Roman generals— attracts hyperbole. In Rome the stories about her exploits excited loathing and terror. She formed a subject for the contemporary poets Horace (*Odes; Epodes*) and Virgil (*Eclogues*). Unfortunately, the earliest historical accounts that have been preserved are those of Appian (*Bella civilia*) and Plutarch (*Lives*, chiefly *Antony*), written about a century after her death. She is mentioned by Ovid, Lucian, and Pliny. Strabo, Josephus, and Dio Cassius provide some of the elements of her legend.

The early historical sources are in the main unsympathetic to Cleopatra, for they are based on Roman presentations of the case, and Rome had nearly been defeated by this woman. Plutarch's account is the most complete, and it served as the basis for Shakespeare's *Antony and Cleopatra*. (In *Notes to Caesar and Cleopatra*, George Bernard Shaw excused his play *Caesar and Cleopatra* from any attempt at delineating historically true personalities.) With fresh evaluation of old sources and the use of evidence hitherto unrecognized, the historian W. W. Tarn has written eloquently in Cleopatra's defense (*The Cambridge Ancient History*, vol. 10, chaps. 2 and 3).

The popular 20th century image of Cleopatra as a sex-mad siren is due to ignorance. The stories of her sexual exploits, aside from the liaisons with Caesar and Antony, were almost certainly fabricated as part of the propaganda campaign to discredit Antony. (Tarn has called attention to the fact that the outrageously exaggerated charges and countercharges in this propaganda campaign were accepted as fact by the Classical historians and have distorted our picture of Roman history ever since.) In her relationships with the two great generals, Cleopatra used her body as well as her mind to achieve political ends. Her standards of conduct differed widely from Roman custom and law and are generally repugnant to present-day Europeans and Americans, so largely the heirs of Rome. But it was for her determination and intelligence that she was feared at Rome, and Cleopatra deserves to be remembered as a nearly successful contender for control of the Hellenistic world.

CAROLINE NESTMANN PECK, *Brown University*

**CLEOPATRA'S NEEDLES,** klē-ə-pat′rəz, are Egyptian obelisks now standing in London and New York City. They were originally erected as a pair before the sun temple at Heliopolis by King Thutmose III in the 15th century B. C. In 22 B. C. they were removed by order of the Roman emperor Augustus to Alexandria, where they remained until the middle of the 19th century A. D. The London obelisk was offered to King George IV of Britain by Mehmet Ali, viceroy of Egypt, in 1820 and was actually set up on the Victoria Embankment of the Thames River in 1878. The New York obelisk was a gift of the Khedive Ismail Pasha to the city of New York and was erected in Central Park in 1881.

Each of these obelisks is a monolithic shaft of Aswan granite nearly 70 feet (21 meters) tall and tapering from an almost square base about 7.5 feet (2 meters) on a side. The weight of the New York obelisk is 224 tons. (The London obelisk now measures and weighs somewhat less than its "twin" because it is more severely weathered and chipped, having lain on the ground from some time after the 12th century A. D. until its removal to London.) Each side of each shaft bears three columns of hieroglyphs. The central column in each case is the original inscription of Thutmose III, giving his official names and telling of his devotion to the gods of Heliopolis. The flanking columns were added by Rameses II in the 12th century B. C. In antiquity the pyramidions at the top were covered with electrum to catch and reflect the first and last rays of the rising and setting sun.

It is not known how these obelisks received their popular name. Medieval Arab writers called them "Pharaoh's great needles," and in 19th century colloquial Arabic, *Misallah,* "big needle," could mean "obelisk." Cleopatra was perhaps the best known of the pharaohs who ruled in Alexandria; it was evidently not realized that she reigned nearly 1,500 years after the obelisks were made.

CAROLINE N. PECK, *Brown University*

**CLEOPHON,** klē′ō-fon (died 404 B. C.), was an Athenian politician who continued the demagogic tradition of Cleon and Hyperbolus. He was originally a lyre maker. Having become leader of the restored democracy after the oligarchic revolution of 411 B. C., Cleophon persuaded the Athenians not to make peace when it was offered by the Spartans after the Spartan defeat at Cyzicus in 410. He ably directed Athens' financial recovery but advocated that money needed for the war be used for salaries and public works, such as the Erechtheum on the Acropolis. He also introduced the *diobelia,* a dole of two obols per day paid to all citizens impoverished by the war.

Cleophon seems to have been out of favor in 406 at the time of the Battle of Arginusae with Sparta and so was not one of the demagogues responsible for the condemnation of the victorious generals. But he reemerged as leader of the war party, stoutly opposing negotiation even after the fate of Athens was sealed by the loss of its fleet at Aegospotami. Finally, when the resistance of many Athenians was weakened by starvation, brought on by the siege of the city, Cleophon was condemned to death on a trumped-up charge by those wishing to negotiate, and Athens surrendered to Sparta in 404.

DONALD W. BRADEEN
*University of Cincinnati*

I. DONALD BOWDEN

Cleopatra's Needle, in New York's Central Park.

**CLEPSYDRA,** klep′sə-drə, or *water clock,* an instrument for measuring time by letting water drip through a small opening in the bottom of a vessel. The oldest preserved water clock is an Egyptian bucket-shaped vessel dated about 1400 B. C. The Egyptians used water clocks to determine the time during the day and the night. The time it took for the water to drip out of a vessel was a measuring unit. The Greeks used this simple form of water clock to measure the time allotted to speakers in Athenian courts. Ctesibius, an engineer in Alexandria, invented a constant-flow water clock about 250 B. C., using a vessel in which the water level was kept constant. This vessel released water into a second vessel at a constant rate. The elapsed time was measured by the amount of water in the second vessel, using a float as a gauge. The Romans introduced a float with a fixed pointer that registered against a graduated scale. By about 25 B. C. there existed at least one elaborate water clock with rods, gears, and dials. The water clock, with further improvements, remained in use until the 1600's.

**CLERC,** klàr, **Laurent** (1785–1869), French educator of the deaf. Clerc was born in La Balme, France, near Lyon, on Dec. 26, 1785. An accident in early childhood resulted in his becoming deaf. He was educated at the Institute for the Deaf and Dumb in Paris, one of the earliest of such schools in Europe. In 1815, Clerc met the Rev. Thomas Hopkins Gallaudet (q.v.) and accompanied him back to the United States. In 1817 they established a school at Hartford, Conn., now known as the American School for the Deaf. Because of its success, Congress in 1819 granted the school 20,000 acres (7,685 hectares) of land in Alabama. The land was later sold for $30,000.

Clerc was the first deaf teacher of the deaf in the United States. It is largely because of him and Gallaudet that the manual alphabet and the language of signs were introduced into schools for the deaf. Clerc died in Hartford on July 18, 1869.

Powrie V. Doctor
*Editor of "American Annals of the Deaf"*

A **CLERESTORY** in the nave of the Cathedral of Notre Dame, Paris.

FRENCH GOVERNMENT TOURIST OFFICE

**CLERESTORY,** klir'stôr-ē, in architecture, that part of a structure, pierced by windows, that rises above an adjoining roof of a lower part of the building, as in a church or hall. The term is also spelled *clearstory.*

The most highly developed of the many types of clerestories are found in Gothic churches. In these the central aisle or nave is lighted by clerestories above the roofs of the side aisles. The earliest known example of the use of the clerestory is the hypostyle hall in the great temple of Amon-Ra at Karnak, Egypt. The lofty bath halls and palaces of the ancient Romans were lighted by huge semicircular clerestory windows.

Clerestory windows admit light, and sometimes air, to the central portion of the building. They range from very small (sometimes mere spherical triangles) to very long and large, as in the Decorated and Perpendicular styles.

**CLERGY,** in the Christian church, the ordained ministers, representatives, or officers of the church, as distinguished both from unordained lay leaders or officers and from the main body of the faithful (the laity). The term is sometimes used of the officers or ministers of established or state churches, viewed in their relation to the state or to society in general. It is in use in Eastern Orthodox churches and in the West, in the Roman Catholic, Anglican, and established Protestant churches. Ordinarily it connotes priesthood, but not in those Reformed churches that maintain "the priesthood of all believers." Although "clergy" has special uses in some churches, in the modern world it is a convenient term for any group of Christian priests or ministers. The term is sometimes used of the leaders in other religions, as in Islam, but this usage is misleading and often disliked—as for example in Judaism.

**Development of the Ministry.** The existence of the ministry in one or more forms is evident in the records of the Christian church from earliest times. The influence of Greek religious societies is scarcely to be denied, though the main antecedents, examples, functions, and even titles were derived from the Jewish synagogues of the western or Greek-speaking Diaspora. For example, *bishop* meant "overseer"—one responsible for the welfare of the congregation, its faith and morals, its protection from persecution, even its finances. *Deacon* meant "minister"—helper or servant of the bishop or of the congregation. *Priest* was Jewish "elder" (*presbyter*) abbreviated, not pagan priest (*hiereus,* an officiant at sacrifices and a steward or administrator of sacred things). The New Testament reflects the earliest stage in the development of the ministry, when the office of apostle and evangelist was making way for the settled ministry of following generations. See also Archbishop; Bishop; Deacon.

By the Middle Ages the term *clericatus* (Old French *clergie*) was in use. It included not only clerks in holy orders—that is, priests, deacons, and subdeacons (the office of bishop was viewed as a fuller form of priesthood)—but also those in the four minor orders (doorkeeper, lector, exorcist, and acolyte). Ordination did not imply membership in a religious order, though many priests were and are members of orders (for example the Jesuit order).

The "simple cleric," or clerk, in medieval England was one who had received the ecclesiastical tonsure and as a man of learning—able to read and write—was entitled to various benefits, privileges, and immunities. He was also liable to be called into the king's service. Out of this situation grew the "benefit of clergy," which entitled members of the clergy to trial in ecclesiastical rather than in civil courts. In 1350 this privilege included those in minor orders, the secular clerks.

In 1972 the Roman Catholic Church abolished tonsure, the minor orders, and subdiaconate. Admittance to the clerical state was attached to ordination to the diaconate.

In the Roman Catholic Church, a rule of long standing requires priests above the rank of deacon to be unmarried. The Eastern Orthodox Church allows married men to be ordained but forbids marriage after ordination. Bishops, on the other hand, are selected from the celibate orders. In the Anglican and all Protestant churches there are no bans on marriage of priests or ministers. See Celibacy.

**Anticlericalism.** By the Middle Ages, clergy in both East and West formed the chief learned class. Thus they were in great demand as officials for the secular government, and many churchmen held high offices at the Byzantine court and the court of the Holy Roman Empire. This identification of church and state created grave problems, and by the time of the Reformation there was strong opposition to the involvement of the clergy in secular affairs and government. The full tide of anticlerical reaction could be seen in the French Revolution and other movements inspired by it. Yet tensions persisted. In Europe, the 19th century saw a strong movement of clericalism in the Roman Catholic Church, and an equally strong anticlerical movement. Both movements, and the tension between them, affected the rise of modern secularism and communism in European political circles.

Among Protestants, outside the established or state churches, there has been little occasion for the rise of such movements, though the revulsion against an official ministry has been characteristic of certain groups, chiefly the Friends (Quakers) and some sects of the Baptists. See also ANTICLERICALISM; CHURCH AND STATE.

FREDERICK C. GRANT
*Union Theological Seminary*

**CLERGY, Benefit of.** See BENEFIT OF CLERGY.

**CLERGY RESERVES.** See CANADA—*46. British North America, 1815–1857.*

**CLERK.** See CLERGY.

**CLERK-MAXWELL, James.** See MAXWELL, JAMES CLERK.

**CLERMONT,** kler-môn′, a town in France, in the department of Oise, 16 miles (26 km) southeast of Beauvais. It was a military post in the Middle Ages, and the remains of its fortress still exist. The Church of St Samson dates from the 13th century, and the town hall was built by Charles IV, who was born in Clermont in 1298. The town was sacked by the English in 1359 and 1415.

**CLERMONT-FERRAND,** kler-môn′ fe-rän′, a city in central France, is the capital of Puy-de-Dôme department and the largest city and historical capital of the Auvergne region. It is the economic and cultural focal point for much of the region, which is a rich agricultural area. The produce of the Auvergne is used in the agricultural processing industries that form an important part of the industrial activities that take place in the city.

One of France's major manufacturing cities, Clermont-Ferrand has varied manufactures, including rubber goods (especially tires), canned fruits and preserves, leather, linen, footwear, chemicals, and many engineering products. The local hydroelectric power of the Central Massif has been a strong stimulant to manufacturing. There are excellent rail and road connections in all directions, and an airport that has regular service to other French cities as well as to Algeria and Corsica.

Clermont-Ferrand is also the principal tourist crossroads for central France, especially in summer, when visitors can enjoy excursions into the beautiful Auvergnois countryside. Puy-de-Dôme Mountain, the popular health resorts of Royat and Châtel-Guyon, and the interesting old town of Riom are a few of the attractions nearby. The city itself has a number of monuments and churches of note, as well as a university. Population: 136,181 (1990 census).

HOMER PRICE
*Hunter College, New York*

**CLERMONT-GANNEAU,** kler-môn′gà-nō′, **Charles** (1846–1923), French Orientalist. He was born in Paris on Feb. 19, 1846. He studied Oriental languages and made expeditions to Jordan, Syria, the Red Sea, Egypt, and Cyrenaica. In 1870 he discovered the Moabite Stone, the stele of King Mesha, which bears the oldest known form of Semitic writing. The site of Gezer was identified by him in 1873–1874.

After entering the French diplomatic service, he held various posts, including vice consul (1880–1882), consul general (1896), and minister plenipotentiary (1906) in Palestine. He was also a director of the School of Oriental Languages in Paris and a member of the French Academy. Clermont-Ganneau helped expose as forgeries the Hebrew texts offered for sale to the British Museum in 1883 and, in 1903, the "tiara of Saïtapharnes" in the Louvre. His published works include *Les fraudes archéologiques en Palestine* (1885) and *Recueil d'archéologie orientale* (1885–1924).

**CLEVE,** klā′və, **Joos van** (c. 1485–c. 1540), Flemish religious and portrait painter. He was possibly born in Cleves. The earliest work ascribed to him is dated 1507. In 1511 he became a master in the Antwerp painters' guild. In 1515, in Cologne, he painted the triptych *Death of the Virgin*, introducing the Flemish tradition to that city. Joos, who served twice as dean of the Antwerp guild, was summoned by Francis I to France, where he painted several portraits of Francis and his Queen, Eleanor of Austria. In his last years Joos visited England (about 1536) and probably Italy. He died in Antwerp about 1540.

Many of Joos' paintings were derivative: the calm realism of his portraits suggests the influence of Quentin Massys and Holbein, and his religious paintings include deliberate imitations of Massys, Dürer, Jan van Eyck, Rogier van der Weyden, and Leonardo. Joos' best works are two *Madonnas*, one of which is now at Ince Hall, Lancashire, England, and the other in the Kunsthistorisches Museum, Vienna. His religious paintings are characteristically Flemish in their coloring and wealth of symbolic detail, but his use of chiaroscuro is Italianate.

**CLEVE,** klā′və, **Per Teodor** (1840–1905), Swedish chemist, who is known for his work on the rare-earth elements. Cleve was born in Stockholm, Sweden, on Feb. 10, 1840. He graduated from the University of Uppsala in 1863, studied in Paris, and joined the Uppsala faculty as professor of chemistry in 1874, holding that post until shortly before his death there on June 10, 1905.

Cleve first showed that the hypothetical eka-boron of Dmitri Mendeleyev is in reality scandium, first extracted by Lars Nilson. In 1879, after Nilson and Jean Charles Galissard de Marignac had extracted scandium and ytterbium, respectively, from erbium, Cleve resolved erbium into three oxides, those of erbium, holmium, and thulium. The latter two were named after Stockholm and Thule. In 1886, however, Paul Émile Lecoq de Boisbaudran separated Cleve's holmium into true holmium and dysprosium.

R. J. FORBES, *University of Amsterdam*

**CLEVELAND, Duchess of.** See VILLIERS—*Barbara Villiers.*

G. Cleveland

## 22d and 24th President of the United States (1885–1889; 1893–1897)

**Born**—March 18, 1837, in Caldwell, N. J.
**Higher Education**—None.
**Religion**—Presbyterian.
**Marriage**—June 2, 1886, to Frances Folsom (1864?–1947), in the White House.
**Children**—Ruth Cleveland (1891–1904); Esther Cleveland (1893–    ); Marion Cleveland (1895–    ); Richard Folsom Cleveland (1897–1974); Francis Grover Cleveland (1903–    ).
**Political Party**—Democratic.
**Position When Elected**—Governor of New York.
**Principal Writing**—*Presidential Problems* (1904).
**Died**—June 24, 1908, in Princeton, N. J., at age 71.
**Burial Place**—Princeton, N. J.

**CLEVELAND,** klēv′lənd, **Grover** (1837–1908), 22d and 24th president of the United States. Historians have judged Cleveland one of America's greatest presidents and his presidency as the most distinguished one between Lincoln's and Theodore Roosevelt's. Four achievements are generally associated with his name. He restored honesty and impartiality to government; he planted deep in the American mind the idea that the evils of the protective tariff system ought to be abolished; he saved the nation from the abandonment of the gold standard at a time when abandonment might have produced economic chaos; and he taught the American people that in their handling of foreign affairs conscience should always be the one dominant force.

Yet Cleveland's greatness as a president rests more on his character than on his accomplishments or brilliance. For honesty and independence alone he would stand out as a major president in the Gilded Age. Many historians have praised Cleveland for his courage, firmness, uprightness, self-direction, and common sense. "It is as a strong man, a man of character, that Cleveland will live in history," wrote Allan Nevins, who has made the most exhaustive study of Cleveland.

Stephen Grover Cleveland, the son of a Presbyterian minister, was born in Caldwell, N. J., on March 18, 1837. Several years later his family moved to Fayetteville in western New York, and he spent his childhood there and in nearby Clinton. Shortly after his father died in 1853, Cleveland went to stay near Buffalo, N. Y., with his uncle, who was able to place him in one of the best law offices in the city. For the next 26 years Cleveland remained in Buffalo.

**Rise to National Prominence.** Soon after Cleveland was admitted to the bar, he began his political activity as a Democratic ward worker. He served as assistant district attorney and, after the Civil War, as sheriff of Erie county. Then a series of chance events pushed him into the political limelight. A group of Buffalo citizens, aroused over the corruption and inefficiency that had characterized their city government for many years regardless of the party in power, persuaded Cleveland to run for mayor in 1881, and he won by a comfortable majority. He had campaigned on a platform of honesty and economy, and when he carried out his promises once in office,

Cleveland began to win recognition in New York state as an able administrator.

He now developed the ambition to become governor. He was successful in this venture in 1882 chiefly because of a stroke of good luck. With few outstanding Democratic leaders in the state, with the party leadership unable to unite on a candidate, and with the public in a mood to vote against machine politicians, Cleveland's reputation for independence won him the nomination. He went on to win the election mainly because of a split in Republican ranks.

As governor, Cleveland showed little understanding of the broader and more positive role the government could play. He was a vigorous proponent of the prevalent view of his day that government should not intervene in the economic and social life of the people except to maintain law and order and to protect property rights. He was known principally as a veto governor, and while he underscored the technical flaws of the bills he returned unsigned, he rarely recommended remedial action. With such a reputation Cleveland endeared himself to the conservatives and businessmen in both parties, who increasingly began to regard him as their best hope in the White House. As a result, the Democrats nominated him for president in 1884.

**The Election of 1884.** The Republicans turned their back on the incumbent president, Chester A. Arthur, and nominated James G. Blaine. Viewing Blaine as an old guard politician inimical to good government, a number of the reformist "Mugwumps" bolted the Republican party and supported Cleveland. There were few real issues, and the campaign degenerated into one of personal abuse and vilification. The Democrats published the "Mulligan letters" to attempt to prove that Blaine, as Speaker of the House, had been guilty of unethical conduct in connection with land-grant railroads, and the Republicans retaliated with the charge that Cleveland was the father of an illegitimate child, the responsibility for which he had accepted. The election of 1884 was close. Cleveland won by fewer than 25,000 popular votes, and his electoral vote was 219 to Blaine's 182.

**The Presidency:** *Philosophy of Government.* Cleveland's election as president ended 24 years of unbroken Republican control of the office. But his victory represented more of a change in spirit than it did in policies, because the Democratic party was largely in the hands of eastern conservatives who did not differ fundamentally from their Republican counterparts. Moreover, while Cleveland had the reputation of a reformer, not many believed he would put forth a progressive program or display vigorous leadership. Instead he was expected to bring greater honesty and sincerity to the presidency. During the campaign, Cleveland had emphasized a new moral attitude and the need for corrective action over that of constructive action. Many Americans agreed with him.

Cleveland's presidency is best understood in terms of his political and economic beliefs, which, it should be noted, were the prevalent ones of his day. He had an intense dislike of "paternalism" in government and therefore opposed the idea of the social service state. He believed Americans were entitled to economy, purity, and justice in their government but nothing more. There were to be favors for no one. His role as president was that of a righteous watchdog looking after other politicians and keeping them from granting favors and taking bribes. Thus he opposed tariff favors to business, pension favors to veterans, land favors to railroads, and economic benefits to farmers and workers. Cleveland's place in history is almost wholly as a negative President who believed it was his duty to prevent bad things from occurring but not to make good things happen.

**The Patronage Problem.** Because the Democrats had been out of power for a generation, one of the first problems Cleveland faced was that of patronage. Loyal and deserving Democrats were eager for positions, but the reformers who had done much to bring about Cleveland's election opposed any complete sweep from office. Cleveland was aware that he had a hungry party behind him, but the horde of office seekers so annoyed and distracted him that he cried in anguish: "My God, what is there in this office [the presidency] that any man should ever want to get into it?"

When Cleveland at first resisted the demands of the spoilsmen he was praised by the reformers, but under unrelenting pressure from office seekers and faced with a revolt within his own party, Cleveland gave in and Republicans were replaced. In his first term Cleveland approved of the removal of two thirds of the federal employees under his immediate control. On the credit side, Cleveland nearly doubled the number of classified civil servants (that is, these with tenure) during his first administration. But neither the reformers nor the Democratic party workers were satisfied, for Cleveland had offended the former by replacing Republicans with "deserving Democrats" and had antagonized the latter by lengthening the civil service list.

**Presidential Powers.** Cleveland's effort to restore the powers of the presidency was a major contribution to American political life. The seat of national political power for most of the post-Civil War generation was in Congress and not in the presidency. Cleveland never took issue with the prevalent viewpoint that the chief executive was subordinate to Congress, but he firmly believed in the doctrine of the separation of powers.

Since the end of the Civil War, Republican senators had dominated the national political scene. They had nearly ousted President Andrew Johnson from office, had gained almost complete possession of Grant, and then strove to put the succeeding presidents at their mercy. The bitter struggle between the executive and legislative branches over the Tenure of Office Act had begun in Johnson's day. Now, Republican senators, reluctant to relinquish their control to a Democratic president, sought to curb Cleveland's appointive power by demanding that he give them full information about his dismissals as well as his nominations for office. Cleveland refused to supply the information for removals. In an important state paper he defended the constitutional right of the president to withhold from Congress all information of a private or confidential nature and to determine what material was to be classified.

The Republican Senate fought back by threatening to block all appointments, but Cleveland knew the real power lay with him and that the public supported his position. This issue was so important to Cleveland that in March 1886 he appealed directly to the people. The Republican Senate subsequently gave in. In March 1887, the Tenure of Office Act was repealed. Cleveland had won both a personal and political victory.

**Pension Policy.** Cleveland is also remembered for his ability to say "no" and to mean "no." A good example of this iron fortitude is revealed in his pension policy. By the time Cleveland became president, nearly 900,000 Civil War pension claims had been filed, and more than a third of them had been approved. If a claim were rejected, congressmen could introduce private pen-

FRANCES FOLSOM married Cleveland in 1886, when she was 22, in the first White House presidential wedding.

sion bills, and great numbers of these were passed by general consent in a perfunctory manner. Because the wounds of a number of claimants were simulated or imaginary, many thoughtful Americans had become disgusted with this raid on the public treasury and regarded the situation as scandalous. No president before Cleveland had ever vetoed a private pension bill, but, while Cleveland signed more of these private pension bills than any previous president, he vetoed hundreds.

The veterans, through the Grand Army of the Republic, a powerful pressure organization in the country, protested these vetoes, and Congress responded by enacting the dependent pensions bill in 1887. It would have given a pension to any veteran who suffered from any disability, regardless of when or how it was received. Also included were dependent parents of soldiers who had died in service. Cleveland had the courage to veto this enormous largesse for veterans, though he predicted it might contribute to his defeat for reelection in 1888—and it did.

**Tariff Reform.** Cleveland's most important reform move in his first administration was his effort to lower the tariff. He believed government aid like government regulation should be kept to a minimum, and therefore he opposed the protective tariff on the grounds that it interfered with the economic natural law and that it was government paternalism as well as a subsidy to one portion of the business community. The protective tariff had also contributed not only to higher prices for consumers but also to the development of trusts. There was also the embarrassing matter of a consistent surplus in the Treasury. By 1887 the surplus had become a public issue. There were many proposals for spending the money, but too many of them smacked of the pork barrel. In Cleveland's view tariff reduction was the logical solution, and he decided to push for it.

In 1887, he did an unusual thing by devoting his entire annual message to Congress to an attack on the high tariff. No other president had ever given over his whole message to a single topic. Cleveland's move focused nationwide attention on the tariff and emphasized his leadership. But this is as far as Cleveland got in his tariff reform efforts, because he lost his opportunity to secure an effective law. The Mills bill, passed by the House in July 1888, contained only moderate reductions in the rates. When it became evident that the tariff would be an important issue in the 1888 election, the Republicans introduced a protectionist measure in the Senate. In these circumstances a satisfactory compromise bill was impossible.

**The Election of 1888.** The Democrats renominated Cleveland in 1888, and the Republicans chose Benjamin Harrison of Indiana. The campaign was waged largely on the tariff issue, with Republicans defending protection and Democrats advocating a reduction in duties. Both parties used money freely, and throughout the country voters were bribed in probably the most corrupt presidential election in U. S. history.

Although Cleveland had a majority of the popular vote, Harrison gained 233 electoral votes to Cleveland's 168. Despite the campaign talk about the tariff, the vote did not indicate a national decision against Cleveland on that issue. Cleveland carried the manufacturing state of New Jersey and increased his strength of 1884 in such pro-tariff states as Ohio, Michigan, and California. The decisive factors in his defeat were probably the efficiency of the Republican organization under Sen. Matthew S. Quay of Pennsylvania and the purchase of votes in some states.

**Between Administrations.** During the four years that Cleveland was out of office he had little to say about the questions then confronting the country, because he thought it was improper for a former president to speak out on public issues. He spent his time as a private citizen in New York City, practicing law with a Wall Street firm. Only once in the interval between his two administrations did he speak out on a public issue. That occurred in February 1891, when, with the free-silver sentiment increasing in the country and shaping up as a key issue in the 1892 campaign, Cleveland challenged the growing silver movement in a public letter in which he said "the greatest peril would be initiated by . . . the unlimited coinage of silver at our mints."

**The Election of 1892.** The appearance of the Populist or People's party, advocating, among a number of reforms, the free and unlimited coinage of silver at the ratio of 16 to 1, was the most exciting and important aspect of the presidential campaign of 1892. Harrison and Cleveland were pitted against one another again. Gen. James B. Weaver of Iowa, the Populist nominee for president, polled more than one million popular votes and won 22 electoral votes, and thus the Populists became the first third party since the Civil War to break into the Electoral College. By appearing as a staunch champion of conservative financial policies, Cleveland attracted much Republican support and defeated Harrison, 277 to 145, in electoral votes.

**Second Term.** Cleveland had the misfortune to have his entire second administration taken up by the most severe depression the country had yet experienced. Within a year after his second inauguration there were 4 million unemployed out of a population of about 65 million. There were acute personal hardships and a deterioration in the government's financial position. This period was Cleveland's real testing time.

Cleveland believed the Sherman Silver Purchase Act and the McKinley Tariff, both passed in 1890, had caused the panic of 1893 and the subsequent depression. In his view whatever else was wrong with the economy resulted from the folly or misfortune of individuals and thus was not the concern of the federal government. Cleveland used effective leadership to bring about the repeal of the Sherman Act, but unfortunately this did not restore prosperity or have any noticeable effect on the depression. To prevent the Treasury's gold reserve from falling below an amount sufficient to remain on the gold standard, Cleveland had the Treasury sell U. S. Government bonds to New York City bankers for gold. This was one of the most unpopular things Cleveland ever did, because many Americans became alarmed over the dependence of the government on a syndicate of Wall Street bankers.

Cleveland failed again to secure tariff reform. The Wilson-Gorman Tariff of 1894 did not fulfill the campaign promises of the Democrats in 1892 to lower the tariff. Although Cleveland refused to sign the bill, he declined to veto it. But worse than this he gave no effective leadership in framing the measure. It was a sad conclusion to the crusade he had launched in 1887.

The reform phase of Cleveland's public career had ended. For the rest of his presidency his role was that of a protector of the status quo. In this he was successful. He vetoed the seigniorage bill aimed at increasing the supply of the currency. Through subordinates he brusquely dismissed the petitions of angry wage earners, such as those who marched to Washington with Coxey's Army of the unemployed in 1894.

In the same year, he sent federal troops to crush the Pullman strike, which was obstructing the railroads and interfering with the mails. The strike soon collapsed, and at the same time Eugene V. Debs and other union leaders were sent to jail for violating a federal injunction. Cleveland's solution of the Pullman strike was costly. The imprisonment of Debs by a court order, without jury trial or conviction, and the use of a blanket injunction in the strike aroused serious concern in many Americans, even conservatives. All over the country advocates of states' rights and supporters of organized labor launched a heavy attack on Cleveland, whose popularity was now definitely on the wane.

The long-standing boundary dispute between British Guiana and Venezuela provided an opportunity for a partial recovery in the President's popularity. In response to Venezuela's appeal, the United States asked Britain a number of times to arbitrate the matter, only to be turned down on every occasion. Cleveland, in his message to Congress in December 1895, asked Congress for authorization to appoint a commission to determine the true boundary between Venezuela and British Guiana. His message and his support of the Monroe Doctrine were widely approved in the country, and Congress responded immediately with the authorization. The British agreed to submit the claim to arbitration. See also VENEZUELAN BOUNDARY DISPUTE.

In two other developments in foreign relations Cleveland stood by his strong anti-imperialist convictions: he refused aid and encouragement to rebel movements in Hawaii and Cuba.

**Later Years.** In 1897, Cleveland settled in Princeton, N. J. The former president remained a public figure, lecturing and writing and engaging in business affairs. He died in Princeton on June 24, 1908.

For all his faults and limitations, Cleveland was a symbol of civic staunchness in his own day. While few regarded him as a great constructive force in public affairs, they looked to him to lead the reform movement in terms of honesty, economy, and efficient government. Cleveland performed his task so well that for his generation and later ones he was the embodiment of this type of reform.

VINCENT P. DE SANTIS
*University of Notre Dame*

**Bibliography**
Cleveland, Grover, *Letters of Grover Cleveland, 1850–1908,* ed. by Allan Nevins (Houghton 1933).
Gillis, J. A., *A Hawaiian Incident* (1897; reprint, Ayer 1977).
Hollingsworth, Joseph R., *The Whirligig of Politics: The Democracy of Cleveland and Bryan* (Univ. of Chicago Press 1963).
Marszalek, John, *Grover Cleveland,* ed. by Carol B. Fitzgerald (Meckler Pub. 1988).
Parker, George F., *Recollections of Grover Cleveland* (1909; reprint, Ayer 1970).
Vexler, Robert I., *Grover Cleveland 1837–1908: Chronology, Documents, Bibliographical Aids* (Oceana Pub. 1968).
Welch, Richard E., Jr., *The Presidencies of Grover Cleveland* (Univ. Press of Kan. 1988).

**CLEVELAND,** klĕv'lənd, **John** (1613–1658), English poet, who had a considerable influence on other 17th century poets, particularly on Samuel Butler (in *Hudibras*) and possibly on Abraham Cowley and John Dryden. Cleveland (also spelled *Cleiveland*) was born in Loughborough, Leicestershire, in June 1613. At the age of 14, he entered Christ's College, Cambridge University. After receiving his bachelor's degree in 1631, Cleveland transferred to St. John's College, where he took his master's degree in 1635. He remained at St. John's as a master. During the next few years he wrote a number of bitterly satiric prose character sketches of Puritans that received wide circulation.

After the beginning of the Civil War in 1642, Cleveland was expelled from Cambridge because of his hostility to Oliver Cromwell. He joined the Royalist army, and in 1645 he was appointed judge advocate for the Royalist garrison at Newark. He held this position until the surrender of Newark to the Puritans in 1646. For the next nine years little is known of his activities, but he must have eked out an existence by tutoring the children of impoverished fellow Royalists. In 1655 he was arrested in Norwich, probably for debt, and jailed at Yarmouth because he had no gainful employment. He was released after writing his *Petition to the Protector,* to Cromwell, and again he must have taught for a living. In 1657 he moved to Gray's Inn, London, but he lived only a short time. He died in London on April 29, 1658.

Most of Cleveland's miscellaneous verse was written while he was at the university. Evidence reveals that by the early 1640's his reputation as a poet was well established, although no volume of his verse was published until 1647. There then followed 22 editions during the next 50 years, a fact that shows Cleveland to have been the most popular English poet of the mid-17th century.

Cleveland's popularity is probably to be explained by the fact that much of his verse, especially that written in couplet form, is polemic satire treating of contemporary issues and persons. Its success certainly cannot be explained by any intrinsic poetic merit in the verse, since he used an exaggerated form of the "metaphysical conceit" so frequently that the epithet "Clevelandism" became synonymous with bad and labored verse.

DONALD B. CLARK
*University of Missouri*

**Further Reading:** Etchells, Ruth, ed., *Early English Poets* (Lion Pub. 1988); Lord, George D., *Classical Presences in 17th-Century English Poetry* (Yale Univ. Press 1987).

**CLEVELAND,** klĕv'lənd, a city in Mississippi, one of the two seats of Bolivar county, is about 100 miles (160 km) north of Vicksburg. (The other county seat is Rosedale.) Cleveland is the trading center for an agricultural area that produces cotton, rice, soybeans, and various grain crops. It manufactures ceramic tile, pharmaceuticals, automobile trim, and tool and die products.

Delta State College, a coeducational institution, was established in Cleveland in 1924. The city is the headquarters for the Bolivar county public library system. Cleveland was first settled in 1884. It was incorporated in 1886, and it became a city in 1930. Government is by a mayor and a city council. Population: 13,841.

The Terminal Tower Building, completed in 1930, is still the centerpiece of the Cleveland skyline.

**CLEVELAND,** klēv′lənd, a city located in northeastern Ohio, at the mouth of the Cuyahoga River, on Lake Erie's southern shore, approximately 30 miles (50 km) north of Akron. Situated about midway between Chicago and New York, Cleveland lies near the center of industrial North America, within easy range of raw materials and markets. The Cleveland metropolitan area—home of some 2.9 million people, including more than 478,000 in the city proper—ranks among the foremost manufacturing centers in the United States. Scattered around the city and its suburbs are diverse industrial enterprises ranging from gigantic steel mills and automobile assembly plants to small shops. Cleveland is also a center for education and research. Long Ohio's most populous city, Cleveland was surpassed by Columbus in the 1990 census.

Cleveland has an intense and diversified cultural life, focusing on the unusual concentration of museums and educational systems in the northeastern part of the city, in an area known as University Circle. Interest in music, theater, and sports runs high, and excellent facilities for these activities center in the downtown district. The city has many fine parks and is surrounded by a suburban park system preserving the woodlands for which Cleveland was named the "Forest City."

From its early days Cleveland attracted immigrants from abroad, especially from Germany, Italy, and central Europe, as well as from many parts of the United States. The result is a population of many ethnic, racial, religious, and socioeconomic strands. In 2000 the city's population was about 51% black and 7% Hispanic.

Cleveland is divided into an east and a west side by the valley of the Cuyahoga River. Just to the east of the Cuyahoga is the Mall, a park extending inland from Lake Erie. Around the Mall are many of Cleveland's public buildings, including the county courthouse, the city hall, the convention center, and the public library. Many of the city's main arteries emanate from the Public Square, also called Monument Park, located close to the Mall. The cosmopolitan downtown gives way to the slum areas of the central city. Cleveland, like many older industrialized cities, has a decayed urban core ringed with prosperous modern suburbs. The Hough area was the scene of riots in the 1960's. Efforts are being made to rebuild such areas.

Cuyahoga county, of which Cleveland is the seat, has become a completely urban area with a high concentration of industrial and commercial establishments. Greater Cleveland, once confined to Cuyahoga county, now extends to Lake, Geauga, and Medina counties as well. The city is part of the Cleveland-Akron-Lorain consolidated metropolitan area, which in 1990 ranked 13th in population among the metropolitan areas of the United States.

Initially, two factors enabled Cleveland to become the metropolis and industrial center of Ohio. First, the Ohio and Erie Canal, completed to the Ohio River at Portsmouth in 1832, attracted mercantile and shipping business to Cleveland. Second, easy access to iron ore (shipped on the Great Lakes from Minnesota and Michigan since 1855) and to coal (transported by canal and rail from West Virginia, Kentucky, and southern Ohio) made the city a shipping headquarters, a steel producer, and a diversified production center.

For the first 125 years of Cleveland's history —from 1796, when the city was laid out—development was mainly within the city itself. In the second half of the 19th century the main thoroughfare, Euclid Avenue, became "Millionaire's Row," lined with the mansions and gardens of the commercial-industrial barons. In the 1920's came extensive rebuilding downtown, in government structures, department stores, office buildings, and theaters. During this decade the city's suburban periphery also built up, mostly in residential development.

From the middle of the Great Depression of the 1930's until the end of World War II, there was little construction. Then, in the years after the war, the major building occurred on an ever-widening semicircle of suburban land, where large acreage was available for home allotments, shopping centers, and industrial use.

In the meantime there was a great shift in the city's population structure. Until World War I, the people who settled in Cleveland had come mainly from the eastern United States or Europe. In 1918, when there was a shortage of labor in Cleveland's factories making war goods, there began a major influx of blacks from Southern rural areas and of whites, mainly from Kentucky, Tennessee, and West Virginia. After World War II, thousands of more newcomers, mostly black, arrived. Almost all of these people were seeking economic opportunities unavailable to them in their home states.

The demand in most Cleveland factories and offices long has been for special skills. When the newcomers of the 1950's and 1960's arrived, generally they did not have the education and capability needed. Frequently they were forced to take temporary work or become relief clients, living in small homes and apartments in the inner city's older neighborhoods. Crowded living conditions and low incomes caused dissatisfaction and despair among many of these residents. These factors contributed to the serious rioting in the Hough section in 1966.

As more prosperous residents drifted to the suburbs after World War II and new suburban shopping centers competed with downtown business, the traditional growth and natural renewal of central Cleveland were interrupted. New buildings that might have gone up near the city's heart were erected elsewhere. Finally, with federal aid, renewal of a part of the downtown area, called Erieview, began in the late 1950's. Thereafter, urban renewal was ongoing, though the pace was often slow.

## 1. The Urban Crisis

While businesses, governmental agencies, and individuals had spent billions of dollars on construction in Greater Cleveland after 1945, the consensus of civic leaders in the late 1960's was that more improvements were needed in the city proper, especially in the older sections. Among the most pressing problems were the needs to construct or remodel office buildings, apartment houses, and hotels, and to clean up the lakefront and Cuyahoga river to reduce pollution. In these respects, it was felt, Cleveland had not matched the progress reflected in the rapid pace of suburban residential building since World War II or the expansion or rebuilding of steel mills and automobile plants in the metropolitan area.

**Downtown Renewal.** One factor that hampers acquisition of land for major projects in the older areas of Cleveland is the manner in which Gen. Moses Cleaveland's surveyors platted the city in 1796. General Cleaveland, whose name was shortened by poor spellers, envisioned the community as a replica of his native Connecticut village (Canterbury), where small houses clustered around a central public square. Lots in downtown Cleveland, therefore, were laid out in small frontages for one-family dwellings. This has imposed the often costly difficulty of dealing with numerous owners when an accumulation of land is needed for a major new development. Some streets in or near the downtown area still have narrow business buildings interspersed with occasional 19th century residences. Many such parcels were done away with only through the right of condemnation in making way for the three major development projects that have changed the face of downtown Cleveland since 1900—the Mall group plan of public buildings (1910's and 1920's), the Union Terminal complex (1920's) facing Public Square, and the Erieview redevelopment (1960's).

In Erieview, a 40-story privately owned office building, a 32-story federal office building, a 12-story privately owned apartment building, and many small structures have been completed since 1964. Several other parts of the Erieview project were not started as soon as their private planners had promised. Elsewhere downtown, since 1955, new office structures have replaced outmoded buildings, while many others have been modernized. The size of the city's Convention Center has been doubled.

Two educational developments have infused young blood in the near-downtown area: creation of the publicly supported 2-year Cuyahoga County Community College in 1963; and transformation of Fenn College, a private institution, into Cleveland State University (CSU), an Ohio-supported school, in 1965. Both, particularly CSU, expect to enlarge their enrollments and the size of their campuses.

**Housing.** Cleveland was among the first major U. S. cities to sponsor, with federal help, urban renewal programs in older residential neighborhoods. In the early 1930's, Msgr. Robert Navin, later president of St. John College, downtown, made a classic study of the cost of slums in terms of extra police and fire protection, delinquency, and disease. Since then, numerous slum clearance or improvement programs have been undertaken, mostly on the southeast and east sides. The city's

---

### INFORMATION HIGHLIGHTS

**Population:** (2000 census) city, 478,403; Cleveland-Akron consolidated metropolitan statistical area (including eight counties), 2,945,831.

**Land Area:** City, 76 square miles (196 sq km).

**Elevation:** 659 feet (201 meters) at Public Square, the city center.

**Climate:** Normal temperatures—January, 20–35° F (−7– +2° C); July, 60–83° F (16–28° C); normal precipitation—35.35 inches (898 mm) annually.

**Government:** Mayor and city council composed of 33 members.

**Date of Founding:** 1796.

share of the cost has been defrayed largely through bond issues approved by referendum.

Unfortunately, for years after World War II, overcrowding was tolerated by city officials; housing regulations were lax and inspections infrequent. Some renewal projects were begun without considering where displaced residents would go, and their moving created overcrowding in other neighborhoods. With many low-income newcomers arriving after World War II, this overcrowding has continued despite the creation of a city housing department, added legislation, and employment of more housing inspectors.

Civic-minded business leaders in increasing numbers have joined in trying to find practical ways of meeting slum problems, through improvement of educational opportunities, through creation of jobs for semiskilled workers capable of learning machinery operation, and through experiments in remodeling deteriorating dwellings. One vital corrective instrument has been the Cleveland Metropolitan Housing Authority (CMHA), a public agency that built five "estates" with 1,541 suites for lower-income families and retired persons between 1961 and 1966. The authority's estates mostly replaced dilapidated structures in older parts of the city.

**Air and Water Pollution.** In the mid-20th century Cleveland developed a reputation for pollution. When there was cloud cover and little wind off Lake Erie, air pollution was serious, and demands were made that industrial operators, apartment landlords, and electric utility owners (including Cleveland itself, which operates a municipal power plant) take corrective measures. Much, though not enough, was done with precipitators and other devices to reduce air pollution in Cleveland, and the city stepped up its efforts to force compliance with legislation long on the books.

While it was customary to blame industry for air pollution in Cuyahoga county and for water pollution in the Cuyahoga River and the parts of Lake Erie near the Cleveland shoreline, another serious cause of the menace was the past failure to twin all sewer systems for purposes of both drainage and sewage disposal. A result was diversion of sewage into sanitary sewers at times of heavy rains. Cleveland and its suburbs spent millions of dollars a year, received from bond issues and sale of water, for better sewer systems and more adequate sewage treatment plants. Some manufacturers responsible for pollution installed expensive equipment to correct conditions. But local, state, and federal planners believed that many millions of dollars were needed to cope with the problems. Programs for improving Lake Erie, sometimes referred to as a "dead" lake because of the absence of fish once plentiful in it, were formulated by the states concerned and by the federal government. Over the decades significant improvements were made.

Cleveland supplies itself and most other Cuyahoga county communities (as well as parts of adjoining counties) with water at low cost. Cleveland was one of the first large cities in the nation to fluoridate its water, starting in the mid-1950's.

## 2. The People

Cleveland's first settlers came from Connecticut, because the area was part of that state's Western Reserve until 1800. The Ohio Canal and railroad construction brought laborers from Ireland and elsewhere. After Cleveland's commercial and

### POPULATION OF CLEVELAND AND CUYAHOGA COUNTY

| Census year | Cleveland | Rest of county | County total |
|---|---|---|---|
| 1820 | 606 | 5,722 | 6,328 |
| 1850 | 17,034 | 31,065 | 48,099 |
| 1900 | 381,768 | 57,352 | 439,120 |
| 1950 | 914,808 | 474,724 | 1,389,532 |
| 1960 | 876,050 | 771,845 | 1,647,895 |
| 1970 | 750,879 | 969,956 | 1,720,835 |
| 1980 | 573,822 | 924,578 | 1,498,400 |
| 1990 | 505,616 | 906,524 | 1,412,140 |
| 2000 | 478,403 | 915,575 | 1,393,978 |

industrial possibilities became understood in the mid-1850s, waves of tradespeople and skilled workers arrived from New England, New York, and other eastern states. To some extent before the Civil War, but especially thereafter, immigrants came in hordes from England, Germany, Ireland, Scotland, Bohemia, Poland, Slovenia, Russia, and other lands.

Although these newcomers frequently settled in neighborhoods "with their own kind," no single ethnic group has dominated the community. In certain areas, however, one nationality still predominates, as in "Little Italy" near University Circle and the Slovenian section along St. Clair Avenue in the East 60s. Irish, German, and Italian immigrants might have argued and scorned each other's habits and dialects, but their children intermarried, and their offspring went into politics as leaders in both major parties.

African Americans have lived in Cleveland since its early decades and never have faced segregation in public schools. An early history of the schools, in fact, states that an African American effort to have a segregated school, in 1843, was refused. As large numbers of low-income African American families from small towns and rural areas of the South moved to Cleveland in 1918 and after, they settled in the older east side, gradually occupying nearly all the living space; in such areas, de facto school segregation exists.

There is no doubt that many white families moved to the suburbs after African American families bought houses on their streets. This condition has continued, aggravated in some cases by "blockbusting," the deliberate inducement of panic selling so that the buyer can make a quick profit by reselling or renting to African Americans.

In the interest of racial harmony and neighborhood stability, private biracial organizations have been formed in Cleveland, in East Cleveland, in the Ludlow section of Shaker Heights, and elsewhere. On a citywide scale, the Cleveland Community Relations Board, created in 1945 as the first such group in the United States formed by municipal ordinance, investigates interracial complaints and has done much good in airing frictions and seeking solutions. In 1967 Carl B. Stokes, a Democrat, was elected Cleveland's first African American mayor.

Cleveland's population peaked in 1950 at 914,808 and then declined by 47.7% over the next 50 years as large numbers moved to the suburbs. The suburban population jumped, but by 1970 the county had also peaked. In 2000 the population of Cleveland was 51% African American, compared with 15% for the rest of Cuyahoga county.

## 3. The Economy

Cleveland has anchored its livelihood in the waters of Lake Erie, which since the 19th century have brought commerce there, and iron ore

A STEEL MILL in the "flats," an industrial area along the Cuyahoga River. Terminal Tower, in downtown Cleveland, can be seen in the distance.

for its basic industry, steel. The metropolitan area is a leading manufacturer of many products dependent on steel: automobile parts, trucks, aircraft engines, machine tools, industrial fasteners, household appliances. In the broader spectrum of its diversified economy, Cleveland ranks as a major printing and publishing center and stands high in output of goods as varied as paints, apparel, light bulbs, and hothouse tomatoes.

**Industrial Growth.** Early farsighted Clevelanders gained control over ore and coal fields in the mid-1800's; they built railroads and ships, steel mills and fabricating plants in the years that followed. John D. Rockefeller was educated in Cleveland and started his business career there. He saw that possession of oil wells was not enough to build a business empire and that control of transportation and marketing was essential. He first incorporated the Standard Oil Company in Cleveland in 1870. His business acumen and his action, often ruthless, created a behemoth monopoly that the nation in self-defense broke up in 1911. The pieces of that monopoly persisted as leading businesses of the city.

Cleveland's early industrial successes attracted skilled immigrants. Their abilities and standards ensured success for their employers and led to the location of more factories in Cleveland. Thomas H. White moved his sewing machine plant there from Massachusetts in 1866, to be near materials and markets; the factory continues to operate, as does an offshoot plant that makes trucks. In 1880, two New Englanders, Worcester R. Warner and Ambrose Swasey, found that Chicago did not have the skilled mechanics they needed for their machine tool and telescope-making business. They were persuaded by Clevelanders to settle in the city, and they led in making Cleveland a machine tool center. Factories producing more than 75 makes of automobiles sprang up in Cleveland after 1895. Some failed quickly, but others were successful until about 1930. They led to the emergence of companies specializing in auto parts; some of these expanded and remained in Cleveland. When the big Detroit auto makers were ready to decentralize, Cleveland was

a natural location for stamping, parts, and assembly plants and for foundries, because of its supply of steel and skilled help.

Traditions of skill have been passed on, generation after generation, but not only in steel mills, assembly lines, and machine tool plants. Cleveland is home for companies that make men's and women's clothing worn in all parts of the nation. Even many Clevelanders do not realize that Cuyahoga county is a principal greenhouse producer of Bibb lettuce and tomatoes; some of this quiet industry's more than 400 acres (160 hectares) under glass is within sight of the Terminal Tower downtown. Excellent trade schools, scientific and business courses, and research laboratories bulwark the technological and productive skills that go back three and four generations.

In the second half of the 1960's, nonagricultural employment in the 4-county Cleveland metropolitan area passed 800,000. About 39% of the workers were in manufacturing (durable goods 29%, nondurable 10%), 21% in wholesale and retail trade, 14% in services, 12% in government (including school) employment, and the remaining 14% in other categories. Value added by manufacture in the Cleveland area was nearing $5 billion a year, about double the figure for the same four counties 10 years earlier.

**Labor Relations.** Since the 1930's, when there was bloodshed during steel strikes, Cleveland, a strong union center, has been generally blessed with intelligent labor-management relations and negotiations, and with less violence than has afflicted some other industrial centers. The longer strikes mostly have been at smaller companies. One tie-up lasted four months in the winter of 1962–1963, suspending publication of the two daily newspapers, the *Plain Dealer* (mornings and Sundays) and the *Press* (afternoons).

**Transportation.** Cleveland's port, dredged to a depth of 27 feet (8 meters), is visited in season (usually April-December) by a continuous flow of shipping. Ore carriers come from Minnesota and Labrador, while freighters bring imports from European and Asian ports and carry Ohio products, often heavy machinery and

THE CLEVELAND MUSEUM OF ART displays objects from its medieval collection in a light, modern gallery.

vehicles, to lands abroad. The municipal department of port control has spent millions of dollars, since its creation in 1954, to meet the demands of St. Lawrence Seaway shipping. The money, from bond issues paid off by real estate taxes, has gone to build new docks and warehousing. Among U. S. Great Lakes ports, Cleveland ranks fifth in cargo handled and stands second in incoming cargo tonnage. It is the leading iron-ore port on the lakes.

Cleveland is served by five major railroads. More than 200 freight-trucking lines have terminals or offices serving the Cleveland-Akron area.

Motor travel improved greatly in the 1960's with the completion of parts of the federal interstate expressway system in the Cleveland area. Of the six interstate routes serving the metropolitan district, all but the Ohio Turnpike (built by the state in the 1950's) are freeways. They include an Inner Belt, completed around the eastern and southern portions of downtown Cleveland, and a partly completed Outer Belt through the suburbs. Interstate 90 now links Cleveland with the New York Thruway, and Interstate 71 runs to Columbus and Cincinnati. Progress has also been made on Interstates 80 (eventually a short route to New York City) and 77 (to Marietta, Ohio).

Public transportation includes municipal and privately operated bus lines and two rapid transit lines using high-speed street cars. The largest bus operator is the municipally owned, self-sustaining Cleveland Transit System (CTS), which serves Cleveland and many suburbs. CTS also runs a rapid transit line from East Cleveland to Union Terminal in downtown Cleveland and from there southwest, with an extension under construction to Cleveland Hopkins International Airport. A rapid transit line run by the city of Shaker Heights connects that community with Union Terminal.

Major airlines operate both propeller and jet planes on regularly scheduled flights from Cleveland Hopkins International Airport. Regular service also is provided to Detroit from Burke Lakefront Airport. Both Hopkins and Burke are municipally owned.

## 4. Points of Interest

Highlighting any list of things to see and do in Cleveland would be a trip to its excellent art museum, a concert by its world-renowned symphony orchestra, and a major league baseball or football game at Municipal Stadium. No visit would be complete without viewing the city from Terminal Tower, Cleveland's tallest building, which rises 708 feet (126 meters) over the downtown section.

**Museums.** Three of the principal museums are located 5 miles (8 km) east of Public Square, in a complex of cultural and educational institutions known as the University Circle. These are the Cleveland Museum of Art, the Natural Science Museum, and the Western Reserve Historical Society Museum. Between the Circle and Public Square are two other museums of great interest, the Health Museum and Dunham Tavern.

The Cleveland Museum of Art is one of the finest in the world. Its paintings by Spanish masters, its medieval Guelph treasure, and its Oriental and Middle Eastern works of art are among the outstanding exhibits. Programs and art classes are presented for children and adults. The annual May Show features local artists' work.

The Natural Science Museum contains fine exhibits of minerals, glacial remnants, beetles and butterflies, birds, mammals, and giant reptile remains, including a haplocanthosaurus uncovered by a museum expedition in Utah. A good collection of Cleveland shale fossils has been enhanced by finds in excavations made in the mid-1960's for an interstate highway in Cuyahoga county. Special classes in sciences are conducted. The museum contains a planetarium and helps operate, with Cleveland, an aquarium in Gordon Park. The aquarium was housed in a new building in 1967.

The museum and library of the Western Reserve Historical Society focus attention on the area's heritage, in paintings, books, sculpture, furniture, housewares, dolls, clothing, and other displays. The society also has an outstanding Napoleonic collection and a top genealogical department. Adjacent to the library is the spacious Automobile and Aircraft Museum, with antique cars and early airplanes.

The Cleveland Health Museum expands the visitor's knowledge of human body processes and of medicine, through transparent anatomical figures and other displays, all designed to promote good health practices. Dunham Tavern, a former stagecoach inn, is now a history museum and contains many antiques.

**Music and Theater.** Severance Hall is the permanent home of the Cleveland Orchestra, generally regarded as one of the best in the world. Long under the baton of George Szell, it has made triumphal tours in the United States and abroad. The Metropolitan Opera Company, of New York, performs a week of operas in Public Hall each spring.

The Play House, operating three repertory theaters, has maintained high standards of cast and play selection since its founding in 1916. Karamu Theater produces excellent performances with local interracial casts. The Hanna Theater houses plays and musicals with professional road casts.

**Sports.** Major participant and spectator sports all are popular in Cleveland—baseball, basketball, boating, football, golf, hockey, horseback riding, horse racing, swimming, and tennis. The city's professional sports teams include the Browns (National Football League), the baseball Indians (American League), and the Cavaliers (National Basketball Association). Skiing and soccer have increased in popularity.

The city of Cleveland operates a score of recreational centers, including swimming pools, and each major suburb has its own. There are eight Cleveland municipal and Cleveland Metropolitan Park System public golf courses and more than a dozen major private courses. International tennis matches have drawn large audiences.

**Parks.** Cleveland's parks total 2,000 acres (800 hectares) and include a large zoo in Brookside Park on the southwest side. Much of the city's scenic acreage was donated by philanthropists such as John D. Rockefeller, Jeptha Wade, and William Gordon from the 1880's on. Surrounding the city is an "emerald necklace" of parkland administered by an independent agency set up in 1917 under Ohio law. The Metropolitan Park System contains 17,000 acres (6,900 hectares) along streams and woodlands. These parks have miles of scenic drives, nature trails and bridle paths, and several trailside museums.

## 5. Education and Research

In the 1960's, Cleveland adopted bond financing for new school construction for the first time in modern decades, as the need for classrooms skyrocketed, particularly in Negro areas. In the second half of the decade, more than 20 major schools were being erected or were planned. Meanwhile, teacher supply had tightened, partly because of the drain of teachers to the suburbs, but this situation was eased by recruiting outside the metropolitan area and by the return of some former teachers whose children had grown up. Many Head Start programs, with federal aid, have broadened the horizons of deprived young Clevelanders.

Until the 1960's all the major institutions of higher learning in Cleveland were operated privately. Western Reserve University, Case Institute of Technology, John Carroll University, Notre Dame, St. John and Ursuline colleges, and Baldwin-Wallace College (in suburban Berea) remain under private auspices. The publicly supported institutions are Cleveland State University (formerly privately operated Fenn College) and Cuyahoga Community (junior) College.

Western Reserve University (founded 1820) and Case Institute (1880), on adjoining campuses in the University Circle, in 1967 took the last legal steps to consummate a consolidation under a new corporate name, Case Western Reserve University. This united many of their operations. With museums and other institutions nearby, they had formed in 1957 the University Circle Development Foundation, which unified programs and land acquisition. With the help of the foundation, construction of research center for industrial and other users was begun in 1966 near Case Institute.

Many companies in Greater Cleveland have research laboratories. Long a model of its kind is General Electric's Nela Park, which is devoted to lighting and electrical research. Much important aircraft, missile, and outer-space research has been carried out at the National Aeronautics and Space Administration's Lewis Research Center near Cleveland Hopkins International Airport. Extensive medical research has been done in Cleveland hospitals, notably on the heart.

The Cleveland Public Library System, created in 1869, has an open-shelf policy that applies to almost all its collections. The downtown main library and adjoining business-science library building cover an entire block. In 1965 the main library instituted a drive-up service, by which borrowers can telephone for books and pick them up without leaving their cars. The John G. White collection's materials on folklore, Orientalia, and chess are among the best of their type. An art gallery in the main library is cosponsored by the Museum of Art. The library has 36 neighborhood branches.

The Allen Memorial Medical Library has a major collection and houses the Howard Dittrick museum of Historical Medicine, much of it pertaining to Cleveland. Long-established suburbs have their own libraries, and the Cuyahoga county system provides books elsewhere. The area's colleges have expanding library collections.

## 6. Government

Cleveland is governed by a mayor and city council. The mayor and councilmen are elected directly by the people, the mayor in a citywide election, the councilmen in wards.

Generally the city has operated with a balanced budget. Limited finances have kept some municipal services at a lower level than many believe they should be. To provide more operating revenues, the council in 1966 authorized a 0.5% municipal income tax. Collections began in 1967.

County government operates courts, hospitals, roads, and jails, runs elections, and administers welfare. Public welfare programs are augmented by a United Appeal program, which receives exceptionally high per capita support.

Periodically, as demands for services in some suburbs have exceeded the ability to provide them, there have been demands for broader county government under a county charter. Voters have defeated each such proposal.

Public revenues in Cleveland have come primarily from real estate taxes, fees, and state and federal matching grants. The principal expenditures are for departmental operations. Cleveland's water and sewage-disposal operations are self-sustaining, through direct billing of local users and master-metering of mains to suburbs, which bill their residents. Municipal, school, and county capital improvements customarily are financed by bond issues, which are paid off from real estate taxes.

Overwhelmingly Democratic since the days of Franklin D. Roosevelt, Cleveland in 1971 elected its first Republican mayor in 32 years, Ralph J. Perk. He succeeded Cleveland's first black mayor, Carl B. Stokes, and was reelected in 1975.

JOHN F. HUTH, JR., *"The Plain Dealer"*

**Further Reading:** Kusmer, Kenneth L., *A Ghetto Takes Shape: Black Cleveland 1870–1930* (Univ. of Ill. Press 1976); Miggins, Edward M., and Campbell, Thomas F., eds., *The Birth of Modern Cleveland* (Western Reserve Univ. Press 1988); Van Tassel, David D., and Grabowski, John, eds., *Cleveland: A Tradition of Reform* (Kent State Univ. Press 1986); id., *The Encyclopedia of Cleveland History* (Ind. Univ. Press 1987).

**CLEVELAND,** an industrial city in southeastern Tennessee, seat of Bradley county, 26 miles (42 km) northeast of Chattanooga. It is in a pine timber and farming area and manufactures stoves, furniture, textiles, clothing, and chemicals. Lee College, a four-year liberal arts and theological institution founded in 1918 and owned by the Church of God, is in Cleveland. A community college was established in 1967. The city is the headquarters of Cherokee National Forest, which adjoins Great Smoky Mountains National Park. Cleveland was founded in 1837 and incorporated the following year. Population: 37,192.

RUTH CHAMBERS, *Cleveland Public Library*

**CLEVELAND MUSEUM OF ART,** an art museum founded in 1913 in Cleveland, Ohio. A world-class repository of art, the museum is distinguished by exceptional collections and a long-standing commitment to scholarship and education. Admission to the museum is free, a rarity among major private art museums.

The original neoclassical building, designed by Hubbell and Benes, opened in 1916. A major addition in 1958 doubled gallery space, and in 1970 Marcel Breuer's three-story wing added two large galleries for special exhibitions, a 750-seat auditorium, two lecture and recital halls, classrooms, and offices. Expansion in 1984 added nine more galleries and a new art reference library. The museum has flourished in large measure through the generosity of its founders and supporters; important bequests include those of Jeptha Wade, John Huntington, Horace Kelley, Elizabeth Severance Prentiss, and Leonard C. Hanna.

The Cleveland Museum's permanent collections represent a wide range of history and cultures, including the ancient Mediterranean, Egypt, Greece, and Rome; Europe; North America; Africa; ancient and Islamic West Asia; India and Southeast Asia; China, Japan, and Korea; and the pre-Columbian Americas. Holdings in medieval European art and Asian art are especially noteworthy. Well-known works include the medieval Guelph Treasure, two 14th-century B.C. heads of the Egyptian pharaoh Amenhotep III, the finest group of Japanese screens outside of Japan, and major Western paintings by Filippo Lippi, El Greco, Caravaggio, Rubens, Poussin, Turner, Church, Degas, van Gogh, Matisse, Picasso, and Kiefer.

The museum's education and public programs department offers classes, gallery talks, and family events and also conducts a joint art history program with Case Western Reserve University. The musical arts department sponsors frequent concerts, and there is a respected film program.

**CLEVELAND ORCHESTRA,** one of the finest—and youngest—of the major American symphony orchestras in the United States. It gave its first concert on Dec. 11, 1918, at Grays' Armory in Cleveland, Ohio. The first conductor was Ukrainian-born Nikolai Sokoloff, and the first manager was Adella Prentiss Hughes, one of the founders. During its initial season the orchestra had 55 players; by 1921–1922 it had 90. In its early years the Cleveland Orchestra played at the Masonic Temple, but in 1931 it moved into its own home, Severance Hall, the gift of industrialist John L. Severance and the people of Cleveland and dedicated to the memory of Mrs. Elisabeth Severance.

Sokoloff retired in 1933 and was succeeded by Artur Rodzinski, who continued to build the orchestra. Erich Leinsdorf was the next music director (1943–1946), but U.S. Army service left him much absent from the post. George Szell became music director in 1946 and further increased the orchestra's size, to 107. Under his leadership it achieved an international reputation for brilliance of tone, virtuosity of execution, and purity and clarity of sound. Following Szell's death in 1970, Pierre Boulez served as musical adviser and principal guest conductor until 1972. Lorin Maazel, music director from 1972 to 1982, continued to maintain the orchestra's preeminence, as did Christoph von Dohnányi, who became music director in 1984, after being music director-designate from 1982.

From its inception the Cleveland Orchestra has played perhaps the most extensive schedule of concerts for schoolchildren of any American orchestra, and it has made many tours of Europe (from 1957) and Asia (from 1970). In addition, it has performed at the prestigious Salzburg Festival (1967, 1990, 1992, 1994). The orchestra has long performed—in concert and on recordings—with the Cleveland Orchestra Chorus, founded by George Szell in 1952. The 170-voice volunteer choir was brought to early brilliance by Robert Shaw, the orchestra's associate conductor (1956–1967). In 1968 the Cleveland Orchestra established its summer home, Blossom Music Center, located in Cuyahoga Falls, between Cleveland and Akron.

ROBERT FINN*
*Cleveland "Plain Dealer"*

**CLIBURN,** klĭ'bərn, **Van** (1934–    ), American pianist who achieved world renown when in April 1958 he won first prize in the first International Tchaikovsky Piano Competition in Moscow. Upon his return home, he became the first classical musician to receive a ticker tape parade in New York City. His performances throughout the United States that year established him as one of the world's leading box-office attractions in music; later, world tours and highly successful recordings placed him among the preeminent concert artists to emerge after World War II.

Harvey Lavan Cliburn, Jr., was born in Shreveport, La., on July 12, 1934. He was brought up in Kilgore, Tex., where his mother gave him his first piano lessons, and in 1947 he made his debut as a pianist in Houston. In 1948, as winner of the National Music Festival Award, Cliburn made his New York debut in Carnegie Hall. In 1951 he continued his piano study with Rosina Lhévinne at the Juilliard School of Music in New York City. He won the Edgar M. Leventritt Foundation award in 1954, which provided a performance with the New York Philharmonic.

A pianist of outstanding technique, with a great command of the Romantic repertoire, Cliburn made many international concert tours from 1958 to 1978, when he retired until 1987. That year he played at the White House for Ronald Reagan and Mikhail Gorbachev, whose invitation to perform in Moscow—Cliburn did so in 1989—brought him out of retirement and back to regular solo concerts. In 1962 the Van Cliburn International Piano Competition was established; it is held every four years in Fort Worth, Tex., Cliburn's home and that of the Van Cliburn Foundation and Cliburn Concerts, which produces performances at Texas Christian University.

DAVID EWEN*
*Author of "Famous Instrumentalists"*

**CLICHÉ,** klē-shā′, literally a stereotyped expression. This definition supplies the key to the origin of the word, which comes from the French verb *clicher*, meaning "to stereotype" in printing. A cliché is a phrase, not a single word. The corresponding phenomenon in single words is the "vogue" word.

Clichés fall roughly into four groups: idioms so overused that they have become clichés; other phrases that have suffered the same fate; stock phrases and quotations from Greek, Latin, and modern European languages; and all-too-familiar quotations from English and American literature.

Idiom clichés include such trite phrases as *far and wide, heart and soul, much of a muchness, pick and choose, ways and means, bag and baggage, slow but sure;* also such metaphors as *lead a dog's life* and *leave a sinking ship;* and similes such as *fit as a fiddle, large as life,* and *old as the hills.*

Almost as dull as the first group and even deadlier is the very large second group of nonidiomatic hackneyed phrases. These are the most overused of all, the mere counters and substitutes of speech. Yet several of them were, at the time of coining, apt and even picturesque. Among this group are *add insult to injury, a fate worse than death, explore every avenue, leave no stone unturned, at the psychological moment, the salt of the earth, speed the parting guest* after *welcoming* [him] *with open arms, the wind of change,* and *the march of time.*

In the third group, the most battered of Latin phrases and quotations are perhaps *de mortuis* (*nil nisi bonum*), and *persona non grata;* the prime offenders in French include *bête noire, cherchez la femme,* and *c'est la vie.*

The final group, quotations from British and American authors, is so large that any arbitrary selection would be fatuous. The archcriminal is Shakespeare's *To be or not to be, that is the question.* Almost as hopelessly hackneyed is Longfellow's *Life is real! Life is earnest!*

ERIC PARTRIDGE
*Author of "A Dictionary of Clichés"*

### Bibliography

Brussel, Eugene F., *Webster's New World Dictionary of Quotable Definitions* (Prentice-Hall 1988).
Ewart, Neil, *Everyday Phrases: Their Origins and Meanings* (Sterling 1985).
Partridge, Eric, *A Dictionary of Catch Phrases,* rev. ed. (Stein & Day 1986).
Partridge, Eric, *A Dictionary of Clichés* 5th ed. (Methuen 1978).

**CLICK BEETLE,** an insect identified by the clicking noise it makes when it rights itself after falling or being placed upside down. After arching its body (by means of a long first thoracic segment that fits into a socket on the underside of the second thoracic segment), it rights itself by vigorously snapping its body straight. The insect is also called *skipjack* or *snapping bug.*

Adults are generally 0.5 to 1.2 inches (1.2 to 3 cm) long, but in the largest species they may reach a length of 1.5 inches (4 cm). Their bodies, which usually are brown, are long and slender, and tapered at each end. The click beetle larvae are brown or yellow and popularly are known as "wireworms" because of their hard bodies and cylindrical shape. They live in soil or under bark and in rotten stumps. Some eat white grubs and the young of other insects. Other wireworms feed on newly planted seeds and the roots of several crops, including corn and beans.

U. S. DEPARTMENT OF AGRICULTURE
A common click beetle is the eyed elater.

Click beetles belong to the family Elateridae, in which there are more than 500 species. One common species, the eyed elater (*Alaus oculatus*), is recognized by two eyelike spots on the top of its thorax.

**CLICK LANGUAGES,** a group of languages spoken in southern and eastern Africa, which received their name because of the characteristic click sounds that are found in all of them. An alternative name is *Khoisan,* composed of the Hottentot word for themselves (Khoi) and their name for the Bushmen (San). The click sounds are also found in a number of Bantu languages (Zulu, Xhosa, and Southern Sotho) of southern Africa as a result of Khoisan influence. They are not known to occur anywhere else in the world.

The Click languages have probably no more than 75,000 speakers in all, the most important being Nama Hottentot, with about 25,000, and Sandawe, estimated at about 23,000. The Click languages occur in two distinct areas: in the southern part of Africa, chiefly in South West Africa and Botswana, but also in Angola and the Orange Free State of South Africa; and farther north in eastern Africa, in Tanzania. Many of the southern languages are extinct or almost so. It is thought that speakers of the Click languages formed the basic population of most of eastern and southern Africa prior to the Iron Age Bantu expansion during the last millennium.

Linguistically the Click languages may be divided into three groups: Sandawe; Hatsa; and South African Khoisan. The first two are spoken in Tanzania. South African Khoisan may in turn be divided into quite distinct northern, central, and southern groups of languages. The Hottentot are included in the central group.

The most conspicuous linguistic feature of the language group is the click sounds, produced by an inrush of air, in contradistinction to most speech, in which sound is made on outgoing breath. A great variety of click sounds occur, as many as 20 different ones in a single language, depending on the point of oral closure and the phonetic type of release that follows.

JOSEPH H. GREENBERG
*Stanford University*

**CLIENT,** klī′ənt, in a legal sense, one who employs an attorney for advice on a question of law or who commits his cause to an attorney for his management in prosecuting a claim or defending against a suit in a court. In advising the client, the attorney is bound to exercise reasonable care and diligence and to conduct himself as one holding a position of highest trust and confidence. This obligates him to maintain the maximum standard of good faith, honesty, and

THE CLIFF PALACE, built under a massive overhanging rock formation in an eroded cliff in Mesa Verde National Park, Colorado, is the largest known prehistoric cliff dwelling. The circular structures are the remains of ceremonial chambers, called kivas. The square buildings were the living quarters.

JOSEF MUENCH

fidelity in all of his relations with the client. The attorney is precluded from having any personal interests adverse to the subject matter of his relationship with the client, and he cannot obtain personal advantage from the relationship without the client's knowledge or consent. At the same time, the client must deal with the attorney in a fair and equitable manner.

Communications between an attorney and his client are confidential and deemed privileged. That is, the attorney is forbidden to testify as to any communications made by the client to him or as to his advice relating to these communications given in the course of his professional employment, without the consent of the client. The secrecy is maintained for the benefit of the client and cannot be unilaterally repudiated by the attorney. The existence of a professional relationship does not necessarily depend on payment of a fee. The principle of privileged communications rests on the client's need to have perfect freedom to say anything to his attorney and on the need for unrestrained communication between them.

PETER D. WEINSTEIN
*Member of the New York Bar*

**CLIFF DWELLERS** are peoples whose dwellings are built in large caves in cliffs or under cliff overhangs. Often these groups are distinguished from their immediate neighbors solely by the location and architecture of their structures.

The custom of using cliff overhangs or rock shelters as places of abode is almost as old as man himself. Partly because of the protection which these places have given to their contents, some of the best archaeological records of early human culture have been found in such shelters. These shelters were variously used, either permanently or temporarily; their temporary use, especially for herds of animals, still persists. In the earliest prehistoric uses, the cliff overhangs were rarely embellished with architectural modifications.

**France.** Two of the best-known areas of cliff dwellings are southwestern France (the departments of Dordogne and Lot, among others) and the southwestern United States. In both areas the dwellings were commonly located on the north side of valleys in order to obtain heat from the winter sun and protection, by overhanging rocks, from the summer sun. The French cliff dwellers built their houses, or occasionally castles, against the cliff walls to utilize the native rock as the rear wall, and often as part of the roof, of the structures. The buildings may be at the level of the valley floor or high on the talus at the base of the cliff proper.

**United States.** The Indian cliff dwellings of the southwestern United States were the end product of a long tradition of use of rock shelters. As early as the Basket Maker period (about 500 A.D.), impermanent structures of poles and brush erected over a shallow pit had been located in caves as well as in the open. The same practices of dwelling location continued into the Pueblo periods, with masonry houses replacing the former type. The cliff dwellings reached their peak in the Great Pueblo period (also known as the Classic Pueblo or Pueblo III), which lasted from about 1050 to 1300. During this time the large multistory buildings commonly associated with the cliff dwellers were built. These consisted of a compact mass of contiguous rooms, numbering from 20 to several hundreds, often terraced toward the cliff wall, the whole complex set in an enormous shallow cave. The individual sleeping rooms were often as small as 6 by 8 feet (1.8 by 2.4 meters) but sometimes as large as 10 by 16 feet (3 by 4.9 meters), with ceilings ranging from a height of 4 feet to 8 feet (1.2 to 2.4 meters). Toward the front of the building mass, ceremonial chambers (kivas) were embedded with their roofs at terrace level. These terraces were probably the locus of everyday life. Complete with living rooms, corn-grinding rooms, storage rooms, and ceremonial chambers, each building actually constituted a single town.

68

The southwestern United States cliff dwellings are concentrated in the Four Corners area (where Utah, Arizona, New Mexico, and Colorado meet). Some of the notable examples are preserved in Mesa Verde National Park, Colorado, and in Canyon de Chelly National Monument, Arizona. In general cultural affiliations they belong to a wider prehistoric area that includes other dwelling styles.

By contrast with the French cliff dwellers, about whom there is no mystery, the cliff dwellers of the southwestern United States have caused speculation. The dwellings, sometimes against vertical cliff walls but more often in huge caves in the cliff face, were found abandoned by the first explorers of the region; most of them showed sign of orderly abandonment. When other Indian pueblos were found still inhabited, what fate overtook the cliff dwellers? The abandonment of these dwellings in the San Juan River drainage area, as well as of those villages in the open, came toward the end of the 13th century. Probably no single factor was responsible. But we know of a serious drought lasting from 1276 to 1299, following years of subnormal rainfall. Possibly, combined with attacks from nomadic non-Pueblo peoples in the area and with internal social dissension, the drought may have been the final blow. The refugees evidently drifted to the southwest and southeast of this area, and their descendants are likely to be found among the Indians of northeastern Arizona and the Rio Grande pueblos.

The American cliff dwellings were first brought to the attention of archaeologists in 1874 by the explorations of the photographer W. H. Jackson. The major ruins in the present Mesa Verde National Park were found in 1888, and some were scientifically excavated in 1891 by Baron Gustav Nordenskiöld. Their value as a record of man's past was formally recognized when the park was established in 1906. See also CAVE DWELLERS; MESA VERDE NATIONAL PARK.

ROBERT F. G. SPIER, *University of Missouri*

### Bibliography

**Bohn, Dave, and Jett, Stephen C.,** *House of Three Turkeys: Anasazi Redoubt* (Capra Press 1977).
**Erdoes, Richard,** *The Rain Dance People* (Knopf 1976).
**Folsom-Dickerson, W. S.,** *Cliff Dwellers* (Naylor Co. 1968).
**Harrington, Mark K.,** *The Ozark Bluff-Dwellers,* 2d ed. (Mus. of the Amer. Indian 1971).
**McGregor, John C.,** *Southwestern Archaeology,* 2d ed. (Univ. of Ill. Press 1982).

**CLIFFORD** is the name of an English noble family that took its name from Clifford Castle, near Hay in Herefordshire, in the 12th century and is represented in the modern peerage by members of two branches.

The founder of the family, Ponz, was probably of Norman origin. His son, Richard Fitz-Ponz, was the father of Walter, who lived in the reign (1154–1189) of Henry II and married Margaret, daughter and heir of Ralph de Toeni, thereby acquiring Clifford Castle. Walter was the first to take the surname de Clifford.

Walter de Clifford had two sons: Walter, his heir, and Richard. He also had two daughters, the elder of whom, Rosamond, was the mistress of Henry II and by him the mother of William Longsword, Earl of Salisbury.

The de Cliffords continued to gain wealth and royal favor in the 13th century, and in 1299, King Edward I summoned Robert de Clifford (died 1314) to Parliament as Lord de Clifford. The peerage of de Clifford dates from that summons. As an officer in the Border Country, Robert fought against Scotland and was killed at the Battle of Bannockburn. His son Roger, 2d Lord de Clifford (1299–1322), was executed as a rebel against Edward II, and the title passed to his brother Robert, 3d Lord de Clifford (1305–1344), whose younger son, Roger, the 5th Lord (1333–1389), fought with distinction in the wars of Edward III.

John, 7th Lord de Clifford (died 1421), grandson of the 5th Lord, married a daughter of the famous Harry "Hotspur," Lord Percy, and their offspring played a prominent part in the Wars of the Roses. Thomas, 8th Lord de Clifford (1414–1454), died in the first Battle of St. Albans, and his son John, the 9th Lord (died 1461), died fighting in behalf of Henry VI. John's cruelties earned him the name "the Butcher" and a place in Shakespeare's *Henry VI* as the murderer of Edmund, Earl of Rutland, the son of Richard, Duke of York, after the Battle of Wakefield in 1460. After his death at the Battle of Ferrybridge, his peerage was forfeited to the new king, Edward IV.

John left a 7-year-old son, Henry (1454–1523), whose birth for reasons of security had been concealed by his mother. He was brought up as a shepherd. On the accession of Henry VII in 1485 the attainder that caused the peerage to be forfeited was reversed, and the Shepherd Lord, as he was called, became 10th Lord de Clifford. He is mentioned in William Wordsworth's poetry.

His eldest son, Henry, 11th Lord de Clifford (1493–1542), acquired both fortune and honor. He received grants of monastic lands during the Reformation and became a Knight of the Garter. Henry VIII created him Earl of Cumberland in 1523.

His son Henry, 2d Earl of Cumberland and 12th Lord de Clifford (1517–1569), married Eleanor, the niece of Henry VIII, and, after her death without issue, Anne, daughter of William, Lord Dacre. Their son George, 3d Earl and 13th Lord (1558–1605), was a scholar at Cambridge as well as a celebrated naval commander under Elizabeth I. He commanded a royal ship against the Spanish Armada and became a minor favorite of the Queen. As a privateer he fitted out 10 expeditions against the Spaniards, in four of which he sailed himself. He died without male issue, and his brother, Francis (died 1641) became 4th Earl.

However, the barony of de Clifford, created in 1299, did not pass to him with the earldom. It remained in abeyance until 1691, when it passed to the grandson of the 3d Earl's daughter Anne, Countess of Dorset. The barony subsequently passed through the Tufton, Southwell, and Russell families to Edward Southwell Russell, 26th Baron (1907–     ), in 1909.

While the original barony was in abeyance, a new one was created in 1628 in favor of Henry Clifford, son of the 4th Earl of Cumberland, who later succeeded as 5th Earl. This barony fell into abeyance between the descendants of his only daughter, Elizabeth, Countess of Cork and Burlington.

A third Clifford barony, Clifford of Chudleigh, was created in 1672 for descendants of Sir Lewis de Clifford (died 1404), third son of Roger, the 5th Lord of the original barony. Hugh Clifford (1916–     ) succeeded to the title as 13th Baron in 1964.

L. G. PINE
*Former Editor of "Burke's Peerage"*

**CLIFFORD, Clark McAdams** (1906–     ), American lawyer and public official who served as secretary of defense and was unofficial adviser to three Democratic presidents. He was born in Fort Scott, Kans., on Dec. 25, 1906, and grew up in St. Louis, Mo., where he received his law degree from Washington University in 1928. He practiced law in St. Louis, joined the Naval Reserve during World War II, and became assistant naval aide to President Harry Truman in 1945. After the war, President Truman named him his general counsel, and in that capacity he helped draft the legislation that created the Department of Defense in 1947.

Clifford left the White House in 1950 to return to private law practice, and in the years that followed he represented many major corporations while continuing to advise government leaders. He served as President-elect John F. Kennedy's liaison with the outgoing Eisenhower administration, and he handled many special assignments for Presidents Kennedy and Lyndon B. Johnson before he was appointed secretary of defense in 1968. He served in that post until 1969, and then returned to his legal practice in Washington, D. C.

Clifford went to the Defense Department with the reputation of being a "hawk" on the Vietnam War. He had counseled against President Johnson's 37-day moratorium on the bombing of North Vietnam in 1966. However, as secretary of defense he publicly stressed the need for American disengagement from the war, and he supported the bombing halt announced by Johnson in November 1968. For his services, he was awarded the Medal of Freedom.

**CLIFFORD, John** (1836–1923), English Baptist clergyman. He was born on Oct. 16, 1836, in Sawley, Derbyshire. Clifford was educated at the Baptist College, Nottingham, and at London University. From 1859 to 1915 he was minister of Praed Street Chapel and of the Westbourne Park Chapel in London. From 1905 to 1911 he served as first president of the Baptist World Alliance, formed to promote international friendship through the church. From 1919 to 1923 he headed the World Brotherhood Federation. Clifford died in London on Nov. 20, 1923.

Clifford's keen social sympathies led to his active association with the radical wing of the Liberal party. He organized the "Passive Resistance" movement against the English Education Act of 1902 to protest against the use of public funds to support denominational schools.

**CLIFFORD, Nathan** (1803–1881), American Supreme Court justice, who is better known for helping to negotiate the treaty that secured California as a part of the United States than for the opinions that he wrote during 23 years on the court. Clifford was born in Rumney, N. H., on Aug. 18, 1803. He was admitted to the New Hampshire bar in 1827 but moved to Newfield, Me., to practice law. In 1830 he entered politics as a Democrat in the lower house of the Maine legislature, serving as speaker from 1832 to 1834. That same year he became state attorney general, and in 1838 and 1840 he was elected to the House of Representatives.

In 1846 he was appointed U. S. attorney general by President Polk, and in 1848–1849 he served as commissioner to Mexico. He helped conclude the Treaty of Guadalupe Hidalgo, which ended the war with Mexico and annexed all or part of seven present Western states.

After the Whigs regained the presidency, Clifford resumed the practice of law, in Portland, Me. In 1858 he was appointed an associate justice of the Supreme Court by President Buchanan. On the bench, he concurred in the first Legal Tender case, *Hepburn* v. *Griswold* (1870), and dissented in *Knox* v. *Lee* (1871), which overruled the former and declared constitutional Congress' issuing of treasury notes to pay earlier debts. He also concurred in the Slaughterhouse cases (1873), wherein the butchering monopoly of one New Orleans corporation was declared constitutional. He died on July 25, 1881, at Cornish, Me.

LEO PFEFFER
*Author of "This Honorable Court"*

**CLIFFORD, William Kingdon** (1845–1879), English mathematician, who is noted for developing the algebra of biquaternions and for advocating the study and application of non-Euclidean geometry. Clifford was born at Exeter, England, on May 4, 1845, and received his early education there. He graduated from Trinity College, Cambridge, in 1867 and in 1868 was elected a fellow of Trinity. In 1871 he was appointed professor of applied mathematics at University College, London, where he remained until his premature death in Madeira on March 3, 1879.

A geometer at heart, Clifford protested the analytical bias of the Cambridge school and urged the use of graphic and geometric methods in preference to analysis. He was much impressed by the hyperbolic non-Euclidean geometry of Lobachevsky, whose revolutionary views he compared with those of Copernicus. Later he came to prefer the elliptic geometry of Riemann, which led him to develop the algebra of biquaternions to represent motions in 3-dimensional, non-Euclidean space.

Clifford's mathematical powers were matched by exceptional ability in classics, oratory, and gymnastics. His work is characterized by great insight and imagination, as exemplified in his best-known book, *Common Sense of the Exact Sciences*, left in fragmentary form at his death but completed in 1885 by Karl Pearson.

CARL B. BOYER, *Brooklyn College*

**CLIFTON,** an industrial city in northeastern New Jersey, in Passaic county, 9 miles (14 km) north of Newark, just west of the Passaic River. The city's industries include the manufacture of electronics equipment, chemicals, cosmetics, plastics, textiles, special machinery, and paper and metal products. The U. S. Animal Quarantine Station was founded here in 1900. Many residents of Clifton commute to New York City.

The history of the area dates back to 1640, when fur trading was begun with the Leni-Lenape Indians, known to white settlers as "Delawares" from the name of the principal river in their territory. The early name of the area was Acquackanonk township. It included a large tract from which Paterson withdrew in 1831, Passaic in 1866, and Little Falls in 1868. The remaining 12 square miles (31 sq km) was incorporated as the city of Clifton in 1917. Industrialization was rapid after 1935. Clifton is governed by a mayor and council, who appoint a city manager. Population: 78,672.

BARBARA A. MEARNS
*Clifton Public Library*

**CLIMATE** is the average weather conditions of a region over a period of several decades or more. The word is used to describe not only the average weather conditions but also all deviations from the average, which can be determined by taking observations over a period of at least 25 years. The probability that a given set of weather conditions will occur in a region can be estimated from the frequency with which those conditions occurred there in the past. The chance for the recurrence of a comparatively rare event, such as a tornado, cannot be calculated without a much longer record or additional records of observations in surrounding areas. Even then there is a measure of uncertainty, for climates are not fixed but are changing constantly.

Climates have had a profound effect on the spread of population throughout the world. Since only small portions of the earth's land areas have climates ideal for human habitation, people are very unevenly distributed; the vast majority of them live in the areas best adapted to human life. The largest of these regions are the eastern United States, Europe, India, China, and Japan. In marginal regions it is climatic change that has, as a rule, controlled the growth or decline of populations.

## CONTENTS

## 1. Kinds of Climates

Although no two places in the world have identical climates, many areas have climates sufficiently similar to fall into the same climatic group. Wladimir Köppen, a Russian-German climatologist, divided all climates into five groups, as follows:

| Group | Name |
|---|---|
| A | Tropical rainy climates |
| B | Dry climates |
| C | Warm temperate rainy climates |
| D | Cold snow forest climates |
| E | Polar climates |

The climatic types are in general identifiable with zones of latitude around the world. The A climates are all in low latitudes. They cover the tropical oceans, northern and central South America, central Africa, southeastern Asia, northern Australia, and the East and West Indies. The B climates are found in dry belts in the subtropical and middle latitudes of both the Northern and Southern hemispheres. They include most of the western United States, North and South Africa, southwestern and central Asia, and most of Australia. The C climates are in temperate latitudes of both hemispheres. They cover the middle latitude oceans, the eastern United States, western Europe and the Mediterranean, much of the Orient, parts of southern South America and South Africa, and the south and east coasts of Australia. The D climates are found only in the Northern Hemisphere over land areas at high latitudes. They cover most of Alaska, Canada, European Russia, and Siberia.

The E climates are in the Arctic and Antarctic regions and also on the highest mountains, particularly in the Andes of South America and the Himalaya of Asia.

The world's population lies mostly in the regions of C and A climates, with progressively fewer people in D, B, and E climates.

**Tree Climates.** The A, C, and D climates are the only climates in which trees grow, since the B and E climates are too dry and too cold, respectively. The tree climates are differentiated from one another by the mean temperature of the coldest month. (The mean temperature is the average of all the daily temperatures.) If the coldest month has a mean temperature higher than 64°F (18°C)—the ideal temperature for comfort—the climate is classified as an A climate. If the mean temperature of the coldest month is lower than 27°F (3°C), snow will usually remain on the ground in the winter, and the climate is called a D climate. If the coldest month has an intermediate mean temperature, the climate is called a C climate.

**Dry Climates.** The determining factors for the B climates are the mean annual precipitation and the temperature, the latter being directly related to the rate of evaporation. If the temperature is high, evaporation is more rapid and precipitation is less conducive to the growth of vegetation. Therefore, the maximum precipitation for a dry climate is greater for a higher temperature. If the average monthly precipitation is roughly the same throughout the year, the annual precipitation for a B climate is defined as less than 10 inches (25 cm) at a mean annual temperature of 42°F (6°C), and less than 20 inches (50 cm) at 65°F (18°C).

The B climates are further classified as desert and steppe climates; in a desert climate the mean annual precipitation is less than half of the previously indicated levels.

**Polar Climates.** The E climates are characterized by a mean temperature of less than 50°F (10°C) in the warmest month. In this they are unlike the A, C, and D climates, which require a mean temperature of more than 50°F in the warmest month if trees are to grow. The E climates are classified as tundra or forest climates, depending on whether the mean temperature of the warmest month is, respectively, above or below freezing (32°F, 0°C).

## 2. Causes of Climates

The underlying factor in the creation of the different climates is the sun, but the relationship between the sun and the climates is complicated. Also involved are the earth's rotation and the resulting winds, and the effects of land and water areas.

### VARIATIONS IN TEMPERATURE

Three kinds of global variation in temperature must be considered in a discussion of climates on an idealized earth with a uniform land surface. The most obvious is the difference in temperature between latitudes, but seasonal and diurnal differences in temperature are also important.

**Latitudinal Differences.** The dependence of the temperature on latitude makes latitude one of the most important factors in determining climate. There are two reasons why temperatures are lower at high latitudes than at low latitudes. One is that the sun is nearly overhead at noon

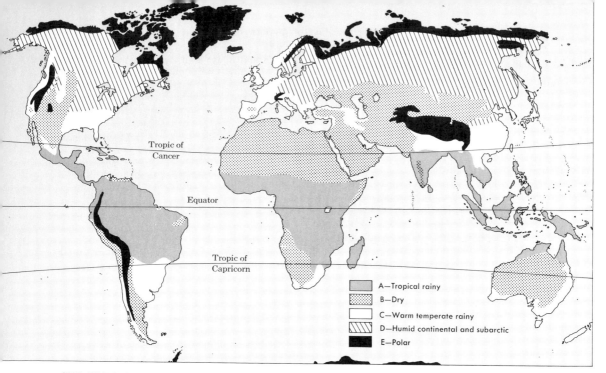

| | |
|---|---|
| ░░░ | A—Tropical rainy |
| ⠿ | B—Dry |
| | C—Warm temperate rainy |
| ⫽ | D—Humid continental and subarctic |
| ■ | E—Polar |

**THE KINDS OF CLIMATES** found around the world are divided into the five groups shown on the map.

in the tropics. A horizontal area in this region would be nearly perpendicular to the sun's rays, and would have about the largest possible cross section of sunshine. An equivalent horizontal area in the polar regions, however, would be at an oblique angle to the sun's rays and would get a much smaller amount of sunshine.

The other reason for the lower temperatures at high latitudes is that the sun's rays, which fall slantingly on the earth's surface at the poles, have to pass through more of the atmosphere before they can reach the earth. At low latitudes the sunlight at noon traverses the atmosphere almost vertically and travels only a short distance before reaching the earth's surface. Because of its longer path through the atmosphere near the poles, the sunshine that reaches the earth's surface there has been robbed of much of its energy through absorption and scattering in the atmosphere.

If both of these reasons are considered, it is not surprising to find that the mean annual temperature, that is, the average of the 12 monthly average temperatures, is much lower in the polar regions than in the tropics.

**Seasonal Differences.** The difference in temperature between the seasons is greater at higher latitudes. Thus the decrease in temperature toward the polar regions is greater in winter than in summer. This winter decrease exceeds the average annual poleward decrease in temperature because of the shortened day toward the poles. The average length of time per day that the sun is above the horizon in winter decreases from 12 hours at the equator to 10 hours at latitude 35° and to 0 hours at the poles. In summer the situation is reversed. The poleward temperature decrease is less than the average annual poleward decrease in temperature because of the extra hours of sunshine; summer days are longer at the higher latitudes than they are at the equator. They increase from 12 hours at the equator to 14 hours at latitude 35°, and at the poles the days in summer are 24 hours long.

The annual temperature range—defined as the difference between the mean temperatures of the warmest and coldest months—therefore increases with increasing latitude. At latitude 60° there is an average annual range of 37°F (21°C), which is about twice as great as the average annual range of 18°F (10°C) at latitude 30°. These differences in the annual temperature range, as with latitudinal temperature variations, are caused by differences in the sun's angular altitude and in the length of day. The angular altitude of the sun at noon changes during the course of a year by 23½° at the equator, by about 35° in the tropics, and by 47° in middle and high latitudes. In the Northern Hemisphere, where the noon sun is highest on June 21 and lowest on December 21, these dates mark the beginning of summer and winter, respectively. In the Southern Hemisphere, where the sun's noon altitude is lower in June than in December, the seasons are reversed.

It is interesting to note that changes in the distance of the earth from the sun are not responsible for the seasons. In January, the coldest month in the Northern Hemisphere, the earth is about 3 million miles closer to the sun than in July, the warmest month in the Northern Hemisphere. In the Southern Hemisphere this change in distances does, it is true, help to make January (summer) warmer than July (winter). The effect is small, however, compared with the effect of the extensive oceans in the Southern Hemisphere. The oceans keep the winter and summer temperatures more nearly alike than in the Northern Hemisphere. At latitude 60°N, for example, the average annual temperature range is greater by 34°F (19°C) than it is at 60°S.

**Diurnal Differences.** Unlike the seasonal differences, the differences in temperature between day and night are generally smaller at high latitudes than at low latitudes. This poleward decrease in the average diurnal temperature range is primarily a result of the poleward decrease in the 24-hour variability of the sun's angular altitude. Another cause is the difference in cloudiness at low and high latitudes. Tropical clouds are usually scattered or broken. The clear spaces allow sunshine to raise the daytime temperature and permit the earth's radiation to escape into space. There is a consequent lowering of the temperature at night, and the result is a large daily temperature range in the tropics. On the other hand, clouds in the polar regions frequently form a continuous overcast, keeping out solar heating during the day and preventing the loss of heat at night. Under these conditions, the daily temperature range at high latitudes is comparatively small.

In the course of a year the earth and its atmosphere must lose by radiation into space about the same amount of heat as they receive from the sun. Otherwise the temperature would change appreciably from one year to the next. This heat balance operates for the earth and atmosphere as a whole, but it does not hold true at most of the latitudes, considered separately. In the tropics the amount of radiation coming from the sun exceeds the outgoing radiation; in the polar regions more heat is lost to space than is gained from the sun. The resulting inequalities produce a gradual warming at low latitudes and a gradual cooling at high latitudes. These temperature trends are counteracted by the currents circulating in the atmosphere and in the oceans. Great movements of air and water carry the excess heat accumulated at low altitudes to the higher latitudes.

## PREVAILING WINDS AND VERTICAL AIR CURRENTS

The primary cause of the great currents circulating in the atmosphere is the gradual decrease in temperature toward the poles. Since warm air is less dense than cold air, a given weight of warm air occupies more space than an equivalent weight of cold air does. Consequently, the warm atmosphere at low latitudes is distributed vertically to greater heights than is the cold atmosphere at high latitudes.

Atmospheric pressure at any height is the weight per unit of horizontal area of all the air above that height. As there is more air above the 10,000-foot (3,000-meter) level in the tropics than in the polar regions, the average atmospheric pressure at 10,000 feet is relatively high at the equator and relatively low at the poles, that is, there is a poleward pressure gradient (from higher to lower pressure) at this height.

**Winds on a Nonrotating Uniform Earth.** If the sun revolved daily around a nonrotating earth, the poleward pressure gradients would cause a flow of high-altitude air from the equator toward the polar regions. If prolonged, these upper-level air flows would diverge at the equator and converge at the poles. The effect would be to decrease the weight of the atmosphere at the equator and increase it at the poles. The resulting difference in sea-level atmospheric pressure would then cause a return flow of air at the earth's surface from the poles toward the equator. Vertical currents moving upward at the equator and downward at the poles would complete closed paths for the air to follow between low and high latitudes.

The fact that such simple steady winds do not occur is primarily a result of two causes: the rotation of the earth and the irregularity of the earth's surface.

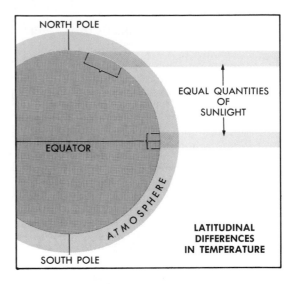

SUNLIGHT strikes the earth almost vertically at the equator. At the poles an equal amount of sunlight strikes the earth at a slant, and must travel farther through the atmosphere and spread over a larger area.

**Winds on a Rotating Earth.** The simple steady north-south winds that would exist on a nonrotating earth are in actuality deflected nearly 90° to the right in the Northern Hemisphere and 90° to the left in the Southern Hemisphere (as would be seen by an observer looking down from above). This deflection is caused by the rotation of the earth, but for convenience it is attributed to the imaginary Coriolis force.

The deflection of the earth's winds in this manner can be explained by the principle of the conservation of angular momentum. The principle states that the absolute speed of rotation about an axis decreases as the distance from the axis increases, provided no torques—forces tending to produce rotation or twisting—are acting about the axis. A familiar example is the skater who whirls faster as he draws his arms in close.

The principle applies to the circulation of the atmosphere. Thus, suppose that there are north winds from the north pole, which is at one end of the axis of the earth's rotation. As the winds proceed, they carry air farther away from the axis of rotation. Therefore, by the principle of the conservation of angular momentum, the rotation of the air about the earth's axis must slow down in both temperate zones and in the tropics. Moreover, as the air moves toward lower latitudes, the earth under it is moving faster toward the east. As a result of the slower rotation of the air and the faster rotation of the earth's surface, the southward-moving air is left behind by the surface. An observer on the ground would interpret the wind as coming from an easterly direction instead of from the north.

By the same reasoning, the high-altitude south winds of the Northern Hemisphere come closer to the earth's axis of rotation as they approach the north pole. In the higher latitudes, therefore, the winds are rotating more swiftly about the earth's axis, while the earth's surface is moving more slowly. The result is that the current of air is interpreted by an observer as a high-altitude westerly wind.

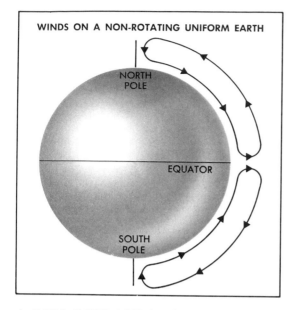

**WINDS ON A NON-ROTATING UNIFORM EARTH**

NORTH POLE

EQUATOR

SOUTH POLE

A SIMPLE CLOSED PATTERN of steady winds would exist in the northern and southern hemisphere of a non-rotating uniform earth around which the sun revolved.

**Trade and Antitrade Winds.** This theoretical description fits the winds actually observed over the greater part of the world. From 30° latitude to the equator are found the northeast trade winds of the Northern Hemisphere and the southeast trade winds of the Southern Hemisphere. Both blow quite steadily and meet to form the International Convergence Zone near the equator. Then the air ascends and starts moving toward higher latitudes. These currents, called the antitrades, blow in the opposite direction from the trades, but they are more irregular than the trades. The antitrades are not restricted to latitudes below 30°, but—as the prevailing westerlies—they exist aloft all the way to the polar regions. They form great whirls high up around the poles in both hemispheres. The strongest winds in these whirls are known as jet streams, and are located in narrow latitudinal belts at the base of the stratosphere. The air from the antitrades descends as it loses heat in the polar regions and starts moving toward lower latitudes as surface winds. These winds, called the polar easterlies, extend to about 60° latitude in both hemispheres.

**Winds at Middle Latitudes.** To complete the circulation cycles, it would seem that the air from 60° latitude would have to move equatorward to 30° as surface winds, from the east-northeast in the Northern Hemisphere and from the east-southeast in the Southern Hemisphere. Observations show, however, that in these middle latitudes a belt of westerly winds prevails at the surface as well as aloft. The apparent discrepancy can be explained by reexamining the theoretical circulation pattern. Suppose that surface winds actually did move in an easterly direction over the entire earth. If such a pattern continued for a long period of time, the frictional force between the earth's surface and the air would tend to bring them to the same speed of rotation. Not only would the east winds disappear as the air speeded up in its rotation from

west to east about the earth's axis, but also the rotation of the earth woud slow down.

The earth, instead, is rotating at a nearly constant rate, though there is a very slight slowdown caused by ocean tides (controlled primarily by the moon). The observed wind pattern at the earth's surface shows an approximate balance between the easterly winds of low and high latitudes and the westerly winds of middle latitudes. Clearly the retarding effect of the easterly winds on the earth's rotation is counteracted by an accelerating effect of the westerly winds. The absence of any significant slowing down in the earth's rotation requires this belt of westerly winds at the earth's surface.

The westerly middle-latitude winds require, in turn, a belt of subpolar low-pressure areas at latitude 60° and of subtropical high-pressure areas at latitude 30°. Because winds blow from high-pressure areas toward low-pressure areas, surface winds at northern middle latitudes start as south winds and then deflect to become winds from the west-southwest. Southern middle-latitude winds start from the north, then deflect to become winds from the west-northwest. The deflection, of course, is a result of the same forces that deflect the trade winds.

**Polar Fronts.** The middle-latitude winds meet the polar easterlies near latitude 60°. Since they are warmer and less dense than the polar easterlies, the two currents of air do not mix. Instead, a discontinuity surface called the polar front forms between them. The polar front slopes upward toward the poles at an inclination of about 1 mile vertically to every 100 miles horizontally. The warmer and lighter prevailing westerlies ascend aloft above the frontal surface, while the polar easterlies remain below the front without rising off the earth's surface.

The large-scale discontinuities called fronts complete the picture of the mean circulation pattern of the atmosphere. This entire pattern shifts several degrees of latitude poleward in summer and several degrees equatorward in winter. However, the pattern described does not account for the variability of the circulation, especially in middle latitudes. There are prevailing winds at all levels from the west-southwest in northern middle latitudes and from the west-northwest in southern middle latitudes. Since these prevailing winds between latitudes 30° and 60° in both hemispheres have components that blow toward higher latitudes—that is, polewards—the result is a gradual transference of air from the tropics to the polar regions. This in turn results in a significantly increasing air pressure in the polar areas, and a more slowly decreasing pressure over the more extensive area of the tropics. This condition could not continue indefinitely without seriously disturbing the distribution of air pressure over the earth.

Instead, the intensification of the polar "highs"—high-pressure areas—by the influx of air from the middle latitudes causes a strengthening of the polar easterly winds (from the northeast and southwest in the Northern and Southern Hemispheres, respectively). Since the polar air is below the polar front and cannot go through the front, the increasing polar winds force the polar front to move toward lower latitudes. The polar air, accompanied by a high-pressure area, advances equatorward behind the moving front. This process continues until the front sweeps all the way into the tropics, causing sudden drops in temperature in these regions. Such a major polar outbreak interrupts the prevailing west-southwest winds of northern middle latitudes, replacing them with north or often northwest winds due to a low-pressure area farther east. When the polar outbreak reaches low latitudes, the direction of the wind shifts to the northeast, strengthening the trade winds prevailing there.

### EFFECTS OF FRONTS ON CLIMATE

Through the mechanism of polar outbreaks, the excess air at high latitudes is carried to the equatorial regions and counteracts the deficit of air there. After a polar outbreak, the prevailing winds again return until another outbreak occurs. These polar outbreaks do not occur at regular intervals of time, but, instead, spasmodically. The outbreaks are more frequent and have stronger winds in winter than in summer. They are responsible for cold waves in winter. They also account for the variability of middle-latitude weather, with migratory high- and low-pressure areas moving generally from the west, as contrasted with the relatively steady trade winds between latitude 30° and the equator.

Other fronts are found in the atmosphere besides the polar front, of course. All fronts lie in troughs of low atmospheric pressure. The Arctic and Antarctic fronts in the subpolar low-pressure belts at high latitudes separate different masses of polar air. The intertropical convergence zone in the equatorial trough of low pressure separates tropical air of the Northern Hemisphere from tropical air of the Southern Hemisphere. It frequently develops frontal characteristics. At any given location, a front is classified as a cold front or a warm front according to whether the temperature falls or rises as the front passes.

**Precipitation.** Fronts may cause rain or snow in addition to producing changes in temperature. Precipitation must always be preceded by condensation (the change of moisture from water vapor to liquid water drops) or sublimation (the change from water vapor to ice crystals). The process takes place around tiny particles called condensation or sublimation nuclei, and it occurs when more than enough water vapor is present to produce saturation. A supersaturated, or "wet," condition is caused, not so much by an increase in the actual amount of water vapor present, but more often by a decrease in the amount that is necessary for saturation. Thus, if the temperature of a parcel of air drops 18°F (10°C), the amount of moisture needed to saturate the air is decreased by about 50%.

Cooling is the most effective method of causing supersaturation, condensation, and then precipitation, provided there is initially a certain amount of water vapor in the air. There are many ways in which cooling can occur in the atmosphere. It may be caused by the convection, radiation, or conduction of heat, or by the evaporation of water drops or ice crystals. The most rapid cooling occurs with convection, which is the transport of heat by vertical circulation. When a parcel of air rises, the pressure acting upon it decreases. The parcel of air expands by pushing back the surrounding air, which is at a lower pressure. The energy for this expansion must come from the parcel's internal energy, since the conduction of heat to the parcel from the surroundings is negligible. In the process of using up energy it loses heat; this process is called adiabatic cooling, or cooling without heat loss to, or gain from, the outside. By the time the parcel of air has risen 6,000 feet (1,800 me-

## WINDS ON A ROTATING EARTH

A complex pattern of winds results from the actual rotation of the earth. Within each hemisphere, this circulation pattern shifts several degrees of latitude equatorward in the winter and poleward in the summer.

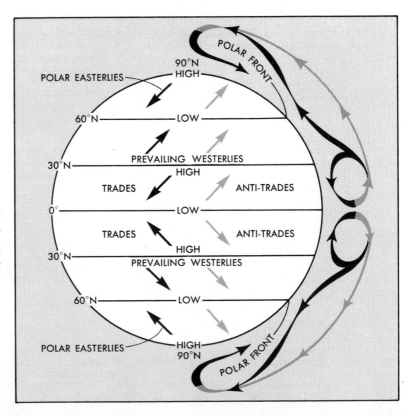

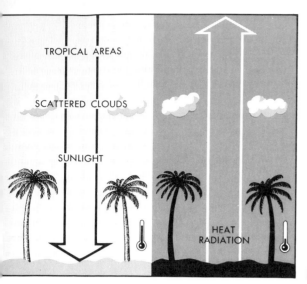
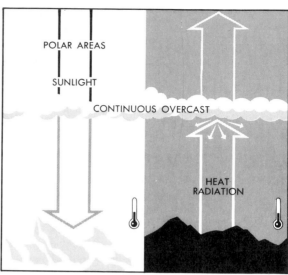

DIURNAL DIFFERENCES in temperature are generally greater at low latitudes than at high latitudes, partly because of the heavier cloud cover in polar regions.

ters) above the condensation level, about one half of the water vapor it contains has condensed as a result of cooling.

**Precipitation Belts and Dry Zones.** Since the most effective method of cooling air is to lift it to a higher altitude, condensation and precipitation are almost invariably to be expected in regions of rising air above the fronts in the low pressure belts, where currents of surface air converge. There are three main precipitation belts: the equatorial belt, along the intertropical convergence zone between the northern and southern tropics, and the two subpolar belts. The maximum precipitation in the subpolar belts occurs closer to 45° latitude than to 60° latitude, because of the greater supply of moisture in middle latitudes than in high latitudes and because of the frequent strong frontal lifting that occurs in middle latitudes.

In each hemisphere there are two dry regions between the belts of precipitation. These correspond to the high-pressure regions, where the air descends rather than ascends. The descending air becomes warmer and its relative humidity decreases, that is, the air becomes less humid. The driest regions are under the polar highs, and near the subtropical highs at about 30° latitude. It is in these regions near the tropics that the most extensive deserts of the world occur in both hemispheres.

The rainy and dry belts are shifted poleward in summer and equatorward in winter, along with the low-pressure and high-pressure belts. This accounts for the rainy summers in the tropics and polar regions and helps to explain the rainy winters over oceans in the middle latitudes.

Precipitation is not restricted to frontal zones, however, but can occur wherever air rises sufficiently high. Thus air is cooled when it flows up a mountain slope, and condensation occurs in the same way as in air ascending over a frontal surface. That is why the windward slopes of high mountain ranges usually have ample precipitation. In the middle latitudes the prevailing westerly winds bring rains to the western sides of continents. At low latitudes the trade winds cause eastern coasts to be rainy and leave the western coasts very dry.

## EFFECTS OF A NONUNIFORM EARTH

The temperature of the lower atmosphere is controlled by the temperature of the earth's surface rather than directly by the sun. This fact is indicated by the normal decrease in temperature of the atmosphere as height above the earth increases. Therefore the factors which affect the temperature of the earth's surface play an important part in the determination of the climate of a region. Thus far, the latitudinal and seasonal variations in temperature, pressure, winds, and precipitation have been discussed for an assumed uniform surface. Once the differences in the physical properties of bodies of land and of water are taken into account, the picture must be modified.

**Temperature Variations over Land and Water.** The temperature of a water surface varies much less than the temperature of a land surface. There are at least six reasons for this. (1) When the sun is near the horizon, water reflects more of the sunlight than bare ground does, provided the ground is not covered with snow. As a result, less of the sunlight is absorbed by the water than by the land. However, when the sun is nearly overhead, water reflects less light than land reflects. (2) Water is semitransparent and land is opaque; thus sunlight reaches down into a considerable depth of water but is absorbed only at the surface of the land. As a result, the absorbed heat is less concentrated in the water than on land. (3) Vertical mixing of the water spreads out the absorbed heat even more thinly, whereas there is no mixing under a land surface. (4) Water, to a greater degree than almost any other known substance, has the capacity to absorb heat without much rise in temperature. This means that if the same amount of heat is added to water and to land, the temperature of the water will increase less than the temperature of the land. (5) Water conducts heat more easily than land does. (6) Part of the sun's heat evaporates the water instead of warming it. This may also happen on moist land, but the water supply on land is limited.

The combination of these factors makes the oceans the world's great thermostats. They regulate the temperatures of all maritime air masses, that is, the air masses above the oceans. These air masses keep temperatures moderate on islands, coastal areas, and even inland on continents where the prevailing winds blow from sea to land.

Land surfaces can grow very hot or very cold. Because of this they are hotter than the neighboring oceans in low latitudes, where more heat is received from the sun than is radiated into space. They are colder than the nearby oceans at high latitudes, where the heat radiated outward exceeds the incoming sunshine. For the same reasons, land areas have greater yearly and daily ranges of temperature than the oceans have. In middle latitudes land areas are hotter than the oceans in summer and colder than the oceans in winter. Moreover, land tends to be warmer than water during the day and colder than water during the night.

**Pressure Variations over Land and Water.** Because of the temperature variations of the atmosphere over land and water, atmospheric pressures also vary. The colder a mass of air is, the greater are its density and weight. Usually its sea-level pressure is higher as well. Consequently, the pressure belts around the world have different intensities, according to whether the air is over oceans or over continents.

Since the total weight of the entire atmosphere is constant, an increase of pressure in one region must be attended by a decrease of pressure elsewhere. In winter, air tends to accumulate in high-pressure areas over the colder continents at the expense of the neighboring oceans, which have low-pressure areas. In summer, the heated air over the continents expands and spills over the nearby oceans, where it is cooled and forms high-pressure areas, leaving low-pressure areas over the continents.

The polar high over the Antarctic continent is stronger than the polar high over the warmer Arctic Ocean. In fact, the highest pressure in the Northern Hemisphere in winter is not over the North Pole but over Siberia, where the air is even colder than the air over the Arctic Ocean. In the Southern Hemisphere the subpolar low-pressure areas lie near 60° latitude in a continuous belt over the relatively mild Antarctic Ocean. In the Northern Hemisphere, on the other hand, there are two distinct subpolar low-pressure areas. One is located approximately over the Aleutian Islands in the north Pacific Ocean, and the other is located between Greenland and Iceland in the north Atlantic Ocean. These lows are most intense in winter, when the difference in temperature between the cold land and the relatively warm water nearby is greatest.

The subtropical high-pressure belt near 30° latitude is broken into high-pressure areas which are located over the oceans; at this low latitude the oceans are not, on an average, as hot as the continents are. Since this contrast in temperature is most marked during the summer, the subtropical highs reach their greatest intensity in summer—particularly in the Northern Hemisphere. The equatorial low-pressure belt is characterized by diffuse low-pressure areas over the hot continents. However, these low-pressure areas are not restricted to the equator but occur in various hot continental areas at low latitudes in summer. They lie, for example, over West Pakistan in Asia, over northwestern Mexico in North America, and over northern Australia.

**Effects of Land and Water on Winds.** The wind belts around the earth vary in intensity in accordance with the variations in atmospheric pressure. Thus the oceanic subpolar lows, which have their maximum intensities in winter, cause the polar easterly winds and the middle-latitude westerly winds to be strongest over the oceans, particularly in the winter. Similarly, the subtropical highs that lie over the oceans cause the trade winds to be strongest and steadiest over the oceans.

While zonal flows—that is, from west or east—are best developed over the open oceans, a different type of circulation characterizes the borders of the continents. It is there that the monsoon winds occur in tropical and middle latitudes. A monsoon is a seasonal wind that blows as a result of a seasonal thermal (temperature-regulated) pressure center over land. Since the continents in middle latitudes have high pressures over them in winter and low pressures over them during the heat of summer, the monsoon blows outward from the continental high in winter and inward toward the continental low in summer. This statement can be generalized by saying that the surface monsoon wind always blows away from the colder surface, or toward the warmer surface.

Higher in the atmosphere there is a countermonsoon, blowing in the opposite direction to the monsoon. Both the surface winds and the higher winds are deflected by the earth's rotation—to the right in the Northern Hemisphere and to the left in the Southern Hemisphere. Thus at the earth's surface the cold winter air circles outward from the continental highs, and the moist summer air circles inward toward the continental lows. (For example, India's rainy season results from the southwest monsoon that blows in over the continent.)

Just as the monsoons are seasonal winds, so are the land and sea breezes daily winds, which result from the same causes. During the heat of the day a slight low pressure develops over the land. This may cause a sea breeze to blow onshore if the prevailing winds of the atmosphere's general circulation pattern are not too strong. At night a slightly higher pressure develops over the cooled land, often causing a land breeze to blow offshore.

**Continental and Oceanic Climates.** The climates of different parts of the world are profoundly influenced by pressure variations, in both space and time, that are caused by the differences between land and water.

*Oceans and Continental Borders.* Because of the strong winds associated with the intense subpolar low-pressure areas, conditions are stormy over the oceans at middle and high latitudes in winter. Rainy winters are also found in the maritime climates on the west coasts of continents at middle latitudes. Since the middle-latitude oceans in summer are dominated by strong subtropical high-pressure areas, summer weather over the oceans is generally serene (with fog occurring at high latitudes). An important interruption in this pattern takes place when tropical hurricanes or typhoons form over low-latitude oceans in summer or fall and move into middle latitudes as severe storms. These tropical disturbances occur in all tropical oceans except the south Atlantic Ocean and the southeastern Pacific Ocean. The coasts of South America do not experience any hurricanes.

## TEMPERATURE VARIATIONS OVER LAND AND SEA

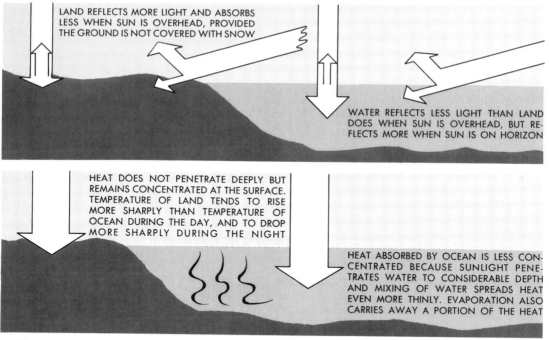

LAND REFLECTS MORE LIGHT AND ABSORBS LESS WHEN SUN IS OVERHEAD, PROVIDED THE GROUND IS NOT COVERED WITH SNOW

WATER REFLECTS LESS LIGHT THAN LAND DOES WHEN SUN IS OVERHEAD, BUT RE-FLECTS MORE WHEN SUN IS ON HORIZON

HEAT DOES NOT PENETRATE DEEPLY BUT REMAINS CONCENTRATED AT THE SURFACE. TEMPERATURE OF LAND TENDS TO RISE MORE SHARPLY THAN TEMPERATURE OF OCEAN DURING THE DAY, AND TO DROP MORE SHARPLY DURING THE NIGHT

HEAT ABSORBED BY OCEAN IS LESS CON-CENTRATED BECAUSE SUNLIGHT PENE-TRATES WATER TO CONSIDERABLE DEPTH AND MIXING OF WATER SPREADS HEAT EVEN MORE THINLY. EVAPORATION ALSO CARRIES AWAY A PORTION OF THE HEAT

*The temperature of water surfaces varies much less than the temperature of land surfaces. Because of the differences in the ways that water and land absorb and reflect light, the oceans act as the world's great thermostats. Temperatures generally are more moderate over islands and coastal areas, and even inland where prevailing winds blow in from the sea. Variations between land and sea temperatures and pressures produce wind and weather patterns both globally and locally.*

When the borders of continental regions are dominated by monsoon winds, the climate there is characteristically cold and dry in winter, with cold, dry winds blowing from the frigid interior. In summer such regions are warm and rainy, with moist tropical air coming in from the sea. This is best illustrated by the large continent of Asia and to a lesser extent by North America.

**Continental Regions.** A heavy summer rainfall is characteristic of most tropical regions, since they come under the influence of the equatorial low-pressure belt in the summer. This summer rainfall is intensified by thunderstorms developed from the moist monsoons and sea breezes that are lifted up the hills and mountain slopes after coming ashore. An excellent example of this climate is found in Burma, northeastern India, and East Pakistan, which have some of the heaviest rainfalls in the world.

The rainy summer may reach into middle-latitude continents, where the maritime air is made unstable by surface heating. The unstable air may then flow up fronts or mountains (as happens in China), causing precipitation. The maritime winter rainy season (associated with subpolar lows) is restricted to the oceans and to the western parts of the continents. This is seen in the climate of western Europe.

At high latitudes, annual precipitation is generally small. Summer is the season when precipitation is greatest, particularly over the continents. A good example of this is the climate of northern Asia.

### EFFECTS OF OCEAN CURRENTS

The oceans have an extensive influence on climates everywhere in the world except at the centers of large continents. Oceanography is of great importance, therefore, in the study of climates. Because of the ocean's thermostatic control over air temperatures, it is essential to know what determines the distribution of ocean temperatures. As with land temperatures, ocean temperatures are highest at low latitudes and decrease to their lowest point at high latitudes. However, the poleward lowering of temperature over the oceans is much more gradual than over the land, because oceanic temperatures at low and high latitudes are not as extreme as land temperatures are. Ocean temperatures vary not only with latitude but also with longitude, because ocean currents have a powerful effect on the temperatures of the seas.

**Prevailing Ocean Currents.** Prevailing winds drive the major ocean currents around the sub-tropical high-pressure centers and the subpolar low-pressure centers. If the currents could be viewed from above it would be seen that, like the winds, the currents around the high-pressure centers are anticyclonic—clockwise in the Northern Hemisphere and counterclockwise in the Southern Hemisphere. Ocean currents move counterclockwise around low-pressure centers in the Northern Hemisphere and clockwise in the Southern Hemisphere.

The anticyclonic oceanic circulations involve more water and cover larger areas than the cyclonic currents do. Over the open oceans the zonal winds—those blowing east and west—drive the zonal ocean currents. The equatorial currents flowing from the east are driven by the trade winds. The west-wind drifts of the middle-latitude currents are urged along by the prevailing westerlies, and the high-latitude currents from the east get their power from the polar easterlies.

There are converging current patterns in the western portions of the oceans, off the east coasts of continents. The equatorial currents from low latitudes move poleward as warm currents. From this poleward movement of warm water arise the Gulf Stream in the northern Atlantic Ocean and the Japan Current (Kuroshio) in the northern Pacific. In middle latitudes these large currents meet the smaller high-latitude currents, such as the Labrador Current, that are moving equatorward. The converging currents then cross the oceans from west to east. Some mixing of their waters occurs, but more water is contributed by the warm than by the cold current.

When the currents reach the eastern sides of the oceans—that is, the western coasts of the continents—they diverge. One branch moves equatorward as a relatively cold current, where eventually it furnishes the beginnings of the equatorial current. A smaller branch of the eastward-flowing current moves poleward as a relatively warm current, where it supplies the high-latitude current. The temperatures of the cold, southward-flowing currents are further lowered by the upwelling of colder water from the oceanic depths along the subtropical western coasts of the continents. Examples of these currents are the relatively cold California Current and the relatively warm Alaska Current in the northern Pacific Ocean and also the cold Canaries Current and the warm Norwegian Current in the northern Atlantic.

**Coastal Climates.** The currents have a considerable influence on two factors that determine climates: temperature and precipitation. The convergence of the currents in the western portions of the oceans and their divergence in the eastern portions lead to a more rapid lowering of air temperature toward the pole on the westward sides of the oceans.

In middle latitudes, with their prevailing westerly winds, the oceanic influences are felt primarily on the western coasts of the continents. Summers are on the whole cooler and winters are milder than on the eastern coasts. On the western coasts, relatively warm air is found at the higher latitudes and relatively cool air at the lower latitudes as a result of the corresponding currents in the eastern parts of the oceans. Consequently, the lowering of air temperatures toward the pole on the western coasts of continents is less abrupt than it is over other parts of the continents.

Precipitation is favored by the heating and moistening of the air over warm ocean currents. As a result, areas of heavy precipitation are found where the prevailing winds blow from warm ocean currents. Areas of scanty rainfall and of a good deal of fog occur in the neighborhood of cold currents. At low latitudes the east-coastal areas of continents receive heavy rains from the trade winds blowing in from the equatorial currents. This kind of climate occurs in the West Indies, Brazil, Madagascar, the East Indies, and the eastern coast of Australia; an exception is the eastern coast of North Africa. The low-latitude western coasts, on the other hand, are virtual deserts with coastal fogs, since they are next to cold currents and exposed to offshore winds aloft. Examples are Lower California, Peru, Morocco, southwestern Africa, and the western coast of Australia.

At middle latitudes the picture is reversed. The prevailing westerlies carry shoreward the warm moist air from the warm currents near western coasts, releasing heavy precipitation on the coastal mountains. This kind of climate is found in British Columbia, southern Chile, and Scandinavia. Middle-latitude eastern coasts, with prevailing offshore winds and exposure to cold ocean currents, generally have less precipitation and more fog than western coasts. They are not deserts, however, since advancing fronts bring rain and there is less evaporation of moisture off the ground because of the lower temperatures. Patagonia is an exception to this rule, but the eastern coasts of Canada and of Siberia are good examples.

The ocean currents also affect the average sea-level pressure of the atmosphere. Warm currents tend to produce low-pressure areas and lead to the development of fronts. This is particularly noticeable off the eastern coasts of continents at about latitudes 30° to 40°, where the Gulf Stream and the Japan Current are found. Since cold currents favor high pressure, the subtropical high-pressure areas are not centered in the middle of the oceans but tend to lie on the eastern sides. For example, the northern Atlantic and northern Pacific high-pressure areas are located, on the average, over the Azores and between California and Hawaii, respectively.

## 3. Climatic History

In meteorology and geology, climatic history is the record of the course, character, distribution, change, and fluctuation of the earth's climates through the ages. The evidence upon which to build up a history of the climates is only fragmentary, and knowledge of the subject is far from complete. Moreover, since still less is known about the causes of climatic changes, it is impossible to verify with certainty any theoretical account of climatic history.

Nevertheless, it is known that climates are variable over a wide range of irregular periods of time. The longest known cycles of climatic change cover hundreds of millions of years, whereas the shortest cycles that could be called climatic run their courses in a matter of decades. Any cycles of still shorter duration are looked upon merely as variations in weather within a more constant climate.

### THE GREAT ICE AGES

The longest periods of climatic change are the climatic cycles revealed by ancient rocks, and the best evidence that the earth's climates have undergone important changes is the record of glaciers. There have been four great ice ages within the past billion years. Spaced about a quarter of a billion years apart, they occurred during the following periods of time: the Lower Proterozoic of Precambrian time; the Upper Proterozoic of Precambrian time; the Upper Carboniferous period in the Paleozoic era; and the Pleistocene epoch in the Cenozoic era. This last ice age took place within the past million years. No major glaciations are known for the Mesozoic era, when semitropical conditions prevailed.

The last great ice age consisted of four major periods of glaciation. The first was the Günz (Nebraskan or Jerseyan), 520,000 to 490,000 years ago. The second was the Mindel (Kansan), 430,000 to 370,000 years ago. The third period of glaciation was the Riss (Illinoian), which took place 130,000 to 100,000 years ago; and the most recent period was the Würm (Wisconsan and Iowan) of 40,000 to 18,000 years ago. Each of these four periods was characterized by several shorter stages of advancing and retreating ice sheets.

Even though glaciers never covered more than a small fraction of the earth's surface, they had a worldwide effect on the climates. In general, the ice ages caused lower temperatures around the world, and they produced more precipitation in the tropics as storm tracks shifted closer to the equator.

**Causes of the Ice Ages.** It seems significant that each of the great ice ages followed a period of mountain building and the raising of land into extensive high continents. The periods, or revolutions, of mountain building that preceded the ice ages were, respectively, the Laurentian and Algoman revolutions; the Huronian, or Killarney, revolution; the Appalachian, or Hercynian (Pennsylvanian), revolution; and the Alpine revolution in the Miocene or Pliocene epoch of the Cenozoic era.

**Effects of Mountain Building.** The connection in time between structural changes in the earth's crust and the occurrence of ice ages suggests that geographical factors were the principal causes of the great glacial periods. Mountain building and the formation of plateaus on the earth's surface, by creating large areas of land and by increasing its altitude, produce great extremes of cold in high latitudes. The mountains and plateaus also increase snowfall, which is produced by moist air that is forced up the mountain slopes. With the increase in the size of continental areas, oceanic expanses are necessarily reduced and divided into separate seas. This reduces or even terminates the flow of warm ocean currents into the polar seas, which then proceed to cool faster than the seas in low latitudes.

The Upper Carboniferous ice age, unlike the other great ice ages, saw widespread glaciation at low latitudes in the Southern Hemisphere. Taking geological factors into account, this southern glaciation can best be explained by assuming the presence of land masses uniting India, Africa, South America, and Antarctica. This great land barrier would cut off the oceans of middle and high southern latitudes from the warmth of the equatorial waters.

The Cenozoic glaciation may in turn have resulted in part from the elevation of the submarine Wyville Thomson Ridge between Greenland and Scotland. This would cut the Arctic Ocean off from warm currents in the adjoining Atlantic Ocean. Eventually the fresh water, which remained at the surface because it is less dense than the saline ocean water, would be able to freeze—at first near the shore, and then farther out. The growth of glacial conditions was then speeded up over both the Arctic Ocean and the continents. According to a recent theory, the earth's poles had been wandering, and reached at that time their present thermally isolated locations in the nearly enclosed Arctic Ocean and the Antarctic continent.

**Effects of Dust and Carbon Dioxide.** Volcanic dust no doubt also had a part in reducing the temperature during glacial periods. Consisting as it does of very small particles, the dust can float in the air for two or three years after an explosive eruption. While in the air, the dust deflects part of the sunlight back into space without letting it reach the earth. Such volcanic activity, which has varied greatly in frequency and intensity through geological time, was probably greatest during the periods when the geological revolutions were taking place.

It is possible that a decrease of carbon dioxide in the atmosphere also played a part in causing the ice ages. Carbon dioxide acts as a blanket in the atmosphere; it absorbs some of the outgoing radiation from the earth, preventing this heat from being lost to space. However, it is not known whether decreases in the thickness of the earth's carbon dioxide blanket actually occurred during or close to the periods of mountain building, since the processes that cause changes in atmospheric concentration of carbon dioxide are themselves not fully known.

**Importance of the Polar Ice Caps.** In estimating the effect of geographical factors on climate, it must be realized that accumulations of ice in the polar regions are very sensitive to small changes in the average temperature over the higher latitudes. Slight variations in temperature can easily be magnified into large changes in climate, because ice and snow, as soon as they appear, have a tremendous cooling effect on the atmosphere. The effect of a heat deficit that is initially small can grow rapidly when a large ice sheet is formed that adds its own cooling effect. Similarly, if a slight warming occurs, the melting of a dwindling ice cap removes the chill that the cap had spread over the surrounding area, with the result that even milder conditions prevail. It has been estimated that if all the world's glaciers suddenly were annihilated, under present climatic conditions they would not be able to reappear unless some new influence caused an increase of snowfall and a resulting cooling at the higher latitudes. Strangely enough, greater snowfall is favored by a temporarily warmer polar ocean, which supplies extra water vapor by greater evaporation.

**Astronomical Factors.** In order to account for the great ice ages and the shorter stages of glaciation, some scientists have turned to astronomical explanations. Since ice sheets at high latitudes can melt only during the summer, their growth or recession depends more on summer temperatures than on winter temperatures. There are three astronomical conditions that would tend to bring low summer temperatures. The first is that the ellipse of the earth's orbit would become longer and narrower. The second is that the earth would reach aphelion in summer, that is, in summer the earth would be at that part of its orbit where it is farthest from the sun. The third condition is that the earth's axis would be, as nearly as possible, perpendicular to the plane of the earth's orbit.

The first factor—the lengthening and narrowing of the earth's elliptical orbit—has been used to explain the four recent glaciations. The earth's orbit is at its longest and narrowest about every 100,000 years, which is approximately the interval of time between the Günz and Mindel glaciations and between the Riss and Würm glaciations. The eccentricity of the earth's orbit, however, cannot account for the long Mindel-Riss interglacial period of about 250,000 years.

According to the third factor just mentioned, the shorter stages of glacial advance within each of the four main periods of glaciations were associated with the periods when the earth's axis was most nearly perpendicular to the plane of the earth's orbit. This occurs about every 40,000 years. It has been computed that there should have been a difference of about 10,000 years in the periods at which the Northern and the Southern hemispheres had their greatest glaciations. This supposed alternation between the hemispheres is based on what is called the precession of the equinoxes, a wobbling of the earth's axis as the earth spins. This movement would carry the aphelion from the summer of one hemisphere to the summer of the other hemisphere in half of the precession period, that is, in about 10,000 years. It should be said that many scientists remain unconvinced by the attempts to account for the ice ages in this manner.

**Other Factors in Smaller Glaciations.** Other causes probably played their roles in the periods and smaller stages of the great ice ages. For example, there may have been larger variations in the intensity of solar radiation than are familiar to astronomers in the 11-year sunspot cycle known today. Variations in atmospheric circulation that would cause cooler summers and a heavier snowfall in winter would also favor glaciation. Besides, a lowering of ocean temperatures would cool the temperature of the air.

On the other hand, a natural cycle in the advance and withdrawal of ice sheets could develop without having to assume that astronomical variations caused it. When a thick ice sheet spreads over a continent, it has sufficient weight —it is about one third as dense as rock—to depress the land under it. The sinking of the land lets in the sea, which in turn tends to break up the glacier by tearing it to pieces and melting the ice. With the glacier gone, the land can rise again, and at its old altitude it is again cold enough for glaciers to form and advance.

Another cycle might well be a result of variations in snowfall. Mountain glaciers can advance when the snow line is below the height at which the maximum amount of snow falls on the mountain sides. If these glaciers invade the neighboring plains and form a continental ice sheet, the resulting cooling of the air might well cause the development of areas of high atmospheric pressure, attended by generally fair weather. Under such conditions, less snow would fall and the level of maximum snowfall would be below the snow line; therefore the ice would melt in the summer. This would end the advance of glaciers in the mountains, and the ice sheet over the plains would dwindle away through lack of reinforcement. Once the ice sheet disappeared, higher ocean temperatures would intensify storms, which could again bring heavy snows to the mountains, and the glaciation cycle would be repeated.

In summary it may be said that the ending of a glacial period may come from a lowering of the land, from a rise in summer temperatures, or from a decrease in snowfall. However, these events do not necessarily bring the end of a great ice age, for the ice may advance again. Consequently, when it is remembered that glaciers are still present in the world today, it cannot be said that an ice age is a thing of the past. Future glacial advances may produce other continental ice sheets in a few ten thousands of years.

## CLIMATES OF THE PAST 10,000 YEARS

Evidence gathered in the Northern Hemisphere concerning the past 10,000 years has revealed that the climate had minor fluctuations of short duration. Signs of these minor changes can be found in a variety of places: in old weather records and literary references in Europe; in the migrations of peoples; in variations in lake levels in Asia; in changes in the levels of lakes and of the Nile River in Africa; and in variations in tree growth shown by studies of annual rings in the sequoias in North America. Changes in precipitation in a given latitudinal zone seem to have taken place at about the same time on different continents. A climate approaching the ideal—that is, a climate characterized by the smallest amount of ice and the highest sea levels—seems to have existed at about 5000 B. C. This ideal climate is called the Climatic Optimum.

The worldwide nature of these climatic changes, and the simultaneous beginning and ending of the Riss and Würm glaciations in all parts of the world, indicate a general rather than a local cause for the advance and recession of glaciers. Variations in solar radiation, which have been mentioned, might be a satisfactory general cause, but there are no accurate records to prove their existence. Another possible cause is a variation in the tide-generating forces, as a result of changes in the distances of the moon and the sun over a period of about 1,700 years. Thus a maximum tidal force computed for 1433 A. D. may have broken up large quantities of ice in the polar seas, thus increasing the amount of drift ice. The great storms and excessive rainfall of the 12th to 14th centuries in Europe were supposed to have been caused by the increase of tidal forces at that time. Solar activity, however, may have been an equally important factor.

The most notable climatic events in modern times were the dry period of the 16th century; the great increase in mountain glaciers about 1600; the dry period in western Europe in the first half of the 18th century; and the worldwide rise of temperatures, along with the recession of mountain glaciers, from 1850 to at least 1940. The chief cause of the warming during the past 100 years is not yet known. The building of cities, the leveling of forests, and the increase in industrial smoke and carbon dioxide in the atmosphere probably contributed to local temperature increases around the earth. It is not yet known what effect they may have eventually on the world's climates.

See also ATMOSPHERE; CLOUD; METEOROLOGY; OCEANOGRAPHY; RAIN; WEATHER; WINDS.

EDWARD M. BROOKS, *Geophysicist*
*Edgerton, Germeshausen and Grier, Inc.*
*Former Professor of Geophysics*
*Institute of Technology, St. Louis*

### Bibliography

Budyko, M. I., and Golitsyn, G. S., *Global Climate Catastrophies* (Springer-Verlag 1988).
Critchfield, Howard J., *General Climatology*, 4th ed. (Prentice-Hall 1983).
Dotto, Lydia, *Thinking the Unthinkable: Civilization and Rapid Climate Change* (Humanities Press 1988).
Gregory, Stanley, ed., *Recent Climatic Change* (Columbia Univ. Press 1988).
Kondratyev, K. Y., *Climate Shocks: Natural and Anthropogenic* (Wiley 1988).
Lamb, Hubert H., *Climate, History and the Modern World* (Routledge 1982).
Lamb, Hubert H., *Weather, Climate and Human Affairs* (Routledge 1988).
Landsberg, H. E., ed., *General Climatology: Heat Balance Climatology* (Elsevier Pub. Co. 1985).
Williams, M., *Climatic Changes in Deserts* (Academic Press 1988).

Climbing perch

**CLIMBING FERN,** any of a small group of mainly tropical ferns that differ from most other ferns in that their fronds (leaves) are borne on long twining stems. One species, *Lygodium palmatum,* sometimes called the Hartford fern, is native to the eastern United States. It has nearly rounded fronds, with 4 to 7 lobes, and is best grown in a shady moist area with an acid soil. The Japanese climbing fern (*L. japonicum*) is planted in the Gulf States and is so vigorous that it can escape cultivation and become a weed pest. Another species, *L. scandens,* is native to eastern Asia but is often grown as a greenhouse ornamental.

DONALD WYMAN
*Arnold Arboretum, Harvard University*

**CLIMBING PERCH,** a freshwater fish that is able to travel overland and to take in oxygen from the air. It is widely distributed in Southeast Asia, from India and Ceylon to the Philippines and from south China to the Indo-Australian archipelago. As climbing perch are tasty and are able to stay alive for long periods of time out of water, they are important food fish in many parts of their range.

A somewhat elongated, compressed fish, the climbing perch has reached a length of 9 inches (23 cm), but it may be mature at 4 or 5 inches (10 or 12 cm). Its color is brown. Its dorsal, anal, and ventral fins have strong, sharply pointed spines, and its opercle, or bony flap covering the gill chamber, bears a series of sharp spines along its rear margin. The climbing perch frequently travels overland between bodies of water.

In 1791, Lieutenant Daldorf of the Danish East India Company reported seeing a climbing perch 5 feet (1.5 meters) above the ground on the trunk of an Indian palm tree during a rainstorm. This report led to the fish's common name and to a controversy regarding the fish's ability to climb. One explanation, offered by an Indian naturalist, Dr. Das, is that the climbing perch cannot climb, but that during its land trips, it is seized by crows and kites and placed in trees. Whatever the answer to the controversy, the climbing perch is famous for its ability to spend long periods of time out of water. It is able to do this because of a special breathing organ situated in a cavity above the gills. This organ allows the climbing perch to take oxygen from the air in addition to the oxygen that fish normally take from water through their gills. In fact, the climbing perch is so dependent on air that it will drown if it is kept from rising to the surface for an occasional gulp of air.

The climbing perch, *Anabas testudineus,* contrary to its common name, is not a perch. It is a member of the family Anabantidae in the order Perciformes. Other members of this family, all of which have the special breathing organ mentioned above, are the paradise fish, the gourami, and the Siamese fighting fish.

DANIEL M. COHEN
U. S. *Fish and Wildlife Service*

**CLINCH RIVER,** klinch, a tributary of the Tennessee River. About 300 miles (480 km) long, it rises in Tazewell county, southwestern Virginia, and flows southwestward into Tennessee. Its waters are impounded by two major dams of the Tennessee Valley Authority: Norris Dam, above which the Powell River joins the Clinch in Norris Lake; and Watts Bar Dam (on the Tennessee River), in whose lake the Clinch unites with the Tennessee. The atomic research and development center of Oak Ridge is on the Clinch River, below Norris Dam.

**CLINGMANS DOME,** kling'mənz, a peak in the Great Smoky Mountains, the highest point (6,642 feet, or 2,024 meters) in Tennessee. It is situated about 35 miles (56 km) southeast of Knoxville, on the Tennessee–North Carolina border. The peak, named for Thomas L. Clingman, U. S. senator from North Carolina, is included in the Great Smoky Mountain National Park.

**CLINOMETER,** klī-nom'ət-ər, any of various simple instruments that are used to measure vertical angles, particularly the dip (degree of slope) of rock strata and other geological features. The most simple form of clinometer consists of a pendulum attached to an arc that is marked off in degrees of a circle. When the clinometer is held horizontally, the indicator points to 0 degrees. When the instrument is aligned with the inclined surface that is being measured, the pendulum remains vertical and indicates the degree of slope of the surface. Other forms of clinometer incorporate an indicator attached to a spirit level—a liquid-filled tube with a bubble trapped inside. A clinometer is often conveniently combined with a compass.

Clinometer

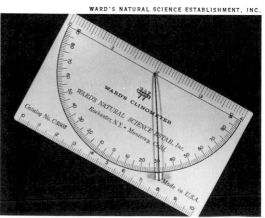

**CLINTON,** klin'tən, **DeWitt** (1769–1828), American politician. As mayor of New York City and as governor of New York state, he made a lasting impact on New York politics and instituted notable political and social reforms. Through his promotion of the Erie Canal, he spurred the nation's growth. He was known for his literary, scientific, and philanthropic contributions.

Clinton's political career was embroiled in controversy and checkered by opposition. His temperament was such that his achievements won him respect rather than affection. He was unwilling to yield to party regularity; Dixon Ryan Fox, in his classic history of New York politics, calls him "Clinton, Divider of Parties."

**Early Career.** DeWitt Clinton was born in Little Britain, N. Y., on March 2, 1769. He was the grandson of Charles Clinton, who emigrated from Ireland and settled in New York in 1731, and the son of Gen. James Clinton, who led New York troops in the American Revolution. His mother, Mary DeWitt, was of Dutch ancestry.

Educated privately in his early years, DeWitt attended Kingston Academy (1782–1784) and Columbia College (1784–1786). While studying law in 1787 he published unsigned letters in the New York *Journal* opposing adoption of the U. S. Constitution and controverting the *Federalist* papers. After admission to the state bar, he became secretary to his uncle, George Clinton, governor of New York, in 1790. When his uncle left that post in 1795, DeWitt then turned to law practice.

Clinton was elected as a Republican to the New York Assembly in 1797 and to the state Senate in 1798. He was one of the senators elected to the governor's council of appointment, and his influence increased as he expanded its role. Although elected to the U. S. Senate in 1802—where he introduced the 12th Amendment to the Constitution—he resigned in 1803 to become mayor of New York City. He held that office for all but two annual terms until 1815. While mayor he also served in the state Senate (1806–1811) and as lieutenant governor (1811–1813).

**Mayor and Governor.** Clinton was one of New York's ablest mayors, distinguished for his decisions in the mayor's court. As a state legislator he left a remarkable record of social legislation. In the Senate, he was a leading spokesman for public education, heading the Free School Society of New York and advocating the monitorial system (q.v.). He championed the Irish immigrants, drafting the law of 1806 that removed voting restrictions against Roman Catholics. He introduced laws against slavery and against imprisonment for debt and helped to establish such New York City institutions as New York Hospital, the Humane Society, and the Orphan Asylum.

Although Clinton embraced Jeffersonian principles and adhered to the Republican party, he shared Federalist interests in land speculation, manufacturing, banks, roads, and canals. In 1812 he gained Federalist support in his bid for the presidency against James Madison. The Federalists were convinced that he would end the war with England, while dissident Republicans felt he would prosecute it more vigorously than Madison. Clinton lost by an electoral vote of 128 to 89. Opposition from his own Jeffersonian-Republican party prompted a council of appointment to remove him from the office of mayor in 1815.

Clinton was elected governor of New York in 1817. His election was closely associated with his promotion of the Erie Canal. As a member of a legislative commission in 1810 he had explored a route for the canal and had sought federal aid. He led the canal movement in 1815, writing a memorial from New York City in which he petitioned the legislature for construction of canals from the Hudson River to Lake Erie and Lake Champlain. His sponsorship led to the enactment of laws in 1816 and 1817 authorizing these works, and identification with the project helped him to be elected governor in 1817. The successful construction of the Erie and Champlain canals brought him increasing recognition.

Opposed by Martin Van Buren and the Republican faction known as "Bucktails," Clinton did not attempt a campaign for reelection to the governorship in 1822. But his subsequent removal from the canal board evoked popular protest, and he was reelected governor as the People's party candidate in 1824. As governor he presided over the canal celebrations in 1825.

Clinton furthered political reform in New York while governor. He supported, if belatedly, the state constitutional convention of 1821, which abolished the councils of appointment and revi-

DeWitt Clinton

(Painting by John Trumbull)

sion, and he advocated abolishing the caucus system for choosing presidential electors.

**Outside Interests.** Aside from his political involvement, Clinton was attracted to an unusually broad range of literary and scientific pursuits. He held, simultaneously, the presidencies of the New-York Historical Society, the American Academy of Art, and the Literary and Philosophy Society. The Historical Society was a result of his patronage; he secured its incorporation in 1809 and gained it state support. In natural history, he discovered a species of fish and an indigenous American wheat. He wrote on swallows, passenger pigeons, and wild rice, and in 1814 he published an *Introductory Discourse* on the progress of American science.

Clinton married Maria Franklin in 1796, and they had 10 children. After her death in 1818, he married Catharine Jones. He died while still governor, in Albany, N. Y., on Feb. 11, 1828.

RONALD SHAW
*Miami University, Oxford, Ohio*

**Further Reading:** Freidel, Frank, and May, Ernest, eds., *DeWitt Clinton, Years of Molding, 1769–1807* (Garland 1988); Shaw, Ronald E., *Erie Water West* (Univ. Press of Ky. 1966).

**CLINTON, George** (1739—1812), American public official, influential in the politics of the Revolutionary and early national periods. Clinton served seven times as governor of New York (1777—1795 and 1800—1804) and was twice elected vice president of the United States (1805—1812), serving under presidents Jefferson and Madison.

Clinton was born in Little Britain, N.Y., on July 26, 1739. He served in the French and Indian War, then studied and practiced law and entered the New York Assembly. During the controversy with Britain he became known as a fiery radical. Clinton was elected to the Second Continental Congress, but, having been commissioned a brigadier general in the militia in December 1775, he was absent for the signing of the Declaration of Independence.

The outbreak of the Revolution saw Clinton entrusted with the defense of the Hudson River valley. By his own admission, however, he was an ineffectual military strategist, and his lack of tactical skill led to the loss of Fort Montgomery and the burning of Esopus in the fall of 1777.

He returned to New York politics in 1777, becoming the state's first governor, and built a powerful political machine. He was respected for his management of finances, astute handling of a dangerous Indian problem, and severe treatment of Loyalists.

Perceiving that a strong national government would shift power from the states, Clinton opposed the U.S. Constitution. He presided over New York's ratifying convention in order to block ratification. However, when the Constitution had been approved by the necessary nine states, he acquiesced in New York's ratification.

In the 1790s Clinton cast his lot with the Democratic Republicans. He retired from the governorship in 1795 but was reelected in 1801. In 1804 he was elected vice president under Thomas Jefferson. Failing in his presidential ambitions in 1808, he accepted the second spot again under James Madison, whom he openly despised. He died in Washington, D.C., on April 20, 1812.

ARTHUR SHAFFER*
*University of Missouri at St. Louis*

**CLINTON, George** (1686—1761), British colonial administrator in America. The son of an English nobleman, he joined the Royal Navy in 1708 and rose to the rank of admiral of the white in 1747. Through the influence of the duke of Newcastle, he was appointed governor of New York in 1741. He arrived in that province in 1743 and served as governor for 10 years. Clinton granted the provincial assembly the right to pass an annual revenue law, to control all appropriations, and even to appoint administrative officers. The British Board of Trade, angered by this loss of "legal prerogative" and by the need to send additional revenues to New York, dismissed Clinton in 1753. He returned to England and sat in Parliament from 1754 to 1760. He died on July 10, 1761.

His son, Henry Clinton, was commander in chief of the British army in America during most of the Revolution.

**CLINTON, George Wylie** (1859—1921), American bishop and educator. He was born in Lancaster county, S.C., on March 28, 1859, the son of slaves. After studying at Brainerd Institute, he attended the University of South Carolina during a period (1874—1877) when blacks were admitted. He then studied theology at Livingstone College, Salisbury, N.C., and in 1879 became a minister of the African Methodist Episcopal Zion Church. He was president of the Atkinson Literary and Industrial College in Madisonville, Ky., for eight years.

In 1896 Clinton was elected bishop of his church. As a member of the executive committee of the Federal Council of Churches of Christ in America and president of the Negro Young People's Educational and Religious Congress, he was prominent in social and educational work. He died in Charlotte, N.C., on May 12, 1921.

**CLINTON, Henry** (c. 1738—1795), British army officer who commanded the British forces in North America when Lord Charles Cornwallis surrendered at Yorktown, Va., ending the American Revolution (1781). He was born about 1738, the son of Admiral George Clinton, later governor of New York. Commissioned a lieutenant in the Coldstream Guards when he was only 13 years old, Clinton rose to the rank of major general in 1772. He served in Parliament in 1772 and 1774.

At the outbreak of the American Revolution, Clinton distinguished himself in the Battle of Bunker Hill (1775) and was subsequently named second in command to Gen. William Howe, the British commander in chief. In 1776 Clinton unsuccessfully assaulted Sullivans Island at Charleston, S.C., shared in the British victory in the Battle of Long Island, and captured Newport, R.I. When General Howe resigned his command in 1778 Clinton was named to succeed him.

Clinton's first step as commander in chief was to move his headquarters from Philadelphia to New York. In 1779 he joined Cornwallis in the South, capturing Charleston in 1780. On Clinton's return to New York, hostility arose between the two generals, which may have contributed to Cornwallis's surrender. Clinton resigned his command in 1781.

In England Clinton sought to vindicate his conduct of the war by publishing his *Narrative*. In 1790 he reentered the House of Commons and in 1794 was appointed governor of Gibraltar. Clinton died in Cornwall on Dec. 23, 1795, before taking up his post as governor.

PAUL C. BOWERS, JR., *Ohio State University*

**CLINTON, James** (1733—1812), American general in the Revolutionary War. He was born in Orange county, N.Y., on Aug. 9, 1733. During the French and Indian War he took part in Lt. Col. John Bradstreet's successful campaign against Fort Frontenac (now Kingston, Ontario) in 1758. When the American colonies revolted, he commanded a New York regiment and accompanied Brig. Gen. Richard Montgomery on the disastrous expedition against Quebec in 1775.

The next year Clinton was commissioned brigadier general in the Continental Army. He was unable to hold Forts Clinton and Montgomery in New York against the British forces in 1777, but he and Maj. Gen. John Sullivan defeated the Loyalists and Indians two years later at Newtown (Elmira), N.Y. In 1781 he participated in the siege of Yorktown. Clinton died in Little Britain, N.Y., on Dec. 22, 1812. He was a brother of George Clinton, vice president of the United States in 1805—1812, and the father of DeWitt Clinton.

# WILLIAM JEFFERSON CLINTON

*Bill Clinton*

**42D PRESIDENT OF THE UNITED STATES (1993–2001)**

**BORN** Aug. 19, 1946, in Hope, Ark.

**HIGHER EDUCATION** Georgetown University (B.S., 1968);
Yale University (J.D., 1973).

**RELIGIOUS AFFILIATION** Baptist.

**OCCUPATIONS** Professor, lawyer, public official.

**MARRIAGE** Oct. 11, 1975, to Hillary Rodham (1947–    ).

**CHILDREN** Chelsea Victoria (1980–    ).

**MILITARY SERVICE** None.

**PARTY AFFILIATION** Democratic.

**LEGAL RESIDENCE WHEN ELECTED** Arkansas.

**POSITION BEFORE TAKING OFFICE** Governor of Arkansas.

**CLINTON, William Jefferson** (1946–    ), 42d president of the United States. Clinton's two terms in office were marked by efforts to create or expand domestic social programs, by attempts to resolve several major crises overseas, and by various scandals of both a political and personal kind that resulted in Clinton's becoming the first president since Andrew Johnson to be impeached and tried.

**Early Years.** Born on Aug. 19, 1946, in Hope, Ark., William ("Bill") Jefferson Blythe IV grew up in a troubled home. His father had died in an automobile accident three months before his son's birth, and his mother later was forced to leave her two-year-old son with his grandparents when she moved to New Orleans to pursue her nursing studies. The family settled in Hot Springs, Ark., after his mother married Roger Clinton, whose surname Bill later adopted. As a young man, Bill Clinton was determined to succeed and frequently earned academic honors, including selection as a delegate to the American Legion Boy's Nation program in Washington, D.C., where the 16-year-old met Pres. John F. Kennedy and determined to embark on a political career.

Attending Georgetown University to study international affairs, Clinton served as an intern for Sen. J. William Fulbright of Arkansas before receiving his B.S. degree in 1968. After winning a Rhodes scholarship to Oxford University, Clinton returned to the United States to enroll at Yale Law School. In 1972 he helped to manage presidential candidate George McGovern's Texas campaign. After graduating from law school in 1973, Clinton returned to Arkansas to teach and to plan his political career. On Oct. 11, 1975, he married Hillary Rodham, a fellow Yale law student.

**Political Career.** After working for Jimmy Carter's presidential campaign in Arkansas, Clinton won his first statewide election in 1976, when he became Arkansas's attorney general. Two years later he was elected the nation's youngest governor. Clinton and his youthful staff were committed liberal activists, perceived as too eager to remold the conservative, Deep South state according to their own image. Clinton angered state leaders when he increased automobile license plate fees and challenged powerful timber and utilities interests. His heavy-handed leadership style led to his biggest political defeat in 1980, when Arkansas voters did not reelect him to a second two-year term as chief executive.

Clinton's defeat motivated him to adopt a more cautious, pragmatic, and moderate approach. This new strategy served him well as he quickly regained the governorship in 1982, a position he retained for five consecutive terms. His agenda focused on education, health care, welfare reform, the economy, and the environment. Under his leadership Arkansas increased teacher salaries, required teacher competency exams, and made admission to high school conditional on successful completion of a standardized examination. By 1992 Arkansas had the highest high-school graduation rate of any southern state, and the percentage of Arkansans going to college had increased substantially. In addition, he initiated school-based health clinics, expanded Head Start programs, and approved home-schooling alternatives.

As governor, Clinton could claim other policy successes as well. State income rose 61%, though it still lagged 25% behind the national average; he enacted a welfare reform program requiring able-bodied persons to undergo job training or schooling and penalizing those who did not.

In 1990 Clinton became chairman of the Democratic Leadership Council, an organization of prominent moderate and conservative Democrats, and was rated the most effective governor in the country by his colleagues. He firmly believed that the party had to adopt a less liberal approach in order to attract broader popular support.

**The 1992 Presidential Campaign.** Clinton was keenly aware of the recession, and his campaign offered change and focused on the economy and the high unemployment rate. He promised health-care reform, tax cuts for the middle class and tax increases for the wealthy, and reductions in defense spending. Although the Bush campaign portrayed Clinton as untrustworthy and inexperienced, the Republican strategy failed to convince the voters to trust a president who had been unable to pull America out of the recession.

Clinton won the presidency with 43% of the popular vote and an electoral college landslide. With one-party control of the legislative and executive branches, he promised an end to governmental gridlock.

**The Clinton Presidency.** After 12 years of Republican control of the presidency, Clinton came to office amid high expectations for fundamental policy change. Early in his administration he reversed a number of Republican policies. He ended the federal prohibition on the use of fetal tissue for medical research, repealed rules restricting abortion counseling in federally funded health clinics, and used his appointment power to fulfill a promise to place many women and minorities in prominent government positions.

Although backed by a Congress controlled by the Democratic party, Clinton found it difficult to change the course of national priorities during his first two years in office. The failure to enact comprehensive health-care reform proved to be a major setback for Clinton. Widespread public concerns over the proposal's complexity, combined with an effective lobbying campaign by opponents, drained congressional support for this major policy initiative, which had been one of the cornerstones of Clinton's campaign.

Clinton's biggest setback came in 1994, when the Democrats lost control of both houses of Congress to the Republicans. In 1995–1996 some Clinton White House activities were subjected to criticism, and several alleged scandals became the target of congressional investigations, most notably the "Whitewater affair," an investigation into alleged improprieties by the president and his wife, Hillary Rodham Clinton, in a 1980s Arkansas land deal. Administration actions that were investigated included White House requests for FBI security files, the White House travel office firings, and fund-raising methods used for the 1996 presidential campaign. Yet Clinton's popularity increased as the strength of the economy continued.

In seeking reelection in 1996, Clinton claimed a number of achievements, among them a deficit-reduction plan, a college-loan payback plan, the Family and Medical Leave Act, an anticrime bill, and a welfare reform bill that ended federal guarantees and shifted the responsibility for these services to the states. His domestic record showed that he had cut the deficit in half, had expanded earned-income credit for the working poor, and had significantly reduced the number of government workers.

During his first term Clinton succeeded in appointing two members to the U.S. Supreme Court. Ruth Bader Ginsburg and Stephen G. Breyer were the first appointments to the high court made by a Democratic president in 25 years.

In the first years of his administration, Clinton experienced many of his greatest difficulties in the foreign policy realm. Indeed, issues involving Bosnia, Haiti, the former Soviet Union, Somalia, Cuba, North Korea, and Iraq seemed intractable, but his inexperience in foreign affairs showed when he appeared unable to establish a consistent U.S. position on these daunting problems.

Nevertheless, Clinton succeeded in some of his foreign policy efforts. Under threat of an imminent invasion, Haiti's military junta agreed to relinquish power in favor of the democratically elected president, Jean-Bertrand Aristide. American troops entered Haiti to keep the peace. A major conflict with North Korea was eased with an agreement offering North Korea assistance with its civilian nuclear program in return for the relinquishment of plutonium-producing nuclear reactors. Clinton used currency funds controlled by the president to grant to Mexico a $40 billion loan guarantee. One of his more controversial decisions was to grant U.S. recognition to Vietnam. In 1994 Clinton deployed troops to Kuwait when Iraq, protesting UN sanctions and the enforcement of a no-fly zone, appeared to threaten its neighbor again. Two years later he ordered air strikes against Iraq for violating the terms of peace agreed to at the end of the Persian Gulf War.

On balance, Clinton demonstrated that he had adjusted to the tasks of the presidency and had become an astute political leader. In 1996, voters chose him by a comfortable margin over Republican nominee Robert Dole, making Clinton the first Democratic president since Franklin Roosevelt to be elected to the office twice.

The president was not able to deliver a Democratic majority back to Congress, but he developed a deft touch at leading a divided government. In 1997 Congress enacted a major tax cut, the first since 1981, and Clinton negotiated a deficit-reduction package that projected a balanced federal budget in 2002. He also had success with a number of targeted domestic programs on education, health, and the environment; won an increase in the minimum wage; and sponsored a welfare reform bill that established time limits for benefits. He claimed credit for the general health of the economy, for a 30-year low in unemployment, and for the fastest real-wage growth in 20 years. The 1998 fiscal year ended with a federal budget surplus of $70 billion, the first surplus in a generation.

In international affairs Clinton's second term was characterized by attempts to support European unity and strength; to deal with the virtual collapse of the Asian regional economy; to nurture peace efforts in the former Yugoslavia, Northern Ireland, Israel, and the Korean peninsula; to encourage Chinese cooperation in world affairs; and to ensure Iraqi compliance with international agreements. Clinton and his foreign policy team, led by Secretary of State Madeleine Albright, achieved considerable successes in Northern Ireland and Israel. With Iraq, however, the administration came to consider that diplomatic measures had been exhausted; on Dec. 16, 1998, Clinton, together with British prime minister Tony Blair, authorized renewed air strikes against Iraq.

The Clinton administration also supplied the bulk of the aircraft and weaponry for NATO's 1999 military campaign against Yugoslav president Slobodan Milošović's troops in the predominantly Albanian province of Kosovo in Serbia.

On the domestic front the Whitewater affair consumed much of the president's final years in office. Independent Counsel Kenneth Starr's investigation of allegations of wrongdoing by Clinton and his wife, begun in 1994, eventually expanded to include charges of perjury, obstruction of justice, and abuse of power, which arose from a relationship between the president and a White House intern, Monica Lewinsky. The ensuing scandal preoccupied the capital from January 1998 on. Clinton adamantly denied any sexual involvement with Lewinsky, but the Starr investigation developed evidence to the contrary. In August Clinton admitted to an "inappropriate relationship." Because Clinton had testified under oath both in a civil case and before the grand jury that he had not had such a relationship, he was open to the charge of perjury. Starr delivered his report to the House of Representatives on Sept. 9, 1998. In November the House Judiciary Committee began impeachment hearings, which ended in mid-December with the refusal to entertain a Democratic motion for censure and the drafting of four articles of impeachment. On Dec. 16, exactly one day before the full House was scheduled to vote on the articles, Clinton launched renewed air strikes against Iraq, causing some of his opponents to claim that the attack was a diversionary tactic—one, moreover, of unprecedented scope. On Dec. 19, 1998, the full House approved two of the four articles (perjury and obstruction of justice). Clinton thus became the first elected president in U.S. history to be impeached. On Jan. 7, 1999, the Senate trial to remove Clinton from office began. It ended on Feb. 6, 1999, with neither article gaining a simple majority (46–54, 50–50). After the vote Clinton returned to efforts directed toward reforming the health-care system and determining how best to handle the budget surplus. (See also IMPEACHMENT.)

In his final year in office, Clinton still had to deal with matters pertaining to the scandal that led to his impeachment. A committee of the Arkansas supreme court, for example, recommended that Clinton's right to practice law in the state should be revoked because of his "serious misconduct" in a sexual harassment case brought by a former state employee, Paula Jones. Clinton had to devote some of his time to fighting the recommendation that he be disbarred in Arkansas.

The president also spent considerable time in his final year in office battling the Republican majorities in Congress over a host of issues. He vetoed GOP-passed bills on the repeal of estate taxes and the "marriage penalty" (so-called because of unfavorable tax outcomes for some married couples). Clinton offered the GOP a trade: marriage penalty relief in return for his prescription drug benefit plan, which would bring relief to consumers of prescription drugs; but the Republicans ignored the offer. Clinton also battled the GOP over a so-called Patient's Bill of Rights (intended to address consumers' grievances regarding health maintenance organizations) and gun control measures. One of the president's more controversial moves was to order the release of oil from the nation's strategic oil reserve in an attempt to lower home heating costs. Clinton justi-

fied the action as necessary given a huge increase in oil prices, but Republicans charged that this was a political ploy designed to aid Vice Pres. Al Gore's chances in the 2000 presidential race.

President Clinton and the GOP-led Congress did come together on one important issue: the granting of permanent normal trade relations with China. The initiative had strong bipartisan support, despite a campaign by human rights advocates to quell the effort because of China's poor rights record. Elsewhere, Clinton's efforts to broker a Middle East peace began to crumble as that region became embroiled in renewed violence. Some criticized the president's efforts as having only exacerbated the tensions in the region.

Historians will debate for years the meaning of the Clinton legacy. Was he a president who benefited politically from a strong economy, or was he the architect of policies that created economic growth? Was he a visionary leader who redefined the Democratic party, or was he a political chameleon who changed ideological stripes whenever it was in his interest to do so? And was his impeachment a partisan travesty for which Republicans will be shamed in history, or was it the justified rebuke of a president who truly committed high crimes? Regardless of the answers to these questions, there is no doubt that Bill Clinton was the towering political figure of his era and that his impact on the country will be analyzed and debated for generations to come.

MARK J. ROZELL, *Catholic University of America*

### Bibliography

Baker, Peter, *The Breach: Inside the Impeachment and Trial of William Jefferson Clinton* (Scribner 2000).

Burns, James MacGregor, and Georgia J. Sorenson, *Dead Center: Clinton-Gore Leadership and the Perils of Moderation* (Scribner 1999).

Hitchens, Christopher, *No One Left to Lie To: The Triangulations of William Jefferson Clinton* (Verso 1999).

Hyland, William G., *Clinton's World: Remaking American Foreign Policy* (Praeger 1999).

Maraniss, David, *First In His Class: The Biography of Bill Clinton* (Touchstone Bks. 1996).

Posner, Richard A., *An Affair of State: The Investigation, Impeachment, and Trial of President Clinton* (Harvard Univ. Press 1999).

Renshon, Stanley A., *High Hopes: The Clinton Presidency and the Politics of Ambition* (N.Y. Univ. Press 1996).

Rozell, Mark J., and Clyde Wilcox, eds., *The Clinton Scandal and the Future of American Government* (Georgetown Univ. Press 2000).

Schier, Steven E., *The Postmodern Presidency: Bill Clinton's Legacy in U.S. Politics* (Univ. of Pittsburgh Press 2000).

**CLIO,** klī′ō, in Greek mythology, the daughter of Zeus and Mnemosyne (Memory). The muse of history, she is usually depicted seated, crowned with a laurel wreath and holding a half-open inscribed parchment in one hand, with a box holding more manuscripts beside her. She was said to have fallen in love with Peirus, king of Macedonia, and to have been punished by giving birth to Hyacinthus, whom Apollo accidently killed with a discus.

**CLIPPER,** a sailing merchant ship designed primarily for speed. Clippers were usually square-rigged ships with three or more masts, but there were also clipper barks, brigs, and schooners. Considerations of large carrying capacity and economical operation were subordinated to fine hull lines and heavy sparring in order to carry maximum sail. A swift clipper needed a hard-driving captain and a large crew to handle sail quickly.

The great age of the American clipper ship was 1845 to 1860. Speed was demanded in the

China tea trade and also for the fast delivery of cargoes at San Francisco and Melbourne during the California and Australian gold rushes. Among the most famous of American clipper designers and builders were John W. Griffiths, Donald McKay, Samuel H. Pook, and William H. Webb. Between 1845 and 1859 nearly 500 clippers were built in American yards. The largest clipper ship was Donald McKay's *Great Republic* of 1853 (4,555 tons register). British yards built 27 tea clippers between 1859 and 1869. Unlike the wooden-hulled American clippers, most of the British vessels were of "composite" construction, with iron frames and wooden planking. Clippers became obsolete as freight rates declined and steamships provided competition. The British tea clipper *Cutty Sark*, fully rigged and equipped, is preserved in a permanent dry dock at Greenwich, England.

JOHN HASKELL KEMBLE
*Pomona College*

**CLIVE, Kitty** (1711–1785), British comedic actress and soprano who had her greatest success in ballad operas. She was born Catherine Raftor, probably in London, in 1711. She began to act in 1728 at the Drury Lane Theatre, London, then run by Colley Cibber, in whose *Love in a Riddle* she had her first theatrical triumph in 1729. In 1731 she gained popularity as a comedian and singer in *The Devil to Pay*, Charles Coffey's farce-opera. She married a barrister, George Clive, in 1733, but they soon agreed to part. From 1746 until she retired in 1769, Clive was a leading member of David Garrick's Drury Lane company. She also wrote the libretto of the 1750 burlesque *The Rehearsal, or Boys in Petticoats*. Among her notable friends was Horace Walpole, who presented her with a small house, Clive's-Den, in Twickenham, London, where she died on Dec. 6, 1785.

**CLIVE, Robert** (1725–1774), British soldier, administrator, and pioneer of empire. Clive was born on Sept. 29, 1725, near Market Drayton, Shropshire. The son of a lawyer and small landholder, he was appointed a writer in the East India Company's service at the age of 18 and was sent to Madras, India, arriving in 1744.

**South Indian Background.** Clive sought to demonstrate his abilities in the outbreak of hostilities between the British and French in southern India during the War of the Austrian Succession. He was promoted to the rank of ensign in 1747. The peace of Aix-la-Chapelle ended the war in Europe but not the rivalry between the British and French East India companies. Two phases of the contest were significant to the future balance of power in India, and Clive was active in both. The first phase was European involvement in the internal power struggles of India; the second was European use of small numbers of well-trained troops to gain allies, influence, and power.

In 1751, when the French position was at its strongest in the south, Clive led a diversionary expedition against Arcot, capital of the Carnatic, in order to relieve the British in Trichinopoly. For 53 days Clive, with a force of 500, held Arcot. In June 1752 he relieved Trichinopoly, accepted the surrender of the French, and installed a British puppet as ruler of the Carnatic.

**Success in Bengal.** Following a three-year interval in England, Clive went again to Madras, then as a lieutenant colonel in the Royal Army. He served briefly as deputy governor of Fort St. David

and then in 1756 was called on to retrieve the British position in Bengal. There, Sirajuddaullah, the new nawab, had captured the British factory (trading station) at Kassimbazar and marched on Calcutta, which fell on June 16. Clive set out from the south on October 16 with 2,400 troops, five men-of-war, and five transports. The city was recovered on Jan. 2, 1757.

Sirajuddaullah restored and extended the company's privileges, but Clive, seeing that the nawab was surrounded by disaffected officers and nobles, determined to take advantage of this dissension and sponsored a new ruler well disposed to the company. An agreement was reached with the elderly general Mir Jafar whereby vast compensations would be paid for the loss of Calcutta, including large considerations to the chief officers of the company. At Plassey, on June 23, 1757, Clive, with an army of 800 Europeans and 2,200 Indians, faced the nawab's 80,000 disorganized and treasonous troops. Mir Jafar withheld his men and cavalry and Sirajuddaullah quickly fled. On June 28, 1757, the British puppet was placed on the throne, beginning an era of public and private corruption. Clive himself took £234,000 ($1,170,000) and an estate worth £30,000 ($150,000) a year. Vast personal fortunes were made in this period, an injustice Clive himself recognized.

**The Greatest Nabob.** After serving his first term as governor of Fort William (Calcutta), Clive left India in February 1760 and returned to England a man of wealth and fortune. He purchased a controlling interest in the company and a seat in Commons from Shrewsbury. In 1762 he was given an Irish peerage as Baron Clive of Plassey and in 1764 was made a knight of the Bath.

**The Second Governorship and Reform.** In 1764 Clive returned again to Bengal and on May 3, 1765, began his second governorship. He undertook the immense task of controlling chaos and corruption and did so with typical vigor. The Battle of Buxar (Baksar or Baxar) in 1764 had confirmed the British position in Bengal. In the settlement following Buxar the company was granted the *diwani*, or revenue collecting rights, for all of Bengal, while the nawab, in theory, remained in control of the enforcement of law and order. In fact, the administration of Bengal was in the control of the company and its Indian agents.

Clive's most difficult task was his effort to control peculation. Immediately on his arrival he struck out at corruption by demanding resignations, cutting swollen allowances, crushing the "White Mutiny" of discontented officers, limiting the size of gifts that could be accepted, and regulating private trade. Financial reform was far from complete, but it was Clive's achievement to have initiated reform.

**Parliamentary Defense.** Clive retired from the governorship in February 1767 and left for England. In 1772, when the company was threatened with bankruptcy, Clive was charged with corruption during his first governorship. In 1773 Parliament passed a unanimous resolution that found Clive "to have rendered great and meritorious service to his country." Both censure and recognition were perhaps warranted. Nevertheless, in the acquisition of Bengal, Clive's leadership created the basis of a vast colonial empire.

Apparently the pressures of 1772 and 1773 were too great; in London, on Nov. 22, 1774, at the age of 49 and in poor health, Clive took his own life.

WALTER HAUSER, *University of Virginia*

Plaster cast of a c. 1400 B.C. Egyptian water clock (*left*). Water fills the bowl to the topmost mark of a scale on the inner surface; as it leaks out a hole below, the water level falls at a uniform rate. Time intervals on the 17th-century Spanish sandglass (*right*) were measured by how long it took sand to fall from the top to bottom bulb.

**CLOACA,** klō-ā′kə, a body chamber into which the intestinal tract and urogenital ducts open. From the cloaca, sperm cells, egg cells, and waste products are discharged from the body through a single opening, the cloacal aperture. A cloaca is present in all birds, reptiles, and amphibians, as well as in many fishes. In most mammals a cloaca is present only during the early stages of embryonic development. The only mammals that have a cloaca in the adult stage are the echidna (spiny anteater) and the platypus.

JEFFREY WENIG, *ENDO Laboratories*

**CLOACA MAXIMA,** klō-ā′kə, the main drain or sewer of ancient Rome. Its construction is traditionally ascribed to Tarquinius Priscus, the fifth king of Rome, who died in 578 B.C. The Cloaca Maxima is built of three tiers of arches made of stone blocks laid together without cement; it has an opening 14 feet (4.3 meters) high and 11 feet (3.4 meters) wide. Originally the drain was built to carry water from streets in the Forum area to an outlet at the Tiber River; the drain was later extended between the Forum and Subura. The Cloaca Maxima is still used for drainage.

**CLOCK,** a machine that indicates or records the time of day by dividing the earth's period of rotation as accurately as possible into equal time intervals. Conventionally the period is divided into 24 hours, each hour into 60 minutes, and each minute into 60 seconds. All clocks do this by means of some kind of regular motion that governs the indicating or recording elements so that they make equal movements in equal intervals of time.

## EARLY NONMECHANICAL CLOCKS

**Egypt.** The earliest extant timekeepers are sundials and water clocks, or clepsydras, of ancient Egypt. A fragment of a sundial of about 1500 B.C. is in Berlin's Neues Museum, and a water clock of about 1380 B.C. is in the Cairo Museum. Sundials divided the period from sunrise to sunset into 12 equal intervals, and water clocks were used to divide the period from sunset to sunrise into 12 equal parts. In general, a day "hour" was not the same length as a night "hour," and both varied with the season. (See also CLEPSYDRA; SUNDIAL.)

The Egyptian water clock consisted of an alabaster bowl with sloping sides and a small hole in the bottom, from which a small metal outlet pipe protruded. It relied on uniform water flow through the hole to indicate passage of time. On the bowl's interior surface are 12 hour-scales, one for each month of the year. The vessel was filled with water to the topmost hour mark; water was then allowed to leak out through the outlet pipe. Because of the shape of the bowl, the water level fell at an almost uniform rate.

**Greece and Rome.** In the great Greek and Roman civilizations, sundials and water clocks continued to be the only timekeepers available. Though still made of stone, sundials became more sophisticated in design and varied in form. One of the best and most common types was the so-called hemicycle of Berosus, invented about 300 B.C. The hollowed-out bowl was placed so that it faced due south. Lines on its inner surface corresponded to the 12 hours of the day from sunrise to sunset. A horizontal gnomen projected from

The works can be seen on this English 18th-century brass lantern clock (*right*), known as such because of its resemblance to portable medieval lanterns. Lantern clocks were a variation on heavier German and Dutch chamber clocks, and their single hands and weight-driven movements were often altered in the 19th century to include eight-day spring-driven movements and minute hands.

The American block-and-shell-carved mahogany tall clock (*left*), c. 1760–1780, retains its original movement by Edward Spalding of Providence, R.I. Its handsome case was made by the Goddard-Townsend cabinetmaking family of Newport, R.I., whose furniture was distinguished for its block fronts, shell motifs, and other neoclassical elements, such as the flame finials here.

COURTESY ISRAEL SACK INC.

the center of the top edge of the sundial so that the shadow of its tip fell on the hour scales.

Greek and Roman water clocks were generally cylindrical vessels into which water flowed at a uniform rate from a constant-head device. The time indicator was attached to a rising float. None of these water clocks has survived, but it is believed that some were quite elaborate and may have incorporated striking or alarm mechanisms.

**China.** A remarkable series of water clocks was constructed in China between about the 8th and 11th century A.D. These clocks were large structures with moving figures. They drove celestial globes and sounded the time by gongs or bells. Their timekeeping was controlled by the steady flow of water through a pipe, but the motion of the wheelwork was intermittent.

**Europe.** Sandglasses originated in Europe in the 14th century. They are essentially two glass bulbs, connected by a narrow neck, that contain a certain amount of sand. Intervals of time, usually small, are measured by the time it takes for all the sand to fall from the top bulb through the narrow neck to the bottom bulb. The sandglass is turned over for reuse.

Candle or oil-lamp clocks were also used to a very limited extent. The hour scales were marked on the side of the candle or on the glass oil reservoir. The shortening of the candle or the fall of the oil level indicated passage of time.

Sundials continued to be used in medieval Europe. Some were made portable and were equipped with a compass.

### MECHANICAL CLOCKS

**Weight-Driven Clocks.** The first all-mechanical clocks known were probably made about 1300. They were large iron-framed structures, driven by weights. The cyclic motion they utilized was produced by an escapement known as the verge and foliot. A horizontal iron bar with adjustable weights at its ends (the foliot) was suspended at its center on a vertical spindle (the verge). The foliot was pushed first in one direction of rotation and then in the opposite direction by the teeth of the crown wheel, which "escaped," one by one. The crown wheel itself was driven, through one or more stages of gearing, by a weight suspended from a rope that was coiled on a drum.

The function of these first European mechanical clocks was not to indicate the time on a dial, but to drive dials that gave astronomical indications, and to sound the hour. They were located in monasteries and public bell towers. The earliest surviving example, constructed in 1386, is in Salisbury Cathedral, England. By this time, clocks for civil use in Europe were designed to divide the day-and-night period into 24 equal hours.

According to a contemporary manuscript, Richard of Wallingford made an elaborate clock, with many astronomical indications, for St. Alban's Abbey in England in 1330. An equally elaborate clock was made by Giovanni Dondi in Italy. He completed it in 1364, and it survived for nearly

200 years. A reconstruction of it was made in England in 1961 and is now a permanent exhibit in the Smithsonian Institution in Washington, D.C.

Domestic clocks were scaled-down versions of public clocks, but without astronomical indications. They had iron frames and wheels, and usually a striking mechanism or an alarm. The weighted bar controlling the timekeeping was soon replaced by a balance wheel, but the verge escapement was the same. The clock could then be regulated only by varying the driving weight. The earliest extant illustration of such a clock is in an illuminated manuscript of 1406 in the National Library of France, Paris.

From the mid-14th to the mid-17th century, the mechanism of weight-driven clocks underwent surprisingly little alteration in principle, but the construction of both the mechanism and the case became much more refined. After about 1600, brass took the place of iron for frames and wheels.

**Spring-Driven Clocks.** Springs were first used instead of weights for the driving power of clocks in the second half of the 15th century. Their disadvantage was an inconstant drive; the pull, or torque, was greater when the spring was fully wound than when it was nearly unwound. Since the timekeeping ability of the verge and foliot escapement depends on a constant driving force, some form of compensation was needed.

Early French spring-driven clocks employed a device called a fusee to equalize the force of the uncoiling spring. The spring is contained in a drum, and its power is transmitted through a gut cord or chain wound on the drum. The other end of the chain is wound round a spiral groove in a pulley, which then passes the drive on to the clock mechanism through gearing. When the spring is fully wound, the cord or chain unwinds from the narrow end of the pulley, where its radius and consequently its leverage are small; but as the spring runs down, the cord unwinds from increasingly wider parts of the pulley. Therefore the leverage increases, compensating for the weakening pull of the spring. Spring-driven clocks were often regulated by allowing the single crossbar of the balance wheel to strike two short pieces of gut that projected from an adjustable arm.

The earliest German spring-driven clocks employed a kind of friction brake called a stackfreed, which reduced the spring power markedly when it was fully wound, but only slightly toward the end of its run.

The earliest spring-driven clocks were in the form of metal drums a few inches in diameter, with the dial on the top. About the middle of the 16th century, clocks in the form of small vertical towers, with the dial on one side, took their place. They were often elaborately decorated.

Early domestic clocks had only one hand, but in the 16th and the early 17th century a few minute hands appeared. They were, however, hardly justified by the accuracy of the clocks, which erred by at least a quarter hour a day.

Watches were first made in about 1500. For their history and development, see WATCH.

**Pendulum.** Great accuracy in time measurement was first made possible when the pendulum was applied as a regulator in clocks. Galileo, in 1582, had noticed that, as timed by his pulse, a swinging lamp in the cathedral of Pisa seemed to have the same time of swing for large as for small arcs. This observation was used in reverse by physicians, who timed their patients' pulses

PRIVATE COLLECTION, U.S.A., PHOTO COURTESY OF ROSENBERG & STIEBEL, INC.

French Louis XIV globe clock, c. 1710, A.-C. Boulle; works by Jacques Thuret, design by G.-M. Oppenord.

by a simple pendulum, or pulsilogium, which they carried. Toward the end of his life, Galileo attempted to apply the pendulum to clocks as the timekeeping element. However, he died in 1642, before the clock he designed was constructed.

Christian Huygens, working independently in Holland, completed a preliminary model of a pendulum clock in 1656. In the following year his clockmaker Salomon da Coster began making spring-driven pendulum clocks in The Hague. The escapement was the same, but the pendulum, with its characteristic period, replaced the foliot balance or balance wheel. The use of pendulums improved the timekeeping of clocks so much that all new clocks incorporated them, and many older clocks were converted to employ one.

Coster's first pendulum clocks were housed in very simple wooden cases. In Holland and England these evolved into the typical wooden longcase, or grandfather, clock and the bracket clock. In France the evolution was to the mantel clock, which became very ornate in the 18th century.

**Balance Spring.** An innovation in clocks parallel to that of the pendulum was the application of the balance spring to the balance wheel, which gave the regulating system a characteristic beat. Robert Hooke was the first to experiment with a straight spring, but it was again Huygens who, in 1675, first successfully applied a spring. He used a spiral spring in an arrangement that persists in

French art deco mystery clock by Cartier, 1920s. An optical device seems to make the hands rotate without works.

Smaller portable clocks, whose timekeeping element is a balance and spring, require escapements of a different type, since in these clocks the balance may have quite a large arc of swing. For these, Graham devised his cylinder escapement in about 1720. It had properties similar to the deadbeat for pendulum clocks. Although it was difficult to make, it achieved considerable success and was widely used in watches and small clocks. It was later superseded by Thomas Mudge's detached lever escapement, in which the balance wheel receives an impulse at the center of its swing and is entirely free of outside interference for the rest of its swing. It was invented in 1765 but was not in general use until much later. Since about the mid-19th century it has been almost universally employed in small clocks and watches.

Other types of escapements have been devised for use in large tower clocks, which have their hands exposed to the wind and precipitation. The varying forces on the hands lead, with an ordinary escapement, to a varying impulse to the pendulum. In a gravity escapement the force at the escape wheel is not applied directly to the pendulum, but lifts gravity arms, which, on their subsequent fall give a constant impulse to the pendulum. The first wholly successful escapement of this type was invented by Baron Grimthorpe in England and applied by him in 1854 to Big Ben, the tower clock of the new Houses of Parliament.

**Temperature Compensation.** A pendulum rod expands or contracts with a rise or fall of temperature according to the material of which it is made. This change of length alters the time of swing, and for a brass rod will produce a losing rate of five seconds per day for a temperature rise of 10° F (5.5° C). The corresponding change in a steel rod is 2.5 seconds per day.

Devices compensating for the effects of temperature were invented by George Graham in London in 1721 and by John Harrison in Lincolnshire in 1726. Graham attached to the lower end of the pendulum rod a jar of mercury, which acted as the pendulum bob. The upward expansion of the mercury compensated for the downward expansion of the rod as the temperature rose. Harrison's gridiron pendulum was a more complex device of brass and steel rods that had the same effect. These two types of compensation were used for all precision long-case clocks in Europe until the 19th century, when a combination of zinc and steel tubes was occasionally employed.

The problem was finally solved by Charles Guillaume, working in Paris in 1895, who produced a nickel-steel alloy called invar. Rods of invar effectively remain the same length over a wide temperature range. Methods used to compensate timekeepers controlled by a balance and spring involve the use of two metals fused together for the balance wheel, moving weights inward or outward to compensate for the change in stiffness of the balance spring with temperature.

**American Clocks.** In colonial America domestic clocks bore a close resemblance to their European counterparts, particularly the English long-case clock. After 1776, however, American clockmaking began to diverge into various new forms.

The "case on case" clock, from around 1790, was an attempt to produce an apparent bracket clock (which is a portable spring-driven clock) that was, in fact, driven by weights; and in 1802 Simon Willard patented an improved timepiece

clocks and watches to this day. Clocks employing spring-controlled balance wheels are regulated by varying the effective length of the spring.

**Escapements.** Pendulums, used in conjunction with the verge escapement, made clocks accurate enough for normal domestic requirements, but for observatory or other scientific purposes considerably higher accuracy was required. Efforts were next directed toward improving the verge escapement mechanism, which gave an impulse to the pendulum on every swing and allowed the escape wheel to move through the pitch of one tooth for each double swing of the pendulum.

Huygens had discovered that the ideal curve of the pendulum swing for regular, or cyclic, motion is similar to, but not exactly the same as, the arc of a circle. He devised a mechanical means of changing the actual curve traced by the pendulum. However, other inventors found that the error introduced by allowing the pendulum to swing in a circular arc was more easily minimized by simply shortening the arc of swing. Attempts were also made to make the pendulum swing as free as possible from external interference. Pendulum clocks are usually regulated by raising or lowering the pendulum bob with a screw arrangement.

In about 1670 the recoil, or anchor, escapement was devised by William Clement in England. It allowed the pendulum to swing with a smaller arc than the earlier verge allowed, and became the standard for domestic clocks. More accurate clocks were made possible by the deadbeat escapement, introduced by George Graham in England in about 1715. With the deadbeat escapement, the pendulum received an impulse near the center of its swing and was subject to only slight friction for the rest of its swing. A good pendulum clock with a deadbeat escapement is accurate to a few seconds per day.

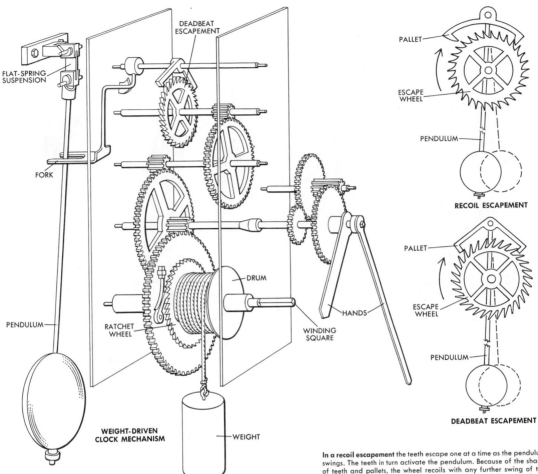

**DEADBEAT ESCAPEMENT**

**FLAT-SPRING SUSPENSION**

**FORK**

**PENDULUM**

**RATCHET WHEEL**

**DRUM**

**HANDS**

**WINDING SQUARE**

**WEIGHT**

**WEIGHT-DRIVEN CLOCK MECHANISM**

**PALLET**

**ESCAPE WHEEL**

**PENDULUM**

**RECOIL ESCAPEMENT**

**PALLET**

**ESCAPE WHEEL**

**PENDULUM**

**DEADBEAT ESCAPEMENT**

**The pendulum clock** (above) is driven by a weight suspended from a drum. As the weight descends, power flows through a system of gears to the escape wheel, one tooth of which "escapes" with each swing of the pendulum, thus regulating the speed of the gears that drive the clock hands. The pendulum is driven by the impulses from the escape wheel teeth.

**In the verge and foliot** escapement (below) one tooth of the crown wheel escapes at each swing of the foliot. As each tooth escapes, it strikes the pallet, swinging the foliot.

**In a recoil escapement** the teeth escape one at a time as the pendulum swings. The teeth in turn activate the pendulum. Because of the shape of teeth and pallets, the wheel recoils with any further swing of the pendulum after the pallet and wheel are engaged. The deadbeat escapement is designed to eliminate this recoil, and the pendulum is impulsed near the center of its swing, making it more accurate than the recoil escapement.

**The fusee** compensates for the changing force of the uncoiling spring in spring-driven clocks. When the spring is fully wound, the chain unwinds from the narrow end of the pulley where its radius and leverage are small. As the spring runs down, the chain unwinds from wider parts of the pulley, where the leverage increases and thus compensates for the weaker pull of the spring.

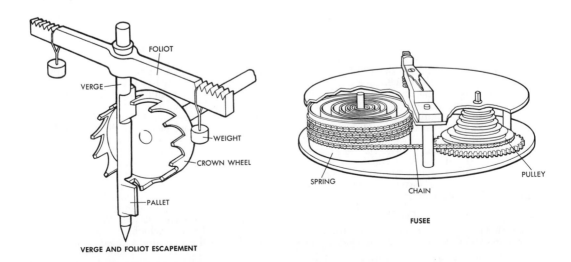

**FOLIOT**

**VERGE**

**WEIGHT**

**CROWN WHEEL**

**PALLET**

**VERGE AND FOLIOT ESCAPEMENT**

**SPRING**

**CHAIN**

**PULLEY**

**FUSEE**

Eli Terry type pillar and scroll shelf clock with 30-hour wood movement; Ephraim Downs, Bristol, Conn., about 1826.

Brewster & Ingraham's shelf clock with a gothic twin steeple, designed by Elias Ingraham, Bristol, Conn., about 1847.

Terry & Andrews clock with an ogee style case and a 30-hour stamped brass works; Bristol, Conn., about 1840.

AMERICAN CLOCK AND WATCH MUSEUM, INC., BRISTOL, CONN.

—now well-known as the banjo type—in which a heavy weight with limited fall acted on a small-diameter drum, to which was attached a large gear wheel. This developed later into the lyre and girandole types.

The next important American development was the mass production of wooden clock movements by Eli Terry, which led to the establishment of clockmaking as an industry in Connecticut. Terry introduced many of the well-known designs of shelf clocks that are now sought after by collectors. In the 1840's Chauncey Jerome began the manufacture and export to Europe of mass-produced clocks with brass movements.

### STRIKING MECHANISMS

The train of gears that drives the striking mechanism of a clock is called the striking train. The striking train of early clocks was impelled by a separate driving weight, which was released each hour by the timekeeping mechanism. From the 14th to the late 17th century the striking train was of the count-wheel, or locking-plate, type. In this type, the number of blows struck is determined by a set of notches in the outer rim of a wheel, into which a pallet falls. With locking-plate striking, the hours must follow in their normal sequence.

In 1676, Edward Barlow, in England, introduced the rack, a striking mechanism in which a stepped cam, or snail, is attached to the axis of the hour hand. The number of blows struck is then determined by the depth of the step opposite the controlling pallet. In the rack type it is possible to utilize a repeating mechanism with which the nearest hour is struck "on request" as well as, or instead of, the automatic release at exactly the hour.

### ELECTRIC CLOCKS

Electricity is used both to replace the springs and weights as a power source in clocks and to supply the regular motion necessary for time-keeping. It has enabled a single central master clock to control the dials of a number of remote clocks, and thus supply a unified timekeeping service to a whole building or institution. When used to give impulse to the pendulum, it greatly increases accuracy, because the impulse can be applied less frequently and with greater precision than in wholly mechanical clocks.

The earliest inventors of electric clocks were Alexander Bain in Scotland and Sir Charles Wheatstone in England, who worked independently and in some rivalry in 1840. Their master clocks sent a signal every second or two seconds to secondary clocks and thus controlled the time indicated on their dials. The system of synchronization that is most widely employed is that in which a master clock sends out a signal every minute or every half minute to advance the hands of remote clocks.

Other inventors between 1850 and 1890 tried systems in which each distant-controlled clock had a pendulum of its own, which was synchronized by signals from the master clock. Some incorporated systems of hourly correction.

In 1898, Robert James Rudd in England realized that it was possible to transfer the impulsing and counting functions of the escapement to a "slave" clock, which released an impulse to the "free" master pendulum every minute. The "slave" clock then received a synchronizing signal from the "free" master pendulum. Rudd built an all mechanical clock on this principle.

William Hamilton Shortt, in 1921, devised a clock similar in principle to Rudd's, in which the linkage between the master pendulum and the slave clock is electrical. Shortt clocks have an accuracy of a few thousandths of a second per day. They were the standard timekeepers of the Greenwich Observatory from 1924 to 1942.

**Synchronous Electric Clocks.** Wheatstone devised a system in 1869 in which the electric circuit was closed, and the pendulum acted as a dynamo. A more practical system of this type was developed by Henry E. Warren in 1916 in the United States. He used a small electric motor to drive the hands of a clock, through reduction gearing. It operated on commercial alternating current. Warren also developed a suitable master clock for use at power stations. The frequency of the power distributed could be controlled accordingly. The system was soon widely adopted in the United States and in Europe. Ordinary electric clocks are usually accurate to within a few seconds.

### QUARTZ CRYSTAL AND ATOMIC CLOCKS

The Shortt free-pendulum clock appears to have reached the limit of accuracy that is attainable utilizing the pendulum for regular motion. Greater accuracy is obtainable by utilizing the vibrations of a quartz crystal. Quartz is a piezoelectric material. When it is compressed, small electric charges and voltages appear on its surface; these can be amplified and fed back to the crystal to maintain it in oscillation. The frequency of vibration of quartz is very high. It is on the order of 100,000 vibrations per second, but it can be reduced by various forms of electrical "gearing" to frequencies such as 60 vibrations per second. At this level it can drive a common synchronous electric clock.

Walter G. Cady, in 1922, was the first to employ a quartz crystal as a frequency standard, but it was W. A. Marrison who first worked out the full possibilities of quartz crystals for timekeeping. By 1929 he had constructed a ringcrystal timekeeper that was accurate to a hundredth of a second a day and 10 times as accurate for short periods of seconds or minutes. By 1938, L. Essen at the National Physical Laboratory in England had increased this accuracy by five times, which made the quartz clock more accurate than the Shortt clock. In 1942 the Greenwich Observatory replaced its Shortt clocks with quartz crystal clocks.

The most accurate clocks utilize the oscillations of atoms and molecules for regular motion. These extremely high-frequency oscillations are used to synchronize a lower-frequency quartz clock. Atomic clocks are accurate to one part in $10^{11}$ or in $10^{12}$. This is equivalent to an error of only one second in 3,000 years or in 30,000 years, respectively. For a detailed discussion of atomic clocks, see ATOMIC CLOCK.

F. A. B. WARD, *Science Museum, London*

#### Bibliography

Baillie, G. H., *Clocks and Watches, 1344–1800* (Saifer 1981).
Britten, Frederick J., *Britten's Old Clocks and Watches and Their Makers*, ed. by Granville H. Baillie and others, 3d ed. (Apollo Bks. 1980).
Cipolla, Carlo M., *Clocks and Culture, 1300–1700* (Norton 1978).
DeCarle, Donald, *Watch and Clock Encyclopedia*, 3d ed. (State Mutual Bk. 1985).
Jagger, Cedric, *The Artistry of the English Watch* (Tuttle 1988).
Kahlert, H., and others, *Wristwatches* (Schiffer 1987).
Lloyd H. Alan, *Some Outstanding Clocks Over Seven Hundred Years: 1250–1950* (Antique Collector's Club 1981).
Maurice, Klaus, and Heuer, Peter, *European Pendulum Clocks* (Schiffer 1988).
Rose, Ronald E., *English Dial Clocks*, 2d ed. (Antique Collector's Club 1981).
Tait, H., *Clocks and Watches* (Harvard Univ. Press 1983).
Tardy, *French Clocks, Clocks the World Over*, ed. and tr. by Alexander Ballantyne (Seven Hills Bks. 1982).
Ward, F. A. B., *Time Measurement: part I, Historical Review*, 4th rev. ed. (Science Museum, London, 1961).

**CLOCK PARADOX.** See RELATIVITY.

**CLODION,** klô-dyôn', **Louis** (1738–1814), French sculptor, who is especially remembered for the small statuettes of satyrs, fauns, and nymphs. He was born Claude Michel on Dec. 20, 1738, at Nancy, and studied sculpture with his uncle Lambert-Sigisbert Adam. Awarded the Prix de Rome, Clodion lived and worked in Italy from 1767 to 1771. There, the charm of his small, romantic terra-cotta and marble figures attracted the attention of such important patrons as Catherine II of Russia.

In 1771, Louis XV demanded that Clodion return to France. A marble portrait of Montesquieu (1779–1783; Versailles) is, however, the only royal commission Clodion received in France. The aristocratic frivolity of his work earned him severe criticism during the French Revolution, but he recaptured critical favor by switching to monumental sculpture in the Greek or neoclassic style favored by the new regime. One of the best of his small terra-cottas is the *Satyr Crowning a Bacchante* (Louvre). Clodion died in Paris on March 29, 1814.

**CLODIUS,** klô'dē-əs, **Publius** (died 52 B.C.), Roman political leader. He was of the patrician Claudius family, but his whole career shows him to have been an independent and reckless politician. In 68 B.C. he stirred mutiny among Roman troops in Asia. In 62 he was caught posing as a woman in the religious festival of Bona Dea and barely escaped conviction for sacrilege. At that trial Cicero testified against him, thus earning Clodius' undying enmity.

Shunned by the conservative nobility, Clodius catered to popular tastes. As tribune in 58, he provided for free grain distribution and legalized private clubs. Through the clubs he organized gangs of thugs with which he drove Pompey off the streets. Another of his measures secured the exile of Cicero. But Clodius' use of violence brought retaliation. Pompey's henchman Milo collected mobs of his own to check Clodius, and in 57 they effected the recall of Cicero.

Clodius' influence waned thereafter. Ever an opportunist, he attached himself to Pompey, but the street fights with Milo's gangs continued until Clodius was killed in a brawl on Jan. 18, 52. Loyal followers burned down the Senate house as Clodius' funeral pyre.

ERICH S. GRUEN
*University of California at Berkeley*

**CLOETE,** klōō'tē, **Stuart** (1897–1976), South African writer, noted for his vivid novels portraying the complexities of African life. Edward Fairly Stuart Cloete was born in Paris on July 23, 1897, of a family that had lived in South Africa for generations. Educated in France and England, he joined the British army in World War I and was a company commander at 19. Wounded twice, he was retired in 1925 and went to South Africa to farm.

Becoming interested in writing, Cloete returned to England in 1935 and produced *Turning Wheels* (1937), a disapproving picture of a Boer family, and *Congo Song* (1943), also set in Africa. In *Against These Three* (1945) he drew the biographies of three giants of South African history—Kruger, Rhodes, and Lobengula. After World War II, Cloete returned to South Africa. Later novels include *Storm over Africa* (1956) and *The Abductors* (1966). He died in Cape Town, South Africa, on March 19, 1976.

**CLOG DANCE,** a kind of solo step dance performed with clogs (wooden-soled shoes) to emphasize the rhythm. Although French peasants did a clog dance in wooden *sabots* during the time of the Renaissance, the form is most characteristic of the industrial areas of northern England and southern Scotland in the 19th century. The Lancashire hornpipe is a well-known example of a clog dance. The clog dance is a forerunner of tap dancing.

**CLOISONNÉ,** kloi-zə-nā´, is the technique of applying brass wires to the surface of a copper or bronze object, forming compartments to be filled with powdered enamel that is subsequently fused by heating. Cloisonné is sometimes combined with the champlevé technique, in which the enamel is confined by cells scooped directly into the metal itself.

Both cloisonné and champlevé techniques were extensively employed in China, beginning in the 14th century with the Yüan dynasty. Knowledge of enameling probably reached China from Byzantium through Arab merchants, although it might also have come from the 14th century Mongol court at Karakorum, where a French silversmith was employed. On the basis of emperors' reign marks, a few of the earliest surviving specimens of cloisonné are attributed to the 15th century. The reign of Emperor Ching T'ai (1450–1457) of the Ming dynasty is especially noted for work of this kind. However, examples of cloisonné enamel from the Ming dynasty (1368–1644) are usually less refined in workmanship than work of the Ch'ing (or Manchu) dynasty (1644–1911).

The finest of the Ch'ing cloisonné vessels were made for the royal household at a workshop established in 1680 inside the palace of Emperor K'ang Hsi (1662–1722) in Peking. Eventually, cloisonné vessels of large size and considerable elaboration of form became common. Ornamentation was more profuse, overdetailed, and pedestrian, with too great a variety of colors. Many existing specimens of cloisonné that date from the Ch'ing dynasty belong to this later style.

In Japan during the 19th century, cloisonné enamels were made in large quantities. However, they are rarely of much artistic importance. For a discussion of European cloisonné, see ENAMEL.

GEORGE SAVAGE<br>
Author of "Pottery Through the Ages"

**CLOISONNÉ BOWL** made in China during the Ming dynasty, with a mark of the Wan Li period (1573–1619).

THE METROPOLITAN MUSEUM OF ART—GIFT OF EDWARD G. KENNEDY, 1929

**CLOISTER,** kloi′stər, in architecture, a courtyard that is open to the sky in the center and lined by four arcaded walks. Most cloisters, though not all, are attached to monastic churches.

Cloisters were designed to provide a charming, sheltered, private retreat for monks. There they could contemplate, study, hear lectures, or take recreation, as well as pass with some protection from the weather from one part of the monastery to another. The cloister at Gloucester Cathedral gives evidence of the variety of purposes a cloister served. One walk has a lavatory with several basins where the monks could wash before or after meals. In another walk the wall of each bay between columns forms a cubicle for study.

Some scholars trace the origin of the cloister to the peristyle of the ancient Roman house, which was also open to the sky and surrounded by walks. Cloisters developed during the Middle Ages, when the monastic movement was a dominant part of European life. Most of those that are architecturally interesting date from the Romanesque period (10th to 12th century) and the Gothic period (12th to 16th century).

**Ground Plan.** A cloister, rarely more than one story high, is normally surrounded by other, often higher, monastic buildings. Usually it is in the angle formed by the nave and the south transept of the church. The other two sides are generally formed by the chapter house, refectory, or other buildings. The open area, known as the cloister garth, is usually planted in grass and may be crossed by two paths, with a well or fountain at the central intersection. The French Gothic cloister of Mont St. Michel (13th century) is unique is being situated on top of its monastic buildings instead of beside them. Its garth is the paved roof of the Salle des Chevaliers.

**Columns.** The arcades surrounding the garth are formed by light columns or piers on a low wall or parapet. The columns may be arranged in a variety of ways. For example, the short slender columns of the Romanesque cloisters of St. John Lateran and St. Paul's Outside the Walls, both in Rome, are set in pairs and support small arches. The cloisters of Mont St. Michel are edged by two rows of colonnettes staggered so that each shaft in the outer row is midway between those of the inner row.

In Italian cloisters the design of the shafts of columns may also vary. In St. John Lateran and St. Paul's Outside the Walls, some shafts are smooth and round, some are octagonal, and some are spiral. Also, many of the columns are fluted in vertical or spiral lines; some flutes are continuous, others are composed of short grooves alternating with solid spaces. The flutes of the columns of these cloisters, and of those attached to the cathedral of Monreale in Sicily, are filled with Cosmati work, sparkling mosaics of gold, red, blue, and green named for a family of Roman craftsmen. Most French and Spanish cloisters of Romanesque period lack the playful variety of the Italian ones.

Because the capitals of low cloister columns are more easily seen than those of the lofty columns inside dark churches, their decoration assumed a special importance. They might be adorned with a wealth of sculpture, sometimes foliate, suggesting Roman motifs, but often representing scriptural themes or other complex religious symbolism. Those at St. Pierre Moissac (12th century) are an example.

**Ceilings.** Cloister columns often supported a vault. Sometimes, as in the heavy barrel vaults of French and Spanish Romanesque cloisters, an occasional buttress was needed. The lighter, ribbed vaults of English Gothic cloisters are particularly outstanding. That of Westminster Abbey has the rich tracery of the Gothic Decorated style (14th century). The fan vaults of the cloister of Gloucester Cathedral is a striking example of the Gothic Perpendicular style (late 14th to mid-16th century). The rib moldings radiate from the tips of the columns like an open fan. Fan vaulting is especially suited to cloisters because it fits better structurally in the smaller spans of an arcade than in the vast spans of a church nave.

EVERARD M. UPJOHN
*Coauthor of "History of World Art"*

**CLOISTER AND THE HEARTH, The,** a historical novel by the English writer Charles Reade, published in 1861. It gives a broad picture of European life during the Renaissance. Gerard, a Dutch boy intended by his father for the church, and Margaret are formally betrothed, but Gerard's father prevents their marriage. Gerard flees to Rome, intending to return after he has made his fortune. While in Rome, he hears that Margaret is dead, and he becomes a Dominican friar. He returns to Holland and finds that she is still alive and the mother of his child. But Gerard has given himself to the church, which permits no union between the cloister and the hearth. The son of Margaret and Gerard was the scholar Erasmus.

**CLOISTERS, The,** a branch of New York City's Metropolitan Museum of Art, housing the museum's medieval collection. The building, suggestive of a medieval cloister, is situated on a bluff overlooking the Hudson River, in Fort Tryon Park, Manhattan.

In 1938 the Cloisters was opened to the public in its present building, which incorporates parts of five medieval monasteries, a Romanesque chapel, and a 12th century Spanish apse. The medieval art collection of George Grey Barnard, purchased in 1925 by John D. Rockefeller, Jr., and given to the Metropolitan Museum, forms the basis of the Cloisters' collection. Among the later acquisitions of the museum are the 15th century tapestry series *The Hunt of the Unicorn;* the 14th century tapestries *The Nine Heroes;* and the 15th century *Mérode Altarpiece.* The Cloisters' collection also includes sculpture, paintings, and stained glass windows.

**CLONE,** klōn, a group of genetically identical cells or whole organisms derived from a single original cell or organism. Clones arise naturally in a number of ways. The body of an adult animal or plant is typically a clone of cells, having arisen by mitosis from a single cell, the fertilized egg. Within the body, a single cell may divide many times to produce a clone of cells with the same function—as, for example, when a single human lymphocyte gives rise to a group of plasma cells all of which synthesize the same kind of antibody. A group of genetically identical plants may arise from a single original plant that is reproducing by vegetative (asexual) rather than sexual means. In human beings a set of identical twins represents a small clone of two individuals, both of whom originated from the same fertilized egg.

**THE CLOISTERS** in Fort Tryon Park, New York City, include this one from the Abbey of Saint-Michel-de-Cuxa.

Cloning is of actual and potential economic importance for propagating organisms without the time-consuming and expensive methods of selective breeding. Many varieties of fruit trees and flowering shrubs, for example, are produced by cloning, and the procedure is potentially applicable to the raising of livestock. Medical and biological research could benefit from having large numbers of genetically uniform laboratory animals, such as mice, available for testing or experimental uses.

Single cells are routinely cloned in laboratories simply by isolating them in a suitable culture medium and allowing their descendants to form colonies of cells. Muscle cells, pigment cells, and cartilage cells, among others, have been cloned in this way. Many plants can be cloned simply by taking cuttings of leaves, stems, or roots and replanting them. Plants also have been cloned by first dissociating the cells of stems or roots and then culturing the individual cells to obtain complete plants. Small clones of adult frogs have been obtained by transplanting the nuclei of several cells from a single embryo into a series of frog eggs whose own nuclei had been removed and allowing the eggs to develop in ordinary pond water.

The cloning of mammals, including man, is theoretically possible, but it is more difficult to achieve because of the smaller size of the mammalian egg and the more complex conditions required for normal embryonic development. Some of the technical problems have been overcome in the case of the mouse egg, and clones of laboratory mice may soon become a reality. Because of the importance of learning and experience in the early development of mammals, the individuals that make up a mammalian clone, while genetically identical, need not always be exact copies of one another, especially in the area of behavior.

PETER LUYKX, *University of Miami*

**CLOOTS,** klōts, **Baron de** (1755–1794), German-born leader in the French Revolution. Popularly known as Anacharsis Cloots, he styled himself the "orator of the human race." Cloots was born Jean Baptiste du Val-de-Grâce on June 24, 1755, near the city of Cleves in Prussia. His family were Prussian aristocrats of Dutch origin. At the age of 11, as a student in Paris, Cloots fell in love with the city. However, his parents forced him to return to Prussia to attend the Royal Military School in Berlin.

In 1776, Cloots was able to return to Paris, where he associated with philosophers who were in the intellectual vanguard of Europe. On the outbreak of the revolution in 1789 he joined the Jacobin Club, and the following year he represented the Committee of Foreigners at the bar of the National Constituent Assembly. He was elected to the National Convention in September 1792 and voted for Louis XVI's execution.

The key to Cloots' politics was his concept of a universal republic of men devoted to freedom. The republic was to be achieved by a war of propaganda against tyrants. Eventually he gravitated toward the ultrarevolutionaries and became associated with the Hébertists, followers of Jacques Hébert, a proponent of the dechristianization of France. The revolutionary leader Robespierre opposed the Hébertists and linked the movement's leaders with a foreign conspiracy. As a result, Cloots went to the guillotine with the Hébertists on March 24, 1794.

RICHARD M. BRACE, *Oakland University*

**CLOQUET,** klō-kā', a city in eastern Minnesota, in Carlton county, on the St. Louis River, 19 miles (30 km) west of Duluth. The city's leading manufactures are paper, matches, and other wood products. Fond du Lac Indian Reservation is just west of the city. Cloquet is governed by a mayor and council. Population: 11,201.

**CLOSED-CIRCUIT TELEVISION.** See TELEVISION —*Special Applications of Television.*

**CLOSED SHOP,** a place of employment where the employer hires only union members and continues to employ them only as long as they remain members of the union. The closed shop is normally based on a provision in a collective bargaining contract.

The closed shop is a union security arrangement that can be traced to English guilds of the 16th and 17th centuries whose rules prohibited members from working with nonmembers. Unions in the United States developed comparable rules in the early 1800's. Many hard-fought strikes of the 19th and 20th centuries were waged over this issue.

In the United States the Labor-Management Relations Act of 1947 (Taft-Hartley Act) outlawed closed shops in industries in or affecting interstate commerce. However, closed shops are generally legal in intrastate commerce in the absence of prohibitory legislation in a given state. Many informal, illegal closed shops are maintained, based on oral agreements. Employers in casual industries or in highly skilled trades where there is a shortage of workers will enforce a closed shop and use the union as a hiring agent.

Closed shops generally have been condemned when coupled with *closed unions*—that is, unions that restrict membership by setting arbitrary standards for membership. Closed unions are prohibited by the Civil Rights Act of 1964 if workers are excluded from membership because of race, creed, color, or ethnic origin.

Closed shops are relatively rare outside the United States except in a few countries such as New Zealand, where they are legally enforced and combined with compulsory arbitration.

HARVEY L. FRIEDMAN
*University of Massachusetts*

**CLOSTER,** klos'tər, a borough in northeastern New Jersey, in Bergen county, 3 miles (5 km) west of the Hudson River and 20 miles (32 km) northeast of Newark. The borough is a residential and manufacturing center. Local factories produce textiles, curtains, windows, and paper containers. Oradell Reservoir is just to the west. Closter was incorporated in 1903. It has a mayor-council form of government. Population: 8,383.

**CLOSURE.** See CLOTURE.

**CLOTAIRE I** (died 561), klō-târ', ruler of the Franks, who expanded the domain of his father, Clovis I, first king of all the Franks. On Clovis' death in 511, the Frankish kingdom was divided among his four sons—Clotaire, Theodoric I, Clodomir, and Childebert I. Clotaire received the region around Soissons.

In 523, Clodomir and Clotaire invaded Burgundy. On the death of Clodomir in 524, Clotaire murdered Clodomir's children and seized their lands. He fought the Thuringians in 531 and divided Burgundy in 534 with his surviving brothers. The Ostrogoth rulers of Italy ceded Provence to the Franks as the price of an alliance against Byzantium in 536. In 542–543, Clotaire invaded Visigothic Spain with his brother Childebert, pushing as far as Saragossa.

Clovis' policy of expansion thus matured under Clotaire. By eliminating rivals weaker than himself and by outliving others, he became sole ruler of the Franks in 558. His surviving sons divided the kingdom again when he died.

K. F. MORRISON
*University of Chicago*

**CLOTAIRE II,** klō-târ' (died 629), king of the Franks. Like his ancestors Clovis and Clotaire I, he succeeded in uniting the Christian but still barbarian Franks under one rule. Clotaire II was the son of Chilperic I of Neustria (northwestern France) and his concubine, Fredegund. On Chilperic's death in 584, Clotaire became king, under Fredegund's regency.

When, after protracted struggles, Austrasian and Burgundian nobles overthrew their ruler, Queen Brunhilde, they accepted Clotaire as their king. With supreme cruelty, Clotaire humiliated and executed Brunhilde. The price Clotaire paid for the support of these noblemen was the reduction of his own royal powers, set forth in a decree of 614, which led to the virtual autonomy of each of his realms. The fragmentation of Clotaire's domain became especially clear when he made his son, Dagobert, king of Austrasia in 623. Clotaire encouraged the arts, especially favoring large, ornamental works in gold and silver.

K. F. MORRISON
*University of Chicago*

**CLOTBUR.** See COCKLEBUR.

**CLOTH.** See TEXTILE.

**CLOTHES MOTH,** a common name of any of three species of moths that are closely associated with man and are serious economic pests. They are worldwide in distribution. All three species are small, averaging about ½ to ¾ of an inch (1.3 to 1.9 cm) across the wing. The adult moths, which have reduced mouthparts, do not feed; hence all damage by clothes moths is done by their small, whitish larvae, which feed on nearly all animal products, particularly wool, hair, feathers, furs, leather, and upholstered furniture. Fabrics damaged by clothes moth larvae usually have holes eaten through them and may be partly covered by tiny silk threads extending over the surface of the material.

**Life History.** Female moths usually lay from 100 to 150 tiny whitish eggs on some material that the larvae will feed on. These eggs hatch in about 5 days. The length of the larval stage is extremely variable, taking from 6 weeks to almost 4 years for completion, depending largely on food supply and humidity. The entire life cycle of a clothes moth may require from 2 months to over 4 years.

**Types of Clothes Moths.** The casemaking clothes moth (*Tinea pellionella*) is probably the most destructive clothes moth species. The adult moth is brownish, with three tiny dark dots arranged in a triangle near the center of its forewing. The larva constructs a small, portable case out of its food material, and it lives and eventually pupates in this case. As the larva grows, the case is correspondingly enlarged.

The larva of another clothes moth, the webbing clothes moth (*Tineola bisselliella*), makes no case but feeds exposed or partly concealed in a fold or crevice of the material it is eating and usually under a web of silk, which it spins wherever it goes. The adults of this moth are yellowish brown and without markings.

The third species of clothes moth, sometimes referred to as the carpet moth (*Trichophaga tapetzella*), is less common than the first two. In the adults the base of the forewing is black, and the remainder of the wing is white.

Clothes moths are in the order Lepidoptera, family Tineidae. They are controlled by the use of paradichlorobenzene or naphthalene crystals.

DON R. DAVIS
*Smithsonian Institution*

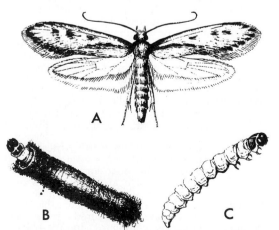

U. S. DEPARTMENT OF AGRICULTURE

CASEMAKING CLOTHES MOTH: A—adult; B—larva inside its portable case; C—larva outside its case.

**CLOTHING,** in its widest sense, includes a great range of materials that man wears or applies to his body. In addition to garments made of woven fabrics, clothing is made from such varied materials as body paint, fur, feathers, and jewels.

Just when man began to wear clothing cannot be known, because the perishable materials that early man would have used for clothing have not survived for archaeologists to study. At some point in man's evolution, however, he began to adorn himself with flowers, seeds, bones, and other objects, as do some primitive tribes today.

During the last glacial stage of the Pleistocene period, about 25,000 years ago, man had the skill to make pendants of stone and carved ivory, some of which have survived. Until this fourth and last glacial period, man had no need to wear clothing for protection against the elements, for with each descent of the ice cap over northern and central Europe, he moved southward into warmer areas. It was only with the beginning of the fourth glacial period that he was technologically advanced enough to live in a cold climate just south of the glaciers. Bone needles have been found in association with ivory pendants, figurines, and other artifacts of Late Stone Age man, and it is inferred that these needles must have been used to make skin or fur clothing for protection from the cold. Indeed, archaeologists have discovered in the Soviet Union a Late Paleolithic figurine carved from mammoth tusk showing clearly a hooded fur costume similar to that worn by modern Eskimos.

Aside from its function of protecting the wearer from the elements, clothing has at least three other important uses: those of maintaining modesty, furnishing adornment, and fixing status. The functions are frequently combined, and a costume may represent all four functions.

### PROTECTION FROM THE ELEMENTS

**Tailored Clothing.** The men and women who remained in northern Eurasia during the last glacial period wore clothing of fur. The garments were tailored to follow the lines of the body and to protect the limbs, torso, head, feet, and hands. In the intense cold of the Arctic winter, man would be unable to survive without such protection. The classic Arctic costume had a snug-fitting hood, sometimes attached to the upper garment as in the Eskimo parka. Mittens, trousers, leggings, and boots completed the costume, with each garment tucked into the adjoining one to keep out icy air. This costume, with regional variations in style, was worn all across Arctic Eurasia and North America. When Russian colonists settled in Siberia in the 17th and 18th centuries, they adopted the tailored garb of the Siberian aborigines. In Alaska, the U. S. Army hired Eskimo women before World War II to make fur clothing until cold-resistant synthetic materials were perfected for troops stationed in the Far North. Even when such new materials were adopted, however, the tailoring followed traditional Arctic lines.

> This article describes the methods used by man to clothe and adorn his body since prehistoric times. For a history of the costumes worn in major civilizations, see DRESS. See also such articles as COSMETICS, HAIRDRESSING, and JEWELRY, and the Index entry *Dress*.

Antarctica had no human population before the arrival of European explorers and scientists, who wore garments similar to those designed for the Arctic. The southernmost aboriginal population, the Indians of Tierra del Fuego, lived in a climate where the temperature, though cold, is usually above freezing. These Indians had no tradition of tailored clothing. They kept warm by smearing their bodies with mud and wrapping themselves in the pelts of the guanaco, an animal similar to the llama. Genetic research has disclosed that the Indians of Tierra del Fuego are biologically adapted to the climate and withstand cold better than do Europeans.

In the Northern Hemisphere, the principle of tailored clothing spread southward from the Arctic. In the steppes of Central Asia, where the winters are frigid and summer nights cold, the inhabitants tailored their garments of skin or fur. They wore caps with flaps that could be turned down over the forehead, ears, and back of the neck in cold weather. Leather tunics with long sleeves were tucked into the full tops of the trousers, and trouser legs were fitted into the tops of boots. For winter they wore fur overcoats with long sleeves that extended over the hands. While Central Asian costumes are now usually made of woven fabrics, nomads still prefer skin and fur for winter wear.

In areas of North America south of the Arctic, tailoring was less fully developed. The feet were protected by tailored moccasins, but other garments were not so carefully shaped. Among the Northern Plains Indians, for example, who lived in a climate similar to that of Central Asia, both men and women wore tailored leggings in winter, but the upper garment had a minimum of cutting and shaping. The man's shirt was of the poncho type, made of two skins of deer or mountain sheep. The woman's longer dress, made of two elk skins, had a yoke at the shoulders and a capelike extension that fell loosely over the arms. A Plains Indian protected his head with a skin cloak or a tailored fur cap.

To be comfortable in a hot, humid, tropical climate, man needs free movement of air over his body. For this reason primitive man traditionally wore little covering in the tropics. His clothing served the functions of modesty, adornment, or status-fixing rather than of protection from the elements.

**Draped Clothing.** In warm, dry regions where the sun is hot, a loose covering best serves the needs of protection. Thus, in the area between the humid tropics and the temperate zone, draped clothing became established. In this area of draped clothing, weaving was invented independently in both the Old and New Worlds.

Draped clothing is characteristically made of one piece of material instead of several pieces cut and stitched together. It is draped loosely around the body, giving protection from the sun or from chill, but allowing a cooling flow of air.

The form of draped clothing varies according to regional tradition. In the New World, in an area extending from New Mexico to southern Peru, the upper garment was woven in one piece with a slit for the neck, and there was no fitting. The lower garment consisted of a single piece of fabric wrapped around the middle of the body as a loincloth. Among women of the Pueblo Indians, two strips of cloth were sewed together to form a tube, and the garment was fastened over one shoulder.

In India, the garment consists of a single length of woven fabric. For women, the sari is wrapped around the waist to form a full skirt, with one end draped over the shoulder or over the head. For men, the dhoti is wrapped in voluminous folds around the waist and thighs, with one end passing between the legs and tucked into the waist. In Southeast Asia and the islands of the Pacific, the garment consists of either a tubular skirt or a wraparound sarong skirt, folded over and tucked in at the waist.

The ancient Mesopotamians and Egyptians also wore draped clothing, and the draperies of the classic Greek costume and of the Roman toga are familiar from statuary and written descriptions.

Each geographical region had its distinctive fiber for the manufacture of clothing. The ancient Egyptians wove their clothing of linen, and the Mesopotamians used wool. The people of India and those of Middle America raised cotton for textiles. In Japan and the Philippines other plant fibers were used, while the Chinese used silk for luxury garments. In Southeast Asia and the islands of the Pacific, as well as in parts of Africa, the traditional fabric was bark cloth, made by pounding and felting the bark of certain trees. Bark cloth was usually worn as a loincloth or a short wraparound skirt.

In the areas where draped clothing is worn the characteristic footwear is the sandal, a flat piece protecting the sole and attached to the foot by straps. Where head covering is worn, it is draped. In the Muslim Middle East, for example, men wrap a length of cloth around the head to form a turban, while women cover the hair with a shawl that can also be pulled over the face.

**Mixed Styles.** In the temperate zone, where winters are cold and summers warm, no distinctive type of clothing came into being. Instead, the peoples of the temperate zone borrowed from the zones of tailoring and draping, with tailoring exerting the greater influence.

Tailoring was minimal in Japan before the introduction of European clothing, and the classic kimono was made by sewing together strips of fabric. Sandals were worn on the feet, but with tailored cloth stockings. In China, clothing is tailored, and the Chinese popular garb of loose cotton blouse and trousers spread southward through Vietnam. Elsewhere in Southeast Asia and Indonesia acceptance of tailoring was more limited. Tubular or wraparound skirts continue in vogue, and though some peoples of the area have adopted a tailored blouse, many hill people of Southeast Asia wear an unshaped poncho type of upper garment. In India in the 20th century, women of fashion have begun to wear a tailored blouse with the sari, while upper-class Indian men wear a tailored jacket and trousers in public and a loose tailored shirt with their dhoti at home.

In Southwest Asia and in North Africa, clothing represents a compromise between the draped form traditional to the area and the tailoring introduced from the north at various times over the millennia. On the Iranian Plateau and in Turkey, where Central Asian influence has been strong and the climate is tempered by the high altitude, tailoring is complete. In West Pakistan, a popular warm-weather costume is the loose-hanging pyjama. Among the Arabs in their warmer climate, however, draped clothing has

Bodily adornment is the purpose of a ritual costume worn by natives of northwestern Australia. Their headpieces are designed to approximate the shape of their totem pole.

# CLOTHING

Anthropologists, who study clothing as an aspect of human culture, find at least four factors affecting the amount and style of clothes people wear. Garments are designed to protect against the weather, to meet standards of modesty, to decorate the body, and to show rank or status. One costume may serve several or all of these purposes. Some peoples living in hot climates, where there is little need for protective clothing, still cover themselves with loosely draped robes. In Arctic climates, clothes, whether decorated or not, are designed for warmth and are tailored to fit snugly.

Loosely draped robes worn in Saudi Arabia serve to cover the body completely and at the same time allow cool air to circulate freely over it.

(Above) The tailored clothing of Finnish Lapps fits snugly at the wrists and ankles in order to hold body heat in a cold climate.

(Right) Status is indicated by the feathered headdress and bone necklace of a 19th-century American Indian.

persisted. Through most of the Muslim area a draped turban is worn over a tailored skullcap.

The European pattern of tailored clothing has been carried over most of the world. For informal occasions, Europeans living in warm climates wear short trousers and short-sleeved shirts, without jackets. This abbreviated costume has become popular for sportswear, particularly in the United States. For formal wear, however, Europeans and Americans continue to wear the conventional attire of tailored trousers, jacket, shirt, hat, shoes, and stockings. This style has become a symbol of high status in other parts of the world, however unsuited it may be to the local climate.

## CLOTHING AND MODESTY

Cultural values concerning modesty vary widely from one people to another and may change with time. In the 19th century, New England missionaries, accustomed to seeing their own women fully covered, were greatly shocked at the costume of Polynesian women, who wore nothing above the waist. Although the Polynesians felt quite modest in this attire, converts to Christianity were required to wear the enveloping holoku, a garment inspired by New England dress.

In the United States values of decency have changed greatly since the 19th century. Only 150 years after Americans introduced the holoku into Hawaii, women in the United States were accustomed to appearing in public in scanty dress that would shock many people in other parts of the world. Among the people of the Muslim Middle East, for example, modesty requires that both men and women cover the whole body, from neck to wrists and ankles, and women must also cover their hair and face. For women brought up in such societies, uncovering the face in public is as indecent as appearing naked. When the veiling of women was first forbidden in Iran in the 1930's, many older women never left their homes because the act of showing their faces on the street was too indecent to be endured.

Primitive tribes who often wear no covering at all in the usual sense, have their own ideas of modesty. Among the Botocudo of South America, for example, women go naked but wear a labret, or circular plate of wood, held in the distended lower lip. One Botocudo woman, on removing the labret that she had agreed to sell to an anthropologist, was so overcome by her immodest condition that she fled into the forest in shame. Among the Witoto of the Amazon Basin the women also go naked, and the men wear a meager loincloth of bark cloth, which they never remove in the presence of another person. In Africa south of the Sahara, where women usually wear only a short apron or loincloth, girls are taught from an early age to make sure that the tiny garment is in place and that modesty is at all times satisfied. A man of the Trobriand Islands off New Guinea, where the costume consists of a palm leaf, is equally careful to see that his leaf is always precisely and securely arranged. Some men of the Comanche, a Plains Indian tribe, who formerly wore only a small loincloth, still feel indecent if they do not wear this garment under their modern trousers.

While the Comanche retained their old sense of modesty after adopting a new kind of clothing, some peoples have acquired new values of decency along with new clothes. Among the Lamet of Laos in Southeast Asia, for example, women traditionally wore only a cloth wrapped around the hips and extending to the knees. Forty years after the adoption from the Thai of blouse and skirt at the beginning of the 20th century, Lamet women were ashamed to bare their breasts except when nursing an infant.

## CLOTHING AND ADORNMENT

**Primitive Decoration.** However fully or scantily people cover their bodies, almost everywhere they have some form of adornment. Among the adornments worn by many primitive peoples with limited technological resources are seeds, teeth, bones, shells, and leaves, through which holes can be drilled for stringing on fiber strands. It is probable that prehistoric men wore such ornaments long before they acquired the skill to carve and drill holes in the Late Stone Age stone pendants that are the earliest ornaments known to archaeologists.

The primitive Arunda of Australia wear armbands, headbands, and necklaces of strips of fur twisted into a cord and greased and dyed. The Polynesians make necklaces of flowers, and wear flowers in the hair. Shell beads have been worn by many peoples, some of them living far from the sea, such as the Crow Indians of the North American plains. Crow Indian men also wore necklaces of bear claws, more readily available, while the Gururumba of New Guinea wore as ear pendants not only shells but the bodies of iridescent green beetles.

**Paint.** Body paint is probably also very old, for late Stone Age burials have been found in which the corpse had been smeared with red ocher. Among living peoples, the Australian Arunda, like the Witoto, the Hopi of Arizona, and a number of other peoples, paint their bodies for ceremonial occasions. For everyday embellishment, young Pygmy women in the eastern Congo region of Africa spend a good deal of time decorating the lower part of the body with a vegetable dye. In the Hadhramaut area of South Arabia, men stain their skins blue with indigo, and women use a base of yellow turmeric on which, particularly for the face, they paint designs in henna and in black, red, and green mineral pigments.

**Other Cosmetic Effects.** In addition to color, other cosmetic effects are obtained. Among the Hottentots of South Africa, for example, the women first smeared their bodies with moist cow dung, which has adhesive properties; then, when the dung was nearly dry, they scraped it off and rubbed fat into the skin. Finally, sweet-smelling herbs were rubbed over the body. Every Hottentot woman kept a bag of such powdered herbs at hand for grooming. Polynesians kept their skin soft and glistening by rubbing in coconut oil, while both the Todas of south India and various peoples of East Africa used butter for this purpose.

**Hair.** The hair is another feature that has been treated in many cultures. Among the Arunda, for example, the men dyed their hair with red ocher. In Fiji the hair was bleached with lime, while Samoan women stiffened their hair with scented oil and gum. The presence or absence of facial and body hair is subject to varying cultural values. In India, where the people's hair tends to be naturally luxuriant, Sikh men make a religious principle of not cutting their hair, and they take pride in the richness of their beards and moustaches. In areas where the natural growth of body hair is sparse, however, the presence of any hair may be regarded as unsightly. The Witoto remove all facial and body hair with latex. The Tinguian of the Philippines pluck out all body hair, and in some parts of Indonesia people even pluck out their eyebrows.

The teeth are also subject to enhancement. In parts of Southeast Asia and Indonesia it was the custom to enamel the teeth black. Tooth blackening gradually went out of fashion in the 20th century, but an expensive alternative used in some regions is a gold covering.

**Mutilations.** Mutilations are also regarded as enhancing to the appearance. The Witotos pierced the lobes of their ears and enlarged the hole until they could insert a wooden plug, often decorated with feathers. They also pierced the nasal septum (the cartilage that divides the nostrils) and wore feathers or wooden pins in the hole. The piercing of the ear lobes is a widespread practice. In parts of Southeast Asia, Indonesia, and Melanesia, holes in the ears were also distended to accommodate plugs or tubes in which flowers, leaves, and other ornaments were worn. The piercing of the nasal septum and the insertion of quills, feathers, and small rods of wood or bone is particularly favored in Australia and the islands of Melanesia. In India, women often wear jeweled studs in the pierced alae, or wings of the nostrils.

Tattooing and cicatrization are practiced in many parts of the world. In tattooing, tiny holes are pierced in the skin, and a dye is rubbed in to create a permanent colored design. In cicatrization, the skin is gashed with a knife, and salt is rubbed into the wound so that, in healing, raised welts are formed.

The area of the body adorned varies from group to group. The Crow Indians had some tattooing on the face, while the Haida of British Columbia decorated the lower legs, forearms, and chest. Among the Ainu of Japan the women had tattooed designs on the forehead, arms, and hands, and most distinctively, black tattooing around the mouth that gave the appearance of a moustache. In Thailand some men have their legs tattooed from the hips to the knees.

That tattooing is a practice of some antiquity is evidenced by an archaeological discovery made in Central Asia. In a mountain tomb a frozen body was found in which the extensively tattooed skin had been preserved by the cold for some 2,000 years.

An unusual form of deformation was practiced by a Karen group in the highlands of Burma. Girls wore rings of brass wire around the neck, with more rings added as the girl grew. This structure forced up the chin and gradually elongated the neck until the rings were needed for support.

**Decorating Textiles.** Although even primitive people have ample means of ornamenting themselves with simple materials, societies with a more developed technology develop new sources of adornment. The people of the Arctic, for example, decorated their fur clothing with insets of contrasting furs. The skin garments of the Plains Indians were adorned with leather fringe and with designs painted on or embroidered with dyed porcupine quills. In Asia, south of the Arctic, appliqué designs in contrasting color and texture were favored. When woven fabrics came into use in this area, the appliqué motifs were further embellished with embroidery, particularly in northern China and Mongolia.

Elsewhere, woven garments were given color by dyeing either the yarn or the woven fabric. Yarns of different colors could be woven together to give patterns of stripes or plaids, a favorite method in both Southeast Asia and highland Scotland. In India, gold threads are used in the borders of fine saris.

In addition to the use of color, textiles can be enhanced by the use of various weaving techniques. The pre-Hispanic Peruvians had all the basic weaving techniques known to the modern textile industry, including brocade, gauze, and velvet, and these were also used in the Old World. The textile fiber may itself be ornamental. Silk, because of its lustrous appearance, was carried from China, where it originated, to Europe.

**Jewelry.** Technological advance also brought into use new ornamental materials. One of the first metals to be worked by man was gold. Because of its softness it is unsuitable for tools and weapons, but it was used as a jewelry material in ancient times both in Mesopotamia and Middle America, as it is today. Silver was also used for jewelry and is still widely used for that purpose in Mexico and Central Asia.

In Neolithic times early man attained considerable skill in the working and polishing of stone. When metal began to replace stone for tools and implements, some craftsmen applied their stoneworking techniques to semiprecious stones for luxury items such as jewelry. Among these stones were turquoise, lapis lazuli, jade, and coral.

Pearls were already used for jewelry in the Mediterranean area in the 1st century B. C., the time of Cleopatra. They were also carried to India, where interest in precious stones reached a high development. The earliest diamond mine known was in India; rubies came from Burma, and sapphires from Ceylon, Kashmir, and Thailand.

## CLOTHING AND STATUS

An important function of clothing is that of defining a person's status and position in his society. For example, in some societies small children wear no clothing at all, and the adoption of clothing by a child marks a change in age status. In Turkistan small boys wear clothing like that of their fathers except that they do not wind a turban over their skullcap until they become men. In East Africa a boy's developing status is indicated through a number of stages: at one age a front tooth is knocked out, later he undergoes scarification, and when he becomes eligible to look for a bride, the regalia he wears at once identifies this status. Among the Ainu of Japan the tattooing of a woman's moustache was done just before her marriage. Tattooing and scarification, which are usually completed by the time of marriage, may have other status significance. Among Australian aborigines the scars on a man's back indicated the totem group to which he belonged, while in Borneo the symbols tattooed on a Dayak's legs were supposed to identify him to his ancestors in the afterworld when he died.

Hairdress serves as a status symbol almost everywhere. Men and women dress their hair differently, and girls often change their hairdress after marriage. In Turkistan, for example, a girl wears her hair in 40 tiny braids until marriage, changing to two large braids after the birth of the first child. In a number of societies a widow shaves her head, rubs ashes in her hair, or leaves it unkempt to denote her bereaved status. Among the Iroquois Indians, the warrior shaved his head except for a scalp lock.

Among the Witoto a necklace of human teeth denoted the successful warrior, and chiefs wore a necklace of jaguar teeth. In the Philippines, Mandaya warriors were distinguished by their red clothing, as were women shaman mediums.

Local group affiliations are often indicated by variations in costume. Among the Plains Indians each tribe had its own conventions in making the traditional skin clothing. In the Burmese highlands each locality had its own colors and patterns of stripes or plaids, and a woman's locality could also be identified by her headdress. Originally, the Scottish tartan indicated the locality in which the wearer lived. Later the clan tartan denoted membership in a larger kin group and could be worn by clan members who had left the highlands.

As societies become more complex, class differences develop and are reflected in the people's clothing. Among the authoritarian Incas of Peru, only officials, nobles, and priests were allowed to wear fine fabrics of alpaca and vicuña. Also forbidden to commoners were gems, feathers, and ornaments of gold and silver. In 19th century Turkistan, a man's status was measured by the number of robes he wore in public and by the elaborateness of his silver girdle.

Precious jewels usually symbolize economic status because of their rarity and cost. In Burma a well-dressed woman wears diamond jewelry both day and night, and would be ashamed to be seen without it.

In Europe and the United States expensive jewelry is not so essential to the well-dressed woman as in Burma, but precious gems, particularly diamonds, are status symbols. In the Western world expensive furs are also worn to indicate high economic or social status.

In many parts of the world, European clothing, particularly that of men, has become a status symbol. Even in tropical climates, men of standing wear tailored clothing in public. An exception is that of African representatives in the United Nations who, though they may wear European clothing for official functions in Africa, wear distinctive robes in New York to distinguish themselves from American blacks. Women have been less ready to accept European clothing. Most Indian women, for example, continue to wear the sari, and Indonesian women tend to wear the sarong wherever they go. Chinese and Pakistani women also often wear native clothing abroad. At home the social and economic status of the wearer is indicated by the richness of the material used for the costume, while abroad the dress identifies nationality.

ELIZABETH E. BACON
*Michigan State University*

### Bibliography

Horn, Marilyn J., and Gurel, Lois M., *The Second Skin: An Interdisciplinary Study of Clothing* (Houghton 1981).
Kaiser, Susan B., *The Social Psychology of Clothing* (Macmillan 1985).
Nordquist, Barbara K., and others, *Traditional Folk Textiles and Dress* (Kendall/Hunt 1986).
Storm, Penny, *Functions of Dress: Tool of Culture and the Individual* (Prentice-Hall 1987).

## CLOTHING INDUSTRY.

The factory system of clothing production that flourishes today is of fairly recent origin. Until the middle of the 19th century all garments were individually crafted by hand. Those who could afford it had their clothing made by others; those who could not invested time and energy in producing their own. Either way it was expensive.

The introduction of the sewing machine changed all that. While there had been a clothing industry before the invention of the sewing machine, there was no factory production of apparel. It was this invention that revolutionized the way people dressed.

Society, which for centuries had been limited to made-to-order clothes, became within little more than one generation accustomed to ready-to-wear apparel. And as clothing is the most visible indicator of social class, the widespread availability of presentable, even fashionable, clothing tended to democratize society. Few technical innovations have surpassed the sewing machine in their social impact. Few industries have been so totally altered in so short a time.

**Development of Technology in the Clothing Industry.** The Frenchman Barthélemy Thimonner developed a chain-stitch sewing machine that was patented in 1830. He recognized that a machine could not simply mimic handsewing. Stitches of an entirely new type were needed. The American Elias Howe patented the first practical machine in 1846, which employed a double continuous thread. It was left for Isaac Singer to develop and successfully market the first practical domestic sewing machine.

The sewing machine was the only great revolutionary innovation in the history of clothing manufacture. Thereafter all developments in technology dealt essentially with the difficulties that were inherent in handling and processing limp fabrics.

From the mid-19th century to the 1890's there were no radical improvements in equipment until advances in electric motor construction made possible small, portable rotary or reciprocating electric knives capable of cutting through many layers of fabric. Around the turn of the century the steam pressing iron and the pressing machine were introduced. Of far more recent origin have been computer-aided pattern design equipment, laser fabric cutters, robotics, and automated warehouse facilities. Most modern production innovations, however, are best suited to large-scale operations.

**Development of the Clothing Industry in Britain.** The British clothing industry existed long before the Industrial Revolution and the emergence of the factory system. An artisan industry in which retail tailors made menswear to measure and seamstresses or retail dressmakers made women's clothing was functioning in the mid-18th century. In the early 19th century there was increased demand for ready-made clothing on the part of the emerging class of professionals, businessmen, farmers, and shopkeepers. In response, retail tailors began to produce ready-made clothing in their workrooms for both men and women. Seamstresses could buy commercially prepared patterns in fashionable styles. Men's tailored clothing was of a superior cut and fit, due largely to the British tailors' long experience with fine woolens.

By 1830 the London tailors were almost completely unionized. Yet over the next 30 years, as the industry evolved, the unions were effectively destroyed. Piecework replacing work paid by the day, homework replacing work done on the premises, and cheap female labor employed at the newly introduced sewing machines were the undoing of British labor in the clothing trades. By 1860 the British industry was a "sweated" trade, characterized by long working hours, low wages, substandard working conditions, and the shifting of work into unregulated, crowded, unsanitary lofts or living quarters. Most of these sweated clothing workers were women, joined in the second half of the 19th century by immigrant Jewish men from continental Europe. Throughout the second half of the century the production of ready-made menswear increased more rapidly than women's ready-to-wear, but by the end of the century both were being factory produced in large quantities.

The sweatshop system in the early 20th century spawned a myriad of small factories, primarily in London but also in Manchester and Leeds. After more than half a century of decline, efforts were made to revive the unions, but the industry had so dramatically changed that it was virtually impossible to do so. Women made up a majority of the work force, and they were difficult to organize because marriage, low pay, homework, apathy, and the opposition of male workers isolated them. Throughout this period in British labor history the work force in the clothing trades was highly stratified and disorganized.

In 1909 the British government, through the Trades Board Act, fixed minimum wages in a number of industries including men's tailoring. This legislation encouraged the industry to move work back into the factory that had previously been done in lofts or in workers' homes. In fact, by the 1930's there was also a well-established factory system manufacturing women's ready-to-wear in Britain.

Although the Depression and World War II disrupted the clothing industry, it rebounded after the war chiefly because the large number of small firms declined and the larger remaining firms adopted more efficient cost-effective factory techniques. The British clothing industry, together with that of West Germany, is one of the most highly developed in the world.

**Development of the Clothing Industry in the United States.** At the beginning of the 19th century, two thirds of all garments in the United States were produced in the home, the remainder by seamstresses or in the shops of custom tailors. The technology that would permit factory production had yet to be developed, and there was little demand for ready-made clothing on the part of the general public. It was, however, being produced for sailors who, because they were in port for only a short time, could not wait to have their clothes made to measure. It was also produced for slaves, who had little choice in the matter. Because it was cheap and unfashionable, such clothing came to be known generically as "slops." Men's leather breeches, widely worn in Colonial America, were also ready-made.

As the country grew, demand for relatively fashionable ready-made clothing at affordable prices increased. In response, a true garment manufacturing industry developed with its center in New York City. Tailors, who were the prime source of clothing before the late 1820's, divided their shops to do custom work and to produce ready-to-wear for both men and women. Although the plentiful supply of seamstresses and the complexity of women's dress retarded the growth of the women's ready-to-wear industry, such clothing was, in fact, being produced before the Civil War. Women passing through New York on their way West could buy dresses made up beforehand, rather than to measure, by tailors and dressmakers. These garments were either sold to the customer directly or to department stores that, in turn, resold them to country stores or peddlers. During this period, secondhand clothing dealers specializing in the repair and renovation of used clothing proliferated. This trade in used clothing was perhaps more extensive than that in ready-to-wear.

By the 1830's a clearly recognizable clothing industry was functioning in New York City, and to a lesser extent in Philadelphia, Boston, and Baltimore. It was so well established that some businesses were producing ready-to-wear exclusively. Generally, pattern making and cutting were done on the premises (often a tailor shop), and the cut goods were contracted outside as homework to be sewn and finished.

Clothing being sewn in a loft in New York City at the turn of the century. Such sweatshops were staffed largely by recently arrived immigrants, who provided the clothing industry with cheap labor.

The clothing industry in the United States at midcentury, made up of over 4,000 manufacturing establishments, prospered on the strength of four factors: (1) the rapid development of the domestic cotton and wool textile industries; (2) the arrival in the 1840's and 1850's of large number of Irish and German immigrants who provided a supply of labor; (3) the impetus the Civil War gave to the production of military uniforms; and (4) the development and successful marketing of a practical sewing machine invented by Isaac Singer.

In the period 1860 to 1920 the industry continued its rapid expansion, becoming, more properly, an industry of industries, each segment with its own pattern of organization turning out a multiplicity of products. The Civil War had provided experience in the mass production of garments, which led to the next stage in the industry's development, namely the contracting system. This scheme (in which cut goods are sent out to be sewn in lofts or at home) became more prevalent and marked the emergence of the sweatshop in the United States much as it already existed in Britain. The arrival of millions of poor and industrious Jews and Italians between 1890 and 1920 further reinforced the system. These immigrants provided the clothing industry with more than a source of cheap labor; they provided it with a character and style that was uniquely American.

By the turn of the century the menswear industry was dispersed in a number of cities including Rochester, Philadelphia, and Chicago. But New York was indisputably the center of the women's ready-to-wear trade. Its large work force was organizing itself into unions, the most famous and successful of which was the International Ladies' Garment Workers' Union. The highly competitive labor-intensive nature of the New York garment industry made conflict between workers and manufacturers inevitable. In 1909 the first significant strike in the industry was settled inconclusively. But an outgrowth was the introduction of collective bargaining the next year.

The 1920's saw the movement of the New York ready-to-wear industry uptown to Seventh Avenue and the beginning of a period in which garments were mass produced in such astonishing quantities and varieties that it has been called a "ready-made miracle." The clothing industry by this time was fashion-driven, which is to say it was characterized by constant change. As never before, inexpensive and stylish clothes were available to all Americans. This was partly a result of Seventh Avenue's efficiency and economy and partly a result of the remarkable distribution system exemplified by such retailers as Sears, Roebuck & Company and the J.C. Penney Company.

The Great Depression of the 1930's reduced many apparel manufacturers to bankruptcy. Late in the decade the attrition rate for New York City dress firms had reached an annual rate of 20%.

Despite government restrictions on production, World War II brought great prosperity to Seventh Avenue. Profits were earned in meeting the needs of the armed forces and from the increased demand for clothing by a private sector now fully employed. This prosperity carried over into the postwar period and was given further impetus by the Korean War in the early 1950's.

**The Functioning of New York's Garment Center.** During this period of New York's ascendancy, a system of production developed that still governs the women's ready-to-wear industry on New York's Seventh Avenue. To understand how it works, one must understand clustering. Seventh Avenue's agglomeration of manufacturers makes possible a high degree of specialization, with firms making similar clothing clustered together in the same building and the various buildings clustered to form the garment center. Such concentration facilitates communication between buyers and sellers and makes accessible a wide variety of fabrics and services. Market signals are transmitted quickly in such an environment.

Garments, although they may be organized into lines or collections, are created individually. In a typical Seventh Avenue dress house the process commonly begins with the designer choosing fabric swatches, then deciding how the fabric

© MARVIN E. NEWMAN

A model touches up her makeup moments before a famous designer's showing of her evening wear to prospective buyers. Publicity and glamour are essential ingredients in the promotion of a designer's seasonal collection.

One machine can cut through many layers of fabric, an operation that results in major production economies.

might best be employed in a garment. The design, represented in a sketch, may be original or it may be inspired by the work of others (referred to as a "knockoff").

Designers frequently work six to eight months ahead of the retail selling season, beginning with a series of decisions regarding fabric and color. A sample of each garment is made up together with a cost sheet detailing the expenses to be incurred for fabric, trimmings (belts, buttons), findings (linings, zippers), as well as labor and shipping expenses. A wholesale price is calculated by adding total cost to an amount representing profit. A third of the cost will generally represent labor, a third materials, and a third overhead (rent, administrative salaries, showroom expenses, electricity and telephone service, corporate taxes) and profit.

The production department is responsible for making the production pattern, grading it for the size range in which the garment is to be produced, and for making the marker (the outline of the pattern pieces that is placed on top of the fabric to be cut). The fabric is laid out in multiple layers and cut by machine. The cut goods are bundled together and moved to the sewing room, where they are assembled. It is rare today for one person to sew a complete garment. Section work, in which the garment is passed down an assembly line, is much more common. After sewing operations are completed the garments are pressed, then packed or hung on racks, and shipped to the retailer.

**Shift of the Industry from New York.** After enjoying a period of post-World War II prosperity, the New York ready-to-wear industry began a period of gradual decline. A number of factors contributed to this condition, but the industry's unremitting search for cheap labor must be counted as the most important. Union wages as well as high rents for manufacturing space, traffic congestion, crowding, and garment center racketeering have encouraged flight from the city. Unlike steel mills and oil refineries, clothing factories are easy to move. In fact, many have been moved to the Southern states and abroad.

Additionally, the clothing industry is now composed of larger organizations, many engaged in the manufacture of staple apparel like jeans. This has, as a result, increased standardization and made possible economies of scale unattainable by the smaller firms so typical of the New York garment center. Across the country even larger multiplant operations now exist.

Finally, apparel imports, especially those from low-wage countries, have become increasingly troublesome to the domestic industry and have contributed to New York's decline as a manufacturing center. Much of the world's apparel production has shifted to the Caribbean Basin and the Far East where labor costs are much less than in North America and Western Europe.

**The Clothing Industries in Western Europe.** Although France for many years has been the creative center of the European clothing industries, its ready-to-wear industry has lagged behind those of Britain and West Germany. Distracted by its rivalry with the designers of Italy, France has failed to develop its basic apparel manufacturing industry, which has actually shrunk in the face of competition from West Germany. France's strength still lies in its small dress companies, which are adept at catching trends and filling orders quickly.

West Germany's ready-to-wear manufacturers are better able to mount strong export campaigns than France because they are larger and because 60% of their production is carried out in low-wage East European countries. About 20% of West German production is in the hands of only four firms, a much greater concentration than that found in any other nation. As in the British industry, German clothing manufacturers are organized to sell to large, national chain stores.

Italy excels in the manufacture of fine knits and other sophisticated, fashionable ready-to-wear for export, much of it to the United States.

SWEETMAN R. SMITH, *Fashion Institute of Technology, State University of New York*

**Further Reading:** Ghadar, Fariborz, and others, *U.S. Industrial Competitiveness: The Case of the Textile and Apparel Industry* (Lexington Bks. 1987); Schmiechen, James A., *Sweated Industries and Sweated Labor: The London Clothing Trades, 1860–1914* (Univ. of Ill. Press 1984); Waldinger, Roger D., *Through the Eye of the Needle: Immigrants and Enterprise in New York's Garment Trades* (N.Y. Univ. Press 1986).

**CLOTILDA,** klō-til′də, **Saint** (475?-545), Frankish Catholic queen. She was born about 475, probably in Lyon, France, the daughter of Chilperic, king of Burgundy. In 492 she married the Frankish king Clovis I (q.v.), who, though a pagan, permitted his first two children to be baptized and finally accepted baptism himself. As the conversion of Clovis was a key event in Christian history, Clotilda's religious influence was of incalculable importance. She was left a widow in 511, and the remainder of her life was saddened by the power struggle among her three sons for the Frankish kingdom. She retired to Tours, where she retained her sovereign power, devoting herself to prayer and the founding of churches and monasteries and other good works. Clotilda died in Tours on June 3, 545. Her remains were transported to the Church of St. Leu, Paris, in 1793. Her feast day is June 3.

JOHN F. BRODERICK, S.J.
*Weston College*

**CLOTTING.** See BLOOD–*Clotting*.

**CLOTURE,** clō′chər, also called *closure*, is any parliamentary device for ending debate in a deliberative assembly. It differs from the *previous question* motion in that the latter is a specific procedure to bring about cloture. The previous question can be moved by one member, must be voted on immediately without debate, and is decided by a simple majority.

Cloture is invoked in the U. S. House of Representatives by a motion for the previous question. Similarly, only a majority vote is needed for shutting off debate in the British and Canadian Houses of Commons and in the French National Assembly, but there are procedural difference. In Canada a motion for cloture is introduced by a member of the government, while in Britain the support of 100 members of Commons is needed before a vote is called. In France the governmental majority may call for the imposition of cloture by majority vote when, in its view, "the case for and against has been adequately presented."

**Cloture in the U. S. Senate.** Invoking cloture in the U. S. Senate is a far more difficult matter. The Senate cloture rule requires that a motion to invoke cloture be supported by a petition signed by 16 senators before it can be considered; the motion's fate is decided two days later. An affirmative vote of three fifths of the total Senate membership (until 1975, two thirds of those present and voting) is required.

Many senators repeatedly have urged that cloture be permitted in the upper chamber of Congress if a simple majority approves. But this move has been resisted by those who claim that such limitation would destroy the Senate's deliberative function and make it a mere annex of the House, where legislation can be gaveled through at breakneck speed with a minimum amount of debate.

Indeed, except for the period between 1789 and 1806, when the previous question could be moved, the Senate had no provision for limiting debate until 1917—a unique distinction among the free world's legislative assemblies. It was a hallmark of America's democratic experiment that any senator could speak as long as he wished on any subject he chose. Unlike the procedure in the House of Representatives, a senator did not have to seek a place on the speaking calendar

from the Rules Committee, but could seek recognition from the chair.

This privilege of unlimited free speech frequently led to long-winded discourses called *filibusters*—usually by senators on the minority side of an issue—calculated to prevent a controversial matter from reaching a vote. Filibustering is defended as having the useful function of calling the public's attention to a controversial bill and bringing all sides of a question to full consideration. Above all, it is supported as a vital protection of minority rights. Opponents, however, insist that the filibuster not only fails to contribute positively to the quest for useful information, but also fails even to address itself to the subject under consideration; in effect, it represents only minority obstruction of the majority will.

The Senate tradition of unlimited debate was modified in 1917 by the adoption of Rule XXII, which, as revised in 1949 and 1959, provides that:

> [At] any time a motion signed by sixteen senators, to bring to a close the debate upon any measure, motion, or other matter pending before the Senate, or the unfinished business, is presented to the Senate, the Presiding Officer shall at once state the motion to the Senate, and one hour after the Senate meets on the following calendar day but one, he shall lay the motion before the Senate and direct that the Secretary call the roll, and, upon the ascertainment that a quorum is present, the Presiding Officer shall, without debate, submit to the Senate by a yea-and-nay vote the question:
> "Is it the sense of the Senate that the debate be brought to a close?"
> And if that question shall be decided in the affirmative by two thirds of the senators present and voting, then said measure, motion, or other matter pending before the Senate, or the unfinished business, shall be the unfinished business to the exclusion of all other business until disposed of.
> Thereafter no senator shall be entitled to speak in all more than one hour on the measure, motion, or other matter pending before the Senate, or the unfinished business, the amendments thereto, and motions affecting the same . . . . Except by unanimous consent, no amendment shall be in order after the vote to bring the debate to a close, unless the same has been presented and read prior to that time. No dilatory motion, or dilatory amendment, or amendment not germane shall be in order. Points or order, including questions of relevancy, and appeals for the decision of the Presiding Officer, shall be decided without debate.
> The provisions [prohibiting debate on motions made before two o'clock] . . . shall not apply to any motion to proceed with the consideration of any motion, resolution, or proposal to change any of the Standing Rules of the Senate.

In 1964 the Senate adopted another rule to the effect that three hours of each day's debate must be confined to the business at hand.

Despite provision for cloture, the Senate invoked the rule only 7 times in 35 attempts between 1917 and 1967. Civil rights legislation was blocked consistently by filibustering Southern minorities until June 10, 1964, when, after 75 days of dilatory debate, the Senate invoked cloture by a vote of 71 to 29 on the subsequently enacted Civil Rights Act of 1964.

Support for a stronger Senate cloture rule persisted among members anxious to expedite legislative business. The legislature's tasks had become so vast as to cause concern that unless legislative procedure were streamlined, the role of legislatures would be diminished. On March 7, 1975, the Senate, after prolonged debate, voted 56–27 to amend its cloture rule. Henceforth a vote by three fifths of the full Senate membership (that is, 60 of the 100 senators) to end debate would suffice to invoke cloture.

HENRY J. ABRAHAM
*University of Pennsylvania*

# CLOUD

VAN BUCHER, FROM PHOTO RESEARCHERS

**CLOUD,** a collection of a large number of tiny water droplets or ice crystals in the air. The droplets fall through the air, like fine dust, with such slowness that they may be thought of as following the air motion. Only by growth or coagulation do they become large enough to fall out as rain, hail, or snow. The fallout is replaced as vapor by evaporation from the earth's surface.

### SYSTEMS OF CLASSIFICATION

When Luke Howard, an English chemist, gave Latin names to a few obviously different cloud forms in 1803, the proper study of clouds in their own right may be said to have begun. His names for the three main forms of cloud—*cumulus* (Latin for "heap"), *cirrus* ("curl" or "hair"), and *stratus* ("layer")—are firmly established. His synthesis of four more types of cloud by combinations of these names, however, is not of use because the names do not correspond to fundamental mechanisms in cloud formation and development.

Latin names were proliferated by many writers, sometimes to a ridiculous degree, to describe what were supposed to be distinct cloud types. Some of these names have been preserved in the international classification adopted by the World Meteorological Organization. The clouds are classified in genera and species—like vegetation—so as to enable a name to be given to any particular cloud. The classifications, however, are generally ignored by meteorologists (except as a source of impressive captions for cloud photographs)

**Meteorological Codes.** The classification most widely used today is represented by the numerical reporting codes adopted by all observers in state meteorological services throughout the world. The aim of this system is to give information about the characteristics of air masses, the degree of development of shower clouds, and the probable position of the observer in relation to fronts and other large-scale weather systems. Clouds are divided into *low,* with a base below 7,500 feet (2,500 meters); *medium,* between 7,500 and 21,000

feet (2,500 to 7,000 meters); and *high* clouds, above 21,000 feet (7,000 meters). High clouds are called *cirro—*because most fibrous clouds are at that level, and medium clouds are named *alto—*.

This system of coding has been based mainly on the needs of aviation weather forecasters. It is helpful to the forecaster in piecing together the various kinds of information on a weather chart to make what he calls his analysis, in which he describes the positions, movements, and characteristics of air masses, fronts, and pressure systems. Since this code came into use, however, man's knowledge of how clouds are formed has greatly increased, mainly through research with aircraft and radiosonde balloons. The older names and

**STRATOCUMULUS clouds form in layers when rising air reaches an equilibrium and spreads out horizontally.**

LOUIS D. RUBIN

ALTOCUMULUS in foreground is a wave cloud that has become unstable and broken into cloudlets. Some of the cloudlets are arranged in billows by the change of wind within the cloud. In the background are evening cumulus.

R. S. SCORER

codings have been found not to correspond entirely to the basic physical cloud mechanisms. Some outdated names nevertheless are preserved in popular literature. *Nimbus* (a rain cloud), for example, is not really a kind at all, because many quite different kinds of clouds produce rain; furthermore, clouds of the same kind may or may not produce rain, depending on slightly different conditions that do not affect their formation. Another example is *altocumulus*, which is differentiated from the same cloud in the low or high range (stratocumulus and cirrocumulus) by the coding system, while many essentially different medium-height clouds are given the same name.

**Revised Classifications.** Aviators are now concerned with problems quite different from those of their predecessors, and methods of chart analysis are being computerized. Meteorologists are becoming more interested in a classification of clouds that corresponds with what is now known about cloud physics and mechanics. It is necessary to use only such names as fit the new approach. English names are generally given when new ones are required.

Most notable among the omissions in all earlier classifications are *wave clouds*. Although they were understood clearly by some writers, they had not been generally recognized as a separate kind of cloud. It is also probable that with the rapid development of satellite photography, new names will be coined for much larger-scale cloud structures that will become recognizable to the earthbound observer who can view them only in part.

### FORMATION OF CLOUDS

Clouds are formed when the air is cooled by one of the mechanisms described below. It is then necessary that there should be condensation nuclei on which cloud droplets may form. These may be tiny dust, salt, or other particles, and they are normally plentiful in the atmosphere.

**Convection Clouds.** The cooling may be brought about by thermal convection. This occurs when the air is cooler than the earth's surface below—for example, when the ground is warmed by sunshine, or when air flows from cool to warm sea areas. The convection causes bodies of air to penetrate upward to regions of lower pressure; and, as a result, they expand. This expansion al-

ways causes cooling; and, since the air cannot contain as much water (in the form of vapor) at lower as it could at higher temperatures, continued cooling eventually produces saturation (when the dew point is reached). This is followed by condensation of vapor into cloud droplets.

There are always enough nuclei present in the air, so that the condensation is not delayed beyond the dew point. Therefore, every sample of rising air has a definite condensation level at which a cloud first appears. This level is at about 1,800 feet (600 meters) over the ocean but is usually higher over land, and it may be as high as 9,000 feet (3,000 meters) in hot arid regions. The cloud, when it forms, is always dense enough to be visible. The droplets are so numerous and small that the speed at which they fall through the air—a few inches, or centimeters, per second—is negligible compared with the up-and-down motion of the air, which may range up to a few meters per second.

Penetrative convection produces cumulus (heap) clouds with a typical cauliflowerlike structure. If the supply of warm air into the bases of these clouds is not maintained, they evaporate in a few minutes because of mixing with drier air. They are quickly replaced, however, so that the general appearance of the sky changes slowly as the clouds come and go.

Cumulus clouds may reach up to the tropopause (about 43,000 feet, or 14,000 meters, in warm climates), and occasionally the larger clouds penetrate temporarily up to 6,000 feet (2,000 meters) higher, into the stratosphere. The continual ascent of cumulus clouds, and the rainfall from them, is the chief means of warming the air as it moves from cool to warm latitudes; and their evaporation supplies the moisture needed to produce rainfall in other parts of the world.

**Wave Clouds.** When air flows over a hill it follows wavy streamlines, with the positions of the waves themselves remaining almost stationary. If the air is lifted above its condensation level in the crest of such a wave, a stationary cloud is formed. Condensation occurs where the air flows into the wave, and evaporation takes place at the wave's lee edge.

Wave clouds are common over land areas and are best developed near mountains in high latitudes, where the high-level winds are more often found

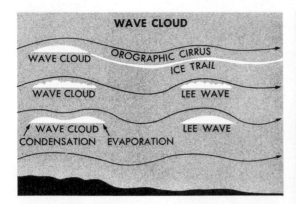

## WAVE CLOUD

WAVE CLOUD    OROGRAPHIC CIRRUS
ICE TRAIL

WAVE CLOUD                         LEE WAVE

WAVE CLOUD                         LEE WAVE
CONDENSATION    EVAPORATION

H. KLIEFORTH

(*Above*) Mountain wave clouds (*left*) are larger than lee wave clouds at high levels. Low cloud is stable; middle one is unstable but unfrozen; and highest is ice trail. (*Right*) Three-layered cloud in a wave crest, with cumuliform cloud below. A strong wind blows through this type.

to be stronger and to move in the same direction as low-level winds. They have a smooth outline, particularly when the layer of air in which they are formed is stably stratified. Clouds in such layers may also be formed above cumulus clouds, which push up the air above them as they rise; these are called *pileus* ("cap") clouds.

**Layer Clouds.** Extensive layers of cloud may be formed at a level where penetrating buoyant air reaches its equilibrium level and then spreads out horizontally as at a ceiling. These layers are called *stratocumulus*. Extensive layers also may be formed by the more or less uniform ascent of air over a wide area, particularly at the warm fronts of temperate-latitude cyclones (large low-pressure systems). The rate of ascent is usually less than 3 feet (1 meter) per second, and is not measurable by direct observation. At first the clouds appear as formless layers, called *stratus*, but they are rapidly transformed by the mechanisms described later. Stratus may be formed at many altitudes, and warm fronts often have several thin layers of cloud with clear air between them.

When smaller-scale motions within a layer cloud turn it over, the cloud becomes lumpy. It is then called *alto*cumulus because the lumps are formed at a high level and not (as in ordinary cumulus) by penetration from below.

**Fogs.** Fogs differ from other layers in that they are formed by cooling as a result of proximity to a cold surface. If there is no wind, moisture is condensed as dew on the cold surface and not as cloud. Fogs are rare in strong winds because the cooling is reduced in magnitude by being distributed, on account of the intense mixing, through a deep layer of air. Therefore a light wind is required; and then the air close to the ground is cooled to a temperature below its dew point and then stirred into air higher up. The mixing of two masses of air at different temperatures, the warmer of which is not saturated, often produces a supersaturated mixture. The colder mass need not be, but often is, already saturated.

When the cold surface is ground that has lost heat by radiation into space at night, the fog is called *radiation fog*. *Sea fog* formed over a cool sea is common in the warm sectors of cyclones and near west coasts of continents in lower latitudes where cold ocean currents are found.

Sea fogs are evaporated when the surface beneath is warmed by sunshine, or when mixed into a deeper layer of air as the wind increases.

*Steaming fogs,* which are always very shallow, are produced in cold air over a hot wet surface, such as a river warmed by a power station or a wet road in sunshine. They occur naturally over warm seas in high latitudes, typically in cold airstreams near the coast of Norway (where they are called *arctic smoke*). In this case the warm damp air near the surface is mixed with the colder air higher up. (Condensation trails, or *contrails*, produced by aircraft are formed by the same mechanism; for the exhaust, which contains much water vapor, is mixed into very cold surroundings. The steaming of the breath of animals in frosty weather is similar, but the air is generally cold enough for contrails only high in the troposphere or in the stratosphere. The contrails may persist for hours if the droplets freeze, particularly ahead of warm fronts.)

*Hill fog* is cloud on high ground, and its origin is not usually the same as genuine fogs.

HILL FOG is a cloud on high ground. Here, warm moist air of clearing sky covers the cold hillsides with fog.

R. S. SCORER

**Clouds Outside the Troposphere.** Occasionally clouds are found very much higher above the earth's surface than clouds are usually found. *Mother-of-pearl clouds* occur in the stratosphere between about 13 and 19 miles (19 to 27 km) altitude, but only in high latitudes in wintertime; otherwise the air is too dry. They are seen frequently in mountainous areas such as Norway, Alaska, and Iceland. Although the temperature of the clouds is about $-130°F$ ($-80°C$), freezing appears to be prevented by their sulfuric acid nuclei, which are formed from dissociated $H_2S$ and $O_2$ molecules. The drop size is very small—0.00015 mm—and the iridescence gives the cloud its name; the colors are very clear when these high clouds are still in sunshine after sunset.

The only other place outside the troposphere where clouds could be formed is in the cold layer at a height of about 50 miles (80 km). These ice clouds, called *noctilucent clouds,* usually show a billowed structure. Although they may be common they are very difficult to see; they are invisible when sunshine reaches the troposphere below them or when the light illuminating them has passed through the troposphere. Consequently, they can be seen easily only in high latitudes in summer, and it is not really known whether they occur in low latitudes.

## MODIFICATION OF CLOUDS

Once a cloud has been formed by one of the basic mechanisms, one or more of the several subsidiary mechanisms described below may radically change its structure and appearance.

**Radiation.** Clouds lose heat by infrared radiation from their tops. The base of the clouds may be warmed a little from below, however, if the

surface or lower clouds are warmer. (Clouds do not absorb a significant amount of sunshine.) This temperature difference causes convection within a layer of cloud soon after its formation, and as a result the layer acquires a cellular structure. Therefore, from above, sea fogs have a similar appearance to altocumulus.

**Latent Instability.** Some layers of air are stable until cloud forms, after which the latent heat released by condensation of water vapor causes thermal convection. This may (as with temperature differences caused by radiation) produce cellular structures—in wave clouds, for example—or it may produce small, rapidly growing towers called *castellanus.*

**Wind Shear.** A change of wind direction or magnitude with height tends to arrange cloud cells into billows, which lie like rollers across the direction of the shear. If there is no latent instability in the layer of air, the billows often are smooth and arched and occasionally behave like breaking waves. Shear near the ground often arranges cumulus into *streets,* with lines of cloud along the shear direction.

**Glaciation.** Clouds are not formed until the air is saturated with respect to water. When saturation is reached, the water vapor is in equilibrium with the water droplets present. However, since the vapor pressure over ice is less than it is over water, condensation will occur on any ice crystals present in the cloud. Thus, if a cloud is composed of supercooled droplets—colder than $32°F$ ($0°C$)—the droplets will grow rapidly if they become frozen. The freezing, or glaciation, of a supercooled cloud therefore delays evaporation as the cloud mixes with clear air. The cloud edge becomes silky and less well defined, and cloud elements may become drawn out or curled by the air motion and acquire a fibrous appearance. The cloud is then called cirrus.

*Effects of Glaciation on Different Clouds.* If some or all of the droplets in a wave cloud become frozen, their evaporation is delayed; a trail, or plume, of *orographic cirrus* is thus produced that may extend a mile or two, or in some cases hundreds of miles, downwind. Mother-of-pearl clouds also exhibit such trails.

Layer clouds may remain supercooled for many hours at temperatures as low as $-13°F$ ($-25°C$), but below $-22°F$ ($-30°C$) glaciation soon sets in. At $-31°F$ ($-35°C$) it occurs in a

few minutes, and at or below −40°F (−40°C) it is almost instantaneous. The upper parts of cumulus soon become glaciated at temperatures below 5°F (−15°C) because of the presence of large droplets that freeze more readily. (Rising cumulus that spread out are called *anvils;* the higher anvils are usually glaciated, and because evaporation is halted they are much better developed than unglaciated anvils.)

In stratus clouds, if almost all the droplets freeze, their growth may be very slow, and the cloud form is not much altered. It is then called *ice stratus* and only merits the name *cirrostratus* if it begins to assume a fibrous appearance.

### RAIN, SNOW, AND HAIL

If a few of the droplets of a supercooled cloud become frozen, they grow rapidly. When the frozen droplets grow larger than about 0.008 inch (0.2 mm), they acquire a falling speed of about 3 feet (1 meter) per second and begin to accrete smaller droplets by collision. Hailstones are sometimes formed in cumulus, where freezing occurs in a plentiful water supply, if such droplets freeze on contact. Updrafts of about 90 feet (30 meters) per second, or about 60 mph (95 km/hr), are required to support hailstones long enough for them to grow as large as grapes or golfballs. In layer clouds or small cumulus the majority of droplets, if they freeze, form snowflakes, instead, by the entanglement of several crystals having dendritic (treelike) growths on their corners.

This aggregation of cloud particles as a result of glaciation is important in temperate and cool climates, but most tropical and much temperate-latitude rain does not depend on freezing. In clouds at these latitudes, the collection of particles begins when droplets grow larger than about 0.0008 inch (0.02 mm), most cloud particles being in the range of 0.001 to 0.01 mm. At 0.2 mm

**GLACIATION** of water clouds often produces falling trails of ice crystals. The "fibers" contrast with the former woolly appearance of the water-droplet cloud.

**OROGRAPHIC CIRRUS** may extend downwind from a wave cloud that freezes. The edge at which uppermost cloud forms is at right, with "fibers" aligned along wind.

APPROACHING WARM FRONT (*top*) may fill sky with cloud lines lying along direction of jet stream. Waves commonly form under the stream's strong winds. Line of shower (*center*) often has characteristics of a cold front; some mamma fall from the anvils at left.

HALO is often seen in the thickening layers of ice cloud in an approaching warm front. (A contrail left by an aircraft appears in the rising moistened air.)

(drizzle) the particles grow rapidly and soon fall out of the smaller updrafts to form rain.

**Related Formations.** Several cloud forms are visible evidence of falling rain or snow. As an example of this, trails of falling crystals from glaciated altocumulus or castellanus are common. These falling crystals often form hairlike clouds known as *mare's tails*.

The first rain from a shower often appears to descend as bulbous masses called *mamma* (breast). Similar forms are more easily seen on the underside of the anvils of large cumulus, which are often glaciated. The rain in mamma usually evaporates before reaching the ground.

The aggregation of cloud water into larger particles causes a *downdraft* of air by the very weight of the water accreted. In addition, the partial evaporation of the rain (or hail or snow) as soon as it falls into cloud-free air causes sufficient cooling to intensify the downdraft greatly—occasionally to as much as 60 to 90 feet (20 to 30 meters) per second. Heavy rain reaching the ground from a *cumulonimbus* (a raining cumulus, or shower cloud) brings with it a downdraft that spreads over the ground ahead of the advancing rain. One of the main mechanisms for prolonging the life of a shower is the scooping up, by this advancing cold air, of fresh, warm, moist air that continuously feeds the updraft in the cloud. The process is most effective when wind shear is present; the shear makes the cloud lean over and causes the rain to enter cloud-free air far above the base level of the cloud. Evaporation begins higher up and the downdraft is much more intense; it also has a different velocity from the air at the ground, and therefore scoops it up more effectively.

If the air that enters a growing updraft in such rain clouds possesses some rotation, the converging motion intensifies the rotation and produces a funnel cloud. If the low-pressure region in the vortex center is intense enough, the funnel cloud may extend down to the ground. Over land, such a cloud is called a *tornado;* over the sea it is called a *waterspout*.

**Artificial Stimulation of Rain.** Methods of artificially producing rain can be of use only where nature is least efficient—namely, in cumulus over land surfaces where large condensation nuclei (such as the salt crystals over the sea) are absent, or where cloud temperatures are too high for natural freezing nuclei to be effective. Thus, salt particles may sometimes be used to induce rain in warm cumulus. Lumps of "dry ice"—solid carbon dioxide—thrown into a supercooled cloud leave trails of frozen cloud particles in their paths. Minute silver iodide particles can be introduced into the updraft of a cumulus through its base and may induce the freezing of supercooled droplets. If the updraft is too strong, the seeded elements reach the evaporating parts of the cloud before there is significant particle growth.

The best prospect of inducing useful artificial rainfall is in cumulus clouds that remain almost stationary in light winds, or possibly in wave clouds over a range of hills. In other situations individual clouds may be obviously modified in appearance by seeding, but the scale of operations required to achieve useful amounts of rainfall is then almost prohibitive.

## OPTICAL PHENOMENA IN CLOUDS

The colors, arcs, and bright spots often seen in clouds are useful in giving the observer imme-

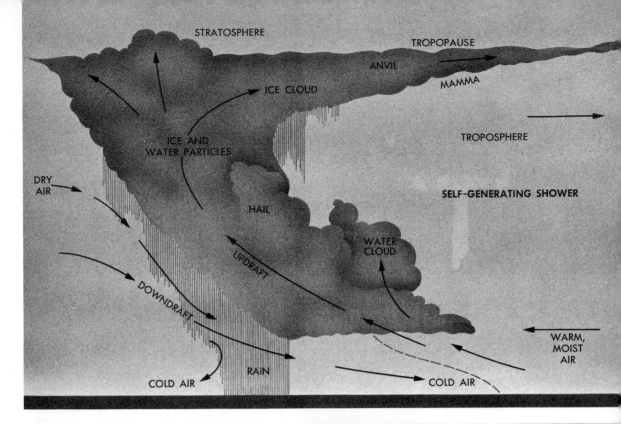

STRATOSPHERE

TROPOPAUSE

ANVIL

MAMMA

ICE CLOUD

ICE AND
WATER PARTICLES

TROPOSPHERE

DRY
AIR

SELF-GENERATING SHOWER

HAIL

WATER
CLOUD

UPDRAFT

DOWNDRAFT

WARM,
MOIST
AIR

COLD AIR

RAIN

COLD AIR

(Above) The mechanics of a shower are maintained continuously if the wind at high levels differs from that below. The updraft leans over so that dry air from higher levels is rain-cooled and forms a wedge of cold air that scoops up more warm moist air into the cloud. Most of the frozen top is carried forward, and a carpet of cold air is left behind. (Right) The anvil of a large raining cumulus spreads overhead; mamma fall from the anvil.

diate information about the cloud particles, such as their size, shape, and orientation.

**Water Droplets.** The colored rings, or *corona*, closely centered around the sun or moon are produced by diffraction of light by small spherical droplets. The droplets also produce the rings, or *glory (Brocken specter)*, seen around the observer's shadow when it falls on a cloud, as when an airplane casts its shadow on a cloud below. The colors of the corona or glory are intensified by a uniformity of drop size, which also produces a greater number of concentric rings. When drop size varies from one part of a cloud to another, iridescent colors may be observed in patches rather than rings.

Rainbows are produced by the refraction of light through larger droplets of rain or drizzle. (In the *primary* bow, produced by one internal reflection, the order of colors in the bow is reversed; in other refraction phenomena, the red band is closest to the line from the sun or moon to the observer.)

**Ice Crystals.** The most common ice crystals are hexagonal prisms. If they are randomly oriented in a cloud, they may produce rings, or *halos*, by refraction, around the sun or moon. If they are vertically oriented, however, the halo is concentrated as a bright spot of light called a *mock sun* or *sun dog*, located at the altitude of the sun but at an angular distance of about 22° on either side. White horizontal arcs are produced by reflection, while refraction in the ends of vertical crystals

R. JENSEN

produces the *circumzenithal arc*, which is often more brightly colored than the rainbow. Horizontally floating crystals produce various noncircular arcs or vertical "pillars." There is a great variety of rare optical phenomena. See also ATMOSPHERE; METEOROLOGY.

R. S. SCORER, *Imperial College of Science and Technology, London*

**Bibliography**

*Cloud Types for Observers*, 2d ed. (Kraus 1983).
**Howard, Luke,** *Clouds: The Realm of the Air* (St. George Bk. Serv. 1987).
**Mason, B. J.,** *Clouds, Rain, and Rainmaking*, 2d ed. (Cambridge 1976).
**Moffill, G. E., and Scholer, M.,** eds., *Physical Processes in Interstellar Clouds* (Kluwer 1987).
**Scorer, R. S.,** *Cloud Investigation by Satellite* (Halsted Press 1986).
**Scorer, R. S., and Wexler, H.,** *A Colour Guide to Clouds* (1964; Pergamon 1976).
**Steiner, Ralph,** *In Pursuit of Clouds* (R. Steiner 1986).

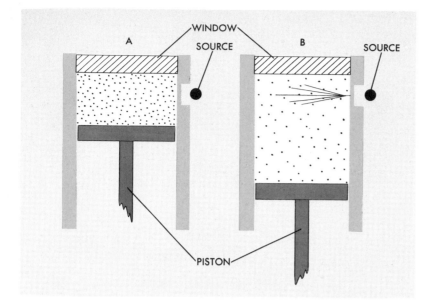

**CLOUD CHAMBER**

Fig. A shows the chamber before expansion. In Fig. B the piston has been pulled down suddenly. This rapid expansion of the gas cools it, leaving it in a supersaturated state.

**CLOUD CHAMBER,** a device used to make visible the paths of subatomic particles. It consists of a container of a gas and liquid, arranged so that at certain moments or in certain regions the gas is supersaturated.

There are two main types of cloud chamber. The original kind, developed by C. T. R. Wilson during the early years of this century, is a pulsed instrument. At regular intervals, or when triggered, a flexible wall of the chamber is abruptly moved a short distance. The sudden expansion produces cooling, leaving the gas supersaturated at the new, lower temperature. If the chamber and gas are clean, the liquid cannot immediately condense to form droplets. However, in this unstable condition the charged ions left by the passage of a subatomic particle can serve as seeds for the formation of fog drops. The viewer, or a camera, can see white droplet trails, showing the paths of the particles.

The second type of cloud chamber, the "continuous" or diffusion type, was developed during the early 1950's. In these devices, the bottom of the chamber is kept very cold and the top very warm. Liquid, usually an alcohol-water mixture, evaporates from a storage at the top. The vapor diffuses downward into the cold region, thus passing through a zone where it supersaturates the gas. In this unstable region, which may be several inches high, condensation can be triggered by the presence of ions left by the passage of subatomic particles, leaving white droplet trails which slowly settle to the bottom.

Cloud chambers were widely used until the invention of the bubble chambers and spark chambers in the middle 1950's, when attention turned to very high-energy particle events. Since the gas of a cloud chamber has low density, only small portions of the tracks of high-energy particles can be contained in a chamber of reasonable size. Many ingenious arrangements of cloud chambers, electronic detectors, and shielding barriers were used to detect and identify for the first time various subatomic particles, such as the positron and many of the mesons.

CLIFFORD E. SWARTZ
*State University of New York at Stony Brook*

**CLOUD SEEDING** usually refers to the introduction into supercooled clouds of materials that cause the formation of ice crystals, which may result in precipitation in the form of rain or snow. Supercooled clouds are a common occurrence. They consist of minute water drops that remain unfrozen even at temperatures below 32° F (0° C), and sometimes as low as −40° F (−40° C). This condition is quickly changed by the presence of ice crystals. Because the crystals have a lower vapor pressure than the water drops, they cause the drops to evaporate. The moisture then condenses on the ice crystals, which increase in size until they fall as snow or rain. Cloud seeding occurs naturally when ice crystals that have formed at higher altitudes fall into the cloud or when ice-forming dust particles are present in the atmosphere.

**Methods.** Artificial cloud seeding is accomplished both from the air and the ground. An airplane can be used to drop granules of solid carbon dioxide (dry ice) into the cloud. Because of their very low temperature, the granules generate enormous numbers of ice crystals. Another method is to release "smokes" or submicroscopic silver iodide particles or other substances, either from the air or the ground. The particles, when they fall into or are drawn up into the cloud, serve as centers for ice crystal formation. Because a few ounces of material are sufficient to seed many cubic miles of supercooled clouds, the treatment of large volumes of atmosphere is economically feasible.

**Uses.** Cloud seeding can produce significant changes in a cloud; it releases heat, changes the nature, size, and number of the water particles, and alters the humidity and circulation. It may therefore serve as an important tool for modifying the weather. It has been used to open holes in supercooled layers of cloud and to dissipate supercooled fogs over airports; if clouds are present, it can help to increase rain and snowfall over a region, to reduce crop and property damage from hail.

See also CLOUD.

BERNARD VONNEGUT
*State University of New York at Albany*

**CLOUDBERRY,** kloud′ber-ē, a hardy wild flower widely distributed in the high mountains of northern temperate regions. The cloudberry grows only in cool moist climates. In North America it ranges as far south as the mountainous regions of Maine and New Hampshire. It is sometimes grown in rock gardens.

The cloudberry ranges in height from 3 to 10 inches (70 to 250 mm) and has a creeping rootstock. The shallow flowers are white and borne singly. Some plants bear both male and female flowers; others bear only male flowers or only female flowers. The leaves of the cloudberry are rounded, with three to five lobes. The female flowers ripen into reddish or yellowish tasty raspberries that were prized by early settlers. The cloudberry is known technically as *Rubus chamaemorus,* and it belongs to the rose family (Rosaceae).

DONALD WYMAN
*The Arnold Arboretum, Harvard University*

**CLOUDED LEOPARD,** lep′ərd, a medium-sized member of the cat family. It is rather heavily built, with strong paws, and stands 16 to 20 inches (40–50 cm) at the shoulder. Head and body are about 50 inches (130 cm) long, and the tail measures about 35 inches (90 cm). The upper canine teeth are exceptionally big. The ground color of the striking fur is pale gray to bright yellow. The undersides are white. Black spots and stripes mark the face, and black bands run down the neck. Large black-rimmed patches of gray to brown cover the back and flanks; and black blotches are dotted over the limbs, belly, and tail, which is also marked with incomplete rings.

The range of the clouded leopard extends from Sikkim and Nepal eastward through the Himalayan foothills to southern China, and down through southeastern Asia to Sumatra, Java, and Borneo. A smaller race with a much shorter tail lives in Hainan and Taiwan (Formosa).

Clouded leopards live chiefly in trees and prey mainly on birds, but also on smaller mammals. Little is known of their life in the wild, however. The cat has been bred successfully in zoos, usually with two to four young in a litter.

There is a single species, *Neofelis nebulosa,* which is classified in the family Felidae, order Carnivora.

PAUL LEYHAUSEN
*Max Planck Institute for Behavioral Physiology
Wuppertal, Germany*

THE CLOUDED LEOPARD, which lives mainly in trees in its wild state, has been bred successfully in zoos.

NATIONAL ZOOLOGICAL PARK

**CLOUDS, The,** a comedy by Aristophanes, first performed in Athens in 423 B.C. (The text was revised from an earlier, unsuccessful version.) The play's chief target of ridicule is the philosopher Socrates, who is represented as instructing pupils for pay in a Phrontisterion (Thinkery). Old Strepsiades (Twister), anxious to cheat his creditors, sends his son Pheidippides to Socrates to learn how to argue on either side of a case. Socrates corrupts Pheidippides by showing him how to make wrong appear more plausible than right, and the play ends with the disappointed Strepsiades leading an attack on the Phrontisterion.

In this notoriously unfair portrayal, Socrates is pictured as being guilty of the very faults he criticized in his opponents, the Sophists: teaching for money, confusing physical with philosophical investigation, and emphasizing rhetorical glibness over ethical integrity.

RICHMOND Y. HATHORN
*Author of "Handbook of Classical Drama"*

**CLOUET,** kloo-e′, **François** (c. 1510–1572), French painter, a follower of the school of Fontainebleau (q.v.), who was the official painter to the court of Francis I. He was born at Tours sometime before 1520, and succeeded his father, Jean Clouet (q.v.), as painter to the king about 1540. His style, somewhat more detailed than his father's, combines a Flemish meticulousness with Italian mannerist elegance; it set the style for French court portraiture for many years.

Of Clouet's few surviving paintings, most are portrait drawings of members of the court. His earliest known work is a portrait of a friend, the apothecary Pierre Quthe (Louvre, Paris), painted in 1562. His *Lady at Her Toilet* (National Gallery, Washington, D. C.) was one of the first paintings on this theme, which became a favorite of the 16th century. Clouet's other paintings include the *Bath of Diana* (in several versions, one of which, now in the Louvre, depicts the king's mistress Diane de Poitiers), and portraits of Francis I (Uffizi, Florence) and of Charles IX (Kunsthistorisches Museum, Vienna). Clouet died in Paris in 1572.

**CLOUET,** kloo-e′, **Jean** (1485?–?1540), Flemish painter in France who refined the art of portraiture. His birthplace was probably in Flanders; his father, also a painter, was Michel Clouet (or Clawet) of Valenciennes, Flanders (now France). Jean Clouet became chief painter at the court of the French king, Francis I, with the title Painter and Valet of the King's Bedchamber. He died at Paris.

No signed works of Jean Clouet survive, but the museum at Chantilly, France, has about 130 drawings attributed to him. These were apparently sketches from life, and give evidence of his exceptional powers of observation. He is also celebrated as a painter of miniatures, several of which are in the Bibliothèque Nationale, Paris, and in the British Museum, London.

The great contribution to art of Jean Clouet's attributed works is the lively characterization and polished stylization of his portraits. The most famous are likenesses of Francis I (two in the Louvre, Paris); one of the most engaging is that of the future Francis II at the age of 2 or 3 (Antwerp); and one of the most expressive is the *Portrait of a Man with a Book by Petrarch* (Hampton Court, England).

**CLOUGH,** kluf, **Anne Jemima** (1820–1892), English pioneer in the education of women. She was born in Liverpool, England, on Jan. 20, 1820. She and her brother, Arthur Hugh Clough (q.v.), spent most of their childhood in Charleston, S. C., where she was educated at home. After their return to Liverpool in 1836, she continued her education. In 1852, having maintained her own school for some years, she moved to Ambleside, where she opened a school for the children of farmers and tradesmen.

In 1862, Miss Clough turned her attention toward reforms in the education of middle-class women. Her activities led to the founding of the North of England Council for Promoting the Higher Education of Women, of which she was president in 1873–1874. This council later developed the Cambridge higher local examination for women.

In 1870, lectures for women were instituted at Cambridge University, and Miss Clough took charge of a resident group of five female students. This was the beginning of the present Newnham College, of which she was principal from its organization in 1880 until her death, in Cambridge, on Feb. 27, 1892.

         RICHARD E. GROSS, *Stanford University*

**CLOUGH,** kluf, **Arthur Hugh** (1819–1861), English poet, whose work was inspired by an intense involvement in the social, political, and spiritual problems of 19th century England. He is commemorated in Arnold's elegiac poem *Thyrsis.*

**Life.** Clough was born in Liverpool on Jan. 1, 1819, and spent his childhood in the United States, returning to England to study at Rugby. He entered Oxford in 1837 with the intention of becoming a clergyman, but found that he could not accept the dogmas of the Church of England and in 1848 resigned his fellowship at Oriel College.

Clough was appointed head of University Hall, London University, in 1849. Three years later, with the encouragement of Ralph Waldo Emerson, he visited and lectured in the United States. He returned to England in 1854 to accept an appointment as examiner in the government education office. He later served as secretary to a commission reporting on military schools on the Continent. During this time he helped Florence Nightingale, the cousin of his wife, Blanche Smith Clough, in her philanthropic works. He contracted malaria on a trip to Italy and died in Florence on Nov. 13, 1861.

**Writings.** In its tone and its attitude toward Victorianism, much of Clough's work is closer to the modern temper than to that of his own day. The form of his poetry is rough, even in his best works—*The Bothie of Tober-na-Vuolich* (1848) and *Amours de Voyage* (1858).

Clough's posthumous *Poems* (1862) enjoyed immense popularity and were reprinted 16 times before the end of the 19th century. This vogue died down at the start of the 20th century. There was later a revival of interest in the work, particularly among academic critics, who admired the adventurousness of Clough's style and his grasp of the intellectual concerns of his time.

         DAVID GALLOWAY
         *Author of "The Absurd Hero"*

**CLOUZOT,** kloō-zō', **Henri-Georges** (1907–1977), French film director. He was born on Nov. 20, 1907, at Niort, and attended the University of Paris, from which he received a law degree. His early positions in films included work with director Anatole Litvak and with German film companies in Berlin. He began directing motion pictures in the 1940's and gained international renown with the thrillers *Wages of Fear* (1951) and *Diabolique* (1954). For the latter he was awarded the Prix Louis-Delluc. Clouzot's later films included *Le Mystère Picasso* (1956; Cannes film festival special award); *Les Espions* (1957); *La Vérité* (1960; Grand Prix du Cinéma Français); and *L'Enfer* (1965). His first wife, Véra Amado, appeared in *Diabolique;* she died in 1963. He was married again, to Inès de Gonzales, in 1965. He died in Paris on Jan. 12, 1977.

**CLOVE,** klōv, the dried, unopened flower bud of the clove tree (*Syzygium aromaticum*). Cloves have long been valued for their spicy flavor. They were used in China as early as the 3d century B. C. and were introduced into Europe during the Middle Ages.

Cloves, either whole or ground, are used as a pickling spice as well as a flavoring in many foods. They are also used in flavoring vermouth and in the Orient as an ingredient in some chewing and smoking tobaccos. Clove oil is a colorless or pale yellow to amber-colored oil obtained by the distillation of broken cloves, leaves, and unripe fruits. It is used as a clearing agent in the preparation of slides for microscopic examination and as an antiseptic in dentistry. About 85% of clove oil is eugenol, a product that may also be obtained from the oils of other trees, including

**CLOVE BUDS** are picked before the flowers open (*top photo*) and are dried (*bottom photo*) before marketing.

AMERICAN SPICE TRADE ASSOCIATION

WALTER DAWN, FROM NATIONAL AUDUBON SOCIETY

the cinnamon and the bay, or laurel, tree. Eugenol is used in the manufacture of perfumes and synthetic vanillin.

The clove tree is an evergreen tree with smooth gray bark. Cultivated trees usually range in height from 25 to 40 feet (7.5–12 meters), but wild trees may attain a height of 60 feet (18 meters) or more. The trees are grown from seed and begin to produce flowers when about 8 or 9 years old. They continue to produce flowers for 50 years or more. The buds are picked by hand and are dried in the sun until they shrivel and turn dark brown. Clove trees thrive in fertile loamy soils at altitudes up to 2,000 feet (600 meters) in tropical regions having an annual rainfall between 50 to 70 inches (1,300–1,800 mm).

It is believed that the trees were originally native to the Moluccas (Spice Islands) and were later introduced into many other tropical regions. Now, however, clove trees are extensively cultivated only in a few areas of the tropics. The world's leading producer of cloves and clove oil today is the island of Zanzibar. It and the neighboring island of Pemba produce about 90% of the world's total clove supply. Other exporters of cloves and clove oil are Indonesia, Madagascar, and the Indian Ocean islands of Seychelles and Réunion.

LAWRENCE ERBE
*University of Southwestern Louisiana*

**CLOVER,** klō'vər, is the common name for plants of the genus *Trifolium* of the pea, or legume, family (Leguminosae). *Trifolium* derives its name from the Latin words *tres* (three) and *folium* (leaf), since most *Trifolium* species normally exhibit leaves composed of three leaflets. Such leaves are known botanically as "trifoliolate leaves." The term "clover" is also used as part of the common name for some plants closely related to *Trifolium* that have similar trifoliolate leaves.

**General Characteristics.** True clovers are herbaceous annual or perennial plants and thrive under cool, moist conditions. Many annual species of clover behave as winter annuals (they germinate in the fall and live through winter) in areas with mild, moist winters and as summer annuals at northern latitudes and high elevations. Perennial clovers persist best at more northern or southern latitudes or at higher elevations. Some species, especially those from Africa, lack winterhardiness.

Clovers are dicotyledonous (the embryo plant has two seed leaves, or cotyledons). The germinating seedling characteristically produces a tap root and, in sequence, the two cotyledons, a unifoliolate ("one leaflet") leaf, and the first of many trifoliolate leaves.

All true clovers have flowers in dense clusters (heads) and one or a few seeds per seed pod. Taxonomy (classification) of species is based on the structure of flowers and seed pods. Flowering occurs only under proper conditions of growth, photoperiod (relative proportions of daylight and dark), and temperature. Flower color of species varies from white to yellow to pink, red, and purple and includes the intermediate shades. The number of flowers (florets) per flowering head varies from 3 to 200, depending on the species.

Species of clover may be self- or cross-fertilized. Cross-pollination is by insects, mostly bumblebees and honeybees. Clover seed, depending on the species, varies greatly in size and seed color varies from pale yellow to purple to black.

**Cultivation and Use.** Clovers are grown alone or in combination with other legumes or grasses and are used for hay, pasture, soilage (green fodder), silage ("fermented" fodder), and soil fertility and conservation purposes. Establishment (seeding and cultivation) of plants in culture is in early spring or fall, depending on climatic conditions and competition with weeds. Methods of culture and harvest are similar to those of most small-seeded forage legumes.

**Origin.** All clovers of major economic importance appear to have originated in the Mediterranean and Middle Eastern regions. Distinct groups of species also appear to be native to the highlands of eastern Africa and to western North America. A few species are indigenous to eastern North America and to South America. Most authorities cite the genus as containing 200 to 300 species.

**Mediterranean and Middle Eastern Species. White Clover.** White clover (*T. repens*) is a perennial that grows by means of stolons, or runners. It is of great value as a grazing plant. It is probably the most nutritious of all forage legumes and is adapted to all areas of the world with adequate moisture and temperate climate. Its ecotypes (groups that are genetically adapted to certain environments), which range in height from 2 to 20 inches (5 to 50 cm), vary in shape and size of leaves. The trifoliolate leaves have long leafstalks (petioles) and are without hairs (glabrous). The stolons root at their joints, or nodes, and each node is capable of producing a flower stalk or stolon branch. In the largest ecotypes, branching of stolons produces a radial growth of 3 feet (1 meter) or more from the plant's center, resulting in 6-foot-wide (2-meter) clumps. The leaflets are stalkless (sessile), with finely toothed margins; they may exhibit white V-shaped marks, red pigments, or no markings. Flowers are white to pinkish, with 20 to 150 florets per head. The seed pod of a floret may contain 1 to 7 yellow or, occasionally, brown to red, seed. *T. occidentale* is similar to a small ecotype of *T. repens* but is self-fertile and a diploid species.

**Red Clover.** This species (*T. pratense*) is an upright perennial of great value as a hay plant and is used to a lesser extent for grazing. The species is adapted to temperate climates from the Equator to the Arctic. Its pattern of growth form varies from a rosette of basal leaves to upright, flowering stems. Ecotypes in America exhibit hairy (pubescent) stems and leaves, while those of northwest Europe are glabrous: this difference is attributed to natural selection for resistance to leafhopper insects in America. The plant may be 3 feet (1 meter) in height, with many stems and flowering heads. Flowering heads usually contain 50 to 125 florets of rose-purple or magenta color. The mitten-shaped seed varies from yellow to purple in color. Leaflets are oblong, usually with a light-colored marking in the center.

**Alsike Clover.** An upright perennial hay and pasture plant, alsike clover (*T. hybridum*) is especially adapted to cool climates and to wetter, more acid soils. Stems and leaves are glabrous; flower heads resemble those of white clover, but with more pinkish flowers; seeds vary in color from yellow to green. The taxonomist Linnaeus thought the species originated as a hybrid between white and red clovers; hence the name *hybridum.*

**Other Perennial Species.** Among the other perennial species of some economic value or poten-

THREE SPECIES OF CLOVER: (Left) rabbitfoot clover (*Trifolium arvense*); (center) red clover (*Trifolium pratense*); (right) hop clover (*Trifolium agrarium*).

tial to the United States are strawberry clover (*T. fragiferum*), which is stoloniferous (has stolons) and somewhat like white clover, with flower heads resembling those of a strawberry. It is adapted to extremely wet, alkaline, and saline soils of the western United States; kura clover (*T. ambiguum*), which is the only known species of the genus failing effectively to nodulate (form bacteria-filled root swellings) in the field and which spreads by vigorous rhizomes (underground stems); and zigzag clover (*T. medium*), which is also rhizomatous (bears rhizomes), similar to red clover in many ways, and distinctive by the zigzag (bent at every node) habit of the stems.

**Crimson Clover.** Crimson clover (*T. incarnatum*) is an upright, winter-annual hay, pasture, and soil conservation plant adapted to areas of humid and mild winters such as the southeastern United States. Leaves and stems are very pubescent. Flower heads are pointed and conical in shape, with 75 to 125 florets per head; flower color is characteristically crimson. Seeds are yellow and roundish. Arrowleaf clover (*T. vesiculosum*) is a late-maturing winter annual, and derives its common name from the pronounced white V-markings on its leaflets. Leaflets and flower heads are large, and plants may exceed 3 feet (1 meter) in height. Stems are solid, often purple, and fibrous and hard at maturity. Florets, 150 to 170 per head, are white to purple, and each produces 2 to 3 brown seeds.

**Other Winter Annuals.** Other winter-annual species include small hop (*T. dubium*), hop (*T. agrarium*), and large hop (*T. campestre*) clovers. These species, which are characterized by small, round, yellow flower heads resembling the pistillate (female) cones of the hop plant (*Humulus lupulus*), grow to a height of 10 to 20 inches (25 to 50 cm) and are primarily pasture plants on infertile soils. Many authorities consider *T. dubium* to be the original "Irish shamrock."

Rose clover (*T. hirtum*) is adapted to Mediterranean-like climates and is used primarily for grazing. Plants are pubescent and are characterized by rose-colored flower heads.

Subclover (*T. subterraneum*) is an especially important pasture plant of Australia; ripening seed heads develop fishhook-shaped appendages which bury some of the seed heads into the soil, hence the name. Its seed, the largest of any clover, are blueblack in color. Stems are decumbent (reclining); the heads have a few cream-colored or pink flowers.

Berseem clover (*T. alexandrinum*) is a winter-annual species of importance in the Nile Valley and resembles alfalfa in growth form. It is winterhardy only in the mildest climates of the United States.

Persian clover (*T. resupinatum*) is of importance in the Middle East and is also adapted to the heavy, moist soils of the Gulf States of the United States. Stems may be 3 feet (1 meter) in height; flower heads are small and flat; flowers are purple; seed pods are inflated, balloonlike capsules easily shattered; and seed are olive-green to black.

Lappa (*T. lappaceum*), knotted (*T. striatum*), and cluster (*T. glomeratum*) clovers are winter-annual pasture plants, adapted to the blackland (alkaline, heavy, and wet) soils of Mississippi and Alabama, the alkaline, heavy clay soils of the Gulf States, and the lighter, moist soils of southern Mississippi, respectively.

Rabbitfoot (*T. arvense*) and narrow-leaved clover (*T. angustifolium*) are common, weedy, annual species with erect, hairy stems, long narrow leaflets, and small pink flowers; they lack leaf markings. Rabbitfoot clover heads appear silky and grayish.

**Native North American Species.** Clover species native to eastern North America, none of commercial importance, include Carolina clover (*T. carolinianum*) and buffalo clover (*T. reflexum*). Carolina clover is extremely short, resembling white clover, and its purplish red flowers give a cast to the associated turf. Buffalo clover is characterized by large light-brown seed heads with reflexed (bent sharply down) florets, giving an umbrella effect. Western North American species of importance on grazing lands include seaside clover (*T. willdenovii*), a rhizomatous perennial tolerant to saline soils; whitetip clover (*T. variegatum*), an annual with purple flowers tipped with white; long-stalked clover (*T. longipes*), similar to alsike clover in appearance and habitat; Fendler clover (*T. fendleri*), a perennial adapted to wet mountain meadows at less than 7,000 feet (2,000 meters); and hollyleaf clover (*T. gymnocarpum*), adapted to semiarid conditions, extremely palatable to sheep, and often found growing beneath sagebrush. Bighead clover (*T. macrocephalum*) and certain other North American species have 5 to 9 leaflets per leaf rather than characteristic trifoliolate leaves.

American alpine species, all located in the high altitude zone of the Rocky Mountains of the United States include *T. dasyphyllum*, *T. attenu-*

*atum, T. brandegei, T. parryi,* and *T. nanum.*
These species are found at altitudes ranging from
7,000 to 13,500 feet (2,000 to 4,000 meters)
above sea level; they are small plants with relatively large flowers, and are exclusively perennial.
A closely related species, *T. lupinaster,* is the
only species known to be indigenous to Japan,
Korea, Manchuria, and northern Asia.

**African Tropical Species.** Species indigenous to
tropical Africa are cited as valuable forage plants
under natural conditions, but conclusions about
their future value in more intensive agriculture
are lacking. Of this group, *T. usambarense* shows
the greatest adaptation to the tropics, occurring
at elevations as low as 2,700 feet (850 meters) at
the Equator. *T. semipilosum,* a perennial species
resembling *T. repens,* holds most promise for the
more temperate regions of the world. *T. bur-
chellianum* is a rhizomatous perennial African
species of promise.

Annual African species of possible economic
importance include *T. tembense,* which is noted
for extreme vigor and rapidity of growth, and *T.
rueppellianum,* which is adapted to poorly
drained areas.

ROBERT C. LEFFEL
*U. S. Department of Agriculture*

**CLOVIO,** klô'vyō, **Giulio** (1498–1578), Italian
painter, who is considered the greatest of Italian
miniaturists and illuminators. He was born in
Grižane, Croatia. He went to Italy to study in
1516 and remained there. He studied art in Rome
and learned illumination from Girolamo de' Libri
in Verona.

Clovio received commissions from kings,
popes, and cardinals. He was a master of both
color and graphic technique, but in his attempt
to create dramatic scenes he sometimes exceeded
the limits of miniature painting.

Clovio's greatest work, the 26 illuminations
for the *Book of the Hours of the Blessed Virgin,*
with covers by Cellini, took nine years to complete. Twelve miniatures of the victories of Emperor Charles V are in the British Museum. The
Vatican Library has an illuminated life of Frederick, Duke of Urbino, and the Pierpont Morgan
Library in New York City has the Farnese *Brevi-
ary.* Clovio died in Rome in 1578.

**CLOVIS I,** klō'vis (466?–511), king of the Franks,
who raised his people to preeminence among the
barbarian tribes of Europe. The early life of
Clovis (a Gallicized form of the Frankish name
*Clodovec*) is almost entirely unknown. In 481,
on the death of his father, Childeric, he became
king of the Salic Franks, who were centered
about Tournai in northeastern Gaul. After extinguishing the last trace of Roman control in this
region, Clovis conquered the Franks along the
Loire and Seine rivers, including those in Paris,
despite resistance there by the Christian population, led by St. Geneviève.

**Religion and Politics.** In 493, Clovis sealed an
entente with Burgundy, his neighbor to the south,
by marrying Clotilda, a niece of Burgundy's joint
kings, Godegisil and Gundebald. The effects of
this marriage went beyond the immediate diplomatic purposes it served. Clotilda was a Catholic,
or orthodox, Christian (although many Burgundians and one of her royal uncles, Gundebald,
were followers of the Arian heresy). Although
Clovis allowed his children to be baptized, he
himself remained pagan until 496. In that year,
while engaged in a battle with the Swabians at
Tolbiac, Clovis vowed to accept Clotilda's God if
He would give him victory. When the Franks
routed the Swabians, Clovis and some 3,000 of
his subjects were baptized.

Political shrewdness as well as piety may have
prompted Clovis' acceptance of Christianity. His
conversion to orthodox Christianity established a
bond between him and the Gallo-Roman Catholics of Burgundy. However, rivalry between Burgundy's two kings tore the realm apart. In 500,
King Godegisil allied himself with Clovis against
the pro-Arian Gundebald. Despite initial victories,
Clovis had to retreat. Gundebald killed Godegisil and reunited the kingdom.

Religion and politics combined more favorably for Clovis in the Visigothic south. Theodoric, the Ostrogothic king of Italy, had evidenced
interest in this region by giving his daughter in
marriage to the Visigothic king, Alaric II. From
506 on, after permanently subduing the Swabians, Clovis launched a series of campaigns against
the Visigoths, ending in the battle of Vouillé, in
which Clovis killed Alaric in hand-to-hand combat. Alaric's grandson retained Septimania, and
Theodoric seized Provence. But the rest of southern Gaul fell to Clovis.

**The Frankish Kingdom.** The victory at Vouillé
brought Clovis from the level of tribal warfare to
that of world politics. The Byzantine emperor,
Anastasius I, who wished to restore his direct
control over Italy, saw that the Franks might be
powerful allies against Theodoric. He therefore
conferred upon Clovis the honorary title and insignia of consul in 508. Under this inducement,
Clovis campaigned in 509 and 510 against Theodoric, who nevertheless kept Provence with
Narbonne.

By war and assassination, Clovis removed
rival Frankish kings, united the Franks, and extended their territories from northern France to
the Mediterranean. However, this achievement
was ephemeral. On his death in Paris on Nov. 27,
511, Clovis' four sons divided his kingdom.

**Clovis and the Church.** Of more permanent importance than Clovis' territorial aggrandizement
was his conversion to Christianity. He was not
the first Frankish convert—Christianity had existed
among the Franks long before this time. Clovis'
conversion did not instantly change his religious
practices or those of his people. Moral and
ethical conversion lagged far behind acceptance
of a new creed.

But the bond between Frankish kings and the
See of Rome was one of the most critical and
lasting elements in medieval history, involving
both antagonism and cooperation between them.
Clovis assumed control over the administration of
the church in his realm. This beginning of a national Frankish church, later incorporated into
the Gallican church, was to lead to centuries of
conflict between the papacy and Frankish and,
later, French kings.

Clovis' precedent for the control of the church
was critical in German history, too. For the
Franks were responsible for the conversion of the
tribes along their eastern frontiers, and these
tribes ultimately adopted Clovis' ideas of the
king's headship over ecclesiastical administration.
The crises of church and state that marked
French and German history until recent times
began on the battlefield of Tolbiac.

K. F. MORRISON
*University of Chicago*

MYLES J. ADLER

RAPHO GUILLUMETTE

CLOWN EMMETT KELLY (above) gained fame as a sad-faced hobo dressed in tatters.

CLOWN LOU JACOB amused audiences by emerging from a small, comic automobile.

**CLOVIS,** klō′vis, a city located in central California, in Fresno county, 7 miles (11 km) northeast of Fresno. Clovis is situated in the San Joaquin Valley, in an agricultural area that grows grapes as well as other fruits. The city has fruit processing plants and manufactures forest products and concrete pipe. Clovis was incorporated in 1912 and is governed by a mayor and a council. Population: 68,468.

**CLOVIS,** klō′vis, a city in eastern New Mexico, the seat of Curry county. Located 178 miles (286 km) southeast of Santa Fe, near the Texas border, the city is a railroad division point and has railroad repair shops. Clovis is a trade and distribution center for wheat and cattle; it manufactures flour and dairy products and has a meat-processing plant. Cannon Air Force Base is nearby.

Clovis was settled in 1907 and incorporated in 1909. It has a commission-manager form of government. Population: 32,667.

**CLOWN,** a comic entertainer who generally depends on elements of visual humor to evoke laughter. An important part of the clown's act is his colorful, often exaggerated, costume and his frequently grotesque makeup. Clowns are usually featured in circuses, where they are great favorites, especially with children.

**Types of Clowns.** There are three basic types of clowns. The neat-faced *traditional clown* wears white makeup that is compounded with a zinc oxide base. The makeup used by the French mime Marcel Marceau is typical of that worn by traditional clowns. The "Auguste," or *grotesque clown,* may be distinguished by his usually ill-fitting, outlandish, and riotously colored costume. The Fratellini brothers of France and the German performer Lou Jacob, with their huge crater-like smiles, highly arched eyebrows, and bulbous noses, are examples of grotesque clowns. *Character clowns* include such types as cops, "rubes," and tramps. Two well-known character clowns are the film comic Charlie Chaplin and the circus performer Emmett Kelly. Kelly's characterization of a sad, wistful tramp has made him world-famous.

**Development of the Art of Clowning.** Clowns learn their art through a purely oral tradition passed down by older members of the profession. They are a living embodiment of the spirit of the great 15th and 16th century Italian *commedia dell' arte,* an improvised form of comedy. The modern clown is a descendant of the *zanni,* or comic servants of the *commedia,* such as the sly and witty Harlequin and the awkward Pedrolino, whose costume of baggy trousers, loose fitting blouse, and wide brimmed or peaked hat is still worn by most clowns.

The English pantomime theater that rose to prominence in the 18th century used these and other *commedia* characters. Gradually the role of "Clown" emerged, first as a stock supporting figure and later as a leading character with words and music in his part. "Clown" became important largely through the English actor Joseph ("Joey") Grimaldi (1778–1837), who gave the character a central position and also devised a special whitefaced makeup, accented with red paint for the part. Both the role of "Clown" or "Joey" and the makeup Grimaldi developed were copied and introduced into the circus.

**Circus Clowns.** The early circus clowns were either skilled equestrian or acrobatic performers, or talking comics. Perhaps the most noted 19th century American circus clown was the witty entertainer Dan Rice, who performed in a one-ring circus. As the American circus departed from the traditional European one-ring show in the latter part of the 19th century, becoming a three-ring entertainment with several acts performed simultaneously, the talking clown could no longer be heard. Clowns then resorted to visual humor, including sight gags, pantomime, and slapstick. The familiar "walk-around," or moving parade of clowns doing gags and stunts, was inspired by the addition of the race course or Hippodrome track that surrounded the three rings in many American circuses.

The clowns of the classic one-ring circus in Europe still offer musical or "talking" gags, generally based on situations in which a clumsy clown tries to emulate a clever clown. The clumsy clown does nothing right and his bumbling, knockabout antics are often hilarious to the appreciative audience.

MEL MILLER
*Ringling Museum of the Circus, Sarasota, Fla.*

**CLUB,** an association of individuals who share some common interest and meet periodically for pleasure or cooperation. Social clubs emphasize eating, drinking, and relaxation in good company and comfortable surroundings; political and professional clubs stress the advancement of the common interest that brings their members together.

Clubs generally have a test of membership, usually acceptability by existing members, who vote on admission and, in the case of social clubs, may exclude, or "blackball," candidates; a hierarchy of elected officers; and a set meeting place. Normally, dues are paid to finance the club's operations.

Men have always gathered into groups outside their own families for cooperation and companionship. Religious, occupational, social, and political groups can be traced back to the ancient world, particularly the urban civilizations of Greece and Rome. During the Middle Ages, religious orders, confraternities, trade guilds, and universities also served social purposes. Although there were antecedents in 15th century and Elizabethan England, the idea of the modern club dates from 17th century England. From English models, clubs of all kinds—social, professional, political, women's, workingmen's, and service clubs—spread throughout the world, especially in the United States.

### ENGLISH CLUBS

The club as a place for eating, drinking, conversation, and sociability developed in England out of the coffeehouse, after coffee was introduced around 1652, but particularly after the Restoration. In 1660 the diarist Samuel Pepys referred to a tavern, the Coffee Club, where he and his friends often gathered for "clubbing." Besides drink, the coffeehouse offered news and the chance to discuss it in days when it was hard to come by. Charles II, complaining of the freedom of speech enjoyed in coffeehouses, issued a proclamation in 1675 that declared them to be resorts of "idle and disaffected persons" who produced "very evil and dangerous effects," and suppressed them. But the resulting public outcry forced him to rescind the decree.

**Social and Specialized Clubs.** As coffeehouses spread throughout London, they gradually acquired different kinds of customers. Merchants who wished to talk business gathered at Lloyd's, soldiers met at Young Man's, stockbrokers at Old Man's, lawyers at the Grecian, and clergymen at Child's. Literary men, who sought a quieter atmosphere, gathered at Will's, where John Dryden often held forth, or Button's, where Joseph Addison ruled. Admission to the coffeehouse was at first open to anyone who paid his entrance fee, but in time the older and more important customers dominated, so that the house grew more private, lost its informality, and became a class or professional stronghold. Older members passed judgment on the acceptability of the new, subscription fees and other rules were fixed, and the coffeehouse transformed itself into a club.

Boodle's, which opened in 1762, devoted itself to fine eating and card games. Less sedate was Brooks', a gaming place from its beginning in 1778. It numbered both eminent literary figures like Edward Gibbon, Richard Sheridan, and Horace Walpole and political rakes such as Charles Fox and the Prince of Wales (later George IV).

Not all 18th century clubs resembled these, however. The Literary Club grew out of casual but frequent meetings of literary men with the artist Sir Joshua Reynolds. It was founded formally in 1764 and its select membership included Samuel Johnson, Edmund Burke, and Oliver Goldsmith.

In the 19th century social and professional clubs multiplied and grew even more specialized. The Athenaeum, founded in 1824, was intended as a club for established authors, scientists, artists, bishops, and judges. It constructed an impressive building and housed an important library.

Other specialized clubs still in existence include the United Service, established in 1816 for military officers; the Travellers' (1819), a meeting place for British and foreign diplomats; the Oriental (1824), for returning East Indian officials; the Cambridge and Oxford University (1830), for graduates of those schools; the Garrick (1831), organized by actors; the Farmers' (1842), for agriculturalists; the St. James's (1859), for members of the diplomatic corps; the Naval and Military (1862), for officers; the Arts (1863), gathering those in art, literature, and science; the Authors' (1891), a meeting place for writers; and the Royal Air Force (1919), for aviators.

Clubs devoted to specific pastimes also appeared. The Portland Club (1816) devotes itself to bridge, while the London Fencing (1848), Alpine (1857), Turf (1868), Cyclists' Touring (1878), Royal Cruising (1880), Flyfishers' (1884), Golfers' (1893), Bath (for swimming, 1896), Royal Automobile (1897), Royal Aero (1901), and Roehampton (for polo, 1902) clubs advance their special interests.

Though English club life was severely affected by World War II and the postwar austerity, it regained much of its glamour and vigor with the revival of prosperity in the late 1950's and the 1960's. The Betting and Gaming Act of 1961 also stimulated the appearance of new gambling clubs. Another significant change was the admittance of women for the first time to some formerly all-male establishments.

**Women's Clubs.** At the outset, women were excluded from English club life. Only in 1883 was a separate ladies' club, the Alexandria, established. It excluded men from its premises. (Even the future Edward VII was forced to wait outside for his wife, Princess Alexandra.) Later women's clubs include the University Women's (1887); the Pioneer (1892); the Ladies' Empire (1902); the London Lyceum, for arts and literature (1904); the Ladies' Carlton (1906); the Women's United Services (1920); the Cowdray, for professional women and nurses (1922); and the Women's Press Club (1944).

**Workingmen's Clubs.** Special clubs for workingmen also developed in the 19th century. Except for mechanics' institutes designed to educate the worker, and public houses, which encouraged drunkenness, no facilities existed for workingmen until the Rev. Henry Solly founded the Working Men's Club and Institute Union in 1862. At first a temperance organization supported by wealthy philanthropists, its democratic membership eventually voted to serve beer and liquor. Besides offering quiet relaxation, it promoted adult education. Political reform acts and the growth of labor unions increased the number of workingmen's clubs in major industrial towns, which offered both indoor and outdoor activities for members.

**Political Clubs.** Almost from the beginning, conversation at coffeehouses included discussion of politics, and the houses became meeting places for political and conspiratorial gatherings. The Rota, or Coffee Club, founded in 1659, served as a kind of debating society for spreading republican opinions. Members included James Harrington, author of *Oceana,* who lectured on the advantages of a commonwealth.

The king's Head Club, a rowdy group dedicated to combating "papism," appeared during the Restoration. Members identified each other by green ribbons worn in their hats. The Treason Club, composed of opponents of James II, met at the Rose Tavern and was instrumental in helping to overthrow the King and install William of Orange. The Glorious Revolution of 1688 crystallized Whig and Tory factions and their separate clubs.

The Kit-Cat Club, formed around 1700 by supporters of the House of Hanover, included such Whig leaders as the dukes of Somerset, Richmond, Grafton, and Marlborough. During Queen Anne's Tory ministry (1710–1714), it was considered an opposition stronghold. Their Tory rivals, more rural and churchly, were less prominent in club activity. But the October and Saturday clubs, dating from 1710, brought Tories together for enjoyment and to plan common action. Two other contemporary clubs, the Brothers and the Scriblerus, while not purely political, were made up of Tory men of letters, notably Jonathan Swift, who wrote and patronized polemical literature in their cause. Political clubs faded away during the long period of Whig supremacy following the accession of the Hanoverian line.

Only in the last quarter of the 18th century did the stimulus of parliamentary reform revive real club activity. Groups like the Society for Promoting Constitutional Information, to which members were elected by ballot and paid a large subscription, were active in the 1780's. The centennial of the Revolution of 1688 and the outbreak of the French Revolution the next year prompted the growth of numerous new clubs throughout England and Scotland. Many of them corresponded with and sent delegates to the French Jacobin club. But events in France, growing government fears of domestic unrest, and finally the outbreak of war in 1793 led to prosecutions and repressive legislation. Even more effective in stifling political clubs was the resurgence of popular patriotism, which turned against reform and lasted through the Revolutionary and Napoleonic wars.

True political parties and their clubs developed as a result of the movement for parliamentary reform in the late 1820's and early 1830's. The Reform Club, established by Whig members of Parliament in 1832, was intended to rally support for the Great Reform Bill. Its quarters, opened in 1837, surpassed all others in size and magnificence and served as the meeting place for Whig and Liberal adherents throughout the century. The rival Carlton Club was formed in 1832 around the Duke of Wellington and his friends and became a citadel of Toryism. Through its elegant halls passed the leaders of the party, notably Disraeli and Lord Salisbury. An offshoot for younger members, the Junior Carlton, appeared in 1864. The destruction of the Carlton Club building by German bombs in 1940 and the triumph in 1945 of the Labour party, which had no club tradition, reduced the power and prestige of the club. After World War II the Conservative party relied on the annual party conference, but the club spirit still prevailed, especially in the choice of leadership.

## CONTINENTAL EUROPEAN POLITICAL CLUBS

Elsewhere in Europe political parties and clubs evolved out of the French Revolution. Numerous reading societies, smoking clubs, Masonic lodges, and literary salons had existed earlier. But these were largely confined to the upper classes and served primarily social functions, although discussion of the issues of the day did take place.

The meeting of the Estates-General in May 1789 precipitated the formation of political clubs. At Versailles deputies from Brittany met in a Breton Society. When the royal family was taken to Paris, the deputies followed. There the club established itself as the Society of the Friends of the Constitution, but soon became known as the Jacobins (q.v.). It gradually acquired branches in the provinces and acted as a center for news, propaganda, and action. By 1793 it had become the dominant club, with some one million members, largely respectable lawyers, shopkeepers, and independent craftsmen who had time and interest for politics.

After the fall of Robespierre, clubs lost their influence; the Jacobin club was closed in 1794, its members persecuted. The French constitution of 1795 specifically banned political clubs. But under the Directory, both neo-Jacobin organizations and royalist clubs appeared to carry on the work of left and right respectively. The government closed the former in 1796, while the latter vanished after the coup of 18 Fructidor (Sept. 4, 1797).

The spread of the Revolution brought political clubs to Holland, Belgium, the Rhineland, Switzerland, and Italy after 1792. They served as meeting places for radical patriots and republicans. None survived Bonaparte's rise to power in 1799, and clubs as such disappeared from France for half a century.

The success of the February Revolution of 1848 saw a proliferation of political clubs in Paris and the provinces. Sparked by the acute social and economic crisis, they served as forums for debate and aroused popular action. But they were closed in the repression following the workers' uprising in June. Revolutionary clubs emerged simultaneously in Germany, Austria, and Italy, and suffered the same fates in 1849.

Political clubs reappeared in France after the proclamation of the Republic in 1870. Varying from Blanquist to Jacobin and Socialist, all became the focus for debates on political, social, and military questions. However, the collapse of the Commune in 1871 ended political club activity in France.

## AMERICAN CLUBS

Development of clubs in America was slower than in England because of the small and rural population. The earliest social club, the "State in Schuylkill," or Fish House Club of Philadelphia, was formally organized in 1732. In New York City, the Social Club (1776) gathered the town's leading Tories and British officers on duty there. Club life began to flourish after the Revolution. Besides benevolent groups like the Society of the Friendly Sons of St. Patrick (1784) appeared the aristocratic, hereditary Society of the

Cincinnati (1783) and the more democratic Sons of St. Tammany (1789). Purely social were the Krout Club, its members descendants of early Dutch settlers, and the Turtle Club, composed of "solid men" of New York City, who met annually to feast in the groves of Hoboken, N. J. The Sans-Souci Club of Boston (1785) held "tea assemblies" for drinking and dancing.

Political clubs appeared during the 1790's as a result of popular support for the French Revolution. The French ambassador Edmond Genêt capitalized on this, helping to establish several clubs. One, the Democratic Society of Philadelphia, became a mother society for some 40 clubs dedicated to the extirpation of aristocracy and monarchism. Their "Jacobin" activity frightened the Federalists and was partly responsible for the passage of the Alien and Sedition Acts in 1798.

**Social and Specialized Clubs.** It was not until the 19th century that various specialized clubs, based on English models, appeared in the United States, notably in New York. There the Union Club, for socially prominent gentlemen, was founded in 1836. It was followed by the Century Club, for arts and letters (1847); the University Club (1865); the Knickerbocker Club (1871); the Salmagundi Club, for artists (1871); the Lambs Club, for actors (1874); the Racquet Court Club (1875); the United Service Club (1889); the Metropolitan Club (1891); and the Explorers' Club (1912). The Civil War period saw the establishment of the Union League Club (1863), formed to support the Union war effort, and it became a Republican stronghold; the Manhattan Club (1865) supported the Democratic party.

Boston in the same era witnessed the rise of the Handel and Haydn Society, for choral music (1815); the Temple Club, a social organization (1829); the Tremont and its successor, the Somerset Club (1851), patterned on English examples; the Union Club, a patriotic organization (1863); the Boston Yacht Club (1866); the St. Botolph, for literary and artistic figures (1880); and the Algonquin, Tavern, and Puritan clubs, all formed in 1886. The Country Club of Brookline, Mass., was organized in 1882; with its outdoor recreational facilities, it became the prototype of thousands of similar clubs in the United States and elsewhere.

Washington, D. C., has its Metropolitan Club (1872); Cosmos Club, for scientists, men of letters, and artists (1878); Army and Navy Club (1885); Gridiron Club, for correspondents (1885); and University Club (1904.

**College Clubs.** In addition to Greek letter societies, fraternities, and sororities, virtually every American college and university possesses club organizations on campus devoted to specialized activities. These include glee clubs, sports clubs, dramatic societies, as well as religious and denominational groups.

Social clubs outside the fraternity system are rare except at a few older institutions. At Harvard ten "final" clubs evolved out of chapters of fraternities that dropped their national ties and became independent. The oldest, Porcellian, dates from about 1791. In addition, the Hasty Pudding Club (1770) stages amateur theatricals each year. At Yale there are secret societies for seniors, the oldest being Skull and Bones (1832). At Princeton, eating clubs, with membership limited to juniors and seniors chosen by the "bicker" sys-

tem of interviewing to weed out and select candidates, came to dominate social life at the university. Their restrictive policies were attacked by the university's president, Woodrow Wilson, in 1907, but his plan to abolish them failed, and the clubs remained an integral part of Princeton undergraduate life. Graduates of major colleges and universities also maintain clubs in principal cities, offering lodging and hospitality to their members.

**Social Service Clubs.** More widespread and representative than purely social clubs are clubs devoted to community service. Usually composed of professional and businessmen, these are generally national, if not international, in scope and have impressively large memberships. Oldest of these is Rotary International (q.v.), founded by Paul P. Harris in 1905. It began as a weekly luncheon club to foster sociability and contacts among business and professional men in Chicago. By 1907 community service was made an integral part of its activities. The organization took as its motto "Service above self—He profits most who serves best." As the clubs spread to foreign countries, Rotary also devoted itself to promoting international goodwill.

The success of Rotary led to the establishment of other such clubs. Kiwanis International (q.v.), organized in 1915 by a group of professional and businessmen, also has its weekly luncheon, but its chief purpose is to render service in the fields of vocational guidance, social welfare, public affairs, and business organization. Kiwanis sponsors Key Club International for high school boys (1925) and Circle K International for college men (1955).

The Lions International (q.v.), begun by Melvin Jones in 1917, is the nation's largest service organization. It emphasizes citizenship and civic improvement, education, safety, and aid to underprivileged children, the blind, and other handicapped persons.

**Women's Clubs.** As in England, special clubs for women developed in the 19th century. The Sorosis Club of New York (1868) and the Ladies' New York Club, "of women, for women, by women," (1889), were among the first. The National Federation of Women Clubs, formed in 1890 to unite and promote the common interests of such organizations, had some 11,000,000 members in the late 1960's.

Women's social service clubs are a product of the 20th century. Notable examples are Zonta International (1919) and the Soroptimist Federation of the Americas (1921), for executive women; and the American Woman's Association (1922), for business and professional women. The National Federation of Business and Professional Women's Clubs (1919) promotes the interests of women in the professions.

See also FRATERNAL SOCIETIES; FRATERNITIES AND SORORITIES; SECRET SOCIETIES.

JAMES FRIGUGLIETTI
*Case Western Reserve University*

**Bibliography**
Christen, Dorothy, *How to Survive Belonging to a Club* (Tolvan 1979).
Leibers, Arthur, *Leiber's Guide* (Morrow 1977).
Martin, Theodora P., *The Sound of Our Own Voices: Women's Study Clubs* (Beacon Press 1987).
White, Ted, *Club Operations and Management* (Van Nostrand Reinhold 1983).
Whiteman, Maxwell, *Gentlemen in Crisis* (Union League of Pa. 1975).
Wolfers, E. E., and Evansen, Virginia B., *Organizations, Clubs, Action Groups* (St. Martin's 1981).

CLUB MOSS

The two species shown are
(left to right) Lycopodium
complanatum and L. obscu-
rum (the ground pine).

**CLUB,** a cudgel or heavy, blunt weapon made of any of a variety of materials and used to deliver a crushing blow. The club is probably the most primitive of all weapons, and hunters through the ages have used it in various forms to kill small animals caught in snares or large ones wounded by spears or arrows. It is also used for throwing or for close-combat fighting.

Clubs may differ greatly, and range in form from the plain, fire-hardened wooden ones used by the American Indians of the Southwest, to complicated ones such as the elaborately carved clubs of Polynesia and the Pacific Northwest. Frequently a single material—traditionally wood, bone, horn, or stone—is used in making a club. A club can, however, have a stone or metal head with a hole in it hafted onto a wooden handle. Aztec clubs were set with blades of volcanic glass, and those of the Maori often had sharp-edged insets of bone and nephrite.

The club has frequently been used as a throwing weapon. The Tasmanians hunt with a fire-hardened throwing stick, and throwing clubs are widespread in Africa, Polynesia, and among the Eskimos. The Australian fighting boomerang and the returning boomerang, which is used for hunting birds, are varieties of throwing clubs. See BOOMERANG.

In the more advanced cultures that have more sophisticated methods of hunting and fighting, the club has ceased to be an implement in daily use and has taken on a more symbolic or ceremonial function. In Scandinavia, even as long ago as the Viking era, the club was not in ordinary use, but was regarded as a legendary weapon. In Norse sagas, for example, it is often mentioned as used by giants.

With the progress of the Iron Age and the wide range of metal battle arms which were developed, the club became less effective as a fighting weapon. Its use in warfare was continued only in single combat between similarly armed adversaries.

PRISCILLA C. WARD
*The American Museum of Natural History*

**CLUB MOSS** is the common name for a group of about 200 species of nonseed plants constituting the genus *Lycopodium* of the order Lycopodiales. Club mosses are not true mosses, but are related to the quillworts and to a large number of extinct plants. Most club mosses are tropical but some are widespread in northern temperate regions. The plants grow in moist, shady places,

either on soil or as epiphytes (attached, but non-parasitic) on the bark of trees.

Modern club mosses are the remnants of a group, the subphylum Lycopsida, that was extremely important during past geological ages. The Lycopsida included large trees (Lepidodendrales), some more than 100 feet (30 meters) tall, with well-developed woody tissues. They dominated the earth's landscape during the Carboniferous period, about 300 million years ago, when the great coal deposits were being formed. Only four or five genera of the Lycopsida have survived to the present—among them the modern club moss genus.

Club mosses are small plants, generally less than 12 inches (30 cm) high, with either erect or pendent stems or prostrate stems that bear erect branches. The leaves are small and evergreen and in many species are numerous enough to obscure the stem.

In some species the leaves near the tip, or apex, of the stems look like ordinary vegetative leaves, but in others the terminal leaves are smaller and more compactly arranged to form a cone-like structure called a strobilus. Spore cases (sporangia) develop in the axils (upper angle between leaf and stem) of these terminal cones or in the axils of the ordinary vegetative leaves toward the stem apex. The contents of the sporangia develop into spores, which drop to the supporting surface and begin to grow. The new plants are known as the gametophyte stage because they produce gametes—sex cells—instead of spores. The gametophytes are very small, ranging from pinhead size to about 1 inch (25 mm). They may lie on the surface of the ground, contain green chlorophyll, and mature within months; or they may be partially or completely below ground, colorless, and mature after 6 to 15 years of funguslike existence. In either case, development depends on the entrance into the minute plants of a microscopic fungus (a phycomycete) that helps them obtain nourishment.

Male sex organs (antheridia), which produce sperm cells, and female sex organs (archegonia), which develop one egg cell each, are borne on the same gametophyte near its apex. The sperm cells are equipped with whiplike flagella that enable them to move through a film of water into the egg case and effect fertilization. The plant that develops as the result is the familiar club moss (technically the sporophytic stage) of northern forests.

RICHARD S. COWAN, *Smithsonian Institution*

**CLUBFOOT,** the most common of all orthopedic congenital deformities involving the foot. The name is derived from the clublike appearance of the foot because of its inward and downward twisting. In medical terminology, the deformity is known by the Latin designation *talipes equinovarus.*

There are three component deformities of a clubfoot: an inward turning of the front of the foot, an inward turning of the heel, and a downward tilt to the entire foot at the ankle joint. The foot is held tight in this position and resists manual efforts made to push it into a normal position.

**Causes.** In most instances, a clubfoot is a congenital deformity, that is, present at birth. It is estimated that it occurs in about one out of every 1,000 births, and it affects males more frequently than females. There is some evidence to support a genetic basis for the disorder; a definite family history of the deformity has been noted. Although clubfoot usually occurs as an isolated deformity affecting one foot or both, it may also be only one of many deformities in a single patient.

Occasionally a clubfoot is not congenital but occurs after birth. It may be due to a muscle imbalance caused by a neurological disease, such as poliomyelitis, or by a disorder of the spinal cord, such as meningomyelocele. (Meningomyelocele is a hernial protrusion of the meninges and part of the spinal cord through a defect in the spinal column.)

**Treatment.** The treatment of a clubfoot is based on complete correction of the three component deformities, using plaster casts to keep the foot in its proper position until the danger of a recurrence is past. Treatment should begin as soon after birth as possible. A very resistant clubfoot may require surgery to release soft tissue contracture (stiffening) or to redirect abnormally placed tendons so that they pull in a normal direction. In older children, surgery involves operating on the bones to correct deformity and fuse the joints together to keep the foot in a straight position.

JOHN J. GARTLAND, M.D.
*Jefferson Medical College*

**CLUBROOT,** a serious disease of plants of the mustard family (Cruciferae), which contains the cabbage, turnip, kale, and rutabaga. It is caused by the slime fungus, or slime mold, *Plasmodiophora brassicae.* The disease is often called finger-and-toe or Anbury disease.

Clubroot attacks only the underground portions of the plant. The root's vascular system undergoes repeated cell division (hyperplasia) to form knobby, clublike shapes on the roots, which give the disease its name. The attacked plant is not immediately killed, but becomes stunted and weakened, wilting on hot days. The swollen roots rot, giving off an unpleasant odor.

Planting of specially resistant strains is the main control measure. Soil fungicides are also used.

ROBERT W. SCHERY
*Lawn Institute, Marysville, Ohio*

**CLUJ-NAPOCA,** kloozh-nä-pô′kä, a city in northwestern Romania, situated in the foothills of the Apuşeni mountains on the Someşul Mic River. Cluj-Napoca (Hungarian, Kolozsvár; German, Klausenburg), which is the administrative center of the Cluj region, underwent great changes following 1945 with the growth of industry in and around the city. In the 1970s the city of Cluj was united with its neighbor, Napoca. The city's economy is fueled principally by heavy and light industries.

Lying on the main road from the Hungarian plain through Transylvania to Wallachia and the Black Sea, Cluj was historically the most important city in Transylvania. It was the site of Stone Age, Dacian, and Roman settlements. The establishment of the present-day city is ascribed to a German settlement in the 13th century. Although Cluj-Napoca now has a predominantly Romanian character, it has had in the past strong Hungarian political, cultural, and social influences. In the 17th century, Cluj, with the rest of Transylvania, was incorporated into the Habsburg empire; after 1867 the city and the province passed under direct Hungarian control. After 1918, Cluj became a part of Romania; however, during World War II, the city was once more placed under Hungarian rule.

Cluj-Napoca is one of the most attractive cities in eastern Europe and has a vigorous cultural life. It is an educational center; a branch of the Romanian Academy and the Babeş-Bolyai University are located there. The principal architec-

Cluj-Napoca is the second-largest city in Romania and an important cultural, historical, and industrial center.

tural monument is the 14th-century Gothic Cathedral of St. Michael, which dominates the central square of the city. Population: city, 328,008 (1992 census); region, 735,100 (1992 census).

BARBARA JELAVICH and CHARLES JELAVICH
*Indiana University*

**CLUMBER SPANIEL,** klum'bər span'yəl, the heaviest of the field spaniels in the working group of dogs. The long, low, heavy body of the clumber spaniel has power rather than speed; the dog works slowly but steadily in the field and can be trained to be a good retriever. Its body stands 16 to 21 inches (40 to 50 cm) at the shoulder and weighs 35 to 65 pounds (16 to 30 kg). The straight and fairly silky coat is white with lemon markings. The ears are long and the tail is very short.

The breed originated in the kennels of the Duke of Newcastle, whose country estate—Clumber Park, in Nottingham—gives the breed its

EVELYN M. SHAFER

Clumber spaniel

name. The dog was once a royal favorite and was known as "the aristocrat of the spaniel family." It is a relative curiosity in the United States, the other, faster-moving breeds of spaniel having gained greater popularity. However, although the clumber spaniel lacks the pace, the agility, and the range of the springer spaniel, it is good-tempered and easily trained.

WILLIAM F. BROWN
*Editor, "The American Field"*

**CLUNY,** klü-nē', a town in the department of Saône-et-Loire, France, 12 miles (19 km) northwest of Mâcon. In the Middle Ages, Cluny's Benedictine abbey was one of the most powerful Christian centers in Europe. Though much of the abbey has been destroyed over the centuries, enough of the structure remains to indicate its former glory.

In the early 10th century, William the Pious, Duke of Aquitaine, founded a monastery in this southern part of Burgundy. The fact that it was placed under the direct jurisdiction of the pope permitted the abbey to grow without interference from bishop or king. In time the abbey ruled over a great number of houses and priories that it had established in other parts of Europe, and Cluny's abbots spoke with an authority that

sometimes exceeded that of the popes. As the order spread over Europe, the abbey became richer and in time lax in observing the Benedictine rule.

The abbey church of St. Peter and St. Paul, begun in 1088, was the largest church in Europe until the construction of St. Peter's in Rome. This basilica was one of the finest examples of Romanesque architecture. Following the French Revolution, the abbey was sold to a speculator, and most of the buildings were slowly demolished. Today only the south transept remains. Other buildings still standing include the 13th-century Gothic building known as the façade of Pope Gelasius, the 18th-century cloistral buildings, the 13th-century granary in which some of the abbey's sculptures have been placed, and the 15th-century abbey palace, now the Ochier Museum.

**CLUNY, Hôtel de,** klü-nē', an edifice in Paris, France, housing the Cluny Museum of medieval art. Located on the site of Roman ruins of the 3d century B.C., it was built between 1485 and 1500 by an abbot of the great Benedictine abbey at Cluny in Burgundy and is in the Gothic Flamboyant style.

Used by successive abbots, by royalty, and by papal nuncios, it was sold by the state during the French Revolution. Alexandre du Sommerard, a collector of medieval art, lived there from 1833 until his death in 1842, when the state bought the building and his collection and in 1844 opened the museum.

**Cluny Museum.** One of the museum's greatest treasures is its early 16th century tapestry *The Lady with the Unicorn.* Other celebrated tapestries include a series on courtly life and on the life of St. Stephen. There are also fine altars, including the golden altar of Basel, and stained-glass windows, jewelry, sculpture, and ceramics.

**CLURMAN,** klûr'mən, **Harold** (1901–1980), American director, drama critic, and author. He was born in New York City on Sept. 18, 1901. He graduated from the University of Paris in 1923 and studied with Jacques Copeau in Paris in 1923 and 1924. He returned to New York in 1924 and took a job as an actor at the Greenwich Village Playhouse. He then joined the Theatre Guild as an actor and stage manager, and from 1929 to 1931 he was their play reader. He also studied directing with Richard Boleslavsky.

In 1931, Clurman helped found the Group Theatre, a noncommercial company dedicated to the "group acting" methods of Stanislavsky, and was its managing director until the company dissolved in 1941. He staged most of Clifford Odets' plays for the Group Theatre, and later directed the Broadway productions of plays by Eugene O'Neill, Tennessee Williams, William Inge, and Arthur Miller.

Clurman also reviewed plays for the *Nation,* the *New Republic,* and other periodicals. *Lies Like Truth* (1958), *The Naked Image* (1966), and *The Divine Pastime* (1974) are collections of his reviews and essays. He also published *The Fervent Years* (1945), about the Group Theatre; *On Directing* (1972); *All People Are Famous* (1974), his memoirs; and *Ibsen* (1978). He died in New York City on Sept. 9, 1980.

OSCAR BROWNSTEIN, *University of Iowa*

**CLUSIUM.** See CHIUSI.

**CLUTCH,** a coupling that can be engaged and disengaged as required and used to transmit torque (rotational force) from a driving shaft to a driven shaft. Most clutches are designed to drive an initially stationary shaft from a continuously rotating shaft. Thus, the matching members of the clutch are designed to allow slippage until the driven member is brought up to speed. However, in *positive clutches,* where the matching members are interlocking jaws or teeth, no slippage is possible. The most common positive clutch is the *square-jaw clutch,* which can be engaged only when both members are stationary or moving slowly. *Spiral-jaw clutches* can be engaged at low to moderate speeds, but not without a high shock load being transmitted to the driven member.

**Friction Clutch.** The most common type of clutch is the friction clutch, which is generally placed between an engine and its load. In automobiles, a friction clutch is located to connect the engine to a transmission and the drive shaft.

The *plate,* or *disk, friction clutch,* the type used in automobiles, consists of two sets of disks, or plates, faced with high-friction materials, that rotate around the same axis. One set is attached to a shaft (usually the driven shaft). The driven and driving disks are mounted alternately. When the clutch is engaged, a spring compresses the disks together so that they are brought into contact with the rotating plates. As the driven member is brought up to speed, heat is generated by the slippage between parts. In most automobile clutches, which are run dry, the heat escapes through the clutch housing to the atmosphere. In heavier machinery, the parts of a friction clutch are immersed in circulating oil, which carries off the heat.

Other widely used friction clutches are the *cone clutch* and the *rim clutch.* The members of a cone clutch are matching sections of a cone faced with high-friction materials. As one member is inserted into the other, contact is made and the driven member turned. Cone clutches are used to drive machinery such as hoists from a constantly rotating shaft.

In rim clutches, one member is the rim of a wheel, and the other member consists of shoes that grip either the interior or the exterior of the rim. The shoes are brought into contact with the rim by springs, hydraulic pressure, or rotational forces.

Materials for friction clutches should have a high and uniform coefficient of friction, an ability to withstand the high temperatures and to dissipate the heat generated by slippage, a low response to environmental changes, and a resistance to abrasion. Typical pairs of surfaces are woven asbestos or bronze with chromium-plated steel, molded asbestos with cast-iron or steel, hard steel with hard steel, or powder metal with cast iron.

**Hydraulic Clutch.** Hydraulic clutches, or *fluid couplings,* provide a smoothness of operation not possible with friction clutches or positive clutches. The matching members of a hydraulic clutch are hollow halves of a doughnut shape lined with vanes. The space between them is filled with a viscous fluid that transmits torque from the vanes of the driving member to the vanes of the driven member. A third set of vanes, with adjustable pitch, is placed between the members, and it acts to disrupt the flow of fluid when the clutch is to be disengaged. About 3% to 5% of

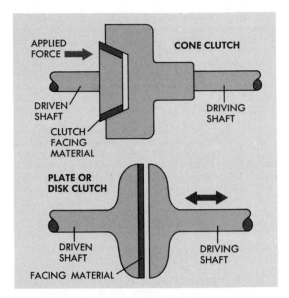

Driven member of the cone clutch turns when it is inserted into driving member. Driven member of the plate clutch turns when driving member is forced against it.

the power input is lost in the form of heat, which must be dissipated to prevent clutch failure.

**Electromagnetic Clutch.** Electromagnetic forces are utilized in a number of clutches. Disk clutches that are engaged by electromagnetic attraction between disks and plates are sometimes called "electromagnetic clutches." *Magnetic powder clutches* are simple disk clutches in which the space between disk and plate is filled with a powder that coalesces into a friction-bearing mass when a magnetic field is applied. A *magnetic fluid clutch* is similar, except that the powder is in an oil suspension. In *eddy current* and *hysteresis clutches,* the mating members are kept together by electromagnetic effects and are not in physical contact.

DONALD N. ZWIEP
*Worcester Polytechnic Institute*

**CLUTHA RIVER,** klōō′thə, in New Zealand, the longest river on South Island. It flows southeast for 210 miles (338 km) to the Pacific Ocean.

The Clutha River drains an agricultural area and supplies water for irrigation. It is navigable by small boats as far as Roxburgh, about 45 miles (72 km) from its mouth. A dam near Roxburgh is an important source of hydroelectric power.

**CLYDE, Baron.** See CAMPBELL, SIR COLIN.

**CLYDE,** Scotland's third-longest river and economically the principal one, flowing through Glasgow. Its source is on the north side of Queensberry Hill (2,285 feet, or 698 meters), Dumfriesshire. Numerous burns (streams) join to form the upper Clyde. Its main headstreams, the Daer and Potrail waters, meet before their confluence with the Clyde Burn, 2 miles (3 km) below Beattock Summit. From here the stream is known as the River Clyde, and after meandering for miles over glacial deposits it forms the four Falls of Clyde—Bonnington, Corra, Dundaff, and Stonebyres Linns, now harnessed for electric power.

Between Glasgow and the sea the river was virtually choked with sandbanks until 1768, the depth of water at Broomielaw in the center of Glasgow being 15 inches (38 cm) at low tide. Extensive dredging began in 1768, but until 1818 no foreign trade vessels came farther than Port Glasgow, about 20 miles (32 km) down the river. In 1836 the river was dredged from Glasgow to Port Glasgow and is now maintained by the Clyde Port Authority as a navigable river with 25 feet (7.6 meters) of water at low tide between Kingston and King George V docks and 20 feet (6 meters) at Broomielaw. Shipbuilding has developed on both banks of the Clyde between Glasgow and Greenock. Below Dumbarton the river is called the Firth of Clyde.

CHARLES W. BLACK
*Mitchell Library, Glasgow, Scotland*

**CLYDEBANK,** klīd′bangk, an industrial burgh and river port in West Dunbartonshire, Scotland, on the north bank of the Clyde, about 7 miles (11 km) northwest of Glasgow. In the latter part of the 19th century it became highly industrialized after the relocation of shipyards downstream from Glasgow. In addition to shipbuilding and ship repair, which are the major activities, there are sewing machine works, engineering works, and other plants. The ocean liners *Queen Elizabeth* and *Queen Mary* were built and launched at Clydebank. Population: 51,832 (1991 census).

**CLYDESDALE,** klīds′dāl, in South Lanarkshire, Scotland, the valley of the upper reaches of the Clyde River. The Clydesdale Valley is about 50 miles (80 km) long. The district is chiefly agricultural and is noted for its orchards and coal and iron mines. Clydesdale is the name of a breed of heavy draft horse that was developed there in the early 18th century. (See also HORSE.) Population: 57,078 (1991 census).

**CLYMER,** klī′mər, **George** (1739–1813), American patriot, who signed both the Declaration of Independence and the U. S. Constitution. He was born in Philadelphia, Pa., on March 16, 1739, and was educated at the College of Philadelphia (later the University of Pennsylvania). He was a prosperous merchant, and he ardently supported the drive for independence. He served as a militia officer, a member of Pennsylvania's committee of safety, a Continental treasurer, and a representative in the Continental Congress (1776–1777 and 1780–1782). First appointed to the Congress to replace a member who had refused to sign the Declaration of Independence, Clymer welcomed the chance to sign the document, and he also served the Revolutionary cause in administrative and fiscal matters. In the Pennsylvania legislature (1784–1788), he worked to bring about penal reform.

At the federal Constitutional Convention of 1787, Clymer was a strong nationalist. He served in the first U. S. Congress (1789–1791). Later he was a federal excise collector in Pennsylvania, which involved him in the Whiskey Rebellion of 1794, and a member of a commission that negotiated a treaty with the Cherokee and Creek Indians in 1796. He then retired from public life and devoted himself to the fine arts and scientific agriculture. He died in Morrisville, Pa., on Jan. 23, 1813.

DON HIGGINBOTHAM
*University of North Carolina*

**CLYNES,** klīnz, **John Robert** (1869–1949), English labor leader and politician. He was born at Oldham on March 27, 1869, and began working in a mill at the age of 10. He rose to power through the General and Municipal Workers Trade Union and was a founding member of the Labour party. Clynes became minister of food (1918) in the Lloyd George government and served under Ramsay MacDonald in the first Labour government (1924) as lord privy seal and deputy leader of the House of Commons. From 1929 to 1931 he was home secretary. He died in London on Oct. 23, 1949.

**CLYTEMNESTRA,** klī-təm-nes′trə, in Greek legend, was the daughter of Tyndareus, king of Sparta, and Leda. She married Agamemnon, king of Mycenae, by whom she had two daughters, Iphigenia and Electra, and one son, Orestes.

During her husband's absence in the Trojan War, Clytemnestra took as her lover Aegisthus, Agamemnon's cousin, who had been entrusted with the management of the kingdom. On Agamemnon's return from the war, Clytemnestra and Aegisthus plotted to kill him. They arranged a banquet in his honor, but before the festivities began they had him killed in his bath.

Clytemnestra and Aegisthus ruled Mycenae for seven years, after which Orestes returned and killed them both. Clytemnestra's story is told in Aeschylus' *Agamemnon* and in the *Electra* plays of Sophocles and Euripides.

**CNIDUS,** nī′dəs, an ancient Greek city on the coast of Caria, in southwestern Asia Minor. Its original site was on the eastern part of the long Triopian peninsula, near modern Datça, Turkey, but in the late 4th century B. C. the city was moved to the isthmus just behind Cape Krio (Tekir), the southwestern tip of Asia Minor. The city had a harbor on either side of the isthmus, one military and one commercial; these were vital to its prosperity since it lay on an important shipping route and ships often had to wait there for a favorable wind to round the dangerous cape. Cnidus also profited from the export of local wine.

Major excavations in 1857–1859 revealed a regular street plan, theaters, temples, and civic buildings. The temple of Aphrodite, which housed the famous statue by Praxiteles, was not found. Excavation recommenced in 1967.

The Cnidians were members of the Dorian Hexapolis, which held regular festivals at Triopion (probably modern Kumyer, east of Cape Krio). Cnidus had to submit to Persia after 546 B. C. and in the 5th century was a member of the Delian League. In 394 the Athenian admiral Conon defeated the Spartan fleet off Cnidus in a famous battle. In the 3d century B. C., Cnidus came under the rule of Egypt, and later perhaps under that of Rhodes. After 48 B. C., Cnidus was a free city within the Roman province of Asia. It possessed a famous school of medicine as well as the observatory of the astronomer Eudoxus.

D. J. BLACKMAN
*University of Bristol, England*

**CNO BI-CYCLE.** See CARBON-NITROGEN-OXYGEN BI-CYCLE.

**CNOSSUS.** See KNOSSOS.

**CNUT.** See CANUTE.

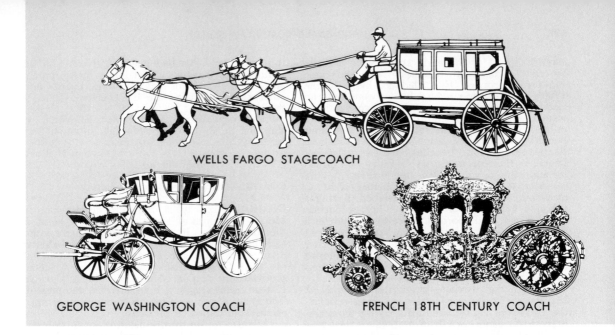

WELLS FARGO STAGECOACH

GEORGE WASHINGTON COACH

FRENCH 18TH CENTURY COACH

**COACH,** a 4-wheeled, closed carriage for the conveyance of passengers, having a roof that forms an integral part of the body. Thus a coach may be distinguished from other vehicles that have folding tops or canopy tops supported by rods or pillars. For greater comfort the body of a coach is suspended on springs that separate it from the wheeled framework of the carriage. Before carriage springs were invented, the earliest coach bodies were suspended from leather straps attached to posts on the framework, or they lacked any form of suspension, merely resting on the carriage.

**European Coaches.** The term "coach" is believed to come from the name of the Hungarian town Kocs (pronounced "kôch"), where a primitive form of coach is said to have developed from a kind of German agricultural wagon. As early as 1457 one of these carriages was sent by King Ladislas of Hungary to the Queen of France, and the fact that it was described as *branlant* ("shaking" or "trembling") causes historians to believe the body was suspended in some manner. During the next 100 years the use of the coach spread throughout Hungary and into Germany, Italy, and the Netherlands. France and England were slow to make use of coaches. In 1560 there were only three coaches in Paris, and the first coaches had been introduced into England only a few years previously. During this early period coaches belonged mainly to royalty and the aristocracy.

During the 17th century, while the coach continued to be a mark of rank or wealth, it also began to be used as a public conveyance between towns and was eventually known as a *stagecoach*, or *stage*. About 1610 a stage service began operating in Scotland between Edinburgh and Leith. About the same time *hackney coaches* (those available for hire) were introduced in London, and in mid-century similar coaches, known as *fiacres*, began service in Paris.

About 1660 another method of suspension was developed in Berlin, Germany, and the name of the city was given to that type of carriage. The front and rear portions of the running part of the *berlin* were connected by two perches, or shafts, in place of the single, very heavy perch formerly employed. Leather thoroughbraces extended from front to back of the berlin, with the

body resting upon them. This construction, however, did not come into extensive use for nearly a century.

Shortly after 1670, elbow springs began to be used to support coach bodies. These were fastened underneath the four corners of the body, and leather braces, hung from posts on the carriage framework, were attached to the ends of these springs. About the same time coach bodies began to depart from the traditional squareness of wagon design. The bodies were carved, paneled, and generally more tastefully designed. Glass windows came into use for both private and public coaches in the late 17th century.

*Refinements.* Improvements during the 18th century produced more attractive and more comfortable coaches. About mid-century the four upright posts to which the leather braces had been attached were replaced by whip-springs or S-springs and by the end of the century by the popular C-springs, which were to continue in use until the end of the 19th century. The coach body, which had been excessively heavy, could then be made much lighter, since the springs, replacing the posts, decreased the effect of road shocks on both the body and the carriage part of the vehicle. For greater maneuverability crane-necked perches were devised to allow the front wheels to pass under the perches, thus permitting sharper turns.

**American Coaches.** In America the first coaches appeared in the last quarter of the 17th century and were used almost exclusively by some of the colonial governors, apparently as a mark of their high office. Gradually, after 1700, other persons of wealth or high rank began to own coaches but the vehicle never came into popular use in America, even in the 19th century. In Massachusetts, in 1753, there were only 6 coaches and 18 chariots (smaller coaches), but there were over 1,300 2-wheeled carriages (chaises and chairs). Coaches were more commonly used in Virginia than in the other American colonies.

Public transport began early in America but developed slowly. As early as 1696 a hackney coach was in operation along the Bowery, in New York City, and in 1716, stages ran from Boston to Newport, R. I. Public coaches, however, were not common in America until after the mid-18th century. Most of the early stages were actually covered wagons with benches inside, and these could not properly be called coaches. By the 1760's some of these wagon bodies were hung on leather thoroughbraces, and the conventional wagon tops were replaced by flat roofs on slender pillars. The driver still sat inside on the front bench. Most of these stage-wagons seated about 12 people on four benches, and only the last bench, in the rear, had a back. Entry was gained through the open front of the wagon.

**Later Developments.** Shortly before 1820 an oval-bodied stagecoach was developed, having a rounded top, a door in one side, an outside driver's seat, and thoroughbrace-suspension on a 3-perch running gear, somewhat reminiscent of the berlin carriage. About a decade later the famous American mail coach was developed almost simultaneously by J. S. Abbot, then employed by Lewis Downing of Concord, N. H., and by several carriage builders in Troy, N. Y. Known as *Concord coaches* and *Troy coaches,* the two were almost identical, having thorough-brace-suspension, swell-sided bodies, flat tops equipped with a luggage rail, an additional luggage rack behind, and a driver's seat high on the front of the coach. Both sides of the coaches had doors, and the passengers faced one another on two transverse seats, with one or two cushioned benches in between for additional passengers. These coaches held from 6 to 16 passengers, exclusive of those who might occupy seats on the roof. Decoration of the exteriors was lavish and brilliant.

After 1800 nearly all the principal cities as far west as Pittsburgh, Pa., were connected by stage lines, and from 1800 to 1840, stagecoaches provided the only means of cross-country travel for a large percentage of the population. In 1832, 106 stage lines ran out of Boston alone. Even after the development of the railroad, in the mid-1800's, coaches continued in importance. There were thousands of them serving beyond and between the railroads, particularly in the west where the railroads were widely separated. Most of these coaches also carried the U. S. mails. During the 19th century the speeds and fares for coach travel varied according to the period and locality, generally running between 4 to 12 miles (6–20 km) an hour at a fare of 3 to 15 cents per mile. Production of coaches did not cease in the United States until about 1910, and service in some remote areas continued as late as the 1920's.

DON H. BERKEBILE, *Smithsonian Institution*

**COACHWHIP SNAKE,** a harmless snake of the southern United States and much of Mexico. Normally it is from 3 to 5 feet (1 to 1.5 meters) long, but it sometimes reaches 8 feet (2.4 meters). In the eastern half of the range, the adult is black or dark brown in the front part of its body and light brown toward the rear, or black all over. Elsewhere, the color and pattern vary greatly. The young are always cross-barred.

The coachwhip inhabits many types of country, but in general it likes hot, dry places. It is active by day. It is agile and alert and sometimes climbs. Coachwhips nearly always make their escape when surprised but will defend themselves vigorously if cornered. As they bite, some jerk their heads, so that lacerations result. The common belief that coachwhips "whip" an adversary, however, is entirely false.

Rarely, a bold coachwhip may advance on an intruder, but it cannot inflict injury by whipping. Small mammals, birds and their eggs, lizards, and other kinds of snakes are the preferred food of the coachwhip.

The coachwhip, *Masticophis flagellum,* is classified in the family Colubridae, suborder Serpentes (Ophida), order Squamata.

CLIFFORD H. POPE
*Author of "The Reptile World"*

**COAGULATION.** See BLOOD–*Clotting.*

**COAHUILA,** kō-ä-wē′lä, the third largest state in Mexico, lies south of Texas along the big bend of the Río Grande. Its area is 58,522 square miles (151,571 sq km). The Sierra Madre Oriental divides the state into a northeastern section, in the Gulf Coastal Plains, and a larger western-southwestern section, within the North Mexican Plateau. Hot steppe and desert climates prevail. The state is rich in minerals and produces most of the coal mined in Mexico.

Manufacturing is the leading sector of the state's economy. The principal activities are the smelting, refining, and processing of metals; the production of chemical fertilizers, sulfuric acid, and coke; food processing; and the manufacture of farm machinery and clothing. Coahuila accounts for about half of Mexico's iron and steel output, with production concentrated at Monclova (1960 population, 43,077). The most populous cities are Torreón (179,901) and Saltillo (98,839), the capital.

Irrigation of the rich silt soils of the Laguna district in the southwest, together with areas of dry farming, give Coahuila an intermediate position in Mexican agriculture. The chief crops are cotton, wheat, maize, grapes, beans, alfalfa, and sorghum. Coahuila is the leading state in production of grapes, wine, and brandy. Cattle and goat raising are also important.

During the colonial period Coahuila was a sparsely occupied ranching, farming, and mining frontier. In 1824 it became one of the original 19 Mexican states. The advent of railroads in the 1880s resulted in the founding of Torreón and a boom in mining. From Coahuila came the first two leaders of the Mexican revolution—Francisco I. Madero and Venustiano Carranza. Population: 2,172,132 (1995 est.).

DONALD D. BRAND
*The University of Texas*

**COAHUILAN SERIES,** kō-ə-wē′lən, the lowest series of rocks in the Cretaceous system. It is named for the Mexican state of Coahuila. The series, laid in the Coahuilan epoch about 130 million years ago, is succeeded by the Comanchean series and is about equivalent to the Neocomian stage of Europe. The term "Coahuilan" is provincial; the equivalent series in California and northward, and in northeastern British Columbia, is called Neocomian.

The typical Coahuilan rock of the Mexican geosyncline in Chihuahua and southeastern Arizona is basal sandstone overlain by limestone. The series is absent farther to the east, but reappears on the coast of the Mexican state of Tamaulipas on the Gulf of Mexico. Coahuilan rocks are not exposed in southern United States, but they have been penetrated by deep wells in northern Louisiana and eastern Texas.

MARSHALL KAY, *Columbia University*

BUREAU OF MINES AND JOY MANUFACTURING COMPANY

MINING with a self-propelled cutter, the operator of this machine can use it to under-cut coal seams as low as 30 inches or to make bottom cuts ranging from 9¾ inches be-low the floor to 21 inches above. Each of the driving wheels has a separate transmission.

# COAL

**COAL** is a rock derived from wood and other plant tissues that flourished several hundred million years ago. Apparently the plants partially decayed and then were covered, preserved, and ultimately compacted by the other sediments that were deposited upon them. Although coals are sometimes described as forms of carbon, this is not strictly true; they are actually intricate mixtures of complex compounds of carbon. Coals differ from one another in composition and properties, and even the various constituents of any one coal may be quite unlike.

Coal as a fuel has played a vital part in the development of industry during the past few centuries. Coke obtained from coal has been used to reduce iron ore to iron for the large-scale manufacture of machinery, and coal has produced power to operate these machines. Today coal is used mainly for generating electric power and making coke for the steel industry, while petroleum-derived fuels and natural gas have displaced coal for some other purposes. In the United States, for example, the railroads have been completely converted to diesel or electric power since the 1930's, and gas has rapidly taken over the burden of domestic heating. Methods for converting coal to liquid and gaseous fuels are known, however, and it seems certain that such manufactured fuels will become important as supplements to petroleum and to natural gas.

## 1. How Coal Was Formed

There is no doubt that coal was formed from the remnants of plants that once flourished in some areas of the earth, since examination of coal through a microscope shows various kinds of plant cell structure. But any description of the circumstances under which these plants grew, died, and were converted to coal, or any attempt to tell just when these events occurred, must of necessity involve some speculation.

**Accumulation of Plant Debris.** Millions of years ago (perhaps about 300 million years for Carboniferous, 100 million for Cretaceous, and somewhat less for Tertiary deposits) the earth's climate and atmospheric composition were particularly favorable for profuse plant growth. There were large areas of level, swampy land or very shallow bodies of water where plants thrived. Generation after generation of swamp plants grew, died, and fell into the shallow waters. There, although they underwent partial rotting, they were preserved against complete decay. The resulting plant debris, called peat, accumulated until in some places it was many feet thick. Ultimately it was inundated—because the land subsided or the sea rose, or possibly for both reasons. Clays, sands, or lime muds containing seashells were then deposited upon this organic matter; such sediments became the shales, sandstones, and limestones that are found above seams of coal. The weight of these sediments compacted the peat, which during the ensuing millennia became more dense and was gradually converted to coal. (It is believed that these changes are still going on and that, given enough time and the proper conditions of temperature and pressure, present-day soft coal might become anthracite or perhaps even graphite.)

Some mineral matter found its way into the peaty material as wind-blown dusts, water-borne sediments, or soluble compounds that penetrated the plant mass by means of the water that permeated the mass. Traces of mineral elements (which are a normal occurrence in growing

133

## THE FORMATION OF COAL

Coal is derived from the tissues of plants that flourished several hundred million years ago in swamps. As generations of plants grew and died, their debris accumulated as peat until in many areas it was several feet thick. Such areas sometimes subsided for long periods beneath shallow seas. Sediments settling on the sea bottom formed sandstones and other sedimentary rocks; their weight compressed the peat and converted it into coal. This cycle might be repeated several times, as the land reemerged and new layers of peat were formed.

SWAMPLAND

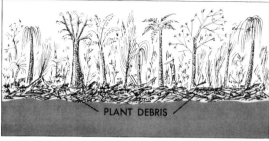

PLANT DEBRIS

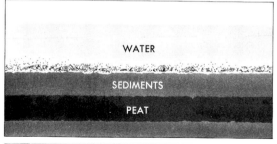

WATER

SEDIMENTS

PEAT

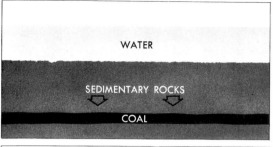

WATER

SEDIMENTARY ROCKS

COAL

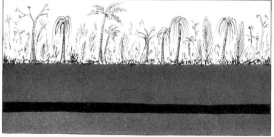

plants) were in part retained in the plant debris. Along with the wind- and water-borne impurities, they remained to become the ash that is left when coal burns.

In some places, after the seas had covered the deposits for some time, the water receded (or the land rose again). Conditions favorable for plant growth were reestablished, and the cycle was repeated, perhaps a number of times. In such regions several seams of coal are found, separated by layers of other rocks.

In subsequent geologic periods additional sediments that may have been many hundreds of feet thick were deposited. In some regions the coal-bearing strata have remained relatively undisturbed; they form extensive, fairly uniform coal seams of the kind found in the midwestern United States. In other areas, such as the anthracite regions of eastern Pennsylvania, the strata have been involved in mountain-building deformations of the earth's crust and have been bent, tilted, and faulted.

Probably most deposits were formed in the locations where the coal-forming plants grew. This "in situ" origin appears particularly likely for coal seams that extend for many miles with relatively little variation in thickness. Other coal deposits have been explained by the theory that tree or plant fragments were transported by water and laid down in large masses elsewhere.

**Appearance of Coal Seams.** Most coals are banded or laminated in appearance, and the laminations are approximately parallel to the bedding plane, or surface upon which they were deposited. If the above views of the manner in which the coal-forming debris accumulated are correct, this would be expected. The wood of a tree trunk differs from the bark, both differ from leaf fragments, and all differ from spore and pollen grains. Therefore it is to be expected that the coalified log would differ in appearance from a mass of coalified twigs and leaf fragments or other plant residues. The water level of the swamp may have fluctuated, giving some portions of the mass an opportunity to dry out and perhaps undergo dry rot before being submerged, while others were immediately covered by water. At times unusually large quantities of clays or silts were introduced; these became the shale or "bone" layers often found in coals.

There are several systems of nomenclature for the different-appearing bands of coal. Perhaps the best system for those who cannot examine coals by means of a microscope is the one proposed early in the 20th century by the British scientist Marie Stopes, because it is based on what may be seen by the naked eye. In the Stopes system, *vitrain* is the shiny, black, glasslike material that is clean to the touch; it was derived from wood. *Fusain*, sometimes called mineral charcoal, is the friable, dusty, charcoal-like substance. It also was derived from wood, but under somewhat different conditions. One theory ascribes its origin to dry rot prior to submergence, and another holds that it was charcoal formed in forest fires. *Durain* is the dull, hard material, often granular in appearance; it is made up of fine plant fragments of various types, including such things as spores and pollen grains. *Clarain* is the finely laminated portion that is predominantly bright and lustrous. It may be made up of all of the above types of material deposited intimately together, but with enough of the vitrain to give it a shiny appearance.

## ANALYTICAL DATA FOR VARIOUS COALS

| Rank[1] | Proximate Analysis and Calorific Value—"as received" basis | | | | | Ultimate Analysis—"moisture and ash-free" basis | | | | |
|---|---|---|---|---|---|---|---|---|---|---|
| | Moisture | Ash | Volatile matter | Fixed carbon | Calorific value (calories per gram)[2] | Carbon | Hydrogen | Nitrogen | Sulfur[3] | Oxygen |
| | % | % | % | % | | % | % | % | % | % |
| Cellulose | ... | .. | ... | ... | .... | 44.4 | 6.2 | .. | .. | 49.4 |
| Lignin (approx.) | ... | ... | ... | ... | .... | 63 | 6.0 | .. | .. | 31 |
| Lignite | 32.5 | 5.0 | 30.8 | 31.7 | 4237 | 72.4 | 5.3 | 1.1 | 0.7 | 20.5 |
| Subbituminous B | 20.7 | 3.9 | 30.7 | 44.7 | 5572 | 77.7 | 5.2 | 1.6 | 0.5 | 15.0 |
| High-volatile Bituminous C | 11.9 | 8.5 | 36.9 | 42.7 | 6268 | 79.2 | 5.9 | 1.5 | 2.9 | 10.5 |
| High-volatile Bituminous B | 4.2 | 6.4 | 34.6 | 58.8 | 7281 | 82.4 | 5.7 | 1.5 | 1.6 | 8.8 |
| High-volatile Bituminous A | 3.0 | 2.4 | 36.3 | 58.3 | 7959 | 85.0 | 5.7 | 1.6 | 0.8 | 6.9 |
| Medium-volatile Bituminous | 1.4 | 1.8 | 26.0 | 70.8 | 8384 | 89.5 | 4.9 | 1.7 | 0.4 | 3.5 |
| Low-volatile Bituminous | 0.6 | 7.4 | 18.2 | 73.8 | 7989 | 91.4 | 4.6 | 1.2 | 0.7 | 2.1 |
| Anthracite | 4.2 | 2.4 | 3.1 | 90.3 | 7662 | 94.9 | 1.8 | 0.7 | 0.8 | 1.8 |

1) Definitions of these rank designations are given in American Society for Testing and Materials, *Book of Standards, Part 19: Gaseous Fuels—Coal and Coke* (Philadelphia 1967). Each rank covers a range of analytical values; this table gives actual analyses that fall within their respective ranges. Several rank designations are omitted for the sake of simplicity.
2) Multiply by 1.8 to get British thermal units per pound.
3) Some of these values are atypically low; 3 to 5% sulfur values are not uncommon.

The use of the microscope has led to interesting and important developments in coal petrology. Studies of the various coal constituents have yielded fundamental information about the origin of coal and produced results that are finding practical applications in coal utilization.

## 2. Kinds of Coal

When the wide variety of plants that exist and the striking differences in appearance and properties of the parts of any one plant are considered, it is obvious that they must contain many different chemical substances. It is not surprising, then, that the coals derived from such materials are complex and heterogeneous.

**Composition of Coals.** The two substances that predominate in plant structures and make up almost the entire composition of wood (exclusive of the water that all organisms contain) are cellulose and lignin. Both are complex, high-molecular-weight compounds of carbon, hydrogen, and oxygen. Both may have contributed importantly to the coal substance, although because cellulose is more readily attacked by bacteria than is lignin, some investigators believe that it may have been largely destroyed in the peat swamp.

As partial decay took place in the peat bog, and as the slower chemical metamorphosis continued after the peat was buried and compacted, one trend in the overall change is particularly evident: the percentage of oxygen progressively decreased. As this occurred, the percentage of carbon increased, but the percentage of hydrogen did not vary greatly until the later stages of the process were reached. The oxygen decrease did not come about by the loss of oxygen as such but rather by the loss of groups of atoms that formed such volatile compounds as carbon dioxide ($CO_2$) and water ($H_2O$). These compounds contain more oxygen by weight than carbon or hydrogen, respectively, so the net effect was a lowering of the oxygen content of the residue. The ultimate lowering of the hydrogen content doubtless resulted from the loss of methane ($CH_4$).

This progressive change in composition of the organic material is called coalification, and as it occurs the coal is said to increase in rank. The accompanying table shows the compositions of various ranks of coals. The names used in the table are those of the classification scheme adopted by the American Society for Testing and Materials (ASTM). Somewhat different classification systems are used in other countries.

**Analysis and Testing of Coals.** Various analytical and testing procedures are used to evaluate coals for commercial and research purposes.

*Proximate Analysis.* The laboratory procedures used in proximate analysis are empirical, and strict adherence to standardized methods must be observed. Heating a weighed sample for a specified time a little above 100° C (212° F, the boiling point of water) gives a loss in weight reported (as percent of the original weight) as moisture content. Burning a weighed sample in an open crucible at 700° to 750° C (1292° to 1382° F) leaves a residue that is weighed and reported in percent as ash. Heating dry coal to about 950° C (1742° F) in the absence of air decomposes it. The loss in weight in percent represents the volatile matter of the coal; the residue, corrected for ash, is the fixed carbon.

*Ultimate Analysis.* The determination by chemical means of the percentages of the major elements in the coal is known as ultimate analysis. Some laboratories use a direct method for determining the amount of oxygen, whereas others obtain this value by subtracting the sum of all other percentages from 100.

*Calorific Value.* The amount of heat obtained by burning coal is of obvious interest to users of fuel. This calorific value is determined by burning a weighed sample in pure oxygen in a calorimeter; the heat produced is absorbed in a known amount of water, and the rise in temperature of the water is noted. The results are expressed as calories per gram or as British thermal units (Btu) per pound of coal.

*Other Special Tests.* Some of the more commonly used tests of coal measure the extent to which it softens or melts as it is heated, its specific gravity, and its amenability to grinding. Chemical analyses are sometimes made to determine such constituents as sodium and chlorine, which are related to slag formation and corrosion in power plant installations.

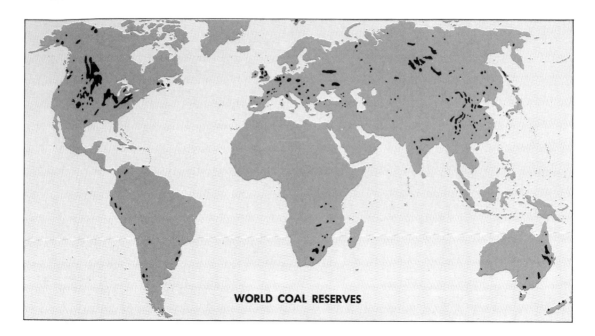

**WORLD COAL RESERVES**

**Uses of Various Coals.** Although all coals may be burned to generate heat or power, the differences between them in composition and properties are important factors in determining under what circumstances a coal will be used.

The combustion of most fuels is accompanied by flame, and improper firing or the use of unsuitable equipment may result in incomplete combustion and the production of offensive smoke. The flame in coal combustion is actually the burning of combustible gases that form when the fuel is decomposed by heat. The coals of high "volatile matter" content are therefore the potential smoke-producers, whereas anthracite is a "smokeless" fuel. However, high-volatile coals can be burned with relatively little production of smoke in properly designed furnaces.

One very important use, for which only a limited number of coals are suitable, is the manufacture of metallurgical coke for smelting iron ore. Coals that undergo partial melting when heated in the absence of air are the only ones that will fuse together into the strong, hard, blocky coke that blast furnaces require. The coals of this description are mainly the bituminous coals that range from the high-volatile B bituminous to the low-volatile bituminous in the rank classes mentioned in the table. Coals of lower and higher ranks undergo decomposition when heated, but the product is a weak coke or a loose, powdery "char" that cannot be used in smelting. Coking coals must also have a low sulfur content and should have a reasonably low but uniform ash content.

G. R. YOHE
*Illinois State Geological Survey*

## 3. World Coal Resources

Coal is by far the most abundant fossil fuel, both in the United States and in the world. The energy of the recoverable mapped and explored coal resources of the world amounts to about 100 quintillion ($10^{18}$) Btu, while the energy of proven petroleum reserves amounts to only about 4 quintillion Btu. Allowing for continuing growth in population and energy use, it has been estimated that this coal could meet the entire growth in energy demand to the year 2000 and there would then be enough remaining to meet all energy needs for another 150 years. If coal were consumed only at the rate at which it was used in the early 1970's, this coal supply would last more than 1,000 years.

Estimates of the world's coal resources, total as well as those actually mapped and explored, are given in the following table, which is based on studies by Paul Averitt (see bibliography).

**WORLD COAL RESOURCES**
(In billion metric tons)

| | Mapped and explored | Estimated total[1] |
|---|---|---|
| Soviet Union | 5,900 | 8,620 |
| North America | 1,560 | 4,080 |
|   United States | 1,420 | 2,910 |
| Europe[2] | 560 | 750 |
| Asia[2] | 450 | 1,360 |
| Africa | 70 | 220 |
| Oceania | 50 | 120 |
| Latin America | 20 | 30 |
|   World total | 8,610 | 15,180 |

[1] Mapped and explored resources plus probable additional resources in unmapped and unexplored areas. [2] Less the Soviet Union.
*Source:* Darmstadter, Joel, and others, *Energy in the World Economy* (Johns Hopkins Press 1971).

Data in the table take account of high-grade and low-grade coal seams that are at least 1 foot (0.3 meter) thick and that occur mostly at depths of less than 4,000 feet (1,220 meters). In the first column, only about 5% to 10% of the 8,610 billion ton total consists of "measured" resources, which have computed tonnages judged to be accurate within 20%; the remainder consists of less well-defined "indicated" and "inferred" resources. For the United States, only about 8% of the 1,420 billion tons are measured resources.

Of the 8,610 billion ton total given in the preceding table, only about 4,305 billion tons, or 50%, are considered to be recoverable by current mining technology. These coal resources are distributed as shown in the following table.

Western Europe accounts for most of Europe's total of 280 billion tons, and the People's Republic of China accounts for most of Asia's total of 225 billion tons.

## RECOVERABLE COAL RESOURCES
### (Mapped and explored)

|  | In billion metric tons | Percent of world total |
|---|---|---|
| Soviet Union | 2,950 | 68.5% |
| North America | 780 | 18.1 |
| United States | 710 | 16.5 |
| Europe | 280 | 6.5 |
| Asia | 225 | 5.2 |
| Africa | 35 | 0.8 |
| Oceania | 25 | 0.6 |
| Latin America | 10 | 0.2 |
| World total | 4,305 | 100.0 |

*Source:* Darmstadter, Joel, and others, *Energy in the World Economy* (Johns Hopkins Press 1971).

Only a very small portion of the world's coal stock is anthracite (hard coal), which ranks at the top in the order of coals. The bituminous (soft) coals constitute less than half of the world stock. China, the Donets region of the Soviet Union, western Europe, and Britain have important shares of high-rank bituminous coals, as does the eastern United States, which has the largest single concentration of carboniferous coals. The largest portion of the world coal stock consists of lignitic coals—the lowest level of the developed-coal family. Most of the lignitic coal is in the Soviet Union, East Germany, Canada, and the western United States.

C. L. CHRISTENSON, *Indiana University*

## 4. Coal Mining and Production

Coal has been used by man since prehistoric times, but coal mining did not become a major industry until the 18th century and the Industrial Revolution. In the United States, coal was discovered by explorers in 1673, but coal mines were not operated until as late as the 1740's in Virginia and about 10 years later in Ohio. Anthracite mining started in Pennsylvania about 1790; initially the coal was taken from outcrops, or near-surface deposits. Three kinds of coal are mined today: lignite, bituminous, and anthracite.

**Kinds of Mines.** Mines may be classified by the method of entry into the coal seams. Where coal lies close enough to the surface and the costs of removing the overlying material are sufficiently low to permit a profit to be made, the coal is mined by *opencut* or *strip mining*. Other coal is mined by *underground* methods.

The details of mining are adapted to local conditions. Coal seams of moderate depths may be entered by a *slope mine,* an opening excavated to the coal through the overlying rock at a gradual incline to permit truck, rope, or conveyor haulage of the coal out of the mine. Where coal outcrops and the seam can be entered directly, the workings are known as *drift mines.* Where steeply sloping or vertical openings are driven to the coal, usually at greater depth a *shaft mine* results.

**Underground Mining.** Most underground mines require at least two openings to the surface for ventilation purposes. In a shaft mine, one shaft is also used for bringing coal to the surface, transporting workers, for electric cables and compressed air lines, and so forth. The second shaft is primarily for ventilation, with a fan located at the surface to draw in air.

Vertical shafts may serve more than one working level, although bituminous coal that can be mined seldom occurs in multiple beds. Shaft mines in the United States average between 200 to 500 feet (60-150 meters) in depth, while those in Britain are over 1,000 feet (300 meters) deep.

The common underground procedures of extracting bituminous coal are known as (1) the *room-and-pillar,* (2) the *long-wall,* and (3) the *bord-and-pillar* methods. All three systems have variations in layout, method of operation, and sequence of mining of sections of the coal seam. The highest percentage of extraction is achieved with the latter two methods, however.

The room-and-pillar method is employed in most of the mines in the United States. Two parallel galleries (tunnels), with joining crosscuts for ventilation and haulage, are mined in a

## COAL MINING PROCEDURES

### SURFACE MINE

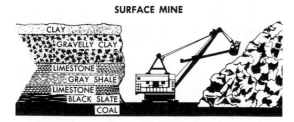

Coal that lies sufficiently near the surface is reached simply by removing the overlying layers of rocks.

### SLOPE MINE

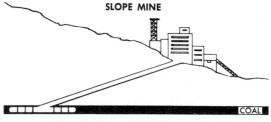

When the coal seam lies at moderate depths, an opening that slopes gradually permits easy haulage from the mine.

### DRIFT MINE

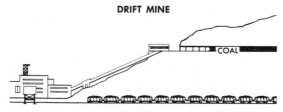

In rugged terrain, a seam of coal sometimes outcrops on the surface, and can be entered and mined directly.

### SHAFT MINE

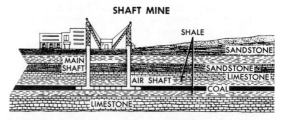

Coal that lies deep beneath the ground is reached by steeply sloping or vertical openings called shafts.

chosen direction. "Rooms" are excavated perpendicular to these galleries, leaving about 50% of the coal in pillars between the rooms. The rooms and pillars are laid out systematically in blocks, with crosscuts between rooms for ventilation; the pillars are from 20 to 40 feet (6-12 meters) wide and 40 to 90 feet (12-18 meters) long. Where possible, the pillars are mined, or "robbed"; the miners retreat from the end of a completed room or groups of rooms and pillars as they proceed. When pillars are removed, the roof is allowed to cave; where caving is not permissible because of possible damage to the earth's surface, 30% to 50% of the coal is left behind. Where roof support is required (as is often the case in weak shale), the overhead rock may be held in place by timber props, rock bolts, or other means. Artificial support is limited where possible to permanent openings.

The long-wall system has limited use in the United States. The coal is "won," or mined, from a face of coal which may be a few hundred feet to several thousand feet in length. The face is continuously advanced outward from a shaft around which a substantial pillar is left. Entries called *mail roads* and *gates* are driven out from the shaft in a branching, radial pattern; thus, the coal working face is roughly circular, with the shaft as a center of the circle. Coal is broken onto a conveyor that runs along the face where the roof is temporarily supported. As the face advances, the roof is allowed to cave, except over haulage ways (roads) and air passageways.

The bord-and-pillar system is used largely in Britain. In this system the coal seam is divided into very large rectangular blocks by means of narrow openings. Pillars as large as 130 to 200 feet (40-60 meters) square are then extracted by retreating procedures. This is a variation of the long-wall and room-and-pillar methods.

A weak mine roof may be supported by props, timber sets, or rock bolts. A prop (post) is a single-piece timber support that is set on solid floor to give a firm footing. A headboard is placed on top and wedges are driven between the rock and board to tighten the prop in place. Rock bolts are usually made of round steel; they have an anchor on one end and are threaded on the other. The anchor end is fastened in a hole drilled in the rock, and a nut on the other end tightens a steel plate against the rock. This plate may support the rock by suspension, beam building, or reinforcement.

**Surface Mining.** When man first began to mine coal, he took the coal that lay at the surface of a deposit. When such surface coal was depleted, man moved the earth and rock back and followed the coal into the ground. Shallow coal usually has weak rock overlying it and is dangerous to mine by underground methods. Hence, until large power excavation equipment was developed, only very shallow coal or coal overlain by sufficiently strong rock could be mined.

Before stripping is begun, information is obtained on the topography of the area, depth of the coal, thickness and grade of the coal seam, and nature of the overlying rock, or "overburden." The ratio of overburden to coal may be as high as 20:1. The maximum depth of coal for strip mining is about 100 feet (30 meters).

Large shovels and draglines are used for stripping the overburden and moving it to a "spoil pile." Small shovels are then employed to excavate the coal, which is hauled out of the pit by truck or similar means. Usually both the coal and the overburden must be drilled and broken with light explosive charges. Computers are often used to determine the size of equipment needed, as well as to calculate costs and profits and predict future operations.

In Germany and in some places in the United States, *wheel excavators* are used for stripping. German wheels are used for both stripping and coal excavation; the machines are electrically powered and have a digging wheel on the end of a boom that excavates earth onto an internal conveyor. The machines may vary in weight from 55 to 5,500 tons and have the capacity to move from 260 to 13,000 cubic yards (200-10,000 cubic meters) per hour. They are usually crawler-mounted for operation on soft ground.

Coal is hauled by trucks of sizes from 2½-ton standard dump trucks to 110-ton tractor-trailer units. A diesel tractor and bottom-dump semi-trailer unit with a capacity of 40 to 60 tons is also used. Haulage and excavator units should be matched in operating capacity. Labor and maintenance costs, as well as the cost of roads, are important items in selection and operation of equipment.

Another surface mining method, *coal augering*, is used (1) when coal lies under high walls that were prepared for this operation or were left by stripping or (2) when coal outcrops to the surface. Up to 8 million tons per year have been produced by coal augering. To be mined by this method the coal seam must lie flat and be free from rock inclusions and from rolls and undulations. The mining machines consist of large single and double augers, 16 to 84 inches (about 40–213 cm) in diameter, which drill into the coal in much the same manner as a wood auger cuts into wood. The larger machines produce up to 35 tons per minute. When stripping and augering operations are performed together, the high wall over the coal to be augered must not be disturbed by blasting. One or two holes may be drilled to remove the coal, depending on seam thickness. One is drilled vertically above the other, and small pillars are left between the holes. Some augering machines of recent design are operated by remote control.

The stripping of land destroys the usefulness of the surface for agriculture and other purposes. The residue and spoil may also lead to acid run-off water. Many states have laws that require the reclamation of land after strip mining. In some cases the land is leveled, soil may be placed back on top, and the ground may be planted with trees. Acid runoff water is prevented by proper drainage and other means.

**Mining Machinery.** Operations in both underground and surface mines may be highly mechanized, in order to increase the rate of production and to lower operating costs per ton.

The kinds of equipment used underground include small auger-type drills for drilling coal, coal cutters for the undercutting or sidecutting of coal face, ripper-type and other continuous mining machines, and coal loaders, such as gathering-arm loaders, duckbill or shaker loaders, overshot or rocker loaders, and slusher or scraper loaders. The various kinds of conveyor systems include chain-type, rubber belt, steel section, and other conveyors. The coal is hauled by means of shuttle cars—mine cars with locomotives. Turret overcutters, mushroom jibs, coal ploughs, and similar kinds of machines are used

## LONGWALL MINING TECHNIQUE

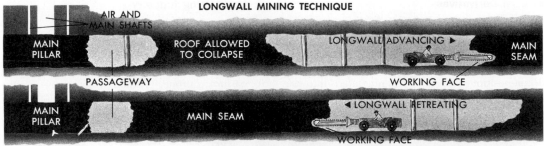

## COAL MINING PROCEDURES

In the longwall mining technique, bituminous coal is worked from a face that may be several thousand feet long. The face is advanced by retreating toward or advancing from a shaft around which a substantial pillar is left. The roof is allowed to cave except over haulage ways and air passageways. In the room-and-pillar technique the coal is excavated in rooms perpendicular to mined galleries. Where permissible the supporting pillars between rooms also are mined and the roof allowed to cave as the miners proceed. The British bord-and-pillar method is a variation of these methods.

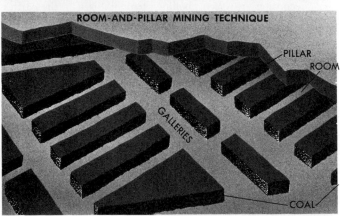

ROOM-AND-PILLAR MINING TECHNIQUE

in long-wall mining in Britain, as well as shearing machines, self-advancing roof jacks for advancing roof support, and road-ripping machines.

The kinds of equipment used in surface mining include draglines and large power shovels for stripping, smaller power shovels for excavating the coal, and drills for drilling and blasting the overburden and coal. Haulage equipment includes conveyors, trucks, and bottom-dump semitrailers. Coal augers for auger mining and wheel excavators for the removal of soft overburden have already been mentioned; among the other kinds of equipment used is the Joy pushbutton miner, a mobile borer and conveyor train.

**Mining Hazards and Mine Safety.** Although mine explosions are greatly publicized when they occur, they cause only a minor portion of coal mine fatalities. It is statistically safer to work in a coal mine than to travel on a main highway. Thus in a typical year in the mid-1960's, the number of fatalities in bituminous and lignite mines decreased from the previous year by 14%. There were 216 fatalities, of which 187 occurred underground, 13 on the surface, 15 at strip mines, and 1 at an auger mine. Three general types of accidents caused 89% of the deaths. The major cause—falls or cave-ins of face, roof, or ribs (elongated pillars of coal or overburden) —killed 113 men (53%). Haulage accidents were responsible for 53 deaths (24%), and machinery accounted for 25 fatal accidents (12%). The other fatalities were due to a variety of causes, such as electrical shock, explosions, and so forth. In anthracite mines during the same year the major causes of fatalities were likewise falls of roof, face, and ribs.

The increase in safety has been due to intensive safety programs and the use of many safety devices. Reliable, adequate ventilation and rock dusting prevent mine explosions. The use of rock bolts, timber, and other supports has reduced accidents due to roof falls. Safety shoes, hard hats, and explosion-proof lights are standard equipment. Increasing mechanization and the use of permissible explosives have also helped. Intensive research into mine safety, carried out by the United States Bureau of Mines and other agencies, has laid the groundwork for much of the safety improvement.

**Coal Preparation.** Before coal mines became mechanized, miners sorted out large pieces of waste material visually, and coal was sold as a run-of-the-mine product. Mechanization made underground sorting uneconomical, however, and the demand for sized coal led to the development of methods of coal preparation. Treatment accomplishes two important objectives: (1) refining coal by elimination of rocky waste material and (2) sizing for particular market demands.

Because the density of coal is less than that of the rock materials that occur as impurities, coal is separated from such waste largely by gravity-controlled processes. Coal washing devices are of various shapes; some are inverted cones. The separation media may be sand and water or similar materials that together have an average density greater than coal and less than the waste material. The coal is ground or crushed and fed into the separation device. The coal floats while the slate and rock sink. Jigs and tables similar to those used in ore preparation may accomplish the same separation. Chemicals are often added to assist in the process.

The coal is then sized, usually by shaker screens, and is stockpiled for market. Various sizes have differing uses, such as the heating of homes, the generation of electricity, the manufacture of coke, and so forth. Some companies add oil to the finer sizes intended for home use, to reduce the formation of coal dust.

GEORGE B. CLARK
*University of Missouri at Rolla*

## 5. Coal Derivatives

Many chemical products are derived from coal. Most of them are obtained by more or less tortuous routes that involve several or many successive transformations.

When coal is converted to coke, the volatile decomposition products are separated into the readily condensed liquid (tar), the more volatile liquids (light oil), and gas. The gas (predominantly methane and hydrogen) is used as a fuel.

The light oil is refined principally by fractional distillation, which separates volatile liquids according to their boiling temperatures. The most important products are benzene ($C_6H_6$), toluene ($C_7H_8$), and a mixture of the three xylenes ($C_8H_{10}$). These find use as solvents and as intermediates for other chemicals.

The tar is distilled to remove the portion that boils below about 350° to 400° C (662° to 752° F), leaving a residue of pitch that is used as a fuel or in the manufacture of such products as road and roofing tars. The distillate is further refined by extraction methods to separate it into neutral portions (largely hydrocarbon compounds—that is, containing only hydrogen and carbon), acidic portions (phenol-type compounds), and basic portions (nitrogen-containing compounds). From these, individual compounds are separated by distillation, crystallization, or other methods. A few of the important compounds thus isolated are naphthalene ($C_{10}H_8$), anthracene ($C_{14}H_{10}$), phenol ($C_6H_5OH$, commonly called carbolic acid), the three cresols ($C_7H_7OH$), and pyridine ($C_5H_5N$). Numerous other compounds are produced commercially.

Many of the materials familiar in modern life are made by the chemical industry from these raw materials; the list includes medicines, dyes, explosives, pesticides, and plastics. For example, phenol will combine with formaldehyde under suitable conditions to give a synthetic resin of the bakelite type. Phenol may also be converted to salicylic acid, from which either aspirin or oil of wintergreen can be made easily. However, many of these chemical intermediates also are made from petroleum.

If coal is treated with hydrogen at high temperature and pressure and in the presence of a suitable catalyst, a significant portion of it is converted to a petroleumlike oil from which motor fuels and lubricants can be made. During World War II, Germany kept her air force and mechanized army operating on fuel manufactured by this process.

Coal, or preferably coke made from coal, will react with steam at high temperatures to give a mixture of carbon monoxide (CO) and hydrogen. This is called synthesis gas, and it is used to make certain compounds that find application as solvents or chemical intermediates. Methanol ($CH_3OH$, commonly known as wood alcohol) is an example. Synthesis gas can also be converted to petroleumlike hydrocarbons; this process is a potential source of motor fuel for the future. Several promising processes for converting coal to gas of high heating value by treating it with hydrogen at elevated temperatures and pressures are being actively developed in pilot plant laboratories. Such gas may well be supplementing natural gas within a relatively few years.

See also COAL GASIFICATION; COAL LIQUEFACTION.

G. R. YOHE
*Illinois State Geological Survey*

## 6. Coal-Mining Industry

Coal, the creation of aeons of geological development, is an important source of energy in the modern industrialized world. Coal satisfies more than 50% of the energy requirements in Britain and western Europe and more than 70% in eastern Europe. Although its share of the energy market has declined in the United States for decades, coal contributes significantly to the operation of electric utilities and steel mills—its two largest customers—and to other industries.

**Development of the Industry.** The twisting of the earth's crust compressed coal—densely packed vegetable matter—into different degrees of thickness and determined its location at numerous points below the surface of the earth. Primitive man's mining to convert coal into economic resources began with mere hand extraction of outcroppings. Exhaustion of these outcroppings led to man's crawling underground with simple picks and shovels. The product was then pulled to the surface in tubs by human effort or with aid from horses and mules.

Centuries of development still leave coal mining a handling industry. Modern mechanization, however, has added greatly to the complexity of mining. Innovations early in the 20th century included machines to slice a cut several inches thick at the base of the exposed coal seam, drills to make holes in the coal face (to be filled with explosives to shatter coal in masses by blasting), and improved cars and hoists for lifting coal to the surface. Loading into cars remained a task for human effort until after 1925, when various mechanical devices began to appear. In the 1950's continuous mining machines were introduced along with extensive hauling by conveyor belts. Continuous mining machines combine several operations: shattering coal from the face by boring or ripping, scooping it up, and passing it back to either shuttle cars or conveyor belts. The coal may then be transferred automatically to the mine cars of the main haulage system.

No recognition was given to ranks or grades of coal when it was first used in making pottery, forging iron, and heating houses. The coming of industrialism and urban life led to the development of refined classification for specific purposes. The low-volatile coals with the capacity of separating coke from gas contributed to steelmaking and gas heating. The high-volatile coals were generally used by electric generating stations and became known as "steam coal."

Competition with oil and natural gas after World War II sharply reduced the use of coal for transportation and home heating. Uses for cement and brick manufacturing, electric-power generation, and steelmaking were emphasized. In steelmaking, coke ovens separate coke and gas from coal, and chemical byproducts are created.

**World Production.** The annual world coal production in the mid-1970's was estimated at about 3.1 billion metric tons. About 75% was of anthracite or bituminous coal, and 25% was of lignitic coal, which ranks lower.

A large part of the lignitic production is in the Soviet bloc of eastern Europe. The USSR alone produces about 160 million metric tons of lignitic coal annually. Less than 75% of the USSR's output was of anthracite-bituminous rank, compared with about 99% of U. S. production in this class. Annual coal production in the United States is about 550 million metric tons.

In order of rank, the ten leading coal-producing countries in the mid-1970's were the Soviet Union, the United States, China, East Germany, West Germany, Poland, the United Kingdom, Czechoslovakia, Australia, and India. The Soviet Union accounts for about 22% of the world production of coal; the United States, about 18%; China, about 14%; and the two Germanys, about 15%. Each of the ten leading countries produces more than 75 million metric tons of coal per year. Countries that produce lesser amounts of coal include South Africa, North Korea, France, Yugoslavia, Japan, Bulgaria, and Hungary.

**U. S. Coal Market.** In the United States, coal furnished 90% of the national energy up to 1900, even though important reserves of oil and gas had been developed in the 19th century. From 1900 to 1920 the expansion of the oil market was largely at the expense of anthracite; bituminous coal continued to provide 70% of U. S. energy through World War I. Since 1920, bituminous coal has been in continuing retreat; in the mid-1930's it provided only 45% of the country's mechanical energy. World War II raised that share back to 52% temporarily. The retreat through the 1950's and 1960's was irregular, but the downward trend was clear. In the late 1960's indications were that bituminous coal may continue to represent at least a quarter of energy used, in the face of competition from oil and gas and the longer-range prospect of nuclear power. The sources of strength for the U. S. bituminous coal industry lay in expansion of the market for energy and in developments in mining technology.

Electric generating plants buy about 60% of the coal sold annually in the United States. General industries—including steel, chemical, and cement plants—account for about 33% of U. S. consumption. Retail dealers supplying households account for only about 2% of annual sales. In addition to households, the other major market lost to the coal industry was the railroads, which converted from steam to diesel locomotives after World War II.

Since 1962 about 10% of the U. S. coal output has been exported annually. Canada is the largest single foreign buyer, but improved ocean shipping has made coal from the United States commercially attractive to Brazil, Japan, and the countries of the European Coal and Steel Community.

**Industry Structure in the United States.** The U. S. coal industry is divided into anthracite and bituminous mining. The anthracite segment is limited almost entirely to northeastern Pennsylvania and operates under a state control board that schedules production and assigns shares to the separate operators. The far larger bituminous segment contains about 7,000 privately owned operating mines. West Virginia is the leading state in annual production of bituminous coal, followed in descending order by Pennsylvania, Kentucky, Illinois, Ohio, Virginia, Indiana, and Alabama.

More than 15% of the annual bituminous production is by "captive" mines for use of parent companies. Steel companies account for most of the captive production, but some electric utilities and a few chemical plants operate mines. Captive production in steel companies represents about 60% of that industry's consumption, but not more than 5% of the coal used by electric plants come from their own mines.

The tendency toward concentration in the industry is growing: the 50 largest firms produced 45% of the total output in 1950, but the "top 50" produced 64% in 1966. There remains, nevertheless, substantial diversified operation. About 80% of the U. S. mines are small, each producing less than 100,000 short tons (about 90,000 metric tons) annually, and they account for almost 20% of output.

The counterpart of the large producing mine is the large buyer. Concentration in mining is in part the result of steam electric plant purchases that have reduced the volume of open market sales. Long-term contracts for delivery of millions of tons over a period of 5 or 10 years are common. Some 6,000 small mines participate as partial subcontractors furnishing supplements to production of larger companies. The other portions of the small-mine output go to satisfy the demands of homes and commercial users.

Since 1960 important transformations have taken place in the coal industry in the United States. These are in part due to the continued expansion in the use of coal by electric generating stations, which in turn has encouraged further strip mining to lower costs and greater use of cleaning plants to purify the raw product.

Federal support of research dealing with conversion of coal to oil or gas has encouraged the mergers of coal mining companies with oil refining and processing organizations. This has also led to the direct purchase of large tracts with undeveloped coal reserves by leading oil companies. Thus the competition between different forms of fuel has been replaced by alliances in the general energy market.

**Industry Structure in Europe.** In the Communist countries of the Soviet bloc, all mining is government controlled, and a substantial part of western European mining is also under government control. Most important are the nationalized sectors in the British and French coal areas and West Germany's Saar area. The very small amount of Italian coal mining is also done by the government, as is more than half of the much larger Netherlands production. In contrast, four fifths of the mine output in West Germany, the most important coal producer of the European Coal and Steel Community (ECSC), is in the hands of private companies. Belgium, which is perhaps the least efficient coal producer of all the ECSC countries because of the extreme depth of its deposits, is also the only country in which the government does not own any mines.

The private ownership of coal mines in West Germany does not mean an entirely open market. A substantial part of production, especially in the Ruhr, is by steel corporations for their own use. Moreover, the High Authority of the ECSC and the individual governments of the member states endorsed the practice of selling coal through agencies at administered prices.

**The Economics of Production.** The expansion of electric utilities in the United States placed that industry's large, steady buyers in the position of leadership in the coal market. Steam plants, with fuel the principal element of variable costs, seek to purchase heat units at the least expense per million Btu (British thermal units). The large quantities of fuel needed must be continuously available. With supplies of oil and gas becoming increasingly available and with cheaper nuclear power in the offing, coal operators had strong competitive reasons to keep costs and prices low by raising productivity.

The increasing refuse that accompanies mechanization requires the processing of coal to satisfy large-scale, discriminating buyers. Cleaning plants as adjuncts to the larger mines processed two thirds of the U. S. output in 1965.

**Economical Deliveries.** The growing concentration of steady service to small numbers of large customers emphasizes the importance and possibility of economical deliveries. Underground mobile bridge conveyors and large stripping shovels have been employed along with delivery trucks that haul over 200 short tons (about 180 metric tons) in single loads. A similar large-scale innovation was the unitized train with interlinked 100-ton cars traveling at passenger train speeds without stops. The unitized train enables steam generating plants to stockpile inventories in 10,000-ton deliveries at a saving in freight charges. European coal mines have also attempted extreme economies in fuel deliveries to serve electricity customers. In Britain, 6 miles (about 10 km) of interlocked underground conveyor belts deliver coal from four mines to a generating plant at the waterfront.

**Coal Revival.** World production of coal rose steadily in the early 1970's. Severe energy shortages stemming from disruptions of international trade in crude oil were evident by late 1973, and shortages of petroleum products and natural gas sent their costs upward sharply. Under these conditions, interest in coal production and coal research was stepped up considerably, and the outlook was that coal would become an increasingly important energy source.

See also ENERGY; FUEL; MINING.

C. L. CHRISTENSON, *Indiana University*
*Author of "Economic Redevelopment*
*in Bituminous Coal"*

### Bibliography

**Alm, Alvin L.,** *Coal Myths and Environmental Realities: Industrial Fuel-Use Decisions in a Time of Change* (Westview Press 1984).

**Andrews, William H., and Christenson, C. L.,** *Manpower and Technology in Bituminous Coal Mining* (USGPO 1971).

**Christenson, Carroll L.,** *Economic Redevelopment in Bituminous Coal* (Harvard Univ. Press 1962).

**Edgar, Thomas F.,** *Coal Processing and Pollution Control* (Gulf 1983).

**Elliot, Martin A.,** ed., *Chemistry of Coal Utilization*, vol. 2 (Wiley 1981).

**Ellington, R. T.,** ed., *Liquid Fuels from Coal* (Academic Press 1977).

**Gordon, Richard L.,** *World Coal: Economics, Policies and Prospects* (Cambridge 1987).

**James, Peter,** *The Future of Coal* (Crane, Russak 1982).

**Klein, Ralph, and Welleck, Robert,** *Sample Selection, Aging and Reactivity of Coals* (Wiley 1988).

**McAteer, J. David,** *Coal Mine Health and Safety: The Case of West Virginia* (Praeger 1973).

**Schobert, Harold H.,** *Coal: The Energy Source of the Past and Future* (Am. Classical College Press 1987).

**Tompkins, Dorothy C.,** *Strip Mining for Coal* (Institute for Government Studies Berkeley 1973).

## COAL GASSIFICATION

**COAL GASSIFICATION** is the chemical transformation of solid coal into fuel gas. Gas made from coal had its first commercial success in the early 1800's when coal gas was used in the cities of London and Baltimore to light streets. Producer gas, water gas, and other gases derived from coal were developed and used in the 19th and 20th centuries, but their role in commerce and industry became small after World War II when natural gas resources began to be exploited rapidly. See also GAS, FUEL—*Manufactured Gas* and *History of the Gas Industry.*

By the early 1970's natural gas supplied about 33% of the total energy used in the United States, oil supplied about 43%, while coal supplied only about 17%. At the same time, the United States had reached a plateau in natural-gas production and become seriously dependent on imported as well as domestic oil, even though it had enormous reserves of coal. Consequently, interest in coal gasification underwent a strong revival, because gasification promised to help relieve the country's dependence on imported fuels and to provide a substitute for the nation's rapidly dwindling supply of natural gas.

Two principal types of coal-gasification process are now under development. Coal gasification processes of one type yield a gas with a high heating value; it is called *substitute natural gas* (SNG) or *pipeline-quality gas.* Processes of the other type yield a gas with a low heating value; it is called a *low-Btu gas.*

### SUBSTITUTE NATURAL GAS (SNG)

A coal-derived gas that could be used interchangeably with natural gas is particularly desirable because it could be distributed along with natural gas in the nation's 1 million mile (1.6 million km) network of interstate pipelines. Natural gas in a pipeline consists of about 93% methane ($CH_4$) and has a heating value in excess of 1,000 Btu per cubic foot. To be interchangeable with natural gas, a coal-derived gas must have a heating value of at least 900 Btu per cubic foot. Such a gas consists mostly of methane.

**Research and Development Efforts.** The American Gas Association (AGA) sponsored research by the Institute of Gas Technology (IGT) on the conversion of coal to SNG as early as 1946, and this program has been funded by the AGA and the Department of the Interior's Office of Coal Research (OCR) since 1964. From 1964 to 1971 the annual budget of the OCR for coal-gasification research and other coal research rose from about $4 million to about $20 million. Since then, government and industry efforts have been accelerated greatly.

The AGA and the OCR in the mid-1970's had a $30 million per year program to use large pilot plants to study several existing processes for converting coal to SNG. These processes include the Hygas process developed by IGT, the Consolidation Coal Company's $CO_2$ (carbon dioxide) Acceptor process, and Bituminous Coal Research's Bi-Gas process. Also, the Bureau of Mines was studying a process of its own called Synthane, and the gas industry was investigating a modification of the Lurgi process developed in West Germany. Plants using the Lurgi process for intermediate Btu gas—400 to 500 Btu per cubic foot—and the Koppers-Totzek process (low-Btu gas) operate commercially in Europe and elsewhere. However, such gases can be converted to SNG by additional steps that greatly increase its methane content at additional cost. These steps have not yet been demonstrated commercially.

**Processes.** Investigation of various coal-gasification processes was necessary for several reasons. One is that different kinds of coal may require different conditions to convert them to SNG. Another is that no process was a clear choice for production of SNG on a commercial scale.

The basic steps for converting coal to SNG have been established. Generally, they include:

(1) *Pretreatment*, required for certain coking coals, to improve the physical behavior of the coal during the gasification process.

(2) *Gasification* of coal at a pressure of about 1,000 pounds per square inch (70 kgs/sq cm) and at a temperature in the range from 1200° F to 1900° F (650° C–1090° C) in a hydrogen-rich atmosphere, producing a raw gas that has a methane content ranging from about 8% to about 26%.

(3) *Shift conversion* increases the hydrogen to carbon dioxide ratio to about 3.3 to 1 as feed for the methanation step.

(4) *Purification* of the raw gas, including removal of carbon dioxide, hydrogen sulfide, and other sulfur compounds.

(5) *Increasing the methane content* of the raw gas by converting its carbon monoxide (CO) and hydrogen ($H_2$) components to methane in a step called methanation, in which a nickel catalyst also is used to form SNG.

(6) *Removing water* from the methanation reaction to meet dryness specifications for pipeline use of SNG.

The pilot plant for studying the Hygas process was put in operation in Chicago, Ill. This plant could produce 1.5 million cubic feet (42,000 cu meters) of SNG per day from 75 tons of coal per day. In 1973, it became the first plant in the world to achieve large-scale conversion of coal to SNG. The pilot plant for studying the $CO_2$ Acceptor process was put in operation in Rapid City, S. Dak., and the pilot plant for studying the Bi-Gas process was in Homer City, Pa. In addition, the Bureau of Mines studied its Synthane process at a large pilot plant at Pittsburgh, Pa. If experiments there were successful, it planned to build a full-scale Synthane plant for producing 250 million cubic feet (7.1 million cu meters) of SNG per day from about 15,000 tons of bituminous coal per day.

Construction of one SNG plant with an output of 250 million cubic feet per day, and consuming 15,000 to 20,000 tons of coal per day, would cost about $500 million. Six such plants were planned for sites in New Mexico, Wyoming, Montana, and North Dakota to convert western coal to SNG by using Lurgi gasifiers.

## LOW-BTU GAS

Energy shortages and environmental concerns in the United States in the early 1970's led to a renewed interest in producing a low-sulfur, low-Btu gas from coal. Such a gas, with a heating value of 150 to 300 Btu per cubic foot, could be used by electric power plants and certain industries that had used nonpolluting natural gas or highly polluting coal. Thus, nonpolluting low-Btu gas from coal could reduce both the demand for natural gas and other clean fuels and pollution by former coal-burning plants.

The Bureau of Mines operated a low-Btu pilot plant at Morgantown, W. Va. It gasified 18 tons of coal per day, producing a gas with a heating value of about 150 Btu per cubic foot. Also, the Commonwealth Edison Company and the Electric Power Research Institute planned to build a low-Btu coal gasification plant that would use three Lurgi gasifiers. When completed near Pekin, Ill., about 1977, this plant will be the first large-scale coal gasification station to be used for generating electric power in the United States.

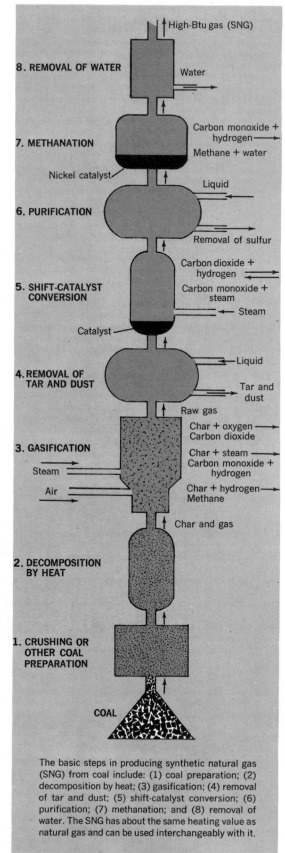

The basic steps in producing synthetic natural gas (SNG) from coal include: (1) coal preparation; (2) decomposition by heat; (3) gasification; (4) removal of tar and dust; (5) shift-catalyst conversion; (6) purification; (7) methanation; and (8) removal of water. The SNG has about the same heating value as natural gas and can be used interchangeably with it.

## UNDERGROUND GASIFICATION OF COAL

The United States, Britain, and the Soviet Union have made tests to gasify coal underground to obtain a low-Btu gas. In this approach, input- and output-bore holes are drilled down to a coal bed at selected points, an oxidizing agent is pumped down the input holes, the coal is ignited, and the gaseous combustion products, including $H_2$, $CO$, and $CO_2$, are obtained from the output-bore holes. Where air is used as the oxidizing agent, methane forms only about 5% of the output-gas volume. This percentage can be increased, for example, by using oxygen rather than air as the oxidant. So far, only the Soviet Union is believed to have practiced underground gasification of coal on a commercial basis. However, this technique may prove to be the most practical way to obtain energy from coal in very deep seams and other seams where mining is impracticable.

**Further Reading:** Gray, Robert H., and others, *Toxicology of Coal Conversion Processing* (Wiley 1988); Penner, S. S., ed., *Coal Gasification: Direct Applications and Synthesis of Chemical and Fuels*, vol. 12 (Pergamon 1987).

**COAL LIQUEFACTION** is the conversion of coal to a liquid hydrocarbon such as synthetic crude oil (syncrude) or low-sulfur fuel oil. The pioneering work in this field was done by the German chemist Friedrich Bergius, who patented a process for converting coal to oil in 1913, and the German chemists Franz Fischer and Hans Tropsch, who developed another conversion process in 1923. See also BERGIUS, FRIEDRICH; FISCHER-TROPSCH PROCESS.

Plants that produced coal-derived liquid fuels were established in Germany, Japan, England, and other countries having poor petroleum resources, but these fuels generally played a temporary minor role because they cost considerably more than petroleum products. In the 1970's, however, petroleum costs and energy shortages led to renewed interest in coal liquefaction.

**Processes.** In the Fischer-Tropsch process a coal-derived gas consisting of carbon monoxide and hydrogen is passed through a catalytic reactor, yielding liquid hydrocarbon products. This process is in limited use for commercial production of liquid hydrocarbons.

Pilot-plant studies of other processes can be divided into two classes—coal hydrogenation processes, in which coal is reacted with hydrogen; and coal pyrolysis processes, in which coal is decomposed into liquids by heat.

In the Synthoil process developed by the U. S. Bureau of Mines, crushed coal is slurried with a coal-derived oil. The slurry and turbulently flowing hydrogen are fed to a fixed-bed catalytic reactor, in which the coal is liquefied and desulfurized. The yield is about three barrels of low-sulfur fuel oil per ton of coal. Other coal hydrogenation processes include the H-coal process developed by Hydrocarbon Research, Inc.

In the Coed process developed by the FMC Corporation, crushed coal is heated to successively higher temperatures in a series of fluidized-bed reactors. After further processing, the main products are syncrude, fuel gas, and residual char. The syncrude yield is about one barrel per ton of coal. Another coal pyrolysis process is the Oil Shale Corporation's Toscoal process.

**Further Reading:** Pierce, T. J., ed., *Coal Liquid Mixture* (Hemisphere 1988).

**COAL TAR** is a heavy, dark viscous liquid obtained from the destructive distillation, or carbonization, of coal. The primary product of the carbonization of coal is coke, while the secondary products are coal tar, light oil, ammonia liquor, and coal gas.

**Production.** Modern coke ovens are equipped for the efficient recovery of coal tar and the other by-products of the coking process. The ovens, which are erected together in batteries, are long, narrow brick chambers. The coal is coked by the combustion of a fuel gas in flues in the walls. In the commonly used high-temperature carbonization process, the oven walls are at a temperature of from 870° to 1205° C (1600° to 2200° F). As the coal carbonizes, the tar and other compounds are separated from the generated gas by cooling in a collecting main; the liquid stream passes to a decanter where the tar and ammoniacal liquor form two layers and are separated. The coal tar is then distilled to give light and middle oils, methylnaphthalenes, and three creosote portions. The residue remaining from the distillation is refined coal tar or coal tar pitch. The term *pitch* is used to designate the semisolid or solid residues of distillation, while *tar* is used to refer to the liquid residues. See also COKE.

**Composition and Properties.** Coal tar is a complex mixture of organic compounds, most of which are aromatic hydrocarbons. Light oil, which is the fraction that distills off at temperatures of up to 200° C (392° F), contains benzene, toluene, xylene, and various tar acids and bases. The middle oil, which distills off at from 200° to 250° C (392° to 482° F), is primarily composed of tar acids and bases and naphthalene. Heavy oils are recovered at temperatures of from 250° to 300° C (482° to 572° F). This fraction includes the methylnaphthalenes and the creosotes, which contain various aromatic compounds such as phenanthrene, chrysene, and pyrene. At temperatures of from 300° to 350° C (572° to 662° F), phenanthrene, anthracene, carbazole, and quinoline distill off, and the residue of this distillation is the coal tar pitch.

Coal tar pitch has been shown to contain approximately 93% carbon, 4.5% hydrogen, and small amounts of nitrogen, oxygen, and sulfur. More than 100 different compounds have been identified in the coal tar pitch. The molecules found in pitch are relatively small, with molecular weights of from 200 to 2,000. Pitch residues usually exhibit a great change in viscosity with changes in temperature. Both coal tars and coal tar pitches have been found to be extremely resistant to water absorption and to moisture vapor permeation.

**Modification of Pitch.** Depending on the degree of reduction by distillation and other treatments, the flow properties and the hardness of the pitch can be varied greatly. Thus, properties can be changed by the addition of oils or solvents or by additional polymerization. Modification of the pitch can also be effected by the addition of coal fines. Upon heating, the fines are "digested" and this process lowers the susceptibility of the pitch to alterations in viscosity due to changes in temperature.

**Uses.** Coal tar is used in the production of chemically cured thermosetting mixtures. It has been used with epoxies, urethanes, and polysulfides in the preparation of various chemically resistant and antiskid coatings and sealants. Coal tars are used in road construction and maintenance, although their use for these purposes has decreased since World War II because of the increased use of petroleum asphalts. Coal tars are also used on airport surfaces because they are very resistant to jet fuels and other petroleum oils. In addition to wearing well, surfaces containing coal tars maintain their skid-resistant qualities over long periods of time.

The importance of coal tar pitches has increased tremendously in recent years because of the growing number of useful chemicals recovered and derived from them. However, the single most important use of coal tar pitch itself in the United States is as a fuel. It is widely used in steel manufacturing as the fuel for open-hearth furnaces. Another important use of pitch is in the manufacture of carbon electrodes, which are widely used in dry cell batteries and in certain metallurgical processes.

Pitch is also used as a foundry core binder and as a binder for the briquetting of coal and coke. Further uses are: in the construction of certain types of roofs; for waterproofing; as a saturant for fiber pipes used to drain water or sewage; as a coating for other types of pipe; as a base in the preparation of various protective coatings; for protection of metals and structures against a marine environment; and to prevent corrosion in underground water, oil, and gas lines.

Creosote, which is one of the heavy tar oils, is of great and long-standing importance as a preservative for wood. It is used to protect objects such as telephone poles, railroad ties, and dock pilings.

While a great number of chemicals may be recovered from the distillation of coal tar, relatively few of these compounds are obtained in large enough quantities to be of real industrial importance. Naphthalene, quinoline, and tar acids, including phenol, cresols, and xylenols, are the most important of the chemicals. Anthracene is also recovered from the coal tar, but in smaller quantities than the other chemicals.

Naphthalene is an intermediate used in the production of dyes, synthetic resins, and other chemicals. It is also used in fungicides, moth repellents, lubricants, and explosives and as a preservative and solvent. Quinoline is used for the production of dyes and niacin and as a preservative and solvent. The coal tar acids are used as insecticides and wood preservatives and in disinfectants. Anthracene is used in the manufacture of dyes.

**History.** The first reference to tar obtained from coal appeared in a British patent in 1681. However, it was not until 1781 that any commercial uses of coal tar were realized, and even then most recovered coal tar was dumped into the sea. In 1881 the Germans successfully introduced the by-product coking oven for the production of metallurgical grade coke. With the advent of these ovens, it became possible to recover coal tars and pitch in large quantities.

It was gradually realized that important solvents and wood preservatives could be obtained from coal tars and that the residue could be used for highway pavement binders and for specialized coatings. Extensive use of the refined coal tars, and especially of coal tar pitches, developed concurrently with the derivation of chemicals and dyes from the distilled fractions of coal tar.

ARNOLD J. HOIBERG
*The Flintkote Company, Whippany, N. J.*

NORWEGIAN INFORMATION SERVICE
Fjords—deep arms of the sea extending far inland—are characteristic of the glaciated coast of Norway.

FAIRCHILD AERIAL SURVEYS
The barrier coast at Lloyd Neck, Long Island, N. Y., is a sand spit separated from the mainland by a lagoon.

**COAST,** the land bordering an ocean or a sea. Coasts vary considerably according to local geology and geomorphology and the stability of the sea level. Under stable conditions the sea tends to erode the softer rocks and form bays, while the harder rocks remain to form headlands.

## FORMATION OF COASTS

Coasts are subject to constant change because of the action of waves, currents, rivers, ice, and winds. They are also subject to occasional change as a result of movements in the earth's crust.

In calm weather, the sea has little erosional effect on the coast, instead making shoreline deposits of sand and gravel. In stormy weather, great waves hurl sand, gravel, and rocks against the land, causing erosion of the coast.

The material torn loose from the land by the sea is graded according to size. Gravel and sand remain close to shore, forming beaches, spits, and bars, while the fine material is swept out to sea. The speed with which the sea erodes the coast depends on the frequency of powerful onshore winds, the resulting waves, and the resistance of the coastal rocks.

This delta coast was formed by deposits of the Mississippi River where it empties into the Gulf of Mexico.

This submergent coast is at Boothbay Harbor, Maine. The river valley is almost totally inundated by the sea.

The irregular coast at Emerald Bay, California, consists of jutting headlands formed by the eroding surf action.

The two main problems in protecting coasts are the destructive power of the waves and their ability to transport materials in the nearshore area. The energy for nearshore processes comes from the sea and is produced by winds, the gravitational attraction of the moon, and disturbances at the atmospheric and terrestrial boundaries of the ocean. Also, rivers and winds transport erosion products from the land to the coast.

### COAST PROTECTION

Beaches can exist only where there is a balance between the amount of sand supplied to a beach and the losses caused by wave erosion. Various activities of man, such as dam building, have upset this balance, making it necessary to take measures to protect coastal lands.

**Structures.** Various kinds of structures are built to decrease coastal erosion. Seawalls are built at the edge of the shore facing ocean waves. Breakwaters are built offshore parallel to the coast to reduce the rate of shifting sand while building sand deposits on their downwind side. Groins are rocks or pilings placed perpendicular to the coast that act as a barrier to sand transport. Jetties are built perpendicular to the coast to confine currents and prevent silting at a harbor entrance.

**Artificial Beaches.** Beaches are the most effective protection for adjoining upland coastal areas. The building up of an artificial beach directly remedies any deficiency in the natural sand supply, thereby halting erosion and benefiting the whole shore area. However, the building up of an artificial beach generally has to be done in conjunction with the use of groins or other structures. Otherwise the beach buildup will be only temporary and must be rebuilt often.

**Artificial Dunes.** Artificially formed sand dunes, located landward of the beach, prevent waves from reaching the coastal upland. A belt of sand dunes will protect upland coastal property so long as the tops of the dunes remain beyond the limit of the high tides. When used with natural sand formations, a belt of artificially formed sand dunes can provide greater protection at less cost than a bulkhead or seawall.

The sand dune surface can be protected from wind by planting beach grass. A snow fence on the dunes will retard the drifting of sand.

### TYPES OF COASTS

Coasts that have been influenced mainly by nonmarine processes are called primary coasts. They include land-erosion coasts, as in Maine; volcanic coasts, as in Hawaii; deposition coasts, as in Egypt; and fault coasts, as on the Red Sea.

Coasts that have been shaped mainly by marine processes are called secondary coasts. They include wave-erosion coasts, barrier coasts, and coral-reef coasts.

Another classification consists of submergent, emergent, and compound coasts. A coast is submergent if it resulted from a rise in the relative sea level and emergent if it resulted from a decline in sea level. A coast that was both raised and lowered is a compound coast.

**Further Reading:** Godschalk, David R., and others, *Catastrophic Coastal Storms* (Duke Univ. Press 1989); Shih-Ang Hsu, ed., *Coastal Meteorology* (Academic Press 1988).

**COAST AND GEODETIC SURVEY.** See NATIONAL OCEANIC AND ATMOSPHERIC ADMINISTRATION.

AT THE U. S. COAST GUARD ACADEMY in New London, Conn., a color guard passes in review.

**COAST GUARD, United States,** kōst gärd, a military service that has many distinct duties in peacetime and in war. Its missions as described in federal statutes fall into five general categories. On the high seas and waters over which the United States has jurisdiction, the Coast Guard is charged with (1) enforcing or assisting in enforcing all applicable federal laws; (2) administering laws and promulgating and enforcing regulations for the promotion of safety of life and property; (3) developing, establishing, maintaining, and operating aids to maritime navigation, rescue services, and ice-breaking facilities; (4) performing oceanographic research; and (5) maintaining its readiness at all times to operate as a service of the Navy.

In peacetime the Coast Guard operates under the Department of Transportation. In time of war, or when the president so directs, it is under the Navy Department.

In performing its missions, the Coast Guard operates ships (called *cutters*), small boats, aircraft, and lifesaving stations. Coast Guard officers and enlisted men have the same ranks and ratings as those of the U. S. Navy. Uniforms are similar to those of the Navy, with distinguishing Coast Guard insignia.

From its establishment in 1790 until 1967, the Coast Guard served in peacetime under the Treasury Department. On April 1, 1967, the service became a part of the newly formed Department of Transportation. The commandant of the Coast Guard, a USCG admiral, is appointed by the president.

The United States Coast Guard is unique among nations because of its military character and the broad scope of its responsibilities. Its closest parallels are the Canadian Coast Guard and the Japanese Maritime Safety Agency. Most European maritime countries have volunteer life-boat associations. Britain has Her Majesty's Coastguard, which is essentially a beach patrol.

**Law Enforcement.** The Coast Guard is the maritime police agency of the federal government. Laws enforced by the Coast Guard fall roughly into two groups: those relating to navigation and merchant shipping for which the Coast Guard is primarily and directly responsible; and those relating to customs and revenue, immigration, quarantine, protection of fish and game, and other matters within the jurisdiction of other federal agencies. These require the Coast Guard's authority and marine facilities for effective enforcement.

Enforcement of the Motorboat Act and the Federal Boating Act, which relate to motorboats and recreational boating, are strictly Coast Guard responsibilities. In connection with these laws, the service conducts an educational program on boating safety. Through the Coast Guard Auxiliary, a course in recreational boat handling is provided. For other agencies, the Coast Guard enforces the Oil Pollution Act, the Fur Seal Act, the fishery treaties and law, and many others.

**Merchant Marine Safety.** The many disasters in early steamboats caused Congress to pass regulatory laws to improve maritime safety. Laws governing relationships between seamen and shipowners also became necessary. The Coast Guard is the federal agency charged with their enforcement. Its merchant marine safety responsibilities include: inspection and regulation of vessels and equipment; regulation of marine personnel; engineering and technical supervision over safety standards; and investigation and review of marine casualties.

**Aids to Navigation.** In further recognition of its responsibility for maritime safety, the Coast Guard is the federal agency charged with devel-

147

oping, maintaining, and operating United States aids to maritime navigation. These include lightships, offshore light structures, lighthouses, buoys, and electronic navigational aids such as loran and radio beacons.

Transoceanic aviation during World War II needed navigational aids, accurate weather observations, and strategically located rescue facilities. This need was met by stationing ships at various locations (ocean stations) in the Atlantic and Pacific oceans. After the war, through international agreement, some of these stations were continued for the support of civil aviation. Ships at these stations, which are furnished by participating nations, provide navigational services, communications, weather observations, and if necessary, rescue facilities. The Coast Guard operates the stations for which the United States is responsible.

Shortly after the sinking of the S. S. *Titanic* in a collision with an iceberg in 1912, the first International Conference on the Safety of Life at Sea was held in London. Attended by representatives of 13 nations concerned with North Atlantic Ocean commerce, the conference established the International Ice Patrol, to be conducted where icebergs threatened shipping lanes. The cost was met by assessments on various maritime nations using the North Atlantic. The United States was asked to conduct this patrol, and the Revenue Cutter Service, forerunner of the Coast Guard, was given the task. The patrol was originally conducted entirely by surface vessel, but scouting for icebergs is now done by aircraft. During the ice season, ice information is broadcast to all shipping.

*Search and Rescue.* In carrying out its search and rescue mission the Coast Guard uses its cutters, aircraft, and lifesaving stations. It also calls upon other vessels and airplanes that may be in the best position to aid a ship or aircraft in distress. The Coast Guard conducts a computerized program, to which merchant vessels of all nationalities voluntarily contribute position reports to determine instantly the location and rescue capabilities of all nearby craft when a distress call is heard.

*Icebreaking.* Icebreaking began as a corollary of search and rescue, as simply assistance to a vessel in the ice. During the extremely cold winters of the mid-1930's the Coast Guard provided icebreaking services in northern rivers and harbors of the United States. An executive order of 1936, officially recognizing the custom, directed the Coast Guard to continue ice operations. During World War II the service performed polar icebreaking. By agreement between the Treasury and Defense departments in 1965, the Coast Guard assumed responsibility for all major icebreaking for the armed forces.

*Oceanographic Research.* From 1867, revenue cutters recorded hydrographic observations in the Bering Sea. Vessels of the International Ice Patrol were ordered to collect oceanographic data. The Coast Guard's basic law since 1961 has required it to conduct oceanographic research, and nearly all of its larger cutters do so.

*Military Readiness.* The Coast Guard is required always to be ready to serve as a part of the Navy. All cutters have armament and equipment similar to what would be carried in wartime. Organization, training, and communications are compatible with those of the Navy. Major vessels undergo periodic training periods under Navy supervision. In the event of mobilization, the Coast Guard has its own trained reserve.

*Associated Organizations.* The United States Coast Guard Reserve was established in June 1939. The enabling act provided for a nonmilitary, voluntary, self-governing organization of men and boats. Its mission was to assist the Coast Guard in various activities, including Search and Rescue. On Feb. 19, 1941, the name was changed to Coast Guard Auxiliary, and a military Coast Guard Reserve was established, patterned after the Naval Reserve. Soon the reserve members were called to active duty, many continuing to serve until the end of World War II. A women's reserve was authorized on Nov. 23, 1942, as a part of the Coast Guard Reserve, to release male officers and enlisted men for sea duty. For the women's reserve the name adopted was SPAR, standing for the Coast Guard's motto: *Semper Paratus* (Always Ready). During World War II the Reserve was used as an instrument for expansion, with wartime volunteers coming in as members of the Reserve. The Coast Guard Reserve like the reserves of the other armed forces, consists of three elements: the Ready Reserve, the Standby Reserve, and the Retired Reserve.

The Coast Guard Auxiliary, administered by the commandant, assists the Coast Guard in various activities. Through educational programs it fosters a wider knowledge of the laws, rules, and regulations governing the operation of motorboats and yachts. Auxiliary members must be citizens of the United States and preferably owners of motorboats, yachts, aircraft, or radio stations. These facilities, as well as the services of the members themselves, may, when offered, be used by the Coast Guard.

The Coast Guard League is a nonprofit organization devoted to the advancement of the Coast Guard's interests. It was begun in 1944 with Coast Guard sponsorship. Members are former Coast Guardsmen and others interested in the service.

THE COAST GUARD ICEBREAKER *Eastwind* clears a channel in thick ice by repeatedly pushing on top of the ice and crashing down with the weight of its bow.

U. S. COAST GUARD

SEA RESCUE performed by a boat from the Coast Guard cutter *Rockaway* in December 1964 saved crewmen from the American freighter *Smith Voyager*, listing dangerously in the North Atlantic. Later the *Smith Voyager* sank while it was under tow by a British salvage tug.

## HISTORY

The United States Coast Guard was established by Act of Congress on Jan. 30, 1915, when two organizations, the Revenue Cutter Service and the Lifesaving Service, were merged. The new service was made a part of the military forces of the United States and continued under the Treasury Department.

**The Revenue-Marine.** The first Congress of the United States, seeking operating funds for the new republic, established a protective tariff. To enforce it, Alexander Hamilton, first secretary of the treasury, requested 10 cutters, properly manned and armed, and by an act of Aug. 4, 1790, Congress authorized the acquisition of these vessels. The service came to be called the Revenue-Marine. At Hamilton's insistence, officers were given military rank. During the hostilities with France (1798–1800) and the War of 1812, cutters operated with the Navy.

In 1831, Secretary of the Treasury Louis McLane, recognizing the cutters' potential for rescue work, directed seven cutters to cruise during the winter months on the lookout for vessels in distress. Cutters began to enforce other laws, such as navigation laws and prohibitions against wrecking, plundering, piracy, and the slave trade. The cutters operated with the Union Navy during the Civil War. One of them, the *Harriet Lane*, in an expedition to relieve the besieged Union troops at Fort Sumter (Charleston Harbor, S. C.), fired the first shot from any vessel in the war, across the bows of the Confederate ship *Nashville*. In the Spanish-American War (1898–1899) the cutter *McCulloch* was Commodore Dewey's dispatch boat at Manila. During the years that followed, the Revenue-Marine came to be known as the Revenue Cutter Service.

**The Lifesaving Service.** This service was established much later than the Revenue Cutter Service. After years of shipwrecks with attendant losses of life, Congress in 1844 acknowledged a federal responsibility by appropriating $5,000 to the secretary of the treasury for lifesaving purposes. Congressional interest grew, and by 1854 there were 137 lifeboat stations along the coasts. They were, however, manned by volunteers who were often not available when the need arose.

Beginning in 1871, full-time crews were employed, and in 1878 Congress created the United States Lifesaving Service under the Treasury Department. The Lifesaving Service worked closely with the Revenue Cutter Service; frequently, cutter officers were detailed to duty with it. In 1915 the two were merged to form the United States Coast Guard. See also LIFESAVING APPARATUS; LIFESAVING SERVICE.

**World War I.** Two years later the United States entered World War I. The Coast Guard was immediately transferred to the Navy. Six cutters were sent to Gibraltar, to escort merchant convoys between that port and the United Kingdom. One, the *Tampa*, was lost with all hands, apparently the victim of a German torpedo. In the United States, under the Espionage Act of 1917, the Coast Guard supervised loading of ex-

AIR RESCUE of a fisherman stranded by rising tides is effected by a Coast Guard helicopter. The Coast Guard maintains its own weather and rescue aircraft.

plosives and munitions in major ports, thus beginning its port security function.

**Enforcing Prohibition.** Following demobilization, the Coast Guard resumed its peacetime duties, including the International Ice Patrol, which had been inactive during the war. Almost immediately the Coast Guard became involved in prohibition, enforcing antismuggling laws. The service was doubled in size to more than 10,000 officers and men. It also acquired many new vessels, operating more than 300 additional patrol boats and 25 former Navy destroyers.

**Bureau of Lighthouses.** On July 1, 1939, the Bureau of Lighthouses was transferred by executive order from the Department of Commerce to the Coast Guard. The Lighthouse Service, like the Revenue Cutter Service, dated from the earliest days of the republic. An act of the first Congress accepted title and jurisdiction over all existing lighthouses and aids to navigation, placing authority and responsibility for their maintenance in the secretary of the treasury. The Lighthouse Establishment was organized rather loosely. In 1852 the Lighthouse Board took it over and administered it until 1910, when a reorganization directed by Congress abolished the board and established the Bureau of Lighthouses under a commissioner. The bureau operated under the Department of Commerce and Labor, and then under the Department of Commerce from 1903 to 1939. See also LIGHTHOUSE.

**World War II.** To assist transatlantic flying, the Coast Guard in 1940 established two weather stations in the Atlantic Ocean between Bermuda and the Azores. World War II had started in Europe, and port security was again inaugurated. Late in 1941 the Coast Guard was transferred to the Navy. During World War II all large cutters were engaged in convoy duty. The Coast Guard manned many Navy ships, including transports, destroyer escorts, and landing craft. After the close of hostilities, the Coast Guard on Jan. 1, 1946, was returned to the Treasury Department.

**Ship Inspection.** The Bureau of Marine Inspection and Navigation (BMIN) was temporarily transferred from the Department of Commerce to the Coast Guard on March 1, 1942. BMIN was itself an amalgamation of two agencies, the Steamboat Inspection Service and the Bureau of Navigation. After many serious shipboard fires and boiler explosions in the early 1800's, Congress had become determined to regulate steamboats. A law passed in 1838 required licensed engineers aboard steamers, also boiler and hull inspections. In 1852 the Steamboat Inspection Service was organized under the Treasury Department. In recognition of federal responsibility for the safety and well-being of seamen, Congress in 1872 authorized shipping commissioners to supervise relationships between merchant seamen and their employers.

Twelve years later, Congress created the Bureau of Navigation, which absorbed the shipping commissioners and was charged with enforcement of all navigation laws. Both agencies started in the Treasury and moved to the Department of Commerce. Congressional dissatisfaction with both services resulted in their amalgamation and the creation, in 1936, of the Bureau of Marine Inspection and Navigation (BMIN). On July 16, 1946, transfer of BMIN to the Coast Guard was made permanent.

**Korean War.** The Coast Guard continued to operate ocean stations (weather vessels) under an international agreement. Meanwhile, the cold war was intensified, and in 1950 the Korean War broke out. The Coast Guard launched an intensified port security program and built new loran stations to provide navigational facilities to aircraft and surface vessels that might become involved in the war.

**Later Activities.** In 1956, at the direction of the president, the National Search and Rescue Plan was promulgated. Under this SAR plan the Coast Guard's responsibility for the maritime regions of the United States was reaffirmed.

Coast Guard barque *Eagle* leads "Operation Sail" in New York Harbor, observing U. S. Bicentennial, July 4, 1976.

THE COAST RANGES rise spectacularly along the coast of California between Monterey and San Luis Obispo. The Big Sur Scenic Highway, cut into the slopes, follows the shoreline for 72 miles.

The Coast Guard became involved in the Vietnam War in 1965, when a number of small patrol boats were ordered to duty with the Navy, constituting an inshore patrol force against the smuggling of arms and other munitions.

### A CAREER IN THE COAST GUARD

The Coast Guard's military structure is similar to that of the other armed services. The majority of its commissioned officers are graduates of its professional academy (see UNITED STATES COAST GUARD ACADEMY). Each year a few officers enter by direct commission from the merchant marine. Others come from the Coast Guard Officer Candidate School at Yorktown, Va. This school is attended by selected regular enlisted personnel and by reservists appointed from civilian life or already members of the Reserve. Upon graduation they go on active duty as officers—regulars with temporary commissions, reservists with Reserve commissions. They all may ultimately have the opportunity of becoming regular commissioned officers. There is also a warrant officer corps.

Coast Guard recruiting offices are maintained in major cities, and information may be obtained directly from the commandant's office, Washington, D. C. Enlisted personnel are sent to one of the training stations for basic training, then to their first duty stations. Advancement in certain specialties follows on-the-job training, while in others a course must be completed at a training center. The Coast Guard Institute provides correspondence courses. A career in the Coast Guard will usually include many years at sea and in lifesaving stations.

WALTER C. CAPRON
*Captain, U. S. Coast Guard (Retired)*
*Author of "The U. S. Coast Guard"*

**COAST MOUNTAINS,** a range in British Columbia and southeastern Alaska, extending for 1,000 miles (1,600 km) parallel to the Pacific coast. Throughout much of the range's length the mountains drop steeply to the coast, which is indented by many fjords. The highest peak is Mt. Waddington (13,260 feet; 4,042 meters) in British Columbia. The mountains are continued on the north by the Alaska Range and on the south by the Cascade Range. Although sometimes popularly called the Coast Range, they are not an extension of the Coast Ranges (q.v.) of the United States, which continue into Canada.

**COAST RANGES,** long, narrow ridges and valleys paralleling the Pacific coast of the United States and Canada. They extend from the vicinity of Santa Barbara, Calif., into the Queen Charlotte Islands, British Columbia. They are interrupted, however, by the Klamath Mountains in northwestern California and southwestern Oregon, and by the Olympic Mountains of northwestern Washington, both of which are of different character; by Juan de Fuca Strait, between Washington and Vancouver Island, British Columbia; and by Queen Charlotte Sound, between Vancouver Island and the Queen Charlotte Islands.

The Coast Ranges consist mainly of sedimentary rocks that have been folded and in some cases faulted. The faults, or rifts, have produced some violent earthquakes in the California section and lesser ones farther north. In some areas igneous intrusions are fairly common also. Although a few peaks stand out, such as the Golden Hinde on Vancouver Island, elevation 7,219 feet (2,200 meters), Marys Peak in Oregon, 4,097 feet (1,249 meters), and Mt. Linn in California, 8,083 feet (2,464 meters), much of the Coast Ranges can be described as rough hill land rather than mountains.

The valleys between the California ranges are in some cases intensively cultivated with irrigation for fruits, grapes, and vegetables. Here the ranges are covered with either grass, brush, or forest. In the northerly areas, forest is dominant on the ranges and constitutes an important resource, with such trees as the redwood, Douglas fir, and spruce. The climate in the south consists of long, dry summers and mild, moderately rainy winters. To the north the rainfall is greater, reaching over 150 inches (3,810 mm) annually in places, and is heavy both in summer and winter on the British Columbia coast. The coastal margin includes many miles of beaches separated by rugged headlands, capes, and promontories but has few deep harbors, except on San Francisco Bay and Puget Sound.

SAMUEL N. DICKEN, *University of Oregon*

**COAT OF ARMS,** a heraldic insignia that was originally embroidered on the tabard, a short coat worn by knights over their armor. Coats of arms originated in the 12th century; their devices usually symbolized the name or status of the bearer or his achievement or aspiration. Coats of arms were useful as a means of identifying visored knights, although they were not originally developed for that purpose. Coats of arms came to distinguish families as well as individuals, and the terms used to describe their designs gave rise to the language that is used in the science of heraldry.

Modern nations have adopted coats of arms. In monarchical countries these are often adaptations of the heraldic insignia of dynasties. The coats of arms of other countries, such as the United States, and of the individual states are arbitrarily adopted emblems without true heraldic significance. Some cities have adopted coats of arms, which may represent their leading industries. See also HERALDRY.

**COATBRIDGE,** kōt'brij, an industrial burgh in south central Scotland, in Strathclyde region, on the Monkland Canal, 8 miles (13 km) east of Glasgow. Situated in a coal- and iron-mining district, the burgh has blast furnaces and manufactures cast iron, tinplate, firebrick, steel rolls, and paper. Coatbridge became a burgh in 1885. Population: 50,866 (1991 census).

**COATES,** kōts, **Albert** (1882–1953), English conductor and composer. He was born in St. Petersburg, Russia, on April 23, 1882. His father, an Englishman, intended that he follow a business career, but he preferred music and entered the Leipzig Conservatory in 1902, where he was profoundly influenced by the conductor Arthur Nikisch. Coates was successively chief conductor for the operas of Elberfeld, Dresden, and Mannheim. An invitation in 1911 to conduct *Siegfried* in St. Petersburg led to a 5-year appointment as first conductor of the Imperial opera there. In St. Petersburg he met the composer Aleksandr Scriabin, who also influenced him. Forced to leave Russia by the revolution of 1917, Coates then conducted in western Europe, England, and the United States and taught at the Eastman School of Music, Rochester, N. Y. His works include the symphonic poems *The Eagle* (1925) and *Launcelot* (1930) and the operas *Samuel Pepys* (1929), *Pickwick* (1936), and *Van Hunks and the Devil* (1952). Coates died in Cape Town, South Africa, on Dec. 11, 1953.

**COATES, Eric** (1886–1957), English violist and composer, who was best known for light, conventional songs, fantasies, ballets, and suites. Coates was born in Hucknall, Nottinghamshire, Aug. 27, 1886. He studied violin with George Ellenberger and composition with Ralph Horner. He won a scholarship in 1906 to the Royal Academy of Music, where he studied viola and composition. As a violist Coates toured with the Hambourg String Quartette in 1907 and later played with the Cathie and Walenn string quartettes. In 1912 he was appointed principal violist in the Queen's Hall Orchestra, London.

By 1918, the popularity of Coates' early works enabled him to devote his whole time to composition. His music includes such song cycles and songs as *The Mill o' Dreams, The Green Hills o' Somerset, Four Shakespeare Songs,* and *A Song Remembered,* and the *Miniature, Countryside,* and *Summer Days* suites. Coates also published *Suite in Four Movements, an Autobiography* (1953). He died in Chichester, Sussex, on Dec., 1957.

**COATES, Joseph Gordon** (1878–1943), New Zealand statesman, who was prime minister from May 30, 1925, to Dec. 10, 1928. He was born at Pahi, near Paparoa, New Zealand, on Feb. 3, 1878. He became aligned with the Reform party after his election to the New Zealand Parliament in 1911.

His political career was interrupted by World War I, during which he served with the New Zealand Army in France. Shortly after his return to New Zealand in 1919, he was appointed to the cabinet of William F. Massey as postmaster general and minister of telegraphs (1919–1925) and minister of justice (1919–1920). Subsequently he showed his administrative ability by improving the country's road and rail systems while serving as minister of public works (1920–1926) and minister of railways (1923–1928).

When Prime Minister Massey died in 1925, Coates became leader of the Reform party and led it to victory at the polls. With the approach of a worldwide depression, the Reform party lost control of the government in 1928. Coates later served in the coalition government of George W. Forbes, and as minister of public works (1931–1933) and minister of finance (1933–1935) he contributed to improved economic conditions in New Zealand. He served in the War Cabinet from 1940 until his death in Wellington on May 27, 1943.

HOWARD J. CRITCHFIELD
*Western Washington State College*

**COATES, Robert Myron** (1897–1973), American author, whose novel *The Eater of Darkness* (1929) was the first Dada novel in English. He was born in New Haven, Conn., on April 6, 1897, and graduated from Yale University in 1919. From 1921 to 1926 he lived in Europe. Later he joined the staff of the *New Yorker* magazine, for which he wrote fiction, book reviews, and art criticism, and, for a while, edited its "Talk of the Town" column. Coates' other books include *The Outlaw Years* (1930), a sociological study of land pirates on the Natchez Trace; *Wisteria Cottage* (1948) and *The Farther Shore* (1955), novels dealing with criminal psychology; *The Hour after Westerly* (1957) and *The Man Just Ahead of You* (1963), volumes of short stories; and *Beyond the Alps* (1961), an account of Coates' travels in Italy. Coates died in New York City on Feb. 8, 1973.

**COATESVILLE,** a city in Pennsylvania, in Chester county, 30 miles (48 km) west of Philadelphia. The city's economy is centered around steel manufacturing. Textiles also are manufactured. The city is the site of a U.S. Veterans Administration hospital, established in 1932.

Coatesville obtained its city charter in 1915. It is governed by a mayor and a city council. Population: 10,838.

**COATI,** kə-wä'tē, a raccoonlike carnivore, with an elongated body, a long mobile muzzle, and a long tail. Coatis are generally reddish brown to black in color, with whitish areas on the chin and throat, but some individuals may be almost orange red. The tail is banded with dark rings. Coatis can grow to 54 inches (136 cm) in length, are 12 inches (30 cm) high at the shoulders, and weigh from 7 to 13 pounds (3 to 6 kg).

Coatis are forest animals and are primarily diurnal. They feed on lizards, insects, birds, fruit, and roots. Females and their young travel in bands of 4 to 20 animals; adult males are solitary, joining the band only during mating season. Coatis nest in trees, where two to six young are born in the spring, after a gestation period of about 77 days.

There are two species: *Nasua nasua,* found from Arizona to Argentina, and *N. narica,* which ranges from the southwestern United States into South America. The coati is a member of the family Procyonidae, in the order Carnivora, class Mammalia. Another species, *Nasuella olivacea,* is known as the mountain coati.

FERNANDO DIAS DE AVILA-PIRES*
*Universidade do Brasil*

ZOOLOGICAL SOCIETY OF PHILADELPHIA

Coati.

**COATICOOK,** ko-at′i-kō͝ok, a town in southern Quebec, Canada, on the Coaticook River. It is about 95 miles (152 km) southeast of Montreal and about 8 miles (12 km) north of the United States border. Wood products, woolens, bricks, and milk products are made in Coaticook. The town was founded late in the 18th century by Levi Baldwin, an American Loyalist. Population: 6,653.

**COATSWORTH, Elizabeth Jane,** kōts′wûrth (1893–1986), American author. Born in Buffalo, N.Y., on May 31, 1893, Coatsworth was educated at Vassar College and Columbia University. In 1929 she married Henry Beston, a naturalist and fellow author. She died in Nobleboro, Maine, on Aug. 30, 1986.

Coatsworth is best known as a prolific author of children's books. *The Cat Who Went to Heaven* (1930), a poetic story about a Japanese artist and his cat, won the Newbery Medal in 1931. Notable among her many other children's books are a series of five "Sally" books with historical settings, beginning with *Away Goes Sally* (1934), and *Door to the North* (1950). Her most acclaimed novels for older readers include *Here I Stay* (1938) and several "Incredible Tales" (*The Enchanted,* 1951; *Silky,* 1953; and *Mountain Bride,* 1954). Volumes of Coatsworth's verse include *Fox Footprints,* her first published book (1923); *Country Poems* (1942); *Summer Green* (1948); *Poems* (1957); and *The Sparrow Bush* (1966). *A Personal Geography: Almost an Autobiography* appeared in 1976.

**COAXIAL CABLE,** an electric cable with a tubular outer conductor that encircles a concentric inner conductor; the two conductors are separated by a dielectric. See CABLE.

**COBALT,** kō′bält, a mining town in northeastern Ontario, Canada. It is located in the Timiskaming district, 330 miles (530 km) north of Toronto. From 1903 to 1911 Cobalt was one of the richest silver-mining camps in the world. The town was named for the cobalt that was a by-product of the ore in the mines. After 1920, mining activity slackened as the ores became depleted; however, it was revived in the 1950s as new recovery processes were perfected. The town of Cobalt is situated in picturesque hunting and fishing country on the perimeter of the immense Provincial Forest Reserve. Population: 1,401.

**COBALT,** kō′bält, a magnetic, silvery-blue metallic element, symbol Co. The pure metal was first isolated by the Swedish chemist Georg Brandt in approximately 1735. The element's name was derived from *kobold,* the German word for "goblin" or "evil spirit." Salts of cobalt have been used since before 1000 B.C. for the production of brilliant and permanent blue colors in porcelain, glass, pottery, tiles, and enamels.

**Properties.** Cobalt is a hard, silvery-blue metal that closely resembles iron and nickel in its appearance, properties, and behavior. Its melting point is about 1495° C (2723° F), and its boiling point is roughly 2927° C (5301° F). There are two allotropic forms of cobalt. One is a close-packed hexagonal crystal structure that is stable below 417° C (783° F); the other has a face-centered cubic crystal structure that is stable up to the melting point of the metal. Pure cobalt is about as hard as pure iron; it has a tensile strength of about 34,500 pounds per square inch (237,877.5 kilopascals) and a hardness of 224 on the Brinell hardness scale.

Cobalt is located in Group VIII of the periodic table and is a typical transition metal. Its oxidation number can be either +2 or +3. The atomic number of cobalt is 27, and its atomic weight is 58.9332. Its known isotopes range from $^{50}Co$ to $^{70}Co$, but $^{59}Co$ is the only one found in nature; the others are synthetic. The isotope $^{60}Co$, which is prepared by bombarding $^{59}Co$ with thermal neutrons in a nuclear reactor, has a half-life of 5.271 years. Its effects are similar to those of radium, and it is widely used in medicine for radiation therapy. It is also used in food sterilization and radiography, as well as in radiochemistry.

Although finely divided cobalt ignites spontaneously in air, in the massive state the metal is not attacked by air or water at temperatures that fall below 300° C (572° F). At higher temperatures oxidation proceeds much the same as in iron. However, cobalt can be made passive by exposure to strong oxidizing agents, such as, for example, the dichromates, and in the passive state it is resistant to corrosion. Through chemical reactions with dilute mineral acids, the metal is rapidly converted to the respective soluble divalent mineral salts, such as the chlorides, nitrates, and sulfates. Cobalt forms complex ions with ammonia, halogens, and cyanides. (See also METAL; TRANSITION ELEMENTS.)

**Occurrence.** Cobalt, which is considered a rare metal, is found in the earth's crust in concentrations of about 0.0029%. However, because of certain natural concentration processes, ores from the Congo, Zambia, Morocco, and Canada may yield as much as 40% cobalt. The most important ores fall into three classes—the arsenides, such as skutterudite; the sulfides, such as carrollite, linnalite, and cattierite; and oxidized minerals, such as heterogenite, asbolite, and sphaerocobaltite. Nickel, silver, and gold are generally found with the arsenides, while the other ores are associated with copper.

**Production.** Only a small percentage of the cobalt that is produced comes from the smelting of cobalt ores. Generally, the desired cobalt mineral must first be separated from the residue of the processing of another metal. This separation may involve hand sorting, flotation, or, on occasion, magnetic separation. The extraction of the cobalt minerals is usually a complicated process because of the presence of numerous contaminating elements that are difficult to remove.

**Uses.** The principal use of cobalt is in alloys, particularly the superalloys that have been developed since 1960. These alloys are employed where resistance to high temperature and to stress is of primary importance; for example, superalloys are widely used in jet engines. There are three groups of superalloys, classified according to the major element in the alloy. They are nickel-base alloys and iron-nickel-base alloys (each of which may contain up to 20% cobalt) and cobalt-base alloys. Although the cost of the superalloys is relatively high, the need for them justifies the expense.

Another major use of cobalt is in the preparation of alloys of high magnetic strength for permanent magnets. Such alloys generally contain iron, aluminum, and nickel in addition to cobalt. Cobalt is also employed in high-speed tool steels, hot-work tool steels, and high-carbon, high-chromium, cold-work steels. Cobalt concentrations range from 3 to 25% in these alloys. In the pure state, cobalt is used as a binder for cemented carbides such as the tungsten carbide—cobalt composite used in steel-cutting operations.

Metallic cobalt is used in cobalt hard-facing (rock drill tools), wear-resistant alloys, low friction surfaces, protective electroplates, expansion alloys (glass-metal seals), and dental alloys. Also, small quantities of cobalt are a nutritional requirement for many animals. Cobalt salts are used to correct mineral deficiencies in livestock and are also used in varnish additives and inks.

DOUGLAS V. KELLER JR., *Syracuse University*

**Bibliography:** Emsley, John, *The Elements*, 2d ed. (Oxford 1991); Greenwood, N. N., and A. Earnshaw, *Chemistry of the Elements* (Pergamon 1984); Lide, David R., ed., *CRC Handbook of Chemistry and Physics*, 75th ed. (CRC Press 1994).

**COBALT BLUE,** kō'bält, one of the most permanent of the blue pigments. It is also known as Thénard's blue, cobalt ultramarine, azure blue, and king's blue. It is essentially cobalt aluminate and is nonpoisonous and resistant to acids and alkalis. The cobalt blue colors also include the range of blues known as matte blues. These contain cobalt oxide, potash or ammonium alum, and varying quantities of zinc oxide. From 20% to 30% zinc oxide helps weld the color in ceramics. An excess of cobalt in the pigment will give a slightly greenish tinge.

Cobalt blue is made by heating alumina with cobaltous oxide, cobalt phosphate, or cobalt arsenate. The pigment may be added to either oil or water, and it is used in cosmetics.

ALVIN S. COHAN, *Scientific Design Company, Inc.*

**COBALTITE,** kō'bäl-tīt, a mineral compound of cobalt, arsenic, and sulfur. It is an ore of cobalt. The mineral occurs in granular form and is also found as well-formed cubic crystals. The crystals are brittle, have a metallic luster, and are a silvery white. A considerable amount of iron (up to about 10%) is usually present in cobaltite.

Cobaltite is a rather rare mineral despite its use as an ore. Its usual occurrence is in sulfide veins in association with other cobalt and nickel ores, or dispersed through metamorphic rocks. The most significant deposits are in Sweden, the Congo, and Canada.

Composition, $(Co,Fe)AsS$; hardness, 5.5; specific gravity, 6.33; crystal system, isometric.

**COBÁN,** kō-vän', a city in the highlands of Guatemala, north of Guatemala City. It is the capital of Alta Verapaz department. Cobán is in a major agricultural district with a subtropical climate, heavy rainfall, and rich soil. The hills surrounding the city are covered with extensive coffee plantations that make it the northern center of the country's coffee industry.

Cobán was founded in about 1538 by the Dominican friar Bartolomé de las Casas and was named for the Indian chief Cobaón. High on a hill is the Church of the Calvary, which dates from 1559 and contains the *Christ Crucified* of the colonial artist Evaristo Zúñiga. More accessible is the cathedral, built in the mid-17th century. The area about Cobán abounds in ancient Mayan mounds. Population: 33,996 (1994 est.).

**COBB, Frank Irving** (1869—1923), American journalist. He was born in Shawnee county, Kans., on Aug. 6, 1869. In 1896, after beginning his newspaper career in Grand Rapids, Mich., he went to the Detroit *Evening News* as a political correspondent and editorial writer, and in 1900 to the Detroit *Free Press* as chief editorial writer. His terse editorials caught the attention of Joseph Pulitzer of the New York *World*, who was attacking corruption in business and politics. In 1904, Cobb became confidential adviser to Pulitzer and was soon given control of the *World*'s editorial page. After Pulitzer's death in 1911, Cobb became the newspaper's editor in chief.

In the presidential campaign of 1912, Cobb gave the paper's full support to Woodrow Wilson and was offered a position in Wilson's cabinet, which he declined. Cobb died in New York City on Dec. 21, 1923.

**COBB, Henry Ives** (1859—1931), American architect of the functionalist school, who was noted for his use of steel. Cobb was born in Brookline, Mass., on Aug. 19, 1859, studied at Massachusetts Institute of Technology, and graduated from Harvard University. In 1881 he went to Chicago, where he joined a brilliant coterie of American architects who were openly breaking with traditional European design and following their own belief that "form follows function."

Cobb was soon recognized as an expert on steel construction. He was one of the first architects to introduce the steel skeleton, which shifted the emphasis in design from the horizontal to the vertical and made modern skyscrapers possible. Cobb's most notable works are the original buildings of the University of Chicago, for which he was chief architect. His best-known designs include those for the Opera House and the Newberry Library, both in Chicago, and the American University in Washington, D.C. Cobb practiced in New York City from 1902 until his death there on March 27, 1931.

**COBB, Howell** (1815–1868), American politician, who shifted from strong support for the Union to secessionism in the critical pre–Civil War period. He was born in Jefferson county, Ga., on Sept. 7, 1815, into a wealthy family with a tradition of public service. After graduating from the University of Georgia (1834), he was admitted to the state bar (1836) and was elected to Congress (1842) at the age of 27.

In Congress, Cobb exhibited a broad national spirit, supporting the annexation of Texas and the Mexican War and opposing efforts to form a Southern party. He was elected speaker of the House in 1849. In Georgia, Cobb's Union Democrats split with the Southern-rights wing of the Democratic party and joined the Whigs to win the state convention's approval of the Compromise of 1850. The next year the Unionists and Whigs merged forces as the Constitutional Union party and elected Cobb governor. Later he sought unsuccessfully to reunite the state's Democratic party. He was reelected to Congress in 1855, and in 1857 he became secretary of the treasury under President Buchanan.

Surprisingly, in view of his former Unionism, he advocated immediate secession after Lincoln's election in 1860. Cobb was chairman of the convention that organized the Confederacy in 1861 and was a contender for its presidency. In the Civil War he became a major general. He died in New York City on Oct. 9, 1868.

GERALD M. CAPERS, *Tulane University*

**COBB, Irvin Shrewsbury** (1876–1944), American journalist and humorist, who, with keen insight and colloquial style, capitalized on his experiences in the South after the Civil War. Cobb was born in Paducah, Ky., on June 23, 1876. At

Irvin S. Cobb

WIDE WORLD PHOTOS

the age of 16 he was a reporter for the Paducah *News*, and at 19 he was editor. He later reported for the Louisville *Evening Post* and the New York *Evening Sun*, and from 1905 to 1911 he wrote for the New York *World*, reputedly as the highest-paid reporter in the country.

A regular contributor of humorous articles to the *Saturday Evening Post*, Cobb was a member of the magazine's staff from 1911 to 1922. For another decade he was a staff writer for *Cosmopolitan* magazine. He also wrote plays, acted in films, and was a popular speaker. Cobb died in New York City on March 10, 1944.

As a writer, Cobb is known for his tales of the kindly old Confederate veteran, Judge Priest, in the collection *Old Judge Priest* (1915). Other collections of Cobb's humorous writings include *Speaking of Operations* (1916) and *Incredible Truth* (1931). Cobb also wrote the autobiography *Exit Laughing* (1941).

ROBERT W. DESMOND
*University of California, Berkeley*

**COBB, John Rhodes** (1899–1952), British racer and fur broker, who was the first man to attain a speed of 400 miles per hour on land and 200 mph on water. In achieving his top land mark, with an average speed of 394.196 mph for the 1-mile distance at the Bonneville Salt Flats, Utah, on Sept. 16, 1947, he sped at 403.135 mph on the north run. He was killed at Loch Ness, Scotland, on Sept. 29, 1952, after his jet-propelled boat had been clocked at 206.89 mph on the first of two heats required to set a new record.

Cobb was born in Esher, Surrey, on Dec. 2, 1899. He graduated from Eton and Trinity Hall, Cambridge, and became interested in racing to aid in technical improvements of automobiles. Between 1932 and 1939 he broke all world's records for time and distance up to 24 hours. In 1939 he averaged 368.85 for a 1-mile run, 326.7 mph for 5 miles, and 270.4 for 10 miles.

During World War II, Cobb was a member of the Royal Air Force (1940–1942) and a ferry pilot in the Air Transport Auxiliary (1943–1945).

BILL BRADDOCK, *New York "Times"*

**COBB, Ty** (1886–1961), American baseball player, known as the "Georgia Peach," who was one of the greatest and most dynamic figures in the game. In a 24-year career in the American League, Cobb set numerous records for batting and stolen bases that stood for decades after his retirement. Although many of his batting records were finally eclipsed by Pete Rose and Hank Aaron, and his stolen-base records by Lou Brock, Maury Wills, and Rickey Henderson, certain marks seem destined to remain intact. Among these are his lifetime batting average, consecutive years of batting over .300, and number of years as a league batting champion. A left-handed hitter, Cobb spread his hands apart well up on the bat handle, which afforded him excellent control for placing hits all over the field.

Tyrus Raymond Cobb was born in Narrows, Ga., on Dec. 18, 1886. His father, an educator and state senator, was fatally shot by his mother, who said that she had mistaken him for an intruder. Many believe that this event caused Cobb to be a loner and of irascible temperament. After playing with a club in Augusta, Ga., he was sold at age 18 for $750 to the Detroit Tigers in 1905. He starred with the Tigers for 22 seasons,

UNITED PRESS INTERNATIONAL

Ty Cobb in his Detroit Tigers uniform.

doubling as manager for the last six. He played his last two years with the Philadelphia Athletics, retiring in 1928 at the age of 42.

Cobb led the American League in hitting 12 times, 9 in a row, and had a .367 lifetime average. Only once (his first year) did he fail to hit above .300, and three times he hit above .400. His high was .420 in 1911. In 1922 he made 5 or more hits in a game four times during the season. In 1925, at the age of 38, he went 6-for-6, including 3 home runs and a double. An intrepid baserunner, he stole 96 bases in 1915 (long a record) and had a career total of 892. Once he scored from first on an infield out without an error in the field. Under Cobb as manager (1921–1926), the Tigers finished second once, third twice, fourth once, and in the second division twice.

Cobb was the first player elected to the Baseball Hall of Fame in 1936. He died in Atlanta on July 17, 1961.

MICHAEL QUINN*, "Sports Illustrated"

**COBBETT,** kob'ət, **William** (1763–1835), English journalist, publisher, political radical, and agriculturist. Known in his day as the most forceful English radical in the reform movement, Cobbett now is recognized for his burly prose in *Rural Rides* (1830) and *Advice to Young Men* (1829), his archetypical English personality, and his knowledge of rural life.

The son of a farmer and innkeeper, Cobbett was born on March 9, 1763, at the sign of The Jolly Farmer in Farnham, Surrey. In 1783 he became an attorney's copyist in London and after a few months, he enlisted in the infantry and became copyist to the commandant. His regiment was sent to Canada in 1785, where he stayed until 1791, having risen to the position of sergeant major.

As sergeant major, Cobbett knew of the corruption in the army and, after his honorable discharge in England in 1791, he tried to get a court-martial to expose abuses. Becoming aware of the official malice his action had aroused, he went with his bride to France in March 1792. He lived there until August, learning the language, and then, seeing the trend of the French

Revolution and the inevitability of war between England and France, he went to America where he enjoyed a short interval from controversy.

Settling first in Wilmington, Del., he became popular as a teacher of English to French refugees. He then moved to Philadelphia, continuing to teach until, with the arrival of Dr. Joseph Priestley, recently driven from England for his pro-French views, he found his vocation as a pamphleteer and champion of Britain against Jacobin sentiment. His attack on Priestley, *Observations on the Emigration of Dr. Joseph Priestley* (1794), brought him notoriety and a public following.

In 1796 he founded an antiradical periodical, the *Political Censor,* which was superseded by his *Porcupine's Gazette* (1797)—Cobbett's pseudonym being "Peter Porcupine." He became known as an anti-Jacobin and anti-Democrat and a journalist of alarming skill. He attacked Dr. Benjamin Rush, the famous physician and politician, as a killer rather than a healer. Rush sued him for libel and won the suit. In spite of the fine of $5,000, Cobbett continued his harassment in public print, and as a result had to depart for England in 1800 to avoid severe punishment.

The British government offered him the editorship of, and shares in, a political paper, the *True Briton,* but Cobbett refused and started his own publication, *Cobbett's Weekly Political Register* (1802), which eventually turned into a radical antigovernment journal. After 1806, Cobbett, having seen the misery of the rural workers, turned to reform radicalism. He was charged with sedition in 1810 for protesting in the *Register* the flogging of militiamen in Ely. The government won its case, and he was sentenced to two years in Newgate Prison and heavily fined.

On his release, he again fought for working-class demands through a cheap *Register,* selling for two pence. The government, fearful over the workers' unrest, in 1817 suspended the Habeas Corpus Act. This action caused Cobbett to fear arrest as an enemy of the government, and he escaped to a farm in Hempstead, Long Island, N. Y., where he lived until 1819, when he returned to England, bearing with him the bones of Thomas Paine, whom he now regarded as a hero. After the Reform Act of 1832, Cobbett was elected to Parliament. He died on June 18, 1835, of an attack of influenza, at his farm near Guildford.

ARTHUR C. YOUNG
*Russell Sage College*

**COBDEN,** kob'dən, **Richard** (1804–1865), British political leader and reformer. He was born at rural Midhurst, Sussex, on June 3, 1804, the fourth of 11 children. In 1828 he set up business as a calico merchant in the developing industrial district of Lancashire in the north of England. Thereafter, although he never prospered as a businessman, he became increasingly preoccupied with the problems and opportunities of his own and other countries in an industrializing world. In two pamphlets—*England, Ireland, and America* (1835) and *Russia* (1836)—he described the economic and political contours of the United States and Russia and argued strongly against traditional concepts of British foreign policy, particularly the concept of intervention to maintain the balance of power. At the same time he advocated free trade, a cause that he took up enthusiastically in 1838 and 1839 as one of the founders of the

Anti-Corn-Law League (see CORN LAWS).

Between 1841, when he was elected to Parliament from Stockport as a Leaguer, and 1846, when the corn laws were repealed, Cobden was the chief parliamentary spokesman of the movement. He succeeded in introducing a moral factor into what had been a largely economic debate, and the Prime Minister, Sir Robert Peel, paid him a deserved tribute when the victory was won. After 1846, however, Cobden was unable to win large-scale public support for further measures of financial reform, and his cogent but passionate critique of the English landed interest, which he called "a feudal governing class," went much further than most businessmen liked. Finally, as a result of his opposition to the Crimean War and his increasingly frank advocacy of far-reaching social change, Cobden lost his parliamentary seat at the general election of 1857. He was elected two years later by a different constituency, Rochdale, but refused an invitation from Lord Palmerston, the prime minister, to serve as president of the Board of Trade. Despite his long-standing objections to Palmerston's foreign policy, Cobden agreed to represent Britain in the laborious discussions that led in 1860 to the commercial treaty with France that bears his name. Thereafter, his immediate interest in foreign affairs was the welfare of the Union in the American Civil War.

Cobden died in London on April 2, 1865. In his last years, while continuing to support free trade, international understanding, and the extension of democracy, he became disillusioned about the prospects of his own country. His hopes that "our mercantile and manufacturing classes," which had played a decisive part in the politics of the 1840's, would gain in wisdom and power were never realized. Although free trade seemed secure, the Cobden Club, a political club founded in his memory, had to deal with new demands for protection as early as the 1880's. Cobden's writings, nevertheless, remain persuasive and powerful.

ASA BRIGGS, *University of Sussex, England*
*Author of "The Age of Improvement"*

**COBH,** cōv, an urban district in southwestern Ireland, on the south side of Great Island, in Cork harbor, 9 miles (14 km) southeast of Cork. A seaport with extensive docking facilities, it is an important port of call for ocean liners and mail steamers. In the 19th century it was a military and naval center and a point of embarkation for British troops. In 1849, Cobh was renamed Queenstown to honor Queen Victoria's visit to the city. The ancient name was resumed in 1922. Population: 6,200 (1991 census).

**COBHAM, Lord.** See OLDCASTLE, SIR JOHN.

**COBIA,** kō'bē-ə, a mackerel-like, fighting game fish with tasty, fine-textured meat. It lives in warm seas around the world, especially offshore near the mouths of bays and rivers. It is not a common fish, and it is not commercially important.

The cobia is a large fish; it usually weighs 10 to 20 pounds (4.5 to 9 kg) but may reach 100 pounds (45 kg). It has a large mouth, a long, flat head, and a spindle-shaped body with long, soft anal and dorsal fins. The dorsal fins are preceded by short spines. The cobia has a dark brown body, silvery white underside, and two or three sometimes indistinct dark bands on the sides. Two or three cobia school together in the open sea or lie under floating debris, seaweed, or drifting boats. A swift fish, it feeds voraciously on crustaceans, mollusks, and small fishes.

The cobia, *Rachycentron canadus*, is the only species in the family Rachycentridae, which is in the order Percomorphi.

EDWIN S. IVERSEN
*University of Miami*

**COBLENTZ,** kō'blentz, **William Weber** (1873–1962), American physicist, who was a pioneer in the measurement of infrared radiant energy. Coblentz was born in North Lima, Ohio, on Nov. 20, 1873, and was educated at the Case Institute of Technology and Cornell University. During his 40-year tenure at the National Bureau of Standards, he verified experimentally Planck's law of radiation and supervised the establishment and maintenance of radiation standards for worldwide use. His great skill in devising and using delicate apparatus was employed in measuring radiation emitted by terrestrial sources, such as furnaces, and by extraterrestrial sources, such as stars. He determined the sensitivity of the normal human eye to the various parts of the visible spectrum and developed standards for eyeglasses tinted to absorb harmful radiation.

Coblentz was the author of more than 400 scientific articles and of two books, *From the Life of a Researcher* (1951), an autobiography, and *Man's Place in a Superphysical World* (1954). He died in Washington, D.C., on September 15, 1962.

DEANE B. JUDD
*National Bureau of Standards*

**COBLENZ,** kō'blents, a city in Germany in the state of Rhineland-Palatinate. Coblenz (also spelled *Koblenz*) is situated at the confluence of the Mosel and Rhine rivers, 56 miles (90 km) southeast of Cologne. The city of Coblenz marks the beginning of the most picturesque segment of the Rhine, the 44 miles (71 km) to Bingen. The scenic route up the Mosel to Cochem and Trier also begins here.

The city has a chemical industry, printing plants, canning factories, textile mills, and a large trade in bottling and shipping champagne and other wines. River traffic is important to Coblenz; several million tons of freight are shipped annually on this part of the Rhine, and additional tonnage passes up and down the Mosel. The city is an important tourist center.

**Description.** The focal point of the city is the German Corner (German, *Deutsches Eck*), the point of land where the Rhine and Mosel rivers meet. A broad promenade leads from the German Corner up the Mosel, past the Blumenhof (where outdoor concerts and operas are given in summer), past the Mosel River harbor, to the Balduin Bridge and the 13th century castle, which holds the municipal library.

Across the Rhine from the German Corner, on a commanding height, is the historic fortress of Ehrenbreitstein. Destroyed and rebuilt many times, it was begun in the 11th century. Another broad, shaded promenade leads up the Rhine from the German Corner past the steamer docks to St. Castor's, the oldest church in Coblenz, which was consecrated in 836. The 18th century Electoral Palace (now a museum) is close by. The Pfaffendorf Bridge, the main Rhine crossing at Coblenz, is near the palace.

The Asian cobra (*Naja naja*), which grows 4 to 5 feet long, is commonly used by Indian snake charmers.

**History.** The Roman general Drusus built a fortress on the site of Coblenz in 9 B.C. The Latin name was *Confluentes*. The city came under the control of Trier in 1018 and later became a favorite residence of the archbishop-electors of Trier. French armies occupied Coblenz in 1794, and in 1815 the Congress of Vienna awarded the city to Prussia. The city was rebuilt after four-fifths of it had been destroyed in World War II. Population: 108,733 (1991 est.).

A. G. STEER, JR.
*University of Georgia*

**COBOURG,** kō′bûrg, a town in southern Ontario, Canada, the seat of the united counties of Northumberland and Durham. It is situated on Lake Ontario, 70 miles (110 km) east of Toronto, Cobourg has an excellent harbor and is the center of a summer colony. Its industries include a large food products plant, woolen mills, a carpet and matting factory, a brass foundry, a tannery, a sporting rifles factory, and chemical plants. Cobourg formerly was the seat of Victoria University, which was moved to Toronto. The former university buildings are used as a provincial mental hospital. Population: 16,027.

**COBRA,** kō′brə, a venomous snake of the Eastern Hemisphere. When excited, it raises the forepart of its body in an erect position and spreads its neck into a "hood." The Asian cobra is the best known, but most cobras are found in Africa. Cobras belong to the family Elapidae, which also includes coral snakes, mambas, kraits, and many Australian species.

Found in Africa, southern Asia, and the East Indies, cobras are not a well-distinguished group. They share many anatomical features with other elapids that are not cobras, but only cobras assume the erect "candlestick" pose when they spread their necks. True cobras—that is, cobras belonging to the genus *Naja*—range from 5 to 9 feet (1.6 to 3 meters) in length as adults.

Cobras have short fangs on the front end of the bones of the upper jaw. Their venom is neurotoxic, that is, it has its main effect on the nervous system. The death of a victim of cobra bite usually results from the venom's interference with the nerve impulses that control the action of the diaphragm or heartbeat, and the victim dies of suffocation or of heart failure. The venom may have effects on other body systems as well.

Like most members of its family, the cobra tends to feed on cold-blooded vertebrates—frogs, lizards, and other snakes. Some species eat small mammals as well. Young cobras are hatched from eggs. A clutch of 12 to 15 eggs is laid in a protected place and is hatched by the heat of the sun. Some species are believed to guard their eggs during the entire 40 to 60-day incubation period.

**The Asian Cobra.** This species (*Naja naja*) is the main tool of the Indian snake charmer's trade, and, as such, is one of the best-known snakes in the world. It is also known as *cobra de capello*, the *Indian cobra*, and the *spectacled cobra*. This cobra has a broad geographic range; it is found from the Philippines, Taiwan, and southern China, through the East Indies and Southeast Asia westward to Iraq and Iran. As an adult, it is 4 to 5 feet (1.3 to 1.6 meters) long. Its color pattern varies widely over its range. For example, the Philippine cobra, a geographic variety of the Asian cobra, is a dark brown snake, but in other parts of its range, the Asian cobra may be light tan, speckled, banded, or solid black. The hood of the Asian cobra also varies. In India it is spectacle-shaped; in Burma and Thailand it is monocled; and in other parts of its range it may assume other shapes or be absent.

A rodent eater, the Asian cobra lives near towns and villages where mice and rats abound. It is not an especially aggressive snake, but because of its proximity to a largely bare-legged and bare-footed population, it probably causes more deaths than any other snake. It is estimated that 20,000 to 40,000 people in Southeast Asia die from snakebite each year—most of them from cobra bite—and it is suprising that there are not more fatalities. A moderate-sized cobra may have enough highly toxic venom to kill 10 men; yet many people survive cobra bite, probably because cobras inject only a small part of their venom when they bite defensively.

**The King Cobra.** The most impressive of all cobras, and perhaps the most impressive of all snakes, is the king cobra (*Ophiophagus hannah*) of Southeast Asia. It is the largest of all venomous snakes, attaining a length of 18 feet (5.5 meters) and a weight of over 20 pounds (9 kg). The king cobra is the only known nest-building snake. The female builds an 18-inch (46-cm) high, two-compartmented nest of grass and leaves on the forest floor. The lower compartment contains the eggs, and the upper houses the female, who guards the clutch until it hatches.

The king cobra is a snake-eating snake. Unlike the rodent-eating Asian cobra, it is not attracted to populated areas. Perhaps for that reason and also because it is large and easily seen, few king cobra bites are reported. However, none of the few victims reported survived for even an hour unless they received immediate treatment with antivenin.

**The Egyptian Cobra.** The Egyptian cobra (*Naja haje*) is closely related to the Asian cobra. It may attain a length of 8 feet (2.6 meters) and is highly variable in color, ranging from a uniform brownish yellow to tan or black. Found from the Arabian Peninsula and North Africa through the drier regions of tropical Africa, it is best known as the sacred snake (*uraeus*) of the ancient Egyptians. It appears in many temple drawings, and Egyptian rulers wore its image on their foreheads as a symbol of authority. The Egyptian cobra was probably the "asp" that Cleopatra used as an instrument of suicide. If so, it was an excellent choice—this cobra possesses a highly toxic venom that can cause a relatively painless death within minutes.

**Spitting Cobras.** Perhaps the most unusual of the African true cobras is the spitting cobra (*Naja nigricollis*), a 6- to 7-foot (2- to 2.3- meter) snake that ranges over most of the dry open territory of tropical Africa. Ordinarily, this snake does not bite in defense but squirts its venom toward a presumed aggressor through specialized fangs. It can spray twin jets of venom a distance of 8 feet (2.6 meters). Another cobra of South Africa, the ringhals cobra (*Haemachates haemachatus*) has a similar adaptation. A relatively small snake which averages a length of less than 4 feet (1.3 meters), the ringhals cobra can spray its venom to a distance of 7 feet (2.3 meters) or more.

The fangs of these spitting cobras are modified so that the opening of the venom duct is more to the front of the fang than in nonspitting cobras. The opening is narrowed to produce a "nozzle" effect, and the venom is ejected upward and outward under considerable pressure; the pressure gives the venom its range. The venom is harmless to the skin, but if it gets in the eyes, it causes immediate and intense pain—effectively causing blindness. The eyes may be permanently affected if the venom is not washed out immediately. Presumably, this adaptation provides the snakes with protection against being stepped on by antelopes or other hoofed animals of the African plains.

**Other African Cobras.** Other African cobras are also modified and have unusual habits. The speedy, glossy-scaled, frog-eating tree cobras (genus *Pseudohaje*) of West Africa have assumed a slender form typical of snakes living in trees, while the water cobras (genus *Boulengerina*) have retained the typical cobra form and hood but have taken up an aquatic existence and feed on fish. There is also a burrowing cobra (genus *Paranaja*) in western Central Africa. Another important African cobra is the "yellow cobra" (*Naja nivea*) of South Africa; this cobra has the most toxic venom of all cobras.

H. G. DOWLING
*The American Museum of Natural History*

**COBURG,** kō'bŏŏrKH, a city in Germany, in the Upper Franconian region of Bavaria. Located 55 miles (89 km) north of Nuremberg (Nürnberg), near Germany's eastern border, the city is situated on the banks of the Itz river. The economic life of Coburg and the surrounding area is characterized by agriculture and diversified light industry. Since there are extensive forests in the region, woodworking of various kinds accounts for almost a third of the city's total industrial output. There is also a variety of metalwork done in Coburg. Ceramics, glass, toys, and Christmas tree ornaments are also manufactured there.

Coburg was first settled in 800 A.D. as a station on the trade route running from Nurem-berg in the south and Frankfurt in the west to Leipzig in the north. The picturesque old city is dominated by a medieval fortress called the Veste, which dates from the 12th century. Never taken by storm, the fortress has had a long and eventful history. Martin Luther was sheltered there in 1530, during the Diet of Augsburg. The fortress was also the seat of the ducal family of Saxe-Coburg-Gotha, who ruled the area until 1918. Prince Albert, the consort of England's Queen Victoria, was a member of this family. Through judicious marriages the family also managed to place representatives, at various points in history, on the thrones of Belgium, Bulgaria, Portugal, Russia, and Sweden. Part of the ducal fortress is maintained as a museum, housing valuable collections of wood carving, painting, engravings, and antique weapons gathered over a long period by the dukes of Saxe-Coburg-Gotha.

Coburg's location in the heart of Germany and its lack of strategic importance protected it from severe damage in World War II. The city has, therefore, retained its prewar appearance and is justly famed as a tourist attraction. Population: 44,246 (1991 est.).

A. G. STEER, JR.
*University of Georgia*

**COBURN,** kō'bərn, **Charles Douville** (1877–1961), American actor-manager, who was popular with more than three generations of the theater- and movie-going public. Coburn was born in Macon, Ga., on June 19, 1877. He started in the theater as a program boy at age 14; by 18 he was theater manager, and by 22, an actor. He made his first New York appearance in 1901.

With Ivah Wills, whom he married in 1906, he formed the Coburn Players, a repertory company presenting classical and modern plays, such as *Yellow Jacket* and *The Better 'Ole*—both major successes on Broadway. Until 1937, when he left Broadway for the movies, Coburn was active in every theatrical season—a record achievement. He often coproduced or directed in addition to his acting.

In 1943, Coburn won an Oscar as the best supporting actor, for his role in the movie *The More the Merrier*. He continued to act in movies and on television, until his death in New York City on Aug. 31, 1961.

**COBWEB.** See SPIDERS.

**COCA,** kō'kə, is a drug that consists of the dried leaves of the coca plant (*Erythroxylon coca*). Native to the Andes mountains in western South America, the coca shrub has inconspicuous yellowish flowers and small reddish fruits. It normally grows to a height of about 12 feet (4 meters), but during cultivation its growth is restricted to 3 or 4 feet (1.0 or 1.3 meters) to facilitate the harvesting of its small, elliptical-shaped leaves, which are collected three or four times a year. Most of the alkaloids are now obtained from plants grown at elevations ranging from 1,500 to 6,000 feet (500 to 2,000 meters) on the moist eastern slopes of the Andes. Bolivia accounts for about half the world's coca leaf crop, Peru for somewhat less.

Coca leaves contain a complex mixture of alkaloids. Of these, cocaine is certainly the most important, accounting for much of the physiological activity of the leaves, although other alkaloids as well as tannins and a volatile oil contribute to the overall effects of coca leaf chewing. In the United States, all use of coca and its preparations and derivatives is under regulation of the federal narcotic laws.

**Coca Leaf Chewing.** For centuries, natives of the central Andes have chewed wads of coca leaves, mixed with lime or vegetable ashes, to induce a feeling of well-being and to alleviate hunger. The leaves stimulate the central nervous system and produce effects of euphoria. The effects are not, however, accompanied by visual or auditory hallucinations. Archaeological findings indicate that coca leaf chewing was prevalent among the Incas as early as 500 B.C., and the characteristic bulged cheek produced by a coca leaf quid is a recognizable feature of the faces portrayed in various artifacts of these people. In the earliest period coca chewing was a privilege of royalty, but by the 16th century the practice had spread to the common man. Today, the practice is an integral part of the native culture and is followed by approximately eight million people in the mountainous areas of northwestern Argentina, Bolivia, Colombia, and Peru and also in the adjacent lowlands of the Amazon Valley.

Authorities do not agree on the ill effects of the prolonged practice of coca leaf chewing. It cannot be compared in seriousness to injection or inhalation of cocaine. Some authorities assert that untoward effects have not been observed in persons who have chewed coca leaves for 50 years, while others maintain that the habit promotes premature senility. However, it is difficult to separate the effects of this practice from the effects of other conditions, such as inadequate nutrition, poor environment, and poor sanitary practices. The habit is not necessarily physically or socially dangerous. It does not lead to addiction, and it is probably less harmful than the tobacco and alcohol habits.

VARRO E. TYLER
*Purdue University*

**COCAINE,** kō-kān', a naturally occurring alkaloid, extracted from the leaves of the coca plant, that is both an excellent local anesthetic and a widely abused illicit drug. Like amphetamine and related stimulants of the central nervous system, cocaine increases heart rate and blood pressure, produces intense euphoria (a "high") and a sense of well-being, increased energy, and mental clarity, and decreases appetite. Paradoxically, the euphoria may coexist with anxiety and suspiciousness. The many street names of cocaine include "coke," "snow," "lady," and "gold dust."

The euphoric effects of cocaine are powerfully reinforcing. In a laboratory setting, for example, animals that have learned to inject themselves with cocaine by pressing a lever will press the lever as often as 6,000 times in order to obtain a single dose. If they are allowed unlimited access to the drug by this means, many continue to inject themselves with cocaine until they are dead or seriously poisoned. Given a choice between food and cocaine, they will choose cocaine to the point of total starvation.

In humans, cocaine produces addiction or dependence. Cocaine use becomes more important than all other aspects of the users' lives, and they will sacrifice health, safety, friends, money, and freedom for it. While chronic use of cocaine does not produce the type of physical dependence and withdrawal symptoms produced by opioids, such as heroin, it does produce a distinct withdrawal syndrome that typically includes craving for cocaine, fatigue, drowsiness, and depression. These symptoms may be due to depletion of dopamine, one of the brain's neurotransmitters.

**Patterns of Use and Abuse.** The use of cocaine for mood effects is illegal in most countries. In the United States pure cocaine was not readily available for nonmedical purposes for most of the 20th century. Consequently, users tended to take the drug only intermittently and in low doses, and there were very few cases of cocaine dependence or toxicity. In the early 1980's, however, this pattern began to change as the drug became much more available and its cost declined. By 1985 about 22 million Americans (12%) reported use of cocaine at some time in their lives, and 5.8 million had used it within 30 days prior to the survey. But in the following years there was some evidence that use was on the decline. Despite this downturn, as a larger proportion of continuing users became heavy users and shifted to more hazardous routes of administration (intravenous injection and freebase inhalation), demand for treatment, medical complications, and deaths from cocaine escalated.

The effects of cocaine are felt within a few minutes, but euphoric effects begin to decline after about 40 minutes. Thus frequent doses are necessary to maintain a high.

Cocaine is most commonly used in the form of a fine powder of its hydrochloride salt. Users inhale ("snort") the powder through a straw or rolled up paper. The cocaine is absorbed through the mucous membrane of the nose and passes into the bloodstream. Often cocaine is mixed with other substances, such as the local anesthetics procaine and lidocaine, that produce similar effects on the membranes; sometimes it is mixed with amphetamine. Cocaine powder can also be injected, and it is sometimes combined with heroin ("speedballs") for this purpose.

Some users (especially in Peru, Ecuador, and Bolivia) smoke cocaine in the form of coca paste (cocaine sulfate) mixed with marijuana or tobacco. The paste is formed during the processing of coca leaves to obtain pure cocaine hydrochloride. In the United States some cocaine users convert the cocaine hydrochloride back to the pure alkaloid—the "free base." The free base is then smoked, or "freebased." Freebasing very rapidly produces high blood concentrations of the drug as the vaporized cocaine comes in contact with the large surface of the lung. Some users claim that freebasing is even more pleasurable than snorting but that craving for more cocaine is intense within minutes as the effects of the drug decline.

In time, traffickers began to produce freebase cocaine using ordinary sodium bicarbonate (baking soda). Generally referred to as "crack," the material was sold in relatively inexpensive, small dosage units, making it more accessible to both poor and young people.

**Medical Complications.** Frequent snorting of cocaine causes a chronic runny nose ("cocaine sniffle") due to damaged mucous membranes. Heavy use of cocaine—snorted, freebased, or injected—can result in serious behavioral symptoms. These include restlessness, anxiety, irritability, and paranoid or psychotic states similar to those seen in amphetamine psychoses. Hallucinations involving the senses of smell, hearing, and touch can occur. For example, heavy users sometimes hallucinate that insects are crawling under their skin ("cocaine bugs"). Even single doses of cocaine can cause myocardial (heart) damage or stroke. Deaths from such cardiovascular toxicity or from cocaine overdose, characterized by convulsions and cardiovascular collapse, are becoming more common as the use of the drug spreads and doses become larger.

**History.** In the 16th and 17th centuries, Spanish physicians adopted the coca leaf as a remedy for a variety of ailments. In 1860 the German scientist Albert Niemann succeeded in isolating a pure active drug, which he called cocaine, from coca leaves. The new substance at first was thought to have great therapeutic potential. In 1884 the Viennese surgeon Carl Koller discovered the value of cocaine as a local anesthetic—thereby greatly facilitating eye surgery—and by the late 1800's it was widely used for this purpose. Cocaine was also used to treat fatigue, alcohol and morphine addiction, impotence, stomach disorders, asthma, and many other complaints. Sigmund Freud believed it was useful in treating depression. Despite mounting evidence that cocaine could be habit forming, it was an ingredient in many popular patent medicines, and until 1903 it was the stimulant contained in Coca Cola.

Since 1912 production and sale of cocaine have been regulated by international narcotics treaties. Most countries prohibit its use except for limited medical purposes.

See also COCA; DRUG ADDICTION AND ABUSE.
JEROME H. JAFFE, M.D.
*National Institute on Drug Abuse*
*Addiction Research Center*

**COCCIDIOIDOMYCOSIS,** kok-sid-ē-oi-dō-mī-kō'-sis, an infectious disease caused by the fungus *Coccidioides immitis.* The fungus is normally present in the soil in various parts of the world, notably in the drier desert areas of the southwestern United States. When dust from the soil is carried by the wind and inhaled, fungal spores enter the lungs and may germinate, forming tiny, round fruiting bodies. These bodies then break open, releasing many spores, which may spread through the bloodstream to other organs.

Symptoms of coccidioidomycosis frequently include coughing, fever, aching joints, and raised tender areas beneath the skin of the lower legs. In Mexican Indians, Filipinos, blacks, and less frequently in Caucasians, the infection spreads to produce inflammation and abscesses of the soft tissues beneath the skin, occasionally producing draining lesions on the skin. A less common but more serious manifestation of the disease is meningitis.

Because the symptoms of coccidioidomycosis resemble those of tuberculosis, other fungal diseases, and certain chronic bacterial infections, care must be taken to distinguish coccidioidomycosis from these diseases. This is done by examining some of the diseased tissue under a microscope for the spore-filled fruiting bodies. The diagnosis is confirmed by growing and identifying the fungus in the laboratory.

In regions where coccidioidomycosis occurs most frequently, the great majority of its victims may recover spontaneously or have no symptoms at all. When there is evidence that the disease has spread or when it persists, drugs are administered—usually the antibiotic amphotericin B. Destroyed tissue must be removed surgically, and infected abscesses must be drained. Unless treated, the spreading infection is generally fatal.
JOHN P. UTZ, M.D.
*Medical College of Virginia*

**COCCIDIOSIS,** kok-sid-ē-ō'-sis, a contagious disease that affects all young domestic animals except horses. It is found most commonly in cattle, sheep, goats, pigs, dogs, cats, poultry, and rabbits. The disease is caused by a group of organisms (coccidia) that belong to the lowest phylum (Protozoa) of the animal kingdom.

Animals become infected through the ingestion of food and water contaminated with coccidia-laden droppings of infected animals. When adequate numbers of coccidia are consumed, extensive destruction of intestinal cells results. The coccidia penetrate the intestinal cells, causing them to lyse and die. The affected animal develops diarrhea and may become anemic and die. Mortality rates are very high in young chickens and rabbits with acute infections. Animals that have recovered from the disease are immune carriers of the organisms. The disease is controlled by proper sanitation and by certain medications, such as the sulfa drugs.
KEITH WAYT
*Colorado State University*

**COCCOLITH,** kok'ə-lith, the minute disk- or button-shaped plates of calcium carbonate that form the spherical shells of coccolithophores. Coccolithophores are floating marine, one-celled organisms commonly classed as golden brown algae in the phylum Chrysophyta. When the organisms die, their shells (the coccoliths) form a large part of the globigerine ooze found at the ocean bottom. The shells also have been found in bedded rocks, such as foraminiferal marl. The term "coccolith" was coined by the British biologist T. H. Huxley.

**COCCUS.** See BACTERIA AND BACTERIOLOGY—*Bacterial Anatomy.*

**COCCYX,** kok'siks, the terminal portion of the spinal column. In man, the coccyx is composed of four vetebrae. Often they are fused together, but sometimes the first vertebra is separate while the other three are fused. In fishes, reptiles, and other vertebrates that have a tail, the coccyx (or caudal) vertebrae are not fused and extend partway, if not entirely, along the length of the tail.

JEFFREY WENIG, *ENDO Laboratories*

**COCHABAMBA,** kō-chä-väm'bä, a city in Bolivia, 150 miles (240 km) southeast of La Paz. Surrounded by mountains of the Eastern Cordillera of the Andes and situated at an elevation of 8,389 feet (2,550 meters), Cochabamba has a pleasant valley climate. The temperature of the coldest month averages 57°F (14°C). The city is set in the Cochabamba basin, on a level stretch measuring 15 miles (24 km) long and 6 miles (10 km) wide. With the help of some irrigation to compensate for scanty rainfall, the basin's rich alluvial soil produces maize (corn), barley, alfalfa, and fruit. Cattle are grazed in the valley, and the city is a leading dairy center.

CARL FRANK

Cochabamba's cathedral faces a tree-lined plaza.

Cochabamba's location enables trade to be conducted by rail and road with La Paz, 150 miles (241 km) to the northwest, and with the newly opened tropical agricultural area of Santa Cruz, to the east, by means of the 312-mile (502-km) trans-Andean highway. Nearby highland mining communities depend upon the city for food supplies and other essentials. Among Cochabamba's industrial installations are a flour mill, a large government-owned powdered milk factory, and several canneries.

Founded in 1574, the city was called Oropeza until 1786. It is the seat of the University of San Simón, a technical institute, and several other specialized institutions. Among its many colonial structures is the cathedral, noted for its stonework, and the community is also widely known for its luxuriant gardens. Most of the people are of European immigrant or mixed ancestry (*Cholo*). Population: 448,756 (1993 est.).

LAURENCE R. BIRNS
*The New School for Social Research*

**COCHET,** kô-she', **Henri** (1901–1987), French tennis player, who scored one of the most famous victories on record when he dethroned Bill Tilden in the quarterfinal of the U.S. championship in 1926, ending Tilden's six-year reign. Cochet was an artist with a racquet. His touch and skill in manipulating the ball with a minimum of effort enabled him to return the powerful strokes of players like Tilden.

Cochet was born in Villeurbanne on Dec. 14, 1901. He was one of the "Four Musketeers" (with René Lacoste, Jean Borotra, and Jacques Brugnon) who won the Davis Cup for France for the first time in 1927, and he helped defend the trophy until France lost to Britain in 1933. He won the British singles in 1927 and 1929, the U.S. singles in 1928, and the French singles five times between 1922 and 1932. Cochet died in Paris on April 1, 1987.

ALLISON DANZIG, *New York "Times"*

**COCHIN,** kō'chin, is a city on the Malabar Coast of southwestern India. It is in the state of Kerala and is part of the Cochin-Ernakulam-Alwaye town group. Cochin has extensive backwaters to which an approach canal was dredged, and in 1930 the harbor was opened to ocean-going vessels. The city became the major port of the Malabar Coast and an important rail terminus.

Cochin was the earliest European settlement in India. Vasco da Gama established a trading post in 1502, and St. Francis Xavier began his missionary work here in 1530. The Dutch captured the town in 1663, and the British took it in 1795 but allowed the Dutch to retain their administration. The city remained a British possession of the former princely state of Cochin until 1947. Cochin is noted for its Dutch houses and for two Jewish groups: the "Black" Jews, who claim to have settled here in the 3d and 4th centuries, and the "White" Jews of European descent, who arrived much later. Population: 564,038 (1991 census). See also KERALA.

**COCHIN CHINA,** kō'chin, is a former name for six provinces in South Vietnam (Giadinh, Dinhtruong, Bienhoa, Vinhlong, Angiang, and Hatien). Part of the empire of Funan to the 6th century, Cochin China was afterward ruled by the Khmers and the Vietnamese. When the name was introduced to the West in the 16th century it meant all of Vietnam, but after the 17th, referred only to the Mekong delta.

The area was torn by wars between the Trinh and Nguyen families until 1802, when Nguyen Anh unified it. The French gained the three eastern provinces in 1863 and the three western ones in 1868. They ruled the colony until 1945 and their subsequent attempts to retain it precipitated the Indochinese War. Cochin China became part of South Vietnam in 1954. See also INDOCHINA; VIETNAM.

**COCHINEAL DYE.** See COCHINEAL INSECT.

**COCHINEAL INSECT,** koch'ə-nēl, a scale insect that feeds on opuntia cacti (prickly pears) and has long been used in Mexico as a source of crimson dye. The adult female cochineal is approximately ⅛ inch (0.3 cm) long and normally is reddish or crimson in color. She either is covered by or rests upon masses of cottony white wax secretions in which she lays her eggs. Several generations seem to be produced annually. The cochineal insect (*Dactylopius coccus*) belongs to the family Eriococcidae of the order Homoptera.

Cochineal dye, which consists of the dried bodies of the insects, originally was used by the Aztec Indians for making body paint, for medicine, and for dyeing textiles a luxuriant crimson. Today, cochineal dye is produced on a small scale on plantations in Oaxaca, Mexico, and in Peru, other Central and South American countries, the Canary Islands, southern Spain, and Algeria.

The cochineal insects are brushed from the cacti, dried, cleaned, and packaged for market. The once substantial market for cochineal dye almost disappeared after the discovery of aniline dyes in the late 19th century, but it has revived to some extent because of the possible detrimental effects of aniline dyes in cosmetics and food products.

HOWARD L. MCKENZIE
*University of California, Davis*

**COCHISE,** kō-chēs' (1812?–1876), American Indian chief of the Chiricahua Apache of southeastern New Mexico, who terrorized the Southwest during the 1860's and early 1870's. With Magnus Colorado, chief of the Mimbrano Apache, Cochise warred against the Mexicans in the 1850's, but he refused to fight the Americans until 1860. Then, while living in the Apache Pass of the Chiricahua Mountains and supplying the stage station with firewood, he was falsely accused of kidnapping an American child. Coming to a parley with federal troops to deny the charge, he was arrested. He managed to escape but was wounded, and five of his followers were hanged.

Cochise rallied his people to avenge the deed and, as he said, to defend his homeland against the invaders. His greatest battle took place in September 1861, when he and Magnus Colorado ambushed the advance party of General James H. Carleton's troops marching from California to take New Mexico from the Confederates. With 500 to 700 warriors he commanded the heights of Apache Pass, and only after an all-day fight was he dislodged by howitzer fire.

For a decade Cochise raided and plundered. In September 1871, when the government embarked on a policy of conciliation, he accepted peace with a guarantee of the Chiricahua country. But shortly afterward the government ordered his people onto a distant reservation, and he returned to the warpath. Before his death he was again promised the Chiricahua reservation, but the government later reneged.

DAVID H. CORKRAN, *Author of*
*"The Cherokee Frontier"; "The Creek Frontier"*

**COCHLEA,** kok'lē-ə, a coiled, snail-shaped structure of the inner ear. See EAR.

**COCHLEARIA,** kok-lē-âr'ē-ə, is a small genus of plants, one species of which, the scurvy grass (*Cochlearia officinalis*), is cultivated in the United States. The scurvy grass is native to Arctic regions of the Northern Hemisphere. It ranges in height from 6 to 12 inches (15 to 30 cm) and has heart-shaped leaves, borne on long stalks from the base of the plant. The small white flowers, only about ¼ inch (6 mm) wide, are borne in a cluster during the spring. The plant's name was derived from the belief that it could be used to treat scurvy.

DONALD WYMAN
*The Arnold Arboretum, Harvard University*

**COCHRAN,** kok'rən, **Sir Charles Blake** (1872–1951), English theatrical manager and producer. He was born in Lindfield, Sussex, on Sept. 25, 1872. After several unsuccessful years as an actor in England and the United States he turned to producing plays in New York City. His first production was Ibsen's *John Gabriel Borkman* (1895). He was also Richard Mansfield's secretary and shared in Mansfield's great success as the star of *Cyrano de Bergerac* (1898). In 1902, Cochran began his career as a London producer and manager, and during the next half-century he introduced many famous entertainers to London audiences. He produced and promoted plays, revues, ballets, circuses, rodeos, and boxing and wrestling matches. Forced into bankruptcy in 1924, Cochran reestablished himself in the next few years. He died in London on Jan. 31, 1951.

PICTORIAL PARADE INC.

Jacqueline Cochran

**COCHRAN,** kok'rən, **Jacqueline** (1910?–1980), American pilot, who held more speed, distance, and altitude records than any other contemporary flier. In 1964 she flew at more than twice the speed of sound. Miss Cochran was born in Pensacola, Fla. She was orphaned in infancy and was reared in a foster home in Columbus, Ga. She left school at the third grade to work in a cotton mill. At the age of 14 she got a job in a beauty shop. After learning the trade, she went to New York City to enter the cosmetic industry.

Miss Cochran received a pilot's license after three weeks' training in 1932. The first woman to fly in a Bendix transcontinental race (1934), she won this race in 1938. The International League of Aviators voted her the world's foremost aviatrix in 1937, 1938, and 1939. She was the first woman to ferry a bomber to England. She organized and headed the Women's Airforce Service Pilots (WASP) in World War II.

Miss Cochran wrote *The Stars at Noon* (1954) and served as board chairman of Jacqueline Cochran, Inc., a cosmetic firm. She died in Indio, Calif., on Aug. 9, 1980.

C. R. ROSEBERRY
*Author of "The Challenging Skies"*

**COCHRANE,** kok'rən, **John** (1813–1898), American public official. He was born in Palatine, N. Y., on Aug. 27, 1813 and graduated (1831) from Hamilton College. A New York City lawyer, he campaigned for Franklin Pierce in 1852 and became New York port surveyor. He served two terms in Congress as a Democrat (1857–1861). A states-righter favoring conciliation, he opposed secession, raised a regiment in the Civil War, and retired a brigadier general in 1863 because of poor health. As a war Democrat on the Republican-Union ticket, he was elected New York attorney general.

Dissident Republicans at the Cleveland convention in 1864 nominated him for vice president to run with John C. Frémont, but both candidates withdrew, and Cochrane campaigned for Lincoln. As a Liberal Republican at the Cincinnati convention of 1872, he promoted Horace Greeley's nomination. Thereafter, Cochrane held local offices and was a collector of internal revenue. He died on Feb. 7, 1898, in New York City.

**COCHRANE,** kok'rən, **Mickey** (1903–1962), American baseball player, who was one of the game's outstanding catchers. Gordon Stanley Cochrane was born in Bridgewater, Mass., on April 6, 1903. Originally an infielder, he began his career as a catcher with Dover (Md.) in 1923. He played with Portland in the Pacific Coast League in 1924, and the same year Connie Mack of the Philadelphia Athletics bought his contract.

Cochrane sparked the Athletics to three straight pennants (1929–1931) and two world championships (in 1929 against the Chicago Cubs and in 1930 against the St. Louis Cardinals). In 1928 he was voted the American League's most valuable player. In 1934 he became playing manager of the Detroit Tigers and again was voted the league's most valuable player. With Cochrane the Tigers won two straight pennants (1934 and 1935), defeating the Chicago Cubs in the World Series in 1935. In 1937 he was hit in the head with a pitched ball, and his playing career ended; he continued as Tiger manager midway through 1939. In 13 seasons he compiled a .320 batting average.

Cochrane served in the U. S. Navy in World War II and later coached and scouted for several ball clubs. In 1947 he was elected to the Baseball Hall of Fame. He died on June 28, 1962, in Lake Forest, Ill.

MICHAEL QUINN
*"Sports Illustrated"*

**COCHRANE,** kok'rən, **Thomas** (1775–1860), 10th Earl of Dundonald, British naval officer who also commanded revolutionary navies of Chile, Brazil, and Greece. He was born Dec. 14, 1775, in Lanarkshire, Scotland, the son of Archibald Cochrane, 9th Earl of Dundonald, whom he succeeded as 10th Earl in 1831.

Cochrane began his naval career in 1793 in a frigate commanded by his uncle Alexander Cochrane. From his first command, a gun brig, his fame spread as a superb commander, aggressive and intrepid. In the Mediterranean, 1799–1801, he captured more than 50 vessels, one a large Spanish frigate. In 1806 he entered the House of Commons but soon was ordered to sea for agitating for naval reform. In one of his most conspicuous feats, he inflicted heavy damage by fire ships on a French fleet at Basque Roads near Rochefort in 1809.

In 1814 he was arrested for alleged connection with stock market manipulation that involved false rumors of Napoleon's death. Convicted, apparently through a miscarriage of justice, he was fined, imprisoned, and ousted from the navy and Parliament. Thereafter he accepted invitations to serve as commander in chief of revolutionary navies—of Chile (1818–1823), Brazil (1823–1825), and Greece (1827–1828). He became involved in repeated troubles with the new governments, took part in many actions with improvised flotillas, and pioneered in the use of steam warships.

In 1832 he was reinstated in the British Navy as a rear admiral, and in subsequent years he received many promotions and honors. In 1847 he was appointed to command the North America and West Indies squadron. Cochrane engaged in many experiments, notably in the use of steam power and screw propulsion, and produced several inventions. He wrote two volumes of memoirs. He died on Oct. 31, 1860, and was buried in Westminster Abbey.

ROBERT G. ALBION, *Harvard University*

**COCHRANE,** kok'rən, a town in Ontario, Canada, 400 miles (640 km) northwest of Toronto. It is the seat of Cochrane district and is the trading center for a large mining region. Cochrane produces lumber, machinery, and lumber and dairy products. It was founded in 1908. Population: 4,443.

**COCK OF THE ROCK.** See COTINGA.

**COCKATOO,** kok'ə-tōō, a parrotlike bird that inhabits forests and open woodlands from the Solomon Islands west through New Guinea to Timor and from Tasmania north through Australia to Celebes. One species is also found in the Philippines.

The characteristic that sets cockatoos apart from other parrots is a long erectile crest. Cockatoos range in size from the 25-inch (63-cm) great black palm cockatoo of Australia and New Guinea to the slender 13-inch (33-cm) cockatiel of central Australia. The cockatoo's head is very large, and its curved, narrow bill is sharply pointed. The best known cockatoos (genus *Kakatoe*) are white with yellow or pink tints on the body or crest. Other species are gray or black with red or yellow heads or tail bands.

Cockatoos screech noisily, but they can be taught to talk well. Because of this ability and their striking appearance and docile nature, they have been popular cage birds for nearly 300 years. They are also long-lived; some captive birds have lived for over 100 years. Most cockatoos eat hard nuts, which they break with their powerful bills. Some cockatoos also feed on grains, fruit, vegetables, roots, and tree-boring beetle grubs. The more gregarious species are serious agricultural pests.

Like all parrots, cockatoos nest in a natural hollow high up in a tree or rock crevice. The female lays one to four white eggs. The young are fed regurgitated food by their parents.

There are 16 species of cockatoos classified in the parrot family, Psittacidae.

GEORGE E. WATSON, *Smithsonian Institution*

**COCKBURN,** kō'bərn, **Sir Alexander James Edmund** (1802–1880), lord chief justice of England. He was born on Dec. 24, 1802, into an old Scottish family. Cockburn had a highly successful career in law and politics (he was a member of Parliament and served as solicitor general and attorney general) before becoming lord chief justice (1859), an office he held until his death.

A small, sociable man and a connoisseur of music, literature, and the natural sciences, Cockburn was also a brilliant advocate. He proved a great judge whose versatility, patience, and powers of analysis allowed him to range over the whole field of the law. Learned in commercial law, libel, and tort, he demonstrated his knowledge of international law in his dissenting report on the *Alabama* arbitration (1872). In *R.* v. *Nelson and Brand* (1867), he gave a classic definition of martial law. The most celebrated trial over which he presided was that of the claimant to the Tichborne title and estates in 1873–1874. (See TICHBORNE CASE.) He may be criticized for not disguising his belief in the claimant's guilt, but his summing-up, lasting 20 days and dealing with the evidence of 400 witnesses, was a masterpiece of clarity and cogency. He died in London on Nov. 20, 1880.

ANGUS MACINTYRE, *Oxford University*

**COCKCROFT,** kok'krôft, **Sir John Douglas** (1897–1967), British physicist, mathematician, and engineer, who is best known for his work in nuclear physics and for his leading role in the release of atomic energy on a large scale. In 1951 he was awarded the Nobel Prize for physics (jointly with E. T. S. Walton) for "their pioneer work on the transmutation of atomic nuclei by artificially accelerated atomic particles."

In 1919, Rutherford had succeeded in transmuting nitrogen into oxygen by bombarding the nitrogen nuclei with alpha particles emitted by radioactive substances. However, the number of alpha particles emitted by available radioactive sources was too small and their energy was too low for their use in research on the heavier nuclei. Further, it was highly desirable that other types of bombarding particles should be available. To produce suitable beams of such particles appeared to require the use of voltages many times higher than seemed possible at the time. That the problem was not as formidable as was expected was shown by Cockcroft by applying to the penetration of nuclei by various particles the theory of alpha particle emission, put forward independently by George Gamow and by E. U. Condon and Ronald Gurney. After discussions with Gamow, Cockcroft pointed out that beams of protons accelerated by relatively low voltages would be expected to penetrate in adequate numbers the nuclei of light elements. With the approval of Rutherford, Cockcroft, together with E. T. S. Walton, began development work that led to the production of fast protons with energies up to 700,000 electron volts. Bombardment of light nuclei with these particles was found to produce disintegration reactions of types previously unknown. This work, carried out in the early 1930's at Cambridge, England, opened up a large new field of nuclear study.

Following the discovery of nuclear fission, Cockcroft played an important part in directing the research and development efforts to produce nuclear reactors for scientific research and for the production of power. In 1944 he took charge of the Canadian Atomic Energy project and was director of the Montreal and Chalk River Laboratories. In 1946 he was appointed Director of the Atomic Energy Research Establishment at Harwell, England, where experimental nuclear reactors were built and used to obtain basic information for the design of the British nuclear power stations.

Cockcroft's knowledge of engineering and mathematics enabled him to design improved equipment that was of much help to others. In collaboration with Peter Kapitza, at Cambridge, he designed apparatus for the production of intense magnetic fields and of very low temperatures. When suitable cobalt steels became available, he helped in the design of a large permanent magnet for use by C. D. Ellis in his studies of beta-ray spectra.

Born at Todmorden, Lancashire, on May 27, 1897, Cockcroft studied electrical engineering at Manchester and mathematics at Cambridge university. He became a Fellow of the Royal Society in 1936 and was knighted in 1948. He died in Cambridge on Sept. 18, 1967.

E. T. S. WALTON, *University of Dublin*
*Nobel Prize Winner in Physics*

**COCKCROFT-WALTON ACCELERATOR.** See PARTICLE ACCELERATOR.

EVELYN M. SHAFER

American cocker spaniel

**COCKER SPANIEL,** kok'ər span'yel, the smallest breed of hunting spaniel. Originally bred to hunt woodcock, from which the name "cocker" is derived, the cocker spaniel has long been a favorite as a show dog and house pet in the United States.

The cocker stands from 14 to 15½ inches (35–39 cm) at the shoulder and weighs from 22 to 28 pounds (10–12.5 kg). The coat is soft and dense. Popular colors are black, red, liver, and lemon; these colors also may be combined with white.

The cocker spaniel was developed from the general spaniel group by selecting the smaller "field" spaniels and blending them with the small, round-headed "Marlborough" types. Though it was originally a fine hunting dog, the sporting qualifications of the cocker spaniel were submerged when it became the most popular purebred in the United States, a rank it held for 17 years. Its displacement in 1953 by the beagle (in total registrations) resulted from temperament changes, such as increased nervousness, brought about by ill-advised breeding to meet the high demand. Properly bred, the cocker spaniel has an affectionate and playful personality, which makes it an ideal family pet.

A similar but somewhat larger breed is known as the English cocker spaniel.

WILLIAM F. BROWN
*Editor of "American Field"*

**COCKERELL,** kok'ər-əl, **Theodore Dru Allison** (1866–1948), American naturalist, whose major areas of interest were the geographic distribution of life, the nature of variations in species populations, the natural history of geographic regions, and fossil plants and insects. He made expeditions to Asia, Africa, and South America, gaining many insights into the natural history of these areas, and wrote over 3,000 articles describing his findings.

Cockerell was born in Norwood, England, on Aug. 22, 1866. After studying in England and the United States, he served on the faculty of the University of Colorado from 1904 to 1934. He died in San Diego, Calif., on Jan. 26, 1948.

DAVID A. OTTO
*Stephens College*

RALPH BUCHSBAUM

COCKLES, like other clams, have two tubular siphons—one for taking in, the other for expelling, water.

**COCKFIGHTING** is the sport of matching fighting roosters (gamecocks) and setting them at each other until one is the acknowledged victor. Considerable wagering almost always accompanies any cockfight.

Gamecocks are naturally pugnacious. They have been bred for thousands of years for fighting, and only those produced by the blending of strains of the most courageous birds are regarded as fit for championship honors. Gamecocks weigh from 3 to 9 pounds and are usually between 1 and 2 years old when they are first entered in matches, or bouts.

Before they enter the fighting pit, they receive special exercises to develop and strengthen their muscles. Their skin is toughened by massage. Their feathers are trimmed and the comb cut to reduce it as a target for the opposing fowl.

Some roosters have longer spurs (bony, sharp spines on the legs, used in fighting) than others; hence, to equalize a contest, metal spurs, or gaffs, sometimes called heels, are often slipped over the natural spurs of the fighters. (In India cocks are always fought in natural spurs.) Gaffs range from 1¼ to 3 inches in length, depending on the size of the gamecock and local regulations. If knife-edged 3-inch gaffs called slashers are used, only one may be placed on a rooster. Birds are matched for the fight by weight.

Each cock has a handler, or pitter. Fights are staged in pits often enclosed by walls. The pit management regulates the contest and selects the referee who presides over the battle. The referee's decisions in anything relating to the main (match) are final. The mains usually consist of contests between an agreed number of pairs of birds, the majority of victories deciding the main. Some fights last until one or the other cock is killed; some permit the handler to withdraw a badly hurt cock at any time; in still others a time limit is fixed. Surviving cocks may fight many times; sometimes they are retired to the brood yard.

One of the most ancient sports, cockfighting originated in the Orient and was introduced into Europe in the 5th century B.C. Themistocles is said to have brought the sport to Greece, and the Romans spread it throughout their empire. A national pastime in early England, cockfighting had become a royal sport by the time of Henry VIII. The Spaniards carried the sport to their possessions in the New World, and the English to North America. By the late 1960's contests were still popular in Asia and in many Spanish-speaking areas of the world, but were illegal in England, Canada, and most of the United States.

RUTH DeCAMP McMILLAN
*Editor of "Grit and Steel"*

**COCKLE,** a marine clam that lives in all parts of the world, from the Arctic to the tropics and from the intertidal estuaries to depths of over 1 mile (1.6 km). Its shells, which range in length from about ½ inch (1.2 cm) to 6 inches (15 cm), are heart-shaped, with serrated or scalloped edges and many raised radial ribs. The cockle has a strong muscular foot and moves about easily.

In western Europe, cockle species such as *Cerastoderma edule* are collected by the ton from shallow sandbanks and are sold in fish markets as food. The dozen American cockle species are edible, but they are generally too tough for eating unless ground or pounded. Cockles are also a food source for important market fish.

Cockles belong to the bivalve family Cardiidae; there are about 200 species. The beautiful, ribbed shell of *Cardium costatum* from West Africa is a collector's item and commands a high price. Several of the Florida species, such as the rose cockle (*Trachycardium egmontianum*), are used to make various shell craft items.

R. TUCKER ABBOTT
*The Academy of Natural Sciences of Philadelphia*

**COCKLEBUR,** kok′əl-bûr, any of several weedy plants of the genus *Xanthium*, in the composite family. Cockleburs range throughout the United States and south Canada. They are coarse annual plants that grow about 3 feet (90 cm) tall and have alternate, heart-shaped, bristly leaves with coarsely toothed edges. The flower heads are rather inconspicuous, but the fruits are round, bristly balls that stick to any cloth or fur that comes in contact with them. Cockleburs are best controlled by cutting them close to the ground so that they cannot produce flowers and thus cannot reproduce.

DONALD WYMAN
*The Arnold Arboretum, Harvard University*

**COCKNEY,** a native of the East End of London; traditionally, one born within the sound of "Bow bells," the bells of St. Mary-le-Bow Church, which was badly damaged in World War II. The word was originally spelled *cokeney* and meant "cock's egg," the name applied to malformed eggs supposedly laid by cocks. It later came to mean a pampered child, then any city dweller; its present meaning has been current since 1617.

"Cockney" also refers to the dialect common to Londoners of the East End. This dialect, which probably dates from the late 15th century, is marked by various peculiarities of pronunciation, such as pronouncing "ï" for "ā" ("shyme" for "shame"), "ä" for "ou" ("abaht" for "about"), "w" for "v" ("wery" for "very"), and "f" or "v" for "th" ("fink" for "think"). Dropping or adding an initial "h" is characteristic of cockney speech but not peculiar to it. Cockney also possesses a slang consisting mostly of rhyming slang; an example is "trouble and strife" for "wife."

ERIC PARTRIDGE, *Author of "A Dictionary of Slang and Unconventional English"*

**COCKROACH,** kok'rŏch, one of the world's commonest insects. It occurs in almost every habitable land from the Arctic to the Antarctic. There is a word for cockroaches in almost every language: in German they are called *Schaben,* in French *blattes,* and in Spanish *cucarachas.* In English they are often called simply "roaches."

Cockroaches are flat and oval and have long antennae. They range in color from brown to gray and black, but many tropical species are brilliant green, yellow, red, or orange. Some have contrasting markings.

Most cockroaches vary in length from ¼ inch to more than 3 inches (0.6 to 7.6 cm). The largest roaches are found in the tropics, and it is there that they are most abundant. A few roaches are so tiny that they are able to live as "guests" in the nests of the leaf-cutting ants.

**Types of Cockroaches.** Most kinds of roaches are wild; that is, they live in forests among decaying vegetables, under the bark of rotten logs, or in similar situations where they usually feed as scavengers on plant and animal material. A few types of roaches damage living plants by feeding upon them.

However, long ago several kinds of roaches took up life in human habitations and became pests, especially in the warmer parts of the world. Many kinds have been carried as stowaways in ships to almost all parts of the world. These include such pest species as the German cockroach (*Blattela germanica*), the brown-banded roach (*Supella supellectilium*), the Oriental roach (*Blatta orientalis*), and others. The largest cockroach found in North America is the native American roach (*Periplaneta americana*), which is nearly 2 inches (5 cm) long.

**Habits and Control.** Most roaches are scavengers and will eat nearly anything. The kinds that infest kitchens consume almost any food left exposed. While roaches often have been accused of spreading disease by walking over filth and then onto food, this has never actually been proved.

Because roaches are elusive in their habits, their presence is often unsuspected. They are often difficult to eliminate, especially the small German roach. In many cases, they are not noticed until lights are turned on late at night, revealing roaches scurrying into cracks where their flattened bodies make concealment easy. Being negatively phototropic (repelled by light), they always seek darkness.

In guarding against infestation by roaches, cleanliness is important. Food should be protected and garbage disposed of. Cockroaches can be controlled by using chlordane, dieldrin, or Malathion in the cracks and crevices in which they hide. Yellow phosphorus paste is used to eliminate heavy infestations of the American roach.

**Natural History.** While most insects deposit their eggs individually on food plants or in other places, cockroaches' eggs are usually enclosed in purselike capsules, or oötheca, that may be carried by the female, attached to her abdomen, for several days before being dropped. In the different species these egg cases vary in size and in the number of eggs they contain. Usually there are from 15 to 40 eggs arranged side by side in a double row. There are exceptions, however; for instance, there is a tropical roach that bears living young.

When newly hatched, young cockroaches resemble the adults except that they lack wings.

PHILIP GENDREAU       BLACK STAR

American cockroach (*left*) and German cockroach (*right*)

During growth they molt several times and eventually acquire wings. Some kinds of roaches remain wingless even as adults. Roaches vary considerably in the time required for development from egg to adult—in some species several years is required, while others complete their growth in a few weeks.

**Experiments and Behavior.** Because of its large size and ease of rearing, the American roach is often used as an experimental animal in biological laboratories. It serves as a subject for the study of insect physiology and for the testing of insecticides.

Roaches are also ideal subjects for studying insect behavior. It has been found, for example, that American roaches have limited ability to learn their way through a simple maze, as contrasted with ants, which can learn their way through a much more complicated maze. On the other hand, some tests indicate that roaches have better memories than ants. It was found that roaches soon learned to avoid dark cracks into which they normally would have retreated if they were given a weak electrical shock each time they tried to hide in them.

**History.** Cockroaches and their relatives are among the most ancient of all insects. Their remote ancestors probably crawled through the early land plants, which lived about 400 million years ago during the Silurian period.

While there are more than 2,000 different species of roaches living at present, their heyday occurred during the Carboniferous period, which began about 345 million years ago and lasted for 65 million years. During that period, cockroaches were much more abundant than they are today. These ancient cockroaches saw the rise of the seed ferns (pteridosperms) and the primitive conifers, as well as the coming of the first reptiles.

The cockroaches of these ancient forests were winged, and from them were evolved all the later types of flying insects. Thus they were the first animals to fly, for more than 100 million years were to pass before the first flying reptiles took to the air.

**Classification.** Cockroaches are classified in the family Blattidae of the order Dictyoptera.

ROSS HUTCHINS
*State Plant Board of Mississippi*

ARTHUR AMBLER, FROM NATIONAL AUDUBON SOCIETY

R. A. SCHLEGEL

COCKSCOMBS produce dense flower clusters that may be flattened and crested *(left)* or open and feathery *(right)*.

**COCKSCOMB,** a popular annual garden plant often cultivated for its brightly colored summer flowers, which are similar in shape to a cock's comb. The cockscomb ranges in height from 1 to 2 feet (30–60) cm) and bears alternate, entire leaves. The flowers are mostly red, yellow, purple, green, or white, and may be from 3 to 6 inches (7.5–15 cm) wide.

Cockscombs may be propagated by seed or by cutting off the top of a young plant just below the flower and inserting it in moist sand as a cutting. In early spring the plants are grown in a greenhouse, but by May they may be planted outdoors. They grow best in full sun and have few, if any, pests.

The cockscomb is known technically as *Celosia argentea* var. *cristata.* It is a member of the amaranth family.

DONALD WYMAN
*The Arnold Arboretum, Harvard University*

**COCKTAIL PARTY,** a play by T. S. Eliot (q.v.), first performed at the Edinburgh Festival in 1949. It opened in New York on Jan. 21, 1950, and in London on May 3, 1950. With *Murder in the Cathedral* (1935), *The Cocktail Party* ranks among Eliot's most effective dramatic works.

Both plays are concerned with the difficulty of knowing and accepting one's spiritual vocation. Unlike the earlier play, however, which is set in medieval England, *The Cocktail Party* seeks to be thoroughly contemporary. Much of the first act could pass as conventional drawing-room comedy, and the entire play is cast in and performed against this convention. Moreover, the primary source of spiritual guidance in the play is represented by a fashionable London psychiatrist. He is part of a worldwide organization of guardians, but it is not made clear just what these guardians are. They seem to belong to a semireligious order and to have limited mystical powers.

In *The Cocktail Party,* Eliot attempts to justify his theories about modern poetic drama. He uses a poetry of contemporary speech, thus providing a subtle rhythmic structure that intensifies the action and heightens the play's emotional impact.

OSCAR BROWNSTEIN, *University of Iowa*

**COCO-DE-MER,** kō-kō-də-mâr′, also called *double coconut* and *sea coconut,* is the huge coconutlike fruit of the giant, 100-foot (30-meter) palm *Lodoicea maldivica,* native to the Seychelles Islands of the Indian Ocean. The fruit, which weighs up to 50 pounds (22.5 kg) and takes 6 to 10 years to ripen, consists of a fibrous husk enclosing a 2-lobed "nut" containing a single seed, the largest known. The fruit was long known from specimens washed ashore on the Maldive Islands, but their origin remained a mystery until the discovery of the Seychelles in 1743.

LAWRENCE ERBE
*University of Southwestern Louisiana*

**COCO PLUM,** an evergreen plant of the rose family (Rosaceae), native from southern Florida to Brazil. It grows as a shrub or a tree, sometimes reaching 30 feet (9 meters) in height. The coco plum (*Chrysobalanus icaco*) has rounded, leathery leaves and bears small clusters of white flowers. Its edible plumlike fruits are small, yellowish, and rather dry and pulpy.

DONALD WYMAN
*The Arnold Arboretum, Harvard University*

**COCOA,** kō′kō, a city on the east coast of Florida, is in Brevard county, 42 miles (68 km) east of Orlando, on the Indian River, a segment of the Intracoastal Waterway. The economy of the Cocoa area is based on aerospace industries, the year-round tourist trade, livestock raising, citrus fruit, and commercial and sport fishing industries. Cocoa is the seat of Brevard Junior College, a 2-year coeducational institution.

A causeway of 8 miles (13 km), crossing Indian River, Merritt Island, and Banana River, links Cocoa with the barrier beach on which are situated the space-oriented city of Cocoa Beach, Cape Kennedy Air Force Station and launching site, and Patrick Air Force Base, headquarters of the Air Force Eastern Test Range. The John F. Kennedy Space Center is located on Merritt Island.

Settled in 1860, Cocoa was incorporated as a town in 1895 and as a city in 1911. Government is by a mayor and council, who appoint a city manager. Population: 16,412.

JOSEPHINE BEERY GOODRICH, *Cocoa Public Library*

**COCOA,** a fine, dark brown powder obtained by subjecting chocolate liquor to hydraulic pressure. Cocoa is also a beverage made by mixing the powder with milk or water. See CHOCOLATE.

**COCONUT,** kō′kə-nut, the most valuable palm of the moist tropics. The coconut palm is indispensable to the economy of some areas and supplies many products for local use, especially on islands in the South Pacific where it may be the only important crop. The green coconuts supply a nutritious drink; the ripened nuts furnish food and oil, the latter being used for cooking and for lamp fuel. Coir, a fiber obtained from coconut husks, is used in brushes and rope. Coconut shells serve as cups and as fuel. An alcoholic drink, syrup, and sugar are made from the sap of the unopened flower cluster. The leaves are used for thatching and for baskets, and the trunk serves as a building material.

**Distribution and Origin.** The coconut palm grows along coastal areas, and occasionally inland and at elevations up to about 2500 feet (750 meters), throughout the humid tropics. Coconut palms are grown to some extent in the subtropics, but productivity of these palms is low. An annual rainfall of at least 60 inches (150 cm), distributed fairly uniformly throughout the year, is essential for maximum productivity unless underground water is available.

There is some question as to the coconut's place of origin. Most authorities believe the coconut is native to tropical America and became dispersed in prehistoric times through the Pacific islands and adjacent areas. How dispersal occurred is not known, but man was probably partly responsible. The coconut, however, is well adapted for dispersal by ocean currents. The fruits (the coconuts) can float for months, and when cast ashore they are capable of producing trees if conditions are favorable. About half the world's coconut production comes from noncultivated palms.

**The Tree.** The cylindrical trunk of the coconut palm (*Cocos nucifera*) is 60 to 100 feet (18–30 meters) and is ringed with leaf scars. About 25 to 30 large pinnate leaves are clustered near the top of the trunk. Each leaf, which may grow to a length of 20 feet (6 meters), consists of a strong fibrous leaf stalk (petiole) and a midrib (rachis) from which extend many leaflets.

Flowering usually begins when the tree is 7 to 10 years old. A flower cluster, classified botanically as a spadix, is produced in the axil (the angle between the upper surface of the leaf-stalk and stem) of each leaf.

The coconut palm is threatened by "lethal yellowing"—a disease caused by a mycoplasmalike organism carried by the *Myndus crudus.* It is widespread in Florida, the Caribbean, and the Yucatán Peninsula. A similar, if not identical, strain has occurred in Africa.

**The Coconut.** The immature nuts contain a copious quantity of coconut milk. By the 12th month the fruit has little milk and may be 9 to 10 inches (23–25 cm) long. A thick husk surrounds the nut, which encloses a single large seed. The seed coat is pressed close against the nut.

Coconuts may be collected after they fall, or harvesters may climb the trees about every three months to cut the ripened fruits. Harvesting also can be done from the ground by means of a knife attached to a long pole.

RUSS KINNE, FROM PHOTO RESEARCHERS

COCONUTS grow in clusters in the coconut palm leaves.

**Commercial Products.** Copra, the dried meat of the coconut, is the principal export product derived from this plant. Coconut oil, one of the most important vegetable oils, is extracted from copra. Other major commercial products are the fresh nuts, coir fiber, and shredded coconut.

The principal areas of production and export of coconut products are the Philippine Islands, Indonesia, Sri Lanka, Oceania, and the Malay Peninsula.

The increasing importance of the coconut in world trade is due primarily to the extensive demand for coconut oil. Formerly, the oil was used mostly for making soaps and candles. All

COCONUT PALMS may reach a height of 60 to 100 feet.

JOHN J. SMITH

floating soaps were made from coconut oil, until it was discovered that other oils could be used if air was mixed with the soap during manufacture. Because of its high lauric acid content, which imparts a quick-lathering property, coconut oil is used in quick-lathering soaps.

Refined coconut oil is odorless and colorless; when solidified, it is white to yellowish in color and melts at about 72°F (22°C). Coconut oil serves as a butterfat substitute in margarine, chocolate, and other foods. It is also used in cosmetics and synthetic rubber and as a plasticizer in many products.

LAWRENCE ERBE
*University of Southwestern Louisiana*

**COCOON,** kə-kōōn, a body covering constructed by certain kinds of insect larvae to protect themselves during the resting, or pupal, stage. The pupal stage immediately follows the last larval molt, and it is the most vulnerable period of an insect's life. During this stage the insect is completely helpless, protected only by its cocoon. The length of time spent in the cocoon varies greatly depending on the species. In some insects it may last only a few days, while in others it may last several months. While inside the cocoon the insect undergoes many changes, and at the end of this stage it emerges as a fully developed adult.

During the course of insect evolution various methods of protecting the pupa have developed. Many insect larvae simply retreat to some crevice where the pupal stage will be passed. Other species burrow into the ground and pupate inside earthen cells. A third, more advanced, method is the construction of a cocoon. Cocoon building occurs in several orders of insects. It is particularly common in the Lepidoptera (butterflies and moths), but may also be observed in the Coleoptera (beetles), Hymenoptera (ants, wasps, bees, and others), Diptera (flies and mosquitos), Trichoptera (caddisflies), and the Neuroptera (ant lions, lacewings, and others).

**Structure.** A typical cocoon consists either entirely or partly of silk or some similar material. These substances are usually secreted from glands located in the larva's head and they may be used to form the entire cocoon or as a glue to hold foreign materials together. The substance comprising the major part of the cocoon varies according to species and often depends on the kind of food the insect eats or on its immediate surroundings. For example, many wood-boring insects construct cocoons largely of wood chips, and a number of species that pupate either in or on the ground make considerable use of sand or soil particles. Larvae that live and feed on leaves often roll the leaves up or cut a small flap from one edge of a leaf and pupate inside the resulting cavity. Most hairy caterpillars remove their hairs just before pupating and weave them into a flimsy cocoon.

In many species, particularly wasps and moths, the cocoon is made entirely of silk. However, the texture and architecture of these silken cocoons vary considerably. Some cocoons are fragile and lacelike, functioning as tiny cages to keep out predators and parasites. Others are firm and consist of many layers. Many silkworm moths construct this kind of cocoon.

**Methods of Emergence.** Just as there are many different types of cocoons, there are also different methods by which the adult insects emerge from them. In species that have chewing mouthparts, the adult simply chews its way out. Insects with sucking mouthparts emerge in various other manners. In some of these species the head is equipped with a prominent crest or beak that functions as a knife in tearing an opening in the cocoon. Most remarkable of all are those species whose larvae deliberately weaken one end of the cocoon to form a kind of valve, or trap door, through which the adult insects can later escape.

DON DAVIS, *Smithsonian Institution*

**COCOS ISLANDS,** kō'kōs, two Australian atolls in the Indian Ocean, 1,720 miles (2,768 km) northwest of Perth. Also known as the Keeling Islands, they consist of 27 coral islands, islets, and reefs with a combined land area of 5.4 square miles (14 sq km). The tropical climate is tempered by southeast trade winds.

In 1982 the population was 551, distributed between two islands of the larger, southern atoll. The 314 Malay-speaking Muslims, mostly of Indonesian and Malayan heritage, lived on Home Island. Nearly all of the 237 people of European stock were Australians on West Island.

The economy is based on extensive groves of coconut palms, and copra (dried coconut meat) is exported to Australia. Malays work mainly in the coconut industry, whereas white residents are employed chiefly by the Australian government. The local food supply is limited largely to fish, fruit, and garden produce. Other foods, as well as fuel, lubricants, and consumer goods, must be imported. The islands have air and sea connections with Perth. An underwater oil pipeline runs from the main anchorage in the southern atoll's lagoon to West Island, which is also the site of the airport.

The Cocos Islands were discovered in 1609 by William Keeling, an English naval commander on a voyage for the East India Company. The first permanent settlement was made on Home Island in 1827 by a Scottish sailor, John Clunies-Ross, and his party of mostly Malay laborers. More Malays and other Asians soon followed. The Cocos group was annexed by Britain in 1857, and perpetual title to all its land was granted to the Clunies-Ross family in 1886.

Early in World War I, the German cruiser *Emden* attacked the islands' cable station, but the warship was forced aground by the Australian cruiser *Sydney* on Nov. 9, 1914. During World War II the Japanese shelled and bombed the station. Between 1948 and 1951 some 1,600 islanders—two thirds of the population—were resettled in Sabah and elsewhere because the economy could not sustain them.

When Britain relinquished responsibility for the islands in 1955, they became a dependency of Australia. In 1978 the Australian government bought most of the land from the Clunies-Ross family, thus ending the hegemony of the "kings of the Cocos." The next year, for the benefit of the Cocos Malays, Australia entrusted the property it had acquired on Home Island to a newly established local government council. In 1984 the Australian government sponsored a referendum, supervised by the United Nations, on the islands' future status. Cocos citizens chose integration with Australia over the alternatives of free association or independence. Home islanders gained full Australian citizenship and have control over local affairs.

**COCTEAU,** kŏk-tō', **Jean** (1889–1963), French writer, artist, and film maker, whose work includes poetry, fiction, drama, criticism, ballet, cinema, and paintings. In all these forms he thought of himself as a "poet," and of his works as "poetry."

**Life.** Cocteau was born at Maisons-Laffitte, near Paris, on July 5, 1889, the son of a successful lawyer. His mother's interest in the arts, especially in the theater and the opera, determined the course of his life. While a student at the Lycée Condorcet from 1900 to 1904, Cocteau met and admired many prominent theatrical personalities of the time, including Sarah Bernhardt and Isadora Duncan. He also admired the virtuoso performers of the circus and music hall.

In 1909, Cocteau published his first volume of poetry, *La lampe d'Aladin.* In the same year he met the Russian impresario Diaghilev, at whose suggestion he made his first venture into ballet, writing part of the scenario for *Le dieu bleu* (1912), choreographed by Fokine for Nijinsky.

Rejected for military service at the outbreak of World War I, Cocteau organized an ambulance unit, flew with his friend, the French ace Roland Garros, and had many extraordinary experiences at the front, most of which he used later in his poetry and in his novel *Thomas l'imposteur* (1923; Eng. tr., *Thomas the Impostor,* 1925). In 1917 he returned to civilian life, gaining recognition through the production of his modernistic ballet *Parade,* with score by Eric Satie and scenery by Picasso. Also in 1917, Cocteau helped to bring together in Paris a group of young composers later known as "Les Six" (Auric, Durey, Honegger, Milhaud, Poulenc, and Tailleferre). Cocteau's later ballets included *Le boeuf sur le toit ou the Nothing Doing Bar* (1920), with score by Milhaud, and *Les mariés de la tour Eiffel* (1921), with score by "les Six."

In 1918, Cocteau formed an intimate friendship with the 15-year-old novelist Raymond Radiguet, whose death from typhoid fever in 1923 was a severe blow to Cocteau and drove him to the use of opium. Nevertheless, during the 1920's he produced considerable poetry, drama, fiction, and criticism. His recovery from addiction is described in *Opium* (1930; Eng. tr., 1932).

In the 1930's Cocteau devoted himself largely to the theater. During World War II he was primarily engaged in film making, and after the war he adapted some of his plays for the screen. In the last decade of his life he turned his attention largely to painting, including the decoration of several chapels.

In 1954, on the death of his friend Colette, the novelist, Cocteau took her place in the Belgian Academy, and in 1955 he was elected to the French Academy. He died of a heart attack at his château, Milly-la-Forêt, near Fontainebleau, on Oct. 11, 1963, after hearing the news of the death of another friend, the singer Edith Piaf.

**Works.** Cocteau began as a poet. His early verse was influenced by Edmond Rostand and the Comtesse Anna de Noailles, but with the volume *Le Cap de Bonne Espérance* (1919) it took on freer forms reflecting aspects of cubist, futurist, and dadaistic art. Cocteau's main poetic works are *Plain-chant* (1923), *Opéra* (1927), and *Clair-obscur* (1954). His poetry is often elusive, embodying the relationship between sleep and waking, between life and death.

Cocteau's best novels include *Thomas l'imposteur,* a subtle, moving account of an adolescent's

Jean Cocteau

HENRI DE CHATILLON, FROM BLACK STAR

involvement in war; and *Les enfants terribles* (1929; Eng. tr., *Enfants Terribles,* 1930), probably his masterpiece, which describes four adolescents whose attempt to escape the realities of life leads to their destruction.

Cocteau's most important artistic contribution was to the theater. His scenarios for ballets were strongly surrealistic, poeticized treatments of the events of everyday life. His earlier plays reversed this technique, modernizing and deflating ancient legends, as in *Antigone* (1922; Eng. tr., 1961), *Orphée* (1925; Eng. tr., 1935), *La machine infernale* (1934; Eng. tr., *The Infernal Machine,* 1936), and *Les chevaliers de la table ronde* (1937); Eng. tr., *The Knights of the Round Table,* 1963). Cocteau's later plays include the romantic melodrama *L'aigle a deux têtes* (1946; Eng. tr., *The Eagle Has Two Heads,* 1948); and more conventional plays presented in modern dress, such as *La voix humaine* (1930; Eng. tr., *The Human Voice,* 1951); *Les parents terribles* (1938; Eng. tr., *Intimate Relations,* 1951); and *La machine à écrire* (1941; Eng. tr., *The Typewriter,* 1948).

Cocteau was best known outside France for his films. They include, in addition to adaptations of his own plays, *Le sang d'un poète* (1932; *The Blood of a Poet*), an experimental classic of the early cinema; *L'éternel retour* (1944; *The Eternal Return*), based on the legend of Tristan and Iseult; and *La belle et la bête* (1945; *Beauty and the Beast*), a surrealistic treatment of the fairy tale.

**Cocteau's Art.** Cocteau, although always in the avant-garde, was less an innovator than a popularizer in that he introduced to a given art various modes and techniques already developed in another. His art sometimes rests on trick effects and mechanical surprises, but this fault is outweighed by the wealth, variety, and profundity of his work.

PIERRE E. BRODIN, *Director of Studies*
*Lycée Français de New-York*

**Further Reading:** Ashton, Dore, and others, *Jean Cocteau and the French Scene,* ed. by Arthur Peters (Abbeville Press 1984); Cocteau, Jean, *Cocteau on the Film: Conversations with Jean Cocteau Recorded by André Fraigneau* (Garland 1985); id., *Journals,* ed. by Wallace Fowlie (Criterion Bks. 1956; Crossland, Margaret, *Jean Cocteau* (1955; reprint, Darby Bks. 1981); Steegmuller, Francis, *Cocteau: A Biography* (Godine 1986).

**COD,** a marine, primarily bottom-living fish found in cool waters. It is also known as *codfish*. The most important and most common species of cod is the Atlantic, or common, cod (*Gadus morhua*), found in the northern Atlantic Ocean.

**Distribution.** On the North American side of the Atlantic Ocean, the Atlantic cod inhabits cool temperate waters from inshore areas to the edge of the continental shelf. It ranges from the Hudson Strait off western Greenland to Cape Hatteras, North Carolina; it is most abundant off the coasts of Newfoundland and Labrador. On the European side, the Atlantic cod ranges southward from Iceland and other Arctic islands off the coast of Europe to the Bay of Biscay. It is also found in the Baltic Sea as far east as Finland.

**Description.** A heavy-bodied fish, the Atlantic cod has a large head that constitutes about one fourth of the total length of the fish; it also has an overhanging snout and a single barbel on the midline of the lower jaw. Its three dorsal fins and two anal fins are soft-rayed and its tail fin is square. Its scales are small. The fish may grow to a large size; in fact, there is one report of a codfish that weighed over 200 pounds (90 kg). However, the weight of fish taken offshore does not usually exceed 60 pounds (27 kg), and the average weight of inshore fish is from 5 to 12 pounds (2–6 kg). These smaller fish make up the greatest proportion of the commercial catch. The color of Atlantic cod varies, depending on the type of bottom and the locality. It may be various shades of gray to green or of brown to red. The sides and back are liberally sprinkled with round, brown to red spots, and the lateral line, arched in the first two fifths of the fish, is noticeably paler than the rest of the body. The underside is whitish.

**Behavior—Habitat.** Cod live between the surface and depths of at least 250 fathoms (1,500 feet, or 500 meters) in temperatures ranging from 32° to 55° F (0°–13° C). They normally live close to the bottom, except when they are pursuing food or in seasonal migration. When migrating, they move both horizontally and vertically. Large numbers of cod have been tagged and much has been learned of their movements. For example, the cod stocks from Labrador move north and south along the coast, but remain in cold waters. They tend to remain in deep water during winter and to move into shallower inshore waters in summer. In fact, cod migrations in general show an inshore movement in summer and an offshore movement in fall and winter.

Atlantic cod

There also is evidence to suggest that there is little mixing of stocks over wide areas.

**Diet.** Atlantic cod are voracious feeders. As fry, they eat copepods and many other small crustaceans; as young adults, they add shrimp, small lobsters, crabs, and shrimplike crustaceans including euphausiids and mysids to their diets. After the young cod reach a length of 20 inches (50 cm), fish becomes their principal food. They feed heavily on capelin and often come into surface waters in pursuit of them. They also take large numbers of herring. Sand lance, small cod, and a wide variety of other animals are also included in their diet. The size of the prey seems to be the only factor that limits their diet. In turn, cod fry are eaten by pollock and other fishes and adult cods are preyed upon by sharks and seals.

**Reproduction.** Spawning occurs on both sides of the Atlantic chiefly in the winter, but it is dependent on water temperatures. Atlantic cod spawn over a wide area of the continental shelf; therefore, generalizations concerning spawning grounds and times of spawning are misleading. On the Grand Bank of Newfoundland, Atlantic cod spawn from April to June, probably reaching a peak in late May. Farther south, ripening fish are caught from late October to mid-February. The Atlantic cod is prolific; females about 40 inches (100 cm) long produce approximately 5 million eggs a year. There is a record of a 52½-inch (133-cm) fish producing over 8 million eggs in a year.

The eggs are spherical, 1.2 to 1.8 mm in diameter. They are buoyant and float near the surface during incubation. The length of time required for hatching depends on the temperature of the water; it may be several weeks. The young grow at different rates in different areas; cod on the Grand Bank grow much more quickly than those off northern Laborador. In colder waters, growth is slower than in warm water.

**Commercial Importance.** Atlantic cod is of great commercial importance. It is considered one of the leading food fishes of the world, and it supports the most valuable fishery in the northwest Atlantic. Cod has been sought on the banks of the North Atlantic for hundreds of years. It is caught by otter trawls, line trawls, pair trawls, hand lines, Danish seines, traps, and gill nets from vessels of the United States, Canada, Portugal, the USSR, Germany, France, Spain, and other countries. In a typical year in the mid-1960's nearly 3 million metric tons were landed.

Cod flesh is used in a variety of ways. It is sold fresh, smoked, salted, canned, and frozen. Special parts of the cod, such as cheeks and tongues, are delicacies among certain maritime peoples. Salted cod is especially popular in Spain, Portugal, and the West Indies. Cod-liver oil, once considered an important source of vitamins, is obtained from the liver of cod.

**The Cod Family.** The Atlantic cod belongs to the family Gadidae of the order Gadiformes. The family Gadidae contains 59 species, including, besides the Atlantic cod, such other food fishes as the Pacific cod, the haddock, the pollock, the hakes, and rocklings.

The Pacific cod (*Gadus macrocephalus*) is closely related to the Atlantic cod. It occurs from central California to the Bering Sea. Other species of cod include the Arctic cod (*Boreogadus saida*), found in salt waters in the polar region and differing from related species in its forked tail and slender body, and the Greenland cod (*Gadus ogac*), which ranges from western Greenland to Point Barrow, Alaska, and south along the Arctic and Atlantic coasts to the Gulf of St. Lawrence and Cape Breton Island. The Greenland cod is very similar in shape to the Atlantic cod, but it lacks the characteristic round spots of the common cod, and its eye is slightly larger.

W. B. SCOTT
*University of Toronto*

**COD, Cape.** See CAPE COD.

**COD-LIVER OIL,** a pale yellow oil obtained from the fresh livers of the cod. A valuable source of vitamins A and D, cod-liver oil is used to prevent rickets in children and for other nutritional purposes. It has also been used as an auxiliary therapy in the treatment of tuberculosis. Applied externally, it may also hasten the healing of burns and wounds.

Although cod-liver oil has been used as a folk remedy by the Dutch peasants for centuries, it was not until the middle of the 19th century that it was introduced into scientific medicine and not until the 1920's that it was recognized as a source of vitamins A and D.

Separated from fresh cod livers by low-pressure cooking, cod-liver oil is often prepared in an emulsion form flavored with volatile oil or malt extract, and also in capsules.

GEORGE B. GRIFFENHAGEN
*American Pharmaceutical Association*

**CODAZZI,** kō-dät′tsē, **Agostino** (1793–1859), Italian geographer, who explored and mapped parts of northern South America. He was born at Lugo, Italy, on July 11, 1793. Between 1831 and 1838 he served the government of Venezuela and published *Resúmen de la geografía de Venezuela* and *Atlas físico y político de la República de Venezuela*. In 1849 he accepted an invitation from the government of Colombia to prepare an atlas. The *Geografía física y política de los Estados Unidos de Colombia*, which was nearly completed at his death, appeared posthumously under the names of his collaborators. Codazzi died at Espíritu, Colombia, on Feb. 7, 1859.

**CODDINGTON, William** (1601–1678), American colonial leader, who founded Portsmouth and Newport, R. I. Born in Lincolnshire, England, he became a commissioner of the Massachusetts Bay Company and sailed for Boston in 1630. A religious dissenter himself, he defended Ann Hutchinson before the Puritan magistrates, then went to Providence, R. I., in 1638. That year he established a settlement called Pocasset (later Portsmouth) in the northern region of the island of Aquidneck. However, William Hutchinson and Samuel Gorton established a rival colony there, and in 1639 Coddington and his adherents moved to southern Aquidneck and founded Newport. Late that year the two settlements were combined with Coddington as governor.

In 1644, Coddington's domain was officially united with the mainland provinces of Providence and Warwick. Determined to regain control, Coddington in 1651 secured a Parliamentary patent making Aquidneck a separate colony and himself governor for life, but this was revoked in 1652. Later, in the 1670's he was several times chief magistrate of the combined Rhode Island colonies. He died in office on Nov. 1, 1678.

**CODE.** See CRYPTOGRAPHY.

**CODE, Legal.** See CODIFICATION.

**CODE Napoléon.** See CODIFICATION.

**CODE OF HAMMURABI.** See HAMMURABI, CODE OF.

**CODEBALL** is a kicking game for two to four persons, played with a highly inflated rubber ball. *Codeball in the court,* the indoor version, utilizes a standard 4-wall handball court for the playing area. The outdoor game, *codeball on the green,* is played on a 5- to 20-acre course. The ball has a 6-inch diameter and weighs 12 ounces.

In the court game, handball rules prevail, except that the ball is kicked and, after the service, may be kicked on the fly or after the first or second bounce. Game is 21 points.

The game on the green combines features of golf and soccer. Each of the 14 holes in the playing area has for its cup a light metal cone-shaped basin, or bowl, 40 inches wide at the base, rising 7 inches from the turf to an opening 18 inches wide. The object is to advance the codeball from each of the 14 kick-off lines into the bowls, which are anywhere from 50 to 300 yards apart, in the fewest possible kicks.

Codeball was invented in 1927 by William E. Code, a Chicago physician, and was sanctioned by the Amateur Athletic Union in 1929.

HAROLD T. FRIERMOOD
*National Board of YMCA's*

**CODEINE,** kō′dēn, is a narcotic drug derived from opium. Although codeine can be produced from morphine, it is a much weaker narcotic than morphine, and it is much less likely to cause euphoria or addiction. Therefore, it is the most widely used narcotic drug.

Codeine has two main therapeutic actions. First, it can relieve mild to moderate pain more effectively than aspirin and similar medications but less effectively than morphine. There is a limit to the pain-relieving ability of codeine, and if pain is severe, increasing the dose of codeine beyond the usual therapeutic range does not help. The pain-relieving effects of a usual single dose of codeine last about two to three hours. The second therapeutic action of codeine is the relief of cough by an action on the brain. If the cough is a dry, nonproductive one that is tiring the patient for no good purpose, the effect of codeine is beneficial. However, if the cough is a productive one that is helping the patient to get excess mucus out of his lungs, codeine can, by reducing or eliminating the cough, worsen the patient's condition. Codeine may also be dangerous in some cases of asthma.

Addiction to codeine is rare, although addicts to other narcotic drugs such as morphine, heroin, and meperidine will sometimes take codeine if they cannot obtain a stronger narcotic. In the United States, codeine is subject to federal narcotic laws. However, the sale of cough medicines that contain less than a specified concentration of codeine per ounce is permitted without a doctor's prescription.

Toxic effects of codeine are rare, but convulsions have been reported in children receiving large doses.

SOLOMON GARB, M.D.
*University of Missouri Medical School*

**CODEX,** kō′deks, a handwritten, hand-bound volume of pages made of various materials. The English word comes from the Latin *caudex* or *codex,* meaning a tree trunk or stem stripped of bark. Later, the term denoted a wooden tablet coated with a layer of wax on which one could write with a stylus. Such tablets could be hinged together to form larger units used as account books, ledgers, or school books.

The term "codex" also refers to a collection of laws, such as the *Codex Theodosianus;* a constitution, such as the *Codex Justinianus;* or church regulations, such as the *Codex Juris Canonici.* Some of the most noted codices, however, are Biblical manuscripts, including the 4th century *Codex Sinaiticus* and *Codex Vaticanus* and the 5th century *Codex Alexandrinus*—the oldest and most complete manuscripts of the Greek Bible. The *Codex Sinaiticus* was discovered on Mt. Sinai in 1844. It was acquired by Czar Alexander II of Russia in 1869, but in 1933 the Soviet government sold it to the British Museum in London, where it remains.

Other important codices include the 3d century *Chester Beatty Papyri,* containing several Greek codices of Old and New Testament books; the *Bodmer Papyri* (2d–7th century), with codices of Biblical and classical works in Greek and Coptic; the 10th century *Ben Asher* and *Aleppo* codices, two of the earliest and best extant copies of the Hebrew Bible; the 12th century *Codex Dresden,* a Mayan work on divination, astrology, and mythology; and the 12th or 13th century *Codex Paris,* another Mayan work on divination, ceremonies, and rituals.

Until recent times, codices in the Orient often took the form of bark or wood strips folded like an accordion. In Southeast Asia bamboo strips or palm leaves were strung together in parallel strips like a modern bamboo shade and folded. This type of accordion-fold codex was used in China before the 10th century. Usually only one side of the page was written on, and sometimes the blank backs of the folded pages were pasted together, closely resembling modern books. Before the 15th century, Central American Mayas also used the accordion-fold type of codex, with pages made of skin or paper made from plant substances enclosed between two boards. The Aztecs prepared similar books of coarse cloth coated with a kind of white varnish to provide a smooth writing surface.

See also BIBLE—3. *Manuscripts and Versions of the Old Testament; 12. Manuscripts and Versions of the New Testament;* PALEOGRAPHY.

ROBERT P. MARKHAM
*American Bible Society*

**CODFISH.** See COD.

**CODICIL,** kod′ə-səl, an addition to, qualification of, or change in a will. It must be in the same form as a will, and be executed with the same formalities. All the laws applying to wills apply to a codicil. A codicil properly executed is a republication of the will and makes the will speak from the date of the codicil. The will and codicil are read together as one instrument. There may be more than one codicil to a will. It is also important to note that if there is a discrepancy between the will and the later-executed codicil, the codicil controls even in the absence of expressly revocatory text.

See also WILL (in law).

**CODIFICATION** is the process of collecting and arranging laws into a code. A code may be defined as a complete, written system of law unified and promulgated by legislative action in the jurisdiction (sphere of authority) concerned. The formulation of a code implies (1) a compilation of existing laws and their systematic arrangement according to logical principles, and (2) a thorough revision in order to harmonize conflicts, supply omissions, and clarify and make complete the body of laws designed to govern the subjects to which they relate. A code differs from a mere compilation, which is a collection of the statutes in force, logically arranged according to subject matter, with all the laws relating to a given subject brought together under one head. The compilation only rearranges existing laws into logical order. The code, however, is an act of positive legislation, proclaimed as one new law to cover the whole field embraced in its title and to replace preexisting laws in that field.

### HISTORICAL SURVEY

The concept of codification is much older than was once thought. In 1901 the Code of Hammurabi (21st century B. C.) was discovered, and Hammurabi, a Babylonian monarch, was credited with the first codification. More recent discoveries, however, have extended the history of codified law by centuries. The first code to which contemporaneous reference has been discovered is that promulgated by Lipit-Ishtar, King of Isin in ancient Sumer (about 2210 B. C.). But it is known that even earlier codes existed, notably that of Ur-Nammu, King of Ur (25th century B. C.). A copy of the code made around the time of Hammurabi has been discovered.

Development of the codification concept in the ancient world marks a fundamental step in the attempt to form a government of laws, not of men. The early stage in this evolution is usually a demand for definite written law, by which every man knows what he may and may not do. The code ensures that the magistrate must act according to preestablished precepts, rather than according to his arbitrary will. In early systems, justice itself meant merely the decision of cases according to settled written rules. Hence, both Lipit-Ishtar and Hammurabi could say, in the prologues to their codes, that they "established justice in the land."

Other ancient peoples, too, had written codes, usually associated with the names of lawgivers such as Draco (about 621 B. C.) or Solon (about 594 B. C.) in Athens, or Lycurgus (9th century B. C.) in Sparta. The oldest surviving Greek example is an inscription in Gortyna, Crete (450 B. C.).

**Roman Codes.** Roman law begins and ends with a code. The Twelve Tables, in 450 B. C., fulfilled the same basic need as did other ancient codes—to meet the demand for definite written laws. They marked the change from uncertain custom to fixed laws known to all and binding all equally. The underlying goal was to avoid the method later attributed to Emperor Caligula of writing his laws in very small characters and hanging them up on high pillars "the more effectively to ensnare the people."

If the need at the beginning of Roman law was to reduce essential principles to binding written form, a similar need existed for different reasons during the maturity of the Roman system. After full legal development it was necessary to simplify the unwieldy developed law, which was obscured by obsolete rules, and to systematize and harmonize its elements. As early as Julius Caesar, projects for reducing the *ius civile* to a code were unsuccessful. From Marcus Aurelius to Diocletian, collections of imperial legislation were published. The Codex Theodosianus (438 A. D.) was also an authoritative compilation of legislation, comparable to the United States Code or the codes of state laws in the U. S. system.

It was not until Emperor Justinian I (reigned 527–565 A. D.), a century after Theodosius II had planned a complete codification, that the goal of a complete restatement of the whole body of Roman law in statutory form was realized. Known as the *Corpus Juris Civilis*, the Code of Justinian was given statutory authority in 533–534 A. D. It contained a complete revision of imperial legislation, omitting obsolete enactments, eliminating contradictions and repetitions, and making necessary additions and consolidations, as well as a digest of the Roman juristic writings. Justinian's code was a landmark in legal history. Stating in systematic form the results of a millennium of Roman law, it has served as the basis for modern civil-law (as distinguished from common-law) systems.

The Byzantine maritime code of Leo III (8th century) was based on the famous maritime regulations of Rhodes. These regulations also became the source of other codes governing medieval commerce, notably those of the Hanseatic League.

**Development in Western Europe.** The fall of Rome created a legal vacuum filled in part by codes of the different barbarian tribes that succeeded to the Roman *imperium*. Most famous of these were the Salic Law, the *Breviarum* (summary) of Gothic laws of Alaric II, and the code enacted by the Burgundian kings, all formulated during the 6th century. These codes were the result of the same need that had led to ancient codes like the Twelve Tables: to reduce basic customary principles to written form, binding on rulers and ruled alike.

With the reception of Roman law, beginning in the Italian universities during the 12th century, the development and sophistication of European law progressed to the point where new codifications were needed. Local laws and customs had grown so complex and diverse that codes were required to systematize and unify the law. In the French States-General of 1484 and 1560, the third estate (bourgeoisie) formally requested restatements of binding rules and customs. Similar wishes were expressed later, although they were not to achieve full satisfaction before Napoleon.

The first modern legislation that may be called a code is the penal code of Emperor Charles V (1532), which remained the basis of German criminal law for more than three centuries. In France the Great Ordinances of Colbert, Louis XIV's chief minister, codified admiralty, criminal, and commercial law. By the 18th century, juristic theory had come to believe in the possibility of a complete code worked out from the law of nature. In Prussia, Frederick the Great, strongly influenced by this theory, ordered a code drawn up. This code, completed after his death in 1786, was put in force in 1794 and governed in Prussia until 1900.

## MODERN NATIONAL CODES

**Code Napoléon.** One of the immediate results of the French Revolution was the impetus given to the movement to unify French law in a single modern code. The Constituent Assembly of 1790, the Convention in 1793 and 1794, and the Directory in 1796 all promised that they would draw up such a code. Finally, in 1800, Napoleon, then First Consul, appointed and led the commissions that drew up the civil code. Adopted in 36 statutes successively enacted, it was formally consolidated as a single *Code Civil* in 1804.

The French civil code is the first great modern codification of the law. It abrogated the law of the old monarchy—which, based largely on local custom, failed even to approach the unified system demanded by a large national state—and substituted a coherent code, logically arranged and clear and precise in its terms. The framers of the code were dominated by the desire to present the law in a form readily accessible to all. Like Jeremy Bentham, they wanted to be able to say: "Citizen, what is your condition? Are you a farmer? Then consult the chapter on Agriculture."

The drafters of the code did not wholly succeed in their aim. But the instrument they drew up as a codification of all the private law is remarkable for its brevity and lucidity of style. The entire code contains only 2,281 sections and, even in its modern form, can readily be printed in a convenient pocket-size volume. The code itself, after six short preliminary sections, is divided into three parts. The first deals with persons, the second with property, and the third with the different ways whereby property may be acquired.

The French civil code today is in its essentials what it was when Napoleon ordered it drawn up. Its dominant characteristic was the spirit of moderation with which it was drafted. Although a product of the French Revolution, its provisions were anything but revolutionary. But neither was it a reactionary document seeking to undo the work of the men of 1789. On the contrary, it sought to preserve the sound portions of their work—such as the equalitarian ideal, so vital to a democratic legal and economic system—while renouncing the radical, violent measures of the later Revolution. See also FRANCE—8. *Law*.

The Napoleonic code has served as a model for similar codes in most countries outside the Anglo-American world. In countries so diverse as Belgium and Japan, Italy and Egypt, the French code has served as the basis for analogous codifications. More recent codes of particular interest have been the German civil code of 1900 and the Swiss civil code, in force since 1912. Not modeled as directly on the Napoleonic code as other enactments, they carry forward into the 20th century the codification concept upon which that code was based. See also CIVIL LAW.

**Codifications in British Law.** The 16th-century proposals for codification in France inspired a proposal in 1614 in England by Francis Bacon, then attorney general, to codify the common law. Bacon's idea was not implemented, and there was no substantial movement for codification in England until the 19th century. In 1860, Lord Westbury proposed a government plan for revision and compilation of statute law. In 1866 a royal commission endorsed the idea of codification, but nothing came of the project. Thereafter, the movement for law reform focused upon reorganization of courts and reform of procedure and criminal law. Instead of complete codifications of the Napoleonic code type, English law has stressed codifications of particular branches of the common law. Thus the needs of modern commerce led to three statutes in which the principal parts of commercial law were codified: Bills of Exchange Act (1882?), Partnership Act (1890), and Sale of Goods Act (1893). Such partial codification, amounting to legislative restatement of particular fields of law, has continued during the present century, as in the Law of Property Act (1922) and the Administration of Estates Act (1925).

The movement for broad-scale codification has never gotten far in England because of the strength of the common-law tradition of judge-made law, with legislation serving only to fill in gaps in the common law. Even when modern conditions made it increasingly necessary to resort to statute law, the basic goal was to supplement, not supplant, the common law. The common law tradition has not been as strong in other British countries, and codification efforts in them have been more successful, notably in the codes enacted in British India (1837–1886).

**Codification in United States Law.** Codification in American law starts with the adoption by Louisiana in 1824 of a comprehensive civil code based upon the *Code Napoléon*. In 1836 a Massachusetts commission under Joseph Story recommended codification of the state's common law, but its report was not adopted. In New York, largely because of David Dudley Field's agitation, the 1847 constitution provided for commissioners to codify the law. That commission and one appointed in 1857 drafted five codes, usually called the Field codes. New York adopted the penal code and codes of civil and criminal procedure. The Field codes were widely adopted in other states, with some 30 enacting the criminal procedure code, 16 adopting the penal code and code of criminal procedure, and 4 (including California) enacting all 5 Field codes (including the most controversial, the civil code).

The Field codes were a product of the legislative reform movement of the early 19th century, as well as the hostility toward English law and institutions that followed the Revolution and the favor toward things French that accompanied Jeffersonian democracy. The codification movement lost impetus after the Civil War. Instead of broad-scale codification, there were compilations and revisions, such as the revised statutes in many states, and the United States Code (1926), which in annual revisions of federal law organizes it systematically and classifies it according to subject matter.

There have also been partial codifications of the English type, starting with the pioneer New York Real Property Law of 1828. Such codification of particular branches of law has been stimulated by the work of the National Conference of Commissioners on Uniform State Laws organized in 1890–1892. It has drafted more than 100 "uniform" and "model" acts, which have been widely adopted in the states. Among them have been the Negotiable Instruments Act (1896), Sales Act (1906), Stock Transfer Act (1909), Bills of Lading Act (1909), Partnership Act (1914), and Conditional Sales Act (1918). The most important attempt at partial codification has been the Uniform Commercial Code drafted jointly by the uniform state-law commissioners and the American Law Institute (1951). Adopted in whole or in part by all of the states, this has been the most ambitious American codification attempt since the Field codes.

The American Law Institute, set up in 1923, has also drafted 10 "restatements" of different branches of the law, ranging from torts and contracts to foreign relations law. They present the basic principles governing the law in the fields covered and are, in substance, codifications of American common law. As drafts prepared by a private body, they have no legal authority, but they are widely followed by the courts and may ultimately pave the way for legislative codifications. See also COMMON LAW.

**Codification of Soviet Law.** In czarist Russia, there was a compilation of legislation, called the Code of Statutes of the Russian Empire. After the Revolution of 1917, codes were promulgated, including a criminal code in 1922 and a civil code a year later. Although revolutionary jurists had called for completely new codes, the Soviet civil code was actually patterned on Western and czarist models. After the 1936 constitution, the drafting of new codes was undertaken. The new codifications culminated in a civil code in 1964, as well as codes of criminal law and criminal procedure.

**Prospects.** Two principal problems for the future of codification are a civil code of English and American law and a code unifying the world's legal systems. Codification of English and American law is complicated by the common lawyer's continuing hostility toward codification. Unification of the world's law appears even more remote than codification of the common law. The differences between the great legal systems are still too pronounced to make the possibility of one comprehensive code, to govern throughout the world, more than a utopian ideal.

BERNARD SCHWARTZ
*New York University School of Law*

**Further Reading:** Graveson, R. H., *One Law, Comparative Conflict on Law: On Jurisprudence and the Unification of Law*, Vol. 2 (Elsevier Pub. Co. 1977); Schwartz, Bernard, ed., *The Code Napoleon and the Common-Law World* (1956; reprint, Greenwood Press 1975).

**CODLING MOTH,** kŏd'lǐng môth, a small widespread moth whose larvae are among the most destructive insect pests of apple trees. Codling moths are also one of the most difficult insect pests to control, and in some regions they have become so abundant that they prohibit the commercial cultivation of apples.

The adult codling moth is grayish with a large dark brown, somewhat iridescent spot at the tip of both front wings. About 2 to 6 weeks after the trees have begun to blossom, the female deposits her eggs on the upper sides of the tree's leaves and twigs. The eggs hatch in about 6 to 20 days, and the tiny white larvae burrow into the developing fruit. Before the apples fall from the tree, the larvae leave the fruit to build their cocoons. The thick silken cocoons are usually built beneath loose bark or on the ground. The larvae pass the winter inside the cocoon, and around midspring they change into dark brown pupae. About 2 to 4 weeks later the adults emerge and the cycle is repeated. In warm climates there may be 3 or 4 generations each year.

Among the insecticides that are useful in controlling codling moths are DDT, parathion, lead arsenate, diazinon, and methoxychlor.

The codling moth (*Carpocapsa pomonella*) belongs to the family Olethreutidae of the order Lepidoptera.

DON R. DAVIS
*Smithsonian Institution*

**CODRINGTON,** kod′ring-tən, **Sir Edward** (1770–1851), British admiral, who commanded the Allied fleets that won the Battle of Navarino. He was born on April 27, 1770, and joined the navy as a midshipman in 1783. He was a captain in the Napoleonic Wars and the War of 1812.

As a vice admiral, Codrington led the British, French, and Russian warships that destroyed the Turkish and Egyptian fleets in the Bay of Pylos (Navarino), Greece, on Oct. 20, 1827. The victory hastened the end of Turkish rule over Greece. Codrington retired in 1842 and died in London on April 28, 1851.

Sir William John Codrington (1804–1884), his son, commanded a brigade in the Crimean War in 1854–1855 and served with distinction at the Alma River and Inkerman.

**CODY,** kō′dē, **John Patrick** (1907–1982), American Roman Catholic cardinal and archbishop of Chicago. He was born in St. Louis, Mo., on Dec. 24, 1907, and was ordained a priest in 1931. After serving in many high-ranking posts, he was appointed auxiliary bishop of New Orleans in 1961. He implemented the desegregation of the Catholic school system there. He was named archbishop in 1964. In 1965 he became archbishop of Chicago and immediately effected church reforms, making a particular drive for racial justice. Pope Paul VI elevated him to cardinal in 1967. He died in Chicago on April 25, 1982.

**CODY,** kō′dē, **William Frederick** (1846–1917), American frontiersman, known as *Buffalo Bill*, who was a scout for the U. S. Army in the Indian wars and the showman largely responsible for romanticizing the cowboy West. His legendary image as Buffalo Bill, the hero of hundreds of dime novels and the actor who dramatized himself in his Wild West show, has somewhat obscured his able services as a scout.

Cody was born in Scott county, Iowa, on Feb. 26, 1846. He attended several sessions of country schools organized by his father, Isaac Cody, and grew up in Kansas, where the family moved in 1854. After his father's death in 1857, young Will worked for the firm of Russell, Majors & Waddell, making wagon-train trips across the Plains and riding for the Pony Express. In the Civil War he served in the 7th Kansas Cavalry.

In 1867–1868, Cody hunted buffalo to feed workers building the Kansas Pacific Railroad, and from then on he was known as Buffalo Bill. After carrying dispatches through hostile Indian country for Gen. Philip H. Sheridan, he became chief of scouts for the 5th U. S. Cavalry and was employed in this work for more than four years. As a scout he took part in 16 Indian fights, including the defeat of the Cheyenne at Summit Springs, Colo. (1869), and at Hat Creek, Wyo. (1876), famed for his "killing of Yellow Hand."

Ned Buntline (E. Z. C. Judson) in 1869 made Buffalo Bill the hero of a dime novel that was later dramatized, and in 1872 he persuaded Cody to appear on the stage. Cody broke with Buntline after a year but remained an actor for 11 seasons. The first and most authentic of his many autobiographies appeared in 1879. Buffalo Bill was also an author of dime novels, as well as the hero of some 1,700 of these publications, most of them written by Prentiss Ingraham.

In 1883, inspired by the success of a July 4th celebration at North Platte, Nebr., Cody organized Buffalo Bill's Wild West, an outdoor ex-

THE GRANGER COLLECTION

**William F. Cody (Buffalo Bill)**

hibition that dramatized the contemporary Western scene. It remained on the road as an attraction for 30 years. Its showing in London in 1887 for Queen Victoria's Jubilee made it an international success. Other European tours followed. The show's stars included Buck Taylor, "King of the Cowboys," the first cowboy hero; Annie Oakley, "Little Sure Shot"; Johnny Baker, "the Cowboy Kid"; and, for one season, Sitting Bull. Its acts included the Pony Express, the attack on the Deadwood stagecoach, the "Rough Riders of the World," and the roping, the bucking broncos, and the "cowboy fun" that developed into the rodeo.

Buffalo Bill's show scored its greatest U. S. success at the Chicago World's Fair of 1893. Previously, in the last Sioux outbreak of 1890–1891, Gen. Nelson A. Miles had asked for Cody's services, and Indians who had toured Europe with the show proved useful as peacemakers.

Cody died in Denver, Colo., on Jan. 10, 1917. While he had sometimes been denounced for portraying Indians as savages in his show, he had offered Indians employment at a time when their opportunities were few, and many of them for the first time thus learned of a world beyond the limits of their villages. His use of buffalo in the show helped preserve the species from extinction. Above all, he had been able to see as historic an aspect of life in his own time and to make the cowboy West appear forever romantic.

Don Russell
*Author, "Lives and Legends of Buffalo Bill"*

**CODY,** kō′dē, is a resort city in northwestern Wyoming, the seat of Park county. It is on the Shoshone River, 185 miles (298 km) northwest of Casper, in a sheep and cattle ranching area. Nearby is the Shoshone National Forest, for which Cody serves as the headquarters. The city's chief industries are tourism and oil refining.

Cody was named for its founder, Col. William F. Cody (Buffalo Bill), American scout and showman. Attractions include the Buffalo Bill Museum and the William Cody House. The latter, Cody's birthplace, was moved from Iowa. Government is by mayor and council. Population: 8,835.

**COEDUCATION,** kō-ej-ə-kā′shən, is the practice of having both sexes attend the same school or college. Historically, it is a relatively recent development. The spread of coeducation has been closely related to changes in the attitude of society toward women and to their success in the long struggle to achieve equal rights.

**Historical Background.** Plato expressed high regard for the capacities of women, but Aristotle held that their distinctive function necessitated a different kind of education for them. The latter view prevailed and was widely held over the years. In ancient Greece and Rome, formal education was predominantly for boys.

Throughout the Middle Ages, what educational opportunities girls enjoyed were separate. With the Reformation came a demand that girls as well as boys be taught to read the Bible. To achieve this purpose Protestant communities in western Europe and colonial New England began to provide elementary instruction in mixed classes. The Dutch parochial schools of New Netherlands provided joint instruction in reading, as did the Quakers, who were early advocates of coeducation.

## COEDUCATION IN THE UNITED STATES

**Public Schools.** Leaders of the American Revolution stressed the importance of education in a democracy. The new free public elementary schools, which began to supplant parochial schools in the late 18th and early 19th centuries, were usually coeducational.

Coeducation at the secondary and higher levels was practically unknown in most countries until it began in the United States in the early part of the 19th century. While the first high schools for girls were separate, the need to keep costs down and the demand for equal educational opportunities favored the development of coeducation, especially in the vast new areas of the country beyond the Appalachians.

During the second half of the 19th century, interest in coeducation in public schools reached a peak as the movement for education of women became national in extent. In public addresses and printed documents school officials discussed the problem. For example, William Torrey Harris, in his report for 1872–1873 as superintendent of the public schools of St. Louis, asked for an end to opposition to coeducation at all levels.

Arguments advanced for coeducation were: (1) It is more economical to operate a single system of schools. (2) Women are not inferior to men in coping with intellectual tasks. (3) Discipline is better in mixed classes. (4) Including girls in the schools promotes a "higher standard of moral thought and feeling." (5) Coeducation is a "natural system." As one zealot exclaimed, "What God hath joined together in the family why should we separate in the school?"

In 1891 a national survey of public school systems was made, to which the superintendents of instruction in 40 states and 4 territories replied. The survey showed that 28 states and 3 territories had coeducation in all public schools; 12 states and 1 territory reported coeducation in all schools except those in a few cities (Boston, New Orleans, Atlanta, Louisville, and Columbia, S. C.). In the 5 states and 1 territory that did not reply to the survey, coeducation was apparently the general policy.

In reporting a total public school enrollment of 15,341,220 in 1900–1901, the U. S. commissioner of education wrote: "The great body of these young people are instructed together, without distinction of sex. . . . In the elementary grades coeducation is practically universal and excites no comment." At the high school level, coeducation is "of later origin"; separate schools are found mainly in cities because of the location and structure of school buildings or a belief that separation is desirable. At this time, the U. S. commissioner of education was able to describe coeducation as a "marked characteristic of public education in the United States."

**Coeducation in Higher Institutions.** Higher education for women became a reality in the United States in 1837, when Oberlin College, in Ohio, admitted four women as full students to the freshman class. Founded in 1833, Oberlin from the beginning had admitted women to its preparatory department, but four years later this modified form of coeducation gave way to equal status with men in the regular classes of the college. When three of the women graduated in 1841, they became the first of their sex to receive bachelor's degrees that were fully equivalent to those granted to men.

Under the leadership of Horace Mann, Antioch College, in Yellow Springs, Ohio, began a program of coeducation in 1852. The new state universities of the West were pioneers in education for women. Iowa was coeducational from its opening in 1856. As early as 1850 the regents at Wisconsin proposed a normal department to which both men and women would be admitted, but it was not until 1860 that women actually enrolled. The University of Michigan admitted its first women students in 1870, twelve years after the first petitions were presented. By 1879 there were women studying in every department of the university.

The arguments against coeducation at the collegiate level seem strange today. Chief among the reasons for opposing it was what was believed to be the "difference between the male and the female mind." Many leaders felt sincerely that women were mentally inferior to men and were unable to meet the standards set for men's higher education. A corollary to this argument was that the quality of instruction would be diluted, standards of achievement lowered, and the nature of higher education itself would deteriorate under the distracting influence of women students.

The "diversity of pursuit and mission" was also mentioned frequently. Woman's place, according to this argument, was in the home, in her role as rearer of children and helpmate to her husband who was the wage earner and career person of the partnership. Another argument involved differences in physical strength. Many leaders asserted that women did not have "the stamina to endure a course of education as thorough and as extensive as men." This objection seems to have caused some apprehension among administrators, even of women's colleges, who emphasized their concern for the health and physical fitness of women students.

Still other opponents of coeducation feared a moral decline if mixed schooling became the practice. To refute this argument, proponents of coeducation pointed out the success of the practice in secondary schools and the wholesome results of Oberlin's experiment. In fact, many advocates felt that the association of the sexes was "an invaluable feature in restraining indecorum" and "an incitement to every virtue."

The number of "mixed colleges" increased rapidly, especially in the West. By 1870, women had been admitted to 30% of all colleges (excluding technical schools and women's colleges as such). Ten years later, the proportion of coeducational institutions was 51%. By 1890 the percentage was 65 and by 1900 it had reached 71.

In the 1890's even the Eastern universities reacted to the demand for women's education. Tufts College opened all departments to women in 1892–1893. Yale began admitting women to its graduate school in 1891–1892. By the turn of the century the question of coeducation was regarded by many leaders as a dead issue. Newer institutions, such as Stanford and Chicago, were coeducational from the start.

Coeducation established the right of every woman to share in the benefits of education, from the grades through the graduate school. Admission to universities on an equal footing with men was an advantage to individual women. Society as a whole also benefited from women's contributions to scholarship and the professions.

**Coordinate Colleges for Women.** The coordinate college for women, a new type of institution, developed in the eastern United States in the 1870's and 1880's, when proponents of coeducation were seeking its extension into the older universities. The concept of setting up a branch college for women was a compromise, as President Henry Barnard of Columbia recognized in his report to the trustees in 1879. A precedent was found in England, where Queens College, in London, began offering in 1853 a program for women similar to that of Kings College. In 1883, Columbia established "a course of collegiate study" for young women, which eventually resulted in the chartering of Barnard College in 1889. As time passed, courses at Columbia were opened to Barnard juniors and seniors.

Harvard began taking some responsibility for the education of women in 1879. However, it was not until 1894 that the Society for the Collegiate Instruction of Women, which had begun granting degrees in the late 1880's, was incorporated as Radcliffe College. In 1947, Harvard and Radcliffe abandoned separate classes as a permanent policy. Other early coordinate colleges were Sophie Newcomb of Tulane University (1887) and Pembroke of Brown University (1891).

**Women's Colleges.** Beginning about 1775, female seminaries spread rapidly, especially in the eastern and southern parts of the United States. While the seminary did offer women a more liberal education than they could get through such means as private reading, it often had inferior standards. One of the critics of the shortcomings of the seminaries was Emma Willard. In 1814 she opened the Troy Female Seminary (now the Emma Willard School) at Troy, N. Y. This school made no pretensions to collegiate rank. However, Mrs. Willard set high academic standards. This example and her ardent advocacy of higher education for women did much to stimulate public support for women's colleges.

Wesleyan Female College, Macon, Ga., chartered in 1836, was a pioneer in education for women and was the first women's college with authority to grant academic degrees. Also in 1836, Mary Lyon obtained from the Massachusetts legislature a charter for Mount Holyoke Seminary, where her administration of the institution and her active concern about educational opportunities for women did much to further the cause. Seminaries for women multiplied rapidly between 1836 and 1860, and they played an important part in establishing the need for and the feasibility of higher education for women. By 1861, when Vassar College was chartered, the idea of a college education for women similar to that for men was becoming well established. When Smith College opened in 1875, it had from the start a course of study almost identical with that of the leading men's colleges.

The Morrill Act of 1862, which established the land-grant colleges, provided unexpected stimulus and support for the higher education of women. With few exceptions, the land-grant colleges of the West were coeducational from the start. Consequently, there was not the incentive to establish separate colleges for women that was found in the East.

**20th Century Trends.** In the 20th century there has been a marked increase in the number of women attending high school and college and in the number receiving bachelor's or first degrees in the United States. The number of girls graduating from high school grew from 57,000 in 1900 to 367,000 in 1930 and to 1,430,500 in 1975. After 1900, girl high school graduates consistently outnumbered boys, but the proportion dropped from 60% girls in 1900 to 50.8% in 1975.

Historically, fewer girls than boys graduating from high school attended college. However, the percentage of female college students steadily increased, and by 1980 there were more women enrolled in college than men.

In 1940 about 1,400,000 women 25 years of age or over in the United States were college graduates. By the mid-1970's this figure had risen to about 6,165,000, representing about 5.7% of the total female population.

The proportion of institutions admitting only one sex decreased sharply after mid-century. In 1950, of 1,808 U. S. colleges and universities, 1,313 were coeducational (70% of the total), while 267 were for women only, and 228 were for men. Of 2,573 institutions of higher learning in 1970–1971, 2,226 (or 87%) were coeducational, 193 were for women only, and 154 were for men only. Thus, in a 20-year period the number of coeducational institutions increased by 913, including such venerable institutions as Vassar, Princeton, and Yale, while those for men or women only decreased by 74 each.

## COEDUCATION IN OTHER COUNTRIES

In western Europe, education is usually coeducational at the elementary school level, separate at the scondary level, and coeducational on the university level. There are exceptions to this rule. Nondenominational and Protestant education in the Low Countries is predominantly coeducational at all levels, and the same is true of Scandinavia. Roman Catholic education in Europe is still typically separate for the sexes, although there is a trend toward coeducation.

The Latin American countries have until recently tended to separate the sexes at the elementary and secondary levels, with coeducation generally prevailing in the institutions of higher learning. In countries such as Mexico, where great progress in public education has been made, the new schools are usually coeducational, certainly at the elementary level.

Coeducation has become the general practice in much of the non-Western world, especially at the elementary school level, with the exception of the Muslim countries, where separate schools below the university are the custom. Among the countries of the Middle East, Israel stands out in that its educational program gives women equal opportunities.

**Britain.** After a long tradition of private schools and separate education, Britain began to educate boys and girls together in the 1900's in its publicly supported elementary schools, mainly for reasons of economy. However, coeducation at the high school level was still the exception until the development of the "secondary modern school" in the 1950's. This is a state-aided institution similar to the American comprehensive high school. It is coeducational, offers a broad program of studies, and draws its pupils from a variety of educational sources.

**Canada.** The public system of education in English-speaking Canada has always been coeducational. However, there are a number of private schools for boys or for girls. Most of the English-language universities have been coeducational from the beginning. The Royal Victoria College of McGill University, originally a separate college for women, is now merely a residence, as the women students now attend lectures with the McGill men. The same is true of St. Hilda's College, now a residence for women students of Trinity College of the University of Toronto.

In French-speaking Quebec, where separation of the sexes in schools was once customary, there is now extensive coeducation. However, there are a number of private Roman Catholic liberal arts colleges for men or for women.

**Soviet Union.** Systematic education of women in Russia was initiated by Catherine II in the 18th century. She had girls admitted to elementary schools and established Russia's first secondary school for girls. When the empress died in 1796, the total school enrollment was 176,730 boys and 12,595 girls. Only a small number of girls (1121) were in coeducational schools, most of them in St. Petersburg and vicinity. During the 19th century, enrollments increased greatly. However, coeducation was frowned upon, and many parents—especially in rural areas—preferred to keep their daughters at home.

In 1917 the Bolsheviks abolished separate education on the grounds that it was a device for keeping women in a subordinate position. However, in 1943, in the midst of World War II, this position was reversed and coeducation below the university level was abolished throughout the Soviet Union. The reason given was that girls develop more rapidly than boys; therefore, mixed classes of equal age tend to slow down the work and retard the progress of the girls.

In 1954 this position was again reversed, and coeducation was made the practice in all Soviet schools. Equal education opportunities for both sexes has been an important principle of Communism. The proportion of women prepared for careers in government, technology, and the professions, especially medicine and dentistry, is high.

**China.** In the Orient educational opportunities for women were not available until the 1850's, when schools for girls were begun by the Christian missionaries in China. The Nationalist government took steps in the 1920's to provide schooling for both boys and girls and opened the universities to women. When the Communists took over the government in 1949, coeducation at all levels became mandatory. Extensive efforts were made to educate all Chinese youth, especially to teach them the ideology of the regime.

**India.** Before 1900 there was little provision in India for the formal education of girls; in 1901 the percentage of literacy among women was 0.8. Progress since then has been phenomenal.

At the lower primary stage, the number of girls enrolled per 100 boys increased from 12 in 1901 to 39 in 1950 and to 55 in 1965. At the secondary stage, the corresponding figures are 4 in 1901, 15 in 1950, and 26 in 1965. In higher education, the enrollment of women increased from a mere 264 in 1901 to 40,000 in 1950 and to 240,000 in 1965.

According to the report of the education commission of the government of India (1964–1966), education in mixed schools was more readily accepted at the lower primary stage, where 85% of the girls enrolled were in mixed schools, and at the higher primary stage, where the proportion is 78%. There was still considerable resistance to coeducation at the secondary stage, where only 40% of the girls enrolled were in mixed schools. These resistances tended to soften at the university stage.

## HIGHER EDUCATION FOR WOMEN AROUND THE WORLD

Indications of changing attitudes toward the education of women can be found in UNESCO's *World Survey of Education*, vol. 4 (1966). According to the survey, the number of women students in higher institutions increased a median of 10% between 1930 and 1959 in 28 countries for which comparative figures were available. In no instance was there a decrease. The percentage increase was small in countries such as the United States, Britain, and Canada, where the proportion of women attending college was already large at the start of the period covered.

The most striking increases were in the non-Western countries. For example, in China enrollment of women students increased 87% in the 29-year period surveyed; in India, 129%; in Thailand, 252%; in Japan, 509%; and in the United Arab Republic, 614%. The numerical as well as the percentage increases were striking. For example, the number of women in higher education in Japan went from 883 to 113,235; in China, from 5,777 to 131,311; and in the United Arab Republic, from 70 to 12,203.

The UNESCO information revealed that countries which had once virtually excluded women from colleges had moved toward giving them equal opportunities. Higher education has become increasingly open to women, primarily through coeducation.

EDWARD ALVEY, JR., *Dean*
*Mary Washington College*
*University of Virginia*

### Bibliography

Acker, Sandra, *The World Yearbook of Education, 1984: Women and Education* (Nichols 1984).
Deem, Rosemary, ed., *Coeducation Reconsidered* (Taylor & Francis 1984).
Fennema, Elizabeth, and Ayer, M. Jane, *Women and Education: Equity or Equality?* (McCutchan Pub. 1984).
Howe, Florence, *Myths of Coeducation: Selected Essays 1964–1983* (Ind. Univ. Press 1984).
Kelly, Gail P., and Elliot, Carolyn M., eds., *Women's Education in the Third World: Comparative Perspectives* (State Univ. of N.Y. Press 1982).
Lasser, Carol, ed., *Educating Men and Women Together* (Univ. of Ill. Press 1987).
Newcomer, Mabel, *A Century of Higher Education for American Women* (1959; reprint, Zenger Pub. 1976).
Perun, Pamela J., ed., *The Undergraduate Woman: Issues in Educational Equity* (Lexington Bks. 1982).
Solomon, Barbara M., *In the Company of Educated Women* (Yale Univ. Press 1985).

**COEFFICIENT,** kō-ə-fish′ənt, a term used in mathematics to denote a number or other quantity placed before an algebraic expression as a multiplier of the expression. For example, in the polynomial $x^3 + 7x^2 - 4x + 2$ the algebraic expressions are the powers of $x$ $(x^3, x^2, x^1, x^0)$, and the coefficients are the numbers 1, 7, $-4$, and 2. The so-called binomial coefficients are the coefficients in the expansion of $(x + y)^n$ and are denoted by the symbol $\binom{n}{r}$, which is equal to

$$\frac{n(n-1)(n-2)\cdots(n-r+1)}{r(r-1)\cdots 1}.$$

Thus $(x + y)^n = x^n + \binom{n}{1} x^{n-1}y + \cdots + \binom{n}{r} x^{n-r}y^r + \cdots + y^n$.

In physics, the term coefficient is applied to any of a number of constants, such as the coefficient of sliding friction—the ratio of the frictional force between two surfaces sliding across one another to the force that is perpendicular to the surfaces.

**COEHOORN,** kōō′hōrn, **Menno van** (1641–1704), Dutch military engineer and general. He was born in Leeuwarden, Friesland, in March 1641. He entered military service at 16. At the siege of Grave in 1673, his engineering genius became evident when he harassed the French garrison with a small mortar that he had invented. A larger model, called a *cohorn*, was used as late as the American Civil War.

Baron van Coehoorn excelled in design and construction of fortifications and in siege techniques. His *Nieuwe Vestingbouw* (New Fortification, 1685) and other books were studied widely. During the wars of William of Orange against the French, Coehoorn was often called upon to defend a city or to capture one. The battles for Kaiserswerth, Bonn, Fleurus, and Namur showed him a worthy adversary of the great French military engineer Vauban (q.v.). Each general took and lost Namur to the other. While Vauban was slow and certain in a siege, Coehoorn tried to shorten it with heavy artillery fire and open attacks. During the War of the Spanish Succession he commanded a corps in Marlborough's army. He died of apoplexy at The Hague on March 17, 1704.

JOHN D. BILLINGSLEY, *Colonel, U. S. Army*
*United States Military Academy*

**COELACANTH,** se′lə-kanth, a group of very primitive bony fishes that are often called "living fossils." They are closely related to the living fossil lungfishes (Dipnoi) and to the group of fossil fishes from which, over 300 million years ago, the first land-dwelling vertebrates (Amphibia) evolved. The only living species of coelacanth is *Latimeria chalumnae*, and it is this fish with which the name "coelacanth" is most famously associated. This species lives in the water off the coast of southern Africa.

**Discovery.** Some 25 genera of fossil coelacanths have been discovered. The oldest fossils are of the Devonian period (which began about 405 million years ago), while the youngest are of the Cretaceous period (which ended about 70 million years ago). Since no fossil coelacanths from a more recent period were known, the group was long thought to be extinct.

The first living coelacanth was caught in the trawl of a fishing boat off South Africa on Dec. 22, 1938. J. L. B. Smith, who described the fish,

COELACANTH is one of the oldest living fishes.

named it in honor of Miss Courtenay-Latimer, who had the specimen saved for study, and the Bay of the Chalumna River near East London, South Africa, where the specimen was caught. No further specimen was discovered until Dec. 20, 1952, when one was taken off Grand Comoro Island, northwest of Madagascar. Since then, more than 20 specimens have been caught, all off the Comoro Islands.

**Zoological Importance.** Apart from the novelty of being such rare fish, coelacanths have very great zoological importance. First, they are "living fossils"—a life form that has been preserved almost unchanged for many millions of years. As such, they offer the scientist a view of the biology of an earlier stage in the history of life. Second, the group of fishes to which the coelacanth belongs occupies an extremely important place in the history of vertebrate life. They include the ancestors of all land forms, including man himself.

**Description.** Coelacanths have several characteristic features, including a hollow spine in the first dorsal fin (coelacanth is Greek for hollow-spined). They also have lobe-shaped, highly mobile, paired fins that are unlike normal fins in that they have a muscular and skeletal axis that enables the fish to use them as props or primitive legs; because of this unusual feature, the coelacanth was named "old fourlegs" by Smith. Coelacanths also have a lung filled with fat that is used as a flotation device; a specialized jaw mechanism with a joint in the middle of the skull that enables the snout region to be moved up and down as the lower jaw moves; and large, rough bony scales.

Most fossil coelacanths were small, but *L. chalumnae* reaches a length of 6 feet (2 meters) and a weight of over 90 pounds (40 kg). It is usually purple brown and blue with irregular pink blotches.

**Natural History.** The earliest fossil coelacanths almost certainly lived in freshwater, but later they entered the oceans. They probably live in quiet deep waters, coming nearer to the surface at night. They are usually caught at about 200 feet (70 meters) with a long line and a single hook baited with a chunk of fish. Coelacanths are active carnivores; they have many sharp teeth, and they fight fiercely when hooked.

**Classification.** The coelacanth genus (*Latimeria*) is classified in the family Coelanthidae in the order Coelacanthini.

KEITH THOMSON, *Yale University*

**COELE-SYRIA,** sē'lē sir'ē-ə, is the name of a region of the ancient Middle East whose limits were variously defined at different periods in history. In the Hellenistic period Coele-Syria was the name applied to a province of Ptolemaic Egypt which covered most of southern Syria and part of Palestine. In its narrower sense, Coele-Syria identifies the Marsyas (Massyas) valley with the adjacent Lebanon and Anti-Lebanon mountain ranges and the city of Damascus, an area included in present-day Lebanon and Syria.

Coele-Syria as a Ptolemaic province was one of the richest tax revenue sources of the Egyptian dynasty that emerged following the death of Alexander the Great in 323 B. C. In the Syrian wars, fought in the 3d century B. C. between the Ptolemies and the Seleucid kings, Coele-Syria was a coveted prize. Strong fortresses such as Brochi and Gerrha at the southern entrance to the Marsyas valley made victory over an opponent in this region a major accomplishment. The loss of Coele-Syria to the Seleucid empire in 200 B. C. was a disaster for the Ptolemies.

Under Seleucid rule, Coele-Syria was divided into administrative units known as *merides,* each based on a city where Hellenic Greek culture prevailed. This culture declined, however, with the conquest of the region in the first century B. C. by Jannaeus, the "Jewish Alexander," who held Coele-Syria for the Hasmonaean dynasty almost until the coming of the Romans under the leadership of Pompey (63 B. C.).

**COELENTERATE,** si-len'tə-rāt, any of a large phylum of invertebrates that includes the sea anemones, jellyfishes, and corals. All coelenterates have a centrally located mouth surrounded by one or more whorls of tentacles. The tentacles are studded with characteristic "thread capsules," or nematocysts, specialized cells each containing a long, coiled thread. The nematocysts are used to entangle and inject poison into small prey.

The phylum has been given the name Coelenterata, meaning "hollow intestine," because the main body cavity of the coelenterate is a hollow digestive cavity. However, some authors prefer the name Cnidaria for the phylum because this name emphasizes the coelenterate's distinctive cnidoblasts, the cells that produce the nematocysts.

**Habitat.** Almost all coelenterates are marine, and they are found mostly in warm, shallow oceans along the shores. For example, the true reef-building corals cannot grow in waters that have a yearly average temperature below 70° F (21° C). Coelenterates such as the sea fans, sea plumes, sea whips, and organ-pipe corals are restricted to either tropical or subtropical shallow waters. However, hydroids, sea anemones, jellyfishes, and extensive beds of tall, branching coral colonies are found in cold waters. Only a few coelenterates live in freshwater habitats. These coelenterates include the tiny freshwater hydras that are found in ponds, lakes, and streams.

**Structure.** There are two types of coelenterate bodies: an attached, fragile polyp, and a more gelatinous, free-swimming medusa, commonly known as a jellyfish. Both types have a number of more or less well-developed tissues but few organs.

The polyp type, which is seen in hydroids, sea anemones, and corals, is a cylinder with an adhesive disk at the bottom used for attaching the animal to the ocean or lake bottom or to a hard object. At the tip of the free end is the mouth opening and its surrounding tentacles.

The medusa, or jellyfish, type is a convex umbrella, or bell, that swims with the convex surface upward. A stalk (manubrium), with a mouth at its tip, hangs from the undersurface of the bell. Often, the corners of the mouth are drawn out into long lobes that help to capture prey and direct it into the mouth.

The outside of the coelenterate body is covered by a layer of cells called the epidermis, and the gastrovascular cavity (the inner digestive and circulatory sac) is lined with a cell layer called the gastrodermis. Between these two layers is a middle layer called the mesoglea. In delicate hydroid polyps, the mesoglea is a thin gelatinous membrane and is noncellular. In the large jellyfishes, this gelatinous material forms the bulk of the animal and has fibers and scattered ameboid cells.

Nerve cells coordinate behavior in coelenterates. In the free-swimming medusas there are one or more kinds of sense organs around the margin of the bell. These sense organs are used to capture small living animals, such as crustaceans and fishes, that make up the food of almost all coelenterates. The prey is captured with the aid of certain nematocysts that entangle the victim while other nematocysts immobilize it with poisoned threads.

The food is then brought through the mouth, into the gastrovascular cavity, which partially digests the food and also distributes it through branching canals to all parts of the body. The digestion is completed in the food vacuoles of the cells of the digestive lining (gastrodermis). Since there is no anus, body wastes must be ejected through the mouth.

**Evolution and Reproduction.** The primitive coelenterate ancestor is believed to have been a sexually reproducing medusa that shed eggs and sperms into the sea. The fertilized eggs developed into small ciliated larvae, called planulas, and then through another free larval stage into a new sexually reproducing medusa. In some cases, the larva began to multiply asexually by budding off the other larvae that developed into medusas. In time, the habit of larval budding, combined with settling to the bottom of the sea, produced the present hydrozoan polyp types. The hydrozoan polyps budded off little sexually reproducing free medusas. The juvenile polyp stage became predominant and eventually produced groups like the freshwater hydras and the marine anemones and corals. In these forms, the polyp reproduces sexually.

**Importance.** The coelenterates are not an important source of food for man. The sea anemones, the fleshiest group, are eaten in Greece, Italy, France, and in some Pacific islands. Certain jellyfishes are part of the diet on the shores of China, Korea, and Japan.

The hard inner skeleton of the red "precious coral" has been used for many centuries by the artisans of the Mediterranean shores for jewelry, and the Japanese also use red coral to make jewelry and ornaments. In ancient times, black corals were used widely on the Mediterranean, Red Sea, Persian Gulf, and South Pacific shores for ornamental and therapeutic bracelets.

Most coelenterates have stinging capsules

## ANATOMY OF THE COELENTERATES

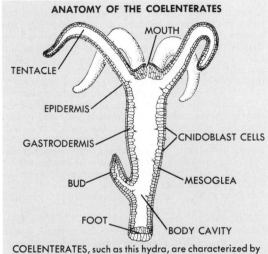

TENTACLE
MOUTH
EPIDERMIS
GASTRODERMIS
CNIDOBLAST CELLS
BUD
MESOGLEA
FOOT
BODY CAVITY

COELENTERATES, such as this hydra, are characterized by a hollow body cavity and centrally located mouth surrounded by one or more whorls of tentacles. In addition, they have special cells, called cnidoblasts, which produce nematocysts, structures used in capturing and killing prey.

**2. JELLYFISH**

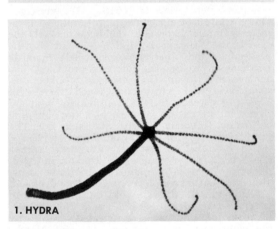

**1. HYDRA**

**3. SEA ANEMONE**

ALL PHOTOS ANNAN PHOTO FEATURES

COELENTERATES ARE DIVIDED INTO THREE CLASSES. The hydra (1) belongs to the class Hydrozoa, while the true jellyfishes (2) make up the class Schyphozoa, and the sea anemone (3) is a member of the class Anthozoa.

that are too small to penetrate human skin, and one gets no more than a sticky feeling even when the tentacles of large sea anemones are touched. However, the 12-inch (30-cm) *Cyanea* that is found off cold Atlantic shores in summer, can inflict painful red welts on swimmers. In the Pacific and Indian oceans, the cuboidal jellyfish, known as the sea wasp, has been reported to cause death in 3 to 8 minutes. Also the bluish or pinkish bladderlike float of the colonial coelenterate known as the Portuguese man-of-war, which is found in warm waters, can inflict painful stings than can cause a swimmer to drown. In some cases the swimmer may die of allergic shock if he has been sensitized to the poison through earlier contact.

**Classification.** The phylum coelenterate has about 9,000 species, which are grouped into 3 classes. The class Hydrozoa (over 2,100 species) is almost entirely marine, but also includes the truly freshwater forms. Polyps are solitary or colonial, and the life history of various groups may have only polyps, both polyps and medusas, or only free-swimming medusas. Among the

members of the class Hydrozoa are the hydras, obelias, stinging corals, and the Portuguese man-of-war.

The class Schyphozoa (200 species) is entirely marine and includes all the true jellyfishes.

The class Anthozoa (more than 6,000 species) is the largest coelenterate group. It includes the corals, sea anemones, sea whips, sea fans, and sea pens. All are fully marine except for a few anemones in brackish waters. The adult is a cylindrical polyp, which is either solitary or colonial. The animal may be delicate and with a supporting limestone skeleton, as in the corals, or it may be fleshy and with no skeleton, as in anemones. There is no medusa stage. A few anthozoans, like the anemones and sea pens, may move about at times, but most live permanently attached.

RALPH BUCHSBAUM AND MILDRED BUCHSBAUM
*University of Pittsburgh*

**Further Reading:** Buchsbaum, Ralph, and Milne, Lorus, *The Lower Animals*, chap. 3 (Doubleday 1960); Simpson, T. L., *The Cell Biology of Sponges* (Springer-Verlag 1984).

**COELOM,** sē'ləm, the large body cavity formed during the embryological development of nearly all multicellular (metazoan) animals, including annelids, arthropods, mollusks, and all vertebrates. In many of these organisms the coelom remains a single large cavity throughout the animal's development. In others the coelom develops into several smaller body cavities (For an explanation of how the coelom is formed during embryonic development, see EMBRYOLOGY–*Mesoderm;* for a discussion of the importance of the coelom as a characteristic used as a basis for animal classification, see ANIMAL–*Animal Diversity.*)

In the development of a human embryo, two coelom cavities are formed. One, the *extraembryonic coelom,* is the cavity in which the embryo itself develops. The second, the *intraembryonic coelom,* is a large cavity within the embryo's body. The front portion of the intraembryonic coelom is the precursor of the pericardium, the sac that will enclose the heart. Next to the pericardial region, the coelom forms a paired cavity, the pleural cavity, around the embryo's two developing lung buds. The back portion of the coelom becomes the peritoneal cavity, the main body cavity in which most of the other organs will lie. During the early stages of development, these three cavities are interconnected, but as the embryo develops, the openings between them close, and by the time the baby is born, its pericardial, pleural, and peritoneal cavities are completely separate from each other.

JEFFREY WENIG, *ENDO Laboratories*

**COELOSTAT,** sē'lə-stat, a device that follows the apparent motion of a celestial object across the sky and reflects the object's image into a stationary telescope. An advantage of the coelostat is that the reflected image does not rotate. Because of this, the coelostat is often used for observations of the sun.

The telescope of a coelostat usually points toward the zenith. Above the telescope is an

LIGHT FROM A STAR

MIRROR

MIRROR

**THE COELOSTAT**

The coelostat mirror is mounted on a movable platform and can rotate to follow the apparent passage of a star across the sky. The platform's position is adjusted according to the star's declination. Light from the star is reflected to an adjustable mirror and thence to a telescope.

adjustable flat mirror, which intercepts the light from the coelostat mirror and reflects it into the telescope. The coelostat mirror is mounted so that it can rotate on a polar axis—parallel to the earth's axis—at the rate of one turn approximately every 48 hours, thus compensating for the apparent rotation of the celestial sphere.

For any given adjustment of the two mirrors, a constant declination is maintained. (Declination is the angular distance of a celestial object from the celestial equator.) The image does not rotate, and long exposures on photographic plates can be obtained. To work at a different declination, the coelostat mirror is moved backward or forward, and the adjustable mirror is reset accordingly. See also TELESCOPE.

LAURENCE W. FREDRICK, *University of Virginia*

**COEN,** kōōn, **Jan Pieterszoon** (1587–1629), Dutch governor-general in the East Indies, who was a major European empire builder in Asia. Coen was born on Jan. 8, 1587, at Hoorn, the Netherlands. In 1607 he entered the service of the Dutch East India Company.

Through great drive and ability Coen rose to become governor-general of the Dutch East India Company territories in 1618. He envisaged Dutch control of all Asian trade through a commercial empire that would dominate not only the East Indies (present-day Indonesia) but also the Philippines and other territories where Spanish, Portuguese, or English interests prevailed. To achieve this dream, Coen, a man of imperious, sometimes cruel, nature, envisioned the use of Japanese mercenaries, the transplanting and enslavement of native peoples, and the founding of Dutch settlements. His first step was the conquest in 1618 of the Javanese port of Jacatra, which he renamed Batavia (it is now named Djakarta). In the Bandas, in 1621, Coen conducted a "transfer of population" with so many atrocities that his employers reprimanded him.

Although Coen twice held the high office of governor-general (1618–1623 and 1627–1629), his plans for conquest were repeatedly vetoed by the company's directors, who objected to the cost of his military adventures. During his second term, on Sept. 21, 1629, Coen died suddenly of cholera while fighting off a Javanese attack on Batavia. Although frustrated in his grand ambitions, he had laid the foundations of a long-lasting Dutch colonial empire.

ROBERT C. BONE, *Florida State University*

**COENZYME,** kō-ən'zīm, a complex organic molecule that is necessary for the functioning of enzymes. Also known as *cofactors,* coenzymes are the nonprotein components of enzymes, and they can be separated easily from the enzymes.

Coenzymes are involved in all aspects of cell metabolism, including the synthesis and degradation of proteins and amino acids, carbohydrates and sugars, lipids, and nucleic acids. One important example of coenzyme action is their role as electron carriers in oxidative phosphorylation, the process by which organisms derive energy from foodstuffs.

**Coenzyme Activity and Regeneration.** Coenzymes serve in enzymic reactions by carrying certain chemical groups from one substrate (substance activated by the enzyme) to another. In doing so, the coenzyme shuttles between two or more enzymes and unites them in a coupled enzyme system. In coupled reactions, the coenzymes

## TABLE OF COENZYMES

| Coenzyme | Vitamin | Carrier for | Enzymic and metabolic function |
|---|---|---|---|
| **COENZYMES IN COUPLED ENZYME SYSTEMS** | | | |
| Adenosine triphosphate (ATP) | None | Phosphate | Energy transfer and distribution, trans-phosphorylations; metabolism of proteins, amino acids, carbohydrates, lipids, and nucleic acids |
| Ascorbic acid | Ascorbic acid (vitamin C) | Electrons | Electron transport (?), collagen biosynthesis |
| Cobamide | Cobalamine (vitamin $B_{12}$) | Methyl groups | Methyl transfer, methionine, thymidine, coenzyme Q biosynthesis |
| Coenzyme A | Pantothenic acid | Acyl groups | Amino acid, carbohydrate, lipid, and nucleic acid metabolism |
| Coenzyme Q (ubiquinone) | None | Electrons | Electron transport, oxidative phosphorylation (energy transfer and ATP production) |
| Lipoic acid | None | Electrons and acyl groups | Oxidative decarboxylations in carbohydrate metabolism |
| Nicotinamide adenine dinucleotide (NAD or DPN) and its phosphate derivative (NADP or TPN) | Niacin | Electrons | Electron transport, oxidative phosphorylation; general redox (reduction, oxidation) reagents in amino acid, carbohydrate, lipid, and nucleic acid metabolism |
| Tetrahydrofolic acid | p-amino-benzoic acid, folic acid | Methyl and other one carbon groups | Biosynthesis of sulfur amino acids, serine purines, and pyrimidines |
| Vitamin K | Vitamin K | Electrons | See coenzyme Q |
| **PROSTHETIC GROUPS** | | | |
| Biotin | Biotin | Carbon dioxide | Carboxylations in fatty acid, purine, carbohydrate metabolism |
| Flavin adenine dinucleotide (FAD) and flavin mononucleotide (FMN) | Riboflavin (vitamin $B_2$) | Electrons | Amino acid, carbohydrate, and nucleic acid and lipid metabolism; see coenzyme Q |
| Heme (iron-porphyrin complex) | None | Electrons | Prosthetic group for cytochromes; see coenzyme Q |
| Pyridoxal phosphate | Pyridoxine (vitamin $B_6$) | Amino groups | Transamination; amino acid and nitrogen metabolism |
| Thiamine pyrophosphate | Thiamine (vitamin $B_1$) | "Active acetate" | Biosynthesis of valine, isoleucine; see lipoic acid |

are regenerated; therefore, minute amounts of coenzymes are sufficient for metabolism in living organisms.

The regeneration of coenzymes is illustrated in the process of yeast fermentation. In fermentation, sugar is converted to glyceraldehyde-3-phosphate. The further reaction of this compound requires the simultaneous reduction of the coenzyme nicotinamide adenine dinucleotide (NAD). Sugar metabolism soon would be blocked if all the NAD were reduced. However, the final reaction in fermentation, the reduction of acetaldehyde to ethanol, requires the reoxidation of reduced NAD, thus regenerating the coenzyme.

**Prosthetic Groups.** Coenzymes that are not easily separated from their enzymes are called prosthetic groups. They have a high affinity for an enzyme and cause the entire reaction sequence to take place on a single enzyme.

**Coenzymes and Vitamins.** Many coenzymes have a vitamin as a structural component. Although the enzymatic role of coenzymes generally is well understood, it is not yet possible to explain the symptoms of vitamin deficiency in terms of specific enzyme reactions.

KENNETH D. LUNAN, *Stanford Research Institute*

**COERCION,** kō-ûr′shən, means unlawfully compelling a person to do that which he would not otherwise do. It may be effected through force, threats of physical injury to the person or his loved ones, or through psychological pressures. In many circumstances, proof of coercion invalidates the legal effects of certain acts. For instance, a will executed under duress is nullified and the decedent's property distributed among his heirs as if no will existed. Coerced confessions are inadmissible in evidence against the accused. Also, acts otherwise regarded as criminal may be justified on a showing that the defendant was under immediate threat of grievous bodily harm.

Under some penal codes, however, the defense of coercion is not available where the charge is murder of an innocent person.

DOV GRUNSCHLAG, *Member, New York Bar*

**COERCIVE ACTS,** kō-ûr′siv, four measures passed by Britain's Parliament in the spring of 1774 that were designed to reinforce the authority of the crown in Massachusetts Bay Colony. They were the Boston Port Act, the Massachusetts Bay Regulating Act, the Impartial Administration of Justice Act, and the Quartering Act. Together with the unrelated Quebec Act (q.v.), the measures became known as the *Intolerable Acts.*

Shocked by the defiance of law and the destruction of private property in the Boston Tea Party (q.v.), most factions in Parliament supported King George III's fighting speech of March 17, 1774, in which he urged coercive action. Either the colonies were subordinate to constituted law and authority as vested in crown and Parliament or the empire was faced with disintegration and anarchy. Further retreat after the repeal of the Stamp Act of 1765 and the Townshend Acts of 1767 was deemed impossible. Assertion of authority appeared essential.

**The Acts.** Prime Minister Lord North introduced the first measure, the Boston Port Bill, on March 18, 1774; it passed both houses of Parliament without serious opposition and was signed by the King at the end of the month. The port of Boston was ordered closed until restitution for the tea was made and until royal officials were compensated for personal damages; the Massachusetts capital was moved to Salem; and Marblehead was made the customs port of entry.

The North ministry then sought to redress what it considered to be defects in the administration of Massachusetts Bay. The Massachusetts Bay Regulating Act made the Council royally appointed rather than elected and made all law officers subject to the governor's appointment. To restrain the liberty-minded, no town meetings in the colony could be held without royal approval, and freemen could no longer elect juries. To secure fair trials for British subjects and to prevent rioting, North proposed the Impartial Administration of Justice Act, permitting the governor to move trials to other colonies or to England and to call for aid from the British Army to put down civil disturbances. Both measures were introduced on April 15, 1774. Despite strong opposition to these acts from Edmund Burke, Isaac Barre, William Pitt (Lord Chatham), and the Marquis of Rockingham, they passed Parliament in mid-May and were signed by the King on May 20.

The fourth measure, the Quartering Act, permitted the billeting of British troops in private homes in addition to public quarters, inns, and warehouses. It passed on May 28 without very much debate and then received the royal assent on June 2.

**The Reaction.** A fleet blockaded Boston Harbor, and troops under Maj. Gen. Thomas Gage maintained order. But the Bostonians remained firm despite the threat of economic disaster, and surrounding towns and colonies sent in abundant food supplies.

British opponents had predicted that the Coercive Acts would defeat their purpose by alienating colonists who had previously been unsympathetic with Bostonian rashness. They were proved right. Americans of all classes, political persuasions, and interests, whatever their misgivings about the Boston Tea Party, saw a general threat to their liberty in these four acts. The colonies united and responded quickly to a call from Virginia for a Continental Congress that was to meet in Philadelphia in September 1774 to seek a redress of the colonists' grievances. Coercion provoked rebellion.

DAVID ALAN WILLIAMS
*University of Virginia*

**COEUR,** kûr, **Jacques** (c. 1395–1456), French merchant-financier and royal councillor. Coeur was born a commoner at Bourges. His first quest for wealth brought him imprisonment in 1429 for fraudulent speculation in coinage. After being pardoned he sailed to the Levant to seek his fortune in the spice trade. Misfortune struck on the return trip when his ship foundered and his cargo was stolen, but Coeur's experience had shown him where potential riches lay.

During the next 10 years Coeur built up at Montpellier a commercial empire that controlled France's trade with the East. He prospered by supplying the court of Charles VII with silver plate, fabrics, and other luxuries of the East. Ennobled in 1441, he used royal favor to gain control of Languedoc as collector of the *gabelle* (salt tax) and as royal commissioner to the provincial estates. Backed by his wealth and offices, Coeur undersold or absorbed his rivals. He expanded his investments into the slave trade, silver mines, silk manufacture, and dye works.

Coeur's fabulous wealth and proximity to Charles VII brought him entrance into the king's council in 1442. His loans to the impoverished monarchy enabled Charles to recover Normandy in 1450. Loans to impecunious court nobles and purchase of their estates enabled Coeur to live as a *grand seigneur.* But his new status aroused the envy of the nobles, and his disgrace soon followed.

In 1451, Coeur was charged with poisoning the king's mistress, Agnes Sorel. It was a mani-

festly false accusation, and at his trial the charges were reduced to trading with the "Infidel," bribery, peculation, sale of a Christian into slavery, and exporting specie from France. Although these charges were largely true, the sentence was delivered against him chiefly because he had grown too rich and powerful. His property was confiscated and plundered by the crown and the nobility, and Coeur was sentenced to prison until he paid a fine of 400,000 livres. He escaped in 1454 and died on the island of Chios on November 25, 1456, while leading a papal fleet against the Turks.

EDMUND H. DICKERMAN
*University of Connecticut*

**COEUR D'ALENE,** kôr də-lan, is a city in northern Idaho, the seat of Kootenai county, on the north shore of Coeur d'Alene Lake, 280 miles (451 km) north of Boise. It is the trade center for a rich agricultural and lumbering region and for a mining area 45 miles (72 km) to the east. Irrigated land produces fruits, vegetables, and grains; dairying and cattle raising are important activities. The city has lumber mills, and plants that produce dairy foods and wood products. North Idaho Junior College and the headquarters for Coeur d'Alene National Forest are located here.

Coeur d'Alene was founded in 1878 as a military outpost. In 1882 silver and lead were discovered in the area. The mines were the scene of widespread labor violence in the 1890's and early 1900's. Incorporated as a city in 1906, Coeur d'Alene is governed by a mayor and council. Population: 34,514.

**COEUR D'ALENE INDIANS,** kûr-də-lān', a name given by the French Canadian *voyageurs* to a North American Indian tribe. The name means "awl heart" and denotes an Indian's opinion of the size of a trader's heart. More correctly called Skitswish, the tribe is of Salish stock, closely related to the Kalispel (q.v.).

The Coeur d'Alene lived near the headwaters of the Spokane River, around Coeur d'Alene Lake, Idaho, and on the upper Clearwater River. When first encountered by Meriwether Lewis and William Clark, who called them Skitzoomish, there were about 2,000 persons living a sedentary life, subsisting on fish, small game, and roots. Father Pierre Jean de Smet visited them in 1841, and a Catholic mission was established the following year; it is still active.

The Coeur d'Alene attempted to live in peace with their neighbors after becoming Christians, but encroaching white settlers caused an outbreak in 1858, when Chief Vincent and his band attacked the white settlements in the area, only to be defeated by Col. George Wright after two sharp battles at Four Lakes and Spokane Plains. In 1867 part of the tribe was placed on the Coeur d'Alene Reservation in Idaho, and in 1872 the rest were removed to Colville Reservation, Wash. Numbering about 800 in the mid-1960's, they made a better adjustment to white culture than many other Indians.

FREDERICK J. DOCKSTADER
*Museum of the American Indians
Heye Foundation, New York City*

**COEUR DE LION.** See RICHARD I, king of England.

**COFFEE,** kô'fē, the seeds, or beans, of any of a group of tropical evergreen shrubs of the genus *Coffea*, in the Madder family (Rubiaceae). Coffee is the second most important product in international commerce on the basis of volume traded, and it is estimated to be the first on the basis of value. The value of coffee imports is estimated to be about $2 billion a year, or 1% of total world trade. Most coffee is consumed in the form of a beverage, although large quantities are used in flavors and extracts. Very small amounts are made into diverse products such as perfume (from blossoms rather than beans) and

BRAZILIAN COFFEE INSTITUTE

COFFEE flowers and berries in various stages of maturity may appear on a single coffee plant at one time.

animal feed. Research indicates that coffee beans can be used to make many other items such as tar, pitch, fuels, plastic, antiseptics, and wall and floor materials.

Coffee contains two principal chemical compounds that provide its familiar qualities as a beverage. The first, caffeine, has a stimulating effect; the second, caffeol, supplies flavor and aroma. See also CAFFEINE.

### HISTORY

The coffee tree is believed to be indigenous to Ethiopia. According to legend, a goatherd in that country watched his animals as they ate the bright red berries from a tree growing wild in the pasture and then was surprised to see the goats cavort about in an unusually frisky manner. He too tried the berries and enjoyed their stimulating effect. It is not clear whether the coffee tree was brought from Ethiopia to Arabia or whether it was also native to Arabia. The Arabs cultivated the plant as early as 600 A. D., and the first mention of coffee in literature was by the Arab physician Rhazes about 900 A. D.

Coffee was a food and a medicine long before it became a beverage. At first the coffee berries, which contain the seeds, or beans, were dried, crushed, and mixed with fat to form a ball that was eaten. Later, the skins of the berries were mixed with the green beans and allowed to ferment to create a wine.

Coffee became a lucrative article of trade following the discovery in Arabia, in the 13th century, that a delicious beverage could be made from the roasted beans. The beverage made from roasted beans was introduced from Arabia into Turkey in 1554, from Turkey into Italy in 1615, from Italy into France in 1644, and soon thereafter into other European countries.

**Introduction of Coffee Plants into the West.** The Arabs long maintained coffee as a national monopoly. For centuries they exported large quantities of beans but did not permit a fertile seed or seedling to leave their territories. However, in 1690 the Dutch managed to obtain a few plants and placed them in botanical gardens in the Netherlands. Then they began cultivation in Java and sent plants to other botanical gardens in Europe.

The story of the introduction of coffee plants into the Western Hemisphere from Europe in 1723 centers on Gabriel Mathieu de Clieu, a young French officer who served in Martinique and believed that coffee could be raised there. While on leave in Paris, he stole a coffee plant from the Jardin des Plantes. De Clieu managed to keep the plant alive during the voyage back to Martinique in spite of an attempted kidnap, an attack by Barbary pirates, violent storms, and a serious water shortage aboard ship. The plant flourished in Martinique and its progeny spread throughout the West Indies and eventually reached the mainland of South America.

**Introduction of the Coffee Plant into Brazil.** The coffee plant did not reach Brazil until 1727. In that year Brazil sent one of its army lieutenants, Francisco de Melo Palheta, to arbitrate a boundary dispute between French and Dutch Guiana. Both were cultivating coffee, but neither allowed the export of seeds or seedlings. Palheta handled the arbitration adroitly and so endeared himself to the wife of the governor of French Guiana that on his departure she presented him with a bouquet; hidden in the bouquet were fertile coffee beans and cuttings. Palheta brought them to Brazil, where they flourished.

YOUNG COFFEE TREES are carefully thinned and tended. Coffee must be grown in a rich, well-drained soil.

BRINTON, FROM PIX

COFFEE is harvested by hand so that only fully ripened berries are selected. In some localities the harvest season continues through nearly all of the year.

### THE COFFEE TREE

Although usually referred to as a tree, coffee is actually an evergreen shrub. If left unpruned, it would reach a height of 14 to 30 feet (3–9 meters). Its leaves are dark green and glossy on top and a lighter, duller green underneath. They are 3 to 6 inches (7½–15 cm) long and grow opposite each other along the branches. At the points where the pairs of leaves join the branches, many small white blossoms appear at the time of flowering and give the coffee plantation the appearance of being covered with light snow.

The fragrant blossoms fall within a few days and small berries develop that change from dark green to deep crimson as they ripen. The berries ripen about 6 to 7 months after the tree has flowered. Beneath the skin of the berry is a fleshy pulp and within the pulp is a parchmentlike covering that encloses the green beans—usually 2 in each berry. The green beans have a delicate, tight-fitting, almost transparent skin.

Coffee trees usually bloom once a year, although they may bloom more often in very rainy climates. The trees often have flowers, green berries, and ripe berries on their branches at the same time.

Coffee trees normally begin to bear within 5 years of their initial seeding, and yield good commercial quantities of beans within 8 years. The trees produce at an optimum level for 15 to 20 years, but may continue to bear commercial amounts for many more years where soil conditions are favorable. Annual yields of 1 to 1½ pounds (0.5–0.7 kg) of green beans per tree are considered adequate, but they are frequently higher.

While there are 20 or more commercial species of the genus *Coffea*, only 2 coffee trees, *C. arabica* and *C. robusta*, are raised in quantity for beans. Very few *C. liberica* are raised because of the poorer taste qualities of the bean. *Arabica* generally is preferred to other types of coffee because of its mild, rich flavor. Until the middle of the 19th century it was the only variety cultivated. But because *arabica* is subject to attacks by insects and disease, the more resistant *robusta* and *liberica* species were subsequently developed.

### CULTIVATION

The coffee tree requires a stable environment. It cannot tolerate frost, nor can it survive prolonged periods of extremely high temperature. It requires at least 40 and preferably 70 or more inches (100 to 180 or more cm) of rain per year and it cannot survive drought. It is desirable to have heavy rainfall when the beans are developing, but light when they are ripening.

*Arabica* grows best at altitudes between 2,000 feet above sea level and the frost line, which is about 6,000 to 6,500 feet (600–2,000 meters). *Robusta* and *liberica* thrive between sea level and 2,000 feet (600 meters).

**Soil.** Coffee trees grow best in soils that are rich in potash and have good drainage. Some of the most productive trees are found on the slopes of extinct volcanoes. Organic debris, such as coffee pulp and manure, is preferred to commercial fertilizers.

**Propagation.** Although trees may be propagated from cuttings or shoots, most are started from seeds. Cuttings are made from the upright branches and planted directly in the field or in nursery beds. Seeds are planted directly in the field or in seedbeds.

**Planting.** When sown directly, the seeds are planted in hills about 15 to 20 feet (4½–6 meters) apart. The young plants are thinned to 8 or fewer plants per hill. If sown in seedbeds, the seedlings are transplanted after a few months to larger nursery beds. After a year or two, they are placed singly in the field. In some regions shade trees are used to shield the shorter coffee trees from direct sunlight. However, the need for shade trees has not been definitely established.

**Maintenance.** Coffee trees are usually pruned to 6 feet (2 meters) or slightly taller to expedite harvesting. The plantations must be weeded from 2 to 5 or more times per year. This is usually done by hand because of the hilly terrain, although mechanical weeders can be used where the ground is level. Insecticides and fungicides are sprayed on the trees to prevent damage by insects and diseases. Sometimes diseases can be controlled only by stripping the trees of their fruit and blossoms in the affected zones. The debris is then burned and the ground thoroughly raked.

**Harvesting.** The ripening season varies throughout the world, depending on local conditions of climate and altitude. In São Paulo, Brazil, harvesting continues from about May through September. In Java three crops are produced each year, requiring almost continuous harvesting. In

Ethiopia the harvest extends through two periods, October through March and May through June.

Harvesting is often a festive affair, involving whole families. Each member, with a basket slung over his shoulder, handpicks the ripened berries. Since only thoroughly ripened berries should be picked, harvesting is a selective process. It is difficult, therefore, to use mechanical harvesters.

## PROCESSING

After the berries are harvested, the leaves, sticks, and other debris are removed. The berries are then prepared for market by either the wet or the dry method. Where water is scarce, the dry method is used. It consists of spreading the berries out in thin layers on flats to dry in the sun. The berries are raked and turned several times each day so that evaporation will be uniform. After about three weeks, the hulls are removed. On smaller plantations this is done by hand threshing and pounding; on larger estates, hulling machines are used.

In the wet method, the berries are soaked overnight in large tanks to soften the outer skins. Pulping machines remove the skins and pulp surrounding the beans. A fermentation process rids the beans of the gummy coating that clings to them. Then the beans are washed and dried.

The thin parchmentlike covering and the silvery skin must be removed from the beans after hulling. This is done by polishing the beans in revolving cylinders, after which dust is removed by air blasting. The beans are then separated according to size by means of automatic sorters and inspected by hand. Broken or discolored beans are discarded.

The green coffee then is graded on the basis of quality, packed in bags, and transported to ports where coffee merchants blend varieties to meet market requirements.

**Roasting and Grinding.** Most coffee is roasted in the country where it will be consumed. Most processors blend different types of green beans before roasting. Roasting is performed in revolving, perforated, metal cylinders that are heated by gas or light fuel oil. The older batch roasters operate at about 400° F (200° C) for 16 to 17 minutes. The modern, continuous-process roasters operate at 500° F (260° C) for 5 minutes. A large roaster can turn out 5,000 to 10,000 pounds (2,300 to 4,500 kg) of roasted coffee per hour.

Medium roasts are preferred in the United States. French and Italian roasts are much darker, and Turkish roasts are darkest of all.

The roasted coffee is cooled before grinding. Grinding machines break the whole beans into particles with a series of rollers that produce from 1 to 10 grind sizes at rates up to 4,000 (1,800 kg) pounds per hour. The ground coffee is then packaged in vacuum cans or paper bags in sizes from ½ to 3 pounds (0.2 to 1.3 kg).

**Soluble (Instant) and Decaffeinated Coffee.** The possibility of preparing an extract from coffee was considered as early as 1838, when the United States Congress substituted coffee for rum in the rations of soldiers and sailors. Probably the first powdered instant coffee was invented by Sartori Kato, a Japanese chemist living in Chicago. He first sold his soluble coffee at the Pan American Exposition in Buffalo in 1901. Soluble coffee was first marketed on a broad scale in the United States by the American chemist G. Washington in 1909. However, the demand for the product remained small until World War I when the entire output of all soluble coffee in the United States was purchased by the War Department for troops in the field. During World War II the government bought almost 260 million pounds (118 million kg) of instant coffee. By 1953 one cup of coffee in 10 was instant; a more recent estimate is one cup in five.

Soluble coffee is produced by brewing coffee in a series of giant coffee pots. The extract moves from pot to pot until it reaches optimum strength. Then the water is removed, usually by drying. A spray nozzle atomizes the liquid in a current of hot air. The hollow spherical particles known as "beads" then are packaged.

Decaffeinated coffee is made by several methods; each treats the green coffee to remove the caffeine. The decaffeinization processes provide a major source of caffeine for the chemical and drug industries.

## MAKING COFFEE

Each brand of coffee represents a different blend of coffee beans. A brand should be selected for its flavor, and the grind for the type of coffee maker used. For a percolator, use regular grind; for a drip pot, drip or all-purpose grind; for a vacuum style coffee maker, fine grind.

Regardless of the brand, grind, or personal preference as to whether coffee should be full-

AFTER CLEANING by the wet method, coffee beans move through sluices to a drying area. In the sluices, the last of a gummy coating is removed from the beans.

PAN-AMERICAN COFFEE BUREAU

DRYING the cleaned beans takes from four to eight days. The beans are turned frequently to assure thorough drying.

PAN-AMERICAN COFFEE BUREAU

bodied or light, coffee must be made full strength to obtain optimum flavor. For less than full-bodied brew, dilute the coffee with hot water after making it with the recommended coffee-to-water ratio.

For each serving, use 1 coffee measure or 2 level measuring tablespoons of coffee and ¾ of a measuring cup, or 6 ounces (170 grams), of water. Both the coffee and the water should be fresh. Coffee should be purchased in amounts that can be used within a week and should be stored in a tightly closed container in a cool, dry place. Freshly drawn cold water is desirable because the flavor of coffee is sometimes affected by mineral deposits in hot water pipes.

The coffee maker should be clean and should not be used at less than three fourths of its capacity. If a percolator is used, perk gently for 6 to 8 minutes. If a drip or cone type coffee maker is used, dripping is usually completed in 4 to 6 minutes. In vacuum pots, boiling water that rises into the upper bowl should be allowed

DRIED COFFEE BEANS are sorted for size automatically, and then inspected by hand. They will be graded and blended while still green, and then roasted.

to mix with the ground coffee for about 1 minute and then be removed from heat. The brew will return to the lower bowl within 2 minutes. In electric coffee makers, the timing is automatically controlled.

Experts regard the filter-type coffee maker, which is really a kind of drip-type brewer, as the optimum. Its advantages are that the water passes through the grounds only once and the grounds never pass into the cup. Lower water temperatures are not considered to convey any special qualities to coffee.

Once brewed, coffee should not be allowed to boil because boiling causes an undesirable change in flavor. Coffee should be served immediately after brewing.

*Café au lait* is made by simultaneously pouring equal quantities of freshly-brewed coffee and hot milk. *Viennese coffee* is made with extra strength coffee, poured into tall cups, sweetened to taste, and topped with whipped cream. *Caffè espresso* is traditionally made in an espresso machine by forcing live steam through French- or Italian-roast, drip grind coffee. However, it can be approximated at home by using espresso coffee in a regular drip pot or an Italian *macchinetta*. It should be served black in demitasse cups with a twist of lemon peel and sugar.

## THE COFFEE TRADE

**Major Producers and Consumers.** Brazil exports more coffee than any other country in the world, although its share of the total has declined somewhat. Other major coffee-exporting countries in the Western Hemisphere in order of importance are Colombia, El Salvador, Guatemala, Mexico, Costa Rica, Ecuador, Peru, Nicaragua, Honduras, Haiti, the Dominican Republic, and Venezuela. Coffee is extremely important to the economies of many Latin American countries. Of the value of all exports from those nations almost 20% is represented by coffee. The percentage in some countries is much higher. It is over 60% for Colombia, 55% for Haiti, 50% for El Salvador, and 40% to 50% each for Guatemala, Brazil, and Costa Rica.

The principal coffee-exporting countries of Africa and Asia are the Ivory Coast, Angola, Uganda, Ethiopia, Indonesia, Cameroon, Madagascar, Kenya, Congo (Kinshasa) Tanzania, India, and Burundi.

The United States imports more green coffee than any other nation. Other major importers are western Europe and Canada.

In terms of per-capita consumption of green coffee, Sweden has been first, with Denmark, Finland, Norway, Switzerland, Belgium, the Netherlands, the United States, and Germany following in order of magnitude. It may surprise many persons in the United States that, in spite of the much heralded "coffee break," they fall far behind citizens of seven other countries in the amount of coffee consumed per person.

**Commercial Varieties.** Of all coffee marketed, 72% is *arabica* and most of the remaining 28% is *robusta*. In the Western Hemisphere, *arabica* is grown almost to the exclusion of other types. The coffees grown in Brazil are called Brazils; those from other Latin American countries are called Milds. The Brazils are also traded under the names of the principal ports of export: Santos, Rio, Victoria, and Paraná. Each of the four classes is further divided according to the characteristics of the beans and by the districts in which they originate. Usually a number is used to designate the subdivision. Thus a Brazil coffee might be known as Santos 2 or Santos 4.

The Milds are designated by their country of origin and a few words of description that indicate either quality, district, or state of preparation. Typical names are Guatemala Prime Washed, Costa Rica Hard Bean, and Dominican Republic Cibao. Coffee from Colombia is known as MAMS, derived from the initial letters of the departments or cities of Medellín, Armenia, Manizales, and Sevilla.

Most African and Asian coffee is *robusta*. Typical names are Ivory Coast Superior, Uganda Washed Cleaned, and Portuguese West Africa Ambriz No. 2 AA.

Preferences in coffee vary throughout the world. *Arabica* is favored in the United States and Scandinavia. But in other countries, notably France and Italy, *robusta* is in great demand.

**The International Coffee Organization.** In order to bring production into better relation with demand, and thereby maintain more stable prices, the International Coffee Organization was founded in 1962. About 60 countries participate in the organization. Its headquarters are in London, England.

The ICO has been faced with huge surpluses of green coffee since its formation. To prevent the surpluses from lowering prices to levels that would hurt the producing countries, it restrains shipments of coffee in excess of demand and attempts to increase demand. The ICO also limits the amount of coffee that can be shipped from each country, and it encourages crop diversification, especially in countries whose economies rely heavily on coffee.

WILLIAM C. STRUNING
*Pan-American Coffee Bureau*

### Bibliography

Akiyama, Takamasa, and Duncan, Ronald C., *Analysis of the World Coffee Market* (World Bank 1982).
Clarke, R. J., and Macrae, R., eds., *Related Beverages* (Elsevier Pub. Co. 1988).
Clifford, M. N., and Wilson, K. C., eds., *Coffee* (AVI 1985).
DeGraaff, J., *The Economics of Coffee* (Unipub 1988).
MacMahon, Brian, and Sugimura, Takashi, eds., *Coffee and Health* (Cold Spring Harbor Lab. 1984).
Marshall, C. F., *The World Coffee Trade* (Longwood 1983).
Palacios, Marco, *Coffee in Colombia, 1800–1970* (Cambridge 1980).
Pieterse, M. T., and Silvis, H. J., *The World Coffee Market and the International Coffee Agreement* (Unipub 1988).
Schapira, Joel, and others, *The Book of Coffee and Tea*, rev ed. (St. Martin's Press 1982).
Sivetz, Michael, and Foote, H. Elliott, *Coffee Processing Technology*, 2 vols. (AVI 1963).
Ukers, William H., *All About Coffee*, 2d ed. (1935; reprint, Gale Res. 1975).

**THE COFFEE TESTER, or cupper, tastes but does not swallow the brew.**

**COFFEEHOUSE,** a place where people meet for companionship and to exchange ideas and conversation over a cup of coffee. Coffeehouses followed the spread of the coffee-drinking habit from the Middle East to Italy and then to the rest of the European continent, England, and, later, the Americas. Notable examples of the continental coffeehouse are the French café and the Viennese coffee shop. In Leipzig Johann Sebastian Bach directed (1729–1737) an ensemble that gave weekly concerts at a "coffee garden" in summer and at Zimmermann's coffeehouse in winter. (See CAFÉ.)

The first English coffeehouse was established about 1650, at Oxford, and a second in London in 1652. The houses quickly grew in number, and Charles II, who suspected them of being centers of seditious opinion, tried to outlaw them in 1675. Near the middle of the 18th century, the golden age of the English coffeehouse, there were over 2,000 of the houses in London. Certain shops became noted for special types of clientele and conversation. Will's and Button's were the gathering places for the literary intelligentsia and were frequented by Dryden, Dr. Johnson, Boswell, Pepys, Addison, Steele, Congreve, and Swift. The fashionable world resorted to White's, depicted in Hogarth's famous series of paintings *A Rake's Progress* (1735). Other houses, such as Garraway's and Lloyd's, were centers for commercial interests.

Coffeehouses began to decline in the last half of the 18th century; private clubs, pubs, and newspapers had largely taken over their functions. But the mid-20th century witnessed a vigorous revival in their popularity. The modern coffeehouses have a literary flavor and serve as gathering places for poetry readings, music performances, and exhibitions of classic films, among other activities.

CARROLL CAMDEN*, *Rice University*

**COFFERDAM,** kô'fər-dam, a temporary watertight enclosure built in water and then pumped dry so that construction of bridge piers, building foundations, or other structures can proceed under dry, open-air conditions. Several kinds of cofferdams are used; they are usually built of earth, wood, steel, or concrete.

A single-wall sheet-pile cofferdam, used to enclose a small area, is built by driving guide piles (cylindrical posts) into the subsurface and fastening wood or steel sheet-piling to the posts. The sheet-piling provides watertightness, and the posts provide resistance to outside water pressure.

A cellular sheet-pile cofferdam, used to remove water from a large area, is built by driving steel sheetpiling into the subsurface to form a series of connected cells. After the water is removed, the cells are filled with soil to provide a base for building a dam or large structure.

ALBERT H. GRISWOLD, *New York University*

**COFFEYVILLE,** kôf'ē-vil, a city in southern Kansas, in Montgomery county, 105 miles (169 km) southeast of Wichita, on the Verdigris River. The city is a trade and industrial center in a grain and cattle raising area. Its varied manufactures include oil well equipment, refined oil, aircraft parts, house trailers, furniture, clothing, flour, paint pigments, and evaporated milk. Natural gas, oil, and clay are found nearby. Coffeyville College, a two-year coeducational institution, is in the city.

Laid out in 1871, Coffeyville was originally a busy frontier cattle town. On Oct. 5, 1892, the Dalton gang held up two banks here. The Dalton Defenders Memorial Museum commemorates the incident, in which four of the five outlaws were killed. Population: 11,021.

**COFFIN, Robert Peter Tristram** (1892–1955), American poet and teacher best known for his poems about Maine life. Descended from a Nantucket whaling family, Coffin was born near Brunswick, Maine, on March 18, 1892. He studied at Bowdoin College and Princeton University and in 1916 was a Rhodes Scholar at Trinity College, University of Oxford. Coffin became professor of English at Wells College in 1921 and Pierce Professor of English at Bowdoin in 1934. He was a Fulbright lecturer at Athens University in Greece in 1953. Coffin died in Portland, Maine, on Jan. 20, 1955.

Coffin's poetry, chiefly inspired by his Maine boyhood, is vigorous and cheerful. His volumes of verse include *Ballads of Square-Toed Americans* (1933), *Strange Holiness* (1935; Pulitzer Prize, 1936), and *Apples by the Ocean* (1950). Among his novels and sketches, also about Maine life, are *Lost Paradise* (1934), *John Dawn* (1936), and *Maine Doings* (1950). Coffin wrote the critical works *New Poetry of New England: Frost and Robinson* (1938) and *The Substance That Is Poetry* (1942).

DAVID GALLOWAY, *Author of "The Absurd Hero"*

**Bibliography:** A recording of Robert P. Tristram Coffin reading his work was made in August 1937: *Robert P. Tristram Coffin Reads from His Poetry* (Brander Matthews Dramatic Museum Collection, Library of Congress; playback copy 1978).

**COGGAN, Donald,** kog'ən (1909–2000), 101st archbishop of Canterbury. Frederick Donald Coggan was born in Highgate, a London suburb, on Oct. 9, 1909. He studied at St. John's College, University of Cambridge (B.A., 1931; M.A., 1934). Ordained a deacon in 1934 and priest in 1935, he served as curate of the Church of St. Mary in Islington, London (1934–1937). He was professor of the New Testament at Wycliffe College from 1937 until 1944, when he became principal of the London College of Divinity. He later was named bishop of Bradford (1956–1961) and archbishop of York (1961–1974). On Dec. 5, 1974, Coggan succeeded Arthur Michael Ramsey as archbishop of Canterbury. He resigned in January 1980 and

A massive cofferdam surrounds a pier being laid to support the Throgs Neck Bridge in New York City.

LITTON INDUSTRIES—AERO SERVICE DIVISION

thereafter was made chaplain of the Merchant Taylors' Company (1980–1981) and life president of the Church Army (1981). In 1980 Coggan was created a life peer. He died near Winchester, England, on May 17, 2000.

A highly respected theologian and biblical scholar, Coggan chaired the joint committee that oversaw the translation and publication of the New English Bible (1970), and after his retirement he supervised its revision. His own books include *The Ministry of the Word* (1945), *Christian Priorities* (1963), *Sinews of Faith* (1969), *Word and World* (1971), *The Heart of the Christian Faith* (1978), *Paul: Portrait of a Revolutionary* (1984), *God of Hope* (1991), and *The Voice from the Cross* (1993). An early supporter of the ordination of women, he was an energetic spokesman for the evangelical movement within the Church of England and for ecumenism.

**Bibliography:** Pawley, Margaret, *Donald Coggan: Servant of Christ* (SPCK 1987).

**COGNAC,** kô-nyȧk', a town in France in the department of Charente, on the Charente River, 23 miles (37 km) west of Angoulême. The famed Cognac brandy is distilled from wines of the Charente and Charente-Maritime departments. Grand Marnier liqueur is also made at Cognac.

Cognac's Church of St Léger, though originally a Romanesque edifice, was greatly altered in the 16th century. Several 15th- and 16th-century buildings also survive. The town received its charter in 1352. Francis I was born here in 1494. Cognac was one of the four Protestant strongholds in the 16th-century wars of religion. In 1685 the revocation of the Edict of Nantes, which had granted toleration to Protestants, undermined the town's earlier prosperity. Cognac's fortunes revived from 1787, however, with the growth of its brandy industry. Population: 19,528 (1990 census).

**COGNITION,** kog-nish'ən, any mental process by which an organism becomes aware of objects of thought or perception, or gains knowledge of the world. Cognition thus is knowing in the most general sense. It involves perceiving, recognizing, conceiving, judging, and reasoning and is, with feeling (emotional experience) and conation (volition), one of the three functions of consciousness operating at once in humans.

The essence of cognition is judgment—the process by which an object is distinguished from other objects and is characterized by concepts. The development of cognitive (or judging) processes, particularly in the child, is a subject of great interest to both psychologists and educators. To Swiss psychologist Jean Piaget, cognition is an orderly, clearly structured process by which the child "apprehends reality." It involves multiple interrelationships, both among "cognitive acts" on the one hand and between these acts and the meanings and concepts they reflect on the other. Since these relationships are subject to change, cognition becomes an ongoing, fluid process in which the child is continually amending his inner representation of and response to the environment on the basis of new experiences. Thus, cognitive growth occurs.

Jerome S. Bruner and other modern learning theorists conceptualize cognition in terms of a mastery in achieving and utilizing knowledge. An individual gains knowledge of something by doing it, by depicting it, by imagining it, or by organizing it symbolically (for example, through language). These may be called the "systems of representation." When these systems conflict, the child changes his or her way of solving problems—a manifestation of cognitive growth.

Bruner describes three stages of cognitive growth. In "enactive representation," which begins soon after birth, experience and action are fused; there is no separation of the child from his environment. In "iconic representation" the child can represent the world by an image relatively independent of his own action. In "symbolic representation," the child learns that things have names and thus acquires linguistic skills. Bruner contends that the categories into which man organizes his world are really the inventions and tools of science, which is constantly modifying cognitive structure much as the infant does to meet the demands of an increased range of experiences. (See CHILD DEVELOPMENT; CONCEPT.)

MICHAEL G. ROTHENBERG, *Columbia University*

**COGSWELL, Joseph Green,** kogz'wəl (1786–1871), American librarian and bibliographer. Born in Ipswich, Mass., on Sept. 27, 1786, Cogswell graduated from Harvard University in 1806. He returned to Harvard to teach geology and mineralogy in 1820 and became librarian there (1821–1823). He left to help found the Round Hill School in Northampton, Mass. (discontinued in 1834). Cogswell next helped plan the Astor Library in New York City (now part of the New York Public Library). As superintendent of the Astor Library from 1848 until he retired in 1861, Cogswell spent several years abroad, acquiring books for the Astor collection. He also prepared a catalog of the collection that later served as a basis for the present catalog of the New York Public Library. He died in Cambridge, Mass., on Nov. 26, 1871.

**COHABITATION,** kō-hab-ə-tā'shen, primarily the state of two persons dwelling together. More specifically, it connotes the act of a man and woman living together as husband and wife, in a durable status, not merely sojourning or visiting. Whereas cohabitation only indicates a marital state and does not create one, it nevertheless may ratify a marriage. In this context, it means more than living in the same house and includes sexual intercourse. Thus, when a party to a marriage voidable by reason of fraud cohabits with the other party, although having full knowledge of the fraud, the marriage is reaffirmed.

PETER D. WEINSTEIN, *Member, New York Bar*

**COHAN, George Michael,** kō-han' (1878–1942), American playwright, actor, producer, director, and songwriter who was one of the most versatile figures in the history of the American theater. He is considered the father of American musical comedy. For his patriotic World War I song *Over There* (1917), he was awarded a congressional medal in 1941. A statue of him, erected in Duffy Square, New York City, was unveiled in 1959.

George M. Cohan was born in Providence, R.I., on July 3 (not July 4, as he claimed), 1878. The son of vaudevillians, he made his first stage appearance at the age of 9 in his parents' act. In 1888 he became a regular part of the family act "The Four Cohans" (his parents, his sister Josephine, and himself), and by the time he was 13 years old he was contributing songs and other

GEORGE M. COHAN, playing Franklin D. Roosevelt in the 1937 Rodgers and Hart musical *I'd Rather Be Right*.

material to the act. His first published song was *Why Did Nellie Leave Home?* (1894), and his first song hit was *I Guess I'll Have to Telegraph My Baby* (1898). In these, as in all his songs, he was his own lyricist.

In 1901, Cohan expanded one of his vaudeville skits into the musical comedy *The Governor's Son*. In 1904 he wrote book, lyrics, and music for *Little Johnny Jones*, in which he also starred. This production marked a turning point in the American musical theater, away from operettas with foreign settings and characters and toward a thoroughly American product. Out of this show came such song standards as *Yankee Doodle Boy* and *Give My Regards to Broadway*. His other important musicals include *Forty-Five Minutes from Broadway* (1905) and *George Washington, Jr.* (1906).

Cohan also distinguished himself as a playwright with such nonmusical productions as *Get Rich Quick Wallingford* (1910), *Broadway Jones* (1913), *Seven Keys to Baldpate* (1913; based on a novel by Earl Derr Biggers), and *The Tavern* (1920). Great Cohan songs include *You're a Grand Old Flag* and *Mary's a Grand Old Name*.

As an actor he starred in the 1932 film *The Phantom President*. In 1933 he won critical acclaim for his performance on the Broadway stage in Eugene O'Neill's *Ah, Wilderness!*, and in 1937 he starred in the Rodgers and Hart stage musical *I'd Rather Be Right*. Cohan, with Sam Harris, formed a producing company that flourished from 1904 to 1920. He died in New York on Nov. 5, 1942.

DAVID EWEN, *Author of "The Story of America's Musical Theater"*

**COHASSET,** kō-has'it, is a residential town in eastern Massachusetts, in Norfolk county. It is on the Atlantic Ocean, 15 miles (24 km) southeast of Boston. Its industries are tourism, lobster fishing, and the manufacture of furniture. Cohasset was incorporated in 1770. Government is by town meeting. Population: 7,075.

**COHEN, Hermann** (1842–1918), German philosopher, who was a leader of the neo-Kantian Marburg school of philosophy and a major Jewish religious thinker. Cohen was born in Coswig, Anhalt, on July 4, 1842, and studied at the Jewish Theological Seminary in Breslau and at the University of Berlin. He was professor of philosophy at Marburg from 1876 until his resignation in 1912, when he went to teach at the School of Jewish Studies in Berlin. He died in Berlin on April 4, 1918.

Cohen took a new approach to Kantianism by trying to rid it of Hegelian accretions. In such works as *Kants Theorie der Erfahrung* (1871) and *Kommentar zu Kants Kritik* (1907), he denied Kant's transcendent "thing in itself" (*Ding an sich*) and emphasized instead "pure thought" as a creative process that does not merely organize what is given but is the source from which existing things derive. In his principal work, *System der Philosophie* (1902–1912), Cohen unified the three Kantian areas of inquiry—logic, ethics, and aesthetics—by seeing them as areas of culture consciousness, which develops over time. He defended Judaism against anti-Semitism in *Religion der Vernunft aus den Quellen des Judentums* (1918), maintaining that genuine religion is concerned entirely with ethics and that Judaism defines God primarily in ethical terms.

STEPHEN J. NOREN
*Wesleyan University*

**COHEN, Morris Raphael** (1880–1947), American philosopher. He was born in Minsk, Russia, on July 25, 1880, and went to the United States in 1892. He was educated at City College, New York, and at Harvard University. Between 1902 and 1938, Cohen taught mathematics and philosophy at City College, where he became a professor of philosophy in 1912. In 1913 he organized the Conference on Legal and Social Philosophy, and he served as president of the American Philosophical Association (1929) and of the Conference on Jewish Relations (1933–1941). From 1938 to 1942 he taught philosophy at the University of Chicago.

Cohen was too critical to join any philosophic school of thought; his philosophy unites pragmatism with logical positivism and linguistic analysis. He exercised great influence on legal philosophy, in which he specialized. His works include *Reason and Nature* (1931), *Law and the Social Order* (1933), *An Introduction to Logic and Scientific Method* (with Ernest Nagel; 1934), *Faith of a Liberal* (1946), and *The Meaning of Human History* (1948). Cohen died in Washington, D. C., on Jan. 28, 1947.

**COHESION,** kō-hē'zhən, is the force of attraction acting between the particles of any given mass. The cohesive forces interact between adjacent parts of a single body and are present throughout the interior of the body. Because of them the particles resist separation; that is, the mass resists physical disintegration.

"Adhesion" also refers to forces of attraction between particles, but it is used only when these forces act across a surface separating two different masses. Thus the forces between molecules in a drop of water are cohesive, while the mutual attraction between water and glass represents adhesion.

Cohesion in gases is always much less than in liquids or solids, and cohesion in liquids is usually less than in solids. The forces of cohesion in gases are known as Van der Waals forces, and they are short-range electrostatic dipole interactions between closely neighboring molecules. In nonpolar liquids and solids, the cohesion is also of the Van der Waals type. In substances made up of polar molecules (molecules in which the centers of positive and negative charge do not coincide), the positive end of one molecule is attracted to the negative end of a close neighbor, thus setting up cohesive forces different than those of the Van der Waals type.

The nature of cohesion in crystalline solids depends on the type of crystal structure present. In a molecular crystal lattice, such as that of carbon dioxide in the form of dry ice, the structural unit is the molecule, and the cohesive forces are Van der Waals forces. In an ionic lattice, such as that of sodium chloride, the structural units are ions of opposite charge, and the forces of cohesion are electrostatic coulomb forces. In a covalent lattice, such as that of diamond, cohesion results from the sharing of electrons between atoms, while in metallic lattices, it results from electrostatic attraction between metallic ions and a sea of valence electrons.

The ultimate strength of a material is not a reliable measure of the true strength of its cohesive forces. A typical sample of quartz, for example, consists of many crystals, each of which is held together by strong cohesive forces. However, the separate crystals are bound to each other by relatively weak adhesive forces, and it is these forces that limit the strength of the whole sample.

HERBERT LIEBESKIND
*The Cooper Union, New York*

**COHN, Edwin Joseph** (1892–1953), American chemist, who developed the classic method of separating the different proteins found in blood plasma. After working for several years on the chemistry of proteins, Cohn began his attempts to fractionate blood plasma and obtain as many of the pure components of plasma as possible. Using simple reagents such as ammonium sulfate and alcohol and carefully regulating all the physical constants, Cohn succeeded in separating albumin, globulin, and fibrin factors from blood plasma. These components, subsequently known as "Cohn fractions," became very important in the treatment of many diseases and disorders, especially during World War II. For example, albumin was used to treat shock, gamma globulins to prevent infections, and fibrins to treat hemorrhage and other blood disorders.

Before beginning his work on the fractionation of blood plasma, Cohn investigated the solubility and acid-base behavior of proteins and found an equation that described the conditions under which proteins dissolve or precipitate as salt is added to their solution. Later, working on amino acids and peptides, he discovered the relationship between the chemical structure of a peptide and its solubility characteristics.

Cohn was born in New York City on Dec. 17, 1892. After studying at Amherst and the University of Chicago, he did postdoctorate work on egg albumin at the University of Copenhagen. In 1920 he joined the department of physical sciences at Harvard University's Medical School. He spent his entire academic career there. He died in Boston on Oct. 1, 1953.

**COHN, Ferdinand Julius** (1828–1898), German botanist, who is often considered one of the founders of bacteriology. Cohn was the first scientist to treat bacteria as plants, and during his lifetime he was known as the leading student of bacterial systematics. He believed that bacteria, like other plants, could be classified into species and genera based largely on their structural differences. He also pointed out, however, that structure alone should not determine bacterial classification. Cohn was among the first biologists to recognize that structurally similar organisms may differ drastically from each other in their physiology and biochemical makeup.

In 1877, Cohn discovered bacterial spores, a finding that shed much light on the question of spontaneous generation, the theory that living organisms can arise from nonliving matter. That same year, while working with Robert Koch, Cohn helped prove that anthrax is caused by a specific bacterium, *Bacillus anthracis.* Through Cohn's efforts, Koch was appointed to the Imperial Health Office of Germany where he conducted his other well-known studies.

Cohn was born in Breslau on Jan. 24, 1828. He was educated at the universities of Breslau and Berlin and became a professor at Breslau in 1859. During his lifetime he was awarded many honors for his teaching ability as well as his scientific findings. He died at Breslau on June 25, 1898.

DAVID OTTO, *Stephens College*

**COHN, Gustav** (1840–1919), German economist, who wrote extensively on economic theory, transportation, and public finance. He was born in Marienwerder, East Prussia, on Dec. 12, 1840. He studied at the universities of Berlin, Jena, and Leipzig. From 1869 to 1875 he taught at the Polytechnical Institute in Riga and from 1875 to 1884 at the Politechnikum in Zürich. In 1884 he was appointed to the faculty of the University of Göttingen, where he remained until 1918. He was a cofounder of the *Verein für Sozialpolitik* (1872), an association of professors and other persons who advocated social reform.

As an economic theorist Cohn rejected a number of the basic assumptions of the so-called English classical school. He denied that self-interest is the underlying force of economic activity and that all economic behavior can be explained with reference to it. He also rejected the postulate that free competition is an essential part of scientific economics. Cohn considered economics an ethical science and advocated the historical approach to and inductive methods in its study. His writings included *The Science of Finance* (1889; tr. by T. B. Veblen, 1895) and *System der Nationalökonomie*, 3 vols. (1885–1898). Cohn died in Göttingen on Sept. 17, 1919.

RAMON KNAUERHASE
*University of Connecticut*

**COHOES,** kō-hōz, is a city in eastern New York, in Albany county, at the confluence of the Mohawk and Hudson rivers, 10 miles (16 km) north of Albany. Power from the 70-foot (21-meter) falls of the Mohawk made it an important manufacturing center. The first power-operated knitting machine was installed here in 1832, and textiles have been made here since 1840. Industries also include shipbuilding and the manufacture of electrical appliances and fine papers. Places of historic interest include the Van Schaick House, built in 1735 and used as Revolutionary War headquarters by General Horatio Gates.

Settled in 1665 by the Dutch Van Schaick family, Cohoes was incorporated as a village in 1848 and chartered as a city in 1870. Government is by mayor and council. Population: 15,521.

PORTERFIELD-CHICKERING, FROM PHOTO RESEARCHERS

THE UNIVERSITY OF COIMBRA, in Coimbra, Portugal, is centered upon these 18th century baroque buildings.

**COHOSH,** kō'hosh, the common name for several North American perennial herbs bearing one or a few large leaves, each divided in such a way that it seems to be many individual leaves. The cohoshes of the buttercup family (Ranunculaceae) are better known as bugbane or black snakeroot (*Cimicifuga racemosa*), white baneberry (*Actaea pachypoda* or *A. alba*), and red baneberry (*A. rubra*). The blue cohosh (*Caulophyllum thalictroides*), of the barberry family (Berberidaceae), grows to 3 feet (1 meter) high and produces a cluster of small greenish purple flowers. Its seeds, which break through the fruit and develop a fleshy blue coat, resemble berries.

**COIL, Electrical.** See ELECTRICITY—4. *Electromagnetism.*

**COIMBATORE,** koim-bə-tōr', one of the largest cities in the Madras state in southwestern India. It is situated on the Noyil River, about 1,400 feet (425 meters) above sea level. Coimbatore commands the eastern entrance to the Palghat Gap, the only natural break in the western coastal mountains between the Tapti River and Cape Comorin, a distance of 900 miles (1,450 km). This strategic pass figured prominently in Indian history and gave the city importance in the 19th century British wars with Hyder (Haidar) Ali and Tipu Sultan. The pass is now crossed by a highway and by the Southern Railway which links Tamil land with Kerala and the upper Malabar Coast. A railroad line runs from Coimbatore south to Madurai and Tuticorin, and air service connects it with Madras, Bangalore, and Cochin.

Coimbatore became a municipality in 1866 and is the headquarters of its district. Its economic development was spurred by a hydroelectric complex on the Pykora River, and the city became an important industrial and commercial center. It is the largest cotton-milling center south of Bombay, and also has cement works, tanneries, and coffee-processing plants.

Most of the population is Hindu and speaks Tamil. The well-known Hindu-Dravidian-style Temple of Perur is located in Coimbatore, and just north of the city and linked by railroad are the attractive Nilgiri Hills, famous for their tea and coffee and for Ootacamund ("Ooty"), queen of south Indian resort towns. Population: 853,402 (1991 census).

ROBERT C. KINGSBURY, *Indiana University*

**COIMBRA,** kwēNm'brə, is a city in Portugal and seat of the University of Coimbra, one of Portugal's major institutions of higher education. The city, which is the capital of Beira Litoral province, is situated on the right bank of the Mondego River, 139 miles (224 km) northeast of Lisbon. The main industries of Coimbra are tanning and the manufacture of pottery, fabrics, beer, wine, and paper.

The name "Coimbra" derives from Conimbriga, the ancient Roman name for what is now Condeixa, 8 miles (13 km) away. Modern Coimbra is built on the site of ancient Aeminium. The name was changed when the episcopal see of Conimbriga was moved to Aeminium.

Coimbra was a Moorish stronghold during the Moorish occupation of Portugal and Spain. It was recaptured by Ferdinand I of Castile in 1064. For many years it was the headquarters of the Reconquest of Portugal. Six kings were born there as well as the poet Sá de Miranda (1481–1558). It was a focal point in the insurrection of the followers of Dom Miguel in the 19th century.

The national university was established permanently at Coimbra in 1537 and has since been the most important feature of the city. Its buildings are among the city's outstanding architectural monuments. In the old city, which is on a hill overlooking the river, are the Romanesque cathedral (1170) and the Church of São Salvador. Many of the buildings have been rebuilt on Roman or medieval bases. Population: 97,140 (1991 census).

GREGORY RABASSA
*Columbia University*

**COIMBRA, University of,** the oldest, and for over five centuries the only, institution of higher education in Portugal. It was founded in Lisbon in 1290 by King Diniz and transferred to Coimbra in 1308, alternating between the two cities until 1537, when it was settled permanently at Coimbra. The university's influence subsequently declined until 1772, when the Marquess de Pombal, then Portuguese prime minister, effected major reforms, including the introduction of faculties in mathematics and philosophy.

Now operated under the jurisdiction of the Portuguese ministry of education, the university has faculties of letters, law, medicine, and sciences, and a school of pharmacy. A library of over 1.2 million volumes is supplemented by special libraries for each faculty, and there are museums of natural history and zoology. Average enrollment is about 7,000.

**COINS** are pieces of metal, usually disk-shaped, that bear lettering, designs, or other inscriptions attesting to their value, weight, or fineness (metallic content). A coin possesses a value that makes it useful as a medium of exchange. The word comes from the Latin *cuneus*, meaning "die," later "coin."

---

## CONTENTS

---

Until the 18th and 19th centuries most coins were assigned monetary worth based on the concept of *intrinsic value*. For example, the value of a gold coin would be equal to the current value of the metal it contained. This necessitated weighing and reevaluating the coin every time it reached a bank or merchant. As the price of a metal fluctuated so did the value of coins made of that metal.

Modern coins usually pass at the *face value* stamped on them. The face value may bear no relation to the intrinsic value. For example, United States 25-cent pieces are made of copper and nickel alloys sandwiched together. These coins in commerce have a face or monetary value of 25 cents apiece, although their intrinsic or metallic value is just a small fraction of that.

Coinage—the process of coining—is performed at a *mint,* a place equipped with coining presses, weighing instruments, and other specialized equipment. Coinage in modern times has been a government function and has been closely regulated. The government guarantees the face value of coins. Prior to the 20th century hundreds of nongovernment agencies issued coins for various purposes. Thus, in the California goldfields, hundreds of thousands of gold coins were privately issued by banks and assay offices from 1849 to 1855 to enable miners to convert raw gold into convenient coins. (A U. S. government mint was established in San Francisco in 1854, and within a few years it supplanted entirely the private mints.) In England a flood of privately issued coins appeared from about 1787 to 1796 after widespread public hoarding caused nearly all government issues to disappear from circulation. See also MINT.

**Numismatics.** Numismatics is the science and study of coins, tokens, paper money, and other objects that have served as mediums of exchange, as well as of medals. Although medals resemble coins in appearance, they differ in that they are issued to commemorate an event and are not a medium of exchange. Tokens are generally issued by a private (nongovernment) agency and have a value limited in area and function. Thus, gambling tokens are issued by many of the world's casinos and have value only in those casinos. Transportation tokens have value only on a particular railroad, subway, or bus line. Paper money, scrip and emergency currency, military orders and decorations, and a variety of related items are all encompassed by the field of numismatics.

## UNUSUAL COINS

Chinese bell money.

Chinese key money, 5th century B.C.

Alaskan Indian copper plate money.

East Indian coin tree of 1897.

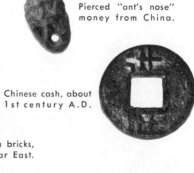

Money made of compressed tea bricks, used in some areas of the Far East.

Pierced "ant's nose" money from China.

Chinese cash, about 1st century A.D.

Silver money in various shapes, including (*upper right*) Laotian coins known as tiger tongues.

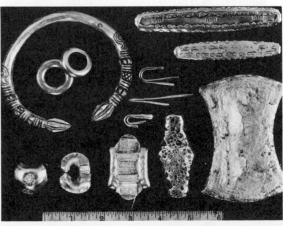

## GREEK CLASSICAL COINS

The coins of the various Greek city states can frequently be identified by a symbol struck on the reverse. The Athenian owl is the best known, but the horse-drawn chariot of Syracuse, the eagles slaying hares of Agrigentum, the eagle of Elis, and the goat of Aenus are also important. The winged horse, Pegasus, usually a symbol of Corinth, also appears on some Carthaginian coins. The dolphins around the head of the nymph Arethusa on the obverse of Syracusan coins symbolize the sea surrounding the island of Ortygia, her home.

Decadrachm of Agrigentum, about 413 B.C.

Syracusan decadrachm, about 480 B.C., showing head of Arethusa.

Athenian tetradrachm, 550 to 100 B.C.

Decadrachm commemorating Syracusan victory, about 413 B.C.

### ORIGIN OF COINAGE

Items such as metallic bars and bullion—and, in primitive societies, shells and stones—served in commerce as mediums of exchange for many millenniums before the Christian era. The first metallic coinage as such is attributed to the Chinese in the 2d millennium B. C. In the Western world the first coinage dates from the 7th or 8th century B. C. in Asia Minor. The historian Herodotus attributed the first Western coinage to the Lydians of Asia Minor, who placed marks on unrefined gold bars or ingots to avoid repeated weighing during subsequent exchanges. These early pieces were made of *electrum*, a natural alloy of gold and silver occurring in widely varying proportions.

From early times to the present era, gold coins were used mainly to facilitate large transactions, as in real estate and banking and in foreign exchange between countries. They were not common in everyday use because their values were too high to make them useful in small transactions. Gold became a virtually worldwide standard of coinage values in the 19th century. Significant changes, however, occurred in the 20th century. For example, the United States ceased the minting of gold coins in 1933. See also GOLD STANDARD—*Traditional Gold Standard*.

The main coinage metal for commerce since the days of ancient Greece and the Roman republic has been *silver*. The largest actively circulating silver piece of a country is known as a "crown" by numismatists. Generally, crown-size pieces are about the size of an American silver dollar, although wide variations occur. See also SILVER—*Silver as a Monetary Metal*.

*Copper* and its alloys (mainly bronze and brass) traditionally have filled the need for "small change"—small fractional values of the main monetary unit. For example, in Britain the penny, halfpenny, farthing, and fractional farthing issues have been in copper or bronze; in Canada 1-cent pieces (issued since 1858) have been of bronze; United States half cents (1793–1857), 1-cent pieces (coined continuously since 1793 with the exception of 1816), and 2-cent pieces (1864–1873) have been of copper or its alloys.

Nickel has emerged as a major coinage metal since the mid-19th century. It was first used in the United States for regular coinage in 1865 for 3-cent pieces. (Before that, the copper-nickel alloy of the U. S. cents of 1857–1858 contained only 12% nickel.) Nickel presented early difficulties because its hardness caused excessive die wear and breakage; however, improved technology has eliminated the problem. The last widespread use of silver-alloy coins in the United States was for the dimes, quarters, and half dollars dated 1964. Later 10-cent and 25-cent coins have been made of alloy containing nickel (the "clad" coinages) as have half dollars (although half dollars have retained a small silver content). Nickel has also supplanted the role of silver in Canadian coinages beginning in 1968. Prior to that time it had been used solely for 5-cent pieces (nickel was first used in Canada for this denomination in 1922). Nickel alloy is also the main coinage metal for the higher-denomination British coins—sixpence, shilling, florin, half crown, and crown. It appears probable that silver will disappear almost entirely from the world coinage scene and that its use will be relegated only to limited-issue commemorative pieces.

Over the centuries many other metals have been tried for coinage. Imperial Russia produced an illustrious series of *platinum* coins, mainly in

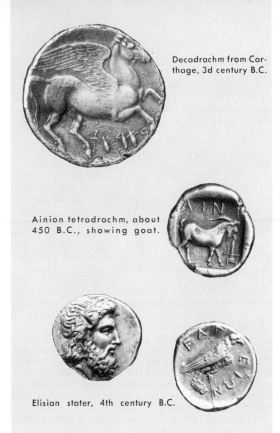

Decadrachm from Carthage, 3d century B.C.

Ainion tetradrachm, about 450 B.C., showing goat.

Elisian stater, 4th century B.C.

the 1830's; the United States experimented with platinum for coinage in the late 19th century, but only pattern (experimental) pieces were produced. *Zinc-coated steel* was used by the United States for 1-cent pieces struck during the wartime exigencies of 1943. *Aluminum* was extensively tested by the U. S. mint during the late 19th century; several hundred patterns of various designs were made but no coins were issued. During the 20th century, aluminum has been used by certain African and European countries, but the softness of the metal caused the coins to wear quickly, and their lightness made them difficult to use in coin-operated machines.

*Lead* has been used sporadically for coinage but without consistently successful results. Perhaps its greatest use for "coinage" has been by counterfeiters seeking to simulate silver coins. However, lead and lead alloys—for example, pewter—have been used for tokens, such as the 18th and 19th century Scottish communion tokens,

certain tokens of 1862–1863 in the United States, and the U. S. continental dollar of 1776.

Nonmetallic substances used for coinage have included porcelain (certain German issues of the post-World War I period), pressed fiber (a multitude of tokens, including Office of Price Administration food tokens in the United States in World War II), plastic, and even pressed blocks of tea leaves (China).

### COINS OUTSIDE THE UNITED STATES

**Classical Greek Coinage.** In its broadest definition the classical Greek coinage covers the monetary issues of the many Mediterranean lands as well as those early settlements as far north as Britain and as far east as India. All these countries were either under Greek political control or, in the case of the far-flung areas, under the influence of Greek culture as spread by sailors and traders. Ancient Greek coinage represented a high point in artistic achievement.

Greek coinage had its beginnings in the electrum (gold-silver alloy) pieces of the Lydians. Early pieces were impressed with a die only on one side; the reverse side was blank. Early motifs were predominantly animals, notably the stag, lion, and turtle.

The silver coinages of Aegina, Corinth, Chalcis, and Eretria arose about 650 B. C. The early pieces of Athens (about 594 B. C.) with the head of Athena on the obverse and an owl on the reverse, are among the first coins to have devices on both sides. Lettered inscriptions in addition to a central motif did not become common until several centuries later.

As coinage spread, figures of certain animals or other designs, sometimes in combination with a brief inscription, came to represent specific localities. An early piece of Ephesus bearing an inscription in Greek meaning *I Am the Badge of Phanes* was an exception to the rule of brief inscriptions. Among the motifs of the time were the seal (Phocaea), Pegasus (Corinth), the turtle (Aegina), the owl (Athens), the silphium plant (Cyrene), the mythological griffin (Abdera). The human head was used rarely. When it was used, the head was usually in profile but with the eye shown as though in a front view.

The first period of Greek coinage, from about 650 to 480 B. C., is known as the archaic period. The second period, 480 to 415 B. C., is the transitional. This period represented a refinement both in the artistic aspects of coinage and in the mechanical process of minting.

The third period, the Greek classical period

### ROMAN COINS

Aureus of Augustus, 27 B.C. to 14 A.D.

Gold solidus of Theodosius, 383-388 A.D.

Silver denarius of Emperor Augustus.

Denarius of Geta, 209 A.D.

Roman *aes grave*, 3d century B.C., showing head of Janus on the obverse; bow of a galley on the reverse.

Archaic silver decadrachm from Athens.

Tetradrachm from Aenus, 5th century B.C., showing Hermes.

Reverse of a Syracusan coin showing horse-drawn chariot.

Carthaginian coin showing a head of the Phoenician goddess Tanit.

Macedonian gold stater, 3d century B.C., with a head of Philip II on the obverse, a chariot on the reverse.

Arabian gold dinar, 7th century A.D., bearing inscription but no images, which are forbidden by the Koran.

AMERICAN NUMISMATIC SOCIETY

415 to 336 B. C., marked the height of Greek artistry in coinage. The latter part of this period is considered by many to represent the high point in the history of coinage with respect to beauty and artistic achievement. Among the finest pieces from this period are the decadrachms of Syracuse, struck in Sicily about 413 B. C. Issued to celebrate the defeat of the Athenians by the Syracusans, these masterpieces of die cutting are the work of artists who proudly signed their names to their products. Two famous examples are the decadrachm of Cimon signed KIM (Kimon) on the bandeau of the nymph's head on the obverse, and a similar piece signed EYAINET (Euainetos) beneath the head on the obverse. The identity of these and other master sculptors and engravers of the period might have been lost to history were it not for their signed coinages. Most issues between 415 and 336 B. C. were in silver metal. The use of the gold-silver alloy electrum dwindled as nearly pure gold took its place. Outstanding among the gold issues of this era were the gold staters of Philip II of Macedon.

The fourth Greek period, 336 to 280 B. C., represented a continuation of the classical art. The figures of gods and goddesses and allegorical beings were supplanted by portraits of contemporary leaders. The seated figure became the dominant motif for the reverse of a coin. This tradition is continued in the modern coinage of certain countries, as in the seated figure of Britannia on the current English pennies.

The fifth period, 280 to 146 B. C., marked the decline of many of the city and state coinages. The individuality of coin designs declined as stereotyped motifs were adopted. The coinage of the new Hellenistic monarchies of Egypt, Macedonia, Rome, and Syria took the ascendancy. The sixth period, 146 to 27 B. C., continued the decline. Coinage of the seventh and final period, which falls under the classical Greek grouping, is the imperial coinage in use from 27 B. C. to 268 A. D., which was produced in Rome or at Roman branch mints.

**Roman Coinage.** The earliest issues of the Roman series, produced for the Roman citizens of Italy, consisted of rather crude cast bronze pieces. The earliest pieces were the crudest—merely irregular lumps of bronze known as *aes rude*. The next coinage was the *aes grave*, a cast piece of bronze, round, and bearing a portrait. The largest of these weighed about one pound. The *aes grave* currency consisted of six denominations: uncias (ounce or twelfth); sextans (sixth), quadrans (fourth), triens (third), semis (half), and the as. During the period from about 335 to 89 B. C., the as was steadily reduced in weight, down finally to about 10% of its former standard.

The silver denarius was issued first in 268 B. C., along with its half (quinarius) and quarter (sestertius). Together with the bronze as currency, these silver pieces formed the chief coinage of the Roman republican period. The republican silver coins are often known as consular (or "family") coins because they bear the family names (sometimes in abbreviated form) of Roman officials. These officials were monetary magistrates. Some museums, including the British Museum, arrange the Roman coinages chronologically, but most collectors and sale catalogers retain the family system.

The Roman Empire, beginning with Augustus in 29 B. C., issued gold coins infrequently. Silver was the main coinage metal. Besides the gold aureus and the silver denarius, the coinage included the large brass sestertius (of four asses), the middle brass, or dupondius, and the copper as, semis, and quadrans. Portraits of the emperors and the imperial family were placed on the obverses of coins. The appearance of the portraits of women on coins was more a compliment to the imperial family than a manifestation of the coinage right of a given empress or an emperor's daughter.

Beginning with the coinages of Pompey and Caesar, 49 to 44 B. C., events were portrayed on coins with great frequency, providing a valuable historical record. This portrayal was continued to varying degrees by succeeding emperors.

A decline in Roman coinage, through debasement of the various denominations and a deterioration in the artistry of the designs, occurred in the early centuries of the Christian era. The successive debasements by Nero, Caracalla, and Gallienus reduced the value of Roman coins to the point where the public completely lost confidence, and prices rose to inflationary heights.

After Rome fell, Britain, Gaul, and other western European countries began their own coinage systems, using the Roman system as a starting point on which to base denominations and designs. The coinage of the Eastern Roman Empire passed into the coinage system of the Byzantine Empire.

**Oriental Coinage.** The Chinese coinages date from the 2d millennium B. C. The first issues consisted of cast bronze pieces in the shape of implements, such as knives and spades. "Cash" pieces—round coins with square center holes so that they could be suspended—were issued at an early period to serve as small units of money.

India began producing square silver and copper coins about 350 B. C. These coins were punchmarked with symbols such as the swastika and the sun. The Bactrian Greek invaders brought coinage of Greek characteristics to the Kabul Valley in the 2d century B. C. Their successors,

the conquering Kushan tribes, then blended Greek and Oriental coinage.

Arabic coins differ from others in that, complying with Muslim religious practice, they bear no images. From 695 A. D., the designs on Muslim coins consisted of Arabic inscriptions. These coins were usually thin, flat, well executed, and of even standard. However, the earliest Arabic issues, from about 661 to 695, were gold and copper imitations of the designs used by the Byzantine emperors of Constantinople. During the Persian medieval period, the Arab rulers of Persia issued Sassanian-type coins, thin and flat in relief. The Persian shahs began about 1520 to strike coins that were unusually thick and had a particularly flowing style of inscription.

Japan's earliest coinage dated from about the 5th century and was similar to that of the Chinese "cash." Long silver ingots were struck during the 17th and 18th centuries. Small 1 bu and 2 bu pieces of silver were struck in the 19th century. Large and small oblong gold obans and kobans were also struck during the 19th century. Since 1869 the country's coinage has been patterned on the Western style.

**Medieval Coinage.** The Byzantine coinage is intertwined with the Roman coinage to the extent that the late Roman and early Byzantine pieces are virtually identical. Byzantine coinage began in 491 A. D., and its influence spread to Italy, Russia, France, Germany, and Denmark. European coinage from the fall of the Roman Empire to the time of Charlemagne was a largely imitative coinage by the Ostrogoths, Visigoths, Vandals, Lombards, and others.

A distinct medieval coinage began to arise in 800 with the issuance of the silver denarius of Charlemagne. In the Renaissance, coinages assumed an independent character as portraits were introduced, and the first pieces of the mid-15th century rank high in artistic merit. Antonio Pisano, Matteo da Pasti, Benvenuto Cellini, and other Italian artists produced large, beautiful medals.

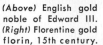

(Above) Carolingian denier struck for Pepin the Short. (Below) Silver Denier struck for Charlemagne.

(Above) English gold noble of Edward III. (Right) Florentine gold florin, 15th century.

English silver penny, 14th century, showing Edward III on the obverse.

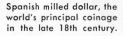

Spanish milled dollar, the world's principal coinage in the late 18th century.

British coins (*clockwise, from Royal Mint medallion at top center*): ½ penny, 2 pence, 1 penny (all bronze); 50 pence, 20 pence (issued in 1982), 10 pence, and 5 pence (all cupro-nickel); and, at center, 1 pound (nickel-brass, issued in 1983). The ½ penny was discontinued in 1985.

BRITISH ROYAL MINT

The coinage and medallic art became stereotyped in the 16th century. This led to the development of the standard in use today throughout the world: coinage of a particular country consists of set designs that are changed little from year to year except for the date numerals.

**Spanish and Spanish American Coinage.** Spanish coinage followed the regal portrait design pattern used throughout medieval Europe. The Spanish conquests in the New World in the 15th and 16th centuries led to the adoption of the Spanish dollar (8 reals) and its counterparts throughout North and South America. The gold doubloon (8 escudos—equal in worth to about $16 in U.S. money) was the standard of large monetary transactions in the Western Hemisphere until the 19th century. A Spanish real was worth about 12½¢ in U.S. money and was known as a "bit." The term "two bits" for our 25-cent piece today is a reflection of the Spanish coinage heritage.

As the Spanish-speaking American countries developed their own coinages they patterned them after the Spanish standard, so that the denominations resembled one another from country to country. To an extent—particularly in the earlier years—the designs of Mexican, Bolivian, Chilean, Ecuadorian, and other coinages also were similar.

**Canadian Coinage.** Until 1858, Canada used a wide variety of tokens and provisional coinages as well as the predominant regular French and English pieces. In 1858 the country instituted a decimal coinage patterned on the U.S. system. The smallest unit was the cent, and the largest was the dollar (although, with the exception of a 1911 pattern, silver dollars were not coined until 1935). Denominations included the 1-cent, 5-cent, 10-cent, 20-cent (coined only in 1858 and then discontinued), 25-cent, 50-cent, $1, $5, and $10 pieces. Coinage was not continuous; pieces were struck sporadically to meet the needs of commerce. In 1935 the first silver dollar, a commemorative design, was issued. Since 1935, Canada has issued a series of beautiful commemorative dollars depicting events in Canadian history. In 1967, for the first time, Canada issued a $20 gold piece as a commemorative.

Canadian coinage has been produced at the Royal Mint in London, England; at the private Heaton Mint in Birmingham, England; and at the Canadian Royal Mint in Ottawa, Canada. At present the Royal Mint in Ottawa fills all the coinage requirements, including special yearly sets for collectors. Various provinces, including Nova Scotia, Prince Edward Island, New Brunswick, and Newfoundland, have issued coins.

**African Coins.** Before the 20th century most African areas, as colonies of European powers, either used coins of the mother country or coins with legends and devices similar to those of the mother country. The newly independent African nations of the 20th century, including Ghana, Malawi, and Zambia, have issued their own coinages, but only the largest ones have established their own mints. Most of the smaller countries have their coins produced in non-African mints on contracts. Most of this business goes to the Royal Mint in London.

Q. DAVID BOWERS
*Author of "Coins and Collectors"*

A set of commonly circulated coinage of Canada (*left to right*): 1 dollar, 50 cents, 25 cents, 10 cents, 5 cents, and 1 cent. These coins are now minted at the Royal Canadian Mint in Ottawa.

## UNITED STATES COINS

The United States traces its coinage system to the Spanish milled dollar of eight *reals*, known as the "piece of eight." The Spanish dollar was the predominant coin in circulation in the American colonial era and in the early years of the new nation, and the exchange rate for other currencies was commonly expressed in terms of it.

Thus the U. S. Congress chose an already familiar standard on July 6, 1785, when it passed a resolution declaring that "the money unit of the United States of America be one dollar." In the same resolution Congress adopted the decimal system by declaring, "The several pieces shall increase in decimal ratio." In contrast, Spain's "piece of eight" had eight parts—one real ("one bit"), two reals ("two bits," or a quarter dollar), and four reals ("four bits," or a half dollar).

Over the years the denominations of coins minted by the United States have ranged from a half cent (in copper) to a $20 piece (in gold). However, the U. S. mints now issue only six coin denominations for general circulation to meet the small-change needs of a vast economy. They are the cent, one hundredth of a dollar; the 5-cent piece, or nickel; the 10-cent piece, or dime; the 25-cent piece, or quarter dollar; the 50-cent piece, or half dollar; and the dollar.

In the past, U. S. mints have also issued coins in the following denominations:

Half cent, copper (1793–1857).
Large cent, copper (1793–1857).
One cent, copper-nickel (1857–1864).
Two-cent, bronze (1864–1873).
Three-cent, silver (1851–1873).
Three-cent, copper-nickel (1865–1889).
Half dime, silver (1794–1873).
Twenty-cent, silver (1875–1878).
Trade dollar, silver (1873–1885).
Dollar, silver (1794–1873, 1878–1935).

### Gold Pieces
Dollar (1849–1889).
$2.50, or quarter eagle (1796–1929).
$3 (1854–1889).
$5, or half eagle (1795–1929).
$10, or eagle (1795–1933).
$20, or double eagle (1849–1933).

With the exception of the trade dollar, all U. S. coins remain redeemable at face value by the Treasury. (Obviously, however, coins no longer being minted have greater value as collectors' items.)

**Current Designs.** Most U. S. coins now being minted bear the portrait of a president and the initials of its designer. In addition, the motto "In God We Trust," which has appeared on many coin denominations since 1864, is required by an act passed in 1955. As the result of a law passed in 1890, no change in design is permitted oftener than once in 25 years, unless authorized by Congress.

**Lincoln Cent.** Victor D. Brenner designed the Lincoln cent, issued in 1909 to commemorate the centenary of Abraham Lincoln's birth. Originally Brenner's initials, V. D. B., appeared on the reverse of the coin, but in 1918 the initials were placed in the truncation of Lincoln's shoulder on the obverse. The Lincoln cent succeeded the Indian-head cent, issued in copper-nickel (1859–1864) and in bronze (1864–1909).

**Jefferson Nickel.** The Jefferson 5-cent piece appeared in 1938, replacing the Indian-buffalo nickel. The design by Felix Schlag, chosen after open competition, showed Thomas Jefferson on the obverse and Monticello on the reverse. Schlag's initials were placed on the coin in 1966.

**Roosevelt Dime.** The portrait of Franklin D. Roosevelt was placed on the dime in 1946, the year after his death. John R. Sinnock, chief engraver of the U. S. mint, designed this coin. The Roosevelt dime replaced designer Adolph Weinman's Mercury dime, which was minted from 1916 to 1945 and took its name from the wings on the cap of Liberty.

**Washington Quarter.** A new 25-cent piece was issued in 1932 to commemorate the 200th anniversary of the birth of George Washington. The design was by John Flanagan, who used as his model the famous Washington bust by Jean Antoine Houdon. The Washington quarter replaced the standing Liberty quarter, designed by Hermon A. MacNeil, which circulated from 1916 to 1930.

**Kennedy Half Dollar.** In 1964, the year after the assassination of President John F. Kennedy, a half dollar bearing his portrait was issued. The portrait of Kennedy on the obverse was designed by Gilroy Roberts. The U. S. presidential seal on the reverse was designed by Frank Gasparro. The Kennedy coin succeeded Sinnock's 50-cent piece bearing the portrait of Benjamin Franklin on the obverse and the Liberty Bell on the reverse. The Franklin-Liberty half dollar was minted from 1949 to 1963. It followed Weinman's "Liberty walking" coin, issued from 1916 to 1947.

**Eisenhower Dollar.** A dollar coin portraying Dwight D. Eisenhower (obverse) and an eagle landing on the moon (reverse), issued from 1971 to 1975, was not popular because of its bulk and weight. It was designed by Frank Gasparro.

**Anthony Dollar.** The Susan B. Anthony dollar, also designed by Frank Gasparro and with the moon-landing eagle on the reverse, was issued in 1979. It weighed only one third as much as the Eisenhower coin but was criticized for looking too much like a quarter.

**Bicentennial Coins.** Dollars, half dollars, and quarter dollars showing a colonial drummer on the reverse and the dates 1776–1976 under Washington's portrait on the obverse were issued after July 4, 1975, for the Bicentennial celebration.

**Colonial Coins.** Before the United States became a nation, the colonists were confronted with a lack of small coins. The coins in circulation came mostly from trade with England, Holland, Spain, France, and the West Indies.

England did not sanction a mint in her colonial empire, but the Massachusetts Bay Colony established one at Boston in 1652 with John Hull as its mintmaster until 1682. The first coins produced at Hull's mint were plain New England shillings, sixpence, and threepenny pieces that have on the obverse the letters "NE" and on the reverse the denomination in Roman numerals. Some of the silver could be clipped off without impairing the design, so the design soon was changed. The succeeding issues were known as Willow Tree, Oak Tree, and Pine Tree coins. On the obverse of these pieces is a tree in the center of a beaded circle surrounded by the word "Masathusets." The reverse carries the date 1652 and the denomination in Roman numerals within a beaded circle surrounded by the words "New England. An. Dom." The Pine Tree coins in the shilling, sixpence, and threepenny denominations were minted for about 30 years, but they all have the same date, 1652. The Pine Tree shilling is

The Spanish dollar, the silver "piece of eight," was the money unit on which the U. S. coinage was modeled. Considered as having eight parts, the Spanish dollar could be cut into halves and quarters to make pieces called "four bits" and "two bits."

The Pine Tree shilling was minted in Boston from 1652 to 1686, but all coins bear the 1652 date.

The Rosa Americana copper penny, minted in 1722, was produced in England for use in the colonies.

The 1787 Fugio copper cent was the first coin issued under authorization of the U. S. government.

The Excelsior cent, designed for New York state in 1787, carried the image of the state seal.

The profile of George III decorated the obverse of the gold spade guinea, minted in England in 1789.

A half cent, issued from 1793 to 1857, was one of the first coins produced by the Philadelphia mint.

probably the most noted coin of early America.

The Higley, or Granby, copper was minted in 1737 and 1739 by John Higley, who owned a copper mine near Granby, Conn. The first type had the inscription "Value of Threepence." The quantity soon exceeded the demand, so that Higley changed the legend to read "Value Me as You Please."

Before the Revolutionary War many coins, mostly coppers, were produced abroad and sent to the colonies for circulation. These pieces included the St. Patrick halfpence and farthing brought to New Jersey from Ireland by Mark Newby in 1681; the Hibernia, or William Wood's coinage of 1722–1724, in the halfpence and farthing denominations, which had been rejected for use in Ireland; the Rosa Americana twopence, penny, and halfpenny, manufactured by Wood especially for the colonies under a patent obtained by him from George I in 1722; the Lord Baltimore shilling, sixpence, and fourpence, in silver, for use in Maryland about 1659; the Carolina and New England tokens of 1694; and the Virginia halfpenny of 1773, the only coin sanctioned by George III for circulation in the colonies. The tokens were made of copper and brass and were issued unofficially for monetary or advertising purposes.

**First Coins After Independence.** A large variety of English-made tokens, some bearing George Washington's portrait, circulated in the United States shortly after it became a nation. When the United States authorized its own coinage, it was proposed that Washington's portrait appear on the coins. He refused to permit this, however, on the premise that the practice would not be in accord with the principles of the new democracy.

The Articles of Confederation, adopted in 1778, gave the states the authority to coin money. Connecticut, New Jersey, and Massachusetts did so. Although Vermont was not one of the 13 original colonies and did not become a state until 1791, its assembly became, in 1785, the first to authorize a regular issue of copper pieces. Although New York did not authorize a coinage, several types of cents were manufactured by individuals for use in that state. The right to coin money was taken from the states by the Constitution in 1787, and Congress since 1789 has had the power to coin money and to regulate its value.

**Establishment of the Coinage System.** Under the Articles of Confederation, Congress appointed a committee, headed by Robert Morris, to prepare a report on a coinage system for the United States. In January 1782, Morris recommended that the monetary standard be affixed to silver with a ratio of 14.5 to 1 between silver and gold; that the decimal system be established; that the monetary unit be $\frac{1}{1440}$ of a dollar, which would standardize the different valuations of the Spanish milled dollar; and that a mint be established. These recommendations were approved by Congress on Feb. 21, 1782, and Morris was requested to make a further report on his plans. In April 1783, Morris submitted to Congress specimens of silver coins in denominations of 1,000 units (a mark), 500 units (a quint), and 100 units (a bit). However, his plans for a coinage and a mint were referred to a committee and died there.

Thomas Jefferson, then a member of the House of Representatives, disapproved the Morris plan as being too confusing and complex. He favored the decimal system but thought that a monetary unit based on the dollar would be easier to understand. Jefferson's proposals were made in 1784 and accepted on July 6, 1785, when Congress passed a resolution making the dollar the nation's monetary unit and adopting the decimal system.

In 1787 the Fugio cent became the first coin issued by authorization of the national government. This coin was minted in New Haven, Conn., by James Jarvis, who contracted with the Board of Treasury to make 300 tons of copper coin. The Fugio cent has on the reverse a circle of 13 links (representing the 13 original colonies), a small circle in the middle with the words "United States" around it, and in the center the words "We are one." On the obverse there are: a dial with the hours expressed on the face of it; a meridian sun figure above, on one side of which is the word "Fugio"—"I fly," referring to the sun—and on the other side the year in figures, 1787; below the dial the words, "Mind your business." Because the inscriptions have been attributed to Benjamin Franklin, the piece is frequently called the Franklin cent.

In 1789 Congress directed Alexander Hamilton, secretary of the treasury, to prepare a report on how to establish a national coinage. Hamilton's report, presented in January 1791, endorsed the decimal subdivisions and the dollar as the monetary unit, as suggested earlier by Jefferson, and the use of both gold and silver in the standard money. After much debate Congress passed the Coinage Act on April 2, 1792. It authorized a mint, specified the coin denominations to be minted, and established two units of value: the gold dollar of 24.75 grains of pure gold and the silver dollar of 371.25 grains of pure silver.

**Establishment of Mints.** The first mint was established in Philadelphia in 1792. It was authorized to operate only for 5 years. During the first 10 years of the mint's existence, several bills to abolish it were introduced into Congress, and one such resolution passed the House of Representatives. However, the life of the mint was renewed for 5-year periods until 1828, when an act was passed to operate the mint in Philadelphia until otherwise provided by law. The Philadelphia mint is considered the "mother" mint, because dies for all United States coins are made there.

The United States also has mints in Denver (established in 1906) and in San Francisco (1854–1955, reactivated in 1965 for a limited period). It also has had the following mints, none of them now in operation: Dahlonega, Ga. (1838–1861); Charlotte, N. C. (1838–1861), for gold only; New Orleans, La. (1830–1861, 1879–1909); and Carson City, Nev. (1870–1893). See also MINT.

**Coinage and Coinage Regulations.** Regular U. S. coinage commenced at the Philadelphia mint in 1793. In that year only half cents and cents were produced. The mint began making half dimes, half dollars, and silver dollars in 1794 and dimes and quarters in 1796. Gold coins were not minted until 1795, when the 5-dollar and 10-dollar pieces were issued. The first 2½-dollar piece or quarter eagle was coined in 1796.

Nevertheless, the Spanish dollar and its fractions continued to be the predominant currency in circulation in the early 1800's. The use of Spanish coins gradually declined until an act in 1857 repealed the legal tender power of all foreign coins.

*Metallic Content.* In 1864 the composition of the cent was set at 95% copper and 5% tin and zinc, and its weight was reduced to 48 grains. In 1943 a zinc-steel combination was minted, and in 1962 the alloy was changed to 95% copper and 5% zinc. The rising cost of copper led Congress in 1974 to authorize a coin of 97.6% zinc and 2.4% copper, but such pennies were not minted in quantity until 1983.

Bronze was employed in a 2-cent piece that was first issued in 1864. However, the 2-cent piece was never popular and was discontinued in 1873. It was the first coin to bear the motto, "In God We Trust." Salmon P. Chase, secretary of the treasury, authorized the placing of this motto on the coin.

In response to calls for the use of more nickel in coinage, Congress in 1865 authorized 3-cent and 5-cent coins composed of 75% copper and 25% nickel. (Never popular, the 3-cent coin was discontinued in 1889.) From 1942 to 1945, when nickel was needed for World War II, the 5-cent piece contained no nickel. It was minted with an alloy of 56% copper, 35% silver, and 9% manganese. But in 1946 the 5-cent piece was restored to its original composition.

Because of a silver shortage, Congress in 1965 authorized the minting of dimes and quarters without silver and reduction of the silver content in the half dollar from 90% to 40%. The dimes and quarters become composite, or "clad," coins having a core of pure copper (which shows as a red line on the edge) sandwiched between layers of a white alloy of 75% copper and 25% nickel. The half dollar has a cladding and a core that are composed of alloys of silver and copper.

A number of gaps occur in the minting of the silver dollar, first struck in 1794. Coinage ended

During the 1830's and 1840's, "Hard Times" tokens containing political slogans were widely issued.

An octagonal gold piece, worth 50 dollars and called a "slug," was legal tender in California during the gold rush.

A privately issued Civil War token, dated 1863, shows the Union ironclad *Monitor* on its obverse.

A bronze 2-cent piece, issued in 1864, was the first U. S. coin with the motto "In God We Trust."

The trade dollar, weighing more than the U. S. dollar, was issued to compete with Mexican dollars in the Orient.

in 1804, resumed in 1840, ended in 1873, resumed in 1878, ended in 1904, resumed in 1921, and ended in 1935. (From 1836 to 1839, only patterns were struck.) President Jefferson ordered the first suspension because speculators were shipping U. S. dollars to the West Indies, where they were exchanged for Spanish dollars at a profit. A special trade dollar of greater weight, authorized in 1873, was intended for export to the Orient in exchange for goods in competition with the Mexican dollar. The trade dollar was coined for general use until 1878, but proof pieces were struck for collectors until 1885. An act of 1887 discontinued the coinage of trade dollars and provided for their exchange, within six months, for standard silver dollars. After that, they ceased to have any redemptive value, except for bullion, making the trade dollar the only U. S. coin not redeemable at face value by the Treasury.

The U. S. mints discontinued gold coinage on May 19, 1933. A 1934 act provided that gold coins—aside from those held by collectors—be withdrawn from circulation and formed into bars.

Since 1933, all U. S. coins have been legal tender in all amounts. Up to that time, cents and nickels were legal tender up to 25 cents, and dimes, quarters, and half dollars were legal tender up to $10. See also LEGAL TENDER.

*Early 20th Century Designs.* In 1907, Augustus Saint-Gaudens, one of the leading sculptors of the time, introduced a new design for the 10-dollar and the 20-dollar gold coins. These designs set a high standard in medallic art. Many think that the 20-dollar piece, with the high relief of a full figure of Liberty on the obverse and

the eagle in flight on the reverse, is the most beautiful and most artistic U. S. coin. The 10-dollar piece also is a beautiful coin, with the head of Liberty crowned with an Indian war bonnet on the obverse and majestic eagle standing on the reverse.

The 5-dollar and 2½-dollar gold coins of 1908 were designed by Bela Lyon Pratt. The designs on these two coins, of an Indian with a feather headdress on the obverse and a standing eagle on the reverse, are unique in U. S. coin types, as the designs and lettering are incused, or sunk below the surface of the coin.

The peace dollar of 1921 was designed by Anthony de Francisci and was approved over eight others by the director of the mint, the secretary of the treasury, and the Commission of Fine Arts. At the time there was much criticism of the design, as the young head of Liberty was referred to as the "flapper head." The coin is known as the peace dollar because it was issued to commemorate the peace following World War I.

**Commemorative Coins.** Commemorative coins depict some event or occasion of historical significance. The coins are authorized by special acts of Congress and are not minted for general circulation. The sponsors pay all coinage expenses and distribute the coins to the public. Commemorative pieces are sold at a price in excess of the face value of the coin; the difference is used by the sponsors to meet expenses of the celebration or to erect a memorial to commemorate the person, place, or event being so honored. All commemorative coins are legal tender, but because they are sold at a premium, most of them remain in collectors' hands.

The 1892 Columbian half dollar was the first U. S. commemorative coin.

CHASE MANHATTAN BANK MONEY MUSEUM

CHASE MANHATTAN BANK MONEY MUSEUM

In 1907 the sculptor Augustus Saint-Gaudens designed a striking 20-dollar gold piece.

The peace dollar of 1921 was issued until 1935, when silver-dollar minting ceased.

AMERICAN NUMISMATIC SOCIETY

The first U. S. commemorative coin was the Columbian half dollar issued in 1892 in connection with the World's Columbian Exposition in Chicago. A commemorative quarter dollar, issued during the second year of the World's Columbian Exposition (1893), is the only U. S. coin with a portrait of a foreign monarch, that of Queen Isabella. The Washington-Lafayette silver dollar, issued in 1900 to commemorate the unveiling of the Lafayette statue in Paris, is the first coin bearing a portrait of a U. S. president.

The portrait of a living person has never been authorized to appear on a coin for general circulation. However, four commemorative coins bear the likeness of persons who were living at the time of minting. These are the Alabama half dollar of 1921, commemorating the centenary of the admission of the state of Alabama into the Union, with portrait of Thomas E. Kilby, the governor in 1920; the Sesquicentennial half dollar in 1926, commemorating the 150th anniversary of the signing of the Declaration of Independence, with portrait of President Calvin Coolidge; the Lynchburg (Virginia) Sesquicentennial half dollar of 1936, with portrait of Sen. Carter Glass; and the Arkansas Centennial half dollar, 1936 issue, with portrait of Sen. Joseph Robinson.

A complete set of commemorative half dollars minted since 1892 contains 48 types, with a total of 142 pieces, because some issues were struck in more than one mint, in different years, and some with a slight variation in the design. The commemoratives include the half dollar minted from 1951 through 1954 to honor Booker T. Washington and George Washington Carver. Also in the commemorative series are five types of gold dollars, two types of quarter eagles, and two types of 50-dollar gold pieces—one round, and one octagonal. The latter were issued in 1915 for the Panama Pacific Exposition, held in San Francisco, to commemorate the opening of the Panama Canal. For this occasion there were also issued a commemorative half dollar in silver and a dollar and a quarter eagle in gold. A complete set of gold commemorative coins from 1903-1926 contains nine 1-dollar pieces, two 2½-dollar pieces, and two 50-dollar pieces.

**Proof Coin.** Primarily a collector's piece and a souvenir, the proof coin is minted by the U. S. government with great attention to detail. The dies and planchets undergo special polishing so that a proof coin is given a brilliant mirrorlike surface differing from the regular coinage. Because of the time and care given to the striking and handling of proof coins, extra charges are made for them.

Proof coins encompassing all metals were first struck in 1855. (Before that, some copper half cents and silver dollars were struck in proof.) There have been several intervals in which no proof coins were minted: 1916–1935, 1943–1949, and 1965–1967.

**Private Coins.** From 1830 to 1861, in certain sections of the United States, private individuals, assayers, or firms issued gold coins, or ingots, that were accepted as a medium of exchange even though not coined by authority of the government.

In 1830 the first private gold pieces were struck by Templeton Reid, assayer, in Lumpkin county, Ga., in the 2½-dollar, 5-dollar, and 10-dollar denominatons. Because the gold content made the coins worth more than their face value, most of them were melted for bullion.

In the early 1800's the principal source of gold in the United States was around Rutherfordton, N. C. The miners in that area used gold dust as a medium of exchange, as most of them did not want to risk its transportation to the mint in Philadelphia. This was one of the reasons the government in 1838 established mints in Charlotte, N. C., and in Dahlonega, Ga., for the coinage of gold. Before the establishment of these mints Christopher Bechtler and his son August, who in 1830 had come to Rutherford county, N. C., from Baden, Germany, had started striking gold coins in 1831. These coins were issued in 2½-dollar and 5-dollar denominations. The weight of each piece was stamped on the coin, together with "C. Bechtler," "Rutherfordton," and "Carolina Gold." The Bechtlers produced the first gold dollar in the United States in 1832; the government did not mint such pieces until 1849. In about 1842 Christopher Bechtler transferred

The Kennedy half dollar was first issued in 1964, the year after President John F. Kennedy was assassinated.

In 1965 the minting of quarters containing a copper core between layers of an alloy was authorized.

Since 1946, Franklin Roosevelt's portrait has been on U. S. dimes.

An open competition decided the design of the Jefferson nickel.

The Lincoln cent replaced the famous Indian Head cent in 1909.

WHITMAN PUBLISHING COMPANY

his coinage operations to his son, who then minted 1-dollar and 5-dollar Carolina gold pieces bearing the name "A. Bechtler." Between 1831 and 1840, Christopher Bechtler coined over $2 million in gold pieces.

The discovery of gold in California in 1849 caused an influx of population into that territory and a resulting shortage of a circulating medium for business transactions. As the use of gold dust was inconvenient, several firms began producing gold coins before the end of 1849. In 1850 the State Assay Office of California was established with F. D. Kohler as state assayer. It was Kohler's duty to convert the mined gold into ingots and to stamp the weight and fineness onto the ingot. In 1851 the United States Assay Office was established with August Humbert as assayer. Humbert placed his name and the government stamp on gold ingots issued by Moffat and Company. One of the pieces bearing his name was the 50-dollar, octagonal coin dated 1851. This coin was accepted as legal tender at the custom house and was called a "slug."

It is estimated that there were as many as 15 private mints operating in California from 1849 to 1855. Wass, Molitor, and Company and Kellogg and Company each issued 50-dollar gold pieces as late as 1855.

In 1849 gold coins were also struck in the territories of Oregon and Utah. The Oregon pieces were minted by the Oregon Exchange Company in Oregon City in the 5-dollar and the 10-dollar denominations. The Mormon coinage under the supervision of Brigham Young in Salt Lake City consisted of 2½-, 5-, 10-, and 20-dollar denominations. The Mormon 20-dollar coin was the first of that denomination to be issued in the United States; the government did not begin to strike the 20-dollar piece for circulation until 1850.

In 1860 and 1861 private gold coins were issued in Colorado. The gold for these coins came from Pike's Peak. Clark, Gruber, and Company, Denver, minted 10- and 20-dollar pieces dated 1860, and in 1861 issued coins in the 2½-, 5-, 10-, and 20-dollar denominations. In two years this company put about $3 million in circulation.

Other companies to issue gold coins in Colorado were John Parsons and Company, Tarryall Mines, and J. J. Conway and Company, Georgia Gulch. The last issue of private gold coins was in Denver in 1861.

**Tokens.** When a shortage of coins developed due to hoarding in the severe economic depression of 1837–1838, copper pieces of the size of the large cent, and in many varieties, were placed in circulation by individuals and corporations. These pieces were called "Hard Times" tokens because conditions were especially hard during the 12-month period after May 10, 1837, when specie payments were suspended and the banks were unable to meet their obligations. The situation had been agitated by President Andrew Jackson's veto of a bill to continue the Bank of the United States after its charter had expired in 1836. Consequently, many of the tokens bore political slogans and designs. There was no way to tell who issued some of these pieces. Others were issued as advertising and bore the name of the merchants. By 1840 most of these tokens had disappeared from circulation.

Because of the scarcity of minor coins in the Civil War, there was issued a large quantity of private, copper coins, equivalent in value to one cent. They were of various sizes and metallic composition. These tokens were of two types: those issued by merchants, advertising their product, with a promise to redeem the piece in goods or in money; and those issued with patriotic designs, without any reference to the issuer. It is estimated that between 1862 and 1864 there were more than 50 million tokens, issued in 22 states, with more than 8,000 varieties.

The legality of these tokens was questioned by government officials, but at that time no law prohibited the issuance of these private coins. In April 1864, Congress passed a law prohibiting the issue of any 1- or 2-cent coins, tokens, or devices for use as money. Private coinage of every description was abolished by another law in June 1964.

VERNON L. BROWN
*Former Curator, Museum of Moneys of the World*
*Chase Manhattan Bank*

## COIN COLLECTING

Coin collecting is the orderly assembling of a set or group of coins with a specific purpose. Many millions of persons collect coins; in the United States alone the number is estimated at 5 to 10 million. Coin collectors, also known as numismatists, concern themselves with the origins, history, rarity, and value of coins.

**Groupings.** One person may wish to collect by *dates and varieties.* For example, he would obtain a specimen of each U. S. Indian head cent dated from 1859 to 1909, the last year of issue. He would have over 50 coins in his collection, mostly alike except for dates.

Another collector may prefer to group coins by *types*—an approach that has achieved great popularity. This collector limits his interest to major changes in design, and he obtains a representative example of each type. He would have only three Indian cents in his collection: (1) the 1859 Indian cent, the only year with the laurel wreath reverse; (2) a specimen of any year 1860 to 1864 of the thick copper-nickel alloy type with a shield on the reverse; and (3) a specimen of the thin bronze type in any year from 1864 to 1909.

A third collector may prefer a *topical* grouping in which all coins have a particular theme, such as animals or cathedrals. Other ways to collect coins are by *metals* (all gold coins or all copper coins, for example), by *historical periods* (coins of George Washington's presidency, for example), by *design* (all coins of the 1838–1891 Liberty seated type, for example), or by some other facet of interest. Some numismatists specialize to the extent that they collect only misstruck or error coins.

**Caring For a Collection.** The beginning collector will house his coins in inexpensive coin folders and albums, some of which have protective acetate slides. More valuable coins may be stored in plastic holders that protect the coins from air and moisture.

Coins may be acquired in two main ways: by looking through "change" in the hope of finding scarce pieces in circulation; and by purchasing desired pieces from other collectors and from dealers.

Coins are graded by quality in the following terms: *Poor* (most features obliterated); *Good* (badly worn but most major features still visible); *Very Good; Fine* (evenly worn but most details still sharp); *Very Fine; Extremely Fine; AU* (almost uncirculated); *Uncirculated* (in "new" condition, as fresh as the day it was minted). A special condition, *Proof*, describes coins that have a mirrorlike surface from having been slowly struck from highly polished dies using specially prepared metal blanks or *planchets*.

**History.** Coin collecting in the United States started as a major hobby in the 1850's. Before that time there were fewer than two dozen serious collectors in the country. In 1858 the American Numismatic Society was formed to promote the interchange of coin knowledge. In 1891 the American Numismatic Association was formed for the same purpose. Its monthly magazine, the *Numismatist*, keeps collectors up to date on prices and events. The American Numismatic Association numbers about 25,000 members and is the largest coin collectors' organization in the world. Its headquarters building, dedicated in 1967, is in Colorado Springs, Colo.

Additional information is supplied to U. S. collectors by several hundred local coin clubs, by an estimated 3,000 to 5,000 rare coin dealers, and by several dozen general and specialized newspapers and magazines. Leading publications of interest to collectors include *Coin World*, Sidney, Ohio; *Numismatic News*, Iola, Wis.; *Numismatic Scrapbook*, Chicago; and the *Numismatist*, Colorado Springs, Colo.

**Educational Aspects.** Because coins are closely related to history, coin collecting is an educational hobby. The triumphs of the Roman legions, the California gold rush of the 1850's, the 18th century victories of the British Navy—these and thousands of other historical events are recorded on coins.

Often a special coin, or *commemorative*, is prepared to honor a specific event. In the United States 48 types of commemorative half dollars were issued from 1892 to 1954 to mark such diverse events as the Columbian Exposition (1892–1893), 250th anniversary of the charter of Albany, N. Y. (1936), 300th anniversary of the founding of Connecticut (1935), and the achievements of educator Booker T. Washington (coins issued 1946–1951).

Beginning with the issuance of its first silver dollar in 1935, Canada has been especially active in the commemorative coin field. Many aspects of Canadian history have been displayed on coins.

As an aid to education many universities and museums have outstanding displays. The National Coin Collection, formerly the Philadelphia Mint Collection, is housed in the Smithsonian Institution in Washington, D. C. Its displays are arranged to illustrate the history of U. S. coinage from the opening of the first mint in Philadelphia in 1792 (coinage for circulation began in 1793) to the present. On view are many rarities, including the only known 1849 $20 gold piece, the only two 1877 pattern $50 gold pieces in existence, and an 1804 silver dollar (valued at about $35,000 for a comparable specimen on the collectors' market).

Other outstanding public collections of coins include the Chase Manhattan Bank Money Museum, New York City; the American Numismatic Society, New York City; the Byron Reed Collection, Omaha, Nebr., City Library; and the Garrett Collection, Johns Hopkins University, Baltimore.

**Investment Aspects.** Coins have become popular as an investment in a period in which many people have more money and more leisure for hobbies. The supply of old coins remains static, but prices tend to increase as demand increases. Selected rare coins increased in value on the average of 10% to 20% per year during the 1950's and 1960's. Some persons collect coins strictly for investment, often by saving bank-wrapped rolls of mint-condition coins as they are issued. Others put away choice sets of earlier issues.

Q. DAVID BOWERS
*Author of "Collecting Rare Coins for Profit"*

**Bibliography**

Banks, F., *Coins of Bible Days* (S. J. Durst 1985).
Bowers, Q. David, *Collecting Rare Coins for Profit* (Harper 1975).
Needleman, Saul B., *Perspectives in Numismatics*, ed. by Chicago Coin Club Staff (Ares 1988).
Orosz, Joel J., *The Eagle That Is Forgotten: Pierre Eugene Du Simitiere, Founding Father of American Numismatics* (Bower & Merena 1988).
Yeoman, R. S., *Current Coins of the World*, 8th ed. (Coin and Currency 1987).
Yeoman, R. S., *A Guide Book of U.S. Coins*, 41st ed. (Western Pub. 1988).

**COIN'S FINANCIAL SCHOOL** is the title of a book, published during the hard times of 1894, that sought to convert its readers to bimetallism, or specifically the free and unlimited coinage of silver at a ratio of 16 to 1 in relation to gold. Its author was William Hope ("Coin") Harvey, a promoter who had been active in silver mining in the West. *Coin's Financial School* contains a fictional account of a young financier named Coin, whose lectures won over leading bankers, professors, and senators to the cause of free silver. Up to one million copies were sold, and many readers, accepting the tale as factual, became convinced that free silver would restore prosperity.

**COINSURANCE** is a method of insurance in which an insured party shares in the losses. In property insurance, for example, the insured absorbs a proportion of the loss to the extent that his total insurance is less than the value of the property. In some cases, the insurer's payment is limited to a fixed percentage of the total value. The purpose of coinsurance, like the use of deductibles, is to reduce the amount of the premium.

**COINTREAU,** kwän'trō, is the proprietary name of an 80-proof liqueur whose flavor comes primarily from dried orange peels. Cointreau is one of the finest of the triple secs, which are colorless Curaçao liqueurs. The dominant flavoring of all Curaçaos is obtained from the aromatic bitter peels of green oranges of a type grown on the island of Curaçao.

**COIR,** koir, is the commercial fiber derived from the husk (mesocarp) of the coconut. Most coir comes from Sri Lanka and India. Its tensile strength is not so great as that of various other fibers, but it has relatively high elasticity and is resistant to decay, especially in salt water. For centuries it has been used in the Asian tropics as cordage—for ropes and fishnets—and for caulking boats. Coir is also made into doormats, hall mats, and brushes, and it is used as stuffing in mattresses and cushions.

Coir is ordinarily removed from the coconut before the nut is shipped. Fruits harvested for the highest grade coir must be picked somewhat earlier than those collected for the best yield of copra, or dried coconut meat. When the fiber is processed by hand, the husk is removed and then soaked in water for at least a few days; preferably it should be soaked for several months or even a year. The residual reddish brown husk is then beaten, repeatedly cleaned, hackled into fibers, carded, and dried. When processed by machinery, the husk, soaked for about a week, is crushed between iron rollers and separated into fibers by spikes on a rotating drum before being cleaned and dried.

**COIT,** koit, **Margaret Louise** (1919–    ), American author, who won the 1951 Pulitzer Prize for her biography *John C. Calhoun: American Portrait.* She was born in Norwich, Conn., on May 30, 1919, and grew up in Greensboro, N. C. While still in high school she became interested in Calhoun, and after graduating from the Women's College of the University of North Carolina (B. A., 1941) she spent nine years of research and writing on the life of the Southern statesman. At the same time she began a career in journalism, moving to Massachusetts where she became

Margaret Louise Coit, about the time she won the 1951 Pulitzer Prize for her biography of John C. Calhoun.

a correspondent for the Lawrence *Daily Eagle.* Later she worked for papers in Haverhill and Newburyport and contributed feature articles to the Boston *Sunday Globe.* In 1948 she was a fellow at the Breadloaf Writers' Conference. She joined the faculty of Fairleigh Dickinson University in 1955 and later became an author-in-residence.

Coit's first book, published in 1950, was hailed by critics as a "new illumination" of Calhoun's career. The prizewinning work was cited for its scholarship, readability, and for the skill with which the author humanized Calhoun and other political giants of his era. In 1957 she published a biography of Bernard Baruch, followed by the historical studies *The Fight for Union* (1961), *The Sweep Westward* (1963), and *Andrew Jackson* (1965).

**COIT,** koit, **Stanton** (1857–1944), American social leader, who pioneered in the American settlement movement and was a leader of the English Ethical movement. Coit was born in Columbus, Ohio, on Aug. 11, 1857, graduated from Amherst College in 1879, and received a Ph. D. from the University of Berlin in 1885. In 1886 in New York City he established a "neighborhood guild," or settlement, for which he organized lectures, theatricals, a kindergarten, gymnasiums, and clubs.

An ardent promoter of the Ethical Culture Society, Coit became minister of the London Ethical Church in England in 1888. He created and directed the West London Ethical Society (1894), the Union of Ethical Societies (1895), and the Moral Instruction League (1897). He also organized the International Foundation for Moral and Religious Leadership, which trained Ethical leaders. Coit died in Birling Gap, England, on Feb. 15, 1944.

**COJUTEPEQUE,** kō-hōō-tā-pä´kä, a city in El Salvador, 22 miles (35 km) east of San Salvador by the Inter-American Highway. It is the capital of Cuscatlán department and a marketing center for a region producing rice, sugarcane, and coffee. The city has an important annual fair and is known in El Salvador for its cigars and smoked meats. The chief points of interest are a church in Palladian style and Lake Ilopango near the city. Population: 43,564 (1992 census).

**COKE,** kŏŏk, **Sir Edward** (1552–1634), English legal scholar and parliamentarian, who first reduced the common law to an orderly system and laid the cornerstone for the English constitution. About 1642 the General Court of Massachusetts Bay ordered "two copies of Sir Edward Cooke on Magna Carta" to be purchased in London as aids in drafting the colony's own Body of Liberties. The order attests to the authority that his *Institutes* on the common law enjoyed.

**Intellectual Training.** Born at Mileham, Norfolk, on Feb. 1, 1552, the son of a wealthy attorney, Edward became impatient as a youth to pursue the study of law. Although he stayed for four years at Trinity College, Cambridge, he left without taking his degree to enroll at the Inns of Court in London. He completed his preparation in a year less than the usual seven and was called to the bar on April 20, 1578.

As a neophyte law student, Coke established a habit, which remained with him all his life, of retiring to bed at 9 P. M. and rising at 3 A. M. for five or six hours of intensive, uninterrupted study of all available sources of the ancient English law. This habit and a prodigious memory equipped him with an encyclopedic knowledge of the details of feudal and early modern legal precedents that overpowered opposing counsel and judges alike. He enjoyed immediate success in practice. Even more significantly, the voluminous knowledge of early English procedures and substantive rules became the basis for his landmark works—his own reports of decided cases and his four volumes on the common law of the realm. Although he seems on oc-

**Sir Edward Coke, English legal scholar.**
THE BETTMANN ARCHIVE

casion to have stretched certain precedents to meet his desired rule of decision and to have exaggerated the meaning of some ancient judgments and charters, his contemporaries ratified most of his holdings and accepted them as first principles. It may be said with accuracy, therefore, that the English common law after the first quarter of the 16th century was largely what Coke said it was.

**Professional Success and Marriages.** Coke's reputation for learning in the law spread rapidly in the 15 years after he began practice. First, the town of Coventry elected him as its recorder, a position somewhat equivalent to city counsel today; then the larger municipality of Norwich elected him to the same position; and finally he was elected recorder of London. In private practice he also settled a point of property law with a rule that became a classic with lawyers for generations afterward. Known as the "rule in Shelley's case," it held that when a title to land went to one party for life and the rest was to go to his heirs, an absolute title was created in the first party and he could dispose of the land without liability. It was a striking illustration of Coke's ability to adapt an ancient feudal principle to a contemporary need —particularly the need of a client.

Coke's first marriage, in 1582, was to Bridget Paston, daughter of a wealthy attorney at Norwich. Ten children were born of this union before she died in 1598. By then Coke had become, successively, speaker of the House of Commons —having been elected to the Parliament of 1589 from Aldeburgh, Suffolk, and that of 1592–1593 from Norfolk—solicitor general, and finally attorney general to the queen.

Coke's second marriage, shortly after Bridget's death, was purely opportunistic on both sides; Lady Elizabeth Hatton, a 20-year-old widow, had wealth and position at court, while the 46-year-old lawyer represented for her a prestigious connection with the legislative and judicial branches of the government. Historians have speculated whether this clearly incompatible union did not account in part for the vehemence with which Coke thereafter prosecuted many of the courtiers—the earls of Essex and Southampton and Sir Walter Raleigh, among them—who had fallen from favor. Certainly he was known throughout Queen Elizabeth's remaining years as an unswerving vassal of the crown, whether in Parliament or in the courtroom.

**Confrontation with the Throne.** This made all the more dramatic Coke's change of character in 1606, when James I made him lord chief justice of the court of common pleas. Although a judge held office only at the crown's pleasure, Coke almost immediately acknowledged that he had but one sovereign—the common law itself. He saw it as the supreme authority in English life, to which even the king was subject.

Coke's unrivaled knowledge of the common law from its earliest beginnings gave him a substantial advantage, as always, and his determination to stand by his principles suddenly imparted new strength to the courts and the rule of law. He revived ancient writs of prohibition (orders to lower courts not to take particular cases) and habeas corpus (a process for removing a defendant and his case to another court). Although habeas corpus had not yet become the means of setting a person at liberty until his case was tried, its revival as a procedural device made it easier to apply it to civil rights when the English Revolution came about.

Coke's law reports, written while he was lord chief justice, provided an authoritative basis both for the skilled practice of law and for the growing constitutional argument in Parliament over James' claim for the royal prerogative. The king is "under no man, but under God and the law," said Coke in a famous confrontation. James sought first to reduce Coke's effectiveness by transferring him in 1613 to the court of King's Bench, which was concerned primarily with criminal cases. But Coke merely converted this position into an unofficial kind of chief justiceship of all courts. Finally, finding him unbending in the matter of prerogatives, the king dismissed him from the bench in 1616.

**Promulgation of the Rights of Man.** James' troubles were just coming to a head, but Coke's career was still to reach its climax. Returning to Parliament in 1620, Coke drafted the famous Protestation of the Commons, in which the lower house declared to the Crown that from the time of the Magna Carta "the liberties, franchises, privileges and jurisdictions of Parliament are the ancient and undoubted birthright and inheritance of the subjects of England." James dissolved the session and tore the Protestation from the official journal; but four years later when his brother Charles succeeded him that king, too, found Parliament as adamant as ever. Outraged at the crown's summary imprisonment of many persons who had refused to pay special taxes levied by executive decree rather than by legislative authority, the Parliament in 1628 adopted Coke's draft of a Petition of Right. This great document, incorporating the provision of the Magna Carta against depriving persons of liberty or property without due process of law (a provision later to appear in the 5th and 14th Amendments to the United States Constitution), was ultimately acquiesced in by the crown.

**Publication of the Institutes.** The previous year, Coke's first volume of his *Institutes* of English law, which has been known ever since as *Coke upon Littleton*, had been published. It was a modernization of Thomas Littleton's ancient treatise on land tenures, a fundamental work on property law. Coke's volume setting forth some of the basic rights of an individual in a stable legal order and his authorship of the Petition of Right represented his great contribution to the constitutional system that was in the making. The other parts of his *Institutes*, including a volume on Magna Carta, were considered so incendiary that Charles impounded the manuscripts for almost a decade after Coke's death at Stoke Poges at Sept. 3, 1634.

The fundamental documents of the English constitution that emerged from the revolution against the Stuarts—Magna Carta, as embodied in the Petition of Right, the Habeas Corpus Act of 1679, the Bill of Rights in 1689, and the limited monarchy established by the Act of Settlement in 1701—had been initiated by the work of Sir Edward Coke. They would be cited as the "rights of Englishmen" by American revolutionists a century and a half later.

WILLIAM F. SWINDLER
*School of Law, College of William and Mary*

**Further Reading:** Seagle, William, *Men of Law* (1947; reprint, Hafner Pub. Co. 1971); Swindler, William F., *Magna Carta: Legend and Legacy* (Bobbs 1965); White, Stephen D., *Sir Edward Coke and "The Grievances of the Commonwealth"* (Univ. of N. C. Press 1979).

**COKE,** kōk, **Richard** (1829–1897), American public official and first post-Reconstruction governor of Texas. He was born in Williamsburg, Va., on March 13, 1829, and educated there. In 1850 he settled permanently in the frontier town of Waco, Texas, and began to practice law. Coke consistently advocated what he conceived to be his state's interests. He favored secession and fought in the Civil War. In 1866 he was elected to the state supreme court, but he and other Texas officials, deemed impediments to Reconstruction, were removed by the military governor.

In 1873, Coke ran for governor as a Democrat against the incumbent Radical Republican Edmund J. Davis and won by a 2 to 1 margin. Coke resigned during a second term to become a U. S. senator. In the Senate from 1877 until 1895, he favored free silver, opposed a protective tariff, and sought federal aid in policing the Mexican border and in deepening Texas harbors. Coke died in Waco on May 14, 1897.

**COKE,** kook, **Thomas** (1747–1814), British Methodist leader. He was born at Brecon, Wales, on Sept. 9, 1747, and was ordained an Anglican priest in 1772. Reproved for certain practices leaning toward Methodism, he openly cast his lot with the Methodists in 1778. In 1782 he presided over the first Irish Methodist conference.

Ordained a superintendent by John Wesley, Coke traveled to America in 1784 to help organize the Methodist Episcopal Church, and he worked actively to commit American Methodists to the antislavery cause. Against the desires of Wesley, Coke was styled "bishop" by the American church but was unable to have this term adopted in England. Coke made nine trips to America, maintaining some leadership, but after 1803 stayed in England. He served for many years as a leader of the English Methodist conference.

His greatest contribution, however, was as a missionary. As founder and president of its missionary committee, he influenced British Methodism in developing a vital foreign program, raising vast sums in its behalf. Called the "Foreign Minister of Methodism," he did a great deal of work in the West Indies and also established a mission in Africa. He died on May 3, 1814, while going to India to establish a mission, and was buried in the Indian Ocean.

ALBEA GODBOLD
*Former Editor of "Methodist History"*

**COKE,** kook, **Thomas William** (1752–1842), English agricultural reformer, who improved breeds of sheep, cattle, and hogs, as well as land for the growing of crops. Coke, known as Coke of Holkham, was born in London on May 4, 1752. After attending Eton, he traveled abroad until 1774. On his father's death in 1776, he was elected to his seat in Parliament, retaining it for more than 50 years until he retired in 1833. In Parliament he favored reform but always voted for agricultural interests. He was made earl of Leicester and Viscount Coke in 1837.

Soon after inheriting estates in 1776, Coke began farming. He improved the land so much that wheat could be grown in his region. In all his leases he laid down rules for cultivation of crops instead of allowing the tenants to cultivate the land as they chose.

Coke also bred Southdown Sheep, Devon cattle, and Suffolk pigs. In each case he improved the breed.

White-hot coke, a by-product of high-grade bituminous coal, pours from the coking oven into a quenching car.

**COKE** is the solid residue, consisting chiefly of carbon, that is left behind when bituminous coal or petroleum or other liquid hydrocarbons are distilled in the absence of air. Coke made from coal and used as a fuel is by far the most important type of coke commercially. *Pitch coke,* which is made by distilling coal tar, is about 99% carbon and is used chiefly for making carbon electrodes. *Petroleum coke,* the final distillation product from petroleum, contains about 99% carbon and is used in the production of molded carbon compounds. *Calcined coke* is petroleum coke that has been heated to 1315° C (2400° F) to remove the remaining volatile matter, and it is used when an extremely pure form of carbon is needed.

### COKE FROM COAL

Coke made from bituminous coal is a reliable fuel that consists chiefly of fixed carbon with less than 10% ash. It is gray in color, coherent, infusible, cellular, and porous. In the production of coke, a process called "carbonization of coal" or "coking," most of the volatile matter is removed by heating the coal in a closed chamber to retard or prevent burning. Carbonite, a natural coke found in Virginia and England, possesses the same properties as manufactured coke; it is formed by the heating action of igneous rock on layers of bituminous coal.

Nearly 90% of the coke produced from coal each year is used by the iron and steel industry for the production of pig iron. Most of the remainder is used for making gas and other products, including "semicoke" or "smokeless fuel," which is usually briquetted for use as a household fuel, particularly in Europe.

In most modern coking operations, a large number of valuable by-products are recovered from the volatile matter distilled off from the coal. Among the more important of these by-products are coal gas, coal tar, ammonium sulfate, and benzol.

**History.** The development of a primitive coal carbonization process began in England toward the end of the 16th century as a result of the depletion of the forests that had provided wood for charcoal. The first coke "ovens" were simply conical piles of bituminous coal, which were ignited and then covered with earth or coke dust to retard the entrance of air. About 1620, English coke producers began to use permanent ovens, known as "beehive ovens" from the rounded shape of their masonry walls. Although these ovens generally wasted nearly all of the potential by-products, their construction was simple, and their cost was low. The first beehive coke oven in the United States was built in Pennsylvania in 1841.

Coke was first successfully used in a blast furnace by Abraham Darby in Shropshire, England, in 1709. The resulting pig iron could be cast into various ironware objects, but it was made so brittle by impurities that it could not be worked at a forge. In 1748, however, Darby's son, Abraham Darby II, discovered how to make a pig iron suitable for conversion to wrought iron in coke-fired blast furnaces by proper selection of ores. Further improvements in coke making and iron making led to the gradual adoption of coke-fired furnaces, and by the beginning of the 19th century nearly all of England's blast furnaces were coke-fired. The change from charcoal to coke in the iron industry allowed the use of much larger furnaces because coke, with its hard porous structure, is able to carry a much heavier burden than charcoal without being crushed.

The first true by-product coke ovens, designed especially to facilitate recovery of coke by-products, were constructed by Albert Hussner at Gelsenkirchen, Germany, in 1881. These ovens supplied the rising German chemical industry, which was largely based on coal-tar derivatives. The first by-product coke oven in the United States began operation in Rochester, N. Y., in 1895.

**Coal for Coking.** Coal that is used for coking is seldom of one particular type or rank. A coal is classified as coking or noncoking depending on its reaction when heated in the absence of air. If the coal becomes soft during heating and then solidifies into a solid mass or cake, it is classed as coking coal; if upon heating the coal crumbles or solidifies into a noncoherent mass, it is classed as noncoking. The cell structure of the coke must also be considered. Some coals coke upon heating but have an undesirable cell structure; in others the ash content or the concentration of sultur and phosphorous (both of which are deleterious in iron and steel) may be too high.

Volatile matter in coking coal ranges from 16 to 40%. The yield of coke from a particular coal increases roughly as the content of volatile matter of the coal decreases. Coking coal that is to be used for the production of metallurgical grade coke may contain between 23 and 32% volatile matter. Low volatile and high volatile bituminous coals behave differently during coking operations. A high volatile coal usually expands upon heating, while low volatile coal contracts when heated. This characteristic is of particular importance because of possible sticking and damage to coking equipment. Most often low and high volatile coals are blended to produce a mixture with optimum properties. In the United States, the Appalachian coal region, including the strip from western Pennsylvania and Ohio through Tennessee, Georgia, and Alabama, produces most of the coal used for coking. Coal from Indiana and Illinois has poorer coking characteristics.

Although the known coal deposits in the United States are greater than those of any other country, every continent, including Antarctica, contains coal of a quality suitable for coking and in quantity great enough to satisfy local needs.

**Production of Coke—Beehive Coking Ovens.** The beehive process is normally used near the source of a coal that is suitable for the process. The beehive oven is about 12 feet (3.6 meters) in diameter and 6 feet (1.8 meters) high, with brick walls and a hole at the top for charging and gas exit. A side door permits charge leveling, quenching, and coke removal.

The charge of 6 to 8 tons (5.4 to 7.2 metric tons) is leveled to a depth of about 2 feet (0.6 meter), the door is bricked nearly to the top, leaving only a small opening for the entrance of air. Burning of the coal starts on top of the charge, and as the gases and volatile matter are burned, the resulting heat causes the coking process to continue. Coking time depends upon the charge depth, and the process is controlled by regulation of the amount of air that is permitted to enter. At the end of the coking operation (2 to 3 days) the door is broken down, and the coke is quenched by spraying with water. In 1914, beehive coke accounted for 75% of coke production, but with depletion of coal suited to the beehive process and the increased use of the more efficient "retort" or "by-product" equipment, the process is used chiefly during peak periods as a standby method of production.

**By-Product Ovens.** By-product coking is classified as a true distillation process because all the constituents of the coal are recovered. One of the chief differences between by-product ovens and the beehive ovens is in the source of heat. Instead of burning part of the coking coal, as in the beehive oven, the by-product oven is heated by an external fire. Several types of coking ovens are used in this process, but the basic design is similar for all types, and they differ chiefly in the method of heat application. The coking

chambers into which the coal is charged are rectangular and range from 30 to 42 feet (9 to 12.6 meters) in length, from 6 to 14 feet (2 to 4.2 meters) in height, and from 12 to 22 inches (30 to 55 cm) in width. For maximum efficiency, the ovens are arranged in batteries of 10 to 100 so that a single furnace unit and handling system can serve all the retorts in a battery. Coking chambers are alternated with heating chambers so that every coking chamber has a heating chamber on each side. Fuel for heating may be gas from the coking process, producer gas, or blast furnace gas. The coke oven batteries are equipped with units to recover heat from flue gases.

At the start of the coking operation, doors on each end of the retort are sealed, and the coal is charged through openings in the top. At the top and the ends of the coking chambers are openings for collection of the volatile matter as it evolves during the heating cycle. These openings are fitted to offtake pipes that carry the gases to chemical recovery units where the byproducts of coking are obtained.

The temperature of the carbonization process determines both the reaction rate and the distillation products. Below 200° C (390° F), the volatile products are mainly methane, water, and carbon dioxide. Between 200 ond 400° C (390 and 750° F), carbon monoxide, carbon dioxide, and water are evolved. In the range from 350 to 450° C (660 to 840° F), larger volumes of gas begin to appear; hydrogen is present in small amounts, which increase with rising temperatures until hydrogen becomes the main constituent at temperatures above 800° C (1470° F). All of the phosphorus and a large percentage of the sulfur from the coal remain in the coke.

The coking coal, which entered the retort as individual particles, begins to soften at about 400° C (750° F), and as the temperature rises the coal fuses into a plastic mass. Depending on the volatile matter content, the coal expands or contracts during the plastic range and gas evolution period until it resolidifies into the characteristic cellular coke structure at about 500° C (930° F).

Coke is classified according to reaction temperature as low-temperature or high-temperature coke. Low-temperature coke, which is produced at temperatures ranging from 450 to 700° C (840 to 1300° F), is used chiefly for the production of gas, although some is used for making fuel briquettes. For metallurgical use, only high-temperature coke, which is produced at temperatures of from 800 to 1000° C (1470 to 1830° F) and has a lower content of volatile matter, can be used. In a typical high-temperature coking retort, the flue temperature is in the range of 1425 to 1485° C (2600 to 2700° F), while the actual temperature of the block of coke adjacent to the oven walls is between 1040 and 1095° C (1900 to 2000° F). Coking time is generally from 17 to 18 hours.

At the end of the coking cycle, both end doors of the chamber are opened, and a "pusher" mechanism shoves the block of incandescent coke into a quenching car. The car then advances to a spray system that rapidly cools the coke to prevent combustion. The quenching operation is precisely controlled so that the final moisture content of the coke will average 2.5%. After quenching, the coke is crushed and screened for proper sizing for specific applications.

**By-Products of Coking.** As the name implies, the recovery of coal chemicals is an important aspect of the by-product coking process. The recovery system is extremely complex, but essentially it involves the condensation or extraction of the desired products from the gases of the coke-oven exhaust stream. The gases and vapors leave the ovens at a temperature ranging from 315 to 370° C (600 to 700° F). Water sprays at strategic locations in the collecting system reduce the temperature to a range of 145 to 215° C (295 to 420° F).

The carbonization of a ton (0.9 metric ton) of coal produces an average yield of about 0.7 ton (0.63 metric ton) of coke; 11,500 cubic feet (345 cu meters) of gas; 12 gallons (45.6 liters) of tar; 27 pounds (12 kg) of ammonium sulfate; 50 gallons (190 liters) of benzol; 0.9 gallon (3.4 liters) of toluol and naphtha; and 0.5 pound (0.2 kg) of naphthalene.

Coal tar, which is the source of a great number of chemical compounds, including creosote, pitch, toluene, and naphthalene, is extracted from the stream of gases evolved during coking. This is done by means of water spray cooling towers, mechanical impingement of tar particles, and electrostatic precipitation. See also COAL TAR.

Ammonia, a gaseous compound, is used in products ranging from smelling salts to agricultural fertilizers. Of three processes used to extract ammonia from coke-oven gas, the most common involves concentration of ammonia-bearing vapors by use of a still and an ammonia absorber. In the absorber, the rising gases are sprayed with dilute sulfuric acid to form ammonium sulfate, which, when dried, contains about 26% ammonia.

Phenol ($C_6H_5OH$) is recovered from coal tar and ammonia liquor. Sometimes called carbolic acid, phenol is used in the manufacture of plastics (Bakelite), perfumes, picric acid, salicylic acid, cutting oils, antiseptics, and wool preservatives. One method of recovering phenol uses benzol as a solvent to remove the phenol from the ammonia liquor. Caustic soda is then used to extract the phenol from the benzol, and the final product is sodium phenolate.

Cresols ($C_7H_8O$) are used extensively in insecticides, weed killers, resins, pharmaceuticals, and photographic compounds. They are in the phenol family and are extracted by a process using sulfuric acid as a converter and benzene as an extracting agent.

Toluene ($C_6H_5OH_3$) is recovered both from the coke-oven gas and from coal tar. It is used in the manufacture of chemicals, explosives, detergents, solvents, and dyes, and it is also converted to benzene.

Light oil, which is one of the components of coke-oven gas contains more than a hundred compounds. The most important constituents recovered from light oil are benzene, toluene, xylene, and solvent naphtha. Benzene is used in the production of styrene (a component of polystyrene resins and synthetic rubber), phenol, nylon, DDT, and many other compounds. The xylenes (there are three isomers) are derivatives of benzene that are used in the preparation of solvents, plasticizers, resins, and synthetic fibers.

**Coke in Blast Furnaces.** The physical and chemical properties of metallurgical-grade coke make it an ideal fuel for blast furnaces and foundry cupolas. In a blast furnace, iron ore is converted

To control air pollution, emissions from the hot coke as it comes from the oven are captured and passed through a scrubbing and cleaning process. The cleaned effluent (*left foreground*) is then released into the air.

to pig iron as it descends through a rising stream of hot reducing gases. The role of coke is threefold. Added to the furnace in alternating layers with ore and flux, the porous and infusible coke supports the hundreds of tons of charge and keeps it permeable; as coke burns, it supplies the heat necessary for the reactions in the furnace; and it provides the reducing gases required in these reactions. Prior to the use of coke, blast furnaces used charcoal as the fuel and supporting medium, and they were limited to a height of 60 feet (18 meters). Coke permits blast furnaces in excess of 100 feet (30 meters) in height because its greater strength can support a larger charge.

Several routine tests are employed in the control of the physical properties of coke used in blast furnaces. One important test is of the porosity, or volume of cell space, of the coke. Porosity is important because the reaction rate of the coke is a function of the surface area available for the reaction with oxygen.

Since the coke must be strong enough to support the charge of a blast furnace, its strength must be measured. In the "shatter test" a sample of standard size coke is dropped onto a steel plate. The shattered coke is screened and the percent by weight that remains on the 2-inch (5-cm) screen is taken as a measure of shatter strength. With blast furnace coke, 70 to 80% is retained.

The "tumbler test" measures the resistance of coke to abrasion as the charge descends through the furnace. Coke that breaks due to abrasion can clog the furnace. Coke to be tested is rotated in a steel drum and then screened.

PAUL B. EATON, *Purdue University*

**Further Reading:** Albright, Lyle F., and Baker, R. T., eds, *Coke Formation on Metal Surfaces* (Am. Chemical Soc. 1982); *Petroleum Products, Lubricants, and Fossil Fuels:* Vol. 05.05 (ASTM 1986).

**COL,** kol, in geography, a saddle-shaped depression or gap across a ridge or between the peaks of a mountain range. It is derived from a French word meaning "neck." A depression or gap of this nature occurs in a divide at a point where two streams, flowing down opposite sides of the divide, gradually erode the land between them until a groove is formed in the separating ridge. The term "col" is most often used to designate mountain passes in the predominantly French sections of the Alps.

**COLA,** kō′lə, a genus of trees of the chocolate family (Sterculiaceae), from which cola nuts are obtained. Cola nuts contain caffeine and are chewed as a stimulant, despite their bitter taste, by natives of tropical Africa. Dried cola nuts are widely used in combination with coca (not to be confused with cocoa) in the manufacture of cola beverages and to a minor extent for medicinal purposes. *Cola nitida* and *C. acuminata* are the main sources of cola nuts.

The genus comprises some 50 species and is native to the rain forests of western tropical Africa. Cola trees are cultivated in the West Indies, where they were introduced during the period of slavery, and also in Brazil, India, Sri Lanka, and the Malay Peninsula.

Mature cola trees vary in height from 40 to 65 feet (12 to 20 meters), depending on the species and growing conditions. The trees grow best on rich, well-drained sandy loams at elevations of up to 2,000 feet (600 meters). They are propagated by seed or cuttings. Warty, green pods, 5 to 7 inches (13 to 18 cm) long, are first produced when the trees are about 5 years old. Full bearing starts at about the 12th year. Each pod contains 6 to 12 white, pink, or purplish seeds that turn brown after drying. Each seed, depending on the species, consists of two to five fleshy cotyledons (seed leaves), which on drying separate into the so-called cola nuts of commerce. Approximately 40 to 50 nuts are in each pound (90–110 in each kg).

Cola nuts contain about 2% caffeine, plus kolanin (a heart stimulant), traces of theobromine, and other substances. The nuts are much in demand, and tons of them are imported annually into the United States.

LAWRENCE ERBE
*University of Southwestern Louisiana*

**COLA DI RIENZO.** See RIENZO, COLA DI.

**COLAC,** kō-lak′, a city in Australia, in the southwestern part of the state of Victoria. It is situated on the southern shore of Lake Colac, 95 miles (153 km) southwest of Melbourne, capital of the state.

The city is a commercial and processing center for the surrounding agricultural area, where dairying is the most important industry. Other industries include sawmilling, which utilizes timber from the nearby Otway Ranges, and the manufacture of agricultural tools. Colac, which is a rail junction, grew up along an old coach route. Population: 10,241 (1991 census).

**COLBERT, Claudette,** kōl′bâr (1903–1996), French-born American stage and film actress who was best known for her feisty, stylish roles in classic 1930s' film comedies. She was born Lily Claudette Chauchoin on Sept. 13, 1903, in Paris, and went to the United States with her family in 1910. She studied at the Art Students League in New York City, where she made her stage debut, as Claudette Colbert, in 1923, in *The Wild Wescotts.* She also appeared on Broadway in *The Barker* (1927), as a seductive snake charmer; in Eugene O'Neill's *Dynamo* (1929); and in Elmer Rice's *See Naples and Die* (1929).

Among Colbert's early box-office hits were *The Lady Lies* (1929) and *The Smiling Lieutenant* (1931). Soon after, she was cast by Cecil B. DeMille as a vamp, most notably in *The Sign of the Cross* (1932), as the empress Poppaea, and as Cleopatra in the eponymous film (1934). But in 1934 Colbert established an immediate reputation for sophisticated comedy in Frank Capra's Oscar-winning film *It Happened One Night,* for which she, her director, and her costar, Clark Gable, also won Academy Awards.

For the next two decades Colbert acted steadily on screen, largely alternating between light comedy and tearful melodrama, in films such as *Imitation of Life* (1934), *The Golded Lily* (1935), *Private Worlds* (1935), *Tovarich* (1937), *Midnight* (1939), *Drums along the Mohawk* (1939), *The Palm Beach Story* (1942), *Three Came Home* (1950), and *Parrish* (1961), her last feature film. She periodically returned to the stage, where she starred in, among other plays, *Janus* (1956), *The Marriage-Go-Round* (1958), *The Irregular Verb to Love* (1963), *The Kingfisher* (1978), and *Aren't We All?* (London, 1984; Broadway, 1985).

In 1988 Colbert was named an officer in the French Legion of Honor, and in 1989 she received a Life Achievement Award at the Kennedy Center in Washington, D.C. Colbert, who made a total of 65 movies, last performed on stage in 1987, the year she also shared the title role with Ann-Margret in the television miniseries *The Two Mrs. Grenvilles.* Colbert suffered a serious stroke in 1993 and was confined to a wheelchair until her death, at her home in Barbados, on July 30, 1996.

Claudette Colbert won an Oscar for *It Happened One Night* (1934), as did her costar Clark Gable.

MUSEUM OF MODERN ART STILLS ARCHIVE

**COLBERT,** kôl-bâr', **Jean Baptiste** (1619–1683), French statesman, who was finance minister to Louis XIV and the first controller general of France. He was born in Reims on Aug. 29, 1619. In 1640, through the efforts of his cousin, Jean Baptiste Colbert de St. Pouange, young Colbert obtained a position in the ministry of war, then directed by Sullet des Noyers. His rise in government was rapid. On the death of Cardinal Richelieu in 1642, the new minister of war, Michel Le Tellier, father-in-law of Colbert de St. Pouange, appointed Colbert first commissioner of the ministry, then first secretary. In 1649 he became a counselor of state. In 1651, Cardinal Mazarin, the prime minister of France; invited Colbert to assume the duties of his personal intendant without, however, possessing title to the office. Colbert rendered enormous services to his new superior during the Fronde rebellion, and his appointment was made official in 1655. Three years later he entered the higher ranks of aristocracy by purchasing the baronetcy of Seignelay in Burgundy.

**Colbert and Fouquet.** Rivalry between Colbert and the *surintendant des finances* of France, Nicolas Fouquet, developed into open and intense hostility during the last two years of Mazarin's life. Colbert worked tirelessly toward Fouquet's ruin. He finally convinced Louis XIV, when the monarch assumed personal rule in 1661, that Fouquet, by his immense fortune and by his personal position in the state, best symbolized the odious past of political and financial disorders associated with the tradition of "first ministers." Fouquet was arrested on Sept. 5, 1661, and the office of *surintendant des finances* was abolished. The controller generalship, established in its place, was awarded to Colbert. Determined to prevent Fouquet's return to power by having him executed, the controller general brought him to trial. Since prosecution of Fouquet as an isolated case would have revealed Colbert's motives, the controller general made his trial part of a general investigation of people suspected of profiteering under Mazarin.

Fouquet's trial lasted for four years. Despite enormous pressure from Versailles, 13 out of 22 judges voted for exile rather than the death penalty demanded by the crown. (The crown later changed the penalty to life imprisonment.) Public rejoicing over the more lenient sentence was widespread, since Colbert's often hysterical campaign for honest government and his vast programs for industrial and commercial expansion had won him many enemies. Animosity toward Colbert became indistinguishable from opposition above all to his mercantilist programs. Moreover, a profound economic depression, lasting the entire period of his ministry, compounded the controller general's difficulties, strengthening the opposition, who insisted France's ailing affairs were the consequence of his misconceived policies.

**Cultural Patronage.** Colbert waged a truly titanic struggle against both political hostility and economic dislocation. In the course of these endeavors he not only extended his authority in government but, in part to parry opposition from intellectuals, he also dominated educational, artistic, and scientific institutions, placing himself at the head of a vast network of cultural patronage. Colbert established the Académie des Inscriptions et Belles-Lettres (1663), the Académie des Sciences (1666), the Académie de France in Rome (1666), the Académie Royale d'Architecture

(1671), and the Paris Observatory (1667–1672). He greatly enlarged the Bibliothèque Royale, founding the collection now deposited in the Bibliothèque Nationale. Moreover, in 1667 he established the great factory-school, the Gobelins, for training artisans in the manufacture of fine tapestries and furniture. By these and other means Colbert placed a significant portion of French intellectuals and artists on the royal payroll.

**Economic Policies.** The controller general's principal project, however, was to transform France into the greatest industrial and maritime power on earth. Toward this end, as minister of marine, Colbert built a huge fleet and established naval schools and new systems of marine recruitment. At the same time he promulgated the commercial (1673), marine (1681), and colonial (1685) codes. The founding of the East India, the Northern, the West Indian, and the Guinea trading companies was part of the French mercantilist effort to deprive other maritime powers, particularly the Dutch, of overseas commerce. The trading company was an important adjunct of Colbert's protectionist system, exemplified above all by the tariff of 1667 (not, as is often said, by that of 1664).

This policy of maritime regulation led logically toward administrative regulation in all spheres of economic endeavor. The building of canals throughout the realm, including the great one in Languedoc connecting the Atlantic with the Mediterranean, and the undertaking of a major road-building program were all part of an enormous system of subventions and controls whereby Colbert hoped to achieve economic self-sufficiency at home and French hegemony abroad. Colbert failed to achieve these ends. But by the time of his death in Paris on Sept. 6, 1683, his organizing genius and prodigious energy had contributed much toward national integration.

LIONEL ROTHKRUG, *University of Michigan*

**Further Reading:** Murat, Ines, *Colbert,* tr. by R. F. Cook and J. Van Asselt (Univ. Press of Va. 1984); Rothkrug, Lionel, *Opposition to Louis XIV* (Princeton Univ. Press 1969).

**Jean Baptiste Colbert**

METROPOLITAN MUSEUM OF ART
(GIFT OF WILDENSTEIN FOUNDATION, INC.)

**COLBORNE,** kōl'bərn, **Sir John** (1778–1863), British general, who commanded the forces that put down the Mackenzie-Papineau rebellion in Canada in 1837. He was born at Lyndhurst, England, on Feb. 16, 1778, and joined the army in 1794. He was knighted in 1814. As a colonel, he led a regiment at the Battle of Waterloo.

Colborne was lieutenant governor of Upper Canada from 1828 to 1836, and as commander in chief of the army in Canada, he suppressed the 1837 rebellion. He was governor in chief of British North America in 1839 and was created 1st Baron Seaton in the same year. Later he held administrative positions in the Ionian Islands and in Ireland. He was made a field marshal when he retired in 1860. He died in Torquay, England, on April 17, 1863.

**COLBY,** kōl'bē, **Bainbridge** (1869–1950), American lawyer and secretary of state. Born in St. Louis, Mo., on Dec. 22, 1869, Colby graduated from Williams College in 1890 and subsequently received a law degree from the New York Law School. After nine years of practice in New York City, he served a term in the New York Assembly (1901–1902). A man of independent convictions, he broke from the Republican party in 1912 to support Theodore Roosevelt and the Progressive party. In 1914 and again in 1916 Colby ran unsuccessfully for the U. S. Senate on the Progressive ticket, although in the latter year he supported President Woodrow Wilson for reelection. During World War I, Wilson appointed him commissioner of the U. S. Shipping Board.

From March 1920 to March 1921, Colby served as secretary of state under Wilson. The major diplomatic concerns of his secretaryship, which he handled with ability, were the improvement of relations with Latin American countries, problems relating to League of Nations mandates, and the development of the U. S. position toward Communist Russia. After he left the cabinet, Colby practiced law in New York City and wrote for newspapers. He died in Bemus Point, N. Y., on April 11, 1950.

KEITH W. OLSON, *University of Maryland*

**COLBY COLLEGE,** kōl'bē, is a private, coeducational, liberal arts college in Waterville, Me. It was established in 1813 as the Maine Literary and Theological Institution, and classes were begun in 1818. Renamed Waterville College in 1821 and Colby University in 1867, it adopted its present name in 1899. Women were first admitted in 1871. The college was transferred in 1952 to a new campus on Mayflower Hill, in Waterville. Student enrollment numbers approximately 1,700.

Colby offers the bachelor of arts degree in over 20 majors. Class schedules are suspended during January, which is set aside as a period of independent study. The library includes collections on British and American writers and the papers of Edwin Arlington Robinson.

**COLCHESTER,** kōl'ches-tər, is a municipal borough in Essex, England, on the Colne River, 48 miles (77 km) northeast of London. It is a river port, and the trade center of a rich agricultural area. It also has oyster fisheries.

The Belgic king, Cunobelinus, made his capital here about 10 A.D. Colchester was the site of the first Roman colony in Britain, founded by Emperor Claudius in his conquest of Britain in 43 A.D. It was known to the Romans as Camulodunum and to the Saxons as Colneceaster. Points of interest are the remains of the Roman wall, the ruins of the 11th century St. Botoloph's priory, and the Saxon tower of the church of the Holy Trinity. A Norman castle here houses the Colchester and Essex Museum, a collection of British, Roman, and medieval antiquities. Colchester was heavily bombed in World War II. Population: 149,621 (1994 est.).

**COLCHICINE,** kol'chə-sēn, an alkaloid found in the roots, seeds, and leaves of many plants. It has two main actions: the relief of acute attacks of gout in humans and the interruption of mitosis, or cell division, in plants and animals.

The effectiveness of colchicine in the treatment of gout has been known for centuries, but how the drug acts is still unknown. Gout is a disease of uric acid metabolism that causes acute localized attacks of arthritis which produce severe swelling, inflammation, and pain in the joints, most commonly in the big toe. Colchicine does not have any effect on uric acid metabolism, and it is not an analgesic, yet it is uniquely capable of relieving the symptoms of gout. Given in small doses every four hours soon after the start of an attack, colchicine will relieve more than 90% of the cases. It may, however, cause side effects such as vomiting and diarrhea, and in some cases, other drugs, such as the adrenal cortical hormones, must be used to treat the gout.

Colchicine also produces effects on mitosis (q.v.). When cells are placed in a solution of colchicine (as little as one part per billion), cell division is interrupted at metaphase when the chromosomes (q.v.) have divided and are lined up in matched pairs of new chromosomes. Colchicine apparently destroys the spindle fibers that serve to pull apart the pairs of chromosomes so that they can form two new nuclei. Thus the resulting individual cell—if it survives—will be a polyploid with twice the original chromosome number. The effect of colchicine on mitosis is also reversible. If the tissue containing the multiplying cells is removed from the colchicine solution, normal cell division is usually resumed.

Colchicine-induced polyploids, called colchiploids, are difficult to produce in mammals, and they do not breed true. However, many varieties of plants with enlarged flowers or fruits have been easily produced with the use of colchicine. It has also been used in the study of cancer.

The usual commercial source of colchicine is the autumn crocus (*Colchicum autumnale*). Chemically, colchicine ($C_{22}H_{25}O_6N$) is unusual. Its basic molecular structure has three interlocking rings, two of which have seven atoms per ring instead of the usual six.

FRANK C. FERGUSON, JR., M. D.
*Albany Medical College of Union University*

**COLCHICUM,** kol'chə-kəm, a genus of hardy, autumn-flowering bulbs belonging to the lily family. The most popular species is the autumn crocus (*Colchicum autumnale*), a native of Africa. Its narrow leaves rise from the base of the plant and may be from 8 to 10 inches (20–23 cm) long. The purple, crocuslike flowers each consist of 6 segments and are from 3 to 4 inches (7.5–10 cm) wide. They are borne atop a stalk 6 inches (15 cm) tall. When properly harvested in the summer the bulbs can be kept dry inside the house and still produce flowers in the fall. Another popular species, *C. bornmuelleri,* is native to Asia Minor and produces flowers 5 inches (12.5 cm) wide. It may be propagated by seed but takes 2 years to germinate.

In addition to being raised as ornamentals, colchicums are important as a source of colchicine, a poisonous alkaloid that has long been used in medicine and has recently become important in plant breeding. See also COLCHICINE.

DONALD WYMAN
*The Arnold Arboretum, Harvard University*

J. J. SMITH

Colchicum

**COLCHIS,** kol′kis, was the name given in ancient times to a roughly triangular area at the eastern end of the Black Sea. It consisted of the valley of the Phasis River (modern Rioni River) and was bounded on the northeast by the Caucasus mountains and on the south by the Moschic Mountains (modern Surami Mountains). It now forms the western part of the Georgian republic of the USSR.

Colchis is first mentioned in an 8th century B.C. Urartean inscription. From at least the 7th century B.C. the Greeks located there the fabulous land of Aea, home of Medea and the Golden Fleece and goal of the Argonauts (q. v.).

The area was long under Persian rule. In the 6th century B.C., Greeks from Miletus established two colonies on the coast: Phasis, at the mouth of the Phasis River (near modern Poti); and Dioscurias, to the north (near modern Sukhumi). Neither site has yet been found. The rest of the country was occupied by native tribes, many of whom went to Dioscurias to trade.

The main product of the area was linen; materials for shipbuilding (timber, pitch, wax, hemp, and flax), medicinal herbs, skins, and slaves were also exported. Pheasants were first brought to Europe from Colchis. Herodotus described the Colchians as dark skinned, curly haired, and related to the Egyptians (not an impossibility); Hippocrates said they were yellow, fat, and lazy from living in a sultry, marshy valley and drinking the stagnant water of Phasis.

Colchis was ruled by Mithridates VI of Pontus from 89 to 65 B.C. and thereafter by kings owing allegiance to Rome. By the 6th century A.D. the semi-independent state of Lazica, which incorporated Colchis, had grown up and was a bone of contention between Byzantium and Persia. Later Colchis formed part of Abasgia and then of Georgia.

D. J. BLACKMAN
*University of Bristol, England*

**COLD** is the absence of heat. The term is relative and is generally applied to anything at a lower temperature than an observer or his surroundings. See HEAT; HEAT TRANSFER.

**COLD, Common,** a mild, contagious virus infection of the upper respiratory tract (nose, throat, and larynx). The common cold is most prevalent during the winter. It is estimated that about 50% of all people acquire colds during the winter, while only about 20% are infected during the summer. The disease is also more prevalent among certain age groups. The incidence of upper respiratory infections, most of which are common colds, is highest in small children. Preschool children average from 6 to 12 colds a year, while their parents have about 6 colds a year. Other adults average only 2 or 3 a year.

The importance of the common cold is measured by its contribution to absenteeism. About one-third of all industrial absenteeism is related to respiratory infections, chiefly the common cold. In the United States it is estimated that the cold and other respiratory illnesses account for an average loss of 3.67 working days each year for every employed person, while every child loses an average of 5.65 school days.

**Causes.** The popular belief that chilling alone leads to a cold lacks scientific evidence. However, it is possible that the warm, dry air inside homes and other buildings during the winter affects the nasal membranes and enhances a person's susceptibility to this virus infection. Arctic explorers are notably free of colds during the coldest months of the year. The common cold returns when their contact with civilization (and viruses) is reestablished.

The principal cause of the common cold is a group of viruses known as rhinoviruses. These 50 to 60 viruses are members of a larger category of viruses, the picornaviruses. Closely related to the rhinoviruses and also members of the picornavirus group are the enteroviruses, including the polioviruses. The picornaviruses are among the smallest viruses known, measuring from 15 to 30 microns in diameter. (One micron equals about $\frac{1}{25,000}$ of an inch.) The rhinoviruses differ from the enteroviruses in that they are less stable in an acidic environment and require a more precisely controlled environment when grown in tissue culture.

In addition to the rhinoviruses, which seem to account for the majority of common colds, certain enteroviruses have been associated with the disease. The common cold has also been associated with other respiratory viruses, including the myxoviruses (those causing influenza and parainfluenza) and the adenoviruses (those usually associated with sore throat and fever). The reovirus, another respiratory disease virus, is also believed to be associated with the common cold.

Once a person is infected with a cold-producing virus, the disease may be easily spread from person to person through close contact or association. It is probable that coughing and sneezing facilitate this spread, but it is not yet known whether clouds of very small airborne droplets (aerosols) or larger, short-range drops are principally involved in the transmission of the viruses.

**Symptoms.** The principal and most characteristic manifestation of the common cold is an inflammation and obstruction of the nose. Other frequent symptoms include sore throat, hoarseness, and coughing.

The systemic, or generalized, symptoms of the common cold include fatigue, malaise, generalized aches and pains, and a feeling of chilliness that may precede the nasal symptoms. Except in small children, the systemic symptoms are not severe, and fever is unusual. Although the common cold is a self-limiting disease, usually lasting less than 10 days, it may be complicated by or lead to bacterial infections of the throat, middle ear (otitis), or lungs (pneumonia).

**Treatment and Prevention.** There is no specific treatment for the common cold, but the patient may be made more comfortable by various drugs, including antipyretics (drugs that reduce fever), analgesics (drugs that relieve pain), and decongestants. Antihistamines and antibiotics have been advocated in the past, but they have not been found to be effective in treating colds. Also, the popular home remedy of drinking a lot of liquids, especially citrus juices, has not been found effective.

The prevention of the common cold is not feasible at the present time. Isolation and quarantine measures are neither realistic nor appropriate approaches in controlling this infection, particularly because the virus may be transmitted by persons who are infected but have no symptoms of the disease.

Because so many viruses cause the common cold, it is unlikely that artificial immunization will be feasible for some time. A natural form of immunity does exist; but an individual must be infected with all of the many cold-producing viruses before he is truly immune to the disease. Evidence of natural immunity is the fact that colds occur less frequently in older persons. This is the result of immunity acquired from cold infections in the past. It also reflects their lessened contact with small children, a major source of infection.

**Research.** Modern research on the common cold has increased greatly since the 1940's and is directly related to the development of methods of isolating and growing viruses in tissue cultures. Early studies of the common cold strongly suggested that the disease is contagious, and in 1914 the German physician W. Kruse demonstrated that colds could be transmitted experimentally from man to man through nasal washings that had been filtered to remove bacteria.

More definite evidence that the common cold is caused by a virus was found in the 1950's. One of the problems faced by researchers was that except for the chimpanzee, animals other than man are not susceptible to human rhinoviruses and therefore could not be used for laboratory studies. It was not until the perfection of tissue and cell cultures that viruses could be successfully isolated and propagated. In 1953, workers at the Common Cold Research Unit in Salisbury, England, succeeded in propagating an infective agent in human embryonic lung tissue. The results of any studies, however, were irregular until more appropriate tissue cultures were devised in 1960. Before that, however, American workers in 1956 had isolated and grown in human and monkey tissue cultures a virus that was later identified as the first continuously propagated rhinovirus.

Scientific research on the common cold is now being conducted on many fronts. Scientists are studying the growth and structure of the causative viruses, testing various kinds of vaccines, and studying the course of the disease and its epidemiological nature.

EDWIN D. KILBOURNE, M. D.
*Cornell University Medical College*

**Further Reading:** Castleman, M., *Cold Cures* (Fawcett Bks. 1987); Wagenvoord, J., *Beat the Common Cold* (Morrow 1984); White, Arthur, *Catarrh* (Sterling 1988).

**COLD-BLOODED ANIMAL,** an animal whose body temperature varies with the temperature of its surroundings. Fish, insects, snakes, and frogs are cold-blooded animals. See also ANIMAL HEAT.

**COLD CREAM.** See COSMETICS.

**COLD FRAME,** a bottomless box used to provide protection for seedlings and other delicate plants or to serve as a sheltered wintering site for bulbs and hardier plants. A cold frame generally consists of a low, 4-sided, wooden frame with a removable top. The top is most often made of glass or other transparent material, set into a suitable sash, to allow the entry of light and the development of warmth.

U. S. DEPARTMENT OF AGRICULTURE

COLD FRAMES are used to extend the growing season of vegetables, and also to protect seedlings before planting outside.

**COLD FRONT,** the forward edge of a mass of cold air that is moving toward and displacing a warm air mass. The cold frontal surface slopes upward and back over the cold air mass, which thus forms a thin wedge underlying the warm air. The cold frontal surface rises a vertical distance of about 1 mile over a horizontal distance of about 150 miles. On a weather map, a cold front is represented by a blue line or, in black and white, by the symbol

When a cold front passes a given point, the pressure at that point falls and then rises. The wind abruptly shifts direction clockwise (for example, from southwest to northwest) in the Northern Hemisphere and counterclockwise in the Southern Hemisphere. The weather that occurs during the passage of the front may be quite variable. Typically, however, it changes from muggy and partly polluted air, with showers, to colder, drier, and cleaner air, with clearing skies. A series of cold fronts, each one bringing colder air than its predecessor, ushers in the winter season in the United States.

See also METEOROLOGY—*The Weather Map;* WEATHER.

JAMES E. MILLER
*New York University*

**COLD HARBOR, Battle of,** in the American Civil War, fought on June 3, 1864. The direct frontal assault against Confederate entrenchments cost the Union Army 6,000 men killed and wounded in less than one hour.

In March 1864, Lt. Gen. Ulysses S. Grant had been appointed to command the armies of the United States. For the first time, a coordinated plan was prepared for all the Union forces. The Virginia campaign began on May 4, 1864. The principal antagonists were Gen. Robert E. Lee's Confederate Army of Northern Virginia and Maj. Gen. George G. Meade's Union Army of the Potomac. General Grant accompanied Meade's army. Two great battles were fought: the Wilderness (May 5–6); and Spotsylvania (May 8–19). After each battle, General Grant marched by his left flank, making a turning movement, and in each instance, found Lee's army facing him, at the North Anna River (May 23–24), and again at Totopotomoy Creek (May 30).

Another turning movement brought the opposing forces together at Cold Harbor, Va. There, on June 1, heavy fighting occurred. On June 3, at 4:30 A. M., the great assault was delivered. The principal effort was made by three Union corps: the 2nd and 6th from the Army of the Potomac; and the 18th Corps from Maj. Gen. Benjamin F. Butler's Army of the James. In less than an hour the assault collapsed, although sporadic fighting continued until early afternoon. The attackers entrenched, in some places within 30 yards (27 meters) of the Confederate works. Total Union losses for the day were 7,000 men, whereas the Confederate casualties numbered only 1,500. Several days of costly, miserable trench warfare ensued. On June 12, Grant withdrew to make a crossing of the James River, surprising Lee and almost capturing Petersburg, which was saved by the prompt action of Gen. P. G. T. Beauregard.

JOSEPH B. MITCHELL
*Author of "Decisive Battles of the Civil War"*

**COLD LIGHT.** See CHEMILUMINESCENCE.

**COLD SORE,** the common name for a small sore known medically as *herpes simplex.* Cold sores usually occur on or around the lips, although the cheeks, ears, or genitals may also be affected. A very painful condition known as a *herpetic whitlow* occurs when the palmar surface of a finger is involved.

Cold sores, sometimes called *fever blisters,* appear first as groups of tiny blisters, each group set on a small patch of red skin. These blisters are at first filled with a clear fluid and may later develop into pus-filled pimples. Within several days the blisters dry up and form yellowish or brownish crusts that drop off a week or two later.

Cold sores are caused by viruses that infect the nuclei of the cells of the epidermis. As indicated by their name, they are more likely to appear in a person afflicted with the common cold. However, they also occur in association with other febrile (fever-producing) diseases, such as influenza or pneumonia. In addition, they frequently follow a severe sunburn or occur with each menstrual period. It is believed that these conditions somehow lower the body's resistance and allow the virus particles, which presumably have been dormant in the body, to become reactivated.

STEPHEN E. SILVER, M. D.
*University of Oregon Medical School*

**COLD STORAGE** is the storage of perishable products, especially food, at temperatures sufficiently low to require refrigeration. Cold storage is also used to preserve furs, photographic film, and drugs. It is customarily used for keeping food products in unfrozen condition in the range of 32° to 45° F (0° to 7.2° C). Although water freezes at 32° F, many products have sugars or salts in their cells and thus will not freeze at a few degrees below 32° F. Therefore many cold storage rooms can be maintained at 28° to 31° F (−2.2° to 0.6° C) to store unfrozen products. Freezer cold storage refers to holding products in a frozen state, commonly in the range of 10° to −20° F (−12 to −29° C). Freezers should be operated at −10° to −15° F (−23° to −26° C) for good storage life of frozen foods and reasonable operating cost.

**Causes of Food Spoilage.** Decay organisms such as fungi and bacteria are always present on unsterilized products. The growth and development of these organisms are retarded as the temperature is lowered. Freezing in most cases does not kill bacteria, but their inactivation is so complete that freezer storage for long periods is possible. Spoilage also results from the activity of enzymes that cause nonliving cells to disintegrate. The rate of enzyme activity is halved for each 18° F (10° C) drop in temperature. Freezing does not stop enzyme activity, but it effectively retards it, particularly at temperatures below 0° F (−18° C). A third type of storage deterioration is due to oxidation. In fresh vegetables or fruits, which are living organisms, oxygen is absorbed by the product and acts to ripen it or carry out other changes. In nonliving materials, such as the fats in meat or the oils in nuts, oxidation occurs and contributes to rancidity. Oxidation reduces rapidly as temperatures are lowered, but continues at below-freezing temperatures.

**Food Storage Conditions.** The temperature range employed depends upon the food, the length of time it will be stored, and the acceptable diminution in quality resulting from storage. Apples can be stored from 2 to 7 months, with temperatures held in the range of 30° to 32° F (−1.1° to 0° C). Beef can be stored for 1 to 6 weeks in the range of 32° to 34° F (0° to 1.1° C) or for 9 to 12 months if frozen and held between −10° and 0° F (−23° to −18° C). Eggs, in their shells, can be kept 6 to 9 months at temperatures of 29° to 31° F (−1.6° to −0.6° C). Fish can be held for 5 to 15 days at 31° to 33° F (−0.6° to 0.6° C) or for 8 to 10 months when frozen and held below 0° F (−18° C). Lettuce at 32° F (0° C) can be held 3 to 4 weeks, milk at 33° F (0.6° C) for 7 days, and ice cream at −15° F (−26° C) for 6 to 8 months. Bananas require special treatment. They are picked unripe and are allowed to ripen slowly at temperatures of slightly above 55° F (13° C).

BURGESS H. JENNINGS*
*Northwestern University*

**COLD WAR,** an extended conflict between the communist states led by the Soviet Union and the western states led by the United States, which lasted from 1945 to 1990. The struggle had political, ideological, military, and economic dimensions. The Cold War began in Europe, where, in the aftermath of World War II, the Soviet Union extended its control into Eastern and central Europe by imposing communist regimes on Poland, Romania, Bulgaria, Hungary, Czechoslovakia, and East Germany (which had been created out of the Soviet zone of military occupation). The establishment of the People's Republic of China in 1949, followed by the North Korean invasion of South Korea, extended the Cold War to Asia. By the mid-1950s the Cold War became global as the West and the Soviet Union, and to a lesser extent China, competed for influence throughout much of the Third World.

An important component of the conflict was ideological. The Soviet Union justified its expansionist policies with the rhetoric of Marxist-Leninist ideology, which viewed global politics as a struggle between the progressive forces of communism and the reactionary forces of imperialism. In 1947 the Soviet Union established the Communist Information Bureau (Cominform) to promote communism in Europe and to ensure that European communism remained under Soviet control.

The United States countered Soviet expansion and propaganda with a policy of containment, initially with the Truman Doctrine of aid to Greece and Turkey in 1947, the Marshall Plan (1948) for Europe's economic reconstruction, the airlift (1948–1949) to the blockaded city of Berlin, and the creation of the North Atlantic Treaty Organization (NATO) in 1949. During the Eisenhower administration the United States and its allies sought to build a worldwide system of military pacts to contain communism. These included the Southeast Asia Treaty Organization (1954) and the Baghdad Pact (1955).

Throughout the Cold War, relations between the Soviet Union and the West alternated between periods of tension and crisis and periods of reduced tension and even limited cooperation. Though the two superpowers never engaged each other militarily, they were periodically caught up in major political crises that had the potential to become open warfare. Such crises included the Soviet blockade of Berlin (1948–1949), Soviet threats to cut off access to West Ber-

lin (1958, 1961), the Cuban missile crisis (1962), crises in the Middle East (1970, 1973), and the U.S. bombardment of Hanoi and Haiphong (1972). After the mid-1970s the number and severity of crises declined sharply, owing in large part to the powerful nuclear deterrents possessed by each side.

Although they never engaged each other militarily, the United States and the Soviet Union each were involved in combat operations to keep smaller states within their camp or to prevent them from falling into the other side's camp. Thus the Soviet Union sent troops into Berlin (1953) to quell a workers' uprising, into Hungary (1956) to crush a national revolution against communist rule, into Czechoslovakia (1968) to bring down a reformist government, and into Afghanistan (1979) to keep a communist government from being overthrown. In the mid-1970s Moscow assisted the sending of Cuban troops to Angola and Ethiopia to help keep Marxist regimes in power. In the early 1980s Moscow threatened to use force to keep the Solidarity movement from overthrowing the communist regime in Poland.

For its part, the United States assisted the overthrow of a leftist government in Guatemala (1954) and sent troops to the Dominican Republic (1965) to prevent a communist government from coming to power. In 1961 the United States supported an abortive effort to overthrow the government of Fidel Castro in Cuba. It covertly aided a military coup against a leftist government in Chile (1973). In 1983 the United States invaded the island of Grenada to displace a Marxist regime. In the 1980s it organized and supported the *contra* movement opposing the leftist Sandinista government in Nicaragua, and it funded the campaign of the opposition leader who eventually defeated the Sandinistas in free elections.

The United States fought two major wars against communist forces. One was in Korea (1950–1953) to resist an invasion of South Korea by North Korea. The war in Vietnam (1965–1975) failed to prevent North Vietnam from bringing South Vietnam under communist rule.

After the death of Stalin there was a brief period of improved relations between the United States and the Soviet Union, reflected in the "spirit of Geneva" (1955) and the "spirit of Camp David" (1959) in the Khrushchev-Eisenhower years. In the latter part of Khrushchev's administration a policy of "peaceful coexistence" prevailed, which produced two arms-control agreements with the Kennedy administration: the "hotline" agreement and the partial nuclear test-ban treaty (both in 1963). During the Brezhnev-Nixon years a policy of "détente" (1969–1974) prevailed, leading to several important agreements and a series of Soviet-American summit meetings. The most important of the agreements reached during détente was the SALT I agreement, which outlawed nationwide antiballistic missile defenses and established a five-year moratorium on the construction of new strategic ballistic missiles.

A major change in Soviet-Western relations took place during the administration of Mikhail Gorbachev. In the face of a profound collapse of the Soviet economy and growing social malaise, Gorbachev instituted a number of domestic reforms, expressed by the terms *perestroika* (reconstruction), *glasnost* (openness), and *democra-*

*tization.* In order to transform the Soviet political system and economy, Gorbachev committed his regime to restoring a new détente with the West. Beginning in 1987 he reversed Soviet foreign policy in virtually every area of conflict with the West. He agreed to abolish intermediate nuclear missiles worldwide; he withdrew Soviet forces from Afghanistan and reduced or eliminated Soviet support for regimes or activities in the Third World (notably in Angola, Nicaragua, and Cambodia). He also articulated a set of ideas ("new thinking") that implicitly repudiated the classical Marxist-Leninist doctrines stressing class conflict and socialist-imperialist conflict, replacing them with ideas emphasizing global interdependence and cooperation.

One of the unexpected by-products of Gorbachev's policies was the collapse of the communist regimes in Europe between 1989 and 1990. A series of spontaneous popular upheavals in Eastern Europe and Germany led to the establishment of noncommunist political parties, free elections, and the first genuinely democratic governments in the region in more than four decades. By not intervening in these revolutions, Gorbachev in effect abandoned the Brezhnev Doctrine, which asserted Moscow's right to use military force to keep communist governments in power. In October 1990 the German Democratic Republic was abolished, and East and West Germany became one democratic state. In 1991 the Warsaw Pact was disbanded. Presidents Bush and Gorbachev both proclaimed the end of the Cold War and the birth of a "new world order."

Fundamentally, the Cold War ended because the Soviet Union ceased to be a superpower, and the bipolar configuration of the international system gave way to a complex, multipolar world in which the United States was the dominant global power.

JOSEPH L. NOGEE, *Coauthor of "Soviet Foreign Policy since World War II"*

**COLDEN,** kōl′dən, **Cadwallader** (1688–1776), American physician, politician, and botanist. Colden was born in Dunse, Scotland, on Feb. 17, 1688, and received his M.D. from the University of Edinburgh in 1705. He practiced medicine in Pennsylvania from 1708 to 1715 and then returned briefly to England, where his first work on animal secretions was published. In 1716 Colden returned to the New World permanently, settling first in Pennsylvania and then in New York. There he soon entered public life, being named surveyor general in 1718 and a member of the king's council in 1720.

In 1727 Colden published his *History of the Five Indian Nations of Canada,* probably his most popular, though least scientific, work. His interest in science included physics and medicine, but his real passion was botany. He introduced the Linnaean system of plant classification into America and sent a description of more than 300 plants to Linnaeus, who published it in 1743. In gratitude, Linnaeus named the plant genus *Coldenia* after him.

Colden's political views were increasingly out of tune with the times. He was a staunch royalist and supported the unpopular Stamp Act. With the colonies' Declaration of Independence, he retired from public life. He died at his Long Island estate on Sept. 28, 1776.

L. PEARCE WILLIAMS, *Cornell University*

**COLDSTREAM GUARDS,** kōld′strēm, a regiment in the Foot Guards of the Household Brigade, the oldest in the British Army, except for the Royal Scots. Descended from a force raised by Oliver Cromwell in 1650, it marched in 1660 under Gen. George Monck from Coldstream, a burgh on the Scottish border, into England to effect the restoration of Charles II. Originally called "Monck's regiment," it was included under the name of Coldstream Guards in a brigade of guards given to Charles by Parliament. The military record of the Coldstream is brilliant.

**COLDWELL,** kōld′wəl, **Major James William** (1888–1974), Canadian political leader; a founder and eventually the national leader of the Cooperative Commonwealth Federation (CCF), a left-wing Canadian political party. ("Major" is not a military title but his first name.) Born on Dec. 2, 1888, in Devonshire, England, he emigrated to Canada in 1910 and became a teacher and school principal in Regina. Active in teachers' organizations and local affairs, he was leader of the Saskatchewan Farmer-Labour party in 1932–1935 and played an important role in the formation of the CCF during that time. Attempts on his part to enter either provincial or federal politics met with disappointment until 1935, when he won the federal seat of Rosetown-Biggar, which he held until 1958. He became CCF leader in the House of Commons in 1940 and was national president and parliamentary leader in 1942–1960. In 1961 he became honorary president of the newly-formed New Democratic party. *Left Turn, Canada* (1945) summed up his political viewpoint. High personal integrity, clarity of thought and expression, parliamentary skill, and strong idealism made him an effective leader. He died in Ottawa on Aug. 25, 1974.

D. G. G. KERR
*University of Western Ontario*

**COLE,** kōl, **Albert McDonald** (1901–      ), American public official. He was born in Moberly, Mo., on Oct. 13, 1901, and grew up in Topeka, Kans. After graduating from the University of Chicago (1925), he practiced law in Kansas. A county attorney, then state senator (1941–1944), he was elected to the U.S. House of Representatives as a Republican in 1944 and reelected three times. He opposed federal subsidies for low-rental housing, arguing that the government should not supplant the housing industry.

Appointed head of the Housing and Home Finance Agency by President Dwight Eisenhower in 1953, he supported low-rental housing, slum clearance, urban redevelopment, and research in prefabrication. He established a national, voluntary mortgage credit extension commission to facilitate loans to potential homeowners. In 1959 he left the government to become a business corporation executive.

**COLE,** kōl, **Fay-Cooper** (1881–1961), American archaeologist and anthropologist. Cole was born in Plainwell, Mich., on Aug. 8, 1881, and studied at Northwestern University and the University of Chicago. He served on the staff of the Field Museum of Natural History in Chicago from 1906 to 1923. He conducted two expeditions among the tribes of the Philippines, and from 1922 to 1923, he was the leader of the Field Museum expedition to the Malay Peninsula. In 1924, Cole joined the University of Chicago, where he became chairman of the department of anthropology. He retired in 1948

In the 1930's, Cole was closely identified with the development of Midwestern archaeology. One of his works, *Kincaid: A Prehistoric Illinois Metropolis,* provided the first archaeological dating for the Midwest based on tree rings. Cole died in Santa Barbara, Calif., on Sept. 3, 1961.

**COLE, George Douglas Howard** (1889–1959), British economist, who was a leading intellectual of the British Labour party and the author of books and articles on the philosophy and history of the labor movement. He was born in Ealing, a London suburb, on Sept. 25, 1889, and was educated at St. Paul's School, London, and Oxford University. He was appointed reader in economics at Oxford University in 1925 and Chichele professor of social and political theory there in 1944, a position he held until 1957.

Cole was one of the originators of guild socialism in England and helped found the National Guilds League in 1915. He opposed state socialism as too bureaucratic and antilibertarian. Instead he proposed a decentralized democratic socialism in which all the members of the society were to be organized along occupational lines. His voluminous publications, some written in collaboration with his wife, Margaret Isabel Postgate Cole, cover the following: historical studies of the working-class movement since the Industrial Revolution; the organization of the modern labor movement; studies of working conditions, strikes, and industrial organization; philosophical studies in socialism; and essays in social and political theory. In addition he coauthored with his wife over 30 detective stories. He died in London on Jan. 14, 1959.

RAMON KNAUERHASE, *University of Connecticut*

**COLE, King,** a legendary British king and the subject of the traditional nursery rhyme *Old King Cole Was a Merry Old Soul.* The 12th century chronicler Geoffrey of Monmouth identified the monarch with a duke of Kaercolvin (probably modern Colchester) named Coel, who made himself king in the 3d century. A later opinion is that the name is derived from a clothier of Reading named Cole-brook who, apparently, was familiarly known as "Old Cole."

**COLE, Margaret Isabel Postgate.** See COLE, GEORGE DOUGLAS HOWARD.

**COLE, Nat "King"** (1919–1965), American singer and pianist, who was noted for his intimate, relaxed singing style and for the distinctive husky quality of his voice. He was born Nathaniel Adams Coles in Montgomery, Ala., on March 17, 1919, and was brought up in Chicago, where he received piano instruction. In 1936 he left Chicago to tour as a pianist with the Negro revue *Shuffle Along.* He later worked as a solo pianist in Hollywood nightclubs, and in 1939 formed the King Cole Trio. (At that time he dropped the "s" from his name and adopted the nickname "King.") The trio recorded its first national hit, *Straighten Up and Fly Right,* in 1943. By the late 1940's, Cole was featured as a singer rather than as a pianist, recording mainly with big bands. Among his hit songs were *Nature Boy, Mona Lisa,* and *It's Only a Paper Moon.*

Cole also appeared in several motion pictures, including a short subject entitled *The Nat "King" Cole Musical Story* (1955). He died in Santa Monica, Calif. on Feb. 15, 1965.

**COLE, Thomas** (1801–1848), American painter, who was a founder of the Hudson River school of landscape painting. The most distinguished American landscape painter of the first half of the 19th century, Cole was largely responsible for making landscape an acceptable subject for serious painters. He was a master of the intimate, detailed view of nature, as well as of wild, romantic vistas that show man as the victim of nature's overwhelming forces. His reputation, which faded after his death, rose again in the 20th century with the revival of interest in romantic interpretations of nature.

Cole was born at Bolton-le-Moors, Lancaster, England, on Feb. 1, 1801, and went to America with his family in 1818. He learned the rudiments of painting from an itinerant artist in Steubenville, Ohio. In 1823 he went to Philadelphia, where he studied briefly at the Pennsylvania Academy.

In New York City, where he moved in 1825, Cole soon found patrons for the landscapes he painted on trips up the Hudson River valley and into the Catskill Mountains. The National Acad-

**THOMAS COLE'S** *Expulsion from the Garden of Eden* (1827–1828) contrasts a peaceful, luminous Eden *(right)* with the dark, ominous world of turbulent nature into which the fallen Adam and Eve are made to flee.

emy of Design, which he helped found in 1826, frequently exhibited his work. From 1829 to 1832, Cole traveled and painted in Europe, where he was particularly impressed by the English landscape painters William Turner and John Martin and, during his stay in Italy, by the romantic ruins of ancient Rome.

Soon after his return to the United States in 1832, Cole married Maria Barton and settled at Catskill, N. Y. The large historical and allegorical canvases that he painted during this period became widely popular through engraved reproductions. Two of his best-known allegorical cycles are a series of five canvases representing *The Course of Empire* (1832–1836) and another series of four paintings, *The Voyage of Life* (1839–1840). The latter, usually considered his masterpiece, is painted with great dignity in a direct and unsentimental manner. Just when he had reached full maturity and was painting the most powerful and impressive compositions of his career, Cole died of pneumonia at Catskill on Feb. 8, 1848.

FREDERICK A. SWEET
*The Art Institute of Chicago*

**COLE, Timothy** (1852–1931), American engraver. He was born in London, England, on April 6, 1852. His parents took him to the United States in 1857, and at 16 he became an apprentice wood engraver in Chicago. Cole lost everything in the great Chicago fire. In 1871 he began working as engraver-illustrator for New York periodicals, and he developed new methods of using wood engravings to copy paintings.

In 1883, *Century Magazine* (then *Scribner's*) sent him to Europe to make engravings of works of old masters. These appeared in a series of volumes between 1892 to 1907. His stay in Europe, originally intended for one year, lasted until 1910. After his return to the United States he was commissioned to copy masterpieces belonging to both public and private collections. Cole was acclaimed as the foremost wood engraver of his day. He wrote *The Magic Line* (1917). Cole died in Poughkeepsie, N.Y., on May 17, 1931.

**COLE, William Sterling** (1904–    ), American public official, who represented the United States in international efforts to control atomic energy. He was born on April 18, 1904, in Painted Post, N. Y. He earned degrees at Colgate University (1925) and the Albany Law School (1929). After teaching in public schools and practicing law, he was elected as a Republican to Congress in 1934. A member of the Joint Committee on Atomic Energy (1947–1957), he became an expert on the control of atomic energy.

When the International Atomic Energy Agency, based on President Dwight D. Eisenhower's "atoms for peace" program, was founded in 1957, Cole resigned his congressional seat to become its first director general. The agency, with headquarters in Vienna, was a United Nations-sponsored body designed "to seek to accelerate and enlarge the contribution of atomic energy to peace, health, and prosperity throughout the world." Cole headed the agency until 1961, when Eisenhower's term as president ended. He then engaged in private law practice in Washington, D.C.

WALTER DARNELL JACOBS
*University of Maryland*

**COLEBROOKE, Henry Thomas** (1765–1837), English Orientalist, who was the first great Sanskrit scholar in Europe. He was born in London on June 15, 1765, and in 1782 entered the British East India Company, where his father was an official. Soon promoted, Colebrooke went to Bengal where he began studying the agriculture of the region, as well as Indian law and Sanskrit. By 1794 he was contributing essays on Indian poetry, religion, and science to *Asiatic Researches*, a journal of the Asiatic Society of Calcutta. He became a magistrate in Mizapur in 1794, and in 1801 was appointed judge of the court of appeals in Calcutta. Colebrooke wrote *Digest of Hindu Law on Contracts and Successions* (1798); *Sanskrit Grammar* (1805), based on the works of native scholars; and *Two Treatises on the Hindu Law of Inheritance* (1810). He died in London on March 10, 1837.

**COLEMAN,** a city in Texas, the seat of Coleman county, situated 150 miles (240 km) northwest of Austin. It is a commercial and shipping center, and it has livestock-processing plants, grain elevators, machine shops, a fabricating iron and saddle plant, a brick and tile plant, and factories that produce boots and Western wear. Government is by council-manager. Population: 5,127.

**COLEMANITE,** kōl′mə-nīt, is a hydrous calcium-boron oxide mineral, and a source of borax. The prismatic crystals are transparent to translucent, have a glassy luster, and are colorless to white. Deposits of colemanite are found only in the United States, in California and Nevada. Colemanite was the most important source of borax until the discovery of kernite in 1926. Composition, $Ca_2 B_6 O_{11} \cdot 5H_2O$; hardness, 4–4.5; specific gravity, 2.4; crystal system, monoclinic.

**COLENSO,** kō-len′zō, **John William** (1814–1883), English Biblical scholar and Anglican bishop of Natal. In 1846 he became vicar of a parish in Norfolk, from which, in 1853, he was appointed first bishop of Natal in South Africa. Colenso provoked wide criticism almost at once because of his lenient policy towards the practice of polygamy by native African converts. A storm of protest greeted the publication in 1861 of his *Commentary on the Epistle to the Romans*. In it he displayed liberal views on the question of eternal punishment and rejected much of the traditional sacramental theology. In the years following 1862 he published successive parts of *The Pentateuch and the Book of Joshua Critically Examined*, in which he challenged the accepted views of the authorship and historical accuracy of these books.

Colenso was censured by a large number of Anglican bishops, including a majority of those at the Lambeth Conference of 1867. Robert Gray, archbishop of Capetown, declared him deposed in 1863. However, Colenso denied Gray's claim of metropolitan jurisdiction over him, appealing to the letters patent by which the crown had appointed him to Natal. After considerable litigation he was supported by the privy council, and until his death in 1883 he remained the excommunicate bishop of Natal, in legal possession of the property of the diocese of Natal.

POWEL MILLS DAWLEY
*The General Theological Seminary, New York*

**COLEOPTERA.** See BEETLE.

**COLERAINE,** kōl-rān', a district in Northern Ireland. Coleraine is located on the estuary of the Lower Bann, about 4 miles (6 km) from its mouth and 52 miles (84 km) northwest of Belfast. Situated at the head of navigation, it is a seaport and marketing center. Coleraine's economy depends on whiskey distilleries and salmon and eel fisheries. St. Patrick is said to have given the name Cûil Rathain to the site in the 5th century. Population: 48,600 (1990 est.).

**COLERIDGE,** kōl'rij, **Hartley** (1796–1849), English writer, who was the eldest son of Samuel Taylor Coleridge. David Hartley Coleridge was born at Clevedon, Somersetshire, on Sept. 19, 1796. After the estrangement of his parents he was brought up in the Lake District by Robert Southey. Coleridge graduated from Oxford in 1819 and was awarded a fellowship at Oriel College, Oxford, but he was dismissed in 1820 for intemperance. As a child he had been indulged as a genius, and his tendencies toward unreliability and procrastination, which he shared with his father, filled him with self-reproach and melancholy.

For some years Coleridge lived successively in London, Ambleside (Westmorland), and Leeds, contributing poems to the *London Magazine* and writing hack biographies. In 1833 he published a small volume of poetry. In the same year he returned to the Lake District, where he spent the rest of his life in teaching, writing, dreaming, and dissipation. He died at Rydal, Westmorland, on Jan. 6, 1849.

Coleridge's best works are his graceful and sensitive sonnets. His critical works are sound, although his prose is labored. He also wrote an unfinished lyrical drama, *Prometheus*.

**COLERIDGE,** kōl'rij, **Samuel Taylor** (1772–1834), English poet, philosopher, and critic. As a poet he greatly influenced such contemporary romantics as Wordsworth, Byron, Keats, and Shelley. His most famous poem is *The Rime of the Ancient Mariner* (1798). As a philosopher and theologian who attempted to reconcile reason and religion, he was one of the inspirers of 19th century English and American idealism and also of the Broad Church movement. Coleridge was among the greatest English literary critics, seeing literature as an organic unity achieved by the reconciliation of opposites, and his critical thought has continued to be of major importance.

## LIFE AND WORKS

**Early Years.** Coleridge was born at Ottery St. Mary, Devonshire, on Oct. 21, 1772, the youngest of the 10 children of John Coleridge, vicar of Ottery St. Mary, by Ann Bowdon (Bowden), his second wife. Coleridge was a precocious, dreamy, introspective boy, set somewhat apart from his brothers and sisters by his age and his unusual qualities. "So," avowed Coleridge himself, "I became very vain, and despised most of the boys that were at all near my own age, and before I was eight years old I was a *character*. Sensibility, imagination, vanity, sloth, and feelings of deep and bitter contempt for all who traversed the orbit of my understanding, were even then prominent and manifest." When his father explained to him the motions of the heavenly bodies, he accepted the explanation without difficulty. "For from my early reading of fairy tales and genii, etc., etc., my mind had been habitu-

ated *to the Vast*, and I never regarded *my senses* in any way as the criteria of my belief. I regulated all my creeds by my conceptions, not by my *sight*, even at that age." These accounts are doubtless highly colored and do some injustice to the natural amiability of Coleridge's character, but they contain an essential truth. The death of his father in 1781 deprived him of a sympathetic friend.

In 1782, Coleridge was sent to the famous charity school of Christ's Hospital, where he remained for eight years. There he formed a lifelong friendship with Charles Lamb, read the Neoplatonists, became an accomplished Greek and Latin scholar, and came under the fearsome but salutary tutelage of the Rev. James Boyer, to whom, in his *Biographia Literaria* (q.v.) Coleridge attributes the foundation of his poetic creed. He entered Jesus College, Cambridge, on a Christ's Hospital scholarship in 1791, with the intention of taking orders. Free of the strict discipline of school, however, he involved himself in such financial and ideological difficulties that in 1793 he ran away and enlisted as a trooper of the 15th Light Dragoons, under the name of Silas Tomkyn Comberbacke—"and verily," he says, "my habits were so little equestrian, that my horse, I doubt not, was of that opinion." After some time his relatives discovered his whereabouts and arranged his discharge, to his undisguised relief. The authorities of his college so highly respected his abilities that they made no difficulty about taking him back. His meeting with Robert Southey in the summer of 1794, however, put an end to his Cambridge career; association with Southey, then a vigorous young radical, destroyed in the inflammable Coleridge all thought of orthodoxy and the priesthood. He returned to the university in the autumn, but stayed there only a few months.

**Literary Friendships.** The next couple of years Coleridge spent in Bristol. With Southey, Robert Lovell, and others he threw himself wholeheartedly into a scheme to establish a pantisocracy, or community based on ideal equality, on the banks of the Susquehanna River in Pennsylvania. As a more or less direct result of this plan he married Sara Fricker, the sister of Southey's fiancée, in 1795. Pantisocracy itself came to nothing.

In 1796, Coleridge attempted a periodical publication, the *Watchman*, which failed after 10 numbers, as did his later venture, the *Friend*. In the same year he published *Poems on Various Subjects*. At the end of the year he moved to Nether Stowey, a village at the foot of the Quantock Hills, so that he could be near his friend Thomas Poole.

*Poems* appeared in 1797. In addition to Coleridge's work, it included verse by Lamb and by Coleridge's protégé Charles Lloyd. The same year saw the beginning of Coleridge's intimate and fertile association with William and Dorothy Wordsworth, one of the great literary friendships of all time and one that was enormously profitable to both men. From it arose the epochal *Lyrical Ballads* (1798), for which Coleridge wrote *The Rime of the Ancient Mariner*, the tale of a superstitious sailor on an ill-fated voyage. (See ANCIENT MARINER, RIME OF THE.) In 1797 and 1798 he also wrote *Christabel* (q.v.), an unfinished romantic poem involving a pure maiden and an evil power, and *Kubla Khan*, a fragmentary poem that describes the exotic setting and the magnificence of the khan's palace.

In 1798–1799, Coleridge and the Wordsworths visited Germany, where Coleridge attended the University of Göttingen and read intensively in German metaphysics. From this period came his first significant acquaintance with the work of Immanuel Kant, whose influence upon him was undoubtedly large, although difficult to estimate precisely.

In July 1800 the Coleridges settled at Greta Hall, Keswick, near Wordsworth and his family. During this year Coleridge translated two plays of Friedrich von Schiller's dramatic trilogy *Wallenstein*, a task he found so distasteful that he believed it prevented his finishing *Christabel*. In 1801 two misfortunes occurred to him: he began to take opium in serious amounts, and he fell in love with Sara Hutchinson, a sister of Wordsworth's wife-to-be, to whom, in 1802, he addressed his notable *Dejection: An Ode*, lamenting the loss of his poetic powers, his "shaping spirit of Imagination." Opium, taken to relieve severe neuralgic and rheumatic pains and at the time freely prescribed by physicians, dominated him in varying degrees for many years. In April 1804 he sailed for Malta in search of better health and peace of mind, and did not return to England until 1806. His stay in Malta, where he was for a time secretary to the governor, did not fulfill the purposes for which he went. During the next few years he separated entirely from his wife and family, the care and maintenance of whom devolved largely upon Robert Southey, with intermittent help from Coleridge.

From 1808 to 1818, Coleridge's principal literary activity was lecturing. He gave a number of lecture courses, chiefly in London—on William Shakespeare, on the English poets, on education, on the principles of taste, on classicism and romanticism, and on philosophy. As a lecturer, Coleridge was profound, often fascinating, sometimes irritatingly digressive, occasionally baffling, but on the whole successful. He can be considered the greatest of Shakespearean critics, the creator of a new appreciation of Shakespeare's genius. There has always been some question about his indebtedness to contemporary Germans, especially to A. W. von Schlegel, but in the most reasonable opinion Coleridge's essential originality remains unchallenged. He made another attempt to establish a periodical in the *Friend*, which appeared weekly (with some gaps in continuity) from June 1809 to March 1810. It failed from practical difficulties of distribution and from Coleridge's inability to adapt himself to his readers, in particular to write self-contained weekly essays. The *Friend* is known today in the revised version of 1818.

In October 1810 came a serious breach with Wordsworth, some of whose remarks about Coleridge's domestic habits as a guest were incautiously repeated and exaggerated to Coleridge by a tactless friend. This misunderstanding was healed after protracted and complicated negotiations by the diarist Henry Crabb Robinson, but it left a scar. The two poets never fully returned to their happy relations of earlier years. From 1810 to 1816, Coleridge lived primarily in London. Along with his lecturing he occupied himself at times with literary and political journalism, and achieved considerable success at the Drury Lane Theatre in 1813 with his tragedy *Remorse*, a revision of an earlier play, *Osorio*. He was befriended and cared for in his frequent illnesses and difficulties by the merchant John Morgan.

PORTRAIT BY WASHINGTON ALLSTON
NATIONAL PORTRAIT GALLERY, LONDON

Samuel Taylor Coleridge in 1814

**The Sage of Highgate.** Morgan himself fell into misfortune, and in 1816 Coleridge placed himself under the care of James Gillman, a physician, at Highgate, a suburb of London. He had planned to stay for a few months only, but the arrangement was so successful that he remained in the Gillman household until his death. Under Gillman's regime the opium habit was effectively brought under control, and Coleridge led a relatively tranquil and happy existence.

In 1816 the unfinished poems *Christabel* and *Kubla Khan* were at last published, after many years of oral circulation. In particular, the poetry of Sir Walter Scott and Lord Byron had already shown the influence of *Christabel*. In 1817 appeared *Sibylline Leaves*, including *The Ancient Mariner* with the prose gloss of all modern editions, and *Biographia Literaria*, Coleridge's literary life and opinions. The *Biographia* employs irregular narrative and casual reminiscence to introduce, as Coleridge says, "my principles in Politics, Religion, and Philosophy, and an application of the rules, deduced from philosophical principles, to poetry and criticism." He wishes "to effect, as far as possible, a settlement of the long continued controversy concerning the true nature of poetic diction; and at the same time to define with the utmost impartiality the real *poetic* character of the poet [Wordsworth], by whose writings this controversy was first kindled...." In the *Biographia Literaria*, Coleridge sets forth his famous distinction between imagination and fancy, and provides an admiring but judicious account of Wordsworth's poetical theory and practice. Chapter 14 of the *Biographia* is only less influential in English criticism than Aristotle's *Poetics*.

After 1817, Coleridge devoted himself principally to a great effort to effect a definitive reconciliation of religion with philosophy and reason. He became the Sage of Highgate, who held open house on Thursday nights for an admiring group of disciples, mainly younger men, including Keats, John Sterling, and J. H. Green. Two *Lay Sermons* were published in 1816 and 1817, and an abortive association with an encyclopedia produced his notable *Treatise on Method*. In 1817 there also appeared *Zapolya*, "a dramatic entertainment." Coleridge contributed haphazardly to *Blackwood's Edinburgh Magazine* during 1819–1821, and more significantly in 1825 published *Aids to Reflection*, a defense of Trinitarian Christianity (Coleridge had once trembled on the brink of becoming a Unitarian minister), both as a practical rule for conduct and politics and as a necessity of metaphysical thought. *On the Constitution of Church and State* (1830) was the last work published in Coleridge's lifetime. The posthumous *Table Talk* (1835) and *Confessions of an Inquiring Spirit* (1840) date from this final period of Coleridge's life. During the 1820's he worked upon his *Logosophia* or *Opus Maximum*, which was to expound the nature of reason in its metaphysical aspect, and in so doing arrive at the ultimate justification of the doctrine of the Trinity. His disciple J. H. Green worked on the *Opus Maximum* for the rest of his life, and left his version of it in *Spiritual Philosophy* (1865). Coleridge died in Highgate on July 25, 1834. He was survived by his wife, his sons Hartley and Derwent, and his daughter, Sara, who later with his nephew H. N. Coleridge edited his critical works.

Coleridge's contemporaries were accustomed to lament the discrepancy between his capabilities and his actual achievement. This habit has persisted even in the scholarship of the mid-20th century, but it might well be given up at last. Coleridge's self-acknowledged weakness of will, as he pictured it in his analysis of Hamlet's character, is celebrated. Much of his work, like the *Opus Maximum*, is unfinished; many of his texts, posthumously revised by others, are uncertain; and the charge against him of plagiarism from German philosophy and criticism cannot be wholly laid. Yet it would be hard to overestimate what remains after these qualifications. The incredible comprehensiveness of Coleridge's mind is in itself sufficient to explain his failure to complete his many literary projects.

## THOUGHT

Coleridge's critical thought is inseparable from his philosophy and his psychology. Its chief emphasis, indeed, is psychological. Imaginative creation is the fullest activity of man's mind, and to understand a literary work one must look to the qualities of the mind behind it. His psychology, however, is organically one with his philosophy, which assumes an ultimate reality and attempts to explain it. The faculties of imagination, reason, and understanding are not only components of mind, but also organs of objective knowledge. Coleridge's aesthetics are psychological insofar as they are concerned with effect, the mind's reaction to an aesthetic object (the criticism of Edgar Allan Poe bears his hallmark); he describes by introspection the pleasure that the object can give. This pleasure, however, is the subjective counterpart of a beauty that objectively exists.

Coleridge's criticism is based upon the idea of unity as the necessary principle of reality. He would assign to the individual literary work its appropriate place in a total structure of literature. This structure is an organic whole, but to the intellect it is composed of literary types or genres, arranged according to their relative value. These genres have the familiar Aristotelian names of tragedy, epic, comedy, pastoral, but Coleridge's conception of genres is distinct from Aristotle's

and from the neoclassical theories derived from Aristotle.

Coleridge differs from Aristotle and from neoclassicism in his larger allowance for individuality. According to Coleridge, every work of literature is unique and subject only to laws proper to itself, so that no predetermined code can wholly deal with it. Recognition of the uniqueness of a work does not, however, mean critical anarchy. It merely points to a fact that consideration shows to be self-evident. Every piece of literature must be unique, or must possess aspects that are unique; this uniqueness, however, does not prevent rational classification of a work. Coleridge seeks a perfect balance between the particular and the universal, and tries to describe a work according to its individuality, its kind, and its universal significance.

His conception of genre is based upon the "reconciliation of opposites," the characteristic method of his thought. Kind can be reconciled on the one hand with individuality, on the other with the universal. Definition can be reconciled with the judgment of value by careful distinction, since kind is distinguished from degree. The reconciliation of opposites is, indeed, the Archimedes lever of Coleridge's thought. His procedure and terminology are dialectical or polar. Reality is always an organic, inseparable unity, yet this reality can only be discursively revealed as two, in the form of polar opposites reconciled, or centripetal and centrifugal forces in equilibrium. In aesthetics and criticism this principle involves the full acceptance of the doctrine of organic unity of form and content, but at the same time it preserves their distinctness as concepts, for without their twoness organic unity would be unintelligible.

The reconciliation of opposites is the organizing principle of Coleridge's psychology. The imagination is the mind's unifying agency, which mediates between reason and understanding. Reason apprehends truths beyond the reach of our senses. It is immediate in action and indemonstrable by argument: itself the starting point of thought, nothing in the mind can explain it. From the reason comes our idea of God, our idea of unity. Reason's opposite, the understanding, is the discursive intelligence, by which we deal with phenomena. The understanding organizes the evidence of the senses for practical use. It is the generalizing and abstracting power by which we classify, the faculty of scientific method. The understanding cannot perceive living reality, but only the world as mechanism.

Coleridge distinguishes between the primary imagination common to all, which is the instrument of his psychology and his philosophy, and the secondary or poetic imagination, the instrument of his criticism. It would be hard to overemphasize the importance to him of imagination's unifying, vitalizing force. Without the conception of its cohesive power his system can be seen in fragments only. Difficult to grasp and therefore liable to be set aside as chimerical, the unifying power of imagination is central and indispensable to his thought.

To Coleridge organic unity is a means of describing both the work of imagination and the mind that creates it. Its symbol is the living plant or tree, whose life is not in roots, or trunk, or branches or leaves, but pervades them all and is "all in each." "The organic form . . . is innate; it shapes as it develops itself from within, and the fullness of its development is one and the same with the perfection of its outward form. Such as is the life, such the form." The principle of organic unity includes (1) the process of growth, whereby the parts develop simultaneously from a seed in which the mature organism is already potentially contained; (2) the inseparability of form and content; (3) the inseparability of the part and the whole; and (4) the copresence of conscious and unconscious, willed and spontaneous elements.

By means of his principles of the reconciliation of opposites and organic unity, Coleridge was able to solve the basic contradictions of previous English criticism. He perceived that nature and art, genius and judgment, were merely different aspects of the same whole, and could be reconciled. Shakespeare's "judgment is equal to his genius," because one is necessary to the other. Genius cannot be realized unless judgment directs it; whereas without genius judgment is mere vacuity. Shakespeare is not lawless, although not susceptible to the predetermined rules of neoclassical criticism. He is instead the very embodiment of law, but of an organic law, which cannot be imposed from without.

Coleridge's method of critical analysis can be deduced from his doctrine of organic unity. He looks for an informing principle, corresponding to the pervasive life of an organic body—the seed or germ that contains potentially the completed form, as the acorn contains the oak. This principle appears intelligibly (since reality is intelligible only in the form of polar opposites) as an opposition: in drama, for example, it appears as a dislocation in the hero's mind, which is the source of the drama's action. Thus in *Hamlet* the tragic action is said to arise from an imbalance between the hero's mind and external reality. Hamlet is a giant of intellect who is without the will to action. Satisfied with the rich reality of his inward life, he finds the outer world unreal, dim like the pictures that pass for a moment before closed eyes. Clearly discerning the moral necessity for action, he yet cannot act. His mind is a richly figured curtain, but he needs a window.

RICHARD HARTER FOGLE
*Author of "Idea of Coleridge's Criticism"*

### Bibliography

#### Editions

Coburn, Kathleen, ed., *The Notebooks of Samuel Taylor Coleridge*, vol. 1, 1794–1804 (Princeton Univ. Press 1957).
Coleridge, Ernest H., ed., *The Complete Poetical Works of Samuel Taylor Coleridge*, 2 vols. (Oxford 1912).
Greggs, Earl, ed., *Unpublished Letters of Samuel Taylor Coleridge*, 2 vols. (Arden Library 1983).

#### Biography and Criticism

Barfield, Owen, *What Coleridge Thought* (Wesleyan Univ. Press 1983).
Bloom, Harold, ed., *Samuel Taylor Coleridge* (Chelsea House 1986).
Chambers, Edmund K., *Samuel Taylor Coleridge: A Biographical Study* (1967; reprint, Greenwood Press 1978).
Coleman. Deirdre, *Coleridge and the Friend* (1809–1810) (Oxford 1989).
Fogle, Richard H., *Idea of Coleridge's Criticism* (1962; reprint, Greenwood Press 1978).
Goodson, A. C., *Verbal Imagination* (Oxford 1988).
Hamilton, Paul, *Coleridge's Poetics* (Stanford Univ. Press 1983).
Jackson, H. J., ed., *Samuel Taylor Coleridge* (Oxford 1985).
Magnuson, Paul, *Coleridge and Wordsworth: A Lyrical Dialogue* (Princeton Univ. Press 1988).
Roe, Nicholas, *Wordsworth and Coleridge: The Radical Years* (Oxford 1988).
Tak, A. H., *Coleridge and Modern Criticism* (Apt. Bks. 1986).
Yarnall, Charlton, ed., *Forty Years of Friendship* (1911; reprint, Telegraph Bks. 1981).

**COLERIDGE-TAYLOR,** kōl'rij tā'lər, **Samuel** (1875–1912), English composer. He was born in London on Aug. 15, 1875, of an English mother and an African Negro father from Sierra Leone. From childhood he showed exceptional talent for music, playing the violin and singing in a church choir. While attending the Royal College of Music (1890–1896), he studied composition with C. V. Stanford. From 1904 to 1912 he conducted the Handel Society. However, he spent most of his life teaching and composing in Croydon, near London, where he died on Sept. 1, 1912. His two children, Hiawatha and Gwendolen, also became professional musicians.

Coleridge-Taylor composed several large choral works, incidental music for plays, and a quantity of vocal and instrumental pieces. He is best known for his trilogy *The Song of Hiawatha*, after Longfellow, for soli, chorus, and orchestra. In much of his music, including *African Suite* for orchestra, *Symphonic Variations on an African Air*, *African Dances* for violin and piano, and *24 Negro Melodies* for piano, he recalled his African heritage.

GILBERT CHASE, *Tulane University*

**COLES,** kōlz, **Edward** (1786–1868), American abolitionist and political leader. He was born in Albemarle county, Va., on Dec. 15, 1786. He was educated at William and Mary College, and served as private secretary to President James Madison from 1809 to 1816. He championed the antislavery cause on moral and humanitarian grounds and corresponded with Jefferson on the subject. In 1819, Coles moved to the free soil of Illinois and there liberated the slaves he had inherited. He was appointed register of the land office at Edwardsville, Ill., and organized the first state agricultural society. He soon became prominent in the antislavery party in Illinois and in 1822 he was elected governor, serving until 1826. While governor, he led the antislavery forces in vigorous opposition to a proposed state constitutional amendment that would have legalized slavery. The proposal was defeated in 1824, thereby preventing the extension of slavery into the Northwest. Coles died in Philadelphia, Pa., on July 7, 1868.

**COLET,** kol'ət, **John** (1466–1519), English educator, clergyman, and humanist, who founded St. Paul's School in London. He was born in London. His father was a wealthy merchant who was twice lord mayor of London. John graduated from Oxford University in 1483 and left England about 1493 to study in France and Italy. While studying law and Greek on the Continent he became acquainted with several eminent humanists, including the French royal librarian Guillaume Budé. Colet became an enthusiastic advocate of the revival of interest in classical learning, and he was particularly interested in new theories of education.

Colet returned to London in 1496 and later took up residence as a lecturer at Oxford and was ordained a priest. In 1504 he was appointed dean of St. Paul's Cathedral.

In establishing St. Paul's School in London in 1510, Colet had an important influence on education in England. The school was endowed for the free education of poor children, and its statutes specified that the Greek and Latin classics be combined with traditional moral and religious training. Erasmus, the Dutch scholar who taught at Cambridge (1509–1514), drew up a Latin phrase book, *Decopia*, for use by students at the school.

Colet advocated church reforms that helped pave the way for the Protestant Reformation. In particular he accused the bishops of self-indulgence and ignorance. Although for a time he was suspected of heresy in some quarters, Colet did not advocate a break with the Roman Catholic Church, and he remained in favor with the Church in Rome.

Colet's writings were not numerous, and many of them remained unpublished until J. H. Lupton produced an edition of his works in the late 19th century. In the lest year of his life he wrote the final statutes for St. Paul's School. He died at Sheen, Surrey, on Sept. 16, 1519.

**COLET,** kô-le′, **Louise Revoil** (1810–1876), French author. She was born in Aix-en-Provence on Sept. 15, 1810. In 1835 she married the composer Hippolyte Colet and went with him to Paris, where in 1836 her first book of verse, *Les fleurs du midi*, was published. Her beauty and passionate nature, rather than the quality of her poetry, soon made her popular, and her salon was frequented by such literary figures as Alfred de Musset, Victor Hugo, Mme. Récamier, Abel Villemain, and Alfred de Vigny.

Mme. Colet became notorious for her love affairs with Victor Cousin and Gustave Flaubert; after her stormy separation from Flaubert she published *Lui* (1859), a scandalous account of their relationship. Her works include plays, among them *La jeunesse de Goethe* (1839); novels and other prose works; and numerous volumes of poetry. Mme. Colet died in Paris on March 8, 1876.

**COLETTE,** kô-let′ (1873–1954), French author, who was known for her uniquely feminine treatment of the emotions. She belongs, in time, to the illustrious generation of writers that includes Marcel Proust, Paul Valéry, André Gide,

COLETTE in her apartment in Paris.

RAPHO GUILLUMETTE—PHOTO BY ROBERT DOISNEAU

and Paul Claudel; but the differences between her writing and theirs are striking and revealing. The major preoccupations of her contemporaries were aesthetics, metaphysics, and morality. But Colette was not an intellectual, and she had no sense of sin; her preoccupations were pleasures, people, and things.

**Life.** Sidonie Gabrielle Claudine Colette was born on Jan. 28, 1873, in the small Burgundian village of St.-Sauveur-en-Puisaye. She spent her childhood and early adolescence in her native province, where her artistic sensibility was nurtured by the earthy wisdom of her mother, "Sido," by the shadowy figure of her one-legged father, Jules Colette, and by the animals, flowers, trees, scents, and sights of the countryside around her.

In 1893, Colette married Henry Gauthier-Villars, a 34-year-old writer. The couple lived in Paris, and Colette became acquainted with the writers, journalists, and members of the *demimonde* among whom she was to spend her early adult years. In this world, at her husband's prompting and with his help, she began to write her spicily fictionalized reminiscences of her school days. These books, published under Gauthier-Villars' pen name, "Willy," include *Claudine à l'école* (1900; Eng. tr., *Claudine at School*, 1930), *Claudine à Paris* (1901; Eng. tr., *Claudine in Paris*, 1931), *Claudine en ménage* (1902; Eng. tr., *The Indulgent Husband*, 1935), and *Claudine s'en va* (1903; Eng. tr., *The Innocent Wife*, 1934).

After divorcing "Willy" in 1906, Colette worked successively as a music-hall dancer, actress, journalist, drama critic, and beautician. But writing had become a habit for her, and she finally devoted all her energies to it. She was married twice again: in 1912 to Henry de Jouvenel, a journalist and diplomat, whom she divorced in 1924, and in 1935 to Maurice Goudeket, a journalist. In 1936 she became a member of the Royal Belgian Academy, and in 1944 Colette was named as the first woman member of the Goncourt Academy. In 1953 she was named a grand officer of the Legion of Honor.

During the last 20 years of her life Colette suffered from a painful and crippling form of arthritis. She died on Aug. 3, 1954, in Paris, where she was accorded a state funeral by the French government.

**Writings.** Colette's life is the subject matter of everything she wrote. All her works—novels, short stories, plays, drama criticism, chronicles, prefaces, personal reminiscences and meditations, and portraits of men, animals, and flowers—are invigorated by her vibrant, sensuous presence. Her voice, whether telling of lovemaking, cooking, gardening, suffering, aging, or dying, speaks with an appropriateness of vocabulary, rhythm, and tone that is nearly infallible.

Colette wrote more than 50 novels and scores of short stories. Her best works include the novels *Chéri* (1920; Eng. tr., 1929), *Le blé en herbe* (1923; Eng. tr., *The Ripening*, 1932), *La fin de Chéri* (1926; Eng. tr., *The Last of Chéri*, 1932), and *Gigi* (1945; Eng. tr., 1952), and the autobiographical reminiscences *La maison de Claudine* (1923; Eng. tr., *My Mother's House*, 1953), *La naissance du jour* (1928; Eng. tr., *A Lesson in Love*, 1932), and *Sido* (1929; Eng. tr., 1953).

ELAINE MARKS
*Author of "Colette"*

**COLEUS,** kō′lē-əs, a genus of annual and perennial plants widely grown as house and garden plants. *Coleus* belongs to the mint family (Labiatae) and is native to Java and tropical Africa, although many species have become naturalized in the American tropics.

Most cultivated coleuses are derivatives of *Coleus blumei* or it variety *verschaffeltii.* These plants range in height from 2 to 3 feet (60 to 90 cm) and have showy, often toothed, leaves in various combinations of red, yellow, and green. Their small flowers are bluish and are borne in terminal spikes.

Coleuses grow well in any normal soil but must be kept at temperatures above 55° F. (13° C) to flourish. They are among the easiest plants to propagate and are rooted by placing tip cuttings in moist soil or sand. To produce compact plants with dense foliage, the end buds of young shoots should be pinched when the shoots are from 4 to 6 inches (10 to 15 cm) long. If coleuses are grown out of doors, they should be moved indoors during the winter and replanted outside in the warm weather. The chief pest of coleus is the mealy bug, which can be controlled by spraying infested plants with the chemical insecticide malathion.

DONALD WYMAN
*The Arnold Arboretum, Harvard University*

PAUL E. GENEREUX

Coleus (*Coleus blumei*)

**COLFAX,** kŏl′faks, **Schuyler** (1823–1885), American public official. He was born on March 23, 1823, in New York City and in 1836 moved with his family to Indiana, where he served in minor political offices and began a career as a journalist. In 1845 he purchased the South Bend *Free Press,* renamed it the *St. Joseph Valley Register,* and turned it into the leading organ of Whig politics in northern Indiana. He was defeated for Congress on the Whig ticket in 1850.

Colfax helped establish the new Republican party and in 1854 was elected to the U.S. House of Representatives. Although his service was not distinguished, he became speaker of the House in 1863 and continued in that capacity until he left the House in 1869. After the Civil War his liberal ideas on Negro suffrage commended him to Radical Republican leaders, who nominated him for vice president in 1868. His candidacy contributed little to the electoral victory of his running mate, Gen. Ulysses S. Grant. The party failed to renominate Colfax in 1872.

His involvement in the Crédit Mobilier of America (q.v.) scandal brought disrepute to Colfax and the party. Apparently he had agreed to accept 20 shares of stock and had received a substantial sum in dividends. His muddled efforts to exonerate himself were not very convincing, but he escaped censure or impeachment because his alleged misconduct had occurred before his election to the vice presidency. Colfax died in Mankato, Minn., on Jan. 13, 1885.

WILLIAM E. DERBY
*State University College, Geneseo, N.Y.*

**COLGATE,** kŏl′gāt, **William** (1783–1857), American manufacturer and philanthropist, who founded what became Colgate-Palmolive Co., a giant of the soap and perfumery industry. He was born in Hollingbourne, England, on Jan. 25, 1783. His family moved to the United States in 1795. After some schooling, William was apprenticed to a New York soapboiler in 1804. Two years later he established a laundry soap factory in New York City. His son Samuel Colgate (1822–1897) joined him in 1838, when the firm of Colgate and Co. was founded. The firm moved to Jersey City in 1847, added toilet soap to its products, and in 1870 set up a perfumery department.

After William Colgate's death in New York on March 25, 1857, the business was greatly expanded by Samuel. By the early 1900's the Jersey City plant occupied two city blocks, had huge boiling vats of 600,000 pounds (about 272,000 kg) capacity each, and employed 800 men. For its perfumery business, it used hundreds of tons of rose leaves and other blossoms, all grown for Colgate in France.

William, his son Samuel, and another son, James B. Colgate (1818–1904), all leading Baptist laymen, were benefactors of religious and educational projects. Their many donations to an academy in Hamilton, N.Y., enabled it to emerge as Colgate University in 1890. James B. Colgate headed an important New York banking house and was president of the Gold Exchange.

COURTNEY ROBERT HALL
*Author, "History of American Industrial Science"*

**COLGATE UNIVERSITY** is a private, nonsectarian, liberal arts institution for men, located in Hamilton, N.Y. It was founded in 1819 as the Hamilton Literary and Theological Institution and renamed Madison University in 1846. The present name was adopted in 1890 to honor the benefactions of the Colgate family, William and his sons Samuel and James. The theological seminary separated from Colgate in 1928.

Part of the study course is directed toward orientation to the world and society. Early phases deal with the natural sciences, philosophy, religion, and fine arts. Upperclassmen concentrate on American institutions and their relation to the world community, with some emphasis on special world areas. Some upperclassmen spend a semester in government study in Washington, D.C. Others share in cooperative studies at Argentine universities. A third group concentrates on economic study at home and abroad. Master's degrees are offered in some subjects notably teaching which is open to women students. Enrollment in the mid 1960's averaged about 1,700.

**COLIC,** kol′ik, is a spasmodic, cramplike pain in the abdomen. Colicky pains tend to build up to a severe pitch of intensity and then rapidly subside, only to recur. They usually result when there is an obstruction within a body tube or passage. In young infants, the causes of colic are generally unknown.

One of the most common types of colic is *biliary colic,* an intense pain in the region of the gall bladder (upper right portion of the abdomen). It is usually caused by a gallstone that has impacted, obstructed, or passed into one of the ducts leading from the gall bladder or liver. Another common type is *renal colic,* which is usually caused by a stone or blood clot in the kidney or in a ureter, one of the tubes leading down from the kidneys into the bladder. This pain characteristically occurs on the side of the abdomen and radiates down the groin. *Intestinal colic,* another fairly common type, is often associated with an obstruction in the intestine or with abnormal contractions or spasms of intestinal muscles.

Sometimes colic may arise from the appendix, especially when there is an obstruction at the mouth of this slender, hollow structure. *Ovarian colic* is often due to a ruptured or twisted cyst, and *tubal colic* is usually due to spasmodic contractions of the oviducts. In some cases, tubal colic results from the implantation of an embryo in an oviduct. Other types of colic may result from certain kinds of metal poisonings.

LOUIS J. VORHAUS, M. D.
*Cornell University Medical College*

**COLIGNY,** kô-lē-nyē′, **Gaspard II de** (1519–1572), French Huguenot noble, who was prominent in the wars of religion in Valois France. He was born at Châtillon-sur-Loing on Feb. 16, 1519. A member of the powerful Châtillon family, he held the title of Count de Coligny. Coligny grew up at the court of Francis I, where he was the companion of the future King Henry II. After Henry was crowned in 1547, he made Coligny lieutenant general, governor of Paris and the Île-de-France, and in 1552 admiral of France. Coligny served the crown heroically against Emperor Charles V and negotiated the Truce of Vaucelles in 1556.

Coligny was captured by the Spaniards at St. Quentin in 1557, and his subsequent imprisonment marks a turning point in his career. His reading of Scripture during this period, and perhaps a prior inclination, brought about his conversion to Calvinism. He deferred his public profession of faith, however, until 1559. That year Henry II was killed in an accident, and France was left with a boy king, Francis II. French Calvinism faced a zealously Catholic party headed by the Duke de Guise, and civil war seemed imminent. For the next 13 years Coligny sought to protect Calvinism while preserving the peace. Unlike many of his peers, the admiral had no feudal ambitions and sought honestly to serve both the monarchy and his faith. But religious antipathies, unchecked by the weak monarchy, made his task impossible.

Francis II was dominated by his Guise advisers, so Coligny's appeals for religious toleration went unheeded. Guise's massacre of Huguenot worshipers at Vassy in 1562 precipitated the first war of religion, in which Coligny reluctantly fought. The Peace of Amboise (March 1563) only temporarily soothed religious passions. The assassination of François de Guise by a Hugue-

not was unjustly blamed on Coligny by Guise's son, who swore vengeance against the admiral.

Coligny withdrew to his estates while Charles IX and the queen mother Catherine de Médicis toured France (1564–1566). But the bad faith of both parties in the religious struggle revived the civil war in 1568, and Coligny fought ably as the lieutenant of the Prince de Condé. When Condé was killed at Jarnac in 1569, Coligny assumed leadership of the Huguenot party. His perseverance in the face of continued defeat finally forced a stalemate. The Peace of St.-Germain (1570) granted the Calvinists freedom of conscience, freedom of worship in two cities of each province, and also four fortified cities.

In September 1571 Coligny was recalled to court. He soon acquired influence over Charles IX, who was uncomfortable under the domination of his mother, Catherine de Médicis. The admiral persuaded Charles to try to unite the nation by supporting the Low Countries in their revolt against Spain. Catherine and the Duke de Guise were opposed to this move since it involved the danger of renewed war with Spain and challenged Catherine's influence over her son. Before the new royal policy could be implemented, Catherine and Guise planned Coligny's assassination. When the assassin succeeded only in wounding him (Aug. 22, 1572), Catherine panicked. Fearing disgrace if her plot were revealed to the admiral, she persuaded her weak son that the Huguenots were planning his, his brother's, and her own death. Charles then authorized the Saint Bartholomew massacre (Aug. 24, 1572). In the massacre Coligny was murdered and his body mutilated by followers of the Duke de Guise.

EDMUND H. DICKERMAN
*University of Connecticut*

**COLIMA,** kō-lē′mä, is a small state in southwestern Mexico, between the Pacific Ocean and the high massif of Colima. Its area is 2,106 square miles (5,455 sq km). Dominating the 70-mile 110-km) coast are Manzanillo Bay (one of the best natural harbors in Mexico) and the Laguna de Cuyutlán. Tropical agriculture, livestock raising, and agricultural industries characterize the economy. Iron ore and salt are also produced. Tourism is increasingly important, especially in the Manzanillo Bay area and along the long sandy beach from Cuyutlán to the Boca de Apiza.

Colima city, the largest urban center and the capital of the state, is located in a tropical valley near the southern foot of the Colima massif, which includes the active volcano of Colima. The city is a market and processing center, and is the home of the state university.

In 1523 the Spaniards conquered the area and founded Colima city, one of the oldest Spanish settlements in Mexico. For several centuries Colima was known mainly for its salt, its groves of coconut palms (Colima was the part of Mexico into which the Spaniards first introduced the coconut), and its volcano and frequent earthquakes, tsunamis, and hurricanes. A railroad from Manzanillo via Colima city to Guadalajara (completed, 1908), a paved highway from the coast to the highlands (built in the 1950s), irrigation of the fertile coastal Tecomán Valley, and elimination of malaria as a killer have helped make Colima one of the leading Mexican states in population percentage growth. Population: of the state, 487,324 (1995 est.); of the city, 106,967 (1990 census).

DONALD D. BRAND, *University of Texas*

**COLITIS,** kō-lī′tis, is an inflammation of the mucous membrane lining the colon, the part of the digestive tract between the small intestine and the anus. There are many types of colitis, all characterized by a change in bowel habits, usually diarrhea. Often they are associated with cramplike pains in the abdomen, and frequently the stools contain mucus, blood, or pus.

**Types.** Some types of colitis, known as *acute colitis,* are of brief duration. They are usually caused by an infection or by a toxic material, as in food poisoning. *Chronic colitis* occasionally results from a chronic infection, but more often it is caused by emotional stresses or strains. In such cases, the symptoms often come and go over the years and are likely to be troublesome when the individual is under stress. In mild forms, the stool is often loose and contains mucus, a condition known as *mucous colitis.* Sometimes, the disorder is associated with considerable cramping, in which case it is known as *spastic colitis.* All these types of colitis are known collectively as *adaptive colitis,* in reference to a possible relationship between the disorder and the patient's adaptation to his environment.

A severe form of chronic colitis is known as *chronic ulcerative colitis,* and it usually starts early in adult life. Its cause is unknown, but many doctors feel that it, too, is related to emotional problems. In chronic ulcerative colitis the diarrhea is more severe, and the feces often contain blood. The mucous membrane lining the colon becomes eroded by small ulcers that often become infected. Occasionally, the colon wall becomes so thin that it perforates, and sometimes the patient may hemorrhage.

**Treatment.** The treatment of colitis depends on its cause. If it is due to an infection, it often clears up spontaneously in a matter of a few days. If the infection lingers, an antimicrobial or antibiotic drug may eradicate the causative organism. In forms of colitis related primarily to emotional stress, symptomatic treatment along with psychotherapy are often effective. In chronic ulcerative colitis, particularly in more severe cases, treatment with adrenal steroids may be necessary. Sometimes, however, the patient gets worse despite all treatment. In such cases the colon must be removed.

Louis J. Vorhaus, M. D.
*Cornell University Medical College*

**COLLAGE,** kə-läzh′, a work of art made by composing fragments of paper, cloth, cardboard, newspaper and magazine clippings, photographs, illustrations, and other printed material, and pasting them to a flat surface. "Collage," the French word for pasting, sticking, or gluing, is applied to the method as well as to the work produced. Often regarded as a subcategory of assemblage (q.v.), collage has been widely practiced by 20th century artists, both as an independent medium and in conjunction with drawing and painting. Among the variations of the collage technique are *décollage,* compositions made by tearing away papers already pasted, and *découpage,* cleanly cut collages made of new materials.

**Early Collage.** Although pasting had been a common technique used in decorative and folk art for centuries, its adoption by modern artists began with Picasso's *Still Life with Chair Caning* (1912), an oil painting to which the artist added a fragment of oilcloth printed to simulate chair caning. Later in 1912, Braque incorporated

COLLECTION WASHINGTON UNIVERSITY, ST. LOUIS, MO.
COLLAGE, *Bottle of Suze by Picasso (1912–1913)*

in his charcoal drawing *The Fruit Dish* three rectangular pieces of wood-grain paper. This was the first *papier collé* ("pasted paper"), a term that refers specifically to the paper collages made by the French cubist painters in 1912–1914.

In the development and aesthetics of 20th century art, collage was much more than a substitute for drawing and painting. It made possible sharp, unexpected, and often disquieting juxtapositions of forms, materials, images, words, and phrases. Picasso, Braque, Gris, and other cubists introduced a new kind of realism into their works by inserting lettering, news clippings, labels, calling cards, and even bits of mirror and other materials. Picasso went further to make three-dimensional assemblages.

**Later Developments.** For the futurists, among them Umberto Boccioni and Carlo Carrà, collage served to represent the strident confrontation of forces in the modern world. Dadaists such as Hannah Höch and Raoul Haussmann used collage and photomontage (collage of cut or torn photographs) for shocking effects of discontinuity. For the surrealists, collage symbolized nonrational and "convulsive" juxtapositions drawn from the unconscious. Max Ernst created complex Dada and surrealist compositions from old engravings and prints. Kurt Schwitters, following Picasso, expanded collage into assemblage and large architectural environments incorporating a great variety of materials and objects.

American artists who have done collage include Joseph Stella, Arthur Dove, Man Ray, Joseph Cornell, Robert Motherwell, Landès Lewitin, Willem de Kooning, Anne Ryan, Conrad Marca-Relli, Robert Nickle, William Getman, Leo Manso, Esteban Vicente, Robert Goodnough, Robert Rauschenberg, Larry Rivers, Bruce Conner, James Dine, and Saul Steinberg.

William Seitz
*Author of "The Art of Assemblage"*

**COLLAGEN.** See Connective Tissue.

**COLLAGEN DISEASES,** kol'ə-jən, are disorders marked by significant changes in the cellular structure and ground substance of the body's connective tissue. The disorders usually included in this group are rheumatic fever, rheumatoid arthritis, systemic lupus erythematosus, scleroderma, dermatomyositis, polyarteritis, and thrombotic thrombocytopenic purpura. The two most common of these disorders, rheumatoid arthritis and rheumatic fever, are discussed separately in the articles ARTHRITIS and RHEUMATIC FEVER. This article deals mainly with the disorder known as systemic lupus erythematosus but also includes brief descriptions of some other, rarer, collagen diseases.

**Systemic Lupus Erythematosus.** This disorder, commonly known as SLE, is probably as common as rheumatic fever but often remains undiagnosed. It is related to rheumatoid arthritis and to a skin disease, discoid lupus erythematosus. About 10% of the patients with the latter two diseases may eventually develop SLE.

The number of diagnosed cases of SLE has greatly increased during the past 20 years owing to the discovery of blood tests that confirm the diagnosis early in the course of the disease. Although the symptoms of SLE may be quite varied, the disease most often begins as a form of arthritis or with the appearance of skin eruptions on areas exposed to the light. At some time, over 90% of all patients have polyarthritis (inflammation in many joints), 80% have fever, 70% have various types of skin changes, 60% have lymph node enlargement, 55% have anemia, 50% have disorders of the stomach and intestinal tract, 45% have pleurisy, and 40% have a low white blood cell count. About half of all SLE patients have abnormalities in their blood proteins and suffer muscle aches and kidney damage. The course of the disease is characterized by periods of spontaneous remission contrasted with frequent flare-ups. Infections and exposure to sunlight may worsen it.

The treatment of SLE is quite similar to that of rheumatoid arthritis, particularly in the milder forms in which joint pains are the major manifestation. The vast majority of patients respond well to treatment. Skin lesions may be controlled by the use of creams and ointments containing cortisone derivatives; antimalarial drugs, such as quinacrine (Atabrine), chloroquine, and hydroxychloroquine, are useful for more extensive lesions. The most serious complication of SLE and the major cause of death is progressive kidney involvement. Patients with this form of the disease usually respond initially to cortisone and other anti-inflammatory steroids. If they become resistant to this treatment, certain immunity-blocking agents, such as nitrogen mustard, are of value.

**Other Collagen Diseases.** *Dermatomyositis* is a rare disorder with extensive skin and muscle damage and symptoms resembling SLE. *Polyarteritis* is an inflammation of the small and medium-sized arteries that causes damage to organs because of impaired circulation. *Scleroderma* is due to an excessive growth of connective tissue, producing localized or generalized thickening of the skin and often involving the internal organs. *Thrombotic thrombocytopenic purpura* is a very rare disorder in which there is a clotting of the blood platelets in the small capillaries.

EDMUND L. DUBOIS, M.D.
*Collagen Clinic, Los Angeles General Hospital*

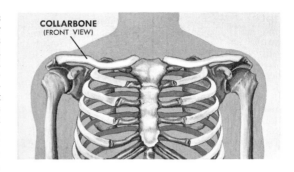

COLLARBONE
(FRONT VIEW)

**COLLARBONE,** one of the major bones that form the shoulder girdle of a vertebrate, or backboned, animal. The collarbone, also known as the *clavicle,* is generally a long narrow bone. In humans it lies above the first rib on either side of the neck and resembles an elongated letter S lying on its side. In birds the two collarbones are fused together, forming the structure commonly known as the *wishbone.*

**COLLARD.** See KALE.

**COLLARED LIZARD,** kol'ərd liz'ərd, a common lizard of rocky country and gullies of the plains of northern Mexico and southwestern United States. From 8 to 12 inches (20–30 cm) in overall length, the collared lizard has a robust body, a large head, large limbs, a long tail, and a conspicuous black and white collar across its shoulders. A variegated pattern of spots and bars tends to fade with age. It is brighter in males, but during the breeding season, females develop spots and bars of orange on their sides.

A diurnal species, the collared lizard is swift and pugnacious. It usually feeds on insects, but it may also eat other small lizards and invertebrates and even some plants. It attains sexual maturity in about a year. The female may lay up to 24 eggs at a time, but usually about 8.

The collared lizard, *Crotaphytus collaris,* belongs to the family Iguanidae. It is closely related to the leopard lizard (*C. wislizeni*).

CLIFFORD H. POPE
*Author of "The Reptile "World"*

**COLLECT,** kol'ekt, a short form of prayer used in Western Christian liturgy. It originated in the custom, probably begun in Gaul, of collecting the petitions of a congregation into one prayer. The collect was used in Gregorian, Gelasian, and Leonine Roman sacramentaries as early as the 6th century. In the Roman sacramentaries, collects were said before the Epistle, after the offertory and after the Communion.

The collect developed a specific structure and includes an invocation to God (for example, "Almightly God"); a reason for the petition ("unto whom all hearts are open, all desires known, and from whom no secrets are hid"); a petition ("Cleanse the thoughts of our hearts by the inspiration of Thy Holy Spirit"); a desired benefit ("that we may perfectly love Thee, and worthily magnify Thy holy name"); and an ascription of glory to the Trinity or a pleading of the merits of Christ ("through Christ our Lord. Amen."). Most English collects have been translated from earlier prayers.

JAMES H. SMYLIE
*Union Theological Seminary, Richmond, Va.*

**COLLECTIVE BARGAINING,** kə-lek'tiv bär'gən-ing, between employers and unions establishes formal rules governing work and conditions of employment. The term applies to negotiations about wages, hours, conditions of work, and fringe benefits, and to the processes by which agreements on these matters are maintained.

In the United States collective bargaining is inseparable from trade unionism. From its inception the trade union movement in the United States has sought recognition from employers so that unions might enjoy the right of representation and might negotiate an enforceable contract, the culminating point in collective bargaining.

In many countries, however, the forms of collective bargaining have undergone considerable change since the Industrial Revolution. For example, in the early days of industrialism in Britain, questions on specific issues were often adjudicated through bargaining between an employer and an employees' committee set up for the occasion. Later, however, the trade union provided the machinery for a collective bargaining procedure that was continuous rather than casual.

**Patterns Around the World.** Collective bargaining in a given country is shaped by special factors. Because legal, economic, political, and cultural restraints vary from one country to another, each country develops its own particular forms of collective bargaining.

In Britain, trade unions developed freely only after repeal of the Combination Acts in 1824. Nevertheless, it was not until 1871 that unions could utilize so-called coercive weapons, such as a threat to strike, without fear of conspiracy charges. In certain industries, employers took the initiative in introducing such instrumentalities as local boards of conciliation to reduce tension over wage fixing and to eliminate unions as bargaining agents. Nevertheless collective bargaining continued to develop in Britain mainly on a voluntary basis. State intervention did occur in both World Wars I and II, when compulsory arbitration was temporarily enforced. Wage councils are also used to establish wages in those industries that are not well organized. The decisions of the wage councils are enforceable by the minister of labour.

In Scandinavia, collective bargaining is more centralized than in the United States. Negotiations in Sweden, for example, take place between the employers' association and the central trade union organization and then filter down to local bodies. Matters of interpretation are referred to a labor court, established in 1938.

In France, government intervention is more extensive. Work conditions are governed by statute, and a national minimum wage may be set by the government.

In African countries, collective bargaining may be found in the oil extraction industry, in mining establishments, on plantations, and among government employees. Although major employers in Africa have not always recognized unions as bargaining agents, management has moved cautiously toward negotiation as a way of reaching settlements.

In Japan, trade unions have resorted to political pressures. Much reliance is placed on legislative action plus an annual ritual of "struggles" to achieve wage gains.

**Participants and Scope.** In the United States the chief participants in the collective bargaining system are the employers (represented by managers); unions and their representatives; government officials; and, on occasion, private individuals, such as mediators and arbitrators. Under collective bargaining in the United States the roles played by participants in governing wages, hours, and working conditions are explicit and are usually written into a labor-management agreement. Such a document specifies union security and management rights—questions that revolve about the determination of representation and authority.

Central to the agreement is a specification of wages, production standards, and contingent (fringe) benefits. In addition, the agreement spells out grievance machinery, including arbitration procedures. The "bargains" arrived at through negotiations may apply at the level of individual firms, at regional and industrial levels, or at national levels. In a sense, the agreement delineates the ground rules in a geographic and industrial framework.

Prior to the New Deal of President Franklin D. Roosevelt, collective bargaining relationships functioned within a framework of common law and local ordinances. Employers generally did not bargain with unions unless compelled to do so by the union's economic strength. The National Labor Relations Act of 1935—known as the Wagner Act—substantially altered the legal environment of collective bargaining. The Wagner Act protected the worker's right to join a union of his own choice (blacklisting of workers for union membership had been a common practice). It provided election machinery to determine the representative union. It compelled the employer to recognize and bargain with the union selected by the employees. Certain devices that had been utilized to coerce workers were declared unfair labor practices. Although some matters were referred to the National Labor Relations Board (established by the act), it was clear that the scope of bargaining extended beyond wages, hours, and conditions of employment to the whole range of contingent benefits, such as health and welfare programs, retirement, merit ratings, and the like.

The Taft-Hartley Act of 1947 and the Landrum-Griffin Act of 1959 altered somewhat the relationships established between labor and management by the Wagner Act, but basically there was not much change in specifying the scope of collective bargaining. The effect of Taft-Hartley and Landrum-Griffin has been to make more explicit the conditions under which the federal government may inject itself into the collective bargaining process. Thus, whenever a strike affecting the national interest is threatened, the federal government may impose a cooling-off period. Picketing and secondary boycotts were subjected to further statutory limitations, although in many instances specific determinations still had to be made by the NLRB.

**Procedures and Strategy.** Some writers have described collective bargaining negotiations before a new contract as a "ritual," implying that somehow the results are predetermined and need only be verified across the bargaining table. This appears to be a simplistic view of the process, for collective bargaining has many more attributes of diplomacy in action than the term "ritual" would suggest.

The common practice on the union side has been to establish a negotiating committee composed of union officers and rank and file members. If the negotiations are conducted through a local union, a representative of the international union often will be present. Frequently, the international representative, as the union's "professional," will have consulted with the committee well in advance of the negotiations.

For the employers, especially if they are large firms, labor relations specialists or personnel directors often are designated representatives. There may be variations in the composition of the employer side that result in a limited delegation of authority: this condition often develops in multi-employer or employer association bargaining.

Because the union committee must function with provisional authority, it will generally feed back information to its constituency. Initially the union formulates demands to reflect what the members are requesting, assembles data regarding these demands, and publicizes them. Demands may be based on the union's perception of the needs of employees as well as on an attempt to duplicate what some other union may have achieved. The latter has a tendency to create a pattern of bargaining within an industry and even across industry lines. For example, in the late 1950's supplementary unemployment insurance programs spread from the auto workers to the steelworkers. The initial demands obviously tend to represent an estimation of the higher limit of the bargaining situation.

Most companies also actively prepare for negotiations. A purely defensive strategy tends to be negative and may lead to seemingly irreconcilable differences between the parties. The company may want to define the area of bargaining, excluding from negotiations what it calls management prerogatives, such as production and sales policies.

The negotiations customarily take place privately in order to maintain an atmosphere of freedom from external pressure. Seated on opposite sides of a bargaining table, management and labor engage in the sort of strategy that appears to them most effective under the circumstances. A company may adopt a position of resistance or it may assume a more flexible bargaining posture. In some instances, a company has insisted that its first offer is its final offer, but the NLRB declared this strategy to be an "unfair labor practice."

Union negotiators use a number of factors in evaluating their demands. These include improvements in productivity, ability to pay, effects of a wage increase on purchasing power, and wages and fringe benefits paid elsewhere. Productivity increases pose difficult technical issues revolving about measurements. Unions argue that employees are entitled to share in productivity gains. The ability-to-pay issue relates to a company's financial capacity and implies a comparison of profit trends with wage trends. In periods of rising prices, unions point to changes in purchasing power as a relevant factor.

Management, on the other hand, contends that wage increases contribute to further price increases, and implies that price stability is the desirable course. Or the company may insist that gains in productivity stem from improvements in capital equipment and overall production rather than from labor effort. Frequently, the company insists that it cannot afford to pay higher wages, but this contention, under NLRB rules, has to be substantiated by relevant data.

**Strikes and Lockouts.** Should an impasse develop, the union's final recourse may be a refusal to work—that is, a strike. Negotiations may cease, perhaps to be resumed under pressure from the government and with the participation of a conciliator. The decision to strike is seldom taken without serious consideration, because heavy costs and risks are involved. To add to its arsenal of bargaining weapons during negotiations, a union frequently will poll its membership on whether to strike or not. Should a strike develop, the objective is to deprive the company of production and force it to come to terms. Such action involves picketing, a form of union activity that has been increasingly limited by government regulations. The restrictions, for instance, include limits on the number of pickets. The ability to maintain a strike depends largely on the union's resources and its ability to extend financial aid to its striking members.

Employers have similar weapons, such as the lockout—simply shutting down the plant. Or in some cases employers may attempt to generate a back-to-work movement among union members to break the strike. Some writers have described these aspects of collective bargaining in military terms: "negotiations," "strikes," and "agreements" appear to have their parallels in "diplomacy," "war," and "treaties." However, in view of the fact that in the United States lost time due to strikes has been about ½ of 1% of all time worked in the average year, it appears that collective bargaining is a relatively peaceable arena.

Some strikes have a great impact on matters of public concern. In an interdependent economy, for example, the transportation of food from farmers and processors to central markets is of crucial importance. Nevertheless, not all strikes manifest such effects, and a distinction needs to be made between "public interest" and "public inconvenience." Some writers contend that strikes in such areas as the newspaper field may create only a public inconvenience, because there are alternative sources of information.

**Size of Bargaining Units.** In the United States collective bargaining functions through "bargaining units," which may be single-employer or multiemployer in structure. A Bureau of Labor Statistics study in 1956, based on more than 1,700 agreements covering units of 1,000 or more employees, revealed that 68% of the agreements, covering 57% of the workers, were of the single-employer type. Only a third of the agreements covered multiemployer units. In manufacturing, the percentages for single-employer units are even higher: about 80% of all agreements, covering 82% of the workers, were with single-employer bargaining units.

An analysis of bargaining units by size, made by Neil Chamberlain for the year 1953, showed that the single-employer unit was generally small. Usually a unit consisted of fewer than 500 employees. On the other hand, larger units, both of the single-employer and multiemployer type, although small in number, included the larger part of the work force. Thus units of 10,000 or more employees made up 1.4% of all employer units but covered 30.4% of all employees.

Just as employer bargaining units include many small companies and a few large ones, so a similar variation exists on the union side. About 25% of the unions in the United States have fewer than 5,000 members. Only three unions—the United Auto Workers, the Steelworkers, and the

Teamsters—have more than 1 million members.

**Coordinate Bargaining.** A development in collective bargaining in the 1960's has been described as "coordinate bargaining." The term stems from the electrical equipment manufacturing industry, where 11 AFL-CIO unions negotiated jointly with the General Electric and Westinghouse companies. At G. E., for instance, bargaining had been conducted individually with some 90 unions, mainly on a local basis with local managements. The unions contended that this was a policy of "divide and rule," and that they were weakened further when the policy was coupled with staggered expiration dates for the various contracts. Beginning in 1965, the 11 unions agreed on national bargaining goals and planned a coordinated bargaining strategy. Protracted negotiations, involving proceedings before the NLRB and in the courts, led in 1966 to contracts at both firms that created a broader form of collective bargaining.

**The Contract and Its Enforcement.** Some writers prefer to call a collective bargaining contract an "agreement," on the ground that an employer does not contract for labor with the union but with employees. The distinction is pedantic, for the essentials of a collective bargaining agreement are those found in the law of contracts. There must be a meeting of minds, acceptance of an offer, and a definite agreement on terms. In addition the subjects covered must be such that the contract does not violate the law. A collective bargaining contract is enforceable in the courts and need not be reduced to writing to be enforceable. The terms "agreement" and "contract" appear to be interchangeable.

Generally the terms of a collective bargaining agreement are written. The agreement spells out the following: the bargaining unit (that is, the job or job categories to which the contract applies); the form of recognition (usually exclusive bargaining rights); duration of contract and date of renewal; labor grades and pay rate ranges; pay steps within grade; crew sizes and work rules; premium pay (overtime and shift differentials); contingent, or fringe, benefits, such as pensions, severance pay, and health and welfare plans; and coffee breaks, holidays, and vacations. Unions also have paid particular attention to seniority clauses and grievance and arbitration procedures.

Unions seek to "police" the contract during its life. For this purpose local union members may elect a shop steward, who derives his authority from the contract. Normally, arrangements are made to allow stewards to leave their work to confer with management and affected employees.

Collective bargaining in the United States operates within a statutory framework embodied in the Taft-Hartley Act and the Landrum-Griffin Act, successors to the Wagner Act. However, many complexities of the law are so interpreted by the NLRB that its decisions do have the effect of law. In Britain, however, the common law, as modified by Parliament, provides the legal background. It is essentially pragmatic and based on notions of fair play. In western Europe, many rules governing collective bargaining stem from the Napoleonic code, which tends to inhibit in that region the sort of relationships that exist in Britain and the United States. Consequently, unions in France, West Germany, and Italy have stressed political activity as a means of attaining their objectives.

BEN B. SELIGMAN, *University of Massachusetts*

**COLLECTIVE SECURITY,** in international relations, is the commitment of a group of states to maintain the security of each member by cooperating in measures to prevent or frustrate aggression against any of them by another member of the group. It implies acceptance by all members of rules of international law defining and prohibiting aggression and of the procedures for applying them. The Rio (1947), NATO (1949), and Warsaw (1955) pacts are collective security agreements in so far as each signatory pledges that it will take measures to prevent aggression within the group. Their primary purpose, however, is not collective security, but collective defense of each against attack by an outside state.

**How Collective Security Works.** A collective security system implies legal rules and procedures to maintain the security of all. By establishing commitments of law and procedure before aggression occurs, it seeks to make the system preventive and not merely remedial. It assumes that common action will be taken against any member of the group that is found to have committed an act of aggression within the group as defined by the law and procedure that all have accepted. The system differs from a balance of power in that it rests on interpretation of law rather than on calculation of power. It differs from world government because there is no central authority with material power capable of preventing a member state from violating international law. Collective security implies that physical power in the group is divided among the member states. The assurance of their cooperation in an emergency depends, like most rules of international law, upon their sense of obligation to observe the law that they have all accepted in the common interest.

**History.** There were elements of collective security in the commitments of the great powers, after the Napoleonic wars, to maintain the "public law of Europe" as set forth in the Treaty of Vienna (1815). Treaties among the great powers guaranteed the neutralization of Switzerland in 1815, of Belgium in 1839, and of Luxembourg in 1867. The concept was set forth more precisely and comprehensively in the League of Nations Covenant in 1920, supplemented by the Kellogg-Briand Pact in 1928–1929. They were amplified by the United Nations Charter in 1945. By these instruments the member states agree to settle their disputes peacefully and to respect the territorial integrity, political independence, and jurisdiction of each state. The use of force is forbidden in international relations except in individual or collective self-defense or under the authority or with the consent of the United Nations. Each state agrees to act through the organization to bring about a cease-fire if hostilities occur and to cooperate in measures to determine the aggressor and to frustrate his action if the cease-fire is not successful.

**Failure of Collective Security.** Although the system of collective security has operated successfully on a number of occasions, it failed during the League period to prevent aggression in Manchuria and Ethopia, and it failed to prevent World War II. During the United Nations period it brought about peace in Indonesia, but its operation in Korea resulted in serious hostilities and it was unable to prevent aggression in Hungary, the Middle East, and Vietnam. These failures of collective security were due to a number of circumstances. Some important states never became members of the League of Nations or the United Nations, and member states sometimes failed to carry out their collective security obligations. States often relied for security on collective defense arrangements that were not controlled by the collective security system.

Since the end of World War II civil and colonial strife have tended to escalate into international hostilities. While individual states are forbidden to intervene in civil strife, the United Nations may do so if, as in the Congo in 1961, it finds that the situation threatens international peace. The frequency of civil strife since the end of World War II, the disposition of states to intervene in it, and the difficulty of effective UN action in such situations have been serious obstacles to the effective operation of collective security.

QUINCY WRIGHT
*Professor Emeritus of International Law*
*University of Chicago*

**COLLECTIVISM** is a plan of social or political organization in which the means of production and distribution belong to the people collectively. Ownership is vested in a group, most often the state. The term is also applied to the theory that society should be so organized. For examinations of varying forms of collectivism, see COMMUNISM, FASCISM, and SOCIALISM. For discussion of a contrasting system in which capital and the means of production are privately owned and used, see CAPITALISM.

**COLLECTOR.** See TRANSISTOR.

**COLLEGE** is a general term used to designate several kinds of educational institutions above the high school level. In the United States, the terms "college" and "university" are frequently used interchangeably, as in references to college entrance requirement, or college football. There are, however, several specific meanings of the term "college." One important type of college is an institution that forms a major division of a university, granting undergraduate or graduate degrees, or both, in a particular field. A second type is the independent 4-year institution that grants bachelor's degrees in liberal arts or science or both. A third type is the technical or professional college offering bachelor's or master's degrees. Teachers colleges are examples of the professional classification. Junior or community colleges, offering associate degrees, constitute a fourth category.

In England, as in the United States, the term "college" may mean a division of a university. Oxford and Cambridge universities, for example, are composed of an affiliation of independent corporate colleges furnishing undergraduate and graduate study. Some secondary schools in England are called colleges. In France, the term "collège" always refers to a secondary school. Canadian colleges correspond generally to those in the United States, with the exception of the *collège classique*, which is a secondary school.

See also COLLEGE, LAND-GRANT; COLLEGES AND UNIVERSITIES; JUNIOR AND COMMUNITY COLLEGES.

**COLLÈGE CLASSIQUE,** kô-lej' klå-sēk', or *classical college*, a kind of private secondary school in Quebec, Canada, for French-speaking students.

These schools are financially supported by the provincial government and controlled for the most part by the Catholic Church, though voluntarily affiliated with Laval University, the University of Montreal, and the University of Sherbrooke. Two of the colleges were founded in the 17th and 18th centuries. Sixteen more were started in the 19th century, and more than 70 have been opened since 1900.

In the late 1960's there were 94 classical colleges attended by approximately 52,000 pupils, of whom about 85% were boys. The average age of admission for both boys and girls is 12. The course of study is eight years long. The first five years, equivalent to a secondary school education, end with matriculation examinations. The last three years are at the college level and end with baccalaureate examinations. The curriculum comprises classical studies, religion, rhetoric, philosophy, and science. This classical training is a prerequisite for entrance to almost all professional courses that are offered in the parent universities.

**COLLEGE ENTRANCE REQUIREMENTS.** See COLLEGES AND UNIVERSITIES—8. *Admissions Requirements.*

**COLLEGE OF CARDINALS, SACRED,** the senate or advisory arm of the pope of the Roman Catholic Church. Its most important function is to elect the pope. See CARDINAL; CATHOLIC CHURCH, ROMAN—4. *Organization.*

**COLLEGE PARK,** a city in west-central Georgia, in Clayton and Fulton counties, about 8 miles (13 km) southwest of Atlanta. It is a residential suburb of Atlanta. The Georgia Military Academy is located there. The community was incorporated as Manchester in 1891 and was renamed College Park in 1895.

The city has a council-manager form of government. Population: 20,382.

**COLLEGE PARK,** a city in south central Maryland, in Prince Georges county, 7 miles (11 km) northeast of Washington, D.C., of which it is a residential suburb. The city is the administrative seat and the site of the main campus of the University of Maryland.

It was originally the site of the Maryland Agricultural College, chartered in 1856 which was consolidated with the University of Maryland in Baltimore in 1920. The campus at College Park includes the university's administrative division, as well as its colleges of agriculture, education, engineering, arts and sciences, business and public administration, home economics, and physical education, and the Glenn L. Martin Institute of Technology.

College Park was incorporated in 1945. It has a council-manager form of government. Population: 24,657.

**COLLEGE STATION,** a city in east-central Texas, in Brazos county, adjoining the city of Bryan on the northwest, situated 84 miles (135 km) northwest of Houston. It is the seat of Texas A&M University, founded in 1871. The university was originally known as the Agricultural and Mechanical College of Texas.

College Station was incorporated in 1938. It has a city manager form of government. Population: 67,890.

**COLLEGES, Land-Grant.** The land-grant colleges are U.S. institutions of higher education established under the provisions of the Morrill Act of 1862 or financed to some extent by this and related federal laws. This legislation granted to each state 30,000 acres of federal land for each congressman from the state. The land was to be sold to provide an "endowment" for "at least one college where the leading object shall be, without excluding other scientific and classical studies and including military tactics, to teach such branches of learning as are related to agriculture and the mechanic arts . . . in order to promote the liberal and practical education of the industrial classes in the several pursuits and professions in life."

The climate within which the legislation was passed was conditioned by the growth, during the first half of the 19th century, of effective democracy, the influence of the middle class, industry, and commerce, and an increasing awareness of the importance of science and technology. These forces led to a significant protest against a system of higher education inherited from England that aimed almost solely at preparing well-to-do young men for careers as ministers, lawyers, teachers, and civil officers.

Important among those protesting was Jonathan Baldwin Turner, a New England farmer's son, who settled in Illinois as a college teacher and farmer after his graduation from Yale. From 1859 he vigorously advocated the establishment of universities for the "industrial classes" and detailed a blueprint for such institutions.

**The First Morrill Act.** A bill to provide federal aid in the form of 20,000 acres of public lands to encourage the establishment of such institutions was introduced into the U.S. Congress by Representative Justin Smith Morrill of Vermont in 1857. Passed by the House (1858) and the Senate (1859) by narrow margins, the bill was vetoed by President James Buchanan, chiefly on the grounds of cost and constitutionality. It was reintroduced by Morrill in 1861, with a larger acreage allotment and the addition of military science and tactics to the previously proposed agricultural and mechanical arts curriculum requirements. This second bill passed both houses by large margins and was signed into law by President Abraham Lincoln on July 2, 1862.

Within a year of its passage, nine states had established colleges under the act, largely by assigning land-grant functions to existing institutions. These pioneering institutions included Iowa State, Kansas State, Michigan State, Rutgers (N.J.), and Pennsylvania State universities and the universities of Vermont, Minnesota, Missouri, and Wisconsin. By 1929, 20 states and territories had established colleges of agriculture and mechanic arts, and 31 others had assigned the functions to state or other institutions. Two states allotted federal funds to private institutions—New York to Cornell and Massachusetts to Massachusetts Institute of Technology. Following the passage of the Second Morrill Act in 1890, 17 agricultural and mechanical colleges for blacks (one of which has since voluntarily relinquished its land-grant status) were established in the Southern states.

**The Second Morrill Act.** This act authorized continuing federal appropriations for the support of land-grant institutions. The framework for federal-state cooperation in establishing and operating these institutions was broadened with the passage, in 1887, of the Hatch Act, which provided federal aid for agricultural experiment stations at land-grant institutions. It was rounded out in 1914 by the Smith-Lever Act, which established the Cooperative Extension Service in agriculture and home economics at these institutions in association with the U.S. Dept. of Agriculture. Over the years annual federal appropriations have grown.

**Growth of Land-Grant Institutions.** The new institutions developed slowly over the latter half of the 19th century. During this time they pioneered in a break with classical traditions. Beginning about 1900 land-grant institutions developed rapidly, partly as a result of direct federal support through the Second Morrill Act and an increasing acceptance by the states of their obligation to support such institutions. The programs were broadened and extended, with many agricultural and mechanical institutions developing into comprehensive state universities.

Often cited as the United States' single greatest contribution to higher education, the land-grant institutions, together with the state universities, pioneered important innovations in American higher education. These include the establishment of such concepts as public higher education at low cost; research as a legitimate function of higher education; public service and continuing education; and the elevation of the "useful" arts, sciences, and professions to academic respectability.

**Recent Progress.** Since World War II the land-grant institutions have taken the lead among American institutions in international cooperative programs, especially in agricultural and university development in the emerging nations. Through their international, research, and extension programs in agriculture, land-grant institutions have also been significantly responsible for the development in the United States of the world's highest agricultural productivity. In 1953 the National Manpower Council concluded that "the most important single governmental step in connection with the training of scientific and professional personnel was the Morrill Act of 1862, which laid the basis for the country's extensive state college and university system."

In 1887 representatives of land-grant institutions formed the Association of American Agricultural Colleges—the first association for institutions of higher education in the United States. Together with the National Association of State Universities (formed in 1895), it has played a leading role in higher education and was one of the founders of the American Council on Education in 1918. The two associations were merged in 1963 to form the National Association of State Universities and Land-Grant Colleges, which represents state universities and all of the land-grant institutions.

CHRISTIAN K. ARNOLD
*National Association of State Universities and Land-Grant Colleges*

**Bibliography**

Anderson, Lester G., *Land-Grant Universities and Their Continuing Challenge* (Mich. State Univ. Press 1976).
Geiger, Louis G., *Higher Education in a Maturing Democracy* (1963; reprint, Greenwood Press 1977).
Nevins, Allan, *The State Universities and Democracy* (1962; reprint, Greenwood Press 1977).
Ohles, John F., and Ohles, Shirley M., *Public Colleges and Universities* (Greenwood Press 1986).
Parker, William B., *Life and Public Services of Justin Smith Morrill* (1924; reprint, Da Capo 1971).
Ross, Earle D., *Democracy College* (1942; reprint, Ayer 1969).

# COLLEGES AND UNIVERSITIES

## CONTENTS

**COLLEGES AND UNIVERSITIES.** Since the Middle Ages, universities have been valued and respected as centers for intellectual life. They have provided places for scholars to work for the advancement of the arts, letters, and sciences. Traditionally, society has valued scholarly contributions whether or not they had direct practical applications. At the same time, universities have performed the more immediately useful service of training leaders for the professions and for public life. As society has become more complex, the value of higher education has become more evident.

Conditions that make higher education essential to society also make it essential to the individual. Society needs professional men and women in increasing numbers. Anyone who wants to become a microbiologist, engineer, physicist, teacher, lawyer, or librarian, for example, must have training in college and often in graduate school.

Moreover, even less specialized careers call for education beyond high school. A college degree is replacing a high school diploma as a ticket of entry for hundreds of occupations. For example, office jobs eliminated by computers have often been clerical, but new jobs created by computers are for the better educated. This trend reflects the declining importance of unskilled labor in the economy and the movement toward professionalism in the middle and upper levels of business and industry.

Beyond the practical matters of jobs and income, college is important for personal development. It offers opportunities for enriching patterns of thought, for developing taste in art, literature, and music, for expanding the uses of leisure, and for finding social and political guidelines. College is a time for accelerated growth of the mind and spirit, a stirring of new powers, a choice of directions. When college opens up new opportunities for individuals, it also benefits the society in which these individuals live.

### 1. The Establishment of Schools for Higher Education

The intellectual traditions of higher education can be traced back to the schools of ancient Athens, Rome, and Alexandria. The history of the modern university, however, begins with medieval centers of learning. In the 12th and 13th centuries a number of European universities

Students wearing robes and mortarboard caps participate in commencement exercises at Cornell University.

grew up to meet demands for instruction in law, theology, and medicine. Some of these are still among the world's greatest centers of learning. The University of Bologna, which developed from the intellectual guilds, specialized in law. The University of Paris, growing out of a complex of guildlike corporations formed by teachers, gained eminence in theology. Migrations of students led to the founding of universities at Oxford and Cambridge in England.

Universities founded later, and still well known, include the German Universities of Halle, founded in 1694, and Göttingen, founded in 1737 and renowned for the study of mathematics; and Scotland's University of Edinburgh, founded in 1583 and noted for its teaching of medicine.

Graduates of English universities founded the first colleges in the North American colonies. Other scholars carried the traditions of European higher education, particularly of the German and Scottish universities, to the New World.

**Colonial America.** The founders of Harvard College, the first institution of higher education in what is now the United States, had as their major concerns the advancement of learning and the training of clergymen. These concerns continued to be the dominant purposes of higher education throughout the colonial period. Except for the College of Philadelphia (now the University of Pennsylvania), all of the colonial colleges were founded and supported by religious groups, were staffed and led mainly by the clergy, and had as one principal function the training of ministers. Even the College of Philadelphia, with no sectarian requirement for membership on the board of trustees, had unofficial ties with the Church of England. Its provost was an Anglican clergyman, and three fourths of its board were of that denomination.

The process of establishing institutions of higher education in America was sporadic and slow. After the founding of Harvard in 1636, there followed a period of about 60 years in which no new institutions were established. Around the turn of the 17th century, first William and Mary and then Yale came into being, but then another 45 years passed with no additions. In contrast, during the next 23 years (1746–1769), six new colleges were founded—twice the number established in the previous 110 years. Four were in New England, one in the Middle Atlantic States, and one in the South.

The American colleges took for their pattern the English college, not the university, and remained small. In 1775 the graduating class at Harvard numbered 40; at Yale, 35; at Columbia (then King's College), 13; at Dartmouth, 11; and at Pennsylvania, 8.

Recent historians have attempted to correct the misconception that America's early colleges were roughly equivalent to the divinity schools of today. Theology was never taught to the exclusion of other subjects, for it was assumed that the clergy, who were the educated leaders, needed a broad, general background. Classical languages, Hebrew, logic, rhetoric, ancient history, and mathematics usually were in the curriculum for all students. Training in applied sciences, modern history, or modern languages was rare. Students were also admitted to prepare for professions other than the ministry, and usually students who were not members of the denomination that governed the institution were not excluded from it.

During the colonial period the emphasis on theological training as a primary concern of higher education steadily diminished. The record shows that 70% of Harvard's graduates during the 1640's became ministers, but a hundred years later less than half did so. By 1750 the profession for which most college students trained was rapidly shifting to the law. The secularization of undergraduate training was accelerated by the establishment of separate theological schools during the early 19th century.

Many leaders of the new nation were products of the colonial colleges even though two thirds of the colleges were less than 30 years old when the Revolutionary War broke out. Of the 56 signers of the Declaration of Independence, 17 were graduates of American colleges. Three of the five members of the committee to draft the Declaration had graduated from American colleges; so had four of the five members of Washington's first cabinet. Although the curricula of the early colleges may seem antiquated today, the colonial institutions clearly were effective in training leaders for the young United States. The college, with emphasis on the ideal of developing the gentleman scholar, who knows the "best that is said and thought in the world," remained the most potent force in American higher education until the rise of the universities in the late 19th century.

**Development After Independence.** With the end of the Revolutionary War, efforts toward the establishment of new colleges were quickly resumed. By 1800, 17 new colleges had been added to the 9 colonial institutions.

The population increase in the North, the recognition of educational needs in the South, and the expansion to the West combined to create demand for many more institutions. When the Civil War began in 1861 the number of colleges had grown to 182.

Graduates of colonial colleges founded many of the new colleges. Yale alumni, for example, founded 16 new colleges before the Civil War. Thus it is not surprising that many new institutions adopted the classically oriented curricula of the colonial colleges. Proposals for new subjects and new ways of teaching met resistance then, as they do now.

Attempts were made in the first half of the 18th century to establish graduate education formally, but they failed. The highest degree given was the master's degree, and it was virtually an unearned degree awarded by the colleges to alumni who met certain minimal requirements. No true universities existed in the United States prior to the Civil War.

**The First Professional Schools.** The ideal of educating the scholar-gentleman soon was challenged, however, by demands for more specific training that would produce the skilled professional. When the established institutions did not respond quickly to pressures to make their programs more practical, the second distinct structure of American higher education came into existence—the separately organized professional school.

Although America was beginning a vast program of industrial expansion and building of railroads, canals, and highways, there were practically no technical training centers. When the Erie Canal was opened in 1825, West Point was the only institution with a program in engineering. A year earlier (1824) Rensselaer Polytech-

THE GRANGER COLLECTION AND DARTMOUTH COLLEGE

William and Mary College, Williamsburg, Va., about 1740.

Harvard College about 1725 (engraved in 1740).

Princeton, or "Nassau Hall" (engraved in 1764).

Dartmouth College in the early 19th century.

nic Institute (R.P.I.) at Troy, N.Y., had been founded primarily to train teachers who could help farmers apply scientific knowledge to agriculture. Some 10 years later R.P.I. began to offer a course in engineering that immediately attracted students. During the 1850's the new schools of applied science included Polytechnic Institute in Brooklyn, Cooper Union in New York City, and state schools of agriculture in Maryland, Pennsylvania, and Michigan. In 1861 the Massachusetts Institute of Technology was chartered. Meanwhile, the established colleges began to offer alternate programs emphasizing scientific training. Harvard and Yale established such schools in 1847, and in 1851 the Chandler School of Science and Arts was instituted at Dartmouth.

The success of the separately organized technical schools tended to limit their own further spread, for they demonstrated so much need for their educational programs that the established institutions could no longer stay out of the field. Furthermore, when the Land-Grant College Act of 1862 was passed, it specifically required that participating institutions teach, among other things, "such branches of learning as are related to agriculture and the mechanic arts. . . ." Thus the curriculum of the technical institutions was increasingly incorporated into the programs of the private and public universities and of the colleges as well.

Another separately organized professional structure that appeared about this time was the normal school, the prototype of the present-day teachers college. The primary function of these institutions was to train teachers for the rapidly expanding elementary schools. Normal schools developed in great number during the mid-19th century, but as the high schools began to grow it became obvious that a more comprehensive training for teachers was needed. The normal schools either closed or else became teachers colleges.

**Higher Education for Women.** College training for young women was first offered in several sections of the country between 1825 and 1875. Initially this was provided in separate colleges for women, but in 1833, Oberlin Collegiate Institute (later Oberlin College) opened as the first coeducational degree-granting college. After the Civil War a number of separate colleges for women were established, particularly in the South, but coeducation gradually became the trend. The coordinate college, separately organized for women but operating parallel with a college for men, appeared toward the end of the 19th century. Examples were Radcliffe College

Yale College (engraved in 1749).

(Harvard), Barnard College (Columbia), and Newcomb College (Tulane).

**Rise of the Universities.** With the founding of Johns Hopkins in 1876 the first true university was established in the United States. Within a few years the university as an institution began a rapid rise to its present position of leadership in American higher education. One reason for this rapid and successful emergence of the university was that it could be built upon an already existing base in many of the oldest and best-known liberal arts colleges, such as Yale, Columbia, and Harvard. Several of the better established and more aggressive public institutions, such as Michigan, Wisconsin, Minnesota, and California, also assumed the status of universities.

A remarkable number of institutions were founded as universities and endowed with grants of considerable magnitude from the possessors of business fortunes. These grants included $1 million from Cornelius Vanderbilt, $3.5 million from Johns Hopkins, $20 million from the Leland Stanford estate, and $30 million from John D. Rockefeller, Sr., to establish the University of Chicago. In no other period of American history have so many major private institutions come into existence on so grand a scale.

Leaders of the university movement were divided on what the new structure should be. In the absence of university training in the United States, many Americans had gone to Germany to study, and there were powerful advocates of universities along German lines. Presidents Daniel Coit Gilman of Johns Hopkins, G. Stanley Hall of Clark, and William Rainey Harper of Chicago wanted to see what is now known as a graduate school of arts and sciences established as a separate structure devoted primarily to the increase rather than to the transmission of knowledge. They thought the graduate school should be oriented primarily toward research rather than toward teaching, as was traditional. Johns Hopkins, in fact, was opened without an undergraduate college. But there were too many pressures against such a structure—the long tradition of the liberal arts college as the core of higher education, the need for providing pregraduate training to prospective graduate students, and the financial necessity of having an undergraduate college to help support the more expensive graduate schools.

A compromise between graduate and undergraduate emphases produced a peculiarly American structure, unlike any other existing university system. An essentially German graduate school emphasizing research was placed structurally on top of an English-style college devoted to general education. Professional schools, which in Europe have usually been separate structures, increasingly were incorporated into the university, some paralleling the graduate schools (for example, schools of law, medicine, and divinity) and others paralleling the liberal arts college (for example, engineering, forestry, and music schools). Many professional schools were founded originally as proprietary institutions, then became loosely associated with universities, and finally became part of them.

The demand for graduate education was partly a response to the increase and diversification of human knowledge. The rather rigid single curriculum of the old liberal arts colleges was no longer acceptable in an age that seriously questioned what an educated man should know. It was apparent that a student could go through college many times without mastering more than a small fraction of human knowledge. As a consequence, the elective system was followed in more and more universities, to the point of almost complete student freedom in choosing courses. The practice of majoring in a specific subject also became common.

A professor (wearing a silk top hat) supervises fieldwork during an 1883 Yale University surveying class. Engineering programs were not generally offered by U.S. colleges until the middle of the 19th century.

***Land-Grant Colleges.*** One of the most significant legislative acts in the history of American higher education was the Land-Grant College Act of 1862, usually referred to by the surname of its sponsor, Justin S. Morrill. While the federal government was already making specific grants of land to the states in order to foster higher education, the Morrill Act, because of its scope and magnitude, had a more continuous influence than any previous legislation. The bill granted to each state 30,000 acres (12,000 hectares) of land (or its equivalent) for each senator and representative in Congress, based on the census of 1860. Proceeds from the sale of the land were to help support at least one college whose principal aim was to provide training in "agriculture" and the "mechanic arts" though the law specified that such an emphasis should not exclude "other scientific and classical studies." Participating institutions were also to offer military training.

The states were given considerable latitude in implementing the act. Twenty-eight states elected to establish new "A and M" (agricultural and mechanical) colleges. Confronted with the problem of staffing so many institutions offering courses that had rarely been taught, a number of institutions were forced to hire instructors who were trained entirely in the classical disciplines. The result was that more than one former language teacher undertook the teaching of agriculture. This may explain in part the contempt of practicing farmers for the early agricultural colleges and the general reluctance of prospective farmers to attend them. It was not until the 20th century that agriculture became well established, but from the beginning the "A and M" colleges were successful in engineering.

In states where a public university or college had already become well established, these institutions broadened their programs to meet the course provisions of the Morrill Act. Some states elected to apportion part or all of the money to private institutions. Massachusetts, for example,

established what is now the University of Massachusetts for the teaching of agriculture, but gave a third of its income from the Morrill Act to strengthen the Massachusetts Institute of Technology, a private school. In other cases, private institutions undertook the fulfillment of public functions, as when Cornell, a private university, undertook the operation of the New York State College of Agriculture and the New York State Veterinary College.

The states did not always show acumen in managing their grants. More than half of them failed to obtain the then average sales price of $1.25 per acre. (Cornell, however, sold its million acres for over $5.50 per acre.) It became obvious that the original grants would not provide sufficient income for the operation of the institutions, and within 10 years Morrill sponsored another bill to provide additional federal support. By the time the measure passed in 1890, the states had come to realize that regular support was necessary if their institutions were to survive.

The land-grant colleges began to incorporate schools of education into their structure during the last decade of the 19th century. In the 20th century, they became increasingly active in this area and assumed some functions of the separately organized teacher-training institutions.

The land-grant colleges and universities have been a major influence in developing the structure and curriculum of American higher education. They gave official academic recognition to disciplines that had previously been isolated in separate professional schools. Their administrators realized that if education was to be offered to the agricultural and industrial groups it must be placed within their economic means. This philosophy contributed to the development of a peculiarly American concept of the university—what Ezra Cornell called "an institution where any person can find instruction in any study." See also COLLEGES, LAND-GRANT.

Oberlin, founded in 1833, was the first U.S. college to offer coeducation to women; the women below graduated in 1855. Vassar College for women was chartered in 1861; an astronomy class of 1878 is shown at right.

VASSAR COLLEGE

OBERLIN COLLEGE NEWS BUREAU

The two-year college, often called a junior college when in private hands and a community college when public, also came into being in the late 19th century, the first ones being founded in the 1890's. Yet it was not until the next century that they became a significant part of the system of higher education. See JUNIOR AND COMMUNITY COLLEGES.

For further details on the establishment of institutions of higher learning, see EDUCATION.

## 2. Control and Support of Present-Day Colleges and Universities

Today's colleges and universities in the United States can be grouped into two categories in terms of control and support, private and public. Public institutions can be further subdivided into those under state, municipal, and federal jurisdiction. An important fact about American education is that the federal government has no direct control over educational institutions or their standards, except in the case of the few federally administered schools, such as the service academies. All other public institutions and all private ones are subject to state laws.

**Private Colleges and Universities.** Private institutions are usually corporations operating under state charters. In some states, the authority to grant charters is assigned to the state department of education and the board of regents. The responsible agencies set up standards that must be met before a new institution can obtain a charter. In many states, however, few standards are imposed and any group that can afford to incorporate, or that can induce the legislature to issue a charter, can obtain authority to grant a variety of degrees.

Private colleges are financed by tuition and fees, gifts from individuals, business, and foundations, endowment earnings, and certain governmental appropriations. The relative amount of support from these sources varies among institutions, and from time to time. The proportion of governmental support has increased substantially at many institutions, though some colleges reject funds from government.

**State Colleges and Universities.** State institutions are established by provisions of the state constitution or, more often, by acts of the legislature. Institutions are usually under the general direction of a state board of higher education and are governed by trustees, who may be appointed by the governor.

State colleges receive their basic financial support from the government of the state. Other sources are tuition and fees, gifts, and federal grants.

**Municipal Colleges and Universities.** Some cities have their own colleges, and a few maintain major universities. These are established under state law or charter and administered by local governing boards. Board members usually are named by the mayor, the board of education, or the city commission.

There are two principal sources of income—local tax funds and student fees. Private gifts and state support are important in some cases, but endowment income is negligible. There has also been federal assistance.

**Federal Institutions.** The federal government is directly engaged in a program of higher education, chiefly related to national defense. The service academies—the United States Military Academy at West Point, N.Y., the United States

THE BETTMANN ARCHIVE

Tuskegee Institute was founded in 1881 to train black students as teachers; an algebra class is shown above.

Naval Academy at Annapolis, Md., and the United States Air Force Academy at Colorado Springs, Colo.—combine undergraduate programs with officer training. Specialized institutes such as the Air Force Institute of Technology and the Naval Postgraduate School enroll thousands of officers for advanced study.

Other branches of government are also engaged in providing college-level programs. For example, the Treasury Department is responsible for the United States Coast Guard Academy at New London, Conn., and the Department of Commerce controls the United States Merchant Marine Academy at Kings Point, N.Y.

## 3. Patterns of Organization

No single description can cover the patterns of organization of all colleges and universities. The summary that follows notes features that may be regarded as typical of American institutions.

**President and Trustees.** The control of colleges and universities in the United States customarily is by a board of trustees, sometimes referred to as a board of regents or board of directors. The members usually are informed laymen, chiefly in the fields of law, finance, industry, and (in church-related colleges) the ministry. An institution's charter commonly provides for the naming of the first board of trustees and sets forth procedures for selecting their successors. The method by which board members are selected provides the clearest test for classifying an institution as public or private. If a majority of the trustees are elected by the people or are chosen by some governmental official (such as the state governor) or agency, then the institution is a publicly controlled college or university. In some privately controlled (and a few publicly controlled) institutions, the board members choose their own successors; this is known as a self-perpetuating board. In church-related private institutions, trustees are elected or appointed by the religious organization with which the college is affiliated. It is common practice for alumni also to select some trustees.

Within the limits of the charter and such general state laws as may apply, the board of trustees usually has complete power to manage the institution as it sees fit. In practice, the board nearly always delegates most of its executive functions

245

to one or more full-time administrative officers, whom it selects. The title of the chief administrative officer usually is president, but occasionally it is chancellor.

American presidents or chancellors have far greater responsibility and authority than their European counterparts. In the United States their tenure is not limited, their executive functions are less restricted, and their opportunities for exercising initiative are wider.

The president is usually assisted by one or more vice presidents and a staff of general administrative assistants. Some of the larger universities delegate all strictly educational activities to a provost or academic vice president; in smaller institutions the officer in charge of the educational operations is usually the college dean. The provost or dean is directly responsible to the president for such matters as selection of faculty members, organization of the curriculum, quality of instruction, and academic budget. Other administrative officials usually include the registrar, who is in charge of keeping official records; the director of admissions, who determines the eligibility of candidates for admission; and the business officer, who is concerned with financial management.

**Schools and Departments.** A university, which has the most complex organization of all American institutions of higher education, is usually composed of a number of degree-granting schools and colleges at undergraduate and graduate levels, grouped in one administrative system. A university typically has a liberal arts college as its core, a graduate school (stressing academic training), and professional schools (emphasizing the application of theory; for example, law and medicine) at the top of its structure. The schools, headed by deans, are organized into departments, under chairpersons.

A university may be a physical and administrative unit, having its main divisions on one campus. Some very large universities, however, have divisions that require their own administrative hierarchies. The University of California, for example, has a president with statewide jurisdiction plus chancellors, each heading a campus that is a major institution in its own right. The term "multiversity" has been applied to very large and complex institutions such as the Universities of California and Illinois.

Colleges have comparatively simple structures. The principal officers below the president and dean are the chairpersons of subject departments.

**Faculty.** In a college or university the ranks to which a member of the faculty may be appointed are instructor, assistant professor, associate professor, and professor. The master's degree is normally the minimum requirement for appointment as instructor or assistant professor, but the trend is toward requiring the doctorate. The Ph.D. is usually required in the ranks of associate professor and professor.

Some institutions, chiefly the larger universities, demand that faculty members carry on research and publish articles and books in order to qualify for promotion. This "publish or perish" policy is widely believed to cut back the time and energy a faculty member can devote to teaching. The issue has probably been exaggerated, for studies show that in all but a few leading institutions less than 10% of the faculty account for 90% of the published research.

## 4. Accreditation

An aspect of higher education in the United States is the procedure known as accreditation. As applied in education, accreditation is the process whereby an organization or agency recognizes a college or university as having met certain qualifications or standards. In higher education, accreditation is largely a responsibility of independent cooperative agencies, although certain state agencies have the legal authority to perform this function.

The accrediting agencies have been a significant influence in improving the quality of American higher education. They have stimulated improvement in the qualifications of faculty members, the conditions under which they work, the provisions and services for students, and the financial support of higher education.

The agencies of greatest scope are the regional accrediting associations, which cover every section of the United States. The membership of these associations consists of institutions adjudged as meeting the standards for membership; admission to membership constitutes accreditation. Regional accreditation usually applies to an institution as a whole, without differentiation among the institution's various curricular and professional schools.

Professional schools, whether divisions of universities or independent, are accredited by associations of members of a profession, by associations of professional schools, and by joint councils representing various interests of a given profession.

When an institution applies for membership in a regional association, a committee from the association considers the following factors: admissions policy, curriculum, faculty (academic preparation and working conditions, such as instructional load, salary, and tenure), physical plant, library, students' extracurricular activities, student personnel services, and finances.

Accrediting agencies do not rank or grade institutions; they either accredit or refuse to accredit. A few, however, provide probationary accreditation for institutions that are deficient in minor respects, with a stipulation that the deficiencies must be remedied by a certain time.

LOGAN WILSON* and CHARLES G. DOBBINS*
*American Council on Education*

### Bibliography

Barzun, Jacques, *The House of Intellect* (Univ. of Chicago Press 1975).
Bender, Thomas, ed., *The University and the City: From Medieval Origins to the Present* (Oxford 1988).
Bess, James L., *College and University Organization* (N.Y. Univ. Press 1984).
Blits, Jan H., ed., *The American University: Problems, Prospects, and Trends* (Prometheus 1985).
Boyer, Ernest L., *College: The Undergraduate Experience in America* (Harper 1988).
Chapman, John W., ed., *The Western University on Trial* (Univ. of Calif. Press 1983).
Clark, Burton R., ed., *The School and the University: An International Perspective* (Univ. of Calif. Press, 1985).
Diener, Thomas, *Growth of an American Invention: A Documentary History of the Junior and Community College Movement* (Greenwood Press 1986).
Eyerman, Ron, and others, eds., *Intellectuals, Universities, and the State in Western Modern Societies* (Univ. of Calif. Press 1987).
Giamatti, A. Bartlett, *A Free and Ordered Space: The Real World of the University* (Norton 1988).
Hofstadter, Richard, and Smith, Wilson, *American Higher Education: A Documentary History*, 2 vols. (Univ. of Chicago Press 1968).
Kerr, Clark, *The Uses of the University*, 3d ed. (Harvard Univ. Press 1982).
Nevins, Allan, *The State Universities and Democracy* (1962; reprint, Greenwood Press 1977).

**COLLEONI,** kŏl-lā-ō′nē, **Bartolomeo** (1400–1475), Italian soldier of fortune. Born near Bergamo, of a noble family, he early became a soldier and served under the greatest captains of the day, fighting at first in southern Italy and later for the rulers of Milan and Venice. In 1454 he was appointed general-in-chief of the Venetian republic for life.

Proud and resolute, Colleoni was a worthy representative of the *condottieri,* who fought the confused wars of the Italian Renaissance. Like them he customarily served the highest bidder, but once engaged he was a resourceful and determined fighter. Several heroic exploits, the introduction of artillery, and the patronage of art are connected with his name. He and his class were idealized in Verrocchio's powerful equestrian monument to him, which still stands on the Piazza of San Giovanni and San Paolo in Venice. Colleoni died at Malpaga, his castle near Bergamo, in 1475.

RANDOLPH STARN
*University of California at Berkeley*

**COLLETT,** kŏl′let, **Camilla** (1813–1895), Norwegian writer. She was born Jakobine Camilla Wergeland, in Kristiansund, on Jan. 23, 1813, the sister of the great poet Henrik Arnold Wergeland. Camilla grew up in a cultured household and developed an intense interest in literature and the emancipation of women. In 1841 she married Peter Jonas Collett, a professor of law and literary critic, who encouraged her to write. In 1855 her most famous work, the novel *Amtmandens Døtre* (*The Sheriff's Daughters*), appeared. The first novel in Norwegian literature to picture life realistically, *Amtmandens Døtre* dramatically presented its author's views on women's rights and social reform. The work influenced Ibsen and other Norwegian writers.

Other writings by Camilla Collett include *I de lange naetter* (1863; *In the Long Nights*), *Fra de stummes leir* (1877; *From the Camp of the Silent*), and *Mod strømmen* (1879; *Against the Stream*). She died in Kristiania (now Oslo) on March 6, 1895.

**COLLIE,** kŏl′ē, a large breed in the working group of dogs. The collie is a lithe, strong, active dog with a firm, straight stance. The body is well balanced, although a trifle long in proportion to height. It stands 24 to 26 inches (61 to 66 cm) at the shoulder and weighs 60 to 75 pounds (27 to 34 kg). Bitches are slightly smaller. The lean head, never massive, is smooth and clean in outline and tapers toward the nose. The expression of the collie is alert, confident, and intelligent.

Two varieties of collie are recognized: the rough-coated and the smooth-coated. Below the thick, rough outer coat of the former is a soft, furry undercoat. The four accepted colors of the coat are sable and white, tricolor (black, white, and tan), blue merle, and white.

The breed was first developed in Scotland. The ancestry of the rough-coated variety can be traced to the hardy canines that for hundreds of years aided Scottish shepherds in caring for their flocks. Early specimens were black or black and tan, and were referred to as "coally" dogs—thus giving rise, it is assumed, to the present name of the breed. The smooth-coated variety of collie was used as a cattle driver, and supposedly originated in northern Britain.

EVELYN M. SHAFER

THE COLLIE, a breed developed in Scotland as a working dog, is an intelligent, loyal, and handsome pet.

Although there is little doubt that breed characteristics were established hundreds of years ago, pedigree records and other standards were not established until late in the 19th century, when Queen Victoria's admiration for the collie stimulated interest in the breed. There have been refinements in head characteristics and overall conformation since then, and its aristocratic appearance has been further enhanced; it is now rated as one of the most beautiful and intelligent of all dogs. It continues to be one of the most popular breeds in Britain and the United States.

WILLIAM F. BROWN
*Editor of "American Field"*

**COLLIER,** kol′yer, **Arthur** (1680–1732), English philosopher, who developed the first system of absolute idealism, denying the possibility of an external world. Collier was born at Langford Magna, Wiltshire, on Oct. 12, 1680. He was educated at Pembroke and Balliol colleges, Oxford, where his study included the works of Descartes, Malebranche, and John Norris. In 1704 he became rector of Langford.

The theories advanced in Collier's *Clavis Universalis, or a New Inquiry After Truth,* written in 1703 and published in 1713, coincided remarkably with those in George Berkeley's *Treatise Concerning the Principles of Human Knowledge,* which was published in 1710, seven years after Collier had written his *Clavis Universalis.* Collier, observing that mutually incompatible properties had been predicated of the physical world, asserted that physical objects could have no existence outside the mind and that the material world is merely a manifestation of the divine will. The *Clavis Universalis,* because of its inferior style and later publication, gained much less attention in England than Berkeley's work. However, a translation published in Germany in 1756 won its author high repute there. Collier later published *A Specimen of True Philosophy* (1730) and *Logology, a Treatise on the Logos or Word of God in Seven Sermons on St. John's Gospel* (1732). He died at Langford Magna in September 1732.

**COLLIER,** kol'yər, **Constance** (1880–1955), English stage and screen actress. She was born Laura Constance Hardie on Jan. 22, 1880, in Windsor, Berkshire, the daughter of professional actors. From 1901 to 1908 she played important Shakespearean roles in Sir Herbert Beerbohm Tree's company in London. In 1915 she scored a notable success in *Peter Ibbetson*, a play adapted from George du Maurier's novel. She wrote the libretto for Deems Taylor's opera (1931), based on *Peter Ibbetson.*

During most of her career, Constance Collier acted in both London and New York, making her last New York stage appearance in *Aries is Rising* (1939). Her first screen role was in D.W. Griffith's *Intolerance* (1916), and she continued to act in motion pictures into the 1950's. She died in New York City on April 25, 1955.

**COLLIER,** kol'yər, **Jeremy** (1650–1726), English moralist and historian. He was born in Cambridgeshire on Sept. 23, 1650. Collier entered Caius College, Cambridge, where he received both B. A. and M. A. degrees. He was ordained a priest in 1677, and moved to London in 1685 to lecture in Gray's Inn. Loyalty to the deposed Stuarts, coupled with refusal to swear allegiance to William and Mary, led to his imprisonment in 1688 and again in 1692. Outlawed in 1696 for opposition to the crown, Collier was nevertheless able to return to London a year later.

In London he turned his attention to the licentiousness of the Restoration theater, and in 1698 he published the *Short View of the Immorality and Profaneness of the English Stage,* a scathing denunciation of contemporary dramatic standards. Efforts of such notable playwrights as Congreve and Vanbrugh to refute Collier's arguments proved insubstantial.

The first volume of Collier's major work, *An Ecclesiastical History of Great Britain . . . ,* appeared in 1708 and the second in 1714. The historical importance of this work, whose notes are still consulted frequently, lies in the break with the traditional Anglican interpretation of the medieval church. In his last years Collier assisted in drawing up a communion service for nonjurors (q. v.) and made the final revisions of his more than 40 published works. He died in London on April 26, 1726.

JOHN FERGUSON, *Columbia University*

**COLLIER,** kol'yər, **John** (1884–1968), American sociologist and ethnologist. He was born in Atlanta, Ga., on May 4, 1884, and received his education at Columbia University and the Collège de France. After some years in social service work, in 1923 he became executive secretary of the American Indian Defense Association.

In 1933 he was appointed U.S. commissioner of Indian affairs, serving until 1945. During this time he was largely responsible for the passage of the Indian Reorganization Act, which gave far greater consideration to Indian needs.

Collier was one of the founders of the Interamerican Indian Institute and president of the Institute for Ethnic Affairs. From 1947 until his retirement in 1954 he was professor of sociology at City College, New York. His books include *Indians of the Americas* (1947) and *Patterns and Ceremonials of the Indians of the Southwest* (1949). He died in Taos, N. Mex., on May 8, 1968.

FREDERICK J. DOCKSTADER
*Director, Museum of the American Indian*

**COLLIER,** kol'yər, **John** (1901–1980), English-born American author, who is known for the sardonic blend in his fiction of humor, fantasy, and horror. Collier was born in London on May 3, 1901, and was educated at home.

He began to write poetry in 1920, and his poems were first published in magazines in 1921. Collier's first book was a novel, *His Monkey Wife, or Married to a Chimp* (1930), written in a deft and gracefully ironic style that has been compared to that of H. H. Munro ("Saki"). Thereafter, except for two collections of poetry— *Gemini* (1931), containing early verse, and *Defy the Foul Fiend* (1934)—Collier devoted himself to fiction, characterized by wit, ingenuity, and grotesque whimsy. He published the novels *Epistle to a Friend* (1931) and *Full Circle* (1933) and collections of short stories. He settled in the United States in 1942 and died in Pacific Palisades, Calif., on April 6, 1980.

**COLLIER,** kol'yər, **William Miller** (1867–1956), American lawyer and diplomat, who was an eminent authority on the law of bankruptcy. He was born in Lodi, N. Y. on Nov. 11, 1867. Upon graduation from Hamilton College in 1889, he attended Columbia College Law School and in 1892 was admitted to the bar. He was referee in bankruptcy for the Northern District of New York (1898–1899) and lectured on the law of bankruptcy at the New York Law School (1903–1905). Collier's chief work, *Collier on Bankruptcy* (1898), has remained the outstanding reference source in its field. The 14th edition, in 12 volumes with supplements, was published in 1940– 1950. Collier later served at various times as U.S. minister to Spain, as president of George Washington University, and as ambassador to Chile. He died in Caldwell, N.J., on April 15, 1956.

**COLLIER TROPHY,** kol'yər, an award presented annually to a person, group, or organization in the United States for the greatest achievement in improving the performance, efficiency, or safety of air or space vehicles during the preceding year. The value of the achievement must have been thoroughly demonstrated in that year.

The trophy, established in 1912 by Robert J. Collier under the auspices of the Aero Club of America, was first awarded to Glenn H. Curtiss for developing the hydro-airplane (seaplane). The winner is now selected by a committee appointed annually by the president of the National Aeronautics Association. A replica of the trophy is usually presented to the winner by the president of the United States. The trophy, with the names of the winners inscribed on it, is on display at the Smithsonian Institution.

EDWARD H. HEINEMANN
*General Dynamics Corp.*

**COLLIER'S,** kol'yərz, a popular magazine founded in 1888 by Peter F. Collier. Its original title was *Once a Week,* which was changed in 1895 to *Collier's, the National Weekly.* Under the editorship of Norman Hapgood, *Collier's* was one of leading crusading journals of the first decade of the 20th century, but after World War I it emphasized popular articles, fiction, and cartoons. Although *Collier's* ultimately attained a circulation of more than 4 million, it was forced to suspend publication in 1956 for financial reasons.

**COLLINGDALE,** a borough in southeastern Pennsylvania, in Delaware county. It is about 5 miles (8 km) southwest of Philadelphia, of which it is a residential suburb. The borough, which was incorporated in 1891, has a mayor-council form of government. Population: 8,664.

**COLLINGSWOOD** is a borough in southwest New Jersey, in Camden county, 3 miles (5 km) southeast of the city of Camden. Although it is primarily a residential borough, it has some industry, notably the manufacture of leather goods and thermometers.

The community was settled by Quakers in 1682 and originally named Newton. A reminder of this Quaker background is the Friends Burying Ground. Collingswood was incorporated as a borough in 1888. Government is by a commission. Population: 14,326.

**COLLINGWOOD, Cuthbert** (1750—1810), British admiral, who was second-in-command to Lord Nelson at the Battle of Trafalgar. Collingwood was born at Newcastle-upon-Tyne, England, on Sept. 26, 1750, and went to sea at the age of 11. After serving in the naval brigade that fought in the Battle of Bunker Hill (1775) in the American Revolution, he was promoted to lieutenant for his gallantry.

He was assigned the next year to the West Indies, where he met Nelson, under whom he served intermittently in wars against France. Collingwood took part in many major engagements. In the victory of Trafalgar (Oct. 21, 1805), as a vice admiral he performed brilliantly under Nelson's orders and, when Nelson was killed, took command of the British fleet. For his conduct in this battle he was created Baron Collingwood.

Collingwood subsequently commanded in the Mediterranean area until his death at sea on March 7, 1810.

**COLLINGWOOD, Robin George** (1889—1943), English philosopher and historian. Although his vividly written books abound in interesting ideas, Collingwood generally has been dismissed as a latter-day idealist because he rejected the main developments and theories of contemporary philosophy.

Collingwood was born at Cartmel Fell, Lancashire, on Feb. 22, 1889. Trained at University College, Oxford, as a philosopher and archaeologist, he spent most of his life teaching at Oxford, where he became Wayneflete professor of metaphysical philosophy. He wrote on many of the main problems of philosophy and produced important work on the history of Roman Britain. Seriously ill after 1932, he died at Coniston, Lancashire, on Jan. 9, 1943.

**Work.** History is central to Collingwood's thought. His *Essay on Metaphysics* (1940) argues that metaphysics is the historical study of changes in the "absolute presuppositions"—the most basic, unquestioned assumptions—of the thought of the past. In *The Idea of History* (1946) he presents the theory that to understand a historical event is to think again the thoughts of the historical agents. His widely read *Principles of Art* (1938) and his tense, brilliant, and irascible *New Leviathan* (1942) apply methods derived from these views to the study of art and politics.

J. B. SCHNEEWIND
*University of Pittsburgh*

**COLLINGWOOD,** a town in southern Ontario, Canada, in Simcoe county, about 70 miles (110 km) northwest of Toronto. Situated on Nottawasaga Bay, an inlet of Georgian Bay on Lake Huron, it is an important lake port and a summer resort. Collingwood has steelworks, shipyards, two dry docks, a grain elevator, flour mills, sawmills and planing mills, potteries, canneries, and furniture and clothing factories. Population: 15,596.

**COLLINS, Anthony** (1676—1729), English philosopher and deist. He was born in Heston, England, on June 21, 1676, and was educated at Eton and King's College, Cambridge. Influenced by a friendship with John Locke, Collins lived in an intellectual atmosphere in which natural theology and freethinking deism were popular. His writings are among the best examples of this school of thought (see DEISM). In 1707 his *Essay Concerning the Use of Reason* challenged the idea that human reason was limited in its capacity to attain knowledge of God.

In his chief work, *A Discourse of Freethinking* (1713), he argued that free inquiry was the means of acquiring full knowledge of truth and, far from being at variance with Christian principles, was actually enjoined by Holy Scripture. The *Discourse*, widely regarded as a defense of deism, provoked answers from a number of churchmen, including Dean Swift's caricature and Richard Bentley's serious and scholarly reply. Collins died in London on Dec. 13, 1729.

POWEL MILLS DAWLEY
*The General Theological Seminary, New York*

**COLLINS, Eddie** (1887—1951), American baseball player. Edward Trowbridge Collins was born in Millerton, N.Y., on May 2, 1887. While a student in Columbia University, he played for the Philadelphia Athletics under an assumed name, and when this fact was discovered he became ineligible for further collegiate sports. With the Athletics, Collins played several infield positions until Connie Mack, the manager, assigned him to second base in 1908, and Collins became a member of the "$100,000 infield" (with "Stuffy" McInnis, "Home Run" Baker, and Jack Barry). In 1915 he was sold to the Chicago White Sox, and for 12 seasons he was their regular second baseman, as well as manager in 1925 and 1926. He played for the Athletics again in 1927 and 1928, remaining with the team as a pinch hitter and coach in 1929 and 1930.

Collins' 25-year batting average was .333, his best years being 1911 (.365) and 1923 (.360). He topped both leagues in scoring runs in 1912 (137), 1913 (125), and 1914 (122) and in stolen bases in 1910 (81). His lifetime number of assists totaled 7,629. He played in six World Series.

In 1933, Collins became general manager and vice president of the Boston Red Sox. Relieved of the managership in 1948, he remained as club vice president until his death on March 25, 1951. He was elected to the Baseball Hall of Fame in 1939.

MICHAEL QUINN
*"Sports Illustrated"*

**COLLINS, J. Lawton** (1896—1987), American general, who commanded an army corps in western Europe in World War II. He was born Joseph Lawton Collins in New Orleans, La., on May 1, 1896. He was graduated from the United States

Military Academy in 1917 and served in World War I.

His first notable service in World War II was as a major general commanding the 25th Division in the Guadalcanal campaign. When the Allies invaded France in June 1944, Collins commanded the 7th Corps. His troops captured Cherbourg and led in the breakthrough near St.-Lô in July. They took part in the drive across Belgium and into Germany. Collins' army nickname was "Lightning Joe."

Collins was chief of staff of the Army from 1949 to 1953 (during the Korean War). He was then U.S. representative to the North Atlantic Treaty Organization (NATO) and special envoy to Vietnam until his retirement in 1956. Collins died in Washington, D.C., on Sept. 12, 1987.

**COLLINS, Michael.** See ASTRONAUTS.

**COLLINS, Michael** (1890–1922), Irish patriot, who was a leader in the Irish war for independence (1919–1922) and in the creation of the Irish Free State. He was born on Oct. 16, 1890, near Clonakilty, County Cork, the youngest of eight children. At the age of 17 he went to work as a postal clerk in London, and it was there that he soon joined the revolutionary Irish Republican Brotherhood.

After the outbreak of World War I, Collins returned to Ireland to participate in the Irish Volunteer movement. He fought in the abortive Easter Rising of 1916 and was captured and interned for eight months at Frongoch in Wales. He emerged as a nationalist leader, and in the sweeping Sinn Fein electoral victory of December 1918 he was elected to Parliament from West Cork. When in January 1919 the Sinn Feiners, instead of taking their seats at Westminster, met in Dublin and proclaimed themselves Dail Eireann (the Assembly of Ireland), Collins was appointed minister of finance and head of intelligence for the Irish Republican Army.

From the outset of the Irish revolution Collins was brilliantly successful in raising money in Ireland to finance the war for independence. At the same time he organized a superb intelligence service that enforced the loyalty of Irishmen while it successfully cultivated sympathizers and informers among the British. In 1921, British authorities, realizing that Collins was their most formidable enemy, offered £10,000 for him dead or alive. In the few remaining months of fighting Collins narrowly escaped capture on several occasions. He displayed the most extraordinary courage and became an almost legendary figure in Ireland.

A truce ended hostilities on July 11, 1921, and Collins accompanied Arthur Griffith and three other delegates to London in September to discuss the final settlement with Britain. He played a prominent part in persuading his colleagues to accept the British terms that established the Irish Free States as a self-governing dominion of the British Commonwealth, and he was largely responsible for engineering the Dail's ratification of the treaty in January 1922. As chairman of the provisional government and commander of the Free State army during the ensuing civil war between proponents and opponents of the treaty, Collins took vigorous action to end the fighting. He had almost succeeded when he was killed in ambush at Beal-na-Blath, County Cork, on Aug. 22, 1922. In a life of only 32 years, he had become the most popular Irish leader after Charles Stewart Parnell.

GIOVANNI COSTIGAN
*University of Washington*

**COLLINS, Wilkie** (1824–1889), English author, who has been called the father of the English detective story. William Wilkie Collins was born in London on Jan. 8, 1824, the son of the painter William Collins. His education in private schools was followed by a two-year stay with his father in Italy (1836–1838). He spent some time as an apprentice to a tea company. He then studied law at Lincoln's Inn and was called to the bar in 1851, the year he met Charles Dickens. The two formed a relationship based largely on their similar views of the novel as an art form.

Collins abandoned the profession of law and devoted all his time to writing. He contributed heavily to Dickens' periodicals *Household Words* and *All the Year Round*. In the latter he published installments of what was to become his best and most popular novel, *The Woman in White* (1860). In 1873–1874 he made a reading tour of the United States, after which he began to retire from social life. In his last years his talent diminished, and he was affected by failing eyesight and declining health, but he continued to write. Collins died in London on September 23, 1889.

**Works.** Wilkie Collins' novel *Antonina, or the Fall of Rome* (written when he was a boy, but not published until 1850), represents the first stage in his development. He used personal observations of settings (in *Antonina*, Rome, from his visit with his father) and he adopted a style suggesting an admiration for the historical romances of Bulwer-Lytton. Other early works were a biography of his father, which appeared in 1848, a year after the subject's death, and *Rambles Beyond Railways* (1851), an account of a summer in Cornwall.

Collins' second and best period, dating from his acquaintance with Dickens, is represented by *The Woman in White* and *The Moonstone* (1868). These two novels are prototypes of the genre of detective fiction. In them Collins combined his genius for involved, yet believable plot with his talent, perhaps nurtured by Dickens, for creating distinctive characters.

Collins' style was enhanced by his technique of having different characters give their own versions of events; thus, the characters are neither unique, since they must serve the rigorous demands of the intricate plot, nor mere types, since they must present the events from a distinctive point of view. Such characters as the villain Count Fosco in *The Woman in White* and the detective Sergeant Cuff in *Moonstone* strike a perfect balance between the unique and the typical; however, when separated from their respective plots and imitated by later writers, they become only stereotypes.

In his third period Collins turned more toward didacticism and social criticism, as in the novels *Man and Wife* (1870) and *The New Magdalen* (1873), which criticized, respectively, the English overemphasis on athletics and the unsympathetic attitude of society toward the "fallen woman." In such works as these, his talent for contrived plots does not well serve his didactic purposes.

Collins collaborated with Dickens on a number of books, none of which is important. He also wrote approximately nine plays, mostly dramatic versions of his fiction.

THOMAS J. ASSAD, *Tulane University*

### Bibliography

**Beetz, Kirk,** *Wilkie Collins* (Scarecrow 1978).
**Lonoff, Sue,** *Wilkie Collins and His Victorian Readers: A Study in the Rhetoric of Authorship* (AMS Press 1982).
**O'Neill, Philip,** *Wilkie Collins: Women, Property and Propriety* (Rowman 1988).
**Page, Norman,** ed., *Wilkie Collins: The Critical Heritage* (1974; reprint, Routledge 1985).
**Parish, Morris L.,** *Wilkie Collins and Charles Reade* (1940; reprint, Century Bookbindery 1983).
**Robinson, Kenneth,** *Wilkie Collins: A Biography* (1951; reprint, Greenwood Press 1973).
**Taylor, Jenny B.,** *In the Secret Theatre of Home: Wilkie Collins, Sensation Narrative, and 19th Century Psychology* (Routledge 1988).

**COLLINS, William** (1721–1759), English poet, noted for lyrical odes that exhibit strains of both neoclassicism and romanticism. The son of a prosperous hatter, he was born on Dec. 25, 1721, at Chichester, Sussex. After attending Winchester, where he formed a lifelong friendship with the poet and critic Joseph Warton, Collins studied at Magdalen College, Oxford, from 1741 to 1744. He then went to London, where he mingled with leading literary men of the day, including David Garrick and Dr. Johnson, and to Richmond, probably to escape London creditors, where he met the poet James Thomson, who became his intimate friend. Collins' indebtedness was relieved by inheritances, but about 1750 be began to suffer from a debilitating disease that apparently affected his mind. He died at Chichester on June 12, 1759.

Collins' poetry reflects a transitional period in English literature. Like the neoclassicists of the 17th and 18th centuries, he wrote in genres derived from the classics. In his odes he vividly personified abstract concepts and asserted, though he did not always practice, a devotion to simplicity. At the same time, he anticipated aspects of romanticism in the antididactic spirit of his poetry, in his emphasis on imagination and invention, and in his attraction to Spenser, Milton's minor poems, and fanciful aspects of Shakespeare's plays.

Collins was best known during his lifetime for his *Persian Eclogues* (1742), but his reputation today rests chiefly on *Odes on Several Descriptive and Allegorical Subjects* (1746), of which the outstanding poems are *Ode Written in the Beginning of the Year 1746* ("How Sleep the Brave") and *Ode to Evening*. Other notable poems are *Ode occasion'd by the Death of Mr [James] Thomson* (1749) and *An Ode on the Popular Superstitions of the Highlands of Scotland* (1788), published posthumously from a faulty manuscript.

J. K. JOHNSTONE, *University of Saskatchewan*

**COLLINSVILLE,** a city in southwestern Illinois, in Madison county, 75 miles (120 km) south of Springfield. A former coal-mining center, it has developed since the 1940s as a residential suburb of St. Louis, Mo., and East St. Louis, Ill. There is some local industry, notably the manufacture of ladies' garments. The Edwardsville campus of Southern Illinois University is located 5 miles (8 km) north of Collinsville. Cahokia Mounds State Park, with its great pyramid and various other Indian earthworks, is 5 miles to the west. The city has a commission form of government. Population: 21,808.

**COLLIP,** kol'ip, **James Bertram** (1892–1965), Canadian biochemist, who is best known for his work in endocrinology. Collip was born in Belleville, Ontario, on Nov. 20, 1892. After graduating from the University of Alberta in 1921, he studied at the University of Toronto, where he joined the Canadian scientists Frederick G. Banting and Charles H. Best, who had recently discovered the hormone insulin. Collip aided them in their work to increase the yield and purity of the hormone, and when the 1923 Nobel Prize was awarded to Banting and John Macleod (who provided the facilities for this work), Banting divided his share with Best, and Macleod shared his portion of the prize with Collip.

Returning to the University of Alberta as a professor of biochemistry, Collip turned his attention to the parathyroid gland and developed excellent techniques for extracting and purifying its active proteins, including the hormone Parathormone. In 1928 he became chairman of the biochemistry department at McGill University and in 1933 succeeded in isolating the hormone ACTH.

While at McGill, Collip and his associates published some 200 scientific reports, but as his administrative duties increased, Collip found he had little time for research. He retired from his chairmanship in 1941 to become director of the newly created Institute of Endocrinology. He also became chairman of the National Research Council, where he and his staff investigated medical problems that arose during World War II. In 1947, Collip was appointed dean of medicine at the University of Western Ontario, where he established the department of medical research, housed in a building named the Collip Research Laboratory in his honor. He died at London, Ontario, on June 19, 1965.

CHARLES H. BEST
*The Best Institute, University of Toronto*

**COLLISON,** kol'i-sən, **Wilson** (1893–1941), American playwright and novelist. He was born in Gloucester, Ohio, on Nov. 5, 1893. With Avery Hopwood he was coauthor of the plays, *The Girl in the Limousine* (1919) and *Getting Gertie's Garter* (1921). He collaborated also with Otto Harbach in *Up in Mabel's Room* (1919). Among the plays of which he was sole author were *Desert Sands* (1924) and *Vagabond* and *Red Dust* (both 1927). Collison's novels include *The Murder in the Brownstone House* (1929). He died in Beverly Hills, Calif., on May 24, 1941.

**COLLODI,** kôl-lô'dē, **Carlo** (1826–1890), Italian journalist and author, who created the celebrated children's story *Pinocchio*. He was born Carlo Lorenzini in Florence, Italy, on Nov. 24, 1826. In 1848 he founded *Il Lampione,* a satirical journal, which was suppressed the next year. Another periodical, *La Scaramuccia,* established in 1853, was longer-lived, and in 1860 he revived *Il Lampione.* Meanwhile, he wrote comedies and edited newspapers and reviews, assuming the pseudonym "Collodi" from the name of the town where his mother was born. He died in Florence on Oct. 26, 1890.

Collodi's most famous work was *Le avventure di Pinocchio, storia di un burattino,* first published in a children's magazine in 1880. An English translation appeared in 1892. Walt Disney's cartoon *Pinocchio* (1939) was based on this tale of a puppet so very like a little boy.

**COLLODION,** kə-lō′dē-ən, is a solution of cellulose nitrate in a mixture of ethyl ether and ethyl alcohol. Evaporation of the solvent leaves a cellulose nitrate film. Plain collodion contains 5 parts cellulose nitrate by weight in 63 parts ether and 32 parts alcohol.

In the mid-19th century, collodion solutions were used to apply light-sensitive chemicals to glass plates in the "wet process" of photography. They were used also as decorative finishes for paper and fabrics. However, the high volatility of the ether and alcohol in collodion solutions was a disadvantage, and less volatile solvents and plasticizers were substituted in these applications. Collodion is now used only for pharmaceutical and cosmetic purposes—for example, to protect minor wounds or as an adhesive for false eyelashes. A collodion solution with small amounts of camphor and castor oil added is called *flexible collodion*, and the further addition of salicylic acid forms an antiseptic solution used in the treatment of warts and corns.

HARRISON H. HOLMES
*E. I. du Pont de Nemours & Co.*

**COLLOID,** kol′oid, a homogeneous mixture of substances, at least one of which is very finely dispersed. The term also may be used to refer to the dispersed particles themselves. Colloids occur widely in nature; fogs are colloids, and protoplasm itself is a complex colloidal system. Many colloids are economically important—for example, foodstuffs such as butter and homogenized milk. Soaps and synthetic detergents form colloidal solutions in water.

**What Colloids Are.** Early in the 19th century the British chemist Michael Faraday and a few other scientists recognized and studied individual colloidal compounds. However, it was the Scottish chemist Thomas Graham, in 1861, who first applied the term "colloid" (meaning "gluelike") to an entire class of materials (solutions of some vegetable gums). He distinguished the behavior of these substances from solutions of what he called "crystalloids."

It is now recognized that colloids are not distinguished from other classes of materials by their chemical composition. Instead, the characterizing feature of a colloidal substance is the degree of subdivision of its particles. Individual particles should have at least one dimension in the range between $4 \times 10^{-8}$ and $4 \times 10^{-5}$ inches ($10^{-7}$ to $10^{-4}$ cm). This size is between that of most simple molecules and the size of small particles that are readily visible in an ordinary light microscope.

The dispersed component of a colloid has a very large surface area compared to its volume. A single ounce may have 100,000 square feet of surface (about 300 sq meters per gram). Approximately 1 out of every 100 of a colloidal particle's atoms or ions either is exposed to the surrounding medium or is close enough to the surface of the particle to be subject to forces arising from interaction with the medium.

It is therefore apparent that the term colloid refers to a special physical condition rather than to a group of specific chemical substances. Colloidal particles may be large molecules, or they may be aggregates of smaller molecules or ions. Indeed, the only materials that cannot be prepared in colloidal form are materials both of which are entirely gaseous under the specified conditions of temperature and pressure.

**Classification.** Colloids commonly are classified according to whether the particles (the *dispersed phase*) and their medium (the *continuous phase*) are solids, liquids, or gases. Thus, the general term for a liquid or a solid dispersed in a gas is *aerosol*. If the particles are liquid, the colloid is a fog; if they are solid, it is called a dust or a smoke.

A liquid dispersed in a liquid (homogenized milk, for example) is an *emulsion*. A solid dispersed in a liquid forms a *sol*, or sometimes a *gel* (in which both phases are continuous, such as gelatin in water). A solid medium may contain liquid in colloidal form (crude oil in porous rock) or may itself consist of a network of colloidal particles (bone) or contain solid particles (lead-copper bearing metal).

A liquid or a solid in which a gas is dispersed is called a *foam;* whipped cream and foam rubber are examples. In some foams, both the continuous and dispersed phases are colloidal. Fibers and films that are of appropriate thickness are also colloids (for example, soap fibers in grease and soap bubbles).

**Lyophilic and Lyophobic Colloids.** It is often useful to classify colloids as either lyophilic or lyophobic.

In a lyophilic colloid there is a strong affinity between the dispersed material and the medium. The system is stable. For example, a lyophilic colloid forms spontaneously when its components are placed in physical contact. The dispersed material consists either of large molecules (macromolecules, such as DNA) or of colloidal aggregates of smaller molecules or ions (micelles, as in soap solutions). The latter were first called "colloidal electrolytes" but are now called "association colloids" since they do not all conduct electricity well.

If aggregation is made to occur in a lyophobic system (a phenomenon that is known as *coagulation* or *flocculation*), the process is not simply reversible. However, lyophobic colloids can be maintained for very long periods of time (even as much as 100 years) under properly controlled conditions.

**Preparation.** Lyophilic colloids form spontaneously when their components are brought into contact. Examples include soaps and detergents in water and rubber in benzene. Lyophobic colloids generally require development of colloidal-sized units through molecule-by-molecule addition to subcolloidal units called *nuclei*. Once appropriate nuclei are introduced or formed within the system, their growth to colloidal size requires a suitable ratio in the number of molecules (or ions) to nuclei, but otherwise it is spontaneous. In principle, lyophobic colloids may also be formed by mechanical subdivision of bulk material, a process once called *peptization;* however, this process is useful for only a few types of systems, notably emulsions.

All preparation processes for lyophobic colloids require the presence of a stabilizing agent during the formation of the particles. The stabilizer becomes adsorbed onto the surface of the particles and acts by preventing permanent cohesion between them when contacts occur. Some stabilizers act by giving all the particles an identical electrical charge so that they repel each other. Some form an adherent coating of material which is itself lyophilic in the particular medium. Colloids that are formed in this way are known as *protective colloids*. An example of a colloid of this type is the light-sensitive coating of photographic film, in which the gelatin serves as both medium and stabilizer. Other kinds of stabilizers are believed to act by interfering with the freedom of motion of the adsorbed molecules when the particles approach each other. Such a restriction requires an expenditure of energy and is thus equivalent to mutual repulsion between particles.

**Dispersion.** Many kinds of grinding devices, called *colloid mills*, have been designed for the preparation of solid colloidal particles from bulk material. The mechanical disruption of liquids to colloidal droplets is also a simple process. However, preparation of a lyophobic colloid by means of dispersion becomes more difficult as the particle size desired grows smaller, and it is sometimes difficult to achieve stability in the resulting colloidal system.

Aerosols may be formed by the rapid injection of a liquid through a fine orifice or through a screen. Often the aerosols remain stable as a result of electrical charges that they have acquired through friction produced during the formation of the droplets. In other cases, airborne ionized particles or charged colloidal dusts are adsorbed by the droplets. Agricultural sprays, as well as garden sprays, are commonly prepared by the use of this technique.

In the preparation of emulsions, which are the only type of lyophobic system usually prepared by mechanical dispersion, both liquids are broken up into fine droplets in the presence of a stabilizing agent, which is often called an *emulsifying agent*. The liquid for which the rate of drop coalescence is most rapid becomes the medium in which droplets of the other liquid remain suspended.

**Aggregation.** As previously mentioned, the formation of lyophobic colloidal particles occurs by the joining of ions or molecules to subcolloidal "nuclei." The composition of these nuclei may be chemically identical with that of the aggregating substance (homogeneous nucleation), or it may be chemically distinct (heterogeneous nucleation). The latter type is the more common; indeed, it is unlikely that homogeneous nucleation has been achieved except in the condensation of vapor to form fog.

A further requirement for aggregation is that the medium must be "supersaturated" with respect to the aggregating species. That is, the concentration of the aggregating species per unit volume must be greater than the equilibrium concentration. In homogeneous nucleation, the greater the degree of supersaturation, the smaller the colloidal particles.

Supersaturation can be obtained by the cooling of a vapor or a solution or by chemical reaction. Lubricating greases may be formed by cooling a solution of the thickening agent (to form collodial particles) in the base oil. Colloidal carbon, which is widely used to reinforce rubber products, is usually made by forcing smoke from a luminous flame to impinge on a cold surface. Bredig metal sols are formed by condensation of vaporized metal produced by an electric arc beneath the surface of a nonconducting liquid.

**Properties and Uses.** The useful applications and biological activity of materials that result from their being in a colloidal state are determined largely by the size, shape, and flexibility of the individual particles.

**Adsorption.** The adsorption of molecules or ions at the surface or interface between two phases is of both theoretical interest and practical importance in many situations. In the case of colloids, in addition to stabilizing lyophobic systems, adsorption plays a role in de-watering ore slimes, water purification, stabilization of soil, soil conditioning for agricultural use, and catalysis. Adsorption is also important in the decolorization of crude syrup in sugar refining, the transport of material through biological and other membranes, chromatography, protection of metal parts against corrosion by adsorption of water by silica, the "cracking" of oil to increase the yield of high octane number gasolines, and the purification of air.

**Light Scattering.** Light scattered from a colloid is much more intense relative to the light source than light scattered by small molecules. The conspicuous scattering by airborne dust or by fog) can be readily observed in the path of a beam from a searchlight. It is often called the *Tyndall effect*. Light is absorbed by individual atoms and molecules in the particles and then re-emitted. Rays from different atoms in the same particle interfere with each other, sometimes leading to increased net intensity and sometimes decreased. Information regarding the size, shape, electrical charge, and other characteristics can be obtained from a careful study of this complex process. The ultramicroscope is an instrument that is used to detect the presence of colloidal particles from flashes of scattered light, even though particles of this size are too small to be seen directly.

**Wetting.** Good wetting properties of a liquid are desirable for degreasing wool, detergency, dyeing, ore flotation, and many other processes. The same substances that function as wetting agents in solution also form association colloidal micelles. The two properties are essentially unrelated except that the micelles act as reservoirs supplying additional single molecules (by dissociation) as fast as those originally present in the liquid are used up by adsorption on the wetted surface.

**Electrokinetic Behavior.** The word "electrokinetic" suggests a reciprocal relation between electricity (flow of charge) and flow of matter or, alternatively, between the electrical and mechanical forces causing these flows. Many liquid colloidal systems exhibit electrokinetic effects. In *electrophoresis*, charged particles move in response to the application of an electric field. Their velocity within the field makes possible an approximate calculation of the magnitude of the interaction between the particles. The same information can be obtained if a mechanical force induces flow of liquid relative to the charged particles (electroosmosis). Electrophoresis is of great practical importance and has been widely used, particularly in the study of proteins.

**Rheological Properties.** The term "rheological properties" refers to the type of flow or deformation exhibited by a substance under mechanical stress. The viscosity of a colloid under stress can be used to infer the approximate shape of either suspended particles or macromolecules in solution, or the extent of their swelling (solvation in the case of molecules), or the average size (weight per macromolecule); however, information about all these characteristics together cannot be determined without auxiliary data from other types of experiments.

Charged colloidal particles have a higher viscosity than neutral particles at the same concentration in the same liquid. This effect is called *electroviscosity*. Some colloidal systems, such as napalm, or ammonium oleate in water, have elastic properties. Some show lower viscosity with increased speed of stirring but become almost solid when stirring stops. This phenomenon, called *thixotropy*, occurs in substances such as oil well drilling mud and nondrip paint. Other substances show the opposite effect and become solid when stirred rapidly. This phenomenon is called *dilatancy*, and it is found in "Silly Putty" or in a solution of cornstarch in cool water.

**Ultracentrifugation.** Spinning a colloidal sol or solution at high speeds, corresponding to nearly a million times the acceleration due to gravity, causes the sedimentation of macromolecules according to their size and relative density. Many useful types of data can be obtained from ultracentrifugation, depending on the specific techniques employed. Among the characteristics that may be determined are the anhydrous apparent molecular weight, molecular weight in solution, density in solution and extent of solvation, and particle-particle interaction.

ROBERT D. VOLD
MARJORIE J. VOLD
*University of Southern California*

**COLLOQUIALISMS** are expressions appropriate to informal spoken language but ordinarily inappropriate to more formal (usually written) language. Colloquialisms (from Latin *colloqui*, to speak with, converse) abound in spoken or familiar English and do not reflect unfavorably on the speaker's education. In this respect they are distinguished from slang, which is less widely acceptable and usually more ephemeral, and from cant, which is ordinarily unacceptable as well as obscure. See SLANG.

The distinction between colloquial language and dialect is one not of degree but of kind: colloquial language is standard for a broad level of usage, whereas dialectal language is standard only for a geographical region. In English, all usages were once dialectal; ultimately one dialect, the Midland, was promoted at the expense of the other dialects and became Standard English. See DIALECT.

Colloquialisms are often promoted to the rank of Standard English. This process is especially likely if the colloquial expression has no true equivalent in Standard English, if its equivalent is somehow inferior, or if the colloquialism exists only as a slightly different sense of an accepted word. Similarly, slang or dialect expressions may become colloquial. Any of these processes may be reversed.

Colloquialisms may be single words, such as "folks" for "relatives" ("Did you meet my folks?") or "tremendous" for "excellent" ("The movie was tremendous"); clipped words, such as "lab," "ad," or "bike"; short picturesque words for technical terms, such as "bugs" for "insects" or for "mechanical faults"; contractions, such as "we'll" or "can't"; and verb-adverb combinations, such as "put out" for "expel," "extinguish," "publish," "inconvenience," "embarrass," or "retire" (in baseball). Colloquial usage may also differ from Standard English in grammar, pronunciation, or connotation.

ERIC PARTRIDGE, *Author of "A Dictionary of Slang and Unconventional English"*

**COLLOR DE MELLO,** kōō-lôr' di me'lōō, **Fernando** (1949–     ), Brazilian political leader. He was born in Rio de Janeiro on Aug. 12, 1949. After studying economics at the University of Brasília, he went to work for his family's media group in Alagoas, becoming its president. As governor of Alagoas in 1986–1989, he slashed the salaries of the "maharajahs," or government elites.

On March 15, 1990, Collor became the first directly elected president of Brazil in 29 years. At his inauguration, he reiterated his pledge to attack inflation, revamp the inefficient education system, and advance social justice and environmental protection. The next day he unveiled an economic "shock plan" that included a one-month price freeze, limits on bank withdrawals, sharply higher prices on publicly provided goods and services, and a floating exchange rate. He also abolished 24 ministries, state firms, and foundations. He later announced a new industrial policy keyed on urging business competition. In 1992 impeachment proceedings were brought against him (on grounds of corruption); he resigned in December of that year. He was later cleared of the charges.

GEORGE W. GRAYSON
*College of William and Mary*

**COLLOT D'HERBOIS,** kô-lō' der-bwȧ', **Jean Marie** (1750–1796), French revolutionist. An actor who turned to politics, he was a Parisian by birth. First holding office in the Commune of Paris in 1792, he soon represented the capital in the National Convention, where he voted death for Louis XVI and arrest for the moderate Girondists. A member of the Committee of Public Safety from 1793 to 1794, he usually sided with the radicals Jean Nicolas Billaud-Varenne and Bertrand Barère de Vieuzac. In 1793 he accepted the difficult assignment of suppressing a revolt in Lyon. By November 3, he had mastered the city. Moderate opponents criticized him sharply for his severe reprisals against the insurgents. He helped defeat Robespierre in the stormy debate of 9 Thermidor (July 27, 1794), but during the Thermidorian reaction, he was arrested and sentenced to deportation to French Guiana. He died there of fever in Sinnamary on Jan. 8, 1796.

RICHARD M. BRACE, *Oakland University*

**COLLUSION,** in law, is an agreement between or a concert of action by two or more persons. The term usually connotes fraud and secrecy. It is often defined as an agreement to defraud another person of his rights by the forms of law or to obtain an object forbidden by law. Collusion is less inclusive than, but substantially the same as, conspiracy.

In judicial proceedings there is collusion where two or more persons, apparently in an adversary position in relation to each other, improperly conspire to defraud or to injure another person or to deceive the court. However, a proper act of cooperation or common effort by persons having similar or identical interests does not constitute collusion.

In the law of divorce, collusion is a conspiracy of a husband and wife to suppress evidence, to present false or manufactured testimony, or for one of them to commit or appear to commit an act in order to lead the court to grant a divorce. The mere fact that both parties desire to obtain a divorce is not of itself collusion.

RICHARD L. HIRSHBERG, *Attorney at Law*

**COLMAN,** kōl′mən, **George,** the Elder (1732–1794), English dramatist and theater manager. He was born in Florence, Italy, to British parents. He practiced law briefly in England. Then, partly through his friendship with the actor-manager David Garrick, he became attached to the theater.

Although Colman wrote, coauthored, or adapted more than 30 works in various dramatic forms, and also published many essays, he is best known for his comic plays. *The Jealous Wife,* one of his most successful comedies, was produced by Garrick at the Drury Lane, London, in 1761. Colman and Garrick collaborated on *The Clandestine Marriage* (Drury Lane, 1766); this comedy inspired Domenico Cimarosa's popular opera *Il matrimonio segreto.*

From 1767 to 1789, Colman managed playhouses in London, first Covent Garden and then the Little Theatre in the Haymarket. Meanwhile he continued to write plays and to adapt works by dramatists such as Shakespeare, Jonson, and Beaumont and Fletcher. He translated the comedies of Terence and Horace's *Ars poetica.* His son, George Colman the Younger (1762–1836), also was a dramatist and theater manager.

**COLMAR,** kôl-mȧr′, is a city in northeastern France. The capital of the department of Haut-Rhin (Upper Rhine) in Alsace, it is situated on the Lauch River, 43 miles (69 km) southwest of Strasbourg. Although Colmar is noted for its many cultural attractions and as the trade center for Alsatian wine, it is also a manufacturing city. Its chief industry is textile milling; metalworking and food processing are important as well.

Typical of the old town are narrow, winding streets leading to attractive squares and lined with Renaissance houses (often half-timbered) or offset by courtyards containing small shops. Among the places of interest are the Church of St. Martin (13th-14th century) at the town center, the Old Custom House (1480), the Tanners′ Quarter, "Little Venice" with its canals, the wooden-galleried Maison Pfister (1537), the Dominican Church with 14th-15th century stained glass, the Maison des Têtes (1609) covered with small sculptured heads, and the Unterlinden Museum with its magnificent altarpiece (about 1515) by Mathis Grünewald.

Frankish in origin, Colmar became a free Imperial city in 1226. It passed to France in the 17th century, and its history thereafter was that of Alsace. Population: 63,498 (1990 census).

**COLOBUS MONKEY,** kol′ə-bəs, a genus of thumbless monkeys that live mostly in tropical rain forests and mountain forests of Africa, from Senegal to Ethiopia and south to Angola. The four species have head and body lengths ranging from 20 to 30 inches (50–80 cm), with tails of 25–40 inches (60–100 cm). The many subspecies of black-and-white colobus monkeys, or guerezas (*Colobus abyssinicus* and *C. polykomos*), have a variety of striking black-and-white facial ruffs and other white fur markings. One subspecies, *C. p. satanas,* is entirely black.

The green colobus monkey (*C. verus*) is the smallest, most primitive species. Its face is naked or sparsely furred. It has the trait, unusual for monkeys, of carrying its young in its mouth. The red colobus monkey (*C. badius*) includes many subspecies differing widely in appearance, but most have some reddish fur.

**COLOCYNTH,** kol′ə-sinth, is the dried pulp of the unripe but fully grown bitter apple. It was once widely used as a powerful cathartic.

Bitter apple (*Citrullus colocynthis*) is a herbaceous perennial vine that is indigenous to the warm, dry regions of Africa and Asia. It now grows wild in many areas and is also cultivated in the Mediterranean region.

The fruit of the bitter apple vine resembles a small orange. Its rind is removed and the whitish, bitter pulp contained in the fruit is dried. The dried pulp is then shipped as whitish globular berries called "apples." These "apples" are from 2½ to 3 inches (6 to 7 cm) in diameter, and they are very light and spongy. Commercial supplies of colocynth come mainly from Turkey (the finest grade), Spain, and Sudan.

As a cathartic, colocynth pulp can produce copious watery evacuations within two to three hours. In large doses, however, its action may be accompanied by violent cramping, bleeding, prostration, and dangerous inflammation of the intestine. It is infrequently used in medicine.

JOHN C. KRANTZ, JR., *U.S. Pharmacopeia*

**COLOGNE,** kə-lōn′ (German: Köln, kûln), one of the largest cities in Germany, a nodal point of west German commerce and industry, and a leading cultural center. It faces the Rhine River, mainly along the left (west) bank, between Düsseldorf and Bonn.

Situated at the crossing of historic east-west and north-south trade routes, Cologne is a major rail junction and river port and is served by several autobahns (express highways). Its harbor traffic includes vessels of many nations, and

The twin spires of Cologne Cathedral soar above the Rhine River. At left is Gross St. Martin Church.

© E. GEBHARDT/FPG

small seagoing ships as well as rivercraft. The city shares a busy airport with the West German capital, Bonn. Industries in Greater Cologne produce motor vehicles, machinery, electrical equipment, chemicals, steel, pharmaceuticals, beer, and eau de Cologne toilet water. The city is also an insurance center.

Cologne is noted for its great Gothic cathedral and its Romanesque churches, for its international trade fairs, and for its pre-Lenten carnival. Foremost among the city's educational institutions is the University of Cologne, established in 1388; closed by the French in 1798, it was refounded in 1919 by Konrad Adenauer, who was then lord mayor of the city.

**Description of the City.** After suffering severe damage during World War II, Cologne was rebuilt in the postwar decades with foresight and taste. City planners grasped the opportunity to cut new streets and widen old ones. Historic structures were restored—landmarks such as the cathedral, many other churches, the Gürzenich (a 15th century banquet hall), and the 14th-16th century Rathaus (the Old Town Hall), as well as quite ordinary old buildings. New structures of handsome modern design were erected, notably the municipal theater and opera house, several churches and bridges, and various commercial, industrial, and civic buildings.

Compact central Cologne—the Altstadt, or Old City—is bounded on the east by the gently curving Rhine and on the other sides by a semicircular boulevard, the Ring, which traces the course of the former medieval city wall. West of the Ring is a wide concentric greenbelt of parks and sports fields occupying the site of 19th century fortifications. Directly across the river lies the Deutz section, containing the splendid Rhine Park with fair and exposition buildings and the Tanzbrunnen (Dancing Fountain), a plaza surrounded by water displays.

The focal point of the city is the cathedral. Nearby are the main railroad station, bus station, and post office, the headquarters of Westdeutscher Rundfunk (the regional broadcasting corporation), and some of the city's best stores, hotels, and restaurants. Also close to the cathedral is the riverbank, with attractive promenades.

Cologne Cathedral is one of Europe's most imposing edifices, its two towers rising more than 515 feet (157 meters) and its nave reaching an interior height of 141 feet (43 meters). Construction began in 1248 under Master Gerhard. It proceeded fitfully, stopping altogether between 1559 and 1842, but the work was finally completed in 1880 to the original plans. The main shrine, a masterpiece of goldwork, is the reliquary (1181–1220) of the Three Kings,' or Magi, by Nicholas of Verdun. The beautiful stained-glass windows in the choir date from about 1275. Two chapels contain remarkable works—the monumental Gero Cross (about 970) and a mid-15th century altarpiece by Stephan Lochner depicting the adoration of the Kings.

Cologne's dozen Romanesque churches by themselves would have made the city a noble center of religious architecture. Some, such as St. Gereon's (mainly 11th–12th century), were built over Roman structures. New churches, by distinguished architects, were erected mostly in outlying districts of the city after the war.

Just south of the cathedral is the Roman-Germanic Museum, completed in 1974 and built mainly to house a large mosaic floor from a Roman villa of about 200 A.D. The mosaic, discovered on the museum site in 1941, depicts the drunken god Dionysus. Chief among the city's other museums is the Ludwig (Wallraf-Richartz), a gallery of Western paintings that range from the medieval Cologne school to contemporary idioms.

**History.** Cologne was the chief Roman city on the Rhine and the key to the Rhine defenses of Gaul against Germanic invaders. It began as a settlement of the Ubii in the 1st century B.C. The Romans based legions there and colonized the town with Roman army veterans. About 50 A.D. the Emperor Claudius granted the town municipal rights and named it Colonia Claudia Ara Agrippinenisum after his wife, Agrippina, who was born in the area. Shortened to Colonia, the name became Köln in German and Cologne in French and English.

Cologne remained important after it passed to the Franks in the 5th century, and in the late 8th century under Charlemagne it was made the seat of an archbishopric. In the 10th century the archbishops of Cologne combined ecclesiastical authority with temporal rule over their extensive church province. In 1164 the Emperor Frederick I (Barbarossa) presented the archbishop with the presumed relics of the Three Kings. Placed in their magnificent new shrine, the remains made Cologne a great pilgrimage center.

By the 10th century, Cologne was becoming an important center of North European commerce and industry. It reached the height of its premodern prosperity after joining the Hanseatic League in 1201. Its burghers were long in conflict with the archbishops, and in 1288 they gained complete independence, the archbishop removing to Bonn. Cologne was the largest and wealthiest city in Germany from the 11th to the 16th century, after which economic decline set in. The city stoutly resisted the Reformation, remaining as it had been since the 13th century—and is today—the spiritual capital of German Catholicism.

Under the German Empire (1871–1918), Cologne emerged as a modern industrial center and absorbed suburbs in all directions. During World War II it was one of the first targets of mass Allied air raids. About 90% of the inner city was destroyed. The cathedral, though damaged, survived.

Following the postwar division of Germany, Cologne was included in the West German state of North Rhine—Westphalia. Reconstruction, planned by the architect Rudolf Schwarz, was accompanied by new economic and demographic growth. The population of the city proper peaked in 1980 at 976,800, with 1.8 million in the city and suburbs. Population: 963,300 (1997 est.).

**COLOMBE,** kô-lôɴb', **Michel** (c. 1430–c. 1513), French sculptor. Little is known of his early life, but he spent productive years in Tours. Perhaps the last great sculptor of the French Gothic tradition, Colombe is known primarily for two works. In 1502–1507 he completed the tomb of Francis II, duke of Brittany, and his wife, Marguerite de Foix, carving the recumbent effigies and the four corner figures representing the virtues. This work is now in the cathedral of Nantes. In 1508–1509 he executed a marble relief panel commissioned by the Cardinal of Amboise for the chapel of his château at Gaillon. Displayed today in the Louvre, it depicts St. George slaying the dragon.

© BOUTTIN/LEO DE WYS

Bogotá, the capital of Colombia, is situated on a high plain in the eastern Andes.

# COLOMBIA

State Arms

## CONTENTS

**COLOMBIA,** kə-lum′bē-ə, the country named for Christopher Columbus, occupies the northwestern corner of South America. It is both an Andean and a Caribbean nation and the only one on the continent with Atlantic and Pacific coastlines. Colombia is larger than France and Spain combined, but over half of its territory is virtually inaccessible and uninhabited.

Economically, Colombia occupies a middle rank among the Latin American nations. It is neither as richly endowed in natural resources nor as fully developed as Argentina or Venezuela, yet it is far more modernized than Paraguay, Bolivia, Ecuador, and most of Central America. Its population is of mixed ancestry, and its social structure has changed only slightly with industrialization and urbanization. Internally fragmented by three Andean mountain chains—a condition that has promoted a deep-seated sense of regionalism and isolation—Colombia has responded to challenges of the 20th century in an uneven fashion.

Colombia was conquered and settled by the Spaniards in the first half of the 16th century. It gained its freedom in 1819 under the South American liberator Simón Bolívar, who preserved a shaky union of Colombia, Venezuela, and Ecuador until 1830. A two-party political system, unusual in Latin America, emerged in the 1840's, and the second half of the 19th century was marked by frequent armed conflicts between factions of the Liberal and Conservative parties. Toward the end of that period, however, Colombia began to emerge from its long isolation by entering world trade as an exporter of coffee.

In the first half of the 20th century Colombia enjoyed relative political stability until the late 1940's, when brutal partisan conflict broke out again. Like the earlier fighting it was begun by party leaders, but subsequently it seemed almost to feed on itself and escaped the control of its initiators. In 1958, to end the fighting and the military dictatorship to which it had led, representatives of the two parties embarked on a

265

© LOREN McINTYRE

Colombia's highest mountain range is the snowcapped Sierra Nevada de Santa Marta, near the Caribbean Sea.

bipartisan experiment in "qualified democracy." Although this power-sharing agreement ended in 1974, as planned, it left a constitutional imprint on the nation's political institutions.

## 1. The Land and Natural Resources

Colombia lies in the "Ring of Fire," an area of seismic instability that surrounds the Pacific Basin and is subject to frequent volcanic eruptions and earthquakes. The country's most notable surface feature is the Andes mountain system, which breaks up the national territory into regions that are isolated from one another and have distinctive characteristics. The three major regions are the Andean mountains and valleys, the Caribbean coast, and the eastern plains.

**The Andean Highlands and Valleys.** The Andean region occupies about a quarter of Colombia. In the southern part of the country the Andes divide into three separate ranges, which continue northward toward the Caribbean Sea. The western range (Cordillera Occidental) is the lowest. Its highest peak is about 4,400 meters (14,436 feet), but most of the other high peaks are between 3,600 and 4,000 meters (11,811–13,123 feet). Its mountains are worn by erosion and are thickly vegetated. The central range (Cordillera Central) is the loftiest and includes permanently snow-covered peaks. The highest of these is 5,429 meters (17,812 feet). The eastern range (Cordillera Oriental) is somewhat lower on average than the central, although its tallest peak—at 5,493 meters (18,022 feet)—is higher than any in the central range.

The basins that separate the three Andean ranges contain Colombia's most important rivers. The Magdalena, which flows northward between the central and eastern ranges and empties into the Caribbean Sea, has been called "the lifeline of Colombia." Between the central and western Andean ranges the Cauca River flows north into the Magdalena.

Climate in the Andean region depends on elevation. The *tierra templada*, or "temperate" zone, extending from 1,000 to 2,000 meters (3,281–6,562 feet), is warm, with Cali having an average temperature of 73°F (23°C) and Medellín of 68°F (20°C). Bogotá, in the *tierra fría*, or "cold" zone above 2,000 meters, has an average temperature of 57°F (14°C). Rainfall in the Andean region is moderate.

The region has extensive level areas that are suitable for agriculture. Among these are the *sabana* (plain) of Bogotá and the Cauca Valley. In many places, however, the land is either too high and cold or too steep for farming. Many inclines are gentle enough for cultivation but are quickly eroded if deprived of their natural ground cover.

The Andes contain much mineral wealth: coal near Bogotá and Medellín, some of it of coking quality; emeralds near Bogotá; gold in the Medellín area; iron ore near Tunja; and petroleum, especially in the Magdalena River valley. The mountain rainfall makes the region the center of Colombia's hydroelectric potential.

**The Caribbean Coastal Region.** The coastal area bordering the Caribbean makes up about an

### INFORMATION HIGHLIGHTS

**Total Area:** (land and inland water) 439,621 square miles (1,138,914 sq km).
**Boundaries:** *North*, Caribbean Sea; *northeast*, Venezuela; *southeast*, Brazil; *south*, Peru, Ecuador; *west*, Pacific Ocean; *northwest*, Panama.
**Elevations:** *Highest*—Pico Cristóbal Colón (18,947 feet, or 5,775 meters); *lowest*—sea level.
**Population:** 39,309,422 (1999 est.).
**Capital and Largest City:** Santa Fe de Bogotá.
**Name of Nationals:** Colombians.
**Major Language:** Spanish (official).
**Major Religion:** Roman Catholicism.
**Monetary Unit:** Peso (= 100 centavos).

For Colombia's flag, see under FLAG, both illustration and text.

eighth of the country. This northern region consists for the most part of broad lowlands, including extensive swamps. However, an isolated mountain group—the Sierra Nevada de Santa Marta—contains the nation's highest peaks, reaching 5,775 meters (18,947 feet).

The climate of the Caribbean lowlands is hot and harsh, and tropical diseases are common. The seaport of Barranquilla has an average temperature of 82°F (28°C). The region's rainfall is adequate and seasonally heavy.

The varied coastal terrain includes some good lands for plantation agriculture and grazing. Coal is abundant in the department of La Guajira and near Barranquilla. Nickel is found in the department of Córdoba.

The Caribbean lowlands connect with the narrow Pacific (western) lowlands at the Gulf of Urabá. Much of this hot, wet zone is separated from the Pacific by mountains known as the Serranía de Baudó. The west coast is cut off from the interior by the Cordillera Occidental.

**The Eastern Region.** The hot, isolated, and thinly populated eastern plains account for almost three fifths of the national territory. This region consists of two quite distinct zones of vegetation. The southern, wetter part lies within the tropical rain forest of the Amazon River basin. Rubber was an important product during the early part of the 20th century. Now, tourist potential and wild animals for zoos are the most important resources. From Leticia, shipping down the Amazon through Brazil to the Atlantic is possible. Agricultural development is difficult because of the tree cover, and the heavy rainfall causes nutrients to leach from the soil when the land is cleared.

The northern part of the eastern region is made up of the open plains (*llanos*) of the Orinoco River basin. The *llanos* are tropical grasslands that undergo seasonal flooding. They are suitable for livestock grazing and, in some areas, the cultivation of crops.

Major petroleum discoveries have been made in the eastern region. These include some in the Amazon near Ecuador and others in the Orinoco area near Venezuela.

## 2. The Economy

Colombia has a mixed economy, with separate functions for the government, private Colombian business, and foreign multinational corporations. The government is considered to have a primary role in leading the nation to full development. Besides owning the railroads, roads, and telecommunications, it engages in costly but important activities such as the generation of electricity. Since subsoil rights are the patrimony of the nation, the government is expected to develop energy resources, but the way that this is done varies. At times the government is also expected to begin manufacturing industries. It does so when the private sector will not invest in an enterprise that is regarded as essential to national development. However, once such industries are established on a profit-making basis, the government typically sells them to private companies. In addition to its direct role in development projects, the state is deeply involved in the economy through its control of taxation, tariffs, and exchange rates, and through its policies toward other countries and multinational corporations.

Private enterprise is stronger in Colombia than in most Latin American countries. One of the most dynamic capitalist developments in the history of Latin America was centered in Medellín at the beginning of the 20th century. Since that time the assumption has generally been that the private sector can operate the economy more efficiently than the government can. As a result, many of the economic activities that are government-run in other Latin American countries are in the hands of private business in Colombia.

Multinational corporations, on the other hand, have never had the importance in Colombia that they have had in neighboring states. They have invested principally in banana plantations, petroleum, and coal mines.

**Historical Background.** The development of the Colombian economy falls into four distinct periods. The first lasted until 1880, during which the country had no stable exports that would consistently earn foreign exchange to buy imported

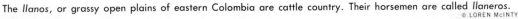

The *llanos*, or grassy open plains of eastern Colombia are cattle country. Their horsemen are called *llaneros*.
© LOREN McINTYRE

# COLOMBIA

MERCATOR PROJECTION

SCALE OF MILES

0   50   100   150   200

KILOMETRES

0   50   100   150   200

Capitals of Countries ............... ✦
Other Capitals ............................ ◉
International Boundaries ........... —··—
Other Boundaries ........................ —·—
Canals ........................................... ·········

© Copyright HAMMOND INCORPORATED, Maplewood, N.J.

CARIBBEAN SEA

PANAMÁ

VENEZUELA

PACIFIC

OCEAN

ECUADOR

Quito

PERÚ

BRAZIL

**Main cities and places:**

Panamá, Gulf of Panamá, Acandí, Turbo, Chigorodo, Ríosucio, Jurado, Dabeiba, Antioquia, Urrao, Bolívar, Pto. Mutis, Nuquí, Quibdó, Itsmina, Pizarro, Cabo Corrientes, Punta Churambirá, I. Gorgona, Guapi, Mosquera, Iscuandé, Rada de Tumaco, B. de Ancón de Sardinas, Tumaco, Barbacoas, Túquerres, Ipiales, Tulcán

Cartagena, Barranquilla, ATLÁNTICO, Soledad, Sabanalarga, Baranoa, I. Barú, San Onofre, Is. de San Bernardo, G. de Morrosquillo, Arjona, Turbaco, Sincelejo, SUCRE, Lorica, Sahagún, Corozal, Cereté, Montería, CÓRDOBA, Ciénaga de Oro, Planeta Rica, Tierralta, Caucasia, Nechí, Simití, San Carlos

Santa Marta, Cabo de Aguja, Ciénaga, Ríohacha, LA GUAJIRA, Uribia, Maicao, Pta. Gallinas, Guajira Pen., Pta. Espada, Gulf of Venezuela, Pto. López

MAGDALENA, Pico Cristóbal Colón 19,029 ft. (5800 m.), Sta. Marta, Nev. de Sta. Marta, El Plato, Magangué, El Banco, Mompós, Majagual, Ayapel, Convención, NORTE DE SANTANDER, Ocaña, Cúcuta, Pamplona, San Cristóbal

CESAR, Agustín Codazzi, Villanueva, Valledupar, Chiriguaná, Maracaibo, Cabimas, Lake Maracaibo, El Vigía, Mérida, Barinas, San Fernando de Apure

ANTIOQUIA, Ituango, Segovia, Yarumal, Cisneros, Barrancabermeja, Zapatoca, SANTANDER, Socorro, San Gil, Bucaramanga, Piedecuesta, Málaga, Bello, Medellín, Itagüí, Envigado, Sonsón, Pto. Berrío, Andes, La Dorada, Chinchiná, Vélez, Duitama, Tunja, BOYACÁ, Chiquinquirá, Sogamoso, Yopal, CASANARE, Nunchía, Pto. Nuevo, Puerto Carreño, Maipures, Amanavén, Pto. Inírida

CALDAS, Manizales, RALDAS, Pereira, Cartago, Armenia, QUINDÍO, Ibagué, TOLIMA, Nev. del Tolima 17,110 ft. (5215 m.), Honda, Facatativá, Zipaquirá, CUNDINAMARCA, Girardot, BOGOTÁ, DISTRITO ESPECIAL, Guateque, Villavicencio, Acacías, San Martín, META

VALLE DEL CAUCA, Buenaventura, G. de Tortugas, Buga, Palmira, Cali, Tejada, Pto. Tejada, CAUCA, Santander, Popayán, Miranda, Aipe, Nev. del Huila 18,865 ft. (5750 m.), Neiva, Vol. Puracé 15,243 ft. (4646 m.), Bolívar, Campoalegre, Garzón, Pitalito, San Agustín, Chaparral, Espinal, Chafurray, Guayabero, Angostura Falls, San José del Guaviare, GUAVIARE, Serrania de La Macarena

NARIÑO, Sandoná, Pasto, San Pablo, Mocoa, Sibundoy, Las Casas, Pto. Asís, PUTUMAYO, Belén de los Andaquíes, Tres Esquinas, Florencia, CAQUETÁ, Cuñaré, Miraflores, Mitú, VAUPÉS, San José, GUAINÍA, San Felipe

Puerto Leguízamo, Pto. Pizarro, Puerto Toledo, Salto Grande, Cachorras, La Pedrera, AMAZONAS, Barras, Arica, Tarabacá, Leticia, Benjamín Constant

Iquitos, Napo, Amazon

**Inset (lower left):**

CARIBBEAN SEA

Banco de Serranilla, Banco Alicia, Bajo Nuevo, Roca que Vela, Banco de Quitasueño, Banco de Serrana, I. Sta. Catalina, Sta. Isabel, I. de Providencia, Cayos de Roncador, San Andrés, I. de San Andrés, Vigía, Cayos del E.S.E., Cayos de Albuquerque

INTENDENCIA DE SAN ANDRÉS Y PROVIDENCIA

Same scale as main map.

Longitude West 72° of Greenwich

goods that Colombia did not manufacture. In the second period (1880–1930) a stable product, coffee, was exported to pay for manufactures from abroad. During this period, however, some industry developed around Medellín.

Industrialization on a national scale, which began during the Great Depression, characterized the third period (1930–1967). Economic policy stressed this process, and revenues from coffee exports were used to purchase imports of capital and intermediate goods for the new factories. The fourth period began in 1967, after which governments encouraged "minor" exports (those other than coffee and refined petroleum). Minor exports were to supplement coffee, not replace it, as a source of foreign currency.

**Agriculture.** Approximately one fourth of Colombia's territory is used for agricultural purposes, about a tenth of the land being devoted to crop production and the rest to pasture for livestock. In some cases farming takes place on inclines that are quickly eroded. This practice and widespread deforestation in the Andean region have made erosion a serious problem.

While coffee makes up only about 4% of the gross domestic product, it is the leading legal export. (For illegal exports, see under *History*.) Coffee had entered the country's foreign trade by 1850 and reached a high of 80% of exports in 1924. Dependence on this commodity decreased mainly after 1967.

Coffee is subject to great demand when the crop fails in Brazil. During such "bonanzas," as they are called in Colombia, foreign exchange is much more available. This is a mixed blessing, since inflation normally results when production of consumer goods cannot increase as rapidly as demand. Colombian governments typically reduce tariff barriers at the times of bonanzas, thus lessening inflationary pressures but also harming domestic industry.

The *tierra templada* is the coffee zone. The center of production is the western Andean departments of Antioquia, Caldas, Risaralda, and Quindío, but coffee is also grown in other Andean areas between 1,000 and 2,000 meters (3,281–6,562 feet). This is a labor-intensive crop and is typically cultivated on small farms, which are

© LOREN McINTYRE/WOODFIN CAMP & ASSOC.

Coffee is sometimes grown in the shade of banana trees. Both coffee and bananas are important exports.

either owned or rented by the growers.

Another important cash and export crop is bananas, grown particularly in the Caribbean coastal plain. Foreign multinational corporations were the first in banana production, but private Colombian firms have entered the market also. Fresh-cut flowers are a third agricultural export. Grown in the *sabana* of Bogotá, this product has generated many new jobs. Raw sugar is a fourth major farm export. None of these products, however, has ever had more than 25% of the export value of coffee.

Subsistence agriculture is practiced in all parts of Colombia, the crops depending on elevation. Potatoes, wheat, and other grains are grown at higher elevations, while maize (corn) is grown almost everywhere. Livestock raising is similarly scattered through the country, with major concentrations in the *sabana* of Bogotá and in the eastern plains.

A fishing industry is developing along both the Caribbean and Pacific coasts, as well as in the Magdalena River valley. With the growth of population, many of the Andean forests have been cut for fuel. The Amazon forests, although a source of commercially valuable products, have been difficult to exploit.

**Mining and Energy Production.** Colombia has long produced great mineral wealth. It has mined gold and emeralds since pre-Hispanic

times. During the colonial period it was the largest contributor of gold to the Spanish coffers, and it is the world's leading present source of emeralds. Among the modern industrial minerals, nickel has been developed in the department of Córdoba. But Colombia's most important minerals today are petroleum and coal.

By world standards, the country is not a major producer of petroleum, but the development of oil resources has been a major economic objective. For most of the 20th century, Colombia was self-sufficient in this fossil fuel and even exported crude oil. The government hopes that new discoveries, as in the eastern plains, will at least eliminate dependency on foreign sources for part of the nation's petroleum needs.

Possessing the largest coal reserves in Latin America, Colombia derives about a quarter of its national energy from that fuel—by far the greatest proportion for any country in the region. Moreover, production is conveniently located near the major cities of Bogotá, Medellín, Cali, and Barranquilla.

Because of its rivers and mountains, Colombia ranks high among Latin American producers of hydroelectricity. But despite an ambitious program of hydropower development, supply has lagged behind demand. In part this insufficiency was due to increases in demand at a rate that made doubling of generation capacity necessary every eight years.

Closely linked to Colombia's energy needs are a series of ecological changes: increased shortfalls of electricity and its high cost have led to increased cutting of the Andean forests for fuel. Deforestation has, in turn, led to greater erosion and less rainfall.

**Manufacturing.** The manufacturing sector contributes a little over 20% of the gross domestic product. Consumer nondurables (clothing and foodstuffs) are the leading category, meeting in some years nearly half of national demand.

Medellín has been one of the leading textile centers in Latin America, and the local industry became the largest manufacturing employer in the country. Partly because of a loss of exports to foreign competitors, its position in the Colombian economy has declined somewhat. The Bogotá area tended to stress mechanical and chemical products, while the Cali area specialized in the manufacture of sugar and paper products.

**Transportation.** Colombia's geography creates major obstacles to transportation. In the populous highlands, the Andean terrain and landslides due to heavy rainfalls make road and rail communication difficult. In the eastern region, the seasonal flooding of the *llanos* and the dense forest cover of the Amazon area are barriers.

Formerly the rivers were the best arteries of surface transportation. Of the 14 navigable waterways, the most important was the Magdalena River, which carried nearly 95% of all commercial inland water transport. Coastal shipping has centered on the Caribbean ports of Cartagena, Barranquilla, and Santa Marta. On the Pacific, Buenaventura has grown in importance.

Rail facilities were greatly expanded in the 1940's and 1950's until the network connected major highland population centers with both coasts. Passenger and freight traffic reached its apogee in the 1960's. Afterward, air and truck services began to supersede rail movements.

The effort of the government to extend roads and highways made the major cities more accessible to one another. However, transportation between Bogotá and Medellín still takes a day by land, though only a half hour by plane. Feeder roads have increased in number but are still inadequate or even nonexistent in many places. Colombia shares with Panama the only gap in the Pan American Highway, through the forbidding Darién swamps.

**Foreign Trade.** Colombia's imports are predominantly raw materials and intermediate goods. Exports are led by coffee, coal, and fuel oil.

The United States has long been Colombia's chief trading partner. However, the relative importance of U.S. trade declined greatly after the mid-1950's, when it represented more than 70% of Colombian exports and over 60% of imports. Besides opening new markets in Europe, Colombia has played an active role in the Andean Common Market. One of the major goals of this group was to increase trade among the member nations. Neighboring Andean countries now are significant in Colombian exports and imports.

### 3. The People and Education

Colombia is remarkable for its ethnic diversity. European, Amerindian, and African strains, pure and intermingled, make up the complicated ethnic pattern. While racial characteristics are important in the country, they have less salience than in the United States.

The government makes no attempt to estimate racial makeup, and one must guess at the percentages. Surely no more than 20% are of unmixed European ancestry, while the National Indigenous Council states that 1% are "pure-blooded" Indians. Probably no more than 4% are pure black. Therefore the predominant strain is the Indian-European *mestizo*, with smaller numbers of mulattoes and of individuals with ancestry in all three races.

The numerically dominant *mestizos* are found in every social stratum and walk of life, although they are still underrepresented at the highest levels of the society. Blacks are still largely engaged in farm labor on the plantations, although urbanization has brought more to Barranquilla, Cartagena, and Cali. Unacculturated Indians pursue traditional ways in isolation.

**The Peopling of Colombia.** A variety of Indian cultures existed prior to the arrival of Europeans early in the 16th century. Most of the indigenous peoples were essentially nomadic. The most advanced were the Muiscas (Chibchas), who practiced agriculture in the high basins of the eastern Andean range, maintaining permanent settlements and dominating nearby tribes. The coming of the Spaniards was quickly followed by a decline of the Indian cultures, owing to deaths from combat and disease as well as to miscegenation.

Black slaves from Africa were first introduced in the 16th century, and throughout the colonial period this infusion continued. Slaves were brought particularly to the coastal regions. Some escaped their masters and fled to the mountainous interior, while others were taken to plantation regions of the Cauca Valley and to mining areas of Antioquia. Most blacks remained in slavery until it was abolished in 1851.

Sporadic waves of European immigration followed. However, these did little to alter the main features of Colombian society.

**Regional and Ethnic Distribution.** Nearly three fourths of the Colombian people live in the Andean highlands and valleys. Most of the remainder are in the Caribbean coastal region, which in the 1980's became the fastest-growing section of the country. The increased importance of this region was due in part to exploitation of its mineral resources, particularly coal.

Ethnic variations are most common in the Andes. Some parts, as around Bogotá, were originally populated by large groups of Indians, and their typical makeup today is *mestizo*. Other parts, such as Cali, became the center of sugar plantations, with resulting black and mulatto populations. Still others, as in the case of Medellín, had both Indian occupants and black slaves for mining, leading to a population with various mixtures of the three racial strains. The majority of blacks and mulattoes still reside in the coastal lowlands. The largest concentrations of Indians are outside the highlands as well.

**Cultural Characteristics.** Colombia is distinctive among Andean countries in having few citizens who do not speak Spanish. A maximum of 4% speak an indigenous language, and many of these speak Spanish also. Colombians take pride, especially in Bogotá, in preserving the best Spanish in Latin America. Regional accents exist, however. The most notable is the Caribbean coastal speech, which is more like that of Cuba or the Dominican Republic than that of interior Colombia.

A small-town market in the Andes of southern Colombia features articles of clothing and religious pictures.
© WELDON KING/FPG

© VICTOR ENGLEBERT

Finding new uses for old assets: the Museo Nacional is housed in a former prison in Colombia's capital city, Bogotá.

The country is mainly Roman Catholic, and most Colombians are at least nominal members of the church. Yet the religious fervor of the people varies greatly. The most religious are women, especially in Antioquia department (Medellín); the least are men, particularly in the Caribbean coastal region. There are small numbers of Protestants, especially fundamentalists in the lower social strata, and of Jews.

One prominent cultural division centers on the urban-rural split. In general, the urban middle and upper sectors have cultural characteristics not unlike those of the United States and western Europe. Rural dwellers, and also the poorer classes of the cities, differ in maintaining traditional Colombian dress, food and beverages, and music, with regional variations. Mass communications, however, are blurring urban-rural distinctions.

Another cultural division concerns social status. Colombia has a rigid class system, which has shown some signs of mellowing. The upper class, probably no more than 5% of the population, consists largely of Colombians who can claim an unmixed European ancestry. The very top of the upper class, commonly called the "oligarchy" by other Colombians, takes pride in its family background. Economic growth, both legal and illicit, has produced new groups with greater income but lacking the social status of the "old families."

The middle-income sector, perhaps as much as 20% of the population, has increased with economic growth. Like the upper group, these Colombians earn their living through nonmanual work—especially in the civil service, teaching, and other white-collar occupations. They aspire to upper-class status, but the likelihood of their obtaining enough wealth is slight.

The working class, about 75% of the population, has one thing in common: manual occupations. In other respects, this group is quite varied. Al-though it includes most nonwhites, its members come from all racial backgrounds. In income they range from fairly well-to-do members of labor unions down to the "marginals," who improvise a livelihood as street vendors and the like and live in self-constructed shanties. The more affluent of the working class can aspire to middle-sector status for their children through education. The marginals lack this possibility.

**Population Trends.** Colombia experienced dramatic shifts in population growth during the second half of the 20th century. Rising income levels and the adoption of modern methods of disease control produced a rapid decline in death rates starting in the late 1940s; birthrates remained high into the early 1970s. The population grew over 3% a year from the late 1950s through the late 1960s—one of the highest rates in the world. Increased urbanization and an aggressive family-planning program then led to a rapid drop in fertility. In 1997 the population was estimated at 40,214,723 and growing at only 1.6% a year.

Urban migration has been another important trend. By 1994, 74% of the population was urban, in contrast to about 30% in 1950. In the 1980s, however, the rate of urbanization leveled off. The three largest cities were in the Andean region: Bogotá (Santa Fe de Bogotá), in the eastern range; Medellín, in the central range; and Cali, in the Cauca Valley. The Caribbean coast had the fourth largest city, Barranquilla. Each of these urban centers contained more than 1 million people.

A third population trend has been external migration, primarily to Venezuela and the United States. Many of the emigrants have entered foreign countries illegally. By comparison, immigration is negligible. Net emigration amounts to approximately 0.01% of the population each year.

**Education.** In 1958 the Colombian constitution mandated that a minimum of 10% of the national budget be spent on education. Free public education is most common for the lower-income groups. On some occasions, however, especially in the countryside, not enough places are available in the schools. Furthermore, poor people sometimes need the meager income their children can earn. Some children of the working class do receive higher education, almost always in the public universities. The largest of these, and the country's largest university, is the Universidad Nacional. The main branch of the university is in Bogotá.

Within the middle and upper groups, private education is most common at the primary and secondary levels. Parents seek to enroll their children in the best private *colegios* in preparation for their placement in a prestigious private university, such as Bogotá's Universidad de los Andes and Universidad Pontífica Javeriana.

## 4. Culture

Colombians take great pride in their cultural achievements. Bogotá has been called the "Athens of Latin America," in reference especially to appreciation of the arts.

**Literature.** During the 19th century, Jorge Isaacs gained fame with his novel *María* (1867), a characteristic work of the Romantic school. French literary influences grew in the later part of the century and helped provide impetus for the evolution of the Modernist movement, from which José Asunción Silva and Guillermo León Valencia were most notable. See MODERNISMO.

Twentieth century literature moved in the direction of realistic social commentary. Novelist Tomás Carrasquilla wrote of the mountain people of Antioquia, while José Eustacio Rivera won

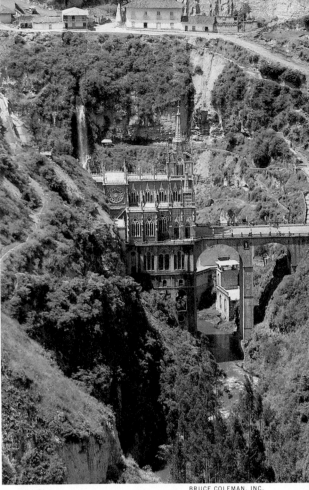
BRUCE COLEMAN, INC.
The Sanctuary of the Virgin of Las Lajas, in Ipiales, is built over a canyon. The church attracts many pilgrims.

Treasures of the pre-Hispanic cultures of the Colombian highlands are preserved in the Gold Museum in Bogotá.
© JEAN-MARIE JRO/VALAN PHOTOS

hemispheric attention in 1924 with *The Vortex*, dealing with life in the Amazon jungles. Widespread partisan violence in the 1950's and 1960's was the basis of Daniel Caicedo's *Dry Wind* (1954) and Eduardo Caballero Calderón's *Christ With His Back to Us* (1953).

Gabriel García Márquez was a leader of Latin America's literary "boom" in the 1960's. His novel *One Hundred Years of Solitude* (1968) chronicled the mythic Buendía family of the imaginary town of Macondo. García Márquez received the 1982 Nobel Prize in literature, the selection committee citing him "for his novels and short stories, in which the fantastic and the realistic are combined in a richly composed world of imagination, reflecting a continent's life and conflicts." The committee noted also that each new work of his was translated into many languages and published as quickly as possible in large editions.

**Art and Architecture.** Colonial art followed Spanish trends in technique and subject matter. It was characterized by strong, rich colors, firm delineation, and a sense of dignity. Painting received relatively little attention in the 19th century, but *costumbristas* (documentors of local customs and manners) such as Ramón Torres Méndez depicted the dress, occupations, and hobbies of the working class. Toward the end of the century, interest was spurred by French realism and impressionism.

271

In the 20th century a group of progressive artists introduced works representative of international trends, and several became world famous. Alejandro Obregón initiated the modern movement. Fernando Botero painted pneumatic nudes and overdressed children; Eduardo Ramírez Villamizar attained fame as an expressionist; Enrique Grau worked with geometric forms; and the sculptor Edgar Negret led the avant-garde by fashioning "magic machines," combining metal, stone, and plaster materials. In a completely different vein, Alfonso Ramírez Fajardo rendered mountain scenes in primitive watercolors, and the Indian artist Francisco Tumiñá created pencil sketches to illustrate the landscapes and legends of the Andean people.

Colombia's colonial architecture adapted many Spanish styles. It varied according to the climate of a particular site and the provinces of Spain from which the colonists came. One style, from southern Andalusia, has many Moorish details as seen in elaborate paneled ceilings, screens, arched windows, and portals. Another, the Castillian style, came with the northern Spanish colonists. Colonial architecture is best seen in Santa Marta, Cartagena, Popayán, Tunja, and Bogotá's old section.

**Performing Arts.** Colombia's music is highly distinctive. The country's folk music reflects the people in a variety of moods and from many different areas. Many of the rhythms are derived from a combination of Indian music with Spanish and African music brought to the New World. Among the typical native folk instruments are the tiple, bandola, cuarto, and maracas.

Plays are the most developed of the dramatic arts, though dozens of movies have been filmed by Colombian companies. Television has been popular since the mid-1950s, but critics have complained that Colombian television has yet to find its niche in the arts.

## 5. Government

The second constitution of the Republic of Colombia came into effect on July 5, 1991, replacing the original constitution of 1886. It maintained a unitary form of government and preserved the institutional framework of a president and a bicameral legislature. It also strengthened the power of the judiciary and guaranteed certain civil liberties, including rights to equality for women and young people, to social welfare, and to education.

The president, who is head of both state and government, is elected by direct vote for a term of four years and may not serve consecutive terms. Congress, whose members are also elected to serve four years, consists of the Senate and the House of Representatives, reduced in size to 102 senatorial seats and 161 house seats (down from 116 and 199 seats, respectively). The indigenous population was also given the right to elect some congressional representatives. The new structure and its electoral provisions encourage greater political participation and seek to restrict corruption and misrepresentation. The Supreme Court and a restructured network of lower tribunals still constitute the judiciary, but the post of public prosecutor and defender of the people was created to strengthen the judicial branch. The greatest controversy arose over the provision that prohibits extradition of Colombian nationals. While the new constitution was welcomed by most Colombians, concerns remained related to the armed forces and the rights of indigenous groups.

# HISTORY

## 6. Colony and Nationhood

Alfonso de Ojeda in 1500 was the first Spaniard to reach the shores of what today we call Colombia. At that time at least eight different Native-American linguistic groups lived in the country. Some were warlike hunters and fishers, but many had developed agriculture. By far the most advanced were the Muiscas (Chibchas) of Cundinamarca and Boyacá. In 1509, Ojeda established a settlement on the Carribbean coast near today's Cartagena.

**The Spanish Colony.** The first permanent settlements were made at Cartagena (1533) and Santa Marta (1535). Cali and Popayán, near the Pacific coast, were established in 1536 by Spanish navigators who had crossed the Isthmus of Panama.

Pre-Hispanic stone figures of unknown origin abound in the Valley of the Statues near San Agustín. Above is the entrance to a tomb.

The colonial town of Villa de Leiva has been preserved as a national monument by the Colombian government.

In 1538, Bogotá was founded by Gonzalo Jiménez de Quesada. In 1549 a royal court (*audiencia*) was set up in Bogotá, and in 1564 the colony was upgraded to a captaincy general.

The colonial years were a period of ineffectual government. The captaincy general was formally part of the Viceroyalty of Peru, but distance made it difficult for the viceroy in Lima to maintain effective control over the captain general in Bogotá. Further, Bogotá had great difficulty in maintaining effective control over the leaders in the other parts of the country.

The captaincy general, while not a center of Spanish colonization like Mexico or Peru, was not a backwater either. Cartagena developed into the major port through which all trade with South America was supposed to flow. In 1739, Bogotá became the capital of the new viceroyalty of Nueva Granada (New Granada), combining today's countries of Colombia, Panama, Venezuela, and Ecuador.

In May 1810, Cartagena was the first city of the viceroyalty to declare independence. Bogotá did so also in the next month, and six years of independence followed, although some parts of the country never declared it. The Spaniards reconquered the territory in 1815–1816. Final independence came in August 1819 when the Venezuelan Simón Bolívar defeated the Spaniards at the Battle of Boyacá.

**The First Years of Independence: 1819–1903.** In 1821 the Constitution of Cúcuta formally set up an independent federation consisting of Colombia (including Panama), Venezuela, and Ecuador. The federation was called the Republic of Colombia, and within it the present-day Colombia was known as Nueva Granada. Only in 1863, long after the federation was dissolved, did Nueva Granada take the name Colombia. Subsequently, to avoid confusion, historians adopted the convention of calling the former federation Gran Colombia (Greater Colombia).

Bolívar was elected president of Gran Colombia but continued south to fight for the liberation of Ecuador (1822) and the independence of Peru (1824). He left behind his vice president, Francisco de Paula Santander, to govern the new nation.

The federation was doomed from the start because of regional differences. In 1827, Bolívar returned to Bogotá. Finding that unity was breaking down, he established a dictatorship in 1828 but resigned in March 1830 in despair of holding the federation together. He died in December of that year.

After the breakup of the federation in 1830, Colombia was on its own as an independent country. Politics in the early years were personalistic and volatile, with constant regional conflicts. The first of eight civil wars of the 19th century took place between 1838 and 1842.

The personalist nature of politics abated under the government of Gen. Tomás Cipriano de Mosquera from 1845 to 1849. In it, political representatives of the merchants started to play a role. The social basis for the creation of two political parties was laid by 1849. On one side were the traditional landholders and the Roman Catholic Church; on the other, the merchants and the artisans. The government of Gen. José Hilario López (1849–1853) took actions that destroyed the colonial institutional structure and, in the process, gave permanence to the new social cleavage. Among the major reforms was the free cultivation and commercialization of tobacco, which was the country's main crop and a government monopoly. Other changes included the suspension of mortgages given by the church, the elimination of Indian reservations, the introduction of a direct form of taxation, and, in 1851, the emancipation of slaves.

The Liberal and Conservative parties were established in 1849. The Liberals were for federalism and free trade and were anticlerical; the

Conservatives favored unitary government and protectionism and were proclerical. In the end the most important difference between them was the one concerning the church. In 1861 a Liberal government under Mosquera confiscated church lands, which were estimated to constitute one third of the nation.

The parties soon developed other characteristics. They became multiclass, with membership among both the elite and the dependent peasants. They engaged in civil wars in which the peasants were little more than cannon fodder. As a result, Colombians developed intense party loyalties. Many could point to family "martyrs" who had been killed by the other party. The elites, however, were more pragmatic, at times forming coalitions with leaders of the other party when it suited their interests.

The country experimented with both extreme federalism and centralism during the 19th century. Through the constitutions of 1853, 1858, and 1863, Colombia had one of the most federalist systems of the world. The extreme federalism continued until 1885, when Rafael Núñez led an independent party to power. While the party did not last long, the Núñez reforms did, becoming institutionalized through the centralist constitution of 1886.

After Núñez left office in 1894 the Conservative Party held power until 1930. A Liberal revolt in 1899, however, led to the Thousand Days' War, which claimed some 100,000 lives. Although this was Colombia's last major armed conflict for more than 40 years, no sooner had peace been restored than Panama seceded in 1903 with U.S. connivance, an event that embittered Colombian-American relations for many years.

## 7. Stability, Conflict, and Coalition

During the unusually stable Conservative period, from 1903 to 1930, Colombia entered foreign trade consistently for the first time with the development of coffee exports. In the 1920's multinational corporations began to invest in the country, particularly in petroleum and banana production. Workers started to unionize, and peasants who had no land became restless.

**The Liberals in Power: 1930–1946.** In 1930 the Conservatives were divided, and the Liberal candidate for the presidency, Enrique Olaya Herrera, won the election. Under the constitution of 1886 the Liberals were able to replace almost all public officials. Violence broke out between Liberal and Conservative peasants, often instigated by party leaders, but it soon ended when nationalist feelings were aroused by a border incident with Peru.

The Liberals stayed in power until 1946. During that period new ideological cleavages appeared both between and within the two parties. The main issue concerned the role of the government in the economy. Part of the Liberal Party had come to support government intervention in the economy and controlled social change. Olaya's status quo government was followed in 1934 by the innovative administration of Alfonso López Pumarejo. During his four-year "Revolution on the March," the government was given a constitutionally guaranteed role in economic development and diversification of exports. Legal means of protecting domestic industry were enacted, and a graduated income tax was introduced. Labor was granted the special protection

of the state. The right to strike was guaranteed, and a series of laws gave unions firmer guarantees in collective bargaining. Property was to have a social function, and property not being used effectively could be expropriated. The first agrarian reform took place. Government expenditures on education increased fourfold.

Neither the next president, Eduardo Santos, nor López himself, when he was reelected in 1942, had the inclination or the ability to continue the impetus of the first López government. The Revolution on the March had crystallized the differences between moderate Liberals who wished to maintain the new status quo and radical Liberals who wanted to continue the peaceful revolution. By 1946 the division was so complete that there were two Liberal candidates for the presidency. The Conservative hopeful, Mariano Ospina Pérez, thus won the election.

**"La Violencia" and Dictatorship: 1946–1958.** With the return of the Conservative Party to power, violence in the countryside broke out almost immediately, at least in part instigated by the leaders of the parties. The incipient violence was aggravated by the assassination of popular Liberal leader Jorge Eliécer Gaitán on April 9, 1948.

For the next several days considerable conflict raged in the cities, especially Bogotá. But the long-term *violencia*, which continued until 1966, was primarily a rural phenomenon involving peasant members of the two parties. With the exception of Nariño department, all of Andean Colombia was engulfed, as were the Orinoco plains. The Caribbean coast was little affected. At the beginning Liberals and Conservatives attacked each other. The affected group fled to the mountains, from which they plotted revenge against the members of the attacking party. Because the Conservatives held power, the law-enforcement agencies—the national police and the army—took the Conservative side. *La violencia* had certain religious overtones as well, with some parish priests taking the side of the Conservatives.

The breakdown of order led to Colombia's first military dictatorship since the 19th century, that of Gen. Gustavo Rojas Pinilla (1953–1957). The Rojas regime took immediate steps to bring the conflict to an end. Many of the guerrilla bands ceased fighting in return for amnesty and state aid. The government began an extensive series of public-works projects, made possible by high prices for coffee on international markets. Nevertheless the violence recurred in 1954, and by 1956 it was obvious that General Rojas intended to stay in power indefinitely. Press censorship increased; on occasion the government itself instigated violence. On May 10, 1957, top military commanders, with the support of the leaders of most economic interest groups, persuaded Rojas to step down. A caretaker military junta governed for the next year.

**The National Front: 1958–1974.** As early as 1956, Liberal and Conservative leaders had begun discussions toward setting up a coalition government with two goals—to end the military dictatorship and to halt the violence. Once Rojas was gone, the primary task was to address the problems of the countryside. In 1957, therefore, the leaders of the two parties formed a coalition called the National Front, which was endorsed overwhelmingly in a constitutional plebiscite. The agreement specified, first, that for 16 years from 1958 the presidency would alternate between the Liberals and Conservatives every four years. Second, during that time all elective and appointive governmental positions would be divided equally between the two parties. Third, no other parties could legally contest elections until the National Front ran its course.

Accordingly, Liberals and Conservatives rotated in the presidency from 1958 to 1974. All National Front presidents faced serious problems. Ending rural violence, the primary goal, was largely achieved by 1966 after at least 200,000 peasants had lost their lives. Ironically, though, as the partisan violence ended, leftist guerrilla organizations emerged. The first was the pro-Castro Army of National Liberation (ELN) in 1962, which was followed two years later by the Armed Forces of the Colombian Revolution (FARC), a Communist-oriented group that became the largest guerrilla organization in the country.

Land distribution was another goal, and three agrarian reform laws were enacted under the National Front. The Colombian Institute of Agrarian Reform (INCORA) was set up. Land was redistributed, but analysis suggests that by the end of the period there were actually fewer *minifundios* (very small holdings) and more *latifundios* (very large ones) than before.

During the Liberal presidency of Carlos Lleras Restrepo (1966–1970) two important policies were initiated. One was Decree-Law 444, which established a tax credit for "minor" exports (those other than coffee and petroleum). It also regulated multinational corporations for the first time. Foreign investments above U.S. $100,000 would have to be approved by the government. Profit remittances were limited to 14% of investment. Finally Decree-Law 444 set up a "crawling peg" for small devaluations of the peso, in hope of avoiding a radical devaluation.

The second notable policy begun by Lleras Restrepo concerned population control. The 1964 census showed that the population had been growing at a rate of 3% a year since 1951. In 1966 the ministry of health signed a contract for family-planning training and research. The results of the new program were impressive. By 1972, 164,000 women were participating in programs in family planning, and by mid-1973 half of the women in Bogotá were using some form of contraception. The government was said to have adopted the most thorough antinatalist policy in Latin America, despite the power of the Roman Catholic Church.

Misael Pastrana, a Conservative, was the last president of the National Front. Notable among his government's policies was the indexing of housing-loan interest rates with inflation. The goal was to channel savings toward the housing market, in which there was a notable shortage.

A third guerrilla group, M-19, emerged in 1970. This group contended that the 1970 presidential election had been stolen from former dictator Rojas Pinilla. M-19 began its activities in the cities, but organized bands in the mountains as well. A fourth guerrilla group, the pro-Chinese People's Army of Liberation (EPL), was founded in 1974.

## 8. The Contemporary Period

Although the National Front ended in 1974 as planned, parts of the bipartisan agreement were extended by constitutional means. Thus the equal distribution of appointive positions in the government lasted until 1978. Presidents after that date were required to offer "adequate and equitable" participation in the government to the other party.

**The López Administration: 1974–1978.** The first president of the post-National Front period was Alfonso López Michelsen, a Liberal. In his first year he concentrated on tax reform, trying to increase the progressivity of the system, while simplifying it and increasing its yield.

In 1975 three phenomena came together, causing the López government to shift its policy to inflation control. These were Colombia's new status as a petroleum importer, the enormous amounts of foreign currencies coming into the country through the illicit drug trade, and a coffee "bonanza" after a 1974 frost in Brazil.

Petroleum production had begun in 1921 with the entrance of a subsidiary of Standard Oil of New Jersey; Gulf followed a few years later. Exports of crude began in 1922, and by the time they ended in 1974, when internal demand became greater than production, over 1 billion barrels had been exported. The typical contract was a "concession," in which the multinational corporation (MNC) had complete control of production and the government received royalties and taxes.

In 1951 the first Standard contract ended, and the area that the MNC had exploited for 30 years reverted to the government. The government of Laureano Gómez (1949–1953) founded the Colombian Petroleum Enterprise (Ecopetrol) to continue production. Ecopetrol later developed petroleum on its own in areas declared by the government to be "national reserves."

During the rule of military dictator Rojas Pinilla, Cities Services offered an alternative contract to the concession model. This was the "association" contract, a joint venture in which the MNC does the exploration at its own cost and risk. If an economically worthwhile amount of petroleum is found, the MNC and Ecopetrol invest equally in production activities. The government receives royalties from the MNC, as well as other taxes, and 50% of the petroleum. Actual production is run by the MNC as "operator," and the entire enterprise is governed by an executive committee composed of one representative of the MNC and one of Ecopetrol.

In 1975, President López decreed that there would be no new concessions, although the existing ones would be allowed to run their contracted periods. Association contracts were favored by López and his successors. As a result, by 1978 petroleum was being produced in three ways: directly by Ecopetrol (39% of production), by MNC's in concession agreements (37%), and by association contracts between Ecopetrol and MNC's (24%). Subsequently, as the concession agreements slowly ran out, the share of production by association agreements grew more rapidly than that of Ecopetrol.

A related matter was coal development. The López government divided the immensely rich El Cerrejón coal deposit, discovered in 1872 in the Caribbean department of La Guajira, into three parts. The central part was being explored by Peabody Coal; the southern zone was not awarded for production. The northern area, closest to the coast and richest in reserves, was chosen for an association contract. The International Colombia Resources Corporation (Intercor), a subsidiary of Exxon, won the bidding and signed an association contract with the state Coals of Colombia (Carbocol) in 1976.

Colombia's role in the international drug market developed rapidly during the 1970s. In 1979 the country exported an estimated 37 metric tons of cocaine and 15,000 metric tons of marijuana, with foreign earnings of U.S.$3 billion. Figures were comparable during the López years.

Estimates of amounts of cultivation and earnings are guesses, at best. It is certain, however, that the Sierra Nevada region became the world's largest area of marijuana production. Most cocaine was processed in Colombian cities, with most of the coca coming from other Andean countries.

The López administration's response to the growing narcotics trade was to open in the Banco de la República a window at which anyone could exchange dollars for pesos without questions being asked. No major effort was taken to destroy the crops or prohibit refining.

Meanwhile, international coffee prices had risen from $0.78 per pound in 1974 to $2.40 in 1977. This jump increased inflationary pressure, since the productive capacity of the economy was not similarly raised. It also detracted from the emphasis on minor exports, which by 1974 had reached 59% of total exports.

The López government responded by withdrawing some of the dollars from the economy. Import restrictions were loosened, thereby harming Colombian manufacturing industry. Coffee taxes were increased, and a waiting period for changing dollars at full market price was instituted. Government expenditures were either delayed or canceled completely.

**The Turbay Government: 1978–1982.** The same major policies were followed during the Liberal presidency of Julio César Turbay Ayala. In the petroleum sector the association contracts led to increases in production for the first time in more than a decade.

For the central part of El Cerrejón, after Peabody Coal had left the country, the Turbay government awarded a contract in 1981 to a consortium of one Colombian and two Spanish firms. The Intercor contract for North Cerrejón became final in 1980 and was to run until 2007. Between 1981 and 1985, Intercor contracted the building of two towns for workers, a railroad, and a deepwater port on Portete Bay. Total investment was about $3 billion, shared equally by Intercor and Carbocol. After production from North Cerrejón began in 1985, coal was expected eventually to equal or surpass coffee as Colombia's most valuable export.

By June 1981 the international coffee price was down to $1.27 per pound. Earnings from the drug trade were also down because of a coordinated program of the U.S. and Colombian governments to combat the illicit traffic. During the last year and a half of the Turbay government, the balance of trade declined. In 1980 a general recession hit the Colombian economy. It was caused in part by the recession in the world's industrial countries.

**The Betancur Initiatives: 1982–1986.** In 1982 Conservative Belisario Betancur seemed to hold forth new promise for Colombia. He had campaigned on a populist platform, offering government housing with no down payment, university education by correspondence, and a better life for the poor. Further, he had promised to work for a solution to the guerrilla problem.

Betancur granted more than half a million "housing solutions" without down payment and initially pursued fiscal policies beneficial to middle and lower strata. He also involved himself, along with the presidents of Mexico, Venezuela, and Panama (the Contadora Group), in peace efforts in war-torn Central America.

The president made a dramatic attempt to end leftist insurgency. In the first six weeks of his presidency he appointed a peace commission. In November 1982 he signed a law that granted amnesty to all guerrillas at large or in jail. Then on April 1, 1984, he announced an agreement with FARC. It included a cease-fire for a period of one year, a program of rehabilitation of the peasant areas affected by the violence, and political reform to establish full democracy and permit the emergence of new political groups. A similar truce was agreed to at the end of May 1984 with the EPL and the M-19. These agreements came to be called the National Dialogue. In the following years the guerrilla organizations were allowed to form political parties and to use the mass media.

The international lending community obliged Betancur to abandon his early protectionist policies and to lower tariffs, devalue the peso (50% in 1985 alone), and decrease government spending, which led to new growth in the gross domestic product by 1985. Foreign-exchange reserves increased as a result of another coffee bonanza, owing to a 1984 drought in Brazil, and of new exports of coal and anticipated ones of petroleum. The Colombian-Spanish consortium left Central Cerrejón in 1985, and the value of North Cerrejón exports was not so great as Exxon had projected in 1980, because of the world petroleum glut and its effects on coal prices. Nonetheless coal had taken a promising role in foreign trade.

In 1984 Occidental Petroleum, in the exploration stage of an association contract with Ecopetrol, found the largest oil deposit in the history of Colombia—a field in the Cravo Norte area of Arauca in the eastern plains. As a consequence, Colombia in 1986 became a crude-petroleum exporter for the first time since 1973. During the entire 1973–1985 period the country had continued exporting residual fuel oil, which was second only to coffee during those years in value of exports. Unemployment, however, remained high.

Crime had become a serious problem, with the 1985 census reporting that murder was the fourth leading cause of all deaths. Some of the crime was related to the guerrilla conflict. But a significant part was nonpolitical, including the drug trade, which continued to flourish despite the U.S.-Colombian campaign.

The M-19 and the EPL abandoned the cease-fires by mid-1985, charging that the National Dialogue was getting nowhere and that the government was not abiding by the truces. In November 1985 the M-19 seized the Palace of Justice in downtown Bogotá, stating their intention to try Betancur for not complying with the cease-fire agreements. Before the 28-hour fight between the M-19 and the armed forces ended, about 100 civilians had died, including 11 of the 24 members of the Supreme Court. FARC abandoned its truce in August 1986.

**From Barco to Pastrana.** In 1986 the Liberal Party's Virgilio Barco was elected president. Terrorism by narcotics traffickers continued, culminating prior to the 1990 elections in the assassina-

Cartagena and other Caribbean ports grew rapidly with the region's economic development in the late 20th century.

tions of three presidential candidates by the Medellín drug cartel. Elected president in 1990, César Gaviria of the Liberal Party promised freedom from extradition to the United States, reduced sentences, and human rights guarantees to drug traffickers who surrendered. A new Colombian constitution that banned the extradition of nationals took effect in July 1991. Meanwhile the M-19 disarmed and became a legal party in 1989. The EPL and some smaller groups followed suit in 1991 but failed to win enough votes in elections that year to sustain their party status.

Liberal candidate Ernesto Samper was elected president in 1994, but soon afterward his campaign was accused of having accepted $6 million in donations from the Cali drug cartel. The charges embroiled his administration and disrupted relations with the United States, which cut off most economic aid for the rest of Samper's term. The economy, nevertheless, continued fairly strong growth through most of the period, despite persistent inflation and unemployment, and petroleum surpassed coffee in export earnings.

In the 1990s the guerrilla war became increasingly violent and took on new dimensions. FARC and the ELN, ever more intertwined with narcotics traffickers, financed their operations with money from drugs, kidnappings, and the extortion of multinational corporations, especially oil companies with pipelines in disputed or guerrilla-controlled areas. The United Self-Defense Forces of Colombia (AUC)—a privately financed paramilitary organization beyond the control of the army, but maintaining some level of unofficial contact—began vigilante operations against the guerrillas and, in the process, committed extensive abuses against the civilian population.

In 1998 Andrés Pastrana of the Conservative Party became president with a platform of fighting corruption and negotiating with guerrillas. Following a pattern established in the 1980s, he established demilitarized zones that were to func-

tion as "safe havens" for the guerrillas and ensure an atmosphere conducive to dialogue. FARC and the ELN took possession of their respective areas in 1998 and 2000, but the anticipated cease-fire did not result. For their part, the guerrillas complained of the government's failure to curb the AUC, which had virtually exterminated the legal political party established by M-19. The AUC, on the other hand, demanded its own seat at the negotiating table.

Operations against the giant drug cartels of Cali and Medellín were more successful in that the cartels were largely dismantled. The narcotics flow, however, continued as traffickers innovated more flexible and efficient organizational forms. Colombia continued to be the world's largest producer and exporter of cocaine and had also become a coca grower and a heroine supplier. In 2000 the U.S. Congress approved a $1.3 billion aid package to support Colombia's war against drug traffickers; but critics claimed that the package was overly militarized and could lead to U.S. involvement in the guerrilla war.

HARVEY F. KLINE*, *University of Alabama*

### Bibliography

Bergquist, Charles W., *Coffee and Conflict in Colombia, 1886–1910* (1978; reprint, Duke Univ. Press 1986).

Bergquist, Charles, et al., eds., *Violence in Colombia, 1990–2000* (Scholarly Resources 2001).

Berry, R. Albert, ed., *Economic Policy and Income Distribution in Colombia* (Westview Press 1980).

Bushnell, David, *The Making of Modern Colombia: A Nation in Spite of Itself* (Univ. of Calif. Press 1993).

Fluharty, Vernon Lee, *Dance of the Millions: Military Rule and the Social Revolution in Colombia, 1930–1956* (1957; reprint, Greenwood Press 1975).

Henderson, James D., *Modernization in Colombia* (Univ. Press of Fla. 2001).

Kline, Harvey F., *State Building and Conflict Resolution in Colombia, 1986–1994* (Univ. of Ala. Press 1999).

McFarlane, Anthony, *Colombia before Independence: Economy, Society, and Politics under Bourbon Rule* (Cambridge 1993).

Sowell, David, *The Early Colombian Labor Movement: Artisans and Politics in Bogota, 1832–1919* (Temple Univ. Press 1992).

**COLOMBO,** kə-lum′bō, the largest city and chief port of Sri Lanka (formerly Ceylon), is on the southwestern coast of the island. The city's original name, Kalantotta, was corrupted by Arab traders to Kolambu, which in turn was altered by the Portuguese to Colombo. Situated only 6° north of the equator, the city has a warm, humid climate the year round. Its average temperature, however, is kept at 80°F (27°C) by the cooling influence of the Indian Ocean and monsoon winds from the southwest and northeast.

The oldest section of the city, the Pettah, is still a crowded, colorful quarter of narrow streets and tiny shops and stalls. The big stores and office buildings and the expensive boutiques are concentrated just to the west in the Fort area, site of a 16th century Portuguese outpost. In the Cinnamon Gardens residential district to the southeast are the houses of many of the well-to-do, occupying land where once grew the spices for which Sri Lanka was famous. Numerous parks adorn the city: one of the most popular is the Galle Face promenade green along the seafront south of the Fort. In the southern suburb of Dehiwala–Mt. Lavinia are an excellent beach and one of the world's finest zoos.

Reflecting the city's cosmopolitan culture are its many temples (Buddhist and Hindu), churches, and mosques. The National Museum contains much material on Sri Lanka's early history and art. The University of Colombo is the foremost center of higher education in the country, and there are technical, Buddhist, and other universities in the metropolitan area. Also in the city is the central bureau of the Colombo Plan for Asian economic development.

Greater Colombo dominates Sri Lankan industry, trade, and transportation. Its industries encompass, on a modest scale, a broad range of activities—from food processing and clothing manufacture to oil refining, iron and steel production, and motor-vehicle assembly. Gem cutting is a Colombo specialty. The city's gem merchants enjoy a wide market for their star sapphires, star rubies, cat's-eyes, aquamarines, garnets, topazes, and moonstones. The port of Colombo, one of the largest artificial harbors in the world, handles 80% of the nation's trade. Katunayake Airport, 21 miles (34 km) north of the city, is a crossroads of international traffic, and a second airport serves domestic flights.

**History.** Colombo was probably a trading station even before Prince Vijaya founded the Sinhalese dynasty in Sri Lanka in the 6th or 5th century B.C. Kotte, now a suburb of Colombo, was a capital of Sinhalese kings in the 15th and 16th centuries, after they were forced to abandon their splendid city of Polonnaruwa. The Portuguese settled at Colombo about 1517; the Dutch captured it in 1656; and the British occupied it in 1796.

In 1885, when the first of Colombo's large breakwaters was completed, the city replaced Galle as the principal port of Sri Lanka. In 1950 the city hosted the international conference that produced the Colombo Plan. With the establishment of an extensive free-trade zone on the northern outskirts of the city in 1978, the Greater Colombo Economic Commission attracted substantial foreign investment in industries such as clothing and electronics. Afterward the commission developed an investment promotion zone near the international airport and a container marshaling yard at the harbor.

Colombo was the capital of Sri Lanka under the British and after independence in 1948. The city retains that distinction de facto, pending the completion of a new capital-designate, Sri Jayawardenepura. Population: city, 612,000 (1989 est.); metropolitan area, 2,050,000 (1989 est.).

ARGUS TRESIDDER*, *Author of "Ceylon: An Introduction to the Resplendent Land"*

**COLOMBO PLAN,** kə-lum′bō, a regional development program known formally as the Colombo Plan for Co-operative Economic and Social Development in Asia and the Pacific. Founded in 1950 by Great Britain and other Commonwealth states (Australia, Canada, India, New Zealand, Pakistan, and Sri Lanka), it was later expanded to include many other countries, including the United States and Japan. The plan's executive arm is the permanent Colombo Plan Bureau, with headquarters in Colombo, Sri Lanka. The highest deliberative body, the Consultative Committee, consists of ministers who represent member governments and meet regularly in a member country.

The plan was designed to promote and support development projects in agriculture, industry, transportation, education, public health, and related fields, originally in South and Southeast Asia but afterward in the Pacific as well. Member states furnish or receive grants, loans, and personnel training. Technical experts and equipment are provided for training and research facilities established in recipient countries. In 1975 the Colombo Plan Staff College was founded in Singapore to train senior technical educators and planners.

The Colombo Plan takes a coordinated approach to reviewing the regions' economic and social progress and to identifying and discussing developmental problems. Assistance, however, is arranged bilaterally between donor and recipient members.

**COLÓN,** kô-lôn′, is a city in Panama, on Limón Bay at the Atlantic (Caribbean) end of the Panama Canal. Adjacent to the former Canal Zone port of Cristóbal, it is connected with the city of Panama by the canal, the Panama Railroad, the Trans-Isthmian Highway, and air service. Colón is a processing and distribution center of international importance as well as a residential and commercial adjunct of the canal.

The Limón Bay area originally was rife with yellow fever and malaria. Nevertheless a settlement was founded there in 1850 as the Atlantic terminus of the Panama Railroad and in 1852 was named Aspinwall for one of the line's builders. Panamanians preferred to call the town Colón, the Spanish name of Columbus, and in 1890 that designation was officially adopted.

Colón prospered while the Isthmus of Panama provided the main link between the eastern United States and California. But after a transcontinental railroad was completed in the United States in 1869, isthmian rail traffic declined and Colón became a shanty town. Its fortunes revived in 1904 as work on the Panama Canal began and mosquito-borne diseases were brought under control. The opening in 1948 of a duty-free zone for the import and subsequent processing and reexport of goods made Colón a great entrepôt port. Population: 158,935 (1996 est.).

LAURENCE R. BIRNS
*New School for Social Research*

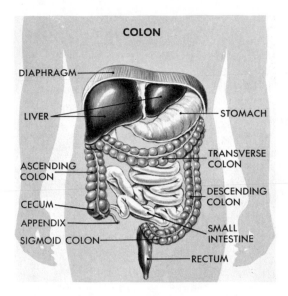

**COLON**

DIAPHRAGM

LIVER

STOMACH

TRANSVERSE COLON

ASCENDING COLON

DESCENDING COLON

CECUM

APPENDIX

SMALL INTESTINE

SIGMOID COLON

RECTUM

**COLON,** kō'lən, the part of the digestive tract located between the small intestine and the rectum. The human colon is about 4½ feet (1.3 meters) long. Together with the rectum it makes up the large intestine.

The colon is subdivided into four sections: the ascending colon, the transverse colon, the descending colon, and the sigmoid colon. At the point where the small intestine empties into the colon is a large pouch, called the cecum. Extending from the cecum a little below this point is a slender tubular sac, the appendix.

**Description.** The ascending colon is located on the lower right side of the abdomen and passes upward from the cecum to the liver, where it bends to the left to become the transverse colon. This bend is called the right colic flexure. From this point the transverse colon, which is the longest segment of the colon, sweeps across the abdominal cavity below the stomach and bends downward on the left side of the spleen to become the descending colon. The juncture of these two segments is called the left colic flexure, and from this point the descending colon, the narrowest segment of the colon, extends downward along the left side of the abdomen to the brim of the pelvis, where it joins the sigmoid colon. The sigmoid colon is an S-shaped segment, whose lower end is continuous with the rectum.

**Structure and Function.** The wall of the colon consists of three separate layers. The innermost layer is a smooth mucous coat containing many small glands. Beneath this layer is the submucosa coat, containing many blood and lymph vessels embedded in loose connective tissue. The third layer consists of three longitudinal strips of muscle, the taeniae coli. Because these muscle bands are shorter than the other layers of the colon, the colon wall is thrown into many folds, forming a series of pouches, called haustra.

By the time food material enters the colon, it consists largely of unusable matter. The major function of the colon is to absorb water and inorganic salts from this matter and to move it to the rectum, from where it is eliminated.

JEFFREY WENIG
*ENDO Laboratories*

**COLON,** in grammar. See PUNCTUATION.

**COLONEL,** kûr'nəl, is a senior military rank, above lieutenant colonel and below brigadier general. Colonels historically have commanded regiments and still do in the U. S. Marine Corps and in most armies. The U. S. Army, which no longer has the regiment, usually assigns a colonel to head a brigade of infantry under peace conditions or a brigadier general to lead it in war. A colonel may also head a division's artillery or support group. In the U. S. Air Force a colonel may command a wing or an airbase, which may be composed in turn of wings, service groups, and squadrons of aircraft. Colonels fill important staff positions in most military forces. In most countries navy captains rank with colonels. The British Royal Air Force's group captains rank with colonels.

**COLONIA,** kə-lō'nē-ə, a community in the township of Woodbridge, in east central New Jersey. It is situated in Middlesex county, 12 miles (19 km) southwest of Newark. Colonia is primarily a residential center in an industrial area. Edison State Park, 3 miles (5 km) to the southwest, marks the site of one of Thomas A. Edison's laboratories. Colonia is governed by the township. Population: 17,811.

**COLONIAL AGENT,** a person who represented the interests of an American colony in England. For much of the 17th century agents normally were sent only on special missions, but in the late 17th and in the 18th centuries some colonies maintained permanent representatives. Famous Americans who served as colonial agents included Miles Standish, Roger Williams, William Byrd, John Winthrop, Jr., Increase Mather, and Benjamin Franklin.

The colonial agent gave information to the English colonial office about the colony and defended its interests in such matters as commercial regulations, disputes over colonial boundaries, and taxation and finance. To inform the British public about the colony, a few of the agents contributed to newspapers or published pamphlets. Familiarity with personnel and procedures in the various government offices was important for the successful representation of colonial interests; for this reason and also to minimize expense, the men chosen as agents sometimes were permanent residents of England. Agents were not well paid, and, because they dealt with a cumbersome bureaucracy, they encountered numerous and lengthy delays. In addition they sometimes suffered abuse from the colonial legislature when a decision in England went against the interests of the colony.

GEORGE D. LANGDON, JR., *Vassar College*

**COLONIAL ART AND ARCHITECTURE.** See LATIN AMERICA—*Culture* (Art and Architecture): Colonial Era; UNITED STATES—*Art and Architecture* (Colonial Period).

**COLONIAL HEIGHTS,** a city in east central Virginia, situated in but independent of Chesterfield county. It is across the Appomattox River from Petersburg and 21 miles (35 km) south of Richmond. The city is in an industrial section and produces boats and dairy products.

During the siege of Petersburg in 1864, Confederate Gen. Robert E. Lee's headquarters were nearby. The city is governed by a mayor, city manager, and council. Population: 16,897.

Agriculture was the primary colonial enterprise. Large farms, such as this Southern plantation depicted by an unknown artist, were generally located near rivers because of the easy transportation of crops to market.

**COLONIAL LIFE.** The colonial period in United States history, from 1607, when the first permanent English colony was established, to 1776, when the colonists declared their independence from Britain, saw rough wilderness settlements grow into prosperous and sophisticated provinces. Colonists upon arriving were preoccupied with personal goals such as family and farm, but they left descendants who possessed broader visions. In time they established distinctly American customs so pervasive as to overcome regional differences and to enable those of European descent to consider themselves a new people. For blacks and Indians, however, the American experience led to bondage and oppression rather than to freedom and independence.

Within a generation after Columbus' arrival in America, Spain, Portugal, England, and France had each staked a claim to parts of the New World. For more than a century, Spain was the only European nation strong enough to exploit its claims in the Caribbean Sea and South America. Then at the beginning of the 17th century, France established several fishing stations and fur-trading posts along the North American coast and in the valley of the St. Lawrence River. Neither the Spanish nor the French settlements attracted many Europeans, however, and England became the major colonizing power in the New World.

Before 1600, Englishmen concluded that their nation should plant colonies in America to develop raw materials for the mother country and become markets for its manufactures. Undoubtedly its spirit of international competition in commerce was partly responsible for England's ultimate success. The primary reason for the empire's greatness, however, was the thousands of Englishmen who left their homeland to settle in the New World. Some were adventurers, who returned to England when their dreams of an easy fortune came to naught. But most sought religious freedom or improvement of their lot in life. Throughout the colonial period they were joined by thousands of other Europeans with similar goals. In pursuing their individual livelihoods these colonists, without realizing it, laid the foundations for a new nation.

The territory settled by Englishmen varied from the chilly, granite coasts of Maine to the verdant, semitropical lands of the Carolinas and Georgia. Poor farming conditions and the hostile interior led many New Englanders to earn their living from the sea. Others turned to the northern woods for timber and furs. The geography south of New England was kinder to the prospective farmer. The river valleys of the Hudson, Mohawk, and Delaware yielded thousands of acres of rich, rolling farmland. Here, too, milder climate and gentler topography encouraged large-scale farming. Even more significant differences prevailed in the Chesapeake Bay region, where broad rivers opened up a rich interior all the way to the fall line nearly 100 miles (160 km) inland. Still farther south, in the Carolinas and Georgia, coastal plains protected by offshore islands provided ideal conditions for plantations.

Despite wide differences between geographical regions and ways of earning a livelihood, American colonists had much in common. The stark reality of survival in a harsh environment gave them one important bond. And because most white Americans were farmers, the abundance of land gave them the opportunity to improve their economic position. Most colonists shared as well a belief that a man could better himself by his own efforts. This willingness to work hard made colonists increasingly self-sufficient. By the mid-18th century, 150 years of shared experience in the New World created a new man in America—a man largely independent of European authority and tradition.

## SOCIETY

**National Origins.** The men and women who settled in the English colonies came from a wide variety of backgrounds. While most New England inhabitants could trace their roots to the mother country itself, the middle colonies attracted numerous immigrants from Germany, northern Ireland (the Scots-Irish), and the Netherlands (from the days when New York had been a Dutch colony), and a scattering of settlers from Finland and Sweden. To the back country of Virginia and the Carolinas came additional groups of Germans and Scots-Irish as well as Highlanders. New York City and Newport, R. I., became homes for small numbers of Jewish immigrants, and French Huguenots settled in several colonies from Massachusetts to South Carolina.

The largest single minority group at the end of the colonial period were blacks from Africa, while the English represented the dominant majority (about 60 percent) of the population. Except for the Germans, most immigrants abandoned their native language within a generation, but such words as "boss" and "cruller" (from the Dutch), "bureau" (from the French), and numerous terms from the native Indians ("canoe," "moccasin," and "skunk") became a part of the American language. The blacks made a considerable imprint on pronunciation in the Southern colonies.

**The Extended Family.** For most Americans life centered around the family. In addition to his parents and several sisters and brothers, a colonial child was likely to share his home with at least one grandparent, an unmarried uncle or aunt, and perhaps a cousin or two whose mother had died. In time, his older brother might bring a wife into the household, and soon after nephews and nieces would join the family group. It was not unusual to find households numbering 12 or more as generation succeeded generation. The large, extended family served an important economic function, for without laborsaving devices, many hands were needed to make a household self-sufficient.

**Class Structure.** Most colonial Americans lived out their lives within a vaguely defined social class. Among the bottom third stood the blacks, both slave and free, along with white indentured servants and other landless whites, including apprentices and other laborers both urban and rural. But the poorest white held one distinct advantage over the less fortunate blacks—no burden of racial prejudice prevented him from improving his lot in life. At the other extreme were the wealthy planters, merchants, and professional men whose property and personal prestige commanded respect, however grudgingly, from those less fortunate. Less than 10 percent of the population could claim such distinction.

The majority of colonists, around 60 percent, comprised an amorphous middle class—farmers for the most part, along with the artisans and shopkeepers of urban communities. Within this class could be found a wide variety of men. At one end of the scale were subsistence farmers owning a few acres of inferior soil, semiskilled carpenters with a little property, and small entrepreneurs struggling to make a living. At the other end were well-to-do craftsmen or successful farmers who produced a surplus for market.

The gulf between these classes varied according to location. It was less pronounced in rural areas than in the seaports, in Northern colonies less than in the South. In all regions the middle class was relatively large and possessed considerable political and economic strength. Among freemen, property was distributed far more evenly in America than in European countries of the era.

What particularly struck commentators about colonial America was the high degree of social and economic mobility. While the proportional distribution of people among the lower, middle, or upper ranks remained more or less stable throughout the period, a family's place on that scale might vary considerably through the course of two or three generations. Several factors account for this relatively high degree of social mobility. For one, America had no titled aristocracy monopolizing positions of political and economic power. For another, labor was constantly in great demand, and a man willing to work hard was relatively well rewarded. Still more significant was the availability of cheap land in the unsettled interior to which people discontented with their lot in established communities could move in search of new opportunity.

Still another factor was the steady increase in population, which doubled every 25 years. The frontier could not absorb this growth all at once, and therefore small villages became towns,

The Chandler Wedding Tapestry depicts a New England wedding in 1765. The clothes reflect English styles.

Colonial families were large, representing several generations. This group portrait of his own family is by Charles Willson Peale, a leading painter of the period.

and towns grew into cities along the Eastern Seaboard. As a result, new demands for the services of blacksmiths, millers, and other artisans created new opportunities. Another result was the revolution in agriculture brought on by the rising demand for foodstuffs in the urban centers. Rapid increase in population meant social dislocation as well, for family farms could not be divided indefinitely among three or four sons. But the opportunities generally outweighed the drawbacks. Furthermore, the steady influx of impoverished immigrants and the rapid growth of slavery as the primary labor system of the Southern colonies improved the relative standing of the native-born whites.

**Government.** The most important political development during the colonial period was the tradition of self-government. With slight regional variations, the basic principle was that local political decisions should be made by the property owners residing in the area. In most farming communities this meant that perhaps three quarters of all adult white males had a voice in political matters if they cared to exercise their right. In urban communities property qualifications usually restricted the franchise to about two thirds of the adult males.

**Local.** In New England with its pattern of condensed settlement, the town was the local unit of government. At the town meeting voters determined such matters as local taxes; appropriations for schools and highways; and the choice of selectmen, assessors, and overseers of the poor. In the 17th century, town meetings had attempted to operate on the principle of consensus, but increasing differences between villagers and "outlivers," farmers and artisans, rich and poor eroded the earlier spirit of community, with the common result that dissident groups left to form their own settlements or forced a permanent partition of the original town.

In the relatively thinly settled Southern colonies, the parish or the county was the local political unit. In all regions both law and custom often restricted candidates for elective office to men of more than average economic and social position. Many artisans or small farmers did not aspire to office because they could not afford

the time. Besides, many colonists looked to men of wealth and status for leadership in civic affairs. This "habit of deference," though on the wane throughout the 18th century, meant that not every white freeman had an equal opportunity to become a political leader.

**Provincial.** On the provincial level, towns, parishes, and counties were represented in the legislature through the delegates they elected to lower houses of assembly. Generally speaking, law and customs likewise restricted membership in these bodies to the more well-to-do colonists. But they had to stand for election annually and were often specifically instructed by their constituents to support particular local interests. Provincial politics were characterized in the 18th century by a "chaotic factionalism," by which various groups struggled for domination over their political rivals. These battles rarely centered on ideological differences. Rather, their object seemed to be the attainment of power for such self-serving purposes as land grants, military contracts, or simply prestige.

Although colonial politicians squabbled among themselves within the legislature, they usually formed a united front against royal authority as represented by the governor and other crown-appointed officials. In colonies such as Pennsylvania and Maryland the governor represented the interest of the hereditary proprietors, the Penns and Calverts. Battles between governors and the legislatures were likewise fought for political rather than ideological ends, for few colonists seriously challenged their sovereign's right to appoint administrative officials. But they did view executive authority with considerable suspicion and strove to strengthen the power of their assemblies at every opportunity.

By the mid-18th century, colonists had attained a large measure of self-government in almost all of the provinces. Yet the political system remained something far less than democratic—if that term is taken to mean government *by* the people. For significant numbers of inhabitants—women, servants, and blacks, as well as adult males without property—could not participate in governmental affairs.

**Religion.** One of the strongest influences on

the daily lives of colonial Americans was religion. Throughout the colonies one could find, by the mid-1700's, a wide range of religious groups including Quakers, Pietists, Catholics, and Jews in addition to the more common Protestant denominations. Encouraged by the abundance of free land and by the religious toleration in most colonies, other persecuted Europeans continually migrated to the New World.

**Denominations.** Religion, in fact, had provided the prime motivation for the founding of several colonies. As the Puritans approached the shores of New England in the spring of 1630, their leader, John Winthrop, reminded them of their holy mission: "We shall be as a City upon a Hill, the Eyes of all People are upon us; so that if We shall deal falsely with our God in this Work We have undertaken ... We shall open the mouths of enemies to speak Evil of the ways of God. ..." The Puritans had made a covenant with God to establish a community governed by his holy laws as revealed in the Bible. Their church was therefore of central importance because the minister helped his followers interpret the word of God, and the members of the congregation strengthened each other in the continuing battle against sin. Many New Englanders must have experienced the guilt to which Michael Wigglesworth confessed in 1653: "This morning God let in some comfortable persuasion of His love to me; yet after, vain thoughts prevailed. ... Instead of admiring God I admire myself; for this I loath myself."

Although the Puritans founded their New England colonies so that they could practice their religion without interference, they saw no reason to extend toleration to other groups. Accordingly, Catholics, Quakers, and Baptists found asylum in other colonies such as Maryland, Pennsylvania, and Rhode Island. Quakers were particularly vulnerable to persecution by other colonists, for they maintained that God communicated directly to man through an inner voice, a belief that Calvinists considered heresy. Furthermore, they were pacifists, and when Quaker leaders in Pennsylvania refused to raise arms to defend the colony against Indian attacks, the frontiersmen, who bore the brunt of the fighting, were understandably bitter. Finally, the Quakers believed in perfectionism and would make no compromises to accommodate the views of those around them. But they ruled well in Pennsylvania, and the province prospered both spiritually and materially.

Throughout the tidewater regions of the Southern colonies the Church of England had the largest number of followers, but the influence of Anglicanism in America was never very strong. Plantations and settlements were widely scattered in this area, making it difficult for a parish minister to establish cohesion among his followers. Furthermore, the dominant characteristic of the Anglican Church was conservative respectability, and its religious currents, therefore, tended to run quietly. In the piedmont and backcountry areas of the Southern colonies, religion played a more direct role in the lives of the inhabitants. Most of the settlers were Presbyterians, Methodists, or members of a variety of evangelical sects. There were few resident

Colonial society differed markedly between South and North. (*Left*) Charles Calvert, a Maryland aristocrat, was portrayed by John Hesselius in fashionable dress, attended by a body slave. (*Right*) Rev. Ebenezer Devotion, as painted by Winthrop Chandler, reflects New England Puritanism in his severe expression and scholarly surroundings.

BALTIMORE MUSEUM OF ART; HERBERT VOSE

The Puritan religious heritage is preserved in New England by white, spired churches, such as this graceful Congregational church on the green in Litchfield, Conn.

ministers, and church services depended on the visits of itinerant preachers. On arriving at a backcountry settlement, the minister generally had much business to conduct, including baptisms, weddings, and funerals. Because many months often would have passed since the inhabitants had attended church, services tended to be highly emotional.

Emotionalism occasionally swept through the more staid communities of the Eastern Seaboard as well. During a particularly bleak period in the history of Massachusetts at the end of the 17th century, a severe wave of witchcraft mania broke out in Salem Village. Before the charges and countercharges of consorting with the devil had ended, 19 inhabitants had been hanged as witches and yet another pressed to death for refusing to deny the accusations against him.

*Revival.* On a happier note, a religious revival known as the Great Awakening swept through the colonies in the 1730's and 1740's. English evangelists such as George Whitefield exhorted audiences of 8,000 or more, often twice a day for weeks on end. A Connecticut farmer later recorded his reaction to the news that Whitefield was to preach in nearby Middletown. "I was in my field at work. I dropped my tool that I had in my hand and ran to my wife, telling her to make ready quickly.... I with my wife soon mounted the horse and went forward as fast as I thought the horse could bear." Hearing Whitefield preach, the farmer recalled, "gave me a heart wound. By God's blessing, my old foundation was broken up, and I saw that my righteousness would not save me."

As a result of the Great Awakening, many colonists were divided thereafter into "old light" adherents to what had become orthodox practices and "new lights," who had embraced the more expressive practices of the revivalists. Yet another result of the Great Awakening was to increase the participation of the common people in religious activities.

**Education.** Like religion, education was more firmly established in the North than in the South. Not only did the compact settlements of New England make the founding of schools more practical, but the Puritan doctrine that God's will was revealed in the Bible put a religious premium on literacy. Massachusetts and Connecticut enacted laws requiring the town fathers to provide for the education of youth by tax-supported, public elementary schools. Attendance was compulsory unless the parents made alternative arrangements for the instruction of their children with a private tutor.

Public schoolmasters were expected to instruct their pupils "both in humane learning and good literature, and likewise in point of good manners and dutiful behavior towards all, especially their superiors." To assist in this latter goal *The New England Primer* taught the young scholar by such rhymes as "In *Adam's* fall/We sinned all," and "The Idle *Fool*/Is Whipped at school." Under the heading "The Dutiful Child's Promises" were found such precepts as "I will honor my father and mother" and "I will submit to my elders." Among the "Lessons for Youth" was the doctrine "Foolishness is bound up in the heart of a child, but the rod of correction will drive it from him." School was usually kept in one-room buildings, where pupils of various ages demanded the attention of the teacher in recitation and came under his strict discipline. The younger pupils studied their alphabet from "hornbooks," while the older scholars struggled through more advanced readers.

More promising students were often sent to grammar schools in preparation for college. Here they learned the basics of Latin grammar, classical history, and the rudiments of Greek over the course of six or seven years. Pupils who were willing and able to continue their education might then, at the age of 16 or so, enter one of the several colonial colleges, such as Harvard, Yale, or the College of William and Mary. A few were sent to England for further training at Oxford or Cambridge. Harvard's curriculum offered a broadly liberal education in "good literature, arts and sciences and all other necessary provisions that may conduce to the education of English and Indian youth of this Country in knowledge and godliness." Most of the books and all of the instruction was in Latin at first, although by the mid-18th century the introduction of new subjects required a relaxation of this pattern.

Next to Massachusetts, Pennsylvania took the most active role in education. Here the primary purpose was utilitarian rather than religious. When Benjamin Franklin proposed the establishment of an academy in 1749, he suggested that the pupils be taught "those things that are likely to be most useful and most ornamental," by which he meant arithmetic, geometry, geography, and gardening as well as the more obvious skills of reading and writing. South and west of Philadelphia, however, educational institutions were few in number, mainly because of the pattern of scattered settlement.

By no means did all education take place in schools. Through the system of apprenticeship inherited from Europe, many a colonial youth acquired a trade or craft by working under contract to a master artisan for a period ranging from three to seven years. The apprentice generally lived in his master's household and received clothing and other necessaries in addition to his keep. The master instructed his charge in "the art and mystery of his craft" and at the end of the apprenticeship period usually gave him enough tools or other equipment to set him up in business for himself. Girls often were indentured as household servants, learning how to cook and manage the multitude of other tasks necessary to keep a family fed and clothed. Masters generally took their obligations seriously and instructed their servants in reading and writing as well as in the practical arts. It was not uncommon for apprentices and servants to marry into their masters' families at the end of their period of service. At the other end of the scale, men interested in learning a profession such as medicine or law usually studied with an established doctor or lawyer for several years until pronounced ready by their mentors to set up for themselves.

**The Military Establishment.** Self-defense was a fact of life in colonial America, not only against hostile Indians, who resisted the European invasion of their homeland, but against the French and Spaniards as well. A few professional soldiers in each colony helped to train all white males 16 and older in local militia units, which in time of war became the components of companies and regiments. Some local units elected their own officers, while the governor, who served as commander-in-chief of his colony's forces, appointed the higher officers. Each man was expected to provide his own weapon, a small quantity of powder and ball, and a few other necessaries, but in time of emergency the legislature usually appropriated sufficient funds to supplement these supplies.

The colonists balked at maintaining large standing armies, for few farmers were willing to spend long months of garrison duty in frontier fortresses. Some of these posts were manned by as few as eight or ten men during peacetime. Not surprisingly, they were quickly overrun whenever the French or Indians made a surprise attack. The authorities then hastily organized an expedition of militiamen to retaliate. Under the circumstances, only by superior numbers and equipment did the English settlers prevail over their opponents in wilderness warfare.

At the end of the 17th century there began a series of wars between England and France that taxed the resources of the colonists to the very limit. During a span of nearly 80 years the mother country assisted its colonies by sending regiments of troops, providing arms and other military supplies, and compensating the various assemblies for much of their expenditures. Fighting side by side often created more friction than friendship between British regulars and colonial militia, however, particularly because the redcoats tended to look down upon their provincial cousins. For their part, the colonists were understandably skeptical of the kind of tactics that led to the ambush of Gen. James Braddock in 1755. By the end of the colonial period, thousands of colonists had acquired sufficient military experience to face the British regulars with some confidence in the battles that marked the outbreak of war in 1775.

From the 1740's on, American shipowners outfitted vessels to attack the merchantmen of

Princeton University, originally called the College of New Jersey, was chartered in 1746. Nassau Hall is at the left, and the president's house is at the right.

Punishment in the colonies was often cruel. As this broadside proclaims, a criminal might be condemned to the pillory, to have an ear cut off, and to be whipped.

Spain and France. The valuable prizes were divided among successful owners and crews, and the enemy's commerce was seriously disrupted as well. But privateers cannot attain command of the sea, and the ultimate triumph over France in America depended on the power of the British fleet, which time and again prevented the enemy from bringing in fresh troops and supplies to its land forces. Few Americans willingly served in the British Navy, although during wartime a number of hapless mariners were impressed into service by desperate British captains. Working toward the common goal of ousting the French from America, Americans and Britons succeeded by 1763. By that time as well, the danger of Indian attack had been drastically reduced. Thereafter, military defense to most Americans meant defense against the British Army itself.

**The Legal System.** In most colonies the governor, and his council sat as the highest court of justice. In some they were also authorized to establish inferior courts, and in most they appointed justices and other officials to the various tribunals. Governors in the 17th century often complained about the lack of trained lawyers qualified to serve on the bench, although matters improved somewhat in the 18th century. Colonial courts were expected to make rulings according to English common law, which most Americans viewed as a means of maintaining public order. Beyond this, virtually every colony adopted its own code of laws governing personal conduct, proscribing numerous misdeeds, and establishing punishments.

The criminal codes, like other laws, were derived for the most part from English precedents, and the full range of corporal punishments, including branding, mutilation, and whipping, remained on the books throughout most of the colonial period. However, in some respects the penal system in America was more humane than in England. Because labor was so scarce in the colonies, offenders were less likely to be left languishing for months or years in a crowded, filthy, disease-ridden prison. Rather, it was hoped that public humiliation in the stocks or at the whipping post would reform the offender and serve as a warning to others.

Whether because of or in spite of this system of punishment, there seems to have been comparatively little crime in colonial America. Most people, of course, lived in rural areas, traditionally less troubled by public disorder. On the frontier, however, lawlessness occasionally reached serious proportions. Attacks on peaceful Indians, occupation of land without proper title, and theft of livestock were not uncommon. In the seaports, bands of unruly sailors sometimes got out of hand. But it is a wonder that the cities were not more tumultuous, for there were no policemen in the modern sense. Part-time constables maintained law and order as best they could, calling on the general citizenry to lend assistance when necessary. By and large, the American colonists were law-abiding people. Wages were relatively high, land was cheap, and the opportunities for an honest living were sufficiently numerous to make a life of crime unappealing.

## ECONOMY AND TECHNOLOGY

**Agriculture—Landholding.** In several parts of the American colonies during the 17th century large landholders attempted to attract Europeans to settle as tenant farmers paying rent. Wealthy Dutch patrons in the Hudson Valley had a little success for a while, as did some of the Calverts and their followers in Maryland. But for the most part, Europeans saw no reason to exchange their dependent status at home for a similar dependence in the New World. Every attempt to restrict the tenure of land in America inevitably failed because so much land was available on a freehold basis.

In the Southern colonies anyone paying for the passage of an immigrant to America received a "headright," or title to 50 acres (20 hectares) of land. Although later modified, this system enabled planters, shipmasters, and others to amass large tracts of land during the 17th century. In New England the various legislatures granted entire townships to approved groups of immigrants, who then distributed some of it to prospective inhabitants while reserving the rest for common use or for later grants as the population grew. If one failed to acquire land by headright or outright grant, he might be able to purchase it from a colonial proprietor or speculator. Failing that, a man might brave the wilderness and carve out a holding without benefit of legal title by simply "squatting" on the tract of his choice.

**Plantations and Farms.** In the Southern colonies, where an individual could acquire several thousand acres, the plantation system soon emerged as the most suitable means of agricultural production. Devoted almost entirely to the cultivation of a single marketable crop, plantations around Chesapeake Bay became the world's largest producers of tobacco. In South Carolina, rice and indigo were the staple crops. This one-crop system rapidly depleted the soil, however, and required a constant search for new lands. Few tidewater planters knew or cared about methods of soil conservation until late in the colonial period. The existence of a seemingly inexhaustible supply of land had already begun to make an impact on Americans as "the people of plenty." In addition to land, tobacco and rice plantations required a large labor supply for efficient operation. After initial efforts to enslave the Indians failed and white indentured servants discovered how easy it was to escape into the wilderness, Southern planters increasingly relied upon Africans imported against their will and forced into permanent slavery.

In contrast, farmers in the Northern colonies developed different methods of production. Climate, soil conditions, and the method of land distribution itself all contributed to the predominance of the small family farm in New England. The township system perpetuated for several generations an emphasis on general farming rather than specialization in a marketable crop. Thus each settler held a small tract for pasturage, several small fields for cultivation, and perhaps another tract for an orchard. Not until the 18th century did many New England farms begin to produce a surplus marketable in a nearby town such as Boston, Newport, or Hartford. Still, diversification rather than specialization remained characteristic of Northern farming, and a marketable surplus was more a welcome dividend to the year's labors than a planned goal.

The New England farm was almost entirely self-sufficient. It provided a wide variety of foodstuffs for the family and the materials necessary to house and clothe it. The skills needed to preserve food for winter and to make furniture, utensils, and warm clothes were taught by father to son and by mother to daughter down through successive generations. The family was dependent on the outside world only perhaps for a plow from the blacksmith, boots from the shoemaker, and imported English iron pots from the storekeeper.

In Pennsylvania still another kind of agriculture developed. Palatine Germans, with their conservative use of land, rotation of crops, and loving care of livestock, were by far the best farmers in America. As they prospered, they turned to wheat as a marketable commodity. By the mid-18th century the middle colonies produced enough of this and other grain to feed most of the major settlements along the Atlantic seaboard. The Germans took their methods with them as they spread southwest. There they grew wheat, barley, and corn and raised cows and pigs. Flour and whiskey, made from grain, along with beef and pork from grain-fed animals, became the chief cash products of the interior.

***Methods and Markets.*** Most farm implements were made of wood. Harrows had teeth of tough hickory or oak, and scythes were later equipped with wooden "cradles" to catch the stalks. Scythe blades, of course, were of metal as were plowshares to break the sod. Other wooden implements included rakes, pitchforks, flails for threshing, and woven baskets for winnowing. Not surprisingly, such tools broke easily and required constant repair or replacement. Most farms had a two-wheeled cart hauled by a yoke of oxen, but much of the heavy work was done by sledge.

Farming in the 18th century as in the 20th required long hours of hard toil, for animals required constant care and feeding, and crops had

Bethlehem, Pa., was founded in the mid-1700's by the Moravians, who, like many others, sought religious freedom.

The kitchen was the living center of the colonial home. In this New England kitchen a weighted clockwork device rotates the fireplace spit. At the table are a Windsor highchair (*left*) and armchair.

to be planted, cultivated, and harvested according to nature's schedule, not personal convenience. Even a wealthy planter such as George Washington spent many hours a day overseeing the work of his laborers, experimenting with new crops and methods, and arranging to market his produce to the best advantage. With the possible exception of the rice and indigo planters of South Carolina, few colonial farmers enjoyed much leisure time.

Farming was a risky venture in the 18th century. In addition to natural disasters such as drought and pestilence, which could destroy a season's crop, the farmers who raised a commodity such as wheat or tobacco for market were at the mercy of the merchants and factors who purchased their crops. Overproduction was a major problem, for it drove down prices and tempted the farmer to plant more the season following, which resulted in still greater overproduction. Wealthy Southern planters were habitually in debt to English merchants, just as Northern farmers were to seaport merchants who supplied them with the manufactured articles they had come to consider necessary for a comfortable living. Only the subsistence farmer could remain free of this dependence on others, but his standard of living improved more slowly as a price for his independence.

**Trade.** Trade had been the chief interest of the various companies that had founded several of the American colonies in the 17th century. Englishmen hoping for profits invested capital in these New World enterprises but without much success. Individual settlers took up where the joint-stock companies left off, and by the end of the 17th century a number of settlers had begun to amass considerable fortunes.

The New England fisheries formed one important cornerstone to this enterprise. In addition to the cod and herring banks of Newfoundland, the broad Atlantic also became the scene of the Nantucket whaling industry, for oil was a valued fuel for lamps. Another basic resource was found in the Northern woods, where timber abounded for sawn lumber, shingles, barrel staves, and ship timber and masts (the largest pine trees being reserved for the Royal Navy). From Albany the Dutch (and later the English) carried on a flourishing fur trade with the Iroquois, although they could not compete with the French trade that reached out from Montreal into the Great Lakes region and beyond. Hunters in the Southern colonies brought in quantities of deerskins for sale in local and foreign markets as well. The abundance of the North American continent offered the basis for commercial prosperity.

Because England had little use for the fish and timber of the Northern colonies, however, New Englanders were forced to build sturdy vessels and carry the produce of forest and sea to the Southern colonies and the West Indies. There they exchanged their fish and timber for tobacco, rice, and sugar—all marketable in England. These exports, in turn, permitted the Northern merchants to purchase the manufactured articles so necessary to their expanding economy. They also carried dried and salted fish to the Atlantic islands and the Mediterranean to exchange for wine, fruit, and salt. The importation of molasses from the West Indies fed the distilleries of New England. Rum not only helped keep Northern farmers and fishermen warm through the long winters but also was a staple in both the fur trade with the Indians and the infamous slave trade with Africa. The middle colonies carried on a lively coastal trade with the other continental colonies, providing flour and breadstuffs to all regions.

The goal of all this commercial activity was to provide the American colonies with the commodities they needed most—manufactured articles from the mother country, labor from Africa, and sugar and molasses from the West Indies. Thousands of mariners and shipwrights, hundreds of merchants and captains, and scores of customs officials all made a livelihood from the burgeoning commerce of colonial America. As the result of this trade throughout the Atlantic world, the colonies grew steadily richer.

**Manufacture.** The shipyard was in one sense America's first factory, for here on one site were assembled the various materials and craftsmen needed to build a fine vessel. The work of many specialists and many kinds of materials went into the process, and in a large yard more than one vessel could be built at a time.

Another highly developed colonial industry involved the manufacture of iron. An operation such as Alexander Spotswood's works in Virginia required a capital investment of £ 12,000, thousands of acres of ore-field, and 2 square miles (6 sq km) of woodland for fuel. Water-powered bellows brought the blast furnace to a high temperature to drive out the impurities from the ore. The Spotswood furnace could produce almost 20 tons of iron a week, some of it exported to England but most of it used in America itself.

Still another heavy industry was the merchant mill that ground wheat and other grains for flour. Many of these mills were located along the rivers around Philadelphia and Wilmington, for water-power drove both the big grinding stones and the auxiliary machinery as well. On a smaller scale almost every village had its local sawmill powered by waterwheel. Paper mills, fulling mills, and other factories appeared along the fast-flowing streams of the Northern colonies in increasing profusion.

On a still smaller scale was the master craftsman, who owned his own shop. At first many basic crafts, such as baking and weaving, were carried on in each colonist's home. Special products such as clocks and furniture were imported. This pattern continued in rural areas. But the increasing population and specialization of labor made possible the establishment of professional craftsmen in towns and villages. Such a man required only his tools, materials, and place to work, often the ground floor of his house. He worked by hand, with the help of his family and perhaps an apprentice or two and usually made his own designs. Craftsmen in a typical 18th century town included bakers, cabinetmakers, clockmakers, potters, weavers, dyers, hatters, tailors, and cordwainers (shoemakers). Other skilled artisans, such as housewrights and bricklayers, did their work on site.

In smaller villages, craftsmen usually made goods on order only, but in larger towns the artisan was a shopkeeper as well. He publicized his wares by a sign over his door and perhaps by advertising in the local newspaper, but his best advertisement was the quality of his work. The most successful craftsmen enjoyed a market well beyond the limits of their own communities.

Colonial America was far from the free-enterprise paradise that modern businessmen like to think it was. British regulations attempted to restrict the exportation of certain American-made goods, such as hats and woolens. Far more effective a restraint were the various local regulations, which held artisans to high standards of quality in their work, thus affording the buyer some protection from shoddy produce, underweight goods, and unscrupulous practices. A further check on colonial manufacture was the fact that many colonists preferred imported to

Much of the industry in the colonies was limited to artisans with small workshops. Shown (*left to right*) are a cabinetmaker; a cutler, who made knives, razors, and scissors; and a brazier, who manufactured household utensils.

native goods. For example, Americans bought English woolens and Irish linens whenever they could afford them. The importation of these fabrics continued to be the mainstay of Anglo-American commerce even after the colonists had declared political independence from the mother country. So strong was this habit of reliance on English goods that French and continental textiles could never offer serious competition.

**Urban Life.** While most colonists lived in the country, by the mid-18th century, America boasted cities such as Philadelphia, New York, Boston, and Charleston that offered a stimulating cultural and economic environment. It was no accident that of the 20 largest urban centers all but Lancaster, Pa., were located on tidewater, for the 18th century city was first of all a seaport. For this reason, however, cities were confined to rather narrow peninsulas or strips along the waterfront. Land became expensive, and, as nearby timber resources disappeared, building costs soared. Crowded into these cities were artisans and their apprentices, shopkeepers, sailors and merchants, longshoremen, and professional men.

Many of the problems of urban life so familiar to later generations plagued the city dwellers of the 18th century. Sanitation was poor and public health problems a constant threat to life. Streets were poorly lighted at best, law enforcement difficult, and fire an ever-present danger. Nevertheless, the cities of colonial America offered a dynamic and exciting alternative to rural drudgery and attracted increasing numbers of sons and daughters from the farms.

**Transportation.** Despite the attraction of the cities, the average colonist had little opportunity to travel beyond a semiannual trip to the nearest market town. As a result, he knew nothing about his fellow settlers in other colonies except what he might occasionally read in newspapers in the village tavern. The main barrier to better communications, beyond the fact that farmers had little time for travel, was the abominable condition of roads. Most were only wide enough to permit passage of a single man on horseback and too rough for any vehicle resembling a stagecoach, at least until the mid-18th century. Even then it took three days to journey from New York to Philadelphia. Small streams were crossed by fording and larger rivers by ferries.

Travel was so slow by land that overnight facilities became a necessity. Yet the American roadside inn was legendary for its bad food, surly keeper, and spartan accommodations, which one had to share with other guests. The wise traveler booked passage on a coastal sailing vessel, on which accommodations were at least no worse than at most inns, and distant points often could be reached more quickly by sea than by land. Regular (if slow) post roads linked the larger communities by mid-18th century, especially after Benjamin Franklin improved the service. Even so, Americans remained rather isolated, not only from each other but more particularly from their European origins. While one could cross the Atlantic in four to six weeks, the passage was tedious, often dangerous, and always expensive.

**Food, Drink and Clothing.** At the outset of settlement, colonists lived extremely simple lives by necessity. Foodstuffs such as corn, squash, and wild game—turkey, deer, pigeon, and rabbit —provided the principal fare at most dinner tables. Along the northern coast and by the rivers of the middle colonies, fish offered variety to the main meal, while backcountry people relied on pork. Later generations of settlers

Taverns furnished the nightlife for colonial men. In this painting by John Greenwood, American sea captains, far from prying neighbors, carouse in Surinam.

Shops and houses lined John Street in 18th century New York, one of the thriving ports along the Atlantic coast.

could afford beef on occasion, along with oysters, crabs, and other shellfish in season. Preserving food for the long winter was a constant challenge. Meat was smoked or salted; fish, dried or pickled. Many vegetables could be stored in the root cellar, and potatoes, reintroduced to America in the 18th century, were a good vegetable for winter consumption. By then, orchards produced apples and other fruit that could be dried for the winter months. In addition to cornmeal, ingenious housewives used flour from a wide variety of grains for baking bread and mixing with other foodstuffs.

Many farm families kept a cow for milk. In addition, beer (in the middle colonies), rum (in New England), and cider (in the backcountry) were all popular beverages. In the homes of the Southern planters and urban merchants, wine, tea, chocolate, and coffee had begun to be common by the 18th century. Sugar was rarely found outside of such wealthy households, the ordinary people relying on molasses or honey. Spices were also rare but sought-after commodities.

Most American colonists dressed much as they had in England. Men wore coats, vests, shirts, kneebreeches, and long stockings. Women wore long, full dresses and shawls. People who could afford them imported clothes from England—in linen, wool, velvet, and silk. Common folk used coarser domestic materials such as linscy-woolsey and homespun. The middle class copied the fashions of their social "betters" whenever possible. Sumptuary laws prohibiting such aspirations were difficult to enforce. On the frontier, people dressed in deerskins and furs. "Buckskins" became a term of opprobrium for the simple backcountry folk. At the other extreme, overdressed city dandies were disparagingly known as "macaronis."

**The Household.** Throughout most of the colonial period the fireplace provided the only means of cooking food as well as of heating the house.

Since coal was not available until the very end of the period, every household required considerable quantities of firewood. In the Northern colonies the central chimney heated the entire house. In the more elaborate Southern plantations where the kitchen was in an outbuilding, the main house had end-chimneys, which permitted a central hallway to carry refreshing breezes through the structure. Germans in Pennsylvania constructed iron heating stoves, which stood out into the room. From these models Benjamin Franklin developed his famous Pennsylvania fireplace, known as the Franklin stove. Long-handled warming pans and other portable heating devices were also relied on to fight the bitter cold of American winters. Women secreted small metal footwarmers filled with hot coals beneath their skirts during church services, an idea originating with the Dutch in New York.

Iron pots hung from cranes over the open fire, while meats turned on spits. Brass and iron pots, kettles, skillets and other utensils were costly items, much prized by the housewife. Meals were served in wooden platters and bowls for the most part, sometimes in painted tinware, although pewterware was common in richer homes. Planters and merchants could afford silverware made by English or colonial craftsmen, and expensive china plates and teacups were the pride of well-to-do ladies.

Colonial houses were poorly lighted by modern standards. Not only was window glass expensive but so were spermaceti candles and whale-oil lamps. Most homes were lighted by tallow candles, rush and betty lamps, or simply the flames of a roaring fire. Few colonists in rural areas stayed up after dark anyway, their daily routine being regulated by sun time through most of the year. The absence of running water meant considerable labor for the women and children of the family, whose task it was to keep the water buckets filled from nearby wells or springs. Inside toilet facilities were unknown, and the backyard privy, or necessary house, was a common structure.

Because the colonists made so much of their own clothing and utensils, the well-equipped household required a number of specialized tools. Spinning wheels for the preparation of yarn and looms for weaving were only the largest of these pieces. The housewife had need for a wide variety of vats and pans for preparing dyes, curing hides, and processing cloth. The husband required a workbench at which he could fashion the various household and farm tools needed for the season ahead. From attic rafters herbs hung to dry, and shelves held seeds for next year's kitchen garden. If the farmer made maple syrup, he needed many buckets to collect the sap and a large vat in which to boil it. If he cut ice from a nearby pond, he needed different sets of implements. Husband and wife together had to master a score of techniques and to improvise when conditions or materials were not quite right. These circumstances were reflected in the country adage "make do or do without." By the mid-18th century, life in the New World had made the American an ingenious jack-of-all trades.

## CULTURAL LIFE AND LEISURE PURSUITS

Colonial American cultural life was largely underdeveloped until well into the 18th century. Even then it depended heavily on the mother country for its sources and standards.

Furnishings of the beamed 17th century parlor from the Job Wright house, Oyster Bay, Long Island, include a gateleg table, a Hadley chest, and an Oriental carpet.

HENRY FRANCIS DU PONT WINTERTHUR MUSEUM

**Literature.** Although few Americans possessed extensive libraries, many households had an almanac and a Bible. Some households might also have a book on home remedies, perhaps a classical history, and a work or two on law. The more affluent might own several religious tracts, a collection of poems or essays, and perhaps a practical guide such as *The Complete Gentleman* or *Of Domestical Duties*. City dwellers unable to afford their own books might join a subscription group such as Franklin's famous Library Company of Philadelphia.

One of the most popular subjects for ambitious American authors was the history of their colony. The goal of these works was often to encourage further immigration or to justify a particular pattern of behavior in the past. Among the best of these works were Robert Beverley's *History and Present State of Virginia* (1705) and Thomas Hutchinson's *History of the Colony of Massachusetts Bay* (3 vols., 1764–1828).

The better-known ministers published many of their sermons along with other tracts extolling the virtues of a Christian life. During such periods of religious fervor as the Great Awakening, major disputes were fought out in books and pamphlets. Political arguments found similar expression, especially at the end of the colonial period. Another favorite theme was the "Indian captivity" tale. Mary Rowlandson struck horror into her readers as they relived her experiences during King Philip's War. The Reverend John Williams made the account of his capture at Deerfield into a religious tract as well as a historical description. The colonial period produced several talented poets, such as the Puritans Anne Bradstreet and Edward Taylor and, later, the black slave Phillis Wheatley.

Surely the most widely read works of the era were almanacs and newspapers, the popularity of which attested to the colonists' preference for practical works. Almanacs were filled with all sorts of useful (and some useless) information concerning phases of the moon, sunrises, high and low tides, and various astronomical orbits and juxtapositions. In his famous *Poor Richard's Almanack*, Benjamin Franklin treated his readers to numerous aphorisms and other sayings for their moral and practical guidance. Newspapers carried the "freshest advices," often months old by necessity, on the doings of the colonial legislature and the arrival of vessels at the waterfront. One of their most valuable features was the myriad of commercial advertisements for goods and services offered by local craftsmen and shopkeepers. By the mid-18th century, more than 20 newspapers circulated through the colonies, each copy avidly devoured by numerous readers in taverns, inns, and private homes.

**Architecture and Art.** The evolution of American architecture illustrates the pattern of cultural development in the colonial period. Houses built by the earliest inhabitants had to be simple to construct with the materials at hand. Often they had to provide shelter from severe weather conditions and protection against Indian attack. These first homes were crude huts or even tents and caves. Log cabins appeared only when the Scandinavians settled along the Delaware River in the mid-1600's. As soon as possible, each group of settlers built a heavily timbered garrison house for protection.

Pioneers who survived several seasons could build more permanent homes. These later houses

In Williamsburg, colonial capital of Virginia, parishioners attend Bruton Church,
built in the early 18th century. Only the wealthy owned coaches and carriages.

reflected the general lines of 17th century European architecture, but gradually each region went its own way in architectural styles. By the early 1700's the wooden New England farmhouse, with its center chimney, four rooms on each floor, and lean-to attached behind took on its characteristic "saltbox" appearance. In the middle and Southern colonies a large number of houses were of brick. There, too, Georgian architecture appeared in the 1730's. As planters and merchants of the Chesapeake Bay area accumulated wealth, they sought, in architecture as in other matters, to follow the model of the English ruling class. So also did their counterparts in the North. These substantial houses copied the Georgian styles of the most up-to-date English books. But here and there an American touch appeared, such as the widow's walk atop New England seaport houses or the separate summer kitchen in many Southern homes. Indigenous American architecture was much more common in country villages and on farms. In some rural areas true improvisation took place, as planters such as Thomas Jefferson designed their own mansions. But such departures from English models were unusual.

Other art forms grew more slowly in America because practical demands precluded the early emergence of a leisure class with the wealth to become patrons. Even so, itinerant, self-taught portrait painters roamed the colonies looking for business. By the eve of the Revolution two artists of major importance, John Singleton Copley and Benjamin West, were at the peak of their careers. Generally speaking, however, American art took a more practical path. Colorful designs on walls, furniture, and even buildings themselves brightened the home. The Pennsylvania Germans were also skilled in the art of *fraktur*, illuminating documents and other papers with brilliant decorations. Other common art forms were carved weathervanes and figureheads, the gaily painted signs advertising shops and taverns, and fancifully carved gravestones.

Leading furniture makers of 18th century America depended heavily on English design books such as Thomas Chippendale's *The Gentleman and Cabinetmaker's Directory*. The best American craftsmen, such as Benjamin Randolph of Philadelphia and the Goddard brothers of Newport, put something of their own design in each piece. For the middle class, Boston joiners turned out chairs and tables by the hundreds for export to the rural areas of many colonies, but Philadelphia's craftsmen remained preeminent.

Many merchants and planters converted their profits into silverware. Much of it was imported from the mother country at first. By the mid-18th century, however, such silversmiths as Joseph Richardson, John Coney, and Paul Revere had established reputations far beyond their own towns. Pottery, easily made from local clays, was popular. Especially decorative types were Pennsylvania German slipware and Bennington stoneware. Glassware, requiring costly equipment and highly trained workers, was less common. By the mid-18th century, however, the rich could buy glassware of great beauty from glassworks such as those of John Frederick Amelung in Maryland and Henry William Stieglitz in Pennsylvania. Textiles gave the housewife, especially in the countryside, the opportunity to display her skill and ingenuity in dyeing, weaving, embroidery, and quilting. In her leisure time she made blue-and-white woven coverlets, gay crewel-embroidered hangings, and patchwork and appliqué quilts.

**Drama and Music.** Of all art forms, probably drama suffered most from New World conditions. The first settlers had little time for such diver-

Architecture in the colonies varied regionally. Many Southern plantations had stately mansions, such as the graceful, 18th century Georgian-style Carter's Grove (*above*) in Tidewater Virginia. In New England, domestic architecture tended to be simpler. The 17th century John Ward House (*left*) in Salem, Mass., has austere clapboard siding.

sion. Besides, Puritans strongly opposed theatrical entertainment, as did the Quakers. By the beginning of the 18th century, however, traveling theatrical companies began to receive increasing public approval, particularly in such seaports as New York and Charleston. Philadelphia's Thomas Godfrey was America's only accomplished playwright in the colonial period. Other forms of public entertainment included waxworks, the display of elephants and other exotic beasts, and performances by trapeze artists. Scientific demonstrations and lectures on intellectual topics were also popular.

Americans enjoyed singing perhaps more than any other form of public entertainment. Every

major religious denomination except the Quakers gave an important place in their services to the singing of hymns, and the first book printed in English America was in fact the Puritans' *Bay Psalm Book* (1640). The organ, introduced by the Anglicans, was resisted at first by stricter groups but gradually gained acceptance by the 18th century. The music of backcountry folk was not only a form of entertainment but also a means of recalling their past and preserving it for future generations. The blacks similarly relied on singing, for song gave them a solidarity, which the plantation system constantly threatened, and helped them to retain through note and rhythm the rich heritage of their native Africa. American music owes much of its musical tradition to blacks.

On a more formal plane, cities such as Boston, New York, and especially Charleston, where interested citizens formed the St. Cecilia Society in 1762, offered professional concerts on a regular basis by the eve of the Revolution. As for composition, however, hymns were about the only kind of music actually written by colonists with any degree of skill.

**Science.** Given the conditions of frontier life in America, it is not surprising that intellectual life should be dominated by utilitarian interest. Both Europeans and early colonists shared a compelling curiosity about the natural history of the New World. As time and circumstances permitted, a number of 17th century Americans examined their environment by the best scientific methods available, not so much for the sake of

## COLONIAL SITES

Three kinds of colonial sites represent the colonial period in U. S. history. First are buildings that have been preserved intact, usually on their original sites. They rank first in authenticity, and most cities and towns along the Eastern Seaboard have fine examples. However, often these buildings remain in private use and are not open to the public. Second are the museum "villages" comprising restored and reconstructed buildings, at least some of which have been moved from other locations. A restored building is basically the original structure with the necessary repairs and replacements; reconstructions are structures newly built according to original specifications. A third kind of historic site comprises totally reconstructed buildings. These categories should not be confused with commercial amusement parks in colonial settings.

Of the hundreds of colonial sites open to the public, the following, arranged geographically, are among the most authentic and interesting:

**Shelburne, Vt.** The Shelburne Museum includes a number of houses dating from the late 1700's and exhibiting an outstanding collection of antiques.

**Portsmouth, N. H.** The original settlement at the mouth of the Piscataqua River, known as Strawbery Banke has restored historic buildings dating from 1695 to 1830. In addition, there are a number of fine homes in their original settings along Pleasant Street.

**Salem, Mass.** The Essex Institute has restored one 17th and several 18th century houses with authentic furnishings. The House of Seven Gables is another good example of early architecture. Pioneer Village is a modern reconstruction of the original settlement at Salem. Chestnut Street has many fine late colonial and early Federalist homes.

**Boston, Mass.** Within the city are many 17th and 18th century houses. Many of the historic structures are indicated on maps of the "Freedom Trail."

**Plymouth, Mass.** On the outskirts of modern Plymouth is "Plimoth Plantation," a reconstruction of the Pilgrims' first village.

**Deerfield, Mass.** As a result of cooperation among the townspeople, the local historical society, and the privately endowed Heritage Foundation, Deerfield has become one of the most impressive "lived in" historic sites. The main street has been restored to very nearly its 18th century appearance.

**Sturbridge, Mass.** "Old Sturbridge Village" is one of the most authentic of the museum villages. Houses, shops, and other buildings are arranged in a natural setting, and visitors may travel by horse-drawn wagon.

**Newport, R. I.** Newport is carrying out a major restoration campaign that promises to preserve many of its 18th century buildings from further decay.

**Mystic, Conn.** "Mystic Seaport" is a skillful re-creation of an early 19th century seaport village with many colonial buildings and vessels. Most of the houses have been moved to the site and restored. The overall effect is highly authentic.

**Cooperstown, N. Y.** The "Village Crossroads," a reconstructed farming village, and the Farmer's Museum have preserved many relics of early country life.

**Philadelphia, Pa.** In the Independence Hall area are many well-known public buildings that have been preserved, while the "Society Hill" section of the city is composed of privately owned town houses restored to their 18th century exterior appearance.

**Wilmington, Del.** Within a small radius are three important historic institutions: The Hagley Museum, a group of restored and reconstructed mill buildings along the Brandywine River; the Eleutherian Mills, the du Pont family's first powder factory in America; and Winterthur, a museum housing the antiques collection of Henry F. du Pont.

**Alexandria, Va.** George Washington's estate, Mount Vernon, has been carefully preserved and gives the observer a graphic idea of an 18th century plantation.

**Williamsburg, Va.** The most famous historic site in America, "Colonial Williamsburg" includes more than 80 original buildings preserved from Virginia's colonial capital and many skillful reconstructions. Guides in costume complete the authentic setting. At the nearby site of Jamestown, the first permanent English settlement in America, the Jamestown Festival Park includes replicas of 17th century buildings.

**Charlestown, S. C.** Many buildings from the colonial era, both public and private, have been preserved, and some are open for inspection.

pure knowledge as in the hope of making practical discoveries. Botany aided the search for medicinal herbs, metallurgy the quest for iron ore and other useful metals. Before the end of the century, Harvard College was offering courses in astronomy and physics, as well as in the more traditional subjects of algebra and geometry. In Boston the Reverend Cotton Mather championed the new technique of inoculation against smallpox, and other ministers, too, were interested in practical science.

In the early 18th century, Mark Catesby and later John Bartram advanced the frontiers of natural history by their studies of American species of animal, bird, and plant life. The founding by Benjamin Franklin of the American Philosophical Society in 1743 for the "promotion of useful knowledge" symbolized his own primary interests along with those of other American scientists. Franklin's experiments with electricity, while fraught with theoretical value, were turned to practical application by his invention of the lightning rod. Another Philadelphian, David Rittenhouse, was a self-taught astronomer who built America's first orrery (a working model of the universe) in 1767. His contributions to the field were second only to Harvard's John Winthrop in the New World and demonstrated that even an amateur could advance the frontiers of knowledge. By the eve of the Revolution at least two score Americans had been elected to the Royal Society in London, and all colonists could take pride in the honorary degrees conferred on Benjamin Franklin by Edinburgh University in 1759 and Oxford in 1762.

A number of Americans applied their scientific knowledge to the field of medicine, experimenting with a wide variety of herbs and other remedies to combat the deadly effects of dysentery, measles, diphtheria, and smallpox. The vast majority of practitioners were self-taught, however, and could do little to cure the seriously ill. But by the Revolution two medical schools had

In the middle colonies—New York, Pennsylvania, New Jersey, and Delaware—stone was an important building material, as in the Chadd house in southern Pennsylvania.

JANE LATTA

*Mrs. Thomas Boylston*, by John Singleton Copley. Portraiture was the principal form of colonial painting, and Copley was one of the period's major artists.

been established along with numerous hospitals, and the practice of quarantine for the crews of incoming vessels helped prevent the spread of contagious infections. Superstition continued to hamper major medical advances throughout the period. Many colonists, for instance, objected to smallpox inoculation as an interference with God's will. Change came slowly even in America.

**Leisure Pursuits.** The seriousness of purpose that brought most immigrants to America com-bined with the challenge of settling the wilderness left little leisure time during the 17th century. Almost all Americans had to work hard six days a week, and Sunday was reserved for rest and worship. Every colony adopted laws severely restricting social activities on the Sabbath, the most effective bans being observed in Puritan New England. In addition to actual recreation, household work, travel, and even a family stroll were prohibited at first. Sunday was the Lord's day, and the good Puritan spent most of it in church or in meditation at home. Gradually these standards fell out of favor, and by the 18th century most New Englanders gave them token recognition at best. In the Southern colonies, where population remained relatively dispersed, visiting became a favorite leisure-time activity. George Washington's diary records numerous callers at Mount Vernon, who threatened to drink and dine him into bankruptcy. The American custom of hospitality had firm roots in the colonial era.

Simpler folk everywhere made a party out of every possible occasion, from quilting and spinning bees for the women to barn raisings and community construction projects for the whole family. Another necessary activity that was a source of recreation as well as hunting. Fishing too gave pleasure as well as the possibility of food for the table. In New York the Dutch introduced the sport of ice skating, and Benjamin Franklin urged his fellow Americans to learn how to swim for the sheer pleasure of it (as well as for its practical value, of course). But outdoor sport in the colonial period had not yet become the great American diversion it proved to be for later generations.

Men who lived in the towns and cities of the Northern colonies had the opportunity to enjoy each other's company at the local inn or tavern, where they smoked, played cards, and gambled. Billiards and backgammon were favorite games. In the Southern colonies especially, gentlemen aped the English aristocratic love for horse racing,

Pennsylvania Dutch birth certificate. Colonial folk art had its roots in European tradition, and the decoration on this document is based on manuscript illumination of the Middle Ages.

Neoclassical parlor from Port Royal, a mansion in southern Pennsylvania. Colonial craftsmen copied fine European furniture, and most of the furnishings in this room were made in Philadelphia in the Chippendale style.

which gave them an opportunity to display their favorite mounts and bet a little money on the outcome. Cockfighting was also popular, although often outlawed, along with bearbaiting and other brutalities.

Colonial children, like their descendants, found ingenious ways to amuse themselves, not always with parental approval. The boys of Boston devised a kind of stickball game played in the street, and a primitive form of football was also popular. As usual, country children had even greater opportunity for recreation, exploring the endless challenges of farm life such as rat hunting and turtle "gigging," as well as hunting and fishing. By the mid-18th century, newspapers advertised toys for sale, although most children made do with homemade hoops, balls, and other devices for their games.

Perhaps the most popular pastime for colonial Americans was dancing. Rich merchants and planters held assemblies either in their own spacious ballrooms or in a suitable public room in the larger cities. In many communities professional dancing masters instructed the youth in the steps and formations of this graceful accomplishment. A dance might mark almost any of several public festivities, such as muster day, the king's birthday, or a thanksgiving day. In Boston, Harvard's commencement day was celebrated by the entire community, while Southerners made a public festivity of elections. Sometimes these public celebrations dissolved into drunken brawls. Pope (Guy Fawkes) Day in Boston, for instance, became the occasion for a pitched battle between gangs of the rival north and south

end. For the most part, however, colonial Americans enjoyed the company of their fellows without reaching such extremes.

### LEGACY

The colonial period saw the establishment of many institutions, attitudes, and values that differentiated Americans from other peoples of the era and have since found a permanent place in the American way of life. Many have been altered through the years, and others are no longer appropriate to the realities of the late 20th century, but the basic shape of American national institutions was discernible by the mid-18th century.

**Self-Government.** Largely because of the dispersal of population, political authority rose from the grass-roots level, where most important decisions were made. English sovereignty was felt through the presence of the royal governor, but colonial legislatures derived great strength from the fact that they represented local, not imperial, interests. Although not very democratic at first, this structure encouraged the later development of democracy throughout the political system after the Revolution. Since then, the scope of such national problems as defense, the economy, and social justice has grown so large as to reduce the power of local authority, but the American government nevertheless remains more closely tied to the grass roots than that of any other industrialized nation.

**Public Education.** The most significant social institution established in the colonial period was the system of public education first founded in

New England. The colonists' insistence on at least a minimum education for their children had far-reaching effects on both the economy and the social structure of the nation-to-be. Education became a principal route upward, especially for the children of later immigrants.

**Religious Toleration.** Despite a slow start in New England, religious toleration became firmly established in Pennsylvania, New Jersey, and other colonies in the 17th century. By the mid-18th century a host of small denominations flourished in all the provinces under principles of religious freedom that became a cornerstone of the future nation.

**Faith in Progress.** Perhaps the most common belief shared by the colonists was their faith in progress. Americans continually made short-term sacrifices and took great risks in the hope of long-term gains, as evidenced by the men and women who moved to the frontier. The continent's bountiful natural resources imbued Americans with a fervent faith in the future. The fertile soil, forests of virgin timber, and rich grazing lands seemed to stretch endlessly westward. Even in colonial days the West held the promise of future greatness for America so richly fulfilled in the 19th century.

**The Model American.** Out of the colonial heritage there emerged a symbolic ideal citizen for the new nation—the yeoman farmer, embodying the virtues that colonists had come to cherish. He was free and independent, owning his own farm and calling no man lord and master. Of a practical bent, he devised tools and techniques to meet every challenge. He was not afraid of hard work, so eager was he to improve his lot and that of his children. Above all, he was an individualist, determined to make it on his own, somewhat wary of outsiders, particularly of city folk, who seemed to him almost "un-American."

The yeoman farmer served as the model for more than a century after the Revolution. Although the ideal American is no longer a farmer, the virtues embodied by the yeoman of the mid-18th century remain largely intact. The American still prides himself on his independence, his willingness to work hard, his practicality, and his individualism. His belief in progress may now be somewhat restricted by the problems of modern-day society—dwindling natural resources, recurring business recessions, and persistent racial discrimination; but through it all, Americans have continued to display that buoyant faith in the future that gave birth to a new nation 200 years ago.

BENJAMIN W. LABAREE, *Author of*
*"America's Nation-Time, 1607–1789"*

#### Bibliography

Cassara, Ernest, *The Enlightenment in America* (Univ. Press of Am. 1988).
Hoffer, Petrer C., ed., *Commerce and Community* (Garland 1987).
Kammen, Michael G., *Colonial New York: A History* (Scribner 1975).
Katz, Stanley Nider, comp., *Colonial America: Essays in Political and Social Development* (Little 1976).
Labaree, Benjamin W., *America's Nation-Time, 1607–1789* (Allyn & Bacon 1973).
Millar, John F., *Country Dances of Colonial America* (Thirteen Colonies Press 1988).
Miller, John C., *The First Frontier: Life in Colonial America* (Dial 1968).
Nash, Gary B., *Red, White, and Black: The Peoples of Early America* (Prentice-Hall 1974).
Wright, Louis B., *The Cultural Life of the American Colonies* (Harper 1957).
Wright, Louis B., *Everyday Life in Colonial America* (Putnam 1966).

**COLONIALISM** defies simple definition, for its usage has tended to reflect changing moral judgments. In the late 1800's the term was applied only to colonies of white settlers and was used in either of two ways, both morally neutral: (1) a trait characteristic of such colonies, and (2) the political status of a dependency as distinct from the metropolis (parent state) or another sovereign state.

Actually, the term colonialism rarely was used in the sense of a colonial system. Its later usage resulted from its adoption as part of the verbal ammunition of the age of decolonization. In this it suffered the fate of "imperialism," which after 1900 was adopted by critics of European expansion to serve ideological purposes and used imprecisely to suggest both the annexation of territories and their subsequent state of subordination—in each case to serve the economic interests of the capitalist powers of Europe and North America. By the mid-1900's, colonialism also began to be used in this derogatory sense.

The two terms were gradually refined and distinguished. Whereas "imperialism" came to indicate the dynamics of European empire building and, for Marxists, the special character of the capitalist societies that acquired empires, "colonialism" described the resultant complex of political and economic controls imposed on dependencies. Colonialism, therefore, must now be taken to denote the colonial system in its post-expansionist phase, with the implication that it constituted a system of controls that was constructed by the imperial powers to subordinate and to exploit their dependencies.

This article will examine the character of the colonial system in modern European colonial empires in the light of this implication. Two questions are fundamental: (1) How were these empires organized? (2) Did the colonial system exploit the dependency to benefit the metropolis?

In considering these questions, one should bear in mind a general historical point: although the term "colonialism" has been applied mainly to conditions of the 1900's, colonial systems have existed throughout history wherever empires have arisen. The character of these systems varied immensely over time and place. The colonialism denounced by critics of the recent colonial empires was not uniform, and it differed substantially from patterns of colonialism in the past.

### HISTORY OF COLONIZATION

The special feature common to most modern colonial systems was that dependencies were geographically separated from their metropolis, although they remained under some degree of imperial control. The only power of which this was not true was Russia, whose "colonies" stretched without a break from its territory in Europe to the borders of India and to the Bering Strait. Although contiguous, these outlying provinces were true colonial dependencies, for they had been distinct ethnic and economic units with which Russia's initial relations were those of conqueror or colonizer.

**Early Continental and Maritime Empires.** The Russian Empire provides a conceptual bridge between the modern colonial empires and other territorial empires at earlier periods, most of which were continental and contiguous to the metropolis. Most of Europe, Asia, Africa, and Central and South America at one time fell under the authority of an imperial dynasty or state. The greatest ancient imperial powers—Egypt, Babylonia,

Assyria, Persia, Rome, Byzantium, the Carolingians, the Arabs, China, the Incas, and the Aztecs —were essentially continental.

Maritime empires were few and unspectacular before modern European overseas colonization. In classical times the Phoenicians, Greeks, Carthaginians, and Romans established overseas colonies. Later, Hindus and Muslims from India and Arabia settled territories of the Indian Ocean and Indonesia, and the Chinese colonized much of Southeast Asia. However, these settlements generally lacked central control or even continuing contacts with the parent state.

For the most part, neither the great continental empires nor earlier maritime settlements had much in common with modern colonial systems— the former because they were territorially contiguous, the latter because they lacked central control. However, then, as later, both the motives that led to the creation of the systems, and the patterns of government, trade, or culture that emerged, were infinitely varied.

Continental empires were the product of multiple factors, notably dynastic ambition, frontier insecurity, religious fanaticism, or the need for land or slave labor. The same variety of motives is seen in earlier maritime colonization in which trade, surplus population, dynastic ambition, and religion figured. Colonial systems were equally varied. Some empires attempted to impose cultural uniformity; others did not. Some were highly centralized administratively; others consisted of essentially autonomous provinces.

**European Colonial Empires.** Modern European expansion can be dated from the Portuguese conquest of Ceuta (in Morocco) in 1415 to the Italian occupation of Abyssinia (Ethiopia) in 1936. Within this period there were two overlapping cycles, the first ending with the independence of the majority of the original colonies in the Americas in the 1820's, the second beginning with the British conquest of Bengal in and after 1757. During the first cycle most of the European colonies were in the Western Hemisphere. During the second cycle the colonial empires encompassed much of Asia, the Pacific, and Africa. Behind these geographical contrasts lay fundamental differences in the character of colonialism.

**The First Cycle.** The paradoxical feature of the first cycle was that the states of western Europe established vast empires in America almost by accident. Columbus intended to find an oceanic route to the East, not to found colonies. He failed, but Spain found compensation in the gold and silver resources of parts of Central and South America. Colonization there was the result of the first overseas gold rush by Europeans. In the wake of the first conquistadores came missionaries, administrators, settlers, and craftsmen. By 1650, Spain, Portugal, France, England, and the Netherlands all had colonies in America.

The motives of the colonizers varied, and their enterprises at first were experimental. Many hoped to find gold or silver. The search for a northwest passage to China continued. French and English fishermen needed bases near the Newfoundland Banks. Emigrants were attracted by free land or hoped to escape political or religious persecution at home. American colonization was an unforeseen and largely uncontrolled reaction to the challenge of discovery.

In other parts of the world the character of European expansion was quite different and to some extent was the result of deliberate planning.

The general pattern was set by Portugal, which from the 1400's aimed to exploit the discovery of a route to the East round the Cape of Good Hope for commercial rather than colonizing purposes. Portugal did establish territorial possessions in certain parts of Africa and Asia, but on the whole it chose to limit its commitments to coastal bases, relying on naval power and treaties with indigenous rulers to provide suitable conditions for a profitable trade. The French, English, and Dutch followed this example.

Colonization on the American plan was impractical and unnecessary. In Asia and Africa, Europeans found civilized societies and powerful states that possessed frameworks of government and commerce into which Europeans could fit. Only when political conditions in Asia altered and when rivalries between Europeans became more intense, did this pattern change significantly. During the 1700's territorial empires grew slowly from British involvement in Indian politics and Dutch commitments in Java. Earlier, the European involvement in Africa and Asia was not colonialism in its true sense.

**The Second Cycle.** From the 1760's to the mid-1820's the European colonies in America coexisted with the first large territorial possessions in the East. But by 1825 the former had dwindled to comparative insignificance. Most of British North America achieved independence through revolution by 1783. Spain lost all its continental possessions in America by 1824, and in 1825 Portugal recognized the independence of Brazil, and France that of Haiti. Britain, however, remained a major colonial power. It retained part of North America, including French Canada; it had acquired many foreign colonies through war, notably Trinidad, the Cape of Good Hope, Mauritius, Ceylon, and Malacca; it was the ruler of vast territories in India, and its convict settlement in Australia was dispersing settlers throughout that continent and into the South Pacific. The Netherlands retained its hold in Indonesia, but for Spain, Portugal, and France the age of colonialism seemed to be over.

In the 1830's there seemed little reason for countries to build new colonial empires. America was closed to European intervention by the Monroe Doctrine and the British navy, Africa offered few immediate attractions, and the Far East consisted of apparently impregnable empires and states. Britain was adopting free trade, and other countries gradually followed its lead, so that colonies no longer would be commercial monopolies. Furthermore, there were fewer obstacles to European overseas enterprise independent of formal colonization. Emigrants could go to the United States, Latin America, or British colonies in Australia or South Africa. Traders, missionaries, planters, and prospectors could try their luck almost anywhere. The principle of the "open door" and the practice of influencing non-European peoples by diplomacy seemed preferable alternatives to empire.

**The "New Imperialism."** Nevertheless, European colonial empires expanded anew in the later 1800's. This "new imperialism" is conventionally explained in terms of changing European economic needs and interests. Sources of raw materials, fields for investment, and ever-larger markets were needed, and fear of exclusion from regions controlled by other states forced each country to establish colonies in order to protect its interests. An alternate explanation holds that, with intensified international rivalries, each state claimed colonies to increase its strategic power, to defend its trade routes, or to use pawns in diplomacy. Finally, it has been suggested that colonization reflected a new aggressive nationalism in Europe, produced partly by international rivalries and partly by racist theories.

All these explanations focus in Europe, but while there were elements of truth in each, the evidence suggests that the dynamics of European expansion once again lay outside Europe: that imperialism was a reaction to crises and opportunities in Asia, the Pacific, and Africa rather than the product of needs and calculated policies within Europe. Crises might result from the frontier problems or expansionist tendencies of existing colonies, from the disintegration of indigenous political or social systems, or from rivalries between Europeans on the spot. Such situations might induce a European government to annex.

Between 1880 and 1910 the tempo of annexation was quickened partly because crises occurred simultaneously in many areas and partly because Germany, Belgium, the United States, Italy, and Japan joined the existing group of maritime nations and Russia as colonial powers. The outcome was virtually complete partition of Africa and the Pacific region and an increase of colonial territory in Asia. By 1914, Europe dominated every continent except the Americas, which in turn were dominated, indirectly, by the United States.

The period from 1914 to 1939 was the apogee of the modern colonial empires. After World War I, German, Japanese, and Ottoman territories were assigned mainly to European powers. These territories technically were League of Nations mandates, but they were administered like other dependencies. With the Italian occupation of Abyssinia (Ethiopia) in 1936 the colonial empires reached their territorial peak. Most western European countries were colonial powers, as were the United States and Japan. Russia, by this time a Socialist state, disclaimed colonies, but retained those parts of central and eastern Asia that the Czarist regime had acquired, technically as autonomous republics.

*Decolonization.* World War II marked the beginning of the end. Europe lost control of most possessions in the Pacific and Southeast Asia to Japan, and other colonies were isolated from their metropolises. Although most ties were restored after 1945, the dissolution of empires had begun.

The reasons are not entirely clear. Hostility to alien rule sprouted or increased. Changing attitudes in Europe weakened faith in the moral basis and the practical advantages of colonialism. Russia and then China supported revolutionary movements. The first dependencies to gain independence—India, Pakistan, Ceylon, Burma, and Indonesia—inspired nationalists elsewhere.

By the late 1960's only a few colonies remained, notably Portuguese and Spanish territories in Africa, and some British, U.S., and French dependencies, which could not easily be set adrift or which still provided useful military facilities. Colonialism in the formal sense was dead.

There remained, however, a complex of economic and political influences exercised by the advanced over the less advanced world. Labeled "neocolonialism" by its critics, this predominance became the focus of anti-European and anti-American complaint. Whether it differed in substance from the predominance exercised by the USSR over the eastern European states and how the imbalance of power could be redressed were open questions.

## COLONIAL ECONOMIC SYSTEMS

The most common interpretation of colonialism is that it was a calculated system for exploiting the economic potential of dependencies in the interests of the parent states. Methods varied rather than aims. Until the mid-1800's empires were "mercantilist" (see MERCANTILISM). Thereafter, all countries experimented with virtual free trade before adopting "neo-mercantilist" economic systems. Allegedly, each system, in differing degrees, provided "superprofit" for the metropolis, while it harmed the economic and social interests of the colonies. Such an interpretation, however, is misleading.

**Mercantilism.** Colonialism in its mercantilist phase before 1830 was not a rational system contrived to exploit colonies. Monopolistic restrictions were adopted merely from existing practice within the nations of Europe. The aim was to treat distant colonies as extensions of the parent state, rather than as autonomous communities open to international trade. Foreigners were excluded from colonial ports; colonies had to send all or most of their exports to the metropolis and to buy all imports from or through its merchants; attempts were made to ban colonial industries if they competed with those of the metropolis, while the production of colonial staples wanted by the parent state was stimulated by preferential tariffs and bounties.

The intention of these controls was to create economies in which metropolis and colonies played complementary parts, with the balance of advantage on the metropolitan side. In practice, results varied according to the severity of the restrictions and the economic efficiency of each parent state. During the 1700's, for example, Spanish and Portuguese colonies in America suffered from the economic decadence of the metropolises. However, the British colonies benefited from Britain's industrial, commercial, and maritime superiority over potential rivals.

It is broadly true that mercantilist controls did less harm to the colonies and provided less artificial advantage to the metropolis than supporters or critics of the system had supposed. The colonial economy largely reflected the natural endowment of these colonies, which depended on exports of specialized staples. Their economic character would have differed little had there been no imperial monopoly. Equally, the net value of imperial profit is dubious. Adam Smith showed that monopoly had serious economic effects on the metropolitan economy.

**Free Trade.** Colonial free trade grew in the period from 1825, when Britain threw open its colonial ports and trade on a reciprocal basis, to about 1870, when the trade of virtually all colonies was open. In principle, free trade should have provided colonies with economic justice because empire no longer meant monopoly. On the other hand, imperial free trade, arbitrarily imposed, had corresponding disadvantages for dependencies because it kept their markets open to technically more advanced European producers and barred the way to industrial growth through protection.

Again, the balance of advantage is difficult to draw. The market economy benefited some colonies and some people in all colonies, although it may have damaged others. Significantly, most British self-governing colonies adopted protection as soon as they were permitted.

**Neo-mercantilism.** Imperial free trade began to ebb in the 1880's as the European states adopted protection at home and extended it to their possessions. Their motives were pragmatic: colonies were expensive to maintain, and the metropolis had a right to compensation.

However, there was no return to monopoly. Colonies were not closed to foreign trade or capital, nor were they forbidden to produce particular commodities. Neo-mercantilist devices included preferential tariffs on intraimperial trade; subsidies on shipping on imperial routes; and, from the 1930's, quotas on foreign imports to colonies and on colonial exports to the metropolis.

Although these devices accentuated the tendency for colonial trade to flow along imperial routes, they did so effectively only when economic realities coincided with political boundaries. (Thus, the French West African colonies tended by the 1930's to trade almost exclusively with France, but French Indochina, depending heavily on trade with China, never had more than half its external trade with France.)

The attraction of the preferential metropolitan market tended to stimulate those segments of the colonial economy that fitted the needs of the metropolis. Hence, the existence of specialized economic enclaves in otherwise nonwesternized economies gave support to the view that colonial economic growth was deformed by subordination to European needs. In addition, the fact that most colonies received substantial capital investment, primarily from the parent state, suggested that they were being exploited by European capitalists.

To some extent these criticisms were justified. Empire, whether free trade or protectionist, was an obstacle to economic autarky and perhaps to balanced growth in some dependencies, and the profits of investment went to the overseas investor rather than to the colony. Yet both factors must be seen in proportion. Very few non-European states, however politically independent, succeeded in developing advanced or diversified economies in this period. Even for them a specialized export staple was a valuable thing. Investors in general did not receive higher profits from capital invested in colonies than in sovereign states of similar economic character. It is impossible to say with confidence that empire was generally harmful to dependencies or profitable to imperial powers.

## COLONIAL ADMINISTRATION

Although colonialism tended to produce roughly similar economic patterns, it developed significant differences on the political side. An initial distinction must be made between colonies of European settlement and other types of dependencies, mainly those acquired during the 1800's. In the first case, each imperial power governed its settlements according to metropolitan principles and practices, which varied widely. In the second, all powers acted pragmatically and tended to move toward similar systems under pressure of common problems.

**Settlement Colonies.** The original European colonies in the Americas and most later British settlement colonies were treated very much as existing possessions of each metropolis in Europe. Modifications were necessary to take account of special colonial conditions, but these did not affect the general principle that colonists carried with them whatever legal and political rights they possessed at home. The major exception to this was the power given to chartered companies or individual proprietors, but in time these settlements reverted to direct royal government.

The result was that colonial governments and laws differed as widely as those between countries in Europe. Because Britain had a representative parliament and limited monarchy, its original colonies were relatively autonomous; its later settlement colonies acquired cabinet government, and after 1931 they became sovereign states, merely owing allegiance to the crown. Such voluntary association was the basis of the post-1945 Commonwealth of Nations, to which other former dependencies could belong after independence if they chose. By contrast, the political traditions of most continental powers were autocratic, at least until 1789. So, therefore, was government in their colonies, though the asperities of the *ancien régime* were generally softened across the Atlantic.

Colonists of any nationality were usually freer politically and legally than fellow subjects in the metropolis; their main grievance was the preponderance of expatriates in the highest government posts. Revolutions normally did not so much reflect intolerable oppression as they did the influence of liberal ideas in Europe and concurrent changes in the previously accepted political and economic system.

**Foreign Dependencies.** Little of this applied to the majority of foreign colonies acquired during the 1800's and 1900's, which primarily were not settlement colonies and were not treated as if they were extensions of the metropolis. In Africa, Asia, and the Pacific it seemed inexpedient to impose systems of government and law evolved by and for European societies. New forms had to be contrived that suited local conditions but left effective authority with the metropolis.

Central government in these colonies commonly took the form of a governor, a small administrative council of expatriate officials, and in some cases a larger council with legislative powers, which might contain representatives from the indigenous people. The extent of local autonomy varied. Colonial rule became increasingly benevolent, but before 1945 it could be characterized as despotic.

***Assimilation or Preservation.*** What general policy these central governments were to apply remained a problem. Fundamentally, all empires had a choice between two opposing principles: to assimilate non-Europeans to the civilization of the metropolis or to preserve the indigenous society as nearly as possible in its original form.

The common assumption of most states before the 1800's was that European civilization was so superior that assimilation was in the best interests of non-Europeans. Consequently, only where Europeans were merely traders on sufferance did they respect ways alien to them. In the 1800's, however, the problem became more acute. The majority of new colonies could not be assimilated effectively because they were too large and contained too few European settlers. It was simpler to maintain native laws and act through indigenous agents than to impose radical changes and govern through expatriate officials. Generally speaking, this was done by all powers.

***Direct or Indirect Rule.*** In India and Ceylon

the British moved from indirect to direct rule, gradually modifying law and society. Neither country was ever fully assimilated into European civilization, but no other substantial European possessions were more affected by colonialism. The same general tendency occurred in most other European dependencies as government became more complex and European education and example eroded indigenous cultures. France, Russia, Portugal, and the United States positively aimed at assimilation, regarding it as an essential aspect of imperial policy to mold dependencies on the model of the metropolis.

In the early 1900's, however, the British reacted against assimilation, notably under the influence of Lord Frederick Lugard (q.v.), whose principles of indirect rule were set forth in his book *Dual Mandate* (1922). According to these principles, indigenous political and social forms should not merely be tolerated but preserved where possible; central governments should act through native rulers; European civilization should permeate slowly; and above all, the interests of the native people should predominate.

However, too much should not be made of contrasts between direct and indirect rule. By 1939 most indigenous subjects in European colonies had little effective control over government in their own countries, and assimilation had barely begun. In retrospect, political colonialism appears unprogressive rather than inherently bad. In most colonies the initial period of occupation was the worst; thereafter, government was increasingly humane and constructive. The weakness of colonialism was that it lacked viable ultimate objectives. Gradual assimilation leading to eventual incorporation with the metropolis never was practical. No power planned for the future independence of its dependencies before 1939, except possibly Britain in the case of India.

The European presence generated a class of people in each dependency that was detached from its native culture by education and experience. A minority of this class was satisfied by the fruits of collaboration with the imperial power, but the majority found that the colonial situation provided inadequate rewards. After 1945 independence became a universally attractive alternative to colonialism, both because it promised progress and because the imperial powers had nothing better to offer.

### APPRAISAL OF COLONIALISM

An objective evaluation of colonialism is impossible, for everything depends on the criteria adopted. By contemporary standards, based on the sanctity of self-determination, colonialism was morally indefensible because one society dominated another. On Marxist-Leninist grounds, colonialism was wrong because it allegedly involved the economic exploitation of the dependencies. To the new states, their colonial period was one of servitude, an unforgivable insult by Europe to other continents and races.

But these criteria are invalid historically because they assume the existence of a better alternative to empire and colonialism—a world of independent states pursuing their own best interests within the security of an assumed international order. This was not always so. All colonial systems arose, virtually unplanned, from the compulsions of the historical process. Colonialism as a historical fact must be assessed morally as part of a world order constantly changing over many

centuries. The criteria used must relate to the period under consideration.

**Advantages to the Metropolis.** The effects of colonialism can be considered from the point of view of either the metropolis or its dependencies. Many independent states, as well as colonies, offered European citizens opportunities for emigration, trade, or capital investment, but the special reward of empire was the ability of a colonial system to provide better conditions for these activities than would otherwise have existed in a particular place. Thus, Europeans settled in New Zealand before it was made a colony, but only annexation gave them stable titles to land and sound government. Europeans could trade with Africa without occupying the continent, but by the later 1800's expanding trade was hampered by the character and multiplicity of local governments, alien laws, and mutual rivalries. Colonialism provided a better framework for economic activity at that time—though in many cases this was not the deliberate reason for annexation.

In addition, some imperial states derived special advantages. Spain, Portugal, and the Netherlands at times transferred surplus revenues from colony to metropolis. Economically weak states could obtain an artificially large share of colonial trade through monopoly or other preferential policies. Expatriates commonly paid low taxes in colonies. But these factors were of marginal importance. Fundamentally, the economic role of colonialism was to make the world virtually one economic system centered on Europe and North America.

**Effect on Dependencies.** In our consideration of whether dependencies, as well as the metropolitan states, derived measurable benefits from colonialism, a distinction must be drawn between settlement colonies and non-European societies subjected to alien rule. For the first, colonialism was a necessary preliminary to nationhood. None of these countries subsequently renounced the cultural, economic, or the legal and political endowment they received.

For nonsettlement colonies, however, colonialism meant, to some degree, enforced changes in native forms of government, society, culture, religion, and economic organization. Colonialism was a traumatic experience, changing the course of their history and generating what has been called a "colonial mentality"—consciousness of defeat and inferiority.

As compensation, colonialism brought them the political and social equipment of advanced European countries. Large territorial units and improved administration replaced a multiplicity of small kingdoms or tribes; recurrent wars and slave trading were ended; public utilities were constructed; European currency and banking were introduced; rudimentary educational and medical services were established; and standards of living were improved. An increasing number of non-Europeans became qualified—though they were not always permitted—to play leading roles in all these fields. It became possible to conceive of these countries as capable of surviving unassisted in the contemporary political and economic world.

**Balance Sheet.** Any appraisal of colonialism must turn on two questions: (1) Was it desirable for non-European societies to have been brought forcibly within the mainstream of European and American development? (2) Could this have been done without colonialism?

To the first question, the initial answer might have been negative. Yet the new states have chosen to preserve much of their colonial inheritance, though many adhere to European socialism rather than European capitalism. Few have renounced the West. Most former British dependencies have remained in the Commonwealth, and most former French West African colonies have retained special economic relations with France and the Common Market. For all new states the economic goal is to achieve a system of industrialization modeled on European lines.

Could these opportunities have been taken without a period of colonial apprenticeship? It is undeniable that Japan, China, and some other states have achieved spectacular economic and political advance without ever having been European colonies. Others might have done the same—notably the countries of Islamic Africa and southern Asia—but it seems doubtful that the precolonial societies of sub-Saharan Africa and the Pacific could have achieved so much by the mid-1900's on their own account. For them colonialism was a shortcut, even if a morally reprehensible one, to intellectual, political and economic advance. See also IMPERIALISM.

DAVID K. FIELDHOUSE, *Oxford University*

**Bibliography**

Brett, E. A., *Colonialism and Underdevelopment in East Africa* (Heinemann 1973).
Fieldhouse, David Kenneth, *Colonialism, 1870–1945: An Introduction* (Weidenfeld & Nicolson 1981).
Huttenback, Robert A., *Racism and Empire: White Settlers and colored Immigrants in the British Self-Governing Colonies, 1830–1910* (Cornell Univ. Press 1976).
Jones, Dorothy V., *License for Empire: Colonialism by Treaty in Early America* (Univ. of Chicago Press 1982).
Voeltz, Richard, *German Colonization and the South West Africa Company* (Ohio Univ. Press 1988).
Von Albertini, Rudolf, and Wirz, Albert, *European Colonial Rule, 1880–1940: The Impact of the West on India, Southeast Asia and Africa,* tr. by John G. Williamson (Greenwood Press 1982).

**COLONIE,** kol-ə-nē′, a village in eastern New York, in Albany county, about 5 miles (8 km) northwest of downtown Albany, of which it is a residential suburb. The village has light industries. Incorporated in 1921, it has a mayor-council form of government. Population: 7,916.

**COLONNA,** kō-lōn′nä, an ancient and noble Roman family, first among Roman houses in historical importance. Most famous for its soldiers and churchmen, the family has figured prominently in the history of Italy and of Europe since the Middle Ages.

The Colonna trace their descent from Pietro, son of the Count of Tusculum. The family name is taken from the castle of Columna in the Alban hills. The castle was inherited by Pietro in about 1064. Like their rivals the Gaetani and the Orsini, the Colonna gained power and wealth from their feudal estates in the Roman countryside, from their private armies, and from the favor of the papacy. By the 13th century they were furnishing churchmen, soldiers, and senators to Rome. Thereafter, their turbulent history was practically inseparable from the history of the city and the church.

From the beginning of the 14th century until the late 16th century the family was embroiled in a continuous struggle to dominate Rome. Pope Boniface VIII, of the Gaetani family, attempted to destroy the power of the Colonna through excommunication and a crusade. But allied with France, and led by Sciarra Colonna (died 1329),

the Colonna were revenged in 1303 when they besieged the Pope at Anagni; he died shortly thereafter. Under Sciarra the Colonna completely dominated Rome.

In 1347 they suffered a bloody defeat at the hands of the popular dictator, Cola di Rienzi. Again the setback was only temporary. With Oddone Colonna (1368–1431), who, as Pope Martin V, enriched his kin with territories in the Papal States and southern Italy, the family rose to new heights. Nevertheless, for well over a century longer the Colonna were repeatedly condemned by the popes and just as frequently reinstated in papal favor.

One of the last battles of the long struggle was fought between Marc'Antonio Colonna, Duke of Paliano (1535–1584), and Pope Paul IV. Exiled from Rome, his possessions confiscated by the Pope, the duke led a Spanish army against the Papal States in 1556. After the death of Pope Paul in 1559, however, he returned to Rome, and in 1571 commanded the papal galleys in the great naval victory over the Turks at Lepanto. From about this time the Colonna enjoyed unbroken peace with the papacy, serving as prelates, soldiers, and statesmen in Italy and elsewhere, particularly in Spain and Germany.

The Colonna have also contributed notable figures to literature and learning. Egidio Colonna (about 1247–1316), a scholastic theologian and the tutor of Philip IV of France, wrote a popular textbook on government as well as the most thoroughgoing medieval defense of papal power. Fabio Colonna (1567–about 1650) is remembered for his botanical compilations and discoveries. Most famous is the poetess Vittoria Colonna (1492–1547), daughter of the general Fabrizio Colonna, and the friend of Michelangelo. After her husband's death in 1525, she lived in convents and sought consolation in the composition of amatory and religious verse.

Three branches of the family survive today. The great Colonna palace (15th to 18th centuries) in Rome testifies to the importance of the family. It houses the Colonna Gallery, one of the most celebrated private art galleries in Europe.

RANDOLPH STARN
*University of California at Berkeley*

**COLONNA,** kō-lōn′nä, **Vittoria** (1492–1547), Italian poet. She is best remembered for her platonic friendship with Michelangelo, who greatly admired her piety and addressed sonnets to her.

She was born at Marino, near Rome, the daughter of Fabrizio Colonna, later grand constable of the Kingdom of Naples. In 1509 she was married by arrangement to Fernando Francisco de Avalos, Marquess di Pescara, a Spanish-Neapolitan soldier in the service of the Holy Roman Empire. After Avalos died in 1525, having achieved fame earlier that year by capturing Francis I of France at the Battle of Pavia, his wife turned to religion, living in convents and working for religious reform. She died in Rome on Feb. 25, 1547.

Many of her poems are elegiac, inspired by her husband's death; others, published as *Rime spirituali* (1538), have religious subjects. Their Neoplatonism reflects the influence of Petrarch. Conventionality and repetitiousness impair her work, which is important, nevertheless, for its influence on later Italian poets.

**COLONNA, Cape.** See SOUNION, CAPE.

**COLONNADE,** kol-ə-nād', in architecture, a line or range of columns. A court lined with colonnades, as in Egyptian temples or Roman houses, is called a peristyle. An edifice surrounded by a row of columns (for instance, the larger Greek temples) is called a peripteral structure. A line of columns, usually four or six, set along a side or end wall, but not necessarily extending the full length of the wall, is called a portico.

Colonnades vary in the style of columns used and in the placement and grouping of the columns. The peristyle of the Temple of Amon (14th century B.C.), in Luxor, Egypt, is composed of clustered columns. The Parthenon (447–432 B.C.), in Athens, is a peripteral temple with columns in the Doric style. The Romans inherited the colonnade from the Greeks, and used it for porticoes, as at the front of the Maison Carrée (4 A.D.), Nîmes, France. (The side colonnades are formed by engaged columns.) The elliptical piazza (1656–1663) designed by Giovanni Lorenzo Bernini for St. Peter's, Rome, is defined by colonnades of four parallel rows of columns.

EVERARD M. UPJOHN, *Columbia University*

**COLONNE,** kô-lôn', **Édouard** (1838–1910), French violinist and orchestra conductor, who introduced and helped popularize the works of many eminent composers of his time. He was born Judas Colonne in Bordeaux, France, on July 23, 1838. Colonne studied at the Paris Conservatory, where he won first prize for harmony in 1858. From that year until 1867 he was first violinist at the Paris Opera.

In 1873 Colonne helped establish a series of concerts, the Concert National, at the Théâtre de l'Odéon. These concerts, which were transferred to the Théâtre du Châtelet in 1874, eventually became known as the Concerts Colonne and were conducted by him until his death. As leader of these concerts, he introduced the works of such contemporary composers as Berlioz, Wagner, Tchaikovsky, Grieg, Massenet, and Franck. He also was guest conductor in England, Russia, Portugal, and the United States. Colonne died in Paris on March 28, 1910.

**COLONUS,** kə-lō'nəs, a farm tenant in the Roman Empire. Originally the *coloni* leased the land they farmed, usually for a period of five years. In the 4th century A.D., however, the *coloni* were bound to the soil and became almost "slaves of the land." Moreover, the status of *colonus* became hereditary. Eventually, a distinction was made between *adscripticii*, who were indeed rural slaves, and *coloni*, tied hereditarily to the land, but having the status of freemen.

TOM B. JONES, *University of Minnesota*

**COLONY.** See COLONIALISM.

**COLOPHON,** kol'ō-fon, was an ancient Greek city in central Ionia, near modern Değirmendere in Turkey, 35 miles (56 km) south of Smyrna (Izmir) and 9 miles (14 km) from the Aegean Sea. It flourished from the 8th century B.C. Conquered by Gyges of Lydia about 665 B.C., it was ruled by Persia after 545. Colophonian exiles seized Smyrna before its conquest by Lydia in the early 6th century B.C. Colophonians also seized Notion, which became the port for Colophon.

The city, ruled by a wealthy oligarchy, was famous for its luxury. It was also noted for its cavalry. The poets Mimnermus, Xenophanes, and Antimachus were born in Colophon, which also claimed to be the birthplace of Homer.

Colophon was conquered in 302 by Lysimachus, a general of Alexander the Great; later, most of the inhabitants were moved to his new city of Ephesus. Colophon continued to be inhabited but was superseded in importance by Notion, which became known as New Colophon. At Claros, near Notion, was the famous shrine of Apollo, whose temple and oracle have been excavated since 1950.

Excavations at Colophon itself were cut short after one season (1922). The ruins include an acropolis, a theater, and baths. A "beehive" tomb that was discovered in the area nearby indicates that there was settlement in Mycenaean times.

D. J. BLACKMAN
*Bristol University, England*

**COLOPHON,** kol'ə-fən, originally, an inscription on the last page of a book or manuscript, giving the name of the printer or scribe and the date and place of publication. (The word means literally "finishing stroke.") Often, additional designs or devices were added to the basic colophon, such as the armorial bearings of the printer or of the town in which he worked, or a message of thankfulness for having completed the work. In modern publications, the colophon generally appears on the spine or title page as the emblem of a publishing house or author.

The earliest printed book containing a colophon was the Mainz Psalter of 1457, in which the colophon gave the date of publication and the names of the printers, Johann Fust (a partner of Gutenberg) and Peter Schoffer. The printers added two shields at the end of the colophon to their Vienna edition of the Psalter, and used the more elaborate colophon for their edition of the Latin Bible (1462) as well.

From about 1520, the information contained in the colophon, often with an identifying design, was printed on the title page of publications. Colophons occasionally appear on the last page of modern publications in limited or fine editions.

COLOPHON used by the printer William Morris for an edition of the works of Chaucer.

ÞERE ENDS the Book of the Works of Geoffrey Chaucer, edited by F. S. Ellis; ornamented with pictures designed by Sir Edward Burne-Jones, and engraved on wood by W. H. Hooper. Printed by me William Morris at the Kelmscott Press, Upper Mall, Hammersmith, in the County of Middlesex. Finished on the 8th day of May, 1896.

The hearty thanks of the Editor and Printer are due to the Reverend Professor Skeat for kindly allowing the use of his emendations to the Ellesmere MS. of the Canterbury Tales, and also of his emended texts of Chaucer's other writings. The like thanks also the Editor and Printer give to the Delegates of the Oxford University Press for allowing them to avail themselves of Professor Skeat's permission.

**COLOR** provides us with much of our information concerning the world in which we live. Color is what we see or, more important, what we think we see.

In the past there has been much confusion over the precise meaning of the word, but gradually, at least in technical fields, the meaning has become more carefully defined. Color is usually defined in one of two ways, either subjectively, as an aspect of visual appearance, or objectively, as the property of light by which we are made aware of objects or light sources. Formerly the term "color" was also applied to substances used to modify the colors of objects, such as dyes and pigments. To avoid confusion, such substances are now called colorants.

Thus, for purposes of this discussion, we confine ourselves to a consideration of color in relation to its two related definitions, one referring to the color of an object as part of visual experience, and the other referring to color as a property of light that can be described in terms derived from the spectral characteristics of the light emitted, reflected, or transmitted by an object.

The appearance of color can be described in terms of hue, lightness, and saturation for objects, and hue, brightness, and saturation for light sources. This is the psychological, or subjective, approach, which is widely used in practical color work because it is relatively easy for persons to visualize colors that are specified in these terms.

The objective aspect of color may be described in terms of dominant wavelength, luminance, and purity. More often, however, this aspect of color is described in terms of the standard coordinates of an internationally adopted system of values, which are based on the color-matching functions of a "standard observer." This is a psychophysical approach and forms the usual basis for modern colorimetric studies.

Through standard procedures the subjective and objective aspects of color are today so completely interrelated that it is possible for the color of a new paint or textile sample to be given a common descriptive name that can be obtained by either a subjective or an objective method. The subjective method is based on visual comparisons to standard color charts, while the objective method involves measurements of the sample, which may either be made directly or be derived from computations based on spectral reflectance. By either method it is possible to arrive at the same name for the sample.

It has taken many years of study and the adoption of international standards to make such precision in color specification feasible, for color is a complex subject. The phenomenon of color is the result of a sequence of processes that involve several fields of science: the physics of light, the chemistry of colorants, and the physics, physiology, and psychology involved in studying the eye and brain. These fields are all brought in, since, for an individual to experience or measure color the following are necessary: a stimulus, usually light; an object which emits, reflects, or transmits light; and some sort of receptor and response mechanism to receive and interpret the light. Studies of all three phases are necessary in order to understand all aspects of color.

## LIGHT AND COLOR

While color may be experienced from memory, in dreams, or from pressure or electrical stimulation of the eyeball or optic nerve, the usual stimulus is light. Light is a very small portion of the electromagnetic spectrum, the radiant energy that travels through space in the form of waves. These waves extend in length (or frequency) from the very, very short gamma and X rays that are less than a billionth of a meter in length, through the ultraviolet, visible, and infrared, to the short and then longer radio waves that may be as long as, or even longer than, 1,000 meters. The minute part of this spectrum that is visible includes wavelengths that measure from about 380 to 780 nanometers (nm; billionths of a meter).

**The Spectrum.** If the light from a source containing wavelengths from 380 to 780 nm (that is, white light) is dispersed through a prism, or by a grating, the result will be a spectrum of rainbow colors ranging from reds at the longer wave end, through orange, yellow, green, cyan, and blue, to violet at the shorter wave end. Observers with normal color vision usually see blue at about 480 nm, green at 515 nm, yellow at 575 nm, and red at 650 nm.

Basic data for defining the color of a light source are given in terms of measurements of the energy at each of the wavelengths, or groups of wavelengths, of which the light is composed. For example, different light sources emit energy in relatively different amounts in different parts of the spectrum. An object illuminated by a light source can reflect or transmit only such parts of the spectrum as are contained in the source by which it is illuminated. Thus, in order to see objects in their true colors (usually this means the color they appear to have in daylight), it is necessary that the source contain all portions of the visible radiant-energy spectrum.

The instrument used to determine the spectral composition of radiant energy is a spectroradiometer, a two-part instrument. One part is a device, usually a prism or diffraction grating, to disperse the radiant energy into its component spectral parts. The other part contains a meter to measure the amount of energy radiated at each of the dispersed wavelengths. Thus, the spectral composition of a light source may be measured and expressed as either the actual or the relative amounts of energy radiated for each wavelength in the visible spectrum.

**White Light.** From the foregoing explanation it is clear that the light source must contain energy for all wavelengths in the visible spectrum if it is to be used as an all-purpose light source. Thus, the concept of white light is important to color. It may be defined as radiant energy with a wavelength distribution that evokes a neutral, or hueless, sensation in the observer with normal color vision. Yet the color range of white light may vary considerably, particularly in the yellow-blue direction. For example, sunlight coming in through a south window may be white when one is adapted to it, but it is quite yellow when compared to the color of daylight from a blue north sky. Yet each has a continuous spectrum, and each may be considered for some purposes as within the range of white light.

For colorimetry and photography it is especially important to be able to identify any par-

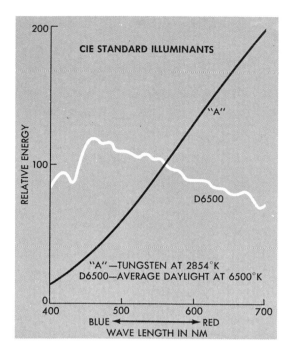

CIE STANDARD ILLUMINANTS

"A"—TUNGSTEN AT 2854°K
D6500—AVERAGE DAYLIGHT AT 6500°K

RELATIVE ENERGY

BLUE ◄────► RED
WAVE LENGTH IN NM

ticular "white" reference source. For this purpose the concept of *color temperature* is useful. It is the absolute, or Kelvin (K), temperature of a perfect radiator, called a blackbody, whose chromaticity (color without regard to brightness) is the same as that of the body in question.

At a temperature of 800° K to 900° K a blackbody is red; as the temperature becomes higher, the color becomes yellow at about 3000° K, white (neutral) at about 5000° K, a pale bluish color at 8000° K to 10,000° K, and a more brilliant sky blue at 60,000° K to 100,000° K. Yet light sources whose color temperatures range from the 3000° K of tungsten light to the 6500° K of so-called average daylight are all considered in the range of white light when used as sources of illumination.

The spectral energy distribution of light from incandescent lamps follows a blackbody distribution very closely. General-purpose incandescent lamps used in the home are usually about 2820-3000° K. The color of average noon sunlight at ground level in Washington, D. C., based on measurements made by Charles G. Abbot of the Smithsonian Institution, is reported to be 5035° K, while the color of the sun above the atmosphere is reported to be 6085° K. In 1966 relative spectral energy distributions were adopted as an international standard for average daylight at a correlated color temperature of 6500° K. At the same time, standardized spectral distributions for 5500° K and 7500° K were recommended for representing somewhat yellower and bluer phases of daylight. For general use in color science, standards for "CIE illuminant A" (an incandescent lamp operated at 2854° K) and "CIE illuminant D6500" (representing average daylight) are thought to suffice. (The CIE standards are those of the Commission Internationale de l'Éclairage.) Relative spectral-energy curves of these two standards are illustrated in Fig. 1.

While there are exceptions, the colors of objects show considerable constancy under white light sources that vary in relative amounts of energy, just as they show constancy, for example, under various phases of daylight. Even under tungsten light, while colors shift somewhat from their daylight color, they do so in a regular manner to which we have become accustomed, as we have to the familiar changes in daylight color from the reddish light of dawn or sunset, through the yellowish white of noon sun, to the deep blue of north skylight. In the Northern Hemisphere, light from a lightly or moderately overcast sky from the north is the "white light" preferred for use by artists and professional color matchers.

There are, however, many light sources commonly used today that depart considerably from a blackbody type of spectral distribution. The colors of objects illuminated by such light sources do not always retain their expected constancy but often shift in a manner to which we are not accustomed by our daylight-trained eyes. Yet the color of these light sources may still lie in the range of what is considered white light. For example, it is quite possible for two light sources to match in color, yet vary importantly in their spectral composition. As a consequence, the color of many objects seen under one and then the other of such light sources will differ considerably. This is a result of the very important fact that objects reflect or transmit light at the various parts of the spectrum only in the proportion in which these wavelengths are present in the light source. Thus, the spectral energy distribution of a light source, not simply its "white" color, is the basis for its effect on the color of objects.

The fluorescent lamps available today come in several different whites: Warm White, White, Cool White, and Daylight, and in both standard and deluxe types for some. The deluxe types emit more energy in the red end of the spectrum, thus making their relative energy distributions more like those of a blackbody or daylight-type lamp of the corresponding color temperature. Relative spectral energy curves for four white fluorescent lamps in current production are illustrated in Fig. 2. The correlated color temperature for Warm White is about 3000° K, for White about 3500° K, for Cool White about 4200° K, and for Daylight about 6500° K.

The light source, whether it be "white" or chromatic, is one of the three important requirements for seeing color. Upon its spectral distribution much depends.

### COLOR VISION

To experience color vision, there must be some sort of receptor and response mechanism to receive and interpret light. In the human visual system this starts with the eye, which has an optical system to direct the incoming light to the point at which receptors may be stimulated. These lie in the retina, which contains among other things a layer of rods and cones that contain chemicals sensitive to light. The rods are spindle-shaped cells that are found only outside the fovea, or central portion, of the retina. They are sensitive to small amounts of light and are most useful at night. The cones are somewhat larger than the rods and are sensitive to color. It is possible that because of the different pigments that they contain, some of the cones may be predominantly sensitive to blue light, others to green light, and still others to red light. As a group the cones are sensitive to the entire visible spectrum.

# COLOR

## THE COLORS OF THE SPECTRUM

The colors of the spectrum may be produced by passing white light through a prism. As shown in the schematic diagram above, the light from the source is first passed through a narrow slit and then through a glass prism. The colors are formed when the prism refracts, or bends, the different wavelengths that make up white light by different amounts, the shorter violet and blue wavelenghs being bent more than the longer red wavelengths. The light extending toward the bottom of the figure is part of the original light that has been reflected from, rather than refracted by, the prism.

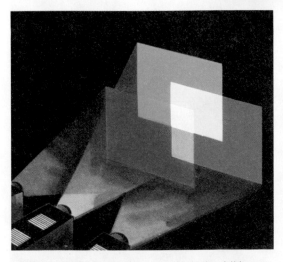

ADDITIVE PRIMARIES. Nearly every color in the visible spectrum can be produced by mixing (adding) lights of the primary colors green, blue, and red. In pairs, for example, they combine to produce blue-green, red-blue, and yellow. All three primary colors in combination make white light.

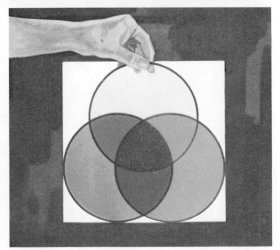

SUBTRACTIVE PRIMARIES. A wide range of colors can be produced by using colorants to subtract part of the spectrum from white light. Here, filters tinted with the subtractive primaries yellow, magenta, and cyan combine in pairs to produce red, blue, and green. All three together make black.

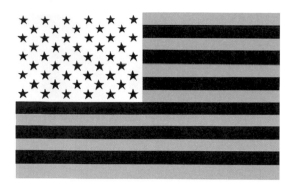

AFTERIMAGE. A red, white, and blue flag will be seen if one stares at the lower right-hand star for 30 seconds and then focuses on the black dot at the right.

COLOR CONTRAST. The appearance of a color is affected by its surroundings. Thus the same blue appears to change when seen against different backgrounds.

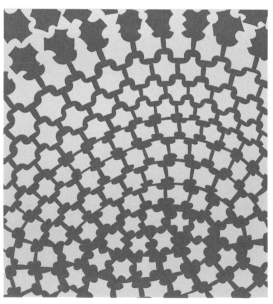

LEGIBILITY. Letters that differ from their background only in lightness can be read more easily than those that differ from the background only in hue or saturation.

VIBRATION. Patterns made by combining highly saturated colors that differ from each other in hue but not in lightness seem to vibrate as you look at them.

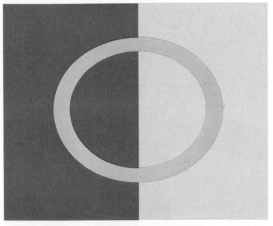

SIMULTANEOUS CONTRAST. If a pencil is placed on the border between the red and blue areas, the two halves of the gray circle will seem to differ slightly in color.

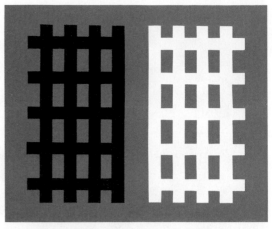

SPREADING EFFECT. The red background under the black grid appears to differ from the identical red under the white grid. Note the ghostly red dots on the white grid.

ADVANCING AND RECEDING COLORS. The ends of the two corridors are equally distant, but the red ("advancing") wall seems to be nearer than the blue ("receding") wall.

COLOR FROM BLACK AND WHITE. If the pattern is held a few inches in front of your eyes, colored streaks will appear above and below the black lines.

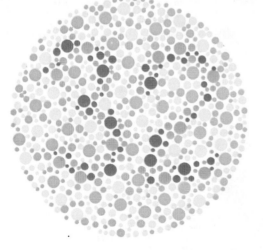

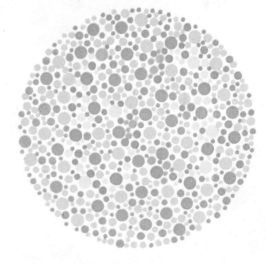

DEFECTIVE COLOR VISION can often be diagnosed through the use of special visual tests. The plates shown above are used for determining whether the subject can distinguish between reds and greens. People with normal color vision see the number 32 and 63 while those with red-green blindness do not see any numbers at all.

Sections of the Munsell color solid are shown in these two views of a model. Each leaf contains chips of the same hue but of different chroma and value.

## THE MUNSELL COLOR SOLID

The dimensions of the Munsell color solid are shown in the larger, three-dimensional figure. The *value*, or lightness, of a color is measured vertically along the central, neutral pole. The *chroma*, or saturation, of a color depends on its radial distance outward from the pole, and the different *hues* are arranged in a circle around the pole. For practical purposes, the Munsell system is often considered as having five primary hues and five intermediate hues, as in the Munsell color wheel (*bottom right*).

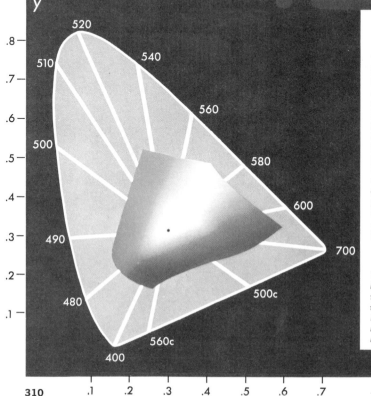

## THE CIE CHROMATICITY DIAGRAM

The wavelengths of the visible spectrum, in nanometers (nm), are marked off around the horseshoe-shaped border. Along the straight bottom line are the wavelengths of colors complementary to the purples. The dot in the center represents the source of "white" light selected, and the colored area represents those colors reproducible by today's printing inks. Colors of the same hue lie on straight lines connecting the source to the wavelength of that color on the spectrum line; they increase in purity as they approach the border. The *x* and *y* axes are two of the three CIE chromaticity coordinates of the different colors shown in this diagram.

*With the exception of the Dvorine color blindness tests, the illustrations in the preceding plates have been adapted from source materials developed by Interchemical Corporation and the Eastman Kodak Company. The use of these materials is gratefully acknowledged.*

There is little doubt that light is absorbed in the rods and cones and is converted into nerve impulses by a process not yet understood. The activity set off in the nervous system by activity in these receptors completes the physiological circuit needed to see colors. This activity must reach the occipital cortex of the brain, which is the anatomical end of the nerve pathways related to color vision. The entire process is very complicated; in fact, it is not known precisely how light is perceived, although there are many theories, beginning with those of Hermann von Helmholtz and Thomas Young and including those of G. E. Müller. Scientists are still hard at work on many phases of the problem. To be successful, a color theory must account not only for the facts of normal color vision but also for all facts of abnormal color vision. See also COLOR BLINDNESS.

## PRIMARY COLORS

A set of primary colors is one from which nearly all other colors may be derived or mixed, with the restriction that no one primary color may be matched by any combination of the other two. In practice, some primaries are capable of producing a wider gamut of colors than others.

From the aspect of *appearance,* four hues are known as unitary hues. These are the psychological color primaries: red, yellow, green, and blue, each having in its appearance no tinge of any other hue.

From the aspect of *light,* any color may theoretically be matched with a mixture of no more than three colors. These are the additive color primaries: red, green, and blue. In practical use, as in color television or in tristimulus (three-stimulus) colorimeters, the particular red, green, and blue chosen as primaries will depend on the gamut that is preferred out of those that it may be feasible to produce. Primaries are selected to produce as many as possible of the colors important to include within the limits of the gamut. In any real situation, a few extreme colors will lie outside the gamut.

In the color illustration of additive mixture of light from three sources, red and green light added together produce yellow; green and blue produce cyan; blue and red produce magenta; and red, green, and blue produce white.

The additive method of producing colors from primaries may be based on space or time. In space, lights of different colors may be superimposed on the same spot, or small areas of color may be juxtaposed. Such methods are the basis of television and of pointillistic painting. In time, colors may be added together, or averaged, by presenting them in rapid succession in the same place, a method used for early systems of color television, in some older forms of motion pictures, and in colorimeters using disk mixtures. If they are presented rapidly enough to avoid flicker, the result will appear as a steady, uniform color.

From the aspect of *colorants,* primaries are magenta (bluish red), yellow, and cyan (blue-green). These are known as subtractive color primaries, since the substances of which they consist have the property of absorbing from the spectrum of incident light some wavelengths that the other primaries would reflect or transmit. With colorants are included filters, since they also are used to modify the color of light. It can be seen that the subtractive primaries are

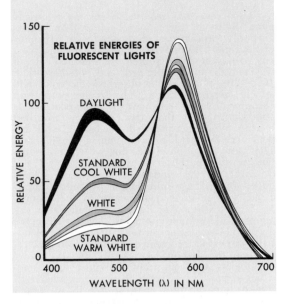

generally complementary in color to the additive primaries. A magenta filter will subtract the green part of the spectrum, and thus is sometimes called minus-green; and similarly, yellow is known as minus-blue and cyan as minus-red. Because magenta subtracts green and yellow subtracts blue, a magenta filter over a yellow filter leaves only the red wavelengths; similarly, yellow over cyan produces green; cyan over magenta produces blue; magenta over yellow and cyan filters produces black.

*Complementary colors* are colors that, when mixed additively in suitable proportions, produce an achromatic (neutral) color. In general, blues are complementary to yellows, reds to blue-greens, and greens to red-purples.

## PRODUCTION OF COLOR

Light sources *emit* energy that makes it possible to see color. Objects, on the other hand, *absorb, transmit,* or *reflect* light, and sometimes do all three. In each case, a particular proportion of light for each wavelength is emitted, absorbed, transmitted, or reflected. It is this property of an object—to be selective about the relative degree of light that it will reflect or transmit at each wavelength—that is the principal reason that color is so often considered a property of the object itself, quite apart from the light source that illuminates it.

An object that *absorbs nonselectively,* that is, absorbs the same proportion of daylight at each wavelength, produces a neutral, or achromatic, color, one with no distinguishable hue. (It is also possible, but not usual, for objects that are spectrally selective to appear achromatic, for example, when the spectral selection is such that it can be balanced by use of a particular light source.) If very little light is absorbed, the color will appear white when the remainder is reflected, and transparent when the remainder is transmitted. If most of the light is absorbed, and very little is either reflected or transmitted, the color will appear black. For intermediate amounts of light absorbed nonselectively as to wavelength, an object will appear as one of a series of grays, its lightness depending upon the proportion of light it absorbs.

An object that *selectively absorbs* relatively more light at some wavelengths than others generally produces a chromatic color. If most of the light (90 or 95%) from daylight or almost any common light source is absorbed at all wavelengths except the red, and not more than 10 or 20% of the red is absorbed, the color will appear as a saturated red. If the proportion absorbed by the red part of the spectrum is only slightly less than the proportion absorbed by the remaining parts, the color will still appear red but of low saturation, a grayish red. The same principle holds for selective absorption in other parts of the spectrum.

Any full explanation of how color is produced by the use of colorants is quite complicated, but in general it relates to the absorption and scattering of light in colorant layers by pigments (insoluble particles that usually produce light-scattering layers) or dyes (molecularly dispersed substances that most frequently produce transparent layers).

Objects that transmit or reflect light may either *diffuse* it without change in wavelength composition, or they may *scatter* it, in which case there is a change in wavelength composition. When light passes from a medium containing small particles that differ in refractive index from the medium, the direction of the light that strikes each particle is changed. If the diameters of the particles are many times greater than the wavelengths of light and if the particles consist of a substance that is nonselective, there is essentially only a directional change, an action called diffusion. When light is not diffused by an object, its reflectance or transmittance usually is called *specular*, as in objects we describe as glossy. When light passes through a medium that contains many particles that are as small as or smaller than the wavelength of light, the light is scattered—the short wavelengths more than the long wavelengths.

It is the scattering of the shorter, blue wavelengths of light from the sun by particles (clumps of air molecules) in the atmosphere that is responsible for the blue appearance of the sky. Also, the sunlight, as we see it in relation to a blue sky, is yellow because it lacks some of the blue end of the spectrum that the air has scattered. To an observer situated above the air layer that envelops the earth and looking out toward space, the sky appears black, for in space there are too few particles to scatter the sunlight. On earth, as the sun approaches the horizon, sunlight travels a longer path through the air and through an increasing amount of water and small dust particles. As it does, the color of the sun gradually changes to orange and then red. Selective scattering also accounts for the blue color of opals, skim milk, and blue eyes.

The *surface reflection* characteristics of metals differ from those of most objects. Most surfaces reflect nonselectively, reflecting a certain percentage of the light at each wavelength unchanged; only that part of the energy distribution of the light is altered that passes through the outer surface and is reflected within or from the layers below the surface. This can be observed in most highly chromatic objects that have a smooth, polished, or glossy surface. Highlights from the surface of such objects usually reflect the color of the light source. In metals and a few other materials, however, se-lective reflection takes place at the surface according to wavelength. Copper and gold are good examples. Similar effects are shown by some dyes and printing inks.

The *refraction* of light, a change of direction when light passes from one medium to another, varies with wavelength according to the difference in refractive indices between the two media, and thus also gives rise to colors. It is refraction of light that results in the rainbow formed from raindrops in the air, and in the spectrum produced when white light passes through the plane, nonparallel sides of a glass prism.

*Diffraction* of light, a bending of waves around the edge of an obstacle or around a small aperture, results in the separation of light by wavelength. A very bright spectrum can be produced by means of a good diffraction grating, one on which many thousands of parallel lines per inch are ruled.

*Interference* of light waves from the same source will produce a redistribution of light that depends on the amplitude of the combined wave. Light from one wave may be added to that of another so that the amount of light is doubled to form a bright spot or line, or it may be subtracted so that one wave cancels another and produces a dark area of no light at all. Interference may be caused by refraction or diffraction or by reflection from the front and back surfaces of films that are suitably thin. The colors of a soap bubble, an oil film on water, butterfly and bird wings, and of some beetles are produced by interference.

*Fluorescent* objects are self-luminous. They absorb energy at one wavelength and emit it at another, usually longer, wavelength. Phosphors that are used to produce fluorescent colors may vary widely in the distribution of spectral energy that each emits. One of the reasons that fluorescent lamps do not provide better color rendering is that inexpensive, safe phosphors covering the reds in the long-wave range of the spectrum are not currently available. For color-matching purposes a few fluorescent lamps are made with special phosphors.

## SYSTEMS FOR SPECIFYING COLORS

Any description of the characteristics of color depends upon the point of view from which color is considered. In the following paragraphs the subject is considered from the subjective and objective points of view separately, then in terms of their own interrelations.

**Subjective Description of Color.** When color is considered subjectively, it may be described in terms of three attributes of sensation; hue, saturation, and brightness, or lightness. The attributes of extent and duration add factors such as size, shape, location, texture, glare, flicker, sparkle, and glitter, which are important to color experience and must be considered in any total examination of color perception. But from these experiences the basic responses of hue, saturation, and brightness may be abstracted and scaled. *Hue* is that attribute by which colors are classed as red, yellow, green, blue, or intermediate between any contiguous pair of these. *Saturation* is the attribute that describes the vividness of hue, or the degree of difference from a gray of the same lightness or brightness. *Brightness* is the attribute by which color may be referred to a scale of dim to very bright for light sources, black to colorless for transparent objects, and black to white for opaque objects. The term "lightness" frequently replaces the term "brightness" when it refers to the relative brightness of opaque or transparent objects.

These three attributes are often considered as dimensions and are represented by a three-dimensional model in which brightness is the vertical dimension, hue is cyclical, and saturation extends in a radial dimension horizontally from a vertical neutral axis.

**Subjective Classification Systems.** Colors may be classified according to different systems by use of this three-dimensional concept. Such systems will be varied, each depending on the method of scaling. Of systems intended to relate to appearance, or to naming or identifying colors, several have been developed that are illustrated by large collections of samples. The best known probably are the Ridgway, Lovibond, Ostwald, and Munsell systems. The *Ridgway* system is a system of 1,115 named colors, published in 1912 and widely used for many years in biological sciences. The *Lovibond* system is exemplified by glasses colored to provide scales of red, yellow, and blue, each marked with a number of units on the corresponding scale, so that samples may be matched and specified by light coming through a combination of glasses. The *Ostwald* system describes colors in terms of color content, white content, and black content. It is usually exemplified by triangular color charts. In each chart, one vertex represents white, one vertex represents black, and one vertex represents a "full" color. The *Munsell* system specifies colors on scales of hue, value, and chroma, exemplified by a collection of color chips forming an atlas of charts. These charts show scales intended to represent equal visual intervals for a normal observer under daylight and viewing colors against a gray to white background, so that under these conditions the hue, value, and chroma of the color correlate closely with its description in the subjective terms, hue, lightness, and saturation.

*Notation of the Munsell System.* The notation of the Munsell system has found wide acceptance for specifying color in terms of appearance attributes. This is because the scales of the Munsell system correlate closely with the attributes of color perception, because the notation is based upon uniform spacing within each attribute, and because a smoothed set of curves, based on colorimetric studies of samples in the *Book of Color* (1929), enables one to assign a Munsell notation to any color sample.

The Munsell hue scale contains five principal hues, red (R), yellow (Y), green (G), blue (B), and purple (P); and five intermediate hues, YR, GY, BG, PB, and RP. The value scale contains ten steps from black to white: 0 to 10. Chroma scales contain up to 16 or more steps from the neutral gray of equivalent value. This 3-dimensional concept is described in terms of a color solid, a world of color in which color charts become maps of color space. Such a concept may be illustrated with a 3-dimensional model of a Munsell Color Solid cut open to display one hue. The system is sometimes described in terms of a color tree. This corresponds to stripping the solid to a skeleton of its hue, value, and chroma coordinates—the central neutral pole becoming the tree trunk, chroma scales reaching out like branches, and the individual colors be-

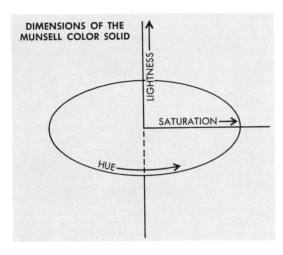

DIMENSIONS OF THE MUNSELL COLOR SOLID

coming leaves. The Munsell notation gives hue, value, and chroma, in that order, for example, 5R 4/10. Each scale can be expressed decimally to provide as precise a color notation as may be needed. One widely used approximation of equivalence between scales of hue, values, and chroma units is 1 value step ≡ 2 chroma steps ≡ 3 hue steps (when hue is at chroma 5).

**Objective Description of Color.** When color is considered objectively, as a property of the light by which we are made aware of objects or light sources, it may be described in terms of a color classification system which indicates the amounts of the three real or imaginary primary colors that are required to match the color of a given object or light source. This match can be made directly, or it can be derived indirectly from calculations based on the spectral energy distribution of the light from the source or object in question. It can be expressed in terms of tristimulus values (one stimulus for each of three primaries), or it can be put into terms of dominant wavelength, luminance, and purity, terms that are more suggestive of color appearance attributes but do not correspond with them exactly.

*The CIE system* is an international method for specifying color in this objective sense. It was recommended in 1931 by the Commission Internationale de l'Éclairage and since then has found wide use and acceptance. It is doubtful whether modern colorimetry could have developed without it. The 1931 resolutions covered recommendations for a standard observer, standard illuminants for colorimetry, and standard conditions of illumination and viewing.

The *CIE standard observer* is based on the smoothed mean of observations made for each wavelength from 380 to 780 nm to obtain the amounts of the three primaries needed by a normal observer to match each of the colors of an equal-energy spectrum. The color-matching properties of the 1931 standard observer are defined in tables of $\bar{x}(\lambda)$, $\bar{y}(\lambda)$, and $\bar{z}(\lambda)$, which define the color-matching functions and their corresponding chromaticity coordinates when the white of a spectrum of equal energy has chromaticity coordinates 1/3, 1/3, 1/3. The color-matching data of the standard observer have been mathematically transformed from a basis of real primaries, R,G,B, in order to provide CIE tristimulus values $X,Y,Z$, in which the Y value is made equal to luminance (analogous to brightness for subjective systems), and only positive numbers are required for the specification of a color. As converted, the primaries of the CIE system are imaginary.

To represent chromaticity, it is usual to employ ratios of each of the standard CIE coordinates (that is, the tristimulus values $X,Y,Z$) to the sum of the three. Since the sum of these chromaticity coordinates, $x,y,z$, is 1, only two ordinates, usually $x$ and $y$, are needed to describe chromaticity. One of the tristimulus values must also be specified, usually $Y$. Thus, a CIE specification can be given in terms of $X,Y,Z$, or in the derived terms of $Y,x,y$.

Except for differences in luminance, $Y$, the relationship of colors can be shown on a CIE $x,y$–chromaticity diagram, where the $x$ and $y$ are the horizontal and vertical coordinates, respectively. On the color illustration on Plate IV, the horseshoe-shaped line represents the locus of spectrum colors as seen by the CIE standard observer, and each point within the line thus represents a particular color. The straight line that connects the ends of the spectrum and completes the horseshoe-shaped region is the purple locus. The wavelength designation for the purples is that of the complementary wavelength, which will depend upon the reference neutral color in the center region of the diagram. When the color of an object is to be designated, the light source under which the object is illuminated serves as the central reference point. One of the important advantages of the CIE chromaticity diagram is that it is a mixture diagram; mixtures of colors lie along the path of the straight lines that connect them.

Three *CIE standard light sources* were recommended in 1931: A, an incandescent lamp at 2854° K; B, a lamp and liquid filter to represent direct sunlight, at 4870° K; and C, a lamp and liquid filter to represent average daylight, at 6770° K. As light sources, B and C have found little direct use, but the tables of data based on them, for the range of 380 to 780 nm, have found wide use, particularly that based on C. In 1966, CIE recommendations provided data for calculating the spectral energy distribution in the range of 300 to 830 nm, corresponding to any given correlated color temperature of daylight from 4000° K to 25,000° K. Illuminant D6500 was designated for standard use in colorimetry, and D5500 and D7500 for use when daylight substitutes of lower or higher correlated color temperature are required. It is expected that eventually CIE D6500 will replace standard source C as a substitute for average daylight in colorimetry.

CIE standard conditions for illuminating and viewing were recommended in 1931 for illuminating the object at 45°, and viewing normally, but this recommendation has found little acceptance. There has been as much or more interest in other conditions, such as illuminating the object diffusely and viewing normally.

*Dominant wavelength, purity,* and *luminance,* terms more suggestive of color appearance than a $Y,x,y$–specification, may be derived from $Y$ and an $x,y$–diagram. The *dominant wavelength* of the color of any object is the wavelength indicated on the horseshoe-shaped spectrum locus by a straight line that passes through the $x,y$–points representing the color of the object and of the light source. The *excitation purity* of a color is the ratio of the distance of its $x,y$–point

from the point representing the light source, to the total distance from the light source along a straight line to the point where it intersects the spectrum locus. The excitation purity of colors that lie on the spectrum locus is 100%; colors with an excitation purity of 50% lie halfway along a line connecting the points representing the light source color and the spectrum locus. The *luminance* of a color is represented by CIE tristimulus value $Y$. If $Y$ is 1.00, it represents complete reflectance or transmittance; at 0.00 it represents zero reflectance or transmittance.

The CIE chromaticity diagram lacks uniform spacing of colors. Several projective transformations have been made in order to improve the uniformity of spacing, but none has yet equaled the spacing provided by the Munsell system. Nevertheless, some improvement on the 1931 $x,y$–diagram is shown by a projective transformation of this diagram made in 1937 by David L. MacAdam, which has recently been approved as a CIE 1960 UCS (Uniform Chromaticity Scale) diagram. An extension to three dimensions forms the basis for a CIE 1964 Uniform Color Space ($U^*,V^*,W^*$) system. This recommendation makes it possible to provide a color-difference formula based on CIE coordinates.

**Interrelation of Color Specifications.** It is frequently desirable to convert from one system of specification to another, or to convert samples of one chart or color card into terms of another. Specifications given for any system or sample in terms of either Munsell or CIE may be converted or compared to samples or specifications of any other system for which a similar conversion is available. It is becoming more and more usual for specifications of color standards to be provided with either Munsell or CIE specifications, or both.

Diagrams of the Munsell system, overlaid on CIE diagrams for value levels 1 through 9, are available for making conversions from one system to another, as are computer programs. The name blocks of the Inter-Society Color Council–National Bureau of Standards method of designating colors specify the limits of each name block in terms of the Munsell system; the centroid samples are specified in both CIE and Munsell terms. Use of the ISCC–NBS naming method makes it possible to convert numerical specifications to a commonly understood descriptive color name for any sample specified in either Munsell or CIE notation.

## PHYSIOLOGICAL AND PSYCHOLOGICAL PHENOMENA

The following color-related phenomena are selections from a wide range of topics. For further details the reader is referred to the literature on color vision and color psychology, particularly the periodical literature of color science.

**Color Constancy.** Color constancy, discussed briefly in the section on white light, is a phenomenon under which object-color perceptions remain largely independent of ordinary changes in illumination. In other words, an apple is red in daylight and remains red under the much yellower light of an incandescent lamp. Color constancy is aided by a low degree of spectral selectivity in the illumination, by high reflectance in surroundings, and by familiarity of objects. It requires an awareness of illumination, and may be greatly affected by attitude, that is, by the direction of attention. Under experimental conditions the measured ratios for color constancy have been found to vary from zero to one, depending upon observers and viewing conditions. Color constancy breaks down for unfamiliar conditions of illumination, particularly for conditions in which there is a high degree of spectral selectivity.

**Color Adaptation.** Studies in the field of color adaptation have led to a theory that involves the background, or frame of reference, against which color perceptions are made. According to the theory, in every viewing situation an average adaptation level is established; objects with reflectances above that level, those that are lighter than that level, tend to take on the hue of the light source, and objects that are darker or below that level tend to take on the hue of the afterimage complementary. This theory implies that the color of any object, regardless of its actual spectral composition, may under suitable conditions appear hueless, with other colors appearing chromatic in relation to the neutral adaptation point.

While many facts of color constancy and adaptation are known, it is not yet possible to compute their precise effects for objects under a change of illumination. When this precision is achieved, it will be possible to compute the daylight color of any object and know just how the color of that object will appear after a change to another light source. This is one of colorimetry's unsolved problems.

**Color Contrast.** This is an area concerned with the effect of adjacent areas of color upon each other, either in space (simultaneous contrast) or time (successive color contrast). Usually the color differences between objects are accentuated when they are juxtaposed. Brightness differences usually appear respectively brighter and darker than they would if separated. For saturation differences in the same hue, the higher saturation appears more saturated and the low saturation less saturated than when the samples are separated. Complementary hues when juxtaposed generally appear more saturated than when seen alone in a neutral situation. When they are of equal lightness and high saturation, the colors may even seem to vibrate, which can prove quite a disturbing effect. By successive contrast, large changes can be produced in brightness and saturation. Sharply defined contours separating two areas tend to increase both saturation and brightness contrast, while fuzzy contours tend to reduce them.

A phenomenon known as the *spreading effect,* a reversal of large-area color contrast, was noted by Wilhelm von Bezold prior to 1880. For certain complicated patterns, the changes that occur among colors of small juxtaposed areas appear more alike than different, which is contrary to what is expected from the usual contrast effects for large areas. For example, small areas of a colored ink overprinted with a pattern of fine black lines usually appear darker than small areas of the same ink overprinted with fine white lines. Related to this is the observation that a light object viewed against a dark background seems larger than a dark object viewed against a light background. The stimulation of a bright image on the retina seems to spread into the darker surroundings. This is why a black dress makes a girl appear smaller than a white dress does. The phenomenon could be caused by narrow-angle scattering of light within the eyeball, or by imperfect imagery by the lens of the eye, or a spreading of the pattern of nerve impulses caused by the light patch into the unstimulated area of the retina.

**Afterimages.** Afterimages may be positive or negative, but are usually negative. The color of the afterimage produced by staring at a color sample for a short time and then looking at a neutral area is complementary to the color of the sample, as in the color illustration of the American flag. This can be explained by assuming that there are three color receptors in the eye, for red, green, and blue light. Staring at any color causes adaptation of the receptors to that color. If it is a red color, the red receptor is decreased in sensitivity, so that when the eyes are shifted to a neutral area, which sends about equal amounts to the three receptors, the blue and the green receptors will be more affected than the red, and so produce the complementary color on the gray area until such time as the receptors regain an equilibrium. An example of negative afterimage is shown in the color plates.

In positive afterimages, the brightness and hue relationships are about the same as in the original. Positive afterimages are produced by brief, relatively intense stimulation, as in motion pictures.

**Advancing and Retreating Colors.** These colors seem to separate into different planes, reddish colors seeming to advance and bluish colors to retreat. Chromatic aberration in the eye may cause this, for there are different focal lengths in the eye for different colors. These effects apply to viewing with one eye, and are relatively unimpressive. With binocular vision, a phenomenon known as *color stereopsis* may be quite startling. Red and blue luminous signs that are actually at the same distance may appear to be widely separated; or, in modern abstract paintings, colors sometimes appear to leave the plane of the picture. The effect is due to chromatic aberration of the eye lens combined with a slight decentering of the eye pupil so that a red image is formed on the retina slightly displaced from the blue image; to some the red may advance, to others the blue, depending on the direction of the lateral decentering of the pupil.

*Warm* and *cool colors* have been shown by experimental studies to refer to hue more than to brightness or saturation. Orange seems to be the warmest hue, the coolest ranging through blues and greens.

DOROTHY NICKERSON
*Consultant in Color Technology*

**Bibliography**

**Albers, Josef,** *Interaction of Color: Unabridged Text and Selected Plates,* rev. ed. (Yale Univ. Press 1975).

**Babbitt, Edwin D.,** *The Principles of Light and Color* (Lyle Stuart 1980).

**Billmeyer, Fred W., Jr., and Saltzmann, Max,** *Principles of Color Technology,* 2d ed. (Wiley 1981).

**Birten, Faber,** *Light, Color and Environment,* rev. ed. (Schiffer 1988).

**De Grandis, Luiginia,** *Theory and Use of Color* (Prentice-Hall 1987).

**Judd, Deane B., and Wyszecki, Gunter,** *Color in Business, Science and Industry,* 3d ed. (Wiley 1975).

**Kelly, K. L., and Judd, Deane B.,** *The ISCC-NBS Method of Designating Colors and a Dictionary of Color Names,* National Bureau of Standards Circular 553 (USGPO 1955).

**Kobayashi, S.,** *A Book of Colors* (Kodansha Intl. 1987).

**Nassau, Kurt,** *The Physics and Chemistry of Color: The Fifteen Causes of Color* (Wiley 1983).

**Stiles, W. S.,** *Mechanisms of Color Vision* (Academic Press 1978).

**COLOR BLINDNESS** is a somewhat inaccurate term referring to a great variety of defects of color vision. A great deal is still unknown about color blindness, and research scientists are continuing to discover new facts and formulate new theories concerning it.

## TYPES OF COLOR DEFECTS

**Red and Green Defects—Anomalous.** The most common defects in color vision are those which pertain to red and green vision, and the most common of these are the anomalous defects. These defects are present in about 6% of the white male population, but this percentage varies greatly in other populations studied.

Anomalous defects are often insignificant, and the color-anomalous person is similar to the normal individual in that he has trichromatic vision; that is, he uses three spectrum samples to match any hue in his spectrum. He can see all four of the primary colors: red, green, yellow, and blue.

The red and green responses of the color-anomalous person do not, however, correspond to those of the person with normal color vision. On the basis of the varying wavelengths at which certain colors are seen, scientists have distinguished two types of red and green anomalous vision: the *protanomalous* and the *deuteranomalous*. In both types of anomaly, colors in a small area of the spectrum are desaturated (less intense than normal). This area occurs in different places for protanomalous and deuteranomalous people, but both types of individuals see green poorly. The protanomalous individual, moreover, is further limited by the fact that he sees the long red wavelengths as somewhat darkened. The deuteranomalous individual is particularly unaware of his deficiency, and his color vision functions quite well in the judgment of traffic lights and color-coded objects. The color judgments of both protanomalous and deuteranomalous individuals are variable, and several factors, such as fatigue and contrasting colors, may influence their color judgments.

Of those individuals who have red and green anomalous vision, about one sixth are protanomalous, while about five sixths are deuteranomalous. Thus deuteranomaly occurs much more frequently, and it is interesting to note that of the less than 0.5% females who have defective color vision, the majority are deuteranomalous.

*Red and Green Blindness.* Red and green blindness is the other major type of defective red and green vision, and it is found in about 2% of the white male population. These individuals lack all red and green responses. They do not see red or green, and for them the main difference between these colors is in their luminosity, or brightness. They see the world in shades of yellow, blue, and gray, and thus cannot see any of the mixed hues containing green or red, such as orange, blue-green, and violet. The red and green blind do, however, use the terms "red" and "green" just as people with normal color vision do. They speak of "red" berries and "green" vegetables, but for them these are merely names, not perceptions of color.

The red and green blind, unlike normal people or even people with red-green anomalous vision, have dichromatic color vision; that is, they can match any hue in the spectrum with only two spectrum samples. These dichromates are divided into two groups: the *protanopes* and the *deuteranopes*. Each type sees a small, but differ-

ent, colorless area in the spectrum which corresponds to the area in which the normal person sees pure green. The protanope is further distinguished by the fact that his entire spectrum is shortened; thus the longer red wavelengths are nearly invisible to him.

*Causes.* Defects of red and green vision are most often inherited. Protanomaly, protanopia, deuteranomaly, and deuteranopia are inherited as sex-linked recessive traits. In most cases, these deficiencies appear in males. This is because a male has only one X-chromosome, and if this carries a color-defect gene, he will certainly have a color vision defect. A female, on the other hand, has two X-chromosomes, and because the color-defect genes are recessive, a woman can inherit defective color vision only if the same defect is carried in both her X-chromosomes. This is a coincidence that occurs very infrequently.

Although most red and green defects are inherited, they may also result from diseases of the optic nerve or the optic cortex, the part of the brain concerned with vision.

**Yellow and Blue Blindness.** Yellow and blue blindness is a rare form of defective color vision. The yellow and blue defective individual has dichromatic color vision. He lacks all yellow and blue responses and sees the world in shades of red and green as well as black, white, and gray. Unlike the person with a red-green defect, a person with yellow and blue blindness sees two neutral, or colorless, areas in the spectrum.

The person who has the yellow-blue type of color blindness generally has acquired it through a disease of the retina or by the development of a cataract. Less often, this color defect appears as a hereditary condition. The exact genetic pattern of inheritance, however, is unknown.

**Monochromatism.** The most severe form of defective color vision is monochromatism. It is extremely rare, but when present it occurs in one of two forms: the *typical* and the *atypical*. A person with typical monochromatism has very poor visual acuity, accompanied by nystagmoid eye movements (rapid, involuntary movements of the eyeball). He is hypersensitive to light and sees the world only as varying intensities of neutral light, a world without color. In the atypical form of monochromatism, the individual has normal visual acuity, suffering only the loss of color vision. Like the typical monochromat, he sees only black, white, and shades of gray.

Monochromatic defects are inherited, although scientists do not yet know the genetics involved. There are also cases in which complete color blindness comes about as the result of eye disease.

## DIAGNOSIS OF COLOR DEFECTS

**Anomaloscope.** The diagnosis of protanomaly, protanopia, deuteranomaly, and deuteranopia may be made by means of a delicate spectrum instrument called the Nagel anomaloscope, which was first devised in 1907 by the German physiologist Willibald Nagel. This instrument is based on the research of the English physicist Lord Rayleigh, whose findings were published in 1881. Rayleigh discovered that most people use a specific proportion of green and of red to match a specific hue of yellow. This concept is called the *Rayleigh match* or the *Rayleigh equation*, and the task of the individual being tested with the anomaloscope is to make this match.

The subject is presented with two adjacent viewing fields. One field is a nearly pure yellow light, and the other contains both red and green light in variable proportions. The subject must, by turning knobs, mix the red and green light to match the yellow. The proportions that he uses to make the match indicate the accuracy of his perception of red and green. Typically, the deuteranomalous individual will arrive at a match that contains more green than that of the normal person, and the protanomalous person will arrive at a match that contains more red.

**Pigment Tests.** In addition to the anomaloscope there are various pigment tests that are very widely used as diagnostic aids in the testing of color vision. Among the most widely used pigment tests are the pseudoisochromatic plates, such as the Ishihara, Hardy-Rand-Rittler, Velhagen, and Dvorine plates. These plates are printed by means of special techniques and show colored figures on a contrasting background in a pattern of dots. The task of the person being tested is to distinguish the figure from its background.

A second type of pigment test involves the arrangement of a group of colored samples. Examples of this type of test are the Farnsworth D-15 Test and the Farnsworth-Munsell 100 Hue Test.

RICHARD S. KOCHMAN, M.D.
*St. Luke's Hospital, New York City*

**COLOR GUARD,** a guard of honor that carries and escorts the flag, ensign, or standard of a country or of an organization, usually military. In the U.S. military services it usually consists of one noncommissioned or petty officer bearing the national colors and another bearing the regimental, battalion, brigade, or squadron color or standard, flanked by two armed enlisted men. A mounted or motorized cavalry unit, following old traditions, might call its color guard the "guard of the standard." In the British and Canadian armies the "colour party" is two subaltern officers bearing the "King's (or Queen's) Colour" and regimental color, with a warrant officer between them and two enlisted men following.

**COLOR INDEX,** in astronomy, a quantity derived from the magnitudes of stars. In stellar photography, astronomers may use both blue-sensitive plates (the so-called *photographic* region of the spectrum) and yellow-sensitive plates (the so-called *visual* region). Magnitudes obtained on the different plates may vary widely for a given star, according to its spectral type. Subtraction of the photovisual from the photographic magnitude provides the color index of the star (c.i. = $m_{pg} - m_{pv}$). For example, a hot bluish star is brighter in the photographic than in the visual region of the spectrum; its photographic magnitude therefore is a smaller number than its photovisual magnitude, and its color index has a negative value. The system, calibrated so that the color index of an AO-type star is zero, was first defined by the American astronomer William Pickering in the early 1900's.

LAURENCE W. FREDRICK
*University of Virginia*

**COLOR ORGAN,** an instrument designed to produce changing effects of color. One of the earliest color organs, Louis Bertrand Castel's "Clavecin Oculaire" (about 1720) synchronized a color (made by light passing through a colored tape) with each key on a harpsichord. The investigation of light wavelengths in the 19th century led to attempts to relate certain colors and sounds through similarities in vibration ratios. A. Wallace Rimington's color organ, demonstrated in London in 1895, produced "color music" on this principle.

Most later experiments abandoned attempts to analogize sound and color, aiming instead to produce an artistic composition in color patterns. The elaborate color projector built by the English color expert Adrian Bernard Klein in the 1920's was a forerunner of various later efforts to utilize changing color such as the many "environmental art" works featuring colored light in the 1960's.

**COLOR PHOTOGRAPHY.** See PHOTOGRAPHY—3. *Technology of Photography.*

**COLOR PRINTING.** See PRINTING.

**COLOR TEMPERATURE,** of a hot object, the temperature of a perfect, or "black body," radiator that has the same color as the object. The temperature of a perfect, or black body, radiator determines the intensity at all wavelengths of the radiation that it emits. At each temperature there is a unique wavelength, or "color," for which this radiation is most intense, and this wavelength characterizes the color of the black-body radiator. When the temperature is above about 500°C, a substantial portion of the radiation is in the visible-light range, and as the temperature changes the color of the light changes correspondingly.

Many objects, including the sun and other stars and various hot solids (such as a current-carrying metal filament), are good approximations to black-body radiators occurring at high temperatures, and the color of such objects is a convenient way of measuring their approximate temperatures. Fluorescent and phosphorescent objects, however, do not approximate black-body radiators, and so the concept of color temperature is not applicable to them.

MICHAEL McCLINTOCK
*University of Colorado*

**COLOR VISION.** See COLOR—*Color Vision;* COLOR BLINDNESS.

**COLORADAN SERIES,** kol-ə-rad'ən, a series in the Cretaceous System of rocks. The term, derived from the name of the state of Colorado, applies to the middle Upper Cretaceous rocks of the Rocky Mountains and Great Plains of the western United States and Canada.

The Coloradan Series was laid about 100 million years ago. On the east, in the Dakota region, the Coloradan is composed of a few hundred feet of shale and marly (clayey) limestone. The rocks increase to a few thousand feet in western Wyoming and Alberta, where they are principally sandstone containing nonmarine, coal-bearing strata. The base of the Coloradan Series is equivalent in age to the upper Albian Stage in Europe, and the higher parts are equivalent to the Cenomanian.

See also CRETACEOUS PERIOD.

MARSHALL KAY
*Columbia University*

© TOM ALGIRE/TOM STACK

Colorado, the Rocky Mountain State, is famous for its scenic ranges, such as the San Juan in the southwest.

# COLORADO

The State Seal

## CONTENTS

**COLORADO,** kol-ə-rad′ō, a west central state of the United States, situated about midway between the Pacific Ocean and the Mississippi River and between the Canadian and the Mexican borders. In shape Colorado is almost a perfect rectangle. It is approximately 385 miles (620 km) from east to west and 275 miles (443 km) from north to south. Often it is called the top of the nation because its average elevation is the highest of all the states. The nickname "Centennial State" signifies that Colorado achieved statehood in 1876, the 100th anniversary of the Declaration of Independence; but above all, Colorado is "the Rocky Mountain State."

The Rocky Mountains, backbone of the continent, extend through west central Colorado, occupying two fifths of the land area. The crest of the Rockies, which is known as the Continental Divide, runs through Colorado in a line shaped like a giant reverse S. The highest point is Mt. Elbert (14,433 feet, or 4,399 meters) in the Sawatch Range near Leadville, but Colorado has more than 50 "fourteeners," peaks exceeding 14,000 feet (4,267 meters). The most spectacular is Pikes Peak, which rises abruptly from the eastern foothills. Its alliterative name and the fact that it inspired the "Pikes Peak or Bust" slogan of Colorado's gold rush days make it known to almost every schoolchild.

318

The Continental Divide separates Colorado into sections known as the eastern slope, which descends through foothills and vast stretches of fertile but semiarid plains, and the western slope, where rushing rivers have cut the tablelands into steep-sided, flat-topped hills, called mesas. Of these, the best known is the Mesa Verde in the southwestern part of the state. There, in the rimrock, prehistoric Indians (Colorado's first known residents) built their fortress homes during the final period of their occupancy of the mesa. Modern man, in contrast, has chosen to build his cities and urban complexes along the eastern foothills, and there an overwhelming majority of Coloradans live today.

The rugged Rocky Mountains have determined the direction and pace of Colorado's growth. Gold, discovered in the mountains in 1858, brought the first rush of settlers, chiefly gold seekers. These were followed by a steady stream of miners, tradesmen, and farmers, as well as engineers and railroad builders who were determined, if not to conquer the Rockies, to make them a less formidable barrier to transportation. When gold and silver resources began to dwindle, Colorado experienced a steady growth in agriculture, made possible in part by expansion of irrigation systems fed by the rivers that rise high in the mountains.

Agriculture remains a basic industry, as does mining. In the 1950's manufacturing, together with space-age research and related activities, began to overtake these older industries as a source of income and employment. Tourism also has become a major factor in the economy, for the Rocky Mountains has attracted an ever-growing number of visitors, whose goals are to ski, fish the trout streams, hunt, climb the mountains, or simply enjoy the views.

## 1. The Land

Colorado's land area encompasses parts of three major physiographical regions of the western United States—the Great Plains, the Rocky Mountains, and the Colorado Plateaus. A fourth region, the Wyoming Basin (elevated plains, mainly in Wyoming), extends into northwestern Colorado. This basin separates the upper part of the Southern Rocky Mountains (which are chiefly in Colorado) from the lower section of the Middle Rocky Mountains (which lie to the west and run through Utah, Wyoming, and Idaho).

The plains of eastern Colorado are well suited for winter wheat, the state's most valuable crop.

© CRAIG AURNESS/WEST LIGHT

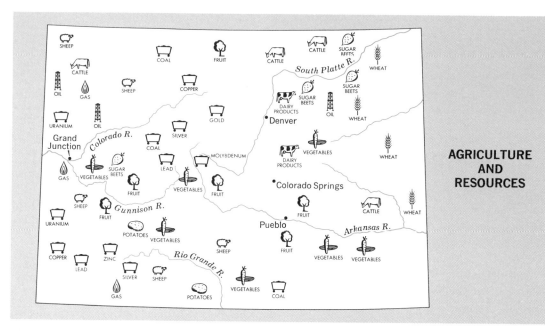

**AGRICULTURE AND RESOURCES**

**Major Physical Divisions.** The High Plains section of the Great Plains enters Colorado from Kansas and Nebraska and rises gently to the foothills of the mountains. This part of the state, about two fifths of the total area, is generally level, although it is broken in places by rolling hills and bluffs.

The Southern Rocky Mountains begin in northern New Mexico, sweep northward through Colorado in two major belts, and end in southern Wyoming. The eastern belt includes the Front Range, the Wet Mountains, and the Sangre de Cristo Range. Such prominent landmarks as Pikes, Longs, and Blanca peaks are in this belt. The western belt includes the Park Range, the Sawatch Range, and the San Juan Mountains.

Both mountain belts, or folds, extend generally north and south, but the western fold is characterized also by numerous spurs and extensions that help form the parks (high level valleys, or basins, between mountain ranges) that are a prominent feature of Colorado's Rockies. North Park, in Jackson county, is bounded on the west and south by the Continental Divide (which runs through the Park Range and then is carried abruptly eastward by the Rabbit Ears Range). South of the Rabbit Ears Range and within the great eastward bulge of the Continental Divide is Middle Park, the headwaters area of the Colorado River. To the south of this bulge is South Park, enclosed by mountains except where the South Platte River flows out to the plains. The largest and southernmost park is the San Luis Valley, a vast basin between the Sangre de Cristo Range on the east and the parts of the San Juan Mountains that carry the Continental Divide in a sharp westward bulge.

The Colorado Plateaus region is divided into the Uinta Basin and the Canyon Lands, which Colorado shares with Utah, and the Navajo section, extending into New Mexico. The Uinta Basin is an arid plateau deeply eroded in places by the White River and its tributaries. The Canyon Lands include the Book Plateau between the Colorado and the White rivers, the Grand Mesa between the Colorado and the Gunnison, and the Uncompahgre Plateau between the Gunnison

and the Dolores rivers. The Navajo section is divided into mesas by the San Juan River and its tributaries.

**Rivers and Lakes.** Several major rivers of the western United States have their sources in Colorado's mountains. The Colorado River drains much of the western slope and affords valuable water resources to states throughout the Southwest. The Rio Grande rises on the eastern slope of the San Juan Mountains and flows southeastward through the San Luis Valley to New Mexico. The Arkansas River, from its origin near Leadville in the central part of the state, breaks through the mountains in the Royal Gorge near Canon City and flows eastward across the plains to Kansas. The South Platte River, which also rises near Leadville, flows southeastward, then northward past Denver to Greeley, and northeastward over the plains to Nebraska. The North Platte River has its source in the North Park area, from which it flows into Wyoming.

Hundreds of beautiful natural lakes, most of them small, are nestled high in the mountains. In addition, Colorado has more than 1,900 artificial lakes, or storage reservoirs, which have been built on rivers and streams.

**Climate.** An inland location, far from major sources of moisture, together with a high elevation and mountains oriented in different directions, produces significant variations in Colorado's climate. For this reason it is impossible to make generalizations for the state as a whole, other than to identify such features as low relative humidity, abundant sunshine, and wide daily and seasonal ranges in temperatures.

In the high mountains, alpine conditions prevail, characterized by moderate daytime temperatures in the summer and extreme cold and abundant snowfall in the winter. On the eastern plains and the western plateaus, the climate is more uniform, with light precipitation. Temperature extremes in the state vary from well over 100°F (34°C) to well below −50°F (−46°C).

The prevailing winds are the temperate westerlies, but these often are interrupted by the intrusion of polar air from the north or tropical air from the south. The weather of the eastern foot-

# COLORADO

# TOPOGRAPHY

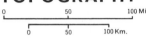

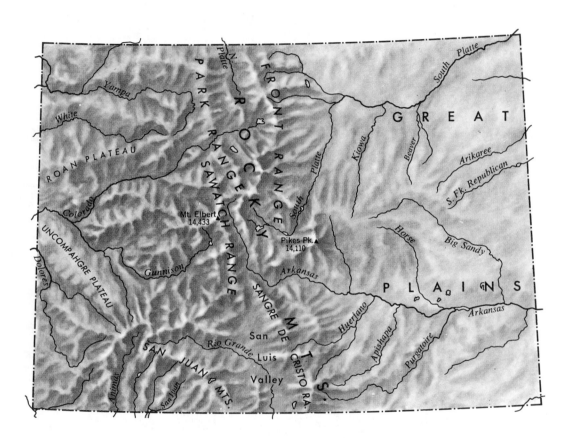

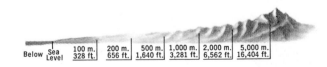

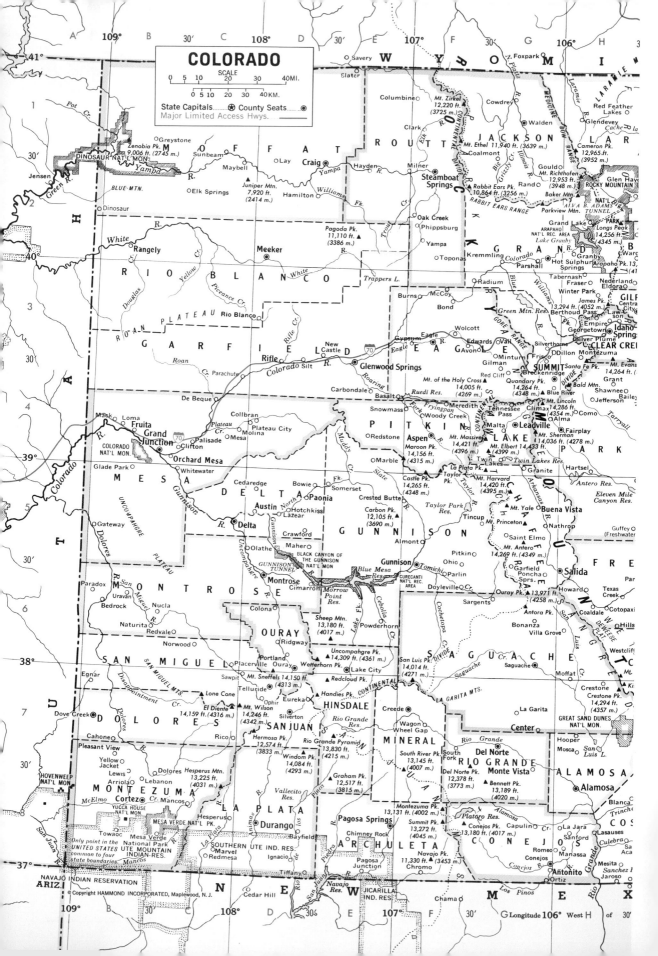

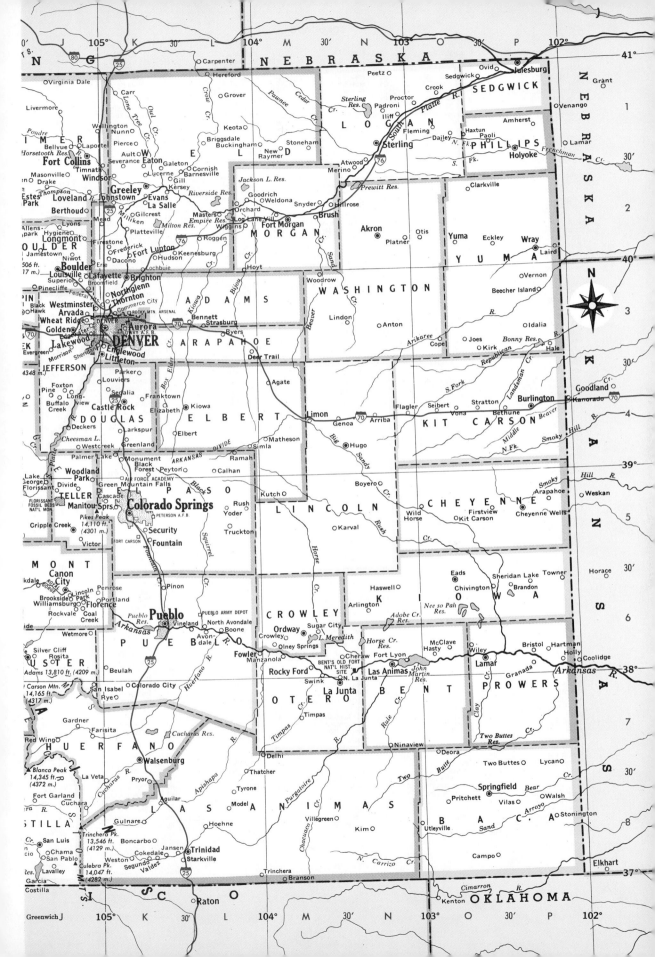

# COLORADO

## COUNTIES

Adams 363,857 .....L3
Alamosa 14,966 .....I17
Arapahoe 487,967 .....L3
Archuleta 9,898 .....E8
Baca 4,517 .....O8
Bent 5,998 .....N7
Boulder 291,288 .....J2
Chaffee 16,242 .....G5
Cheyenne 2,231 .....O5
Clear Creek 9,322 .....H3
Conejos 8,400 .....G8
Costilla 3,663 .....J8
Crowley 5,518 .....M6
Custer 3,503 .....J6
Delta 27,834 .....D5
Denver 554,636 .....K3
Dolores 1,844 .....C7
Douglas 175,766 .....K4
Eagle 41,659 .....F3
Elbert 19,872 .....L4
El Paso 516,929 .....K5
Fremont 46,145 .....J5
Garfield 43,791 .....C3
Gilpin 4,757 .....H3
Grand 12,442 .....G2
Gunnison 13,956 .....E5
Hinsdale 790 .....E7
Huerfano 7,862 .....K7
Jackson 1,577 .....G1
Jefferson 527,056 .....J3
Kiowa 1,622 .....O6
Kit Carson 8,011 .....O4
Lake 7,812 .....G4
La Plata 43,941 .....D8
Larimer 251,494 .....H1
Las Animas 15,207 .....L8
Lincoln 6,087 .....M5
Logan 20,504 .....N1
Mesa 116,255 .....B5
Mineral 558 .....F7
Moffat 13,184 .....C1
Montezuma 23,830 .....B8
Montrose 33,432 .....C6
Morgan 27,171 .....M2
Otero 20,311 .....M7
Ouray 3,742 .....D6
Park 14,523 .....H4
Phillips 4,480 .....P1
Pitkin 14,872 .....F4
Prowers 14,483 .....P7
Pueblo 141,472 .....K6
Rio Blanco 5,986 .....C3
Rio Grande 12,413 .....G7
Routt 19,690 .....E1
Saguache 5,917 .....G6
San Juan 558 .....D7
San Miguel 6,594 .....C6
Sedgwick 2,747 .....P1
Summit 23,548 .....G3
Teller 20,555 .....J5
Washington 4,926 .....N3
Weld 180,936 .....L1
Yuma 9,841 .....P2

## CITIES and TOWNS

Aguilar 593 .....K8
Akron▲ 1,711 .....N2
Alamosa▲ 7,960 .....H8
Allenspark 496 .....J2
Alma 179 .....G4
Almont 135 .....F5
Amherst 85 .....P1
Anton 875 .....N3
Antonito 873 .....H8
Arapahoe 300 .....P5
Arriba 244 .....N4
Arriola 5,672 .....B8
Arvada 102,153 .....J3
Aspen▲ 5,914 .....F4
Atwood 195 .....N1
Ault 1,432 .....K1
Aurora 276,393 .....K3
Austin .....D5
Avon 5,561 .....F3
Avondale 754 .....L6
Bailey 150 .....H4
Basalt 2,681 .....E4
Bayfield 1,549 .....D8
Bellvue 250 .....J1
Bennett 2,021 .....L3
Berthoud 4,839 .....J2
Bethune 225 .....P4
Beulah 1,164 .....K6
Black Forest 13,247 .....K4
Black Hawk 118 .....J3
Blanca 391 .....H8
Blue River 685 .....G4
Bonanza 14 .....G6
Boncarbo 200 .....K8
Boone 323 .....L6
Boulder▲ 94,673 .....J2
Dowic 10 .....D5
Breckenridge▲ 2,408 .....G4
Briggsdale 85 .....L1
Brighton▲ 20,905 .....K3
Bristol 200 .....P6
Brookside 219 .....J6
Broomfield 38,272 .....J3
Brush 5,117 .....M2
Buena Vista 2,195 .....G5
Buffalo Creek 150 .....J4
Burlington▲ 3,678 .....P4
Burns 100 .....F3
Byers 1,233 .....L3
Cahone 200 .....B7
Calhan 896 .....L4
Campo 150 .....O8
Canon City▲ 15,431 .....J6
Capulin 600 .....G8
Carbondale 5,196 .....E4
Cascade 1,709 .....K5
Castle Rock▲ 20,224 .....K4
Cedaredge 1,854 .....D5
Center 2,392 .....G7
Central City▲ 515 .....J3
Chama 239 .....J8
Cheraw 211 .....N6
Cheyenne Wells▲ 1,010 .....P5
Chimney Rock 76 .....E8
Chromo 115 .....F8
Cimarron 50 .....D6
Clifton 17,345 .....C4
Climax 975 .....G4
Coal Creek 2,323 .....J6
Coaldale 153 .....H6
Cokedale 139 .....K8
Collbran 388 .....C4
Colorado City 2,018 .....K6
Colorado Springs▲ 360,890 .....K5
Columbine 24,095 .....E1
Commerce City 20,991 .....K3
Conejos▲ 200 .....G8
Cope 110 .....O3
Cortez▲ 7,977 .....B8
Cotopaxi 250 .....H6
Craig▲ 9,189 .....D2
Crawford 366 .....D5
Creede▲ 377 .....E7
Crested Butte 1,529 .....E5
Cripple Creek▲ 1,115 .....J5
Crook 128 .....O1
Crowley 187 .....M6
Dacono 3,015 .....K2
De Beque 451 .....C4
Deer Trail 598 .....M3
Del Norte▲ 1,705 .....G7
Delta▲ 6,400 .....D5
Denver (cap.)▲ 554,636 .....K3
Dillon 802 .....H3
Dinosaur 319 .....B2
Divide 700 .....J5
Dolores 857 .....C8
Dove Creek▲ 698 .....A7
Doyleville 75 .....F6
Drake 300 .....J2
Durango▲ 13,922 .....D8
Eads▲ 747 .....O6
Eagle▲ 3,032 .....F3
Eaton 2,690 .....K1
Eckley 278 .....P2
Edgewater 5,445 .....J3
Edwards 8,257 .....F3
Elbert 200 .....L4
Eldora 170 .....H3
Elizabeth 1,434 .....K4
Elk Springs 18 .....C2
Empire 355 .....H3
Englewood 31,727 .....K3
Erie 6,291 .....K2
Estes Park 5,413 .....J2
Eureka 25 .....D7
Evans 9,514 .....K2
Evergreen 9,216 .....J3
Fairplay▲ 610 .....H4
Farisita 116 .....J7
Federal Heights 12,065 .....J3
Firestone 1,908 .....K2
Flagler 612 .....N4
Fleming 426 .....O1
Florence 3,653 .....J6
Florissant 130 .....J5
Fort Collins▲ 118,652 .....J1
Fort Garland 432 .....J8
Fort Lupton 6,787 .....K2
Fort Lyon 500 .....N6
Fort Morgan▲ 11,034 .....M2
Fountain 15,197 .....K5
Fowler 1,206 .....L6
Franktown 99 .....K4
Fraser 910 .....H3
Frederick 2,467 .....K2
Freshwater (Guffey) 24 .....H5
Frisco 2,443 .....G3
Fruita 6,478 .....B4
Galeton 200 .....K1
Garcia 75 .....J8
Gardner 100 .....J7
Gateway 7,510 .....B5
Genoa 211 .....N4
Georgetown▲ 1,088 .....H3
Gilcrest 1,162 .....K2
Gill 250 .....L2
Gilman 160 .....G3
Glade Park 100 .....B5
Glendevey 50 .....H1
Glen Haven 110 .....H2
Glenwood Springs▲ 7,736 .....E4
Golden▲ 17,159 .....J3
Goodrich 85 .....M2
Granada 640 .....P6
Granby 1,525 .....H2
Grand Junction▲ 41,986 .....B4
Grand Lake 447 .....H2
Granite 47 .....G4
Grant 50 .....H4
Greeley▲ 76,930 .....K2
Greenland 21 .....K4
Green Mountain Falls 773 .....K5
Grover 153 .....L1
Guffey 24 .....H5
Gunnison▲ 5,409 .....E5
Gypsum 3,654 .....F3
Hamilton 100 .....D2
Hartman 111 .....P6
Hartsel 69 .....H4
Hasty 150 .....O6
Haswell 84 .....N6
Haxtun 982 .....O1
Hayden 1,634 .....E2
Hereford 50 .....L1
Hesperus 50 .....C8
Hillrose 254 .....N2
Hillside 79 .....H6
Hoehne 400 .....L8
Holly 1,048 .....P6
Holyoke▲ 2,261 .....P1
Hooper 123 .....H7
Hotchkiss 968 .....D5
Hot Sulphur Springs▲ 521 .....H2
Howard 200 .....H6
Hoyt 60 .....L2
Hudson 1,565 .....K2
Hugo▲ 885 .....N4
Hygiene 450 .....J2
Idaho Springs 1,889 .....H3
Idalia 125 .....P3
Ignacio 669 .....D8
Iliff 213 .....N1
Jamestown 205 .....J2
Jansen 267 .....K8
Jaroso 50 .....H8
Joes 100 .....O3
Johnstown 3,827 .....K2
Julesburg▲ 1,467 .....P1
Karval 51 .....N5
Keenesburg 855 .....L2
Keota 5 .....L1
Kersey 1,389 .....L2
Kim 65 .....N8
Kiowa▲ 581 .....L4
Kit Carson 293 .....O5
Kremmling 1,578 .....G2
Kutch 2 .....M5
Lafayette 23,197 .....K3
La Garita 10 .....G7
Laird 105 .....P2
La Jara 877 .....H8
La Junta▲ 7,568 .....M7
Lake City▲ 375 .....E6
Lake George 500 .....J5
Lakewood 144,126 .....J3
Lamar▲ 8,869 .....O6
Laporte 2,691 .....J1
Larkspur 234 .....K4
La Salle 1,849 .....K2
Las Animas▲ 2,758 .....N6
Lasauces 150 .....J8
Lavalley 237 .....J8
La Veta 924 .....J8
Lawson 108 .....H3
Lay 40 .....D2
Lazear 60 .....D5
Leadville▲ 2,821 .....G4
Lebanon 50 .....B8
Lewis 150 .....B8
Limon 2,071 .....N4
Lincoln Park 3,904 .....J6
Lindon 60 .....N3
Littleton▲ 40,340 .....K3
Livermore 150 .....J1
Lochbuie 2,049 .....K2
Log Lane Village 1,006 .....M2
Loma 265 .....B4
Longmont 71,093 .....J2
Longview 10 .....J4
Louisville 18,937 .....J3
Louviers 237 .....K4
Loveland 50,608 .....J2
Lucerne 135 .....K2
Lyons 1,585 .....J2
Mack 380 .....B4
Maher 75 .....D5
Malta 200 .....G4
Manassa 1,042 .....H8
Mancos 1,119 .....C8
Manitou Springs 4,980 .....J5
Manzanola 525 .....M6
Marble 105 .....E4
Marvel 176 .....C8
Masonville 200 .....J2
Masters 50 .....L2
Matheson 120 .....M4
Maybell 130 .....C2
McClave 125 .....O6
McCoy 62 .....F3
Mead 2,017 .....K2
Meeker▲ 2,242 .....D2
Meredith 47 .....F4
Merino 246 .....N2
Mesa 120 .....C4
Mesa Verde National
  Park 45 .....C8
Mesita 70 .....H8
Milliken 2,888 .....K2
Milner 196 .....F2
Minturn 1,068 .....G3
Model 200 .....L8
Moffat 114 .....H6
Molina 200 .....D4
Monte Vista 4,529 .....G7
Montezuma 42 .....H3
Montrose▲ 12,344 .....D6
Monument 1,971 .....K4
Morrison 430 .....J3
Mosca 100 .....H7
Nathrop 150 .....H5
Naturita 635 .....B6
Nederland 1,394 .....H3
New Castle 3,440 .....E3
New Raymer 80 .....M1
Ninaview 2 .....N7
Niwot 4,160 .....J2
North Avondale 110 .....L6
Northglenn 31,575 .....K3
North La Junta 1,076 .....N7
Norwood 438 .....C6
Nucla 734 .....B6
Nunn 471 .....K1
Oak Creek 849 .....F2
Ohio 100 .....F5
Olathe 1,573 .....D5
Olney Springs 389 .....M6
Ophir 113 .....D7
Orchard 2,880 .....L2
Orchard Mesa 6,456 .....C4
Ordway▲ 1,248 .....M6
Ortiz 163 .....H8
Otis 534 .....O2
Ouray▲ 813 .....D6
Ovid 330 .....P1
Padroni 97 .....N1
Pagosa Junction 15 .....E8
Pagosa Springs▲ 1,591 .....E8
Palisade 2,579 .....C4
Palmer Lake 2,179 .....J4
Paoli 42 .....P1
Paonia 1,497 .....D5
Parachute 1,006 .....C4
Paradox 250 .....B6
Parkdale 21 .....H6
Parker 23,558 .....K4
Parlin 100 .....F6
Parshall 80 .....G2
Peetz 227 .....N1
Penrose 4,070 .....K6
Peyton 250 .....K4
Phippsburg 300 .....F2
Pierce 884 .....K1
Pine 100 .....J4
Pinecliffe 375 .....J3
Pinon 50 .....K6
Pitkin 124 .....F5
Placerville 50 .....D6
Plateau City 35 .....D4
Platteville 2,370 .....K2
Pleasant View 300 .....B7
Poncha Springs 466 .....G6
Portland .....D6
Portland 17 .....K6
Powderhorn 100 .....E6
Pritchett 137 .....O8
Proctor 25 .....N1
Pryor 50 .....K8
Pueblo▲ 102,121 .....K6
Radium 22 .....G3
Ramah 117 .....L4
Rand 50 .....G2
Rangely 2,096 .....B2
Raymer (New Raymer) 91 .....M1
Red Cliff 289 .....G4
Red Feather Lakes 525 .....H1
Red Mesa 100 .....C8
Redstone 115 .....E4
Redvale 300 .....B6
Red Wing 200 .....J7
Rico 205 .....C7
Ridgway 713 .....D6
Rifle 6,784 .....D3
Rio Blanco 4 .....C3
Rockvale 426 .....J6
Rocky Ford 4,286 .....M6
Roggen 100 .....L2
Romeo 375 .....G8
Rush 40 .....L5
Rye 202 .....K7
Saguache▲ 578 .....G6
Saint Elmo 75 .....G5
Salida▲ 5,504 .....H6
San Acacio 50 .....J8
Sanford 817 .....H8
San Isabel 8 .....K7
San Luis▲ 739 .....J8
San Pablo 150 .....J8
Sargents 31 .....F6
Sawpit 25 .....D7
Security-Widefield 29,845 .....K5
Sedalia 211 .....K4
Sedgwick 191 .....O1
Segundo 200 .....K8
Seibert 180 .....O4
Severance 597 .....K1
Shawnee 100 .....H4
Sheridan 5,600 .....J3
Sheridan Lake 66 .....P6
Silt 1,740 .....D4
Silver Cliff 512 .....J6
Silver Plume 203 .....H3
Silverthorne 3,196 .....G3
Silverton▲ 531 .....D7
Simla 663 .....M4
Slater 10 .....E1
Snowmass 1,822 .....E4
Snyder 200 .....M2
Somerset 200 .....E5
South Fork 604 .....F7
Springfield▲ 1,562 .....O8
Starkville 128 .....L8
Steamboat Springs▲ 9,815 .....F2
Sterling▲ 11,360 .....N1
Stoneham 35 .....M1
Stonington 27 .....P8
Strasburg 1,402 .....L3
Stratton 669 .....O4
Sugar City 279 .....M6
Sunbeam 19 .....C1
Superior 9,011 .....J3
Swink 696 .....M7
Tabernash 165 .....H3
Telluride▲ 2,221 .....D7
Tennessee Pass 5 .....G4
Texas Creek 80 .....H6
Thatcher 50 .....L7
Thornton 82,384 .....K3
Tiffany 24 .....D8
Timnath 223 .....J2
Timpas 25 .....M7
Tincup 8 .....F5
Toponas 55 .....F2
Towaoc 1,097 .....B8
Towner 61 .....P6
Trinchera 20 .....M8
Trinidad▲ 9,078 .....L8
Truckton 10 .....L5
Twin Lakes 6,301 .....G4
Two Buttes 67 .....P7
Tyrone 9 .....L8
Uravan 500 .....B6
Utleyville 2 .....O8
Vail 4,531 .....G3
Valdez 12 .....K8
Vernon 50 .....P3
Victor 445 .....J5
Vilas 110 .....P8
Villa Grove 37 .....G6
Villegreen 6 .....M8
Vineland 100 .....K6
Virginia Dale 2 .....J1
Vona 104 .....O4
Wagon Wheel Gap 20 .....F7
Walden▲ 734 .....G1
Walsenburg▲ 4,182 .....K7

▲ County seat.

hills and plains is influenced also by the chinook, a warm surface wind from the west that descends the eastern slopes and brings sudden rises in temperature.

**Plant Life.** Within the state there are five distinct life zones. On the eastern plains, native grasses abound, as do flowers that thrive in a semiarid climate, such as prickly poppy, cacti, and yucca. Juniper and piñon, with cottonwood along the watercourses, are the common trees on both the eastern plains and the western plateaus. In the foothills, the predominant flowers include the mariposa lily, pasqueflower, larkspur, and Indian paintbrush. Juniper and piñon are the chief trees in the south and west, while in the north ponderosa (western yellow) pine and Douglas fir are interspersed, especially along the streams, with aspen and spruce.

The mountain zone, from 8,000 to 10,000 feet (2,438 to 3,048 meters), contains anemone, yellow lady's slipper, and columbine. The coniferous forest, beginning in this zone, consists of lodgepole pine and aspen, which give way at higher elevations to spruce and fir. The subalpine zone, from 10,000 to 11,500 feet (3,048 to 3,505 meters), features the glacier lily, shooting star, and fringed gentian. The alpine zone, above 11,500 feet (3,505 meters), displays dwarf shrubs and such flowers as the globeflower and the alpine forget-me-not.

**Animal Life.** The lower elevations of Colorado, once inhabited by the American bison, antelope, and coyote, are now the habitat of small animals such as the jackrabbit and the cottontail. The mountainous regions contain most of the mammals peculiar to the plains and plateaus as well as numerous game animals—black bear, black-tailed and white-tailed deer, elk, and mountain lion.

Birds common to the plains include the lark bunting, oriole, brown thrasher, and song sparrow. Ring-necked pheasant and duck are the most numerous game birds. In the foothills, the blue jay, bluebird, meadowlark, and mountain chickadee are among the birds frequently seen. The Rocky Mountain jay and hermit thrush inhabit the forest regions at higher elevations.

The mountain streams and the lakes and reservoirs contain approximately 90 varieties of fish. The most popular, from the angler's view, is the trout family, especially the rainbow trout, which is found in most streams having their sources in the mountains, and the brook trout, which inhabits the deep cold-water lakes. Ponds, lakes, and reservoirs throughout the state yield tasty panfish, particularly bluegill, black crappie, and yellow perch.

**Mineral Resources.** Colorado abounds in minerals. Large amounts of gold and silver still exist in the form of low-grade ores. The more common metals, including copper, lead, and zinc, are found throughout the state. Rare metals, especially molybdenum and vanadium, occur in the mountain regions, as do tungsten and uranium.

© GRANT HEILMAN

Sheep are herded from horseback in the Colorado Plateau region in the western part of the state.

Other minerals of commercial value include gypsum, fluorspar, mica, limestone, sandstone, granite, gemstones, sand and gravel, and the fuels—coal, petroleum, natural gas, and oil shale. Vast reserves of bituminous coal exist in both northern and southern counties. Oil and gas are found in western Colorado as well as in the east.

Potentially, the rock known as oil shale is Colorado's richest mineral resource. This rock contains kerogen, a gummy, bituminous substance that yields oil when heated. The richest deposits are in the Piceance Creek basin of Rio Blanco and Garfield counties, in the northwestern part of the state. According to estimates by the U.S. Geological Survey, these deposits and others that extend into Utah and Wyoming contain well over 50 times the proven oil reserves of the United States.

**Conservation.** Colorado long has been aware of the need to conserve its vast natural resources. The need for effective utilization of land, water, timber, and minerals has prompted a variety of programs to prevent losses through neglect or wasteful consumption.

Water resource development has occurred largely under federal auspices. The John Martin Reservoir on the Arkansas River near Las Animas was built by the U.S. Army Corps of Engineers for flood control and irrigation purposes. The U.S. Bureau of Reclamation operates huge water storage facilities on the major rivers. Some of these, such as the Colorado–Big Thompson and the Fryingpan–Arkansas projects, are designed

to correct nature's seeming error in placing most of the fertile farmland on the eastern slope, while most of the moisture collects on the western slope.

The Colorado–Big Thompson Project, completed in 1959, collects Colorado River water in the vicinity of Rocky Mountain National Park, stores the water in Lake Granby and other reservoirs, and diverts some of it through a tunnel under the Continental Divide to the Big Thompson River and the South Platte Valley. The tunnel serving this project, the Alva B. Adams Tunnel, is 13 miles (21 km) long. The Fryingpan–Arkansas Project was authorized in 1962 and completed in the 1980's. Key units include the Ruedi Dam and Reservoir on the Fryingpan River (a tributary of the Roaring Fork) and a tunnel beneath the Continental Divide to carry water to the Arkansas River valley for agricultural and municipal use. In addition to storage, diversion, and flood control, the many water projects generate large amounts of hydroelectric power and provide recreational areas of inestimable value to residents and tourists.

Other conservation programs under the direction of the federal government encompass the management of national forests, grasslands, wildlife refuges, and parks. The U.S. Soil Conservation Service assists the state's soil conservation districts in promoting watershed protection and flood control. The state maintains continuing programs for the conservation of land, timber, mineral, and wildlife resources.

## 2. The Economy

The economy of Colorado has developed in three rather distinct phases—the mining era of the latter half of the 19th century, the agricultural period of 1900–1940, and the present era, in which manufacturing, governmental activities, trade, and services are dominant factors, although agriculture and mining continue to be important. Agriculture employs less than 10% of the labor force, and mining less than 3%.

**Agriculture.** When settlers started to grow crops in Colorado, they irrigated their fields by the simple method of diverting water from streams. Two decades after the gold rush, large community irrigation enterprises began to hasten the growth of farming. The success of the cooperative Union Colony in developing fertile lands in the Greeley area stimulated other projects

### PERSONAL INCOME IN COLORADO

| Source | 1960 | 1970 | 1980 |
|---|---|---|---|
| | (Millions of dollars) | | |
| Farms | 177 | 295 | 527 |
| Mining | 104 | 157 | 1,085 |
| Construction | 253 | 499 | 1,682 |
| Manufacturing | 535 | 1,077 | 3,717 |
| Transportation, communications, and public utilities | 279 | 536 | 1,919 |
| Wholesale and retail trade | 633 | 1,234 | 3,868 |
| Finance, insurance, and real estate | 181 | 376 | 1,408 |
| Services | 457 | 1,063 | 3,973 |
| Other industries | 12 | 25 | 81 |
| Government | 601 | 1,589 | 4,132 |
| | (Dollars) | | |
| Per capita personal income | 2,272 | 3,887 | 10,590 |
| Per capita income, U.S. | 2,216 | 3,945 | 9,910 |

Source: U.S. Department of Commerce, *Survey of Current Business.*

throughout the South Platte Valley and elsewhere. By the early 1900's, the South Platte and the Arkansas river valleys were extensively developed, and irrigation flourished in the San Luis Valley as well as in fertile valleys on the western slope. Advances in dry-farming techniques also made agriculture potentially profitable on the plains. In 1909 one fifth of the land in Colorado was devoted to farming. Thirty years later that proportion had doubled, and it has remained constant since then.

Colorado's cattle industry had its beginnings in herds driven northward from Texas shortly after the Civil War. At present cattle and calves alone account for about half of the total cash farm income. Other livestock and livestock products are milk, poultry and eggs, sheep, and hogs.

Winter wheat is the most valuable single crop. The other major crops, according to cash return, are commercial vegetables, especially potatoes, dry beans, onions, lettuce, and tomatoes.

**Mining and Mineral Extraction.** During the 20th century approximately 40 minerals have been extracted commercially in Colorado. Until 1900, gold and silver, together with zinc and copper, constituted more than 75% of the total output. From 1905 (when accurate records first became available) until the present, the proportion of gold, silver, and related metals has declined to a point of insignificance. Molybdenum's share of Colorado's mineral output was about 65% until the decline of steel production, in which the rare metal is used as a hardening agent, caused cutbacks in mining operations. Other metals produced in Colorado are uranium and vanadium.

Fuels, in terms of value, comprise more than half of Colorado's mineral production. Petroleum, the leading fuel, is extracted on both the eastern and western slopes, as is natural gas. Coal is mined principally in northwestern Colorado, and in the southern portion of the state near Trinidad. Other important nonmetals are sand and gravel and stone.

**Manufacturing.** Although Colorado is not heavily industrialized, manufacturing is the foundation of its economic well-being. In the second half of the 20th century, growth in manufacturing has reflected the development of military and other governmental installations within the state, with emphasis on armaments and aerospace programs. But food processing, long one of Colorado's major industries, still leads in value added by manufacture. Denver has been an important livestock market and packing center since the early 1900's. The manufacture of sugar from beets began in Colorado in 1899 with the opening of a processing plant near Grand Junction. Soon beet cultivation spread to the South Platte and the Arkansas valleys, where new plants were established.

Another important manufacture is machinery, especially mining machinery, which once was the state's leading export commodity. The major companies also produce machinery and equipment for the construction, petroleum, metallurgical, sugar, and other industries.

The U.S. Army maintains an ordnance depot near Pueblo. Private ordnance enterprises also build rocket-powered vehicles, process fissionable materials, and act as subcontractors for military constructors. Other large manufacturing units in Colorado make rubber products, luggage, and computers. Numerous smaller units turn out textiles and apparel, furniture and wood

© DOUG LEE/TOM STACK

Aspen, one of Colorado's leading resorts, attracts vacationers in both winter and summer.

products, chemicals, and stone, clay, and glass products.

Colorado's economy is powered by electricity. Although private companies are the major producers and distributors of electricity to domestic consumers, cities, commerce, and industry, municipal and cooperative enterprises also serve the state's population. The federal government sells to distributors (public and private) power from its hydroelectric facilities throughout the region. Nuclear power is significantly less important as a source of energy.

**Tourism.** Tourism is Colorado's third-largest industry. Several million people from other states and countries visit Colorado annually. Most of these are tourists, vacationists, or winter-sports enthusiasts, but a growing number attend conventions held each year in Colorado.

**Transportation.** Colorado, with its inland location far from the nation's major industrial centers and a mountainous terrain that acts as a barrier to the movement of people and goods, always has valued the expansion of various modes of transportation. Denver is the transportation hub of the Western mountain and plains states. Railroads, which first linked the state with the rest of the country, are still the principal means of moving bulk goods. Modern highways, including interstate routes, afford excellent thoroughfares for common carriers and private automobiles. Numerous airlines, including national and international, regional, and local carriers, serve Colorado's cities, with operations centering at Denver's Stapleton International Airport.

© BLAINE HARRINGTON

The 16th Street Mall in downtown Denver is a major shopping center in the Mile High City.

## 3. The People

At the time of the Louisiana Purchase in 1803, Colorado was inhabited by a number of Indian tribes. Several bands of the Ute Indians occupied the mountainous area, as they had for generations. To the east, the Arapaho (or Arapahoe) and Cheyenne, having moved southward from the headwaters of the Yellowstone and the Missouri rivers, held most of the land north of the Arkansas River. The Kiowa, under pressure from the advancing northern tribes, moved southward, sharing the hunting grounds south of the Arkansas River with the Comanche.

Encroachment on the Indians' hunting grounds occurred from two directions. Soon after the close of the Mexican War in 1848, Spanish-speaking colonists from New Mexico moved northward to occupy parts of the San Luis Valley. Migration from other parts of the United States, chiefly from the east, began on a significant scale in 1859, spurred by the discovery of gold. According to the federal census of 1860, the future state of Colorado contained 34,277 residents. By 1880 (four years after statehood), the population exceeded 194,000, and by 1900, there were about 540,000 Coloradans, of whom 16% were foreign born.

**Components of the Population.** Colorado's population increased nearly eightfold in the 20th century. Following the collapse of precious-metal mining about 1910, growth was slow, declining to less than 10% during the Great Depression. During World War II the rate accelerated and remained high, averaging over 20% for the next five decades. Most of the population growth has been confined to cities in the urban corridor along the eastern foothills from Denver northward to Fort Collins and southward to Colorado Springs.

Less than half of the population is Colorado born. Of the foreign born, many are from Mexico, Canada, Japan, and European countries.

Caucasians make up about 82.8% of the population. The non-Caucasians are predominantly African Americans. Others include Japanese, American Indians, Chinese, and Filipinos. The American Indians represent two branches of the Ute tribes—the Southern Ute and the Ute Mountain. The Southern Ute Indian Reservation is wholly within Colorado. A small part of the Ute Mountain Indian Reservation is in New Mexico.

**Way of Life.** In the 20th century, Coloradans had experienced marked changes in their way of life. Until around 1900, a large percentage of the people resided in remote mining communities

### RESIDENT POPULATION SINCE 1870

| Year | Population | Year | Population |
|------|-----------|------|-----------|
| 1870 | 39,864 | 1940 | 1,123,296 |
| 1880 | 194,327 | 1950 | 1,325,089 |
| 1890 | 413,249 | 1960 | 1,753,947 |
| 1900 | 539,700 | 1970 | 2,209,596 |
| 1910 | 799,024 | 1980 | 2,889,735 |
| 1920 | 939,629 | 1990 | 3,294,394 |
| 1930 | 1,035,791 | 2000 | 4,301,261 |

**Gain, 1990–2000:** 30.6% (U.S. gain, 13.2%). **Density,** 41.5 persons per sq mi of land area (U.S. density, 79.6).

### URBAN-RURAL DISTRIBUTION

| Year | Percent urban | Percent rural |
|------|---------------|---------------|
| 1920 | 48.2 (U.S., 51.2) | 51.8 |
| 1930 | 50.2 (U.S., 56.1) | 49.8 |
| 1940 | 52.6 (U.S., 56.5) | 47.4 |
| 1950 | 62.7 (U.S., 64.0) | 37.3 |
| 1960 | 73.7 (U.S., 69.9) | 26.3 |
| 1970 | 78.5 (U.S., 73.6) | 21.5 |
| 1980 | 80.6 (U.S., 73.7) | 19.4 |
| 1990 | 82.4 (U.S., 75.2) | 17.6 |

### LARGEST CENTERS OF POPULATION

| City or metropolitan area | 2000 | 1990 | 1980 |
|---------------------------|------|------|------|
| Denver | 554,636 | 467,610 | 492,365 |
| Metropolitan area | 2,581,506 | 1,848,319*| 1,618,461 |
| Colorado Springs | 360,890 | 281,140 | 214,821 |
| Metropolitan area | 516,929 | 397,014 | 309,424 |
| Aurora | 276,393 | 222,103 | 158,588 |
| Lakewood | 144,126 | 126,481 | 113,808 |
| Fort Collins | 118,652 | 87,158 | 65,092 |
| Metropolitan area | 251,494 | 186,136 | 149,184 |
| Arvada | 102,153 | 89,235 | 84,576 |
| Pueblo | 102,121 | 98,640 | 101,686 |
| Metropolitan area | 141,472 | 123,051 | 125,972 |
| Westminster | 100,940 | 74,625 | 50,211 |
| Boulder | 94,673 | 83,312 | 76,685 |
| Thornton | 82,384 | 55,031 | 40,343 |
| Greeley | 76,930 | 60,536 | 53,006 |
| Metropolitan area | 180,936 | 131,821 | 123,438 |
| Longmont | 71,093 | 51,555 | 42,942 |
| Loveland | 50,608 | 37,352 | 30,215 |

*Consolidated Metropolitan Statistical Area.

throughout the Rocky Mountains. Many others dwelt in cities that bordered the eastern foothills and extended out onto the plains, providing smelting and commercial operations on which the mining towns depended. Still others cultivated the fertile valleys and raised livestock.

During the period 1900–1940, Colorado became a center for the production and processing of foods for a wide market. Industrial diversification and general economic growth thereafter afforded Coloradans greater opportunity for employment, while attracting a large volume of labor from other states.

Today most of Colorado's inhabitants live in centers of 2,500 or more people. This feature of the population, which was peculiar to the mining era of an earlier day, has been accentuated in the second half of the 20th century. A steady decline in the number of farms has prompted a rural to urban migration within the state. At the same time, newcomers have tended to settle in the cities.

**Largest Centers of Population.** The Denver metropolitan area is the principal economic and population center of the state. The city and county of Denver (which are coextensive), together with adjoining Adams, Arapahoe, Jefferson, and Boulder counties, contain more than half of all Coloradans. By the year 2000, if present trends continue, two thirds of the population will be in the Denver metropolitan area.

Denver, Colorado's capital and largest city, is known as the mile-high city because of its elevation (5,280 feet, or 1,609 meters, above sea level). It is the financial, manufacturing, marketing, and transportation center of the entire Rocky Mountains region. Colorado Springs, the second-largest city, is situated at the base of Pikes Peak about 65 miles (105 km) south of Denver. It was founded as a residential resort in the early 1870's. In 1916 it annexed Colorado City, first territorial capital of Colorado. Pueblo is the industrial and commercial center of the Arkansas Valley. Boulder, situated 30 miles (48 km) northwest of Denver, is the home of the University of Colorado and the state's leading scientific research center.

## 4. Education and Culture

Colorado's educational system had its origin in private schools that appeared during the height of the gold rush. These soon were augmented by public facilities first authorized under the territorial government.

**Elementary and Secondary Education.** In the mid-1950's, Colorado began centralizing its public schools. As a result, the rural schoolhouse all but disappeared from the state. The number of districts declined radically, as directed by state law, resulting in stronger districts, centralized educational facilities, reformed curriculums, and higher standards of teaching and learning.

**Higher Education.** Colorado's institutions of higher learning include one of the nation's service academies, a rapidly growing system of public higher education, and several private universities and colleges. The U.S. Air Force Academy occupies a tract of more than 25 square miles (65 sq km) in the shadow of the Rampart Range, 8 miles (13 km) north of Colorado Springs.

The University of Colorado, with its main campus at Boulder, is the largest university in the Rocky Mountains region. Colorado State University is at Fort Collins, and the Colo-

© STEWART M. GREEN/TOM STACK

The ultramodern Denver Center for the Performing Arts houses a concert hall and theater complex.

rado School of Mines is at Golden. The state-supported four-year schools include Northern Colorado University at Greeley, Adams State College at Alamosa, Western State College at Gunnison, Southern Colorado University at Pueblo, Fort Lewis College at Durango, and Metropolitan State College at Denver.

Communities throughout Colorado have junior college facilities, financed by local districts and the state. These include Grand Junction, Trinidad, Lamar, Sterling, La Junta, Rangely, Greeley, Glenwood Springs, Leadville, and Pueblo.

**Research Centers.** Colorado's principal universities and colleges maintain extensive research programs in the social sciences, sciences, business, and engineering. The School of Medicine of the University of Colorado promotes research at its Denver campus in conjunction with the Colorado General Hospital. Colorado State University specializes in research related to agriculture, homemaking, forestry, and veterinary medicine. The state's major institutions of higher learning—the University of Colorado, Colorado State University, and the University of Denver—are members of the National Center for Atmospheric Research (NCAR), which is located at Boulder.

**Libraries.** Public libraries in Colorado have increased in number and size because of growing support from all levels of government. The Colorado State Library, a division of the state department of education, provides a wide range of services to localities and individual citizens and maintains a branch in Grand Junction to serve remote areas of the western slope. The Denver Public Library, founded in 1869, is the largest of its type between Kansas City, Mo., and the Pacific coast.

Special libraries include the library of the Colorado Historical Society, the Western history department of the Denver Public Library, and the many collections maintained at the universities and colleges, such as the military and aerospace collection of the U.S. Air Force Academy and the Western history collections of the University of Colorado.

**Museums.** Public and private museums are numerous in Colorado, many of them serving as important tourist attractions. The Colorado Historical Society operates the Colorado State Museum in Denver as well as regional units that include Healy House and Dexter Cabin in Leadville; Fort Garland Museum at Fort Garland; El Pueblo Museum in Pueblo; Baca House, Bloom Mansion, and the Pioneer Museum in Trinidad; Fort Vasquez (a reconstructed adobe fort) at Platteville; and the Ute Indian Museum in Montrose. Other well-known museums are the Denver Art Museum, the Denver Museum of Natural History, and the Colorado Springs Fine Arts Center and Taylor Museum.

**Other Cultural Activities.** Colorado offers a growing variety of theatrical, musical, and other cultural attractions. Denver has three nationally known theaters—the Elitch Gardens Summer Theater, in west Denver; the Denver Center for the Performing Arts; and the Red Rocks Theater, west of Denver, near Morrison, a natural amphitheater where concerts, ballet, and stage extrava-

ganzas are presented each summer. The Denver Symphony Orchestra features distinguished guest performers throughout the winter season. The Opera House in Central City, founded in 1878, offers summer opera and plays.

---

**PROMINENT PEOPLE IDENTIFIED WITH COLORADO**

**Bent, William** (1809–1869), fur trader and pioneer; builder, with his brother **Charles Bent** (1799–1847) and Ceran St. Vrain, of Bent's Old Fort.

**Boettcher, Charles** (1852–1948), merchant and industrialist; early supporter of Colorado's beet-sugar industry.

**Bonfils, Frederick Gilmer** (1860–1933), and **Tammen, Harry Heye** (1856–1924), purchasers, 1895, and publishers of the *Denver Post;* widely known as "Bon" and "Tam" (characterized in Gene Fowler's *Timberline,* 1933).

**Chaffee, Jerome B.** (1825–1886), banker, mine-owner, and one of Colorado's first U.S. senators.

**Evans, John** (1814–1897), physician, teacher, and railroad builder; second territorial governor; founder of Colorado Seminary, later the University of Denver.

**Iliff, John Wesley** (1831–1878), cattleman; one of Colorado's best-known cattle kings.

**Mears, Otto** (1840–1931), road and railroad builder, who constructed first toll road over Poncha Pass in Sangre de Cristo Mountains.

**Meeker, Nathan Cook** (1817–1879), agricultural editor of Horace Greeley's New York *Tribune* and founder, with Greeley's support, of the Union Colony of Colorado at Greeley, 1869–1870.

**Moffat, David Halliday** (1839–1911), banker, mine-owner, and railroad builder, for whom Moffat Tunnel was named.

**Ouray** (?1820–1880), Ute Indian chief, who devoted his last years to promoting peace between Indians and settlers.

**Palmer, William Jackson** (1836–1909), soldier, railroad executive, and industrial promoter, long identified with Colorado Springs.

**Tabor, Horace Austin Warner** (1830–1899), mine-owner, merchant, and politician; referred to as "silver king of the Rockies."

**Teller, Henry Moore** (1830–1914), U.S. senator; U.S. secretary of the interior, 1882–1885; champion of free silver.

---

The National Center for Atmospheric Research, overlooking Boulder, is involved in advanced meteorological research.

Ice fishing, a popular wintertime sport, on Antero Reservoir, which forms part of Denver's water-supply system.

The old mining town of Aspen has revived as an all-season cultural center, as well as a winter sports area. The Aspen Institute for Humanistic Studies, founded in 1949, presents seminars and lecture programs. The Aspen Music School and Festival is held annually from June through August. The University of Colorado holds a summer Shakespeare Festival.

**Communications.** Colorado's first newspaper, the *Rocky Mountain News*, appeared at the Cherry Creek diggings (near present Denver) early in 1859. The *Denver Post* was established in the 1890's. These two morning papers are the most widely read among Colorado's many daily and weekly newspapers. Several television stations and scores of radio stations are licensed to operate in the state. Every community of any size has one or more cable television systems.

## 5. Recreation and Places of Interest

Colorado is one of the nation's major outdoor recreation areas. Its varied landscape and wide range of temperatures permit activities to suit almost any taste. The rivers and artificial lakes of the eastern plains afford excellent camping and fishing sites. The foothills and mountains, with their unexcelled scenic beauty, offer active sports to the energetic and sightseeing to all.

Skiing is a major winter sport. River-running (white-water boating) is fast becoming an important summer activity. Hiking and mountain climbing attract sportsmen and amateurs during all seasons of the year.

**National Areas.** The National Park Service administers a variety of areas in Colorado. Mesa Verde National Park, west of Durango, preserves prehistoric Indian ruins, including excavated pit houses, pueblos, and cliff dwellings. Rocky Mountain National Park, lying between Estes Park and Granby, is a wilderness recreation area dominated by high mountain peaks.

The Black Canyon of the Gunnison National Monument, near Montrose, is located in a spectacular gorge of the Gunnison River. Colorado National Monument, near Grand Junction, fea-

White-water rafting on the Arkansas River. The summer sport provides exciting challenges to the daring.

tures a colorful variety of canyons and other erosional forms. Great Sand Dunes National Monument, north and east of Alamosa, contains the largest and highest inland sand dunes in the United States. Dinosaur National Monument preserves an area in northwestern Colorado and northeastern Utah that is rich in deposits of the skeletal remains of prehistoric reptiles. Hovenweep National Monument, also shared by Colorado and Utah, contains four groups of prehistoric pueblos and cliff dwellings. Yucca House

The rock formations of Colorado National Monument were created by erosion of the area's red sandstone plateau.

National Monument, west of Mesa Verde National Park, contains unexcavated ruins of a prehistoric pueblo.

Bent's Old Fort National Historic Site, located on the Arkansas River between La Junta and Las Animas, re-creates the trading post erected on that site in the early 1830's.

Shadow Mountain National Recreation Area, at the western entrance to Rocky Mountain National Park, includes Shadow Mountain Lake and Lake Granby. The Curecanti Recreation Area, established around Blue Mesa, Morrow Point, and Crystal reservoirs, lies just southeast of the Black Canyon of the Gunnison National Monument.

National forests, covering about one fourth of the total land area, provide extensive recreational facilities. The popular Arapaho Basin, Berthoud Pass, and Loveland Pass ski areas, little more than an hour's drive west from Denver, lie within the Arapaho National Forest. The forests are notable also for areas in which no development is permitted. These include the Mount Zirkel–Dome Peak Wild Area in Routt National Forest and the Maroon Bells–Snowmass Wild Area in the White River National Forest.

**State Areas.** The state operates Lathrop State Park near Walsenburg and numerous other sites at reservoirs throughout the state for camping, boating, and, in season, fishing and hunting.

**Other Points of Interest and Events.** Many of the former mining towns have been preserved or restored. These include Central City, Leadville, Georgetown, Cripple Creek, and Silverton. The nation's last steam-operated narrow-gauge railroad with passenger service, the Durango-Silverton branch of the Denver and Rio Grande Western Railroad, operates excursion trains daily during the summer months. Lookout Mountain, west of Denver, contains a scenic high drive and the grave of William F. ("Buffalo Bill") Cody. The Garden of the Gods, a park near Colorado Springs, is noted for grotesquely eroded masses of red sandstone.

Annual events include almost everything from grand opera to rodeos and fairs. Each New Year is celebrated by a display of fireworks on Pikes Peak.

## 6. Government and Politics

The state constitution implemented at the time of statehood remains in effect, although it has been amended frequently. It provides that the state share political power with the 63 counties and numerous municipalities. Each level of government faces the problems of raising sufficient revenues to expand desired services, while competing with the other levels and the federal government for the tax dollar.

**Structure of State Government.** The executive branch is headed by the governor, who is responsible for the faithful execution of the law. The governor also exercises general supervision over a large number of agencies, boards, and commissions.

Legislative functions are performed by the General Assembly, made up of the Senate and

---

**GOVERNMENT HIGHLIGHTS**

**Electoral Vote**—9.
**Representation in Congress**—U.S. senators, 2; U.S. representatives, 7.
**Legislature**—Senate, 35 members, 4-year terms; House of Representatives, 65 members, 2-year terms.
**Governor**—4-year term, may serve successive terms.

the House of Representatives. The General Assembly meets annually. To provide for a continuing study of state problems, it has created three permanent joint committees—the legislative council, the committee on education beyond the high school, and the joint budget committee. In carrying out its functions, the legislative council depends on a full-time professional staff.

The state constitution, as amended, vests the judicial power in the Colorado Supreme Court, a probate court and a juvenile court in the city and county of Denver, district courts, county courts, and municipal courts.

**Political Divisions.** The counties perform local functions on behalf of the state and also provide services as a local government independent of the state. Each county, except Denver, is governed by a board of commissioners and other elected officials. The effectiveness of county government varies. In about two thirds of the counties, where the population is below 10,000, administration is inefficient due to too small a population and tax base. In the populous eastern foothills, the counties are well organized but for the most part incapable of solving their problems of urbanization.

First-class cities (those with more than 70,000 inhabitants) are required by law to govern themselves under the mayor-council system. Second-class cities (those with populations of 2,000 to 70,000) may adopt either the mayor-council or the council-manager plan.

**Public Finance.** The state's expenditures fall into six major categories—education, health, and welfare; highways; institutions; capital construction; recreation; and regulatory and scientific activities. The counties finance police protection, courts, highways and roads, and social services. Cities, towns, and special districts provide police and fire protection, water and sanitation, libraries, streets, recreation, education, and other services.

To produce revenues, the state taxes the incomes of individuals and corporations, inheritances and gifts, gas and oil, retail sales, cigarettes, and liquor. It also levies other special taxes and receives substantial federal grants-in-aid. Local governments derive revenues from property and excise taxes, sales taxes, and a variety of fees. School districts obtain most of their revenues from property taxes and state aid.

**Social Services.** The state and the counties, assisted by federal grants-in-aid, maintain extensive social services. Public health programs are administered through county agencies. The state department of public welfare is responsible for uniform and equitable administration of welfare programs. County welfare departments conduct programs pertaining to child welfare, old-age pensions, and aid to dependent children, the blind, and the tubercular. The state department of rehabilitation provides medical and vocational diagnosis, training, and other forms of aid leading to eventual employment of the handicapped.

The state department of institutions operates a variety of facilities. The Colorado State Hospital in Pueblo and the Fort Logan Mental Health Center in Denver care for the mentally ill. State homes and training schools for the mentally retarded are maintained at Grand Junction and Wheatridge. Community centers for the retarded operate in Boulder and elsewhere. Correctional units include the penitentiary and a women's facility at Canon City.

**Politics.** Traditionally the two-party system has prevailed in Colorado, with political power balanced between Republicans and Democrats.

The Colorado State Capitol, in Denver, is modeled on the U.S. Capitol in Washington, D.C.
© JOHN J. SMITH

These cliff dwellings, preserved in Mesa Verde National Park, were built by pre-Columbian Indians.

Third parties have had little influence since the agricultural and mining depressions of the late 19th century, which gave rise to Populism and the crusade for bimetallism, and the reform-oriented Progressive movement of the early 20th century.

The Republican party tended to dominate the state from 1876 to 1909; the Democratic party was dominant from 1909 to 1919; and since 1920, the two parties have both enjoyed periods in power. Colorado voters are independent and unpredictable, and neither party enjoys their support in state and national elections for long periods of time.

## 7. History

From about the beginning of the Christian era to 450 A.D., a primitive people lived on or near the Mesa Verde in caves, subsisting on cultivated corn and squash, augmented by game. From 450 to 750 they attained a higher standard of living, as indicated in part by the construction of homes known as pit houses. The period from 750 to 1100 was a time of town building, with structures that suggest peace and prosperity. The next two centuries marked the emergence of a complex culture, with larger villages, irrigated agriculture, and trade with Indians to the southwest.

About 1300, the prehistoric civilization of Mesa Verde began to decline. The turning point was the abandonment of the dwellings on the tableland for homes in the caves and walls of the mesa. Students of prehistoric peoples attribute the change to drought, internal strife, or the appearance of nomadic war bands. Whatever the reason, the cliffs were temporary residences; within a few generations the people had moved southward, and the area was abandoned. For nearly five centuries Colorado was uninhabited except by nomadic Indians who hunted over the plains and mountains.

**Exploration and Early Settlement.** Three years after the Louisiana Purchase, in 1803, Zebulon M. Pike led a party of 22 men into Colorado, seeking the headwaters of the Arkansas and the Red rivers. Pike's report described the wonders of the West, including such landmarks as the peak that bears his name and the Royal Gorge of the Arkansas River. Other explorers followed the trail blazed by Pike, but the true explorers of Colorado—indeed, of the whole Rocky Mountains region—were the mountain men, who searched for beaver and other pelts and harvested furs for more than three decades.

During the 1840's the Mexican government made large grants of land to individuals to encourage settlement in the San Luis and the Arkansas valleys. The Mexican War delayed this colonization work, and the Treaty of Guadalupe Hidalgo (1848) transferred all of Mexico's claims to the United States. Permanent settlement of southern Colorado began soon afterward. Migrations from New Mexico to the San Luis Valley led to the founding of San Luis in 1851, followed in quick succession by other towns. For a time the area was an extension of the old Spanish agricultural and pastoral communities to the south.

**The Gold Rush.** The discovery of gold near Denver in 1858 altered the course of settlement in Colorado. The mining towns and the commercial centers, populated largely by migrants from other parts of the United States, fixed upon the future state a predominantly Anglo-American culture. The presence of gold and silver, acting as a magnet to attract new settlers, focused attention on the need for effective government and the removal of Indians.

**Territorial Days.** At the time of the gold discoveries, Colorado was Indian land, divided politically between the territories of Utah, Kansas, Nebraska, and New Mexico. The goldfields were far from the settled parts of those territories, and in 1858 a handful of miners, determined

## HISTORICAL HIGHLIGHTS

**c. 1500** Ute peoples established in southern Rocky Mountains.

**1541** Francisco Vásquez de Coronado, searching vainly for the fabled Seven Cities of Cíbola, becomes first Spanish explorer to enter Colorado.

**1682** René Robert Cavelier, sieur de La Salle, claims for France all of Colorado east of the Rocky Mountains.

**1706** Juan de Ulibarri claims southeastern Colorado for Spain.

**1803** Through the Louisiana Purchase the United States acquires most of eastern Colorado.

**1806** Lt. Zebulon M. Pike explores Colorado; discovers peak that will ultimately bear his name yet fails in attempt to climb it.

**1819** Under the Adams-Onis Treaty, eastern Colorado is established as a U.S. territory.

**1820** Dr. Edwin James leads first recorded ascent of Pikes Peak.

**1848** By the Treaty of Guadalupe Hidalgo, Mexico cedes western Colorado to the United States.

**1850** U.S. government purchases Texas's claims in Colorado, fixing what will become the present boundaries of the state.

**1851** First permanent white settlement in Colorado, Conejos, is founded in San Luis Valley.

**1859** First newspaper in region, *Rocky Mountain News,* begins publication (April 23).

**1861** Colorado Territory is established with present-day boundaries; Colorado City named capital.

**1862** Territorial capital moved to Golden.

**1864** More than 150 Cheyenne and Arapaho killed in Sand Creek Massacre (November 29); Colorado Seminary, now the University of Denver, established.

**1867** Denver becomes the permanent capital.

**1870** Denver Pacific and Kansas Pacific railroads are completed.

**1876** Colorado enters Union as the 38th state (August 1).

**1877** University of Colorado opens at Boulder.

**1881** The White River and Uncompahgre Ute relinquish their lands in western Colorado.

**1890** Sherman Silver Act raises price of silver, bringing considerable wealth to state.

**1893** Repeal of Sherman Act and panic of 1893 result in Colorado mine closings; Colorado gives women the right to vote (November 2).

**1906** U.S. Mint at Denver produces its first coins; Mesa Verde National Park established.

**1915** Rocky Mountain National Park established.

**1924** Colorado becomes second state to ratify child labor amendment to federal Constitution; Klu Klux Klan–endorsed candidates are elected governor and senator.

**1927** 6.4-mile (10.3-km) Moffat Tunnel completed, linking eastern and western portions of the state.

**1932– 1937** "Dust bowl" conditions (prolonged drought and high winds) cause tremendous damage in southeastern Colorado.

**1958** The U.S. Air Force Academy opens its campus near Colorado Springs.

**1959** The Colorado–Big Thompson Project, approved in 1937, completed, providing irrigation for 720,000 acres (291,600 ha) of land in the eastern part of the state.

**1966** The North American Aerospace Defense Command (NORAD) completes its underground center in Cheyenne mountains.

**1967** Colorado becomes first state to liberalize abortion laws (for therapeutic reasons or to end pregnancy from rape or incest).

**1974** Desegregation of Denver schools launched through busing program.

**1977** U.S. Solar Energy Research Institute opens near Denver.

**1985** The Frying Pan–Arkansas River Project completed, bringing water from western Colorado to eastern plains.

**1992** Taxpayer Bill of Rights (TABOR) amendment to state constitution limits expansion of state and local governments.

**1998** Militant environmentalist group claims responsibility for an arson fire that caused millions of dollars of property damage at a resort complex in Vail.

---

to have a government on the scene, met and organized the goldfields as "Arapahoe County" of Kansas Territory. The next year the residents of the mining camps petitioned Congress to establish a separate territory in the mountain region to be known as the Territory of Jefferson, and without waiting for congressional approval, they drafted an organic act and elected a governor. This extralegal government was dissolved in February 1861, when Congress authorized the creation of Colorado Territory, with boundaries essentially those of the future state.

Indian troubles plagued the mining region for more than a decade. During the 1860's the Cheyenne and Arapaho, after destructive warfare against the settlements, ceded all lands east of the mountains and agreed to leave that area. The western slope remained in control of the Ute tribes, whose rights were recognized by treaty in 1868. The discovery of silver in the San Juan Mountains, followed by a rush to the area, led to warfare as the Ute fought for their lands. In 1873, mainly because of the influence of Chief Ouray, the Indians abandoned the region and, in 1881, were removed to reservations.

During the territorial period the population increased rapidly. After 1870 the construction of railroads—particularly the Denver Pacific between Denver and Cheyenne, Wyo., and the Kansas Pacific between Kansas City and Denver—spurred immigration and economic growth.

**Early Statehood.** After admission to the Union in 1876, Colorado continued to prosper. Its economy was dependent largely on the production of precious metals. When high-grade gold ores became

scarce, silver advanced in importance; however, silver proved to be a precarious economic base. Increased output of silver, together with its demonetization in the United States in 1873 and

An abandoned mine near Victor is a mute reminder of Colorado's gold rush in the 19th century.

subsequently throughout Europe, caused supply to exceed demand, with sharp decreases in price. For a time, the U.S. Treasury artificially supported domestic silver by monthly purchases, but following the panic of 1893, when Congress repealed the silver purchase law, Colorado's mining industry entered a slump.

**Economic Diversification.** After the turn of the century, Colorado concentrated on agriculture, food processing, and production of a variety of minerals. During World War I, large areas of the plains were plowed up and planted to wheat, coal output increased sharply, and there was a demand for Colorado's molybdenum and tungsten. Oil production became significant in the 1920's and 1930's. The voters approved a bond issue for construction (1923–1927) of the 6.4-mile (10 km) Moffat Tunnel beneath James Peak on the Continental Divide, west of Denver. This tunnel, together with the Dotsero Cutoff, completed in 1934, put Colorado for the first time on a direct transcontinental rail route.

**The Depression Years.** When the prosperity of the 1920's gave way to depression in the 1930's, Colorado turned to the federal government for help. In 1933, relief, public works, and conservation programs were inaugurated on a vast scale. The public lands, which include national forests and parks, were revitalized. Water storage and transmountain diversion projects augmented water supplies for Denver and for farmers in the South Platte Valley. Streets, highways, airports, and other public facilities were constructed or improved.

**A New Era.** Colorado emerged from the depression with the mobilization of its economic resources for World War II. Military training facilities were constructed throughout the state, and the economy was geared toward war production. Mining activities expanded, especially the production of fuels and metals, and manufacturing grew rapidly.

The wartime reorganization of Colorado's economy, with emphasis on defense manufacturing and military-related services, opened a new era in the history of the state. After the war, manufacturing continued to expand until it surpassed agriculture in importance. This trend was accompanied by rapid urbanization, in part the result of changes occurring in the coal industry and in farming.

Faced with rapid growth, urban centers in eastern Colorado had to find water to sustain burgeoning populations and the variety of enterprises on which city dwellers depended for their economic well-being. Traditionally, those communities had drawn their water supplies, as did farmers, from the mountain streams that emptied onto the plains. When watercourses that drained eastward from the Rockies proved inadequate, the state's most populous area underwrote, usually with financial aid from the federal government, transmountain diversion projects that shifted water from the western to the eastern slope. Cities along the eastern front range have encountered fierce competition from within as well as from outside the state for dwindling water reserves.

Today Colorado has a diversified economy. Manufacturing, agriculture, and tourism are its principal money earners, in that order. An invigorating climate, progressive government, and excellent educational institutions continue to attract new industries, particularly those related to science and modern technology.

LEE SCAMEHORN, *University of Colorado*

## Bibliography

Abbott, Carl, and others, *Colorado: A History of the Centennial State*, rev. ed. (Colorado Assoc. Univ. Press 1982).

Athearn, Robert G., *The Coloradans* (1977; reprint, Univ. of N. Mex. Press 1982).

Dallas, Sandra, *Colorado Ghost Towns and Mining Camps* (Univ. of Okla. Press 1985).

Dorsett, Lyle W., *The Queen City: A History of Denver* (Pruett 1986).

Griffiths, Mel, and Rubright, Lynell, *Colorado: A Geography* (Westview Press 1983).

Marsh, Charles S., *People of the Shining Mountains: The Utes of Colorado* (Pruett 1982).

Mills, E. A., *Wild Life on the Rockies* (Univ. of Neb. Press 1988).

Rohrbough, Malcolm J., *Aspen: The History of a Silver Mining Town* (Oxford 1988).

Ubbelohde, Carl, and others, *A Colorado History*, 5th ed. (Pruett 1982).

Vandenbusche, Duane, and Smith, Duane A., *A Land Alone: Colorado's Western Slope* (Pruett 1981).

## GOVERNORS OF COLORADO

| Territorial | | |
|---|---|---|
| William Gilpin | | 1861–1862 |
| John Evans | | 1862–1865 |
| Alexander Cummings | | 1865–1867 |
| A. Cameron Hunt | | 1867–1869 |
| Edward M. McCook | | 1869–1873 |
| Samuel H. Elbert | | 1873–1874 |
| Edward M. McCook | | 1874–1875 |
| John L. Routt | | 1875–1876 |
| **State** | | |
| John L. Routt | Republican | 1876–1879 |
| Frederick W. Pitkin | " | 1879–1883 |
| James B. Grant | Democrat | 1883–1885 |
| Benjamin H. Eaton | Republican | 1885–1887 |
| Alva Adams | Democrat | 1887–1889 |
| Job A. Cooper | Republican | 1889–1891 |
| John L. Routt | " | 1891–1893 |
| Davis H. Waite | Populist | 1893–1895 |
| Albert W. McIntire | Republican | 1895–1897 |
| Alva Adams | Democrat | 1897–1899 |
| Charles S. Thomas | " | 1899–1901 |
| James B. Orman | " | 1901–1903 |
| James H. Peabody | Republican | 1903–1905 |
| Alva Adams | Democrat | 1905 |
| James H. Peabody | Republican | 1905 |
| Jesse F. McDonald | Republican | 1905–1907 |
| Henry A. Buchtel | Republican | 1907–1909 |
| John F. Shafroth | Democrat | 1909–1913 |
| Elias M. Ammons | " | 1913–1915 |
| George A. Carlson | Republican | 1915–1917 |
| Julius C. Gunter | Democrat | 1917–1919 |
| Oliver H. Shoup | Republican | 1919–1923 |
| William E. Sweet | Democrat | 1923–1925 |
| Clarence J. Morley | Republican | 1925–1927 |
| William H. Adams | Democrat | 1927–1933 |
| Edwin C. Johnson | " | 1933–1937 |
| Ray H. Talbot | " | 1937 |
| Teller Ammons | " | 1937–1939 |
| Ralph L. Carr | Republican | 1939–1943 |
| John C. Vivian | " | 1943–1947 |
| William Lee Knous | Democrat | 1947–1950 |
| Walter W. Johnson | " | 1950–1951 |
| Dan Thornton | Republican | 1951–1955 |
| Edwin C. Johnson | Democrat | 1955–1957 |
| Stephen L. R. McNichols | " | 1957–1963 |
| John A. Love | Republican | 1963–1973 |
| John Vanderhoof | " | 1973–1975 |
| Richard D. Lamm | Democrat | 1975–1987 |
| Roy Romer | " | 1987–1999 |
| Bill Owens | Republican | 1999– |

**COLORADO,** kol-ə-rad′ō, **University of,** a coeducational state institution of higher education located in Boulder, Colo. It is part of the University of Colorado System, which also includes campuses at Colorado Springs and Denver and a Health Sciences Center at Denver. Founded in 1876, the university began instruction in 1877 and awarded its first degree in 1882.

The university has five colleges and four professional schools. It offers a broad curriculum leading to bachelor's, master's, and doctoral degrees and professional degrees in law and pharmacy. In addition, it provides special facilities for research in such fields as environmental sciences, behavioral science, behavioral genetics, cognitive science, arctic and alpine studies, high altitude environment, atmospheric and space physics, and economic analysis and participates in the National Bureau of Standards' institute for laboratory astrophysics.

The university is widely known for such annual events as the Colorado Shakespeare Festival, Conference on World Affairs, and Writers Conference and programs in opera, drama, dance, and fine arts.

The Boulder campus, situated at the base of the Rocky Mountains at an elevation of 5,000 feet (1,524 meters), comprises 600 acres (240 hectares). The buildings are picturesque with rough-cut sandstone and red tile roofs.

**COLORADO CITY,** kul-ə-rā′də, a city in western Texas, the seat of Mitchell county. It is on the Colorado River, about 240 miles (385 km) northwest of Austin. The city is a center for shipping cattle, dairying, oil production, and the growing of cotton, grains, and grain sorghums. It has cotton gins and compresses, a cottonseed-oil mill, and refineries for oil and asphalt. Two lakes provide water and recreational facilities.

Colorado City was founded in 1881 and was incorporated in 1907. Government is by city manager. Population: 4,281.

**COLORADO DESERT,** kol-ə-rad′ō, an area of arid lowlands adjacent to the lower Colorado River where that stream leaves the United States and enters Mexico. The mountain and hill ranges that rise above the lowlands are excluded. Commonly understood as part of the Colorado Desert are the Colorado River valley from Parker Dam southward to the border, the lower Gila River valley of southwestern Arizona (sometimes called the Gila Desert), and the Salton Trough of southeastern California.

The Salton Trough stretches 125 miles (200 km) northwestward from the Colorado River at the Mexican border. It consists of three parts: the Imperial Valley, which slopes gently away from the Colorado River to the surface of the saline Salton Sea; the Salton Sea, which covers the lowest part of the trough, with its surface about 240 feet (73 meters) below sea level; and the Coachella Valley, which narrows as it rises gradually northwestward to end against the steep slopes of the San Bernardino and San Jacinto mountains. In the Coachella and Imperial valleys irrigation allows intensive farming. Lettuce, dates, and citrus fruits dominate the agricultural scene. At the northwestern end of the Coachella Valley and at the base of Mount San Jacinto lies the desert resort of Palm Springs.

HENRY M. KENDALL
*Miami University, Ohio*

**COLORADO NATIONAL MONUMENT,** kol-ə-rad′ō, is a scenic reserve 12 miles (19 km) by road west of Grand Junction, Colo. It consists of canyons formed by wind and water erosion of a red sandstone plateau flanking the Grand Valley of the Colorado River. Standing in many of the canyons are unusual monoliths, one of which—Independence Rock—is 500 feet (150 meters) high. A forest of piñon pine and juniper covers much of the area. A 22-mile (35-km) road skirts the canyon rims, from which footpaths descend into the eroded area. The monument, 27 square miles (70 sq km) in area, was established in 1911.

**COLORADO PLATEAU,** kol-ə-rad′ō, a major surface region in the western United States. It is characterized by high elevation, essentially horizontal sedimentary rock materials, and deeply trenched river canyons, including the Grand Canyon of Colorado River in northwestern Arizona, which is the most renowned. The plateau includes the southeastern two thirds of Utah, the southwestern quarter of Colorado, the northwestern quarter of New Mexico, and the northern third of Arizona, encompassing approximately 50,000 square miles (130,000 sq km). To the east the southern Rocky Mountains rise over 14,000 feet (4,300 meters), while to the west the Great Basin region lies at lower elevations.

Elevations on the plateau range from over 12,000 feet (3,600 meters) in central Utah to less than 2,000 feet (600 meters) at the Grand Canyon. The greater part of the surface is monotonously flat. Over most of the plateau, rainfall is sufficient to support summer grazing. Population is sparse and is predominantly dependent on cattle grazing and mining.

See also GRAND CANYON.

HENRY M. KENDALL, *Miami University, Ohio*

**COLORADO POTATO BEETLE.** See POTATO BEETLE.

**COLORADO RIVER,** kol-ə-rad′ō, one of the great rivers of North America. It rises in north central Colorado, in the 14,000-foot (4,300-meter) snow-capped peaks of the Continental Divide, and flows 1,400 miles (2,250 km) southwest into the Gulf of California.

The Colorado drains an area of 246,000 square miles (637,140 sq km)—about one fifteenth of the continental United States (excluding Alaska) and a small part of Mexico. In its upper basin lie portions of Wyoming, Colorado, Utah, and New Mexico; in its lower basin, parts of Nevada, Arizona, and California; and in its delta, segments of Sonora and Baja California, Mexico.

More than 50 rivers make up the Colorado's complex river system. Its main tributaries include the Green River from Wyoming, the Gunnison and Dolores of Colorado, the Dirty Devil of Utah, the San Juan of New Mexico, the Virgin of Nevada and Utah, and the Little Colorado, Williams, and Gila rivers of Arizona.

The river extends through five life zones, each with a different climate, plant life, and animal life. It slashes its way through a wilderness of mountains, plateaus, and deserts, which offer some of the most dramatically beautiful scenery to be found anywhere in the world. The river is cliff-bound nine tenths of its way and travels 1,000 miles (1,600 km) through deep canyons.

**Grand Canyon.** Grand Canyon, in Arizona, is the largest, deepest, and most spectacular gorge

JOE MUNROE FROM PHOTO RESEARCHERS

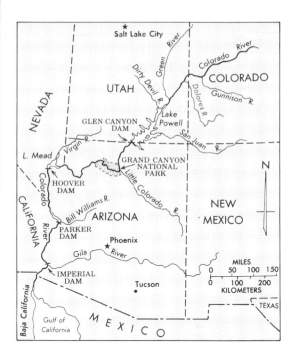

COLORADO RIVER has cut deep canyons through the desert country of the Southwest. Great dams, such as Hoover Dam (at left), direct its energy to man's use.

of the Colorado. It is 217 miles long (349 km), 4 to 18 miles wide (6 to 29 km) from rim to rim, and 1 mile deep (1.6 km). For the million and a half people who view it each year, Grand Canyon is an inexpressible wonder. For geologists it is the world's largest and oldest book. Its pages consist of 15,650 feet (4,770 meters) of compressed and folded rock formations, weirdly eroded and strikingly colored. At the bottom of the gorge is bared part of the earth's original crust—vertical layers of gneiss formed before the earth had cooled, and blocks of granite forced into them in a molten state by heat and pressure. Nowhere else in the world is there such a comprehensive record of the 2-billion-year history of the earth. For more than 12 million years the Colorado has been writing it—eroding primeval mountains level, depositing their rock in ancient seas, and cutting through new upthrusts of land during successive uplifts and submergences.

**Exploration.** Deep in the canyons of the Colorado and high on neighboring mesas are the ruins of the prehistoric cliff dwellings and pueblos of America's first people. Throughout the Colorado Plateau their descendants and successors live in the Indian tribes of Ute, Paiute, Hopi, Navaho, Havasupai, Mohave, and Apache. The first white man to explore the Colorado was Hernando de Alarcón, who in 1540 pushed his tiny Spanish galleon upriver to a point near the present city of Yuma, Ariz. García López de Cárdenas, an officer on the simultaneous land expedition led by Francisco Vásquez de Coronado, discovered Grand Canyon. Over 200 years later the Franciscan missionary Francisco Tomás Hermenegildo Garcés named the river the Colorado ("discolored").

In 1826, Lt. R. W. H. Hardy of the British Navy explored the mouth of the river. In 1858, Lt. Joseph C. Ives of the U. S. Army forced his boat up to Black Canyon, the present site of

Hoover Dam. Meanwhile, trappers, prospectors, explorers, and adventurers were trying to run the rapids downstream. John Wesley Powell, in 1869, led the first expedition through Grand Canyon (by boat) and was the first to explore the Colorado scientifically. With the U. S. Geological Survey expedition of 1923 the surveying and mapping of the river were completed.

**Development.** The Colorado River is a major factor in the lives and future of all the people in the great Southwest. In 1922, when the 7-state Colorado River Compact was drawn, modern efforts to control and use the river began. The first unit in the Colorado River Project was Hoover Dam, between Nevada and Arizona. Completed in 1936, its hydroelectric power plant supplies southern California with industrial power. Downstream, just north of Yuma, Ariz., Imperial Dam was completed in 1938. From here the All-American Canal, 80 miles long (130 km), was constructed to carry water into the Imperial Valley of California, below sea level. With 2,900 miles (4,670 km) of lateral canals, the valley is the largest irrigated area in North America. In 1948 a branch canal, 125 miles long (200 km), was completed to California's Coachella Valley.

Parker Dam, between Imperial and Hoover dams, was completed in 1938. From its 717,000 acre-feet of storage water, the Colorado River Aqueduct (1939) carries water 242 miles (389 km) to supply Los Angeles, San Diego, and other cities in the Metropolitan Water District of Southern California. Davis Dam, between Parker and Hoover dams, was completed in 1949. Its power plant and transmission lines eased power shortages in Arizona.

The mammoth Glen Canyon Dam, just above Marble Gorge of Grand Canyon, was completed in 1964. The federal Bureau of Reclamation then proposed erection of two other power dams on the Colorado: Bridge Canyon Dam in Lower Granite Gorge at the lower end of Grand Canyon, and Marble Gorge Dam at the upper end of Grand Canyon. Bridge Canyon Dam would back up water 80 miles (130 km) through Grand Canyon National Monument and 13 miles (21 km) into Grand Canyon National Park. Marble Gorge Dam would back water 55 miles (88 km) to the foot of Glen Canyon Dam, and from the reservoir created the Colorado River would be channeled underground for 104 river miles (167 km) through a proposed Kanab Diversion tunnel to another hydroelectric plant.

Introduction of bills into Congress for these dams aroused wide public protest. Opponents insisted that the dams would irretrievably destroy the present natural state of Grand Canyon. A counter-bill was introduced in Congress to provide for the inclusion of all Grand Canyon in Grand Canyon National Park, established in 1919 "to be preserved unimpaired for future generations." Proponents of the dams claimed that they are necessary to the comprehensive Southwest Water Plan, which will supply central Arizona with Colorado River water.

FRANK WATERS, *Author of "The Colorado"*

**COLORADO RIVER,** kul-ə-rā'də, one of the longest rivers in Texas, rises in Dawson county in the plain known as the Llano Estacado. It flows generally southeastward for about 600 miles (965 km) to the Gulf of Mexico. Its chief tributaries are the Concho, Pedernales, and San Saba rivers, Pecan Bayou, and Beals Creek. The river is navigable as far as Austin. Under the control of three river authorities a number of dams, among them the Colorado River's 278-foot-high (85-meter) Marshall Ford Dam, northwest of Austin, have been built for power and irrigation.

**COLORADO RIVER AQUEDUCT.** See AQUEDUCTS —*Modern Aqueducts.*

**COLORADO SPRINGS,** kol-ə-rad'ō, is a city in central Colorado, the seat of El Paso county, 65 miles (105 km) south of Denver. It is situated at an altitude of 6,035 feet (1,840 meters), east of the Rocky Mountains and just east of Pikes Peak. The city is a noted vacation center.

The economy has three main bases: military establishments—the U. S. Air Force Academy, Fort Carson, and Ent Air Force Base, headquarters of the North American Air Defense Command (NORAD)—tourism; and industries that include electronics and printing.

The city is the seat of Colorado College, a 4-year coeducational institution; the Colorado Springs Center of the University of Colorado; and the Colorado School for the Deaf and Blind. The Colorado Springs Fine Arts Center and Taylor Museum has an art collection and operates an art school jointly with Colorado College.

Scenic attractions in the region include the Garden of the Gods, the Will Rogers Shrine on Cheyenne Mountain; Pike National Forest, and Pikes Peak, whose summit is reached by highway and cog railway.

Founded in 1871, the settlement was known originally as Fountain Colony. It was incorporated as Colorado Springs in 1872. It is a home rule city with a council-manager government. Population: 360,890.

MARGARET G. REID
*Pikes Peak Regional District Library*

**COLORADO STATE UNIVERSITY** is a public coeducational university and landgrant college in Fort Collins, Colo. It was established in 1870 as the Agricultural College of Colorado, although instruction did not begin until 1879, when the local citizenry was able to provide the land and the first buildings. The college was subsequently renamed Colorado State College of Agriculture and Mechanic Arts (1935) and later Colorado Agricultural and Mechanical College (1951). In 1957 it received its present name. The graduate school opened in 1896.

The university comprises colleges of science and arts, agriculture, engineering, forestry and range management, home economics, and veterinary medicine. It administers and maintains a graduate school of engineering in Bangkok, Thailand, and provides assistance for programs in agriculture, engineering, and home economics at the University of Peshawar, Pakistan. It also participates in National Science Foundation and National Institutes of Health research programs. Enrollment has risen from just over 2,000 in 1945 to almost 18,000.

**COLORADO TICK FEVER** is a virus disease transmitted through the bite of the wood tick (*Dermacentor andersoni*). Despite its name, Colorado tick fever is not limited to the state of Colorado but occurs throughout all the Western states. It is by far the most common of all the tick-borne virus diseases and usually occurs in the spring and early summer, when the ticks are most active.

**Symptoms.** The onset of the disease is sudden, with the symptoms first appearing from 4 to 6 days after the person has been bitten. At first he feels chilly and is often bothered by bright lights (photophobia). He soon develops an aching in his muscles and joints and often a severe headache with a pain behind the eyes. Low backache is another common symptom. Frequently, the patient loses his appetite and becomes nauseous. In addition, his temperature rises

OVERLOOKING COLORADO SPRINGS, the Will Rogers Memorial Shrine is on a knoll on Cheyenne Mountain.

BURLINGTON ROUTE

ROCKY MOUNTAIN LABORATORY, U. S. PUBLIC HEALTH SERVICE

**COLORADO TICK FEVER is transmitted by wood ticks. Above are a male (left) and a female (right).**

rapidly, sometimes to 104° F (40° C) or more. Unlike Rocky Mountain spotted fever, which is a more serious disease, Colorado tick fever does not produce a rash.

The patient remains ill for about two days and then appears to have recovered. However, the remission of symptoms lasts only a day or two and is usually followed by a second attack. This episode may be more or less severe than the first and it generally lasts a day or two longer. Occasionally there is also a third attack, but most often the symptoms disappear quickly after the second attack and the patient soon recovers.

**Treatment.** There is no specific treatment for Colorado tick fever. Aspirin may be given to reduce the fever and aching, but there are no drugs that are effective against the disease-producing virus.

LOUIS J. VORHAUS, M. D.
*Cornell University Medical College*

## COLORATION IN ANIMALS. See MIMICRY; PRO-TECTIVE COLORATION.

## COLORATURA, kul-ə-rə-tōōr′ə, is a musical term
most frequently applied to sopranos who sing highly embellished music. The term can also be used to describe music containing rapid runs, trills, and other ornaments—so-called "coloratura" passages.

Although the term "coloratura" is ultimately derived from an Italian word meaning "colored," its more immediate ancestor is the German word *koloratur*, which first came into common use in Germany during the 16th century. Then it meant, primarily, embellished music, either vocal or instrumental. With this meaning, the German word was equivalent to the Italian terms *musica colorata* or *musica figurata*.

Before about 1850, when coloratura took on its current specialized usage, all singers, male and female, regardless of range, were trained as virtuosos capable of executing rapid ornaments. With the decline of the *bel canto* tradition and with the entrance into the repertory of more and more operas requiring vocal stamina rather than finesse, the art of coloratura singing became associated almost exclusively with light, flexible soprano voices.

Operatic passages requiring unusual coloratura technique include the two arias of the Queen of the Night in Mozart's *Magic Flute*, the Mad Scene in Donizetti's *Lucia di Lammermoor*, and Zerbinetta's aria in Strauss' *Ariadne auf Naxos*.

WILLIAM ASHBROOK, *Author of "Donizetti"*

## COLORIMETER, kul-ər-im′ə-tər, an optical instrument for the measurement of color. In *visual colorimeters*, the unknown color is presented beside a comparison field into which may be introduced any one of a range of known colors from which the operator chooses the one matching the unknown. To be generally applicable, the comparison field must be continuously adjustable in color in one of three ways. Additive colorimeters mix red, green, and blue lights of adjustable amounts; subtractive colorimeters use yellow, cyan, and magenta filters of adjustable thickness. A third type of colorimeter has a rotating sectored disk whose four differently colored sectors are adjustable in relative area. Most colorimeters, however, provide only a single series of comparison colors and are limited to specimens known in advance to have one of these colors.

*Chemical colorimeters* measure the concentration of a known constituent in solution by comparison with colors of solutions of known concentrations of that constituent. Photoelectric chemical colorimeters use a photocell to measure the light transmitted by the unknown. Maximum sensitivity is obtained by using a filter over the photocell to isolate the part of the spectrum where the known constituent has its maximum absorptance. The readings of the photocell are converted to concentration by means of a calibration curve obtained by measuring a series of solutions of known concentration.

*Photoelectric tristimulus colorimeters* of general applicability employ three filter-photocell combinations adjusted to approximate either the three color-matching functions of the normal human eye directly or some weighted average of them. The three readings obtained from the colorimeter may be converted into an approximation of the unknown. The degree of approximation obtained depends on the photocell response and on how well the filter-photocell combinations duplicate the color-matching functions of the normal human eye. The principal application of photoelectric tristimulus colorimeters is the measurement of how much a manufactured component departs in color from the standard. See also COLOR.

DEANE B. JUDD
*National Bureau of Standards*

## COLOSSAE, cə-los′ē, was an ancient city of Asia Minor in the Roman province of Phrygia. It was situated about 4 miles (6 km) east of the modern city of Denizli in southwestern Turkey, at the head of a precipitous gorge into which the Lycus River (modern Curuksu River), a tributary of the Maeander (modern Menderes River), plunges. The city was on the route from Antioch to Ephesus and in the 5th century B. C. was a flourishing commercial center with an important woolen industry. However, its fortunes dwindled as the neighboring city of Laodicea prospered.

The population of Colossae was mainly Jewish, Greek, and Phrygian. Along with nearby Hierapolis and Laodicea the city was the focus of missionary activity and was especially famous because of its connection with the writings of St. Paul. The city was a Christian bishopric until the 8th century, when it was abandoned because of earthquakes. The ruins of an aqueduct, an acropolis, and a theater near the modern village of Honaz remain. See also COLOSSIANS, EPISTLE OF PAUL TO THE.

THE COLOSSEUM, impressive even as a ruin, stands as a reminder of the tastes and the power of imperial Rome.

**COLOSSEUM,** kol-ə-sē′əm, the popular name of the Flavian amphitheater, built by the emperors Vespasian and Titus. It was constructed after Nero's death on the site of his famous Golden House and opened to the public for the first time in 79 A. D. by Vespasian. In a later age it acquired the name Colosseum because of a large statue (colossus) of Nero which was placed at its entrance by the Emperor Hadrian.

Although the Colosseum was used as a quarry by architects of the Middle Ages and Renaissance, enough of it still stands today to testify to its greatness. It was elliptical in shape, could hold approximately 45,000 to 50,000 people, and covered about 6 acres (2½ hectares) of ground. In its completed form the seating was in three tiers, with standing room above the third tier. The three tiers were decorated with Doric, Ionic and Corinthian columns, respectively. Above the third tier there was a windowed wall.

Beneath the timber floor there was a maze of dens where animals in movable cages were kept. In addition, the arena could be flooded for sea fights, and an awning could be raised to protect the audience during inclement weather. The seats were supported by a vaulted substructure. Ventilation was good, and the large crowds were accommodated by an excellent system of staircases, entrances, and exits. Originally the Colosseum had a marble facing and marble seats and was decorated with statues.

The Colosseum was a place for games and the exhibition of rare, wild beasts. Usually, the animals were made to fight with one another or with men. The most popular events were the gladiatorial contests, man against man. In many ways the Colosseum stands as the symbol of the cruel and barbaric element in Roman civilization. But it is also the symbol of the grandeur that was Rome. No other structure characterizes the spirit of Roman civilization as well as the Colosseum.

ARTHER FERRILL
*University of Washington*

**COLOSSIANS, The Epistle of Paul to the,** kə-losh′ənz, the 12th book of the New Testament, written by St. Paul while he was imprisoned in Rome toward the end of his life. Paul had never been in Colossae and was not known personally to the Colossians (2:1). Undoubtedly they had received the news of Christianity during Paul's stay in Ephesus, when the whole province of Asia was evangelized (Acts 19:10).

Colossae was one of three cities in the Lycus River valley of the Roman province of Asia (part of Anatolia in modern Turkey). The others, Hierapolis and Laodicea, were on opposite sides of the river. All three were wealthy cities, located in a center of the clothing trade.

**Reason for Paul's Letter.** Paul always wrote to meet a particular situation. In this case, we learn from his admonitions that the Colossians were evidencing a tendency toward certain false teachings that could undermine their faith. There was much good in the Colossians. They had faith and steadfastness and love (1:4,8; 2:5). They were producing the harvest of a Christian life (1:6). But Paul stresses a present threat to their faith. If we note the things he emphasizes, we can perhaps find the sources of that threat.

Paul first speaks of the total adequacy of Jesus Christ, who is the very image of God and in whom all fullness dwells (1:15,19; 2:2,9). The apostle also emphasizes the part that Jesus played in the Creation (1:16,17), while at the same time noting his total humanity: he was a flesh and blood man (1:22; 2:9).

Then, since the Colossians leaned toward astrology, Paul speaks of the elemental spirits of the stars that, according to Colossian belief, controlled the lives of men (2:8,20). Like others of their time the Colossians believed in demons, principalities, and powers (1:16; 2:10,15).

The particular heresy that Paul saw threatening the Colossians emphasized the worship of angels and fear of demons (2:18). It had a philosophical character, too (2:8), as well as ascetic elements, notably in its laws on food and drink (2:16,21). The heresy also had an aspect that made men careless of purity, chastity, and morality (3:5,8). It produced an intellectual snobbery against which Paul set the Christian conviction that Christianity is for every man (1:28).

We now must ask what had gone wrong at Colossae. For the answer we must take into consideration the fact that traces of Judaic law still lingered there, particularly in dietary practices. These, combined with certain aspects of a Greek tendency of thought called Gnosticism, were probably responsible for many non-Christian practices.

**The Gnostic Heresy.** The basic belief of Gnosticism is that matter and spirit existed from the beginning. All things were made from matter, and this matter was and is essentially flawed and evil.

If matter is evil, then God—who is spirit—cannot himself have touched it. Instead, from God there came a long line of emanations until one was reached that was so distant from, and so ignorant of, God that it could touch matter, and it created the world: the world was made by an inferior, an ignorant, and a hostile god.

Paul rejects this theory. He states that behind creation is Christ. The principles of redemption and of creation are the same.

Gnosticism had its repercussions on belief in Jesus. According to Gnostic belief, Jesus was not unique; he was simply one—even if the greatest—of a long chain between the world and God. Since it requires philosophical knowledge to encompass the elements of that chain and arrive at God, real religion is only for the philosopher.

Concomitantly, if matter is evil, the body is evil. Therefore, to the Gnostics Jesus had no real body: he was not a man; he was simply a ghost in human form. Further, if the body is evil, it must be despised and contained by asceticism. Or, since the body is evil, desires can be indulged in with impunity even if the result is uncontrolled immorality.

It can be readily be seen how these ideas could have destroyed Christianity. In his epistle Paul meets them, shows their error, and affirms the truth. See also PAUL, SAINT.

WILLIAM BARCLAY
*The University of Glasgow*

**COLOSSUS OF RHODES,** kə-los'əs, rōdz, one of the Seven Wonders of the World (q.v.). It was a bronze statue of Helios, god of the sun, that stood overlooking the harbor of the island of Rhodes. The statue, over 105 feet (32 meters) high, was completed about 280 B.C. and was destroyed by an earthquake in 224 B.C. It was designed by the sculptor Chares.

**COLOSTRUM,** kə-los'trəm, is the protein-rich milk secreted by the female breasts for a period usually lasting from a few days before to one or two weeks after childbirth. After this period, normal milk is secreted.

Colostrum differs from normal milk in that it is more yellow in color and contains more proteins and minerals with less fat and sugar. The high protein content of colostrum is due largely to the presence of globulins similar to the gamma globulins of blood plasma. A normal milk protein not found in colostrum is casein.

JEFFREY WENIG
*ENDO Laboratories*

**COLQUHOUN,** kō-hōōn, **Patrick** (1745–1820), British police magistrate, civic reformer, and economist-statistician, who contributed to the administrative reform of the London police. He also eased the condition of the London poor and gained administrative reforms favorable to the industry and commerce of the city of Glasgow and of Scotland.

He was born in Dumbarton, Scotland, on March 14, 1745, and spent several years in Virginia. He settled in Glasgow in 1766 and was elected lord provost of Glasgow in 1782 and 1783. In 1783 he founded the Glasgow Chamber of Commerce. In 1789 he moved to London, and from 1792 to 1818 he served as magistrate in the City of London. In his reform of the London police system Colquhoun suggested crime prevention methods and more efficient supervision of police. To aid the poor he established soup kitchens and an elementary school. In addition he published treatises proposing reforms designed to improve the condition of the poor. The statistics published by Colquhoun are today an important source on the economic conditions during the early part of the Industrial Revolution in England. Colquhoun died in Westminster on April 25, 1820.

RAMON KNAUERHASE, *University of Connecticut*

**COLT, Samuel** (1814–1862), American inventor of the Colt revolver. Colt was born in Hartford, Conn., on July 19, 1814. He went to sea at 16 and, while on a voyage to Singapore, constructed a wood model of his famous revolver. He made several models after his return to the United States and obtained his first U. S. patent in 1836. Colt's revolver was the first practical revolving firearm. The cylinder was automatically revolved when the gun was cocked. A plant was established to manufacture his revolver at Paterson, N. J., but it failed in 1842. When the Mexican War (1846–1848) began, however, the U. S. Army ordered 1,000 of Colt's revolvers. They were first manufactured at Eli Whitney's factory at Whitneyville, Conn. Colt set up his own factory in 1847, at Hartford, Conn.

Colt also invented a submarine battery and experimented with a submarine telegraph cable in New York Harbor in 1843. He died in Hartford on Jan. 10, 1862.

**COLTER,** kōl'tər, **John** (1775?–1813), American fur trader and guide. Colter was born near Staunton, Va. In 1803 he enlisted in the army to join the Lewis and Clark expedition, and stayed with the party until it was homeward bound from the Pacific. But at the Mandan Indian villages in present North Dakota, he again turned westward in company with two white trappers, spending more years in the wilderness.

Colter accompanied trader Manuel Lisa up the Missouri in 1807, and was sent on a trading expedition across the mountain ranges of Wyoming to the Yellowstone National Park region. His notable explorations in this area are mainly unrecorded, as he was illiterate, but he did give some valuable geographical information to his old commander, William Clark, on his return. After guiding a party from the St. Louis Missouri Fur Company to the Three Forks of the Missouri in 1810, Colter returned to civilization, spending his last years on a farm near Dundee, Mo. He died there in November 1813.

DONALD JACKSON, *University of Illinois*

**COLTON, Walter,** kōl'tən (1797–1851), American clergyman and writer. Colton was born in Rutland, Vt., on May 9, 1797. After studying at Yale University and Andover Theological Seminary, he taught philosophy and letters at Middletown Academy in Connecticut (1825–1830). He served briefly as editor of the *American Spectator* in Washington, D.C., and was commissioned a navy chaplain in 1831. In 1846 he was appointed chief judge of Monterey, Calif., where he established California's first newspaper, the *Californian*. Colton's books include *Ship and Shore* (1835), *Three Years in California* (1850), and *Deck and Port* (1850). He died in Philadelphia on Jan. 22, 1851.

**COLTRANE, John,** kōl'trān (1926–1967), African American jazz saxophonist, composer, and bandleader whose harmonic, melodic, and rhythmic contributions were so comprehensive that his influence transcended his particular instrument and affected the concepts of players of all instruments. Coltrane's musical career was characterized by lifelong study and practice and by a restless evolution in musical style and content.

John William Coltrane was born in Hamlet, N.C., on Sept. 23, 1926. He grew up in High Point, N.C., where he learned to play the E♭ alto horn and then clarinet and alto saxophone. After high school he moved to Philadelphia, where he studied saxophone formally. In Hawaii during his 1945–1946 U.S. Navy duty, he played in a band with other servicemen. Nonprofessional recordings from this period show Coltrane grappling with the innovations of Charlie Parker, whom Coltrane succeeded in meeting and playing with in 1947. After military duty he returned to Philadelphia and played both alto and tenor saxes in the bebop style when possible and in a rhythm-and-blues style when the job required.

Coltrane's first national exposure came in 1949, when he joined Dizzy Gillespie's band, where he soon concentrated on tenor sax. In 1955 he was hired by the trumpeter Miles Davis, who was forming a group playing in what would soon be called the hard bop style, to which Coltrane's timbre and hard-driving attitude were well suited. On early recordings he is heard struggling to articulate complex melodic lines based on the rapid outlining of a song's basic and "substitute" harmonies. Critics were divided on Coltrane, but musicians generally admired him.

In 1957 Coltrane joined a group led by pianist-composer Thelonious Monk, whose music challenged Coltrane harmonically, melodically, and rhythmically; the few recordings they made together are high points of modern jazz. By the time Coltrane rejoined Miles Davis in 1958, the saxophonist had reached new levels of both technical prowess and musical individuality with his virtuosic melodic lines, called "sheets of sound." During this period he perfected improvisation over a characteristically difficult chord progression (soon known as "Coltrane changes") that formed the basis for his classic 1959 composition *Giant Steps*. In 1959 he also played on Davis's innovative *Kind of Blue*, which influenced Coltrane to de-emphasize the difficult chord progressions he had mastered and begin improvising according to scales, or "modes."

After Coltrane left Davis's band, the saxophonist assembled the "classic quartet" that would be his primary musical format for some five years. A 1960 modal arrangement of Rodgers and Ham-

John Coltrane, December 1962.

merstein's *My Favorite Things* featured his first released work on soprano sax. As his quartet developed, he improvised for longer stretches—some pieces ran 30 to 45 minutes. Much of the power and complexity of this group is captured in Coltrane's suite *A Love Supreme*.

Coltrane's quartet dissolved as he began adding to it wind players and percussionists often associated with the free jazz movement. An important work of his group in transition is the high-energy *Ascension*. He never fully embraced stream-of-consciousness, free improvisation, usually including some type of underlying organization in his music, which was still evolving when he died in New York City on July 17, 1967.

CARL WOIDECK, *University of Oregon*

**Bibliography:** A selected Coltrane compact-disc discography includes *Giant Steps* (Atlantic 1311–2), *My Favorite Things* (Atlantic 1361–2), *A Love Supreme* (GRP GRD-155), and *The Major Works of John Coltrane* (GRP GRD 2-113). For a complete discography and balanced biography, see, respectively, **Fujioka, Yasuhiro,** *John Coltrane: A Discography and Musical Biography* (Scarecrow 1995); **Nisenson, Eric,** *Ascension: John Coltrane and His Quest* (St. Martin's 1993).

**COLTSFOOT,** a small, weedy plant whose large, oval or heart-shaped leaves are similar in shape to the hooves of a colt. Known botanically as *Tussilago farfara*, coltsfoot belongs to the family Compositae. Although it was originally native to Europe and Asia, it now also ranges throughout eastern North America, growing chiefly on dry banks.

Coltsfoot grows about 18 inches (46 cm) tall and bears yellow flower heads similar to those of dandelions. The leaves, which appear only after the flowers have faded, have toothed edges and are about 7 inches (18 cm) wide. Extracts from the leaves were formerly used in cough medicines. Although coltsfoot spreads readily and has sometimes been used as ground cover, it is not often grown as a garden plant.

DONALD WYMAN
*Arnold Arboretum, Harvard University*

**COLUM, Padraic,** kol'əm (1881–1972), Irish-American poet and dramatist, and member of the group that founded the Irish National Theatre. Colum was born in Longford, Ireland, on Dec. 8, 1881, and spent his early years in Dunleary, near Dublin. After moving to Dublin about 1900, he took an active part in the Irish literary revival. The Irish National Theatre (later the Abbey Theatre) produced his first play, *Broken Soil* (1903). In 1911 Colum was one of the founders of the *Irish Review*. (See IRISH LITERARY REVIVAL.)

Colum married Mary Maguire, a critic and author, in 1912, and from 1914 the couple lived in the United States. In the 1920s Colum served as drama critic of *The Dial* magazine. Elected to the American Academy of Arts and Letters, he received the 1952 fellowship for poetry from the Academy of American Poets. In 1953 the Irish Academy of Letters awarded him the Gregory Medal. He died in Enfield, Conn., on Jan. 11, 1972.

Colum's first book of poems, *Wild Earth*, appeared in 1909 (enlarged ed., 1916). Other books of verse followed: *Dramatic Poems* (1922); *Creatures* (1927), a collection of poetry about animals; *Old Pastures* (1930); *Flower Pieces* (1939); and *Collected Poems* (1953). In March 1967 *Carricknabauna*, a dramatization by Colum and Basil Burwell of a number of Colum's poems, was produced off-Broadway in New York. Colum also wrote many children's stories and adapted Homeric and other mythological tales for children. He retold Irish sagas in *The Frenzied Prince* (1943) and edited *An Anthology of Irish Verse* (1948) and *A Treasury of Irish Folklore* (1954).

HORACE V. GREGORY*, *Coauthor of "History of American Poetry, 1900—1940"*

**Bibliography:** Colum's work has been edited by Sanford Sternlicht for Syracuse Univ. Press: *Selected Short Stories of Padraic Colum* (1985), *Selected Plays of Padraic Colum* (1986), and *Selected Poems of Padraic Colum* (1989).

**COLUMBA**, kə-lum′bə (521?—597), Irish abbot and missionary regarded, with St. Patrick and St. Brigid, as the patron saint of Ireland. Columba, later known as Columcille ("Dove of the Church") was born in Gartan, Donegal, about 521. A member of the O'Neill dynasty, he received his literary and monastic training largely at Clonard, under St. Finnian. He was ordained a priest in 551. By 563 he had founded many churches and several monasteries, notably those at Durrow, Derry, Kells, and Raphoe.

Columba's most famous monastery was founded in 563 on Iona, a small island in the Inner Hebrides. Strategically located near the boundary between Christian and pagan lands, the Iona monastery was both a center for Irish Christian immigrants to nearby Dalriada (now Argyll) and the point of departure for the greatest missionary achievement of the early Irish—the permanent Christianization of much of Britain.

Columba's visit to King Brude in the Scottish highlands in 565 initiated the conversion of the Picts north of the Grampian Hills. The Iona monks not only penetrated the Orkneys and the Hebrides but also revived the faith among the Lowland Picts. Columba's mission to the Picts had political consequences: it set in motion the gradual consolidation of Scotland into a unified nation. In 575, Columba demonstrated outstanding political ability in his mediation of the differences among the chieftains at Druim-Cetta in Ireland.

Columba organized the Scottish church along the monastic lines characteristic of the Irish church. He and the succeeding abbots of Iona, although only priests, headed the church in northern Ireland and Scotland. After his death, on Iona, on June 9, 597, monks from Iona founded the monastery at Lindisfarne and from there carried out the conversion of the Northumbrians and the Anglo-Saxon conquerors of Britain.

Ancient but not entirely convincing tradition attributes to Columba several poems in Gaelic and Latin. His biographer, St. Adamnan, described this greatest of Irish missionaries as "angelic in aspect, refined in speech, excellent in ability, great in counsel." His feast is observed on June 9.

JOHN F. BRODERICK, S.J.
*Weston College*

**COLUMBANUS**, kol-əm-bā′nəs (c. 540—615), Irish missionary and monastic founder, and saint of the Roman Catholic Church, known also as Columban or Columba the Younger. He was born in Leinster, Ireland, and studied at Bangor, Ireland, under its founder, Comgall. After his ordination Columbanus remained at Bangor as a teacher for about 30 years and during this time reputedly composed poems and a commentary on the Psalms.

A completely new phase of his career began about 591, when Comgall sent him to engage in those apostolic labors that made him one of the most influential ecclesiastics of his time and the most famous of the many medieval missionary Irish monks on the Continent. When the rulers of the divided Frankish kingdom welcomed him, he settled in Burgundy. During the next two decades he succeeded in raising the level of religious life among clergy and laity. He reinvigorated and popularized monastic life through the abbeys he founded at Annegray, Fontaines-en-Vosges, and most notably, at Luxeuil; some 200 other abbeys arose from these.

Columbanus gave new direction to Gallic monasticism by sending his monks outside the cloister to engage in pastoral work. His monastic rule, modeled on the severe Irish ones, was widely influential until it was replaced by the 8th century by the milder Benedictine rule. He promoted frequent private confessions of sins, and his famous *Penitential* cataloged penances.

His insistence on retaining Irish customs—particularly in regard to the tonsure, the date of Easter, and the superiority of abbatial over episcopal authority—and his excoriations of the corrupt royal court brought Columbanus into conflict both with the ecclesiastical hierarchy and with the Merovingian kings, who exiled him from Burgundy in 610. He moved east to work among the Alamanni but was forced to flee in 613. He went to Lombardy and established a monastery at Bobbio that became one of the greatest of medieval monasteries. Columbanus died at Bobbio on Nov. 23, 615. His feast is November 23.

JOHN F. BRODERICK, S.J.*, *Weston College*

**COLUMBIA**, a city in central Missouri, the seat of Boone county. It lies about 30 miles (48 km) north of Jefferson City, the state capital, and about midway between St. Louis and Kansas City.

Columbia is one of the state's major educational centers, containing the University of Missouri at Columbia, which was established in 1839; Columbia College, which was founded as Christian Female College in 1851; and Stephens College, which originated as the Columbia Female Academy in 1833.

Columbia was established in 1821, the year in which Missouri attained statehood. It had been planned two years earlier under the name of Smithton but soon was renamed and was incorporated in 1826. Population: 84,531.

MARION L. ALBRECHT*
*Daniel Boone Regional Library, Columbia*

The undergraduate library of the University of South Carolina in Columbia.

**COLUMBIA,** the capital of South Carolina and seat of Richland county, is situated in the central part of the state. It is on the fall line at the head of navigation on the Congaree River, about 100 miles (160 km) northwest of Charleston. Columbia is the center of a two-county metropolitan area (population, 1960 census: 260,828) and is surrounded by a number of municipalities and many unincorporated suburbs. The Congaree, which flows near the western edge of the business district, divides the city from its neighbors in adjoining Lexington county. The population of the metropolitan area is increasing rapidly, but substantial population gains within the city boundaries are not likely.

**Economy.** Geographically and economically the area is expanding in all directions. Industries of long standing, chiefly textile mills and plants making clay products have been supplemented by many light industries, including those that produce cameras, electronic equipment, fibers, and boats. Many of these have located outside the city, where they provide hundreds of industrial jobs in the two-county area.

Government is the dominant activity of Columbia. Most of the state offices are within the city, as are the University of South Carolina, the state mental health hospital, and several other state institutions. Major federal agencies in or near the city include a U.S. veterans' hospital, internal revenue offices, a Federal Land Bank, and Fort Jackson, a large U.S. Army base.

Columbia also is the chief banking, insurance, financial, and communications center of the state and is a leading retail and wholesale area. To promote both agriculture and trade, the state maintains in Columbia all the year a large and colorful farmers' market where farm produce of all kinds is sold. Many statewide organizations have offices in the city.

**Urban Planning.** In facing urban problems, the city has done comprehensive planning and has instigated many programs of its own, including provision of downtown parking garages, public housing for the elderly and other low income groups, and fire and water protection. Activities in cooperation with other units of government are perhaps more significant. These include metropolitan planning, joint tax collections with Richland county, construction of waste treatment facilities on a multiunit basis, urban renewal over a wide area in cooperation with the University of South Carolina, and a metropolitan traffic and transportation plan.

Racial relationships are generally good, having been influenced by a biracial committee, established prior to enactment of major civil rights laws. Many Negroes voted before the laws were passed and integration has been accepted in many areas without overt antagonism. The Negro population represents about 30% of the total.

**Education and Culture.** Columbia is the educational center of the state. Educational institutions include the University of South Carolina, Lutheran Theological Southern Seminary and several other church-related colleges, Richland Technical Education Center, the South Carolina Trade School, the State Opportunity School, the Hall Psychiatric Institute, and several business colleges.

The city supports an art museum, which is being expanded into a major cultural and educational center, and there is an active "little theater" group. Historic buildings, maintained as museums or having museum features, include the handsome State House, begun in 1851 and completed in 1907; the South Caroliniana Library (built in 1840) of the University of South Carolina; the Ainsley Hall Mansion with gardens, which has been restored and renamed the Robert Mills Historic House and Park, in honor of its architect; and the Woodrow Wilson Boyhood Home.

**History.** Political controversy between the up-country and the coastal region of South Carolina led the General Assembly in 1786 to select the present site of Columbia for a new state capital, replacing Charleston. The assembly first met in Columbia in 1790. During the Civil War the State House was shelled (Feb. 16, 1865) by the Union general William T. Sherman, but it escaped the fire that broke out the next night, destroying most of Columbia. Rebuilding, although slow, resulted in a more beautiful city.

Columbia has a city-manager form of government, with a mayor and councilmen. Population: 115,876.

ROBERT H. STOUDEMIRE
*University of South Carolina*

**339**

**COLUMBIA,** kə-lum'bē-ə, a city in south central Tennessee, seat of Maury county, situated on the Duck River, 40 miles (64 km) south of Nashville. It is a trade and shipping center in a dairy farming region and is an important center for the mining of calcium phosphate rock. Manufactures include food processing and the production of elemental phosphorus, electrodes, fertilizer, work clothing, and hosiery.

The city is the home of the Columbia Military Academy, a private school for boys. The President James K. Polk home, built by the father of the 11th president of the United States, is maintained as a museum in the city. Columbia is governed by a city manager and commissioners. Population: 33,055.

**COLUMBIA, District of.** See DISTRICT OF COLUMBIA.

**COLUMBIA HEIGHTS,** kə-lum'bē-ə, a city located in eastern Minnesota, in Anoka county, situated 0.5 mile (0.8 km) east of the Mississippi River. It adjoins Minneapolis, of which it is a residential suburb. The first village plat was recorded on the site in 1893, and the village of Columbia Heights was incorporated in 1898. Now a municipal corporation under a home rule charter, Columbia Heights has a council-manager form of government. Population: 18,910.

**COLUMBIA PLATEAU,** kə-lum'bē-ə, a region covering more than 200,000 square miles (518,-000 sq km) in Washington, Oregon, and Idaho. It is bordered on the west by the Cascade Range, on the south by the Basin and Range region, and on the east and north by the Rocky Mountains. The plateau derives its name from the fact that it is drained by the Columbia River and its tributaries, which in many cases flow in deep gorges and canyons. The Snake River, on the eastern margin, flows through a canyon one mile (1.6 km) deep.

The surface of the region is not a simple plateau. It includes plains and basins at low elevations; small plateaus, some level and some sloping; hill lands, both gently rolling and rough; and rugged mountain ranges rising above 10,000 feet (3,000 meters). The names of some of the subdivisions suggest the variety of landforms: the Yakima Folds, central Washington; the Channeled Scablands, eastern Washington; the Deschutes-Umatilla Plateau, north central Oregon; the Wallowa Mountains, northeastern Oregon; the High Lava Plains, central Oregon; and the Snake River Plain, southern Idaho.

The climate is generally warm in summer and cold in winter. Precipitation ranges from less than 10 inches (254 mm) in the south to more than 50 inches (1,270 mm) on the slopes of the higher mountains. The lower plains are cultivated intensively with irrigation from the rivers, producing fruits, sugar beets, potatoes, grains, forage crops, and many others. The semiarid areas produce winter and spring wheat and other small grains. In many of the rougher and drier areas grazing is the principal land use. The slopes of the mountains furnish lumber, principally from ponderosa and other pines.

The chief cities of the plateau are Spokane and Yakima, Wash.; Pendleton, Ore.; and Boise, Pocatello, and Idaho Falls, Idaho.

SAMUEL N. DICKEN
*University of Oregon*

**COLUMBIA RIVER,** kə-lum'bē-ə, a stream in Canada and the United States. It drains an area of 259,000 square miles (671,000 sq km), of which 219,000 square miles (567,000 sq km) are in the United States. The river is first in North America in hydroelectric development and potential. It is also used for irrigation, city water supply, transportation, and recreation.

The river rises in British Columbia on the western slope of the Rocky Mountains. It flows first northwestward, then generally southward through British Columbia and Washington, and finally westward to the Pacific Ocean. In its lower course it forms the border between Washington and Oregon. Its drainage basin also includes portions of Idaho, Montana, Wyoming, and Utah.

The Columbia River has a length of 1,210 miles (1,947 km), and its principal tributary, the Snake, has a length of 1,000 miles (1,609 km). Other important tributaries are the Kootenay, Okanogan, and Willamette rivers. The volume of the Columbia's flow is second only to that of the Mississippi, among U. S. rivers. Although the flood stage comes in summer, the flow is remarkably uniform because melting snows feed the southern tributaries earlier than the northern tributaries.

**Hydroelectric Development.** Besides the large volume and fairly even flow, the chief assets of the Columbia River for hydroelectric development are its low percentage of silt, a relatively steep gradient, and numerous dam sites favorable for building because of the strength of the bedrock. These advantages enable the Columbia basin to produce more than one third of the hydroelectric energy of the United States, and, with the addition of some supplementary fuel power in certain areas, to attract a great many industries. Although the region as a whole is not highly developed industrially, some industries that use large amounts of hydroelectric energy are quite important, especially aluminum refining.

On the main river and its tributaries, dozens of large multipurpose dams are in operation, and more are under construction or in the planning stage. Besides having power plants that produce electricity, the dams regulate the rivers' flow to reduce flooding and to provide better transportation for barges, while their reservoirs store water during the period of heavy flow for use later in the season and are used for recreation. The most important dams are Bonneville, The Dalles, John Day, McNary, Priest Rapids, Rock Island, Rocky Reach, Chief Joseph, and, the largest dam of all on the Columbia River, Grand Coulee. The last backs up the waters of the Columbia River to create Franklin D. Roosevelt Lake, which extends to the Canadian boundary.

In the Canadian portion of the river, dams reinforce the natural storage properties of Upper Arrow, Lower Arrow, and Kootenay lakes. These dams also provide additional hydroelectric power, most of which is consumed in the United States.

**Irrigation.** The rivers of the Columbia system flow through many nearly level basins and low plateaus. Some of these areas are farmed successfully without irrigation; others produce bountifully with additional water. Several large areas of irrigation occur in the Snake River Plain of Idaho, in east central Washington, in north central Oregon, and in the Willamette Valley of western Oregon. These areas produce large

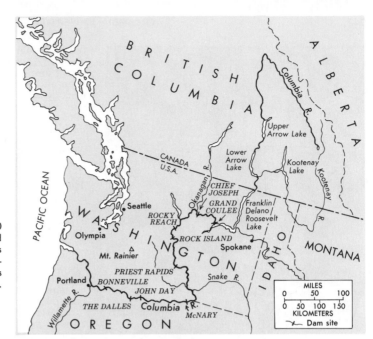

## COLUMBIA RIVER

The river drains a vast area (259,000 square miles) in northwestern United States and southwestern Canada. Its power has been harnessed for hydroelectric developments, and its waters have been drawn to irrigate farmland.

quantities of forage crops, sugar beets, potatoes, fruits, and various other crops.

**Transportation.** One of the chief uses of the Columbia River is for transportation. From the Fraser River in British Columbia to the Klamath River in California, the Columbia is the only stream that crosses the barrier of the Cascade Range. Portions of the Columbia River and its tributaries are followed by mainline railroads and through highways. The river itself is navigable by ocean freighters as far as Portland, Oreg., and Vancouver, Wash., and above these cities by barges. The completion in 1975 of the Columbia-Snake Inland Waterway, which includes parts of the Willamette River and stretches from the Pacific Ocean inland to Lewiston, Idaho, created the West's longest navigable waterway.

Constant dredging of the Columbia is required. At the mouth of the river, long jetties help to keep the channel open. However, at low tide in rough weather, the passage still is hazardous.

**Recreation.** The rivers, natural lakes, and reservoirs of the Columbia basin are used extensively for recreation including boating, water skiing, and fishing. The salmon run has declined with the construction of dams, in spite of fish ladders. Commercial fishing for salmon is restricted, but the Columbia is still very important for sports fishing. Also, the various reservoirs are stocked with other varieties of fish. Although the dams have destroyed many scenic rapids on the river, the reservoirs behind them provide miles of quiet, safe water for recreation.

**Exploration.** The exploration of the Columbia River began when Capt. Robert Gray entered it by ship in 1792. Prior to this time many coastal navigators had passed by the entrance to the Columbia without observing it. Later in 1792, Capt. George Vancouver explored the lower 100 miles (160 km) of the river, the part that is reached by the tide. In 1805–1806, Lewis and Clark explored the middle and lower portions of the river. The published report of their expedition gave rise to a keen interest in the Columbia River and encouraged the United States to claim the territory. By 1807 a fur-trading post was established on the Columbia in what is now the

southwestern part of British Columbia. This was followed by other fur-trading posts, including the one at Astoria, Oreg., at the mouth of the river in 1811 and the post at Fort Vancouver, Wash., in 1825. The fur traders traversed all of the Columbia and most of its tributaries in their search for furs and did more than any other group to explore the river.

See also OREGON QUESTION.

SAMUEL N. DICKEN
*University of Oregon*

THE COLUMBIA RIVER flows past Crown Point in Oregon. The far bank is in the state of Washington.

RAY ATKESON

COLUMBIA UNIVERSITY campus in New York City. Low Memorial Library (large dome) is in the foreground.

**COLUMBIA UNIVERSITY,** kə-lum′bē-ə, a private, nonsectarian university located in New York City. The fifth-oldest degree-granting educational institution in the United States, it comprises Columbia College (the undergraduate facility); graduate faculties of political science, philosophy, and pure science; schools of medicine, law, engineering and applied science, architecture, journalism, business, library service, social work, oral and dental surgery, international affairs, and general studies; the School of the Arts; and the Summer Session. Corporations connected with Columbia but separately administered and financed are Teachers College and Barnard College. Except for Barnard (for women), all of the components are coeducational. Women were admitted to Columbia College for the first time in 1983. Enrollment, apart from the affiliated corporations, averages over 18,000, and the teaching staff numbers more than 5,000. Of Columbia College's graduates, well over 80% go on to professional or other graduate schools, and the university as a whole has conferred more Ph.D. degrees than any other American institution of higher education.

Columbia aims at excellence at all levels of study, hence its total size is of less significance than the fact that most of its parts are relatively small. Emphasis is on small classes, carefully selected and taught by a distinguished faculty. Its integrated courses at the undergraduate level, particularly that in contemporary civilization taught jointly by the economics, government, history, and philosophy departments, have been widely imitated. A similarly comprehensive course in the humanities combines the study of literature, philosophy, the arts, and music.

More languages (71) are taught at Columbia than at any other American university. Since 1948 the university has opened institutes in East Asian, European, Near and Middle Eastern, East Central European, African, Latin American, and Communist affairs. There is an international fellows program, an institute of war and peace studies, a center of Israel and Jewish studies, and a foreign student center. Institutes also have been added in air flight structures, nutrition, and geology (Lamont Geological Observatory). A computer center was opened in 1962, and in 1966 an institute of urban development was organized to study the problems peculiar to city life. In association with the Archaeological Institute of America, Columbia contributes to the support of schools in Athens, Rome, and Israel. The university also maintains working relations with Union Theological Seminary and many other centers of scholarship in New York City.

**History.** Columbia's history dates from July 1754, when Samuel Johnson, first president of the school, undertook the instruction of eight students in the schoolhouse vestry of Trinity Church, in lower Manhattan. On October 31 of the same year, the school was granted its first charter as King's College by King George II of England. In 1760 the college moved to its own quarters nearby.

Classes continued until 1776, when the New York Committee of Safety requisitioned the building during the Revolutionary War. The institution remained suspended until 1784, when it was revived by the New York state legislature, which vested control of the school in the Regents of the State University of New York and changed its name to Columbia College. Control reverted to private auspices in 1787, and in 1857 the college moved to larger quarters in midtown Manhattan. As new faculties were added and enrollment increased, the college was moved again, in 1897, this time to permanent quarters on a 28.5-acre campus in upper Manhattan. Columbia's status as a university was officially recognized by New York state in 1912.

The original liberal arts college was augmented by a school of medicine in 1767 (merged with the College of Physicians and Surgeons in 1813 and reaffiliated with Columbia in 1860); a school of law in 1858; a school of mines in 1864 (renamed the School of Engineering and Applied Science); and graduate faculties of political science (1880), philosophy (1890), and pure science (1892). The School of Architecture opened in 1896 (although instruction had begun in 1881), and the School of Social Work was started in 1898 (affiliated with Columbia in 1940 and made a university division in 1959). The Summer Session was initiated in 1900. A school of journalism was established in 1912 (given graduate status in 1935); of business in 1916 (graduate since 1949); of dental and oral surgery in 1917; of library service in 1926 (first instruction in 1887); of international affairs in 1946; of general studies in 1947 (replacing University Extension, dating from 1904); and the School of the Arts in 1965 (replacing three schools dating from 1948). Teachers College (founded in 1887) affiliated with Columbia in 1898, Barnard College (1889) affiliated in 1900, and the College of Pharmaceutical Sciences (1829) affiliated in 1904.

Columbia has been fortunate in its presidents. Notable among them was Seth Low (1889–1901), who reorganized the graduate and professional schools and initiated the move to the present campus. Frederick Barnard (1864–1889) had instituted elective courses and provided for graduate study and research. His interest in education for women brought about the founding of Barnard College in 1889, a liberal arts college for women named in his honor. Nicholas Murray Butler (1902–1945) brought Columbia to the forefront of American education Dwight D. Eisenhower headed the university (1948–1951) before becoming president of the United States. He was succeeded in 1953 by Grayson Kirk, who had been acting president for two years.

Among the outstanding alumni of Columbia have been Carlos Romulo, a president of the United Nations General Assembly; Frances Perkins, first woman member of a presidential cabinet; and Charles Evans Hughes and Harlan Fiske Stone, U. S. Supreme Court chief justices.

Nobel Prize winners among the alumni and faculty have included Nicholas Murray Butler, Robert A. Millikan, Irving Langmuir, Thomas H. Morgan, Harold C. Urey, Enrico Fermi, I. I. Rabi, Hideki Yukawa, and Konrad E. Bloch.

FLOYD M. SHUMWAY, *Columbia University*

## COLUMBIAN EXPOSITION OF 1893. See WORLD'S COLUMBIAN EXPOSITION.

**COLUMBINE,** kol'əm-bīn, a stock character in Italian *commedia dell'arte*, French comedy, and English pantomime. In early *commedia dell'arte*, Columbina, as she was called in Italian, was a pert maidservant, a character derived from ancient Roman comedy. Later she was the daughter of old Pantalone and the delicate sweetheart of Arlecchino (Harlequin), forming with Harlequin the traditional pair of lovers.

**COLUMBINE,** kol'əm-bīn, is the common name for a genus of perennial plants valued for their brightly colored flowers. There are about 70 species of columbines and many additional garden hybrids. They belong to the crowfoot family (Ranunculaceae) and range throughout the northern Temperate Zone.

Columbines vary in height from 6 inches to 4 feet (15 cm to 1.2 meters). Their flowers, which are either erect or hanging, have 5 petals, each with a long backward-projecting spur containing nectar. The so-called long-spurred hybrids are probably derivatives of *Aquilegia caerulea* and *A. chrysantha,* both native to the Rocky Mountains. They have large flowers, which are white, pink, yellow, blue, or multicolored, and are often grown in rock gardens. The European columbine (*A. vulgaris*) is a species with white, blue, or purple flowers 2 inches (5 cm) wide.

DONALD WYMAN
*The Arnold Arboretum, Harvard University*

**COLUMBITE,** kə-lum'bīt, is a mineral oxide of niobium, tantalum, iron, and manganese. The name derives from columbium, the old name for niobium. The ratio of niobium to tantalum varies; when the former predominates, the mineral is called columbite; when the latter, *tantalite.*

The mineral commonly occurs as crystals in granitic rocks. The short, prismatic, and often tabular crystals are brownish-black to black, have a submetallic luster, and may be iridescent. Significant locations of the mineral are in the Republic of the Congo, Nigeria, Brazil, Norway, and the Soviet Union. In the United States it occurs in most of the Appalachian Mountain states and in Colorado, South Dakota, and California. The mineral is a source of the rare elements niobium and tantalum.

Composition, $(Fe,Mn)(Nb,Ta)_2O_6$; hardness, 6; specific gravity, 5.2–7.9, increasing with percent of tantalum; crystal system, orthorhombic.

**COLUMBIUM.** See NIOBIUM.

**COLUMBUS,** kə-lum'bəs, **Bartholomew** (1432?– ?1514), Italian navigator, brother of Christopher Columbus. He was born in Genoa; little is known of his early years. He was probably in Lisbon in 1477 as a mariner and map maker, and he may have accompanied Bartholomeu Dias to the Cape of Good Hope. Christopher sent him to England in 1488 to solicit the aid of Henry VII for a voyage of discovery. Failing there, he went to France in 1490 and found Charles VIII even less interested, though the king's sister, Anne de Beaujeu, became his patroness. He was at Fontainebleau as a cartographer when he learned of his brother's landfall in the New World.

He returned to Spain in 1493, and Queen Isabella gave him command of three supply ships bound for Hispaniola where his brother had already gone on his second voyage. On his arrival there, Bartholomew became lieutenant governor of the Indies. He administered Hispaniola from 1496 to 1498 in his brother's absence and founded the city of Santo Domingo. Troubles caused by Francisco Roldán prompted the crown to send Francisco de Bobadilla to restore order in 1500, and both Christopher and Bartholomew were returned to Spain in chains. The monarchs freed them and confirmed Bartholomew's title. He sailed with Christopher on his fourth voyage (1502–1504), and again with his nephew Diego in 1509. He held government office in Santo Domingo, where he died.

R. A. SCHLEGEL

J. J. SMITH

Wild columbine
(*Aquilegia canadensis*)

Columbine (long-spurred hybrid)

Sebastiano del Piombo's 1519 portrait was painted years after Columbus's death. No authenticated portrait exists.

**COLUMBUS,** kə-lum′bəs, **Christopher** (c. 1451–1506), Italian navigator in the service of Spain. Columbus commanded, in 1492, the first recorded European expedition to cross the Atlantic Ocean in warm or temperate latitudes.

He was not the first European to land in the Americas: adventurers from Norway, Iceland, or Greenland, in the late 10th and early 11th centuries, had almost certainly settled briefly in Newfoundland and may have landed elsewhere on the Atlantic coast of North America. "Vinland," the Norse name for the part of America that they knew, appears in Adam von Bremen's 11th-century ecclesiastical history, as well as in several works produced in the 14th and 15th centuries.

There is also some evidence to the effect that fishermen from the western part of England may have sighted some part of northern North America at about the same time as Columbus's first voyage, or possibly earlier. But there is no evidence—indeed, it is unlikely—that Columbus knew of these Bristol voyages or of the earlier Norse discoveries.

His achievement, moreover, is distinguished from the earlier adventures not only by the latitudes in which it was made and by the much longer ocean passages that it entailed, but also by its consequences. The early northern voyages were without significant result. His discoveries in the West Indies were followed by rapid, widespread, and permanent settlement. In this sense it may be said that he discovered "America."

**Early Years.** There is little doubt, though there has been much discussion, about Columbus's nationality and origins. Attempts have been made to prove that he was a Spaniard, a Catalan, a Jew of Spanish or Catalan descent, even a Greek. But the overwhelming weight of evidence and the opinion of almost all serious scholars support the statements made by his early biographers and by contemporary commentators. He was Cristoforo Colombo, a Ligurian, born in or near Genoa, probably in 1451. He remained a loyal citizen of Genoa all his life and at his death bequeathed several legacies to families or individuals resident there. Though he and his son and biographer Ferdinand indulged in fantasies of remote noble ancestry, there is no doubt that members of his immediate family were comparatively humble folk. His father was a master weaver, who also seems to have kept a wineshop for a time.

Christopher received little or no formal education in his youth. So far as is known he never wrote in Italian and probably never had occasion to do so. His native Ligurian dialect was not then, and is not now, a written language. All his surviving writing is in Castilian, just as all his major achievements were in the service of Castile, but he used many Portuguese spellings and tricks of phrase, which suggest that he learned to read and write in Portugal. (The Spanish form of his name is Cristóbal Colón.)

Columbus appears to have spent much of his youth working at his father's trade. By his own account, however, he began to follow the sea at a "tender age," and his periods of work at the loom may have been interspersed with coasting voyages, possibly to collect supplies of wool or wine. In his early twenties he began to make longer voyages: one to Marseille and Tunis, at least one to Chios—then a Genoese colony—and, in 1476, one intended for Flanders and England that got no farther than Cape St. Vincent. The ship in which Columbus sailed—presumably as a deckhand—was sunk by French privateers, and Columbus landed penniless in Portugal. From Lagos he made his way to Lisbon, where he was taken in by one of the many resident Genoese.

**Preparation at Sea.** Columbus's fortuitous arrival in Portugal was probably the chief turning point of his career. Lisbon was then the principal European center of overseas exploration. Columbus learned to read and write, picked up Portuguese, Castilian, and a smattering of Latin, gained experience in oceangoing seamanship, and acquired most of his knowledge of navigation and hydrography. He may, indeed, have been concerned, with his brother Bartholomew, in a chart-selling business in Lisbon. Fire and earthquake have destroyed records, and the outlines of his life in Portugal have to be inferred from his own allusions and his son's account.

In 1477 he shipped on a voyage to Ireland and Iceland. In 1478 he was sent by one of the Genoese merchants resident in Lisbon to Madeira to buy sugar and deliver it in Genoa. Trusted by the leaders of the Genoese community, he evidently prospered, and contracted, in about 1479, an advantageous marriage. Felipa Perestrello e Moniz was the daughter of a widow of distinguished family, who had inherited property in Madeira and an interest in the hereditary captaincy of Pôrto Santo. Columbus apparently went with his wife to live in Madeira, possibly as a merchant, and remained there for two or three years. Diego, his only legitimate son, was born there in 1480. From his wife's family he probably learned much of the recent—and continuing—story of island discovery and settlement and caught the optimistic enthusiasm for new islands that was characteristic of the time. In Madeira also he would have had the opportunity to observe some of the peculiarities of the northeast trade wind.

In the early 1480s Columbus went to sea again for at least one voyage to the Gulf of Guinea, possibly in the fleet of Diogo d'Azambuja, who established the trading station and fortress of São Jorge da Mina on the Gold Coast. It is not known in what capacity he sailed. He was evidently impressed by West Africa; in later years he often compared the indigenous inhabitants of the islands he discovered with those of Guinea and repeatedly spoke of his intention of discovering a "mine" in Hispaniola. The Guinea voyage or voyages, indeed, completed his preparation for the task of discovery.

**The Enterprise of the Indies.** Though not a professional seaman, Columbus had acquired during his Portuguese years comprehensive seagoing experience in precisely those areas in which ocean exploration was most vigorous at the time. One may reasonably infer that in the same years he formed, from talk, reading, and speculation, his basic cosmographical ideas, and worked out, at least in outline, the project of western discovery that in later years he always called the Enterprise of the Indies.

The nature of Columbus's proposals is not precisely known, and his intentions have been the subject of considerable controversy. Some scholars think that he originally intended no more than the discovery of some Atlantic island, possibly Atlantis or Antilla, the legendary Isle of the Seven Cities. This hypothesis, with its implication of widespread lying or forgery on the part of Columbus's early biographers, raises more difficulties than it solves. The agreement under which he eventually sailed in 1492 commanded him to "discover islands and mainland in the Ocean Sea." This was a standard general formula, which in this instance probably included Antilla, if such a place existed. Almost certainly, however, the phrase "islands and mainland" was also understood to mean Cipangu and Cathay, the names by which Marco Polo, in the early 14th century, had described Japan and China.

There was nothing fantastic, in theory, about a proposal to reach Asia by sailing west. Because the earth was known to be round and because there was no suspicion of an intervening continent, the practical possibility depended on winds, on currents, and above all on distance. In believing that the distance might be relatively short, Columbus was following respected authorities, especially Pierre d'Ailly, whose *Imago mundi* (*Image of the World*) he had studied. His conviction was apparently strengthened by correspondence with a distinguished contemporary, the Florentine physician and cosmographer Paolo Toscanelli, who had long advocated, on theoretical grounds, the feasibility of a western route to Asia and who had, indeed, advised the Portuguese government on the subject.

**The Search for Support.** Not unnaturally, it was to the Portuguese Crown that Columbus first applied for support, in 1484, and according to the chronicler João de Barros, Cipangu was specifically mentioned in his proposals. Portugal, however, was already heavily committed to West Africa and to the search for an African route to India. Diogo Cam (or Cão) had returned from his first voyage to the Congo and had left, or was about to leave, on the second. Columbus's proposal for an expedition at royal expense was declined after a careful hearing, and in the next year he left Portugal to try his luck in Castile.

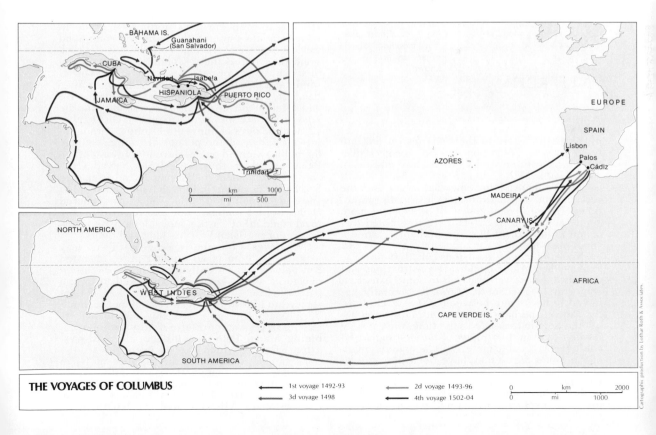

**THE VOYAGES OF COLUMBUS**

1st voyage 1492-93   2d voyage 1493-96
3d voyage 1498   4th voyage 1502-04

The disappointment of Cam's second voyage may have caused Portuguese second thoughts, for in 1488 negotiations were reopened on a hopeful note. The triumphant return of Bartholomeu Dias from the Cape of Good Hope late in that year, however, put an end to them.

Columbus, having in the interval tried England without success, turned finally to Spain. There, after many importunities, he succeeded in enlisting the support of a great officer of state, Luis de Santángel, keeper of the privy purse to King Ferdinand and treasurer of the Santa Hermandad, a police force. Santángel himself raised a considerable part of the money needed to finance the enterprise. Through him the consent and participation of the Spanish monarchs was secured. In the expansive mood induced by the capture of Granada, they agreed to all of Columbus's terms, including the handsome rewards that he was to receive in the event of success. They provided his ships and paid their crews. They furnished him with letters of credence to any sovereign princes whom he might encounter, including Marco Polo's "Great Khan." The detailed negotiations took three months. The expedition eventually sailed from Palos on Friday, Aug. 3, 1492.

**Ships and Crew.** Columbus's fleet consisted of three vessels. Two were caravels of the type commonly used in the coasting trades of Portugal and western Andalusia and on the African coast—light single-decked vessels with a minimum of superstructure and cabin accommodation. The *Pinta* had the combination of square and lateen rig recently made popular by the Portuguese. The *Niña* was lateen-rigged originally,

Columbus's enigmatic signature: The Greek and Latin elements signify "Christ-bearing," or Christopher. The meaning of the other letters is unknown.

THE GRANGER COLLECTION

but during his stay in the Canaries on the outward passage Columbus had her rerigged like the *Pinta*, with crossed yards on fore and main. The *Santa María*, the flagship, was almost certainly a *nao*, a ship somewhat larger than the caravels but still small for her class, with proportionately more beam and with higher and more ample superstructures. Her rig resembled that of the *Pinta*, except that she probably carried a small main-topsail.

None of the dimensions of the ships is known; the various modern reconstructions and models are necessarily based to some extent on conjecture. The *Santa María* is generally believed to have been between 100 and 120 tons, the caravels perhaps 60—the ton in question being the Seville *tonelada* of the time, the capacity needed to stow two pipes of wine: roughly 60 cubic feet (1.7 cubic meters). The overall length of the *Santa María* may have been between 80 and 85 feet (24 and 26 meters); that of the caravels, between 65 and 70 feet (20 and 21 meters).

Columbus thought his flagship too unwieldy for coastal exploration and preferred the caravels,

especially the *Niña*, but all three were well-found vessels, perfectly adequate, by the standards of the time, for long ocean passages, though doubtless vilely uncomfortable. They were lightly armed, for normal self-defense rather than for war. Their cargoes were the normal "trade goods"—brightly colored cloth, knives, glass beads, hawks' bells, and other trinkets—commonly used by the Portuguese for barter on the Guinea coast.

The fleet carried 90 men, of whom 40 sailed in the flagship. Except for a few clerks and officials, most of them were professional seamen recruited in the Río Tinto ports. Members of some of the leading shipowning families of the district were among the officers, and they probably did most of the recruiting. Some of these officers, especially the brothers Martín Alonso and Vicente Yáñez Pinzón, captains of the *Pinta* and the *Niña*, respectively, subsequently disputed with Columbus the principal credit for the success of the voyage.

**First Voyage.** Columbus's first transatlantic voyage can be followed in some detail from his own journal, which survives in an abstract made by the missionary and historian Bartolomé de Las Casas. Las Casas knew and admired Columbus, and there is no good reason to think that he took undue liberties with the text. The outward passage, apart from its alarming distance out of sight of land, was prosperous. A stop was made at Gomera, in the Canaries, for wood and water and some refitting. Columbus was fortunate here in that if he had sailed under Portuguese colors instead of Castilian, his last call would have been not the Canaries but the Azores, and the prevailing westerly winds in the Azores would probably have prevented his success.

His course from the Canaries lay due west, with an alteration to west-southwest 31 days out. He was thus in the most northerly latitude in which, in late summer, the northeast trade wind can be expected. In that latitude it is, indeed, somewhat unreliable. Columbus, discovering this, made his later passages considerably farther south, and this became the normal Spanish practice. In 1492, however, he was fortunate. He had a fair wind nearly all the way out, and he missed the late summer hurricanes. On October 12, after 33 days of uneventful sailing, with nothing but gulfweed and pelagic birds to encourage them, they sighted one of the outlying cays of the Bahamas, which they named San Salvador. It was probably modern Watling Island (renamed San Salvador in 1926), though a number of other sites have been proposed. The ships anchored at dawn. Columbus went ashore, bearing the royal standard of Castile, and solemnly took possession of the island for his king and queen.

Whatever Columbus's original object may have been, there is no doubt that he regarded San Salvador as an outlying island in the archipelago of which Japan was supposed to form a part—such an archipelago as is marked, for instance, on Martin Behaim's 1492 globe. Columbus apparently supported this conclusion by relying in general on Pierre d'Ailly and by combining Marco Polo's estimate of the east-west extent of Asia, which was an overestimate; the same traveler's report of the distance of Japan from the Asian mainland—1,500 miles (2,400 km), a gross overestimate; and Ptolemy's estimate of the size of the world, which was an underestimate. He assumed the length of an equatorial degree of longitude to be shorter than Ptolemy had taught, about 25% shorter than the true figure. This calculation would make the westward distance from Europe to Japan less than 3,000 nautical miles (5,550 km). The actual great circle distance is 10,000 nautical miles (18,500 km). According to Columbus's reasoning, San Salvador was near to where Japan ought to be; he seems, indeed, to have thought that the fleet had missed Japan on the outward passage, that San Salvador was farther west, and that the coast of "Cathay" was within ten days' sailing.

The next step, then, was to find Cathay itself. The expedition, threading its way to the southwest between the cays, found the northeast coast of Cuba and the north coast of Hispaniola, clothed in high forest. The indigenous peoples lived by rudimentary agriculture and by fishing and gathering mollusks. Initially they offered the Europeans little resistance. The native peoples collected small amounts of gold from streams, and the Spaniards obtained from them a few gold bracelets and nose plugs by barter. These gold trinkets sealed the ultimate fate of their owners; they indicated the potential value of the discoveries and ensured that the Enterprise of the Indies would be pursued.

Immediately, however, the search for Cathay had to be postponed. Off Hispaniola, Columbus lost his flagship, wrecked by grounding, and decided to return home, taking with him a small party of Arawak captives. He left some of his own men behind, at the harbor that he called Navidad, with instructions to build houses and search for gold mines.

On the return passage in the *Niña* Columbus made one more important discovery. To get clear of the islands he had to stand far to the north, beating against the trade wind. About the latitude of Bermuda he found a westerly wind and ran down before it to the Azores. This, like the trade-wind passage out, became standard Spanish practice. He then, however, ran into heavy weather, became separated from the *Pinta*, and was obliged to put in for shelter, first in the Azores and then in the Tagus River at Lisbon.

Here the Portuguese authorities demanded an explanation of his activities. They were skeptical of his story, contemptuous of his geographical reasoning, and unimpressed by his captive Arawaks. On the other hand, with a valuable and vulnerable trade monopoly in West Africa, and with an expedition to India under discussion, they were suspicious of all Spanish maritime activity in the Atlantic. John II decided to lay claim to Columbus's discoveries on the ground that they came within the provisions of the Treaty of Alcáçovas of 1479. With that warning he allowed Columbus to proceed to Spain.

The court was at Barcelona, and there Columbus, who had already sent letters overland from Lisbon, received a hero's welcome. Whether Ferdinand and Isabella entirely accepted his geographical reasoning is impossible to say. Some intelligent contemporaries did not; and skepticism was reflected in the early application of the name "Antillas," from Antilla or Atlantis, to the Caribbean islands. The gold and the docile natives, however, were genuine. Columbus received his titles of admiral and viceroy, his coat of arms, and the promise of a substantial share of the revenue that the discoveries were expected to yield. He was commanded to make immediate preparations for a second voyage.

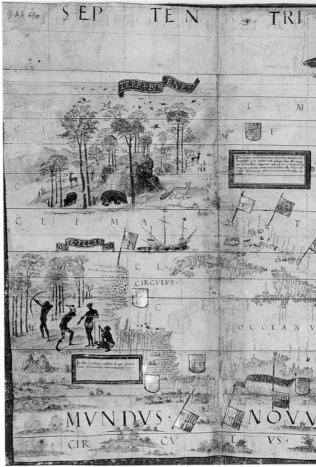

The Miller Atlas (c. 1519) imaginatively depicted the riches of the New World and its inhabitants' activities.

Meanwhile, Ferdinand and Isabella moved to counter the claim of Portugal by seeking the support of the papacy. Pope Alexander VI, himself a Spaniard, was induced to issue a series of bulls in favor of the Spanish claims, each bull successively strengthening and extending provisions of the preceding one, in accordance with successive demands by the sovereigns, on Columbus's advice. The most important of these bulls, *Inter Caetera*, divided the Atlantic into eastern and western areas of exploration and allocated the western area to Spain. This principle of demarcation, in a modified form, was finally accepted by the Portuguese government and embodied in the definitive Treaty of Tordesillas of 1494.

**Second Voyage.** Columbus was back in the West Indies long before the treaty was signed. He sailed from Cádiz on his second voyage on Sept. 25, 1493. The fleet was a large one—17 sail. It carried tools, seed, livestock, and more than 1,000 passengers: priests, gentleman-soldiers, farmers, artisans—a whole society in miniature. The purpose was to settle the island of Hispaniola and to found a mining and farming colony that would produce its own food, pay the cost of the voyages by remitting gold to Spain, and serve at the same time as a base for further exploration in search of Cathay and India. There had been no lack of volunteers, and the fitting-out, which took five months, was efficiently done. The only serious mistake was failure to provide the colony with enough food for the first year. Overoptimism about the extent to which Europeans could live off the country in the tropics was a common feature of these early explorations and one of the chief causes of the difficulties that Columbus encountered.

The fleet made an auspicious passage and a good landfall at Dominica. It sailed along the arc of the Lesser Antilles, through the Virgin Islands, past Puerto Rico, and came to the northern coast of Hispaniola. There Columbus and his men found that the settlement of Navidad had been destroyed. In selecting as the site for his second settlement the unprotected, unhealthy shore that he named Isabela, Columbus made his first serious blunder. Isabela never prospered, and Columbus paid it little attention. His energies, during this second visit to the Indies, were concentrated on the exploration, in the *Niña*, of the southern coast of Cuba—which island he declared to be a peninsula of mainland Asia—and on the discovery of Jamaica. Early in 1496 he returned to Spain to report progress and to deal with complaints carried there by malcontents from Isabela. In his absence, but with his approval, his brother Bartholomew, whom he had left in charge, organized the removal of the settlement from Isabela to a better site on the south coast, where the colonists began to build the town of Santo Domingo.

The Spanish monarchs still had no adequate return on their investment. Little gold had been collected, and systematic panning in the streams had scarcely begun. Columbus had rounded up and shipped a number of native peoples to Spain for sale as slaves, but many of them died in passage, and the rest were released by the queen's order and sent back home. The sovereigns still trusted Columbus's judgment, however, and respected their agreement with him.

**Third Voyage.** Columbus was dispatched on a third expedition at royal expense in 1498, but this time there were no volunteers, and men had to be pressed or released from prison to sail with the admiral. He steered south of his former courses and discovered the island of Trinidad, the Gulf of Paria with its two dangerous mouths and its freshwater currents issuing from the Orinoco, the beautiful Paria Peninsula, the Pearl Coast, and Margarita Island. According to Las Casas, he appreciated the continental character of the coast, but to the sovereigns he later reported that he had found the terrestrial paradise, lying at the end of the Orient. He coupled this statement with an even wilder report of a vast pear-shaped protuberance on the surface of the globe. He missed the pearl fisheries for which Margarita later became famous and sailed directly from the Venezuelan coast, by a remarkable feat of navigation, to Hispaniola, to the new settlement that his brother had established.

Columbus found the colony in an uproar. The Arawaks in the neighborhood of the settlement, long parted from their accumulation of gold trinkets, had been exasperated to the point of war by incessant demands for food and women. Half the settlers, disillusioned and hungry, were in open revolt against Bartholomew's authority. Columbus bought off the rebels with pardon and restoration to office, with land grants, and—more significant still—with a general division of the "Indians" of the island among the Spanish settlers as estate laborers or "miners."

This *repartimiento* system, imported from the Canaries, later became general in a modified form throughout the Indies. Rebellious discontent among the Spaniards was, for a time, appeased, but the damage had been done. In the spring of 1499 the sovereigns appointed Francisco de Bobadilla to supersede Columbus and to investigate the complaints against him. Bobadilla sent the admiral home, in irons. Though his sovereigns restored his titles and revenues and treated him with courtesy, Columbus was never again allowed to exercise his offices of admiral and viceroy or to intervene in the government of the Indies.

**The "High Voyage."** Columbus encountered difficulty even in securing permission and financial backing to return to the Indies, and when permission was granted and ships provided, it was on the condition that he keep away from Hispaniola, where a new governor, Nicolás de Ovando, had been appointed. Columbus—then 51, and failing in health but not in spirit—sailed in May 1502, with four caravels, on his fourth and last transatlantic voyage, the *alto viaje* ("high voyage"), as he called it, the trip that would restore his fame and fortunes. With him sailed his son Ferdinand, his brother Bartholomew, and many old friends and shipmates from Palos.

For the purpose of exploration, this was the best equipped of all the fleets he commanded. He made the fastest crossing of his career and reached Martinique in 21 days. He disobeyed instructions and approached Santo Domingo, but Ovando refused to let him land or anchor, despite the signs of an imminent hurricane. The great fleet that had brought Ovando out was on the point of sailing for Spain; it put to sea, disregarding Columbus's warning, and was almost totally destroyed. Columbus's four ships succeeded in riding out the storm, refitted in a lonely bay in southern Hispaniola, and sailed into the western Caribbean, then unexplored.

Apparently his intention, when he reached land, was to follow it to the south, in the track of Marco Polo, in search of the Golden Chersonese (the Malay Peninsula) and India. His own earlier observation of the easterly set of the equatorial current encouraged the hope of an ocean channel. Passing south of Jamaica, the ships made land on the coast of Honduras, which barred their passage to the south. They coasted slowly, first beating to the east in the teeth of the trade wind, then reaching south along the shores of Nicaragua and Costa Rica, then east along the Isthmus of Panama.

Ferdinand's eyewitness account gives many details of this careful exploration, including a major battle with the native inhabitants and the loss of two of the ships. The relatively high quality of the clothing and artifacts of the Honduran peoples was noted—the first record of European contact with any of the more developed Amerindian cultures. Much gold was obtained by barter—the Isthmus region was soon to be named Golden Castile by Spanish settlers—but no seaway was found, and in April 1503 the fleet left the coast on a northerly course for Hispaniola. It made the south coast of Cuba—according to Ferdinand, Columbus still called it "Mangi, which is part of Cathay"—and from there sailed to the north coast of Jamaica.

By this time the ships, worm-riddled after more than a year at sea, were sinking under the men. The trade wind was still impeding their progress to the east, and Columbus made the desperate decision to beach his ships in the lagoon that he called Santa Gloria, now St. Ann's Bay. Here he composed his last major dispatch to the sovereigns of Spain, the so-called *Lettera rarissima,* in which the rambling incoherencies betray the extent to which disappointment and ill health had upset the balance of his mind. A message was sent to Hispaniola by canoe. Ovando, however, made no haste to rescue Columbus and his people, and another year elapsed, during which the admiral had another mutiny to deal with, before a ship arrived. Some of the survivors elected to remain in Hispaniola, but Columbus, his brother, his son, and 22 companions finally reached Spain in November 1504.

**Last Days.** In Spain a further disappointment awaited Columbus. The fourth voyage had been a notable achievement. He had brought back a great deal of valuable information and a rich haul in gold. He might reasonably expect further recognition and reward. But the queen was dying, and the king showed little interest. Not until the spring of 1505 was Columbus granted a courteous but noncommittal audience. Columbus's interpretation of the rights that had been granted him after the first voyage differed widely from the king's and was, indeed, excessive. He pressed his claims, repeatedly, and the king wearied of his importunities.

Columbus passed the remaining year of his life, not indeed in poverty—his share of the profits of the Indies, though much less than he claimed, gave him a substantial income—but in comparative obscurity and litigious discontent. He died at Valladolid, still following the court, on May 20, 1506. His hereditary, and empty, titles of admiral and viceroy descended to his son Diego, who retained the royal favor and was appointed three years later to succeed Ovando as governor of Hispaniola. Ferdinand, the younger and illegitimate son, inherited his father's books, which he later bequeathed, along with his own substantial library, to the cathedral chapter of Seville. Some of them, with Columbus's marginal notes, may still be seen there.

Columbus was buried in Valladolid. In 1509 his body was removed to Seville. In 1541, in accordance with a wish expressed in Diego's will, the remains were shipped to Santo Domingo and interred in the cathedral there. The site has since been excavated several times. The subsequent history of the remains has been from time to time fiercely disputed, and the matter is still uncertain. No contemporary monument survives, nor any portrait of proven authenticity.

**The Man and His Achievements.** Columbus made the initial discovery from which the entire exploration and settlement of the Americas began. No disinterested contemporary doubted this, so far as we know, and no proof to the contrary has ever been produced. He discovered also the best way to make use of the North Atlantic wind system for transatlantic sailing. He began the European settlement of the West Indies, discovered the continental coast of South America, and explored the western Caribbean and revealed its landlocked outline. He first noted the equatorial current and made the first known observations of westerly compass variation.

His achievements were his own; he had loyal friends and capable lieutenants, but no intimate partners. He was a self-taught and persuasive geographical theorist, a bold and pertinacious explorer, a capable sea commander, and a careful and accurate navigator. To portray him as an unpractical visionary is mere caricature. His geographical theories were never precisely defined and, insofar as they were defined, were in some respects wildly wrong. Columbus's characteristic obstinacy and feeling of divine guidance led him to persist in them and to reject all evidence that contradicted them. But at the time he first sailed, in the light of the knowledge of that time, the theories were not absurd; they were supported by respected authorities. It was only when failing health, disappointment, and a sense of grievance began to affect the balance of his mind that he fell into fanciful and extravagant self-deception.

As a navigator he was conservative, indeed old-fashioned. He employed only the simplest method of celestial navigation, the use of the altitude of Polaris to determine latitude, and that only occasionally. There is no record of his taking sun sights; the method was new in his day, and he was probably unfamiliar with it. On the other hand, his dead reckoning had an uncanny accuracy. Once he had visited a place he could always find it again.

Gold obsessed him. Avarice apart, he knew that his credit at court depended largely on his ability to discover sources of precious things, and sometimes the immediate search for gold diverted him from major tasks of exploration. It also led him on occasion to use great cruelty toward the Amerindians. Though he was certainly not alone in brutalizing and enslaving the native peoples he encountered, he failed to check the abuses of those under his command and was directly responsible for thousands of deaths and for the imposition of the *repartimiento* system.

His undoubted powers of leadership at sea often deserted him ashore. His humble birth and foreign origin were serious handicaps. Probably, also, his intellectual and spiritual loneliness and his sense of personal mission made him arbitrary and inflexible. He had little of the

A woodcut in a 1493 Florentine edition of Columbus's letter announcing his discovery dramatizes the moment of first contact between the Old World and the New.

tact needed to handle the undisciplined individualists who first went to settle in the New World. In Hispaniola he was universally unpopular. His incompetence as an administrator led directly to his supersession.

In general, contemporary judgment of him was informed and fair. Chroniclers and officials took pride in his discoveries, which gave Spain title to a new world, but they could not ignore his limitations and failures. It was Ferdinand's filial piety that created the legend of a great man brought down by his jealous enemies.

**Sources.** Columbus's achievements were described in detail by four major writers who knew him personally: Peter Martyr, Oviedo, Las Casas, and Ferdinand Colón. Good modern editions are Peter Martyr Anghiera, *De orbe novo*, edited and translated by F. A. MacNutt, 2 vols. (New York 1912); Gonzalo Fernández de Oviedo y Valdés, *Historia general y natural de las Indias*, edited by Juan Pérez de Tudela Bueso (Madrid 1959); Bartolomé de Las Casas, *Historia de las Indias*, edited by L. Hanke and A. Millares Carlo (Mexico City 1951); Ferdinand Colón, *The Life of the Admiral Christopher Columbus by His Son Ferdinand*, edited and translated by Benjamin Keen (New Brunswick, N. J. 1959).

The principal collections of documents concerning Columbus are Martín Fernández de Navarrete, ed., *Colección de los viajes y descubrimientos*, 5 vols. (Madrid 1825–1829); *Raccolta di documenti e studi pubblicata dalla R. Commissione Colombiana*, 6 parts in 14 vols. (Rome 1892–1894); Cesáreo Fernández Duro, ed., *Pleitos de Colón*, 2 vols., being vols. 7 and 8 of second series *Colección de documentos inéditos relativos al descubrimiento . . .* (Madrid 1892–1894).

The journal of Columbus's first voyage, in Las Casas's abstract, is published in a good English translation by Oliver Dunn and James E. Kelley, Jr., revised as *The* Diario *of Christopher Columbus's First Voyage to America, 1492–1493* (Norman, Okla. 1991). *The "Libro de las Profecías" of Christopher Columbus*, translated and edited by Delno West and August Kling (Gainesville, Fla. 1991) presents his notebook of prophecies, compiled after the third voyage, which reveals his religious and millenarian concerns.

JOHN H. PARRY*, *Harvard University*
*Author of "The Spanish Seaborne Empire"*

### Bibliography

**Bedini, Silvio A.**, ed., *Christopher Columbus Encyclopedia*, 2 vols. (Simon & Schuster 1991).
**Colón, Ferdinand**, *The Life of Admiral Christopher Columbus by His Son Ferdinand*, tr. by Benjamin Keen (1959; reprint, Greenwood Press 1978).
**Crosby, Alfred W., Jr.**, *The Columbian Exchange: Biological and Cultural Consequences of 1492* (Greenwood Press 1973).
**DeVorsey, Louis, and Parker, John**, eds., *In the Wake of Columbus* (Wayne State Univ. Press 1985).
**Fagan, Brian M.**, *Kingdoms of Gold, Kingdoms of Jade: The Americas Before Columbus* (Thames & Hudson 1991).
**Fernández-Armesto, Felipe**, *Columbus* (Oxford 1991).
**Morison, Samuel Eliot**, *Admiral of the Ocean Sea*, 2 vols. (1942; reprint, Northeastern Univ. Press 1983).
**Morison, Samuel Eliot**, ed. and tr., *Journals and Other Documents on the Life and Voyages of Christopher Columbus* (Heritage Press 1964).
**Russell, Jeffrey Burton**, *Inventing the Flat Earth: Columbus and Modern Historians* (Praeger 1991).
**Ryan, S.**, *Christopher Columbus in Poetry, History, and Art* (Gordon 1976).
**Sale, Kirkpatrick**, *The Conquest of Paradise* (Knopf 1990).
**Viola, Herman J., and Margolis, Carolyn**, eds., *Seeds of Change: A Quincentennial Commemoration* (Smithsonian Press 1991).
**Wilford, John Noble**, *The Mysterious History of Columbus* (Knopf 1991).

**COLUMBUS, Diego** (1450?–1515), Italian voyager, brother of Christopher Columbus. He was born in Genoa, Italy. He sailed on his brother's second voyage to the New World in 1493 and was placed in charge of the settlements of Isabela and Santo Domingo on the island of Hispaniola. A poor administrator, he succeeded only in making a difficult situation worse by his inept handling of rapacious soldiers. Christopher, though ill, was obliged to take over the presidency of the colony's council. Diego returned to Spain in 1500 and entered the priesthood. In 1509 he sailed to Santo Domingo with his nephew Diego, but soon departed. He died in Seville, Spain, on Feb. 21, 1515.

**COLUMBUS, Diego** (c. 1480–1526), the only legitimate son and heir of Christopher Columbus. His mother was the daughter of the governor of the island of Pôrto Santo. He was born in Lisbon, Portugal. After instruction at the monastery of Santa María de Rábida, near Palos, Spain, he served as attendant to Prince Juan in the Spanish court from 1492 to 1506. He claimed his father's hereditary rights and honors and won them only after a long legal contest with King Ferdinand, largely through the influence of his wife, who belonged to the powerful Alba family.

Confirmed admiral of the Indies in 1509, he sailed to the New World and became governor of Hispaniola, where he ruled in great splendor. His enemies prompted his recall to Spain in 1523 to answer charges that were never proved. He died on Feb. 23, 1526, at Montalbán, near Toledo, Spain.

**COLUMBUS, Ferdinand** (1488–1539), the illegitimate son of Christopher Columbus. His mother was Beatriz Enríquez de Arana. He was born in Córdoba, Spain, on Aug. 15, 1488. He accompanied his father on the fourth voyage to the New World (1502–1504), and he sailed to Santo Domingo in 1509 with his half brother Diego and stayed six months. In Spain Ferdinand received large grants from the Crown, became wealthy, and collected a library of approximately 20,000 volumes. Bequeathed to the cathedral chapter of Seville, the library, now known as the Biblioteca Colombina, was greatly diminished through neglect.

Ferdinand wrote a life of his father. The original manuscript in Spanish, now lost, was taken to Italy in 1568 by Christopher's grandson Luis before a Spanish edition was printed. It was translated into Italian by Alfonso Ulloa and printed in Venice in 1571. Most of Christopher's biographers, including Bartolomé de Las Casas, drew heavily on Ferdinand's work. He died in Seville on July 12, 1539.

**COLUMBUS, Luis** (c. 1521–1572), grandson of Christopher Columbus and son of Diego Columbus. He was born in Santo Domingo and fell heir to the titles of viceroy and admiral of the Indies. The former was confirmed, but he had to relinquish the latter in 1530. In exchange, he received the island of Jamaica and an estate in Veragua (now Panama). Luis—duke of Veragua, Marquis of Jamaica, and the recipient of a large pension—was captain general of Hispaniola from 1540 to 1551. Arrested in 1559 for having three wives, he was prosecuted, imprisoned, then banished in 1565 to Africa. He died in Oran, in present-day Algeria, on Feb. 3, 1572.

**COLUMBUS,** a city in western Georgia, 100 miles (161 km) south of Atlanta, on the Chattahoochee River, opposite Phenix City, Ala. It is the seat of Muscogee county.

The city is the commercial center of Georgia's second-largest metropolitan area and the Chattahoochee Valley, and is the distribution point for farm produce of southwestern Georgia and eastern Alabama. It is a port city with docking facilities for commercial and pleasure craft. The city's industries produce cotton-processing machinery, fabricated iron and steel, concrete pipe, storage batteries, upholstery fabrics, clothing, hosiery, processed foods, packed meats, soft drinks, lumber products, and fertilizer.

Columbus is the seat of Columbus College, a four-year coeducational institution of the University System of Georgia. The Columbus Museum has an art gallery and relics of the Yuchi Indians, who originally inhabited the area. The city is also the seat of the Confederate Naval Museum, which houses the hulk of the gunboat *Muscogee*, built in Columbus and sunk in the Chattahoochee River in 1865. The Springer Opera House is a restored two-balconied Victorian theater built in 1871.

Just south of the city is Fort Benning, one of the largest infantry bases in the world, where a million officers and troops were trained during World War II. The Infantry Museum here was opened in 1960. The "Little White House," the Georgia home of President Franklin D. Roosevelt, is 32 miles (51 km) north, at Warm Springs.

Columbus was founded in 1828 when 632 lots were sold at public auction from what had been the Coweta (Indian) Reserve. The city was incorporated the same year. Columbus was active in arms manufacture and as an arsenal during the Civil War. On April 16, 1865, it was captured by Union forces; because of poor communications at the time, it was not known that Robert E. Lee had surrendered a week earlier on April 9. Population: 186,291.

JOHN R. BANISTER
*Bradley Memorial Library*

**COLUMBUS,** a manufacturing city in Indiana, the seat of Bartholomew county, 40 miles (64 km) southeast of Indianapolis. It is situated on the East Fork of the White River, in a diversified farming area. Columbus has a tannery, and its manufactures include automobile parts, diesel engines, appliances, cement products, furniture, and textiles.

Columbus is celebrated for its wealth of modern architecture. Partly as a result of the philanthropy of the Cummins Engine Foundation, which pays the architects' fees for the designs of new public schools and other public buildings, it has more buildings by distinguished architects than any other U.S. city of comparable size.

Among the architects represented by buildings in Columbus are Cesar Pelli; Roche, Dinkeloo and Associates; Robert Venturi and John Rauch; Myron Goldsmith and Charles Bassett of Skidmore, Owings, and Merrill; Harry Weese; John Carl Warnecke; Edward Larrabee Barnes; James Stewart Polshek; Eliot Noyes; Hardy Holzman Pfeiffer Associates; and I. M. Pei. In addition, Eliel and Eero Saarinen designed two churches, a bank, and a private house.

Columbus was settled in 1820 and incorporated as a city in 1854. Population: 39,059.

**COLUMBUS,** a city located in eastern Mississippi, seat of Lowndes county, situated on the Tombigbee River, 78 miles (126 km) north of Meridian. It is the trade, industrial, and shipping center for a farming and dairy region. Important manufactures are chemicals, lumber, garments, rubber, marble, bricks, and soft drinks. The city has many pre–Civil War houses. Franklin Academy, the first public school in the state, was founded here in 1821. Mississippi State College for Women, founded in 1884 as Columbus Industrial Institute and College, was the first state-supported college in the United States exclusively for women. A trading post called Possum Town was established there in 1817. Columbus was incorporated in 1884. Population: 25,944.

**COLUMBUS,** the capital of Ohio and its largest city, situated in central Ohio on the Scioto River. Columbus is the seat of Franklin county and the home of The Ohio State University. It has a sophisticated service economy.

Columbus is a planned state capital, created by an act of the General Assembly in 1812. The newly designated capital, platted into a rectangular grid and provided with a capitol, an arsenal, and a penitentiary, stood alone on the flat Central Ohio Till Plain. State government and geographic location were important factors shaping early development.

**Layout.** The intersection of Broad and High streets marks the heart of Columbus, now dominated by government buildings, high-rise offices, and corporate headquarters. City Center, established in the early 1990s, helped revitalize retailing in the downtown area. The Ohio State University's 3,300-acre (1,330-hectare) campus is about 3 miles (5 km) north of the city's core. Columbus is a city of single-family homes, with good residential areas in the city and its adjacent suburbs. Port Columbus international airport lies about 6.5 miles (10.5 km) to the east.

**Places of Interest.** The state capitol is one of the finest Greek Revival buildings in the United States. Nearby are the Center for Science and Industry, the Columbus Museum of Art (1878), and the Ohio Historical Society Museum and Village, with excellent collections depicting early Native American cultures and historical Ohioana. The Columbus Zoo, about 14 miles (23 km) north along the Scioto River, is noted for its successful breeding of gorillas. At Ohio State are the Wexner Center for the Arts and Ohio Stadium (home to the Big Ten's Buckeyes). The city has an excellent and extensive system of metropolitan parks.

In addition to Ohio State, Capital, Ohio Dominion, and Franklin universities are situated in Columbus. Ohio Wesleyan University is nearby. A rich research environment is offered by these institutions, along with the Battelle Institute (one of the largest private research organizations in the world), Chemical Abstracts, and various producers and distributors of computerized information. Cultural amenities include the Columbus Symphony, Ballet Met, Opera Columbus, and Players Theater.

**History.** Columbus grew slowly, reaching a population of 3,500 in 1834, when the city was incorporated. Early manufacturing was limited by local resources and markets. With improved transportation—turnpikes, the Ohio and Erie Canal feeder (1831), the National Road (1833), and the coming of the railroads (1850s)—manufactur-

© D. R. GOFF/QUICKSILVER PHOTOGRAPHY

Columbus's location on the Scioto River and its role as Ohio's capital, the two critical factors in its early growth, continue to influence its development.

ing expanded, drawing on the natural resources of the region. In the late 1800s Columbus became a major rail center with a distinctive industrial economy based largely on mineral resources from southeastern Ohio, such as coal, natural gas, iron ore, clay, and sand. Several nationally prominent companies produced buggies, mining machinery, cement mixers, fire engines, oilcloth, and steel castings.

With the federal government's 1941 choice of Columbus as the site of the Curtis-Wright aircraft plant, the city's economy expanded. At war's end, the large labor force, partly drawn from Appalachia and the South, helped attract manufacturers of auto parts, appliances, and electrical equipment. In succeeding decades, the city's location and its excellent interstate service and Outerbelt attracted large distribution and warehousing facilities.

An aggressive annexation program was begun in the early 1950s, whereby Columbus, which was then 52 square miles (135 sq km) in area, provided water and sewage service to suburban areas in exchange for annexation. In the 1980s Columbus, by then approximately 200 square miles (520 sq km), increased in population by 12%, which was the eighth-highest increase among the United States's top 25 cities. The city's metropolitan area grew from one county in 1950 to seven counties in 1990, making Columbus the fastest-growing metropolitan area in Ohio, in population and employment. Continued employment growth could be anticipated in the service industries, such as finance, insurance, real estate, professional and general services, retail and wholesale trade, and government. Manufacturing was expected to account for about 15% of the labor force. The city's largest employers are the state government and Ohio State University.

Population: city, 711,470; metropolitan area, 1,540,157.

HENRY L. HUNKER
*The Ohio State University*

**COLUMBUS, Knights of.** See KNIGHTS OF COLUMBUS.

**COLUMBUS DAY,** celebrated the second Monday, or the 12th, of October to honor Columbus's landing in America. It is observed annually with parades, church services, and school programs in most of the United States, parts of Canada, and many Latin American countries. The holiday was first celebrated in the United States, in 1792, the 300th anniversary of Columbus's arrival in the New World, on the initiative of the Tammany Society in New York City. A notable celebration took place in 1893, at the Columbian Exposition in Chicago.

**COLUMELLA,** kol-ū-mel′ə, **Lucius Junius Moderatus,** Roman writer of Spanish origin, who lived in the first half of the 1st century A.D. Under Emperor Tiberius (reigned 14–37 A.D.) he had a military career. Later he bought an estate in Italy and became a farmer. His works on agriculture contain much practical advice. The best known is the *De re rustica* in 12 books (one in hexameters), in which he deals with land management, viticulture, livestock, poultry and birds, fish, wild beasts, beekeeping, gardening, and the care of the farmhouse and the duties of its staff. He also wrote a book on arboriculture, a treatise against astrologers, and *De lustrationibus*, which deals with religious rites concerning agriculture. The last two of these are lost.

ARTHER FERRILL, *University of Washington*

**COLUMN,** kol′əm, in architecture, a vertical support consisting of a base, an approximately cylindrical shaft, and a capital. The term "column" is loosely used in a general sense for any isolated support, such as a post (a slender support without capital or base) or a pier, which may have a rectangular shaft or a cluster of small shafts and may lack a capital.

The earliest columns were simply tree trunks. Later, in ancient civilizations columns came to be made of stone. In modern times columns are sometimes wooden copies of stone columns. The shaft of a column is usually composed of drums or cylinders superimposed on one another, although it may be one solid piece. The unit of measurement of the height of a column is the diameter of the shaft at the base; thus, a column may be said to be ten lower diameters high.

The chief purpose of a column is to support a roof beam, entablature, or arch. Most columns are free standing; some, however, are engaged, that is, part of the circumference is embedded in a wall. Occasionally a column may stand alone as a monument, perhaps with a statue on its capital. Examples of monumental columns are the commemorative columns of Trajan and Marcus Aurelius in Rome and the Monument in London, recalling London's great fire of 1666.

**Egyptian Columns.** Many ancient Egyptian columns are derived from plant forms. A common style has a shaft grooved to look like a bundle of stems of lotus or papyrus plants. The shaft broadens slightly just above a disklike base, as do the stems of these plants above their roots. The shaft then narrows slightly toward the top, ending just below the capital in horizontal moldings that look like cords binding several stems together. (The columns of the side aisles of the Temple of Amon-Ra at Karnak keep the stem cluster's outline but have abandoned the sug-

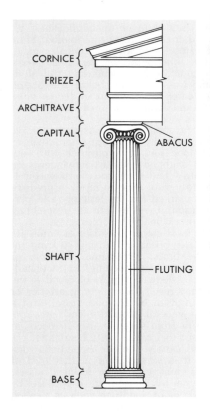

CORNICE

FRIEZE

ARCHITRAVE

CAPITAL

ABACUS

SHAFT

FLUTING

BASE

Thomas Jefferson used Ionic columns for his design of the capitol at Richmond, Va.

Drawing of an Ionic column and of the entablature, the section above the abacus.

gestion of individual stems in favor of a cylindrical shaft.) Some Egyptian capitals are shaped like a bud, bulging out above the cord and then tapering to hold a square stone block supporting the roof beam. Other capitals, suggesting a bell-shaped, open lotus, flare out to hold the block. Leaves are painted on the base of the shaft, and sepals and petals adorn the capital.

**Greek Columns.** Classical Greece developed three types of columns—*Doric, Ionic,* and *Corinthian*—that have influenced architecture ever since. A Doric column has no individual base; it rests on the stylobate (top step of the temple), which serves as a collective base for the shafts of all the columns. A Doric column is relatively short—only four diameters high in early temples, about five and a half diameters high in the Parthenon of the 5th century B.C. The shaft tapers in a flat curve, called *entasis,* but is never wider than at the bottom. The height of the shaft is accented by *fluting* (vertical grooves). In Doric columns the flutes are relatively shallow and meet in an *arris* (ridge), and their number varies from temple to temple. (The columns of the Parthenon have 20 flutes.) The Doric capital consists of a *necking,* in which the flutes terminate, a cushion-like *echinus* that bulges beyond the top of the shaft, and an *abacus,* a square block to support the entablature.

The Ionic column has a base that is usually composed of a *torus* (convex-molding), a *scotia* (concave molding), and another torus. There are variations. The Ionic shaft is taller and more slender than the Doric, with 24 semicircular flutes separated by fillets (narrow bands). The Ionic capital is distinguished by two pairs of scrolls, on the front and the back, each joined by a graceful curve under a very thin abacus. As a result, the front view of the capital differs from the side

view. Therefore, in order to give the capital at the corner of a temple a unified appearance with the capitals extending in either direction from the corner, Greek architects bent the corner scroll outward to an angle of 45 degrees.

The Corinthian column has a base and shaft similar to the Ionic. Its capital, however, is bell-shaped with two staggered rows of acanthus leaves and four small diagonal scrolls under the corners of the abacus.

**Roman and Later.** Rome inherited the Greek forms of columns and added to them the *Tuscan,* a plainer version of the Doric, and the *Composite,* whose capital combines Ionic scrolls and Corinthian leafage. The Romans also modified some other details of the older forms. For example they provided separate molded bases for the Doric column and converted the free-hand curve of its echinus into a quarter-round molding. Sometimes fluting was omitted, especially on columns made of colored marbles. According to the canon of mathematical proportions prescribed by the Roman architect Vitruvius in the 1st century B.C., the Tuscan column should be seven lower diameters in height, the Doric eight, the Ionic nine, and the Corinthian and Composite ten.

During the Middle Ages the classical orders were modified and mixed, with Byzantine, Moorish, and regional influences leading to a great variety of styles in columns. In the Renaissance such architectural theorists as Alberti, Palladio, and Vignola revived the classical orders of columns which persisted into the baroque period and the late 18th century. These forms continued to be used in the 19th and 20th centuries, especially for public buildings. See also CAPITAL; GREEK ARCHITECTURE.

EVERARD M. UPJOHN, *Columbia University*

**COLUMNIST,** the writer or editor of a *column*—a regular newspaper feature, usually with fixed title, style, and format, and with content ranging from Hollywood gossip to political opinion. The columnist, often nationally syndicated, is independent of, and possibly opposed to, the editorial policies of the newspaper in which he appears.

The practice of including articles of independent opinion in newspapers dates back to the 18th century, to the newspaper publication of such series of essays as the *Journal of Occurrences* (1768) and the famous *Federalist Papers* (1787–1788), both dealing with early American affairs. In the 19th century the emphasis turned to wit, and a number of writers, including Artemus Ward (Charles F. Browne) and Mark Twain, wrote journalistic features that evolved into humorous "colyums" of the late 19th and early 20th centuries. The best of the columns were brilliant miscellanies of quips, anecdotes, and commentary on personal or political affairs. Outstanding "colyumists" were George Ade (*Fables in Slang*) and Finley Peter Dunne (*Mr. Dooley*); Eugene Field, who wrote the famous *Sharps and Flats;* Field's successors Bert Leston Taylor, best known as B. L. T. (*Line o' Type or Two*) and Franklin P. Adams (*The Conning Tower*), who carried the Field-Taylor style from newspapers in Chicago to New York City; and Don Marquis, who created the famous cockroach "archie" in his *Sun Dial* column.

By the 1920's, the age of the political opinion column had been launched by such widely syndicated political "pundits" as Mark Sullivan, David Lawrence, and Walter Lippmann (all of whom continued writing their views for several decades). A bolder political columnist was the humanitarian Heywood Broun, with his *It Seems to Me* column.

In 1931, Drew Pearson and Robert S. Allen started an exposé column on Washington politics and political figures that made significant disclosures of graft and scandal, ending what had become too cozy a relationship between the press and politicians, and initiating a new style of sharp, aggressive political reporting. Pearson, one of the most durable and prominent of all columnists, continued writing in this vein, as did Paul Mallon, in his *News Behind the News.*

However, the main trend of Washington reporting was toward interpretation of events rather than exposé. During the Depression, and in the period following, scores of commentators rushed to explain or berate the New Deal. Notable were Raymond Clapper for objective analysis, Eleanor Roosevelt for her liberality, and the vitriolic, anti-New Deal Westbrook Pegler. Later famous political columnists included Joseph and Stewart Alsop, Marquis Childs, Doris Fleeson, Ernest K. Lindley, Dorothy Thompson, and James Reston.

Columnists in other areas included Hearst editor Arthur Brisbane, who established the abbreviated mode of later tabloid editorials in his widely syndicated *Today* column; such Broadway and Hollywood gossip writers as Leonard Lyons, Dorothy Kilgallen, Louella Parsons, and Hedda Hopper, who wrote their columns in the usually flamboyant style set by Walter Winchell in the 1920's; sports columnists Grantland Rice and Arthur Daley; and the advice-to-the-lovelorn specialists, Dorothy Dix and the sisters Ann Landers and Abigail Van Buren.

**COMA,** kō′mə, is a state of unconsciousness resulting from either temporary or permanent brain injury. A comatose state always indicates major damage to the functioning of the many nerve cells that, in complex ways, maintain full alertness. The affected cells may be in the brain's surface layers (cerebral cortex) or in deeper areas (diencephalon and brainstem) near the brain's midline.

A person in a comatose state is unresponsive to stimuli that normally interrupt sleep, such as a bright light, loud sound, or pinprick, although he may show slight automatic movements in response to pain. The transition from wakefulness to a comatose state may be rapid or gradual. Generally, it is marked first by lethargy and perhaps by confusion, then by stupor resembling light sleep, before it finally becomes coma.

Among the most common causes of coma are head injuries that produce bruising, tearing, or bleeding of the brain; intracranial bacterial or viral infections that cause meningitis, encephalitis, or both; an inadequate supply of blood to the brain, which may result from clots in arteries or veins or by a rupture of a blood vessel, and a drastic drop in general arterial blood pressure, which may result from severe injury or occur in shock or a myocardial infarction ("heart attack"). Other common causes include metabolic disorders leading to a severe drop in the level of blood sugar or causing liver or kidney failure; and various types of poisoning, especially by carbon monoxide or by sedatives such as alcohol.

Early diagnosis and treatment are essential if irreparable brain damage is to be averted. The urgent need is to care for any impairments in circulation or respiration while a diagnostic examination and laboratory tests are carried out.

E. CHARLES KUNKLE, M.D.,
*Maine Medical Center*

**COMANA,** kō-mä′nə, was the name of two ancient religious centers in Asia Minor. One of them, an ancient city of Cataonia in Cappadocia, was located on the upper Sarus River (now the Göksu) in the Anti-Taurus Mountains, on the site of present-day Sar. It eventually came to be also known as Hieropolis. This Comana was famous in antiquity for its temple of Ma-Enyo, a version of the mother goddess of Anatolia, who was worshiped with wild and ecstatic rites. The sanctuary's foundation was supposedly connected with Orestes. The adjoining settlement grew greatly as a result of the sanctuary's fame. Strabo relates that there were over 6,000 temple slaves, both men and women; that the sanctuary owned estates that provided large revenues; and that the high priest held complete power there, ranking second to the king in Cappadocia, and was usually a member of the royal family.

The other Comana, an ancient city in Pontus, was located on the Iris River (modern Yesilırmak), on the site of modern Gümenek, 6 miles (10 km) northeast of Tokat. Said to have been colonized from Comana in Cappadocia, it too had a sanctuary of Ma-Enyo, the richest sanctuary in the kingdom of Pontus, with a high priest of high rank, large estates, and many temple slaves. In 34 A.D. the settlement was made a city and incorporated into what was then the Roman province of Pontus, thus losing its previous state of near-independence.

D. J. BLACKMAN
*University of Bristol, England*

**COMANCHE INDIANS,** kə-man'chē, a North American Indian tribe living entirely on the Southwestern plains. The name Comanche means "enemies" in the Ute language. The traditions and language of the Comanche so closely resemble those of the Shoshoni of Wyoming that it is probable that the two tribes were formerly one.

In the 18th century the Spanish explorers Ulibarri and Valverde reported that the Comanche were replacing the Apache in eastern Colorado and eastern New Mexico. Valverde also learned that the French were approaching New Mexico from the east. The almost continuous wars between the Comanche and their traditional enemies, the Apache, were partly to determine who would trade with the French. Apparently the Comanche won, for in 1719 the French trader Du Tisne was visited only by that tribe during his visit in eastern Colorado. In 1739 only Comanche Indians were seen, and in 1744 a group of Frenchmen traded guns with them.

The Comanche were famed as the finest horsemen of the West, and their rise to power depended on their having many horses, most of which they stole from Spanish settlements. They obtained an abundance of firearms and ammunition from the French. A warlike tribe, the Comanche grasped their opportunities and enlarged their area of influence, plundering settlers and Indians alike from Colorado to northern Mexico. This continued until 1786, when a peace treaty was signed with the New Mexican governor, Juan Bautista de Anza.

In 1795, after a war with the Kiowa Indians, the two tribes formed a close confederation, and their center of activity shifted to Texas and Oklahoma. Treaties were signed by the United States and the Comanche in 1835 and 1865, and in 1875 the Comanche finally surrendered and agreed to remain on a reservation in Oklahoma.

From lowly cultural beginnings, the Comanche became typical Plains Indians in their material culture. They were wealthy in horses, firearms, skin tepees and clothing, and food. Horses, essential as beasts of burden and for personal transportation, were frequently used as gifts or payment and as tokens of prestige. Because horses had a practical and emotional value, Comanche herds were immense. One Indian was reputed to have owned more than a thousand horses.

Before 1875 the Comanche were chiefly a nomadic tribe, and their food, fuel, clothing, and shelter came from buffalo, which were run down by individuals or in great communal hunts. Dried meat was stored in rawhide boxes or envelopes, called *parfleches*. Their vegetable food consisted of wild seeds and berries, as well as corn (maize), obtained by trade or plunder from Spanish and Mexican Indians.

Although the Comanche developed an efficient military organization and acquired an exaggerated interest in individual war honors, they never attained the complex social and political institutions characteristic of other Plains tribes. Their 12 divisions, or bands, were politically autonomous, bound only by friendship.

The earliest population estimate, probably exaggerated, was 25,000 Comanche in 1780. An epidemic reduced the figure to 9,000 in 1816. In 1910 the figure had shrunk to 1,500. In 1960 there were estimated to be 3,000 Comanche on the Kiowa Reservation in Oklahoma.

OMER C. STEWART, *University of Colorado*

**COMANCHEAN SERIES,** kə-man'chē-ən, a series in the lower Cretaceous System of rocks, formed in the Comanchean Epoch about 120 million years ago. The typical exposure of the series, named for the Comanche Indians, is on the Gulf Coast of Texas. Comanchean sedimentary rocks overlie those of the Coahuilan Series in the deep subsurface, but on the outcrop they overlap on Paleozoic rocks. They are overlain (with regional unconformity) by Woodbine Sandstone of the Upper Cretaceous.

The Comanchean Series contains the Trinity, Fredericksburg, and Washita Stages. These rocks consist of marine shales and limestones that pass northwards into sands that were deposited on the shore of an advancing sea. The rocks outcrop eastward along the Gulf Coast to Alabama, where they pass into the subsurface and their thickness reaches several thousand feet. In northern Mexico, Comanchean limestones (with associated gypsum) overlap the Coahuilan Series of rocks in the state of Coahuila.

Comanchean rocks are equivalent to the European Aptian and Albian stages of the Cretaceous System, and are classified under these names in much of North America. Among the frequent and distinctive fossils that are found in Comanchean rocks are rudistids, which were very thick-shelled mollusks that formed reefs and were related to oysters.

See also CRETACEOUS.

MARSHALL KAY
*Columbia University*

**COMAYAGUA,** kō-mä-yä'gwä, the former capital of Honduras, is a small city about 65 miles (100 km) northwest of Tegucigalpa by road. A community of cobbled streets and low whitewashed buildings, it has many buildings of architectural interest including 16th century churches and the early 18th century cathedral.

Comayagua was founded around 1540, and it developed as the administrative center of what is now the republic of Honduras. When Honduras became independent in 1838, the city was made the capital, but in 1880 the government moved to Tegucigalpa. Comayagua is now the capital of a department of the same name and is the trade center of a farming region that produces coffee and staple food crops. Population: of the city, 39,500 (1989 est.); of the department, 257,000 (1991 est.).

**COMAYAGÜELA,** kō-mä-yä-gwä'lä, is the twin city of Tegucigalpa, which is the capital of Honduras. The two communities, of about equal population, form contrasting halves of a single urban area administered since 1938 as the Central District, in Francisco Morazán department. They are separated by the steep-banked Choluteca River, spanned here by three bridges including the Puente Mallol, which was constructed in colonial times.

Comayagüela, which is located south and west of Tegucigalpa, stands on level terrain and was laid out in the 19th century with a checkerboard street plan; Tegucigalpa, by contrast, is much older, is built on hilly ground, and has many winding, narrow streets. There is a large central market in Comayagüela, some light industry, and a school of arts and crafts. An obelisk on the southern outskirts commemorates the first 100 years of Central American independence. Population: city, 36,414 (1988 census); department, 239,859 (1988 census).

Combs have been used both for practical and for decorative purposes since prehistoric times. They may have either one or two rows of teeth, as illustrated by the examples on this page.

Ancient combs: *(right)* archaic Greek, 7th century B.C.; *(below)* Egyptian Coptic, 324–640 A.D.

MUSEUM OF FINE ARTS, BOSTON

MUSEUM OF FINE ARTS, BOSTON

COOPER UNION MUSEUM, NEW YORK

Decorative comb *(above),* probably of Spanish origin, meant to be used with a lace mantilla headcovering.

**COMB,** a toothed implement for arranging or adorning the hair. The word probably derives from the Greek *gamphos* ("peg") or *gamphē* ("jaw"). Combs are used by most peoples. They may be of wood, bone, shell, ivory, metal, rubber, or synthetic materials such as plastic. Combs may have one row of teeth of two rows on opposite edges, and they may be highly decorated.

Combs for unsnarling and smoothing the hair, called small-toothed combs, usually are long with short teeth; half of a single row or one of two rows of teeth is often coarser. Combs for holding the hair in place and ornamenting it are generally shorter with a single row of longer teeth.

**Early Combs.** The earliest combs, dating from the Stone Age, are of wood or bone with a simple curved back and a single row of triangular teeth. Undecorated double-edged combs appeared in the Bronze Age. It is difficult to tell whether some of these early combs were used for arranging hair or for weaving cloth.

The first decorated combs were produced after 1000 B.C., especially in Egypt, where thick wigs were fashionable, and in Assyria, where men wore heavily curled hair and beards. Some of these wood or ivory double-edged combs were elaborately carved on both sides with the center design cut out. Others had incised or relief decoration.

**Combs in the West.** In the Middle Ages (and still today in the Roman Catholic Church) ivory combs were liturgical objects used during the consecration of a bishop. Such combs, usually double-edged, might be intricately carved with foliage, figures, or typical Christian symbols such as chalices and crosses, or they might be inlaid or jeweled. The same richness characterized secular combs used by the nobility, especially those of the 14th, 15th, and 16th centuries, which were decorated with floral scrolls, pastoral scenes, and legendary characters.

In the 17th century and later periods, whenever women wore their own long hair uncovered and elaborately dressed, they sometimes used combs as ornaments; for example, Spanish women wore a high, carved tortoiseshell comb to support a mantilla. In the late 17th century and early 18th century, when fashionable men and women wore long curled wigs, they combed them in public. The short hairstyles of the 20th century have sharply reduced the use of ornamental combs.

**Combs in the Non-Western World.** In the East the traditional dress of Chinese, Indonesian, and Japanese women often included one or more ornamental, single-edged combs. Pronglike teeth surmounted by a carved panel held a bun or locks of hair in place. Such combs were made of tortoiseshell, ivory, or metal, the material and decoration, sometimes inlaid, indicating the wearer's rank or the occasion. In the South Sea Islands, men wear ornamental combs. In Melanesia these combs are made of long sticks of wood or bamboo in a whisk broom shape, the tops adorned with beads, shells, or feathers; on other islands high wooden combs are decorated with geometric cutouts (Samoa), inlaid mother-of-pearl (northern Celebes), or carved handles representing ceremonial headdresses (Admiralty Islands). Ornamental wood or ivory combs with carved figures are traditionally worn by some African Negroes. American Indian tribes made wood or bone single- or double-edged combs, some richly carved with figures, as in the Pacific Northwest.

PENELOPE TRUITT
*Museum of Fine Arts, Boston*

**COMB JELLY,** any of a small phylum of delicate, gelatinous invertebrate animals that inhabit all seas, from the Arctic to the Antarctic. Also called *ctenophores*, they are so transparent that they are all but invisible as they drift or swim slowly at the surface of the water.

Comb jellies range in size from small oval or rounded animals less than an inch (less than 2.5 cm) in length to ribbonlike forms 4¼ feet (113 cm) long. The most prominent feature of the comb jelly is the rippling iridescence of eight vertical rows of beating combs that radiate from the upper to the lower pole of its body and propel it through the water. Each comb consists of large cilia fused at their attached ends like the teeth of a comb. At night, the iridescence is replaced by luminescence.

Another unique feature of the comb jelly is the adhesive cells (colloblasts) that stud its tentacles, which are found on each side of the body between two comb rows. Small struggling prey adhere to the protruding sticky heads of these cells and cannot pull themselves loose because each cell is attached at its inner end to a yielding, spirally coiled filament. The extended tentacle then is shortened, and the prey is swept through the mouth into the gastrovascular cavity, a large branching sac, that serves both for digestion and distribution of food. Between the digestive lining and the delicate outer covering is a mass of jelly containing muscle fibers. The swimming movements of the comb jelly are coordinated by a network of nerve cells that connect at the upper pole to a small sense organ, the statocyst, which acts as a balancing device.

Comb jellies are hermaphroditic; that is, each individual has both eggs and sperm. The sex cells are released through the mouth into the sea, where fertilization and development occur.

The phylum Ctenophora is divided into two classes, the Tentaculata which have tentacles, and the Nuda, which lack tentacles.

RALPH BUCHSBAUM AND MILDRED BUCHSBAUM
*University of Pittsburgh*

**COMBAT NEUROSIS,** noo-rō′sis, is a special type of traumatic or transient neurosis. It has been called by several names, including *combat fatigue, operational fatigue,* and *shell shock.* It is delineated more by the special circumstances under which it occurs than by any unique and specific symptoms.

In combat neurosis the individual, prior to the development of his neurosis, has often undergone prolonged, violent emotional experiences. He has been excessively fatigued. He has lacked emotional supports to relieve pent-up feelings. He has a general feeling of helplessness, a feeling that he has no control over what will happen to him. Also, he has been in an ego-thwarting situation for a good many weeks. He has had to lay aside his personal plans, and his own style of living.

Even in such conditions, most military personnel and civilians in a war zone do not become psychiatric casualties. U.S. Army experience in World War II was that only an estimated 10% of men in combat developed combat neurosis. Those who do develop symptoms do not break down because of a single battle episode. Their neurosis is a consequence of the special factors associated with the combat zone over a period of time, plus a critical incident.

**Symptoms.** The symptoms of combat neurosis

JACK DERMID

COMB JELLIES, such as these "sea gooseberries" (*Pleurobrachia*), inhabit every sea throughout the world.

are extremely varied: some patients lose all feelings in a limb, while others may display hysterical paralysis, hysterical blindness, or hysterical deafness. Some patients become mute and appear to be in a stupor. Others are agitated and unable to be still. Some seem depressed, but others appear to be overexcited. The symptom picture is so varied that it is not possible to diagnose combat fatigue on the basis of the symptoms presented by the patient. The diagnosis is made after consideration of the suddenness of the onset of the disorder, the special circumstances under which the individual had been existing, and certain secondary character changes more or less common to all patients who exhibit the disorder. Almost all of these patients have terrifying battle dreams. Most patients also exhibit decreased control as manifested by irritability, oversensitivity to noise or to being startled by any means, and over-reaction to minor irritations. They also show inability to concentrate and a restriction of interest.

**Treatment.** Experience during World War II demonstrated that best results in treating combat neurosis occur if the patient is treated as close to the combat zone as possible and within a few days of the terrifying critical incident. Many men were able to return to combat duty after two or three days of rest and psychotherapy. When men who had had slight combat experience prior to the breakdown were treated close to the combat zone, approximately 90% recovered and returned to duty; but only 35% of those who had undergone prolonged combat experience recovered and returned to combat duty. When men were treated several hundred miles from the combat zone, only 10% recovered and were returned to combat duty. Thus, a delay in treatment and the removal of the men from the combat zone appeared to fixate the symptoms.

AUSTIN E. GRIGG, *University of Richmond*

**COMBE,** ko͞om, **William** (1741–1823), English writer, who is best remembered as the author of the "Dr. Syntax" series. He was born in Bristol, England, in 1741 and was educated at Eton College and Oxford University. In 1762 he received a legacy, which he squandered so recklessly that he became known as "Count Combe." Constantly in debt, he served as a cook, waiter, and private soldier. About 1771 or 1772 he began to write anonymously for London booksellers to avoid recognition by his creditors.

Combe's three Dr. Syntax books were written in verse to accompany the drawings of Thomas Rowlandson. The series, which depicts the adventures of Dr. Syntax, clergyman and teacher, includes *The Tour of Dr. Syntax in Search of the Picturesque* (1812), *The Tour of Dr. Syntax in Search of Consolation* (1820), and *The Tour of Dr. Syntax in Search of a Wife* (1821). Combe died in London on June 19, 1823.

**COMBES,** kônb, **Émile** (1835–1921), French politician, who was premier of France from 1902 to 1905. Justin Louis Émile Combes was born on Sept. 6, 1835 at Roquecourbe. In preparation for the priesthood he took a doctorate in theology and taught for a time in Catholic schools. Later, breaking with the church, he trained in medicine and became a practicing physician.

Combes began his career in national politics when he was elected to the Senate. He was an active member of the left wing and a staunch opponent of church influence in education and politics. An ardent believer in the innocence of Alfred Dreyfus, the French officer who had been convicted of high treason in a case fraught with overtones of anti-Semitism and conspiracy, Combes firmly supported René Waldeck-Rousseau's cabinet (1899–1902), which, in the aftermath of the Dreyfus affair, attempted to curb the influence of the church and army. In June 1902 he succeeded Waldeck-Rousseau as premier, also heading the ministries of the interior and of religions.

Whereas Waldeck-Rousseau had sought to bridge the divisions created by the Dreyfus affair, Combes gave his ministry a belligerently anticlerical tone. He rigorously enforced earlier curbs on church schools and under a 1904 law forbade the religious congregations to teach. He also severed diplomatic relations with the Vatican in 1904. He resigned in January 1905 when his former war minister, Gen. Louis André, was revealed to have used secret reports on the reactionary political views and religious sympathies of army officers to block their promotions. He returned to the Senate but never regained importance. He died in Pons on May 24, 1921.

JOEL COLTON, *Duke University*

**COMBINATIONS AND MERGERS.** "Combination" is a general term meaning an association between two entities by set agreement in order to accomplish some aim by joint operation such as, a combination of labor or capital. The term "merger," more precisely, denotes an absorption, so as to involve a loss of identity. Thus, the property of the merged corporation is transferred to the surviving corporation, and the former ceases to exist. In a "consolidation," however, both corporations end their existence and become parties to a new one. See also ANTITRUST LAWS; CARTEL; CONSPIRACY; MERGER; MONOPOLY.

PETER D. WEINSTEIN, *Member, New York Bar*

**COMBINATIONS AND PERMUTATIONS,** kom-bə-nā′shənz, pər-mū tā′shənz. In the branch of mathematics known as combinatorial analysis, a combination is a grouping of objects that is made without respect to their order, while a permutation is an ordered grouping. For example, the sequences of letters *abc, acb,* and *bca* all represent the same combination of letters, but each sequence represents a different permutation. Combinatorial analysis is used widely in the mathematical theory of probability and statistics and has many applications in the modern theory of games. There are, in fact, important applications in just about every field of modern science —mathematical, physical, biological, and social.

**History.** The great Hindu mathematician Brahmagupta (born 598 A.D.) gave many of the rules for combinations and permutations. The Jewish scholar Levi ben Gershon (born 1288) determined the number of simple permutations of *n* objects by use of mathematical induction, perhaps the first use of this method, which was not formally stated until more than four centuries later. In the 15th century there began to appear a systematic interest in the mathematical problems of combinations and permutations with various applications, such as the throwing of dice. In the 16th century the Frenchman Johannes Buteo discussed the mathematics of dice games and the theory of a type of combination lock that could be opened only when the letters stamped on movable cylinders were lined up in a certain order.

Serious research in the general mathematical theory of combinations and permutations came in the 17th and 18th centuries with the great mathematicians Fermat, Pascal, and Pierre Rémond de Montmort in France, de Moivre and John Wallis in England, Jacques Bernoulli and Euler in Switzerland, Huygens in Holland, and Leibniz in Germany. In most cases the study was prompted by questions in probability and games of chance. The theory was further developed by Laplace in the early 19th century and later by the British mathematicians Augustus de Morgan and Percy A. MacMahon, among others. Today, combinatorial analysis is developing rapidly through new mathematical techniques, aided by the use of computers.

### PERMUTATIONS

An arrangement of a set of objects in some linear order (that is, in a straight line), is called a permutation of these objects. Given a set of *n* objects, the linearly ordered arrangement of *r* of them is called a permutation of *n* objects taken *r* at a time. For example, given the set *a,b,c,d* of four letters, how many different ordered arrangements of three letters can be formed? Think of the problem in terms of three boxes, numbered by their order from left to right (Fig. 1) into each of which one letter is to be placed. In the first box we can put any one of the four letters. For each such choice we can put any one of three into the second box and, lastly, any one of two into the third box. The result then is $4 \cdot 3 \cdot 2 = 24$ different arrangements:

| | | | |
|-----|-----|-----|-----|
| abc | bac | cab | dab |
| abd | bad | cad | dac |
| acb | bca | cba | dba |
| acd | bcd | cbd | dbc |
| adb | bda | cda | dca |
| adc | bdc | cdb | dcb |

A handy technique for finding all the permutations is the following. Write down the letter *a*.

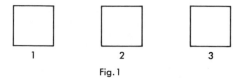

Fig. 1

From *a* draw three prongs. After each prong write one of the remaining letters in order. From each of these letters draw two prongs. After each of these prongs write the remaining letters in order, omitting those connected to *a* by a prong. Repeat the same process starting with *b,c,d* in turn. (Fig. 2)

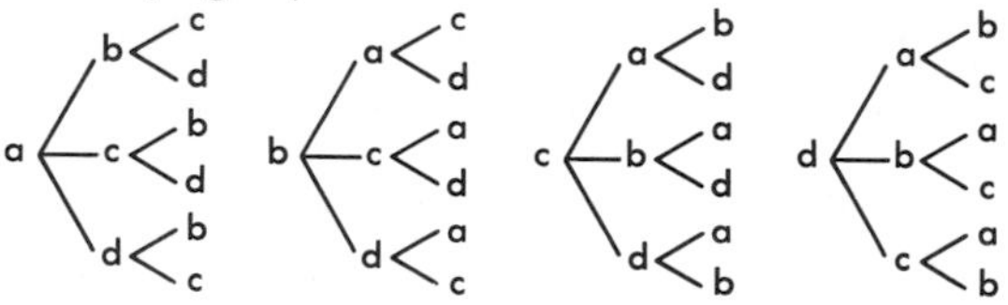

Fig. 2

If $P(n,r)$ denotes the number of permutations of *n* objects *r* at a time, where $n \geq r$, a generalization of the example above gives:

$$P(n,r) = n(n-1) \cdots (n-r + 1)$$
$$= \frac{n(n-1) \cdots (n-r + 1) \ (n-r) \ (n-r-1) \cdots 1}{(n-r) \ (n-r-1) \cdots 1}$$
$$= n!/(n-r)!$$

Thus, in the example of the letters, $P(4,3) = \frac{4!}{(4-3)!} = \frac{4 \cdot 3 \cdot 2 \cdot 1}{1} = 24$. The expression $n!$, called *n*-factorial, represents the product of all integers from 1 to *n*. The factorial notation was introduced by the German mathematician Christian Kramp in 1808.

By definition, $0! = 1$. Thus, if $r = n$, then $P(n,n) = \frac{n!}{0!} = n!$. As *n* increases, the value of $P(n, n)$ grows rapidly. For example, the number of ways the 30 volumes of *The Encyclopedia Americana* can be arranged on a shelf—$P(30,30)$ —is $30! = 265,252,859,812,191,058,636,308,480,-000,000$. At the rate of one permutation every 5 seconds, working 24 hours a day, 7 days a week, it would take more than $4.2 \times 10^{25}$ years to complete the task—vastly longer than the age of the universe, estimated by scientists to be less than $1.0 \times 10^{10}$ years.

If, of the *n* objects, *p* are of one type and *q* of another type, the number of permutations of the *n* objects is given by $P = \frac{n!}{p! \ q!}$. For example, the number of different arrangements of the five letters *a,a,a,b,b* is $P = \frac{5!}{3! \ 2!} = \frac{5 \cdot 4 \cdot 3 \cdot 2 \cdot 1}{(3 \cdot 2 \cdot 1) \ (2 \cdot 1)} = 10$. The formula may be arrived at by noting that if all the objects were distinct each arrangement above would produce $p!q!$ times as many ordered arrangements.

The above cases have the restriction that each object can appear just once in a given permutation. If this condition is removed, then each of the *r* places can be filled in *n* different ways. For example, if a zero or one is put in each of the three boxes in Fig. 1, the number of permutations is equal to the product $2 \cdot 2 \cdot 2 = 2^3 = 8$.

In general if repetition is allowed, the permutation of *n* objects taken *r* at a time is given by $n^r$.

**Circular Permutations.** If the objects are arranged in a circle, then only the relative order as the circle is traversed in a definite sense is significant. To solve this type of problem, fix one object arbitrarily and calculate the number of permutations of the remaining objects as if they were in a straight line. Thus *n* distinct objects can be arranged in a circle in $(n-1)!$ ways. For example, five people can be arranged at a circular table in $4! = 24$ ways. Given 10 beads of different colors, how many different necklaces can be formed by stringing all the beads together? Here the answer is not 9!, for if the beads are arranged in a particular order, another order identical to the first but counted as distinct in the 9! is obtained by turning the necklace over. Thus the answer is $\frac{1}{2}(9!) = 181440$.

**Derangements.** Given a set of *n* distinct objects in a determined order, a derangement is a permutation such that exactly *k* objects are in their original positions. The number of derangements for the set is given by

$$D(n,k) = \frac{n!}{k!} \left(1 - \frac{1}{1!} + \frac{1}{2!} - \cdots + \frac{(-1)^{n-k}}{(n-k)!}\right)$$

The number of ways five numbered balls can be drawn from a box so that no ball is drawn out in its proper order is $D(5,0) = \frac{5!}{0!}(1 - 1 + \frac{1}{2!} - \frac{1}{3!} + \frac{1}{4!} - \frac{1}{5!}) = 44$. By noting that the series in parentheses is a truncated form of the expansion of $e^{-1}$, where *e* is the base of the natural logarithms, we find that $D(n,k)$ is the nearest integer to $\frac{n!}{k! \ e}$. This is often a help in computation, since the value of *e* is known (approximately 2.718).

A problem related to that of derangement is the famous problem of Latin squares, first studied by Euler. A Latin square is a *n* x *n* square in which objects 1,2, ..., *n* are placed so that each object appears exactly once in each row and exactly once in each column. Two Latin squares are called *orthogonal* if, when one square is superimposed on the other, each object of the first square occurs once and only once with each object of the second square, that is, every element of the combined square is distinct. The two 4 × 4 Latin squares in Fig. 3 are orthogonal. Latin squares are so called because in Euler's time they were written with Latin letters as elements. Euler conjectured that there are no orthogonal Latin squares of order $4n + 2$ for $n > 1$. Only in 1959 was this shown to be false. But no general closed formula for the number of distinct Latin squares of arbitrary order *n* has been found.

Two orthogonal Latin squares and their superpositions.

Fig. 3

| 1 | 2 | 3 | 4 |
|---|---|---|---|
| 2 | 1 | 4 | 3 |
| 3 | 4 | 1 | 2 |
| 4 | 3 | 2 | 1 |

| 1 | 2 | 3 | 4 |
|---|---|---|---|
| 3 | 4 | 1 | 2 |
| 4 | 3 | 2 | 1 |
| 2 | 1 | 4 | 3 |

| 11 | 22 | 33 | 44 |
|----|----|----|----|
| 23 | 14 | 41 | 32 |
| 34 | 43 | 12 | 21 |
| 42 | 31 | 24 | 13 |

## COMBINATIONS

A set of $r$ objects selected from a given set of $n$ objects, without regard to order is called a *combination* of $n$ things taken $r$ at a time. The number of combinations is denoted by $C(n,r)$.

Since each combination of $r$ objects can be ordered in $r!$ ways, we can find $C(n,r)$ by ignoring the order of objects in $P(n,r)$, that is,

$$C(n,r) = \frac{P(n,r)}{r!} = \frac{n!}{r!(n-r)!}.$$ The four letters

$a,b,c,d$, can be put in sets of two in six different

ways, since $C(4,2) = \dfrac{4!}{2!\,(4-2)!} = \dfrac{4 \cdot 3 \cdot 2 \cdot 1}{(2 \cdot 1)\,(2 \cdot 1)} =$

6. The six ways are: $ab,ac,ad,bc,bd,cd$. Note

that $C(n,r) = \dfrac{n!}{r!\,(n-r)!} = C(n,n-r)$. *Thus,*

for example, given five objects the number of ways three may be selected is the same as the number of ways two may be selected, for every time three are selected, two are left behind. Another important relation is given by $C(n,r) = C(n-1,\ r-1) + C(n-1,r)$, where $n \geq r$. This relation can be shown algebraically or by noting that the combinations may be divided into two classes, those which contain a certain object and those which do not contain it. The number of combinations containing the object is $C(n-1,r-1)$ since one element is fixed. The number of combinations that do not contain the object is $C(n-1,r)$, since there is one less object in the set from which the objects are selected.

If unlimited repetition of objects is allowed, the number of combinations of $n$ objects taken $r$ at a time is given by $C(n+r-1,r)$. With repetition allowed, the four letters $a,b,c,d$, can be formed into ten different combinations of two

since $C(4+2-1,2) = C(5,2) = \dfrac{5!}{2!\quad 3!} = 10.$

**Relation to Binomial Theorem.** An interesting and important connection exists between com-

| n＼r | 0 | 1 | 2 | 3 | 4 | 5 | 6 | 7 | 8 | 9 | 10 |
|---|---|---|---|---|---|---|---|---|---|---|---|
| 0 | 1 | | | | | | | | | | |
| 1 | 1 | 1 | | | | | | | | | |
| 2 | 1 | 2 | 1 | | | | | | | | |
| 3 | 1 | 3 | 3 | 1 | | | | | | | |
| 4 | 1 | 4 | 6 | 4 | 1 | | | | | | |
| 5 | 1 | 5 | 10 | 10 | 5 | 1 | | | | | |
| 6 | 1 | 6 | 15 | 20 | 15 | 6 | 1 | | | | |
| 7 | 1 | 7 | 21 | 35 | 35 | 21 | 7 | 1 | | | |
| 8 | 1 | 8 | 28 | 56 | 70 | 56 | 28 | 8 | 1 | | |
| 9 | 1 | 9 | 36 | 84 | 126 | 126 | 84 | 36 | 9 | 1 | |
| 10 | 1 | 10 | 45 | 120 | 210 | 252 | 210 | 120 | 45 | 10 | 1 |

Fig. 4

binations and the coefficients of the terms in the expansion of $(x+y)^n$. The table in Fig. 4 gives the values of $C(n,r)$ for values of $n$ up to 10. The table is actually a form of what is generally known as Pascal's triangle. Each row gives the coefficients of terms in the expansion of $(x+y)^n$, for example, $(x+y)^4 = x^4 + 4x^3y + 6x^2y^2 + 4xy^3 + y^4$. The triangle is easily extended since

any term is the sum of the term immediately above it and the one to the left of this term. Thus, the first 15 in row six is the sum of $5 + 10$. This is due to the relation $C(n,r) = C(n-1, r-1) + C(n-1,r)$ noted above.

For $n$ a positive integer, the binomial theorem is: $(x+y)^n = C(n,0)x^n + C(n,1)x^{n-1}y + C(n,2)x^{n-2}y^2 + \ldots + C(n,r)x^{n-r}y^r + \ldots + C(n,n)y^n$. By setting $x = y = 1$ in the binomial theorem, we get $2^n = C(n,0) + C(n,1) + C(n,2) + \ldots + C(n,n)$. Given a set of $n$ elements, $C(n,r)$ is the number of subsets having $r$ elements, so $2^n$ is the total number of possible subsets, including the set itself and the empty set (the set having no elements). Often the

symbol $\begin{pmatrix} n \\ r \end{pmatrix}$, introduced by the German math-

ematician Andreas von Ettingshausen in 1827, is used in place of $C(n,r)$.

FRANCIS A. GREENE, S. J.
*Xavier University, Cincinnati*

**COMBINE,** a machine that combines harvesting with threshing. As it moves across the field, it divides the crop into bunches by projections on the cutter bar, cuts it with a reciprocating knife, and feeds it into a threshing cylinder. The straw is laid on the ground and the grain poured into sacks, a tank, or a truck.

Designs for a combine were patented in the United States in 1828 by Samuel Lane and in 1838 by Hiram Moore and J. Hascall. From about 1875 the combine was used on farms in California, where it enabled four men with a team of 24 or more mules or horses to harvest 25 acres (10 hectares) a day. Its use spread, but it was not widely employed on the Great Plains until 1920. Animal power was replaced successively by steam- and gasoline-engine tractors. In 1935 the one-man combine was introduced for the smaller farm, and the self-propelled combine came into vogue during the agricultural boom of World War II.

**COMBUSTION** is a chemical process that liberates heat. The word carries the connotation of fire or flame. Combustion can be described as the combination of an oxidizer with a fuel, for example, oxygen with petroleum, to produce compounds such as carbon dioxide and water. Processes of this type are important in home and industrial furnaces, various engines, and also in harmful fires. Combustion processes involving different oxidizers or fuels, for example, rusting of metals, have long been recognized and are important in chemical industries. Some "fuels," such as nitrocellulose, are capable of experiencing combustion in the absence of an oxidizer because they contain atoms of fuel and atoms of oxidizer within the same molecule. These substances form common ingredients of explosives and of propellants for rocket motors. Thus, combustion encompasses a wide class of chemical phenomena in nature and has various uses.

**History of the Science of Combustion.** The early history of the study of combustion is closely related to the history of chemistry and of the molecular theory of matter. Perhaps because fire is spectacular and superficially mysterious, studies of combustion enjoyed undeserved prominence in the development of the foundations of chemistry until the end of the 18th century. During the Middle Ages the idea persisted that fire was one of the four basic elements of matter. Discussions of combustion later played a prominent role in Georg Ernst Stahl's erroneous "phlogiston" theory of matter, which delayed the progress of chemistry during the first 75 years of the 18th century. On the other hand, mutual reinforcement of chemistry and combustion studies arose from the careful 17th century investigations of Jean Rey, Robert Boyle, Robert Hooke, and John Mayow concerning changes in weight and volume produced by combustion. Combustion also entered the later studies of Antoine Laurent Lavoisier (discovery of oygen), Joseph Priestley, and Karl Wilhelm Scheele that began in the decade 1770–1780 and established the basis of modern chemistry. By 1800 the overall chemical changes associated with common processes of combustion were well understood. Later studies focused on mechanisms of combustion and led to the recent emergence of combustion as an identifiable scientific discipline.

The present discipline of combustion draws on the fields of chemical kinetics, thermodynamics, fluid mechanics, and transport processes. These four subjects, particularly the first and last, did not begin to flourish until the middle of the 19th century. Therefore, the seeds of the modern science of combustion were not sown until the last half of the 19th century, notably by the experiments of Robert Bunsen (1866), of Claude Louis Berthelot and Paul Marie Eugène Vieille (1881) and of Ernest Mallard and Henry Louis Le Chatelier (1881, 1883) on the propagation of combustion waves, and by theoretical explanations offered by Vladimir Aleksandrovic Mikhel'son (1890), David Leonhard Chapman (1899), and Émile Jouguet (1905, 1917). Combustion as a scientific discipline has grown steadily in the 20th century.

## PRINCIPLES OF COMBUSTION

**Materials for Combustion.** Most substances can participate in combustion, either as fuels or as oxidizers. Those that cannot are the noble gases (for example, helium), molecular nitrogen, and a large class of compounds—including many oxides, sulfides, fluorides, and chlorides—that exist in their most stable chemical configurations and that can be formed as products of combustion.

The list of known oxidizers is much shorter than the list of known fuels. The most common oxidizer is oxygen. Others include sulfur, all of the halogens, compounds made solely from halogens (for example, chlorine trifluoride), ozone, nitrogen tetroxide and other oxides of nitrogen, hydrogen peroxide, nitric acid, and potassium nitrate. Oxidizers also include, among a number of oxygen-rich salts, ammonium perchlorate, which is the most common oxidizer in solid-propellant rocket motors.

Fuels encompass hydrogen, boron, carbon, silicon, phosphorus, sulfur, all metals, all hydrocarbons, and essentially all organic molecules. Among other fuel substances are ammonia, hydrazine, and metal hydrides. In the past, many of these materials have not been classified as fuels; for example, metallic aluminum is often used in construction and is commonly considered noncombustible, but it will burn with oxygen and release more heat than conventional fuels if it is brought to sufficiently high temperatures (approximately 2300°K). Degrees Kelvin (°K) are units of measurement on the Kelvin scale of absolute temperature. Temperature given on the Kelvin scale may be converted to centigrade by subtracting 273 or to Fahrenheit by multiplying by 1.8 and then subtracting 460.

The impetus for lengthening the lists of fuels and oxidizers comes largely from the field of rocket propulsion; all of the fuels and oxidizers cited above have been investigated as potential rocket propellants, and the most powerful combination that has been discovered is a mixture of hydrogen and the metal beryllium as fuel with oxygen as the oxidizer.

Most of the energy that man consumes today is produced by the combustion in air of organically derived fuels. The three primary types of natural fuels are coal, petroleum, and natural gas. Fuels manufactured from them include such gases as coal gas, carbon monoxide, hydrogen, acetylene, and propane; the liquids benzene, kerosine, gasoline, and alcohol; and the solid coke. Other natural fuels are wood, peat, and lignite, a solid whose properties are intermediate between those of peat and coal.

**Heat of Combustion and Flame Temperature.** A basic thermodynamic property of a fuel, relevant to its usefulness in combustion, is its heat of combustion, which is the energy released when a given amount of fuel reacts with an oxidizer to form specified combustion products at constant pressure and temperature. The heat of combustion with oxygen ranges from very low values for poor fuels to 34,000 calories per gram of fuel for hydrogen. For natural fuels, the values are 4,000 to 4,500 cal/gm for wood, 6,500 to 8,500 cal/gm for coal, 10,000 to 11,000 cal/gm for petroleum, and 11,000 to 14,000 cal/gm for natural gas.

An important thermodynamic property of a combustible system is its adiabatic flame temperature, the maximum temperature achieved if all of the heat of combustion is used to increase the temperature of the combustion products. Adiabatic flame temperatures range up to about 2100°K for natural fuels burning in air and to 3000°K for natural fuels burning in pure oxygen.

**Ignition.** The *ignition temperature* is the temperature to which a fuel must be raised before it begins to burn. Ignition temperatures depend on rates at which chemical reactions take place, on the rate at which the system can lose heat and materials to its surroundings, on the shape of the fuel and its container, and on the method of ignition that is employed. Approximate values of ignition temperatures for common fuels in air are 650°–750°K for coal, 500°–650°K for newspaper, dry wood, and gasoline, and 850°K for hydrogen.

Ignition criteria have been expressed in terms of many quantities besides ignition temperature. Examples include the minimum rate of addition of energy and the minimum amount of energy needed for ignition. After the energy or temperature necessary for combustion to occur is imparted to a combustible system, a certain amount of time elapses before observable combustion begins; this is the *ignition delay time*, ranging from small fractions of a second to many days.

*Spontaneous Combustion.* In this process, piles of certain materials, such as oily rags, react slowly with trapped oxygen. The heat produced by the reaction is lost slowly enough for the temperature of the materials to increase to a point at which flaming combustion begins.

**Flammability.** Some fuel-oxidizer mixtures cannot be made to burn, either because the pressure is too low or because too little fuel or oxidizer is present; these mixtures lie outside the *limits of flammability* of the system. At atmospheric pressure, the upper and lower values of the percentage (by volume) of fuel in air between which the concentration must lie for combustion to be possible are 6 and 1 for gasoline vapor, and about 75 and 4 for hydrogen.

**Arrangements of Fuel and Oxidizer.** Central to the science of combustion is the fact that there are two basic arrangements of fuel and oxidizer. They are premixed systems, wherein the fuel and oxidizer are intimately mixed before combustion begins, and nonpremixed systems, wherein fuel and oxidizer are separated initially and mix as they burn. An example of premixed combustion is the inner flame cone of a Bunsen burner, in which gaseous fuel is thoroughly mixed with air at the base of a tube that holds a flame at its upper exit. An example of nonpremixed burning is a wood fire. Fuels such as explosives that burn "without" an oxidizer are intrinsically premixed. Liquid and solid fuels that require an oxidizer are usually nonpremixed, although fine spray or dust (for example, pulverized coal) suspensions in air sometimes burn as premixed systems. In such cases, the premixed flame may have a nonpremixed substructure.

**Combustion in Nonpremixed Systems.** In nonpremixed systems combustion is nonexplosive, and chemical heat release occurs in a flame into which fuel and oxidizer are transported from opposite sides. Such flames are called diffusion flames, because fuel and oxidizer diffuse into the flame zone while combustion products and heat diffuse out. Pertinent measures of combustion quality in diffusion flames include the *flame height* or *flame length* (the linear extent of the flame in the direction in which fuel is fed into the system) and the rate of heat release per unit area of a fuel bed.

**Combustion in Premixed Systems.** In premixed systems, combustion reactions can proceed in a transient process nearly homogeneously throughout the entire system, or thin combustion waves can develop that consume fuel by propagating into unburned combustibles. The homogeneous mechanism tends to occur in small systems and the wave mechanism in large ones.

**Explosions.** Premixed systems experiencing homogeneous combustion are often observed to react slowly under certain conditions of pressure, temperature, composition, and chamber dimensions, and to explode under other conditions. Two qualitatively different mechanisms can produce explosions in homogeneous combustion systems. One mechanism is that of a thermal explosion, in which heat released by the reactions raises the temperature, which in turn accelerates the rate of heat release. The other mechanism is that of a branched-chain explosion, in which large numbers of highly reactive intermediate chemical species (free radicals) are produced in the combustion reactions and further accelerate the rates of these reactions. The destructive phenomenon of "knock" in internal combustion engines is believed by many experts to be caused by high pressures resulting from a branched-chain explosion.

**Combustion Waves.** For any temperature, pressure, and composition (within the limits of flammability), two distinct types of combustion waves occur in premixed systems: deflagrations and detonations.

**Deflagrations.** Deflagration waves propagate slowly, typically at *flame speeds* of 50 cm per second. At atmospheric pressure their thicknesses are of the order of a millimeter. Combustion is completed within the wave, causing the temperature behind the wave to be much greater than the temperature ahead of it. The wave propagates by conducting enough heat to the combustible gases ahead of it to raise their temperature to a point at which they begin to burn rapidly. Deflagrations provide a useful means for achieving hot flames and high rates of heat release per unit volume without producing damaging pressure waves. Bunsen burner flames and oxyacetylene torches are deflagrations, as are the combustion processes in jet engines and in solid propellant rockets.

**Detonations.** Detonation waves propagate rapidly, at velocities of approximately 5,000 meters per second. They consist of a very thin shock wave, across which the pressure and temperature both increase by a factor of ten or more, followed by a combustion zone, in which chemical reactions proceed rapidly to completion. The strong shock wave serves to ignite the combustible gases in a detonation. The pressure pulses associated with detonations are highly destructive, and therefore detonations usually must be avoided in engines and furnaces. High explosives are purposely constructed to support detonations. Concepts of detonative combustion form the basis of some novel theoretical designs for jet and rocket engines.

FORMAN A. WILLIAMS
*University of California at San Diego*

**Further Reading:** Buckmaster, J. D., and Takeno, T., eds., *Mathematical Modeling in Combustion Science* (Springer-Verlag 1988); Chomiak, Jerzy, *Combustion* (Abacus 1988); Iinuma, K., *Laser Diagnostics and Modeling of Combustion* (Springer-Verlag 1988).

**COMÉDIE FRANÇAISE,** kô-mā-dē′ frän-sez′, the oldest French state theater. Founded in the 17th century, the Comédie Française, also called the Théâtre Français, Société des Comédiens Français, or Maison de Molière, is famous for its traditions, its classical and modern repertory, and the high quality of its productions.

**Character.** The Comédie Française is a cooperative association subsidized by the government. It has 30 *sociétaires*, who serve 15 to 30 years, share profits according to years of service, and vote on the budget and new members. Forming a reservoir of trained talent are the *pensionnaires* (salaried actors) and the *stagiaires* (young probationers) chosen annually from among students of the Paris Conservatory. The company is run by a *comité d'administration* composed of eight *sociétaires,* working with an *administrateur général* appointed by the state, who plan the production schedule, hire *pensionnaires,* cast plays, and choose directors. A *comité de lecture* selects new plays.

The core of the repertory is the works of Molière, Racine, Corneille, Marivaux, and Musset. (Molière's *Tartuffe* has been given nearly every year since 1680.) Noteworthy modern productions include Henri de Montherlant's *Reine morte* (1942), Paul Claudel's *Soulier de satin* (1943), André Gide's *Retour de l'enfant prodigue* (1963), Armand Salacrou's *Comme les chardons* (1964), and Eugène Ionesco's *La soif et la faim* (1966). The company also makes phonograph records, radio and television broadcasts, and films. It conserves a rich collection of paintings, sculpture, furniture, costumes, and priceless archives.

**History.** In 1680, Louis XIV united two companies of actors, including some members of Molière's former troupe, to form a single company, the Théâtre Guénégaud. The new company had a constitution based on that of a 15th century Parisian acting guild, and, like the guild, had a monopoly on all French plays. In 1689 the company moved to the Rue des Fossés-St.-Germain-des-Prés (now the Rue de l'Ancienne

Comédie) and took the name Comédie Française to distinguish it from the Comédie Italienne, a troupe of Italian actors. Other moves followed. During this early period outstanding members of the Comédie Française included Baron and Mlle. Champmeslé, both from Molière's company, and, later, Lekain, Mlle. Clairon, and Préville.

During the Revolution the Comédie Française split along political lines. In 1799 it was reconstituted in a theater named the Théâtre Français, on the Rue de Richelieu, near the Palais Royal, where it has since remained. In 1804 the Comédie Française signed a new charter which is still in force.

In the early 19th century the classics of the Comédie Française were interpreted by such great actors as Talma, Mlle. Mars, and Rachel. Eminent administrators added new works. Baron I. J. S. Taylor introduced romantic plays; later, Arsène Houssaye added problem plays and historical spectacles. In the 20th century, Édouard Bourdet encouraged untraditional productions. Famous performers of this expanded repertory included Constant Coquelin, Sarah Bernhardt, Mounet-Sully and, later, Cécile Sorel, Denis d'Inès, Jean Yonnel, Maurice Escande, Marie Bell, Madeleine Renaud, Pierre Dux, Louis Seigner, Robert Hirsch, Jacques Charon, Georges Chamarat, and Annie Ducaux.

EDITH MELCHER, *Author of "The Life and Times of Henry Monnier"*

**COMÉDIE HUMAINE,** kô-mā-dē′ ü-men′, the name of a series of nearly 100 novels and short stories by Honoré de Balzac (q.v.). The English title is *The Human Comedy.* The first volume, called *Le dernier Chouan,* appeared in 1829, but it was not until 1842 that the author adopted the general title. Balzac divided the stories into groups depicting life in Paris, in the provinces, and in various milieus and professions—the whole designed to form a panorama of contemporary French life. Among the best-known works in *La comédie humaine* are *César Birotteau, Eugénie Grandet* and *Le père Goriot.*

**COMEDY** is a form of dramatic literature designed to amuse and often to correct or instruct through ridicule. It generally ends happily. To achieve its effects, it exposes incongruity, absurdity, and foolishness, and its treatment of characters frequently has elements of exaggeration and caricature.

Like tragedy, comedy grew out of early Greek religious festivals honoring the god Dionysus, in which joyful tribute was paid to the natural world. Traces of ritual elements still existed in the comedies of Aristophanes (about 400 B.C.), the greatest Greek writer of comedy, who added to the form the element of satire of men and institutions. The Greek Menander, followed by the Roman playwrights Plautus and Terence, devised the "New Comedy," using stock characters to exploit life's absurdities.

Since the Renaissance, comedy has taken many forms in Western literature: the artifice of the Italian *commedia dell'arte;* the broad humor of Molière and the English Elizabethans; the Restoration comedies of manners; the genial realism of Goldoni; the intricate high comedy of Chekhov; the witty farces of Oscar Wilde; and the comedies of ideas of George Bernard Shaw.

C. HUGH HOLMAN
*Coauthor of "A Handbook to Literature"*

**COMEDY OF ERRORS, The,** an early, perhaps the first comedy written by William Shakespeare. It was presented at Gray's Inn on Dec. 28, 1594. When *The Comedy of Errors* was actually written is a subject of scholarly controversy. However, most critics feel that about 1590 seems to be a reasonable date for the play's composition, with some revisions made before the private performance of 1594. The text, as first published in the Folio of 1623, shows a remarkable diversity of styles. Although *The Comedy of Errors* is unmistakably early Shakespeare in choice and treatment of material, it already evidences a playwright with sureness of touch in adaptation and with technical skill in knitting and unraveling complications.

**Plot.** *The Comedy of Errors* is Shakespeare's shortest play, however, no brief summary can do justice to the complexity of its plot. The play is set in Ephesus. The enveloping action concerns Aegeon, an elderly merchant of Syracuse, who, parted by a series of dreadful misfortunes from his wife, his twin sons (the Antipholi), and their twin attendants (the Dromios), has been condemned to death by the Duke of Ephesus unless he provides ransom by evening. One Antipholus, with his Dromio, resides in Ephesus with his wife, Adriana, and her sister Luciana. The second Antipholus, who is unmarried, lands there with the other Dromio in search of his brother. In the central part of the play the two pairs of twins become entangled in an elaborate series of mistaken identities involving money, a necklace, a dinner engagement, the jealous wife and her unattached sister, a kitchen wench, and a courtesan, to a point where they are assumed to be utterly mad or think themselves bewitched. One pair takes refuge in a priory, and the exasperated Adriana appeals to the Duke for justice. In the process of explanations both pairs of twins appear together for the first time, and the confusion is finally resolved. Aegeon is reprieved; the abbess of the priory turns out to be his long lost wife; the whole family is at last joyfully reunited; and the unmarried Antipholus is free to continue his romance with Luciana.

So farcical a play clearly provides little opportunity for depth or breadth of characterization, and by the nature of the plot the twins must be pretty much alike. Adriana does become a brief but neat portrait of a violently jealous woman, and the gentle and patient Luciana is drawn in dramatic contrast to her. Also, some serious tones are given to the tragic plight of the sorrowful and resigned Aegeon. In general, however, the characters remain merely suitable to the plot, exemplifying bewildered exasperation rather than high or subtly varied emotions.

**Sources.** Renewing his grammar school acquaintance with Latin comedy, Shakespeare adapted his basic source, the *Menaechmi* of the Roman playwright Plautus, by means of the same writer's *Amphitruo,* the popular tale of Apollonius of Tyre, other minor sources, and his own brilliant dramatic invention and ingenuity. He developed his plot by creating two sets of twins in place of Plautus' one pair, thereby increasing the "errors" of mistaken identity. Shakespeare also provided for an enveloping action by adding a modicum of romantic love interest and heightened the gentility of the central characters.

**Performances.** In countries where the translation of Shakespeare has proved especially difficult, *The Comedy of Errors*, with its emphasis on situations, has been popular on the stage. Productions in translation include those given in Norway, Germany, Switzerland, Bulgaria, Czechoslovakia, Yugoslavia, and Russia.

In England there was a court performance at Whitehall in 1604, but there are no further records of production until 1734, when an adaptation was presented at Covent Garden. Adaptations, including an "operatic" revision in 1819, were indeed the rule until 1855, when Samuel Phelps revived the play at Sadler's Wells. Another revival by Charles and Harry Webb at the Princess' Theatre during the Shakespeare Tercentenary celebrations of 1864 was remarkable both because the play was acted continuously without lowering the curtain and because the Webbs, as the two Dromios, were so identical in appearance that the audience itself was delightfully confused. In the United States the most memorable performances have been by William H. Crane and Stuart Robson, who began playing the Dromios in 1878. A musical adaptation, *The Boys from Syracuse*, by Richard Rodgers and Lorenz Hart, was a Broadway success of 1938–1939.

ROBERT HAMILTON BALL
*Queens College of the City of New York*

### Bibliography

**Anderson, Linda,** *A Kind of Wild Justice: Revenge in Shakespeare's Comedies* (Univ. of Del. Press 1987).

**Baldwin, Thomas W.,** *On the Compositional Genetics of The Commedy of Errors* (Univ. of Ill. Press 1965).

**Frye, Northrup,** *A Natural Perspective* (1969; reprint, P. Smith 1988).

**Smidt, Kristian,** *Unconformities in Shakespeare's Early Comedies* (St. Martin's Press 1986).

**Williamson, Marilyn L,** *The Patriarchy of Shakespeare's Comedies* (Wayne State Univ. Press 1986).

**COMENIUS,** kō-mē′nē-əs, **John Amos** (1592–1670), Czech educator and theologian, who is sometimes called the "grandfather of modern education." Comenius, whose name in Czech is Jan Amos Komenský, was born in Nivnitz, Moravia, on March 28, 1592. A key thinker during the transition from medieval to modern education, Comenius' educational reforms reflected his experiences as a leader of the persecuted Protestant Unity of Czech Brethren (the Moravian Brotherhood sect) during the religious dissensions that were both the cause and the expression of the Thirty Years' War. Comenius viewed world tensions as stemming from religious differences, and his reforms were aimed at eliminating these tensions by organizing knowledge so that it could be taught to everyone. This universalization of knowledge, based in part on the development of a universal language, would make education relevant to everyday life and to the common man. His philosophy of universal education, known as pansophism, marks him as one of the first modern advocates of education for women.

**Works.** Comenius was forced by the Thirty Years' War to emigrate to Leszno, Poland, where he wrote many of his great works. One of the first of these was *Labyrinth of the World*, written about 1623, a religious allegory similar to John Bunyan's later work, *Pilgrim's Progress*. *Janua linguarum reserata* (1631; Eng. tr. *Gate of Tongues Unlocked*, 1659), an introduction to Latin grammar, outlined his method of teaching languages through the vernacular and of relating

## Orbis Sensualium Pictus,

### A World of Things Obvious to the Senses drawn in Pictures.

| Invitation. | I. | Invitatio. |

| *The Master and the Boy.* | *Magister & Puer.* |
|---|---|
| M. **C**ome, Boy, learn to be wise. | M. **V**eni, Puer, disce sapere. |
| P. What doth this mean, *to be wise?* | P. Quid hoc est, *Sapere?* |
| M. To understand rightly. | M. Intelligere recte, |

Page from *Orbis pictus* (1658) by Comenius (taken from Ernest Eller's edition of Comenius' *School of Infancy*, published by University of North Carolina Press, 1956).

Latin to the vernacular through parallel passages and illustrations. An illustrated reworking of this book, *Orbis sensualium pictus* (1658; Eng. tr. *The Visible World*, 1659), became his most famous work. One of the first picture books designed to provide children with reading material at their own level, it was a milestone in the history of education. *Didactica magna* (*The Great Didactic*), written between 1628 and 1632, was his great educational work and was unequaled as a guide to educational theory and practice for many years.

In 1641, Comenius went to England to serve on a Parliamentary commision to reform education, but the political agitation of the English Civil War prevented these reforms from being carried out. Nevertheless, the creation of the British Royal Society is said to have grown from Comenius' inspiration.

He helped plan a reform of the Swedish educational system and established a demonstration school in Hungary. Because of strife between Poland and Sweden, he was forced to flee Leszno, and from 1655 to the end of his life he lived in Amsterdam, devoting his time to educational reform and to the care of his fellow religionists scattered by the war. He died in Amsterdam on Nov. 15, 1670.

Although he derived much of his thinking from others, none of his predecessors had his ability to communicate, and this was the essence of his success. His last years were marked by an increasing and less effective mysticism, but his detailed organization of a broad curriculum based on principles of natural order in learning remain a lasting philosophical legacy that shaped the development of education in modern times.

RICHARD E. GROSS, *Stanford University*

Comet West speeds past the earth on March 8, 1976, showing tails of gas and dust extending for millions of miles.

**COMET,** kom′ət, an astronomical body of small mass, moving about the sun in a more or less elongated orbit. When it is sufficiently close to the sun, icy materials in the main mass, or *nucleus*, are vaporized by sunlight and form a hazy envelope of gases and finely divided dust particles. The presence of this diffuse envelope, which tends to obscure the nucleus, is a characteristic and defining feature. The dust and gases may then form one or more *tails*, which are always directed more or less away from the sun. The term comet derives from a Greek word meaning "long-haired," which is descriptive of the flowing appearance of the tail of a bright comet.

Comets were formerly of interest to astronomers principally because of problems connected with their motions. They are now recognized as representing probably the least-changed available sample of the primordial material from which the sun and planets were formed. Thus they are studied today in order to understand their physical and chemical characteristics.

### PROPERTIES

**Orbits.** Comets are generally classified, according to the size and shape of their orbits, into *short-period* and *long-period* objects. The former move in elliptical orbits that require less than 200 years per revolution. Some of them have been observed repeatedly for many revolutions as they pass by the earth and sun. The long-period comets move in much larger and more elongated orbits that are nearly parabolic in shape. Such comets come to the vicinity of the sun only at intervals of thousands or millions of years. A recent catalog of orbits listed 135 short-period comets and 613 that moved in nearly parabolic orbits.

The great majority of short-period comets have periods between 3 and 9 years long. Of these, over 120 comets known as the Jupiter family have aphelia that are located close to the orbit

of Jupiter. (Aphelion is the orbital point most distant from the sun.) Essentially all the remaining comets of short period appear to have passed close to Jupiter at one time or another. Although associations of similar comet families with other planets have been suggested, their reality is doubtful. The probability of the dominance of Jupiter in shaping the smaller orbits seems overwhelming.

The orbit planes of short-period comets also show a concentration toward the average plane of motion of the major planets. Practically all these comets revolve about the sun in the same direction as do the planets. Comet Halley, which revolves in the retrograde direction in an orbit inclined some 18° to the plane of the earth's orbit, is one noteworthy exception.

The orbits of the long-period comets, on the other hand, reach far beyond the domain of the major planets and out toward interstellar space. Such orbits are distributed essentially at random with respect to the inclination of the orbit planes to the plane of the earth's orbit around the sun. The apparent distribution of orientations of the long axes of the comet orbits in their planes is more complex, being affected by such factors as the motion of the sun in the Milky Way Galaxy and effects of observing conditions on comet discoveries.

In both groups of comets the observed tendency is for the orbits to have perihelion distances—the points of closest approach to the sun—that are not far from the orbit of the earth. However, since comets are made visible by reflected and scattered sunlight, they appear brightest when they are close to the sun and to the earth. Thus comets that remain far from the sun are fainter and may escape detection; and, unless it is very luminous, a comet may also escape detection in the bright sky near the sun. The observed distribution of perihelion distances therefore must be strongly influenced by selection effects.

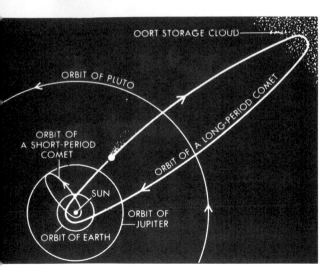

Most short-period comets have periods of less than 9 years; long-period comets may travel far beyond Pluto.

**Structure.** A typical comet, when it first brightens enough to be detected with a large telescope, looks like a faint star embedded in the weakest trace of nebulosity. Depending on the size of the nucleus, a few comets may be observed as far from the sun as the distance of the planet Saturn, but more average ones can be detected only to about one third that distance. As the comet approaches the sun the hazy envelope, or *coma*, becomes brighter and larger, and a tail may have begun to develop by the time the orbit of Mars is reached. When the comet moves still closer to the sun, the coma generally shrinks as the increasingly intense solar radiant energy more rapidly tears apart the gas molecules of which it is composed. At the same time the tail may lengthen and brighten quite dramatically until the nucleus and coma become quite insignificant in comparison. These comets that penetrate closest to the sun generally are the ones that become most spectacular, especially if they should move in such a way as to pass fairly close to the earth before or after perihelion passage.

As confirmed by direct observations from spacecraft of the nucleus of Halley's comet in 1986, most of the material of a comet is contained in a compact nucleus no more than a few miles in diameter. The structure of this nucleus resembles that of a large, dirty snowball. Water ice is the dominant component, but many compounds of hydrogen, carbon, ozygen, and nitrogen are present. Dust grains composed of silicates with traces of various metals are embedded in the icy material. A very dark crust covers much of the surface.

With decreasing distance from the sun, the intensity of sunlight increases, causing icy material exposed at the surface to vaporize. Jets of gas and entrained dust emanate from vents, mainly on the sunward side of the nucleus. The jets blend together as they flow outward, forming the coma. Although the material contained in the coma at any one time is only a small fraction of that in the nucleus, the volume of the coma is very much larger than that of the nucleus. Coma diameters more than 500,000 miles (800,000 km) have been observed, but the size is always some-

what indefinite and depends on whether dust or gas is observed and exactly how the observations are made.

The gases of the coma absorb and reemit sunlight at wavelengths that correspond to resonant frequencies of the molecules of which they are composed, while the dust scatters sunlight less selectively. Finely divided material is far more efficient in scattering and reflecting light than is an equivalent mass in one or a few solid chunks. Thus it should not be surprising that the total light of the coma of a bright comet near the sun may be a hundred times greater than the light reflected from the nucleus.

As sunlight (especially its ultraviolet component) continues to act on the material of the coma, the gas molecules are gradually broken down to simpler fragments. Some of them become electrically charged through loss of an electron. The weak pressure of electromagnetic radiation emitted by the sun, combined with the gravitational attraction on each molecule and grain, causes some of the diffuse material to be pushed from the coma in a gently curved tail. The motion of the charged particles, however, is determined by much stronger forces. These forces derive from the streams of charged particles and associated magnetic fields known as the *solar wind*, which flow constantly from the sun. As a result, the charged particles of the comet are driven almost directly away from the sun and form a nearly straight tail.

Some of the detailed effects of the interaction with the solar wind can be recognized through the complex and constantly changing structures of comet tails. Such structures include sharply defined *rays*, and clouds of charged particles moving rapidly (some tens of miles per second). A comet may have two tails at the same time, or even several, representing a sorting of the tail material according to the forces by which each type is affected. Light, ionized molecules undergo the greatest acceleration and form the straightest, most active tails. Neutral molecules and dust are the usual components of those tails that are more strongly curved and nearly structureless.

**Composition.** At great distances from the sun the small nucleus of the comet reflects only a meager amount of sunlight. Upon spectroscopic analysis, this light shows the same basic characteristics as does sunlight. However, as the comet approaches the sun and the coma develops, a process of absorption and reemission of sunlight by molecules in the coma becomes increasingly important. In a dominant process, known as *resonance fluorescence*, atoms and molecules absorb sunlight at characteristic frequencies. They then reemit the light at about the same frequencies. Many molecules and a number of atoms present in the coma have been identified through observation of their characteristic emission bands and lines in the spectrum.

The strongest emission band in photographs of cometary spectra—one that becomes prominent almost immediately upon development of the coma—is the band produced in the blue region by the cyanogen radical CN. Generally the next bands to develop, and the next in prominence, are those in the yellow part of the spectrum produced by the two-carbon radical $C_2$. Observations from spacecraft above the earth's atmosphere prove, though, that hydrogen atoms and hydroxyl radicals (OH), both of them fragments of water molecules, are in fact the dominant constituents of cometary comae. A number of other molecules, including water itself, have been observed in the infrared and radio portions of the spectrum of several bright comets. Many of the observed molecules are composed of atoms of hydrogen, carbon, oxygen, and nitrogen in various combinations.

If a comet moves much closer to the sun than the orbit of the earth, emission lines produced by atomic sodium often appear, sometimes in great strength. Lines corresponding to a number of metals and other atomic species, including iron, nickel, copper, chromium, cobalt, manganese, vanadium, calcium, potassium, and silicon were observed in 1965 in comet Ikeya-Seki. This comet was one of an interesting group that nearly graze the surface of the sun at perihelion and are subject to intense radiation. Sulfur was observed in a comet that made an unusually close approach to the earth in 1983.

The emission bands observed in the spectrum of straight comet tails are characteristically those of ionized molecules. The pairs of bright lines of $CO^+$ and emissions of $N_2^+$ and $CO_2^+$ (positive ions of carbon monoxide, nitrogen, and carbon dioxide, respectively) are the strongest contributors. The light reflected and scattered by finely divided dust particles in curved tails is continuous and difficult to analyze in terms of the composition, size, and shape of the grains.

## THE STUDY OF COMETS

Although some new comets are discovered by professional astronomers, a considerable number are still found by skilled amateurs who search for them visually with small telescopes. The comets discovered by professionals are generally found on photographic plates taken with wide-field telescopes for programs not connected with comet research. Included are practically all known comets of large perihelion distance and a portion of those that come closer to the sun. Amateurs tend to concentrate their searches in the parts of the sky relatively neglected by professionals—the low western sky in the evening and especially the eastern sky just before dawn. These are the regions in which relatively bright comets are most likely to be found.

A number of comets have been discovered from spacecraft, including six during the sky survey made in 1983 by the Infrared Astronomy Satellite (IRAS). Six small sungrazers were found by the SOLWIND spacecraft in 1979–84 and two by the Solar Maximum Mission (SMM) spacecraft in 1987.

**The Cataloging of Comets.** Newly discovered comets and returning periodic comets are assigned a temporary designation as soon as the first observations are reported. This consists of the year of discovery, or of recovery, followed by a small letter indicating the sequential order in the year—for example, 1975n, 1982i, 1987a. If more than 26 comets come under observation in a year, as happened in 1987, the alphabet is recycled and a number added, preferably as a subscript, as 1987b$_1$. A permanent designation is assigned according to the order of perihelion passage of the comets during each year. It consists of the year followed by a Roman numeral—for example, 1976 VI, 1986 III, 1986 XVII. Since comets may be discovered in one year and pass perihelion in another, assignment of the permanent designations is usually deferred for a

year or two to minimize the chance that new discoveries will upset the assigned numbering sequence.

Each newly discovered comet is identified also by the name or names (up to three) of independent discoverers. Examples are several comets Shoemaker, comet Sugano-Saigusa-Fujikawa, and comet Churyumov-Solodovnikov. Very occasionally a comet has been named for a person who did extensive computational work on its orbit. Such well-known comets as Halley's and Encke's were named in this way.

**History of Comet Study.** Bright comets have been subjects of historical record since at least the 3d century B.C. Their sudden and unexpected appearance was a source of puzzlement and alarm, and they were often interpreted as signs of impending danger, war, or famine. Although some early philosophers, such as the Roman Seneca, recognized the astronomical nature of comets, they were regarded in Europe for many centuries as atmospheric phenomena unworthy of serious scientific study.

The Danish astronomer Tycho Brahe's demonstration that the great comet of 1577 was appreciably more distant than the moon marked a significant step forward. Later, after the development of the law of gravitation by Isaac Newton, the applicability of the new law to the observed behavior of comets was recognized. Newton himself studied the motion of the bright comet of 1680, and in 1705 the English astronomer Edmond Halley published orbital elements for 24 comets calculated by the use of Newton's theory. The sudden appearances and apparently erratic motion of comets could now be understood in terms of their motion in elongated ellipses or parabolas, the comets being visible only while they traversed those portions of their orbits that lay closest to the sun.

**Notable Comets.** Nearly all the comets that become bright enough to be easily visible move in large orbits that require thousands of, even several million, years to traverse. The most notable exception is the comet whose appearances in 1531, 1607, and 1682 were included in studies of orbits by Edmond Halley. Halley recognized the near 76-year periodicity of the appearances and attributed them to a single comet that might be expected to return in 1758. The comet, now known by Halley's name, did appear as expected and was subsequently observed in 1835, 1910, and 1986. No other comet whose reappearances are reliably predictable becomes bright enough to be seen regularly with the unaided eye. Because of its relative brightness coupled with its well-known orbit, Halley's comet at its return in 1986 was the target of an intensive international campaign of scientific investigations from the earth, from spacecraft in both earth and solar orbit, and from spacecraft directed to intercept the comet.

The brightest comets are first-timers, or ones that pass unusually close to the sun. Their appearance can be anticipated only in the sense that discovery may occur some weeks, or even months, before they reach peak luminosity upon their closest approach to the sun. Among the comets that have been easily visible with the unaided eye in recent decades are Arend-Roland in April–May 1957, Mrkos in August 1957, Ikeya-Seki in October 1965, Bennett in March–April 1970, Kohoutek in January 1974, and West in March 1976.

Comet Halley travels past the earth on March 7, 1986. Flybys confirmed that its nucleus resembles a large, dirty snowball made up mainly of water ice.

Occasionally a small comet may become visible to the unaided eye for a few days at the time of an unusually close approach to the earth. An example is comet IRAS-Araki-Alcock, which in May 1983 made the closest approach to the earth of any comet since Lexell's in 1770.

Bright comets offer outstanding opportunities for scientific study, and important advances in understanding the nature of comets have been coupled with their relatively infrequent appearances. They are not suitable objects for *in situ* study from spacecraft, however, because missions cannot be planned in advance.

**The Life History of Comets.** While they are in the vicinity of the sun, comets suffer a continual loss of material as gases and dust stream from the nucleus into the coma and tail. The known densities of interplanetary material are much too low for this loss to be made good by accretion while the comets are in more remote parts of their orbits. The lifetimes of comets in orbits that carry them close to the sun must therefore be limited. Efforts have been made in the past to measure a rate of gradual fading. But it is now realized that, because of the dark crust, gas and dust flow from the nucleus, and hence during their active phases the brightness of comets is erratically variable. Light outbursts have been observed, sometimes in conjunction with the splitting of the nucleus, in many comets presumably as fresh material is exposed to sunlight. More recently, estimates of the lifetimes of comets in the inner solar system have been based on rates of mass loss compared with the total mass of the nucleus. Conclusions are still uncertain, but lifetimes may be as short as some hundreds to a few thousand revolutions—very much less than the age of the solar system. The population of comets now observed is clearly a temporary one.

**Comets and Meteors.** Several comets are known to be associated with showers of meteors that occur when the earth passes through streams of solid material that move around the sun in the same orbits as the comets. Dust trails, which are meteor streams seen at a distance in space, have been recognized in data from the infrared sky survey by IRAS. Some of these trails also have been identified with known comets. Collisions between asteroids contribute as well to streams of meteoroids in space. The prominent Geminid shower seen annually in December is now known to have an asteroidal source. But the possibility exists that a comet nucleus can become so thickly crusted over that no gas or dust can escape. In such a case no coma could form, and

the object would be classified as an asteroid. A number of asteroids in fact have orbits that are much like those of short-period comets.

Comets thus may follow one of several tracks as they age. The nucleus may gradually disintegrate as ices are lost, coexisting with a meteor stream until too little of the nucleus is left to be observed. The nucleus may become crusted over and inert. Or the nucleus may suffer a catastrophic disruption, leaving only a swarm of particles to follow the orbit of the lost comet. Such apparently was the fate of the short-period comet Biela, discovered in 1772, rediscovered in 1805 and again in 1826, and eventually reobserved in 1832 according to prediction. In January 1846 the nucleus was seen to be double. Both parts returned in 1852, but neither of the little comets was ever seen again. Instead there was a tremendous rain of faint meteors on Nov. 27, 1872, from a point in the constellation Andromeda that indicated an association with comet Biela. Another great shower of meteors occurred in 1885. Subsequent showers were, however, much weaker.

**Theories of Comet Structure.** The association of several comets with meteor streams led to a picture of a comet nucleus as composed of a compact swarm of meteoroids, the *sandbank* model. This idea was accepted for some time because it was so hard to detect the true nucleus hidden in the bright coma of an active comet. As the behavior to be expected from a swarm of separate particles in interplanetary space was studied more carefully, however, serious difficulties became apparent. How could a cloud of particles continue to release large amounts of gas and dust? And how could a comet so composed survive a very close approach to the sun?

*Icy-Conglomerate Model.* It had been suggested early on that comets might be composed of ices. Studies of spectra obtained to the 1940's supported the idea that the observed fragments of molecules might derive from stable ices of water ($H_2O$), methane ($CH_4$), ammonia ($NH_3$), and carbon dioxide ($CO_2$). In 1950, F. L. Whipple proposed a model of a comet nucleus that resembled a large dirty snowball. A comet constructed according to Whipple's model could survive even the very close approaches to the sun that are characteristic of the group of sungrazers of which comet Ikeya-Seki is a member. Only surface layers would be lost during each perihelion passage, while the inner portion would remain frozen. In addition, the fact that some comets were regularly a little early to perihelion (comet Encke) or a little late (comet Halley) could be understood if the nucleus was rotating and the loss of gas and dust took place preferentially on the afternoon side. The slight jet effect would either add to or subtract from the orbital energy, making the period either longer or shorter than expected by allowing only for the gravitational attractions of the sun and planets.

Whipple's model has been supported by many aspects of cometary behavior observed over the years. Pictures of the nucleus of Halley's comet obtained by three spacecraft in March 1986 established its basic correctness beyond doubt. The spacecraft also observed that a dark crust permitted vaporization of ices only locally and obtained evidence that the average density of the nucleus is substantially less than that of solid ice. Hence the structure of the nucleus probably resembles a moderately compacted snow, mainly of water, in which dust grains and complex carbon-bearing molecules are embedded.

**Storage Clouds of Comets.** From a study of the sizes and shapes of the best-determined nearly parabolic orbits, freed from the disturbing effects of the major planets, the Dutch astronomer Jan Hendrik Oort concluded in 1950 that fresh comets must come from a vast storage region, later called the Oort cloud, at the far outer edges of the solar system. He supposed that large numbers of comets move slowly in a sort of deep freeze in this region, continually stirred by gravitational disturbances produced by passing stars. Occasionally a comet would be so deflected as to be sent into the inner solar system, where it could be observed. To account for the frequency with which such comets were seen, Oort calculated that there must be some 100 billion comets in this distant, nearly spherical, cloud. Later calculations showed that galactic tides and giant interstellar clouds, as well as passing stars, disturb the motion of the distant comets. Their number must be even larger than Oort supposed, and their total mass is likely to be at least several times the mass of the earth.

Many comets would have been lost from the distant cloud over time to interstellar space. Further, there are difficulties in capturing comets from nearly parabolic orbits into small elliptic ones efficiently enough to match the observed numbers of short-period comets. These, and some other considerations, led to the idea of an inner storage cloud. Such a cloud is thought to extend from just beyond the planets to merge into the distant Oort cloud. The inner portion probably is substantially flattened to the average plane of the planetary system. Almost certainly the inner storage cloud contains a mass of comets substantially larger than that of the distant Oort cloud. On relatively rare occasions the inner cloud might be disturbed by the passage of a star unusually close to the sun. As a consequence, showers of comets could be sent into the inner solar system, some of them to be captured by Jupiter and the other large planets into short period orbits. Others would be thrown outward to repopulate the Oort cloud.

As comets repeatedly penetrate the part of the solar system closest to the sun, their orbits are gradually changed by the gravitational attraction of the planets, especially Jupiter. Some are ejected from the solar system into interstellar space. Some return to the Oort cloud. And some, especially those that move in planes close to those of the principal planets, may be deflected into small,

distinctly elliptical orbits like those of the short-period comets.

**Formation of Comets.** Comets probably formed in the outer portions of the solar nebula, either in the vicinity of the outermost planets or perhaps as far from the sun as the proposed massive inner cloud of comets. Some solid grains that condensed in dense cold parts of interstellar clouds may have survived the formation of the solar nebula to be incorporated virtually unchanged into the nuclei of comets.

The early history of the solar system is very hard to decipher from the properties of the highly metamorphosed planets and asteroids that have long stayed close to the sun. If comets were formed at the same time as the planets but in the cold outer portions of the solar nebula, it seems very probable that some of the record of those early times is locked in the present chemical and physical structure of the comets. Thus they have become targets for intensive scientific investigation from earth and from spacecraft.

ELIZABETH ROEMER, *University of Arizona*

### Bibliography

Brandt, John C., and Chapman, Robert D., *Introduction to Comets* (Cambridge 1982).

Hillebrandt, W., and Meyer-Hofmeister, E., eds., *Physical Processes in Comets, Star and Active Galaxies* (Springer-Verlag 1987).

Marsden, Brian G., *Catalogue of Cometary Orbits*, 5th ed. (Enslow 1986).

Whipple, Fred L., *The Mystery of Comets* (Smithsonian Institution Press 1985).

**COMFORT, Alex,** kum'fərt (1920–2000), English-born physician and author who made important studies of sexual behavior and aging. Alexander Comfort was born in London, England, on Feb. 10, 1920. He studied at the University of Cambridge and qualified as a physician at the Royal London Hospital in 1944. A conscientious objector during World War II, he campaigned against militarism and centralized government and in favor of anarchism.

Comfort wrote much fiction and poetry but made his reputation with books such as *Sexual Behavior in Society* (1949); *The Biology of Senescence* (1956); *Sex in Society* (1963); *Aging* and *The Process of Aging* (both 1964); and the enormously popular *The Joy of Sex: A Gourmet Guide to Lovemaking* (1972) and the sequel *More Joy of Sex* (1974). In the latter two books Comfort argued that greater freedom in sexual activity promotes improved human relations. Other published works include *I and That: Notes on the Biology of Religion* (1979); *Reality and Empathy: Physics, Mind and Science in the Twenty-First Century* (1984); and *The New Joy of Sex* (1991).

In 1974 Comfort moved to California, where, until 1983, he was a lecturer in Stanford University's psychiatry department and, from 1980 to 1991, served as a professor at the Neuropsychiatric Institute and Hospital, at the University of California at Los Angeles. He died in Banbury, England, on March 26, 2000.

**COMFREY,** kum'frē, the common name for the coarse plants making up the Eurasian genus *Symphytum*. Several species are cultivated, but in the United States the most popular is the common comfrey (*S. officinale*), a perennial plant sometimes grown in flower borders. Reaching about 3 feet (90 cm) in height, members of this species bear lance-shaped, alternate or nearly opposite leaves from 3 to 6 inches (7.5 to 15 cm) long. The plant's small flowers may be white, yellowish, purplish, or rose colored and are borne in drooping clusters.

Hardy plants, comfreys can be grown outdoors in all but the coldest parts of the United States. They are easily propagated by seeds or by division of the somewhat tuberous roots. *Symphytum* belongs to the borage family, Boraginaceae, in the order Lamiales, class Magnoliopsida.

DONALD WYMAN*
*Arnold Arboretum, Harvard University*

**COMICS,** kom'iks, cartoons arranged either in a single panel or in several boxes (in which case they are called comic strips), which are a popular feature of most American newspapers. Generally, comic strips have a continuing cast of characters. Depending on the nature of the strip, these characters may appear either in short humorous incidents or in longer narratives employing suspense, drama, and adventure. The term *comics* is also applied to comic books, a carryover from the cartoon strips from which they developed. A distinctive feature of most comic strips and comic books is the enclosure of the dialogue in "balloons" that seem to emerge from the speakers' mouths.

Daily and Sunday comic strips are read by millions of Americans from all segments of society. The comics, with their use of familiar folk themes and motifs, may be likened to modern versions of fairy tales, myths, and fables, drawing upon the folklore of American life and creating their own gallery of folk characters. The comics are an American institution, and from their beginning they have influenced the American language. Cartoonist Thomas A. Dorgan, for example, created many expressions that became part of American slang. Dorgan's strips *Indoor Sports* and *Judge Rummy* introduced phrases such as "twenty-three skiddoo," "cat's pajamas," "drugstore cowboy," and "yes, we have no bananas."

In his book *The American People: A Study in National Character* (1948), the British anthropologist Geoffrey Gorer made the observation that "With the notable exception of the *New York Times*, almost every American newspaper carries comic strips. They are one of the few important bonds (the films being another and the presidential elections a third) uniting all Americans in a common experience."

From their beginning in the 1890s, the comics have appealed both to young readers and to adults. Research conducted by Charles Swanson indicated that in the period from 1939 to 1950 the comic strip page was by far the most widely read section of the newspaper. Analyzing the appeal of about 40,000 news and feature items that appeared in 130 American newspapers, Swanson found that the comics ranked highest, with an average male readership of 56.3% and an average female readership of 56.6%. The next highest category was war (World War II, of course, occurred during the time of these surveys), with an average readership of 34.6%. Swanson did not conclude that the comics were more important to the average American newspaper reader than news about World War II. But this study did indicate that comic strips have a very great appeal.

A strong case could be made for the comics as the most widely read mass medium in the United States. For example, a comic strip such as

UPI

Cartoonist George McManus, creator of *Bringing Up Father*, designed U.S. aircraft insignia in World War II.

*Blondie*, a popular strip for decades, has probably been read hundreds of billions of times. This estimate is based on the assumption that 40 or 50 million *Blondie* devotees have habitually read this strip each day. By reestablishing itself daily with its reader, a comic strip reinforces its hold on him or her.

American comic strips have been widely circulated throughout the world. In turn, the success in the United States of strips such as Britain's *Andy Capp* signifies that the medium is an agent for the exchange of mass culture. American comics have achieved wide popularity in Latin America, where in Buenos Aires the prestigious *La Prensa* has carried several American strips. They have been accepted in Europe, even in eastern European countries, including Yugoslavia, Poland, and Hungary. Australia and South Africa also have proved to be good markets for American comics.

### ORIGINS AND HISTORY

Newspaper comic artists are the spiritual descendants of the Egyptian artists of 3000 B.C., who drew amusing animal cartoons on papyrus, and of the ancient Romans, who hawked satiric cartoons on tabulae. In England broadsheets and pamphlets of Punch and Judy characters were sold at fairs in the 17th century and thus might be called the first comic books. By the early 1880s two satiric comic weeklies, *Judge* and *Life*, had been started, each utilizing cartoon humor.

**The First Phase.** From their beginning in the 1890s, the comics passed through four distinct periods. The initial period, ending in 1914, when syndication began, marked the emergence of the first great newspaper comic artists. Cartoonists such as James Swinnerton and Richard Felton Outcault began to apply their talents to the needs of a press seeking mass readership. In 1892 Swinnerton created the first continuing characters to appear in a daily newspaper—*Little Bears*, in William Randolph Hearst's San Francisco *Examiner*. On Nov. 18, 1894, Richard Outcault became a

LISTEN TO DE WOIDS OF WISDOM WOT DE PHONOGRAFF WILL GIVE YER

YELLOW KID
© KING FEATURES SYNDICATE — NEWSPAPER COMICS COUNCIL INC.

**EARLY COMIC STRIPS** enjoyed sufficient popularity to be used as newspaper circulation builders by many American publishers at the turn of the century.

BUSTER BROWN
©1967 KING FEATURES SYNDICATE INC.

HAPPY HOOLIGAN
©1967 KING FEATURES SYNDICATE INC.

THE KATZENJAMMER KIDS
© UNITED FEATURES SYNDICATE INC.

MUTT AND JEFF
© BELL SYNDICATE INC.

major figure in the medium when his *Origin of a New Species* appeared in Joseph Pulitzer's New York *World*. With the appearance of the *Yellow Kid* a year later in the Pulitzer paper, Outcault achieved nationwide fame. This strip probably marks the real beginning of the comics.

As part of his intense circulation war with Pulitzer, Hearst lured Outcault away from the *World* to the New York *Journal* in 1896. The expression "yellow journalism," which later came to categorize this whole flamboyant period in American journalism, derived its meaning from the acrimonious struggle that developed as both papers vied for Outcault and his *Yellow Kid*. See YELLOW JOURNALISM.

Also in 1896, Hearst's *Journal* initiated the first newspaper section devoted to color comics. This section was advertised as "Eight pages of polychromatic effulgence that makes the rainbow look like a lead pipe." Besides Outcault, the New York *Journal* had Swinnerton, who moved east from San Francisco and called his strip *Little Bears and Tigers;* Frederick Burr Opper, whose *Happy Hooligan* became a comics classic; and Rudolph Dirks, who based his *The Katzenjammer Kids* on Busch's *Max und Moritz.*

Newspaper publishers welcomed the comic strip as a circulation-builder and encouraged additional artists to enter the field. Thus, scarcely more than a decade after its beginning, the comics world included such strips as Carl Schultze's *Foxy Grandpa* (1900), Swinnerton's masterwork, *Little Jimmy* (1905), and Fontaine Fox's famous *Toonerville Folks* (1908). Outcault's *Buster Brown*, created in 1897 for yet another paper, James Gordon Bennett's New York *Herald,* was a favorite of the reading public for many years.

During this early period, the idea of having strips appear daily began with Clare Briggs' *A Piker Clerk* (1904), which ran in the Chicago *American*. Three years later in the San Francisco *Chronicle,* Bud Fisher started *Mutt and Jeff.* Other notable cartoonists of this first period were Winsor McCay, who created the brilliant fantasy *Little Nemo in Slumberland,* and Harry Hershfield, who drew *Desperate Desmond*. By 1912, as the period was ending, George McManus conceived probably the most popular characters in all comics history—Maggie and Jiggs of *Bringing Up Father*. Great numbers of Americans, including millions of immigrants who were just becoming accustomed to American culture, either empathized with Jiggs and his shrewish wife Maggie or laughed at them, and McManus' strip became a favorite of an immense reading public.

**The Golden Age.** Comics entered a second phase in 1914, when they became syndicated. Within a few years virtually every newspaper in the United States carried a comics page. For the next three decades the medium flourished, as outstanding new artists joined such established cartoonists as McManus, Opper, and Outcault. One of the greatest cartoonists of the period, George Herriman, had begun a strip titled *The Family Upstairs* in 1910. In it there appeared the redoubtable Krazy Kat. By 1913, *Krazy Kat* was a distinct strip, and during the next 30 years, until Herriman's death, the antics of Krazy Kat, Offisa Pup, and Ignatz Mouse were enacted against the surrealistic background of Coconino County, Arizona.

Gilbert Seldes, in his book *The Seven Lively Arts* (1924), recognized *Krazy Kat* as an enduring contribution to American art. As with such

371

KRAZY KAT
BY GEORGE HERRIMAN —
©KING FEATURES SYNDICATE —
THE NEWSPAPER COMICS COUNCIL INC.

POPEYE
©1967 KING FEATURES
SYNDICATE INC.

LITTLE ORPHAN ANNIE
©1967 NEWS SYNDICATE CO. INC.,
WORLD RIGHTS RESERVED

DICK TRACY
©1967 CHICAGO TRIBUNE, WORLD RIGHTS RESERVED

DAGWOOD AND BLONDIE
©KING FEATURES SYNDICATE

THE GOLDEN AGE OF COMICS introduced characters popular with readers of all sorts for over 40 years. *Krazy Kat* was a favorite of 1920's American intellectuals; *Dick Tracy* was a literary discovery for French intellectuals in the 1960's.

later comic strips as *Li'l Abner* and *Peanuts*, *Krazy Kat* could be read on several levels of enjoyment. More than any other strip, it appealed to intellectuals and the literary minority who at first rejected comics as a subliterary form not worthy of their attention. It is said that President Woodrow Wilson read *Krazy Kat* before holding his cabinet meetings. In 1921, John Alden Carpenter composed a ballet about Krazy Kat. When a collection of the strips was published in a hard-cover edition, the distinguished poet E. E. Cummings wrote an appreciative introduction to the volume.

During this golden age of comics art, many other famous cartoonists began long-enduring strips. Harry Hershfield created *Abie the Agent*; H. H. Knerr took over the drawing of *The Katzenjammer Kids*; and Sydney Smith began *The Gumps*, a strip conceived and named by Joseph Patterson, the founder of the New York *Daily News*. Between 1919 and 1925, Patterson acquired other top-level cartoonists, who produced such popular strips as *Harold Teen, Little Orphan Annie, Gasoline Alley*, and *Moon Mullins*. (To this array, Patterson later added *Smitty, Winnie Winkle, Dick Tracy, Terry and the Pirates*, and *Smilin' Jack*.)

Other noted cartoonists of this period included Billy DeBeck, who originated *Barney Google* (1919); Elzie C. Segar, whose *Thimble Theatre* (1919) featured Olive Oyl and a scrawny, spinach-eating sailor named Popeye; and Murat (Chic) Young, whose first strip success was titled *Dumb Dora* (1924).

Newspaper comics sections could still be called the "funny papers" throughout the 1920's. The gifted cartoonists Rube Goldberg and Milt Gross presented humor that was at once broad and raucous, yet sharply barbed with satire on American society. Gross' *Nize Baby* was enjoyed by such disparate personalities as President Calvin Coolidge and Justice Oliver Wendell Holmes. Rube Goldberg's zany inventions in *Boob McNutt* became a hallmark of cartoon ingenuity.

**The Third Period.** Until the 1930's the comics were essentially humorous exaggerations of American life and manners, although such relatively

serious strips as Harold Gray's *Little Orphan Annie* had already become successful. The trend from 1934, when Milton Caniff created *Terry and the Pirates*, until the end of World War II was toward adventure strips. There emerged such new heroes as Roy Crane's *Captain Easy* and *Buz Sawyer*. This was also the decade of the science-fiction adventures—*Superman, Flash Gordon, Buck Rogers*, and *Brick Bradford*. Strips such as *Apple Mary* (1932), thematically similar to the radio soap operas of the 1930 depression days, began to appear on the comics page. When *Apple Mary* became *Mary Worth* in 1938 under Allen Saunder's sophisticated hand, it became one of the most widely read comic strips.

The trend in the 1930's was generally toward comics that treated themes of adventure or domestic problems. But in 1934 the public quickly accepted what soon became one of the most famous of all humor strips, Al Capp's *Li'l Abner*.

**Postwar Comics.** After World War II there was a fairly sharp return to humorous comic strips. This may have been stimulated by the creation of two of the most enjoyable comic strips in the history of the medium, Walt Kelly's *Pogo* (1949) and Charles Schulz' *Peanuts* (1950). From 1956 to 1960, 32 of the 39 new comic strips introduced were purely humorous. These included Frank O'Neal's *Short Ribs*, Johnny Hart's *B.C.*, Mel Lazarus' *Miss Peach*, and Mort Walker's *Beetle Bailey*.

After 1960 new humor strips continued to outnumber new story strips more than two to one. Such single-panel cartoons as Jerry Robinson's incisive *Still Life* and Morrie Brickman's *Small Society* combined humor and topical satire that required the reader to be in touch with the day's news. *Andy Capp*, a British import, quickly gained a large following among American readers, who found the antics of the diminutive Cockney extremely amusing. Although such long-time serious favorites as *Dick Tracy, Steve Canyon*, and *Mary Worth* retained their millions of daily readers, there was a clear indication that new comics, such as the *Wizard of Id, Miss Peach*, and *Peanuts*, once again had made the cartoon strips "the funnies."

BATMAN AND ROBIN
©1967 NATIONAL PERIODICAL PUBLICATIONS INC.

MUSCULAR COMIC STRIP HEROES of the 1930's have survived both on their own merits and through their affectionate reappraisal in the works of several pop artists.

DAISY MAE AND LI'L ABNER
©NEWS SYNDICATE CO. INC., WORLD RIGHTS RESERVED

SUPERMAN
©1967 NATIONAL PERIODICAL PUBLICATIONS INC.

## COMIC BOOKS

The comic book developed from the newspaper comic strip. Although the comic strip had expanded to include a wide range of nonhumorous subject matter—family life, romance, fantasy, science fiction, the West, detective adventures—the name "comics" remained. This subject matter carried over to the comic book, whose name is descriptive of a format rather than an editorial content. The many comic books published monthly, bimonthly, or quarterly include cartoon comics in the broadly humorous category, but the majority of titles feature fantasy, romance, or adventures in space, the American West, or the military.

Comic books might have been more appropriately called magazines, since almost from the beginning they were published on a periodical basis. Some were geared to very young readers, and others to the specific interests of teenagers. Some were aimed at boys' love of action and adventure, and some, with heavy emphasis on fashions and romance, were directed toward female audiences. The heaviest readership of comic books appeared to be in the 7-to-14 age group, although there was a substantial readership in the preschool and high school age groups. During World War II, comic books outsold *Life* and the *Reader's Digest* ten to one at U. S. Army post exchanges. Comic books sold at the rate of millions of copies per month, with a probable "pass on" readership of at least three for each copy sold.

**History of Comic Books.** Primarily an American product, the comic book is a relative newcomer to publishing. Although the Chicago *American* reprinted a group of its old *Mutt and Jeff* plates and bound the pages together in a book in 1911, the first comic book in its familiar format did not make its appearance until 1933. This pioneer, *Funnies on Parade*, consisted of reruns of Sunday newspaper comic strips reduced to standard magazine size. It was conceived initially as a sales promotion device. When the enterprising publisher decided to experiment with some copies by placing them on a few newsstands with a 10-cent price tag, they were sold in a weekend.

The first comic books to use original material began in 1935, but it was not until 1937, with the publication of *Detective Comics*, that a publication devoted itself entirely to a single theme or predominant character. This subsequently became the standard format. The industry moved ahead quickly with the appearance in 1938 of a personality named Superman, who "flew" through the pages of the first issue of *Action Comics*.

The great success of *Action Comics* brought many other publishers into the field. By 1940 there were 60 titles, and a year later there were 168. Some publishers specialized in horror comics with such titles as *Tales from the Crypt* and *The Vault of Horror*, some specialized in crime comics in which violence became an end in itself, and others concentrated on offensive themes that disturbed the parents of many young readers.

**Reform of Comic Books.** By the early 1950's there was considerable demand for some form of censorship of the offensive comic books. The most severe critic of the comic books was Frederic Wertham, a New York psychiatrist. In his book *The Seduction of the Innocent* (1954) Wertham described the effects of the particularly brutal and perverted horror comics he studied as the "psychological erosion of children." However, his material was gathered from the clinical study of disturbed children and contained little empirical evidence regarding the influence of horror comics on the normal child. Nevertheless, Wertham's account increased the anxiety of certain groups over the possible effects of comic books on children.

Facing the prospect of lengthy litigation throughout the United States, the comic book publishers formed an association in 1954, and later set up a comics code authority. The code covered both the editorial content and the advertisements in comics magazines. Members of the association agreed to adhere to the terms of the code, and to submit all material intended for publication to the code authority for advance review and judgment. The code worked well, serving to allay most of the fears of those who once termed comic books "the marijuana of the nursery." Publishers who could not abide by the code did not join the association and gradually left the field. As a consequence of the elimination of much of the gore and horror elements from comic books, the number of readers diminished.

With the adoption of the Comic Authority Code in 1954, the major anxieties in relation to comic books were allayed. However, in 1967 the Comics Magazine Association warned that another flood of comic books featuring horror and other objectionable material had been seen on newsstands. Since the code could be applied only to members of the association as a self-regulating force, there was little to thwart the unscrupulous publisher of objectionable material.

Also in 1967, social scientists at Oxford University made a study of 40 weekly comic books in England. It indicated that young readers acquire prejudiced stereotypes of foreigners through reading war comics. Their report expressed concern that these stereotypes would shape later attitudes.

The influence of comic books on young readers is a recurrent and hotly debated subject. However, the value of the comic book technique as a highly effective communications medium is shown by the increasing number of comic booklets sponsored by government and private agencies and by leading industrial firms. The U.S. Atomic Energy Commission used a comic book to describe what an atom is, how it is split, and what happens when it is split. The General Electric Corporation published a number of comic booklets dealing not only with electricity, atoms, and other scientific subjects, but also with historical topics. Public welfare organizations, such as the Anti-Defamation League, used comic books to spread the principles of tolerance and brotherhood. Archie Comics in 1967 produced *What Happened to Joe and His Drinking Problem* for Alcoholics Anonymous, and the U.S. Department of Health, Education, and Welfare used a comic booklet called *Hooked* in its drive against narcotics addiction.

## COMICS AND OTHER MEDIA

The comics, from their earliest decades, contributed to the other arts, ranging from serious music to (more obviously) Pop Art.

**Music.** In the 1920's Billy Rose wrote two songs derived from the comics—*Yes, We Have No Bananas* and *Barney Google with the Goo-Goo Googly Eyes*—that became standards in the popular repertory. In the 1930's there were musical tributes to *Popeye, the Sailor Man* and *Little Lulu*. In 1956, *Li'l Abner* was turned into a successful Broadway musical, which in turn became a Hollywood film in 1959. In 1966 the Broadway musical *It's a Bird . . . It's a Plane . . . It's Superman* attempted to satirize the comic strip *Superman*. One of the most successful off-Broadway musical productions of 1967 was *You're a Good Man, Charlie Brown*, based on the comic strip *Peanuts*. Its cast included Lucy, Linus, Schroeder, and even Snoopy, Charlie's extraordinary dog.

Comics also inspired serious music; for example, John Alden Carpenter's score for the 1921 ballet *Krazy Kat*. In the Contemporary Music Festival held at Geneva, Switzerland, in June 1967, the soprano Cathy Berberian performed her own composition *Stripsody*, based on themes from the comic strips.

**Films.** There was an immediate and continuing interplay between the comics and the movies. In 1897, Opper's engaging *Happy Hooligan* was adapted into the first movie serial series, with J. Stuart Blackton playing the incorrigible Happy. One of the first animated cartoons, *Humorous Phases of Funny Faces*, was filmed by Blackton in 1906. In 1909, Winsor McCay, the cartoonist of *Little Nemo in Slumberland*, produced an animated cartoon titled *Gertie the Dinosaur;* and a few years later the first animated cartoon in color, *The Debut of Thomas Cat*, was based on a comics character. Walt Disney turned some of his animated cartoon characters, such as Mickey Mouse and Donald Duck, into comics. See also CARTOON, ANIMATED.

From 1931 live actors were used in feature films about *Skippy, Blondie, Red Ryder, Captain Midnight, Dixie Dugan, Jungle Jim,* and *Joe Palooka.* George McManus' famous Jiggs was the central figure in a popular play called *Father* and in some 11 movies. Later, the derring-do of *Superman* and *Steve Canyon* moved from the newspaper to the screen. In 1967, Jane Fonda starred in a film version of the French comic strip *Barbarella.*

**Radio and Television.** The broadcast media made considerable use of the comics, particularly during the heyday of radio serials. Among the afternoon adventures that beguiled youngsters of the 1930's were *Dick Tracy, Terry and the Pirates, Little Orphan Annie, Buck Rogers,* and *Mickey Finn.* Television used both live actors and cartoon figures as it drew upon the comics for various programs. The indestructible *Superman* early became a popular television series, and *The Flintstones*, a television cartoon show, became a comic strip. *Dennis the Menace, Batman,* and *Steve Canyon* also were successful evening television shows for a number of years. In 1967, Charles Schulz' *Peanuts* characters were animated for two programs shown during prime evening hours on nationwide telecasts.

**Art.** The influence of comic art on the so-called Pop Art of the 1960's may be closely allied to the cult of camp (q.v.). During this period Roy Lichtenstein, a major contemporary artist, painted canvases that were like comic strips "because of their anti-artistic image and because they are such a modern subject." At first art critics laughed at Lichtenstein's pop paintings as outlandish examples of the "King Features school." This did not trouble the artist. "I was serious about the comic strips," he said, "yet I also expected them to look funny, because the whole idea of doing a comic strip is humorous." In 1967, with three major showings of his paintings, including one at the Stedelijk Museum in Amsterdam, Lichtenstein's canvases were much in demand.

There have been exhibitions of comic art in major galleries throughout the world. In Paris in 1967 the Louvre set aside three rooms for such an exhibit. It attracted much critical attention and a number of comics art devotees.

**Other Influences.** The influence of the comics on American culture also has been felt in such mundane things as eating habits. In Crystal City, Texas, for example, the grateful citizens of that spinach-growing community erected a statue of Popeye in honor of the comic strip character who made America spinach-conscious. There were numerous other instances of comic strip characters endorsing various foodstuffs and thus

NO ONE UNDERSTANDS US CRABBY PEOPLE!

LUCY

© UNITED FEATURES SYNDICATE, INC.

MAX EISEN, NEW YORK CITY

*Peanuts,* an "intellectual" comic strip by Charles Schulz, features the lovable Charlie Brown *(below, left),* the ill-tempered Lucy *(right),* and the philosophical dog Snoopy *(below, right).* Peanuts has been published in hard-cover books and has inspired television shows and a musical comedy, *You're a Good Man, Charlie Brown,* with *(left to right)* Reva Rose as Lucy, Bill Hinnart as Snoopy, and Gary Burghoff as Charlie Brown.

I NEVER WORRY ABOUT HOW I START THE DAY... IT'S HOW IT ENDS UP THAT BOTHERS ME!

CHARLIE BROWN

© UNITED FEATURES SYNDICATE, INC.

DETERMINED PRODUCTIONS, INC.

IF YOU CAN'T DANCE, YOU SHOULD AT LEAST BE ABLE TO DO A HAPPY HOP!

SNOOPY

© UNITED FEATURES SYNDICATE, INC.

influencing American tastes in food. In the 1930's the sale of cheese rose so impressively when the comic strip heavyweight Joe Palooka trained on this food that the National Cheese Institute bestowed on Palooka's creator, Ham Fisher, the title of Cheese King of 1937. Corned beef and cabbage became a favorite preparation for millions partly because of Jiggs' fondness for it. Readers of a comic strip have written to newspapers to ask for the recipe of a dish enjoyed by an entirely fictional character: there were more than 85,000 requests for a recipe after the title character of *Gordo* made it popular.

Comics have also affected styles. At the turn of the century, a whole generation of American boys were dressed like the cartoon character Buster Brown. The influence on teen-age girls was more pervasive. *Penny* inspired first a group of hats, then a complete collection of teen-age fashions, and *Brenda Starr* also wielded considerable influence on styles.

Merchandise, particularly dolls and other toys, inspired by comic strip characters became immensely successful. One year after their introduction, more than $3 million worth of Sparkle Plenty dolls had been sold. There were dolls based on Cookie and Alexander (*Blondie*), Clovia (daughter of Skeezix and Nina in *Gasoline Alley*), and Bonny Braids (daughter of Dick Tracy). Al Capp's "Shmoos" promoted the sales of some 60 products, such as glassware, underwear, soap, fishhooks, egg cups, coin banks, birthday cards, and household deodorizers. One company sold some 5 million glass containers of cottage cheese with the Shmoo likeness on them.

## COMICS AND EDUCATION

Sidonie Mastner Gruenberg, an educator, observed in the 1940's that the only thing unique in the emergence of the comics as a social phenomenon of 20th century America is that they "came upon us silently and grew to considerable proportions before the 'guardians of culture' were aroused by them." Yet the comics were the targets of some criticism almost from their very beginning, when the raucous antics of the *Yellow Kid* elicited moral indignation.

Educators, in general, have not been overly concerned about the great attraction comics (both newspaper and comic books) hold for young readers. From the advent of comic books, 9 out of 10 children probably had comics as their first exposure to print, and continued to read them habitually through their high school years. The comics were enjoyed by generations of readers, and the fears once expressed that they would drive out the "classics" have proved groundless. (In fact, a number of classics read in school were adapted to a comic book format.) Furthermore, sociologists discovered that high readership of comics is not incompatible with equally high exposure to books. Educational researchers found that comic books, which use a vocabulary of some 10,000 words, help stimulate interest in reading on the part of new readers.

From their beginning in 1895 the comics have mirrored American life. They have also affected American culture in a variety of ways, from influencing dress or eating habits to providing their readership with an unending series of culture heroes. The comics may contribute to the development of a national ethos; their creators, in seeking the widest possible audience, reflect that audience and its thinking.

David Manning White, *Boston University; Coeditor of "The Funnies: An American Idiom"*

**Bibliography**

Barker, Martin, *A Haunt of Fears* (Longwood 1984).
Barrier, Michael, and Williams, Martin, *A Smithsonian Book of Comic Book Comics* (Abrams 1982).
Horn, Maurice, *Women in the Comics* (Chelsea House 1981).
Lorenz, Lee, *The Golden Age of Trash: Cartoons for the Eighties* (Chronicle Bks. 1987).
Schodt, Frederick, *Manga! Manga! The World of Japanese Comics* (1983; reprint, Kodansha Int. 1986).
Scott, Randall W., *Comic Books and Strips* (Oryx Press 1988).
Van Hise, James, *Comics Feature History of Comic Books* (Borgo Press 1986).
White, David M., and Capp, Al, *From Dogpatch to Slobovia* (Little 1964).
White, David M., and Abel, Robert, eds., *The Funnies: An American Idiom* (Glencoe 1963).

**COMINFORM,** kom'in fôrm, the abbreviated name of the Bureau of Information of the Communist and Workers' Parties, an agency of the Soviet and Soviet-dominated Communist parties of eastern Europe. It was formed in September 1947 at Sklarska Poreba near Wrocław, Poland, by the Communist parties of the USSR, Poland, Czechoslovakia, Hungary, Yugoslavia, Bulgaria, Rumania, Italy, and France. Its avowed aim was "to meet the need for an exchange of experiences and a voluntary coordination of the activities of the individual parties." It set up headquarters in Belgrade, Yugoslavia (shifted to Bucharest, Rumania, in 1948) and published a weekly bulletin.

The real aim of the Cominform was to increase Communist militancy in Europe and to strengthen Soviet control over the satellite countries at a time when the Soviet Union fell back upon extreme Stalinism for its security and cohesion. Andrei Aleksandrovich Zhdanov, the chief agent of Stalinism at the time, was the principal Soviet spokesman at Sklarska Poreba.

The creation of the Cominform marked the end of the wartime alliance between the Soviet Union and the Western powers and the beginning of the Cold War. The Cominform fomented vigorous anti-Americanism in Italy and France; in eastern Europe, its center of activity, it established the exclusive rule of Communist leaders subservient to Moscow in place of the "National Front" governments (which had permitted non-Communist participation).

The first major effect of the new policy was the Communist take-over of Czechoslovakia in February 1948. Purges of leading Communists suspected of nationalist leadings soon followed. These were relatively mild in Poland, where Władysław Gomulka (later the head of the Polish Communist party) was demoted. Elsewhere there were show trials and executions: Traicho Kostov in Bulgaria, László Rajk in Hungary, and later, Rudolph Slansky in Czechslovakia.

In Yugoslavia, however, the new policy met with disaster. Under Marshal Tito's leadership, the Yugoslav Communist party resisted Soviet penetration and preserved its independence. Stalin's wrath led to an open break with Tito and Yugoslavia's expulsion from the Cominform in June 1948. With the reassessment of Soviet policy after Stalin's death in 1953, the Cominform gradually declined. In 1955, Khrushchev reversed the Soviet policy toward Tito, and after the 20th Congress of the Soviet Communist party in 1956, the Cominform was officially dissolved.

THEODORE H. VON LAUE
*Washington University, St. Louis*

**COMINTERN,** kom'in-tûrn, an abbreviation for Communist (Third) International. This worldwide organization of Communist parties existed from 1919 to 1943. It was controlled by the Soviet Communist party. See also COMINFORM; INTERNATIONAL.

**COMITIA,** kə-mish'ē-ə, a meeting of all the citizens of the Roman state, both patrician and plebeian. A meeting of only part of the citizens —the plebeians—was called the *concilium*. Summoned by an official of state, a *comitia* met to transact state business. In the *comitia* the citizens voted approval or disapproval of matters put before them, or they elected officials. The people voted as units, the majority in each unit determining the unit's vote.

The *comitia curiata*, the most ancient of the Roman assemblies, consisted of citizens grouped into 30 gentilic units (*curiae*)—10 from each of the three ancient tribes. The *comitia curiata* confirmed the civil and military power of the kings and later confirmed the power of consuls, praetors, and dictators, the same officials who had the right to convene the assembly. The *pontifex maximus* could call this assembly to inaugurate certain priests. The assembly also dealt with citizens who wished to transfer from the patrician to the plebeian order and settled wills and adoptions. Probably in the late 3d century B. C., as a result of the assembly's loss of power, the people stopped attending its meetings and the *curiae* were instead represented by 30 lictors.

The *comitia centuriata*, established in the 6th century B. C. by King Servius Tullius, originally was made up of military units (*centuriae*, or centuries); in the course of the 5th century B. C., these developed into voting units. Citizens were assigned to classes according to their wealth. In addition to the wealthiest citizens who served as cavalry and voted in 18 centuries, there were five classes of citizens divided into 170 centuries, with the wealthier citizens having the greater number of centuries under their control. There were also 5 centuries of supernumeraries. The *comitia centuriata* could be convened by a consul, praetor, or dictator. It elected these same officials as well as censors and curule aediles. This assembly declared war and heard citizens' appeals of the death sentence. It also served as the chief lawmaking body until superseded by the *comitia tributa* in the 3d century B. C.

The Roman people were divided into territorial tribes for administrative and census purposes, and these tribes were the voting units in the *comitia tributa*. This assembly met under a consul, praetor, or perhaps a tribune, and elected the latter official, the plebeian aediles, and the quaestors. Because it was easier to call the people together in tribes, the *tributa* soon replaced the centuriate assembly in lawmaking. Once the assembly of the plebeians (*concilium plebis tributa*) obtained power to pass legislation (287 B. C.), the difference between the *comitia* and *concilium tributa* became insignificant. The *comitia* lost all importance under the emperors.

RICHARD E. MITCHELL, *University of Illinois*

**COMMA.** See PUNCTUATION.

**COMMAGENE,** kom-ə-jē'nē, was the ancient name of a district on the west bank of the Euphrates River between the Taurus Mountains and the Syrian plain. Now a part of Turkey, this area in ancient times was bordered on the west by Cilicia and on the west and north by Cappadocia. It was an important strategic area where several routes across the Taurus reached the Euphrates, and was coveted by many major powers. It formed the Neo-Hittite state of Kummuhu, which gradually came under Assyrian control in the 9th and 8th centuries B. C.; it paid tribute of cedar, cattle, silver, and gold, an indication of its natural resources.

Although little is known of the area thereafter for some centuries, the survival of its name as Commagene implies the survival of its culture. It passed from Persian to Armenian to Seleucid kingdoms, and under the Seleucids was ruled by local princes, one of whom, Ptolemy, declared himself an independent king (about 162 B. C).

His successor, Samos, reputedly founded the later capital Samosata (now Samsat). His great-grandson Antiochus I (reigned about 69–34 B.C.) submitted to Pompey and was recognized as a client king of Rome in 62 B.C. Rome thus gained a useful buffer state between its empire and Parthia.

Antiochus built a splendid tomb-sanctuary on the peak of Nemrud Dağ for the cult of himself, his ancestors, and his family's patron gods; he built a similar one for his father, Mithridates Kallinikos, at nearby Arsameia on the Nymphaios River. Both sanctuaries were excavated in the 1950s and 1960s.

On the death of Antiochus III in 17 A.D., Germanicus annexed the kingdom. Caligula returned it to his friend Antiochus IV in 38, but Vespasian finally took it from him in 72. The four cities of Commagene were Samosata, Doliche (near Gaziantep), Caesareia Germaniceia (now Maraş), and Perrhe (now Pırun Adıyaman).

D. J. BLACKMAN
*Bristol University*

**COMMAGER, Henry Steele,** kom′ə-jər (1902–1998), American historian and educator. Commager was born on Oct. 25, 1902, in Pittsburgh, Pa., and grew up in the Midwest. He received his undergraduate and graduate training (Ph.D., 1928) at the University of Chicago. His teaching career began at New York University (1926–1938); later he taught at Columbia University (1938–1956) and at Amherst College, where he was a professor of American history (1956–1972) and then Simpson Lecturer (1972–1992). Commager died in Amherst, Mass., on March 2, 1998.

Commager exercised wide influence on the study of American history. With Samuel Eliot Morison he wrote (1930) and later revised (through its tenth edition in 1987) *The Growth of the American Republic,* an unusually successful textbook that exhibited fine critical judgment, wit, and literary grace. In scholarship Commager showed remarkable versatility: as a biographer, in *Theodore Parker* (1936); as a constitutional historian, in *Majority Rule and Minority Rights* (1943) and *Freedom, Loyalty, Dissent* (1954); as a historiographer, in *The Search for a Usable Past* (1967); as an intellectual historian, in *Jefferson, Nationalism, and the Enlightenment* (1974), *The Empire of Reason* (1977), and *Commager on Tocqueville* (1993); as an editor, in *Documents of American History* (1934 and later editions), *Immigration and American History* (1961), and *Lester Ward and the Welfare State* (1967); and as a coauthor of popular histories with Allan Nevins and others.

All of Commager's work, which includes scores of articles, mostly on issues of social justice, demonstrates his Jeffersonian liberalism, owing in part to his admiration for Vernon L. Parrington, Justice Oliver Wendell Holmes, and Pres. Franklin D. Roosevelt. Perhaps his most enduring achievement is *The American Mind* (1951), in which he treats the social problems of the 1890s and their solutions as the great cultural divide in American life.

BERTRAM WYATT-BROWN*
*Case Western Reserve University*

**Bibliography:** Garraty, John, *Interpreting American History: Conversations with Historians,* 2 vols. in 1 vol. (Macmillan 1970); **Hyman, Harold, and Leonard W. Levy,** eds., *Freedom and Reform: Essays in Honor of Henry Steele Commager* (Harper 1967); **Jumonville, Neil,** *Henry Steele Commager and Midcentury Liberalism: The History of the Present* (Univ. of N.C. Press 1998).

**COMMANDO,** kə-man′do, a word adopted by the Boers in South Africa to designate a command or military unit and eventually by the British to denote a military unit trained for swift hit-and-run raids on enemy territory. The Boers originally used the term specifically for military and quasi-military expeditions against native Africans. By the time of the South African War (1899–1902) a commando was the local Boer militia unit.

In World War II the British organized commandos that were the size of an infantry battalion. Specially trained for raiding the coasts of German-held Europe, the first unit was created in June 1940 of army volunteers who learned the tactics of hand-to-hand combat, night infiltration, and surprise. Later, commando units were established in the Royal Marines. Commandos participated in the Dieppe raid of August 1942, in Mediterranean campaigns, notably the Salerno invasion, and in campaigns in northwestern Europe. The U.S. Army Rangers, from which developed the Special Forces, were modeled on commandos.

After the war the commando role in Britain was reserved for the Royal Marines, and one commando unit fought in Korea. Always ready, the commandos are used chiefly to quell disorders.

MARTIN BLUMENSON
*Office of Military History, U.S. Army*

**COMMEDIA DELL'ARTE,** kō-mâ′dyä del-lär′tä, a form of improvised Italian comedy that flourished from the mid-16th to the mid-18th century. It was performed by wandering troupes of professional actors, hence the term *arte,* meaning profession. Improvisation and the use of masks are the two salient and distinguishing features of commedia dell'arte, and these have given rise to alternate designations, including "improvised comedy" and "comedy of masks."

The commedia dell'arte was a true theater of the people—original, spontaneous, and often quite racy. Companies of actors traveled from place to place, erecting their small stages in marketplaces and at fairs and festivals. From Italy the commedia spread throughout most of Europe.

**Acting Techniques.** Instead of memorizing a set play (the written drama of this time was known as *commedia erudita*), the actors worked with a plot outline or scenario, usually a story about true love. They implemented these sketches with improvised dialogue, music, dancing, acrobatics, and buffoonery, including stage tricks, or *lazzi.* From time to time they recited stock passages from their notebooks or *zibaldoni.*

**Commedia dell'Arte Characters.** The various characters in the commedia dell'arte spoke in prescribed local Italian dialects. The central and most constant figures in the commedia dell'arte were the comic personages, notably those that have been referred to as the "four masks"—two older men and two servants, or *zanni.* Many plays also employed a captain, or *capitano,* another masked figure. The other staple characters in a typical cast included the two or more pairs of lovers, or *innamorati,* and the serving maid, or *servetta,* all of whom acted without masks. The basic traits, personalities, and costumes of the characters were constant in all the plays.

One of the older stock characters was Pantalone, a merchant from Venice who spoke in the Venetian dialect. He was habitually the head of a household, astute in business, but woefully inadequate in other matters. His companion and neigh-hor was the Dottore, a native of Bologna, who was either a lawyer, scholar, or medical doctor. The doctor, generally called Dottor Graziano, was usually presented as a lustful, garrulous, boastful and bumbling old man.

The chief of the *zanni,* or zanies, was Arlecchino (Harlequin), who spoke with the Bergamasque dialect in the early period. He was a lithe, athletic fellow—amoral, witty, and shrewd. However, in matters of love he was a fool. He had several equally zany companions, most of whom have now been forgotten with the exception of Brighella and Scapino, the embodiments of the crafty clown. Arlecchino's Neapolitan counterpart, Pulcinella, who was unscrupulous and coarse as well as a good quipster, developed later than the Bergamascan and soon vied with him in popularity. He was the ancestor of the English puppet known as Punch.

The *capitano* was portrayed as a typical braggart soldier, or *miles gloriosus.* Like his Roman comedy prototype, he was a coward and a liar. When he was used in a play, he always had a conspicuous part in the plot, usually as an unsuccessful or deceived lover. He is perhaps best known under the name Scaramouche.

The *innamorati* always appeared on stage in elegant dress, speaking a refined Tuscan dialect. Their only distinguishing trait was that they were in love. However, they were essential to the action of the plays, which opened with them and ended in their marriage. The *servetta* was a sprightly young lady, always loyal to her mistress. She was amorously inclined, and in the course of the play she became the bride of one of the zanies.

**History.** Attempts to trace the origins of the commedia dell'arte through various forms of drama from antiquity to the Renaissance have been largely unsuccessful. Whatever its beginnings, the commedia was an established theatrical genre by the mid-16th century. One of the most famous of the early companies was known as I Gelosi and was led by Francesco Andreini and his wife Isabella. Traveling Italian troupes toured Europe and gradually the influence of the commedia dell'arte made itself felt in the works of such prominent dramatists as Molière, Shakespeare, Lope de Vega, and Goldoni. It is still felt in the 20th century in circus clowns, who are the direct descendants of the *zanni,* in Punch and Judy shows, and in comic skits that feature stock characters.

JOSEPH C. FUCILLA, *Northwestern University*

**COMMENCEMENT,** the occasion at colleges and universities on which students receive a degree in recognition of having completed a prescribed course of study. The word, often used synonymously with graduation, has been extended to include the closing exercises of secondary or even elementary schools. In the early universities commencement exercises signified that the graduate was recognized by his profession and was ready to commence teaching.

The commencement ceremonies are sometimes divided into two parts. The baccalaureate ceremony, usually held on Sunday, is essentially a religious service at which a sermon is delivered to the graduates. On graduation day earned and honorary degrees are conferred and there is frequently an address by a public figure. Although many speakers intend only to give good advice, others take the opportunity to issue statements on the arts or on politics and world affairs.

**COMMENSALISM,** kə-men′səl-iz-əm, the association of two organisms of different species in a living relationship that is beneficial to one member (the commensal) and neither harmful nor beneficial to the other. The species benefiting from the association usually receives transport, food, shelter, or physical support from the other.

One good example of commensalism is provided by certain species of fish that live among the tentacles of sea anemones, which capture and eat other fish species. The commensal fish are thus protected from predator fish, and they also share in the sea anemone's prey. In some cases, the fish live even in the digestive cavity of the sea anemone and come and go as they please.

In a peculiar commensal relationship, the tropical fish *Fierasfer* lives in the cloacal chamber (the last part of the intestine) of a species of sea cucumber. The fish leaves the cloaca to feed. When it returns, the fish pokes the sea cucumber in the cloacal area with its head and then immediately turns around to be drawn into the cloacal chamber tail first.

Commensalism may be imposed upon some animals, as in the case of a very small crab species. While they are larvae, these crabs enter oysters. As the crabs mature, they become too large to escape through the narrow opening between the oyster's valves. As a result, the crab is trapped within the oyster's shell for life, but it is fed when the oyster takes in food.

Some barnacle species are found attached only to the backs of whales, and other species of barnacles are found attached only to the barnacle species found on whales. The benefits in this relationship are not clear; however, it appears that the barnacles are being transported from one rich feeding ground to another.

Plants also demonstrate commensalism. For example, orchids, and bromeliads (a common example is Spanish moss) are supported on tree limbs in tropical forests. Such plants are called epiphytes.

DAVID A. OTTO
*Stephens College*

**COMMENTARII,** kom-en-târ′ē-ī, Roman memoranda, which were often used as source material by historians. Initially, in the Roman Republic, commentarii were informal, personal, written materials that served as an aid to the memory, such as notes for speeches, legal notebooks, private memoranda, household records, or the memoirs of families or of individuals recording the deeds and accomplishments of which they were proud. Public commentarii, kept by priestly colleges, were not records of performance but rather handbooks of method, describing the technicalities of ceremonies and rituals, to be passed down from one priest to another. Roman magistrates also kept commentarii concerning the procedural aspects of their office and protocol. Provincial governors kept commentarii in order to write the reports required by the Senate. Technically such commentarii were not intended for publication.

Although they were originally not history in themselves, the commentarii were important sources for the writing of history. But with their development as memoirs by such men as Sulla and Cicero in the 1st century B.C., the commentarii began to be more than merely records of facts. This trend reached its logical conclusion with the writings of Caesar, who called his works on the Gallic and civil wars "commentaries" because he professed to be merely setting down the facts for someone else to use in writing a history. However, his plain, simple style was skillfully designed to present his own case in a most favorable light while making it appear that his presentation was above self-interest.

In the Roman Empire a record of the daily occurrences in court, commonly called the *commentarii diurni*, was kept, and there was also a record of the official decisions of the emperors and the accusations brought before them, the *commentarii principis*.

RICHARD E. MITCHELL, *University of Illinois*

**COMMERCE.** See TRADE.

**COMMERCE, Chamber of.** See CHAMBER OF COMMERCE.

**COMMERCE, United States Department of,** an executive department of the U.S. government, created to promote the country's international trade, economic growth, and technological advancement.

With the growth of U.S. industry in the late 19th century, many business leaders came to feel that the federal government should do more to promote their special interests and that they should have formal representation in the president's cabinet. On Feb. 14, 1903, Congress authorized the creation of the U.S. Department of Commerce and Labor, and on March 14, 1913, the agency was divided into separate departments. The primary responsibility of the new Department of Commerce was to promote business enterprise at home and American trade with foreign nations abroad. At the same time, Congress gave the secretary of commerce responsibility for fostering commercial shipping and the nation's merchant marine.

**The Department's Expanding Role.** The increasing involvement of government in the national economy in the course of the 20th century has been reflected in the expanding activities of the Department of Commerce. The department was created at a time when Americans were keenly interested in expanding foreign trade. Although this has continued to be a major function, the department over the years has assumed greater responsibilities for aid to domestic business. This trend first became evident in the decade of the 1920s, when Secretary of Commerce Herbert Hoover attempted to make the Commerce Department dominant in the cabinet.

If the department's influence in national affairs has fluctuated, reflecting the personality of individual secretaries as well as the prevailing business environment, the general trend in its history has been one of expansion. Although it has undergone innumerable changes in organization and functions, its primary goal of contributing to a strong economy has remained constant.

**Administrative Organization.** The organization of the Commerce Department has become increasingly complex. In 1981 the Reagan administration made various administrative changes, designed particularly to strengthen the department's ability to undertake economic analysis and economic policy development.

Attached directly to the secretary of commerce and the deputy secretary are seven important offices. These include the general counsel of the agency and assistant secretaries for congressional affairs and for administration. In addition, the associate deputy secretary, inspector general, spe-

cial assistant for regional development, and director for public affairs are directly responsible to the secretary. Important also is the undersecretary for international trade, who supervises policies in this vital sphere.

Other functions of the department are in the hands of seven assistant secretaries, in charge, respectively, of tourism, communications and information, economic affairs, economic policy, trade administration, trade development, and productivity, technology, and innovation. In 1981 the functions of an assistant secretary for maritime affairs were shifted, with the Maritime Administration, to the Department of Transportation.

Many of the department's important activities, such as the Minority Business Development Agency, the National Bureau of Standards, the Patent and Trademark Office, and the National Technical Information Service, are administered by directors. The administrator of the National Oceanic and Atmospheric Administration is in charge of one of the agency's most important divisions. Under the assistant secretary for economic affairs are the directors of the Bureau of the Census, the Bureau of Economic Analysis, and the Bureau of Industrial Economics.

**Principal Functions of the Department.** To carry out its broad mandate of encouraging American business at home and overseas and fostering economic growth, the department engages in a wide range of activities. Some of these provide information, others directly promote or regulate business, and some perform research functions.

One of the traditional promotional functions has been the advancement of technology in the United States, not only through the granting of patents and trademarks, but also by the dissemination of a vast fund of information concerning technological developments throughout the world. Among significant fact-gathering activities are the collection and analysis of data relating to business activity and the measurement of their impact on the national economy. The department closely monitors variables such as personal income, the gross national product, government purchases, and capital investment as indexes to the pace of the nation's economic activities. Such information is vital not only to many other federal agencies concerned with the formulation and implementation of economic policies but also to state and local units of government and to business people in the private sector. The administration of a census every ten years is a crucial aspect of this function.

The department also has responsibility for assisting economically depressed areas in the United States and for alleviating unemployment. It has performed these functions by extending loans to business and by providing direct grants and loan guarantees. Related are programs to assist minority businesses with direct grants and loans and with counseling aid.

As tourism has become increasingly important in the U.S. economy, the department has provided extensive programs designed to increase the flow of foreign visitors to the United States.

Among the department's research functions are the activities of the National Bureau of Standards, the National Weather Service, and the National Oceanic and Atmospheric Administration, which is involved in numerous projects dealing with atmospheric, oceanic, and outerspace programs.

## SECRETARIES OF COMMERCE

| Name | Term | Under President |
|------|------|-----------------|
| George B. Cortelyou* | 1903–1904 | T. Roosevelt |
| Victor H. Metcalf* | 1904–1906 | T. Roosevelt |
| Oscar S. Straus* | 1906–1909 | T. Roosevelt |
| Charles Nagel* | 1909–1913 | Taft |
| William C. Redfield | 1913–1919 | Wilson |
| Joshua W. Alexander | 1919–1921 | Wilson |
| Herbert C. Hoover | 1921–1928 | Harding, Coolidge |
| William F. Whiting | 1928–1929 | Coolidge |
| Robert P. Lamont | 1929–1932 | Hoover |
| Roy D. Chapin | 1932–1933 | Hoover |
| Daniel C. Roper | 1933–1938 | F. Roosevelt |
| Harry L. Hopkins | 1938–1940 | F. Roosevelt |
| Jesse H. Jones | 1940–1945 | F. Roosevelt |
| Henry A. Wallace | 1945–1946 | F. Roosevelt, Truman |
| W. Averell Harriman | 1946–1948 | Truman |
| Charles Sawyer | 1948–1953 | Truman |
| Sinclair Weeks | 1953–1958 | Eisenhower |
| Lewis L. Strauss | 1958–1959 | Eisenhower |
| Frederick H. Mueller | 1959–1961 | Eisenhower |
| Luther H. Hodges | 1961–1965 | Kennedy, L. B. Johnson |
| John T. Connor | 1965–1967 | L. B. Johnson |
| Alexander B. Trowbridge | 1967–1968 | L. B. Johnson |
| Cyrus R. Smith | 1968–1969 | L. B. Johnson |
| Maurice H. Stans | 1969–1972 | Nixon |
| Peter G. Peterson | 1972–1973 | Nixon |
| Frederick B. Dent | 1973–1975 | Nixon, Ford |
| Rogers C. B. Morton | 1975–1976 | Ford |
| Elliot L. Richardson | 1976–1977 | Ford |
| Juanita M. Kreps | 1977–1980 | Carter |
| Philip M. Klutznick | 1980–1981 | Carter |
| Malcolm Baldrige | 1981–1987 | Reagan |
| C. William Verity, Jr. | 1987–1989 | Reagan |
| Robert A. Mosbacher | 1989–1993 | G. H. W. Bush |
| Ronald H. Brown | 1993–1996 | Clinton |
| Mickey Kantor | 1996–1997 | Clinton |
| William Daley | 1997–2000 | Clinton |
| Norman Y. Mineta | 2000–2001 | Clinton |
| Donald L. Evans | 2001– | G. W. Bush |

*Secretary of commerce and labor.

The department is also closely involved with stimulating the nation's foreign trade. It provides aid to the Department of State in formulating national commercial policies and also alerts U.S. businesspeople to opportunities for exports around the world. It accomplishes this function through maintaining its own trade representatives abroad, publishing a wide assortment of special publications, helping U.S. business representatives at international trade expositions, sponsoring conferences with businesspeople, and working with personal contacts.

Finally, the department serves as an important lobbyist for business interests in Congress by advocating specific legislation considered to be desirable or by opposing policies thought to be harmful. As the watchdog for U.S. business, the department monitors discriminatory trade or tariff policies of other nations and alerts Congress and the president as to their influences on the U.S. economy.

GERALD D. NASH, *University of New Mexico*

**COMMERCE CITY,** an industrial and residential city in north-central Colorado, in Adams county, on the east bank of the South Platte River. It is about 7 miles (11 km) northeast of downtown Denver, of which it is a suburb. Stapleton International Airport is to the southeast. Commerce City is a transportation center. The Rocky Mountain National Wildlife Refuge borders the city.

The community was incorporated as Commerce Town in 1952 and as Commerce City in 1962. Population: 20,991.

**COMMERCIAL ART.** In the broadest sense of the term, commercial art includes all art that is intended to help industry or business sell a product or service or present a point of view. It may be regarded as any illustrative or design function applied to advertising, display, publishing, visual education, or manufacturing. Because the burgeoning of commercial art in the 20th century has given rise to numerous subdivisions within the field, the term no longer is in popular use. Such branches, or specialized areas, of commercial art as "advertising design," "book design," and "package design" are now used as specific designations within the commercial field. The term "communication art" increasingly is accepted as a synonym for commercial art.

**History.** During much of the past, the common distinctions between fine arts, crafts, and commercial art did not exist. All art forms were then considered utilitarian to some degree. Most art objects were made by craftsmen to the order of a patron, rather than at the artist's inspiration, and many art objects made for aristocratic or religious patrons embodied a persuasive message. One of the few examples of ancient art made for purely commercial purposes was the carved or painted signs marking the shops in ancient Egypt, Greece, and Rome. Because most of the public was illiterate, traditional symbols designated the nature of the shop; for example, in ancient Rome a painting of a cow marked a dairy shop, and a flying cherub with a shoe marked a shoe shop.

A distinguishing characteristic of most modern commercial art is that it is designed for reproduction. The invention of the printing press in the 15th century, because it offered almost limitless opportunities to reproduce illustrations, may be said to mark the birth of modern commercial art. Especially in England, known as the "nation of shopkeepers," printed advertising and advertising art increased with growing trade. Handbills and circulars, sometimes with woodcut illustrations, were common by the end of the 15th century. The first advertisement in an English newspaper appeared in 1625. In Britain's American colonies a similar respect for trade gave a brisk start to advertising art in the form of signs, circulars, and advertising symbols such as the wooden cigar-store Indian.

The Industrial Revolution was a tremendous stimulus to the growth of commercial art, which is a natural ally of mechanical and technical progress. Among the most influential inventions in the 19th century were photography, photoengraving, and the rotary press. Motion pictures, television, and improved color printing opened new fields in the 20th century, and commercial art continued to expand with the introduction of technical developments such as continuous-tone color printing, electronic laser scanning used for color reproduction, computerized typesetting, and computer-directed systems for editorial layout and elaborate graphic displays.

**Scope of Commercial Art.** Advertising, packaging and product design, publishing, and corporate-design programs are the major fields in which the commercial artist works. In many instances, designers and artists working in these fields coordinate their specialties with those of experts in industrial and architectural design. This is particularly true in the areas of product design, packaging, and corporate design.

Advertising art includes advertisements in

newspapers and magazines, commercials on television, large billboards, point-of-purchase displays, and exhibits in trade shows. These are the creations of the combined efforts of designers, artists, and photographers in collaboration with copywriters, consumer researchers, and account managers or executives. Visual impact, judicious use of color, and readability are primary requirements of the design.

Packaging and product design utilizes many of the techniques and devices of the advertising designer. The containers, wrappers, and labels for canned foods, bottled beverages, and cosmetics are designed for immediate sales appeal—a striking combination of color, distinctive typography, and usually an identifying trademark. The jackets for books and records are popular examples of packaging art. The shape as well as the decorative aspects of the package are intended to reflect the form and function of the product inside.

Product design is usually the domain of the industrial designer. However, an advertising designer may be involved on a consulting basis to coordinate the styling of a product with an overall corporate-design system. In planning a commodity that must be primarily functional as well as attractive, the designer strives for consumer appeal without dependence on packaging or other promotional aids. See also INDUSTRIAL DESIGN.

Publishing employs the skills of the editorial designer and the talents of specialized illustrators and photographers. Editorial design involves planning the format and the typographic styling of a book, magazine, or newspaper. In book and magazine publishing, when the format and style have been established, the designer creates layouts for individual pages, coordinating text and pictorial material in a logical and visually appealing manner that best communicates an idea or story to a reader.

Designers and illustrators for children's books and textbooks have the greatest opportunity for varied creative development in publishing. Periodicals specializing in fashion, decoration, travel, and science offer similar creative prospects for the artist in magazine publishing.

In newspaper publishing, the designer's work usually is finished with the creation of a format and typographic style. The pages of a daily paper are laid out by a makeup person following an editor's rough layout. Here speed and readability supersede aesthetics. The magazine sections of Sunday editions tend to follow the creative techniques of quality periodicals.

Corporate design, or a corporate-identity program, creates a distinctive image for a corporate enterprise. It requires a full range of design disciplines expressing the policies, purpose, and activities of an organization. The trade-mark is the basis of the program. This can be a word, a symbol, or a combination of the two that identifies the company in a simple configuration of line, mass, and color.

The essence of this basic motif is extended throughout the styling of products, advertising media, architecture, office decor, transport vehicles, employees' uniforms, and company literature. It is a cooperative effort of advertising designers, environmental designers, textile designers, and architects. The project may be developed by the corporation's internal design staff or by an outside consultant. Upon completion of

COURTESY OF CONGDON MACDONALD INC.

A designer and art director discuss creating a trademark or logotype that will identify a company or organization.

the program, a director or manager of corporate identity is retained to maintain consistency of style for future implementation.

**Careers in Commercial Art.** The principal functions that are basic to most areas of commercial art are design, photography, illustration, and production. Within these categories, artists and technicians with diversified talents and specialties work individually or in teams to produce a finished commodity. Most commercial art is guided through the successive steps from conception to finished product by an art director, who is responsible for the visual quality of a project, and by a production manager, who is in charge of the technical aspects of the process.

**Design.** There are two kinds of designers. One creates the product to be sold—greeting cards, textiles, wallpaper, clothes, rugs, appliances, automobiles, housewares, books, and every other product. Another promotes the sale of these products by designing labels, packaging, displays for counters and store windows, and various kinds of printed advertising.

After an advertising or editorial designer has planned a promotional brochure, for example, the layout artist executes the specific placement of pictures, text blocks, and other elements in the design. In some instances a sketch artist or renderer may make comprehensive drawings of any picture required. The typographer specifies the typefaces to be used and provides type proofs for makeup. The mechanical artist or paste-up artist is then responsible for assembling the finished art and typography into a "mechanical," from which reproductions are made.

To create animated graphics for film or television, an artist-writer prepares a storyboard—a series of sketches depicting the action and dialogue of a story. Layout artists then develop drawings showing individual scenes, specific backgrounds, and characters in the film. With these drawings as a guide, background artists and animators, working separately, render the finished art, which then is combined photographically by technicians in the camera department. See also CARTOON, ANIMATED.

In designing a new product, industrial designers develop sketches illustrating a variety of ideas. When one design is selected for development, a three-dimensional model is prepared by a model maker. After necessary modifications are approved, a draftsman and an illustrator prepare detailed working drawings from which a prototype model is built.

*Photography and Illustration.* One of the basic trends in 20th century advertising and publishing has been toward the use of more illustrative material and fewer words. This trend also is apparent in label designs, book and record jacket designs, and many other areas of commercial art. All of this illustrative material, planned by the art director or designer, is provided by a photographer or an illustrator. Most photographers and illustrators specialize in specific fields of illustration such as fashion, housewares, industrial products, science, or architecture.

Photography is used extensively in almost all areas of commercial art. Some large companies have photographic facilities in their art departments. In other instances photographs are bought from photograph agencies and other suppliers, such as a specific industry, or are produced by a photographer as a special assignment. In any case, art directors, artists, and layout men must have a good knowledge of photography, photographic techniques, print quality, and reproduction requirements. They must also be able to choose or plan a photographic shot with taste and flair.

For most people, the commercial artist is an

JOHN DUNIGAN FOR FREDERIC LEWIS/MAIL & MEDIA, INC.

A rough sketch, usually made by the art director, is normally the first step in planning a promotional booklet.

illustrator—the person who draws or paints the pictures for magazine articles and for various advertising media and who, in short, provides virtually all the "art" in commercial art. Indeed, illustration is perhaps the most glamorous and creative aspect of commercial art. It is also the most difficult for the beginner to break into. Topflight illustrator have a striking personal style that marks their work as their own. But for the beginning illustrator, who holds a subordinate position as boardman, sketch artist, or art director's assistant, it is often more important to have the ability to work in a variety of styles. As in other fields, greater freedom of personal expression is given to people of experience and proven ability.

Because commercial art is made for reproduction, an illustrator's success depends on how well the work will reproduce. Only broad experience in the field can provide the required knowledge of art techniques and printing methods. Illustrators and photographers, having acquired experience in their fields, may choose to work on a free-lance basis rather than as salaried employees of an agency or firm.

Animated television commercials usually begin with an idea outlined on a storyboard by a layout person.

JOHN DUNIGAN FOR FREDERIC LEWIS/HAL SEEGER PRODUCTIONS

Package design is an important field of commercial art. Here a designer creates cartons for cosmetic products.

© TYRONE HALL/STOCK BOSTON

*(Left)* Comprehensive layouts, to be shown to the client, are prepared from the sketches made by a layout artist. *(Right)* Press proofs of the printed booklet are checked for accuracy by the art director and production manager.

Television has greatly increased the need for artists who can work with the additional element of motion. The animated art used in motion pictures and in television is a highly demanding and specialized form of illustration. Hundreds of separate drawings often are required for even one minute of animated film. Television also uses unanimated forms of art, as, for instance, in title designs, visual inserts, and weather charts.

***Typography and Reproduction.*** The responsibility for typesetting and good reproduction is in the hands of the production manager and his staff in the larger art departments. Some lettering is done by hand, especially in the initial layout stages, but prepared lettering (such as phototype and paste-up letters) and set type are most commonly used in the final stages. Large firms may have specialists in the various aspects of production, but more commonly a single production manager oversees all technical aspects of the commercial-art product. The production manager must have an up-to-the-minute knowledge of typography, paper stock, methods of reproduction, and comparative production costs.

***Education for Commercial Art.*** Commercial artists generally are trained in art schools or in the art departments of colleges and universities. Art schools generally stress a strong foundation in design, drawing, and rendering techniques; most university programs maintain curricula with a balance between art and the humanities.

Most art schools and college art departments permit the student to specialize in the aspect of commercial art that particularly interests him—fashion illustration, photography, or industrial design, for instance. Art majors at many colleges and universities augment their art courses with special classes in marketing, business administration, computer science, and basic engineering.

Art schools require a high-school diploma and offer a two- or three-year course in general commercial art, or in some field, such as illustration or advertising design. Some offer a four-year program with a broader liberal-arts background leading to the bachelor's degree. A few universities offer graduate courses in communication arts leading to a master's degree. A sound background in the basic elements of art—design, color, and drawing—are fundamental necessities for all commercial artists.

***Employment Opportunities.*** Beginners in com-

mercial art often start as paste-up artists, sketch or layout artists, or assistants to senior staff members. Salaries for beginners are not high because most art departments look for experienced artists. However, talent also determines how far the commercial artist can rise. Top art directors, illustrators, production managers, and others in the most responsible positions achieve income levels comparable to those of professionals in law or medicine. Most commercial artists work for advertising departments of large corporations, advertising agencies, department stores, television or motion-picture studios, printing firms, or publishing companies.

The highest salaries and greatest number of opportunities in commercial art are in the major cities—New York, Chicago, Los Angeles, Dallas, Denver, Atlanta, and Toronto. In Europe and Asia, London, Paris, Milan, Dusseldorf, Tokyo, and Hong Kong are the leading centers for commercial art. In Australia, Sydney and Melbourne offer some specialized opportunities for the artist. Positions in advertising, trade-magazine publication, and in teaching commercial art are available in many parts of the United States and Canada.

FRANKLIN N. SAYLES
*Art Director, Young People's Publications*
*Grolier Incorporated*

**Bibliography**
**Dalley, Terence, and others,** eds., *A Complete Guide to Illustration and Design* (QED Pub. 1980).
**Doherty, M. Stephen,** *Developing Ideas in Artwork* (Watson-Guptill 1988).
**Gorb, P.,** ed., *Living by Design* (Pentagram Press 1979).
**Saxton, Colin,** ed., *Art School: An Introductory Guide* (Chartwell Pub. 1981).
**Snyder, John,** *The New Commercial Artists Handbook* (Watson-Guptill 1986).
**Ward, Dick,** *Creative Ad Design and Illustration* (North Light Bks. 1988).

**COMMERCIAL BANK.** See BANKS AND BANKING — *Commercial Banks.*

**COMMERCIAL COURT,** a court with jurisdiction over disputes relating to trade and commerce. Commercial courts appeared in medieval England and continental Europe when most commerce took place at public fairs. See COMMERCIAL LAW—*The Law Merchant.*

**COMMERCIAL EDUCATION.** See BUSINESS EDUCATION.

**COMMERCIAL LAW,** kə-mûr′shəl lô, is that branch of the law dealing with the rights of property and the relations of persons engaged in commerce. In most areas of the world, professionals understand the term "commercial law" to include 10 bodies of law: (1) the law of contracts, (2) the law of agency and business organization, (3) the law of sales, (4) the law of commercial paper and banking, (5) the law of bulk sales and fraudulent conveyances, (6) the law of documents of title, (7) the law of investment securities, (8) the law of secured transactions, including the law of suretyship, (9) the law of bankruptcy, and (10) the law of admiralty.

It is sometimes maintained that there is a universal or general commercial law. However, this is only a convenient way of saying that because men engaged in commercial ventures frequently have business relations throughout the civilized world, various governments have naturally taken into account this international factor in developing their commercial laws. As a result, commercial law is more uniform throughout the world than any other system of law except international law itself. In this sense it is true that commercial law is general and universal, but it should be remembered that "law" is traditionally defined as a rule prescribed by a sovereign power. Thus there can be no such thing as a general commercial law separate from and irrespective of the particular state or government it represents.

### THE LAW MERCHANT

Modern commercial law is often said to have begun with the Industrial Revolution in 18th century England. It is true that most commercial rules were not established before this period. Nevertheless, a number of commercial principles, particularly in the area of commercial paper and banking, can be traced to earlier times, particularly to the ancient "law merchant."

The law merchant, which had a profound impact on the development of modern commercial law, was a body of rules that grew up in medieval England, following similar practice in the rest of Europe, to govern the dealings of merchants. During the Middle Ages many international merchants, as well as itinerant peddlers, traveled from town to town selling wares to the local people and merchants at fairs that they set up in those towns.

Disputes frequently would arise between these roving merchants and the local residents over sales of merchandise and other matters. The traveling merchants could not stay in a town long enough for the slow and cumbersome procedures of the local courts to dispose of their cases. Moreover, they feared that they might not receive justice at the hands of local judges in their claims against the townspeople. The town judges knew little or nothing about the customs and rules of international trade. Therefore, the roving merchants insisted that the disputes be handled by courts they set up and be tried according to the rules administered by these courts. Otherwise they would refuse to bring their fairs to that town. The traveling fairs were popular because they provided a welcome change from the dull life of medieval towns and were an important source of revenue to the burgomasters by way of license fees. Rather than lose the fairs, the local authorities consented to have the disputes settled by the merchants' courts instead of by the local justices.

In 1353 the English crown established "Staple Courts" to hear merchants' complaints in accordance with the usages and customs of trade. Their decisions accumulated in a body of law known as the law merchant. For a long time the law merchant was not recognized as part of the common law, but recognition finally came in the latter part of the 18th century when two distinguished judges, Lords Holt and Mansfield, incorporated the law merchant into the body of the common law.

The law merchant is continually evolving, and in modern practice it still provides the common law with a valuable source of new thinking and new business and banking procedures. In fact, many common law rules have been changed when judges were informed of new commercial practices. U. S. Supreme Court Justice Benjamin N. Cardozo once made a statement to the effect that the law merchant still operates in the 20th century. In the case before him he held that the law merchant (in regard to certain practices carried on by the New York Stock Exchange) could be used to fill gaps in statutory law as well as to provide sound working rules for the common law (*Manhattan Co.* v. *Morgan,* 1926).

See also COMMERCIAL COURTS; LAW MERCHANT, THE.

### COMMERCIAL LAW IN THE UNITED STATES

There are 11 main areas, or subdivisions, of commercial law in the United States. These are similar to, but not all identical with, the 10 bodies of law listed in the first paragraph of this article, which constitute commercial law as it is understood in most regions of the world. The main areas in the United States may be grouped under the following headings: *contracts; agency and business organizations; areas covered by the uniform commercial code; bankruptcy;* and *admiralty.*

**Contracts.** The law of contracts is the most basic of all commercial laws. Because many other branches of commercial law are simply bodies of special contractual rules, this article concentrates its principal attention on contract law.

Although "contract" has been defined in many ways by the courts, the definition that has gained the greatest general acceptance is the one given in the restatement of contracts by the American Law Institute: "A contract is a promise or set of promises for the breach of which the law gives a remedy, or the performance of which the law in some way recognizes as a duty."

This definition deals with two ideas: promises and the legal effect of promises. In short, there is no contract unless a promise has been made, and even if a promise is made, a contract does not exist unless the law recognizes the promise as being enforceable. These points may perhaps be best illustrated by some examples.

*Example 1.* A tells B that he might give B $1,000 if B names his son after A. B names his son after A, but A refuses to pay B the $1,000. B sues A.

There is no contract, so B loses the lawsuit. A did not promise to pay B $1,000 if B named his son after A. A merely indicated that he *might* pay B. Any statement that according to its terms makes performance optional with the person making the statement, whatever may happen or whatever course of conduct in other respects he may pursue, is no promise, although it is often called an "illusory promise."

**Example 2.** *A* promises that he will go to the football game with *B*. Subsequently, *A* refuses to go to the game. *B* sues *A*.

Judgement is awarded to *A*, for this is not a contract. Although *A* made a promise, the promise is not the kind the law will enforce. His promise contemplated social, not legal, relations.

**Example 3.** *B*, a regular customer, enters the store of *A*, a fruit dealer. *A* is busy waiting on a customer. *B* is in a hurry. *B* holds up a melon so that *A* can see it. *A* sees it and *B* walks out of the shop with it. *A* does not object.

*A* and *B* have thereby made a contract under which *B* is liable to *A* for the price of the melon. The conduct of the parties shows a promise on the part of *B* to pay for the melon, and this kind of promise the law will enforce.

The law usually will not enforce a promise unless it is supported by "consideration" (something to be done) and has a legal objective. No legal system in any country has gone so far as to declare that all promises must be performed. The law of contracts permits one to change his mind with respect to promises made foolishly or on the spur of the moment through an impulse, or as a token of generosity, courtesy, or gratitude to persons who have given nothing for such promises. Consideration is the price for the promise. It is either an act of forbearance, or a return promise bargained for and given in exchange for a promise. The fact that the promisee relies on the promise to his injury, or that the promisor gains some advantage by merely making the promise, does not establish consideration without the element of bargain or exchange.

Textwriters usually have defined consideration in terms of legal detriment or legal benefit, although courts have generally employed only the legal detriment theory in determining whether there is consideration for a contract. The promisee sustains legal detriment when, at the request of the promisor and in reliance on the promise, he does something he was not already legally bound to do, or refrains from doing something he had a legal right to do. A few more examples will illustrate these points.

**Example 1.** *A* promises *B* that he will repair *B*'s car free of charge. He afterwards refuses to do so. There is no consideration for *A*'s promise, and hence it is unenforceable. *B* sustained no detriment in relying on *A*'s promise, because he did not obligate himself to do something he was not legally bound to do, or refrain from doing something he had a legal right to do.

**Example 2.** *A* promises *B* that he will repair his car for $5 and *B* promises to pay this price for the work. There is consideration for both promises and each party is legally bound to a contract. Each party suffers a legal detriment: *A* by being obligated to do something he was not legally required to do, the repair of *B*'s car; *B* by being obligated to do something he was not legally required to do, that is, to pay $5 to *A*.

The fact that $5 is not adequate compensation for *A*'s work, if such is the case, is irrelevant. The law of contracts does not concern itself with adequacy of consideration, unless the consideration for mutual promises is of the same kind. Thus a promise by *A* to give $5 to *B*, in return for a promise by *B* to give $10 to *A*, would not be supported by consideration. But a promise to pay $5 for repair work having a value of $100 would be supported by consideration. The law of contracts will assume where it can that mutual promises involve the exchange of equal economic value. It can make this assumption where promises involve different kinds of consideration, but it cannot make the assumption where the promises are of the same kind.

**Example 3.** A father writes to his son, "I will give you $1,000 if you refrain from smoking for one year." The son gives up smoking for one year. He may enforce the promise, inasmuch as he suffered a legal detriment in refraining from smoking, because he had a legal right to smoke. The fact that giving up smoking may have been a physical benefit to the son does not prevent it from being a legal detriment.

Except for special kinds of contracts covered by the statute of frauds (q.v.) oral contracts are just as binding as written contracts. The statute of frauds, so called because it was intended to prevent fraud and perjury in the proving of contracts before the courts, was enacted by the English Parliament in 1677 and has been substantially reenacted in most states of the United States. It provides that certain types of promises are enforceable only if made in writing and signed by the person to be charged. The types of promises included are: (1) promises by executors and administrators to pay a debt of the deceased out of their own pockets; (2) promises made in consideration of marriage; (3) agreements which by their terms cannot be performed in one year; (4) promises to answer to the debt of another; (5) contracts for the sale of land; and (6) contracts for the sale of goods above a value, usually $500, fixed by statute.

Certain persons, because of immaturity of judgment or other reasons of public policy, are, for their own protection, unable to make binding contracts. These persons are: infants (that is, persons under 21 years of age); insane people; drunkards; and married women (to some extent, in certain states). Additionally, contracts may be avoided because of fraud, coercion, mistake, undue influence, or illegality. See also CONTRACT.

**Agency and Business Organizations.** In a modern commercial society most businessmen are not doing business for themselves but are acting as agents for others. Agency (q. v.) is the body of commercial law regulating the legal relationships established when one man represents or acts for another.

One may conduct his business as a sole proprietor in person or through agents, but most larger businesses are either partnerships or corporations. Different legal results flow from activities of sole proprietorship, partnerships, and corporations, and a body of commercial law known as "business organizations" has been developed to regulate and establish these results.

**Areas Covered by the Uniform Commercial Code.** The Uniform Commercial Code, drawn up in 1952 by the commissioners on uniform laws and the American Law Institute, is a unified, comprehensive set of laws that covers the following areas, or subdivisions, of commercial law: sales, commercial paper and banking, letters of credit, bulk sales, documents of title, investment securities, and secured transactions.

The Uniform Commercial Code encompasses all business transactions from the time raw materials are purchased until finished merchandise is sold to a consumer. It also deals with many related transactions, such as the movement of the merchandise from one point to another, the storage of goods, and the financing of commercial transsactions. Finally, its provisions cover payments for merchandise and the deposit and collection of checks, notes, and drafts.

The Uniform Commercial Code, generally considered the most important legislative measure in the history of U. S. commerce, has been enacted in every state except Louisiana. Of its 10 articles, the 1st contains general principles of construction and definitions. The 2d, dealing with sales, is the longest and perhaps most radical article of the code, completely repealing and replacing the Uniform Sales Act. The 3d and 4th articles are particularly significant to bankers because they deal with checks, drafts, and notes and their collection in the United States. The 5th article codifies for the first time the law of letters of credit. The 6th covers situations where a person or business transfers in bulk a major portion of its assets. It contains provisions that are designed to protect creditors of the transferor. The 7th article deals with bills of lading and warehouse receipts and is especially important to shippers and storers of goods. Collectively the documents it covers are known as documents of title, and that is the name given to the article. The 8th article governs certain problems involved in the issuance, transfer, purchase, and registration of investment securities such as shares of stock, bonds, and the like. The 9th sets forth the law relating to personal property security, completely repealing and replacing the old law of chattel mortgages, conditional sales, trust receipts, and factor's liens, as well as other chattel security rules. The 10th article is not substantive in nature but contains the effective date of the statute and a list of prior laws that it has repealed.

**Bankruptcy.** The law of bankruptcy provides an important method of settling the estate of an insolvent debtor and discharging him from his debts so as to give him an opportunity to start his commercial life afresh, unencumbered by past debts. Jurisdiction over bankruptcy proceedings is vested exclusively in the federal courts, and the National Bankruptcy Act, passed by Congress, supersedes all state laws on the subject. See also BANKRUPTCY.

**Admiralty.** Sometimes called "maritime law," admiralty consists of a body of commercial rules governing the carriage of goods and passengers by water. The subject constitutes the most important part of the private law that deals with shipping. See also MARITIME LAW.

WILLIAM D. HAWKLAND, *School of Law,*
*State University of New York at Buffalo*
*Author of "A Transactional Guide*
*to the Uniform Commercial Code"*

### Bibliography

Brennan, Bartley A., and Kubasek, Nancy, *The Legal Environment of Business* (Macmillan 1988).
Corman, Calvin, *Commercial Law: Cases and Materials* (Little 1983).
Hall, Kermit L., ed., *The Law of Business and Commerce* (Garland 1987).
Hawkland, William D., *A Transactional Guide to the Uniform Commercial Code*, 2 vols. (Am. Law Inst. Pub. 1964).
Hawkland, William D., *Uniform Commercial Code Series*, 6 vols. (Callaghan & Co. 1982).
Kudej, Blanka, *International Trade Law* (Oceana Pub. 1984).
Lyden, D., and Reitzel D., *Business and the Law* (McGraw 1985).
Senn, Mark A., ed., *Negotiating Business Transactions* (Wiley 1988).
Stone, Bradford, *Uniform Commercial Code in a Nutshell*, 2d ed. (West Pub. 1984).
Trakman, Leon E., *The Law Merchant* (Rothman 1983).
Whitman, Douglas, and Stoltenberg, Clyde D., *Commercial Law*, 2d ed. (Wiley 1985).

**COMMERCIAL TREATIES** are agreements between states that establish rights and regulate conditions of navigation and trade between, and of residence within, the territories of the contracting parties. The difference between commercial treaties and political treaties, with which they are often contrasted, is exemplified in the first two treaties made by the United States, both with France and both signed on Feb. 6, 1778. One was called "a treaty of alliance" and provided for common action and mutual assistance in the war against England, for U. S. independence, for title to conquests, for cooperation in making peace, for accession of other allies, and for mutual guarantees of territory after the war. The other was called a "treaty of amity and commerce" and was four times as long. It provided for permanent peace between the parties, reciprocal conditional most-favored-nation treatment, and mutual protection of vessels. It dealt with such other matters as rights of neutrals in time of war, fisheries, rights of residence, assistance in case of wreck, asylum, consuls, and free ports.

In the long history of commerce, the content of such treaties has varied greatly. They have become increasingly specialized, increasingly changeable, and increasingly multilateral as they have become increasingly numerous. While today most states have a general commercial treaty with each of the other states with which they have important commercial relations, they also have numerous special agreements, often of less formal and durable character, dealing with tariff rates, navigation dues, customs formalities, air-transport clearance arrangements, quantity restrictions on special commodities, and similar matters. Furthermore, most states are parties to many multilateral agreements regulating commercial, financial, transportation, and communication facilities, and establishing standards of commercial and maritime law, weights and measures, rights of residence, commercial arbitration, patents, trademarks, copyrights, and the like.

In 1906 the United States had in force some 300 treaties and agreements bearing on commercial matters, and there were some 8,000 such treaties and agreements in force in the world. By 1930 the United States had some 1,000 such agreements and there were over 20,000 in the world. Both of these figures should be more than doubled for the 1960's. The number of bilateral commercial obligations would also be greatly increased if all of those involved in each multilateral treaty were calculated. For example, the General Agreement on Tariffs and Trade (GATT)—over 2,000 printed pages in length, signed by 23 states at Geneva in 1947, and revised in 1967 after a long series of negotiations, known as the Kennedy Round, among 70 states—regulates four fifths of the world's international trade and is the equivalent of 2,415 bilateral agreements.

**History.** The earliest commercial treaties were usually brief, merely reciprocally extending the right to trade. The ancient empires of Mesopotamia, Egypt, Athens, Carthage, and Rome exacted the right to trade from the barbarians on the peripheries of their territories and bargained for that right among themselves. The Bible records an agreement permitting Israelite traders to conduct bazaars in Damascus (I Kings 20:34). Commercial treaties of 509 B.C. and 348 B.C. between Carthage and Rome have been preserved. In the Middle Ages rulers often gave foreign merchants personal permission to trade.

The modern commercial treaty system, which not only extends rights of trade but also defines conditions of trade, can be dated from treaties made in the 12th century by Italian commercial cities. During this century, Genoa, Pisa and Venice made such treaties with Valencia, Morocco, the Balearic Islands, and Sultan Saladin. The Netherlands, Sweden, the Hanseatic towns, England, and Norway made similar treaties in the 13th century. By the 16th century such treaties were numerous, and the system of capitulations by which France and other states gained the right to trade and to exercise extraterritorial jurisdiction over their merchants in the Ottoman Empire was established.

**Reciprocal and Unilateral Obligations.** Between European states commercial treaties were generally reciprocal—that is, each gave to the other whatever advantages it received. But following the precedent of the commercial agreements (capitulations, q.v.) with Turkey, European states generally gained trading privileges with Asian countries that they did not reciprocate. Schedules of maximum tariff rates, binding the Asian country, were frequently included in these treaties. Unilateral commercial obligations also were sometimes imposed by the victor in a war against a European enemy, but these were usually short-lived. The Treaty of Versailles in 1919 (Articles 264–281) required Germany to grant certain commercial privileges to the Allied powers, but only for a period of five years.

In the 20th century, non-Western powers have increasingly resented the unilateral character of their commercial treaties with Western nations. Japan escaped this discrimination in 1894 and has since made only reciprocal treaties. Turkey has made only reciprocal treaties since extraterritoriality was abolished by the Treaty of Lausanne, concluded in 1923 and made effective in 1924. Other Asian countries have followed such suit until, with the reciprocal treaties made by China with the United States, Britain, and other countries in 1943, the system of unilateral commercial treaties practically came to an end.

**National and Most-Favored-Nation Treatment.** The negotiators of commercial treaties have often sought to obtain special privileges, but the modern tendency has been to seek only equality of opportunity.

In regard to acquisitions of property, access to courts, civil rights, internal taxes, and other rights of residence, equality of aliens with nationals has been sought and to an increasing extent accorded. The United States and France in the treaties of 1778 reciprocally accorded each other's nationals "national treatment" with regard to property, taxes, and inheritance. A U.S. treaty with Germany in 1923 went further, providing that "the nationals of each of the High Contracting Parties shall be permitted to enter, travel, and reside in the territories of the other"; to enjoy civil liberties, engage in professions and trade, and acquire property; "and generally to do anything incidental to or necessary for the enjoyment of any of the foregoing privileges upon the same terms as nationals of the state of residence, or as nationals of the nation hereafter to be most favored by it, submitting themselves to all local laws and regulations duly established." "National treatment" in regard to internal taxes, access to courts, and police protection as "required by international law" was then provided (Article 1). The commercial treaty of 1948 that the United States concluded with Italy went further still, extending national treatment even in respect to tonnage dues and navigation rights, with the exception of coasting trade (cabotage) and inland navigation.

With reference to commerce and navigation, states usually reserve freedom to give their own nationals special advantages. Consequently, "most-favored-nation treatment" has been the usual standard in these matters, although the standard of "international law" or even the treatment of the national has sometimes been accorded to other states in regard to navigation. The first most-favored-nation clause in a reciprocal commercial treaty appears to have been that in a treaty between the Netherlands and Portugal in 1641, soon followed by a clause in the treaty between England and Sweden in 1654. Even earlier, European states had obtained most-favored-nation treatment in their nonreciprocal treaties with Turkey.

Most-favored-nation clauses have appeared in three forms: conditional, unconditional, and general. The first may be illustrated by Article 2 of the treaty of 1778 between the United States and France: "The Most Christian King and the United States engage mutually not to grant any particular favour to other nations, in respect of commerce and navigation, which shall not immediately become common to the other party, who shall enjoy the same favour, freely, if the concession was freely made, or on allowing the same compensation, if the concession was conditional." Under such a clause a privilege given by either party to a third state in exchange for advantages did not have to be extended by the most-favored-nation clause. The most that could be claimed was an opportunity to bargain, but as each reserved the right to decide whether the compensation offered was equal to that given to the third state, this might not produce results.

The unconditional form of the most-favored-nation clause is illustrated by Article 7 of the treaty between the United States and Germany of 1923. It provides that "each of the High Contracting Parties binds itself unconditionally to impose no higher or other duties or conditions and no prohibition on the importation of any article, [that is] the growth, produce, or manufacture, of the territories of the other than are or shall be imposed on the importation of any like article, [that is] the growth, produce, or manufacture, of any foreign country." Under this clause each party is bound to give the other any other commercial advantage it may give to a third state, whether by legislation or treaty. Such a clause precludes special reciprocity treaties.

The general form of the most-favored-nation clause is illustrated by Article 8 of the treaty between the United States and Switzerland of 1850. "In all that relates to the importation, exportation, and transit of their respective products, the United States of America and the Swiss Confederation shall treat each other, reciprocally, as the most favored nation, union of nations, State, or society." This type of clause leaves it uncertain whether conditional or unconditional treatment is intended and has led to controversy. In 1898, Switzerland demanded the tariff rate on its imports into the United States that the United States had given to France by a special reciprocity treaty just concluded with that country. The United States contended that since it had traditionally followed the policy of conditional most-favored-nation treatment, the Swiss treaty must be so interpreted. The Swiss, however, were able to show that the negotiations of 1850 indicated an intention to interpret this clause unconditionally. The United States acquiesced and authorized the lower duty on Swiss goods, but at the same time it took advantage of a provision in the treaty of 1850 to denounce this clause on a year's notice. It was clear that since the United States gave Switzerland the lower rates without any compensation, it would be obliged to extend these rates to all other countries with which it had conditional most-favored-nation clauses, thus doing away with the system of special reciprocity treaties that it had pursued and wished to continue.

In 1923 the United States abandoned the policy of conditional most-favored nation treatment in an agreement with Brazil in pursuance of the Tariff Act of 1922. Subsequently, as manifested in the German treaty of 1923, the United States has been a leading advocate of unconditional most-favored-nation treatment. This system has been followed in the numerous agreements negotiated under the Reciprocal Trade Agreements Act of 1934, including the General Agreement on Tariffs and Trade of 1947. Consequently, all states with which the United States has commercial treaties, and in practice all that do not discriminate against U. S. trade, gain the tariff advantages extended to any country by reciprocal trade agreements. Each of these agreements, therefore, has the effect of lowering the general tariff.

**Multilateral Treaties.** Equality in commercial relations can be promoted by multilateral treaties as well as by unconditional most-favored-nation clauses. Before World War I, multilateral treaties dealt with the navigation of straits and canals, such as the Danish sounds, the Turkish straits, and the Suez Canal; with postal, telegraphic, and other forms of communication; with standards of weights and measures, commercial and maritime law, sanitary and safety regulations, patents and trademarks; and with prohibited articles of commerce such as slaves, white slaves, obscene publications, and narcotic drugs. The number and scope of such treaties have greatly multiplied since World War I under the auspices of the League of Nations and the United Nations. The General Agreement on Tariffs and Trade (GATT), and the United Nations Conference on Trade and Development (UNCTAD), which had its first session, in Geneva in 1964, were organized to regulate the conditions of international trade with a view to greater freedom and equality.

**Imperial Preferences, Reciprocity Agreements, and Customs Unions.** Commercial agreements have frequently sought to create special advantages for trade within empires or regions or between states with special geographical or political relationships. The question has been raised as to the compatibility of such arrangements with most-favored-nation clauses. The United States has in its history made special reciprocity treaties with Canada, Cuba, and other countries. Under its conditional interpretation of the most-favored-nation clause the United States did not extend the advantages of these treaties to other countries. After adopting the unconditional interpretation in 1923, however, it did so, except in the cases of Cuba and the Panama Canal Zone, which, because of geographical relations were expressly excepted from the operation of unconditional most-favored-nation clauses.

When Britain entered into the Ottawa Agreements with Canada and other dominions in 1932, creating a system of imperial preferences, the United States, which then adhered to the unconditional, most-favored-nation clause, objected, but Britain argued that members of the Commonwealth were in a special political relation, as were the states of a federation such as the United States, and that they were free to extend special favors to one another without extending them to outside states. In more closely knit empires this argument has always been accepted. The same argument was accepted in regard to customs unions such as the German *Zollverein* of the period before formation of the German Empire in 1871; the European Coal and Steel Community (Schuman Plan), established in 1951 among West Germany, France, Italy, the Netherlands, Belgium, and Luxembourg; and the European Economic Community (EEC), or Common Market, among the same states.

There has been a great deal of discussion as to whether the formation of large imperial or regional free trading blocs—such as the Common Market; the European Free Trade Association (EFTA), including most of the remaining non-Communist states in Europe; and free trade associations in Latin America, Central America, and the Arab states—will tend toward a general equalization and freeing of trade or the reverse. It has sometimes been the case that the increase of trade within such blocs has in even greater measure diminished the trade of the bloc as a whole with outside countries. Recent regional agreements, however, may not have this effect. Following agreement on agricultural imports in 1966, members of the Common Market reduced tariffs with one another. The association as a whole then reduced its tariffs with outside states, on many items as much as 50%, in the GATT negotiations concluded in 1967. The same has been true of the other regional groups. There has also been a tendency for Western states to make agreements reducing barriers to trade with the Communist states and to make agreements to meet the commercial needs of many of the underdeveloped countries.

**Interpretation.** Commercial treaties, like all treaties, are in the first instance interpreted by the respective governments, but under international law, neither party can give a final interpretation. If the parties fail to agree on an interpretation, it is recognized that the matter should, in principle, be submitted to some form of international adjudication. Specific obligations for such submission have frequently been included in a "compromissary" clause of the commercial treaty itself. States that are parties to the optional clause of the statute of the International Court of Justice are obliged to submit to that court the interpretation of all treaties with states that are also parties to the optional clause if negotiations fail to achieve agreement.

Since commercial treaties usually include a provision for a unilateral denunciation on six months' or a year's notice, one of the parties often denounces the treaty if there is a failure to agree on interpretation and if there is no obligation to submit to adjudication. In 1911 the United States thus denounced the commercial treaty of 1832 with Russia because of failure to agree on the application of the treaty in respect to the rights of residence in Russia of U. S. citizens of Jewish faith.

**Termination.** Apart from denunciation, commerial treaties often come to an end through expiration of the period of time for which, according to their own terms, they were made; through the negotiation of another treaty dealing with the same subject between the same parties; through absorption of one of the parties in another state; or through change of political relations, such as the outbreak of war. The modern practice has been to recognize that war does not terminate the operation of commercial treaties but merely suspends them for the duration of the war, insofar as their application is incompatible with the state of war. Treaties of peace following war often determine which commercial treaties shall continue and which shall be terminated.

**Foreign Policy and Commercial Treaties.** Commercial treaties have sometimes been used for the political purpose of unifying friends and injuring enemies. Commercial reciprocity has sometimes led to political unions, as in the case of the German *Zollverein* and the U. S. reciprocity treaty with Hawaii. Commercial preferences have been used as instruments of political solidarity, as in imperial and regional preferences and customs unions. Commercial agreements diverting the course of trade have been utilized as instruments of political hostility. Hitler so used them and they have been so used by both sides in the Cold War since World War II.

Commercial treaties have been used to gain special commercial advantages as well as to maintain conditions of freedom and equality. This objective was prominent in the period of mercantilism, and it inspired the United States in making special reciprocity treaties under the conditional most-favored-nation clause. Such treaties and the use of penalty duties were authorized by the McKinley (1890) and Dingley (1897) tariffs in the United States. Under these acts higher tariffs were imposed on imports from countries that discriminated against U. S. trade. Such retaliation has led to "tariff wars" that have later been ended by commercial treaties. States have sometimes pursued the policies of "maximum and minimum tariffs" and of "general and conventional tariffs." By the first, a minimum tariff is established by law, higher rates up to the maximum being imposed on countries that discriminate. By the latter, a general tariff is established by law, lower rates being offered to all states with which tariff treaties are negotiated, these being generalized by unconditional most-favored-nation clauses. The United States tariff under the Reciprocal Trade Agreements Act of 1934 is of this type.

Since the modern era of commerce began in the late Middle Ages, the general tendency has been toward freer and more equal trade. This situation reached a maximum in the late 19th century when Britain pursued a policy of free trade in both colonial and foreign relations. World Wars I and II and the rise of new ideologies led to policies of economic nationalism and of Cold War containment that contributed to modifying this long-run tendency, and brought a return to ideas more characteristic of the Middle Ages and the period of mercantilism. Economic policy has been utilized as an instrument of political integration and expansion by totalitarian states. Even the liberal states tend to pursue similar policies in defense. Trade across the Iron Curtain diminished to a mere trickle, and trade among the liberal countries was hampered by currency controls, quotas, customs regulations, and tariffs thought necessary to sustain national employment and national currencies. These tendencies have moderated through the efforts of the United States and the United Nations to promote freer and more equal trade by negotiation of reciprocal trade agreements and multilateral treaties with the unconditional most-favored-nation clause. This suggests that the distortions effected by World Wars I and II and the clash of opposing ideologies may prove temporary, and the long-run trend toward a relatively free world market with equal opportunity will continue under the influence of liberal commercial treaties. See also TREATY.

QUINCY WRIGHT, *Professor Emeritus of International Law, University of Chicago*

**Further Reading:** Baldwin, Robert G., *Multilateral Trade Negotiations* (Am. Enterprise Inst. 1979); *General Agreement on Tariffs and Trade* (Unipub 1980); Glick, Lesie A., *Multilateral Trade Negotiations* (Rowman 1984); Twiggs, Joan E., *The Tokyo Round of Multilateral Trade Negotiations* (Univ. Press of Am. 1987).

**COMMINES,** kô-mēn′, **Philippe de** (c. 1447–1511), French statesman and historian. Born at Renescure in Flanders of noble parentage, Commines (also spelled *Commynes, Comines*) was brought up at the Burgundian court and served as an adviser to Charles the Bold of Burgundy from 1464 to 1472. Commines then switched his allegiance to Charles' foe, Louis XI of France. Commines' property was confiscated, but Louis compensated him handsomely with rich holdings in France. The French King gained a loyal servant; Commines was to be his chief adviser and leading diplomat.

When Louis died in 1483, Commines fell out of favor with the regent, Anne of France (Anne de Beaujeu). He rashly joined the revolt of the Duke d'Orléans in 1486 and was briefly imprisoned. When Charles VIII assumed his majority in 1491, Commines was recalled to court. He cautioned Charles against his ambitions in Italy, which, he warned, would not serve France's interests. But he accompanied Charles on his short-lived conquest of Italy (1495). On Charles' death in 1498, Commines retired from court. He died at Argenton, France, on October 18, 1511.

It is as a memoirist and political theorist that Commines is most famous. His *Mémoires* is a historical narrative of the reigns of Louis XI and Charles VIII. But without an overall historical theory, he often had to fall back on divine causation to explain contemporary events. While unsystematic, his political thought in several ways anticipates Machiavelli's. Commines' ideal prince was Louis XI, whose caution and deceit had enabled him so successfully to outmaneuver his foes and strengthen royal power in France. In contrast, Charles the Bold and Charles VIII emerge as reckless and dull-witted. Commines remained a Christian but tended to play down religious sanctions on kingship. Success was praised, regardless of means. The aim of government was peace, order, and prosperity, for which Commines was almost willing to accept royal absolutism. But he refused to condone royal taxation without the consent of the States-General. Hence Commines did not completely abandon the medieval ideal of limited monarchy, and this places him as a transitional figure in Western political thought.

EDMUND H. DICKERMAN
*University of Connecticut*

**COMMISSION,** in political science, means (1) a document certifying an appointment to office or (2) an official body of relatively small size and independent status. A commission in the first sense is given only to important officers. Thus in the armed forces "commissioned officers" appointed by high authority of the state are distinguished from "noncommissioned officers." Important civil officers also receive commissions. In the second sense, the term "commission" is applied to both national and international bodies, either temporary or permanent, but only to bodies smaller than "conferences," more independent than "committees," more bound by law than "councils," and less bound by law than either "courts" or "tribunals."

**Temporary Commissions.** The United States has made use of temporary commissions to adjudicate claims against the government, to distribute the proceeds of international arbitral awards, and to investigate and recommend on incidents (for example, the Roberts commission on Pearl Harbor and the Hoover commission on government reorganization). In Britain information is often collected by temporary commissions classified as royal, statutory, or departmental.

In international law, temporary commissions are usually investigatory, conciliatory, or technical bodies established by international organizations. Such commissions report on facts or recommend settlements of disputes and are distinguished from international courts and arbitral tribunals with authority to make final decisions on the basis of international law.

Procedures by which states may set up temporary commissions of conciliation are prescribed in inter-American treaties, including the Bogotá pact of 1948, and in the General Act of Geneva that was concluded among many states under the auspices of the League of Nations in 1928 and was later revised by the Leagues' successor, the United Nations, in 1949.

**Permanent Commissions.** The Bryan treaties, concluded by the United States with many countries in 1914 and subsequently, provided for the establishment of permanent international commissions to report on the facts concerning controversies threatening the peace between the two countries involved and to recommend settlements. The General Act of Geneva provides for similar permanent commissions.

Permanent international commissions, of limited membership and prescribed functions, include the commissions on international law, peace observation, and disarmanent established by the General Assembly of the United Nations; the commissions on atomic energy and conventional armaments set up by the UN Security Council; and numerous functional and regional commissions set up by the Economic and Social Council in accord with Article 68 of the Charter of the United Nations.

Permanent governmental commissions operating in the United States include the Interstate Commerce Commission, the Federal Trade Commission, and the Federal Communications Commission. In addition, some municipalities also are governed by commissions.

QUINCY WRIGHT, *Author of "The Role of International Law in the Elimination of War" Professor Emeritus, University of Chicago*

**COMMISSION FORM OF GOVERNMENT.** See URBAN GOVERNMENT.

**COMMITMENT,** the warrant, order, or process by which a court directs that a person be taken to prison, either to await trial or to serve a sentence. One may be committed to await trial either when charged with a nonbailable crime, such as first degree murder or high treason, or when unable to put up bail. If, after commitment, the prisoner posts bail, he is freed.

SAMUEL G. KLING, *Author of "The Complete Guide to Everyday Law"*

**COMMITTEE, Legislative.** See CONGRESS OF THE UNITED STATES — *The Committee System.*

**COMMITTEE FOR ECONOMIC DEVELOPMENT,** a nonpartisan, nongovernmental group of businessmen and scholars in the United States who share an interest in economic problems and policies. Its headquarters is in New York City. CED was formed in 1942 to help make the transition from a high-employment war economy to continued prosperity in peace. Its longer-run objectives are the preservation and strengthening of a free society, maintenance of high employment, increased productivity, greater economic stability, and greater opportunity for all. It conducts economic research, holds discussions, and issues statements and publications on its findings. CED is supported by contribution from business and grants from foundations. Its 200 trustees are board chairmen of business and financial corporations and university presidents. "Statements of National Policy" are issued periodically by the 50-man research and policy committee.

DAVID MCFARLAND *University of North Carolina*

**COMMITTEE OF PUBLIC SAFETY,** the committee elected by the French National Convention in 1793 to enforce the revolutionary law. The committee (French, Comité de Salut Public) was officially constituted on April 6, 1793. Its members were empowered to oversee the work of the provisional executive council and had the right of annulling its ordinances.

During the summer of 1793, when France suffered internal disorder and war abroad, the committee's powers were greatly increased. The famous Great Committee of Public Safety, which was maintained in power for over a year, ruled France together with the Committee of General Security and the Revolutionary Tribunal. The 12 members of this committee were Jean Bon Saint-André, Barère, Couthon, Hérault de Séchelles, Prieur de la Marne, Saint-Just, Robert Lindet, Robespierre, Carnot, Prieur de la Côte d'Or, Billaud-Varennes, and Collot d'Herbois. Robespierre was the chief, largely because of his influence in the Convention, the Jacobin Club, and the Paris Commune.

The Great Committee centralized all governmental authority. Each member performed specific functions as in a modern war cabinet, normally working 16 hours a day. Discussion was free and informal; decrees usually were signed by two or three members. The committee's fears of counter-revolution led it to extend the Terror, with mass arrests and increasing numbers of executions. It was, however, an efficient revolutionary and war government. In the period of reaction after the fall of Robespierre on July 27, 1794, it was abolished.

RICHARD M. BRACE *Oakland University*

**COMMITTEES OF CORRESPONDENCE,** during the pre-Revolutionary period in America, helped mobilize public opinion against Britain. The committees included local groups, county organizations, and standing committees of the colonial legislatures. All acted to spread propaganda promoting the patriot cause.

Every revolutionary crisis saw the formation of such committees. After Britain passed the Sugar Act in 1764, the New York assembly selected representatives of New York county as its committee of correspondence, charged with guarding the colony from the "dangers" of unconstitutional legislation from Parliament. Committee members included the wealthy and prominent New Yorkers John Cruger, William Bayard, and Philip and Robert R. Livingston. The committee organized opposition to the Sugar Act and later to the Stamp Act, and its members served as the colony's hosts and delegates at the Stamp Act congress in New York City in October 1765.

The most famous of the corresponding committees was the one appointed by the city of Boston in November 1772, composed of such patriot leaders as Samuel Adams, Joseph Warren, and James Otis. This committee issued the Suffolk Resolves of Nov. 20, 1772, which declared that the colonists were entitled to all the rights of persons born or residing in England and enumerated the grievances of Massachusetts against custom racketeering, illegal search, and unjust taxation. More than 80 Massachusetts towns responded by forming local committees of correspondence and issuing their own resolves. These committees generated much emotion and, as Gov. Thomas Hutchinson reported, caused colonials to think of independence from Britain.

These local committees were sitting when Massachusetts was agitated by the Tea Act of 1773. The committees around Boston reacted to the new crisis by organizing the Boston Tea Party and justifying their behavior in letters to other colonies.

As the dispute with Britain spread, the local committees served as propaganda bureaus and performed the duties of revolutionary governments. New England committees collected arms for the militia and maintained discipline by tarring and feathering opponents.

The first standing legislative committee was formed by Virginia's House of Burgesses in 1773 to handle correspondence with other assemblies, and in less than a year all the other colonies had similar bodies. After the outbreak of fighting in 1775, the role of the committees of correspondence was taken over and broadened by committees of safety.

JOHN A. SCHUTZ
*University of Southern California*

**COMMITTEES OF SAFETY** carried on certain functions of government within the colonies during the early years of the Revolution. Appointed by the congresses (assemblies) of the colonies, they filled the role of the executive when the congresses were in session and possessed legislative as well as executive powers during congressional recesses. Successors to the committees of correspondence, the committees of safety usually represented the revolutionary leadership of the colonies and frequently were more powerful than the parent congresses. Sometimes, during the turbulent early days of the war, they were the only governing bodies in existence.

The Massachusetts committee of safety came into being on Oct. 26, 1774, under the chairmanship of John Hancock. He soon was succeeded by Joseph Warren, who also held the presidency of the Massachusetts legislature and thus became the single most powerful man in the colony. New York committees of safety had short tenures at first, but they gained power and independence as the war crisis deepened. Influential revolutionaries such as John M. Scott, Gouverneur Morris, and Philip Livingston were members. The Pennsylvania council of safety discharged all executive functions of the state for a period in 1776 and 1777. Its members included the zealous patriots James Cannon and Timothy Matlack.

Many congresses, fearing the committees, attempted to limit their tenure and authority, but the committees usually won the powers they needed to recruit and provision soldiers. On the passage of constitutions or the return of stability in a colony, the committees gave way to state executives or state legislatures. Most committees of safety operated between 1775 and 1777, but New Hampshire's remained in existence until 1784.

JOHN A. SCHUTZ
*University of Southern California*

**COMMODITY CREDIT CORPORATION,** a U. S. government agency, part of the Department of Agriculture that deals primarily with price supports and commodity stabilization programs. The CCC maintains extensive storage facilities. Its other activities include supply and foreign purchases, commodity export, and surplus sales and distribution programs.

Established in 1933, under the laws of the state of Delaware, the CCC was transferred in 1939 to the Department of Agriculture. In the summer of 1948, the Commodity Corporation Charter Act dissolved the existing charter and provided a permanent federal charter. The CCC is managed by a board of directors, under the general supervision and direction of the secretary of agriculture. Because it has no operating personnel, the CCC's programs are carried out through the personnel and facilities of the Agricultural Stabilization and Conservation Service of the department.

Important in its impact on the national economy is the price-support program, which in 1967 covered corn, oats, rye, barley, grain sorghum, wheat, cotton, rice, most types of tobacco, peanuts, milk, butterfat, wool, mohair, tung nuts, and honey.

JAMES E. McMAHON
*Information Division, Agricultural
Stabilization and Conservation Service*

**COMMODITY MARKET,** kə-mod′ə-tē. What the stock market is to listed securities, the commodity market is to a growing list of foods, metals, and hides, as well as rubber. The principal commodity markets in the United States include the Chicago Board of Trade, Chicago Mercantile Exchange, New York Mercantile Exchange, New York Cocoa Exchange, Commodity Exchange (in New York), New York Coffee and Sugar Exchange, and New York Produce Exchange. The items on which traders speculate as to future prices—called *futures*—include wheat, soybeans, corn, oats, rye, live steers and cattle, soybean oil and meal, pork bellies, potatoes, platinum, cocoa, cotton, wool, frozen orange juice, copper, lead, tin, silver, zinc, coffee, sugar, cottonseed oil, mercury, rice, and silver coins. Commodities are added as market demand rises. A commodity market deals only in contracts; no commodities are on the trading floor. See also FUTURES TRADING.

Increasing demands for food and metals aid the commodity markets, as do periodic bear markets in stocks, which tend to divert money temporarily into the commodity markets.

GENE SMITH, *"The New York Times"*

**COMMODORE,** kom'ə-dôr, is a naval rank above captain and below rear admiral, ranking with brigadier general in the army. It also is a courtesy title for a person commanding more than one ship. In the U. S. Navy it was purely a courtesy title until 1862, then was an official rank until 1899. It was restored in 1943 and discontinued after World War II until restored once more by Congress in 1981. Commodores hold major commands, such as convoys, naval bases, or squadrons of warships. Coast Guard commodores command Coast Guard districts, groups of warships, and convoys. U. S. Navy and Coast Guard captains commanding squadrons are often addressed unofficially as "Commodore." It is also the courtesy title for the president of a yacht club.

**COMMODUS,** kom'ō-dəs, **Lucius Aelius Aurelius** (161–192 A. D.), Roman emperor. He was one of the twin sons of Marcus Aurelius and survived Marcus' other male children. Pushed into public affairs when the revolt of Avidius Cassius threatened the throne in 175, Commodus was made co-augustus (joint senior emperor) with his father in 177 and accompanied Marcus to the wars in defense of the Danubian frontier.

After the death of Marcus Aurelius in 180, Commodus ruled alone, changing his name to Marcus Commodus Antoninus. He terminated frontier hostilities by agreeing to pay subsidies to the barbarians along the Danube.

The reign of Commodus (180–192) was troubled by economic decline, barbarian threats, internal discord, palace conspiracies, and finally the insanity of the emperor himself. About 182, Commodus' sister Lucilla plotted his assassination, but the conspiracy was detected and foiled. Somewhat lacking in talent and still too young to exert authority, Commodus relied heavily on his associates for the conduct of state affairs. Consequently, they, rather than the emperor himself, suffered when things went wrong. The praetorian prefect Perennis was sacrificed to appease military discontent in 185. Cleander, the chamberlain who suceeded Perennis, was thrown to the mob when grain ran short in 189.

By 191, Commodus had become insane. He imagined himself the reincarnation of Hercules. He renamed Rome *Colonia Commodiana,* the colony of Commodus. He changed his name back to Lucius Aelius Aurelius Commodus, and he changed the names of the months to correspond to his names and titles, among which were Hercules, Romanus, Exsuperatorius, and Amazonius. On New Year's Eve, 192, Commodus was assassinated by members of his palace staff.

TOM B. JONES, *University of Minnesota*

**COMMON CARRIER,** a company or person that offers to the public the service of transporting passengers or property. Common carriers include railroads, airlines, steamships, buses, taxicabs, express companies, moving companies, truckmen, pipelines, and other similar enterprises. Cases in which the definition of common carrier was extended beyond the more usual means of transportation involved the operation of a chair lift (1959) and a mule train (1962).

The most important difference between a common carrier and a private carrier is that the former offers to perform transportation services for the public generally rather than for particular persons under special contractual arrangements. Although the relationship between the passenger or shipper and the common carrier is essentially contractual, nevertheless the law imposes certain duties and affords certain rights to each, aside from any express or implied agreement between them.

There is generally no legal obligation on the part of a common carrier to continue in business; but so long as he does, he is subject to a certain degree of government control and regulation, on the theory that he has dedicated his property to the public use. In the United States, the federal government may, and to a considerable degree does, regulate the operations of carriers engaged in interstate and foreign commerce. State and local governments may exercise control over intrastate carriers, and over interstate and foreign carriers to the extent that such control does not conflict with federal action.

Government regulation may be exercised directly by the legislature, but it is usually accomplished through administrative agencies and commissions. Control extends not only to the fixing of rates but also to such matters as requiring the furnishing of adequate services and facilities and imposing minimum standards of safety. The regulation of common carriers is subject to judicial review, particularly in establishing rates.

RICHARD L. HIRSHBERG°, *Attorney at Law*

**COMMON CAUSE** is a nonpartisan citizens' lobby founded by John W. Gardner in 1970 for the purpose of effecting political reforms and promoting legislative action on national problems. Its headquarters are in Washington, D. C. Policies are determined by a 60-member governing board elected annually by Common Cause members through mailed ballots and working with the chairman. (John W. Gardner served as the first chairman.)

Common Cause is organized in state, congressional district, and sometimes state legislative district units. Many states have steering committees that determine priorities for action. Groups of volunteers on all levels carry on the active work of the organization. Major goals have been to improve the systems of financing political campaigns, including partial financing by the public; to reform the internal workings of Congress and to improve its code of ethics; to reform state governments; to break down voting barriers and grant the franchise to 18-year-olds; to protect the environment; to open congressional meetings to the public; to revise the congressional seniority system; and to end political corruption at all levels of government.

Common Cause monitors the work of Congress and makes recommendation to its membership for legislative reforms. It also files lawsuits and engages in lobbying. Its members are kept informed and urged to participate in political action through newsletters and special reports. Membership numbers approximately 225,000.

# COMMON LAW

**COMMON LAW** is the term denoting the legal system that developed in England and then spread to many other parts of the world under British domination. Today the common law continues to flourish even where British rule no longer prevails—most notably in the United States, and in most Commonwealth countries including Canada and Australia. Its great rival in Western civilization is the *civil law* which, based on Roman law, developed on the continent of Europe and then spread to Latin America and to various Asian and African countries that were colonized (or at least dominated at some time) by the nations of continental Europe. One of the striking contrasts between these two leading world systems is that the civil law, being primarily legislative in origin, is codified, while the common law, being primarily judicial in origin, is found mostly in court decisions. For this reason the term "common law" is frequently used to describe judge-made law as distinguished from statutory law.

The term "common law" has a curious derivation. It was originally used to describe the law that was common to the entire realm of England —national, rather than local, law; the king's law, rather than that promulgated and administered by the lesser feudal lords. This meaning has now become obsolete, and in the United States it is customary to speak of each individual state as having its own system of common law and of there being no national common law for the country as a whole. Nevertheless, the original meaning of the term is a key to understanding the historical development of the institution.

## THE COMMON LAW IN ENGLAND

The common law developed with the growth of centralized royal power in England. In the Middle Ages power and wealth were based on landholding, and landholding in turn was based on military might. No sharp distinctions were recognized between military power and legislative, executive, or judicial power. All were merged in the hands of feudal lords, each of whom dealt with the affairs of his tenants—that is, those who held their land from him—as he and his advisers saw fit. In theory all land in the realm belonged ultimately to the king as the chief lord and was held at his pleasure by his tenants, but there was no effective apparatus of government to make his power felt below the level of those tenants who held directly from him.

After the Norman Conquest in 1066, William the Conqueror laid the foundation for centralized government when he established his Curia Regis, or king's court. It was not a body that would be considered a court in modern times, but rather a group of men surrounding the king, assisting him generally and exercising the powers he delegated to them. Over the course of the next several centuries legislative and judicial functions became differentiated from executive functions, and there ultimately emerged a legislative body—Parliament—as well as courts in fundamentally the form we recognize today.

**Writs and the King's Peace.** The extension of royal judicial power was accomplished on the basis of two central ideas. First, King Henry II (reigned 1154–1189) and his successors, calling attention to the essential nature of feudalism, asserted that because they ultimately owned all the land in the realm, they were entitled to decide all disputes concerning it. If a dispute arose, the king's chancellor would issue a royal order

(*writ*) directing where the hearing was to be held. Even if the writ specified a lesser tribunal than the Curia Regis, the prerogative of the king to keep jurisdiction was maintained. Second, the king asserted that certain roads, certain places, and certain days were protected by his "peace." Any disturbance in those roads or places or during the specified days was considered a breach of the king's peace and so liable to be dealt with by the king or his court. This was the foundation of royal jurisdiction over crime. In turn such criminal jurisdiction provided the basis for asserting jurisdiction over disputes between individuals involving a breach of the peace, as where one man committed a trespass against another by assaulting him or breaking into his house or making away with his goods. Gradually the idea of the king's peace was extended to all times and places, and the degree of disturbance serious enough to be called a breach of the peace became purely nominal. Crushing a blade of grass by stepping on another man's land was enough. Furthermore, over a period extending from the Norman conquest to about the beginning of the 16th century, royal justice was extended far beyond actions concerning land, crime, and trespass to deal with indirect as well as direct injuries, thus covering the entire area of what today are called *torts* (various "wrongs") as well as all kinds of breaches of contract. See also TORT.

**The Law Courts.** Meanwhile, specialization of function was developing in the Curia Regis. Those of the king's advisers who were most suited to judicial work concentrated on it, while others more suited for legislative or executive work concentrated on their specialties. Thus a legal profession developed in and around the king's courts. Judges became specialists in litigation and so did the lawyers who practiced before them. Ultimately, three distinct courts evolved, manned by professional judges: the Court of Common Pleas, the Court of King's Bench, and the Court of the Exchequer. In the early stages of their development they handled different kinds of cases, but ultimately their jurisdiction became overlapping and concurrent.

Another development that took place during the same period was the extension of royal jurisdiction in such a way as to operate outside the monarch's personal presence. The king's judicial representatives spent some of their time with him in Westminster (part of what is now London); the rest of the time they traveled around the country on circuit to hear and decide cases. This brought royal justice close to the people.

**Trial by Jury.** Closely related to the practice of going wherever cases had arisen was the evolution of a new method of trial in the king's courts. The older methods of trial—ordeal, battle, and compurgation—were in effect in the older local tribunals and were all based on a belief in the supernatural intervention of the Deity to reveal the truth. In an ordeal the person accused of wrongdoing had to plunge his arm into a pot of boiling water, carry a red hot coal in his hand, or perform some similar act. If his wounds healed within a certain time, that proved his innocence; if not, his guilt was established. Trial by battle decided issues by physical strength (either in the person of the litigant or that of a champion hired by him). The man who prevailed in the fight prevailed at law. Trial by compurgation was little better. Various persons would swear in a set ritualistic form of words that a litigant had told the truth; but any slip in repeating the formula destroyed the value of the oath, whereas a letter-perfect recitation (although full of perjury) established the case.

In place of these modes of trial the king's courts offered a more rational inquiry into what had happened by calling on people who had first-hand knowledge of the facts to be decided. This was the beginning of trial by jury. At first the jurors were neighbor-witnesses who decided cases on the basis of their own personal knowledge. Gradually, however, they became judges of fact, hearing evidence from others and basing their verdicts on testimony presented in court. By the middle of the 14th century, there were two types of jury: the grand jury (consisting of a varying number of persons) and the petit jury (consisting of 12 persons). The grand jury heard evidence in secret as to alleged crimes that had been committed and then decided whether to formally charge the accused and bring him to trial. If it did so *indict* him, his case was heard in public by a petit jury. Its function was to determine guilt or innocence. The petit jury, unlike the grand jury, was also used in civil cases to determine issues of fact. Even in its rudimentary form trial by jury was a vast improvement over the supernatural methods of trial that had prevailed earlier. It made for public satisfaction with royal justice and contributed to the ultimate disintegration of the jurisdiction of local courts presided over by the lesser lords. By the time of Edward III (reigned 1327–1377) the process was complete, and royal justice was firmly established to administer law common to the entire realm.

**The Doctrine of Precedent.** In addition to trial by jury, there was another outstanding characteristic of the operation of the royal courts: their decisions became "precedents." The judges were frequently—indeed in the early days of judicial development, usually—confronted with cases for which there was no previously formulated rule of decision. With no statute to guide them, they had to decide such cases as best they could according to their own sense of justice and fair dealing. In doing so, they stated the reasons for their decisions. These decisions were reduced to writing by lawyer-reporters and were carefully collected and preserved. The decisions then became guides for deciding future cases. By the doctrine of *stare decisis*—or precedent—the courts considered themselves bound to follow earlier decisions. In other words, if a case was substantially similar to another that had been decided earlier, it had to be decided the same way. This held true even if, in the present view of the judges, the first case had been decided wrongly. However, if the case at hand could be distinguished—that is, shown to differ from the other case in some significant way—the precedent did not govern and the court was free to fashion a new solution. This, in turn, became a precedent for similar cases in the future. The 19th century jurist Sir Henry Maine explained the doctrine of precedent:

"We in England are well accustomed to the extension, modification, and improvement of law by a machinery which, in theory, is incapable of altering one jot or one line of existing jurisprudence ... With respect to that great portion of our legal system which is enshrined in cases and recorded in law reports, we habitually employ a double language, and entertain, as it would appear, a double and inconsistent set of ideas. When a group of facts comes before an English Court for adjudication, the whole course of the discussion between the judges and the advocates assumes that no question is, or can be, raised which will call for the application of any principles but old ones, or of any distinctions but such as have long since been allowed ... Yet the moment the judgement has been rendered and reported, we slide unconsciously unavowedly into a new language and a new train of thought. We now admit that the new decision has modified the law. The rules applicable have, to use the very inaccurate expression sometimes employed, become more elastic. In fact they have been changed. A clear addition has been made to the precedents, and the canon of law elicited by comparing the precedents is not the same as that which would have been obtained if the series of cases had been curtailed by a single example. The fact that the old rule has been repealed, and that a new one has replaced it, eludes us, because we are not in the habit of throwing into precise language the legal formulas which we derive from the precedents ...

"We do not admit that our tribunals legislate; we imply that they have never legislated; and yet we maintain that the rules of the English common law, with some assistance from the Court of Chancery and from Parliament, are coextensive with the complicated interests of modern society."

Thus the common law grew and expanded constantly. In the process it developed a mode of juristic thinking that was more inductive than deductive and that placed greater emphasis on close comparisons of concrete situations than on the enunciation in advance of broad general principles. In doing so, it also served well the ideal of equal justice under law, treating men in similar situations in the same way.

**The Role of Parliament.** It must be remembered, however, that all English law did not emanate from the courts. Just as the courts had evolved as distinct institutions from the Curia Regis, so also had Parliament evolved as a distinct legislative body. It exercised the power to make law in general terms, unrelated to particular cases. Sometimes Parliament enacted statutes in areas not previously covered by judicial decisions, but sometimes it dealt with areas already covered, and sometimes in such a way as to cancel out earlier judicial decisions that were considered unjust. When it spoke, its command prevailed over any contrary rule enunciated by the courts. Furthermore, Parliament also exercised some direct control over common law decisions, thus laying the foundation for the still existing appellate jurisdiction of the House of Lords.

**The Rise of Equity.** The king himself long continued to be a source of English law. Even after the law courts had developed into distinct institutions, subjects still sometimes petitioned the king for justice. He was regarded as the fountainhead of justice, from whom redress could be sought if the subject felt that he could not get justice in the ordinary courts. The king delegated the hearing of most such petitions to his lord chancellor. As the work increased, it became institutionalized and was delegated to subordinates of the lord chancellor, who began to function as a tribunal called the court of chancery and to administer *equity*. There was plenty of judicial work to be done, because the common law courts were becoming set in their ways. In many situations those courts were unwilling or unable to do justice, mostly in the area of civil litigation. While they gave money judgments for wrongs that had already been committed, they had no machinery for preventing future wrongs or for forcing a defendant to perform a contract or other obligation. Some of the rules that they enforced were excessively harsh and contrary to common ideas of fairness. There was much emphasis on formalism and ritual, particularly in the field of contract and property law, where the tendency was to insist on a literal interpretation of anything in writing. While trial by jury was a much better method of determining facts than the methods it had supplanted, juries were sometimes incapable of understanding complicated transactions and were sometimes subject to corruption or intimidation by powerful men. Finally some institutions and areas of conduct were not covered by the common law at all, notably trusts and the administration of estates of deceased persons. It was because of such inadequacies in the common law that the Court of Chancery came into being.

At first the chancellor decided cases without reference to any fixed rules of substantive law or procedure. His standard was "equity and good conscience"—a fact that gave rise to a famous quip that the only measure in chancery was "the chancellor's foot." Decisions were not systematically preserved and there was no conscious adherence to precedent. During the 17th century, however, it became customary to appoint lawyers rather than ecclesiastics to the post of chancellor, and to report systematically the decisions rendered in chancery. Gradually the doctrine of precedent developed, and came to operate in chancery much the same as it operated in the common law courts.

Just as the court of chancery developed its own body of substantive law, it also developed its own special procedure. It differed from common law procedure in many respects, but the most striking contrast was the fact that no jury was used in equity. Perhaps this was because the chancery's intervention was sometimes predicated on the claim that juries were subject to intimidation and corruption, or perhaps it was because much of chancery's jurisdiction was taken over from the ecclesiastical courts (particularly in connection with the administration of estates of decedents, minors, and incompetents) and so its procedure was modeled to a considerable extent on that which prevailed in those courts, where juries were unknown. In any event all issues of fact as well as of law were determined by the judge alone.

In the beginning the chancellor recognized no limitations on his power to dispense justice. He operated in the same areas as the common law courts and gave the same remedies. Such duplication of effort, however, was not long tolerated. During the 14th century the principle was established that the chancellor would not act where there was an "adequate remedy" at common law. This left the court of chancery a large area of discretion, but established some sort of jurisdictional line, blurred at first, but later becoming sharper as precedents were established defining where chancery would act and where it would leave the common law courts to act. As a result equity never became a complete body of law. It consisted instead of a collection of miscellaneous rules. The point was well made by Frederic W. Maitland, English legal historian. "We ought not to think of common law and equity as of two rival systems. Equity was not a self-sufficient system, at every point it presupposed the existence of common law. Common law was a self-sufficient system. I mean this: that if the legislature had passed a short act saying 'Equity is hereby abolished,' we might still have got on fairly well; in some respects our law would have been barbarous, unjust, absurd, but still the great elementary rights, the right to immunity from violence, the right to one's good name, the rights of ownership and possession would have been decently protected and contract would have been enforced. On the other hand had the legislature said, 'Common Law is hereby abolished,' this decree if obeyed would have meant anarchy. At every point equity presupposed the existence of common law. Take the case of the trust. It's of no use for equity to say that A is a trustee of Blackacre for B, unless there be some court that can say that A is the owner of Blackacre. Equity without common law would have been a castle in the air, an impossibility.

"For this reason I do not think that any one has expounded or ever will expound equity as a single, consistent system, an articulate body of law. It is a collection of appendixes between which there is no very close connexion. If we suppose all our law put into systematic order, we shall find that some chapters of it have been copiously glossed by equity, while others are quite free from equitable glosses . . . The law of contract has been . . . richly provided with equitable appendixes. The power of the Chancery to compel specific performance, and its power to decree the cancellation or rectification of agreements brought numerous cases of contract before it, and then it had special doctrines about mortgages, and penalties, and stipulations concerning time. Property law was yet more richly glossed. One vast appendix was added to it under the title of trusts. The bond which kept these various appendixes together under the head of equity was the jurisdictional and procedural bond. All these matters were within the cognizance of courts of equity, and they were not within cognizance of the courts of common law. That bond is now broken by the Judicature Acts [1873]. Instead of it we find but a mere historical bond—'these rules used to be dealt with by the Court of Chancery' —and the strength of that bond is being diminished year by year."

Although equity generally supplemented the common law, this was not true where the two came into conflict. The chancellor sometimes presumed to say that a legal remedy was inadequate or improper because the substantive rule on which it was based was unjust. In particular he asserted his right to enjoin a litigant from prosecuting an unjust action in a common law court or from enforcing an unjust judgment already recovered. If the injunction was violated, the offender was subject to imprisonment for contempt. The chancellor, following his normal method of enforcing decrees and avoiding the appearance of any direct attack, did not purport to act directly against the common law courts, but only against litigants who resorted to them. Nevertheless, his assertion of power did not go unchallenged by the common law judges. Their spokesman was Edward Coke (1552–1634), chief justice of the court of king's bench; his adversary was Lord Ellesmere, the chancellor. Coke said that he would use the writ of habeas corpus to release any person imprisoned by the chancellor for violating such an injunction. The controversy was bitter and notorious. King James I, anxious to assert his supremacy over all the judges, appointed a committee of distinguished lawyers, including Sir Francis Bacon, to advise him how the dispute should be settled. On the basis of their report, he decided in 1616 in favor of chancery. Thenceforth, whenever an equity rule conflicted with a common law rule, the equity rule prevailed.

### THE MERGER OF LAW AND EQUITY

This solution was neither wholly satisfactory nor permanent. It made little sense to have two sets of courts administering two separate bodies of substantive law by two differing procedures. Sometimes a litigant had to go to both of them in order to fully vindicate his legal rights, and sometimes he went to one only to learn that he should have gone to the other. This caused a wholly unnecessary waste of time, effort, and money. The way out of the predicament was to merge the jurisdiction of the two courts.

Reform, though it was long overdue, was slow in coming. It was, in fact, delayed until the 19th century, and then occurred first in the United States. There the law of England had been adapted along with the bifurcation of jurisdiction between courts of equity and courts of common law. In 1848 the New York legislature enacted a new code of civil procedure drafted by David Dudley Field, a great reformer and enthusiast for codification. The new code was remarkable not only because it marked the entry of the legislature into an area that previously had been almost exclusively the province of the judiciary but also because it inaugurated sweeping reforms. The code vested in a single system of courts the jurisdiction previously exercised by separate courts of equity and common law. It further provided that a uniform procedure should be used in all types of cases, except that juries were to be available only in those cases that would formerly have been tried in common law courts, while juries were not to be available in those that would formerly have been tried in equity. This qualification was thought to be desirable in view of a provision in the New York constitution preserving the right to trial by jury only to the extent that it had existed theretofore.

The uniform new procedure was a copy neither of the system that had prevailed in common law nor of that which had prevailed in equity, but a combination and modernization of the best features of both. By this time both the equity courts and the common law courts had created procedural systems of grotesque complexity, almost unintelligible even to the judges themselves. The rights of litigants were all but forgotten in a welter of technicalities, while judges and lawyers quibbled and split hairs endlessly. In the Field code, all this was swept away in favor of a relatively simple set of rules expressed in plain, clear language. Substantive rights, however, were not affected. The same remedies that had previously been available in the two separate sets of courts were still available, and they were granted or denied on the basis of the same principles of law that had been separately developed in those two sets of courts. The New York code

was quickly recognized as a great step forward and was soon copied in most of the U. S. states. Its basic pattern still prevails, although now in many states procedural rule-making power has been restored to the courts.

### THE ENGLISH LEGAL SYSTEM TODAY

The New York pattern as established by the Field code was also adopted in England with the enactment of the Judicature Act of 1873. This was the last major reform before the English legal system took its present form. It combined the equity and common law courts into the "high court of justice" and established the court of appeal. The two together constituted the "supreme court of judicature." The House of Lords was also retained. Though it is ordinarily thought of as a purely legislative body, the House of Lords is also the highest tribunal of England, performing its judicial functions by delegating them to a small group of "law lords"—men who have been made life peers for the primary purpose of serving as judges. Another body, which like the House of Lords has its background in the old Curia Regis, is the privy council. It functions as the supreme appellate court for such Commonwealth nations as choose to use it.

While the English legal system has continued to grow, its fundamental characteristics today are still those that evolved during the course of the historical development just sketched. The law is still common to the entire realm. The jury is still used in criminal cases and, although only to a very limited extent, also in civil cases. Parliament is still supreme, but the doctrine of precedent still flourishes and provides the mechanism by which the common law continues to grow. Indeed, the tempo of change in the common law may be accelerated in the future, because in 1966 the lord chancellor of England announced that henceforth the judges of the House of Lords would feel free to depart from a previous decision when they deemed it proper and just to do so. Thus far no drastic change in approach has materialized, but at least there is now a prospect of some relaxation of England's rigid doctrine of precedent.

### COMMON LAW IN THE UNITED STATES

The United States, unlike England, has no common law in the most ancient meaning of the term, denoting law uniform throughout the entire nation. Instead, 51 systems of law are in operation, one for each state and another for the federal government. This is because the U. S. Constitution establishes a central government of limited, enumerated powers, leaving all residual judicial and legislative powers to the individual states.

Nevertheless, what is now regarded as the essence of the common law was brought to America by the early English settlers. Although they carried few lawbooks with them and although few persons among them were trained in the law, the fundamental principles of the common law were understood and generally (though not universally) accepted by them, and consequently applied in a hit-or-miss fashion to cases as they arose. In some colonies the common law was formally "received," as in this Virginia enactment (1776):

"Be it ordained by the representatives of the people now met in General Convention, That the common law of England, all statutes or acts of Parliament made in aid of the common law prior to the fourth year of the reign of King James the first, and which are of a general nature, not local to that Kingdom, together with the several acts of the General Assembly of this colony now in force, so far as the same may consist with the several ordinances, declarations, and resolutions of the General Convention, shall be the rule of decision, and shall be considered as in full force, until the same shall be altered by the legislative power of this colony."

The common law so received continued to grow as it had been growing in England, by the accretion of new precedents dealing with new situations. However, it developed independently in the various colonies and states. The judges of New York, knowing little about decisions being made in other states and in any event not feeling bound by them, inevitably reached results that were somewhat different from the results being reached in similar cases in Connecticut and Maryland, and in the process the various courts enunciated differing rules. As the nation moved westward and new states were created, the common law moved westward too. In 1787, Congress passed the Ordinance for the Northwest Territory, providing that judicial proceedings should be conducted "according to the course of the common law," and many new state constitutions provided that the common law should continue in force until modified by legislation. Meanwhile the common law itself was growing and expanding in each state with each new decision. Thus it spread throughout the nation, even into such states as Louisiana, California, and Texas, which had originally started out with legal rules and institutions derived from the civil law.

**Federalism and the Constitution.** The common law in the United States has continued to grow in separate compartments, with much resulting diversity from state to state, but still with some underlying nationwide coherence. The judges of one state often cite decisions from other states, for they are "persuasive" as representing attempts by other judges to solve similar problems even though they have no binding effect as precedents. There are several other unifying factors: the common origin of the judge-made law of every state in the law of England; the constant interaction between people from all parts of the nation in communication, travel, and commerce across state borders; and the methods by which legal knowledge is transmitted from generation to generation. Meanwhile, the unifying influence of Blackstone's *Commentaries on the Law of England* (published shortly after the middle of the 18th century), which formed the basis for the legal education of most American lawyers for the next century, has been replaced by the unifying influence of the so-called "national" law schools—those that do not concentrate on teaching the law of any particular state, but rather on the principles of law generally applicable throughout the nation.

As noted above, the absence of a truly national system of common law in the United States is attributable to its Constitution, which established a federal, as distinguished from a unitary, form of government. The Constitution is also responsible for another major contrast between the legal systems of the two nations: the relative roles of courts and legislative bodies. In England, where there is no written constitution, Parliament is supreme. The courts can interpret its legislation, but they cannot invalidate it. In the United

States, Congress is not supreme, for its acts can be annulled by the Supreme Court as violating the Constitution. Similarly the acts of any state legislature can be judicially invalidated as being inconsistent with either the state constitution or the U. S. Constitution. In 1803 in the famous case of *Marbury* v. *Madison,* Chief Justice Marshall said:

"The powers of the legislature are defined and limited; and that those limits may not be mistaken, or forgotten, the Constitution is written. To what purpose are powers limited, and to what purpose is that limitation committed to writing, if these limits may, at any time, be passed by those intended to be restrained? The distinction between a government with limited and unlimited powers is abolished, if those limits do not confine the persons on whom they are imposed, and if acts prohibited and acts allowed, are of equal obligation. It is a proposition too plain to be contested, that the Constitution controls any legislative act repugnant to it . . .

"It is emphatically the province and duty of the judicial department to say what the law is. Those who apply the rule to particular cases, must of necessity expound and interpret that rule. If two laws conflict with each other, the courts must decide on the operation of each."

Since *Marbury* v. *Madison,* many statutes, both state and federal, have been held invalid by the courts as being unconstitutional.

**Relaxation of Precedent.** The concept of judicial supremacy thus established is probably responsible for a subtle transformation of the doctrine of precedent in the United States, making the American version quite different from that which prevails in England. Because the U. S. Constitution is notoriously difficult to amend, the Supreme Court has felt impelled from time to time to revise its earlier interpretations of the document when they have appeared to be obsolete or mistaken, and in the process has overruled its own prior decisions. In other words, those precedents were no longer treated as having binding force. This approach has spread from constitutional issues to nonconstitutional issues, and from the Supreme Court of the United States to other appellate courts, even when dealing with common law problems having no constitutional implications. A result has been a substantial weakening of the doctrine of *stare decisis.* While lower courts still feel constrained to abide by the precedents established by tribunals above them, those tribunals feel free to depart from their own precedents whenever they seem to have outlived their usefulness. Such overrulings of previous decisions reveal the extent to which many American courts are consciously engaged in determining questions of policy, attempting to correct old errors and to adapt the law to changing conditions and changing ideas.

**Trial by Jury: Current Status.** In addition to the contrasts between England and the United States already discussed, one more deserves particular mention—the role of the jury. In England its use has greatly declined. The grand jury has ceased to exist; its purpose is served by preliminary hearings before *magistrates.* These officials are also called justices of the peace but should not be confused with American officials with that title; English magistrates are respected and responsible judges, although most of them are not formally trained in the law. They have the duty, in any serious case, of inquiring whether there is sufficient evidence to hold the accused for trial.

Petit juries still exist, but they are not used extensively in either criminal or civil cases. As far as criminal cases are concerned, the reason is that the overwhelming majority of such cases—well over 95%—are tried before justices of the peace, who function without the aid of a jury. As a result juries are used only in the very small minority of criminal cases that are serious enough to merit trial in the higher courts. In the adjudication of civil cases, the jury has all but disappeared. During World War II, when England was suffering from an acute shortage of manpower, temporary restrictions were placed on the use of juries in civil cases. Later they were lifted, but by then judges and lawyers had learned that they could get along without juries, and the public acquiesced in this view. Now the right to trial by jury is limited to a few kinds of special cases such as libel; although judges have power in their discretion to impanel juries in other kinds of civil cases, they seldom do so.

In the United States, on the other hand, the jury still flourishes. The right to trial by jury is guaranteed by the federal Constitution for cases in the federal courts and by state constitutions for cases in state courts. These constitutions guarantee the right to trial by jury in all criminal prosecutions, but this is generally interpreted to exclude prosecutions for petty offenses such as traffic violations. For civil cases, they provide, either in specific terms or in effect, that the right to trial by jury shall "remain inviolate," meaning that it exists only in cases "at common law" as distinguished from those "in equity" and new types of cases that have come into existence since the constitutions were adopted. Grand juries are ordinarily regarded as less important than petit juries in the protection of individual liberties, and they are constitutionally guaranteed in some states but not in others. The effect of the constitutional provisions is to make juries available as a matter of right in a wide variety of cases. Not only are they available, they are in fact used very extensively, not only in the vast majority of serious criminal cases but also in civil litigation, particularly the great mass of personal injury claims that arise out of auto accidents.

### TRENDS AND PROSPECTS

The main lines of development of the common law have already been indicated. These trends are likely to continue. In addition, two trends that have not been discussed are worthy of note. One is the tendency toward unifying the law of the United States; the other is the broadening of professional horizons through comparative study.

Although the United States still has no law common to the entire realm and is not likely in the foreseeable future to develop a unitary system of law, there are countervailing forces. The U.S. Supreme Court has exerted a very powerful unifying influence by reason of its power to interpret the federal Constitution. Many subjects that until recently were thought to fall exclusively within the province of the states, notably criminal procedure and voting rights, have now become matters of constitutional law, uniform and binding throughout the nation. The work of the American Law Institute and of the Commissioners on Uniform Laws is also worthy of note. The former, a private organization of judges, lawyers, and law professors, has carried on a mas-

sive project since 1923 to "restate" the common law by extracting from the voluminous mass of case law in each state general principles of nationwide applicability. The Commissioners on Uniform Laws, composed of representatives from every state, has been engaged since the organization began (1890–1892) in drafting and urging enactment, in the states, of uniform legislation, especially in fields such as commercial law, involving many transactions across state lines.

Comparative law study is a relatively recent development in the United States and England (though not for European scholars). In its classic form it involves a comparison of rules and institutions of common law with those of the civil law. In another, narrower form, but one that is no less useful, it involves a comparison of the rules and institutions of one common law nation—such as England—with those of another—such as the United States. Both types of comparative study are growing in popularity, not only with law professors and students but also with judges and practicing lawyers. The long-range effect is to expose the strengths and weaknesses of differing approaches to the same problems and thus allow each nation to improve its own system of law by borrowing proven legal practices and institutions from other nations.

DELMAR KARLEN, *Director, Institute of Judicial Administration, New York City*

### Bibliography

Bodenheimer, Edgar, et al., *An Introduction to the Anglo-American Legal System* (West 1988).
Calabresi, Guido, *A Common Law for the Age of Statutes* (Harvard Univ. Press 1982).
Cosgrove, Richard, *The Anglo-American Legal Community* (Dutton 1986).
Milsom, S. F. C., *Studies in the History of the Common Law* (Hambledon Press 1985).
Reinsch, Paul S., *English Common Law in the Early American Colonies* (1899; reprint, Da Capo 1970).
Scheppele, Kim L., *Legal Secrets: Equality and Efficiency in the Common Law* (Univ. of Chicago Press 1988).

**COMMON-LAW MARRIAGE,** a marriage by agreement of the parties without either a civil or religious ceremony. This kind of marriage is similar to the canonical *matrimonium per verba de praesenti*, or "marriage by means of words referring to the present time." Common-law marriage may be regarded as legal if followed by cohabitation of the partners as husband and wife.

In the United States, common-law marriages were necessary in the early days on the frontier when neither a minister nor a justice of the peace was easily available. But by the early 1990s this type of marriage was valid in only 13 states—Alabama, Colorado, Georgia, Idaho, Iowa, Kansas, Montana, Ohio, Oklahoma, Pennsylvania, Rhode Island, South Carolina, and Texas—and the District of Columbia. Currently, 16 states (Arizona, Arkansas, California, Delaware, Hawaii, Maryland, Minnesota, Missouri, Nebraska, New York, North Carolina, Oregon, Tennessee, Virginia, Washington, and West Virginia) recognize common-law marriages as valid in the states where contracted yet invalid in their own states.

**COMMON MARKET,** a regional grouping of nations organized to facilitate trade among themselves and promote their economic growth. Major examples are the European Economic Community, European Free Trade Association, Latin American Free Trade Association, and Caribbean Community and Common Market.

**COMMON PRAYER, Book of.** See BOOK OF COMMON PRAYER.

**COMMON SENSE,** in philosophy, a mental faculty or an attitude. The term has had different meanings in different periods.

**Ancient Philosophy.** In Greek and Roman philosophy, common sense is that which is common to all the senses, or the ideas common to all humans. According to Aristotle's psychology, the common sense is a general centralizing faculty by means of which one apprehends the "common sensibles"—motion, rest, figure, magnitude, number, and unity. These qualities are not known through any one of the five special senses. Also, since the "togetherness" of the special sense qualities in an object is not discerned by the special senses singly, it is necessary to postulate a common sense that enables one to perceive that a certain color, taste, and sound are all present in the same object at once.

In Stoic philosophy, the view that all rational minds (*pneumata*) are emanations of an identical rational world-stuff (*pneuma*) entailed the further view that all rational minds have innately certain notions in common with each other; therefore, what is common sense to all men may be presumed to be true.

**Early Modern Philosophy.** These notions, or "innate ideas," came under attack in the 17th century by John Locke, who maintained that humans are not born with any ideas at all, that the mind at birth is a "blank tablet," and that our ideas result from sensory experiences and combinations of these. Locke's insight led to the empirical movement, which sought to base all knowledge on experience and which in the 18th century culminated in George Berkeley's denial of material substance and in David Hume's thoroughgoing skepticism regarding the certainty of empirical knowledge.

These consequences, distasteful to some, stimulated a countermovement, the so-called Scottish school of commonsense philosophy, led by Thomas Reid, Dugald Stewart, and James Beattie. Reid urged against Locke that the mind is congenitally furnished with some ideas, the presence of which may be certified by introspection. These are the same for the deepest thinker and the simplest human, and they are not the product, but the prior condition, of experience. Sensations are not the objects of knowledge but are "signs" that unmistakably point to the existence of a real self and of real objects to which our thoughts correspond, in a real world, the existence of which cannot be doubted. The final outcome of this movement was a rejection of philosophy as such, or a reduction of philosophical problems to psychological ones.

**Contemporary Philosophy.** In 19th- and 20th-century thought, *common sense* sometimes denotes a naïve view of reality as contrasted with a scientific view. The term also may denote a set of attitudes and assumptions presumed to be held by those who are untutored in a conscious philosophy. As such, common sense has been defended by such thinkers as John Dewey; George Santayana, who claimed that "common sense, in a rough and dogged way, is technically sounder than the schools of philosophy"; and, particularly, by George Edward Moore. Moore argued that certain statements about the existence and behavior of one's body and of things and other minds in one's environment are everywhere and always understood. The fact that we know these things is proof that they are true; indeed, no other proof of that fact can be given that does not beg the question. The skeptic can have no reason for doubting them, and what is not doubted in common life ought not to be doubted by philosophers.

ARTHUR DANTO, *Columbia University*

**COMMON SENSE,** a famous revolutionary pamphlet by Thomas Paine, published in January 1776, that advocated America's complete independence of Britain. It followed the natural-rights tenets of the British philosopher John Locke, whose writings had justified independence as the will of the people and revolution as a device for bringing happiness. Although the arguments were not original with Paine, Paine's passionate language and direct appeal to the people prepared them for the ideas expressed in the Declaration of Independence. Fighting with Britain had been under way for some nine months before publication of the pamphlet, but the political direction of the revolution was not yet clear. For many, *Common Sense* crystallized the revolution's goals.

In writing the pamphlet, Paine was encouraged by the Philadelphia physician and patriot Benjamin Rush. Rush read the manuscript, secured Benjamin Franklin's comments, suggested the title, and arranged for anonymous publication by Robert Bell of Philadelphia. *Common Sense* was an immediate success. Paine estimated that not less than 100,000 copies were run off and boasted that the pamphlet's popularity was "beyond anything since the invention of printing." Rush noted that its effect on Americans was "sudden and extensive." It was "read by public men, repeated in clubs, spouted in schools." Everywhere, it aroused debate about monarchy, the origin of government, English constitutional ideas, and independence. John Adams, although himself a strong proponent of independence, assailed the governmental principles of *Common Sense* as either "honest ignorance or knavish hypocrisy" and wrote his own *Thoughts on Government* (1776) in rebuttal.

*Common Sense* traces the origin of government to a human desire to restrain lawlessness. But government can be diverted to corrupt purposes by the people who created it. Therefore, the simpler the government, the easier it is for the people to discover its weakness and make the necessary adjustments. In Britain "it is wholly owing to the . . . people, and not to the constitution of the government, that the crown is not as oppressive . . . as in Turkey." The monarchy, Paine asserted, had corrupted virtue, impoverished the nation, weakened the voice of Parliament, and poisoned people's minds. The "royal brute of Britain" had usurped the rightful place of law.

Paine argued that the political connection with England was both unnatural and harmful to Americans. Reconciliation would only cause "more calamities. . . . It is repugnant to reason, to the universal order of things, to all examples from former ages, to suppose that this continent can longer remain subject to any external power." In short, the welfare of America, as well as its destiny, in Paine's view, demanded steps toward immediate independence.

JOHN A. SCHUTZ
*University of Southern California*

**COMMONS, John Rogers** (1862—1944), American labor historian, economist, and political scientist. His investigations and analyses of the social sciences explained and justified business unionism as practiced by American labor.

He was born in Hollandsburg, Ohio, on Oct. 13, 1862, and early exhibited an independence that was to characterize his intellectual endeavors. He was a professor at the University of Wisconsin from 1904 to 1932. Commons investigated, analyzed, classified, and reported on the practical application of economic theories. His ten-volume *Documentary History of Industrial Society* (1909—1911) and his *History of Labor in the United States* (1918) are the definitive works in American labor history, theory, and ideology, and they created the basis for the "Wisconsin School" of labor analysis. Commons died in Fort Lauderdale, Fla., on May 11, 1944.

HARVEY L. FRIEDMAN
*University of Massachusetts*

**COMMONWEALTH,** a term referring both to the public welfare or general good of a people and to a whole political and social body constituting a nation or state. The word is derived from *commonweal*, meaning the common well-being and general prosperity of the community, and came into conventional usage in the 16th century.

In English history the word was associated with reformers who held the public good in high esteem. The term *commonwealth* was later applied to the republican form of government that lasted in England from the execution of King Charles I in 1649 to the restoration of King Charles II in 1660. After the English Civil War the word was often applied to more radical reformers who championed the principle of popular sovereignty and opposed autocracy in any form. The word thus came to represent the exact opposite of despotic or absolutist government.

**COMMONWEALTH GAMES,** a quadrennial series of athletic competitions whose participants must be amateurs and qualified by birth or residence to represent a member of the Commonwealth of Nations. Through the years the competitions underwent several changes of name: British Empire Games (1930—1954), British Empire and Commonwealth Games (1954—1966), British Commonwealth Games (1966—1974), and the present name, in effect since 1978.

The events include athletics (track and field), swimming and diving, gymnastics, and lawn bowls for both men and women; and boxing, cycling, shooting, weight lifting, and wrestling for men. Other sports are sometimes introduced as regular or demonstration events, such as badminton, fencing, lacrosse, rowing, and shooting. Women became participants in 1934.

The idea for imperial games became a reality immediately after the Amsterdam Olympiad in 1928, when athletes of the British empire and the United States staged a dual relay meet in London. Its success led to the formation of an empire games council, with the earl of Derby as president and Sir James Leigh-Wood as chairman. King George V became patron of the games, and the Prince of Wales served as honorary president. The first British Empire Games were held in Hamilton, Ontario, in 1930 under the direction of M. M. Robinson, manager of the Canadian Olympic team in 1928.

**COMMONWEALTH OF INDEPENDENT STATES,** often abbreviated CIS, an association of former republics of the Union of Soviet Socialist Republics. The commonwealth was established in December 1991 and comprises 11 states: Russia (Russian federation), Ukraine, Belarus, Kazakhstan, Uzbekistan, Kyrgyzstan, Tajikistan, Turkmenistan, Moldova, Armenia, and Azerbaijan. The capital of this loose grouping of states is Minsk, Belarus.

By the end of 1990 all 15 of the USSR republics had issued declarations of sovereignty, although definitions of sovereignty differed widely. This breakdown of central authority and the growing assertiveness of the republics prepared the way for the CIS.

Anxious to preserve the union in some form, USSR president Mikhail Gorbachev initiated negotiations with leaders of the republics on a new constitutional framework. At Novo-ogarevo, near Moscow, in April 1991, Gorbachev agreed to recognize the sovereignty of the republics and to transfer the greater part of governmental functions to them.

Despite Gorbachev's concessions, most of the republics were reluctant to join the proposed Union of Sovereign States. When leaders of three of the republics scheduled the signing of a draft treaty in August 1991, hard-line Communists tried to save the old union through a forcible takeover of the government. Russian federation president Boris Yeltsin led the successful resistance to this coup attempt, which left the central government weak and largely under the domination of the Russian federation. Subsequent attempts to organize a reconstructed union foundered because of the opposition of Ukraine, which voted its independence on Dec. 1, 1991.

On Dec. 7—8, 1991, Yeltsin met near Minsk with the leaders of Belarus and Ukraine; they announced the formation of the Commonwealth of Independent States and invited other republics to join. The commonwealth was formally constituted at a meeting in Alma Ata, Kazakhstan, on Dec. 23, 1991. Formation of the CIS rendered the old central government superfluous, and the USSR was dissolved on Dec. 25, 1991.

The immediate concerns of the commonwealth were to remove barriers to economic interaction among the republics and to resolve dangerous political conflicts. Progress on developing institutions for cooperation within the CIS was slow because the members were forced to deal first with the critical issues arising from the breakup of the USSR. These included sharing the foreign debt, controlling nuclear weapons, determining the disposition of the Black Sea fleet and the Soviet Army, and coordinating price reform and monetary policy.

The long-term plan is to create a framework for political and economic cooperation similar to that of the European Community. Divergent political interests make achieving this goal difficult. The government of Ukraine, under Pres. Leonid Kravchuk, treats the CIS as a temporary expedient, and the states of Central Asia see a broad-based commonwealth as a guarantee against Russian domination. Most prominent politicians in the Russian federation regard the CIS as a means for preserving the Slavic core of the historic Russian state and for maintaining Russia's position as a Great Power.

R. JUDSON MITCHELL
*University of New Orleans*

TOURING THE COMMONWEALTH, Queen Elizabeth II and Prince Philip take an elephant ride in Varanasi, India.

**COMMONWEALTH OF NATIONS,** an association of independent countries and their dependencies, linked by a common acknowledgment of the British monarch as Head of the Commonwealth.

**Origin.** The term "Commonwealth of Nations" replaced the term "British Commonwealth of Nations" in 1949. The designation "British Empire" was generally used from the 1600's to the early 1900's but gradually yielded to the less imperialistic-sounding "British Commonwealth of Nations" after World War I.

The number of independent nations holding membership in the Commonwealth has increased significantly, particularly since World War II and most especially during the 1960's and 1970's. In the 1970's alone 14 independent nations became members, many of them small Caribbean or Pacific islands. All of them acknowledge the British monarch as Head of the Commonwealth, although some of them do not give allegiance to the British crown.

The name "Commonwealth of Nations" is often limited to these independent states, but technically it denotes all of their dependencies as well. The United Kingdom of Great Britain and Northern Ireland is the cornerstone of the Commonwealth, and the British monarch is the symbol of its unity. But the Commonwealth nations are not obligated to follow Britain's lead in any act of war or peace. Each is the sole judge of the nature of its association with the other members.

The Commonwealth has no formal or written constitution. Its members are bound together by common ideals and interests that have their source in a shared historical background and political heritage. Member nations may consult one another on common problems and exchange views and information.

### THE COMMONWEALTH TODAY

**Area and Population.** The Commonwealth has a total of about 11 million square miles (28 million sq km), roughly one fifth of the land surface of the earth. Its total population in the early 1980's was about 1,151,000,000, approximately one fourth of the human race. The peoples of the Commonwealth belong to all the major races of mankind, profess many religions, and speak hundreds of different languages and dialects. Culturally, they range from distinguished graduates of the world's greatest universities to primitive jungle aborigines. The peoples of the Commonwealth live on every continent and on islands in every ocean and experience every variety of climate from Arctic cold to equatorial heat. Their economic pursuits range from modern forms of industry and high finance to nomadic hunting and fishing. Their standards of living range from those of the highly industrialized welfare state to those of the village in the African bush.

**The Sovereign States—Government.** The following independent Commonwealth countries give allegiance to the British monarch: Antigua and Barbuda, Australia, Bahamas, Barbados, Canada, Fiji, Grenada, Jamaica, Mauritius, New Zealand, Papua New Guinea, St. Kitts and Nevis, St. Lucia, St. Vincent and the Grenadines, Solomon Islands, Tuvalu, and the United Kingdom. Except in the United Kingdom the crown is represented by a governor-general who occupies fundamentally the same position as the monarch in Britain. In some instances, as in Canada, the governor-general is a national of the dominion.

The Commonwealth also includes among its sovereign states these republics: Bangladesh, Botswana, Cyprus, Dominica, Gambia, Ghana, Guyana, India, Kenya, Kiribati, Malta, Malawi, Nauru, Nigeria, Seychelles, Sierra Leone, Singapore, Sri Lanka, Tanzania, Trinidad and Tobago, Uganda, Vanuatu, Western Samoa, Zambia, and Zimbabwe. It also includes these monarchies: Lesotho, Malaysia, Swaziland, and Tonga. These countries do not give allegiance to the British crown but acknowledge it as the symbol of the free association of the member countries of the Commonwealth of Nations and, as such, Head of the Commonwealth.

Canada and Australia are federal states, somewhat similar in this respect to the United States. New Zealand, like Britain, is a unitary state. Of the nations that achieved independence within the Commonwealth after World War II, India, Malaysia, Kenya, Nigeria, and Uganda adopted the federal system.

Most Commonwealth nations have parliamentary governments patterned after Britain's. The laws of these nations are made by a freely elected parliament after full and public debate. The executive holds office by virtue of the support of a majority in parliament. If he loses the confidence of that majority, the executive must either resign his office or appeal to the people in a general election. In accordance with the British system of cabinet government, ministers are collectively responsible for the actions of the government.

With several exceptions, the Commonwealth parliaments are two-chamber bodies. The lower house is usually elected by secret ballot. For the upper house, the method of selection varies. For example, members of the Canadian Senate are appointed for life, nominally by the governor-general but actually by the prime minister. Members of the Australian Senate are elected for a 6-year term by universal adult suffrage, each of the six states returning an equal number of senators. With the exception of money bills, which must originate in the lower house, legislation may be initiated in either chamber. But in practice the lower house has much greater legislative authority, and it alone can decide the fate of the government.

The rule of law prevails in most Commonwealth nations. Citizens have the right to a fair trial in an open court by an independent judge and an impartial jury, and the writ of habeas corpus is upheld. In the republics, judges are appointed by the president. In Malaysia, judges are appointed by the head of state on the recommendation of a judicial and legal service commission. In the sovereign states of the Commonwealth that owe allegiance to the crown, judges are appointed by the governor-general on the advice of the government concerned, except in Britain where they are appointed by the crown on the advice of the prime minister.

*Intra-Commonwealth Relations.* Each Commonwealth nation is an independent state, exercising sovereignty, both internal and external, in the fullest sense of the term. Each decides its own form of government and its own domestic and foreign policies. Each is free to secede from the Commonwealth at any time, as did Burma on becoming independent in 1947, the Republic of Ireland in 1949, South Africa in 1961, and Pakistan in 1972.

The independent status of the member nations was defined in the report of the Balfour Committee at the Imperial Conference of 1926. Issued at a time when the term "British Empire" was still in use and when the major components of the empire were termed "dominions," the report has been called the foundation stone of the modern Commonwealth of Nations. Its key passage asserts that the dominions "are autonomous Communities within the British Empire, equal in status, in no way subordinate one to another in any aspect of their domestic or external affairs, though united by a common allegiance to the Crown, and freely associated as members of the British Commonwealth of Nations. . . . Every self-governing member of the Empire is now the master of its destiny. In fact, if not always in form, it is subject to no compulsion whatever. . . . The British Empire is not founded upon negations. It depends essentially, if not formally, on positive ideals. Free institutions are its life-blood. Free cooperation is its instrument."

This definition of equal and independent status was enacted into law in 1931, by the Statute of Westminster, often spoken of as the "Magna Carta of the Commonwealth."

The attainment of equal and independent status illustrates the Commonwealth's capacity for change because all of Britain's present Commonwealth partners were once her colonies or dependencies. The Commonwealth is in a continuing process of constitutional evolution, an evolution characterized not only by the growth of its members to independent nationhood but also by the great diversity of their forms of government: unitary and federal, monarchical and republican. So flexible is the structure of the Commonwealth that it could accommodate such an anomaly as the temporary suspension of parliamentary government by a benevolent military dictatorship in Pakistan during the late 1950's and early 1960's. It could also countenance the union of a Commonwealth nation with a non-Commonwealth country, as exemplified by the loose (and short-lived) federation of Ghana and Guinea, a former dependency of France, formed in 1958.

The Commonwealth is not held together by legalities. In legal terms it simply represents "the lowest common denominator of consent." It recognizes no common law applicable to all members. Although the common law of England was established by English colonists in territories acquired by settlement—for example, in the Australian colonies and in Upper Canada—the preexist-

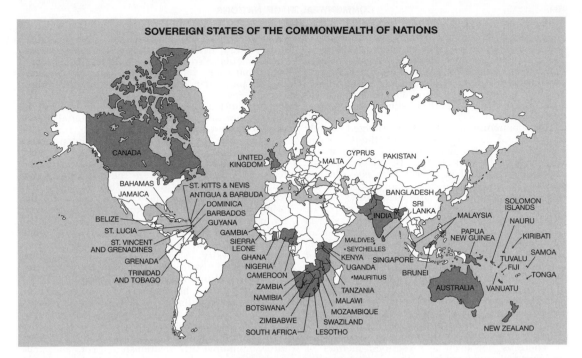

## SOVEREIGN STATES OF THE COMMONWEALTH OF NATIONS

## COMMONWEALTH OF NATIONS

| Component | Status | Component | Status |
|---|---|---|---|
| **Europe** | | St. Kitts and Nevis[2] | Sovereign state |
| Channel Islands | Crown dependency | St. Lucia | Sovereign state |
| Gibraltar | Dependent territory | St. Vincent and the Grenadines | Sovereign state |
| Great Britain | Sovereign state | Trinidad and Tobago | Sovereign state |
| Isle of Man | Crown dependency | Turks and Caicos Islands | Dependent territory |
| Malta | Sovereign state | **Asia** | |
| **Africa** | | Bangladesh | Sovereign state |
| Botswana | Sovereign state | Brunei | Sovereign state |
| British Indian Ocean Territory | Dependent territory | Cyprus | Sovereign state |
| Cameroon | Sovereign state | India | Sovereign state |
| Gambia | Sovereign state | Malaysia | Sovereign state |
| Ghana | Sovereign state | Maldives | Sovereign state |
| Kenya | Sovereign state | Pakistan | Sovereign state |
| Lesotho | Sovereign state | Singapore | Sovereign state |
| Malawi | Sovereign state | Sri Lanka | Sovereign state |
| Mozambique | Sovereign state | **Oceania and Australia** | |
| Namibia | Sovereign state | Australia | Sovereign state |
| Mauritius | Sovereign state | Ashmore and Cartier Islands | External territory |
| Nigeria | Sovereign state | Christmas Island | External territory |
| Seychelles | Sovereign state | Cocos Islands | External territory |
| Sierra Leone | Sovereign state | Coral Sea Islands | External territory |
| South Africa | Sovereign state | Heard Island and the McDonald Islands | External territory |
| St. Helena | Dependent territory | | |
| Ascension | Dependent territory | Norfolk Island | External territory |
| Tristan da Cunha | Dependent territory | Fiji | Sovereign state |
| Swaziland | Sovereign state | Kiribati | Sovereign state |
| Tanzania | Sovereign state | Nauru | Sovereign state |
| Uganda | Sovereign state | New Zealand | Sovereign state |
| Zambia | Sovereign state | Cook Islands | Self-governing state in free association with New Zealand |
| Zimbabwe | Sovereign state | | |
| **America** | | | |
| Anguilla | Dependent territory | Niue | Self-governing state in free association with New Zealand |
| Antigua and Barbuda | Sovereign state | | |
| Bahamas | Sovereign state | | |
| Barbados | Sovereign state | Ross Dependency | Dependent territory |
| Belize | Sovereign state | Tokelau | Dependent territory |
| Bermuda | Dependent territory | Papua New Guinea | Sovereign state |
| British Virgin Islands | Dependent territory | Pitcairn Island | Dependent territory |
| Canada | Sovereign state | Samoa | Sovereign state |
| Cayman Islands | Dependent territory | Solomon Islands | Sovereign state |
| Dominica | Sovereign state | Tonga | Sovereign state |
| Falkland Islands[1] | Dependent territory | Tuvalu | Sovereign state |
| Grenada | Sovereign state | Vanuatu | Sovereign state |
| Guyana | Sovereign state | **Antarctica** | |
| Jamaica | Sovereign state | Australian Antarctic Territory | Dependent territory |
| Montserrat | Dependent territory | British Antarctic Territory | Dependent territory |
| South Georgia and the South Sandwich Islands[1] | Dependent territory | Ross Dependency (New Zealand) | Dependent territory |

[1]In dispute between Britain and Argentina. [2]Officially St. Christopher and Nevis.

ing system of law was allowed to remain in force in regions conquered from or ceded by civilized peoples. Thus, the origins of the civil law of the Canadian province of Quebec go back to pre-revolutionary France; Roman-Dutch law prevails in Ceylon; and in India and Pakistan the law is derived from Hindu and Muslim codes, respectively.

No Commonwealth nation is pledged, merely by virtue of its membership in the Commonwealth, to go to the defense of any of the others. Yet in World Wars I and II, all—except the Republic of Ireland in World War II—rallied to the side of Britain. Today many of them are partners in various international alliances.

The members are not obligated to pursue common policies, to attend regular meetings, or to follow set voting procedures. Nevertheless, all are represented at the frequent meetings of the Commonwealth prime ministers. The Union of South Africa, for instance, made a point of being represented at the Commonwealth prime ministers' meeting in London in May 1960, although the session took place at the height of widespread Commonwealth criticism of South African racial policies. (The criticism led to South Africa's withdrawal from the Commonwealth a year later.)

There is not even a prescribed method of applying for membership in the Commonwealth, nor any precedent for expulsion from membership. The closest approach to the latter was the refusal of the other Commonwealth prime ministers, at their meeting in 1960, to agree in advance to permit the Union of South Africa to retain its membership if it decided to become a republic.

**Citizenship and Nationality.** The unity underlying the diversity of the Commonwealth is indicated by the existence of a large measure of Commonwealth citizenship. Each member country defines the citizenship and nationality of its own people and determines within its own territory the status of the citizens of other Commonwealth nations. Most Commonwealth countries grant the nationals of the other Commonwealth nations common status as citizens of the Commonwealth or as British subjects. Even where there is no provision for common status, the Commonwealth countries grant privileges to citizens of the Commonwealth that are not enjoyed by aliens.

The concept of common citizenship is so persistent that, although the Republic of Ireland withdrew from the Commonwealth in 1949, its citizens are not regarded as foreigners by the nations of the Commonwealth. Although ambassadors, instead of high commissioners, are now exchanged between Ireland and Commonwealth countries, Ireland's relations with Britain are conducted through the Commonwealth relations office, and not, as in the case of foreign countries, through the foreign office.

**Consultation.** An extensive machinery of consultation permits a flow of information and exchanges of views among the members of the Commonwealth. Because of its superior military and economic resources and its longer and broader experience in world diplomacy, as well as for historical and sentimental reasons, Britain is still "first among equals" in the Commonwealth.

The Commonwealth countries are represented in one anothers' capitals by high commissioners who have the status of ambassadors. But unlike ambassadors—who are accredited by their heads of state—the high commissioners are accredited by their governments, because the Commonwealth has a single head. Ministers of Commonwealth governments also visit the various capitals of other member countries from time to time to discuss particular issues with their opposite numbers.

In addition to such visits by individual ministers, there are Commonwealth ministerial meetings or conferences on defense, finance, and other matters. Most important of all are the periodic Commonwealth prime ministers' meetings. These meetings have replaced the earlier imperial conferences, which in turn were the offspring of the colonial conferences of the 1800's. Like the former imperial conferences, the Commonwealth prime ministers' meetings provide an opportunity for personal contact at the highest level of government and for the consideration of a wide range of common problems. Their functions are purely advisory or consultative. The meetings have neither executive nor legislative authority, and their resolutions are not legally binding upon the participants; hence the term "meeting" is preferred to "conference." Nevertheless, a consensus, or near consensus, generally carries considerable moral weight.

Consultation thus has become the essence of the Commonwealth relationship. Yet, so paradoxical is this unique community that Commonwealth nations, without consulting their fellow members, have come into armed conflict with foreign states (for example, Britain's participation in the invasion of Egypt in 1956) or even with each other (for example, the conflict between India and Pakistan over Kashmir in 1948 and in 1965).

The establishment of the Commonwealth secretariat in 1965 has improved the machinery of consultation. The mixed-manned secretariat, headed by a secretary-general selected by and responsible to the heads of government of all the Commonwealth countries, not only stresses the equality of the Commonwealth members but also indicates their desire for closer and more continuous cooperation.

**Defense.** Each sovereign Commonwealth nation is entirely responsible for its own defense. Although no central organization coordinates the defense resources and strategy of the Commonwealth, the governments of the member countries maintain close liaison in defense matters, and there is a substantial measure of practical day-to-day cooperation among their armed services.

When Communist China invaded northern India in 1962, Britain and Canada supplied military aid to the Indian government. In 1963, Britain guaranteed the independence of Malaysia against Indonesian attack, and British troops helped repel Indonesian guerrillas in Sarawak and Sabah. In 1964, at the invitation of the governments of Kenya, Tanganyika, and Uganda, Britain sent troops to quell military mutinies in those countries. As one of the guarantors of the independence of Cyprus, Britain maintained a garrison on that island. In 1964, at the request of the Cypriote authorities, Britain reinforced the garrison to help maintain peace between the Greek and Turkish communities.

The British dependencies contribute to Commonwealth defense insofar as their means permit. They are responsible for the forces necessary for their own security, although in many cases Britain assumes part of the expense. Britain also safeguards Commonwealth sea and air communications, using bases in the dependencies and maintaining garrisons in them for that purpose.

**International Ties.** Each member country is at liberty to assume its own international obligations for the maintenance of peace and security. All have done so to a greater or lesser degree. Most are members of the United Nations. Britain and Canada are members of the North Atlantic Treaty Organization (NATO), and both maintain forces in western Europe under the supreme allied commander of NATO. Britain, Australia, and New Zealand are members of the Southeast Asia Treaty Organization (SEATO). Australia and New Zealand are signatories, with the United States, of the Pacific Security Pact, or ANZUS treaty, for mutual defense in the Pacific. Britain, Australia, and New Zealand also coordinate their defense plans in Southeast Asia. Britain is a member of the Central Treaty Organization (CENTO)—formerly known as the Baghdad Pact—for the defense of the "northern tier" in the Middle East.

The Commonwealth nations also participate in many international economic organizations, including the various specialized agencies of the United Nations. Most are parties to the General Agreement on Tariffs and Trade (GAAT). Britain and Canada are members of the Organization for Economic Cooperation and Development (OECD). Britain, Canada, Australia, New Zealand, India, Ceylon, and Malaysia are active in the Colombo Plan for Cooperative Economic Development in South and Southeast Asia.

**Dependencies.** The Commonwealth nations' dependencies, situated for the most part in the tropical and subtropical zones, are inhabited mainly by people of non-European stock. They include colonies, protectorates, protected states, trust territories, and condominiums.

**Colonies.** Colonies are territories belonging to the British crown. The government of Britain is responsible to Parliament for their effective administration. Some of them have been acquired by treaty and others by settlement or conquest. The colonies exhibit varying degrees of political development. Some, like Hong Kong, are directly governed by British officials appointed by the Colonial Office; others, approaching the goal of independence, have ministers responsible to elected legislatures and enjoy a large measure of internal self-government.

**Protectorates and Protected States.** Protectorates are territories that have not been formally annexed but over which, by treaty, grant, usage, sufferance, or other lawful means, Britain has power and jurisdiction. In some protectorates the system of government is similar to that of a colony; in others, government is conducted by a local administration subject to a measure of control by British officials. Protected states, for example the sultanate of Brunei, are territories governed by a local ruler who enjoys the protection of the British government. The latter exercises control over the external relations of the protected state but has no jurisdiction over its domestic policies.

Most of the older dependencies originally were trading settlements of ill-defined status. In the course of time many of them became colonies directly administered by the British crown, while adjoining territory subsequently came under British control with protectorate status. This explains why a dependency sometimes comprised both a colony and a protectorate, as in the former territory of Aden. However, many colonies have no accompanying protectorate, and there are protectorates without an adjoining colony.

**Trust Territories.** The trust territories of the Commonwealth are rapidly disappearing as the territories gain independence. They are administered under the trusteeship system of the United Nations. Before World War I, they were all German colonies. They comprised the areas later called Tanganyika Territory, British Togoland, the Cameroons, South West Africa, the Territory of New Guinea, Nauru Island, and Western Samoa. After their seizure from Germany in World War I, they became mandated territories of the League of Nations. After World War II, all except South West Africa were reconstituted as United Nations trusteeships. South West Africa—for which South Africa was given a League of Nations mandate—remained under the administration of South Africa, which refused repeated requests by the UN General Assembly to enter into a trusteeship agreement with the territory on the alleged ground that the inhabitants of the territory did not desire it. South Africa, however, agreed to govern South West Africa in the spirit of the former League of Nations mandate.

Tanganyika, which was under the trusteeship of Britain, became an independent republic within the Commonwealth in 1961. In 1964, Tanganyika and Zanzibar joined to form the United Republic of Tanzania.

Australia was responsible (with Britain and New Zealand) for Nauru until Nauru became independent in 1968. Australia also administered the UN Trust Territory of New Guinea and the Territory of Papua until they merged and then became independent in 1975 as Papua New Guinea. Western Samoa, formerly under New Zealand trusteeship, became independent in 1962.

The former British trusteeship territory of Togoland decided by plebiscite, held under United Nations auspices in 1956, to integrate with the Gold Coast Colony, now Ghana. The Cameroons was under the trusteeship of Britain until February 1961, when the northern part decided, by plebiscite, to join Nigeria. The southern section voted to join the Republic of Cameroon.

**Condominiums and Leased Territory.** Britain exercises a condominium in the New Hebrides—a group of islands in the South Pacific Ocean—and in Canton and Enderbury, two small islands of the Phoenix group. In the former, the condominium is shared with France. In the latter, it is shared with the United States. In each case, the British powers are exercised by a resident commissioner who is responsible to the British high commissioner for the Western Pacific.

The only leased territory in the Commonwealth consists of that portion of the mainland of China (called the New Territories, 365½ square miles, or 946.6 sq km) which was leased to Britain in 1898 for 99 years and which is administered by the government of the adjacent colony of Hong Kong.

**Production and Trade.** The economic resources of the Commonwealth nations and their dependencies are vast. They include almost every major natural product useful to man. In minerals, Britain produces coal and iron; Canada, petroleum, natural gas, uranium, iron, coal, copper, lead, nickel, zinc, fluorspar, and gold; Australia, gold, silver, and coal; New Zealand, gold and coal; India, iron, bauxite, aluminum, coal, copper, and lead; Ceylon, graphite; Malaysia, gold, coal, and bauxite; and Ghana, gold, diamonds, manganese, and bauxite. Minerals produced in the dependencies and trust territories include asbestos, tin, gold, diamonds, copper, coal, wolfram, phosphates, lead, zinc, and kyanite.

The range of the Commonwealth's agricultural products is equally impressive. The cultivation of cereals, cattle and sheep ranching, dairy farming, and fruit growing are carried on in many sovereign states. Canada and Australia produce great quantities of wheat. The wool output of Australia and New Zealand is very large. The principal agricultural products of India and Pakistan are rice, tea, cotton, jute, and wheat. Rubber, tea, rice, coconuts, and tobacco are the main produce of Ceylon. Rubber, copra, and tea are produced extensively in Malaysia. Ghana is the world's largest producer of cocoa; its other crops include coffee, rice, tobacco, bananas, and rubber. Britain, although a net importer of foodstuffs, is renowned for its intensive agriculture and its scientific raising of livestock. The dependencies, situated for the most part in the tropics, grow sugarcane, citrus fruits, cocoa, coffee, oilseeds, rice, and rubber.

The Commonwealth includes a number of advanced industrialized nations and others still on the road to industrialization. Canada, with its great hydroelectric resources, has taken giant strides in manufacturing, especially in newsprint, in which it leads the world. Australia has made notable progress in chemicals and textiles. Meat freezing and the manufacture of butter and cheese continue to be of major importance in New Zealand, but to these have been added such factory products as domestic appliances, building materials, tobacco, paints, paper, and chemical fertilizers. India's industrialization has been marked by a steady expansion in steel-making capacity, light engineering, chemical plants, and textile

factories. Britain continues to rank among the leading manufacturing nations of the world. Britain's scientists and technologists have made major contributions in the fields of radar and electronics, and in the development of peaceful uses of nuclear energy.

Industrialization has made comparatively slow progress in the dependencies, handicapped as they are by the lack of skilled labor, the shortage of investment capital, and the scarcity of low-cost power. The dependencies, however, are now being helped, on an increasing scale, to develop their economic resources. Investment capital, both public and private, and technical aid are being supplied under several international projects both by Commonwealth nations and by foreign countries, notably the United States. Especially valuable assistance is given by the government of Britain both in grants-in-aid and through the medium of the colonial development and welfare acts.

Intra-Commonwealth trade is stimulated by several factors, notably by imperial tariff preference, by the accessibility of the London money market, and by the fact that many Commonwealth countries are members of the sterling area. Nevertheless, trade between the Commonwealth nations and other states is normally twice as large as intra-Commonwealth trade.

**The Bonds of Union.** The contemporary Commonwealth is confronted by many problems, the most crucial of which have been raised by the vast changes occurring throughout Africa. Since World War II, Britain has enabled its former colonial peoples in Asia and Africa to achieve their national aspirations within the Commonwealth. However, in those parts of the Commonwealth containing a substantial and powerful minority of white settlers, the racial conflict has at times been acute. Indeed, it has led to rebel-

BRITISH PRIME MINISTER Harold Wilson (*right*) meets other Commonwealth leaders in 1966 during Rhodesia crisis.

lion in the case of Rhodesia, where, on Nov. 11, 1965, Premier Ian Smith's white supremacist government issued a unilateral declaration of independence rather than accept the British government's plans for an extension of equal political rights to the Negroes. Because the nonwhite sovereign nations of the Commonwealth have championed the cause of the subject peoples particularly in Rhodesia, these racial conflicts have threatened to split the Commonwealth. The Commonwealth, however, has shown a remarkable capacity for survival.

The twin threats of external aggression and internal subversion are potent factors in preserving the Commonwealth. Although most leaders of the newly independent Asian and African countries of the Commonwealth follow a neutralist policy in international affairs, they are aware that they cannot stand alone in today's dangerous world. They value the advantages of the Commonwealth relationship which, through Britain, links them with the defense organizations of the free world.

Trade, too, furnishes strong ties. Membership in the Commonwealth yields significant commercial and financial benefits. Most Commonwealth governments and business firms find it easier and more convenient to borrow in London than in New York or other money markets, because British banks are better informed about economic conditions in the Commonwealth nations and dependencies.

Tariff preferences have created a community of interest throughout the Commonwealth while complicating Britain's own trading problems. In June 1971, after ten years of negotiation, Britain and the European Economic Community (EEC, or Common Market) reached agreement on terms of membership, and Britain signed the EEC treaty in January 1972. Most of the problems that had to be worked out involved safeguarding Commonwealth exports, such as New Zealand butter, West Indian sugar, Canadian wheat, and Indian tea. In the long run it is expected that the increased prosperity accruing to Britain from EEC membership will enable it to become a better customer for Commonwealth products, but transitional hardships are possible. Beginning in 1973 the Commonwealth nations, individually, may choose to negotiate either association or trade agreements with the enlarged EEC.

Education provides yet another link. Many leaders of the Asian and African countries within the Commonwealth studied at universities or military colleges in Britain. Mohammed Ayub Khan, leader of Pakistan for 10 years, attended Sandhurst, and Dr. H. Kamuzu Banda, the first president of Malawi, received his postgraduate medical education at Edinburgh. Besides heads of government and leaders of nationalist political parties, many members of the civil service and of the small class of professional men in these countries have a British education. As a result, English has become the common language of the educated elite of the Commonwealth. Many Asian and African leaders speak English more fluently than their own languages.

Perhaps the most important bond of union, the British monarch, as Head of the Commonwealth, stands above all divisions of politics and race. The monarch is at once the symbol of its unity and the pledge of its continuity.

ALLAN M. FRASER*
*Former Provincial Archivist of Newfoundland*

## HISTORY OF BRITISH EMPIRE AND COMMONWEALTH

The English founded the Irish Pale, their first overseas colony, in 1169. As lord of Ireland, the king of England claimed authority over this "plantation" and over the scattering of feudal magnates and Celtic tribal Irish throughout the whole island. He ruled the Pale through a deputy and, from 1295 onward, through an Irish Parliament like that of Westminster. Ireland was full of troubles. Palesmen at once scorned and feared "the wild Irish" and resented control by their lord and his English Privy Council, who presently took power to forbid the Dublin legislature to meet or discuss business without their leave, and even applied English law to Ireland over its head (1494). Once Henry VIII had made himself king of Ireland (1542), the tribesmen were apt to find their lands confiscated because of the too frequent rebellions of their chiefs, and "planted" with English, Welsh, and (in Ulster from 1609 onward) Scottish settlers.

The English gave early promise of moving further afield. In 1497 the Italian John Cabot, sailing westward to find for them a passage to the spice-bearing East Indies, happened upon the Newfoundland cod banks, a nursery for deep-sea ships and seamen. This effort died away, while Tudor England weathered the Reformation, lost her last foothold in Continental Europe, rid herself of the privileged Hansa merchants who had shared control of her commerce and finance, and won the naval war with Spain (1569–1604). But then the English began to hope that colonies might bring them the products for which they had been dependent on foreign rivals, and provide a cure for the poverty that an economic revolution was producing in the country, side by side with considerable monetary wealth.

**Early Settlements Overseas.** Elizabethan attempts to settle Newfoundland and Virginia and the long search for a northeast or northwest passage to the East Indies failed. But English trade flourished so vigorously that the eastern or "company" half of an overseas empire had taken shape between 1554 and the Civil War (1642–1649). The Muscovy Company was active in newly discovered Russia, the Levant Company in the Mediterranean, and the East India Company in Java and India, while the Guinea Company nibbled at the African west coast. The western or colonial half came a little later. Working as a rule through proprietors or companies, the English made good in Virginia, Bermuda, New England, Maryland, the Leeward Islands and Barbados, as well as in the logwood-cutters' haunts on the coasts of Honduras and Yucatan (1607–1642). However, colonies established in Nova Scotia (1627, 1629) failed within a few years, and control passed to the French.

Conquest played a part for the first time when Oliver Cromwell not only united the British Isles for a time but also seized Spanish Jamaica, while Charles II took Dutch St. Helena and New Amsterdam (New York, New Jersey, and Delaware). Charles also presided peacefully over the foundation of Pennsylvania and the Carolinas and over the launching of the Hudson's Bay Company.

Dependent Ireland suffered progressive exclusion from the English home market and the growing colonial system, and it had to endure the wholesale plantations that followed the Cromwellian and Orange conquests. Independent Scotland also suffered exclusion; but once Scotland, like England, had disowned James II and seen its Parliament become an effective legislature, many of its citizens proposed to get rich quickly by founding a company to trade with the Americas, Africa, and Asia, and to plant a colony on the Isthmus of Panama in the heart of the jealous Spanish-American empire. This venture, known as the Darien Scheme (q.v.), failed dismally; the remnant of the Scottish colonists had to be rescued from the outraged Spaniards by an English ambassador, and so heavy was the blow to Scotland's pride and scanty wealth that, combined with various political bickerings, it brought England and Scotland almost to the point of war. Mercifully, legislative and commercial union was preferred to bloodshed. The new kingdom of Great Britain emerged under a single enlarged Parliament, and the English Empire became the British Empire (1707). The Scots, however, retained their own law and courts subject to an appeal to the House of Lords; they themselves safeguarded their Established Presbyterian Kirk (Church), and they received from English taxpayers the money they had lost in the Darien Scheme with 5% interest.

Thus did Britain become a powerful state, the largest free trade area in the tessellated European world of that day, and successor to the Dutch Republic as the chief financial, commercial, and naval power of the West. Britain had also become a Mediterranean power, thanks to its treaty with Portugal which gave it the use of the Tagus estuary (1703), and its seizure of Spanish Gibraltar (1704) and Menorca (1708). By the Treaty of Utrecht (1713) France recognized British sovereignty in Nova Scotia (Acadia) and also, subject to French fishing rights, in Newfoundland. It was not, however, all a matter of conquest nor even of colonization. Britain was still represented on the west coast of Africa by a company that tried to meet the demands of its sugar colonies for Negro slaves, and in Asia by the East India Company, which sought "quiet trade" in the East Indies, Bombay, Madras, and its own recent creation of Calcutta.

**Mercantilism.** The principles upon which this growing empire was to be run had become clear by 1713. On the economic side, Oliver Cromwell and the Restoration Stuarts had been the first to enforce the more or less exclusive mercantilism to which the English had paid lip service from the beginning. Navigation ordinances and acts shut out foreigners and decreed that the empire's trade should be carried in English (including colonial) ships manned by mainly English crews; that colonies must pay English rates of duty; that Continental goods must pass through England on their way to the colonies; and that a varying list of "enumerated" colonial products must only go to other parts of the world through England, where many of them were assured of preferences or even a monopoly. In short, the empire was treated as a unit, whose plantations, trade, and finance were to be regulated in the last resort by the mother country.

The universal framework was even clearer on the constitutional side. When they were planting their first transatlantic colonies in pre-Civil War days, the English, Welsh, Scots, and Irish had long been accustomed to representative parliamentary institutions. Effective rule lay with the king and his ministers, who were organized in a council that did executive, legislative, and judicial

work, heard petitions, and possibly redressed grievances, and that went to Parliament for an increasing number of the laws and the money grants necessary for the carrying on of the king's government. But there was nothing like present-day "responsible government." Neither the personally summoned House of Lords nor the elective House of Commons, nor both together, could influence policy, except by refusing assent to bills or taxes; still less could they get rid of an unpopular minister short of impeachment, attainder, rebellion, or plain murder. The essentials of this system were transplanted first to Virginia in 1619 and thereafter to the other transatlantic colonies. In each there was a governor, appointed as a rule by the crown, but sometimes by proprietors or colonists, a council nominated by the governor, and an elective assembly. Nothing of this applied to the company half of the empire. By 1714, in Britain itself, the balance was changing with the emergence of the party and cabinet systems and with the overshadowing of Lords and crown by the Commons. This process became more marked when the House of Hanover had to depend on the parliamentary-minded and moneyed Whigs. In the colonies, however, there continued a series of representative legislatures dominated by a single executive.

**Empire in the 18th Century.** The third stage (1713–1794) saw the British Empire rise to unprecedented heights, then split, and at the last show marked signs of recovery. The consolidation of the uneasy Anglo-Scottish Union was by no means stopped by the rebellions of the Jacobites (q.v.) in 1715 and 1745. On the other hand, the mass of the Irish were subjected to the oppressive Anglican "garrison" Dublin Parliament, which was too weak, isolated, and corrupt to resist the claim that the British Parliament made to legislate for Ireland over its head (1719). In North America, the British founded Georgia (1732), the last of the 13 original colonies, and set about colonizing Nova Scotia (1750). By the close of the Seven Years' War (1763), the British had swept the French and Spaniards out of almost all North America as far west as the Mississippi, annexed many West Indian islands, and acquired more stations in West Africa, whence the British slave trade rose to its zenith in the interests, particularly, of aggressive Liverpool merchants (1772). The East India Company had destroyed the power of its French rival, assumed wide powers in Bengal, and stood out as a major territorial power, the only European power worth mentioning in chaotic India. Its misrule soon called forth the first governor-general and other reforms under the Regulating Act (1773).

**American Colonies.** The crash came when young George III essayed to awaken in the American colonists a sense of responsibility. Having beaten France and Spain and the Indians at heavy cost to the overburdened British taxpayer, he invited the colonists, who still regarded direct taxes, 17th century fashion, as "impositions," to tax themselves to help to pay the cost of a British garrison, whose presence many of them resented. The garrison would both defend their long Indian frontier and enforce a humane policy toward the tribes that was anathema to traders, lawyers, and land speculators. To crown all, in a land where smuggling was regarded as an almost respectable occupation, he set about enforcing the trade laws.

This unaccustomed enforcement of the Navigation Acts led to uproar in the ports; the request for self-taxation was rejected by the assemblies, and the reluctant passing of the imperial Stamp Act (1765), combined with talk of "giving" the king a revenue, was denounced as a breach of colonial privileges. The quarrel over the trade laws died down once the Stamp Act had been repealed in face of violence and passive resistance; but opposition continued to the overriding powers that Parliament now claimed.

The Boston Tea Party called for punitive acts against Massachusetts. Independence-minded colonists classed the Quebec Act (1774) as such a punitive measure. Except for French and Roman Catholic Canada, all the French and Spanish colonies annexed in 1763 had been given the customary representative institutions. After prolonged delay, which exasperated the go-ahead handful of English-speaking immigrants who alone wanted an elective assembly, the Quebec Act gave the French Canadians and the British officials what they wanted. To the former, it gave the French law and recognition of Roman Catholicism as their lawful religion at a time when punitive anti-Catholic laws were the rule in other parts of the empire; to the latter, it gave a permanent revenue, which was lacking in other colonies, and a large nominated council of British and French which was to help rather than hamper the executive, as too often was the practice elsewhere. Such doings failed to please Puritan New Englanders, while the inclusion in Canada of their hinterland infuriated them and the New Yorkers farther south.

**The American Revolution.** The shooting, begun in 1775, was followed by the Declaration of Independence (1776). The British Renunciation Act failed to mend matters, though it promised that never again would Britain tax any of her transatlantic colonies, except for the regulation of trade, and even then would spend the money thus raised in a given colony on that colony. France, Spain, and the Dutch Republic supported the colonists; presently the armed neutrality of nations of northern Europe loomed up in the background, and the East India Company had to fight hard against the French and many of the potentates of India. Thanks mainly to her navy, Britain finished the war better than had been expected but had to restore Menorca and much else to the Bourbons and had to recognize the independence of the United States, with a territory reaching westward to the Mississippi River (1783).

**Problem of Ireland.** At bottom, the American Revolution had been caused by the prevalence of an independent dominionlike state of mind that the British could not satisfy. Yet a "Dominion" experiment in self-government had to be tried in Ireland. As the redcoats were drafted away to America, power passed to the volunteers raised by leading "garrison" politicians. The Dublin Parliament gave Irish Nonconformists, though not Roman Catholics, full political rights, and by 1783 the British Parliament had freed the Irish legislature and courts from all external control and accorded Irishmen virtual free trade within the empire. George III, meanwhile, had abandoned his attempt to rule, and had accepted the Tory, William Pitt, as the first fully responsible minister in the empire (1784).

Those who foresaw a dreary future for the British Empire and the 13 new North American states were mistaken. Rather than lose heart and go under, the empire began to set its house in order and even extended its borders. Helped by a flourishing agricultural revival and the nascent industrial revolution, Pitt restored Britain's finances and fleet. But neither he nor anyone else could induce two sovereign parliaments to march in step in empire-wide matters, even though they shared one flag and the same person as king. The Irish Parliament refused his offer of full free trade in return for a permanent contribution to the navy; British and Irish opponents wrecked his attempt to clear away the rotten boroughs abounding in both islands. Nor could he stop Wolfe Tone from enrolling Protestant and Catholic United Irishmen to press for the repeal of the penal laws and the full enfranchisement of Roman Catholics, while all the Dublin legislature would do was to give Catholics the vote, but in no wise admit them to its houses (1793). Nor could he then, nor anyone since, find satisfactory answers, short of a treaty or legislative union, to awkward Irish questions. What of the Laws of Trade, the Mutiny Act, and the Naval Code? Why should not Ireland have its own ambassadors, treaties, and fleet? Was the crown, perchance, divisible? Why, asked the Whig Irish Parliament, should not the Prince of Wales be free from the checks which the Tory, Pitt, proposed to lay upon him as regent during the insanity of his father? Why, asked Tone, should not Ireland remain neutral in the event of another "British" war?

**Reform in India.** Pitt had greater success in India. His India Act (1784) set up a dual control whereby the East India Company still dispensed patronage and ruled its growing dominions, while the crown and Parliament exercised a salutary and permanent check on its doings. Lord Cornwallis, the first governor-general (1786–1793) under this act, carried through many fiscal and administrative reforms, acquired much coastal territory, and began the system of subsidiary treaties under which the company guaranteed Indian princes their thrones in return for control of their external policies and an annual subsidy for the company's troops stationed in their principalities. He also leased Penang (1786), the company's first foothold in the Malay Peninsula. The impeachment of Warren Hastings (1788) for high-handed acts as governor-general (1773–1785) ended in his acquittal, but it was a reminder that the East India Company had duties as well as powers in faraway India.

**Slave Trade.** Even before the American Revolution, evangelical principles had largely inspired the attack on the immense British slave trade by poets and Quakers on either side of the Atlantic, and they influenced Lord Mansfield (William Murray) and others who laid down in the courts (1772) that slavery could not exist legally in the British Isles. Presently, Samuel Clarkson and the Tory William Wilberforce opened their campaign against "the Trade," and Pitt carried through Parliament a cautious measure (1792) limiting the number of slaves that might be carried in a British ship of a given tonnage. In the same period, British philanthropists founded a colony at Sierra Leone for freed slaves.

**North America.** Many American colonists who had been loyal to Britain fled to western Nova Scotia and western Quebec rather than face persecution at the hands of their triumphant fellow citizens. Britain, therefore, constituted that part of Nova Scotia the colony of New Brunswick, with the customary representative institutions (1784), and, by the Constitutional Act (1791) cut off loyalist Ontario from predominantly French Quebec and gave both colonies similar institutions.

Meanwhile the new nation created by the American Revolution was finding that its troubles had only begun when the British departed. It had lost its old footing in the British imperial commercial system, especially in the West Indies, which had always been dependent on it. In due time growing bankruptcy, internal unrest, and external threats to its security forced the United States to strengthen its national government. The 13 jealous, diverse, and inexperienced states were driven into giving up some of their cherished sovereign powers to a newly created government. In April 1789, George Washington became president of the first large, federal, and democratic republic the world had ever seen.

The momentous fact that the United States now had a really effective government, and the alliance of many Whigs with Pitt's Tories during the period of the French Revolution, cleared the way for the Jay Treaty (1794). This treaty permitted the tardy withdrawal of the redcoats from the hinterland of the New England and Middle states, and gave the United States most-favored-nation treatment in the British home market for 10 years, and the right, denied even to British subjects, of entry into the East India Company's sphere. Even though the U. S. Senate threw away the proffered right of limited entry into the British West Indies, the French republicans were so angry at this Anglo-American settlement that they denounced their royal predecessor's alliance with *perfide Amérique*.

**Transportation.** Meanwhile, because it could no longer send convicts to its former American colonies, the British government began in 1788 to transport them and "the poor of the parish" to New South Wales, there to lay the foundations of "White Australia." Two years later, British naval deserters sought refuge on Pitcairn Island, even farther away. In 1804 the government began to send convicts to Van Diemen's Land (Tasmania); in 1808 it took over Sierra Leone from the philanthropists; and in 1816 it founded a colony, dependent upon Sierra Leone, on the Gambia River.

**Union with Ireland.** There were very few liberal constitutional developments in the empire until near the close of the next period, 1794–1833, because the British were too busy fighting France, half of Europe, much of India, and, for a time, the United States, to give heed to such things, and thereafter were occupied with licking their wounds. The dominant Tories, shocked by the recent American rebellion and present French democracy, stood by the principles of law, order, and security. They applied them soon enough to Ireland. There matters drifted from bad to worse. After a bloody republican rebellion had been crushed and two French invasions thwarted, Pitt incorporated Ireland in the new United Kingdom of Great Britain and Ireland (1801). Ireland received liberal representation at Westminster, whither she now had to send her appeals, and, at long last, free trade within the empire; but the king damned the union from the start, in the eyes of most Irishmen, by sacrificing his prime minister rather than consent to Roman Catholic emancipation.

**Colonial Expansion.** During the long wars with France, Britain swept up all the colonies of her enemies. She gave most of them back eventually, but kept some, usually because they were good naval stations. Such were Heligoland, Malta and the Ionian Isles, Trinidad, St. Lucia, British Guiana, Ascension, Tristan da Cunha, the Cape of Good Hope, Mauritius, Rodriguez, the Seychelles, and Ceylon.

**East India Company.** In India, the East India Company was gaining widely increased authority. It had become the paymaster of its nominal overlord, the Great Mogul, by 1826; it was direct or indirect ruler of nearly the whole of the subcontinent, and it had secured Singapore, Malacca, and part of coastal Burma. The company and the British administration in Ceylon were also training their servants not as mere clerks but as rulers charged with a sacred trust for the welfare of the governed—rulers, some said, who should probably withdraw for the good of all as soon as they had taught the peoples to stand on their own feet. Further in line with the taking over by the crown of the privileges of the Elizabethan Levant Company in 1825, Parliament transformed the East India Company by stages into a purely political organization. The Charter Act of 1813 took away its monopoly of the India trade, and that of 1833 took away its last monopoly, the China trade. The latter act also gave the company's governor-general at Calcutta wide powers over the other presidencies of Bombay and Madras, and it decreed that no Indian should be debarred from any office in the public service "by reason only of his religion, place of birth, descent, color, or any of these."

**Emancipation of Slaves.** British Tories dreaded democracy and noted that most of Britain's recent colonies were either convict depots, naval bases, or tropical islands, with mixed and foreign populations that hardly knew the meaning of representative institutions. These views were shared by many Evangelicals who were also Tories. In the background, a missionary flood continued to pour out from all Protestant Europe, but mainly from Britain, to Africa, India, and the Pacific Islands. At home, the Evangelicals were vocal in the country and strong in Parliament; they invaded the office of the secretary of war and colonies, a post newly created in 1801. The veteran William Wilberforce was strong enough to induce the great Whig leader Charles James Fox to abolish the British slave trade (1807). This reform was carried further by Lord Castlereagh, who persuaded the statesmen of Europe, assembled at the peace conference in Paris, to condemn this "traffic in human flesh" (1815). Thereafter, successive foreign secretaries strove by political pressure, governmental bribery, and the maintenance of an expensive British "sentimental squadron" off the African west coast to hold to their promises the rulers of France, Spain, Portugal, newly independent Brazil, and, above all, the United States, where increased cotton production had spurred a keen demand for Negro slaves. Some success in restricting the slave trade was achieved, but the efforts of the British government to induce the recalcitrant colonial assemblies to ameliorate the lot of their slaves had small result. In 1833, however, the Westminster Parliament, predominantly Whig at last, carried the Emancipation Act over the heads of the colonial legislatures, thus setting free some 800,-000 slaves in the 17 slave-owning colonies at the cost to the British taxpayers of £20 million in compensation to the slave owners.

**Toward Responsible Government.** There were signs of reviving liberalism toward the end of the period. Emigrants flowed out, especially during the desperate 1820's, to Ontario and the Maritimes of Canada, Cape Colony, Mauritius, New South Wales, Van Diemen's Land, and (after 1829) to Western Australia.

Reform was furthered by investigations by royal commissions. By 1834, councils had been set up in Cape Colony, Mauritius, Western Australia, New South Wales, and Van Diemen's Land, and a magistrate without real authority had been sent to control, if he might, the missionaries, traders, and scalawags in independent New Zealand. Slaves had been freed in all the colonies, and the colored majority at the Cape of Good Hope had been put on a legal equality with whites. Advance overseas was, however, most marked in French Quebec and fast-growing Anglo-American Ontario. In spite of increasing friction, both colonies were given municipal institutions, and their assemblies were granted control of nearly all the already insufficient revenues. This virtual surrender of the purse-strings naturally stimulated the demands of French- and English-speaking reformers there and in Nova Scotia for what some of them began to call "responsible government."

But how could there be any such thing so long as the British Empire was treated as a unit commercially? True, the opening of "free ports" to foreigners on mutual terms and the granting of mutual preferences and reciprocity had shifted the empire from the old rigid mercantilist basis. Even the United States had reestablished its commercial ties in the West Indies. But, flexible though it was, this reciprocity preference was still one centrally controlled system. Only imperial free trade could set colonies free to go their own ways in the all-important fiscal field.

**Imperial Expansion.** Free trade and responsible government came together during the first part of the Victorian period (1833–1874). That period saw, too, great changes in India and on its approaches. To the westward, the East India Company handed over St. Helena to the crown (1834), but it annexed Aden (1839), burned its fingers in independent Afghanistan (1838–1842), annexed Sind and the aggressive Sikh Punjab (1834–1849), and in the process of rooting out piracy built up an informal protectorate over the Persian Gulf sultanates. The end of the Crimean War (1856) saw expansive Russia forbidden to keep warships in the Black Sea—that is, on the flank of the Mediterranean route to the Orient. To the eastward, the East India Company made fast-growing Singapore the capital of its Penang Presidency (1836) and annexed the Irrawaddy delta of Burma (1852). Meanwhile, the crown had gained from China the cession of the barren island of Hong Kong and the opening of Shanghai and other treaty ports to Western merchants (1842), while in western Borneo, the sultan of Brunei had recognized James Brooke as rajah of Sarawak (1843) and ceded to the crown the empty island of Labuan (1846).

**Indian Progress.** In India itself, an economic revolution began in the 1830's. The old exchange of Indian handicrafts for British silver and luxuries gave way to the purchase of Indian raw materials for Lancashire cotton textiles and other manufactures. During the governor-generalship of Lord Dalhousie (1847–1856) the vast country was drawn together and nearer to the outer world by steamships, railways, telegraphs, canals, and the Grand Trunk Road. Improved communications and better administration began to lessen the recurrent threat of famine in the densely peopled subcontinent. Next, after long and prudent delay, the East India Company began to repress the fanatical and barbarous Thugs. It also imbued the class-conscious Indians with Western legal principles and made slave owning a punishable offense (1860). Similarly, during the 1830's it began a revolution by freeing the press and by imposing English as the official language of government and higher education. It then centralized India's finances, unified its coinage, instituted cheap postage, and set up nominee municipal councils in the larger cities with powers similar to those that the three Presidency capitals had long enjoyed. The Charter Act (1853) created an official legislative council at Calcutta, divided the immense Bengal Presidency into provinces (each under a lieutenant governor or chief commissioner to relieve the governor-general), renewed the 20-year-old promise that there should be neither social nor color bar in the public service, and limited the company's powers of patronage by the introduction of competitive examinations for the higher posts. So that Indians might be able to compete in the English language, the company opened universities on the new London model at Calcutta, Madras, and Bombay (1857).

**The Indian Empire.** These sweeping changes were interrupted by a mutiny (1857) of many of the company's Indian troops, who greatly outnumbered the Europeans. The British suppressed the mutiny, deposed the last Mogul emperor, and transferred the authority of the East India Company to the crown. A secretary of state and a council for India replaced the president and board of control in London, and, in Calcutta, the governor-general Lord Canning reigned also as Queen Victoria's viceroy. The army in India was reorganized on the basis of one British to two Indian soldiers, and the field artillery was concentrated in British hands.

During the 1860's a beginning was made in the dilution of purely bureaucratic rule by giving nonofficial British nominees seats on the central legislative council, while similar councils for Madras, Bombay, and Bengal, all of them with very limited powers, were created. At the same time, Indians were admitted to the civil service examinations, though the requisite preliminary attendance at a British university debarred many. This reform was extended to the civil services of Ceylon, of Hong Kong (enlarged in 1861 by the leasing of Kowloon from China), and of Singapore, Malacca, and Penang which the crown now grouped together as the Straits Settlements free from control by the East India Company (1869).

Meanwhile the British were troubled by the ambitions of Napoleon III. They had, however, built up a powerful new steam and iron navy, modernized the Gibraltar and Malta dockyards, handed over the Ionian Isles to Greece on condition that the minor base of Corfu be dismantled, and seen to it that the canal which a French company was cutting through the Egyptian isthmus of Suez should be internationalized and open to the passage of ships of all nations at all times. The British, also, had hoisted the Union Jack over part of Delagoa Bay (1861) and successfully invaded mysterious and mountainous Abyssinia (Ethiopia) with an Anglo-Indian force (1868). Empress Eugénie of France duly opened the Suez Canal in 1869, thus bringing the Indian Empire, now part of the British Empire, much closer to Westminster and the English Channel.

**The Colonial Empire.** Comparatively few people in Britain had any systematic plan for getting rid of the colonies, however strongly the House of Commons aborigines committee (1837) and West African committee (1865) might counsel caution in annexing new territories or even in making embarrassing treaties with tribal chiefs. But many, usually old Tories, disliked the worry and expense of maintaining colonies, and could not forget that most of the American colonies of Britain, Spain, and Portugal had won their independence between 1775 and 1825. Many more, among them the ardent free traders, held with Adam Smith that it was a good thing that those colonies had become republics, if only because British trade with them was greater than it ever had been. They noted, too, that British trade with the independent parts of West Africa was greater than that with the few British colonies in that region. On the other hand, the rank and file of the British public took colonies for granted, and emigrated to them freely. The small group of colonial reformers, headed by Lord Durham, advocated that colonies of settlement could be and ought to be retained; while most colonials, forbearing to ask whether Britain could carry on without her colonies, were sure that the colonies would not last for long without British support. Finally, there was a widespread feeling that Britain must do the best it could for its colonies of settlement, so that, if and when they did break away, there would neither be mutual recriminations nor a sense of duty shirked. This belief found expression in the idea of trusteeship for the more backward parts of the empire, a concept that was held by men like Earl Grey, Henry Lawrence, Sir Thomas Buxton (Wilberforce's successor), and the West African committee of 1865.

**Tariff Policies.** Such expansion as there was, and the remarkable experiments in colonial government that were carried through, were due, in the main, to the Industrial Revolution and the adoption of a free trade policy, which enabled Britain to retain its naval supremacy to such a degree that there were no global conflicts between Waterloo (1815) and the outbreak of World War I in 1914. The fiscal crisis came when Robert Peel abolished the Corn Laws (the keystone of the reciprocity-preference system), repealed the remaining navigation acts, and permitted colonies with representative institutions to cancel the British trade preferences in their own markets (1846–1849). Successive finance ministers, notably William Ewart Gladstone, pursued like policies until, by 1874, all the British preferences were gone, and Britain was levying duties merely on a few luxuries, filling the gap in her revenues with the income tax.

The repeal of these protective laws did not bring the disasters that opponents had foretold. Flourishing British agriculture combined with new supplies of gold from California, British Columbia, New South Wales, and Victoria stabilized prices and wages. British steam-driven iron ships soon surpassed the old wooden sailing ships as carriers of cargo. And if the British free trade policy did not put an end to wars, as many had hoped, it did, by its example, encourage the Western world to become, from the 1840's until 1879, a freely trading world with currencies linked to the British golden pound sterling.

**West African Developments.** Under these changing circumstances a fringe of protectorates emerged, primarily in West Africa. The only British colonies in those parts in 1830 were Sierra Leone and its dependency of Gambia. The remaining British stations were in the feeble and impecunious hands of a committee of London merchants. During the 1830's Capt. George Maclean, the committee's president on the Gold Coast, made peace with the neighboring and truculent Ashanti and, by treaty, exercised jurisdiction over the coastal Fanti tribes. This bold and unauthorized policy, coupled with extensions of consular authority in the Levant (1825) and the Chinese treaty ports (1842), led to the passing of the Foreign Jurisdiction Act (1843), which empowered Queen Victoria to exercise, on the spot, any jurisdiction she might have or might acquire in a foreign country as fully as if that jurisdiction had arisen by the cession or conquest of territory.

The crown took over the Gold Coast at once, and presently enlarged it by purchasing (1850) the Danish stations with which its shores were dotted. Meanwhile, farther east, Macgregor Laird and other members of the African Steamship Company had opened up trade in palm products (1832) on the Oil Rivers (in the Niger delta), but a subsequent attempt to found a model farm and settlement on the Lower Niger failed (1840). Nevertheless, the crown annexed the neighboring island of Lagos (1861), thus closing the chief native slave market on the coast and laying the foundations of the future Nigeria. A little later, Britain extended consular jurisdiction over its subjects on the Oil Rivers, acquired the old Dutch stations on the Gold Coast, and defeated the Ashanti soundly when they tried to upset this arrangement (1874). Meanwhile, British pertinacity and naval patrols had combined with President Lincoln's abolition of slavery in the United States (1863) to end slaving by white men (except, perhaps, by the Brazilians) and enabled Britain to concentrate on abolition of the Arab slave trade in East Africa and on the Indian Ocean.

**West Indian Stagnation.** British compensation for the freeing of the slaves did little more than pay off the debts of West Indian estates that were already impoverished by generations of primitive cultivation. The projected apprenticeship system for former slaves broke down so completely that most of the Caribbean colonies, besides Mauritius and, after 1860, Natal (and several French and Dutch sugar colonies also), imported swarms of indentured East Indian coolies who were utterly alien and ignorant of elective legislatures. The disappearance of the time-honored sugar tariff preference (1854) left the Caribbean colonies unprotected to face the competition of Mauritius, India, and slave-owning Cuba and Brazil. Hence between 1859 and 1874 one after the other of the West Indian colonies had to accept strict crown colony rule.

**Political Advancement.** Britain had not lost faith in the old representative system. It gave these institutions to New Brunswick and Newfoundland in the 1830's, and, encouraged by the privy council's recommendation (1849) that they should be given wherever they would do more good than harm, Britain extended them to British Honduras, Malta, and the Ionian Isles. Even Grenada and St. Vincent were brought within measurable distance of responsible government by the appointment of elected assembly members to their executive councils (1856). At the same time, the governor of the Hudson's Bay Company in Vancouver Island summoned an elective assembly.

The main advances along the traditional line were made in South Africa and Australasia. In the former area, the Great Trek of Cape Colony's Boer frontier farmers (1835–1848) scattered Europeans over the huge expanses between the Orange and Limpopo rivers and led others into Natal. The British government first extended its inoperable criminal law to British subjects *in partibus* (1836), and then, to safeguard the colonial frontiers, preserve the peace of South Africa, and ward off dreaded French, Dutch, or even U. S. intervention, annexed republican Natal as a detached portion of the Cape Colony (1843). It also gave the governor at the Cape the status of high commissioner with wide powers over British interests in southern Africa, proclaiming the Orange River Sovereignty between the Vaal and Orange rivers (1846–1854). The government in London then changed its mind. It hurriedly recognized the independence of the Transvaalers (Sand River Convention, 1852), withdrew from the Orange River Sovereignty— most of which became the Orange Free State (Bloemfontein Convention, 1854)—and made isolated Natal a separate crown colony with a strongly elective assembly (1856). The new Boer republics based their constitutions on the institutions at the Cape, the principle of color bar, and the U. S. Constitution. The Cape Colony, which had received further egalitarian reforms and elective municipal institutions, was given a completely elective Parliament based on a "color-blind" franchise (1854); in the following year, this legislature gave the rural areas elective divisional councils.

Australasia progressed rapidly. "Free" South Australia was founded (1836), and transportation of convicts to New South Wales ceased. Mainly elective legislatures were then given to the latter colony and to Van Diemen's Land (Tasmania), South Australia, and Victoria (a new colony, formerly the southern part of New South Wales). After 1852 no convicts were sent to any part of the continent except Western Australia, and the practice ceased there when that crown colony was granted representative institutions in 1867. Meanwhile, New Zealand had been annexed in 1840, and it received similar legislative institutions with a "color-blind" franchise in 1852.

**Responsible Government.** Britain had learned from experience that elected members of colonial bodies often rendered unworkable those institutions headed by irremovable British officials. Britain had found a solution to this difficulty by evolving the party and cabinet systems, and (almost alone at first) the colonial reformers in the British House of Commons proposed to give analogous powers to certain colonies, primarily as a means of training their peoples in the responsibilities of citizenship.

Factors other than an overwhelming navy and reforming zeal made this startling experiment possible. Growing world trade and local re-

sources, natural increase, and emigrants gave some of the colonies the indispensable revenues and populations. Soon, the biggest obstacle to the introduction of responsible government in socially advanced colonies was swept away by the adoption of free trade within the British Empire. The crucial first step in extending self-government was taken in North America. Petty rebellions in Quebec and Ontario led to the suspension of the Quebec constitution and the sending in 1838 of Lord Durham as governor-general of British North America. Durham, supported by Charles Buller and Gibbon Wakefield, aimed at counteracting the strong southward pull of the United States and saw much of his advice embodied in Lord John Russell's Union Act (1840). This act united Upper and Lower Canada so that the combined British vote would outweigh that of the French Canadians and it gave the elective Assembly full control of all revenues. But only by implication did Russell concede Durham's other chief proposal by instructing the governor-general to allow his permanent heads of departments to retire whenever public policy demanded this. It was only after the settlement of the New Brunswick and Oregon frontier disputes with the United States (1842 and 1846) and rioting in Montreal, that responsible government was fully worked out in Canada and Nova Scotia (1848–1849), and in Newfoundland (1855). New Zealand and all the colonies of eastern Australia, including Queensland, had achieved the system of responsible government by 1859; but Cape Colony did not attain it until 1872, when ostrich farming, the discovery of diamonds at Kimberley, and imperial pressure gave her the necessary revenue and impetus.

In all this evolution, Durham's proposed reservations of certain powers to the authorities in Britain figured little. Central control of trade had begun to pass in 1846, well before the achievement of responsible government. The Australian colonies were forbidden even to offer preferences to one another (1850–1873), but the British North American colonies gave striking proof that colonies could exercise this "external" power without implicating the rest of the empire. Their governor-general, Lord Elgin, arranged a reciprocity treaty for all of them with the United States (1854–1866), and Canada itself levied substantial duties on British imports, replying to protests that Britain must make Canada a crown colony again if Britain wished to tell Canada how to raise its own revenues. There was (and is) no reply to that except some form of legislative union. Control of crown lands and, with it, of immigration, passed at once to the self-governing colonies; so, gradually, did control of native policy, which Durham had not mentioned. By 1874 the imperial government was trying to hand over such problems even to colonies with merely representative institutions.

Durham's third reservation, the exclusive right to change colonial constitutions, was whittled away. New Zealand was given fairly wide powers in this respect in 1857. By the Colonial Laws Validity Act of 1865, New Zealand and many other colonies with representative institutions were allowed to amend their constitutions, powers, and procedures provided that the amendments did not conflict with British legislation that was still in force. The result was that self-governing colonies could do whatever they liked at the diminishing risk of seeing their handiwork

COMMONWEALTH PRIME MINISTERS consider mutual problems at formal meeting in Marlborough House, London.

vetoed by the governor or the British sovereign.

Defense and control of foreign policy remained much on the old footing. Self-governing colonies could have no foreign policy of their own without breaking up the formal unity of the British Empire. Nor was any colonist anxious to deprive the taxpayers of Britain of their privilege of providing the redcoats and the navy. Rather the reverse. It was Britain that began to insist that self-governing colonies must provide for their own local defense, and began to withdraw the imperial garrisons from such colonies, partly on the sound strategic and financial principle of concentrating them at the center, and partly to prevent autonomous New Zealand and some other colonies (about 1869) from fighting their own native wars with British soldiers.

**Federations of Colonies.** The next development in this peculiar mid-Victorian empire was a trend toward the federation of contiguous self-governing colonies. This was no new idea. Nothing indeed had come of proposals to federate the British North American colonies. Earl Grey had failed to federate Australia, and Sir George Grey, governor of the Cape Colony, had been recalled in 1859 for trying to federate the South African colonies and the Orange Free State. But now conditions were far more favorable. The disjointed elements of both Germany and Italy were far on the road to closer union, and a Civil War in the United States resulted in victory for the Union cause. The widely dispersed British North American colonies were finding, as their southern neighbors had found before them, that autonomy was not enough. Poverty, lack of credit, intercolonial friction, the desire for railways, deadlock

in the constitution of spiritually divided Canada, and the ambitions of a few farsighted men combined to drive them together. With the encouragement of the British government, a federation of Quebec, Ontario, New Brunswick, and Nova Scotia, styled the "Dominion of Canada," was effected (1867). The purchase of Russian Alaska by the United States impelled the new Dominion of Canada to buy, with imperial aid, the vast and almost vacant intervening territories of the Hudson's Bay Company, out of which it carved Manitoba, the first of its prairie provinces (1870). The federation was joined by isolated British Columbia (1871) and little Prince Edward Island (1873); but Newfoundland stood out until 1949.

**Imperial Federation.** The Colonial Society, ancestor of the Royal Empire Society, was formed to study colonial problems (1868); there was even public talk of imperial federation. The internal development of the empire, however, was destined to be in the direction of separation rather than unification. Britain had to face competition such as it had not known since the 18th century. Britain now had to reckon with vast military powers, which were soon grouped in the Triple Alliance of Germany, Austria-Hungary, and Italy, and in the rival Dual Alliance of Russia and republican France; while in the background, loomed the rising might of the United States and westernized Japan. It was only in 1902 that Britain allied with Japan, and then, in 1904, swung over informally to the side of the Dual Alliance. All this time the advancing industrial revolution and deepening medical knowledge helped Britain to conquer the tropics, move swarms of people and masses of cheap, bulky goods over long distances as never before, and hold together colonies of unprecedented size. But these changes helped Britain's rivals to these same ends, besides enabling them to swamp Britain's unprotected home market with floods of wheat, and, by 1900 at latest, to press upon its industries with their artificially fostered manufactures and subsidized shipping. From 1914 onward, when its scattered empire was only one among many, Britain was caught up in a world revolution, which was to reduce its strength relatively to that of immense and geographically compact European and American powers.

The imperialistic scramble for dependencies, which Britain entered with enthusiasm, has of course been severely criticized, but it was surely better that lands, which were going to be opened up in any event, should be opened up by organized home governments or by the new galaxy of chartered companies than by irresponsible white adventurers. During the first stage (1874–1917), the empire gained much in population by dint of immigration and natural increase, but it secured little new territory apart from Upper Burma (1885). It did, however, take charge of the foreign policies of Afghanistan and Brunei, and it accorded protection to independent Sarawak and the chartered British North Borneo Company (1878–1888). Britain also formed the Federated Malay States (1895) and established a protectorate over the unfederated Malay States (1909). In the Pacific, it annexed Fiji (1874) and gave its governor wide powers over British subjects in adjacent independent islands as high commissioner of the western Pacific. It also gained various small island groups in return for leaving Samoa to be partitioned by Germany and the United States (1890). It agreed to an Anglo-French condominium in the New Hebrides (1898 and 1907) and, having acquired part of New Guinea (Papua), handed it over to newly federated Australia (1906). Finally, after helping to put down the rebellion of the Boxers in China, it secured the potential naval base of Weihaiwei and formed an alliance with Japan (1902). After its ally's victory over Russia, it withdrew the bulk of the China squadron to face the growing threat of the German High Seas Fleet nearer home (1905).

**Developments in Africa.** Britain and its European rivals made far and away their greatest territorial gains in Africa, which they virtually partitioned before 1914. In the north, the British government bought from the spendthrift Egyptian khedive 40% of the Suez Canal shares and assumed with France control of Egypt's finances. Britain was empowered by the Turkish sultan, first to administer Cyprus, and then to put down a military revolt in his nominal Egyptian dependency (1875–1882). Britain had to let the flimsy Egyptian Empire in the Sudan pass into the hands of the Dervishes, the fanatical followers of the Mahdi (1885), but it annexed Socotra, set up a protectorate over part of Somaliland, and ruled Egypt under the khedive in face of persistent French obstruction.

In the south of the African continent, the British recrossed the Orange River, behind which they had withdrawn in 1854, by annexing Basutoland and the diamond-bearing lands in Griqualand West (1868–1871). Their subsequent efforts to federate South Africa (1871–1888) involved them in native wars and a rebellion in the Transvaal, which they had annexed. The Transvaal

regained its independence subject to some control by Queen Victoria over its foreign policy, and the Cape absorbed unwanted Griqualand West. Thereupon, to ensure a free road to central Africa by keeping the expansive Transvaalers apart from the Germans (who had just acquired South West Africa), the British annexed part of intervening Bechuanaland and set up a protectorate over the remainder (1885).

Despite failure in South Africa and entanglement in Egypt, Britain received international recognition of its exclusive interests in the Lower Niger and Benue rivers. This area was entrusted to the chartered Royal Niger Company (1886), but once mutual frontiers in those parts had been fixed with France and Germany, Britain took it over and organized the protectorates of Northern and Southern Nigeria (1900), which were combined in 1914. Meanwhile, the international Brussels Conference forbade the slave trade in those parts of eastern Africa, the Red Sea, and the Persian Gulf that were covered by British treaties with their Muslim rulers (1890–1892). Events in East and North Africa were closely connected. In the east, Anglo-German rivalries were ended by the recognition of a British protectorate over Zanzibar, in exchange for the cession of Heligoland to Germany (1890), and of the chartered British Imperial East Africa Company's acquisitions in Uganda and British East Africa. That company presently made way for the crown, which built a railway from the coast to Uganda and, in 1902, opened the Kenya highlands of East Africa to white settlement. Meanwhile, having reorganized the Egyptian finances and army, the British overthrew the Sudanese dervishes, and, having peaceably ejected an unexpected French exploring party from Fashoda on the Upper Nile, set up an Anglo-Egyptian condominium in the Sudan (1896–1899). Better still, the Anglo-French Entente Cordiale not only settled long-standing fisheries disputes in Newfoundland, but it promised the British an end to French intransigence in Egypt, and the French a free hand in the tottering Sultanate of Morocco—subject to Spanish rights (1904).

In central and southern Africa, where the British self-governing colonies were taking charge of many adjacent native territories, Britain acquired Nyasaland; Cecil Rhodes' chartered British South Africa Company founded Rhodesia; and the Cape Colony, of which Rhodes was premier, absorbed British Bechuanaland (1890–1895). The failure of an unauthorized raid by Leander Starr Jameson into the Transvaal, in an attempt to force that republic into a federation, ruined Rhodes politically and paved the way for the South African War (1899–1902). This war ended with the annexation by Britain of the Transvaal and its ally, the Orange Free State. The risk of intercolonial war over railways and customs, which arose from the speedy grant of self-government to the two new colonies, was only averted by their legislative union with Natal and the Cape Colony (1910). However, Southern Rhodesia stood out from the new Union of South Africa, and the High Commission Territories of Basutoland, Bechuanaland Protectorate, and Swaziland were excepted from it by the British government, though procedure was laid down for their possible future inclusion.

**Constitutional Changes.** The years 1874-1917 saw the acquisition of several protectorates. These are not colonies in strict law, but because the colonial office usually took over administration of them from the foreign office they were treated in nearly every way as colonies. Above all, neither they nor the colonies were taxed for the benefit of Britain, though help from the British treasury meant cutting local expenditure to the bone for all alike. The colonial office, separated from the war office since 1854, was responsible in varying degrees for the administration of the whole empire, other than the Sudan and India. Its members, as well as those of the colonial service generally, were recruited after 1877 by examination; and separate examinations for services of Ceylon, Hong Kong, and Malaya were presently merged with the general one for the colonial civil services. A relaxation of this rule was made, however, about 1900, when recruits for the arduous Nigerian and Sudanese services were chosen for their general records, like candidates for Rhodes scholarships. Joseph Chamberlain, as colonial secretary from 1895 to 1903, reorganized the working of the colonial office, helped found the London and the Liverpool schools of tropical medicine, the department of tropical agriculture, and, connected therewith, what has since become the Imperial College of Agriculture, in Trinidad. He saw to it that all colonies might register their loans as gilt-edged securities and enabled crown colonies to raise loans on easy terms for improvement of their communications. Neither of these privileges, however, applied to protectorates. Soon after Chamberlain's resignation, various expert committees were appointed, the forerunners of many such, and in 1907 a dominions division was formed within the colonial office.

Tentative liberal constitutional reforms began during the 1880's in crown colonies, protectorates, and the provinces of British India. These changes were tempered, however, in tropical Africa especially, by the doctrine that the interests of a large native population must not be sacrificed to the will of a minority, whether of Europeans or of educated native inhabitants. Rather, in Northern Nigeria, first, and then in other parts of tropical Africa, the British relied on Lord Lugard's "indirect rule," which, with all its risks of favoring conservative chiefs above westernized native commoners, did build on what was already there by combining British and native ideas and institutions. In all dependencies the executive, responsible to the British government at Westminster, still had the last word.

**Reforms in India.** Queen Victoria ruled India as empress after 1877. Few changes were made in the numerous princely states, but many were made in British India, that is, in the provinces that contained three fourths of the rapidly increasing population. The Indian problem was complicated by widespread poverty and ignorance and by the radical division between Hindus and the Muslim minority. On the other hand, the spread of English as the common language of the educated, a vigorous vernacular press, and improving communications made possible common political action by an Indian elite. Elective municipal and rural councils, set up between 1873 and 1883, did not answer well; but the Indian National Congress (predominantly Hindu), formed on the advice of a retired British official, had much more success. Its early demands were soon met, in a measure, when the Imperial Indian Civil Service, still recruited solely in Britain, was separated from a provincial civil service recruited

locally—as in so many British colonies; and as a next step, minorities of nonofficial nominees were included in the central and provincial councils, whose powers were somewhat extended. Desirable official reforms were then greeted with sporadic violence, during which parties formed, with the Congress party splitting into the moderates and the left, and many Muslims forming the Muslim League (1897–1908). The Morley-Minto reforms (1909) marked a great advance toward real parliamentary government, for Indians were given seats on the councils of the secretary of state in London and the governor-general in India; the central and provincial councils were empowered to vote on any matter (including even the budget); nominated and elective members achieved a majority in each of the provincial councils; and (prophetic of what was to come) elective members were given a clear majority in restive Bengal. None of these legislatures could, however, control its executive.

**Progress Toward Dominion Status.** Indian ambitions had been encouraged by the rapid rise of Japan and of some favored British colonies. Responsible government had been given to weak and, as far as Europeans were concerned, sparsely peopled Western Australia (1890), Natal (1893), the Transvaal (1906), and the Orange Free State (1907). Further, the six Australian colonies had federated as a commonwealth (1901) from which New Zealand held aloof; Canada had created the new provinces of Saskatchewan and Alberta (1905); and the four South African colonies had formed a union (1910).

More remarkable was the advance of these groups toward dominion status, an advance governed by the practice that whatever was given to one member of a class of colony should be given to the others. As a rule, the lead was taken by Canada, most rapidly advanced along the economic line. In 1879 Canada not only sent to London a high commissioner with quasi-diplomatic powers, instead of a mere trade commissioner but also adopted a national policy of fiscal protection and was given leave to contract out of British commercial treaties. Similar powers of contracting out were given to all the dominions by 1911. Meanwhile, Canada had waged a private tariff war with Germany and, armed with full powers, had negotiated a commercial treaty with France (1907). Britain indeed maintained the formal unity of the empire by having this treaty countersigned by a British ambassador. But Britain then went on to emphasize the growing individuality of the dominions by persuading foreign powers that, in spite of Britain's most-favored-nation treaties, it was right and proper for the dominions to give preferences to Britain, for Canada to exchange preferences with the West Indies, and for the dominions to give one another preferences.

Political differentiation was less rapid. The designation "dominion" was adopted for this class of colony, with a claim to "a very disproportionate equality" with Britain (1907). The dominions were not to be included against their will in Anglo-American arbitration and conciliation treaties; and they might send their own representatives to conciliation committees whenever their interests were involved as well as to nonpolitical international conferences. But Britain reserved the right to reject international agreements signed by them; and though, in 1911, Britain promised to consult them where possible on grave political matters, they agreed readily that Britain must continue to conduct day-to-day imperial foreign policy and decide on peace or war. In 1914, at the outset of World War I, Britain declared war on Germany for the whole British Empire without consulting the dominions.

This step proved that the dominions had no recognized power of deciding matters of life and death for themselves, and that really effective means had yet to be devised for ensuring common action. Knowledge of the British Empire, and even enthusiasm for it, had grown since the 1880's when it had been "discovered" by John Robert Seeley in his *Expansion of England.* Tennyson, Swinburne, Stevenson, W. E. Henley, and above all, Kipling had hymned its glories; the Imperial Institute had been founded as a center of research into its industrial and commercial resources; Queen Victoria's Diamond Jubilee (1897) and the South African War (1899–1902) had signalized the highwater mark of this new and short-lived imperialism. In 1907, Oxford, first of British Empire universities, founded a chair of colonial history; and in 1910 the *Round Table,* a quarterly, was founded to work, among other things, for federation. There had been vague talk of federation since Disraeli's time, notably by the Imperial Federation League (1884–1893). Little practical result had come of the talk beyond the inclusion of the federal idea in the abortive Home Rule bills of 1893 and 1914—which were to have given the Irish representation at Westminster as well as in the projected Dublin Parliament. More effectively however, colonial and Indian judges were appointed to the judicial committee of the Privy Council—the final court of appeal for the empire outside the United Kingdom (1897).

**Intra-Commonwealth Cooperation.** The nearest approach to machinery for common action was the periodic and purely consultative colonial and imperial conferences (1887, 1894, 1897, 1902, 1907, and 1911). Starting as an amorphous assemblage of British Empire notables, these became meetings of the premiers of Britain and the dominions with no power to bind one another nor even themselves beyond an undertaking to press on their respective parliaments whatever had been resolved. Free trade within the empire was out of the question, for the dominions feared nothing so much as the consequent competition of the highly developed British industries. The dominions might give fiscal preferences to one another, and even to Britain, if only by raising their tariffs against foreigners, but free-trading Britain could not give them preferences, for which Canada and Australia pressed, without penalizing its much larger foreign trade. Britain, supported sometimes by New Zealand, held that binding measures for mutual defense should come first; but most of the dominions would not hear of it. By land, they did indeed welcome an imperial general staff, dominion representation on the committee of imperial defense, and the organization of home defense everywhere on the same lines (1907). By sea, the Cape Colony and Natal gave small unconditional naval subsidies, and Australia a larger subsidy on condition that Britain maintain a considerable squadron in Pacific waters (1887 and 1897); but Australia, at the last, began to build its own private navy (1909). This awkward breakaway, reminiscent of 18th century Irish "dominion" aspirations, was overcome successfully when war came in 1914; even so, Canada and most of the others would never accept suggestions of true federation put forward by British or New Zealand statesmen.

**Mandated Territories.** The Ottoman sultan joined the Central Powers during World War I, whereupon the British made Egypt a protected state and Cyprus a protectorate. Presently, they recognized Egypt's independence, subject to a treaty that gave them the right to maintain a few troops in Egyptian territory, and gave Cyprus, on its annexation (1925), an elective majority in its legislature. Meanwhile, the British Empire had gained a new class of dependencies. At the end of the war, the principal Allied and associated powers entrusted former German colonies and Arab areas formerly subject to Turkey to some of their own members under mandate from the newly created League of Nations. Britain volunteered to keep the "open door" commercially in its Class A mandates, and acknowledged the fact that their independence had been recognized provisionally. Britain did not treat Iraq or Transjordan as mandatory territories, but bound them by treaty to admit a few troops to vital points. Britain allowed the world-wide Zionists to set up a national home in Palestine, which Britain henceforward tried to lead along the paths of peace and self-government in the face of growing Arab and Jewish antagonism. Militarization was forbidden, and the open door was assured to League members and associated powers in Britain's Class B mandates, comprising parts of Togoland and the Cameroons and almost the whole of former German East Africa (renamed Tanganyika Territory). The Class C mandates of South West Africa, Western Samoa, and New Guinea (and in practice, Nauru) fell to South Africa, New Zealand, and Australia, respectively, who ruled them as virtually integral parts of their own states.

Britain gave liberal institutions to its dependencies where it could; for instance, responsible government to Southern Rhodesia on taking it over from the British South Africa Company (1923), and a near approach thereto to Ceylon, Malta, and Cyprus. But it was not all democratic advance. Malta and Cyprus were deprived of their privileges (1931); the Dominion of Newfoundland, fallen on evil times, had to accept rule by an official Anglo-Newfoundland Commission (1934); a scheme for the federation of some of the West Indies was rejected and all that came of white agitation for the federation of some or all of the British central African territories was provision for official departmental cooperation (1929–1939).

**Progress in India.** On the other hand, British India advanced rapidly. Having rendered good service in World War I, India was treated very much as a dominion in the matter of separate representation in the Imperial War Conferences, the Paris Peace Conference, and the Assembly of the League. India sent a high commissioner to London, saw the long-desired end of coolie recruiting for work in tropical colonies, and was promised the Indianization of the civil services and responsible government by stages. These hopeful changes brought the left back to the Indian National Congress, which agreed with the Muslim League on their respective shares of representation in the coming Indian legislature. Unfortunately, the promised British reforms had to be launched in a stormy India. Mahatma Gandhi, an astute and saintly Hindu politician of great influence, proclaimed nonviolent civil disobedience against certain disciplinary governmental measures. Inevitably, he let loose violence that was answered by unaccustomed official violence at Amritsar. In the confusion Afghanistan, a Muslim state, attacked the British in India and, though their forces were repulsed, the Afghans regained control of their foreign policy (1919). Nevertheless, the British promises were largely fulfilled by the Government of India Act (1919), which set up a consultative chamber of princes, gave Indians nearly half the seats on the governor-general's executive council, which was deprived of much of its control over provincial administration, and reduced the officials to a minority in each house of the bicameral legislature. "Dyarchy" was prescribed for each province, thus constituting a division of powers that gave certain departments under Indian ministers almost complete self-government. Almost, but not quite; for at the center and in the provinces, the governor-general or governor responsible to "the Great Mogul in Whitehall" could resolve deadlocks or carry rejected measures by certification.

In spite of sporadic violence and occasional political bycotts by the Indian National Congress, the reforms marched. The Indianization of the services proceeded swiftly, and British India, which had gained virtually complete control of its fiscal policy, ranked by 1931 eighth among the industrialized powers of the world. Even so, another Government of India Act (1935) failed to check the growth of division. Aden was separated politically from India; Burma was placed under its own secretary of state (though he was also secretary of state for India); and self-government, subject only to the rare exercise by a governor of his "emergency powers," was given to the provinces of British India, as a rule Congress ministries taking office. The fact remained, however, that the projected dyarchy at the center had to be deferred because this depended on the federation of the princely states with India; and for this the princes had no desire. Congress, against Gandhi's advice, repudiated dominion status and demanded downright independence (*purna swaraj*). Mohammed Ali Jinnah, head of the Muslim League, envisaged a Muslim "Pakistan" separate from Hindu "India."

### Sovereign Status of Dominions.

Dominion powers and status, which the Congress party thus despised, had long since amounted to sovereignty within the British Empire. The turning point had come during World War I, when some Nationalist Irishmen had rebelled, but dominion leaders, led by Robert Borden, prime minister of Canada, and Jan Smuts, South Africa's minister of defense, had sat in the imperial war cabinets and conferences, and gained an equal voice with Britain in foreign policy. Each dominion had its separate representation at the Paris Peace Conference, and, together, they held one of the seats on the empire delegation. Each signed the peace treaties in its own right, and each except Newfoundland was given separate representation on the League Assembly and the right of election to the more powerful League Council; three of them received mandated territories. In 1920, Northern Ireland was given its own Parliament at Belfast but retained its representation at Westminster as part of the United Kingdom. The next year, in terms of the treaty that ended the civil war, the remainder of the island became the Irish Free State, with its Parliament at Dublin and powers equal to those of Canada.

The problem then arose, as it had arisen between Britain and Ireland (1782–1800), of keeping a group of mutually independent parliamentary governments in step. The dominions showed what was coming when the Imperial Conference of 1921 for the first time advised the king (actually, the British government) on imperial policy —and then left the taxpayers of Britain to foot the bill. Under pressure from some of them and the United States, Britain abandoned its Japanese alliance and submitted to such a limitation of its battle fleet that naval supremacy in the Western Pacific passed to Japan (1922). This done, the dominions, with "Canada first," relapsed into an almost United States isolationism. Behind the bulwarks of the attenuated British Navy and the even less effective League of Nations, the dominions asserted their individuality as states with such success that the old dominions division of the colonial office became the separate and distinct dominions office (1925); and the Imperial Conference of 1926 accepted the Balfour Declaration, which proclaimed the equality of status between Britain and the dominions. However, because status is one thing and function another, the dominions paid too little heed to the fact that the major share of responsibility for defense and foreign policy "rests now, and must for some time to come continue to rest, with His Majesty's Government in Great Britain." The Statute of Westminster (1931) merely gave legal precision to this declaration by abolishing Britain's power to legislate for a dominion, except at its own request, by relieving the dominions of the Colonial Laws Validity Act and certain other acts of the British Parliament, and by empowering them to repeal such other British legislation as affected them. Australia and New Zealand, little interested in such things, only implemented this act some 10 years later; but the rest, with the exception of Newfoundland, did so at once, and the Irish Free State, renaming itself "Eire," became as nearly a republic as it could consistently with remaining a member of the Commonwealth (1937).

### Economic Problems.

The Imperial Conference met from time to time, but got no nearer than before to giving the fissiparous Commonwealth effective legal unity. Nor did attempts to draw the economic bonds closer really succeed. Britain had begun to swing in the direction of fiscal protection, rather than free trade, during World War I. From 1929 on, Britain offered loans or grants to dependencies, including even protectorates, for capital expenditure that might help British trade and manufacturers. During the world slump that followed the Wall Street crash in 1929, Britain adopted protection frankly, and, at the Ottawa Economic Conference (1932), Britain, nearly all the dominions, and India exchanged preferences, while Canada and the Irish Free State did the like. Britain also secured for many of its dependencies privileges in Commonwealth markets similar to those Britain itself received, and induced those comparatively few dependencies that were not debarred by international or other agreements to give Commonwealth members privileges in their markets. But "the retreat from Ottawa" soon began. India withdrew; Canada and Australia soon got their hands free; and Britain (with dependencies) modified its concessions by agreement with the United States (1938).

### World War II.

In 1939, Britain took Newfoundland, India, and its dependencies into World

ELIZABETH II, with Prince Philip at her side, presides over the opening of Parliament in New Zealand in 1963.

War II. Not so the dominions. The parliaments of Australia and New Zealand simply confirmed the fact that, when the king went to war, they also went to war. But Canada declared war formally after a week's delay, South Africa came in by only a narrow margin of votes, and Eire declared neutrality. The British Fleet, which by then was only "a one-hemisphere Navy for a two-hemisphere Empire," could not save what lay between India and New Guinea from falling to Japan; but, once the U. S. Navy had recovered from its early disasters, all was regained. Meanwhile, by the terms of the colonial development and welfare acts (1940 onward), the overburdened British taxpayer had wiped out many colonial debts and was providing increasingly large sums annually for research and for social and economic improvements in the dependencies—without which the grant of liberal institutions would have been in vain. After World War II ended (1945), Britain, Australia, and New Zealand agreed to hold their mandates henceforth as trusteeship territories under the nominal and distant supervision of the United Nations, the successor to the defunct League of Nations; but South Africa refused to accept the new status for South West Africa.

**Postwar Commonwealth.** One after another of Britain's dependencies were caught up in a postwar tide of nationalism that altered drastically the structure of the Commonwealth. Britain gave Burma independence, withdrew from bloodstained Palestine, helped Newfoundland to become the tenth province of Canada, and saw Eire unexpectedly vote itself a republic outside the Commonwealth. Britain quietly withdrew the last

of its troops from Egypt and the Suez Canal zone, and was unable to prevent Egypt, by that time a republic, from seizing the canal itself and laying claim to the Sudan. Sudan, however, gained its independence in 1956. Meanwhile, the East Indian dependencies had been reorganized. The Straits Settlements were broken up; Singapore became a separate colony, and Penang and Malacca were incorporated in the newly constituted Federation of Malaya. North Borneo, including Labuan, became a colony, while in Sarawak a colonial governor superseded the last of the European rajas and assumed the powers of a high commissioner over neighboring Brunei.

The really significant development, however, was the transformation of the bulk of the old empire into the British Commonwealth, a kind of political "club" consisting of Britain and an increasing number of dominions, or, as they are now termed, member states. In 1947 the British marched out of India peaceably, and Pakistan was severed from India, both states becoming dominions. India remained a parliamentary state, but Pakistan was soon obliged to submit to a mild military dictatorship. Both set a bad example to the rest of the Commonwealth by fighting each other for control of Kashmir on the vital northwest frontier and by bickering continually over the division of the Indus waters on which the life of Pakistan depended.

India became a republic in 1950, Pakistan in 1956. They both remained in the Commonwealth and continued to send representatives to the periodic conferences of Commonwealth prime ministers, which had been inaugurated in 1949.

Ceylon, meanwhile, had become a sovereign

**419**

member state in 1948. Ghana (Gold Coast) and the Federation of Malaya became member states in 1957. In 1960, Ghana became a republic. Nigeria attained full status in the Commonwealth as a sovereign state the same year, as did Cyprus. Sierra Leone and Tanganyika achieved independence within the Commonwealth in 1961, Uganda in 1962, and Zanzibar and Kenya in 1963. However, in 1960 the Somaliland Protectorate left the Commonwealth, joining former Italian Somalia in the new Republic of Somalia. The Federation of Rhodesia and Nyasaland, a grouping of dependencies (Northern Rhodesia, Southern Rhodesia, and Nyasaland) formed in 1953, was dissolved in 1963. Both Nyasaland and Northern Rhodesia gained their independence within the Commonwealth in 1964. Nyasaland took the name of Malawi, and Northern Rhodesia, Zambia.

In 1965, Southern Rhodesia, now Zimbabwe, declared its independence unilaterally. The white-controlled government was unwilling to share political power with the black majority.

The West Indian Federation was dissolved in 1962 after Jamaica and Trinidad and Tobago declared their independence. Meanwhile, South Africa, under attack by other Commonwealth states for its apartheid policies, withdrew from the Commonwealth in 1961. In 1963 the Federation of Malaya expanded into the Federation of Malaysia, including Malaya, Singapore, Sarawak, and North Borneo (renamed Sabah), but not Brunei. Singapore withdrew from the federation in 1965.

Tanganyika and Zanzibar were united in April 1964 and took the name of Tanzania six months later. Malta gained its independence in 1964, Gambia in 1965. In 1966, Guyana (formerly British Guiana), Botswana (Bechuanaland), Lesotho (Basutoland), and Barbados became sovereign states of the Commonwealth; and in 1968, Mauritius, Swaziland, and Nauru. Aden and South Arabia withdrew in 1967 when they combined as the People's Republic of Southern Yemen. Bahrain, Qatar, and the United Arab Amirates left the Commonwealth in 1971.

Many newly independent states joined the Commonwealth in the 1970's and 1980's. Tonga, Fiji, and Western Samoa joined in 1970. Bangladesh joined in 1972 following Pakistan's withdrawal. Subsequently joining were the Bahamas (1973); Grenada (1974); Papua New Guinea (1975); Seychelles (1976); Solomon Islands, Tuvalu, and Dominica (1978); St. Lucia, Kiribati, and St. Vincent and the Grenadines (1979); Vanuatu and Zimbabwe (1980); Belize and Antigua and Barbuda (1981); and St. Kitts (or Christopher) and Nevis (1983).

Despite the crown's unifying force, the increasing variety of states with so many sovereign governments puts a severe strain on Britain, chiefly in its formation of external policy. If the crown, advised by its ministers, signs a treaty or makes war or peace, it takes with it the peoples of the mother country and its dependencies. But it does not automatically take those of the member states. None of these was directly affected when Britain and Canada joined the North Atlantic Treaty Organization (1949); none of them had been bound to follow Britain into war in 1939, unless their respective governments so wished. In quite another manner, two Commonwealth members, Australia and New Zealand, joined the United States in a Pacific Defense Pact in 1951, a pact from which Britain was excluded. However, Britain became a charter member of the Southeast Asia Treaty Organization in 1954, as did three other Commonwealth members.

Old formal bonds of union have been weakened or broken. The crown means little to the republican member states; the judicial committee of the privy council has lost much of its influence as the final court of appeal for the overseas Commonwealth; the proud title of "British subject" has been emptied of much of its meaning since Canada drew a marked distinction between "British subject" and "Canadian citizen." In another move away from familial ties, Britain itself in 1948 issued a decree under which former British subjects must be either citizens of one of the overseas member states or else "citizens of the United Kingdom and Colonies."

Comparatively little survives of the empire that once included one fifth of the human race. The Commonwealth still stands, however, and, as a fair cross section of mankind, it can help greatly in the solution of problems relating to racial differences and economically underdeveloped areas.

See also individual articles on the sovereign independent nations and their dependencies.

Eric A. Walker*, *Cambridge University*

### Bibliography

Andrews, Eric, *The Writing on the Wall: The Commonwealth and the Manchurian Crisis* (Allen & Unwin 1987).

Austin, Dennis, *The Commonwealth and Britain* (Routledge 1988).

Ball, M. Margaret, *Open Commonwealth* (1971; reprint, Books on Demand 1978).

Barnett, Correlli, *The Collapse of British Power* (1972; reprint, Humanities Press 1986).

Carrington, Charles E., *British Overseas*, 2d ed. (Cambridge 1968).

Cook, Chris, and Paxton, John, *Commonwealth Political Facts* (Facts on File 1979).

Cowen, Zelman, *The British Commonwealth of Nations in a Changing World* (Northwestern Univ. Press 1965).

Cumpston, I. M., ed., *The Growth of the British Commonwealth, 1880–1932* (St. Martin's Press 1973).

De Smith, Stanley A., *The New Commonwealth and Its Constitutions* (Stevens 1964).

Griffiths, Percival, *Empire into Commonwealth* (Intl. Pub. Ser. 1969).

Hall, Hessel D., *Commonwealth: A History of the British Commonwealth of Nations* (Van Nostrand Reinhold 1971).

Hamilton, William B., and others, eds., *A Decade of the Commonwealth, 1955–1964* (Duke Univ. Press 1966).

Huttenback, Robert A., *The British Imperial Experience* (1966; reprint, Greenwood Press 1976).

Jennings, William Ivor, *The British Commonwealth of Nations* (1961; reprint, Greenwood Press 1978).

Jennings, William Ivor, *Problems of the New Commonwealth* (Duke Univ. Press 1958).

Judd, D., and Slinn, P., *Evolution of the Modern Commonwealth, 1902–1980* (Humanities Press 1982).

Laundy, Philip, *The Office of Speaker in the Parliaments of the Commonwealth* (Intl. Spec. Bk. 1986).

Louis, William R., *The British Empire in the Middle East, 1945–1951: Arab Nationalism, the United States and Postwar Imperialism* (Oxford 1986).

Low, Alaine M., *British Commercial Banking and Commonwealth Development: An International Survey* (1986; reprint, Routledge 1988).

Mansergh, Nicholas, *The Commonwealth Experience*, 2 vols., rev. ed. (Univ. of Toronto Press 1982).

Miller, John D. B., *The Commonwealth in the World*, 3d ed. (Harvard Univ. Press 1965).

Moore, R. J., *Making the New Commonwealth* (Oxford 1987).

Morgan, D. J., *The Official History of Colonial Development*, 5 vols. (Humanities Press 1980).

Ovendale, Ritchie, *The English Speaking Alliance: Britain, the United States, the Dominions and Cold War, 1945–1951* (Unwin Hyman 1985).

Underhill, Frank H., *British Commonwealth: An Experiment Among Nations* (Duke Univ. Press 1956).

Walker, Andrew N., *The Commonwealth: A New Look* (Pergamon 1978).

Walker, Eric A., *The British Empire: Its Structure and Spirit, 1497–1953* (Harvard Univ. Press 1956).

Williamson, James A., *The British Empire and Commonwealth*, 6th ed. (Macmillan 1967).

**COMMONWEALTH PRESS UNION,** an independent organization designed to promote the welfare of the Commonwealth of Nations press and to oppose measures inhibiting its freedom. The CPU, which was founded in 1909 as the Empire Press Union, has its headquarters in Fleet Street, London; it holds an annual meeting in the United Kingdom and an additional meeting every fifth year in another Commonwealth country.

The CPU guards the interests of the Commonwealth press by opposing all proposals likely to affect freedom of expression, by striving to secure improved telecommunications and other reporting facilities, and by supporting plans for the education and training of journalists.

**COMMUNE,** kom'ūn, the lowest administrative district in some countries. In France the commune is governed by a mayor (*maire*), his assistants (*adjoints*), and a municipal council, although this characteristic organization has been altered in a few instances to meet the special requirements of large cities like Paris.

Essentially, a commune is a union of the inhabitants of a limited area, whether urban or rural. Some communes thus comprise an urban center with the open country immediately surrounding it; others consist mainly of open land, with perhaps several small settlements located within its boundaries.

The communal organization is found in Belgium, Italy, France, and in other countries. Since these nations are officially subdivided into communes, census returns are usually given for communes rather than for cities, towns, or villages. A more detailed breakdown of the census returns would be required to obtain the population figures on the municipalities within the commune's borders.

**COMMUNE,** kom'ūn, the name for a type of medieval town government established on the basis of an oath of mutual aid among the participants. More generally, however, the name may be applied to any medieval town regime which possessed privileges that set it apart from the surrounding countryside. The commune's rights were recognized, or at least tolerated, by the nominal ruler, and were often, but not always, expressed in a formal charter. Where central authority was strong this system might result in nothing more than local self-government in the modern sense; where the central authority 'was weak, particularly in the region stretching from southern Italy to the Baltic Sea, where imperial power was crumbling, towns might enjoy virtual independence.

Communes appeared in Europe at the time of the commercial revival that followed the end of the barbarian invasions of the 10th century. The underlying causes for the communes' appearance were the need for protection and the need for a legal and economic system better adapted to new commercial conditions. The inhabitants of the growing centers of population no longer fitted into a relatively simple agricultural and feudal pattern of rule by local bishops or powerful families. They wrested recognition of their new status from their overlords either by money or by force of arms. By the end of the 11th century the towns of Europe were playing a vital economic and political role.

Although they differed widely in the details of their organization, the medieval communes did have features in common. Townsmen were obliged to put loyalty to their fellows above all else, and they were also expected to share in common expenses, such as those for the upkeep of fortifications. Political authority was usually vested in a group of elected officials, known variously as *boni homines, jurés, échevins, consuls, signori*. Sitting in the town hall and using the communal seal, these officials represented the body politic. The whole structure of authority was directed toward keeping the peace and protecting the members of the community. Disputes were judged in communal courts, and economic affairs were regulated in the community's interest. These areas might have included the regulation of trade and the collection of taxes.

**Decline.** As time went on, however, the towns became more self-centered and their economic regulations became more and more detailed and cumbersome. Political power tended to fall into the hands of a few wealthy families, who often abused it. The 14th century was a time of widespread civil strife within the towns. Out of this grew a tendency toward dictatorship in the independent towns, while elsewhere the previously nominal ruler intervened in local political issues with greater and greater authority. By 1400 the communes had for the most part given way to the larger territorial states in political importance. However, their importance as economic and social units remained and has continued to the present.

R. T. McDONALD
*Smith College*

**COMMUNE OF PARIS (1789–1795),** kom'ūn, the Parisian municipal government during the French Revolution. Created in 1789, it was to play a vital role in the government of the whole nation from 1792 to 1794.

When the Bastille fell on July 14, 1789, the electors who had chosen the Parisian deputies to the States-General formed themselves into a revolutionary municipal government at the Hôtel de Ville, the city hall of Paris. Most of the original leaders were political moderates. Their government was constituted as the Commune on July 25, and it survived numerous changes of organization and membership until it was finally swept away by the great Jacobin uprising of Aug. 9–10. 1792. On the night of August 9, radical delegates from 28 of the 48 sections of Paris took possession of the Hôtel de Ville, with the help of the National Guard, and quickly suspended the legal Commune, proclaiming a new one in its stead.

**The Insurrectional Commune.** Such was the weakness of the Legislative Assembly in the interval before the meeting of the National Convention that for a short time this Jacobin Commune was the most powerful body in France, numbering among its members Georges Jacques Danton, Maximilien Robespierre, Jean Paul Marat, Jacques René Hébert, and Gaspard Chaumette. The insurrectional Commune imprisoned Louis XVI in the Temple and pressed the Legislative Assembly and the Provisional Executive Council for more vigorous revolutionary action. Step by step the commune increased its power, despite the opposition of conservative sections of Paris and the Legislative Assembly. It assumed extraordinary police powers; abolished the status of "passive citizenship," whereby persons of lower economic rank had until that time been prevented from participating in politics; and reorganized the National Guard so that each section of Paris had a military force that could be placed at its disposal.

In June 1793 the Commune crushed the moderate Girondists, who had tried to reduce its influence. Armed men of the sections and the National Guard surrounded the Convention, which meekly voted to approve the arrest of 29 Girondists. Even the great Committee of Public Safety yielded to pressure from the Commune, and it was Robespierre's greatest asset that he could often walk the bridge between the committee and the Commune.

In late March 1794, Robespierre crushed the followers of the extremist Hébert both inside and outside the Commune and replaced them with his supporters. Yet when opposition to him mounted and he was attacked in the National Convention on the 9th of Thermidor (July 27, 1794), the Commune lacked the organization and zeal to save him. With Robespierre's downfall the administration of the city of Paris came under the control of various executive commissions of the Convention, and the members of the Commune were outlawed.

**Dissolution of the Commune.** From 1792 to 1794 the Commune of Paris had represented more fully than any other institution the hopes of the ordinary man. However, during the Thermidorian Reaction the government's emphasis was on decentralization. The new leadership resolved to dismantle municipal administrations that might play a rival national role. In this spirit the Constitution of the Year III (1795) broke the administration of large cities into separate units, each responsible to a different departmental administration.

RICHARD BRACE
*Oakland University, Mich.*

**COMMUNE OF PARIS (1871),** kom'ūn, an insurrectionary Parisian government established after France's defeat in the Franco-Prussian War. In September 1870, when the armies of Napoleon III were defeated at Sedan by the Germans, the Emperor abdicated, and a provisional republic was proclaimed. The French armies fought on, however, and Paris was cruelly besieged for four months until it finally surrendered in January 1871. The German chancellor, Otto von Bismarck, then encouraged the French to elect a national assembly, which would write a constitution for the new regime and sign a final peace treaty. To the dismay of republican elements, especially in Paris, the elections returned a conservative monarchist assembly.

There was concern in Paris, which was still recovering from the dreadful siege, that the new assembly would restore some form of monarchy and accept an onerous peace. These suspicions were heightened when the assembly resolved to meet in Versailles, outside of Paris, in order to avoid pressure from the population of the city. The assembly further irritated the Parisians by ordering the payment of rents and debts suspended during the siege and by demanding the return of artillery still located in the city to the government.

**Creation of the Commune.** On March 18 fighting broke out in the Montmartre district when the regular armies tried to remove cannon from that district. A central committee proclaimed itself in control of Paris and held elections for a revolutionary municipal government, the Commune. The name recalled the radical municipal government of Paris which governed during the French Revolution.

The leaders of the Commune were a mixed group, lacking coherence in their political outlook and programs but united in opposition to the Versailles government headed by President Adolphe Thiers. Men like Louis Charles Delescluze and Félix Pyat were ardent patriots who denounced the surrender to the Germans and called for a revolutionary Jacobin revival and renewed struggle under the leadership of Paris. Others were followers of Auguste Blanqui, a veteran conspirator and social revolutionary, others of Pierre Joseph Proudhon, who believed in a federation of small, autonomous, self-governing units (like communes) as a remedy for social oppression. Some, like Leo Frankel, were Marxists affiliated with the First International; but despite popular misconception, the Marxist, or Communist, group was definitely in the minority. In fact, the social measures adopted while the Communards prepared to fight the Versailles government were quite mild. Their decrees did not go beyond restoring the moratorium on debts and rents and the abolition of night work in bakeries; there was no attempt made by Commune leaders even to seize the gold that was then held by the Bank of France.

The military efforts of the Commune against the regular armies failed, but its leaders refused to surrender. In the final days of the Commune, May 21–28, the *semaine sanglante* or "bloody week," the regular armies forced their way into the city and ferocious street fighting resulted. The Communards shot hostages, including the archbishop of Paris, Georges Darboy, and in an act of desperation, set fire to several public buildings.

When the Versailles troops conquered the city they took a fearful revenge. More persons were killed than in the fighting with the Germans or in the Terror of 1793–1794. Thousands were denounced and arrested, an estimated 20,000 Communards and suspects were shot, and some 7,500 were tried and deported to New Caledonia in the Pacific. The last of the Communards died fighting in the Père Lachaise cemetery where, ever since, working-class organizations have made an annual pilgrimage in the last week of every May.

**Results.** The entire episode left a bitter heritage of class antagonism and internal division in France. It also entered into socialist mythology, especially through the writings of Marx (*Civil War in France,* 1871) and later of Lenin, as the first example of a proletarian uprising and proletarian dictatorship. This interpretation, which served to frighten the upper classes of Europe for many years, was not exactly accurate. The Commune had arisen primarily out of the resentment of republican Paris at the defeat and capitulation of France. Although it had definite overtones of class struggle, the Commune was primarily patriotic, Jacobin, and republican in character rather than socialist. The repression accompanying the overthrow of the Commune crippled the socialist movement in France for many years. Not until 1879, when an amnesty for those involved was proclaimed, was a revival of the French socialist movement possible.

JOEL COLTON
*Duke University*

# COMMUNICATION

**COMMUNICATION,** in its most general sense, is a chain of events in which the significant link is a *message*. The chain connects a source that originates and a destination that interprets the message. The process also involves the production, transmission, and reception of messages. In its broadest humanizing sense, communication is a source and extension of imagination in forms that can be learned and shared. It is the production, perception, and understanding of messages that bear man's notion of what is, what is important, what is right, and what is related to something else.

Messages are events that signify other events. How they accomplish this is a subject of philosophical and psychological controversy, but it is generally agreed that the significance of messages stems from form, pattern, or structure rather than from other causally or naturally determined connections with other events. Where there is smoke there may be fire; but the smoke is a causally determined event and not a message unless it is a smoke signal coded to convey significance. Similarly, dark clouds may portend rain, but they are not messages for rain in the same sense as the word "rain" or pictures of rain are. Messages may represent events, as pictures do; they may encode meaning associated with events as smoke signals, words, or numbers do; and they may symbolize other things in the way that verbal and visual languages or graphic patterns do.

Messages are formally coded, symbolic, or representational patterns of some significance in a culture. Culture itself may be broadly conceived as any system in which messages cultivate and regulate relationships. In human culture, and in the conduct of man's life and society, communication plays its most complex and distinctive part.

## THE DEVELOPMENT OF COMMUNICATION

Men's hands, brains, eyes, ears, and mouths are the chief organic means of communication and intelligence. The questions of when and how their teamwork resulted in speech, drawing, and writing, and why other species with similar organs did not share in this development have long puzzled mankind. The puzzle includes, of course, man's ability to puzzle over the origins of his ability to puzzle, and thus to become so far as we know the only self-conscious creature in the universe.

The center of the human intelligence system is the cerebral cortex of the brain. There millions of nerve cells specialize in storing an immense number of memories and associations. The abilities to remember and to make associations enable humans to learn from experience. This frees them from rigidly following instincts only and enables them, instead, to respond flexibly to new situations.

AMERICAN MUSEUM OF NATURAL HISTORY

**EARLIEST RECORDS** of human communication are the prehistoric drawings on cave walls in France and Spain.

Man's relative insulation from the disturbances buffeting the more limited response mechanisms of other organisms provides him with the mental calm necessary for reflection. Storage capacity and reflective ability make it possible to generate language and to extend communications into the collective memories called culture.

**Speech.** No one knows how speech began. The amusing names, perhaps more than the evidence supporting them, served to popularize and perpetuate such theories of speech origin as the "bow-wow" theory (imitation of animal sounds), the "dingdong" theory (of harmony between sound and substance), the "pooh-pooh" theory (of derivation from instinctive or other intense feelings and sensations). Other theories claim that speech arose as the accompaniment of movement, gesture, or ritual, and that the first more or less articulate sounds were attached to behavior in specific situations.

The great social changes of Neolithic times created speech and language as they are now. Such specialized occupations as weaving and pottery required greatly enlarged vocabularies. The change from the nomadic life of food gathering and hunting to a more settled and sedentary life of food raising and cultivation brought about greater social stratification, surpluses (and wars over them), and thus civilization (derived from the Latin word for "city"). Language was adapted to fulfill new needs—for keeping

PRINTING PRESSES, for newspapers (*above*), magazines, and books, are essential factors in communication.

state stores (literally "statistics"), for observing seasons and weather, and for constructing elaborate mythologies to explain and perpetuate the art, science, and religion of the newly developed civilizations.

**Cave and Home Arts.** The craftsman can use his skills and his implements to give concrete shape and form to what animates his mind and stirs the imagination of his tribe. The flowering of the visual and plastic arts among the late Paleolithic people (who were also versed in ceremonial dancing and some verbal arts) left its mark on the caves of Europe and the rocks of Africa and the Arctic, and scattered its figurines and ornaments in graves and campsites in many parts of the world. The intense excitement of the cave art of Paleolithic hunters merged into the more decorative, abstract, schematic, and utilitarian pottery and home art of the more settled cultures of the Neolithic herdsmen and farmers.

The cave and home arts of up to 30,000 years ago exhibited the same aesthetic tastes and basic handicraft techniques of drawing, painting, stenciling, engraving, modeling, and sculpting known to modern man. Much of it was undoubtedly produced by specialists. Although their subject matter was mostly limited to animals and fertility and their purposes encompassed magic, wish fulfillment, and decoration as well as sheer enjoyment, the art of nonliterate peoples served the functions of all artistic communication: to relate individual imagination and vision to the common consciousness of a culture.

**Writing.** Rulers and priests accumulated private property that needed branding, marking, and counting for inventory and trading purposes. The builders and keepers of temple observatories had to record the movements of the heavens to predict the rhythm of seasons, birth, life, and death. Calendars, seals of property, and precious metals stamped with the mark of trading value (money) became the first forms of sign or picture writing. The more schematic forms of writing that could be broken down into interchangeable parts and combined into novel patterns had to await new styles of life.

Pictograms, the pictorial accounts and records of the preliterate age, denoted things but could not make statements, issue commands, convey instructions, record contracts, or embody abstract concepts of action, time, or function. The essential requirement for the new tasks of written language was that the sign lose its purely representational character and come to encode a meaning, an abstracted fragment of experience, an idea (such as a number), a word, a syllable, and eventually the basic unit of speech, the sound.

As far as is known, the people of Sumer who inhabited Mesopotamia about 3000 B.C. first bridged the gap between sign writing and sound writing, although not without the help of their Indian, Egyptian, and Semite neighbors. The Sumerians invented a wedge-shaped (in Latin, *cuneiform*) stylus to stamp their signs on soft clay, and, fortunately for history, made the signs virtually imperishable by baking the clay. Cuneiform script employed over 600 distinct characters and required a special caste of professional scribes. It greatly influenced the sign language of Egyptian hieroglyphics ("sacred writing") and the scripts of other trading partners of Sumer, who spoke different languages and recognized different imagery. These cultural developments and contacts eventually led to the further simplification and syllabification of script, the association of signs with the sounds and meanings of any language, and thus to phonetic writing and the development of the alphabet (see also ALPHABET).

## DEVELOPMENT OF THE NEW TECHNOLOGIES

Movable type, paper, ink, and the handpress are ancient Far Eastern inventions that reached Europe (or were reinvented there) in the 15th century. Laurens Coster, a printer in Holland, and the better known Johann Gutenberg in Germany applied movable type to the handpress about 1450. Soon the new process spread to other countries. An academic press was set up at the Sorbonne in Paris, and in 1470 printed romances were published in Lyon, France. William Caxton established his press in England in

1477. Within some 70 years, a tract by Martin Luther sold more copies in 5 days than 1,000 scribes could have produced in the same time.

Mexico had its first press in the 1530's, and the American colonies had one 100 years later. Occasional newssheets printed in Venice sold for a small coin called a *gazzeta;* the first English newspaper was the London *Gazette* (1665). Similar organs of mostly commercial intelligence, called *coranto*, appeared in Amsterdam and England around 1621, and the first English daily paper was the *Daily Courant* (1702). After an abortive start in 1690, American newspaper publishing began with the Boston *News Letter* in 1704, and achieved daily continuity and success in Philadelphia in 1784 with the *Pennsylvania Packet and Daily Advertiser.*

The increasing speed and decreasing unit cost of printing from movable type made production for an enlarged market a commercially attractive proposition. The "wisdom" of the priest, the king, the scholar, the lord of the manor, and, eventually, an entire ruling class or even a generation of elders could be challenged by younger men and women, who now had access to essentially the same sources of wisdom—and power.

The next big technological leap forward came with the application of steam power. During the lifetime of James Watt (1736–1819), the inventor of the steam engine, steam drove the German-made presses of the London *Times,* printing 1,100 copies an hour, an amazing figure at the time. Soon even faster presses printed from type cast in molds (stereotype). But the type was still set by hand until Ottmar Mergenthaler introduced the first Linotype typesetting machine to commercial use in 1886. French-made equipment used a German process to produce low-cost newsprint from wood pulp, replacing paper made by hand from rag stock. By the end of the 19th century, giant paper rolls fed electrically driven rotary presses printing 96,000 copies of a 12-page New York paper in one hour.

Printing served to standardize written communications and spread them everywhere roads, rails, and ships would reach. Its standardizing effects were applied to private communication through the practical development about 1866 of the typewriter (invented in England about 1714). Typewriting and typesetting by machine speeded the process of writing or composing type by hand. Rapid printing compressed the time needed to mass-produce written messages, and to make them readily available for public distribution in millions of copies.

**The Conquest of Signaling-Time.** The invention of typewriting and typesetting did not affect the time needed to deliver the message. Ancient methods of transportation had become more reliable but not much faster until the steamship and the steam locomotive began the real conquest of signaling-time, and, with that, of new empires.

Signaling-time is the time it takes a message to go from its source to its destination. Historically, the conquest of signaling-time meant speeding a response or compliance from a distance (the Greek word for distant is *tēle*); thus it meant increasing effective control across space.

Rapid signaling at a distance began with hand signs, smoke signals, flags, drumbeats, hornblowing, flashing mirrors and lanterns, cannon shots, beacons, carrier pigeons, and signaling positions (semaphores) of various kinds. Most early uses of telesignaling were adapted to the needs of identification and of traffic by sea and land (Napoleon spanned 1,000 miles with a relay of 224 semaphore stations). In the last conflict between distant enemies in the pretelegraph era, the U.S. Congress declared war in 1812 not knowing that the British had already revoked their offending ban on neutralist shipping to French-held Europe. In the last battle of that war, Andrew Jackson's men shot nearly 2,000 British soldiers storming New Orleans, neither side knowing that the Treaty of Ghent ending the war had been signed two weeks earlier. News still crossed the ocean by sailing ship. The high cost of signaling over distance was still measured in human time—and lives.

*Telegraph.* Experimenters from the early Greeks to Benjamin Franklin knew how to store and discharge electricity, but not how to control or use it. The work of Volta, Galvani, Ampère, Joseph Henry, Faraday, Clerk Maxwell, Heinrich Hertz, and others led to the basic understandings on which the electric age rests. Several people tried the voltaic battery as a source of current for transmitting signals. But Samuel F. B. Morse, a professional painter, scholar of literature and design, and inventor, first hit upon the idea of sending long and short impulses, coded to represent letters, through 10 miles of wire strung around and around in his workshop, and patented his invention in 1837. The first telegraph, which was built in 1844 on a government grant, tapped out Morse's historic message: "What hath God wrought?"

*Telephone.* Alexander Graham Bell invented the telephone in 1876 while working toward a harmonic telegraph designed to send several distinct signals over the same wires (a problem Edison was the first to solve). The American Telephone and Telegraph Company was founded in 1885 to build long-distance lines, and service between New York and Chicago opened in 1892. Coded signals and the human voice could now travel between distant points.

**TELEGRAPHY, introduced in 1844, was a vital step on the road to instantaneous, worldwide communication.**

*Radio.* Communication by wire is essentially private, personal, and confined. Communication by means of the wireless radiation of signals may be cast more broadly—that is, broadcast. Radio waves were the subject of intense interest and speculation after Heinrich Hertz demonstrated that they could pass through solid objects. Guglielmo Marconi used his understanding of both Hertzian waves and the Morse code to send the first wireless message in 1895, and Aleksandr Popov of Russia reported a similar experiment in the same year. In 1906, Reginald Fessenden, a Canadian who had worked for Edison, first transmitted the human voice by radio. Lee De Forest invented an improved vacuum tube that made "wireless telephony" an instant sensation, and in 1910 a Caruso performance was broadcast from the Metropolitan Opera House to astonished radio "hams" and ship operators. De Forest delivered the first newscast when he announced the presidential election returns of 1916.

Strangely, radio's "lack of privacy" was considered more a nuisance than a historic opportunity. But when Frank Conrad, a Westinghouse researcher, sent out test signals of music and his own patter (what would later be called a disc-jockey program), he was impressed by the audience response he received. And when a department store began to advertise the sale of radio receivers for "those who want to tune in to Dr. Conrad's popular broadcasts," Westinghouse stumbled into the future. In 1919 it joined General Electric in the formation of the Radio Corporation of America (RCA; later, the courts ordered both General Electric and Westinghouse to rid themselves of RCA stock). RCA decided to use radio broadcasts to boost the sale of its receivers. Regularly scheduled broadcasting began with reporting Harding's victory over Cox in the presidential election of 1920. Once constrained by the need for privacy, radio now became harnessed to the demands of publicity. From two stations in Pittsburgh and Detroit in 1920, the number of U. S. radio stations grew to 571 in five years, to more than 2,000 in 30 years, and to 5,800 in 60 years.

**Recording Image and Sound.** Signals sent as quick as a flash may be no more lasting than a flash, and signaling time saved at the expense of a durable record was not all gain. While some technicians worked on shrinking time, others took on the problem of storing the sound message and visual image for reproduction at a later time.

*Photography.* But much had to happen before the visual image could be recorded and transmitted. Even before sound was captured by electricity, the ancient projecting devices of "camera obscura" and "magic lantern" acquired a new significance. Alchemists had known that silver compounds darken on exposure. In 1802, Thomas Wedgwood, an Englishman, used a lens to focus an image on paper coated with fresh silver nitrate. The image lasted until further exposure to light blackened the entire picture. Could the picture be preserved? Could it be copied, printed, or transmitted by wire? Could motion be captured, projected from a visual record, joined with sound, and sent through the air? All these questions were answered within about 100 years of the first fleeting glance at a recorded image. The answers required not only further optical and chemical progress, but also a convergence of all communication arts and techniques.

The French chemist Joseph Nicéphore Niepce became interested in lithography. In 1822 he succeeded in obtaining a durable image on a glass plate and etching it onto pewter. His partner, a Parisian artist named Louis Daguerre, used mercury vapor to develop an image on a copper plate treated with iodized silver, and fixed the picture with a warm solution of salt. An Englishman, William Henry Fox Talbot, found a way to reduce the time of exposure and to produce positive paper copies. Both Daguerre and Talbot announced their inventions in 1839, and within a year, the American artist-inventor Samuel F. B. Morse was taking pictures on a Manhattan rooftop. Soon dozens of "daguerreotype galleries" opened in New York and spread over the country. A man no longer had to be rich to have his likeness immortalized or to send it to the folks back home. A new tool enlarged man's power to record momentary, faraway, inaccessible events; to produce images; and to reduce, enlarge, and store pictures and information of all kinds. (Mathew Brady photographed leading Americans and some 3,500 Civil War battle scenes.) In 1888, with processes and emulsions greatly simplified, George Eastman marketed his Kodak camera. Frederic E. Ives produced a photoengraving of a line drawing for the Cornell student paper in 1877. The next year he created halftone engravings by using tiny dots to indicate shadings. By 1897 the fast rotary presses could use halftone photographs, line cuts on wood, or zinc etchings, and photography was launched as a popular art, a branch of science, and a form of journalism.

No sooner had photography become practicable than it joined the already developed art of pictorial animation. Animation is image fused with imagination to give the illusion of motion. The key to motion pictures is the persistence of an image on the eye's retina just long enough for a quick series of still pictures to merge into continuous action in the brain. A complex web of inventions, experiments, trials, and errors, in search of suitable light sources, cameras, films, emulsions, and projection machines, led in 1894 to the first commercial showing of motion pictures using Edison's Kinetoscope. The film of the Corbett-Fitzsimmons fight of 1897 toured the United States and made rich men out of its exhibitors. English and French technicians improved projection machines and techniques. Operators of penny arcade peep shows, vaudeville "flickers," and nickelodeons grew rich on an American market of uprooted humanity massed in the city slums, immigrants speaking many languages but endowed with a common vision, who were, as a contemporary account put it, "below the reach of even the yellow journals." With sound added in 1926, with improvements in technique, color, scope, and dimension, and with their entry into television, films became the most international of the popular arts and the most personal and least literary medium of mass communication.

*Phonograph.* One of those who experimented with solutions to the problem of recorded sound was Thomas A. Edison. As a telegraph operator, he invented the automatic transmitter and the "quadruplex" capable of sending four messages at once. In 1877, Edison used a diaphragm telephone transmitter to record sound vibrations on a rotating wax cylinder and then to reproduce the spoken word by picking up the vibrations from the groove on the cylinder with a needle.

The phonograph was a success in the penny arcades. Edison even tried to link sound and image in his Kinetoscope peep show. A practical system for coupling recorded sound with moving image came in the late 1920's, when a narrow optical track on the side of the motion picture film was used to reproduce the sound by means of a photoelectric cell in the projector. After World War II, magnetic means for recording sound gradually replaced phonographic.

**Television.** Recorded image followed signal and sound in instantaneous transmission when, in 1904, the first wirephoto was sent from Munich to Nuremberg. Less than 20 years later pictures were televised between New York and Philadelphia. Regular television broadcasts began over the General Electric station in Schenectady, N. Y., in 1928. Daily broadcasting of a facsimile newspaper began in St. Louis, Mo., in 1938, but this form of electronic journalism was never commercially exploited. Television reached its highest pre-World War II development in Britain. After the war it swept the United States; the number of American TV stations rose from 11 in 1947 to nearly 800 by 1980, penetrating 98% of American homes.

Nothing has dramatized the speed, reach, and international scope of modern communications more than the events following the assassination of President John F. Kennedy in 1963. Jack Ruby's shooting of Lee Harvey Oswald was viewed not only in Dallas, Texas, but also in the living rooms of America. Margaret L. Coit's account (*Saturday Review*, April 15, 1967) of the aftermath of the assassination tells of the greatest single simultaneous experience that the United States, and the world, had ever shared:

"Often the participants in the tragedy did not know as much as those who watched their television sets through the four harrowing days. Even Lyndon Johnson tuned in Walter Cronkite to find out what was going on. Seventy-five million people knew before the Kennedy party knew it that priests, the harbingers of death, were on their way to Parkland. The Kennedys did not realize that hundreds of millions were grieving with them, that flags were falling all over the world, that the House of Commons had adjourned, and services were being held at Westminster and St. Paul's, that the Russian radio was playing dirges, that all Ireland was bowed in prayer, that the youth of Berlin was moving through the streets, their torches blazing against the night."

Instantaneous magnetic recording and playback of video and audio signals serve well television's unique capacity to witness the spontaneous and fix it in memory as it happens, and thus to make history. Lighter and cheaper videotape recorders, telephones equipped to provide sight, sound, and even a permanent record at the push of a button, and giant computers capable of retrieving image, sound, and text have closed most of the technological gaps that had fragmented communication ever since man's personal vision was first given expression on a cave wall.

**World Communication.** Global news agencies, with headquarters in a few world centers, serve most newspapers by teletype. In 1962 the *New York Times* transmitted pages by photo facsimile to its Paris edition, anticipating the "global newspaper." A subscriber to this paper of the future would dial a number on his telephone, and the first page of his paper (selected from any country) would appear on a screen. If he wanted a copy, the "videophone" could produce a facsimile.

Photocomposition has largely replaced conventional printing, and facsimile broadcasting can connect art galleries or libraries. Xerography, chemical and photoreproduction methods, and microphotography can copy, reduce, and store almost all visible (and some invisible) forms. Printed text, spoken words, drawings, and diagrams can be coded into forms a machine can read and store in computer memories for indexing and retrieval. Computers can use their immense signaling capacity to edit, correct, retype, print, and even deliver or otherwise transmit proofed and paginated text with justified lines and to construct and insert charts, graphs, and line drawings. They can also perform certain translation chores and either reply to spoken queries or instruct the speaker to frame his questions more clearly. These and similar developments are potentially disturbing both socially and economically because they upset traditional trades; the established concepts of organization, publishing, and copyright; and all communication systems based on the ownership of information as a scarce resource.

The transmission of millimeter waves through wave guides makes it technically possible to send 200,000 one-way television signals or 100,000 two-way telephone channels through a single 2-inch (5-cm) tube, easily mounted in a satellite and powered by solid-state devices of low energy consumption. Through microelectronics hundreds of circuit configurations may be printed on the surface of a tiny silicon wafer, and coherent light generated by lasers holds out the possibility of circuits of almost unlimited band width.

Communication satellites permit the beaming of programs to any one or all of the thousands of television stations broadcasting in more than 130 countries to millions of sets. By means of satellites, continental networks can exchange programs any time they find it commercially or politically feasible to do so.

International in origin, time-binding in essence, and global in implications, communication has made "one world" out of the shrinking globe. International and national agencies have intensified their efforts to exchange and share cultural values and even more often, to reach new audiences and new markets with their messages. It also has been argued that the subject matter introduced along with new communication technologies often has imposed systems of thought and social organization inimical to the self-chosen goals of a nation or culture. In a world of massive commercial, political, and military pressures, voices have pleaded for the preservation of some social distance and cultural integrity to permit or assist the developing nations to find their own ways.

**Regulation.** Until the end of the 17th century, literature generally was supported by patrons or encouraged as a political weapon; indeed, all art was produced under sponsorships independent of popular taste or purchasing power. But cultural production became increasingly dependent on popular acceptance. The development of a new middle-class reading public created a market for romantic literature, sensational newspapers, and consumer products. The intellectual controversy about mass culture and its regulation started in 18th century England and has been raging since.

**Printing.** In England, strict censorship of printing was relaxed with the abandonment of the Licensing Act of 1694. The flourishing arts of printing and rising commercial pressures led to the enactment of the Copyright Act of 1710, whose protection made it possible to publish profitably for a larger public.

The sale of books was combined with the peddling of drugs and nostrums. The growing public of readers and consumers made cultural mass production possible, and advertising made it profitable. By 1759, Dr. Samuel Johnson could say that "the trade of advertising is now so near to perfection that it is not easy to propose any improvement," a remark that has not failed to amuse later generations.

As increasing production costs forced the newspapers to seek new sources of revenue, advertising subsidy and dependence on a market replaced patronage. Newspapers, always organs of commercial as well as political intelligence, now had to sell and entertain as well as to inform general publics. The fraudulent, the morbid, the comic, the personal, the scandalous, the violent, the catastrophic, and the trivial all became news. Already accused of subversion and self-seeking, newspapers now were charged with hoax, sensationalism, libel, irreverence, immorality, invasion of privacy, and distortion of public values. Attempts were made to continue or reimpose official controls. In America, licensing of the press persisted until about 1730. Later, special taxation was attempted through the Stamp Acts of 1765, but they were quickly abandoned.

The pamphleteers, editors, and commercial publishers of Colonial and Revolutionary America settled mostly along the New England seaboard, where news was available, commerce was booming, and readers were hungry for information and entertainment. At first, postmasters, who already owed allegiance to the government, were the favored recipients of licenses to engage in publishing.

With the coming of independence, universal suffrage, public education, and rapid industrialization, the class press and the party press were transformed into a mass press selling lively "yellow" newspapers on the crowded streets at a penny a copy. Newspaper chains, news and feature syndicates, and advertising agencies emerged. Magazines also turned to national mass audiences, or to specialized (but wealthier) publics, to survive the competition for media markets. The emergence of widely distributed paperback books helped to popularize book reading after World War II. In the 20th century, through failures, bankruptcies, acquisitions, and mergers, publishing enterprises became larger but fewer.

In 1931 the U. S. Supreme Court interpreted the First Amendment as forbidding prior restraint (that is, censorship before publication) and extended this immunity to include censorship by states. But some constraints on publishing are imposed by the threat of possible antitrust action; copyright, libel, and obscenity statutes; rules limiting pretrial publicity; the deliberations of some public as well as private policy-making agencies; and rarely enforced industry canons and codes (such as the comics code). Certain types of unorthodoxy may still place writers and journalists in jeopardy, and seditious-libel statutes exist in many states. However, self-interest on the part of publishers tends to regulate most mass communication by print and keep it generally acceptable to advertisers and readers alike.

**Films.** The motion picture was born as a commercial enterprise catering to the lower classes and to uneducated or immature minds. It was considered entertainment rather than publication and was subjected to state and local censorship almost as soon as it moved from the penny arcade to the movie theater. State and municipal film censorship still prevails in many localities. But a series of U. S. Supreme Court decisions in the 1950's extended the protection of the First Amendment to the films and weakened the authority of the local censorship boards.

The major regulatory mechanism affecting commercial motion pictures in the United States is the Production Code of the Motion Picture Association of America. The pressures that led to the adoption of the code in 1930, and to its more rigorous enforcement from 1934, were exerted chiefly by moralistic agitators and persons in the industry who feared federal censorship. As movies became a major middle-class medium, standards of acceptability became the standards of middle-class morality. But after antitrust action loosened the hold of the production companies on the exhibition of films, foreign films began seriously to compete with the Hollywood product, independent production increased, and as cultural mores changed after World War II, standards of acceptability also changed, and the Production Code was somewhat liberalized.

**Broadcasting.** American broadcasters operate on a limited number of radio frequencies that, as a national natural resource, are in the public domain. Unregulated broadcasting in the 1920's led to chaos on the airways, and the broadcasting industry turned to the federal government for help. The eventual result was the Communications Act of 1934, which created the Federal Communications Commission(FCC) to license stations, assign frequencies, and regulate broadcasting in the "public interest, convenience, and necessity."

While these terms have never been precisely defined, the development of broadcasting as a major marketing arm of American business and the ever-present possibility of FCC or government regulation of content led to the establishment of network self-censorship and to the code of the National Association of Broadcasters (NAB). This code is broad and sweeping; but its day-to-day operation is concerned mostly with protecting the credibility and effectiveness of broadcast commercials, and its influence is limited because cooperation is voluntary. Network self-censorship codes are binding at least on the network-owned and affiliated stations. Major advertising agencies and sponsors also have codes suited to their own requirements of effectiveness and acceptability. This structure of self-regulation, based mostly on commercial interest, requires occasional FCC intervention on behalf of the fairness and diversity of public discussion protected by the First Amendment.

Television cut into movie theater attendance but extended the audience for motion pictures into the home and subjected televised movies to the more stringent codes of the broadcasting industry. These codes were originally modeled after the motion picture code, but through revisions they came to reflect the broad penetration of radio and television into everyday life and to take cognizance of the structure of the broadcasting industry.

## THE STUDY OF COMMUNICATION

Man has altered the symbolic environment that gives meaning and direction to his activity, but he has only begun to inquire systematically into these meanings, these directions, and their alternatives. The study of communication processes and their effects has become a necessary part of policy making in business, education, industry, and government. There are perennial problems to be scrutinized, including the structure and logic of meanings and the measure of their validity. How does a message, image, or story evoke and elicit, unite and divide, bind and release? How is information processed, transmitted, and integrated into given frameworks of knowledge? How do societies and technologies produce symbol systems and assign value and weight to the issues and choices inherent in these systems? These are some questions involved in the study of communications. What are the answers?

The historic impulses that led to the study of communication as an independent discipline are both ancient and diverse. Much of philosophy deals with such fundamental aspects of communications as the relationship of existence (or reality) to consciousness, the acquisition of representation of knowledge, the nature of the mind, and the logical organization and analysis of symbols and the way in which symbols are related to action.

Physiology, psychiatry, and psychology contributed to the study of perception, cognition, learning, association, and other aspects of signaling behavior. Anthropologists, linguists, and communications-media scholars have taken the cultural communications-media patterns into their field of inquiry. Psycholinguistics arose in the 1950's to study the behavioral (as distinct from formal grammatical) aspects of verbal language. Social psychologists and sociologists have been concerned with interpersonal and group communication, with collective behavior, public opinion, the social aspects of literature and the arts, and the social functions of mass communications. Historians, economists, legal scholars, and students of communications-media techniques also inquired into communication economics, law, organization, history, and decision making. They also have conducted studies of communication development, technological and institutional change, and the history of concepts and laws relating to communication. Political scientists have dealt with the allocation of attention and power through communication, the analysis of political symbols and documents, and international political communications. The work of literary and art critics necessarily involves communication, usually from a stylistic or aesthetic point of view. Experts in the educational uses of new media and of other communication technologies (such as programmed instruction and learning), specialists in electrical and human engineering, and students of administration and management have contributed additional knowledge.

A convergence of some of these efforts after World War II led to the establishment of centers of advanced study and research specifically devoted to communications. Some of these centers grew out of schools of journalism; others developed from departments of advertising, public relations, engineering, or the social sciences; and still others were founded on fresh interdisciplinary effort. Because they made communication the focus of their inquiry, and the production, transmission, reception, and meaning of messages their intellectual domain, the approach of such centers usually differed from the approaches of the related disciplines. Systematic research in communications became a field of academic specialization, whose contributions were equally useful to scientists, humanists, media professionals, artists, businessmen, and social critics.

As an essentially post-World War II development, the study of communication bears the traces of its multidisciplinary origin. Its literature is scattered. Its organizations are adjuncts of such related fields as journalism, speech, education, linguistics, public-opinion research, media arts and techniques, electrical engineering, the information sciences (see CYBERNETICS), and the older social sciences.

## THEORIES OF COMMUNICATION

The nature, process, and effects of social communication have been the subject of endless theorizing and a vast amount of research. No single or unified approach to the diverse phenomena of symbolic production and of interpersonal, group, and mass communication has found general acceptance. The following survey of the historically, scientifically, or culturally more significant theories is intended merely as a starting point for further reference and more systematic organization by the interested reader.

**Meaning.** Studies of meaning and its relation to language have led Alfred Korzybski, Wendell Johnson, S. I. Hayakawa, and others to develop general semantics as a science promoting understanding and cooperation among people. Semantics is the study of the relations between symbols and the objects or concepts to which they refer, including the changes and history of these "meanings." These studies influenced literary and philosophical theories relevant to communication such as those put forth in Charles K. Ogden's and I. A. Richards' *The Meaning of Meaning* (4th ed., 1937), Ernst Cassirer's *An Essay on Man* (1944), and Suzanne Langer's *Philosophy in a New Key* (3d ed., 1957).

Charles Morris, in *Signs, Language, and Behavior* (1946), proposed a "semiotic" science to study how signs acquire significance. The three branches of this science he designated as *syntactics* (relations among signs), *semantics* (relations between signs and their referents), and *pragmatics* (relations between signs and their interpreters).

Studies by cultural anthropologists and linguists led Edward Sapir and Benjamin L. Whorf to develop a theory of the impact of language on thought. The "Whorfian hypothesis" that men codify reality in patterns given to them in the structure of the languages they speak was modified by Charles E. Osgood, and extended by Marshall McLuhan into a theory of sensory determination through modern media.

Charles E. Osgood, George Suci, and Percy H. Tannenbaum developed the concept of "semantic space" in *The Measurement of Meaning*

(1957). They found that the connotations of most concepts in the English language clustered in the three relatively independent dimensions of evaluation, potency, and activity. Their research contributed to the rise of psycholinguistics and to its convergence with the new modes of linguistic analysis.

**Political Theories.** Political scientists concerned with the allocation of attention and power, and aware of the strategic significance of the control of communication, pioneered in the development of theories of propaganda and political symbolism. Harold Lasswell defined propaganda as "the management of collective attitudes by the manipulation of significant symbols." Lasswell also described the functions of mass communications as surveillance of environment, correlation of the parts of society, and transmission of the sociocultural heritage. He proposed the first communication model: "Who—Says What—In Which Channel—To Whom—With What Effect?" Lasswell and his collaborators initiated studies in quantitative semantics, comparing the distribution of significant political symbols in the major news organs of different times and places. Other social scientists developed communication theories of government and the political process and applied them to the study of public opinion, social change, and international communications.

Walter Lippmann, in his classic *Public Opinion* (1922), first used the term "stereotype" to relate communications to "the picture in our heads." The study of public opinion later served the needs of business and government and figured prominently in the political theories of such scholars of communication as Harold Lasswell, Herbert Blumer, Bernard Berelson, and V. O. Key, Jr. Studies by Paul F. Lazarsfeld and others defined the significance of mass communications in voting as forcing attention through news coverage in a way that cultivates existing tendencies, at least in the short run.

**Psychological Theories.** The contributions of psychology have been essential to a better understanding of how individuals perceive and integrate messages into given frameworks of knowledge. Psychological theories of perception, cognition, attitude formation, and behavioral effects have been especially influential. Some psychologists investigated such variables of persuasion as the credibility of the source, the order of presentation, one-sided versus two-sided presentation, and personality factors, while others focused on resistance to persuasion. Prior decisions, prior commitments, and prior knowledge affect the kind of information persons will seek or accept and the way in which they will act on it. There is greater consonance, balance, stability, and resilience in human thought and action than was expected by investigators, who were fearful and suspicious of the "power of propaganda."

**Sociological Theories.** Some sociological theories view mass communications as the "cement of social cohesion" and the "wholesalers" of public conceptions and the models of identity. The classical tradition, stemming from the work of Auguste Comte, Herbert Spencer, Ferdinand Tönnies, and Émile Durkheim, led to a conception of mass society in which organic solidarity gave way to psychological isolation because the specialization of labor had been elaborated to the point where individuals could not effectively relate to each other. David Riesman suggested the term "the lonely crowd" (in a 1950 work of that name) to describe such a syndrome. The role of the mass media was seen as supplying direction to individuals who have lost their social moorings. Contemporaries of Riesman documented the ways in which mass communications tend to channel attention, confer social status, enforce social norms, reinforce existing attitudes, and serve as opinion leaders in different areas of life in different ways.

The most comprehensive summaries of sociological and social-psychological theories of mass-communication process and effects, taken together with the findings of psychological research, suggest that mass communications cultivate the dominant perspectives of society in forms acceptable to the largest numbers of people. They form as well as inform their publics. Individuals are selective, choosing a communications medium generally to reinforce or confirm what they already think, know, or want. Past communications shape dispositions that subsequent communications may trigger into action in generally predictable ways. Single campaigns or messages rarely evoke responses that have not been previously cultivated except perhaps in new situations and at times of general cultural breakdown.

Harold A. Innis suggested that communication technologies confer control over knowledge, social organization, and collective consciousness. Marshall McLuhan extended this concept, claiming that the "grammar" of a medium (that is, the particular mixture of the senses it activates) determines ways of sensing and organizing experience. According to McLuhan, phonetic writing transformed the oral into the visual; printing imposed visual and private, individualized logic on consciousness. The medium of television engages the viewer more actively than the medium of print engages the reader; reading encourages passivity as well as relative isolation. Each medium seems to encourage some styles and reject others. Hence, regardless of what it talks "about," for McLuhan the "medium is the message." Other communications theorists consider this concept technological overdeterminism, at the very least.

GEORGE GERBNER, *Annenberg School of Communications, University of Pennsylvania*

### Bibliography

Bittner, John R., *Fundamentals of Communication*, 2d ed. (Prentice-Hall 1988).
Budd, Richard W., and Ruben, Brent D., eds., *Beyond Media: New Approaches to Mass Communication*, rev. ed. (Transaction Bks. 1988).
Comstock, George, ed., *Public Communication and Behavior*, vol. 2 (Academic Press 1989).
DeFleur, Melvin L., and Ball-Rokeach, Sandra, *Theories of Mass Communication*, 4th ed. (Longman 1981).
Gerbner, George, and others, *The Analysis of Communication Content: Developments in Scientific Theories and Computer Techniques* (1969; reprint, Krieger 1978).
Greenbaum, Howard H., *Organizational Communication*, vol. 9 (Sage Bks. 1984).
Handel, Warren, *Ethnomethodology: How People Make Sense* (Prentice-Hall 1982).
Katz, Elihu, and Lazarsfeld, Paul F., *Personal Influence: The Part Played by People in the Flow of Mass Communications* (Free Press 1964).
Koch, Arthur S., and Felber, Stanley B., *What Did You Say: A Guide to the Communications Skills*, 3d ed. (Prentice-Hall 1985).
Larson, Charles U., *Communication: Everyday Encounters* (Waveland Press 1981).
Lowenthal, Leo, *Literature and Mass Culture* (Transaction Bks. 1984).
McLuhan, Marshall, *The Gutenberg Galaxy: The Making of Typographic Man* (New Am. Lib. 1969).

**COMMUNICATIONS SATELLITE,** a space vehicle that relays electromagnetic signals from one or more transmitters to one or more receiving stations, usually at long distances. In principle these relays can be *passive*, wherein the relay is accomplished by reflection without amplification, or *active*, in which amplifying repeaters function on the satellite. Because the large information-handling capacities required for practical commercial and government communication systems can be attained only by active relay, communications satellites have been of the active type since 1960, when the U.S. Army Courier 1B was launched.

**Types of Satellites.** Commercial communications satellites have evolved into two main types, providing point-to-point service. The leading example of the first type is the Intelsat series, which provides global trunk-line communications to 135 user countries. The need to handle trunk-line traffic from a limited number of earth stations over a wide area has increased the complexity and capacity of each successive generation of Intelsat spacecraft.

The second principal type is the domestic or regional satellite. Especially in North America this type of communication has grown rapidly, providing mostly television distribution and private-line telephone traffic. Domestic satellite designs have followed different trends from the Intelsats, incorporating power levels generally less than 1 kilowatt, compared with several kilowatts generated by larger solar arrays on the Intelsat spacecraft.

Direct-broadcast devices form a third category of commercial communication satellite design. In the United States and Canada, as many as 50,000 earth stations equipped to receive signals only, with antennas ranging in diameter from 3 to 5 meters (10–16.5 feet), are in use to receive television signals at the frequency of 4 gigahertz (4 GHz, or 4 billion cycles per second). Transmission at 12 GHz with higher effective radiated power can make it possible to have smaller receiving antennas, as successfully demonstrated by the Canadian satellite Anik-B, which attained effective television distribution to antennas as small as 1.2 meters (about 4 feet) in diameter.

Government communications satellites, such as the Defense Satellite Communication System (DSCS), are relied upon heavily as the primary means of maintaining continuous contact between military command authorities and far-flung strategic and tactical forces. Tracking and Data Relay Satellites (TDRS) are deployed to provide support to U.S. Space Shuttle flight operations as they become less dependent on the global network of ground stations. The TDRS system consists of two satellites 130° apart, providing communications and tracking services in the Ku and S frequency bands to low earth-orbit spacecraft. The ground terminal is at White Sands, N. Mex.

Search and Rescue Satellites (SARSATs) have been launched as a result of a cooperative program of the same name among the United States, Canada, France, and the Soviet Union. Rescues of downed aircraft and crews have been achieved and lives saved on several occasions.

**Satellite Technology.** Communications satellites can be sized and configured in a variety of ways, involving different capacities and power levels, alternate means of on-board propulsion and stabilization, varying useful lifetimes (in-

NASA

Communications satellite Palapa B, for Indonesia and the Association of Southeast Asian Nations, is launched from the Space Shuttle *Challenger* on June 19, 1983.

cluding the possibility of manned or unmanned maintenance), adaptation to different boosters, and, for military satellites, incorporation of various survivability measures against hostile environments. In this discussion, communications satellite technology is described in terms of Intelsat VI, the largest commercial communications satellite program to have been undertaken by the early 1980's and a useful example of the state of satellite technology. Nearly all international television and about two thirds of intercontinental telephone service are carried by the several Intelsats operating in geostationary orbit (an orbit in which the satellite remains over a fixed point on the surface of the earth). The Intelsat VI fleet of 5 to 16 satellites is expected to be the backbone of international telecommunications through the rest of the 20th century.

Intelsat VI is designed with a diameter of 3.6 meters (12 feet), a length of 11.7 meters (38.4 feet) when in orbit with antennas deployed, and a dry mass of 1,780 kilograms (3,924 pounds). It is compatible for launch by either the U.S. Space Shuttle or the Ariane 4 European launch vehicle. Once in orbit, the outer concentric solar panel is extended downward, the antennas and their mounting shelf are made to stop spinning, and their reflectors are unfolded and pointed toward the earth. The rest of the satellite spins at 30 revolutions per minute throughout its 7–10-year lifespan to provide gyroscopic stability. Other satellites, including large military craft, employ three-axis body stabilization without spin.

The Intelsat VI configuration is dominated by the two C-band antennas and their two large reflectors. Each antenna must provide two fixed beams for hemispheric coverage and four isolated beams for zone coverage. Antenna reconfiguration required for the Atlantic, Pacific, or Indian

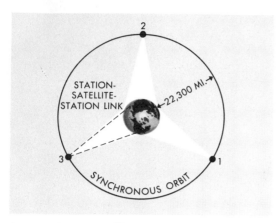

A geosynchronous satellite appears to remain stationary above a point on the equator. Three such satellites are able to provide worldwide communication service.

Ocean service areas is done by a mechanism that allows switching of distribution networks in orbit. Intelsat VI also carries two K-band spot-beam antennas that can be steered in orbit, as well as C-band earth-coverage horn antennas and telemetry and command antennas.

The satellite communications subsystem provides 50 distinct transponders operating at C-band and K-band frequencies. The C-band payload includes two hemispheric-coverage repeaters and six spot-beam repeaters, and the K band includes two spot-beam repeaters. The transponders are interconnectable, using either static switch matrices or a dynamic switching network. Spacecraft power is provided by the solar panels backed up by nickel-hydrogen batteries, and power loads are equally divided between two independent preregulated power buses. Basic power output is between 2 and 3 kilowatts. The attitude determination and control subsystem maintains the spacecraft altitude without ground intervention.

The Intelsat VI level of technology permits a communications capacity per satellite of 33,000 telephone circuits, compared with 12,000 for Intelsat V in 1979 and 240 for Intelsat I in 1965. If advanced signal-switching techniques are employed, the number of voice circuits can be increased to 100,000.

**International Systems.** The successful operation of synchronous satellites in 1963 opened the way for the use of geosynchronous orbits for voice communications. The placing of Intelsat I ("Early Bird") in geostationary orbit over the Atlantic Ocean on April 6, 1965, was the first step in the commercialization of intercontinental space telecommunications. It was built by Hughes Aircraft Corporation for the Communication Satellite Corporation (Comsat), a partly private, partly government corporation established by Congress in the Communications Satellite Act of 1962 as the agency to spearhead the opening of the international satellite communications era.

Comsat later became a leading member of the 98-nation International Telecommunications Satellite Consortium (Intelsat), formed in 1964 to establish a global system as a joint international venture. By the early 1980's more than 30 Intelsat spacecraft of progressively greater capacity, series II through V, had maintained a global operational system in conjunction with more than 150 earth stations in the 135 user nations.

In 1976 a 20-nation Arab Satellite Telecom-

munication Organization was formed to generate the Arabsat program, which by 1984 would provide telephone and television coverage to 22 Arab nations.

On June 30, 1977, 20 countries signed an agreement to form the European Telecommunication Satellite Commission (Eutelsat). By 1982, two geosynchronous satellites were providing telephone relay, television, and business communication services.

On July 16, 1979, several nations signed an agreement to form the International Maritime Satellite Commission (Inmarsat). Maritime communications are served by three Marisat satellites and will be joined by Marecs and Intelsat V units. These will be used in conjunction with six coastal earth stations and 1,500 stations on ships to provide intership telephone, telex, data, and facsimile service.

The Soviet Union launched the first of its series of Molniya communications satellites on April 23, 1965, and since then has launched more than 100 Molniya 1, 2, and 3 spacecraft into highly inclined elliptical orbits. Subsequent Raduga, Ekran, and Gorizant satellites have been launched into geostationary orbits. The geostationary devices are referred to generically as Stationar satellites. The reason for the inclined elliptical Molniya orbits (65° inclined to the equator; perigee, 500 kilometers, or 311 miles, in the Southern Hemisphere; and apogee of 40,000 kilometers, or 24,850 miles, over the USSR) is to get better coverage of high north latitude areas. These satellites are all used in the Intersputnik system for television, telephone, and telegraph.

The Soviet Union in 1971 signed an agreement with eight Socialist-bloc countries to establish the Intersputnik International Communications Network, later to be joined by five additional Socialist-bloc nations. Each member is to construct an Orbita ground receiving station in compliance with set specifications, including a 12- or 25-meter (40- or 80-foot) parabolic antenna. In addition to the Orbita ground station network, a Dubna station, built near Moscow for the 1980 Olympics, houses three earth stations.

**National Systems.** Numerous national communications satellite systems were initiated in 1966 by the Applications Technology Satellite (ATS 1), which provided direct communication with a minimal number of ground stations.

**Canada.** The North American domestic satellite communications traffic is increasing faster than the international. It was pioneered by Canada's Telesat organization in 1972 with the launch of Anik 1 (Eskimo for "brother"), the world's first synchronous communications satellite to be used by a single nation. Three more Anik satellites were placed in orbit, including Anik C-3, launched from the U.S. Space Shuttle *Columbia* in November 1982. They provide television, telephone, and data-relay services across Canada. Anik D carries 24 transponders, each capable of transmitting 960 one-way voice circuits or one color television program. The Telesat control center is in Ottawa.

**United States.** The United States entered the domestic communications satellite activity with the launch of Western Union's Westar 1 in 1974. The five-satellite Westar system provides continuous video, facsimile, data, and voice communications service throughout the continental United States, Alaska, Hawaii, Puerto Rico, and the Virgin Islands. The control station is located in

Glenwood, N.J., and the system includes seven major earth stations.

The RCA three-satellite Satcom system, which began operating in 1975, provides all 50 U.S. states and Puerto Rico with television, voice channel, and high-speed transmission coverage. More than 4,000 earth stations have direct access to these spacecraft.

Comsat General Corporation placed Comstar 1 in operation in 1976, and others emplaced since then provide telephone and television services to the continental United States, Hawaii, and Puerto Rico.

Satellite Business Systems (SBS), a partnership of Aetna Life and Casualty, Comsat General, and International Business Machines, operates a geostationary two-satellite system—the first domestic U.S. commercial satellite to operate in the relatively uncrowded K-band frequency range. It provides intercompany networks for the largest communications users. The SBS satellites, having useful life spans of seven years, extend voice, video, high-speed data, and electronic mail services to business and industry throughout the United States.

**Japan.** Japan in April 1978 became the third nation to place a satellite in geostationary orbit with the launch of the Broadcasting Satellite for Experimental Purposes (BSE), a three-axis controlled satellite operating at 1 kilowatt and providing two-channel color television for Japan.

**Indonesia.** Indonesia, with its thousands of islands and without groundline communications, is solving its growing communication problem by use of satellites. Its first Palapa satellite was launched in 1976. In 1983 the geostationary Palapa B was one of the first communications satellites to be launched from the Space Shuttle.

**India.** India, with its thousands of isolated villages and sparse groundline communications, also addresses its communication problems by using satellites. Insat 1 was launched in 1982, providing telecommunication, television, and weather information to rural areas of India. The system consists of two body-stabilized geosynchronous satellites and 34 earth stations, and provides radio networking of audio programs, standard time and frequency signals, disaster warning, and emergency communication service.

**France.** France is served by the TELECOM system, providing telecommunications to the French mainland, Martinique, and French Guyana.

**Australia.** The Australian National Satellite System (AUSSAT) planned to be operational in 1985 with three satellites in geostationary orbit at about latitude 160° E. They will offer Australia and Papua New Guinea television broadcasts to remote areas, telephone service, a centralized air traffic-control system, and maritime service.

**Brazil.** In Brazil, Sistema Brasiliero de Telecomuncacoes por Satelites (SBTS) will cover the country with an advanced telecommunications network operated by Embratel.

**Colombia.** In Colombia the TELCOM agency planned to operate a national satellite starting in 1985.

**Military Satellites.** National-security interests around the world are increasingly dependent on satellite communications. Operational U.S. military communications satellites began with the launch of Tacsat in 1969 by the Department of Defense to provide service both to ships and to

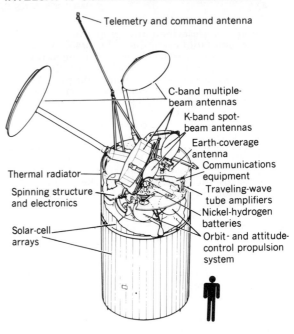

Telemetry and command antenna

C-band multiple-beam antennas

K-band spot-beam antennas

Earth-coverage antenna

Communications equipment

Traveling-wave tube amplifiers

Nickel-hydrogen batteries

Orbit- and attitude-control propulsion system

Thermal radiator

Spinning structure and electronics

Solar-cell arrays

HUGHES AIRCRAFT COMPANY

airplanes. Fleet Satellite Communications (FLTSATCOM) satellites are the spaceborne portion of a worldwide U.S. Navy, Air Force, and Department of Defense communications system linking naval aircraft, ships, submarines, ground stations, the Strategic Air Command, and the Presidential Command Network. Four spacecraft form the constellation required for continuous global coverage.

Leasat, a series of four geosynchronous satellites for relay, serving U.S. Navy ships, is leased by the Department of Defense and is used also by the U.S. Army, Marine Corps, and Air Force. About 4 meters (14 feet) in diameter, the cylindrical Leasat can be placed in orbit only by the U.S. Space Shuttle. It is the first satellite designed to be launched exclusively from the shuttle.

The Milstar system will include as many as 4,000 ground terminals. It is intended to provide the military with a jam-resistant encoded communication system that would function even in a nuclear war.

The NATO III network, operated by the NATO Integrated Communication System (NICS), began in 1970 to provide voice, telegraph, and data services to eligible military and civilian authorities of NATO.

The Soviet Union since 1970 has launched several hundred clusters of eight military communications satellites per launch into near-circular random orbits. The orbits are at about 1,440 km (895 miles) altitude at 74° inclination, and the satellites are estimated to weigh about 40 kilograms (88 pounds). The low orbit allows use of small low-power ground terminals, and interception of signals is difficult for other nations.

**History.** Global communications by space technology is one of the most important political and commercial developments of recent times. Its physical basis was established in the 17th century by Isaac Newton, who pointed out that man-made objects could be made to orbit the earth. In 1929 the Austrian engineer Hermann

Noordung described the properties of the 24-hour geostationary orbit. In 1945, Arthur C. Clarke, then a radar officer with the Royal Air Force, suggested that three relay satellites operating in a geostationary orbit could provide continuous worldwide communication coverage. And in 1955, J. R. Pierce of the Bell Telephone Laboratories described long-distance communication systems based on orbiting radio relays of various types and altitudes.

The first voice transmission from a satellite occurred on Dec. 19, 1958, when President Eisenhower's Christmas message was carried to the world by an orbiting Atlas rocket with signal-repetition facilities aboard. This was a unique initial demonstration of the promise of satellite communications.

In 1962, Bell Telephone Laboratories launched Telstar 1 into a low orbit and first demonstrated the feasibility of wideband transoceanic communications via satellite. Also in 1962, RCA provided for NASA the Relay low-orbit experimental active repeater satellites.

The first attempt to orbit a satellite in geosynchronous orbit ended in failure with the explosion in February 1963 of the Syncom 1. Syncom 2 achieved a geosynchronous inclined (but not equatorial) orbit. The first equatorial geostationary orbit was attained in 1964 by the Hughes Syncom 3. It carried television transmissions of the Tokyo Olympic Games across the Pacific.

NASA's Applications Technology Satellite (ATS) was a historic milestone. ATS 1 was launched on Dec. 6, 1966. It took the first pictures of the full disk of the earth, and 15 years later it was providing Pacific region people with a communications link for medical emergencies and classroom instruction.

Communications through the space medium are the basis of a growing commercial industry, as well as a linchpin in the structure of strategic and tactical military systems around the world. It is a multibillion-dollar enterprise commercially and of inestimable value to the military.

Projections show sharply increased global communications traffic, both commercial and military. The growth via the Atlantic basin information transfer is projected to continue at about 15% per year. The growing requirements for communications capability in geostationary orbit are leading to interference problems, both in regard to orbital placement and to use of the electromagnetic frequency spectrum. A possible solution is to combine the functions of many satellites on large integrated geostationary platforms having multibeam spot antennas to service individual regions on earth. This evolution in communication will lead not only to expanding commercial opportunities but also to defense satellite communications that may result in improved world security.

GEORGE E. MUELLER, *Chairman and President,*
*and* ROBERT J. SALKELD
*System Development Corporation*

### Bibliography

Binkowski, Edward, *Satellite Information Systems* (Knowledge Industry Pub. 1986).

Brown, Martin P., Jr., ed., *Compendium of Communication and Broadcast Satellites* (Inst. of Electrical & Electronics Engineers 1981).

Douglas, Robert L., *Satellite Communications Technology* (Prentice-Hall 1988).

Mueller, George E., and Spangler, E. R., *Communication Satellites* (Krieger 1964).

Tydeman, John, and Kelm, Ellen J., *New Media in Europe* (McGraw 1988).

**COMMUNION,** a term in the Christian vocabulary that has a number of special uses. The one most frequently met is its attachment to the sacrament of the Lord's Supper, sometimes called the Eucharist, or, in ordinary Roman Catholic usage, the Mass. This central act of Christian worship is widely known as the "celebration of the Holy Communion," emphasizing that the act of receiving the consecrated elements is the climax of the worshipers' participation in the liturgy. "Communion," therefore, may refer to the sacramental service of worship or to the reception of the elements therein.

Usages in Holy Communion vary among the Christian churches almost as widely as do doctrines or convictions in respect to the full meaning of the sacrament, the manner in which the Lord's presence is apprehended by the participants, or the spiritual benefits conferred thereby. Whatever their differences, however, there are few Christians who are not faithful to the command of Jesus at the Last Supper: "This is my body which is broken for you. Do this in remembrance of me," and "This cup is the new covenant in my blood. Do this, as often as you drink it, in remembrance of me." (I Corinthians 11:23–26). Bread and wine are the elements of Holy Communion, though a number of Protestant churches use grape juice in place of wine.

The Roman Catholic Church normally administers the elements to the people in one kind, that is, the consecrated bread alone. Protestants returned to the more ancient use of both kinds in the peoples' communion, though there is variety in the manner of receiving. In Anglican churches, for example, the chalice is used for all communicants at the altar rail, but some Protestant churches use individual communion cups that are distributed throughout the congregation. In Eastern Orthodox churches communion is given in both kinds by intinction; that is, fragments of the consecrated bread are placed in the chalice, and the two species are administered together with a spoon.

In those churches where reception from the chalice is practiced, a method of intinction is sometimes employed in which the communicant or the officiating clergyman touches the bread to the consecrated wine in the chalice. See also EUCHARIST; MASS.

The word "communion" is also used to denote a group of churches bound together by common faith, principles of church order, and ways of worship. The Anglican churches throughout the world are thus often spoken of as the Anglican Communion. An extended use of the term that derives from this application is made when it is said that certain churches are "in full communion" or "in intercommunion." These churches permit the adherents of each to receive the sacraments in the other. This practice is also sometimes called "table fellowship."

In the phrase "The Communion of Saints," which appears in the Apostles' Creed, the word refers to the union of all Christian souls as members of the mystical Body of Christ. In traditional Roman Catholic thought this includes all on earth, in purgatory, or in heaven. This conviction of the unity of all Christians in Christ can be expressed more simply as the fellowship of all believers, living and departed. See also APOSTLES' CREED.

POWEL MILLS DAWLEY
*The General Theological Seminary, New York*

Karl Marx (1818–1883), Communist philosopher, and V. I. Lenin (1870–1924), who made Russia a Communist state.

# COMMUNISM

**COMMUNISM** is the term used broadly to designate a theory or system of social organization based on the holding of all property in common. Specifically and currently, it refers to the doctrines underlying the revolutionary movement that aims to abolish capitalism and ultimately to establish a society in which all goods will be socially owned and all economic activities socially planned and controlled, and in which distribution will be in accordance with the maxim "from each according to his capacity, to each according to his needs." It is to be distinguished from socialism, which aims, by constitutional and democratic methods, to nationalize gradually only the essential means of production and to organize distribution on the basis of a just reward to each person for the amount and quality of his or her work.

**Early Forms.** In its specific sense, the term "communism" first came into use in France after 1840; but the general idea—that private property is the source of all social ills, which can be cured only by community of goods and interests—has been held in one form or another by individuals and groups at various times in the past. In the Greco-Roman world, Plato expounded the idea in the *Republic* in the 4th century B.C., and the Stoics implied it in their doctrine of natural right *(jus naturale),* according to which nature created all men free and equal, and private property was unknown in the original state of nature.

The early Christians applied the idea in some of their communities, which shared all things in common. Some of the Fathers of the Church approved it, and various heretical sects clung to it after it had been repudiated by the main body of the church. In more modern times, it was preached by certain Christian dissidents, notably by the Anabaptists during the Reformation in Germany. It found expression during the first half of the 16th century in Sir Thomas More's *Utopia,* inspired by Plato, and it was restated in terms of the natural right doctrine by Morelly, one of the French *philosophes,* who outlined an ideal communist society in his *Code de la nature* (1755).

The idea also became the basis of an idealistic, peaceful communism expounded by Étienne Cabet, whose *Voyage en Icarie* (1840) had wide influence, and it provided a stimulus for numerous unsuccessful experiments in communistic settlement made by followers of Cabet and others in North America in the second quarter of the 19th century.

The origins of *revolutionary* communism may be traced to "Gracchus" (François Noël) Babeuf, who headed a conspiracy that failed against the French Directory in 1796, for which he was sent to the guillotine a year later. Babeuf's belief that the French Revolution would be followed by another revolution, which would "emancipate the class of proletarians," was propagated by Louis Auguste Blanqui between 1836 and 1839 in the secret societies of Paris, where the term "communism" was coined. Blanqui urged the workers to organize insurrections and to establish a dictatorship for the purpose of reorganizing France on a republican and communist basis.

**Marx and Engels.** The theoretical foundations of modern communism were laid by the Germans Karl Marx and Friedrich Engels in *The Communist Manifesto* (1848; see COMMUNIST MANIFESTO) and in such later writings as Marx's *Class Struggles in France* (1850), *Das Kapital* (first volume, 1867; see KAPITAL, DAS), *The Civil War in France* (1871), and *Critique of the Gotha Programme* (1875), and Engels' so-called *Anti-Dühring* (1877).

Marx and Engels took over and modified the then current concepts of materialism, the Hegelian view of historic evolution as a dialectical process moving from thesis through antithesis to synthesis, the labor theory of value of David Ricardo, the critique of capitalism of the "utopian" French socialists, and the tactics of Blanqui. The synthesis of Marx and Engels consisted in formulating these

FRIEDRICH ENGELS (1820–1895), a German Socialist, coauthored the *Communist Manifesto* with Marx.

LEON TROTSKY (1879–1940), who became second to Lenin in authority, was later exiled by Joseph Stalin.

ideas into a *general* theory of historical evolution and a *specific* theory of capitalist development. These theories, it should be remembered, were evolved under the conditions of 19th century industrialism.

According to the Marxian general theory, all historical changes are ultimately determined by changing relations of production caused by changes in technical conditions. As economic systems changed from slavery to serfdom to capitalism and free labor, there was progress in the production of material goods; but, again according to the theory, each economic system had an exploiting class that owned or controlled the means of production—patricians in Rome, feudal lords in medieval times, the bourgeoisie (employers and property owners) in an industrial society—and a class of exploited that made efforts to bring about a more equal distribution of wealth and income. All history, according to Marx and Engels, is thus a history of class struggles.

According to the Marxian specific theory, capitalism, which was based on the exploitation of the worker through the appropriation by the employer of surplus value (that is, in simplified terms, the appropriation of the difference between the value produced by the worker and the value that he received in wages), was doomed by its own inner contradictions: capitalism was increasing the productive powers of society but at the same time was condemning the workers to lives of ever-increasing misery; the concentration of industry in fewer and fewer hands was eliminating the middle class, merging it with the workers, and bringing employers and workers into ever sharper conflicts; the capitalist economy was subject to recurrent crises and depressions, which made factories idle while there was need for their products, and which would become increasingly severe. The ultimate

result of this historical process, according to Marx and Engels, would be that as production reached a stage where it could satisfy the material needs of society, the workers organized in a political party would establish a "dictatorship of the proletariat," abolish capitalism, and substitute for it a social system based on the collective ownership of the means of production.

In their later writings, Marx and Engels described the ideal communist society only in general terms as a system of social ownership under which production would be carried on by voluntary associations of workers, distribution would be in accordance with needs, the state would cease to be an instrument of force and "wither away," and the individual would live in freedom and in harmony with society. Marx and Engels thought that the social revolution they aimed at could be carried out by peaceful means in some countries, for example in England and the United States.

Marx and Engels used the term "communism" to distinguish their program from socialism, which in the 1840's meant economic and social reform. From about 1875 to 1917, the term ceased to be used, the Marxian doctrines being described as "scientific socialism," but it was revived in 1918-1919 by the Russian Bolsheviks.

The socialists of Western countries vigorously repudiated the violent and dictatorial methods of the Bolsheviks and stressed the democratic character and aims of socialism, continuing to honor Marx and to interpret his theories in a democratic sense. See also SOCIALISM.

**Later Elaborations.** The Russian Bolsheviks declared themselves to be the "true heirs" of Marx. The Bolshevik leader Lenin undertook to "bring Marx up to date" (in his essays *The State and Revolution* and *Imperialism*) by analyzing the so-called "last phase of capitalism" or "imperialism"

BOLSHEVIKS in Petrograd (Leningrad), after the fall of the czar, are fired on by provisional government police.

and the dynamics of "world revolution." After Lenin's death, Joseph Stalin added to Communist doctrine his special ideas that socialism could be built in one country, particularly Russia, and that the Soviet Union was the base of the "world revolution."

In 1928 the 6th Congress of the Third International systematized these ideas into a program that became official for world communism. The congress declared Lenin's work to be of equal importance with that of Marx, justifying the designation of Communist theory as Marxism-Leninism. Lenin, and especially Stalin, gave their own definitions of the future Communist society, but these were essentially the same as that given by Marx. Declarations by Stalin and others after the end of World War II did not affect the basic tenets of communism, except that Russian Communists subsequently stated that until the "capitalist encirclement" is totally "liquidated" a Communist society will have to maintain the state instead of letting it "wither away."

According to these Communist elaborations, the present stage of world history is that of "finance capitalism" or "imperialism," marked by the growth of monopoly and the control of industry by finance. It is the epoch of the decay or "general crisis" of capitalism on the one hand, and of the "world revolution" on the other. The "general crisis" of capitalism, say the Communists, began with World War I. It is to be a prolonged process, during which there may be brief periods of world economic stabilization and development; but every such period will be followed by a new crisis and

decline, bringing the final collapse of capitalism nearer. The "general crisis" of capitalism cannot be overcome, argue the Communists, because "finance capitalism" aggravates the disparity between the growing productive forces of society and the restrictive methods of distribution, between the capacity to produce and the ability of the people to purchase the products of industry. The Communists view these disparities as the cause of industrial and social conflicts within each country, and as the cause of increasing struggles between nations for the control of raw materials and markets. International animosities are further accentuated, they maintain, by political antagonisms between the great powers and the colonial and underdeveloped countries.

World War II, according to their theory, sharpened these antagonisms in such a way as to divide the world into two opposing camps—the "capitalist-imperialist" states led by the United States on one side, and the "socialist" countries led by the USSR on the other side. Between these two camps struggle is inevitable, though for temporary periods the peaceful coexistence of the two systems and an easing of international tensions are possible.

As a result of the "general crisis" of capitalism, the "world revolution," which, the Communists maintain, began with the Russian Revolution of 1917, is "maturing." This "world revolution" is conceived by the Communists as a whole epoch of class struggles, national wars, revolutions, and proletarian dictatorships in different countries, some of which may fail temporarily while others are

MAO TSE-TUNG *(center)*, chairman of the Chinese Communist party, reviewing troops during the Sino-Japanese War.

successful. For an indefinite period, therefore, the Communists expect the world to present a spectacle of conflicting socioeconomic systems existing side by side.

Though their ultimate aim in each country is the establishment of a Communist society, the achievement of this aim, according to their theory, must be preceded by a transition period, during which industry will be nationalized, a planned economy organized, and the people accustomed to collective ways of living. The Communists call this period the "building of socialism" as the "first phase of communism." During the transition period the government will be organized as a "proletarian dictatorship," that is, as the class rule of the workers under the control of the Communist party, which claims to be the "vanguard of the proletariat." Such a government will use all the powers of the state to crush resistance to its program. Thus, though the Communists claim that in some countries the revolution may initially be carried through by peaceful means, the fulfillment of the program involves the employment of violent and dictatorial methods.

JOSEPH STALIN (1879–1953) succeeded Lenin as Russian ruler in 1924. Here his coffin is carried by members of the Soviet hierarchy.

**Communism Versus Socialism.** The use of the term "socialism" by the Communists is the cause of much confusion. Though both derive from Marx, socialism and communism parted ways in 1917–1919 and are now farther apart than ever. To the extent that they still hold to Marxian ideas, the democratic socialists have revised them to fit modern conditions of democratic freedom and social progress. The democratic socialists consider Leninism a Russian distortion of Marx and denounce Communist methods as antidemocratic and immoral. Nor do they regard the Soviet Union as a socialist country simply because it has nationalized its industries and introduced economic planning.

**Criticism.** From an objective point of view and in the light of actual developments, the Communist doctrine is untenable on both theoretical and practical grounds; its claim to scientific status is part of its Marxian pretentiousness, which has been amply refuted by various writers. It may be, and has been, criticized specifically on the following grounds:

(1) Earlier Marxian predictions as to capitalist development were not borne out by experience, and later Leninist and Stalinist analyses of "finance capitalism" and world political developments have repeatedly proved faulty.

(2) The Communist doctrine of class war ignores group cooperation and peaceful change.

(3) The "dictatorship of the proletariat" in practice means the rule by force of the Communist party and its leaders, which destroys individual freedom and true representative government.

(4) The idea of "world revolution" is an apocalyptic myth subservient to the imperial aims of the major Communist powers and inimical to peace.

(5) The Soviet Union itself shows trends toward group inequalities and social stratifications, as well as toward increasing centralization of political power, which contradict Russian claims as to their progress toward, and the possibility of, an ideally envisaged Communist society.

See also COMMUNIST PARTIES.

LEWIS L. LORWIN
*Author of "The International Labor Movement"*

**Bibliography**
Burkharin, Nikolai, and Preobrazhensky, Evgeny, *The ABC of Communism*, rev. ed. (Univ. of Mich. Press 1988).
Daniels, Robert V., ed., *A Documentary History of Communism*, 2 vols. (Univ. Press of New England 1984).
Daniels, Robert V., *Red October: Bolshevik Revolution of 1917* (Beacon Press 1984).
Lenin, V. I., *Complete Collected Works*, 45 vols. (1927–1945 Imported Pub. 1980).
Marx, Karl, and Engels, Friedrich, *The Communist Manifesto* (1848; Regnery 1982).
Meyer, Alfred .G., *Communism*, 4th ed. (Random House 1984).
Pankov, Y. N., *Communists and the Youth* (Imported Pub. 1984).
Pryer, Peter, *The New Communism* (State Mutual Bk. 1988).
Smith, Dorothy E., *Feminism and Marxism: A Place to Begin, A Way to Go* (Riverrun Press 1985).
Sowell, Thomas, *Marxism* (Morrow 1986).

**COMMUNIST MANIFESTO,** the earliest authoritative exposition of Marxism as a socioeconomic doctrine, with an explicit political program founded on that doctrine. It was written by Karl Marx and Friedrich Engels in 1847 and published the next year in London as *Manifest der Kommunistischen Partei* (*The Manifesto of the Communist Party*). It is one of the most famous documents in the history of Marxism and communism.

The Communist Manifesto, the title by which it is known in English-speaking countries, is a booklet of fewer than 40 pages divided into four sections. The first section is a pointed appraisal of socioeconomic orders in Europe from the time of ancient slave civilizations. Each order is treated as a system in which a ruling class derives its power from private ownership of the principal existing means of economic production. The discussion is designed to show that the exercise of such power by the ruling class inevitably results in the economic exploitation and political oppression of other classes and that new epochs in history appear only when a ruling class is displaced by another class with a new relationship to new and more powerful means of production. Hence, the class struggle—that, for instance, between feudal lords and the capitalists at the end of the Middle Ages—is seen as the chief dynamic of past history. Economic factors are seen as the chief determinants of political developments. On this basis it is argued that for the first time a scientific understanding of historical forces and a realistic conception of politics are made possible.

All this points to what is concluded to be the only practicable way to communism as a new epoch in human history, as a socioeconomic order with unrestricted abundance of productivity but no private ownership of the means of production, an order without classes, class struggle, exploitation and oppression. That is, when capitalist private ownership and private competition become obstacles to the full utilization of new forces of production, so great in scope that they demand a collectivist approach, the working class will come to power on the basis of a collectivist program that eliminates the class system.

The second section of the *Manifesto* continues the development of these ideas in terms of political strategies, ideological polemics, and psychological attitudes. The third section is devoted to a critique of other schools of thought claiming to be socialist or communist, and the fourth is a brief comment on other political groups of the period.

Some of the *Manifesto's* references to the parties then in existence and to their platforms and ideological positions have only historical interest, and some of the specifics of the political program presented in the work were soon outdated. One especially important example is contained in the concluding paragraph of the *Manifesto*: "They (the Communists) openly declare that their ends can be attained only by the forcible overthrow of all existing social conditions." Some 25 years later, in 1872, Marx cited both England and the United States as "countries in which the workers may hope to secure their ends by peaceful means." Marx based his judgment on the emergence in those countries of a parliamentary democratic system capable of carrying out the will of the majority even if that will were for a radical change.

The first two editions of the *Manifesto,* both published in London in 1848, appeared in German. Translations into French, Polish, Danish, and Swedish followed rapidly. The first English translation appeared in London in 1850, and the first Russian one in 1869. The first three American editions were published in 1871. Thereafter editions and translations multiplied. By 1964 more than 1,000 editions in more than 100 languages with total printings in excess of 14 million copies had appeared.

JOHN SOMERVILLE, *California Western University;*
*Author of "The Philosophy of Marxism"*

PHOTO M. RIBOUD—B. BARBEY, FROM MAGNUM

Fiftieth anniversary of the Bolshevik Revolution is celebrated in Moscow on Nov. 7, 1967.

**COMMUNIST PARTIES.** In the wake of the Bolshevik Revolution in Russia in 1917, communist parties emerged in a number of political systems throughout the world, both as ruling and as nonruling parties. With the demise of the Soviet Union in 1991, their fate, goals, and strategies were dramatically affected. The entry that follows discusses the history, ideologies, distinguishing features, and current status of communist parties around the world. The entry itself comprises four subentries. "An Overview" examines the ideology, structure, and functions characteristic of communist parties worldwide. "The Communist Party of the Soviet Union" focuses on the vicissitudes of this, the original communist party. An assessment of the Chinese Communist Party and a discussion of its current state are the focus of "The Communist Party of China." The entry concludes with "The Communist Fringe of the Postcommunist World," a comprehensive survey of communist parties in other areas of the world, most of which have altered their strategies either to maintain control of their respective states or to remain viable in states where they compete with other parties for power and influence.

### 1. An Overview

The Communist Party of the Soviet Union (CPSU) was by far the major formative influence

in the development of the communist movement, even if its power of direct intervention was restricted to countries on its western periphery. The first communist parties were those groups that joined the Third (Communist) International—the Comintern—separating themselves from other socialist parties in June 1919. This cohesive organization brought together those socialist parties that shared the Bolsheviks' revolutionary goals. The Bolsheviks themselves, having started life as one wing of the Russian Social Democratic Workers' Party, had changed their name in 1918 to Russian Communist Party (Bolshevik) to distinguish themselves from the socialists who favored a reformist strategy.

**Evolution.** The power struggle that followed Lenin's death in 1924 involved a conflict between two views of the Soviet Union's future development, encapsulated in the opposition between the terms *socialism in one country* of the Stalinist faction and the *permanent revolution* promoted by Trotsky and his followers. Although the internationalist Trotskyist opposition was defeated in this struggle, Trotskyism remained a persistent rival to Soviet orthodoxy within the communist movement, but only in very few ephemeral cases did it produce a ruling party. The first ruling communist party, the Communist Party of the Soviet Union (CPSU), developed the ideology, structure, and role in society that others would initially try to follow.

After World War II the orthodox movement expanded with a series of communist parties coming to power under Soviet patronage in Eastern Europe but autonomously in Albania and Yugoslavia. This expansion was followed by schism in 1948, when the Yugoslav party embarked on an independent path of development based on "social self-management." The same pattern of expansion and schism was repeated after the accession to power of the Chinese Communist Party in 1949. For a while, after the Sino-Soviet split climaxed in 1970, pro-Chinese parties existed in many countries. Despite this trend the Communist Party of the Soviet Union remained by far the major formative influence in the communist movement. This influence waned after Stalin's death, but in 1960, when the CPSU sought to ostracize the Chinese party, the Soviet party was still capable of summoning a worldwide conference of 81 communist parties. By the 1970s it was no longer possible to hold such conferences.

**Distinguishing Features.** Among the political parties of the world, communist parties have been distinguished by three features. First, in their ideology, they bequeathed to the world one consistent and, for a time, very widespread version of Marxism, to which the term *Marxism-Leninism* has been attached. In his treatment of the general Marxist notion that the working class plays a historic role by achieving class power and bringing the class war to a close, Lenin developed the idea that if the working class is to achieve this goal, its political consciousness must be promoted and sustained by a "vanguard," the communist party. Lenin's theory of the party is central to communist thinking and practice, but the actual form the leading role of the party was to take historically was determined by the tasks of economic and cultural development the CPSU addressed during the Stalinist period.

A second distinguishing feature of communist parties—or at least of those that have exercised state power—can be held to have followed from this. Through the exigencies of a revolutionary struggle and through the rigors of a drive for economic development at a forced pace, the ruling communist parties acquired a monopoly of economic and political power that had distinct characteristics. It rested on two key mechanisms in the hands of the party's apparatus: control of appointments to responsible positions (the so-called *nomenklatura*) and control over communications. The way in which the apparatus was structured and functioned resulted in a dual bureaucracy— that of the party duplicating that of the state administration. Structurally the two were distinct, but functionally they were fused. This monopoly of power enabled the party to pinpoint developmental targets and to pursue them without distraction from rival priorities, which it was able to drown out through its control of communications. But this obliteration of rival signals spelled starvation of information within the system itself, which was to prove fatal in the Soviet case.

Many of the features of communism in the case of the ruling parties therefore reflected the developmental tasks that faced those parties. Starting in the 1960s, this connection to the evolution of political systems led certain Western political scientists to analyze communist politics as a variety of the politics of development.

The third distinguishing characteristic of communist parties is also applicable to the nonruling communist parties. Democratic centralism, a guiding organizational principle that all communist parties adopted, has involved a strong notion of unity in pursuit of a common purpose and the conviction that the interest of the organism—be it the party or society—transcends that of the individual or of a group. Where a communist party is in power, democratic centralism encapsulates the "leading role of the party" in all its detail. In the case of the nonruling parties, it has been interpreted as "freedom of discussion, unity in action," in which action has taken priority over discussion. As the French communist Louis Althusser pointed out in a celebrated polemic in 1978, the principle of democratic centralism has resulted in the isolation of the leadership group and in the degeneration of party congresses into platforms at which the leadership proclaims its policies. A traditional disdain for discussion has gone hand in hand with a high value placed on militancy. This directive expects the party member to militate in society for the party's goals but to refrain from militating inside the party in support of positions that conflict with those of the leadership. Ever since the Bolsheviks' 10th congress in 1921, such fractionalism has had pride of place in the demonology of communism.

It has been traditional in communist parties for a regularly held congress to elect, on a list system, a central committee that in turn elects a political bureau. In both ruling and nonruling communist parties, the central committee has had a powerful secretariat attached to it. This secretariat, in the case of the ruling parties, headed up the apparatus, which consisted of the substantial number of people who were on the party's payroll. Communism thus described took its full form during the Stalinist period, from the first five-year plan in 1928 to the death of Stalin in 1953.

Thereafter a gradual process of de-Stalinization began, developing first in certain Western European communist parties, with the Italian Communist Party (PCI) in the vanguard and providing the impulse for a number of challenges to the Soviet Union's control in Eastern Europe (notably the Prague Spring of 1968). But this trend could not culminate until there had been movement in the Soviet Union itself. This occurred when the Gorbachev leadership undid the power monopoly in an attempt to secure a future for the CPSU in a society that had socially and culturally outgrown its Stalinist origins.

The term *Eurocommunism* attaches to those moves by the PCI and other Western European communist parties to distance themselves from the CPSU and to accept the political norms prevailing in their own societies. Until that point (and afterward in those communist parties, such as the French, the Portuguese, and the Greek, that maintained an orthodox position), striving for electoral success was seen as but one part of the party's activity—political militancy in the workplace and in trade unions claiming equal, if not greater, weight.

The CPSU fell from power in 1991, two years after the withdrawal of Soviet support had led to the collapse of the Eastern European regimes in 1989. Communist parties remained in power in China, Vietnam, North Korea, and Cuba. At that time the first two of these were already strug-

## ORGANIZATION OF A COMMUNIST PARTY

**NATIONAL LEVEL**

- Presidium or Politburo
- Control Commission
- Central Committee
- Secretariat
- All Union or National Party Congress
- Administrative agencies and social organizations

**REPUBLIC OR PROVINCE LEVEL**

- Republic Party Conference
- Committee
- Bureau

**CITY AND DISTRICT LEVEL**

- City Conference
- Committee
- District Conference
- Committee
- Bureau
- Bureau

**PRIMARY UNITS**

- General Meeting
- General Meeting
- General Meeting
- General Meeting
- Bureau
- Bureau
- Bureau
- Bureau

## 2. The Communist Party of the Soviet Union

From 1917 until early 1990, the Communist Party of the Soviet Union (CPSU) was the central institution in the Soviet political system. Founded in 1898 as the Russian Social Democratic Workers' Party, the CPSU ruled with virtually unrivaled power for more than seven decades following the revolution of October 1917, first as the self-styled embodiment of the "dictatorship of the proletariat" and from 1961 as "the party of the whole Soviet people."

**The Vanguard.** According to the 1977 Soviet constitution, the party was the "leading and guiding force of Soviet society and the nucleus of its political system, of all state organs and public organizations." It supposedly "determined the general perspectives of the development of society and the course of the home and foreign policy of the USSR, directed the great constructive work of the Soviet people," and imparted a "planned, systematic and theoretically substantiated character to their struggle for the victory of communism." Its membership of 19,487,822 in January 1989, the last year before its decline, embraced almost a tenth of the adult population; the so-called "best" 45.4% were classified as workers, 11.4% as collective farm peasants, and the remaining 43.2% as white-collar employees, including the intelligentsia, drawn from a wide range of professions and occupations; it had representatives of over 100 nationalities, with members in practically all workplaces.

**Party Monopolies.** The party controlled a complex set of offices and committees that overlapped with those of the state, economic management, and the trade unions and offered a career structure for the politically ambitious. Party membership was, indeed, a necessary qualification for a career in administration, and millions of Soviet citizens depended on the party in their working life—some for their very livelihood. The party constituted an enormous organization that functioned through thousands of local offices. As an important employer, it offered jobs to politicians at all levels and to thousands of auxiliary staff: secretaries and office workers, janitors, and chauffeurs, computer operators, office managers, and even social scientists.

**The Economy.** The CPSU also played a wider economic role. It charted the course of economic development via the state planning mechanism, to which it issued control figures establishing development priorities, and it was an economic force in its own right. The party owned or used large amounts of office space and other property; it possessed fleets of vehicles; it ran publishing houses, hotels, and vacation homes; and it consumed office furniture and equipment, paper, ink, typewriter ribbons, and floppy disks.

Its members' entrance fees and earnings-related monthly subscriptions, plus profits of its 11 publishing houses and other subsidiary enterprises, enabled the party to draw from colossal funds to cover salaries of party officers and employees and the upkeep of various party facilities. In 1988 running the central apparatus alone cost 50.4 million rubles (3% of the party's total budget).

**Membership.** As an institution, the party made enormous demands on its members. Individuals were not free to join or to leave; rather, they were identified at their place of work as potential recruits, invited to apply, and then subjected

gling with the problems of reform that had brought down the CPSU, while the beleaguered orthodoxy of the last two regimes was becoming necessarily exposed and vulnerable. Despite the demise of the CPSU itself and the decline or transformation of other communist parties, the remaining ruling parties still hold on to the features that long have distinguished them from other political parties, their vanguard role, and their organization.

MICHAEL WALLER
*Keele University*

### Bibliography

Fischer-Galati, Stephen, *The Communist Parties of Eastern Europe* (Columbia Univ. Press 1979).
Hill, Ronald J., and Peter Frank, *The Soviet Communist Party*, 3d ed. (Allen and Unwin 1986).
Kautsky, John H., *Communism and the Politics of Development: Persistent Myths and Changing Behavior* (John Wiley 1968).
Tiersky, Ronald, *Ordinary Stalinism* (Allen and Unwin 1985).
Waller, Michael, *The End of the Communist Power Monopoly* (Manchester Univ. Press 1993).
Waller, Michael, and Meindert Fennema, *Communist Parties in Western Europe: Decline or Adaptation?* (Blackwell 1988).

to a complex admissions procedure, including a year's probation, to screen out undesirables—those who were insufficiently devoted to the cause. Regular study of the classic Marxist texts and a willingness to accept binding discipline were part of the life of the ordinary member, as were paying subscriptions and attending monthly branch meetings. And, while under Leonid Brezhnev in the 1970s, the party elite—the *nomenklatura* officials, appointed through the party-based nomination mechanism—exploited the system for their own private benefit, ordinary members were subject to disciplinary proceedings, up to and including expulsion, for "losing contact with their organization" or other misdemeanors. Without such an apprenticeship, however, a career of responsibility, authority, or power was unthinkable.

**Ideology.** The party claimed its authority on the basis of its supposed understanding of the "scientific" ideology of Marxism-Leninism, which had allegedly identified the dynamic of human society in class relations and mapped out the way toward the classless society of communism. However, even before the Bolshevik Revolution the ideology had become a means of political struggle and control. In later years this ideology was manipulated by leaders and imposed on their subordinates as a test of loyalty. From Joseph Stalin onward it proved almost infinitely malleable and was invoked to support surprisingly unsocialist principles of inequality and privilege, not to mention the horrors of the purges and forced labor, the show trials, and the 1939 pact with Nazism.

This flexibility in practice, coupled with the assertion of universal correctness and applicability, rendered the ideology a powerful weapon in the political struggle and led, in Mikhail Gorbachev's words, to the party's "infallibility complex." Advances in the ideology were signaled in the speeches of party leaders and in the resolutions of the quinquennial congresses that laid down the official line or current interpretation. This ideology was binding on all party members and organizations and was converted into state policy for application by all citizens.

**Institutions.** The CPSU was, for all intents and purposes, a permanently ruling organization that deployed its members in strategic positions in the institutions of rule: legislatures, the courts, economic management, state administration. It was in a dominant position, able to have its policies adopted and applied, subject only to inefficiencies in the system and resistance among those responsible for their implementation. As became clear in the Gorbachev era in the late 1980s, however, those inefficiencies and that resistance were powerful antidotes to the authority conferred on the center by democratic centralism. The need to rely on an apparatus whose interests lay in perpetuating its members' own comfortable lifestyle was a fundamental weakness of a reforming general secretary, as Nikita Khrushchev in the 1950s and Mikhail Gorbachev in the 1980s discovered. Those two leaders, along with Yuri Andropov (Brezhnev's immediate successor in 1982), attempted to return the party to its more puritan spirit and image, ultimately with little success.

The party's dominance extended to the Soviet state, which was politically subordinate to the party whose policy it dutifully implemented. The relationship was often seen as one of party dictatorship, and from the earliest years *podmena*, or party interference in the work of state and other bodies, was a problem that prevented effective administration. The opportunities for this were enhanced by the overlapping or interlocking membership of state and party bodies and further entrenched by career patterns that embraced both sets of institutions.

**Democratic Centralist Structure.** The CPSU ruled through a complex network of structures, from the quinquennial congresses down through conferences and committees at the republic, province, city, and district levels and ultimately to the branches, or primary party organizations (PPOs), in almost every place of employment in the country. Every party member—including state officials—belonged to such an organization. Monthly meetings discussed the admission of new members and allocated party assignments. District or city conferences formally elected the party committee and delegates to the provincial or republican conference, rising on up the hierarchy to the All-Union Party Congress. Although acquiring the quality of a rally, this forum discussed broader policy matters and formally elected the Central Committee, which in turn elected the Politburo and the general secretary, the highest party office. Such indirect party elections, guided by the superior organs, deprived rank-and-file members of any say in selecting the leadership, and democratic centralism ensured that power lay in the hands of officials at whatever level.

Locally, the district committee performed a crucial coordinating role. The first secretary was the most powerful politician in a given locality, and a substantial apparatus conducted the party's work, its various departments supervising both internal party matters and the administrative areas that were nominally the state's responsibility. The occupants of such positions, who also controlled recruitment, extended their privileges and perquisites in the 1970s and later resisted Gorbachev's attempts to simplify the structure and define the party's role more precisely, delineating it from the state.

In short, the CPSU created the system and directed it, using its own officers and members to ensure the compliance of other institutions, including the political security agencies, through which the population was controlled. The party administrators, or apparatchiks, dominated the system and were responsible to their superiors through patronage links; through *nomenklatura* they in turn could dispense patronage by arranging appointments for associates. Corruption, nepotism, cronyism, and other antidemocratic practices invaded the apparatus and became endemic but were hidden from the public by official party and state secrecy.

Nevertheless, the apparatchiks performed vital functions, unblocking bottlenecks in the economy and generally lubricating the administrative wheels of Soviet society. It was widely understood that the party committee, rather than the state office, was the place to turn to get things done. This boosted the apparatchiks' power and prestige. They set the tone of the system, and their understanding of how society was actually run, together with their own self-defensive networks, repeatedly proved a significant obstacle to reform. The image of the faceless bureaucrat proved correct, and the leaders of the abortive coup of Aug. 19, 1991, were drawn from such a background: they hoped to maintain the system of rule based on administrative and command methods, for which a privileged and comfortable lifestyle was a highly desirable reward.

By that stage, Boris Yeltsin, who had resigned from the CPSU in July 1990, had subsequently won election to the Russian presidency as an independent. He moved to destroy the party's power by banning its operation in state economic and administrative enterprises in Russia. At the time of the coup, he nationalized the party's assets on the territory of the Russian republic and subsequently forced Gorbachev to resign as general secretary and to recommend the disbanding of the Central Committee; Yeltsin formally banned the party in Russia in November 1991 (although later this was partially rescinded by the Constitutional Court).

**Conclusion.** As the evolution of the power and influence of the CPSU shows, in the 1920s a machine for winning power in a revolutionary situation was converted into the central element of power for rapidly modernizing a backward, politically inexperienced society. In the 1930s an elite of committed radicals became a mechanism for imposing discipline on the new managerial class, and from the 1960s onward that class used the party as a means of establishing its own control over a society whose increasing complexity and sophistication led it to make demands for which the CPSU was unprepared. Although various successor parties claimed the mantle—undoubtedly with a view to obtaining access to the former institution's substantial wealth—and although a "Revival-Unification" congress was held outside Moscow in February 1993, the chances of a return to power by the CPSU are remote. A dozen or more successor parties reorganized during 1993, but they too were banned following the constitutional crisis of September-October 1993 and forbidden to participate in the elections to a new state Duma (parliament). The CPSU, in attempting in the conditions of the 1930s to build communism—a model society characterized by wealth, freedom, harmony, and social homogeneity, according to the official rhetoric of decades past—but having signally failed to satisfy the most basic wants and needs of a complex and demanding society, undermined not only its own position but also the very idea of socialism and communism based on Marxist principles.

RONALD J. HILL, *Trinity College, Dublin*

### Bibliography

Armstrong, John A., *The Politics of Totalitarianism: The Communist Party of the Soviet Union from 1934 to the Present* (Random House 1961).

Hill, Ronald J., and Peter Frank, *The Soviet Communist Party*, 3d. ed. (Unwin Hyman 1986).

Hough, Jerry F., *The Soviet Prefects: The Local Party Organs in Industrial Decision-Making* (Harvard Univ. Press 1969).

Lowenhardt, John, et al., *The Rise and Fall of the Soviet Politburo* (UCL Press 1992).

Rees, E. A., ed., *The Soviet Communist Party in Disarray* (St. Martin's 1992).

Schapiro, Leonard, *The Communist Party of the Soviet Union*, 2d ed. (Methuen 1970).

## 3. The Communist Party of China

The Communist Party of China (CPC) is the largest and one of the last ruling communist parties in the world. It was founded in 1920 from the small radical study groups that had sprung up in metropolitan centers. Following a long armed struggle, the CPC seized state power in 1949 and established the People's Republic of China (PRC). It has remained in power ever since.

**Unique Features.** Unlike in Russia, where the party suddenly found itself in power, or in Eastern Europe, where most communist regimes were installed as baggage-train governments, the CPC derived legitimacy from an extensive struggle to gain national power. It fought a protracted guerrilla war against the Japanese (1937—1945) and was twice engaged in a civil war with the nationalist party of China (1927—1937 and 1945—1949). This experience before seizing state power had a number of implications for the post-1949 system.

First, the revolution was homegrown. Mao Tsetung (Mao Zedong), who effectively led the CPC from 1935 until his death in 1976, made it clear that he was not leading the fight in a war of liberation simply to bring the CPC under Soviet tutelage. The perception of many Chinese that the CPC rather than the nationalist party was at the forefront of the nationalist struggle was important in undermining the latter's position in the subsequent civil war.

Second, from 1937 onward the CPC controlled a number of areas with a total population of between 80 and 100 million people. This enabled the CPC to experiment with its own policies of social and economic transformation before it gained state power. These two factors meant that the CPC's leaders were quite willing to reject Soviet advice when they felt it ran counter to China's national interest. This background proved to be valuable in the late 1950s, when the Chinese leaders became aware of the inherent problems in the Soviet model (the yawning gap between rural and urban development, the excessive attention paid to heavy industry as opposed to light industry and agriculture, and the emergence of new elites based on the party officials and new technocrats). In 1958 the CPC embarked on its own course of development in the Great Leap Forward. This precipitated the split with the Communist Party of the Soviet Union, and even though the policies proved too ambitious and ended in economic disaster, it is important to note that the CPC did not turn back to the Soviet model of development but continued to seek its own path to socialism.

Third, the guerrilla and civil wars meant that most senior party leaders also played a significant military role, thus blurring the civil-military distinction. Functional overlap has continued in the People's Republic of China, with leaders often holding top party, army, and state positions. While a major thrust of the reforms has been to produce a clear separation between organizational lines, this problem persists. For example, the current secretary-general of the CPC, Chiang Tse-min (Jiang Zemin), is also the nation's president and the chair of the central military affairs commission.

Fourth, the need to fight against the Japanese not only provided the CPC with legitimacy but also forced the adoption of the tactic of the united front to appeal to a broad section of the population for support. This policy of class collaboration rather than class conflict was pursued after 1949 until policy, radicalized in the late 1950s, culminated in the large-scale class struggle launched by Mao Tse-tung in the Cultural Revolution (1966—1976). This movement tore the party apart and undermined its credibility and legitimacy in the eyes of many. With the emphasis on economic modernization since 1978, however, the CPC has revived the emphasis on class harmony and the united front. Indeed the *Work Report* adopted by the 14th party congress (October 1992) referred to the new policies as amounting to "another great revolution" under which China's senior leader, Teng Hsiao-p'ing (Deng Xiaoping), has put together a new coalition of classes to modernize China's still-backward economy.

**Democratic Centralism.** Since the mid-1920s the CPC has been governed in theory by the principles of democratic centralism that subordinate the lower to the higher levels and the individual to the collective. On this basis, 3 million primary organizations in the workplace or neighborhood form the bottom of a pyramid of power that leads up to the National Party Congress, which convenes in Beijing once every five years. According to the party statutes, this is the CPC's supreme decision-making body, but its unwieldy size (nearly 2,000 delegates) and its infrequent meetings mean that real power lies elsewhere—among the various patron-client relationships and the informal groupings of elderly party veterans at the top who control the political agenda.

**The Vanguard of Economic Reform.** At the 14th National Party Congress, convened in 1992 to set policy direction for the 21st century, nearly 2,000 delegates representing 51 million party members ratified the decisions of China's senior leaders, many of whom hold no official position. The congress proclaimed a victory for Teng Hsiao-p'ing's program of rapid economic transformation accompanied by tight political control. Teng's theory of "socialism with Chinese characteristics" became the cornerstone of the newly revised party statutes. This theory is intended to remove ideological objections to the continuation of wide-ranging economic experimentation by claiming that, in the current phase of development, both capitalist and socialist techniques are valuable. The end result is to allow the market to play a greater role in the economy than that offered by any other ruling communist party to date.

In line with this emphasis on economic modernization, significant changes have taken place in the composition of the party membership as Teng and his supporters have tried to replace hard-line ideologues with better trained, reform-oriented officials. A clear Politburo majority favors increased reliance on market forces and supports decentralization. These economic reforms have resulted in a devolution of power to the provinces. This trend can be observed in the marked increase in the representation of the provinces in the CPC's central organs. Some 70% of the delegates to the 14th National Party Congress were drawn from the provinces with representation from the central party and government apparatus dropping to 16.5%. Further, while there were fewer military delegates to the congress than in 1987 (13th National Party Congress), their representation on the Central Committee has increased, reflecting the growing importance of the People's Liberation Army to the continuation of party rule since the repression of the student-led protests of 1989.

The emphasis on economic reform has also affected party membership as a whole. The criteria for membership have changed over the years, reflecting changes in ideology and recruitment policies. In the 1990s the emphasis was on recruiting better-educated members rather than "workers, soldiers, and peasants," as was the case during the Cultural Revolution. In the early 1990s some 30% of party officials had received a college education as opposed to only 18% in the late 1970s. Party membership remains important in China, although other avenues to wealth and power have opened up. It is probably true to say that whereas in the past young people may have been attracted to join because of the party's prestige, in the 1990s it was seen as a necessary step for career advancement or for laying the necessary connections to smooth the wheels of finance and speculation.

**Threats to Party Rule.** While the CPC's clear commitment to rapid economic reform may offer it one last chance to position itself at the forefront of reform rather than appearing as an antique body engaged in increasingly irrelevant ideological polemics, a number of serious problems persist that threaten its continued rule. The process of institutionalization has not progressed far enough despite the repeated mention in party publications. Individual prestige and length of service to the party are far more important than any formal position one might hold. Thus it is known that the real decision-maker in China is Teng Hsiao-p'ing even though he holds no formal leadership position. The reform drive of the 1990s is tightly linked to Teng's name and his prestige and capacity to prod other leaders to support his initiatives. This personalization of the program, while understandable over the short term, reveals one of the enduring problems of the Chinese political system: the incapacity to institutionalize policy-making and the consequent need to invoke the name of the "supreme individual" to legitimize policy choice. To this extent Teng has behaved in precisely the same way as Mao Tsetung. This opens up the prospect of a tenacious power struggle after Teng's death. Overreliance on the individual and the cavalier way in which the formal structures are treated mean that the main mechanism for leadership change remains the purge, making succession and policy management extremely unstable.

Finally, the CPC has always been hostile to political activity that takes place beyond its direct control and has generally sought to crush it. Yet the CPC's own policies of economic modernization are creating an increasingly complex society in which many different interests seek to coexist. The party, however, has rejected any meaningful political reform that might seek to accommodate these new interests and groups. Consequently, many either ignore the party, engage in political activities beyond the formal structures, or become increasingly opposed to the system. Unless the CPC is willing to overhaul its administrative structure, its grip on rule will remain fragile and it might have to rely increasingly on the use of force against China's citizens.

TONY SAICH
*Sinologisch Instituut, Rijksuniversiteit Leiden*

**Bibliography**

Manion, Melanie, "The Cadre Management System, Post-Mao: The Appointment, Promotion, Transfer and Removal of Party and State Leaders," *China Quarterly* 102 (1985).

Saich, Tony, "Much Ado about Nothing: Party Reform in the Eighties," in *The Chinese State in the Era of Economic Reform: The Road to Crisis,* ed. by Gordon White (M. E. Sharpe 1991).

Saich, Tony, "The Fourteenth Party Congress: A Programme for Authoritarian Rule," *China Quarterly* 132 (1992).

Saich, Tony, *The Rise to Power of the Chinese Communist Party: Documents and Analysis, 1920–1949* (M. E. Sharpe 1994).

Teiwes, Frederick C., *Leadership, Legitimacy, and Conflict in China* (M. E. Sharpe 1984).

White, Gordon, *Riding the Tiger: The Politics of Economic Reform in Post-Mao China* (Basingstoke 1993).

Young, Graham, "Party Reforms," in *China: Modernization in the Nineteen Eighty's*, ed. by Joseph Y. S. Cheng (St. Martin's 1990).

## 4. The Communist Fringe of the Postcommunist World

The collapse of communism in Eastern Europe and the Soviet Union has had a considerable effect on communist parties and groups elsewhere. The ruling communist parties in Eastern Europe and most of the 26 communist parties outside Europe had looked to the USSR as a model of social, political, and economic development, and they had depended on the "mother country of revolution and socialism" for ideological, financial, military, and diplomatic backing. With very few exceptions, the nonruling communist parties also relied on the Soviet state and the Communist Party of the Soviet Union. But the degree of dependency varied between countries and parties and even between ruling and nonruling communist political elites. The demise of communism at its source deprived all of them of important structural and ideological connections.

**Eastern Europe.** The decline of the Eastern European communist parties actually started in the spring of 1989, when Mikhail Gorbachev let it be known that he considered the Brezhnev doctrine of limited sovereignty to be defunct. This doctrine, which was used as a justification for the Warsaw Treaty Organization's invasion of Czechoslovakia in 1968, contained the threat of Soviet military intervention against any substantial challenges to communist power. Once the doctrine was removed, the Eastern European communist regimes began to collapse.

The once-ruling communist parties not only suffered from identity problems but, more important, also experienced a substantial credibility gap. They swiftly embraced a reformed socialist posture and ideology and promptly abandoned the cornerstones of communist doctrine: dictatorship of the proletariat, democratic centralism, and the party's vanguard role in the society. Instead, they began advocating multiparty democracy, a free-market economy, and a rapprochement with the rest of Europe, with a view toward membership in the European Community. At first all the former ruling communist parties, with the exception of those of Albania and Bulgaria, were reduced to isolation, but they recovered somewhat during 1992 and 1993.

The Polish United Worker's Party (PUWP) was the first to lose power. In the semidemocratic elections of June 1989, the PUWP did not win a single seat in the newly established Senate, and the humiliated communists found themselves unable to form a government. The marginalization of the Polish communists was obvious. After the formation of the Solidarity government in August 1989, the PUWP was faced with virtual extinction unless it transformed itself into a broadly based left-wing party. It attempted to do so in January 1990, when it changed its name to Social Democracy of the Polish Republic, but it opted for yet another change in October 1991, when it formed the Democratic Left Alliance and garnered 11.7% of the vote in subsequent elections. Its fate changed again in 1993, when the former communists once again became the governing party by winning the majority of the seats in parliament.

The former ruling Hungarian Socialist Workers' Party (HSWP) was the first communist party in Eastern Europe to alter its outlook while still in power. The increasingly organized discontent throughout 1988 motivated the party to accept that Hungary would become a multiparty democracy. In October 1989 the HSWP changed its name to the Hungarian Socialist Party (HSP) and adopted social-democratic principles and a commitment to mixed forms of property and a socialist/market economy. These changes were clearly aimed at presenting the renamed party as a new organization not tainted by the legacy of communist rule. Despite these changes, the HSP received only 10.89% of the vote during the first free elections in 1990, but it attracted a much larger percentage of votes in several by-elections held since.

The Bulgarian Communist Party became the Bulgarian Socialist Party (BSP) in April 1990 and declared itself a party of democratic socialism and a part of the world socialist Left. The once-homogeneous communist movement in Bulgaria split into numerous factions. In addition to the BSP, a dozen groups and political parties displayed the entire spectrum of Marxist, Leninist, Trotskyite, and neo-Marxist variations. Although the BSP remained popular, its support declined from 47% to 33% in the early 1990s.

In Czechoslovakia the communist party expelled most of its leaders associated with the post-1968 regime after the Velvet Revolution of 1989 and professed a policy of "national understanding," indicating its readiness to work with the new democratic forces. The Communist Party of Czechoslovakia underwent a number of transformations before its collapse prior to the decisive parliamentary elections of June 1992. The Communist Party of Bohemia and Moravia (KSCM) was established alongside the already existing Communist Party of Slovakia. Before the election the KSCM together with a smaller group, the Democratic Left, formed the Left Block and emerged as the second-strongest party in the Czech Republic in 1992. The Slovak Communist Party, renamed the Party of Democratic Left, became one of the principal exponents of Slovak nationalism. It won a considerable measure of support by advocating more state intervention, increased government subsides for industry, and larger welfare benefits. In the early 1990s it became the second-strongest party in Slovakia.

The Albanian Socialist Party (ASP), formerly the Albanian Party of Labor, was returned to power in the first free elections in 1991, but it suffered a decisive loss in 1992, when the newly created opposition party, the Albanian Democratic Party, won by a landslide. As the sole opposition force, the ASP launched a sharp offensive against the ruling Democrats and made impressive gains in the subsequent local elections of July 1992.

In the 1980s the once-powerful Romanian Communist Party claimed membership equaling 24% of the Romanian population, the highest percentage of party membership per population anywhere in the communist world. The party was overthrown during a bloody revolution in December 1989 and collapsed in its wake. Although declared illegal by the new government in January 1990, the party reappeared in late 1990 as the Socialist Party of Labor.

**The Third World.** For a generation of Third World leaders, Soviet communism represented an alternative model of political, social, and economic development and a successful example of effective social control. The USSR and its Eastern European allies were also an important source of military and technical support for the newly independent countries. The post-1989 Eastern European pattern of disintegration of communist party rule or fundamental ideological adjustment has not, by and large, been repeated in the Third World. Most of the communist parties, with the exception of those of North Korea and Cuba, were quick to adjust their ideas to the post-Soviet circumstances. In some cases where the party lost power, it managed to retain considerable dominance over the directions of political and economic developments through its control of the army and the bureaucracy.

**Asia.** The Asian ruling and nonruling communist parties proved to be remarkably resilient to substantial modifications. Although collapse of communism around the world left it without allies, the Korean Worker's Party (KWP) has been the most resistant to change. The KWP, in power since 1949, still adheres to the North Korean version of the communist doctrine designed by its leader, Kim Il Sung. Based on extreme nationalism and xenophobia, the so-called *chuch'e* ideology (philosophy of self-reliance) is still the basis for the political, social, and economic structures of the country. The party has shown no willingness to make any compromises by accelerating the process of grooming Kim Il Sung's son Kim Jong Il as his successor.

The Communist Party of Vietnam (CPV) still monopolizes power. Although its 7th congress (1991) backed a "renovation program," progress toward political reforms was effectively halted in 1990 as apprehension spread within the party over events in the Soviet Union and Eastern Europe. The Vietnamese communists argued in stereotypical fashion that, while the socialist countries faced a profound crisis, the Vietnamese people "had resolved not to accept any path other than the socialist one." They opposed the establishment of a multiparty system on the grounds that it would create conditions for the growth of internal and foreign reactionary forces. With the suspension of Soviet aid, the CPV increasingly emphasized the need for economic reforms and allowed a slight liberalization of the economy including some private ownership and joint ventures with foreign companies. As the government promotes an economic system with a market mechanism managed and regulated by the state, Vietnam's leaders increasingly argue that communist rule can be combined with capitalist development.

In Cambodia the Kampuchean People's Revolutionary Party (KPRP), installed by Vietnam in 1979, radically transformed itself in anticipation of the signing of the Paris peace agreement. Just prior to the signing of this accord, which brought to an end 13 years of civil war and created the UN Transitional Authority in Cambodia in October 1991, the KPRP changed its name to the Cambodian People's Party and endorsed a multiparty liberal democracy and a free-market economy. The day-to-day running of the country remained largely in the hands of a coalition government dominated by the former communists until a new constitution was adopted and Norodom Sihanouk was installed as king in September 1993. The Party of Democratic Kampuchea (Khmer Rouge) that controlled the government of the notorious Pol Pot regime between 1975 and 1979 still retained control over large parts of northern and central Cambodia and showed no signs of changing its ideological platform or policies.

In Mongolia the Mongolian People's Revolutionary Party (MPRP), voted out in 1990, returned to power in June 1992, after it had streamlined its structure and modified its ideology in an attempt to distance itself from its communist roots. A similar scenario unfolded in Afghanistan, where the former communist party became the Homeland Party in 1990. It has not disappeared in the wake of the mujahedin victory of 1992 in Afghanistan. The divisions within the mujahedin ranks and the continuing cohesion of the former communist regime's military, political, and administrative structures have allowed the communists a place in the new coalition that runs the fragmented country. In Laos the Lao People's Revolutionary Party (LPRP) remains dominant but shares power with other parties. In 1991 it further improved its position when the LPRP party president, Kaysone Phomvihane, became president of Laos, a powerful position established under the newly approved constitution.

The demise of communism in Eastern Europe and the former Soviet Union had little impact on the nonruling parties in Asia. In Sri Lanka the two most important communist groups, the Communist Party of Sri Lanka and the historically Troskyite Lanka Sama Samaja Party, merged in January 1993 to form a single communist party, the United Socialist Alliance. Nepal is one of the few countries where the communists have increased their popular support and gained access to the centers of power since 1989. The country's constitutional transformation from an absolute monarchy into a multiparty democracy in 1990 brought about the unification of the Nepalese communists.

**Latin America and the Caribbean.** Little substantive change has taken place among the ruling and nonruling communist parties in Latin America and the Caribbean. The Cuban Communist Party (PCC) retains its Marxist-Leninist orthodoxy and the monopoly of power. Fidel Castro has firmly repudiated the developments in Eastern Europe and the former Soviet Union as events with no consequence for Cuba, even though Russian and Eastern European economic subsidies on which the country relied extensively have been cut off. Although faced with enormous difficulties, the PCC has closed ranks behind Castro and has shut down any serious debate on the country's future. The February 1992 elections, heralded by the Castro regime as free and democratic, offered a single list of candidates, some 70% of whom were Communist party members. The nonparty members were not outright opponents of the regime, but the election did introduce a direct secret ballot instead of election by party-dominated municipal and regional councils.

In Nicaragua the Sandinista National Liberation Front (FSLN) lost power to the National Opposition Union (UNO), led by Violeta Barrios de Chamoro, in 1990, but the FSLN retained considerable influence in the military and the state bureaucracy. The UNO government therefore had to rely increasingly on Sandinista leadership and the Sandinista Popular Army to maintain political stability. In fact, since 1991 the FSLN has been in unofficial coalition with the UNO and may regain power in future elections.

Despite communism's demise elsewhere, the fringe revolutionary movement, basing its activities on a mixture of Marxism-Leninism, Maoism, and Che Guevara's writings, has remained virtually intact. The notorious Shining Path movement (Sendero Luminoso), which began its "people's war" in June 1980, plans a world revolution from the Peruvian Andes. The movement, terrorizing Peru for over a decade and claiming more than 25,000 victims, has financed its campaign from cocaine deals in the jungle. But Shining Path has declined somewhat since the 1992 arrest of its leader, Abimael Guzmán Reynoso.

**Africa.** Africa once boasted nine ruling Marxist parties and a similar number of regimes guided by principles of "scientific socialism." Events in Eastern Europe and the former Soviet Union had important implications for many African countries that had close connections with the old regimes. In two of the former communist regimes, Angola and Mozambique, the erstwhile communist parties remain intact albeit in coalition with former opponents.

Since its independence from Portugal in November 1975, Angola has been ruled by the Popular Movement for the Liberation of Angola (MPLA), reconstructed in 1977 as the MPLA Worker's Party (MPLA-PT). Prompted by a deteriorating economy and by the 15-year civil war between the MPLA and the American-backed National Union for the Complete Independence of Angola (UNITA) forces, the MPLA-PT in 1990 replaced its Marxist-Leninist ideology with a commitment to democratic socialism, agreed to relinquish its monopoly on power, and promised to implement a multiparty democracy. The withdrawal of Cuban forces and advisers who had fought alongside the MPLA-PT since 1975 also contributed to this change in attitude. On May 31, 1991, Pres. Jose Eduardo dos Santos and the UNITA leader, Jonas Savimbi, signed a cease-fire agreement in Lisbon to end hostilities. In the first multiparty elections of September 1992, the MPLA-PT secured a majority of seats in the National Assembly.

In Mozambique, Guinea Bissau, Cape Verde, São Tomé and Príncipe, the Congo, Benin, Burkina Faso, and Zimbabwe, where ruling communist parties had been in power since the 1970s, multiparty politics and legalized opposition parties were approved in the early 1990s. The communist parties abandoned their adherence to Marxism-Leninism and frequently adopted new names and new organizational structures. The situation in Benin presents a typical example of the flow of events since the demise of the communist parties of Eastern Europe and the former Soviet Union. Following mass demonstrations in January and February 1990, the ruling People's Revolutionary Party (PRP) dropped its commitment to Marxism-Leninism. The National Conference of Active Forces of the Nation, convened in February 1990, proclaimed itself a sovereign body, suspended the 1977 Marxist constitution and all existing state institutions in order to provide for multiparty politics, and appointed an interim government headed by Nicephone Soglo, an economist and former World Bank administrator. A draft constitution establishing a multiparty democracy and direct presidential elections was approved in a nationwide referendum on Dec. 2, 1990. In the subsequent parliamentary elections (1991), the newly formed Union for the Triumph of Democratic Renewal (a three-party coalition that included the communists) secured only 12 seats in the 64-seat National Assembly.

In Ethiopia the ruling but minuscule communist Ethiopian Worker's Party also tried to shed some of its communist identity by renaming itself the Democratic Unity Party, but it was ousted from power and outlawed in 1991 in a move to allow wider political participation. Its ouster, however, was achieved not by the triumph of democratic values and aspirations, as in Eastern Europe, but by the victory of former Maoist guerrillas of the Ethiopian People's Revolutionary Democratic Front, armed largely by Iraq and also supported by the United States.

The South African Communist Party (SACP) is one of a very few communist parties to be legalized after the demise of communism at its source and one of the few whose popularity is increasing. Founded in 1921, it was declared illegal in 1950 and operated underground until it was legalized in February 1990. During its clandestine years the party received political, financial, and diplomatic support from the Soviet Union, the Eastern European regimes, and Cuba. Despite the changes in the communist world, the 1991 SACP congress rejected proposals to adopt a social-democratic program and voted to continue the party's adherence to Marxism-Leninism and to maintain its traditional structure based on party cells. Most of the SACP recruits since 1989 are young, unemployed black males. The SACP maintains close alliance with the African National Congress and the Congress of South African Trade Unions. Many among its leadership also hold high-ranking positions in these two organizations.

The Yemeni Socialist Party, the only Marxist party ever to rule an Arab country (South Yemen), has through the unification of South Yemen and the Yemen Arab Republic (May 22, 1990) become one of the two ruling parties of the new Republic of Yemen, with political machinery, army, and intelligence forces intact.

**Western Europe.** Some of the most profound and far-reaching changes have occurred among the nonruling but traditionally powerful communist parties of Western European nations. One of the most interesting examples of adaptations to postcommunist realities is that of the Italian Communist Party (PCI). The party, which has been in the process of transformation for at least two decades, was dissolved at its 20th congress in February 1991. The decision marked the culmination of a bitter 15-month internal struggle over the nature and place of a distinct communist party within the Italian political system and the postbipolar world.

As it dissolved the PCI, the party congress launched the Democratic Party of the Left (PDS), abandoned the goal of constructing socialism, and instead called for the comprehensive democratization of society. PDS also dismantled the traditional communist structure based on party cells and replaced it with a loose organizational framework. A group of PCI hard-liners broke away to establish the Communist Refoundation (RC). It claims a membership of 100,000, including 9,000 members of the Proletarian Democracy, a left-wing party that merged with the RC in 1991. In the April 1992 elections, the first nationwide electoral test, all the communists combined drew fewer votes (21.7%) than the PCI had before the communist transformations.

Two other Western European communist parties have disintegrated since 1989. The Communist Party of the Netherlands, the second-oldest communist party in the world, dissolved in 1991. It merged with the Pacifist Socialist Party and the Radical Political Party to form the Green Left. The Belgian Communist Party, which was always very weak (polling only 2% to 3% of the national vote), lost its two remaining members of parliament in the 1980s and ceased to exist in November 1991.

The Communist Party of Finland (SKP), once one of the strongest communist parties in Western Europe, has been deeply divided between the Eurocommunist and hard-line factions since the 1960s, but the collapse of communism in Eastern Europe brought the factions together in 1990 when the SKP, the hard-line Finnish Communist Party-Unity, and the Democratic Alternative formed the new Left Alliance. They adopted a vague program advocating a just society, "red" and "green" values, and social and ecological management of the market economy. In 1991 the Left Alliance won approximately 10.1% of the vote and gained about the same number of seats in parliaments as the combined figure for all the communist groups in 1987.

The primary communist groups in Spain formed the United Left (IU) in 1986. In addition to several left-wing and independent groups, it incorporated the Communist Party of Spain (PCE) and the Communist Party of the Peoples of Spain. In joining the IU coalition the PCE sought to overcome its isolation and the electoral decline it suffered during the early 1980s. The alliance increased its electoral support during consecutive elections in 1989 and 1993. The PCE itself has made little if any attempt to adjust to the postcommunist world. At its 13th congress (1992), proposals to initiate ideological and structural changes similar to those adopted by the Italian Communist Party were defeated. The congress reiterated the party's adherence to revolutionary Marxism and other traditional tenets of communist doctrine.

The communists in Greece, split since 1968 into several distinctive organizations, continue to maintain their respective ideological positions and to attract virtually undiminished electoral support. The traditionalist, pro-Soviet Greek Communist Party—Exterior (KKE-Exterior), standing as a part of the Left coalition, received 10.97% of the vote in 1989 and 10.28% in 1990. The Eurocommunist Communist Party of Greece—Renewal Left polled 0.2% in 1989 and 0.1% in 1990. The KKE-Exterior congress (1991) reaffirmed the party's adherence to the traditional communist tenets, Marxism-Leninism, democratic centralism, and the theory of class struggle, making it one of the few unreformed Stalinist parties in Europe.

The French Communist Party (PCF), which in the 1970s and 1980s devoted much energy to promoting the success of the Soviet and Eastern European communist regimes, has also not altered its commitment to Marxism-Leninism. It continues to claim that the collapse of the Soviet Union did not discredit Leninism. The long-standing hard-line leader of the PCF, Georges Marchais, was reelected its secretary-general. But, despite appearances, the party has been in turmoil for several years. While the political bureau continues to support Marchais, a small reformist wing has been advocating change.

The importance of the hard-line, pro-Soviet Portuguese Communist Party steadily declined during the 1980s, when its support dropped from approximately 18% in 1983 to 12% in 1987. Such decline did not occur in Cyprus, where the hardline Cypriot communist party, the Progressive Party of the Working People, increased in strength. In the May 1991 parliamentary election, it reemerged as the second most powerful party on the island, polling 30.6% of the vote (an increase of 3.1% since 1985).

BOGDAN SZAJKOWSKI, *University of Exeter*

**Bibliography:** East, Roger, ed., *Communist and Marxist Parties of the World*, 2d. ed. (Longman 1990); Szajkowski, Bogdan, ed., *New Political Parties of Eastern Europe and the Soviet Union* (Longman 1991).

**COMMUNITY,** in sociological and anthropological terminology, a relatively small, isolated center with a stable population, in which all economic and social services necessary to life can be maintained. The community is one of the oldest forms of human social organization. In the hypothetical community, social relations are primary, direct, and personal, and common values are reinforced and supported by a rich ceremonial life and by folkways and mores, rather than by legislation or police. The individual has little value apart from the group. The family is responsible for an individual's behavior, and this behavior is determined by clearly defined traditional roles based on age, gender, lineage, and family position. Thus individual choice and rational decision-making are precluded.

In a less technical sense, the term *community* generally denotes any small, localized, political, economic, and social unit whose members share values. Thus hamlets, villages, towns, and cities are often considered communities.

The ideal type of community emerges as an intellectual concept when social change threatens to destroy a locality's isolation, traditionalism, and solidarity. The decline of the community has been a recurrent theme in theories about society from ancient to modern times. This decline has been attributed to contacts with other cultures because of depletion of natural resources, trade, conquest, the growth of city and national states, industrialism, transportation and communication, and the emergence of mass society. The ideal type of community is considered to place social and psychological limits on individuals that constitute boundaries within which they can comfortably live. The decline of the community is alleged to destroy these boundaries of self and create a sense of loss that results in personal alienation or social disorganization.

The rise of modern industrial urban society has undoubtedly destroyed the natural boundaries created by social isolation. But the need for a sense of limits within which personal identity and response can be expressed has led to the construction of voluntaristic communities, where the psychological benefits of community life can be gained without recourse to the social isolation of an ecological community. These newer forms—including occupational and professional groups, neighborhood groups, and ethnic and political groups—become the functional equivalents of the older, ecological, isolated community, and they make it possible for their members to avoid the problems of a multidimensional mass society. Their members can find a focus for their social relations, loyalties, and interests.

JOSEPH BENSMAN*
*City College, City University of New York*

**COMMUNITY,** in ecology, a term that refers to all the plant and animal populations within a given area or habitat. A community, representing the living organisms, or biota, of an area, together with its physical environment constitute an ecosystem. For example, a pond, a coral reef, or a forest could each be called an ecosystem. All ecosystems together constitute the earth's biosphere. Communities undergo constant change but nonetheless have certain definable properties, including the occurrence of species dominance, species diversity, and succession.

Species dominance refers to a situation in which the size or biological activity of one or a few of the community's populations becomes greater than that of other species. Communities are often named for these dominant species, as exemplified by the ponderosa pine, spruce-fir, or oak-hickory forest communities.

Communities vary considerably in species diversity, that is, the number of different species they possess. The degree of diversity depends primarily on the state of environmental factors such as light, heat, moisture, food, and shelter because these elements determine the number of available niches, or means of existence, within the community.

Each community has several standard niches. Green plants, for example, occupy a niche as primary producers because they use energy from sunlight for photosynthesis, the process through which they manufacture basic foodstuffs. The herbivores, which can, within a single community, range from plant lice and caterpillars to rabbits and antelope, feed on the primary producers. First-level carnivores, in turn, feed on herbivores, as when ladybird beetles feed on plant lice and lions feed on antelopes, and may themselves be eaten by second-level carnivores.

Parasites feed on other species without killing them, as when ticks feed on mammals, while scavengers feed on dead matter; and decomposers, mainly comprising microorganisms, break down the bodies and excreta of other organisms to less complex substances that can be reused in the food-energy cycle. Organisms can also be described as generalists or specialists, meaning that they are, respectively, able or unable to exist on a highly varied diet or able or unable to live in a wide range of habitats. Humans, for example, are generalists, while koala bears, which feed exclusively on eucalyptus leaves, are specialists.

A community that is self-perpetuating and has attained a stable equilibrium with its physical environment is termed a climax community. If the equilibrium of the climax community is disturbed by factors such as fire, flood, drought, predator plague, or disease, a series of changes immediately begins within the community that may require years, decades, or even centuries to complete. Such changes bring about the replacement of one community with another, until a new climax community develops. This process is known as succession.

DAVID A. OTTO*, *Stephens College*

**COMMUNITY ANTENNA TELEVISION** (CATV), a system that used a strategically located central antenna, an amplifying system, and cables connected directly to a large number of receivers to provide extended and improved reception of commercial television programs. It differed from regular television reception in that television owners shared a central antenna rather than having individual antennas, and they paid to receive programs rather than getting them free. CATV, which evolved into what is now known as cable television, was initially introduced in 1948 by John Walston of Mahanoy City, Pa., in an effort to increase television set sales in his appliance store.

**Growth of Service.** In the early 1950s, CATV systems provided service only to rural areas or small towns that had no local television at all or, at best, poor reception from one or more stations. CATV systems were also implemented in areas where reception was poor or limited by mountain interference or long distances. Besides relaying regular programs from local stations, CATV companies sometimes offered extra services, such as weather reports, stock quotations, and information on amusements.

Eventually CATV service spread to metropolitan areas where television reception was often limited, due to tall buildings in cities that reflected directly transmitted signals, which resulted in a poor picture with a multiplicity of horizontally displaced images, or "ghosts." Underground cable transmission from a central antenna avoided such sources of interference. Service in metropolitan areas also gave the CATV subscriber a wider range of programs; in most localities an extensive choice of channels could not be provided by local broadcasting stations because of interference from other stations that transmitted on the same channels.

**Program Reception.** The central, or master, antenna was located at a point of relatively high elevation atop a high mast that had one or more highly directive antenna arrays directed toward individual television transmitters, which could be hundreds of miles away. The signals received by an antenna array were amplified and fed by coaxial cable to individual television receivers; usually the cable was strung on poles owned by local telephone or utility companies. Each receiver connected to the cable obtained programs on the regular channel positions of the receiver in the same manner that it would from its own antenna. With the towering central antenna, the subscriber received programs that otherwise could be received only by installing a prohibitively costly individual antenna.

**Service Agreements.** Usually CATV service was provided by a private corporation that was granted an exclusive franchise by a local governing body; in turn, the corporation agreed to furnish programs from a specified number of stations and to provide satisfactory monochrome and color picture quality. Each subscriber paid a monthly fee for the cable service. See also TELEVISION—*Broadcasting in the United States—(Cable TV).*

GLENN M. GLASFORD*, *Syracuse University*

**COMMUNITY CHURCH,** one of several kinds of Christian congregations, independent of denominational control, that developed in the 20th century, chiefly in the United States. Generally a community church is composed of two or more congregations of different denominations that had insufficient members or funds to continue separately but are able to support one minister, Sunday school, and service program between them. When such a church retains denominational affiliations, it is called a federated church. Sometimes a community church is formed of individuals of different denominations in areas that had no previous church groups. Because community churches include people of various religious traditions and aim to encourage Christian unity, they have no uniform standard of doctrine or practice. In the United States, the Council of Community Churches has about 200 member churches and many associates.

**COMMUNITY COLLEGE.** See COLLEGES AND UNIVERSITIES; JUNIOR AND COMMUNITY COLLEGES.

**COMMUNITY PROPERTY,** the term used for possessions held mutually by husband and wife under the laws of some states of the United States. The legal concept of community property is based on the assumption that spouses work for their mutual benefit and so share equally in everything acquired after marriage, except property that either receives by gift or inheritance. In the late 1960s, this method of holding property, deriving from old French and Spanish systems, prevailed only in Arizona, California, Idaho, Louisiana, Nevada, New Mexico, Texas, and Washington.

**General Procedure.** Property owned before marriage remains separate. Income from separately owned property is separate except in Idaho, Louisiana, and Texas, where it becomes community property. The parties, by written contract made before or after marriage, may hold their property separately. On the couple's divorce or separation, the courts can dispose of all property, community or separate, on a fair basis.

Critics of the system note that each spouse may manage and control his or her separate property but only the husband may control community property. The system formerly had some usefulness under the old federal tax laws, because it permitted spouses to split their incomes, thus effecting tax savings, but it has no utility under present law, which permits joint returns.

**Varying Laws.** Most of the community property states permit a surviving spouse to retain only half the community property; but in some states if a wife predeceases the husband, he receives all the community property, while if he dies first she receives only one half. In some states property bought during marriage with separate funds becomes community property, in other states it does not. There is no uniform policy on community property as regards creditors.

Since the passage of married women's property acts about 1850, all common-law states have recognized a wife's right to hold and dispose of her own property. However, except in community property states, she has no vested interest in her husband's earnings or assets acquired during marriage. See also ALIMONY.

JULIA PERLES, *Chairwoman*
*Special Committee on Matrimonial Law*
*New York County Lawyers' Association*

**COMMUTATION OF SENTENCE,** the reduction of punishment or sentence after a person has been convicted of a crime. This power is generally vested in either the pardoning board of a state or the governor. A reduction in sentence, after conviction, is not a matter of right but of grace, or favor.

The power to commute or reduce a sentence after imprisonment is broad. Thus, a death sentence may be commuted to imprisonment for life or for a term of years, or a 10-year sentence may be reduced to one year. One commutation of sentence does not necessarily preclude further reduction. For example, a person originally sentenced to death may have that sentence reduced to life imprisonment and later, on further application, may have it reduced still further. A sentence can even be commuted so that the prisoner is discharged from serving any more time.

A commutation does not remove the stigma of guilt or restore civil privileges, such as the right to vote or hold public office, except by operation of a specific law. Commuted sentences may be revoked where they have been obtained by fraud. Also, a commutation of sentence may be conditioned on the prisoner's future behavior. The commission of a new crime, after commutation, ordinarily revokes the commutation, so that the prisoner may be compelled to serve the full original sentence as well as another sentence for the new crime.

SAMUEL G. KLING
*Author of "The Complete Guide to Everyday Law"*

**COMMUTATIVE LAW,** a mathematical law which states that when two objects are combined by any of certain operations, the order in which they are taken does not affect the result. Operations that satisfy the commutative law are said to be "commutative." In arithmetic the operations of addition and multiplication are commutative (for example, $7 + 4 = 4 + 7$) but subtraction and division are not commutative (for example, $4 - 2 \neq 2 - 4$).

The precise definition of the commutative law is based upon sets and operations on sets, as follows. Let $S$ be any set of elements. A binary operation in the set $S$ is a rule, or operation, which assigns some element of $S$ to every pair of elements of $S$. If $*$ is a binary operation, then we let $x * y$ be the element assigned to the pair $x,y$ by $*$. The binary operation is called commutative; that is, $*$ satisfies the commutative law, if, for every pair of elements $x,y$ of $S$, the equality $x * y = y * x$ is true.

FRANCIS A. GREENE S.J.
*Xavier University*

**COMMUTATOR.** See MOTORS, ELECTRIC—*Direct-Current Motors.*

**COMNENUS AND ANGELUS,** kom-nē'nəs, an'jə-ləs, the names of two important and related families that furnished a number of Byzantine emperors.

The first Comnenus to become a Byzantine emperor was Isaac I (reigned 1057–1059), but it was with Alexius I (reigned 1081–1118), a nephew of Isaac, that the Comneni established themselves as the ruling dynasty of the empire. Alexius successfully passed on the throne to his son John II (reigned 1118–1143), who in turn was succeeded by his son Manuel (reigned 1143–1180). When Manuel died, his position was inherited by his son Alexius II (reigned 1180–1183), a minor, whose mother, Mary of Antioch, served as regent. But this arrangement was disturbed by a revolution that brought to the throne Manuel's cousin Andronicus (reigned 1183–1185), a brilliant and tempestuous personality.

Andronicus was also overthrown by a revolution, and he was succeeded by Isaac II Angelus (reigned 1185–1195), grandson of Theodora, the youngest daughter of Alexius I Comnenus, and her husband, Constantine Angelus. Isaac was in turn put aside, blinded and imprisoned by his

Lake Como, showing the town of Bellagio at the left and one of its villas on the promontory.

brother Alexius III (reigned 1195–1203), whose rule was ended when his nephew Alexius, with the aid of the Fourth Crusade, reinstated his father Isaac and, as Alexius IV, shared the throne with him in 1203–1204. The imperial tenure of the Angeli was terminated with the conquest of Constantinople by the crusaders in 1204. A branch of the family, however, founded the Despotate of Epirus. At the same time a branch of the Comneni established the empire of Trebizond.

The period of the Comneni marks the last phase of the Byzantine Empire as a power of importance. When Alexius I became emperor, the empire was surrounded by enemies, the Seljuks in Asia Minor and the Normans and the Patzinaks (Pechenegs) in the Balkans, and was on the brink of dissolution. A skillful diplomat and an able soldier, Alexius dealt successfully with the Patzinaks and the Normans and then, aided by the First Crusade, recovered much of Asia Minor. He was the subject of the *Alexiad*, written by his daughter Anna Comnena.

John II continued his father's work and enhanced still more the position of the empire. Manuel extended the influence of the empire in the Balkans as far as Hungary. However, he suffered a disastrous defeat in Asia Minor. In the meantime, his partiality for Westerners and Western ways had alienated his people, a situation that helped Andronicus to overthrow Manuel's son. During the reign of Andronicus the Normans of Sicily took and sacked Thessalonica.

Under the Angeli the empire lost Bulgaria and Cyprus, and Serbia rose to full independence. Meanwhile the squabbles of the Angeli weakened the empire internally and helped create the conditions that led to the destruction of the empire by the Fourth Crusade and the end of Greek rule in Constantinople for 57 years.

PETER CHARANIS
*Rutgers—The State University*

**COMO,** kô′mô, a town in Italy at the southwestern end of Lake Como, 24 miles (39 km) north of Milan. The town, the capital of the province of Como, is a bishop's see and has a cathedral built in the 14th to 18th century, combining Gothic and Renaissance architecture. The town hall (the Broletto), of rose, white, and gray limestone, was built in 1215; there are also several fine Romanesque churches.

Although the beauty of the surrounding country attracts a considerable tourist trade, Como depends chiefly on industry for its livelihood. Its silk spinning and weaving industry, begun in 1510, has been famous for centuries. Como is a rail junction on the line between Switzerland and Milan. Population: 85,955 (1991 census).

**COMO, Lake,** kô′mô, a large lake in northern Italy in the southern portion of the Alps of Lombardy. It is glacial in origin, with a characteristically steep profile and great depth (1,350 feet, or 410 meters, at the deepest point). Lake Como resembles a Y turned upside down: the northern part is referred to as Lake Colico, the southwestern as Lake Como, and the southeastern as Lake Lecco.

The lake is so well protected by the surrounding arc of the Alps that its climate resembles that of the Italian Riviera. Since Roman times the sheltered shores of the lake have provided popular resort sites. There is also a local fishing industry.

The two principal cities on Lake Como are situated on its southern branches. Como, in the southwest, is an important industrial center and port of entry for rail and road traffic from Switzerland. The beautiful marble cathedral, built in the 14th to 18th century, fuses Gothic and Renaissance styles. There is also a town hall (Broletto) completed in 1215. Lecco, in the southeast, is located on the lake shore beneath the jagged ridge of the Monte Resegone.

Of the many resort centers, the best known and possibly most beautiful are Menaggio, near the point where the lake divides into two branches, and Bellagio, on the tip of the peninsula that separates the two branches. Near Dongo, close to the northern end of the lake, the dictator Benito Mussolini was taken prisoner by Italian partisans while attempting to flee to Switzerland. He was subsequently executed there in April 1945.

GEORGE KISH
*University of Michigan*

**COMODORO RIVADAVIA,** kō-mō-thō'rō rē-vä-thä'vyä, a seaport in southern Argentina, on the Gulf of San Jorge, an arm of the Atlantic Ocean. It is important because Argentina's oil production is concentrated in the vicinity. The wells are administered by an autonomous federal agency, Yacimientos Petrolíferos Fiscales. Tankers from the port deliver oil to refineries in northern Argentina, and pipelines supply natural gas from the region to Buenos Aires and La Plata.

Oil was discovered near Comodoro Rivadavia in 1907, six years after the city's founding. During the Perón era, the region was under army jurisdiction, but in 1955 the Comodoro Rivadavia military zone was abolished and the city was included in the newly created province of Chubut. Population: 123,672 (1991 census).

**COMONFORT, Ignacio,** kō-môn-fôrt' (1812–1863), Mexican general. He was one of the major political leaders of the mid-19th-century movement in Mexico known as *La Reforma.*

Comonfort was born in Puebla in 1812 and educated in law. As a young man he joined Gen. Antonio Santa Anna to drive President Anastasio Bustamante from office. In 1855 he emerged as a leader of the Liberal Revolution of Ayutla, together with Juan Álvarez, Benito Juárez, Melchor Ocampo, and the brothers Miguel and Sebastián Lerdo de Tejada. Succeeding Álvarez as provisional president (1855–1857), he reestablished the federal system, suppressed the Society of Jesus, and abolished the system of inalienable church lands. A new constitution (1857) incorporated the Liberal Revolution principles.

These reforms provoked violent opposition in the military, landholding, and ecclesiastical oligarchy. A series of uprisings culminated in the bloody War of Reform. Discouraged by the opposition, Comonfort collaborated with the conservative Gen. Ignacio Zuloaga in a coup in December 1857 and in suspending the constitution of 1857. Driven from office into exile in the United States the following month, he was succeeded by the president of the supreme court, Benito Juárez. In 1862 Comonfort returned to Mexico to fight against the French invaders. He was assassinated near Celaya the following year by a group of bandits reputedly supporting Gen. Tomás Mejía who sympathized with the French.

HAROLD E. DAVIS, *American University*

**COMORIN, Cape,** kom'ō-rin, the southernmost point of India. It is a rocky headland in Tamil Nadu state and lies about 10 miles (16 km) south of the Cardamom Hills. The Temple of Kanya Kumari the Virgin, an attribute of the goddess Devi, is located in Comorin village at the cape's tip. The temple is a much-frequented place of pilgrimage.

**COMOROS,** kom'ə-rōz, an archipelago of four islands and some small islets between Madagascar and the eastern coast of Africa. Three of the islands—Njazidja (formerly called Great Comoro), Nzwani (Anjouan), and Mwali (Mohéli)—constitute the Federal Islamic Republic of the Comoros. The fourth island, Mayotte (Mahoré), is a dependency of France.

**The Land.** The islands, all of volcanic origin, cover an area of 863 square miles (2,236 sq km). They are mountainous, with the highest elevation being 7,746 feet (2,361 meters), on Mt. Karthala, an active volcano on Njazidja. Mangrove swamps are found along the shorelines, and forests occur at heights of 1,300 to 5,800 feet (400–1,770 meters). The climate is tropical, tempered by sea breezes.

**The People.** The four islands had a population of 645,200 in 1994. The people are of mixed Arab, Malay, and African stock. Most speak Comorian (a mixture of Arabic and Swahili) and are Islamic, except on Mayotte, which is largely Roman Catholic. The capital and largest city is Moroni on Njazidja, with a population estimated at 22,000. Mutsamudu (on Nzwani) and Fomboni (Mwali) are the other principal towns.

**Economy.** Agriculture is the main economic activity, with bananas, rice, cassava, and sweet potatoes the principal crops. About a third of the land consists of plantations introduced by the French.

**History.** The Comoros came under Arab influence in the 8th century and were explored by Europeans in the 16th century. France took possession of Mayotte in 1843 and the other islands in 1886. The Comoros were attached administratively to Madagascar in 1914 but became an overseas territory of France in 1947. They were granted internal autonomy in 1961.

In December 1974 the islanders (except on Mayotte) voted for independence, while Mayotte asked to remain a French overseas territory. The French Parliament arranged for a referendum, but on July 6, 1975, the Comoros's Chamber of Deputies declared the islands to be independent and elected Ahmed Abdallah president. The government was overthrown in a coup in August 1975 and then again in May 1978, the latter led by a French mercenary named Bob Denard. A federal Islamic republic was proclaimed that May, and Abdallah was elected president under a new constitution in October. In January 1979 the Comoros became a one-party state.

President Abdallah was assassinated in November 1989 by Denard, who briefly held power until he was expelled in December by French troops. Multiparty presidential elections held early in 1990 introduced democratic government. In September 1995 Denard, with several mercenaries and 300 rebels, staged another coup but was again removed from power by French troops.

In 1997 the leaders of Nzwani and Mwali, suffering from high unemployment and complaining of discrimination by the central government on Njazidja, requested the return of French rule to those two islands. When France refused, they declared themselves the Republic of Anjouan but

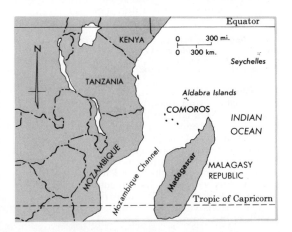

failed to acquire international recognition. Negotiations between the government and the secessionists produced an agreement on autonomy in April 1999, but that was nullified when the government was overthrown by the army ten days later.

HUGH C. BROOKS*, *St. John's University*

**COMPACT DISC,** or CD, a thin plastic disk 12 centimeters (5 in) in diameter that can store text, images, graphics, sound, and any other information expressed in digital form. Total CD capacity is over 500 megabytes of data, sufficient to store about 74 minutes of high-fidelity stereo sound. A CD stores data in a single spiral track roughly 5.6 kilometers (3.5 mi) long. This spiral track has shallow depressions, called pits, in a reflective layer that are read optically. CDs spin at about 500 rpm when read near the center, decreasing to approximately 200 rpm when read near the circumference. This produces a constant linear velocity, resulting in a constant data rate.

The "ones" and "zeroes" of binary information are encoded by modifying the lengths of the pits and of the "land" between them. During playback, a low-power laser beam is focused on the track and reflected back into a detector. The quantity of reflected light varies depending on whether the beam is on land or in a pit. This modulated light is converted into a data stream by a photodetector. The data are then reorganized to reproduce the original digital information.

In addition to the stored data, a CD contains data conveying information about synchronization, display, and error correction. To facilitate playback synchronization, an encoding scheme called eight-to-fourteen modulation is used. During playback, data errors can originate from defects in or damage to the disk. Most of these errors can be corrected by a powerful data correction scheme, originally used in digital communications systems, called cross-interleaved Reed-Solomon coding. This error correction produces a playback data stream virtually identical to the original source.

Digital audio data are generated by sampling an analog audio signal at a high rate. Each sample is a 16-bit numerical representation of the instantaneous voltage of the audio signal. An audio CD reproduces 44,100 samples per second $\times$ 16 bits per sample $\times$ 2 channels, or 1,411,200 bits per second. With the reproduction of sound, a digital-to-analog converter transforms these samples back into an audio voltage. This signal is then applied to the listener's amplifier and speakers.

ALDO G. CUGNINI, *Philips Laboratories*

**Bibliography:** Brewer, B., and E. Key, *The Compact Disc Book: A Complete Guide to the Digital Sound of the Future* (Harcourt 1987); Carrasso, M., et al., "Compact Disc: Digital Audio," *Philips Technical Review* 40 (1982):151–180.

**COMPANY TOWN,** a living area built for industrial workers and usually controlled by a company to assure a constant labor supply. Such towns came into existence near large-scale industrial operations in the United States about 1850. They appeared in the western mining states and soon afterward near large oil strikes and around giant steel mills. After World War I hundreds of company towns appeared in the southern states, to which part of the textile industry had moved.

Conditions varied from one company town to another, but company control of the town was the rule. Kannapolis, N.C., with approximately 30,000 population in 1990, could be called a typical company town. Almost everything in it is owned by the Cannon textile firm. With no regular corporate existence, the town functions only as an area to house workers employed in Cannon mills.

Some early industrialists tried to alleviate the unrest of their workers by constructing attractive model towns. In 1880 George Pullman established such a town for his palace car workers near Chicago, but he exercised excessive control over the town's affairs, and the experiment was abandoned after riots occurred during the Pullman strike of 1894.

Later efforts to improve conditions were more enlightened. The copper town of San Manuel, Ariz., is well managed and has schools, churches, shopping centers, attractive houses, and well-paved streets. Not all the miners choose to live in San Manuel, and the town is usually operated at a loss. Burlington Industries began in 1964 an elaborate multimillion-dollar plan for the improvement of its plant and residential area in Cramerton, N.C. The Kennecott copper firm decided in 1955 to sell its town of Hayden, Ariz., to its workers, who organized an independent town government. The operators of the Climax, Colo., molybdenum mine, who had housed their workers alongside the mine for 40 years, moved the town in 1961 to a site near Leadville, refurbished the houses, and sold them to their workers. For this work the employer engaged a "town mover" who moves, builds, and improves company towns.

By and large the company town has come into disfavor with companies and workers. The companies have become embarrassed by the bad reputation that such towns have acquired, and workers continue to resent the close control of their housing and community life. The general tendency among companies now is to discontinue responsibility for the living arrangements of industrial workers.

COURTNEY ROBERT HALL, *Author of "History of American Industrial Science"*

**COMPANY UNION,** technically, a union whose members are all employed by the same company and whose local organization is not affiliated with a national union or organization. Practically, the term "company union" has come to stand for a company-dominated union—that is, a union whose operations and goals are controlled or strongly influenced by the very company with whom the union has established a collective bargaining relationship.

Company unions are primarily a 20th-century American phenomenon. Faced with a rising tide of unionism, employers formed employee groups whose purpose was to provide a facade of democratic representation for the workers without the economic independence of the trade unions. Participants in these groups or associations frequently included management personnel who effectively controlled organizational activities. The idea—which is also known as an "employee representation plan"—was first introduced in 1912 by the Colorado Fuel and Iron Co.

Company unions grew during the 1920s and flourished when the National Industrial Recovery Act was in effect in 1934 and 1935. After the passage of the National Labor Relations Act of 1935 (Wagner Act), the unions were often found to be in violation of a section that prohibited company influence, control, or domination of a union. When the National Labor Relations Board found a violation, its remedy was an order to the company union and the company to break their collective bargaining relationship. As a result, company-dominated unions became less significant factors in labor relations, but they still exist in some sections that are less well unionized.

HARVEY L. FRIEDMAN
*University of Massachusetts*

**COMPARATIVE ANATOMY.** See ANATOMY, COMPARATIVE.

**COMPARATOR,** kəm-par′ə-tər, is a device that measures a dimension of an object by matching the dimension with a known or standard reference value.

A *mechanical comparator* has a standard gauge for measuring the length, diameter, or other dimensions of parts produced by machine tools. This device automatically sorts parts into as many as 30 different groups on the basis of how accurately the parts were made, and it can compare as many as 20 different dimensions against reference values. For rapid testing on a production line, it compares a dimension and a standard and shows a red or green light to indicate acceptance or rejection.

An *optical comparator* for precision measurements has a microscope and a standard scale that enable a user to measure dimensions of an object to a tolerance of 0.000020 inch (0.0005 mm). The contour of an object, such as a gear or small part, can be measured to a tolerance of 0.0002 inch (0.005 mm) by projecting the magnified image of the object on a screen to see if the contour matches a standard drawing.

E. NORMAN LURCH
*State University of New York, Farmingdale*

**COMPASS,** kom′pes, a 2-legged instrument for locating a point or describing an arc. The legs are pointed and meet at a joint. They are adjustable so that the distance between the points can be varied.

Draftsmen use the term "compass" only for an instrument in which one of the points is a pencil or pen used for drawing an arc. They apply the term "dividers" to the compass when it is equipped with two sharp points (without pen or pencil) for use in stepping off equal units of space on their drawings or for transferring measurements from one sheet to another. Compasses, usually in the style of the draftsman's dividers, are essential tools for many other craftsmen also, including carpenters, machinists, pattern makers, tinsmiths, and toolmakers. As used by such craftsmen, one point serves to establish the center point and the other to scribe an arc or mark a point by scratching the working surface. In mathematics, the compass and ruler are used to construct geometrical figures.

Compasses were found in the ruins of Pompeii, but they were used by mathematicians centuries before the eruption of Vesuvius buried Pompeii in 79 A. D. Early records of compasses antedate the writings of Ahmes (c. 1650 B. C.).

In the plain-hinge style of compass, the legs retain their relative positions because of friction at the joint. A handle, extending above the hinge, may be provided to permit easy and rapid turning of the compass. Ingenious arrange-

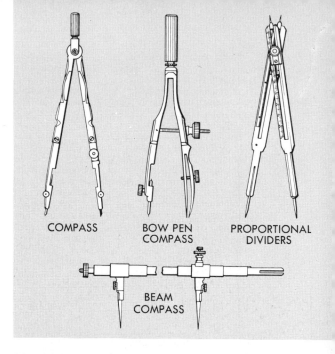

COMPASS    BOW PEN COMPASS    PROPORTIONAL DIVIDERS

BEAM COMPASS

COMPASSES AND DIVIDERS are basic tools for draftsmen and are also widely used by most craftsmen.

ments have been devised to ensure that the handle will bisect the angle between the legs. Friction-joint dividers are sometimes provided with a flat spring device in one leg to provide a minute adjustment of the angle between the legs.

To extend the capacity of the ordinary compass by 2 or 3 inches (5.1 to 7.6 cm), provision is made for the insertion of an extension bar in one leg. Compass legs more than 5 inches (12.7 cm) long usually are provided with a knee in each leg to permit setting the points at right angles to the working surface, no matter what angle the legs may make. Such a device is essential when using a pen to ensure that both blades of the pen will make proper contact with the surface.

When a drawing requires much work to be done from a single center, there is a tendency for the center point of the compass to make a sizable hole, causing the compass leg to be positioned off center. This disadvantage can be avoided by means of a small transparent disk fixed in position on the drawing by three sharp points mounted on the metal rim of the disk. A depression in the upper surface of the disk receives the compass point, which can be placed repeatedly at the precisely desired center point.

**Special Types of Compasses.** *Bow pen compasses* are instruments with spring-opened legs. In one design, the two legs of the compass are joined at the upper ends by a hinge, and the compass is equipped with a separate spring to open the legs. In another design, the legs are formed as integral flat springs from a single piece of metal. In both designs, the tendency of the springs to open the legs is restrained by a screw that controls the opening between the legs. In bow instruments, the handle always bisects the angle between the legs.

A *drop compass* is a special form of short-radius bow compass for drawing many small circles rapidly. It is useful, for example, in structural drawings where many rivets are represented.

A *beam compass* is for use where relatively large distances are involved. It is essentially a bar with two movable members attached. One member carries a point for the center; the other carries a point, pencil, or pen, depending on the intended use. The two members can be slid along the bar to the desired positions.

A *bullet compass* has one leg with an enlarged, round end shaped like a bullet. It is used for shop work where arcs are often scribed around a central hole instead of around a point.

A very useful form of compass is the *proportional divider,* used for enlarging or reducing in a desired ratio. Its two legs cross, forming an X, and there are points at all four ends. The joint, which is movable, can be shifted at will to selected positions. Thus the distance between the two points at one end will be in a fixed ratio to the distance between the two points at the other end. This permits transferring distances measured at one end to a proportionately greater or shorter distance at the other end.

ALEXANDER W. LUCE, *Norwich College*

**COMPASS, Magnetic,** kom'pəs, a device for determining direction by allowing a balanced and pivoted bar magnet to align itself with the earth's magnetic field.

**History.** In its most primitive form, a compass was a piece of magnetic ore (lodestone) attached to a piece of floating wood. The compass was first mentioned in writing by Alexander Neckam (1157–1217), an English monk, but the magnetism of lodestone was known to the ancient Greeks. The magnetic compass, which has been used by mariners since the Vikings, is convenient to steer by and is usable when the more accurate method of celestial navigation is not possible due to an overcast sky.

**Points of the Compass.** Since the 12th century, the compass rose has been subdivided by repeated bisection into compass points named in the order: north, north by east, north-northeast, northeast by north, northeast, northeast by east, east-northeast, east by north, east, and so forth. The $11\frac{1}{4}°$ interval between the 32 named points was about the accuracy with which an old mariner's compass could be read. As accuracy improved, it became customary to give directions in degrees from north or south; for example, northeast became north 45° east, and southeast became south 45° east. Since the 1920's it has become universal practice to indicate direction, called azimuth, by a single number representing degrees measured clockwise from the north.

**Construction.** In its simplest form, a compass consists of a magnetized steel needle balanced to pivot above a circular dial; the dial indicates correct directions when it is rotated so that its north direction coincides with the north-seeking end of the needle, which is usually colored for identification.

In most modern compasses, such as a mariner's compass, the compass needle is attached out of sight on the bottom side of the dial; the entire dial, then called the card, is balanced and pivoted on a jewel bearing in a nonmagnetic case filled with oil to damp oscillations. A compass often is equipped with a sighting device, or alidade, which permits measurement of direction, or magnetic bearing, to a distant object.

**Land Compasses.** Scouts, explorers, soldiers, and hikers use a small pocket compass by holding it level in the hand. The most accurate land compass is mounted on a tripod; when also provided with a sighting telescope for measuring elevation angles, the instrument is called a transit or theodolite, and is used in surveying.

**Marine Compasses.** A ship rolls and pitches while at sea, and thus it is necessary to make a marine compass self-leveling. The card of a marine compass usually is pivoted in a round-bottom case or bowl that is weighted at the bottom and mounted in a hollow pedestal (binnacle) by using two concentric rings (gimbals) pivoted in perpendicular directions. The glass top of the bowl is marked with the lubber line, which points along the ship's keel and thus indicates the magnetic heading of the ship.

**Aircraft Compasses.** In the simplest type of aircraft compass the card is a cylinder, rather than a disk, with degree markings on the outside surface. The card is pivoted in an oil-filled case behind a vertical glass window marked with a vertical lubber line. To minimize compass error, the compass usually is mounted as far as possible from electrical instruments in the cockpit.

It is not necessary to mount an aircraft magnetic compass in gimbals because in all normal maneuvers the bank of an airplane (like a bicycle or motorcycle) is coordinated with its turning radius, and so the gravational force and the centrifugal force on any object add up to a resultant force that always remains perpendicular to the cabin floor. However, these acceleration forces are another source of compass errors.

### COMPASS ERRORS

**Deviation.** The simplest compass error, deviation, is caused by the presence of steel or current-carrying wires that produce a local magnetic field. This causes the compass needle to deflect from the direction of magnetic north by an angle known as compass error or deviation. It is necessary from time to time to swing a ship or airplane into accurately known directions and to make the compass error as small as possible by moving a set of adjustable compensating magnets inside the compass case. Because it is rarely possible to reduce error to zero in all headings, the remaining errors at various headings are

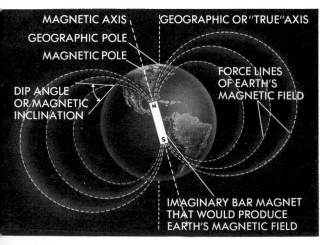

THE EARTH'S MAGNETIC FIELD is thought to be created by currents deep within its liquid core. These currents produce the same effect as would a bar magnet aligned approximately with the earth's geographic axis.

MAGNETIC AXIS
GEOGRAPHIC POLE
MAGNETIC POLE
GEOGRAPHIC OR "TRUE" AXIS
FORCE LINES OF EARTH'S MAGNETIC FIELD
DIP ANGLE OR MAGNETIC INCLINATION
IMAGINARY BAR MAGNET THAT WOULD PRODUCE EARTH'S MAGNETIC FIELD

THE MARINE COMPASS is gimballed to offset the roll and pitch of a ship at sea. The compass card is marked in degrees and with the major compass points.

AIRCRAFT COMPASS card and index (marker at top) show the magnetic heading. Pointers indicate direction to a radio beacon or ground path to a radio range station.

written on a compass correction card and posted next to the compass.

**Declination or Variation.** The earth's magnetic field is far from simple. Its vertical component is zero only very near the equator; elsewhere it points downward at a steep angle, called magnetic inclination or dip. At polar latitudes greater than 65° north or south, its horizontal component is too weak and erratic for navigational purposes; elsewhere, it points east or west of true north, or geographic north, by an angle called magnetic variation or declination. In the United States, this angle ranges from about 30° east to about 15° west; its local value changes slowly with time.

**Turning Errors.** A compass needle balanced to swing horizontally before being magnetized would point downward at a steep angle after it was magnetized. Since a compass is intended to indicate only the horizontal component of the earth's field, its card must be weighted on the north or south direction, depending on whether it is to be used in the Southern Hemisphere or Northern Hemisphere, respectively. When statically balanced in this way, the compass card becomes dynamically unbalanced and will start spinning when the compass is subjected to acceleration forces. These acceleration or turning errors make an aircraft magnetic compass nearly useless as a flight instrument because it will give a correct indication only after the plane has been flying straight and level for several minutes. It has therefore been the practice, since the early days of all-weather flight, to use a gyroscopic compass for steering. In level flight the magnetic compass is used to correct drift errors of the gyroscopic compass caused by bearing friction. See also GYROSCOPE—*Gyroscopic Instruments;* TERRESTRIAL MAGNETISM.

HENRY H. KOLM
*Massachusetts Institute of Technology*

### Bibliography

Denne, W., *Magnetic Compass Deviation and Correction,* 3d ed. (Sheridan 1979).
Fleming, June, *Staying Found: The Complete Map and Compass Handbook* (Random House 1982).
Jacobson, Cliff, *Map and Compass Use: The Basic Essentials* (ICS Bks. 1988).
Kaganov, M. I., and Tsukernik, W. M., *Nature of Magnetism* (Imported Pub. 1985).
Mayaud, P. N., *Derivation, Meaning, and Use of Geomagnetic Indices* (Am. Geophysical Union 1980).

**COMPASS PLANT,** kom'pəs, a hairy, perennial North American plant, so named because leaves on young shoots tend to point north and south. The compass plant ranges in height from 6 to 12 feet (1.8–3.6 meters), and its leaves, which grow about 1 to 2½ feet (30–75 cm) long, are composed of lance-shaped segments. The yellow flower heads, which resemble those of the sunflower, are about 5 inches (13 cm) across.

The compass plant is easily grown in any good garden soil and blooms best when grown in full sunlight. It may be propagated by sowing seed in a hotbed or in the garden when there is no danger of frost. Because of the height and coarse texture of this plant, it is best to place it at the rear of the flower border.

The compass plant (*Silphium laciniatum*) belongs to the composite family (Compositae).

DONALD WYMAN
*The Arnold Arboretum, Harvard University*

**COMPENSATION** is a broad legal term that denotes the balancing of one thing against another; for example, payment against services rendered or benefits against loss or damage. It implies making whole or giving an equivalent or substitute of equal value.

In an employer-employee relationship, compensation is salary or wages from the employer for work performed. Compensation also covers remuneration for services such as those rendered by a repairman or professional man; payment made to a supplier for goods; reimbursement for expenses or an outlay made in behalf of one person by another; and the amount paid by the owner of one ship to the owner of another ship that salvages or prevents the destruction of the first vessel.

In yet another sense, compensation is the remuneration required by court order to be paid by one person to another who has sustained loss or injury through the act or omission of the first person. Thus, the seizure of property through the condemnation process to make room for a highway or a public building must be accompanied by compensation paid by the seizing authority equivalent in value to the appropriated property.

Compensation is also the remuneration necessary to restore an injured person to his former position—the damages for pain, for loss of wages, and for medical expenses—paid by a person guilty of negligence to the injured party. The area in which compensation becomes payable continues to be broadened by statute and by judge-made law—for example, the recognition by many courts that a person's privacy is valuable and that invasion of that privacy, as by use of his name for advertising purposes, is the subject of compensation.

Examples of the general trend toward statutory expansion of compensation are workmen's compensation laws awarding money for injuries sustained during employment, and laws requiring payments to aged, ill, and unemployed persons. A number of states of the United States and some other countries have enacted laws compensating blameless victims of crimes of violence, on the theory that the state owes a duty to protect and make whole those of its citizens victimized by crime.

M. MARVIN BERGER
*Associate Publisher, "New York Law Journal"*

**COMPENSATION** is the tendency of an organism to make up for deficiencies of structure or function. For example, the heart may become enlarged in order to perform its function more satisfactorily if there is an initial impairment; or if one eye is injured the other eye may assume part of its function and perform more efficiently than originally.

The idea of compensation was discussed by Alfred Adler in a 1907 publication. Sigmund Freud considered Adler's paper very important, and the notion of certain kinds of behavior representing compensations for deficiencies in other behavior became widely accepted. Adler further theorized that a child has feelings of weakness and insignificance in relation to adults who are larger, stronger, and more competent. Adler later saw neurotic symptoms as compensations for lack of self-esteem. He held that many neurotic symptoms represented attempts to make up for feelings of inadequacy or inferiority.

The notion of compensation is sometimes regarded as an elaboration of the physiological principle of homeostasis, which holds that the organism maintains an optimal equilibrium in its functions. Living organisms exhibit a tendency to master or compensate for internal defects. Adler extended this notion to the realm of psychological functioning, especially as related to personality. The mechanism of compensation is a defense against feelings of inferiority that grow out of real or imagined personal defects or weaknesses. The need to compensate does not usually come as the result of a single failure or frustration, but occurs after a recurring chain of thwarting and frustration. Compensation is the overemphasis of one type of behavior in order to hide or defend against deficiencies the individual feels in other areas of behavior.

People often compensate by developing the function associated with an impaired body part. This type of compensation is common among individuals who are not neurotic. For example, Demosthenes, who was a stutterer, became a great orator; Theodore Roosevelt, a childhood weakling, became a rough and robust adult; Lord Byron, who had a clubfoot, became an expert swimmer.

AUSTIN E. GRIGG
*University of Richmond*

**COMPETITION,** in economics, refers to a variety of market relationships. *Pure* (or *perfect*), *imperfect, free, fair* or *unfair, workable*—these and many other terms are employed to describe the competitive pattern of actual or theoretical economic markets. In its broadest sense, competition means a condition of rivalry among buyers or sellers; but when analysis of a specific market is undertaken, agreement on terms and concepts disappears. This is particularly true of general business usage as against that of economic theory.

**Perfect Competition.** The basic purpose of economic analysis is to provide an answer to the question of how individual satisfactions may best be achieved with a limited quantity of productive resources. Different market situations are analyzed to determine the extent to which they foster the achievement of this basic goal. Economic theory has demonstrated that a market characterized by perfect competition will provide the optimum level of individual satisfactions. The conditions of perfect competition are: large numbers of small independent buyers and sellers; homogeneity of product; perfect mobility of all resources; an informed market; and freedom of entry. These conditions have rarely been satisfied in an actual market situation, but perfect competition serves as a model of optimum market conditions, against which other situations may be assessed.

Variants of perfect competition, ranging from slight deviations to pure monopoly, are also described and analyzed in economic theory. In each instance, the effects of specified market conditions on the allocation of resources and the distribution of income are appraised and compared with the ideal of perfect competition.

**Workable Competition.** When the economic theorist refers to competition, he has in mind a market in which large numbers of relatively small firms operate—a small firm being defined as one that is not large enough to exert a measurable influence on price or any other term of trade on the market. The businessman, however, uses "competition" in a broader sense. He means essentially the existence of rivalry among buyers or sellers, or no exercise of monopoly power. In this interpretation, competition exists whenever a firm is restricted in its actions by possible reactions on the part of either its customers or its competitors. This condition prevails in varying degrees throughout all national economies, whether they are called capitalistic, socialistic, communistic, industrial, or agrarian.

A serious need exists for bringing these two concepts of competition into closer harmony. In the first place, theory can be more meaningful when its terminology closely approximates that of the business world. Then business can appreciate the terminology. In the United States economy a second reason is even more immediate. The U. S. antitrust laws are founded on the orthodox economic idea that atomistic competition is most consistent with the economic aims of a democracy. The courts, however, have generally chosen to interpret antitrust laws in purely legal terms. The result has been that although abuses of monopoly power have tended to be punished by the courts, the competitive ideal of economic theory has not been fostered. However, after World War II antitrust decisions took a slightly new tack and placed some emphasis on market conditions rather than on overt monopoly practices alone.

In the search for a meeting ground for theory, business, and the courts, the concept of "workable competition" has been developed. This idea recognizes that conditions of perfect competition cannot be met in a modern industrial society. Technological advance, social legislation, and the growth of the corporation have all contributed to this recognition. Competition among business firms is still considered essential to the best possible level of individual satisfactions, but in a highly industrialized country in particular it cannot be the atomistic competition of pure economic theory. Workable competition will exist whenever the consumer has sufficient choice among rival sellers to ensure that he is protected from exploitation by sellers. This is the social function of competition.

The United States economy has a record of production unrivaled in history. It is largely because the American economy has been competitive that this record has been possible. In a competitive economy, producers always risk the loss of business to rivals, yet workable competition provides the best opportunity to achieve maximum well-being for both the individual and the society.

WILLIAM N. KINNARD, JR.
*University of Connecticut*

**Bibliography**

Auerbach, Paul, *Competition: The Economics of Industrial Change* (Basil Blackwell 1988).
Peston, M. H., and Quandt, R. E., eds., *Prices, Competition and Equilibrium* (B&N Imports 1986).
Tucker, Ken, and Baden-Fuller, Charles, eds., *Economics of Firms and Markets* (St. Martin's Press 1986).
Whicker, M. L., and Moore, R., *Making America Competitive: Policies for a Global Future* (Praeger 1988).

**COMPIÈGNE,** kôn-pyen', is a town in north central France, about 45 miles northeast of Paris, in the department of Oise. Set in beautiful forested countryside on the banks of the Oise, it is an elegant country retreat for wealthy Parisians and is famous for its rich history and its palace. It is well known for its late Gothic *hotel de ville*, the churches of St. Antoine and St. Jacques, and for the remains of St. Corneille abbey, now the municipal library. Compiègne and its environs house a variety of manufacturing industries, including engineering, tires, matches, food processing, and chemicals.

The complete restoration of the Compiègne Palace, which dates from the time of Charles V, was begun under Louis XV. The architect Jacques Gabriel designed the buildings in a rather severe classical style. The King and his court frequented Compiègne on hunting excursions. During the French Revolution and afterward it served as a military training school and then as a crafts school. Napoleon I took the palace over and restored it. It was the favorite residence of Napoleon III. Apart from its fine views of the adjoining parks and forests, the palace's most interesting features are the apartments, with their elaborate decoration and the displays of tapestries, furniture, and memorabilia of the royal personages who occupied the palace in the late 18th and 19th centuries.

In ancient times, Compiègne was a Roman outpost. Later it was a royal residence under the Merovingian kings. It was here that Joan of Arc was captured by the Burgundians on May 24, 1430. The armistice ending World War I was signed in a railway car in Compiègne forest on Nov. 11, 1918. The same car was used for the Franco-German Armistice in 1940. Population: 41,896 (1990 census).

HOMER PRICE, *Hunter College*

**COMPLAINT,** in states that have a code of civil procedure, the initial pleading by which a plaintiff states his cause of action—similar to the "declaration" in common law. The primary purpose of a complaint is to inform the defendant of the material facts that give rise to the claim against him. To this end, it must include a statement of the jurisdictional facts, that is, those that determine the court's authority to act in the case; a statement of the operative facts, or principal facts that form the basis of the claim; and a demand for judgment for the relief to which the plaintiff deems himself entitled.

LINDA ALDEN RODGERS
*School of Law, Columbia University*

**COMPLEAT ANGLER,** kəm-plēt', one of the most admired treatises of 17th century English literature, written by Izaak Walton (q.v.). *The Compleat Angler* was first published in 1653 and went through five editions in Walton's lifetime, with substantial sections added to the 5th edition (1676) by Walton's friends Charles Cotton and Robert Venables. While Walton has a considerable reputation as one of the finest English biographers, readers have found the humanity and idyllic pastoralism of *The Compleat Angler* the best index to the gentle and compassionate nature of the man.

The book is not easily categorized: it is a practical treatise on the art of fishing; an early example of the informal essay; a discourse on the virtues of solitude; and a defense of the contemplative life. Walton's narrative begins with a meeting between Piscator (Fisherman), Venator (Hunter), and Auceps (Falconer), who discourse on the values of their various sports. Piscator paints such an idealized portrait of the delights of fishing that Venator temporarily surrenders his blood-letting sport and stays with his new companion for five days. During this time, while they fish and converse in the charmingly portrayed English countryside, Piscator points out that there is an analogy between fishing and the true Christian life (Christ was a "fisher of men"), discourses on such details as bait and game fish, and regales his friend with savory recipes that can transform the meanest fish into a gourmet's delight.

Walton's *Compleat Angler* is an imaginative reconstruction of Eden, a world still filled with simple pleasures, companionship, song, and peace. To understand the full significance of this idyll, it must be remembered that Walton wrote his book about the time of the English Civil War. Most of the works of the period reflect despair and disillusionment with the ruptured condition of the kingdom, and, no doubt, Walton offered his imaginary world of quiet (the last line of the treatise is the Biblical quotation, "Study to be quiet") as a counterbalance to the noisy and disturbed world around him. It is this gentle pastoralism that has endeared it to many generations of readers.

Excellent editions of *The Compleat Angler* include those by John Buchan (1935) and by Geoffrey Keynes in the latter's *Compleat Walton* (1929).

RICHARD E. HUGHES
*Author of "Literature: Form and Function"*

**COMPLEX,** in psychology, means an idea or attitude with strong emotional overtones that may lead to abnormal behavior. The Swiss psychiatrist Carl Jung introduced the notion of complexes in 1906 as part of his analysis of schizophrenic thinking. He later elaborated the concept to apply to neurotic as well as psychotic reactions and even to normal reactions.

Jung defined a complex as a group of ideas that share common emotional associations. Because the feelings or thoughts or memories making up the complex have been repressed and exist in the unconscious mind, Jung had to devise an indirect means of studying them. He used a word association technique: a stimulus word is given, and the patient is told to respond with the first word that occurs to him. When a long list of stimulus words is used, individuals show characteristic response times. Some words, however, disrupt the response times, and these disruptions indicate complexes.

It is assumed that there is a connection between a complex and early emotional experiences. Complexes are experienced by the individual as something foreign to his self or are unrecognized. Typically some original event precipitates feelings. Later these feelings are experienced again when some partial element of the original event occurs. In this manner feelings or moods may appear that at first seem unintelligible to the person experiencing them.

When the associative link between the original event and the current event is discovered, a normal individual recognizes the reasons for his current feelings. In an abnormal personality, however, the associative linkage between the original arousal of the feelings and the current circumstances is difficult to trace. Typically the original circumstance has been repressed or forgotten by the individual, although the feelings may be triggered by presently occurring events. Complexes are, thus, irrational consequences of experiences that are long past.

Complexes tend to become dominant in the personality. In Jung's conception of a complex, more and more of the individual's personality becomes controlled by the complex. In the case of schizophrenia, Jung felt that the patient becomes completely absorbed by his complexes and thus has no energy left for making adjustments to the objective demands of reality. In the case of neurosis, the complexes exert less control over the entire personality functioning, but there is still an undue concern with the moods and associations of the complex. Thus a man with a mother complex will become so preoccupied with what his mother thinks, values, and wishes that he will act more in accordance with herself than with his own self.

The term "complex" was widely accepted in psychology and psychiatry until about the middle of the 20th century. For example, during the early part of the century Freudians made much of the Oedipal, or Oedipus, complex, wherein a boy is alleged to feel sexual desire for his mother and hostility to his father. The term is less often used in more recent writings by American psychologists and psychiatrists. They prefer "Oedipal situation" for the son-mother relationship. Instead of inferiority complex, many psychologists use the simpler expression "feelings of inferiority."

AUSTIN E. GRIGG
*University of Richmond*

**COMPLEX NUMBERS** are expressions of the form $a + ib$, where $a$ and $b$ are any real numbers and $i$ is the square root of minus 1; $a$ is called the real part and $b$ is called the imaginary part of the complex number.

**History.** After negative numbers were accepted as numbers in their own right, mathematicians tried to find a number which, when multiplied by itself, is equal to a given negative number. Early mathematicians who attempted to deal with this question concluded that no such number could exist, and even though the Italian mathematician Girolamo Cardano used square roots of negative numbers in some computations in 1545, he referred to these as *ficta*, that is, imaginary or false numbers. René Descartes in 1637 referred to numbers of the form $a + ib$ as imaginary, although the modern symbol $i$ for the imaginary unit was not introduced until 1777 by Leonhard Euler. Gauss in 1832 made a distinction between numbers of the form $ib$, in which the real part is zero, and those of the form $a + ib$ where $a$ is not zero. Gauss called the latter "complex numbers." Complex numbers became very important with the development of a mathematical theory of electricity and magnetism in the 19th century.

**Operations with Complex Numbers.** Two complex numbers $a + ib$ and $c + id$ are said to be equal if, and only if, $a = c$ and $b = d$. Addition, subtraction, multiplication, and division are defined according to the same rules which govern polynomials of the form $a + bx$, that is $(a + ib) + (c + id) = (a + c) + i(b + d)$, and $(a + ib) - (c + id) = (a - c) + i(b - d)$. For multiplication and division we use the rule for multiplying $i$ by itself: $i^2 = -1$, $i^3 = i^2 \cdot i = -i$, and so on. Thus, $(a + ib)(c + id) = (ac - bd) + i(ad + bc)$ and, if $c$ and $d$ are not both zero,

$$(a + ib) \div (c + id) = \frac{(a + ib)}{(c + id)} \cdot \frac{(c - id)}{(c - id)} = \frac{(ac + bd)}{(c^2 + d^2)} + i\frac{(bc - ad)}{(c^2 + d^2)}.$$

With these definitions of addition and multiplication, the complex numbers satisfy all the axioms of a field, so that all the ordinary operations and characteristics generally associated with the real numbers are valid also for complex numbers, with one very important exception: they cannot be ordered as to magnitude.

If $z = x + iy$ is any complex number, the *complex conjugate* of $z$ is the complex number given by $\bar{z} = x - iy$. From the definitions above it is seen that the complex conjugate of the sum, difference, product, and quotient of two complex numbers is equal, respectively, to the sum, difference, product, and quotient of their complex conjugates.

The *modulus,* or *absolute value,* of a complex number $z = x + iy$ is written $|z|$ and is given by $|z| = \sqrt{x^2 + y^2}$. From the definition of complex conjugate it is easily seen that $|z|^2 = z \cdot \bar{z}$. For any two numbers $z_1 = x_1 + iy_1$ and $z_2 = x_2 + iy_2$, we have $|z_1 \cdot z_2| = |z_1| \cdot |z_2|$, and $|z_1 + z_2| \leq |z_1| + |z_2|$.

**Complex Numbers as Ordered Pairs.** It is possible to define complex numbers, and all the concepts above, without using the imaginary unit $i$. Since all complex numbers have the form $a + ib$, we can consider a complex number as an ordered pair of real numbers, written $(a,b)$. Two such pairs of real numbers, $(a,b)$ and $(c,d)$, are called equal if and only if $a = c$ and $b = d$. Addition and multiplication are defined by $(a,b) + (c,d) = (a + c, b + d)$ and $(a,b) \cdot (c,d) = (ac - bd, ad + bc)$, while $i^2 = -1$ becomes $(0,1) \cdot (0,1) = (-1,0)$. Such pairs of real numbers then have all the properties of complex numbers. Notice also that any real number $a$ can be represented by the complex number $(a,0)$, or $a + i0$, so that the real numbers form a subset of the set of complex numbers.

**The Complex Plane.** Ordered pairs of real numbers can be represented as points in the plane using ordinary rectangular Cartesian coordinates and therefore complex numbers can also be represented as points. The real part, $x$, of the complex number $z = x + iy$ is taken as the abscissa, and the imaginary part, $y$, as the ordinate of the point. The plane itself is called the *complex plane*, or the *z*-plane, with the *x*-axis and the *y*-axis being called the *real* and *imaginary axis*, respectively. In Fig. 1 the complex numbers $6 + 4i$, $-2 + 7i$, and $4 + 11i$ are represented by the points $(6,4)$, $(-2,7)$, and $(4,11)$, respectively.

A point in the plane also determines a unique line segment directed from the origin of the coordinates to the point. This directed line segment is a vector and offers another representation of the complex number $x + iy$. In Fig. 1 the complex numbers $z_1 = 6 + 4i$ and $z_2 = -2 + 7i$ have as their sum the number $4 + 11i$, which corresponds to the geometric vector sum of their respective vectors. This vector sum is obtained by the parallelogram law; that is, through $P_1$ we draw the directed line segment from $P_1$ to $P_3$ equal and parallel to the segment $OP_2$. The vector $OP_3$ represents the sum $z_1 + z_2$, and it is a diagonal of the parallelogram formed by the vectors of $z_1$ and $z_2$. Note that the other diagonal, as a directed line segment from $P_1$ to $P_2$, is equal to $z_2 - z_1$ and as a directed segment from $P_2$ to $P_1$ is equal to $z_1 - z_2$.

The complex conjugate of a number is the reflection of the number with respect to the *x*-axis and thus, in Fig. 1, $6 + 4i$ and $6 - 4i$ are conjugates. The absolute value $|z| = \sqrt{x^2 + y^2}$ is interpreted as the length of the vector $z$, that is, the distance from the origin to the point $z$, which is always a nonnegative real number.

**Polar Coordinate Representation.** Another very useful representation of complex numbers uses polar coordinates. In this representation a complex number $z = x + iy$ is uniquely determined

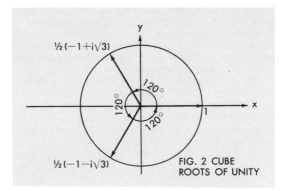

FIG. 2 CUBE ROOTS OF UNITY

by its vector length $r$ and the angle $\theta$ from the *x*-axis to the vector. $\theta$ is called the *argument*, or *amplitude*, of $z$ (written $\theta = \arg z$). For $\theta$ in radians, the interval $-\pi < \arg z \leq \pi$ is taken as the *principal value* of $\arg z$ since adding any whole number multiple of $2\pi$ to $\theta$ will not change the value of $z$. The point $z$ has the equations

$$x = r \cos \theta, \quad y = r \sin \theta, \quad \text{and } r = |z|, \quad \tan \theta = \frac{y}{x}.$$

Thus, the polar form of $z$ is $r(\cos \theta + i \sin \theta)$. In Fig. 2, the point $\frac{1}{2}(-1 + i\sqrt{3})$ has $r = 1$ and $\theta = \frac{2\pi}{3}$ and may be written as $\cos \frac{2\pi}{3} + i \sin \frac{2\pi}{3}$.

In 1748, Leonhard Euler developed the important relation $e^{i\theta} = \cos \theta + i \sin \theta$, where $e$ is the base of the natural logarithms. Using this form, we can write $z = re^{i\theta}$. This expression greatly simplifies calculation with complex numbers. For example, $z_1 z_2 = (r_1 e^{i\theta_1}) \cdot (r_2 e^{i\theta_2}) = r_1 r_2 e^{i(\theta_1 + \theta_2)}$ and if $z_2 \neq 0$, $z_1 \div z_2 = \frac{r_1}{r_2} e^{i(\theta_1 - \theta_2)}$. If $r = 1$, we have $1 = |z| = |e^{i\theta}|$ so that for $\theta$ real, $e^{i\theta}$ represents a point on the unit circle, that is, $e^{i\theta}$ represents a vector of length 1 forming an angle $\theta$ with the *x*-axis. For $\theta = \pi$, the remarkable relation $e^{i\pi} + 1 = 0$, involving five fundamental numbers in mathematics, results. Powers and roots of complex numbers are also simplified by this notation. If $n$ is a positive integer, then $z^n = (re^{i\theta})^n = r^n e^{in\theta}$. If $r = 1$, we have $(e^{i\theta})^n = e^{in\theta}$, which gives the famous relation of De Moivre: $(\cos \theta + i \sin \theta)^n = (\cos n\theta + i \sin n\theta)$. The $n$ nth roots of $z = re^{i\theta}$ are given by $z^{1/n} = r^{1/n} e^{\frac{i(\theta + 2k\pi)}{n}}$, where $k = 0, 1, 2, \ldots, n-1$. There are exactly $n$ such roots, since any $k$ greater than $n-1$ will only reproduce one of the roots already obtained. These roots all lie on a circle whose center is the origin and whose radius is $r^{1/n}$. The angle between successive roots is $\frac{2\pi}{n}$. Since $1 = e^{i2k\pi}$, the *nth roots of unity* are given by $e^{\frac{i2k\pi}{n}}$, where $k = 0, 1, 2, \ldots, n-1$. For example, the three cube roots of unity are given by $e^{\frac{i2k\pi}{3}}$, where $k = 0, 1, 2$; that is, $e^{i \cdot 0} = 1$, $e^{\frac{i \cdot 2\pi}{3}} = \frac{1}{2}(-1 + i\sqrt{3})$, and $e^{\frac{i \cdot 4\pi}{3}} = \frac{1}{2}(-1 - i\sqrt{3})$. These are shown in Fig. 2.

Francis A. Greene, S. J. *Xavier University*

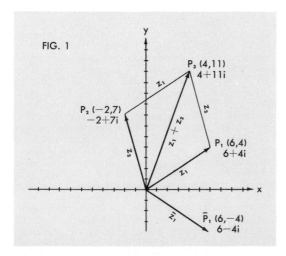

FIG. 1

**COMPLEX VARIABLE,** theory of functions of a complex variable, basically a product of the 19th century. Along with many totally new ideas, the theory gave new insights into old problems of analysis and found many important applications in physics and technology.

In analysis a complex variable is a variable of the form $z = x + iy$ where $x$ and $y$ are real variables and $i = \sqrt{-1}$, that is $z$ is a complex number. Thus functions of a complex variable are a generalization of functions of a real variable. An example of a simple function of $z$ is given by $w = f(z) = z^2$. This may be written as $f(z) = z^2 = (x + iy)^2 = x^2 - y^2 + 2ixy$. The real part of this function is $x^2 - y^2$ and the imaginary part is $2ixy$. In general, $f(z)$ is equivalent to a pair of functions of real variables, or in symbols, $f(z) = u(x,y) + i\,v(x,y)$.

The power of the theory of functions of a complex variable comes from restricting consideration to what are called analytic (or holomorphic or regular) functions. The French mathematician Augustin Cauchy (1789–1857) was the first to develop a successful theory of analytic functions of a complex variable. In the plane a domain (or region) is an open connected set; for example, the interior of a circle is a domain. The derivative $\frac{dw}{dz}$ of a function of a complex variable is defined by analogy with a function of a real variable. Then a function $f(z)$ is said to be analytic on a domain $D$ if it is differentiable at every point of $D$. One remarkable property of such a function is that the existence of the first derivative implies the existence of all successive derivatives. Another property is the equivalence of $f(z)$ being analytic on a domain $D$ and $f(z)$ having a power series expansion at every point of $D$, that is, $f(z)$ can be uniquely represented in the form $f(z) = a_0 + a_1(z - z_0) + \ldots + a_n(z - z_0)^n + \ldots$, where $z_0$ is a point in $D$ and $a_0, a_1, \ldots$ are complex numbers. Such properties are not true for functions of a real variable.

A very important theorem on integration bears Cauchy's name: If $f(z)$ is a single-valued analytic function in a simply connected domain $D$, then $\int_C f(z)\,dz = 0$, where $C$ is any simple (nonintersecting) closed curve of finite length in $D$. A simply connected domain is one which, if it contains a simple closed curve, also contains all points interior to the curve. This theorem implies that for any two points $z_1$ and $z_2$ in $D$, $\int_{z_1}^{z_2} f(z)\,dz$ will always be the same no matter what path is taken in $D$ between the two points.

The German mathematicians Bernhard Riemann (1826–1866) and Karl Weierstrass (1815–1897) emphasized the importance of considering singular points, the points where a function $f(z)$ fails to have a derivative. Many essential properties of a function can be deduced from a study of the singular points. One property is that if $f(z)$ has a power series expansion $a_0 + a_1 z + a_2 z^2 + \ldots$, then the power series expansion must converge and be equal to $f(z)$ for all points inside a circle with center at the origin and radius equal to the minimum distance from the origin to the points where $f(z)$ fails to be analytic. The power series will diverge for all points outside this circle.

FRANCIS A. GREENE, S.J.
*Xavier University*

**COMPLEXION.**   See SKIN.

**COMPOSITE MATERIALS,** produced by combining two dissimilar materials into a new material that may be better suited for a particular application than either of the original materials alone.

The most common example of a composite material is the fiberglass-reinforced plastic commonly used in household goods and in many industrial applications. The plastic alone, which may be any one of a large number of organic polymers, is relatively weak and has a low elastic modulus—that is, it bends and stretches easily. However, it is very stable chemically and constitutes an excellent matrix for the composite. The strength and stiffness in the fiberglass/plastic composite are provided by glass fibers, which are extremely strong; their modulus of elasticity may be 50 times greater than that of the plastic. Since the glass fibers can withstand a much higher tensile stress before strain or yielding occurs, they assume most of the load when the composite is stressed. This principle applies to most high-strength composites—the strong fiber has the high stiffness and therefore assumes a greater proportion of the load than its cross-sectional area would suggest.

**Structural Types.**   The structural arrangement of the components of a composite material can vary widely. Long, continuous fibers of glass or other high-strength material may be embedded in a matrix in either an oriented or random pattern; short high-strength crystal "whiskers" may be dispersed in the matrix; the materials may be combined in alternate layers; or a metal honeycomb may be filled with a matrix material. Glass fiber is a particularly versatile material for reinforcing plastics, since it may be used in the form of yarn, tape, or cloth, as well as in the form of fibers.

**Whiskers and Short Fibers.**   A large amount of research has been devoted to the reinforcement of metals, such as aluminum, nickel, and titanium, with short, single-crystal whiskers. These whiskers are most commonly composed of alumina ($Al_2O_3$) or silicon carbide (SiC). Single crystals have strengths on the order of several million pounds per square inch, and when the whiskers are embedded in a metal matrix, the composite has a much higher strength than the base metal alone. The simplest method for making such a composite is to mix fine metal powder with the crystal whiskers, press the mixture into a shape in a die under high pressure, and sinter it. In sintering, the mixture is heated (but not melted) until its components become merged in the form of a solid, coherent mass.

Inorganic ceramic materials may be reinforced by the addition of short refractory metal fibers. Tungsten and molybdenum metals are available as wire 0.002 inches (0.050 mm) in diameter. This wire is very strong and stiff and can be cut to $\frac{1}{8}$-inch (3-mm) lengths. Composites of this type may be produced by mixing the short lengths of wire with the fine ceramic powder and then hot-pressing the material to form the desired shape. The thermal expansion of the ceramic must be matched to that of the fiber so that the ceramic does not crack when the composite cools after hot-pressing. A typical system of this type is a ceramic, strontium zirconate ($SrZrO_3$, reinforced by molybdenum wire or fiber. Strontium zirconate is normally quite weak, but a composite containing 20% by volume of wire has a strength approximately three times that of the ceramic. The composite is not so brittle as the ceramic alone and may display considerable mechanical-deformation prior to complete failure. The thermal shock resistance of the composite greatly exceeds that of the ceramic alone.

**Continuous Filaments.** The availability of glass fiber yarns of unlimited length has made possible a new technique for producing large, lightweight rocket fuel casings and other high-strength vessels. This process, which is known as filament winding, involves drawing yarn off many spools simultaneously, dipping it in liquid plastic, and winding it on a mandrel, which determines the shape of the vessel's interior. Complicated patterns of winding are used to orient the fibers in the directions of maximum stress. After the curing of the plastic matrix the mandrel is removed.

Because filament winding provides greater reinforcement than can be obtained with whiskers and short fibers, there has been much emphasis on the development of new kinds of continuous filaments. Continuous boron fibers, for example, are of growing industrial importance. To make a continuous boron fiber, a fine tungsten wire, tightly stretched, is passed through a tube that is sealed with mercury baffles at each end. The baffles also serve as electrical contacts so that the wire may be heated to a high temperature. A mixture of boron trichloride and hydrogen gases is passed through the tube; the boron trichloride decomposes and deposits boron metal on the hot tungsten wire. The boron filament, therefore, has a tungsten center, and it is very stiff and strong. One typical composite consisting of an epoxy plastic reinforced by 70% by volume of boron fibers has a flexural strength of 300,000 pounds per square inch (21,000 kg per sq cm). Boron filaments are also being used to reinforce other metals such as aluminum. Besides being strong and stiff, boron has the advantage of being very light in weight, an important factor in aerospace technology.

Graphite, a crystallized form of carbon, is normally used in bulk form for high-temperature electrodes in arc and resistance electric furnaces. Fibrous graphite filaments that have high strength and a high modulus of elasticity can be produced by the pyrolysis of an organic fiber. As it passes through the furnace, the fiber is heated to approximately 2300° C (4170° F) in the absence of oxygen. Volatile substances are driven off as gases, and the residual carbon is converted to graphite. Experimental fibers thus produced have a very high degree of stiffness. Continuous graphite fibers and yarns available commercially have a somewhat lower degree of stiffness. The use of these graphite yarns to reinforce plastics and metals is in the early stage of development; however, it is anticipated that such composites will have interesting and useful properties.

The pyrolysis of rayon is used to produce carbon cloth and felt. When these materials are laminated with resin, a composite is produced that is an excellent heat shield. It may be used for protection against extremely high temperatures, such as those encountered in the reentry of space vehicles into the atmosphere.

Many of the new fibers and whiskers used in the production of reinforced composite materials are very expensive. Therefore, these composites are used only in very critical applications in aerospace. However, fiberglass and a few other fibers are inexpensive, and the composite materials made from them are in common use.

JAMES R. TINKLEPAUGH
*College of Ceramics, Alfred University*

**COMPOSITES,** kəm-poz′its, members of the family Compositae, the largest of all plant families. There are nearly 20,000 different species and innumerable varieties of composites, including many familiar wildflowers as well as garden and crop plants. Among the best-known wild species are daisies, dandelions, sunflowers, ragweed, and cockleburs. Popular garden types include asters, marigolds, camomiles, and chrysanthemums. Among the composites that are raised chiefly as crops are lettuce, chicory, endives, and artichokes. Other species contain compounds that are used in industry. The safflower, for example, yields both an edible oil and a yellow dye.

Composites are generally herbaceous (nonwoody) plants, although the family does contain a few shrubs and trees, such as the sagebrush. Composites are native to all parts of the world and differ considerably in growth and appearance, varying greatly in height and bearing leaves that may be opposite, alternate, or whorled.

About the only thing that all composites have in common is the structure of the blossoms. In popular usage the blossom of a daisy, sunflower, or chrysanthemum is known as a flower. This, however, is not correct. Close examination reveals that rather than comprising a single flower, the blossom is actually a cluster of many tiny individual flowers, which is why the composite's blossom is called a flower head.

In daisies, sunflowers, coneflowers, and most other kinds of composites, the flower head is made up of two different kinds of flowers. In the center of the flower head are many minute flowers known as disk flowers. Disk flowers have both male and female reproductive structures but lack petals. Around the margin of the flower head are the ray flowers. Unlike disk flowers, ray flowers, which are either female or sterile, are made up of petals. The combined ray-flower petals, or corolla, may assume a straplike shape and resemble

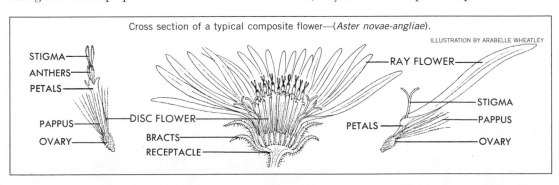

Cross section of a typical composite flower—(*Aster novae-angliae*).

ILLUSTRATION BY ARABELLE WHEATLEY

STIGMA — ANTHERS — PETALS — PAPPUS — OVARY — DISC FLOWER — BRACTS — RECEPTACLE — RAY FLOWER — STIGMA — PETALS — PAPPUS — OVARY

a single large petal. The daisy has yellow disk flowers and white ray flowers.

Unlike the daisy, many composites have flower heads made up of just one type of flower. For example, the flower head of a dandelion, endive, or salsify consists solely of ray flowers.

DONALD WYMAN
*Arnold Arboretum, Harvard University*

**COMPOST,** kom'pōst, a mixture of various components used to fertilize and improve the structure of soils. The principal ingredient of compost—also called artificial manure—is decomposed organic matter. Composts are prepared in ricks (stacks) or pits by alternating layers of plant residue 6 to 12 inches (15 to 30 cm) thick with layers of soil about 1 inch (2.5 cm) thick. Each layer is dampened as it is laid down. In addition, nitrogen and phosphorus are usually added to the plant residue in the form of commercial fertilizer.

Plant residues, such as lawn clippings, tree leaves, and weeds, possess very large quantities of carbon-containing substances. Microbes attack these substances, with the consequence that most of the carbon is either incorporated into the microbial cells or liberated into the air in the form of carbon dioxide. During a period of several months, microbes by this process convert the originally dry, tough plant material into a crumbly substance that is relatively easy to manipulate. The use of microbial conversion of municipal wastes into marketable compost can reduce waste disposal costs and diminish air pollution caused by incineration.

JOHN R. EDWARDSON, *University of Florida*

**COMPOUND,** a substance consisting of molecules composed of atoms or ions of two or more different elements. The composition of compounds is fixed—that is, the relative amount of each element in the compound is constant. For example, water always contains two atoms of hydrogen for each atom of oxygen. In addition to the constant chemical composition, the physical properties of compounds, under a given set of conditions, are the same for any sample tested. These properties differentiate a compound from an element or a mixture. An element consists of only one type of atom, while a mixture contains two or more compounds. The composition and properties of mixture, such as soil, may vary greatly from one sample to another.

Compounds are formed by chemical reactions in which the reactants may be other compounds or elements or both. The stability of a particular compound depends on the chemical activity of its component elements. The more active the elements, the more stable the compound. The stability of a compound can be measured by determining the amount of energy (usually in the form of heat or electricity) required to decompose it. The more stable the compound, the more energy that is needed to decompose it.

The chemical and physical characteristics of a compound cannot be predicted from the characteristics of its component elements. For example, two gases may combine to form a liquid, as in the case of water.

**COMPOUNDING A FELONY,** in law, the making of an agreement, especially by the victim of a felony, with the offender not to inform against or prosecute him, in consideration of the payment by the criminal of a reward, bribe, or reparation. Under early common law, compounding made the victim of the crime an accessory after the fact. In modern times, however, compounding a felony is recognized as a separate offense and is usually prohibited by statute.

Since this crime involves no active assistance in the commission of the principal offense, it is distinguishable from being an accessory. Because an agreement to forbear from prosecution is essential to constitute compounding, the taking back of stolen or embezzled property without such an understanding is not punishable, even though a compromise of civil liability is involved.

RICHARD L. HIRSHBERG, *Attorney at Law*

**COMPRESSIVE STRENGTH,** the unit load required to cause a material to fracture or deform permanently. Compressive strength is measured by subjecting a specimen to axial loading in unconfined compression.

When plastic materials and soft metals are tested in compression, the specimen deforms and no fracture occurs. The compressive strength is the unit load that is required to cause permanent deformation. With brittle materials, such as concrete, cast iron, and ceramics, the specimens fracture along shear planes. In this case, compressive strength is the resistance to shearing stresses within the specimen and, by definition, is the total load applied to the specimen divided by the cross-sectional area of the specimen. This quotient is equal to the unit load.

The compressive strength of concrete, about 5,000 psi (350 kgs/sq cm), is approximately 10 times as great as its tensile strength. Because concrete is weaker in tension, steel reinforcing bars are typically used to carry the tension stresses in structural concrete.

Wood is not homogeneous throughout the length or cross section of structural member. The compressive strength of wood is much greater when the load is applied parallel to the grain than when it is applied perpendicular to the grain.

WILLIAM A. CORDON
*Utah State University*

**COMPRESSOR,** kəm-pres'ər, a machine generally used to compress air and other gases from atmospheric pressure to some higher pressure. Compressors are also used, to a small extent, to maintain a partial vacuum, or pressures below atmospheric pressure, by pumping gases out of an enclosed area.

### TYPES OF COMPRESSORS

Low-pressure compressors—particularly those operating below about 2.5 kilograms per square centimeter ($kg/cm^2$; 35 lb per square in, or psi)—are sometimes referred to as blowers. Compressors that raise the pressure only a fraction of a pound per square inch are usually called fans. Compressors can be classified as reciprocating, centrifugal, axial-flow, rotary, and jet. (See FAN.)

**Reciprocating Compressors.** Reciprocating compressors are positive-displacement devices in which air is compressed by a reciprocating piston in a cylinder equipped with intake and discharge valves. Such devices generally consist of a crank, attached to the crankshaft and rotating with it; a connecting rod; and a crosshead, which guides the end of the piston rod in a straight line. In small, single-acting compressors, the crosshead and

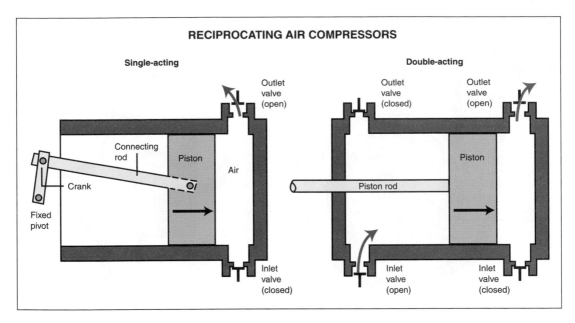

## RECIPROCATING AIR COMPRESSORS

**Single-acting**

Outlet valve (open)

Connecting rod

Piston

Air

Crank

Fixed pivot

Inlet valve (closed)

**Double-acting**

Outlet valve (closed)

Outlet valve (open)

Piston

Piston rod

Inlet valve (open)

Inlet valve (closed)

In the single-acting compressor (*left*), air is admitted and compressed on alternate strokes of the piston. In the double-acting compressor (*right*), air is admitted and compressed on each individual stroke of the piston.

piston rod are often omitted, and the connecting rod is attached directly to an elongated hollow (trunk) piston. In any case, the piston moves back and forth inside the cylinder. The working fluid is admitted to the cylinder through the intake valve on the suction stroke. The valve closes at the end of the stroke, and the piston then moves in the opposite direction, compressing the fluid. It is expelled through the discharge valve at the end of the compression stroke, when the pressure is sufficient to open the valve. The compressor may be single acting (that is, the gas is compressed on only one side of the piston), or it may be double acting (that is, compression takes place first on one side of the piston and then on the other). (See PISTON.)

Older compressors followed the steam-engine practice of using a few cylinders of large bore and long stroke, low-speed and double-acting operation, and a horizontal construction. The automotive internal-combustion engine has led, however, to the development of compressors with many cylinders of small bore and short stroke, high-speed operation, and a vertical construction. (See INTERNAL-COMBUSTION ENGINE.)

Air gets very hot when compressed to high pressure. The temperature may be so high that it causes trouble with the lubrication of the cylinder and piston. For this reason, and also to save considerable power, multistaging may be used, which means that compression is carried out in two or more cylinders. After the air leaves the first, or low-pressure, cylinder, it generally flows through an intercooler, where it is cooled by circulating cold water before it goes to the high-pressure cylinder for more compression. Cooling affects the power saving.

The reciprocating machine is generally most suitable for supplying small amounts of air at rather high pressure. It operates at high efficiency and, when running at constant speed, will deliver a fixed amount of air at any discharge pressure. It does, however, introduce oil vapor from the cylinder lubricant into the gas being compressed, which is objectionable in some applications—for

example, if the gas is to be used in the processing of food.

Reciprocating compressors are widely used to supply the high-pressure air needed for work such as operating tools and cleaning castings when units of only small capacity are required. For many years the reciprocating blowing engine, driven by gas or steam, was also the accepted machine for supplying the large amount of air needed to make pig iron from iron ore in the blast furnace. Similar engines of smaller capacity were also used to supply air to the Bessemer converter, which is used to make steel. The centrifugal blower has, however, almost completely supplanted the piston blower in the last two applications.

**Centrifugal Compressors.** In the centrifugal compressor, the air (or other gas) flows radially through an impeller within a scroll-shaped housing. The impeller, a bladed wheel, rotates rapidly, drawing air in at its center. The wheel rotation is imparted to the air, which is thrown outward by centrifugal force into the diffuser, a narrow ring-shaped space fitted with stationary curved vanes. As the air passes through the wheel, its speed is increased. In the diffuser its speed is decreased, causing an increase in the pressure of the air in accordance with Bernoulli's principle. From the diffuser, the compressed air is discharged into the collector ring, which leads to the outlet. Because these machines rotate at high speeds, the impeller must be perfectly balanced. Even the slightest imbalance would cause vibration, which might wreck the machine. For air pressures of $0.4$ kg/cm$^2$ (6 psi) and under, a single impeller is generally sufficient. Higher pressures usually require multistage compressors having two or more impellers in series. (See BERNOULLI'S PRINCIPLE.)

As a result of their high speed, centrifugal compressors are able to handle large volumes at low pressures. The fluid is delivered in a steady stream, so no receiver is required to even out the flow pulsations (such as is needed with a reciprocating machine). Centrifugal compressors are compact, simple, use no internal valves, need no internal lubrication, and do not introduce oil

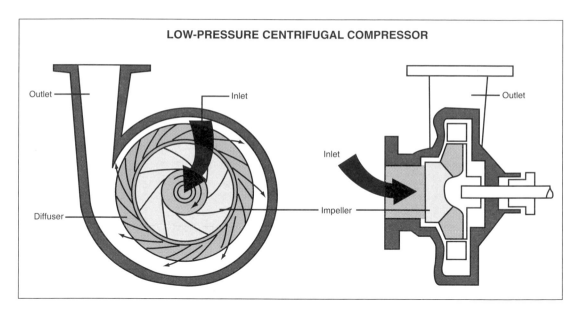

## LOW-PRESSURE CENTRIFUGAL COMPRESSOR

Outlet — Inlet — Outlet

Inlet

Diffuser — Impeller

In the centrifugal compressor, air enters the center of the impeller. The impeller increases the speed of the air as it whirls it radially. The air then strikes the diffuser, which slows it, causing an increase in pressure.

or grease into the air being compressed. The absence of rubbing parts, except for the bearings, keeps costs of their operation fairly low.

For pressures up to 2.1 to 2.5 kg/cm² (30 to 35 psi), multistage centrifugal compressors are generally uncooled. For higher pressures intercoolers are used to lower the gas temperature as it passes from stage to stage. Water-cooled multistage centrifugal compressors can supply large volumes of compressed air at 2.8 to 8.8 kg/cm² (40 to 125 psi) for mining operations, large manufacturing plants, chemical plants, and the like. Using water jackets or intercoolers, these units cool the air during compression.

The modern trend is to use air cooling exclusively, even for the highest compression ratios. This reliance on air cooling recognizes the relative ineffectiveness of any jacket from a heat-transfer point, and the increased investment and operating cost of a water-cooling system. Likewise, the potentialities of intercooling on multistage machines were formerly looked upon with greater favor than they are today. Both the increased cost and the pressure drop of the gas limit intercooling to those few cases where multiple-cylinder construction is substituted for the more usual single-barrel unit.

**Axial-Flow Compressors.** The axial-flow compressor is distinguished by the ring-shaped passage through which the working fluid flows in a direction parallel to the rotor, or impeller, axis and by the alternate rows of stationary and moving blades that increase the pressure level of the fluid. It is the reverse of a turbine. A typical axial-flow compressor consists of a rotor, bearing supports, and a stator housing. The rotor supports the moving-blade rows (rotor blades) and often forms the inner wall of the ring-shaped duct through which the air passes. The rotor may be of hollow, drum-type construction; or the disk type of rotor may

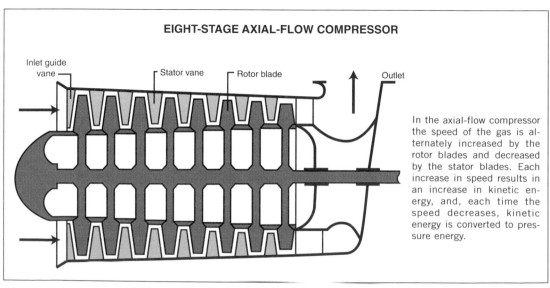

## EIGHT-STAGE AXIAL-FLOW COMPRESSOR

Inlet guide vane — Stator vane — Rotor blade — Outlet

In the axial-flow compressor the speed of the gas is alternately increased by the rotor blades and decreased by the stator blades. Each increase in speed results in an increase in kinetic energy, and, each time the speed decreases, kinetic energy is converted to pressure energy.

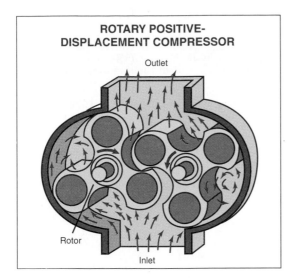

## ROTARY POSITIVE-DISPLACEMENT COMPRESSOR

Outlet

Rotor

Inlet

Roots blowers are widely used in superchargers. As the rotors turn, air is drawn in at the inlet and is carried to the outlet where it undergoes compression.

be used, in which the blade rows are mounted in disks shaped to minimize centrifugal stress. The bearing supports (generally two) form sections of the entrance and exit ring-shaped ducting and provide spokes that transmit loads from the bearings to the outer casing. A balance piston is frequently used to reduce thrust loads. The stator housing supports the stationary-blade rows (stator blades or vanes) and forms the outer wall of the ring-shaped duct. It may be made in two semicircular sections to facilitate assembly and disassembly.

The first row of moving blades accelerates the air (or other gas) that enters the inlet, giving it an increase in speed. The first row of stationary blades then decreases the air's speed, resulting in an increase in pressure according to Bernoulli's principle. The air is then accelerated again by the second row of moving blades and the process is repeated to increase the pressure further.

Axial-flow compressors have several advantages. Fluid leaving one stage enters the next stage without long connecting ducts or change in direction, thus permitting staging for higher pressure ratios. (Each moving-blade row with its adjacent stationary-blade row is called a stage.) The arrangement is compact, so that only a small size is needed for a given flow capacity. The moving blades lie along radial lines, which permits high rotative speed without excessive centrifugal stress. Because an axial-flow compressor has a higher efficiency than a centrifugal device, it is especially attractive for use in gas turbine engines. (See GAS TURBINE.)

**Rotary Positive-Displacement Compressors.** In rotary positive-displacement compressors, a confined volume of air is moved by lobes, gears, or an eccentric pump to successively smaller spaces. As the volume decreases, the pressure increases.

One of the most well-known of the many different kinds of rotary positive-displacement compressors is the Roots blower. It has two two-, three-, or four-lobed rotors. The rotors fit together like gear teeth. As the rotors turn, the fluid is drawn in at the inlet, carried around the outer side of the rotors, and compressed against the gases at higher pressures at the outlet. The Roots blower

is much used in the gas industry, for it can readily handle tar-laden gases and operate simultaneously as a gas meter. It is also used for scavenging and supercharging internal-combustion engines. The Roots blower is limited to pressure ratios of less than two to one, with capacities up to 1,400 cubic meters per minute (50,000 cu ft per minute). Two units may, however, be placed in series to give a higher overall ratio of compression. Among the advantages of Roots blowers are their simple construction and nonuse of intake and discharge valves.

**Jet Compressors.** There are two general types of jet compressors. Hydraulic compressors utilize falling water or water under pressure to compress air without the use of any mechanical moving parts. One of the oldest hydraulic methods of compressing air was the trompe, or water bellows. Water was led from a higher to a lower level through a pipe or hollow bamboo pole having openings in the side through which air entered to mingle with the descending water. This air was then separated from the water at a pressure. One of the most successful of several improved versions developed from this early apparatus is the Taylor compressor. A hydraulic compressor offers a very simple way of utilizing waterpower for compressing air. Although the first cost of the installation is relatively high, operating expenses are low and efficiencies are very high.

A gas and vapor compressor consists essentially of a nozzle in which high-pressure gas or vapor is allowed to expand. The high-velocity jet serves as the actuating fluid to entrain air or other gas and deliver the mixture to the diffuser tube in which kinetic energy is regained as pressure energy. The load may be imposed on either the suction or the discharge, with the jet compressor serving as exhauster or blower, respectively. Steam is frequently used as the actuating medium. Such apparatus finds use for forced and induced draft service, as air supply for processes where the steam is not detrimental, as air ejectors for vacuum applications, and as thermocompressors for heat pumps and air conditioners. (See JET ENGINE; AIR CONDITIONING.)

In the jet compressor a gas is first drawn in and accelerated by the high-velocity motive fluid. It is then compressed in the diffuser, where its kinetic energy is converted to the form of pressure energy.

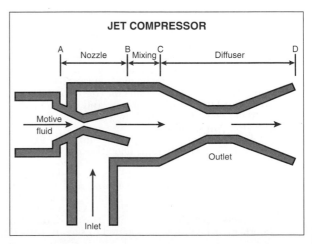

### JET COMPRESSOR

A | Nozzle | B | Mixing | C | Diffuser | D

Motive fluid

Inlet

Outlet

HISTORY

The ordinary bellows, used by blacksmiths and early smelters of iron and other metals, was perhaps the first form of air compressor. The intake valve usually consisted of several holes in the wooden frame, over which were placed flaps of cloth or leather. Some sort of rudimentary check valve was provided on the discharge to prevent air from being taken in from the wrong direction on the suction stroke. By the time of Greek engineer Hero of Alexandria (c. 250 A.D.), the water trompe was being used to provide the blowing air needed in smelting and forging. About 1650 German physicist Otto von Guericke made great improvements in both compressors and vacuum pumps. Then, in 1829, William Mann patented the compound compressing of air (then called stage pumping). It effected greater economy and employed lighter weight machines. (See HERO OF ALEXANDRIA; GUERICKE, OTTO VON.)

Not until 1872 was cooling during compression adopted. The method used—spraying jets of water into the cylinder—was effective enough, but it led to other complications such as corrosion. For this reason it was soon discarded in favor of the water-jacketed cylinder, although some compressors of the wet type were still in use during the early 20th century. The first compressor used in large-scale work in the United States was a four-cylinder unit built in 1866 for the Hoosac Tunnel in Massachusetts.

ELEANOR ALLEN
*Managing Editor of "SAE Transactions"*

**Bibliography:** Bloch, Heinz P., *A Practical Guide to Compressor Technology* (McGraw-Hill 1995); Brown, Royce N., *Compressors: Selection and Sizing*, 2d ed. (Gulf 1997); Japikse, David, *Centrifugal Compressor Design and Performance* (Concepts ETI 1996); McKenzie, A. B., *Axial Flow Fans and Compressors: Aerodynamic Design and Performance* (Ashgate 1997).

## COMPROMISE OF 1820. See MISSOURI COMPROMISE.

## COMPROMISE OF 1850,
the name given to five statutes enacted separately by the U.S. Congress in September 1850 with the collective aim of settling a sectional quarrel over slavery that had developed during the preceding two decades. Henry Clay, the chief architect of the Compromise, saw it as the means of preserving the Union, but the peace it brought was short-lived.

**The Controversy.** The long-standing conflict over slavery was accentuated in the late 1840s by the question of the status of slavery in the territories acquired after the Mexican War. The Wilmot Proviso of 1846, which declared that slavery should never exist in any territories obtained from Mexico, had not become law, but it remained a rallying cry for the Northern opponents of human bondage. Southern demands for a more stringent fugitive slave law, Northern clamor for excluding slavery from the District of Columbia, and a border dispute between Texas and New Mexico further complicated the situation.

When Congress met in December 1849, disputes over these questions filled the air. The House of Representatives consisted of 112 Democrats, 105 Whigs, 12 Free Soilers, and 1 Native American. The parties split over the issues, and no party had a stable parliamentary majority. For example, it took 63 ballots to elect Howell Cobb of Georgia speaker of the House, and the election of a doorkeeper favorable or opposed to slavery caused

days of debate. A Southern convention was scheduled for Nashville in June 1850, and many feared that it would result in the secession of a number of Southern states. The Union seemed to be in the process of dissolution.

Political leaders offered a variety of proposals for dealing with this situation. President Zachary Taylor, a Louisiana slaveholder, took a national point of view and proposed the immediate admission of California, which wished to come in as a free state. John C. Calhoun demanded equal rights for slavery in the new West and its full protection in the East, and Southern extremists declared that if such demands were not met, the Union must be dissolved. Clay, supported by Daniel Webster and Stephen A. Douglas, took the lead in proposing a compromise settlement. Salmon P. Chase and William H. Seward opposed any compromise with slavery.

**Clay's Compromise.** On Jan. 29, 1850, Clay proposed in the Senate a plan of adjustment that eventually resulted in five statutes. One admitted California as a free state. Another created the Territory of New Mexico without reference to slavery and provided that Texas would relinquish some 125,000 square miles (324,000 sq km) of territory claimed by New Mexico, receiving $10,000,000 as compensation from the federal government. A third bill created the Territory of Utah, also without reference to slavery. A fourth bill was designed to facilitate the return of fugitive slaves. (There would be no jury trial; affidavit by a claimant would establish his title to the slave; the federal commissioner who presided at the hearing would receive $10 if he remanded the fugitive to slavery, $5 if he ordered the slave's release.) The fifth measure prohibited bringing slaves into the District of Columbia for transportation or sale.

In reporting out these bills on May 8, a Senate committee of 13, headed by Clay, combined the provisions relating to the territories of California, New Mexico, and Utah in a so-called "Omnibus" in order to facilitate their passage. Southern senators and representatives feared that if the California bill passed separately, Northerners would refuse to pass the measures favored by the South. The fugitive slave and District of Columbia measures were offered separately.

All the bills encountered stormy weather. Prospects for passage heightened after the death of President Taylor on July 9, because the new president, Millard Fillmore, was friendly toward Clay and toward the Compromise; but opposition remained strong. On July 31 the "Omnibus" went down to defeat. Clay, exhausted, went off to Newport, R.I., for a rest. In his absence Douglas took charge and succeeded in gaining separate passage of all the measures except the District of Columbia bill, and when Clay returned, he steered that bill through Congress on September 17. The enactment of the five bills owed more to Democratic than to Whig votes.

**Results.** Many Americans believed that the Compromise would end the sectional strife over slavery. Webster declared that it was the most important legislation in 30 years. Others were not so certain. In the North the Fugitive Slave Law produced deep resentment, and there were a number of spectacular rescues of escaped bondsmen. By and large, the country accepted the Compromise as a finality, but events proved that it merely furnished a respite. The Kansas-Nebraska Act of

1854, by repealing the Missouri Compromise of 1820, provoked a new outburst of antislavery feeling and took the country a giant step along the road to war.

GLYNDON G. VAN DEUSEN
*University of Rochester*

**Bibliography:** Hamilton, Holman, *Prologue to Conflict* (Norton 1966); Holt, Michael F., *The Political Crisis of the 1850's* (Norton 1983).

**COMPROMISE TARIFF OF 1833.** See NULLIFICATION.

**COMPSOGNATHUS,** komp-sog′na(nə)-thəs, a small carnivorous bipedal dinosaur. The first *Compsognathus* specimen was discovered in the late 1850s in a limestone deposit near Kelheim, Bavaria. The same deposit, from the Late Jurassic Period (which ended about 144 million years ago), is also well known for having yielded the first specimen of *Archaeopteryx*, the oldest known bird. *Compsognathus* is classified, together with all other carnivorous dinosaurs, in the group Theropoda.

In a report published in 1859, German paleontologist Andreas Wagner contended that *Compsognathus* ("elegant jaw," a reference to the lightly built skull) had been an ancient lizardlike animal. It was not until 1868 that the dinosaurian characteristics of the 28-inch- (70-cm-) long specimen were recognized, by British biologist Thomas Henry Huxley. He believed that *Compsognathus* represented a link between birds and reptiles. The idea that birds evolved from dinosaurs, however, would not gain favor with the majority of paleontologists for approximately another century.

Owing to the presence of tiny polygonal structures in the belly region of the skeleton, *Compsognathus* was initially thought to have borne extensive armor, in the form of a horny skin. This theory has since been discounted, the patterns having been recognized as flaws caused by natural mineral solutions circulating through the fossil's surrounding rock. The same explanation has also been offered for what initially appeared to be preserved muscle fibers on the specimen.

Although there is some disagreement regarding hand structure, *Compsognathus* apparently had only two, rather than three, functional fingers on each hand. This characteristic was shared with only the much larger tyrannosaurids, including *Tyrannosaurus rex.*

*Compsognathus* was probably well suited to hunting, possessing not only sharp, serrated teeth but also the long slender legs and powerfully built thigh bones needed to outrun prey. Nonetheless, because the only known skeletons of this dinosaur have been found in marine rock, *Compsognathus* has commonly been portrayed as a scavenger, feeding on dead sea animals that washed ashore. According to a second view, however, the dinosaur lived inland, where it pursued live prey, with its bones becoming fossilized in marine rock only after being swept downriver and out to sea.

The notion that *Compsognathus* was an active hunter is supported by the fact that the German specimen contained the well-preserved skeleton of a tiny land-dwelling lizard, *Bavarisaurus* ("Bavarian lizard"), within its stomach area. *Compsognathus*'s small size suggests that insects also may have been an important food source.

A second complete *Compsognathus* skeleton was discovered in 1972, near Nice, France. The specimen, from the end of the Jurassic or beginning of the Cretaceous Period, was slightly younger than the German fossil. Because the French dinosaur was almost 50% larger than the other find, it has been suggested that either the second skeleton represents a different species of *Compsognathus* or the initial fossil did not belong to a fully grown adult. The latter idea is supported by the German specimen's long legs, sizable skull, and large eyes, all features of an immature animal. However, the skeleton also bears adult characteristics, including well-ossified bones and closed vertebral sutures.

A close relative of *Compsognathus* has further bolstered the theory that birds evolved from dinosaurs. A fossilized *Sinosauropteryx* ("Chinese dragon feather") taken from Early Cretaceous lake deposits in Liaoning, a Manchurian province in northeastern China, reveals a covering of featherlike structures. Although these feathers, some of which were more than 1 inch (2.5 cm) long, could not have been used for flight, they probably served as insulation against extreme temperatures. This suggests that *Sinosauropteryx* was endothermic, since warm-blooded animals use insulation to prevent the loss of internally produced body heat. The Chinese fossil may also indicate that other small theropods, including *Compsognathus*, bore feathers.

Both *Compsognathus* and *Sinosauropteryx* belong to the theropod subgroup Coelurosauria, which also includes the Tyrannosauridae, Dromaeosauridae, and several other types of dinosaurs as well as, according to the previously discussed theory, Aves (birds). The coelurosaurs shared certain features, including an expanded, circular

Although remains of *Compsognathus* have been found only in marine rock, opinions differ as to whether it was a coastal scavenger or an active inland predator.

eye socket and specializations of the pelvis, ankle, and tail that gave these animals greater speed and agility than earlier dinosaurs had. (See also DINOSAUR; JURASSIC PERIOD.)

JAMES I. KIRKLAND
*Utah Geological Survey*

**Bibliography:** Ackerman, Jennifer, "Dinosaurs Take Wing," *National Geographic* 194 (1998):75–99; Callison, George, and Helen M. Quimby, "Tiny Dinosaurs: Are They Fully Grown?," *Journal of Vertebrate Paleontology* 3 (1984):200–209; Currie, Philip J., and Kevin Padian, eds., *Encyclopedia of Dinosaurs* (Academic Press 1997).

**COMPTON, Arthur Holly,** komp′tən (1892–1962), American physicist whose discovery and explanation of the Compton effect, named for him, provided an important confirmation of the quantum theory. For this work, Compton was awarded a share of the 1927 Nobel Prize for physics.

Compton embarked on his career at a time of great excitement in the world of physics. Max Planck had theorized in 1900 that energy was not continuous but granular, being emitted and absorbed in packets called quanta. In 1911 Ernest Rutherford (later 1st Baron Rutherford of Nelson) had suggested an atomic model that had the interesting property of being totally impossible according to classical electrodynamic theory. In 1913 Niels Bohr applied Planck's concept of quanta to Rutherford's nuclear atom with striking success. Bohr's theory relied, however, on a number of questionable assumptions and arbitrary hypotheses which perturbed scientists. The basic question was: "Do quanta really exist, or are they merely convenient mental constructions of physicists?" Compton's first major research seemingly had little to do with this fundamental question, but the result, which was called the Compton effect, was to be used as important proof of the quantum theory.

In 1920 Compton was attracted to the strange behavior of X rays when directed at substances of low atomic weight. Most of the radiation was simply scattered, but part of the secondary radiation differed considerably from the primary, having a longer wavelength. In 1923 Compton showed that this effect could be explained in terms of the collision of an X-ray quantum with an electron, the X-ray quantum continuing on with diminished energy (longer wavelength) and the electron recoiling from the collision. C. T. R. Wilson of England soon detected these recoiling electrons, and Compton's explanation was validated. The quantum theory had received impressive confirmation.

Using X rays, Compton later devised a method of determining the distribution of electrons in atoms. In the 1930s he also did important work on cosmic rays.

Compton was born in Wooster, Ohio, on Sept. 10, 1892. His home environment provided him with an unusual background for an American scientist. His father was both a Presbyterian minister and a professor of philosophy at the College of Wooster. For Compton, religion, with a deep philosophical tinge, and science were essentially one. This feeling particularly marked his later writings, when he and his generation confronted the problems involved in the unleashing of atomic power. He was educated at the College of Wooster and at Princeton University, where he received a Ph.D. degree in physics in 1916. In later years he recalled that it was the discovery of radium

by Pierre and Marie Curie that first aroused his interest in the study of the atom.

During World War II, Compton played a leading part in the development of the first nuclear chain reaction and was instrumental in setting up the Manhattan Project, which created the first atomic bomb. Thereafter he served as an adviser to the United States government. He held many teaching positions and from 1945 to 1953 was chancellor of Washington University in St. Louis. Compton died in Berkeley, Calif., on March 15, 1962.

L. PEARCE WILLIAMS
*Cornell University*

**COMPTON, Fay,** komp′tən (1894–1978), English actress, noted for her roles in a great variety of productions, ranging from Shakespearean tragedies to London music hall revues. She was born in London on Sept. 18, 1894, into a family of actors. She made her professional debut in London in 1911 and her American debut in 1914. Her first appearance on the London music hall stage was in 1939. Later she appeared with the Old Vic and the Chichester Festival Theatre.

Compton's Shakespearean roles included Ophelia in *Hamlet* (opposite John Barrymore in 1925 and John Gielgud in 1939), Paulina in *The Winter's Tale* (1937), Volumnia in *Coriolanus* (1954), and Queen Margaret in *Richard III* (1957). Some of her other leading roles were in *Mary Rose* (1920), *Autumn Crocus* (1931), and *A Month in the Country* (1965). She died on Dec. 12, 1978.

**COMPTON, Henry,** komp′tən (1632–1713), English bishop. He was born at Compton Wynyates in Warwickshire. Compton studied at Queen's College, Oxford, and after brief service in the army he was ordained in the Church of England in 1666. He became bishop of Oxford in 1674 and bishop of London in 1675.

Compton was conciliatory toward Protestant dissenters, and so displeased the Roman Catholic King James II that he was denied his seat on the privy council. When Compton refused the royal command to suspend John Sharp, rector of St. Giles in the Field, who had preached against Roman Catholicism, Compton himself was then suspended. He was restored to his see after the Revolution of 1688, and with the bishop of Bristol voted to place the Protestants William and Mary on the throne. He performed the coronation ceremony and was appointed one of the commissioners to revise the Anglican liturgy. During the reign of Anne he was on the commission for the union of England and Scotland. Compton died at Fulham, London, on July 7, 1713.

**COMPTON, Karl Taylor,** komp′tən (1887–1954), American educator and physicist. Compton was born in Wooster, Ohio, on Sept. 14, 1887. He was educated at the College of Wooster and Princeton University, where he received a Ph.D. degree in 1912. Although he contributed a number of papers in the fields of thermionics and spectroscopy, his greatest talent was as an administrator and educator. It was especially as president of the Massachusetts Institute of Technology (MIT) from 1930 to 1948 and as chairman of the corporation of MIT from 1949 to 1954 that he left his mark. Compton realized that American institutes of technology, not excluding MIT, had a tendency to view the engineering profession narrowly. He felt that the engineering curriculum needed widening and he led the movement to introduce more of pure science and of the humanities into technical training. After his arrival at MIT in 1930 he worked a quiet revolution that affected all higher technical training in the United States. During World War II Comptom set up and headed the radiation laboratory at MIT where most of the American work on radar was accomplished. After the war he was active on a policy level in coordinating scientific research with national defense. Compton died in New York City on June 22, 1954. He was the older brother of Arthur H. Compton.

L. Pearce Williams,
*Cornell University*

**COMPTON,** komp'tən, a city in southern California, in Los Angeles county, about midway between downtown Los Angeles and Long Beach. It was an agricultural center until the Los Angeles area entered a period of greatly accelerated population growth during World War II. It has since become primarily a residential and industrial city, with more than 150 manufacturing plants producing electronics equipment, aircraft parts, oil tools, pipe, nonferrous castings, roofing, heaters, structural steel, and other products. Compton College, a publically controlled 2-year college, is situated there.

The area was settled in 1867 by a Methodist farming group led by Griffith Dickinson Compton, for whom the agricultural community was named. Most of the city lies on land that was formerly part of the vast Domínguez landholdings known as the Rancho San Pedro. Called the "Hub City," Compton was incorporated in 1888 and has a city-manager government. Population: 93,493.

Lloyd R. De Garmo
*Head Librarian, Compton College Library*

**COMPTON-BURNETT, Ivy,** kump'tən bûr-net' (1892–1969), English author who wrote witty novels about family relationships in the British upper middle class. She was born in London and studied at the University of London, where she received a degree in 1906. She lived most of her life in London. In 1951 she became a Commander of the Order of the British Empire, and in 1956, Compton-Burnett was awarded the James Tait Black Memorial Prize for her novel *Mother and Son* (1955). She died in London on Aug. 27, 1969.

I. Compton-Burnett, as she signed herself, was an innovator in the novel form, writing almost entirely in dialogue to the exclusion of narrative and description. Her settings, late-Victorian, usually a country house, are backdrops for conversations that reveal her characters as they dominate their families or are dominated by them, and as they react to incidents, usually shocking, in their family lives. Her plots have some affinity with Greek tragedy, her dialogue with the comedy of manners, and her subjects with the novels of Jane Austen. Her first major novel was *Brothers and Sisters* (1929). Compton-Burnett's works also include *Dolores* (1911), *Men and Wives* (1931), *A House and Its Head* (1935), *Elders and Betters* (1944), *Two Worlds and Their Ways* (1949), and *A God and His Gifts* (1963).

J. K. Johnstone
*University of Saskatchewan*

**COMPTON EFFECT.** See Compton, Arthur Holly; and Quantum Theory—*The Compton Effect.*

**COMPTROLLER OF THE CURRENCY.** See Treasury Department, United States.

**COMPULSION,** in psychology, the necessity to carry out a seemingly illogical, unwanted action. Compulsions range from seemingly trivial rituals or habits, such as licking one's lips or hunching one's shoulders repeatedly, to more serious ones, such as compulsive stealing (kleptomania) or compulsive washing and rewashing of the hands (handwashing mania).

Compulsions may be divided into two broad types: antisocial impulses, such as kleptomania, and self-corrective impulses, such as handwashing mania. Compulsions are usually regarded as a sign of neurosis. The traditional term in psychiatry is *obsessive-compulsive neurosis.*

**Freudian Theories.** When the Austrian psychoanalyst Sigmund Freud tried to explain this form of neurosis, he encountered a difficulty. His general theory of neurosis held that undesired ideas or drives are repressed and not available to conscious awareness and that the end result of this repression is a set of symptoms representing the repressed drives seeking expression in disguised form. In compulsive behavior, however, the individual is aware that he or she is carrying out some unwanted behavior. Despite wishing not to behave this way, the person is aware that he or she is unable to remove the impulse from his or her mind.

Freud and other early psychoanalysts were forced to expand the general theory of neurosis in order to account for obsessions (morbid, recurring, unwanted thoughts) and compulsions. Freud decided that the unacceptable idea, while it does intrude into awareness, lacks the normally expected associations and emotional ramifications. Thus, although the impulse or idea is not repressed, its rich emotional accompaniments are repressed. For example, a patient may engage in compulsive handwashing in order to act out guilt feelings, but the actual feeling of guilt is not experienced during the handwashing ritual. This process, in which the impulse is divorced from the usual feelings and emotional associations, is called isolation. Freud and his followers related compulsions to the sadistic anal stage of personality development and alleged that the predisposition to this kind of behavior is related to very strict toilet training by a parent or other caregiver.

**Non-Freudian Explanations.** Many modern American authorities on child development feel that the psychoanalysts overstressed the role of toilet training in the forming of compulsions. The critical factor, they believe, is the perfectionistic, demanding approach the parent had toward the child in the child's early years. Many authorities have commented on the personality traits of people who tend to develop compulsions: they are exacting and pedantic thinkers, perfectionistic, and emotionally rather cold and aloof, with a good deal of hostility in their general attitude toward others. There is often a history of difficult relations with the parent of the opposite sex. It is generally agreed that compulsions represent defenses against some impulse that arouses anxiety in the individual. Although some people experience compulsions but do not have obsessions, the traditional finding is that a patient suffers both obsessions and compulsions.

Austin E. Grigg*
*University of Richmond*

## COMPUTER-AIDED DESIGN AND COMPUTER-AIDED MANUFACTURING,

**COMPUTER-AIDED DESIGN AND COMPUTER-AIDED MANUFACTURING,** or CAD/CAM, the process of electronically linking computer systems and personnel who perform design and manufacturing functions. Individually, CAD represents computer-aided design, while CAM stands for computer-aided manufacturing.

Prior to the widespread use of computer technology, companies often treated design and manufacturing as distinct and separate entities. By the 1990s global economic competition required companies to implement higher product quality, faster market response time, and lower product costs. CAD/CAM has enabled companies meet these challenges by providing an integrated systems approach in which design and manufacturing engineers can interact and communicate with each other, their customers, and other components within a company.

**Computer-Aided Design.** Computer-aided design (CAD) can be defined as the use of computer systems to help in the creation, modification, analysis, or optimization of a design. CAD computer programs are capable of generating geometric models of basic components, for example, mechanical parts such as gears, racks, springs, bushings, and bearings. Applications programs are used to simplify and verify the functionality of engineering designs before working models are created. Other programs translate drawing parameters for use by manufacturing equipment including machine tools and robots.

Designers use CAD systems to create models that may be viewed on a computer monitor. Electronic designs are constructed by manipulating basic sets of geometric components, such as lines and circles, splines, or surfacing representations. These basic elements are generated on a screen, where designers size and orient them appropriately and then trim or adjust the elements to create drawings of components. In other words, drawings of complex parts can be built by using basic geometric elements to create a model. Several different methods may be used to represent an object in geometric modeling.

Wire frame geometric modeling is classified into three types; two-dimensional, two-and-one-half dimensional, and three-dimensional modeling. Wire frames are used in this format to represent the object, which is displayed by interconnecting lines. The type of modeling used depends on the capabilities of the interactive computer graphics system and the object being pictured. Two-dimensional representation is used to represent flat objects. Two-and-one-half dimensional models permit a more thorough representation than a two-dimensional view in that a three-dimensional object may be represented as long as it has no side wall details. Three-dimensional representations allow the modeling of all surfaces of more complex geometries.

The most advanced method of geometric modeling is called solid modeling. Solid basic geometrical shapes called primitives are typically used in this method to construct the object in three dimensions. A logical relationship among elements of the design is maintained so that new shapes may be rapidly created.

CAD models also enhance the clarity of a design because the user is allowed to rotate complex parts and view them from multiple angles. Many complex coordinate transformations must be calculated to do this, and these repetitive math-

© JOHN ZOINER/UNIPHOTO

Rendering models using CAD systems allows engineers to test for potential weaknesses in a design well before a structure is built.

ematical processes that can be quickly performed by a computer would take a human hours, days, or months to calculate. Some CAD systems also allow the designer to simulate the movement of a part, for example, a piece that is hinged, which allows the user to perform tests (such as tests for clearance) without actually building a prototype. Most computer-aided design systems currently available offer extensive capabilities for developing engineering drawings. These capabilities include automatic crosshatching of surfaces in drawing from wire frame models, the ability to write text on drawings, the semiautomatic dimensioning of drawings, and the automatic generation of a bill of materials needed to manufacture the item pictured. Additional features such as color, shading, and textures are available on some CAD systems in order to enhance the visualization of geometric models. For instance, color helps to clarify components grouped in an assembly or to highlight dimensions of a single component. Graphics systems with these capabilities are used for a wide range of applications outside of computer-aided design or manufacturing. Applications include color illustrations in magazines and technical publications, film animation, and training simulators such as flight-training simulators.

Application programs aid designers in performing stress analysis of components or computer-aided engineering (CAE), dynamic response of mechanisms, and heat transfer calculations. For example, given the finite elements, boundary conditions, and engineering theory, an applications program can determine factors such as the maximum load the components can withstand before failure, or the rate of heat transfer through a component. Furthermore, applications programs may aid in the numerical control part programming used to direct the motion of factory equipment. To accomplish this, a part programmer plans the process for the portions of the job to be accomplished by numerical control. The machining instructions are prepared on a form called a part programmer manuscript, which is a listing of the cutter/workpiece positions that must be followed to machine a part. In computer-assisted part programming, much of the tedious computational work required by manual part programming is transferred to the computer. Use of the computer for complex workpiece geometries and jobs with many machining steps results in significant savings in part-programming time. Many of these techniques, historically available only to component designers, are now widely available to people responsible for planning and performing manufacturing operations such as machining. These techniques replace intuitive decision-making with a more scientific approach, leading to higher product quality and improved production rates.

**Computer-Aided Manufacturing.** Computer-aided manufacturing (CAM) can be defined as the use of computer systems to plan, manage, and control the operations of a manufacturing plant through either direct or indirect computer interfacing with the production resources of the plant. In CAD/CAM systems, information developed in the design phase is delivered electronically to the manufacturing site. The applications of CAM fall into two broad categories: (1) computer monitoring and (2) computer control or manufacturing support.

Computer process monitoring requires a direct computer interface with the manufacturing process to obtain information from the process and associated equipment. For example, a technician may rely on a detection sensor connected to a computer to monitor tool wear. Typically the monitoring process analyzes a given input, such as cutting force, and makes a decision about the impending failure of the tool. Thus, an increasing cutting force can be monitored by an indicator of increased tool wear. By using computer process monitoring, a responsible technician, guided by information collected by the computer, controls the process.

Computer process control goes one step further than monitoring by automating the process. During equipment operation, computers use sensed information from the process, analyze it, and modify the operation based on previously written computer programs. In computer process monitoring, the flow of data between the manufacturing process and the computer is in only one direction, that is, from the process to the computer. However, with computer process control, the computer interface allows a two-way flow of data. Signals are transmitted back and forth between the computer and the manufacturing process.

In addition to applications involving a direct computer process interface, CAM includes indirect applications wherein the computer serves a support role in the manufacturing operations of a plant. With indirect applications the computer is not directly linked to a manufacturing process. Instead, networked computers provide access to process plans, production schedules, tooling information, a variety of forecasts, processing estimates, and information that will enhance the effective management of production resources. (See also ROBOT; ARTIFICIAL INTELLIGENCE.)

**Computers Used for CAD/CAM Applications.** Mainframes historically have been the computers used for CAD/CAM applications; however, by the 1990s many CAD/CAM applications were also operating on engineering workstations and personal computers. Often employed in applications requiring very large data-processing and memory capacity, mainframes typically support many peripheral devices and can drive several devices simultaneously.

Multiple workstations are often networked to facilitate the concurrent development of new products by using many functions within a single CAD/CAM application. Workstations provide powerful computing capabilities with advanced operating systems that harness the power of their CPUs (central processing units) and hardware architectures. Basic CAD/CAM applications are frequently run on high capability personal computers. Personal computers typically provide lower graphical resolution and operate more slowly than workstations. (See PERSONAL COMPUTERS AND WORKSTATIONS.)

**CAD/CAM Applications.** CAD/CAM applications have become an integral part of design and manufacturing industry process. Traditionally, designers created a design for the product; passed on the paper output to the manufacturing engineers, who often modified the design model and then sent it back for approval. Thus the product design entered into a loop, ended only by time constraints and the customer's need for a final product. Even minor modifications meant delays while the model was completely redrawn. During this long and tedious process, critical factors were sometimes overlooked, to the detriment of the final product.

A CAM system can be used to optimize and manage industrial processes that involve, for example, this IRB 6000 industrial robot.

COURTESY ABB FLEXIBLE AUTOMATION INC.

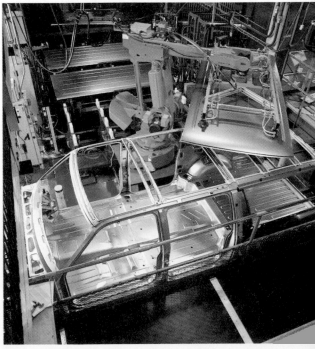

In contrast, design and manufacturing engineers using an online CAD/CAM system provide one another with continuous feedback, thus accelerating and enhancing the design process. Consequently, the modification time is significantly reduced. For example, analysis of inputs including the efficiency or tolerance parameters in automotive parts such as engines or transmissions can swiftly be performed. With the help of application software, manufacturing engineers can generate tool paths required for cutting components from basic metal shapes, material requirements, and production schedules in a matter of minutes, whereas such tasks previously required days to complete.

A host of specialized design and manufacturing firms have been formed to take advantage of these methodologies. With the help of electronic data links, firms remain in close contact with their clients, while concentrating on their field of specialization at the same time. CAD/CAM applications have become an integral part of the design and manufacturing process for automobile manufacturers. Auto companies can significantly reduce design costs by modeling vehicle designs on computers because this method eliminates the need for multiple prototypes. Using computer technology, designers can improve aerodynamics, evaluate safety features through crash simulations, or implement process monitoring of paint finishes to meet the expectations of a global market.

CAD/CAM technology also has extensive applications in the architectural field. Architects use CAD systems to design structures and view these designs three-dimensionally; they and their clients use CAD applications to observe building models from many angles, both internally and externally, to detect flaws and fine-tune plans before construction begins. Further applications add construction details for air ducts, utility paths, computing the amount of structural materials required, and estimating the deflection of building elements under varying loads from snow, vibration, or earthquake in planned buildings. Other industries in which CAD/CAM technology has been invaluable include fashion design, where directions for cutting a pattern are sent electronically to a computer-driven machine once a clothing pattern has been laid out. In the electronics industry CAD/CAM applications have been employed to aid in the design of printed circuit boards, components, and computer peripherals.

See also AUTOMATIC CONTROL; AUTOMATION—*Types of Automation*; MACHINE TOOL—*Automation*; MASS PRODUCTION—*Numerical Control*; MICROPROCESSOR; AIRPLANE.

EMORY ZIMMERS
*Lehigh University*

**Bibliography**

Epsito, Anthony, "Computers for CAD/CAM," *Machine Design* (June 1991):724–731.
Erisman, Albert M., and Kenneth W. Neves, "Advanced Computing for Manufacturing," *Scientific American* (August 1991):163–169.
Groover, Mikell, and Emory W. Zimmers, *CAD/CAM: Computer-Aided Design and Manufacturing* (Prentice-Hall 1984).
Halton, Richard, *Making CAD/CAM Work* (Prentice Hall 1993).
Kochan, D., ed., *Integration of CAD/CAM* (Elsevier Pub. Co. 1993).
McMahon, Chris, and James J. Brown, *CAD/CAM: From Principles to Practice* (Addison-Wesley 1993).
Toriya, H., and H. Chiyokura, eds., *Three-D CAD Principles and Applications*, tr. by Hiromi Yaguchi (Springer-Verlag 1993).
Zachary, William B., "Building an Operations Management Foundation That Will Last: TQM, JIT and CIM," *Industrial Engineering* (August 1993):39–43.
Zimmers, Emory W., Jr., "CAD/CAM Applications in Machining," *Metals Handbook*, 9th ed., vol. 16, ed. by Joseph R. Davis et al. (1989):627–636.

**COMPUTERS AND COMPUTER SCIENCE.** A computer is a device that automatically performs calculations and sorts, files, edits, or otherwise processes information. The term now is applied especially to electronic digital computers, whose operation is based on the processing of discrete quantities of information such as digits or characters, in contrast to analog computers, whose operation is based on continuously variable quantities such as lengths, weights, or voltages. Electronic digital computers are the culmination of a long line of computing devices, including knotted strings, tallying pebbles, the abacus, and the adding machine. In the latter part of the 20th century, computers, along with their associated technologies, changed the way people communicate, work, and learn, thus transforming society worldwide. The four articles that follow—"Computer Science," "History of the Computer," "Computer Architecture and Design," and "Computer Systems and Methodologies"—constitute a well-rounded look at the principles behind mechanical and electronic components created to form computers, as well as the events that led to technological innovations. An extensive discussion of computer science, which may be defined as the study of the ways computers are utilized both to collect and to disseminate information, is included in this group of articles. For further information regarding the impact computers have made on the way people live and work in the 20th century, see COMPUTERS AND SOCIETY. Other related articles include MICROPROCESSOR; COMPUTER-AIDED DESIGN AND COMPUTER-AIDED MANUFACTURING; and ROBOT.

## 1. Computer Science

The discipline of computing has been characterized by the Association for Computing Machinery as "the systematic study of algorithmic processes—their theory, analysis, design, efficiency, implementation, and application—that describe and transform information. In Europe the discipline of computing is called informatics, a name that directs attention to the central role of information. The fundamental question underlying all of computing is, What can be efficiently automated?" Some computer scientists summarize this by saying that the field studies digital computers and the phenomena surrounding them.

The discipline of computer science has broadened to include not only computers but also the ways in which people have utilized computers. The story of the development of computer science is intimately interwoven with the story of how human beings work and socialize together. The computing profession comprises the people and the institutions that are devoted to taking care of people's concerns for information processing and coordinated work through worldwide communication systems. The profession contains various specialties such as computer science, software engineering, computational science, information systems, and computer-aided design.

### ORIGINS

The roots of computing can be traced back many centuries, extending deeply into the fields of mathematics, science, and engineering. Mathematics imparts analysis to the field; science im-

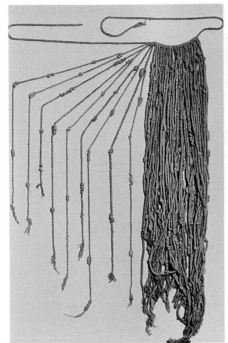

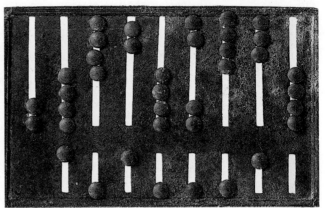

The Inca kept numerical records by tying knots on strands on quipu (*left*); the size and placement of the knots indicated specific decimal numbers. The counters on this Roman abacus (*above*) were used to perform the four basic arithmetic operations.

parts experimental method and modeling; engineering imparts design. Like many physical science disciplines, computing embraces its own theory and experiment. Unlike those disciplines, computing embraces the applications of computing and the design of useful computer systems.

The explicit and intricate intertwining of the ancient threads of calculation and logical symbol manipulation, together with the modern threads of electronics and electronic information codes, has given birth to the discipline of computing. For thousands of years, calculation has been a principal concern of mathematics. Many models of physical phenomena have been used to derive equations whose solutions yield predictions—such as calculations of planetary orbits and weather forecasts. Many general methods for solving such equations have been devised—for instance, algorithms for solving linear systems or for integrating functions. For almost the same period, a primary concern of engineering has been calculations that aid in the design of mechanical systems. Examples include algorithms for evaluating stresses in bridges; measuring distances, much larger or smaller than our immediate perception; and determining the power of an engine.

One product resulting from the long symbiotic relationship between engineering and mathematics has been mechanical aids for calculating. Some surveyors' and navigators' instruments date back a thousand years. Both Pascal and Leibniz built arithmetic calculators in the mid-1600s. In the 1830s Charles Babbage conceived of an "analytical engine" that could mechanically and without error evaluate logarithms and other general arithmetic functions. His machine, which was never completed, served as an inspiration for later work. In the 1920s Vannevar Bush constructed an electronic analog computer for solving general systems of differential equations. During the same period, electromechanical calculating machines capable of addition, subtraction, multiplication, division, and the calculation of square roots became available.

Logic is a branch of mathematics concerned with the validity of inference and formal principles of reasoning. Since the days of Euclid, logic has been a tool for rigorous mathematical and scientific argument. In the 19th century a search began for a universal system of logic that would allow anyone to determine mechanically whether any given statement is true or false. Such a system was perceived as the epitome of human rationality and would have guaranteed a permanent place in history for its inventor. In 1931 Kurt Gödel published his "incompleteness theorem," showing that no such system can be possible. In the late 1930s Alan Turing explored the idea of a universal computer that could simulate any step-by-step procedure of any other computing machine. His conclusion was similar to Gödel's: Some well-defined problems cannot be solved by any mechanical procedure. Even before the first general-purpose computing machines were built, these theorems provided deep insights into the limits of automatic calculation.

In studying deduction and, later, universal computation, logicians developed methods for encoding statements as strings of symbols. Those strings could sometimes be interpreted as meaningful statements and sometimes as data to be manipulated. Today we call this flexibility of interpretation the "interchangeability of data and instruction." This insight has been the key idea distinguishing the stored-program computer from calculating machines. The steps of the algorithm have been encoded in a machine representation and stored in the memory for later decoding and execution by the processor. The machine code can be derived mechanically from a higher-level symbolic form, the programming language.

### FOUNDATIONS

The digital computer plays the central role in discussions regarding computer science because it is a universal computing machine. With enough memory a digital computer has the capability of simulating any information-processing system, provided the task can be specified as an unambiguous set of instructions. One machine model has the capability of exploring and studying a great variety of concepts, schemes, simulations, and techniques of information processing. Three skills have become necessary to deal effectively with these digital computers in practice: algorithmic thinking, representation, and programming.

**Algorithmic Thinking.** Algorithmic thinking can be described as an interpretation of the world in which one understands and formulates actions in terms of step-by-step procedures that give unambiguous results when carried out by a person or by a suitable machine. Algorithmic thinking resembles standard scientific thinking, which seeks to invent standard ways of observing that allow anyone to see and reproduce physical effects. Algorithmic thinking emphasizes procedure, modeling, and observation.

**Representation.** Representation addresses the way in which data are stored so that the questions one may ask about them can be answered efficiently. For example, a standard phone book may be organized in a computer database for quick answers to questions such as "What is the phone number assigned to person $N$?" The machine goes quickly to the alphabetic part of the list containing the name $N$. However, this would not be an efficient organization to answer the question "To whom is the phone number $N$ assigned?" because the standard book would then have to be searched entry by entry until the given phone number was found. A data organization more suited to the second question might be a listing of phone numbers in their numeric order, accompanied by the names of their owners.

The skill of representation reaches beyond knowing how to organize data for efficient retrieval or processing. It involves inventing ways of encoding phenomena to allow algorithmic processing. Examples include representing a mathematical expression so that it can be differentiated; representing a document so that "what you see (on the computer screen) is what you get (on the printout)"; representing handwritten ZIP codes for automatic recognition and sorting by the Postal Service; representing encoded speech so that one can talk to a computer; and creating the representation of an engine part so that it can be shown on the display screen and then manufactured.

**Programming.** Programming has enabled people to embody algorithmic thinking and representation concepts in software that will cause a machine to perform in a prescribed way. This skill includes working knowledge of different programming languages (each having its own strengths and limitations), program-development tools (which aid in testing, debugging, modularity, and compatibility), and operating systems (which control the internal operations of computers). Though everyone in the computer science field is expected to have this basic skill, it would be a mistake to equate computer science with programming. Many aspects of the discipline do not involve programming, even though they involve algorithmic thinking and representation.

### RELATIONSHIP WITH OTHER DISCIPLINES

A number of other disciplines have close relationships with computing, notably mathematics, biology, management, economics, engineering, physical science, library science, linguistics, and philosophy; each of these disciplines claims information as a central or important principle. In the future it seems likely that the interconnections between computing and other disciplines will continue to grow. The role of computing in the sciences, engineering, professions, business, and humanities may become similar to the role of mathematics in the physical sciences.

**Mathematics.** For the historical reasons noted earlier, the bond between mathematics and computing has been strong—stronger possibly than the bond between mathematics and physics, chemistry, or biology. This has been due largely to the strong mathematical heritage of computer science, including mathematical logic, the theorems of Turing and Gödel, Boolean algebra for circuit design, and algorithms for solving equations and other classes of problems in mathematics. Computer science has also brought algorithmic thinking to mathematics—many proofs nowadays have been structured as algorithms for constructing or identifying a mathematical object. In the case of the four-color conjecture, which was unproved for over a hundred years, algorithmic thinking led to a proof in the late 1970s in which the computer was utilized to examine a large finite number of cases to search for any counterexamples.

**Biology.** One of the most widely discussed analogies between computing and nature comes from the field of molecular biology, in which the mechanisms of cell growth and reproduction have been seen as controlled by the genetic information encoded in DNA sequences. A long-standing question, dating back to the 1940s, has been the relation between the cognitive processes of humans and the structure of the nervous system. This question has provoked people to model cognitive processes with digital simulations of neural networks and to seek from these models new insights for cognitive psychology and biology. The phenomenon of natural selection in biology has inspired new classes of "genetic algorithms" that are very good at locating solutions to problems requiring a search through many alternatives.

**Management.** Beginning in the 1950s with Herbert Simon's invention of decision science, management of organizations has been seen as an information-processing activity. Simon proposed that the job of a manager consists of selecting among a set of competing alternatives; thereafter many people began studying how to use computer models to enumerate alternatives and locate the one with the greatest payoff. In the early 1960s Jay Forrester proposed modeling organizations as feedback systems with many different parts interacting by exchanging information; computers could evaluate the models and help forecast the future evolution of the organization's market position. Today people commonly refer to most organizations as knowledge organizations because they can be modeled as large information-processing systems. Management Information Systems (MIS) departments keep track of company records in databases and deliver, on request, reports to managers. Computer scientists and management scientists frequently collaborate as they develop and extend such models and systems.

**Economics.** For many of the same reasons, economics has now become regarded as an informational science. Like organizations, economic systems can be modeled as many interconnected parts exchanging information. Econometric computer models have been used regularly to forecast national and international conditions that might follow from new policy proposals. Although few of these models have been successful, the research continues to find a reliable, all-inclusive model.

**Engineering.** Most branches of engineering now regard themselves as information technologies.

Many designs can now be done with the aid of a computer, which can store a representation of a structure, perform simulations (a form of testing) on it, show still and animated pictures of it, and even drive a manufacturing process. This paradigm has been used in civil engineering for bridges and buildings, in aeronautics for aircraft design, in electrical engineering for simulations of logic circuits and of communication systems, in chemical engineering for simulation of molecules and bondings, in materials engineering for simulation of materials under various stresses, and in manufacturing for process control and machine-tool control. The widespread use of computers in the field of engineering has made the acronyms *CAD* (computer-aided design) and *CAM* (computer-aided manufacturing) common jargon.

**Physical Sciences.** A new bond has formed between computer science and the physical sciences. Leading figures in physics, chemistry, biology, geology, astronomy, and meteorology have stated that certain "grand challenge" problems will succumb to massive high-speed computations performed on new generations of massively parallel computers controlled by new kinds of algorithms. Problem topics under study include the formation of atomic particles from quarks, calculation of chemical properties of materials from the Schrödinger equation, simulation of aircraft in flight, exploration of space, global climate modeling, oil exploration, cosmology, earthquake prediction, and human genome sequencing. Some people have become fond of saying that computation has emerged as a new paradigm of science, joining theory and experimentation. The business of studying science through computation has been named computational science. In 1991 the U.S. Congress passed the High Performance Computing and Communications Act, which set aside $1.7 billion to further this science and encourage more interdisciplinary collaborations.

**Library Science.** Library science is concerned with archiving texts and organizing storage and retrieval systems to give efficient access to texts. Digital library systems have been built and attached to the worldwide high-speed networks, meaning that libraries will change from storage places for books to electronic data centers that will grant wide-ranging access to their communities. Libraries have a special concern with the problem of migrating data from older storage media onto newer ones.

**Linguistics.** Linguistics is concerned with understanding languages, and computational linguistics is concerned with natural language recognition, machine translation, and speech recognition. The relationship between human speech syntax and machine syntax has been an absorbing field of study for scientists searching for the source of human thought processes. Linguistics has been a crucial area of study for researchers in artificial intelligence.

**Philosophy.** Philosophy is concerned with the way people use language to design and interpret realities and values. Philosophers have contributed much to the debates on whether machines can think or whether formal models are sufficient for dependable software systems. Some philosophical work, such as speech act theory, has contributed to the design of computers that help people in organizations get their work done. Recent work on virtual realities (realistic situations) has given philosophers much to think about.

## THEORY, ABSTRACTION, AND DESIGN

To understand the discipline of computing, one must understand the three skills previously discussed—algorithmic thinking, representation, and programming—and the 11 major subareas into which the discipline is divided. The work in the discipline of computing tends to be conducted within one of three major paradigms or processes:

(1) Theory—Building conceptual frameworks and notations for understanding relationships among objects in a domain and the logical consequences of axioms and laws.

(2) Abstraction—Exploring new systems and architectures by means of models and measurements guided by those models. This paradigm is sometimes referred to as modeling or experimentation.

(3) Design—Constructing computer systems that support work in given organizations or application domains.

These three paradigms derive from the historical roots of the discipline of computing. Theory comes from applied mathematics; experimentation comes from the scientific method; design comes from engineering. All three have become important. Continuous interaction between people in the three paradigms has become important for vigorous progress in the discipline. Many controversies in the field have been associated with someone in one paradigm criticizing the work of someone in another without being aware of the difference in paradigms.

**Theory.** The theoretical side of computing has reached maturity. Theoretical work has often been aimed at bringing order to a rapidly accumulating mass of experience; this work focuses on introducing broad conceptual frameworks, taxonomies, and analytic methods. Work in databases, human interfaces, and hypertext retrieval systems has been of this kind. In a few areas, theoretical work focuses on comprehensive analysis of phenomena for which formal models exist. Work in data structures, formal languages, and switching theory has been of this kind. Regardless of domain, much theoretical work has had limited impact on the complex problems of systems and applications that are encountered in practice. Exceptions to this statement include logical design, graphics, and analysis of algorithms.

**Abstraction.** The abstraction side of computing has reached early adulthood. It has been concerned with constructing and using models of phenomena that are accurate but much simpler than the phenomena themselves. Abstraction requires extensive use of computers and laboratories, and it often stimulates new developments in computer design and use. Typical experimental and modeling activities include logic simulation, simulations of other systems and of physical processes, testing of protocols, measurement of algorithm and system performance, and comparisons of different architectures.

**Design.** The design side of computing can still be considered in late adolescence. It has registered many significant accomplishments, such as simulators, microchip design systems, CAD/CAM, and supercomputers. The most successful design work has been with hardware and self-contained software packages, all proceeding from formal specifications of what the machine, device, package, or system is to do. The least successful design work has been with software systems, many of which are too large, unreliable and undependable, too costly, too difficult to change, and too complex to understand. Many designers believe that the reason for this has been that the same formal approaches that work for hardware do not work for software; the designer must become aware of the nature and practices of work in the organization that will use the system of machines, devices, networks, and packages. They have advocated design approaches that resemble those used in architecture. These holistic approaches take into account all physical systems as well as human concerns about form and function.

## SUBDISCIPLINES

The discipline of computer science may be broken down into 11 commonly recognized subdisciplines. The three paradigms—theory, abstraction, and design—mentioned earlier may be applied to each subdiscipline. Each subdiscipline has an underlying unity of subject matter, a considerable theoretical component, essential abstractions and models, and substantial design and implementation issues. Significant industries and institutions have been established in each of these areas. The last two subdisciplines, computational science and organizational informatics, can be considered both new and multidisciplinary. Their influence on computing grows greater each year.

The subsequent discussion forms a summary of the principal questions and concerns dealt with in each of the 11 subdisciplines. This discussion should be viewed as a general guide, enabling navigation through the discipline's elements and processes. It is not a plan for a curriculum but a framework in which a discussion of curriculum can be conducted, subject to change as the understanding of the territory increases.

**Algorithms and Data Structures.** Algorithms and data structures address specific classes of problems and their efficient solutions. Examples of problem classes are the sorting of arrays of elements or the removal of hidden lines in a two-dimensional projection of a three-dimensional object. Fundamental questions include the following: For given classes of problems, what are the fastest algorithms? What is the trade-off between storage and time? What is the best way to arrange the data in memory or throughout the nodes of a computer network? Will algorithms apply to general classes of problems?

Algorithmic theory, sometimes called computability theory, defines what machines can and cannot do. Algorithms can be subjected to various tests by applying them to sample cases and analyzing their performance. When theoretical analysis has proved too daunting, experimental testing using models has helped determine the characteristics of efficient, near-optimal algorithms for important classes of problems. Guidelines have been developed to assist programmers to select, implement, and test algorithms for important classes of problems such as searching, random-number generation, and textual pattern matching. Algorithms that use heuristics to find approximate answers have been tested extensively to locate the cases in which they do well or poorly. Results of theory have also been widely applied in practice, for instance, in cryptographic protocols for secure authentication and secret communication.

**Programming Languages.** Programming languages have provided notations for virtual machines that execute algorithms and notations for algorithms and data; the sets of strings of symbols generated by such notations have been called languages as well. This area also deals with efficient translations from high-level languages into machine codes. Fundamental questions are these: What are possible organizations of the virtual machine presented by the language? How can these abstractions be implemented on computers? What notation can be used effectively and efficiently to specify what the computer should do? How do we associate functions, or semantics, with language notations? How can machines translate between languages?

The theory of programming languages studies models of the virtual machines that may be used as the bases of languages and of the grammars for expressing valid strings in the languages. The theory deals with semantics, the study of the relationships between strings of the language and states of the underlying virtual machines. Testers and modelers have developed classifications of languages based on their syntactic and semantic models (for example, object-oriented and data-flow models) as well as classifications according to intended application (for instance, business-data processing or simulation). Designers have produced programming environments—systems that help users develop programs in a given language.

**Architecture.** Architecture has been concerned with methods of organizing hardware (and associated software) into efficient, reliable systems. The fundamental questions are these: What are good methods of integrating processors, memory, and communication in a machine? How does one design and control large computational systems and demonstrate that they work as intended despite errors and failures? What types of architectures can efficiently incorporate many processing elements? How does one measure performance?

The theory of architecture includes discussion of Boolean algebra, a notation system proposed by Claude Shannon in the early 1940s that permits designers to express when circuits are open (transmitting) or closed (not transmitting) in terms of binary input variables; coding theory, which studies optimal ways to encode information; and finite-state machine theory, which deals with the specifications and optimizations of machines. Computer architects have been heavy users of models. Their favorites include finite-state machines that relate function to behavior; optimizing instruction sets for various models and workloads; and identification of "levels of abstraction" at which the design can be viewed. A large number of components and systems have been systematically designed and tested, including hardware units for fast computation; the so-called von Neumann machine, a model of the single-instruction sequence stored-program computer; RISC (Reduced Instruction Set Computers) implementations; CISC (Complex Instruction Set Computers) implementations; and supercomputers, such as the CRAY machines.

**Numerical and Symbolic Computation.** Numerical and symbol computation includes general methods of efficiently and accurately solving equations resulting from mathematical models of physical systems; these may be airflow around wings, water flow around obstacles, petroleum flow in the earth's crust, or galactic collisions. Fundamental questions are these: How can continuous or infinite processes be accurately approximated by finite discrete processes? How can algorithms minimize the effects of errors arising from these approximations? How rapidly is it possible for a given class of equations to be solved for a given level of accuracy?

Number theory deals with representations of numbers in binary machine codes, their manipulations, and algorithms for performing arithmetic calculations. Numerical analysis deals with the analysis of algorithms for solving systems of equations for the propagation of errors due to finite representations. Nonlinear dynamics deals with the behaviors of chaotic physical systems that are not accurately described with linear equations. Models and experiments in this area have tended to be used as guides to practical implementations and have usually been backed by well-developed theory. Models have been concerned with formulations of physical problems such as discrete approximations to continuous physical problems. Major implementations of design include high-level problem-formulation systems such as Chem and symbolic manipulators such as Mathematica.

**Operating Systems and Networks.** Operating systems and networks are control mechanisms that allow multiple resources to be efficiently coordinated in the execution of programs on computer systems consisting of a variety of devices and resources and connected by local or wide-area networks. Fundamental questions are these: For each class of resource, what is a minimal set of operations that permit their effective use? How can interfaces be organized so that computer users deal only with abstract versions of resources and not with physical details of hardware? What are effective control strategies for job scheduling, memory management, communications, reliability, and security?

Major elements of theory in operating systems include concurrency theory; scheduling theory, especially processor scheduling; program behavior and memory-management theory; and performance modeling and analysis. Major models include abstraction principles that permit users to operate on idealized versions of resources without concern for physical details, models for important subproblems such as memory management and performance analysis, models for secure computing, and networking models. This field has yielded standard methods for efficient design implementations of common components, including time-sharing systems, memory managers, and hierarchical file systems.

**Software Methodology and Engineering.** Software methodology and engineering include the design of programs and large software systems that meet specifications and are safe, secure, reliable, and dependable. Fundamental questions include the following: What are the principles behind the development of programs and programming systems? How does one develop specifications that do not omit important cases and can be analyzed for safety? How do software systems evolve through different generations? How can software be designed for understandability and modifiability? What methods reduce complexity in designing very large software systems? How can the user interface be organized to minimize the possibility of human misinterpretation of information?

The three kinds of theory used for software engineering have been program verification and proof, which treats forms of proofs and efficient algorithms for constructing them; temporal logic, an extension of predicate calculus, which allows one to state that certain events precede others; and reliability theory, which relates the overall failure probability of a system to the failure probabilities of its components over time. Models and measurements guided by them have played significant roles in software engineering. Methodologies for organizing the software-development process may be listed under generic names, such as HDM or the surnames of their inventors (for example, Edsger Dijkstra, or Edward Yourdon). These process methodologies have been augmented with procedures and practices for testing, quality assurance, and overall project management. In some cases, such as for systems implemented by the U.S. Department of Defense, additional criteria and testing methods have been used by designers to certify that a system meets standards for secure computing.

**Database and Information Retrieval Systems.** This area addresses the organization of large sets of persistent, shared data for efficient query and update. The term *database* has been used for a collection of records that can be updated and queried in various ways. The term *retrieval system* has been used for a collection of documents that will be searched and correlated; updates and modifications of documents are infrequent in a retrieval system. Fundamental questions are these: What modeling concepts should be used to represent data elements and their relationships? How can high-level queries be translated into high-performance programs? What machine architectures lead to efficient retrieval and update? How can data be protected against unauthorized access, disclosure, or destruction?

Theories that have been devised to study and design database and information-retrieval systems include relational algebra and relational calculus, which give notations for the entities and relationships among them that are represented in the database; concurrency theory, especially as it relates to serializable transactions and "deadlock" prevention; sorting, search, and indexing large files; performance analysis of query and retrieval systems; and cryptography as it relates to ensuring privacy of information.

Models used to represent the logical structure of data and relations among the data elements include the relational model and the entity-relationship model. A rich set of practical design techniques has been evolved that forms a tool kit for the database or retrieval-system designer. These techniques include general approaches to relational, hierarchical, network, and retrieval systems. The methods have been used in commercial database systems such as dBase, in commercial retrieval systems such as Lexis, and in commercial hypertext systems such as HyperCard.

**Artificial Intelligence and Robotics.** Artificial intelligence and robotics involve the modeling of human cognitive behavior in order to build machine components that mimic these behaviors. Behaviors of interest include recognizing sensory signals, sounds, images, and patterns; learning; reasoning; problem solving; planning; and understanding language. Fundamental questions include the following: What are basic models of cognition, and how might machines simulate them? How can knowledge of the world be represented and organized to allow machines to act reasonably? To what extent is intelligence described by rule evaluation, inference, deduction, and pattern computation? What limits constrain machines that use these methods? How are sensory and motor data encoded, clustered, and associated? How can robots be designed so that they see, hear, speak, plan, and act?

One of the six branches of theory that have been developed thus far for artificial intelligence, neural networks, was inspired by the structure of biological nervous systems. It was based on the hypothesis that machines that mimic cognitive behaviors must imitate natural neural structures. The theory deals with the neural structures, computing their responses to stimuli, how they store and retrieve information, and how they form classifications and abstractions. All branches of the theory draw heavily on the related disciplines of structural mechanics, graph-theory linguistics, philosophy, and psychology.

Models have been used to understand and develop design principles in various subdomains of intelligent systems and learning machines. Because problem solving is regarded as an intelligent human activity, substantial effort was devoted to algorithms for searching large spaces of alternatives, leading among other things to efficient machines for games of strategy. Artificial intelligence has fostered many implementations and its own design principles. In this area, techniques for designing software systems for logic programming that are based on efficient theorem proving and rule evaluation have been perfected. Expert systems, which use rules stored in a database to deduce and propose actions for a given situation, have been successful in a number of well-focused, narrow domains, such as the medical diagnostic system Mycin.

**Human-Computer Communication.** The area of human-computer communication addresses the coordination of action and transfer of information between humans and machines by way of various humanlike sensors and motors, and with information structures that reflect human conceptualizations. Important parts of this field are computer graphics and user interfaces. Fundamental questions are these: What are effective methods for receiving input or presenting output? How can the risk of misperception be minimized? How can graphics and other tools be used to understand physical phenomena through information stored in data sets?

Major areas of theory used in the area of human-computer interaction include color theory, cognitive psychology, and geometry. Geometry has been particularly important in graphics, where it yields algorithms for projecting objects onto the viewing surface, showing reflections, and rendering translucent surfaces. Models have been used in extensive studies that have yielded efficient algorithms for displaying pictures, including methods for color maps, fractals, and animation. Sophisticated image processing and enhancement methods have been developed that facilitate interpretation of photographs ranging from those of deep-space probes to human CAT (computerized axial tomography) and MRI (magnetic resonance imaging) scans. Many of these models have been implemented commercially.

**Computational Science.** Computational science supports explorations in science and engineering that cannot proceed without high-performance computation and communications. Computation has been seen as a third approach to science, joining the traditional approaches of theory and experiment. It is used to address very difficult problems, sometimes called "grand challenges," in physics (for example, demonstrating the existence of certain quarks), chemistry (for example, designing enzymes and proteins that selectively attack viruses), geology (for example, predicting earthquakes), meteorology (for example, long-term weather forecasting), and earth sciences (for example, charting the relation between ocean currents and world climate). The fundamental questions in this area relate to the other disciplines and not to computing.

Each of the other areas of theory contributes to a collaboration in computational science, notably parallel algorithms, optimizing compilers, numerical methods, differential equations, linear algebra, organization of large data sets, graphics, and statistics. Computing theory has been mixed with the theory in another area of science to form the theoretical side of the exploration in that specific area. As in theory, the abstractions of areas of computing have been joined with abstractions from a particular area of science to form models. Computational science influences the design of machines, languages, algorithms, compilers, and networks. Modern supercomputers have been built explicitly to help solve problems in scientific areas.

**Organizational Informatics.** Organizational informatics provides information and systems that support the work processes of organizations and coordination among people participating in those processes. Information systems have been seen as essential to the success of businesses in the growing global marketplace. Because most of the work of organizations occurs in human processes—in which agreements must be made about what work will be done, who will do it, and who must be satisfied by the results—information systems must be designed with an understanding of work. This has been a major area of collaboration among computing people, systems-engineering people, and people in organization disciplines such as marketing. The fundamental questions come from the organizational disciplines, not from computing, but give considerable inspiration to the associated areas of computing.

Many parts of computing contribute theory to organizational informatics, notably languages, operating systems, networks, databases, and artificial intelligence. Linguistics has provided theories, such as speech acts, which have been used to map work processes. Models, abstractions, and measurements have been more dominant than theories in this area. Because most of the theories in this area have been descriptive, they do not provide the means for calculating future conditions of organizations; therefore models and simulations have been needed to obtain such forecasts. Management Information Systems (MIS) has been a long-standing commercial arena in which computing systems consisting of workstations, databases, networks, and reporting systems have been deployed in organizations to assist them in their work. Many decision-support systems have been available commercially; they range from simulation and mathematical models that forecast market, economic, and competitive conditions to cooperative work systems that assist people in reaching decisions as groups or in collaborating together over a network.

[*Editor's note:* Portions of this article appear in the *Encyclopedia of Computer Science*, 3d ed., published by the Institute of Electrical & Electronics Engs. Inc.]

PETER DENNING, *George Mason University*

### Bibliography

Amarel, S., "Overview of Computer Science," in *Encyclopedia of Computer Science*, 3d ed., ed. by A. Ralston and E. Reilly (Institute of Electrical & Electronics Engs. 1993).

Arden, B., ed., "What Can Be Automated?" in *The Computer Science and Engineering Research Study* (MIT Press 1980).

Denning, Peter, "Internal Structure of Computer Science," in *Encyclopedia of Computer Science*, ed. by A. Ralston and E. Reilly (Institute of Electrical & Electronics Engs. 1993).

Denning, Peter, et al., "Computing as a Discipline," *Communications of ACM 32,1* (January 1989):9–23.

Drucker, Peter, *Post Capitalist Society* (Harper Business 1993).

Hartmanis, Juris, et al., *Computing the Future* (National Acad. of Sciences Press 1992).

Kurzweil, Raymond, *The Age of Intelligent Machines* (MIT Press 1990).

## 2. History of the Computer

Perhaps the biggest surprise in the history of electronic computers is the number of them now in use. In 1945, experts thought that merely a dozen machines would satisfy all practical needs for computers worldwide for 50 years. Today there are over 50 million personal computers (PCs) in use, not counting supercomputers, minicomputers, and the myriad of special computers, or microprocessors, integrated into washing machines, automobiles, videocassette recorders (VCRs), and virtually all machines. Personal computers today are much more powerful and flexible than any of the mainframe computers of 1945 and immensely more powerful than the early calculating machines of the 1600s. While as recently as 100 years ago, most computations and correspondence were performed by hand, today both are frequently performed with the aid of a computer. Technological innovations such as the computer, and their effect on the world around us, have changed the way people learn, communicate, and do work.

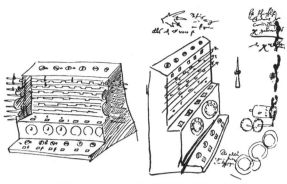

COURTESY PROFESSOR B. BARON VON FREYTAG LÖRINGHOFF, UNIVERSITY OF TÜBINGEN

Wilhelm Schickard built the first known mechanical calculator to aid Johannes Kepler in his efforts to analyze Tycho Brahe's copious astronomical calculations.

### ORIGINS

The earliest devices used for computations include the abacus, the tally stick, and the slide rule. Though these simple devices were suitable and effective, as calculations grew more complex and the speed of calculation became more important, the need for mechanical computing devices became greater.

**Early Mechanical Computing Aids.** The abacus, known as the first mechanical computing device, dates from ancient times and is still used today. The first mechanical calculator capable of performing the basic arithmetic operations of addition, subtraction, multiplication, and division was built about 1623. Wilhelm Schickard, a professor at the University of Tübingen in Germany, constructed a device called the Calculating Clock as an aid for astronomical calculations. Schickard began building a copy for the astronomer Johannes Kepler, but all of Schickard's work was destroyed during the Thirty Years' War. All knowledge of his machine was lost until the early 1930s, when his correspondence with Kepler, including sketches of the machine, was discovered by Franz Hammer. A working copy of Schickard's machine was built by Dr. Bruno Baron von Freytag Löringhoff, curiously enough also a mathematics professor at the University of Tübingen, which was completed in 1960.

In 1642, when he was just 19, the French mathematical genius Blaise Pascal began to develop a mechanical calculator to aid his father, a lawyer and the local tax collector. This successful machine was best suited to performing addition, and Pascal presented a copy to Louis XIV. Around 1673 Gottfried Wilhelm von Leibniz conceived

and developed a calculating machine that was intended to perform all four basic arithmetic operations, an improvement over Pascal's machine. The machine, called the Stepped Reckoner, was exhibited at the Royal Society in London in 1673. Unfortunately, however, it did not work. Still, this machine was in a sense a forerunner of the mechanical desk calculator, the Arithmometer, invented by Charles X de Colmar in 1820. All these machines were designed to perform multiplication by repeated additions. In 1887 Leon Bollee built a multiplication table into a calculating machine, making unnecessary the repeated additions of the machines Leibniz and Colmar invented.

**Babbage Computers.** A major theoretical step forward occurred early in the 19th century, when Charles Babbage, an Englishman, embarked on the project of automating the calculation of mathematical tables to aid astronomers. He first conceived of the idea for a "difference engine" that would automatically calculate and print mathematical tables, but he was unable to build it.

In 1833 Babbage began work on a more significant machine that he called his "analytical engine." This machine consisted of a "store," or memory, and a "mill," or central processing unit. Because his machine used two sets of punch cards, in a sense it was a stored-program computer. Its instructions were stored on one set of punch cards, and its data on another. His innovative idea to use punch cards came from his observation of the card-controlled Jacquard loom, which used punched cards to weave intricate damask patterns on table linens.

For the next ten years Babbage devoted much time, effort, and money to his project. The British government also contributed considerable funds, but the machine was never completed. His work is known mainly because of the efforts of his colleague, Augusta Ada, the countess of Lovelace, the only legitimate child of the English poet Lord Byron. A modern woman, Ada was trained in mathematics, which was very unusual for ladies of nobility. She met Babbage at a social function and became fascinated with his work, preparing a detailed description of his "analytical engine." By programming the calculation of Bernoulli numbers for the machine, she earned the title "the first programmer in history." But she and Babbage also shared a disastrous interest in betting

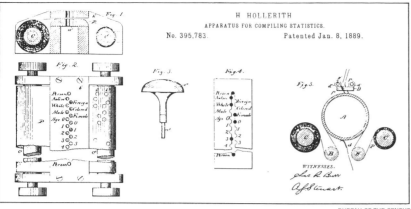

Herman Hollerith's tabulating machines were used by the U.S. government to automate the census of 1890. This patent drawing (*above*) illustrates Hollerith's first tabulator. His punch-card systems were featured on the 1890 cover of *Scientific American* (*right*).

on horses using mathematical methods. Her losses led her husband Count Lovelace to forbid her from having any further contact with Babbage.

**Hollerith System.** Near the end of the 19th century, Herman Hollerith, a young engineer working in the U.S. Census Office, designed machines to automate the census of 1890. These machines were extraordinarily successful, deftly handling the records of 63 million people. The machines used a punch-card system, and the staff hired to complete the 1890 census punched more than a billion holes.

Soon these machines were being used worldwide by governments and industries. In 1896 Hollerith formed the Tabulating Machine Company. In 1911 this company became the keystone of the Computing-Tabulating-Recording Company, which eventually was renamed International Business Machines Company (IBM).

By the early part of the 20th century, machines existed for handling a variety of business data-processing applications. In 1906–1907, the Census Bureau authorized the newly formed National Bureau of Standards to develop equipment competitive with Hollerith's. The head of the new bureau was James Powers, who subsequently founded the Powers Tabulating Machine Company, which merged in 1927 with the Remington Rand Company.

In 1928 the astronomers Wallace J. Eckert in the United States and Leslie John Comrie in England independently conceived of the idea of using punch-card machines for astronomical calculations and adapted these machines to carry out the preparation of nautical almanacs. Their work helped scientists realize the value of applying computing machines to uses other than commercial applications.

**Analog Devices.** One of the earliest analog machines to be widely useful was the slide rule, an ingenious device for automating the use of logarithms. Analog machines depend on some physical model of a mathematical principle; the principle governing the slide rule is that the sum of two lengths is proportional to the sum of two logarithms. In 1620 Edmund Gunter, an English mathematician, drew up a physical scale that was a physical analog of logarithms. This device became extremely popular with navigators because it made fast and relatively accurate calculations possible. William Oughtred, another English mathematician, created a circular slide rule employing Gunter's scale.

In the period between Babbage and Hollerith, the class of machines known as analog devices became increasingly important. The harmonic analyzer, a key analog machine, was built in 1876 by the English physicist Lord Kelvin to measure tidal motion. This machine contained apparatus for forming eight terms in a Fourier series. The American physicist Albert A. Michelson built a substantially improved analyzer in 1897. The main devices appearing in both Kelvin's and Michelson's machines were called integrators, instruments capable of finding the area under a curve—that is, of calculating the value of an integral in the calculus. James Clerk Maxwell is credited with inventing the first precision instrument of this sort in 1855.

Kelvin also tried unsuccessfully to build an analog machine for solving differential equations, particularly those that arise commonly in mathematical physics. He was frustrated by the lack of a device that would not be invented for another 50 years, the torque amplifier, which was invented in 1927 by the American engineer C. W. Niemann. Vannevar Bush seized upon this invention and in 1930 built the first operable differential analyzer at the Massachusetts Institute of Technology (MIT) to meet the needs of electrical engineers there.

Analog instruments such as these were of great importance to the physicist and the engineer who urgently needed to perform very fast but not necessarily very accurate calculations. The computational pattern, therefore, in the first half of the 20th century was one in which the needs of the astronomer or the entrepreneur were met by either extensive hand or punch-card machine computations, and the needs of the physicist or engineer were met by analog computations.

**Electromechanical Computers.** In the late 1930s several pioneers developed electromechanical calculators possessing some kind of automatic control. Electromechanical computer components typically included mechanical switches and relays.

**Zuse.** In the early 1930s Konrad Zuse, a German aircraft engineer, designed a machine having the main features of a modern computer—an arithmetic unit, a memory, and a control. Zuse eventually built four computers, although he was greatly hampered by World War II; his second machine was destroyed in an air raid. After the war he designed several other machines as well as an advanced programming language called Plankalkul. This term was taken up by a German computer manufacturer in the 1970s as the name for another system.

**Stibitz.** George R. Stibitz, a physicist at Bell Telephone Laboratories, developed a large relay computer in response to the need for tabulating vast amounts of military data during World War II. He built the Complex Number Calculator, a small special-purpose machine that became operational in January 1940. It was the first computing machine with the ability to service more than one terminal, and it was the first to be used remotely over telephone lines. The machine's internal registers used telephone relay switches for memory. It operated on a binary-coded decimal system in which four switches were used to encode each decimal digit.

In 1946 Stibitz completed a large computer made entirely from standard telephone and teletype components, such as relays, paper-tape punches, and paper-tape readers. In this computer, sequences of instructions were read from looped paper tapes. The majority of instructions took one to two seconds, and 20 numbers of seven digits could be stored. This was the first computer system to feature self-checking and unattended operation.

**Aiken.** In 1937 Howard H. Aiken of Harvard University conceived of the first large-scale automatic digital computer. It was built to his specifications by the IBM corporation under a U.S. Navy contract and was named the Automatic Sequence Controlled Calculator, or Mark I. The Mark I, which became operational in 1943, contained more than 750,000 parts in a chassis measuring 51 feet (16 meters) long and weighing 5 tons. Its components, such as switches and counter wheels, were mostly mechanical. The input medium was punch cards or punched paper tape. The Mark I, first used for calculating tables of Bessel functions, performed a multiplication in about 6 seconds.

Aiken continued to build four more machines, each with a different technology. The Mark II computer, a large relay machine, was completed in 1947. IBM built a relay computer called the Selective Sequence Electronic Calculator (SSEC) in 1948. The machine contained about 23,000 relays and 13,000 vacuum tubes. The top speed of a relay computer was about one multiplication per second. By the early 1940s the relay as a computer component was being made obsolete by electronic circuits that could provide much higher operating speeds.

**Commercial Success.** Commercially, the most successful of the electromechanical calculators were those built to augment IBM's punch-card accounting machines. In 1935 IBM started manufacturing the 601 multiplying punch. By 1948 the IBM 604 used all-vacuum-tube technology, containing more than 1,400 vacuum tubes. In 1949 several accounting machines were connected to form the Card Programmed Calculator (CPC), which permitted users to program the computer without rewiring.

Vannever Bush's mechanical differential analyzer was used during World War II to calculate the trajectories of ballistic weapons.

## EARLY ELECTRONIC COMPUTERS

Research money was granted to universities by several government agencies to support war efforts such as the computation of ballistic firing tables during World War II. If not for the war and the need for fast information processing, funding for computer projects might never have reached such a high level. Several similar projects were ongoing simultaneously during the war.

**Atanasoff-Berry Computer.** The first experimental all-electronic binary computer was built by John V. Atanasoff, a professor of physics at Iowa State University, working with a graduate student, Clifford E. Berry, between 1939 and 1942. They built a prototype that first operated successfully in October 1939, followed by the ABC (Atanasoff-Berry Computer) in 1942. All development on the ABC ended in May 1942, when both men left Iowa to engage in war efforts.

This pioneering effort might have been forgotten had it not been for a famous lawsuit in the early 1970s in which Sperry Rand sued Honey-

Grace Murray Hopper, inventor of compilers and programming languages, uses a tape punch to code programs for the Mark I computer.

The first general-purpose digital computer, ENIAC, weighed 30 tons and occupied an area 50 feet long by 30 feet wide (15 by 9 meters).

The Colossus computer was successfully employed by the British to break German Enigma and Fish codes during World War II.

well for infringement of the ENIAC-UNIVAC patents. Honeywell brought forward Atanasoff as a witness to challenge the validity of the patents, stating that physicist John Mauchly had been influenced by the ABC since he had both seen and discussed it with Atanasoff before applying for the ENIAC-UNIVAC patents. The court ruled that "John Vincent Atanasoff was the inventor of the first electronic computer."

**ENIAC.** Shortly after the entrance of the United States into World War II, a substation of the U.S. Army's Ballistic Research Laboratory was opened at the Moore School at the University of Pennsylvania to help produce firing and bombing tables for the U.S. Army. Lieutenant Herman H. Goldstine, a mathematician, was placed in charge of this project. The university appointed J. G. Brainerd to be its liaison officer with the army. In the winter of 1942–1943 Brainerd brought to Goldstine's attention a memorandum by physicist John W. Mauchly proposing the construction of an all-electronic computer.

This proposal was accepted by Goldstine and his superiors, and work started on the development of the first all-electronic, general-purpose computer in the spring of 1943. A young graduate student, J. Presper Eckert, Jr., was made the chief engineer, with Mauchly as his consultant. The machine, called ENIAC (Electronic Numerical Integrator and Computer), was completed in the winter of 1944–1945. It successfully carried out an extensive calculation for the Manhattan Project's Los Alamos Laboratory, in New Mexico, on its initial test run.

ENIAC had a computing speed of about 5,000 additions per second and about 300 multiplications per second. All other digital machines of this era had multiplication speeds of about one per second. This meant that previously infeasible tasks could be successfully carried out. In other respects, however, the machine was not very satisfactory. Its roughly 18,000 vacuum tubes required virtually constant attention. ENIAC had a high-speed memory of only 20 words of 10 decimal digits each, together with a read-only memory of 450 words. Its control was decentralized and contained in a myriad of switches, plugs, and cables. The time needed to convert from one problem to another was measurable in hours or days.

**Colossus Project.** While ENIAC was under development in the United States, a series of special-purpose computers were built in England under conditions of great secrecy for use by British military cryptanalysts. The program, known as the Colossus project, was supervised by the mathematician M. H. A. Newman. The first Colossus, designed and constructed in Bletchley Park by the mathematician Alan Turing and his colleagues to decode German military messages enciphered by the German coding device, the Enigma, became operational in December 1943. The Colossus machines, special-purpose vacuum-tube machines, contained a single tape that carried the input data. By the end of World War II, about ten computers were being used to decipher messages produced by the Enigma.

**EDVAC.** In August 1944 Goldstine introduced the mathematician John von Neumann to the ENIAC staff. Von Neumann was captivated by the ENIAC and by the electronic computer in general. A study group consisting of A. W. Burks, J. Presper Eckert, A. K. Goldstine, H. H. Goldstine, Mauchly, von Neumann, and several others was formed, and discussions of a successor to the ENIAC began. In late August 1944 these discussions gave birth to the stored-program concept and other basic ideas that were to govern computer development for the next two decades. Among these ideas were separation of storage, arithmetic, and control; random-access memory; stored program; arithmetic modification of instructions; conditional branching; binary number and decimal number representations; and consideration of serial and parallel machines. It was also von Neumann's idea to represent the computer's output on a cathode-ray-tube (CRT) screen.

Von Neumann wrote up the results of this activity in a report entitled "First Draft of a Report on the EDVAC" in 1945. In it he described in detail the architecture and logic of the projected machine, the EDVAC (Electronic Discrete Variable Computer), and gave an instruction set for the machine. Shortly afterward he programmed a novel way to sort data by repeated mergings. Because it was a draft report, von Neumann did not include references to the origin of the ideas presented. When the report was reproduced and widely circulated, von Neumann was commonly given credit for all the ideas, and the term *von Neumann machine* became synonymous with computers having the traits listed in this report.

**EDSAC.** Although the war ended before their machine was finished, a group of English engineers headed by Maurice V. Wilkes built a machine, the EDSAC (Electronic Delay Storage Automatic Computer), at Cambridge University modeled on ideas generated in von Neumann's report. This machine, placed in operation in June 1949, was the first true stored-program computer with significant calculating ability. The EDVAC-type machine had a mercury delay-line memory. In this technology binary bits were stored as sound pulses traveling through a tube filled with mercury. The storage time was only a few milliseconds, but this was long when compared with the electronic cycle time of the machine. Delay lines provided an inexpensive cost per bit at a reasonable speed in comparison with other available storage devices.

**The IAS Machines.** In 1946 von Neumann and H. H. Goldstine set up a project at the Institute for Advanced Study (IAS) in Princeton, N.J., to build a machine having a CRT memory and operating on all pairs of digits simultaneously. The result of this project was a machine, completed in 1952, that became the prototype for the modern electronic computer. The project was very successful, partly because it concerned itself not just with engineering but also with machine architecture, programming, numerical analysis, and numerical meteorology. The IAS prototype was widely copied by universities and national laboratories, although each unit built was unique.

**Whirlwind.** The next major advance was made simultaneously in 1949 by Jay Forrester of MIT and Jan Rajchmann of the Radio Corporation of America (RCA). Forrester worked on an early computer at MIT called Whirlwind, for which he developed a magnetic-core memory that increased the speed of the machine and decreased the maintenance time needed. Rajchmann also invented the magnetic-core memory and developed many computer circuits. The Whirlwind was the first real-time computer completed.

**Index Register.** Another significant development was the "B-tube," or index register, invented by Tom Kilburn at the University of Manchester in England. The index register provides a way automatically to change the address portion of an instruction. When many such registers are attached to a machine, they markedly increase its efficiency.

## COMMERCIAL ELECTRONIC COMPUTERS

Commercial computers are often classified by "generations" and distinguished by the technology used in their construction. Because of the speed of technological breakthroughs during the 1950s and 1960s, there is some overlap between machine generations. Technological advances that later became acknowledged as characteristics of certain computer generations were not used uniformly by manufacturers during the prescribed time periods.

**First-Generation Machines.** Computers with first-generation characteristics appeared from 1952 through 1958. Machines manufactured during this period have vacuum-tube circuits and individual processors. First-generation computers may be distinguished by their form of main memory storage. Storage media used during this period included electrostatic storage, magnetic-drum storage, and

The EDSAC, developed at the Mathematical Laboratory in England, was the first working stored-program computer.

magnetic-core memories. Because of their cost and size, first-generation machines were mostly designed for and used by large scientific customers, such as government-sponsored laboratories.

**UNIVAC.** J. Presper Eckert and John W. Mauchly left the Moore School and founded America's first start-up company for the commercial exploitation of computers. They focused on scientific and data-processing applications mainly for large scientific customers. They eventually designed a whole line of computers under the generic name of UNIVAC (*universal automatic computer*). The Census Bureau commissioned the first UNIVAC in August 1947; it became operational in March 1951. The Eckert-Mauchly organization was taken over by Remington Rand in March 1950; Remington Rand later became Sperry Rand, which is now Unisys. The UNIVAC was the first large commercially available computer produced.

**Mercury Delay-Line Storage.** Over the next few years about a dozen other single-copy delay-line computers were built, including Ferranti, Wilkes's EDSAC, Leo, and BINAC. Computers with delay-

John von Neumann is pictured with the general-purpose electronic computer he built at Princeton's Institute for Advanced Study.

THE SCIENCE MUSEUM/SCIENCE & SOCIETY PICTURE LIBRARY

Alan Turing (*far right*) is known worldwide as one of the founders of the field of artificial intelligence.

line memories had a number of features in common. The memory delay time, usually several hundred microseconds, limited their speed. Multiplication, which was performed by repeated addition, was completed in a few milliseconds. Memory capacity was only approximately 1,000 words. Most of these computers worked in the binary system; only UNIVAC used a decimal representation. Most initially used punched paper tape as input, but UNIVAC had an elaborate magnetic-tape system to input data.

**Electrostatic Storage.**  The least reliable part of the IAS machine was its Williams-tube memory. This device was an adaptation of a cathode-ray tube that stored charges on its face and was developed by the British physicist Frederic C. Williams, an associate of Colossus project head M. H. A. Newman. The Williams tube was used in several computers built in the United States, including the IBM 701 and 702. These machines, along with UNIVAC, were the earliest machines that were produced commercially. Their memo-

J. Presper Eckert shows television reporter Walter Cronkite the UNIVAC, which was used to predict the result of the 1952 U.S. presidential election.

COURTESY UNISYS

ries were soon replaced by the more reliable magnetic-core storage.

**IBM 701 and IBM 702.**  In 1950 the Korean War generated a great expansion of defense-related industries and a greatly increased need for computation. IBM delivered its first Defense Calculator, later named the IBM 701, to Los Alamos Scientific Laboratory in 1953. The IBM 701 was a binary computer, similar in design to the IAS machines. In 1955 IBM delivered the 702, a computer developed for the burgeoning commercial data-processing field. However, its unreliable memory soon made it obsolete for data-processing functions.

**Magnetic-Drum Computers.**  In the early 1950s several companies began marketing smaller and slower computers using magnetic drums as primary memory. Magnetic drums, originally recommended by J. Presper Eckert in 1944 for use in the EDVAC, provided large amounts of medium-speed storage at a very low price per bit and were among the earliest devices considered for use in digital computers. In 1955 the IBM 650, a magnetic-drum computer, was released. Its advantages over its competitors included a drum that rotated at higher speeds and a sleek card-handling design, with buffered-card equipment integrated into the system. IBM grossly underestimated the size of the market for 650s, planning to produce only about 50, mainly for scientific users. Eventually, over 1,000 computers were sold to commercial users.

**Magnetic-Core Memories.**  Magnetic-core memories were initially developed for the Whirlwind computer, doubling its operating speed. The magnetic-core technology was the first to offer a basis for fast, reliable, large-scale memories at a reasonable cost. These were rugged, and the individual cores did not lose their information in a power failure. The IBM 704, a successor to the 701, debuted in 1956 with a magnetic-core memory. It was outstanding for its time and achieved a near-monopoly for IBM in the field of large-scale scientific computers. The main competition was Sperry Rand's 1103 series. Large computers with magnetic-core memories were introduced commercially by Burroughs, RCA, Control Data Corporation, General Electric, Philco, and Honeywell, though the IBM series was the most successful of these machines because of its excellent software and IBM's strong sales support.

**Second-Generation Machines.**  Second-generation machines appeared between 1959 and about 1963. Distinguishing characteristics included the use of individualized transistor circuits rather than vacuum tubes and the exclusive use of magnetic-core storage systems for main memory. Among other new features were the use of index registers for addressing and built-in floating point arithmetic. Magnetic disks were introduced by IBM during this period and became widely used.

**Transistors.**  The transistor was invented by John Bardeen, William Shockley, and Walter Brattain at Bell Laboratories in 1947; they received the Nobel Prize in physics for this invention in 1956. Though it was soon clear that transistors would be more advantageous to use than vacuum tubes, it took more than ten years for the semiconductor industry to perfect mass production and testing processes.

Transistors had many advantages over vacuum tubes, including size, speed, and reliability. Even the earliest transistors were only 0.5% the size of the bulky vacuum tube. Because the transistor was smaller, electrical impulses had a shorter distance to travel within it and could be made to switch much faster than in a vacuum tube. Because the transistor was a solid monolithic unit, it was far more rugged and more reliable, and it generated much less heat than a vacuum tube.

**Stretch (IBM 7030).** In 1956 IBM, with partial funding from the Atomic Energy Commission at Los Alamos and the National Security Agency, undertook the project of building the world's fastest computer. The project, headed by Stephen W. Dunwell, had as its goal "to stretch the state of the art by a factor of 100" (hence the project's name). The machine created was huge, containing over 150,000 transistors. During its development period, from 1956 to 1961, Stretch became a test bed for many new hardware and programming features used in the next generation of transistorized machines. Although Stretch was not a marketing success, due to its astronomical cost, its technological advances led to the development of the more profitable IBM 7090.

**IBM 7090.** The first IBM 7090 was built in response to the need for a computer for the Ballistic Missile Early Warning System. A project group headed by George Monroe built the 7090, a transistorized version of the vacuum-tube IBM 709, in the record time of 18 months by using electronic hardware already developed for the Stretch project. The key technology for the 7090 was the Stretch 2-microsecond memory. The Stretch word, which contained 64 information bits and 8 check bits (72 bits total), was easily adapted to handle pairs of 36-bit 7090 words. The 7090 was delivered in June 1960; its follow-on 7094, in September 1962.

The relative ease of software implementation decided the success of the 7090. Programming new software and systems for machines like Stretch was a formidable task. The 7090 was able to leapfrog over Stretch by using programs written for the 704 and 709 that could run unchanged on the 7090. This flexibility gave the 7090 a significant advantage over other computers available at the time.

**Philco Transac.** While under contract to a government agency, Philco built a small, high-speed, transistorized computer called the Transac S-1000. The high-speed transistors, developed by Philco, made the Transac S-1000 valuable as a scientific computer. In late 1957 a new version of the Transac S-1000, the Transac S-2000, was launched as a major commercial effort. The Transac S-2000, Model 211, and Model 212 were all moderately successful second-generation machines because of their number-crunching abilities.

**Control Data.** In 1957 the Control Data Corporation was founded by a group of former UNIVAC employees to build transistorized computers. Their first machine, the CDC 1604, was delivered in early 1960. Although not as powerful as the IBM 7090 or the Philco 2000, it was much lower in price, which made it very popular with customers. The more powerful CDC 3600, delivered in 1963, was also very successful. Control Data continued to grow and later became a force in the supercomputer field.

**Other Commercial Machines.** Using transistor circuits, it was possible to build much more complex machines at a lower cost. This encouraged many companies to go into the field in the early 1960s. Remington Rand introduced a series of machines following its pioneer effort, UNIVAC-I. Its first transistorized machine was the UNIVAC 1107, delivered in 1962. Other early machines included the National Cash Register 304, the RCA 501, the Honeywell 800, and the Burroughs 5000. By 1960 roughly 5,000 stored-program computers were in operation in the United States.

**Third-Generation Machines.** Third-generation computers appeared from 1964 to about 1975. The distinction between the second and third generation of computers is not always clear. This generation is sometimes characterized by the introduction of integrated circuits (ICs) and large-scale integration. However, by 1965 all new computers, and older machines still on the market, were called "third generation" by their manufacturers whether they used integrated circuits or not. Another characteristic of the third generation was the introduction of families of computers that were of different sizes but could run the same programs, thus making it easier to upgrade to a higher-powered machine without having to reprogram all existing applications. Auxiliary devices were also being continuously upgraded during this period.

**Integrated Circuits.** William Shockley, one of the inventors of the transistor, left Bell Laboratories in 1955 and started his own semiconductor company near Palo Alto, Calif. Two years later, eight of his brightest employees, including Robert Noyce, left and founded Fairchild Semiconductor.

Jack Kilby, an engineer for Texas Instruments, demonstrated the world's first integrated circuit in September 1958. It consisted of five electrical components on a thin, 1-cm- (⅖-inch-) long wafer of germanium. Texas Instruments soon built a computer for the Air Force using integrated circuits that was $\frac{1}{150}$ the size of the machine it replaced.

Working independently, Robert Noyce of Fairchild designed a similar device of silicon in 1959. His model had key advantages over Kilby's design; in particular, it was easier to manufacture. In 1962 mass production of ICs was started. The U.S. Patent Office awarded a patent to Noyce in 1961, but the agency subsequently recognized Kilby as coinventor and awarded him a patent in 1964. Noyce went on to found Intel, one of more than 50 companies eventually founded by former Fairchild employees. The area between San Francisco and San Jose became the center of the integrated-circuit industry known as "Silicon Valley."

**IBM System/360.** Early commercial computers were all uniquely designed, and a customer wishing to convert to a new machine was faced with a massive reprogramming task, placing a great burden on any manufacturer trying to sell a new machine. IBM was particularly vulnerable to this problem because it marketed so many computer models. In 1961 IBM began designing a family of compatible computers that merged the requirements of both their scientific and commercial customers.

On April 7, 1964, six new computers were officially announced as members of the System/360 family. Although the physical and logical hardware was quite different for each model, they all presented the same instruction set to the programmer. A program could run on any member of the 360 family without reprogramming, provided the machine had sufficient memory. The program would simply run faster on the larger, more expensive models. This compatibility was achieved using the technology of microprogramming in read-

IBM designed the compatible System/360 family to allow companies to easily upgrade their systems.

only memory. A different microprogram on each model simulated the same System/360 instruction set. The S/360 used SLT (solid-logic technology) integrated circuits, which could be manufactured, like ceramic chips, in large quantities.

**Other Computer Families.** Many features of the 360 architecture were soon accepted as standards by other manufacturers in the mid-1960s. Shortly after the introduction of the 360, RCA brought out its SPECTRA 70 series, which used the 360 instruction set. In December 1963 Honeywell announced its 200 computer, which was compatible with the IBM 1401 series; General Electric announced its GE 600 series, which was almost compatible with the IBM 7090 series; and Burroughs had a very successful family of computers, starting with its 5500 computer, which had built-in virtual memory hardware.

**PDP Minicomputers.** Beginning in 1959 Ken Olson and his coworkers at the Digital Equipment Corporation (DEC) built what is considered to be the first commercial minicomputer, the PDP-1 (Programmed Digital Processor-1). It was the first member of a very successful family of PDP processors. In addition to their small size and relatively low cost, the PDPs did not need an air-conditioned environment, which made them ideal for installation almost anywhere. They also permitted program compatibility over a very wide range of computer models. Starting in 1975 the DEC VAX, an advanced member of the PDP series, swept the academic computing world. Its operation mainly involved remote terminals, so many students could use it at once.

**Time-Sharing and Virtual Memory.** Meanwhile, extensive research was under way on "time-sharing," a process in which many small programs can be in a computer, sharing its resources one after another in small time segments, making it unnecessary for users to be physically in the machine room while their programs ran. They could even use remote terminals over telephone lines. Early research on this subject was done at Manchester University and at Massachusetts Insti-

tute of Technology (MIT). In 1959 the Ferranti Atlas computer was the first to solve the problems of allocation of main memory to multiple programs and the automatic swapping of data between main memory and disk storage. Each programmer wrote programs assuming access to a large "virtual memory."

In the early 1960s Project MAC was formed at MIT to study the problems of multiprogramming and time-sharing. In mid-1964 Project MAC ordered a dual processor GE 645, which had the required special hardware built in. The operating system to manage the system was called MULTICS, a joint effort of General Electric, MIT, and Bell Telephone Laboratories.

In 1967 IBM released the System/360 Mod 67 for time-sharing. It used a concept known as "virtual machines." Each user not only had a large virtual memory but also had the effect of owning a stand-alone virtual S/360 machine to use without having to worry about disturbing other users. Other time-sharing systems of this period included the Datanet 30, the SDS 940, the RCA Spectra 70 Mod 46, and the DEC PDP-10.

**Fourth-Generation Machines.** The fourth generation began in the mid-1970s with the development of very-large-scale integrated (VLSI) circuits, multiprocessors, and networks; it was characterized by a great expansion in numbers and types of computers, made possible by the design and manufacture of VLSI circuits. A drop in the cost of memory chips made possible high-resolution displays, which made many image-oriented applications practical. VLSI also made it possible to develop minicomputers, which led to high-performance personal computers and workstations. One of the most significant breakthroughs of this period was the advent of the personal computer, which made computers accessible to and affordable for the general public.

**Microprocessor.** In 1972 a major innovation in the computer industry was made by Marcian "Ted" Hoff, Jr., of Intel. He combined several integrated circuits onto a single chip. The result was a microcomputer that performed arithmetic and logic functions and could be programmed to carry out almost any function previously done by special wired circuits. Because it dramatically cut manufacturing costs while adding value and capabilities to the product, the microprocessor was quickly integrated into many existing and new products. Intel introduced 8-bit chips, such as the 8008 in April 1972 and the 8080 in April 1974. The 16-bit 8086 chip was introduced in 1978. The latter was adopted for the IBM personal computer in 1980 and quickly became the industry standard in the early 1980s. Other 8-bit chips were the Motorola 6800, the Zilog Z80, and the Texas Instruments 9980, followed by 16-bit families, and then 32-bit families. The Intel 80286, 386, 486, and Pentium were all released within ten years. The Motorola MC 68000 and the National Semiconductor NS 3200 were also popular 32-bit chips.

Computer manufacturing became a "commodity" business during the 1980s. Changes came so quickly that it was hard for the marketplace to absorb them all. Many companies could not keep up with the trends. Even IBM experienced serious difficulties.

**VLSI.** Very-large-scale integration (VLSI) technology, which combines 20,000 or more transistors on a single chip, first appeared in the late 1970s. This innovation was of major importance, not just because it made machines smaller, but because it greatly shortened the distances between the active elements, reducing time delays and thereby increasing the speed of the whole system. The cost of a VLSI chip can be much lower than that of the multiple chips it replaces, but only if the VLSI chip can be manufactured and sold in very large numbers.

**Personal Computers.** Early personal computers (PCs) were characterized by proprietary machine languages and programs. Manufacturers attempted to keep customers loyal by making it difficult to use application programs on other computers. As the sales of PCs skyrocketed and the exchange of information between people with different computer systems became more important, efforts were made to standardize both the computer architecture and the applications software.

The availability of cheap Intel microprocessor chips made it possible for manufacturers to offer the market inexpensive computers. The first widely used personal computer, the Altair 8800, was introduced in late 1974 by MITS, a small electronics firm. It was offered to hobbyists as a $399 do-it-yourself kit. The Commodore PET computer was announced in January 1977. Radio Shack's Tandy, with its widespread system of distribution, soon surpassed Commodore in sales; however, within a year both Commodore and Radio Shack were overtaken by a new company, Apple Computer.

Stephen Wozniak and Steven Jobs founded Apple Computer in 1976 and became two of the most successful entrepreneurs of all time. The Apple II personal computer was announced in 1977. By 1980 Apple had $117 million in sales. Later, Apple's Macintosh became the computer of choice for nonprofessional computer users. Apple followed a strategy of keeping a "closed architecture," that is, they did not allow other manufacturers to add to or duplicate their machines or programs.

In early 1981 IBM unveiled the IBM personal computer, based on the Intel 8086 chip. IBM quickly released information about the computer architecture and encouraged IBM employees as well as independent software developers to write applications software for the IBM PC. Within a very few years the IBM PC became the industry standard, with several manufacturers, including Dell, Hyundai, and Gateway, selling inexpensive "clones" of the IBM PC. The abundance of IBM-compatible machines ensured that there would be a substantial amount of software applications for the machines.

Perhaps one of the most amazing stories in the history of computing is the rise of Bill Gates and Microsoft. In 1977 Gates dropped out of Harvard College to start Microsoft with the purpose of writing a BASIC-language compiler for the Altair microprocessor. By 1980, when Gates was 24 years old, Microsoft was a small, 32-person company in Bellevue, Wash. Gates got the contract from IBM to provide BASIC and an operating system (DOS) for the as-yet-unannounced IBM PC. Through a combination of hard work, good luck, and brilliant negotiating, Gates rode the dramatic PC revolution during the next decade. He guided Microsoft from nowhere in 1980 to its status as one of the top ten companies in the United States in the 1990s and became the richest man in America. (See PERSONAL COMPUTERS AND WORKSTATIONS.)

**Other Developments.** Major changes in computing have been assisted by advances in related technologies that contribute to reductions in cost, size, and weight. One such modern advance is the modem, which allows computer data to be sent over telephone lines. In the 1990s faster channels enabled thousands of computers of all sizes to network in a multimedia mode. The development of lightweight storage batteries and liquid-crystal displays made small, portable computers called "laptops" or "notebooks" practical. Laser printers, which were originally expensive mainframe components, are now common desktop components; CCD (charge-coupled device) scanners make low-cost facsimile (fax) machines possible; and consumer computer networks, such as Prodigy and CompuServe, reach hundreds of thousands of subscribers. The industry continues to expand, driven by increasingly higher-speed transmission technology.

**Fifth-Generation Machines.** In 1982 the Japanese government began funding a ten-year, fifth-generation computer systems project. Its goal was to further the research and development of computers, focusing on nonnumerical data processing, such as symbol manipulation and applied artificial intelligence. The fifth-generation machine was to achieve inference logic, use knowledge bases, and develop intelligent interfaces. The program at the Institute for New Generation Computer Technology (ICOT) ran 12 years before the project's demise was announced and the software given away. During the same 12-year period, several European and U.S. groups also participated in the activities. The fifth-generation project was not deemed a success, but the problems it tried to solve were formidable. It did generate many technological advances in natural-language processing, image processing, and networking. In 1993 the Japanese government began funding a new ten-year, sixth-generation project, known as the Real World Computing Program (RWC). The goal of the sixth-generation project was to produce prototype parallel-processing machines using natural-language queries and image interpretation.

## CONTEMPORARY DEVELOPMENTS

Several technologies, projects, and ideas that span more than one computer generation are discussed in this section. New information about these technologies may be found in contemporary computer journals.

**Parallel Processors.** Parallel processing is a means of increasing speed by having multiple computers operate on one problem or a set of problems at the same time. Two common classes of parallel processors are called SIMD (single instruction, multiple data) and MIMD (multiple instruction, multiple data) for the ways in which they are controlled. Developing operating systems and applications to make efficient use of parallelism has been very difficult.

ILLIAC IV was the first of the "parallel processors." It had 256 processing elements that operated on a single problem. Westinghouse began work on the machine, but it was completed at Burroughs. It was operational at NASA Ames Laboratory in 1968. The Denelcor HEP in 1981 was the first commercial parallel machine on the market. In 1985 it was followed by the Connection machine, the Cosmic Cube, and the BBN Butterfly. Many manufacturers, such as MasPar, offer parallel or multiprocessor options. They face increased competition from networks of high-speed RISC (Reduced Instruction Set Computers) workstations.

**Supercomputers.**  A *supercomputer* is defined as the most powerful scientific system available at any given time. In 1956, when transistors made much larger and faster machines possible, two major supercomputer projects were begun, the Remington Rand LARC and the IBM Stretch. LARC was delivered to the Atomic Energy Laboratory at Livermore, Calif., in May 1960, and Stretch to Los Alamos, in New Mexico, in May 1961.

By 1964 the CDC 6600 had become the undisputed leading supercomputer. It used multiple arithmetic and logical units and had ten peripheral processors, each a small computer handling specific tasks. It averaged 3 million instructions per second in 1965. In 1967 IBM unveiled the System/360 Mod 90 Series. CDC countered with the 6800 in 1967 and the 7600 in 1968.

In 1972 the designer of CDC's supercomputers, Seymour Cray, left CDC to form his own company. His first machine, the CRAY-I of 1975, was a great success. There followed a series of CRAYs that were the leading supercomputers until 1990, when parallel processors and nets of RISC machines began to take the lead. In the late 1980s several supercomputers were available, including the CRAY X-MP, the NEC SX-l, the Amdahl 1200, the CDC Cyber 205, and the IBM 3090 vector processor.

The increasing power of VLSI technology created a new category of computer called the "mini-supers." These machines were priced as medium-size computers but had the power of a small supercomputer. In 1982 Floating Point Systems FPS M64/40 released the first mini-super. Other mini-super machines include the Alliant FX/8, which was released in 1985; the Gould NPl, released in 1987; the Multiflow Trace 7/200, released in 1987; and the SC5-40, designed to be a CRAY-compatible workstation.

The future of supercomputers seemed unlimited, but in the late 1980s challenges came from two directions: from powerful RISC workstations and from parallel network machines. By the mid-1990s lack of demand had forced many supercomputer manufacturers to withdraw from the field.

**RISC Machines.**  The trend in high-performance computer design for two decades was toward more and more hardware complexity. However, building truly fast machines in the 1980s and 1990s required a return to the instruction-set simplicity of the 1950s. This permitted commonly used instructions to be executed in one machine cycle with simpler decoding and made possible more efficient compilers to translate the application programs into the simpler machine code.

John Cocke, of IBM Research, headed the first project, which resulted in the IBM 801 in 1979. David Patterson at the University of California at Berkeley began a project in 1980 and coined the name *RISC* for this architectural approach. Several machines, including the RISC-I and RISC-II, were built at Berkeley. John Hennessy at Stanford University developed a 32-bit microprocessor called MIPS (millions of instructions per second) using RISC architecture. Results of Hennessy's research project, published in 1981 by Hennessy and his colleagues at Stanford, showed that RISCs had a performance advantage of two to five times over other designs.

RISC machines are particularly well suited to high-speed workstations. Examples of RISC machines include the IBM RT PC workstation series, introduced in 1986; the Motorola 88000, introduced in 1988; and the Hewlett-Packard Spectrum series of machines, first introduced in 1986 as part of a plan to convert all of its machines to RISC-architecture machines. In a few years Hewlett-Packard had surpassed IBM in the workstation market.

At the high-performance end, the computing power of RISC machines of the 1990s reached a level of performance that had been possible only in the largest supercomputers of the early 1980s, resulting in the replacement of many expensive mainframe computers with smaller but more powerful workstations.

**Virus Attacks.**  As with any other human endeavor, computing has its share of individuals who attempt to destroy what others have built. "Virus" programs, "worms," and "Trojan horses" are penetrating, sometimes self-replicating, secret programs that are introduced into both private and public computer systems in order to cause annoyance or destruction.

In 1982 Jim Hauser, of California Polytechnic State University, and one of his students developed the first computer virus. Because he was using an Apple computer, Hauser called the program a "worm." Although his program was harmless, he saw the potential destructive capability and published an article to alert the computer community. On Nov. 2, 1988, a program created by Robert T. Morris immobilized an estimated 6,000 computers linked to the unclassified Internet research computer network in the United States. Morris was found guilty of federal computer-tampering charges. Steps taken to guarantee computer security have become increasingly important as more and more personal computers and computer systems are networked together.

There is concern that the Bill of Rights can be trampled by overzealous investigators who do not understand the difference between a "hacker," a highly skilled programmer with a passion for tinkering with technology, and a computer criminal. (Another term sometimes incorrectly used is *computer nerd*, usually a socially inept person obsessed with computers. *Nerd* is from *If I Ran the Zoo*, the 1950 children's book by Dr. Seuss.) Nevertheless, with sufficient effort any computer security system can eventually be broken into. The goal of security is to make the effort required not worth the value of any information gained.

### SOFTWARE

Software, or the set of instructions used by programmers to direct computers to perform particular tasks, has become increasingly sophisticated over the years. A brief overview of computer languages and operating systems follows.

**Computer Languages.**  The earliest computers could be programmed only by experts using machine language. Assembly-language programs were written that permitted the use of symbolic names instead of numerical addresses, which are very prone to human copying errors. Higher-level language programs, at the time called "automatic programming," were written by several groups. The first truly successful higher-level language was a result of the IBM FORTRAN project, headed by John Backus and released in 1957. COBOL, sponsored by Grace Hopper of the U.S. Navy, was introduced soon after and was designed as a common language for business data processing. COBOL and FORTRAN are still widely used but have

COURTESY INTEL CORPORATION

The first 8-bit microprocessor chip was designed to control video display terminals and keyboards.

evolved greatly since the 1950s.

ALGOL, an algorithmic language developed in the early 1960s for education and documentation, served as a prototype for many later languages. Dozens of computer languages have been developed. Some important ones in use are Pascal, developed by Niklaus Wirth and used in education; APL, a scientific system invented by Kenneth Iverson; LISP, a list-processing language developed by John McCarthy; and BASIC, developed by Tom Kurtz and John Kemeny at Dartmouth College for student use. Others include FORTH, developed by C. H. Moore and used for control programs; and PROLOG, developed by A. Colmerauer, R. Kowalski, and D. Warren and used for knowledge systems.

Some languages were decreed by organizations. The first was COBOL, mentioned above. Another was PL/1, started in 1964 by IBM with two IBM customer groups. PL/1 was a combined scientific and commercial language, intended to replace COBOL and FORTRAN. In 1977 the U.S. Department of Defense issued proposals for the Ada language, named after Lady Ada Lovelace, which was intended to replace all older languages. It was in heavy use in the 1990s for defense projects. However, the existence of millions of lines of old programs has made it hard to replace COBOL and FORTRAN.

One of the most successful languages has been C, originally developed by Brian Kernighan and Dennis Ritchie for writing operating systems. It rapidly became the language of choice for microprocessors and workstations. "C++" is its object-oriented version.

**Operating Systems.** Operating systems are supervisory programs that provide for automatic transition from one computer program to the next and manage the disk-storage and peripheral devices. Early computers were limited by how fast human operators could throw switches on the console. Simple control programs were then developed to sequence from one short job to another (called "batch processing"). The next step was to "time-sharing," in which many independent users had access to big computers remotely. This was followed by "multiprogramming," in which many independent programs could be executed at the same time on one or many processors.

The first true operating system was MCP (Master Control Program) for the Burroughs B2500 and B3500. IBM's OS/360 in 1961 was an elaborate system supporting language processors, input/output devices, and application programs. The simpler disk operating system (DOS/360) could execute three programs concurrently.

The UNIX system has, since the mid-1980s, become one of the most widely used operating systems in the world. The first version of UNIX was developed at Bell Laboratories in 1969 by Ken Thompson and Dennis Ritchie. The name *UNIX* was a pun on MULTICS, the large operating-system project of MIT's project MAC. Initially UNIX was just an internal tool for developers, but a major UNIX project at the University of California at Berkeley in the early 1980s led to its widespread use. For microprocessors a key step was the development of CP/M (Control Program for Microprocessors) in 1978 by Digital Research Inc. It was eclipsed in popularity by Microsoft's PC-DOS and MS-DOS, mentioned earlier (in the personal computer section). (See the section "Computer Systems and Methodology.")

HERMAN H. GOLDSTINE
*Institute for Advanced Study*
HARWOOD G. KOLSKY
*University of California at Santa Cruz*

### Bibliography

Almasi, George S., and Allan Gottlieb, *Highly Parallel Computing* (Benjamin/Cummings Publ. 1991).

Augarten, Stan, *Bit by Bit: An Illustrated History of Computers* (Ticknor & Fields 1984).

Bashe, Charles J., et al., *IBM's Early Computers* (MIT Press 1986).

Burks, Alice R., and Arthur W. Burks, *The First Electronic Computer: The Atanasoff Story* (Univ. of Mich. Press 1988).

Carroll, Paul, *Big Blues: The Unmaking of IBM* (Crown 1993).

Dertouzos, Michael L., and Joel Moses, eds., *The Computer Age: A Twenty-Year View* (MIT Press 1979).

Eames, Charles, and Ray Eames, *A Computer Perspective* (Harvard Univ. Press 1973).

Goldstine, Herman H., *The Computer from Pascal to von Neumann* (Princeton Univ. Press 1980).

Hodges, Andrew, *Alan Turing: The Enigma* (Simon & Schuster 1983).

Ichbiah, Daniel, *The Making of Microsoft* (Prima Publ. 1991).

Lundstrom, David E., *A Few Good Men from UNIVAC* (MIT Press 1987).

McAfee, John, *Computer Viruses, Worms, Data Diddlers, Killer Programs and Other Threats to Your System* (MIT Press 1987).

Miller, Richard K., *Fifth Generation Computers* (Prentice-Hall 1987).

Pinkert, James, and Larry Wear, *Operating Systems* (Prentice-Hall 1989).

Slater, Robert, *Portraits in Silicon* (St. Martin's 1989).

Stein, Dorothy, *Ada, a Life and a Legacy* (MIT Press 1985).

Watson, Thomas J., Jr., and Peter Petre, *Father, Son & Co.* (Bantam 1990).

Williams, Michael R., *A History of Computing Technology* (Prentice-Hall 1985).

### 3. Computer Architecture and Design

The history of the development of computing can be traced through three interlaced factors—technology, computer architecture, and algorithms. The computational aids used by humankind have increased in complexity and sophistication as have the mathematical techniques conceived of in order to solve increasingly complex problems. Computer architects use the basic building blocks provided by technology to organize a computational problem-solving engine to execute algorithms. The original concept behind computer architecture was to provide a level above which the user, or programmer, could ignore the implementation of the computer. Programmers could then assume that the computer architecture was fixed as they developed software. As the search for higher performance continues, the software becomes more and more "aware" of the implementation of the computer architecture.

## EARLY TECHNOLOGY

Early computational aids include tally sticks, or carved wooden sticks first used for counting more than 20,000 years ago; the abacus, known as the first mechanical computing device, used to perform the four basic arithmetic functions beginning in the Middle East around 500 A.D.; and the slide rule, an analog device that used logarithms to perform multiplication and division, first developed in the early 1600s.

Charles Babbage's proposed "analytical engine" of the mid-1800s incorporated mechanical gears to allow the sequencing of arithmetic operations. The analytical engine did not work properly, partially because the parts needed for the engine could not be machined precisely enough at that time—the computational machines envisioned required precision-made parts beyond the capabilities of machinists using available technology. The necessary basic building blocks were finally provided, first in the form of vacuum tubes, and soon followed by the solid-state transistor and the integrated circuit in the electronics age. This led to a revolution in computing machines in the second half of the 20th century. Today integrated circuit chips may incorporate more than 10 million transistors, and the number of transistors used on integrated chips continues to increase at a 40% to 60% annually compounded rate.

Technology has been such a critical distinguishing factor that computer historians define generations of computers by the technologies in which they were implemented. Computer generations are dated beginning with the electronic age of computers, even though mechanical and electromechanical computers predated electronic computers. During the first generation (1945–1958), vacuum tubes were used in computers as active components; in the second generation (1958–1966), discrete transistors were used, and computers had magnetic-core memories; during the third generation (1966–1972), computers were distinguished by the use of small-scale and medium-scale integrated circuits; in the fourth generation (1972–1978), computers incorporated large-scale integration with 100 to 10,000 transistors per chip; and in the fifth generation (1978–    ), computers used and continue to use very-large-scale integration with over 300,000 transistors per chip.

## COMPUTER HIERARCHY

While modern technology provides the physical building blocks, computer architecture provides the logical organization necessary to build a structure with the ability to perform computations. Since a single computer may incorporate hundreds of millions of transistors, the concept of hierarchy was introduced to segment the computer into components that could be more easily understood. Basic building blocks at one hierarchical level are organized into structures, which in turn become the basic building blocks for the next higher level, as depicted in figure 1.

The lowest level in the computer hierarchy is usually defined as the circuit level, where the basic building blocks are circuit components such as transistors and capacitors, which are then organized into logic components such as an OR gate. An OR gate combines two binary values so that the output of the OR gate is true only if input A or input B or both are true. Gates are organized into data paths and controllers at the logic level. At the computer architecture level, data paths, controllers, and memories combine to form an instruction set embodied in a processor. The processor retrieves and executes instructions stored in memory. The processor is described in greater detail in the section "The Basic Computer."

At the programming level, instructions are combined into software modules that perform application programs such as spreadsheets or word processing. Software and processors can be interconnected to form networks of cooperating computers at the system architecture level. Thus, at each level in the hierarchy, building blocks from the previous, lower level are used to implement the architecture at the current level. This architecture, in turn, becomes a basic building block at the next higher level to be organized into an implementation of yet a higher level architecture.

## COMPUTER ARCHITECTURE

The importance of abstraction and levels of hierarchy was not fully understood during the development of the first two generations of computers. Until the early 1960s, computers were not designed to be compatible with one another. When a company replaced its old computer with a new one, all software applications were completely rewritten, because each machine was uniquely designed, and software could not be transferred from one machine to another. Therefore, incorporating new applications software onto a new computer and readying it for normal daily use took a great deal of time. Peripherals, such as printers and tape readers, were also replaced or completely rewired to accommodate a new computer. The introduction of the IBM System/360, a family of computers all executing the same software while spanning a factor of 25 in performance, was an architectural innovation that allowed compatible software to be written for different models of similar computers. Performance is measured in units of time, and the fastest computer in the family could execute the program 25 times faster than the slowest machine.

The concept of architecture and implementation was introduced in a 1964 paper by Gene Amdahl, Gerrit Blaauw, and Frederick Brooks, three of the team leaders on the IBM/360 project, describing their role in the design of this line of compatible computers. The term *architecture* refers to the function the system provides to the user, and the term *implementation* refers to the way in which the architecture is constructed. Consider a watch. The architecture of a watch can be analog, where hours, minutes, and seconds are indicated by hands on a dial; or digital, where numbers on a display indicate hours, minutes, and seconds. The watch architecture can be implemented in several technologies, such as mechanical gears or electronic chips. A person wearing a watch can operate the watch without understanding the implementation. For example, some digital clock architectures were implemented by mechanical gears during the Middle Ages, whereas some contemporary wristwatches are implemented by electronic chips but display analog architecture, with hour, minute, and second hands on a liquid-crystal display.

Amdahl, Blaauw, and Brooks defined architecture and implementation only at the computer

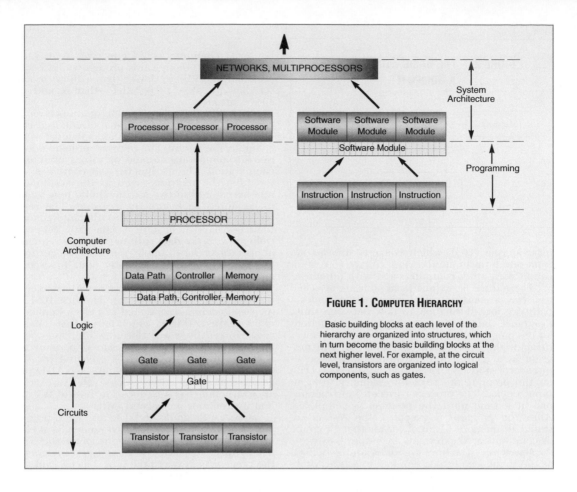

**FIGURE 1. COMPUTER HIERARCHY**

Basic building blocks at each level of the hierarchy are organized into structures, which in turn become the basic building blocks at the next higher level. For example, at the circuit level, transistors are organized into logical components, such as gates.

architecture level. Architecture was defined as the attributes of a computer as seen by the programmer. Implementation was defined as the actual electronic structure. Since 1964 the concept of architecture and implementation has been extended to all levels in the computer hierarchy. For example, at the systems architecture level, data files can be transferred using a common protocol (TCP/IP) over many different physical networks, such as Ethernet or Token Ring.

Because of the cost and complexity of hardware, initially the implementation of a computer as depicted in figure 3 had to be simple. The instruction sets produced by computer architects were also simple. As the capacity of the hardware increased, the implementation became more complex; this higher level of sophistication was translated into a comprehensive instruction set, sometimes referred to as the Complex Instruction Set Computer (CISC).

An instruction set comprises several components. The first issue an architect must decide is how data are to be represented by bits (binary digits). What format should be used for integers, floating point numbers, text characters, and instructions? Next, the architect determines how the data types are to be represented in main memory, and the number and the organization of the processor registers. Finally, the instruction set must be designed.

An instruction is composed of two parts, or fields. The first field is often called the operation code, or op code, which defines the particular function the instruction will perform. Operation codes are divided into classes such as arithmetic

(add, subtract, multiply, divide); memory reference (load data from main memory, store data into main memory); program control (looping, testing conditions, jumping to new segments of code); input/output; and communications with the operating system program. The second field defines the number and location of the operands used by the operation code. The operand field specifies the algorithm for combining data from the processor registers into addresses for the operands in main memory.

The growing length of the data path and the complexity in decoding the bits of the instruction to determine the operation and the location of the operands led computer architects in the late 1970s to return to simpler instruction formats, as in Reduced Instruction Set Computers (RISC). Though the resulting simplified data paths can be run at higher clock frequencies, other hardware and software techniques, such as memory hierarchy and concurrency (described in this article, in the section "Performance Enhancement"), are employed to further increase computer performance.

### THE BASIC COMPUTER

Computers resulted when calculators were combined with a modifiable memory in which sequences of operations, representing algorithms, could be stored. In the earliest days of the stored-program computer, three separate units were identified. As depicted in figure 2, these units were the processor, which retrieves and executes instructions stored in memory; the memory, which contains the instructions and the data; and the

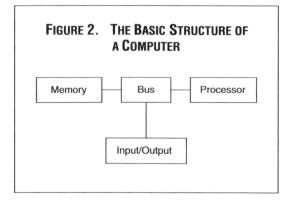

## FIGURE 2. THE BASIC STRUCTURE OF A COMPUTER

Memory — Bus — Processor

Input/Output

input/output (I/O), which converts information from one form to another to facilitate communication with other computers and with humans.

These three basic functional units are attached to a bus, a common set of wires that provides a pathway for information to flow between units. Programs, composed of a sequence of instructions for the processor, are loaded into the main memory through the input hardware. Consider the program as a recipe, and the instructions as a sequence of steps for combining ingredients. Data for the program are read into memory from an input device. The processor executes instructions one at a time until the program is completed. After the program is executed, the results are stored in memory as input for another program, or communicated externally by output hardware.

**Algorithms.** The term *algorithm* can be defined as the sequence of steps required to solve a problem. An algorithm can be considered a detailed plan for resolving a situation. For example, a recipe can be considered an algorithm for combining the ingredients to produce a cake. The order and timing prescribed in the recipe must be accurately followed if the result is to be successful. Algorithms are utilized throughout the computer hierarchy. Some algorithms are implemented in electronic hardware such as the computer's instruction set. Other algorithms, such as the operating system, are implemented as software.

**Processor.** A processor retrieves and executes instructions stored in memory. Processor complexity is typically measured by the number of transistors incorporated on the chip, where a transistor is a primitive on/off switch. The on/off switch implements a binary system composed of the two symbols 0 and 1, which are referred to as *binary digits*, or bits. Another measure of the complexity of the processor is the number of bits that are manipulated in a single operation. A 16-bit processor can represent $2^{16} = 65,536$ unique integers. Similarly, a 32-bit processor can represent $2^{32}$, or approximately 4.3 billion integers. Because of the high cost of hardware and the relatively low level of component sophistication, early computers operated on a single bit at a time; known as bit serial processing, operations such as addition occurred on individual digits. This is similar to the way humans add multidigit numbers. For example, consider two three-digit numbers: first, the two units digits are added; then the tens digits are added, followed by the digits in the hundreds position. By using a software algorithm to add individual bits in sequence, arbitrary numerical precision could be achieved in exchange for longer program-execution time. For example, a

bit serial computer could add two 16-bit numbers bit by bit, though this process would be approximately 16 times slower than a 16-bit processor that operates "in parallel"—that is, adds all 16 bits at once.

A simplified implementation of a processor incorporates registers, an arithmetic unit, and controller building blocks from the logic level of the computer hierarchy. The registers provide a location for temporary storage of values used in a computation. The arithmetic unit combines values from the registers (such as the addition of numbers stored in two registers) into new values to be stored back into the registers. The registers, the arithmetic unit, and the interconnections between them form a data path. The controller directs the data path to perform a sequence of operations (for example, move an integer from the registers to the arithmetic unit) to execute an instruction.

A rough gauge of processor performance is the processor clock frequency. The first IBM PC (personal computer) operated at a clock frequency of 5 megahertz (MHz), which means that the processor internally was performing 5 million operations per second. Another measure of performance is the number of instructions executed per second by the processor. For example, a 5 MHz processor that requires ten clock cycles to execute an instruction has an execution rate of 0.5 million instructions per second (MIPS).

**Memory.** Programs and data are stored in main memory, which can be accessed randomly, at close to the performance speed of the processor. Thus it may take 1 clock cycle to add two integers in the process, or it may take 2 or 3 clock cycles to access memory. Main memory is often called random-access memory (RAM). Typically, programs that cannot be stored in main memory are stored on an electromechanical disk, a spinning platter coated with a thin film of magnetic material that acts as secondary memory. The response time of secondary memory is usually several orders of magnitude slower than main memory (for example, over 10,000 clock cycles on average to access disks) because of the rotational delay of secondary memory. The capacity of memory is typically measured in bytes; a byte is composed of 8 bits.

**Input/Output.** The third major component of a computer is input/output (I/O). A user typically interacts with a computer through a keyboard (input) and a display screen (output). The clarity, or resolution, of the display is measured by the number of picture elements (pixels) that may be displayed on the screen. Each pixel may be represented by 1 bit, which turns the picture element on or off, for a black-and-white display; 4 bits, which incorporates $2^4 = 16$ shades of black and white, sometimes called gray scale; or 24 bits, which incorporates $3 \times 8 = 24$ bits for a color display, where red, blue, and green are each represented by $2^8 = 256$ shades.

Finally, computers also communicate with other computers using modems (*modulate/demodulate*) connected by telephone lines, and network interfaces for wires dedicated to carrying digital information. Examples of computer-to-computer communications include bank/money transfers, paying for groceries with an ATM card, and accessing information from remote sites over computer networks such as the Worldwide Web. Performance of electronic communications is measured in bits transmitted per second.

## PERFORMANCE ENHANCEMENT

Algorithms exhibit temporal and spatial locality. The term *temporal locality* refers to the observation that recently accessed items are likely to be accessed again in the near future. The term *spatial locality* means that items close to one another in an array of data tend to be referenced close together in time. The computer architect can utilize locality to increase the performance of all three functional units in the basic computer.

**Memory Hierarchy.** The memory is one of the first places to exploit locality, as in the structure in figure 2. Because technologies with widely varying capabilities are available for memory use, ranging from electromechanical disk drives to semiconductor chips, a balance between cost and performance must be decided on. Application programs exhibit locality in accessing main memory. For example, a program loop repeatedly executes the instructions within the loop exhibiting both temporal (same memory access pattern while the loop is being executed) and spatial (same sequence of instructions in the loop) locality.

Memory performance hierarchies are based on the principle that slower memory costs less than faster memory, and that the locality of programs may be captured with small amounts of high-speed memory. A typical memory hierarchy is composed of several levels. At the top of the hierarchy are the processor registers that are the fastest in performance but smallest in capacity; they reside on the same semiconductor chip as the processor, and the overall size of a semiconductor chip is limited. Processor registers are directly manipulated by the software program.

On the next level down in the memory hierarchy is the cache memory, which is intermediate in speed and capacity between the processor registers and the main memory. Cache memory contents are controlled by hardware that retrieves data requested by the processor from main memory and then stores a copy in the cache. A second request is supplied by the faster cache rather than by the slower main memory, thus yielding a faster average memory access time.

The lowest level in the memory hierarchy involves secondary storage. Frequently, the combi-

Figure 3. Inside a personal computer system unit. The motherboard is a circuit board that houses the microprocessor, RAM, connectors, and ports. The microprocessor (CPU) is an integrated circuit that controls and performs each computer instruction. Within the CPU, the arithmetic logic unit is the microprocessor's calculator; the prefetch unit organizes instructions for processing; and the bus interface unit acts as the link between the units in the CPU and other components, including the RAM cache. Extra RAM, packaged as SIMM modules, enables a PC to perform faster. CMOS (complementary metal oxide semiconductor) memory stores the current date and time, as well as system configuration data. The basic input and output system (BIOS) enables the computer to communicate with devices such as a disk drive or printer. Expansion slots hold cards such as video or sound cards, which increase the versatility of a PC. Parallel ports connect printers to the system. The hard drive contains several platters that can hold millions of bytes of data, and software programs loaded onto the hard drive run faster. Floppy disks and CD-ROMs store data.

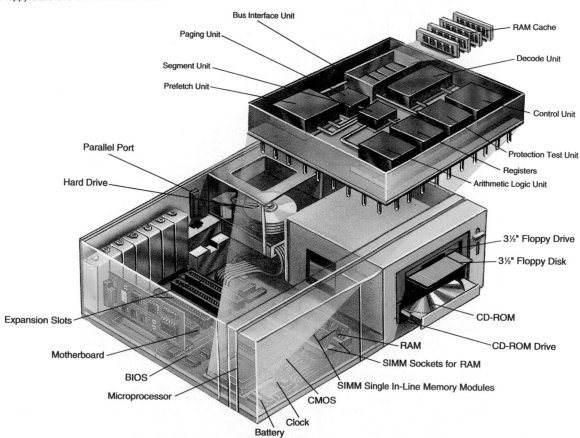

nation of a program and its data set is too large to fit into main memory, especially in the case of large scientific programs. Virtual memory solves this problem by providing a mapping table that transforms a program's logical memory address into an actual address in main memory. The principle of operation is very similar to that of the cache memory, except that the most recently accessed portions of the program and data reside in main memory, while unused portions of a program are "migrated" to secondary storage (for example, disk) by operating system software. A further advantage of using virtual memory is that programs do not rely on having a certain amount of main memory installed on the computer, so the hardware configuration may change without requiring a change for programs that would not originally fit entirely in main memory.

**Concurrency.** Another approach for increasing performance is allowing concurrency of operation of one or more of the functional units shown in figure 2. There are two major ways to accomplish concurrent program execution—concurrency through overlap of operations (concurrency in time) and concurrency through replication (concurrency in space). Overlap allows phases of different computations that use separate resources to execute concurrently. Replication provides multiple copies of the same resource so that several sections of the same computation can proceed concurrently.

Consider the execution of an instruction. The instruction and any data the instruction is to operate on is retrieved from memory. The processor determines which function the instruction is to perform (this process is called instruction decode) and then performs, or executes, the instruction. With a little extra hardware, the processor and memory units can proceed independently. The memory could be used to retrieve the next sequential instruction while the processor executed the current instruction. Another opportunity for concurrency is between the processor and the I/O. With a small amount of extra hardware, the processor can start an I/O operation and then continue non-I/O processing. When the I/O device finishes, it notifies the processor by means of an interrupt. This allows data for one program to be loaded while a second program is executed and the results from a third program are printed.

The concept of concurrency can be extended into each of the functional units. By breaking down an operation into smaller steps, the steps can be executed concurrently on different hardware in a production-line fashion. Consider an automobile assembly line, where something is added to the automobile at each station, and then the automobile is passed on to the next station. Every minute, a separate subassembly (for example, a bumper, windshield, or engine) enters at one end of the assembly line, and a car is driven off the other end. The "throughput" is thus one car per minute, but the time to convert subassemblies into a completed product is about 8 hours (the latency). This arrangement is often called a pipeline because material progresses uniformly from one stage to the next.

In a computer a simple instruction execution might be composed of five steps: an instruction retrieval, instruction decode, execute, write to memory, and write to registers. If each stage could be completed in one clock period, and if the clock frequency is 100 MHz, each clock period would be 10 nanoseconds (that is, a period is the recip-

rocal of the frequency). Though the processor could execute 100 million instructions per second, each instruction would execute in 50 nanoseconds (that is, five stages at 10 nanoseconds per stage). By providing extra hardware to turn a computer as schematized in figure 2 into a five-stage pipeline, the throughput of the processor could be increased by a factor of five (one instruction completes the pipeline every clock period, or 10 nanoseconds), while the instruction latency would remain the same (each instruction would still take 50 nanoseconds to execute).

Although concurrency through overlap is a powerful technique, it is eventually limited by the fact that the peak processing rate is achieved when all hardware resources are busy. The only way to improve performance beyond this point is to introduce concurrency through replication of resources, the simplest form being identical copies of resources that are explicitly controlled by software. For example, if a second arithmetic unit is added to the data path, two arithmetic instructions could be executed in one clock period, yielding a further factor of two increases in throughput if the rest of the pipeline hardware can handle two instructions per clock period.

If a processor has extra functional units that allow more than one operation per clock period, it is called a superscalar processor. However, the potential speedup is not always achieved because most programs introduce data dependencies that must be preserved. For example, if the second instruction uses the results of the computation of the first instruction, an explicit mechanism must be provided to ensure that the first instruction is completed prior to the execution of the second instruction. The mechanism can be built into the hardware or accomplished by rearranging instructions through the software so that adjacent instructions are independent.

If the entire data path is replicated several times but there is only one controller, the result is called a single-instruction-multiple-data (SIMD) organization. The controller broadcasts the same instruction to all the data paths, which operate on different subsets of data. SIMD architectures are effective when there are large data sets to which the same algorithm is applied. Satellite image enhancement, weather prediction, and simulation are examples of applications that effectively use SIMD architectures.

If the processor and memory in figure 2 are replicated, the resulting architecture is a multiple-instruction—multiple-data (MIMD), or multiple-processor, organization. If any processor can access any memory, the organization is called a multiprocessor. If processors can communicate only by way of messages under software control, the organization is called a multicomputer. Applications composed of independent programs can make effective use of the replication in MIMD organizations to increase system throughput. Conversely, applications that require high reliability can use the replication to tolerate failures. Transaction-processing systems, such as bank teller machines, can make effective use of MIMD systems.

Note that even when the throughput in the transaction-processing systems increases, the latency for each program remains unchanged. If the goal is to speed up the latency of a single program, the programmer must reorganize the algorithm to take advantage of the opportunities for concurrency. With the large variety of speed-up

FERRANTI ELECTRONICS/H. STERNBERG/SCIENCE PHOTO LIBRARY/PHOTO RESEARCHERS

This microprocessor chip has more computing power than early computers' circuitry, which filled large rooms.

techniques available, one might think that any program could be made to process more quickly by any arbitrary amount simply by adding enough pipeline stages and replicated processors. Unfortunately, most programs have only a limited amount of code that may be processed in parallel. Amdahl's Law states that the performance improvement is limited by the fraction of code on which the speed-up technique can be used. In other words, speeding up only a portion of a program brings diminishing returns as that one portion of a program runs faster and faster. For example, if two-thirds of the code can be made to run in parallel, the program cannot be made to execute in less than one-third the time of the original program, using even an infinite amount of concurrency, since the original one-third of the code remains unchanged.

### RATE OF TECHNOLOGICAL CHANGE

The rapid rate of technological change is one major factor that determines which economically feasible features to include in a computer system. Techniques that might have been prohibitively expensive only a decade ago may become profitable because of rapid technological advances. A comparison indicating the rate of technological change during the first 30 years commercial electronic computers were available is depicted in table 1. The Univac I, the first commercial computer, was introduced by Remington Rand Corporation in 1951. The IBM PC, IBM's first personal computer, was introduced in 1981. Processor performance increased from 20,000 instructions per second to 400,000 instructions per second, an improvement factor of 20. The cost fell from $250,000 (in 1951 dollars) to $5,000 (in 1981 dollars), for an improvement factor of 50. If inflation had averaged 5% over that 30-year period, then the cost improvement would have been a factor of almost 2,000. Power consumption fell from 50,000 watts to less than 500 for an improvement factor of 100. By way of comparison, if the automotive industry had had the same rate of technological improvement as that of the computer industry over that same period, cars built in 1981 would have traveled at over 2,000 miles per hour and

**TABLE 1. FIRST 30 YEARS OF COMMERCIAL ELECTRONIC COMPUTERS: TECHNOLOGICAL COMPARISONS**

|  | Univac I | IBM PC |
|---|---|---|
| Year of Introduction | 1951 | 1981 |
| Speed (instructions/second) | 20,000 | 400,000 |
| Cost (dollars) | 250,000 | 5,000 |
| Power Consumption (watts) | 50,000 | 500 |

cost less than $10, and mileage would have increased to over 1,500 miles per gallon.

For nearly three decades computer engineers have been plotting the time-rate of change of technology; they found that a rough approximation of capacity, performance, and cost can be modeled by using a simple compounding relationship. Table 2 gives the rate of change for a microprocessor, a complete processor contained on a single semiconductor chip; main memory, a group of memory bits contained on a single semiconductor chip; and secondary memory.

**TABLE 2. TIME-RATE OF CHANGE OF COMPUTER TECHNOLOGY**

| Processor | Complexity per chip (transistors) | Performance (MIPS) |
|---|---|---|
| Rate of Change | +40% | +35% |
| Main Memory | Complexity per chip (bits) | Cost/bit (cents) |
| Rate of Change | +64% | −25% |
| Secondary Memory (disks) | Capacity per disk (bytes) | Cost/byte (cents) |
| Rate of Change | +14% | −21% |

From this table we see that processor complity is increasing by 40% per year compounded and performance by 35% per year compounded. By way of contrast, the performance improvement between the Univac I and the IBM PC was only about 10.5% per year compounded. Main memory chips have been increasing in complexity at a rate of 64% per year compounded (that is, increasing by a factor of four every three years), while cost is decreasing at a rate of 25% per year. Note that the microprocessor and memory-chip time-rate of change projections are for first availability of these chips. Another two years may pass before new chips are designed and implemented in a system and before that system is manufactured and is then made available to buyers.

DANIEL P. SIEWIOREK, *Carnegie-Mellon University*

### Bibliography

Amdahl, Gene M., "Validity of the Single Processor Approach to Achieving Large-Scale Computing Capabilities," *Proceedings AFIPS 1967 Spring Joint Computer Conference* 30:483–485.

Amdahl, Gene M., et al., "Architecture of the IBM System/360," *IBM Journal Research and Development* 8(2):87–101.

Bell, C. G., "The Mini and Micro Industries," *IEEE Computer 1* 17(10):14–30.

Bell, C. G., "The Future of High Performance Computers in Science and Engineering," *Communications of the ACM* 32(9):1091–1101.

Blaauw, Gerrit A., and Frederick P. Brooks, Jr., *Computer Architecture*, vols. I and II (Addison-Wesley 1992).

Dubois, Michel, and Shreekant S. Thakker, eds., *Cache and Interconnect Architectures in Multiprocessors* (Kluwer 1990).

Flynn, Michael J., "Very High-Speed Computing Systems," *Proceedings IEEE* 54(12):1901–1909.

Hennessy, John L., and David A. Patterson, *Computer Architecture: A Quantitative Approach* (Morgan Kaufmann 1990).

Huck, Jerome C., and Michael J. Flynn, *Analyzing Computer Architecture* (IEEE Comp. Soc. 1989).

Siewiorek, Daniel P., and R. S. Swarz, *Reliable Computer Systems: Design and Evaluation*, 2d ed. (Butterworth 1992).

Stone, Harold S., *High-Performance Computer Architecture*, 3d ed. (Addison-Wesley 1993).

UPI/BETTMANN

In a 1946 contest pitting an abacus against an electronic calculator, the abacus won in four out of five categories.

## 4. Computer Systems and Methodologies

The mechanical and electronic components of a computer system, including the various input and output devices, are termed *hardware*. The contrasting term, *software*, refers to computer programs—the set of instructions that prompt the computer to perform some action. The concept of a program, of a "machine built out of software"—of a machine that is "powered" by the computer on which it executes—is one of the subtlest and most elusive in modern technology. It is also, arguably, the most important idea in modern technology. This article presents the basic principles of computer software, with special reference to operating systems, programming, and languages.

### PROGRAMMING METHODOLOGIES

The machine we call a digital computer becomes productive precisely to the extent that we equip it with programs, commonly known as software. A computer without software is like a power shovel without an operator. The power shovel is capable, in principle, of accomplishing much useful work, but without an operator it can do nothing. The power-shovel operator, like the computer program, makes the machine useful and determines which tasks it will perform. Although the power shovel has limited functions, whether it digs a hole, knocks over a building, or loads sand into a dump truck depends on the actions of the operator. Likewise, the computer sets certain limits on what a program can do, but within those limits, it is the program and not the computer that is in control.

Consider the computer as a device that causes programs to be executed. An observer watching a program execute on a computer—watching the solution of a numerical problem, the creation of a document on the screen, the display of a picture—may believe that a machine is busily at work. But the program, not the computer, determines which numbers are computed, how the document appears on the screen, how the picture is composed. In a sense the program is the machine whose activities are being observed, and the physical computer is merely its "power source." A "machine built out of software" is an unconventional kind of machine, an intangible machine that exists inside a computer. It cannot be seen or touched directly, but like any other machine, a software machine has real and observable effects on the outside world.

The computer is indispensable if the program is to run—in roughly the sense that gasoline is indispensable if an automobile is to run. But the influence of the gasoline on the automobile's performance, or the computer on the program's performance, is minimal at best. It is the program and not its power source (that is, the car and not its fuel) that determines the character of the computation (of the transportation) that is delivered to the user.

**Machine-Language Programs.** The primitive instructions that a computer is capable of executing directly are the raw material of software. These instructions are collectively referred to as machine language. Although each type of computer has its own machine language, all machine languages have a similar purpose.

Machine language reflects the physical structure of computers. A computer consists, in essence, of two parts: a memory and a processing unit. The memory is divided into cells, and each cell holds a number. The cells themselves are numbered, so that instructions may refer to the number or information in a particular cell. The memory of a modern computer typically has millions of cells.

The processing unit is capable of executing primitive instructions. An instruction may perform an arithmetic operation on numbers chosen from memory. For example, it might add together the numbers currently found in cells 200 and 201 and put the sum in cell 500. Or an instruction may examine a number chosen from memory and reach some decision based on the value of the number. For instance, it might examine the number in cell 12 and halt the program if the number is 0. Finally, instructions may cause information to be transferred from the outside world into memory, or from memory to the outside world. For example, if a computer is connected to a keyboard and a display screen, which is typically the case, such an instruction might take a number typed in at the keyboard and place it in cell 137, or take the number in cell 15 and display it on the screen.

Each simple instruction is itself represented by a number. Numbers representing instructions are stored in the memory, along with numbers that represent data. After a list of instructions has been placed in memory—in the simplest case, this can be accomplished by a person manipulating switches on a front panel—the computer may be told to start executing, beginning with the instruction in cell 12 and continuing in sequence.

In order to extract useful work from the computer, the programmer must present it with an appropriate list of instructions. Suppose the set task is for the computer to read two numbers typed in at a keyboard and to respond by printing the sum of the two numbers on the screen. The programmer must create a list of instructions roughly as follows:

(1) Read a number typed at the keyboard; store that number in memory cell 1.

(2) Read another number typed at the keyboard; store it in memory cell 2.

(3) Add the number in cell 1 to the number in cell 2; store the sum in cell 3.

(4) Take the number in cell 3 and display it on the screen.

This is a paraphrased list of instructions rather than an actual program; each written instruction must be translated into code recognized by the computer. The details of the program—the exact nature of each instruction, and the numbers that represent the instructions—depend on the computer for which the program was designed. A version of this program written for a Macintosh computer, for example, would differ from a version written especially for execution on an IBM or IBM-compatible machine, even though the logic of the two programs would be similar. Although this is not a functional program, this paraphrased program captures the spirit of a machine-language program.

**Programming Languages.**  Building programs in machine language is a poor way to get the computer to perform useful work. Programmers prefer to build programs using a notation that reflects their own way of thinking rather than the physical capacities of the computer.

Consider the following analogy. A composer thinks in terms of musical phrases. To compose the beginning of *The Star-Spangled Banner* ("O say can you see ..."), she thinks in terms of a certain sequence of six musical notes. The composer would like to write these six notes down in the form of six symbols, one symbol per note. A violinist, on the other hand, is physically capable of moving his bow back and forth and the four fingers of his left hand up and down. If a composer were forced to compose music using a notation that reflected the physical capacities of the violinist rather than her mental picture of the musical notes, her musical notation would be a list of primitive instructions for bodily motions, such as "first, move the bow this way, arrange the left hand that way, and keep it up for an eighth of a second; then, do this with the bow and that with the left hand, for the next quarter second; then ..."

This system is untenable. The composer wishes to use a notation that represents musical phrases, not the physical capabilities of the violinist. The violinist must learn how to translate the musical phrases listed on the page into the physical movements that enable music to be generated on the violin. The violinist seeing a series of symbols on the page representing a specific musical phrase, such as the six notes denoting the opening phrase of *The Star-Spangled Banner*, must then translate those symbols into the detailed physical maneuvers necessary to get a violin to make the desired sounds.

In the same way, the programmer does not wish to formulate a process in terms of the low-level operations executed by the computer. Whereas a composer thinks in terms of musical phrases, a programmer thinks in terms of "information machines." An information machine accepts information from the outside world and transforms it—creating documents, making pictures, solving numerical problems, accomplishing all the tasks of which software is capable.

An information machine does not work unless it is "plugged into" a computer; an information machine as the programmer creates it is a passive shell that "comes to life," or becomes active, when a computer begins to execute it. But an information machine, unlike a machine-language program, is not designed with the details of any particular computer in mind. In general, it may be executed by any computer, just as a musical phrase may be played by a musician on any instrument. An information machine is expressed in a language appropriate to its basic character, just as musical notation is appropriate for expressing music, not the physical device executing it.

A programming language is a notation used for specifying the design of an information machine. The programming language provides the programmer with rules for creating a document. This document is the specification for an information machine, in the sense that a musical score is the specification for a piece of music, or a blueprint is the specification for a building.

Pascal is a programming language whose simplicity and clarity have made it popular for teaching programming concepts to students. Using Pascal, we could specify an information machine that reads two numbers, adds them together, and then displays their sum. The program would read as follows:

```
Program Add(input, output) ;
Var FirstNumber, SecondNumber, Sum: integer;
Begin
  readln(FirstNumber) ;
  readln(SecondNumber) ;
  Sum := FirstNumber + SecondNumber;
  writeln(Sum)
End.
```

The line-by-line explanation of the program, which omits a few unimportant details, is as follows: (1) The name of the program is Add. It performs both input and output operations—that is, it will read numbers that a user types in at the keyboard, and it will display the numbers on the screen. (2) The program is concerned with three numbers, or variables (which is what Var stands for). Their names are FirstNumber, SecondNumber, and Sum. The numbers are integers, that is, each variable equals either 0, a positive whole number, or a negative whole number. (3) The computer is instructed to begin executing the program. (4) When the program is executed, it reads values for FirstNumber and (5) SecondNumber as they are typed by the user at the keyboard. (6) The program adds the two numbers together and calls the result Sum. (7) The value of Sum is then displayed on the screen. (8) The computer is finally instructed to halt the program.

This Pascal program carries out the same activities and achieves the same results as the machine-language program. However, some of the differences between the two programs are important. The machine-language program must be tailored to a specific computer, but the Pascal program can be executed on any computer. A related but more significant point is that the Pascal program is concerned with high-level concepts, the machine-language program with low-level operations. The Pascal program deals with numbers that have names; and it handles arithmetic expressions such as FirstNumber + SecondNumber. In the machine-language program, there are no names; we refer merely to cell 2 or cell 3. There are no numbers per se; we refer merely to the contents of particular cells. There are no arithmetic expressions, merely instructions to the computer to "add" or "store."

The high-level concepts in this sample Pascal program—numbers, names, and arithmetic expressions—are important to anyone trying to solve a particular problem. These concepts are not specifically related to any particular computer, or even linked to computers in general. High-level concepts have been important ever since people began attempting to solve problems. A larger or more complex example would reveal other key ideas in Pascal that have nothing to do with computers—ideas that are taken directly from the language and methods that are natural to problem solving, which precede the computer by centuries or even millennia. These concepts are "musical phrases" to the programmer; they are the stuff of information machines.

**Translation from Programming to Machine Language.** The words and symbols in the programmer's information machine must be translated into the proper machine language for the computer on which the program will execute. The same information machine might be executed on an IBM-compatible computer or on a Macintosh, but in the first case it will be translated into the IBM-compatible's machine language, in the second case into the Macintosh's machine language. The translation from programming language to machine language could be carried out by a human translator, in the same fashion that a human might translate from French to Japanese. But it is much faster and more convenient to accomplish this translation through a special translator program called a compiler.

The creation of software proceeds as follows: The programmer designs an information machine and specifies it, using a programming language. A special program, the compiler, then translates this information-machine specification into the appropriate machine language. The computer executes the machine language.

An important variant of this procedure uses a different kind of translator, called an interpreter. Whereas a compiler translates an essentially complete information machine into machine language, an interpreter translates the programmer's information machine piece by piece and executes each piece immediately. The programmer may type in a few phrases and execute them right away to see if they work. Interpreters allow programs to be developed incrementally rather than all at once—a technique that many programmers find convenient as well as conducive to improvisation and creativity.

**The Programming-Language Spectrum.** A programming language is a way of specifying an information machine. However, the world of information machines is independent of the world of programming languages, in the sense that the world of buildings is independent of the world of drafting tools. Programmers have many programming languages to choose from. Their choice of language is similar to the architect's choice of drafting tools: colored pencils may be best in one case, drafting pens in another case, a sophisticated computer drafting program in a third case. The appropriate choice is decided by the aptness and convenience of the tools in the context of a particular job.

*Development of Programming Languages.* The development and proliferation of programming languages in this century—indeed, in the last quarter of the 20th century—beggars the imagination. Yet most of the major characteristics of today's programming-language picture had emerged within five years of the advent of programming languages on a large scale, with IBM's FORTRAN language developed by a team headed by John Backus in 1957. Direct descendants of that first FORTRAN (*For*mula *Trans*lation) continue to be the most widely used languages for scientific and engineering software.

The publication of the ALGOL 60 language in 1960 may well have been the most important event in the history of software. ALGOL 60, developed by an international committee, is no longer used, but Pascal, which was developed by Niklaus Wirth in 1973; C, the widely used language developed by Brian Kernighan and Dennis Ritchie at Bell Labs in 1972; and many other useful languages are ALGOL 60's direct descendants. LISP (short for List Processing), versions of which remain the principal vehicle for artificial intelligence and related applications, was introduced in 1960 by an MIT team headed by John McCarthy; COBOL (short for Common Business-Oriented Language), versions of which are the main vehicles for commercial data-processing applications, was introduced in 1962 and promoted by Rear Adm. Grace Hopper of the U.S. Navy.

*Object-Oriented Programming.* The most significant programming-language innovation in recent times is object-oriented programming. The basic techniques used were introduced in 1967 in the programming language Simula 67. Its popularity expanded with the introduction of the influential Smalltalk language in a series of versions during the 1970s. Object-oriented programming represents an attempt to move programming even closer to the programmer's natural view of problem solving, and further from the details of a particular computer, by conceiving of an information machine as a collection of separate and essentially self-sufficient objects, rather than as a single unit.

In object-oriented programming, commands are directed at entities in the program itself. For example, instead of commanding the computer to add two numbers, the command is directed at one number to add itself to another. The various rules and routines for accomplishing that are already in the machine and are the responsibility of the number.

## COORDINATION SYSTEMS

The discussion so far has focused on only one of the two basic elements that make up software. These two elements are computation and coordination. The activity of step-by-step problem solving is known as computation. Connecting separate activities together so that they constitute a single integrated ensemble rather than a mass of unrelated actions is known as coordination. An operating system is necessary to enable a human programmer to get usable information from a computer.

**Coordination.** An information machine specified by using Pascal can execute inside a computer. But a program inside a computer is of no use unless that program can be coordinated with the user's feeding information into the program in order to get information from the program. Transferring information from the user to the program and vice versa is an important coordination issue. In the Pascal program listed previously, this coordination is specified through the use of special "read" and "write" instructions. Carrying out these instructions—accomplishing the sequence of steps that actually transfers information into or out of the computer—is the job of a special coordination program discussed in the following paragraph. Accomplishing each of these transfers using a single instruction of machine language is possible in principle, but rarely in practice.

Coordination implies multiple activities. In this case, the program and the user are both active. When the program wants information, it may have to stop and wait until the user is ready to provide it, that is, until the user types a number on the keyboard. A user wanting information must wait until the program has finished computing it. This stop-and-wait procedure is a basic part of coordination; making coordination possible means making it possible to synchronize many separate activities.

In another important example, if a user executes the same program on Tuesday and on Thursday, the Tuesday execution may need to pass information on to the Thursday version. In other words, a program may have to coordinate with a later execution of itself. For example, the program might be a word processor, designed to create and manage documents. The program might be used on Tuesday to create a document; on Thursday, it might be necessary to add new material to the original document. The Tuesday version must transfer information to the Thursday version, just as the add-two-numbers program must transfer information to the person using the program. Both examples involve the coordination of separate activities. In one case, the activities are separated by time (Tuesday versus Thursday); in the other case, the activities are separated by space (inside and outside the computer). But the underlying issues are the same.

Coordination of separate-in-time activities is usually accomplished by a "file" system or a database. A computer file is simply an aggregate of information (words, numbers, pictures—any kind of information the computer is capable of generating) that is stored in such a way that the information outlasts the execution of any particular program. A database is exactly the same as a file, although a database is often designed to coordinate two separate-in-time users rather than two separate-in-time programs. A program might put information in a file on Tuesday and retrieve it on Thursday; a person might put information in a database on Tuesday and retrieve it on Thursday. Thus the file and the database both achieve the coordination of separate activities.

When a Pascal program executes inside a computer, it will sometimes share that computer with other programs. Before the widespread availability of desktop computers, time-sharing allowed many programs to share a single computer, thus allowing many programmers to work simultaneously. Time-sharing is still practiced today, although only to a limited and diminishing extent. A powerful modern desktop computer may have only one user at a time, but that user's program might still share the computer with many other programs—programs that may keep the computer's memory well organized, receive electronic mail, manage the display on the screen, and so forth. When many programs need to share a single computer, the computer switches its attention rapidly back and forth between them. The computer may switch so frequently that many programs appear to be executing simultaneously, although in fact the computer can execute only one program at a time. When many programs share a single computer, we have a problem of coordination. We must ensure that this cohabitation works smoothly—that no program destroys another program's data, for example.

**Operating Systems.** Managing the sorts of coordination just described is the job of a special coordination program called an operating system. The role of an operating system is to coordinate an executing program with other activities, with people outside the computer, with later executions of itself, and with other programs inside the computer.

To this end, the operating system provides the input and output routines that transfer data between the computer and the outside world. It knows how to accomplish the physical transfer of information. The operating system provides a file system that allows programs to communicate with later versions of themselves. It provides the scheduler and the communication routines that allow many programs to share the computer simultaneously. It is, in short, a kind of life-support system that makes an individual program viable. Without the operating system, a program is adrift in a sea of unorganized and self-immolating bits of information.

**The Operating-System Spectrum.** There are almost as many operating systems as there are programming languages. Three systems that are especially important and widespread today are UNIX, MS-DOS, and the Apple Macintosh operating system.

UNIX was developed for minicomputers at Bell Labs during the 1970s. UNIX is particularly useful for programmers because of its elegant yet powerful and flexible utilities and tools. In a number of related versions, it has become one of today's most popular operating systems.

The Apple Macintosh operating system, dating from the early 1980s, popularized an invention of the Xerox Corporation in the 1970s: the use of a "window-based" display and a "mouse." The window-based display is intended to allow the computer's screen to be treated like a desk on which documents are scattered; each window on the computer's screen corresponds metaphorically to a document on the desktop. The mouse makes it possible to control the computer, to some extent, without recourse to typing at the keyboard. This device can be used to direct the computer's attention to the information appearing in a particular portion of the screen.

MS-DOS (MicroSoft—Disk Operating System) was developed by the Microsoft Corporation in the 1980s. Unencumbered by any major technical innovations, MS-DOS rose to popularity with the IBM PC, the machine for which it was originally designed. Windows, an exceptionally widely used interface, was built to work with MS-DOS. Windows was designed to allow an IBM PC to mimic the ease and simplicity of use of the Apple Macintosh.

## CURRENT TRENDS

Two issues have emerged as clear trends in the software field: graphic images and software ensembles. These areas of intense investigation are likely to remain important research topics in the future.

**Graphic Images.** The issue of graphic images is concerned with the use of pictures in software development. Displaying graphic images on a computer's screen requires a reasonably powerful computer, because the programs that produce graphic images can be quite complicated; on a slow computer these programs may take an inconveniently long time to compose the graphic image and display it on the screen. The use of graphic images also necessitates an electronic display system that is fairly sophisticated, and preferably in color. As powerful computers and sophisticated screens become progressively cheaper and more widely used, the use of pictures (graphics) grows accordingly.

One use of graphic images is concerned strictly with applications of software; software-generated pictures are increasingly important to scientists and engineers as well as in advertising, publishing, entertainment, and art. However, pictures are important as well to the developers of software, for two major reasons. First, the design of good user interfaces has always been a primary concern for software developers. The user interface is the part of the program that determines how users control the program—that is, how the user makes the program perform a task. Second, the user interface determines the format in which information may be entered or displayed by the program.

Another major application of graphic images is in designing reliable software, since software code can be very complicated, and reliability has always been a major problem in software development. The process of debugging a program—of finding and fixing the errors, or "bugs," that prevent the program from working properly under certain circumstances—can be an intensely difficult and time-consuming task. Graphic images play an increasingly significant role here; a display that shows programmers the "shape" of a program as it executes, or displays information about the execution of a program in the form of graphs or other abstract pictures, can be invaluable.

**Software Ensembles.**  The increasing focus on ensembles is another major software trend. A software ensemble is a collection of programs all working together on a single problem. Software ensembles are important for many reasons, but the two that are most significant today have to do with networks and with parallelism.

A computer network is a group of computers connected together, just as a telephone network is a collection of telephones connected with one another. In both cases, the connections allow the separate elements to communicate with one another. Computers communicate with one another so that their users can send messages by way of electronic mail, to move useful information back and forth, to share machinery such as printers (many computers might share a single printer; they communicate with the printer using the network), and for other purposes. To make a network of computers function as an integrated whole, a "software ensemble" is required—in concept, a single program with "branch offices" on every computer of the network. All of these branch offices are open, meaning that all programs are simultaneously active, and they serve to tie the computers on the network into an integrated whole.

In parallel programming, many computers participate in the execution of a single program. The individual computers must be interconnected, but the intention in this case is to execute a complicated program quickly by focusing the power of many computers on the program simultaneously.

The program must be structured as a software ensemble; it must be made up of many pieces, each one a separate program, with all pieces capable of operating simultaneously. Building software ensembles is precisely the same problem of coordination discussed previously. Builders of software ensembles and of operating systems face the same kind of issues and problems. Parallel programming dominates the future of "supercomputing," the area of the computing field that is concerned with the largest and most difficult computing problems.

DAVID GELERNTER, *Yale University*

### Bibliography

Abelson, Harold, and Gerald Jay Sussman, with Julie Sussman, *Structure and Interpretation of Computer Programs* (McGraw-Hill 1985).

Athey, Thomas H., and Robert W. Zmud, *Introduction to Computers and Information Systems with BASIC*, 2d ed. (Scott Foresman 1988).

Cox, Brad C., *Object-Oriented Programming* (Addison-Wesley 1986).

Gelernter, David, and Suresh Jagannathan, *Programming Linguistics* (MIT Press 1990).

Hafner, Katie, and John Markoff, *Cyberpunks: Outlaws and Hackers on the Computer Frontier* (Simon & Schuster 1991).

Huber, Peter, *Orwell's Revenge* (Free Press 1994).

Levy, Steven, *Hackers: Heroes of the Computer Revolution* (Doubleday 1984).

Tanenbaum, Andrew S., *Operating Systems: Design and Implementation* (Prentice-Hall 1987).

Wexelblat, Richard L., ed., *History of Programming Languages* (Academic Press 1981).

Wirth, Niklaus, *Algorithms + Data Structures = Programs* (Prentice-Hall 1976).

**COMPUTERS AND SOCIETY.**  Just as the tools people invented transformed the societies in which they lived, so the needs of these societies inspired inventions, of which computers are a cornerstone in the 20th century. Throughout the world, computers have become a source as well as a conduit of information. This article takes a discursive look at computers, related technological developments, and social issues affected by the inclusion of computers in everyday life, with particular reference to issues of privacy.

**The Information Revolution.**  Information technology has long been acknowledged as a revolutionary social force. In medieval times the invention of the printing press by Gutenberg eventually broke down the monopoly of the church over written knowledge. Previous to the printing press, handwritten manuscripts, approved and edited by the church, were the only texts available; easily available books unapproved by the church were viewed by some monks as a threat to their control over learning. Printing presses were initially banned from medieval universities in an attempt to control the dissemination of knowledge. However, once a valuable technology has been experienced, it cannot easily be completely suppressed. More important, since printing permitted the efficient documentation of knowledge, learning became a cumulative process, with each new discovery or insight building on all previously understood kernels of knowledge. Thus, printing, and the resulting rapid exchange of ideas contributed materially to the explosion of and the exponential increase in discoveries in art and science during the Renaissance period.

The advent of printing also helped to fuel the Industrial Revolution in Europe in the 18th and 19th centuries by creating more productive ways to learn and making accumulated knowledge readily accessible. This was the first "information revolution" of modern times. For instance,

THE BETTMANN ARCHIVE

Printed, mass-produced books, scorned by possessors of scarce handwritten texts, gave many people their initial access to written knowledge.

new technologies for generating and harnessing energy to mills helped bring about the Industrial Age, accelerating the growth of cities and aggregating economic, political and military power into the modern nation state.

***Information versus Energy as a Revolutionary Force.*** Nuclear fission power and the digital computer emerged in the United States as the most dramatic new technologies developed and honed during World War II. Nuclear energy, with its promise of infinite amounts of cheap energy, was initially thought to be the more revolutionary of the two developments, since energy technology is essential for the growth of modern industrial economies. However, the digital computer has, in fact, made a far more significant social impact, and the technical discontinuity represented by the modern computer is no less dramatic than that of nuclear energy. Whether one measures technical progress by speed of computation, by data rate of telecommunications, or by volumetric density of data storage, the increase in capabilities, starting with the early digital computers of the late 1940s and ending with the supercomputers of the early 1990s, is measured in factors of magnitude ranging from a million to a billion.

***Transformation of the U.S. Economy.*** In 1976 Sociologist Daniel Bell recognized that information, not energy, would be the new bellwether of economic progress and agent of social change. His book, *The Coming of Post-Industrial Society,* mapped the social changes associated with the emerging transformation of industrial economies. Information technologies responsible for this social transformation include computers, telecommuni-

cations, the software that controlled their functions, and the information they created, processed, stored, and retrieved. The "Age of Information" may be said to have arrived when the majority of the people become engaged in the creation, gathering, storage, processing, or distribution of information, rather than in agriculture or manufacturing. By the early 1990s more than 60% of the U.S. workforce was estimated to be engaged in such activities, and perhaps 40% of the world's population was so employed. Since much of the information-intensive activity occurs in the service sector, it was not surprising that during the 1980s two-thirds of the U.S. workforce was engaged in services, nearly one-third in manufacturing, and only 2% in agriculture. The facilities and institutions that support these information-intensive services may be collectively called the information infrastructure, by analogy to the transportation services and facilities that dominate the physical infrastructure of a modern state. Legal scholar Anne Wells Branscomb defined *information infrastructure* in 1982 as "the lifeline through which we sustain our business and commerce, amuse ourselves, exchange our gossip, console our friends, and cry out for help in emergencies."

In the 1990s the U.S. computer and telecommunications industries represented the largest manufacturing sector in the U.S. economy, outpacing the auto industry. In the period from 1965 to 1995, computer hardware of a given speed and power fell in cost by about 15% per year, an unprecedented rate of industrial productivity improvement. The creation of software that gives the hardware its useful function has proved more resistant to productivity growth, resulting in a shift of economic activity from hardware to software. The best estimate of the total size of all segments of the U.S. software industry, made for the year 1988 by C. A. Zraket, president of Mitre Corporation, was an annual revenue of $100 billion, or roughly three times official government estimates for that period. This represented about a 60% share of world software revenue. Despite very rapid growth of the Japanese computer industry and a strong position in Japan and Europe in digital telecommunications, the United States was still the dominant industrial power in information technology in the early 1990s. Though the industry's growth rate for hardware and software slowed in the early 1990s, the pace of technological change has itself become a source of economic as well as social change, for when individuals and institutions have difficulty accommodating change, it becomes a source of social stress.

***Effects of Computers on Society.*** The social effects of the computers that surround us, seen and unseen, in our daily lives are of two kinds: immediate effects on each individual who uses a computer or encounters services delivered by computer, and aggregate effects on society as a whole. (These societal issues will be addressed in the following section.) Residents of the United States find the effects on individuals most visible, since they have become immersed in a society in which virtually every activity has become dependent on the reliable functioning of information technology and the people who manipulate it.

Perhaps the most dramatic evidence for the extent of computer use is seen in the fact that by the early 1990s over 20 million personal computers (PCs) were installed in homes across the United States. The U.S. installed base of PCs in business,

During a 1946 labor dispute, supervisors ran the switchboards, since halting communications in New York City would have caused considerable disruption.

government, and education (excluding homes) is expected to continue to grow throughout the 1990s. These projections do not encompass imbedded microprocessors, which have been installed in the hundreds of millions in automobiles, appliances, timepieces, television sets, videocassette recorders (VCRs), telephones, and fax machines, and which have countless other uses in business, agriculture, education, and the military. Products that have their functions controlled by microprocessors have often been referred to as *smart* products. Since they are more energy efficient and responsive to user's needs, they have changed the way people live and work in many ways.

Perhaps the most pernicious social effect of the contribution information technology makes to economic productivity is the economic disenfranchisement of those who receive an inadequate education. Manual tools can be learned by apprenticeship; information tools require formal education. Increasingly, the tools of a modern economy incorporate computer intelligence and require educated users. Because they are more productive, their operators command higher compensation. This leaves the educationally deprived even more disadvantaged. Thus the poor state of U.S. public school systems in the last decade of the 20th century became a serious threat to equal opportunity in the information age.

Generally, computers perform functions long familiar to people in other forms. Why has the shift from file cabinets, adding machines, and voice telephones to digital computers, telecommunications, and software made such a big difference in our lives? Digital information-handling is fundamentally different from analog, or uncoded information, in five crucial respects: (1) retrieval, copying, storage, and transmission of information, once digitally encoded, can be made completely error free by using mathematical "tricks" such as

parity checking; (2) computers can perform operations with extraordinary speed and can inexpensively store incredibly large amounts of information in a very small space. This facility introduces great economies of scale and scope to information applications and makes possible cross-comparison of enormous databases for consistency, activities that would be inconceivably complex operations using paper records; (3) since electronic communication has become virtually instantaneous, computer communications create affinities of interest that are independent of distance. This was the idea behind Marshall McLuhan's concept of a "global electronic village"; (4) digitally encoded information can be exactly recognized by a machine, which allows information to be searched, compared, and logically processed and then used to create new information and automatically trigger further actions; (5) intelligent machines, such as those implementing "neural networks," which emulate the wiring of synapses in the brain, can be designed and programmed so that the machines "learn" from repeated experience with a task.

Realization of the elusive promise of artificial intelligence has been long delayed. The hope of automatic language translation in the 1960s remained unrealized in the 1990s, but other areas of artificial intelligence research—expert systems, image and sensory recognition, and robotic activity—have been integrated into many applications. Expert systems, pioneered by Professor Edward Feigenbaum, create logical conclusions by processing a large store of expert knowledge. Other computer systems can "see," "hear," "feel," and manipulate objects. These two lines of investigation are coming together in new tools for exploring artificial or "virtual" reality. (See ARTIFICIAL INTELLIGENCE.)

Despite their extraordinary capabilities and promise, and a quarter-century of research on artificial intelligence, computers are deterministic machines; they do not think for themselves but instead doggedly follow the instructions in their programs, using the data in their stores. This fact has produced a great deal of frustration on the part of those computer users who expect a computer to respond to their instructions in the same way a human being might. This frustration has been perhaps best expressed in a poem posted anonymously on the bulletin board of the University of Wisconsin computer center:

I'm sick and tired of this machine
I wish that they would sell it.
It never does just what I want,
But only what I tell it.

Millions of citizens who use personal computers take satisfaction in their mastery of the new technology, but their frustrations also color their attitudes toward the use of computers by government, merchants, banks, and other institutions they encounter. People complain that computers can be hard to understand, and that messages created by them can be sometimes inappropriate or incomprehensible. Human factors and ergonomics experts continue to attempt to overcome these difficulties; the object of their efforts has been a "user friendly" machine—a phrase used more often in irony than in admiration.

**Computers and Privacy.** Citizens continue to be deeply concerned about threats—both real and perceived—to their personal liberty and privacy. Government agencies and commercial firms operate a vast array of computer systems and databases that contain information about individuals, usually created to provide people with services or benefits. Each time a credit card is used, a computer record is created, which, when combined with records of mail order purchases, magazine subscriptions, bank transactions, hotel and airline reservations, makes it possible to paint a picture of an individual's tastes, preferences, buying habits, and ability to pay. But the records contained and algorithms inherent in these machines have been largely invisible to the individuals whose actions created them. These records can be used to improve service; they can also be used to bombard individuals with unwanted solicitations for business and "junk" mail. Errors in these records, whether created accidently or through mal-intent, can create serious difficulties for individuals, such as the loss of financial credit, improper billings, or even accusations of illegal behavior.

**Privacy Concerns.** Privacy concerns became a national issue in the 1960s with the publication of Alan Westin's book *Privacy and Freedom* in 1967. They peaked during the Ford administration when Vice President Nelson Rockefeller chaired a national commission to develop the legislative response to the issues raised, since in the United States, government behavior had been the focus of concern. The computer industry responded early to these concerns and promulgated voluntary privacy principles. The industry insisted, successfully, that these principles should also apply to all records of personal data, whether in electronic or paper format. The Right to Privacy Act of 1974, amended in 1976, was its primary achievement. It provides citizens with access to computer records pertaining to them and limits government agency authority in the use of these records.

However, substantial exceptions for national security requirements have been made. Regulation of private-sector data activities has been quite limited in the United States; the primary regulations require citizen access to and the right to correct financial credit records. In the United Kingdom and in Europe generally, the emphasis of public concerns about privacy has been focused not on governments so much as on private firms. In some countries all commercial databases with personal information must be registered; in others special ombudsman offices have been established to protect citizens' interests.

Many privacy issues remain unresolved, for they involve trade-offs between desirable and undesirable attributes of the same application. Citizens must cooperate in the creation of some national statistical data collections, such as the U.S. Census, if their value to society is to be realized. For example, the National Crime Information Center (NCIC), operated by the Department of Justice, has banks of computers in which state and local police records are stored, along with federal data. Citizens may approve FBI use of the NCIC to track the activities of suspected, but unindicted, drug dealers through surveillance by local police and tracking credit card use and hotel reservations electronically. But the same people strenuously object to the idea that their own travels and buying activities might be revealed to the FBI. During Judge Robert Bork's Supreme Court confirmation hearing in 1987, the record of his choices of videotaped movies, contained in the video store's computer, was published. The

© DAVID BALL/THE STOCK MARKET

At the New York Stock Exchange, communication devices such as computers are used to gather data quickly, enabling traders to make fast, informed decisions.

public outcry against this blatant invasion of his privacy was so intense that Congress almost immediately passed a law making such records confidential.

Confidentiality of medical records is another such example. Should records of HIV- (human immunodeficiency virus-) positive individuals be disclosed to prospective employers or insurance companies? Should a national data bank of genetic information, analogous to the Federal Bureau of Investigation's fingerprint files, be created?

Nation-states assert a national right to privacy, often referred to as cultural sovereignty. Satellites broadcast television signals across national borders; networks facilitate the flow of culture-sensitive information across national borders as well. Nations seeking to minimize political or culture intrusion from their neighbors and hoping to protect national markets for their artists and producers, find little in international law to assert their cultural sovereignty. Similar concerns surround the prospect of earth-observing satellites acquiring information from across borders.

**Data Encryption.** The growth of computer networks and data banks in the 1960s and 1970s created a need for good encryption. The best way to protect electronic messages and records has been to encrypt, or encipher, them. In 1976 the U.S. government promulgated a Data Encryption Standard (DES) for communicating and storing nonnational-security data, based on a strong computer cipher invented by IBM. Because cryptography in the United States, as well as in other countries, has been closely regulated by government as a matter of national security at the highest level, the commercial introduction of the DES was accompanied by considerable controversy. The export of products incorporating DES was, and is, tightly regulated. This presented the government with a dilemma, since, while it wishes to ensure the privacy of U.S. computer messages and records, it also wishes to obtain intelligence by reading the secret messages of foreign governments, terrorists, and other criminals. Some academic and commercial cryptologists therefore wondered whether the government had weakened the DES so that the government, with its immense resources, could crack it even though private entrepreneurs could not; some people even questioned whether IBM, lured by the promise of government contracts, had connived with the government to leave a "trap door" in the DES algorithm. However, the DES has stood the test of time; no evidence that the DES is not sufficiently robust for personal and commercial use has ever been publicly documented. The U.S. government has sought to resolve its dilemma by prohibiting the export of the DES and convincing other countries to do the same. In the 1980s and 1990s, with encryption becoming ever cheaper, better, and more common, another threat loomed—the government might no longer be able to understand the wiretapped telephone calls of criminal suspects. It proposed that two organizations hold the encryption keys to telephone scramblers sold commercially and make those keys available to law-enforcement agencies upon court order. The system, called key escrow, was not immediately adopted. Opponents felt that criminals would not use the escrowed scramblers even if they were conveniently available and that more good encryption beneficially enlarged citizen's privacy.

The laws in some Asian and European countries restrict the right of private persons and business firms to use cryptography to protect messages communicated across their borders. Some require that the encryption key be divulged to government security authorities. Private firms, suspicious of government complicity in industrial espionage, often circumvent these regulations. (See CRYPTOLOGY.)

**Social Effects of Information Technology.** It has become commonplace to think of technological change as creating social consequences, for good or ill. The anticipation of social effects of technology has become a field of study in social science called technology assessment. While it can hardly be described as an exact science, it has become a useful guide for monitoring the effects of a technology and planning regulations, training, and other interventions to mitigate the undesired consequences and maximize the benefits from a new technology. However, technological change has itself become a product of social forces. Thus the character of social change resulting from a technology may be quite different in different societies, and the evolution of the technology in those societies may also be quite different. Indeed, the fact that transnational computer networks link societies with quite different laws and customs and create legal questions about jurisdiction and accountability has become a major source of conflict arising from the global spread of information technology.

The explosive growth of information technologies raised concerns on two counts: the possibility of technological abuse by authoritarian and bureaucratic governments intent on exercising political control of their citizens, and concern that computers could displace human beings in clerical jobs as well as in other forms of employment. The first of these concerns may be best illustrated by George Orwell's apocalyptic novel *1984*, first published during the Cold War era, in which authoritarian governments use new information technologies to deprive individuals of their humanity and their freedom. (See also ORWELL, GEORGE.)

When the year 1984 arrived, reassessments were made of Orwell's warning; most scholars found evidence for his fears but on balance concluded that (1) illicit access to technological advances such as copying machines and to foreign computer networks and (2) transnational diffusion of audiocassettes, radio and television broadcasts contributed substantially to the erosion of control by the USSR's Communist party. During the abortive counterrevolution in Moscow in August 1991, an international computer network used by elementary school children was used to exchange messages in support of democracy. The American KIDNET, over which thousands of children perform cooperative science experiments, had been linked to an elementary school in Moscow. Russian teachers were in the process of testing the network when the coup occurred. The messages they sent to the United States during the crisis were later circulated on the KIDNET, providing a graphic experience of history in the making.

In the 1990s these technologies have been rapidly expanding, creating links between reformers in Russia and other republics and supporters of democratic government. An estimated 100,000 modems were installed on computers in Moscow City alone, which allowed their owners to connect with other computers in Russia and to networks reaching around the globe. The Moscow Telephone network has sought the registration of these modems, many of which were installed without official approval. A new computer network in Moscow, GLASNET (its name derived from *Glasnost*, or "openness"), has been associated with PeaceNet, Econet, GreenNet, and many others. It has provided contact between ordinary Russian citizens and foreigners sharing their interest in peace, human rights, and environmental protection. Supporters of Russian president Boris Yeltsin made use of GLASNET during the August 1991 coup.

**Global Computer Networks.** The largest collection of interconnected networks in the world is the Internet—a collection of over 4,000 networks among which electronic mail messages flow. In 1995 over 100 countries were connected directly or indirectly to the Internet. In 1994 Anthony Rutkowski, president of the Internet Society, estimated that at least 10 million people had access to the Internet worldwide, and the Internet traffic level during the early 1990s increased exponentially. In the United States some 28 million personal computers, or 56% of all PCs installed in the United States, were attached to others through local area networks (LANs) by the mid-1990s. Many more can be expected to be eventually linked to the Internet.

*Transborder Data Flow.* When commercial applications of computer networks began to span national boundaries in the 1970s, with American companies in the lead, Europeans became concerned about foreigners controlling their domestic information resources and threatening their national sovereignty. For example, the fire department in Malmo, Sweden, purchased an interactive database providing information about the city of Malmo from an U.S. firm. Concerns about vulnerability of Swedish citizens to a possible breakdown of the computer in Columbus, Ohio, where the data were stored, were widely publicized. Economies of scale and scope accelerated the formation of information services that crossed national boundaries. Governments reacted by creating constraining regulations. For instance, the Brazilian government has required all commercial databases to be moved inside Brazilian borders before they can be used. However, in the 1990s the level of public concern about transborder data flow subsided.

**Intellectual Property.** A second, unresolved information trade issue being discussed in the General Agreement on Tariffs and Trade (GATT) concerns national differences in the way intellectual property has been protected and traded. In the 1990s a major international effort was under way to bring more uniformity to various nations' rules. This discussion has taken place in the GATT and both regionally in the European Economic Community and bilaterally among the industrialized countries. The existence of so many transnational information networks means that intellectual property embodied in documents, images, and multimedia circle the globe with the speed of light. Unless these ideas, inventions, and creative works have been protected in foreign lands, as well as in the United States, their originators could lose the opportunity to appropriate the benefits, reducing the incentive to create.

This problem has become particularly acute for computer software, where copyright and patent law have proved a less than perfect fit to the nature of software. Software has become very expensive to develop and produce but costs almost nothing to duplicate electronically. The software industry in the United States and Canada estimated in 1990 that $2.4 billion worth of commercial software was illegally copied and distributed. This figure was equal to nearly half of the $5.7 billion in sales of end-user, commercial software for the same year.

**Developing-Country Interests.** At the same time, the developing countries, concerned that they have been left behind in the rush to construct a global information infrastructure, have been seeking concessions from technologically richer countries. Strident calls for a "New World Information Order" that dominated many United Nations meetings in the 1970s and 1980s have given way to more sophisticated efforts to obtain foreign investments to create information resources under favorable conditions. Are the new electronic information technologies widening the gap between rich and poor nations, or are they providing the very tool developing countries need to overcome their isolation? The spread of computer networks around the world can accelerate a developing country's access to the world's knowledge resources. At the same time, because their information infrastructure is weak, their economies tend to lag behind those of industrial societies. The net result seems to be islands of modernity, such as Singapore and Hong Kong, amid oceans of poverty and ignorance.

**Organizational Behavior.** Early in the institutional use of computers, commercial firms used centralized computer systems to increase efficiency, reduce waste, protect assets, and monitor operations. As interactive computer networks became commonplace, transaction processing replaced the more labor intensive manipulation of paper documents. The result was increased efficiency and control, emphasizing the hierarchical structure of organizations. The ARPANET, a computer network developed by university scientists working with the Defense Department's Advanced Research Projects Agency, had the opposite effect—empowering individuals at all levels in an organization to share ideas, plans, and solutions. The hierarchical structure of the institution was thus flattened. ARPANET quickly gave rise to commercial computer

networks. By 1985 some 80,000 IBM employees were interconnected through a simpler peer network, called VNET. Renamed BITNET by universities in 26 nations around the world, this store and forward network is also connected through a gateway to the Internet. By 1992 over 10,000 IBM personnel, three-quarters of them in the United States, had Internet addresses, with the number continuing to rise rapidly. The coexistence of both hierarchical and peer-to-peer networks, often using the same physical communications facilities, gives organizations a remarkable combination of creativity with control, with the virtues of both vertical and horizontal organizational relationships.

In the 1980s private corporate networks began linking themselves to one another to provide electronic data interchange (EDI). A manufacturer's orders to its suppliers are transmitted electronically, allowing the supplier to adopt "just-in-time" manufacturing efficiencies. Similarly, the manufacturer's internal network may be connected to those of its customers, providing quicker service and feedback. Each firm may have many such information relationships with its customers, suppliers, banks, stock exchanges, regulatory agencies, universities, and other institutions. Many of these links circle the globe. The result is the interlinking of the economies of many nations, with a geographic dispersion of economic activity that makes nationalistic policies increasingly inappropriate and ineffective. This intricate web of electronic information relationships is of such enormous complexity that many people have become concerned about its vulnerability to technical instabilities as well as industrial espionage.

**Revolution in Engineering and Industrial Innovation.** Computers have revolutionized engineering and science and their use in industrial innovation. Since production processes and the properties of materials have been quantitatively characterized, the pace of industrial innovation has been accelerated, productivity enhanced, and quality of production greatly increased. These new industrial methods are called computer-integrated manufacturing (CIM). Product designs created using computer-aided design (CAD) can be tested and refined through computer simulation. Automated production tooling can then be programmed

Researchers use weather simulators to visualize and model storm activity.

NCSA/UNIVERSITY OF ILLINOIS AT URBANA-CHAMPAIGN

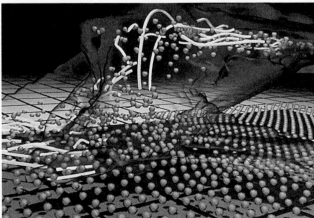

Robots on this cylinder-head assembly line have replaced many human workers.

COURTESY ABB ROBOTICS INC.

through computer-aided manufacturing (CAM) tools. The logistics of manufacturing, including just-in-time deliveries of essential components by suppliers, are managed by materials-control and process-flow-control computers. The whole of this process is CIM. Firms using it successfully often gain a substantial competitive advantage. Thus one important social impact of the information age has been a radical change in the way in which manufacturing is performed. With the aid of these new tools, it has become much easier to distribute manufacturing activities in many different locations, to introduce new products and processes simultaneously worldwide. Cooperating firms gain the advantages of vertical integration, without the inflexibility and bureaucratic impediments of aggregating all the needed capabilities within a single firm, by using electronic data interchange. (See COMPUTER-AIDED DESIGN AND COMPUTER-AIDED MANUFACTURING; AUTOMATION.)

The negative side of this revolution, especially for inhabitants of wealthy countries, in the nature of work has been a permanent alteration in the global division of labor. The geographic dispersion of the locus of production, made possible through computer control of processes and logistics, means that U.S. workers compete with others in faraway places. Even service jobs have been exported to low-cost locations. People in the Caribbean island of Barbados, for example, have been employed to enter the data on gasoline credit slips into massive banks of computers, connected to America by satellite dish. From the perspective of the developing countries, this phenomenon provides significant economic opportunity.

### Telecommuting and Collaborating at a Distance.
Just as industrial firms have used computer networks to create geographically distributed industrial alliances, individuals have begun to use computer networking as an alternative to commuting to work. In 1991 there were 31.2 million American households in which one or more person worked at home at least part-time, up 12.6% from the previous year. This figure represents one-third of all U.S. households. These households use information technology to make work at home feasible; two-thirds of them have an electronic answering machine, and nearly half have a personal computer. The annual growth rates of home

computers, facsimile (fax) machines, and modems for telecommuting have been estimated at 28% per year. Computer networks have also made it possible for individuals at widely separated locations to collaborate in a common task. As applied to scientific and engineering research, the National Science Foundation refers to this arrangement as a "collaboratory." It has been extensively used in software design and development and is spreading to many other fields of endeavor.

### Computer Crime and Sabotage.
Computers give rise to problems that have proved a challenge to the U.S. legal system. Courts traditionally look to precedent to resolve conflicts and to create appropriate codes of behavior. However, when radical technological change occurs, the old models on which cases have been based can no longer be stretched to cover new situations, and new laws must be written. A new legal specialty has arisen: computer law. Thousands of attorneys now specialize in it.

It was not until 1980 that Congress determined that computer software could be covered by copyright protection. The legal basis for controlling unauthorized entry into computers is complex. Wiretapping of computer communications was not illegal until enactment of the Electronic Communication Privacy Act in 1986. The Computer Fraud and Abuse Act of 1986 makes deliberate unauthorized computer penetration a felony, and inadvertent entry a misdemeanor. Every state but one (Vermont) had, by 1991, passed a similar statute dealing with computer crime.

Computer systems are vulnerable to destructive activities ranging from deliberate sabotage, to theft or alteration of data, to computer vandalism, or to relatively harmless pranks by "hackers." One particularly pernicious form of unauthorized intrusion is a self-replicating software program that moves throughout a network (a computer "virus"), which may destroy data or clog networks or only post unexpected messages (a computer "worm"). One example of such a "worm" was that inserted into the Internet in 1988 by Robert T. Morris, Jr. Although he insisted he had no intention of causing havoc, networks became hopelessly clogged all across the United States, and computers had to be shut down and restarted, seriously disrupting hundreds of institutions. He was convicted under the 1986 federal statute.

Most deliberate attempts to steal, alter, or destroy data can be prosecuted under existing criminal laws, where intent to do harm can be shown. When an intrusion takes place in a country other than the country from which the data was stolen, the jurisdiction in which the offense should be prosecuted may be unclear. The hazards of computer terrorism, that is, deliberate attempts to wreak havoc against a nation or an institution, are considerable, although the number of clearly identified instances of terrorism is small, mostly associated with disgruntled former employees rather than with foreign agents. The information systems most critical to national security are rigorously protected from outside attack. Most of the press reports of intrusions into computers on military installations relate to access to mail systems or other applications at relatively low security levels.

So-called computer hackers represent quite a different phenomenon. The term *hacker* is generally applied to young people with a special talent for computers, a distrust of all large institutions and their bureaucracies, and a deep conviction that information should be treated as a public good, open to all. Sometimes a hacker's motivation is simply to demonstrate that the security of computer installations is not as great as authorities claim; they justify their intrusions by asserting that they contribute to deeper understanding of computer security. Four hackers from a group called the Legion of Doom, once arrested for entering a commercial computer, have now created Comsec Data Security, a computer security company created to protect computer owners from other would-be intruders. The fact that hacker culture is creative, if disrespectful of authority, does not excuse the unauthorized tampering with systems used by others. But many individuals who practiced "hacking" in their youth have become major contributors to technical advances in computer software.

**Future Prospects.** As the use of computers and other digital information technologies become commonplace in many countries, the nature of concerns about the social effects change. In Europe during the 1970s, concerns about computers displacing human employment were high on the political agenda, and undoubtedly contributed to Europe's loss of competitive position in the world computer industry. Automation of both clerical and manufacturing tasks is now widely accepted as a necessary tool for remaining competitive in world markets, even as Europe and North America struggle with high unemployment levels in the 1990s. Early science fiction stories, in which computers escaped human control and through "artificial intelligence" reduced humans to a position inferior to the machine, are no longer a source of serious concern.

However, there is another way computers may be reducing human autonomy even as they empower people to leverage their intelligence. As the applications of computers get more complex, and computers are asked to help make decisions when events are moving too fast for humans to track, the human individual must cede control of events to the computer. In this process, the opportunity for human instinct to intervene when unwanted outcomes seem in prospect is lost; the human becomes in that sense a victim of the machine. Consider, for example, the destruction of an Iranian commercial airliner by the U.S.S. *Vincennes* in 1988. Its automatic weapons were computer controlled, designed to intercept missiles such as the Exocet that sank HMS *Sheffield* in the Falklands war. The people operating the weapons on *Vincennes* were in a room full of computers with no windows; everything happened far away, too quickly to be seen by human eyes. The reality confronted by the human beings was an artificial reality; the complexity of the real world was filtered by the algorithms built into the radars and computers. Unexpected consequences of the assumptions built into such systems were no longer susceptible of challenge; the humans were surrounded by a sterile world largely devoid of the subtleties that make real events intelligible. As Gary Chapman, the leader of the Century 21 project to define goals for U.S. science, has written, "We seem to be moving away from the concept of the rational citizen who can examine the world and assess and implement proposals for improvement, and toward a society of spectators, people in a state of suspended animation with a cognitive inability to penetrate the

© PHOTRI/THE STOCK MARKET

Pilots can test their reactions to potential extreme weather scenarios by using flight simulators.

fast-paced phantasmagoria of mediated experience presented to them."

People have become concerned about the vulnerability of societies dependent on networks of computers too complex for most humans to fully understand. For example, can one be certain that world financial markets might not become unstable when so much computer-programmed trading drives market activity? A second issue is the unemployability of undereducated people in an information society. If even the simplest tasks become automated, what jobs await those who drop out of school? A third issue concerns the loss of an individual's anonymity in a world where merchants, government officials, and possibly criminal elements can learn so much about an individual's preferences and activities if they gain access to computer data records available for purchase without any legal restraint. Finally, in a world where information linkages cross political boundaries and create self-defined communities of interest not based on geography or nationality, what will be the future of the nation-state? As global interdependence is replaced by global connectivity, will the result be the resurgence of democracy and individual liberty or a chaotic situation in which ethnic and religious factions, unconstrained by stable political systems, are at war with one another? Experiences in the last decade of the 20th century give evidence of both.

LEWIS BRANSCOMB, *Harvard University*

### Bibliography

Bell, Daniel, *The Coming of Post-Industrial Society* (Basic Bks. 1976).
Branscomb, Anne W., *Who Owns Information?* (Basic Bks. 1994).
Feigenbaum, Edward, ed., *Building Blocks of Artificial Intelligence, 1956–1986*, 2 vols. (Addison-Wesley 1993).
Gore, Al, et al., "Computers Networks and Public Policy," *Scientific American* (Sept. 1991). Special issue includes articles by Al Gore, Lee Sproull, Nicholas Negroponte, Mitchel Kapor, and Anne W. Branscomb.
Kelly, Kevin, *Out of Control* (Addison-Wesley 1994).
Marcus, George E., ed., *Technoscientific Imaginaries: Conversations, Profiles, and Memoirs* (Univ. of Chicago Press 1995).
McLuhan, Marshall, and Bruce R. Powers, *The Global Village: Tranformations in World Life and Media in the 21st Century* (Oxford 1992).
Schorbach, Karl, *The Gutenberg Documents*, ed. by D. C. McMurtie (R. S. Barnes 1949).
Westin, Alan, *Privacy and Freedom* (Atheneum Press 1967).

**COMSAT (COMMUNICATIONS SATELLITE CORPORATION),** a private U.S. company authorized by Congress in 1962 and incorporated in 1963 to establish a commercial communications satellite program.

In 1964 the International Telecommunications Satellite Consortium (Intelsat) was established by 14 countries, with Comsat as managing agent and principal shareholder, to develop an international communications system. Comsat launched the first of several satellites, Early Bird, or Intelsat I, in 1965. See also COMMUNICATIONS SATELLITE.

**COMSTOCK,** kom′stok, **Anthony** (1844–1915), American reformer. A controversial crusader against every form of vice, he boasted of tons of materials destroyed and thousands of people arrested, often by his own hand. Many prominent people supported his wars against pornographers, abortionists, birth controllers, and gamblers, and even some opponents praised his drives against swindlers and medical quacks. But progressive-minded persons assailed his methods of entrapment and his alleged persecution of advocates of unpopular social and religious ideas. His attacks on the works of several prominent authors and artists made him the symbol of a prudery termed "comstockery" by George Bernard Shaw

Comstock was born in New Canaan, Conn., on March 7, 1844. He served in the Union Army during the Civil War and then worked in New York City as a clerk and salesman. Convinced of his duty to ban what he regarded as obscene books and pictures, he won the sponsorship of the Young Men's Christian Association and drove out of business the city's principal publishers of erotic books. Striking at the distribution of objectionable matter, he gained national notoriety by attempting to stop the mailing of a published account of a scandal involving the Rev. Henry Ward Beecher (q.v.). In 1873 he induced Congress to bar from the mails various "obscene" items, among which he included birth control instructions. Thereafter he became an enforcer of these so-called "Comstock laws." He served as an inspector for the U. S. Post Office department (unpaid until 1907) and as secretary of the New York Society for the Suppression of Vice, which he helped organize in 1873. His books include *Frauds Exposed* (1880), *Traps for the Young* (1883), and *Gambling Outrages* (1887). He died in Summit, N. J., on Sept. 21, 1915.

FRANK L. BYRNE
*Kent State University*

**COMSTOCK LODE,** kom′stok lōd, a rich vein of silver spangled with gold in the Virginia Range of western Nevada. It was discovered in 1859 by several prospectors and named for one of them, Henry T. P. Comstock, who was known as "Old Pancake." The town that sprang up there was named Virginia City, for another of the discoverers, James Fennimore, known also as "James Finney" and as "Old Virginny." After rich strikes, the mines produced prodigiously, then for a dozen years had alternate booms and recessions. After a slack period (1869–1871) a revival was climaxed in 1873 by discovery of the Big Bonanza, the richest silver strike in America.

To bring water from the Sierra Nevada to Virginia City, Henry Schussler in 1873 built long flumes and a 7-mile (11-km) pipeline forming an inverted siphon across the Washoe Valley. In 1875 a larger line, including a 3,000-foot (900-meter) tunnel, brought water 31.5 miles (50 km) from Marlette Lake. To ventilate and drain lower levels of the mines, Adolph Sutro in 1859–1878 built a 4-mile (6-km) tunnel into a mountain. Mining output declined again in the late 1870's, and by 1900 Virginia City's population, nearly 30,000 in its heyday, had shrunk to 2,700. The mines yielded more than half a billion dollars in silver and gold. They made several of the owners multimillionaires, made Virginia City a place of wealth and luxury for a time, and contributed to the business growth of San Francisco.

WAYNE GARD
*Author of "Frontier Justice"*

**COMTE,** kôNt, **Auguste** (1798–1857), French philosopher, who is noted as the founder of the positivistic school and an originator in the development of sociology as a science. Isidore Auguste Marie François Xavier Comte was born in Montpellier, France, on Jan. 19, 1798. His Catholic Royalist background influenced his philosophy, which reflected the rise of science and technology, and the social turbulence resulting from the French Revolution. The central themes of his work were the evolution of the human mind and the necessity of devising scientific foundations for social rule. These themes, one a scientific doctrine, the other a political program, became the component parts of the positivistic philosophy that he founded.

Comte's genius lay in his ability to synthesize ideas from the most disparate sources. From Saint-Simon (q.v.), his mentor, he took the notion of a scientifically directed society. From clericalist thinkers he took the notion of a hierarchical and obedient society. From the philosophers of the 18th century Enlightenment he adopted the idea of historical progress. These various philosophic strains were combined with Comte's own encyclopedic knowledge of the natural sciences in his *Cours de philosophie positive* (1830–1842), one of the most influential philosophic works of modern times.

The rudiments of his thought were largely formed during his association with Saint-Simon, between 1816 and 1824. Comte broke with Saint-Simon shortly before the latter's death, and in 1825 he took the first of a series of minor academic positions. He was subject to intense depressions, and an unhappy marriage ended in separation in 1842. Yet he developed the lectures out of which the *Philosophie positive* grew.

**Philosophy.** Comte based the development of positivism on a historical classification of the sciences, according to which the thought process proceeds from the understanding of simple and abstract principles to the analysis of complex and concrete phenomena. The order of the development of the sciences—mathematics, astronomy, physics, chemistry, biology, and sociology—reflected the necessities of this mental development, which Comte viewed as having passed through three (sometimes overlapping) stages: a theological stage, a metaphysical stage, and ultimately, a triumphant positivistic stage. In the initial theological stage, all thought was dominated by religious conceptions, including fetishism, polytheism, and finally monotheism. In each of these conceptions, man attributed power and will, and thus the functioning of the world, to various specifically represented forces. In the metaphysical stage, the functioning of the world was attributed to forces of a disembodied and hypothetical kind. Finally, in positivism, man attained intellectual maturity, and science became possible. The world was described by laws based on observable relations of phenomena. Comte's objective was to complete the positivistic stage by eliminating metaphysics from sociologic reasoning, and thus to make sociology a science of its own.

Comte's sociology had practical aims. Envisaging the reorganization of society on scientific principles, he divided sociology into a statics, which studied the forces that held society together, and a dynamics, which studied the causes of change. Statics taught that individual egoism, encouraged by the division of labor, could endanger cohesion in the social body. This divisive force in society could be controlled if the family, which was the basic social institution, were strengthened. The strengthening of the family, however, required knowledge of the scientific laws governing society.

Social dynamics taught that such knowledge could come only when society entered the positivistic phase of human evolution. Comte's social dynamics was thus the application to all human history of his depiction of the evolution of the mind through the three stages. The emergence of the positivistic stage, he believed, would concentrate spiritual and intellectual power in a corporation of positivistic philosophers, who in turn would give society knowledge, moral discipline, and cohesion. The actual conduct of the business of economics and politics would be left to the propertied classes.

**Comte's Influence.** The *Philosophie positive* was the great work of Comte's life. In it were united all the tendencies that later characterized positivism as a movement: its belief in both the progress of the human spirit, and in a social science as an applied technology, and its subsequently unacknowledged elitism. In Comte's later works, including *A General View of Positivism* (1848; Eng. tr., 1865) and *The Catechism of Positive Religion* (1852; Eng; tr., 1858), he promulgated a "religion of humanity," which showed his debt to Catholicism in its spiritual and social reorganization of mankind along somewhat clericalized lines. This working of religion into his sociology was sharply criticized by some of Comte's great contemporaries who, like John Stuart Mill, nevertheless declared themselves indebted to him. Comte died in Paris on Sept. 5, 1857.

Comte's philosophy was an effort to set the theory of knowledge on rational foundations consonant with the natural sciences. Modern philosophers now honor Comte more as a precursor than as a direct influence. His sociologic doctrines influenced the first great British sociologists, Sir Edward Burnett Tylor and Herbert Spencer, but his conceptions of social statics and dynamics were first systematically utilized by Emile Durkheim, whose reputation as a founder of the modern French school of sociology does not obscure his great dependence on Comte. Indeed, many, if not most, contemporary sociologists are unconscious Comtians, following his ideas even if they no longer bother to read his writings.

NORMAN BIRNBAUM
*The New School for Social Research,*
*New York City*

**COMUS,** kō'məs, in Greek and Roman mythology, was the god of revelry, drunkenness, and mirth. He is first mentioned by the 3d century Greek rhetorician Philostratus, who describes him as a winged youth, dressed in white and carrying a torch. The Greeks believed that he presided over all festive occasions and was in charge of entertaining the Olympians. He had a similar role in Roman mythology. John Milton, in his masque *Comus*, described him as the son of Bacchus (Dionysus) and Circe, the wily goddess who turned Odysseus' (Ulysses') men into swine.

The name Comus is derived from the Greek word meaning revelry or company of revelers, and is associated with festive occasions.

**COMUS,** kō'məs, is a masque written by the English poet John Milton. It was produced by Henry Lawes at Ludlow Castle on Sept. 29, 1634, for the inauguration of Sir John Egerton, 1st Earl of Bridgewater, as lord president of the council of Wales. Three of Bridgewater's children took part in the performance. Lawes himself, who had been a music tutor in the family, composed settings for the songs (five of which have been preserved) and appeared in the important role of the Attendant Spirit. *Comus*, the first of Milton's poems to be written in blank verse, is marked by the richness, charm, and vividness of its language. The style of the work is quite different from the grand epic sweep of *Paradise Lost*. However, the total effect is highly individual, and the poem exemplifies the grace, delicacy, and moral fervor of Milton's early work.

**Plot.** The theme of *Comus* is the struggle between pure virtue and sensual delight. A Lady and her two brothers are lost in a wood. Her brothers leave her to seek aid, and she encounters the enchanter Comus, who in the guise of a countryman tries to persuade her to accept his hospitality and that of the wild band of monsters who follow him. The brothers are informed of her danger by the Attendant Spirit, also in disguise, and are guided to the castle of Comus, where they find her under a spell but stoutly resisting every effort to subdue her will. They drive Comus out and summon up the local nymph Sabrina, who frees their sister from her enchantment. The Spirit then reveals his heavenly origin and takes farewell with an exhortation of the love of virtue.

**Literary Allusions and Background.** In late Roman mythology, Comus, the son of Bacchus and Circe, was regarded as the god of sensual pleasure. (The name comes from the Greek word *komos*, meaning "revelry.") Milton's *Comus* is an allegory in which the various characters personify abstract thoughts and ideals. The Lady is a personification of purity; Comus is vice in its seductive form; the monsters that surround him are vice in its true brutishness; and the Attendant Spirit is the divine power that protects true virtue against harm.

The plot of *Comus* has various analogues in literary tradition, among them George Peele's play *The Old Wives' Tale*. The character of Comus, in its original personification of revelry, had appeared in Ben Jonson's masque *Pleasure Reconciled to Virtue* and in a neo-Latin play by Erycius Puteanus. The mythological groundwork of Milton's poem is to be found in the Circe story in the *Odyssey*, already interpreted Platonically in ancient times as an allegory of the degrading effects of sensuality. The most essential literary

CONAKRY'S Place de la République, with the Republic of Guinea's presidential palace in the background.

relationship, however, is with Edmund Spenser, whose poetic symbolism in the *Faerie Queene* fused in Milton's mind with Platonic idealism and with Christianity.

**Historical Background.** *Comus* was published anonymously in 1637. It had a preface by Lawes, who undoubtedly arranged for Milton to write the poem, as he had probably also done with the earlier *Arcades*, an entertainment in honor of Bridgewater's stepmother, the Countess of Derby.

*Comus* appeared under Milton's name with a commendatory letter by Sir Henry Wotton in the collected *Poems* of 1645. The poet himself called it simply "A Maske," but the title of *Comus*, first used in an 18th century stage version, has been generally adopted. Milton's original copy is preserved as part of the Trinity College manuscript of the minor poems. There exists also a manuscript in a scribal hand, representing the masque as originally performed and as it stood before Milton made extensive additions with an eye to publication.

JAMES H. HANFORD
*Author of "John Milton, Englishman"*

**COMYN,** kum′in, a Scottish baronial family that figured prominently in the troubled history of Scotland during the late 13th and early 14th centuries. The earldom of Buchan (q.v.) was first held by members of the Comyn family.

John Comyn (died 1274) was justiciar of Galloway and the nephew of two powerful Scottish nobles. He took an important part in Scottish affairs and fought for Henry III at Northampton and Lewes.

John Comyn the Elder (died c. 1300), the son of the justiciar, was appointed a guardian of Scotland (1286) and shared in diplomatic negotiations between Edward I and the Scots. When Margaret, the Maid of Norway, died in 1290, he was a claimant for the Scottish throne but also supported his brother-in-law John de Baliol. After supporting Baliol's rising against Edward I, Comyn submitted to Edward in 1296.

John Comyn the Younger (died 1306), also called "the Red," was the son of John the Elder. He also supported Baliol's claim to the throne and in 1298 became a guardian of Scotland. He led resistance to the English but in 1304 submitted to Edward I. Subsequent rivalry led to his murder by Robert the Bruce at Dumfries.

**CONAKRY,** kon′ə-krē, is the capital and leading seaport of Guinea. It is situated on Tombo Island, 328 yards (300 meters) from the mainland, with which it is connected by a rail and road bridge.

The port city receives 170 inches (430 cm) of rain a year, mostly in the period from June to November. Humidity is high throughout the year, and temperatures range from 70° to 90° F (20° to 30° C).

Conakry is divided into several distinct quarters, many showing the influence of the French. Wide boulevards, lined with palm and mango trees for shade, cut across the city. Handsome villas overlook the Atlantic Ocean from the wealthy sections. The newest quarter of Conakry is the commercial center, which is the site of the city's modern shops. The administrative section dates almost exclusively from after World War II. Conakry has spilled over from the island to the mainland in a suburban sprawl, and most of its industries are located on the mainland.

Conakry has an excellent natural deep-water harbor that handles some 800 ships each year. The principal exports are agricultural products including bananas, coffee, and palm kernels. Iron, mined near Conakry, and bauxite, from some small-scale deposits on Los Islands four miles (6 km) west, are also exported. Imports include petroleum products, machinery, food (wheat and rice), and manufactured goods.

Conakry is the terminus of a railroad that runs 310 miles (499 km) east to Kankan, the head of navigation on the Niger River. An international airport 9½ miles (15 km) from the city is served by major worldwide airlines.

Conakry was settled by the French in 1887. The city grew rapidly after 1945, and its population rose commensurate with that growth. Population: 1,508,000 (1995 est.).

HUGH C. BROOKS
*St. John's University*

**CONAN DOYLE, Sir Arthur.** See DOYLE, SIR ARTHUR CONAN.

**CONANT,** ko′nənt, **James Bryant** (1893–1978), American university president, diplomat, author, and influential critic of American educational practices. He was born in Dorchester, Mass., on March 26, 1893. Educated at Harvard University, he taught chemistry there from 1919 to 1933 and was president of the university from 1933 until 1953. For the next five years he held diplomatic posts in Germany, first as U. S. high commissioner and then as ambassador to West Germany.

In 1957, Conant began a comprehensive study of American public high schools under a grant from the Carnegie Corporation. Although this study was formally completed in 1962, he continued to observe and comment upon educational patterns in American high schools. The results of a study of teacher education in the United States, also made under a Carnegie grant, were contained in *The Education of American Teach-*

ers (1963) and included proposals for reforms in the professional training of teachers. Between 1963 and 1965, Conant acted as an educational adviser to the Ford Foundation, serving in West Germany.

Active also in military and scientific fields, Conant served in the U. S. Army's Chemical Warfare Service between 1917 and 1918. During World War II he was an adviser to the Manhattan Project, which developed the first atomic bomb, and from 1946 until 1962 he was an adviser to the Atomic Energy Commission.

Conant's prodigious output of books includes several texts on high school and college chemistry and a 2-volume work of case histories in experimental science. In addition, he wrote on the broader relationships of science to society and education in *Science and Common Sense* (1951), *Modern Science and Modern Man* (1952), and *Two Modes of Thought* (1964), and on foreign affairs in *Germany and Freedom* (1958).

Nevertheless, it is in the area of education that Conant has made his most notable contribution. In numerous reports including *Education in a Divided World* (1948), *Education and Liberty* (1953), *The Citadel of Learning* (1956), and *The Child, the Parent, and the State* (1959), he highlighted the role of public education in a democracy and sought to unify conflicting views in education. His study *Thomas Jefferson and the Development of American Public Education* (1962) documented the continuity of past and present trends in American educational patterns. His reports on American high schools and junior high schools in the late 1950's and 1960's, which stemmed from the Carnegie study, supported the concept of large, comprehensive schools under local community control. The importance of decentralizing control of education while promoting interstate cooperation was particularly pointed up in *Shaping Educational Policy* (1964). *Slums and Suburbs* (1961) was a pioneering work on upgrading the education of underprivileged children in metropolitan areas and warned that inadequate educational and vocational guidance for disadvantaged youth amounted to "social dynamite." Some of Conant's ideas have been criticized, but he nevertheless exerted a deep influence on American educational practice. He died in Hanover, N. H., on Feb. 11, 1978.

WILLIAM W. BRICKMAN
*University of Pennsylvania*

HARVARD UNIVERSITY

James B. Conant

**CONBOY,** kon'boi, **Sara Agnes McLaughlin** (1870–1928), American labor leader, who was the first woman to attain an elective position of national influence in the American labor movement. She was born in Boston on April 3, 1870. On the early death of her husband, Mrs. Conboy went to work as a carpet weaver. After directing food relief in a textile strike in Lawrence, Mass., in 1912, she became a staff organizer for the United Textile Workers.

Upon the death of Albert Hibbert in 1915, she was chosen secretary-treasurer of the union and held the position for the rest of her life. She reorganized the union's finances and administration and then turned her attention to national social problems. She frequently represented the American Federation of Labor at public conferences and was considered to be labor's spokesman in affairs of particular interest to women. She died in New York City on Jan. 8, 1928.

HARVEY L. FRIEDMAN
*University of Massachusetts*

**CONCEIT,** kən-sēt, in literature, an elaborate poetic metaphor expressing an analogy or parallel between two things or situations that seem totally unlike. Though it can be brief, a conceit often forms the basis for an entire poem.

The term, which originally meant "concept" or "idea," came, during the Renaissance, to be applied to a special type of poetic metaphor, first used in the love sonnets of Petrarch. The Petrarchan conceit compares the beloved in great detail to some natural or familiar object. Shakespeare's Sonnet 130, which begins, "My mistress' eyes are nothing like the sun," is almost a satiric catalog of Petrarchan conventions.

The conceit was widely used in the 17th century by the English metaphysical poets, including John Donne, Henry Vaughan, and Richard Crashaw. The metaphysical conceit was highly intellectualized, with analogies drawn from science, religion, and scholarship as well as everyday life. Its goal was to be witty and startling. Often, analogies were drawn with such exaggerated attention to detail as to seem deliberately grotesque.

Severely condemned in the 18th century by Dr. Johnson, and in bad repute in the 19th century, the conceit again became a respected poetic device in the 20th century. Some of the best examples of its use in modern verse are found in the works of Emily Dickinson, T. S. Eliot, and Allen Tate.

C. HUGH HOLMAN
*Coauthor of "A Handbook to Literature"*

**CONCENTRATION CAMP,** a guarded enclosure set up by a government for the confinement of special categories of people. Assignment to a concentration camp usually follows a roundup or mass arrest without judicial trial. Men, wommen, and children may be sent to a camp, where their quarters are generally barracks or tents surrounded by barbed wire. The camp guards may have the power of life and death over the inmates. The concentration camp differs from other places of detention, in that its prisoners do not retain basic human rights and do not have to be released under definite conditions. Ordinarily, penitentiaries, prisoner-of-war camps, immigration stations, or reservations are not concentration camps. However, the official designation of an enclosure does not always indicate its true nature.

Concentration camps have been employed for several purposes. Western countries have established them during emergencies for temporary internment. Totalitarian states have built them as integral components of government. The Soviet variety has been used for general terrorization of the people and special exploitation of the prisoners. The Nazis maintained camps for large-scale killings as well.

**Western Camps.** The modern concentration camp first appeared at the turn of the century. In the Boer War the British commander, Lord Kitchener, decreed on Dec. 27, 1900, that the families of Boer guerrilla fighters be gathered in "concentration camps." By February 1902, 117,-000 Boers were interned in 46 sites. Overcrowding, unhygienic conditions, and a sparse diet led to many cases of pneumonia, measles, dysentery, and typhoid fever. The death toll in these camps is variously estimated from 18,000 to 26,000.

More recently, concentration camps have emerged on several continents during upheavals or insurrections. In 1942, during World War II, 110,000 persons of Japanese ancestry were removed from Pacific coast areas in the United States to 10 "relocation centers" in the interior. The evacuation, which was demanded by Lt. Gen. John L. DeWitt of the Western Defense Command, was approved by executive order and made enforceable by law. The camps, which had schools and newspapers, were guarded by military police and controlled by the War Relocation Authority.

In the course of the Mau Mau rebellion of Kikuyu tribesmen in Kenya during the 1950's, the British general Sir George Erskine decided upon the arrest and detention of persons suspected of supporting or supplying the rebels. Some 80,000 Kikuyu were thereupon concentrated in "emergency detention camps" to be "cured" of "lawless violence" and prepared for "rehabilitation." By February 1959, all but 1,100 had been released.

**Communist Camps.** Russia has long sent its political prisoners to remote, cold regions for forced labor. In imperial times this mode of imprisonment was known as the "galley" (*katorga*); later, the Communists designated their installations as "corrective labor camps."

Shortly after the Bolshevik Revolution "class enemies" were dispatched to camps on the Solovetski Islands in the White Sea. Later, the Soviet regime established an elaborate legal and administrative framework for a concentration camp system. The criminal code provided, in articles 58 and 59, for punishment of "crimes against the state." Article 58 dealt with "counterrevolutionary crimes," including "wrecking," "diversion," and "propaganda and agitation" against the regime. Article 59 defined "crimes against the administration" such as "pillage" and breach of labor discipline. The interpretation of these articles was elastic: they could be applied retroactively, and they could be made effective against acts not specifically mentioned in the code. One of the punishments for "crimes against the state" was detention in a camp.

Mass arrests followed in waves during the 1930's and 1940's. The first wave engulfed independent peasants (*kulaks*) and "wreckers." The second was an indiscriminate roundup in the purges. Following the annexation of new territories by the USSR in 1939 and 1940, the police picked up a number of Lithuanians, Latvians, Ukrainians, and Poles. After 1943 there was an infusion of persons suspected of collaboration with the Germans, plus Axis prisoners in the Soviet Union and Soviet prisoners of war returning from captivity. At least five million people were swept into the camps during these years.

The Soviet state police had overall control of the camp network. Known first as the Cheka, the police apparatus was renamed the GPU in 1922 and the OGPU in 1923. In 1934 the OGPU gave way to the NKVD, which was restyled the MVD in 1946. On the eve of the great camp expansion in 1930, the OGPU formed as one of its departments the Central Administration for Corrective Labor Camps (GULAG). The GULAG—which later became part of the NKVD and MVD—operated the installations through its "production" organs (inmate employment), "administrative" organs (housekeeping), and "regime" organs (guards, or VOKHR).

By the late 1940's there were five major camp complexes: the Dalstroi in the Far East, ranging along the Kolyma River to Magadan; the Taishet-Komsomolsk cluster, covering the Lake Baikal-Amur River region; Pechora in the European far north, including the Kotlas and Vorkuta camps; the White Sea aggregation at Archangel; and Karaganda in Kazakhstan. Well over 100 individual camps have been identified.

For more than two decades the camps played an important role in the Soviet economy. The state plan of 1941 allocated to the NKVD 17% of all capital construction, as well as 1.2% of all industrial output, including 3% of the coal mining, 12% of the timber, almost half of the chrome, and two thirds of the gold production. Most of the forced labor took place in stark surroundings. Often prisoners worked long days in icy areas, wearing ragged clothes and guarded by dogs. In 1953 and 1954, strikes and mutinies broke out in the camps. Conditions began to improve and on Oct. 25, 1956, the GULAG was transformed into GUITK (Central Administration for Corrective Labor Colonies) to indicate the withering away of the forced labor system.

After World War II, the institution of the corrective labor camp spread to several other Communist countries, from Albania to mainland China. Their criminal codes and general offices for "reform through labor" closely resembled the Soviet prototype. In China alone several million "reactionaries," "bandits," and "illegal landlords" appear to have become slave laborers.

**Nazi Camps.** Immediately after the rise to power of the German Nazis in 1933, eager Nazi party regional chiefs (*Gauleiters*), the State Police, the SA (storm troopers), and the SS (Hitler's elite guard) set up concentration camps. After a while, one man emerged in sole charge: the *Reichsführer*-SS Heinrich Himmler. The nucleus of Himmler's camp organization was Dachau, and an early Dachau commander, Theodor Eicke, became the first inspector for concentration camps.

In prewar days two principles were employed for the imprisonment of inmates in a camp. One was the "security arrest" of persons suspected of "tendencies" against the state, flexibly applicable to Communist or socialist functionaries, purged Nazis, Jehovah's Witnesses, opponents in the clergy, and Jews. The other criterion was the "preventive" arrest of "asocials" such as Gypsies, prostitutes, and homosexuals, and of "habitual criminals," that is, persons who had served sentences for crimes and might commit them again.

CONCEPCIÓN, Chile, is the home of the University of Concepción. The university's main entrance is shown here.

When war broke out in September 1939, the camps contained 21,000 people, but in the next few years a new and much greater influx began that included: members of resistance movements, removed to concentration camps under the "night and fog" decree; convicts from German and Polish prisons; and Soviet prisoners of war. By far the largest transports, however, consisted of Polish, Ukrainian, and Russian workers impressed in the occupied east for forced labor, and Jews who were to be gassed.

The camp network grew with the number of arrivals. There were now three kinds of authorities in control of camps. The first was the Economic-Administrative Main Office (WVHA), in which the old Inspectorate functioned as Office Group D. By August 1944 the WVHA centrally administered 20 concentration camps and 165 satellite labor camps in Germany and occupied Europe. The inmate count in the WVHA camps jumped from 88,000 at the end of 1942, to 224,-000 in August 1943, 524,000 in August 1944, and 714,000 in 1945. The second group of camps was set up by regional SS chiefs—the Higher SS and Police Leaders—for temporary or pressing needs. The third group consisted of camps erected by Axis satellite states under German influence.

Inmates were usually worked to the point of death in camp maintenance, SS construction projects, SS industries, and private enterprises such as the I. G. Farben chemical company. Invalids and the sick were intermittently killed. In several camps, notably Dachau, Buchenwald, and Auschwitz, doctors performed often fatal "medical experiments" on prisoners.

The systematic gassing of Jews took place in Auschwitz, Treblinka, Belsen, Sobibor, and Chelmno in German-occupied Poland. Mass shootings of Jews occurred in Lublin as well as the Rumanian camps Bogdanovka, Dumanovka, and Akmecetka.

About 4 million inmates died in Nazi camps. Three quarters of these victims were Jews, and almost half of all the deaths were accounted for by Auschwitz and Treblinka alone. But none of these figures includes another 5 million victims who died under other circumstances.

RAUL HILBERG, *University of Vermont*

### Bibliography

Abzug, Robert H., *Inside the Vicious Heart* (Oxford 1985).
Axford, Roger W., *Too Long Silent: Japanese Americans Speak Out* (Media Prod. & Marketing 1986).
Eitinger, Leo, *Psychological and Medical Effects on Concentration Camps* (Norwood Eds. 1982).
Gesensway, Deborah, and Roseman, Mindy, *Beyond Words* (Cornell Univ. Press 1988).
Greife, H., *Jewish-Run Concentration Camps in the Soviet Union* (Revisionist Press 1982).
Herling, Gustav, *A World Apart: The Journal of a Gulag Survivor* (Arbor House 1986).

**CONCEPCIÓN,** kôn-sep-syôn', a city in south central Chile, the capital of Concepción province and one of the country's largest cities, is situated on the Bío-Bío River, 6 miles (10 km) from the Pacific Ocean. It is a manufacturing, commercial, and rail center, with extensive shipping facilities at Talcahuano, its port on Concepción Bay, about 8 miles (13 km) to the northwest. Near the port are the sites of Chile's principal steel plant (the Huachipato plant) and of a major oil refinery, completed in 1966. These serve as the nucleus of an expanding industrial complex. Concepción's older industries include textile mills, tanneries, shoe factories, and glass, cement, and pulp and paper plants. Agricultural communities surround the city.

The University of Concepción, which was founded in 1919 and financed by municipal lotteries, contains numerous faculties and schools. Its School of Agriculture is southern Chile's most important center for agronomical studies. The hub of Concepción's public life is the Plaza de Armas, around which are government buildings and the cathedral. Concepción was founded by Pedro de Valdivia in 1550 on a site situated several miles from its present location. Several times during its history, notably in 1570, 1730, 1751, and 1939, it has been devastated by earthquakes and tidal floods and subsequently rebuilt. As a result, the city has few relics of the past. Population: 350,268 (1995 est.).

LAURENCE R. BIRNS
*New School for Social Research*

**CONCEPCIÓN,** kôn-sep-syôn', the chief commercial center of northern Paraguay and the capital of Concepción department. It is on the Paraguay River about 125 miles (200 km) north of Asunción, which is reached from Concepción by air or by river streamer. The city has sawmills and is an outlet for products of the Chaco region—cattle, yerba maté, and quebracho. Part of its trade is with Brazil, to which it is linked by road to the border town of Ponta Porã, Brazil. Population: 35,485 (1992 preliminary census).

**CONCEPCIÓN DEL URUGUAY,** kôn-sep-syôn′ del ōō-rōō-gwī′, an agricultural center and river port located in eastern Argentina, in Entre Ríos province, about 160 miles (250 km) north of Buenos Aires. It ships grain and beef down the Uruguay River to Buenos Aires and also is a center of trade with Uruguay. Food processing and sawmilling are the chief industries. Its National College, a secondary school, is one of the best known in Argentina. The city, sometimes called simply Concepción or Uruguay, was founded in 1778 and twice during the 19th century was the capital of Argentina. It was also for a time the capital of Entre Ríos province. Population: 46,065 (1980 preliminary census).

**CONCEPT** may be defined as a thought or an idea. In philosophical terms a concept is an idea that includes everything characteristically associated with or suggested by a class of logical species. The history of philosophy has been characterized by the conflict over the nature of reality: is the general idea or the particular object more real? The conceptualist school held that universals—ideas held everywhere to be valid—have real existence only in the mind, where they exist as concepts uniting individual things. See CONCEPTUALISM.

In psychology, the problem of defining reality —whether as the group of objects, the quality they share in common, or their unifying concept —has lost much of its relevance. The significance of understanding what a concept is lies, rather, in its relation to the learning process. For the psychologist, a concept is knowledge not directly perceived through the senses, but which results from the manipulation of sensory impressions. It includes in it the isolation of a property and its application to several different objects. The general idea or ideas used for a group of objects is a concept; the process by which a person comes to give the same response to all those objects that share certain common qualities is called concept formation.

**Concept Formation.** Among the most notable researches into the nature of the process of concept formation is the work of the Swiss psychologist Jean Piaget starting in the 1920's. By applying techniques of naturalistic research and extensive interviews with children of all ages, Piaget ascertained four stages in the formation of a concept.

In the first stage, the child demonstrates his ability to discriminate objects by his characteristic reactions to particular objects. These first "preconcepts" are action-ridden, imagistic, and concrete. All members of a particular class of objects are seen as reappearances of the same member of that class. In the second stage, the child employs words to stand for particular objects but cannot yet use them to represent whole classes. In the third stage, the child responds symbolically to an entire class of objects but is unable to give an adequate explanation of the rationale for his concept. Finally, in the last stage, the child is able to give an acceptable definition of his concept.

It is clear′ that while some concepts are grasped early in life, others are not grasped until much later. The factors involved here include the complexity of the concept and the degree of abstraction required. Research by other psychologists has demonstrated that even adults learn new concepts without first being able to give adequate verbal expression to their rationale,

thus providing empirical verification for some of Piaget's work.

A critical study by the American psychologist Edna Heidbreder indicates that concepts involving concrete objects are more readily learned than those involving spatial forms or abstract numbers. Indeed, it has been demonstrated that even lower animals are capable of rudimentary concept formation in concrete situations. For example, rats have been trained to respond to triangular shapes in preference to other shapes in a discrimination task. A related line of research indicates that injury to the frontal lobe of the cortex will impede the development of abstract concepts, but has less effect on an individual's ability to deal concretely with particular objects.

These facts have been utilized in the development of psychological tests for the detection and diagnosis of brain damage. An example is the "object sorting test." The material here is simply a variety of objects encountered fairly frequently in daily life. The subject is instructed to group the objects on the basis of some common characteristic. The objects can be grouped on fairly concrete grounds, such as color or use, or higher levels of abstraction may be used to categorize them. Normal adults are quite capable of categorizing on both levels, but children, brain-damaged adults, and schizophrenics usually deal with the objects only in very concrete ways. In fact, once many brain-damaged patients have settled on a particular means of organizing the material, they find it difficult if not impossible to shift to a new mode. Additional research findings tend to support clinical evidence for the notion of regressive deterioration in the thinking processes of brain-damaged and schizophrenic patients.

**Creativity in Concept Formation.** Many contemporary learning theorists and educators view the process of concept formation in a new light, as evidence of creativity. Most of the concepts that people learn and use are those they cull from the culture in which they are brought up. The individual does not invent them. Rather, he acquires them in his interactions with others. The invention of new concepts is far more difficult, and it is here, in the ability to formulate novel combinations not previously considered, that creativity plays a critical role.

There are several general classes of concepts, and it is clear that some require more creativity in their formulation than others. The first type is the *conjunctive concept,* in which is found the joint presence of several attributes, as in the concept of red circles. A second general type is the *disjunctive concept,* in which there must be at least one of several possible attributes present for an object to be considered part of a class, as any organization having as its membership requirement such different contingencies as "anyone who lives or pays taxes in this district". This is a difficult type because of the lack of apparent relation between attributes that can be substituted for each other. A third type is the *relational concept,* defined as any specifiable relationship between the defining variables. Thus income tax brackets are defined in terms of the relationship between number of dependents and level of income. It is in this third class that there is the greatest need for creativity and the most potential for the development of concept formation.

It seems evident that the old philosophical debate about the concept as a universal is irrelevant, and the answer, if there is one, to the question of where reality resides will be of no apparent practical value in helping us to better understand our world. For in operational terms, concepts are networks of relational inferences that may be sent into play by an act of categorization. Here, it seems, is the next fruitful direction for theoretical consideration and empirical investigation. See also COGNITION; LEARNING; PSYCHOLOGY.

MICHAEL G. ROTHENBERG
*Columbia University*

**Further Reading:** Neisser, Ulric, ed., *Concepts and Conceptual Development* (Cambridge 1987); Schwartz, David, *Concept Testing* (Am. Management Assn. 1987); Weltz, Morris, *Theories of Concepts: A History of the Major Philosophical Tradition* (Routledge 1988).

**CONCEPTION,** the fertilization of an egg cell by a sperm cell. See EMBRYOLOGY—*Fertilization*.

**CONCEPTUALISM** is a philosophical position about the existence of universals. It holds that universals, or general concepts, such as "humanity" or "true," exist in the mind rather than in nature.

Conceptualism stands midway between two extreme views on the question of universals: realism and nominalism. A realist—for example, Plato—believes that universals exist objectively in nature outside of the individual subjective mind. He would say, "The universal 'tree-ness' is a substance or essence common to all trees." The conceptualist would agree that general concepts exist, but only in individual minds.

Nominalists, such as William of Occam, do not believe in the existence of universals, either in nature or in the mind. They believe that members of a given class or group of entities—for example, individual trees—have in common only the name men give them. The word "tree" names neither "tree-ness" nor some identical property every tree has. Each tree is distinct in everything but name from every other tree. A conceptualist would agree that common names are general but would add that they stand for general ideas.

In the conceptualist view, only particular things and events exist in nature. But common words do name something—a universal— that exists in another way. A universal, or a general concept, is common to all minds. Universals permeate the ways in which men experience, think about, and talk about the particulars of nature.

A particular object cannot be experienced (sensed) as what it is if the perceiver is restricted to the particular sense experiences he has while confronting it. He must have a general concept to refer to in order to identify his perception; he must, for example, subsume the green-leaf, brown-trunk thing in front of him under the general concept "tree" or "tree-ness." Only by linking his particular experience to the abstract concept can he perceive a particular tree as a tree.

Thinking about objects also requires universal concepts, so that a particular object can be understood in terms of a larger class of objects. In order to think about a tree, one must have a general idea of what a tree is, a general idea of "tree-ness."

Similarly, the act of talking about particulars requires the use of common names. To make sense as a common (not proper) name, "tree" must indicate the general idea "tree-ness"—that which is conceived to be characteristic of all things

called a tree—rather than a particular tree. A key assumption of conceptualism is that common names do name something. That something is a universal that is common to all minds—a general concept.

John Locke is the major philosopher who comes closest to being a conceptualist. He claims that, while all ideas are particular, a particular idea of a particular tree might stand also for all other particular ideas of the class "trees." In thus allowing certain ideas to have a general function (that of standing for other particular ideas), Locke substitutes, in terms of conceptualism, the notion of function for concept.

JOHN P. DREHER
*Lawrence University*

**Further Reading:** Aaron, Richard I., *Our Knowledge of Universals* (Haskell 1975); Berkeley, George, *A Treatise Concerning the Principles of Human Knowledge* (Open Court 1985); Canfield, John V., ed., *The Philosophy of Wittgenstein: Psychology and Conceptual Relativity* (Garland 1987); Scholnick, Ellin K., *New Trends in Conceptual Representation: Challenges to Piaget's Theory?* (L. Earlbaum 1983).

**CONCERT OF EUROPE,** a concept of the 19th century that the leading powers in Europe should supervise or settle, through negotiations and agreement, problems threatening the peace of Europe. The concept is restricted by some historians to the period from 1815 to the Crimean War (1854–1855), but in a broader sense it prevailed until World War I. The Concert of Europe had its origin in the Treaty of Chaumont (March 1, 1814) by which Britain, Russia, Austria, and Prussia, allied against Napoleon I, agreed that their sovereigns or their representatives should meet periodically to ensure continued good understanding.

The Chaumont agreement was repeated in the subsequent peace treaties, notably in Article 6 of the Quadruple Alliance Treaty (Nov. 20, 1815), of which Viscount Castlereagh, the British foreign minister, was the moving force. This article called for periodic ". . . meetings consecrated to great common objects and to the examination of such measures as at each one of the epochs shall be judged most salutary for the peace and prosperity of the nations and the maintenance of the tranquility of Europe." It thus reinforced the foundation of the new system of congresses, meetings, and multilateral diplomatic negotiations designed to establish agreed policies among the powers.

At the Congress of Aix-la-Chapelle (1818), France was admitted to the Quadruple Alliance. Further congresses were held at Troppau (1820), Laibach (1821), and Verona (1822) to deal with the revolutionary situations in Italy, Spain, and Greece. But Britain did not accept the Protocol of Troppau, which called for intervention by the powers to suppress revolutions that might disturb the peace of Europe, and the Concert never developed a regular organization.

The problems that drew the attention of the powers varied, but the Near Eastern question in particular led the powers to concert their actions on numerous occasions. The London Ambassadorial Conference, where the ambassadors of the great powers met regularly to "take in hand" the many issues arising out of the Balkan Wars of 1912–1913, is one of the best instances of the effective functioning of the Concert of Europe.

ERNST C. HELMREICH
*Bowdoin College*

**CONCERTGEBOUW ORCHESTRA,** kən-särt'KHə-bou, of Amsterdam, the outstanding orchestra of the Netherlands and one of the finest in the world. The orchestra was founded in 1883, and the Concertgebouw ("Concert Building") for which it was named was dedicated five years later. The orchestra was at first privately supported; it is now subsidized by Amsterdam, the province of North Holland, and the national government. Its conductors have included Willem Kes (1883–1895), Willem Mengelberg (1895–1945), and Eduard van Beinum (1945–1956); after Beinum's retirement the orchestra was conducted jointly by Bernard Haitink and Eugen Jochum.

The Concertgebouw gives about 90 performances a year in Amsterdam and about that number in other Dutch cities; it made its first international tour in 1898 and has since played in many countries, including the United States.

**CONCERTINA,** kon-sər-tē'nə, a small, portable musical instrument invented in England in the early 19th century as an improvement on the accordion ( q.v.). The concertina consists of pleated bellows connecting two hexagonal end pieces, each of which contains a keyboard of "studs," or finger pistons. The concertina's sound is produced by the vibration of metal "reeds" set in motion by the bellows' action. The same note sounds whether the bellows are expanded or contracted (double action), and the most frequently used type, the treble concertina, has a complete chromatic scale of four octaves.

The concertina was perfected in 1884 by Charles Wheatstone, an English physicist. It used the intricate reed mechanism that Wheatstone had developed for his mouth-blown *symphonium*, patented in 1829. The first concertina was small, but its sound was capable of filling a large hall. Wheatstone's firm manufactured three sizes—treble, tenor-treble, and baritone. There is also a quartet family that covers roughly the same range as the classical string quartet.

The concertina was particularly popular with the English aristocracy. One of the most renowned concertina virtuosos, an Englishman named Alexander Prince, astonished listeners in the late 19th century by performing the overture to *Tannhäuser*. Tchaikovsky wrote parts for four concertinas in the score of his second *Orchestral Suite*, and the instrument is still used by orchestras for special effects.

SHIRLEY FLEMING
*Editor of "Musical America"*

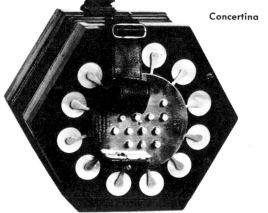

**Concertina**

C. WHEATSTONE & CO., LTD.,
LONDON, ENGLAND

**CONCERTO,** kən-cher'tō, a musical composition for instrumental soloist or soloists and orchestra. If it has more than one soloist, it is sometimes called a *concertante*. The concerto usually has three (or sometimes four) movements, though Franz Liszt, among others, wrote concertos in only one movement, a symphonic entity consisting of a single theme in many disguises.

**Early Forms.** The earliest forms of the concerto, dating from about 1540, were called *concerti ecclesiastici* or *concerti da chiesa* (church concertos) and consisted of various instrumental parts alternating with each other. Gradually, short solo passages (*concertino obbligato*) emerged and led eventually to the *concerto grosso,* a kind of concertante. The greatest masters of the concerto grosso were Antonio Vivaldi (1678?–?1741) and George Frideric Handel (1685–1759). Johann Sebastian Bach (1685–1750) based many of his violin and harpsichord concertos on themes by Vivaldi, but Bach's most celebrated works in this genre are the Brandenburg concertos, which derived from the concerti grossi.

**Classical Concerto.** Although others made good use of the concerto form, the next great composer of concertos was Wolfgang Amadeus Mozart (1756–1791). In his 28 piano concertos, 6 violin concertos, and many concertos for other instruments (such as flute, clarinet, bassoon, French horn), he brought a new approach to the form. Usually, in a Mozart concerto, the orchestra opens alone with an exposition of the thematic material. It builds up suspense for the entrance of the solo instrument. Mozart gave the orchestra greater importance than it had had in previous concertos, and he made the minor keys and chromaticism more significant parts of the music's texture.

**Romanticism.** Extreme brilliance, smoothness, and velocity of execution marked the works of the French-Italian virtuoso school that followed Mozart. The most durable representative of this school is Niccolò Paganini (1782–1840), whose violin concertos are the first real virtuoso concertos in the modern sense.

Ludwig van Beethoven (1770–1827) added several novel touches to the concerto form. His first three piano concertos are based on the classical pattern, but the last two and the violin concerto reveal some fresh approaches. The Fifth Piano Concerto (*Emperor*), for example, begins with a quasi-improvised cadenza by the pianist (previously, cadenzas had always been placed at the ends of movements) followed by the entrance of the full orchestra.

Robert Schumann (1810–1856) expanded the melodic material of the concerto, gave a new physiognomy to its modulations, and attempted to make the solo and orchestra parts more integrated. This integration was carried even farther by Johannes Brahms (1833–1897), whose concertos are actually complex symphonies, with soloist and orchestra interweaving thematic developments as equal partners.

**The 20th Century.** Paul Hindemith (1895–1963) introduced the neoclassic chamber concerto (*Kammermusik*), marking a return to the concertante style. Other 20th century developments include the exploration of untapped potentialities in the sound and pitch of solo instruments, and the writing of concertos for solo instruments never before used for this purpose—trombones, saxophones, double basses, and percussion instruments.

CARL BAMBERGER
*Editor of "The Conductor's Art"*

**CONCESSION,** in international law, means the act of granting or the thing granted. In diplomatic negotiations each party concedes advantages within its control to the other until agreement is reached. A government makes a *political concession* when it grants political rights in its territory to a foreign government. It makes an *economic concession* when it gives a grant, franchise, license, patent, charter, or monopoly for use of land, exploitation of resources, or conduct of an enterprise within its territory to one of its own nationals or corporations, or to a foreign individual, corporation, or state.

A concession has the character of a contract. Its terms are established in a formal instrument usually involving burdens as well as advantages to the concessionaire. Concessions have generally been given for a term of years but may be perpetual. They usually concern matters deemed to be of public interest by the law of the conceding state but may involve only private interests.

**History.** Under the feudal system in the Middle Ages, concessions for use of land or establishment of municipal corporations were given by the crown in European countries. Early in the 17th century, Lord Coke, an English jurist, remarked that the great English estates "were nothing but concessions of the crown." In the 17th and 18th centuries, chartered companies such as the British and Dutch East India companies and the Virginia, Massachusetts, and Hudson's Bay companies and proprietors such as William Penn and Lord Baltimore were given concessions by the crown to operate with governmental powers in colonial areas. In the 19th and 20th centuries, underdeveloped countries have given concessions to foreign governments and corporations for canal construction, naval bases, residential areas, railroad building, public utility development, agricultural development, mining, oil extraction, and many other purposes.

Economic concessions have contributed to the development of underdeveloped countries by providing public utilities, such as railroads, lighthouses, airports, and hospitals, and by leading to the discovery and development of natural resources. Such concessions usually give the conceding state at least 50% of the profits and include provisions concerning duration, the law applicable, and arbitration of disputes. Since World War II, however, the conceding governments, especially in Asia and Africa, have shown increasing dissatisfaction with these concessions. The underdeveloped countries, on achieving independence, have tended to identify concessions with exploitation and imperialism. They often have demanded renegotiation to obtain more favorable terms or have nationalized the concessions by exercising the right of eminent domain.

A United Nations commission established in 1958 suggested that nationalization, expropriation, and requisition of foreign concessions may be justified on grounds of public utility, security, and national interest, but that appropriate compensation should be paid. In 1966 the UN General Assembly approved two covenants of human rights, each of which provided for the right of self-determination for all peoples and of permanent sovereignty of peoples and nations over their natural wealth and resources.

QUINCY WRIGHT, *Professor Emeritus of International Law, University of Chicago*

**CONCH,** kongk, a large marine snail with a heavy coiled shell, found in temperate and tropical seas. The most common conch in Florida and the West Indies is the pink conch (*Strombus gigas*). It is about 1 foot (30 cm) long with a large flaring, pink lip. The flesh is used in chowders and salads, and the shell is a tourist item.

There are several species of conch belonging to the genus *Busycon*, which are found in the northeastern United States. Members range from 3 to 10 inches (7.5–25 cm) long. These conchs are noted for the long, snakelike strings of horny, button-shaped capsules laid by the female; each of the capsules contains hundreds of young. The foot of the snail is sometimes sliced, pounded, and cooked in tomato sauce. Parts of the shell of the left-handed conch were used by the American Indians in making wampum.

In the western Pacific, the largest conch is the Triton's trumpet of the genus *Charonia*. It reaches a length of 18 inches (45 cm) and is popular as a collector's item.

Conchs belong to several families, including Strombidae, Melongenidae, and Cymatiidae, in the class Gastropoda.

R. TUCKER ABBOTT
*The Academy of Natural Sciences of Philadelphia*

THE PINK CONCH is common in Florida and the Caribbean. Photo at right shows animal emerging from shell.

**CONCHOID,** kong′koid, a shell-shaped curve whose invention is credited to the Greek mathematician Nicomedes, who lived about 200 B. C. Given a point O at a perpendicular distance a from a fixed line AB; call Q the moving point on AB cut out by a line pivoted on O; from Q in both directions along the line OQ measure out a fixed distance b so that QP = QP′ = b. As the line OQ rotates on point O, the points P and P′ will trace out a conchoid. The relative sizes of a and b determine the three types of conchoids shown in the figure below.

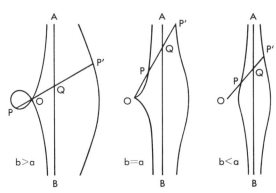

If b is longer than a, the curve has a loop with a node at O; if b equals a, there is a cusp at O; if b is shorter than a, the conchoid does not pass through O. The equation in rectangular coordinates is $(x - a)^2 (x^2 + y^2) = b^2 x^2$; the polar equation, with O taken as the origin (pole) and the polar axis as horizontal, is $r = a \sec \theta \pm b$. Both branches of the curve are asymptotic to line AB in both directions.

**CONCIERGERIE,** kôN-syerzh-rē′, a famous prison in Paris, part of the Palais de Justice. In the Middle Ages the building was an adjunct of the royal residence. In 1392, after the royal residence was moved from the Île de la Cité, the Conciergerie was converted into a prison.

During the French Revolution, the prison housed many notable inmates awaiting execution, including Marie Antoinette, Mme. du Barry, Danton, and Robespierre. It now holds prisoners awaiting arraignment by examining magistrates.

**CONCILIAR THEORY,** kən-sil′ē-ər, a concept in theology that holds that a general or ecumenical council is the supreme authority in a church. The term usually is specifically applied to the Western historical development of the 13th and 14th centuries. During this period the Western Schism (1378–1417) divided the Catholic Church into factions supporting different claimants to the papacy. The conciliar theory thus gained widespread popularity as the solution to the schism. The Catholic Church teaches, however, that no council can be above or against the pope because, without his presence or approval, a general, or ecumenical, council cannot be validly held.

After the Reformation the conciliar theory was almost entirely disregarded in Catholic circles. Since the Second Vatican Council (1962–1965), however, the related concept of collegiality has come to the fore. This theory holds that the bishops of the church, as successors to the apostles, collectively form a "college" which shares in the authority of the pope.

C. J. McNaspy, S. J., *"America" Magazine*

**CONCORD,** kong′kərd, a city in western California in Contra Costa county, is situated at the base of Mt. Diablo, 15 miles (24 km) northeast of Oakland. The city is in the San Francisco metropolitan area and is the Contra Costa county terminus of the Bay Area rapid transit district system that links major cities of the Bay Area in a 75-mile (120-km) rail network. Concord is a residential, commercial, and industrial community with a rapid growth rate; the population increased more than fivefold in the decade 1950–1960. Diablo Valley Junior College is situated in Concord.

The site of the city was first settled in 1846 by Don Salvio Pacheco, whose adobe ranch house still stands in the downtown area. The town, originally named Todos Santos ("All Saints"), was surveyed in 1868.

The influence of settlers from New England led to the renaming of the community, and it was incorporated as Concord in 1905. Concord has a council-manager form of government. Population: 121,780.

**CONCORD,** kong′kərd, in northeastern Massachusetts, is one of the most famous towns in American history. It is situated in the Boston metropolitan area, in Middlesex county, about 19 miles (31 km) northwest of Boston. The town lies on the Concord River, which is formed by the confluence of the Sudbury and Assabet rivers.

The community remains semirural and suburban, but there are firms manufacturing electronic test equipment, furniture, iron, bronze and aluminum sand castings, and precision machinery.

After the middle of the 19th century, Concord became a literary and cultural center, the home of such personages as Ralph Waldo Emerson, Henry David Thoreau, Louisa May Alcott, Amos Bronson Alcott (her father), Nathaniel Hawthorne, Franklin Benjamin Sanborn, Elizabeth Peabody, Harriett Mulford Lothrop (Margaret Sidney), and Daniel Chester French. The homes of some of these notables have become public shrines. They include the Old Manse, associated with Emerson and Hawthorne; Orchard House and the Wayside, where Miss Alcott lived; and the Ralph Waldo Emerson House, where Emerson lived from 1835 until his death in 1882.

Other places of interest include the Antiquarian House, which contains exhibits of period rooms and furniture, the Concord Free Public Library, and the Thoreau Lyceum. Walden Pond, made famous by Thoreau in his book *Walden*, is in Concord.

Concord was incorporated in 1635. The First Provincial Congress of Massachusetts met in 1774–1775 in the First Parish Meetinghouse. Harvard College held sessions in Concord while the British occupied Cambridge during the Revolutionary War.

The second skirmish of the war was fought at the North Bridge on April 19, 1775, where the Minute Men met British soldiers sent from Boston to destroy stores of powder and munitions. The Minute Man statue by Daniel Chester French stands at the battle site. The Minute Man National Historical Park (750 acres, or 303 hectares) includes the Battle Road from Lexington to Concord, North Bridge, and the Wayside.

Concord has a town meeting and town manager form of government. Population: 16,993.

Edward J. Diffley
*Concord Free Public Library*

**CONCORD,** kong'kərd, a city in south central New Hampshire, is the capital of the state and its third-largest city. It is the seat of Merrimack county. It is situated on the west bank of the Merrimack River, about 15 miles (24 km) north of Manchester. The city is a financial, administrative, industrial, and transportation center and an important distribution point for a dairying and general farming area.

Concord's industries include printing and publishing, railroad shops, electronics, and the manufacture of leather and wood products. Just north of the city are granite quarries that produce the famous white Concord granite, which is used in the Library of Congress in Washington, D. C., Concord's State House, as well as in many other public buildings.

The domed State House, at the heart of the city's civic center, is a fine neoclassic structure, the front portion of which was completed in 1819. Other buildings in the civic center are the state library, the state historical society, the city library, and city hall. The New Hampshire Historical Society has collections of early American furniture, silverware, glassware, china, paintings, and state manuscripts and artifacts.

Concord is the seat of the New Hampshire Technical Institute, established in 1965, and St. Paul's School, an Episcopal preparatory school for boys. Franklin Pierce, the 14th president of the United States, lived in the city from 1857 until his death in 1869, and his house is maintained as a museum. The birthplace of Mary Baker Eddy, founder of Christian Science, is marked by a small granite pyramid at the village of Bow Center, 5 miles (8 km) to the south. There is a Shaker village 9 miles (14 km) north of Concord at Canterbury.

The site of the city was originally called the Plantation of Penny Cook (from the English version of an Indian word that referred to the bend of the Merrimack River here) in a grant from the Massachusetts Bay Colony in 1659. Settlement did not begin until 1727. The town was incorporated as Rumford by Massachusetts in 1733 and as Concord by New Hampshire in 1765 following settlement of a boundary dispute. Citizens of Concord were among those who supported Massachusetts' rebellion against the British, and they fought in the battles of Concord, Lexington, and Bunker Hill.

Concord became the state capital in 1808 and was incorporated as a city in 1853. The firm of Lewis Downing and Stephen Abbot, which began business at Concord in 1813, had, before 1860, the largest stagecoach factory in the United States. The sturdy Concord coaches were a vital mode of overland transport, and they were especially popular in the American West. The vehicles were also marketed in Mexico, South America, South Africa, and Australia.

Concord has the mayor-council form of government. Population: 40,687.

**CONCORD,** kon'kó'rd, a city in central North Carolina, the seat of Cabarrus county, situated 18 miles (29 km) northeast of Charlotte. The city is a cotton textile center with a number of hosiery mills, and it also manufactures foundry and machine-shop products and soft drinks. Concord became the center of a rich gold-mining region for a short time after gold was discovered nearby in 1799. Government is by mayor and council. Population: 55,977.

THE STATE HOUSE in Concord, N.H. The statue is of Franklin Pierce, the state's only U.S. president.

**CONCORD, Battle of.** See American Revolution—*Important Battles of the American Revolution;* Lexington and Concord, Battles of.

**CONCORD,** kon'kord, **Formula and Book of.** The Book of Concord, which includes the Formula of Concord, states the basic doctrines of the Lutheran Church. At the time of the Augsburg Confession, presented in 1530 to Emperor Charles V, the Lutherans in Germany were united in opposition both to the papal church and to the followers of the Swiss reformers. However, the Lutherans were not agreed among themselves on the doctrines of justification by faith, the relationship of faith and good works, the freedom of the will, the reality of the presence of Christ in the sacrament, and the significance of inherited rites and ceremonies. The princes, anxious to preserve peace, turned to theological leaders in the search for agreement. A consensus was achieved in 1577 in a Formula of Concord, drawn up under the leadership of Jacob Andreae, Martin Chemnitz, and Nikolaus Salnecker. The Formula, together with the Augsburg Confession, the Apology, the Smalcald Articles, and Luther's Catechisms, made up, in 1580, the Book of Concord, which became the doctrinal constitution of the Lutheran Church. See also Lutheranism.

Conrad Bergendoff
*Augustana College, Rock Island, Ill.*

**CONCORD GRAPE,** kon'kərd grāp, the foremost native American grape variety, grown mainly for the grape juice industry. It is a medium-to-large, black, strong-flavored grape; its thick, easily removable skin is covered with a delicate powdery coating (bloom). The Concord grape and many other varieties, such as the Catawba, cultivated in eastern North America are descendants of the fox grape (*Vitis labrusca*), native to that area. The native grapes are relatively resistant to the parasites that make cultivation of the European grape, *V. vinifera*, extensively grown in California, impracticable in eastern North America.

From the time of its development from a wild grape seed planted in 1843 by Ephraim W. Bull, of Concord, Massachusetts, the Concord grape has played a dominant role in the expansion of grape growing in eastern North America. Its continued popularity is principally the result of its ability to thrive in many soil types, its consistently high productivity, and the high quality of its pasteurized juice. The Concord has been used in the development of many other varieties.

LAWRENCE ERBE
*University of Southwestern Louisiana*

**CONCORD SCHOOL OF PHILOSOPHY,** an informal summer school in Concord, Mass., founded in 1879 by Bronson Alcott and William Torrey Harris. The school, conducted on Alcott's farm, was devoted to the exposition of transcendentalism, Hegelianism, and educational theory. Its speakers included William James, John Fiske, Noah Porter, and James McCosh. The school's sessions were discontinued in 1887.

**CONCORDANCE,** kon-kôr′dəns, an alphabetical arrangement of key words, context lines, and the place where they are found in a book or collection of writings. Concordances were first compiled to versions of the Bible and later to the works of noted authors.

The first recognized concordance to the Latin Vulgate was compiled by Hugh of St. Cher about 1230. Rabbi Isaac Nathan ben Kalonymus compiled the first Hebrew Bible concordance, published in Venice in 1523. Other Hebrew concordances are those of Solomon Mandelkern (3d ed. 1955) and Gerhard Lisowsky (1958). The first Greek Bible concordance was that of Sixt Birck (1546). Others include the standard work of Edwin Hatch and H. A. Redpath (1897) and the *Concordance to the Greek [New] Testament* of H. Moulton and A. S. Geden (4th ed. 1963).

John Marbeck prepared the first English Bible concordance (1550). Alexander Cruden's classic concordance to the King James Version (1737) is still in use. Later ones include R. Young's (1879) and J. Strong's, which was keyed both to the King James and to the Revised Version (1894). N. W. Thompson and R. Stock compiled a concordance to the Rheims-Douay Version (1942), and using an electronic computer, J. W. Ellison compiled one to the Revised Standard Version (1957).

ROBERT P. MARKHAM
*American Bible Society*

**CONCORDAT,** kon-kôr′dat, a solemn agreement entered into between the Roman Catholic Church and a sovereign civil state. It has the nature of a public treaty and the force of international law. A concordat may concern strictly temporal affairs, such as the ownership, administration, and disposition of church property, the taxation of such property, or the salaries of the clergy. It may also deal with chiefly spiritual questions, such as the appointment of bishops and pastors, the division of dioceses, or public liturgical functions. Sometimes it treats of so-called mixed matters, having both a temporal and spiritual content, such as questions concerning marriage, education, schools, or Catholic youth activities.

A concordat is usually entered into to settle an argument or to prevent one. In this sense, it can be compared to a peace treaty or a nonaggression pact. A concordat may grant a civil power certain rights and privileges in ecclesiastical affairs in order that the church may freely exercise what it believes to be its own most basic and essential rights without fear of interference from the civil authority. There have also been concordats of friendship that gave legal status to an already satisfactory church-state relationship, but these are relics of the past. Most modern concordats resulted from friction between the church and civil authorities. The universal Catholic Church, personified by the Holy See and represented by the pope as the supreme head of the church or by a general council is one of the contracting parties in a concordat; the other is a sovereign state, represented by its chief executive or official spokesman. The sovereign principality known as Vatican City is not the ecclesiastical party in a concordat. However, parts of the concordat known as the Lateran Accord (1929) between the Holy See and the Italian government had the character of a civil treaty between Italy and the newly created Vatican City; by it, the temporal claims of the Papal States were settled and the areas of papal temporal sovereignty were established.

The first formal concordat was probably the Concordat of Worms, negotiated on Sept. 23, 1122 by Pope Callistus II and Emperor Henry V, which settled the investiture struggle. By it the Emperor renounced the right of spiritual investiture of bishops with ring and crosier, and in turn, was given the right of lay investiture with the scepter as a sign of temporal authority. Since that time more than 150 formal concordats have been entered into by the Holy See. The most notable are the concordats of Pius VII with France and Napoleon Bonaparte in the early 19th century; the concordat of 1929 between Pius XI and Benito Mussolini; and the concordat with Germany in 1933.

Concordats cease to bind in the same way as treaties between states. They may not be renounced or changed unilaterally, but may be altered, amended, or rescinded by mutual consent.

DAMIAN J. BLAHER, O.F.M.
*Holy Name College, Washington, D.C.*

**CONCORDE.** See under SUPERSONIC TRANSPORT.

**CONCORDIA,** kông-kôr′thyä, a trading center in northeastern Argentina. It is on the Uruguay River opposite Salto, Uruguay, 225 miles (360 km) north of Buenos Aires. Concordia is one of the largest cities in Entre Ríos province. It ships grain, fruit, and other agricultural products downriver to Buenos Aires and also has a considerable trade with Uruguay and Brazil. Food processing is its main industry. The city, which was founded in 1832, is modern. It has a golf course, a race track, a theater, and pleasant parks. Population: 138,905 (1991 preliminary census).

**CONCORDIA,** kon-kôr′dē-ə, in Roman mythology, was the goddess of peace and harmony. As Concordia Augusta, she presided over the peace of the imperial household. In 367 B.C., when the plebeians of Rome won political equality, a temple on the Capitoline Hill was erected in her honor, symbolizing the union of citizens. Her closest equivalents in Greek mythology were Aphrodite Pandemos, symbol of earthly or common love, and Harmonia, wife of Cadmus.

Concordia is represented as a matron, bearing an olive branch and a cornucopia.

**CONCRETE,** kon' krēt, is a composite material whose key ingredient is a binding medium in which small pieces of rock or other materials are embedded. The small pieces are called aggregate; the binder is a cementing material. In portland-cement concrete, the binder is a mixture of portland cement and water. Asphalt and other cements are used to make some types of concrete, but the term "concrete" generally refers to portland-cement concrete.

Concrete is the most versatile and widely used building material. It is used in dams, canals, and aqueducts; in highways, pavements, and sidewalks; and in buildings, bridges, and other structures, both as a structural and as a decorative material.

Where concrete is not used as the primary structural material, it may be used for fireproofing, waterproofing, or soundproofing. Concrete also acts as a shield against damaging nuclear radiation.

Concrete is of such importance that almost every civil engineering structure uses it. On a worldwide basis the yearly production of concrete amounts to approximately one ton per capita.

### CONTENTS

### HISTORY

Some form of concrete has been used by man for the past 5,000 years. The Egyptians used lime mortar in building the pyramids. The mortar was made by heating off limestone ($CaCO_3$) in primitive kilns, driving off carbon dioxide ($CO_2$) gas. The resulting calcium oxide (lime) was mixed with aggregate and used as mortar. The lime hardened as it absorbed $CO_2$ gas from the air and returned to the original $CaCO_3$, or limestone, form.

The Romans are credited with the discovery of hydraulic cement, which is a cement that will set in the presence of water. The Romans made hydraulic cement by mixing lime paste with a pozzolanic volcanic ash from Mt. Vesuvius. A pozzolan is an amorphous silica that hardens as a silica gel by reacting chemically with alkalis in the presence of water. The name is derived from Pozzuoli, an Italian town, where a pozzolan composed of glassy tuff was found. Pozzolanic cement was used in such notable structures as the Pantheon and the Colosseum, and it was used in aqueducts and the Appian Way. Many of these structures are still in existence, which indicates the high quality and durability of concrete made by the Romans.

The art of making cement was lost after the fall of the Roman Empire, and it was not until 1756 that hydraulic cements were used again.

PORTLAND CEMENT ASSOCIATION

**RIPPLING DESIGN** of the Benedictine Priory at Creve Coeur, Mo., demonstrates the versatility of concrete.

John Smeaton was commissioned to rebuild the Eddystone lighthouse off the coast of Cornwall, England. After he found by experiment that better limes could be made from limestone containing considerable clay, he built a sturdy lighthouse using hydraulic lime. Smeaton is credited with being the first to reestablish the use of hydraulic cement, which was the forerunner of natural cement.

A patent was issued to James Parker of England in 1796 for a natural cement made by burning impure limestone. His product, called Roman cement, was widely used in concrete structures. Natural cements were made from clay-bearing limestones that were burned, cooled, and then ground into a fine powder; these impure limestones, called cement rocks, naturally contained suitable amounts of lime, silica, and alumina. Natural cements were used quite extensively in the United States in the 1820's; the most important concrete structure built during this period was the Erie Canal.

In 1824 an English brickmason, Joseph Aspdin, patented a cementing material that he produced by burning limestone and clay together. He named his product portland cement because its color resembled that of a limestone quarried on the Isle of Portland, a peninsula on the English coast. Aspdin is commonly considered to be the inventor of modern portland cement, but it is recognized that portland cement, a hydraulic cement, was a natural development from hydraulic lime, natural cements, and similar products.

The first portland-cement plants in the United States were established in Pennsylvania in 1875, and the first mile of concrete road was laid in Michigan in 1909. The use of portland cement

**507**

## HYDRATION OF COMPOUNDS IN PORTLAND CEMENT

$$2(3CaO \cdot SiO_2) \quad + \quad 6H_2O \quad \longrightarrow \quad 3CaO \cdot 2SiO_2 \cdot 3H_2O \quad + \quad 3Ca(OH)_2$$
(TRICALCIUM SILICATE)    (WATER)    (TOBERMORITE GEL)    (CALCIUM HYDROXIDE)

$$2(2CaO \cdot SiO_2) \quad + \quad 4H_2O \quad \longrightarrow \quad 3CaO \cdot 2SiO_2 \cdot 3H_2O \quad + \quad Ca(OH)_2$$
(DICALCIUM SILICATE)    (WATER)    (TOBERMORITE GEL)    (CALCIUM HYDROXIDE)

$$4CaO \cdot Al_2O_3 \cdot Fe_2O_3 \quad + \quad 2Ca(OH)_2 \quad + \quad 10H_2O \quad \longrightarrow \quad 6CaO \cdot Al_2O_3 \cdot Fe_2O_3 \cdot 12H_2O$$
(TETRACALCIUM ALUMINOFERRITE)    (CALCIUM HYDROXIDE)    (WATER)    (CALCIUM ALUMINOFERRITE HYDRATE)

$$3CaO \cdot Al_2O_3 \quad + \quad Ca(OH)_2 \quad + \quad 12H_2O \quad \longrightarrow \quad 3CaO \cdot Al_2O_3 \cdot Ca(OH)_2 \cdot 12H_2O$$
(TRICALCIUM ALUMINATE)    (CALCIUM HYDROXIDE)    (WATER)    (TETRACALCIUM ALUMINATE HYDRATE)

$$3CaO \cdot Al_2O_3 \quad + \quad CaSO_4 \cdot 2H_2O \quad + \quad 10H_2O \quad \longrightarrow \quad 3CaO \cdot Al_2O_3 \cdot CaSo_4 \cdot 12H_2O$$
(TRICALCIUM ALUMINATE)    (GYPSUM)    (WATER)    (CALCIUM MONOSULFOALUMINATE)

TRANSFORMATION OF COMPOUNDS occurs when water is added to portland cement. As shown in the top two lines, the two calcium silicates, which constitute about 75 per cent of a portland cement by weight, react with water to produce two new compounds: calcium hydroxide and a calcium silicate hydrate called tobermorite gel. Next two lines show how the other two major compounds in portland cement react with water. The bottom line shows the reaction involving gypsum, a fifth compound in cement.

made it possible to produce high-quality concretes at a relatively low cost and led to the wide use of concrete as a structural material.

Modern portland cements are a vast improvement on the product patented by Aspdin, even though they are still made from the same basic ingredients. Because of the abundance of these ingredients, there is a portland cement plant in practically every convenient location in the world where a market is available. Standardization, careful selection of raw materials, and quality control in manufacturing provide uniformity of product among the many portland cement plants throughout the world. Approximately 65 million tons of portland cement are used annually.

## MATERIALS

**Portland Cement.** Portland cement is composed essentially of two of the most abundant elements of the earth's crust, silica and calcium. To make it, a lime-containing material (such as limestone, shell, or chalk) and a claylike material (such as shale, slate, or clay itself) are finely ground, carefully proportioned either dry or in a wet slurry, and fed into a rotary kiln. When the temperature in the kiln reaches about 2700°F (1682°C), the clay-bearing components become molten. In the meantime, the limestone, $CaCO_3$, has been reduced to calcium oxide (CaO) and carbon dioxide ($CO_2$). The calcium oxide reacts chemically with the molten clay material, forming silicates of calcium. Portland-cement clinker, which is the fused product formed in the kiln, is cooled and ground to a fine gray powder.

Calcium silicates ($CaO \cdot SiO_2$) make up about 75% of the total weight of portland cement. The remaining 25% is composed of tricalcium aluminate ($3CaO \cdot Al_2O_3$), tetracalcium aluminoferrite ($4CaO \cdot Al_2O_3 \cdot Fe_2O_3$), and small amounts of minor components. The properties of portland cement are largely determined by the relative proportions of these compounds.

### AVERAGE PERCENTAGES OF MAJOR COMPOUNDS IN FIVE BASIC TYPES OF PORTLAND CEMENT

| Type and Characteristic | Tricalcium Silicate | Dicalcium Silicate | Tricalcium Aluminate | Tetracalcium Aluminoferrite |
|---|---|---|---|---|
| Type I, normal general use | 53 | 24 | 8 | 8 |
| Type II, modified general use | 47 | 32 | 3 | 12 |
| Type III, high ecrly strength | 58 | 16 | 8 | 8 |
| Type· IV, low heat of hydration | 30 | 46 | 5 | 13 |
| Type V, sulfate resistant | 43 | 37 | 2 | 12 |

In chemical reaction with water, tricalcium silicate ($3CaO \cdot SiO_2$) sets relatively rapidly, producing high early strength and high heat of hydration. Dicalcium silicate ($2CaO \cdot SiO_2$) is slower setting and produces lower heat of hydration. Tricalcium aluminate produces very high heat of hydration; it has poor durability because it reacts with sulfate alkalis found in soil and water. Tetracalcium aluminoferrite is produced when iron is added to the kiln; this is the principal method for reducing undesirable aluminates.

**Aggregates.** Aggregates are usually inert materials that, when bound together into a conglomerated mass by portland-cement paste (the mixed portland cement and water), form concrete, mortar, or plaster. Aggregates make up about 75% of the total mass of concrete. Aggregates are classed as coarse or fine, depending on size.

*Coarse aggregate* is that portion of an aggregate that is retained on a No. 4 (4.76 mm) sieve. Coarse aggregate comes from natural gravel deposits, which are formed by water, wind, or glacial action. Coarse aggregates are also manufactured by crushing rock, stone, boulders, and large cobblestones.

Suitable concrete aggregates can be formed from nearly all of the minerals found in the earth's crust. The aggregates should be free from harmful materials such as clay, soluble salts, and organic materials.

*Sand, or fine aggregate,* is generally the product of natural disintegration of silica-bearing or calcium-bearing rock. Almost all of the sand should pass through a No. 4 sieve and be predominantly retained by a No. 200 (74-micron) sieve. Fine aggregate is sometimes manufactured from larger pieces of aggregate by crushing, grinding, and rolling. The four common kinds of coarse-aggregate minerals are: (1) limestone or calcium-bearing material; (2) basalts, granite, and related igneous rocks; (3) sandstones and quartzites; and (4) rocks, such as opal and chert, composed mainly of amorphous silicon dioxide.

**Water.** For concrete mixtures, water should not contain substances that harm the concrete. In general, water that is acceptable for drinking purposes is also satisfactory for use as mixing water in concrete. Excessive amounts of silt, oil acids, alkalis, salts of alkali, organic matter, or sewage in water have an injurious effect upon concrete.

**Admixtures.** As defined by the American Society for Testing and Materials, an admixture is a material other than water, aggregate, or portland cement that is used as an ingredient in concrete and is added to the batch immediately before or during its mixing. Admixtures are used in cements, mortars, and concretes to improve workability or consistency, improve durability, increase strength, accelerate strength development, retard or accelerate the initial setting, retard or reduce the evolution of heat, control alkali-aggregate expansion, and increase density and reduce permeability.

Air-entraining admixtures greatly improve the durability of concrete by entraining billions of microscopic air bubbles, which are distributed throughout the matrix of the concrete. These tiny air bubbles are very large compared with the capillary voids and the gel pores in portland-cement paste. The air bubbles provide space for the relief of pressure built up in the smaller cavities when they are filled with water, which expands when it freezes.

Water-reducing admixtures minimize the amount of mixing water that is needed. These admixtures are adsorbed onto the surface of particles of portland cement and give each particle a negative charge. The cement particles, consequently, repel each other, and they disperse when they are mixed with water rather than being attracted to each other. The dispersion of the cement releases approximately 10% of the mixing water entrapped by clusters of cement particles. This released water provides additional workability and consistency without an increase in the original amount of the mixing water. A higher quality paste is achieved with the reduction in the water requirement.

Pozzolans are added to concrete because of their ability to react with soluble alkalis that are produced as a hydration product when portland cement is mixed with water. Pozzolans provide an additional cementing material which has a lower heat of hydration and, in addition, they react with any free alkalis in concrete, thus inhibiting chemical reaction between reactive aggregates and cement with a high alkali content.

Accelerating admixtures are added to increase the rate of hydration of portland cement when early strength is desired. Retarding admixtures decrease the rate of hydration in hot weather or when a delayed set is desirable.

## HOW CONCRETE IS MADE

The steps in the manufacture of concrete are handled by different organizations. Portland cement, the cementing ingredient, is manufactured by the portland-cement industry. The sand and gravel industry provides aggregates for concrete. The final step in manufacture, proportioning the concrete mixture, is controlled by the purchaser or final consumer of concrete. Proportioning of the concrete ingredients is the most difficult manufacturing step to control, and it is one of the most important in producing high quality, economical concrete.

**Proportioning Concrete Mixtures.** Proper proportioning of the ingredients of concrete provides a balance between the requirements of economy and those of workability, strength, durability, and appearance. The required characteristics are usually governed by specifications for the properties of concrete desired for a particular use.

Numerous methods for proportioning concrete mixtures have been proposed, based on relationships between the grading of aggregates, volume of voids within the mixture, amount of water, and quantity of portland cement. In 1918, Duff A. Abrams, an American research scientist, discovered that the ratio of the amount of water to the amount of cement in a concrete mix (the water-cement ratio) is related to the strength and quality of the concrete. Since that time it has been found that many other variables influence the strength of concrete, but the water-cement ratio law still provides a basis for predicting strength and, to some extent, other desirable properties of concrete.

In the early 1940's it was found that the durability of concrete can be increased tenfold by the use of small amounts of an air-entraining agent in a concrete mixture.

The discovery of the water-cement ratio law and the use of entrained air are considered to be the two major turning points in concrete technology in this century.

**Consistency.** In proportioning, mixes of the stiffest consistency that can be placed efficiently should be used. Slump, or subsidence, is a measure of the consistency.

FLOATING CONCRETE BRIDGE over Lake Washington, Seattle, Wash., is the world's longest pontoon bridge.

HERBERT LANKS, FROM BLACK STAR

**Aggregate.** In general, the largest size of aggregate that is consistent with the dimensions of the structure and the limitations of the mixing and placing equipment should be used.

**Mixing Water.** The amount of mixing water per cubic yard of concrete influences the consistency of the concrete. The proper amount of mixing water to produce a given consistency varies with the textures and sizes of the aggregates, the cement used, and factors such as temperature.

**Air Content.** Besides some air that is normally entrapped in a concrete mix, entrained air is added to obtain maximum durability of concrete. The entrapped-air content ranges from about 0.3 to 3% by volume; with entrained air, the average total air content ranges from about 3.5 to 8% by volume.

**Water-Cement Ratio.** The required water-cement ratio is usually determined by strength requirements, although other properties, such as durability, may govern it. In general, concrete with low water-cement ratios is more durable than concrete with high water-cement ratios.

**Mixing.** The ingredients should be mixed thoroughly to produce uniform concrete. The mixing action of a concrete mixer blends all ingredients and works the cement paste into the surface of the aggregate particles.

**Mixing on the Job.** Mixing is usually done in the field with revolving mixers. A tilting mixer usually has a conical or bowl-shaped drum, whereas a nontilting mixer usually has a cylindrical drum and a manually operated, swinging discharge chute. Mixers in the field are equipped with a loading skip and are charged by means of a feed hopper.

In rare cases where concrete is mixed manually in the field, the ingredients are measured by weight or by volume. The aggregates are usually weighed; but water is measured in gallons, and cement is measured by sacks.

**Centralized Ready-Mix Plants.** The suppliers of ready-mix concrete are among the newer members of the concrete industry. Until recently the contractor or consumer purchased the various ingredients of concrete, moved them to the site of construction, and proportioned and mixed them in a concrete mixer. Now, concrete of any desirable proportions or quality for numerous special purposes can be ordered directly from the ready-mix concrete producer; the desired type and quantity of concrete is delivered to the project site very rapidly. In a modern ready-mix concrete plant the production of the various concrete mixes is programmed by an electronic computer, and batches of concrete of any desired size are proportioned automatically by electronic control. All ingredients are measured by weight.

In ready-mix plants concrete is mixed either in mobile mixers or in stationary mixers. When a batch of concrete is placed in a mobile mixer at the plant, the mixing takes place from the time the mixer leaves the plant until it reaches the job site. When a ready-mix concrete plant uses a stationary mixer, the concrete is mixed before it is placed in a truck mixer, where the concrete is only agitated. Mixing at the plant provides more accurate control of the consistency and other properties of the fresh concrete.

Tilting mixers are one type of mixer used in central mixing plants. The large tilting mixers are tilted upward to receive the charge of mix ingredients, are held approximately level during the mixing cycle, and are then tilted downward to discharge into the truck mixers.

**Hand Mixing for Home Use.** Anyone can produce good concrete by obtaining portland cement from the local lumberyard and mixing it with water, sand, and gravel. If the sand and gravel are clean and sound, and if about one half as much water as cement by weight is used, the product will be a high-quality concrete. A good mix proportion is 1 pound (0.45 kg) of water, 2 pounds (0.91 kg) of cement, 4 pounds (1.8 kg) of sand, and 5 pounds (2.3 kg) of coarse aggregate.

In order to help the home user, the ingredients of concrete mix, with the exception of water, are prepared and sold as dry-mix concrete. All that is necessary to produce concrete is to add water to this mixture.

**Placing.** One of the most important characteristics of concrete is the ease with which it can be molded into any desired shape.

Ready-mix concrete is poured into a form (mold) by means of chutes at the back of the mixer truck. The blades in a truck mixer are designed so that, when the drum rotates in the opposite direction from that used for mixing or agitating, the concrete is lifted and discharged from a high opening in the back of the mixer.

When concrete is to be placed in a location inaccessible to ready-mix trucks, the concrete is discharged from the truck into a concrete bucket, lifted by a crane to the point of placement, and then discharged from the bucket.

In recent years concrete has sometimes been pumped to the point of placement through steel pipelines and rubber hoses. A strategically located pump can supply concrete to all parts of a structure, including those inaccessible to a truck or crane.

After the concrete is placed in its final location, it must be compacted to fill all the corners and recesses of the form. Compacting is also desirable to release all entrapped air. Compaction is most effectively accomplished by concrete vibrators—rapidly turning eccentric rods encased in a flexible shaft—which are placed in the concrete and cause it to consolidate to maximum density. A great advantage of the internal-vibration method is that a relatively low-consistency concrete can be used. This permits the use of low water content and results in concrete of higher quality.

**Curing.** The last step in the manufacture of concrete is curing, or hardening. Hardening of concrete is produced by the hydration of portland cement. Moist conditions must be maintained for a sufficient time to ensure adequate hydration of the portland cement. A common method of preventing the loss of moisture from a concrete surface is to keep the surface damp by sprinkling or covering it with water or by covering it with wetted burlap. An alternative method is to cover it with a membrane that acts as a barrier to evaporation.

During the mixing of concrete, more than enough water is added to hydrate the portland cement. If this water can be retained within the concrete mass, there will be more than sufficient moisture for curing. The evaporation of water within the concrete can be prevented by using membrane-curing compounds, which are sprayed on the surface of concrete immediately after it sets. Alternatively, waterproof paper or plastic coverings can be used to prevent evaporation.

POURING CONCRETE to build the Nimbus Dam across the American River near Sacramento, Calif. Framework for one of the buttresses is shown rising at the right.

Long curing periods are desirable to produce more complete hydration of portland cement. Sprinkling, water covering, or other methods of keeping the surface of concrete moist usually are discontinued after approximately seven days.

**Chemistry of Concrete.** The chemical reaction between portland cement and water is the principal action in the chemistry of concrete. Portland cement by itself does not provide a cementing binder; the cementing gel is formed by the reaction of portland cement and water. The setting of the cement paste takes place as the compounds that collectively make up portland cement are converted into their hydration products. The cement paste becomes hard within a week, but the hardening process may continue to some extent for months or even for years.

It is a common misconception that concrete hardens upon drying by evaporation. This is not true, because without water there is no reaction and no hardening. The water seems to disappear only because it combines (by hydration) with the portland cement. Only the excess water should be allowed to evaporate.

The chemical reactions that take place in the hydration of the compounds of portland cement are complex, and until recently no attempt was made to write a precise chemical formula for them. The presentation of the reactions shown in the table on page 508 is the first attempt to establish quantitative measures of the amount of water used in the hydration of cement.

### PROPERTIES

**Workability.** Concrete is said to be workable when it is (1) properly proportioned for transport and placed without segregation (nonuniform distribution of the particles of aggregate), (2) easily molded into desired shapes that completely fill the space it is to occupy, and (3) easily

finished. Other terms used in describing workability are consistency, plasticity, and mobility. Consistency is the degree of wetness or slump of a concrete mix; it varies directly with the amount of water in the mix. Plasticity is the ease with which fresh concrete can be molded or deformed without segregation. Mobility is the capacity of concrete for movement or flow, particularly during vibration.

Concrete should be proportioned to produce the workability required for the structure. Fairly stiff concrete can be placed for pavements, because the concrete can be vibrated and tamped. The workability of this concrete would not be suitable for thin wall structures, where concrete must be compacted with a minimum of vibration. A semifluid consistency is required for concrete in applications where it must flow in order to fill all of the space it is to occupy.

**Strength.** Concrete in structures is subjected to compressive, tensile, flexural, and shearing forces. The strength of concrete is its ability to resist the stresses caused by these forces. This important property determines the load-carrying capacity of concrete structures.

Many factors influence the strength of concrete. The principal factor is the water-cement ratio used in the concrete mix. In general, a low water-cement ratio makes a high-quality portland-cement paste. Because this paste is the binder in concrete, it has the most important influence on the strength of concrete. Low water-cement ratios also produce other desirable properties of concrete, such as watertightness, abrasion resistance, and durability.

In mixes that have low water-cement ratios, the strength of concrete can be increased significantly by increasing the total surface area of the aggregates. This is accomplished by using smaller aggregates. Strength can also be increased by using aggregates having a surface texture that improves the bond strength between portland-cement paste and the aggregate particle.

**Durability.** The durability of concrete is its ability to resist the forces of deterioration. The forces that cause concrete to deteriorate include freezing and thawing of water-saturated concrete, expansion caused by the reaction between reactive aggregates and alkalis in cement, reactions between soil and water sulfates and the hydrated portland cement, and expansion and shrinkage caused by wetting and drying, respectively.

*Freezing and Thawing.* The freezing of water in the pore structure of concrete causes it to expand about 9% in volume. If the concrete is saturated and the pore structure cavities are filled, freezing water is forced into the surrounding hydrated portland-cement gel structure. The pressures caused by expansion of freezing water may be sufficient to damage the gel structure and cause deterioration of the concrete. The danger can largely be overcome by the entrainment of air bubbles, which provide for relief of the pressure in freezing concrete.

Another deterioration mechanism is the growth of ice crystals under the surface of pavements, causing the concrete to scale. The growth of ice crystals can be inhibited by entraining air in the concrete. Water forced into the larger air voids will freeze and compete for available water, thus depriving the capillary ice of sufficient moisture for dangerous growth.

*Reactions Between Aggregates and Cement Alkalis.* Chemical reaction between reactive aggregates and a portland cement with a high alkali ($K_2O$ and $Na_2O$) content causes expansion, which can lead to cracking and deterioration of the concrete. When there is an indication that the aggregates are reactive, a cement with a low alkali content is used.

*Reactions Between Sulfates and Cement.* Unprotected concrete is actively attacked by sodium and magnesium sulfates that are present in alkali soils and some corrosive waters. These sulfates react with the hydrated portland cement. As a result, the concrete corrodes and disintegrates. Sulfate-resistant cements have been developed for use in such conditions. Low water-cement ratios and an increase in watertightness provide added protection from sulfate attack.

*Shrinkage and Expansion.* Concrete tends to swell upon wetting and to shrink upon drying. Swelling takes place when moisture enters the gel structure of the hydrated portland cement. The tiny crystals of the hydrated portland cement are long and thin and resemble a pile of matches in which the matches of each layer are at right angles to the matches of the layer below. As moisture enters, these crystal layers tend to be forced apart, causing swelling of the cement gel. As concrete drys out, this layered structure becomes more compact, causing shrinkage of the concrete.

Shrinkage also occurs because the volume of the portland cement and water gradually decreases as chemical combination proceeds during hydration. The hydration product, therefore, does not occupy all the space originally required for the fresh paste.

An increase in temperature will cause thermal expansion of concrete due to the increased energy in the atomic structure. This increased activity decreases as the concrete cools. A large difference between the temperature of the outside surface of the concrete and the temperature of the interior mass will cause fine cracks in the concrete.

**Watertightness.** Although concrete is used extensively in dams, water tanks, aqueducts, and other structures, it is not completely watertight, since the excess water used to obtain workable mixes creates capillary voids in the portland-cement paste. Because the capillary voids in concrete are very small, the resulting permeability of concrete is not significant for most uses.

However, the ingress of water into a porous or permeable concrete can cause it to reach the critical saturation point for freezing and thawing actions that deteriorate it. If the concrete is porous or permeable, harmful salts and acids also may permeate the inner structure of the concrete matrix. There is also a slow weakening of concrete structures when pure water from rain or snow slowly dissolves the soluble components of hydrated portland cement.

The watertightness of concrete can be improved by use of the minimum amount of mixing water that is practical for placement of the concrete. Density-increasing agents, which permit a reduction of the amount of mixing water, are sometimes used for this purpose.

**Unit Weight.** The weight of concrete per unit volume (specific gravity) depends on the weight per unit volume of the ingredients, the mix proportions, and the amount of compaction used to consolidate the concrete. The weight of freshly mixed concrete per unit volume is important in computations pertaining to proportioning the mix.

The total weight of all the ingredients in a concrete mix must equal the weight of concrete per cubic yard, or one cubic yard of concrete will not be obtained from the batch. Therefore, the mix proportions must be adjusted so that the total weight of the mix ingredients per cubic yard will equal the weight of concrete per cubic yard.

Heavy concrete for shielding atomic reactors contains heavy ores as aggregates to obtain a concrete with a unit weight of more than 200 pounds per cubic foot (3,200 kg per cubic meter). For heat-insulating concrete, lightweight aggregates are used to obtain a concrete with a unit weight as low as 50 pounds per cubic foot (800 kg per cubic meter).

**Chemical Resistance.** Because hydrated portland cement is chemically a base, it will react with most acids; this reaction causes concrete to disintegrate.

Concretes of low water-cement ratio and high density are more resistant to chemical attack than the more porous concretes of high water-cement ratios. In some cases, however, even the highest quality concrete must be protected from direct contact with corrosive chemicals. For this reason concrete in areas subject to chemical attacks is given a protective coating.

Magnesium fluorosilicate or zinc fluorosilicate hardens the surface of concrete by chemical action and makes it more impervious to chemical attack. Sodium silicate (water glass), linseed oil, synthetic resins, paints, and varnishes have also been used as protective coatings for concrete.

**Fire Resistance.** Concrete is used extensively to fireproof steel beams because it has a low thermal conductivity. The gel structure of hydrated portland cement does not break down until a temperature of approximately 2000°F (1093°C) is reached; and the point of fusion of most aggregates is reached only at very high temperatures.

The kind of aggregate that is used affects the fire resistance of concrete. Limestone or other calcium-bearing aggregates are the least effective in their resistance to fire. The basalts and related igneous rocks are more resistant than limestone but are less resistant than granites and sandstones. Aggregates made of quartz and quartzites have the highest resistance to fire.

## TYPES OF CONCRETE CONSTRUCTION

**Reinforced Concrete.** The tensile strength of concrete is usually only about 10% as great as the compressive strength. In order to make practical use of concrete, steel reinforcement is placed within the concrete member to carry the tensile stresses.

Concrete and steel work well together in reinforced concrete because they have similar coefficients of thermal expansion, and a suitable bond can be made between the concrete and the steel rods. Concrete also protects the reinforcing steel from fire and corrosion. Reinforcing is placed in a structural member so that all tensile stresses are transferred from the concrete to the steel. In concrete beams between two supports, steel is placed in the lower portions of the beam where tension stresses due to bending are concentrated. Where beams or floors extend continuously over several supports, concrete may be subjected to tension in the upper side of the member. In this case it is necessary to use steel reinforcement in a position to withstand these tensile stresses. In columns, poles, and chimneys, it is necessary to reinforce all portions that may be subjected to tensile stress. (For weight saving and efficiency, reinforced concrete now is used sometimes as a substitute for cast iron or steel in the structures of heavy machines.)

**Historical Background.** Some structures in ancient Greece show that the builders knew something about reinforcing stonework for additional strength. In modern times, concrete reinforced with iron bars was developed in France. Joseph L. Lambot built a small reinforced concrete boat in 1849 and exhibited it at the Paris Exposition in 1855. Lambot also suggested the use of reinforcement in a concrete beam. A patent for a reinforced concrete floor was issued to W. D. Wilkinson of England in 1854. François Coignet published a book in 1861 in which he described many uses for reinforced concrete.

The first practical use of reinforced concrete is credited to Joseph Monier, who, in 1867, acquired his first French patent for iron-reinforced concrete tubs for use in his nursery in Paris. Monier continued his work in reinforced concrete, obtaining patents for reinforced concrete tanks, bridges, and stairways.

Pioneering work with reinforced concrete in the United States was done by Thaddeus Hyatt, who experimented with reinforced concrete beams in the 1850's and published his findings in 1877. Ernest L. Ransome used some form of reinforced concrete as early as 1870; he also placed wire rope and hoop iron in many structures, and he patented a deformed reinforcing bar in 1884. During the 1890's various theories and test results were published in Europe. The first textbook on reinforced concrete appeared in 1899.

GENERAL DYNAMICS

PREFABRICATING concrete units speeds construction. Here a prestressed member is swung into place.

Since 1900 there have been vast improvements in reinforced concrete design and construction. Only a few tons of reinforcing steel were used in the United States in 1900, whereas reinforced concrete is now a major structural material. The first building built wholly of reinforced concrete in the United States was the William E. Ward House (1876) in Port Chester, N. Y. The first reinforced concrete skyscraper was the Ingalls Office Building (1902) in Cincinnati, Ohio. Reinforced concrete now is used in the largest and most complex engineering projects and is also used for a wide variety of purposes.

**Prestressed Concrete.** The basic principle of prestressed concrete is that the reinforcing steel is under tension, while the concrete is under compression. When a prestressed concrete member is stretched by an applied tensile force, the stress is carried by the steel, which has very high tensile strength. In the concrete part of the member, the stretching relaxes the preexisting compression but does not ordinarily place the concrete under tension. Since concrete is about 10 times as strong in compression as it is in tension, prestressing thus makes use of concrete's characteristic strength. Also, because all of the concrete in prestressed members is in compression, there is negligible cracking due to shrinkage.

Prestressing is applied to steel or concrete for two purposes: first, to induce desirable strains and stresses in the structure, and second, to counterbalance undesirable strains and stresses. In prestressed concrete, the steel reinforcement is prestretched to avoid later excessive lengthening under service loads. The concrete is precompressed to prevent later cracking under tensile stress. This is an ideal combination of the compressive strength of concrete with the tensile strength of steel, and is responsible for the basic desirability of prestressed concrete.

Prestressing has made it possible to increase the span length of concrete members in bridges, roofs, floors, and other structural members. It also enables architects and engineers to design shallower, lighter, and more graceful concrete structures.

**Methods of Prestressing.** Two methods are used to prestress concrete: pretensioning and posttensioning.

In pretensioning, steel-wire cables are stretched between two abutments to a predetermined stress; concrete is then placed around the steel-wire cables and is allowed to harden. Tensile forces in the steel are transferred to the concrete by bonding between the steel reinforcement and the concrete. After the concrete has reached a predetermined strength level, the cables are cut off at the ends of the concrete member.

In posttensioning, concrete is placed with ducts left in the concrete for the steel-wire cables. After the concrete has reached a predetermined strength level, the steel-wire cables are threaded through the ducts left in the concrete member, are stretched to a predetermined tension stress with hydraulic jacks, and are then attached to anchorages on the ends of the member. Stress is transferred to the concrete by the end anchorages. Bonding between the cables and the concrete may also be prevented by greasing or wrapping the cables, which permits posttensioning. With this type of construction, anchorages on the ends of the members must be left in place permanently.

**Historical Background.** Prestressing was first used on an experimental basis by P. H. Jackson of San Francisco about 1886. However, early development of prestressing in the United States was concentrated on circular prestressing. In this case, the prestressing rods act like metal bands applied on wooden barrels.

The first practical development of prestressed concrete is credited to Eugène Freyssinet of France; he was the first to use high-strength steel wires for prestressing (about 1928). In 1939, Freyssinet developed a conical wedge for anchoring prestressing wires and used a double-acting jack to apply tension to the wires. Prestressed concrete was widely used in Europe, particularly in France and Belgium, shortly after World War II. During the period 1949–1953, 350 prestressed bridges were built in European countries. The first major prestressed concrete bridge in the United States was the Walnut Lane Bridge in Philadelphia, built in 1950. Since then the use of prestressed concrete has spread to every developed country. Prestressed concrete structural members now compete with structural steel for use in bridges, columns, roofs, floors, and other structures.

**Concrete Shells.** One of the more recent developments in concrete is the use of shells—thin slabs formed into various curved surfaces. The various surfaces that are readily fabricated as concrete shells are cylindrical, hyperbolic, elliptical, and parabolic curves. More complex forms, some resembling seashells, have been used to produce unusual shapes for architectural beauty and grace. Reinforced concrete is quite suitable for shell structures, because the concrete in the shell needs to resist only compressive stresses. All tensile forces are carried by reinforcing steel in the supporting plane surrounding the shell.

The common egg illustrates the tremendous load-carrying capacity imparted by curved surfaces. The egg has exceptional strength in compression with a uniform load bearing around its surface. If an eggshell were to be formed in a thin sheet of the same thickness, however, it would break under a very light load.

In 1920, Franz Dischianger and Ulrich Finsterwalder of Germany first applied the principle of shells to reinforced concrete construction. The use of shells in reinforced concrete construction has become common in modern building, particularly where the architect wants to create the unusual graceful and pleasing effects which are possible with the use of curved surfaces.

## SPECIAL KINDS OF CONCRETE

**Precast Concrete.** The versatility of concrete as a construction material permits its use for many purposes. Precast concrete, which is coming into more common use, is manufactured as concrete members of various sizes and shapes. The members are hauled to the site of construction and placed in a structure. There was no definite discovery of precast concrete because precasting is an adaptation of regular construction methods. The use of precast concrete has been limited by construction equipment capable of lifting the members into place. As better lifting equipment became available, larger precast concrete members were constructed and used.

The most notable example of precast concrete is precast, prestressed concrete. Large members are transported from the prestressing yard to the construction site. Precast concrete with conventional reinforcement is sometimes used to fabricate beams, columns, culverts, and bridge sections.

Concrete pipe is another important use for precast concrete, and it is built in a wide variety of sizes for a wide variety of uses. The principal uses for concrete pipe are conveyance of water or sewage. Thin-walled concrete pipe can be built with prestressed reinforcing; this pipe can withstand high pressures without leakage.

**Precast Concrete Wall Panels.** The use of precast concrete wall panels has grown rapidly because they speed construction and add to the beauty of completed structures. Exposed decorative aggregates of various shapes and textures provide the architect with numerous possibilities for creative art in buildings. Large-size precast curtain-wall panels and window units permit a simplified and more rapid construction of finished walls.

Precast concrete panels can be given an unusual and attractive appearance by the use of special aggregates of various colors and textures that are exposed in the panel face. These special aggregates include naturally occurring aggregates, such as gravels, limestone, quartz, marble, and granite, as well as manufactured materials, such as glass and ceramics. Decorative aggregates, because of their higher cost, are generally mixed in the facing concrete, which is backed up with concrete using regular aggregates.

**Concrete Building Blocks.** Concrete building blocks, which are usually compacted from a dry, coarse mixture of lightweight aggregate and portland cement, are one of the most important ma-

CRISSCROSSING concrete roads in a Los Angeles, Calif., freeway interchange.

terials in the building construction industry. A building block usually is constructed as a block that has a hollow core area greater than 25% of the overall cross-sectional area. Building blocks are constructed in modular dimensions in multiples of 4 inches (10.16 cm). Actual dimensions usually allow for a joint ⅜ inch (0.95 cm) wide.

**Lightweight Concrete.** The use of lightweight aggregates to reduce the weight of concrete is not new to the concrete industry. Cinders from commercial furnaces have been used for years to produce cinder blocks, which are made of portland cement and cinders.

During World War II great emphasis was placed on producing high-quality lightweight aggregates for use in constructing concrete ships; a shortage of steel during the war made it mandatory that other materials be used in shipbuilding. Since then, many different types of aggregates have been investigated. Lightweight aggregate for structural concrete now is usually composed of expanded shale, clay, or slate products. Oil shales or materials containing some organic material are crushed to desired sizes and expanded in a rotary or sintering kiln at high temperatures. The organic materials form gases at these high temperatures; these gases cause the aggregate to expand.

The strength of structural lightweight concrete made with expanded slate, shale, or clay is comparable to the strength of concrete made with natural aggregates, but the weight is reduced approximately one third. Lightweight aggregate concrete permits construction of longer spans, more slender members, and taller buildings. The deck of the San Francisco-Oakland Bay Bridge was one of the first major structures in which lightweight concrete was used to reduce the dead load of the bridge.

**Prepacked Concrete.** Prepacked concrete is a special type of concrete that is used primarily for repairing deteriorated concrete. Aggregates are prepacked or preconsolidated into the void space of the faulty concrete; portland cement grout is then pumped into the voids of the aggregates. This type of construction is particularly advantageous for underwater repairs. Prepacked concrete provides a tight bond to the original concrete and minimizes shrinkage.

**Terrazzo.** Terrazzo is used in decorative floors and walls. Concrete containing colored aggregates is ground and polished on the job. In most terrazzo floors, white portland cement and decorative aggregates are placed only in the upper surface of concrete floors. After the concrete has been compacted and allowed to set sufficiently, the floors are ground until the decorative aggregate particles are exposed. After sufficient concrete has been taken from the surface to expose the aggregate, the floors are polished. Terrazzo floors are very durable and beautiful.

WILLIAM A. CORDON
*Utah State University*

### Bibliography

Eglinton, M. S., ed., *Concrete and Its Chemical Behavior* (Am. Soc. of Civil Engs. 1987).
Iegel, Leonard S., and Limbruner, George, *Reinforced Concrete Design*, 2d ed. (Prentice-Hall 1986).
Neville, Adam M., *Properties of Concrete*, 3d ed. (Halsted Press 1981).
Peterman, M. B., and Carrasquillo, R. L., *Production of High Strength Concrete* (Noyes, 1986).
Wilby, C. B., *Structured Concrete* (Butterworths 1983).
Wittmann, Folker H., ed., *Concrete and Concrete Structures* (Brookfield Pub. Co. 1987).
Wynne, G., *Reinforced Concrete* (Reston 1981).

**CONCRETE,** in philosophy, refers to a particular thing exactly as it is, without analysis, abstraction, or any other mental operation. It is contrasted with *abstract,* which refers to an isolated quality shared by a general class of things. The term is used by such anti-positivistic and Hegelian philosophers as Bergson and Croce, who distinguish between an intuited (or immediately apprehended) object, which is concrete, and a conceptualized object, which is abstract. According to these philosophers, for an object to be correctly (concretely) understood, it must be grasped on its own terms through intuition. A conceptualized (abstract) object is necessarily distorted because it is understood in terms other than itself—that is, it is understood only in terms of concepts.

JOHN P. DREHER
*Lawrence University, Appleton, Wis.*

**CONCUBINAGE,** kon-kū′bə-nij, is the practice of cohabitation without legal marriage; the concubine being a mistress, paramour, or female dependent whose sole function is the entertainment and sexual gratification of her master. In the past, many different kinds of polygynous marriage in non-European and primitive cultures were mislabeled "concubinage" by missionaries and early anthropologists who interpreted them in terms of their own Judeo-Roman monogamy. What they called a concubine was actually a secondary wife.

Ancient Hebrew and Roman law decreed that a man could have only one wife at a time. However, both codes provided a certain legal status for the concubine. She usually came from a lower social class and brought no dowry, but there was no stigma attached to her position. The chief difference between the concubine and the wife was that the children of the concubine had either no inheritance rights or extremely limited ones. This pattern lasted in Europe until the Middle Ages despite church law which forbade concubinage.

Under Koranic law, a man might have four wives, but no provision was made for additional women. The concubines in the Muslim harems had no legal status, being little more than slaves. However, their children had certain rights and often inherited equally with legitimate heirs. This major difference between the Islamic and the European patterns of concubinage reflects the different positions of women in these two cultural traditions.

PRISCILLA C. WARD
*American Museum of Natural History*

**CONCUSSION** is a temporary disorder in brain function caused by a sudden forceful blow to the head. Its essential feature is a loss of consciousness lasting a few seconds or minutes with no residual neurological damage. It is not yet understood why unconsciousness occurs. It may be due to an interruption of the normal activity of the nerve cells in both the superficial and deep regions of the brain. It may also be due to a momentary separation of the connections between the nerve cells as the wave of pressure transverses the brain.

The major danger of a concussion lies in the more ominous and lasting forms of injury that may accompany it and at first may not be obvious. Such injuries include a contusion (bruise) or a laceration (tearing) of the brain or bleeding from a tear in one of the small veins or arteries lying between the brain and the skull.

The symptoms of a simple concussion are temporary, usually clearing up within a few hours. If the concussion is more severe, they may last several days. The most common symptoms are intermittent headache, occuring mostly when the person is active; brief giddiness when getting up from a recumbent position; and a slight difficulty in concentrating. A transient loss of memory is common.

The treatment of a concussion consists of rest for at least a few hours, combined with close observation of the patient for any neurological symptoms or signs that denote brain injury. To ease the headache pain, simple nonnarcotic drugs may be administered.

E. CHARLES KUNKLE, M. D.
*Maine Medical Center*

**CONDÉ,** kôN-dā, the name of one of the most important cadet branches of the French house of Bourbon. The seignieury of Condé-sur-l'Escaut was an ancient fief under the counts of Flanders. Marie de Luxembourg–St. Paul brought it to the house of Bourbon when she married Count François de Vendôme (1470–1495). Their son became Charles IV, Duke de Bourbon, after the death of his distant cousin Charles III, Duke de Bourbon, in 1527. Charles IV's third son, Louis, became the first Prince de Condé in the Bourbon line. The title remained in the family, descending through the male line for 10 generations, until 1830.

### THE CONDÉ LINE

François de Vêndome (d. 1495)
m. Marie de Luxemburg-St. Paul

Charles de Vêndome (1489-1537)
Duke Charles IV de Bourbon

Antoine (1518-1562)
Duke de Bourbon
King of Navarre

**HENRY IV** (1553-1610)
Duke de Bourbon
King of Navarre
King of France

Bourbon Kings of France

LOUIS I (1530-1569)
Prince de Condé

HENRI I (1552-1588)
Prince de Condé

François
(1558-1614)
Prince de Conti

HENRI II (1588-1646)
Prince de Condé

LOUIS II, the Great Condé
(1621-1686), Prince de Condé

HENRI JULES (1643-1709)
Prince de Condé

Armand (1629-1666)
Prince de Conti

The Conti Line

LOUIS III (1688-1710), Prince de Condé
m. Mlle. de Nantes, daughter of Louis XIV

LOUIS HENRI (1692-1740), Prince de Condé, Duke de Bourbon
m. (1) Marie Anne de Bourbon-Conti
(2) Charlotte von Hesse

LOUIS JOSEPH (1736-1818), Prince de Condé, Duke de Bourbon

LOUIS HENRI JOSEPH (1756-1830), Prince de Condé, Duke de Bourbon
m. Louise Marie d'Orléans

Louis Antoine Henri (1772-1804), Duke d' Enghien
Executed under Napoleon I. Last of the male line.

Louis I de Condé was the leader of the Huguenot (French Calvinist) party in the first years of the civil and religious wars; he was assassinated in 1569. His son Henri I also became a Huguenot leader, and like his cousin, Henri, Duke de Bourbon and king of Navarre (later Henry IV of France), he renounced his Huguenot faith to save his life at the time of the St. Bartholomew's Day massacre (1572). Henri I was succeeded by a posthumous son, Henri II, whose career as critic and rebel during the regency of Marie de Médicis was quite unheroic; his one great claim to fame was the fact that he fathered Louis II, better known as the Great Condé. The Great Condé won great renown as a soldier in the latter part of the Thirty Years' War (1618–1648). He married a niece of Cardinal Richelieu, the prime minister of France. She was both hunchbacked and very short, and her genes marked the family for the next two generations. Their son Henri Jules was debauched and dissolute. His son, Louis III, married one of the illegitimate daughters of Louis XIV.

In the 18th century one prince de Condé, Louis Henri, became first minister under the regency of the Duke d'Orléans. Another Condé, Louis Joseph, distinguished himself as a soldier in the Seven Years' War, and later formed the so-called "Army of Condé," made up of émigré noblemen, to wage war on the French Revolution. The next in the line, Louis Henri Joseph, fought under his father's banner against the revolution. His son, the Duke d'Enghien, was executed by Napoleon's orders in 1804. After the defeat of Napoleon, Louis Henri Joseph returned to France with Louis XVIII to become grand master of the royal household. He committed suicide in 1830 when Charles X was driven from the throne. The Condé princes were better educated than most noblemen of the day, and several of them toyed with literature.

JOHN B. WOLF
*University of Illinois at Chicago Circle*

**CONDE,** kôn-dä, **Henri II de** (1588–1646), French nobleman and intriguer. Henri II de Bourbon, Prince de Condé, was born at St.-Jean-d'Angély on Sept. 1, 1588, nearly six months after the death of his father, Prince Henri I de Condé. King Henry IV married the young prince to Charlotte de Montmorency, the beautiful daughter of the *Connétable* of France, with the intention of making the young lady the royal mistress, but his plan was foiled when the couple fled to Brussels.

After Henry IV was murdered in 1610, Henri de Condé returned to France and demanded a place in the regency government. He was refused. When the queen mother, Marie de Medicis, persisted in marrying the young king Louis XIII to a Spanish princess, Condé rallied a party of the great nobles and a large section of the Huguenots (French Calvinists) in opposition to the queen and her favorite, the Marquis d'Ancre. Although he was unable to stop the marriage, Condé did force the court to make concessions by the Treaty of Loudun (May 1616) and to grant him a huge sum of money. But in the fall of 1616, the queen's ministers persuaded her to have Condé arrested.

After emerging from three years' imprisonment Condé became a faithful servant of the crown. He supported Cardinal Richelieu and even persuaded his son, the Duke d'Enghien (later Prince Louis II, the Great Condé), to marry one of Richelieu's nieces. Prince Henri spent the remaining few years of his life pressing for favors for his famous son. He died in Paris on Dec. 26, 1646.

JOHN B. WOLF
*University of Illinois at Chicago Circle*

**CONDE,** kôn-dä, **Louis I de** (1530–1569), French nobleman of the house of Bourbon who was the founder of the Condé line. Born Louis de Bourbon at Vendôme on June 7, 1530, the third son of Duke Charles IV de Bourbon, he was the first of his line to carry the title Prince de Condé. Like his elder brother Antoine, the father of Henry IV of France, he was converted to Calvinism early in the period of the French Reformation. After the death of King Henry II in 1559, Louis emerged as one of the most important of the Huguenot (French Calvinist) chiefs.

Condé's personal and religious hostility to the Duke de Guise and his brother, whom Francis II had placed in control of the French government, led him to take part in the conspiracy of Amboise, a plot to capture the young king. The Duke de Guise discovered the plot, arrested and executed a number of the lesser members, and imprisoned Condé with the intention of having him executed. However, before Condé could be convicted, Francis II suddenly died. Condé's life was ultimately spared, for Catherine de Médicis, the queen mother and regent for Charles IX, felt she could not execute a prince of royal blood without danger of great difficulties for her government.

In 1563, by the pacification of Amboise, Condé secured religious toleration for the Huguenot nobility at the expense of the other groups in the Huguenot community. Three years later armed conflict again broke out, and Prince Louis became the leader of the Protestant forces. He was murdered on March 13, 1569, shortly after the Battle of Jarmac, by order of the Duke d'Anjou.

JOHN B. WOLF
*University of Illinois at Chicago Circle*

**CONDE,** kôn-dä′, **Louis II de** (1621–1686), French nobleman and general, Prince de Condé, who was known as the *Great Condé*. Born Louis de Bourbon in Paris on Sept. 8, 1621, he was given the title Duke d'Enghien at his birth. His parents were Prince Henri II de Condé, who was first prince of the blood, and Charlotte de Montmorency. Louis inherited the Condé title and the rank of first prince of the blood on the death of his father in 1646.

In order to secure a military command, Louis married Mlle. de Maille-Brézé, the niece of the prime minister of France, Cardinal Richelieu. His first military victory came in 1643, when he was only 22 years old; he practically annihilated the Spanish army at Rocroi. In the last years of the Thirty Years' War he added to his reputation by his exploits at the battles of Freiburg, Nördlingen, and Lens. In the first Fronde rebellion Condé sided with Cardinal Mazarin, Richelieu's successor, and the court, but subsequent disagreements with the cardinal led to Condé's arrest and imprisonment (1650). Within a year the tables were turned, and Mazarin retired to the Rhineland after freeing Condé and his brother, the Prince de Conti. Yet the princes were unwise, and Mazarin was able to undermine

GIRAUDON

THE GREAT CONDÉ (Louis II), in a painting by Juste d'Egmont that hangs in the Palace of Versailles.

their position. As a result Condé became the center of the revolt known as the Fronde of the Princes (1651–1652).

When the second Fronde collapsed, Condé joined the Spanish and served with Philip IV's armies in the Netherlands, though with somewhat less success than he had shown in the previous decade. By the Treaty of the Pyrenees (1659), which ended the war between France and Spain, Condé was restored to his French titles, fiefs, and rank as first prince of the blood, which he had lost as a result of his treason.

Condé was not given a new military command until 1668, when he directed a campaign into Franche-Comté. In the Dutch Wars, Condé served with the army that invaded the Rhineland and the United Netherlands in 1672. His part in the war was not particularly brilliant; at the crossing of the Rhine he was wounded and lost the king's confidence by a foolhardy act. In a rearguard action against the Dutch Imperial troops at Seneffe (1674), Condé turned what would have been a modest victory into a bloody, indecisive action.

In 1675, Condé was given the French command in Alsace. He was old and indecisive by this time, but so was the imperial commander, Raimund Montecuccoli, and the Prince's defensive campaign was a success.

Condé retired in the winter of 1675 to his beautiful estate at Chantilly, where he spent the last decade of his life following the career of his son, Henri Jules, reading books, and living the life of a country gentleman. Louis XIV never really forgave Condé for his part in the Fronde and his subsequent treason, but the King's hostility did not extend to Condé's family. Louis XIV gave his legitimatized daughter, Mlle. de Nantes, in marriage to Condé's grandson. Condé died at Fontainebleau on Dec. 11, 1686, after writing a humble letter to Louis XIV begging the king to forget and forgive his past actions.

JOHN B. WOLF
*University of Illinois at Chicago Circle*

**CONDELL,** kun'dəl, **Henry** (died 1627), English actor. His name is also spelled *Cundell*. He began his acting career probably about 1590 and was, along with Shakespeare, who mentioned him in his will, a member of the lord chamberlain's company of players. He was a partner with the Burbages in the Globe and Blackfriars theaters. With John Heminge he edited the famous first folio of Shakespeare's plays (1623). Condell retired about 1623 and died at Fulham, England, in December 1627.

**CONDEMNATION PROCEEDINGS,** are the means whereby the governmental power of eminent domain is implemented. (See also EMINENT DOMAIN.) To condemn land is to set it apart for public use on payment to the owner of just compensation.

These proceedings typically involve such issues as whether the use for which the property is intended is indeed public in nature, and whether adequate compensation is offered. As a result of a land condemnation proceeding, the private owner is divested of title to his property, and that title is vested in the governmental authority empowered to appropriate. The conveyance, or transfer, thus effected is generally deemed to bind all parties interested in the property, even those not directly participating in the proceeding. The owner and the government may avoid the necessity for the proceeding by entering into a contract conveying the property. Statutes generally require that the prescribed procedures be followed strictly, and noncompliance may void the condemnation. Some statutes require that the proceeding precede the taking of the property; others authorize the taking and then allow the owner to challenge it or petition for compensation.

In admiralty law, condemnation is the judgment of a court by which a vessel is forfeited to the government. Vessels may be condemned if they have engaged in piracy, if they have been seized at sea as a prize of war, if they have violated revenue, navigation, or neutrality laws, or if they are unfit and unsafe for navigation.

DOV GRUNSCHLAG
*Member of the New York Bar*

**CONDENSATION** applies to various physical and chemical transformations of matter. From the physical standpoint, condensation usually refers to the transformation of a substance from the gaseous to the liquid or solid state. In order to condense a gas, it must be compressed and cooled. Above a certain temperature, known as the critical temperature, the gas can be subjected to pressure without any condensation occurring. Below the critical temperature, the gas is commonly referred to as a vapor. In the condensation of a vapor to a liquid, the heat of vaporization must be removed. An apparatus used to effect this heat transfer is called a condenser.

Clouds (which consist of tiny particles of water) and precipitation are clear evidence that water vapor in the atmosphere condenses into the liquid or solid state. Condensation is greatly facilitated by the presence of condensation nuclei, such as smoke particles, ions, and minute salt crystals. In the absence of such nuclei, a gas may become highly supersaturated before condensation occurs.

In chemistry, the term condensation refers to a reaction in which two or more molecules combine, with the separation of water or some other simple substance such as hydrogen chloride, ammonia, or alcohol. An example of a condensation reaction is that between hexamethylenediamine, $H_2N-(CH_2)_6-NH_2$, and adipic acid, $HOOC-(CH_2)_4-COOH$, in which a hydrogen from $-NH_2$ reacts with an OH from adipic acid to form water. Upon elimination of the water molecule, a bond is formed between the two molecules. When the condensation reaction occurs continuously at both ends of the two molecules, the polymer nylon-66, $[\ldots-CO-NH-(CH_2)_6-NH-CO-(CH_2)_4-CO-NH-\ldots]_x$, is formed.

HERBERT LIEBESKIND
*The Cooper Union, New York*

**CONDENSED MILK.** See MILK—*Manufacturing Milk.*

**CONDENSER,** a device employed to condense a vapor to its liquid phase. In steam power plants condensers are used to reduce back pressure on turbines or engines. In refrigeration systems condensers are used to remove from the refrigerant the heat that it extracted from the cooled area. In various processing systems condensers are used to selectively recover certain components of a fluid.

Condensers can be classified as surface or contact. In surface condensers the vapor condenses on the tubing or other heat transfer surface, which in turn is chilled by the coolant (usually water). In contact condensers the vapor and coolant come into direct contact and are removed together.

The surface condenser is made in many forms but most are of the shell-and-tube type and employ water as a coolant. In its simplest form it is a shell (length of pipe of suitable diameter) to the ends of which previously drilled tube sheets are welded. Tubes are positioned lengthwise in the drilled holes of the tube sheets. Gasketed water headers are then bolted outside the tube sheets. These guide the circulating water into the tubes to make one or more passes through the bank of tubes. The vapor enters an opening made in the top or side of the shell and it condenses on the water tubes. The condensed liquid leaves at a low part of the condenser.

Contact condensers are classified as barometric or jet. In barometric condensers the vapor to be condensed (usually steam) passes into a chamber into which the coolant (water) is sprayed. When the vapor condenses and mixes with the coolant, the pressure in the chamber is reduced. The outlet is a long column called a barometric leg, which conserves the low pressure in the chamber. In jet condensers a high-velocity stream of the coolant entrains the condensed steam and carries it to the outlet where the reduction in velocity of the mixture results in increased pressure.

BURGESS H. JENNINGS
*Northwestern University*

**CONDENSER,** in electrical engineering. See CAPACITOR.

**CONDILLAC,** kôn-dĕ-yȧk', **Étienne Bonnot de** (1715–1780), French philosopher. A contemporary of Jean Jacques Rousseau and Denis Diderot, Condillac was the only philosopher of the Encyclopedist era to create a systematic theory of knowledge. He was strongly influenced by John Locke and was instrumental in introducing Lockean psychological orientation into French 18th century thought.

**Life.** Condillac was born at Grenoble on Sept. 30, 1715. He attended the Seminary of St. Sulpice, where he became an abbé. His official ties to the church were of little importance in his career, however, and he devoted his time to writing philosophical tracts. From 1758 to 1767 he was tutor to Ferdinand, son of the Duke of Parma, and in 1768, after his return to France, he was elected to the French Academy. He died at Flux, near Beaugency, on Aug. 3, 1780.

**Writings.** Condillac's early works, such as the *Essai sur l'origine des connaissances humaines* (1746), manifested an almost complete agreement with Lockean epistemology. However, with the publication of his famous *Traité des sensations* (1754), Condillac parted with Locke in claiming that sensations alone (rather than sensations and reflection) dictate the workings of the mind and are the source of all knowledge. Accordingly, all mental operations, including such "higher" faculties as comparing, judging, and willing, are reducible, in the long run, to sensation. Though many scholars considered this theory deterministic, with man as the sum of his sensations, Condillac in his *Extrait raisonné*, appended to later editions of the *Traité*, also argued for freedom of the will.

Condillac's other works include *Traité des systèmes* (1749) and *La logique* (1780, issued posthumously). His collected works were published in 23 volumes in 1798.

STEPHEN J. NOREN
*Wesleyan University*

**CONDITIONED RESPONSE.** See CONDITIONING.

**CONDITIONING,** in psychology, is a term that applies to two objectively different forms of simple learning. The first of these stems from the work of Ivan Pavlov and is called Pavlovian or, more often, *classical conditioning.* The second is often traced to the work of Edward L. Thorndike and is called Thorndikean, operant, or, more often, *instrumental conditioning.*

**Classical Conditioning.** Pavlov's work involved the conditioning of the reflex of salivation. The experimental animals were dogs that received a minor surgical operation to bring a duct of a salivary gland to the outside of the cheek so that saliva could be collected and measured. The typical Pavlovian procedure was to present some neutral stimulus, such as a light or a tone, and a few seconds later to present food or dilute acid that made the dog salivate. After a number of such pairings, salivation began to take place in response to the neutral stimulus.

The Pavlovian demonstration has provided us with a conventional vocabulary. Reflex salivation to the food or acid is called an *unconditioned reflex;* the food or acid itself, an *unconditioned stimulus.* Salivation to the neutral stimulus is a *conditioned reflex;* the neutral stimulus, *a conditioned stimulus.* Actually, the terms "conditioned" and "unconditioned" are the result of a mistranslation of Pavlov's writings. A more proper translation from the Russian would be "conditional" and "unconditional." There is a developing tendency in psychology and physiology to use the latter terminology.

The distinctive feature of classical conditioning is that the animal is subjected to an experimental treatment over which it has no control. The conditioned stimulus appears and the unconditioned stimulus follows no matter what the animal does.

**Instrumental Conditioning.** In instrumental conditioning, by contrast, rewards and punishments are contingent upon the animal's behavior. Thorndike's early studies were ones in which cats learned to escape from a cage, usually called a "puzzle box," by operating a latch or pulling a string. For each successful escape, the cat received a bit of fish as a reward. It is important to note that such reward was dependent upon the response in question. In more recent times, students of instrumental conditioning have begun to use devices invented by B. F. Skinner and usually called "Skinner boxes." In these experiments the subjects are most often pigeons or rats that learn to peck an illuminated key or to press a lever to obtain food or water or to escape from punishment. Students of instrumental conditioning have applied the terminology of classical conditioning to their procedures; accordingly, they speak of the act of pecking at a key or pressing a lever as a conditioned response.

**Conditioning in Humans.** Although the study of classical and instrumental conditioning began with work on lower animals, the procedures were quickly adapted to the study of conditioning in human subjects, particularly by the American experimental psychologists. The most famous of these applications of classical conditioning was the study of John B. Watson and R. Rayner who conditioned a fear reaction in an 11-month-old infant. These investigators presented the infant with a white rat and, a few seconds later, presented a sudden loud sound which made the infant cry. Prior to the experiment the infant had shown only positive reactions to the animal, but pairings of the rat (conditioned stimulus) and the loud sound (unconditioned stimulus) led to a change in the child's behavior so that: "The instant the rat was shown the baby began to cry." Following this experience, the infant seemed to be afraid not only of the rat but also of objects resembling a rat, such as a fur coat, a ball of absorbent cotton, and a dog. This example reveals the major importance of classical conditioning. It appears to be the process by which emotional reactions are modified and learned. Classically conditioned responses are characteristically automatic and "involuntary." Instrumentally conditioned responses, by contrast, are deliberate, purposeful, "voluntary" reactions.

**Features of Conditioning.** In spite of these differences between classically and instrumentally conditioned reactions, the two forms of learning possess certain features in common. Both display a process of gradual *acquisition* which depends upon *reinforcement*. The term "reinforcement" refers to the rewards and punishments used in instrumental conditioning and the unconditioned stimulus in classical conditioning. If reinforcement ceases (if food no longer follows the ring of the bell or if the rat no longer receives food for pressing the lever), the conditioned reaction disappears or, more technically, *extinguishes*. At least in part, this process of extinction is the result of the development of some fatiguelike inhibitory mechanism. The evidence for this is that, following a rest, an extinguished response will often reappear or, again technically, show *spontaneous recovery*. Both classically and instrumentally conditioned responses exhibit *gen-*

*eralization*. The fear reaction in the experiment of Watson and Rayner appeared not only in response to the rat but also to other similar objects. The term "stimulus generalization" is used to describe such spreading of conditioned reactions to similar stimuli. Finally, both types of conditioning display *discrimination*. The procedure for producing discrimination is to present two different stimuli that are to be discriminated, reinforcing one stimulus but not the other. In this way, the strength of the conditioned response is maintained to the reinforced stimulus and extinguished to the nonreinforced stimulus. These are, perhaps, the most basic phenomena associated with simple conditioned reactions. Any standard text on learning will, however, list as many as a dozen others.

**Factors in Conditioning.** Scientists interested in conditioning are to be found in many different fields: psychology, physiology, psychiatry, pharmacology, and neuroanatomy. Such scientists are concerned with two general types of question: the neurophysiological mechanisms associated with conditioning, and the circumstances that favor or hinder the development of conditioned responses. We now know that the biological mechanism of conditioning is extremely complex and that many levels of the nervous system are involved. There is even some evidence that a primitive form of conditioning may take place at the level of the spinal cord. In the second category, some of the circumstances related to conditioning are:

(1) The magnitude of the reward or punishment used as a reinforcer. The greater the reward or punishment, the better is the conditioning.

(2) The time between the conditioned and unconditioned stimuli in classical conditioning and between response and reinforcement in instrumental conditioning. Delays greater than a few seconds usually interfere with learning.

(3) The schedule of reinforcement. Particularly in instrumental conditioning, if the subject learns under conditions of partial reinforcement (receives reward or punishment for less than 100% of his responses), the effect upon performance will depend on the type of schedule. There is also this important effect: a schedule of partial reinforcement produces slower conditioning and responses extinguish much more slowly than responses reinforced on every occurrence. This is called the "partial reinforcement effect."

(4) Individual differences. Even in lower animals, there are greater differences in the ease with which conditioned responses can be established in individual organisms. The same thing is true at the human level. For example, young people condition more readily than old people; women more easily than men; suggestible people more readily than resistant people; anxious people more readily than nonanxious ones.

**Conditioning and Abnormal Behavior.** The study of classical conditioning has always been somewhat related to the study of abnormal behavior. Pavlov, for example, reported that it was possible to establish an "experimental neurosis" by subjecting a dog to a very difficult discrimination. In one experiment a dog was trained to salivate at the presentation of a circle. After the conditioned response had been established, a discrimination was obtained between the circle and an ellipse. The shape of the ellipse was then changed by stages until it was almost that of the circle. During this phase of the experiment, the discrimination training continued: the circle was followed by reinforcement but the ellipse was not. When the positive and negative stimuli became so similar that the animal could not distinguish between them, the dog began to sequeal and bark, kept wriggling about, and destroyed much of the experimental apparatus with its teeth.

**Behavior Therapy.** In recent years the methods of classical and instrumental conditioning have been extended to the treatment of psychiatric disorders. The name applied to these extensions is "behavior therapy." Joseph Wolpe, for example, has developed a form of therapy called *systematic desensitization.* If a patient comes to treatment because he experiences anxiety reactions, Wolpe may have him list the stimuli that evoke anxiety in order of strength. Then (sometimes under hypnosis) the weakest stimulus in the list is presented to him. Gradually stimuli capable of eliciting more and more intense anxiety are presented; the "desensitization" (extinction) of anxiety in response to the weak stimuli assists in extinguishing anxiety over the strongest ones.

The following case is typical of Wolpe's procedures. A 23-year-old bus driver was brought to the physician in a state of great anxiety after hitting a pedestrian. Although the victim had not been seriously injured, she bled profusely. The patient's fear of the sight of human blood dated back to age 13 when his father had been killed in an accident.

To desensitize the patient, he was hypnotized and instructed to visualize stimuli that aroused increasingly intense anxiety. A weak stimulus was a bloodtinged bandage; a strong stimulus was a ward full of injured bloody and hospitalized patients. After visualizing a series of such stimuli, the patient's fear of blood disappeared. As evidence of this, later on, he helped a man knocked over by a motorcycle and was absolutely unaffected by the blood.

Therapies based on instrumental conditioning come in a variety of forms. In general, however, they involve rewarding desirable behavior or punishing undesirable behavior. Procedures involving punishment seem to work particularly well in cases of addiction and sexual deviation. Typically, an aversive stimulus, such as a severe electric shock or an emetic that induces nausea and vomiting, is presented following the undesirable behavior. In one case, an intellectually superior 33-year-old man was cured of transvestism, the abnormal habit of dressing as a member of the opposite sex and appearing in public. The treatment consisted of requiring the patient to stand before a full-length mirror on an electrified grid that permitted electric shocks to be delivered to the soles of his feet. The patient was instructed to begin dressing in his favorite women's clothing while standing on the grid. As he dressed, he received a series of shocks and a buzzer sounded to indicate that he should divest himself of the woman's clothing. These stimuli continued until he had removed his feminine attire. A series of 400 such trials over a 6-day span cured the patient of this neurotic behavior. A follow-up six months later indicated that the cure was permanent.

GREGORY A. KIMBLE
*Duke University*

**Further Reading:** Kimble, Gregory A., ed., *Foundations of Conditioning and Learning* (Irvington 1967); Kimble, Gregory A., and others, *Principles of Psychology*, 6th ed. (Wiley 1984); Schwartz, Barry, *Psychology of Learning and Behavior*, 3d ed. (Norton 1989).

**CONDOMINIUM,** kon-də-min'ē-əm, in international law, is the joint sovereignty maintained by two or more states over a territory. It usually is a compromise settlement arising from conflicting claims to a territory, and usually is established by a treaty between the claimants that defines the administrative authority of each. Condominiums have included those of Britain and the United States over the Oregon territory (1818–1846); the United States, Britain, and Germany over the Samoan Islands (1889–1899); Britain and Egypt over the Sudan (1899–1956); and Britain and France over the New Hebrides (established in 1906). The United States and Britain agreed in 1939 to create a condominium over Canton and Enderbury islands for 50 years.

QUINCY WRIGHT, *Professor Emeritus of International Law, University of Chicago*

**CONDOMINIUM,** kon-də-min'ē-əm, in real estate, is an arrangement by which property is jointly owned. It involves joint ownership of multiple-occupant buildings with each occupant having title to a separate, divided interest in the property.

Condominiums have long been used in Latin America for owner-occupancy of apartments, offices, or commercial buildings. Condominium ownership emerged in the United States in the late 1950's, when the Federal Housing Administration altered its regulations to permit FHA insurance on condominium apartment units. State enabling legislation was necessary to legalize condominium ownership.

In a real estate condominium, each apartment or commercial unit is owned separately. Unlike a cooperative unit, it may be sold or leased without the approval of the other owners. Each condominium unit is mortgaged and taxed individually. Default on one unit does not oblige other unit owners to make good. The condominium owner also has an undivided interest in all common facilities, such as halls, elevators, or heating equipment. An association of owner-tenants usually provides for their maintenance.

WILLIAM N. KINNARD, JR.
*University of Connecticut*

**CONDON,** kon'dən, **Edward Uhler** (1902–1974) American physicist, who made important contributions to modern theoretical physics, particularly to quantum mechanics. At the time Condon was doing his graduate work at Berkeley, Calif., the insufficiencies of the older quantum theory of Niels Bohr had become clearly evident, and there was a great deal of ferment in theoretical physics. The German physicist James Franck had given a paper in 1925 in London, in which he discussed the dissociation of iodine vapor by the absorption of light. Condon was given proof sheets of this paper by one of Franck's students, and in a few days he was able to generalize Franck's ideas. The result was the Franck-Condon principle and Condon's dissertation, an analysis of the mechanics of photochemical dissociation.

After receiving his doctorate, Condon studied in Göttingen, Germany, where Heisenberg and Born, at the same time as Schrödinger, were laying the foundations of quantum mechanics. With Philip H. Morse he wrote a textbook, *Quantum Mechanics* (1929), that served as a guide to a whole generation of American physicists.

Condon's contributions to the new mechanics were fundamental. Together with R. W. Gurney and independently of George Gamow, he used the new wave mechanics to describe the "tunneling" effect by which particles that, in classical mechanics, could not either enter or escape from a nucleus because of their low energies, could be shown to have a definite probability of doing both. The first "atom smashers" were built on the basis of this effect. In 1938, Condon also showed that photoelectrons from semiconductors should behave in a peculiar way, thus opening investigation into the nature of semiconductors.

Condon was born in Alamogordo, N. Mex., on March 2, 1902. He received his Ph.D. from the University of California at Berkeley in 1926, and taught at several universities. He died in Boulder, Colo., on March 26, 1974.

L. PEARCE WILLIAMS, *Cornell University*

**CONDOR,** kon'dər, either of two species of very large American vultures. The California condor, *Gymnogyps californianus,* is nearly extinct and almost entirely restricted to the coastal mountain ranges at the southern end of the San Joaquin Valley in California. The Andean condor, *Vultur gryphus,* is widely distributed in the mountains of western and southern South America from Colombia to Cape Horn.

Both species of condors are huge, from 43 to 54 inches (1.1–1.4 meters) long, and have broad wings, extending over 9 feet (2.8 meters) in the California condor and 10 feet (3 meters) in the Andean species. They weigh from 20 to 25 pounds (9-11 kg). The California condor is a dark gray-brown and has white underwings and a white bar on its upper wing. The feathers of its ruff and underparts are lance-shaped and streaked with light gray, and the relatively smooth skin of its head is orange, becoming red on the neck. The Andean condor is glossy black with a large dirty white area on its upper wing and a white downy ruff around its neck. Its bare head and upper neck are wattled and waxy red. The male has a fleshy outgrowth on its forehead. The young of both species are duller and grayer than the adults; they have no white on the wings

or ruff, and the head is covered with down.

Condors feed largely on carrion, especially on the carcasses of grazing animals but also on dead rabbits and rodents. Both species have heavy bills and can tear live flesh as well as rotten carcasses; in fact, the Andean condor sometimes kills wounded or young animals.

Condors search for food while soaring high over open terrain. They breed in caves or on mountain ledges. The female lays 1 or 2 white eggs that take 45 to 55 days to hatch. The California condor may breed only once every other year.

Both American condors belong to the family Cathartidae in the order Falconiformes.

GEORGE E. WATSON, *Smithsonian Institution*

**CONDORCANQUI, José Gabriel.** See TUPAC AMARU.

**CONDORCET,** kôn-dôr-sā', **Marquis de** (1743–1794), French mathematician and philosopher, who was one of the outstanding figures of the Enlightenment. A liberal and a humanitarian, he took an active part in the French Revolution. His writings on the progress of man deeply influenced the political and social thought of the 19th century.

**The Enlightenment.** Marie Jean Antoine Nicolas Caritat, Marquis de Condorcet, was born into a noble family in Ribemont, Picardy, on Sept. 17, 1743. Educated by the Jesuits and at the Collège de Navarre in Paris, he became an able and precocious mathematician. He published his first essay on the integral calculus in 1765 and was elected to the Academy of Sciences in 1769, at the age of 26. As assistant after 1771 to its permanent secretary, Grandjean de Fouchy, and later as his successor, Condorcet wrote a series of well-received *Éloges* on its deceased members. He married the beautiful Sophie de Grouchy (sister of the Marquis de Grouchy) in 1786; subsequently their popular salon attracted especially the young *philosophes.*

But it is as an exponent of Turgot's economics and Voltaire's humanitarianism that Condorcet is best known. As a physiocrat he wrote numerous pamphlets advocating free trade and the elimination of the *corvée,* a form of compulsory labor that greatly harassed the French peasant. His humanitarianism found a ready outlet in his campaign to abolish slavery, his opposition to capital punishment, and his pacifist analysis of war. His constitutionalism was reflected in his advocacy of free speech and in his vigorous support of the American Revolution, on which he wrote *De l'influence de la Révolution d'Amerique sur l'Europe* (1786) and *Lettres d'un bourgeois de Newhaven à un citoyen de Virginie* (1787).

**The Revolution.** When the French Revolution broke out in 1789, Condorcet was probably the most prominent of the *philosophes* still alive. He served in the Legislative Assembly as a member for Paris from October 1791 to September 1792, having previously startled public opinion with his *Sur l'admission des femmes au droit de Cité* (1790), in which he had advocated the enfranchisement of women. In April 1792 his report to the Assembly on proposed reforms in education, *Sur l'instruction publique,* envisaged a national system of public education designed to develop the natural talents of all, thus making real equality possible.

California condor

CARL KOFORD, FROM NATIONAL AUDUBON SOCIETY

As a member of the National Convention, Condorcet wrote a constitution that was close to the moderate, Girondist views. Presented on Feb. 15–16, 1793, it was rejected in favor of a hastily drawn, more radical, Jacobin document. After the expulsion of the Girondist deputies (June 2, 1793), the Jacobins proscribed him. He went into hiding for nine months.

While in hiding, Condorcet wrote his most famous work, the *Esquisse d'un tableau historique des progrès de l'esprit humain*, a summing up of his views concerning the development of the human spirit and his hopes for the future of humanity. The work divides human history into ten stages, the last depicting man's possible progress in the future, which may consist of the destruction of inequality among nations, the destruction of inequality among classes, and the intellectual, moral, and physical perfection of individuals. It is a secular and radical document—most misfortunes of mankind are traced to ignorance imposed by priests, kings, and selfish professional men. However, a careful reading will modify the general impression that the book springs from an unlimited optimism. Early in April 1794, Condorcet left his sanctuary and was apprehended and imprisoned several days later. On the morning of April 8, he was found dead in his cell, probably from exhaustion.

PETER GAY, *Author of "The Enlightenment"*

**Bibliography**

Baker, Keith M., *Condorcet: From Natural Philosophy to Social Mathematics* (Univ. of Chicago Press 1975).
Cahen, Leon, *Condorcet et la Révolution française* (1904; reprint, B. Franklin 1976).
Gay, Peter, *The Enlightenment* (Norton 1977).
Gay, Peter, *The Party of Humanity: Essays in the French Enlightenment* (Norton 1971).
Schapiro, J. Salwyn, *Condorcet and the Rise of Liberalism* (1934; reprint, Hippocrene Bks. 1963).
Williams, Charles G., ed., *Literature and History in the Age of Ideas* (Ohio State Univ. Press 1975).

**CONDOTTIERE,** kōn-dôt-tyȧ'rā, is the Italian name for a mercenary captain who commanded his own military company and fought for hire. The condottieri were prominent in the incessant Italian wars of the 14th and 15th centuries. In the 14th century they were mostly foreigners, such as Sir John Hawkwood. In the 15th century, however, the profession passed to Italian military adventurers such as Colleoni and the Sforza, whose object was often to carve out a state for themselves. After the late 15th century they came under severe and sometimes unjust criticism for treachery, greed, and incompetence. The condottieri passed from the scene with the consolidation of the Italian states and the foreign invasions after 1494.

RANDOLPH STARN
*University of California at Berkeley*

**CONDUCTING** is the art and technique of guiding a musical performance by instrumentalists, singers, or both. The duties of a modern conductor include selecting the repertoire to be performed, interpreting the music, impressing his interpretation on the musicians in rehearsal, and directing them in performance.

**Historical Development.** The derivation of the word "conducting," from the Latin *conducere*, meaning "leading together," indicates the conductor's original function—to ensure precision and indicate basic tempi. In the baroque era (1600–1760), when instrumental music was scored for small orchestras or ensembles and the orchestration was simple and the pulse or meter coincided with the stream of the melodic line, these tasks were entrusted to the first violinist, the organist, or the harpsichordist. The larger ensembles used in operas and oratorios required a leader, but for organizational rather than interpretative purposes. The conductor-interpreter, as known today, did not exist in this period.

One of the first musicians to attempt to raise the level of musical performance as a conductor was Jean Baptiste Lully (1632–1687), a Florentine who was the leading composer at the court of Louis XIV of France. Lully used a wooden staff to pound out the beat on the floor during public performances. In addition, he insisted that the string section use a strict bowing technique to ensure precise playing.

The reforms proposed by the French composer Jean Philippe Rameau (1683–1764) in his *Traité de l'harmonie* (1722) slowly took effect, signaling the end of the *basso continuo,* or thorough bass (the practice of indicating an accompanying part by the bass notes only, rather than writing out the whole chord). Gradually, melodic structure started to change, becoming more independent of meter, and orchestration soon reflected this. The complexities in the music of Joseph Haydn (1732–1809), Wolfgang Amadeus Mozart (1756–1791), and other composers led to the assumption of new and greater duties by the conductor.

**Modern Conducting.** The modern orchestra was created, in effect, by Ludwig van Beethoven (1770–1827), whose demands on the performers made a conductor mandatory. Without leadership, musicians could not negotiate Beethoven's drastic tempo changes, pauses, *ritardandi,* and *accelerandi,* or interpret his intensely personal expression.

As music became more subjective and complex, conducting became increasingly important. Romanticism brought the era of the modern conductor, exemplified by Carl Maria von Weber (1786–1826)—who conducted with the orchestra at his back—and by Hector Berlioz (1803–1869) —who was able to master extremely large orchestras.

The Italian conductor Gasparo Spontini (1774–1851) insisted on countless section and *tutti* rehearsals, and Louis Spohr (1784–1859), a German violinist and composer, brought delicacy and imagination to conducting. Felix Mendelssohn-Bartholdy (1809–1847), composer and leader of the famous Leipzig Gewandhaus Orchestra, was one of the first conductors to stand facing the orchestra and use a baton in the modern manner.

This early modern period came to a climax with Richard Wagner (1813–1883), the composer who created the *Gesamtkunstwerk* (the total work of art) in his operas. He achieved additional fame as a conductor with his remarkable interpretations of Beethoven's works.

Conductors of the Wagner circle included his famous father-in-law, Franz Liszt (1811–1886), a great pianist and composer as well as director of the Weimar orchestra; Felix Mottl (1856–1911); Hermann Levi (1839–1900); Franz Wüllner (1832–1902); and Hans Richter (1843–1916). The first of the towering virtuoso conductors was Hans von Bülow (1830–1894), who led the premieres of Wagner's *Tristan und Isolde* and *Die Meistersinger.* Bülow founded the Meiningen court orchestra, which became famous for its ability to achieve subtle shadings of tone and freedom of tempo.

SANFORD H. ROTH, FROM RAPHO GUILLUMETTE

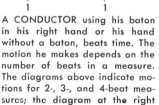
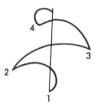
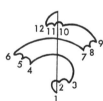

A CONDUCTOR using his baton in his right hand or his hand without a baton, beats time. The motion he makes depends on the number of beats in a measure. The diagrams above indicate motions for 2-, 3-, and 4-beat measures; the diagram at the right is for a measure with 12 beats.

CONDUCTING WITHOUT A BATON, and using his left hand to indicate a tonal gradation, the late Dimitri Mitropoulos leads an orchestra in a rehearsal session.

Arthur Nikisch (1855–1922) created a new splendor of orchestral sound by giving proper value to the hitherto neglected middle voices accompanying the leading melodies. Gustav Mahler (1860–1911) brought a dramatic intensity to his performances. As an opera conductor, he fused all the elements—acting, scene design, costuming, and music—into completely unified productions. Another masterly composer-conductor was Richard Strauss (1864–1949), whose exploitation of orchestral complexities required entirely new rehearsal techniques.

Felix Weingartner (1863–1942) reinterpreted Beethoven with a new clarity and simplicity, and Bruno Walter (1876–1962) revived Mozart with sensitive artistry. The great Italian maestro Arturo Toscanini (1867–1957) was noted for the meticulousness with which he followed the composer's text and for his sense of precision in musical dynamics and coherence. Wilhelm Furtwangler (1886–1954) gave classical masterpieces an abstract sound and color, and Pierre Monteux (1875–1964), Sir Thomas Beecham (1879–1961), and Dimitri Mitropoulos (1896–1960), besides giving lucid interpretations of the standard repertoire, were virtuoso trailblazers of contemporary music, championing many modern composers.

**Rehearsal.** Rehearsal techniques vary with the conductor and the quality of the orchestra. String sections usually require more extensive work than other sections to achieve clean intonation. Bowings have to be meticulously organized so that the string players project the style and atmosphere the conductor sees in the music.

For works in the standard repertoire, woodwind and brass players need little special rehearsing and usually join the string players after the string section has been thoroughly trained. But for much contemporary music, it is often advisable and sometimes mandatory to have wind, brass, and percussion sections rehearse separately before joining the strings. Intricate avant-garde pieces may demand long rehearsal sessions for just a single instrument.

After this preparatory work is done, the conductor holds rehearsals with the full orchestra. These rehearsals are devoted chiefly to establishing the proper balance of sound among the various groups, assuming that each group has been solidly prepared beforehand.

**Performance.** In the performance, the conductor establishes the tempo with a clear, assured beat. Modern conductors usually indicate the important first beat of each musical measure by a strong downward stroke of the right hand (the downbeat), and the usually weak final beat of a measure by an upward stroke (the upbeat). With his left hand he may control loudness and softness or other dynamic qualities. Conductors of very large orchestras, choruses, and opera frequently use additional signals.

The abilities of the modern orchestra have reached unprecedented heights. It is capable of producing sound elements new to the musical lexicon. And rhythmical demands on the orchestra have changed considerably; for example, compositions are now written in $5/8$, $7/8$, $11/8$, and other unusual meters. All this has made the tasks of the conductor enormously more difficult in both rehearsal and performance. See also ORCHESTRA.

CARL BAMBERGER
*Editor of "The Conductor's Art"*

### Bibliography

Bamberger, Carl, ed., *The Conductor's Art* (McGraw 1965).
Boult, Sir Adrian, *A Handbook on the Technique of Conducting*, 7th rev. ed. (Scholarly Press 1975).
Bowles, Michael, *The Art of Conducting* (1959; reprint, Da Capo 1975).
Croger, T. R., *Notes on Conductors and Conducting* (Scholarly Press 1976).
Ensor, Wendy-Ann, *More Heroes and Heroines in Music* (Oxford 1982).
Galkin, Elliott W., *The History of Orchestral Conducting* (Pendragon Press 1988).
Garretson, Robert L., *Conducting Choral Music*, 6th ed. (Prentice-Hall 1988).
Hart, Philip, *Conductors: A New Generation* (Scribner 1983).
Inghelbrecht, Désiré E., *The Conductor's World*, tr. by G. Prerauer and S. Malcolm Kirk (Hyperion Press 1979).
May, Robin, *Behind the Baton* (Merrimack 1983).
Robinson, Paul, *The Art of the Conductor: Bernstein* (Vanguard Press 1982).
Rudolf, Max, *The Grammar of Conducting* (1950; reprint, Schirmer Bks. 1980).
Taubman, H. Howard, *The Maestro: The Life of Arturo Toscanini* (1951; reprint, Greenwood Press 1977).
Wood, Henry J., *About Conducting* (1945; reprint, Am. Biog. Serv. 1988).

**CONDUCTION OF HEAT.** See HEAT TRANSFER.

**CONDUCTIVITY, Electrical,** kon-duk-tiv′ə-tē, a measure of the ability of a material to carry an electric current. In solid materials, conductivity is measured by the ratio of the current per unit area to the voltage per unit length, and it is expressed in units of mhos per meter. Conductivity (in mhos) is the reciprocal of resistivity (in ohms).

Solid materials, generally classified as metals, semiconductors, or insulators, exhibit differing abilities to carry electric current. Metals have a conductivity of $10^6$ to $10^8$ mhos per meter when their temperature is 68°F (20°C); their conductivity decreases with increasing temperature. Semiconductors have a conductivity of $10^{-7}$ to $10^5$ mhos per meter; their conductivity increases with increasing temperature. Insulators have a conductivity less than $10^{-7}$ mhos per meter; their conductivity increases with increasing temperature.

**CONDUCTOR, Electric.** See ELECTRICITY—6. *Conduction of Electricity.*

**CONDYLARTH,** kon′də-lärth, any member of the extinct mammalian order Condylarthra, which flourished during the early Tertiary period about 60 to 50 million years ago. The animals lived primarily in the Northern Hemisphere, particularly in North America. Members of the most ancient condylarth species, of the *Protungulatum,* existed in North America at the end of the Cretaceous period as contemporaries of the dinosaurs.

**Characteristics.** Condylarths probably were both herbivorous and omnivorous. Their dental patterns were considerably varied by early Eocene time, but originally the cheek teeth had low, rounded cusps which perhaps indicate feeding habits broadly similar to those of modern pigs. One such group, typified by the genus *Hyopsodus,* consisted of squirrel-sized mammals abundant during the Eocene in North America. Another group, typified by the genus *Meniscotherium,* included species that were about the size of a fox terrier. Their teeth resembled those of some of the earliest relatives of horses, which suggests they were adapted for browsing on forest leaves.

Members of *Phenacodus,* a characteristic genus of the Paleocene and early Eocene, were about the size of a sheep but had a much more primitive body, with a large, long tail and a comparatively small skull and braincase. The modern African aardvark, with its shuffling gait, sparse hair, and large, cumbersome tail, perhaps resembles *Phenacodus.*

**Descendants.** Various members of the order Condylarthra gave rise to most of the living orders of hoofed, plant-eating mammals called ungulates, including horses, cattle, deer, and pigs. It is also likely, although the evidence is less clear, that condylarths in Africa gave rise to the elephants, hyraxes, and sea cows. South American condylarths were ancestors of several orders of plant-eating mammals that are now extinct. The earliest condylarths are also close to the forerunners of the modern carnivores, and the two orders presumably had a common ancestry in the late Cretaceous period.

ELWYN L. SIMONS, *Yale University*

**CONE,** in botany, a reproductive structure consisting of many open scales that bear either voules (in female cones) or pollen (in male cones). See CONIFER; EVERGREENS.

**CONE,** in geometry, a figure defined by a closed curve *C* (the *directrix*) lying in a plane and a point *V* (the *vertex*) not in the plane of *C,* and formed by joining *V* to each point of *C.* The lines joining *V* to each point of *C* are called *elements* of the cone and may be considered as infinitely extended in one or both directions or as line segments lying between *V* and *C.* In this last case, the cone consists of the lateral surface formed by all line segments from *V* to *C* along with the interior of *C* (the *base*). The perpendicular line segment from the vertex to the plane of the base is the *altitude* of the cone. A *circular cone* has a circle as directrix; a *convex cone* has a convex curve as directrix. If the base has a center, the line segment from the vertex to the center is the *axis* of the cone. The cone is called a *right cone* if the axis is perpendicular to the base; otherwise it is called *oblique.* The volume of a right circular cone is $\frac{1}{3}\pi r^2 h$ where $h$ is the altitude and $r$ the radius of the base; the lateral area is $\pi r \sqrt{r^2 + h^2}$

FRANCIS A. GREENE, S. J.
*Xavier University, Cincinnati*

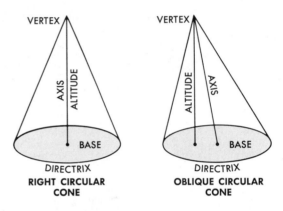

RIGHT CIRCULAR CONE    OBLIQUE CIRCULAR CONE

**CONE COLLECTION,** an important collection of late 19th and early 20th century French art in the Baltimore Museum of Art. The collection includes works amassed by Dr. Claribel Cone, who died in 1929, leaving her collection to her sister, Etta Cone, who in turn left it to the museum in 1949. The Cone sisters lived in Baltimore but spent much time in Paris. They were friends of Gertrude Stein, who introduced them to Picasso, Matisse, and other young artists still relatively unknown. The Cone sisters were particularly friendly with Matisse, and they became owners of 42 oil paintings and 18 bronze sculptures by him. The collection ranges from Delacroix's *Perseus and Andromeda* (1847) to Matisse's *Two Girls, Red and Green Background* (1947) and also includes works by Renoir, Cézanne, Derain, Bonnard, and Marie Laurencin. Outstanding is Picasso's *Woman with Bangs* (1902).

**CONE SHELL,** a marine snail with a heavy, colorful, cone-shaped shell. It is found among the rocks and corals in shallow tropical seas and is popular with shell collectors, but it has a venom, that is fatal even to man.

Adult cone shells vary in length from ½ inch to 8 inches (1.3–20 cm), and they may be variously colored, with spots, bands, or lines. gray, or yellow, with varying shades and patterns of brown. The snails are carnivorous and feed on worms, small fish, and other mollusks. They kill their prey with the neurotoxic venom, which they inject through their tiny, harpoon-shaped teeth. Six species from the Indo-Pacific area have inflicted serious stings in man, and the geography cone (*Conus geographus*) and textile cone (*Conus textile*) have killed several shell collectors in the Pacific. Death occurred within four hours after injection of the venom. No American species are known to be fatal, but collectors should handle live specimens carefully.

A few cone shell species are very rare and have brought prices of many hundreds of dollars among shell collectors. Among the most desirable shells are the glory-of-the-seas (*Conus gloriamaris*), the glory-of-India (*Conus milneedwardsi*), and the rhododendron cone (*Conus adamsoni*). These species are from the Indo-Pacific area.

The cone shell belongs to the family Conidae in the class Gastropoda. There are about 450 species; of these, about 20 species occur in the southeastern United States and only one on the Pacific coast.

R. Tucker Abbott
*The Academy of Natural Sciences of Philadelphia*

**CONEFLOWER,** a name commonly applied to three related groups of plants of the composite family native to North America. The most common is *Rudbeckia*, a genus of about 25 annuals, biennials, and perennials, including the black-eyed Susan, *R. hirta*, and the brown-eyed Susan, *R. triloba*. The orange coneflower, *R. fulgida*, is a 2-foot (⅔-meter) perennial that has orange daisylike flowers with purplish-black centers. The golden glow, *R. laciniata hortensia*, has double yellow flowers and grows 12 feet (3⅔ meters) tall. The closely related genus *Echinacea* includes the purple coneflower, *E. purpurea*, which grows 3 feet (1 meter) tall and bears purple daisylike flowers. The small genus *Ratibida* includes yellow-to purplish-flowered species of coneflowers. Coneflowers are widespread throughout the United States and are easily propagated by seeds or division of roots.

Donald Wyman
*The Arnold Arboretum, Harvard University*

**CONESTOGA, INDIANS,** kon-əs-tō′gə, a once-numerous tribe of Iroquoian Indians who lived along the lower Susquehanna River in Pennsylvania and Maryland and on the eastern bank of the Potomac River and Chesapeake Bay. In early colonial times the Conestoga were at war with the Mohawk and had nearly exterminated them, but in 1675 they were overcome by other Iroquois tribes and later were forced to settle near the Oneida in New York. Eventually allowed to return to their old homeland in present-day Lancaster county, Pennsylvania, they declined rapidly, and in 1763 the remaining 20 individuals were massacred by white settlers.

The tribe was always friendly with the Dutch and Swedish settlers but remained a constant source of trouble to the English, with whom they carried on intermittent warfare. They made a treaty ceding some of their land to William Penn in 1701. The name of the tribe was derived from the Indian Kanastóge, meaning "at the place of the submerged pole." They were also known as Susquehanna Indians, from Susquehannock, a name applied to them by the neighboring Powhatan tribes. In early colonial accounts they are also often referred to as Minqua Indians.

Frederick J. Dockstader
*Museum of the American Indian
Heye Foundation, New York City*

**CONESTOGA WAGON,** kon-ə-stō′gə, a type of covered wagon for overland freight hauling, used extensively in America between 1750 and 1850. The box or bed of a Conestoga was gracefully shaped and gently curved, so that the front and rear were higher than the middle and the two ends were raked somewhat like a boat. Eight or more wooden bows supported a large canvas or homespun cover over the bed. A team of four, five, or six horses, specially bred for the purpose and known as Conestoga horses, pulled the wagon. Loads of three or four tons were typical.

The Conestoga wagon had its origin in southeastern Pennsylvania in the early 18th century, when Lancaster county became a center for fur trading. By 1717, wagons were in use hauling furs to Philadelphia and trade goods back to the region then called Conestogoe. This name, slightly altered, remains in the name of the village of

**CONESTOGA WAGONS** carried freight across the mountains of the eastern United States (1750–1850) and helped open the West.

Conestoga, near Lancaster. The wagons were named after the region. They were also called "Dutch wagons." German and Swiss immigrants who settled Lancaster and neighboring counties prior to 1750 developed the wagon to suit their needs for hauling produce and manufactured goods over the poor roads.

After the Revolutionary War, the Conestoga became the chief freight link across the Appalachian Mountains between centers of commerce on the eastern seaboard and the newly settled Ohio Valley. As trans-Appalachian freighting became increasingly important, and roads improved, the Conestoga evolved into a large and handsome vehicle. Conestoga freight wagoning ended abruptly about 1850 when railroads crossed the mountains.

GEORGE SHUMWAY
*Author of "Conestoga Wagon, 1750-1850"*

**CONEY,** kō'nē, is a name applied to several different small mammals of similar general appearance. The Biblical coney (Psalms 104:18 and other references) was actually the Syrian rock hyrax (*Heterohyrax syriacus*). Rabbits, especially the European rabbit (*Oryctolagus cuniculus*), were formerly called conies and are still referred to by this name in heraldry. The name coney is sometimes used for the pikes (*Ochotona*), also called little chief hares. See also HYRAX; RABBIT; PIKE.

**CONEY ISLAND,** kō'nē, a section of the borough of Brooklyn in New York City, is a popular recreation area. The name "island" persisted after a channel was partly filled in to make it a peninsula. Facing the Atlantic Ocean, Coney Island has a fine beach and a boardwalk. Formerly characterized principally by garish amusement enterprises, by the late 1960's it was becoming an area of high-rise apartment buildings. Scattered among these buildings are one- or two-family homes, housing some 100,000 persons of diverse ethnic and national origin. This housing ranges from slum to middle class.

Besides the beach and boardwalk, many carnival amusement features, centered on Surf Avenue, draw hosts of visitors, especially on summer weekends. It is estimated that 45 million persons visit Coney Island annually. The New York Aquarium, with about 7,000 specimens of marine life, is on the oceanfront.

Coney Island probably derived its name from the Dutch *Konijn Eilandt* (Rabbit Island). It was part of the land sold to Lady Deborah Moody in 1643 by the Dutch West India Company. The first hotel was opened there in 1829, and a pavilion and bathhouse were erected in 1844. Late in the 19th century, sports followers were attracted by prizefights and by horse racing at Brighton Beach nearby. Three famous amusement parks—Steeplechase Park, Luna Park, and Dreamland Park—were opened between 1897 and 1905. All are closed now. Subway lines reached Coney Island in 1920, and by the 1960's the Belt Parkway facilitated access by automobile.

LEO HERSHKOWITZ
*Queens College; City University of New York*

**CONFALONIERI,** kōn-fä-lō-nyå'rē, **Federico,** (1785–1846) Italian patriot and social reformer, who was the leader of a revolutionary secret society. He was born in Milan on Oct. 6, 1785. A liberal aristocrat, he first appeared on the political scene in 1814 as a leader of the anti-French party of the Italici, who sought to dislodge Prince Eugène Beauharnais, the stepson of Napoleon I, from the viceroyalty of Italy. Later that year he went to Paris to plead, unsuccessfully, the cause of Lombard independence before the assembled chiefs of the victorious anti-Napoleonic coalition.

From 1816 to 1819 he traveled extensively throughout Italy and western Europe, sponsored the cultural review *Il Conciliatore*, and experimented with a series of economic, social, and artistic innovations in Milan. Correctly suspected of connections with the secret society of the Federati, or Federazione—the most active affiliate of the Supremi Maestri Perfetti, a north Italian offshoot of the Carbonari—he was arrested on Dec. 13, 1821, at his palace in Milan.

Charged with direct participation in the Federati's plan to link a Lombard revolt with the Piedmontese revolution of that year and later accused of active attempts to foment a "war of liberation" against Austria, Confalonieri was tried by the Lombardo-Venetian Senate and on Jan. 21, 1824, was condemned to death for high treason. The sentence was later commuted to life imprisonment.

He remained in prison until 1836, when an imperial amnesty again commuted his sentence, on condition that he never set foot again within the Habsburg realm. After spending two rootless years in the United States, he returned to Europe, but not to Italy. He died in Geneva on Dec. 10, 1846.

A. WILLIAM SALOMONE
*University of Rochester*

**CONFARREATION,** in Roman law, was a religious form of marriage reserved for patricians. See MARRIAGES, LAW OF.

**CONFECTIONERY.** See CANDY.

**CONFEDERATE MEMORIAL DAY.** See MEMORIAL DAY.

CONEY ISLAND'S fine beach on the Atlantic Ocean provides a recreation area for millions of visitors.

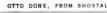
OTTO DONE, FROM SHOSTAL

CONFEDERATE MUSEUM, RICHMOND, VA.

CONFEDERATE PRESIDENT JEFFERSON DAVIS and his cabinet in 1861. *(From left to right)* Stephen R. Mallory, Judah P. Benjamin, Leroy Pope Walker, Davis, Robert E. Lee, John H. Reagan, Christopher G. Memminger, Alexander H. Stephens, and Robert Toombs.

**CONFEDERATE STATES OF AMERICA,** a secessionist republic within the territory of the United States, established by Southern states that broke away from the federal Union. It existed from 1861 to 1865. The Confederacy (South) fought the United States (North) in the American Civil War. When the war ended in victory for the North, the Confederacy was dissolved, and its member states were gradually readmitted to the Union.

Delegates from six states that had seceded from the United States before the outbreak of hostilities—South Carolina, Georgia, Florida, Alabama, Louisiana, and Mississippi—met for the first time at Montgomery, Ala., on Feb. 4, 1861, to form a new republic dedicated to the principles of states' rights and individual liberty. Subsequently, five additional Southern states joined the Confederacy—Texas, Virginia, Tennessee, Arkansas, and North Carolina. Jefferson Davis and Alexander H. Stephens were, respectively, President and Vice President of the Confederate States. Its "permanent" capital (after May 29, 1861) was at Richmond, Va.

**Constitution.** The delegates at the Montgomery meeting showed great moderation when they began to draft a constitution for the Confederacy. None of them considered secession illegal or revolutionary; hence they saw no need for radical innovations. The convention stressed continuity and worked to build a new government much like the old.

A provisional constitution was adopted on Feb. 8, 1861, creating a temporary administration to run the Confederacy for one year. A permanent constitution was adopted on March 11, 1861. Both documents were close copies of the U. S. Constitution, with some important differences.

The provisional charter created a unicameral congress and gave the president of the Confederacy the right to veto specific items in an appropriation bill and sign the remainder into law.

Under the permanent constitution, the president's term was six years, and he could not succeed himself; he retained the item veto. The international slave trade was prohibited, but domestic slavery was protected. Cabinet members were given Congressional seats with debating, but not voting, privileges. Congress could make no appropriations for internal improvements and could not levy protective tariffs or grant special bounties. All appropriations not specifically requested in the executive budget had to be approved by two thirds of both houses of Congress.

**President and Cabinet.** Having completed the job of constitution-making, the convention moved to fill the posts of president and vice president. Many presidential candidates were close at hand in Montgomery. William L. Yancey of Alabama possessed the qualities of leadership but was considered too radical to suit the border states. Georgia's Robert Toombs coveted the presidency, but his fiery tongue disqualified him. A temperate man of experience and national reputation was needed. The final choice was Jefferson Davis of Mississippi, U. S. senator, Mexican War hero, and planter.

As vice president, the Confederate Congress selected Georgia's Senator Alexander H. Stephens, a fiercely competitive politician of boundless ambition. Stephens might well have become president had he defied the Union sooner, before his state seceded. The vice presidency was a sop to Georgia and proper penance for a tardy patriot. But Stephens was not satisfied with a subordinate role, and he spent most of the war years in Georgia plotting secession from the Confederacy.

Davis and Stephens were inaugurated for provisional terms on Feb. 18, 1861, and for six-year terms on Feb. 22, 1862.

President Davis lacked President Lincoln's gift of language and warm appeal. He presided over a lost cause and reaped the loser's share. Consequently, he appears in history as an aloof, remote man. A majority of Confederates fixed the failure of the Southern cause squarely on Davis, and by the end of the Civil War he was resented throughout the South. His apparent devotion to scrupulous observance of detail suggested that he was a small, uninspired leader, unable or unwilling to cope with the fearsome problems facing the Confederacy.

But Davis did better than his contemporaries knew. With dauntless courage he faced the grim facts of too few men, too little money, scant munitions, diplomatic ostracism, and unbridled states' rights. He advocated a hard war. He supported political and social policies repugnant to the South but essential to sustain a war of unprecedented proportions. He developed an overall strategy of offensive defense, which made the best use of Confederate strength and minimized weakness. Measured on the scale of success and against Lincoln's lengthening shadow, Davis received a harsh judgment from history. But judged by his growth in the presidency, his character and increasing wisdom, Davis ranks as an able leader.

Davis' administrative experience led him to select a sound cabinet, which generally provided vital assistance and ably managed the various executive departments. During the Confederacy's four years, Davis made frequent cabinet changes, but several members exerted lasting influence. Judah P. Benjamin of Louisiana served first as attorney general, then as secretary of war, and finally as secretary of state. While head of the State Department, he won deserved acclaim as an urbane, crafty diplomat.

Of the six war secretaries, James A. Seddon served longest. A Virginian, Seddon proved an enterprising administrator with more initiative than Davis sometimes appreciated. Christopher G. Memminger, a South Carolina financier, accepted the Treasury portfolio and the almost hopeless task of providing money for the South. He remained in office until 1864, working for firm taxation and novel revenue measures. He failed largely because the whole South did not understand the incredible stresses imposed by modern war.

Two cabinet members held office throughout the war. Stephen R. Mallory, a Floridian, presided over the Navy Department and gained fame as a staunch advocate of such ironclad warships as the *Virginia* (*Merrimack*) and such commerce raiders as the *Alabama*. John H. Reagan, a Texan, headed the Post Office Department effectively, and fulfilled a constitutional obligation to make his organization self-sustaining by early 1863.

**Resources.** Davis' government faced staggering problems from the beginning, but especially after fighting began at Fort Sumter on April 12, 1861. Although the Confederacy had reached its total membership of 11 states by the spring of 1861, it gained too little material strength from its increased size. The South simply was no match for the North in war potential. Out of a total population of 9 million, the South had to deduct 3.5 million slaves, who did not count as martial resources. Financial resources were almost nonexistent. Only $27 million worth of specie could be found within Confederate borders, and a lapse in foreign trade was to shrink this reserve rapidly. Few factories existed outside of Virginia, and although minor manufacturing miracles were wrought by Brig. Gen. Josiah Gorgas and the Ordnance Bureau, Confederate industry remained weak. Southern railroads counted 9,000 miles (14,500 km) of track but were plagued by multiple gauges, short lines, limited rolling stock, scarce, badly equipped repair shops, and few facilities for making locomotives or cars.

Cotton, land, and courage were virtually the only Confederate assets. King Cotton mythology blinded the Confederates. The popular delusions were these: so vital a commodity as cotton—two thirds of the world's supply—would make all textile nations potential Confederate allies; abundant land would make the South agriculturally independent and feed its armies without stint; and cavalier courage would make up for inferiority in manpower and weapons. These assets failed the test of war.

**Diplomacy.** Faced with overwhelming odds, the Confederate government tried to avoid war through diplomacy. Southern agents worked to win peaceful secession from the North and, failing that, moved to gain foreign recognition. Relying first on Southern "white gold," the Confederacy offered cotton to England and France in return for recognition and aid. When it became clear by 1862 that cotton had lost its luster because of unexpected European surpluses, Davis and Benjamin turned to coercion through a cotton embargo and an offer of trade concessions.

Napoleon III of France had Southern sympathies, but he hesitated to anger the North by aiding the rebels unless England joined him. Britain maintained a difficult neutrality. Many influential Britons openly favored the Confederates. Popular opinion, however, ran strongly for the North, even in the textile midlands where the cotton shortage worked great hardships. English workers tightened their belts in the cause of abolition, and their self-denial did much to keep England uninvolved. The flabby state of British defenses was another factor. A shortage of cotton meant severe privation, but war with the United States might mean national disaster. Skillful Southern efforts to influence English opinion through the columns of the London *Index*, a Confederate-financed paper, were partially successful, and several times Britain came close to recognizing the Confederacy, especially when Confederate military fortunes rose. But as victories grew scarce, chances of foreign intervention faded.

Peripheral diplomatic activities in Canada and Mexico proved more dramatic than helpful. In the end Confederate diplomacy failed in the prime objective of obtaining recognition and intervention from abroad.

**Blockade-Running.** In one area, however, Southern diplomats succeeded. Secretary Benjamin pursued an active secondary diplomacy, centering on trade and blockade-running. Fleets of small, light-draft vessels plied between Southern coasts and Cuba, Nassau, Jamaica, and Bermuda. These islands became busy ports of entry for the embattled South, receiving European cargoes and shipping cotton in return. Private ventures in this lucrative business convinced Gen. Josiah Gorgas, chief of ordnance, of its potential, and he won government approval of regulations that sanctioned official trips and reserved one half the tonnage of all blockade-runners for Confederate cargo.

Careful organization of blockade-running in the Confederacy and abroad brought excellent results: at least 600,000 rifles imported, plus large quantities of coffee, saltpeter, and lead.

THE CONFEDERATE STATES were established in convention at Montgomery, Ala., in February 1861, by delegates from the six states that had seceded from the United States. Later, five more states joined the Confederacy, whose capital was Richmond from May 1861. Part of Virginia repudiated that state's secession from the United States and in 1863 was admitted to the Union as West Virginia.

Confederate states

Area that became West Virginia in 1863

**Finances.** As a means of sustaining foreign purchasing power, the Confederate Congress hesitantly approved in 1863 a $15 million loan from Emile Erlanger and Company of Paris. Even though the loan did provide some funds for purchases abroad, it virtually failed, since manipulations on European exchanges cut proceeds to about $6 million and saddled the South with a large debt.

The Erlanger fiasco was only a small part of Southern financial chaos. A $15 million domestic loan floated in February 1861 lagged for lack of money; a second one of $50 million launched in May did little better, and Congress sought to stimulate it with a "produce loan." This allowed planters to pledge income from unharvested produce as security for bonds. Although highly touted by the Treasury and initially popular, the produce loan failed, and Congress turned to the printing presses. But paper currency only confused the crisis, and Congress at length took a difficult step. On April 24, 1863, it passed the harshest tax law yet seen in the South. This law not only increased the regular rates, but it also levied an income tax, which many Southerners regarded as proof of Confederate despotism. But beyond that, the act assessed a profits' tax on farm products and also required farmers and planters to contribute one tenth of their annual crop yield. The latter so-called "tax-in-kind" clause angered agriculturists and caused endless legal wrangling.

Laws and taxes could not create money, and the government had to keep the presses running at a feverish rate. In mid-1863, Secretary Memminger finally advocated a funding act, which would take one third of the currency out of circulation. Congress reluctantly agreed in February 1864, but the new act was riddled with loopholes. Southerners could not accept stringent taxation, whatever the emergency. A brief respite from inflation, following passage of the new act, gave way to a fantastic price and money spiral, which brought bankruptcy in 1865.

In fact, the government never had any money. It lived entirely on the willingness of Southerners to accept promissory notes. In the early frenzy of patriotism, everyone gladly took Confederate money: it symbolized a nation. And even as late as 1863 and 1864, years of hard privation, hope sustained the currency. When hope faded toward the end of the war, the currency collapsed. Finances posed problems that the Confederate government fended off for four years but never solved.

**Impressment and Conscription.** Penury affected all facets of Confederate life, and forced stern centralization. With money chronically scarce, the government had to resort to impressing private produce, livestock, machinery, and transportation equipment. A desperate measure, impressment ranked second to conscription as the worst invasion of privacy committed by President Davis' administration. Sanctioned by law in 1863, impressment existed from the earliest days of the war and was often harshly and unjustly imposed. Despite its obvious evils, Davis urged it and Congress approved. Without it the armies probably could not have been fed, clothed, sheltered, or moved after 1862.

Conscription was equally essential. Fearing the collapse of the armies at the end of the first year of war, the administration moved to centralize control over manpower. In April 1862, Congress passed the first draft law in American history, which took into Confederate service all white men between 18 and 35. Some cries that this was unconstitutional were heard, but in general Southerners accepted the draft as a war necessity. Even when the law grew more stringent in 1864 and conscription included men between 17 and 50, there was little outcry. Although conscription could not produce enough men to sustain the huge armies required in a total national effort, it did keep the armies together in 1862, and garnered some 400,000 soldiers—almost half the Confederate total.

Negroes were used as teamsters, laborers, and, toward the end of the war, as soldiers. But the full potential of Negro manpower was never developed.

**Centralization.** Without the pressure of conflict, Southerners would never have submitted to impressment, conscription, and the rest of Davis' hard program. Yet much of what Davis advocated and Congress enacted represented a trend to centralization already present in the North. Increasing control over private enterprise, rudimentary management of the national economy, and comprehensive taxation marked the path of the old Whig party. Many Confederates were Whigs in attitude if not in name, and they welcomed a chance to transform the South. War forced much of the change, but not all. More important, peace and Reconstruction did not wipe it all away. What was learned of new management techniques, of modern logistics, of labor's importance, of the Negro's reliability and skill, of Southern strength in adversity would not be completely forgotten.

The achievements of the Confederacy's military heroes—Robert E. Lee, Stonewall Jackson, Nathan Bedford Forrest, Jeb Stuart—on fields forever famed—Manassas, Sharpsburg, Chancellorsville, Gettysburg, Chickamauga, Atlanta, Appomattox—were possible because the Confederacy finally waged modern war. Davis and the Confederate Congress learned modern lessons and applied them as rapidly as possible in the face of strong opposition from such states' righters as Gov. Joseph E. Brown of Georgia and Gov. Zebulon Vance of North Carolina.

Again and again Davis preached the need for central authority and for complete cooperation by all the states. Often he received bitter tirades in reply. By 1864 violent states' rights sentiments in Georgia generated a movement to withdraw the state from the Confederacy. Peace societies, too, did their insidious work in North Carolina and other states. But Davis remained in control of the government and the government largely in control of the shrinking Confederacy until the final exhaustion of the country and surrender of the armies in April 1865.

**Defeat and Collapse.** In the end, attrition defeated the Confederacy. Victorious almost continuously in 1861 and 1862, Confederate armies began to taste the gall of defeat in 1863. General Lee's second invasion of the North came to grief at the Battle of Gettysburg, July 1–3, 1863. On July 4, Gen. John C. Pemberton, commanding the defense of Vicksburg, the rebel bastion on the Mississippi, gave up the fight and surrendered his forces. The first week of July 1863 saw the South lose some 50,000 men and 70,000 arms—at a time when men and arms were irreplaceable.

Throughout the remainder of 1863 the Confederates stood on the defensive, parrying here and there, yielding ground grudgingly. In March 1864, Gen. Ulysses S. Grant became general-in-chief of the Armies of the United States and designed a crusher offensive in Virginia and through Georgia to pin down and erode the South's main field armies. Grant stayed with the Army of the Potomac as it pushed Lee back toward Richmond through May and June; William T. Sherman took charge of the western armies hurled at Confederate Gen. Joseph E. Johnston and his Army of Tennessee. After bloody encounters in Virginia's famed Wilderness area, the Army of the Potomac opened a siege of Petersburg and Richmond, which was to last nine grueling months and end in the surrender of Lee's Army at Appomattox, Va., on April 9, 1865.

Sherman, meantime, shoved Johnston's army inexorably toward its Atlanta base, though he suffered a major defeat at Kennesaw Mountain on June 27, 1864. For a variety of mistaken reasons, President Davis removed Johnston from command and replaced him with Gen. John B. Hood. Hood took the remnants of the Army of Tennessee on a long and fruitless campaign to Nashville, which ended in an ignominious rout on December 15. The army, returned to Johnston's charge, could only strike feebly at Sherman in the last days of the war. On April 26, 1865, a few days after Lee's surrender, Johnston surrendered the Army of Tennessee at Durham Station, N. C.

Military defeat, of course, finished the Confederacy. But military defeat came with total national exhaustion. At the end there were almost no men left with the colors, no munitions, no food, no transportation. Even the dauntless Confederate spirit had vanished. The ragged few who marched to stack arms at Appomattox and Durham Station were the last, the starved, tattered, bone-weary last, who stayed for the honor of the end.

Could the South have won the war? Possibly. Quicker and better mobilization might have resulted in the capture of Washington in July 1861, following the Battle of First Manassas. Retention of General Johnston in command of the Army of Tennessee before the Battle of Atlanta in July 1864 might have resulted in Sherman's defeat and the election of Gen. George B. McClellan as president of the United States. But this is speculation.

In a war of attrition against the North, the South was foredoomed to lose, and the Civil War was the first modern war of attrition. The Confederacy was first exhausted, then defeated. The surprising thing is not that the Confederacy lost, but that it lasted for four years.

See also CIVIL WAR; SECESSION; UNITED STATES—*Sectional Conflict.*

FRANK E. VANDIVER, *Rice University*
*Author, "Basic History of the Confederacy"*

**Bibliography**

Ballard, Michael B., *Long Shadow: Jefferson Davis and the Final Days of the Confederacy* (Univ. Press of Miss. 1986).

Cannon, Devereaux D., Jr., *The Flags of the Confederacy,* ed. by Roger Easson (Peachtree Pub. 1988).

Faust, Drew G., *The Creation of Confederate Nationalism* (La. State Univ. Press 1988).

Freeman, Douglas S., *Lee's Lieutenants,* 3 vols. (1942–1944; reprint, Scribner 1986).

Harter, Eugene C., *Lost Colony of the Confederacy* (Univ. Press of Miss. 1988).

Hattaway, Herman, *General Stephen D. Lee* (Univ. Press of Miss. 1988).

Shackelford, George G., *George Wythe Randolph and the Confederate Elite* (Univ. of Ga. Press 1988).

Vandiver, Frank E., *Basic History of the Confederacy* (1962; Krieger 1980).

Vandiver, Frank E., *Their Tattered Flags: The Epic of the Confederacy* (Harper's Mag. Press 1975).

Von Borcke, Heros, *Memoirs of the Confederate War for Independence* (1866; reprint, Butternut Press 1987).

**FIRST CONFEDERATE FLAG**
**1861**

**CONFEDERATE BATTLE FLAG**
**AND NAVY JACK       1861**

**CONFEDERATE FLAG**
**1863**

**CONFEDERATION,** kən-fed-ə-rā′shən, a form of political organization of component states, less centralized than a federation but more centralized than a league, alliance, or international organization.

All large political organizations composed of groups of varied cultures and interests face the problem of relating the component groups to each other and to the central government. Many solutions have been attempted. At one extreme is the empire or unitary government, which seeks to eliminate all direct relations between its component groups, to concentrate political authority in the center, and to permit the groups to exercise political authority only by delegation from the center. At the other extreme is the international organization, league, or alliance in which the relations of the sovereign states to each other and to central agencies are defined by rules flowing from their express, tacit, or presumed consent.

Between these extremes are confederations and federations. Their constitutions, which define the relations of the component states to the central government and to one another, many derive their authority from the government of the whole, from all of the people, or from the constituent states. A more complex process than legislation by the central government is needed to alter the constitution of a federation or confederation.

When the central government acts only upon the component states, as in the Swiss Confederation of the Middle Ages and the United States under the Articles of Confederation, the organization is usually called a confederation. When the central government acts on individuals in regard to certain matters and the component states act upon them in other areas, as in the present Swiss, United States, Canadian, Brazilian, Australian, Soviet, and Indian constitutions, the system is generally designated a federation.

**Confederation and Secession.** It is sometimes said that in confederations, but not in federations, the member states may secede. The right of secession, however, was asserted in the United States, clearly a federation, not only by the Southern states that exercised the "right" in 1861 but also by New England dissidents during the War of 1812. The constitutions of neither the Australian nor the Canadian federations refer to secession, but Western Australia and Quebec have discussed secession. Canada is sometimes called a confederation because the British North America Act of 1867, its constitution, guarantees extensive rights to the provinces. This was done to placate the demands of the French-speaking population of Quebec.

The Confederate States of America modeled its constitution on that of the United States, though the congress was expressly forbidden to enact a protective tariff or to interfere with slavery in the territories. There was, however, no express reference to a right of secession, though such a right may have been implied. The Soviet Union, a federation closely knit by the authority of the Communist party, is unique in expressly providing for secession of the member states. The right of secession from the British Commonwealth, a very loose confederation, is clearly recognized and was exercised by Ireland and South Africa.

**Integration and Disintegration.** There are forces for integration and disintegration in all political organizations. The Swiss moved from a loose alliance in the Middle Ages to confederation and, after 1848, to federation. The United States progressed from the Articles of Confederation to the Constitution and then, with the post-Civil War constitutional amendments and the Supreme Court's interpretations of the Constitution during the New Deal period, to increasing centralization. These developments resulted from the dominance of forces of integration, in both cases, however, broken by brief periods of civil war. On the other hand, the forces of disintegration led to the breakup of such political entities as the Holy Roman Empire, the 14th century Scandinavian Union of Kalmar, the Habsburg and Ottoman empires after World War I, and the British, French, and Dutch overseas empires after World War II.

Apart from the coercive power of central authority and the need for defense against external aggression, major integrating forces include the desire to resolve conflicts and to enjoy the advantages of free trade and economic cooperation, and the influence of abundant internal communications and a common culture and language. But factors leading to disintegration have been the desire of each locality to solve its own problems, great differences in the cultures, languages, and religions of component groups, limited communication between the various peoples, historic rivalries and conflicts, and protectionist demands of special interests. These factors are likely to be active when united defense against an external enemy is not imperative and central coercive authority is weak. Wartime alliances have usually collapsed as soon as the common enemy is defeated, as did the alliance between France and Sweden after the Thirty Year's War (1618–1648) and the coalition of the Western powers and the Soviet Union after World War II. Both the North Atlantic Treaty Organization (NATO) and Warsaw Pact alliances experienced strains of disunity after fear of the "cold war" had subsided in the 1960's.

While there has been a general tendency for small, isolated tribes of primitive peoples to develop into large nations, empires, federations, and international organizations, this process has not been a continuous one. Great empires have risen and fallen in all periods of history. Whether the United Nations and its specialized agencies move toward more effective confederation or even toward federation will depend upon the influence of technology, historical contingencies, the activities of statesmen and the course of public opinion. Large political organizations based on consent have developed in recent times, but at the same time empires based on coercion, which in the past maintained the largest political systems, have dissolved into individual national states.

See also FEDERALISM.

QUINCY WRIGHT, *Professor Emeritus of International Law, University of Chicago*

**Further Reading:** Creighton, Donald G., *The Road to Confederation: The Emergence of Canada, 1863-1867* (1965; reprint, Greenwood Press 1976); Forsyth, Murray G., *Unions of States* (Holmes & Meier 1981).

**CONFEDERATION, Articles of.** See ARTICLES OF CONFEDERATION.

**CONFEDERATION, Canadian.** See CANADA—47. *The Canadian Confederation, 1857–1914.*

**CONFEDERATION OF THE RHINE,** an association of German states created by Napoleon I in 1806. After the defeat of Austria at the Battle of Austerlitz in 1805, Napoleon wished to organize southern and western Germany as an area federated with the French Empire. He raised Bavaria and Württemberg to kingdoms and Baden and Hesse-Darmstadt to grand duchies; created new states such as the grand duchies of Berg and Frankfurt; and subordinated most of the free imperial cities and free counts and knights to modern governments that were bound to the interests of France. On July 12, 1806, 16 German princes signed the 40 articles of confederation that Talleyrand had drafted. The princes renounced the authority of the German emperor and seceded from the empire. They proclaimed Napoleon protector of the confederation and accepted the obligation to support France with troops in any Continental conflict. As a result, Francis II abdicated the imperial throne on Aug. 6, 1806.

After the defeat of Prussia in the fall, the confederation was extended to the Elbe. Twenty North German princes, among them the kings of Westphalia and Saxony, joined the group, but although the act of confederation envisaged the creation of a diet, no confederate organ came to life. In the fall of 1813, with the defeat of Napoleon's armies, the confederation was abolished, together with most of the German states that Napoleon had called into being. In southern Germany, however, the new states were preserved. Many internal reforms aimed at the destruction of German feudalism also survived the confederation.

HAJO HOLBORN
*Author of "A History of Modern Germany"*

**CONFESSION,** in criminal law, a statement by someone that he has committed a crime. If made under appropriate conditions, it can be used as evidence at a trial, whether it is oral or written, signed or unsigned. A *full confession* is one in which the person admits not only that he has done certain acts (pointed a gun at the victim and pulled the trigger) but also that he possessed the mental state (intent to kill, rather than believing the gun was not loaded) required to constitute a crime (murder). Often, however, the term "confession" is applied to statements or admissions that fall short of being full confessions but that are almost as incriminating.

**U.S. Bill of Rights.** Because a trustworthy confession is the easiest, the most reliable, and sometimes the only way to solve a crime, interrogation of a suspect is naturally the most desirable tool of law enforcement. Nevertheless, severe restrictions have been imposed by Anglo-American law from at least the early 17th century. In the United States the basic limitation is embodied in the Constitution—the privilege against self-incrimination found in the 5th Amendment: no person "shall be compelled in any criminal case to be a witness against himself." To many, it is one of the most distinctive characteristics of the relationship of government to the individual in a free society, a recognition that government itself should act nobly and with a proper regard for the dignity of the individual. To others, it is a shield for traitors and criminals, which it is proper to pierce under conditions not amounting to undue coercion. At present this privilege can be taken away, where authorized by law, only by a grant of immunity from prosecution for any crimes revealed by the answers.

Since adoption of the Bill of Rights, most restrictions on interrogation by law enforcement officers have been imposed by judges, partly through their power to accept or reject confessions as evidence in criminal trials and partly in their decisions as to when a person can be punished for refusing to answer questions before a grand jury, a court, or a legislative investigating committee.

For many years restrictions imposed on interrogation by law inforcement officers were aimed not only at brutality, such as torture, but also at more subtle coercive techniques that might induce an unreliable confession. However, even when a suspect refused at first to answer and, in effect, asserted his 5th Amendment privilege, questioning could continue. Thus the privilege was mostly effective in formal proceedings, where a person subpoenaed as a witness could rightfully refuse to answer questions and a defendant need not testify in his own behalf. The test of admissibility as evidence was whether the confession had been voluntary or involuntary. The courts took into account not only physical exhaustion and discomfort ("the third degree") but also psychological pressures.

**Supreme Court Rulings.** Some of the most controversial cases decided by the U.S. Supreme Court in the mid-20th century have added to restrictions on interrogation. With the McNabb-Mallory rule (from cases in 1943 and 1957) the court shifted to a different plane: a confession or admission, even though voluntary, would be excluded from evidence if federal officers violated the requirement that an arrested person be taken before a judge without unreasonable delay. In *Escobedo* v. *Illinois* (1964) both federal and state officers were required to permit a suspect to consult his attorney while being interrogated. Since *Miranda* v. *Arizona* (1966), all officers are required to advise a suspect in custody that he may remain silent and that he may consult an attorney and, under certain circumstances, be provided with one. If he asserts his privilege or requests an attorney, questioning must cease. If he decides to answer, it must be clearly established that he knowingly waived his rights.

Critics urge that the test should revert to whether a confession is voluntary and suggest that the 5th Amendment be amended. Supporters of the Miranda rule contend that the rule merely requires advising every suspect of rights he has always had.

RICHARD A. GREEN
*Director, American Bar Association Project
on Standards for Criminal Justice*

**CONFESSION,** an account written in 1878–1879 by the Russian novelist Leo Tolstoy (q.v.) of the intense spiritual crisis through which he passed for several years beginning about 1874. Tolstoy, who had been raised as a Russian Orthodox Christian, had long been troubled by his acquaintances' hypocritical behavior that ran counter to their religious professions. Tolstoy was driven ultimately to question the meaning of life. In *A Confession* he based his answer on the New Testament, strongly urging nonviolence, love, and physical work. This powerful, sincere, and moving record was followed by *What I Believe* (1884), a more didactic statement of Tolstoy's doctrines.

**CONFESSION, Sacramental,** in the Catholic Church, the act wherein a penitent accuses himself of his sins to a priest who is duly empowered to grant absolution (q. v.). This confession is likewise designated as *auricular,* for though it is made within the public view, it is committed by the penitent to the ear (Latin *auricula*) of the minister of the sacrament of penance. Even if the confession were made as an open and public admission, the priest would still inherently, that is, in the absence of any regulation to the contrary, possess the power of absolving the penitent.

The law of the Catholic Church requires the faithful, at least once in the course of the year, to confess whatever mortal sins they, upon a diligent examination of their consciences, recall since their last worthy confession, or since their previous baptism, in the event that they are making their initial confession. The penitent is also advised, but not commanded, to confess all his venial sins, in their kind and in their number, as he can recall them. Any willful concealing of a mortal sin, or also of what the penitent may erroneously deem a mortal sin, will render the act of absolution null and void. Accordingly, a new act of confession and absolution would be needed for the forgiveness of sins thus concealed in previous confessions. If after a due examination of his conscience a penitent lacks memory of an earlier committed mortal sin, then upon a later recollection of it he is under obligation to confess that sin to receive direct absolution granted by a priest.

Confessions usually are heard in a small enclosed compartment, called a *confessional,* in churches or oratories. In appearance the confessional resembles a sentry box. The priest sits inside; the penitent kneels outside and communicates with the priest through a finely perforated grating or a lattice of closely spaced crossing bars. Some confessionals have three compartments: the center one serving the priest and the flanking ones accommodating the penitents. The priest establishes communication with the penitent by moving a slide that covers the small grating that is in the wall between him and the penitent.

The word "confessional" may also designate the tomb of a martyr or confessor saint and the altar erected over it. If a church was built over the tomb, its altar usually lay directly over the tomb and the first altar, and was thus included in the title of confessional.

CLEMENT BASTNAGEL
*Catholic University of America*

**CONFESSION D'UN ENFANT DU SIÈCLE,** kôN-fe-syôN' dən näN-fäN' dü syəkl, an autobiographical novel published in 1836 by the French poet Alfred de Musset. Its title in English is *Confession of a Child of the Century.* It owed its immediate, great success to the fact that it was a thinly veiled history of the poet's love affair with George Sand, which she had already used as literary material in her *Lettres d'un voyageur.* Written shortly after their stormy affair, the *Confession* is very generous to the heroine of the romance and lacks the bitterness that later marked the references of the principals to each other.

For the sincerity of its self-revelation, the *Confession* is a personal document of great interest. But it is more. It is a wonderfully striking expression of that peculiar state of mind, often called "Byronic" in English, that was so common among the youth of the generation coming after the French Revolution and the Napoleonic wars, and known in France as *mal du siècle.* The book's opening pages contain a famous description of that malady together with an analysis of the conditions out of which it grew. Thus, the document is even more important for what it tells of the century than for what it reveals of the "child."

ARTHUR G. CANFIELD
*Author of "Poems of Victor Hugo"*

**CONFESSION OF FAITH, Westminster.** The Westminster Confession is the basic theological formula, together with the Longer and Shorter Catechisms, in the Presbyterian churches. It was drawn up in England by the Westminster Assembly of Divines, which was summoned by the Long Parliament in 1643. Episcopacy had been abolished by Parliament in January; the work of the assembly was to formulate a confession in accordance with the word of God and the doctrines of the best Reformed churches as a basis of religious uniformity in England, Scotland, and Ireland. Originally intended as a revision of the Thirty-nine Articles, the Confession became a substitute for it. A purely Calvinistic theology was set forth; upon its basis the Longer Catechism of 1648 was issued and, soon after, the Shorter Catechism.

Though the Confession lost its authority in England with the restoration of the monarchy, it has remained the standard of the Church of Scotland (Presbyterian) and has continued to be of fundamental theological significance for most Congregationalists and Baptists. Some modifications have been adopted in the 20th century. See also PRESBYTERIANISM.

FREDERICK C. GRANT
*Union Theological Seminary*

**CONFESSIONS, Les.** See ROUSSEAU, JEAN JACQUES.

**CONFESSIONS OF AN ENGLISH OPIUM EATER,** a combination of autobiography and fantasy, is the most famous work of the English Romantic essayist Thomas De Quincey. The *Confessions* appeared in two installments in the *London Magazine* in 1821 and in book form in 1822, and was extensively revised by De Quincey in 1856. Although the relatively diffuse revision is inferior to the original, both editions are valuable, not only for their fine prose style, but for their psychological insights in a period well before the advent of modern psychology.

The *Confessions* of 1856 begins with an *Introductory Narrative,* which gives a full account of De Quincey's life up to the time he became a "regular and confirmed" opium user. It includes a moving account of his friendship with a London prostitute and digressions on literature. Middle sections, *The Pleasures of Opium* and *The Pains of Opium,* describe the heightened sensibility and the terrifying hallucinations that occur under the influence of the drug. The *Confessions* concludes with exaggerated accounts of opium-inspired dreams, including *The Daughter of Lebanon,* a dream fantasy in the highly wrought style of the 17th century English prose masters.

THOMAS J. ASSAD
*Tulane University*

## CONFESSIONS OF SAINT AUGUSTINE.

Among the few immortal autobiographies, probably the work that has had most influence, in the intellectual world at least, is *The Confessions of Saint Augustine* (397–401). He wrote it shortly after he became bishop of Hippo, just before 400, when he was in his early 40's. The fact that the book has maintained its popularity for over 1,500 years shows from how close to the human heart it is written. For the *Confessions* is the history of Augustine's heart. We have two other sets of autobiographical documents from his hands: the *Retractationes*, which is the story of his mind, and his letters, which give an account of his activities.

St. Augustine's *Confessions* is not, as so many people imagine, an account of past deeds and, above all, not an avowal of youthful transgressions as such. The word confession is used in the Biblical sense of the Latin word *confiteri* as an acknowledgment. Augustine's *Confessions* is quite literally the acknowledgment of a soul forced to admire the action of God within itself, though it has to admit the many obstacles that it placed in the way of Divine influence. It is full of the psychology of human conduct, though so many people seem to think that only in comparatively recent years have men begun to reflect thus carefully on their inner activities. It has been said of the book, "Neither in respect of penetrating analysis of the most complex impressions of the soul nor communicative feeling, nor elevation of sentiment, nor depth of philosophic views, is there any book like it in all literature."

As Augustine was one of the profoundest intellectual geniuses of human history, famous above all for his marvelous insight into human motives and his capacity to describe the various states of the soul and the facts of the spiritual world, it can be readily understood why this little book in which he set no barriers in his desire to reveal for God's honor and glory all that had gone on within him in the motivation of his life should be of supreme human interest.

The excursions into child psychology in the first book of the *Confessions*, exemplifying that a child has definite tendencies away from law and order toward neglect of study and precept, learns not by rules but by example, and observes closely the inconsistencies of elders, have drawn many to reading the rest of the book. The boy Augustine was very human, hated Greek and liked "the empty tales of the poets," blames, like everyone else, the method of his education, and yet confesses how much more of good than of ill came to him from it. He went through a certain period when he liked to pity himself and has a chapter "On Weeping and Why It Is Pleasant to Be Wretched." Above all he shows very clearly how much personal affection meant to him. The death of a friend overwhelms him, but companions serve to console him; it is his mother who rescues him, not his principles; he comes under the personal influence of Ambrose; always it is personality that draws him. Augustine soon came to realize that the claims of his intellect for satisfaction were incapable of fulfillment, and his *Confessions* will probably continue to be a favorite book for those who like himself have learned the lesson that the heart life of man is much more important than his intellectual life. See also AUGUSTINE, SAINT.

JAMES J. WALSH
*Author of "Catholic Churchmen in Science"*

## CONFESSOR,

in the Roman Catholic Church, has two meanings. It may denote a canonized male saint outside the classes of the apostles, evangelists, and martyrs. In earliest times the only saints who on their death received public veneration in the church were the Blessed Virgin (Mary), the apostles, and the Christian martyrs, and it is these saints who receive mention in the Roman canon of the Mass, though the Milanese canon (Ambrosian rite) carries the names of other saints as well. The second meaning of confessor is the priest who hears confessions. In this sense it corresponds to the Latin word *confessarius*.

CLEMENT BASTNAGEL
*Catholic University of America*

## CONFIDENCE GAMES.

The swindles known as confidence games entered Europe in the 15th century with the Gypsies, who brought them from the East. Non-Gypsies adopted them in the burgeoning European underworld, where they were played for very small *scores* by today's standards. As criminals migrated—or were deported—to America, the *con-games* came along and *con-men* flourished on the westward-moving frontier, using the rather limited European techniques that eventually became the numerous and profitable *short-con* games of today.

The *big-con* is an American phenomenon. It branched off about 1875 with the development of a *store* or dishonest gambling establishment against which *marks* were *steered*. An *inside-man* handled the *mark*, the game being supported by *shills* to stimulate play, character actors as needed, convincing props, and effective fiscal arrangements with the law. The *mark* was supplied funds for initial phases of the *play*, directed against the *store* (which had obviously liquid assets) instead of against an individual. *Mitt-stores, monte-stores, gold-brick-stores,* and *fight-stores* spread rapidly, and in 1902 a *score* of $50,000 caused a sensation in the underworld. Good minds went to work to perfect this principle and by 1906 produced the most effective swindling operations ever invented.

Modern *big-con* games are *the wire* (now obsolescent), *the pay-off,* and *the rag*. *The wire* convinced the *mark* that, with the connivance of a corrupt Western Union official, race results could be delayed long enough for him to bet on the winner after the race was won. An elaborate form of *past-posting*, it involved a dummy Western Union office and a fake gambling club where *shills* won and lost large bets to arouse the larceny in the *mark*. *Scores* of $50,000 to $100,000 were not unusual by 1910.

The *pay-off* convinces the *mark* that he can share information being used to break the big-time bookmakers. He is allowed to win consistently on funds advanced by the *con-mob*, then sent home to liquidate enough of his assets to make a real killing. When he returns, he is wiped out. An elaborate *store* (private gambling club), capable of being swiftly dismantled and moved from place to place, is used. A staff of experts, directed by a skilled *inside-man*, manage the final stages of the play. As many as 40 or 50 *ropers* travel the world over in search of wealthy *marks* who can be moved to the *store* for a *play*, while a *boost* of off-duty *ropers* posing as financiers, millionaire sportsmen, or industrial executives control the tempo of the *action* with deadly precision. Psychologically sound devices discourage the *mark* from reporting his loss, and the *fix* is pushed into very high places, including banks, to handle the *mark's* checks. *Scores* may go to $250,000.

*The rag* resembles the *pay-off*, except that stocks are used and a fake brokerage replaces the fake gambling club, while the *con-men* become "investment brokers." Recent federal laws intended to outlaw the sending or taking of funds across state lines are only partially successful, since subterfuges are readily invented by *con-mobs*, especially those operating internationally. Prosecution of *big-con men* is difficult, expensive, and seldom successful, largely because the *mark* must virtually admit to criminal involvement if he prosecutes. It is literally true that "you can't cheat an honest man" on the *big-con*.

D. W. Maurer, University of Louisville<br>Author of "The Big Con"

**CONFIDENCE-MAN: HIS MASQUERADE,** a satire by Herman Melville (q.v.) published in 1857. It was Melville's last full-length work. The book, laid on a Mississippi riverboat on April Fools' Day, lacks the continuity of action of a novel; instead, it is a series of parables unified by one central character, the Confidence-Man. This scoundrel, appearing in various disguises, dupes a number of his fellow passengers by gaining and abusing their trust, and the one attempt to unmask him fails. *The Confidence-Man* is a bitter attack on both trust and distrust and on the greed, hypocrisy, and soft-heartedness that make swindles possible.

**CONFIDENTIAL CLERK,** a comedy by T.S. Eliot, first produced at the Edinburgh Festival in August 1953. It had its London premiere later in 1953 and its first American production in New York in 1954.

Based on the device of mistaken identity and constructed on a series of recognition scenes of mounting complexity, *The Confidential Clerk*, is one of Eliot's most skillfully plotted plays. The hero, Colby Simpkins, is first identified as the illegitimate son of Sir Claude Mulhammer, then as the illegitimate son of Lady Elizabeth, and finally as the legitimate son of Mrs. Guzzard. Rather than remain the confidential clerk of Sir Claude, Colby chooses to become cleric to the world through a musical and, possibly, a religious vocation. Colby's search for identity is at once a search for his origins and for his role in life. Deliberate overloading of the convention unraveling in Act III produces a comic and magical quality in the revelation of Colby's past.

Oscar Brownstein<br>University of Iowa

**CONFIRMATION** is one of the seven sacraments of the Roman Catholic Church. Though usage is not entirely consistent, it is described by the Lutheran, Anglican (including Episcopal), and some other churches as a rite rather than a sacrament. At confirmation the candidate renews publicly the promises made on his behalf by his sponsors in baptism, and is admitted to the status of a communicant at the Lord's Supper, with full privileges of church membership.

Confirmation originated as the second and completing part of baptism: the "sealing" of the newly baptized with chrism (oil), symbolic of anointing by the Holy Spirit. In the Greek and Oriental churches the two parts are still united. In the West they have been separated, and con-

firmation is usually not administered until at least the eighth year. In the Lutheran and Anglican churches it is administered when the child has reached "years of discretion," and is able to take his baptismal vows upon himself.

In the Latin rite the bishop marks the sign of the cross with consecrated oil on the forehead of the candidate, saying, "(Name) receive the seal of the Holy Spirit, the Gift of the Father." The candidate replies, "Amen." This anointing with chrism, and the words that accompany it and constitute the sacrament, give the candidate the character, or indelible seal, of the Lord.

Among Anglicans the signing with the cross takes place at baptism. At confirmation the following formula is used when the bishop places his hands on the head of the candidate: "Defend, O Lord, this thy child [or servant] with thy heavenly grace; that he may continue thine for ever; and daily increase in thy Holy Spirit more and more, until he come unto thy everlasting Kingdom. Amen."

Frederick C. Grant<br>Author of "Basic Christian Beliefs"

**CONFISCATION** is the compulsory expropriation of property by a governmental authority without compensation. Hence, expropriation (seizure) with fair compensation does not constitute confiscation, but if compensation is inadequate this procedure contains elements of confiscation. *Annexation*, in turn, is the acquisition, usually by occupation, either of no-man's-land or, by force or treaty, of territory of one international entity by another. Confiscation must also be distinguished from *sequestration*, the putting of property (such as enemy property in wartime) into the hands of custodians who administer it on behalf of the owner until its final disposition; and from *freezing* of assets (especially bank accounts of foreigners) by a governmental order preventing the owner from disposing of them until they are "unfrozen." The term *forfeiture* is sometimes used synonymously with confiscation but also means termination by a private party of another party's rights because of violation of a contract.

**Historical Background.** Confiscation has played a great role in history, and the views about its permissibility have undergone many changes. For example, from the 4th century on, pagan (and subsequently Muslim) religious property was dispossessed on behalf of the Roman Catholic Church. During the Reformation, Protestant rulers confiscated Catholic church property; for example, England's Henry VIII expropriated abbey lands. Church property was confiscated in France during the French Revolution, in other European countries as a result of Napoleon's reforms, and in Mexico early in the 20th century. A major aim of the Russian Revolution was "the expropriation of the expropriators."

Confiscation has been used as a weapon of religious or ethnic discrimination and persecution. In past centuries various European countries imposed frequent confiscation measures, especially on Jews, sometimes in connection with expulsion, sometimes as a prize for permission to stay. Nazi Germany imposed increasingly confiscatory taxes or huge collective fines as steps toward physical extermination.

Revolutionary governments (including all the states after the American Revolution; see Loyalists) have confiscated goods of their adversaries, as a penalty for treason or to secure their regimes. The U. S. Constitution authorizes Congress to punish treason by forfeiture.

Especially since the end of World War II, Britain, France, and other non-Communist countries have "nationalized" or "socialized" some sectors of the economy, such as large industries, railroads, mines, banks, and insurance companies. "Nationalization" or "socialization" means that the property, for which (except in rare instances) compensation is paid, is then owned and operated by the government for the benefit of the nation.

**Foreign Assets.** Since World War II, foreign economic entrenchment has come under fire in developing territories. Expropriation is argued on nationalistic grounds—that foreigners should not be allowed to run important aspects of a nation's economy; and on economic grounds—that foreign investments, especially if made long ago, have yielded such high profits that the investors have been amply repaid. The counterargument is that the recipient country has obtained much larger benefits from the investments, and that in any case indemnification must be computed on the basis of the current value of the assets. In principle, international law acknowledges the right of states to take over foreign assets. It is sometimes argued that in case of particular hardship, this can be done even against existing treaty obligations, either because the treaty was "unequal" or because the situation the treaty was intended to regulate no longer prevails. However, the latter doctrine, *rebus sic stantibus*, is controversial. Also, economic and political considerations militate against confiscation of foreign assets; the capital-exporting countries are also politically stronger, so that their countermeasures (which must never include military threats or action) can really be damaging. Furthermore, the country contemplating confiscation may depend on trade and other contacts with the capitalist world. For such reasons, even Communist governments have preferred to negotiate some compensation.

**Domestic Laws.** Harmful goods can be confiscated in exercise of the police power—for example, certain addictive drugs and other objects that are dangerous to public health, morals, or safety.

**Enemy Territory.** Plundering ("pillage") was formerly considered permissible in occupied enemy territory during war. By the 19th century, abhorrence of such looting had become general, and under an international convention of 1907 (Hague Regulations Regarding the Laws and Customs of War on Land) pillage is formally forbidden. Military equipment and other movable property owned by the enemy state can still be taken as booty, provided it is to be used for military operations; such confiscations must never disrupt unreasonably the economy of the occupied territory or cause its population to starve. Privately owned goods usable for war purposes can be seized, but not as free booty; the owner must be given a receipt, and the goods must, unless returned, be paid for. Immovable property, whether public or private, may never be confiscated but may be utilized by the occupant. Any movable object owned by any hospital, school, religious institution, museum, scientific institution, and the like may not be touched. Any violation of these rules constitutes a war crime. Thus the Nuremberg Tribunal (1946) condemned the plunder of occupied countries by Germany in World War II.

JOHN H. E. FRIED
*The City College, New York*

**CONFLICT,** in theories of personality, is usually considered a state of discomfort or stress caused by an individual's experiencing two or more desires or needs that are incompatible.

**Theories of Conflict.** Conflict has been a major concept in the theories of most authorities on neurosis and personality disturbance, from the pioneering work of Sigmund Freud and Alfred Adler to the later American behavioristic writings of John Dollard and Neal Miller. Freud felt that conflict is basically between sexual motivation and the prohibitions against sexual wishes, thoughts, and actions imposed by society. Other psychoanalysts have not agreed with Freud as to the nature of conflict, but all agree that at the root of personality disturbance there is conflict and the discomfort aroused by conflict. Karen Horney, for example, felt that neurosis resulted from a conflict between impulses to hostility and aggression and the prohibitions against hostile impulses and actions. In Carl Rogers' view, personality disturbance is an aftermath of a conflict between what the individual learns about himself and what he had hoped to believe about himself.

Modern stimulus-response theorists (Dollard, Miller, and others) hold that conflict results whenever drives or responses compete significantly with one another. In this view, personality maladjustment is the result of conflicting drives that block the individual from gaining a satisfying state of affairs for a relatively prolonged period of time. Thus, a young man may want very badly to enjoy the company of girls, but he may also be very much afraid of young women. His fear conflicts with his wish to mingle freely with girls and may even prevent him from going near them; that is, his wish to be popular is blocked by his fear. There is little hope that he can satisfy his need for female companionship as long as fear blocks an approach to women. Thus his desire for companionship is frustrated and continues at a high level. In technical terms, the young man is described as being in a state of "chronic high drive." This chronic high drive causes feelings of tension and discomfort.

**Major Types of Conflict.** Conflicts are classified into three major types. In *approach-avoidance conflicts*, the individual experiences both the desire to have and the desire to avoid a certain object or goal, as in the example of the young man and girls. In *double-approach conflicts*, the individual is torn between a desire to gain two equally attractive but mutually exclusive goals. An example is the problem of a man who is very happy with his home but who also is anxious to gain a promotion in his job. He is offered the promotion if he will transfer to a much less desirable town. In *double-avoidance conflicts*, the invidual is surrounded by nonsatisfying conditions with little hope of achieving the things he desires, as in the example of a man who must choose between the boredom of unemployment and the monotony of a menial job. There is one other condition that commonly frustrates: a barrier that blocks or prevents the achievement of goals, as when lack of money prevents a student from continuing in school.

AUSTIN E. GRIGG
*University of Richmond*

**CONFLICT OF INTEREST.** Any interest or loyalty of an individual may conflict at times with another of his interests or loyalties. In common usage, however, the term "conflict of interest" concerns only two interests: the interest of an official or fiduciary in the responsible discharge of his duties and the official's or fiduciary's private economic interest. An example would be an internal revenue agent auditing his own tax return. Regulation of conflicts of interest seeks to prevent such situations of temptation from arising. Laws and regulations against conflicts of interest are peculiar in that they are directed not against actual injury but against potentially injurious situations.

Although Plato stripped his philosopher-kings of personal assets and although the Sermon on the Mount warned against serving two masters, subsequent generations did not think it shocking that a king should own a part of governmentally granted monopolies, that a baron should be landlord, governor, judge, and tax collector, that warships should be privately owned and operated, or that Sen. Daniel Webster should be on retainer from the National Bank.

**Executive.** In the United States, procurement scandals in the Civil War and abuses in handling claims against the government led to enactment of the statutes that, overhauled and modernized during the administration of President John F. Kennedy, make up the body of law governing conflicts of interest of federal employees.

These statutes regulate federal executive employees in four problem areas: the employee who undertakes to work for outsiders in their dealings with the government; the official who acts on behalf of the government in a transaction in which he has a personal economic interest; the former government employee who later appears on the other side of the table from the government to represent himself or others in matters with which he was engaged while a government employee; and the employee who accepts pay from outsiders for his government work. The statutes are both limited in focus and technical in their drafting, so that administrative regulations often provide the critical guidelines to conduct by government officials, as in the matter of gifts.

Part of the pattern of federal regulation of conflicts of interest is the practice of some Senate committees to inquire into the personal economic positions of presidential appointees before senatorial confirmation. For example, in 1953 the Senate Armed Services Committee required Charles E. Wilson, the former president of General Motors Corporation — a major government contractor — to divest himself of his stockholdings in that company before the committee would act favorably on his appointment by President Eisenhower as secretary of defense.

Overstringent restraints imposed in the name of avoiding conflicts of interest can be and have been a significant deterrent to the enlistment in public service of men of high competence and experience when, as a concomitant to accepting governmental appointment, they must dislocate their personal business affairs not only while they are in office but for a period thereafter. This problem has been even more acute for the part-time consultant to a government agency. Furthermore when, as in the science fields, government, industry, and educational institutions are increasingly operating on a partnership basis, it is not workable to insist that a man may not work "for" government unless he ceases to work "for" industry or "for" an educational institution.

**Legislatures.** Members of Congress have been forbidden by statute since 1864 to receive compensation for services rendered before a federal agency (but not before a court), and an increasing number of states have adopted a similar rule. But the conflict of interest problem in the legislative branch is distinct from that in the executive. To prevent a senator who is a farmer and who is elected by farmers from voting on farm subsidies because he will personally benefit from them runs afoul of the basic premises of American representative government.

Efforts have been made to tighten restrictions on the personal economic affairs of legislators. But until new ways are found to generate the large sums required for modern political campaigns, and until legislators receive reasonable compensation, legislators — who often serve only part time in their official capacities and whose jobs are always in political jeopardy — are not likely to impose on themselves stringent conflict of interest restraints that cut off their outside economic affiliations and forbid outside donations.

**Judiciary.** When, as seldom happens, a case comes before a judge who has a personal economic interest in its outcome, the judge will by tradition disqualify himself, and the case is either reassigned to another judge or heard by the other members of the court. There is no current agitation for additional conflict of interest regulation of the judiciary.

**Confidence in Government.** Public confidence in the government is vital, especially in a democracy. To preserve that confidence, government officials not only must be honest but also must be believed by the public to be honest. A president may feel that he must ask an official to resign, not because he is corrupt, and not even because his economic interests are in fact in conflict with the duties of his office, but because circumstances are such that it would appear to outsiders that such a conflict exists. Perhaps in part because overt graft and corruption are rare in contemporary American public administration, the charge of "conflict of interest" has become a death-dealing weapon in American political life.

**Conflicts in the Private Sector.** Conflict of interest problems calling for regulation arise in the private sector as well as the governmental. Corporate officers are liable where they personally avail themselves of an economic opportunity that should properly have gone to the collective enterprise; trustees have long been held liable for any gains realized or losses sustained from transactions in which they dealt personally with the subject of the trust; and the canons of the legal profession demand that a lawyer hold undivided loyalty to but one party in a transaction.

Common practice of the general marketplace, however, is more lax; the brokerage function obviously implies a different tradition; and there is evidence that in business activities involving sales and procurement conflicting interests are not uncommon.

BAYLESS MANNING
*Dean, Stanford University School of Law*

**Further Reading:** Manning, Bayless, *A Concise Textbook on Legal Capital*, 2d ed. (Foundation Press 1981); Williams, Sandra, *Conflict of Interest: The Ethical Dilemma* (Gower Pub. 1985).

**CONFORMAL PROJECTION.** See PROJECTION.

**CONFORMITY,** kən-fôr′mə-tē, in sociology, is a concept used by members of a society to evaluate their own behavior and that of others. It can best be understood in relation to other such concepts, including regularity, consensus, norm, alienation, rebellion, and revolution.

In describing the recurring uniformities or lack of uniformities in social behavior objectively, without giving them a normative, or moral, evaluation, we are describing the *regularity* or *irregularity* of that behavior. One of the major goals of sociology is to describe these uniformities, or regularities, or patterns, or structures, as they are variously called. Thus we can say, for example, that Americans drive on the right, the British on the left. This is an objective description of an actual regularity. All societies are made up of these objectively observable regularities, but no society is without some irregularity, some disorder, and at times some chaos. The everyday functioning of society is largely a mixture of a good deal of regularity with some irregularity, or deviance. At times the irregularity in society may become so great that the society dissolves; with less deviance it may undergo fundamental change resulting in new patterns of regularity. A *rebellion* may be defined as an unsuccessful attempt to establish such new patterns, and a *revolution* as a social movement that succeeds in establishing new basic regularities.

In addition to what "is" in a society, there is an "ought to be," a moral construct, called a *norm.* The norms and values set up by members of a society to define how people ought to behave constitute a chief source and support for regular societal patterns. General agreement among the members of a society on these norms, or rules of behavior, is known as a *consensus.* Insofar as social behavior is based on such a consensus, on shared norms or values, it is said to be *institutionalized.* Institutionalization, or *normative consensus,* is a source stressed by modern social scientists as of regularity in social behavior.

**Modern Attitudes.** In light of these explanations, the meaning of conformity becomes clear. As noted above, conformity is not an objective concept used by social scientists. Its moral overtones stem from the consensus among the members of a society that individuals must give up some of their individual freedom and conform to generally accepted norms for the good of society. Thus some people use the term "conformity" as praise, and "nonconformity" as dispraise. Others however, approve of "nonconformity" and disapprove of "conformity." These terms are likely to be used much more frequently in modern Western liberal society, often even by professional social scientists, than in other types of contemporaneous society or in earlier societies. Modern Western society very highly values individualism, liberty, originality, and creativity. All these values approve of a certain amount of irregularity of behavior, and therefore irregularity itself may become highly valued. Indeed an absolute, perhaps a utopian, emphasis on irregularity sometimes becomes valued, leading to a total moral condemnation of conformity and approval of nonconformity. On the other hand, those in modern society whose values or social positions make them fearful of novelty or irregularity, such as those termed "radical rightists," and certain religious fundamentalists, are likely to strongly disapprove of any type of nonconformity.

One of the social variables that seems to determine attitudes toward conformity, particularly in modern society, is the conflict between youth and age. Youth is likely to use the notion of conformity in a dispraising way, judging irregularity to be a valuable means of expressing independence of the parental generation as well as enthusiasm and creativity not yet dampened by experience. In fact some "liberal" older people think there is something a little wrong with a young person who does not want to be at least somewhat nonconformist. Other older people, constrained by experience, knowing the often dysfunctional effects of youthful irregularity even when these effects are unintended, and acknowledging the necessity for social order, often condemn irregularity as foolish, childish, or wicked nonconformity. The different ways in which youth and age view irregularity and the consequently different moral views they take of conformity and nonconformity are part of the inevitable societal conflict of generations, which sociologists have recently recognized and tried to analyze. This conflict is less in some societies than in others, perhaps particularly where the amount and rate of social change is less, but some minimum conflict seems to be endemic.

**Alienation.** The phenomenon of alienation is closely related to conformity and nonconformity. Karl Marx used the term "alienation" to mean both the physical separation of the workers from the instruments of production, and the moral disgust of the workers with the established regularities of their society. This latter sense is most commonly used by present-day social scientists. In some cases, such alienation may result in irregular behavior, in deliberate or nondeliberate nonconformity. This irregular behavior may consist of not working, or violating sexual norms, of being revolutionary, or of escaping by taking drugs. But alienation is also expressed in less overt ways. Despite his disgust, the worker or citizen may go through his routines obediently, woodenly, all the while in silent moral protest against the social bonds he despises. There is not yet much solid research, however, on the types, social sources, and consequences of alienation in this sense.

Social irregularity, variously approved of or disapproved of as nonconformity, is sometimes segregated in particular communities or in particular parts of a community. This is known as ecological or spatial patterning. Thus sociologists have described the social irregularities in the so-called bohemias—Greenwich Villages, skid rows, hobohemias, red light districts, and the like. In these enclaves, those who practice various forms of irregular behavior can find instruction and moral support from their peers, and structured insulation from those who despise their nonconformity. Such ecological enclaves as Greenwich Village are more likely to be inhabited by young and often temporary nonconformists, while areas like the Bowery in New York City are more likely to be inhabited by older and more permanent ones. Some of these nonconformist enclaves are visited for short periods by conformists seeking a temporary opportunity for irregularity. Thus here as elsewhere, social regularity and irregularity, conformity and nonconformity, function interrelatedly, and must be viewed together. See also CONSENSUS.

BERNARD BARBER, *Barnard College*

**Further Reading:** Gillespie, Marcia, and others eds., *But Thinking Makes It So* (Irvington 1977); Kirk, Russell, *Enemies of the Permanent Things* (Sugden 1984).

CONFUCIUS, as depicted in an ink rubbing from a stele of 1734 in the Peilin, Sian, in Shensi, China.

**CONFUCIUS,** kən-fyōō'shəs (551–479 B. C.), was a sage of ancient China and its greatest philosopher. In the course of China's long history Confucius stands out as the most prominent figure. Without any claim to divinity or reference to the supernatural, the teachings of Confucius have exercised such a molding influence that if the Chinese way of life were to be characterized in one word it would be "Confucian." He is revered among the Chinese as their Supreme Sage and Foremost Teacher, and his temple is found in every one of China's some 2,000 counties. Few civilizations of the world can cite a comparable historical figure.

**Life of Confucius.** Confucius was born in 551 B. C. to the K'ung family in the state of Lu, in today's Shantung province. At the time, the imperial court of the Chou dynasty had lost its power and the empire virtually disintegrated into a number of feudal states. Born into an impoverished noble family, the boy was named Ch'iu, meaning a hill, because there was a noticeable protuberance on his head. His literary name was Chung-ni. These names have been rarely used, however, because of the Chinese practice of showing reverence by avoidance, and K'ung Futzu, meaning K'ung the Grand Master, has been throughout the ages the most popular reference. Confucius is the Latinized form of K'ung Fu-tzu, first introduced to the West by Catholic missionaries in China during the early 17th century.

His father died when Confucius was only three years old, and the boy was brought up by his mother who was his father's second wife and his father's junior by a wide margin. Even in his childhood Confucius liked to play ceremonials, which are a prized expression of the religious and cultural tradition. At 15 he became seriously interested in learning. Reflecting on his intellectual and spiritual progress, Confucius, late in life, said: "At 15, I set my heart on learning. At 30, I was firmly established. At 40, I had no more doubts. At 50, I knew the will of Heaven. At 60, I was ready to listen to it. At 70, I could follow my heart's desire without transgressing what was right" (*Analects of Confucius*, chap. 2, section 4).

Confucius grew to unusual height and people called him "long fellow." He had to go to work early in life, and he did a creditable job of attending to a nobleman's granaries and flocks. Confucius was given an opportunity to travel to the imperial capital, where he was able to immerse himself in the cultural tradition of the nation at its source. The experience was greatly enjoyed by Confucius, and some later historians even insisted that Confucius called upon Lao Tzu, who was then serving as the keeper of imperial archives. Confucius' earnestness and diligence in learning made him probably the most learned man of his day, even though he was mostly self-educated. Many younger men were attracted to him as their teacher.

To Confucius, as to Socrates, knowledge meant wisdom, particularly the kind of wisdom that would contribute to a better life for the individual and society. That is, Confucius was foremost a reformer—a reformer of men and governments. It was a time of chaos and Confucius' ambition in life was to restore order. His political platform included such items as avoidance of needless war, reduction of taxation, and mitigation of severe punishment. But to totally restore the order that Confucius thought had prevailed in the Age of Grand Harmony would be a major operation—both the personal attitude of the rulers and their public policies would have to be redirected. Confucius hoped earnestly to be appointed to a high office in order to launch his reform programs. He was eventually given such an opportunity with his appointment as a high minister in the state of Lu.

But Confucius' successful efforts were cut short by the jealousy and intrigue of a neighboring state. Sense of honor prompted him to resign from his post, but not without reluctance. Now in his 50's, he set off on what turned out to be a 13-year sojourn and travel among various states. The travel was arduous and sometimes dangerous. On the whole, Confucius was received with politeness and decorum by the princes but was never given any confidence or power. Once or twice his service was sought, but he spurned the offers because they came from unprincipled pretenders.

The number of disciples and pupils grew with Confucius' reputation as the sage-teacher of the day. Tradition speaks of 3,000 pupils of whom 72 had mastered the 6 arts—rituals, music, archery, charioteering, literature, and mathematics. A number of his disciples obtained responsible positions in government on Confucius' recommendation. At 67, Confucius was welcomed back to Lu by the reigning prince at the suggestion of a minister who was a disciple of Confucius. He spent his remaining years editing the classical texts and continuing his teaching. In 479 B. C., Confucius died at 72 and was buried in Ch'üfu.

**The Works of Confucius.** The most reliable work on the life and teaching of Confucius is the *Lun-yü,* or *Analects of Confucius,* a volume consisting of notes and journals on Confucius' sayings and activities kept by the disciples and put together after the master's death. Confucius is said to have written the *Ch'un-ch'iu* or the *Spring and Autumn Annals* (of the State of Lu), and to have edited the *Shih Ching* or the *Classic of Poetry,* the *Shu Ching* or the *Classic of History,* the *Yi Ching* or the *Classic of Changes,* and the *Li Chi* or the *Classic of Ceremonials.* This group of ancient texts is known as the Five Classics. During the Sung dynasty (960–1279) Confucian scholars brought together the *Analects,* the *Mencius,* the *Ta Hsueh,* or the *Great Learning,* attributed to Tseng Shen, a disciple of Confucius, and the *Chung Yung,* or the *Doctrine of the Mean,* attributed to Tzu Ssu, the grandson of Confucius. They named the collection the Four Books. The Four Books and the Five Classics are the Confucian texts and have for centuries served as the syllabus for education in China—the Four Books at the primary level and the Five Classics at the secondary level.

**Confucius, the Teacher.** The tremendous influence that Confucius has exercised is due to his personality as much as to his teaching. Combined with an easy manner Confucius had a keen sense of mission—a sense of an appointment by heaven to restore order out of chaos and to relieve the people from their suffering. Confucius wanted to be a statesman, but he had to be content with being a teacher for most of his life. Down to the time of Confucius, education had been the special privilege of the nobility, and instructors were government officials. Confucius was the first private teacher in China, and the first to engage in teaching as a means of reform as well as livelihood. Confucius might be said to be the founding father of a new class in Chinese society, namely the powerful class of literati, or scholars, which eventually replaced the imperial court and aristocracy as the seat of the cultural authority of the nation.

Confucius is revered as the Foremost Teacher of China, because basically he had a deep conviction in the native integrity and dignity as well as the equality and educability of all men. The well-known Confucian saying, "In education there are no class distinctions" (*Analects of Confucius,* chap. 15, section 38) follows naturally from the penetrating observation, "By nature all men are pretty much alike; it is by custom and habit that they are set apart" (*Analects of Confucius,* chap. 17, section 2). Confucius kept an open-door school, and young men were admitted on the sole consideration of their eagerness to learn. He saw abundant potential in each of the students, and in each he sought to develop the total man. The objective was to help each student to develop his virtue and talent to the full, and to provide society and government with leaders.

Confucius' method of instruction was personal and informal. Conversation with individual students or small groups seemed to be the favorite practice. Sometimes the same question was given different answers when different pupils asked it. When his students disagreed with him, he was not affronted and, sometimes, acknowledged that they could be right. In spite of his open-minded approach, however, he did insist on intellectual honesty and alertness. Confucius said: "Yu, shall I teach you what knowledge is? When you know

a thing, say that you know it; when you do not know a thing, admit that you do not know it. That is knowledge" (*Analects of Confucius,* chap. 2, section 17). Confucius did not try to provide all the answers, even if he had them. Occasionally he merely raised the questions and required the students to find the answers. He said, "If I hold up one corner of a square and the student cannot work out the other three for himself, I won't go any further" (*Analects of Confucius,* chap. 7, section 8).

Confucius readily won the affection and respect of his students, and an inner circle of disciples stood by him through good and bad fortune. Evidently tuition was collected from each student according to his financial circumstance. As it happened, the master's favorite disciple was Yen Hui, who was so poverty-stricken that he had "a single bamboo bowl of millet to eat, a gourdful of water to drink, living in a back alley" (*Analects of Confucius,* chap. 6, section 9). Yen Hui died before Confucius. When the news was broken to Confucius, he burst forth, as he rarely did, "Heaven has bereaved me, Heaven has bereaved me!" Upon Confucius' own death, his disciples mourned him as they mourned the death of their parents. This teacher-student rapport and intimacy became a general pattern in China. When a teacher's day was instituted in modern China a few decades ago, September 28, Confucius' legendary birthday, was chosen as the day.

**Teachings of Confucius.** Confucius claimed to be "a transmitter and not an innovator" (*Analects of Confucius,* chap. 7, section 1). This is true only in the sense that he adopted certain ideas and ideals from antiquity, but actually he was very much of an original thinker, even a revolutionary thinker, without advertising himself as such.

*On Humanity and Decorum.* At the center of the Confucian system is humanity, or *jen* in Chinese. "*Jen* is to love men," Confucius said (*Analects of Confucius,* chap. 12, section 22). *Jen* might also be translated as benevolence, love, manhood, or human-heartedness. To Confucius, *jen* is the essence of humanity, that element in man which makes a man man and which distinguishes him from an animal. *Jen* is endowed by nature but should be cultivated by man, and the greatness of man is measured by the extent of the development of *jen* in him. *Jen* is so essential to man that the preservation of one's *jen* is considered more important than the preservation of one's life, and it is so central in the teaching of Confucius that the system might be said to be the philosophy of *jen.*

The virtue of filial piety and those of loyalty and reciprocity were also stressed by Confucius, and they might be regarded as expressions of *jen* within the family and in social relations respectively. The Confucian golden rule has become well known—"Do not do to others what one does not wish to be done unto"—(*Analects of Confucius,* chap. 12, section 2), and Confucius also said, "Wishing to be established oneself he assists others to be established; wishing to be successful oneself he assists others to be successful" (*Analects of Confucius,* chap. 6, section 28). The teachings of Confucius underline the kinship of all men and advocate the expression of the spontaneous goodwill toward one another. "*Jen* is to love men joyously and from the innermost of one's heart," runs an ancient commentary on the *Analects.* The famous saying, "Within the four seas, all men are brothers," (*Analects of Confucius,* chap. 12, section 5) comes from a disciple of Confucius.

Coupled with the basic concept of *jen* and the several related virtues was Confucius' emphasis on the cultivation of decorum and music —a twofold emphasis representing the master's dual feeling for the moral and the aesthetic. Speaking of the development of one's personality, Confucius said, "It is by poetry that one's mind is aroused; it is by ceremonials that one's character is regulated; it is by music that one becomes accomplished" (*Analects of Confucius,* chap. 8, section 8). The cultivation of decorum and music would afford an element of grace in the individual and civility in society. The proper cultivation and combination of *jen* and decorum were the requisites to the perfection of the individual and the restoration of order out of chaos, according to Confucius. Just as a house with a solid foundation should have a pleasing facade, so should a man with an abundance of goodwill take care to express it with thoughtfulness and good manners.

**On Religion.** Although Confucianism has sometimes been called a religion, Confucius was not a founder of religion in the usual sense. He possessed a keen sense of a universal moral force, which he spoke of as heaven and the will of heaven, but talked very little about traditional religion. When a student asked about the worship of ghosts and spirits, Confucius said, "We don't know yet how to serve men, how can we know about serving the spirits?" In reply to the next question about death, Confucius said, "We don't know yet about life, how can we know about death?" (*Analects of Confucius,* ch. 11, sect. 2).

Because of this note of avoidance, Confucius has been marked as a skeptic or an agnostic by some, and upheld as a thoroughgoing humanist by others. It is true that Confucius regarded much of formal religion as superstition, and showed an eagerness to steer clear from the prevalent practices of witchcraft and occultism. But he had a profound feeling and appreciation for the genuine religious sentiment and spirit in life, just as he also found much aesthetic enjoyment in religious ritual.

Even though Confucius never wanted to pose as prophet or messenger of God, it was to a heavenly mission that he dedicated his life. In times of frustration he placed his reliance on heaven; in times of grief he cried out to heaven, as he did when he heard of the death of Yen Hui. Confucius did not discourse on God in anthropomorphic terms and had little to do with organized religion, but he was himself what might be called a God-filled man. His reticence regarding religious matters might at least be partly explained by his saying, "Look at Heaven there. Does it speak? The four seasons run their course and all things are produced. Does Heaven speak?" (*Analects of Confucius,* ch. 17, sect. 19).

**On the Superior Man.** The full development of the Confucian virtues is exemplified by the *chün-tzu,* or the superior man. *Chün-tzu* means literally the son of a prince, and it signified just that at the time of Confucius. Confucius, however, shifted the meaning from "nobleman" to "a man who conducted himself nobly." The new class of *chün-tzu* might still be regarded as constituting an aristocracy, but membership is based on one's merit rather than one's birth. Here is another instance in which one finds Confucius

teaching daringly new thoughts while he proclaims himself a "transmitter and not an innovator."

The superior man, according to Confucius, is the man in whom inborn humanity is harmoniously blended with cultivated decorum. His life is internally directed and not externally controlled. The superior man has neither anxiety nor fear, because when he looks into himself he finds no cause for self-reproach. Putting it another way, being humane he has no anxiety, being wise he has no perplexities, being brave he has no fear. The superior man is distressed by his lack of ability, but not by his lack of fame.

Confucius clarified some of the qualities of the superior man by contrasting them with those of the inferior man. He said: "The superior man is always calm and at ease; the inferior man is always worried and full of distress" (*Analects of Confucius,* chap. 7, section 36). "The superior man understands what is right; the inferior man understands what is profitable" (*Analects of Confucius,* chap. 4, section 16). "The superior man makes demands on himself; the inferior man makes demands on others" (*Analects of Confucius,* chap. 15, section 20).

With a deep sense of confidence and serenity, the superior man is not easily swayed or ruffled or affected by the fortunes of the day. But it does not mean that he may live a life of self-contentment, keeping aloof from the everyday concerns of society. In fact, like the Platonic philosopher, the Confucian superior man is destined to take responsibility in government. Since men are not actually equal either by birth or training, good government will prevail when the superior men lead and the others follow. It is on the basis of this broad Confucian assumption that the renowned civil service examination system was developed in China.

**On Government.** Confucius' thoughts on government are grounded on his assumption of the inviolable sanctity of the individual. He believed that "The commander of a great army may be carried off, but the will of a common man cannot be taken from him" (*Analects of Confucius,* chap. 9, section 25). Governments are formed not for the comfort and enjoyment of the rulers, or even for the maintenance of law and order in the state, but for the happiness and enlightenment of the people. Thus government becomes inseparable from education, and the state may be compared with a schoolhouse, and the ruler with a schoolmaster. And the most effective type of instruction comes from the personal example on the part of the ruler.

When a high minister asked about government, Confucius, employing a pointed pun, said, "To govern (*cheng*) is to set things right (*cheng*). If you begin by setting yourself right, who will dare to deviate from the right?" (*Analects of Confucius,* chap. 12, section 17). Confucius was convinced that self-rectification on the part of the ruler is the key to good government. With it all will go well; without it no matter what orders are given they will not be obeyed. Therefore, the first duty of a nobleman is "to cultivate himself so as to give peace and comfort to all the people" (*Analects of Confucius,* chap. 14, section 45), a kind of *noblesse oblige.* The Confucian political ideal might be called government by virtue. In practical terms, hereditary rulers should delegate all administrative power to ministers selected for their talent and virtue.

For the proper conduct of government, the element of decorum should also be employed in support of the element of virtue or humanity. Confucius said, "Lead the people by laws and regulate them by penalties, and the people will try to keep out of jail but will have no sense of shame. Lead the people by virtue and restrain them by the usage of decorum, and the people will have a sense of shame, and moreover will become good" (*Analects of Confucius*, chap. 2, section 3). If a ruler loves decorum, righteousness, and good faith, according to Confucius, the people will not permit themselves to be vulgar, obstinate, or insincere. Confucius considered the restoration of the proper performance of social rites of public worship and festivals, which had fallen into neglect, as important to promoting social order. The same motivation made Confucius eager to correct the disparity between name or title and reality. This situation had come about because men in high places failed to fulfill their obligations, while underlings usurped the rights and prerogatives belonging to their superiors. Confucius said, in reply to a prince's question about government, "Let the prince be prince, the minister be minister, the father father, and the son son" (*Analects of Confucius*, chap. 12, section 11).

**Confucius' Influence.** The supremacy of Confucius and his teaching among the "hundred philosophers" of the classical age was established shortly before the beginning of the Christian era. For more than 2,000 years Confucianism served as the official creed or state cult and has even been regarded by some as a religion of China. The so-called Confucian classics became the corpus of learning studied by all scholar-administrators through the ages. If there is such a thing as eternal verity, the Chinese have found it in the teachings of Confucius. The way of life and conduct of society in China manifest the molding force of a system of teaching that might be called idealistic humanism. While Confucius' dream of universal peace and harmony has not come true, Confucian China enjoyed considerable peace and prosperity and achieved an incomparable degree of cultural unity and continuity. For centuries China's neighbors, such as Korea, Japan, the Ryukyus, and Vietnam, have also chosen to adopt Confucius as their sage and teacher.

Confucius' family lineage is traceable for over 2,000 years—a social phenomenon rare even in China—from the Eastern Chou dynasty (770–256 B.C.) to the present. K'ung Te-ch'eng (1920–     ), a lineal descendant of Confucius of the 77th generation, was residing in Taiwan in the late 1960s. The house in which Confucius lived and taught during his last years is in the city of Ch'üfu. During the time of Shih Huang Ti of the Ch'in dynasty (270–221 B.C.), when Confucian texts were ordered destroyed, a descendant of Confucius hid books in the walls of the house. Later, during the Western Han dynasty (202 B.C.–9 A.D.), books were recovered, and the house was given the name Lu-pi, meaning "the wall of Lu."

Confucius was buried by his disciples in the northern suburb of Ch'üfu near the Ssu River. The burial grounds, K'unglin, including the tomb of Confucius, have been preserved.

Y. P. MEI, *University of Iowa*

**Bibliography:** Eber, Irene, *Confucianism* (Macmillan 1986); Hall, D. L., and Ames, R. T., *Thinking through Confucius* (State Univ. Press of N.Y. 1987).

**CONGER EEL,** kong'gər, any of 14 kinds of closely related eels found almost all over the world. The name, however, is most often applied to the American conger, which is found along the Atlantic coast from Massachusetts to Florida and in the eastern part of the Gulf of Mexico. It generally lives close to the shore.

The conger is an ordinary looking eel. It is long and slippery and has a jaw that extends back under the eye, a dorsal fin that begins far ahead of the anal fin, and somewhat oval-shaped eyes. It is usually grayish on the back and dirty white on the underside. American congers are known to reach a length of 7 feet (2.3 meters) and a weight of 22 pounds (10 kg), but those most frequently taken are about 4 feet (1.3 meters) long and weigh 4 to 12 pounds (2–5 kg).

At the onset of sexual maturity, the conger stops feeding and moves into deeper water. It is thought to breed in the West Indies. Its transparent larva, the leptocephalus, is about 6 inches (15–16 cm) long. The larva drifts in the plankton of the open seas, gradually changing into a small, bottom-dwelling eel.

The American conger eel, *Conger oceanica*, is a member of the family Congridae, which includes many kinds of eels.

DANIEL M. COHEN, *U.S. Fish and Wildlife Service*

**CONGESTION,** the presence of an increased amount of blood in the blood vessels of a body tissue. It may result from an increased amount of blood flowing through the arteries that supply the tissue. It may also occur when the veins leading from the tissue are obstructed, preventing proper drainage of blood. Sometimes congestion occurs when the capillaries in the tissue become distended (widened). Virtually any part of the body may become congested if an injury or infection occurs. In such instances, congestion serves to hasten the removal of harmful substances and to promote healing. Congestion of the lungs may occur during heart failure when the heart cannot remove the blood from the lungs at the normal rate. When this happens, medicines are prescribed to hasten the removal of the excess fluid.

ERNEST BEUTLER, M.D.
*City of Hope Medical Center, Duarte, Calif.*

**CONGLOMERATE,** kən-glom'ər-ət, a sedimentary rock composed of a detritus of rounded rock fragments cemented in a matrix of sand, silt, or clay. The cementing action probably took place after the rock fragments were buried beneath a layer of other sediments.

Conglomerate is similar in appearance to breccia, except that in breccia the fragments are less waterworn and rounded. The detritus in conglomerate may range in size from pebbles to boulders; as the fragments become finer and finer, conglomerate shades off into sandstone. The fragments are usually quartz or chert, but sometimes are limestone or other rock materials.

Conglomerate may be considered as a consolidation of ancient gravels, such as pebble or cobble beaches. The rock is also known as puddingstone because of its physical appearance; the color contrast between the embedded fragments and the matrix often is quite striking. The ratio of detrital to matrix material may vary widely in different conglomerates.

**CONGO, Democratic Republic of the.** See ZAIRE.

The Plateau section of Brazzaville is comfortably modern, with a low profile. The city is the Congo's capital.

**CONGO, Republic of the,** kong'gō, a country in central Africa. Formerly Middle Congo, a territory of French Equatorial Africa, it became independent in 1960. For a few years the new nation was commonly referred to as Congo (Brazzaville) to distinguish it from its larger neighbor, the former Belgian Congo, conventionally called Congo (Kinshasa). The names in parentheses denoted their respective capitals. From 1971 until 1997 Congo (Kinshasa) changed its name to Zaire, thereby temporarily ending the confusion. After 1997 the countries were differentiated by the use of their full names—Republic of the Congo (Congo Republic) and Democratic Republic of the Congo (the Congo).

## 1. The Land

The Congo Republic is shaped somewhat like a boot, with the seaport of Pointe-Noire at the toe and Brazzaville near the heel. The country has five distinct natural regions.

**Physical Features and Climate.** Along the Congo Republic's western edge is a grassy, treeless coastal plain extending 40 miles (65 km) inland from the Atlantic Ocean. Behind the plain rises the Mayombé Escarpment, a succession of sharp ridges that run parallel to the coast and reach an elevation of 2,600 feet (800 meters). This densely forested area, deeply cut by river gorges such as that of the Kouilou, is difficult to penetrate. To the east stretches the valley of the Niari River, a tributary of the Kouilou. The grassy valley contains the country's best soils, permitting a variety of agricultural pursuits. To the northeast ex-

tend the Batéké Plateaus, a less favored grassland. In the far north are vast forests and swamps.

The country's major rivers are the Ubangi (Cubangui) and the Congo. The Ubangi is a tributary of the Congo, as are the Sangha and other large rivers of the north. Together the Ubangi and the Congo form most of the border between the Congo Republic and the Congo.

With its territory extending across the equator, the Congo Republic has a tropical climate marked by high temperatures and humidity. Torrential rainstorms are frequent, and precipitation averages 80 to 100 inches (2,000—2,500 mm) a year. The country also experiences two dry seasons, which run from January to March and from June to September.

---

### INFORMATION HIGHLIGHTS

**Total Area:** (land and inland water) 132,000 square miles (342,000 sq km).
**Boundaries:** *North,* Cameroon and Central African Republic; *east,* Democratic Republic of the Congo; *south,* Democratic Republic of the Congo and Angola; *west,* Atlantic Ocean and Gabon.
**Population:** 2,716,814 (1999 est.).
**Capital and Largest City:** Brazzaville.
**Major Languages:** French (official), Monokutuba, Lingala, Kongo.
**Major Religions:** Indigenous local systems, Roman Catholicism, Islam.

For the Congo Republic's flag, see under FLAG, both illustration and text.

**Natural Resources.** The Congo Republic was long thought to be poor in exploitable natural assets other than its prime location on the Ubangi-Congo waterway, the major outlet for the products of much of Equatorial Africa but obstructed by falls near its outlet. Possessing a seacoast as well as access to this trade route, the country was favorably positioned to provide overland transshipment and port services vital to landlocked Chad and the Central African Republic (CAR).

Generally infertile soils made commercial agriculture in the Congo Republic unpromising except in the Niari Valley. Large areas of the country's extensive hardwood forests were not easily accessible. The excellent hydroelectric potential required parallel development of mining and manufacturing. Although a wide variety of minerals were known, including valuable deposits of potash and high-grade iron ore, most were too limited in quantity. In the 1970s, however, substantial reserves of petroleum were found offshore, radically altering the nation's economic prospects.

## 2. The Economy

Petroleum production is the most important aspect of the Congolese economy, as measured in contribution to the gross domestic product (GDP) and exports. Agriculture is oriented toward mainly subsistence production, but the country cannot supply all of its food needs.

**Production.** In 1969 mining contributed less than 5% of the value of Congolese exports. Afterward, with the development of offshore oil resources, this figure rose rapidly to 90%. Petroleum extraction and refining came to dominate the modern sector of the economy, accounting for about 40% of the GDP. Although oil pushed the Congo Republic into the middle-income range of developing countries, it made the economy highly vulnerable to downswings in world demand and prices for petroleum products.

Natural gas is exploited in conjunction with oil, and small amounts of lead, zinc, copper, and gold are produced. Large-scale mining, as of potash and iron ore, has been hampered by various problems, including shortages of investment capital and technical and marketing difficulties.

Congolese farmers produce cassava, plantains, and sweet potatoes, mainly for their own consumption. The Congo Republic's cash crops include sugarcane, tobacco, palm kernels, coffee, cocoa, and peanuts.

Forest products formerly contributed more than 60% of the value of exports. The most important export woods are okoumé, limba, and mahogany. The cutting of trees for timber has caused serious depletion of the more accessible forests. Commercial fishing is conducted in Atlantic waters on a small scale.

Extractive industries account for most of the manufacturing done in the Congo Republic. Oil refining and sawmilling are major activities. Industrial output also includes small quantities of sugar, flour, vegetable oils, beer and soft drinks, tobacco products, textiles and footwear, canned fish, and cement. Hydroelectric plants generate most of the country's electricity.

**Transportation and Trade.** Rivers, notably the Congo and Ubangi, are the Congo Republic's major lines of communication. Brazzaville, on the Congo River, is connected with Pointe-Noire, the principal seaport, by the Congo-Océan Railroad. Traversing difficult terrain, the line was begun in 1921 and completed in 1934 with 92 bridges and 12 tunnels. A large proportion of the freight carried has been CAR and Gabonese bulk trade, straining the line's capacity. The Congolese road system is little developed because of forest growth, swamp, and rugged terrain.

Besides oil and wood, the Congo Republic exports some coffee and cocoa. It reexports diamonds from the Democratic Republic of the Congo. Major imports are machinery (including transportation equipment), food, iron, steel, and consumer goods.

## 3. The People

About four-fifths of the Congolese people live in the southern third of the country. Population is sparse in the vast northern rain forests and swamp wastes. As a result of migration by villagers in search of salaried employment, at least two-fifths of the people are urban. Brazzaville is by far the largest city, and Pointe-Noire ranks second.

**Ethnic, Linguistic, and Religious Groups.** The Congo Republic has more than 70 ethnic groups and subgroups and nearly as many languages. The largest ethnic divisions are the Kongo, Teke, Mboshi, and Vili. About half of the people are Christians.

The Kongo, who occupy the area west of Brazzaville, constitute more than half of the population. They take pride in the glory of their Kingdom of Kongo, which extended into the Democratic Republic of the Congo and Angola. The Teke, nearly a quarter of the total population, inhabit the plateaus north of Brazzaville. They are noted for their handicrafts. The Mboshi live in the north, where the grasslands and forests meet. The Vili, many of whom are fishermen, dwell around Pointe-Noire.

Most languages spoken in the country belong

CENTRAL AFRICAN REPUBLIC — Bangui

CAMEROON

GABON

CONGO REPUBLIC

Sangha R.
Likouala R.
Ubangi R.
Alima R.
Congo R.
LEKETI MTS.
Batéké Plateaus
Kouilou R.
Niari R.
Brazzaville
Malebo Pool
Kinshasa
Pointe-Noire
CABINDA (ANGOLA)
ANGOLA
DEM. REP. OF THE CONGO

CONGO REP.
0    200 Mi.
0    200 Km.

to the Bantu family. Besides the numerous ethnic languages are two that were developed to facilitate trade. LiNgala, the lingua franca spoken north of Brazzaville, shows the influence of several ethnic tongues. Monokutuba, used west of the capital, has a strong Kongo base. The official language of the country is French, which is taught in all the schools.

The population is about evenly divided between Christians and followers of traditional African religious beliefs, although these categories are not mutually exclusive. A tiny percentage of the people are Muslims.

**Education.** The French administration emphasized quality education for both Africans and Europeans, and this policy resulted in the formation of a small African elite. After independence the Congolese government broadened the base of its educational system in order to reach many more children.

# HISTORY AND GOVERNMENT

After the Portuguese navigator Diogo Cam (Cão) discovered the mouth of the Congo River in 1483, Portugal established friendly relations with the Kongo kingdom, which had been founded at least a century earlier. Although this state controlled territory north of the river, its center of gravity lay southward in Angola. Another African kingdom, Loango, ruled the Kouilou and Niari valleys in the present-day Congo, and on the plateaus to the east the Teke kingdom held sway.

## 4. French Presence and Rule

French traders interested in slaves and ivory made frequent stops along the coast during the 17th and 18th centuries. After the abolition of the slave trade, the Congo served as a base for French ships seeking to prevent the illegal transport of captives. Although European ships touched along the Congo coast, no penetration of the interior took place until the 19th century.

Pierre Savorgnan de Brazza, exploring for France, founded the town of Brazzaville in 1880. He signed treaties with African kings, placing the area under French protection. The Berlin Conference of 1884–1885 established the boundaries between the French and Belgian Congos.

The colony of French Congo was created in 1891. It became known as the Middle Congo in 1903, and in 1910 it was linked with Gabon, Chad, and Ubangi-Shari (now the Central African Republic) in a federal organization known as French Equatorial Africa. Brazzaville was made the capital of the federation.

France granted large concessions to companies to exploit the colony's scant removable wealth, such as rubber, ivory, and gold. The people were largely ignored or their rights blatantly violated. There were no roads in the entire country until 1925. Head-carrier porters were recruited as compulsory labor, an abuse finally terminated in 1946. However, the French rulers educated a small African elite, who repeatedly demonstrated a warm attachment to France.

During World War II the French governor-general of French Equatorial Africa, Félix Eboué, rallied the Congo's people to the banner of the Free French movement. This loyalty won recognition from France, and a conference was held in Brazzaville in 1944 to define a new colonial policy in the face of rising African nationalism.

The result of the conference was a recommendation that French colonies be given more self-government.

In 1946 the Congo became an overseas territory of France with representation in the French parliament and an elected territorial assembly. The Congo voted to become an autonomous republic within the French Community in 1958. It became fully independent on Aug. 15, 1960.

## 5. The Independent Congo

The Congo's first president was Abbé Fulbert Youlou, a Catholic priest who had switched to politics. He was the founder of the country's principal political party, the Union Démocratique pour la Défense des Intérêts Africains (UDDIA), and had been mayor of Brazzaville.

**The Pro-Western Regime.** Youlou's government retained close ties with France. His strong pro-West policies as well as his support of Moïse Tshombe's attempt to lead Katanga province into secession from Congo (Kinshasa) aroused hostility in his country. The constitution of 1961 had given the president extensive powers, and Youlou attempted to create a one-party state. However, the government was unable to relieve widespread poverty and unemployment, and Youlou shared in the conspicuous extravagances of members of his government.

Youlou was forced to resign on Aug. 15, 1963, after three days of strikes and demonstrations by workers and students. A provisional government of technocrats was established, headed by Alphonse Massamba-Débat. The National Assembly was dissolved, and all political parties were outlawed.

**The Assertion of Radicalism.** In a referendum held on Dec. 8, 1963, the voters approved a new constitution protecting the powers of the National Assembly and dividing executive authority between the president and a premier. On December 19, Massamba-Débat was elected to a five-year term as president by the electoral college. In July 1964 the Mouvement National Révolutionnaire (MNR), headed by Massamba-Débat, was made the country's sole political party.

Massamba-Débat took a hostile attitude toward the Western powers. Brazzaville recognized the People's Republic of China in 1964 and was accused by Kinshasa of aiding rebels against its government. In 1965 the United States withdrew its diplomatic and consular representatives because of alleged mistreatment of them by the Brazzaville regime. China sent advisers and technicians and provided financial assistance. Distrusting pro-French elements in the regular army, Massamba-Débat established a palace guard of Cubans in 1965.

In June 1966 the army staged a coup while Massamba-Débat was out of the country. Resentment against the government's close ties with China and Cuba as well as sympathy with the ethnic supporters of Capt. Marien Ngouabi, who was to be transferred to the interior, provoked the revolt. Government officials were forced to take refuge in a Brazzaville sports stadium. But loyal elements in the army and the special Cuban presidential guard were able to regain control.

The political situation grew increasingly tense throughout 1966 and 1967. Massamba-Débat took the post of premier in January 1968; however, the army removed his government in August of that year. Ngouabi, who was now in control, forced Massamba-Débat from the presidency in Septem-

In 1960 the Congo became independent from France. Congolese and French officials watch the parade in Brazzaville.

ber and became president himself in January 1969.

**The People's Republic.** In December the newly formed Marxist-Leninist Parti Congolais du Travail (PCT) replaced the MNR. It drew up a constitution giving its Central Committee the decisive role in national affairs. Ngouabi, as party chairman, headed the Council of State, which was to govern through local, district, and regional people's councils. The country became the People's Republic of the Congo.

In line with its policy of "scientific socialism," the new government increased the already substantial participation of the state in the economy. One of its first steps was to nationalize the Congo-Océan Railroad and the ports of Brazzaville and Pointe-Noire. Ngouabi, after weathering an unsuccessful coup in 1972, was assassinated in 1977. A party military committee assumed control and soon announced the execution of several persons, including ex-premier Massamba-Débat, for complicity in the assassination.

The military named Col. Joachim Yhombi-Opango as the new president. More moderate than Ngouabi, he favored a mixed economy, and he normalized relations with the United States. Amid growing factionalism in the PCT and an economic downturn caused in part by an accident that led to the cessation of potash production, Yhombi-Opango was forced to resign in February 1979. He was replaced by the vice president and defense minister, Col. Denis Sassou-Nguesso.

In July elections were held for the People's National Assembly and regional, district, and local councils; a new socialist constitution was approved by popular referendum. An amnesty for political prisoners and exiles was followed by increasing respect for human rights. The economy soon recovered as oil production rose and the Congo obtained a loan from the International Monetary Fund in conjunction with a program of economic stabilization. Oil revenues permitted greater investment in development projects. However, the dangers of overdependence on one product became evident when oil prices slumped in the early 1980s, slowing the pace of economic growth.

While the Sassou-Nguesso government remained outwardly dedicated to the Congolese brand of Marxist-Leninist socialism, it developed closer ties with the West and more pragmatic economic policies. The president had to walk a precarious line between PCT champions of orthodoxy and those favoring liberalization. Meanwhile, ethnic rivalries persisted between the north and south under the PCT's northern-dominated government and within the north itself.

In 1990, under domestic and foreign pressure for reform, the PCT ended its one-party monopoly of power. It also renounced Marxism. Opposition parties became legal in January 1991. A broadly based national conference on the political future of the Congo, ending in June, transferred most of the president's powers to a new premier, who formed a transitional government pending general elections. The conference, which was called a "democratic coup," also renamed the country Republic of the Congo.

A national referendum followed in 1992, leading to the acceptance of a new constitution, which called for a multiparty political system.

Presidential elections were held in August 1992, and Pascal Lissouba of the Union panafricaine pour la démocratie sociale (UPADS) won the election. UPADS won the legislative elections held the following year. Ethnic and regional rivalries, however, could not be controlled, and the country continued to experience civil unrest.

In preparation for the presidential elections scheduled for July 1997, the government banned private militias and moved to disarm them. On June 5 an attempt to disarm the Cobras, a militia group maintained by former ruler Denis Sassou-Nguesso, was met with stiff resistance. The situation deteriorated into open warfare between the forces of Sassou-Nguesso and Lissouba in the city of Brazzaville. A cease-fire was signed October 9, but it was not observed. On October 15 the forces of Sassou-Nguesso aided by at least 1,000 Angolan troops gained full control of Brazzaville, the nation's capital, and Lissouba fled.

SANFORD GRIFFITH*, *New York University*

**CONGO EEL,** kong′gō, a species of eel-like sala-
mander, sometimes erroneously called the congo
snake, found in the southeastern lowlands of the
United States. It is about 2 ½ feet (75 cm) long
and has a cylindrical body and two pairs of tiny
legs with two or three toes. Its back is brown
and its sides and belly are slate-colored. The congo
eel is distinguished externally from eels by having legs rather than fins. It is so similar in appearance to the siren—which has only a single pair
of legs and external rather than internal gills—
that the siren is often called a congo eel.

These amphibians usually live in quiet or sluggish water, but they occasionally move overland
from one aquatic site to another. They are active
at night, and they feed on the most readily available small animals, especially crayfish and earthworms, which are usually abundant in the regions
frequented by congo eels.

Little is known about the mating and nesting
habits of congo eels. Copulation, almost unknown
among salamanders, takes place in shallow waters
after a lively courtship during which the female
repeatedly nudges the male. The female lays scores
of eggs. The eggs, resembling a string of large
beads several feet long, form a roughly spherical
mass in a shallow nest. The female coils around
the eggs and protects them.

The congo eel, *Amphiuma means*, is a member of the family Amphiumidae, order Urodela.

CLIFFORD POPE
*Author of "The Reptile World"*

**CONGO RIVER,** kong′gō, the established name for
the longest river in central Africa, flowing 2,900
miles (about 4,700 km) from Zambia to the Atlantic Ocean. During the time that the Democratic
Republic of the Congo—or Congo (Kinshasa)—
adopted the name *Zaire* (1971–1997), it also
changed the name of the Congo River, which
flows chiefly through its territory, to Zaire River.
*Zaire* was the name applied to the river by early
Portuguese explorers, and it was based on their
rendering of the Kikongo word *nzadi* (river). However, *Congo River* was still widely used elsewhere.

In length the mighty Congo is second in Africa
only to the Nile, and in its volume of water flow
it is second in the world only to the Amazon.
The Congo River has the greatest drainage basin
in Africa. Its basin covers an area of 1,600,000
square miles (4,144,000 sq km), including all the
territory of the Democratic Republic of the Congo
as well as parts of Angola, Zambia, Burundi,
Rwanda, Central African Republic, Republic of
the Congo, and Cameroon.

Because the Congo Basin lies astride the equator, one section of the basin is always receiving
rainfall, and the many tributaries flowing into
the Congo River keep the volume of water relatively constant. This evenness of flow makes the
river extremely useful for navigation. The various tributary systems gather water during different periods, however, and they contribute flood-
water at different times of the year.

The Congo River is the home of crocodiles
and hippopotamuses and many species of fish.
Wild animals such as lions, chimpanzees, elephants,
jackals, and leopards abound in the thick forests
along the river, and wild birds, including parrots
and ibis, live on its banks.

**Physiography.** The Congo River crosses a base
of Archean crystalline rocks, covered in most areas
by recent sediments, in a basin measuring some
800 miles (1,300 km) in diameter. Its principal
source, the Lualaba, most likely formerly discharged its waters into the Nile River or the Indian Ocean. Earth movements associated with the
Great Rift Valley system caused the Lualaba to
change its course and flow into the Congo Basin.
The basin was once a vast lake, which emptied
into the Chad Basin and later through Cameroon
into the Gulf of Guinea. The present mouth of
the Congo River is of very recent origin. Earth
movements that created the Luanda Swell, Cameroon Mountain, and the Ubangi-Shari Ridge
blocked up the outlets of the "Congo Lake," causing water in it to increase into early postglacial
times. Eventually the lake was tapped west of
present-day Kinshasa and began cutting a great
gorge through the Crystal Mountains.

**Upper Congo.** The Upper Congo is the Lualaba River. Also the main headstream of the Congo,
it rises in the Democratic Republic of the Congo
south of Likasi at about 4,600 feet (1,400 meters).
Working its way north across the Katanga Plateau, the Lualaba has cut a gorge that drops it
1,500 feet (460 meters) in 45 miles (70 km). There
dams have been built to produce power for the
copper mines of Katanga (later called Shaba).

The Lualaba's major tributary is the Chambe-
shi River, which rises in northeastern Zambia between Lakes Malawi and Tanganyika. After flowing southwest into Lake Bangweulu, the river
becomes the Luapula and forms part of the border between the Democratic Republic of the Congo
and Zambia before flowing into Lake Mweru. It
then flows on as the Luvua.

At Ankoro the Lualaba is joined by the Luvua,
which emerges from Lake Mweru. The combined
river forms the upper reaches of the Congo, which
is generally known in this stretch as the Lualaba.
Continuing north it receives the Lukuga River,
bringing water from Lake Tanganyika. Other major
tributaries of the Upper Congo include the Luama,
Elila, Ulindi, and Lowa rivers. All these rivers
enter from the eastern rim of the Congo Basin.

The Lualaba is navigable for almost 400 miles
(640 km) from Bukama to Kongolo. After Kon-

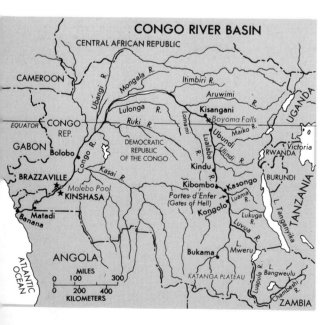

CONGO RIVER BASIN

The Congo River and its tributaries provide an excellent transportation system for central Africa.

golo the river passes through the Portes d'Enfer (Gates of Hell) rapids, extending for 75 miles (120 km). The river is again navigable for 68 miles (110 km) between Kasongo and Kibombo, where rapids interrupt its course. Below this second series of rapids, the river is navigable from Kindu for 191 miles (308 km) to Ubundi and the series of rapids that crosses the equator and ends in Boyoma (Stanley) Falls.

At Boyoma Falls, in a series of seven cataracts, the Lualaba River drops 200 feet (60 meters) in 60 miles (97 km) before reaching the almost level floor of the basin. The river widens to half a mile across near Kisangani and becomes known as the Middle Congo.

**Middle Congo.** For the next portion of its course, the river is mostly a wide, sluggish stream, averaging 4 miles (6 km) in width, although in places it is as much as 9 miles (14 km) across. Some 4,000 low, sandy islands lie in this 1,000-mile (1,600-km) stretch.

As a result of the vast amount of soil and debris carried by the river, its channel shifts frequently and constant dredging and channel marking are necessary for navigation. A 5-foot (1.5-meter) draft is maintained in low-water periods during February, July, and August.

As the Congo River moves west across the Democratic Republic of the Congo, it passes through rich equatorial forests. On this stretch the river receives the Lomami, Aruwimi, Itimbiri, and Mongala tributaries. Turning south, the Congo is joined by the Lulonga and Ruki rivers, draining the center of the basin.

The Ubangi, the Congo's largest tributary, enters the river near Irebu, soon after the Congo crosses the equator at Mbandaka. As the Ubangi cuts into the Congo, it creates a delta 9 miles (14 km) wide. The Congo banks in this area are so low that in flood period the river expands about 5 to 6 miles (8–10 km) over the shore.

Near Bolobo the Middle Congo changes from a river with very low banks to one only 1.5 miles (2 km) wide, racing between cliffs. For 125 miles (200 km) the river, joined by the Kasai at Kwamouth, runs 100 feet (30 meters) deep before breaking out to Malebo (Stanley) Pool, 906 feet (276 meters) above sea level.

Malebo Pool, a shallow lake 22 miles (35 km) long and 14 miles (23 km) wide, is divided at its western end by Bamu Island. On the north shore of the lake is the city of Brazzaville, capital of the Republic of the Congo, and on the south shore is Kinshasa (formerly, Léopoldville), capital of the Democratic Republic of the Congo.

**Lower Congo.** The Lower Congo begins at the outlet of Malebo Pool. In a series of 32 cataracts, the river cuts its way through the Crystal Mountains to the Atlantic Ocean. In 210 miles (338 km) the river drops over 900 feet (275 meters) to sea level and is compressed from its 18-mile (29-km) width at Kinshasa to as little as 1,650 feet (500 meters). Near Matadi the river drops over 500 feet (150 meters). Inga Falls, 25 miles (40 km) upstream from Matadi, is the site of the huge Inga hydroelectric project.

**Estuary.** The fourth and final portion of the Congo River begins at Matadi. The river's estuary is 100 feet (30 meters) deep at this major port, but by the time it reaches Boma, river deposits require constant dredging to keep a 6-foot- (2-meter-) wide channel open. The estuary ends at Banana, where the river enters the Atlantic Ocean, a distance of 86 miles (138 km). The river has cut a canyon beneath the sea from 2 to 8 miles (3–13 km) wide, nearly 1 mile (1.6 km) deep, extending about 100 miles (160 km) offshore.

**Transportation.** The Congo River and its tributaries form an excellent system of some 8,700 miles (14,000 km) of navigable waterways. Those sections of the main river that cannot be navigated because of rapids or waterfalls are circumvented by railroads. The Congo River has long been envisioned as the main source of transportation and communication for the region. The noted explorer Henry Morton Stanley believed that the river would be the great waterway for all trade in the Congo Basin.

The first and most important rail link between the ports of Matadi and Léopoldville (Kinshasa) was begun in 1890. Later a railroad was built around Stanley (Boyoma) Falls, 1,000 miles (1,600 km) upstream from Kisangani to Ponthierville (Ubundi), and then one from Kindu to Kongolo. Bypassing obstacles, the river could be used to transport the mineral wealth of Katanga to the sea. Another railroad was built from Katanga across the Congo Basin to the Kasai River, where goods could be transshipped to Léopoldville.

In the mid-1950s the old wood-burning sternwheelers were replaced by diesel tugs. Constant dredging is needed to keep the often shifting channels open. Radar is used to avoid drifting logs.

Kinshasa is the principal river port of the Congo Basin. It is connected with Matadi, the main ocean port, by 227 miles (365 km) of railroad track. Matadi, situated at the head of the estuary, is really an outport of Kinshasa.

**History.** Diogo Cam, a Portuguese explorer, was the first European to visit the Lower Congo, in 1482. He named it the Zaire and set up a stone column commemorating the event. Bartolomeu Diaz entered the mouth of the Congo River in 1486 and explored the estuary as far as the present-day port of Matadi. British Capt. J. K. Tuckey explored the lower course of the Congo as far as Isangila in 1816. His expedition was wiped out by disease and famine, however.

Various Arab traders traveled and explored in the eastern highlands of the Congo Basin during the first half of the 19th century. Then David Livingstone explored the area of the Upper Congo from 1867 to 1873, discovering the Luapula River and the headstream of the Lualaba. Henry Morton Stanley began an expedition down the Congo River in 1874. After 999 days he reached Boma and thus was the first European to traverse the basin to the mouth of the river, opening up the interior of central Africa.

HUGH C. BROOKS, *St. John's University*

**Bibliography:** Bently, W. Holman, *Pioneering on the Congo,* 2 vols. (1900; reprint, Johnson 1970); **Harms, Robert W.,** *River of Wealth, River of Sorrow* (Yale Univ. Press 1981); **Okolo, Julius, and Wright, Stephen,** eds., *West Africa* (Westview Press 1988).

**CONGREGATION,** a religious assemblage. In its broadest application the term refers to worshipers gathered for a religious service. In the Roman Catholic Church the term is used to qualify several distinct religious bodies.

Monastic congregations are groups of several monasteries united under a common superior who is responsible directly to Rome. The Benedictines, for example, are divided into some 21 loosely organized federations.

Religious congregations are church-approved societies of religious who profess "simple" rather than "solemn" vows of poverty, chastity, and obedience (simple vows are more easily dispensed than solemn vows). Until the 16th century the church had recognized only religious "orders" whose members took solemn vows.

Sacred congregations are the administrative bodies of the Roman Catholic Church, headquartered in Rome and composed of papal-appointed cardinals and other high-ranking ecclesiastics. In the 1990s there were nine such congregations, with functions ranging from the supervision of papal seminaries to jurisdiction over liturgy.

**CONGREGATIONAL CHRISTIAN CHURCHES (NATIONAL ASSOCIATION),** the largest of four groups of Congregational churches in the United States that did not take part in the 1957 merger that formed the United Church of Christ. These churches organized independently in Detroit, Mich., in 1955. (See CONGREGATIONALISTS; UNITED CHURCH OF CHRIST.)

**CONGREGATIONALISTS,** members of a Protestant denomination that took form during the later period of the English Reformation and became dominant in America in colonial and 19th-century New England. Like the Baptists, Disciples of Christ, and American Unitarians, the denomination is organized on a congregational rather than an episcopal or a presbyterian pattern of government. That is, each congregation is autonomous, or self-governing. Congregationalism is a direct spiritual descendant of Calvinism, but from its beginnings it has been animated by a spirit of inquiry that has resulted not only in the founding of educational institutions such as Harvard and Yale universities but also in ready acceptance of advanced thought.

Congregationalism was carried by British and American mission boards to many countries of the world and found association with churches of like character in Europe, such as the Dutch Remonstrant Church and the Mission Covenant Church of Sweden. However, it has grown to its greatest strength in English-speaking countries, especially the United States. Having established itself in New England, Congregationalism may be said to have gone wherever New Englanders have gone and to be strongest in the states they settled. In 1957 the denomination, with the exception of a minority of dissenting churches, entered into union with the Evangelical and Reformed Church to form the United Church of Christ, which has over 2 million members.

### DOCTRINE

Fundamental to Congregational churches is the revelation of God in Jesus Christ. By this fact Congregationalists declare themselves to be one in basic doctrine with other Christian communions. Within the church universal they make their own particular witness by emphasizing the importance of the congregation gathered for worship and ministry in the name of Christ.

The relationship between God and God's people in a congregation is felt to be sacred, since all of the saving powers available in the church are focused there. Hence no outside ecclesiastical or political authority, whether bishop or presbytery, another congregation, or magistrate, is allowed in theory or practice to intervene. Here the doctrine of the priesthood of all believers, which unites Congregationalists to all other Protestants, is expressed in starkest simplicity, for in the presence of Christ in the congregation there is thought to be only one spiritual status for any human being: that in which one receives God's grace and in the Holy Spirit shares it with others. This relationship raises believers to such dignity that they do not need to await the authorization of any higher church authority to unite with like-minded believers to form or maintain a congregation. For this reason a Congregational church is often spoken of as being of the "gathered" type—a company of believers gathered directly by Christ.

Various groups within Christendom with a congregational polity exhibit differing theories as to the right relation to be maintained by any congregation with other Christians. Some have held extreme independence. The Congregationalists, however, are at the other end of the spectrum: they are ready to balance the importance of the congregation with the importance attached by others to any other part of the great church and to cooperate with them fully, always provided that there is no interference with the rule of the congregation over itself under Christ. They hold that a representative body, such as a council or synod, has the right of a congregation: the right to govern itself. It is this openness to other ecclesiastical emphases that has made this denomination particularly responsive to, and kept it in the van of, the ecumenical movement.

Congregationalism is not without its credal standards, however. The denomination has announced its beliefs in a series of statements and confessions, beginning with the Cambridge Platform of 1648. Later came the Confession of Faith of 1680—a redaction of the Westminster Confession of 1647, which was repeated in the Saybrook Platform of 1708—the Burial Hill Declaration of Faith of 1865, the Kansas City Statement of Faith of 1913, and the United Church of Christ statement of 1959; but these announcements have never had the binding authority of Koranic texts. They have simply expressed the conviction of the majority and so provided a center of gravity for the whole, but it has not been expected that all minorities would conform.

These statements of faith disclose at once their roots in Calvinism and their growth away from Calvinism. They give up the idea, for instance, that human nature is depraved from birth and that the Bible is inerrant, but they still declare that the chief end of man is to learn the will of God and to do it.

## PRACTICES

**Worship.** Together with the rest of Protestantism, Congregationalism regards Holy Communion and Christian baptism as the two sacraments of the church, but to all intents and purposes other rites, such as marriage and confirmation (which until the present was usually known as "joining the church"), are completely sacramental. Infant baptism is practiced, as is adult baptism when necessary. The regular form is by water, sprinkled, using the trinitarian formula—in the name of the Father, the Son, and the Holy Spirit.

Regular Sunday morning worship, uniting adoration of God, confession of sin, singing of God's praise, supplication for His mercies, reading of His Word and interpretation of it in preaching, and blessing of the people, is relatively simple in form but not so nakedly simple as that of the Puritan churches of a century or more ago.

Formerly hymns, responsive reading, and the Lord's Prayer were usually the only parts of worship inviting vocal congregational participation. Today, printed services with prayers and responses to be spoken in unison are being more and more utilized. In the United States, as distinct from Britain, responses are almost never sung or chanted by the congregation. Once a year the Sunday morning service in many churches is conducted by laymen or young people trained for the occasion. In U. S. practice, unlike British practice, laymen do not celebrate Holy Communion except by special authority.

**Organization.** Basic to the government of the denomination is the local church with the protections of its autonomy, and basic to the local church is its convenant, whereby members bind themselves "in the presence of God to walk together in all his ways" (as the Salem Covenant of 1629 has it). Local church government resides in the adult members. These members choose their own officers—deacons, the ranking lay authorities of the church, who are responsible for

its spiritual affairs, and trustees, to whom is assigned the care of the church's material properties. In consultation with denominational leadership in the state, the adult members also choose and "call" the minister who is to serve the church. Today local government is likely to be adjusted to the needs of the particular parish, often through a council consisting of the heads of recognized groups within the church serving to correlate their work.

Government is graduated from the local church through the communion as a whole by a system of representative assemblies. At the level of the county or comparable geographical unit the assembly is called an association; at the state level, a conference. At the national level, before the union with the Evangelical and Reformed Church, the assembly was known as the General Council. It is now called the General Synod.

The special responsibility of the association is to sanction the standing of the churches and ministers within its boundaries on behalf of the communion. When ministers of other recognized denominations transfer their standing to a Congregational association, they are not required to be reordained. When a person is ordained into the Congregational ministry the association asks him to write and read an extended statement of his theological views instead of requiring him to subscribe to some symbol of belief already in the tradition of the denomination. Judgment as to whether or not to admit him to the ministry is made on the basis of his statement.

The conference nurtures the churches under its care and serves as a liaison between them and the national synod and mission boards. In recent years the conferences have greatly strengthened their authority, partly because each has a full-time minister, usually called a superintendent or conference minister, to perform the necessary episcopal duties.

The United Church General Synod, like its Congregational predecessor the Council, guides the work of the entire communion. Its chief executive, formerly known as the minister of the general council, is now the president of the church.

These various bodies take seriously the principle of subsidiarity, according to which no larger body usurps the responsibility for any task that can be done equally well by a smaller body within it. When tension between two or more of these bodies occurs on any issue, its resolution is left to the influence of the Holy Spirit. Meanwhile, each body pursues the course dictated by its own majority. If any group considers a situation to be intolerable (as has happened twice at the national level since 1776: at the time of the Unitarian departure and again when a minority refused to accompany the majority into the United Church of Christ) it simply breaks the bond of union.

All offices within the denomination, including that of parish ministry, are open to men and women alike, but women have not been ordained in great numbers.

## HISTORY

Congregational forces, maintaining the inviolable relationship to Christ and to one another that unites the worshipers gathered about His altar in any local church, have been active in the Christian church from its beginning, but it is only since the 17th century that they have been incorporated into an independent movement within the church called "congregational." This word first occurs in this connection in a tract entitled *A Collection of Sundry Matters,* published in 1616 and written probably by John Wing, pastor of the English church in Flushing, the Netherlands: "Every Christian is bound in conscience . . . to walke in that forme of a Church . . . which is set by Christ . . . which indeed is eyther Catholike, or Congregational independent."

**Founding.** The rise of Congregationalism begins with such Puritans as Henry Jacob, born in 1586 in Kent, England, who was obliged by his nonconformity to move to the Netherlands about 1604, and who died in Virginia in 1624; William Ames, born in Suffolk in 1576, who was also forced to leave for the Netherlands, about 1610, and who died there in 1633; Robert Parker, born in Wiltshire (probably in 1564), who fled with Ames to the Netherlands and died there in 1614; and Paul Baynes, born in London, who was silenced in England but not forced to leave, and who died in Cambridge in 1617.

None of these men reached New England, but their thought dominated the churches there through the next generation of leaders. Among these were John Cotton, born in Derby, England, in 1585, who emigrated to New England in 1633 and was chosen teacher of the First Church in Boston, where he remained until his death in 1652; Richard Mather (1596–1669), born in Lancashire, England, who arrived in New England in 1635, became the teacher at Dorchester, Mass., and remained at Dorchester until his death; Thomas Hooker (1586–1647), the skilled preacher of Hartford, Conn., born in Leicestershire, England, who went to New England in 1633; and John Davenport (1597–1670), an émigré from Warwickshire, England, who made his fame as a minister in New Haven, Conn.

Congregationalism as a theory had been presented to the world previously in the writings of Robert Browne (about 1550–1633) but had not caught on as a movement in history. There was one striking difference between Browne and those cited above: he was a separatist, ready to withdraw (in 1582) from what he regarded as the diseased Church of England in order to establish a new, reformed, pure church "without tarying for anie." Browne was a Congregationalist who believed it to be a sin to be associated in any way with the prelacy of the Church of England, whereas the fathers of New England, although equally insistent on their Congregationalism, thought the Church of England to be possessed of many parishes and ministers blameless in God's sight. They felt the separatists, or Brownists, as they were called, to be lacking in generosity and denounced them. This difference in spirit led the New Englanders along a nonseparatist course.

Browne is important to American Congregationalism because his theory was espoused by John Robinson (1575–1625), the pastor of the Pilgrim Fathers. This congregation, leaving Robinson behind in Leiden in the hope that he would rejoin them later, crossed the Atlantic in the *Mayflower* in 1620 to settle at Plymouth (now in Massachusetts) and establish the first Congregational church on American soil. Their leaders were laymen—William Brewster (1567–1644), William Bradford (1590–1657), and Edward Winslow (1595–1655)—who had moved from their strictly separatist disposition before setting sail. On coming to know the Puritans, who entered Massachusetts in great numbers after 1629,

these Congregational leaders found it easy to cast their lot with the newcomers.

**Development.** The Massachusetts settlements prospered from the first, and Congregationalism with them. The "Association and Agreement" known in history as the Mayflower Compact, although directed to the good ordering of the body politic rather than of a church congregation, was drawn up like one of the church covenants with which the Pilgrims were familiar. It served as a basis for the government of the Plymouth Colony and is regarded by some as the beginning of democracy in America. Both at Plymouth and in the Massachusetts Bay Colony there was reproduced in many towns the type of government and ways of society that the colonists had known in England, except that the established church was Congregational, not Anglican.

That there could be more than one recognized church in a state was a possibility foreign to Congregational philosophy, as it was in general to that age, although Congregationalists in Britain were among the first to question the validity of this rule. In mid-17th century England, Congregationalists as a minority had led in pleading for the toleration of more than one church in the realm. A Congregational minister, Henry Burton, in *The Protestation Protested* (1641), was the first to outline a plan for church-state relations that presently became the order in England and has persisted to this day—to have an established church, with freedom of worship permitted to other churches. In New England, however, where the Congregationalists formed the great majority, they made it as difficult as possible for others to gain a foothold in the fear that the Congregational polity would be overturned.

The Cambridge Platform, adopted in 1648, was the first ecclesiastical constitution to be drawn up in America. It guided the churches until the dissolution of the connection between church and state in Massachusetts (1834) and Connecticut (1818). The pioneering constitution of Connecticut, adopted in 1639 as the Fundamental Orders, owed its democratic ideas in large part to the Congregationalists who established the colony. Eventually, these ideas influenced the shaping of the federal constitution. *A Vindication of the Government of New England Churches* (reprinted in 1770) by John Wise (1652–1725), the Congregational minister of Ipswich, Mass., came to be known as the Primer of the Revolution. In it Wise singled out the democratic principles in Congregationalism and set them forth as standards for the state.

**Expansion.** Congregationalism was also in the vanguard of education. In 1636 the Massachusetts General Court voted to give £400 toward the establishment of an academy, which presently became Harvard College. Yale followed in 1701, nine of its ten trustees being Congregational ministers. The many colleges that later took form under Congregational initiative, as the population frontier advanced westward, established themselves as all Congregational churches did—that is, with complete control over their own affairs.

The emigrants from New England to upper New York and the Middle West carried Congregationalism with them, supported by missionaries such as those who made up the Yale Band of 1829–1830 and the Andover Band of 1842. These emigrants met and merged with groups of Presbyterian settlers making their way west. Here a striking experiment in ecumenicity took place:

church leaders of both denominations, instead of competing with one another as to the location and government of their churches, entered into a Plan of Union that united the memberships and left them to choose either the Presbyterian or Congregational structure.

Since in New England the state had largely supplied the connectionalism for Congregational churches above the county or association level, there had been little need to develop strict ecclesiastical relationships, and Congregationalists moving to western areas found themselves without firm denominational unification. Under the Plan of Union, therefore, the great majority of them turned to the more tightly knit polity of Presbyterianism. This caused a great numerical loss to Congregationalism, but one of which they could hardly be ashamed from an ecumenical standpoint.

Congregationalism was the pioneer Protestant denomination in the new domain established west of the Alleghenies in 1787 as the Northwest Territory. Under the influence of Samuel J. Mills and others, missionary groups were established to carry the Gospel not only to these newly opened lands but around the world.

**Missionary and Social Work.** Mills entered Williams College in Massachusetts in 1806. While there, he was a leader in the forming of a prayer society that on one occasion retreated to the shelter of a haystack during a thunderstorm. This Haystack Meeting is regarded as the beginning of the foreign mission movement in the United States. In 1810, carrying on the commitment made at that meeting, the American Board of Commissioners for Foreign Missions, the first in North America, came into being. In 1826 the American Home Missionary Society was formed, as a consequence of whose work the broad advance of Congregationalism into the West was assured.

In the 19th century, Congregationalists felt the force of the evangelical revival on many fronts. In Massachusetts, Mary Lyon started the first academy for women, which subsequently became Mount Holyoke College. Oberlin, in Ohio, was the first coeducational college. The American Missionary Association, which began as a society for the legal defense of a shipload of slaves who had seized their vessel in 1839 while en route from Africa to the United States, became by 1863 the ranking organization for the betterment of freed slaves. It founded hundreds of schools and colleges that trained Negroes for leadership.

Meanwhile, the same return to evangelical activity had a corresponding effect upon Congregationalism in Britain, reviving its zeal and increasing its numbers. This manifested itself in the establishment of academies, concern for the poor, the gathering of Sunday schools, and missionary work at home and abroad. In the political arena, Congregationalists inaugurated a crusade for prison reform and the extermination of slavery and against such narrowing legislation as the Test and Corporation acts, repealed in 1828.

**Changing Concepts.** The early Massachusetts settlers brought with them the conviction that the children of church members—those who had taken the church covenant as consciously "saved" believers—were also members of the church, baptism being only the outer sign of a relationship established by birth. Although these children, as they reached maturity, were without the privileges of taking communion and voting at church meetings, they were none the less "covenanted" members. The question then arose as to whether the child of such a member was also a covenanted member and therefore eligible for baptism. The answer given by the Synod of 1662 gave assurance that he was, provided the parent would "own the covenant"—that is, publicly accept the outer church membership into which he had been born. This practice was nicknamed "the Half-way Covenant," and was utilized by the churches until the day of Jonathan Edwards.

Jonathan Edwards was without doubt the greatest thinker the colonies produced. In the American colonies the vast riches of Calvinism had been concentrated to a great extent into a theology based on the doctrine of human depravity and the action of God in saving some human beings and not others. Writing in this field in his book *The Freedom of the Will,* Edwards moves with relentless logic to a divine determinism. His artistry in theology was matched by his artistry in preaching, since he believed emotion to be one vehicle for truth. It was as a result of his preaching in Northampton, Mass., on the necessity for conversion that not only the thought of any halfway decision in the matter of church membership was discredited but also the remarkable religious revival of the mid-18th century, called the Great Awakening, which began in New Jersey in 1726, was fed mightily. This movement spread throughout the country, being continued in the Baptist and Methodist churches.

Followed by Joseph Bellamy (1719–1790), Samuel Hopkins (1721–1803), Jonathan Edwards the younger (1745–1801), and Nathanael Emmons (1745–1840), Edwards influenced theological development for almost a century in what came to be known as New England theology. While the conservative Calvinists (the "Old Lights," as they were named) stood firm on the sovereignty of God and the inability of man to save himself, these newer thinkers (the "New Lights"), stressing the necessity for human decision within the framework of that very sovereignty, opened the way to methods of revivalism. These methods kept Connecticut Congregationalism an undivided whole.

In eastern Massachusetts, however, a radical break with the concept of underemphasizing man in the God-man relationship was made, resulting in the division, and so in the weakening, of Congregationalism. Those who sought change eventually moved toward acceptance of Unitarianism.

There was never any formal separation between Unitarians and other Congregationalists, but the growth of anti-Calvinistic feeling among those who magnified the place of man in the world made it impossible for them to live comfortably with those who felt this to be an overemphasis. So the division came, and the American Unitarian Association, which included some of the oldest of the colonial churches, was organized in 1825. Early Unitarianism was influenced by such British thinkers as Wordsworth and Coleridge, and it tended to represent religion as a social principle of human betterment.

In the middle years of the 19th century, Unitarianism responded to the appeal of German idealism, and here it was followed by Congregationalism. Congregationalists were in general ready to entertain the idea of a doctrine of evolution as Charles Darwin expounded it. After early misgivings they took over Horace Bushnell's

(1802–1876) theory of Christian nurture as a counterbalance to, although not a denial of, revivalism; and in Washington Gladden (1836–1918) and others, drawing on British and Continental as well as incipient American social Christianity, they stood strongly for political and industrial changes to provide justice for all classes. This zeal for a better society received organized expression in 1934 in the founding of the Council for Social Action, the first of its kind among the denominations.

**Congregationalism Today.** Although Congregationalism is one of the oldest communions in the United States, it is one of the most recent to organize itself denominationally. The first meeting of its national council was not held until 1871, and autonomous state conferences were not recognized until 1913. In spite of denominational crystallization and subsequent growth, however, the ecumenical bent of Congregationalism continues to be evident.

There is no council of churches devoted to interdenominational cooperation in any area where Congregationalism exists in which the denomination does not participate. In 1888 it united with about one third of the Congregational Methodist churches, a group in the South that had given up the episcopal system. In 1925 it united with the Evangelical Protestants, a liberal group of German extraction centering in the Ohio Valley. In 1931 the General Convention of Christian Churches and the National Council of Congregational Churches united to form the General Council of Congregational Christian Churches. The convention represented about 100,000 communicants of Baptist, Methodist, and Presbyterian backgrounds in New England, the southern Middle Atlantic states, and the Ohio Valley.

Since 1957, Congregationalism has been represented in the United Church of Christ. The churches that did not enter this union, chiefly in the fear that they might lose their congregational freedom, continued under the name of the National Association of Congregational Christian Churches. The United Church of Christ made available to them all of its services, but they also had their own boards for organized ministries. Their churches numbered about 300; those of the United Church of Christ, approximately 7,000. In the United States the United Church of Christ was one of 10 churches seeking unity through the Consultation of Church Union.

In Britain the Congregational churches appeared to be ready to unite with the Presbyterian Church on both sides of the Tweed—in England, to become the Reformed Church of England; in Scotland, to be a member of the Church of Scotland. Congregationalism, still maintaining its witness as a protector and strengthener of the congregation, preferred to do so from within an ecumenical church. See also CAMBRIDGE PLATFORM; UNITED CHURCH OF CHRIST.

DOUGLAS HORTON
*Former Dean, Harvard Divinity School*

### Bibliography

Dexter, Henry Martyn, *The Congregationalism of the Last 300 Years as Seen in Its Literature*, 2 vols. (1880; reprint, B. Franklin 1970).
Oliver, Egbert S., *Saints and Sinners: The Planting of New England Congregationalism in Portland, Oregon, 1851–1876* (Hapi Press).
Pruter, Hugo R., *The Theology of Congregationalism* (Borgo Press 1985).
Youngs, J. William, *God's Messengers* (Johns Hopkins Univ. Press 1976).

**CONGRESS,** in diplomacy, a meeting of heads of state or their representatives to discuss and resolve international problems. The term derives from a Latin word meaning "to come together." The outstanding example of such a gathering was the Congress of Vienna (1814–1815). Traditionally, the difference between a conference and a congress was that the representatives at a conference were the ordinary ambassadors to the host country, while envoys to a congress were specially deputed for the purpose. This distinction faded after World War I, however, with the holding of the Paris Peace Conference (1919–1920), as it is generally called.

**CONGRESS, Continental.** See CONTINENTAL CONGRESS.

**CONGRESS, Library of.** See LIBRARY—*Libraries of the United States and Canada* (Special Libraries); LIBRARY OF CONGRESS.

**CONGRESS OF INDUSTRIAL ORGANIZATIONS,** a body of unions formed in 1935 to organize the mass production industries. The CIO merged with the American Federation of Labor in 1955. See AMERICAN FEDERATION OF LABOR AND CONGRESS OF INDUSTRIAL ORGANIZATIONS.

**CONGRESS OF RACIAL EQUALITY,** an interracial organization dedicated to promoting civil rights in the United States. Founded in Chicago in 1942 by James Farmer (q.v.), the organization envisioned a national movement based on the ideas and tactics of nonviolence and direct action as propounded by Mahatma Gandhi. Its earliest efforts were directed toward the area of segregated public accommodations. Staging sit-ins at restaurants in the 1940's, CORE initiated tactics that were further developed and effectively utilized in the 1960's.

During the 1950's CORE expanded its efforts to combat discrimination in employment. Experimenting with direct action techniques, such as picketing and boycotting target stores, CORE attempted to open up new job opportunities for blacks in retail stores in black neighborhoods. In 1958 the organization conducted what may have been the first successful black boycott campaign. It was directed against a St. Louis bread manufacturer.

In 1961, CORE gained national attention as a major civil rights group with its sponsorship of the Freedom Ride into the Deep South. Directed by Farmer, biracial members of CORE participated in a bus ride through Alabama and Mississippi with the purpose of challenging segregation in interstate bus travel. The Freedom Ride represented a continuation of the policy of direct action and confrontation. CORE members were received with open hostility and encountered violence and jail sentences.

After the first Freedom Rides, CORE was involved with other civil rights organizations in voter registration drives and "Freedom Schools" in the South and in establishing projects in urban black ghettos in the North. In 1966, Farmer was succeeded as national director of CORE by Floyd B. McKissick. The organization became more militant in its approach to racial problems under McKissick, who endorsed the concept of "black power." See also BLACK POWER.

JOSEPH BOSKIN
*University of Southern California*

WIDE WORLD

Congressional committees often seek information from the executive, in this case from a secretary of defense.

**CONGRESS OF THE UNITED STATES,** kong'grəs, the legislative branch of the national government. It consists of two houses, a Senate having 100 members (2 from each state) and a House of Representatives having 435 members. The members of the House represent districts that within each state, by requirement of the Supreme Court, must be nearly equal in population.

The Congress was created by Article I, section 1, of the U. S. Constitution (adopted 1787, effective 1789), which enumerates the powers invested in Congress, including the powers to assess and collect taxes, regulate interstate and foreign commerce, coin money, establish post offices, declare war, and maintain the armed forces. Each chamber also has special powers. For example, the Senate must ratify treaties, and the House initiates all revenue bills. (For a complete enumeration of Congress' powers and of the personal prerogatives of its members, see CONSTITUTION OF THE UNITED STATES. See also HOUSE OF REPRESENTATIVES; SENATE.)

Congress itself determines the size of the House (the Senate customarily respecting the House's wishes in this matter), and although the House has grown with the admission of new states to the Union and with population increases, an upper limit of 435 has been maintained since 1913 except for a temporary suspension to accommodate the admission of Alaska and Hawaii in 1959.

**Qualifications and Elections.** Representatives must be at least 25 years old, must be residents of their states (and also, by custom, of the districts they represent), and must have been citizens of the United States for 7 years. They are elected by popular vote for 2-year terms from districts established by the legislatures of their states. (For a discussion of circumstances under which all representatives from a state may be elected at large, see CONGRESSMAN-AT-LARGE.) Senators must be 30 years old, residents

of their states, and citizens of 9 years' standing. Senators are also elected by popular vote; before the adoption of the 17th Amendment to the Constitution in 1913, they were chosen by their state legislatures or according to provisions laid down by their legislatures. Senate terms are for six years, one third of the terms expiring every two years. Elections for both houses are held on the first Tuesday after the first Monday in November of even-numbered years or on special dates set by state laws to fill seats that become vacant between terms. Political parties emerged during the First Congress, and members of both houses have customarily been nominated by parties. In the 18th and early 19th centuries, nominees were selected in conventions; now, with few exceptions, they are chosen by popular primary elections.

**Sessions.** Under terms of the 20th Amendment, adopted in 1933, both houses meet at noon on the 3d day of January after the November elections (unless Congress fixes a different date) to organize for the forthcoming 2-year period. One session is held each year, extending continuously from January until adjournment. In recent years the length of sessions has increased, until now Congress usually remains in session until fall. Each biennium is designated a Congress, the First Congress meeting in 1789 and 1790, and the 100th in 1987 and 1988. The Constitution permits neither house to adjourn for more than three days without the concurrence of the other. Once a session or a Congress adjourns *sine die* (indefinitely), it meets again only if the president calls a special session of one or both houses.

### OFFICIALS AND LEADERS

The Constitution provides that the House shall elect a speaker to preside over it; legally he need not be, but by custom he always is, a member. The speaker is the leader of the party

THE HOUSE, which has a total membership of 435 representatives, meets in the south wing of the U. S. Capitol.

having the greater membership in the House, and he commonly attains leadership only after many uninterrupted terms of service. Except, of course, for the first speaker, Frederick Muhlenberg, only Henry Clay in 1811 and William Pennington in 1859 were elected to the speakership in their first terms.

The Constitution designates the vice president of the United States as president of the Senate; it permits him to vote only when senators' votes are equally divided. In recent years vice presidents have usually presided only on ceremonial occasions or at meetings of special importance. A president *pro tempore*, by tradition the senator having the longest continuous service in the majority party, presides or, more typically, rotates the role of presiding officer among new senators of both parties.

In both House and Senate the party with larger membership takes major responsibility for managing formal leadership positions. Usually the same party commands a majority in both houses, and that party, more often than not, occupies the presidency also. The participation of parties is wholly traditional and extralegal; parties are not mentioned in either the Constitution or the rules of either house. Party caucuses in each house elect majority and minority leaders and their deputies, the party whips. The speaker and the leaders enjoy certain emoluments, notably large offices and chauffeured automobiles.

**Changing Role of the Speaker.** During the speakerships of Thomas B. Reed (1889–1891,

1895–1899) and Joseph G. Cannon (1903–1911), House leaders appointed committees, sometimes ignored seniority in designating chairmen, and set the agenda for debate to suit their policies. First Reed and then Cannon commanded the Republican party and, therefore, the House. In the first decade of the 20th century "insurgent" Republicans, led by George Norris of Nebraska, rebelled against Cannon and joined the Democrats to remove the speaker from the Rules Committee, strip him of his power to appoint committees, and adopt other reforms that made the speaker less powerful and more responsive to a majority of the House—not necessarily a partisan majority. Since then speakers have relied more on informal influence than on formal authority. They have preferred to work privately, hence flexibly, rather than to consolidate power publicly and thus restrict their latitude for compromise. Sam Rayburn, whose 17 years as speaker (1940–1947, 1949–1953, 1955–1961) far exceeded any previous tenure in that office, epitomized the informal leader.

**Senate Leadership.** Senate leaders too have relied almost exclusively on informal influence. Indeed, the formal leadership positions, such as those of majority and minority leader, have occasionally been filled by relatively junior senators selected through a compromise among senior party figures. Not until Lyndon B. Johnson became Democratic leader in 1953 and majority leader in 1955 did a formal party leader centralize power in the Senate. Although chosen by

THE SENATE, meeting in its chamber in the Capitol's north wing, consists of 100 members, 2 from each state.

a traditional compromise and while serving only his first Senate term, Johnson soon defined his role in quite untraditional ways. He acquired the largest staff any leader ever had by drawing together assistants from his several other positions as chairman of committees and subcommittees. Johnson made himself the center of Senate activity, sometimes talking with every Democratic senator every day. Within a few years he became the acknowledged authority on what was acceptable to the Senate. He proved himself a consummate parliamentarian without precedent in Congress or in any other legislature. Nevertheless, when Johnson resigned in 1961 to serve as vice president, he had not yet so consolidated his authority and institutionalized his role that his successor would automatically inherit the accouterments of power. Senate leadership soon reverted to its customary decentralized style.

### THE COMMITTEE SYSTEM

The fate of most proposed legislation rests in the hands of the congressional committees. In 1913 the two houses had 135 committees. Some reduction occurred in the 1920s, but by the end of World War II, 81 committees still existed. The committee system was streamlined by the Legislative Reorganization Act of 1946.

In the 102d Congress the House had 22 standing committees: Agriculture; Appropriations; Armed Services; Banking, Finance, and Urban Affairs; Budget; District of Columbia; Education and Labor; Energy and Commerce; Foreign Affairs; Government Operations; House Administration; Interior and Insular Affairs; Judiciary; Merchant Marine and Fisheries; Post Office and Civil Service; Public Works and Transportation; Rules; Science, Space, and Technology; Small Business; Standards of Official Conduct; Veterans' Affairs; and Ways and Means. The Senate had 16: Agriculture, Nutrition, and Forestry; Appropriations; Armed Services; Banking, Housing, and Urban Affairs; Budget; Commerce, Science, and Transportation; Energy and Natural Resources; Environment and Public Works; Finance; Foreign Relations; Governmental Affairs; Judiciary; Labor and Human Resources; Rules and Administration; Small Business; and Veterans' Affairs.

Most House members serve on only one committee; all Senators serve on several. Each may sit on one or more subcommittees. When bills are introduced in either house, they are referred to a committee. Experience and precedents have been codified to make reference virtually automatic, thus reducing the discretion and influence of the leaders; in rare cases of uncertainty the presiding officer, advised by the parliamentarian, designates the committee having jurisdiction.

The majority party holds a majority of the seats on every committee. The distribution of committee seats is usually adjusted when the ratio of majority to minority changes.

**The Committee's Work.** The chairman of the committee (the majority party member whose continuous service is longest) to which the bill is

569

referred decides whether to refer the bill to a subcommittee, hold hearings in the full committee, or ignore the bill. Some committees have adopted rules to govern the chairman, but in most he proceeds with considerable latitude. Certain sections of the nation, in which one party consistently defeats the other, return the same members of Congress for many years; hence, Southern Democrats and Midwestern Republicans, representing areas that, in the past, have undergone the least social change and that, consequently, have remained relatively conservative, have captured a high proportion of committee chairmanships. Chairmen appoint subcommittees, and subcommittee assignments depend less on seniority considerations and more on the chairman's preferences than do committee appointments. A sympathetic chairman can hasten a bill's passage by scheduling hearings or by affecting the composition of a subcommittee; an unsympathetic chairman can delay action, while his colleagues are reluctant to force his hand.

By custom, chairmen are respected for their positions—acquired through seniority, not through election by the House or party nor by appointment by the party leaders—and members will not readily impinge upon their power even when they differ with them on issues. Leaders can entreat but not command action on bills in committees or subcommittees. Once scheduled, hearings may last from hours to weeks, months, even years, depending on the amount of controversy. After hearing witnesses, public and private, committees or subcommittees vote to report the bill, with or without amendments. Subcommittees respect each others' recommendations: members of full committees hesitate to reverse actions of subcommittees of which they are not members, lest decisions of their own subcommittees in turn suffer reversal.

If the committee's decision is negative, a bill is virtually dead for that Congress. Representatives are disinclined to sign a discharge petition whereby a House majority may take a bill from a committee, lest they encourage similar actions against their own committee, and senators likewise are reluctant to remove a bill from a committee's jurisdiction.

**Acting on Bills Approved by a Committee.** If the committee vote is affirmative, the bill is reported to the House or Senate and is placed on one of the *calendars*. Because the Senate is small, its calendar is simpler than the House's. In the Senate bills are taken from the calendar of business by unanimous consent on recommendation of the majority leader after consultation with his fellow party leaders and with the minority leader. Only rarely is a vote needed to remove a bill from the calendar and to make it pending Senate business. In the House bills are referred to the private calendar, consent calendar, union calendar (revenue and appropriation measures), or House calendar. For the House, taking action on a controversial bill is itself controversial. Because of the large number of House members desiring to participate in debate, leaders are reluctant to debate in the full House bills that are not likely to pass. Occasionally, for reasons of partisan advantage or as a favor to a member or a president who wants an issue for an election campaign, leaders will bring to a vote a bill that they expect to be defeated. Hence, voting to debate a bill is itself a key decision in the House, and opponents try to finish their work by preventing consideration.

Controversial bills come to the floor of the House on recommendation of the Committee on Rules (consisting, since 1961, of 10 majority and 5 minority members). Neither approval nor prompt decision is automatic at this point. Since Speaker Cannon's dominance of House procedure was broken in 1910 by enlarging the Rules Committee from 5 to 10 and by removing the Speaker from the committee, the committee has sometimes been closely attuned to the majority party's leadership and sometimes more representative of House bipartisan majorities. On highly controversial and innovative bills, Rules occasionally delays decision until it is too late in the session for both the House and Senate to complete action. When the Rules Committee recommends debate on the floor, the House votes on Rules' proposal in the form of a simple House resolution. Then, on adoption, it resolves itself into the Committee of the Whole House on the State of the Union.

Under *open rules,* amendments are in order in the Committee of the Whole but, if added, must be affirmed again after the committee rises and reports to the House. If defeated, they cannot be offered again. On tax and occasional other complicated bills, the Rules Committee recommends (and the House almost invariably adopts) a *closed rule* that limits or prohibits amendments. When the House passes a bill, the measure is referred to the Senate (unless, of course, the Senate has already passed it), where similar procedures are followed.

Delay in the Senate has one additional possibility: the filibuster. Unlike the House, the Senate does not limit debate by majority vote. Unanimous consent or a two-thirds majority of those present and voting are required to close Senate debate. A lone senator or a coalition of senators can postpone a vote, perhaps long enough to compel compromise if not defeat.

If the Senate passes a bill in the precise form of the House measure, it is delivered to the president for signature. If both houses do not pass the same version of a bill, one house must agree to the other's; otherwise, the bill is referred to a conference committee of members of both House and Senate whose jurisdiction extends only to resolving differences between the two houses. Compromises adopted by conference committee must be approved by both houses before the bill is sent to the president. At each of these many stages, a bill must win in order to become law. Defeat at any point, except by a presidential veto that is overridden by a two-thirds vote of each house, is permanent, at least until another Congress convenes. Moreover, if a Congress adjourns before a bill has passed through all stages, the bill dies and must begin the enactment process anew in the next Congress. Hence, the iron law of parliaments: it is easier to defeat a motion than to pass it.

## CONGRESS AND THE EXECUTIVE BRANCH

The decisions of the Constitutional Convention to establish a bicameral Congress and to separate it from the executive illustrate a major theme of 18th century American political thought. The Founding Fathers emphasized checks and balances as means of assuring individual freedom and avoiding governmental tyranny. Similar principles had been stressed by classical political philosophers, including Solon, Plato, and Aristotle, in whom the Founding Fathers were well read, and also by contemporary theorists, among them Blackstone, Hume, and Voltaire, who were im-

# HOW A BILL INTRODUCED IN THE HOUSE OF REPRESENTATIVES BECOMES LAW

(Similar procedure is followed for bills introduced in the Senate.)

The administration inspires much legislation. The president usually outlines broad objectives in his State of the Union address.

Members of the president's staff may draft bills and ask congressmen who are friendly to the legislation to introduce them.

Other bills originate independently of the administration, perhaps to fulfill a campaign pledge made by a congressman.

Each bill must be introduced by a member of the House. The speaker then assigns the bill to the appropriate committee.

The committe conducts hearings during which members of the administration and others may testify for or against the bill.

If it is reported out of committee, the bill goes to the Rules Committee, which decides whether to place it before the House.

A bill submitted to the House is voted on, with or without debate. If a majority approves it, the bill is sent to the Senate.

The Senate assigns the bill to a Committee, which holds hearings and then approves, rejects, rewrites, or shelves the bill.

If the bill is reported out of committee, it is submitted to the Senate for a vote, which may be taken with or without debate.

If the Senate does not change the House version of the bill, and a majority approves it, the bill goes to the president for signing.

If the bill the Senate approves differs from the House version, the bill is sent to a House-Senate conference for a compromise solution.

If the conference produces a compromise bill, and it is approved by both House and Senate, the bill goes to the president for signing.

The bill becomes law if the president signs it. If he vetoes it, two-thirds of both House and Senate must approve it again before it can become law.

pressed by Newtonian analogies to the physical and natural order of the universe. Montesquieu thought he observed a nicely honed balance among English political institutions, especially in the separation of powers among legislative, executive, and judicial branches. Although Montesquieu's description was found inaccurate for the British system, his *De l'esprit des lois* (*The Spirit of the Laws*) nevertheless served the Founding Fathers as a model in writing the Constitution of their new nation.

The separation of legislative from judicial and executive functions led not merely to investing Congress with all legislative power; it also charged each house of Congress with checking and balancing the other. Many theorists feared, not political power per se, but power unchecked by countervailing power. Indeed, many contemporaries regarded the Articles of Confederation as a failure because the government they created had insufficient power. The framers of the Constitution, therefore, intended to create a viable government, one vested with sufficient power to fulfill the responsibilities assigned to it. Increasing governmental power required new checks and balances on each source of power. As the federal government was to be balanced by the governments of the states and each house of Congress by its fellow, so each branch of the federal government was to be balanced by the others.

**Separation of Powers, in Practice.** Strict separation of legislative, judicial, and executive functions, however, cannot in fact be drawn or maintained. Although Congress is the principal legislative branch, the judiciary interprets the meaning of acts of Congress and has assumed power to review their constitutionality. The Constitution obliges the president to report to Congress annually on the "State of the Union" and thereby to recommend legislation. His signature is required for a bill to become law, unless each house of Congress passes the bill by a two-thirds majority after the president has withheld his signature. The Constitution empowers the Senate to participate in executive actions by confirming presidential appointments (including appointments to the federal courts) and by consenting to treaties through a two-thirds majority.

Thus, from the beginning of the new government, each branch involved itself in performing functions of another. Accordingly, each branch soon became expected not only to check and balance the others but also to create new practices and institutions for fulfilling the high aspirations of the Founding Fathers. Chief Justice John Marshall established the Supreme Court's acquisition of the power of judicial review (*Marbury* v. *Madison*); President Thomas Jefferson extended the executive's power in ill-defined situations (for example, the Louisiana Purchase); and Speaker Henry Clay and other congressional leaders competed with the other branches to design programs and policies affecting national expansion, roads, tariffs, and slavery. Congress soon was expected (by itself and others) to be a full and active participant in the widest range of problems that concern national government.

**Efforts to Achieve Balance and Retain Initiative.** As an instrument of checks and balances, Congress has changed little since its inception. Through annual appropriations, legislative authorizations, committee investigations, Senate approval of appointments and treaties, and intimate daily contacts, Congress (often acting through its leaders or committees rather than as House and Senate) continues to check executive and judicial power, either by direct action or by others' anticipation of its action. While many other national legislatures have assumed merely ceremonial status or have been subjugated by the executive, Congress remains a fully active, working part of the system of checks and balances. Indeed, compared with the rise of one-party governments in many new nations, the decline of parliaments in the older western European governments, the impotence of the United Nations General Assembly, and the weaknesses of legislatures in the American state governments, Congress ranks indisputably as the world's most powerful and effective legislature.

The influence of Congress rests in its checking, balancing, delaying, questioning, amending, and negating actions of the executive without rendering the government inoperative or ineffective. The executive branch anticipates congressional reaction to its major moves and so acts to win legislative support. Though the Senate rarely fails to confirm a presidential appointment, the president usually inquires privately whether a nominee is acceptable and withdraws his name if he is not. Similarly, the president attempts to anticipate the reaction of Congress to legislation that he plans to request and usually adjusts his proposals so as to increase the probability of a favorable congressional decision.

The most fundamental changes in Congress have occurred with respect to policy innovation. Throughout the 19th century new policies came as often from Congress as from the executive. Positions of congressional leadership, especially in the House of Representatives, were prominent national offices nearly comparable to the presidency in prestige and power. Speaker James K. Polk and Ways and Means Committee Chairman William McKinley achieved the presidency, and Speakers Henry Clay and James G. Blaine were nominees for it. At the turn of the century Speakers Reed and Cannon justly earned their reputations as powerful national party figures. After Reed and Cannon, however, Congress waned as an effective initiator of policy proposals.

**Initiative Taken by the Executive.** Increasingly, Congress relied on its check and balance function —delaying, vetoing, amending, approving executive initiatives—to exercise its influence. It became less concerned with identifying national problems and inventing and prescribing policies to deal with them. The years of Theodore Roosevelt's and Woodrow Wilson's presidencies (1901–1909, 1913–1921) marked the first sustained shift of initiative from Capitol Hill to the White House. From 1921 to 1933 neither the executive nor the legislative branch asserted itself often. From Franklin D. Roosevelt's inauguration in 1933 dates the routine expectation that the president will initiate legislative programs. That this was an institutional change, not merely a difference between Democrats and Republicans, was confirmed by Dwight D. Eisenhower's two terms as president (1953–1961). He also took the initiative; when he did not, some congressional leaders criticized the want of presidential leadership, and Congress itself made no attempt to innovate. It was resigned to awaiting executive action.

That Congress has lost initiative is true for almost every stage of policy making. Policy has come to be recognized as inexorably bound with administration. In all aspects of policy making—gathering intelligence, formulating and recommending alternatives, selecting among alternatives, implementing the prescribed choice, and appraising the effectiveness of the decision—the executive branch has won initiative from the legislature. Congress has not staffed itself with a legislative intelligence network. Its sources of information are largely executive. Sometimes it temporarily employs experts from the other branch; always, it relies heavily on executive officials' reports, testimony, and informal consultation. Virtually every congressional hearing opens with a witness from the executive branch. Committees refer every bill introduced in Congress to one or more executive departments for an opinion. No legislative authorization or monetary appropriation is made until the Bureau of the Budget has reported that the measure is consistent with the president's program. Not infrequently, executive officials call problems to the attention of individual congressmen, usually members of the committee with pertinent jurisdiction. The president supplements his State of the Union address (required by the Constitution) with an annual budget (required by the Budget and Accounting Act of 1921), an annual economic report (required by the Employment Act of 1946), personal appearances (required by custom since Woodrow Wilson restored the precedent that had lapsed with Jefferson) before joint sessions of the House and Senate, and numerous special, written messages.

Even when committees or individual members of Congress undertake their own analyses of issues, they rely extensively on executive documents. Similarly, the Legislative Reference Service of the Library of Congress depends principally on executive sources of information, as the footnotes to its tables and reports often acknowledge. When lobbyists for organized interests testify before congressional committees, their information, whatever their interpretation of it may be, often derives from official publications. (For a discussion of the lobbying tactics used by special interest groups, see LOBBY.)

The executive's near monopoly of information is the product of its vast intelligence network, which embraces the Bureau of the Budget, the Bureau of the Census, the Bureau of Labor Statistics, the Central Intelligence Agency, and other investigative bureaus and research facilities. Information brings problems to politicians' attention, indicating who is deprived, who indulged. Information points the way toward the most practicable courses of action.

Executive officials draft legislation and then arrange its introduction by a member. In his messages to Congress the president establishes the agenda for much public discussion and congressional deliberation. Almost every issue centers on "the Administration's bill." What the president will not support is unlikely to be considered seriously, much less passed. Neutrality may be overcome, but outright executive opposition is rarely defeated.

**Executive-Legislative Liaison.** To facilitate the executive's dominance of the information and recommendation aspects of congressional decision making, elaborate procedures of legislative-executive liaison have developed. In 1937, President Franklin Roosevelt, at the suggestion of House Majority Leader Sam Rayburn, initiated weekly meetings with legislative leaders. The regular exchanges, usually held over breakfast at the White House, are supplemented by many informal contacts. In the administrations of John F. Kennedy and Lyndon B. Johnson, they were augmented by a larger staff for the special assistant to the president for congressional relations.

Every executive department and agency has a team of liaison officers who faithfully respond to congressional requests for information and assistance and who regularly consult with individual members, committee chairmen, and party leaders. Liaison officials at the departmental levels are coordinated at the White House by the special assistant to the president. White House emissaries cooperate with legislative tacticians in mapping plans for congressional votes and proceedings. Although prohibited by House and Senate rules from entering either chamber, presidential aides are available in the galleries above the chambers, in the lobbies just outside, or in leaders' offices. They participate in decisions concerning when bills should be brought to the floor for debate, when votes should be scheduled, and when amendments should be supported by the administration's coalition.

**Reasons for Loss of Initiative—The Industrial Revolution.** The decline in congressional initiative and the concentration of innovation in the executive branch resulted from a fundamental change in the character of public policy making. The Industrial Revolution caused an increase in the number of problems that reach the attention of governments. The Industrial Revolution radically rearranged population centers, opened roads, invented new forms of transport, created unforeseen modes of communication, developed previously unused natural resources, organized bigger markets, enlarged international commerce, stimulated wave after wave of immigration, demanded acquisition of new skills and adaptation of old ones, replaced many small firms with a few immense industrywide organizations, accentuated problems of public health and private welfare, increased rates of birth, and diminished rates of death.

The acceleration of social change that these developments symbolized confronted governments with demands for services that heretofore had been accommodated by private sectors of society or not at all. Statesmen who had been experts on virtually every one of the few major public issues could not command expertise on the greatly extended range of social questions. As the number of problems demanding attention increased, so did the availability of information about them. No longer was personal experience in commerce, agriculture, law, or war sufficient to equip a congressman for almost every contingency. Science, scholarship, and journalism expanded beyond the capacity of single minds to encompass all knowledge. Institutions became unable to process the increased inputs of information without specialization and bureaucratization.

One may date these developments from about 1880, when the decennial census had become such an enormous undertaking that the Bureau of the Census confronted the prospect of being unable to complete analyzing one census before taking the next. A census official, Herman Hollerith, thereupon invented punched-hole cards for machine tabulation to facilitate processing data for the 1890 census. Simultaneously, executive branches of government began to formalize

SENATE LEADERS and executive officers watch President Kennedy sign the Nuclear Test Ban Treaty (1963).

UPI

bureaucratic procedures; indeed, for the first time, bureaucracy, or public administration, became a subject for study, training, and professional employment.

**Failure to Bureaucratize.** Congress' reaction to these developments differed from the executive's. The legislative branch did not specialize or bureaucratize. To this day it has not expanded its staff and supporting facilities to any degree approaching the growth and diversification of the executive branch. Congress still operates from the two wings added in 1857 and 1859 to the same Capitol building it has occupied since 1800. The House built separate office buildings in 1908 when it had 386 members, in 1933, and in 1965; the Senate acquired a separate building for offices in 1909 (when its membership numbered 92) and added another in 1958. This expansion is modest compared with the growth in the number and size of executive buildings in the District of Columbia and in nearby areas of Virginia and Maryland.

**Congress Not Altogether Representative.** The culture, class, and interest of Congress is not that of the nation in miniature. The backgrounds and experiences of individual congressmen selectively determine the sources of influence that reach the focus of their attention. Members typically spring from middle- and upper-class backgrounds, belong to high-status religious denominations, derive from families of relatively high income, and possess more than average education. Although minority groups constitute approximately 16% of the national population, minority membership of the House stood at about 8% in 1991; women, who account for more than half the total population, had less than 7% representation. In contrast to the national population, the average age of which is declining, the average age of members of both houses is increasing. The electoral base of Congress depends more on small states than does that of the presidency, whose "effective constituency" consists rather of populous urban states.

Granting individual exceptions, most congressmen are members of and represent social classes preferring moderate, gradual change. Moreover, the predominant interests of congressmen—law, commerce, agriculture—provide Congress few

specialists in some of the emergent or growing professions—science, technology, social science, communications, medicine—that are increasingly relevant to contemporary public problems. The most common previous political activity of congressmen is service in a state legislature, an experience that breeds generalists rather than specialists and that provides no training in using a staff of specialists. The disinclination to employ staffs with contrasting specializations further reinforces Congress' disadvantages. Congressional staff positions usually fall to lawyers and journalists notable more for their adeptness at arguing a case or at summarizing a body of information than for their expertise on specialized issues.

## TOWARD AN EFFECTIVE CONGRESS

Influential and effective congressmen are those whose colleagues respect them for their hard work, their loyalty to the social life of the institution, their preference for recognition as congressmen over ambition for the presidency, their knowledge of parliamentary procedure, and their devotion to committee responsibilities. Members who observe the "rules of the game" are those most likely to attain positions of influence in Congress and to secure favorable dispensation of bills and resolutions that they propose. In short, a legislator's most valuable asset is the respect of his peers, acquired by learning and adhering to subtle but identifiable folkways of congressional conduct. The apprenticeship that the seniority traditions require a member to serve before he gathers much influence inculcates the personal qualities of respect and the observance of institutional mores.

**Strategies for Action.** In using his assets to achieve his legislative objectives, a congressman has various strategies available. The clublike norms dictate that contests for leadership positions and contests over legislative issues be resolved inside the House and inside the Senate. The "inside strategy" gives preference to personal qualities, discounts ideology, rewards service to Congress as an institution, and pays little heed to demands of special interest groups, constituents, and the executive. Vacancies in positions of official leadership are ordinarily settled by contests in which all candidates adhere to an inside strategy; to resort to an "outside strategy" of appeals for presidential endorsement, national editorial support, and organized lobbying signifies a candidate's weakness and foreshadows his defeat. Presidents rarely express preferences in contests for speaker or floor leaders. On legislative measures, conversely, outside strategies are frequently employed when one side can improve its chances of success by evoking greater public attention. Use of an outside strategy increases the salience of issues in some constituencies and thus increases constituency demands, thereby restricting a representative's or senator's latitude for compromise. The issues on which Congress is most likely to triumph over the presidency are those of relatively low salience.

In addition to choosing between inside and outside strategies, party leaders may choose between strategies that build inclusive coalitions of diverse interests or those that build exclusive coalitions of narrow interests. Many effective party leaders are renowned for their "inclusive" tactics—for winning support of farm groups for legislation favored by unions and for attracting votes of urban representatives for reclamation and irrigation projects demanded by representatives from Western states. The once-powerful Southern Democratic-Republican coalition, based on opposition to federal civil rights legislation and on fiscal conservatism, foundered in the 1960's, when Republicans could no longer afford the political costs of voting against civil rights measures. The success of the inclusive strategy partly explains the Democratic party's control of Congress during most of the mid-20th century.

**Outlook for Congressional Influence.** The future of Congress depends partly on whether current trends and conditions continue or change. The two principal sources of congressional decline—increasing number of public problems and increasing information about them—will flourish rather than diminish. The society served by government evidences more complexity, not less. And complexity produces deprivations and demands for power and economic realignments. Similarly, the variety and number of sources of information relevant to these problems is certain to grow. As these developments become increasingly acute, the participation of Congress in national decisions will continue to be less that of initiator and more that of reactor to executive intelligence and recommendations.

Such a prospect is reinforced by experience in other nations whose legislative branches are losing influence to the executive. In western European democracies, executives dominate parliaments. The same condition obtains in emerging, underdeveloped countries in which political talent is too scarce to staff a legislature with competitive parties. In these the executive, allied with a one-party system, rules parliament at its will, or at the party's will.

**Doctrine of Responsible Parties.** Given this probable future, political theorists have turned their efforts not to ways of rejuvenating Congress as an innovative body but principally to ways of guaranteeing its continued success as a check and balance instrument. The doctrine of party responsibility, popular among political scientists, would adapt the British parliamentary model to the American scene. Majority party leaders and chairmen in Congress would be more closely associated with the president, and minority party leaders would be more closely affiliated with national party figures of the "loyal opposition." Chairmen would be expected to support the party platform adopted at quadrennial national conventions and to follow presidential leadership to enact it. Members unwilling to adhere to the party program would be denied party endorsement and financial support in subsequent elections. Establishing competitive programmatic parties and permitting the electorate to choose between them would give the winning party a mandate for action. Success or failure in enacting a party program could be rewarded, or punished, at the next ballot.

In the unlikely event that programmatic parties emerged to compete with and to check each other, Congress would become merely a stage for party government, not an institution for checking and balancing the executive. To a much lesser degree would it be an initiative-taking institution.

**The "Oversight" Function.** Other theorists expect, and some recommend, that Congress will concentrate more on its "oversight" function, that is, on using its investigating committees to monitor and appraise executive performance. Through hearings, investigations, and staff studies, committees would highlight public discussion of the execution of broad programs enacted by Congress and assigned to the executive for detailed specification and implementation.

Such a role for Congress is most likely to develop first with respect to the policies in which the executive has the greatest informational advantage. Among these are foreign relations and the closely associated policies pertaining to national defense and the military applications of science and technology. Congress has always been at a constitutional disadvantage in affecting foreign policy, and the new characteristics of policy making have further strengthened the executive.

If Congress cannot initiate major foreign and defense policies, its members and committees can make Congress a forum in which conflicting arguments can be focused on executive officials. Occasionally a speech or hearing may prod the executive to take an initiative that it would not otherwise assume or may induce it to withhold or retract an action, either contemplated or already undertaken. At other times Congress may restore a consensus by thorough exposure of an issue, event, or decision through an investigation or a great debate. Indeed it is not impossible that debate, which declined in quality and importance when committees became the principal loci of legislative work, will once again offer dramatic opportunities for resolving political conflicts.

JAMES A. ROBINSON
*Mershon Professor of Political Science*
*The Ohio State University*

### Bibliography

Baker, Richard A., *The Senate of the United States* (Krieger, 1988).

Brenner, Phillip, *The Limits and Possibilities of Congress* (St. Martin's Press 1983).

Clapp, Charles L., *The Congressman: His Work as He Sees It* (1963; reprint, Greenwood Press 1980).

Congressional Quarterly Service, *Congress and the Nation, 1981–1984* (CW Press 1985).

Dahl, Robert A., *Congress and Foreign Policy* (1950; reprint, Greenwood Press, 1983).

Egger, Rowland, and Harris, Joseph P., *The President and Congress* (1963; reprint, Greenwood Press 1988).

Feld, Werner J., and Wildgen, John K., *Congress and National Defense* (Praeger 1985).

Goehlert, Robert U., and Martin, Fenton S., *Congress and Law-Making*, 2d ed. (ABC-CLIO 1988).

Hale, Dennis, *The United States Congress* (Transaction Bks. 1984).

Hinckley, Barbara, *Stability and Change in Congress*, 4th ed. (Harper 1987).

Jennings, Bruce, and Callahan, Daniel, eds., *Representation and Responsibility* (Plenum Pub. 1985).

Keefe, William J., *Congress and the American People*, 3d ed. (Prentice-Hall 1985).

Keefe, William J., and Ogul, Morris S., *The American Legislative Process: Congress and the States*, 6th ed. (Prentice-Hall 1985).

Maass, Arthur, *Congress and the Common Good* (Basic Bks. 1985).

Matthews, Donald R., *United States Senators and Their World* (1960; reprint, Greenwood Press 1980).

Miller, J. A., *Running in Place* (Simon & Schuster 1986).

Murphy, Thomas, *Politics of Congressional Committees* (Barron's Educ. Ser. 1978).

Reedy, George E., *The U.S. Senate: Paralysis or a Search for Consensus?* (Crown 1986).

Rieselbach, Leroy N., *Congressional Reform* (CQ Review 1986).

Robinson, James A., *Congress and Foreign Policy-Making* (1962; reprint, Greenwood Press 1980).

Seltser, Barry J., *The Principles and Practice of Political Compromise* (Mellen Press 1984).

Shields, Johanna N., *The Line of Duty: Maverick Congressmen and the Development of American Political Culture, 1836–1860* (Greenwood Press 1985).

Vogler, David J., *The Politics of Congress*, 5th ed. (W. C. Brown 1988).

Weatherford, J. McI., *Tribes on the Hill: The U.S. Congress—Rituals and Realities* (Bergin & Garvey 1985).

**CONGRESS PARTY,** officially called the Indian National Congress, is a political party of India. It was formed by an Englishman, Allan Octavian Hume, and met for the first time in Bombay on Dec. 28, 1885. Proclaiming its loyalty to the Crown, the newly formed organization prayed for greater participation by Indians in the colonial government. For two decades the party agitated for its goals, but always within consitutional bounds. But the partition of Bengal in 1905 aroused fierce nationalist sentiment, and the Congress supported a boycott movement. Its president, Dadabhai Naoroji, known as the Grand Old Man of India, demanded at Calcutta in 1906 *Swaraj*, or self-rule. In 1918 the Congress urged at Delhi that the Wilsonian principle of self-determination be applied to India.

Repressive measures by the British after World War I and the return of Gandhi from South Africa helped transform the Congress into a mass movement. At Nagpur in 1920 the Congress approved Gandhi's nonviolent noncooperation program. The Lahore session of 1929 marked a historical watershed. Jawaharlal Nehru, inheriting the presidency from his father, declared complete independence as the new goal.

The early 1930's witnessed Gandhi's *Satyagraha*, or civil disobedience. When the Government of India Act of 1935, conceding a measure of provincial autonomy, went into effect, Congress governments were formed in six of the eleven provinces. But the Congress disapproved of Britain's unilateral declaration of war on Germany in 1939, and the provincial ministries resigned. On Aug. 8, 1942, when the Congress adopted the famous "Quit India" resolution, the disobedience movement was suppressed with unparalleled severity. On Aug. 15, 1947, the dream of independence became reality for the Congress. The party, espousing moderately socialistic principles, controlled the central government and all but one of the state governments of the new Republic of India and continued to do so until 1967. India's fourth general election, in 1967, gave Congress control of the central government but of only eight of India's 17 states.

ANAND MOHAN, *Author of "Indira Gandhi: A Personal and Political Biography"*

**CONGRESSIONAL RECORD,** issued daily when Congress is in session, reports the debates and proceedings in both houses of Congress. It also prints annual messages of the president to Congress, inaugural addresses, petitions and memorials, speeches delivered outside Congress, correspondence, and newspaper articles and editorials. Because Congress grants members "leave to revise and extend" remarks, legislators may alter the *Record* by expunging or adding material.

The *Register of Debates in Congress,* begun in 1824 by Gales and Seaton, publishers, preceded the *Record.* Although the Jackson administration placed its printing patronage with the firm of Blair and Rives, which began publication of a rival *Congressional Globe* in 1833, Gales and Seaton from 1834 to 1856 brought together materials from newspapers and other sources to issue the *Annals of the Congress of the United States,* a record of the first 18 Congresses. Their *Register,* however, expired in 1837. The *Globe* continued until 1873, when Congress required the Government Printing Office to publish the *Congressional Record.*

MARTIN GRUBERG, *Wisconsin State University*

**CONGRESSMAN-AT-LARGE,** a representative to the U. S. House of Representatives elected by his entire state rather than a given district within the state. Until 1842, each state could choose to elect its congressional delegation either in single-member districts or in an at-large election. A law passed by Congress in 1842 required that representatives be elected by state districts, with each district containing as nearly as possible the same number of persons as every other district. This law was changed in 1929 to allow each state to decide how to lay out its districts, subject to court challenges of unacceptable disparities in population. When a state receives an increase in its quota of representatives, it may choose the additional legislators by election at large.

A small state that has only one representative elects him at large. In the late 1960's, Hawaii and New Mexico were each still electing their two representatives at large. Until 1962 this was also true of North Dakota's pair of representatives. Because of a failure to reapportion to the satisfaction of the federal courts, Alabama's 8-man delegation to Congress had to run at large in 1964.

MARTIN GRUBERG, *Wisconsin State University*

**CONGREVE,** kon'grĕv, **William** (1670–1729), English author, who was one of the last and greatest Restoration comic playwrights. He was born at Bardsey, Yorkshire, on Jan. 24, 1670, and was educated in Ireland, where his father was the commander of the British garrison at Youghal. While a student at the Kilkenny School, and later at Trinity College, Dublin, Congreve was a contemporary of Jonathan Swift, with whom he formed a lifelong friendship. In 1691, Congreve was admitted to the Middle Temple, London, to study law. However, he gave up his legal studies after the publication of his first literary work, *Incognita* (1692), a slight but talented prose romance. At this time he became friendly with Dryden, who remained one of his admirers.

**Career as Playwright.** In 1693, Congreve began a brilliant seven-year career of dramatic writing, by which he achieved his literary fame. His earliest, and perhaps greatest success came with the production of his first play, *The Old Bachelor* (1693), a clever mix-up of marriages and intrigues. The central roles were played by the leading actor and actress of the period, Thomas Betterton and Ann Bracegirdle. Mrs. Bracegirdle was the object of a long infatuation on Congreve's part, and his most remarkable female characters were created for her. If Congreve's initial success owed something to her considerable acting talent, her career was also indebted to the brilliant roles he designed for her.

In his next comedy, *The Double Dealer* (1694), which did not have the success of his first play, Congreve temporarily succumbed to the fashion known derogatorily as "sentimental comedy." In this tradition, which constituted a reaction against the ribaldry and amorality of Restoration comedy, laughter was less important than the triumph of morality and the discomfiture of villainy. Whereas *The Double Dealer* was not so unabashedly moralistic as some of the works of the genre, it did not have the uninhibited comic spirit of the best of Restoration comedy.

*Love for Love* (q.v.), played by Betterton's company in 1695, almost duplicated the success of *The Old Bachelor,* and it has remained one of Congreve's most popular works. It marked a return to the Restoration medley of laughter, satire, and clever ribaldry and is especially rich in its array of characters, ranging from the supremely clever heroine, Angelica, to the gallery of droll types in Miss Prue, the country wench; Tattle, the consummate dandy; Jeremy, the clever servant; and Mrs. Frail, the easy prey of any man with a pleasing appearance and a glib tongue. Congreve's characters were not new in literature —Jeremy was as old as the clever servants in the Roman comedies of Plautus; Tattle and Mrs. Frail, under different names, dated back at least to the first Restoration comedy, Etherege's *Comical Revenge* (1664); Angelica resembled such Shakespearean heroines as Rosalind in *As You Like It* and Viola in *Twelfth Night.* But Congreve so successfully crystallized these traditional comic types that they seemed finally and unmistakably defined in his work.

Turning briefly from comedy in 1697, Congreve wrote his only tragedy, *The Mourning Bride,* a well-received version of the Restoration "heroic play," with its characteristic elements of exotic setting (Granada), violent and improbable passion (the lovers Almeria and Alphonso forcibly separated by the enraged emperor of Granada, who dies, by mistake, under his own orders), and a triumphant if incredible happy ending. Written in verse, *The Mourning Bride* contains several well-known passages, including "Heaven has no rage, like love to hatred turned,/Nor hell a fury, like a woman scorned," and the usually misquoted "Music hath charms to soothe a savage breast."

In 1698, Congreve was bitterly attacked by Jeremy Collier, a clergyman, in *A Short View of the Immorality and Profaneness of the English Stage.* Though the *Short View* was of negligible value as dramatic criticism, it was most significant as the expression of a change in the social and moral climate of the age—the days of rowdy satiric comedy were numbered.

Congreve's last play, *The Way of the World* (q.v.), produced in 1700, might be described as a splendid obituary of Restoration comedy, the last and most polished utterance of the tradition. As in *Love For Love,* Congreve presented ideal specimens of traditional comic types—the salacious hypocrite (Lady Wishfort) and the witty and clever heroine (Millamant) have become classics of the theater.

**Last Years.** Though *The Way of the World* is one of the most frequently revived of early English comedies, for all its brilliance it was not a success, and Congreve thereafter ceased to write plays. He wrote occasional works, such as the masque *The Judgment of Paris* (1701) and the libretto for the opera *Semele* (1710), both with music by John Eccles, as well as poems, such as *A Hymn to Harmony* (1703), which were collected posthumously in 1781.

Congreve spent most of his time in leisure, enjoying the affluence his plays had brought him and holding minor government posts, mostly sinecures, including that of commissioner for wine licenses and secretary of the island of Jamaica. He was a friend of the highly placed Duchess of Marlborough, to whom he left most of his fortune, and of such famous persons as Swift, Sir Richard Steele, and Alexander Pope, who dedicated his translation of Homer's *Iliad* (6 vols., 1715–1720) to Congreve. Congreve

NATIONAL PORTRAIT GALLERY

William Congreve, from a portrait by Godfrey Kneller.

died in London on Jan. 19, 1729, and was buried in the Poet's Corner of Westminster Abbey.

RICHARD E. HUGHES
*Author of "Literature: Form and Function"*

**Bibliography**

Bartlett, Laurence, *William Congreve: A Reference Guide* (G. K. Hall 1979).
Gosse, Edmund, *Life of William Congreve* (Folcroft 1973).
Hodges, John Cunyus, *William Congreve the Man* (Kraus 1941).
Jantz, Ursula, *Targets of Satire in the Comedies of Etherege, Wycherley, and Congreve,* ed. by James Hogg (Longwood 1978).
Kelsall, Malcolm, *Congreve* (Arnold 1982).
Mann, David D., *A Concordance to the Plays of William Congreve* (Cornell Univ. Press 1973).
Perry, Henry Ten Eyck, *The Comic Spirit in Restoration Drama: Studies in the Comedy of Etherege, Wycherley, Congreve, Vanbrugh, and Farquhar* (1925; reprint, Russell & Russell 1962).
Whibley, Charles, *Literary Studies: Shakespeare, Raleigh, Congreve* (1919; reprint, Telegraph Bks. 1983).
Williams, Aubrey I., *An Approach to Congreve* (Yale Univ. Press 1979).

**CONGREVE,** kon'grĕv, **Sir William** (1772–1828), British artillerist, whose artillery rocket of 1805 was an important step in the development of the rocket. He was born at Woolwich, England, on May 20, 1772, and was educated at Trinity College, Cambridge. His father was comptroller of the Royal Laboratory at Woolwich, and it was there that the younger Congreve developed the 3.5-inch-diameter (8.9-cm) incendiary rocket, using black powder, an iron case, and a 16-foot (4.9-meter) guide stick. This rocket was demonstrated in 1805 before the Prince Regent.

In 1806, Congreve's rockets set Boulogne afire. In 1807, Congreve directed a rocket attack against Copenhagen; about 25,000 rockets were fired, leaving much of the city burned.

Congreve succeeded to the baronetcy and to his father's position at the Royal Laboratory in 1814. That same year he published *The Details of the Rocket System,* in which he described and illustrated uses for his rocket in land and sea warfare. In 1820 he was elected to Parliament, and he served as a member until his death, at Toulouse, France, on May 16, 1828. See also ROCKETS—*Historical Background.*

**CONIC PROJECTION.** See MAP—*Projections.*

**CONIC SECTIONS,** kon'ik, or *conics*, are curves formed by the intersection of a plane with a double circular or elliptic cone. They are the ellipse, the hyperbola, and the parabola, shown in Fig. 1.

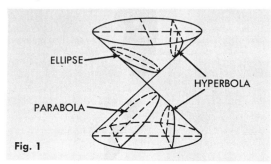

**Fig. 1**

**Ellipse.** The ellipse, shown in Fig. 2, can be defined as the locus of a point $P$ for which the sum of the distances $PF_1$ and $PF_2$ to two fixed points $F_1$ and $F_2$, called *foci*, is constant. If $PF_1 + PF_2 = 2a$ and $F_1F_2 = 2c$, then $a > c$. The ellipse is an oval curve with two perpendicular symmetry axes passing through the *center M* of $F_1F_2$; one of these axes, the *major axis* $A_1A_2$, passes through $F_1$ and $F_2$. The other axis, $B_1B_2$, is called the *minor axis* and the points $A_1$, $A_2$, $B_1$, and $B_2$ are the *vertices*. When we take the symmetry axes as the axes of a Cartesian coordinate system, with $M$ as origin, then the equation of the ellipse is

$$x^2/a^2 + y^2/b^2 = 1, \text{ where } b^2 = a^2 - c^2.$$

The normal at $P$, that is, the line perpendicular to the tangent at $P$, bisects $\angle F_2PF_1$. When $c = 0$, then $F_1$, $F_2$, and $M$ coincide, $a = b$, and the ellipse is a circle with center $M$ and radius $a$. See also ELLIPSE.

**Hyperbola.** The hyperbola is shown in Fig. 3 and can be defined as the locus of a point $P$ for which the difference $2a$ of the distances $PF_1$, $PF_2$ to two fixed points $F_1$ and $F_2$ (*foci*), is constant. If $F_1F_2 = 2c$, then $a < c$. The hyperbola consists of two separate branches and has two perpendicular symmetry axes passing through the *center M* of $F_1F_2$. The axis through $F_1$ and $F_2$ is the *real axis*. The other axis is often called the *imaginary axis*. When we take the real axis as the $X$-axis and the imaginary axis as the $Y$-axis of a Cartesian coordinate system, with $M$ as origin, then the equation of the hyperbola is

$$x^2/a^2 - y^2/b^2 = 1,$$

where $b^2 = c^2 - a^2$.

The other hyperbola shown in Fig. 3, which has the equation $x^2/a^2 - y^2/b^2 = -1$, has $B_1B_2$ as real axis and $A_1A_2$ as imaginary axis. The two hyperbolas $x^2/a^2 - y^2/b^2 = \pm 1$ are called *conjugate*. The two lines $y = \pm bx/a$ are called *asymptotes* and approach both hyperbolas as closely as we like by taking $P$ sufficiently away from $M$ on the curve. See also HYPERBOLA.

**Parabola.** Figure 4 illustrates the parabola, which can be defined as the locus of a point $P$ for which the distance $PH$ to a fixed line $AB$, the *directrix*, is equal to the distance $PF$ to a fixed point $F$, the *focus*. The parabola is a curve stretching to infinity with one axis of symmetry, the *axis* of the parabola, through $F$ and perpendicular to $AB$. The parabola intersects the axis at the *vertex V* so that $VR = VF$. The tangent at $P$ bisects the angle $FPH$. In rectangular Cartesian coordinates, with the axis of the parabola as $X$-axis and the origin at $V$, the equation of the parabola is $y^2 = 2px$, where *parameter* $p = 2FV = FR$. See also PARABOLA.

**General Equation of the Conics.** It can be shown that in Cartesian coordinates $(x,y)$, the general equation of the second degree

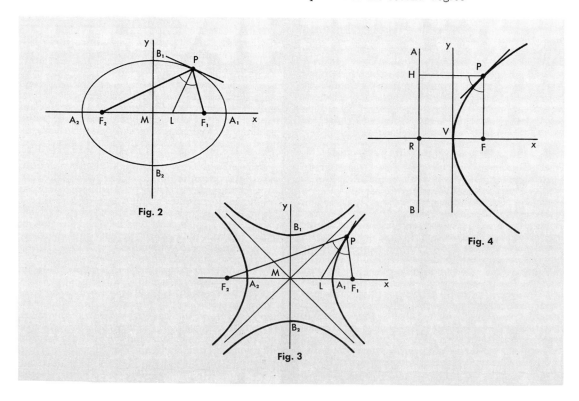

**Fig. 2**

**Fig. 3**

**Fig. 4**

**Fig. 5**

$$a_{11}x^2 + 2a_{12}xy + a_{22}y^2 + 2a_{13}x + 2a_{23}y + a_{33} = 0,$$

where not all $a_{11}$, $a_{22}$, and $a_{33}$ vanish, represents a conic section. In this case, however, the conic section may also be *degenerated*, that is, it may consist of two intersecting, two parallel, or two coinciding lines, which can be represented by $b^2x^2 - a^2y^2 = 0$, $x(x + a) = 0$, or $x^2 = 0$. It is also possible that the conic section is *imaginary*, for instance $x^2/a^2 + y^2/b^2 = -1$. Such conics cannot be represented by a curve in an $x$-$y$ diagram. Introduction of imaginary points and lines allows us to cast theorems into simple forms. For instance, we can now state that 2 conics always intersect in 4 points. In the case of Fig. 5A these 4 points are real and different, in Fig. 5B they are real, but two coincide, and in Fig. 5C two points of intersection are real and two imaginary.

**History.** The theory of conic sections was an achievement of Greek geometry. The first mathematician known to have studied them was Menaechmus (about 350 B. C.) in an attempt to duplicate the cube. The first known to have written a book about them was Euclid (about 320 B. C.), and the first treatise to have survived (at any rate seven books out of eight) was the *Conics* of Apollonius (about 225 B. C.). His older contemporary, Archimedes (287–212 B. C.), was well acquainted with conics and even studied their surfaces of revolution.

To Apollonius we owe our names of the conics. If we study conics by means of the equation $y^2 = 2px + ax^2$, then $a > 0$ gives the hyperbola (Gr. *hyperbolē*, "excess"); $a < 0$ gives the ellipse (Gr. *elleipsis*, "defect"); and $a = 0$ gives the parabola (Gr. *parabolē*, "application"). Apollonius did not have our algebraic notation; his definitions were geometric and dealt with application of areas. In the case of the parabola the application was exact, and in the other cases there was a defect or excess.

The Renaissance revived interest in conics, especially after Kepler had discovered the elliptic orbits of the planets (*Astronomia Nova*, 1609). After Descartes' discovery of coordinate geometry in 1637, algebraic methods more and more supplemented the ancient geometric methods. The systematic study of conics, as we know it from our present textbooks on analytic geometry, dates from the instruction of Gaspard Monge, Jean Baptiste Biot, and Jean N. P. Hachette at the Paris École Polytechnique about 1800.

DIRK J. STRUIK
*Massachusetts Institute of Technology*

**Further Reading:** Bobe, N., and others, *H-Cones* (Springer-Verlag 1981); Coxeter, H. S., *Projective Geometry*, 2d ed. (Univ. of Toronto Press 1974); Hogemdijk, J. P., *Ibn-Al-Haytham's "Composition of the Conics"* (Springer-Verlag 1984); Salmon, George, *Analytical Geometry of Three Dimensions, vol. II* (Chelsea Pub. Co. 1979).

**CONIFERS,** kon'ə-fərz, are trees and shrubs that characteristically bear cones and have evergreen leaves shaped like needles or scales. Conifers are worldwide in distribution, but are most common in temperate regions, though they also occur at high elevations in the tropics. The group includes both the redwood, which is the tallest known tree, reaching a record 364 feet (111 meters) in height, and the bristlecone pine, which is the longest-lived of all trees, with authenticated records of more than 4,500 years of age. The smallest known conifer is the pygmy pine (*Dacrydium laxifolium*), of New Zealand, which produces cones when only 3 inches (8 cm) high.

There is much scientific disagreement regarding their classification, but the conifers may be considered as constituting the order Coniferales (of the class Gymnospermae), with nearly 600 species grouped into more than 50 genera, usually placed in 7 different families: Podocarpaceae, Phyllocladaceae, Taxaceae (the yews), Araucariaceae, Pinaceae (the spruces, hemlocks, pines, firs, cedars, and larches), Taxodiaceae (the bald cypresses), and Cupressaceae (the cypresses, arborvitae, and junipers).

The conifers make up more than 30% of the forested areas of the world. Because they occur widely and usually in extensive stands, and because their wood offers the best ratio of weight to strength, tree conifers have played an exceedingly important role in the development of human cultures. For thousands of years they have furnished fuel and building timber, and in recent decades they have been the chief source of wood pulp for papermaking.

**Characteristics.** There is great diversity among the conifers with respect to structure, and even the common characteristic of bearing seeds in cones is lacking in the yews and in members of the family Podocarpaceae, in which the seed is borne singly in a fleshy cup (aril). Some conifers, like several of the junipers, are creeping shrubs, but most are stately trees of pleasant form. The lower branches are generally longer than those at succeeding levels, giving the tree a graceful, tapered appearance. Unlike the situation in broadleaf trees, removal of the upper part of the main shoot (the leader) reduces or eliminates further increase in height. The lateral, or side, branches usually do not assume the function of the leader in most conifers, as is often true among broadleaf forms.

A common, but not universal, feature of conifers is the presence of resin canals in many of their tissues. These are microscopic ducts that secrete and transport resinous materials. Turpentine and similar products are derived from this resin.

The leaves of conifers have a well-developed epidermis (surface layer) and are usually needlelike or scalelike, but those of plants in the families Podocarpaceae and Araucariaceae may be oval-shaped (variations of elliptic, ovate, and lanceolate). Except in the case of a few kinds of conifers, such as the larch and bald cypress, leaves are not shed annually, but ordinarily persist for several years and are gradually replaced by new ones.

**Reproduction.** Conifers characteristically bear their reproductive structures in cones (stroboli), with the male (staminate) and female (pistillate) structures contained in separate and distinct cones. In contrast to the yew's arillate fruit, which is generally not regarded as a true cone, the

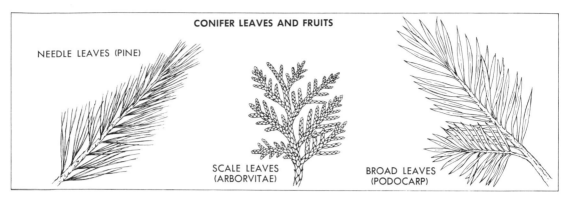

The leaves of conifers vary in shape from needlelike in the pines (*left*) and scalelike in the arborvitae (*center*) to lance-shaped in the podocarps (*right*).

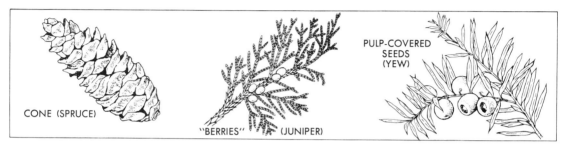

Conifer fruits range from the scaly, dry cones of the spruce (*left*) and the berrylike cones of the juniper (*center*) to the fleshy seeds of the yew (*right*).

berrylike fruits of the junipers and several other forms are modified, fleshy, female cones. Most conifers are monoecious; that is, they bear both male and female cones on the same plant. A few, such as the junipers, may be dioecious, bearing the male and female cones on separate plants.

The rather inconspicuous male cones consist of closely overlapping scales (microsporophylls) borne on a central axis. Each scale bears at its base two pollen cases (microsporangia) containing pollen grains in great numbers.

The conspicuous cones are the female, seed-producing ones. Their overlapping scales (megasporophylls) are borne on a central axis, and each in turn bears two immature seeds (ovules) on the upper surface of its base.

The male cones develop in one season and then shed their clouds of yellow pollen. The female cones may require two years to mature and remain on the plant for several years after they have dropped their seeds.

Prior to the discharge of the pollen, each ovule secretes a droplet of sticky resin. The pollen grains, carried by air currents to the female cones, fall among the cone scales and adhere to the droplets of resin at the opening (micropyle) to the interior of the ovule. Fertilization occurs when the pollen grain germinates, producing a tube which grows into the ovule and discharges the sperm cells in the vicinity of the egg cell. The time required for fertilization varies from a few weeks to more than a year.

The conifer embryo is in many cases unique among seed plants in having multiple seed leaves (cotyledons); the number varies from 2 to 15, in contrast to the flowering plants, which have 1 (monocotyledonous) or 2 (dicotyledonous).

**Cultivation.** There are few plant groups more important in horticulture than the conifers. Being evergreen makes them extremely valuable for gardens, and the several hundred horticultural varieties provide many opportunities for choice of plant form, leaf color, habitat flexibility, height, and other factors.

Many conifers are rather inflexible with respect to shade. Yews, hemlocks, and firs are the most tolerant of shade; most pines are unable to grow in shady places; and bald cypresses and larches are totally intolerant of shade.

Conifers are generally propagated from seed. Large commercial nurseries grow them for several years, until they are large enough to transplant. Though they may be transplanted at any season of the year, in temperate regions it is generally better to move them in the early spring or fall, when plant dormancy, even among the evergreen conifers, is greatest. It is especially important that they be transplanted with a ball of soil around the roots or, if bare-rooted, to keep the roots wet during planting.

In addition to seriously affecting the normal growth of conifers, pruning often destroys their natural symmetry of form. Though yews are often clipped to produce formal hedges, most other conifers need no more than slight pruning, if any. However, if young plants develop more than one leader (main shoot), the extra ones should be removed early. In general, lateral branches should not be pruned except when they die and must be removed altogether.

**History of the Conifers.** The conifers first appeared on the earth during the early Permian period, some 270 million years ago, and became increasingly abundant in the two geological periods that followed (Triassic, 225 to 180 million years ago; Jurassic, 180 to 135 million years ago). With the steadily expanding appearance of the flowering plants in the Cretaceous period (135 to 70 million years ago), the conifers lost some of their dominance, but they still remain one of the most common groups in modern floras. The logs in the Petrified Forest of Arizona are fossilized trunks of ancient conifers.

## THE COMMON CONIFERS

Because many conifers are cultivated for ornament, and because there is much variation among the several groups, a description of several types will be helpful in distinguishing them.

**Pines (Pines).** The pines have clusters of 2 to 5 needle leaves, which, except for the single-leaf piñon (*P. monophylla*), is typical of the true pines. In all the pines, the base of the cluster of leaves is enclosed in a dry, membranelike sheath. The leaves of all species have resin canals and are evergreen, remaining on the tree for periods of up to 10 years. Pine cones are often produced in clusters and require 2 years to ripen. Among the conifers, only pine cones are spiny when mature.

Pine trees are among the most important timber sources. Enormous quantities of various species provide construction lumber. "Hard" pine lumber comes from the southern longleaf pine (*P. palustris*), and "soft" pine lumber is cut principally from white pine (*P. strobus* and *P. monticola*). Resin collected from pine trees is the source of turpentine, tar, pitch, and resin.

**Spruces (Picea).** These are all evergreen trees with straight, tapered trunks and rigid, usually four-sided needle leaves that lack resin ducts. The leaves are not clustered, but instead develop from all sides of the stem. Sharp needle scars (the base of the leaf) are left on these stems when the leaves fall. Spruce cones are borne pendent ("hanging"), almost entirely at the topmost part of the tree. The cones mature in a single season's growth.

Spruce timber is one of the most important timbers in the northern United States and in Canada. Spruces are especially valuable for producing paper pulp, and they are unsurpassed among the conifers for ornamental use, especially the blue spruce (*P. pungens*).

**Firs (Abies).** Fir needles, like spruce needles, are borne singly and arise from all sides of the stem. For this reason, the firs are sometimes confused with the spruces. They differ, however, in that the firs have less rigid, flattened needle leaves that produce an inconspicuous circular scar on the branchlets when they are shed. In addition, fir needles, like pine needles, contain resin canals. The cones are borne erect near the top of the tree and mature in one season's time.

In addition to being important timber trees, the firs are the source of balsam, a resinous material contained in conspicuous blisters under the bark of young trees.

**Hemlocks (Tsuga).** The hemlocks have short, flat needle leaves, usually arranged on two sides of the stem. This arrangement gives the branches the appearance of flat sprays, contrasting in this respect with the pines and firs. As with the spruces, the basal part of the needles remains on the stem when they fall. The leaves have a solitary resin canal through their center. The trees have gracefully drooping branches, at least until they are about 50 years of age. They are

Each of these small cones of the Japanese black pine contains many separate pollen-bearing organs.

common forest trees in dark, deep ravines in the eastern United States. The small cones, which hang downward from the stem and occur over the entire crown of the tree, mature in a single season.

Hemlock bark is rich in tannins and has been an important source of these materials for the tanning industry. The lumber cut from hemlock is not important because it is coarse grained.

**False Hemlocks (Pseudotsuga).** Frequently confused with the true hemlocks, pines, firs, and spruces, the false hemlocks differ from all of these by the presence of three-pointed scales (bracts) that extend out from between the cone scales. The leaves, like those of the spruces and hemlocks, are flat and soft, and two resin ducts run the length of each leaf. Like the spruces, false hemlocks produce leaves on all sides of the stem, and the base of the needle remains on the stem after the needle falls. The cones hang downward, and their seeds mature in one season.

The Douglas fir (*P. menziesii*) is one of the false hemlocks. It reaches heights of 300 feet (90 meters) and is one of the most important timber trees in the United States.

**Larches (Larix).** One of the exceptions among the conifers because they shed their leaves each autumn, the larches are easily recognized by the arrangement of their short, soft leaves. These are borne in clusters of 10 to 40 on short spurs of mature branchlets. The leaves are variable with respect to resin canals: some species have them; others do not. The cones either hang or are borne almost erect. In some species, such as the western larch (*L. occidentalis*), bristlelike scales (bracts) protrude from between the cone scales. Larch wood is durable and is an important lumber material.

**Bald Cypresses (Taxodium).** The bald cypresses, like the larches, lose their leaves each year. In addition to the leaves, the bald cypresses annually shed their slender, immature twigs as well. The

leaves are slender and flat, usually less than ½ inch (13 mm) long, and are arranged featherlike on two sides of the twigs. The cones are round, with the scales closely and flatly pressed against each other. The trunks are swollen at the base, and erect "breathing organs," called knees, are produced from the roots when the tree is growing in water or in waterlogged soil.

The wood is soft, fine-grained, and durable, even in contact with the soil. The bald cypress is an important timber tree in the southeastern United States.

**Sequoias (Sequoia).** The two redwoods of the Pacific coast of the United States are the only American species of this group. Sequoia specimens may exceed 300 feet (90 meters) in height and 10 feet (3 meters) in diameter. The bigtree (*S. gigantea*) is restricted to the western slopes of the Sierra Nevada mountains in central California; the redwood (*S. sempervirens*) has a wider distribution, extending as far north as Oregon. Both species have some of the oldest known individuals; some of the bigtrees have upwards of 2,500 annual growth rings, implying ages exceeding 2,000 years.

The leaves are scalelike, flat, and sharp-pointed. The cones ripen in one or two seasons. Lumber from the redwoods is soft but very durable and fine-grained.

**Junipers (Juniperus).** These are evergreen, erect or prostrate, small trees. Two kinds of leaves occur in this group, sometimes both types on the same tree: overlapping scalelike leaves or short, sharp-pointed needle leaves. The pea-size blue of red cones are fleshy and berrylike. Juniper "berries" are used as a flavoring agent in gin.

Although the wood is hard and durable, it is not economically important because the trees are so small and the trunks crooked and twisted. The wood of the eastern red cedar (*J. virginiana*) is used for making fence posts, pencils, and to some extent in cabinetry.

RICHARD S. COWAN
*Smithsonian Institution*

Beams of sunlight breaking through a towering forest of Douglas fir (*above*) convey the impression of an immense medieval hall. The present natural distribution of the Monterey cypress (*below*) is a narrow strip of California coast about 2 miles (3 km) long and 200 yards (180 meters) wide. The western juniper (*right*) often grows from the cracks in the solid granite of the higher mountains of California. These wind-swept trees are at an elevation of 8700 feet (2600 meters).

**CONINGHAM,** kun'ing-əm, **Sir Arthur** (1895–1948), British aviator and air war strategist. He was born in Brisbane, Australia, on Jan. 19, 1895, and began his career in the New Zealand Army in 1914. He joined the British flying corps as a fighter pilot in 1916. He remained in the Royal Air Force as a squadron commander and later became a staff officer at Middle East headquarters. Coningham led a 5,000-mile (8,000-km) trans-Africa survey flight in 1925.

Coningham achieved his greatest fame in World War II. He was the original architect of the tactical air force, the cooperation of air and ground units, and formed the 1st Tactical Air Force in 1943. Coningham was commander of the 2d Tactical Air Force, comprising all Allied air units, during the invasion of Normandy in 1944. He died in a plane crash on a flight between the Azores and Bermuda on Jan. 30, 1948.

R. M. YOUNGER
*Author of "Australia and the Australians"*

**CONINXLOO,** kō'ningks-lō, **Gillis van** (1544–1607), Flemish landscape painter. He was born on Jan. 24, 1544, probably in Antwerp. In his youth he studied painting in Flanders and traveled in France, returning in 1570 to Antwerp, where he became a member of the painters' guild. In 1585, to escape religious persecution by the Spanish, Coninxloo fled Antwerp, staying in Frankenthal, Germany, until 1595. He then settled in Amsterdam, where he was buried on Jan. 4, 1607.

Coninxloo's landscapes are among the best of his time. The fantastic treatment of landscape in his early paintings is characteristic of 16th century Flemish painting, but his later landscapes are more realistic, combining attention to natural detail with a concern for depth. His work is thus transitional between the landscapes of Pieter Bruegel the Elder and those of Jacob van Ruisdael.

**CONISTON,** kon'is-tən, a former town in northeastern Ontario, Canada, in Sudbury district, 8 miles (12 km) east of Sudbury. It was founded in 1910 as a company town by the Mond Nickel Company and was incorporated as a town in 1934. It was maintained by the International Nickel Company, which has a nickel smelter there, and is now part of Nickel Centre.

**CONJUGATION,** kon-jə-gā'shən, is a primitive form of reproduction that occurs in lower forms of plant and animal life. Hereditary materials are exchanged during conjugation, but true sex cells (sperm and eggs) are not involved. Thus, conjugation can be considered only as either a modification of, or a primitive step toward, sexual reproduction.

Bacteria are the most primitive forms of life that conjugated. During conjugation, two bacterial cells position themselves very close to each other, and a bridge of cytoplasm forms between them. Once the bridge is formed, genetic material passes from the cytoplasm of one bacterium to the cytoplasm of the other bacterium. Bacterial conjugation can occur only between cells of different mating types, which are known as positive and negative strains.

Some algae also conjugate. *Spirogyra*, one of the green freshwater algae, is a classic example. The plant is a multicellular, unbranched filament. Each cell of the filament has a nucleus suspended in the center of the cell by cytoplasmic strands. During conjugation, two filaments of *Spirogyra* line up so that they are in contact with each other along their entire lengths. Protuberances form from points where cells of the two filaments come into contact. Openings develop at the points of contact, forming cytoplasmic bridges between the cells of the two filaments. Then the contents of the cells in one filament migrate through their respective cytoplasmic bridges, or conjugation tubes, into the cells of the other filament. The cellular contents fuse, completing fertilization and forming a series of zygotes (cells formed by the fusion). Later, the zygotes germinate to form new algal filaments.

Some of the ciliated protozoa, such as *Paramecium*, also demonstrate conjugation. Two paramecia attach themselves temporarily along their oral grooves. A cytoplasmic conjugating tube then is formed between them, and nuclear material is exchanged. After the mutual exchange, the two paramecia separate and usually undergo binary fission (cell division into two equal parts with identical genetic material).

DAVID A. OTTO
*Stephens College*

**CONJUNCTION,** kən-junk'shən, in astronomy, is the configuration of two celestial bodies when they are at the same azimuth and have their least apparent separation in the sky. Thus, when the sun and a planet lie in the same direction in the sky—that is, on a straight line with the earth as seen on the plane of the solar system—the planet is described as being in conjunction with the sun.

Specific terms are applied to conjunctions of the so-called inferior planets that lie closer to the sun than does the earth. When the configuration is earth-planet-sun (see diagram), the planet is in *inferior* conjunction; when the configuration is earth-sun-planet, it is in *superior* conjunction. When an inferior planet is at its greatest angular distance from the sun in the sky, it is said to be at its *greatest elongation*.

The planets beyond the earth's orbit are called *superior planets*. When the configuration with a superior planet is earth-sun-planet, the planet is in conjunction; when the configuration is planet-earth-sun, the planet is in *opposition*. When a superior planet is located 90° from the earth-sun line, the planet is in *quadrature*.

LAURENCE W. FREDRICK
*University of Virginia*

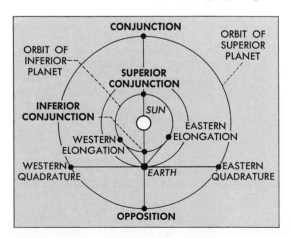

**CONJUNCTION** is the name used in grammar for any of a small class of function words used only as connectives between other words or groups of words. Conjunctions are traditionally divided into three subclasses: *coordinating, subordinating,* and *correlative* conjunctions.

(1) Coordinating conjunctions stand between and join words or groups of words that are grammatically equivalent. The chief coordinating conjunctions in English are *and, but, or, nor, for, yet,* and *so.* (Examples: hot *and* cold; he went *but* I stayed; sharply *yet* kindly).

(2) Subordinating conjunctions, a more numerous group, introduce dependent clauses and join them to main clauses. Some common subordinating conjunctions in English are *after, although, because, before, if, since, that, though, when,* and *whether.* (Examples: I heard *that* she jumped; we hesitated *because* it was raining).

(3) Correlative conjunctions are coordinating conjunctions used in pairs. (Examples: *not* a bird *but* a plane; *either* sit down *or* get out).

Transitional adverbs (conjunctive adverbs), such as *however, therefore,* and *besides,* also function as connectives, but unlike true subordinating conjunctions they need not come at the beginning of the clause.

ROBERT L. CHAPMAN
*Drew University*

**CONJUNCTIVITIS,** kən-jungk-tə-vī′təs, is an inflammation of the conjunctiva, the mucous membrane covering the inside of the eyelids and the outside of the eyeball except for the cornea. Conjunctivitis may be acute or chronic. Although it is often caused by bacteria or viruses, it may also be due to chemicals, drugs, or mechanical irritation. Sometimes it occurs as an allergic reaction.

In *acute catarrhal conjunctivitis,* the inflamed membrane usually secretes a pussy discharge. When caused by the Koch-Weeks bacillus, the condition is self-limited but should be treated because of its contagious nature. Treatment consists of irrigating the eyes with a mild salt solution and administering antibiotic eyedrops. When this type of conjunctivitis is caused by the gonococcus, the bacterium that causes gonorrhea, the inflammation may lead to the loss of the eye. It must be treated with local eye medications as well as systemic antibiotics.

A viral form of conjunctivitis is *epidemic keratoconjunctivitis,* which usually involves the cornea and occurs in only one eye. It is caused by a type of adenovirus and is self-limited but occasionally leaves some opacities in the cornea. *Inclusion conjunctivitis,* also known as *swimming pool conjunctivitis,* is also caused by a virus. In newborn infants it is thought to be contracted from the mother's birth tract during delivery. In adults it is often contracted in swimming pools that are contaminated by vaginal discharges.

*Chronic conjunctivitis* is characterized by a low-grade infection of the conjunctiva, with tearing and a slight granular or mucous discharge. It is often associated with blepharitis (inflammation of the eyelashes and sebaceous glands of the eyelid) and may be caused by a variety of bacteria and other organisms. Treatment consists of applications of an antibiotic and an astringent, such as zinc sulfate.

*Allergic conjunctivitis* may be due to foods, cosmetics, or other allergy-producing agents. Eyedrops containing cortisonelike drugs are used for short-term treatment, but the best method of cure is to eliminate the offending antigen. Occasionally, patients may have to be desensitized to the antigen involved.

BERNARD KRONENBERG, M.D.
*New York Medical College*

**CONKLIN,** kongk′lin, **Edwin G.** (1863–1952), American biologist, who is best known for his research in the fields of embryology, cytology, genetics, and evolution. Conklin was born in Waldo, Ohio, on Nov. 24, 1863. He spent most of his academic career as professor of zoology at Princeton University (1908–1933). He died in Princeton on Nov. 20, 1952.

In addition to his research interests, Conklin was concerned about the effects that scientific achievements have on human society, and he became an advocate of international scientific cooperation. His writings include *Heredity and Environment in the Development of Man* (1915), *The Direction of Human Evolution* (1922), and *Man, Real and Ideal* (1943).

DAVID A. OTTO
*Stephens College*

**CONKLING,** kongk′ling, **Roscoe** (1829–1888), American lawyer and public official. He was born in Albany, N.Y., on Oct. 30, 1829, the son of Alfred Conkling, a distinguished lawyer, judge, and author of several legal studies. Conkling attended school in New York City, studied law under his father, and in 1850 was admitted to the bar. Originally a Whig in politics, he soon became a staunch member of the Republican party. In 1858, Conkling was elected to Congress where he served (except for one term, 1863–1865) until his election to the Senate in 1867.

Tall, with a commanding appearance, he earned a reputation as a picturesque orator. As a member of the Joint Committee on Reconstruction, he advocated a radical policy for Southern Reconstruction. Aided by President Grant's award for all the federal patronage in New York, Conkling became the undisputed boss of his state's political machine. He soon became involved in bitter power struggles within the Republican party, quarreling with James G. Blaine and eventually breaking with President Rutherford B. Hayes when the latter refused to recognize his claims to the control of all federal appointments in New York. In 1880, Conkling was a leader in the unsuccessful move to nominate Grant for a third term and was very disappointed when the nomination went to James A. Garfield. When Garfield followed Hayes' policies regarding New York appointments, Conkling fought the confirmation of the President's appointees, and finally resigned his Senate seat in 1881 in protest.

It was clear by this time that Conkling's power had declined. His attempt to persuade the New York legislature to reelect him in vindication of his leadership failed. Returning to private life, he continued to practice law until his death in New York City on April 18, 1888.

In 1882 in an argument before the Supreme Court, he contended that the drafters of the 14th Amendment intended to protect corporations as well as Negroes, a theory for which little positive evidence has been discovered but one that has persisted in many accounts of post-Civil War politics.

ROBERT W. JOHANNSEN
*University of Illinois*

**CONNACHT,** kon'ǝkHt, in western Ireland, the poorest of the four provinces of the country and the one that has suffered most from depopulation. It consists of five counties, Sligo, Mayo, Galway, and Leitrim on the Atlantic coast and one inland county, Roscommon. It was at one time the seat of the O'Connors, high kings of Ireland. After the 17th century, Catholics could own land only in Connacht and the county of Clare.

Sheep and cattle are raised. Oats and potatoes are the main tillage crops, but beets are grown around Tuam, where there is a sugar refinery. Connacht is famous for its scenery—sea, lake, and mountain—but above all for the mysterious charm of Connemara in western Galway, with its variety of colors beloved of poets and painters.

Galway city, the capital of Connacht, was an important trading center in the Middle Ages and had many links with Europe, particularly Spain. It has a University College of the National University of Ireland, is an important tourist center, and has many small industries.

The province's second-largest town is Sligo, a seaport and manufacturing town. An annual festival is held in Sligo in honor of the poet William Butler Yeats, who spent his summers there. Population: 432,551 (1996 est.).

THOMAS FITZGERALD
*Department of Education, Dublin*

**CONNALLY, John Bowden, Jr.,** kon'ǝl-ē (1917–1993), American political leader. He was born in Floresville, Tex., on Feb. 27, 1917. Connally earned a law degree at the University of Texas (1941) and was general manager of radio station KVET in Austin, Tex., from 1946 to 1949. In 1949 he served as administrative assistant to Sen. Lyndon B. Johnson. Connally reentered law practice in Texas in 1950 and was attorney to Sid W. Richardson and Perry R. Bass, prominent Texas oilmen, from 1952 to 1961. He was secretary of the navy under Pres. John F. Kennedy (1961–1962) and governor of Texas (1963–1969). Connally was riding with Kennedy in Dallas on Nov. 22, 1963, when the president was shot. Connally, wounded badly, recovered.

A conservative Democrat, Connally was secretary of the treasury for Republican president Richard M. Nixon. He helped implement Nixon's program of wage and price controls and represented the United States in international monetary negotiations. In the 1972 presidential race, he headed a Democrats for Nixon committee, and in 1973 he joined the Republican party. He sought the Republican presidential nomination in 1980 but withdrew after defeats in the primaries and instead endorsed candidate Ronald Reagan.

Connally's subsequent business ventures brought him to bankruptcy in 1988, which he blamed on poor real estate and oil investments. He died in Houston on June 15, 1993.

**CONNALLY, Tom,** kon'ǝl-ē (1877–1963), American public official. Thomas Terry Connally was born in McLennan county, Tex., on Aug. 19, 1877. He received degrees from Baylor University (1896) and the University of Texas law school (1898). Admitted to the bar in 1898, he entered practice in Marlin, Tex., and served two terms in the Texas legislature (1901–1904). In 1916 Connally was elected to the House of Representatives as a Democrat, and he was reelected five times. Elected to the Senate in 1928, he remained there until he retired in 1953. He served as chairman of the Senate Committee on Foreign Relations (1941–1947 and 1949–1953).

On domestic questions Connally frequently opposed the Roosevelt and Truman administrations. He voted against the National Industrial Recovery Act in 1933, played a leading role in 1937 in the defeat of Pres. Franklin D. Roosevelt's plan to reform the Supreme Court, opposed federal legislation against lynching and the poll tax, and voted for the Taft-Hartley labor law in 1947. In foreign policy matters he was a loyal administration supporter, favoring the reciprocal Trade Agreements Act of 1934 and its subsequent extensions and backed lend-lease.

Connally helped secure Senate ratification of the United Nations Charter and approval of U.S. participation. He was a member of the U.S. delegation to the UN General Assembly in 1946. At the same time, he pushed through the Connally Reservation, which restricted the World Court's jurisdiction in cases involving the United States to cases approved by the Senate.

Connally lost his committee chairmanship when the Republicans gained a Senate majority in 1946, but he gave strong support to the Greek-Turkish aid bill and the Marshall Plan. Regaining the chairmanship in 1949, he supported the North Atlantic Pact treaty and massive European aid. After he retired, he lived in Washington, D.C., where he died on Oct. 28, 1963. His autobiography, *My Name Is Tom Connally,* was published in 1954.

JOHN BRAEMAN, *University of Nebraska*

**CONNAUGHT AND STRATHEARN, Duke of,** kon'ôt, strath'ǝrn (1850–1942), English soldier who from 1911 to 1916 served as governor-general of Canada. Prince Arthur William Patrick Albert was born at Buckingham Palace, London, on May 1, 1850, the third son of Queen Victoria and Prince Albert. In 1866 he entered the Royal Military Academy at Woolwich, becoming two years later a lieutenant in the Royal Engineers. He served for a year with his regiment in Montreal, Quebec.

In 1871 he was made a captain of the Rifle Brigade. He was in action with the Brigade of Guards in the Egyptian campaign of 1882 and commanded the army in Bombay, India, 1886–1890. He became a general in 1893 and in 1902 was promoted to field marshal. From 1904 to 1907 he was inspector general of the forces, then commander in chief in the Mediterranean until 1909. He became governor-general of Canada in 1911, and in the early years of World War I his military knowledge and experience were of great value. His daughter, Princess Patricia, helped to raise the famous "Princess Pat" regiment. He resigned as governor-general in 1916. His wife, Princess Louise Margaret of Prussia, died the next year. Connaught retired from public life in 1928. He died at his country estate, Bagshot, in Surrey on Jan. 16, 1942.

**CONNEAUT,** kon'ē-ät, a port city in northeastern Ohio. Conneaut is located in Ashtabula county, on Lake Erie, 65 miles (105 km) northeast of Cleveland. The city ships large quantities of coal and steel and is an important iron ore–receiving station. Among its diversified industries are railroad repair shops and fisheries.

Settled in 1799, Conneaut became a village in 1834 and a city in 1902. In 1962 it annexed the village of Lakeville. Population: 12,485.

© EDWARD YOUNG/JOAN KRAMER & ASSOCIATES

Connecticut's seafaring past is brought to life at Mystic Seaport, a reconstructed early 19th century town.

# CONNECTICUT

Great Seal of Connecticut

## CONTENTS

**CONNECTICUT,** kə-net′i-kət, is the most southwesterly member of the group of states known as New England states, situated in northeastern United States. The third smallest state in the Union, Connecticut offers an unusual degree of variety in its people, culture, economy, architecture, and topography. Among the oldest of the 50 states, it provides a delightful blend of the very old and the very new. One of the best examples is the Constitution Plaza area in Hartford, the capital city. Almost surrounded and overshadowed by new, gleaming skyscrapers sits the Old State House, a stately building designed by Charles Bulfinch in the 1790's. Attractive town greens lined with white colonial houses and a white Congregational meetinghouse can be seen in many parts of the state, along with contrastingly modern houses and churches. The diversified economy and good living conditions are bringing in far more residents than the state is losing.

The crucial question for the near future may well be: Will material success spoil Connecticut? Will its many attractions produce such pressures of population that the pleasant environment will be destroyed? Will the onrushing megalopolis overwhelm and completely transform the little state? These questions are just beginning to be pondered and seriously discussed by state and local bodies and by some interested private citizens. Undoubtedly they will be studied more intensively as problems of traffic congestion, air and water pollution, land use, access to recreational areas, urban deterioration, and crime become steadily more serious.

Something of the old Puritan spirit of concern for religion, education, and moral conduct has remained an integral part of the Connecticut spirit and mores. Political scandals have been rare. Although the nickname "Land of Steady Habits" possesses a certain validity, the state repeatedly has demonstrated a willingness to embrace innovation, especially in economic and social areas.

In a sense, Connecticut's people have been blessed by the glaring lack of natural resources. The state has no coal, oil, or exploitable precious minerals. Only small sections possess fertile soil. In the beginning there were great forests, but these were quickly consumed. As the population grew, the people were forced either to migrate or to devise new ways of making a living. The Connecticut Yankee became a notable inventor. He was quick, moreover, to apply the discoveries of others in adapting to the system of large-scale factory production.

Litchfield's tree-shaded streets and fine white frame houses preserve the grace and charm of 18th century Connecticut.

## 1. The People

During the colonial period the great majority of Connecticut's settlers came from England. Among the few other groups were scatterings of French Huguenots, Acadians, and Dutch. A census in 1774 recorded about 198,000 people, including 5,101 blacks and 1,363 Indians.

**Components of the Population.** Connecticut's ethnic homogeneity was broken in the mid-19th century, when growing industrialization produced a large demand for factory workers. A location close to New York City, the chief port of entry for immigrants, meant that many could settle easily in Connecticut. A heavy Irish immigration spurred by famine conditions in Ireland began in the late 1840's. The Irish streamed into the cities, especially New Haven and Hartford. A considerable number of Germans also entered the state in midcentury. French-Cana-

dians, attracted by the textile mills of eastern Connecticut, settled in large numbers. A tremendous expansion in such industries as brass, silver, clocks, small arms, and textiles resulted in a flood of new immigrants from the 1890's to 1914. The 1910 census revealed that about 30% of the population was foreign born. Immigration restrictions in the 1920's, a great depression in the 1930's, and World War II contributed to a sharply reduced immigration flow.

The most distinctive immigrants of the post-1945 period included the Puerto Ricans. The northward movement of Southern blacks also has brought many of them to urban areas. The blacks and Puerto Ricans generally have faced the same problems of discrimination encountered elsewhere in the North. Strong antidiscrimination laws and dedicated efforts by both public and private agencies have resulted in social and economic gains by these new immigrants.

---

### INFORMATION HIGHLIGHTS

**Location:** In southwestern New England, bordered north by Massachusetts, east by Rhode Island, south by Long Island Sound, and west by New York.

**Elevation:** *Highest point*—South slope of Mt. Frissell (the peak of this mountain is in Massachusetts), 2,380 feet (725 meters); *lowest point*—sea level; *approximate mean elevation*—500 feet (150 meters).

**Total Area:** (land and inland water) 5,018 square miles (12,997 sq km); rank, 48th.

**Resident Population:** 3,405,565 (2000 census). Increase (1990–2000), 3.6%.

**Climate:** Generally mild winters; warm, humid summers.

**Statehood:** Jan. 9, 1788; order of admission, 5th.

**Origin of the Name:** Probably from Mohegan *quinnitukqut* ("at the long tidal river"), applied first to the river.

**Capital:** Hartford.

**Largest City:** Bridgeport.

**Number of Counties:** 8.

**Principal Products:** *Manufactures*—machinery, transportation equipment, fabricated metal products, primary metals, scientific instruments, foods, plastics, printing and publishing; *farm products*—milk, poultry and eggs, tobacco; *minerals*—stone, sand and gravel, feldspar.

**State Motto:** *Qui transtulit sustinet* ("He who transplanted still sustains").

**State Song:** *Yankee Doodle.*

**State Nicknames:** Constitution State (official); Land of Steady Habits; Nutmeg State.

**State Bird:** American robin (*Turdus migratorius*).

**State Flower:** Mountain laurel (*Kalmia latifolia*).

**State Tree:** White oak (*Quercus alba Linn.*).

**State Flag:** The armorial bearings of the state on a field of azure blue (the three grape vines symbolize the original Connecticut River towns that were settled, or "transplanted," from Massachusetts). (See also Flag.)

About 10% of the population is foreign born. Nonwhites in 2000 numbered 625,210, of whom 309,843 were African Americans.

With the heavy influx of Catholic immigrants the Catholic population has soared, and Catholics outnumber all other denominations.

**Way of Life.** During the colonial period the typical Connecticut family lived on a farm located in an agricultural community, grew crops, tended livestock, and bartered surpluses with the village

### RESIDENT POPULATION SINCE 1790

| Year | Population | Year | Population |
|------|-----------|------|-----------|
| 1790 | 237,946 | 1940 | 1,709,242 |
| 1820 | 275,248 | 1950 | 2,007,280 |
| 1840 | 309,978 | 1960 | 2,535,234 |
| 1860 | 460,147 | 1970 | 3,032,217 |
| 1880 | 622,700 | 1980 | 3,107,576 |
| 1900 | 908,420 | 1990 | 3,287,116 |
| 1920 | 1,380,631 | 2000 | 3,405,565 |

**Gain,** 1990–2000: 3.6% (U.S. gain, 13.2%). **Density,** 2000: 702.9 persons per square mile of land area (U.S. density, 79.6).

### URBAN-RURAL DISTRIBUTION

| Year | Percent urban | Percent rural |
|------|---------------|---------------|
| 1920 | 67.8 (U.S., 51.2) | 32.2 |
| 1930 | 70.4 (U.S., 56.1) | 29.6 |
| 1940 | 67.8 (U.S., 56.6) | 32.2 |
| 1950 | 77.6 (U.S., 64.0) | 22.4 |
| 1960 | 78.3 (U.S., 69.9) | 21.7 |
| 1970 | 77.4 (U.S., 73.5) | 22.6 |
| 1980 | 78.8 (U.S., 73.7) | 21.2 |
| 1990 | 79.1 (U.S., 75.2) | 20.9 |

merchants. A small number of enterprising merchants and shipowners traded along the coast and in the West Indies. Fishing and shipbuilding also were common occupations.

In the early 1800's the industrial revolution came to Connecticut, and businessmen erected many factories. By the 1870's and 1880's the surplus capital was going largely into manufacturing. Agriculture and seafaring were declining rapidly. The heavy movement to cities leveled off by the 1930's, followed by a shift to the suburbs.

Despite a steady overall growth and high density of population, Connecticut has managed to retain a surprising amount of rural charm. Some 60% of the state is forested, and rolling hills, stone walls, and numerous lakes and streams add to the state's picturesqueness. While one's neighbors are always close and the city is near, many people enjoy privacy in their rural or semirural environment. Most of the people living in the country actually earn their living in a nearby city, which also provides shopping, cultural, and recreational opportunities. The combination of rural and urban life has caused a steady influx of new residents.

So far, the megalopolis has not seriously altered the state's happy balance of urban business facilities and suburban semirural home life. The urban sprawl between New York and Boston, however, does threaten to engulf coastal Connecticut. Only northwestern and northeastern Connecticut seem likely to retain their rural charm. Connecticut's great economic success may yet destroy the distinctive Yankee background and setting.

**Main Centers of Population.** Connecticut's largest cities, in order, are Bridgeport, New Haven,

Connecticut's seafaring past is brought to life at Mystic Seaport, a reconstructed early 19th century town.

TSCHIRKY, FROM ANNAN PHOTO FEATURES

One of Connecticut's covered bridges (*above*) spans the Housatonic River in West Cornwall. In Guilford (*right*) the classically proportioned First Congregational Church, which was built in 1829, faces the village green.

TSCHIRKY, FROM ANNAN PHOTO FEATURES

Hartford, Stamford, and Waterbury. Hartford, the capital city, owed its early growth to its strategic location near the head of navigation on the Connecticut River. Before river trade ceased to be important in the mid-19th century, Hartford fortunately turned to insurance and to manufactur-

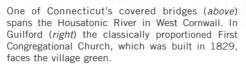

### LARGEST CENTERS OF POPULATION

| City or metropolitan area | 2000 | 1990 | 1980 |
|---|---|---|---|
| Bridgeport | 139,529 | 141,686 | 142,546 |
| Metropolitan area | 459,479 | 443,722 | 395,455 |
| New Haven | 123,626 | 130,474 | 126,101 |
| Metropolitan area | 542,149 | 530,180 | 417,592 |
| Hartford | 121,578 | 139,739 | 136,392 |
| Metropolitan area | 1,183,110 | 767,841 | 726,114 |
| Stamford | 117,083 | 108,056 | 102,466 |
| Metropolitan area | 353,556[1] | 202,557 | 198,854 |
| Waterbury | 107,271 | 108,961 | 103,266 |
| Metropolitan area | 228,984 | 221,629 | 228,178 |
| Norwalk | 82,951 | 78,331 | 77,767 |
| Metropolitan area | 353,556[1] | 127,378 | 126,692 |
| Danbury | 74,848 | 65,585 | 60,470 |
| Metropolitan area | 217,980 | 187,867 | 146,405 |
| New Britain | 71,538 | 75,491 | 73,840 |
| West Hartford | 63,589 | 60,110 | 61,301 |
| Greenwich | 61,101 | 58,441 | 59,578 |
| Bristol | 60,062 | 60,640 | 57,370 |
| Meriden | 58,244 | 59,479 | 57,118 |
| Fairfield | 57,340 | 53,418 | 54,849 |
| Hamden | 56,913 | 52,434 | 51,071 |
| Manchester | 54,740 | 51,618 | 31,058 |
| West Haven | 52,360 | 54,021 | 53,184 |
| Milford | 52,305 | 49,938 | 50,898 |
| Stratford | 49,976 | 49,389 | 50,541 |
| East Hartford | 49,575 | 50,452 | 52,563 |

[1]Stamford-Norwalk.

ing. It is still widely known as the insurance city.

The Puritans chose New Haven as a site for settlement because of its harbor. Like Hartford, it experienced rapid industrialization and a large influx of foreign-born workers. A strategic railroad and distribution hub, New Haven has rivaled Hartford in its economic influence. After New Haven ceased to be a joint capital in 1875, the center of state political power moved to Hartford. Generally, Bridgeport and Waterbury have been the two large cities most dominated by industry. Stamford's growth has been stimulated by its location close to New York City.

### 2. The Land

The pioneer settlers of Connecticut were attracted by glowing accounts of the fertility of the Connecticut River valley. The later settlers tended to spread up the valley from Long Island Sound or along the shores of the sound, where there were many good harbors. The magnificent harbor at the mouth of the Thames River became the site of New London. The Thames gave access to a large hinterland in eastern Connecticut. The rockier and hillier areas in the east and west, which frequently had thin, poor soil, were settled slowly and never very thickly. Nearly all the principal towns of colonial times were established on the sound or on a navigable river. Hence geography had a decisive effect on the pattern of settlement and growth in Connecticut.

**Major Physiographic Regions.** To the naked eye Connecticut's 5,018 square miles (12,997 square km) appear as an irregular rocky land that is punctuated by occasional high hills. Along the

589

Fields of shade-grown tobacco and tobacco-curing barns in the Connecticut River valley near Hartford.

coast lies a narrow, flat coastal plain. On each side of the state, extending north and south, are low ranges of hills called the Eastern and the Western uplands. Between them is the narrow central Connecticut River valley, filled with a deep, rich alluvial soil. The highest and most rugged part of the state is the Taconic section in the northwest. It includes the Housatonic River valley and sharply elevated summits of the Taconic Mountains, which extend into Connecticut from Massachusetts and Vermont.

**Geology.** Through long geologic ages the land surfaces were shaped and reshaped many times. Basically Connecticut is underlain by an upland block of ancient, hard, crystalline rock, especially schist, split down the middle from north to south by a lowland of softer sandstone. The most obvious surface changes resulted from the large sheets of ice that covered Connecticut for thousand of years. Although the large valleys and uplands predated the Ice Age, many secondary effects were produced by it. Drumlins (oval-shaped hills of glacial drift), serpentine ridges, clay beds, and sand plains were created by the glaciers. The glaciers disrupted drainage patterns so thoroughly that hundreds of lakes, large and small, were created. Although the glaciers scarred the land surface, they also enriched it scenically with a variety of lakes, ponds, waterfalls, ridges, drumlins, and boulders.

**Rivers and Lakes.** Connecticut has three major drainage systems: the Connecticut River in the middle, the Quinebaug-Shetucket-Thames in the east, and the Housatonic-Naugatuck in the west.

The Connecticut River, the longest river of New England, rises on the northern boundary of New Hampshire and flows southward about 400 miles (644 km) before it enters Long Island Sound. Its principal tributaries in Connecticut include the Farmington, Scantic, Podunk, Salmon, and Eight Mile rivers. Although its sandbars have troubled mariners since early colonial days, the Connecticut is kept fully naviga-

ble to Hartford by the maintenance of a 15-foot (5-meter) channel.

Most of the streams in eastern Connecticut drain into the Quinebaug-Shetucket-Thames system. The Quinebaug rises in southern Massachusetts and flows southerly until near Taftville it joins the Shetucket River, which in turn soon joins the much smaller Yantic at Norwich to create the Thames River. The Thames is navigable with a 25-foot (7.6-meter) channel from Norwich to the sound. The Housatonic River, in the west, rises in Massachusetts and flows southerly and southeasterly into the sound at Stratford. Roughly paralleling it to the east is the Naugatuck River, which joins the Housatonic at Derby. From there to the sound the Housatonic has been used by small vessels since colonial times. A 14-foot (4-meter) channel is maintained. A few small, short rivers—such as the Pawcatuck (the lower part of Connecticut's boundary with Rhode Island), Mystic, Niantic, Quinnipiac, and Saugatuck—flow directly into the sound.

The state abounds in lakes and ponds—over 6,000 in all. The two largest bodies of water, both man-made, are Lake Candlewood, north of Danbury, and the Barkhamsted Reservoir, north of New Hartford.

**Climate.** Connecticut generally enjoys the temperate four-season climate typical of the northeastern United States. Most of the atmospheric flow is easterly, and except along the coast, Connecticut feels very little effect from polar aid formed over the North Atlantic Ocean. Most low-pressure stormy areas moving across the eastern United States have tracks that bring them over or close to Connecticut. Thus there are frequent changes in weather. Mark Twain (Samuel L. Clemens), a longtime resident, supposedly quipped about New England's weather, "If you don't like it, wait a minute!" This changeability means that extremes of heat or cold usually do not last long. Precipitation is distributed fairly equally through the year, although occasionally droughts do occur, as in 1957 and 1962–1966. Droughts have caused losses to farmers and property owners and have worried water-supply officials, but their effects on Connecticut's economy and mode of living have been only marginal. The state's average precipitation ranges from 44 to 48 inches (112 to 122 cm) yearly—very ample for agricultural and other needs.

Despite Connecticut's smallness there is considerable temperature variation. The coldest weather station—Norfolk, in the northwest—has an annual mean temperature of 45° F (7° C), a January mean of 22° F (−5.6° C), and a July mean of 66° F (19° C). Bridgeport, the warmest, reports an annual mean of 52° F (11° C), with 30° F (−1° C) in January and 71° F (22° C) in July. Annual snowfall, which is relatively light along the coast, becomes moderately heavy in northwestern Connecticut.

Flood and tornado disasters have been rare. The most costly floods were those of March 1936, which caused huge damage in Hartford and other areas along the Connecticut River, and of August and October 1955, which produced major damage along the Shetucket-Quinebaug system. Flood-control projects have helped to prevent further serious floods. The most catastrophic hurricane in modern times, which occurred in September 1938, caused enormous damage in many parts of the state.

Despite irritating qualities at times, Connecticut's temperate climate basically is an asset. Rarely bitterly cold in winter or excessively hot in summer, it permits residents to carry on business and recreational activities with infrequent interference from unpleasant weather.

**Plant and Animal Life.** Connecticut's moderate, moist climate with four distinct seasons encourages the growth of a lush forest cover as well as grasses, plants, and foodstuffs. When the English settlers arrived, they found nearly all the land covered by magnificent virgin forests, broken occasionally by an Indian clearing. The settlers quickly cleared the forests in order to grow crops, but with the decline of agriculture in recent decades, the forest cover gradually has reestablished itself. The forests have low commercial value, but they add immeasurably to scenic values, protect water supplies, and regulate water runoff, so that floods are less likely. The forests are thickest in the hilly, upland areas.

There is little large game remaining in the state except for deer, which are not numerous but are found in various areas. Small game include rabbit, raccoon, and squirrel. Among the game birds are ruffed grouse, pheasant, and some waterfowl.

Saltwater fish found in quantity along the shore and offshore include striped bass, bluefish, and swordfish. The freshwater fish are divided into warmwater species—perch, bullheads, pickerel, largemouth and smallmouth bass—and coldwater species—brook, brown, and rainbow trout and sockeye salmon. In addition, from earliest colonial days shad have migrated each spring from salt water up the Connecticut and other rivers to spawn. A recently introduced species of similar habits is the sea-run brown trout.

**Minerals.** Many of the known minerals, especially metals, have been found in Connecticut, but few in quality and quantity sufficient for profitable exploitation. A high-grade iron ore (limonite) discovered in Salisbury, Sharon, and Kent was mined from the 1730's until after 1900. The Newgate copper mine at Granby (later a prison) operated briefly before the American Revolution. A more successful copper mine in Bristol yielded substantial profits during the periods 1847–1854 and 1888–1895. There were short-lived ventures involving tungsten, bismuth, lead, silver, arsenic, nickel, cobalt, garnet, and graphite. The only mineral deposits that possess any present significance are stone, sand and gravel, and clay.

**Conservation.** Conservation problems stem largely from the pressures of a rapidly growing

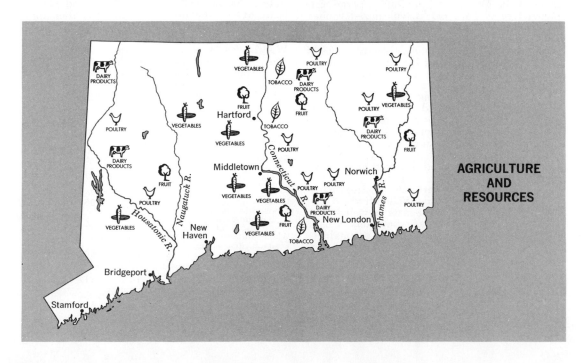

population upon Connecticut's small land area. As in many densely populated areas, there is a growing problem of air and water pollution. The 1967 General Assembly enacted a comprehensive clean-waters bill. Pollution is especially serious in the Connecticut, Thames, and Naugatuck river systems and is growing along the coast. Also along the coast, a related conservation issue is the need to save the rapidly dwindling marshlands, which serve as breeding places for waterfowl.

Other legislation aimed at conservation of Connecticut's environment includes the open-spaces act of 1963, which, coupled with federal open-space grants, has proved helpful in preserving attractive areas for general public use. The 1961 historic-districts act makes it possible for a town or city to preserve choice historic areas from commercial and industrial encroachments. The Connecticut Interregional Planning Program, aided by federal grants, represents an interagency approach to long-range planning for Connecticut's economic and social development, in which conservation is destined to play a major role.

## 3. The Economy

Since the advent of the Industrial Revolution, Connecticut has ranked among the leading states in manufacturing. In agriculture, however, the trend has been one of fairly steady decline. Mining operations now are confined principally to production of traprock, sand and gravel, and feldspar and clays. In terms of the basic factors influencing industrial growth, Connecticut ranks high in skilled labor force, capital, managerial skill, access to materials and markets, and living conditions. Yankee inventiveness and ingenuity have been responsible for many of the manufacturing businesses in the state, ranging from helicopters to Halloween masks.

**Manufacturing.** Several of the nation's major industries started in Connecticut in the early 1800's. Among them was the brass industry, launched in Waterbury in 1802. Large-scale manufacture of hats, clocks, vulcanized rubber, pins, and silverware also began in Connecticut. Modern times have brought steady growth. In every war Connecticut has made contributions of arms and other equipment for the armed forces, and continues to rank among the top states in per capita value of government contracts.

The state is a leading producer of transportation equipment and parts (particularly aircraft engines, helicopters, submarines, and aircraft propellers). Other major manufactures include nonelectrical machinery, fabricated metal products, and electrical machinery, especially household appliances and lighting and wiring devices.

Silverware and copper products are manufactured in Meriden and Wallingford. Other manufactures for which the state is well known are hats, needles and pins, typewriters, clocks, watches, brass, and plastic and rubber products. The principal manufacturing centers in the state are Bridgeport, Danbury, Groton and New London, Meriden, Hartford, New Britain, New Haven, Norwalk, Stamford, Stratford, and Waterbury.

**Agriculture.** With the inflation of land values and the escalation of taxes, farming has become an unprofitable land-use measure. Outside of the small truck farms producing fruits and vegetables,

most of which are sold and consumed locally, the remaining farms in Connecticut produce mainly chickens and dairy products. The leading field crop is tobacco, which is shade-grown and processed in the Connecticut Valley. Other crops in the state include apples, potatoes, peaches, pears, ornamental shrubs, and strawberries.

**Mining.** The most valuable mineral in Connecticut is traprock, a stone that is used in the building of roads. Other nonmetal minerals found in the state include sand and gravel, small amounts of feldspar, lime, barium, calcium, gemstones, clay, and mica. Mining is of relatively little commercial importance in Connecticut, although earlier in its history, iron was mined in Salisbury and copper was produced in Granby.

**Other Economic Factors.** More than 50 insurance companies maintain headquarters in the state. Most of them are centered in Hartford, where they underwrite policies for fire, automobile, traveler's life, accident, and disability insurance.

Although Connecticut has never been a leading tourist state, its excellent highways make it a corridor for out-of-state drivers going to and from the Northeast. The state offers sandy beaches on Long Island Sound and a number of ski areas, but most of its vacationers are either people who stop while passing through to another destination, or dwellers in nearby cities who maintain vacation homes in the area for week-end and summer use.

Expanding corporations in significant numbers are establishing headquarters in Connecticut, particularly in Fairfield county, from Greenwich to Danbury. Small towns are experiencing boomtown symptoms caused by inflated real estate values, congestion, and rapid growth. Even with the influx of corporate headquarters from other states, the county remains one of the most affluent and desirable in the country.

**Transportation.** Connecticut's transportation system began as one largely dependent on water. Gradually the spread of population into the interior sections made the development of an extensive road system necessary. In the post–World War II period the system of superhighways has been rapidly extended. In 1958 the state completed the 129-mile (208-km) Connecticut Turnpike that crosses the state from New York to Rhode Island. Within a decade

### PERSONAL INCOME IN CONNECTICUT

| Source | 1960 | 1970 | 1980 |
|---|---|---|---|
| | (Millions of dollars) | | |
| Farms | 69 | 75 | 97 |
| Mining | 6 | 9 | 75 |
| Construction | 353 | 765 | 1,177 |
| Manufacturing | 2,422 | 4,268 | 9,685 |
| Transportation, communications, and public utilities | 276 | 541 | 1,374 |
| Wholesale and retail trade | 854 | 1,655 | 3,060 |
| Finance, insurance, and real estate | 371 | 682 | 2,124 |
| Services | 727 | 1,753 | 4,834 |
| Other industries | 17 | 38 | 81 |
| Government | 511 | 1,312 | 2,876 |
| | (Dollars) | | |
| Per capita personal income | 2,868 | 4,913 | 11,720 |
| Per capita income, U.S. | 2,216 | 3,945 | 9,521 |

Source. U.S. Department of Commerce, *Survey of Current Business.*

# CONNECTICUT

## TOPOGRAPHY

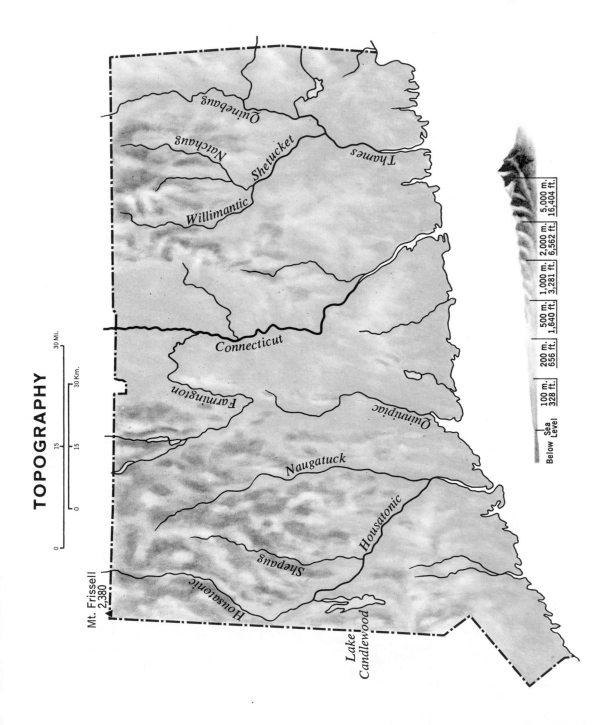

Quinebaug

Natchaug

Shetucket

Thames

Willimantic

Connecticut

Farmington

Quinnipiac

Naugatuck

Housatonic

Shepaug

Housatonic

Lake Candlewood

Mt. Frissell 2,380

30 Mi.
30 Km.
15
15
0
0

100 m. 328 ft. | 200 m. 656 ft. | 500 m. 1,640 ft. | 1,000 m. 3,281 ft. | 2,000 m. 6,562 ft. | 5,000 m. 16,404 ft.

Below Sea Level

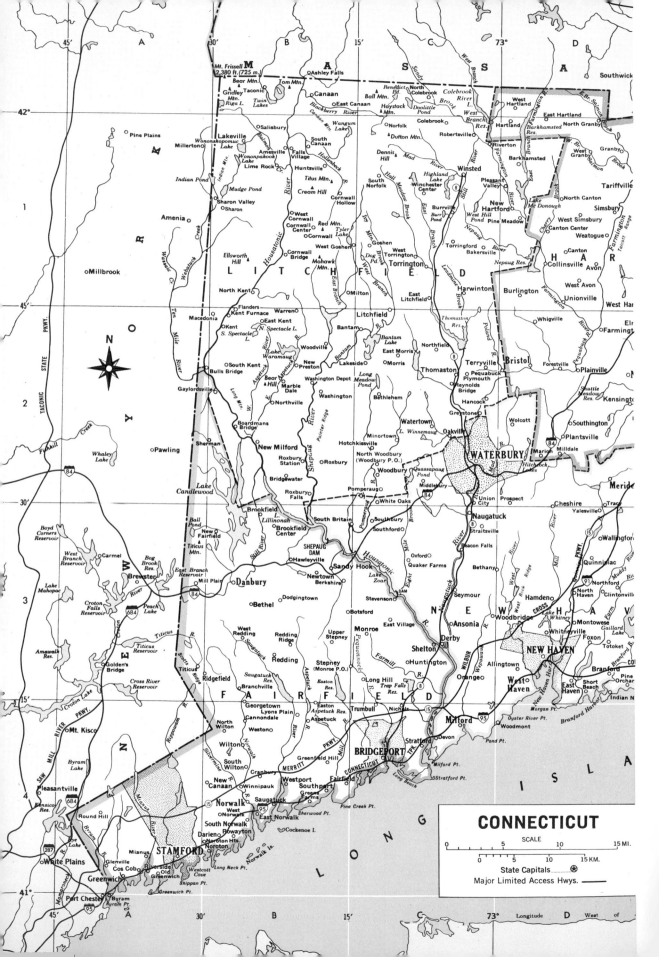

# CONNECTICUT

SCALE

0     5     10     15 MI.

0     5     10     15 KM.

State Capitals ⊛

Major Limited Access Hwys. ——

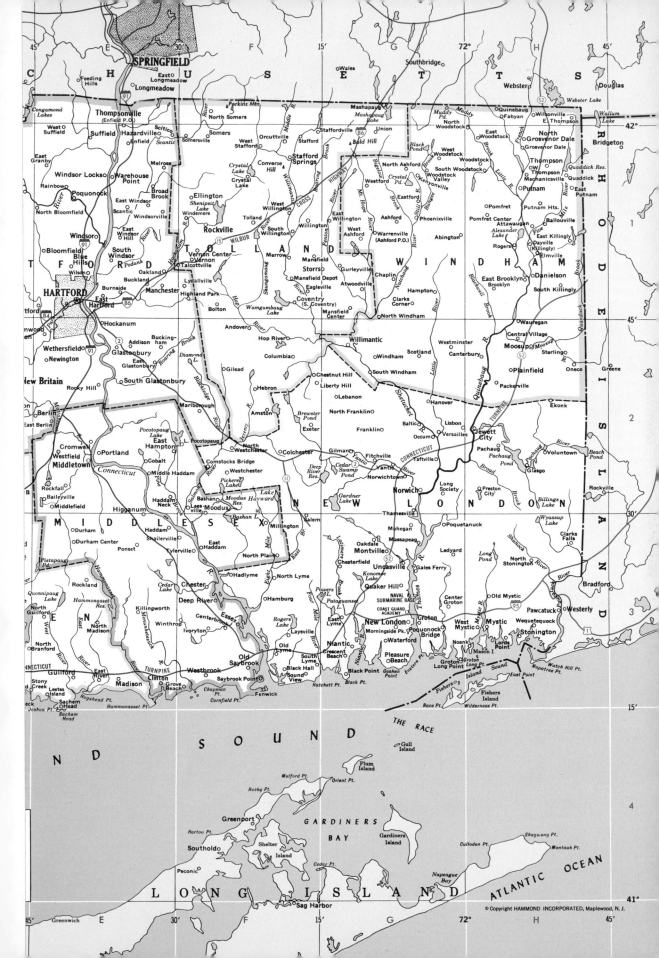

# CONNECTICUT

## COUNTIES

Fairfield 882,567 B3
Hartford 857,183 D1
Litchfield 182,193 B1
Middlesex 155,071 E3
New Haven 824,008 D3
New London 259,088 G2
Tolland 136,364 F1
Windham 109,091 H1

## CITIES and TOWNS

Abington 600 G1
Addison 700 E2
Allingtown D3
Amston 900 F2
Andover• 3,036 F2
Ansonia 18,554 C3
Ashford• 4,098 G1
Ashford P.O. (Warrenville) 500 G1
Attawaugan 400 H1
Avon 1,434 D1
Avon• 15,832 D1
Bakersville 750 C1
Ballouville 800 H1
Baltic G2
Bantam 802 B2
Barkhamsted• 3,494 D1
Beacon Falls• 5,246 C3
Berkshire 500 B3
Berlin• 18,215 E2
Bethany• 5,040 C3
Bethel 9,137 B3
Bethel• 18,067 B3
Bethlehem• 3,422 C2
Bethlehem 2,022 C2
Bloomfield• 19,587 E1
Blue Hills 3,020 E1
Bolton• 5,017 F1
Botsford 400 C3
Branchville 600 B3
Branford• 28,683 D3
Branford 5,735 D3
Bridgeport 139,529 C4
Bridgewater• 1,824 B2
Bristol 60,062 D2
Broad Brook 3,469 E1
Brookfield• 15,664 B3
Brookfield Center B3
Brooklyn• 7,173 H1
Buckingham 800 E2
Burlington• 8,190 D1
Burnside E1
Byram A4
Canaan• 1,288 B1
Canaan 1,081 B1
Cannondale 400 B4
Canterbury• 4,692 H2
Canton• 8,840 D1
Canton 1,565 D1
Canton Center 312 D1
Centerbrook 800 F3
Center Groton 600 G3
Central Village 950 H2
Chaplin• 2,250 G1
Cheshire• 28,543 D2
Cheshire 5,789 D2
Chester• 3,743 F3
Chester 1,546 F3
Clinton• 13,094 E3
Clinton 3,516 E3
Clintonville D3
Cobalt 700 E2
Colchester• 14,551 F2
Colchester 3,212 F2
Colebrook 1,471 C1
Collinsville 2,686 D1
Columbia• 4,971 F2
Cornwall• 1,434 B1
Cos Cob A4
Coventry• 11,504 F1
Coventry 2,914 F1
Cranbury 700 B4
Cromwell• 12,871 E2
Crystal Lake 1,459 F1
Danbury 74,848 B3
Danielson 4,265 H1
Darien• 19,607 B4
Dayville H1
Deep River• 4,610 F3
Deep River 2,470 F3
Derby 12,391 C3
Devon C4
Durham• 6,627 E3
Durham 2,773 E3
Durham Center 500 E3
Eagleville 310 F1
East Berlin 950 E2
East Brooklyn 1,473 H1
East Canaan 800 B1
East Glastonbury 300 E2
Eastford• 1,618 G1
East Granby• 4,745 E1
East Haddam• 8,333 F3
East Hampton• 13,352 E2
East Hampton 2,254 E2
East Hartford• 49,575 E1
East Hartland 900 D1
East Haven• 28,189 D3
East Killingly 900 H1
East Litchfield 300 C1
East Lyme• 18,118 G3
East Morris 800 C2
East Norwalk B4
Easton• 7,272 B4
East Putnam 500 H1
East River 500 E3
East Thompson 350 H1
East Windsor• 9,818 E1
East Windsor Hill 500 E1
East Woodstock 400 H1
Ellington• 12,921 F1
Elmwood D2
Enfield• 45,212 E1
Enfield 8,151 E1
Essex• 6,505 F3
Essex 2,573 F3
Exeter 160 F2
Fabyan 600 H1
Fairfield• 57,340 B4
Falls Village 600 B1
Farmington• 23,641 D2
Fenwick 52 F3
Fitchville 400 G2
Forestville D2
Foxon D3
Franklin• 1,835 G2
Gales Ferry 1,191 G3
Gaylordsville 960 A2
Georgetown 1,650 B4
Gilead 350 F2
Gilman 350 G2
Glasgo 450 H2
Glastonbury• 31,876 E2
Glastonbury 7,157 E2
Glenville A4
Goshen• 2,697 C1
Granby• 10,347 D1
Granby 1,912 D1
Greenfield Hill B4
Greenwich• 61,101 A4
Grosvenor Dale 700 H1
Groton• 39,907 G3
Groton 10,010 G3
Guilford• 21,398 E3
Guilford 2,603 E3
Haddam• 7,157 E3
Hadlyme 450 F3
Hamden• 56,913 D3
Hampton• 1,758 G1
Hanover 500 G2
Hartford (cap.) 121,578 E1
Hartland• 2,012 D1
Harwinton• 5,283 C1
Harwinton 3,293 C1
Hawleyville 600 B3
Hazardville 4,900 E1
Hebron• 8,610 F2
Higganum 1,671 E2
Highland Park 500 F1
Hockanum E2
Huntington C3
Indian Neck D3
Ivoryton F3
Jewett City 3,053 H2
Kensington 8,541 D2
Kent• 2,858 B2
Killingly• 16,472 H1
Killingworth• 6,018 E3
Lake Pocotopaug 3,169 F2
Lakeside 350 B2
Lakeville B1
Laysville 350 F3
Lebanon• 6,907 G2
Ledyard• 14,687 G3
Leetes Island 500 E3
Lime Rock 350 B1
Lisbon• 4,069 G2
Litchfield• 8,316 C2
Litchfield 1,328 C2
Long Hill 3,534 C3
Lords Point 500 H3
Lyons Plain 700 B4
Madison• 17,858 E3
Madison 2,222 E3
Manchester• 54,740 E1
Manchester 31,058 E1
Mansfield• 20,720 F1
Mansfield Center 973 G1
Mansfield Depot 120 F1
Marble Dale 300 B2
Marion 900 D2
Marlborough• 5,709 F2
Marlborough 1,039 F2
Massapeag 350 G3
Mechanicsville 425 H1
Melrose 350 E1
Meriden 58,244 D2
Merrow 290 F1
Mianus 300 A4
Middlebury• 6,451 C2
Middlefield• 4,203 E2
Middle Haddam 325 E2
Middletown 43,167 E2
Milford 52,305 C4
Milldale 975 D2
Mill Plain 750 A3
Milton 600 C1
Mohegan 700 G3
Monroe• 19,247 C3
Monroe P.O. (Stepney) B3
Montowese D3
Montville• 18,546 G3
Montville 1,711 G3
Moodus 1,263 F2
Moosup 3,237 H2
Morningside Park G3
Morris• 2,301 C2
Mystic 4,001 H3
Naugatuck 30,989 C3
New Britain 71,538 E2
New Canaan• 19,395 B4
New Fairfield• 13,953 B3
New Hartford 1,049 C1
New Hartford• 6,088 C1
New Haven 123,626 D3
Newington• 29,306 E2
New London 25,671 G3
New Milford• 27,121 B2
New Milford 6,633 B2
New Preston 1,110 B2
Newtown• 25,031 B3
Newtown 1,843 B3
Niantic 3,085 G3
Nichols C4
Noank 1,830 G3
Norfolk• 1,660 C1
Noroton B4
Noroton Heights B4
North Bloomfield 500 E1
North Branford• 13,906 E3
Northfield 600 C2
Northford D3
North Franklin 500 G2
North Granby 1,720 D1
North Grosvenor Dale 1,424 H1
North Guilford E3
North Haven• 23,035 D3
North Lyme F3
North Stonington• 4,991 H3
Northville 700 B2
North Wilton 900 B4
North Woodbury 900 C2
North Woodstock 400 G1
Norwalk 82,951 B4
Norwich 36,117 G2
Norwichtown G2
Oakdale 608 G3
Oakville 8,618 C2
Occum G2
Old Greenwich A4
Old Lyme• 7,406 F3
Old Mystic 3,205 H3
Old Saybrook 1,962 F3
Old Saybrook• 10,367 F3
Oneco 550 H2
Orange• 13,233 C3
Oxford• 9,821 C3
Pachaug 400 H2
Pawcatuck 5,474 H3
Pequabuck 642 C2
Pine Meadow 400 D1
Plainfield• 14,619 H2
Plainfield 2,638 H2
Plainville• 17,328 D2
Plantsville D2
Pleasant Valley 300 C1
Pleasure Beach 1,356 G3
Plymouth• 11,634 C2
Pomfret• 3,798 H1
Pomfret Center 175 H1
Poquonock E1
Poquonock Bridge 1,592 G3
Portland• 8,732 E2
Portland 5,534 E2
Preston 4,688 H2
Prospect• 8,707 D2
Putnam• 9,002 H1
Putnam 6,746 H1
Putnam Heights 500 H1
Quaddick 400 H1
Quaker Hill 2,052 G3
Quinebaug 1,122 H1
Quinnipiac D3
Redding• 8,270 B3
Redding Ridge 550 B3
Ridgefield• 23,643 B3
Ridgefield 7,212 B3
Riverside A4
Rockfall 900 E2
Rockville F1
Rocky Hill• 17,966 E2
Rogers 650 H1
Round Hill 900 A4
Rowayton B4
Roxbury• 2,136 B2
Roxbury Station 250 B2
Sachem Head 250 E3
Salem• 3,858 F3
Salisbury• 3,977 B1
Sandy Hook B3
Saugatuck B4
Saybrook Point 700 F3
Scantic 500 E1
Scotland• 1,556 G2
Seymour• 15,454 C3
Sharon• 2,968 B1
Shelton 38,101 C3
Sherman• 3,827 B2
Short Beach D3
Simsbury• 23,234 D1
Simsbury 5,603 D1
Somers• 10,417 F1
Somers 1,643 F1
Somersville 750 F1
South Britain 390 B3
Southbury• 18,567 C3
South Coventry (Coventry) 1,381 F1
South Glastonbury E2
Southington• 39,728 D2
South Kent 450 B2
South Killingly 500 H1
South Lyme 250 F3
South Norfolk 400 C1
South Norwalk B4
Southport B4
South Willington 450 F1
South Wilton B4
South Windham 1,278 G2
South Windsor• 24,412 E1
South Woodstock 1,211 G1
Stafford• 11,307 F1
Stafford Springs 4,100 F1
Staffordville 500 G1
Stamford 117,083 A4
Stepney B3
Sterling• 3,099 H2
Stonington• 17,906 H3
Stonington 1,032 H3
Stony Creek E3
Storrs 10,996 F1
Stratford• 49,976 C4
Suffield• 13,552 E1
Suffield 1,244 E1
Taconic 400 B1
Taftville G2
Talcottville 875 F1
Tariffville 1,371 D1
Terryville 5,360 C2
Thamesville G2
Thomaston• 7,503 C2
Thompson• 8,878 H1
Thompsonville 8,125 E1
Titicus 450 A3
Tolland 13,146 F1
Torringford C1
Torrington 35,202 C1
Totoket 950 D3
Trumbull• 34,243 C4
Uncasville 1,597 G3
Union• 693 G1
Union City C2
Unionville D1
Vernon• 28,063 F1
Vernon Center F1
Versailles 540 G2
Voluntown• 2,528 H2
Wallingford• 43,026 D3
Wallingford 17,509 D3
Warehouse Point E1
Warren• 1,254 B2
Warrenville 500 G1
Washington• 3,596 B2
Washington Depot 900 B2
Waterbury 107,271 C2
Waterford• 19,152 G3
Waterford 2,736 G3
Watertown• 21,661 C2
Wauregan 1,085 H2
Weatogue 2,805 D1
West Avon D1
Westbrook• 6,292 F3
Westbrook 2,238 F3
West Cornwall 425 B1
Westfield E2
West Granby 567 D1
West Hartford• 63,589 D1
West Haven 52,360 D3
Westminster 350 G2
West Mystic 3,595 H3
West Norwalk 950 B4
Weston• 10,037 B4
Westport• 25,749 B4
West Reading 500 B3
West Simsbury 2,395 D1
West Suffield E1
West Woodstock 500 G1
Wethersfield• 26,271 E2
Whigville 500 D2
Whitneyville D3
Willimantic 15,823 G2
Willington• 5,959 F1
Wilson• 300 E1
Wilton 15,989 B4
Winchester• 10,664 C1
Winchester Center 350 C1
Windham• 22,857 G2
Windsor• 28,237 E1
Windsor 17,517 E1
Windsor Locks• 12,043 E1
Windsorville 450 E1
Winnipauk 650 B4
Winsted 7,321 C1
Winthrop 750 E3
Wolcott• 15,215 D2
Woodbridge• 8,983 D3
Woodbury• 9,198 C2
Woodbury 1,298 C2
Woodmont 1,711 D4
Woodstock• 7,221 H1
Yalesville D3
Yantic G2

## OTHER FEATURES

Alexander (lake) H1
Aspetuck (riv.) B4
Aspetuck (res.) B4
Bald (hill) G1
Ball (mt.) C1
Ball (pond) A3
Bantam (lake) C2
Bantam (riv.) B2
Barkhamsted (res.) D1
Bashan (lake) F3
Beach (pond) H2
Bear (hill) B2
Bear (mt.) B1
Benedict (pond) C1
Bigelow (brook) G1
Billings (lake) H2
Black (pt.) G3
Black (pond) G1
Blackberry (riv.) B1
Blackledge (riv.) F2
Blackwell (brook) H1
Branford (harb.) D4
Branford (riv.) D3
Brewster (pond) F2
Broad (brook) H2
Bungee (brook) G1
Burr (pond) C1
Byram (pt.) A4
Byram (riv.) A4
Canaan (mt.) B1
Candlewood (lake) A2
Cedar (lake) E3
Cedar Swamp (pond) G2
Chapman (pt.) F3
Cherry (brook) D1
Coast Guard Academy G3
Cockenoe (isl.) B4
Colebrook River (lake) C1
Congamond (lakes) E1
Connecticut (riv.) E2
Converse (hill) F1

• Population of town or township.

most of the 296 miles (476 km) of the interstate highway system also were open to traffic. Connecticut has about 19,000 miles (30,000 km) of roads and highways.

There are about 60 airports in the state, but Bradley International Airport near Hartford handles many times more passengers and freight than all the other airports combined.

Nine hundred and fifty miles (1,549 km) of track provide railroad freight and passenger service in Connecticut. Trains serve the many commuters to New York City.

Water transportation remains important in the state's economy. Bridgeport, New Haven, and New London are principal seaports.

## 4. Government and Politics

In 1662, Connecticut obtained its first legal charter, from King Charles II of England. When the Revolution came, Connecticut declared its independence but retained its original charter until 1818. The new constitution of that year provided for disestablishment of the Congregational Church and complete religious freedom. The basic system of elections, the bicameral legislature, the executive and judicial branches, and the town meeting remained almost unchanged.

**Structure of Government.** As time passed, the system of representation for the lower house of the General Assembly (state legislature) became so disproportionate to population that, in 1950, 10% of the people could elect a majority of the House of Representatives. Senate districts also had glaring inequalities. Finally, under a U. S. Supreme Court ruling, a federal district court in 1964 ordered Connecticut to reapportion and redistrict its legislature. Forced by this order, the leaders of the major parties agreed to have a convention draw up a new constituion. Voters of the state approved the new constitution in December 1965. Major changes included a senate and a house with districts substantially equal in population under federal standards, mandatory reapportionment decennially, easier and more rapid amendment process, and home rule for the townships (called towns in Connecticut).

The General Assembly meets annually, and its members are elected to a two-year term. The judicial branch is headed by the Connecticut supreme court. Other courts include the appellate court (established in 1983), the superior court, and the probate court.

Since 1960, "county" has been little more than a geographical term, for no county government exists. The local units of government are the town, the city, and the borough.

**Public Finance.** After decades of balanced budgets, Connecticut began to experience financial difficulties in the late 1980's. By the 1990's the nation's highest sales tax and a substantial corporate profits tax were not enough to balance the budget. As a result, 1991 saw the passage of a flat 4.5% income tax for Connecticut. The sales tax was reduced, but the number of taxable goods was increased. At the same time, the corporate profits tax was reduced, while the capital gains tax and the tax on income from dividends and interest were eliminated.

Local governments rely on property taxes and state and federal aid for their income.

**Social Services.** The state maintains a comprehensive system of institutions for the care of the ill, aged, retarded, and needy. Large hospitals for the mentally ill are maintained at Newtown, Middletown, and Norwich. The mentally retarded are cared for at training schools at Mansfield and Southbury. For persons with tuberculosis and other serious chronic diseases,

---

**GOVERNMENT HIGHLIGHTS**

**Electoral Vote**—7.

**Representation in Congress**—U.S. senators, 2; U.S. representatives, 5.

**Legislature**—Senate, 36 members; House of Representatives, 151 members; all, 2-year terms.

**Governor**—4-year term; may succeed himself or herself.

the state operates hospitals at Newington, Shelton, Waterford, and Uncasville. Other state-supported institutions include a school for the deaf at Mystic, a hospital for alcoholics at Hartford, a center at Meriden for rehabilitation of patients from mental institutions, and a child study and treatment center at Hamden.

Connecticut has a relatively new state prison at Somers. The state also operates correctional institutions for women and juvenile offenders.

**Political Parties.** Political parties in Connecticut generally have experienced the same evolution as in the country as a whole. The Federalist party remained entrenched until 1817, when it was overthrown by an alliance, the Toleration party, which succeeded in setting up a new constitution the next year. The state went through the usual pattern of the rise of the Jacksonian Democratic and Whig parties, followed in the 1850's by the dissolution of the Whigs and appearance of the Republican party. From 1858 to 1930, the Republicans held the governorship more than three fourths of the time.

The depression and general resurgence of the Democratic party nationally in the 1930's was paralleled in Connecticut by Democratic victories and a kind of "little New Deal." From 1938 to 1954, the two parties competed on relatively even terms, but 1954 signaled the beginning of a new Democratic trend.

The large cities tend to have heavy Democratic registration majorities. Among the suburban towns, formerly overwhelmingly Republican, the Democrats have shown sizable gains. The smaller towns are largely Republican.

## 5. Education and Culture

The Puritans who founded Connecticut were intensely dedicated to the principle of education for their children so they could read the Bible and interpret it. In the first decade, schools were opened in New Haven and Hartford. Ludlow's Code of 1650 (see LUDLOW, ROGER) was intended to defeat the "one chiefe project of that old deluder Sathan, to keep men from the knowledge of the Scriptures." Each town with 50 families was required to hire a schoolmaster to teach children to read and write. When a town reached 100 families, it had to establish a "Grammer Schoole" offering preparation for the "college at Cambridge" (Harvard, at Cambridge, Mass.). Despite the compulsory school laws, there are indications that educational opportunities remained very limited throughout the colonial period.

**Elementary and Secondary Education.** In 1799 the Connecticut School Fund began to yield income, and it still continues to do so. This fund resulted from the sale in 1795 of 3 million acres (1.2 million hectares) of Connecticut's land

(Below) The Phoenix Mutual Insurance Building is one of several strikingly modern buildings in Constitution Plaza, in the business center of Hartford.

© WESTON KEMP, 1967

CARL SCHOLFIELD, FROM RAPHO GUILLUMETTE

(Above) Hills slope gently down to Hamburg Cove, on the Eight Mile River in southern Connecticut. (Below) The American Shakespeare Theatre, in Stratford.

LAURENCE LOWRY, FROM RAPHO GUILLUMETTE

The Capitol in Hartford was designed by Richard Upjohn and completed in 1885. It stands on a hill in Bushnell Park.

I. DONALD BOWDEN

claims in the Northwest Territory. In 1798 the legislature transferred control of public schools from the ecclesiastical societies to new town school societies. But the towns relied too much on the school fund and became indifferent to educational needs and standards.

After 1838 Henry Barnard, secretary of a board of commissioners for common schools and later first principal of the normal school at New Brit-

ain, greatly influenced education in Connecticut. Barnard's educational philosophy was epitomized in his famous statement that the United States ought to have "schools good enough for the best and cheap enough for the poorest."

In 1840, Middletown set up the first permanent public high school in the state. By 1868 all elementary public schools were free, and by 1872 nearly all high schools were.

## GOVERNORS OF CONNECTICUT

### Connecticut Colony

|  | |  |
|---|---|---|
| John Haynes | | 1639–1640 |
| Edward Hopkins | | 1640–1641 |
| John Haynes | | 1641–1642 |
| George Wyllys | | 1642–1643 |
| John Haynes | | 1643–1644 |
| Edward Hopkins | | 1644–1645 |
| John Haynes | | 1645–1646 |
| Edward Hopkins | | 1646–1647 |
| John Haynes | | 1647–1648 |
| Edward Hopkins | | 1648–1649 |
| John Haynes | | 1649–1650 |
| Edward Hopkins | | 1650–1651 |
| John Haynes | | 1651–1652 |
| Edward Hopkins | | 1652–1653 |
| John Haynes | | 1653–1654 |
| Edward Hopkins | | 1654–1655 |
| Thomas Welles | | 1655–1656 |
| John Webster | | 1656–1657 |
| John Winthrop, Jr. | | 1657–1658 |
| Thomas Welles | | 1658–1659 |
| John Winthrop, Jr. | | 1659–1676 |
| William Leete | | 1676–1683 |
| Robert Treat | | 1683–1687 |
| Sir Edmund Andros | | 1687–1689 |
| Robert Treat | | 1689–1698 |
| Fitz-John Winthrop | | 1698–1707 |
| Gurdon Saltonstall | | 1707–1724 |
| Joseph Talcott | | 1724–1741 |
| Jonathan Law | | 1741–1750 |
| Roger Wolcott | | 1750–1754 |
| Thomas Fitch | | 1754–1766 |
| William Pitkin | | 1766–1769 |
| Jonathan Trumbull, Sr. | | 1769–1776 |

### New Haven Colony

|  | |  |
|---|---|---|
| Theophilus Eaton | | 1639–1658 |
| Francis Newman | | 1658–1660 |
| William Leete | | 1661–1664 |

### State

| Name | Party | Years |
|---|---|---|
| Jonathan Trumbull, Sr. | | 1776–1784 |
| Matthew Griswold | | 1784–1786 |
| Samuel Huntington | Federalist | 1786–1796 |
| Oliver Wolcott | Federalist | 1796–1797 |
| Jonathan Trumbull, Jr. | Federalist | 1797–1809 |
| John Treadwell | Federalist | 1809–1811 |
| Roger Griswold | Federalist | 1811–1812 |
| John Cotton Smith | Federalist | 1812–1817 |
| Oliver Wolcott | Toleration Party | 1817–1827 |
| Gideon Tomlinson | Dem. Republican | 1827–1831 |
| John S. Peters | National Republican | 1831–1833 |
| Henry W. Edwards | Democrat | 1833–1834 |
| Samuel A. Foot | Whig | 1834–1835 |
| Henry W. Edwards | Democrat | 1835–1838 |
| William W. Ellsworth | Whig | 1838–1842 |
| Chauncey F. Cleveland | Democrat | 1842–1844 |
| Roger S. Baldwin | Whig | 1844–1846 |
| Isaac Toucey | Democrat | 1846–1847 |
| Clark Bissell | Whig | 1847–1849 |
| Joseph Trumbull | Whig | 1849–1850 |
| Thomas H. Seymour | Democrat | 1850–1853 |
| Charles H. Pond | Democrat | 1853–1854 |
| Henry Dutton | Whig | 1854–1855 |
| William T. Minor | Know-Nothing | 1855–1857 |
| Alexander H. Holley | Whig | 1857–1858 |
| William A. Buckingham | Republican | 1858–1866 |
| Joseph R. Hawley | Republican | 1866–1867 |
| James E. English | Democrat | 1867–1869 |
| Marshall Jewell | Republican | 1869–1870 |
| James E. English | Democrat | 1870–1871 |
| Marshall Jewell | Republican | 1871–1873 |
| Charles R. Ingersoll | Democrat | 1873–1877 |
| Richard D. Hubbard | Democrat | 1877–1879 |
| Charles B. Andrews | Republican | 1879–1881 |
| Hobart B. Bigelow | Republican | 1881–1883 |
| Thomas M. Waller | Democrat | 1883–1885 |
| Henry B. Harrison | Republican | 1885–1887 |
| Phineas C. Lounsbury | Republican | 1887–1889 |
| Morgan G. Bulkeley | Republican | 1889–1893 |
| Luzon B. Morris | Democrat | 1893–1895 |
| O. Vincent Coffin | Republican | 1895–1897 |
| Lorrin A. Cooke | Republican | 1897–1899 |
| George E. Lounsbury | Republican | 1899–1901 |
| George P. McLean | Republican | 1901–1903 |
| Abiram Chamberlain | Republican | 1903–1905 |
| Henry Roberts | Republican | 1905–1907 |
| Rollin S. Woodruff | Republican | 1907–1909 |
| George L. Lilley | Republican | 1909 |
| Frank B. Weeks | Republican | 1909–1911 |
| Simeon E. Baldwin | Democrat | 1911–1915 |
| Marcus H. Holcomb | Republican | 1915–1921 |
| Everett J. Lake | Republican | 1921–1923 |
| Charles A. Templeton | Republican | 1923–1925 |
| Hiram Bingham | Republican | 1925 |
| John H. Trumbull | Republican | 1925–1931 |
| Wilbur L. Cross | Democrat | 1931–1939 |
| Raymond E. Baldwin | Republican | 1939–1941 |
| Robert A. Hurley | Democrat | 1941–1943 |
| Raymond E. Baldwin | Republican | 1943–1946 |
| Wilbert Snow | Democrat | 1946–1947 |
| James L. McConaughy | Republican | 1947–1948 |
| James C. Shannon | Republican | 1948–1949 |
| Chester Bowles | Democrat | 1949–1951 |
| John Davis Lodge | Republican | 1951–1955 |
| Abraham A. Ribicoff | Democrat | 1955–1961 |
| John N. Dempsey | Democrat | 1961–1971 |
| Thomas J. Meskill | Republican | 1971–1975 |
| Ella T. Grasso | Democrat | 1975–1980 |
| William A. O'Neill | Democrat | 1980–1991 |
| Lowell P. Weicker, Jr. | Independent | 1991–1995 |
| John G. Rowland | Republican | 1995– |

In 1865 the General Assembly created the state board of education with powers of "general supervision and control of the educational interests of the state." Gradually the work of this board has expanded with the population increase and the rising expectations of the people for improved educational services.

From early times Connecticut has had one of the most distinguished groups of private preparatory schools in the nation. There is also a very large system of Roman Catholic parochial schools.

**Higher Education.** The Collegiate School (later to become Yale University), Connecticut's oldest institution of higher education, was chartered in 1701 as a conservative reaction to Harvard's growing liberalism. In 1716 the school started its move from Saybrook to New Haven, where it gradually developed into one of the nation's greatest universities. In 1823 the Episcopalians founded the second institution of higher learning, Trinity College in Hartford. The Methodists established Wesleyan University in Middletown in 1831. The U.S. Coast Guard Academy, in New London, is a particular source of pride for Connecticut.

The University of Connecticut has its main campus in Storrs. A system of state-supported two-year community colleges was started in the 1960s.

**Cultural Activities and Institutions.** Not surprisingly, given its traditional emphasis on literacy and its role in American history, Connecticut has long promoted cultural development. The earliest libraries in Connecticut were private. Among the choicest was that of Gov. John Winthrop, Jr. The first public library in Connecticut was organized in Durham in 1733. The Scoville Library in Salisbury, opened in 1803, was the first U.S. library to be supported by taxes. In most cases public libraries have been financed by the local government. Altogether there are about 200 public libraries in the state. Under a 1965 legislative act the state library and the library extension services of the state board of education were combined.

Although all the colleges and universities have libraries, Yale's Sterling Memorial Library ranks among the largest in the nation. Among the outstanding specialized libraries are those of the Connecticut Historical Society, the Hartford Seminary, and the Institute for Living, all in Hartford, as well as the Submarine Library in Groton, and the Mystic Seaport Library.

Connecticut offers a variety of museums. Among its outstanding art museums are the Wadsworth Atheneum in Hartford, founded in 1842; the Yale University Art Gallery and the Yale Center for British Art in New Haven; and the Lyman Allyn Museum at Connecticut College, New London. Smaller art museums of note include the Aldrich Museum of Contemporary Art in Ridgefield, the Mattatuck Museum in Waterbury, the New Britain Museum of American Art, the Slater Memorial Museum in Norwich, and several art centers and galleries at Wesleyan University, the University of Hartford, Trinity College, and the University of Connecticut. Although not primarily art museums, the Florence Griswold Museum in Old Lyme, the Hill-Stead Museum in Farmington, the Litchfield Historical Society, the New Haven Colony Historical Society, and the Connecticut Historical Society in Hartford have art collections.

The Peabody Museum of Natural History at Yale University in New Haven is widely known. Specialized museums include the American Clock and Watch Museum, Bristol; the Barnum Museum,

Bridgeport; the Connecticut River Museum, Essex; the Connecticut Trolley Museum, East Windsor; the Mark Twain Memorial, Hartford; the Mashantucket Pequot Museum and Research Center, Mashantucket; and the Shore Line Trolley Museum, East Haven.

The largest historical museum is Mystic Seaport, re-created by the Marine Historical Association, Inc., which depicts a seaport village of the mid-19th century. The Connecticut Historical Society maintains the Old State House in Hartford as a historical museum. The Henry Whitfield State Historical Museum in Guilford, probably the oldest stone house in the nation, is state-owned, and Gillette Castle, the former home of actor and playwright William Gillette, is the centerpiece of Gillette Castle State Park in East Haddam. Under a 1967 legislative act the Connecticut historical commission was empowered to acquire, restore, and operate important historic structures and to make grants to assist local groups operating them.

Many local historical societies own and maintain early homes as historical museums. Some of these are: the Nathan Hale Homestead, South Coventry; the Tapping Reeve House and Law School, Litchfield; the Putnam Cottage, Greenwich; the Gov. Jonathan Trumbull House, Lebanon; the Harriet Beecher Stowe House, Hartford; and the Webb-Deane-Stevens Museum, Wethersfield.

Important symphony orchestras are based in Hartford, New Haven, New London, Norwalk, Stamford, and Waterbury. Yale, the University of Hartford, and the University of Connecticut have schools of fine arts and music.

Hartford and New Haven have significant theater repertory companies. Musicals are presented at the renowned Goodspeed Opera House in East Haddam and at the Goodspeed-at-Chester/Norma Terris Theatre in nearby Chester. In Waterford the Eugene O'Neill Memorial Theater Center carries on an active theater program.

## 6. Recreation and Places of Interest

Connecticut also offers a wide array of recreational facilities, public and private, for its citizens and visitors. The entire southern coast provides swimming, boating, and fishing on Long Island Sound. Most of the hundreds of lakes and ponds are available for public use, and there are innumerable other areas for picnicking, camping, and hunting. It has a privately developed system of about 400 miles (640 km) of specially marked hiking trails. There are also a few popular ski developments, mostly in the higher hills of the northwest, scores of golf courses, and, at every turn, places of scenic, historical, or cultural interest.

**State Parks, Historic Sites, and Monuments.** There are no national parks or national monuments within the state, but Connecticut has a comprehensive system of more than 100 state parks and state forests. These areas, which are scattered widely, offer varied recreational features. For boaters the state maintains over 80 boat-launching sites, including several on saltwater. Although most of the coast is privately owned, the state operates four large parks on or near the sound—Sherwood Island State Park (Westport), Hammonasset Beach State Park (Madison), Rocky Neck State Park (East Lyme), and Harkness Memorial State Park (Waterford). At Dinosaur Park, located in Rocky Hill, an exhibit center under a geodesic dome features 500 fossilized footprints made by dinosaurs of the Jurassic Period.

The state also maintains monuments commemorating persons, eras, and events such as John Mason, Nathan Hale, Israel Putnam, the early iron industry, the Swamp Fight of the Pequot War, and a British raid led by the traitorous Benedict Arnold.

**Other Points of Interest and Events.** Although there is no state fair, many towns have a local fair, mostly in late summer or early fall. Bridgeport has an annual Barnum circus festival. Several communities have organized fife and drum corps, the one at Deep River probably being the best known. Many well-known golfers compete in the Greater Hartford Open Golf Tournament held annually at Cromwell. Automobile racing at Lime Rock and Thompson attracts many spectators. College football and basketball competition also thrives.

## 7. History

When the first European settlers came to Connecticut in the 1630s, they found 6,000 to 7,000 Native Americans, clustered mostly along the coast. By modern standards the population was very scanty, but the Native Americans were formidable foes of white expansion. The Pequot War of 1637 resulted in complete defeat of the Pequot and opened the way for whites to move freely into all parts of Connecticut.

**Early Settlement.** Connecticut's recorded European history began with the exploration of the lower Connecticut River in 1614 by Adriaen Block, who represented the Dutch West India Company. In 1633 the Dutch erected a small trading fort, the House of Hope (abandoned in 1654) at present-day Hartford. Later in 1633, English settlers from Plymouth, Mass., enticed by reports of the fertile Connecticut River valley, came to Windsor. In 1634 a permanent settlement was made at Wethersfield, and in 1636, Thomas Hooker and Samuel Stone, with members of their congregations, moved from Newtown (Cambridge, Mass.) to Hartford. In 1637 these three towns, known as the River Towns or River Colony, cooperated under Capt. John Mason in fighting and defeating the Pequots. In 1639 they subscribed to the Fundamental Orders of Connecticut. These orders, claimed by some to be the first written constitution used to form a government, more likely were simply a framework of government. Even so, Connecticut earned the nickname of the "Constitution State." Within a few years the separate Saybrook and New London colonies became part of the River Colony.

New Haven, settled in 1638 under John Davenport and Theophilus Eaton, became in the meantime the nucleus of an entirely separate and rigidly Puritan colony. Branford, Guilford, Milford, New Haven, Stamford, and Southold (on Long Island, in present-day New York) made up the membership.

In 1662, through the efforts of John Winthrop, Jr., Connecticut finally obtained a legal charter from King Charles II. This remarkable document granted Connecticut an amazing amount of self-government. It also absorbed the New Haven Colony, which accepted the decision very unwillingly. In 1687 Sir Edmund Andros, as governor-general of all the New England colonies, visited Hartford and demanded the charter. It was concealed from him, probably in the famous Charter Oak tree in Hartford.

**Boundary Disputes.** Unfortunately, the charter opened up a true Pandora's box of troubles with

The Whitman house in Farmington, built about 1660, is one of Connecticut's oldest wood frame houses.

Connecticut's neighbors. The generous and ill-defined boundaries, which carried Connecticut from Narragansett Bay on the east to the Pacific Ocean on the west, were highly unrealistic and were to cause serious trouble with Rhode Island, Massachusetts, New York, and Pennsylvania. Winthrop's great persuasiveness, along with English ignorance of American geography, produced a long-drawn-out series of disputes.

After 80 years of acrimonious discussion and some violence, the Rhode Island line was settled along the Pawcatuck River, much as it is today. Connecticut and Massachusetts experienced less serious differences, although some of these were not resolved completely until 1827. New York, under the duke of York, claimed everything eastward to the Connecticut River, while Connecticut demanded some of the upper Hudson River area. In 1725 the colonies effected an agreement approximately at the present line. Much later, in 1881, minor modifications were made.

The most prolonged and serious conflict developed with Pennsylvania. A group of Connecticut land speculators, organized in 1753 as the Susquehannah Company, sponsored settlements in the Wyoming Valley of northern Pennsylvania on lands claimed under the charter of 1662. Hundreds of Connecticut people moved there. In 1774 Connecticut's General Assembly officially transformed its western outpost into the township of Westmoreland. Meanwhile, Pennsylvanians and their government challenged the legality of Westmoreland, and open skirmishes ensued. After the American Revolution the states agreed to have their quarrel arbitrated. The decision was in Pennsylvania's favor, but it did permit Connecticut families to retain their land and homes. (See PENNAMITE WARS.)

**The Revolutionary Era.** On the eve of the American Revolution, Connecticut had nearly 200,000 inhabitants as well as a reasonably well-balanced economy based upon agriculture and the coastal and West Indian trades. Governor Jonathan Trumbull, Sr., was the only colonial governor to continue as governor throughout the war. The large

## PROMINENT PEOPLE IDENTIFIED WITH CONNECTICUT

**Alcott, Amos Bronson** (1799–1888), educator, transcendentalist philosopher, author.

**Alsop, Richard** (1761–1815), poet; generally identified as the leader of a literary group known as the Hartford Wits.

**Barnard, Henry** (1811–1900), educator, political leader, writer; championed free public education and was first U.S. commissioner of education (1867–1870).

**Barnum, Phineas Taylor** (1810–1891), showman, politician; opened the first public aquarium.

**Bartlett, Paul Wayland** (1865–1925), sculptor known for monumental portrait sculpture.

**Beecher, Lyman** (1775–1863), theologian, pastor, educator, famed preacher.

**Bushnell, Horace** (1802–1876), clergyman and educator.

**Camp, Walter Chauncey** (1859–1925), "father of American football," Yale University football coach.

**Church, Frederic Edwin** (1826–1900), landscape painter.

**Colt, Samuel** (1814–1862), inventor of Colt revolver, manufacturer.

**Cross, Wilbur L.** (1862–1948), educator, public official, state governor (1931–1939).

**Davenport, John** (1597–1670), founder of New Haven.

**Deane, Silas** (1737–1789), Patriot leader; represented state at First and Second Continental Congresses; diplomat.

**De Forest, John William** (1826–1906), author.

**De Koven, Henry Louis Reginald** (1859–1920), composer best known for operettas.

**Dwight, Timothy** (1752–1817), clergyman, theologian, president of Yale College (1795–1817), one of the "Hartford Wits."

**Dwight, Timothy** (1828–1916), clergyman, scholar, president of Yale (1886–1899); during his tenure, Yale was rechartered as a university.

**Edwards, Jonathan** (1703–1758), theologian, philosopher, renowned preacher, missionary, president of the College of New Jersey (now Princeton University; 1757–1758); his preaching gave enormous impetus to the "Great Awakening."

**Ellsworth, Oliver** (1745–1807), jurist and statesman, delegate to the Continental Congress, U.S. senator (1789–1796), 3d chief justice of the U.S. Supreme Court (1796–1800), author of Judiciary Act (1787).

**Gibbs, Josiah Willard** (1839–1903), mathematician who founded discipline of chemical thermodynamics, first person to be named a professor of mathematical physics.

**Gillette, William Hooker** (1853–1937), actor and playwright best known for his 1899 theater adaptation of Arthur Conan Doyle's Sherlock Holmes stories.

**Goodyear, Charles** (1800–1860), inventor of the vulcanization process for rubber.

**Hadley, Arthur T.** (1856–1930), first lay president of Yale University (1899–1921), authority on railroad transportation.

**Hale, Nathan** (1755–1776), patriot of American Revolution.

**Hooker, Thomas** (1586?–1647), founder of Hartford, a framer of the Fundamental Orders of Connecticut.

**Ives, Charles** (1874–1954), composer, important innovator in 20th-century music.

**Johnson, William Samuel** (1727–1819), jurist and educator, influential delegate to the Constitutional Convention, U.S. senator (1789–1791), president of Columbia College.

**Metacom** (c. 1638–1676), known to English settlers as King Philip, sachem of the Wampanoag who led Native Americans against the New England colonists in the conflict called King Philip's War.

**Morgan, John Pierpont** (1837–1913), financier; with his father, Julius Spencer Morgan, and Anthony Drexel, founded the firm that became J. P. Morgan & Co.

**Olmsted, Frederick Law** (1822–1903), landscape architect.

**Phelps, William Lyon** (1865–1943), educator and author; at Yale University, taught first courses in modern drama and the novel.

**Pinchot, Gifford** (1865–1946), forestry expert and early leader of the conservation movement; headed U.S. Forestry Service (1898–1946); governor of Pennsylvania (1923–1927, 1931–1936), professor of forestry at Yale (1903–1936).

**Putnam, Israel** (1718–1790), Revolutionary War general; distinguished himself at the Battle of Bunker Hill.

**Reeve, Tapping** (1744–1823), jurist; established first U.S. law school.

**Ribicoff, Abraham A.** (1910–1998), public official, U.S. representative (1949–1953), state governor (1953–1961), U.S. senator (1963–1981).

**Seabury, Samuel** (1729–1796), clergyman, first bishop of the Protestant Episcopal Church in the United States.

**Seymour, Charles** (1885–1963), educator and historian, president of Yale University (1937–1950).

**Sherman, Roger** (1721–1793), statesman, signer of the Declaration of Independence, first mayor of New Haven (1784); at the Philadelphia Convention, presented the "Connecticut Compromise" of 1787, proposing two houses of Congress.

**Silliman, Benjamin** (1779–1864), chemist and geologist, first professor of chemistry and natural history at Yale University, founder and editor of the journal that became the *American Journal of Science.*

**Stowe, Harriet Beecher** (1811–1896), writer; best known for *Uncle Tom's Cabin* (1852).

**Thomas, Seth** (1785–1859), manufacturer of clocks.

**Trumbull, John** (1750–1831), poet, essayist, judge, one of the "Hartford Wits."

**Trumbull, John** (1756–1843), historical painter of Revolutionary-era scenes; designed original Yale Gallery of Art, of which his collection formed the core.

**Trumbull, Jonathan** (1710–1785), political leader, only colonial governor to remain in office throughout the Revolutionary War (deputy governor, 1767–1769; governor, 1769–1784).

**Twain, Mark** (1835–1910), humorist and writer; while a Hartford resident, wrote *The Adventures of Tom Sawyer* (1876) and *The Adventures of Huckleberry Finn* (1884).

**Webster, Noah** (1758–1843), lexicographer and writer; compiled the "blue-backed speller" (1783) and *American Dictionary of the English Language* (1828).

**Welles, Gideon** (1802–1878), political leader, Pres. Abraham Lincoln's secretary of the navy during the Civil War.

**Wheelock, Eleazar** (1711–1779), clergyman, revivalist preacher, educator; founded Moor's Indian Charity School in Lebanon, Conn., to educate Native Americans (1743); founded (1769) and served as president of Dartmouth College.

**Whitney, Eli** (1765–1825), inventor; pioneered fabrication by machine tools.

**Winthrop, John** (1606–1676), founder of Saybrook (1635), colonial governor (1657–1658; 1659–1676); secured Charter of 1662 from King Charles II.

**Wolcott, Oliver** (1760–1833), comptroller of the United States (1791–1795), U.S. secretary of the treasury (1795–1801), state governor (1817–1827); presided over constitutional convention to replace Charter of 1662.

---

majority of people enthusiastically supported independence in 1776. The relatively few Loyalists lived mostly in Fairfield county.

Connecticut men fought with the Continental Army in nearly all major campaigns, except in the lower South. The militia opposed the British, who made brief raids on Danbury and other places. Connecticut privateers took an enormous toll of British merchant vessels. Nathan Hale, executed as a spy, was the state's most famous Revolutionary hero. Governor Trumbull and his council of safety, working with the General Assembly and many commissaries, collected huge amounts of foodstuffs for the Continental Army and won for Connecticut the nickname "Provisions State."

**The Next Century.** For the next 100 years, Connecticut grew slowly, as thousands of citizens emigrated to nearby areas. They carried the intense Puritan concern for church and education with them and played a very prominent role in shaping the history of states such as Vermont, New York, and Ohio.

Connecticut shared with its sister New England states a bitter dislike for the War of 1812. The notorious Hartford Convention, a gathering of New England Federalists, occurred at the Old State House late in 1814. In 1817 the Federalist monopoly of high office finally was broken by an alliance called the Toleration party, which obtained a new state constitution in 1818. From the early 1800s to the Civil War, Connecticut plunged into the Industrial Revolution. In social welfare, notable achievements included the founding of the American School for the Deaf in 1817 and the Hartford Retreat for the Insane (later, Institute for Living) in 1824.

## HISTORICAL HIGHLIGHTS

**1614** Adriaen Block sails up Connecticut River and claims Connecticut for Dutch.

**1633** English make first white settlement in Windsor; Dutch establish a colony on the site of present-day Hartford; John Oldham and followers establish settlement in Wethersfield.

**1636** Thomas Hooker founds Hartford; Windsor, Hartford, and Wethersfield unite to form the Connecticut Colony.

**1637** Pequot defeated by colonists in bloody "Pequot War."

**1638** Wealthy Puritans found the New Haven Colony at Quinnipiac (New Haven).

**1639** First written constitution—the Fundamental Orders of Connecticut—adopted (January 14).

**1647** Connecticut becomes the first New England colony to convict and hang a woman for practicing witchcraft.

**1654** English drive Dutch from Connecticut after seizing trading posts.

**1662** King Charles II grants Connecticut a legal charter, allowing much self-government.

**1665** Connecticut and New Haven counties united.

**1675–1676** "King Philip's War" between New England colonists and the Wampanoag, Nipmuc, and Narragansett; ends in Connecticut region in early 1675, when colonists defeat Wampanoag.

**1687** Sir Edmund Andros, royal governor of New York, asserts control over Connecticut; "Charter Oak" incident denies him possession of the colony's charter.

**1689** Government under the charter resumes.

**1701** Collegiate School (Yale University) founded, the future nation's third oldest university.

**1755** The *Connecticut Gazette,* the first Connecticut newspaper, is published in New Haven.

**1764** The *Hartford Courant,* the oldest continuously printed newspaper in the United States, begins publication as the *Connecticut Courant.*

**1776** Connecticut passes a resolution of independence from Great Britain (June 14); Nathan Hale executed by the British as a spy (September 22).

**1784** Tapping Reeve founds first law school in the United States, in Litchfield; African Americans born in Connecticut after March 1784 declared free.

**1788** Connecticut ratifies U.S. Constitution and enters the Union as the fifth state (January 9).

**1794** First fire-insurance company opens in Hartford, which becomes known as the insurance center of the United States.

**1817** Thomas Hopkins Gallaudet establishes the American School for the Deaf.

**1818** New state constitution replaces Charter of 1662; eliminates provision for established religion.

**1823** Washington College founded in Hartford; renamed Trinity College in 1845.

**1831** Wesleyan University in Middletown founded.

**1836** Hartford inventor Samuel Colt patents the first successful repeating pistol; pistol first manufactured at Eli Whitney's Connecticut factory; Colt later establishes his own factory (1847).

**1842** Wadsworth Atheneum, America's oldest public art museum, opens in Hartford.

**1844** New York and New Haven Railroad chartered; first east-west rail service (opened 1848).

**1848** Slavery abolished in Connecticut.

**1868** Connecticut gives land at Groton to the U.S. Navy for establishment of a naval station.

**1875** Hartford becomes capital city.

**1878** First commercial telephone exchange in the world is established in New Haven.

**1881** Storrs Agricultural School founded (later called Connecticut State College; in 1939, becomes the University of Connecticut).

**1910** The U.S. Coast Guard Academy moves to New London.

**1917** The U.S. Navy opens submarine base in Groton.

**1939** University of Connecticut created.

**1954** The *U.S.S. Nautilus,* the world's first atomic submarine, launched in Groton.

**1961** Connecticut institutes state circuit court system.

**1965** Connecticut adopts its present constitution.

**1969** Race riots in Hartford.

**1979** Connecticut adopts a law banning the construction of new nuclear power plants.

**1991** City of Bridgeport files for bankruptcy (June); state's first income tax passed, sparking wide-ranging protests (August 22); Hurricane Bob causes $40 million in property damage.

**1997** State of Connecticut takes over the failing Hartford Public School System from the city and its board of education after Hartford High School loses its national accreditation.

---

Internal politics in the late 19th century centered about the issues of apportionment of representatives in the lower house. The over-represented rural areas blocked any change. A population revolution, beginning in the late 1840s and continuing until 1914, brought immigrants from many lands.

**The 20th Century.** In World War I the state sent about 66,000 men into service. Again the small arms, metal, and textile industries worked overtime to produce war goods in large amounts. In Connecticut, as nationally, the 1920s were marked by growing prosperity and Republican domination of politics.

The Depression of the 1930s had a profound impact on the state. The severe economic decline caused enormous unemployment and brought the Democrats to power under scholarly Wilbur L. Cross. A "little New Deal" effected adoption of measures such as old-age pensions, elimination of sweatshops, a minimum-wage law, and reorganization of state government.

During World War II Connecticut again turned into an "arsenal of democracy." It built 75 submarines and 80% of all precision ball bearings. About 210,000 men saw action in the armed forces.

The post–World War II period brought a steady population growth, a high degree of prosperity, and a liberal trend in politics. Under Mayor Richard E. Lee, New Haven launched in 1957 an urban renewal program of such magnitude as to attract national attention. Abraham A. Ribicoff, who served as governor from 1955 to 1961, pushed highway safety and achieved abolition of county government and the replacement of local justice courts by district courts. In 1965 a constitutional convention devised a new constitution to replace the antiquated and much-amended 1818 document.

ALBERT E. VAN DUSEN, *University of Connecticut*

### Bibliography

Buel, Richard, Jr., *Dear Liberty: Connecticut's Mobilization for the Revolutionary War* (Wesleyan Univ. Press 1980).

Bushman, Richard L., *From Puritan to Yankee: Character and the Social Order in Connecticut, 1690–1765* (Harvard Univ. Press 1980).

Horton, Wesley W., *The Connecticut State Constitution* (Greenwood Press 1993).

Kemp, Thomas J., ed., *Connecticut Researcher's Handbook* (Gale Res. 1982).

Lewis, Thomas R., and John E. Harmon, *Connecticut: A Geography* (Westview Press 1986).

Main, Jackson T., *Society and Economy in Colonial Connecticut* (Princeton Univ. Press 1985).

Milne, George McLean, *Connecticut Woodlands: A Century's Story of the Connecticut Forest and Park Association* (Conn. Forest and Park Assn. 1995).

Patton, Peter C., and James M. Kent, *A Moveable Shore: The Fate of the Connecticut Coast* (Duke Univ. Press 1992).

Rose, Gary L., *Connecticut Politics at the Crossroads* (Univ. Press of Am. 1992).

Roth, David M., *Connecticut* (Norton 1979).

Steiner, Bernard C., *History of Slavery in Connecticut* (1893; reprint, AMS Press 1978).

THE CONNECTICUT RIVER, looking south from Gillette Castle State Park at East Haddam, Connecticut.

**CONNECTICUT, University of,** a state university and land-grant college in Storrs, Conn., with campuses at Groton, Hartford, Stamford, Torrington, Waterbury, and West Hartford. It was established in 1881 as the Storrs Agricultural School by the Connecticut General Assembly under a gift of $6,000 and 170 acres of land from Charles and Augustus Storrs of Mansfield, Conn. In 1893 the assembly assigned land-grant funds to the school and renamed it Storrs Agricultural College. Women students were admitted in the same year. The college subsequently became known as Connecticut Agricultural College (1899), Connecticut State College (1933), and the University of Connecticut (1939). The University of Connecticut awards baccalaureate and higher degrees in its colleges of liberal arts and sciences, agriculture and natural resources, allied health professions, business administration, education, engineering, fine arts, and nursing. Only higher degrees are offered in the University's colleges of family studies, pharmacy, law, social work, dental medicine, and medicine.

DONALD W. FRIEDMAN*
*University of Connecticut*

**CONNECTICUT LAKES,** a chain of small lakes in northern New Hampshire, near the border of Canada. They are named, from southwest to northeast, First, Second, and Third Connecticut lakes. A tiny pond, virtually on the Canadian border, sometimes is called Fourth Lake. This pond is the source of the Connecticut River. Lake Francis, southwest of First Lake, sometimes is listed as one of the Connecticut Lakes.

**CONNECTICUT RIVER,** a river of New England, springing from the Connecticut Lakes in northern New Hampshire, near the Canadian border, and flowing 407 miles (655 km) southward to Long Island Sound. It forms the boundary between New Hampshire and Vermont, crosses west central Massachusetts, and bisects Connecticut, emptying into the sound at Old Saybrook. Some 350 towns and 15 cities border the river. Two thirds of the entire watershed of 11,265 square miles (29,176 sq km) is forested, and almost one fourth open farmland. The Connecticut

has 23 principal tributaries, many rapids and falls, and lovely scenery. The lower 60 miles (97 km) is tidal, with a 15-foot (5-meter) channel from Hartford, Conn., to the sound.

**Economic Importance.** For more than two centuries the river was the main artery of trade and travel for Connecticut and western Massachusetts and as such was vital to the prosperity of the valley. Today it is used chiefly for hydroelectric power, industrial purposes, irrigation, navigation (below Hartford), and waste disposal. Commercial fishing is confined to shad.

The total population in the Connecticut Valley exceeds 1,750,000. Some 3,000 manufacturing plants account for most of its wealth, followed by farming and commercial recreation, which steadily increases in importance. Farm income is largely from dairy products (in New Hampshire and Vermont), poultry, and tobacco (shade-grown cigar wrapper). There are parts of two national forests (the White Mountain and the Green Mountain) and well over 100 state parks, forests, and reserves.

**Geology.** The river valley was laid down in alternating layers of sandstone and trap rock during the Triassic period and later fractured into block mountains during the Jurassic period. The upper course flows across complex metamorphic rocks overlaid by terraced deposits formed in lakes. In much of Massachusetts and Connecticut, the river has cut a wider swath in the softer shales and sandstones, and the sandy bottom soils, which are of glacial origin, provide excellent agricultural land. The lower basin has pre-Triassic crystalline rocks.

**History.** The Dutch explorer Adriaen Block discovered the river in 1614, but the valley's first white settlers were English colonists who came from Massachusetts to the vicinity of present Hartford, Conn., in the 1630's. On the river appeared some of the nation's first ferries and canals, first ships to engage in foreign trade, first war vessels, and first factories. Commerce on the Connecticut reached its peak between the American Revolution and the War of 1812.

**Flood and Pollution Control.** Major flooding of the Connecticut has occurred at least 20 times since the first settlement, but the floods of November 1927, March 1936, September 1938, and

August 1955 produced the highest waters and greatest destruction. Dams, especially on the upper reaches of the river, and floodplain zones have helped to control floods.

Generally polluted from the discharge of both industrial and municipal wastes, the river falls below acceptable water quality standards for recreation. It has been classified by the New England Interstate Water Pollution Control Commission to become suitable for swimming by 1982 at best. The four states which the Connecticut River drains have accelerated pollution abatement through state grants, supplemented by federal aid, for constructing or upgrading municipal treatment works.

ELLSWORTH S. GRANT
*Director, Connecticut River Watershed Council*

**CONNECTICUT YANKEE IN KING ARTHUR'S COURT,** a satirical novel by Mark Twain, published in 1889. The Connecticut Yankee, foreman of a Hartford arms factory, is struck unconscious in a quarrel and comes to in King Arthur's England of 528 A. D. He escapes being burned at the stake by "predicting," through his knowledge of the past, a solar eclipse, and his mechanical ability and ingenuity soon gain him authority. As "the Boss" he introduces steam and electricity to the 6th century and attempts to institute democracy, but he is opposed by the church and the magician Merlin, who finally thwarts the Yankee and puts him to sleep for 13 centuries. Through the Yankee's eyes, Mark Twain reveals Arthur's court as a foolish, superstitious oligarchy, opposing to it a sensible New England republicanism. *A Connecticut Yankee* served as the basis for a musical (1927) by Richard Rodgers and Lorenz Hart, as well as for three movies.

**CONNECTING ROD.** See AUTOMOBILE—5. *Modern Automobiles* (Engine).

**CONNECTIVE TISSUE,** the type of body tissue that is largely responsible for binding and supporting the body organs and other structures. Connective tissue is generally divided into three types: bone, cartilage, and connective tissue proper. This article deals only with connective tissue proper. See also BONE; CARTILAGE.

**Composition.** Connective tissue is made up chiefly of cells and fibers embedded in a substance called *matrix*. Matrix ranges from a fluid to a semisolid, or gel, and is composed mostly of polysaccharides. In addition to cells and fibers, matrix also contains many blood vessels and nerves. In some parts of the body it is also well supplied with lymph vessels.

**Cells.** There are two basic types of connective tissue cells: fibroblasts and histiocytes. *Fibroblasts* are concerned with the production of fibers, helping to form new tissue as well as to repair damaged tissue. *Histiocytes*, as part of the body's reticuloendothelial system, act as scavengers in the body. They are concerned with the phagocytosis (engulfment) of cellular debris, foreign bodies, and any blood that has seeped out of the blood vessels into the tissues.

**Fibers.** Of the three types of connective tissue fibers, the *collagenous*, or *white*, *fibers* are the most numerous. Each fiber consists of very delicate fibrils that are held together in bundles by a cementing substance. The fibers are made up of a protein substance called *collagen*.

DR. JEROME GROSS, THE DEVELOPMENT BIOLOGY LABORATORY, MASSACHUSETTS GENERAL HOSPITAL

COLLAGEN FIBRILS, which form the collagenous fibers of connective tissue, as seen in an electron micrograph. The fibrils shown here are from the skin of a calf.

*Elastic fibers* are made up of a substance called *elastin*, and as their name implies, they are highly elastic. *Reticular fibers*, like the elastic and collagenous fibers, divide into many branches but are much thinner than the other two types. Chemically, they are very similar to collagenous fibers and are often continuous with them.

**Types.** Connective tissue is often divided into five basic types based largely on the type and arrangement of the fibers and cells present.

*Loose Connective Tissue.* Loose connective tissue, sometimes called *areolar tissue*, contains all types of connective tissue cells and fibers. It is widely distributed beneath the skin and within and around body organs, supporting them and holding them in place. It also serves as a pathway for nerves and blood and lymph vessels and acts as a carrying medium for drugs and other substances injected under the skin. Loose connective tissue also plays an important role in controlling the spread of local infections. The histiocytes help destroy the invading agents, and the fibroblasts produce a barrier of fibers, contributing to the formation of scar tissue.

*Compact Connective Tissue.* Compact, or dense, connective tissue is characterized by a tight arrangement of its fibers. It forms tendons, ligaments, and fascia, the fibrous sheets that help subdivide the body into compartments containing muscles or organs. Compact connective tissue also forms the aponeuroses, the ribbonlike white structures at the ends of certain muscles.

In most compact connective tissue the chief fiber is the collagenous fiber. In some regions, as underneath the skin, the fibers are irregularly arranged. In tendons, ligaments, and aponeuroses, however, the fibers parallel each other. In some ligaments, elastic fibers are more numerous than collagen fibers. This is especially true for the ligaments between the vertebral arches of the spine, where the elasticity helps save muscular energy in maintaining erect posture.

*Reticular Connective Tissue.* This type of connective tissue is characterized by reticular fibers, and it forms the framework for the lymph tissue, the spleen, thymus, and lymph nodes. It also forms a framework for the bone marrow. A thinner type of reticular tissue is found directly underneath the epithelium of many organs, particularly under the mucous membranes of the respiratory and digestive systems.

*Adipose Connective Tissue.* Adipose, or fat, tissue is the only type of connective tissue in which the cells, not the matrix, form the bulk of the tissue. The cells, believed to be modified fibroblasts, contain large amounts of fat in their cytoplasm. Adipose tissue occurs throughout the body. It serves as a reservoir for fat and helps regulate body temperature by slowing down the loss of heat through the skin. It also acts as a bed for blood vessels and as a padding for the kidneys.

*Pigmented Connective Tissue.* This type of connective tissue occurs in the iris and the choroid, the middle layer of the wall of the eyeball. In dark-skinned peoples, it is also found in the dermis, the deep layer of the skin. Unlike other types of connective tissue, the cells are filled with granules of the pigment melanin.

OTHMAR SOLNITZKY, PH. D., M. D.
*Georgetown University School of Medicine*

**CONNELLY, Marc** (1890–1980), American playwright, director, and actor, who wrote *The Green Pastures,* one of the most successful plays in the history of the American theater. He was born Marcus Cook Connelly in McKeesport, Pa., on Dec. 13, 1890, the son of traveling actors who had settled in McKeesport to manage a hotel. After his father's death in 1902, young Connelly attended a boarding school in Washington, Pa., for five years, and then began working at various newspaper jobs in Pittsburgh. In 1917 he went to New York and became a theater news reporter for the *Morning Telegraph.* He soon met George S. Kaufman, then drama critic for *The New York Times,* and they collaborated on the hit comedy *Dulcy* (1921). Together they wrote a series of light comedies—*To the Ladies* (1922), *Merton of the Movies* (1922), and *Beggar on Horseback* (1924)—and the musicals *Helen of Troy, New York* (1923) and *Be Yourself* (1924).

Connelly assured his place in American drama by writing *The Green Pastures* (1930). Based on Roark Bradford's book of short stories *Ol' Man Adam an' His Chillun* (1928), *The Green Pastures* presents the biblical stories of the Flood and of Moses and Joshua in terms of Negro folk customs. The play had 640 performances in New York. It won the 1930 Pulitzer Prize.

Connelly's other works include a play, *The Wisdom Tooth* (1926); a novel, *A Souvenir From Qam* (1965); his memoirs, *Voices Offstage* (1968); and, with Frank B. Elser, a comedy, *The Farmer Takes a Wife* (1934). He produced and directed plays in New York and London, taught playwrighting at Yale, wrote for motion pictures, and acted in the theater, films, and television. He wrote short stories and humor for *The New Yorker* magazine, which he helped found, and was a member of the famous Algonquin Hotel Round Table group. He also served as president of the National Institute of Arts and Letters and the Authors League of America. He died in New York City on Dec. 21, 1980.

HOWARD SUBER*
*University of California, Los Angeles*

**CONNER, David** (1792–1856), American naval officer, who won a Congressional citation for service in the War of 1812 and commanded the Gulf Squadron during the early part of the Mexican War. Born in Harrisburg, Pa., he served from 1811 to 1817 in the sloop of war *Hornet* and was wounded in battle. He was highly regarded before the Mexican War, but his conduct of operations during the war was criticized as too cautious. He did maintain a blockade of Veracruz with a squadron that included the first steamers used by the Navy in war, and he established a floating base of coal and supply ships in a protected anchorage nearby. His major accomplishment was the landing of 10,000 men of Gen. Winfield Scott's army in 5 hours, in an amphibious operation that compared favorably with those of World War II. Relieved in March 1847 for reasons of health, he died in Philadelphia on March 20, 1856.

JOHN D. HAYES, *Rear Admiral, USN (Retired)*

**CONNERSVILLE,** a city in eastern Indiana, the seat of Fayette county. It is situated on the Whitewater River, 55 miles (88 km) east of Indianapolis. Connersville has factories producing automobile parts, machine tools, dies, castings, dishwashers, refrigerators, blowers, air conditioners, and caskets. The Fayette County Free Fair is held in the city annually.

Connersville was founded in 1813 and laid out in 1817. It has the mayor council form of government. Population: 15,411.

**CONNOLLY, Cyril Vernon** (1903–1974), English writer and journalist, who is best known as the author of *The Unquiet Grave* (1944), an eloquent diary-anthology of maxims, *pensées,* and essays. Connolly was born in Coventry, on Sept. 10, 1903, and was educated at Eton College and Oxford University. In 1927 he took up literary journalism, contributing essays to the *New Statesman* and other periodicals. In the 1930's he published two books: a novel, *The Rock Pool* (1935), and a critical and autobiographical work, *Enemies of Promise* (1938).

In 1939, Connolly founded the English literary monthly *Horizon,* which he edited until it ceased publication in 1950. During this period he published *The Unquiet Grave* and *The Condemned Playground* (1945), the latter a brilliant collection of essays, sketches, and parodies. *The Modern Movement* (1965) lists 100 "key" books in recent literature. Connolly's perceptive, melancholy, inconoclastic works reflect the spirit of his time. He died in London, Nov. 26, 1974.

**CONNOLLY, James** (1870–1916), Irish patriot, who was the first active socialist in Irish history and one of the seven leaders in the Easter Rising of 1916. Born in County Monaghan, he grew up in Edinburgh, Scotland, in extreme poverty. A self-educated Marxist, Connolly worked for socialist causes in Dublin (1896–1903) and New York (1903–1910). He later helped organize unskilled labor in the Irish Transport and General Workers Union. After the Dublin general strike failed in 1913, Connolly founded the Citizen Army and commanded it when it joined the Irish Volunteers in the 1916 Easter Rebellion. For his part in the abortive rising, he was shot by the British in Kilmainham Jail, Dublin, on May 12, 1916.

GIOVANNI COSTIGAN, *University of Washington*

**CONNOLLY,** kon′ə-lē, **Maureen** (1934–1969), American tennis star, who won the U.S. women's singles title three times in the early 1950's. Her victories also included three British, one Australian, and two French championships.

Maureen Connolly was born in San Diego, Calif., on Sept. 17, 1934. Nicknamed "Little Mo," she became a sensation in tennis at the age of 16 by defeating Shirley Fry at Forest Hills for the U.S. singles championship in 1951. A diminutive blonde, she was a killer on the court, hammering her opponents into submission with the power and length of her drives. She won the U.S. singles title again in 1952 and 1953, the Wimbledon (British) crown for three consecutive years in 1952–1954, and the French title in 1953 and 1954. In 1953 she made a "grand slam," taking the Australian, British, French, and U.S. titles. A member of the winning U.S. Wightman Cup team from 1951 through 1954, Little Mo won every match she played. She was named Woman Athlete of the Year (all sports) in a poll of Associated Press sportswriters for the years 1952, 1953, and 1954. A horseback riding accident in 1954 crushed her leg and brought her tournament career to an end. She died in Dallas, Texas, on June 21, 1969.

ALLISON DANZIG, *"New York Times"*

**CONNOR,** kon′ər, **Patrick Edward** (1820–1891), American general, pioneer, and anti-Mormon political leader in Utah. He was born in County Kerry, Ireland, on March 17, 1820, and was brought to New York City as a child. He enlisted in the army to fight the Seminoles and enlisted again in the Mexican War, during which he fought at Palo Alto, Resaca de la Palma, and Buena Vista. He then resigned as a captain to work at mining and business in California.

In 1861, Connor raised a regiment of volunteers in California and, as an army colonel, was given command of the Utah military district. He took California infantrymen and cavalrymen to control hostile Mormons, which he did with tact and firmness; and to kill Indian raiders, which he did with ferocity. Mustered out as a brevet major general in 1866, Connor started Utah's first daily newspaper, built the first steamboat on Great Salt Lake, gave great impetus to mining in Utah, and led the strong anti-Mormon Liberal party. He died in Salt Lake City on Dec. 17, 1891.

THOMAS D. CLARK, *University of Kentucky*
*Author of "Frontier America"*

**CONNORS,** kon′ərz, **Jimmy** (1952–    ), American tennis player, who won five U.S. Open singles titles and was first or in the top five in rank as well as career earnings. A sturdy 5′10″, 150-pound left-hander, he was noted for his aggressive return of service, powerful forehand and two-handed backhand, and dogged determination. At times his good humor was blunted by outbursts of temper.

James Scott Connors was born in East St. Louis, Ill., on Sept. 2, 1952. He was taught to play by his mother and at 16 moved to Los Angeles to be coached by Pancho Gonzalez. As a UCLA freshman he won the NCAA singles title in 1970. Turning professional, he won 75 matches in 1972.

In 1974, Connors laid claim to No. 1 ranking with victories at the Australian Open, Wimbledon, and the U.S. Open, winning 99 of 103 matches in that year. He again won the U.S. Open in 1976, 1978, and 1982 and Wimbledon in 1982. After upset losses in the French Open and at Wimbledon early in 1983, he came back to win a fifth U.S. Open title later that year.

JOHN FORBES, *"New York Times"*

**CONON,** kō′non (died 687), pope from 686 to 687. The son of an army officer in a Thracian detachment, Conon was educated in Sicily and ordained a priest in Rome. After the death of John V in 686, the Roman clergy and militia could not agree on a successor. The clergy, realizing they could not elect Archpriest Peter, offered the aged Conon as a compromise candidate.

His short reign was clouded by prolonged illness and court intrigue. Archdeacon Paschal took advantage of Conon's frailty to bribe the army to support his own succession. Despite the objection of his advisers, Conon appointed Deacon Constantine bailiff of the papal estates in Sicily. The choice proved unwise; Constantine was soon jailed for misconduct. Emperor Justinian II remained friendly and remitted taxes on certain papal lands, returning many serfs to the Holy See. Conon died in Rome on Sept. 21, 687, and was buried in the Basilica of St. Peter's.

THOMAS A. BRESLIN, S.J.
*Loyola Seminary, Shrub Oak, N.Y.*

**CONQUEST, Right of,** in international law, the acquisition of enemy territory by a victorious state in a war. Conquest generally is followed by formal annexation of the territory. Under international law as understood in the 19th century, sovereign states were free to make war for "reason of state" and consequently had the right to annex conquered territory. Title could not, however, be claimed until conquest was complete—that is, until the defeated state surrendered or lost all capability to resist further.

Some international lawyers held that even after conquest was complete, title did not pass to the victor until the defeated state had ceded it by treaty or other states had generally recognized the change. During the War of 1812 neither the United States nor Britain had achieved victory, although the British occupied some U.S. territory. At the peace negotiations in Ghent, Belgium, in 1814, the British argued that the principle *uti possidetis*, or "squatter's right," must be presumed, while the United States argued that the principle *status quo ante bellum* (condition that existed before the war) would apply except insofar as the peace treaty transferred territory. The U.S. opinion prevailed, and the boundaries remained as before the war, with provisions for arbitration to determine their exact location.

The United States held that territory conquered in the war with Mexico (1846) and the Spanish-American War (1898) was acquired only by virtue of the peace treaties. The Permanent Court of International Justice held the same in regard to German territory conquered by Poland in World War I. Britain, however, declared the annexation of the Boer republics in Africa in 1900 even before their conquest was complete.

**20th Century.** The Inter-American Conference in Washington, D.C., in 1890 passed a resolution declaring that the right of conquest did not exist in American international law. The principle of the right of conquest has been rejected by all states as a consequence of the outlawing of aggressive war by the League of Nations Covenant

(1920), the Kellogg-Briand Pact (1928), and the United Nations Charter (1945).

When Japan occupied Manchuria in 1932, the United States declared that it would not recognize changes of territory effected in violation of the Kellogg-Briand Pact. The same principle was asserted soon after by the assembly of the League of Nations. The United States also refused to recognize the Italian conquest of Ethiopia (1935) and Hitler's conquests in Europe during World War II. The Atlantic Charter, signed by U. S. President Franklin D. Roosevelt and British Prime Minister Winston Churchill on Aug. 14, 1941, declared that "their countries seek no aggrandizement, territorial or other" and "they desire to see no territorial changes that do not accord with the freely expressed wishes of the peoples concerned."

The principle of "no fruits of aggression" does not deny the right of the international community as a whole to recognize territorial changes even if initially effected by aggression. The community of nations, acting collectively in the United Nations or in special conferences, may recognize de facto situations even if established by force, if deemed in the best interests of the world community.

QUINCY WRIGHT, *Professor Emeritus of International Law, University of Chicago*

**CONQUEST OF MEXICO, History of the,** the classic English-language account, by William Hickling Prescott, of the initial conquest of the high-culture American Indians of Mexico by the Spaniards. Against the backdrop of Aztec civilization, detailed as fully as knowledge then permitted, Prescott recounted the dramatic campaigns initiated by Hernán Cortés in 1519. Although he depicted two cultures in conflict, Prescott's focus was primarily biographical, featuring Cortés the victor—along with captains Alvarado, Sandoval, and Olid—and the vanquished Montezuma and Cuauhtemoc. Prescott, sensing the epic scope of this theme, structured his account accordingly, while employing the best historical sources. The resultant book, an epic in prose, consciously and successfully combined historical accuracy with literary artistry.

Published initially in 1843 in three volumes in both the United States and Britain, it remains the best and most readable general account of the Mexican conquest. Structurally the finest of Prescott's books, it also is the most popular, having been issued more than 200 times. It has been translated into many European languages. In English it has been continuously available since it first appeared, helping to enshrine Prescott as both historian and man of letters.

C. HARVEY GARDINER
*Author of "Prescott and His Publishers"*

**CONQUEST OF PERU, History of the,** companion piece to *History of the Conquest of Mexico,* by William Hickling Prescott. It is the most widely acclaimed English-language account of the Spanish conquest of the Incas, highlighting the dramatic campaigns led by Francisco Pizarro. A biographical treatment of culture conflict, it focuses on less admirable characters and displays less thematic unity than does the work on Mexico. Strife among the Spaniards themselves further upsets the story line and epic proportions preferred by the author. The book is nevertheless elegantly written, reliable history.

The *History of the Conquest of Peru* was first published in 1847 in two volumes in both the United States and Britain. Third and last of the major histories completed by Prescott (the first was *The History of the Reign of Ferdinand and Isabella the Catholic,* 1837), it was written at the height of his physical and intellectual powers. It has been issued more than 160 times and translated into Danish, Dutch, French, German, Italian, Japanese, Portuguese, Russian, Spanish, and Swedish.

C. HARVEY GARDINER
*Author of "Prescott and His Publishers"*

**CONQUISTADORS,** kon-kwis′tə-dôrz, the Spaniards and Portuguese who went to the New World after Columbus and within about 50 years explored, overran, and settled large areas of the Americas. The name comes from the Spanish word for "conquerors." The story of the conquistadors is thrilling, awe-inspiring, frightening, and at times much too human.

**Their Character.** The conquistadors were rough and rugged adventurers who left a record of fantastic deeds of daring, showed an ability to undergo almost unbelievable hardships, and at times were guilty of many cruelties and injustices toward the Indians whom they met and subdued. They were a curious combination of saint and devil.

The majority were men of common stock or cadets of noble families. All were among the less favored at home; all sought to win fame and fortune in the empires overseas. They came of men who had battled the Muslim invaders for centuries—they were fighters by tradition, hard and harsh. During the Middle Ages their forefathers, in the process of fighting for homeland and religion against infidels, had become belligerent and uncompromising Christian warriors. The conquistadors brought the Crusader mentality to the Americas, and the Indians were often the victims of this dedication. Gold, glory, and Gospel were the three G's that sparked the invaders.

**Individual Accomplishments.** Vasco Núñez de Balboa ranged the Isthmus of Panama and heard of a rich empire to the south, along the shores of the Pacific Ocean, which he discovered. But he fell victim to the jealousy of Governor Pedrarias before he had a chance to go on to the Incas of Peru. Hernán Cortés was the next great conquistador; he won the empire of the Aztecs for Spain and then sent his lieutenants far and wide in search of other rich kingdoms. One of them, the impetuous Pedro de Alvarado, brought what is now Guatemala and El Salvador under Spanish rule.

Álvar Núñez Cabeza de Vaca, after ranging through what is now Texas and the Southwest, went to Mexico with reports of rich cities in the north. Soon Francisco Vásquez de Coronado went north to find the fabled wealth of Cíbola and Quivira, and Hernando de Soto spent the fortune he had won in Peru in a futile search for riches in the southeastern United States. He discovered the Mississippi River, but it brought him nothing more than a watery grave.

In South America, Francisco Pizarro and his brothers won the race to the kingdom of the Incas. They were a ruthless, rapacious, contentious lot. From Peru, Pedro de Valdivia went down to Chile and in the face of fierce opposition from the Araucanians gained another province for Spain. In the northwest, Gonzalo Jiménez de Quesada sought El Dorado (The Gilded Man) among the Chibchas of Colombia. German agents of the commercial and banking house of Welser used Venezuela as their base for a similar quest and, in the process, proved that greed and cruelty were not exclusively the traits of some Spaniards.

In the south, conquistadors first sought to reach Peru from the Atlantic side. When word came that the race had been won by the Pizarros, they laid the basis for settlement on the pampa and in the forests of Paraguay. These men included Pedro de Mendoza, Juan de Ayolas, and Domingo Martínez de Irala. Martim Affonso de Sousa and the even greater Thomé de Sousa, with his Jesuit helpers, enforced Portugal's paper claims to Brazil by occupation.

JOHN FRANCIS BANNON, S. J.
*Saint Louis University*

**CONRAD I** (died 918), known as *Conrad the Salian,* was the first king of Germany not descended from the Carolingian house (the dynasty founded by Charlemagne). Conrad (German, Konrad) was the son of Conrad of Lahngau, Duke of Franconia, and of Glismut, the daughter of Arnulf, the last Carolingian emperor.

On November 10, 911, Conrad was elected king by the German princes at Forchheim. However, he was so weak politically that his rule was never effective over the German duchies of Lorraine, Saxony, Bavaria, and Swabia. When near death, Conrad designated his adversary Henry, Duke of Saxony, as his successor. Conrad died on December 23, 918.

BRYCE LYON
*Brown University*

**CONRAD II** (990?–1039), king of Germany and emperor of the Holy Roman Empire, who founded the Salian dynasty. Conrad (German, Konrad) was the son of Count Henry of Speyer. He was elected king of Germany on Sept. 8, 1024, and was crowned emperor of the Holy Roman Empire on March 26, 1027. According to the chroniclers it was due to Conrad's energetic character and military ability that the German princes elected him to succeed Henry II, the last king from the Saxon house. Conrad followed the policy of Otto the Great (Emperor Otto I) in using the church as a support against the great secular princes. He also employed ecclesiastics as councillors and administrators and worked to gain support from the petty nobles.

In general, the reign of Conrad was successful. Within Germany he maintained peace and zealously protected the rights of his subjects against the nobles. Despite revolts of the dukes, Conrad was able to maintain his authority. For almost five years he campaigned against the Poles who threatened the eastern border of Germany. By 1032 he had forced them beyond the Oder River. In 1034, Conrad acquired the kingdom of Burgundy and in 1035 assumed the crown of Bohemia. In Italy where his imperial authority had first been recognized, Conrad later had to put down revolts. Conrad died at Utrecht, in the Low Countries, on June 4, 1039. More successful than many of his predecessors and successors, Conrad is remembered because he consolidated imperial authority in Germany and prepared the way for the establishment of hereditary monarchy.

BRYCE LYON
*Brown University*

**CONRAD III** (1093–1152), king of Germany, who founded the Hohenstaufen dynasty. Conrad (German, Konrad) was the son of Duke Frederick of Swabia and of Agnes, the daughter of Emperor Henry IV. In 1127, embittered by the election of his opponent Lothair of Saxony as king of Germany, Conrad revolted and had himself elected as antiking, and in 1128 he was crowned king of Italy. He continued his struggle against Lothair until peace was concluded in 1135. Their fight initiated the bitter conflict between Guelph and Ghibelline that paralyzed Italy and Germany until the 14th century. Lothair represented the Guelph interests and Conrad the Ghibelline.

Conrad was elected king of Germany in 1138, after which Henry the Proud, Duke of Saxony and Bavaria, and son-in-law of Lothair, became leader of the Guelphs. During the war that ensued, Henry died and was succeeded by his son, Henry the Lion, who made peace with Conrad in 1142.

Conrad joined the unsuccessful Second Crusade (1147–1149) to Asia Minor. When he returned to Germany in 1149, he had to deal with another Guelph uprising. Shortly before his death, Conrad passed over his son Frederick because of his extreme youth and designated Duke Frederick of Swabia, later known as Frederick I Barbarossa, as his successor. Conrad died at Bamberg, in Bavaria, on Feb. 15, 1152.

BRYCE LYON, *Brown University*

**CONRAD IV** (1228–1254), became Duke of Swabia in 1235, king of Germany in 1237, and king of Sicily in 1251. Conrad (German, Konrad) was born at Andria, in Apulia, Italy, on April 26, 1228. He was the son of Frederick II of Hohenstaufen, Emperor of the Holy Roman Empire, and Isabella of Brienne. Although only nine years old when elected king of Germany, Conrad was given the responsibility for rule over Germany by his father, Emperor Frederick II, because Conrad's half brother Henry VII had revolted and been deposed.

The quarrels of Frederick II with the papacy had weakened Hohenstaufen authority both in Germany and in the Kingdom of Sicily. When, in 1245, Pope Innocent IV declared both Conrad and Frederick deposed, revolt in Germany broke out. In 1246, Conrad was defeated by his opponent Henry Raspe. By 1251 his position was so weak that he went to Sicily to assume its crown, vacant since his father's death in 1250. He died at Làvello, Italy, on May 21, 1254.

BRYCE LYON, *Brown University*

**CONRAD, Barnaby, Jr.** (1922–   ), American writer, artist, and bullfight aficionado. He was born in San Francisco on March 27, 1922. He graduated from Yale University in 1944 and served until 1946 as a vice-consul in Spain, where he studied bullfighting with Juan Belmonte. In 1946 he fought bulls as an amateur in Spain, Mexico, and Peru. He then served for a year as secretary to novelist Sinclair Lewis before beginning his career as a writer in 1948.

Most of Conrad's books concern bullfighting. The best is *Matador* (1952), one of the finest books on the subject in English, which is based on the life of Manolete; this work, which strikingly conveys the atmosphere of the *corrida,* sold nearly three million copies. In 1957, Conrad made a documentary film, *The Day Manolete Was Killed,* which was praised for its technique.

**Joseph Conrad**

**CONRAD, Joseph** (1857–1924), English author, who was one of the great novelists and stylists of modern English literature. Although English was the Polish-born Conrad's adopted language, he used it with a power and mastery that have rarely been surpassed. A sea captain as well as a writer, he is perhaps best known for his works that are closely associated with the sea, including the novels *The Nigger of the "Narcissus"* (1897) and *Lord Jim* (1900) and the short story *The Secret Sharer* (1912).

Conrad, however, was more than a spinner of adventurous sea yarns. He was a student of the human spirit, constantly exploring its complexities, its conflicts, and its essential loneliness and alienation. Whether his setting was the sea or an exotic and remote country, he concerned himself primarily with man's character. He probed beneath the outer layers of men's actions and laid bare the painful struggle of the individual to reconcile himself with his own nature, with his fellow-men, and with his surroundings.

**Life.** Conrad was born on Dec. 3, 1857, near Berdichev, in the Ukraine, in a region that had once been a part of Poland but was then under Russian rule. His original name was Józef Teodor Konrad Nalecz Korzeniowski. Both his parents came from families that belonged to the educated, "land-tilling" Polish gentry and to a long line of zealous Polish patriots. Conrad's father, Apollo Korzeniowski, was a talented poet and translator of French and English literature. Violently opposed to Russian rule, he belonged to the revolutionary Polish National Central Committee. In 1862 he was exiled to Vologda in northern Russia, and his wife and young son went with him. The hardships of exile were too much for Conrad's parents, who died within a few years of each other.

In 1869 the 12-year-old orphan was placed under the guardianship of his maternal uncle Thaddeus Bobrowski in Kraków, Poland. Lonely and unhappy, Conrad read a great deal. He was especially attracted to the rousing adventure stories of Frederick Marryat and the novels of Charles Dickens. Victor Hugo's *Les travailleurs de la mer* may have inspired in the boy his early yearning for the sea. Conrad attended schools in Kraków and also studied under a tutor, Adam Pulman, with whom he made his first trip abroad.

At the age of 16, Conrad finally persuaded his uncle to let him go to sea. He went to Marseille, where he became an apprentice in the French merchant marine and made three voyages to the West Indies between 1875 and 1878. While in Marseille he also mingled in circles that supported Don Carlos de Bourbon as claimant to the Spanish throne. He became part owner of a small vessel, the *Tremolino,* which may have engaged in smuggling arms for Don Carlos.

Impetuous and rash, Conrad had romantic involvements and monetary difficulties. In 1878 his various adventures ended in disaster when he was wounded (in a duel of honor, according to Conrad's version in *The Arrow of Gold* [1919]; in a foolhardy attempt at suicide, according to statements left by his uncle). Conrad then found a berth on an English freighter, the *Mavis,* which was plying the Mediterranean. He landed in England for the first time on June 18 of that year, knowing little of the language but determined to make a career in the English merchant service.

Conrad rose quickly through the ranks from common seaman to first mate. By 1886 he was master of his own ship, and in the same year he also became a British subject and changed his name to Joseph Conrad. He sailed to many parts of the world, including Australia, various ports on the Indian Ocean, Borneo, the Malay states, South America, and the South Pacific islands. During this period he began to write.

In 1890, Conrad went to Africa in the Belgian colonial service and sailed up the Congo River, where fever and dysentery severely undermined his health. In 1894, he reluctantly gave up the sea, partly because of poor health and partly because he had become so fascinated with writing that he decided on a literary career.

In 1896, Conrad married Jessie George, an Englishwoman, by whom he had two sons. Except for several vacation trips to France and Italy, a return journey to Poland in 1914, and a visit to the United States in 1923, he lived thereafter in England.

A highly emotional man, subject to fits of depression, self-doubt, and pessimism, Conrad worked with a feverish intensity, producing a steady flow of books. Although the English intellectual elite recognized his talent, popular success eluded him until 1913, with the publication of *Chance.* This book was well received by both critics and general readers in England and the United States and brought him financial security. For the remaining years of his life, Conrad was the subject of more praise and discussion than any other contemporary writer in the English language. He died at Oswalds, Bishopsbourne, Kent, on Aug. 3, 1924.

**Writings.** Conrad published his first novel, *Almayer's Folly* (1895), when he was 37 years old. This tale of a derelict Dutchman, trading on the jungle rivers of Borneo, was written between 1889 and 1894 during Conrad's spare time on his voyages. The originality and power of the book was praised by such eminent literary figures as Henry James, H. G. Wells, George Gissing, Arthur Symons, and Ford Madox Ford. (Ford collaborated with Conrad on two novels, *The Inheritors*, published in 1901, and *Romance*, which appeared in 1903.)

Other books followed, including *An Outcast of the Islands* (1896); *The Nigger of the "Narcissus"* (1897); *Tales of Unrest* (1898); *Lord Jim* (1900); *Youth* (1902), which included the stories *Heart of Darkness* and *The End of the Tether; Typhoon* (with other stories, 1902); and *Nostromo* (1904). All of these were tales of the sea and of distant countries in Asia, Africa, and South America. But they were more than just adventure stories; they were also compelling narratives that searched with increasing depth and insight into the souls and consciences of their characters, into the conflict of alien cultures, and into the spirit of modern man tested by moral solitude and estrangement, secret guilt, and fear.

In *The Mirror of the Sea* (1906), Conrad wrote a recollection of his experiences at sea. Another memoir of his personal life, *Some Reminiscences* (later called *A Personal Record*) followed in 1912. In *The Secret Agent* (1907), *A Set of Six* (a collection of tales, 1908), *Under Western Eyes* (1911), and *Chance* (1913) he explored social and political themes.

In *Victory* (1915) and *The Shadow-Line* (1917), Conrad depicted in vivid detail the torments endured by alienated souls incapable of love, friendship, and trust. *The Arrow of Gold* (1919) was a novel based on his youthful adventures in Marseille. In *The Rescue* (1920) he returned to the exotic Malay background of his first books, and in his last completed novel, *The Rover* (1923), he wrote a dramatic tale set during the French Revolution. The nonfictional *Last Essays* was published posthumously in 1926.

**Artistry.** Conrad's power as an artist stems both from the experience and vision he brought to his work and from his brilliant use of a language that was not his native tongue. His genius lies partly in his penetrating sense of the human ordeal and in his infusion of physical and romantic experience with psychological insight. He rigorously disciplined his admittedly romantic temperament with an unsparing moral judgment.

Conrad's artistry also lies in an exceptional style and craftsmanship. This style, growing out of an early impressionistic opulence, became steadily firmer, sparer, more specific, and more accurate. He achieved a unique mastery of his craft, combining plot and action, psychic indirection, ingenious manipulation of time sequences, and an intricate use of narrators to produce a powerful and highly dramatic effect. His finest works, containing characterizations that are among the most memorable in modern fiction, are creations of both psychological and poetic strength.

MORTON DAUWEN ZABEL
*Editor of "The Portable Conrad"*

### Bibliography

Conrad, Jessie, *Joseph Conrad and His Circle*, 2d ed. (1935; reprint, Century Bookbindery 1985).
Conrad, John, *Joseph Conrad: Times Remembered* (Cambridge 1981).
Hamner, Robert D., ed., *Joseph Conrad: Third World Perspectives* (Three Continents Press 1988).
Gurko, Leo, *Joseph Conrad: Giant in Exile* (1962; reprint, Century Bookbindery 1985).
Jean-Aubry, Gerard, *The Sea-Dreamer*, tr. by Helen Sebba (1957; reprint, Century Bookbindery 1985).
Ressler, Steve, *Joseph Conrad* (N.Y. Univ. Press 1988).
Sherry, Norman, *Conrad*, (Thames & Hudson 1988).
Wilson, Robert B., *Conrad's Mythology* (Whitston 1988).
Winner, Anthony, *Culture and Irony: Studies in Joseph Conrad's Major Novels* (Univ. Press of Va. 1988).

**CONRAD VON HÖTZENDORF,** kôn′rät fôn hŏŏt′-sən-dôrf, **Count** (1852–1925), Austro-Hungarian military commander, who headed his country's forces at the start of World War I. Franz Conrad von Hötzendorf was born at Penzing (now in Vienna), on Nov. 11, 1852. He became the empire's leading soldier and a force in imperial politics, advocating aggressive expansion and preemptive war against Serbia and Italy. Appointed chief of staff in 1906, Conrad modernized the army's organization, training, and weapons, particularly artillery. Early in World War I his campaigns against the Russians in Galicia were bold, skillful, and successful. Despite his brilliance as a strategist and commander, he was dismissed as chief of staff by the new emperor, Charles I, in 1916. In command of an army group on the Italian front, he contributed substantially to the victory at Caporetto. He died at Mergentheim, Germany, on Aug. 26, 1925.

MARTIN BLUMENSON
*Office of Military History, U. S. Army*

**CONRADIN,** kōn′rä-dēn, (1252–1268), Duke of Swabia, was the last of the Hohenstaufen dynasty. Born on March 25, 1252, at Wolfstein in Bavaria, Conradin (Conrad the Younger) was the son of Conrad IV, king of Germany and Sicily. Upon the death of his father in 1254, Conradin was in line to inherit the kingdom of Sicily. But even before Conrad IV's death, Manfred, a natural son of Frederick II (Conrad IV's father), had laid claim to Sicily. Manfred had himself crowned king in 1258, and Conradin was forced to return to Swabia.

After Manfred had been defeated and killed at the Battle of Benevento in 1266 by Charles d'Anjou, the Ghibelline party of Sicily and Italy requested Conradin to drive out Charles and assume the crown. Late in 1267 Conradin entered Italy and was received by the cities of Pavia, Siena, and Pisa; he occupied Rome in the summer of 1268. But in August 1268, in a closely fought battle at Tagliacozzo, Conradin was defeated by Charles d'Anjou and was forced to withdraw to Rome. However, Rome had been seized by the Guelph party in his absence and he was forced to flee Italy. He was captured at Astura and handed over to Charles D'Anjou. He was executed in Naples on Oct. 29, 1268.

BRYCE LYON, *Brown University*

**CONRAIL,** a railroad providing freight service to the Northeast and Midwest of the United States. The U.S. government sold its 85% share in the railroad in a public offering on March 26, 1987. The remaining 15% of shares were held by Conrail's current and former employees.

In 1973 the Regional Rail Reorganization Act created the United States Railway Association, to operate the Consolidated Rail Corporation (Conrail). The government acted after a number of rail lines in the region declined into bankruptcy. Conrail, a combination of six insolvent carriers, began operations on April 1, 1976.

Within the next five years, the government invested $3.3 billion. The line still lost $1.3 billion. The Northeast Rail Service Act (1981) permitted Conrail to end all commuter service, a small part of its business. Exclusively a freight carrier thereafter, Conrail began to show profits. However, as part of its privatization program, the Reagan administration called for the return of the line to private control.

**CONSALVI,** kŏn-säl′vē, **Ercole** (1757–1824), Italian cardinal and statesman. He was born in Rome on June 8, 1757. In 1783 he began his lifelong career in the papal service. Consalvi was appointed military assessor in 1796 in an attempt to prevent trouble with France. The murder of the French general Duphot in 1797 ruined his efforts and resulted in the French imprisoning him briefly in 1798.

Consalvi was instrumental in securing the election for Pius VII (1800), who made him cardinal-deacon and secretary of state. He negotiated the Concordat with Napoleon in 1801, but lost favor with him for hs firm defense of the church's rights and his refusal to attend the emperor's marriage to Marie Louise. Under pressure from Napoleon he resigned his post in 1806, though he resumed office after Napoleon's fall in 1814. He attended the Congress of Vienna and recovered almost all of the Papal States. Consalvi's attempts to update the papal government were opposed by the reactionary "Zelanti" cardinals. However, he had the support of Pius VII and succeeded in cementing papal relations with the new political order in Europe. Consalvi died in Rome on Jan. 24, 1824.

JOSEPH P. PARKES, S.J., *Fordham University*

**CONSANGUINITY,** kon-sang-gwin′ə-tē, in law, is a relationship by blood, as differentiated from *affinity,* which is the connection existing by reason of marriage between each of the married persons and the relatives of the other. The strict definition of consanguinity is the connection or relation of persons descended from the same stock or a common ancestor; persons so related to each other are described as *kindred.* Consanguinity is *lineal* if the relationship is in a direct line, as with father and son. It is *collateral* if persons are descended from a common forebear, as with brother and sister or cousins.

Consanguinity is significant in the law relating to the descent and distribution of the property of persons who die without leaving a will. It is also important in determining whether two persons are so closely related that marriage between them is prohibited by law. Similarly, the degree of consanguinity between two persons may determine whether sexual intercourse between them constitutes incest. Within certain degrees, consanguinity may disqualify persons from serving as judges or jurors in cases involving their relatives.

RICHARD L. HIRSHBERG*, *Attorney at Law*

**CONSCIENCE,** kon-syän′sə, **Hendrik** (1812–1883), Flemish author, who was the father of Flemish romanticism. He has been called "the Belgian Sir Walter Scott." He was born in Antwerp on Dec. 3, 1812. He began his career as a teacher, served in the army (1830–1836), and for the rest of his life held professorial and minor civil posts. Conscience's first book, *In′t wonderjaer 1566* (1837; *In the Year of Marvels 1566*), was the first modern novel in Flemish and was largely responsible for reviving Flemish as a literary language. It was followed by *De leeuw van Vlaanderen* (1838; Eng. tr., *The Lion of Flanders,* 1867), his most popular novel, based on the Flemish revolt against France in 1302. His more than 100 books include short stories, historical romances, and a series of charming and idealistic moralized tales of rustic Flemish life. Conscience died in Brussels on Sept. 10, 1883.

**CONSCIENCE,** kon′shəns. In traditional theology, conscience is an innate or divinely implanted faculty enabling the individual to make correct judgments about moral issues. In psychoanalysis, the *superego,* though acquired rather than innate, is conceived as functioning in substantially the same manner as the conscience.

The psychoanalytic view of superego formation is as follows: The young child is subject to many frustrations, which contribute to hostile feelings toward his parents. Because of fear of physical retaliation or abandonment by the parent, the child holds back his hostility and makes an active effort to adopt the parents' prohibitions as his own. The child also adopts the capacity to punish himself when he violates a prohibition or is tempted to do so. In this way, the hostility originally directed toward the parents is turned inward. This self-punishment is experienced as guilt feelings, which are dreaded because of their vaguely felt resemblance to earlier fears of punishment. The child avoids guilt by acting in accord with parental prohibitions.

This view has stimulated much research on the effect of child-rearing practices on such aspects of moral development as resisting temptation and behaving in accordance with one's standards even when an enforcing authority is not present, and experiencing guilt after violating standards. Though researchers disagree on details, most accept the basic psychoanalytic premise that the young child uses his parents as models. Thus codes of conduct such as moral standards and values, which were originally externally enforced, become part of the child's own set of standards. The research findings, though inconclusive, suggest that a moral orientation based on fear of detection and punishment is associated with frequent use of disciplinary techniques involving physical punishment and material deprivation, or the threat of these. A moral orientation characterized by an independent attitude toward external sanctions and high guilt following transgressions, on the other hand, is associated with frequent use of methods that are less arbitrary and punitive, and that point up the consequences of the child's behavior for others. This sort of moral orientation is also associated with a generally affectionate attitude on the part of parents. Withdrawal of love as a technique of discipline seems to have little effect except possibly to foster inhibition of hostile impulses.

A second major stream of research, stimulated by earlier theories of the Swiss psychologist Jean Piaget, focuses on the bases for making moral judgments and orienting oneself to society's rules. Current research suggests three stages of development: (1) a premoral level, in which the child obeys rules to avoid punishment or obtain rewards; (2) a conventional morality, in which he conforms to avoid disapproval by others; and (3) a morality of self-accepted moral principles, in which the child conforms primarily to avoid self-condemnation. Each stage is seen as a prerequisite for the next. Individuals and societies vary in how far and how rapidly they advance through these stages. While there is no evidence for the determinants of such advance, the theory is that the major influence is not parental practices but the individual's interactions with others. With increasing interaction the individual becomes able to understand others' viewpoints and the basis for society's rules of conduct.

MARTIN L. HOFFMAN, *University of Michigan*

**CONSCIENTIOUS OBJECTOR,** in general terms, means a person who, on the grounds of principle, is unable to yield to a command of the state. The term has been used most often to denote one who refuses to participate in armed conflict, and thus has been closely associated with pacifism. But persons have also refused on grounds of conscience to be vaccinated, to pay taxes, to go to public schools, and to participate in various forms of compulsory service to the state.

**Early History.** Conscientious objection to war was expressed as long ago as the 6th century B. C. in the teachings of the Chinese philosopher Lao-tse. There is some religious basis for Jewish pacifism in the Old Testament, particularly in Isaiah, but there is no consistent tradition of pacifism in Judaism. The New Testament, most notably the Sermon on the Mount, was the source of early Christian antiwar theology, which remained prevalent until the union of church and state effected by the conversion of Constantine in the 4th century. Pacifism then gave way to the doctrine of the "just war." As developed by Augustine and elaborated centuries later by Thomas Aquinas, this doctrine was more suited to the new secular activities of Christianity and, it provided the theological basis for those who did not condemn all war, as pacifists do, but opposed participation in a particular war.

Pacifism, and with it, widespread conscientious objection, declined during the Middle Ages with the growing secular influence of the church and the predominance of the "just war" doctrine. Only a few heretical sects, including the Albigenses, the Waldenses, and the Lollards, upheld the early Christian teachings, often at the price of persecution. Other sects—the Moravians in eastern Europe, the Doukhobors and Molokans in Russia, the Dunkers in Germany, and the Anabaptists in Switzerland—maintained that tradition through and following the Protestant Reformation.

The United States developed an early familiarity with conscientious objection since many of its original settlers were members of pacifist sects that had been forced out of Europe. As a result, colonial governments frequently provided exemptions from military service for members of those sects that had religious scruples against it. Typically, the laws of a given colony reflected the influence of the sects that settled there. Thus the first New York state constitution, written in 1777, exempted Quakers exclusively, while the first Pennsylvania exemption benefited only the Moravians. An exception to this practice was the very first colonial law providing for conscientious objection—a 1673 Rhode Island statute that applied to all those whose conscience would not permit the bearing of arms. The law was distinctive also in imposing no religious qualifications upon conscience, a feature that made it more liberal than any modern American legislation dealing with conscientious objection.

**Development in the United States.** The bulwarks of pacifism in the United States have been the three religious groups known as the historic peace churches—the Quakers or Friends, the Mennonites, and the Brethren. With the Jehovah's Witnesses, whose position on conscription has led many of its members to reject even nonmilitary compulsory service, they have been primarily responsible for the exemption of conscientious objectors in the United States.

The question of the legal status of conscientious objectors, known as CO's, became crucial with the advent of universal military conscription in the 19th and 20th centuries. During the American Civil War, Southern CO's could pay a fee of $500 to avoid military service, while in the North, CO's often availed themselves of the privilege, accorded to all inductees, of hiring a substitute. The first national legislation regarding CO's was contained in the Conscription Act of 1917. A half-hearted attempt, narrower and harsher than the Russian and British laws then in effect, this law required not only that one be conscientiously opposed to participation in war but that he belong to a "well recognized religious sect or organization" opposed to war. In effect, the law failed to protect the large number of CO's who either were not religious or who belonged to denominations whose tenets did not explicitly forbid participation in war. Moreover, in extending the exemption only to combatant service, the law did not cover members of an exempted sect who believed that compulsory noncombatant service in the armed forces was too closely associated with war for them to serve.

More than a year later, provision was made for CO's adjudged "sincere" to be furloughed for farm service. Those considered "insincere" were court-martialed for refusing to report for noncombatant service. Their sentences were illustrative of the temper of the times: of 500 who faced court-martial, 17 received death sentences, 142 life imprisonment, and 64 jail sentences of 25 years or more. Most of the more severe sentences and all the death sentences were later modified.

**World War II.** Strong pressures from church and civil liberties groups resulted in 1940 in a broadened exemption including all those whose opposition to war was based on religious training and belief. Though the exemption now extended beyond the well-recognized peace sects, the Act excluded nonreligious pacifists. It did, however, provide for those conscientiously opposed to noncombatant service in the armed forces by allowing such persons to perform "work of national importance under civilian direction." Under this provision, almost 12,000 CO's were employed during World War II in Civilian Public Service camps under the supervision of the peace churches. These involved work in governmental agencies, agriculture, forestry, construction, and medicine. The work was often routine and makeshift, however, and unrelated to the skills of many who came to the camps. In addition, CO's and their families suffered severe financial penalties since, unlike those in the military, they received no pay while in service and their dependents received no allotments. After the war, they were excluded from the various benefits for returning GI's. The camps were closed soon after the war. Since that time, alternative service has been performed in a number of approved public and private agencies, where CO's operate under the same working conditions as regular employees.

Approximately 6,000 CO's were prosecuted during World War II, including those whose more absolutist position denied the government's right to compel any public service. Thus some CO's, many of them Jehovah's Witnesses, refused even to register with their draft boards, while others would not report for civilian alternative service.

**Postwar Position.** To an extent, the exemption for CO's reflects the principle that a democratic society, which seeks to strengthen the moral responsibility of the individual, may not compel one to destroy life when it violates his conscience to do so. Nevertheless, because the exemption was largely a response to pressures by the historic peace churches, Congress attempted to limit the exemption to those with traditional religious views. Despite the statute's attempt to exclude from CO status those whose views are essentially moral, philosophical, or sociological, the courts have recognized the complex of experiences and teachings that determine the individual's moral decisions, and they have broadened the statutory definition of religion to include philosophical and humanistic beliefs. No final determination has been made regarding a CO who is avowedly non-religious, but the constitutional prohibition against government favor for one form of belief over another seems to ensure protection for all forms of conscientious objection.

The legal precedents that argue for the protection of the nonpacifist, selective CO are shakier. While not necessarily opposed to all war, such people may conscientiously oppose a particular war, arguing that a society that seeks to protect individual conscience cannot refuse to exempt a person whose own values and reflections on the consequences of a particular war preclude his participation in that war. Moreover, they cite religious basis for their position in the "just war" doctrine. The courts have given limited recognition to this principle in regard to the Jehovah's Witnesses, who claim CO status when conscripted but who proclaim their willingness to fight a theocratic war.

**CO Status in Other Countries.** Provisions for the exemption of CO's vary from country to country. The system of exemption from military service introduced in Russia in 1875 was the forerunner of the American system during World War II. CO's were located in camps administered by church groups, where, for a four-year term, they performed alternative civilian service. Although tolerance of religious CO's declined after the Russian Revolution, legal provisions for their exemption continued into the 1930's.

During World War II, Britain not only recognized all sincere objections, religious or otherwise, but granted exemptions to absolutists who were relieved of all service obligations to the government. Other nations patterned their laws on the American and British systems, with some modifications. Thus Canada often allowed those who qualified to remain at their regular jobs in fulfillment of alternative service requirements during World War II. West Germany followed the British model in its constitution of 1949, providing that a person could not be forced to perform military service with weapons against the dictates of his conscience. During World War II, however, Germany committed many CO's to insane asylums.

In 1964, France exempted CO's for the first time in its history, providing for noncombatant or civilian alternative service. French CO's were still required to serve half again as long as those in ordinary military service, however. Israel, which conscripts both men and women, offers a limited exemption for women of certain orthodox religious groups. Men, however, may not be exempted, and many CO's have been imprisoned. Greece and Italy still deny CO's relief from military service, and many have been imprisoned in those countries.

ALAN H. LEVINE
*New York Civil Liberties Union*

**CONSCIOUSNESS.** The term "consciousness" has been used with a variety of meanings. The two more technical applications are as follows: (1) A person is conscious as long as his mental processes are going on, and he is unconscious when these feelings, ideas, thoughts, desires, and the like are suspended. In this sense, consciousness has the same meaning as *experience* and *awareness*. (2) Consciousness also denotes a person's awareness of his mental processes. By introspection, he can have some knowledge of what he is sensing and thinking and feeling. This article will concentrate on the first meaning.

There are degrees in being conscious in the sense of being aware of what is going on in the world. At one extreme is the condition of a person in a coma, when there seems to be a total absence of experience. At least, there is a total absence of anything that can be recalled later. At the other extreme is the keen alertness of a man who expects danger. Between the states of coma and of maximum alertness are other stages. A person who is asleep is not necessarily unconscious, because he can be aware of dreams and in some degree of factors such as cold and noise.

It is important to point out that consciousness as defined here refers to something that is going on in a person and not to something that exists in itself. Like "happiness," "graciousness," or "thoroughness," consciousness properly refers to some quality of the human being taken in the abstract. However, there is a tendency in human thinking to treat abstractions as if they had actual existence—for example, to speak of "mind" as if it were something located in the head. Since a man may be conscious, it is easy to fall into the assumption that something like a consciousness exists. This tendency has been strengthened by another circumstance. There has been much psychological interest in the description of the individual's experiences when he is conscious, of his feelings, perceptions, emotions, and thoughts. But to arrest such experiences in mid-career, to hold them static for detailed description, incurs the danger of misapprehending these cross-sectional snapshots and treating them as stable and enduring things.

**Study of Consciousness.** It should be pointed out that to deal with how one is conscious, and what one is conscious of, is no less the proper subject matter of natural science than dealing with natural objects. The world of physics is, after all, a standardized and systematized set of constructs derived from comparisons of the original conscious observations of reliable reporters. Such observations are, in the truest sense, phenomena. The afterimage of a bright light that continues to be observed where one knows no real physical light to be, is nevertheless there—as a datum, a phenomenon. And psychologists continue to take a legitimate interest in this phenomenological approach, as witness much of the subject matter of the Gestalt school of psychology.

Although studying what we are conscious of from moment to moment had been the center of interest in man and his mental processes for centuries, it had also been recognized in some quarters that much of what goes on in our own minds goes on without our knowing it.

How can one describe, compare, and formally break down his experiences? To ask, "What is it like to be conscious?" is to word an impossible question. As is true in blindness, unless one has had the experience firsthand, no verbal statements can acquaint him with it. One can, however, recall and compare the different things of which he has been conscious and the different ways in which he has been conscious of them. Psychologists, called *structuralists,* have applied themselves to this analytic work by introspecting. Awarenesses of present things break down, if we are analytic enough, into information derived through the senses—visual, auditory, olfactory, gustatory, cutaneous, kinesthetic, static, and organic. Experiences from any of the senses vary further as to their intensity, extensity, duration, quality, and clearness. Not only may one be aware of things present in these ways, but he may be aware of things absent, through mental images.

What one is conscious of, the so-called contents of consciousness, includes all these variable experiencings. These are combined and rearranged in countless ways, ranging from chance conglomerations of drowsiness or reverie to neat sequences of logical thinking. However, the combining and rearranging are not themselves ordinarily experienced, but only their results.

**Biological Aspects.** Modern thinkers have been much concerned with the functioning of the human being in nature. And as the evolutionary viewpoint became ascendant, the query arose: What is the place of consciousness in the evolving natural world? It must be of survival value. The notion of organismic adjustment to environment, coming to the fore with Darwinism in the mid-19th century, furnished the key: when, in the business of living, an organism meets with a difficulty that it fails to escape or solve at once by automatic reflex-instinctive reactions, it becomes more conscious and more alive and sensitive to the possibilities of the situation. When a difficulty is encountered one "wakes up" or "sits up and takes notice," and thus the range of possibilities for effective reaction is increased. And the various processes of consciousness—such as sensation, perception, conception, and imagination—get their biological significance in terms of their adjustment value.

Just where in the evolution of animal forms consciousness first appeared is a speculative question that can never be answered definitively by direct evidence. However, it has intrigued a number of thinkers, from those who have held that all forms below man have no consciousness and are only elaborate automatic mechanisms, to those who support the view that unicellular organisms have a psychic life. In the ascending order of evolving animal organisms, the modes of behavior observed have led comparative psychologists to speak of two diverging main lines of psychic development. One is in the direction of ever more elaborate mechanical, instinctive adjustments to living conditions, seen in ants, bees, and wasps; the other is toward ever more modifiability, plasticity, and capacity for learning, as exemplified by man. It is supposed that the latter main branch involves more and more conscious experience. These matters are certainly speculative, and they remind a scientist of another fruitless question: Just when in the development of the individual organism does any faintest glimmering of consciousness enter—at conception, at birth, or when?

More related to ascertainable facts is this query: How is a man's being aware, his consciousness, related to his other physiological processes? This question is also difficult to answer. Evidence from embryology, comparative anatomy, and pathology points clearly to some correlation of consciousness with neural functions, particularly of the cerebrum. Complexity of development, as well as healthy integrity of his cerebral structure, seem to go with the ability of a person to report that he is conscious. Injure the head and cerebrum, and the victim loses all consciousness, or is conscious of only some particular kinds of things. Suggestions and feelings are derived from both the external and the internal sense organs.

**Dreams.** There has always been high interest in unusual kinds of conscious experience. The most common form is the dream. The stuff of which dreams are made has some four sources: (1) present sensations occasioned by actual physical stimulations, such as hunger, exposure of the sleeper's feet to cold, sound, or light; (2) fragmentary recalls from experiences in hours preceding the sleep, as of dinner-table conversation or bad news received; (3) persistent lines of motivated interest, as the orphan's dream of going home; and (4) deeper motives that are suppressed as untenable as long as one is awake, but slip into one's dream consciousness sometimes in disguised forms. The latter furnish some of the material with which the psychoanalyst deals as he seeks to revive and reconstruct experiences in his patient's past. The experiences are assumed to leave their traces, though they are beyond voluntary recall.

**Freud's View of the Unconscious.** In disentangling the complex motivations of men—unraveling the peculiarities of their everyday behavior as well as finding the reasons for their neuroses—Sigmund Freud found it useful to assume three levels of awareness: the conscious, the foreconscious or preconscious, and the unconscious. Immediately below the level of full consciousness lie the preconscious ideas that one is not aware of at the moment but can recall to mind more or less readily. Then there are ideas or motives that quite resist any recall under ordinary circumstances and that—to continue Freud's spatial analogy—lie in the great unconscious. The inaccessibility to the individual's recall of these ideas is due to their strong incompatibility with his conscious thoughts and ideals. It is as if a powerful censor—owing its nature to the individual's established thou-shalts and thou-shalt-nots—were acting to suppress and repress them, and so to protect the individual personality from the disruptive effects of realizing them.

**Peculiarities in Experience.** There are many cases of peculiarities in conscious experiences. Examples are: the crystal gazer's recall of things he was not aware of having seen before; the mathematician's or the poet's sudden awareness of an answer to a problem he thought he had put quite out of mind; and the faithful following of an instruction given to a hypnotized subject, but performed some time after the trance is lifted and without any recognition on the performer's part that it was an instruction. Such operations, being outside the person's consciousness, are often called subconscious operations. The great danger is the ready assumption that a "subconscious mind" exists—a daemonlike agency to which all sorts of mysterious powers are popularly attributed. It makes for clearer thinking to insist on using this word (as in the case of "conscious") in its attributive rather than in any substantive sense.

An interesting variation from the workaday consciousness is the mystical experience. Even in deliberative rational thinking, much progress is made not by step-by-step ratiocination but by sudden insights, for which prior thinking only prepares the groundwork. The preliminary diagnosis of a physician and the tentative opinion of a judge, like the inspirations of the scientific research worker or of the author or composer, are only more dramatic than the hunches and insights with which every man is guided in his decisions. Sometimes they come in dreams, and even in waking life they occasionally come as if from without, as "inspirations." Closely allied is the more emotional experience of ecstasy, sought in one form or another by such means as painful self-flagellation, fasting, alcoholic intoxication, mescal or other drugs, or great fatigue. These "Dionysian" experiences have been deliberately sought through all times by peoples in all parts of the world.

There has been a resurgence of interest in the effects of drugs on consciousness. The so-called "consciousness-expanding"—or more critically named "consciousness-distorting"—drugs have been made the center of certain cults. Proponents of using drugs such as LSD have claimed bizarre results in the consciousness of the participants. But such reports are highly subjective; when critically analyzed, they are found to imply little more than increased hallucinatory vividness and excess of feeling rather than originality of thought content. Hallucinatory experiences at times have been followed by prolonged mental illness, attempts at suicide, or attacks on others. See also HALLUCINOGEN.

**Disorders of Consciousness.** Some drug-induced states fall in the category of abnormal forms of consciousness. These are not classified and studied on their own accounts but as symptoms to be understood as parts of whole personality syndromes. Disorders in perceiving and thinking among psychiatric cases include: hallucinations; disorientation or defective perception of place and time; memory failures of many sorts; delusions or paranoidal ideas, especially centering about one's own importance; incoherence in train of ideas; pell-mell flight of ideas; obsessions and compulsions in which the patient cannot escape nagging ideas or seems driven to certain routine actions; phobias in which he is the victim of irrational dreads; anesthesias, or losses of sensibility; and amnesias, or losses of memory. A few of the disorders of emotion include euphoria or exaltation, depression, irascibility, and anxiety and unnamed dreads.

JOHN F. DASHIELL, *University of North Carolina*

### Bibliography

Armstrong, David, and Malcolm, Norman, *Consciousness and Causality* (Basil Blackwell 1984).
Caputi, Anthony, *Pirandello and the Crisis of Modern Consciousness* (Univ. of Ill. Press 1988).
Churchland, Paul M., *Matter and Consciousness*, rev. ed. (MIT Press 1988).
Ellis, R., *An Ontology of Consciousness* (Kluwer 1986).
Gazzaniga, Michael S., *Mind Matters* (Houghton 1988).
Jahn, R. G., *The Role of Consciousness in the Physical World* (Westview Press 1981).
Klein, David B., *The Concept of Consciousness: A Survey* (Univ. of Neb. Press 1984).
McClelland, D., *Roots of Consciousness* (Irvington 1986).
Oakley, D. A., ed., *Brain and Mind* (Routledge 1985).
Stevens, R., ed., *Aspects of Consciousness*, vol. 4 (Academic Press 1984).
Wallace, Benjamin and Fisher, Leslie E., *Consciousness and Behavior* 2d ed. (Allyn 1987).

**CONSCRIPTION,** kon-skrip'shən, is the compulsory recruitment or drafting of men for service in a country's military forces. In some countries women have also been conscripted for military duty, and both men and women have been conscripted for civilian work in wartime.

The idea that all members of a community are obliged to defend it dates back to the beginning of history, and compulsory armed service has existed almost as long. The rationale for modern conscript armies derives from this old idea of universal obligation to defend the community, as well as the newer concept of egalitarianism.

Economic developments have sharpened the competition for men between the military forces and industry. The complexity of weapons and operations requires men of high technical, physical, and mental standards in the armed services. However, rapid social and economic changes are making men of this caliber difficult to obtain. It has thus become necessary for many countries to conscript some men for military service, while allocating others to essential civilian pursuits in order to prevent economic dislocation.

The recruiting system of a country is determined by its special defense problems and the kinds of war it believes it must be ready to wage. International threats and technological developments generally make reserve forces less valuable than forces that are on duty, alert and ready to fight, fully competent, suitably equipped, and poised to travel fast to trouble spots.

Four distinct military systems of recruitment are in general use: voluntary, citizen army or militia, conscript, and mixed.

**Volunteers.** Voluntary recruiting systems are used in countries relatively remote from danger or where the citizens understand international affairs and are willing to participate in the armed forces. A voluntary system saves the trouble and expense of organizing some form of compulsory service, and the military force is well motivated. Pay must be high enough to attract men from civilian life and hold them. The volunteer force fights best, but most countries cannot obtain enough volunteers. A completely volunteer and professional standing army has been regarded as militaristic.

**United States.** Volunteering was the basic U. S. policy for 125 years, based on the belief that in an emergency the nation could rely for its manpower on patriotic response. The enormous numbers of men needed in World Wars I and II proved this position untenable, and legislation based on conscription was enacted. However, early in 1973, the draft ended in the United States, and the all-volunteer concept was restored. To stimulate volunteering, pay and other benefits were improved. One year after the draft ended, the strength of the U. S. armed services was at approximately its programmed level.

**Canada.** Canada, which has a strong tradition of militia service, still relies on the volunteer system. Compulsory service has always been highly unpopular. Conscription was employed only in the last year of World War I. Reintroduced in 1941, universal compulsory service called men for home defense to permit volunteers to serve overseas; late in 1944 conscripts became liable for service abroad. Canada continues to assume that a sizable body of men needs to be kept in actual readiness under arms or immediately available in time of emergency.

PEACETIME CONSCRIPTION was instituted for the first time in the United States to prepare for World War II. President Franklin D. Roosevelt (*left*) looks on as Secretary of the Navy Frank Knox in October 1940 draws the number of one of the first men to be drafted under the Selective Service Act of 1940.

**Citizen Armies.** Citizen armies, or militia forces, are those in which the rights of citizenship automatically carry the obligation for all who are fit to serve in the armed forces for periods of active training and readiness in the reserve throughout every citizen's active life. This system is the most egalitarian and democratic. It distributes the burdens most fairly and ensures the availability of the nation's best minds to the armed forces. Since the whole community is engaged in self defense, no gulf develops between the military and the civilian segments of the nation. The system is low in cost, for the number of men actually serving at any moment in peacetime is comparatively small.

A nation depending on a citizen army, however, tends to be vulnerable to surprise attack. Its armed forces are manned essentially by amateurs. Its weapons and equipment are likely to be obsolescent. Although the system gives sufficient basic training, it provides insufficient time for technical training. The system requires a highly complicated mobilization scheme to call out troops. This may hurt the national economy.

This system is used by countries with few or no external commitments, such as Switzerland, and by those in almost constant danger of attack by neighbors, such as Israel. Citizen armies are unable to deal well with distant disorders that require long periods of military service outside the state but are excellent for nations having wholly defensive strategic objectives.

Citizen armies, then, are effective where the strategic objectives are defensive; they are inexpensive and democratic, but they are weak in technicians, vulnerable to technical changes, and are mobilized only at high national cost.

**Conscripts.** Conscript systems draft physically fit males to spend a period of time in active service, part of it in training, part of it with a regularly constituted unit, and a period of years in reserve status, during which they may be called back into uniform during a general mobilization. Most conscription programs include plans for giving reservists some army training. Short terms of active conscripted service are less useful for naval or air forces, since many of their skills take longer to master.

The conscript system, providing a common experience for practically all the men of a country, can be a powerful political instrument in an authoritarian state. It can act also as a social leveler of class and of regional distinctions. It is egalitarian because all ranks of society go through the same experience. Yet it may put more men into uniform than the nation needs.

Conscription usually depends upon universal military service or universal military training or a compromise between the two. *Universal military service*, generally limited to males and granting an absolute minimum of exemptions for physical and mental handicaps, ensures the equity of universal applicability. If compulsion is unavoidable, it is best applied in a universal and uniform fashion. *Universal military training*, despite its high cost, is socially desirable and produces a trained and ready reserve force. But the usefulness of reserve forces may be questionable considering the drain imposed on regular troops required to conduct the training.

When a country has a potential conscript intake larger than the training staffs can handle or than is needed for national defense, it is often the custom to decide by lot who must serve. Lots have been drawn at one time or another in Denmark, France, Germany, Greece, Portugal, Rumania, Spain, Turkey, and the United States.

*France.* France gave up drawing lots in the 1870's, but its conscriptive system has changed little since then. Colbert, who organized the navy of Louis XIV, set up a "maritime inscription," which ever since has compelled every trained seaman to register with the naval base nearest his home. The air force is also manned in part by conscripts. Most conscripted men go into the army. Everyone is called up, and everyone who is fit serves. There is no provision in the law for conscientious objectors, and exemptions are few. After a period of active training and about 3 years in the reserve, men are free from recall except for general mobilization.

*USSR.* In the USSR, conscription is enforced on everyone reaching military age (18), and the active-duty period of 3 years is used for political indoctrination as well as military training. Conscripts remain in progressively less active reserve components for about 15 years.

**Mixed Systems.** The most practical recruiting method is the mixed system, which combines elements of conscription, volunteers, and a trained citizenry. Volunteers and conscripts are the usual combination, the proportions varying with the urgency of the problems. In a sense, all systems are mixed, except those relying entirely on volunteers, for even a citizen army system requires a few regulars to keep it in operation.

In the United States, for example, the early militia system, a citizen-army concept, gave way in the 19th century to a voluntary system. This was replaced in the 20th century by the use of volunteers and conscripted men. In 1973 a voluntary system was restored.

Mixed systems are helpful to countries needing a force of some size available at short notice to help distant allies or to support distant interests. A nation that tries to operate a voluntary system and cannot obtain enough volunteers has to fall back on a mixed system. The principal disadvantage is that levels of training and readiness are likely to vary widely in the armed forces, and this complicates military planning.

**United States.** The United States, maintaining large forces and making heavy demands on manpower, relied on a mixed system until the draft law expired in 1973. Prior to that date, about 90% of the total forces in uniform were volunteers. The Navy, Marine Corps, and Air Force were usually manned entirely by volunteers, many having volunteered in order to avoid the draft.

The procedure in the United States for deciding who was to be drafted was called the selective service system. Following restoration of the volunteer system, the selective service system was retained in case of an emergency.

**Britain.** The United Kingdom, traditionally dependent on volunteers, instituted its first peacetime draft in 1939, registering men between 18 and 45 and giving 20-year-olds 6 months of compulsory training; in December 1941 the draft was extended to include the registration of women. After World War II a series of National Service acts, passed between 1947 and 1955, established a system under which all young men registered at age 18; if fit and not exempted, they served for 2 years on active duty, then for 3½ years in reserve status with part-time training.

## HISTORY OF CONSCRIPTION

In ancient times warriors usually constituted a separate class in expanding and aggressive communities, while every able-bodied man was expected and compelled to help defend his community in time of emergency. When weapons were costly or difficult to obtain, armies were small and aristocratic, as during the Middle Ages. When weapons became cheap and easily obtainable, armies became large and democratic, as after the general introduction of firearms. Nations too poor to maintain a large professional army depended on citizen militias and hired mercenaries. As early as the 1500's universal compulsory service was suggested, notably by Machiavelli. By the 1700's the soldier's profession had become so poorly paid that men were recruited from the lower strata of society, usually among unemployables. As the human level of armies degenerated, impressment and enticement became the normal methods of recruiting.

**Modern Europe.** The modern idea of conscription stems from the French Revolution. The theory of equality led to universal service, which meant compulsory enlistment. The system of conscription developed in the 1790's was based on registering young men in each department in five classes corresponding to their ages, between 20 and 25. Each year, conscripts were drawn from the first class, the youngest, and others were called if that class failed to furnish enough men. This system made possible the Napoleonic armies based on the *levée en masse,* the nation in arms. Every able-bodied man between 20 and 25 was liable for active service, but each commune selected the men to serve. There was some loss of production because highly skilled civilian workers were compelled to enlist even though many in the military ranks were willing to reengage. Napoleon spoke of "my annual income of 100,000 men."

Prussia in 1808 affirmed the principle of military service without distinction of class or right of exemption by payment and implemented the system fully after 1815. Compulsory training brought all classes into close association during a 3-year period of military service.

Czarist Russia had a system of conscription wherein all men on reaching the age of 21 entered the active army for 5 years. They remained in the reserve for 18 years thereafter.

After about 1870, the value of conscription declined. Compulsory education began to replace compulsory military service, and advances in science and industry made weapons more technical. Wealth increased, conscripts scorned token military pay, and the best men returned to civilian life rather than reengage. The growth of population made it impossible for armies to absorb all men of military age, and abuses in granting exemptions and deferments became common.

When entire populations became vulnerable to attack from the air, the mobilization of industrial resources accompanied the mobilization of manpower, and at least theoretically all the people of a nation became subject to compulsory service in time of war. Out of the simple nation-in-arms concept emerged the idea of the highly complex total-war state, exemplified in the 1930's by the USSR, Germany, and Japan. During World War II conscription was the means by which nations regimented their resources of men and women for military service and industrial production. Total national conscription produced the military machines necessary to wage total war.

**Development in the United States—Colonial Period to Civil War.** The military system in the American colonies was based on the all-embracing, compulsory militia, where every able-bodied man within prescribed age limits, usually 16 to 60, was required to possess arms, be carried on the muster rolls, train periodically, and be mustered into service for military operations whenever necessary. Justices, sheriffs, ministers, physicians, teachers, and others needed to maintain the civilian structure of life were usually exempted from service. Because the militia could not serve outside the home colony without legislative permission, volunteer units were formed to meet emergencies. Some remained in existence and developed proficiency through long training and service. Every colony conscripted for its militia force, but in general only intermittent and part-time service was involved.

The American Revolution was fought by militiamen enlisted for short terms and by volunteers induced to enlist by bounties (cash payments). The difficulties in raising and maintaining a dependable fighting force led some states, notably Massachusetts and Virginia in 1777, to resort to coercion, and they instituted a draft to raise the men requested by the Continental Congress. In most cases the draft involved a drawing by lot from all the eligible men on the militia muster rolls and was usually restricted to unmarried men. The principles of impartiality, selection by lot, and exemption for married men were thus early in force. It was clearly recognized that short-term volunteer enlistment was a poor method of recruiting for protracted war. The abuses connected with the bounty system were also plain. The necessity for national conscription was averted only as the result of aid from France.

The Militia Law of 1792 placed a compulsory and universal military obligation on all free white male citizens between 18 and 45 but granted certain exceptions. An amendment in 1795 limited active service to 3 months in any one year.

During the 19th century voluntary enlistment into the regular forces and into reserve units made the militia system work. Yet despite bounties and bonuses of money, land, and clothing for enlisting, the volunteer system failed to recruit enough men. Congress was considering imposing conscription in the War of 1812 when peace came. By the time of the war with Mexico, the inability of the militia to provide a reservoir of military manpower was shockingly clear; by 1846 the militia was not only inefficient, but verging on extinction.

**The Civil War.** In the Civil War the Northern states furnished men to the Union armies by offering bounties to volunteers. Iowa and Missouri used the threat of a draft in 1861 to accelerate volunteering. The Militia Act of 1862 gave the president authority to draft 300,000 militiamen for 9 months, and the secretary of war drew up the provisions of the system: the governors were to be responsible for conducting the draft through state or county officials; all men between 18 and 45 years of age were to be registered, except for certain exempted classes; draftees could hire substitutes; and the county was to be the local unit of draft jurisdiction. Draft riots in Wisconsin and the threat of violence in Pennsylvania and elsewhere held up the actual implementation of the draft. But the threat of it, together with increased bounties, brought in enough volunteers.

The Draft Act of 1863 was the first federal compulsory recruitment of manpower. It placed the liability of conscription on all male citizens, as well as on all male aliens who had declared their intention of becoming citizens, between 20 and 45. Certain exemptions were granted. Men were divided into two classes: those 20 to 35 years old and those who were unmarried and between 35 and 45. No married man could be drafted until all bachelors had been enlisted. Men were subject to the draft for two years after enrolling; once drafted, they had to serve for 3 years or for the duration of the war. Two draft-evading practices were permitted: substitution, by which a drafted man could hire another person to serve for him; and commutation, by which a drafted man could gain release by paying $300.

The country was divided into enrollment districts, with at least one per congressional district. The president had authority to set quotas for each district, based on population and on the number of men already in service from that district. The provost marshal general of the Army was to be the operating executive.

The enrollment act was designed to intimidate men so they would volunteer, and it applied only in areas that had not produced their quotas of volunteers. Resenting the administration and enforcement of the draft by military officers who went from house to house to enroll men, and outraged by the substitution and commutation privileges, people in many parts of the nation offered sporadic resistance to the draft. This protest culminated in fierce riots in New York City in July 1863 and in violence elsewhere directed against the federal registrars. Yet the measure established the principle that every citizen was obliged to defend the nation and that the federal government could call citizens directly without relying on action by the states. The draft encouraged volunteering, and bounties became high.

The Confederate States had also resorted to the practice of drafting men by the Conscription Act of 1862. The president was given authority to draft for 3 years all white males between the ages of 18 and 35, the system to be administered by state officials under supervision of the central government. The large number of exemptions permitted and the provisions for substitution made the system actually much like a selective service system.

**World War I.** The United States fought the Spanish-American War entirely with volunteer forces. The general mismanagement and inefficiency of that war effort, together with the emergence of the United States as a world power and the outbreak of World War I, led to the National Defense Act of 1916. This established the federally obligated and supported National Guard, a volunteer reserve with units answerable to the state governors but mobilizable as a federal force by the president. National Guard units were mobilized to serve along the Mexican border, and this made clear the inability of the system to produce required amounts of efficient manpower or to provide an equitable manner for the population to share the burden of military service.

On the basis that a voluntary system made military planning uncertain, prevented organized preparedness, destroyed the individual sense of obligation in every citizen, and was excessive in cost, Maj. Gen. Leonard Wood, chief of staff of the U. S. Army in 1915, advocated compulsory universal service based on the Swiss plan, and Maj. Gen. Hugh L. Scott, his successor, recommended universal military training and compulsory military service.

In February 1917, Secretary of War Newton D. Baker, convinced of the necessity for emergency compulsory service imposed equitably, drew up a bill embodying the idea of selective service. President Wilson sent it to Congress and recommended in his war message that men should "be chosen upon the principle of universal liability to service."

The Selective Service Act of 1917 authorized the president to draft up to 500,000 men for the duration of the emergency. All men 21 to 30 years of age (extended in August 1918 to 18 and 45) were required to register. Men could volunteer, and deficiencies would be made up by draftees, but manpower would be reserved for industrial war production. There were to be no bounties or substitutes. Government officials, clergymen, and theological students were exempted; conscientious objectors were exempted from combat duties; and others could be exempted by presidential action. The president was to appoint local boards, none of whose members was to be connected with the military.

The system was administered by the provost marshal general. He linked the 155 district and 4,648 local boards through the state executives to a small federal agency that was the central source of instruction and guidance. It was, in effect, "supervised decentralization."

NEW RECRUITS are sworn into the U. S. armed services during a 1961 U. S.-Soviet crisis over Berlin. Prior to the ending of the U. S. draft in 1973, monthly draft quotas increased during times of international crisis.

UPI

The selective service program consisted of registration, selection (which included classification, deferments, and special categories), and induction. Eligible men registered at their customary voting precincts and received numbered registration cards. In Washington, D. C., numbers were selected by chance, and registrants with those numbers were inducted. The local boards could defer men to avoid undue hardship on dependents and by reason of critical occupations.

In less than 18 months of operation during World War I, the selective service system delivered almost 3 million men to the armed forces, as compared to about 1 million volunteers. The president prohibited volunteering for the Navy and Marine Corps after July 1918, mainly to keep indispensable men in industry. The act established a basic manpower procurement policy that remained in effect: selective conscription to meet manpower deficits resulting from an insufficient number of volunteers.

**Selective Service Act of 1940.** Discontinued after the armistice in 1918, conscription was reinstituted in the Selective Training and Service Act of 1940, the first peacetime U. S. draft. All males from 21 to 35 were required to register with one of 6,443 local boards manned by unpaid civilians; there were 505 appeal boards. Registrants with dependents were exempted, as were those with occupations essential to the national health, safety, and welfare. A lottery by drawings held in Washington, D. C. selected those for training and service. The period of service was initially set for one year, but in August 1941 it was extended to 18 months. When the United States entered World War II, the age limits were expanded to 18 and 65, though only those 20 to 45 were liable for military service. Exemptions were reduced and the period of service was made the duration of the war plus 6 months.

A new feature was job insurance for inducted men. Employers were required by law to rehire men after their military service. In December 1942 voluntary enlistment was stopped, and men with dependents were advised to shift to war-essential work. During World War II, conscription supplied more than 10 million men.

**After World War II.** After the war the military services and President Harry S Truman tried to institute universal military training, at first for one year, then for 6 months, but both proposals failed in Congress.

The selective service system, amended after the war to provide 18 months' service, was allowed to expire on March 31, 1947, and for a year there was no conscription. But when the total strength of the armed forces declined to 1.4 million men, as compared to the 2 million desired by the Department of Defense, Congress enacted the Selective Service Act of 1948, which imposed a 21-month obligation on nonveterans between the ages of 19 and 26, with 18-year-olds permitted to enlist for 1 year only. Beginning in December 1949 all inductees were released upon completing 1 year of service, for the act was due to expire on June 30, 1950. Therefore by February 1950 the armed forces were again on an all-volunteer basis of recruiting. The Communist invasion of the Republic of Korea caused Congress to extend selective service until July 1951.

The Universal Military Training and Service Act of 1951 extended the selective service system to 1955. It laid a military obligation of 8 years on all qualified males between the ages of 18½ and 26; at least 2 years had to be spent on active duty, the remainder in reserve.

The Reserve Forces Act of 1955 provided a 4-year extension of selective service with an active duty obligation of 24 months and a reserve obligation of 5 years. Additional 4-year extensions were passed in 1959, 1963, and 1967.

At the end of 1960, draft calls were negligible, but quotas rose in 1961 for the Berlin crisis, in 1962 for the Cuban missile crisis, and from 1965 for the Vietnam War. The unpopularity of the war brought burning of draft cards, riots at induction centers, and antiwar marches.

Pressure for reform prompted a return in 1969 to a draft lottery, refined in 1970. However, actual inductions ceased in 1973, and registrations were suspended from 1974 until July 21, 1980, when a new registration law came into effect. By Jan. 23, 1976, when the Selective Service System temporarily ceased to function—until the renewal of registrations in 1980—a total of 50,623,715 persons had been registered and 4,894,462 inducted into the armed forces since 1948.

MARTIN BLUMENSON°
*Author of "Breakout and Pursuit"*

**CONSECRATION,** kon-se-krā'shun, is the act by which an object or person is set apart as holy or as dedicated to divine uses. It is closely related to the act of blessing (q.v.), and differs from it chiefly in suggesting a more solemn or definitive act of dedication to God. Among the important consecrative acts are the dedication of altars and churches; the ceremony through which a priest becomes a bishop; and the sacrament of the Eucharist.

**Consecration of Objects.** Rites of consecration are referred to in the records of many ancient civilizations, including the Assyrian, Chaldean, and Hebraic. In the Old Testament there are references to consecration ceremonies for the Ark of the Covenant (Exodus 40) and for the Temple (II Chronicles 5). In the early Christian church, however, no such ceremonies were held. Instead, the celebration of the Eucharist marked the consecration or dedication of altars or churches. From the time of Constantine in the early 4th century, with the general elaboration of liturgy new ceremonies for such consecrations also developed. Some of these, such as the anointing of the altar, seem to derive from practices described in the Old Testament. Others, such as purification of the altar or church with holy water, may be derived from pre-Christian Roman practice. The modern consecration ceremony is elaborate and is normally performed only by a bishop. Among Jewish consecration ceremonies is the *hanukkat habayit,* used in the dedication of a new home.

**Consecration of Persons.** The term "consecration" is applied technically to the ceremony by which a priest receives the highest of the holy orders and becomes a bishop. In a somewhat less technical sense, a person may be consecrated to God's special service in a number of ways. Ever since the early period of the Christian church, the vow of religious virginity has been recognized as a special form of consecration, as are the other vows taken by persons who enter a religious order or congregation. Less officially, a person may dedicate himself to the service of God by a special act of consecration. All these forms of personal consecration are understood as attempts to live up fully to the implications of baptism. Although strictly speaking, consecration means dedication to God, the term is used in a broader sense to express special homage or devotion to God's saints. Some Catholics, for example, consecrate themselves to the Blessed Virgin or to a saint. In the Jewish religion adolescent boys are consecrated to the observance of the commandments through the Bar Mitzvah ceremony.

**Consecration in the Eucharist.** In another specific meaning, the term "consecration" refers to those moments of the canon of the Mass when the priest repeats the words spoken by Christ at the Last Supper. The belief of Catholics and some other Christians is that this act of consecration brings about the Real Presence of Christ, and that He becomes sacramentally present under the appearances of bread and wine. On this point there is some disagreement between Catholic and Orthodox Eastern churches. The orthodox believe that the presence of Christ comes about not at the words of the consecration but at the special prayer to the Holy Spirit known as the epiclesis. In Protestantism, generally, such presence is interpreted as symbolic rather than real.

C. J. McNaspy, S. J.
*"America" Magazine*

**CONSENSUS,** kən-sen'səs, the state of general agreement within a political body with respect to a given issue. There is virtual unanimity of opinion as to which side the body should take and what the common course of action should be. Social scientists use the term "consensus" to refer to the amount and kind of agreement in a given society. Some societies are more consensual than others—there is a greater degree of unanimity of opinion and sentiment, a greater harmony and meeting of minds.

The opposite of consensus is *dissensus.* It is more than a simple lack of consensus, in which many people abstain from committing themselves because they are "of two minds." Dissensus is, rather, a product of agreement within a significant minority that stands positively opposed to the majority view. Dissensus results from the split of opinion into two or more factions.

**Types of Consensus.** The processes through which consensus is achieved differ, and there are at least three types of consensus that illustrate different ways in which general agreement on public issues comes about. These are *spontaneous, emergent,* or *manipulated* consensus.

So-called natural communities, such as the villages of the traditional societies of Latin America, Africa, and Southeast Asia, exhibit only spontaneous consensus. Such communities have few public issues. Change is slow, but when it does occur, the community is viewed as changing its collective mind as one, either abruptly, through magical or divine revelation, or by gradual acceptance of new ways of life made necessary by new circumstances.

Emergent consensus results from the crystallization of opinion after all points of view have been heard in the "marketplace of ideas," and happens only in relatively secular, urbanized, nontraditional societies. The theory is that each individual weighs the evidence and then draws a rational conclusion. The accumulation of judgments constitutes public opinion. If the emergent majority is forceful enough, the minority adopts its view and the result is consensus.

Manipulated consensus is a distinctly modern phenomenon. It requires the kind of social order in which the expression of opinion is formally free and in which emergent consensus can theoretically occur. But over and above that, it requires a sophisticated communications technique that makes it possible for "the message" to reach very large audiences simultaneously. To the extent that people can be persuaded to "buy *X*" or "vote for *Y*" general agreement depends upon who controls the means of persuasion. The candidate with the bigger bankroll, other things being equal, has the better chance of winning the election in a liberal democracy. In a totalitarian state, government censorship and propaganda ensure that the officially sponsored side of an issue gets the best hearing, or even the only hearing. Nevertheless, consensus in both a democracy and a totalitarian state is in part the outcome of a deliberate attempt to "mold public opinion." The limiting factor on manipulated consensus is the effectiveness of technology.

Consensus on norms, beliefs, and traditions validates patterns of action in a given society. It can therefore result in conformity in a society. See also CONFORMITY.

F. William Howton
*The City College of the*
*City University of New York*

A forest in the Canadian Rockies shows the effects of clear-cutting. Conservationists have faulted this technique, saying that it promotes soil erosion and destroys wildlife habitats.

**CONSERVATION,** the concerns and strategies surrounding the protection of natural resources from overuse or degradation. The following article is divided into two subentries, each of which explores a separate set of elements that, taken together, clarify the function and practice of conservation. The first subentry, "An Overview," describes the evolution of the conservation movement, from the nascent environmental awareness of the 18th century through modern responses to global resource issues. The philosophies and goals of the movement are examined as well, bringing into focus the multiplicity of viewpoints that characterize modern conservation. The second subentry, "Sustaining Natural Resources," surveys concerns pertaining to the survival of specific resources and the steps deemed necessary to safeguard their continued existence and use.

## 1. An Overview

The general definition of conservation relates to the overall purpose of the field but conceals the remarkable diversity of intellectual and political interests, some complementary and some contentious, within the conservation movement. Indeed it has been asserted that the term *conservation* has come to have a multitude of meanings.

For example, the word is sometimes used in a relatively narrow sense to refer to a particular subgroup of ideas associated with political progressivism, their emphasis being the scientific development and use of resources to promote both current and future human welfare. In the first three decades of the 19th century, as the American conservation movement took form, conservationists who subscribed to these ideas received their political support from developers and environmental protectionists as well as from consumers (who realized that resource availability drives down the cost of final products). The progres-

sives opposed industrial monopolies and, in the area of resource use, attempted to ensure fair distribution of the benefits of resource exploitation. Concerns over the wise and fair use of resources continue to form an important part of the broader conservation agenda, but some conservationists have come to object to the focus on resource development espoused in management-based approaches, believing that this emphasis results in the neglect of other conservation issues. In the general sense in which it is used here, *conservation* refers to a broad tradition encompassing the original movement as well as its successors and offshoots, including the modern environmental movement.

Despite the philosophical ambiguities of the conservation movement, a wide number of historians agree that it has been, and continues to be, an important force in American politics. Much of the movement's influence extends from the fact that most Americans consider themselves to be conservationists or environmentalists and support a large number of national, regional, and local groups who lobby for particular environmental protections. These groups, in turn, monitor trends and lobby governments to enforce strict laws to protect the environment. Influence is also felt through behind-the-scenes political work and when conservation organizations occasionally galvanize behind an important national cause, such as an attempt to stop a dam or to clean up a large oil spill. On these occasions conservationists help to define national goals.

### CONSERVATION CONCERNS AND GOALS

It is possible to bring some order to the variety of ideas, concerns, and actions associated with conservation by taking a general look at its goals: resource protection and pollution prevention. The former is concerned with the preservation of natural resources, and the latter relates to the outputs of industrial processes in the form of waste or to the unintended impacts of product use, both of which can affect human health and degrade ecological processes.

In the past, conservation focused primarily on resource availability, with concern for pollution more often associated with the related field of environmentalism. In practice, however, the two areas have become difficult to separate. Pollution and environmental degradation can cause at least local resource shortages, as when pollution threatens an area's groundwater supply. Resource conservation and pollution control are likely to become further entwined as a rising world population, coupled with technological growth, intensifies the ecological impact of human activities.

**Designation of Scale.** Sociologists now distinguish between first-generation, second-generation, and third-generation environmental problems. First-generation problems, such as overhunting of a game species or erosion caused by inadequate agricultural practices, tend to be localized and to occur on a relatively small scale. These problems can normally be addressed locally with, for instance, the establishment of hunting regulations or improved farming practices in the affected area. Second-generation problems take place on a larger scale, sometimes involving the contamination or degradation of whole ecological systems, such as the pollution of soil and water by agricultural chemicals. These problems are frequently invisible but widespread, and can pose a health threat. Moreover, second-generation pollution can often be addressed only at a cost of many millions of dollars. Finally, third-generation problems are those that occur on a global scale.

**Nonrenewable and Renewable Resources.** It is also traditional to distinguish between nonrenewable and renewable resources. Nonrenewable resources are those that exist in fixed supply, such as metal ores, or that are replenished far too slowly to be relevant to human planning, such as fossil fuels. Renewable resources are those that, if the processes that produce them remain intact, will survive and can be used indefinitely. Examples include harvestable plant and animal matter as well as clean water and limitless energy supplies, such as solar or wind power. Increasing concern over the vulnerability of certain important ecological processes, such as forest regeneration and topsoil retention, implies that it is also useful to refer to some resources as renewable but fragile.

Many renewable biological resources have proved especially frail in the face of heavy exploitation. A number of the world's fisheries, for example, have become severely depleted or have collapsed altogether as a result of overuse, their fish stocks having fallen too low to reproduce. Tropical rain forests are being destroyed at the rate of millions of acres per year, while the destruction of ancient forests around the globe and other human activities that degrade and fragment traditional plant and animal habitats threaten to destroy perhaps 25% of all species on the earth by the mid-21st century. The necessity to protect natural resources from unimpeded exploitation has given rise to an analogy that compares the stocks and processes required for further resource production to the financial investments that are essential to a nation's economic productivity. Thus natural resources are often referred to as natural capital.

**Physical and Biological Resources.** Natural resources can also be designated as either biological or physical. Biological resources are those comprising living organisms or their products, such as agricultural crops and livestock. Physical resources include soil, water, minerals, and other nonliving substances as well as the physical processes (which in this instance are those that do not directly involve the metabolism of living organisms) that contribute to the survival of life on earth. Physical processes include energy production, the cycling of water through the environment, and natural mechanisms within waterways for diluting aquatic contaminants. The human benefits derived from these processes are customarily referred to as ecological services.

Increased threats to natural resources have led to the rapid growth of such disciplines as conservation biology, which brings the knowledge of modern biology to bear on the monitoring and protection of endangered species and habitats, and restoration ecology, which is concerned with returning habitats already damaged by human activities to their original state. These scientific disciplines are linked to traditional areas of conservation, such as wildlife management, and put into practice the insights of academic, biological research in field projects aimed at protecting the diversity of a habitat's plant and animal species.

## PHILOSOPHIES OF CONSERVATION

A classification of resource-related concerns does not, however, do justice to the intellectual and philosophical diversity of the conservation movement. Conservationists have tended to stress one of at least two broad approaches to protecting nature. Each of these approaches, designated as progressivist resource management and preservationism, can accommodate several worldviews, creating a rich mix of intellectual viewpoints.

**Resource Management.** This approach is based on a philosophy of utilitarianism, which considers an act good if it contributes to a positive balance of human welfare over misery. Early resource managers believed that this moral principle unquestionably supports rapid exploitation of forests and other resources for the building of homes and industry. Those who presently subscribe to a management philosophy, however, do not always agree on the degree to which current resource use should be emphasized in relation to resource protection for future use.

**Preservationism.** The preservationist approach to conservation is often associated with the idea that nature has an intrinsic value, a worth independent of its usefulness to humankind. This viewpoint, referred to as either nonanthropocentrism, biocentrism, or ecocentrism, contrasts with anthropocentrism, the view that a thing is of value only if it is ultimately beneficial to humans.

Thus some preservationists have been highly critical of any view that judges nature by its human value. They insist that the appropriate attitude toward all living things is one of biospecies egalitarianism, in which the value of other species is given equal weight to that of humans.

However, not all preservationists subscribe to an ecocentric philosophy. Indeed, a variety of viewpoints have been used to justify the preservation of elements and processes of nature from destruction through human use. For example, many preservationists adhere to the idea of a stewardship position for humankind, an implicitly anthropocentric view that can be traced to the major religions and that holds that human use of the earth's resources carries with it the responsibility to protect those resources for future generations.

In reality, the differences between preservationism and resource management are not always well delineated. Conservationist philosophies ultimately fall along a wide continuum between the desire to exploit nature and the wish to preserve it. As a result, the values and goals of many resource-management proponents greatly overlap those of many preservationists. At one end of the continuum are the "deep ecologists," a loosely organized group of conservationists who believe that conversion of natural systems for human use has already gone too far. Deep ecologists subscribe to the idea that the human population should be reduced and that attempts must be made to reestablish wilderness and natural areas, with human impact on those areas to be kept to an absolute minimum. These conservationists also reject the political tactics of mainstream environmentalists, arguing for direct action and resistance against the dominant power structure rather than action within the system through political maneuvering and compromise.

At the other end of the continuum is a new and politically powerful group calling itself the "wise use movement." These conservationists emphasize the development of resources for human use and believe in setting aside only small natural reserves within a human-dominated landscape. However, conservationists can also be found at every ideological point between the two extremes, struggling to find a proper balance between the use and preservation of nature.

### HISTORY OF CONSERVATION

To understand how various conservationist worldviews and approaches have led to specific resource-based programs and policies, it will be helpful to trace the history of conservation from its earliest incarnations to its ultimate development into a worldwide movement.

**Early History.** Conservation practices have existed for centuries, as evidenced by the successful strategies against soil erosion and deforestation developed by the indigenous peoples of pre-colonial India, East Africa, and Ghana. Nor have the consequences of resource exploitation been limited to the 20th century. In ancient Greece, for example, evidence suggests that various regions suffered permanent damage as a result of poor agricultural practices. In a section of the Peloponnesus, an analysis of soil layers and intervening erosional deposits was compared with human settlement patterns. Researchers discovered strong signs that clearance of the land for settlement was followed by soil erosion, causing the inhabitants to leave the area. During the subsequent period, with human intrusion at a minimum, a new layer of soil was formed, followed by another pattern of settlement and erosion. The periods of settlement have been dated at about 2500 B.C., 350 to 50 B.C., and 950 to 1450 A.D.

The roots of Western conservationism can be traced back to the 17th and 18th centuries, when European colonial rule was undergoing major expansion. As the French, Dutch, and British East India companies looked to Africa, India, and the Caribbean for valuable minerals and timber, the environmental impact of the indiscriminate harvesting of natural resources became apparent. For example, on the island of Mauritius, located in the Indian Ocean, lumbering activities by 17th-century Dutch settlers caused severe deforestation, greatly reducing the island's population of hardwood trees.

The French took possession of the island in 1721, and over the course of the 18th century, reformers and scientists began to experiment with various conservation strategies. These early conservationists were influenced by a variety of contemporary ideas and social changes, including the teachings of Swiss philosopher Jean-Jacques Rousseau (who maintained that society had corrupted the so-called natural man), the Romantic literary movement, and a trend toward empirical reasoning, which was inspired by the French Enlightenment. Thus conservation activity was motivated at least in part by a growing perception of humankind's responsibility toward nature as well as a very practical understanding of the environmental damage caused by unregulated resource use. In 1769 the French passed an ordinance directing that forests on Mauritius be retained on 25% of all landholdings and that cleared land be reforested. In 1777 a forest service was established on the island, and by the end of the 18th century the French had also enacted laws to regulate factory pollution and preserve Mauritius's shrinking fish populations.

English colonies in the West Indies and the Caribbean began to employ similar conservation strategies. Such efforts were given added validity by British plant physiologist Stephen Hales (1677–1761), who demonstrated the relationship between plant life and the atmosphere, including the influence of trees on rainfall. (See also ENVIRONMENT—An Overview.)

The beginnings of a true, organized conservation movement can be traced to the United States, where burgeoning conservation activities were also inspired by growing resource use. The period following the Civil War was one of rapid economic development, including increased exploitation of standing resources, such as timber. It was during this time that pioneers spread across the country and turned prairies and forests into farms and cities. Consequently, forest preservation became a primary concern of early conservationists. In 1891 Pres. Benjamin Harrison signed a proclamation that turned 1,198,080 acres (485,222 ha) in Colorado into the first national forest reserve. Harrison went on to increase preserved acreage, as did his successors, Grover Cleveland, William McKinley, and Theodore Roosevelt, establishing the basis for the present-day national forest system. In the meantime, the ideas espoused by two leading members of the conservation movement, John Muir and Gifford Pinchot, created a foundation for the development of preservationist and resource-management-based philosophies.

Muir, a naturalist and explorer, had been influential in the establishment of forest reserves; he began urging the formulation of a federal forest-conservation policy in 1876. Yet Muir was as much poet as scientist, espousing a pantheistic view of nature in which he maintained that every fact learned about nature reveals deeper truths about God. Through this philosophy, which presented God and nature as one, Muir was able to unify his scientific and poetic quests.

Muir consequently saw wild places as essential to the health of the human spirit and therefore as a necessity to the spiritual development of modern, urban humans. Despite his occasional comments concerning the rights of other species, however, he never denied a human right to use nature. He instead sought a balanced and harmonious relationship between humans and nature that, when possible, left nature undisturbed. A political outsider, Muir was nonetheless able to gather public support for his views through his skills as a writer and his ability to publicize the growing conservation movement.

Muir's views contrasted with those of Pinchot, a forester who, at the turn of the century, introduced European principles of scientific forest management to the United States. From 1896 to 1910 Pinchot headed the body initially known as the National Forest Commission of the National Academy of Sciences (which in 1905 became the U.S. Forest Service). He favored forest conservation but, unlike Muir, saw the practice as a means of maintaining lumber resources. He never questioned the idea that forests, whether privately or publicly owned, should be used to maximize the material benefits of the expanding U.S. economy.

As a close adviser to Pres. Theodore Roosevelt, himself a conservationist, Pinchot was able to consolidate forest management under his control in the Department of Agriculture. A skilled political operative, Pinchot built support in Washington for Roosevelt's conservation plans by enlisting many interest groups, including timber interests, mining companies, and ranchers seeking additional grazing land, as supporters of forest reserves and Pinchot's management of them. He also created resource development agencies, including the Bureau of Reclamation. The bureau systematically began to dam many of the nation's wild rivers to maintain a constant water supply and, later, to use in generating hydroelectric power. Pinchot ultimately built a powerful force of professionally trained resource managers who accepted his particular vision of natural resource protection and development.

Pinchot's activities, however, inevitably led to a clash with Muir, specifically over agricultural use of public land. Given his emphasis on resource use, and struggling to save the forest reserves from competing efforts to privatize all land, Pinchot angered Muir by recommending that the federal government permit regulated grazing in the reserves.

Friction between the two men was exacerbated in a decade-long battle over a proposal by the city of San Francisco to dam the Hetch Hetchy valley in Yosemite National Park. The municipal government, with the strong support of local taxpayers, sought to remedy San Francisco's water-supply problems by turning the valley into a reservoir. Muir, who had helped to establish Yosemite in 1890, opposed the dam. Treating it as a symbol of greed and human destructiveness, he denounced the dam's proponents as "Godless materialists." In contrast, Pinchot thought it reasonable to put the remote valley to use. Muir's efforts were defeated when, with Pres. Woodrow Wilson's backing, Congress passed legislation in 1913 to dam the Hetch Hetchy. Muir's death the next year was, some said, caused by his heartbreak at the loss of the valley. Subsequently, however, the largely volunteer nature-preservation force he had built campaigned successfully for an independent National Park Service and a prohibition on further large economic-development projects in national parks.

THE BETTMANN ARCHIVE

Pioneering American conservationist John Muir (*left*) with nature essayist John Burroughs.

**Aldo Leopold's "Land Ethic."** The early conservation movement comprised, to a large extent, two factions: those who followed the philosophies of Muir and those who subscribed to the ideas of Pinchot. In time the rhetoric of the two factions became more strident and polarized.

During the first half of the 20th century, however, a partial, and perhaps uneasy, unification of the ideas of Muir and Pinchot was devised by conservationist Aldo Leopold. Educated at the Yale School of Forestry, which had been founded by a gift from Pinchot's wealthy family, Leopold began his career in 1909, at the height of the Hetch Hetchy controversy, in Pinchot's Forest Service. Leopold was rigorously trained in the science of resource management, but he combined this with a strong love of nature and the Romanticist leanings of Muir. He consequently struggled to articulate a conservation philosophy that would integrate both approaches, and it can be argued that he came very close to succeeding.

Best known today as the author of a small but poetically powerful book of environmental essays, *A Sand County Almanac* (1949), Leopold was also a successful and hardheaded resource analyst and manager, who is credited with founding the science of wildlife management. Indeed, Leopold's attitudes toward nature and conservation embodied elements of both Muir and Pinchot.

In his nature essays Leopold stressed the dynamic power and beauty of ecological processes. He argued that natural processes embody different dynamics on different scales and that nature must be understood as a complex system. This view complemented his "land ethic," his belief that "a thing is right when it tends to preserve the integrity, stability, and beauty of the biotic community. It is wrong when it tends otherwise."

Through his scientific knowledge and personal philosophy, Leopold sought to develop both a descriptive science and a prescriptive ethic for the protection of natural communities, which he referred to as land communities. He believed that humans, growing in population and armed with powerful modern technologies, had acquired the ability to alter land much faster, and far more

© CHARLES BRADLEY

American conservationist Aldo Leopold warned of technology's far-reaching environmental effects.

pervasively, than ever before in history. These rapid and far-reaching changes, Leopold maintained, threaten the health and balance, or the integrity, of ecological systems. With this new power to destroy comes new responsibility, he reasoned. In a famous simile Leopold declared that modern humans must learn to "think like a mountain," which meant that they must, in addition to considering nature's short-term economic use, also be cognizant of the environment's changing natural dynamics. Economic use is permissible, said Leopold, provided that its scale and impacts do not threaten these dynamics. In this sense he applied Pinchot's wise-use-of-resources approach on a smaller scale—for example, to forest plots or farms—and Muir's holistic ideas to landscapes and ecosystems.

**Conservation since 1960.** Despite the importance of Leopold's insights, putting them into practice has proved difficult. Ecological science has often lacked the ability to specify which natural processes are most crucial to an ecosystem and how much alteration can take place within the ecosystem before these processes are affected. Moreover, following Leopold's death in 1949, conservation was virtually forgotten in the economic boom that followed World War II.

The conservation movement was reborn in 1962 with the publication of *Silent Spring*, by biologist Rachel Carson. The book, an overnight sensation, used an ecological viewpoint similar to Leopold's to reawaken concerns over environmental degradation. Carson argued that, while pesticides have some uses under carefully controlled circumstances, these chemicals were being applied with far too little care. She maintained that poisons, once placed in the environment, will cycle through it, eventually affecting humans by increasing the population's risk of cancer and other toxin-associated illnesses. While chemical corporations tried to suppress and then ridicule the book, a new era of environmentalism was born, and environmental protection became one of the major social causes of the 1960s and 1970s.

This period saw the regeneration and professionalization of national environmental groups.

Older organizations, such as the Sierra Club and the National Audubon Society, grew rapidly, as did their political influence in the form of lobbying efforts aimed at Congress and at governmental agencies. New environmental groups also formed, some of which specialized in litigation to stop pollution or in efforts to improve the enforcement of existing environmental laws.

Increased public support for conservation helped to encourage the passage of groundbreaking legislation by the U.S. Congress during the late 1960s and 1970s, protecting the nation's resources. The federal government instituted laws to regulate the use of toxic chemicals; regulations to reduce pollution of lakes, streams, and drinking water; and restrictions to reduce air pollution. Wildlife protection much in the preservationist tradition of Muir was enacted through the Wilderness Act of 1964 and the Endangered Species Act of 1973. Even as the country was responding to larger-scale, second-generation problems, however, third-generation problems became a developing concern. In the 1970s and 1980s researchers found evidence that the atmospheric buildup of carbon dioxide may raise global temperatures (a phenomenon known as global warming), that the release of chemicals such as chlorofluorocarbons (CFCs) into the atmosphere is damaging the planet's ozone layer, and that the deposition of acid in polluted rain or snow is destroying wildlife. (See ACID RAIN; GREENHOUSE EFFECT.)

### PROBLEMS OF SCALE

As Leopold predicted, the emergence of successive and expanding waves of environmental threats can be attributed to the growing human population and its rising technological power. Moreover, just as Leopold's concept of nature consisted of multiple levels of stabilities and feedbacks, so modern environmental issues comprise multiple and interlocking layers of first-, second-, and third-generation problems, introducing many difficult issues with regard to ecological priorities. A famous analogy made by American ecologist Garrett Hardin illustrates the interaction between large- and small-scale environmental impacts.

Hardin compared the environment as a whole to a common pasture, one that is equally open to all members of a community. He reasoned that the profits derived from an individual herder's flocks would not be shared with the populace at large, even though the animals were grazing in the common pasture. Yet as each herder increased the size of his or her flock, any degradation costs to the pasture resulting from overgrazing would be borne by the entire community. Thus, according to Hardin's model, individuals acting in their own self-interest are likely to increase their use of a resource-producing system and in the process damage that system. Although Hardin introduced his analogy to articulate his strong views against human population growth, the model has been generalized to apply to virtually all environmental problems, because, like Hardin's pasture, most environmental goods, such as clean air and open space, are universally available.

A debate in the early 1990s surrounding the restoration of the Florida Everglades also illustrates the complex, and sometimes contradictory, issues that conservationists must address. Over the course of the 20th century, increasing development in Florida, and the subsequent need for more land, led the state to drain half of the Everglades for urban and agricultural use. Much of the remaining water was diverted to Miami and to various corporate farms.

These actions severely altered the flow and volume of water through the Everglades and, consequently, had a deleterious effect on wildlife habitats. In 1989 the federal government initiated efforts to restore the natural water flow, an essential element in solving many of the area's ecological problems. In 1990, however, a report from a U.S. Fish and Wildlife Service biologist indicated that the restoration plan would drain a field that had been serving as an important feeding ground for an endangered species, the snail kite, and in the process would make access to the kite's sole food source, the apple snail, more difficult. Ultimately, however, a panel that was assembled by the National Audubon Society concluded that halting the restoration project would provide only a short-term advantage for the kite but that failing to repair the Everglade ecosystem as a whole would, in the long run, prove damaging to the species.

## THE CURRENT SCOPE OF CONSERVATION

In response to the advent of third-generation environmental hazards, the conservation movement itself has also grown globally. During the 1980s environmentalists expressed concern when the federal government, under the administra-

tion of Pres. Ronald Reagan, reduced environmental regulation and sharply curtailed funding for population control in the developing world. Environmentalists responded to these changes by intensifying their efforts to gain public support for their work, thereby increasing the ranks of environmental groups. These organizations, in turn, helped to spur worldwide concern over global environmental problems and to promote international cooperation in addressing these issues.

**International Efforts.** A precedent for such cooperation was set in September 1987, when 24 nations signed the Montreal Protocol. This agreement stemmed from research data, compiled since the 1970s, that revealed a reduction in the layer of ozone gas present in the earth's stratosphere. Ozone, which is composed of oxygen molecules containing three atoms each, absorbs dangerous ultraviolet rays from the sun and is therefore essential to life on earth. Scientific evidence indicates that ozone damage has been caused by certain chemicals released into the atmosphere. These include CFCs, which have been used as coolants and as propellants in aerosol cans. Thus the Montreal Protocol of 1987 stipulated a 50% reduction (from 1986 levels) in the manufacture and consumption of CFCs by 1998. This goal was to be reached through a combination of efforts by both industrialized and developing nations, with the former agreeing to provide alternative, less environmentally harmful technologies to poorer countries. (Developing countries were also given a longer deadline.) In 1990, citing new concerns about ozone depletion, more than 90 countries endorsed an amendment to the protocol, expanding the number of CFCs targeted and calling for their virtual phaseout by the year 2000. In 1992 the agreement was modified again, moving the phaseout deadline up to 1996. Critics have expressed disappointment, however, that the protocol permits companies to continue to use ozone-depleting chemicals for essential uses and for servicing existing equipment beyond the specified deadlines. (See also OZONE.)

Nonetheless, the Montreal agreement is generally considered a success. But not all international efforts have gained such widespread assent. A case in point is the United Nations Conference on Environment and Development (also called

© ROBERT GUSTAFSON

© E. HANUMANTHA RAP/PHOTO RESEARCHERS

Large-scale destruction of wildlife habitats by humans has increased the rate of plant and animal extinctions and placed many species at risk of being wiped out. Two examples of endangered species are the Hawaiian tree *Kokia cookei* (*above*), which apparently no longer exists in the wild; and the Asian elephant, *Elephas maximus* (*right*), which once numbered in the millions but now is found in only a few countries, with the largest population (25,000) in India.

the Earth Summit), held in Brazil in 1992, which placed important issues on the agenda, such as global warming and destruction of biological diversity (the variety of plants and animals present in the environment). Differences in concerns and approaches, both environmental and economic, among industrialized and developing nations limited the extent to which multilateral actions were agreed on by the participants. Environmental protection has become a contentious issue between these parties, with developing nations eager to improve their economies through industrialization but at the same time lacking the pollution-control resources of wealthier nations.

Ultimately, solving the conservation problems of developing nations presents a true puzzle. Environmental damage among industrialized populations can be traced to high per-capita consumption of resources, while in developing nations, where such consumption is only a tiny fraction of that of wealthier countries, overpopulation presents the major environmental threat.

**Conservation Efforts around the World.** Despite the problems inherent in promoting environmental protection among developing nations, many of these countries are benefiting from the work of indigenous nongovernmental organizations (NGOs), that is, local grassroots groups that have in many cases been established to address poverty and environmental degradation. Some NGOs have focused on family planning, exerting an influence on government policies. Grassroots organizations have been particularly active in Africa, Asia, and Latin America.

The evolution of Japan's conservation movement again demonstrates a growing global awareness of environmental issues during the late 20th century. After World War II a combination of industrial expansion and urban population growth provoked increased air and water pollution. The human toll that resulted from severe incidences of industrial pollution, including methylmercury,

cadmium, and arsenic poisoning, led to the establishment in 1971 of a government environmental agency. This new body focused on the prevention of air, water, and soil pollution as well as other environmental disturbances. In addition, the government also instituted a policy requiring industry to pay compensation for pollution-related damage. In order to monitor environmental conditions, Japan developed a nationwide survey, called the Green Census, that is carried out with the assistance of thousands of natural-history experts, a number of NGOs, and more than 100,000 volunteers.

The conservation movement's scope is further evidenced by the growing worldwide market for environmental goods and services, including those for pollution control and disposal of waste or sewage. The bulk of this market, about 80%, comprises the United States, Canada, western Europe, Japan, Australia, and New Zealand. As noted earlier, however, developing nations also represent a market for these goods, albeit a smaller one, with investments in such products growing rapidly in Latin America. Altogether, the worldwide market for pollution and waste treatment may exceed $400 billion by the year 2000.

Historically, conservation has maintained a very weak presence in eastern Europe. In the former Soviet Union, the drive to increase industrial production and the government's lack of environmental consciousness resulted in widespread resource abuse and severe industrial pollution. With the advent of perestroika and the subsequent dissolution of the Soviet Union, environmental issues gained new importance. Russia instituted procedures for environmental damage litigation, adopted the use of environmental impact assessments, and, in 1991, passed the nation's first environmental law. Legislation on forest and underground resource use was later passed as well.

By the mid-1990s, however, such efforts had made little or no impact on Russia's environmen-

A dust storm engulfs a town in the southwestern United States, 1937. Poor farming practices and years of drought caused widespread soil erosion in the so-called Dust Bowl region of the Great Plains.

tal problems. The federal government had proved too weak to enforce the new policies, and local officials had little interest in complying with these laws.

### THE FUTURE OF CONSERVATION

National attention to environmental issues has waxed and waned in an almost cyclical fashion in the United States. The consequences and concerns stemming from major events, such as oil spills and efforts to protect natural areas, are periodically pushed off the federal government's agenda by economic and social issues. At the same time, there has been a steady growth in support and concern for environmental issues among the American population in general.

One important trend, almost certain to continue, is an increasingly broad acceptance of sustainable development. As defined by the World Commission on Environment and Development, this term refers to "development that meets the needs of the present without compromising the ability of future generations to meet their own needs." Development is defined in this instance as all actions that seek to meet human needs.

Another trend that is likely to continue into the future is conflict over both the proper conceptualization of environmental problems and the best route to sustainable development. Many leading economists have contended that depletion of natural resources will not trigger slowed economic growth among industrialized nations because, they argue, technological innovation will produce substitutes for lost resources. Conservationists, on the other hand, tend to believe that ecological systems are resilient up to a point but that these systems can be degraded until they become virtually unexploitable.

The conservation movement will also no doubt see a continuation of the developing conflict between environmental groups over resource control. The first century of environmental action resulted in a national environmental constituency, important federal environmental legislation, and a professionalized cadre of environmentalists acting at the national and international level. Since the 1970s, however, local environmental groups have also proliferated. While these organizations have sometimes appealed to national environmental groups for help in various efforts, such as the rejection of a dam or a toxic waste facility, there has been a trend among local groups to lobby for local government control of natural resources. The upshot has been a growing tension over this issue between national, regional, and local environmental concerns as well as between the nation's federal, state, and local governments.

Environmental concerns about the pace of technological and economic change in developing nations are likewise expected to remain primary issues. Advocates of rapid economic growth will most likely remain in conflict with environmentalists over the appropriate pace of development in these countries and the stress such change places on ecosystems and natural resources. As with similar debates in industrialized nations, this conflict is again often based on differing attitudes toward technology, with those in favor of rapid growth asserting that technological innovations can provide solutions to any new environmental problems that emerge, and environmentalists maintaining that the development and use of increasingly powerful and sophisticated technologies may

© DEDE GILMAN/UNICORN STOCK PHOTOS

The first U.S. forest preserve, now White River National Forest, was created in Colorado in 1891.

result in unforseen environmental problems that will prove costly, or perhaps impossible, to solve.

As conservation-policy questions have come to focus more and more on technology and its impacts, the old, bipolar conflicts that existed between the followers of Muir and the supporters of Pinchot have increasingly been replaced by debates based on far less divergent views. Disagreements among modern conservationists tend to be less concerned with whether or not to exploit a particular resource than with the appropriate degree of such exploitation. For example, whereas Muir cast the fight over the Hetch Hetchy dam as a conflict between the morally righteous and the spiritually bankrupt, current and future environmental debates are likely to involve disagreements over which resource-development technologies will have the most benign effect on an ecosystem.

Environmental and resource questions can also be expected to become more important in the area of international security. With the end of the Cold War, threats to international security now tend to arise from regional conflicts, which are often caused or exacerbated by competition for resources. In the Middle East, for instance, limited access to scarce water supplies has provoked conflicts for thousands of years. Military, economic, and political differences between nations in this region have aggravated the problem, which is expected to become more intense if populations in the Middle East, and consequently the demand for water, continue to grow.

BRYAN G. NORTON
*Georgia Institute of Technology*

### Bibliography

Borelli, Peter, ed., *Crossroads: Environmental Priorities for the Future* (Island Press, Covelo 1988).
Bothe, Michael, ed., *Amazonia and Siberia: Legal Aspects of the Preservation of the Environment and Development in the Last Open Spaces* (Kluwer Acad. Pubs. 1993).
Devall, Bill, and George Sessions, *Deep Ecology: Living as if Nature Mattered* (G. M. Smith 1987).
Fox, Stephen R., *John Muir and His Legacy: The American Conservation Movement* (Little, Brown 1981).
Hardin, Garrett, "Tragedy of the Commons: Adaptation of Address, June 25, 1968," *Science* 132 (Dec. 13, 1968).
Hays, Samuel, *Conservation and the Gospel of Efficiency: The Progressive Conservation Movement, 1890–1920* (Harvard Univ. Press 1959).
Hays, Samuel, *Beauty, Health, and Permanence: Environmental Politics in the United States, 1955–1985* (Cambridge 1987).
Kennedy, Paul, *Preparing for the Twenty-First Century* (Vintage 1987).
Leopold, Aldo, *Game Management* (Univ. of Wis. Press 1933).
Meadows, D. H., et al., *Beyond the Limits: Confronting Global Collapse, Envisioning a Sustainable Future* (Chelsea Green 1993).
Meine, Curt, *Aldo Leopold: His Life and Work* (Univ. of Wis. Press 1988).
Muir, John, *Our National Parks* (Houghton 1901).
Norton, Bryan G., *Toward Unity among Environmentalists* (Oxford 1991).
Pinchot, Gifford, *Breaking New Ground* (Harcourt 1947).
Wilson, E. O., ed., *Biodiversity* (Natl. Acad. Press 1988).

## 2. Sustaining Natural Resources

For much of its history, the conservation movement tended to view natural resources specifically in terms of materials that have a direct economic value, such as minerals, timber, and fossil fuels. This perception has changed, however, in tandem with the development of the science of ecology, the study of the interrelationships between living things and their environment. Ecologists have increasingly clarified the inextricable link that humans share with every part of the earth's environment, and the definition of natural resources has consequently been expanded to include clean air, soil, fresh water, rangelands, and wildlife.

Natural resources can be categorized as nonrenewable and renewable. Nonrenewable resources are those present in fixed supplies that can be depleted by use. Minerals such as copper and aluminum and fossil fuels such as coal, oil, and natural gas are examples of nonrenewable resources. Renewable resources are those that are replaced or replenished by natural processes and, if properly managed, can be exploited indefinitely. Examples of such resources are trees, fresh water, and wildlife. When renewable resources are overexploited or misused, however, the supply can be severely limited or completely lost.

Resource consumption is greatly dependent on both the size and the economic status of a country's population. In developing nations, where population growth is highest, the concentration of people in an area often exceeds the environment's ability to support them. Although resource consumption per person is low in these countries as a result of widespread poverty, population pressures nonetheless contribute to pollution, environmental degradation, and resource depletion. In industrialized nations, population growth tends to be low or even stabilized, but the relative affluence of these countries results in high per-capita resource consumption.

Specific conservation issues and methods exist for each resource and are treated separately in the succeeding discussion. In reality, however, the web of interdependence that exists among earth's natural resources means that no conservation issue can be addressed without considering its impact on the environment as a whole.

**Air Conservation.** Earth's atmosphere is an invisible layer of gases that envelops the planet. It is an essential natural resource that shields the planet's surface from most of the sun's harmful ultraviolet radiation and from lethal amounts of cosmic radiation emanating from outer space. Visible light penetrates the atmosphere, warming the planet and triggering photosynthesis, the process by which green plants synthesize organic compounds, using the sun's energy. Photosynthesis is the initial source of nutrients for almost all life on earth. The atmosphere also contains two gases required by living things: carbon dioxide (used by plants to manufacture sugar during photosynthesis) and oxygen (used by most organisms to break down food molecules during cellular respiration). The production and use of these gases is a cyclical process, with oxygen occurring as a by-product of photosynthesis, and carbon dioxide being expelled during cellular respiration.

The air is often contaminated with pollutants, including particulates, nitrogen oxides, sulfur oxides, carbon oxides, hydrocarbons, and ozone. Some pollutants are discharged into the atmosphere from natural sources such as volcanoes, but others result from human activities. Much of the air pollution caused by humans is concentrated in densely populated urban areas, with the main sources being motor vehicles and industry, particularly the producers of chemicals, metals, paper, and electrical power.

All air-pollution emissions except for carbon dioxide can be controlled by appropriate technologies. For example, electrostatic precipitators, fabric filters, and wet scrubbers remove air pollutants from the smokestacks of electric power plants and many factories. Installing and maintaining air-pollution-control devices, although expensive, is often mandated by legislation, including a 1990 amendment to the federal Clean Air Act.

Carbon dioxide emissions, which occur when fossil fuels are burned, remain a significant problem. The level of carbon dioxide in the atmosphere is increasing, and because carbon dioxide prevents heat from escaping from the earth's atmosphere, the planet's climate may be affected. Many serious environmental consequences could occur during the 21st century as a result of global warming. Food production may be altered, forests destroyed, and, if polar ice melts, coastal areas submerged.

Not all atmospheric experts agree, however, that a serious global-warming threat exists, with some suggesting that current environmental conditions contradict warming predictions based on computer modeling. Nonetheless, most nations have signed the Climate Change Treaty, which is an outcome of the 1992 United Nations Conference on Environment and Development (commonly called the Earth Summit). The treaty, which was ratified by the United States in 1992, requires the signatories to reduce carbon dioxide emissions to 1990 levels by the year 2000.

## EROSIVE EFFECTS OF HUMAN ACTIVITY IN ANCIENT GREECE

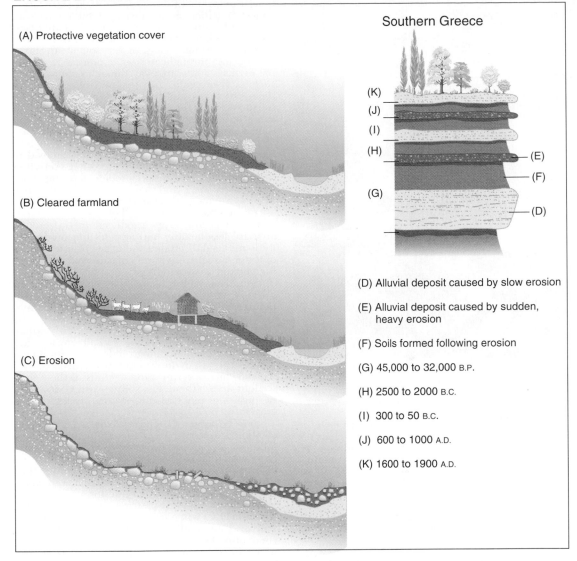

(A) Protective vegetation cover

(B) Cleared farmland

(C) Erosion

Southern Greece

(K)
(J)
(I)
(H)
(E)
(F)
(G)
(D)

(D) Alluvial deposit caused by slow erosion

(E) Alluvial deposit caused by sudden, heavy erosion

(F) Soils formed following erosion

(G) 45,000 to 32,000 B.P.

(H) 2500 to 2000 B.C.

(I)  300 to 50 B.C.

(J)  600 to 1000 A.D.

(K) 1600 to 1900 A.D.

Environmental damage from human activity is not a new phenomenon. Modern technology has widened the scope of such impact, but ancient civilizations also used nature unwisely at times. Research in southern Greece, for example, has pointed to the erosive effects of ancient farming practices there.

The stratosphere, located in the upper atmosphere, contains a thin layer of ozone, a gas composed of oxygen molecules containing three atoms each. Although ozone is considered a pollutant when present in the lower atmosphere, stratospheric ozone serves a valuable function, filtering out much of the sun's harmful ultraviolet radiation. Research indicates, however, that ozone levels in the stratosphere are declining, a phenomenon that has been attributed to the release of chlorofluorocarbons (CFCs) and comparable ozone-destroying chemicals. CFCs have had a number of commercial applications, including as coolants in air conditioners and refrigerators. In 1990 most nations agreed to a total ban on the production of many CFCs by 1999. Soon afterward, scientific evidence pointed to the need for even faster action, and the phaseout date for CFCs and similar compounds was moved up to 1996. CFCs are very stable chemicals with the capability of surviving in the atmosphere for 120 years or more. Consequently, the CFC ban is not expected to bring immediate benefits. (See also AIR POLLUTION.)

**Soil Conservation.** Soil is the complex uppermost layer of most dry land. It consists of organic material, water, air, living organisms, and inorganic minerals from rock. A renewable resource, soil forms continuously as rock in the earth's crust slowly breaks apart through natural weathering processes.

Soil is often not appreciated as a valuable natural resource, yet almost all terrestrial organisms, humans included, depend on it for their survival. It is the medium in which plants grow and from which they extract essential minerals and water. Because humans and other animals obtain food from plants (or from animals that eat plants), soil is crucial to them as well.

© JOHN CALLAHAN/TONY STONE IMAGES

A rice crop in the Philippines. The terraced hillside discourages soil erosion.

A number of human activities cause or intensify various types of soil degradation, such as erosion and reduced fertility. Soil degradation has long been recognized as a local, and sometimes regional, problem, but it must also be considered on a global scale. A three-year assessment of worldwide soil degradation released by the United Nations Environment Program in 1992 stated that almost 5 billion acres (nearly 2 billion ha)—an area constituting 17% of the earth's vegetated land area—have been degraded since World War II.

**Erosion Control.** Some of the soil in any area will be lost through erosion, a process in which soil particles are worn away through natural agents such as wind, rain, and the pull of gravity. Although it takes hundreds of years for a layer of soil 0.4 inch (1 cm) deep to form, that amount can erode in just a few months or years. Vegetation discourages erosion, however, forming a protective covering against the elements and achoring the soil with its roots. Thus the removal of vegetation greatly accelerates erosion. Activities that promote soil erosion include farming, mining, construction, and deforestation, all of which involve removal of the natural plant cover.

Erosion has a variety of ill effects. For example, as topsoil is lost, crops produced in the eroded area are less healthy and agricultural productivity is reduced. If eroded soil is swept into a body of water, aquatic environments also suffer, becoming choked with sediment.

Sound agricultural practices, such as contour plowing, strip cropping, terracing, and conservation tillage, minimize soil erosion and help damaged soil to recover.

**Contour Plowing.** In this method, hilly areas, which are especially prone to soil erosion, are plowed and planted along the land's natural contours rather than in straight rows. Because the plowed furrows run around hills rather than straight across them, less soil is washed downhill by rain. The practice can, in some cases, reduce erosion by 60% to 80%.

**Strip Cropping.** Contour plowing is sometimes combined with strip cropping, the planting of two different crops in alternating rows. For instance, corn, which allows water to travel easily between stalks and therefore offers poor soil protection, can be planted between rows of alfalfa, a so-called cover crop and an effective erosion defense.

**Terracing.** Contour plowing and strip cropping are ineffective when farming takes place on mountains and steep hills. Erosion control in such areas commonly takes the form of terracing, a technique in which a mountain is shaped into horizontal platforms somewhat resembling giant stairsteps. People who farm on steep slopes have built and maintained terraces for centuries.

**Conservation Tillage.** Erosion increases when farmland is plowed in preparation for spring planting. The practice of conservation tillage, or minimum tillage, eliminates such preparation, instead allowing the residue from previous crops to remain and hold the soil in place. Farmers then employ special machines to punch seed holes in the soil. Although conservation tillage greatly reduces soil erosion, sometimes by as much as 90%, it increases the need for weed control via chemical herbicides.

**Maintenance of Soil Fertility.** An important part of soil conservation is the maintenance and improvement of soil fertility, particularly in the case of agricultural land. In natural environments, essential minerals in the soil are incorporated into living organisms and cycle back to the soil when those organisms die and decompose. When crops are harvested, however, the minerals they contain are not returned to the ground, causing soil fertility to decline. The problem is compounded

Without a protective cover of vegetation, tilled land is particularly vulnerable to erosion.

© GRANT HEILMAN/GRANT HEILMAN PHOTOGRAPHY

© GEORGE HOLTON/PHOTO RESEARCHERS

The stone statues of Easter Island. Evidence indicates that this Pacific island once contained a rich subtropical forest. Polynesian settlers apparently overused wood resources for centuries, stripping the land of much essential vegetation and, as a consequence, devastating animal and human populations alike.

when the same crops are grown in the same fields year after year, rapidly depleting the specific minerals required by those plants.

The fertility of agricultural land can be maintained through crop rotation, a process in which different crops are planted in the same field over a period of years. Because the mineral requirements for different crops vary, no one mineral is depleted quickly. If one of the crops in the rotation is a member of the legume family (which includes peas, beans, clover, and alfalfa), soil fertility is actually enhanced. Legumes attract bacteria that convert atmospheric nitrogen into nitrogen fertilizer, which remains in the soil and enhances the growth of other crops in the rotation.

Directly adding fertilizer to soil can also enhance fertility. Organic fertilizers, such as manure, bone meal, and crop residues, slowly release essential minerals as the organic material decays. In contrast, inorganic fertilizers, which are manufactured from chemical compounds, are immediately available to plants but remain in the soil for a short period of time. In addition, inorganic fertilizers are highly mobile and quickly wash out of soil, causing water pollution as they are swept into lakes and rivers.

**Irrigation.** Irrigation of agricultural land in areas with seasonal or sparse precipitation is another means of improving crop growth. Because of the expanding nutritional needs of an increasing global population, the amount of irrigated land worldwide has tripled since 1955. However, because irrigation water contains some dissolved salts, water evaporation leaves behind a salt deposit, which is detrimental to crops. Over a period of years, the amount of salt in the soil increases, a process known as salinization. Therefore excessive irrigation actually causes plant growth to decline and can, in extreme cases, kill crops. Removing excess salt from soil is an expensive and difficult process.

In the United States, extreme salinization has occurred in portions of California where irrigation initially converted desert into rich farmland.

The problem can be minimized, however, through irrigation techniques that utilize small amounts of water sprinkled directly onto the root zone of individual plants rather than large quantities of water sprayed over an entire field.

Drip-irrigation systems can be used to conserve water and reduce irrigation-related soil damage.

© BEN WEDDLE/MIDWEST STOCK

Salt deposits left behind by irrigation water can seriously reduce soil fertility.

**Water Conservation.** Fresh water is a renewable resource that is continually recycled between the land, the atmosphere, and the oceans and other bodies of water. Although water covers the majority of the earth's surface, only 2.5% of the planet's water is fresh, and most of that is frozen in ice caps and glaciers. Fresh water is obtained from surface sources, such as rivers and lakes, and from underground sources called aquifers (underground regions of porous rock).

Because fresh water is unevenly distributed, the amount that is available around the planet varies from region to region. Millions of people live in arid areas where acute water shortages restrict daily water use to several gallons per person. In regions that have adequate fresh water, daily per-capita use can reach several hundred gallons per day. Worldwide, agricultural irrigation accounts for 68% of the fresh water used by humans, while industry uses 24%, and domestic and municipal water usage accounts for the remaining 8%. Water-resource problems include flooding, overdrawing of both surface and groundwater, and water pollution.

**Flooding.** When mountain or hillside forests remain intact, their plant-protected soil absorbs much excess precipitation, which helps to prevent flooding in adjacent areas drained by a river system. By the same token, removal of these forests can exacerbate regional flooding.

Similarly, excess water is also effectively absorbed by wetlands, that is, areas that are transitional between terrestrial and aquatic environments and that are underwater for at least part of the year. Consequently, drainage of wetlands to make way for farming or construction can increase the severity of floods. This factor may have been at work during the extensive flooding that occurred in the midwestern United States in 1993. The greatest flood damage occurred in Missouri, Illinois, and Iowa, which have only 15% of their original wetlands intact.

Flooding is often further provoked by the fact that floodplains, that is, areas that border a river and are prone to flooding, are popular sites for construction. Such development reduces the ability of a floodplain to absorb water, allowing water to rise and spread more extensively and rapidly.

**Overuse.** The demand for fresh water is increasing in response to both the rising world population and the industrialization of developing countries. This growing need can have several deleterious effects on the environment. When too much fresh water is removed from surface sources, wetland areas can dry up, harming wildlife in these habitats. In addition, surface sources typically become saltier when too much water is removed, again posing a threat to wildlife. For example, much of the water in rivers and streams that feed into the Aral Sea in Kazakhstan (formerly part of the Soviet Union) was diverted for irrigation, causing the sea's water level to drop and salt concentration to rise. Many of the Aral's fish died and the local fishing industry was ruined.

The supply of groundwater, that is, water stored in aquifers, is also vulnerable to exploitation. Accessed through wells, the volume of fresh water contained in aquifers is far greater than the amount found in surface sources. Aquifers are supplied by precipitation that is absorbed by the soil and drains through the rock beneath, as well as by seepage from surface bodies of water. However, an aquifer provides a renewable resource only if the amount of groundwater withdrawn does not exceed the amount that replaces it. Otherwise, deeper wells must be drilled as the water supply is reduced. For instance, the water table (the top of an aquifer) of the Ogallala aquifer, a massive groundwater deposit in Texas, Kansas, Nebraska, and surrounding states, has lowered in many places as a result of groundwater withdrawals.

**Water Quality.** A worldwide concern, water quality can be compromised by disease-causing organisms, sewage, chemicals, or sediments from soil erosion. These substances get into surface and groundwater from specific points of discharge, such as pipes or sewers (point-source pollution), or from large areas of land (nonpoint-source pollution). Waste discharged from a factory into surface water is another example of point-source contamination, whereas mining wastes, agricultural runoff, and construction sediments are considered nonpoint-source pollution.

Contamination of groundwater, which occurs when pesticides, fertilizers, and other materials seep downward from septic tanks, landfills, mining operations, and farms, is technically difficult and prohibitively expensive to reverse. Therefore prevention of groundwater pollution is the most effective way to deal with the problem.

Since the 1970s, however, the United States has made substantial progress in cleaning its surface water. Much of the improvement can be traced to the Clean Water Act, which reduced the amount of municipal and industrial pollution reaching surface sources. Under the provisions of this act, which was originally passed as the Water Pollution Control Act of 1972, sewage treatment facilities were built and the Environmental Protection Agency set limitations on the amount of toxic chemicals that can be discharged into waterways. The act was amended in 1977, 1981, and 1987, and in 1995 it was again up for review and reauthorization. (See also WATER POLLUTION.)

**Forest Conservation.** Forests cover about one-third of the earth's total land area. In addition to serving as essential wildlife habitats, they also aid in the cycling of energy and nutrients through the environment and, through absorption and evaporation of water, exercise great influence over world precipitation patterns.

In the United States, the U.S. Forest Service and the Bureau of Land Management oversee forests owned by the federal government. These public forests are managed for multiple uses, including mining and recreation, the harvesting of commercially valuable timber, and as wildlife habitats. Such diverse uses sometimes conflict with one another, with people who want the forests left as wilderness or recreational areas at odds with those who want to exploit at least portions of them for industry.

The maintenance and utilization of forests is further complicated by the fact that in the United States over half of them are privately owned. Consequently, U.S. forests are frequently converted to more profitable uses, including as agricultural land or as business or residential areas. Within the first few decades of the 21st century, the loss of privately owned forests in the United States is projected to be greatest in the South.

Trees may be harvested from forests in several ways. When a forest is clear-cut, all trees are removed from that area. Timber companies prefer clear-cutting because it is the most economical harvesting technique and because it permits the growth of new stands of trees, such as Douglas firs, that cannot tolerate shade. However, this method tends to destroy wildlife habitats and increase soil erosion. Clear-cut areas are often replanted in rows containing a single species of fast-growing tree, similar to the way in which agricultural crops are planted. These reforested areas, which are harvested every 50 years or so, never support the variety of wildlife found in forests containing diverse plant species. Other harvest methods include removal of only the tallest trees, with the trees cut down in stages at intervals of eight to ten years; or the logging of only the largest hardwood trees, or the clearing of diseased ones, at five- and ten-year intervals.

Forests are a renewable resource as long as they are managed for a sustained yield, which means that the amount of timber harvested annually does not exceed the growth of replacement trees. In many parts of the world, however, such principles are not applied. Moreover, many forests, particularly in the tropics, are being permanently cleared to make way for agriculture and cattle ranching as well as for use as timber. The removal of forest without adequate replanting is known as deforestation.

Humans cleared much of the temperate forests of Europe, Asia, and North America over a period of hundreds of years. In contrast, deforestation in the tropics is currently occurring at a pace unsurpassed in human history. Because of conflicting data, the precise rate of tropical deforestation is still under debate. But even the most optimistic figures indicate that millions of acres of rain forest are being destroyed annually.

The Tropical Forestry Action Plan, developed in 1985 by a group that included the World Bank, the United Nations, the United States, and many tropical countries, provides funds to reduce deforestation, establish tree farms on degraded land, and improve forestry research in tropical countries. Other measures that have been adopted to reduce the destruction of tropical forests include debt-for-nature swaps, which forgive some of the massive foreign debts accumulated by developing countries in exchange for their agreement to protect large areas of forest. Conservationists also urge the establishment of tropical reforestation projects in which degraded land would be planted

Fire is used to clear a section of Brazilian rain forest. Millions of acres of tropical rain forest are destroyed annually for timber and to provide land for ranches, farms, mines, and reservoirs.

© M. HARVEY/PANOS PICTURES

Sheep and goats graze on a Kenyan rangeland. Overgrazing can kill rangeland vegetation, leaving the soil vulnerable to erosion. In semiarid, drought-prone regions, the damaged area may deteriorate into desert.

with ecologically (as opposed to commercially) important trees. (See also FORESTRY.)

**Rangeland Conservation.** Grasses and similar plants grow on rangelands, areas that are too arid to support forests or crops. Rangelands occupy about 30% of the total land area of the United States, and their grasses supply forage for both wildlife and grazing livestock. Approximately two-thirds of U.S. rangelands are privately owned, while the remaining one-third is owned by the federal government and managed by the Bureau of Land Management and the U.S. Forest Service. Like public forests, public rangelands are managed for multiple uses, including grazing, mining, and recreation, and as wildlife habitats. Livestock operators pay the U.S. government small fees to graze their animals on public rangelands. The fees, which are heavily subsidized by tax dollars, are used to maintain these areas and to fix any damage done by the livestock. Many conservationists believe that these charges should be increased to cover all costs associated with grazing on federal lands.

Rangeland damage occurs when too many animals graze the vegetation. The maximum number of animals that an area of rangeland can support is known as that area's carrying capacity. If the capacity is not exceeded, rangelands remain a renewable resource. But when too many animals occupy these areas, the grasses and other plants are overgrazed, killing the vegetation and consequently leaving the soil exposed and more susceptible to erosion.

Most rangelands are located in semiarid regions that periodically have extended periods of drought, and the results of overgrazing can be particularly severe in these areas. When drought occurs on a well-managed rangeland, the native grasses die back to the soil line but the underground roots remain alive, holding the soil in place and allowing the plants to make a full recovery once the rain returns. However, when drought occurs on overgrazed rangeland, winds erode the barren soil, leaving the area too damaged to recover when the drought ends. This may cause desertification, a phenomenon in which once-fertile rangeland turns to desert. Millions of acres of new desert are formed worldwide each year as a result of human activities. Desertification can be reversed and rangeland restored through an expensive, time-consuming process in which drought-resistant vegetation is planted (to lessen the impact of wind and stabilize the soil) and the land is permitted to lie fallow (unused) for many years.

**Plant and Wildlife Conservation.** The diverse species of flora and fauna across the globe foster a sustainable environment. Plants, for example, provide food and oxygen for humans and other animals, whereas microscopic bacteria and fungi decompose organic wastes and recycle materials needed by all living things. Living organisms are also the source of many chemicals, medicines, and industrial products.

However, biological diversity is declining worldwide. When the last member of a species dies, those animals are said to be extinct and therefore no longer a renewable resource. Other designations are used to identify the point to which a species' population has declined. A species is classified as endangered when its numbers have declined so much that it is in imminent danger of extinction. A threatened species is one whose population is quite low, but not as perilously low as an endangered group. Each of these designations—threatened, endangered, and extinct—represents a decline in biological diversity.

Although extinction is a natural process associated with the continuing evolution of living organisms, human activities, such as the logging of forests and the draining of wetlands, have greatly accelerated the rate of extinctions, through the alteration and destruction of wild habitats. Pollution of all types also changes habitats, even those in wilderness areas where more obvious changes have not occurred.

Historically, hunting was a major cause of the extinction or near extinction of certain animals, but most countries have come to provide some wildlife protection through the adoption of various hunting and fishing laws. In certain cases, managed hunting can actually benefit a species by ensuring that its population does not exceed its habitat's carrying capacity.

Humans also affect living things by introducing a foreign species into an area where the plant or animal had not previously existed. Such introductions, if successful, may upset the natural balance that has evolved among the organisms living in that habitat. The new species may start killing native plants or animals, successfully competing against other organisms for food and consequently causing native wildlife to decline.

Many countries are developing and implementing a detailed plan, known as a wildlife conservation strategy, to conserve biological diversity. Part of this strategy includes setting aside natural areas for wildlife. Worldwide, more than 3,000 national parks, wildlife refuges, forests, and other protected areas exist, although many of these have multiple uses. Some wildlife refuges in the United States, for instance, have been mined for oil or other minerals, a use that clearly alters the habitat. Certain parts of the world, particularly the tropics, have few protected areas and urgently need more land to be set aside.

Species conservation has been further enhanced by the 1973 Convention on Trade in Endangered Species of Wild Flora and Fauna, which was drafted in association with the United Nations Environmental Program. The agreement, in which most countries participate, bans the hunting, trapping, or selling of any threatened or endangered species. Nevertheless, because enforcement of this treaty is lax in many countries, illegal trade in ostensibly protected species continues.

Another strategy, captive breeding, has also been employed to save endangered animal species. In this, a few members of an endangered species are captured from the wild and bred in zoos or similar facilities to increase their numbers. The ultimate goal of captive-breeding programs is to reestablish small populations of endangered species in the wild. This technique has met with some success, helping to increase, for example, populations of whooping cranes and bald eagles. However, captive breeding is expensive and tends not to be applied to less-conspicuous species, such as plants, bacteria, and fungi, despite their importance to a smoothly functioning environment.

**Mineral Conservation.** Minerals are elements or compounds that occur naturally in the earth's crust. They can be either metals, such as cobalt, copper, and gold, or nonmetals, including quartz, gypsum, and diamond.

Minerals vary widely in distribution and abundance. The United States is rich in copper and molybdenum, for example, but has little chromium or manganese. Because certain minerals are strategically important—chromium, for instance, is used in certain jet parts—the United States and other countries often stockpile these to reduce dependence on politically unstable suppliers.

A mineral deposit is referred to as an ore if it is concentrated enough to be profitably mined. High-grade ores contain relatively large amounts of particular minerals, while low-grade ores contain lesser amounts. Because they are more profitable to mine, high-grade ores are extracted first, and low-grade deposits are developed only after the richer ones have been depleted.

Estimates of worldwide deposits for each mineral are divided into reserves and resources. Mineral reserves are those deposits currently profitable to mine. Mineral resources include known deposits of low-grade ore that are not yet economically worthwhile to extract but may be usable in the future. Economic, political, and technological changes cause estimates of mineral reserves and resources to fluctuate. If a particular mineral's price on the world market increases, for example, some borderline mineral resources may slip into the reserve category.

As with other natural resources, mineral consumption varies widely around the world, with the United States and other industrialized countries consuming a disproportionate share. As a case in point, although the United States has less than 5% of the world's population, it consumes about 24% of the aluminum and 19% of the copper mined annually. Worldwide mineral needs are expected to rise as developing countries, which consume a relatively small share of these resources, become more industrialized. Because minerals are a nonrenewable resource, the prospect of an increased demand raises concerns over the sustainability of these materials.

The estimated amount of time that it will take to exhaust the reserves of a mineral is called the world reserve-life index. Partly as a result of both increased mineral exploration and pricing changes for these resources, rising mineral consumption between the late 1970s and early 1990s was actually paralleled by a growth in world reserve-life indices for various minerals. Coupled with such

Demands for irrigation water have severely reduced the level of the Aral Sea, in Central Asia.

fluctuations is the inherent difficulty in accurately assessing such figures. For example, if the 1972 estimates for copper and lead reserves had been correct, these supplies would have been depleted by 1990. Ultimately, reserve and reserve-life figures are most useful for comparing quantities of minerals in relation to one another rather than for giving a true picture of mineral supplies. With this in mind, world reserves of copper in the early 1990s were estimated at 310 million metric tons and those of lead at 63 million metric tons. If these measurements are accurate, then, at current consumption rates, it is expected that worldwide copper reserves will be exhausted before the year 2024 and lead reserves before 2009.

Concerns over the growing demand for minerals are compounded by the environmental damage produced by the mining and processing of ore. This includes the destruction of wildlife habitats as the land is disturbed and the increased susceptibility of this land to erosion. The latter problem becomes even more severe when soil that has been contaminated with acids and other toxic by-products of mining is swept into the air and nearby waterways.

© THOMAS BRAISE/TONY STONE IMAGES

Chemical waste. Since the 1970s, legislative action has greatly reduced U.S. water pollution.

Ore refinement facilities also contribute to environmental damage. Mineral processing consumes large amounts of energy and emits a great deal of pollution as well. Lead, arsenic, and cadmium are some of the toxic substances that may be discharged into the surrounding environment during refinement.

Several strategies can be employed to reduce environmental damage caused by mineral exploitation and to improve sustainable use of these materials. After a mine closes, for example, degraded land can be restored to a seminatural condition. This process, called reclamation, involves neutralizing the source of pollutants, grading the land to its natural contours, adding topsoil, and establishing a covering of vegetation to hold the soil in place. With the exception of areas that were surface-mined for coal, however, U.S. law

does not currently mandate the reclamation of mining lands.

The release of toxins during the refinement process can be diminished through the use of pollution-control equipment, including scrubbers and electrostatic precipitators. A scrubber, for instance, contains chemicals that react with contaminants as polluted air passes through, causing impurities to precipitate out before they can enter the atmosphere. In lime scrubbers, a chemical spray of water and lime neutralizes sulfur dioxide and other acidic gases, leaving behind a sulfuric slurry. This by-product, however, has itself posed a disposal problem. More recently, scrubbers that utilize magnesium and other chemicals have been developed. These devices remove sulfur from polluted emissions in a form that permits the sulfur to be recycled as a marketable product.

Electrostatic precipitators use electrical charges to remove particulates from polluted air. Emissions pass through an electrically charged area between positive and negative electrodes, causing the particulate matter to become positively charged and therefore to adhere to the precipitator's negatively charged plate. The particulates are disposed of or, in some cases, reused.

Mineral conservation is commonly achieved through recycling, which is the conversion of used materials into new products. The practice greatly increased during the 1980s and 1990s, so that by the mid-1990s approximately 65 million people in the United States were living in areas with curbside collection of materials for recycling, and the average American family of four was recycling more than 1,000 pounds (450 kg) of aluminum and steel cans, plastic and glass bottles, newspaper, and cardboard each year. In addition, more than half of the aluminum cans used in the United States were being collected, remelted, and reprocessed into new cans.

Recycling not only conserves natural resources but also helps to reduce the volume of solid waste in the enviroment, thus lessening the need for sanitary landfills. In areas where solid waste is incinerated, removal of metals and glass for reuse allows the remaining waste products to burn more efficiently. Recycling also produces less water and air pollution than do industrial processes that manufacture products from raw materials.

The recycling of minerals likewise requires less energy than does the mining and processing of virgin ore. Recycling 21 aluminum cans, for instance, saves the energy equivalent of 1.0 gallon (3.8 liters) of gasoline.

Not all recycling projects have been universally lauded, however. In a 1994 study, for example, the Cato Institute, a public-policy think tank, evaluated the results of a mandatory recycling law in New Jersey and concluded that it cost about $100 more per ton to collect, process, and sell recyclables than it did to dispose of them in a landfill. The study also questioned whether recycled products are particularly marketable, since many states are now producing them.

**Energy Conservation.** Fossil fuels—coal, oil, and natural gas—supply most of the energy used by human society. Produced from organic debris over millions of years, they are, for all intents and purposes, nonrenewable resources. Nuclear energy, which is released when the nuclei of atoms are split, is also nonrenewable, because it is fueled by the mineral uranium. However, only small

Smog obscures the Los Angeles skyline. Concerns over pollution, global warming, and the eventual exhaustion of fossil-fuel supplies have led to a search for cleaner, renewable energy sources.

amounts of uranium are required for a nuclear reaction, which makes nuclear power an extremely long-lasting energy source.

There are a variety of renewable energy sources as well.

(1) Solar energy, that is, energy from the sun. This can be utilized by employing photovoltaic cells, which use silicon to transform solar energy directly into electricity.

(2) Geothermal energy, which comes from heat trapped below the earth's surface. The source is granite rock that has been warmed by natural radioactive decay processes. Another form of geothermal power, called hydrothermal energy, is drawn from steam emitted from the ground. Natural steam production occurs in a variety of areas around the world.

(3) Wind power, in which rotating windmills drive electricity-generating turbines.

(4) Hydropower, which uses flowing water to drive turbine generators.

(5) Biomass, which refers to combustible materials, including wood, wood by-products, and agricultural and municipal waste products, that can be used to generate energy.

The production of wind energy, hydropower, and wood are all influenced by the light or heat of the sun. They can therefore also be considered indirect solar-energy sources.

Each form of energy causes some type of negative environmental impact. Problems associated with fossil fuels include damage to the environment at retrieval sites, including coal mines and oil and natural gas wells; accidental spills during transport or storage; and emission of carbon dioxide and other pollutants during combustion. Nuclear-energy use is complicated by the issues of the safety of nuclear power plants and the safe disposal of nuclear wastes, some of which remain dangerously radioactive for thousands, or even millions, of years. While solar-energy technologies are not pollution-free, the negative environmental consequences are less than those resulting from the use of fossil fuels or nuclear energy.

Although energy from renewable sources is currently more expensive to produce than that from fossil fuels or nuclear power sources, substantial price reductions have occurred, and future technological advances are expected to lower costs even further. According to the U.S. Department of Energy, for example, the cost of generating electricity through wind power (taking into account a combination of capital and operating expenses) dropped from about 40 cents per kilowatt-hour in 1980 to less than 10 cents in 1988. Photovoltaic electricity costs shrank from more than $19 per kilowatt-hour in the early 1970s to about 30 cents by the early 1990s. Electricity produced by geothermal plants was estimated to run as low as 4.5 to 6.5 cents per kilowatt-hour in the

Energy from the sun, here being collected by solar dishes, remains costly to harness.

635

early 1990s. By comparison, among fossil-fuel powered steam-electric plants under major investor-owned electric utilities, the cost of electricity production fell from about 2.8 cents per kilowatt-hour in 1985 to approximately 2.3 cents per kilowatt-hour in 1991, taking into account operating, maintenance, and fuel expenses.

However, the deregulation of the U.S. power industry, coupled with the subsequent trend for large utility services to purchase power from small, private suppliers, has been cited as a possible barrier to the use of renewable energy sources. The smaller companies may find it prohibitive to invest the capital needed to fund renewable-technology research, particularly in view of the need to offer their customers competitive prices.

Not surprisingly, industrialized nations use much more energy per capita than do developing countries, with the United States as a whole consuming 25% of global energy supplies. Developing nations are, however, experiencing the greatest increase in energy demands. As with the rising use of other resources by these countries, the change is a consequence of both expanding industrialization and rapidly growing populations.

As worldwide energy use continues to increase, a number of strategies have been proposed to slow the depletion of fossil fuels and the spread of pollution. These include the development of alternative energy sources and the employment of various forms of energy conservation, such as carpooling, reduced use of heat in winter, and even the simple act of turning off lights when leaving a room. In addition, advances have been made in the production of energy-efficient refrigerators, automobile engines, and other products, reducing the amount of fuel needed to power such equipment.

LINDA R. BERG, *Coauthor of "Environment"*

### Bibliography

Anderson, H. M., "Reforming National Forest Policy," *Issues in Science and Technology* (Winter 1993–1994).

Barnett, Vic, and K. Feridun Turkman, eds., *Statistics for the Environment* (Wiley 1993).

Chadwick, D. H., "Roots of the Sky," *National Geographic* (October 1993).

Dreyfus, D. A., and A. B. Ashby, "Fueling Our Global Future," *Environment* 32 (4) (May 1990).

Ehrlich, P. R., and A. H. Ehrlich, *The Population Explosion* (Simon & Schuster 1990).

Endicott, Eve, ed., *Land Conservation through Public/Private Partnerships* (Island Press, Covelo 1993).

Fulkerson, W., et al., "Energy from Fossil Fuels," *Scientific American* (September 1990).

Mitchell, J. G., "Our Disappearing Wetlands," *National Geographic* (October 1992).

Morgan, M. G., "What Would It Take to Revitalize Nuclear Power in the United States?" *Environment* 35 (2) (March 1993).

Owens, Owen, *Living Waters: How to Save Your Local Stream* (Rutgers Univ. Press 1993).

Radetsky, P., "Back to Nature," *Discover* (July 1993).

Raven, P. H., et al., *Environment*, updated ed. (Saunders 1995).

Rolston, H., *Conserving Natural Value* (Columbia Univ. Press 1994).

World Resources Institute et al., *World Resources 1992–93* (Oxford 1992).

Young, J. E., "Mining the Earth," *State of the World: 1992* (Norton 1992).

**CONSERVATION, ART.**   See ART CONSERVATION.

**CONSERVATION OF ENERGY.**   See ENERGY—*Conservation of Energy*; THERMODYNAMICS—*First Law of Thermodynamics*.

**CONSERVATION OF MASS.**   See MATTER.

**CONSERVATION OF MATTER.**   See MATTER.

**CONSERVATIVE JUDAISM,** one of the four branches of American Judaism (with Orthodox, Reform, and Reconstructionist Judaism) and the branch to which the largest number of religious Jews in the United States belong. Conservative Judaism has roots in the 19th-century European Jewish movement called Historical Judaism and like it has striven since its beginnings to balance yearnings for Jewish tradition and identity with the desire to accommodate and adapt to the modern world. Nevertheless, Conservative Judaism in the United States has evolved independently of its European counterpart.

**Origin.**   The beginning of the Conservative movement may be dated to the convening of the first class at the Jewish Theological Seminary of America, in January 1887. At the time the seminary was established, the great majority of American Jewish congregations were affiliated with the Reform movement. Reform's radical Pittsburgh Platform of 1885 had rejected both traditional ritual and the concept of Jewish peoplehood. The 12 men (including Sabato Morais, Henry Pereira Mendes, and Alexander Kohut) who founded the Jewish Theological Seminary in 1886 were seeking (in the words of the seminary's articles of incorporation) to establish a college of "conservative Jewish principles," one that would moderate between the conservative wing of Reform Judaism and the traditionalist (Orthodox) community. The need for such mediation appeared pressing: by the end of the 19th century, the overwhelming majority of Jewish immigrants to the United States were Eastern European and traditional in their religious outlook, while the established American Reform community had its roots in Germany. The seminary's founders themselves represented a spectrum of belief but shared a concern for the successful adjustment of the newcomers to American Judaism.

The seminary's earliest years were difficult. The first class consisted of several teenage boys who received instruction in a decrepit classroom at New York City's Shearith Israel synagogue, and the seminary attracted few students and garnered little distinction during its first 15 years. Then, in 1902, after lengthy negotiations coordinated chiefly by Cyrus Adler, and as the seminary teetered on the verge of bankruptcy, its leaders lured the distinguished Judaica scholar Solomon Schechter (1847–1915) from Cambridge University. They encouraged him to reorganize the institution. He did so with skill and dignity; by the time he died, the seminary had become a prominent institution in the American academic community. (See ADLER, CYRUS; SCHECHTER, SOLOMON.)

**Growth.**   Schechter not only invigorated the seminary but, toward the end of his life, together with representatives of 13 congregations, founded an institution that has come to rank second only to the Jewish Theological Seminary in importance in the Conservative movement: the United Synagogue of America. At its founding in 1913, however, Schechter intentionally rejected the label "Conservative" for this union of synagogues, preferring to call it a Union for Promoting Traditional Judaism. His goal was not only to organize those congregations loyal to the seminary's "conservative" principles but to attract traditionalist congregations as well.

The preamble to the United Synagogue's constitution, reflecting Schechter's hope that all non-Reform synagogues would find a home in the organization, explicitly committed the United Synagogue to embrace all elements loyal to traditionalist (non-Reform) Judaism. But it never did, and the Conservative movement quickly became one of several distinct branches of American Judaism, viewed by the Orthodox as much too radical and by the Reform movement as much too traditional.

Today the Jewish Theological Seminary is an accredited university. Its campus in the Morningside Heights section of Manhattan houses four schools—a college, a cantor's institute, and a graduate school (which includes an extensive teacher-training program) as well as the rabbinical school. Its affiliations with schools in Los Angeles, Jerusalem, Buenos Aires, Budapest, and Moscow give it international connections. Its library contains the largest collection of Judaica in the diaspora. (See JEWISH THEOLOGICAL SEMINARY.)

Struggling to find the right balance between tradition and change occupied Conservative leaders during most of the 20th century. The admission (1983–1984) of female seminarians to the Jewish Theological Seminary and the ordination (1985) of the first women Conservative rabbis, as well as the decision to invest female graduates of the Cantor's Institute with the title *ḥazzan*, seemingly cut off Conservative from Orthodox Judaism permanently. Meanwhile, its ever greater reliance on ritual, ceremony, and Jewish legal precedents (Halakhah) has moved it further from Reform Judaism. Until 1988, Conservative leaders refrained from precise delineation of Conservative Jewish doctrine in order to embrace as many individuals and congregations as possible. The strategy worked well; Conservative Judaism's 850 congregations (in the late 1980s) made it the largest of the four branches of Judaism in the United States. The Conservative movement also was established in Israel, where it became known as the Mesorati, or "traditional," movement.

**Conservative Tenets.** Finally confident of the movement's secure position, rabbis and lay leaders issued the first statement of principles of Conservative Judaism in 1988. The statement continued the Conservative insistence on balancing Halakhah and change, simultaneously advocating accommodation to American culture while trying clearly to distinguish the secular American way of viewing the world from the Jewish way. In contrast to Reform Judaism, which rejected Halakhah, and to Orthodoxy, which (ostensibly) rejected change, Conservative Judaism has articulated a posture of revering the old while embracing the new. The movement has delineated an organic cluster of values that independently determines Conservative Judaism's religious profile, including the nation of Israel, the Hebrew language, peoplehood, Torah, Halakhah, and God.

From the perspective of most American Jews, Conservative Judaism clearly has cast its lot with change. Men and women sit together in prayer; women are called to the Torah, are counted in the *minyan* (the quorum of adult Jews whose presence formally constitutes a congregation for worship), and may rise to presidencies of synagogues. Girls have a Bat Mitzvah nearly identical to the Bar Mitzvah for boys, and Conservative educational programs for women are identical to those for men.

At the same time, wide variations exist in Conservative worship. Sabbath services range from those in which a great deal of English is used to those in which congregants largely chant the service in Hebrew. In accordance with the observance of *kashrut* (dietary laws), some congregations rigorously inspect all food brought into the synagogue, while others rely on members to use good judgment in not bringing nonkosher food to social events. These decisions rest chiefly with the rabbis, who shape (however loosely) the ideology of the movement and the positions of local synagogues, just as they create, edit, and publish all the official liturgy of the movement. The rabbi, more than any other religious professional (such as cantor or educator), is the embodiment of Conservative Judaism in each community.

**Contemporary Issues.** Conservative Judaism thus has attained an explicit statement (1988) of its doctrine and practice, yet areas of considerable concern to the contemporary Conservative movement remain. These include intermarriage, feminism, homosexuality, and spirituality.

Since 1985, one out of every two American Jews who has married has married a non-Jew, and the number of Conservative Jews who are marrying outside their faith continues to increase. Greater numbers of women are emerging in positions of rabbinic and lay leadership; the Conservative prayerbook, *Siddur Sim Shalom,* to the consternation of some Conservatives, removes exclusively male usages for the Divine in selected areas and adds the word *mothers* to some prayers that had previously named only the biblical patriarchs. Increasingly, gay and lesbian Jews are seeking to affiliate with Jewish congregations or are creating their own synagogues, and openly gay and lesbian rabbinical students are eager to become rabbis. Local congregations are struggling to rise to these challenges, as is the national movement.

In the midst of these and other contemporary debates, however, Conservative Jews are continuing to explore dimensions of spirituality. They are looking for enhanced personal and communal prayer, rewriting liturgies to heighten the sense of prayer and communion with God, and searching for new ways to make transcendence or spirituality a more significant part of their lives.

See also JUDAISM.

MARC LEE RAPHAEL
*College of William and Mary*

**Bibliography**

Adler, Cyrus, ed., *The Jewish Theological Seminary of America: Semi-Centennial Volume* (Jewish Theological Seminary 1939).
Cardin, Nina Beth, and David Wolf Silverman, eds., *The Seminary at 100: Reflections on the Jewish Theological Seminary and the Conservative Movement* (Rabbinical Assembly and Jewish Theological Seminary 1987).
Davis, Moshe, *The Emergence of Conservative Judaism: The Historical School in Nineteenth Century America* (Jewish Publication Society 1963).
Ettenberg, Sylvia C., and Geraldine Rosenfield, *The Ramah Experience: Community and Commitment* (Ktav 1989).
Gillman, Neil, *Sacred Fragments: Conservative Judaism: The New Century* (Behrman 1993).
Gordis, Robert, *Conservative Judaism: A Modern Approach to Jewish Tradition* (United Synagogue of Am. 1970).
Greenberg, Simon, *The Conservative Movement in Judaism: An Introduction* (United Synagogue of Am. 1955).
Mandelbaum, Bernard, *Tales of the Fathers of the Conservative Movement* (Shengold 1989).
Nadell, Pamela Susan, *Conservative Judaism in America: A Biographical Dictionary and Sourcebook* (Greenwood Press 1988).
Rosenblum, Herbert, *Conservative Judaism: A Contemporary History* (United Synagogue of Am. 1983).
Sachar, Howard M., *History of the Jews in America* (Knopf 1992).
Sklare, Marshall, *Conservative Judaism: An American Religious Movement* (1955; reprint, Univ. Press of Am. 1985).
Waxman, Mordecai, ed., *Tradition and Change: The Development of Conservative Judaism* (Burning Bush Press 1958).

**CONSERVATISM,** in the broadest sense of the term, is a general disposition to favor the maintenance of things as they are and to be wary of innovations. This attitude distinguishes conservatives from those, often known as radicals or progressives, whose efforts to find new and better ways of doing things may place them in revolutionary opposition to the existing way of life. It also distinguishes conservatives from reactionaries, with whom they are sometimes confused. Reactionaries, believing that the present is inferior to some real or imagined past, are dedicated to the restoration of the good old days. Although their motives are different, their rejection of the existing order may be just as radical as that of the extreme progressives. Both stand poles apart from the conservative position.

Human life is largely a matter of habit, and habits are hard to break. In that sense conservatism always has been, and presumably always will be, a force to be reckoned with. But the conservatism that concerns us here is more specific. It began as a reaction to a particular historical event, the French Revolution of 1789.

The attack on the *ancien régime*, with its far-reaching demands for social and political innovation, was the most concentrated assault on established traditions that the world had seen up to that time. In response to this challenge, defenders of the old order found it necessary to formulate political and social theories of their own. Conservatism in the partisan sense was the product of this conflict. Ever since then it has remained an important factor in the theory and practice of politics.

**The Theory of Conservatism.** The earliest formulations of theoretical conservatism arose in response to the philosophy of the Enlightenment. That philosophy, which had been gathering strength since the end of the 17th century, was the main ideological force behind the French Revolution. Despite their differences, those who adhered to the ideas of the Enlightenment shared a distrust of all established institutions and a confidence in the capacity of "enlightened" reason to solve all human problems. Believing as they did in the progressive perfectibility of mankind, they suspected everything that owed its origin to the unenlightened past. They abhorred above all the web of special privileges that had come in the course of time to constitute the existing political and social system.

As forerunners of the laissez-faire liberalism of the early 19th century, they believed that the maximization of human happiness could best be achieved by allowing men and ideas to compete on terms of absolute legal equality. Their aspirations were most clearly reflected in the French revolutionists' *Declaration of the Rights of Man* (1789), which made a clean sweep of all special privileges and gave all men, as citizens, equal rights in the eyes of the law. In keeping with these aims, the revolutionists abolished all the traditional units of local government. Drastic innovation was the order of the day.

So comprehensive an interference with vested interests was bound to produce a reaction. Opposition theorists soon arose to challenge the basic assumptions of the revolutionists. Of these theorists the most immediately and widely influential was the British statesman Edmund Burke. Profoundly alarmed by the course of events in France, he published in *Reflections on the French Revolution* (1792) a warning to his fellow coun-try men against the dangers implicit in the new revolutionary movement.

The *Reflections* remain the classic statement of conservative political theory. In them, Burke tried to demonstrate that collective experience rather than individual reason is the true agency of human progress. He maintained that the operations of society are too complex to be deduced from the "rights of man" or from any other conceivable set of abstract principles, and that useful forms of social action are not finally derived from general philosophical speculations but from concrete practical experience. Even the best minds are too weak to comprehend the problems of society as a whole, he wrote, but men of ordinary capacity may discover, by trial and error, specific ways of meeting specific needs. Furthermore, these piecemeal discoveries, handed down from generation to generation, harden into tradition, which, as the time-tested product of untold centuries of rational problem-solving, embodies a total range of wisdom and experience far greater than that of any man or even any generation. Thus Burke accused the philosophers of the French Revolution of presuming to reject the collective judgment of the ages in favor of their own individual notions, thereby undermining the rational foundations of progress itself.

Nor did Burke feel that progress alone was at stake. He felt that the very existence of civilized life was threatened. The revolutionists' belief that man is naturally good, and inferentially that corrupt traditions are the source of all evil, seemed to him utterly dangerous because it created both a temptation to destroy tradition and a false confidence in the ability of right reason to bring about a more perfect order. Burke believed that man is passionate and self-seeking by nature, and that rational persuasion has little power to divert him from evil courses. Habit, rather than reason, is the true basis of social order, he maintained. Through habitual acceptance of traditional customs and habitual respect for established authorities and procedures, men gradually learn to discipline their antisocial impulses and live in a civilized fashion. Civilization, in Burke's view, is a great but precarious achievement whose very existence depends on the maintenance of good social habits.

Thus Burke saw the French Revolution as nothing less than a threat to all that is most distinctively human. By challenging the authority of traditional institutions, the revolutionists, in the name of reason, were rashly ushering in an era of irrational and barbarous passion. Writing before Napoleon had even appeared on the French political scene, Burke predicted that military dictatorship would be the final outcome of the revolutionary experiment. Only brute force, he said, would suffice to maintain order in a society where men had lost the habits of civility.

Although the word "conservatism" does not appear anywhere in Burke's *Reflections*, the book is a definite statement of the school of thought now known by that name. From Burke's time on, that school has never ceased to attract influential adherents. Its persistence was assured by the unrelenting dynamism of modern social life. The industrial revolution, the population explosion, and other massive and profound developments made the 19th and 20th centuries outstandingly the age of innovation. As drastic changes in every aspect of human life posed a constant and continuing threat to the maintenance of established institutions, conservative protest became an institution in itself.

The revolution that gave rise to Burke also produced the unique French philosophers Count Joseph Marie de Maistre, Vicomte Louis de Bonald, and many other conservative theorists. During the 19th century Samuel Taylor Coleridge and Thomas Carlyle contributed important writings in defense of conservatism, and such outstanding statesmen at Metternich and Disraeli devoted their careers to its cause. Their 20th century followers are legion.

Conservative theorists in general have continued to follow the main lines laid down in the writings of Burke. Their starting point has always been to protest against the dangers of excessive innovation. In one form or another, faith in progress has been the ideological mainspring of all modern revolutions. Against this faith, conservatives have regularly found it necessary to defend the established order by stressing the organic and gradualist character of social evolution. Their typical mode of argument has been to press the claims of common sense and experience and minimize the creative potential of abstract theorizing.

**Conservative Parties.** The emergence of conservative theory did not lead immediately to the organization of conservative political parties. In the first place, resistance to the French revolutionary and Napoleonic armies, which dominated most of the European continent for nearly two decades, was essentially a military matter. Also, in the period immediately after the Napoleonic era there was little demand for genuinely conservative parties because the official trend of the times was not conservative but reactionary. The new state system set up by Metternich at the Congress of Vienna was an attempt to return as far as possible to the prerevolutionary world. Finally, although most of the restored monarchies found it prudent, as a concession to liberal opinion, to establish parliamentary institutions, the powers of the restoration parliaments were so limited and the electorates so narrow that organized political parties were hardly necessary. The nobility and the clergy, who had suffered most directly from the revolutionary movement, were the most reliable advocates of royal legitimacy, and their influence, rather than that of conservative parties, was generally relied on to secure the allegiance of the rest of the population. The influence of landlords and clerics was generally most effective in rural districts, where traditional ways were least affected by modern innovations. During the first decades of the 19th century, when the industrial revolution was still in its infancy, this state of affairs was an advantage to conservatives, for even in the more advanced countries of western Europe peasants still constituted a large majority of the population.

Nevertheless, within a few years the restoration settlement proved untenable. Because of their greater concentration and mobility the city dwellers tended to be politically more active and influential than the rural population, and among them the progressive sentiments of the revolutionary era were far from dead. Urban discontent with the generally unprogressive character of the restoration regimes festered; moreover, time was running against the countryside, because the absolute and relative size of the urban population continued to increase spectacularly as a consequence of the industrial revolution. In 1830 and, more seriously, in 1848, widespread insurrections threatened the restoration establishment. Once again the forces of innovation were clearly in the ascendant.

Modern conservatism, in the party sense, was an answer to that challenge. In the urban and democratic world that was emerging, the rural conservatism of squire and parson was increasingly outmoded. With the advent of mass electorates, power went to those who could gain the support of popular majorities. This called in turn for the establishment of well-organized political parties. Clearly, if conservatism was to survive and prosper in the modern world, it would have to compete on that basis.

The problem, then, was to find a platform on which conservative parties could appeal to a mass electorate. The social and religious conservatism of most country districts was the surest immediate source of conservative strength, and the agrarian population became and remained the nucleus of most conservative parties. In the dynamic world of the 19th and 20th centuries, however, the support of traditionally minded peasants was a wasting asset, and a good deal more was needed to provide the basis for an effective party.

This need was met primarily by the rise of nationalism. Conservatism first formed its alliance with nationalism when both were threatened by the Napoleonic empire. The alliance was not an easy one, however, either then or immediately after the empire's collapse, for the commitment of the restoration, with its reliance on dynastic legitimacy, to the existing state system in Italy and central Europe flew in the face of ever-rising demands for national self-determination.

Nevertheless, with its emphasis on the preservation of traditional values, conservatism had always been more nearly akin to nationalism than to the cosmopolitanism of the enlightenment, and as the ties of dynastic legitimacy loosened, conservative traditionalism tended more naturally to associate itself with the defense of national traditions. The main obstacle to this association was removed in 1870, when both Germany and Italy finally achieved national unification. By the end of the 19th century, conservative parties had largely succeeded in identifying themselves with the nationalist position. In the following era of strong and often belligerent national feeling, this association greatly broadened the basis of their popular appeal.

Conservatism was still further aided by the emergence of revolutionary socialism, and above all of Marxism, as a major political force. The Marxist position, characterized by dogmatic rejection of religion, nationalism, and private property, challenged a very large group of established sentiments and interests. By presenting themselves as the most determined opponents of this new revolutionary movement, conservative parties were in a position to claim the support of all those who shared one or more of those interests. By the end of the 19th century fear of socialism had driven many new recruits to the conservative camp, and in the 20th century many more were converted by the success of the Russian Revolution of 1917 and by the revolutionary pressures subsequently exerted by the worldwide Communist movement.

The range and variety of contemporary conservative parties is too great to be described in detail. They have no place, of course, in Communist countries, where all non-Communist parties are officially prohibited, and their significance is minimal in most underdeveloped countries, where the organization of competitive parties is rudimentary at best. In the more viable constitutional democracies, however, the political spectrum usually includes one or more explicitly conservative parties that are strong enough to play a substantial and often a leading role in the political life of the nation.

The United States is somewhat exceptional in this respect, for although the early Federalists and the Republicans of the mid-20th century showed certain of the characteristics of conservative parties, the structure of American party politics has been generally unfavorable to the establishment of clear-cut ideological divisions. Major parties of national significance have regularly included a wide variety of ideological tendencies. Under the influence of an intellectual movement known as "the new conservatism," largely associated with William Buckley and the *National Review*, some Republicans in the 1960's determined to turn their party into a strictly conservative, if not reactionary, party. But other Republicans constantly reminded them that no major American party had ever been able to survive on such a basis.

Elsewhere the record is quite different. In countries where the electorate tends to divide its allegiance between two major parties, an overtly conservative party often appears as one of the two contenders. The Conservative party of Britain, which was organized in its present form and under its present name in 1831, has succeeded in maintaining major-party status ever since that time.

In constitutional democracies where the more usual multiparty system prevails, conservative parties, in many cases church oriented, have generally managed to acquire a substantial following and to play an occasionally decisive part in the formation of coalition governments. The most successful of these are the Christian Democratic parties of West Germany and Italy, which emerged in the decade following World War II as majority parties able for a time to exercise exclusive control over the governments of their respective countries. These parties and the postwar victories of the Gaullist movement in France bear witness to the continuing importance of conservatism as a factor in contemporary politics.

**Psychological and Social Factors.** At least since the time of Aristotle, students of politics have tried to account for the fact that men differ so widely in their political attitudes and allegiances. Contemporary social scientists have shown particular interest in this field of investigation, and a number of hypotheses, both psychological and sociological, have been advanced to explain the appeal of conservatism. The validity of many of these hypotheses has yet to be firmly established, and because most of the work has been done in an American context, the general applicability of its conclusions is particularly open to question. Preliminary as these studies may be, however, they are already far enough advanced to warrant some attention.

One line of investigation has been psychological, associating conservatism with something known as the "authoritarian personality." According to this view, the authoritarian personality, formed largely on the basis of childhood experiences, is characterized by such traits as conventionalism, submissiveness to authority, anti-intellectualism, and ethnocentrism. Under normal conditions persons so structured tend insofar as they engage in any sort of political activity to support conservative parties. When their way of life is seriously threatened, however, their desire for security is apt to find expression in the acceptance of some extremist form of authoritarian leadership. The best example of this last reaction is the massive transfer of votes from the German Nationalists to the National Socialists, which took place in the depression years that accompanied the rise of Adolf Hitler.

Bypassing the still thorny question of personality formation, another school of social scientists has investigated the problem of conservatism in terms of the concept of social mobility. One of the basic functions of society has always been to prepare its members for the performance of appropriate social roles. Under the rapidly changing conditions of modern life this has led to unusual difficulties. When roles are constantly changing and social mobility is great, adaptability replaces conformism as the key to social success. Social groups differ greatly, however, in their capacity for adaptation to new circumstances. The less adaptable naturally react to innovation with hostility. Thus the main support for conservative parties can be expected to come from those who are relatively content with their accustomed roles and doubt their ability to maintain or improve their position under conditions of social change.

The conclusions to be drawn are essentially the same. All the available evidence seems to indicate that one of the consequences of the rapid tempo of modern civilization has been an alienation of a substantial number of people from the social system in which they live. The National Socialist experiment in Germany is an extreme but not untypical illustration of the dangers implicit in this particular form of alienation.

In the light of these considerations it is possible to appreciate the significance of contemporary conservatism. Within the context of constitutional democracy it has historically mitigated the dangers of alienation by giving potentially disaffected elements a sense of meaningful participation in the existing political system. Conservative parties, or organizations which, like the all-inclusive American parties, provide conservatives with room to exercise significant political influence, can moderate the tempo and soften the impact of successive innovations. They provide moderate leadership for people who otherwise might panic in moments of crisis. As such they play an indispensable role in the democratic process.

FREDERICK M. WATKINS, *Yale University*
*Author of "The Political Tradition of the West"*

### Bibliography

**Buckley, William F.**, *Up From Liberalism* (Stein & Day 1985).
**Covell, Charles**, *The Redefinition of Conservatism: Politics and Doctrine* (St. Martin's Press 1986).
**Crawford, A.**, *Thunder on the Right* (Pantheon 1981).
**Dye, Thomas R.**, *Who's Running America: The Conservative Years*, 4th ed. (Prentice-Hall 1986).
**Gottfried, Paul, and Fleming, Thomas**, *The Conservative Movement* (G.K. Hall 1988).
**Latch, Rebecca E.**, *Women of the New Right* (Temple Univ. Press 1988).
**Rossiter, Clinton L.**, *Conservatism in America*, 2d rev. ed. (Greenwood Press 1981).
**Watkins, Frederick M.**, *The Political Tradition of the West* (Harvard Univ. Press 1948).
**Will, George F.**, *Statecraft as Soulcraft: What Government Does* (Simon & Schuster 1984).

**CONSERVATIVE PARTY, British,** a major political party in Britain. The defeat of the Tory party in 1832 caused its leaders, not for the last time, to seek a more popular name, and the designation "Conservative" was suggested by John Wilson Croker in the *Quarterly* of January 1833, on the ground that the essential characteristic of the party was to preserve existing institutions. The idea gradually won favor and Sir Robert Peel served as a "Conservative" prime minister until the party split over the question of protection in the 1840's. The word "Tory" was never completely abandoned.

**Disraeli and Salisbury.** Modern British Conservatism really began with Disraeli, whose great achievement was to combine the ideals of 17th century Toryism (See TORY) with the needs of an industrial age. Its aims, he said, were "the preservation of our institutions, the maintenance of our empire, and the amelioration of the condition of the people," while abroad its policy was "peace with honour." These principles formed the basis of Disraeli's last administration (1874–1880), and they were faithfully observed by Lord Salisbury, who led the party for 21 years after Disraeli died in 1881. From 1886 to 1905, Britain gave its allegiance to the Conservative party with remarkable constancy (the Liberals ruled only three years), and its popularity waned only after Salisbury died in 1903.

**Transition.** During the last decades of the 19th century the Liberal party under Gladstone became more radical, and its Whig elements (see WHIGS) began to secede to the Conservatives. Unfortunately for the domestic peace of the British Isles, this development coincided with one of the recurring crises in Irish affairs, and as the Whig magnates were acred up to their eyes in Irish land, they swung their new Conservative friends into opposition to Irish national aspirations. In short, the heirs of the Cavaliers adopted the policy of the Roundheads, and they soon lost popular support as a result.

The early 1900's saw the growth of another influence on Conservative counsels, namely that of finance and industry, which had hitherto been chiefly ranged under the Liberal banner. The advent of big business proved a mixed blessing to the Conservatives, for the Tories had always championed the small man, with the result that the working classes had never identified the party with the "bosses." Furthermore, because wealth is timid at heart it infected its new allies with its own timidity. Having no principles of their own, many industrial and financial magnates endeavored to persuade Conservative leaders to compromise theirs.

**Coalition.** As a result of these infiltrations, the Conservative party became primarily a coalition, and it has since required, though it has not always had, statesmen of the first rank to hold it together. (The disintegration of the Liberal party after World War I gave the Conservatives a temporary advantage.) It has had several internal crises—over tariffs in the early 1900's, and over the government of India and the attitude to be adopted toward Germany in the 1930's. Since 1900 it has experienced periodic defeats but has always recovered.

In 1975 the party chose as its leader Margaret Thatcher, the first woman to become a British prime minister.

SIR CHARLES PETRIE, *Author of*
*"The Powers Behind the Prime Minister"*

**CONSERVATIVE PARTY, Canadian,** one of the two historic political parties of Canada, created in the 1850's by the group of English- and French-speaking leaders who won autonomy for Canada. The Conservative party came to power in 1854 and for most of the next 40 years formed the government of Canada. It played a vital role in the coalition ministry that carried out the union of the British North America colonies in 1867 and embarked afterward on a bold program of nation building. Its founding leaders were the Montreal lawyer George E. Cartier, who died in 1873, and the Kingston lawyer John A. Macdonald, who dominated the party until his death in 1891. Under Macdonald the Conservatives provided economic strength to the young nation through the construction of a transcontinental railway, the settlement of the Western prairies, and through the adoption of a protective tariff.

In opposition during the Liberal premiership of Sir Wilfrid Laurier, the Conservatives, led by a Halifax lawyer, Robert Borden, returned to power in 1911 by successfully opposing reciprocity of trade with the United States. Under Borden the Conservatives directed Canada's participation in World War I. They left office in 1921, returning to power during the stress of the economic depression of the 1930's under a forceful Western lawyer, Richard B. Bennett. However the Conservatives were in decline during the many years of Liberal government under W. L. Mackenzie King. In 1952 the name of the party was changed to Progressive Conservative when John Bracken, the Progressive premier of Manitoba, won the leadership of the Conservative party. But it was not until 1957 that the party regained power. Thereafter Progressive Conservative governments alternated with Liberal governments, though the Liberals held power for longer periods.

D. M. L. FARR*, *Carleton University, Ottawa*

**CONSHOHOCKEN,** kon-shō-hok'ən, a borough in southeastern Pennsylvania, in Montgomery county. It is situated on the east bank of the Schuylkill River, 14 miles (22 km) northwest of Philadelphia. Manufactured products include iron and steel. Conshohocken, an Indian name meaning "pleasant valley," was founded after the building of the Schuylkill Canal in 1825. It became a borough in 1850. Population: 7,589.

**CONSIDÉRANT,** kôn-sē-dā-rän', **Victor Prosper** (1808–1893), French utopian socialist. Born in Salins on Oct. 12, 1808, the son of a teacher, he studied at the elite École Polytechnique, and entered the army as an engineer. Early in his career he met the socialist Charles Fourier, and in 1833 he left the army to devote himself to Fourierist journalism and propaganda. Under Considérant's leadership, the communitarian Socialists sought a reorganized society providing everyone with suitable work and adequate reward through rationally structured communities (phalansteries). After the revolution of 1848, he was elected to the National Assembly. Forced into exile after the abortive insurrection of June 13, 1849, he failed in attempts to found phalansteries in the United States. Returning to France in 1869, he wrote in support of pacifism. He died in Paris on Dec. 27, 1893.

PETER AMANN
*State University of New York at Binghamton*

**CONSIDERATION,** in Anglo-American law, is the requirement that when a contractual promise is made it be supported by an inducement sufficient to render that promise enforceable in a court of law. Consideration is an essential element in a legal contract.

Consideration may consist of doing or forbearance from doing an act, or a reciprocal promise made by the party that seeks to enforce a promise made to it. That party—the *promisee*—must part with something of value; according to one traditional formulation, the promisee must either suffer a detriment or bestow a benefit upon the *promisor*. This element of mutuality is vital. The consideration moving from the promisee to the promisor need not be the reason, or motive, for the promise. One who promises to enrich another, for example, may be motivated by affection or moral commitment, but if his promise is to be legally enforceable, the intended beneficiary must promise to do something that the law calls consideration. [Herein lies the difference between the Anglo-American requirement and that in civil law nations. Their concept of *causa* (inducement) is generally broader in scope and requires only a sufficient reason for making a promise.]

The court will not inquire into the adequacy of the consideration in proportion to the promise, but only into its sufficiency. Thus, a promise to perform a trivial service is sufficient to support a promise to pay a disproportionately high price for it. But if a valuable service has already been rendered, a subsequent promise to pay even a disproportionately low price will not be enforced, because "past" consideration is insufficient. Similarly, if the person seeking satisfaction was under a preexisting legal duty to render the service, his act will not suffice to support a promise to pay because he has not parted with anything that he could have kept.

Dov Grunschlag, *Member, New York Bar*

**CONSISTORY,** kən-sis′tə-rē, an assemblage of church dignitaries meeting in solemn council to determine matters of ecclesiastical significance. The most notable use of the consistory is made by the Roman Catholic Church, which holds three types of assembly: (1) secret, comprising the cardinals and the pope, or his delegate, which decides such matters as canonizations, the creation of cardinals, and the appointment of bishops; (2) semipublic, including bishops as well as cardinals, which gives assent to matters determined at the secret consistory; and (3) public, including bishops, household prelates, and other church dignitaries, at which matters that were initiated and voted on at the earlier consistories are given their final form.

Many other Christian sects use consistories of church or lay officials as advisory bodies. In the Church of England, the bishop of a diocese holds consistorial court to determine ecclesiastical cases arising within his diocese.

**CONSOL,** kon′sol, in the securities trade, a bond or bond issue whose proceeds are used to retire or consolidate two or more outstanding issues. Consols are also called *consolidated annuities;* the term "consol" is a contraction of "consolidated."

British consolidated bonds were first issued in 1751 to refund nine separate government loans. These consols are fixed-interest notes with no set maturity date. They are redeemable on call by the government. Consols are often regarded as a barometer of the British credit position because, with interest payments fixed, they reflect credit market changes through their price fluctuations. British government bonds that are not part of the original consolidated issue are sometimes referred to erroneously as consols.

William N. Kinnard, Jr.
*University of Connecticut*

**CONSOLATION OF PHILOSOPHY,** a treatise by the ancient Roman philosopher and Christian theologian Boethius. See Boethius, Anicius Manlius Severinus.

**CONSOLIDATED SCHOOLS** are schools that have been established by combining two or more schools into one. Public schools in the United States developed as neighborhood institutions, one objective being to have a school within walking distance for every child. The usual pattern was one school for each school district. Consolidated schools have been formed in most instances by uniting small districts. Between the early 1930's and the early 1960's, U.S. public school enrollment grew from about 25 million to about 38 million, yet the number of school districts dropped from 127,531 to 35,676.

Among the factors that have made consolidation possible are the availability of buses and the development of highway systems. With such transportation, students from a wide area can attend one large central school. Consolidation has resulted in broader curriculums, better buildings and equipment, and reduced costs.

**CONSONANCE.** See Dissonance.

**CONSONANTS.** See Phonetics.

**CONSPIRACY** is an agreement to act together by unlawful means or for an unlawful purpose. In the legal sense, it is generally divided into two types, criminal and civil.

The gist of criminal conspiracy is the *act of concert* among the defendants, regardless of whether the objective is ultimately attained. In this respect, criminal conspiracy differs from so-called "civil conspiracy," which requires joint action that actually damages the plaintiff.

**Anglo-American Law.** In the common law of England, and later in the United States, the crime of conspiracy consisted of an agreement or understanding between two or more persons either to commit an unlawful act or to pursue a lawful end by unlawful means. Although the common law crime of conspiracy still exists as an indictable offense in many states, various specific forms of conspiracy are frequently found defined in the state and federal penal codes. The objects of conspiracy in such statutes typically include the common felonies and major misdemeanors, as well as certain otherwise lawful individual objectives obtained by concerted, and hence unlawful, means (for example, collusive trade boycotts).

In some states, a conviction of the crime of conspiracy requires proof of an "overt act" in furtherance of the conspiracy. Mere knowledge of a conspiracy, without actual participation, is insufficient to constitute the offense.

An allegation of conspiracy has important substantive and evidentiary consequences to the defendants named. Admissions of one co-conspirator may be used as evidence against other co-conspirators. In a civil conspiracy case each defendant may be held separately liable for the full damages incurred by the plaintiff.

It is generally held that a corporation and its officer cannot civilly conspire with one another where the act of the officer is performed as part of his corporate duties.

Both at common law and under state and federal statutes it is a crime to conspire to overthrow the government by force; a conspiracy to advocate such overthrow is also illegal under the amended federal Smith Act of 1940. In the civil rights field, conspiracy to interfere with the free exercise of any constitutionally guaranteed right is a federal offense.

**Conspiracy in Restraint of Trade.** A noteworthy area of the U.S. law of conspiracy lies in the field of business regulation, as exemplified by the Sherman Antitrust Act. Common instances of illegal business conspiracies are to be found in express agreements between two or more separate enterprises to maintain fixed prices or to divide markets. So-called "cartels" are in this category. Restrictive provisions in the bylaws of a trade association, binding members not to compete with one another, may supply the consensual element of conspiracy. Patent licenses and interchange agreements also may embody illegal restraints.

**Indirect Evidence.** Where no express restrictive agreements exists, an illegal conspiracy may be shown by testimony or documentary evidence pointing to collusion. Meetings with competitors, code communications, reciprocal reporting systems, minutes of corporate meetings, and parallel marketing activities may indicate a common anticompetitive understanding. On the other hand, a pattern of uniform prices may merely indicate lawful price competition.

**Current U.S. Trends.** Most civil actions and criminal prosecutions under the Sherman Act have been directed against business enterprises as the primary defendants. However, in recent times there has been a trend toward naming individual corporate officers as defendant co-conspirators in criminal cases. Conviction has resulted in substantial fines and occasional prison sentences.

Labor unions and certain federally regulated industries, such as transportation, enjoy ·statutory exemption from the general restrictions of the Sherman Act. The Department of Justice has uniformly disapproved of these exemptions. Special exemptive legislation has also existed in favor of exporter organizations, so-called small business pools, and emergency business pacts such as the codes of the National Recovery Administration in the 1930's.

**Practice in Other Nations.** Foreign attitudes toward the antitrust type of conspiracy have traditionally differed from the U.S. view. Cartel agreements have been tolerated as encouraging orderly production and marketing of goods. However, key industrial nations such as the members of the European Economic Community ("Common Market"), Britain, Canada, and Japan (the last under the influence of U.S. occupation) have begun to adopt antitrust legislation resembling that which has long been in force in the United States.

GEORGE C. SHIVELY
*Member, New York Bar*

**CONSTABLE,** kon′stə-bəl, **Archibald** (1774–1827), Scottish publisher. He was born at Carnbee, Fifeshire, on Feb. 24, 1774. He began publishing periodicals in 1800, and in 1802 founded the *Edinburgh Review and Critical Journal.* From 1802 to 1826 he published most of the works of Sir Walter Scott, including many of his poems and the Waverly Novels. Constable gradually acquired (1810–1814) the *Encyclopaedia Britannica,* to which he added a supplement (1816–1824). The bankruptcy of his firm in 1826 placed Scott, who was connected with it, in enormous debt. Constable died in Edinburgh on July 21, 1827.

**CONSTABLE,** kon′stə-bəl, **Henry** (1562–1613), English poet who is best known for his sonnet sequence *Diana.* He was born in Newark, England, and educated at Cambridge University, graduating in 1580. He then traveled abroad on secret service for the English government, finally settling in Paris. In 1589, Constable converted to Catholicism, remaining in France until 1603 except for a term as papal envoy to Edinburgh in 1598. Returning to England without permission in 1603, he was imprisoned for several months the next year. He left England in 1610 and died in Liège, Belgium, on Oct. 9, 1613.

Constable's *Diana. The praises of his Mistres* (1592) was very popular in his time and contributed to the development of the sonnet. The 23 poems are passionate and melodic but too often derivative and marred by elaborate conceits.

**CONSTABLE,** kon′stə-bəl, **John** (1776–1837), English painter, whose naturalistic style of landscape painting marked the triumph of romanticism over the artificial conventions of 18th century neoclassicism. Constable's work had a great influence in France, where his style and that of his great contemporary J. W. M. Turner helped to lay that foundation of impressionism.

One of the world's leading exponents of naturalism in landscape painting, Constable advanced an artistic theory that was well ahead of his time. He advocated complete fidelity to nature in art, and in his late lectures even urged that landscape be regarded as a branch of natural science. In the early 20th century his work and his theories were criticized as tending too much toward photographic realism. But Constable also believed that an artist should contribute something new to the ordinary man's vision of the world. A comparison of his paintings with the actual scenes represented shows that he did not simply reproduce reality, but created a new way of seeing it. Constable was also a portrait painter of considerable merit, though he regarded this branch of art as little more than an unfortunate financial necessity.

**Early Life.** John Constable was born at East Bergholt, Suffolk, on June 11, 1776. He worked for a time in the offices of his father's mill, but his interest in painting constantly asserted itself in youthful attempts to reproduce the beauties of Dedham Vale on canvas. Encouraged by his mother and by the landscape painter and art patron, Sir George Beaumont, Constable went to London in 1779 to study at the Royal Academy schools. He lived in London for the rest of his life. For some years, however, he spent his summers in Suffolk, gathering material for his work and experimenting with new methods of reproducing the light and shade of trees reflected in

CONSTABLE'S canvas titled *Wivenhoe Park, Essex* (1817) exemplifies the atmospheric effects he achieved in his landscape paintings.

NATIONAL GALLERY OF ART, WASHINGTON D. C. (WIDENER COLLECTION, 1942)

the waters of the Stour. "These scenes," he declared, "made me a painter."

Suffolk scenes formed the principal subjects of the pictures Constable began to exhibit at the Academy in 1802. The size of his paintings gradually increased, and in 1817 he began the series of large paintings that culminated in the *Hay Wain* (1821). Constable's range of subjects was extended by a visit in 1811 to the bishop of Salisbury, one of his early patrons. He also met the bishop's nephew, Archdeacon John Fischer, who became one of Constable's most zealous supporters. Many of Constable's best works were done at Salisbury and at Dorset, where the archdeacon had one of his vicarages.

**Marriage and Later Career.** In 1816, after a protracted courtship, Constable married Maria Bicknell, with whom he had seven children and a very happy life. In 1819, for the sake of his wife's health, he moved his family to Hampstead, where he found a new range of subjects. At Hampstead, Constable made a particular study of cloud formations that eventually became an integral and much-admired part of his landscapes.

Constable's reputation was at first greater in France than in England. In 1824 a Paris dealer bought the *Hay Wain* to exhibit at the Salon of that year. It is said that Constable's style made such a deep impression on Delacroix that he repainted the figures in his own Salon contribution, *The Massacre at Scio.* These two works were the sensation of the year and marked the victory of the romantic movement. The following year Delacroix met Constable in London, and it was through the former that Constable's reputation was kept alive in France after his paintings began to lose their popularity.

In 1828, Mrs. Constable died, leaving her desolate husband to look after their children. He devoted most of his remaining energy to them and to the publication of *English Landscapes* (1833), a collection of mezzotints by David Lucas after landscapes by Constable. Constable was made a full member of the Royal Academy in 1829. A bequest from his father-in-law relieved Constable of the financial anxieties that had plagued him for years. Constable died at his home in London, on March 31, 1837.

Constable's reputation in England did not reach its peak until about 1890, when the small, rough oil sketches owned by his children began to be seen by the public. Many of these sketches were given to the Victoria and Albert Museum. *Constable's Correspondence,* in seven volumes, was published between 1962 and 1967.

RONALD B. BECKETT
*Editor of "Constable's Correspondence"*

**Further Reading:** Cormack, Malcolm, *Constable, His Life and Work* (Cambridge 1986); Rosenthal, Michael, *Constable* (Thames & Hudson 1987); id., *Constable: The Painter and His Landscape* (Yale Univ. Press 1986).

**CONSTABLE,** kon'stə-bəl, in medieval history, a high-ranking dignitary of the Byzantine and Frankish courts, with primarily military functions. The term derives from the Latin *comes stabuli* ("count of the stable"). The office of constable, (French, *connétable*) reappeared under the Capetian kings of France and passed from there to Normandy in the early 11th century, when the title was given also to commanders of castles.

After the Norman Conquest of England a number of barons with the title of constable appeared in England. Among them, members of the Bohun family (see BOHUN) achieved preeminence in the royal household, and in the reign of Edward I, Humphrey de Bohun, Earl of Hereford (died 1298), gained the title of "Constable of England." This office passed by marriage to Thomas of Woodstock, youngest son of Edward III, who became Duke of Gloucester and exercised great political power under Richard II. With his fall and death in 1397 the hereditary office diminished in importance, and on the execution of Edward Stafford, 3d Duke of Buckingham, in 1521, it became extinct. The office is now revived only for coronation ceremonies.

Under the Statute of Winchester (1285), two local constables for keeping the peace were appointed in the jurisdiction of every hundred court. These were the earliest "chief constables" or "high constables"; their subordinate officers were known as "petty constables."

English constables were superseded in the 19th century by paid police forces, but the constable is still the chief local law enforcement officer in many rural areas of the United States.

HENRY GERALD RICHARDSON
*Author of "The Governance of Mediaeval England"*

**CONSTANCE,** kon'stəns, a city in Germany, in the state of Baden-Württemberg, about 35 miles (56 km) from Zürich, Switzerland. Constance (German, *Konstanz*) is located at the point where the Rhine River emerges from the Lake of Constance. The smaller, northern portion of the city lies at the Bodanrück Peninsula, on the German shore of the lake. The larger, southern portion of Constance is a German enclave on the Swiss shore of the lake.

Important railroad lines, shipping routes, and highways radiate from Constance. There are textile, woodworking, metalworking, electrical, chemical, and pharmaceutical industries in the city. Its mild and sunny climate also makes Constance a tourist center.

. One of the city's leading tourist attractions is the lakefront promenade, lined with hotels and parks. The cathedral, begun in the 11th century, is noteworthy, and there are other beautiful churches, including the 13th century Augustinian church, 15th century St. Stephen's, and the Jesuit church (built in 1604). The Konzilium (the building where the Council of Constance was held in 1414–1418), the monument to Jan Hus (the religious reformer who was burned at the stake here for heresy in 1415), the Rosgarten Museum, and the city hall (built in 1589–1594) are also of great interest. The Insel Hotel was once a Dominican monastery and is famous for its beautiful cloisters.

The site of Constance has been inhabited since the Stone Age. The Romans had a fortress here called Constantia. The town became the seat of a bishop about 570 A.D., and in 1192 it was made an imperial city. Annexed by the Austrians in 1548, it remained theirs until 1805, when it became part of the German grand duchy of Baden. Population: 75,089 (1991 est.).

A. G. STEER, JR., *University of Georgia*

**CONSTANCE, Council of,** kon'stəns, an ecclesiastical assembly known also as the 16th General Council of the Roman Catholic Church. It was held at Constance, now in Baden-Württemberg, West Germany, from Nov. 5, 1414, to April 12, 1418. The council was attended by over 300 bishops, 29 cardinals, 33 archbishops, 3 patriarchs, some 100 abbots, a dozen princes, and several hundred doctors of theology and canon law. It was convoked primarily to end the Western Schism but also to repudiate the doctrines of John Wycliffe and Jan Hus and to initiate a reform of the church in its "head and members."

**The Western Schism.** Three months after the election of Pope Urban VI in 1378, the 15 electing cardinals claimed his election invalid. Urban countered by appointing 28 new cardinals; the others thereupon elected Cardinal Robert of Geneva pope. He took the name Clement VII and departed for Avignon, where he established a rival papal court that was to challenge the supremacy of the popes of the Roman line for almost 40 years. In 1409 the situation deteriorated even further when, at the Council of Pisa, a group of cardinals deserted both the Roman and Avignonese popes and elected a third claimant.

Many theologians of the period believed that a general council had final authority in the church. Although this doctrine, known as conciliarism, ran counter to the church's traditional concept of papal supremacy, many moderates accepted it because it appeared to be the only solution to the schism. Consequently Emperor Sigismund prevailed upon John XXIII, the second pope of the Pisan line, to convoke a council in order to restore unity to the church. John finally complied, confident that the support of the Italian cardinals would force the gathering to condemn his rivals, Gregory XII of Rome and Benedict XIII of Avignon. When the council convened at Constance, however, the Germans and the English blocked Italian domination by insisting that voting be conducted by nations. The assembly was divided into four nations— Italian, German, French, and English (a fifth, Spanish, was added in October 1416). Each had one vote at the general sessions, although this system was altered slightly at the council's later session.

In February 1415 the council suggested that a special committee be formed to investigate the alleged crimes of John XXIII. Since John's life had been far from virtuous before his election, he offset this move by promising to abdicate at the next general session. Instead he fled to the court of the Duke of Austria. His departure precipitated a doctrinal crisis: the council could continue only if its members agreed that, even separated from the pope, they enjoyed divine guidance and were in possession of full authority over the church. After much discussion they enacted the controversial decree *Sacrosancta*, which proclaimed conciliar supremacy (April 6, 1415.).

They then turned the full force of their energies to ending the Western Schism. John XXIII was apprehended, condemned, and deposed on May 29, and Gregory XII abdicated on July 4, 1415. In July 1417, Benedict XIII was deposed. A conclave was formed, composed of six deputies from each nation as well as all the cardinals. On Oct. 5, 1417, after three days of deliberation, Odo Colonna was elected pope by a two thirds vote of both the cardinals and the deputies. He took the name Martin V and the church was united under him.

**Heresy.** Attention had been given meanwhile to the problem of the heresies contained in the teachings of John Wycliffe and Jan Hus. These were mainly concerned with the constitution of the church and the sacrament of the Eucharist. Hus, who had been heavily influenced by the condemned Wycliffite doctrines, had succeeded in spreading his ideas throughout Bohemia in the early part of the century. These rapidly became identified with the Czechs' nationalistic aspirations and their rebellion against the imperial authorities. When Hus decided to defend his position at the council, Emperor Sigismund promised him safe conduct. But Hus was denied a proper hearing. Instead he was arrested for celebrating Mass while under censure, interrogated for five weeks, and after refusing to retract, was found guilty of heresy on July 6, 1415. He was burned at the stake on the same day. When news of Hus' death and Sigismund's betrayal reached the Czech people, they became so enraged that by 1420 they were able to revolt against the Emperor and incite a bitter war.

**Reform.** The program for reforming the church was concentrated on the problems raised by papal taxation and the pope's power in making appointments to churches and benefices in individual dioceses. Before the election of Martin V, the prelates had insisted upon the frequent convocations of councils in the decree *Frequens*. On March 20, 1418, Martin V, with the approval of the council, promulgated seven more decrees dealing mainly with papal taxation, benefices, and simony.

Theologians dispute the value of the decree *Sacrosancta,* by which the Council of Constance assumed authority over the pope in matters of faith, and they question the attitude of Martin V toward the council. The council's greatest failure, however, was its inability to deal with the problems Jan Hus posed concerning the spiritual life of the clergy and the people. In a modern perspective, while Constance ended the Western Schism, its petty involvement with political and legislative affairs destroyed the possibility of achieving the needed "reform in the head and members of the Church."

FRANCIS X. MURPHY, C.SS.R.
*Academia Alfonsiana, Rome*

**CONSTANCE, Lake of,** kon′stəns, a large lake bordered by Germany, Switzerland, and Austria. The Lake of Constance (Konstanz; German, Bodensee) has an area of 204 square miles (528 sq km). It is 46 miles (74 km) long at its longest point—the distance from Bregenz, Austria, to Stein-am-Rhein, Switzerland. At its widest point, it is approximately 8 miles (13 km) across. The lake's maximum depth is 827 feet (252 m). At its northwest end, the main lake, or Obersee, is divided by the Bodanrück Peninsula (in Germany) into two arms: The northern arm is called Überlingersee, and the southern arm is divided into the Zellersee and the Untersee.

The Lake of Constance, whose waters are dark green and clear, is subject to sudden risings of its water level caused by the quick melting of snow along the rivers that feed into it. The main lake freezes only in severe winters. It contains a great variety and abundance of fish which are the basis of an important industry.

**CONSTANS I,** kon′stanz (320 or 323–350 A.D.), Roman emperor. Constans I (Flavius Julius Constans) was the youngest son of Constantine the Great and his wife Fausta. In 333, Constans was named a caesar (junior emperor) by his father. After the death of Constantine the Great in 337, the empire was divided among Constans and his brothers Constantine II and Constantius II. Constans' share included Illyricum, Italy, and Africa. In 340 Constantine II invaded Italy and was slain near Aquileia by troops under Constans banner, whereupon Constans became sole emperor in the West.

Constans defended the Nicene Creed against the Arians and the Donatists and closed the pagan temples. But he was also a weak and prolifigate ruler. His misrule eventually led to an insurrection in Gaul under the general Magnentius. Constans fled but was overtaken at the foot of the Pyrenees by the soldiers of the usurper and was killed.

**CONSTANS II,** kon′stanz (630–668), Roman emperor. The grandson of Emperor Heraclius, Constans inherited the throne of Byzantium in 641 at the age of 11. It was a time of acute crisis, since the Muslims were already masters of Syria and virtually masters of Egypt as well. More serious still, under the energetic governor of Syria, Muawiya, they took to the sea, defeated the Roman fleet (655), and began to advance on Constantinople. Only internal feuds checked them for a time.

Constans used this respite to repeople Asia Minor with Slavs from Thrace. His endeavor to reestablish religious unity by a despotic edict, the Typos (648), which forbade discussion between orthodox and Monothelite Christians, was, however, a failure, owing to papal opposition. He left Constantinople in 662, in order to organize the defenses of the West against the Muslims. But when he was murdered at Syracuse on Sept. 15, 668, his empire, both East and West, was still in great danger.

ROMILLY J. H. JENKINS
*Harvard University*

**CONSTANT,** kôns-tän′, **Benjamin** (1767–1830), French author and political leader. As a writer, he is best known for his novel *Adolphe* (1816).

**Life.** Henri Benjamin Constant de Rebecque was born in Lausanne, Switzerland, on Oct. 25, 1767, to middle-class parents of French Protestant stock. He traveled widely in his youth and was educated by tutors and at the universities of Erlangen and Edinburgh. Two marriages did not prevent his having many liaisons, the longest and stormiest of which was with Mme. de Staël, beginning in 1794. He accompanied Mme. de Staël to Paris, obtained French citizenship, and through her influence became a tribune during the consulate of Napoleon. Constant shared his mistress' liberal views and, consequently, went into exile with her from 1803 to 1814. During these years, when he did his best writing, he lived either at Weimar, as one of the Goethe-Schiller circle, or at Coppet, near Geneva, as a member of the famous de Staël salon.

With Napoleon's reverses in 1813, Constant began writing anti-imperialist pamphlets, but he rallied to Napoleon on the latter's return from Elba and was appointed a councillor of state to help liberalize the regime. After Waterloo and a sojourn in England, Constant returned to Paris as a liberal journalist and orator and was elected a deputy. He died in Paris on Dec. 8, 1830, the year of the liberal revolution that he favored.

Map of the Lake of Constance region showing GERMANY, SWITZERLAND, AUSTRIA, and LIECHTENSTEIN, with locations including Ludwigshafen, Überlingen, Radolfzell, Ravensburg, Meersburg, Constance (Konstanz), Friedrichshafen, Stein am Rhein, Kreuzlingen, Lindau, Frauenfeld, Arbon, Bregenz, Wil, Rorschach, Vaduz, Lake of Wallenstadt, Glarus, and the Danube and Rhine rivers.

**Works.** Mercurial, intelligent, and sensitive, Constant was a master of self-analysis. His literary reputation rests chiefly on *Adolphe*. This novel, a faintly disguised account of his relations with Mme. de Staël, is a landmark in the development of the analytical novel. In this and other works Constant's lucidity and style are classical, but his attitude of restless weariness is fully romantic.

Three posthumously published works—*Le cahier rouge* (1907), an elegantly cynical journal of his youth; *Cécile* (1951), an autobiographical novel; and *Journaux intimes* (1952)—have added to his reputation. He also wrote many political, historical, and religious works.

EDWIN JAHIEL
*University of Illinois*

**CONSTANȚA,** kôn-stän′tsä, a city in Romania, on the Black Sea, and the capital of the Dobrogea region and Romania's only port on an open sea. It is particularly important for the export of oil, which is brought in by pipeline from the Ploești oil fields. The city developed new industries in the 1950's and 1960's, in particular plants manufacturing textiles and furniture, as well as processed foods.

Constanța is the site of the former Roman city of Tomis, where Ovid spent the last nine years of his life in exile. It was reconstructed by Constantine the Great in the 4th century and was named Constantiana. The city was under Turkish rule from the 15th to the 19th century. Constanța's commercial significance revived after its acquisition by Romania in 1878. Population: 344,876 (1997 est.).

BARBARA JELAVICH and CHARLES JELAVICH
*Indiana University*

**CONSTANTINE,** kon′stən-tēn, pope from 708 to 715. A Syrian, he was consecrated pope on March 25, 708. Little information about him has survived. It is known that he accepted Justinian II's invitation to go to Constantinople to ratify the Quinisext, or Trullan, Council of 692. Composed of Eastern bishops, the Quinisext Council had enacted canons contrary to Western customs and to which Constantine strongly objected. The council has never been recognized in the West. After the murder of Justinian II, his successor Philippicus, who was a Monothelite, immediately severed relations with Constantine. When Anastasius II succeeded Philippicus in 713, however, emperor and pope were again united. Constantine died on April 9, 715.

JOSEPH S. BRUSHER, S. J.
*University of Santa Clara, Calif.*

**CONSTANTINE (II),** kon′stən-tēn, was antipope from July 767 to July 768. A layman, he acceded to the papacy through the military force of his brother, Toto, Duke of Nepi. After Toto died fighting the Lombards, Constantine was deposed, blinded, imprisoned, and presumably died in a monastery.

The Lateran synod of 769, under Pope Stephen III (IV), decreed that all future papal electors must be clergymen, and that all Constantine's ordinations were nullified. Constantine was actually, if illicitly, consecrated, however, and his actions were valid. His status on the list of popes thus remains undetermined.

JOSEPH S. BRUSHER, S. J.
*University of Santa Clara, Calif.*

**CONSTANTINE I,** kon′stən-tēn (c. 280–337 A. D.), Roman emperor, who is best known for his acceptance of Christianity and his transfer of the administrative center of the empire from Rome to Constantinople. He is usually referred to as *Constantine the Great*.

Constantine (Flavius Valerius Aurelius Constantinus) was born about 280 at Naissus (modern Niš, Yugoslavia) in Moesia. The son of Constantius I and the concubine Helena, he was somewhat older than Constantius' other children, who were the issue of Constantius' marriage to Theodora, daughter of Emperor Maximian.

In 293, Constantius was made caesar (junior emperor) of the West in the tetrarchy established at that time by Emperor Diocletian. Maximian ruled in the West as augustus (senior emperor). In the East, Diocletian served as augustus, and Galerius, completing the tetrarchy, was caesar. When Diocletian and Maximian, the two augusti, abdicated in 305, Constantius and Galerius were elevated to the posts of augusti. Ancient writers suggest that it had been anticipated that Constantine, who had always been a potential heir to his father's position, would be made caesar when Constantius became augustus. However, both Constantine and Maxentius, Maximian's son, were passed over, and the new caesars chosen were Flavius Valerius Severus and Maximinus Daia.

**Civil War.** For some years Constantine had been kept at the court of Galerius, possibly as a hostage. But in 306 he joined his father in Britain at the latter's request, which Galerius was then in no position to oppose. In midsummer of 306, Constantius died, and the British legions hailed Constantine as augustus. Galerius, however, nominated Severus as augustus, giving Constantine the title of caesar to placate him.

The nomination of Severus as augustus of the West did not go unchallenged. A revolution broke out in Rome, and Maxentius, Maximian's son, was proclaimed augustus. When Severus moved to put down the usurper, Maximian himself came out of retirement (307) and defeated and captured Severus. The old emperor then married his daughter Fausta to Constantine and proclaimed Constantine co-augustus with Maxentius. In 308, after an unsuccessful attempt by Galerius to recapture Rome, Maximian turned on his own son Maxentius, and tried to depose him. This move failed, however, because the troops would not support Maximian. In desperation Maximian then attempted to persuade Diocletian to come out of retirement and resume the leadership. Diocletian, however, not only refused to return to power but also ordered Maximian to abdicate a second time.

When Severus was killed in 307, Galerius named his comrade-in-arms Licinius augustus of the West. Constantine was demoted to caesar once more; and Maxentius was declared a rebel. The other caesar, Maximinus Daia, resented the promotion of Licinius and proclaimed himself augustus, as did Constantine. Old Maximian, after a futile conspiracy to overthrow Constantine, committed suicide in 310, while Galerius died in 311, leaving the empire divided among four augusti. When Constantine and Licinius formed an alliance, Maximinus Daia retaliated by concluding a pact with Maxentius. This meant that Licinius and Maximinus Daia would oppose each other in the East, while Constantine and Maxentius would fight it out in the West.

Constantine invaded Italy in 312 and moved on Rome, encouraged by a vision of the cross

CONSTANTINE I, called the Great, was a 4th-century Roman emperor. A Roman marble bust of that period.

against the sun. Maxentius was defeated at the Milvian Bridge and drowned in the Tiber, and Rome was taken. Thus, Constantine was supreme in the West and committed to his alliance with the Christians.

**Constantine and Licinius.** The year 313 was notable for several developments. Licinius and Constantine tried to cement their own rather tentative alliance by the marriage of Constantia, Constantine's half sister, to Licinius. Further, the two augusti made additional bids for Christian support by ordering complete religious toleration and a cessation of the persecutions that had been carried on sporadically since 303. Orders for toleration seem to have been sent to various officials in the empire; these orders are generally known as the Edict of Milan, after the city from which the two rulers issued them. The other major event of the year was the death of Maximinus Daia, who had stoutly resisted the attacks of Licinius. His passing left Constantine and Licinius as the two surviving augusti in a contest in which there had been as many as five claimants at one time.

Now followed a decade of joint rule by Constantine and Licinius. It was marred by mutual distrust and sometimes open hostility. Each emperor secretly aimed at his own total domination of the empire and hoped for the establishment of a single dynasty. In 317, three caesars were created: Crispus, Constantine's son by Minervina, one of his concubines; Constantine II, the infant son of Constantine by his wife, Fausta; and the young Licinius, the illegitimate son of the emperor Licinius. At last, an open break occurred between the two augusti. One of the causes was the mistreatment of the Christians by Licinius. But the final struggle between the two emperors was inevitable in any case. When Licinius was defeated in 324, Constantine became sole emperor and he reigned as such until his death near Nicomedia on May 22, 337.

**Reorganization and Reform.** Although he was the supreme augustus, Constantine could not rule

the whole empire directly and therefore sought to provide for the administration of its parts by members of his family. His son Crispus was, however, put to death in 326 when Fausta, Constantine's wife, alleged that Crispus had attempted adultery with her. Fausta in turn was accused by Helena, Constantine's mother, of adultery with a slave and thus met the same fate as Crispus. After this, Constantine's sons by Fausta were made caesars and given portions of the empire to administer. Constantine II received Gaul, Spain, and Britain; Constantius II, Asia and Egypt; and Constans, Italy, Africa, and territory along the Danube. Delmatius, a nephew, got most of the Balkans, while Hannibalianus, another nephew, was given Armenia, Pontus, and Cappadocia.

In foreign affairs, the reign of Constantine appeared successful. His troops defeated barbarians along the Danube, and at the end of his reign a new Persian war was brought to what seemed at the time a satisfactory conclusion. The victories were partly due to the military skill of Constantine's subordinates and partly to the fact that Constantine had consolidated and extended the reorganization of the army begun by Diocletian. Constantine made increasing use of cavalry, and his army of some 200,000 men, being essentially a field army rather than a garrison force, was capable of being moved from one part of the empire to another.

Constantine also extended the regimentation of the civil population that Diocletian had begun. The latter ruler had been chiefly concerned with the taxes and compulsory services demanded of the rural population, but Constantine's reforms included the town dwellers as well. Certain services were required of the *collegia*, which were the guilds of butchers, bakers, and the like, and membership in these groups was made hereditary. The municipal senators, the *decuriones*, suffered the same fate; they were not only frozen in status, but also they were responsible for the collection and payment of local taxes. In the rural areas Constantine went beyond Diocletian, too, for he decreed that the *coloni*, a class of tenant farmers, should be permanently attached to the soil.

It was necessary for Constantine, as it had been for Diocletian, to wrestle with the currency problem. Diocletian had failed to establish a sound silver coinage. Constantine's efforts, though more realistic, were insufficient in the long run. On the other hand, Constantine did manage to institute a workable system for both gold and bronze coinages. Many new mints were established at key points throughout the empire. As a result, the coinage was standardized to a high degree, and a better distribution was assured.

Constantine, because of his reforms, is entitled to share with the Diocletian the credit for establishing the system characteristic of the "Dominate," the later Roman Empire. But two of the most significant and far-reaching of Constantine's achievements were his transfer of the capital from Rome to Constantinople, and his coalition with the Christians.

**Establishment of Constantinople.** After the defeat of Licinius, which gave Constantine domination over the eastern part of the empire, Constantine began work on a new capital at Constantinople. The old city on this site was Byzantium, which had been founded as a Greek colony nearly 1,000 years earlier. The strategic and commercial advantages of the site were enormous. Rome could not be compared with it in any respect, though Rome was located in the West and had been the capital of the Romans for more than a millennium. Tradition and sentiment, however, cannot have weighed heavily with Constantine or any of his Illyrian predecessors, who were scarcely removed from barbarism.

It was a momentous decision, nevertheless, to move the administrative center of the empire from the West to the East. The ultimate consequence was the abandonment of the western half of the empire and the final Hellenization, or even Orientalization, of the Roman Empire. Diocletian, of course, by situating his own capital at Nicomedia in Asia Minor, had pointed the way for Constantine, but Diocletian had been only one of two augusti—Maximian had maintained an Italian capital—while Constantine was sole emperor. The barbarian pressures along the Danube, the Persian menace in the East, and the greater prosperity and economic resiliency of the eastern province must have been the major considerations in the move, for it is doubtful that Constantine had uppermost in his mind the establishment of a Christian capital.

The abandonment of Rome had a further consequence: at a single stroke the theoretical partnership of the Senate and the emperor, the essence of the "Principate" founded by Emperor Augustus, was terminated. The Roman Senate was relegated to the position of a municipal council, and the new Senate created for Constantinople was little more than a claque for the autocratic emperors of the later empire.

Constantinople, or "New Rome" as it was called, was dedicated on May 11, 330. The size of old Byzantium was quadrupled. A new forum was constructed, and a great palace was built for the emperor. Ultimately, as Christianity became more and more the religion of the empire and of the emperor, many churches adorned the town.

**Constantine and Christianity.** Although Constantine was not baptized a Christian until he lay on his deathbed, he undoubtedly considered himself in some manner a member of the sect and certainly played a major role in the affairs of the church as well as affording its members something more than toleration. In a nontechnical sense, he could be called the first Christian emperor, while many of the members of his family were definitely Christians. His mother, Helena, was extremely devout. She made a pilgrimage to the Holy Land and promoted the establishment of churches both there and in Rome.

Although Constantine attributed his success to the divine message that he believed he had read in the skies just before the battle at the Milvian Bridge in 312, he could not officially—and privately, it seems, did not—abandon paganism at once. He nevertheless threw himself into the affairs of the church. As the "Thirteenth Apostle" he tried to bring unity to the Christian community, torn as it was by doctrinal dissent. Inevitably, the Emperor became more than a referee in these disputes; when he took sides, as he had to, he defined orthodoxy.

No sooner had Constantine embarked on his policy of toleration in 313 than he was drawn into the battle over the Donatist schism in Africa. Then, in 325, Constantine played a leading role in the Council of Nicaea, which was occasioned by the Arian dispute that had divided Christians in Egypt. Probably on the advice of his counselor, the Spanish bishop Hosius, Constantine himself proposed the formula of *homoousion,* the consubstantiality of the Son and the Father, which was inserted in the Nicene Creed. This Alexandrian dispute between Arius and Bishop Alexander—the deacon Athanasius, who was to succeed Alexander in 328, was the chief opponent of Arius—seems to have involved personal antagonisms as well as theological differences.

The alliance of Constantine with the Christians was important for the future of both partners as well as for the Roman government. The immediate advantages were that Constantine became emperor and that the Christians were freed from persecution. In the long run, however, the union of church and state meant that political considerations would influence definitions of orthodoxy; and, again, the political decision of Constantine to abandon Rome for Constantinople was one of the factors leading to the division between the Eastern and Western churches. Further, since the bishops of Alexandria, Antioch, and Rome were resentful of the primacy of the bishop (patriarch) at Constantinople, whose preeminence stemmed directly from the union of church and state, both religious and political harmony were placed in jeopardy. On the other hand, the divinity of the autocratic emperor, the basis for imperial authority under Diocletian, could not be defended once the alliance with Christianity was made; instead the emperor must be considered as divinely chosen for rule.

**Evaluation.** Constantine soon became a legendary figure, and all the stories told about him cannot possibly be accepted. The works of his Christian contemporaries, Eusebius and Lactantius, are manifestly tendentious and frequently inaccurate. Some things have been established with reasonable certainty: Constantine was no intellectual giant; he took himself very seriously with regard to what he considered his mission to promote Christianity; and lacking more than one of the Christian virtues, he was on occasion cruel, ruthless, and even inhumane. On the other hand, his achievements were more than considerable, and, despite some modern evaluations to the contrary, he seems to have deserved his appellation of "the Great."

TOM B. JONES, *University of Minnesota*

Further Reading: Burckhardt, Jacob, *The Age of Constantine the Great,* tr. by Moses Hadas (Univ. of Calif. Press 1983); Upson, Frieda, *Constantine the Great* (Holy Cross Orthodox Press 1987).

**CONSTANTINE II,** kon'stən-tēn (317–340 A. D.), Roman emperor. The eldest son of Constantine the Great and his wife Fausta, Constantine II (Flavius Claudius Constantinus) was a pawn in the game of imperial politics. He was born at Arelate (Arles) in February 317. When only a few weeks old, he was proclaimed caesar (junior emperor) by his father, and he was awarded the consulship at the age of four. Even before he had attained his majority, Constantine II was dispatched to command, at least nominally, troops in the West and was assigned Gaul, Spain, and Britain as his provinces.

When Constantine the Great died in 337, Constantine II became augustus (senior emperor) along with his brothers Constans and Constantius II. This threefold division of the empire proved unworkable. Constantine II soon became involved in a dispute with Constans. He invaded Italy, the domain of Constans, and was killed near Aquileia by his brother in 340.

TOM B. JONES, *University of Minnesota*

**CONSTANTINE III,** kon'stən-tēn (612–641), was Roman emperor in 641. He was born in Constantinople on May 3, 612, the son of Emperor Heraclius by his first wife Eudocia. He reigned for three months, with his half brother Heraclonas as coemperor, and died in Constantinople on May 25, 641.

ROMILLY J. H. JENKINS, *Harvard University*

**CONSTANTINE IV,** kon'stən-tēn (652–685), was Roman. emperor from 668 to 685. He was the eldest son of Constans II. His reign is memorable for the repulse of the Muslim attack on Constantinople (674–678). The Roman victory was assisted by the timely invention of an incendiary weapon known as Greek fire; but the courage and tenacity of Constantine deserve all credit. This, the first major check to Muslim encroachment, was received with profound relief by the empire and Western Europe.

Constantine's statesmanship was shown in his convocation of the Sixth Ecumenical Council at Constantinople (680–681), in which the orthodox doctrine of the two wills and the two energies of the Saviour was upheld and the Monothelite heresy condemned. The one disaster of the reign was a Roman defeat at the hands of the Bulgars (680), which resulted in the establishment of a Bulgar state on Roman soil. Constantine died in Constantinople on July 10, 685, at the age of 33.

ROMILLY J. H. JENKINS, *Harvard University*

**CONSTANTINE V,** kon'stən-tēn (718–775), was a Roman emperor whose reign was remarkable, internally, for the progress of Iconoclasm and, externally, for his victorious campaigns against the Bulgarians. He was the son of Leo III, and came to the throne in 741 at the age of 22.

Constantine, not content with an imperial edict banning icons, summoned an Iconoclast council (754) to condemn the pictures by means of theological argument. Fortified by the council's findings, he began a wholesale persecution of the image worshippers, and especially of the monastic orders, which he wished to extirpate. It has been said that his motives here were economic rather than religious; but modern scholarship rightly diagnoses him as a religious fanatic.

Constantine's Iconoclastic preoccupations prevented him from intervening in Italy, where Ravenna fell to the Lombards in 751, ending Byzantine rule in northern Italy; or in Syria, where the Abbasid dynasty succeeded the Ummayad dynasty in 750. But his repeated campaigns against the Bulgars (763–775) covered him with glory. Constantine died on campaign on Sept. 14, 775.

ROMILLY J. H. JENKINS, *Harvard University*

**CONSTANTINE VI,** kon'stən-tēn (770–c. 797), was Roman emperor from 780 to 797. He was born in Constantinople on Jan. 14, 770, the son of Leo IV and his empress Irene. He came to the throne at the age of 10, but for the next 10 years his ambitious mother ruled in his name. With the assistance of the patriarch Tarasius, she was able to summon the Seventh Ecumenical Council, held at Nicaea in 787, and to restore the use of religious icons, which had been banned since 726.

A military revolt in her son's favor in 790 caused Irene's removal from the administration, but two years later Constantine weakly allowed her to return. She encouraged him to repudiate his wife and take another (795), in order to embroil him with the Church, and her restless in-

trigues finally succeeded in making him generally odious, even to many of his own followers. He tried to escape to the provinces but was seized and, on the order of his mother, blinded (Aug. 15, 797). He died in Constantinople shortly afterward.

ROMILLY J. H. JENKINS, *Harvard University*

**CONSTANTINE VII,** kon'stən-tēn (905–956), called Porphyrogenitus, was Roman emperor of the East from 913 to 959. He was born in Constantinople in September 905. The son of Leo VI by his mistress, later fourth wife, Zoë Carbonopsina, Constantine was legitimized by imperial baptism (Jan. 6, 906).

His early life was clouded by sickness and misfortune. From 912 to 944, he was successively under the domination of his uncle, Emperor Alexander, of his mother Zoë, and of the usurper Romanus I Lecapenus, whose daughter Helena he married (May 4, 919). Only in January 945 did Constantine succeed in gaining possession of the throne that was rightfully his. He died in Constantinople, universally regretted, on Nov. 9, 959.

Constantine's high reputation was won in the realms of literature and the writing of history, and his patronage of all the arts was catholic and beneficent. He became, moreover, in his years of power, an accomplished diplomat. There exist illuminating accounts of embassies to or from Italy, Germany, Spain, Russia, and Hungary. He also tried by law to protect the property rights of small landowners and soldiers.

Among the writings with which Constantine was personally concerned is the *De thematibus (On the Provinces)*, a historical and topographical account of the Roman provinces as constituted in his day. More valuable is his account, in the so-called *De administrando imperio* (compiled 948–952), of the history of the occupants of countries outside the imperial borders; based on information from natives of these countries, this account is surprisingly accurate. His third great work, the so-called *De cerimoniis aulae byzantinae*, is a minute description of imperial ceremonial, one of the most important documents surviving from the Middle Ages. Constantine also wrote a charming and informative life of his grandfather, Basil I. His enforced seclusion during the reign of his father-in-law, though bitterly resented by Constantine, gave him leisure for those pursuits that have put mankind forever in his debt.

ROMILLY J. H. JENKINS, *Harvard University*

**CONSTANTINE VIII,** kon'stən-tēn (960–1028), was Roman emperor of the East from 1025 to 1028. Born in Constantinople, he was the younger brother of Basil II (reigned 976–1025), with whom he nominally served as coemperor. But during these years he had no influence on policy. He was an old man when he came to be sole ruler, and he proved to be a weak, capricious, and cruel despot. He died at Constantinople on Nov. 12, 1028.

ROMILLY J. H. JENKINS, *Harvard University*

**CONSTANTINE IX,** kon'stən-tēn (c. 1000–1055), surnamed Monomachus, was Roman emperor of the East from 1042 to 1055. He was the third husband of the empress Zoë, the daughter of Constantine VIII. He was personally spendthrift and dissolute, and accelerated the decline of Roman power that set in after the death of Basil II in 1025. His throne was shaken by revolt and invasion in 1043 and 1047. And he weakly allowed his patriarch Michael Cerularius to complete the schism with the Catholic Church in 1054. He did, however, encourage education and the arts. But he made no preparation against the imminent perils of the Normans and the Seljuk Turks. Constantine died in Constantinople on Jan. 11, 1055.

ROMILLY J. H. JENKINS, *Harvard University*

**CONSTANTINE X,** kon'stən-tēn (c. 1006–1067), surnamed Ducas, was Roman emperor of the East from 1059 to 1067. He was a typical representative of the civilian aristocracy. By deliberate neglect of the armed forces he reduced the Byzantine Empire to impotence when it was in mortal danger from Normans, Magyars, Uzes, and, most of all, Seljuk Turks. His policy made the disaster of Manzikert (1071), where the Seljuks overwhelmingly defeated the Roman army, inevitable. He died in May 1067.

ROMILLY J. H. JENKINS, *Harvard University*

**CONSTANTINE XI,** kon'stən-tēn (1404–1453), surnamed Dragases, was Roman emperor of the East from 1449 to 1453. He is celebrated as the last Christian emperor of Byzantium.

Born in Constantinople on Feb. 7, 1404, he was the fourth son of Emperor Manuel II Palaeologus. He was an able and resourceful leader and had some success in unifying the Morea under his Despotate (1428–1448). But he was in the end forced to become a tributary of the Turkish Sultan Murad II in 1446.

When Constantine succeeded his brother John VIII as emperor of Constantinople, the capital was already doomed. He died, bravely defending the city against Sultan Mehmed II, on May 29, 1453. His person and his tragic end are thickly overlaid with myth and legend.

ROMILLY J. H. JENKINS, *Harvard University*

**CONSTANTINE I,** kon'stən-tēn (1868–1923), king of the Hellenes, was the son of King George I and Queen Olga. He was born in Athens on Aug. 2, 1868, and named in memory of the 11 Byzantine emperors who had carried the same name. In his youth and early manhood Constantine symbolized for the Greeks their desire to re-create the Byzantine Empire by joining to the kingdom of Greece the Greek-speaking lands held by the Ottoman Empire. In 1889 he married Princess Sophie of Prussia, the sister of Emperor William II.

Though he had studied military tactics in Greece and Germany, Constantine suffered a blow to his prestige in 1897, when, as commander of the Greek army in Thessaly, he was blamed for Greece's defeat in a war with the Ottoman Empire. In 1909 a military revolt caused him to resign from the army and live abroad until August 1910. The post of inspector general of the Greek Army was created for him in 1911; during the Balkan Wars of 1912–1913, he proved to be an effective military leader, thus overcoming the stigma of 1897.

Constantine became king on March 18, 1913, upon the assassination of his father, George I. As a victor in the Balkan Wars and as the first king of modern Greece born on Greek soil, he enjoyed enormous popularity at the beginning of his reign. In 1915 he refused to join the Allies in World War I, and he quarreled with Prime Minister Eleutherios Venizelos, who twice re-signed. Accused of being pro-German, Constantine was the subject of unfavorable propaganda from the Allies. In 1916, Venizelos revolted and set up a pro-Allied provisional government at Salonika. In June 1917 the Allies forced Constantine to leave Greece with his whole family, except for his second son, Alexander, who became king. Following the death of Alexander in October 1920, Constantine was recalled by plebiscite. He returned only to abdicate on Sept. 27, 1922, after a Turkish defeat of the Greek army in Asia Minor ended all Greek hopes for a restoration of the Byzantine Empire. Constantine died in Palermo, Sicily, on Jan. 11, 1923.

GEORGE J. MARCOPOULOS, *Tufts University*

**CONSTANTINE II,** kon'stən-tēn (1940–        ), king of the Hellenes, son of King Paul I and Queen Frederika. He was born on June 2, 1940, at Psychico, an Athenian suburb. His father was then the heir to the Greek throne. Following the German invasion of Greece in 1941, Constantine went into exile with his parents until September 1946. With the death of King George II and the accession of Paul I on April 6, 1947, Constantine became the heir to the throne and the duke of Sparta. After attending a palace school, he went to the National School of Anavryta in 1949, and later to the University of Athens. In 1960 he won an Olympic gold medal in yachting.

Constantine II became king on March 6, 1964, upon the death of Paul I. On Sept. 18, 1964, he married Princess Anne-Marie of Denmark. A daughter, Princess Alexia, was born on July 10, 1965; and a son, Prince Paul, on May 20, 1967.

Constantine quarreled with Prime Minister George Papandreou in July 1965 and dismissed him. A period of political instability ensued. On April 21, 1967, the military, led by George Papadopoulos, seized control and suspended the constitution, though Constantine remained king. In June 1973, Papadopoulos announced the abolition of the monarchy, a decision confirmed by a referendum on July 29, 1973.

GEORGE J. MARCOPOULOS, *Tufts University*

KING CONSTANTINE II and Queen Anne-Marie were married in a Greek Orthodox ceremony in 1964.

BIRNBACK

**CONSTANTINE,** kon′stən-tēn (died 411 A.D.), was usurper of the title of Roman emperor. Constantine (Flavius Claudius Constantinus) was a common soldier who was acclaimed emperor by rebellious troops in Britain in 406 or 407 A.D. Despite his boasts and the opinion of some of his followers, he had nothing in common with Constantine the Great or with the Constantinian dynasty except his name. Constantine the Usurper managed a landing in Gaul, overran the country and defeated marauding German tribes, and repelled attacks mounted against him by the officers of Honorius, Roman emperor in the West.

By 408, after repeated successes, Constantine invaded Spain, where he set up his son Constans as caesar (junior emperor). Following this, the occupation of Italy itself was planned. But matters went awry in Spain, Roman resistance in Gaul stiffened, and Constantine the Usurper was at length captured. Instead of being put to the sword without further ceremony, Constantine was sent to Italy, where he was given a proper trial and received the appropriate sentence for his folly. He was executed at Ravenna in 411.

TOM B. JONES, *University of Minnesota*

**CONSTANTINE,** kôns-tän-tēn′ is a city in northeastern Algeria, the country's largest inland center and the capital of the department of Constantine. It was known in antiquity as *Cirta.* The site of Constantine, on a plateau that has steep cliffs on two sides and a 1,000-foot (305-meter) deep canyon on the other two, is one of the most spectacular in the world. The city center is reached only by a highway that enters where the cliff has been modified to a gentle slope, and by three bridges that span the canyon separating the "Rock of Constantine" from a larger plateau. Part of Constantine has spread from the "rock" to the adjoining plateau.

Constantine is the major trade and administrative center for eastern Algeria. Railroads link the city with the Mediterranean ports of Skikda (fomerly Philippeville) and Annaba (formerly

CONSTANTINE, Algeria, showing one bridge that traverses the canyon and the old city in the foreground.

DIANE RAWSON, FROM PHOTO RESEARCHERS

Bône), as well as with Algiers and Tunis. Tourist attractions include the unusual setting, with routes along the cliff and into the canyon, as well as buildings from the Turkish period, a museum, and a bridge from the period when the city was under Roman rule.

The "Rock of Constantine," which is an easily defended site, has been a trade center from earliest historic times. In the period of the 3d century it was a center of Roman roads, trade, and administration. The Roman Emperor Constantine renamed it after himself in 311 A.D. The city has continued as an important center under the Barbers, Vandals, Arabs, Turks, French, and Algerians. Population: 440,842 (1987 census).

BENJAMIN E. THOMAS
*University of California at Los Angeles*

**CONSTANTINE PAVLOVICH,** kən-stən-tyēn′ pə-vlô′vyich (1779–1831), grand duke of Russia, was born at Tsarskoye Selo (now Pushkin), on April 27, 1779. He was the second son of Czar Paul I and the brother of Alexander I and Nicholas I. Regarded as a possible successor to the Russian throne, he received the same education that was given to his older brother Alexander. During the Napoleonic invasion of Russia, Constantine commanded regiments of the palace guards. He displayed personal courage but his military judgment was limited, and his tactical decisions often led to disaster. In 1816, Constantine was named commander in chief of the Polish army and was soon acting as Alexander's viceroy in the kingdom of Poland. In 15 years he never earned the affection of the Poles. He temporized with Polish rebels in 1830, and military reserves were required from Russia to put down the rebellion.

In 1801, Constantine sent away his wife, a princess of Saxe-Coburg. In 1820 he morganatically married a Polish countess, Joanna Grudzinska. A condition of this marriage was renunciation of his right to the throne in favor of his brother Nicholas, but Alexander's failure publicly to promulgate the new succession led to near revolution (the Decembrist revolt) at Alexander's death in 1825. Constantine died of cholera at Vitebsk on June 15, 1831.

PETER CZAP, JR., *Amherst College*

**CONSTANTINE THE AFRICAN** (c.1015–1087) was a medieval scholar, who translated numerous medical works from the Arabic. His biography is included in the series of lives of famous men associated with the Abbey of Monte Cassino, where he died. Peter the Deacon compiled the biography about 1140, but little confidence can be placed in it. Constantine's name and his familiarity with Arabic point to Muslim origin. It is probable that he traveled extensively before he entered the monastery. He has generally been associated with the great medical tradition of Salerno.

His best-known works are *Pantechne,* a medical handbook; *De melancholia;* and *De coitu liber,* a physiological tract. All are free translations of works by Arabic scholars, some of them based in turn on Galen or the Hippocratic tradition, which Constantine published as his own. He was not the "new shining Hippocrates" of Peter the Deacon's conception; nevertheless, he is an important figure in the recovery of ancient knowledge that preceded the so-called Renaissance of the 12th century.

R. T. McDONALD, *Smith College*

**CONSTANTINOPLE,** kon-stan-tə-nō′pəl, was the former name of the city of Istanbul, Turkey. Located on a promontory between the Sea of Marmara and the Golden Horn, the city was founded as Byzantium in the 7th century B.C. It was renamed Constantinople in 330 A.D. when the Roman emperor Constantine I (Constantine the Great) moved his capital there from Rome. As capital of the Byzantine Empire, Constantinople became a great cultural, economic, religious, and administrative center. In 1453 it was taken by the Ottoman Turks, who had repeatedly besieged the city, and it served as their capital in the succeeding centuries. However, in 1923 the Turkish republic was proclaimed, with Ankara as the capital. In 1930 the name of Constantinople was officially changed to Istanbul. See also BYZANTINE EMPIRE; BYZANTIUM; CONSTANTINE I; ISTANBUL; TURKEY.

**CONSTANTINOPLE, Councils of,** kon-stan-tə-nō′pəl, four councils of the Catholic Church that were held in Constantinople and that have been recognized as ecumenical by the universal church.

**Constantinople I (May–July 381).** Emperor Theodosius I summoned the bishops of the East to his imperial city in May 381 to restore harmony between the Catholic and the Semi-Arian factions in the empire. Presided over by Meletius of Antioch, the council was attended by 150 bishops from Thrace, Asia Minor, and Egypt, as well as 36 Semi-Arian and Macedonian bishops. After Meletius' death, St. Gregory of Nazianzus and Nectarius succeeded to the presidency.

Since the acts of the council have been lost, its proceedings are known only through secondary sources: citations in the letter the synod of Constantinople sent to Pope Damasus in 382, and in the church histories of Socrates, Sozomen, and Theodoret. Of the seven canons ascribed to the council, only the first four are definitely authentic. Canon 1 condemned Arianism, a heresy that denied the divinity of Christ; similiar heresies, such as Macedonianism and Apollinarianism, were also condemned, and the dogmas of the Council of Nicaea (325) were confirmed. Canons 2 and 3 limited the jurisdiction of the powerful see of Alexandria; this established the precedent of confining all episcopal jurisdiction to the civil diocese in which the bishop lived. Canon 3, which gave the see of Constantinople precedence after Rome, was later quoted in the famous Canon 28 of the Council of Chalcedon (451). These two canons were to increase the tensions between these two sees through the centuries. Canon 4 condemned and deposed the Arian bishop of Constantinople, Maximus.

The so-called Nicene-Constantinopolitan Creed is commonly recognized by modern scholars as not originating with this council. Probably formulated by the synod of Alexandria (362) and based on baptismal formula in use in Jerusalem, it was recited by Nectarius during the council, when he was consecrated bishop of Constantinople. Later the Council of Chalcedon accepted it as the expression of faith of Constantinople I. The council of 381 was not accepted as ecumenical until 200 years later, when Pope Gregory I (reigned 590–604) recognized its decrees.

**Constantinople II (May 5–June 2, 553).** Emperor Justinian summoned the fifth ecumenical council to wipe out Nestorianism, a heresy that denied the unity of the divine and human natures of Christ. Justinian saw in the so-called "Three Chapters" (the writings of Theodoret of Cyr, Theodore of Mopsuestia, and the letter of Ibas of Edessa to Mari, bishop of Hardasir, Persia) the last vestiges of Nestorianism and wanted these works condemned. The council was held in Hagia Sophia. Since Pope Vigilius and his Western delegation refused to attend, all but 11 of the 168 bishops at the council were Oriental. Vigilius was held forcibly in the imperial city. He protested, not against the writings, which he himself condemned in a document sent to Justinian (*Constitutum I*), but against the indirect condemnation of the Council of Chalcedon, which had cleared both Theodoret and Ibas of any Nestorian taint. On Dec. 8, 553, however, Vigilius relented and accepted the council's decisions. Although Nestorianism was thus successfully destroyed, Constantinople II's reliance on the Christological terminology of St. Cyril prepared the way for another hersey, monothelitism.

**Constantinople III (Nov. 7, 680–Sept. 16, 681).** Sergius I, patriarch of Constantinople (610–638), with the assistance of Emperor Heraclius, introduced monothelitism as a theological formulation in an effort to unite the Monophysite and orthodox (Chalcedonian) Christians. He taught that Christ had only one will, the divine, while the Monophysites maintained that Christ had a single composite nature. Since Sergius' formulation led to greater political and religious division, Emperor Constantine IV (reigned 668–685), with Pope Agatho, called the bishops together to establish unity.

The council, presided over by three papal legates, met in the imperial palace's domed hall (*trullos* in Greek; hence the council is also called Trullo I). The fathers accepted a document of faith that taught that the two wills and two energies in Christ were distinct, yet inseparable and without confusion, and condemned Sergius, Pope Honorius, and other Monothelites. Pope Leo II, who recognized the council as ecumenical, concurred with the condemnation of Pope Honorius, who, he felt, had acted, not as the living witness of true church tradition, but as an imprudent individual.

**Constantinople IV (Oct. 5, 869–Feb. 28, 870).** Emperor Basil I (reigned 867–886) convoked the council when relations between the sees of Rome and Constantinople were extraordinarily strained. Photius, the patriarch of Constantinople, had anathematized Pope Nicholas I in 867, and was himself condemned by a Roman synod (869) for usurping the see of Constantinople, and deposed by Basil for challenging imperial authority.

With Photius deposed and Nicholas dead, Basil thought unity possible. Pope Adrian II sent three legates to preside over the council, which issued 27 canons. These dealt primarily with the condemnation of Photius and iconoclasm, and the promulgation of laws concerning ecclesiastical discipline. The council fathers claimed ecumenicity for the council, and Adrian II approved its decrees. The Byzantine Church accepted it until Photius regained the patriarchate and rejected Constantinople IV in the synod of 878–880. How universally the Greeks accepted Photius' synod is disputed; nearly 20 years later (885–886), Pope Stephen I reported in a letter to Emperor Basil I that Photius was seeking Greek support for the annulment of Constantinople IV. Byzantine churches in union with Rome recognize it as the eighth ecumenical council.

GEORGE MALONEY, S. J., *Fordham University*

**CONSTANTIUS I,** kon-stan′shē-əs (c. 250–306 A. D.), Roman emperor, nicknamed Chlorus (the Pale). He was the father of Constantine the Great. Constantius (Flavius Valerius Constantius) was of Illyrian stock. In 293 he was appointed caesar (junior emperor) in the tetrarchy established by Diocletian and assigned to Gaul under the augustus (senior emperor) of the West, Maximian. At the same time Constantius put aside Helena, the mother of Constantine, in order to marry Theodora, the daughter of Maximian. After restoring peace to Gaul and turning back an invasion by the Alamanni, Constantius undertook the reconquest of Britain, which had been independent for about a decade.

Constantius was appointed augustus in the West when Diocletian and Maximian abdicated in 305. In July of 306, however, Constantius died at York in Britain. In later times, Constantine the Great attempted to legitimize his dynasty by the claim that his father was related to, or even descended from, Emperor Claudius II Gothicus (reigned 268–270).

TOM B. JONES, *University of Minnesota*

**CONSTANTIUS II,** kon-stan′shē-əs (317–361 A. D.), Roman emperor. Constantius II (Flavius Julius Constantius), the second son of Constantine the Great by his wife, Fausta, was born at Sirmium in Illyricum in 317. After the death of Constantine in 337, the Roman Empire was divided among Constantius and his brothers Constantine II and Constans. Constantius drew the East as his share and for many years was occupied in an inconclusive struggle with the Persians. In the meantime, Constantine II was killed in 340 in a war with Constans, and by 350 the latter had been overthrown by Magnentius, one of his generals. After three years of warfare in Italy and Gaul Magnentius was defeated by Constantius, who then became sole emperor (353).

In his efforts to gain the West, Constantius had appointed his cousin Gallus as caesar (junior emperor) in the East. But Gallus proved unsatisfactory and was executed by Constantius in 354. The latter then returned to the East, leaving his other cousin, Julian (the Apostate), as caesar in the West.

The outbreak of a new Persian war in 359 led Constantius to demand troops in Gaul from Julian. The Gallic soldiers, however, mutinied and proclaimed Julian emperor (360). Before Constantius could confront Julian in battle, he developed a fever at Tarsus, in Cilicia. He died at nearby Mopsucrenae on Nov. 3, 361.

TOM B. JONES, *University of Minnesota*

**CONSTANTIUS III,** kon-stan′shē-əs (died 421 A. D.), Roman emperor. A member of a noble Roman family, he became master of the soldiers under the emperor of the West, Honorius. Constantius distinguished himself in 411 and the years following by overcoming various usurpers in Gaul and forcing the Visigoths to evacuate that region and move on to Spain. The Visigoths also surrendered Galla Placidia, Honorius' sister, whom they had carried off from the sack of Rome in 410. Constantius married Placidia in 417. Constantius was virtual ruler of the West and was finally appointed coemperor by Honorius in February 421, but he died at Ravenna in September of the same year.

TOM B. JONES, *University of Minnesota*

**CONSTELLATION,** any of a number of apparent groupings of stars in the form of imaginary configurations in the sky. The term derives from a Latin word meaning "stars together." The stars of a constellation appear to be projected on the celestial sphere, all at the same distance from the earth, but they may actually be vastly different distances from the earth and from one another. The constellations are helpful guides in navigation, to astronauts in spacecraft orientation, and for star identification.

**Origin.** The practice of naming particular groups of stars stems from remote antiquity. It probably originated about 3000 B. C. with the peoples of the Euphrates River valley and was passed on to later civilizations. The early Greeks and Romans assigned appropriate names to the representations of mythological heroes and other personages, the creatures of fable, and the familiar animals and objects of everyday life that they imagined they saw in the configurations of the stars. These ancient groupings and names, with their wealth of associated folklore, have been carried down to the present day with subsequent additions and modifications.

Constellations such as Orion and the Great Bear were mentioned by the 8th century B. C. or earlier in the works of Homer and Hesiod. In the 3d century B.C. the Greek poet Aratus of Soli listed 44 constellations, as transscribed from a previous list by the Greek scholar Eudoxus. In the 2d century A. D. the Alexandrian astronomer Ptolemy in his famous *Almagest* enumerated 48 constellations, which were probably derived from the earlier star catalog prepared by the Greek astronomer Hipparchus.

The first attempt to represent the constellations on a map of the sky was made by Petrus Apianus (Peter Bienewitz), a German astronomer and mathematician. In 1536 he constructed a constellation map of the northern skies on a planisphere—a reproduction of the dome of the sky on a two-dimensional plane. This single-page sky map incorporated the 48 constellations of Ptolemy with the addition of the constellations Coma Berenices and Canes Venatici. These two figures were later given their exact form by the Danish astronomer Tycho Brahe and the astronomer Johannes Hevelius of Danzig, respectively. In the latter half of the 16th century, star globes containing the constellations were prepared by the Flemish geographer Gerardus Mercator.

**Constellation Atlases.** The first comprehensive star atlas that showed the constellations on separate charts was published by the German astronomer Johann Bayer in 1603. This work, *Uranometria*, contained 51 copper plates depicting the 48 ancient constellations of Ptolemy. To these Bayer added 12 more constellations of the Southern Hemisphere, which were based upon star observations made by the contemporary Dutch navigators Petrus Theodori of Emden and Frederik Houtman. He also added a figure of a dove —the constellation Columbia—and outlined Crux, the Southern Cross, although he made it part of Centaurus. Most importantly, Bayer introduced the modern system of designating stars by the constellations in which they appear. Within a given constellation he assigned each star a Greek or Roman letter prefix in alphabetical order of star brightness (with a few exceptions), followed by the genitive form of the Latin constellation name. For example, Sirius, the brightest star in

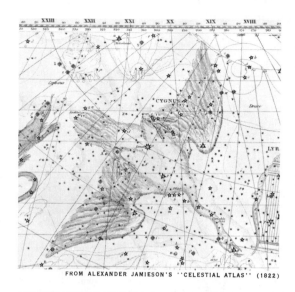

FROM ALEXANDER JAMIESON'S "CELESTIAL ATLAS" (1822)

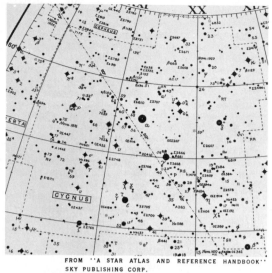

FROM "A STAR ATLAS AND REFERENCE HANDBOOK"
SKY PUBLISHING CORP.

CONSTELLATION CYGNUS shown on an old sky map (*left*) and on a modern map with systematic boundaries (*right*).

Canis Major (the Larger Dog) is designated $\alpha$ Canis Majoris.

The list of constellations was completed during the next two centuries. Jakob Bartsch, a German professor of mathematics and son-in-law of the great astronomer Johannes Kepler, issued a planisphere and star maps in 1661; in them was described a constellation that later became known as Camelopardalis, the Giraffe. A French astronomer, Augustine Royer, published star maps in 1679 in which he added the constellation Mono-

ceros. He also delineated Crux and Camelopardalis more accurately. Seven more constellations were introduced by Johannes Hevelius in his posthumous star atlas *Firmamentum Sobiescianum,* published in 1687–1690. Finally, as a result of a visit to the Cape of Good Hope in 1750, the French astronomer Nicolas Louis de Lacaille added 14 modern constellations to the Southern Hemisphere skies in his *Coelum australe stelliferum* (1763).

**Present Delineation.** The German astronomer

## THE CONSTELLATIONS

The 88 constellations are listed alphabetically by their Latin names, for which the English equivalents are provided. The 47 constellations marked with an asterisk in the Origin column were originally recognized by Ptolemy in the *Almagest,* while the separate constellations Carina, Puppis, Pyxis, and Vela replace Ptolemy's 48th constellation Argo Navis. The remaining 37 constellations are of modern origin as indicated; Columba was also mentioned by Petrus Plancius (1552–1622). The right ascension of the approximate center of each constellation on the celestial sphere is given in hours and minutes, and the declination is given in degrees. The upper culmination is the date on which a constellation reaches (at 9 P.M.) its highest position above the horizon. The column headed Bright Stars provides the number of 1st, 2d, and 3d magnitude stars, respectively, in each constellation.

| Latin Name | English Name | Origin | Right Ascension | Declination | Upper Culmination | Bright Stars |
|---|---|---|---|---|---|---|
| Andromeda | Andromeda (Chained Lady) | * | 0  42 | +43 | Nov. 15 | 0-3-1 |
| Antlia | [Air] Pump | Lacaille | 10  20 | −33 | Apr. 10 | ———— |
| Apus | Bird of Paradise | Bayer | 16  0 | −75 | June 30 | ———— |
| Aquarius | Water Carrier | * | 23  0 | −13 | Oct.  7 | 0-0-2 |
| Aquila | Eagle | * | 19  40 | + 4 | Aug. 30 | 1-0-4 |
| Ara | Altar | * | 17  20 | −52 | July 22 | 0-0-3 |
| Aries | Ram | * | 2  30 | +19 | Dec. 12 | 0-1-1 |
| Auriga | Charioteer | * | 5  40 | +42 | Feb.  2 | 1-1-4 |
| Boötes | Herdsman | * | 14  40 | +34 | June 12 | 1-0-3 |
| Caelum | Graving Tool (Chisel) | Lacaille | 4  40 | −39 | Jan. 13 | ———— |
| Camelopardalis | Giraffe | Bartsch & Royer | 5  20 | +67 | Jan. 31 | ———— |
| Cancer | Crab | * | 8  30 | +14 | Mar. 12 | ———— |
| Canes Venatici | Hunting Dogs (Greyhounds) | Hevelius | 13  0 | +43 | May 21 | ———— |
| Canis Major | Larger Dog | * | 6  45 | −23 | Feb. 13 | 1-4-2 |
| Canis Minor | Smaller Dog | * | 7  30 | + 5 | Feb. 27 | 1-0-1 |
| Capricornus | Horned Goat (Sea Goat) | * | 21  0 | −21 | Sept. 19 | 0-0-2 |
| Carina | Keel (of former Argo) | Lacaille | 9  0 | −62 | Mar. 16 | 1-3-3 |
| Cassiopeia | Cassiopeia (Lady in Chair) | * | 1  0 | +64 | Nov. 20 | 0-4-2 |
| Centaurus | Centaur | * | 12  40 | −44 | May 25 | 2-3-8 |
| Cepheus | Cepheus (the King) | * | 22  30 | +68 | Oct. 10 | 0-0-3 |
| Cetus | Whale | * | 1  30 | − 6 | Nov. 30 | 0-2-1 |
| Chamaeleon | Chameleon | Bayer | 11  0 | −78 | Apr. 13 | ———— |
| Circinus | Pair of Compasses | Lacaille | 14  40 | −65 | June 24 | 0-0-1 |
| Columba | (Noah's) Dove | Bayer | 5  30 | −32 | Jan. 31 | 0-0-2 |
| Coma Berenices | Berenice's Hair | Brahe | 12  44 | +22 | May 17 | ———— |
| Corona Australis | Southern Crown | * | 18  40 | −40 | Aug. 12 | ———— |
| Corona Borealis | Northern Crown | * | 15  48 | +31 | July  2 | 0-1-0 |
| Corvus | Crow | * | 12  20 | −14 | May 13 | 0-0-4 |
| Crater | Cup | * | 11  20 | −13 | Apr. 28 | ———— |
| Crux | (Southern) Cross | Royer | 12  20 | −61 | May 14 | 1-2-1 |
| Cygnus | Swan | * | 20  36 | +48 | Sept. 10 | 1-1-4 |
| Delphinus | Dolphin | * | 20  40 | +18 | Sept. 15 | ———— |
| Dorado | Dorado (a fish) | Bayer | 5  20 | −64 | Jan. 17 | 0-0-1 |
| Draco | Dragon | * | 17  20 | +61 | July 10 | 0-1-5 |

## THE CONSTELLATIONS (Continued)

| Latin Name | English Name | Origin | Right Ascension | | Declination | Upper Culmination | Bright Stars |
|---|---|---|---|---|---|---|---|
| Equuleus | Colt | * | 21 | 12 | + 8 | Sept. 21 | |
| Eridanus | Eridanus (a river) | * | 3 | 40 | −18 | Jan. 2 | 1-0-3 |
| Fornax | Furnace | Lacaille | 2 | 40 | −31 | Dec. 12 | |
| Gemini | Twins | * | 7 | 0 | +18 | Feb. 20 | 1-2-5 |
| Grus | Crane (a bird) | Bayer | 22 | 20 | −41 | Oct. 9 | 0-2-1 |
| Hercules | Hercules | * | 17 | 32 | +22 | July 21 | 0-0-7 |
| Horologium | Clock | Lacaille | 3 | 10 | −53 | Dec. 20 | |
| Hydra | Water Monster (Sea Serpent) | * | 9 | 40 | −16 | Apr. 30 | 0-1-5 |
| Hydrus | Water Snake | Bayer | 3 | 0 | −72 | Dec. 14 | 0-0-3 |
| Indus | Indian | Bayer | 21 | 20 | −54 | Sept. 26 | 0-0-1 |
| Lacerta | Lizard | Hevelius | 22 | 20 | +45 | Oct. 14 | |
| Leo | Lion | * | 10 | 40 | +17 | Apr. 15 | 1-2-3 |
| Leo Minor | Smaller Lion | Hevelius | 10 | 0 | +35 | Apr. 12 | |
| Lepus | Hare | * | 5 | 30 | −23 | Jan. 29 | 0-0-4 |
| Libra | Balance | * | 15 | 0 | −13 | June 25 | 0-0-3 |
| Lupus | Wolf | * | 15 | 30 | −36 | June 19 | 0-0-4 |
| Lynx | Lynx | Hevelius | 8 | 20 | +41 | Mar. 5 | |
| Lyra | Lyre | * | 18 | 50 | +42 | Aug. 18 | 1-0-2 |
| Mensa | Table [Mountain] | Lacaille | 5 | 40 | −78 | Feb. 3 | |
| Microscopium | Microscope | Lacaille | 21 | 0 | −36 | Sept. 19 | |
| Monoceros | Unicorn | Royer | 7 | 0 | − 8 | Feb. 22 | |
| Musca | [Southern] Fly | Bayer | 12 | 40 | −72 | May 14 | 0-0-2 |
| Norma | Square [and Rule] | Lacaille | 16 | 0 | −52 | July 6 | |
| Octans | Octant | Lacaille | 20 | 0 | −79 | Circumpolar | |
| Ophiuchus | Serpent Holder | * | 17 | 0 | − 7 | July 25 | 0-1-7 |
| Orion | Orion (the Hunter) | * | 5 | 30 | + 2 | Jan. 23 | 2-5-3 |
| Pavo | Peacock | Bayer | 19 | 30 | −64 | Aug. 24 | 0-1-0 |
| Pegasus | Pegasus (the Winged Horse) | * | 22 | 30 | +18 | Oct. 15 | 0-1-5 |
| Perseus | Perseus (the Champion) | * | 3 | 40 | +44 | Dec. 21 | 0-2-5 |
| Phoenix | Phoenix (a mythical bird) | Bayer | 0 | 30 | −52 | Nov. 9 | 0-1-2 |
| Pictor | Painter['s Easel] | Lacaille | 5 | 20 | −49 | Jan. 29 | 0-0-1 |
| Pisces | Fishes | * | 1 | 0 | +12 | Nov. 12 | |
| Piscis Austrinus | Southern Fish | * | 22 | 0 | −28 | Sept. 30 | 1-0-0 |
| Puppis | Stern (of former Argo) | Lacaille | 7 | 30 | −39 | Feb. 26 | 0-1-6 |
| Pyxis | Mariner's Compass | Lacaille | 9 | 0 | −32 | Mar. 19 | |
| Reticulum | Net | Lacaille | 4 | 0 | −64 | Jan. 4 | 0-0-1 |
| Sagitta | Arrow | * | 19 | 20 | +18 | Aug. 31 | |
| Sagittarius | Archer | * | 19 | 0 | −32 | Aug. 20 | 0-2-8 |
| Scorpius | Scorpion | * | 17 | 0 | −32 | July 10 | 1-3-11 |
| Sculptor | Sculptor['s Workshop] | Lacaille | 0 | 30 | −32 | Nov. 14 | |
| Scutum | Shield [of Sobieski] | Hevelius | 18 | 44 | −11 | Aug. 12 | |
| Serpens | Serpent | * | 15 | 40 | +10 | July 21 | 0-0-2 |
| | | | 17 | 40 | −13 | | |
| Sextans | Sextant | Hevelius | 10 | 20 | − 5 | Apr. 9 | |
| Taurus | Bull | * | 4 | 30 | +25 | Jan. 15 | 1-1-3 |
| Telescopium | Telescope | Lacaille | 19 | 0 | −51 | Aug. 14 | |
| Triangulum | Triangle | * | 2 | 0 | +32 | Dec. 5 | 0-0-1 |
| Triangulum Australe | Southern Triangle | Bayer | 16 | 0 | −65 | July 4 | 0-1-2 |
| Tucana | Toucan (a bird) | Bayer | 23 | 30 | −63 | Oct. 30 | 0-0-1 |
| Ursa Major | Larger Bear (Great Bear) | * | 10 | 0 | +48 | Apr. 21 | 0-5-7 |
| Ursa Minor | Smaller Bear (Little Bear) | * | 15 | 0 | +73 | June 25 | 0-2-1 |
| Vela | Sails (of former Argo) | Lacaille | 9 | 30 | −46 | Mar. 29 | 0-3-3 |
| Virgo | Virgin | * | 13 | 0 | − 3 | May 25 | 1-0-3 |
| Volans | Flying [Fish] | Bayer | 8 | 0 | −69 | Mar. 1 | |
| Vulpecula | Little Fox | Hevelius | 20 | 0 | +25 | Sept. 8 | |

Johann Elert Bode, in 1801, was the first to draw systematic boundaries to demarcate the areas of the constellations. His boundaries were not universally accepted, however, and there was confusion over the matter for many years. Finally, in 1930, through the efforts of the International Astronomical Union, the constellation boundaries were standardized. All segments of the boundaries were made to lie along hour circles of right ascension and parallels of declination—that is, exactly north-south and east-west on the celestial sphere. The boundaries were drawn in positions corresponding to Jan. 1, 1875, in order to conform with the existing comprehensive star atlas of the Southern Hemisphere, *Uranometria Argentina*, prepared by the American astronomer Benjamin A. Gould in 1879. These boundaries do not change with respect to the stars. With the passage of time, however, the right ascensions and declinations of the boundaries of the constellations do change as a result of the precession of the equinoxes and other factors.

The International Astronomical Union officially recognizes 88 constellations. Of these, 28 are northern, 12 are zodiacal, and 48 are southern constellations. They are listed in the accompanying table, which also provides alternate descriptive or popular titles. The familiar Big Dipper, it should be noted, is part of the constellation Ursa Major; and the Northern Cross is contained within the constellation Cygnus. Further information on several of the more important constellations, or those of historic interest, is provided in separate articles.

FERGUS J. WOOD
*Environmental Science Services Administration*

**Further Reading:** Kippenhahn, Rudolf, *One Hundred Billion Suns: The Birth, Life, and Death of the Stars*, tr. by Jean Steinberg (Basic Books 1985); Motz, Lloyd, and Nathanson, Carol, *The Constellations* (Doubleday 1988); Sanborn, Laura, *Bright Star Guide to the Heavens of the Northern Latitudes* (Search Public 1985).

**CONSTELLATION,** the second frigate built for the U. S. Navy. It was launched at Baltimore, Md., in September 1797. Its most famous exploits were the capture of the *Insurgente* (1799) and an action with the *Vengeance* (1800) during the naval war with France. The frigate was idle for many years but was fully commissioned in 1940 and was a flagship of the Atlantic Fleet in World War II. It was made a National Historic Landmark, anchored at Baltimore, in 1955.

**CONSTIPATION** is an alteration in the normal pattern of defecation, characterized by bowel evacuations that are incomplete or infrequent. In addition, when the stool is passed, it is very hard, making evacuation difficult and sometimes painful.

The normal pattern of defecation may vary considerably from person to person. While most people evacuate their bowel once a day, some people normally defecate twice or even three times a day, while others may move their bowels only once every two, three, or even four days. Thus, a person who normally defecates twice a day is said to be constipated if he moves his bowels every two or three days, a pattern that might be perfectly normal for another individual.

Constipation is not a disease but only a symptom. Unlike diarrhea, which may be a dangerous symptom in itself because of the accompanying loss of body fluids and salts, constipation is not in itself debilitating, although it may cause discomfort and possibly lead to hemorrhoids and other anal disorders. Many people believe toxic substances in the feces are absorbed into the body when a person is constipated, but there is no medical evidence to support this belief.

**Causes.** Constipation may be due to many different causes. Often it is due to a change in an individual's emotional state. Anger, fear, anxiety, and emotional stress are common causes of constipation. Similarly, changes in environment and eating habits may cause changes in bowel function. Constipation may also be caused by drugs, such as codeine and aluminum hydroxide.

Many people have a long history of chronic constipation throughout much of their adult life. Often, this is related to poor bowel habits or chronic emotional problems. Sometimes chronic constipation results from poor toilet training in childhood, especially when there has been too much emphasis on the importance of a daily bowel movement and a tendency to equate regularity with good health. People thus trained in childhood may become upset if they do not defecate every day, and as a result they may use laxatives with excessive frequency. Such an abuse of laxatives, however, may lead to a loss of normal muscle tone in the large intestine and actually impair normal defecation. Sometimes chronic constipation results from weakened or lax abdominal muscles, as in women who have given birth many times.

When constipation occurs suddenly and grows progressively worse, it is most likely caused by an underlying disease. Among the diseases that may cause constipation are tumors of the large intestine and colitis.

**Treatment.** The treatment of constipation depends on its cause. In many patients, longstanding habits are not broken easily, and in patients with chronically weakened or stretched muscles, little can be done to correct the situation though exercises may be of help. Sometimes, a normal pattern of defecation can be attained by increasing the intake of water and certain foods, such as prunes, which naturally stimulate the bowel. Adding bran and salad greens to the diet increases the bulk of the stool, stimulating the intestinal walls to contract. Occasionally, a bulk-forming cathartic, such as methylcellulose, may be prescribed.

LOUIS J. VORHAUS, M.D.
*Cornell University Medical College*

BY PERMISSION WORLD PUBLISHING CO. DRAWINGS © 1954 BY EDWIN TUNIS, FROM HIS BOOK. "OARS, SAILS AND STEAM"
**The Constitution**

**CONSTITUTION,** a 44-gun frigate renowned in the U.S. Navy as *Old Ironsides,* was built in Boston, Mass., in 1797, one of the first six warships authorized by Congress. She was flagship of Commodore Edward Preble in the war with Tripoli. Early in the War of 1812, *Constitution* under Captain Isaac Hull was chased for 60 hours off New Jersey by a British squadron. Using skillful seamanship, including towing with boats and warping ahead with anchors during calms, she escaped to Boston.

Several weeks later on Aug. 19, 1812, about 700 miles (1,130 km) to the east, *Constitution* met the British frigate *Guerrière,* 38 guns, one of those that had chased her. After 30 minutes of action *Guerrière* was a wreck and *Constitution* returned to Boston in triumph. On Dec. 29, 1812, under Captain William Bainbridge, she met the British frigate *Java,* a superior sailer, off Brazil. The U.S. ship, with her heavier armament, forced a surrender after 2 hours. Blockaded in Boston, she escaped to the West Indies in December 1813 and captured several prizes. Again blockaded until December 1814, she made her last cruise under Charles Stewart, and on Feb. 20, 1815, she captured two British sloops of war.

*Constitution* was a lucky ship, at sea more often and winning more battles than any other early American warship. She became a favorite within and outside of the Navy and received the nickname "Old Ironsides" because her hull was so little damaged in her actions. About to be condemned in 1830 as unseaworthy, she was saved by popular clamor stirred by Oliver Wendell Holmes' poem *Old Ironsides.*

In 1860 she was converted to a schoolship for the Naval Academy and a year later some Maryland secessionists hoped to make her the first warship of a new Confederate navy. Instead she transferred the midshipmen to Newport, R.I. Laid up in Boston in 1897, she was restored, beginning in 1925. In 1931 she visited ports on both coasts. She remains moored in Boston as a naval relic.

JOHN D. HAYES, *Rear Admiral, U.S. Navy (Ret.)*

**CONSTITUTION,** a body of fundamental laws and principles according to which a political state is governed. A constitution determines the organization of a government, the functions and powers of the government in general and of its subdivisions and officers, and how these functions and powers are to be exercised. It generally sets forth the substantive and procedural limitations on the government in its relationships with persons within the state, and it provides for change through a specified process of formal amendment.

A constitution is usually a single document; but it may be a group or series of documents, as was the constitution of the Third French Republic; or it may be simply the totality of basic legislation, as is the case in England. But regardless of its form, a constitution, broadly viewed, is a nation's entire legal arrangement, as well as accepted practices and extralegal customs.

By contrast with a constitution, a *charter* is a limited grant of authority, a delegation of power to perform some single action or to engage in a particular field of operation. A *compact* can be distinguished from a constitution in that it is an agreement between equal parties and also covers a very limited scope.

**Written and Unwritten Constitutions.** Regardless of the nature of the national constitution—single document, group of documents, or the totality of fundamental legislation—the law of a land goes beyond these formal basic materials. It includes interpretations of the documents and legislation—by the judiciary in deciding cases, by the legislature in enacting statutes, by the executive in handing down executive orders, and by all citizens insofar as customs become generally accepted. These matters are usually referred to as the "unwritten constitution"; in practice they are as important as any written parts.

The so-called "unwritten constitution" of England differs from that of any other country. It is the cumulative result of all the legal actions over the centuries beginning with the Magna Carta of 1215. As every statute is a part of the legal totality known as the English constitution, each act of Parliament in effect is an amendment to the constitution. Parliamentary discretion is legally unlimited, and judicial review, in the sense of applying fundamental standards to legislation, does not exist.

In all other countries there are basic written constitutions. A typical constitutional document begins with a preamble setting forth the aims and purposes of the constitution and the government it establishes. There follow divisions of the document that establish the legislative, executive, judicial, and administrative areas of operation. Both the organization and powers of these government branches are noted along with limitations on the exercise of their powers. These limitations on the government are frequently further elaborated in the constitution as a bill of rights. The nature of the electorate is determined, and this may involve provisions for direct, popular legislation by the initiative or referendum, or both. There is also a section of the document devoted to detailing the processes of formal amendment. Finally, every constitution contains an ephemeral provision that sets forth the process for the document's adoption and its placement into operation.

**Rigid and Flexible Constitutions.** A constitution is presumed to set down fundamentals, to deal with basic principles. Justice Benjamin Cardozo of the U. S. Supreme Court once said that a constitution should "state principles for an expanding future." When a constitution deals only with basic matters, it lends itself to future interpretation and adaptation to changing conditions; thus it can be classified as flexible.

On the other hand, the more a constitution deals with details, with the application of fundamentals—the more it partakes of the nature of a statute—the more rigid it becomes. Unless a constitution of the latter type provides for an easy method of formal amendment, it becomes rigid to the point of paralysis. The normal distinction between a rigid and a flexible constitution is based on the ease of the amendment process. However, the basic content and phraseology of the document are at least as important in determining its real flexibility or rigidity. A constitution limited to fundamental principles properly expressed rarely needs amendment; it may be considered flexible even if difficult to amend.

**Amendment of Constitutions.** By its nature a constitution is something special and different from ordinary laws. It is the highest legal statement within a political state, the record of the decisions of the sovereign power. It follows that the means by which it is changed must differ from the methods of changing ordinary law. Amendments should be made either by a special body, as a constitutional convention, or by a special process by a regular lawmaking body, as an extraordinary vote of a legislature. Altering a constitution should be difficult. A document that deals with fundamental matters need not and should not be subject to change to conform with the passing whims of the populace.

In the United States amendments may be proposed either by a two thirds vote of both houses of Congress or by a national constitutional convention called by Congress on petition by two thirds of the states. Subsequently the proposals are to be ratified, regardless of how they were introduced, either by a majority vote of the legislatures of three fourths of the states or by a convention in each of three fourths of the states.

In France a proposal for amendment of the constitution is introduced either by the president at the suggestion of the premier or by a member of Parliament; it must then be passed by each house of the national legislature and subsequently ratified by popular referendum. An alternative method is for the president to submit a proposal to a joint session of the national legislature; in this case a three fifths vote is required, but no referendum is necessary. Australia, Switzerland, and Ireland require referendums for the ratification of amendments.

See also CONSTITUTION OF THE UNITED STATES; CONSTITUTIONAL LAW.

PAUL C. BARTHOLOMEW
*University of Notre Dame*

**Bibliography**
Bhagwan, Vishnoo, and Bhushan, Vidya, *World Constitutions,* 2d ed. (Apt. Bks. 1987).
Blaustein, Albert P., *Constitutions That Made History* (Paragon House 1987).
Creasy, Edward, *The Rise and Progress of the English Constitution,* 16th ed. (1892; reprint, Rothman 1986).
Hawgood, John A., *Modern Constitutions Since 1787* (1939; reprint, Rothman 1987).
McWhinney, Edward, *Constitution-Making: Principles, Process, Practices* (Univ. of Toronto Press 1981).
Wiecek, William M., *Constitutional Development in a Modernizing Society* (American Hist. Assn. 1985).

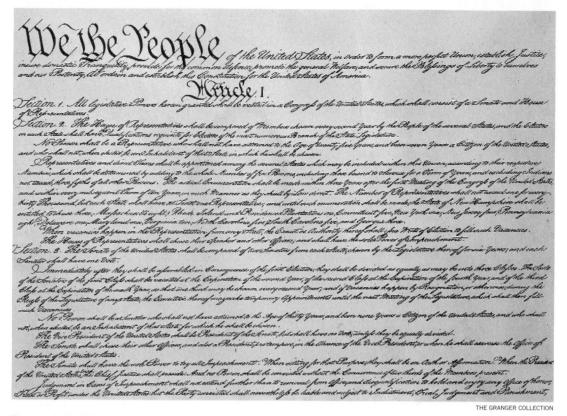

The top half of the original first page of the Constitution of the United States of America, 1787. The complete document, comprising four sheets, is on display in the Rotunda of the U.S. National Archives in Washington, D.C.

**CONSTITUTION OF THE UNITED STATES,** the fundamental law of the United States of America. Drafted by the Constitutional Convention in Philadelphia, Pa., between May 25 and Sept. 17, 1787, it is the world's oldest written constitution still in effect. The document presents a set of general principles out of which implementing statutes and codes have emerged. As such, it embodies the essence of constitutionality—that government must be confined by the rule of law.

The success of the framers of the U.S. Constitution in writing a document geared to serving the varied and changing needs of Americans has been complemented by an ability on the part of successive Congresses and courts to readapt it to these changing demands. The Constitution's 27 amendments, added over a period of 200 years, have in most cases plugged minor loopholes rather than changed the focus or the general structure of the document. As Pres. Franklin D. Roosevelt stated in his first inaugural address on March 4, 1933, "Our Constitution is so simple and practical that it is possible always to meet extraordinary needs by changes in emphasis and arrangement without loss of essential form. That is why our constitutional system has proved itself the most superbly enduring political mechanism the modern world has produced."

**Basic Principles.** The Constitution was a product of the thought of the 18th-century "Age of the Enlightenment." European and American philosophers, such as John Locke, Voltaire, Montesquieu, and Thomas Paine, attacked despotic government and advanced the following ideas: that government comes from below, not from above, and that it derives its powers from the consent of the governed; that individuals have certain natural, inalienable rights; that it is wise and feasible to distribute and balance powers within government, giving local powers to local governments, and general powers to the national government; that all persons are born equal and should be treated as equal before the law.

The framers of the U.S. Constitution sought to do what, as yet, Europeans had not tried: to make these Enlightenment ideas the governing principles of a nation. Hence, the document stressed that the people were forming the government ("We, the People . . . do ordain and establish this Constitution. . . .") and were themselves dividing power in such a way as to afford checks and balances on its use and potential abuse.

The allotting to the federal government of only those powers specifically delegated—a principle that was further bolstered by the addition of the 10th Amendment—made clear that the residual powers would remain with the local units of government. The creation of three separate branches within the federal structure, each in numerous ways dependent upon the others for its healthy functioning, afforded another way to ensure that federal power would not be used indiscriminately. The extensive powers of the president likewise were proscribed in a number of places by designated responsibilities. The judicial power, which the framers clearly intended to "extend to all cases, in law and equity, rising under this Constitution, the laws of the United States, and treaties made . . . under their authority," was to be wielded by judges, "holding their offices during good behaviour"; explicit jurisdiction of the courts was subject to congressional definition and, by implication, redefinition.

Indeed, so impressed were certain of the

framers with the viability of Montesquieu's concepts of separation and balance of power that John Adams counted eight explicit balancing mechanisms and proudly proclaimed them as evidence of the Constitution's republican virtue. These instances of government branches checking one another were as follows: (1) the states v. the central government, (2) the House v. the Senate, (3) the president v. Congress, (4) the courts v. Congress, (5) the Senate v. the president (with regard to appointments and treaties), (6) the people v. their representatives, (7) the state legislatures v. the Senate (in the original election of senators), and (8) the Electoral College v. the people.

**Individual Liberties.** No bill of rights was included in the original document. It was considered unnecessary by many of the framers because of the fact that Congress' powers were delegated and this precluded their being used to deprive man of his inalienable rights. However, a number of basic protections were spelled out. Such traditional guarantees of Anglo-Saxon liberty as habeas corpus and protection against ex post facto laws and bills of attainder were included, along with the assurance that "the citizens of each state shall be entitled to all privileges and immunities of citizens in the several states."

As to the principle that men should have equal rights and opportunities so far as society can assure them, the Constitution was without specific mechanisms for their attainment. But its clear thrust—that men create government to secure their rights; that such a government should be a government of laws and not of men; and that when government fails to serve men well and equally it should be replaced—institutionalized a presumption of equality, which later generations found they could work for within the basic constitutional structure.

## HISTORICAL BACKGROUND

The Articles of Confederation, which had been framed when British armies were in America and hostility to centralized British tyranny was at its peak, had so implemented American anathema to strong national authority as to leave most effective governmental power in local hands. Upon ratification of the Articles in 1781, the problems inherent in the weak confederation structure became apparent. Change was essential.

**Government Under the Articles.** Lacking both a national executive and a national judiciary and with no effective power to raise and utilize national military forces, the central government was unable to enforce its laws. It could not impose its will on its own citizens directly and therefore could not prevent violations by a state of the rights of another, nor could it conduct effective relations with foreign powers. Further, the requirement of unanimous support of all 13 states for amendment of the Articles virtually precluded strengthening the central government through normal processes.

Critical developments in the Confederation period demonstrated the necessity for a sharply different approach to the solving of American governmental problems—the need for a "more perfect union." Obviously, American interests in international relations had to be protected. England had refused to advance diplomatic recognition and was exploiting American weaknesses in world trade and hindering westward settlement through intrigue with Indians. Spain was work-

ing to seize economic control of the lower Mississippi valley, even to the point of encouraging the secession of American communities there.

There also was a pressing need for powers that would enable the central government to promote economic development in an orderly manner. The credit of the new nation was precarious because of the inability of the central government to tax and to redeem its domestic and foreign obligations, and the domestic economy was throttled by a mass of prejudicial interstate commercial barriers and discriminations. Internal domestic antagonisms actually had burst into open revolt in defiance of federal authority, most notably in Shays' Rebellion in Massachusetts (1786–1787).

**Revision Plans.** Talk of revision had grown steadily. Alexander Hamilton, for one, had been dissatisfied with the Articles from the start. Several attempts to amend them failed, and state representatives met at Mount Vernon in 1785 and Annapolis in 1786 to consider various alternatives.

Following Annapolis, the Confederation Congress responded cautiously but favorably to a resolution for a special convention so long as the "sole and express purpose" was revising the Articles. Five states named delegates in 1786. Shays' Rebellion speeded the process in the others. By 1787, 12 states (all but Rhode Island) had named 73 delegates, 55 of whom came to the Philadelphia Convention and 39 of whom eventually signed the Constitution.

## THE CONVENTION OF 1787

The convention delegates agreed that a new constitution was needed. However, many controversies had to be resolved before one could be drafted. A basic issue was the extent of powers to be granted to the national government, and a major obstacle was the conflicting interests of large and small states.

**The Framers of the Constitution.** The activists who sought a new effective national structure were a singular group. Predominantly educated and respected men of affairs, some with considerable wealth, they had in many cases participated prominently in the unified national effort against the British in the Revolutionary years, therein sublimating their local interests to the broader national cause. George Washington (who presided over the convention), James Madison, Alexander Hamilton, James Wilson, John Jay, Rufus King, Edmund Randolph, Gouverneur Morris, and Benjamin Franklin all had served either in the army or as diplomats or key administrative officers of the Confederation government or members of its Congress. These Convention delegates were younger than such apprehensive localists as Samuel Adams, Patrick Henry, Richard Henry Lee, and George Clinton, who still feared the experience of centralized British rule, and whose minds could not embrace the concept of a national interest in which they themselves might share.

The future framers of the Constitution were not so transfixed by the specter of national authority as to feel that any departure from tight local political control would destroy local interests. Conscientious students of comparative government and of America's prior experience, they aimed to create a workable republican structure, strong enough to establish national supremacy and to control "the turbulence and follies of democracy" but limited enough to ensure individual self-determination within a structure of ordered liberty. Their differences lay primarily in means. Their common objectives were summarized by Madison as "the necessity of providing more effectively for the security of private rights and the steady dispensation of justice."

**The Alternatives.** Disregarding its mandate for amendment, the Convention began to consider plans for new governmental structures, developed in advance by various delegates. Edmund Randolph's Virginia Plan, a product of the Virginia delegation in which James Madison took a prominent part, proposed an all-powerful national state allowing only the most limited local authority. This proposal was disturbing to defenders of local interests, especially in the small states, who objected particularly to the failure to provide for state equality in at least one of the houses of the national legislature.

Although Madison and James Wilson of Pennsylvania argued that in a proportionate system the people as such, rather than the states, would be represented, and consequently the people of the small states would have the same representation in Congress as those of the large states, small-state delegates remained unconvinced. Their spokesman, William Paterson of New Jersey, proclaimed that his state would "rather submit to a monarch, to a despot, than to such a fate." Failing to achieve some provisions for representation by states within the context of the Virginia proposal, Paterson put forward a counterproposal. His New Jersey Plan tightened up some glaring weaknesses of the Articles but still made major concessions to state autonomy.

**The Compromises.** The basic issues of government structure and powers had to await settlement of pressing points of friction. First, small-state apprehensions were calmed by the Connecticut, or "Great," Compromise. Every state was conceded an equal vote in the Senate irrespective of its size, but representation in the House was to be on the basis of the "federal ratio"—an enumeration of the free population plus three fifths of the slaves. It was agreed that the same ratio would apply for determining state taxation, and the House was given the prerogative of introducing all money bills.

Other compromises were needed to smooth sectional and economic antagonisms. The merchant-minded North was assured full federal protection of trade and commerce, while the agrarian South was guaranteed permanent relief from export taxes and assurance that the importation of slaves into the United States would not be prohibited for at least 20 years. Similarly, earlier Northern attempts to trade to Spain Southern and Western territorial rights led to successful demands from those sections for a two-thirds Senate ratification of all treaties. The same ⅔ ratio was applied in defining both the proportion of senators necessary to approve executive appointments and that to override presidential vetoes of congressional legislation.

**Basic Decisions.** The settlement of such controversies permitted a return to the two central issues of federalism: (1) granting to the federal government sufficient power to enforce its will and (2) finding ways of limiting popular democracy. Working with the Randolph plan as a point of departure, the convention delegated various explicit powers to the federal government

(Article I, section 8) and left the residue, with some exceptions (Article I, section 10), to the states; certain areas were to be open to concurrent authority. It created a three-branch government, both to implement the new grants of federal authority and to balance local interests when that necessity arose.

Reflecting the general fear of all the delegates of the potential "tyranny of the majority," the convention adopted what Madison called a "policy of refining the popular appointments by successive filtrations." Accordingly, it provided for the indirect election of the president through an electoral college, made senators elective by state legislatures, and assured that federal judgeships be appointive. Originally, only the House was to be elected by direct popular vote.

The new government was afforded what Oliver Ellsworth referred to as the "coercion of the law." It had the power to execute federal authority directly on the people, and all state officials were bound by oath to engage cooperatively in furthering the process (Article IV).

**Other Conflicts.** Many aspects of framing the Constitution produced bitter and detailed controversy, particularly the manner of election of the president and the nature of his office and powers and the proper role and function of the federal courts. A strong-executive party headed by Madison, Wilson, and Gouverneur Morris of New York argued that free government demanded independently constituted executive, legislative, and judicial branches and defeated a move to have the executive chosen by Congress. Thus the possibility of a parliamentary-cabinet form of government was precluded at the outset.

Luther Martin of Maryland, an eloquent champion of states' rights, afforded a way out of a lengthy controversy over the role of the judiciary in maintaining the supremacy of federal legislation by making the state courts an agency for enforcing federal law. This maneuver, however, later was converted into an instrument for nationalism, when state court actions were held to be subject to the surveillance of the U. S. Supreme Court.

**The Document.** On September 8 the rough document was entrusted to a committee on style, where Gouverneur Morris led in polishing the language. On September 17 the finished Constitution was engrossed and signed "By the unanimous consent of the States present." Few, if any, of the framers felt that they had created a perfect instrument of government. But they did feel that the new Constitution was something a majority of people could be persuaded to accept.

As time was to prove, the original document had many flaws. The precise limitations on national power over individual liberties, considered superfluous by the framers, soon had to be spelled out through the amendments constituting the federal Bill of Rights. The authority and power of the federal courts, both in regard to judicial review and in questions of their relations with state courts, was not well defined until a later series of strong rulings by Chief Justice John Marshall. The nature and extent of the implied powers of Congress produced two decades of controversy. The failure to define the precise locus of sovereignty left open a door for a vigorous states' rights movement and led ultimately to the Civil War. It took the same national emergency to clarify many of the powers of the presidency, especially in crises.

On the other hand, the document was remarkable in the boldness with which it sought to extend to the entire nation the heretofore limited and localized American experiment with republicanism. The framers of the Constitution envisaged the conduct of national affairs by all citizens and anticipated that such conduct would result in advancing the welfare of all citizens. This took both breadth of vision and a healthy confidence in the potential wisdom and responsibility of the electorate. It was the boldest step toward government of, by, and for all the people yet undertaken by Western man.

### RATIFICATION OF THE CONSTITUTION

The process of ratification of the new framework of government began immediately after the convention. The required approval of specially elected conventions in nine states was achieved on June 21, 1788, with the acceptance of New Hampshire. However, ratification was not completed for another two years (see table). The organization, enthusiasm, and energy of the Constitution's supporters were major assets in what proved to be a difficult campaign.

**RATIFICATION OF THE CONSTITUTION**

| State | Date of ratification |
| --- | --- |
| Delaware | Dec. 7, 1787 |
| Pennsylvania | Dec. 12, 1787 |
| New Jersey | Dec. 19, 1787 |
| Georgia | Jan. 2, 1788 |
| Connecticut | Jan. 9, 1788 |
| Massachusetts | Feb. 6, 1788 |
| Maryland | April 28, 1788 |
| South Carolina | May 23, 1788 |
| New Hampshire | June 21, 1788 |
| Virginia | June 25, 1788 |
| New York | July 26, 1788 |
| North Carolina | Nov. 21, 1789 |
| Rhode Island | May 29, 1790 |

**The Opposition.** Anti-Federalist opponents of the new Constitution were quick to raise objections to it and equally quick to play on apprehensions, particularly prevalent within the lower classes, that a remote and powerful central government would become an instrument for aristocratic tyranny. The self-proclaimed heirs of the true spirit of the Revolution were convinced that the republican principle, which they embraced locally, could not be extended to encompass all 13 states without the creation of a type of central authority that would suppress individual rights and local interests. The lack of a bill of rights to check such abuse seemed particularly unjustified and suspicious to them. Thus, they launched campaigns against the document, which were sufficiently aggressive to force its champions to produce elaborate defenses.

**The Defense.** Campaigning was especially vigorous in the crucial and pivotal states of Virginia and New York. In support, Virginian James Madison and New Yorkers Alexander Hamilton and John Jay published a series of propaganda pieces on the virtues of the new Constitution. These *Federalist* papers pointed out the reasons for the structure of the new government, the benefits to all Americans from its operations, and the functionalism of the Constitution's explicit solutions to small but perennial governmental problems. The *Federalist* papers accomplished their purpose in Virginia and New York, although they were, respectively, the 10th and 11th states to ratify. Furthermore, by stating the persuasive rationale for a balanced, representative, republican government operating on the federal principle, the *Federalist* papers became a classic treatise in political theory.

### HISTORICAL INTERPRETATION

The view held by Americans of the "Founding Fathers" and the framing and ratification of the Constitution has changed through history, reflecting the values and interests of different periods. During the 1800's, in an era of domestic insecurity and international self-consciousness, most Americans were committed to defending the virtue of their own gallant origins to an extent that virtually necessitated apotheosizing the framers. The Progressive era of the early 1900's, however, found many reformers impatient with a static legal structure operating, they felt, to serve only vested interests. Hoping to provide a new rationale for sweeping constitutional reform, they set out to question the boasted divinity of its origins.

In this spirit, Charles A. Beard's *An Economic Interpretation of the Constitution* (1913) recast the founding fathers as men with decided personal economic interests, framing the Constitution and pushing its ratification with an idea of personal advancement. Beard explored these men's economic status and maintained that their efforts had strongly undemocratic overtones in their desire to put forward an instrument of government under which they would benefit most. Such a view had wide support from liberals for more than three decades, especially in the economically conscious depression years of the 1930's.

Cold War tensions underlay the emergence of a generation of scholars in the 1950's and 1960's who, while not returning to the earlier veneration of the framers, sought to revive their unselfish reputation. Led by Robert E. Brown and Forrest McDonald, these critics questioned Beard's research and assumptions. They argued that there was no evidence to support the contention that supporters and opponents of the Constitution could be divided along lines of economic affluence or economic activity. They also questioned whether the successful ratification struggle represented a devious and undemocratic triumph over the wishes of a majority of the people.

In turn, Jackson T. Main challenged the assumptions and evidence of these men, and Stanley Elkins and Eric McKitrick raised questions as to whether the probing for economic evidence, which had occupied a half century of historical scholars, might not be missing the point. Elkins and McKitrick argued that the struggle for a new governmental framework "was not fought on economic grounds; it was not a matter of ideology; it was not, in the fullest and most fundamental sense, even a struggle between nationalism and localism. The key struggle was between inertia and energy; with inertia overcome, everything changed." The issue of the motivations of the framers of the constitution remains one of the central bones of contention in American historical scholarship.

### THE AMENDMENTS

In its first 200 years of operation, the Constitution proved remarkably flexible. The nature of the government of the United States changed greatly, but most changes evolved from new interpretations of the document. Formal amendment proved necessary in only 27 instances, and these occurred mainly in spurts, as during the Reconstruction and Progressive periods. However, many of the 27 amendments provided for fundamental social and procedural adjustments.

**The Bill of Rights.** During the struggle for ratification critics of the Constitution leaped on the omission of a bill of rights as a serious danger. Richard Henry Lee argued that the Constitution, if adopted unamended, would "put Civil Liberty and happiness of the people at the mercy of Rulers who may possess the great unguarded powers given." He demanded such amendments "as will give security to the just rights of human nature, and better secure from injury the discordant interests of the different parts of this union." When the first Congress convened, it was flooded with some 145 proposed amendments. This number was reduced to 12, which on Sept. 25, 1789, were sent to the states for consideration. Ten were finally ratified and went into effect on Dec. 15, 1791.

The 1st Amendment guaranteed protection of such substantive rights as freedom of speech, press, assembly, and petition, while providing complete religious freedom and separation of church and state. The 2d and 3d amendments guaranteed the citizen's right to bear arms and forbade the government to quarter soldiers in private homes. Amendments 4 through 8 contained basic procedural guarantees long common to Anglo-Saxon justice: freedom from unwarranted search and seizure (4th); guarantees against double jeopardy, self-incrimination, and the loss of liberty or property without due process of law (5th); right to a speedy and fair trial with adequate counsel (6th); trial by jury (7th); and protection against excessive bail and cruel and unusual punishment (8th). The 9th and 10th, dealing with rights held by the states and the people, were included primarily to calm the apprehensions of states' rights advocates who worried about the potential appropriation of reserve power by the national government. In later years, as the federal government did seek to assume more functions, the 10th became a major weapon of laissez-faire interests in their fight for "dual federalism" and against what they considered unwarranted national coercion; it also was cited frequently by opponents of racial desegregation.

**Amendments 11 and 12.** The 11th Amendment (proclaimed Jan. 8, 1798) was enacted to override a Supreme Court decision (*Chisholm* v. *Georgia*, 1793). The product of states' rights protests, it was designed to keep suits between states and their citizens out of federal courts.

The 12th completed the first cycle of revision by amendment. Proclaimed Sept. 25, 1804, in time for the presidential election of that year, it clarified the electoral procedure that had produced a hopelessly confused result in 1800, redefined the vice presidency in its relation to the presidency, and unofficially recognized the existence of political parties (which the framers had not anticipated).

**Reconstruction Amendments.** The 13th Amendment (proclaimed Dec. 18, 1865) represented the first attempt at broad-scale social reform through the amendment process. In abolishing slavery and involuntary servitude, it was the logical culmination of Lincoln's emancipation policies and the legal victory for which two generations of abolitionists had worked.

The 14th Amendment, which has produced more litigation and court interpretation than any other part of the Constitution, originally was enacted to protect the freedman from the abrogation of his rights by the Southern states. By making the Negro a citizen and by making the federal government responsible for his privileges and immunities, it sought to build a wall of federal protection around him. It was proclaimed on July 28, 1868, after a bitter ratification contest in which Southern states that had formally been declared out of the Union were required to ratify the amendment as a condition for return. The amendment subsequently was modified by the Supreme Court in the famous Slaughterhouse cases (q.v.) in 1873. Although the issue at stake did not concern Negro rights, the decision so diluted federal control over state police powers that the 14th Amendment became a virtual nullity as a protection of the rights of Negro citizens. On the other hand, its due process clause was turned into a legal protection for property—especially giant corporations—against state regulatory legislation in the years after 1880. After 1925 the 14th Amendment became the cornerstone of a growing movement to "nationalize" the Bill of Rights against state infringement, and its reinterpretation was the legal heart of the civil rights movement of the 1950's and 1960's.

Another aspect of the program for the newly freed Negro, a federally protected franchise, was embodied in the 15th Amendment (proclaimed March 30, 1870). Again, however, such federal protection was eliminated by judicial ruling, and only in later years did the federal government seek to enforce the amendment against a variety of forms of state disfranchisement.

**Progressive Era Amendments.** Another spate of amendments grew out of the politically active Progressive period. A federal income tax was authorized by the 16th Amendment (proclaimed Feb. 25, 1913), providing an effective revenue source to meet an expanding federal budget. By 1912 many states were nominating senatorial candidates through direct primaries with pledges then obtained from state legislators to support such choices. The 17th Amendment (proclaimed May 31, 1913) made the direct, popular election of senators mandatory.

The 18th and 19th amendments reflected other manifestations of progressivism. With curtailment of alcoholic beverages demanded as part of the war effort in World War I and the moral fervor of the war widespread, temperance advocates succeeded in imposing a "noble experiment"—nationwide prohibition—through the amendment process. The 18th, or Prohibition, Amendment (proclaimed Jan. 29, 1919) proved to be abrasive and was defied openly; the federal government was relieved of the further necessity of enforcing it by the adoption of the 21st, or Repeal, Amendment on Dec. 5, 1933. The 19th Amendment (proclaimed Aug. 26, 1920) extended the suffrage to women.

**Later Amendments.** The 20th, or Lame Duck, Amendment was an important accommodation to modern needs. Proclaimed Feb. 6, 1933, it shortened the period between the election of the president and his inauguration, advancing the latter from March 4 to January 20. It also eliminated the session of Congress that had been held in the interim period and that often had resulted in questionable actions instituted by defeated lawmakers before they left office.

The 22d Amendment (proclaimed March 1, 1951) officially limited the president to two terms or not more than ten years in office. The 23d (proclaimed April 3, 1961) gave residents of the District of Columbia the right to vote for president and vice president. The 24th Amendment (proclaimed Jan. 24, 1964) invalidated the use of the poll tax or other taxes as a condition for voting in federal elections.

The crises caused by the illnesses of President Dwight D. Eisenhower and the assassination of President John F. Kennedy led to the enactment of the 25th Amendment (proclaimed Feb. 24, 1967), which provides for situations of presidential disability and ensures that any vacancy in the office of vice president is filled. By the 26th Amendment (proclaimed July 5, 1971), the legal voting age was dropped from 21 to 18 for all elections. The 27th Amendment, the so-called Madison amendment, first proposed in 1789 (proclaimed May 20, 1992), prohibits midterm changes in the salaries of members of Congress. In addition, to prevent centuries of delay from becoming precedent, Congress also passed a resolution that declared four other long-outstanding amendments invalid.

## JUDICIAL INTERPRETATION

The precise role of the judiciary in interpreting the Constitution and the statutes enacted under it evolved slowly. Acceptance of the Supreme Court as the ultimate and single authority on the subject of constitutionality did not become fully established until the late 1860's. Subsequently, the court's role continued to grow, and judicial interpretation remains the chief means of keeping the Constitution in tune with modern life.

**Judicial Review.** In the early national period congressional debate, executive pronouncements, and even theories of influential statesmen were as significant sources of constitutional doctrine as were court rulings. Nonetheless, the principle of judicial review (the power of the Supreme Court to rule acts of Congress unconstitutional) was claimed for the court by Chief Justice John Marshall in *Marbury* v. *Madison* in 1803.

At the outset, conservatives such as Alexander Hamilton had argued that this power of the court was an essential limit on the elective branch of the government. Marshall enhanced the power and prestige of the court by utilizing fully its accepted function of statutory interpretation. Interpreting constitutional law through relevant state and federal statutes, the Marshall court gave explicit meanings to broad and frequently ambiguous provisions. This judicial practice has enabled justices throughout American history to adjust and adapt the law to the pressing and changing social and economic needs of American society.

Thus, while the theory often prevailed that judges merely interpreted the law, almost from the outset they had the further clear, if not specified, responsibility for assuring its viability. In the words of Woodrow Wilson, the court, in many ways, constituted a "permanent constitutional convention." Charles Evans Hughes once remarked: "We are under a Constitution but the Constitution is what the Judges say it is."

Such judicial prerogative is not unlimited, however. Court actions must have a feeling for contemporary reality, or ways will be found to undermine the further use of judicial power.

**Changing Interpretations.** Supreme Courts have been shaped philosophically by their members, particularly by the chief justice. To preserve the new constitutional experiment, the Marshall court sought protection for men of property who would give the nation stability and permanence. Many legal ways were found to virtually sanctify property rights and ensure federal supremacy. Article I, section 10's proscription of state violation of the obligation of contracts was interpreted to include everything from private contracts to state-granted charters of incorporation to private companies. Interstate commerce, which Congress constitutionally had authority to regulate, was interpreted to include almost every kind of commercial activity. Congress' power over it was complete in itself and could be exercised to its utmost extent, acknowledging no limitations other than those prescribed in the constitution.

In two other areas Marshall set patterns: the supremacy of federal over state courts was established clearly and permanently, and the so-called "necessary and proper" clause (the last of the powers delegated to Congress under Article I, section 8) was interpreted broadly as a positive authorization for Congress to find means to accomplish appropriate national ends.

Jacksonian Democracy placed new emphasis on freer economic competition. As it also placed a new generation of judges on the bench—headed by Roger B. Taney—the law quickly reflected this changed focus. Emphasizing, in his first opinion, that "while the rights of private property are sacredly guarded, we must not forget that the community also have rights," Chief Justice Taney went on to lay a legal basis for freedom of competition, both through encouraging local banking and commerce and by guaranteeing the right of corporations to do interstate business. Corporations were assured of access to federal courts and thereby given protection against the narrow legal localism often used to guard local vested rights. The Taney court also granted the states a new body of police power to better look after the health, safety, and welfare of the citizens. Yet the Taney era ended ingloriously because the dominantly Southern membership of the court sought, as in the Dred Scott decision, to cast the law so as to underwrite Southern assumptions about slavery when the nation was rejecting them.

Under Chief Justice Salmon P. Chase (1864–1873), the court preserved much of the Taney court's attitude toward legal localism, but at times it used the need to protect local sovereignty as an argument against national solutions. Although measures such as the liberal Granger laws of the early 1870's were upheld, much of the liberal Reconstruction legislation, geared toward finding national legal solutions for race relations, was struck down as infringements of local sovereignty.

The courts of the 1880's and 1890's, dominated by such champions of uninhibited property rights as Stephen Field, Joseph Bradley, and Melville Fuller, returned constitutional interpretation to the spirit of the rulings of John Marshall. State legislation was assailed on every side as either a violation of the due process clause of the 14th Amendment or as an improper local infringement on the federal government's commerce power. Federal legislation, such as the Interstate Commerce Act, the Sherman Antitrust Act, and a federal income tax law, similarly was destroyed as unwarranted assault on private property owners.

The Progressive era brought massive demands both for the utilization of government as a prime instrument for social and economic reform and the development of a new sociological jurisprudence that would accommodate the law to the new realities of an industrial, urban, and communal society. The court responded by developing new legal formulas that permitted the validation of broad federal regulatory programs, from the antitrust laws to those of the various new commissions, and evolving a unique body of federal police power through which federal action could be taken to complement the states in the area of health, safety, morals, and welfare. However, at the end of this period the court, confronting the exigencies of a wartime situation, was forced to evolve a new body of law to cope with governmental infringement on various of the guarantees of the Bill of Rights.

The court of the 1920's and early 1930's, while reflecting many of the dominant values of the "normalcy" of the time, seemed curiously out of tune with hard realities. Under Chief Justice William Howard Taft the law once again was restructured so as to give optimum protection to property rights. The "nine old men" of the years before 1937 set themselves the task of continuing such protection, now from the great explosion of New Deal legislation.

However, severely discredited by setting itself so deliberately at odds with the two elected governmental branches, the Court capitulated to presidential pressure in 1937 and charted an entirely new course. It abandoned its traditional role of protecting private property against governmental regulation and instead concerned itself with giving modern, precise meaning to the guarantees of personal liberty in the Bill of Rights and in the 14th and 15th amendments.

Such a role produced a new constituency for the court. Assuming that big government, big business, and big labor had access to the types of political power by which they could protect themselves, the justices sought to provide legal protection for those Americans without such resources. Hence the court sought to "nationalize" various of the guarantees of the Bill of Rights by making them enforceable against the states through the 14th Amendment and to develop new legal ways of guaranteeing civil rights for citizens subject to discriminatory laws and practices.

Many conservatives questioned this new role. One justice in the early 1960's vigorously attacked the view that "every major social ill in this country can find its cure in some constitutional principle, and that this Court should take the lead in promoting reform when other branches fail to act." Nonetheless, this seemed to be the path that the court was launched upon and would continue to follow until public pressure called for a new line of constitutional interpretation.

See also CONGRESS OF THE UNITED STATES; CONSTITUTIONAL LAW; PRESIDENCY, UNITED STATES; SUPREME COURT OF THE UNITED STATES; UNITED STATES—11. *Form and Constitution of the Federal Government* and 16. *The Founding of the Nation, 1763–1815.*

PAUL L. MURPHY
*University of Minnesota*

**Bibliography**

Anastaplo, George, *The Constitution of 1787* (Johns Hopkins Univ. Press 1988).

Cousins, N., ed., *The Republic of Reason* (Harper 1988).

Edwards, George C., III, and Walker, Wallace E., eds., *National Security and the U.S. Constitution* (Johns Hopkins Univ. Press 1988).

Grundman, Adolph M., *The Embattled Constitution: Vital Framework or Convenient Symbol?* (Krieger 1986).

Kammen, Michael, ed., *The Origins of the American Constitution: A Documentary History* (Penguin 1986).

Kipnis, K., and Meyers, D. T., eds., *Philosophical Dimensions of the Constitution* (Westview Press 1988).

Levy, Leonard W., and others, eds., *Encyclopedia of the American Constitution*, 4 vols. (Macmillan 1986).

Thelen, David, ed., *The Constitution and American Life* (Cornell Univ. Press 1988).

# TEXT OF THE CONSTITUTION OF THE UNITED STATES

We the People of the United States, in Order to form a more perfect Union, establish Justice, insure domestic Tranquillity, provide for the common defence, promote the general Welfare, and secure the Blessings of Liberty to ourselves and our Posterity, do ordain and establish this Constitution for the United States of America.

### ARTICLE. I.

SECTION. 1. All legislative Powers herein granted shall be vested in a Congress of the United States, which shall consist of a Senate and House of Representatives.

SECTION. 2. The House of Representatives shall be composed of Members chosen every second Year by the People of the several States, and the Electors in each State shall have the Qualifications requisite for Electors of the most numerous Branch of the State Legislature.

No Person shall be a Representative who shall not have attained to the age of twenty five Years, and been seven Years a Citizen of the United States, and who shall not, when elected, be an Inhabitant of that State in which he shall be chosen.

Representatives and direct Taxes shall be apportioned among the several States which may be included within this Union, according to their respective Numbers, which shall be determined by adding to the whole Number of free Persons, including those bound to Service for a Term of Years, and excluding Indians not taxed, three fifths of all other Persons. The actual Enumeration shall be made within three Years after the first Meeting of the Congress of the United States, and within every subsequent Term of ten Years, in such Manner as they shall by Law direct. The Number of Representatives shall not exceed one for every thirty Thousand, but each State shall have at Least one Representative; and until such enumeration shall be made, the State of New Hampshire shall be entitled to chuse three, Massachusetts eight, Rhode-Island and Providence Plantations one, Connecticut five, New-York six, New Jersey four, Pennsylvania eight, Delaware one, Maryland six, Virginia ten, North Carolina five, South Carolina five, and Georgia three.

When vacancies happen in the Representation from any State, the Executive Authority thereof shall issue Writs of Election to fill such Vacancies.

The House of Representatives shall chuse their Speaker and other Officers; and shall have the sole Power of Impeachment.

SECTION. 3. The Senate of the United States shall be composed of two Senators from each State, chosen by the Legislature thereof, for six Years; and each Senator shall have one Vote.

Immediately after they shall be assembled in Consequence of the first Election, they shall be divided as equally as may be into three Classes. The Seats of the Senators of the first Class shall be vacated at the Expiration of the second Year, of the second Class at the Expiration of the fourth Year, and of the third Class at the Expiration of the sixth Year, so that one third may be chosen every second Year; and if Vacancies happen by Resignation, or otherwise, during the Recess of the Legislature of any State, the Executive thereof may make temporary Appointments until the next Meeting of the Legislature, which shall then fill such Vacancies.

No Person shall be a Senator who shall not have attained to the Age of thirty Years, and been nine Years a Citizen of the United States, and who shall not, when elected, be an Inhabitant of that State for which he shall be chosen.

The Vice President of the United States shall be President of the Senate, but shall have no Vote, unless he be equally divided.

The Senate shall chuse their other Officers, and also a President pro tempore, in the Absence of the Vice President, or when he shall exercise the Office of President of the United States.

The Senate shall have the sole Power to try all Impeachments. When sitting for that Purpose, they shall be on Oath or Affirmation. When the President of the United States is tried the Chief Justice shall preside: And no Person shall be convicted without the Concurrence of two thirds of the Members present.

Judgment in Cases of Impeachment shall not extend further than to removal from Office, and disqualification to hold and enjoy any Office of honor, Trust or Profit under the United States: but the Party convicted shall nevertheless be liable and subject to Indictment, Trial, Judgment and Punishment, according to Law.

SECTION. 4. The Times, Places and Manner of holding Elections for Senators and Representatives, shall be prescribed in each State by the Legislature thereof; but the Congress may at any time by Law make or alter such Regulations, except as to the Places of chusing Senators.

The Congress shall assemble at least once in every Year, and such Meeting shall be on the first Monday in December, unless they shall by Law appoint a different Day.

SECTION. 5. Each House shall be the Judge of the Elections, Returns and Qualifications of its own Members, and a Majority of each shall constitute a Quorum to do Business; but a smaller Number may adjourn from day to day, and may be authorized to compel the Attendance of absent Members, in such Manner, and under such Penalties as each House may provide.

Each House may determine the Rules of its Proceedings, punish its Members for disorderly Behaviour, and, with the Concurrence of two thirds, expel a Member.

Each House shall keep a Journal of its Proceedings, and from time to time publish the same, excepting such Parts as may in their Judgment require Secrecy; and the Yeas and Nays of the Members of either House on any question shall, at the Desire of one fifth of those Present, be entered on the Journal.

Neither House, during the Session of Congress, shall, without the Consent of the other, adjourn for more than three days, nor to any other Place than that in which the two Houses shall be sitting.

SECTION. 6. The Senators and Representatives shall receive a Compensation for their Services, to be ascertained by Law, and paid out of the Treasury of the United States. They shall in all Cases, except Treason, Felony and Breach of the Peace, be privileged from Arrest during their Attendance at the Session of their respective Houses, and in going to and returning from the same; and for any Speech or Debate in either House, they shall not be questioned in any other Place.

No Senator or Representative shall, during the Time for which he was elected, be appointed to any civil Office under the Authority of the United States, which shall have been created, or the Emoluments whereof shall have been encreased during such time; and no Person holding any Office under the United States, shall be a Member of either House during his Continuance in Office.

SECTION. 7. All Bills for raising Revenue shall originate in the House of Representatives; but the Senate may propose or concur with amendments as on other Bills.

Every Bill which shall have passed the House of Representatives and the Senate, shall, before it become a Law, be presented to the President of the United States; If he approve he shall sign it, but if not he shall return it, with his Objections to that House in which it shall have originated, who shall enter the Objections at large on their Journal, and proceed to reconsider it. If after such Reconsideration two thirds of that House shall agree to pass the Bill, it shall be sent, together with the Objections, to the other House, by which it shall likewise be reconsidered, and if approved by two thirds of that House, it shall become a Law. But in all such Cases the Votes of both Houses shall be determined by yeas and Nays, and the Names of the Persons voting for and against the Bill shall be entered on the Journal of each House respectively. If any Bill shall not be returned by the President within ten Days (Sundays excepted) after it shall have been presented to him, the Same shall be a Law, in like Manner as if he had signed it, unless the Congress by their Adjournment prevent its Return, in which Case it shall not be a Law.

Every Order, Resolution, or Vote to which the Concurrence of the Senate and House of Representatives may be necessary (except on a question of Adjournment) shall be presented to the President of the United States; and before the Same shall take Effect, shall be approved by him, or being disapproved by him, shall be repassed by two thirds of the Senate and House of Representatives, according to the Rules and Limitations prescribed in the Case of a Bill.

SECTION. 8. The Congress shall have Power To lay and collect Taxes, Duties, Imposts and Excises, to pay the Debts and provide for the common Defence and general Welfare of the United States; but all Duties, Imposts and Excises shall be uniform throughout the United States;

To borrow Money on the credit of the United States;

To regulate Commerce with foreign Nations, and among the several States, and with the Indian Tribes;

To establish an uniform Rule of Naturalization, and uniform Laws on the subject of Bankruptcies throughout the United States;

To coin Money, regulate the Value thereof, and of foreign Coin, and fix the Standard of Weights and Measures;

To provide for the Punishment of counterfeiting the Securities and current Coin of the United States;

To establish Post Offices and post Roads;

To promote the Progress of Science and useful Arts, by securing for limited Times to Authors and Inventors the exclusive Right to their respective Writings and Discoveries;

To constitute Tribunals inferior to the supreme Court;

To define and punish Piracies and Felonies committed on the high Seas, and Offences against the Law of Nations;

To declare War, grant Letters of Marque and Reprisal, and make Rules concerning Captures on Land and Water;

To raise and support Armies, but no Appropriation of Money to that Use shall be for a longer Term than two Years;

To provide and maintain a Navy;

To make Rules for the Government and Regulation of the land and naval Forces;

To provide for calling forth the Militia to execute the Laws of the Union, suppress Insurrections and repel Invasions;

To provide for organizing, arming, and disciplining, the Militia, and for governing such Part of them as may be employed in the Service of the United States, reserving to the States respectively, the Appointment of the Officers, and the Authority of training the Militia according to the discipline prescribed by Congress;

To exercise exclusive Legislation in all Cases whatsoever, over such District (not exceeding ten Miles square) as may, by Cession of Particular States, and the Acceptance of Congress, become the Seat of the Government of the United States, and to exercise like Authority over all Places purchased by the Consent of the Legislature of the State in which the Same shall be, for the Erection of Forts, Magazines, Arsenals, dock-Yards, and other needful Buildings;—And

To make all Laws which shall be necessary and proper for carrying into Execution the foregoing Powers, and all other Powers vested by this Constitution in the Government of the United States, or in any Department or Officer thereof.

SECTION. 9. The Migration or Importation of such Persons as any of the States now existing shall think proper to admit, shall not be prohibited by the Congress prior to the Year one thousand eight hundred and eight, but a Tax or duty may be imposed on such Importation, not exceeding ten dollars for each Person.

The Privilege of the Writ of Habeas Corpus shall not be suspended, unless when in Cases of Rebellion or Invasion the public Safety may require it.

No Bill of Attainder or ex post facto Law shall be passed.

No Capitation, or other direct, Tax shall be laid, unless in Proportion to the Census or Enumeration herein before directed to be taken.

No Tax or Duty shall be laid on Articles exported from any State.

No Preference shall be given by any Regulation of Commerce or Revenue to the Ports of one State over those of another; nor shall Vessels bound to, or from, one State, be obliged to enter, clear or pay Duties in another.

No Money shall be drawn from the Treasury, but in Consequence of Appropriations made by Law; and a regular Statement and Account of the Receipts and Expenditures of all public Money shall be published from time to time.

No Title of Nobility shall be granted by the United States: And no Person holding any Office of Profit or Trust under them, shall, without the Consent of the Congress, accept of any present, Emolument, Office, or Title, of any kind whatever, from any King, Prince, or foreign State.

SECTION. 10. No State shall enter into any Treaty, Alliance, or Confederation; grant Letters of Marque and Reprisal; coin Money; emit Bills of Credit; make any Thing but gold and silver Coin a Tender in Payment of Debts; pass any Bill of Attainder, ex post facto Law, or Law impairing the Obligation of Contracts, or grant any Title of Nobility.

No State shall, without the Consent of the Congress, lay any Imposts or Duties on Imports or Exports, except what may be absolutely necessary for executing its inspection Laws: and the net Produce of all Duties and Imposts, laid by any State on Imports or Exports, shall be for the Use of the Treasury of the United States; and all such Laws shall be subject to the Revision and Controul of the Congress.

No State shall, without the Consent of Congress, lay any Duty of Tonnage, keep Troops, or Ships of War in time of Peace, enter into any Agreement or Compact with another State, or with a foreign Power, or engage in War, unless actually invaded, or in such imminent Danger as will not admit of delay.

## ARTICLE. II.

SECTION. 1. The executive Power shall be vested in a President of the United States of America. He shall hold his Office during the Term of four Years, and, together with the Vice President, chosen for the same Term, be elected, as follows

Each State shall appoint, in such Manner as the Legislature thereof may direct, a Number of Electors, equal to the whole Number of Senators and Representatives to which the State may be entitled in the Congress: but no Senator or Representative, or Person holding an Office of Trust or Profit under the United States, shall be appointed an Elector.

The Electors shall meet in their respective States, and vote by Ballot for two Persons, of whom one at least shall not be an Inhabitant of the same State with themselves. And they shall make a List of all the Persons voted for, and of the Number of Votes for each; which List they shall sign and certify, and transmit sealed to the Seat of the Government of the United States, directed to the President of the Senate. The President of the Senate shall, in the Presence of the Senate and House of Representatives, open all the Certificates, and the Votes shall then be counted. The Person having the greatest Number of Votes shall be the President, if such Number be a Majority of the whole Number of Electors appointed; and if there be more than one who have such Majority, and have an equal Number of Votes, then the House of Representatives shall immediately chuse by Ballot one of them for President; and if no Person have a Majority, then from the five highest on the List the said House shall in like Manner chuse the President. But in chusing the President, the Votes shall be taken by States, the Representation from each State having one Vote; a quorum for this Purpose shall consist of a Member or Members from two thirds of the States, and a Majority of all the States shall be necessary to a Choice. In every Case, after the Choice of the President, the Person having the greatest Number of Votes of the Electors shall be the Vice President. But if there should remain two or more who have equal Votes, the Senate shall chuse from them by Ballot the Vice President.

The Congress may determine the Time of chusing the Electors, and the Day on which they shall give their Votes; which Day shall be the same throughout the United States.

No Person except a natural born Citizen, or a Citizen of the United States, at the time of the Adoption of this Constitution, shall be eligible to the Office of President; neither shall any person be eligible to that Office who shall not have attained to the Age of thirty five Years, and been fourteen Years a Resident within the United States.

In Case of the Removal of the President from Office, or of his Death, Resignation, or Inability to discharge the Powers and Duties of the said Office, the Same shall devolve on the Vice President, and the Congress may by Law provide for the Case of Removal, Death, Resignation or Inability, both of the President and Vice President, declaring what Officer shall then act as President, and such Officer shall act accordingly, until the Disability be removed, or a President shall be elected.

The President shall, at stated Times, receive for his Services, a Compensation, which shall neither be encreased nor diminished during the Period for which he shall have been elected, and he shall not receive within that period any other Emolument from the United States, or any of them.

Before he enter on the Execution of his Office, he shall take the following Oath or Affirmation:—"I do solemnly swear (or affirm) that I will faithfully execute the Office of President of the United States, and will to the best of my Ability, preserve, protect and defend the Constitution of the United States."

SECTION. 2. The President shall be Commander in Chief of the Army and Navy of the United States, and of the Militia of the several States, when called into the actual Service of the United States; he may require the Opinion, in writing, of the principal Officer in each of the executive Departments, upon any Subject relating to the Duties of their respective Offices, and he shall have Power to grant Reprieves and Pardons for Offences against the United States, except in Cases of Impeachment.

He shall have Power, by and with the Advice and Consent of the Senate, to make Treaties, provided two thirds of the Senators present concur; and he shall nominate, and by and with the Advice and Consent of the Senate, shall appoint Ambassadors, other public Ministers and Consuls, Judges of the supreme Court, and all other Officers of the United States, whose Appointments are not herein otherwise provided for, and which shall be established by Law: but the Congress may by Law vest the Appointment of such inferior Officers, as they think proper, in the President alone, in the Courts of Law, or in the Heads of Departments.

The President shall have Power to fill up all Vacancies that may happen during the Recess of the Senate, by granting Commissions which shall expire at the End of their next Session.

Section. 3. He shall from time to time give to the Congress Information of the State of the Union, and recommend to their Consideration such Measures as he shall judge necessary and expedient; he may, on extraordinary Occasions, convene both Houses, or either of them, and in Case of Disagreement between them, with Respect to the Time of Adjournment, he may adjourn them to such Time as he shall think proper; he shall receive Ambassadors and other public Ministers; he shall take Care that the Laws be faithfully executed, and shall Commission all the Officers of the United States.

Section. 4. The President, Vice President and all civil Officers of the United States, shall be removed from Office on Impeachment for, and Conviction of, Treason, Bribery, or other high Crimes and Misdemeanors.

## ARTICLE. III.

Section. 1. The judicial Power of the United States, shall be vested in one supreme Court, and in such inferior Courts as the Congress may from time to time ordain and establish. The Judges, both of the supreme and inferior Courts, shall hold their Offices during good Behaviour, and shall, at stated Times, receive for their Services, a Compensation, which shall not be diminished during their Continuance in Office.

Section. 2. The judicial Power shall extend to all Cases, in Law and Equity, arising under this Constitution, the Laws of the United States, and Treaties made, or which shall be made, under their Authority;—to all Cases affecting Ambassadors, other public Ministers and Consuls;—to all Cases of admiralty and maritime Jurisdiction;—to Controversies to which the United States shall be a Party;—to Controversies between two or more States;—between a State and Citizens of another State;—between Citizens of different States;—between Citizens of the same State claiming Lands under Grants of different States, and between a State, or the Citizens thereof, and foreign States, Citizens or Subjects.

In all Cases affecting Ambassadors, other public Ministers and Consuls, and those in which a State shall be Party, the supreme Court shall have original Jurisdiction. In all the other Cases before mentioned, the supreme Court shall have appellate Jurisdiction, both as to Law and Fact, with such Exceptions, and under such Regulations as the Congress shall make.

The Trial of all Crimes, except in Cases of Impeachment, shall be by Jury; and such Trial shall be held in the State where the said Crimes shall have been committed; but when not committed within any State, the Trial shall be at such Place or Places as the Congress may by Law have directed.

Section. 3. Treason against the United States, shall consist only in levying War against them, or in adhering to their Enemies, giving them Aid and Comfort. No Person shall be convicted of Treason unless on the Testimony of two Witnesses to the same overt Act, or on Confession in open Court.

The Congress shall have Power to declare the Punishment of Treason, but no Attainder of Treason shall work Corruption of Blood, or Forfeiture except during the Life of the Person attainted.

## ARTICLE. IV.

Section. 1. Full Faith and Credit shall be given in each State to the public Acts, Records, and judicial Proceedings of every other State. And the Congress may by general Laws prescribe the Manner in which such Acts, Records and Proceedings shall be proved, and the Effect thereof.

Section. 2. The Citizens of each State shall be entitled to all Privileges and Immunities of Citizens in the several States.

A Person charged in any State with Treason, Felony, or other Crime, who shall flee from Justice, and be found in another State, shall on Demand of the executive Authority of the State from which he fled, be delivered up, to be removed to the State having Jurisdiction of the Crime.

No Person held to Service or Labour in one State, under the Laws thereof, escaping into another, shall, in Consequence of any Law or Regulation therein, be discharged from such Service or Labour, but shall be delivered up on Claim of the Party to whom such Service or Labour may be due.

Section. 3. New States may be admitted by the Congress into this Union; but no new State shall be formed or erected within the Jurisdiction of any other State; nor any State be formed by the Junction of two or more States, or Parts of States, without the Consent of the Legislatures of the States concerned as well as of the Congress.

The Congress shall have Power to dispose of and make all needful Rules and Regulations respecting the Territory or other Property belonging to the United States; and nothing in this Constitution shall be so construed as to Prejudice any Claims of the United States, or of any particular State.

Section. 4. The United States shall guarantee to every State in this Union a Republican Form of Government, and shall protect each of them against Invasion; and on Application of the Legislature, or of the Executive (when the Legislature cannot be convened) against domestic Violence.

## ARTICLE. V.

The Congress, whenever two thirds of both Houses shall deem it necessary, shall propose Amendments to this Constitution, or, on the Application of the Legislatures of two thirds of the several States, shall call a Convention for proposing Amendments, which, in either Case, shall be valid to all Intents and Purposes, as Part of this Constitution, when ratified by the Legislatures of three fourths of the several States, or by Conventions in three fourths thereof, as the one or the other Mode of Ratification may be proposed by the Congress; Provided that no Amendment which may be made prior to the Year One thousand eight hundred and eight shall in any Manner affect the first and fourth Clauses in the Ninth Section of the first Article; and that no State, without its Consent, shall be deprived of its equal Suffrage in the Senate.

## ARTICLE. VI.

All Debts contracted and Engagements entered into, before the Adoption of this Constitution, shall be as valid against the United States under this Constitution, as under the Confederation.

This Constitution, and the Laws of the United States which shall be made in Pursuance thereof; and all Treaties made, or which shall be made, under the Authority of the United States, shall be the supreme Law of the Land; and the Judges in every State shall be bound thereby, any Thing in the Constitution or Laws of any State to the Contrary notwithstanding.

The Senators and Representatives before mentioned, and the Members of the several State Legislatures, and all executive and judicial Officers, both of the United States and of the several States, shall be bound by Oath or Affirmation, to support this Constitution; but no religious Test shall ever be required as a Qualification to any Office or public Trust under the United States.

## ARTICLE. VII.

The Ratification of the Conventions of nine States, shall be sufficient for the Establishment of this Constitution between the States so ratifying the Same.

done in Convention by the Unanimous Consent of the States present the Seventeenth Day of September in the Year of our Lord one thousand seven hundred and Eighty seven and of the Independence of the United States of America the Twelfth In witness whereof We have hereunto subscribed our Names,

G⁰ Washington—Presid^t
and deputy from Virginia

| New Hampshire | { John Langdon<br>Nicholas Gilman |
| Massachusetts | { Nathaniel Gorham<br>Rufus King |
| Connecticut | { Wm Saml Johnson<br>Roger Sherman |
| New York . . . | Alexander Hamilton |
| New Jersey | { Wil: Livingston<br>David Brearley.<br>Wm Paterson.<br>Jona: Dayton |
| Pennsylvania | { B Franklin<br>Thomas Mifflin<br>Robt Morris<br>Geo. Clymer<br>Thos FitzSimons<br>Jared Ingersoll<br>James Wilson<br>Gouv Morris |
| Delaware | { Geo: Read<br>Gunning Bedford jun<br>John Dickinson<br>Richard Bassett<br>Jaco: Broom |
| Maryland | { James McHenry<br>Dan of St Thos Jenifer<br>Danl Carroll |
| Virginia | { John Blair—<br>James Madison Jr. |
| North Carolina | { Wm Blount<br>Richd Dobbs Spaight.<br>Hu Williamson |
| South Carolina | { J. Rutledge<br>Charles Cotesworth Pinckney<br>Charles Pinckney<br>Pierce Butler |
| Georgia | { William Few<br>Abr Baldwin |

In Convention Monday, September 17th 1787.
Present
The States of
New Hampshire, Massachusetts, Connecticut, Mr Hamilton from New York, New Jersey, Pennsylvania, Delaware, Maryland, Virginia, North Carolina, South Carolina and Georgia.
Resolved,

That the preceeding Constitution be laid before the United States in Congress assembled, and that it is the Opinion of this Convention, that it should afterwards be submitted to a Convention of Delegates, chosen in each State by the People thereof, under the Recommendation of its Legislature, for their Assent and Ratification; and that each Convention assenting to, and ratifying the Same, should give Notice thereof to the United States in Congress assembled. Resolved, That it is the Opinion of this Convention, that as soon as the Conventions of nine States shall have ratified this Constitution, the United States in Congress assembled should fix a Day on which Electors should be appointed by the States which shall have ratified the same, and a Day on which the Electors should assemble to vote for the President, and the Time and Place for commencing Proceedings under this Constitution. That after such Publication the Electors should be appointed, and the Senators and Representatives elected: That the Electors should meet on the Day fixed for the Election of the President, and should transmit their Votes certified, signed, sealed and directed, as the Constitution requires, to the Secretary of the United States in Congress assembled, that the Senators and Representatives should convene at the Time and Place assigned; that the Senators should appoint a President of the Senate, for the sole Purpose of receiving, opening and counting the Votes for President; and, that after he shall be chosen, the Congress, together with the President, should, without Delay, proceed to execute this Constitution.

By the Unanimous Order of the Convention

Go Washington—Presidt

W. Jackson Secretary.

## ARTICLES IN ADDITION TO, AND AMENDMENT OF, THE CONSTITUTION OF THE UNITED STATES OF AMERICA, PROPOSED BY CONGRESS, AND RATIFIED BY THE SEVERAL STATES, PURSUANT TO THE FIFTH ARTICLE OF THE ORIGINAL CONSTITUTION.

### AMENDMENT I.

Congress shall make no law respecting an establishment of religion, or prohibiting the free exercise thereof; or abridging the freedom of speech, or of the press; or the right of the people peaceably to assemble, and to petition the Government for a redress of grievances.

### AMENDMENT II.

A well regulated Militia, being necessary to the security of a free State, the right of the people to keep and bear Arms, shall not be infringed.

### AMENDMENT III.

No Soldier shall, in time of peace be quartered in any house, without the consent of the Owner, nor in time of war, but in a manner to be prescribed by law.

### AMENDMENT IV.

The right of the people to be secure in their persons, houses, papers, and effects, against unreasonable searches and seizures, shall not be violated, and no Warrants shall issue, but upon probable cause, supported by Oath or affirmation, and particularly describing the place to be searched, and the persons or things to be seized.

### AMENDMENT V.

No person shall be held to answer for a capital, or otherwise infamous crime, unless on a presentment or indictment of a Grand Jury, except in cases arising in the land or naval forces, or in the Militia, when in actual service in time of War or public danger; nor shall any person be subject for the same offence to be twice put in jeopardy of life or limb; nor shall be compelled in any criminal case to be a witness against himself, nor be deprived of life, liberty, or property, without due process of law; nor shall private property be taken for public use, without just compensation.

### AMENDMENT VI.

In all criminal prosecutions, the accused shall enjoy the right to a speedy and public trial, by an impartial jury of the State and district wherein the crime shall have been committed, which district shall have been previously ascertained by law, and to be informed of the nature and cause of the accusation; to be confronted with the witnesses against him; to have compulsory process for obtaining witnesses in his favor, and to have the Assistance of Counsel for his defence.

### AMENDMENT VII.

In Suits at common law, where the value in controversy shall exceed twenty dollars, the right of trial by jury shall be preserved, and no fact tried by a jury, shall be otherwise re-examined in any Court of the United States, than according to the rules of the common law.

### AMENDMENT VIII.

Excessive bail shall not be required, nor excessive fines imposed, nor cruel and unusual punishments inflicted.

### AMENDMENT IX.

The enumeration in the Constitution, of certain rights, shall not be construed to deny or disparage others retained by the people.

### AMENDMENT X.

The powers not delegated to the United States by the Constitution, nor prohibited by it to the States, are reserved to the States respectively, or to the people.

## AMENDMENT XI.

The Judicial power of the United States shall not be construed to extend to any suit in law or equity, commenced or prosecuted against one of the United States by Citizens of another State, or by Citizens or Subjects of any Foreign State.

## AMENDMENT XII.

The Electors shall meet in their respective states and vote by ballot for President and Vice-President, one of whom, at least, shall not be an inhabitant of the same state with themselves; they shall name in their ballots the person voted for as President, and in distinct ballots the person voted for as Vice-President, and they shall make distinct lists of all persons voted for as President, and of all persons voted for as Vice-President, and of the number of votes for each, which lists they shall sign and certify, and transmit sealed to the seat of the government of the United States, directed to the President of the Senate;—The President of the Senate shall, in the presence of the Senate and House of Representatives, open all the certificates and the votes shall then be counted;—The person having the greatest number of votes for President, shall be the President, if such number be a majority of the whole number of Electors appointed; and if no person have such majority, then from the persons having the highest numbers not exceeding three on the list of those voted for as President, the House of Representatives shall choose immediately, by ballot, the President. But in choosing the President, the votes shall be taken by states, the representation from each state having one vote; a quorum for this purpose shall consist of a member or members from two-thirds of the states, and a majority of all the states shall be necessary to a choice. And if the House of Representatives shall not choose a President whenever the right of choice shall devolve upon them, before the fourth day of March next following, then the Vice-President shall act as President, as in the case of the death or other constitutional disability of the President—The person having the greatest number of votes as Vice-President, shall be the Vice-President, if such number be a majority of the whole number of Electors appointed, and if no person have a majority, then from the two highest numbers on the list, the Senate shall choose the Vice-President; a quorum for the purpose shall consist of two-thirds of the whole number of Senators, and a majority of the whole number shall be necessary to a choice. But no person constitutionally ineligible to the office of President shall be eligible to that of Vice-President of the United States.

## AMENDMENT XIII.

SECTION 1. Neither slavery nor involuntary servitude, except as a punishment for crime whereof the party shall have been duly convicted, shall exist within the United States, or any place subject to their jurisdiction.

SECTION 2. Congress shall have power to enforce this article by appropriate legislation.

## AMENDMENT XIV.

SECTION 1. All persons born or naturalized in the United States and subject to the jurisdiction thereof, are citizens of the United States and of the State wherein they reside. No State shall make or enforce any law which shall abridge the privileges or immunities of citizens of the United States; nor shall any State deprive any person of life, liberty, or property, without due process of law; nor deny to any person within its jurisdiction the equal protection of the laws.

SECTION 2. Representatives shall be apportioned among the several States according to their respective numbers, counting the whole number of persons in each State, excluding Indians not taxed. But when the right to vote at any election for the choice of electors for President and Vice President of the United States, Representatives in Congress, the Executive and Judicial officers of a State, or the members of the Legislature thereof, is denied to any of the male inhabitants of such State, being twenty-one years of age, and citizens of the United States, or in any way abridged, except for participation in rebellion, or other crime, the basis of representation therein shall be reduced in the proportion which the number of such male citizens shall bear to the whole number of male citizens twenty-one years of age in such State.

SECTION 3. No person shall be a Senator or Representative in Congress, or elector of President and Vice President, or hold any office, civil or military, under the United States, or under any State, who, having previously taken an oath, as a member of Congress, or as an officer of the United States, or as a member of any State legislature, or as an executive or judicial officer of any State, to support the Constitution of the United States, shall have engaged in insurrection or rebellion against the same, or given aid or comfort to the enemies thereof. But Congress may by a vote of two-thirds of each House, remove such disability.

SECTION 4. The validity of the public debt of the United States, authorized by law, including debts incurred for payment of pensions and bounties for services in suppressing insurrection or rebellion, shall not be questioned. But neither the United States nor any State shall assume or pay any debt or obligation incurred in aid of insurrection or rebellion against the United States, or any claim for the loss or emancipation of any slave; but all such debts, obligations and claims shall be held illegal and void.

SECTION 5. The Congress shall have power to enforce, by appropriate legislation, the provisions of this article.

## AMENDMENT XV.

SECTION 1. The right of citizens of the United States to vote shall not be denied or abridged by the United States or by any State on account of race, color, or previous condition of servitude.

SECTION 2. The Congress shall have power to enforce this article by appropriate legislation.

## AMENDMENT XVI.

The Congress shall have power to lay and collect taxes on incomes, from whatever source derived, without apportionment among the several States, and without regard to any census or enumeration.

## AMENDMENT XVII.

The Senate of the United States shall be composed of two Senators from each State, elected by the people thereof, for six years; and each Senator shall have one vote. The electors in each State shall have the qualifications requisite for electors of the most numerous branch of the State legislatures.

When vacancies happen in the representation of any State in the Senate, the executive authority of such State shall issue writs of election to fill such vacancies: *Provided, That* the legislature of any State may empower the executive thereof to make temporary appointments until the people fill the vacancies by election as the legislature may direct.

This amendment shall not be so construed as to affect the election or term of any Senator chosen before it becomes valid as part of the Constitution.

## AMENDMENT XVIII.

SECTION 1. After one year from the ratification of this article the manufacture, sale, or transportation of intoxicating liquors within, the importation thereof into, or the exportation thereof from the United States and all territory subject to the jurisdiction thereof for beverage purposes is hereby prohibited.

SECTION 2. The Congress and the several States shall have concurrent power to enforce this article by appropriate legislation.

SECTION 3. This article shall be inoperative unless it shall have been ratified as an amendment to the Constitution by the legislatures of the several States, as provided in the Constitution, within seven years from the date of the submission hereof to the States by the Congress.

## AMENDMENT XIX.

The right of citizens of the United States to vote shall not be denied or abridged by the United States or by any State on account of sex.

Congress shall have power to enforce this article by appropriate legislation.

## AMENDMENT XX.

SECTION 1. The terms of the President and Vice President shall end at noon on the 20th day of January, and the terms of Senators and Representatives at noon on the 3d day of January, of the years in which such terms would have ended if this article had not been ratified; and the terms of their successors shall then begin.

SECTION 2. The Congress shall assemble at least once in every year, and such meeting shall begin at noon on the 3d day of January, unless they shall by law appoint a different day.

SECTION 3. If, at the time fixed for the beginning of the term of the President, the President elect shall have died, the Vice President elect shall become President. If a President shall not have been chosen before the time fixed for the beginning of his term, or if the President elect shall have failed to qualify, then the Vice President elect shall act as President until a President shall have qualified; and the Congress may by law provide for the case wherein neither a President elect nor a Vice President elect shall have qualified, declaring who shall then act as President, or the manner in which one who is to act shall be selected, and such person shall act accordingly until a President cr Vice President shall have qualified.

SECTION 4. The Congress may by law provide for the case of the death of any of the persons from whom the House of Representatives may choose a President whenever the right of choice shall have devolved upon them, and for the case of the death of any of the persons from whom the Senate may choose a Vice President whenever the right of choice shall have devolved upon them.

SECTION 5. Sections 1 and 2 shall take effect on the 15th day of October following the ratification of this article.

SECTION 6. This article shall be inoperative unless it shall have been ratified as an amendment to the Constitution by the legislatures of three-fourths of the several States within seven years from the date of its submission.

## AMENDMENT XXI.

SECTION 1. The eighteenth article of amendment to the Constitution of the United States is hereby repealed.

SECTION 2. The transportation or importation into any State, Territory, or possession of the United States for delivery or use therein of intoxicating liquors, in violation of the laws thereof, is hereby prohibited.

SECTION 3. This article shall be inoperative unless is shall have been ratified as an amendment to the Constitution by conventions in the several States, as provided in the Constitution, within seven years from the date of the submission hereof to the States by the Congress.

## AMENDMENT XXII.

SECTION 1. No person shall be elected to the office of the President more than twice, and no person who has held the office of President, or acted as President, for more than two years of a term to which some other person was elected President shall be elected to the office of the President more than once. But this Article shall not apply to any person holding the office of President when this Article was proposed by the Congress, and shall not prevent any person who may be holding the office of President, or acting as President, during the term within which this Article becomes operative from holding the office of President or acting as President during the remainder of such term.

SECTION 2. This Article shall be inoperative unless it shall have been ratified as an amendment to the Constitution by the legislatures of three-fourths of the several States within seven years from the date of its submission to the States by the Congress.

## AMENDMENT XXIII.

SECTION 1. The District constituting the seat of Government of the United States shall appoint in such manner as the Congress may direct:

A number of electors of President and Vice President equal to the whole number of Senators and Representatives in Congress to which the District would be entitled if it were a State, but in no event more than the least populous State; they shall be in addition to those appointed by the States, but they shall be considered, for the purposes of the election of President and Vice President, to be electors appointed by a State; and they shall meet in the District and perform such duties as provided by the twelfth article of amendment.

SECTION 2. The Congress shall have power to enforce this article by appropriate legislation.

## AMENDMENT XXIV.

SECTION 1. The right of citizens of the United States to vote in any primary or other election for President or Vice President, for electors for President or Vice President, or for Senator or Representative in Congress, shall not be denied or abridged by the United States or any State by reason of failure to pay any poll tax or other tax.

SECTION 2. The Congress shall have the power to enforce this article by appropriate legislation.

## AMENDMENT XXV.

SECTION 1. In case of the removal of the President from office or of his death or resignation, the Vice President shall become President.

SECTION 2. Whenever there is a vacancy in the office of the Vice President, the President shall nominate a Vice President who shall take the office upon confirmation by a majority vote of both houses of Congress.

SECTION 3. Whenever the President transmits to the President pro tempore of the Senate and the Speaker of the House of Representatives his written declaration that he is unable to discharge the powers and duties of his office, and until he transmits to them a written declaration to the contrary, such powers and duties shall be discharged by the Vice President as Acting President.

SECTION 4. Whenever the Vice President and a majority of either the principal officers of the executive departments or of such other body as Congress may by law provide, transmit to the President pro tempore of the Senate and the Speaker of the House of Representatives their written declaration that the President is unable to discharge the powers and duties of his office, the Vice President shall immediately assume the powers and duties of the office as Acting President.

Thereafter, when the President transmits to the President pro tempore of the Senate and the Speaker of the House of Representatives his written declaration that no inability exists, he shall resume the powers and duties of his office unless the Vice President and a majority of either the principal officers of the executive department or of such other body as Congress may by law provide, transmit within four days to the President pro tempore of the Senate and the Speaker of the House of Representatives their written declaration that the President is unable to discharge the powers and duties of his office. Thereupon Congress shall decide the issue, assembling within forty-eight hours for that purpose if not in session. If the Congress within twenty-one days after receipt of the latter written declaration, or, if Congress is not in session, within twenty-one days after Congress is required to assemble, determines by two-thirds vote of both Houses that the President is unable to discharge the powers and duties of his office, the Vice President shall continue to discharge the same as Acting President; otherwise, the President shall resume the powers and duties of his office.

## AMENDMENT XXVI.

SECTION 1. The right of citizens of the United States, who are 18 years of age or older, to vote shall not be denied or abridged by the United States or any state on account of age.

SECTION 2. The Congress shall have the power to enforce this article by appropriate legislation.

### AMENDMENT XXVII.

No law varying the compensation for the services of the senators and representatives shall take effect until an election of representatives shall have intervened.

**CONSTITUTIONAL CONVENTION,** kon-stə-tōō'-shən-əl kən-ven'shən, a representative assembly called to write a new constitution or to revise or propose changes in an existing constitution. The use of constitutional conventions rather than regular legislatures for these purposes stems from the principle that constitutions are a body of higher law more basic than legislation and that their formulation should be entrusted to representative bodies chosen for that specific purpose.

**Historical Development.** Constitutional conventions are probably one of the United States' most valuable contributions to the art and science of government. They originated during the American Revolution, when the colonies had to establish new forms of government after independence was declared. Although the first state constitutions were framed by existing representative assemblies and were made effective by legislative promulgation without submission to popular vote, pressures for popular approval of state constitutions led to the invention of the constitutional convention. The Massachusetts convention of 1779–1780 was the first constituent assembly to embody all the basic features typical of most modern constitutional conventions in U. S. states: submission of the question of calling a convention to the voters, popular election of delegates, and submission of their work to the electorate for adoption or rejection. By the mid-1780s the constitutional convention was well established as an American governmental institution.

The federal constitutional convention, which met in Philadelphia in 1787, drafted the Constitution of the United States. One method of proposing amendments to this document is by a constitutional convention called by Congress on request of the legislatures in two thirds of the states; this method, however, has never been used. One of the two methods of ratifying amendments to the federal Constitution is by conventions in three fourths of the states; this procedure was used only in ratifying the 21st Amendment. All other amendments have been ratified by state legislatures.

With few exceptions, constitutional conventions have framed U. S. state constitutions since the 1780s. More than 200 such assemblies have been convened by territories seeking admission into the Union and by existing states seeking to alter their basic instruments of government. Many conventions met in the Southern states during and after the Civil War, but many of the resulting constitutions were promulgated without submission to the voters. Growing problems and complexities of government since World War II have resulted in more official attention to modernizing state constitutional structure than during any comparable period. Constitutional conventions were held in a number of states to alter existing constitutions or to write new ones; 2 territories, Hawaii and Alaska, framed new constitutions in preparation for statehood; and another territory, Puerto Rico, wrote a new instrument to provide the basis for commonwealth status.

Although more constitutional conventions have assembled in the United States than in most other countries combined, many nations have employed such bodies to frame their basic laws. Constitutional conventions have often formulated constitutions in the aftermath of revolutions that have overthrown existing political institutions or after other social upheavals. A series of popular assemblies, for example, convened during the French revolutionary period, one of which in 1792 drafted the constitution of the First French Republic. In 1947 a constituent assembly wrote the new constitution that established the Republic of Italy. Other such bodies have formulated basic laws of both new and older states in Asia, Africa, and Latin America, including new states emerging from colonial status to independent nationhood. Notable examples of such countries in which constituent assemblies have been convened are India (1949), Turkey (1960), and South Vietnam (1966–1967). In using constitutional conventions, many nations have followed the basic U. S. pattern.

**Authorization and Powers.** U. S. state constitutional provisions for calling a constitutional convention vary greatly in procedure and other details, but most of them leave initial action to the legislature. Typically, the legislative assembly submits the question of calling a constitutional convention to the electorate. If the required affirmative vote is cast, usually a majority of those voting on the question, the legislature then enacts enabling legislation providing for the selection of delegates, assembling the convention, compensation of delegates and other expenses, organization, and other matters. Eleven state constitutions require periodic submission of the convention question to the voters. Eleven other state constitutions contain no provision for conventions, but the power of the legislature to call them is firmly established.

Constitutional conventions are generally considered to be autonomous bodies that derive their authority from the people and are therefore responsible to no existing organ of government. However, they are limited by the purpose of their creation and are bound by the terms of their popular mandate. If, in submitting the convention question to the electorate, the legislature specifies a function for the convention more limited than total revision, and if the voters approve this limitation, the convention is bound by this mandate unless the existing constitution forbids such restriction.

Constitutional conventions differ from legislative assemblies in both function and form. Conventions are called solely to make or alter constitutions and in no way supersede the existing organs of state government. Conventions are necessarily dependent on legislatures, which frame the enabling acts and provide funds for their operation, but legislative bodies may not encroach on the powers vested in a convention by the people. Unlike the majority of U. S. state legislative bodies, which are bicameral (two chambers), constitutional conventions are unicameral (one chamber). Members of these bodies serve for no fixed term and adjourn when their task has been completed.

**Composition, Organization, and Procedure.** In U. S. states, delegates to constitutional conventions are elected by popular vote, usually from legislative districts. Sometimes, however, delegates are chosen at large or from special districts, or by a combination of these. Delegate elections may be either partisan or nonpartisan; in a few instances both methods may be employed, as in Missouri, where there is equal representation of the two major parties from senatorial districts, and where delegates-at-large are elected on a nonpartisan ballot. The minimum requirement for a delegate is qualification as a voter; in some states, however, delegates must meet the stated requirements for legislators.

After assembling, a convention organizes; it elects officers, selects a staff, adopts procedural rules, and appoints needed committees. Convention officers normally include a president (or chairman), one or more vice-presidents (or vice chairmen), a secretary, and often a sergeant at arms and a parliamentarian. The committee structure is dependent on the convention's purpose; usually the number is small even when a new constitution is to be drafted. Convention committees are generally of two types: procedural and substantive. The former is concerned with general administration, and the latter with the substantive work of the convention. If a new constitution is being written, normally each substantive committee is assigned a particular area of the constitutional system for study and consideration of proposals.

After the organizational period the convention enters the committee phase, during which proposals are received and considered, hearings are held, and draft recommendations are prepared. The final convention stage consists of plenary debate, decision making, and action on proposals. The time required for each phase varies from a few days to many months, depending on the scope and difficulty of the convention's task The product may be one or more proposed amendments, a revision of the existing document, or a new draft constitution.

**Ratification.** American state constitutions written during the Revolutionary period were generally promulgated without popular referendum. During the early 19th century, submission of convention proposals to the electorate became a general practice, but the Civil War and Reconstruction periods produced political stresses that resulted in the promulgation of some constitutions without the voters' approval. Thereafter, submission to the electorate became more prevalent until, by the mid-20th century, it had become a nationwide practice. However, many state constitutions have no express requirement for a popular referendum.

U. S. state constitutions seldom specify the time or the method of submitting proposals. If there is to be a new or a revised constitution, the method of submission is crucial, because the combined votes of numerous dissenting special interest groups may nullify the convention's work. Three principal means have been employed successfully in submitting a new or revised constitution: (1) submission of the entire document to be voted on as a single proposition, (2) presentation of proposals separately, with independent voting on each, and (3) submission of the entire document, but with separate proposals on controversial issues to be voted on independently. The vote required for adoption of convention proposals varies from a majority of those voting on the question to a majority of all the votes cast in the election.

**Preparatory Research.** No group of elected delegates can be expected to have the knowledge necessary to deal with the complex issues and problems that confront them in framing a new constitution or in revising an existing document. Systematic research and preparation of working materials therefore normally precede assembly. The New York convention of 1915 was the first to make such preparation; virtually all states and territories calling constitutional conventions after World War I followed its precedent. Preconvention research has been done by various public and private groups, often by specially designated official commission or by an existing agency. Sometimes the staffs of preparatory research groups are retained to provide research services during the convention.

Typically, the materials prepared for a constitutional convention cover the whole range of subjects with which it must deal, including background data essential for making informed decisions. Sometimes preparatory work includes substantive recommendations. The reports prepared by preconvention research groups compose a large and valuable part of the literature on constitutional reform.

**Conventions and Commissions.** The constitutional convention is one of the three methods of altering constitutions authorized in the basic laws of U. S. states. The two other methods, proposal by legislative action and the constitutional initiative (proposals by a designated percentage of voters, which are submitted to the electorate), are usually employed for relatively minor changes. The great majority of states have used the convention for extensive revision or for writing a new constitution.

Increasingly, U. S. states have employed another technique for changing their constitutions—the constitutional commission. Although not expressly recognized in the basic law of any state, the constitutional commission has served as an auxiliary adjunct of basic legal reform when political difficulties or failures of other means have made it expedient. An appointive body, the constitutional commission's work is purely advisory and preliminary. Its recommendations require action by the legislature, which may accept, modify, or reject them.

Considered as a substitute for the constitutional convention, the constitutional commission has both advantages and disadvantages. Positively, it is smaller, more economical, and more acceptable to legislative bodies than the convention. On the other hand, its appointive members may be less representative than elected convention delegates; it is more likely to be dominated by one party; it stimulates less public interest; and, finally, commissions have been less successful than conventions. The wide use of constitutional commissions may be attributed largely to their subordination to legislative control.

Despite the obstacles to calling a convention—cost, time, opposition of vested interests, and general public inertia—American experience indicates that for constitution making the constitutional convention is unequaled. See also CONSTITUTION; CONSTITUTION OF THE UNITED STATES.

ALBERT L. STURM
*Florida State University*

**Bibliography**
Caplan, Russell L., *Constitutional Brinksmanship* (Oxford 1988).
Collier, James L., and Christopher, *Decision in Philadelphia* (Random House 1986).
Marshall, Geoffrey, *Constitutional Conventions* (Oxford 1984).
Sturm, Albert L., *Methods of State Constitutional Reform* (Univ. of Mich. Press 1954).
Sturm, Albert L., and Craig, James B., Jr., "State Constitutional Conventions: 1950–1965," *State Government*, vol. 39, no. 3 (Univ. of Chicago Press 1966).

**CONSTITUTIONAL LAW,** the fundamental law of a state that defines the powers of the state, constitutes and delineates the organs of government, and limits governmental powers. In addition to dealing with the organization of state and government, constitutional law also concerns itself with the relationship between government and citizens, more specifically with the rights and privileges of the individual vis-à-vis the state.

## SCOPE AND FUNCTION

Because of its fundamental character, constitutional law is legally superior to other types of law. Most commonly, constitutional law is laid down in a special, written document or set of documents, a constitution, that is regarded as the supreme law of the land. A constitution almost always contains a special procedure for amendment in order to prevent facile alteration. (See CONSTITUTION.)

**Separation of Powers.** The idea of separation of powers plays an important role in delineating the powers of the state and the government. Two variants of this theory of politics can be distinguished: one variant concerns the different branches of government; the other relates to a territorial division of state power. The first asserts that liberty can be safeguarded only in a political system in which governmental power is divided into three different functional branches—legislative, executive, and judicial. Each of these branches is assigned different organs that are expected to adhere to their own functions. There is, however, one exception to this rule: under some constitutions the courts (or a special court) are explicitly or implicitly authorized to review statutes in light of the constitution's mandates.

The second variant, called division of powers, refers to the territorial division of state power, which has been established in most contemporary states between a central and a local level. In the constitutional system of the United States (a federal constitutional system), this division of power resulted in a distinction between the organization of power on a national and a state level. In addition to being governed by the Constitution of the United States (the federal constitution), each state adheres to a state constitution in which its official powers are defined. In other constitutional systems, national government can be divided into a central and a decentralized level (such as in France, which has a unitary constitution) or between a decentralized level of states or regions and one central organ with limited powers (such as in Switzerland, which has a confederate system). (See FRANCE —*Government* (National and Local Administration); SWITZERLAND —*Government.*)

**Bills of Rights and Other Sources.** Nations that have written constitutions usually also have an incorporated bill of rights containing basic individual rights, such as freedom of speech and press, freedom of religion and worship, and freedom of association and assembly, among others. These rights aim to protect the individual from state interference. Many modern constitutions have incorporated other rights as well—such as the right to shelter, to employment, and to health care—requiring the state to undertake positive action for their implementation.

The constitutional law of a country is not strictly limited to the rules of the constitution; it also encompasses statutes concerning the structure and functions of central and local governments and their relations with the citizens. In addition, it incorporates judicial decisions (particularly those concerning the interpretation of individual rights and privileges), constitutional conventions, and political practice. In a number of countries certain provisions of international treaties to which these states are a party are now considered part of constitutional law as well.

**Constitutional Law versus Statutory Law.** Certain features distinguish constitutional law from ordinary statutory law. First, constitutional law is the fundamental higher law that governs statutory law. It determines basic matters pertaining to the political system, whereas statutory law applies these matters to specific categories. Second, constitutional law, or rather a specific constitution, springs from a distinct source and is enacted or changed by a special procedure (amendment), either in an extraordinary manner by ordinary bodies or by extraordinary bodies such as constitutional conventions. Sometimes the final adoption of a constitution or its amendment requires the approval of the electorate, to whom it is submitted by referendum. The latter procedure has been and continues to be used in some of the states of the United States. Some constitutions expressly forbid specific constitutional provisions from being amended, such as the principle of the liberal-democratic political order that formed a part of the Federal Republic of Germany's constitution or the republican form of government that is stipulated by the French constitution.

## TYPES OF CONSTITUTIONAL LAW

Two main types of constitutional law are found around the world, the determining factor being whether the constitution is written or unwritten. Although the United Kingdom is usually cited as the classic example of a state without a written constitution, many other countries, including Israel, New Zealand, Oman, and Saudi Arabia, do not have a basic written document. Such countries do, however, have a number of (written) rules pertaining to the organization of government and the rights of citizens. The standard distinction between written and unwritten constitutions is therefore of considerable but nevertheless limited use. Another distinction was introduced by the British legal scholar James Bryce in 1884. He identified flexible constitutions, for which the amending process takes place by simple majority, and rigid constitutions, which involve a special amending procedure. A shortcoming of Bryce's typology is, nevertheless, that it does not take into consideration the fact that constitutions and constitutional law can change not only through formal procedures but also through judicial interpretation and changes in the relationships among political institutions. (See BRYCE, JAMES.)

**Unwritten and Written Constitutions.** Along with its American counterpart, the British constitutional system has been considered the cradle of constitutionalism and an extremely influential model, notably among its former colonies. The sources of British constitutional law are threefold: (1) statutes, such as the Magna Carta (1215), the Bill of Rights (1689), and the Parliament Act (1911); (2) judicial decisions settling aspects of constitutional practice, such as those concerning the interpretation of rights, among them freedom of speech and of assembly; and (3) conventions, practices, or rules that derive from political processes. Thus the principle that a government must resign if defeated on a vote of confidence in the House of Commons is a constitutional custom. (See MAGNA CARTA; BILL OF RIGHTS.)

The 19th-century British constitutional scholar A. V. Dicey distinguished two principles that underlie the British system: parliamentary sovereignty and the rule of law. The first principle refers to the rule that Parliament can legislate on any topic and can pass any laws (including fundamental laws) it sees fit. When laws are passed, the courts must enforce them, which is to say that judicial review does not exist in the United Kingdom. A number of restraints have been placed on the British Parliament, however. (See GREAT BRITAIN AND NORTHERN IRELAND—GREAT BRITAIN: GOVERNMENT.) The second principle of the British constitutional system is the rule of law. This means that every person, including public officials, will be judged according to the ordinary law of the land. A complex body of administrative law has developed in the United Kingdom even though it lacks a regular system of administrative courts, such as that present in France.

The second major type of constitutional law concerns all those states that have adopted a formal written constitution. In this case, too, a further distinction can be made based on the status of the judiciary. In some systems, constitutions explicitly grant the judiciary the power to strike down legislation that is inconsistent with the constitution. In others the judiciary may interpret the constitution in such a way as to invest itself with the power of constitutional review. An example of the first category is the German system; those of the United States and Norway exemplify the second category. (See GERMANY —Government; CONSTITUTION OF THE UNITED STATES; NORWAY—Government.)

**Constitutional Review.** In all systems of constitutional law, the importance of the judiciary in delineating the powers of governments and the scope of individual rights and privileges cannot be overestimated. (See JUDICIAL REVIEW.) Three principal models of constitutional review can be identified. In the first, the "diffuse" or "decentralized" model, all the judges and courts of a given country are authorized to act as constitutional judges. Thus when a dispute that depends on a particular law is brought before them, the courts are permitted to consider the validity of the law and validate or reject it. The most well-known example of a diffuse system of judicial review is that of the United States. Its provisions were largely copied by the majority of the former states of the British Commonwealth: Canada, India, Australia, and Ireland. It was also adopted in Japan and, formally, at least, in a number of Latin American nations.

The second, the "concentrated" or "centralized" model, is characterized by the presence of only a single organ to act as constitutional judge. This institution can be either a supreme judicial court or a special constitutional court organized outside of the ordinary judicial hierarchy. The model finds its origins in Austria and was adopted in many continental European states, such as Germany, Italy, France, Spain, and Belgium.

A further distinction that should be made when discussing constitutional review concerns the method of review. It is possible to distinguish between abstract (*ex ante*) and concrete (*ex post*) review of laws. Concrete review takes place when a lawsuit or some other kind of litigation is brought before the court, as in the case of the U.S. system, in which the Supreme Court hears specific cases. Abstract review, on the other hand, takes place without a specific case or controversy. Such review is the rule in France and occurs to a limited extent in Germany.

Finally, a third type of system distinguishable on the basis of constitutional review is that in which the judiciary is not authorized (more or less explicitly) to review statutes in light of the constitution. Both the Netherlands and Finland have followed this pattern. Since 1953, however, the Dutch courts have been authorized to set aside any constitutional-law provision that may be deemed incompatible with a rule of international law.

### HISTORY OF CONSTITUTIONAL LAW

Whether written or unwritten, based primarily on political or territorial divisions, or encompassing a diffuse or concentrated model of constitutional review, constitutional law has played a fundamental role in the development of political systems throughout history.

**Ancient History.** The roots of modern Western constitutional law stretch back to ancient Greece. Plato originally introduced the notion that government must be guided by law (*nomos*). At the same time, he insisted that lawmaking power should be concentrated in the hands of philosophers, men wiser than ordinary people and therefore more capable of ruling. Aristotle distinguished between a nation's basic governmental structure (*politeia*), its laws, and its changeable policies. His notion of a mixed constitution, a balance of power among monarchy, aristocracy, and democracy, foreshadowed the modern doctrine of separation of powers. Somewhat later, during Roman times, the notion of the equality of all human beings came to the fore, despite the widespread practice of slavery under the Roman Empire. (See PLATO; ARISTOTLE.)

**Middle Ages and the Era of Absolutism.** Building on the ancient heritage, medieval thinkers developed new theories of governance. The king was considered the supreme source of government in the realm. All matters of government were under his control. Unless it fell beyond the physical boundaries of his jurisdiction, or encroached on religious dogma, no edict or rule could be considered illegitimate. The only means to keep the king in check was through resistance. This situation did not change significantly until the advent of the Renaissance and the Reformation. Whereas the king in feudal society was regarded as *primus inter pares* (the first among equals) and had, to some extent, to respect the rights and privileges of his vassals, gradually the monarchy freed itself from these restraints. By about 1600 the era of absolute monarchy had dawned, with even more unfettered control being enjoyed by the crown.

**The Enlightenment.** The next phase in the development of constitutional law occurred in the 17th and 18th centuries, or the Age of Reason (or Enlightenment). During this period important new elements of constitutional law emerged.

First among such new elements were the theories of natural law, which evolved as a reaction to the legal principles of medieval society. The English political philosophers Thomas Hobbes (1588–1679) and John Locke (1632–1704) based their theories on the notion that, before the emergence of state and civil society, human beings lived in a hypothetical state of nature. In this state each human being was a potential threat to others. Locke described the rise of civil society as being the result of a social contract among citizens who agreed to turn over their natural rights to the state in exchange for protection of life, liberty, and property. The notion of natural law became political reality in the constitutions of the British colonies in America. The first of these, the constitution of Virginia of 1776, contained a catalog of natural, inalienable rights. Later, individual rights and privileges became the cornerstone of virtually all constitutions. (See HOBBES, THOMAS; LOCKE, JOHN; CONSTITUTION OF THE UNITED STATES.)

This point serves to introduce a second key trend in constitutional law. During and following the Revolutionary period (1776–1799), many political systems, following the model of the United States, began to lay down the basic structure of government in a special document, a constitution, that was assigned a higher status than ordinary law.

The foundation for the doctrine of separation of powers was laid in the 18th century. The French political philosopher Montesquieu (1689–1755) formulated the doctrine by distinguishing three different branches of government—the legislative, executive, and judicial departments—and assigning each to a separate individual or group. This doctrine was institutionalized in the American and French constitutions of the 18th century and, to this day, remains one of the central ideas of constitutional law. (See MONTESQUIEU, CHARLES-LOUIS.)

**Contemporary Developments.**  The development of constitutional law, and of individual constitutions, in the 20th century has been characterized by paradoxy. On the one hand, constitutions have by now become universally accepted as a means of laying down the law of the land. On the other hand, constitutions are no longer exclusively linked to constitutionalism, or the idea of limited government in service to high principles. Not only do liberal democracies have written constitutions but so too do authoritarian and one-party systems. In some cases a constitution serves primarily as a means of legitimizing the existing political order, as in the case of some Latin American countries. Furthermore, it is not uncommon for discrepancies to exist between constitutional precepts and their exercise in actual circumstances. The constitution of the Weimar Republic (1919), which technically was a model of liberal-democratic principles, proved unfit to prevent the Nazi regime from taking power. Liberal faith in constitutions ended up severely shaken by this event.

The fall of communism in the 1980s brought a revival of constitutional law, with many countries in Eastern Europe and former states of the Soviet Union adopting liberal-democratic constitutions that limited the power of government and, in some cases, restricted or prohibited the participation of communists. The process of transition did not, however, come easily, to which many armed conflicts in the region attested.

In Africa, as many countries gained independence from their former colonial overlords, constitutional developments were initially characterized by a clear commitment to the idea of constitutionalism and the rule of law. At the same time,

however, the notion of limiting the power of the state or its sovereign was rejected, both formally and in practice. Recent developments in Africa have demonstrated a search for adapting European constitutional principles to African political and social circumstances, but the success of such efforts remains unclear.

In the United Kingdom one of the major contemporary questions is whether to adopt a written constitution and enshrine a bill of rights with a system of judicial review. In the United States, discussion has focused on the position of the Supreme Court as a countermajoritarian institution within the constitutional system. The question is whether the judiciary should adhere to a narrow, or strict, interpretation of the Constitution or play a more activist role. This problem is not exclusively American, however. In many European countries the growing importance of the judiciary is a hotly contested issue as well, raising the intriguing question of the politicization of the judiciary or the "judicialization" of politics.

CARLA ZOETHOUT, *Erasmus Universiteit Rotterdam, The Netherlands*

### Bibliography

Abraham, Henry J., *The Judicial Process*, 7th ed. (Oxford 1997).
Alder, John, *Constitutional and Administrative Law* (Macmillan 1994).
Blaustein, Albert P., and G. H. Flanz, eds., *Constitutions of the Countries of the World* (Oceana 1971–1996).
Brazier, Rodney, *Constitutional Reform: Re-shaping the British Political System* (Oxford 1991).
Finer, Samuel Edward, et al., *Comparing Constitutions* (Oxford 1995).
Franklin, Daniel P., and Michael J. Baun, eds., *Political Culture and Constitutionalism: A Comparative Approach* (M. E. Sharpe 1995).
Lane, Jan-Erik, *Constitutions and Political Theory* (Manchester Univ. Press 1996).
Pocock, J. G., *The Ancient Constitution and the Feudal Law* (Cambridge 1987).
Wheare, Kenneth, *Modern Constitutions*, 2d ed. (Oxford 1966).

**CONSTITUTIONAL UNION PARTY,** a political party organized for the United States election of 1860. It comprised old-line Whigs and remnants of the American (Know-Nothing) party. Persuaded that the agitation over the slavery question could lead only to the disruption of the Union, its founders presented no platform other than a vague appeal for adherence to the Constitution, the Union, and the laws of the United States.

Meeting in Baltimore in May 1860, the party nominated John Bell of Tennessee for president and Edward Everett of Massachusetts for vice president. In the November election the Constitutional Union party found its greatest strength among conservatives in the border states, where the effects of civil conflict were especially feared, although the ticket was supported throughout the nation.

Bell trailed the Republican candidate, Abraham Lincoln, and the two Democratic nominees, Stephen A. Douglas and John C. Breckinridge, receiving 591,658 popular votes (only 12.6% of the total). He carried the states of Virginia, Kentucky, and Tennessee with 39 electoral votes. Leaders of the party, in the ensuing months, called for reconciliation of the sections through a compromise of the slavery issue, but without success. With the coming of the Civil War the Constitutional Union Party disappeared from the political scene.

ROBERT W. JOHANNSEN
*University of Illinois*

DELAWARE MEMORIAL BRIDGE UNDER CONSTRUCTION (BETHLEHEM STEEL CORP. PHOTO)

**THE CONSTRUCTION INDUSTRY'S** most dramatic task is the great suspension bridge.

**CONSTRUCTION INDUSTRY.** Construction contributes to economic advancement around the world through both public and private works. Public works involve construction for government departments or agencies at all levels; private construction ranges from large projects in industry to the building or remodeling of a house. The construction industry builds roads, bridges, airports, dams, tunnels, flood control structures, harbors, power plants, pipelines, railroads, water purification and sewage treatment facilities, factories, churches, schools, hospitals, office buildings, apartment houses, and private dwellings.

The industry employs many trades and talents, ranging from trained engineers to common labor. Architects and engineers plan and design structures, and contractors build them. The contractor takes men, materials, and equipment and, by following plans and specifications and applying his special knowledge, completes the work. His force includes supervisory personnel, equipment operators, truck drivers, ironworkers, carpenters, bricklayers, masons, and other skilled and unskilled laborers.

In the United States construction is the largest single industry. Directly and indirectly it employs approximately 15% of the labor force and it accounts for about 15% of the gross national product.

### INDUSTRY STRUCTURE

According to the work they do, contractors are classified as highway, heavy construction, general building (including home builders as a subdivision), and special trade contractors. Some large contractors work in all of the first three categories. Special trade contractors confine themselves to a speciality, such as plumbing, heating, air conditioning, electrical work, painting, tile setting, roofing, plastering, glazing, or pipe fitting.

The construction industry has its roots in the Old World. Settlers from Europe brought to the United States the techniques, methods, and materials to develop an industry. The contract system of building is practiced all over the world, although in developing countries much work is done directly by the government.

**Highway Contractors.** Roads, streets, bridges, and airports are built by highway contractors. They work primarily under contract for some branch of the government—federal, state, county, or municipal. Along with dam builders, highway contractors are big earthmovers. They level hills and fill in valleys in grading a road, because modern highways are built with easy grades and gentle curves. Highway contractors need a wide variety of equipment to do the work. When rock is encountered, the roadbuilders drill, blast, and load the broken chunks into trucks with power shovels. They move dirt with motorized scrapers, bulldozers, and motor graders.

The ideal earthmoving job balances cuts and fills. When the dirt removed from cuts is more than that needed for embankments, it must be "wasted." This may necessitate hauling it to a "spoil" area where superfluous material is dumped. But when material taken from cuts is insufficient to build embankments, the contractor must "borrow" dirt from a pit. Obviously, the material borrowed is not returned.

Road building requires aggregate for base courses and pavements. The contractor may buy this material, blast rock from a quarry, or dig sand and gravel from a bank. When he develops his own material, he crushes and screens it to obtain the gradation of fine and coarse aggregate required by the specifications.

Whether the pavement is to be concrete or bituminous, the contractor mixes batches of the material in a plant and lays it with finishing machines. Materials for cement-concrete pavements are fine and coarse aggregate, cement, and water. Bituminous pavements are made up of fine and coarse aggregate, mineral filler, and bitumen.

When machines are assembled into related groups for a certain task such as grading or

677

A TOPPING-OUT CEREMONY marks the completion of the steel framework of an Atlanta, Ga., office building.

paving, the lineup of equipment is called a "spread." There may be one or many spreads on a job, depending on its size.

**Heavy Construction Contractors.** Big earthmoving jobs are handled by heavy construction contractors in building foundations, dams, and tunnels. In hard-rock tunnels they drill, blast, and muck (dig and load). When tunneling through softer material, miners or sandhogs work behind a shield shaped to the tunnel section. They excavate, advance the shield, and line the tunnel behind it. Tunnel workers are serviced with various lines—high pressure air for drills, low pressure air for ventilation, and water and light.

Underwater tunnels may be bored beneath the bottom of the waterway as in land tunneling. In soft material tunnel crews work under air pressure to prevent cave-ins. The sunken-tube technique is also employed to create underwater tunnels. In this method tunnel sections are prefabricated, floated into position, and sunk into a previously dredged trench.

One group of contractors engages in dredging operations. They employ dipper dredges, clamshell dredges, and hydraulic pipeline cutterhead dredges to move large quantities of earth.

In building concrete dams, contractors mix and place huge quantities of concrete. They divert the waterway and construct temporary sheet-pile cofferdams filled with dirt to enclose the site. Delivered from a central batch-and-mix plant, concrete is placed by crane or cableway. Precautions are taken against cracking because of the great heat of hydration of cement in mass concrete. Aggregate is cooled, ice is used in the mixing water, and cooling water may be circulated in pipes embedded in the lift being placed. The dam is constructed in sections.

Bridge contractors are adapting themselves to

new materials and methods. The on-site spinning of wires to form cables for suspension bridges has met competition from the prefabricating of cables in a shop. The prefabricated cables are pulled into place on top of the bridge towers. Orthotropic decks—steel plates that serve as a bridge floor and as the upper flange of the main longitudinal girders—require new skills in positioning large steel sections of superstructure for welding together. Prestressed concrete members call for new techniques in mixing and casting concrete, and in tensioning the steel wires, rods, or cables.

**General Building Contractors.** Virtually every kind of commercial and industrial shelter is built by general building contractors. The skyscraper or high-rise building is probably the most spectacular.

One type of general builder is the broker-contractor. He does little if any work on a building but invites subcontractors to submit bids on all phases of the work. On the basis of these bids the contractor tenders his own general bid. He owns little equipment but has a permanent estimating crew. He manages the job with a few key men who supervise the subcontractors.

*Home builders* are numerous. Some limit their activities to one- or two-family houses; others erect high-rise apartments. They range from the entrepreneur who, with a few helpers, builds one house at time to the company that builds hundreds or even thousands of homes in large developments. The home builder may work under contract to the eventual owner, supervised by an architect. Or he may build on speculation, buying land and erecting houses to sell to prospective home owners. Low- and middle-priced homes are generally built and sold in this manner.

**Special Trade Contractors.** Although special trade contractors usually work as subcontractors to the general building contractor, they may contract directly with the owner. Once the foundation is completed, the various trades arrive in sequence to do their work. Ironworkers erect the framework for a steel building, followed by form builders for the concrete floors. Then the electricians, plumbers, and steam fitters move in before any concrete is placed so that they can install wiring conduits, pipes, and ducts. After the concrete floor slabs are laid, curtain walls are erected to enclose the building. Glaziers install windows; plasterers and tile setters finish the interior walls and partitions; painters, woodworkers, and other interior craftsmen apply the final touches.

Workers for these special trade contractors are craftsmen skilled with hand tools and machinery. Their subcontractor employer has a limited amount of equipment. He strives to line up successive jobs to keep his men steadily employed.

### LABOR FORCE AND SUPPLIERS

The number of employees engaged in contract construction varies with the seasons and reaches the peak in summer. In the United States about 1.1 million persons work for general building contractors. Heavy and highway construction account for more than 650,000 workers, and the special trades number more than 1.5 million.

**Construction Trades.** A skilled craftsman in the construction trades usually has a high school education and mechanical aptitude, and has advanced through an apprentice training program to achieve the status of a journeyman, a fully qualified worker. The training program normally takes from three to five years. Craftsmen such as bricklayers, carpenters, and cement masons use hand tools or small power tools. Ironworkers formerly used riveting hammers to connect steel members. This operation is now generally done with permanent high-strength bolts that are tightened by air-powered impact wrenches. Bolting is also quieter than riveting. Welding is now used in high-rise buildings, as it is lighter and saves material.

Men who operate the power-driven machinery such as tractors, cranes, shovels, pile drivers, concrete mixers, earthmoving equipment, and derricks are called *operating engineers*. Because of the demand for these equipment operators, there are now special training schools for them.

**Labor Relations.** Most construction workers in the United States belong to unions. These unions have been so successful in their wage demands that the construction industry regularly pays the highest wage rates among major industries. Operating engineers, carpenters, plumbers, bricklayers, electricians, and ironworkers earn high hourly rates, supplemented by overtime pay. Wage rates have climbed steadily, but worker productivity has not kept pace with the wage inflation.

The training of craftsmen from apprentice to journeyman may be sponsored by contractors, by labor unions, or by a combination of management and labor. Contracting companies that have a steady amount of work prefer to hire their own labor forces, train them, and retain them as permanent employees. However, when they are operating away from home or need additional help, contractors use the local union hiring hall—a labor-operated placement office. Unions would prefer that contractors used these hiring halls exclusively, so that unions could exert control over the men being hired and could distribute the jobs evenly. Some unions limit apprentices to sons and other relatives of union members.

**Suppliers.** One half of every construction dollar goes for materials. Building suppliers furnish the basic ingredients: steel, cement, bituminous materials, and lumber.

In purchasing the machinery he needs in his work, the contractor relies on the equipment distributor. The distributor advises on the most efficient machines for a particular job; arranges financing of the purchase; provides field service, skilled mechanics, and a ready supply of replacement parts; and has a maintenance shop available for equipment repair and overhaul. The distributor works closely with the contractor to avoid costly "downtime" (time in which a machine is inoperative during working hours).

Manufacturers of construction machinery spend considerable money on research and development. The trend has been to bigger, faster, and more powerful equipment. Although these improvements result in rapid obsolescence, the contractor needs the more efficient machines so that he can bid lower to win contracts.

## GENERAL CHARACTERISTICS

The gross business of the construction industry in the United States tends to keep rising, but the profit margins have been narrow and average about 2%. Contractor bankruptcies average about 2,500 a year. The business failures may be attributed to low unrealistic bidding, taking on too much work, mismanagement, and inability to finish on schedule, thereby incurring penalties.

MORRISON-KNUDSON COMPANY, INC.

HEAVY CONSTRUCTION can change the potential of the land itself. Work continues through the night on the Hell's Canyon Dam on the Snake River in Idaho.

A contractor must operate efficiently to stay in business.

**Subcontracting.** The subcontracting system enables a company doing a large volume of work to operate with a fairly small staff. The firm also gets along with a minimum investment in equipment and keeps its overhead low. The owner, however, holds the general contractor responsible for the completion of all work, including that of the subcontractors.

The general contractor has a file of subcontractors who give him bids on portions of the work. The work he retains for his own force varies. Usually the general contractor handles the concrete, masonry, and carpentry work, and "subs out"—that is, lets subcontracts to others— the excavation, the pile driving, and many other jobs done by skilled trades. To be sure that the general contractor retains control of the project, the owner may limit the extent of work done by "subs". But the trend is to subcontract more of the specialized operations.

The general contractor supervises the work of subcontractors so that they may operate on a planned schedule. Subcontractors build an organization of skilled labor and provide their men maximum employment by shifting them from job to job.

**Finance.** Few contractors have the working capital needed to finance a project to completion. So they must borrow from banks or other financial institutions. The construction industry depends more on borrowed funds than do most businesses. Because of the large size of units to be put together, such as a bridge, dam, or power plant, the contractor requires considerable financing.

Contracts take many forms, but all describe the work to be done and the amount to be paid for it. Generally all public work construction and much private work is awarded on the basis of competitive bidding, with the lowest bidder getting the job.

There are several types of contracts. *Lumpsum* or *fixed-price contracts* are employed when the quantities of materials and total cost may be accurately estimated in advance. *Unit-price contracts* are employed when the owner cannot es-

BELOW-GROUND construction, as for Montreal's subway system, involves massive excavation before building.

timate precisely the quantities on a large project involving many items. The owner will pay on the basis of unit-price measurements. *Combined lump-sum and unit-price contracts* are useful when part of the project can be clearly defined as to cost and quantities and the rest is made up of variables. *Cost-plus contracts* are awarded when the plans may be changed as the work progresses, when not enough time is available for site investigation or to estimate accurately, or when the work is so unusual that contractors may not care to get involved on the basis of the lump-sum or unit-price method of payment. This type of contract may be cost plus fixed fee, or cost plus a percentage. In private work, particularly in industrial and commercial construction, owners usually contract under the cost-plus system, and may hire the same contractor again and again.

Some owners will issue bid invitations only to construction companies they feel are qualified as *package builders* or *turnkey contractors*. Such firms handle a "package" so complete that when work is finished, the owner simply turns the key and enters to start production. Package builders and turnkey contractors usually do their own engineering as well as the contracting. They acquire the site, design and build the structure, and, in the case of a factory, purchase and install machinery and lay out assembly lines.

The contractor is usually paid on a monthly basis for work completed and for materials inventory on the job site, less 10% to 15% (which is held by the owner until the project is completed and accepted). Many contracts contain clauses penalizing the contractor in money for failing to complete his work on time.

**Planning.** Before he bids on a job, the contractor must decide what personnel and equipment he needs for the work; the methods to use; the logistics of supply for water, fuel, and electric light and power; and the means of transporting materials. A project manager organizes and directs construction activities. Under him a general superintendent supervises actual construction. Job superintendents take charge of specific phases of the work, and foremen supervise the skilled and common labor. Other key personnel include engineers, draftsmen, office manager, accountants,

estimators, purchasing agents, expediters, and master mechanic.

In addition to the bookkeeping associated with any business, a contractor needs a detailed cost-accounting system that relates money to production. The system enables accountants to determine which work items are being completed within the estimated cost figures and which are not. The contractor can then take steps to correct those items getting out of line, for when costs exceed the estimate, he is operating at a loss.

Some contractors avoid the competition of bidding by investing in real estate. They erect a building to rent or lease space but retain ownership. They call themselves *investment builders*. Many large office buildings, apartment houses, and hotels go up in this way.

On especially large projects, a single contracting company may not have the backing and resources to undertake the work by itself. It may then enter a joint venture with one or more other contractors to bid on the big job. In combining their resources for this particular project, contractors pool equipment, men, and money. All share in profits or losses.

**Innovations.** Each year contractors in the United States replace $5 billion in construction machinery. When a machine becomes obsolete, it is generally replaced with a larger and more powerful unit. Preferably the machine is light for greater portability. The contractor wants automatic controls to reduce operator fatigue and to improve machine performance. He is also interested in quality control to meet rigid specifications and tight tolerances.

**Fluctuations.** The construction industry is subject to financial fluctuations caused by cutbacks in government spending, a tight money market, a war economy, and other factors.

The prime variable in the industry, however, is the weather. Rains can halt earthmoving and paving operations, and winter causes slowdowns in northern climates. Technological advances, however, are making much building work feasible during cold weather as contractors use temporary enclosures and heating units to permit the building trades to operate. The increased cost of construction in adverse weather is offset by the advantage of earlier completion of the project.

WILLIAM H. QUIRK
*"Engineering and Construction World"*

**CONSTRUCTIVISM,** kən-strukʹti-viz-əm, was a Russian art movement of the early 20th century. Vladimir Tatlin (1875–1953), generally considered the founder of the movement, was influenced by the tenets of futurism and cubism. His abstract relief constructions (1913–1917) and the model for a *Monument to the Third International* (1919–1920) show his concern with the dynamic interaction of forms and space.

After 1920 the constructivist movement split: Tatlin and Alexander Rodchenko led their followers toward utilitarian art forms—industrial design, architecture, films, and posters. The other faction was led by Naum Gabo and Antoine Pevsner, who in 1920 wrote a "Realist Manifesto" attacking functionalist aims and championing pure art. Constructivist principles, reaching the Bauhaus through Gabo, Vassily Kandinsky, and László Moholy-Nagy, had a great influence on 20th century architecture and design.

**Further Reading:** Milner, John, *Vladimir Tatlin and the Russian Avant-Garde* (Yale Univ. Press 1983).

**CONSUBSTANTIATION,** kon-səb-stan-chə-ā-'shən, is a doctrine of the Lord's Supper, sometimes attributed, erroneously, to Lutheran theology. The official Roman Catholic theory, developed during the Middle Ages, described the mystery of the Mass as a change of the substance of bread and wine into the body and blood of Christ. According to this interpretation the elements ceased to be bread and wine when the words of the ordained priest were pronounced in the act of consecration, and the communicant received, not bread and wine, but the body of Christ. This was the doctrine of *transubstantiation*. Some thinkers, such as Duns Scotus and William of Occam, speculated that instead of a change in the sacrament the substance of bread and of wine remained and coexisted with the substance of the body of Christ. Hence the term *consubstantiation*.

Luther knew of these attempts to rationalize the mystery of the sacrament, but he was less interested in the philosophical "how" of that presence than in the religious fact that Christ said "This is my body, this is my blood" as he gave the disciples the broken bread and the chalice of wine. Against the Roman doctrine Luther insisted that bread remained bread, wine remained wine. Against those who would spiritualize the sacrament he asserted that the eucharist was more than a symbolic act or memorial meal. Those who received the bread and wine were assured of the objective reality of the presence of the Lord "in, with, and under" the earthly elements. The Lutheran doctrine avoids the concepts of "substance" and "change of substance" and concentrates on the personal union promised by Christ. Apart from that promise there are only bread and wine. But the word of the promise accepted in faith reveals to the recipient the living Christ who forgives sin, and offers constant fellowship.

Conrad Bergendoff
*President Emeritus, Augustana College*

**CONSUL,** kon'səl, one of the supreme magistrates in the Roman republic. When the monarchy was overthrown in Rome in 509 B. C., the royal authority passed to two supreme magistrates, first called *praetores* (leaders) and later called *consules*. Consuls were elected in the *comitia centuriata* (the assembly originally based on a military organization of the people and subsequently on property assessment), and their authority was confirmed by the *comitia curiata* (the assembly based on subdivisions of the three ancient tribes). Only twice in republican times were consuls not elected: during the decemvirate (451–450 B. C.) and during the late 5th and early 4th centuries B. C. when military tribunes with consular power were elected.

Less powerful than the kings, consuls did retain marks of royal authority, including the curule chair, *toga praetexta* (purple-bordered toga), and 12 lictors in attendance. The consuls had complete military and civil authority, making them both supreme generals and judges of the state. But their power was limited in several ways. The office was annual, and reelection was prohibited for 10 years. Although each consul had supreme authority, his colleague could veto his acts, and citizens were protected from the consul's jurisdiction within the city's walls by their right of appeal to the centuriate assembly in cases involving capital punishment. Other magistrates had to obey the consul, but the tribunes, whose office was created in 494 B. C., could veto a consul's acts. Also, in emergency situations, consuls might be replaced for six months by a dictator.

In practice the consuls alternated monthly in their civil duties and daily when in the field. Later, when Rome waged many simultaneous campaigns, each commanded his own force. Eventually the demand for officials became so great that, beginning in 326 B. C., their tenure was prolonged as proconsuls, and they were sent to provinces to wage war or to govern. In the Roman Empire, the consulship was an honored office without the authority it had possessed during the republic.

Richard E. Mitchell
*University of Illinois*

**CONSULAR SERVICE,** kon'sə-lər, a branch of a nation's foreign service that deals mainly with commercial functions. A consul is an agent appointed by the "sending state" to perform functions in a designated area of the "receiving state." He can function only if he receives written authorization, known as the *exequatur*, from the government to which he is accredited. An "honorary consul," who is usually a national of the receiving state engaged in business, is differentiated from a "career consul," who is a national of the sending state engaged in its full-time service. Either may enjoy the grade of consul general, consul, vice consul, or consular agent. The grade does not affect the consul's status or immunities under international law, but an honorary consul has fewer immunities than a career consul.

**Consular Privileges.** Consuls do not enjoy diplomatic immunities unless they are provided for by special treaties. Consular archives are immune from officials of the receiving state, as is the consular office if used only for consular purposes. Consuls have the right to designate the consular office by displaying the coat of arms of the sending state. They may not give asylum to persons wanted by the local authorities unless this right is provided for by special treaties. Career consuls are subject to arrest only for serious offenses and are exempt from military and other public service of the receiving state. Their property used for consular purposes is exempt from taxation, and they are exempt from taxes for income earned as a consul or for other services outside the receiving state.

**Functions.** Consular functions include the promotion of commerce and industry and the supervision of navigation. Consuls study commercial conditions in the consular district and make reports to the sending state. They are responsible for the protection of nationals of the sending state. They issue visas, authenticate documents, and perform other legal services in behalf of nationals or others with business in the sending state.

**History.** Officials similar to consuls have appeared in most ages of history. By the Middle Ages consuls were sent by trading cities or groups of merchants to maintain commercial interests abroad and often to exercise jurisdiction in disputes between their fellow citizens abroad.

Modern consular services developed in the 18th century under the iniative of France. The status of consuls, as distinct from diplomats, was recognized, and their functions and immunities often were defined by treaties. Since then, the consular services have tended to become more numerous and more professional and to be assimilated, for purposes of recruitment and promotion, with the foreign service, which also includes the career diplomatic service. The international law concerning consuls was codified in the Vienna Convention of 1963, based on a draft prepared by the United Nations International Law Commission.

There are over 20,000 consuls in the world. The United States, Britain, France, Italy, Spain, and Germany send over 1,000 consuls each and receive an even larger number. Japan, the Soviet Union, and India, on the other hand, send and receive fewer than 200 each.

QUINCY WRIGHT, *Professor Emeritus of International Law, University of Chicago*

**CONSULATE,** kon'sə-lət, the French regime established by Napoleon Bonaparte's coup d'etat of 18 Brumaire (November 9), 1799. The executive branch of the Consulate consisted of three consuls, with Bonaparte holding most of the power as first consul. The consuls worked under some control from the tribunate, legislative chamber, council of state, and senate. The success of the Consulate in solving many of France's internal problems, and in foreign affairs—negotiating peace treaties with Austria and England—paved the way for Bonaparte's proclamation as emperor in 1804.

RICHARD BRACE, *Oakland University, Mich.*

**CONSUMER CREDIT,** kən-soom'ər kred'it, is a lending practice by which a consumer obtains goods, services, or cash for immediate use in return for a promise to repay in the future. If the repayment is made in one lump sum this is called *noninstallment credit.* If the amount owed is repaid in periodic sums (weekly or monthly and usually in equal amounts), this is called *installment credit.* When a family head borrows cash from a small-loan company or a bank, it is a consumer credit transaction. The charge accounts that a family has are another kind of consumer credit. Credit for a home purchase may be regarded as consumer credit, but its character is so specialized that most authorities treat it separately.

Consumer credit is used for personal consumption. This distinguishes consumer credit from *business credit,* which is used for productive purposes.

Consumer credit is largely an American development. Its use can be traced mainly to urbanization, the rise of the working class, the increase of durable goods purchases, and the development of specialized lending institutions. Outside the United States consumer credit is far less important. It has grown mainly in highly developed countries such as England.

Total consumer credit outstanding in the United States increased from about $6 billion in 1945 to about $375 billion by 1979. Over 80% of consumer debt is of the installment type, nearly 30% of which is used to finance automobile purchases. Noninstallment credit makes up nearly 20% of total consumer credit. Single-payment loans, charge account credit, and service credit are virtually equal in importance in this category.

See BANKS AND BANKING—*Installment Lending;* INSTALLMENT BUYING.

DONALD FISCHER, *University of Connecticut*

**CONSUMER PRICE INDEX,** a technical device for comparing the cost of living in different time periods or in different geographical locations. Such information is useful to government agencies as a guide for public policy, to individuals who wish to compare the effective incomes they would receive from jobs at different locations, and to business firms (and labor unions) in which wages are geared to the index.

The U. S. Bureau of Labor Statistics issues its consumer price index monthly after collecting data from 50 cities to cover about 300 goods and services. Its national statistics include special group indexes such as "food" and "services."

The consumer price index shows the percentage by which weighted average retail prices at one time or place differ from those of another time or place. For this, the relative amounts of each good or service consumed must be taken into account. For example, a 10% rise in perfume prices would mean much less to people who spend $1/1,000$ of their income for perfume than would a 10% rise in food prices to people who spend one third of their income for food. The problem of the exact composition of the index is handled by weighting the various items according to their relative importance in the "consumers' market basket."

One difficulty is that the "consumers' market basket" seldom remains constant. For example, fuel is a large element of living costs in northern Wisconsin but is negligible in Florida. Education is a negligible element of living costs in Wisconsin because of the excellent public schools there, but education is an important element of living costs in certain areas where good schools are private rather than public. The same problem exists in making price comparisons in time: television did not exist 50 years ago, and buggies do not exist now. Tastes also have changed because of improved education and generally higher incomes. In short, the index is involved with composition differences as well as with price differences.

So long as the "consumers' market basket" remains fairly constant between the time periods or the locations compared, the error attributable to compositional differences is rather negligible. Where large "market basket" differences are involved, no solution is completely satisfactory. The usual compromise is to weight the commodities according to their average consumption in the places or times being compared.

WARREN J. BILKEY, *University of Wisconsin*

**CONSUMER PROTECTION** is safeguarding the buying public from dangerous or inferior goods and services and from fraudulent and other unfair selling practices. The movement toward increased consumer protection is known as *consumerism.*

**The Consumer in Preindustrial Economies.** Since early times, most societies have had some controls on the form and distribution of goods and services. For example, there were regulations to govern coinage and weights and measures, and restraints were imposed through the issuance of charters and licenses. Such controls were the responsibility of government, often in cooperation with businessmen, or of businessmen and professionals themselves, as in medieval guilds. However, in preindustrial economies, relationships between producer and consumer generally operated on the principle of *caveat emptor* (let the buyer beware), which assumes that the buyer knows what he wants, has the knowledge necessary to choose wisely, and has contact with the producer. It also presupposes that a wrong choice will cause little damage and that one person's choice will not harm another.

**The Consumer in Industrial Economies.** In industrial economies, however, the principle of *caveat emptor* breaks down. The buyer may be manipulated by skillful advertising, and generally he will not have the technical knowledge necessary to compare intelligently, say, various makes of highly complex automobiles or television sets. In other instances, the buyer may be offered only a limited range of choice within the price bracket that he can afford. Also, the buyer is so far removed from the producer that it is difficult to register complaints or trace the source of a fault. Furthermore, an error in manufacturing or marketing can affect millions of consumers and may be physically or financially harmful to some. Finally, in a densely populated urban society, one person's free choice—for example, the unwitting purchase of a defective and potentially dangerous automobile—may cause another's misery.

Industrialized societies have made periodic efforts to solve consumers' problems. As industrialism gathered momentum in the late 19th century, a few governments began to set standards for food and to regulate trusts, and individuals formed cooperatives for mutual protection. In the early 20th century, criticism by the muckrakers—such as the American authors Upton Sinclair and Ida Tarbell, who wrote exposés of the meat-packing and the petroleum industries—encouraged government reforms. The Great Depression of the 1930's resulted in certain protective legislation of the New Deal. After World War II, the rapid growth of industry intensified consumer problems and led to a worldwide consumer movement.

**Areas of Consumer Concern—*Quality and Safety.*** The quality and safety of products are the most obvious consumer concerns. There have been outcries over impure food, such as mercury-tainted fish; unsanitary or faulty packaging, as of soup contaminated by the botulism toxin; and insufficiently tested drugs, such as fetus-deforming thalidomide. Consumers have also complained of food contamination by pesticides, poisonous lead paint on toys, and dangerous or faulty mechanisms in toys, automobiles, and other products.

**Labeling and Pricing.** The great increase in processed and synthetic foods and fibers has made accurate labeling of contents essential. Consumers should be told, for example, if frankfurters contain cereal, if a dessert topping is a nondairy product, or if a coat is imitation or real fur. Food packaging also creates problems when manufacturers use nonstandard sizes in order to maintain competitive prices, thus presenting consumers with difficulty in cost-comparison buying. Fair pricing of essential goods and services, such as electricity and public transportation, which are generally noncompetitive, is also a matter of consumer concern.

**Selling and Credit.** Consumers often complain about fast-talking door-to-door salesmen, who fail to clarify the terms of sale. They also object that the additional cost of buying on credit is not clearly explained or is hidden in contractual agreements. Many consumers are dismayed that personal credit information is recorded without their being able to check or correct it.

Ralph Nader became a leader of consumerism after publishing *Unsafe at Any Speed* (1965), on auto defects.

**Advertising.** Consumers also complain of fraudulent or misleading advertising—for example, a patent medicine that promises miraculous cures or a brand of gasoline that claims to provide more power than another brand with the same octane rating. They object to "bait" advertising that offers a good buy when the merchant has only more costly items to sell or that announces prices "vastly reduced" from those that were too high to begin with.

**Government Protection in the United States—*Federal Measures.*** In the area of quality and safety, the Food and Drug Administration (FDA) sets standards for foods, drugs, and cosmetics; forbids distribution of adulterated products; and requires honest labeling. The Department of Agriculture (USDA) is required to inspect meat and poultry in interstate commerce. It also grades farm commodities, with voluntary compliance. The General Services Administration (GSA) sets standards of government purchases, which indirectly benefit the private consumer. Safety standards are established by such agencies as the National Highway Traffic Safety Administration, the Product Safety Commission, and the Federal Aviation Administration.

In the area of labeling and pricing, the Federal Trade Commission (FTC) requires that food, drug, and cosmetics packaging indicate contents, size, and weight and that clothing labels state fabric content. It also prohibits monopolistic practices, such as price-fixing. Prices of essential goods and services are regulated by the Interstate Commerce Commission, the Civil Aeronautics Board, and the Federal Power Commission. The Antitrust Division of the Department of Justice enforces regulations of various protective agencies.

In the area of selling and credit, the Securities and Exchange Commission oversees trading in stocks and bonds, and the FTC requires that contracts signed with door-to-door salesmen may be canceled by the buyer within three business days. The National Credit Union Administration charters, supervises, and insures credit unions. The Consumer Credit Protection Act (1968) requires that every credit transaction reveal the annual rate of interest, and the Credit Reporting

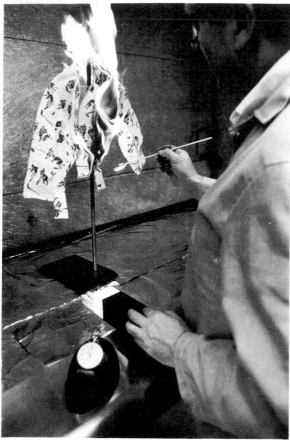

Product safety is among the major consumer concerns. Here, a child's garment is tested for flammability.

Consumers' Research (founded in 1928) in *Consumer Bulletin Annual* and Consumers Union (1936) in *Consumer Reports*. In addition, there are various commercial concerns that publish consumer guides. Local, state, and national consumer groups are represented by the Consumer Federation of America (1967).

One of the most active forces in the American consumer movement is Ralph Nader, a lawyer who has investigated such areas as the automobile industry, intrastate meat-packing, natural-gas pipelines, and nursing homes. He has established several privately funded organizations, staffed by groups popularly known as Nader's Raiders, which check on government protection agencies. Nader and others have formed public-interest law firms, which bring suits and prod sluggish government agencies.

Businessmen themselves have taken affirmative steps, such as warranties and guarantees, to protect consumers from faulty merchandise. They have also formed groups to regulate their industries, including the National Association of Manufacturers, Chamber of Commerce, Council of Better Business Bureaus, and American National Standards Institute. However, the regulations of such groups are suggestive, not obligatory.

**Protection Outside the United States.** Many governments have created protective agencies, such as the British Independent Television Authority, the Swedish Quality Labeling Board, and the consumer affairs ministries of Norway and Canada. In many countries, laws have been enacted to regulate food and drug and door-to-door sales. There are also national-standards institutions, governmental and private.

Many countries have national and local consumer associations concerned with product testing and often with standards, labeling, and complaints. Some are governmental, as in West Germany, Scandinavia, France, and the Soviet Union. Others are private, as in Britain and the Netherlands. In Japan, housewives' groups are active in testing and bringing pressure to bear through boycotts. Private cooperatives, organized to prevent short weight, adulteration, and other abuses, have spread from Britain, Germany, and Scandinavia to developing countries.

On the international level the Committee of Contact makes Euro-tests on Common Market products and represents its consumers. The nonpolitical International Organization of Consumers Unions serves as a clearinghouse for members' problems.

**Continuing Problems.** The growth of consumerism has often been countered by business interests, which object that too much regulation restricts trade and that consumers expect too much. In addition, there are weaknesses within the movement itself. Consumers are considerably less well organized than producers. The responsibilities of many government consumer agencies overlap, and the agencies sometimes fail to enforce regulations or may be influenced by the very industries they are supposed to regulate. Furthermore, with the proliferation of goods and services, it has seemed that for each abuse corrected, new ones spring up.

Act (1971) gives individuals access to credit information about themselves that is made available to others.

Advertising is supervised by the FTC, which, since 1972, has required manufacturers to substantiate advertising claims and correct erroneous or misleading statements. The Federal Communications Commission supervises advertising on television and radio, and the Postal Service protects consumers from such dangers as fraud and hazardous materials.

Consumer information is provided by the USDA Extension Service, the GSA Consumer Information Center, and the Food and Drug Administration Consumer Affairs Offices of the Department of Health and Human Services. The Office of Consumer Affairs, established under the president in 1971, coordinates federal protection agencies.

**State and Local Measures.** Many states, beginning with New York in 1956, have set up offices of consumer affairs to expedite complaints and educate consumers. In addition, some states have enacted laws that require labels to show unit prices. A number of cities also have departments of consumer affairs. Public schools offer courses in consumer education through home economics and adult-education programs.

**Nongovernment Protection.** Private, nonprofit testing organizations examine products and publish the results in monthly magazines—notably

**Further Reading:** Asch, Peter, *Consumer Safety Regulation* (Oxford 1988); Charell, Ralph, *Satisfaction Guaranteed* (Simon & Schuster 1985); Hardine, Roseta R., *Consumer and Patient Satisfaction* (ABBE Pub. Assn. 1988); Pertschuk, Michael, *Revolt Against Regulation: The Rise and Pause of the Consumer Movement* (Univ. of Calif. Press 1982).

**CONSUMPTION,** in economics, is the end utilization, or final use, of goods and services. *Individual,* or *private, consumption* is direct, as in eating food, wearing clothes, or living in a house. *Social consumption* is indirect, as when governments or nonprofit groups make expenditures for weapons, roads, or schools. Business expenditures for equipment and raw materials are not consumption. They are part of the productive process, because they lead to the creation of other goods and services that in turn are consumed.

Social consumption usually is determined by group consensus (via the ballot) or by administrative decree. Such decisions are based largely on political considerations. Individual consumption usually is determined by consumer purchasing acts. In a democracy, social consumption is made, in theory at least, on the basis of "one person, one vote," while individual consumption tends to be made on the basis of "one dollar, one vote."

Liberals usually prefer that a maximum of consumption be social so that low-income people will receive a greater portion of the economic output. Conservatives tend to prefer that a maximum of consumption be private because they dislike the income redistribution that results from social consumption.

Individual consumption may be analyzed by *percent of personal incomes spent,* by *allocation of expenditures,* or by *brand choice.*

**Percent of Personal Incomes Spent.** Studies show that in the aggregate the percentage of total income spent tends to be large where there is a nearly equal income distribution and small where there is a very unequal income distribution (because rich people usually spend a smaller fraction of their incomes than do the poor). Other considerations leading to the spending of a high percent of income are favorable income expectations, expectations of moderately rising or stable price, large families, a high percentage of the population receiving incomes from wages and salaries, and a relatively comprehensive social security system. Experience in the United States has shown that between particular years the percentage of aggregate personal income spent varies considerably, but decade averages have remained remarkably constant for over 70 years.

**Allocation of Expenditures.** Individuals change their allocation of expenditures among broad generic categories, such as food, clothing, and housing, as prices and their incomes change. For example, when interest rates rise and make credit more expensive, the percent of expenditures going to houses and automobiles tends to decline. Expenditure allocations also change with price and income expectations, amount of liquid assets, relative technological developments (better products), relative advertising (more effective appeals), and sequence of disbursements (spending priorities).

**Brand Choices.** Theoretically, consumers select brands by shopping around and comparing alternatives. In practice some shop little. For example, an interview study of 184 families in Madison, Wis., that bought living room furniture showed that 22% visited only one dealer. The extent of shopping tends to be greater for expensive items than for cheaper items. It tends to be greatest among those who have higher education, are younger, have prestige occupations, and have not had a favorable prior experience with a particular brand.

WARREN J. BILKEY, *University of Wisconsin*

**CONSUMPTION.** See TUBERCULOSIS.

**CONSUS,** kon'səs, in Roman mythology, was an earth god, especially identified as the keeper of stored agricultural crops. His altar, which is said to have been discovered under earth by Romulus, was in the Circus Maximus. It remained covered throughout the year, except at the time of the Consualia, festivals in his honor. One of these was held on August 21 in celebration of the harvest; another, on December 15, was in honor of autumn sowing.

Consus, who was often identified with Neptune (Greek, Poseidon), was also associated with horses. On his festival days there were horse races and chariot races, and working horses and other domestic animals were decorated with flowers and not required to work.

**CONTACT LENS,** a small optical device that fits between the eye and the eyelids and can be worn instead of glasses. Under some circumstances, contact lenses provide better correction of defective vision than glasses. This is especially true in certain abnormalities and diseases of the eye, as when the cornea is scarred or very irregular. Contact lenses are also valuable for people who have had cataracts removed. When such people wear glasses, their vision is distorted except at the very center of the lens, but when they wear contacts this problem does not exist. Contact lenses are also particularly useful when a high degree of correction is needed for either farsightedness, nearsightedness, or astigmatism.

**Types.** There are two basic types of contact lenses: the *scleral lens,* which fits over the sclera (white) of the eye, and the *corneal lens,* which covers only the cornea. The scleral lens was first conceived by Leonardo da Vinci in 1508, but it was not until 1887 that the first lens was made. At that time, a German glassblower fashioned a lens for a person with a diseased eyelid to keep the eyelid from touching his eye. The first lenses to correct vision were made the following year. These early lenses were made of glass, and the fitting procedure was very crude. One lens after another was put on the eye until one was found that seemed to fit. Few people could wear these lenses for more than an hour or so.

The first clear plastic scleral lens was made in the United States in 1938 by T. Obrig and F. Muller. This lens was made by pressing a hot sheet of softened plastic over a stone replica of the eye. The major difficulty with this lens was that the person's tears could not circulate beneath it and the lens had to be filled with an artificial tear solution before it could be inserted. Because the cornea cells obtain their oxygen from the tears as well as from the air, and since the oxygen supply in the artificial tear solution was rapidly used up, these lenses had to be removed frequently so that the solution could be changed.

Corneal contact lenses were introduced in 1948 by the American optician Kevin Tuohy. These lenses did not need special solutions or fluids because they were designed to float on top of the thin layer of tears normally covering the eye. Since their inception, corneal contact lenses have been made smaller and thinner, and if fitted properly, they can be worn all day, every day, without discomfort.

CONTACT LENSES: scleral (left) and corneal (right).

Although corneal contact lenses are more widely used than scleral lenses, scleral lenses are being used more and more for therapeutic reasons. Since the 1950's, scleral lenses have been used for patients with chemical burns of the eye, to keep the eyelid from touching the eye. They are also used for people with certain paralytic conditions of the eye and various other disorders.

**Fitting Lenses.** As compared to the crude trial-and-error method used for fitting the early glass lenses, the design and fitting of contact lenses are now very precise. Before a person is fitted with contacts, the contour of each cornea is mapped with optical scanning devices that determine the exact topography of the corneal surface. After the lens is placed on the eye, it is studied with a corneal microscope so that minute modifications can be made if necessary.

LOUIS J. GIRARD, M. D. and JOSEPH SOPER
*Baylor University College of Medicine*

**CONTAGION.** See DISEASE—*Infectious and Contagious Diseases.*

**CONTARINI,** kōn-tä-rē'nē, the name of a prominent noble Venetian family. The Contarini were among the 12 families that elected the first doge in 697, and they subsequently gave the Venetian republic eight doges and many eminent merchants, statesmen, and scholars. Several Contarini palaces remain in Venice as elegant testimony to the family's prominence.

The first Contarini doge was Domenico, under whose rule (1043–1070) Venice subjugated rebellious Dalmatia and began the rebuilding of San Marco. The republic won a decisive victory over its rival, Genoa, under Andrea Contarini (reigned 1368–1382), who patriotically offered his fortune to the state. In the 17th century five Contarini doges occupied the Palazzo Ducale.

Among the other noted representatives of the Contarini, the greatest was Cardinal Gasparo (1483–1542), a humanist, political writer, and theologian, who sought to reconcile Catholics and Protestants at Ratisbon (Regensburg) in 1541. The range of the family's achievements is suggested by the great traveler Ambrogio (died 1499), the painter Giovanni (died 1603), and Marco (died 1689), a celebrated patron of music whose collection of musical manuscripts is now in the Biblioteca Marciana in Venice.

RANDOLPH STARN
*University of California at Berkeley*

**CONTEMPORARY STYLE,** in interior decoration, the style developed in the 20th century to serve the purposes of functionalism, as opposed to traditional style. See FURNITURE, MODERN; INTERIOR DECORATION—*1. Residential Interior Decoration.*

**CONTEMPT OF COURT** is willfully embarrassing or obstructing the court in its administration of justice. Historically, contempt was any act done in violation of a direct order of the king or any direct insult to the king or his government. The purpose of the law of contempt of court is to vindicate the court's authority and dignity by punishing intentional acts in defiance of that authority and to secure compliance with the orders of the court. The first federal statute in the United States regarding contempt of court was passed in 1789.

*Direct contempts* are those committed in the presence of the court, such as insulting language or acts of violence. *Indirect contempts* arise outside the court but usually tend to obstruct the administration of justice through failure to obey a decree of the court to perform or refrain from performing an act. An example of indirect contempt is the refusal of a union leader to obey an injunction against striking.

Contempts (both direct and indirect) are classified as *civil* or *criminal.* Either may be punished by imprisonment. The difference lies in the character and purpose of imprisonment. Civil punishment is designed to compel specific conduct and usually involves imprisonment for an unlimited term, with release conditioned upon compliance with the court order. On the other hand, criminal contempt is aimed at punishing contemptuous acts and deterring others from similarly defying the court. Thus the defendant will be imprisoned for a limited period or will be fined, but the punishment imposed will not be affected by his future conduct.

Another form of contempt, *contempt of Congress,* involves the obstruction of the due course of congressional proceedings. It usually concerns a witness' failure to attend a congressional inquiry or to answer pertinent questions at such an inquiry.

PETER D. WEINSTEIN
*Member of the New York Bar*

**CONTES D'HOFFMANN.** See TALES OF HOFFMANN.

**CONTI,** kôn-tē', is the name of an important cadet branch of the French Bourbon House. The fief of Conti devolved to the Bourbon family when Eleonore de Roye brought it as a dowry for her marriage to the Bourbon Prince Louis I de Condé (1530–1569), the uncle of King Henry IV. Their second son, François, was the first prince of the line to carry the title Conti. He had an undistinguished career in the French wars of religion, and when he died without issue, the fief reverted to the Condé line.

The Conti title was later given to Armand (1629–1666), the second son of Henri II de Condé and Charlotte de Montmorency. Armand played a part in the Fronde rebellion, and was imprisoned with his brother, Louis II de Condé (the Great Condé). Unlike his brother, however, he made peace with the court. He married the niece of Cardinal Mazarin, the prime minister of France, as a token of his good faith. Armand's

### THE CONTI LINE

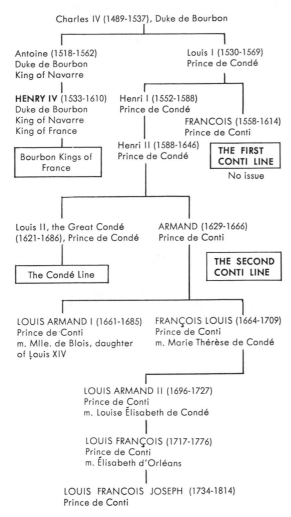

Charles IV (1489-1537), Duke de Bourbon

Antoine (1518-1562)
Duke de Bourbon
King of Navarre

Louis I (1530-1569)
Prince de Condé

HENRY IV (1533-1610)
Duke de Bourbon
King of Navarre
King of France

Henri I (1552-1588)
Prince de Condé

FRANÇOIS (1558-1614)
Prince de Conti

Bourbon Kings of
France

Henri II (1588-1646)
Prince de Condé

THE FIRST
CONTI LINE

No issue

Louis II, the Great Condé
(1621-1686), Prince de Condé

ARMAND (1629-1666)
Prince de Conti

The Condé Line

THE SECOND
CONTI LINE

LOUIS ARMAND I (1661-1685)
Prince de Conti
m. Mlle. de Blois, daughter
of Louis XIV

FRANÇOIS LOUIS (1664-1709)
Prince de Conti
m. Marie Thérèse de Condé

LOUIS ARMAND II (1696-1727)
Prince de Conti
m. Louise Élisabeth de Condé

LOUIS FRANÇOIS (1717-1776)
Prince de Conti
m. Élisabeth d'Orléans

LOUIS FRANCOIS JOSEPH (1734-1814)
Prince de Conti

subsequent career was bizarre: he became an eccentric religious mystic, abandoned his wife, and died unmourned.

Armand had two sons, Louis Armand I and François Louis. Louis Armand served with the French army in Flanders in 1683. In 1684 Louis Armand and his brother left France to join the Emperor's army in Hungary, in spite of the king's orders. But the two Conti princes were forgiven upon their reurn to France. Louis Armand married one of Louis XIV's illegitimate daughters, but died almost immediately, leaving no direct heir. His brother François Louis, who inherited the Conti title, was noted primarily for his failure to win the crown of Poland when he contested it with Augustus of Saxony.

Louis Armand II, the son of François Louis, played a minor role in the Regency government for Louis XV, and he too was an unsuccessful candidate for the throne of Poland. The last in the line, Prince Louis François Joseph, fought in the Seven Years' War (1756–1763), took the Civil Oath of the French Revolutionary government in 1790, was imprisoned in 1792, and was banished from France by the Directory in 1795.

JOHN B. WOLF
*University of Illinois at Chicago Circle*

**CONTI,** kon'tē, **Niccolò de'** (c. 1395–1469), Venetian merchant, who traveled widely in Asia. In about 1414, following a long tradition of Venetian merchant-adventurers, he left Venice to trade in the East. From Damascus he set out on a remarkable journey throughout southern Asia that lasted 25 years. He traveled extensively in Persia and India, and wandered as far north as Ava (the ancient capital of Burma) and as far east as Java. He returned to India through Indochina and eventually found his way home by way of Cochin, Calicut (Kozhikode), the island of Socotra, Aden, Mecca, and Cairo.

During his journey he was forced to renounce Christianity. Consequently, after his return to Venice in 1439, he was ordered by Pope Eugene IV to recount his story to Poggio Bracciolini, the renowned humanist and papal secretary, as a penance. Conti's narrative and observations were incorporated into Book 4 of Poggio's *De varietate fortunae* (1447). The observations of this seasoned traveler on geography, society, religion, and customs provide an interesting human geography of 15th century Asia. The scope of Conti's travels in southern Asia and the quality of his account of the area were unmatched by those of any other European traveler of the 15th century.

RANDOLPH STARN
*University of California at Berkeley*

**CONTIGUOUS ZONE,** kən-tig'ū-əs, in international law, an area of the high seas adjacent to the territorial waters of a coastal state, in which it claims the right to exercise jurisdiction over foreign merchant ships in order to enforce its customs, fiscal, sanitary, or other regulations. A coastal state may claim only limited authority in a contiguous zone while it exercises the right of sovereignty in its "territorial sea." For example, a state may claim the right to regulate fishing activities for the purpose of conservation in a contiguous zone, but it cannot reserve fishing rights there for its nationals to the exclusion of foreign fishermen.

Although the term "contiguous zone" is of recent origin, the practice it denotes goes back at least to the 18th century. In 1736, Britain, the staunchest adherent to the 3-mile (5-km) principle of territorial limit, claimed the right to demand the forfeiture of prohibited cargoes on board a ship hovering within 6 miles (10 km) of its coast. In 1763 the ship itself was made the object of forfeiture, and in 1876 the distance was established at 9 miles (14 km).

Since 1799 the United States has claimed the right to board, examine, search, and punish every ship within 12 miles (19 km) of its coast, which is bound to any port or place in the country. The Soviet Union has not claimed a contiguous zone, but it appropriates 12 miles (19 km) of the high seas as territorial water over which it exerts complete control.

Article 24 of the Convention on the Territorial Sea and the Contiguous Zone, adopted by the UN Conference on the Law of the Sea at Geneva in 1958, authorizes a coastal state to claim contiguous zones for enforcing customs, fiscal, immigration, or sanitary regulations. It limits the zone to a maximum distance of 12 miles measured from the baseline of the territorial sea of the coastline state.

TAO CHENG
*Pennsylvania State University*

**CONTINENT**, traditionally, a landmass larger than an island. A continent is one of the earth's two major geographical elements and one of its most fundamental geological components; the other is the ocean. About 71% of the earth's surface is covered with water, and the remaining 29% is land area. Almost all (96%) of the land area is included in the set of traditionally named continents. In order of decreasing size, the earth's continents include Eurasia (often considered from a historical point of view as two separate continents, Europe and Asia), Africa, North America, South America, Antarctica, and Australia. If Europe is considered a separate continent it would be second smallest, between Antarctica and Australia in size. The next smallest landmass, Greenland, is customarily defined as an island, although its geology is continental, as are other large islands such as New Zealand, Japan, Borneo, and Madagascar.

Continents have both an important geographical significance and a profound geological significance. The evolution of life in general and of humankind in particular was greatly affected by the distribution of land and water, both directly as it bounded and isolated populations and indirectly through the effects of land and water on climate. Our habitation and our most accessible resources of food, minerals, and energy are located on continents, and so their nature is of great practical as well as scientific importance.

**Global Topography.** From a geographic point of view the boundary of a continent is the shoreline separating water from land. This is the obvious boundary in terms of the evolution of life and human history. But continents have a more fundamental geological significance in which sea level (or the shoreline) is not the best continental perimeter, and the traditionally named "continents" do not include all the continental material on earth.

The significance of continents is revealed by study of the topography of the surface of the solid earth (the land area and the ocean floor). Although the difference in height from the tallest mountain (Everest, elevation 5.5 miles, or 8.8 km) to the deepest oceanic trench (Marianas Trench, depths between 6.8 and 7.5 miles, or 11 and 12 km) is about 12 miles (20 km), one of the earth's outstanding characteristics as a planetary body is that most of the surface area is actually confined to only two narrow ranges of elevation. About 26% of the earth's total surface area has elevations between 0.1 mile (0.2 km) below and 0.6 mile (1 km) above sea level, while another 52% is at depths below sea level of between 2 and 4 miles (3 and 6 km). These two areas account for 78% of the earth's surface area and comprise the continental platforms and vast ocean basins, respectively.

The land above sea level is but a part of the larger continental platform that also includes (1) submerged "continental shelves," which are the shallow (depths to 0.1 mile, or 0.2 km), flat areas fringing much of the continental peripheries, and (2) other areas of submerged continent such as the shallow seas linking the islands of Indonesia and Borneo with Southeast Asia, or the islands of Great Britain and Ireland with the continent of Europe. Thus the natural physiographic division between continents and oceans does not occur at sea level but can be associated with the "continental slope" located between depths of the shelf edge (0.1 mile, or 0.2 km) and the

depths of the ocean basins, 2 to 4 miles (3 to 6 km). Depending upon how the "edge" of a continent is defined (the boundary between continental and oceanic structure is not sharp but gradational), up to 41% of the earth's surface is estimated to be continental in comparison to the 25% that is above sea level.

Two critical factors control the division of the earth's outer surface into continental platforms and ocean basins. One has to do with the role of water in eroding the land above sea level and carrying the material to the ocean basins as sediment. This pervasive phenomenon tends to reduce the elevation of the continents toward sea level, and is probably the explanation for the low elevations of the continental platforms. The second factor is the division of the less dense and chemically distinct outer crust of the earth into two basic types, oceanic and continental. The existence of two types of crusts can only be understood in the context of the earth's peculiar dynamics, perhaps unique in our solar system.

**Plate Tectonics.** If the earth were a cooler planet like Mars or Mercury, the strong outer shell (strong because it is cooler than the interior) would remain coherent and stable, punctured only here and there by volcanic emanations from the interior. But the earth's cool outer shell is not thick enough to remain globally coherent; instead, it breaks up into a set of large rigid fragments called "plates," which actually are pieces of the earth's outer spherical shell. Plates can be completely oceanic (for example, Nazca), but most include both oceanic and continental areas (South America). See Fig. 1.

The plates move about as the surface manifestation of the convective motions within the earth's interior. Although solid on the scale of human time, the material beneath the strong outer shell behaves like a viscous liquid over time scales longer than about 10,000 years. The viscous material is continually in motion in a convection system that removes heat from the interior, with hotter material moving upward in some places and cooler material moving downward in others. The motion of one plate relative to another across a common boundary varies from 1 to 8 inches (2.5 to 20 cm) per year. The outer shell is cooler than the interior and maintains its rigidity even on geological time scales of 10 million to 100 million years. The study of the relative motions of the plates and the geological phenomena that take place along their common boundaries is called plate tectonics.

There are three primary types of plate boundaries or margins: divergent, convergent, and transform faults. Where the relative motions of the plates are away from each other, the boundaries are called divergent. Where the relative motions of the plates are toward each other, the boundaries are called convergent. And where the plates move sideways with respect to one another, the boundaries are called transform faults, such as California's San Andreas Fault.

The plates move horizontally away from sites of upwelling of material from the earth's interior and toward sites of downwelling of material into the interior. The upwelling reaches the surface along the globe-encircling submarine mountain system. This system can be traced continuously through all the major oceans, and includes, for example, the Mid-Atlantic Ridge and the East Pacific Rise (see Fig. 1). The upwelling material from the interior spreads out away from the

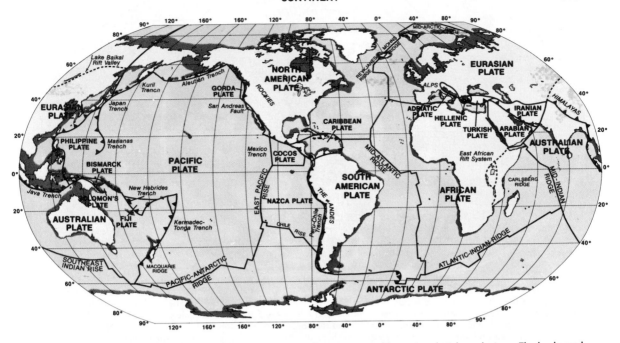

Fig. 1. The major and minor plates of the present-day earth are separated by major plate boundaries. The hachurred lines show convergent boundaries (plates move toward each other), while the "rises" and "ridges" show divergent boundaries (plates move away from each other). "Transform faults" are the third type of primary plate boundary (plates move sideways to each other). The lines with triangles indicate subduction zones where a plate bends downward beneath the other plate and descends into the earth's interior. Each of the continents is embedded in a larger plate that is named for the continent. The shaded areas surrounding the continents represent the continental shelves.

ridges or rises and cools. The two plates move away from the locus of upwelling and away from one another. Oceanic plates are created, and their relative motion is divergent.

Along another globe-encircling system of plate boundaries the relative motions of the plates are toward one another, or convergent. Where at least one of the two plates is oceanic, the convergent motions are accommodated by creating an oceanic trench as the oceanic plate bends downward beneath the other plate and descends into the earth's interior (see Fig. 1). This process is called subduction. The return of the material to the interior compensates for the rise of material from the interior.

Plate thicknesses vary from about zero near the ocean ridges where the upwelling occurs to about 80 miles (130 km) beneath the deepest ocean basins. The plate thickness increases with the "age" of the oceanic plate (the time since the plate was first formed along the oceanic ridge). Thus the lithosphere (solid portion of the earth) beneath the deepest basins is oldest (about 200 million years; all older plates have returned to the interior). The thickness of the continental plates is less well known, but may reach values up to 90 to 200 miles (150 to 300 km).

**Oceanic and Continental Crust.** The bulk of the earth's interior (82% by volume) comprises the "mantle," a region consisting predominantly of magnesium, silicon, oxygen, and iron in forms of silicate and oxide minerals. The mantle encloses the liquid iron "core" of the earth.

Melting of the mantle occurs within its outer 60 miles (100 km). But the melting is partial: only the material with the lowest melting-point temperature becomes liquid. This material percolates upward because it is lighter and more buoyant than the surrounding solid material. Thus a chemical differentiation occurs as the melt (or "magma") moves from the interior upward as volcanic lavas or as intrusions into the surrounding rock. In both cases the melt cools, solidifies, and becomes part of the crust. Along the ocean ridge system of plate divergence, this partial melting of the upwelling mantle forms a crust by volcanism and intrusion that has a remarkably constant thickness of about 3 to 4 miles (5 to 6 km) over nearly the entire area of the ocean basins and ridges. This oceanic crust is chemically distinct from the interior: it is relatively depleted in magnesium and iron and enriched in silicon, aluminum, calcium, sodium, and potassium. It is less dense than the interior material, about 2.8 gm/cc compared to the 3.3 gm/cc for the material just below the crust.

The crust is not to be confused with the plate in which it moves. The crust is a chemically distinct layer within the generally thicker plate, while the plate is a relatively cool and mechanically rigid unit that moves over the hotter, more fluidlike interior of the mantle.

The crust of continents reflects a different and more complex process compared with the formation of oceanic crust. While the oceanic crust is created by a single set of processes acting along the worldwide system of oceanic ridges, the continents are formed and considerably modified over long periods of time by a succession of different processes. By analogy with a pot of boiling soup, the oceanic divergent and convergent zones can be compared with the rising and descending movements of the convecting soup, while the continents can be compared with the froth or scum that accumulates on the surface of the soup.

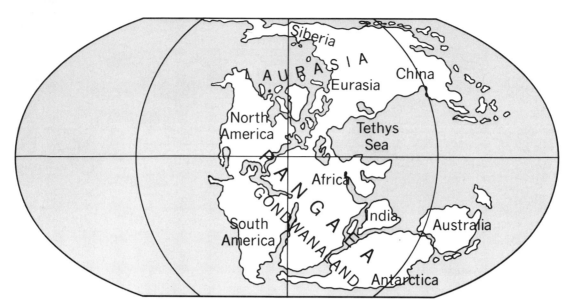

Fig. 2. A reconstruction of the positions of the major continents about 220 million years before the present (early Triassic Period). The Atlantic and Indian oceans are closed, and the Tethys Sea lies between Gondwanaland and the Asian part of Laurasia. During the Cretaceous Period and Oligocene Epoch, the oceanic plate beneath the Tethys Sea largely disappeared back into the earth's interior, and this large body of water no longer exists. In its place are the Mediterranean Sea and various mountain ranges, such as the Alpines of Europe and the Himalayas.

Continental crust ranges in thickness from about 20 to 30 miles (30 to 45 km) except beneath elevated terrains, such as mountain belts or continental plateaus, where thicknesses as great as 40 miles (70 km) have been determined.

The continental crust has a density that on average is not much different than the average density of the oceanic crust, but the rocks exposed at the surface of continents are clearly less dense and chemically different than the oceanic crustal material. The "upper crust" of the continents is enriched in oxides of silicon, potassium, and sodium (feldspar and quartz minerals are particularly abundant) relative to the oceanic crust and depleted in magnesium, calcium, and iron.

The upper part of the continental crust thus represents a further refinement and differentiation of the type of material found in the oceanic crust. This occurs in at least two ways. One is by further partial melting and fractional crystallization of oceanic crust. The other is by erosion and sedimentation, in which some of the material goes into solution in seawater, while the remaining less soluble material, such as quartz ($SiO_2$), forms sedimentary rocks that cover much of the surface of continents. Sedimentary rocks can also be reprocessed by heating and melting when they are thrust beneath other material in mountain belts where the crustal material is pervasively deformed and heated.

The lighter crust "floats" within the denser mantle. The buoyancy of the lighter (lower density) crust causes the crust to rise higher if its thickness (volume) increases. Continental crust is systematically lighter and thicker than oceanic crust and thus floats higher.

The buoyant effect, similar to that of an iceberg floating in water, is a form of "isostasy," or condition of balance. An iceberg floats because it is less dense than water. If the volume of the iceberg increases, it will float higher above the water surface as well as lower below the water surface. Thus a balance is achieved. Likewise, mountain belts, which are composed of large volumes of low-density rock, increase in volume above and below the land surface. The large volume of low-density rock below the land surface, called the root, floats within the denser mantle. Thus continental crust is thicker below mountain belts than below such surface structures as continental plains.

**Age of Continental Crust.** In the oceans the removal of oceanic plate and crust from the surface at the convergent zones keeps pace with the creation of oceanic plates along the divergent margins, so that the oldest oceanic crust still on the surface today is only about 200 million years old. This is a small fraction of the almost 4 billion years of earth history recorded in the continental rocks. The oldest rocks yet discovered on continents are 3.8 billion years old as determined by a study of isotopes produced by the radioactive elements. The continental rocks cover all but the first 800 million years of the earth's 4.6-billion-year history since the planet solidified out of the primitive solar nebula. The continents are thus the primary "history book" for our planet.

The record reveals three great divisions, called geologic "eons": the Archean, older than 2.5 billion years; the Proterozoic, from 2.5 billion to 600 million years; and the Phanerozoic, the past 600 million years. These divisions are based on the structures and compositions of the crystalline rocks and on the evolution of life as recorded in sedimentary rocks. Archean and Proterozoic rocks typically are found in the interior of continents, forming vast continental "shields" or "cratons" where the old rocks have been deeply eroded into a a landscape characterized by low elevations and little topographic relief, such as the Canadian Shield. The shields and sedimentary platforms have suffered little deformation or heating since their formation.

**Continental Drift and Continental Accretion.** The Phanerozoic history recorded by continental rocks reveals a complex sequence of fragmentation and accretion or coalescing of continental pieces that continues today.

The idea of "continental drift," developed by the German meteorologist Alfred Wegener during the first quarter of the 20th century, was based on the remarkable fit of the coastlines of eastern South America and western Africa, and on the similarities of the rocks and fossils on either side of the South Atlantic.

Continental drift is now understood as the movement of the plate in which a continent is embedded rather than as a separate movement of the continent through the surrounding oceanic crust. Africa and South America are parts of two plates that are moving apart or diverging along the Mid-Atlantic Ridge; the ocean basins on either side of this ridge system were created during the past 225 million years since the time when the two continents started to split apart. The margins of the two continents formed on opposing sides of the initial rift and then moved farther and farther apart from one another and from the locus of plate divergence, the Mid-Atlantic Ridge. The margins have since become "passive margins"—that is, continental margins that are no longer active plate boundaries.

In contrast to a passive continental margin, the western side of South America is an "active margin" of the continent. There, one of the Pacific plates (Nazca) and the continental plate containing South America are moving toward one another. The thinner oceanic plate bends downward (subducted) and descends into the mantle beneath western South America, and in so doing forms the Peru-Chile Trench. (See Fig. 1.) The large earthquakes, numerous dormant and active volcanoes, and the Andean mountain belt are all manifestations of this dynamic process.

Fragmentation of continents also occurs. The early stages of fragmentation can be seen in action along the east African rift system, where the African continent is being extended and may be starting to split apart, and along the Red Sea, where the Arabian subcontinent has already split away from Africa.

If a continent, continental fragment, or "island arc" (curved chain of islands enclosing a deap oceanic basin on one side and paralleling a deep oceanic trench on the other) were embedded within the oceanic plate that is moving beneath a continental margin, eventually that place would reach the trench and jam the downward motions because of the buoyancy of the thicker continental crust. (In other words, continents cannot be subducted into trenches because they are lighter than the mantle material and float on it.) Instead, the piece might plow into the continent and become part of it. For example, the Indian subcontinent has collided with Asia during the past 50 million years. The Himalaya mountain chain, the vast Tibetan plateau, and the other spectacular mountain ranges of central Asia are the result of India plowing into Asia.

Geologists think that eastern and southeastern Asia comprises a giant collage of continental fragments that have coalesced to form a larger continental mass. The coalescing of fragments in the region of eastern and northeastern Indonesia, New Guinea, and the Philippines is an ongoing phenomena. Most of western North America including California, Oregon, Washington, British Columbia, and southeastern Alaska has been formed by fragments of continents, oceanic islands, and island arcs that have collided and

"accreted" to the North American mainland.

The separation of South America and Africa was part of the fragmentation of a larger continent called Gondwanaland (Fig. 2) that also included the continents of Antarctica, Australia, the islands of Madagascar and New Zealand, and the Indian subcontinent. Gondwanaland was connected to another large continental mass called Laurasia, which included North America, much of Eurasia, and the island of Greenland. The "supercontinent," including both Gondwanaland and Laurasia, is called Pangaea, which itself had formed from a previous coalescing of fragments.

Ocean basins that are formed by the rifting apart of a continent disappear beneath convergent boundaries that are eventually formed, and the continental fragments then moved toward one another and sooner or later collide. The opening and closing of ocean basins is termed the "Wilson cycle," after the Canadian geologist J. Tuzo Wilson. For example, the Atlantic Basin is still opening, while the Pacific Basin is being subducted on both sides and probably will disappear as Asia collides with the Americas.

Some islands, such as Greenland, Madagascar, New Zealand, and Japan, are known to consist of continental material that rifted away from larger continental bodies and are properly considered to be continental fragments rather than entities distinct from continents.

However, many oceanic islands such as Hawaii and Tahiti form a distinct class of islands different from such continental fragments. These volcanic islands are formed almost entirely by molten material from "hot spots" in the mantle. Hot spots appear to be relatively fixed positions in the mantle where plumes of magma well up and melt holes through the crustal plates like a blowtorch as the plates slowly drift above them. Hot spots have been located in the middle of plates as well as along plate boundaries, which correspond to the ocean ridge system. The specific causes and long-term effects of hot spots have not been resolved.

Another distinct class of islands are those forming the linear archipelagoes paralleling the deep ocean trenches that border parts of the world's oceans. These island arcs are part of the system of convergent plate boundaries. Some arcs appear to be completely formed by volcanism and intrusion of magmas rising upward from the region of the mantle where the oceanic plates reach depths of about 60 to 120 miles (100 to 200 km) in their descent into the mantle.

Convergent plate boundaries generally involve compression and thickening of the continental crust and resultant development of high elevations in mountain belts and high plateaus. Erosion eventually removes the elevated material and deposits it in ocean basins, where it will then be again transported to continents by accretion or by volcanism in another convergent margin. The thickness and elevation of continents relative to the ocean basins is thus maintained by the interplay of plate motions and erosion.

BRYAN L. ISACKS
*Cornell University*

**Further Reading:** Allegre, Claude, *The Behavior of the Earth* (Harvard Univ. Press 1988); Cox, A., and Hart, R. B., *Plate Tectonics, How It Works* (Blackwell 1986); Houston, James D., *Continental Drift* (McGraw 1987); Piper, J. D., *Paleomagnetism and the Continental Crust* (Halsted Press 1987).

**CONTINENTAL CONGRESS,** the body of delegates that spoke or acted collectively first for the American colonies and then for the states during the years 1774 to 1789. The first and second of these congresses, which assembled in September 1774 and May 1775, respectively, served as a kind of advisory council for the colonies because they were extralegal bodies. During the course of the Revolutionary War, subsequent congresses served as the central government of the American union under the Articles of Confederation. These congresses were superseded in 1789 by the new government of the United States established under the federal Constitution.

**Background.** There were precedents for an intercolonial congress before 1774. Earlier in the 18th century both Americans and Englishmen had offered plans for an American union consisting of a congress elected by the individual colonies and an executive appointed by the crown. The purpose of such proposals usually was to provide for a more effective defense against the French and Indians.

In 1754, the Albany Plan of union called for a central government within the colonies to be given certain powers of taxation and controls over western lands and military affairs. But the colonial legislatures that considered the plan rejected it (see ALBANY CONGRESS). The colonies were as much opposed to limitations on their powers by an American central government as by Britain. The intercolonial Stamp Act Congress of 1765 was a temporary body; once its aim of organizing resistance to Parliament's acts had been achieved, it was dissolved.

The calling of the first continental congress resulted directly from a series of repressive measures passed in Britain in the spring of 1774. These were aimed mostly at Massachusetts. To punish that colony for the Boston Tea Party, Britain issued the so-called Coercive Acts (q.v.). Among these were the Boston Port Act, closing that seaport, and the Massachusetts Government Act, which virtually annulled the colony's charter. But instead of isolating that province, as Britain had hoped, these acts ultimately rallied the other colonies to the Massachusetts cause.

Demand for an intercolonial congress came promptly from many quarters. In May 1774, Providence, Philadelphia, and New York City each called for a congress at which common measures binding on all the colonies might be taken. Members of the Virginia House of Burgesses, in an unofficial session on May 27, urged a similar move. On June 17 the lower house of Massachusetts issued a call for a congress to be held in September at Philadelphia. Most colonies responded by choosing delegates. In Georgia, however, the attempt to name delegates was prevented by the governor, and the colony did not participate.

**The First Congress.** The First Continental Congress assembled in Carpenter's Hall, Philadelphia, on Sept. 5, 1774. Twelve colonies eventually sent 56 delegates—a gathering that John Adams termed "a nursery of American Statesmen." Among those attending were George Washington, Patrick Henry, and Richard Henry Lee of Virginia; John and Samuel Adams of Massachusetts; John Jay, James Duane, and Philip Livingston of New York; Roger Sherman of Connecticut; Joseph Galloway, John Dickinson, and Thomas Mifflin of Pennsylvania; and John and Edward Rutledge and Christopher Gadsden of South Carolina.

In organizing the congress as a legislative body, the delegates agreed that each colony should have one vote. Peyton Randolph of Virginia was elected president unanimously, and Charles Thomson of Pennsylvania was elected secretary. It should be noted that the historic choice of the two principal titles in the American system of government—"Congress" and "president"—were made at this time.

The delegates were more interested in gaining a redress of grievances than in declaring independence, but their first major move made difficult any effort at accommodation by the British. On September 17, Congress took a tough stand by endorsing the Suffolk Resolves. These denounced the Coercive Acts as unconstitutional and arbitrary, advised the people to arm and to form their own militia, and recommended stiff economic sanctions against the mother country. A more conciliatory proposal by Joseph Galloway of Pennsylvania then was narrowly defeated. Galloway's plan, like the Albany plan of 1754, provided for an American union and would have given the American colonies something like dominion status within the British Empire.

The Congress next proceeded to issue a series of important state papers. On October 14 the delegates drew up a Declaration of Rights, which listed the personal rights—life, liberty, property, assembly, and trial by jury—to which the colonists felt they were entitled. The document demanded recognition by Britain of these American rights based upon "the immutable laws of nature, the principles of the English constitution, and the several charters or compacts." It called also for the repeal of a long list of laws passed by the Parliament after 1763, including the Coercive Acts.

To bring economic pressure to bear upon Britain, the Congress on October 18 passed a bold measure called the Continental Association, which provided for a boycott of British goods by means of an association formed among the colonies. Nonimportation and nonconsumption of British goods were to go into effect on Dec. 1, 1774, and nonexportation of American products, except rice, to Britain or the West Indies, after Sept. 10, 1775.

As its deliberations drew to a close, the First Continental Congress made an effort to influence public opinion. Petitions were addressed to the king and to the British and American people. Congress adjourned on Oct. 26, 1774, having resolved to meet again on May 10, 1775, if American grievances had not been redressed by that date.

**The Second Congress.** The Second Continental Congress assembled on the designated date at the Pennsylvania statehouse in Philadelphia (later Independence Hall). By that time fighting was under way, for the battles at Lexington and Concord had taken place three weeks earlier. Delegates arrived from all the colonies except Georgia (that colony was not officially represented until autumn). Many members of the Second Congress had attended the first, but there were some new delegates present including Benjamin Franklin of Pennsylvania, John Hancock of Massachusetts, James Wilson of Pennsylvania, and, later on, Thomas Jefferson of Virginia. Randolph and Thomson were reelected, respectively, president and secretary, but Randolph withdrew from the Congress on May 24, and John Hancock was elected to succeed him.

The new Congress gradually assumed the

duties of a provisional government and began to direct the growing American war effort. In June the Congress voted to send military aid to Massachusetts. Congress also moved to assume responsibility for the provincial forces fighting around Boston and to expand them with soldiers from the other colonies. George Washington was appointed commander in chief of the new Continental Army on June 15, 1775. To support the army, money was issued in the form of bills of credit. Congress established a Continental Navy on Oct. 13, 1775.

Although few delegates had advocated the idea of independence in 1774 and 1775, the move for a complete break with Britain began to gather speed in the spring of 1776. Reasons for the change in sentiment were many: a year's bitter fighting, Britain's refusal to offer acceptable concessions, and the use of foreign mercenaries against the colonists. On July 2, 1776, Congress resolved "that these United Colonies are, and of right ought to be free and independent states." Two days later, Congress approved a formal Declaration of Independence.

**After Independence.** The Second Congress adjourned on Dec. 12, 1776, but a new session opened before the end of the year. Holding several sessions then and in 1777, Congress set about drawing up a plan for a more permanent union of the 13 states. This task turned out to be a difficult one in view of the conflicting interests between the large and small states and between those with and those without claims to western lands. On Nov. 15, 1777, however, Congress was able to agree on a framework of government known as the Articles of Confederation, which became the first constitution of the United States.

Ratification of the articles was not completed until March 1, 1781. From that date on, Congress was on a constitutional basis. Though substantially unchanged, Congress under the Articles is sometimes referred to as "the Congress of the Confederation," to emphasize the change to a constitutional regime.

**Under the Articles.** The Articles of Confederation actually did little more than legalize the powers Congress had been exercising since 1775. The Articles provided Congress with an imposing list of powers in foreign, domestic, and military affairs but did not give Congress the power to force the states to comply with its decisions.

**Powers.** In the area of foreign policy Congress had the power to make war and peace, sign treaties, and to send and receive ambassadors. In domestic affairs Congress had authority over many different matters. It could issue paper money, borrow money, and regulate the value of coins minted by the central government and the states; establish a system of weights and measures; create and administer a post office system; manage and regulate trade with Indians outside of state boundaries; and establish courts of final appeal to settle disputes between states. In military affairs Congress had the power to direct operations of the army and navy. To exercise most of the important powers, a vote of nine states was required within the Congress; lesser matters could be settled by a simple majority.

**Limitations.** All powers not enumerated in the Articles remained in the hands of the states, which fact made the state governments very strong. Moreover, the Articles carefully safeguarded the states against encroachment by the central government by granting to them the power of the purse. Congress could requisition the states for money, but it could not force them to pay taxes. The failure to give the central government either coercive power or taxing power proved to be major defects.

**Achievements and Failures.** Despite these limitations, Congress under the Articles was able to accomplish a great deal during the war. It put the army on a more permanent footing by asking the states to enlist men for three years or for the duration of the conflict, and it worked out a pension plan for officers who continued in service until the end of the war. The administration of the central government also was made more efficient. Until early 1781, Congress had functioned through a system of committees. Under the Articles the burden of routine duties was lifted from the shoulders of the congressional delegates and assigned to four executive departments—finance, war, marine, and foreign affairs—operating under strong executives, who were not members of Congress.

During the postwar period, Congress faced serious problems in four major areas—foreign trade, foreign policy, public finance, and currency. In Massachusetts the currency problem and state debt precipitated the uprising known as Shays' Rebellion (1786–1787), which, though it failed, presumably shocked many people into the realization that a stronger central government was needed. This episode, coupled with the growing dissatisfaction over the Articles of Confederation, resulted in the calling of a convention in Philadelphia in 1787, originally for the purpose of revising the Articles.

While this convention was debating, the Congress, still operating under the Articles, registered one of its greatest achievements—the Northwest Ordinance of 1787. This legislation outlined the framework of government for the western territory north of the Ohio River. One of the most striking provisions in the ordinance was that it enabled these western areas, once settled, to be promoted eventually to equal statehood with the older eastern states.

Historians have been prone to criticize the Congress of the Confederation. Such evaluations were based in part on criticisms by Revolutionary War veterans who felt the central government treated them unfairly, and partly on attacks by proponents of the federal Constitution who hoped to make the need for reform seem more urgent. In retrospect, however, the Congress did have certain merits. It successfully prosecuted the war and negotiated the peace, and it issued the Northwest Ordinance. It also managed to carry on the routine administration of matters that were of joint concern to the states, although unusual problems tended to be settled on the state level. The Congress continued to function under the Articles until March 4, 1789, when it was superseded by the government established under the federal Constitution.

See also AMERICAN REVOLUTION—3. *Political, Social, and Economic Developments;* ARTICLES OF CONFEDERATION; DECLARATION OF INDEPENDENCE, UNITED STATES; UNITED STATES—25. *The Founding of the Nation, 1763–1815.*

GEORGE A. BILLIAS, *Clark University*

**Further Reading:** Alsop, Susan M., *Yankees at the Court* (Doubleday 1982); Henderson, H. James, *Party Politics in the Continental Congress* (Univ. Press of Am. 1987); Rakove, Jack N., *The Beginnings of National Politics* (Johns Hopkins Univ. Press 1982); Sanders, Jennings B., *Evolution of Executive Departments of the Continental Congress* (P. Smith 1988).

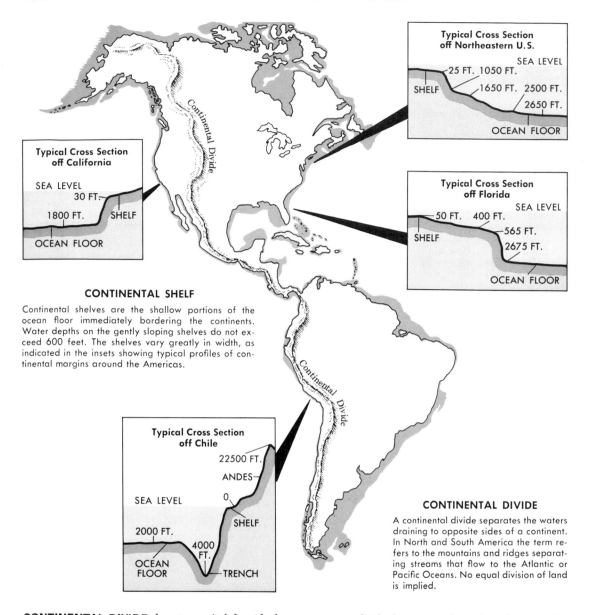

**Typical Cross Section off Northeastern U.S.**

SEA LEVEL

25 FT. 1050 FT.

SHELF

1650 FT. 2500 FT.

2650 FT.

OCEAN FLOOR

**Typical Cross Section off California**

SEA LEVEL

30 FT.

1800 FT.     SHELF

OCEAN FLOOR

**Typical Cross Section off Florida**

SEA LEVEL

50 FT.    400 FT.

SHELF

565 FT.

2675 FT.

OCEAN FLOOR

**CONTINENTAL SHELF**

Continental shelves are the shallow portions of the ocean floor immediately bordering the continents. Water depths on the gently sloping shelves do not exceed 600 feet. The shelves vary greatly in width, as indicated in the insets showing typical profiles of continental margins around the Americas.

**Typical Cross Section off Chile**

22500 FT.

ANDES

SEA LEVEL    0

SHELF

2000 FT.

4000 FT.

OCEAN FLOOR

TRENCH

**CONTINENTAL DIVIDE**

A continental divide separates the waters draining to opposite sides of a continent. In North and South America the term refers to the mountains and ridges separating streams that flow to the Atlantic or Pacific Oceans. No equal division of land is implied.

**CONTINENTAL DIVIDE,** kon-tə-nen′təl də-vīd, the line separating areas that drain to opposite sides of a continent. In the United States, where it is often called the Great Divide, it is the line separating the basins of streams draining to the Atlantic Ocean from those draining to the Pacific. Many portions are low rises of land between headstreams, as in southern Wyoming or east central Arizona; in other sections, the divide follows closely the crestline of the Rocky Mountains. There is no one specific ridge that can be followed from the Canadian to the Mexican boundaries; often the exact position of the divide is not conspicuously marked by any easily observable feature. Three national parks in the United States—Yellowstone, Glacier, and Rocky Mountain—lie across the Continental Divide.

In South America, the divide follows the western portion of the Andes through most of the length of the continent. In Europe it interfingers between streams draining to the Atlantic and Arctic oceans on the one hand and the Mediter-

ranean and Black seas on the other. In Asia the term is usually applied to the separation between Arctic and Pacific drainage and drainage to the Indian Ocean. In Africa separation is made between Indian and Atlantic Ocean drainage. In Australia the continental divide separates Pacific drainage from drainage to the Indian Ocean.

HENRY MADISON KENDALL
*Miami University, Ohio*

**CONTINENTAL DRIFT,** kon-tə-nen′təl drift, the theory that the continental masses have moved across the earth relative to one another. The concept was first proposed by the German geophysicist Alfred Wegener in 1912. The theory has been modified by other scientists and incorporated into the modern theory of plate tectonics. See CONTINENT.

**CONTINENTAL NAVY.** See AMERICAN REVOLUTION—2. *Military Campaigns* (The War at Sea).

**CONTINENTAL SHELF,** the part of the ocean floor that is adjacent to the shores of the continents and is covered by water of shallow depth, less than 80–100 fathoms (480–600 feet, or 145–180 meters). On all ocean floors three distinct kinds of relief features are found: the *continental shelf,* which is a shallow, gently shelving section adjacent to the shore; the *continental slope,* which is a relatively steep slope along the outer edge of the shallow section; and the so-called *abyssal floor,* or *oceanic plain,* where water depths exceed 1,000 fathoms (6,000 feet, or 1,800 meters).

Continental shelves vary greatly in width. Off the coast of New Jersey the continental shelf is 90 miles (145 km) wide; in contrast, off the Pacific coast the average width of the continental shelf is only 18 miles (29 km). Whatever the width, the sea floor plunges abruptly to great depths along the outer edge of the shelf. For example, 90 miles from the New Jersey coast the water depth is only 80 fathoms, while 20 miles (32 km) farther from shore the depth is 1,000 fathoms.

The slope of continental shelves averages 1°. Their relative smoothness is broken here and there by submarine canyons that appear to be seaward extensions of existing or former river valleys—remnants of a geologic period when the land stood at a higher elevation with respect to the sea than it does now.

The continental shelf is the zone of accumulation of sediments derived from the land and then brought to the ocean by rivers and by erosion. Submerged glacial deposits are located on the continental shelf close to the coast of New England. In this respect, deposits on the shelf differ markedly from those on the abyssal floor, which are largely derived from shells and skeletons of various sea organisms.

Most of the world's major fishing grounds are located on continental shelves. Commonly sought varieties of fish congregate in large numbers where the shelves are widest, especially where warm and cold ocean currents meet on the shelves and bring a great diversity of fish food to a relatively restricted area. Where these conditions exist adjacent to densely peopled mainlands, and where commercial fishing is feasible, the waters on the continental shelf take great economic significance. This is true of the Grand Banks of Newfoundland, off the northeastern coast of North America. There the mixing of the cold Labrador Current and the warm Gulf Stream brings a great variety of minute plants and animals (known collectively as plankton) that attract the fish to the shallow waters on the wide continental shelf. This occurs in a location close to the main population centers of North America.

Other important fishing grounds lie on the continental shelves near the Aleutian Islands of Alaska, off the northwestern coast of Europe in the North Sea and adjacent waters, and off the northeastern Asian coast near Japan. The broad continental shelf of southeastern Asia is one of the world's principal pearling areas. The leading fishing nations—Japan, the United States, the Russian Federation, Britain, Norway—all have access to shallow seas on broad continental shelves.

See also MARINE BIOLOGY; OCEANOGRAPHY—*The Oceans and Their Basins.*

HENRY MADISON KENDALL
*Miami University, Ohio*

**CONTINENTAL SYSTEM,** the name given to Napoleon Bonaparte's plan to exclude British commerce from Europe and thereby force peace on his own terms. In control of the coastline from the Baltic to the Adriatic seas, Napoleon tried to close the Continent to British goods by the Berlin Decree (Nov. 21, 1806) and the Milan Decree (Dec. 17, 1807). But contraband traffic and new British markets in South America rendered the plan ineffective.

RICHARD M. BRACE
*Oakland University, Rochester, Mich.*

**CONTINUITY.** See TOPOLOGY—*Basic Concepts of Topology.*

**CONTINUOUS VOYAGE.** See BLOCKADE.

**CONTOUR,** kon'toor, in topography, is a line on a map of part of the earth's surface that connects areas of equal elevation above sea level. A contour is thus a particular kind of isopleth, or line of equal quantity, namely, of elevation.

Contours describe the topography, or configuration, of the ground, and the maps in which they are used are commonly called *topographic maps.* These may range in scale from maps of continents, having contours at each 1,000-foot or 1,000-meter interval, to maps of very large scale showing the path of a projected road, with intervals as small as 1 foot or 5 feet. It is a convention in map making that contour lines are drawn or engraved in brown, as water bodies are shown in blue and cultural features in black.

CONTOUR LINES marking elevations in intervals of 20 feet on a topographic map. Intervals of 100 feet are marked in heavy lines, and their elevations are shown.

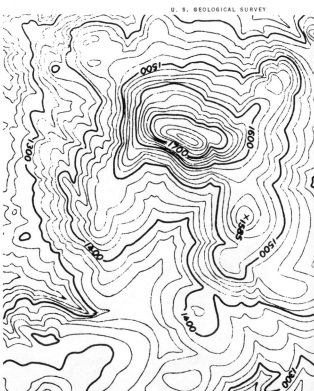

U. S. GEOLOGICAL SURVEY

Contour lines represent the projection to a horizontal plane of the lines that would locate the intersection of the surface of the earth with horizontal surfaces at equally separated intervals. The contour interval depends on the scale of the map, the complexity of the surface forms, and the demand for detail. Contour lines can be visualized as representing the positions of the successive shores of a body of water that is rising by intervals. Since waters extend farthest in valleys, contour lines converge toward the heads of valleys. Tops of hills, which would form islands of diminishing size with rising waters, have closed, encircling contours. Contours are close together on steep slopes, for one moves a shorter distance laterally in climbing the same height on a steep slope than one does on a gentler slope. Depressions are shown by lines having short projections along the lower sides.

Numbers are placed at intervals on the contour lines, and commonly each fifth contour is drawn broader—for example, each 50-meter contour of a map with 10-meter contour intervals, or each 100-foot contour of a map with 20-foot contour intervals. Within the limits of the accuracy of the map, the elevation of points directly on a contour line is given exactly, but the elevations between contour lines can be known only as falling within the contour intervals.

The contour maps of the United States are compiled principally by the U. S. Geological Survey. Known as topographic maps, they can be obtained from the survey in Washington, D. C. British maps are compiled by the Ordnance Survey Department.

Because of their importance in military operations, contour maps are commonly made by military engineers. Formerly they were prepared by means of ground surveys, principally by plane table and telescopic alidade within a triangulation net established by other means. It is now common 'to have photographs taken from the air and, by stereographic methods, to prepare a contour map from the photographs after ground

surveys establish positions and elevations of significant reference points. See also MAP—*Relief Features;* SURVEYING—*Topographic Surveying.*
MARSHALL KAY, *Columbia University*

**CONTOUR FARMING** is farming that involves soil preparation, planting, cultivating, and harvesting across the slope of the land rather than up and down the slope. Severe water and soil losses can result from running rows up and down even gently sloping land. The rate of water movement down slopes is slowed, however, by contour tillage practices, and much of the water is thus able to penetrate the soil rather than running over its surface. The erosion of soil by water movement is likewise reduced by contour tillage since fewer soil particles are transported by the slower moving water. The yields of row crops are increased by contour farming, especially when rainfall is below normal.

Steepness of slope is usually expressed as a percentage derived from the number of feet that the elevation of the land changes in 100 feet of horizontal distance. On slopes ranging from 2% to 8% (that is, changing 2 to 8 feet in elevation per 100 feet of distance), contour cultivation has reduced soil losses as much as 50% and water losses by 10% to 20% in comparison to cultivation up and down the slope.

Though contour cultivation alone reduces erosion and water loss, the combination of contour tillage with *strip-cropping* has been found to be more effective. Strips of a close-growing crop are alternated with strips cultivated for a row crop. The strips are irregular in width, being wider on gentle slopes and narrower on steeper slopes. The rate of water movement is decreased in the strips containing close-growing plants.

**Terraces.** Cultivating on the contour produces ridges and furrows which trap water; however, excess rainfall can break the ridges and induce erosion. Drainage terraces, therefore, are used to catch and divert excess water away from the cultivated slopes. Such terraces are made by

CONTOUR FARMING and the strip-cropping of alternate rows of hay and grass create ribboned patterns on farmland in the hills of the central Wisconsin countryside.

UPI

constructing channels along contours and by forming ridges on the downhill side of the channel with the soil that was removed from the channel. These terraces have gentle grades which permit removal of water at nonerosive rates. The water is then discharged into areas of dense sod or into waterways (diversion terraces) which are covered with erosion-reducing vegetation.

In arid and semiarid regions absorption, or level, terraces are constructed along contours in the form of ridges with little or no grade. Water intercepted on the uphill side of the ridges is absorbed in the soil. If the soil type permits rapid penetration of water, the terrace ends may be blocked to retain all of the impounded water. However, on more impervious soils, terrace ends are open or only partially blocked to allow discharge of the nonabsorbed water.

Loams and clay loams, which are soils of medium texture, are well suited to contour farming. Fine soils with high clay content and coarse soils with high sand content may be contour farmed, but with more difficulty that the medium soils. Maintaining the integrity of ridges and terraces can present considerable problems on clayey soils, which crack on drying, and on sandy soils, which erode rapidly in heavy rains.

**Benches.** Cultural practices involved in contour farming become increasingly difficult when they are applied to steeper slopes. Bench terraces are constructed to accommodate cultivation on slopes steeper than 30%.

Bench terraces in some aspects resemble large stair steps. The cultivated benches (tops of steps), which are leveled or slightly graded across the slopes of steep hills, are separated by uncultivated steep-sloping risers.

Several methods have been used in constructing bench terraces. One is to allow erosion to form steep slopes between high ridges that have been constructed on the contour. As erosion wears down the upper part of the slope, the eroded material collects on the upper side of the ridge—this material slowly builds up over a period of years to convert the ridge into a platform, or bench. Erosion can be increased by plowing up and down the slope in the areas between ridges, thereby increasing the speed of bench formation. In the United States, bench terraces are made with earth-moving equipment.

Benches have been used for growing field crops in some areas of the southern United States. Citrus is produced on bench terraces in parts of Southern California. In Europe, vineyards in many areas such as the Rhine and Moselle valleys have been grown on terraces for centuries.

**History.** Through great expenditures of labor over long periods, man has been able to inhabit inhospitable mountain regions by cultivating food crops on bench terraces. Archaeological findings indicate that Bronze Age (about 3500 B. C.) agriculturalists grew crops with the aid of terrace systems in the British Isles and in the Mediterranean region. The Incas grew corn and potatoes on such terraces in the Andes. Bench-terrace cultivation is now devoted to the production of rice in mountainous regions of India, Indonesia, and the Philippines, and to rice and barley in mountainous areas of China and Tibet.

Contour farming has not been widely practiced in the United States until recently. This lack of interest in an ancient and valuable farming practice was due in part to the availability of abundant good land not situated on slopes.

When land on relatively steep slopes was farmed, it was often improperly managed, its shallow soil became noticeably eroded, and it was abandoned. Most of the good flat land is now in use in the United States as is much of the sloping land. As an increasing population makes increasing demands on arable land, contour farming will be extended in hill and mountain regions.

JOHN R. EDWARDSON, *University of Florida*

**CONTRABAND,** kon′trə-band, in traditional international law, meant goods of military importance destined for the enemy that a belligerent might capture and condemn even though such goods were owned by neutrals and were carried on neutral vessels. The capture of contraband carriers, of vessels attempting to run an effective blockade, of enemy vessels, and of neutral vessels guilty of such unneutral services as carrying troops and dispatches for the enemy were the means accorded to belligerents by traditional international law to cut off the enemy's overseas commerce and sources of supply.

Neutral governments were not required to prevent their citizens from engaging in contraband traffic, although they themselves were prohibited from doing so. They were required to acquiesce in belligerent capture and condemnation of goods that were contraband under international law. Carrying contraband, therefore, was not an international offense but merely an undertaking by a trader that was hazardous in proportion to the sea power of the belligerent that it injured.

The international law of contraband was controversial in respect to the classification of goods as contraband and with respect to permissible penalties. Controversy also centered around the doctrine of "continuous voyage," used by belligerents as rationalization for their destruction or seizure of goods bound for a neutral port but destined ultimately for the enemy. Such maritime powers as Britain usually sought to increase the rights of seizure, while states expecting to be neutral, such as the United States during most of its history, and states inferior in sea power, such as Germany, sought to diminish this right. After the 17th century many treaties dealt with the subject, among them such multilateral treaties as the armed neutralities of 1780 and 1800 (see ARMED NEUTRALITY) and the Declaration of Paris (1856). The position of states on the subject often changed with their changing military and political situations. Many neutral governments have, however, tried to avoid involvement in war by forbidding their citizens to trade with belligerents in such goods as arms, ammunition, and implements of war.

In the later stages of World War I, particularly after the entry of the United States, and in World War II, belligerents tried to control neutral trade. They "blacklisted" neutrals that traded with the enemy, and they agreed not to interfere with neutral vessels carrying a "navicert." This document, issued by a representative of the belligerent state, certified that the vessel would not trade directly or indirectly with the enemy.

In practice, therefore, the traditional concept of contraband, like that of blockade, became in large measure obsolete. Neither concept fits the conditions of modern war or the principles of the Kellogg-Briand Pact and the UN Charter outlawing war of aggression. The "Draft Convention on Rights and Duties of Neutral

States in Naval and Aerial War," published in 1939 by Harvard Law School's Research in International Law, did not use the term "contraband" but permitted belligerents to seize arms, ammunition, and implements of war, as defined by neutrals, if destined for the enemy, and permitted neutrals to embargo the export of such goods. It anticipated that belligerents would control trade at sea, largely by "navicerts" and agreements with neutral states.

QUINCY WRIGHT
*University of Chicago*

**CONTRABASSOON**, kon-trə-bə-sōon', a woodwind instrument with a tube twice as long as the tube of the bassoon and a pitch one octave lower (see BASSOON). It is also called a *double bassoon*. Its range extends from D, two octaves and a seventh below middle C, to F below middle C. Its sound is one octave below the pitch of the notes written for it.

Attempts were made to construct a contrabassoon as early as the 16th century, but the instrument in its modern form took more than 200 years to develop. In the 18th century, the contrabassoon was considered a band instrument rather than an orchestral instrument, but by the end of the 19th century it had become a standard member of the symphony orchestra.

**CONTRACEPTION.** See BIRTH CONTROL.

**CONTRACT**, kon'trakt, in United States law, a promise or set of promises creating a legal duty of performance. Society has largely left to the courts the responsibility for creating and developing the law of contracts, although there is much legislation concerned with particular aspects of contract, such as usury, labor law, and unreasonable restraint of trade.

**Basic Concepts.** Persons often make promises, which are assurances or undertakings that something shall or shall not happen—for example, a promise to build a house or a promise not to assert a claim. Business transactions depend upon such promises. (Although often used, the word "promise" is not actually required.) But unless society creates a *legal duty* to perform a promise, there is no legal compulsion to do so. Thus, a person's promise to pay $100 to another as a gift does not create a legal duty, while a promise to pay $100 for a service subsequently rendered in reliance on the promise creates a legal duty to pay the $100.

A promise can ask for only three things in return: an act, a forbearance (refraining from doing something), or a return promise. A contract is *unilateral* if the promise requests an act or a forbearance. If the promise requests a return promise, the contract is *bilateral*, consisting of mutual promises. A promises to pay $50 for B's services, which B then renders; or C promises to pay $50 to D for services and requests D's return promise to render such services, which D promises. A's promise is a unilateral contract, although both A and B are parties to it. The mutual promises of C and D constitute a bilateral contract.

When one or more of the parties has the right to avoid his duty to perform the contract, the contract is *voidable*. Thus, a contract fraudulently induced is voidable at the discretion of the party defrauded. However, he may waive his power to avoid, keep the contract in force, and hold the defrauding party liable for deceit. When there is no legal remedy to enforce a contract, it is *unenforceable*. Thus, a contract provable only by a writing (the written contract or a signed memorandum) is unenforceable without such a writing; an oral contract to transfer land would be unenforceable.

**Formation.** A promise creates a contract when, with some exceptions, four things are present: two or more parties with legal capacity to contract, agreement between the parties, sufficient consideration, and a legally valid transaction.

**Parties.** Most persons have legal capacity to contract, although anyone adjudged by a court to be incompetent cannot do so. Enemy aliens often cannot contract. Neither can convicts serving long terms of imprisonment. A "person" may be either a *juristic person* created by law (such as a corporation) or a human being. An *infant*, that is, a person under 21 years of age, can contract. However, in the absence of statute or judicial decision to the contrary, an infant may avoid his contracts (1) during his infancy or (2) within a reasonable time after he becomes an adult, unless the contract is one involving land. Where land is concerned, he can avoid only within a reasonable time after he becomes an adult. Because an infant may avoid, businessmen often require an adult as an additional party to the contract. In any case, while under 21, an infant cannot *waive* his power of avoidance.

Parties are jointly liable as a legal entity when they together promise to render the same performance to the same third person. Also, parties are severally liable if they make separate promises to render the same performance to the same third person. Parties may be jointly and severally liable. They may also have joint, several, or joint and several rights.

**Agreement.** The parties must agree on what is to be done, and this they do by offer and acceptance. An offer, made by an *offeror*, is a promise requesting *in exchange* another's act, forbearance, or return promise. It is more than a mere negotiation or an inducement inviting an offer. For example, a statement that an article is for sale is not an offer; it simply invites an offer to buy. Price lists are not offers, and likewise quotations, estimates, and trade inquiries usually are not offers. Bids are offers, with the exception of a bid at an auction where the auctioneer has not reserved the right to accept or reject any bid. In that case a bid is an acceptance of the auctioneer's offer to sell.

An acceptance is made by the *offeree* (the person to whom the offer has been made) and is his manifestation of assent to the offer in compliance with and in reliance on it. However, if *goods* are being sold, provided there is an acceptance of a part of the offer thereby effecting a bargain, there is an agreement. Silence generally is not a manifestation of assent, although the offeree's silent exercise of dominion over the item, as by use, sale, or destruction, implies an acceptance. Also, the parties may agree that silence is an acceptance.

If the offer does not expressly indicate how or when acceptance is to occur, then the offeree can use any proper channel of communication and must assent within a reasonable time. Usually in business transactions time is important, and the acceptance must be made promptly. If the offer requires the offeree to send his acceptance, the sending of it creates an agreement; but if the offer requires that the offeror receive the acceptance, only receipt creates agreement. An offeree's written confirmation, sent within a reasonable time, of an offer to buy or sell *goods* is an acceptance.

An offer is terminated by an acceptance, and both merge into an agreement. Termination may also occur by expiration, revocation, or rejection of the offer. An offer may expire either by its express or implied terms; or by operation of law, as by death of the offeror or the offeree, or by destruction of the thing contemplated by the offer, before acceptance has occurred.

An offeror may revoke his offer before acceptance, but the revocation is effective only when received by the offeree. The offeror's promise to keep the offer open for a time in exchange for consideration (something to be done) by the offeree, which the offeree renders, causes the offer to become an option, which is an irrevocable offer. If the promise to keep the offer open is gratuitous (without consideration), then the promise is not binding on the offeror and the offer is not an option. However, a *merchant's* signed writing offering to buy or sell certain goods and assuring that the offer will be held open is a *firm offer* and is irrevocable, without consideration, for a maximum period of three months. An offeree may reject the offer before acceptance, thereby terminating the offer, by manifesting an intent not to accept the offer. If the offeree requires a change in the terms of the offer, the offeree makes a counteroffer. An offeree's inquiry whether the offeror would change the terms of his offer is not a rejection.

When an agreement has been induced by an intentional misrepresentation, called fraud, or an innocent material misrepresentation of a contracting party, resulting in a contractual mistake, the contract is voidable by the party to whom the misrepresentation was made. Unless otherwise agreed and in the absence of statute or judicial decision to the contrary, contracting parties have no duty to disclose fully what each knows to the other, unless there is a fiduciary relationship between them. That relationship creates a duty to disclose fully and failure to do so makes the contract voidable by the party to whom disclosure should have been made. A fiduciary relationship exists when one party has a duty to act primarily on behalf of another, such as an agent for his principal.

With some exceptions, mistake does not preclude the formation of a contract. When a contract is in writing any oral or written agreement made previously, and any oral agreement made contemporaneously with the written contract, that varies or adds to the contract, are not admissible in evidence.

**Sufficient Consideration.** A promise is unenforceable as a contract unless it is supported by sufficient consideration. Consideration is the price exacted by a promise; it is the act, forbearance, or return promise requested in exchange for the promise. The consideration must have value, in that the person rendering it was under no previous legal duty to do so. For example, A promises $100 to B if B will dig a ditch, which B then does. B's work is the consideration for A's promise, and since B was not under any previous legal duty to A to dig the ditch, B's work was sufficient consideration for A's promise, which is now enforceable. If A and B had a prior contract for B to dig, and later A promised B $20 extra if B would perform his contract (which B then does), A's new promise of $20 is not a contract. It was not supported by sufficient consideration, as B had a previous contractual legal duty to A to dig the ditch. Thus, a promise to pay a debt is not sufficient consideration because the promise does not request anything in return. However, under the Uniform Commercial Code such a promise usually is enforceable as a contract because of the mercantile nature of the transactions covered by it. A creditor's promise to accept a lesser sum from the debtor in full satisfaction of a larger debt is unenforceable when the lesser sum is paid because the debtor was under a previous legal duty to pay the debt. An exception is made when an insolvent or financially embarrassed debtor agrees with some or all of his creditors that, on his payment of a part of his debt to each of them, each shall discharge him of the balance.

Often a claim is disputed because it is honestly and reasonably believed not to be valid by the party against whom it is asserted. A party's promise to discharge his disputed claim, on payment of a compromised lesser amount, is supported by sufficient consideration. Similarly, payment of an unliquidated claim—one which exists when the amount is neither fixed by the parties, certain, nor ascertainable mathematically or by law—is sufficient consideration for a promise discharging the payor's obligation.

There are important occasions when, as exceptions, a promise is enforceable without consideration and without agreement. The statute of limitations limits the time in which a claim may be enforced in the courts. One exception to the consideration rule is a promise, express or implied, to pay money on a debt barred by the statute of limitations. Such a promise is implied from (1) the debtor's mere acknowledgement or part payment of a debt; or (2) his issuance of a negotiable instrument, such as a promissory note or check, or giving collateral security for the debt or interest thereon. Other exceptions are: (1) a promise to pay part or all of a debt discharged or dischargeable in bankruptcy, made after bankruptcy proceedings have begun; and (2) a promise to waive the power to avoid a contract.

**Valid Transaction.** The contract must involve a legally valid transaction. An agreement is illegal when its formation or performance is contrary to law, by being opposed either to statute or to public policy as declared by the courts. Legal relief is denied to a wrongdoer. Thus, an agreement to commit a crime or a tort is void.

**Third Parties.** Only the parties to a contract may enforce it; nevertheless, if a contract is made specifically for the benefit of a third person who is either a creditor or donee of the promisee under the contract, the beneficiary may enforce the contract against the promisor. Thus, if T by contract promises D to pay D's debt to C, C is a creditor of D, and, as the beneficiary of the contract, may enforce it against T. Similarly, if H takes out a life insurance policy with I naming his wife as beneficiary, she is a donee of H and, as the beneficiary of the policy, may enforce it against I on H's death. Also, a party may assign his contract rights and accounts receivable, or delegate his contract duties, to a third person, unless the contract is personal in character, in which case it expressly or impliedly prohibits assignment or delegation. The *assignee* (person to whom assignment has been made) may enforce the assigned right or account against the party who was contractually obligated to his *assignor* (person who assigned). However, the assignee acquires only what his assignor has. For example, S fraudulently induces B to buy goods from S, who assigns the account to T. B may avoid the contract against S and, therefore, against T. Because most assignments of contracts for personal property are made for the purpose of security, they are considered to be secured transactions under the Uniform Commercial Code, which prescribes how the assignee's security interest may be perfected and thereby protected against other persons.

**Statute of Frauds.** In order to prevent fraud, statutes require proof by a writing that certain kinds of contract exist. Unless so proved, these contracts are unenforceable. The writing may be either the contract itself or a memorandum of an oral contract. Examples of contracts when a writing is required are: one for the sale of land or an interest in land; one not performable within one year; and one to answer for the debt, default, or miscarriages of another person.

**Nonperformance.** When the performance required under the contract is not rendered, the legal effect varies. If the nonperformance is *material,* that is, if the main purpose of the contract is not performed or is defeated, the innocent party is discharged from his contractual obligation. If the nonperformance is not material, there is substantial performance and so the innocent party must perform his part of the contract, less the harm he has sustained by the other party's nonperformance. However, nonperformance may be excused or legally justified. A breach on contract is wrongful nonperformance of a contractual duty; unless excused or legally justified, nonperformance is wrongful. Generally, the alternative legal remedies available to the innocent party for breach of contract are (1) the right to damages; (2) in proper cases, the right to have the contract specifically performed; or (3) restitution of what he has previously delivered to the materially nonperforming party.

**Discharge.** The termination of a contractual duty is called a *discharge,* which may occur by act of the parties or by operation of law. Any of the following events causes a discharge: performance; material nonperformance; mutual agreement; assignment; exercise of a power of avoidance; intentional and fraudulent material alteration of a contract by one party without the other's assent; or a judgment, an arbitration award, or an excusable impossibility of performance.

See also COMMERCIAL LAW.

JOSEPH L. FRASCONA
*Graduate School of Business Administration and the School of Business, University of Colorado*

**CONTRACT BRIDGE.** See BRIDGE.

**CONTRACT LABOR** was a system of employment practiced in the United States before 1885. Under this system the worker, usually an immigrant, was in fact indentured to the employer. The passage by Congress of the Contract Labor Law on Feb. 26, 1885, outlawed many of the practices and led to the gradual dissolution of the system.

The contract for employment called for a stipulated period of service at stated wages in return for one-way passage to the United States. As under the indentured servant system, the time period was usually seven years. Wages were generally below those paid native American workers for the same work, and the net effect of the system was to depress wages in manufacturing and in many trades. The system therefore was vigorously opposed by the trade unions that developed in the period of the last quarter of the 19th century.

Several causes contributed to abuses under the contract labor system. Unrestricted immigration into the United States in the 19th century permitted agents of American employers to recruit labor in large masses among workers in Europe. Many of these workers could not read the contract documents, so they could not understand the conditions of their employment. The agents, who often were of the same nationality as the workers, used their native language to make the offers appear to be attractive. Many gullible workers were persuaded by rumors about the abundant life in the United States that the proffered employment would bring them rich rewards in a new land.

The purposes of the 1885 law that made many of these abuses illegal were (1) to protect American labor from foreign competition, (2) to raise the standards for admission of immigrants, and (3) to reduce immigration into the United States of those who were unable to pay their own passage.

The act prohibited prepayment of transportation for immigrants and voided labor contracts made before immigration. It established penalties for violation of the law. Any ship captain who knowingly brought laborers that had signed such contracts into the United States was declared guilty of a misdemeanor. Various amendments later were added to strengthen the act. Eventually, however, certain exemptions were granted. Some persons, such as domestic servants and members of specified professions, were declared admissable to the United States on the basis of a prior contract.

The regulation of immigration became much more direct and restrictive after World War I. Consequently the Contract Labor Law and the system that led to its adoption are now primarily of only historic interest.

WILLIAM N. KINNARD, JR.
*University of Connecticut*

**CONTRALTO,** the female or boy's voice of the lowest range, also called *alto.* Contraltos have a range of about two and a half octaves upward from about E in the bass clef.

See also ALTO.

**CONTRAPUNTAL MUSIC.** See COUNTERPOINT.

**CONTRAST, The,** kon'trast, a comedy by the American lawyer and dramatist Royall Tyler, written in 1787, and traditionally regarded as the first American play. It had its premiere performance at the John Street Theatre in New York City on April 16, 1787, and was the first play by an American dramatist to be professionally produced.

The main plot concerns the amorous adventures and final downfall of the central character, Billy Dimple. But the *The Contrast* gets its title from the subplot, which pits the homespun shrewdness of one servant against the sophisticated wiliness of another.

**CONTREDANSE,** kon′trə-dans, a traditional English country dance that was imported into France in the 17th century and became a popular European ballroom dance in the 18th century. According to some authorities, the name is a French corruption of the English "country dance." According to others, it derives from the position of the two or more couples who stand in opposite lines instead of in a circle. The steps are gay and simple, and the music is in 8-bar phrases in ⅔ or ⅝ time. Contredanse music was written by Mozart and Beethoven, and books of contredanse tunes were published annually in England. The contredanse developed into the quadrille, or square dance, which replaced it in popularity in the early 19th century. See also COUNTRY DANCE.

**CONTROL SYSTEMS.** See also AUTOMATIC CONTROL; CYBERNETICS; SERVOMECHANISM.

**CONTUSION.** See BRUISE.

**CONUS.** See CONE SHELLS.

**CONVALLARIA,** the lily-of-the-valley genus of the lily family (Liliaceae). See LILY OF THE VALLEY.

**CONVECTION OF HEAT.** See HEAT TRANSFER—*Convection.*

**CONVENT,** primarily a community of monks or nuns occupying a monastery or other establishment of a monastic character. The term "convent" is also used to designate the building in which a monastic community is housed. In a popular, but inaccurate, sense the term is used to refer to the building in which women of a religious order reside.

Convents were first given their characteristic form by St. Pachomius (c.292–c.346), an ascetic of upper Egypt. He established communities that successfully combined the asceticism that flourished among hermits of that area with rules that regulated communal life through obedience to a superior.

Conventual life was introduced into western Europe early in the 4th century, beginning a remarkable development in which convents dominated the spiritual and cultural life of the church for centuries. The principal monastic rule of the West was established by St. Benedict of Nursia in the 5th century. The Benedictine order was primarily contemplative, but it also fostered scholarship. In the 10th century, in Cluny, France, centralized control was established over many of the communities of Europe, and the convent of Cluny was among the most elaborate centers of Europe, both architecturally and politically. Other important convents of the medieval period were established by the Cistercians, the Carthusians, the Augustinians, and the Dominicans.

In the 16th century a distinction was established between major and minor convents, the major convent having 12 or more members and the minor having fewer than 12. Within some modern monastic orders a similar distinction is still made. All of the major forms of religious communities have continued to exist in modern times, and convents now engage in a wide range of activities, including charitable, educational, and missionary work.

**CONVENTION,** in sociology, a generally agreed-upon rule of conduct governing social behavior. Since conventions generally standardize behavior within a social group or class, they often tend to mark the differences between social classes and act to reinforce class distinctions. Conventions thus differ from laws or moral precepts, which are generally binding on society as a whole, and which, therefore, have more force. Violation of a convention may result in embarrassment, while violation of a law or moral code may result in punishment and disgrace.

Adherence to conventional conduct is thought to reflect in part a common desire for order and stability. Moreover, conventions are a means of communication; people governed by the same conventions understand each other's actions. On the other hand, as ingrained patterns of action, conventions often act as a barrier to innovation. Often the reason for the development of a particular convention no longer exists, while the convention itself remains as an automatic, customary act. Many conventions are thus attacked as meaningless, stifling rules bolstering a tradition-laden, conforming society. See also CONFORMITY; CUSTOM; TRADITION.

**CONVENTION, Constitutional.** See CONSTITUTIONAL CONVENTION.

**CONVENTION, Political,** a gathering of delegates to conduct business for a political party. National conventions are held during presidential election years by political parties in the United States. Conventions are also held at state and local levels, and in many other nations.

Delegates may conduct internal party business, adopt a declaration of party principles, prepare for election campaigns, and nominate candidates for public office. Each of these tasks is performed at national party conventions in the United States, but some of them—particularly the last—are omitted elsewhere.

**History.** American conventions developed from attempts by parties to unify differing factions and from their desire to extend popular participation in the electoral process. The first organized method for nominations was the caucus, in which legislators with common views met to draw up a list of party candidates. Used at first in state legislatures, the system was quickly extended to Congress. By 1800, the procedure was established, as the Republican and Federalist members of Congress met to nominate Thomas Jefferson and John Adams, respectively, for president.

But if an area did not elect legislators of the party, it was unrepresented. To meet this objection, the "mixed caucus" was instituted, in which legislators and delegates from unrepresented areas were combined. There remained objections to an elite body of legislators making important decisions for the entire party. Moreover, because the legislative caucus chose candidates for executive positions, the practice was seen as a violation of the principle of the separation of governmental branches. Eventually, the caucus lost its effectiveness. See CAUCUS.

The convention emerged as an alternative system early in the 19th century. Delegates were chosen at local party meetings, or "primaries," to attend county conventions. As transportation improved, state gatherings became feasible and were first instituted in relatively small states. The new system permitted wider mass participation, divorced the legislature from control of executive nominations, and facilitated party unity behind a single ticket.

The first national conventions were held in 1831, by the short-lived Anti-Masonic party and by the National-Republican party. More important for historical development was the 1832 meeting of President Andrew Jackson's party, the Democratic-Republicans. The holding of a national convention was a manifestation of the Jacksonian belief in mass democracy. It was also used by Jackson to overcome opposition to his chosen political heir, Martin Van Buren, as the vice presidential choice. The rules of this convention established many important precedents, including delegate apportionment on the basis of electoral votes, the casting of votes by state delegations, and the necessity of a two-thirds vote for nomination. The Democratic party retained the two-thirds rule until after the convention of 1936.

Most contemporary party practices were established before the Civil War, including the writing of a party platform (1840), the selection of a full ticket at the national conventions (1844), and the designation of a national committee to administer party affairs between national elections (1848). Convention practices changed little until the 20th century, when the important innovation of the direct presidential primary was introduced. See PRIMARY ELECTIONS IN THE UNITED STATES.

**National Convention Delegates.** Historically, apportionment of delegates among the states was based on electoral votes, each state receiving one to three votes for each vote in the Electoral College. The basic formula has been modified, however, to give greater voice to those areas from which the party receives its greatest support.

The Democratic party instituted a significantly different apportionment system for its 1972 convention. The new formula aimed at giving more power to the states with large numbers of Democratic voters. The new formula allocated 53% of the seats on the basis of electoral votes, and the remainder on the basis of the average state Democratic vote in the last three presidential elections. Also, the members of the National Committee are automatic delegates. In both parties, the territories are given token representation. Each party chooses up to an equal number of nonvoting alternates.

The delegates from each state are chosen either in direct primary elections or through a series of local, county, and state conventions. Major changes in the process of selection were made in the Democratic party for the 1972 convention, following the recommendations of the special Committee on Party Structure and Delegate Selection. The changes provided for the selection of all delegates in the calendar year of a presidential election, the inclusion of representative numbers of women, young people, and ethnic minorities on delegations; the adoption of formal rules by all state parties; and the prohibition of the unit rule in voting. Under the latter procedure, all votes of a state are cast for the candidate preferred by a majority of the state's delegates. The new rules were not simultaneously adopted by the Republican party, although it has never permitted a formal unit rule.

In 1974 the Democrats adopted a charter to ensure participation in delegate selection by blacks, women, and young people, and proportional representation of candidate preferences.

Some Republicans also considered ways to broaden their party's base. The 1972 convention included bonus delegates for states giving majorities to Republican candidates for president, senator, governor, and the U. S. House. But the same convention rejected a plan to give more voting strength to large states.

Another important change in convention representation has come about through state law. About half of the states chose their convention delegates by direct vote in 1972, and the delegates so chosen comprised about 60% of the total votes. Prior to this, the proportion of directly elected delegates was only about one third of the total. The changes reflected the widespread discontent with the nominating process that had become evident in 1968, particularly after the disruptive Democratic convention.

**Convention Action.** The basic arrangements for a U. S. national convention are made by the party's National Committee, which determines the site, apportions delegates among the states, tentatively chooses officers, and arranges accommodations. The party meeting typically opens on a midsummer Monday in the presidential election year, and continues for four days, but its committees begin work earlier. The major committees are Rules, Credentials, and Platform. In the Republican party, these consist of two delegates from each state. In the 1972 Democratic convention, the committees comprised 150 delegates, apportioned by size of state delegations, but with at least one from each state.

The decisions of the committees may influence the nomination of presidential candidates. The 1952 Republican nomination of Dwight Eisenhower, for example, was critically dependent on the adoption of rules and the settlement of credentials contests in his favor.

The declaration of party principles, or platform, often is the focus of intense disputes. Although platforms are often disparaged as built "to run on, not to stand on," they have considerable significance. Parties have openly divided over their declaration of principles, most notably in 1860, when the Democrats could not agree on the slavery issue. More recent party disputes have involved the civil rights position of the Republican party in 1964 and the Vietnam policy of the Democrats in 1968. Research indicates that platforms are relatively specific in their wording, and that they forecast much of the legislative program of the victorious party. However, the degree of difference between the programs of the two major parties, while observable, is not great.

The first two days of a convention are usually taken up with organization, speeches, settling rules and credentials contests, and adopting the platform. During this time, the candidates seek last-minute support, while the party uses the free coverage by the broadcast media to appeal to the voters. On the third day of the convention, candidates for the presidential nomination are presented. Traditionally, the nomination speech for a candidate was followed by a supposedly spontaneous demonstration on his behalf. But the national television audiences became bored with these outbursts, and both parties have placed strict limits on the procedure. For 1972, the Democrats limited nominations in most cases to candidates with support in at least three states.

State-by-state balloting then begins, with an absolute majority of all votes needed to win nomination. If no candidate receives a majority

POLITICAL conventions, though crowded and noisy, manage to select nominees for office and transact other business.

on the first ballot, successive tallies are taken until a decision is reached. The longest balloting took place at the 1924 Democratic convention, when two weeks and 103 ballots were necessary. The vice president is nominated through similar procedures. The convention closes with acceptance speeches by its candidates.

**Convention Results.** Nominations fall into distinct patterns. The most common is the renomination of an incumbent president. Because of his national prestige and his power within the party, it is extremely difficult to defeat an incumbent. An exception was the decision of President Lyndon Johnson not to seek renomination in 1968 in the face of strong party opposition.

A similar pattern is the nomination of an apparent party leader without a significant contest at the convention. Nearly two thirds of the presidential nominations in the 20th century fall into this pattern. Most frequently, nominees are chosen in a single ballot. Less common patterns are a convention choice among major candidates, or the surprise selection of a relatively unknown dark horse after many ballots.

In vice presidential selections, there has not even been a contest in more than two thirds of the modern nominations. The choice of a running mate is usually prearranged in consultations between the new presidential candidate and other party leaders. An exception came in 1956, when the Democratic nominee, Adlai Stevenson, refused to name a preference, and permitted the convention to select Sen. Estes Kefauver after a spirited two-ballot contest.

The relatively limited choice available to conventions since World War II is due to the greater influence of preconvention factors. Primary elections bind many delegates. Early campaigning exposes the presidential aspirants to the party long before the formal decision. Television coverage also publicizes the candidates more fully, while it makes it more difficult for party leaders to negotiate privately. Convention decisions are also strongly affected by public opinion polls, which indicate the popular favorites. Because

delegates are eager to win the election, they usually select the person leading in the polls. The increasing power of the president and the importance of national issues also makes it difficult for conventions to choose inexperienced candidates unfamiliar with those issues.

For these reasons, it is unlikely that national conventions will again be the storied scene of deals made in smoke-filled rooms in which mediocre but "available" candidates are selected.

**State Conventions.** Party conventions are common among state parties. However, because almost all nominations for state and local office are made through direct primaries, these meetings seldom have a nominating task. More commonly, they exist to write a party platform, to handle official party business, and to provide a forum for campaign rallies. In a few states, preprimary conventions designate an official party choice for nomination, who may then be challenged in the primary. Conventions still designate statewide candidates directly in Delaware and Indiana. In some other states, most notably California and Wisconsin, unofficial party agencies hold their own conventions to select preferred candidates, whom they then endorse in the primary.

**Other Countries.** Although called by other names, party conventions are found in many countries. In Britain, for example, the annual party conference is an important sounding board for the party leaders, an occasion for revitalizing campaign energies, and a forum for the consideration of policy resolutions. Party candidates and leaders are nominated elsewhere—in their local constituencies and in the party caucus in the House of Commons. However, the annual conference resolutions considerably influence the leaders' policy and affect the voters' perception of the parties.

The party conferences in other countries often choose the executive committees, from which leaders of the government are likely to be drawn. If a party directly controls the government, its conventions are of great significance. The most important examples are the Communist nations.

The most important decisions in the former Soviet Union were made at the party congresses, held about every five years, rather than in the formal legislative and executive bodies.

GERALD M. POMPER
*Livingston College, Rutgers University*

**Bibliography**

*Congressional Quarterly's Guide to U.S. Elections*, 3d ed. (1994).

Courtney, John C., *Do Conventions Matter?: Choosing National Party Leaders in Canada* (McGill-Queens Univ. Press 1995).

Kurian, George Thomas, *Encyclopedia of the Democratic Party* (Sharpe 1997).

Kurian, George Thomas, *Encyclopedia of the Republican Party* (Sharpe 1997).

*National Party Conventions, 1831–1996* (Congressional Quarterly 1997).

Rapoport, Ronald B., *The Life of the Parties: Activists in Presidential Politics* (Univ. Press of Ky. 1986).

Sautter, R. Craig, *Inside the Wigwam: Chicago Presidential Conventions, 1860–1996* (Loyola Press 1996).

Shafer, Byron E., *Bifurcated Politics: Evolution and Reform in the National Party Convention* (Harvard Univ. Press 1988).

Smith, Larry David, *Cordial Concurrence: Orchestrating National Party Conventions in the Telepolitical Age* (Praeger 1991).

**CONVENTION OF 1787.** See CONSTITUTION OF THE UNITED STATES.

**CONVERGENCE** is an evolutionary phenomenon in which unrelated organisms or groups of organisms develop structural similarities in their independent adaptation to similar environmental conditions. For example, the squid and octopus, which are mollusks, possess eyes that have the same basic structure as the eyes of whales and other vertebrates. This similarity is due to convergence, and it does not mean that the squid and octopus share a close evolutionary relationship with the vertebrates that have the same basic eye structure.

DAVID A. OTTO
*Stephens College*

**CONVERGENT SERIES.** See SERIES—*Infinite Series.*

**CONVERSANO,** kōn-vär-sä′nō, a town and commune in Italy, in the province of Bari, 17 miles (27 km) southeast of the city of Bari. It is a trading center in a district that produces cherries, olive oil, wine, and grain.

A bishop's seat, it has a fine cathedral, an old Benedictine monastery, and a Norman castle. Population: 20,507 (1981 preliminary census).

**CONVERSE,** kon′vûrs, **Frederick** (1871–1940), American composer. He was born in Newton, Mass., on Jan. 5, 1871, and graduated with honors from Harvard in 1893. He later studied at the Munich Conversatory, where his Symphony in D Minor was played at his graduation in 1898. From 1899 to 1901 he taught harmony at the New England Conservatory, and from 1901 to 1907 he taught composition at Harvard, resigning to devote more time to composing. He was dean of the New England Conservatory from 1931 to 1938. Converse died in Westwood, Mass., on June 8, 1940.

*The Mystic Trumpeter* (1905), an orchestral fantasy, is perhaps Converse's most popular work, but his most noteworthy composition is his one-act opera *The Pipe of Desire*, the first American work given by New York City's Metropolitan Opera (1910). He also wrote chamber music and background music for films.

**CONVERSION** signifies the experience involved in adopting or changing a religious belief out of conviction. This experience is not limited to a particular religion. Both Buddha and St. Francis of Assisi turned from lives of pleasure to what they saw to be spiritual realities—Buddha through renunciation and St. Francis through poverty and love for the world.

In the Bible, conversion is understood as the turning of man to God, and it embodies divine action and human response. The conversions of Isaiah (Isaiah 6) and of St. Paul (Acts 9) are typical, in that they embody conviction of sin, forgiveness, and acceptance of a mission. In the Old Testament, the subject of conversion is often Israel as a whole (Ezekiel 18:30; Exodus 32:30ff.). In the New Testament, conversion of the world is the goal of all preaching. "The kingdom of God is at hand: repent ye, and believe the Gospel" (Mark 1:15) were the words with which Jesus began his ministry.

The Christian church has considered its principal task to be conversion, and such notable preachers as Peter, Paul, Chrysostom, Savonarola, Luther, and John Wesley have stressed it. Both Catholics and Protestants have agreed that the change brought by conversion—called rebirth, regeneration, or faith—is necessary for Christian life. Catholics have held that this change occurs in baptism, whether or not any experience of conversion is present. Protestants, on the other hand, have tended to believe that without such experience one has not became a Christian, whether he has been baptized or not. With the ecumenical movement in the 20th century, there has tended to be a lowering of barriers separating Catholics and Protestants. There seems to be a development of a common view that there cannot be complete conversion and rebirth without the individual's having some relation to the sacramental life of the church.

The development of the science of psychology brought with it much interest in the study of the conversion experience, along with a thorough questioning of any element of divine action in it. Thus William James described it as a natural phenomenon in which "a self . . . consciously wrong, inferior and unhappy, becomes unified and consciously right, superior and happy" (*Varieties of Religious Experience*, 1902). Freud thought that the whole of religious experience to be derived "from the child's feeling of helplessness and the longing it evokes for a father" (*Civilization and Its Discontents*, 1930). There has been a tendency among many theologians to adopt similar language. They note that conversion is no different from other human experiences in which thoroughgoing change in moral outlook and behavior may occur, as in psychotherapy. Some theologians have attempted to describe conversion in terms of a stimulus-response act. Owen Brandon writes: "Conversion means an individual's response to stimulus and suggestion in respect of any particular orientation of mental attitude and/or of behavior" (*Battle for the Soul*, 1959). Still at issue between such theologians, however, and the majority of psychologists, is the question of divine action in conversion experiences.

REV. CHARLES D. BRAND, *Episcopal Church*

**CONVERSION HYSTERIA.** See HYSTERIA.

**CONVERTIPLANE.** See AIRCRAFT—*Vertical/Short Takeoff and Landing.*

**CONVEYOR,** kən-vā′ər, a device for moving loads from one point to another over fixed paths. The conveyor is one of the three basic types of materials-handling equipment used in industry and business. The other two are industrial trucks, and cranes and hoists.

Familiar examples of conveyors include the belt conveyors used on supermarket checkout stands, the chain conveyors that pull cars through automatic car washers, the trolley conveyors used for garment storage and retrieval in dry cleaning establishments, and the cable conveyors of ski lifts.

Conveyors are used throughout industry in nearly every phase of production and distribution, since they promote economy by providing a controlled continuous flow of materials. Many industries depend on conveyors for their very existence. Mining, for example, is nearly 100% materials handling; the construction industry is about 90% materials handling; and in the typical manufacturing industry, 50 to 75% of production cost is materials handling, the exact amount depending on the nature of the processes and products.

The conveyor has become a symbol of mass production. One of the first fully automated factories was Oliver Evans' flour mill, built in Wilmington, Del., in 1785. Evans used belt conveyors, bucket elevators, and screw conveyors to move grain and flour continuously through the manufacturing process. Meat-packing plants were using conveyors during the Civil War. Henry Ford is credited with the first use of conveyors for a moving assembly line in 1912.

### TYPES OF CONVEYORS

There are about 130 different types of conveyors. In choosing a conveyor for a particular job, primary considerations are the characteristics of the materials to be handled, the move to be made, and any building or structural restrictions. The modern trend, however, is away from picking a conveyor to solve an isolated handling task and toward considering materials-handling functions and equipment as aspects of the over-all implementation of production and distribution. In general, conveyors are most useful for (but not limited to) situations in which the loads are uniform and the total load is constant; continuous movement at relatively fixed speeds is desirable; and the path to be followed is fixed.

**Nonpowered Conveyors.** The simplest types of conveyors are those that use gravity or manual power to propel the objects. The most common nonpowered conveyors are chutes, roller conveyors, and wheel conveyors.

**Chutes.** Certain bulk materials, such as coal and gravel, and some solid objects that are not free flowing can be directed and lowered by gravity in troughs called chutes. Chutes may be open or closed, follow straight or curved paths, and have flat or curved beds. Some chutes consist of short slanted sections which permit materials to drop short distances from one section to the next. All chutes depend on sliding friction to control the speed of descent of the materials being conveyed. Chutes are usually used for short moves, such as from one machine to another or from one floor to another.

**Roller Conveyors.** Objects are advanced by gravity or manually on roller conveyors, which consist of a series of rollers supported in a

LINK-BELT COMPANY

A BELT CONVEYOR shaped into a trough between two sets of rollers carries a continuous load of iron ore.

frame. The conveyors can follow straight or curved routes and are usually used over short distances. Level roller conveyors can be used as work surfaces. Workpieces are moved to the next location manually. Inclined roller conveyors depend on rolling friction to control the speed of descent of the materials. The objects moved must have smooth, firm supporting surfaces or be placed in containers. Roller conveyors are extremely common in package-handling operations.

**Wheel Conveyors.** Wheel conveyors are similar to roller conveyors but have skate-type wheels mounted on parallel bars. They are generally less expensive than roller conveyors. However, roller conveyors are usually more durable. Wheel conveyors are commonly used in the unloading of trucks.

**Powered Conveyors.** Most conveyors use power to move materials, and employ a belt, chain, or cable to provide the material movement. A representative group of powered conveyors is described below.

**Belt Conveyors.** Belt conveyors consist essentially of an endless belt of fabric, rubber, plastic, leather or metal. The belt is supported on rollers, troughing idlers, or a flat slider bed and passes over a drive and end pulley. Loads such as cartons, bags, and boxes are carried on the belt. Belt conveyors designed to carry bulk materials like coal, sand, or gravel have idlers that are arranged to form a trough. Belt conveyors may operate on an incline and are frequently used as feeders to other conveyors or for changing elevations between sections of a roller conveyor.

**Live-Roller Conveyors.** The live-roller conveyor is similar to the roller conveyor, but its rollers are power driven. Often power is applied only to sections of the conveyor where it is not

## TYPES OF CONVEYORS

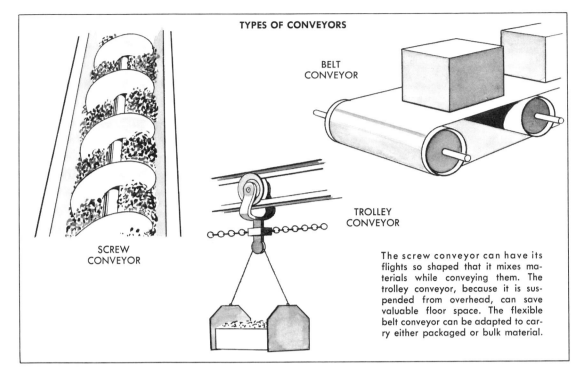

BELT CONVEYOR

TROLLEY CONVEYOR

SCREW CONVEYOR

The screw conveyor can have its flights so shaped that it mixes materials while conveying them. The trolley conveyor, because it is suspended from overhead, can save valuable floor space. The flexible belt conveyor can be adapted to carry either packaged or bulk material.

practical to move objects manually or by using gravity.

*Apron Conveyors.* Apron conveyors consist of a number of overlapping steel plates, aprons, or pans, attached at their ends to two strands of chain that run in steel guides. Apron conveyors are used for moving large quantities of bulk materials under severe service conditions and can handle either fine or lumpy materials. The *slat conveyor* is a variation of the apron conveyor. Its load-supporting surface is nonoverlapping

**SCREW CONVEYORS** are arranged in rows to move wood chips from the base of a lumberyard storage bin.

LINK-BELT COMPANY

and consists of wood or metal slats attached at their ends to two sliding chains. The slats may be molded for a particular purpose such as holding ingots. They may be mounted at working height (bench) or flush with the floor to form a moving floor. Slat conveyors are generally used on the level but can also be used at moderate inclines.

*Bucket Conveyors.* There are many kinds of bucket conveyors, which carry materials in buckets mounted on an endless belt or on one or two chains. Buckets are designed in many shapes and sizes for particular materials-handling jobs. Many bucket conveyors are self-loading and self-unloading. Bucket conveyors are used mostly for moving bulk materials.

*Flight Conveyors.* In flight conveyors, flight or scrapers are attached at spaced intervals to one or more endless chains or cables. Flight conveyors are generally used to push bulk materials along a trough. A common flight conveyor has a single-strand chain with wood flights used for moving small quantities of sawdust, wood refuse, bark, corncobs, and similar nonabrasive materials. By providing gates or openings in the trough bottom, flight conveyors can be employed for automatic distribution of fine or friable bulk materials.

*Trolley Conveyors.* Trolley conveyors consist of a series of trolleys that are supported by a single overhead track. They are connected to and propelled by a chain, cable, or other linkage. The loads are usually placed in carriers that are suspended from the trolleys. Trolley conveyors are very flexible and may follow level, inclined, and curved paths. Trolley conveyors are often used to carry material from one building to another and between floors of a building. Since they can travel near the ceiling, they conserve floor space. Specially designed trolley conveyors can be used for storage, sorting, and automatically releasing and picking up loads.

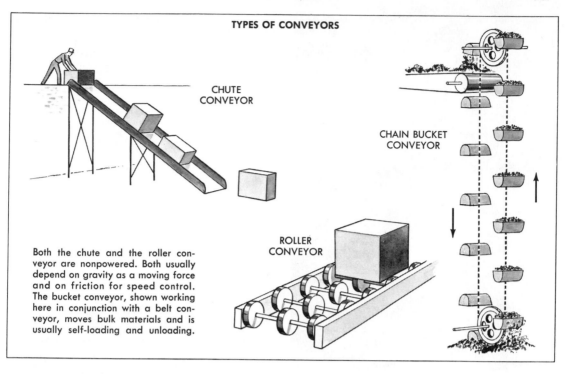

## TYPES OF CONVEYORS

CHUTE CONVEYOR

CHAIN BUCKET CONVEYOR

ROLLER CONVEYOR

Both the chute and the roller conveyor are nonpowered. Both usually depend on gravity as a moving force and on friction for speed control. The bucket conveyor, shown working here in conjunction with a belt conveyor, moves bulk materials and is usually self-loading and unloading.

**Power-and-Free Conveyors.** The power-and-free conveyor is a system in which the load is moved in carriers that are supported by a single rail (monorail). The carriers are connected to and propelled by a trolley conveyor that is directly above the "free" rail. This type of conveyor differs from the trolley conveyor in that the motion of the carriers may be intermittent. Power may be applied to certain sections of the conveyor, with gravity or manual movement in between, or it may be applied along its entire length. This arrangement provides a method of manually or automatically switching the free carriers into and out of adjacent lines. Power-and-free conveyors are used extensively in such mass-production industries as the automobile and appliance industries for feeding assembly lines and for providing a system of automatically controlled selective storage for a number of components.

**Pusher-Bar Conveyors.** Pusher-bar conveyors consist of two endless chains cross-connected at intervals by bars or rotating pushers which propel the load along the stationary bed of the conveyor. Pusher-bar conveyors are used primarily to convey articles of fairly uniform size and with smooth supporting surfaces along inclines ranging to 60°. They may also be used to retard movement along declines. They are commonly used between floors or between levels of other conveyors.

**Sliding-Chain Conveyors.** Sliding-chain conveyors consist of one or more endless chains that slide on tracks. The load is carried on the chain itself. Sliding-chain conveyors are used in the pulp and paper industry for the inspection and sorting of pulp logs and for handling lumber, packages, and crates. Flat-topped attachments on a single strand of chain form an ideal unit to carry bottles, cans, and containers to and from filling machines in the processing industries. A single strand of steel chain equipped with a

pushing device is called a *floor conveyor*. It is commonly used to move dollies that carry automobile bodies for assembly and finishing.

**Tow Conveyors.** Tow conveyors pull floor-supported trucks or carts. They are connected to an endless chain supported by trolleys from an overhead track or running in a track set flush with or in the floor. Trucks are towed along the

A CHAIN CONVEYOR pushes logs under jets of water for cleaning before processing at a newsprint mill.

LINK-BELT COMPANY

LINK-BELT COMPANY

SYSTEM OF BELT CONVEYORS and a 60-foot enclosed bucket conveyor move sand used in making concrete.

and discharged at any point along the path and can be operated in horizontal, inclined, or vertical positions. The flights can be shaped so as to obtain a mixing as well as conveying action. They are usually used for nonabrasive materials.

*Vibrating Conveyors.* Vibrating conveyors are troughs or tubes, flexibly supported and vibrated at a relatively high frequency and small amplitude to convey bulk materials or other objects. The vibratory motion advances the materials along the trough. One type, with a relatively low frequency and a large amplitude of motion, is called an *oscillating conveyor.* It is very satisfactory for handling hot castings.

*Pneumatic Conveyors.* Pneumatic conveyors transport materials in an arrangement of tubes or ducts. Air compressors or blowers are used to create the differences in air pressure in the tubes that cause the materials to move. Sawdust, grain, wood chips, and powdered materials are often carried by this type of conveyor. Objects may be moved in pneumatic conveyors if they are enclosed in carriers. See also PNEUMATIC TUBES.

*Portable Conveyors.* Portable conveyors are any of several types of conveyors that are mounted on mobile supports. They are frequently provided with a means of changing the inclination from the horizontal. Most portable conveyors are apron conveyors, belt conveyors, bucket conveyors, roller conveyors, and flight conveyors. They are commonly used for loading and unloading rail cars and trucks. They are nearly always used to move airplane baggage.

JAMES M. APPLE
*Georgia Institute of Technology*

**Bibliography**

Bhatia, M. V., and Cheremisinoff, Paul N., eds., *Solids and Liquids Conveying Systems* (Technomic 1982).
Colijn, H., *Mechanical Conveyors for Bulk Solids* (Elsevier Pub. Co. 1985).
Conveyor Equipment Manufacturers Association, *Belt Conveyors for Bulk Materials,* 3d ed. (1988).
Conveyor Equipment Manufacturers Association, *Conveyor Terms and Definitions,* 4th ed. (1982).
Conveyor Equipment Manufacturers Association, *Screw Conveyors* (1981).
Stoess, H. A., Jr., *Pneumatic Conveying,* 2d ed. (Wiley 1983).

path prescribed by the track. They may be automatically picked up, switched to auxiliary tracks, and dropped at predetermined locations. They are used extensively in warehouses and manufacturing plants for dispatching and accumulating goods.

*Screw Conveyors.* Screw conveyors consist of a shaft with helically shaped flighting. Bulk materials are moved in open or closed troughs as the screw turns. Screw conveyors may be loaded

TOW CONVEYOR under the floor of an airport cargo terminal moves loaded trucks along a track running from the receiving docks to the airplane runways.

LINK-BELT COMPANY

# CONVICT LABOR

**CONVICT LABOR.** The involvement of prisoners in labor functions has been the policy of almost all nations throughout history. The nature of such inmate labor has been determined by the social philosophy prevalent in a given nation at a given time. Convict, or prison, labor has been instituted as punishment, as a means of rehabilitating offenders into the community, and as a way of offsetting the cost of imprisonment and making a profit for the state.

**Theories of Prison Labor.** Early prison labor programs included many forms of nonproductive, totally punitive labor methods, which only resulted in the greatest possible suffering and discomfort to the prisoner. Some work methods included using the treadmill and carrying a cannonball back and forth in a long hallway. This practice reflected the theory that such punitive labor would deter prisoners from future criminal activity.

In various times, purely punitive prison labor methods or methods involving narrowly limited production were supported by vested interests seeking legal restrictions on the type and amount of inmate employment in order to limit direct competition with private enterprise and "free" labor. Present-day correctional theory, however, emphasizes the development of good work habits and skills that will assist a law violator in leading a socially acceptable life after his release. This theory reflects the view that rehabilitative, productive convict labor is a better deterrent of future crime than punitive labor. Other objectives of contemporary theory include the maintenance or improvement of the physical and mental health of inmates; the reduction of disciplinary problems through active participation in meaningful employment; and the reduction of operating costs of correctional institutions. Thus prison labor in contemporary theory is only one important aspect of a correctional program that includes greater attention to the prisoner's psychological, social, medical, and religious needs as well.

**Types of Employment Programs.** There are six major systems of convict labor in use throughout the world. These include three "private" systems —the lease, contract, and piece-price systems— and three "public" systems—the public-works, public-account, and state-use systems.

The public systems, under which the state controls the custody and employment of the prisoners and the sale of products, are distinguished by restrictions placed on the market. Thus in the public-account system there are no restrictions on the area in which the goods can be sold. In the United States, this system was used in the first quarter of the 19th century and also during the 1880's. It is generally outlawed today in most Western countries. On the other hand, most nations have established the state-use system, under which the market for the sale of goods is limited to the public institutions within the state or country of production. In the United States, some states operating under this system are required to purchase certain prison-made products. The state-use system developed in the United States in the 1880's. The public-works system, the first to develop in the United States, differs from the state-use system in that the "goods" sold are public buildings or roads. Experiments with this system were first made in the 17th and 18th centuries, but its greatest development came after the 1880's and particularly after the invention of the automobile increased the demand for good

roads. Chain gangs represent the use of this system, as do forestry camps that employ prisoners for such projects as fighting fires, controlling insects, and clearing land.

The private systems of inmate labor usually allow private employers the control of employment and the sale of products, while custody and discipline of the prisoners remains in state hands. The contract system, the first of these to develop, appeared first in the United States about 1798. It flourished between 1820 and 1880, when it was fought by a growing labor movement that had to compete with cheap prison labor for jobs. Private employers provided production and market facilities, and the profits were shared by both the employer and the prison. The piece-price and the lease systems are similar to the contract system. In the piece-price system, however, employment was controlled by the state, which sold the product to a contractor who paid per piece for the output, rather than for hours worked. This system first appeared in the United States at the end of the 18th century. It reached its peak in the 1880's and 1890's as a replacement for the much discredited contract system, although in practice the difference was slight. In the 20th century the piece-price system of prison labor has all but disappeared in the United States. Under the lease system, convicts were leased to private employers for work in lumber or other camps. At first often used as a substitute for fines, this system was similar to the indentured-servant system. A somewhat modified version, in which short-term prisoners are employed for a small wage, room and board, sometimes under nearly free conditions, is used in Europe and the United States today.

**Wages and Incentives.** Detailed information regarding wages of employed prisoners is difficult to obtain. According to a survey of prison and parole systems published in 1964, wages in the United States ranged from 5 cents a day to $1.30 a day for all prisoners. The average daily rate for federal prisoners in the 1960's was $1.00 per day. In most countries, prisoners are paid a merely nominal wage, but other incentives are provided to encourage socially acceptable behavior, to keep prisoners occupied, and to ensure the adequate performance of necessary institutional work. In the United States, federal prisoners assigned to industrial functions receive meritorious service awards and have two to five days deducted from their sentence for each month on a given industrial job. The number of state institutions offering reduced sentences for industrial work, however, remains relatively small.

From these few statistics, it is obvious that prisoners are paid wages that are wholly inadequate to sustain their dependents or to sustain themselves for any length of time after release from prison. Moreover, most prison labor does not prepare inmates for a marketable job after release, and a significant number of prisoners in many states are not involved in correctional industries. The partial accomplishments of prison labor, therefore, are the development of work habits, the lessening of idleness, and the maintenance of physical and mental health. Given the current structure of correctional labor programs in the world, it is virtually impossible to develop an employment program that will enable all prisoners to learn productive skills that will enable them to lead normal working lives after they have completed their sentences.

**Current Trends in Prison Labor.** Private prison-labor systems are increasingly being replaced by public ones. Nevertheless, there is increased idleness in prisons both because the work often has little relevance to normal community life and because a greater number of prisoners than necessary are often assigned to a particular job. Therefore, to enable a released prisoner to adjust psychologically and socially to the community —with all the good results to both the prisoner and the community that this involves—contemporary correctional theory more and more stresses the ideal of normal employment for inmates in private enterprise. Thus, looking to the prisoner's adjustment to a noncriminal way of life after his release, increased emphasis is being placed on relating correctional industrial programs to those in free industries where correctional institutions are located. Inmates should not be trained to be textile workers or shoe repair men if these jobs will not be available to them after release.

The American Correctional Association expresses the objectives of contemporary thinking in most advanced nations of the world in its *Manual of Correctional Standards* (1966). The manual states "To hold employable offenders in correctional institutions without the opportunity to engage in productive work is to violate one of the essential objectives of rehabilitation. Without in any way exploiting the labor of involuntary confines for financial gain, or unduly interfering with free enterprise, it is not only possible, but imperative, that all governmental jurisdictions give full cooperation to the establishment of productive work programs with a view to imparting compatible work skills, habits, attitudes, and work discipline."

Current correctional programs of inmate employment therefore reemphasize the value of work, but stress the need for all inmates to work at productive jobs that will enable them to become contributing members of a socioeconomic system. The majority of all prisoners are released to society within two years from the day of commitment. Adequately preparing such prisoners to make useful contributions to society requires that they be trained in prison for a socially acceptable job.

The emphasis is thus on the development of needed vocational skills for life in the "free" community through an increasingly diversified correctional program, rather than on punishment by "hard labor," which contributes little to the vocational rehabilitation of prisoners for life after their release.

Many contemporary techniques in prison employment programs include extensive pre-release training programs in community schools and industrial plants. Increased use is being made of the work-furlough system, under which convicts are released for a short time for the purpose of seeking jobs with future employers. Increased resources for prisoner rehabilitation have enabled highly skilled staffs to develop sound programs in inmate employment that will best restore an imprisoned law violator to a useful life after release from prison.

WILLIAM NARDINI
*Commissioner of Corrections, Delaware*

**Further Reading:** Gildemeister, Glen A., *Prison Labor and Convict Competition with Free Workers in Industrializing America, 1840–1890*, ed. by H. Hyman and S. Bruchey (Garland Pub. 1987); Hawkins, Gordon, *The Prison: Policy and Practice* (Univ. of Chicago Press 1976); Ward, Robert D., and Rogers, William W., *Convicts, Coal and the Banner Mine Tragedy* (Univ. of Alaska Press 1987).

**CONVOCATION,** kon-və-kā'shən, the name given to the legislative assembly of the Church of England in each of its provinces. Though ordinarily referring to the larger Convocation of Canterbury, the term applies as well to a similar assembly of clergy in the northern and smaller province of York. The ancient conciliar activity and authority in the church was exerted through councils or synods, and gradually each province under its archbishop came to have its regional synod or convocation. In Anglo-Saxon England, long before the tribal states had achieved political unity in a single nation, English ecclesiastical unity found expression in the national church synods of the 7th and 8th centuries. These ancient ecclesiastical councils were the remote ancestors of the modern convocations of Canterbury and York, which by the 13th century had begun to assume the form and function they now possess.

Convocations parallel the life of English Parliaments, usually meeting two or three times a year during parliamentary sessions. When a new Parliament is elected, a new Convocation assembles; when Parliament is dissolved, Convocation is dissolved with it. By the laws governing the powers of the crown in relation to the English Church, Convocation may enact and promulgate canons or laws for the church only with royal assent. The chief business of Convocation, however, is not often canonical enactment, but the framing of regulations or declarations expressing the views of the Church of England on matters of doctrine, discipline, and worship, and on subjects of moral, social, and political concern to Christian churchmen. Such formal "acts" of Convocation, constituting synodical decisions made by representatives of the whole body of the clergy and ratified and confirmed by the archbishops of each province, are clothed with solemn spiritual authority.

The Convocation of Canterbury is formed of two houses, an upper house composed of all diocesan bishops within the province, and a lower house made up of the deans of cathedral churches, two archdeacons from each diocese, and a number of proctors, clergy elected from each diocese in proportion to the number of clergymen therein. Somewhat under half the total number of clergy in the lower house, therefore, sit ex officia. There is no representation of the laity in Convocation. Members of the laity are represented, with bishops and lower clergy, in another and much larger church body known as the National Assembly of the Church of England (Church Assembly), a modern synod created by the Enabling Act of 1919. Both provinces meet in this single assembly, which deals largely with the administrative, financial, educational, and promotional activities of the church. See also GREAT BRITAIN AND NORTHERN IRELAND—13. *Religion.*

The name "convocation" is also applied to some regional or diocesan assemblies in the sister churches of the Church of England that form the Anglican Communion. The assembly of the members of a university—sometimes defined as those with a master's degree—is called a convocation.

POWEL MILLS DAWLEY
*The General Theological Seminary, New York*

**Further Reading:** Holloway, R., and others, *The Anglican Tradition* (Morehouse-Barlow 1984); Sumner, D. E., *The Episcopal Church's History: 1945–1985* (Morehouse-Barlow 1987); Sykes, S., and Booty, J., eds., *The Study of Anglicanism* (Fortress 1988); Whitelock, D., and Brett, M., *Council and Synods with Other Documents Relating to the English Church*, 2 vols. (Oxford 1981).

**CONVOLVULACEAE.** See Morning Glory.

**CONVOLVULUS.** See Bindweed.

**CONVOY.** See Submarine—section 5; World War I—section 13; World War II—sections 9 and 12.

**CONVULSION,** kən-vul'shən, an episode in which there is an alteration in the state of consciousness associated with muscular movements or disturbances in feeling or behavior. Such episodes rarely last more than a few minutes and are extremely variable in their outward manifestations. They occur when brain cells become too active and disorganized in their electrical properties.

Convulsive seizures occur in a variety of conditions and diseases involving the nervous system and other organs of the body. In a large number of individuals with recurrent seizures the exact nature of the underlying disease process is not known. In others, seizures have been associated with tumors, blood vessel abnormalities, disturbances in brain metabolism, brain scars, and other conditions. Traditionally, the term "epilepsy" (from the Greek *epilēpsia,* meaning "to be seized") has been used to describe the illness suffered by those with recurrent seizures. As a descriptive term for the type of symptoms that occur it is most suitable. Unfortunately, however, it has come to be used as a term describing a disease entity with many undesirable implications in intellectual capacity which are mostly unrelated to the seizures but which are a result of the underlying disease.

**Types.** The clinical manifestations that occur during a seizure are not necessarily dependent on the nature of the underlying disease process. Instead, their characteristics are determined by the site of origin of the abnormal brain discharge and the rapidity and extent to which the discharge spreads throughout the rest of the brain. Although it may be difficult to classify the attack in an occasional case, most seizures can be classified into one of the following five major categories: grand mal, petit mal, psychomotor, focal, and minor motor.

*Grand Mal.* Attacks of grand mal are one of the most common types of seizures. Although they may begin at any age, they usually start before 25. In an attack there is a loss of consciousness, tongue biting, and urinary and fecal incontinence. There is also a temporary cessation of breathing, causing cyanosis (bluish tinge of the skin) followed by irregular stertorous (snoring-like) breathing. Gradually the patient relaxes, his breathing becomes normal, and he regains consciousness. Afterwards he may be confused, have headaches or gastric disturbances, or fall asleep. The attack may last from less than a minute to 10 minutes, but the post-seizure phase may last for hours. Grand mal seizures may occur as often as several times a day or as infrequently as once every few years. Sometimes, they occur so close together that the patient does not regain consciousness between attacks, a condition known as *status epilepticus.*

*Petit Mal.* Petit mal is not a minor form of grand mal, but a different kind of seizure. Petit mal attacks usually occur in childhood and rarely persist beyond the age of 20. They are characterized by a sudden brief lapse of consciousness, with or without minor motor movements of the eyes, head, or extremities. There may be a drooping of the head, staggering, and, on occasion, urinary incontinence. The attack lasts from 5 to 30 seconds, after which the patient is alert and able to continue his normal activities. Despite their high frequency, attacks rarely occur so close together that they impair consciousness for long periods of time.

*Psychomotor.* In psychomotor attacks there is an alteration in behavior, perception, or mood. Usually, there is a clouding of the mind, total amnesia, and automatic movements during an attack. The movements may be simple and brief, such as clapping the hands or smacking the lips, but they may also take the form of more complex behavior, such as getting out of a chair and walking across a room. Aggressive behavior occasionally occurs, but rarely are violent acts committed. Each episode usually lasts 2 to 3 minutes, and there may be a short period of confusion afterward.

*Focal.* In a focal seizure, the manifestations can be directly correlated to the part of the brain involved. When the attack is limited to one segment or function of the cerebrum, the term focal itself is applied. If the attack starts in one segment but spreads, it is known as a *Jacksonian seizure* (after the neurologist who first described and recognized the importance of these attacks). Typically in this type of seizure, the convulsive movements begin in a finger and spread to the rest of the hand, the arm, the face, and the leg. If these movements spread to the opposite side of the body, the person loses consciousness and a grand mal attack may occur.

*Minor Motor.* Seizures of this type are of brief duration, occur frequently, and lack post-seizure abnormalities. Three distinct types are recognized: (1) *akinetic seizures,* in which there is a sudden loss of tone in all the muscles of the back so that the patient falls and injures his face or head; (2) *myclonic jerks,* sudden involuntary contractions of the muscles of the trunk or extremities; and (3) *massive spasms,* strong contractions of the most of the body's muscles, causing the patient to assume a "jacknife" position, with his arms flung upward, his head forward and down, and his lower limbs pulled up on the trunk. This position may last no longer than 5 to 10 seconds but may be repeated half a dozen times in a few minutes and innumerable times throughout the day.

**Diagnosis and Treatment.** Many diagnostic tests are helpful in determining the exact type of seizure as well as whether there is a definable disease process responsible for the attacks. The most important of these is the electroencephalogram, which records the brain's electrical activities in the form of waves. It has been found that persons with grand mal, petit mal, and psychomotor seizures have characteristic brain waves. Various X-ray techniques are also helpful, including pneumography (injection of air into the brain spaces) and arteriography (injection of dye into the arteries).

The treatment of convulsive seizures consists of eliminating the causative factors, if they are known, and administering anticonvulsant drugs. These drugs suppress the abnormal electrical activity of the brain regardless of the underlying cause. With appropriate treatment, most individuals suffering convulsions are able to lead normal and productive lives.

Melvin Yahr, M.D., *Columbia University College of Physicians and Surgeons*

**CONWAY, Henry Seymour** (1721–1795), British soldier and political leader. He was the second son of Francis, 1st Lord Conway. As aide-de-camp to the Duke of Cumberland, Conway served in the War of the Austrian Succession and at the Battle of Culloden (1746), when the last attempt of the Stuarts to recover the throne was defeated. In 1772 he was commissioned a general and, in 1793, field marshal.

Family influence enabled Conway to pursue concurrently a career in politics, and after the end of the Seven Years' War his connection with the Whig dukes of Devonshire and Grafton and his cousin Horace Walpole drew him into the opposition. For voting against the government on general warrants (see WILKES, JOHN) he lost his regiment and his place as groom of the bedchamber.

Conway's reputation as a Whig martyr was the basis of his political career, but it was chiefly to his patron Cumberland that he owed his appointment in 1765 as secretary of state for the southern department of Europe and leader of the House of Commons. He was efficient in the routine of business, but he proved incapable of managing the House. After the fall of the Marquess of Rockingham's government in 1776, Conway remained in office under William Pitt the Elder (1766–1768) in the hope of reuniting two main sections of the Whig party.

Despite his successful motion for repeal of the Stamp Act in 1766, Conway spoke with an uncertain voice on the American problems of the 1770's. But once the war of American Independence broke out, he condemned it as "cruel, unnecessary and unnatural." In February 1782 he moved the resolution in the House of Commons against continuing the war that brought down Lord North's government. In Rockingham's successor administration, Conway was appointed commander in chief and sat again in the cabinet. Following a violent verbal attack on the younger Pitt in December 1783, however, he lost his seat for Bury St. Edmunds in the election of 1784. He was without political power from then until his death, near Henley, on July 9, 1795.

D. B. HORN, *University of Edinburgh*

**CONWAY, Moncure** (1832–1907), American clergyman and author. He was born near Falmouth, Va., on March 17, 1832. He became a Methodist minister, but turned to Unitarianism and in 1853 entered Harvard Divinity School. In 1854–1855 he was pastor of a Unitarian church in Washington, D. C., from which he was dismissed for his opposition to slavery, and from 1856 to 1861 he was minister of a Congregational church in Cincinnati. He was twice pastor (1864–1884 and 1892–1897) at South Place Chapel, London. In 1860–1861, Conway edited *The Dial*, and in 1862, in Boston, he edited the *Commonwealth*, an antislavery paper. Perhaps his most scholarly work is his *Life of Thomas Paine* (1892). He died in Paris on Nov. 15, 1907.

**CONWAY, Thomas** (1735–?1800), Irish soldier of fortune and American Revolutionary War general, who is best known for his part in the "Conway Cabal," an intrigue to remove George Washington as American commander and put Gen. Horatio Gates in his place.

Conway was born in Kerry, Ireland, on Feb. 27, 1735. At the age of 6 he was sent to be educated in France, where at 14 he joined the Irish Brigade of the French Army. When the American Revolution began, Silas Deane recruited him for the Continental Army. In 1777, Congress made him a brigadier general. Sailing that year, he fought at Brandywine and Germantown.

Washington had scant respect for Conway and opposed his subsequent promotions to major general and inspector general as unjust to more experienced officers. In 1777, Conway became involved in a cabal to make Gates, the victorious commander at Saratoga, commander in chief. The intrigue, in which Conway was supposed to have played a major role but in fact played a minor one, miscarried. Lafayette criticized him severely, and Conway's friends in Congress abandoned him. In 1778 he resigned from the army, and after a duel with Gen. John Cadwalader, in which he was seriously wounded, he apologized to Washington.

In 1779, Conway rejoined the French Army. He was commissioned a major general in 1784, was appointed governor of Pondicherry and all French possessions in India in 1787, and was created a commander of the Order of St. Louis in the same year. He married the daughter of Marshal Baron de Copley and, after the outbreak of the French Revolution, became commander of the Royalist forces in the south of France. Driven into exile by the successful revolutionists, he died in obscurity in England, probably in 1800.

GIOVANNI COSTIGAN
*University of Washington*

**CONWAY,** a city located in central Arkansas, the seat of Faulkner county, 25 miles (40 km) northwest of Little Rock. Conway's manufactures include steel bus bodies, refrigerator cabinets, pianos, furniture, and shoes. Lake Conway, a fishing and hunting area, is 2 miles (3 km) to the south. The city is the home of Hendrix College, the University of Central Arkansas, and Central Baptist College.

Settled in 1871 and named for James S. Conway, the state's first governor, Conway became a city in 1875. Government is by mayor and council. Population: 43,167.

**CONWAY,** a town in eastern New Hampshire, in Carroll county, at the confluence of the Saco and Swift rivers, 62 miles (99 km) north of Concord. The town, situated at the southeastern tip of White Mountain National Forest, is a year-round resort. It includes the unincorporated communities of Conway, Kearsarge, Redstone, and North Conway, famous for its skiing facilities. Conway was founded in 1765. Government is by council and manager. Population: 8,604.

**CONWAY,** a town in northeastern South Carolina, the seat of Horry county, 91 miles (146 km) northeast of Charleston. It is situated on the Waccamaw River and is a shipping point for tobacco, melons, and truck crops. It has light industries, including lumber mills and woodworking plants. A branch college of the University of South Carolina is there. Government is by mayor and council. Population: 11,788.

**CONWAY,** a municipal borough in Gwynedd, Wales, 15 miles (24 km) northeast of Bangor, on the left bank of the estuary of the Conway River. Its castle and town wall, which were built by Edward I during the early 13th century to resist invasion from the east, are well preserved and attract many tourists. Much of the castle is still intact, including the state hall, which is 130 feet (39 meters) long and 32 feet (10 meters) wide. The wall, fortified with battlements and 21 towers, encircles both castle and town.

Conway, once important as a seaport, is a market center for the vale of Conway, with fisheries and an oyster-breeding ground. A suspension road-bridge, built in 1826, spans the river. Robert Stephenson built the wrought-iron tubular railway bridge in 1848. A second traffic bridge was completed in 1959. The borough is also called Aberconway. Population: 13,462 (1981 census).

**CONWAY CABAL.** See CONWAY, THOMAS.

**CONWAY OF ALLINGTON, 1st Baron** (1856–1937), English art historian and mountaineer, who was a pioneer in the exploration of the Andes and the Karakorum ranges. He was born William Martin Conway at Rochester, Kent, on April 12, 1856. Educated at Trinity College, Cambridge, he was professor of art at University College, Liverpool (1885–1888) and Slade professor of fine arts at Cambridge (1901–1904).

In 1892, Conway traveled in the Himalaya and surveyed about 2,000 square miles (5,000 square km) in the Karakorum. He explored the interior of Spitsbergen in 1896–1897, and the Bolivian Andes and Tierra del Fuego in 1898. Among the mountains he climbed are Pioneer Peak in the Karakorum, and, in the Andes, the southern summit of Illimani, Sorata, and Aconcagua, the highest peak in the Western Hemisphere. Conway was the author of many books on art and mountain climbing. He was created baron in 1931. He died in London on April 19, 1937.

**CONWELL, Russell Herman** (1843–1925), American Baptist clergyman and educator, who founded Temple University. He was born in Worthington, Mass., on Feb. 15, 1843, of a poor abolitionist family whose home was a way station of the Underground Railroad. After a few weeks of law studies at Yale, Conwell became a captain in the Union Army during the Civil War. He later graduated from Albany (N.Y.) Law School and was admitted to the bar. He then worked as a journalist, lecturer, and lawyer.

In 1881, Conwell was ordained as a Baptist clergyman and preached at the First Baptist Church in Lexington, Mass. Between 1882 and 1925 he served at the Grace Baptist Church in Philadelphia. He created a thriving congregation and developed it into one of the most important institutional churches in the United States. He founded Temple University out of a night school for young clergymen in 1884 and started Samaritan Hospital in 1891. He wrote numerous books stressing the power of "right thinking."

A gifted and popular lecturer, Conwell was best known for "Acres of Diamonds" (his repertory included nearly 30 formal orations). He gave that talk more than 6,000 times in 55 years, for fees totaling almost $8 million, most of which he used to underwrite his benevolent enterprises. "Acres of Diamonds" reflected the generally materialistic viewpoint prevalent at the time that wealth can be found in everyone's backyard, and stressed that one should attempt to get rich in order to do more good with wealth. Conwell died in Philadelphia on Dec. 6, 1925.

JAMES H. SMYLIE*
*Union Theological Seminary, Richmond, Va.*

**CONY.** See CONEY.

**COOCH BEHAR,** kōōch bē-här', former princely state of India, is now a district in the northeast part of West Bengal state. The 1,289-square-mile (3,339-sq-km) region is one of low plains washed by the tributaries of the Tista and Brahmaputra rivers. The topography causes frequent flooding and shifting of river courses. Communications are mainly by river. Rice and jute are grown in the rich alluvial soil, and sugarcane and tobacco are the chief crops on higher ground.

The towns are small, and none of their populations exceeds 50,000. The largest are Dinhata, Matabhanga, Haldibari, Mekliganj, Tufanganj, and Cooch Behar, the capital of the district. The city of Cooch Behar lies on the east bank of the Torsa River near the ruins of the ancient city of Kamatapur and has beautiful parks, an artificial lake, and Lansdowne Hall, constructed in 1892, which became a local landmark. The majority of the district's inhabitants are Hindu and speak Bengali, and over a third are refugees from East Pakistan.

The princely Koch dynasty was founded about 1510 by Biswa Simha. Cooch Behar, or Koch Bihar, was divided into two rival principalities in the 16th century, and in the 17th century much of the area was annexed by the Mughul (Mogul) emperors. The district came under British control in 1772 and was governed as a princely state until the termination of British rule in India. In 1950 the raja gave up his autonomy, and Cooch Behar was incorporated into West Bengal. Population: 1,771,643 (1981 census).

BRIJEN K. GUPTA, *Brooklyn College*

**COOK, Arthur James** (1885–1931), British labor leader, who through his gifted oratory brought the poor working conditions of the miners to public attention. He was born in Wookey, Somerset, England, on Nov. 22, 1885. In 1905 he joined the labor movement and became active in the South Wales Miners' Federation. As a member of the Federation's unofficial reform committee, Cook was associated with its report, *The Miners' Next Step* (1912). In 1924 he was elected secretary of the Miners' Federation of Great Britain. He was a leader of the general strike of 1926. Although Cook opposed the continuation of the strike by the miners after the Trades Union Congress withdrew its support, he worked with the striking miners until they had to concede defeat. Cook died in London on Nov. 2, 1931.

RAMON KNAUERHASE, *University of Connecticut*

**COOK, Ebenezer** (c.1672–1732), American poet, who was the author of *The Sot-Weed Factor; or, a Voyage to Maryland* (1708). His name is also spelled *Cooke*. The facts of his life are unclear, but he was probably born in England. *The Sot-Weed Factor* represents him as an Englishman visiting Maryland, but he was probably a colonist and seems to have lived in Maryland until his death in 1732.

*The Sot-Weed Factor* is a wittily scurrilous satire attacking the crudities of colonial life. Several later poetic works, published under Cook's name at Annapolis, lack the wit and vigor of his first book. These include two elegies; *Sotweed Redivivus* (1730), a serious treatise on tobacco production; and *The Maryland Muse* (1731), a burlesque on Bacon's rebellion. Cook is the hero of John Barth's *The Sot-Weed Factor* (1960).

Frederick A. Cook

BROWN BROTHERS

**COOK, Frederick Albert** (1865–1940), American physician and explorer, who started a lasting controversy by claiming to have discovered the North Pole on April 21, 1908, nearly a year before Robert E. Peary reached it (April 6, 1909).

Cook was born in Hortonville, N. Y., on June 10, 1865, and graduated from University Medical College, New York City. He was a surgeon on Peary's North Greenland expedition in 1891–1892 and was honored by the King of the Belgians for his medical services on an Antarctic expedition in 1897–1899. His book, *To the Top of the Continent*, in which he claimed the first ascent of Mt. McKinley in 1906, was favorably reviewed in London.

When he cabled from the Shetland Islands on Sept. 1, 1909, en route from Greenland to Denmark, that he had discovered the pole, his statement was accepted and publicized. The Danish royal family honored him, and the University of Copenhagen gave him an honorary doctorate. But within five days, Peary, also returning from the Arctic, cabled that he was the true discoverer of the pole. He observed that two Eskimo who had accompanied Cook said that he "went no distance north and not out of sight of land."

At first Peary's charge was attributed to jealousy and was not widely accepted. Cook was welcomed in New York on Oct. 15, 1909, as the pole's discoverer and received the keys and freedom of the city. On the same day, however, newspapers reported an affidavit by Edward Barrille, Cook's only companion on the Mt. McKinley climb, asserting that they never had been on top of the mountain. In February 1918, Donald B. MacMillan, an American Arctic explorer, reported that Cook's claimed "North Pole" photographs had been specifically attributed by his two Eskimo companions to locations that were hundreds of miles short of the pole. But Cook still had his defenders.

In 1923, Cook was charged with exaggerating claims for Texas oil wells that he was promoting. He was sentenced to 14 years in prison for mail fraud in 1925. He was released within five years and was on parole for five years. In May 1940, President Franklin D. Roosevelt granted him a presidential pardon. Cook died at New Rochelle, N. Y., on Aug. 5, 1940.

TERRIS MOORE
*Author of "Mt. McKinley: The Pioneer Climbs"*

**COOK, George Cram** (1873–1924), American author, who founded the theater group called the Provincetown Players. He was born in Davenport, Iowa, on Oct. 7, 1873. After graduating from Harvard in 1893 and studying in Europe, he taught at the University of Iowa and Stanford University, and was for a time literary editor of the Chicago *Evening Post*.

Cook and his third wife, the author Susan Glaspell, spent several summers in Provincetown, Mass. In 1915 the Cooks with Eugene O'Neill and Ida Rank, founded the Provincetown Players, which produced several of O'Neill's plays. Cook directed the group for several years. With his wife, he wrote the plays *Suppressed Desires* (1914) and *Tickless Time* (1918).

Cook's other publications include the novel *The Chasm* (1911) and *Greek Coins: Poems* (1925). In 1921, Cook settled in Greece. He died there on Jan. 14, 1924.

**COOK, James** (1728–1779), British naval officer, who more than any other navigator added to man's knowledge of the southern Pacific Ocean and the coasts of North America. He was born on Oct. 27, 1728 at Marton-in-Cleveland near Whitby, Yorkshire, England. After a limited education he was apprenticed to a storekeeper at Staithes. In July 1746 he took up an apprenticeship with Walker Brothers, shipowners at Whitby. Cook joined the British Navy as an able-bodied seaman in June 1755 and rose rapidly in rank during the Seven Years' War with France. As a navigator for the British fleet he surveyed the St. Lawrence River and played an important role in the capture of Quebec.

After the fall of Quebec in 1759, Cook became master of the flagship *Northumberland* and spent the summers from 1763 to 1767 surveying the coast of Newfoundland. His observations of a solar eclipse in 1766 were the basis of an accurate calculation of the longitude of Newfoundland and attracted the attention of the Royal Society.

**First Voyage.** In 1768 Cook was made a first lieutenant and appointed commander of an expedition to Tahiti, on behalf of the Royal Society, to observe the transit of Venus between the earth and the sun. Secret orders from the British Admiralty directed him to seek new lands in the southern Pacific Ocean between New Zealand and Chile. He sailed from Plymouth in the *Endeavour* on Aug. 26, 1768. Among the 94 persons on board were 11 members of a scientific party, including the botanist Joseph Banks.

The *Endeavour* rounded Cape Horn to Tahiti, where observations of the passage of Venus across the solar disk were made in June 1769. Cook then sailed south to about latitude 40° S and westward to New Zealand, where he went ashore at Poverty Bay in October 1769. For the next six months he surveyed the coasts of New Zealand. On April 20, 1770, Cook reached the unexplored east coast of Australia, which he named New South Wales. He anchored in Botany Bay, where Banks studied the unusual plant life. Sailing northward along the coast, the *Endeavour* passed inside the Great Barrier Reef and nearly met disaster when dashed onto the coral. After makeshift repairs, Cook moved along the east coast of Queensland. He claimed possession of the east coast of Australia in the name of King George III on Aug. 23, 1770. Discovering a passage between Australia and New Guinea, Cook reached Batavia,

BROWN BROTHERS

JAMES COOK made three voyages to explore the Pacific. During the third, he was killed.

**CAPTAIN COOK'S THREE GREAT VOYAGES**

— FIRST 1768-1771 · –·– SECOND 1772-1775 · ---- THIRD 1776-1779

in Java, in October. The *Endeavour* was repaired with the assistance of the Dutch, but malaria and dysentery, contracted during the 3-month stay, killed 30 men before the ship returned to England in July 1771.

**Second Voyage.** Almost immediately, Cook began to prepare for a second expedition to explore the southern oceans as near to the South Pole as possible in search of a continental landmass. On July 13, 1772, he sailed as captain of the *Resolution* in company with the *Adventure* under Tobias Furneaux. The ships made for the Cape of Good Hope and traversed the southern Indian Ocean, crossing the Antarctic Circle in January 1773. After a rendezvous in Queen Charlotte Sound, New Zealand, in May 1773, the expedition moved eastward and then north to Tahiti for relief from cold and replenishment of supplies. Turning again to New Zealand, Cook lost contact with the *Adventure* at the end of October and missed it at the intended rendezvous in Queen Charlotte Sound. Furneaux subsequently sailed the *Adventure* to England, becoming the first to circumnavigate the world from west to east.

Cook continued his search for a southern continent. He sailed eastward from New Zealand, again crossed the Antarctic Circle, and called at Easter Island, Tahiti, and Tonga on his way to the New Hebrides. In October 1774, he was back in Queen Charlotte Sound, having discovered New Caledonia and Norfolk Island. He again sailed the South Pacific at high latitudes, and finished his voyage by skirting the southern limits of the Atlantic to the Cape of Good Hope. He returned to England in July 1775.

**Final Voyage.** In July 1776 he set out in the *Resolution* on his third and final Pacific voyage. A second ship, the *Discovery*, commanded by Charles Clerke, joined the *Resolution* at the Cape of Good Hope. By December 1777 the ships had revisited New Zealand, Tonga, and Tahiti. In January 1778, Cook discovered and named the Sandwich (Hawaiian) Islands. From Hawaii he sailed to the coast of North America, which he followed through Bering Strait and into the Arctic. Late in 1778 the ships returned to the Hawaiian Islands, where Cook was slain by natives at Kealakekua Bay on Feb. 14, 1779, during a

dispute over the theft of a boat from the *Discovery*. His officers recovered his mutilated remains and buried them at sea. After another unsuccessful attempt to find a northwest passage north of Bering Strait, the *Resolution* and *Discovery* returned to England, first under the command of Clerke and then when he died of tuberculosis, under James Gore. Cook's journal of the third voyage was completed by one of his officers, James King.

Minor indictments against Cook's character and unfounded charges that he was incompetent in dealing with natives have failed to diminish his standing as the greatest British explorer. He was the first navigator to apply scientific method to exploration. On his first voyage he charted the coast of New Zealand and discovered the east coast of Australia, thus laying the foundations for settlement of two great British colonies at a time when the American colonies were in revolt. His second voyage revised the cartography of the mythical southern continent, shrinking it to within the Antarctic Circle. In two broad sweeps of the Pacific Ocean he made important island discoveries and reported at length on the native peoples. Of great significance to the sciences of geography and navigation was his successful use of the chronometer designed by John Harrison for rapid determination of longitude. By persistent use of antiscorbutic foods, such as sauerkraut, he demonstrated their value in the prevention of scurvy on long voyages. In recognition of his work in nautical medicine the Royal Society awarded him its highest distinction, the Copley gold medal. On his last expedition Cook discovered the strategically important Hawaiian Islands, charted parts of the North American Pacific coast, and showed that a northwest passage to the Atlantic did not exist south of the Arctic. Cook's character and contributions to scientific exploration are aptly summarized in the names of his ships: *Endeavour*, *Resolution*, *Adventure*, and *Discovery*.

HOWARD J. CRITCHFIELD
*Western Washington State College*

**Further Reading:** Withey, Lynne, *Voyages of Discovery*, ed. by Harvey Ginsberg (Morrow 1987); Zimmermann, Heinrich, *The Third Voyage of Captain Cook* (Ye Galleon Press 1988).

**COOK, Sir Joseph** (1860–1947), Australian prime minister. He was born in Silverdale, Staffordshire, England, in December 1860 and emigrated to Australia in 1885. In 1891 Cook was elected to the Legislative Assembly of New South Wales, serving until 1901, when he was sent to the Australian House of Representatives as a Liberal. He was Australian minister for defense in 1909–1910. Cook served as prime minister and minister of home affairs in 1913–1914. He subsequently served as navy minister (1917–1920) and treasurer of the commonwealth (1920–1921). Cook was knighted in 1918 and the following year represented Australia at the Versailles Peace Conference. From 1921 until his retirement in 1927 he was high commissioner for Australia in London. Cook died in Sydney on July 30, 1947.

**COOK, Stanley Arthur** (1873–1949), English Semitic scholar. Cook was born at King's Lynn, Norfolk, on April 12, 1873. He was educated at Gonville and Caius College, Cambridge University, where he was a lecturer in Hebrew and comparative religion from 1904 to 1932 and regius professor of Hebrew from 1932 to 1938.

From 1896 to 1903, Cook was a member of the editorial staff of the *Encyclopaedia Biblica*, and from 1902 to 1932 was editor of the Palestine Exploration Fund. He was on the staff of the *Encyclopædia Britannica*, as editorial adviser on Old Testament and Semitic subjects, and was editor of Biblical subjects for the *Cambridge Ancient History*. Among his books on religion are: *The Religion of Ancient Palestine in the Light of Archaeology* (1930); *The Old Testament: Reinterpretation* (1936); and *An Introduction to the Bible* (1946). He died at Cambridge on Sept. 26, 1949.

**COOK, Thomas** (1808–1892), English travel agent, who originated the idea of a travel agency. Cook was born at Melbourne, Derbyshire, England, on Nov. 22, 1808. Leaving school at the age of 10, he worked at gardening and wood turning and at the age of 17 joined the Baptist Church, becoming an ardent temperance advocate. While working for Baptist publishers in Loughborough, Leicestershire, it occurred to him to put the popularity of the new railways to the uses of temperance. In 1841, Cook arranged his first excursion—from Loughborough to Leicester—for a temperance group.

Cook planned other temperance tours in the British Isles, and they proved very popular, particularly with the less well-to-do. As his travel agency developed, it became independent of the temperance cause and served all kinds of travelers. In 1865 he established a London office and also visited the United States. His son, John Mason Cook (1834–1899), specialized in promotion of the firm's American interests and did much to establish Thomas Cook & Son as a worldwide agency. Thomas Cook died at Walton-on-Thames, Surrey, on July 18, 1892.

JOHN PUDNEY
*Author of "The Thomas Cook Story"*

**COOK, Mount,** the highest mountain in New Zealand. It is part of the Southern Alps in the South Island. It rises to 12,349 feet (3,764 meters) and is known by the Maoris as *Aorangi* ("cloud piercer"). The peak was named for the explorer Capt. James Cook.

The mountain is composed of blue-gray sandstone. The summit ridge has three separate peaks, known as High, Middle, and Low. Hooker Glacier on the west slope and Tasman Glacier on the east extend southward toward glacial Lake Pukaki. The alpine peak and its glaciers are the principal features of Mount Cook National Park. The first complete ascent of Mount Cook was made on Dec. 24, 1894, by three New Zealanders, T. C. Fyfe, J. M. Clarke, and George Graham, who approached by way of Hooker Glacier and the steep northern side.

HOWARD J. CRITCHFIELD
*Western Washington State College*

**COOK INLET,** in southern Alaska, is an arm of the Gulf of Alaska. It lies between the mainland and the western side of Kenai Peninsula. Irregular in shape, the inlet is about 150 miles (240 km) long; its maximum width is about 80 miles (128 km). Sudden storms, fogs, and tidal rips caused by high tides along the broken coastlines occasionally make navigation difficult. The important port of Anchorage is near the head of the inlet. The mountain scenery along the coasts is spectacular. On Augustine Island, at the mouth of the inlet, is Mt. St. Augustine, an active volcano, 3,970 feet (1206 meters) high. The inlet was named for James Cook, British navigator, who explored it in 1778 in a search for a passage to the Arctic Ocean.

**COOK ISLANDS,** a group of 15 islands in the South Pacific Ocean, about 1,600 miles (2,600 km) northeast of New Zealand. Their total land area is about 93 square miles (240 sq km). The islands form two distinct groups, about 200 miles (320 km) apart. The seven northern islands are small, sparsely populated atolls. The eight lower, or southern, islands include the volcanic islands of Rarotonga, Mangaia, and Aitukaki, and several atolls. Rarotonga is the largest of the entire group and has nearly half of the total population of 20,519. Avarua, situated on the northern coast of Rarotonga, is the seat of government and the chief port.

The islands have a tropical climate and are occasionally visited by hurricanes. The average

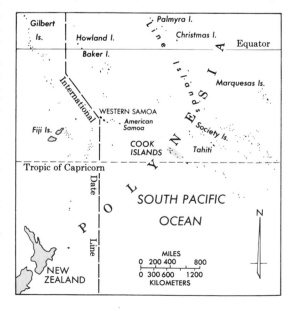

annual temperature on Rarotonga is 75° F and annual rainfall is about 85 inches (215 cm). The northern islands are generally hotter and have frequent water shortages.

The people of the Cook Islands are Polynesians and are closely related to the Maoris of New Zealand. They are citizens of New Zealand, to which large numbers have migrated in recent years without, however, alleviating the population pressure in the islands. Most of the Cook Islanders belong to the Cook Islands Christian Church, an adjunct of the London Missionary Society. Education in the islands is free and compulsory for children between the ages of 6 and 14.

Cook Islands's economy was traditionally agricultural. The principal crops are papayas, coconuts, citrus fruits, bananas, pineapples, and starchy roots. Fish is a dietary staple, and mother-of-pearl shell is collected from the northern atolls. The service industries, including tourism and offshore banking, now comprise the largest sector.

Capt. James Cook discovered several of the islands between 1773 and 1777. They became a British protectorate in 1888 and on June 11, 1901, they were proclaimed part of New Zealand. The Cook Islands Constitution Act of 1965 provided for an elected assembly with complete legislative autonomy in internal affairs. The legislative assembly has 25 members, including a speaker and a cabinet composed of a premier and 8 other members.

HOWARD J. CRITCHFIELD
*Western Washington State College*

**COOK STRAIT,** a channel in New Zealand, is the passage that separates North Island and South Island. Its greatest width is 90 miles (145 km) but it narrows to 16 miles (26 km). Its waters have very strong currents. The strait was named after Capt. James Cook, who discovered it on his first voyage to the Pacific Ocean in 1769. The Maori name is Raukawa.

**COOKBOOKS** are guides to the preparation of food, offering tested recipes that cover the details essential to the creation of many dishes. Cookbooks available today cover almost every type of cuisine, from basic foods to *haute cuisine,* and are among the most popular items published.

**Early History.** Cookbooks go back to antiquity. They were used mainly by professional cooks until the end of the 18th century. The earliest traceable cookbook is a 9th century manuscript of the ancient *De re coquinaria,* believed to have had some connection with Marcus Gavius Apicius, a Roman gourmet of the 1st century A. D. The first printed cookbook, *De honesta voluptate* (about 1475), by the humanist Bartolomeo de' Sacchi (Il Platina), indicates the esteem in which cookery was held in Renaissance Italy.

*Le Cuisinier français* (1651), by Pierre François La Varenne, revealed the refinement French cooking had achieved. However, though the French were plainly better cooks than the English, they published comparatively few cookbooks compared with the large English output.

Cookbooks were written by men until the 18th century, when women began to write them, at least in England. Recipes continued to be sketchy until the development of the classic cuisine of the 19th century. This cuisine's elaborate procedures, which could be followed only by trained chefs, plus the increasing demand among the middle class for housekeeper-cooks (who lacked professional training as cooks), created a sharp division between cookbooks for professional use and those for use in the home. Eliza Acton, recognizing that home cooks needed explicit instructions, supplied such instructions in *Modern Cookery for Private Families* (1845). Probably the first basic cookbook, it gives exact quantities in each recipe, and specifies types of cooking dishes and exact cooking times. In 1859, Isabella Beeton published her *Book of Household Management,* devoted mainly to cookery.

**Cookbooks in America.** Except for Amelia Simmons' *American Cookery* (1796), the first cookbook by an American author, American cookbooks were reprints of English works until the late 1820's. Between 1828 and 1854, Eliza Leslie compiled the numerous volumes that established her as the leading American cookbook writer of her day. Her books contained the best of American regional cookery and such French recipes as she considered adaptable to American kitchens. From the outset, cookbook writing in America was dominated by women, including such 19th century leaders as Sarah Hale of *Godey's Lady's Book* and Lydia Child, Catherine Beecher, and Mrs. Horace Mann, who used cookbooks also to express their views on morals, temperance, and the need for pure food laws.

In the 1880's, cookbooks by cooking teachers brought better recipes to American cooks and, at last, began to print the exact quantities that Mrs. Acton's recipes had given English women 40 years earlier. The Boston Cooking School was probably the birthplace of this improvement; Maria Parloa, Mary J. Lincoln, and Fannie Farmer, principals of the school at different times, all sponsored this reform in their cookbooks. Standard measuring devices were the ultimate result. Mrs. Lincoln, in *The Boston Cookbook* (1883), was one of the first to tabulate ingredients at the head of a recipe. Fannie Farmer published *The Boston Cooking School Cook Book* in 1896. Now called *The Fannie Farmer Cook Book,* it is the longest-lived cookbook in America. Next in longevity is *The Settlement Cook Book,* first published in 1901.

American cookbooks proliferated in the 20th century. Many kitchens now have several cookbooks, but a basic one is essential. In addition to the *Fannie Farmer Cook Book* and *The Settlement Cook Book,* both continuously revised through the years and still among the best, excellent works include *The Joy of Cooking* (1931), by Irma Rombauer; *The American Woman's Cook Book* (1938), edited by Ruth Berolzheimer; and *Picture Cook Book* (1950), published by General Mills, Inc.

Cooks in search of inspiration for family and company dinners will find it offered in many books. Among these are *The New York Times Cook Book* (1961), edited by Craig Claiborne; *Thoughts for Food,* a volume of menus (1938); and Mildred Knopf's *The Perfect Hostess Cook Book* (1950).

**Specialized Cookbooks.** All national cuisines seem to please Americans today, but the favorites appear to be French, Italian, and Chinese, with gourmet cooks drawing heavily from the first two. *Mastering the Art of French Cooking* (1961) by Simone Beck, Louisette Bertholle, and Julia Child, quickly became a classic in its field. *Larousse Gastronomique* (1938) is more an encyclopedia than a cookbook, but it is filled with gourmet ideas and gastronomical information. Italian cooking is covered expertly in *The Talisman Cook Book* (1950) by Ada Boni and *The Art of Italian Cooking* (1948) by Maria Lo Pinto. Chinese cookery, the ultimate in instant cooking, is clearly explained in a longtime favorite, *How to Cook and Eat in Chinese* (1945) by Pu-Weï Chao. An excellent work is *Mrs. Ma's Chinese Cookbook* (1961) by Nancy Chih Ma.

The cookout is typically American. *Better Homes and Gardens Barbecue Book* (1956) covers the subject well. Hazel Meyer's *The Complete Book of Home Freezing* (1953) is one of many books offering recipes and information on another American institution.

Cooking in small quantities receives special attention in *Cooking for One* (2d ed., 1964) by Elinor Parker and in Janet M. Hill's *Cooking for Two* (5th ed., 1951), first published in 1909, often revised and still a favorite. Special culinary arts are covered in such books as *The Art of Cooking with Herbs and Spices* (1950) by Mila Miloradovich, *The Art of Fine Baking* (1961) by Paula Peck, and *Art of Cheese Cookery* (1959) by Nika Standen.

ESTHER B. ARESTY
*Author of "The Delectable Past"*

**COOKE, Alistair** (1908–      ), British-American journalist and broadcaster. Alfred Alistair Cooke was born in Manchester, England, on Nov. 20, 1908. After studying at Cambridge, Yale, and Harvard universities, he began his career in 1934 as film critic for the British Broadcasting Company. Two years later he became London correspondent for the National Broadcasting Company. In 1938 he went to the United States as correspondent for the BBC and the London *Times.* He became an American citizen in 1941.

After World War II, Cooke served as United Nations reporter and, after 1948, as chief American correspondent for the Manchester *Guardian.* His weekly radio program *Letter from America,* which he began to broadcast in 1947 for the BBC, is still a highly popular feature in England. From 1952 to 1961 he served as host of the Ford Foundation's television program *Omnibus.* Cooke wrote several books, including *A Generation on Trial* (1950), *One Man's America* (1952), and *Around the World in 50 Years* (1966).

**COOKE, Elisha** (1637–1715), American colonial leader. Born in Boston on Sept. 16, 1637, he was graduated from Harvard in 1657 and entered the practice of medicine. In 1681 he was elected to the Massachusetts General Court, where he became a leader in the unsuccessful fight to prevent the crown from annulling the Massachusetts Bay Company charter and establishing a new government under Joseph Dudley and later Sir Edmund Andros. He participated in the overthrow of Andros in 1689 and then sailed for England to represent the colony during deliberations about the new charter. On his return Cooke was elected to the Governor's Council, and he was reelected every year until 1715. He was, however, refused his seat by Sir William Phips in 1693; and when Joseph Dudley became governor in 1702, Cooke was not only denied his seat on the council, but his appointments as a justice of the superior and probate courts were revoked. Cooke died in Boston on Oct. 31, 1715.

GEORGE D. LANGDON, JR., *Vassar College*

**COOKE, Jay** (1821–1905), American investment banker, who sold government bonds during the Civil War to thousands of small investors who had never before owned a security. He was born in Sandusky, Ohio, on Aug. 10, 1821, to parents of New England stock. At the age of 14 he left school to clerk in a Sandusky store and then he worked in St. Louis for a time. In 1837 he went to Philadelphia, where he soon joined the firm of E. W. Clark and Co., a private bank specializing in domestic exchange and securities. When the panic of 1857 forced the firm to reorganize he left it, and in 1861 he formed his own banking company in Philadelphia.

Cooke was a religious man and a firm abolitionist. His zeal for the cause as well as his business acumen caused him to offer his aid to Salmon Portland Chase, a friend of the Cooke family and former governor of Ohio, who had become secretary of the treasury under President Lincoln. Chase had found the government credit so low that war bonds were difficult to sell. Instead of depending on banks to buy the bonds, Cooke sent out an army of agents to all parts of the country, used advertising in newspapers, and appealed to the patriotism of the citizens. Hundreds of millions of dollars were obtained in this way. Cooke also aided Secretary Chase in getting the National Bank Act passed in 1863 and in organizing the new national banks that would purchase still more government bonds as security for their notes. His services during the war made his firm one of the best known abroad as well as at home, although some newspapers criticized his large profits.

Jay Cooke and Co. continued to be the largest dealer in government securities after the war. In 1866 a branch was opened in New York. In 1870 a house was opened in London, with Hugh McCulloch, a former secretary of the treasury, as a partner. All went well until the firm became overextended in railroad loans and securities, especially those of the Northern Pacific. The financial strains of 1873 forced the firm into bankruptcy, and it closed that year, never to reopen. Cooke never returned to banking, but he gradually built up a new fortune in mining. He died in Ogontz, Pa., on Feb. 18, 1905.

MARGARET G. MYERS, *Vassar College*

**COOKE, Terence James** (1921–1983), cardinal archbishop of the Roman Catholic archdiocese of New York and military vicar of the United States. He was born in New York City on May 21, 1921. He attended St. Joseph's Seminary and was ordained a priest on Dec. 1, 1945. After serving two years as a parish priest at St. Athanasius' Church, the Bronx, N.Y., he studied at the Catholic University of America and received his master's degree in social work in 1949.

On his return to New York he became assistant director of the Catholic Youth Organization and also taught at Fordham University. In 1954 he was named procurator of St. Joseph's Seminary and in 1957 became secretary to Francis Cardinal Spellman. Appointed chancellor of the archdiocese in 1958, he was named a papal chamberlain by Pope Pius XII in the same year.

Msgr. Cooke was consecrated auxiliary bishop of New York and named vicar general of the archdiocese in 1965. He succeeded Cardinal Spellman as archbishop of New York in 1968, and was named a cardinal by Pope John Paul VI in 1969. He died in New York City on Oct. 6, 1983.

# COOKING

## CONTENTS

**COOKING**, in its strictest sense, is the preparation of food by the action of heat. In its broadest and more modern sense, cooking is the total preparation of food for the table by cleaning, paring, peeling, subjecting to heat or cold, and arranging for service.

Cooking began with primitive man. It is surmised that he tasted the meat of an animal burned in a forest fire and found it palatable. When he learned to make fire by striking a spark from stones, he began to cook food, subjecting his meat to the heat from the fire he created.

As civilization progressed, man learned to grow and cultivate food as well as prepare it better for eating. Cave paintings in France and Spain show how food was cooked in the Stone Age. Carvings and hieroglyphics in many ancient countries, as well as other archaeological artifacts, give evidence of the growth of the art of cookery.

Through the ages, cooking has been strongly influenced by geography and religion. Climate and area determine not only what foods grow best, but also how food is best cooked for safe and palatable eating. In addition, spiritual values attributed to foods and religious food taboos have prescribed methods of slaughter, cleansing, preserving, and cooking.

When man-made and man-controlled fire was moved indoors, the simple earth and stone fireplace that contained it was brought into use for cooking. Gradually, iron utensils were made to facilitate fireplace cooking. The introduction of building bricks improved fireplace design and permitted the addition of a built-in oven. During these ages food was preserved by smoking and by cooling in a stream or spring.

Probably nothing contributed so much to a rapid advance in cooking techniques as the development of a stove to contain the heat from wood or coal. Then came gas and electric ranges and refrigerators, and the continuing development of utensils to use with them. Portable cooking appliances in increasing numbers added to cooking efficiency, and the electronic oven holds promise for the future.

The food industry has kept pace with the trend of the times by producing more and more pre-prepared, frozen, dried, baked, or canned foods of high quality to aid in the cooking of today's meals. New cooking techniques, methods, and improved ingredients tend to make cooking easier and often quicker.

In the following sections are described the best methods for consistently good results in the selection, preparation, and cooking of principal types of basic and familiar foods.

## TYPES OF COOKING METHODS

**BAKING** is the dry heat process of cooking food in an oven, and is the term used for cooking breads, pies, cakes, and pastries.

BOILING

STEWING

STEAMING

**WET HEAT** cooking includes *boiling* foods in a liquid in a saucepan; *stewing* foods in a small amount of liquid in a covered container; and *steaming* foods by setting them in a pan, usually perforated, over a boiling liquid in the lower section of the pan, or by cooking them in a pressure cooker.

FRYING

DEEP FAT FRYING

**FRYING** includes two methods of cooking: *shallow frying* foods in a frying pan, using a little fat or oil, and *deep frying*, in which foods such as potatoes are placed in a meshed frying basket and then immersed in deep fat. The basket is not used for some foods, such as doughnuts and croquettes; as these rise to the surface they are dropped directly into the deep fat.

**BROILING**, also called *grilling*, is a method of cooking in which the food is directly exposed to the heat, either in a broiler or over a charcoal grill.

**ROASTING** includes cooking meat, fish, and fowl in an oven. It is also the term used for cooking these foods on a spit, the oldest method of cooking known and one that has become increasingly popular recently.

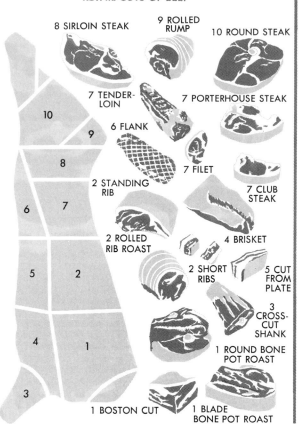

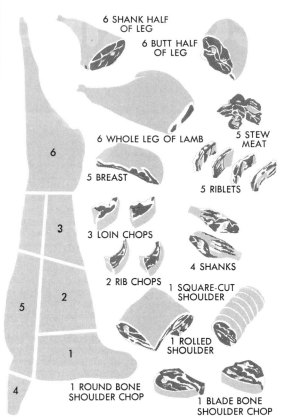

ARMOUR AND COMPANY

## 1. Meats and Furred Game

For the average person, the meat course is the most important part of the meal. Family tradition and regional or nationality meal patterns may dictate the kind of meat dish for certain meals. The selection of the cut to use and its correct preparation, however, determine the eating quality and the enjoyment of the finished product.

**Selection of Meat Cuts.** A number of factors enter into the decision of which meat cut to buy. Setting aside such influences as seasonal or week-end specials in the market, some quality and usability criteria should be applied to all meat purchases.

**Beef.** Of the six official grades for beef, only three are customarily available to the home cook: prime, choice, and good. These three grades carry an inspection mark and a quality stamp. The U. S. inspection mark, which is enclosed in a circle, indicates that the meat was a wholesome product at the time of the inspection. The U. S. grade mark, which is enclosed in a shield, is indicative of the quality of the beef.

*Prime quality* beef comes from young, well-fed cattle. Lean portions are bright red, firm, fine-textured, and liberally marbled with fat. *Choice quality* beef, with good red muscle, has less fat than prime, and is often preferred for that reason. *Good quality* beef has a higher ratio of lean to fat than prime or choice. It is, therefore, not so juicy as the higher grades, although it is relatively tender and has good flavor.

Tender beef cuts such as tenderloin, sirloin, porterhouse, T-bone, rib and top-quality rib eye,

sirloin tip, and rump are best for cooking by dry heat, as in broiling or roasting. Moist heat cooking, such as braising, simmering, or stewing, is best for less tender cuts such as chuck, round, plate, brisket, shank, and most rump. Cuts of beef that have been uniformly tenderized by the controlled application of a natural food enzyme also may be cooked by dry heat.

**Veal.** Veal is the flesh of calves less than a year old. The lean meat is light grayish pink, very finely grained, and fairly firm. The small amount of fat present is firm and white. All cuts of veal are juiciest when cooked in moist heat. Large cuts, such as shoulder, loin, sirloin, rump, and leg, may be roasted and should be larded to provide the fat needed for succulence. Chops, steaks, and cutlets may be panfried or braised.

**Lamb.** Lamb is the meat of young sheep. The lean meat is pink to deep red; the fat is clear, white, and brittle. All lamb cuts are tender enough to cook in dry heat. Shoulder cuts, riblets, and shanks, however, are more flavorful if braised or stewed.

**Pork.** The meat of young hogs has a leaner look than formerly because of new methods of breeding and feeding, and because of closer trimming of fat before marketing. Firm white fat covers the exterior surfaces of pork, and leaner portions are firm and finely grained with a marbling of fat. Large cuts of fresh pork— shoulder, loin, sirloin, tenderloin, and ribs—may be roasted; chops, steaks, and tenderloin may be panfried or braised.

Cured and smoked pork products include ham, smoked shoulder, butt or picnic, loin roast and chops, and both regular and Canadian bacon.

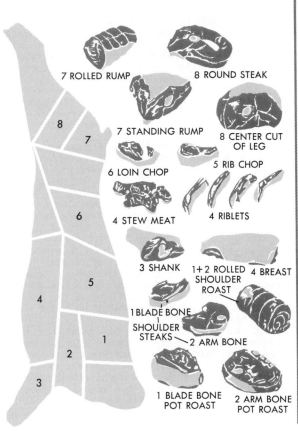

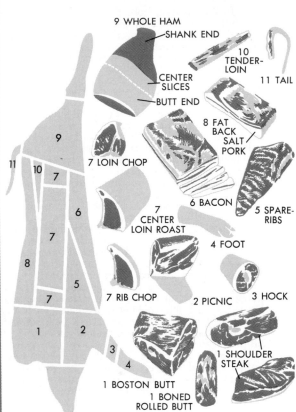

ARMOUR AND COMPANY

How these meats have been processed determines the cooking method to use and the amount of cooking needed.

The cook-before-eating ham or shoulder (also labeled smoked, uncooked, or regular) must be baked thoroughly. The ready-to-eat ham can be served without further cooking, although additional cooking adds to its flavor and texture. The ham with a label indicating that it is fully cooked can be served without further attention. The Virginia or country-style ham is heavily cured and well aged and requires soaking, simmering, and baking before serving. Canned ham in this style, however, is boneless, fully cooked, and ready to slice and serve. Scotch ham is cured or pickled, but not smoked, and requires thorough cooking before eating.

Bacon, or breakfast bacon as it is sometimes called, has clear white fat streaked with lean. It may be broiled, baked, panbroiled, or panfried. Canadian-style bacon, made from boneless pork loin, has a small amount of fat interspersed with the lean. It may be roasted whole; when sliced, it may be broiled, panbroiled, or panfried.

Sausages come in a variety of sizes, shapes, and types. Fresh sausage, in links, casing, bulk, or patties, needs thorough cooking before eating. It is sold as fresh pork sausage, bratwurst, bockwurst, or fresh thuringer-style sausage. Uncooked smoked sausages must be well cooked before eating. Some of these are smoked country-style sausage, mettwurst, kielbasa, and Polish and Italian pork sausage.

Cooked smoked sausages are ready for eating, although they may be simmered or gently panfried and served hot. Among these sausages are frankfurters, bologna, Vienna-style sausage, cocktail-style franks, knackwurst, and German-type mortadella. Cooked sausages, such as liver sausage (liverwurst) and blood sausage, and dry sausages, such as summer sausage, cervelat, salamis, pepperoni, and chorizos, are fully cooked and ready to be served.

**Variety Meats.** Variety meats include liver, heart, kidney, sweetbreads, tongue, brains, and tripe. Beef, veal, calf, pork, and lamb livers are available whole or sliced. If whole, they may be roasted; if sliced, they are best panbroiled or panfried. Veal or calf liver may be broiled; beef liver sometimes is best when braised.

Hearts from the four meat animals vary in size and tenderness. All are composed of strong muscle and require moist heat cooking to tenderize them.

Beef and veal kidneys have many lobes; pork and lamb kidneys are smooth and oval-shaped. If veal and lamb kidneys are cut with the veal or lamb chop, they can be cooked with the chop. Beef and pork kidneys, prepared separately, are best when braised or stewed; lamb and veal kidneys, when broiled, panbroiled, or braised.

Sweetbreads are glands from young cattle or sheep. Spongy in texture and enclosed in membrane, the finest and most delicate are the thymus gland from the neck or throat. The stomach sweetbreads, from the pancreas, are not as good in eating quality. Before sweetbreads can be cooked, they must be blanched to loosen the tubules and membranes and carefully cleaned; then they may be broiled, panfried, braised, or cooked in a sauce.

Beef, veal, pork, and lamb tongues are available fresh, smoked, corned, or pickled. Tongue can be made tender by simmering in liquid for several hours. After the rough covering is removed, the tongue may be served plain or reheated in a sauce. Ready-to-eat canned tongue, sliced or whole, may be served cold or hot.

Brains are tender, soft, and delicate in flavor. Though veal brains are the most popular, those from beef, pork, and lamb have good eating quality. Brains must be blanched before they are fried, scrambled, or cooked in a sauce.

Tripe comes from the first and second stomachs of beef cattle. It is sold fresh, salt pickled, or vinegar pickled. Though the "fresh" type is precooked, it needs further cooking in liquid. Pickled tripe is ready for use. The tripe may be fried, broiled, or sauced.

**Meat Cookery Methods.** Meat is cooked to develop its distinctive taste, to enhance its flavor by browning, seasoning, or combining it with other foods, and to make it safer to eat and more digestible. When it is correctly cooked it is pleasantly moist or juicy, tender, and attractive to look at. A meat thermometer, which indicates temperatures for different stages of doneness, helps the cook prepare a roast properly. With this aid, overcooking that makes meat dry and less tender and flavorful can be avoided, and undercooking for the desired rareness can be properly managed.

*Roasting.* For roasting, meat may be seasoned with salt and pepper. It should be placed fat side up on a rack in an open shallow roasting pan, with the meat thermometer inserted in the center of the large muscle, but not touching the bone. Water should not be added, nor should the pan be covered or the meat basted. A slow oven should be used—300° to 325°F for beef, veal, and lamb, and 325° to 350°F for pork. For roasting frozen meats the same method should be followed. However, the thermometer should not be inserted in the roast until the center of the meat is thawed, when the meat is half done. Hard-frozen roasts need one third to one half as much time to roast as fresh meat. Prethawed roasts are cooked like fresh roasts.

*Broiling.* For broiling, meat should be placed in a broiler pan or grill 3 to 5 inches from the heat, according to the thickness of the cut, and broiled until one side is browned. Then the browned side should be seasoned with salt and pepper and the meat turned and broiled to the desired doneness. A small gash cut in the meat next to the bone or in the center of the piece helps to determine doneness.

*Panbroiling and Panfrying.* For panbroiling, meat should be placed in a heavy skillet, with no fat or water added; it should be cooked slowly, uncovered, and turned occasionally. The fat should be poured off as it accumulates.

For panfrying, meat should first be browned on both sides in a small amount of fat in a skillet. After being seasoned with salt and pepper, the meat should be cooked uncovered over moderate heat and turned occasionally, to the preferred state of doneness.

*Braising and Stewing.* In braising, meat is first browned on all sides in a small amount of fat in a heavy skillet or kettle. The meat is seasoned with salt and pepper, and savory vegetables if desired; a small amount of liquid is added, the kettle is covered tightly, and the meat cooked over low heat until it is fork tender.

In stewing, meat should be browned on all sides in a little fat or in its own fat in a large kettle. After seasoning, enough liquid is added to cover the meat, which is then simmered in a covered kettle until it is fork tender. Vegetables may be added to the stew meat just long enough before serving for them to cook.

Altitudes exceeding 2,500 to 3,000 feet above sea level affect cooking time in braising and stewing. At 5,000 feet, cooking time must be increased by about one fourth over the timing at sea level.

**Furred Game Cooking Methods.** Big game should be hung for two to three weeks for tenderizing before any attempt is made to cook it. If the meat is stored in a freezer after aging, it should be thawed before cooking.

Cuts of deer, bear, elk, antelope, and moose are much like those of beef. Because of the varied eating habits of these large animals, there is considerable variation in the tenderness of the cuts. Some are suitable for broiling or roasting; some may require several days of soaking in a savory marinade for further tenderizing before cooking in dry heat. Many cuts lend themselves best to braising or stewing. Removal of much of the exterior fat before cooking decreases the gamy flavor.

Steaks and chops from big game can be cooked to the state of doneness suiting personal taste. Their flavor is best, however, and they are more apt to be tender if cooked to a medium rare state rather than raw-rare. Overcooking the meat may easily result in dryness and toughness as well as in loss of flavor. In general, the meat of game should be cooked at the same rate as beef.

Since the less tender muscles of big game have been well developed, they need to be cooked carefully in liquid. Marinating before cooking helps to break down connective tissue and tenderize the meat. In braising or stewing, allowing the liquid to boil will toughen long muscle fibers and result in tough, stringy meat despite careful pre-preparation of the meat. The liquid should be kept just below boiling during the entire cooking period. Should the meat become stringy, it can be made more palatable by being carved into diagonal slices.

Small game, such as rabbit skinned and dressed, may be cooked fresh, or it may be frozen and then cooked. Young animals are suitably tender for broiling, panbroiling, or panfrying. Older ones are good for stew or fricassee.

Squirrels, unless very young, need to be parboiled before they are panfried, or soaked in cold salted water for about an hour before they are broiled. All squirrels, however, can be stewed or braised.

Some cooks insist that the meat of opossum should be frozen to make it right for cooking. The thawed meat then is parboiled for an hour in two changes of seasoned water and roasted until brown and tender. The meat of raccoon is handled in much the same way. For roasting, the addition of a flavorful stuffing is often suggested.

Porcupine meat is fatter than that of most of the other small game; when broiled over coals or roasted, the cooked meat is fairly juicy. This meat should be parboiled for about half an hour before broiling or roasting to make it more tender and flavorful.

## 2. Poultry and Feathered Game

Cooked poultry should be golden-brown, moist and juicy, and tender enough to cut with a fork. Whether the finished product turns out that way depends on selection of the right type of bird, its proper preparation for cooking, and use of the correct cooking temperature and time.

**Selection of Poultry.** Today's marketing trend is toward year-round availability of almost every kind of domestic poultry. Fresh or chilled chicken and turkey are supplemented by always-available frozen birds. In addition, frozen turkey parts, duckling, young goose, and Rock Cornish game hens are in plentiful supply. In regional markets frozen domestic pheasants and guinea hens are often available during holiday seasons. Flavor preference, cooking method used, menu needs in relation to number of persons to be fed, and budget limitations determine the type, style, and kind of poultry to buy.

**Guides to Cooking Use.** The appearance of poultry is an indication of age, quality, and tenderness. The best birds for cooking are broad-breasted with short plump legs and pale-yellow, cream-colored, clean, waxy skin evenly spread over the carcass, with streaks of fat showing underneath. There should be few or no pinfeathers, and no cuts, tears, broken bones, or bruises or other discolorations. With cuts and tears the meat will dry out during storage and cooking, lessening the eating quality. In frozen poultry, freezer burn, caused by poor packaging and storage conditions, shows up as small pockmarks on the skin or as dark blistered and dried areas.

U. S. Department of Agriculture (USDA) grades for poultry also indicate quality. Grade A poultry is full-fleshed, meaty, with a good layer of fat. The skin is smooth, unbroken, not discolored; the bones are neither crooked nor broken. Grade B poultry may lack slightly in meatiness and fat, have minor tears or discolorations, and be slightly misshapen. Grade C poultry is likely to be poorly fleshed on breast and leg and have a prominent breastbone; long bones may be broken or misshapen; a scattering of pinfeathers and any number of cuts, tears, and discolorations may be seen.

**Suitability for Use.** The tender, succulent quality of poultry meat lends itself to use in a number of standard cooking methods. For broiling, panfrying, or roasting, a young bird should be chosen, such as a chicken labeled broiler, fryer, roaster, capon, or caponette; a Rock Cornish game hen; a duckling labeled broiler, fryer, or roaster; a goose labeled young or junior; a guinea hen labeled young. For baking in liquid, braising, or stewing the best choice is a mature chicken labeled stewing hen, fowl, stewing chicken, or bro-hen; a mature yearling or old turkey; a mature duck, goose, or guinea hen. If desired, the younger birds may also be baked, braised, or stewed, yielding a more tender and juicy product.

For salads or creamed dishes calling for diced meat, chicken or turkey parts (breasts, turkey roll, or capon) will give a good yield of meat and save cooking time and fuel. Ready-to-cook (dressed and cleaned) poultry costs about one fourth more per pound than a live bird, but the work of preparing it is done. A ready-to-cook turkey loses 25% in boning and 25% in cooking. Thus a ready-to-cook turkey yields half its weight in cooked meat. Therefore, a cooked boned turkey product at twice the price per pound would be an equal meat value. The accompanying table will help the home cook determine the yield to expect in preparing a ready-to-cook bird.

### READY-TO-COOK POULTRY

| Method | Weight Range | Amount per Serving |
|---|---|---|
| **Chicken** | | |
| Broil, Fry | 1½– 3 lbs | ¼–½ bird |
| Roast | 2½– 8 lbs | ½–¾ lb |
| Braise | 2– 5½ lbs | ½–¾ lb |
| Stew | 2– 6 lbs | ¼–¾ lb |
| **Turkey** | | |
| Roast | 6–28 lbs | ½–¾ lb |
| **Duckling** | | |
| Roast | 3– 5 lbs | ¾– 1 lb |
| **Goose** | | |
| Roast | 7–10 lbs | ¾– 1 lb |

**Poultry Cookery Methods.** Dry heat cooking is suitable for young, tender poultry; moist heat methods are best for mature birds. Whatever the method used, slow, even cooking at relatively low heat is advisable for tender, juicy poultry meat.

*Roasting.* Chicken, turkey, duck, and goose may be roasted with or without stuffing. If no stuffing is used, the cavity may be seasoned with a few sprigs of tarragon in chicken, tarragon and whole onions in turkey, whole onions and orange slices in duck, and apple slices with pitted dried prunes in goose. An unstuffed bird roasts in one-third less time than stuffed ones.

If bread stuffing is used, it may be prepared ahead of time and chilled. The bird should never be stuffed, however, until just before roasting time. Since stuffing expands during cooking, it should be piled lightly in the neck and body cavities, but not packed in. Extra stuffing in a covered casserole may be baked as the turkey roasts.

A 1-pound loaf of bread makes about 2 quarts of half-inch-cube bread crumbs. This amount is enough to stuff a 4- to 6-pound bird. A 6- to 12-pound bird requires 2 to 3 quarts of crumbs; a 12- to 16-pound bird 3 to 4 quarts; a 16- to 24-pound bird 4 to 6 quarts. The label directions on packaged dry stuffing suggest the amounts needed per bird.

Turkey may be roasted breast-side down in a V-shaped rack in a shallow pan. It will be juicy but not so attractively browned to serve as turkey roasted breast-side up. A flat rack in a shallow pan will hold all birds well for roasting breast-side up. (In the absence of this kind of rack, a turkey can be supported by several large peeled potatoes.) Roasting of all poultry should be continuous at 325°F until the bird is done. Quality and safety are sacrificed when poultry is partly roasted and cooled, and then reheated to finish cooking.

Roasting is complete when the drumstick can be moved up and down and the thigh meat yields to gentle pressure. A meat thermometer inserted in the meaty thigh muscle, not touching the bone, should register 190°F. Stuffing temperature should be 165°F.

The country-bake method of roasting produces a bird with a tender browned skin and juicy meat. In this method dry-heat and moist-heat cooking are combined by first browning the bird in a 400° F oven, then reducing the heat to 325° F and completing the cooking in a covered pan. Cooking time is shorter this way.

The foil-bake method requires moist heat for the cooking of the bird, followed by dry heat for browning. The foil wrap, though completely covering the bird, must not be sealed airtight or the meat will stew instead of bake in the moisture provided from its own juices. The oven temperature should be 450°F, and the foil should be turned back for 20 minutes at the end of the

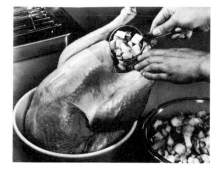

The turkey is first set in a large mixing bowl (*top left*), neck down, and the stuffing is inserted by the cupful. To be sure it is stuffed lightly, shake the legs slightly.

Truss the turkey (*top right*) by pushing the tail under the band of skin into the body cavity. The legs are also pushed under the skin, one at a time, which eliminates the need for skewers or for sewing.

The turkey is then placed on a rack in a shallow baking pan (*bottom left*) and a thermometer is inserted into the thickest part of the inside thigh muscle, avoiding bone.

When the turkey is about half to two thirds roasted, the band of skin is cut and a loose tent of foil is placed on the bird. It is done when the thermometer reads 185° F (85° C).

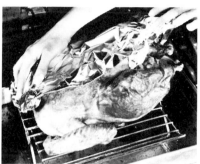

POULTRY AND EGG NATIONAL BOARD

roasting period to allow for browning. Total cooking time is shortened by this method.

Frozen stuffed turkeys are specially prepared under rapid, controlled cold processes for safety. They should be cooked without thawing, according to specific label directions. Small Rock Cornish hens, guinea hens, and domestic pheasant may be roasted from 40 to 60 minutes in a 375°F oven, with or without stuffing. When duckling is prepared for roasting, the free fat should be pulled away from the bird, since there will be enough remaining fat for juiciness. Goose should be treated similarly, and the skin pricked to allow fat drainage.

The pink color that occasionally appears in cooked poultry is harmless. Gases in a heated oven, or in the hot air of an outdoor fire, may react chemically with substances in poultry meat, especially the meat of young, lean birds, giving it a pink tinge. Sometimes there are areas of red color in and around the bones, due to a breakdown of bone marrow blood cells during the freezing and thawing process.

The accompanying table indicates approximate roasting times for the several kinds of poultry.

### POULTRY ROASTING TIME

| Type | Purchased Weight | Approximate Time |
|------|------------------|------------------|
| Chicken | 3–4 lbs | 2–2½ hours |
| Capon | 5–8 lbs | 3¼–5 hours |
| Caponette | 3½–5½ lbs | 2–3 hours |
| Hen Turkey | 8–15 lbs | 3¾–5½ hours |
| Tom Turkey | 16–24 lbs | 5¾–6¾ hours |
| Duckling | 3–6 lbs | 2–3 hours |
| Young Goose | 5–8 lbs | 2¾–3¼ hours |

**Broiling.** For broiling, young turkeys should be split into two parts and set on a rack in the broiling pan; a rack is not needed for chickens. The pan should be placed in the lowest possible position, and the broiler heat set at 350°F for slow cooking. Poultry broiled over live coals is juiciest when cooked 10 inches above the source of heat.

**Panfrying.** One-half inch of fat in a skillet is enough for panfrying chicken or duckling. The pieces should be coated with seasoned flour, then browned and cooked over medium heat, with occasional turning for even cooking.

**Braising and Stewing.** Cooking of all types of poultry in moist heat should be done below the boiling point, at a steady simmer. Braising and stewing may be done by browning the poultry pieces slowly in a little fat, adding some liquid, and cooking until tender in a covered utensil in a 325°F oven.

**Cooking Feathered Game.** Wild birds, a mealtime necessity in pioneer days, are a gourmet's delight today. Roasting, broiling, sautéing, and stewing are the cooking methods used for feathered game, with temperatures and cooking times adjusted to the character of the meat and the size of the bird. Most wild birds need little seasoning to give them flavor. Each has a characteristic taste that should not be disguised.

**Wild Duck, Goose, and Turkey.** To help remove the muddy or fishy taste characteristic of some wild birds, the drawn bird should be rubbed well inside and out with lemon. Then it should be soaked for several hours in water with a little lemon juice or vinegar. Roasting with sliced onion in the cavity will remove some of the fishy taste.

Large wild duck, such as mallard, will serve two persons; small birds, such as teal, one. The duck may be cooked rare, medium, or well done, according to preference, with the oven temperature between 400° and 425°F. Cooking time varies from 15 minutes for rare to 45 minutes for well done. These birds are rarely stuffed. Salt pork strips may be used to moisten the breast, and basting is advised. Rotisserie grilling should be over medium hot coals. Older ducks are braised with vegetables.

Slow roasting at 350°F for 2 to 3 hours is needed to tenderize a wild goose. The bird's cavity may be stuffed with onions or quartered apples.

Rotisserie roasting is the best method to use for wild turkey. The bird should be buttered well inside and out and roasted about 3 hours, or until well done. Whole birds may be simmered in seasoned water, cooking to tenderness in 2 to 3 hours.

**Pheasant, Grouse, and Partridge.** One pheasant will serve two to four persons. Strips of fat on the breast, and butter in the cavity help keep the meat moist, as does frequent basting. The roasting temperature is 350°F; roasting time is about 45 minutes. Pheasant may be sautéed until brown, covered and simmered 15 or 20 minutes, then crisped with the cover off.

Grouse and partridge may be roasted at 400° to 425°F for 15 minutes, basting with butter. For broiling, the birds should be split, cooked with medium heat, and basted often with butter. Each bird serves one person.

**Small Birds.** Doves, snipe, quail, woodcock, and plover may be grilled over coals, and should be basted often. Doves should be roasted at 375°F about 30 minutes; other small birds should be roasted at 425°F for about 15 minutes or broiled flat for 10 minutes. Frequent basting with butter is necessary. Each bird serves one.

## 3. Fish and Shellfish

The value of fish as a food has been known for thousands of years. Edible fish exist all over the world, in fresh and salt waters, and there are many regional favorites.

Today's markets are abundantly supplied with fish in many forms. Fresh, frozen, smoked, salted, canned, cooked, and ready-to-cook fish are available not only in the specialized fish market but also in supermarkets. Which to use depends on personal taste, the way the food is to be cooked, budget limitations, and both seasonal and regional availability.

**Selection of Fresh Fish.** Fresh whole fish are sold just as they come from the water. They must be scaled and eviscerated before cooking. If not baked whole, they may be split or cut into portions, as desired. Drawn fish are sold with entrails removed, but the home cook will have to remove scales, head, tail, and fins. Dressed fish are sold with all these tasks completed.

Fish steaks are cross-section slices of the larger sizes of dressed fish. Fillets are the sides of the fish cut away from the backbone. Butterfly fillets are the two sides or fillets held together by uncut flesh and skin of the underside of the fish. Fish sticks are lengthwise or crosswise cuts from fillets or steaks, uniform in size. All these cuts and slices are ready for cooking.

The flesh of fresh fish should be firm and elastic and should not easily separate from any bones that may be present. The odor should be fresh and mild, not markedly "fishy"; the eyes should be bright, clear, and transparent, not cloudy; the gills should be red and free from slime; and the skin should be shiny and unfaded in color.

Variation in fat content is one criterion for selecting the method of cooking fish. Fat fish—those with dark flesh areas—such as shad, salmon, or Spanish mackerel, are best for baking, broiling, and planking. Their high fat content helps to keep them moist, and little or no fat need be added in cooking. Lean fish such as cod, scrod, and haddock, are best for boiling or steaming because the flesh is firm and flakes nicely but does not fall apart easily during cooking. Both fat and lean fish can be panfried.

**Selection of Frozen, Cured, and Canned Fish.** When using frozen fish in any form, follow label directions for thawing and cooking. Thawing in the refrigerator or in cold running water is acceptable. Thawing at room temperature is quick, but causes an unusual amount of "drip," making the fish dry.

Salt mackerel, haddock, or cod require a long soaking in cold water to get them ready for recipe use. But smoked fish such as whitefish, chub, sturgeon, or salmon, are immediately ready for eating or can be made into a salad or a cooked dish. Sardines, brislings, anchovies, and other cured fishes in cans or jars are ready for eating.

Canned tuna, salmon, mackerel, and white meat fish have many recipe uses, but require no further cooking before eating. These shelf-stored fishes are good bases for both regular and emergency meals.

**Cooking Fresh Fish.** The most serious error in fish cookery is overcooking. When a fish is prepared at the right temperature for the right length of time it will be moist, succulent, tender, and delicate in flavor. The test for doneness, whether the fish is baked, broiled, boiled, or panfried, is easy flaking when tested with a fork.

**Baking and Broiling.** Whole fish stuffed or unstuffed, fillets plain or with a stuffing, and steak cuts are baked at 350°F. Baking time varies from 25 minutes for fillets to 1 hour for whole fish. Fillets are baked quickly in a very hot (500°–550°F) oven after they have been coated with milk and seasoned bread crumbs.

Fish for broiling should be placed in a broiler pan 3 inches from the heat and cooked for 8 to 10 minutes. The fish may be turned at midpoint, but this is not necessary.

**Boiling and Frying.** A fish should be held in a fine wire basket or tied in cheesecloth before plunging it into seasoned boiling water. It then should be cooked at a slow simmer until fork tender.

Panfrying fish requires ⅛-inch of fat in a skillet and should be cooked over moderate heat for about 10 minutes. For deep-fat frying, the fat must be heated to 375°F; the fish then will cook and brown in 3 to 5 minutes.

**Selection and Cooking of Shellfish.** Shellfish may be purchased raw in the shell, shucked, or picked out; cooked; canned; frozen; or ready to cook.

**Lobsters.** The live lobsters have a dark bluish-green shell and are distinguished by large, heavy claws. When they are cooked, their shell color changes to a bright red. Lobsters are marketed live or cooked whole. The cooked meat is available fresh, frozen, and canned, ready for use in salads, sauces, or in many other recipes.

Spiny (rock) lobsters have very small claws; the tail, weighing from 4 ounces to more than a pound, is the edible portion. Frozen lobster tails are marketed in the shell, cooked or uncooked. Some small frozen tails are available cooked and shelled.

Boiled lobsters are prepared by plunging live lobsters headfirst into boiling salted water. When the water resumes boiling, the heat should be turned down to simmer for 20 minutes. After

## MARKET FORMS OF FISH

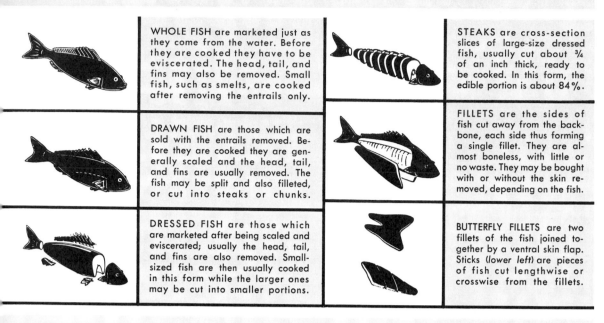

**WHOLE FISH** are marketed just as they come from the water. Before they are cooked they have to be eviscerated. The head, tail, and fins may also be removed. Small fish, such as smelts, are cooked after removing the entrails only.

**STEAKS** are cross-section slices of large-size dressed fish, usually cut about ¾ of an inch thick, ready to be cooked. In this form, the edible portion is about 84%.

**DRAWN FISH** are those which are sold with the entrails removed. Before they are cooked they are generally scaled and the head, tail, and fins are usually removed. The fish may be split and also filleted, or cut into steaks or chunks.

**FILLETS** are the sides of fish cut away from the backbone, each side thus forming a single fillet. They are almost boneless, with little or no waste. They may be bought with or without the skin removed, depending on the fish.

**DRESSED FISH** are those which are marketed after being scaled and eviscerated; usually the head, tail, and fins are also removed. Small-sized fish are then usually cooked in this form while the larger ones may be cut into smaller portions.

**BUTTERFLY FILLETS** are two fillets of the fish joined together by a ventral skin flap. Sticks (*lower left*) are pieces of fish cut lengthwise or crosswise from the fillets.

## MARKET FORMS OF SHELLFISH

Some shellfish are sold fresh in several forms: whole, headless, and shucked, while others are sold in cooked form, either in the shell or just the cooked meat alone.

**IN THE SHELL:** the shellfish that are marketed alive in their shells include the hard- and soft-shelled blue crabs, lobsters, clams, and oysters, with varying edible portions.

**HEADLESS** forms marketed include tail parts of shrimp and the spiny-tail lobsters.

**SHUCKED:** clam, oyster, and scallop meats are sold with their shells removed, in a form called "shucked."

**COOKED MEAT:** edible portions of lobster, shrimp, and crab are sold in cooked form.

draining, the stomach and intestinal vein must be removed. In addition to the meat of the body and claws, the liver and coral roe may be eaten. Rock lobster tails are boiled for 10 to 15 minutes.

Broiled lobsters must be split lengthwise, live or after preboiling. The stomach and vein must be removed and the claws cracked. The lobster then should be opened as flat as possible on the broiler pan, and the exposed meat brushed with butter and seasoned. Broiling should be done about 4 inches from the heat, for 12 to 15 minutes for live lobster, 5 minutes for preboiled lobster, and 10 to 15 minutes for lobster tails.

Baked lobsters, with a stuffing or as lobster thermidor, require a 400°F oven. Baking time varies from 20 to 25 minutes for live lobster to 10 minutes for precooked meat.

**Crabs.** Both hard-shell and soft-shell blue crabs, Dungeness, king, and rock crabs are available in the market. Blues may be purchased live and should be prepared by boiling or sautéing. Boiling takes 15 minutes in seasoned water. Soft-shell crabs should be sautéed for 3 minutes on each side in ¼-inch of melted butter.

King crab claws or frozen whole Dungeness crabs or their claws are marketed cooked, with the meat ready to be picked from the shell. Also,

cooked crab meat (fresh, canned, or frozen) is ready for use in salads, soups, soufflés, or casseroles, or it may be sautéed or broiled in butter.

White lump meat and flake meat come from the legs and body of blue crabs; brownish meat, from the claws. All rock-crab meat is brownish. Body meat from Dungeness crab is white; its claw meat and king crab claw meat are red.

**Oysters and Clams.** Large oysters should be live when purchased in the shell. Shucked oysters should be plump and creamy, in clear liquor. Tiny oysters are generally available canned or smoked.

Oysters may be simmered in their own liquor until the edges curl, baked in a hot oven for 10 minutes, fried for 5 minutes, deep-fried for 2 minutes, or broiled for 5 minutes. Overcooking should be avoided in order to keep the oysters plump and tender.

Hard-shell clams are known as quahogs, littlenecks, cherrystones, or round clams. These are marketed in the shell, shucked, or canned. The smaller ones may be served raw on the half shell, or baked or steamed. The larger ones are good for chowder, stews, and casseroles. Soft-shell clams, with long necks, are sold in the shell as steamers, or are available shucked. These are the clams used for frying, fritters, and clam pie.

For steaming, scrubbed clams should be placed in a large kettle with a small amount of water. With the cover tight, the clams should be cooked over low heat for 15 to 20 minutes, or until the shells open. Overcooking will toughen clams. The broth, once strained, is a bonus taste treat.

**Shrimp and Scallops.** Generally, shrimp are available headless, fresh or frozen in the shell; fresh or frozen cooked, peeled, and cleaned; frozen peeled, cleaned, and breaded; and canned. All ready-to-use shrimp may be heated in sauce, broiled in butter, sautéed, and used in casseroles, salads, and other dishes. Split raw shrimp are good for broiling scampi style. For boiling fresh or "green" shrimp, seasoned water should be used; the shrimp will be tender in 5 minutes.

The meat of a scallop is the muscle that closes the shell. Large sea scallops are white; small bay scallops, creamy or pinkish. Both are available uncooked fresh or frozen. Quick cooking keeps them moist and tender. Scallops may be panfried for 10 minutes, deep-fried for 2 or 3 minutes, broiled for 3 to 5 minutes, baked in a hot oven for 10 minutes, or boiled for 3 to 5 minutes.

## 4. Eggs and Cheese

Both eggs and cheese are cooked best when they are subjected to gentle heat. Overcooking in regard to both time and temperature makes eggs tough and cheese tough and stringy.

**Selection of Eggs.** Eggs are classified in 6 sizes, according to minimum weight per dozen. A dozen jumbos weigh 30 ounces; extra large, 27; large, 24; medium, 21; small, 18; and pee-wee, 15. There are four U. S. Department of Agriculture grades for eggs as marketed to consumers, and the grade mark is in the shape of a shield. Grade AA eggs have clean, unbroken shells, ⅛-inch air cells, clear and firm whites, and well-centered yolks. Grade A eggs have clean, unbroken shells, ⅜-inch air cells, clear and reasonably firm whites, and fairly well-centered yolks. Specifications for Grades B and C eggs are less exacting.

The color of the eggshell varies from white to brown, depending on the breed of hen. The color of the shell has no effect on the flavor or the nutritional value of the egg.

**Cooking with Eggs.** Grades AA and A eggs are best for cooking in the shell, poaching, frying, or for beaten whites. Grades B and C eggs are satisfactory for general cooking and most baking.

**Cooking in the Shell.** For soft-cooked eggs, the eggs should be placed in a saucepan with enough lukewarm water to cover the eggs one inch above their tops. With the pan covered, the water should be brought rapidly to a boil, and then the pan should be removed immediately from the heat. The eggs should stand in the hot water from 2 to 4 minutes, after which the white will be slightly firm, the yolk evenly cooked and hot.

Practically the same procedure should be followed for hard-cooked eggs, except that the eggs are boiled in an uncovered pan. Once the pan is removed from the heat, it should be covered, and the eggs should stand for 15 minutes. To prevent a dark ring from appearing around the yolk, the eggs should be cooled promptly under cold running water.

**Poaching and Frying.** Simmering water is essential for poaching eggs; it must never be allowed to boil. Each egg should be broken into a cup and then poured into the pan of water. To give a poached egg a well-rounded shape, it may be cooked in a ring placed in the pan.

For fried eggs, 1 to 2 tablespoons of butter, margarine, or bacon fat should be heated in a skillet before the eggs are broken and slipped into the pan. In a covered skillet, the eggs should

## STANDARDS FOR QUALITY OF EGGS

| AA QUALITY | A QUALITY | B QUALITY | C QUALITY |

BROKEN-OUT UNCOOKED EGGS (TOP AND SIDE VIEWS)

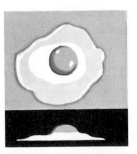 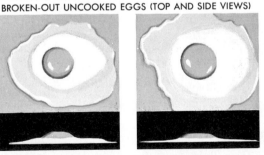 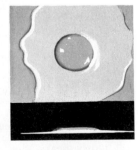

| Egg covers small area, much thick white around the yolk, some thin white, yolk firm. | Egg covers moderate area, much thick white, medium amount thin white, yolk firm. | Egg covers wide area, small amount of thick white, much thin white, yolk flattened. | Egg covers very wide area, has no thick white, a lot of thin white, yolk very flat. |

HARD-COOKED EGGS

| Eggs of AA quality have an air cell ⅛ inch in depth and the yolk is well centered. | Eggs of A quality have an air cell ¼ inch or less in depth, yolk nearly centered. | Eggs of B quality have an air cell ⅜ inch or less in depth and yolk is off center. | Eggs of C quality have an air cell over ⅜ inch deep, yolk off center and flattened. |

## PRINCIPAL TYPES OF CHEESE

| | |
|---|---|
| 1. Cheddar | 12. Swiss |
| 2. Colby | 13. Limburger |
| 3. Monterey | 14. Blue |
| 4. Process | 15. Gorgonzola |
| 5. Cheese Foods | 16. Provolone |
| 6. Cheese Spreads | 17. Romano |
| 7. Club Cheese | 18. Parmesan |
| 8. Gouda & Edam | 19. Mozzarella and |
| 9. Camembert | Scamorze |
| 10. Muenster | 20. Cottage Cheese |
| 11. Brick | 21. Cream Cheese |

be cooked about 3 or 4 minutes. Covering the skillet makes basting unnecessary.

**Omelets.** A proper pan for making omelets should be shallow, with curved sides and a smooth inside surface. A pan 7 or 8 inches wide is adequate for omelets of 2 or 3 eggs. The pan should be moved constantly over moderately high heat as the omelet cooks. For a puffy omelet or a baked omelet, an oven temperature of 350° to 400°F is necessary.

**Eggs Used in Recipes.** Eggs are used to bind ingredients, as in croquettes; to thicken liquids, as in sauces or custards; and to leaven foods such as cakes, soufflés, and fluffy desserts. Correct handling of the eggs assures good results.

When a beaten egg is to be added to a hot mixture, the egg must be warmed first with a little of the hot food so that it can be stirred into the mixture without curdling. The beaten egg may be blended with 2 tablespoons of cold liquid previously reserved from the recipe, then stirred into the hot food.

A soft custard mixture will separate unless it is cooked over the lowest heat or over boiling water. Baked custard, if cooked too long or at too high a temperature, will be watery. Custards served warm tend to "weep" (become watery); well-baked, chilled custards will not weep.

Egg whites can be beaten faster and to greater volume if the eggs are brought to room temperature before beating. When beaten to stiff glossy peaks, the whites will cling to the bowl if it is inverted. Overbeaten egg whites look dull and will slide out of an inverted bowl. Beaten egg whites used for leavening should be folded gently into the mixture.

**Selection of Cheese.** Though more than 400 cheeses have been defined, many are known only locally. However, modern marketing practices have brought to all parts of the United States not only a variety of domestic cheeses but also a number of imported cheeses, such as Promost from Norway, Camembert and Roquefort from France, Cheddar from England, Edam from Holland, Gruyère from Switzerland, and Romano from Italy.

Some cheeses are classified according to flavor or taste, as mild, sharp, or mold-flavored. Some are described by texture, as very hard, hard, semisoft, or soft. Still others are characterized by the milk from which they are made.

Available, then, are very hard cheeses for grating, hard ones for shredding, and softer ones for spreading. There are highly flavored cheeses to complement fruits or pastries and sharply flavored ones that melt easily when combined with other ingredients in dishes such as rarebits or casseroles.

**Cooking with Cheese.** Most cheeses should have an even color throughout and be symmetrical in shape. Color streaks and cracks or splits in a cheese may result in a loss of flavor. Mold that forms on the surface of cheese during storage can be scraped off; the cheese flavor will remain true.

Care must be taken not to overheat cheese when melting it. It should be melted over very low heat on top of the stove or in a double boiler. A moderate temperature must be used when cheese is melted in the oven or broiler. Hard cheeses should be brought to room temperature for faster, smoother melting.

Cheese is also served uncooked. To be enjoyed at the peak of flavor, cheese and cheese spreads or dips should be removed from refrigeration 1 or 2 hours before serving. Crackers or breads served with cheeses should be mild, not heavily salted or seasoned, to let the cheese flavor dominate.

## 5. Vegetables

Much history, legend, and romance surround the use of vegetables as foods. Probably, tender leaves were first nibbled and found pleasing, then roots and bulbs explored for taste. Although it is not known when the cooking of vegetables began, these foods have been enjoyed by many cultures since ancient times.

Great quantities and varieties of vegetables are available today—whether fresh, frozen, canned, or dried—as a result of the efforts of growers, processors, and marketers.

**Selection of Vegetables.** The general rule for selecting good fresh vegetables is to look sharply and feel gently. A fresh, clean color is the first test. Then the vegetable should be felt gently for crispness and firmness. Vegetables with blemishes that have penetrated the flesh should be rejected.

Frozen vegetables should be uniformly hard. Packages with vegetables lumped at one end probably have been thawed and refrozen; this results in deterioration of quality. The buyer should read the label descriptions of canned vegetables to find out whether they are cut up, whole, or seasoned.

**Vegetable Cookery Methods.** In general, all vegetables should be cooked to the tender-crisp stage as quickly as possible in a small amount of water in a covered pan. The cover of the pan should be raised after 4 or 5 minutes of cooking; this permits the volatile acids that destroy natural vegetable coloring to escape, making the cooked vegetables more attractive.

**Preparation for Cooking.** Before cooking, all fresh vegetables should be cleaned and the less tender portions discarded. A leafy vegetable should be washed in a pan of lukewarm water and lifted up and down by hand to let the sand settle to the bottom. Celery stalks should be scrubbed with a brush under cold running water. Root vegetables should also be scrubbed before they are scraped or pared. If the core is removed from lettuce, cold water should be run into the remaining hole; this helps separate the leaves of the head. Tight-growing vegetables, such as Brussels sprouts, broccoli, and cauliflower, should be soaked in cold salted water to remove insects that might be present.

**Boiling.** The smallest amount of salted water consistent with the length of cooking time should be used when boiling vegetables. Once the water has come to a boil, the vegetable should be added to the pan, the pan covered, the water again brought to a boil, and the heat reduced for a slow boil. Timing the cooking should start when the water begins to steam; after about 5 minutes of cooking, the cover of the pan should be lifted for a few seconds.

Asparagus can be boiled upright in a double boiler top or in a glass or ceramic percolator; or it can be cooked flat in a large skillet. Though the nutritive value of potatoes, yams, and sweet potatoes is higher when they are boiled in their skins, peeling them prevents the darkening of these vegetables during boiling.

Frozen vegetables are most pleasing when butter-boiled. This method entails placing the vegetable in a covered saucepan with 1 to 2 tablespoons of water, 1 tablespoon of butter or margarine, and salt. Once the water is brought to a boil, the heat should be slightly reduced, and the vegetables cooked until tender. They should not be drained before being served.

**Steaming and Panning.** Mild-flavored vegetables may be cooked in a rack over steaming water in a covered kettle. Leafy greens are steamed in a tightly covered pan with no water except that which has clung to the leaves after washing.

Shredded or leafy vegetables may be cooked over low heat in a heavy, tightly covered pan with a small amount of fat. They should be stirred occasionally.

**Baking.** It takes nearly twice as long to bake vegetables as to boil them. Potatoes, sweet potatoes, yams, squash, and tomatoes can be baked in their skins in a 400°F oven. When peeled and cut up, they should be baked at 375°F. This same temperature is used for baking sliced or diced vegetables with salt, fat, and little or no liquid in a tightly covered casserole. Frozen vegetables also may be baked with butter and salt in a tightly covered casserole at 350°F.

**Using Canned Vegetables.** It is well to follow the label directions in preparing canned vegetables. In general, the liquid from the can should be poured into a saucepan and simmered until it is reduced to about one third of its volume. Then the vegetable, fat, and seasonings should be heated until the fat melts, stirring once. The vegetable should be served with the liquid.

**Using Dried Vegetables.** Most dried beans, peas, and lentils require soaking before cooking. About 2½ to 3 cups of water will be needed per cup of dried vegetable. The water and vegetable must be brought to a boil, cooked for 2 minutes before being removed from the heat, and soaked for the time required by label directions or recipe. The soaking water may be used in cooking the vegetable at a slow simmer until tender. Hard water slows the cooking. A bit of fat added while dried vegetables are cooking keeps down foaming.

Dried beans that have been precooked before drying need not be soaked. When these are cooked in a liquid or in a thin sauce, the beans become rehydrated and tender after boiling for 15 minutes or baking for 45.

Dehydrated (instant or quick-cooking) potatoes should be prepared according to the package directions. Texture suffers if liquids are substituted, often resulting in gummy instead of fluffy products. Minced dehydrated onions, chives, or shallots may be rehydrated in a little water before use, if liquid is not called for in the recipe.

## 6. Cereals and Cereal Products

It is not known when the fruits of certain grasses were first used as food. Early Chinese writings, however, date the beginning of development of rice from about 3000 B.C. and the eating of macaroni-type products from as early as 5000 B.C. Marco Polo, on his return from the Orient in the latter part of the 13th century, introduced macaroni to Italy. Its growth in popularity since then is evidenced by the 150 or more varieties of macaroni products now available.

During the 17th century the early settlers in America learned from the Indians how to prepare and use cornmeal. The colonists later made hominy from broken and sifted dried corn, and whole hulled corn from corn soaked in water and the lye from the wood ashes.

**Methods of Cooking Cereals.** Cooking in rapidly boiling, salted water is the most common method of preparing a cereal or cereal product. Each kind should be cooked according to the instructions on the package for the best results.

**Rice.** Regular milled white rice is washed, cleaned, and graded during milling; therefore it need not be rinsed or washed before cooking. Long grain rice cooks to separate fluffy grains, and is an excellent accompaniment to other foods.

Medium or short grain rice cooks to a more moist, clinging product; this rice is suitable for puddings, croquettes, and casseroles. One cup of regular rice makes 3 cups of cooked rice.

Parboiled, or converted, rice is specially processed so as to retain vitamins and minerals. It requires more water and longer cooking than regular rice. One cup of this kind of rice yields 4 cups of cooked rice.

Precooked, or instant, rice is completely cooked and needs only to be steamed in boiling water.

Brown rice is whole grain rice with the inedible hull removed. It needs more water and a longer cooking than regular rice and more than doubles its bulk when cooked.

If rice is cooked properly, all the liquid in the pan or kettle will be absorbed. A little fat in the boiling rice keeps down foaming. If desired, rice in boiling salted water can be baked in a covered casserole in 350°F oven until tender. Stirring or fluffing rice with a fork avoids crushing the grains.

Wild rice is not true rice; it is the fruit of a grass that grows in limited quantities in a few swampy areas. This kind of "rice" requires more water and much longer cooking than does other rice.

**Crisp and "Cooked" Cereals.** Ready-to-serve breakfast cereals in flaked, shredded, toasted, and flavored form need not be cooked, of course. But they do lend themselves to many cooking uses. They are fine casserole toppers, ingredients for cookies and quick breads, and garnishes for soups. Crisp cereals can be made into crumbs with a food mill, a rolling pin, or a blender, or by crushing by hand.

"Cooked" cereals are used as hot breakfast food, and in cookies, meat or fish loaves, and casseroles. For best texture and flavor they should not be precooked. Instant oatmeal or other cereal needs only the addition of boiling water, no cooking.

**Fine Cereals and Bulgur.** Cornmeal, and finely ground wheat, rice, or hominy grits are cooked in rapidly boiling water. To prevent lumping, the meal should be well moistened with cold water, then stirred vigorously into the water a little at a time so that the boiling does not stop.

Bulgur, the ancient food of the Middle East, is made today by washing, soaking, cooking, drying, and cracking whole wheat. It is used dry, soaked, or cooked according to recipe need. Though it becomes tender when cooked, it retains its kernel identity.

**Methods of Cooking Macaroni Products.** Macaroni products are available in many sizes and shapes. They include macaroni, which is tubular; spaghetti, which is in solid rod form; and noodles, which are in ribbonlike pieces. Macaroni and spaghetti are made of hard durum wheat and water; noodles contain 5½ percent egg solids.

All macaroni products are best when cooked just before serving. Cooking time in boiling salted water varies, so package directions must be followed. For best eating quality, macaroni and spaghetti should be cooked *al dente,* that is tender but still firm. These products should not be rinsed after cooking, unless they are to be chilled for salad. Hot strands can be kept separate by stirring in a little fat. Cooking doubles the volume of macaroni and spaghetti, but egg noodles do not increase in bulk.

Traditionally, macaroni products have been used with hot spicy sauces, but they are also popular combined with cheese, meat, fish, chicken or seafood in casserole dishes. In addition, noodles may be used in puddings and custards.

## 7. Fruits and Nuts

Many types of fruits and nuts were enjoyed in Asia, Europe, and the Middle East thousands of years before the Christian era. Of course they were not in the succulent forms known today or available the year round. Modern growing, shipping, packaging, freezing, and canning processes have eliminated nearly every seasonal barrier.

**Selection of Fruits.** The nutritive contribution of vitamins, minerals, and soft bulk from fruits makes them important in the daily diet. Nutritive content is highest when all fruits are at their most flavorful. Appearance, aroma, feel, and weight are the subjective tests applied in the selection of fresh fruits.

**Citrus Fruits and Melons.** In general, citrus fruits should be heavy in relation to size; this indicates juiciness. The skin should have a smooth, fine texture and good color for the type. A bit of pale green on an orange indicates full maturity, but on a lemon it may mean immaturity or poor or insufficient curing.

The ripeness of melons can be determined by their color and aroma. A ripe cantaloupe has a raised netting on a light yellow rind, and a depressed scar at the stem end. A ripe Persian melon, which is like a big round cantaloupe, has a fine netting over a green rind, and a smooth stem end. Honeydew melons show waxy, creamy yellow rinds when ripe. A ripe Casaba melon has a deeply ridged yellow rind, often slightly streaked with pale green. The Cranshaw melon, which is a cross between a Persian and a Casaba melon, has a fragile gold and green rind. For all these melons the aroma, ranging from faint and delicate in Casaba to sweet and musky in cantaloupe, is a better criterion of ripeness than softness at the blossom end. Watermelons should show a dark green color and have a yellow underside. Plugging or cutting a melon is the only sure way to test its ripeness and full flavor.

**Apples and Pears.** Apples should be well colored for their type, free of blemishes, evenly shaped, and crisp to the touch. Fruity aroma is evident in ripe fruit. All so-called eating apples can be cooked, but may not always hold their shape. The best apples for baking are Rome Beauty and Stayman. The best all-purpose apples are McIntosh, Stayman, Grimes Golden, Jonathan, and Northern Spy.

Pears are usually harvested before they reach full maturity, in the belief that they ripen best off the tree. Two to four days at room temperature brings them to full flavor. Bartlett pears are bell-shaped with thin, tender, yellow skin and smooth, juicy flesh. Kieffer pears, better for canning than eating fresh, have a dark-green skin and a somewhat gritty flesh. Three late-season pears are Bosc, Anjou, and Comice. Bosc has a long tapered neck and a dark-yellow skin overlaid with russet. This pear can be eaten raw, or it may be baked or stewed. Anjou is oval with slightly unequal sides; it has a thick neck and a yellowish-green skin. It is recommended for salads or for baking and broiling. Comice, a large, rounded pear with a pale greenish-yellow skin, sometimes richly blushed, is very sweet and juicy and is often eaten with a spoon. All ripe pears have a characteristic aroma and should yield to gentle pressure.

**Other Fresh Fruits.** Peaches, apricots, nectarines, plums, and fresh prunes should be well colored for their types, free of blemishes that pierce the skin, and free from bruises. They should yield slightly to gentle pressure and have a typical fruity aroma.

All ripe berries should have a good color and a rich aroma. Crushed, bruised, or moldy berries should not be used.

Avocados should be selected fully ripe or allowed to ripen to velvety smoothness at room temperature before use. At the peak of ripeness, all but those with hard dark skins yield to pressure when they are cupped in the palm of the hand.

**Frozen and Canned Fruits.** Frozen fruits, with or without sugar, regular or quick-thawing, whole or in pieces, should be frozen hard when purchased. Canned fruits should be selected according to heaviness of syrup in relation to their intended use, or for sugar-free pack.

**Methods of Cooking Fruits.** Fresh fruits may be stewed, baked, broiled, or sautéed. Dried fruits should be cooked according to package directions.

**Fresh Fruits.** In stewing, cut-up fruits such as apples and rhubarb develop a better flavor and require less sugar when they are not sweetened until the end of the stewing period. Sliced fruits hold their shape when they are simmered in a sugar and water syrup.

Baked fruits require a moderate oven. Whole apples and pears will cook more quickly and evenly if the pan is covered for the first 20 minutes or so. Sliced, halved, or mixed fruits bake evenly when placed in a single layer in a shallow baking pan.

For broiling, fruits should first be halved and then placed on the broiler rack in a single layer, cut side up. They should be broiled 3 to 4 inches from the flame in order to be heated through before browning.

Generous amounts of butter or margarine are needed for sautéing fruits, and slow cooking is desirable for even cooking and delicate browning.

**Dried Fruits.** Tenderized fruits should be covered with boiling water and soaked for 24 hours to become plump and to make a light, thin juice. For heavy, thick juice, the fruit should be soaked, then brought to a boil, and finally simmered for 5 minutes. To cook dried fruits without soaking, they must be covered with cold water, brought to a boil, and then simmered for 10 to 20 minutes. They should stand in their juice for several hours to become plump.

**Preparation of Nuts.** The nuts most commonly found in the market are pecans, California walnuts, peanuts, almonds, filberts, Brazil nuts, and chestnuts. Nuts in the shell may not be economical for cooking if shelling time must be counted in. Expected yields of nut meats from one pound of nuts in the shell are as follows: walnuts, peanuts, or almonds—2 cups; pecans, 2¼ cups; filberts or Brazil nuts, 1½ cups.

**Shelling.** In shelling nuts the best results are obtained by using a nutcracker. If one is not available, a sharp crack with a hammer may be used to break a shell. For perfect walnut halves, the nut should be placed on the flat end and held by the seam; then a bouncing blow with the hammer should be given on the pointed end. For easy shelling of Brazil nuts, they should

be boiled in water for 3 to 5 minutes, and then drained and covered with cold water before cracking.

**Blanching.** Shelled almonds are easily blanched. This process involves covering them with cold water, heating the water to the boiling point, and draining off the water. Then the skins can be readily slipped off with the fingers. Shelled filberts should be spread in a shallow pan and toasted in a 275°F oven for 20 minutes. While still warm, the thin skins can be rubbed off with the fingers or with a rough towel.

**Toasting and Salting.** A shallow pan should be used for toasting or salting shelled nuts in the oven. Almonds can be toasted in a 300°F oven in 25 to 30 minutes. Walnuts should be boiled in water for 3 minutes and then toasted in a 350°F oven for 15 to 20 minutes, with frequent stirring. For salted nuts, one teaspoon of butter or oil is needed for each cup of nutmeats. The salt should be added after the nuts have been baked (with occasional stirring) at 325°F for about 25 minutes.

**Slicing and Chopping.** Nuts that are moist from blanching can be slivered or sliced easily with a sharp knife on a cutting board. Unblanched nuts should be heated in the oven or in boiling water for a few minutes before slicing.

In chopping nuts, an up-and-down motion with a French (heavy-bladed) knife on a board produces uncrushed pieces of the desired size. Shelled nuts can be put through a food grinder that has a coarse blade, whirled in a blender, or chopped in a mechanical nut chopper.

## 8. Fats and Oils

Few meals are prepared without fats. The kind of fat to use depends upon the purpose for which it is intended. For example, butter may be essential for flavor; margarine or a vegetable oil may satisfy a requirement for an unsaturated fat; shortening or lard may be preferred in baking. Butter and margarine can be used interchangeably in baking. Shortening is the only fat that can be used in one-bowl cakes; vegetable oil is the only satisfactory fat for chiffon cakes and stir-and-roll pastry or cookies. One stick of ordinary butter is equivalent to 1⅓ sticks of whipped butter or margarine.

**Fats Used for Frying.** Fats for frying must be used with care. Every fat has a smoke point, or temperature at which decomposition occurs and smoky fumes are given off. Butter, lard, and most margarines have a low smoke point. They can be used for low to moderate temperature pan-frying but not for deep-frying. Shortenings and vegetable oils have higher smoke points, so they can be used at the 365° to 375°F temperatures required for deep-frying. Fats for deep-frying should be fresh and free of crumbs or food particles. Any fat heated so much as to scorch, or one that has acquired an off-flavor from foods previously cooked in it, should be discarded.

A frying thermometer and a narrow, deep container are desirable for deep frying. The fat should reach the temperature specified in the recipe before any food is added. Food should not be crowded into the fryer because crowding rapidly lowers the fat temperature and delays its reheating to the proper frying temperature. Fat absorption, leading to a greasy taste and texture, is the least at the optimum frying temperature, 365° to 375°F. Absorption increases at temperatures below 365°F. If no frying thermometer is available, the proper temperature can be determined by dropping a 1-inch cube of bread into the hot fat; at 365°F it will brown in just one minute.

Fat used for panfrying should not be overheated. It should be started over medium heat. When a drop of water added to it sizzles and bounces, the fat is hot enough for frying. The same test is used to determine whether a griddle is hot enough to grease for pancakes. When panfrying food in butter, a small amount of vegetable oil may be added to keep the butter from overbrowning or burning.

Shallow frying, in 1 to 1½ inches of fat, requires a 350°F temperature. This is the temperature setting for an electric frying pan. For other skillets the bread cube test can be used. A ⅝-inch cube of day-old bread will brown in 45 seconds at 350°F. If it browns in 35 seconds, the fat is 365°F; at 30 seconds, the temperature is 375°F.

**Fats Used in Baked Foods.** Fats contribute to velvety texture and delicate browning in cakes and cookies; to tender crumbliness and flakiness in high-fat cookies and pastries; to tenderness and good browning in quick breads. All of these effects may be called the shortening power of fats and oils. The shortening power varies according to the composition of the fat and the way in which it mixes with the rest of the ingredients, especially the way in which it separates particles of flour. Solid fats, cut into the dry ingredients, coat the flour just enough to bring about a layering or separation in the baked product, which is called flakiness. When vegetable oils are used in baked foods, the flour particles are more thoroughly coated, and the product tends to be mealy rather than flaky.

## 9. Sugars and Syrups

Sugars and syrups are used in cooking not only to sweeten but also to perform other functions. For example, sugar delays coagulation of custards and impedes curdling. It assists in the proper browning of baked foods and helps produce tenderness in cakes and cookies. It feeds the yeast in bread making, stabilizes egg-whites in meringues, and helps prevent the formation of too-large crystals in frozen fruits and desserts. Corn syrup helps to control crystallization in candy making and to retain moisture in many baked foods. Honey delays baked products from drying out and going stale. Molasses and maple syrup lend color and distinctive flavor to foods.

**Cooking with Sugars and Syrups.** The proper proportion of sugar or syrup in recipes should be carefully observed. Too little or too much of either can spoil the finished product.

**Candy Making.** Fudge and fondant owe their creamy texture to sugar crystals so small they cannot be felt by the tongue. Corn syrup (as well as butter, cream, or chocolate) helps control crystallization, as does correct cooking technique. It is essential to stir only until the sugar dissolves. The pan should be covered for the first 3 minutes of cooking, so that the steam can wash down any crystals on the sides of the pan. The candy mixture must cool to lukewarm before it is beaten and then beating must be continuous.

Chewy or brittle candies are prevented from crystallizing by the use of corn syrup and honey, in addition to milk, cream, or a mild food acid. Cooking to the stage at which caramelization begins is also helpful in retarding formation of crystals.

**Baking.** Too much sugar in cakes makes a too tender product that is likely to sink heavily in the center. Honey can replace up to half of the required sugar in cakes without changing the other ingredients. For crisp cookies honey should replace only up to one third of the sugar. For brownies honey may replace up to one half of the sugar, and for bar cookies, up to two thirds. Baking temperatures for recipes using honey or molasses must be lowered to prevent overbrowning.

**Testing To See if Candy Is Done.** Two tests may be used to determine whether the syrup has cooked sufficiently to reach the consistency required in the recipe. A candy thermometer may be placed in the pan of syrup and the temperature recorded. A cold-water test may be used, in which the pan should be taken from the heat before a sample of the syrup is removed and dropped into a cup of cold water. If more cooking is needed, the pan should be returned to heat. The accompanying table notes temperatures and syrup consistencies for both tests.

### TESTS FOR SUGARS AND SYRUPS

| Thermometer | | Cold Water |
|---|---|---|
| (Temperature at Sea Level) | (Syrup Consistency) | (Description of Test) |
| 230°–234° F | Thread | Syrup spins 2-inch thread from spoon |
| 234°–240° F | Soft Ball | Syrup forms ball that flattens when removed from water |
| 244°–248° F | Firm Ball | Syrup forms ball that holds shape |
| 250°–266° F | Hard Ball | Syrup forms hard but plastic ball |
| 270°–290° F | Soft Crack | Syrup makes hard, not brittle, threads |
| 300°–310° F | Hard Crack | Syrup makes hard, brittle threads |
| 320° F | Clear Liquid | Sugar liquefies |
| 338° F | Brown Liquid | Sugar caramelizes |

## 10. Beverages

Coffee and tea are the beverages most often prepared in the home. Preparation is easy, but the results are often poor. Hot cocoa and chocolate seem to present fewer cooking problems than coffee and tea.

**Brewing Coffee.** Coffee has a full, rich flavor whether it is mild, medium, or strong. A cup of perfect coffee depends on the cleanliness of the coffee maker, the freshness of the water and the coffee, the proportion of coffee to water, and the brewing time.

To ensure the cleanliness of the coffee maker, immediately after use it should be washed with a detergent and rinsed with hot water. Just before it is used again, the pot should be rinsed with boiling water. To preserve its fresh taste, coffee should be tightly covered and stored in a refrigerator. The proper quantity to use is 1 measure of coffee (equal to 2 level tablespoons) to each 6 ounces (¾ measuring cup) of water. For a strong brew, the amount of coffee must be increased. Overlong brewing does not make coffee stronger; it brings out the bitter oils.

Brewing in a drip coffee pot is completed when the dripping stops. In a vacuum coffee maker, the coffee and water should bubble together no more than 2 to 3 minutes. In a percolator, 6 to 8 minutes of slow percolating brings out the full coffee flavor. The "mild" or "strong" setting on an electric coffee maker cannot guarantee full flavor unless the right amount of coffee is used for the desired result.

For iced coffee, freshly brewed, double-strength coffee should be poured onto the ice cubes while it is hot. Regular-strength coffee should be cooled no longer than 3 hours before being poured over ice. Extra flavor may be obtained by using coffee ice cubes made with regular-strength coffee.

For instant coffee, one rounded teaspoon of powder is enough for one cup of coffee; the powder can be measured into the cup or multiplied and measured into a pot. After boiling water is added, the mixture should steep for at least one minute.

**Brewing Tea.** Tea is the tender, young leaves of a plant of the camellia family, which have been dried and processed. The processing of the several kinds of teas gives them different characteristics. Black tea, which makes a copper-colored brew, is fermented; green tea, which makes a light-colored brew, is not fermented. Oolong tea, which is halfway between, also brews to a light color. Pekoe refers to a size of tea leaf, not to flavor or a process.

For best results, tea should be made in a clean teapot, with fresh cold water and the right amount of tea, and should be brewed by the clock. The teapot should be scalded with boiling water just before it is used.

The correct amount of tea is 1 teaspoon of tea leaves or 1 tea bag to 1 cup of water. Fresh, cold tap water should be brought to a full rolling boil and poured over the tea leaves or tea bag. The mixture should brew for 3 to 5 minutes and then be served. For a stronger brew, the amount of tea should be increased rather than the length of the brewing time.

About 50% more tea leaves should be used to prepare the extra-strength brew needed for iced tea. The hot tea should be poured over the ice cubes. If desired, the hot tea may cool up to 3 hours, but it must not be refrigerated or it will cloud. If clouding does occur, a little boiling water may be added to clarify the mixture.

Instant tea should be measured as the label directs, and the cup filled with boiling water and stirred. Instant tea dissolves in cold water and makes good iced tea.

**Making Cocoa and Chocolate.** For the best recipe-made cocoa or hot chocolate, the milk or milk and cream mixture should not be permitted to boil before or after it is added to the other ingredients. The cocoa used may be regular or Dutch process; the chocolate, unsweetened or semisweet. Sweetened cocoa mix dissolves readily in cold or hot milk. Instant sweet-milk cocoa blends very quickly with hot water or hot milk.

Iced cocoa is made by pouring cooled cocoa over ice cubes. It is usually topped with whipped cream or another whipped topping and dusted with a bit of cinnamon or nutmeg.

A few drops of vanilla extract in cocoa or chocolate enriches the flavor.

## 11. Gelatines

Gelatine is a pure food product manufactured from the bones and cartilage of animals approved for use as food. A homemade calf's foot jelly or jellied veal loaf sets because of the gelatine that formed when the bones and meat were cooked. Unflavored gelatine and flavored gelatine mixes are used to make gelatine desserts, salad or main dish molds, chiffon pie fillings, whips, Bavarian or Spanish creams, and other dishes.

**Preparing Gelatine.** The unflavored gelatine

### THE DRIP-POT

**BOILING WATER** trickles slowly down through the coffee grounds, extracting the full essence of the coffee.

### DRIP METHOD

PREHEAT the pot by rinsing with very hot water. Measure drip-grind coffee into the filter section. Place the upper container over the filter section and place it on the pot. Measure fresh boiling water into upper container. Cover. When dripping is completed, in 4 to 6 minutes, remove the upper section of the pot. Stir, brew and serve.

### THE VACUUM COFFEE-MAKER

**STEAM** from boiling water creates pressure and forces most of the water up into the top bowl, where it gently bubbles through the grounds of the coffee. A vacuum is created as the lower bowl cools, thus pulling the brew down through the filter into the lower bowl.

### VACUUM METHOD

MEASURE fresh cold water into the lower bowl. Place the bowl on the heat and bring the water to a boil. Place the filter in the upper bowl. When water boils, measure fine-grind coffee into upper bowl. Remove boiling water from heat. Insert upper bowl with slight twist to ensure tight seal. Return to reduced heat. Most of the water will rise into upper bowl. Allow it to mix with the ground coffee for 1 minute, stirring in a zigzag fashion for first 20 seconds. Remove from heat. Brew will return to lower bowl in 2 minutes. Remove upper bowl and serve.

### THE PERCOLATOR

**A PERCOLATOR** contains a tube through which the water rises in gentle bubbles and sprays the coffee grounds in the basket. The flavor is extracted as the water slowly seeps down through the coffee.

### PERCOLATOR METHOD

REMOVE the basket and stem from the percolator before fresh cold water is measured and put in. (Note: the water level should always be below the bottom of the coffee basket.) Place the percolator on the heat and keep it there until the water boils. Remove it from the heat. Measure regular-grind coffee into the basket. Insert the basket and stem in the percolator, cover, and return to gentle heat. Percolate slowly for 6 to 8 minutes. Remove from the heat, lift out coffee basket and stem, and serve.

called for in many recipes may be dissolved in several ways. Gelatine may be softened by sprinkling it on cold water, using ¼ cup of cold water to an envelope of gelatine; it then can be melted by the addition of boiling water. An alternate method is to mix the gelatine thoroughly with the sugar required in the recipe before adding boiling water; the sugar helps the gelatine dissolve directly without soaking and swelling. Gelatine that has been sprinkled on cold water can also be dissolved over hot water or over a very low surface heat on a modern range. Flavored gelatines dissolve as soon as they are stirred into boiling water.

*Molding.* One envelope of unflavored gelatine or 1 package of flavored gelatine is sufficient to set 2 cups of liquid. This amount of gelatine will support 1½ to 2 cups of solid foods such as meat, fish, fruit, or vegetable—sliced, diced, shredded, or whole—if the pieces are small.

Pineapple, fresh or frozen, contains an enzyme that prevents the setting of gelatine. Therefore, the pineapple has to be brought to a boil before it can be used in molds. Canned pineapple presents no problem.

A gelatine mixture must be chilled to thicken it to the consistency of a raw fresh egg white before solids can be added to it, and before it can be whipped for use in fluffy molds or pie fillings.

The setting of a gelatine can be hastened if half the liquid used in the recipe is ice-cold or in the form of ice cubes. A gelatine can be thickened quickly by stirring it over ice cubes or cracked ice until it mounds up. It is not necessary to grease the mold or rinse it with water before pouring in the gelatine.

*Unmolding.* Before unmolding gelatine, a chilled serving platter should be available; if it is slightly moistened in the center the mold can more easily be centered on the plate.

In unmolding, the tip of a small pointed knife should be run around the edge of the mold and the mold dipped to the rim in warm water for a few seconds. After removal from the water, if a gentle shake does not loosen the contents, the mold should be returned to the water for a few seconds more. Once the gelatine appears to be loosened, the mold should be covered with the serving platter and the platter and mold inverted and set on the table. A slight shake will free the gelatine completely before the mold is removed.

**Kinds of Gelatines.** *Whips* are simply flavored gelatines, chilled until very thick but not set and then whipped with a rotary beater until fluffy and thick. The whip is piled into dessert dishes or molds and then chilled. *Snows* are gelatines to which unbeaten egg whites are added before beating begins. The basic proportion for a snow is 1 egg white to a gelatine made from 1 envelope of gelatine or from 1 package of flavored gelatine. *Bavarians* are composed of a soft custard and a gelatine base, chilled to a slightly thickened stage. Beaten egg white and whipped cream then are folded in, and the mold is chilled until firm. For a *Spanish cream,* a soft custard and a gelatine base are chilled until moderately thick. The mixture is then folded into stiffly beaten egg whites and chilled until firm. *Aspics* are gelatines made with meat stock, tomato juice, or other flavorful liquids, usually highly seasoned. They are served as salads or main dish accompaniments or used as glaze.

## 12. Batters and Doughs

Different kinds of batters and doughs are used for different kinds of cakes, cookies, breads, and pastries. Pancakes, waffles, and popovers are made of thin pour batters. Drop batter is used for muffins and quick-bread loaves. Soft dough makes biscuits, many cookies, and some rolls and coffee cakes, while firmer dough is used for bread, pastries, and other types of cookies. Proportions of ingredients and mixing methods both determine the preparation of the desired kind of batter or dough. See BREAD—*Home Baking* and CAKE AND PASTRY for the preparation of various breads, cakes, cookies, and pastries.

At altitudes of more than 3,500 feet above sea level, the decrease in atmospheric pressure necessitates an adjustment of the ingredients and the baking temperatures used in sea-level recipes to ensure light, moist baked products.

In general, above 3,500 feet, egg whites should be beaten only to soft peaks; whole eggs should be beaten only until slightly thickened. For every 1,500-foot increase in altitude above 3,500 feet, flour in cakes and breads should be increased by 1 tablespoon per cup; baking powder or soda should be decreased by ¼ to ⅓ teaspoonful per cup of flour; in rich cake batters, both sugar and fat should be decreased by 1 to 2 tablespoons per cup of flour; for quick breads, 1 tablespoon of milk per cup of flour should be added.

Above 3,500 feet, baking temperatures for cakes and breads must be increased by 25°F. Label directions should be followed carefully for adjustments to high altitudes when using baking mixes.

## 13. Milk and Milk Products

Milk was probably the first instant food. Many forms of milk and milk products are available in the markets. Much of the milk used in the home is eaten in cooked foods, and special tricks and techniques help produce successful results.

**Whipping.** To whip heavy cream to good volume and stability, it should be well chilled, at least 48 hours old, and placed in a chilled bowl. To prevent separation after whipping, three tablespoons of powdered sugar per cup of cream may be added before beating begins.

Undiluted evaporated milk should be chilled until fine ice crystals form before it is whipped in a chilled bowl with chilled beaters. To stabilize the foam, 2 tablespoons of lemon juice should be folded in after whipping.

To whip nonfat dry milk solids, it is necessary first to combine ½ cup of the solid with ½ cup of cold water and to whip the mixture to soft peaks. Then 2 tablespoons of lemon juice should be added and the mixture beaten stiff. Whipping is completed when ½ cup of sugar has been slowly added and completely beaten in.

**Coagulating.** The addition of rennet pudding mix to milk produces a tender-soft clotted dessert if the milk is heated to lukewarm. If the milk is first boiled and then cooled to lukewarm, coagulation is retarded and the clot is too soft and is breakable.

**Baking.** Most dishes containing milk are best baked at 300° to 350°F. These low to moderate temperatures retard curdling.

To ensure the complete cooking of the starch in scalloped potatoes baked at 350°F, the potato slices should be parboiled before being combined with the other ingredients. When ham is baked in milk, its saltiness and smokiness tend to cause curdling of the milk. This curdling can be retarded by adding ⅓ of the milk at the beginning of the baking period and gradually adding the rest as the baking proceeds. Evaporated milk has less tendency to curdle than fresh milk.

**Substituting and Combining.** One tablespoon of lemon juice or vinegar added to a cup of fresh milk or cream will cause the liquid to sour. Whenever sour milk or cream is substituted for sweet in baking, an adjustment must be made in the leavening—½ teaspoon of baking soda must be added for each cup of sour milk, and 1½ teaspoons of baking powder eliminated. In addition, to adjust for the difference in fat content between sweet and sour cream, the fat called for in the recipe must be reduced by 2½ tablespoons per cup of thin sour cream, or by 6 tablespoons per cup of heavy sour cream.

When used as a liquid ingredient in recipes, ⅞ cup of milk plus 3 tablespoons of butter is equivalent to 1 cup of light coffee cream; about ¾ cup of milk plus ⅓ cup of butter is equivalent to 1 cup of heavy cream. For salad dressings, 1 cup of undiluted evaporated milk plus 1 tablespoon of lemon juice or vinegar may be substituted for 1 cup of sour cream.

Curdling is a problem when milk is combined with tomatoes to make soup. Less curdling is likely to occur if the tomatoes are added very gradually to the milk and if a hot tomato mixture is added to cold milk or if cold milk and a cold tomato mixture are combined and heated together for the shortest possible time and not allowed to boil. The acidity of tomatoes varies; if the acidity is low, curdling may not occur.

## 14. Convenience Foods

Speed is the value of modern convenience foods. Blending of major ingredients is finished, and a tolerance factor is built in to compensate for minor errors in following label directions. Convenience foods need not lead to stereotyped meals; the versatility of the foods and the creativity of the cook can make for individualized uses and cooking shortcuts.

**Ingredients and Mixing Methods.** Many of the basic ingredients used in convenience foods are custom-tailored for the product. The flours used are especially adapted to the mix, and leavenings are selected in relation not only to mixing and baking but also to shelf life. The ingredients that the homemaker must add are carefully specified because of the way they are known to react with the special ingredients. A deviation from directions can adversely affect the finished product. For example, if directions for a cake mix call for water, and milk is used instead, the cake will be coarse and dry. If 2 eggs are stipulated, using only 1 will make a crumbly cake, while using 3 will make a tough cake.

For instant mashed potatoes, exact procedures are also necessary. The proportions of milk and water to use for rehydration are designed to yield a fluffy product. Too much water causes a heavy product, too much milk makes the potatoes sticky and gummy. Lemon pie filling is designed to be smooth when made with water; it curdles if made with milk instead. Instant oatmeal is much like freshly

## SOME BASIC COOKING UTENSILS

COOKING UTENSILS are made of many different materials, including aluminum, copper, tin, enamel, iron, glass, earthenware, and those that have a surface which does not have to be greased. The choice is a matter of personal preference. The utensils illustrated below are the basic ones required.

SAUCEPOT

SAUCEPAN

DOUBLE BOILER

DEEP PIE PLATE

COVERED SKILLET

FRY PAN

GRIDDLE

ROASTING PAN

BREAD OR MEAT LOAF PAN

CASSEROLE

MUFFIN PAN

COOKIE SHEET

**Bake.**—To cook by dry heat in the oven of a range, in a reflector oven before an open fire, in a covered baker on top of a range, or in a portable electric oven.

**Baste.**—To moisten baked, roasted, broiled, or grilled food while it cooks, by spooning on pan drippings, liquid, or savory sauce.

**Beat.**—To use a rapid up-and-down lifting motion with a spoon or whisk to make a mixture light and smooth. A rotary beater, hand driven or electric, accomplishes the same purpose.

**Beurre Manié.**—Equal measures of butter and flour that are kneaded or creamed together. Measured amounts of mixture are used to thicken liquids.

**Blanch.**—To cover first with boiling water for a short time and then with cold water, in order to loosen the skin of a product, set the color, or remove strong flavor elements.

**Blend.**—To combine two or more ingredients by mixing well with creaming, beating, or stirring motion.

**Boil.**—To heat foods over the heat source so that bubbles constantly rise to the surface and break, meanwhile agitating the food mass.

**Boiling Point.**—The moment at which boiling begins. At sea level the boiling point of water is 212° F.

**Bouquet Garni.**—A traditional combination of herbs for seasoning—2 sprigs parsley, 2 sprigs thyme, 1 sprig marjoram, and ½ bay leaf tied together.

**Braise.**—To brown food in a little fat, adding seasonings and a small amount of liquid, covering tightly, and cooking slowly on a range or in an oven until tender.

**Bread.**—To coat food with dry bread, cracker, or cereal crumbs, or with egg, milk or other liquid and then with crumbs, preparatory to frying or baking.

**Broil.**—To cook by direct heat under a broiler or over hot coals.

**Bread Crumbs.**—Dry crumbs made by rolling, grinding, or whirling in electric blender pieces of thoroughly dry bread, or fresh crumbs made by crumbling soft fresh bread slices (crusts removed) with fingers or by tearing them into bits with a fork.

**Caramelize.**—To cook granulated sugar very slowly in a heavy skillet until it melts to golden syrup.

**Chill.**—To let food stand in a refrigerator until it is cold throughout.

**Chop.**—To cut in small pieces with a knife, scissors, or special chopping tool.

**Clarified Butter.**—Clear butterfat that rises to the top (as solids sink to the bottom) when butter is slowly heated over hot water.

**Cream.**—To rub or beat a food, such as butter, with a spoon, fork, whisk, or beater until creamy soft. Also, to blend several ingredients this way until they are soft, well-mixed, and fluffy.

**Crush.**—To press or pound food to break down texture.

**Cube.**—To cut into uniform cube-shaped pieces, usually larger than ¼-inch per edge.

**Cut In.**—To mix fat into a flour mixture with a pastry blender, 2 knives, or a fork, to procure flour-coated fat particles of desired sizes.

**Dice.**—To cut into uniform cube-shaped pieces, usually smaller than ¼-inch per edge.

**Dredge.**—To sprinkle or lightly coat food with flour, sugar, or fine dry crumbs.

**Drippings.**—Meat juices and succulent bits of meat that brown and cook onto a roasting pan or skillet when meat is cooked, together with the small amount of fat that clings to them. Free fat, easily poured from the pan, is not part of drippings.

**Dust.**—To sprinkle the greased surface of a baking dish or pan with fine dry substance such as flour, sugar, crumbs, or ground nuts; particles that do not cling should be shaken out. Also, to sprinkle sugar onto crust of a baked product to decorate it.

**Foamy.**—The appearance of egg white beaten until it takes on a sudsy look with large and small bubbles.

**Fines Herbes.**—A savory combination of herb sprigs or dried herbs, varied to suit the food to be seasoned.

**Flake.**—To break a food, such as cooked fish, gently into pieces by inserting a fork into the natural areas of cleavage.

**Fold.**—To combine beaten egg whites or whipped cream with other ingredients so that air beaten in is not lost. Beaten food is heaped on top of mixture in a bowl. A spatula, spoon, or whisk is plunged through the mass, across bottom of bowl, and up the side to the top. The bowl is rotated ¼ turn as the repeated down-across-up motions combine the ingredients.

**Fry.**—To cook food in hot fat in any of three ways. Cooking in a small amount of fat is *panfrying* or *sautéing*. Cooking in 1 to 2 inches of fat is *shallow-frying*. Cooking in a deep layer of fat in a special deep pan is *deep-fat frying*.

**Garlic Clove.**—One individual bulblet in the cluster that forms a garlic bulb.

**Grate.**—To rub food on a grater to produce desired fine, medium, or coarse particles or shreds.

**Grease.**—To rub a pan or food lightly with softened fat such as butter, margarine, or shortening, or to coat lightly with salad oil.

**Knead.**—To work and press dough with the palms or heels of the hands to develop smoothness and elasticity.

**Larding.**—To lay strips or slices of fat, such as salt pork, bacon, or hard butter, on top of, or in gashes made in, uncooked lean meat or fish to prevent dryness in the cooked product.

**Leavening.**—An ingredient such as baking powder, yeast, or baking soda, used to produce gas during the baking of a food, thus making the baked product light in both appearance and texture. Air beaten into egg whites or whole egg is also a leavening for batters.

**Marinade.**—A flavorful, mildly acid mixture of lemon juice, vinegar, wine, tomato or fruit juice, with savory herbs and spices, and, often, with salad oil. A marinade has a tenderizing effect on collagen and meat fibers and adds flavor to the food.

**Mash.**—To crush or pound to a pulpy mass.

**Meat Extract.**—A seasoned highly concentrated essence of meat including meat juices and extractives. Also called *meat glaze* or *Glacé de Viande.*

**Mince.**—To cut or chop food with a knife, scissors, or mechanical chopper into the smallest possible pieces.

**Mix.**—To distribute ingredients, then blend them into a coherent mass by stirring.

**Mold.**—To give specific shape to a prepared food such as gelatine or dough by the use of a hollow form in which the gelatine is chilled or the dough baked.

**Mounds Up.**—The appearance of a food such as partially set gelatine or beaten eggs or cream when a portion spooned on top heaps up instead of sinking into the rest of the mass. Similarly, when a spoonful dropped on a flat surface retains its shape.

**Panbroil.**—To cook, uncovered, in a hot ungreased or very lightly greased skillet, with the fat poured off from time to time as it accumulates.

**Parboil.**—To boil food in liquid until it is partially cooked, as a preparation for further cooking.

**Pare.**—To cut away the outer covering of foods, such as fruits and vegetables, with a knife.

**Peel.**—To strip or pull off the outer covering of some fruits and vegetables with a knife or the fingers.

**Poach.**—To cook carefully in simmering liquid so that the food retains its shape.

**Purée.**—To press food through a fine sieve or food mill or to whirl it in a blender until it is a homogeneous, nearly liquefied, pulpy mass. Also, the pulp so produced.

**Reduce.**—To decrease the total quantity of a liquid such as broth, stock, or sauce by evaporation. Reduction of broth or stock will be rapid over high heat in an uncovered pan. Reduction of sauce will be slow when simmered over low heat.

**Roast.**—To cook by dry heat in an oven, as in baking. The term is applied especially to baking meats.

**Roux.**—A slowly and thoroughly cooked blend of fat and flour, used as a thickener for liquids. The three color tones of roux, determined by the degree of darkening while cooking, are white, pale, and brown.

**Sauté.**—To cook and brown food lightly in a skillet in a small amount of fat.

**Scald.**—To heat food to a temperature just below the boiling point. Also, to let food stand in boiling water, as in the first step in blanching.

**Score.**—To cut narrow and shallow slits or gashes with a knife in the outer surface or fat of a food.

**Sear.**—To brown the surface of a food very quickly with high heat in an oven, skillet, or broiler, or on a grill.

**Shallot.**—A plant of the onion family with clustered bulbs like garlic, but with a flavor like onion.

**Shred.**—To cut, tear, or grate into small narrow strips or pieces.

**Sieve.**—To purée by pushing food through a fine-meshed utensil. Also, to use a meshed utensil (sieve) to separate the fine and coarse particles of a mixture.

**Sift.**—To put single or mixed dry ingredients through a fine sieve or a mechanical sifter.

**Simmer.**—To cook over low heat, just below the boiling point, so that bubbles form and rise slowly, collapsing just below the surface.

**Steam.**—To cook in steam that rises from a small amount of boiling water in a tightly covered pan.

**Steep.**—To let food stand in warm liquid for a short time to extract its flavor and color.

**Stiff But Not Dry.**—Term applied to egg whites beaten until peaks form when beater is withdrawn and the whites are glossy on the surface. The peaks droop slightly as the beater leaves them.

**Stir.**—To mix foods with a spoon, spatula, wire wisk, or fork, using a circular motion.

**Stock.**—Liquid in which meat, poultry, fish, game, vegetables, or a selected mixture of such foods was cooked slowly until the liquid is rich and flavorful.

**Whip.**—To beat rapidly with a rotary beater, electric mixer, or wire whisk to incorporate air into, and increase the volume of, such foods as heavy cream, egg whites, or gelatine mixtures.

made oatmeal when it is moistened with boiling water, but it becomes sticky when hot milk is used instead.

The correct timing and extent of beating, stirring, boiling, or otherwise manipulating convenience foods are specified on labels. Puddings and pie fillings are firmer if brought quickly to a boil than when cooked slowly. Instant puddings, if beaten too long or stirred while setting, become too soft. Too much boiling gives tapioca puddings a stretchy texture.

Adding individual touches to convenience foods is permissible as long as the basic balance of major ingredients and the mixing methods are not changed. The addition of favorite flavorings or seasonings and the use of garnishes can quickly personalize the product without harming it.

**Use as Shortcuts.** Many convenience foods serve as shortcuts in preparing favorite dishes. Canned soups make quick sauces for use as toppings or binders or as bases for creamed foods. Packaged soup, dressing, or seasoning mixes have a multitude of uses for flavor, texture, and color. Sauce and gravy mixes help in preparing any main dish casserole or loaf in a hurry. Refrigerated biscuits and rolls can be turned into dumplings or casserole toppers.

Dehydrated and freeze-dried minced onions or shallots, chopped chives, and grated orange or lemon peel help cut tedious chores. An envelope of melted chocolate saves measuring, with one envelope replacing 1 square of chocolate or ¼ cup plain cocoa in a recipe.

FREDERICA L. BEINERT
*Author of "The Art of Making Sauces and Gravies" and "The Art of Making Soufflés"*

### Bibliography

Beinert, Frederica L., *The Art of Making Sauces and Gravies* (Doubleday 1966).
Beinert, Frederica L., *The Art of Making Soufflés* (Doubleday 1967).
Bridge, Tom, *The Golden Age of Cookery* (State Mutual Bks. 1983).
Capon, Robert Farrar, *The Supper of the Lamb: A Culinary Reflection* (Harcourt 1979).
Cowenfeld, Claire, *The Complete Book of Herbs and Spices* (Putnam 1974).
Good, Phyllis P., *The Best of Amish Cooking* (Good Bks. 1988).
Grover, Kathryn, ed., *Dining in America, 1850–1900* (Univ. of Mass. Press 1987).
Jones, Ita, *The Grubbag: An Underground Cookbook* (Random House 1971).
Lang, Jenifer H., ed., *Larousse Gastronomique: The New American Edition of the World's Greatest Culinary Encyclopedia* (Crown 1988).
McGee, Harold, *On Food and Cooking: The Science and Core of the Kitchen* (Macmillan 1988).
Morris, Dan, and Moore, Matilda, *The Savor of the Sea* (Macmillan 1966).
Pellegrini, Angelo, *The Unprejudiced Palate* (North Point Press 1984).
Pope, Antoinette and François, *New Candy Cookbook* (Macmillan 1967).
Regis, Alice H., *Cakes and Ale: The Ultimate Food Glossary: A Collection of Two Thousand Five Hundred Foods, Techniques, Tools and Cooking Terms* (Axelrod Pub. 1988).
Rice Council, *Serve Rice and Shine* (Rand McNally 1963).
Riely, Elizabeth, *The Chef's Companion: A Dictionary of Culinary Terms* (Van Nostrand Reinhold 1986).
Shapiro, Laura, *Perfection Salad: Women and Cooking at the Turn of the Century* (Farrar, Straus 1986).
Sokolov, Raymond, *Fading Feast: A Compendium of Disappearing American Regional Foods* (Farrar, Straus 1981).
Stobart, Tom, *The Cook's Encyclopedia* (Harper 1979).
Thompson, Terry, *Cajun-Creole Cooking* (Ballantine Bks. 1987).
Villas, James, *American Taste: A Celebration of Gastronomy Coast to Coast* (Arbor House 1982).
Wheaton, Barbara K., and Kelly, Patricia M., eds., *Bibliography of Culinary History: Food Resources in Eastern Massachusetts* (G. K. Hall 1988).

**COOLEY,** kōō′lē, **Charles Horton** (1864–1929), American sociologist, who was one of the founders of sociology in the United States. He was born in Ann Arbor, Mich., on Aug. 17, 1864. He taught at the University of Michigan at Ann Arbor, but his influence extended far beyond that Midwestern center. He was one of the founders of the American Sociological Society, and his essays on how "human nature" is formed in the context of the individual's group experience did much to demonstrate the distinctive subject matter and approach of sociology.

Cooley's major works, *Human Nature and the Social Order* (1902), *Social Organization* (1909), and *Social Process* (1918), remain important reference sources despite what critics have considered their antiurban, anti-individualist bias. His concepts of the "looking glass self" (self-awareness arising from one's imagination of his appearance to the other) and the "primary group" (characterized by warm, face-to-face relations) continue to be used to explain the development of the self and its social expression. Cooley died in Ann Arbor on May 8, 1929.

LOUISE G. HOWTON, *Brooklyn College*

**COOLEY,** kōō′lē, **Thomas McIntyre** (1824–1898), American judge and public official, who was the first chairman of the U. S. Interstate Commerce Commission. He was born near Attica, N. Y., on Jan. 6, 1824. After studying law in New York and Michigan, he was admitted to the Michigan bar in 1846. From 1859 to 1884 he was a professor of law at the University of Michigan, and from 1864 to 1885 he also was a state supreme court judge.

Cooley became known as a legal authority upon publication of *A Treatise on the Constitutional Limitations Which Rest Upon the Legislative Power of the States of the American Union* (1868). Later works included treatises on the law of taxation (1876), the law of torts (1879), and the principles of constitutional law (1880). In 1887, President Grover Cleveland appointed him to the new Interstate Commerce Commission. Elected chairman, Cooley established the guidelines for the administration of this first important federal regulatory agency. He retired in 1891 and died in Ann Arbor, Mich., on Sept. 12, 1898.

LEWIS G. VANDER VELDE, *University of Michigan*

**COOLEY'S ANEMIA,** kōō′lēz ə-nē′mē-ə, is a blood disorder in which the body does not produce enough hemoglobin. As a result, there is too little hemoglobin in the red cells, and because they appear as tiny targets, they are often described as "target cells." Since the red cells are defective, they remain in the bloodstream for only a relatively short time before they are destroyed by the liver and spleen, the organs responsible for the destruction of abnormal or worn-out red cells. As a result, the person has a low hemoglobin level, and his liver and spleen are enlarged. In addition, there is an accumulation of iron in the body, which may damage the heart and liver.

Cooley's anemia is inherited as a recessive trait. Treatment consists of blood transfusions and the removal of the accumulated iron. Children born with the disease rarely survive past adolescence.

ERNEST BEUTLER, M. D.
*City of Hope Medical Center, Duarte, Calif.*

**30th President of the United States (1923–1929)**

Birth—July 4, 1872, in Plymouth Notch, Vt.

Higher Education—Amherst College (B. A., 1895).

Religion—Congregationalist.

Occupation—Lawyer.

Marriage—Oct. 4, 1905, to Grace Anna Goodhue (1879–1957).

Children—John (1906–     ); Calvin (1908–1924).

Nickname—"Silent Cal."

Political Party—Republican.

Residence When He Became President—Massachusetts.

Position Before Taking Office—Vice President.

Principal Writings—*The Autobiography of Calvin Coolidge* (1929).

Death—Jan. 5, 1933, in Northampton, Mass., at age 60.

Burial Place—Plymouth Notch, Vt.

**COOLIDGE,** ko͞o′lij, **Calvin** (1872–1933), 30th President of the United States. He was a shrewd and taciturn New Englander, who occupied the White House for six years during the prosperous and tumultuous 1920's. The number and variety of Coolidge's accomplishments as president were substantial. Unhappily, wiser ones were needed to meet the growing problems of the time. His major achievements—tax and debt reduction and the Kellogg-Briand Pact renouncing war—were soon made mockeries by the events of the 1930's, and his lesser accomplishments were largely forgotten with time's passage.

**Early Life.** Born on July 4, 1872, in Plymouth Notch, Vt., he was named John Calvin Coolidge, but in early adulthood he dropped the "John." He was descended on his father's side from one John Coolidge, who went from England to Massachusetts about 1630. Coolidge's father, John Calvin Coolidge, was a jack-of-all-trades, teacher, storekeeper, farmer, politician, and even mechanic when necessary. His mother, Victoria Moor Coolidge, a handsome woman and a lover of poetry and natural beauty, died when Calvin was 12.

His upbringing was idealistic. Although Coolidge's ideas of religion were vague, he believed in a divine intelligence and that man had a God-given duty to render public service. Also inculcated in him at an early age were attributes of caution, dependability, fairness, honesty, industry, thrift, tolerance, and unpretentiousness, and a belief in man's perfectibility. These were derived from his homelife and the simple, democratic society of Plymouth Notch. They were reinforced by what he learned in school and at Amherst College in Massachusetts.

Calvin was the first of the Vermont Coolidges to go to college. His years at Amherst gave Coolidge an understanding of culture, strengthened his bent toward civic service, and also persuaded him of the necessity of stability and harmony in the affairs of men. The college made the reserved Vermonter into something of a scholar and a gentleman, graduating him *cum laude* and allowing him to develop into an adequate speaker and an occasionally droll fellow.

After his graduation from Amherst in 1895,

Coolidge decided to become a lawyer. He read law in the offices of John Hammond and Henry Field in Northampton, Mass. Two years later he was admitted to the bar. He decided to build on his beginnings in Northampton and practice law there. Although he never prospered as an attorney, he was able to earn enough in his practice of drawing up legal documents, doing title searches and collection work, managing estates, and whatever else came his way, to become financially independent in a short time.

**Rise in Massachusetts Politics.** His association with Hammond and Field led him into politics, his second profession. Politics came easily to Coolidge because his father was a frequent officeholder in Vermont. In Northampton, Hammond and Field were political leaders and found their young law clerk a willing political apprentice. During 1896 and 1897, Coolidge was active in the Republican party, and in 1898 he was rewarded with nomination and election as a city councilman. From then until his retirement from the presidency he was seldom out of public office. In 1905 he suffered his only election defeat, in a contest for school committeeman.

That year, however, he gained his wife. Grace Anna Goodhue, the daughter of a Vermont mechanical engineer, had been a teacher at the Clarke Institute for the Deaf in Northampton. One of Coolidge's earliest bon mots comes from his courtship, when the quiet young man expressed his hope "that having taught the deaf to hear, Miss Goodhue might perhaps cause the mute to speak." Grace Coolidge was the perfect companion for an affectionate but often cranky husband. She was a woman of natural charm, good humor, and outspoken interest in people, willing to let Calvin take the lead in all things.

The year after their marriage was brightened by the birth of their first son, John, and by Calvin's election to the Massachusetts House of Representatives. During his two 1-year terms in the House, Coolidge made little impression, although his record was mildly progressive. After a short absence from public service, Coolidge was elected mayor of Northampton in 1909 and re-elected in 1910. In 1911 he was sent to the state Senate, where he became a Republican leader. His creed seemed to be "something for everybody," so long as it did not cost much.

After his election to a third Senate term in 1913, Coolidge rounded up sufficient support for election to the presidency of the Senate. In this powerful position he was the most important Republican officeholder in Massachusetts, because Democrats occupied both the governorship and the lieutenant governorship. Advising his colleagues to "Do the day's work" and "Be brief," Coolidge performed effectively as Senate president, producing legislation that was sound and well received. In 1915 he ran successfully for lieutenant governor. Coolidge used his three years as lieutenant governor to acquire more knowledge of government, and in 1918 he was elected governor.

**Governor.** Coolidge made an energetic and effective governor. He worked to settle labor disputes by encouraging reasonable pay increases, and to grant additional home rule to municipalities. Yet his national reputation did not come from such accomplishments, but from the 1919 Boston police strike.

The police of Boston had grievances over pay, hours of work, and working conditions. Receiving little satisfaction from the city, they affiliated with the American Federation of Labor (AFL), and when 19 local police union leaders were suspended from the force, the police voted to strike. Their walkout brought disorder to Boston. Coolidge did not step into the strike until peace had been largely restored, when he took command of the various forces that had been introduced to bring order. He denied the right of the strikers to return to their jobs, and defended the city's and state's actions in a telegram to Samuel Gompers, president of the AFL, in which he asserted, "There is no right to strike against the public safety by anybody, anywhere, any time." Coolidge received the acclaim of the nation, including that of President Woodrow Wilson, for meeting a dire threat to public safety, and that fall he was reelected governor.

**Vice President.** At the 1920 Republican national convention, Coolidge, a favorite-son candidate for president, was passed over as Warren G. Harding was nominated. The delegates, however, spontaneously selected Coolidge for vice president. That fall Harding and Coolidge won a landslide victory.

Vice President Coolidge presided over the Senate without flair or dash, sat quietly at cabinet meetings, and made rather unimpressive speeches over the country. By the summer of 1923 he had little enthusiasm for his job and had developed no power as a national political figure.

**The Presidency.** All that changed during the night of Aug. 2, 1923, when President Harding died. At 2:47 A.M., Coolidge was sworn in by his father in his rural Vermont home by the light of an oil lamp. The new President left for Washington a few hours later to take up his duties.

*First Term.* Coolidge set out to establish a working relationship with the leading members of the Harding administration, and he drew on many people for advice and help. The scandals of Harding's presidency, particularly the Teapot Dome oil affair, were coming to light, and Coolidge spent much of his time defending his party. His relations with Congress were unhappy, but he coped with scandal by prosecuting offenders, and, thanks to that, his integrity, and his self-possession, he retrieved public confidence in the White House.

He gained enough control over the Republican party to be nominated for president in June 1924. Coolidge also gained enough of the people's confidence to be easily elected over his major opposition, John W. Davis (Democrat) and Robert M. La Follette (Progressive). When Coolidge entered the campaign with a series of "nonpolitical" statements late that summer, it was as the apostle of prosperity, economy, and respectability. His opponents exhausted themselves with charges about the government's deficiencies, while the President received credit for his equanimity and the economic upturn. But 1924 was a sad year for Coolidge, for in July his younger son, Calvin, Jr., died of blood poisoning.

*Second Term—Domestic Issues.* Coolidge was fairly successful in getting what he wanted during his full term as president. Heading the list were paring the national debt and reducing income taxes, so that there would be more money for consumer spending. Other measures included orderly growth of civil and military aviation, expansion of the services of the departments of Agriculture and Commerce, regulation of radio broadcasting, development of waterways, flood control, and encouragement of cooperative solutions to farm problems. Twice, he blocked enactment of the McNary-Haugen bill, which pro-

BROWN BROTHERS

PRESIDENT COOLIDGE throws the first ball, opening the baseball season on April 22, 1925. At the left is Mrs. Coolidge, and at right is Secretary of State Frank B. Kellogg, coauthor of the Kellogg-Briand Pact.

posed to dump farm surpluses abroad in the hope of raising domestic market prices, because he objected to its price-fixing features and its cost.

*Foreign Affairs.* In his search for world peace, which absorbed much of his time, Coolidge's course was unsteady. He supported American membership on the World Court, and then, when American participation on the court was rendered impossible by Senate amendments, naval disarmament. When the Geneva Naval Conference of 1927, which Coolidge sponsored, failed because of the refusal of France and Italy to participate and Anglo-American disagreement on what to disarm, the president was discouraged. He supported a multilateral declaration renouncing war as an instrument of national policy and agreeing to settle all disputes by pacific means. This was incorporated into international law through the Kellogg-Briand Pact of 1928.

Coolidge also restored diplomatic relations with Mexico. It seemed for a while, however, in 1927 that the good relations between the two countries might end again as a result of restrictions on foreign oil rights and on the Catholic church in Mexico, and because of the sharp disagreement over recognition of a new government in Nicaragua. Working largely through special representative Henry Stimson in Nicaragua and the new ambassador to Mexico, Dwight Morrow, the Coolidge administration was able to settle the situation. This and other actions anticipated the Good Neighbor policy toward Latin America.

Other distinguishing features of Coolidge's foreign policy were America's insistence on elimination of the treaty rights of many foreign nations to intervene in Chinese affairs and its efforts to settle problems of German reparations to the World War I victors, chiefly through the Dawes Plan, which made reparations manageable for Germany. Regarding foreign debts to the United States government, there was no question of reducing them, but the administration substantially lowered the required interest rates.

As an administrator, Coolidge was most successful. He demanded and got efficient and economical performance in government operations. He was instrumental in releasing the remaining political prisoners convicted under the Sedition Act during the Wilson administration. He also helped by his appointments to raise the level of competence among diplomats and federal judges.

*Later Years.* Coolidge declined to run for reelection. He retired in 1929 to Northampton, where he busied himself writing newspaper and magazine articles. He seldom took an active role in politics. His health declined rapidly, and on Jan. 5, 1933, he died of coronary thrombosis. He was buried in the family plot in Plymouth Notch, where the Coolidge homestead is operated as a museum by the state of Vermont.

The largest collections of Calvin Coolidge's correspondence are in the Library of Congress and the Forbes Library in Northampton.

DONALD R. McCOY, *The University of Kansas*

**Bibliography**

Coolidge, Calvin, *The Autobiography of Calvin Coolidge* (1929; reprint, Tuttle 1972).
Fitzgerald, Carol B., ed., *Calvin Coolidge* (Meckler Pub. 1988).
McCoy, Donald R., *Calvin Coolidge: The Quiet President* (1967; reprint, Univ. Press of Kans. 1988).
Murray, R. K., *The Politics of Normalcy* (Norton 1973).
Ross, Ishbel, *Grace Coolidge and Her Era* (1962; reprint, C. Coolidge Memorial Fdtn. 1988).
Silver, Thomas B., *Coolidge and the Historians* (1982; reprint, Carolina Acad. Press 1986).

**COOLIDGE,** kōō′lij, **Charles Allerton** (1858–1936), American architect. He was born in Boston, Mass., on Nov. 30, 1858. Educated at Harvard and the Massachusetts Institute of Technology, he joined the firm of the noted architect H. H. Richardson in 1883, becoming a partner in 1886. Coolidge subsequently headed the company, and created a new development in architecture—a group office that could handle projects of a size and complexity beyond the capacity of the usual one-man office.

Coolidge's firm, working in a variety of traditional styles, built banks, libraries, museums, and complexes of college buildings. Noteworthy are the classical Art Institute and Public Library in Chicago, a Byzantine quadrangle at Stanford University, and, at Harvard, the Fogg Art Museum, the Memorial Chapel, and the newly conceived college residential "houses," all in a serene Georgian red brick. Coolidge died in Locust Valley, N. Y., on April 1, 1936.

**COOLIDGE,** kōō′lij, **William David** (1873–1975), American physical chemist, who introduced ductile tungsten as a material for light-bulb filaments and X-ray tube components. Born on a farm near Hudson, Mass., on Oct. 23, 1873, Coolidge graduated from the Massachusetts Institute of Technology in 1896. After study in Europe, he returned to M.I.T. to teach. In 1905, Coolidge was invited to join the staff of the General Electric Research Laboratory in Schenectady, N. Y. He spent his career there, serving as director from 1932 until his retirement in 1944. He died in Schenectady, N. Y., on Feb. 3, 1975.

His first assignment at GE was to continue the search for the material best suited for use as a filament in the incandescent lamp to replace the inefficient carbon filaments used by Edison. Tungsten proved to be the ideal material, and it is still used. Coolidge and his associates developed a method of drawing tungsten into the fine wire used to make filaments.

Coolidge later found that tungsten was an excellent material for the generation of X-rays, because of its high atomic number, high melting point, and low vapor pressure. One type of modern X-ray generating tube is called the Coolidge tube in honor of Coolidge's discovery.

LEONARD M. FANNING
*Author of "Fathers of Industries"*

**COOLIDGE,** kōō′lij, a city located in southern Arizona, in Pinal county, 50 miles (80 km) southeast of Phoenix, in the Gila River valley. It is a trade and industrial center in an irrigated cotton- and cattle-raising area. Industries of the city include steel fabrication and the manufacture of fertilizer. Casa Grande Ruins National Monument, which features ruins of a walled pre-Columbian Indian village, is just northeast of Coolidge. The city has a council-manager form of government. Population: 7,786.

**COOLIDGE DAM,** kōō′lij, is on the Gila River in Arizona, about 25 miles (40 km) southeast of Globe. It forms San Carlos Lake, with a capacity of 6 billion cubic feet (170 million cu meters) whose waters are used mainly to irrigate the Casa Grande valley (the basin of the Gila River southeast of Phoenix). The dam, completed in 1928, is a multiple-dome structure and was the first of its type. It is 249 feet (76 meters) high and is crossed by a highway.

**COOLING.** See Air Conditioning; Heat Pump; Refrigeration.

**COOMA,** kōō'mə, is a municipality in New South Wales, Australia. It is situated on the Murrumbidgee River, 65 miles (105 km) south of Canberra. Focal point of the rich Monaro pastoral district, Cooma is an important livestock-selling center.

The region around Cooma produces fine wool, dairy produce, grain, and beef cattle. Cooma is an important highway junction, and air services connect it with Canberra and Melbourne. The town, which is the main entry point to Mount Kosciusko and other alpine snowfields, has developed a considerable tourist trade.

Cooma was chosen as field headquarters for the Snowy Mountains Hydro-electric Authority in 1949. The town soon became the center for major construction companies working on the water conservation and power generation project. Population: (1981) 7,978.

R. M. Younger
*Author of "Australia and the Australians"*

**COOMARASWAMY,** kōō-mä'rə-swä'mē, **Ananda Kentish** (1877–1947), Ceylonese art historian. Coomaraswamy was born in Colombo, Ceylon, on Aug. 22, 1877. He studied at the University of London, where he was awarded a D.Sc. degree in 1904. He directed the mineralogical survey of Ceylon and was among the leaders who revived the ancient Sinhalese culture. In 1917 he went to the United States, becoming keeper of Indian and Muhammadan art in the Museum of Fine Arts, Boston. Being half East Indian and half English by blood and possessing aristocratic tastes and a vast knowledge of many cultures, he was an admirable interpreter of Oriental art to the West.

Coomaraswamy had a special fondness for fine printing and at one time owned the Kelmscott Press in Oxford, printing his own books with great care. He lectured extensively on Oriental art and metaphysics. His enduring monument is the collection of Oriental art in the Boston museum.

Coomaraswamy died in Needham, Mass. on Sept. 8, 1947. Among his numerous books are *Indian Drawings* (2 vols., 1910–1912), *Visvakarma* (1914), *Vidyapati* (1915), *Buddha and the Gospel of Buddhism* (1916), *History of Indian and Indonesian Art* (1927), *Elements of Buddhist Iconography* (1935), and *Hinduism and Buddhism* (1943).

Robert Payne
*Author of "The Splendors of Asia"*

**COON,** kōōn, **Carleton Stevens** (1904–1981), American anthropologist. Coon was born on June 23, 1904, in Wakefield, Mass. He received his Ph.D. from Harvard in 1928, and he taught anthropology there from 1927 to 1948, becoming a professor in 1946. Coon headed the ethnology section of the University of Pennsylvania Museum, where he was also a professor of anthropology from 1948 to 1963. He then became curator of the anthropology section. He wrote *Caravan: The Story of the Middle East* (1951), *The Story of Man* (1954), *The Origin of Races* (1962), and *The Living Races of Man* (1965).

Among Coon's discoveries were the remains of a 50,000-year-old Neanderthal man in North Africa in 1939 and, in 1951, three skeletons of 75,000-year-old human beings in Iran. He died in Gloucester, Mass., on June 3, 1981.

**COON RAPIDS,** kōōn, is a city in eastern Minnesota, in Anoka county, on the Mississippi River. It is situated 14 miles (22 km) north of downtown Minneapolis, of which it is a rapidly growing residential suburb. Coon Rapids was incorporated in 1952. Government is by a council and manager. Population: 52,978.

**COONHOUND,** **Black-and-Tan,** kōōn'hound, a breed of tracking hound in the sporting group of dogs. The coonhound somewhat resembles the bloodhounds but weighs less and lacks the wrinkles. It stands 23 to 27 inches (58–68 cm) at the shoulder and weighs 55 to 70 pounds (25–31 kg). The coat is short and dense.

The coonhound was not recognized as a pure breed by the American Kennel Club until 1945, but its development can be traced back to 11th century England. The modern breed results from the crossing of the Talbot hound and bloodhound with the Virginia foxhound and various other strains. Although primarily a raccoon dog, it can be trained for larger game as well.

William F. Brown
*Editor of "American Field"*

**COOPER, Alfred Duff** (1890–1954), British political leader and author. He was created *First Viscount Norwich of Aldwick* in 1952. Born in London on Feb. 22, 1890, he was educated at Eton and at Oxford University. He served in World War I with the Grenadier Guards, winning the Distinguished Service Order. In 1919 he married Lady Diana Manners, a celebrated beauty and actress of some distinction who played the Madonna in the stage production of *The Miracle* (1923) in the United States.

A Conservative, Cooper served in the House of Commons, first representing Oldham (1924–1929), and then St. George's Division at Westminster (1931–1945). He became financial secretary to the War Office (1928–1929 and 1931–1934) and to the Treasury (1934–1935). From 1935 to 1937 he was secretary of state for war and in 1937 he was made first lord of the admiralty. He resigned that post in 1938 in protest over the Munich settlement; his staunch opposition to "appeasement" caused Adolf Hitler to bracket him with Winston Churchill and Anthony Eden as "one of the principal warmongers." In 1940–1941 he was minister of information in the Churchill government. When the British and French armies met disaster in France in May 1940, Cooper calmly heartened the British people over the radio, quoting Shakespeare's lines about St. Crispin's day from *Henry V*, counseling against not only panic itself but the very thought of panic. He was ambassador to France from 1944 to 1947.

Cooper's nine books include *Talleyrand* (1932) and *Haig* (2 vols., 1935, 1936). He died aboard ship off Vigo, Spain, on Jan. 1, 1954.

**COOPER, Anthony.** See Shaftesbury.

**COOPER, Gary** (1901–1961), American motion picture actor. He was born Frank James Cooper in Helena, Mont., on May 7, 1901. After attending Grinnell College in Iowa, he attempted unsuccessfully to earn a living as a commercial artist. He drifted into motion pictures, acting bit parts in Westerns and rising to stardom as a Western hero in such films as *The Virginian* (1929). He starred in more than 80 films.

GARY COOPER and Grace Kelly in a scene from *High Noon*, a picture that earned him an "Oscar" (1952).

Gary Cooper epitomized the decent, reticent, homespun American led by his principles to a heroism he did not eagerly seek. In *Sergeant York* (1941) and *High Noon* (1952), for both of which he won the Academy Award, he portrayed men of this stamp. However, the early part of Cooper's career especially reveals him as a resourceful and flexible actor, achieving high comedy in Ernst Lubitsch's *Design for Living* (1933) and mastering the cosmopolitan world in Josef von Sternberg's *Morocco* (1930). He died in Los Angeles, Calif., on May 13, 1961.

**COOPER, Gladys** (1888–1971), English actress. She was born in London on Dec. 18, 1888. After making her London stage debut in 1906, she appeared regularly in the British theater. She made her New York debut in *The Shining Hour* (1934) and continued playing both in London and New York. She appeared in several films in the 1940's and 1950's, including *Rebecca* (1940), *That Hamilton Woman* (1941), and *Madame Bovary* (1949). She was seen in New York and London in *The Chalk Garden* (1955) and in New York in *A Passage to India* (1962). In 1965 she was featured on U. S. television in a series called *The Rogues*. She died in London on Nov. 17, 1971.

**COOPER, Henry Ernest** (1857–1929), American public official in Hawaii. He was born in New Albany, Ind., on Aug. 28, 1857, and graduated from Boston University (1878). He took up residence in Hawaii in 1891 and two years later was chairman of the committee of public safety in the revolution that deposed Queen Liliuokalani and established a republican government with a view to eventual annexation of the islands by the United States.

He served as judge in the circuit court of Oahu and became minister of foreign affairs in 1895. From then until 1900, when Hawaii became a U. S. territory, Cooper held most of the important executive offices, including that of acting president. A highly effective public administrator, he was territorial secretary from 1900 to 1903. He worked to establish the College (now University) of Hawaii and was first chairman of its board of regents. Cooper died in Long Beach, Calif., on May 14, 1929.

**COOPER, James Fenimore** (1789–1851), American novelist, historian, and social critic, who was the first great professional author in the New World. He is most famous for the Leatherstocking Tales about the American frontier, of which the best known is *The Last of the Mohicans* (1826; q.v.). As both interpreter of and contributor to the developing national culture, Cooper occupied—as his contemporaries at home and abroad sporadically recognized—a unique and central position. He implicated himself personally, intellectually, and creatively in the American civilization he saw evolving, and committed himself fervently to a magnificent 18th century vision of its possibilities.

**Early Life.** Cooper was born at Burlington, N. J., on Sept. 15, 1789, the son of Quakers, Judge William Cooper and Elizabeth Fenimore Cooper. A representative to the 4th and 6th Congresses, Judge Cooper was a prominent Federalist who attained great wealth by developing large tracts of virgin land. The Coopers moved, when James was about a year old, to the thriving frontier village of Cooperstown, N. Y., which Judge Cooper had founded a few years before. James ("Fenimore" was added later, in deference to his mother) indulged himself—almost too deeply—in the freedom conferred by both wealth and wilderness. He was an undisciplined student and was expelled from Yale in his junior year for frivolity. He was then sent to Europe as a common seaman to prepare for a naval career.

In 1808, on his return to the United States, Cooper received a warrant as a midshipman in the Navy. Three years later he married Susan Augusta De Lancey, who came from a powerful New York Tory family, and shortly thereafter, with his wife's urging, and on the strength of a large inheritance from his father, who had died in 1809, he left the Navy. Cooper took up the comfortable life of a gentleman farmer, first in Westchester county, New York, and then on a fine farm in Cooperstown, overlooking Lake Otsego. However, serious reverses connected with his father's estate destroyed this idyll, and Cooper returned to Westchester in 1817, living modestly on his wife's land.

At the age of 30, inspired by a school of bestselling novels and a need for cash, he wrote his first novel, *Precaution* (1820). Though the work was a failure, Cooper had found his métier, and his next novel, *The Spy* (1821; q.v.), in which he created Harvey Birch, a humble spy for the American revolutionaries, was widely acclaimed.

**Leatherstocking Novels.** Cooper's next work, *The Pioneers* (1823), extended his reputation, both at home and abroad, and marked the start of his Leatherstocking series. These novels, which have become classics of American literature, tell the adventures of the American forester-frontiersman Natty Bumppo (also called Leatherstocking, Hawkeye, and other names) and his Indian companion Chingachgook. The novels were not written in the chronological order of their narrative; their story starts with what was actually the last-published work in the series—*The Deerslayer* (1841; q.v.), which depicts Bumppo in his youth in the Lake Otsego region. *The Last of the Mohicans* follows Natty's exploits against the Huron Indians in the Lake Champlain region; *The Pathfinder* (1840) tells of Bumppo's adventures in the French and Indian War, and portrays him in love; *The Pioneers* shows Natty and Chingachgook as old men in the Lake Otsego region; and *The Prairie* (1827) depicts Bumppo's last days, as a trapper on the Great Plains, where he was driven by the destruction of the forests in the East.

**Sea Novels.** Having created the genre of the frontier tale, Cooper invented, with *The Pilot* (1824; q.v.), the genre of the sea romance, filled, like the forest tales, with rapid action and strongly contrasted characters. His other novels with sea settings include *The Red Rover* (1827; q.v.), *The Wing-and-Wing* (1842), *The Two Admirals* (1842), *Afloat and Ashore* (1844), and its sequel *Miles Wallingford* (1844), and *The Sea Lions* (1849).

**Social Criticism.** Cooper's long conflict with his critics began to erode his popularity in the early 1830's, during the latter part of his residence in Europe (1826–1833). There he continued to write romances but turned increasingly to types of writing in which he could embody his maturing philosophy of political, economic, and social behavior. Cooper's readers had been satisfied with his earlier work, historical romances with recognizable American scenes, characters, and manners. But when he turned his energies to educating his countrymen on their cultural deficiencies, he met with scorn and severe opposition. Deeply persuaded of the necessary co-existence of order and individuality in human affairs, he sought to redress the balance, to suggest the advantages of order to a society impatient of restraints. He was, that is, a constitutionalist in the broad as well as in the narrow sense, an individualist who understood the need for setting bounds to individualism.

Acute though his observations were and faithful though he sought to be to the Founding Fathers' notion of American democracy, Cooper's program proved to be too strenuous, too much at odds with the moving forces of his time. The first of these critical works, *Notions of the Americans* (1828), which was intended to refute what Cooper considered to be false accounts of America by European travelers, was reviewed with hostility in Europe and ridiculed by American journalists. Three new romances with European settings, *The Bravo* (1831), *The Heidenmauer* (1832), and *The Headsman* (1833), also containing social commentary, received harsh treatment in the American press.

Returning to the United States in 1833, first to New York City and later to Cooperstown, Cooper chronicled his ill-treatment by American journalists in *A Letter to His Countrymen* (1834). This was followed by *The Monikins* (1835), a political allegory; five European travel books; *The American Democrat* (1838), which set forth more systematically his views of government and society; and two novels reflecting his bitter disappointment with America, *Homeward Bound* (1838) and *Home As Found* (1838)—all of which were badly received, as was his monumental *History of the Navy of the United States of America* (1839). Cooper challenged his critics, mostly prominent Whig editors, in numerous libel suits designed to expose the tyranny of the press, and won most of his cases.

**Later Years.** Remaining the disappointed, uneasy American, Cooper nevertheless regained some popularity with later publications, among them the final Leatherstocking novels, *The Pathfinder* and *The Deerslayer*. Other late works were *Satanstoe* (1845), *The Chainbearer* (1845), and *The Red-skins* (1846), a trilogy that chronicled the history of the Antirent troubles in New York state; *Ways of the Hour* (1850), a murder mystery with much social commentary; and *Upside Down* (1850), a play ridiculing socialist ideas. Cooper died at Otsego Hall, his home in Cooperstown, on Sept. 14, 1851.

**Significance.** Cooper's permanent value to social and intellectual historians as a sensitive, encyclopedic barometer of his time seems assured. Though his commentary is widely scattered throughout his writings, and some of it is cranky, precipitate, and biased by class associations, his powers of observation were as comprehensive as Tocqueville's, and quite as suggestive.

Literary criticism has yet to give full credit to the richness and complexity of Cooper's art. Critical judgment has too often ended with Cooper's literary faults, especially his carelessness and turgidity, qualities ridiculed in Mark Twain's famous essay, *Fenimore Cooper's Literary Offenses* (1895). Modern critics are beginning to discover the complex internal designs that made Cooper's work admired by such writers as Goethe, Balzac, and Conrad. The full recognition that Cooper was a serious artist will come with the further recognition that, beyond his inventiveness and his pioneering use of American materials, his fiction, at its best, conveys a profound understanding of the human condition.

JAMES FRANKLIN BEARD
*Editor of "The Letters and Journals of James Fenimore Cooper"*

### Bibliography

**Collections of Cooper's Fiction,** though they omit his shorter works, are the W. A. Townsend and Co. edition, 32 vols. (1859–1861) and the Mohawk edition, 33 vols. (1895–1900). The letters and journals were edited by James Franklin Beard, 6 vols. (Harvard Univ. Press 1960–1968). Cooper's nonfiction writings have never been collected.

**Dekker, George,** *Fenimore Cooper: The Critical Heritage* (Routledge 1973).

**Franklin, Wayne,** *The New World of James Fenimore Cooper* (Univ. of Chicago Press 1982).

**Motley, Warren,** *The American Abraham: James Fenimore Cooper and the Frontier Patriarch* (Cambridge 1988).

**Overland, Orin,** *The Making and Meaning of an American Classic* (Humanities Press 1973).

**Railton, Stephen,** *Fenimore Cooper: A Study of His Life and Imagination* (Princeton Univ. Press 1978).

**Ringe, Donald A.,** *James Fenimore Cooper,* rev. ed. (G. K. Hall 1988).

**Thomas, Brook,** *Cross-Examinations of Law and Literature* (Cambridge 1987).

**Wallace, James D.,** *Early Cooper and His Audience* (Columbia Univ. Press 1987).

**James Fenimore Cooper**

Peter Cooper, from a photograph by Mathew Brady.

BROWN BROTHERS

**COOPER, John Sherman** (1901– ), American senator, diplomat, and government official. Born in Somerset, Ky., on Aug. 23, 1901, he graduated from Yale in 1923, attended Harvard law school, and was admitted to the bar in 1928. After a term in the Kentucky legislature, Cooper was a county judge for eight years before running unsuccessfully for governor. During World War II he served in the Army with distinction.

After the war, Cooper devoted himself mostly to his career in the U. S. Senate. He served from 1946 to 1949 and from 1952 to 1955. In 1956 he was elected to fill an unexpired term for a third time, and he was elected to full terms in 1960 and 1966. President Harry S Truman appointed him a delegate to the United Nations (1949–1951) and then adviser to Secretary of State Dean Acheson. During 1955–1956, Cooper was ambassador to India.

A liberal Republican, Cooper supported a bipartisan foreign policy and championed the United Nations. On domestic issues he often bolted his party to back liberal legislation. On civil rights he took what were considered advanced positions for a border-state senator. A friend of President John F. Kennedy, Cooper was a member of the Warren Commission that investigated his assassination.

KEITH W. OLSON, *University of Maryland*

**COOPER, Myles** (1735?–1785), English educator in America. He was born near Millom, Cumberland, England. He attended Oxford University and in 1760 became a fellow of Queen's College, where he distinguished himself as a classical scholar. He was ordained an Anglican priest in 1761. The next year he was appointed assistant to President Samuel Johnson of King's College (now Columbia University) in New York, and he was elected president of the college upon Dr. Johnson's resignation in 1763. During Cooper's administration a grammar school, medical school, and hospital were added to the college.

Cooper was opposed to the colonial movement for independence, and several loyalist pamphlets were attributed to him. In 1775, when the American Revolution began, he fled to Britain, and he spent the last years of his life as senior minister of the Episcopal chapel in Edinburgh.

**COOPER, Peter** (1791–1883), American industrialist and philanthropist, who founded Cooper Union, an adult education institute in New York for the working class. He was born in New York City on Feb. 12, 1791, the son of an unsuccessful small businessman. Peter Cooper received virtually no systematic education and remained almost illiterate, but he showed amazing manual dexterity from an early age and had an inventive turn of mind that enabled him to produce many mechanical devices throughout his life.

After serving as an apprentice to a coachmaker, Cooper tried several lines of business and finally made a fortune manufacturing glue. In addition, he built an experimental locomotive, the *Tom Thumb*, for the Baltimore & Ohio Railroad in 1829–1830 and, realizing the bright future of the iron industry, established several ironworks. The works he established at Trenton, N. J., in 1845 became one of the leading producers in the United States. Later he entered the telegraph industry as president of the American company that helped lay the Atlantic cable.

In 1858, Cooper Union was completed and opened in New York City. It had been Cooper's dream to help workingmen through education, and acting on his belief that wealth is a trust, he provided in his institute free technical courses, public lectures, and a public library.

Besides devoting time to Cooper Union he wrote pamphlets on such public issues as the tariff, abolition, municipal reform, and the national currency. He published these pamphlets collectively in 1833 as *Ideas for a Science of Good Government*. Egalitarian in outlook, Cooper spoke out against corruption and the rising power of the plutocracy, and he was sympathetic to the problems of the farmers and labor. He endorsed civil service, government regulation of the railroads, and government control of the currency, urging that greenbacks be made legal tender. In 1876 he was nominated for president of the United States by the National Independent party, or Greenbackers, but he polled only 81,737 votes.

Cooper died in New York City on April 4, 1883. His funeral was a massive public demonstration of respect for a highly successful businessman who never lost sympathy for the common man.

ELEANOR S. BRUCHEY
*Michigan State University*

**COOPER, Samuel** (1798–1876), American army officer, who was adjutant and inspector general of the Confederate Army in the Civil War. He was born at Hackensack, N. J., on June 12, 1798. After graduating from the U. S. Military Academy, he was assigned to staff duty in the adjutant general's office in Washington, D. C., in 1818. Except for serving against the Seminole Indians in Florida (1841–1842), he remained in the adjutant general's office for 43 years.

At the start of the Civil War in 1861, Cooper resigned from the U. S. Army and offered his services to the Confederacy. He was a friend of Jefferson Davis, the president of the Confederacy, who had been U. S. secretary of war. Cooper was named adjutant and inspector general of the Confederate Army. Throughout the war he was the senior officer and administrative head of the army. When Richmond, Va., was evacuated in April 1865, he accompanied President

Davis on his flight southward but surrendered to federal authorities and gave them his records. He died at Cameron, Va., on Dec. 3, 1876.

**COOPER, Samuel** (1609–1672), English miniaturist, who was one of the first artists to paint fully modeled portraits in miniature, instead of merely tinting an outline drawing ("limning") as had been traditional since the Elizabethan period. Cooper was born in London and trained in miniature painting by his uncle, John Hoskins. Cooper painted most of the eminent Englishmen of his time. The British Royal Collection includes his portraits of Catherine of Braganza (queen consort of Charles II), James II, and the Duke of Monmouth as a boy. A portrait of Charles II is in the collection of the Duke of Richmond, and a portrait of Oliver Cromwell is in the collection of the Duke of Devonshire. Cooper died in London on May 5, 1672.

Alexander Cooper (died 1660), brother of Samuel, was also a miniaturist. He was for many years painter to Queen Christina of Sweden and to her successor, Charles X.

**COOPER, Thomas** (1759–1839), American judge, scientist, educator, and political agitator. An uncompromising radical, he met with opposition throughout his life as a result of his unpopular political and philosophical views.

Cooper was born in Westminster, England, on Oct. 22, 1759, and was educated at Oxford. He left his homeland in 1794 after his support of the French revolutionists horrified prominent English conservatives. Seeking a freer, more congenial atmosphere, he went to America and settled in Pennsylvania. During the next 25 years he practiced law and served as a state judge (1804–1811) and as a professor of chemistry at Dickinson College (1811–1815) and at the University of Pennsylvania (1815–1819).

An early follower of Thomas Jefferson, Cooper wrote pamphlets attacking the Federalist-sponsored Alien and Sedition Acts. As a consequence he was tried and convicted of sedition in 1800, and was sentenced to six months in prison. Years later, Jefferson invited him to join the faculty of the new University of Virginia. However, Cooper's outspoken antireligious beliefs were an obstacle, and the appointment was never concluded. Instead, Cooper accepted a professorial post at South Carolina College (later the University of South Carolina) in 1820. Shortly afterward he was elected its president, and he served as such until 1834, when his unorthodox ideas on religion aroused sufficient opposition to force his resignation.

In his attacks on the clergy, Cooper took the position that freedom of discussion should be unlimited and that all political, philosophical, and theological opinions should be tolerated. Ironically, he later was equally vehement in advocating the suppression of abolitionist literature. As a South Carolinian, Cooper was a militant proponent of states' rights, and during the nullification crisis he favored secession from the Union.

Cooper pursued a number of scholarly subjects. He edited several chemistry texts, wrote a text on political economy, and spent his last years editing the *Statutes at Large of South Carolina* (5 vols., 1836–1839). He died in Columbia, S. C., on May 11, 1839.

JAMES ROGER SHARP
*Syracuse University*

**COOPER, Thomas** (1517?–1594), English lexicographer and bishop. His name is also spelled *Couper*. He was born at Oxford, the son of a poor tailor. He was educated as a chorister at Magdalen College school and became a physician. After the death of Queen Mary, he was ordained in the Church of England and was named bishop of Lincoln in 1571 and bishop of Winchester in 1584. Cooper died at Winchester on April 29, 1594.

Cooper completed a history of the world, begun by Thomas Lanquet, and published the entire work in 1549. His greatest achievement, however, was his revision of Sir Thomas Elyot's Latin-English dictionary in 1552. He eventually incorporated this dictionary into his own *Thesaurus Linguae Romanae et Britannicae* (1565), more commonly known as *Cooper's Dictionary*.

**COOPER CREEK** is an intermittent stream in Australia, which flows for 600 miles (966 km) from central Queensland southwest through arid flatlands into South Australia and on toward Lake Eyre. It is formed by the confluence of the Barcoo and Thompson rivers. The waters of the combined stream quickly dissipate in the gravels of multiple distributaries and generally dry out before reaching Lake Eyre.

Cooper Creek was discovered by Charles Sturt when he crossed its dry channels on his journey to the Simpson Desert in 1845. Later, the Barcoo (or Victoria) River was found to be part of the same stream. The name Barcoo for the whole river was officially recognized in 1860, but subsequently Cooper's Creek was adopted for the lower section. The possessive form is rarely used today.

R. M. YOUNGER
*Author of "Australia and the Australians"*

**COOPER UNION** is a private, coeducational professional school in New York City, offering free tuition to all accepted students. There are additional facilities at Green Camp, N. J. The Cooper Union for the Advancement of Science and Art was founded by the American philanthropist Peter Cooper in 1859 as a free night school for the working class. It is now a selective professional college, offering day and evening courses in schools of art and architecture and engineering and science.

Cooper Union confers baccalaureate degrees in architecture, fine and graphic arts, engineering (chemical, civil, electrical, and mechanical), and physical science; the master's degree in engineering design; and the Ph. D. in engineering research. A program of humanities and social sciences is integrated with the professional courses. The division of adult education offers 35 evening courses for adults and provides free public evening forums each week. These forums, devoted to lectures and performing arts, are held in the Great Hall, where Abraham Lincoln gave a celebrated address on Feb. 27, 1860.

The Cooper Union Library contains 100,000 volumes and 1,000 periodicals. Enrollment in the professional schools between 1945 and the mid-1960's has averaged upward of 1,300 students; in the adult education courses, about 2,000.

FRED H. GRAVES, *The Cooper Union*

**CO-OPERATIVE COMMONWEALTH FEDERATION.** See CANADA—*49. Modern Canada* (Recession).

BROWN BROTHERS

ROCHDALE PIONEERS opened this trend-setting cooperative store in 1844 at Toad Lane, Rochdale, England.

**COOPERATIVES,** kō-op'ər-ə-tivz, are voluntary economic associations in which the members share the "earned dividends"—the financial benefits—that result from doing business at cost or without profits. Service at cost and democratic control are the essential benefits of a cooperative. The net proceeds thus earned and distributed are dubbed the "13th check"—a reward beyond 12 months' income in a year. Western Europe has the largest number of members in sophisticated cooperatives for consumers and producers but the cooperative movement has at least some representation on all continents.

**Types in U.S. and Canada.** The major types of cooperatives, as they have evolved in the United States and Canada, may be classified as follows:

*Sales associations,* which distribute all kinds of agricultural products.

*Purchasing cooperatives,* in two main categories: those specializing in acquiring supplies (such as seed and fertilizer) for productive use in agriculture, and those devoted to assembling and dispensing consumer goods (such as groceries), both in rural and urban areas.

*Service cooperatives,* which operate in many fields, including insurance, electrification, health and hospitalization, housing, and miscellaneous activities—joint farm machine use, artificial insemination of farm animals, rural telephones, grazing, soil conservation, and memorial societies.

*Workers unions,* including labor bargaining associations, industrial associations, and community assistance clubs.

Cooperatives in the United States in the late 1960's included about 500 production credit associations, 750 federal land bank associations, 900 rural electric cooperatives, 1,500 mutual insurance companies, 7,700 mutual irrigation companies, and 22,000 credit unions.

**Principles and Appeals.** The economic cooperative is a distinct form of organization recognized by statute law in a great majority of the democratic societies of the world. Cooperatives are universally governed by principles of equality and justice to all persons who desire to receive the benefits of mutual self-help. These associations present a strong appeal to producers and consumers alike because they provide a "do-it-yourself system." Advocates of the movement contend that cooperatives impart to individuals a sense of solidarity, reduce wastes in human and natural resources by mitigating duplication of efforts in a competitive society, induce initiative for creativity, afford equality of opportunity, and blend self-interest with an awareness of service to their fellow members. The nonprofit cooperatives represent free enterprise—an integral part of the economic and social fabric of the countries wherever they abound.

**History of Cooperative Action.** Cooperative development might roughly be divided into two great periods: the era preceding the machine age, and the years embracing industrialization. For the early period, no positive evidence has been uncovered by historians to reveal the origin of cooperative action, even though various authors have attempted to give credit to some particular country or region. Apparently the act of cooperating with one another has been ubiquitous with mankind in most areas throughout time. Man has learned that his well-being is served best through association with others.

*Antiquity of Cooperation.* In ancient China it was a religious custom for men to undertake a journey to a sacred mountain at least once during a lifetime. To defray the cost of a pilgrimage, these devout souls founded the first known credit or savings societies. Further impetus was given to the spread of these societies through the Asian custom of expending relatively large sums for weddings and funerals. The Chinese also deemed it expedient from primitive times to band together for "crop watching" to stop roving outlaws bent on theft and vandalism.

When nomadic tribesmen became tillers of the soil, they found it necessary to irrigate in arid regions. The construction and management of irrigation systems ordinarily require coordinated effort by those who would be privileged to use them. Consequently, many early cooperative projects were promoted in desert and semi-desert areas to convert barren lands to productive farms. These projects have been notably developed in modern times where relatively little rain falls, including 16 western states of the United States, parts of the west coast of South America, and most of the region around the Mediterranean Sea.

*Medieval Guilds.* The guilds of medieval times represented a conscious movement toward formal organization designed to promote the welfare of selected groups in society. As early as 300 B. C. the Greeks formed associations known as *Eranoi* that possessed many of the characteristics common to the guilds in Teutonic Europe between the 7th and 15th centuries. Members were expected to make annual contributions to a general fund. Each guild carried on certain kinds of business, gave protection to members during periods of illness, arranged for funerals, provided feasts, and aided those in distress.

The first guilds of northern Europe undoubtedly were formed as a defense against invasions. They maintained peace and order within communities that later became the nuclei of cities and other local governments. As the primary purpose of these guilds faded, the guilds were adapted to new functions. The guilds for protection gradually became trade guilds; the trade guilds later became craft guilds; when the communities gained some degree of opulence the various craft guilds became social guilds. The social guilds were the antecedents of the Friendly Societies; the Friendly Societies were the forerunners of the numerous charitable, fraternal, and social organizations that continue to the present.

**Friendly Societies.** In 1793 the British Parliament passed an act that assured the people the right to form voluntary associations to aid one another during times of sickness, need, and bereavement. Prior to this act, these associations had no legal status. By 1800 there were in the British kingdom 7,200 friendly societies with a membership of 600,000.

**Penny Capitalists.** Some of the earliest attempts to conduct business on a cooperative basis in Britain occurred around 1760. Dockworkers in Woolwich and Chatham established their own corn mills to curb the monopolistic practices of millers. It is generally conceded that a small group of weavers in Ayrshire, Scotland, initiated one of the first business ventures on a cooperative basis. This group was formed in 1769 to purchase supplies for handicraft production, including weaver's reeds. It also purchased consumer goods for resale, including flour, sugar, and oatmeal.

A number of similar societies of what were called "penny capitalists" arose and sank into oblivion from 1769 to 1825. Among these was the experiment at New Lanark on the River Clyde in Scotland, where Robert Owen succeeded in a number of social reforms based on cooperative techniques that eventually attracted much attention in Europe and America. See also OWEN, ROBERT.

**Rochdale Pioneers.** Encouraged by these efforts forming self-help cooperatives, the Rochdale Society of Equitable Pioneers took a step in 1844 that had worldwide repercussions in the cooperative movement. Twenty-eight persons, mostly flannel weavers, used accumulated savings of £28 to open a store on Toad Lane, Rochdale, in England. They sold food at current prices, for cash, and distributed the savings periodically to members on the basis of patronage. Each member had a single vote in management regardless of the number of shares he held. This modest society became the springboard for the development of cooperative wholesale movements throughout Europe. See also GREAT BRITAIN—5. *Economic Resources and Activities* (Cooperative Movement).

**People's Banks.** In 1729 the Bank of Scotland hit upon a plan for extending its services to shopkeepers, crofters (small farmers), and others classed as small customers. It made loans based on the character of individuals as distinguished from property collateral. This technique in banking also increased deposits and made the credit institution more useful to the community. Extending credit on the basis of character stimulated thrift, honesty, and industry.

The knowledge of such experience, after a century of success, encouraged residents of Frankford, Pa. (now within Philadelphia), to organize in 1831 the first known credit society in the United States. It was the Oxford Provident Building Association, a modest mutual savings and loan institution that attracted the attention of one of America's earliest economists, Henry C. Carey, who described the enterprise in a tract.

Carey's writings were translated into French, and a German politician economist, Hermann Schulze-Delitzsch, foresaw the possibility of organizing credit banks on a mutual self-help basis. The first German mutual savings society was formed in Eilenburg in 1850. This pioneering organization played a major role in forming similar cooperative credit societies in Germany. Other credit and loan associations were rapidly formed in Saxony between 1853 and 1858. By 1859, a total of 183 people's banks with over 18,000 members had sprung into existence under Schulze-Delitzsch's instructions.

Ten years passed before Friedrich Raiffeisen became aware that mutual self-help associations could be formed on the principles advocated by Schulze-Delitzsch. Raiffeisen became famous as the promoter of people's banks, and through his efforts 425 associations were in existence in 1888, the year of his death. See also BANKS AND BANKING—8. *Mutual Savings Banks;* and 12. *Savings and Loan Associations;* SAVINGS AND LOAN ASSOCIATIONS.

**Cooperatives in the United States.** A common phenomenon in colonial America was the formation of bucket brigades to fight fires. Eventually, these "spur of the moment circles" were formalized as mutual fire insurance companies to provide more positive protection against catastrophe. The first legalized mutual company of this kind on record was formed by New York farmers in 1857. These mutual companies have grown phenomenally in the United States, particularly in the rural communities.

Aside from the many associations formed spontaneously, such as threshing rings, husking bees, and barn-raising get-togethers in pioneer days, the earliest formal business units established on a cooperative basis in the United States date to the beginning of the 19th century. It is reported that a cooperative creamery was built at Goshen, Conn., in 1810. Following this event, a number of cheese rings and cooperative dairies were organized in eastern states and later in Wisconsin and other midwestern states. Progress toward cooperative efforts of this kind, however, was not rapid throughout the first half of the century.

After the Civil War, there were a number of cooperative experiments sponsored by the Grange and other general farm organizations, but the majority of these failed either because of internal or external forces. Late in the 19th century, however, the fruit growers, both on the Atlantic and Pacific seaboards, aggressively formed sales associations, and some of these remain in existence.

The development of the cooperative movement in the United States can be logically divided into three periods: (1) the initial phase when local associations were freely formed; (2) the period in which local associations were federated or united into centralized organizations; and (3) the extension of cooperatives into large regional and national associations.

**Period of Dynamic Growth.** The period of most intensive growth in number of cooperative associations in the United States extended from 1915 to 1930. The major reason for accelerated growth in those years was a transition in legal status: cooperatives were placed under statute laws rather than common law. Many states passed enabling laws in this period. In 1922, the Congress enacted the Capper-Volstead Act that recognized the right of agricultural producers to form voluntary associations for mutual benefit. The act provided that such associations must be democratically controlled by their members and that they either limit dividends on capital stock issues to 8% annually or not deal in the products of nonmembers in amounts greater in value than such as are handled for members.

It is estimated that there were about 1,000 farmer cooperatives by 1900. No estimate of the number of urban cooperatives was given, however, because a very limited number existed. The first nationwide survey of agricultural cooperatives, begun in 1913 and completed in 1915, showed that there were 5,424 cooperatives serving about 651,000 members and handling about $636 million worth of business annually. From 1915 to 1930, the movement surged upward to a total of 12,000 associations. This survey on the eve of the Great Depression indicated that 3.1 million members had joined cooperatives, and that the annual volume of business transacted was about $2.5 billion.

**Fewer Units, Greater Sales.** Since 1930 the number of associations has declined rather steadily. In the late 1960's there were fewer than 9,000 agricultural associations, or a decline of 26%. This decrease in numbers was due primarily to mergers and to an increasing technology in market procedures. In the same period, however, the number of members increased to over 7.2 million, or an advance of 132% even though the number of farms and farmers had declined sharply. In that span of years the net value of farm products sold annually rose markedly from $2.5 billion to about $11 billion, or an expansion of 440%. Some of the increase can be attributed to inflation and other economic factors influencing income.

On the farm as well as in urban centers, there has been a remarkable increase in the gross value of supplies and consumer goods handled by cooperatives. This phase of cooperative business appeared destined to increase rather consistently because of the continuing exodus from farms to urban centers. Cooperatives are composed of people, and if they are to survive, they must go where the people are. Leaders in associationism consider the future bright for three types of cooperatives in the United States —consumer, service, and workers.

**European Cooperatives.** No area of the world has a greater variety of mutual enterprises than Europe. A number of these countries can justifiably claim some credit for motivating other countries to experiment with the utopian ideas and novel schemes conceived by their social innovators. Among the innovators were Robert Owen, Charles Fourier, Louis Blanc, Hermann Schulze-Delitzsch, Bishop Nikolai Grundtvig, Hannes Gebhard, Ole Daley, Friedrich Raiffeisen, Horace Plunkett, Charles Howarth, and William King.

The consumer cooperative movement flowered in England, and its influence has spread all over the earth. France was among the first countries to advocate workers associations, in which employees were to own as well as operate industrial plants. A distinctive form of communal living in *phalansteres* was also advanced to decentralize city populations and create a new social order.

Germany, through its two outstanding leaders,

Schulze-Delitzsch and Raiffeisen, lighted the way to cooperative credit. Denmark evolved folk high schools—for young adults in rural areas—to train its potential cooperators. The influence of this Danish system of education may in some degree account for the many cooperative colleges now sponsored by the various branches of the movement in Europe.

By means of cooperatives, Finland blazed its way to freedom from foreign economic domination; no people in the world has employed the cooperative technique more intensively and extensively than the Finns. Similarly Ireland freed its tenant farmers and inspired them to build and control their own agricultural enterprises. The Scandinavian countries furnish a model for thoroughness in coordination and integration of cooperative organizations. Their wholesale societies have established standards that private competitors are forced to emulate. Almost all dairies in all Scandinavia are owned and operated by the milk producers.

The degree of sophistication attained by the nations of western Europe in the formation of cooperative institutions arises from their long experience as industrial producers of both capital and consumer goods in the milieu of an international market.

The cooperative movement in central and southern Europe was crippled seriously by the Fascist regimes prior to and during World War II. These countries began anew in 1945 to reestablish their cooperative institutions. Communist eastern Europe accords much less freedom of self-determination in the management of mutual associations than is permitted in the western countries.

**South American Cooperatives.** Relatively few cooperatives exist in South America despite the need to improve the standard of living. Deterrents to their development include provincialism, medieval customs, illiteracy, and a paucity of capital. Immigrants from Europe and Japan were instrumental in forming the first South American cooperatives late in the 19th century. Some of these still exist in weak form. Others are reasonably well developed. In the framework of the Alliance for Progress, most South American countries are encouraging proliferation of cooperatives. Argentina, Brazil, Chile, Colombia, Costa Rica, Mexico, Peru, Uruguay, and Venezuela show promise in developing viable units, including consumer stores, credit unions, housing projects, and associations for processing and selling agricultural products.

**Asian Cooperatives.** In Japan cooperatives might be considered indigenous to village societies in rural areas. Much of the cooperative effort elsewhere in Asia assumes the pattern introduced by colonial powers throughout Southeast Asia. The types most prevalent are mutual associations for credit, handicraft industries, fishing, and sales of agricultural products and supplies. All these functions abound in village communities and are commonly combined in the multipurpose units designed to minimize operating costs.

In the extensive Asian areas dominated by communistic forms of government, the main emphasis is placed on mandatory collectives rather than voluntary self-directed associations. The Communists speak of their collectives, or "kolkhoz," as cooperatives, but the collectives are really instruments of the state. The Communists declared ultimate goal is to sequester the reserves and property of the "kolkhoz," in the case of the Soviet Union, for disposition by the state. Whether this type of collective enterprise should be considered and enumerated as cooperative has engendered considerable differences in opinion. Whatever the merits of these collectives may be, they assuredly are prodigious in number.

**African Cooperatives.** Great expanses of Africa are devoid of cooperative institutions. Where they exist, they can be found in all stages of development because of the uneven degrees of social and economic advancement. Many associations are elementary in form and are adapted to simple tasks. In South Africa and some other parts of Africa, the cooperative movement is vibrant and is much like the European model, both in methods of organization and in accomplishments.

**Oceania Cooperatives.** The cooperatives of Australia and New Zealand resemble those of Europe and in many instances have achieved notable success in mitigating the hardships of pioneering in virgin territory.

HENRY. H. BAKKEN
*University of Wisconsin*

**Bibliography**

Axelrod, Robert, *The Evolution of Cooperation* (Basic Bks. 1984).
Bartolke-Bergmann, *Integrated Cooperatives in the Industrial Society* (Humanities 1980).
Jackall, Robert, and Levin, Henry M., eds., *Worker Cooperatives in America* (Univ. of Calif. Press 1985).
Mellor, Mary, and others, *Worker Cooperatives in Theory and Practice* (Taylor & Francis 1988).
Spann, Edward K., *Brotherly Tomorrows: Movements for a Cooperative Society in America* (Columbia Univ. Press 1989).
Taggart, Judy, and Moore, Lynn, eds., *American Cooperation* (Amer. Inst. of Cooperation 1983).
Voorhis, Jerry, *Cooperative Enterprise: The Little People's Chance in a World of Bigness* (NASCO 1975).
Whyte, William F. and Kathleen K., *Making Mondragon: The Growth and Dynamics of the Worker Cooperative Complex* (ILR Press 1988).
Whyte, William F., and others, *Worker Participation and Ownership: Cooperative Strategies for Strengthening Local Economies* (ILR Press 1983).

## COOPER'S HAWK. See HAWK.

**COOPERSTOWN** is a resort village in eastern New York state, 59 miles (95 km) west of Albany. It is situated at the south end of Lake Otsego, where the Susquehanna River has its origin. Cooperstown is the seat of Otsego county.

The site was bought in 1785 by Judge William Cooper, father of the novelist James Fenimore Cooper, who made it the scene of his Leatherstocking Tales. Lake Otsego is the "Glimmerglass" of his novels. Cooper is buried in the village. A statue of him stands on the site of Otsego Hall, the family estate.

Cooperstown is celebrated as the home of Abner Doubleday, who reputedly invented the game of baseball there in 1839. The National Baseball Hall of Fame and Museum, honoring famous players and leaders of the sport, was established in Cooperstown in 1939. An exhibition game and ceremonies to install new members in the Hall of Fame are held annually. Other institutions in the village are the New York State Historical Museum, the Farmers' Museum, the Carriage and Harness Museum, and the Woodland Museum. The Alice Busch Opera Theatre, home of the Glimmerglass Opera, is also found there. Population: 2,180.

SHIRLEY C. FOWLER
*Village Library of Cooperstown*

**COORDINATION COMPOUND,** a compound containing a central atom or ion to which are attached molecules or ions whose number exceeds the number corresponding to the oxidation number (or valence) of the central atom. The central atom, or center of coordination, is usually a transition metal. The coordinated chemical groups may be molecules, such as water or ethylenediamine, or ions, such as chloride, cyanide, or nitrite. Atoms attached directly to the central atom are called *coordinating atoms.*

Attachment is by means of a coordinate bond formed by donation of a pair of electrons from the coordinating atom (donor) to the central atom (acceptor). The entire aggregate of central atom and ligands is known as a *complex.* Ligands may be *unidentate* (one coordinating atom) or *chelate* (two or more coordinating atoms). A complex may be mononuclear (one central atom) or polynuclear (two or more central atoms). Electrically, the complex may be positive, neutral, or negative, depending on the balance between the charges of the central atom and the ligands. Although partial dissociation may occur, the complex tends to remain as a discrete unit, even in solution.

The total number of ligands surrounding a central atom is known as the *coordination number.* Ligands are oriented about the central atom in definite spatial configurations. Because of this orientation, the existence of isomers is possible in certain cases.

Coordinating agents are used in analytical chemistry, solvent extraction, dyeing, leather tanning, electroplating, and water softening.

The coordination theory was proposed in 1893 by the Swiss chemist Alfred Werner. His theory provided an explanation of what were formerly known as molecular compounds or complex compounds. See also CHELATE.

GEORGE B. KAUFFMAN
*California State College at Fresno*

**Further Reading:** Omae, I., *Organometallic Intramolecular-Coordination Compounds* (Elsevier Pub. Co. 1986); Sorenson, John R. J., ed., *Biology of Copper Complexes* (Humana Press 1987).

**COORG,** ko͞org, was an independent kingdom in southwestern India. It is now a district of Karnataka state.

The kingdom was subject to the Gangas from the 2d to the 11th century, to the Cholas and the Hoysalas to the 14th century, and to the Vijayanagars until the 16th century. Ruled by an independent Hindu dynasty during the 17th and 18th centuries, Coorg was conquered by Hyder Ali in 1780. However, its raja entered into a treaty with the British, so that when Hyder's son, Tipu Sultan, was defeated in 1799 the area was returned to its former ruler. Coorg remained independent until the British annexed it in 1834. It became a district of Mysore (now Karnataka) state in 1956.

The district covers 1,584.5 square miles (4,104 sq km) with three subdivisions: Mercara, Somvarpet, and Virarajendrapet. Situated within the Western Ghats, Coorg has a rugged terrain, dense bamboo forests, and an annual rainfall of more than 100 inches (2,500 mm). The Cauvery River rises in its hills and provides irrigation for the rice planted in the valleys. Coffee, wood, and cardamom are among Coorg's chief items of trade. Population: 461,888 (1981 census).

BRIJEN K. GUPTA
*Council on International and Public Affairs*

**COORNHERT,** kōrn'hert, **Dirck Volckertszoon** (1522–1590), Dutch poet, scholar, and humanist theologian. His clear, graceful translations of the *Odyssey,* Cicero, Seneca, and Boethius contributed significantly to the development of the modern Dutch language. His songs, poems, comedies, pamphlets, and the treatise *Zedekunst, dat is wellevenskunste* (1586) express his stoic, humanistic views. His insistence that the individual should develop his rational and moral powers without the interference of a unified church antagonized both Catholics and Calvinists.

Coornhert was born in Amsterdam, the son of a prosperous merchant. He became an engraver in Haarlem and was a commissioner of the city for many years. Firsthand observation of the Inquisition during a tour of Spain contributed to his lifelong hatred for religious fanaticism. Because he held a moderate position in the Dutch struggle for independence from Spain, he was twice imprisoned but escaped both times and went into exile. He finally returned to Haarlem in 1577. Coornhert died in Gouda on Oct. 29, 1590.

**COOS BAY,** kōōs, a city in southwestern Oregon, the state's second-ranking port and one of the world's leading lumber-shipping points. It is situated in Coos county, on Coos Bay, an inlet of the Pacific Ocean, 125 miles (201 km) southwest of Salem. Chief industries are lumber milling, commercial fishing, canning of sea foods, and tourism. Heavy stands of timber and deposits of coal and other minerals are important natural resources of the area. Southwestern Oregon Community College is there. The city of Empire was consolidated with Coos Bay in 1965. Government is by city manager. Population: 15,374.

**COOSA RIVER,** kōō'sə, in northwest Georgia and eastern Alabama. It is formed by the confluence of the Etowah and Oostanula rivers near Rome, Ga., and flows westward into Alabama. Turning south, it joins the Tallapoosa River northeast of Montgomery, Ala., to form the Alabama River. The Coosa River is about 286 miles (459 km) long.

A system of locks and dams built by the federal government makes navigation possible on the Coosa as far as Rome. Lay, Mitchell, and Jordan dams are power dams on the lower course of the river.

**COOT,** kōōt, any of a group of aquatic birds that inhabit freshwater marshes, lakes, and ponds of the Americas, Europe, Asia, Africa, and Australia. The American coot, or mudhen, is found from Canada to Ecuador. It is from 13 to 16 inches (33 to 44 cm) long. It is an overall slate-gray color with a divided white patch under the tail and a white bill. Its legs and feet are green, and its toes are not webbed, as in most aquatic birds, but have a series of lobes. The sexes are identical in appearance.

Although coots are strong swimmers and divers, they are generally sluggish birds and are slow in taking flight from the water. They usually feed in or near water, often coming ashore in flocks to graze on grass. Besides grass, coots also feed on other plant material and on small fishes, tadpoles, and aquatic insects.

The coot's nest is a floating structure, woven of reeds and bulrushes and attached to growing reeds. The female lays 8 to 12 buff-colored eggs

marked with small spots of dark brown. Both sexes incubate the eggs. The young leave the nest the day they are hatched, and they are immediately able to swim and dive.

The American coot, *Fulica americana,* together with other coots, make up the genus *Fulica.* Along with the rails and gallinules, they belong to the family Rallidae, in the order Gruiformes.

KENNETH E. STAGER
*Los Angeles County Museum of Natural History*

**COOTE, Richard.** See BELLAMONT, 1ST EARL OF.

**COOTER,** kōō'tər, a genus composed of 8 species of turtles that abound in various aquatic habitats. They are found chiefly in the central and southeastern United States, but their range also extends through much of Mexico and southward to Panama. One errant species occurs in southern Brazil and adjacent regions. Cooters prefer ponds, streams, and the edges of lakes, but they are also found in brackish and even salt waters. The name "cooter" is used in the southeastern United States, while the name "slider" is used to designate the same group in the Mississippi Valley.

Fishermen often use cooter eggs for bait. Cooters are relished as food in many localities, and they are sometimes seen in markets. Their population was once incredibly large, and hatchlings were sold all over the United States as pets for children. Cooters are, however, very difficult to raise. They must be coaxed to consume necessary calcium, vitamins, and fresh plant food each day. Few children or parents have the time or patience to do this, and almost inevitably the cooters starve. Starvation drags on for months; its first sign is sore eyes.

Cooters are difficult for amateurs to recognize among the many kinds of turtles in the temperate United States. Cooters are typically large turtles with conspicuous yellow stripes along the head and neck and a carapace that is serrated along its rear margin. Females as a rule have a shell about 1 foot (35 cm) long. Males are smaller than females, but males have much longer nails on their forelimbs than do females. During courtship, the males use these long nails to titillate the faces of the females.

Cooters and sliders constitute the genus *Pseudemys* in the family Emydidae, order Chelonia. The two widely distributed species in the United States are *P. floridana* and *P. scripta.* A subspecies of *P. scripta,* the red-eared turtle (*P. scripta elegans*), is popular as a children's pet, generally sold as a hatchling.

CLIFFORD POPE
*Author of "The Reptile World"*

**COPAIS,** kō-pā'is, was the name of a lake, now drained, in northern Boeotia, Greece. Its name in modern Greek is *Kopaïs.* Fed mainly by the Cephissus (Kiphissós) River, it was marshy in character. In ancient times the lake was known for its eels, and several times it was drained into the Gulf of Euboea. In 1883 its drainage was again undertaken by a French company, which after a few years was superseded by the English company that completed the work. By this means approximately 60,000 acres (24,300 hectares) of good land were reclaimed for the cultivation of cotton, tobacco, grain, and vegetables and for pasturage.

**COPÁN**, kō-pän', is an ancient ruined city in Honduras, 35 miles west of Santa Rosa, on the western bank of the Copán River at an altitude of about 2,000 feet (600 meters). The second-largest Mayan city, Copán had an estimated area of 75 acres (30 hectares). Its temples, pyramids, ball courts, and a 63-step hieroglyph stairway are among its most impressive features. The great stone structures were· built in a north-south orientation around five plazas, in typical Mayan layout. The basic material was decomposed trachyte, a light-colored volcanic rock, which was ornately carved in glyphic and anthropomorphic patterns. These were probably originally covered with stucco and fresco designs. Excavations have brought to light marble vases and important ceramics.

From 205 until its abandonment in 800 A. D., Copán was one of the great centers of Mayan genius, particularly in the astronomical sciences. Here the Maya concentrated their mathematical computations, which achieved an unsurpassed precision. An enormous sundial has been found, with stone markers placed 4½ miles (7 km) apart and laid in such a position that the sun set directly in line with them on two specific dates of the year.

The first historical account of the ruins was made in 1576 by Diego García de Palacios. Among the later reporters was John Lloyd Stephens, who in 1839 rediscovered the forgotten city and reported on it. In 1935 the Carnegie Institution of Washington undertook the reconstruction of the site, and this work has aided greatly in unraveling much of the mystery of Mayan culture.

FREDERICK J. DOCKSTADER
*Museum of the American Indian*

**COPE, Edward Drinker** (1840–1897), American naturalist, whose discoveries of vertebrate fossils in the western United States helped to establish the basis for the modern classification of North American fishes, amphibians, and reptiles. Often considered the leader of the American school of neo-Lamarckism, Cope advocated the theory (which he called kinetogenesis) that the movement of the parts of an animal cause heritable changes in them.

Cope was born in Philadelphia, on July 28, 1840. From 1864 to 1867 he taught at Haverford College. Then, for the next 22 years he spent most of his time in strenuous fossil-gathering expeditions. From 1889 he served on the faculty of the University of Pennsylvania, first as professor of geology and then as professor of zoology. He owned and edited the *American Naturalist* for 19 years, and he published more than 12,000 books and papers. He died in Philadelphia on April 2, 1897.

H. CHARLES LAUN
*Stephens College, Columbia, Mo.*

**COPEAU**, kô-pō', **Jacques** (1879–1949), French producer, director, and actor, who greatly influenced modern dramatic art. He replaced naturalistic painted sets lit by footlights with screens on a bare stage lit by projectors. He stressed creative directing and acting and tried to revitalize the classics and to encourage new playwrights.

Copeau was born in Paris on Feb. 4, 1879. While working in an art shop, he became a drama critic, and in 1908 he helped found the

ROBERT S. ANDERSON

COPÁN, Honduras, contains ruins of Maya temples with sculpture, as above, set in the sides of stairways.

*Nouvelle revue française.* From 1913 to 1914, Copeau ran his own small, brilliant experimental theater at 21 Rue du Vieux-Colombier. In 1917–1919, during World War I, he continued his work in New York City under the auspices of the French government. Returning to France, Copeau reopened the Vieux-Colombier in Paris in 1920 and founded a drama school. His outstanding productions included Shakespeare's *Twelfth Night*, Molière's *Avare*, and his own adaptation of Dostoyevsky's *Brothers Karamazov*. Among his disciples, Charles Dullin, Louis Jouvet, and Jean Dasté became notable actor-directors.

In 1924, beset by administrative cares and ill health, Copeau retired to Burgundy, where he directed the Copiaux, a group of young actors, until 1929. Later he lectured and wrote on the theater and was associated in Paris with the Comédie Française, as a consultant-director from 1936 and as administrator in 1940 and 1941. There he started Jean Louis Barrault toward fame. He died at Beaune on Oct. 20, 1949.

EDITH MELCHER, *Author of "The Life and Times of Henry Monnier"*

**COPELAND**, kōp'lənd, **Charles Townsend** (1860–1952), American educator. He was born in Calais, Me., on April 27, 1860, and graduated from Harvard in 1882. After a year at Harvard Law School, he left to work on a newspaper in Boston. Copeland became a lecturer in English at Harvard in 1893, and in 1925 he was made Boylston professor of rhetoric and oratory there.

Copeland's vivid and imaginative readings of great literary works became a Harvard tradition and were attended by the public as well as by students. Among his students who became well-known writers were Malcolm Cowley and John Dos Passos. Copeland retired in 1928. He died in Waverly, Mass., on July 24, 1952.

Copeland's published works include an edition of *Letters of Thomas Carlyle to His Youngest Sister* (1899); *Life of Edwin Booth* (1901); *The Copeland Reader* (1926), an anthology of his favorite selections for reading aloud; and *Anthology of Translations* (1934).

Copenhagen is graced by one of the loveliest and most sophisticated amusement parks in the world, the Tivoli gardens. Beginning at dusk, the buildings and walks of Tivoli are outlined with lights.

BERNARD SILBERSTEIN, FROM RAPHO GUILLUMETTE

**COPENHAGEN,** kō-pən-hā′gən, is the capital and largest city of the kingdom of Denmark. It is called *København* in Danish. The city owes its prominence in the economic and political affairs of the Baltic to its strategic situation at the southern end of the Øresund (The Sound), the strait that separates Denmark from southern Sweden. Geographically, Copenhagen is the principal "crossroads" of Northern Europe, for it commands not only the main water route between the North and Baltic seas but also the land and air routes linking the European mainland with Scandinavia.

**Description of the City.** Copenhagen is located on the eastern shore of the island of Sjælland (Zealand) and on the adjacent small island of Amager. From its original site on a low, sandy embayment between the two islands, the city has spread chiefly westward and northwestward across the rolling plain of Sjælland as well as, to a limited degree, southward over Amager.

*Central Copenhagen.* The life of modern Copenhagen finds much of its focus in the district immediately surrounding the Town Hall Square. Here the main arterial route leading westward across Sjælland and linking Copenhagen with the rest of Denmark intersects H. C. Andersens Boulevard, the principal approach to the island of Amager. This focal point came into being with the destruction of the city's ramparts in 1857 and the subsequent filling of its encircling moat. Thus the Town Hall occupies the site of what was formerly the most important gate to the walled city. Since its completion in 1905, the Town Hall's 346-foot (105-meter) tower has been one of the dominating landmarks of Copenhagen. Adorned by a unique astronomical clock, the Town Hall houses the City Museum as well as the municipal offices.

To the west of the Town Hall lies the world-renowned Tivoli, a summer "pleasure garden," which has perennially delighted Danes and foreigners ever since its opening in 1843. Although many enjoy a daytime stroll through its gardens and along its tree-lined paths, stopping to relax and dine at one of its exotic restaurants, Tivoli really comes to life at dusk. Then the visitor may partake of all manner of amusements and entertainments, ranging from ballet, pantomime, and symphony concerts to dancing, fireworks, shooting galleries, and roller coaster rides.

To the southeast of Tivoli is the Ny Carlsberg Glyptotek, an art gallery built and endowed by one of Denmark's leading brewing families. Its outstanding collections of classical, Near Eastern, and Oriental sculpture are supplemented by many recent Danish and French works. West of Tivoli stands the Central Railway Station, the hub of both long distance and local commuter traffic. Much of the latter moves by an extensive and efficient system of electric express trains, the so-called "S" lines.

Many of Copenhagen's largest hotels and cinemas are located in the district to the west of the station, as well as in the general area leading northeastward toward the Nyhavn and Frederiksstad sections of the city. The principal thoroughfare linking the Town Hall Square with these sections is popularly known as Strøget (The Strip) and is noted for its many large department stores and fashionable specialty shops. The Strip ends at Kongens Nytorv (The King's New Market), which is bounded on the south by the Royal Theater and on the east by the canalized Nyhavn (New Harbor).

*Frederiksstad.* Beyond Nyhavn to the north is the Frederiksttad district, rebuilt following the fire of 1728 on a grid pattern that contrasts sharply with the irregular street plan of the more central parts of the city. Among its more prominent landmarks are the Amalienborg Palace, which was originally constructed as a complex of merchants' mansions between 1749 and 1760 but which has served as the residence of the Danish monarch since 1794; the domed Frederiks Kirke, better known as the Marble Church, built in a Romanesque-baroque style; and the Museum of Decorative Art, whose rococo buildings once served as a hospital and now contain a fascinating collection of handicrafts dating from the Middle Ages to the present. At the northern end of the Frederiksstad section stands the Citadel, first erected in 1619 to guard the seaward approaches to the city. It was rebuilt following a Swedish siege in 1662. The promenade along the harbor side of the Citadel is known as the Langelinie; it leads past the famous statue of the Little Mermaid and the Yacht Club Basin and affords a view of the outer harbor. Beyond the Citadel to the north is Copenhagen's free port.

***Rosenborg and the "Latin Quarter."*** Situated to the west of the Frederiksstad section, along or near the site of the old city walls, are the Rosenborg Palace, built as a summer residence of the king in 1608–1617 and now maintained as a museum of the royal family, with exquisite collections of porcelain, silver, and paintings; the State Art Gallery, which contains works by Rubens and Rembrandt among others; and the Botanical Gardens. The section of the city between Rosenborg and the Town Hall Square is often called the "Latin Quarter," for it is here that the university, founded in 1479, and many associated establishments, including bookshops and student residences, are located. Of the latter, the most notable is Regensen, originally built in 1623–1628 and rebuilt a century later following the disastrous fire of 1728. It faces the famous Round Tower, a structure some 118 feet (36 meters) in height and 50 feet (15 meters) in diameter. The tower is mounted by means of a wide spiral passage, up which Peter the Great of Russia rode on horseback and his wife, Catherine, rode in a horse-drawn carriage during their visit to the Danish capital in 1716.

***Slotsholmen.*** The original center of Copenhagen was located on Slotsholmen (Castle Island), which lies to the east of the present city center across Frederiksholms Canal. The island derives its name from the castle built there in 1167 on a site that has been occupied by six successive castles, including the present Christiansborg Palace, constructed between 1907 and 1915. Christiansborg Palace houses the Danish parliament, supreme court, and ministry of foreign affairs. In close proximity to the palace are the Thorvaldsen Museum, containing many of the most important works of the renowned Danish sculptor Bertel Thorvaldsen; the Arsenal Museum, with its fine collection of weapons, military colors, and uniforms; and the Stock Exchange. Dating from 1619–1640, the latter is readily identified by its ornate spire formed by the intertwined tails of four dragons. Across the canal to the north, one may catch sight of some of the picturesque fishwives during the morning market hours. Overlooking Slotsholmen from the south is the National Museum, whose ethnographic and prehistoric collections are of particular interest to the foreign visitor.

***Christianshavn and Amager.*** East of Slotsholmen and separated from the "mainland" sections of Copenhagen by the Inner Harbor lies the district of Christianshavn. Built on several low islands reclaimed from the sea, Christianshavn is laced by canals and ringed on its southern and eastern sides by a fortified moat. Owing to its ready access to the harbor, it early became the center of numerous industrial enterprises, although some of the best-preserved residential neighborhoods of the 18th century are also located here. The largest enterprise in the district—indeed, the largest

single firm in Denmark—is the Burmeister and Wain shipyard, which is scattered over several adjacent small islands to the north. Architecturally, one of the most interesting structures in Christianshavn is Our Savior's Church, a baroque edifice begun in 1682, which culminates in a 284-foot (87-meter) spire encircled by an open-air spiral staircase.

Southeastward, across the moat from Christianshavn, lies the island of Amager. Although several large industries are found along the shore areas, most of the portion of the island within the administrative jurisdiction of Copenhagen consists of residential districts. Toward the southeast side of the island is Kastrup Airport, Scandinavia's busiest air terminal and the fourth largest in Europe. Much of western and southern Amager is low and poorly drained, but there are plans for building dikes for these areas, to provide the city with an extensive new area for residential development. In addition to such "new towns," Amager will provide the growing metropolis with a stepping-stone toward Sweden by means of the rail and highway bridges that are envisaged as a link between Copenhagen and Malmö. By the year 2000, it is anticipated that the urban agglomerations clustered on both sides of the Øresund will have coalesced into a "supercity," of which Copenhagen will constitute only one part, albeit a major one.

**Economy.** Copenhagen is Denmark's principal center of commerce, industry, and finance, as well as the hub of its transportation system and its most important tourist attraction. Within the city are the country's leading banks, insurance companies, and wholesale firms, in addition to its most exclusive shops and restaurants and largest hotels. About 10 daily newspapers, with a combined circulation of more than 675,000, are published in Copenhagen. One fourth of the country's industrial establishments and 30% of its industrial workers are concentrated in the capital. Ranked according to the size of their labor force, the most important branches of industry in

Copenhagen are metalworking and engineering, food processing, publishing, the manufacture of transportation equipment, and the making of footwear and wearing apparel.

The port of Copenhagen handles one fifth of Denmark's domestic waterborne commerce and nearly one third of its foreign trade. Of the latter, about one fifth moves through the free port. Some 70% of all rail passenger journeys in Denmark either begin or end in the capital, and each year nearly 3 million passengers pass through Kastrup Airport, which is the main traffic center of the Scandinavian Airlines System. Although only one fifth of the country's restaurants and hotels are located in Copenhagen, half of the country's revenues from entertainment are earned in the city—a measure of its great appeal to both Danish and foreign visitors.

**History.** Early in 1167, Bishop Absalon of Roskilde, the ecclesiastic center of Sjælland, erected a castle on the island's eastern shore to protect a small anchorage there from pirate attacks. This anchorage, known simply as Havn (The Harbor), was first frequented by fishermen but gradually grew in importance as Denmark's export trade developed. With this shift in function from fishing to commerce, the place soon came to be called Kiøbmaennehavn (The Merchants' Harbor), from which the city's present name is derived.

Because of its strategic location and growing importance, the incipient coastal town early attracted the attention of both the Danish king and the rising commercial cities of northern Germany, especially Lübeck. As a result, Copenhagen repeatedly served as a pawn in Denmark's internal struggles between church and state as well as in her external relations with the Hanseatic League. On several occasions between 1249 and 1536 the town was besieged, sacked, and burned, first by one, then by another of the opposing forces in this three-cornered conflict. During this period, however, the autonomy of the city was gradually strengthened by successive charters, and since about 1428 the city has served as the royal residence and seat of government. Copenhagen's stature was further enhanced in 1479, when the first university in the double realm of Denmark-Norway was established there.

Although its population was decimated by a half dozen visitations of the plague in the mid-16th century, Copenhagen had become the main commercial and military center of Denmark by the time of Christian IV (reigned 1588–1648). Under this energetic "builder-king," many impressive additions were made to the city, including a new and stronger naval harbor (Christianshavn). During his reign, Copenhagen likewise experienced an unprecedented prosperity, thanks to the mercantile system that gave its merchants a virtual trade monopoly in Norway, Iceland, and other, more distant Danish outposts. At the time of his death, Copenhagen had a population estimated between 25,000 and 30,000.

War with Sweden in 1658–1660 not only brought the city under prolonged siege but also left it on the exposed eastern margin of the country following the loss of the Danish provinces on the Swedish mainland. Although Copenhagen received temporary setbacks by plague in 1711 and fire in 1728, it continued to grow rapidly, and in 1769, when the country's first census was taken, its inhabitants, including the military garrison, numbered over 80,000.

The economic prosperity that Copenhagen enjoyed in the late 18th century was for the most part brought to an end by Denmark's involvement in the Napoleonic Wars, during which much of the city was laid in ruins by an English naval bombardment in 1807. Not until the 1840s was Denmark's economy again on the upswing, and in 1847 the country's first railroad was opened from Copenhagen to Roskilde. Ten years later Copenhagen was given its own constitution. At the same time the fortifications that ringed the city's landward approaches were demolished to permit its expansion inland. In the 1870s industrialization began in earnest, and in 1894, Copenhagen's free port was established. The city's present city council-lord mayor form of government dates from 1938. Population: 476,751 (1996 est.), excluding the communes of Fredericksberg and Gentofte.

VINCENT H. MALMSTRÖM
*Middlebury College*

**COPENHAGEN, Battle of,** kō-pən-hā′gən, a naval engagement fought on April 2, 1801, between British and Danish fleets off Copenhagen, Denmark. Denmark and Sweden in 1800 joined a coalition hostile to Britain's blockade of France. On March 12, 1801, Britain dispatched a fleet commanded by Admiral Sir Hyde Parker to the Baltic Sea. The Danes strengthened the defenses of Copenhagen, while Parker vacillated and Vice Admiral Horatio Nelson, his second-in-command, pleaded that "the boldest measures are the safest," and offered to attack the Danish fleet and forts. The main Danish strength lay in a 1½-mile (2.4-km) line of anchored warships with 634 guns. Nelson lost 3 of his 12 big ships on shoals. The battle had lasted for some three hours when Parker, from a safe distance, ordered Nelson to break off. Raising his spyglass to his blind right eye, Nelson announced, "I really do not see the signal." Both Danes and British fought ferociously, but after four hours so many Danish ships had been burnt and taken that a truce was reached. Copenhagen was a great personal triumph for Nelson, who was only 42. He was created a viscount.

RICHARD A. HOUGH
*Author of "Admirals in Collision"*

**COPENHAGEN, University of,** kō-pən-hägən, a state-supported public institution in Copenhagen, Denmark. The university has five faculties: theology, law and economics, medicine, arts, and science. It is the oldest and largest university in Denmark, and the total student enrollment is more than 16,000. No tuition fees are charged.

The university was founded in 1479 by King Christian I and was reorganized by Christian III in 1537. In 1728 most of the buildings were destroyed by fire. The structures were replaced, only to be severely damaged again by British bombardment in 1807. The present main buildings date from 1837. Also added to the grounds in the 19th century were an astronomical observatory, a zoological museum, and botanical gardens. Facilities added since World War II include new institutes of mathematics, physics, chemistry, zoology, and church history.

The university library, which dates from 1842, contains more than a million volumes, including a notable collection of Persian, Norse, and Icelandic manuscripts. A rector, elected for a two-year period by an assembly of professors, governs the university.

**COPEPOD,** kō'pə-pod, a small to minute crustacean found in fresh and marine waters, where it is an important food source for larger animals. The copepod's elongated, jointed body has a broadened front end with a median eye and a pair of long antennae; underneath are several pairs of mouthparts. The thoracic region has five pairs of bristly legs used in crawling and swimming. The long, tail-like abdominal section ends in two forks armed with long bristles.

Copepods feed by gathering minute organisms and particles of detritus with their mouthparts. Their reproduction is sexual. The male transfers packets of sperm to the underside of the female, and she carries the fertilized eggs in one or two conspicuous egg sacs attached at the junction of her thorax and abdomen. The eggs hatch in a short time into a larval type, the nauplius, which is unlike the adult. The nauplius must pass through several molt stages before reaching the adult stage.

Many copepods are parasites and live attached to other animals, mainly fish. They imbed their front end into the flesh of the victim. These parasitic forms often degenerate into a wormlike state that bears little resemblance to the typical copepod. One parasitic copepod, the fish louse (*Argulus*), has a short, flattened body and a pair of adhesive cups resembling eyes; however, it has retained its swimming legs and can leave the host and swim about.

Copepods form the order Copepoda in the class Crustacea, phylum Arthropoda. See also Crustacea.

L. H. Hyman
*Author of "The Invertebrates"*

**COPERNICUS,** kə-pûr'nə-kəs, **Nicolaus** (1473–1543), Polish astronomer, who founded modern astronomy. Copernicus was born in Toruń on Feb. 19, 1473. He studied mathematics, astronomy, law, and medicine at Cracow, Bologna, and Padua, and received his doctorate at Ferrara. In 1497 his uncle, a powerful prelate, secured his election as canon of the cathedral in Frombork,

and he held this lucrative post until his death.

At an early stage in his career Copernicus became aware of serious defects in the Ptolemaic astronomical system that he had learned as a student. Hoping to get rid of these grave errors, he began to review the older literature of the subject and found that a minority opinion had been long neglected. This opinion placed the sun rather than the earth at the center of the universe, and it was this heliocentric concept that Copernicus chose for the basis of his system.

In removing the earth from its central position, Copernicus made his boldest break with the ideas accepted in his time. His contemporaries still agreed with their primeval ancestors about the nature of the earth. They adhered to the traditional notion that heaven was above and around the earth. In the sky they beheld the sun, moon, stars, and planets, which they put in the category of heavenly bodies, constantly on the move. On the other hand, they perceived no motion of the earth and therefore placed it in an entirely different category. According to this reasoning, the heavenly region had its lowest limit in the moon. This sharp separation between heaven and earth was basic in the view of the universe that was accepted by Copernicus' contemporaries.

Copernicus comprehended the true nature of the earth. He fully understood that it is a planet revolving about the sun, in the company of the other planets. Therefore, like its fellow planets, it too is a heavenly body. Since the earth itself is in the heavens, the contrast between heaven and earth vanished, being replaced by the modern concept of space.

This aspect of Copernicus' thinking unavoidably took him beyond the boundaries of technical astronomy. His pronouncement that the earth is a moving planet was bound to disturb those who had the power to suppress his writings and punish him, even with death, as they often had done to nonconformists. Therefore, as a prudent man, Copernicus circulated his thoughts cautiously. He submitted them in handwritten form to

Nicolaus Copernicus

THE COPERNICAN UNIVERSE, showing the sun at the center, as illustrated in Copernicus' *De revolutionibus orbium coelestium.*

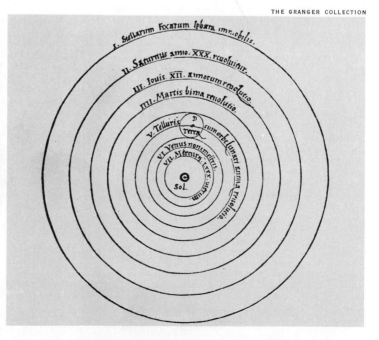

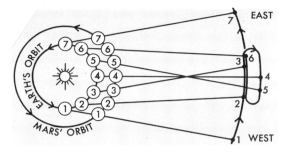

Copernicus explained Mars' "backward" motion as the result of differing periods of Mars and earth (see text).

the scrutiny of a few friends and specialists. Since his brief manuscript could easily be copied and thus fall into the hands of some unsympathetic person, he deliberately withheld his name as author. Nevertheless, the startling news of his magnificent discovery spread steadily. Some of his admirers in high places urged him to put his fears aside and allow his book to be printed. For the purpose of testing public reaction, a summary of his astronomical system was issued by his first and only disciple, Rheticus. When this trial balloon went up without producing an angry explosion, Copernicus finally consented to the publication of his masterpiece. By the time it was printed in 1543 under the title *The Revolutions of the Heavenly Spheres,* he was already on his deathbed. He died in Frombork, Poland, on May 24, 1543, and thus escaped the harsh penalties inflicted on some of his later supporters.

**The Copernican System.** For more than a thousand years before Copernicus' time, the dominant Ptolemaic system of astronomy had taken for granted that what is perceived as happening in the heavens actually occurs as it is seen. For instance, in the daytime the sun is observed rising in the east, climbing toward the south, and setting in the west. Those who were absolutely certain that the earth beneath their feet did not move at all regarded the sun's daily procession as a genuine happening in the heavens. They failed to realize that they were sharing in the earth's motion and therefore did not feel it.

In pointing out this error, Copernicus quoted an ancient poet to the effect that the shore and the port move away from the departing vessel, or so it seems to the passenger on the deck of a ship whose progress is steady. He remains unaware of the motion of a boat that may be carrying him along at a brisk rate and therefore thinks that the land is receding from him.

This principle of the relativity of motion was applied by Copernicus to the earth. When the earth's daily rotation on its axis turns our region of the earth away from the sun, we no longer receive its light, and we say that night is falling. As the earth continues to rotate, it gradually brings our region back again into view of the sun, and we say that day is breaking.

Copernicus assumed that the sun is stationary, and he placed this body near the center of his universe. From this central position it could radiate its light and heat to the earth and the other planets. Its daily rising and setting were properly understood by him to be appearances, due to the real but unperceived rotation of the earth. This distinction between apparent phenomena and actual happenings was extended by

him to the yearly cycle of the seasons. He correctly concluded that the earth revolves in an annual orbit around the sun.

*Planetary Motions.* When a planet is watched night after night, its position constantly changes in relation to the background of the distant stars. It is seen to advance eastward, slow down, stop, reverse its direction briefly, halt again, and then resume its normal eastward course. It thus executes a series of loops, linked by arcs. This endless chain of interconnected curves was deemed to be the actual planetary path. Copernicus, however, showed that the loops were an apparent rather than a real phenomenon. An astronomer has to take into account the motion of the earth from which he observes the stately dance of the planet. His observatory, the earth, is itself moving. This motion of the observer necessarily superimposes itself on the observed motion.

Consider a planet revolving around the sun in an orbit larger than the earth's. Such a planet takes a longer time to complete one orbit than the earth does. If we start with the earth approaching the planet, as shown in the accompanying figure, the planet seems to slow down. As the earth passes the planet, it then appears to stop as it reaches its stationary point, or station, and move in the opposite direction (positions 4 and 5 in the figure). But this backward motion, or retrogression, is only apparent. Actually the planet progresses steadily eastward all the time, as it soon appears to be doing again with increasing speed, and the cycle repeats itself endlessly.

If the observer could escape from the earth and look down on the planetary ballet from a platform mounted high in outer space, he would see the planets travel only in a forward direction. To the earthbound observer, who watches the planets nearly edgewise, their loops, stations, and retrogressions are nothing but a spectacular optical illusion, as Copernicus demonstrated.

Another fundamental concept that Copernicus was obliged to revise was the idea of gravity. The fall of heavy objects toward the center of the earth had been regarded as a movement toward the center of the universe. Copernicus, however, removed the earth from the center of the universe, where his predecessors had stationed it, and had it revolve in the third planetary orbit around the sun. This relocation of the earth had no effect, of course, on the fall of heavy objects, but they could no longer be said to fall toward the center of the universe. Copernicus asserted that there was no single center of gravity in the universe. Every heavenly body, including the earth, has its own center of gravity. This conclusion, so momentous for the development of physics, was an inescapable consequence of Copernicus' reorientation of astronomy.

His reform of established ideas about the universe entailed further changes. Some of these he understood clearly, others only dimly, and still others he missed altogether. In general, he changed only what he had to modify. As a careful thinker, he retained as many past ideas as he could honestly accept. In short, he initiated, but did not complete, what has been aptly called the Copernican revolution.

EDWARD ROSEN, *The City College, New York*

**Further Reading:** Burtt, E. A., *A Critical and Comparative Analysis of Copernicus, Kepler, Galileo and Descartes* (1924; reprint, Foundation for Classical Reprints 1987).

**COPLAND,** kōp'lənd, **Aaron** (1900–1990), American composer, who became one of the most important writers of 20th century music. He was born in Brooklyn, N.Y., on Nov. 14, 1900, and received his first music training from private teachers. From 1921 to 1924 he studied in Paris with Nadia Boulanger, under whose guidance he completed his first compositions. He returned to the United States in 1924, and his first major work, Symphony with Organ, had its premiere in 1925.

From 1940 to 1965, Copland headed the composition department of the Berkshire Music Center at Tanglewood in Lenox, Mass., and from 1957 to 1965 was chairman of the center's faculty. He made frequent world tours as a conductor, and successfully appeared in the USSR in 1960. He also lectured extensively and wrote many articles and books about music. In 1964 he received the Presidential Medal of Freedom.

**Development.** Copland used elements of jazz within a symphonic structure in such early orchestral works as *Music for the Theater* (1925) and Concerto for Piano and Orchestra (1926). From jazz idioms he turned to the use of advanced compositional techniques that resulted in an extremely complex style. Typical works of this period are *Dance Symphony* (1929), Piano Variations (1930), and *Statements* (1935). He then simplified his style, and achieved his first major success, *El Salón México* (1936), an orchestral work that makes use of Mexican popular tunes.

Copland next turned to American folklore and the use of American folk tunes. In the ballets *Billy the Kid* (1938) and *Rodeo* (1942), he utilized cowboy melodies. *A Lincoln Portrait* (1942), for speaker and orchestra, is in a patriotic vein. For the Martha Graham dance company he wrote the ballet *Appalachian Spring* (1944). This work received the 1945 New York Music Critics Circle Award for dramatic music, and an orchestral suite derived from its score won the 1945 Pulitzer Prize in music. Copland's Third Symphony (1946) brought him a second Music Critics Circle prize, and for his score for the film *The Heiress* (1949) he received a 1950 Academy Award.

Later works include *Orchestral Variations* (1957); *Nonet* (1960), for strings; *Connotations* (1962), an orchestral work written for the opening of Philharmonic Hall in New York City; *Music for a Great City* (1964), a symphonic suite; and the tone poem *Inscape* (1967). Aaron Copland died on Dec. 2, 1990, in North Tarrytown, N.Y.

DAVID EWEN, *Author of "Complete Book of 20th Century Music"*

**COPLAS DE MANRIQUE,** kōp'las də män–rē'kä, a lyrical elegy by the Spanish soldier-poet Jorge Manrique (1440?–1479). Manrique wrote the *Coplas por la muerte de su padre don Rodrigo* in 1476, immediately after the death of his father, grand master of the military Order of Santiago, in battle against the Moors. Combining a mixture of medieval and Renaissance themes, the poet considers the vanity of earthly joys, eulogizes his father as a true Christian knight, and likens him to heroes of antiquity.

Manrique used an old Spanish verse form, *pié quebrado* ("limping verse"), in which the full lines of each *copla* (stanza) are regularly interspersed with half lines. The *Coplas* were translated into English by Longfellow in 1833.

METROPOLITAN MUSEUM OF ART—MORRIS K. JESUP FUND, 1924

**JOHN SINGLETON COPLEY'S** portrait of Mrs. Sylvanus Bourne, painted in 1766, while he lived in Boston.

**COPLEY,** kop'lē, **John Singleton** (1738–1815), American colonial portrait painter, who subsequently became a leading painter of portraits and historical subjects in England. During his 21 years of activity in Boston, he produced a remarkable series of realistic portraits that has earned him recognition as the outstanding American artist of the colonial period. In England, Copley and his fellow American, Benjamin West, helped to bring about a revolution in realistic painting of historical subjects.

**Early Career in Boston.** John Singleton Copley was born in Boston, probably on July 26, 1738, to Richard and Mary (Singleton) Copley, recent emigrants from Ireland. His father died during Copley's boyhood, and in 1748 his mother married Peter Pelham, an engraver of mezzotint portraits. Pelham's influence, cut short by his death in 1751, was probably decisive in determining Copley on his future career.

Copley's first dated works were produced in 1753, when he was 15. The early influence of Pelham, John Smibert, Robert Feke, and John Greenwood was followed by that of the more facile, English-trained painter Joseph Blackburn. But Copley soon outstripped them all. The style of his American portraits is characterized by brilliant color, strong chiaroscuro, and realism deepened by his perceptive depiction of his sitters within the context of their role in society. Through his skill in satisfying the then-current taste for realistic portraits, Copley prospered.

In 1766, Copley sent his painting *The Boy with a Squirrel* (1765), a portrait of his half-brother Henry Pelham, to London, where it was exhibited at the Society of Artists. Joshua Reynolds and Benjamin West praised the work and urged Copley to come to Europe to study. Copley delayed, however, reluctant to abandon his lucrative practice, especially after his marriage in 1769 to Susanna Clarke, daughter of a wealthy Bostonian. He settled with his family in an estate on Beacon Hill.

As the political climate worsened in the years preceding the American Revolution, Copley's patronage began to taper off. He was a political moderate, and his clients were divided between Whigs and Tories. After a fruitless attempt to act as a mediator between his Tory in-laws and a Whig mob after the Boston Tea Party, Copley left for Europe in the spring of 1774. He was in Rome when the Revolutionary War broke out in the American colonies. In 1775 he joined his family in London.

**Copley in England.** Although he continued to paint portraits in England, Copley was ambitious to succeed in the most highly regarded branch of his profession—the painting of historical subjects. After an auspicious and popular beginning with *Watson and the Shark* (1778), he won enduring fame with *The Death of the Earl of Chatham* (1779–1781). Realistically set in the House of Lords and incorporating life portraits of 55 peers who had been present at the event, the painting was shocking in its immediacy. His next large historical painting, *The Death of Major Peirson* (1782–1784), is perhaps his masterpiece. Copley's most important commission, *The Siege of Gibraltar* (1784–1791), was painted for the Corporation of the City of London.

He was elected to full membership in the Royal Academy in 1779, but during his later years, Copley was embittered by a declining public regard for his work, by endless squabbles at the Royal Academy, and by debts. He was able, however, to maintain his comfortable home in London, where he died on Sept. 9, 1815.

Copley derived special satisfaction from the success of his brilliant lawyer son, John Singleton Copley, who became 1st Baron Lyndhurst, and who had the distinction of serving three times as lord chancellor of England, in 1827–1830, 1834–1835, and 1841–1846.

JULES DAVID PROWN
*Author of "John Singleton Copley"*

**COPLON CASE,** kop'lən, U. S. criminal proceedings that followed charges of espionage against Judith Coplon; the subsequent dropping of the 17-year-old charges by the Justice Department pointed up the increasing concern about due process and civil rights, spearheaded by rulings of the Supreme Court and lower courts. Miss Coplon (Mrs. Albert H. Socolow), born in Brooklyn in 1921, was convicted in 1949 in Washington and in 1950 in New York of having conspired to pass government secrets to a Soviet spy, Valentin A. Gubitchev.

In 1950 one conviction was reversed because the Federal Bureau of Investigation had searched her purse without a warrant. The other conviction, based on wiretap evidence, was upheld in 1951 but awaited a further hearing on her contention of illegality. On Jan. 6, 1967, the Justice Department dropped the charges, stating that the available evidence was inadmissible in court.

**COPPARD,** kop'ərd, **Alfred Edgar** (1878–1957), English poet and short-story writer. He was born at Folkestone, Kent, on Jan. 4, 1878, and was largely self-educated. After holding several clerical jobs, he began in 1919 to devote himself entirely to writing. He died in London on Jan. 13, 1957.

A. E. Coppard's poetry reveals a unique sensitivity to words and rhythms. His collections of verse include *Hips and Haws* (1922), *Pelagea and Other Poems* (1926), *Collected Poems* (1928), and *Cherry Ripe* (1935).

Coppard's imaginative, observant short stories of country life and characters, many of them modeled on folktales, are written in a poetic style that recalls the verse of Robert Herrick and other Cavalier poets. They are collected in *Clorinda Walks in Heaven* (1922), *The Black Dog* (1923), *Fishmonger's Fiddle* (1925), *The Field of Mustard* (1926), *Ninepenny Flute* (1937), *Tapster's Tapestry* (1939), *Lucy in Her Pink Jacket* (1954), and other volumes. Coppard's autobiography, *It's Me, O Lord!*, was published in 1957.

**COPPÉE,** kô-pā', **François** (1842–1908), French poet and dramatist noted for his sympathy for the poor. He was born in Paris on Jan. 26, 1842. When he was only 13, his father, a minor government official, died, and François had to support the family. Although he held successive jobs—in an architect's office, at the war ministry, as assistant librarian of the Senate, and as archivist for the Comédie Française—he found time to write. He died in Paris on May 23, 1908.

Coppée combined skill with sentiment in his poems and plays. As one of the Parnassian poets, he strove for faultless form in his poetry; his theme was concern for the sufferings of the humble, as reflected in the collections *Le réliquaire* (1866), *Les intimités* (1868), and *Les humbles* (1872). His moral and patriotic verse plays included *Le Passant* (1869) and *Pour la couronne* (1895), both great successes. Coppée was elected to the French Academy in 1884. His personal notes on the Dreyfus affair, in which he was actively anti-Dreyfus, are of significant historical value.

**COPPÉLIA,** kō-pā'lyə, is the most famous comedy classic in ballet. The music is by Léo Delibes, and the book was adapted by Arthur Saint-Léon and Charles Nuitter from a tale by E. T. A. Hoffmann. *Coppélia*, subtitled *The Girl with the Enamel Eyes*, was first presented with choreography by Saint-Léon at the Paris Opéra on May 25, 1870. A restaged and revised version by Marius Petipa was first given in St. Petersburg in 1884. Memorable Coppélias have included the ballerinas Anna Pavlova, Margot Fonteyn, and Svetlana Beriosova.

The three-act ballet revolves around Coppélia, the favorite mechanical doll of the old toymaker Dr. Coppelius. He hopes to bring her to life by infusing her with the blood of the young man Franz, who has seen her at a distance, believes her to be real, and is in love with her. To punish Franz, his sweetheart, Swanilda, mischievously pretends to be the doll.

*Coppélia* was one of the first ballets to popularize doll dances, and it was the first to incorporate the czardas, a Hungarian folk dance, into classical ballet. Among its highlights are the czardas, a mazurka, and the character dancing of Coppelius.

WALTER TERRY, *Author of "Ballet: A New Guide to the Liveliest Art"*

COPPER ORE is usually obtained by strip mining from open-pit mines. The open-pit mine in Bingham Canyon, in north-central Utah, is the largest in the world.

**COPPER,** kop'ər, is a metallic element of great technological and historical importance. It is valued for its strength, malleability, ductility, corrosion resistance, and its ability to conduct electricity and heat. The metal is fairly abundant and has been used by man since prehistoric times for a wide variety of purposes, both by itself and as an alloy with other metals. In the ancient world copper was used for making tools and weapons, and the metal and its alloys have served as building and ornamental materials. Today copper is of importance in such diverse areas as electroplating, plumbing, and the manufacture of electric motors, television sets, airplanes, and satellites. Its compounds are important in agriculture and the chemical industry.

## CONTENTS

## 1. Properties

Copper is the 29th element in the periodic table; it has an atomic weight of 63.54 and is the first in the series of metallic elements that also contains silver and gold. Copper is a relatively heavy metal, with a specific gravity of 8.96. The pure element is salmon pink and has a bright metallic luster when polished. The metal is nonmagnetic, tough, and moderately hard, and it resists wear very well.

**Chemical Properties.** A free atom of copper has an arrangement of electrons which can lead to the formation of a $Cu^{+1}$ ion or a $Cu^{+2}$ ion. A copper ion with a single electron removed is called a cuprous ion, while a copper ion with 2 electrons removed is called a cupric ion. The singly ionized cuprous ion occurs when an electron is removed from the outer electron shell of a copper atom, and the doubly ionized cupric ion results from the additional removal of an electron from an inner electron shell. (An unstable, triply ionized form of copper also occurs.) This difference in the way in which copper can be ionized accounts for the relatively different properties of chemical compounds of copper where different valences are involved. Removal of an electron from a free atom is often referred to as an oxidation reaction. For example, copper with 1 electron removed is said to be in a plus 1 oxidation state, while copper with 2 electrons removed is said to be in a plus 2 oxidation state. (The plus, in this case, refers to the sign of the charge on the ion involved.)

The chemical reactivity of copper in forming compounds involves both the plus 1 and the plus 2 oxidation states; chemical compounds of the plus 2 state are somewhat more stable than those of the plus 1 state. The chemical reaction of copper with basic solutions is minimal, except in the case of solutions containing ammonia. Copper is not replaced by hydrogen in acidic solutions, on the other hand, but it is easily dissolved in oxidizing acids such as nitric acid.

Within a copper crystal, the copper atoms are arranged in a face-centered cubic structure. As a result, each copper atom has 12 equidistant neighbors which are symmetrically distributed around the atom. This arrangement has the highest symmetry of any crystal structure in nature. The actual diameter of a single copper atom is about 2.5 angstrom units or $2.5 \times 18^{-8}$ cm.

**Electrical Conductivity.** One of the single most important properties of bulk copper is its very high electrical conductivity. This property accounts for the extensive use of copper in the electrical industry. The high electrical conductivity of copper is intimately associated with the fact that when free copper atoms are brought together to form bulk copper, the valence electrons of the copper are not restricted to their parent atoms but are free to migrate throughout the solid. On the basis of a unit volume, the electrical conductivity of copper (at room temperature) is exceeded only by the electrical conductivity of silver. Indeed, the electrical properties of copper are the basis of an international standard; the conductivity of a bar of copper 1 meter long and weighing 1 gram, at $20°C$ ($68°F$), is established as 100% conductivity. Even so, modern purification techniques easily produce a grade of copper which is 4% to 5% higher in conductivity than this standard.

**Thermal Conductivity.** Another important consequence of the presence of free electrons in the solid is the very high thermal conductivity of copper, again only exceeded by the thermal conductivity of silver. Many of the extensive commercial applications of copper rely upon this high thermal conductivity. Some of these are refrigerators, evaporators, heating coils, and distilling apparatus in the chemical industry, in which high thermal conductivity is required.

**Mechanical Properties.** Many of the industrial operations involved in the formation of copper into usable shapes involve extensive plastic (permanent) deformation of the metal. Copper, in contrast to iron, can be deformed in this manner —even at temperatures approaching absolute zero—without any serious loss of ductility. This is quite important, since the final forming operation of many products does not require heating the copper during the operation. Heating, if required, would seriously discolor the product. Also, copper would tend to oxidize when heated, and would be seriously embrittled.

The mechanical properties of copper vary over a wide range, depending strongly on the past history of the material. For example, extensive plastic deformation of single copper crystals starts at stresses as low as 15 psi (1 kg per sq cm) in polycrystalline copper, plastic deformation is initiated at 500 psi (35 kg per sq cm). Extensive cold-working of copper can introduce a further increase in the yield stress to a value of 10,000 psi (more than 700 kg per sq cm). However, in contrast to iron, copper shows extensive plastic deformation after extreme reductions in cross-sectional area. In fact, in wire drawing of copper, the material is often reduced to less than 1% of its original diameter.

Cold-worked copper can be annealed at temperatures as low as $392°F$ ($200°C$); extensive softening of the material occurs. Annealing at progressively higher temperatures leads to additional softening of the deformed material. Complete softening is reached at temperatures of about $1200°F$ ($650°C$).

Another important property of copper which lends itself to commercial use is its corrosion resistance, and especially its resistance to oxidation while carrying water. Furthermore, copper tubing, when used for carrying water, does not pick up a mineral deposit (as does iron pipe under similar circumstances). This accounts for the extensive use of copper for making water pipes and water valves and other fittings used in superior plumbing installations. On the other hand, the familiar corrosion product that appears on copper statuary is considered a highly desirable protective coating. This coating, or patina, is a mixture of the basic copper sulfates $CuSO_4 \cdot Cu(OH)_2$ and $CuSO_4 \cdot 3Cu(OH)_2$.

James M. Galligan, *Columbia University*

## 2. Mining and Metallurgy

The primary sources of copper for the mining industry are the mineral copper sulfides (chalcocite, chalcopyrite, bornite), oxides (such as cuprite), and to a lesser extent carbonates (malachite, azurite) that are found in igneous rock. These deposits of copper minerals are distributed throughout the world; very few, if any, known extensive deposits of native elemental copper remain today, although ancient man probably made direct use of such deposits.

**Sources.** About 90% of the world's known reserve of copper is contained in four general areas. Two of the areas are in North America: the Rocky Mountain and Great Basin area, and the central area of Canada (which is associated with a Precambrian shield). One of the areas is in South America, along the western slope of the Andes Mountains in Peru and Chile, while the last is in the upper Katanga region of the Congo (Kinshasa) and the adjacent Copperbelt region of Zambia. The copper deposit at Chuquicamata, Chile, represents today's greatest known reserve of copper ore, but the world center of copper production is the United States —primarily in the Colorado Plateau and the upper Michigan peninsula. Other rich deposits exist in the United States, but they are relatively small. Very little is known of the distribution of copper reserves in the USSR, except that they are thought to exist in the Soviet Asian republic of Kazakhstan.

Another important source of copper is *secondary copper*, or copper obtained from scrap material. This refers not only to material obtained from reclaimed articles but also to such by-products of copper production as "trimmings," "sweepings," and "drosses." About one third of the copper consumed in the United States today comes from scrap; and, because of the high price paid for such materials, many measures are taken to reuse scrap copper.

**Mining.** About 94% of the copper produced throughout the world is obtained through the following series of operations. First the material is strip mined. Concentration of the ore follows, and then the ore is smelted (heated to remove sulfur and oxygen). There is a final refining operation that involves fire or electrolytic refining.

The two major methods of obtaining copper ores from the ground are open-pit mining and underground mining. Of these two methods, open-pit mining is the more extensively used today, since its costs are substantially less than those of underground mining. In open-pit mining, large blast holes are drilled at appropriate places in the ore vein, the material is blasted loose, and it is then removed to the concentrating plant. While the efficiency of each operation has increased greatly throughout history, no substantial change in the sequence has taken place in the process since explosives first began to be used in mining operations. Some recent applications of automatic techniques to the ore handling phase of the mining operation have resulted, however, in significant gains in economy and efficiency. Indeed, in a completely automated mining plant now in operation in the western United States, there is a substantial saving in the costs of obtaining ore from the ground.

**Concentration.** Since the ore obtained from most mines is quite low in copper content (about 1% by weight), the ore is treated to remove a substantial part of the nonessential material before any smelting operations are performed. This operation, called concentration, consists of crushing, grinding, classification (sizing), flotation, and drying of the ore. The usual concentration of copper in the resulting product after this series of steps is about 30% to 40%. The crushing and grinding procedures yield finely divided mineral particles in which some exposure of the copper mineral occurs. The finely divided ore is passed through a series of aerated water cells to which a frothing agent, such as pine oil, is added. Air is then circulated continuously through the flotation cell, producing a heavy froth. An additional chemical, known as a collector, is added to the flotation cell and a selective adherence of the copper sulfide compound to the air bubbles occurs. The unwanted material, called *gangue*, falls to the bottom of the cell.

A simple consideration of the ratio of the output concentration of copper to the input—as large as 100 to 1—shows the distinct advantage of placing concentrating plants as close to the mining operation as possible. Some further processing of the gangue material is performed, which exposes more of the copper; this material is then used in some smelting operations.

**Smelting.** Smelting is concerned with the substantial removal of unwanted sulfur and metallic impurities from the concentrated ore. The removal of the sulfur is accomplished by heating the ore in the presence of air and thereby oxidizing the sulfur, which is released as sulfur dioxide. This particular phase of smelting is often referred to as *roasting*. It yields a product quite suitable for additional smelting, which can then be carried out in an economical manner. The smelting operation also makes use of a silicate flux, which removes some of the iron (present as an oxide) from the ore, by combining with it to form a slag. The slag is less dense than the concentrate, and is periodically removed from the smelting operation.

The material that remains in the furnace—copper, some iron, and smaller amounts of sulfur—is referred to as a *matte*. The matte is fed into another special furnace called a converter, and there it is reduced to relatively pure copper in a two-step process. The first step consists of eliminating any remaining sulfur and iron, again through an oxidation process, after which the remaining copper sulfide is reduced by reaction of the sulfide with air. After this phase of the operation is completed, large poles of green wood are used to stir the melt. The wooden poles reduce any remaining oxides by the reaction of the carbon in the poles with oxygen, leaving a relatively pure copper product.

**Refining.** After the smelting operation is completed, the resulting copper still is not usually suitable for commercial fabrication procedures.

However, a final metallurgical refining operation yields a product that is satisfactory for most commercial use.

An example might help to illustrate what is meant by really "pure" copper. In the product obtained from the smelting operation there are enough impurities to double or triple the electrical resistance of pure copper; thus, if this impure product were used in standard electrical applications, substantial increases in electric power consumption would result. Such material would not be economically competitive with other materials for many applications which involve electrical conductivity. Accordingly, the term "purity" refers to a standard based on applicability.

The small amounts of impurities that remain after the smelting operation are removed either through further fire refining or through electrolytic refining. The fire refining is similar to the process involved in smelting. In the electrolytic refining of copper, the impure copper serves as an anode. Under the action of an applied voltage, it goes into the aqueous copper sulfate solution. The impurities that are contained in the copper and are driven into solution in the copper sulfate are not plated out at the cathode. This occurs because copper is lower in the electromotive series—that is, it gains electrons more readily—than most of the major impurities retained from previous processing operations. The major exceptions to this are the elements gold and silver, which are plated out at the cathode. Indeed, electrolytic refining of copper represents a very important source of gold and silver.

The final purity of the copper after passing through this extensive series of operations is usually about 99.95%, in comparison to a starting purity of less than 1% copper. When the material is to be used for research purposes, additional purification is sometimes undertaken, by a process called zone refining. In this specialized technique a series of molten zones traverses the copper ingot, accumulating impurities along the way. The technique results in additional purification to a level of 99.9999%, with some further increase in electrical conductivity.

JAMES M. GALLIGAN, *Columbia University*

## 3. Alloys and Compounds

When a metal is alloyed (or dissolved) with a second metal, an improvement in certain properties of the metals is sometimes obtained. A great deal of research and development has been undertaken to understand the ways in which specifically desired properties can be influenced and hence obtained by specific alloying treatments.

**Brass and Bronze.** A few copper alloys were known since ancient times to have superior properties, and these properties were extensively exploited; the art of metallurgy preceded the science of metallurgy. For example, bronze (an alloy of tin and copper) was produced in King Solomon's mines on the Sinai Peninsula. Since those early days, however, extensive research has been undertaken to obtain a useful understanding of alloy properties and how they can be controlled.

Undoubtedly one of the more important groups of copper alloys is the one formed by the combination of copper with zinc; this alloy is known as *brass*. The composition of zinc in brass alloys is variable, and many of the properties of the material vary accordingly—in some cases, with highly favorable improvements. One of the striking property changes which accompanies increasing additions of zinc to copper is the gradual transition of colors. The typical salmon pink of pure unoxidized copper changes to a rich bronze (90% copper, 10% zinc), to golden (85% copper, 15% zinc), followed by yellow (70% copper, 30% zinc), until finally a reddish yellow is reached (60% copper, 40% zinc).

The addition of zinc to copper results in an alloy which is easily machined, much stronger than the base metal, and far more corrosion-resistant than copper. Some typical applications of brass include plumbing fixtures and tubing, and decorative items such as brass urns and bases for lamps. However, most brass in the United States is used in industrial applications.

Another well-known alloy employing copper as a base metal is *bronze,* which involves the addition of tin. This alloy was known to the ancients; indeed, the dawn of modern civilization is often called the Bronze Age. As with the zinc in brass, the exact percentage of tin in bronze is variable, and various resultant properties accompany the different compositions. Many uses are known for bronze, although the total production of the alloy is small compared to brass alloys.

**Other Alloys.** Copper is often alloyed with other elements to obtain specifically desired properties. Among these properties is increased corrosion resistance. A classic example of such an alloy is Monel metal, which contains 60% copper and 40% nickel. The commercial product is very corrosion resistant, in some instances more so than stainless steel, and despite its higher cost Monel metal quite often is substituted advantageously for stainless steel in applications which require extreme resistance to corrosion.

A large number of additional alloys of copper with various elements have been developed for special applications. These include alloys with arsenic, beryllium, silver, silicon, aluminum, phosphorus, lead, and manganese. (If ternary —three-member—or still more complex combinations are also considered, the number of possible copper alloys is amazingly large.) The alloy system of copper and beryllium, for example, has interesting and useful properties. The alloy is used quite often in very special springs, since the hysteresis of springs made from this material—that is, their lag in response to the exertion or release of force—is extremely small. This property is very important in highly sensitive electrical instruments such as galvanometers.

Copper is also used as an alloying element in a wide variety of applications in which it is a minor constituent of the resultant alloy. One such industrially important alloy involves the reaction of copper precipitated from solid solution in a matrix of aluminum. The alloy, which also contains small amounts of magnesium and manganese, is known as duralumin. The industrial and commercial importance of aluminum arose when it was shown by the German metallurgist Alfred Wilm in 1911 that aluminum could be strengthened by this process. Before that time, wrought products of aluminum were too soft for most industrial applications.

**Chemical Compounds.** Copper forms a very large number of chemical compounds. The compounds vary from fungicides and insecticides to catalysts in chemical cracking processes, and are used in the refining of copper itself. However, the volume of copper used in such applications is very small compared with the production of the metal itself, amounting to 1% of the total.

The following are only some of the more important copper compounds.

Copper acetate—$Cu(C_2H_3O_2) \cdot H_2O$—is used as a fungicide, as a catalyst in some organic reactions such as the aging of rubber, and as a chemical in textile dyeing. Copper arsenate—$Cu_3(ASO_4)_2 \cdot 4H_2O$—is also used as an insecticide, in snail control, and as a wood preservative. The copper oxides $Cu_2O$ and $CuO$ are used in the coloring of glass and, more important, as a catalyst in many chemical processes. Copper sulfate or blue vitriol—$CuSO_4$—is used extensively in agriculture, principally as a pesticide and as a required trace element in the feeding of plants and animals. Copper sulfide—$Cu_2S$—is one of the most important mineral sources of copper, and is given the name chalcocite. This list of compounds, while by no means complete, illustrates the variety of uses that man has found for copper.

JAMES M. GALLIGAN
*Columbia University*

## 4. History of Copper

Since primitive times copper has played an important role in the technological, industrial, and cultural development of man. Copper's utility has stemmed from its significant number of advantageous qualities—ductility, malleability, formability, strength, corrosion resistance, high electrical and thermal conductivity, and attractive appearance. It has been used by itself and as an alloy with other metals for a wide variety of purposes over thousands of years.

Because of its availability, malleability, and corrosion resistance, copper was first used by primitive man for utensils, weapons, and tools. It was later used in an alloy (bronze) for stronger weapons and implements, for building purposes, and for monuments and objects of art. In modern times, primarily because of its electrical conductivity, copper has been mainly used again as a pure metal for electrical, transportation, and defense purposes.

**Early History.** It is believed that copper was used by man at least as early as 6000 B.C. and perhaps even earlier. Evidence of hammered copper exists among the Chaldean remains dating back to 4500 B.C. There is evidence of more ancient native copper in the Badarian graves of Fayoum in Egypt.

Because copper was found in a native state and could be easily hammered into tools and utensils having sharp and durable edges, it was the first important metal used widely by man. Copper and gold are the only metals having distinct colors other than a shade of gray. Although gold was used earlier than copper, its practical uses are limited. Early man worked copper by the same processes used in working stone or fiber. It was discovered that heat made copper more malleable, and tempering was used as early as 5000 B.C., probably in southwestern Asia and North Africa. Casting and smelting of copper occurred around 4000 to 3500 B.C. and reduction around 1580 B.C.

**Egyptian Developments.** Copper was first worked in Egypt beginning with the 3d dynasty (about

2660 B.C.). An estimated 10,000 tons of copper were produced over a 1,500-year span starting with this period. The greatest supply came from the Sinai Peninsula. The contrast in the extent of use of copper in ancient and modern times is dramatized by the fact that in a typical year in the late 1960's the United States had a copper supply of 2.3 million metric tons (domestic production plus imports).

The English word "copper" is derived from the Greek name (Kypros) of the Island of Cyprus (Latin, Cyprum), where copper was mined beginning around 2500 B.C. These deposits became the primary copper supply for Egypt beginning with the 18th dynasty (1570–1304 B.C.). They are still being exploited.

*Mining Sites.* Copper was used in many places in ancient times by large numbers of peoples. Copper deposits were found, in addition to Sinai and Cyprus, in Syria, Caucusus, Afghanistan, Macedonia, Iberia, and central Europe. In modern times the mining sites have shifted, and the primary copper-supplying areas are the United States, the USSR, Zambia, Chile, Canada, and the Congo.

There is evidence that copper mining existed as far back as 5000 B.C. in North America on the Upper Peninsula in Michigan and on Isle Royale in Lake Superior. Asia Minor was the source of copper for the Sumerians, who used it from 3500 to 3000 B.C., and for the Assyrians later. Copper was used in China in 2500 B.C. It is certain that both open-pit and underground mining were practiced in antiquity.

*Copper Use in Alloys.* Bronze, an alloy of copper and tin, was first used around 2500 B.C. in the second city of Troy for celts (implements shaped like chisels), dagger blades, and objects of art. Bronze was known to be used in Crete around 2000 B.C. Brass, an alloy of copper and zinc, was probably not fully developed until 300 A.D. Biblical mentions of brass probably refer to copper or bronze.

The discovery of copper in a native state and its primitive working by man provided a transition between the industrial time periods known as the Stone Age and the metal ages (Copper, Bronze, and Iron). Because tin was not universally available, a number of cultures moved directly from the Copper Age to the Iron Age without having gone through the Bronze Age, particularly in southern India and South America.

## BASIC STEPS IN MAKING COPPER

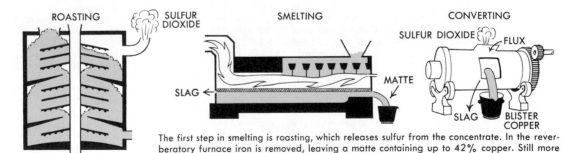

The copper content of ore obtained from most mines is about 1% by weight. Therefore, before smelting, the ore is crushed to small pieces, ground to a powder, and then concentrated in a flotation cell, to yield a product that is about 30% to 40% copper.

The first step in smelting is roasting, which releases sulfur from the concentrate. In the reverberatory furnace iron is removed, leaving a matte containing up to 42% copper. Still more iron and sulfur are removed in the converter. The copper is now 99% pure.

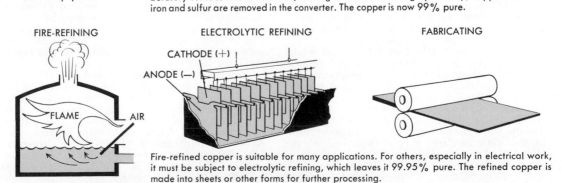

Fire-refined copper is suitable for many applications. For others, especially in electrical work, it must be subject to electrolytic refining, which leaves it 99.95% pure. The refined copper is made into sheets or other forms for further processing.

During the Hellenistic, Roman, Byzantine, and medieval periods, the most important mines in Europe were those of Spain and Portugal, including the Ríotinto ore body, which is still being exploited.

**The 19th Century.** Important new uses for copper were developed in the 19th century, and new ore deposits were found. The greatest new uses of copper came from the development of the electric generator and the transmitting of electricity.

The new age of electricity required a highly developed copper industry. Inventions involving electricity came rapidly in the 19th century. They included the patenting of the telegraph by Samuel F. B. Morse in 1840, the demonstration of the principle of the telephone by Alexander Graham Bell in 1875, and the application by Thomas A. Edison in 1879 for a patent on the incandescent lamp. (It is estimated that about half of the total annual copper consumption in modern-day United States is for electrical purposes.)

The development of the copper industry in the United States, however, predated the surge of electrical discoveries made in the 19th century. Copper was found and produced in the colonies, beginning, on a limited scale, at Simsbury, Conn., in 1709. The discovery of new copper deposits followed the country's expansion westward. Beginning in the early 1850's copper was increasingly mined in the Upper Peninsula of Michigan. From 1850 to 1880 production of Michigan copper—known as lake copper—increased fortyfold. Lake copper, marketed by the Calumet and Hecla companies, was priced low because of the low production costs made possible by the high copper content in the ore.

More impressive copper discoveries were made in 1866 in Montana in the Parrot mine in Butte, later to be worked by the Anaconda Company in the 1880's. By 1886, Montana was the major copper area in the United States. Another important area was developed in Arizona about the same time by the Phelps Dodge Corporation. By 1907, Utah properties were put in operation; eventually they were controlled by the Kennecott Copper Corporation. Few new copper areas have been opened in the United States since the latter part of the 19th century.

Price competition became intense between the older mines in Michigan and the newly opened mines in the West. Competition cut prices in half—from 20 cents a pound to 10 cents a pound. As a result, two major attempts were made to raise copper prices by cornering the market. The French Secrétan corner obtained three fourths of the copper supply and in 1887 succeeded in doubling the price of copper. The rise of independent mines, consumer resistance, and the use of scrap eventually doomed the Secrétan corner, and it ended in 1889.

In 1889, the Amalgamated pool was set up to raise prices. It was organized by U. S. mining and financial interests and was supported by foreign producers. The pool managed to raise prices briefly, but it met the same fate as Secretan's attempt for the same reasons and ended during the financial panic of 1907. Although the demand for copper increased rapidly in the 19th century, supply continued to run ahead of demand. This led to an instability of prices that continued into the 20th century.

PAUL WEINER, *University of Connecticut*

## 5. Modern Copper Industry

The copper industry in the early 20th century was characterized by a high degree of worldwide price instability. By the second half of the century, however, copper prices showed less tendency toward sharp decreases and increases, but there was a movement toward periodic price increases. The copper industry faced a newer problem in competition from an increasing number of substitutes, including aluminum, steel, and plastics.

### INDUSTRY DEVELOPMENT FROM 1900

The instability of prices in the early part of the 20th century led to a number of domestic and international attempts to control both supply and prices (cartelization). Most of these private efforts were unsuccessful. Governmental attempts to control price, however, were generally successful, particularly during World War II.

**Cartels.** New discoveries in Arizona in the early 1900's greatly increased the supply of copper. Increased European demand, particularly from Germany, kept the price of copper up at 18 cents a pound in 1912–1913. The copper industry was given a tremendous impetus during World War I, when the United States supplied 60% of the world's primary copper.

A serious price problem arose in the copper industry after World War I and led to the forming of new cartels. The U. S. Copper Export Association, established under authority of the Webb-Pomerene Act in December 1918, consisted primarily of U. S. producers and gained control of 68% of the world's production of copper. Created to deal with post-World War I problems, the association was able to get prices back to the prewar level. Production controls under this cartel reached a high point in 1921. The resulting higher prices, however, stimulated more production from new mines. So from 1922 to 1929 the swelling production, particularly from Chile, kept copper prices below the prewar level. This cartel was disbanded in 1923 because of internal disagreements about future policies.

A second postwar cartel, operating also within the framework of the Webb-Pomerene Act, was established in 1926 with a broader international base, but it was mainly under U. S. leadership. Called Copper Exporters, Incorporated, this cartel managed to control 95% of the world's copper. The avowed purpose of Copper Exporters was to deal with the problem of increased speculation in copper prices. Rather than acting as a sales agency, the cartel fixed prices and quotas. As a result, prices rose rapidly, and by 1929 copper was up to 18.23 cents a pound. Copper Exporters disbanded in 1933 as a result of European withdrawal from the cartel, expansion of supply, and the stock market crash and ensuing disaster. The copper industry was hard hit by the Depression, and production in 1932 fell 75% below the 1929 level.

Another cartel was established in 1935. Consisting of producers other than American, it became known as the International Copper Cartel and eventually controlled 50% of the copper produced outside the United States. The foreign subsidiaries of Anaconda, Phelps Dodge, and Kennecott participated. Prices were driven so high that many members ignored their production quotas. The outbreak of World War II in 1939 brought this cartel to an end.

HUGE REFINING TANKS are used in electrolytic refining. Sheets of copper are lowered into the tanks to remove the impurities that remain after smelting.

**Price Fluctuations.** General prosperity marked the copper industry during World War II. The price of the metal was primarily stabilized in the United States at 11.87 cents a pound from 1941 to 1946. It jumped to 19.37 cents a pound soon after the wartime ceiling was removed.

The Korean War brought about another dramatic increase in the demand for copper and an increase in copper prices. After the Korean War there were several fluctuations in prices, and in 1956 the price of copper rose to 46 cents a pound—the highest in 90 years. From 1956 to 1962 producer's prices ranged from 46 cents down to 25 cents a pound, with frequent price changes, With formal cartelization the U. S. copper industry was able to maintain a stable price of 31 cents a pound from 1961 to 1964. In the next two years copper made one of the largest price increases among metals by moving up to 36 cents a pound. Because copper is an important contributor to the level of industrial prices, the government intervened under wage-price guidelines and was able to hold the price of the metal down for a time. But in 1967 the price had moved up again, reaching 38 cents a pound.

The causes of price instability in the industry were many: the nature of the markets with multiple sources of prices; the cyclical nature of demand; the concentration of supply; inventory policies of buyers of copper; and government policies.

In the United States, government policies affect supplies because a national stockpile of copper is part of the overall defense program. The Office of Emergency Planning is the policymaking agency for the stockpile. At times in the late 1960's this agency kept an inventory of more than 1 million metric tons of copper for possible use in war emergencies.

**Tariffs.** The United States is a net importer of copper and obtains about one fourth of its supply from foreign sources. Imports of copper come primarily from Chile, followed by Canada, Peru, and Mexico. It exports refined copper primarily to Britain, West Germany, Italy, France, and Japan. In the late 1960's the United States accounted for 20% of the free world output of copper, but it consumed 33% of the world supply.

New sources of ore in the United States will depend on new discoveries. There has not been much change in sources since World War I, but productivity in the copper industry has increased fivefold.

Because of its partial dependence on foreign supplies of copper, the United States has continually modified its tariff arrangements. In 1932 an excise tax of 4 cents a pound was imposed on imported copper. This tax was suspended during World War II and except for a brief period remained suspended until 1950. The tax was then lowered to 2 cents a pound and was immediately suspended until 1958, provided the price of copper remained above 24 cents a pound. The tax in the late 1960's was 1.7 cents a pound and was to remain at that level as long as the price of copper stayed above 24 cents.

### INDUSTRY STRUCTURE

The structure of the copper industry most closely resembles what economists call an "oligopoly." This is a type of market structure in which a few firms control most of an industry's output. The mining, smelting, and refining segments of the U. S. copper industry are highly concentrated among a few firms. The sources of supply are also geographically concentrated. The price behavior of the industry in the 1960's became more typically oligopolistic in that prices either tended to remain stable or increase rather that take up-and-down swings.

There are, however, several thousand dealers and collectors of old copper scrap, and about 25% of the copper consumed in the United States comes from scrap.

The largest copper firm in the world is Kennecott Copper Corporation, which operates the largest open-pit mine in the world at Bingham, Utah. This is the second-largest producing mine in the world. Kennecott alone supplies from 35% to 40% of all the ore mined in the United States.

The second-largest producer in the world is Anaconda Company, which obtains about three fourths of its ore outside the United States, primarily from Chile. Phelps Dodge Corporation is the second-largest domestic producer (that is, in the U. S. mines), and Anaconda is third in this field. These three companies—Kennecott, Anaconda, and Phelps Dodge—mine about 75% of the total U. S. output.

In the smelting segment of the industry, four companies—Phelps Dodge, Kennecott, American Smelting and Refining, and Anaconda—control about 86% of all operations. The same four companies control about 80% of refining capacity.

Concentration is not so evident in fabricating. Anaconda is the largest fabricator, accounting for 10% of the total. In all, there are about 200 firms in the United States engaged in the production and selling of copper. The pattern, especially in the biggest firms, is toward vertical integration—a single firm may mine, smelt, refine, fabricate, and market.

In the United States about 360 mines produce copper, but the largest 25 account for about 96% of all production. Arizona supplies roughly 50% of the U. S. total. Utah, from one mine, produces 18%. The remaining U. S. production, in descending order of importance, comes from Montana, New Mexico, Nevada, and Michigan. Only 2% of the copper is supplied from Eastern states. Most of the smelting of copper is also done in the West.

The grade of copper ore mined in the United States has declined constantly since about 1880, when the ore mined contained an average of 3% copper. By World War I, the ore mined was down to 2% copper, and in the 1950's it was only 0.8%. Improved mining techniques, however, served to keep costs down in spite of the inferior grade of copper mined.

Worldwide, 45 countries produce copper, but five areas contain 93% of the world's measured and indicated reserves of copper. They are: (1) Chile and Peru, where there are large American-owned mines, (2) the western United States, (3) Zambia and the Democratic Republic of Congo (Kinshasa), (4) Kazakhstan in the USSR, and (5) eastern Canada, where three mines supply 75% of the country's copper.

The United States led in the tonnage of copper mined in the late 1960's, followed by the USSR (whose totals are not announced), Zambia, Chile, Canada, and the Congo (Kinshasa). (In some years production in Chile exceeds that in Zambia.) Zambia's mines, which sell most of their copper to Britain, are controlled by Anglo American Corporation and Rhodesian Selection Trust Company.

Estimates vary widely, but the total world reserve of copper is generally considered to be 212 million metric tons. That is enough copper to last 50 years at the usual production rate of slightly more than 4 million tons annually. In North America, the United States is estimated to have a reserve of 32.5 million tons and Canada 8.4 million tons. In South America, Chile is estimated to have a reserve of 46 million tons and Peru 12.5 million tons. The leading reserves found in Europe are in the Soviet Union, 35 million tons, and Poland, 11.4 million tons. In Asia, mainland China's reserves are thought to be 3 million tons. In Africa, Zambia is estimated to have 25 million tons of reserves and the Congo (Kinshasa) 20 million tons.

## COPPER PRODUCTS

It is convenient to classify copper uses by both end use (the product) and by the different industries that buy the metal.

**End Uses.** About 35% of copper consumption in the United States is for electrical equipment. This is followed by fabricated metal products, 32%; machinery other than electrical, 13%; and transportation equipment, 12%. Miscellaneous uses account for less than 8% of the sales. About half of all the copper consumed is for electrical purposes because the listed end uses cut across many lines that involve electrical use. The use of copper for defense-rated orders increases rapidly during wars or military emergencies.

In the electrical equipment industry the four largest end uses consume about 20% of all copper. In descending order these are motors and generators, transformers, switchgears and switchboards, and current-carrying devices.

In fabricated metal products the largest uses of copper are in valves and pipe fittings (the leader at more than 9% of all copper use), and, in descending order, plumbing fixtures and trim, metal stampings, screw machine products, and hardware.

In other types of machinery, refrigeration equipment is the biggest consumer item, accounting for about 3.6% of all copper consumed. This is followed by pumps and compressors and use in machine shops.

In transportation equipment motor vehicles and parts account for almost 10% of all copper consumed. About 40 pounds of copper is required per vehicle. A large airplane uses about 3,000 pounds (1,360 kg) of copper, and a Pullman car uses about 2,000 pounds (907 kg).

**Industry Users.** The largest industry users of copper in the United States include the construction industry, where the metal is bought for building wire, roofing products, plumbing goods, builder's hardware, gutters, flashing, and fittings. In transportation copper is used by many manufacturers: by automobile makers, in radiators, heaters, defrosters, and oil lines; by railroad-equipment makers, in locomotives, passenger cars, and signal devices; and by aircraft makers, in wiring systems. The appliance industry is a large consumer of copper, particularly for washing machines, air-conditioners, refrigerators, and radio and television sets (particularly those with printed circuits). Copper is used extensively for telephone wire and cable.

Copper is also widely used as an alloy. Brass and bronze are used for builder's hardware (locks and knockers), and copper alloys abound in jewelry, furnishings, and cookware.

Paul Weiner, *University of Connecticut*

**Bibliography**

Friedrich, G., and others, eds., *Geology and Metallogeny of Copper Deposits* (Springer-Verlag 1986).
Mazger, Dorothea, *Copper in the World Economy* (Monthly Review Press 1980).
Owen, A., *Biochemical Aspects of Copper* (Noyes 1982).
Sorenson, John R. J., ed., *Biology of Copper Complexes* (Humana Press 1987).
Wagenhals, G., *The World Copper Market* (Springer-Verlag 1984).
West, E. G., *Copper and Its Alloys* (Halsted Press 1982).

**COPPER CLIFF,** a former town in northeastern Ontario, Canada, in Sudbury district, 4 miles (6 km) southwest of Sudbury. The town had large smelting and refining works that process important quantities of nickel, copper, platinum, iridium, osmium, and various rare metals. It was merged with Sudbury in 1973.

**COPPER PYRITE.** See CHALCOPYRITE.

**COPPER RIVER,** a stream in southern Alaska. It rises in the Wrangell Mountains and flows south into the Gulf of Alaska about 30 miles (50 km) east of Cordova, a course of slightly more than 300 miles (500 km). It was named from the rich copper deposits of the region. The greatest of these—in the area around Kennicott—was exhausted in 1938.

The chief tributaries of the river are the Chistochina, Gakona, Gulkana, and Chitina. The Copper is not navigable for any but small boats because of its rapids and the amount of silt and other glacial discharges in the waters.

**COPPER SULFATE** is a common salt of commercial importance. It is also known as *cupric sulfate.* The most commonly used form of copper sulfate is the pentahydrate, $CuSO_4 \cdot 5H_2O$, also known as bluestone, blue vitriol, or blue copperas. In addition, copper sulfate occurs as the anhydrous salt $CuSO_4$ and as the monohydrate $CuSO_4 \cdot H_2O$. Other hydrated forms of the compound are also known.

The pentahydrate crystallizes from aqueous solutions to form large, blue, transparent, triclinic crystals. When heated to 110° C (230° F), they lose water (effloresce) to form greenish white crystals of the monohydrate. Upon continued heating to 250° C (480° F) the monohydrate is converted to the white, powdery anhydrous salt. Above 600° C (1110° F) progressive decomposition occurs until only cupric oxide (CuO) remains. Although the pentahydrate is only moderately soluble in cold water, it is very soluble in hot water.

Almost half the copper sulfate now produced is used for agricultural purposes. It is used as a pesticide to destroy fungi, algae, and other microorganisms and to control weeds and vines. It is added to fertilizers and to animal feeds to provide the trace of copper that is required for the nutrition of plants and animals. In addition, it is used to control the growth of algae in water-treatment ponds.

Other uses of copper sulfate are in the commercial preparation of copper compounds, in textile dyeing, in the preparation of azo dyes, in leather tanning, and in the preservation of wood. It is also used in electroplating solutions, as a battery electrolyte, in marking inks, and in petroleum refining. In medicine it may be used topically as a fungicide and bacteriocide.

Basic cupric sulfate, $CuSO_4 \cdot 3Cu(OH)_2 \cdot H_2O$, is used to control persistent fungus diseases of vegetables and fruits. The green patina that forms on copper that has been exposed to the atmosphere consists for the most part of basic cupric sulfate.

HERBERT LIEBESKIND
*The Cooper Union, New York City*

**COPPERHEAD,** kop'ər-hed, a North American poisonous snake of the pit viper group. Characteristically, the top of the head is coppery red

Eastern copperhead

to yellow. The body is pinkish buff, russet, or orange-brown, with darker crossbands. These crossbands are narrow in the center of the back and wide on the sides in eastern populations but are only slightly narrowed in the back in western populations. The average length of a copperhead is 2 to 3 feet (0.6–0.9 meters); the maximum length is slightly over 4 feet (1.2 meters). Males are larger than females.

Copperheads occur from Massachusetts to southeastern Nebraska and southward to northern Florida and Texas. They inhabit chiefly forested hilly country in the North and East, lowlands in the South, and wooded canyons in the Southwest. They are sometimes plentiful in suburban areas.

In warm weather, copperheads tend to hide during the day and move about after dusk; in cool weather they are also active during the day. In rocky country they often hibernate in ledges with rattlesnakes and various nonpoisonous snakes. Mating usually occurs in the spring but occasionally at other seasons. The young, 3 to 11 in most litters, are born in late summer or early fall. They mature when 2 to 4 years old.

Copperheads feed principally on mice, other small mammals, and some kinds of large insects. They also eat frogs, lizards, birds, and small snakes. Natural enemies of the copperhead include hawks, kingsnakes, and some mammals.

Copperheads usually remain coiled and quiet unless closely approached or touched. They vibrate their tails when angry. They often seem reluctant to strike, but some individual copperheads are very irritable. Copperheads inflict most of the snakebites that occur in the eastern United States outside of Florida and the Mississippi delta. The bite causes considerable pain and swelling, sometimes with signs of general illness, but fatalities are unusual.

**Classification.** The copperhead, *Agkistrodon contortrix,* is related to the cottonmouth, or water moccasin, and to certain Asian pit vipers. There are four subspecies of copperhead: *Agkistrodon contortrix contortrix* inhabits the Southern states except peninsular Florida; *A. c. mokeson* is the familiar subspecies of the North and East; *A. c. laticinctus* occurs in central Texas and Oklahoma; and *A. c. pictigaster* is restricted to parts of trans-Pecos Texas.

The name copperhead is also applied to a venomous Australian snake (*Denisonia superba*) related to the cobras and kraits.

SHERMAN A. MINTON, JR.
*American Museum of Natural History*

**COPPERHEADS** was the name popularly given, as a term of reproach, to elements of the Northern Democratic opposition to the Lincoln administration during the Civil War. Although Republicans charged that the Copperheads were dangerous and guilty of treasonable activities, there is little evidence to support that accusation. Secret societies organized by the Copperheads, such as the Knights of the Gold Circle (q. v.), seemed more eager to promote Democratic party victories than to subvert the government.

Leaders included Horatio Seymour, New York's wartime governor, and Clement L. Vallandigham, member of Congress from Ohio. The Copperheads (or Peace Democrats) urged an end to the Civil War and a reunion of North and South through negotiation. They professed a strong devotion to states' rights and to the Constitution, and opposed the infringement of civil liberties through arbitrary arrests and the suspension of the writ of habeas corpus, the policy of conscription, and the Emancipation Proclamation. Strong in the rural areas of the Middle West, they resented what they regarded as an industrial dominance over the agrarian interests in the government. The peak of their strength came with Democratic successes in the 1862 elections.

ROBERT W. JOHANNSEN
*University of Illinois*

**COPPERMINE RIVER,** a stream in the Kitikmeot region in the territory of Nunavut, Canada. It rises in Lac de Gras and flows northwest about 525 miles (845 km) through Point Lake into Coronation Gulf, an arm of the Arctic Ocean. There are unworked copper deposits in the river basin. The village of Kugluktuk, inhabited mostly by Inuit, lies at the mouth of the river.

**COPRA,** cō′prə, is the dried "meat" (botanically, the endosperm) of the seed of a coconut fruit (see COCONUT) and the principal coconut product of commerce.

In the preparation of copra the thick fibrous husk is usually, but not always, removed before the enclosed ball-like "nut" is split in half. The halves are then exposed to the sun for several days to dry the meat partially and thus facilitate its removal from the nut. Drying is completed in the sun or by heat or heat and smoke.

Copra is used primarily as a source of coconut oil. High-quality copra contains about 3% to 5% water and 60% to 65% oil. During extraction the copra is pulverized between rollers, then steamed, and finally subjected to 3 to 4 tons pressure per square inch (about 500 kg per sq cm) to remove the oil. The residue, sold as livestock feed, contains up to 10% oil and considerable protein.

Copra is the most important export item of the Philippines, the largest exporter. The principal importer is the United States.

LAWRENCE ERBE
*University of Southwestern Louisiana*

**COPROLITES,** kop′rə-līts, are fossilized fecal pellets or castings of animals. They usually have a nodular or pelletlike shape, and many contain phosphates; some coprolites found in coal balls of the Pennsylvanian period (about 280 million years ago) are composed entirely of compacted plant material. Many fossil worms have left castings that closely resemble those produced by modern earthworms. These coprolites are made of compacted soil particles that have been ce-

mented together and excreted. Marine reptiles have left coprolites containing bones, fish scales, and arthropod parts.

When coprolites are found in association with the animal that produced them, they may provide information about the food habits of the animal. Coprolites of plant-eating animals indicate the types of plants that grew during the time those animals lived.

DAVID A. OTTO
*Stephens College*

**COPTIC ART,** kop′tik, is the art produced by the Copts, or Egyptian Christians. In its early period, from the 2d to the middle of the 5th century, Coptic art was strongly influenced by the graceful, realistic Hellenistic style that dominated the sophisticated city of Alexandria. In aristocratic Alexandria, art attained a high level of skill; a degree of Greek elegance and harmony and the use of expensive marble, ivory, and silk persisted at least until the 6th century.

The most characteristic style of Coptic art, however, flourished in a middle period, from the late 5th to the early 8th century. Largely the work of peasant monks from country monasteries, it drew on local Egyptian, and later on Syrian, elements. The monks developed an abstract style that, although rather heavy and crude, forcefully expressed their religious devotion. The emergence of this distinctive Coptic style was accelerated and reinforced by Egypt's isolation from the orthodox Christian world as a result of the Monophysite Copts' refusal to accept the orthodox view of the nature of Christ stated at the Council of Chalcedon in 451. After the conquest of Egypt by the Muslims in the middle of the 7th century, later Coptic art became more decorative and geometric under Islamic influence, and gradually degenerated into a local peasant style.

**Architecture.** The great marble basilicas of Alexandria, such as that dedicated to St. Maenas (begun in 395), were Hellenistic in design with handsome carved capitals imported from Constantinople. Most have not survived. Village and monastic churches, also on the basilica plan, were usually small, mud-brick structures with heavy walls and nave columns suggesting ancient Egyptian temples. The nave was divided transversely into several sections, and the apse might be triconch, or trefoil, in shape and have adjoining chambers, as in the church of the White Monastery at Sohag (440). These churches, unimposing on the outside, especially after the Muslim conquest because the Copts did not wish to call attention to their minority faith, were richly adorned inside with fine stucco carvings, frescoes, and doors and altars of elaborately carved wood.

**Sculpture.** More important than Coptic architecture is Coptic sculpture, both on a large scale in stucco or soft limestone and on a small scale in ivory, bone, or wood. Figures may be on popular pagan themes, which also had a Christian significance, or of Old Testament heroes and Christian saints. Rich floral forms are of Hellenistic origin. The work is in high relief; some figures are stiffly stylized in a frontal position, with emphasis on the head and its deeply set eyes, while others are almost Indian in the sinuous exuberance.

**Painting and Textiles.** Coptic painting may be seen in fresco, as in the monastery at Deir Abu Hennis, and on wooden panels, or icons. Favorite subjects, in addition to mythological characters,

A COPTIC FRIEZE (*at right*), showing carved detail (5th century A. D.).

A COPTIC SCULPTURE (*left*), of limestone and colored gesso (6th century A. D.).

were Christ enthroned, reflecting the Monophysite emphasis on His divinity, scenes from the Bible and apocryphal books, and soldier-saints. The flat figures are generally brightly colored, strongly outlined, and, like the sculpture, shown frontally. In the 6th century, under Syrian influence, as at the monasteries of Bawit, and Saqqara, a more fluent style developed.

The Coptic style is also represented by manuscript illuminations and textiles. The latter, which consist chiefly of woven woolen bands and medallions that decorate linen tunics, employ geometric patterns as well as painting motifs.

D. Talbot Rice
*University of Edinburgh*

**COPTIC CHURCH,** kop'tik. There are two distinct Christian churches in Egypt: the Catholic Coptic and the Monophysite Coptic churches. The word "Copt" is derived from the Greek word for "Egyptian," *Aigyptios,* which the Arabs shortened to *Qubt, Qibt,* or *Qoubt,* and eventually this became "Copt." "Coptic Church" originally referred to the native Egyptian Christian church. In the 5th century a different meaning evolved.

The Council of Chalcedon in 451 defined the hypostatic union of the human and divine natures in Jesus Christ as: "Christ is one person with one nature, yet this resulting union is made up of the two natures that are distinct, not confused, uncommingled, separate though inseparable." Dioscurus, the patriarch of Alexandria, refused to ac-

cept this dogmatic definition, and instead endorsed the Monophysite theory that after the hypostatic union the human nature of Christ is totally absorbed by His divinity; hence Christ has only one nature. For this religious reason, and motivated by political consideration, Dioscurus led the Alexandrian church into obstinate heresy. Since that time the Christians of the Egyptian Monophysite Church have been known as Copts. The Hellenized Christians living in Egypt who remained faithful both to the decrees of Chalcedon and to the Byzantine emperors became known as Melkites, or "king's men."

**Persecution.** Since the rest of Christianity considered Dioscurus and his indigenous church heretical, the Melkites set up a hierarchy in opposition to the Coptic Monophysites. They initiated a war of religious hostility, during which the Byzantines sought to force the Chalcedonian decrees on the Copts through persecution. After two centuries of enduring Greek hostility, the native Egyptians cooperated with the Persians when they arrived in 618–619. By 642, however, the Arab Muslims had subjugated all of Egypt.

The Copts enjoyed a few years of favor under the rule of Amr Ibn al-As (reigned 646–664) but then became the object of economic exploitation and open religious persecution. In the 11th century they were particularly persecuted by Sultan al-Hakim; under Saladin's wise rule, from 1169 to 1193, the persecutions lessened, but the Mamluks (1250–1517) intensified them again. Whether because of the internal strife and disorder within the Coptic Church, or because they hoped to gain political favor from the conquerors, many Copts embraced the Muslim religion during the long years of Islamic rule. The Turkish domination (1517–1798) did not ameliorate the Copts' condition, and they gradually decreased in number and vitality. Under Mohammed Ali (reigned (1805–1848), however, all oppression ceased. From that time on, especially during British rule, the number of Coptic Christians increased from a reported 150,000 in 1830 to an estimated 2,600,000 in the late 1960's.

**Monophysite Coptic Church.** The Monophysite Church, which calls itself "Orthodox," is ruled by a patriarch and other members of the hierarchy, plus an ecclesiastical council primarily made up of laymen. There are 20 Coptic Orthodox bishops in Egypt, 1 in Jerusalem, and 2 in the Sudan. In general, the clergy have been poorly educated, but progress in the intellectual training of the clergy has been made through the efforts of educated Copt lay leaders. The rule set by these leaders (which is more of an ideal) is that each candidate for the priesthood must finish a full course of studies in the modern seminary in Cairo before ordination.

The Coptic Church has had a long history of monasticism. It can justly claim that the first Christian monks, St. Anthony, the father of hermits, and St. Pachomius, the founder of cenobitic monasticism, were Copts. Under Arab and Turkish rule, however, ignorance and illiteracy became widespread in the monasteries and consequently weakened their influence in the Coptic Church. In the 1960's only eight monasteries remained; all are located in the desert, except for the patriarchal monastery of St. Mercurios which is in Old Cairo.

**Coptic Liturgy.** There are three liturgies used in the Coptic Rite: the Liturgy of St. Gregory, celebrated on Christmas, Epiphany, and Easter; the Liturgy of St. Basil, an abbreviation of the Byzantine Liturgy of St. Basil, usually used throughout the year; and the Liturgy of St. Cyril, which is proper to the ancient Coptic Rite and is celebrated only once a year, on the Friday before Palm Sunday.

Until the end of the 19th century, the extinct Coptic language was used in celebrating the Divine Liturgy, but Arabic has since been adopted. The scriptural readings, however, are read in both Arabic and Coptic.

**Attempts at Union.** At the end of the 12th and the beginning of the 13th century, the presence of the Crusaders in Egypt caused the Coptic Church to encounter Latin Catholicism. But rather than effecting a rapprochement, this encounter tended to polarize their theological differences. Serious attempts at reunion with Roman Catholics began in 1714 when Athanasius, the Coptic bishop of Jerusalem, was converted to Catholicism. As a result, six Catholic bishoprics exist in modern Egypt, with authority over 90,000 Coptic Catholics. In general, both the Catholic clergy and the laity are better educated than the Monophysites and engender a vibrant type of Catholicism in Egypt.

Due to the long period of Arab and Turkish domination, few attempts at unity with other Monophysite churches were undertaken. The formation of a more articulate group of theologians, however, has made such contacts possible. The first such meeting was held at Addis Ababa in 1965. The Byzantine Orthodox met with the Coptic and other Monophysite churches at Aarhus, Denmark, in 1964, and representatives initiated a promising rapprochement.

The dogma that in the 20th century still separates the Coptic Church from the Byzantine Orthodox and Catholic churches is the Coptic interpretation of the hypostatic union. Their doctrine concerning the Trinity is orthodox, taken from the Nicene-Constantinopolitan creed. Various theories are taught in regard to souls after death, which still exhibit influences from the ancient pagan religions of Egypt. It is generally believed that souls wander for 40 days after death before appearing before the tribunal of God. During this time of wandering the souls undergo various tests of purification, especially from demons.

GEORGE A. MALONEY, S. J.
*Fordham University*

**Further Reading:** Hutter, Irmgard, *Early Christian and Byzantine Art* (Universe Bks. 1988); Milburn, Robert L., *Early Christian Art and Architecture* (Univ. of Calif. Press 1988), Roberts, C. H., *Manuscript, Society and Belief in Early Christian Egypt* (Longwood 1979).

**COPTIC LANGUAGE AND LITERATURE,** kop'tik. Coptic, descended from ancient Egyptian, is a member of the Hamito-Semitic linguistic family. The term "Coptic" is derived from the Arabic word *qubt,* which means "Egyptian." Coptic was the prevailing language of Christian Egypt from about the 3d century A. D. until it was gradually displaced by Arabic after the Muslim invasion of Egypt in 640. It seems still to have been in fairly common use in the 15th century but was almost extinct by the 17th. It continues in use today only in parts of the liturgy of the Coptic church.

Coptic is written in the Greek alphabet, with seven additional letters derived from the demotic writing (the final form of ancient Egyptian writing), chiefly to represent sounds lacking in the Greek, such as *sh* and *f*. This method of writing the Egyptian language was first practiced to some extent by astrologers and magicians, but both the spelling and the language were crystallized by the translators of the Bible into the various Coptic dialects. Like modern English and German, both language and literary style were profoundly and permanently affected by the Biblical translations.

**Dialects.** Numerous local dialects are known to have existed. Five distinct dialects are represented by considerable literary remains: *Faiyumic* (used in the oasis of El Faiyum; one of a group of subdialects called Middle Egyptian, not to be confused with hieroglyphic Middle Egyptian, the classical language of Pharaonic Egypt; *Akhmimic* (from Akhmim, on the Nile); *Subakhmimic* (probably from Asyut); *Sahidic* (often thought to have originated in or near ancient Thebes, modern Luxor, but according to William H. Worrell's analysis probably between Cairo and the mouth of the Faiyum); and *Bohairic* (probably from the western Delta). Faiyumic, Akhmimic, and Subakhmimic were early displaced by Sahidic, which became the standard language of all Upper Egypt, only to be supplanted in turn by Bohairic and by Arabic. Because Bohairic was the official language of the patriarch of Alexandria, who moved to Cairo in the 10th century, it became the ritual language of the Coptic Church throughout Egypt. Vestiges of traditional Coptic speech recorded near Luxor and elsewhere in the 1930's are of ecclesiastical Bohairic origin, greatly affected by Arabic and other extraneous influences.

The Coptic dialects differ importantly in phonetics and vocabulary, much less in morphology (word formation and inflection), and still less in syntax (grammatical arrangement of words). All of them are derived from Late Egyptian, the standard language of the 19th and 20th dynasties (14th to 12th centuries B. C.). The Coptic language had a strong stress accent that caused the weakening and often the disappearance of unaccented vowels and even words. Many nouns have distinct forms for the plural, but most of them can also use the singular as plural. As in Arabic, the distinct plurals show a bewildering variety of formations. Both definite and indefinite articles have distinct forms for singular and plural; the definite article in the singular also distinguishes between masculine and feminine. Few adjectives exist, adjectival ideas being expressed usually with the help of the preposition *n* "of", as, "a saint of father" for "a saintly father." Verbs are elaborately conjugated, chiefly by means of prefixes that express person, number, tense, and mood. Much use is made of adverbs, prepositions, and conjunctions. Prepositions have distinct forms for noun and pronoun object. Many words are borrowed from Greek.

**Literature.** Coptic literature consists mainly of religious works, chiefly translations from Greek. Only a small number of original writings were produced in Coptic. Not all of the religious writings are Christian: Gnosticism and Manichaeanism, important rivals of early Christianity, are also well represented.

The only writer in Coptic who attained distinction was Shenoute (Shenute). He was abbot of the great White Monastery on the edge of the desert west of Akhmim for more than 60 years, and died, still active, at an extremely advanced age, in about 457. His letters, sermons, and other writings, entirely in Sahidic, show a strong and highly personal literary style, corresponding to the vigorous part he played in the religious and secular life of his time. Although his writings had great influence in Egypt, they were unknown outside that country until the 20th century.

A new growth of popular religious poetry occurred in the 10th century, probably a manifestation of Christian and Egyptian resistance to the Arabic language and the Muslim religion. The dialect of this poetry is Sahidic, and its themes are Biblical. Its poetic forms are largely derived from Byzantine religious poetry. But the compositions themselves are original, and the anonymous authors achieve a degree of freshness and life unusual in Coptic literature. The meter depends on the succession of accented syllables, which is treated with some freedom. There is no rhyme.

WILLIAM F. EDGERTON
*University of Chicago*

**Bibliography**

Budge, Ernest A., *Coptic Biblical Texts in the Dialect of Upper Egypt* (1912; reprint, AMS Press 1977).
Bullard, Roger A., *The Hypostasis of the Archons* (De Gruyter 1970).
Callender, John B., *Studies in the Nominal Sentence of Egyptian and Coptic* (Univ. of Calif. Press 1984).
Cerny, Jaroslav, *Coptic Etymological Dictionary* (Cambridge 1976).
Clarke, Hyde, *Memoir of the Comparative Grammar of Egyptian-Coptic and Ude* (British American Bks. 1987).
MacDonald, William B., *Sketch of Coptic Grammar* (British American Bks. 1987).
Peters, Melvin K., *A Critical Edition of the Coptic* (Scholars Press 1983).
Schiller, A. Arthur, *Ten Coptic Legal Texts* (1932; reprint, Ayer 1972).
Smith, Richard H., *A Concise Coptic-English Lexicon* (Eerdmans 1983).

**COPTIS,** kop′təs, is a small genus of perennial bog plants native to northern temperate and Arctic regions. The plants are commonly known, as *goldthreads* because of their long, slender yellow rootstocks. These rootstocks yield a yellow dye and were once used in medicine as a bitter tonic and as a treatment for mouth ulcers.

Coptis plants range in height from 6 to 12 inches (15 to 30 cm) and bear terminal clusters of small white or yellow flowers. The leaves are basal (growing near the base of the stem) and are composed of small leaflets. They usually remain on the plant throughout the winter. Coptis plants do well in moist, shaded bog areas with peaty soil. They are rarely cultivated as ornamentals.

The genus *Coptis* belongs to the crowfoot family (Ranunculaceae).

DONALD WYMAN
*The Arnold Arboretum, Harvard University*

**COPYING MACHINES** are devices for producing exact copies of written, printed, or drawn original material, which need not be specifically designed for duplication. Generally, copying machines are designed to make a small number of copies, but some can produce hundreds of copies in a short time, and thus compete with duplicating machines, which do require a specially prepared original.

Since the 1950's, copying machines have become standard equipment in practically all business establishments. By the late 1960's, more than 500,000 copiers were in use, producing over 10 billion copies annually. With over 40 firms manufacturing copying equipment, there is a wide variety of machinery, with different capabilities. Some machines require that the original be on translucent material, and almost all require specially coated copy paper. For some machines, the original must be a loose sheet, while other machines can copy pages from a bound volume. Most copiers are limited to copies the same size as the original, but some are capable of enlargements or reductions. In some machines, the copy must be processed in a liquid bath, and then dried; in others, called dry copiers, these steps are not required.

The various types of copying machines can be classified into three general categories according to their basic operating principles: photocopying; thermography; and xerography, or electrostatic copying.

**Photocopying.** All photocopying processes utilize photographic techniques. Copies are produced by the action of light on photosensitive materials.

*Photostats.* First developed in 1906, photostats are simply photographs of the original, made with a special camera on photosensitized paper instead of film. The original can be a bound page, and enlarged or reduced copies can be produced. High-contrast photographic paper is used, usually producing an unreversed, readable negative image (white on black), from which a positive may be made in a separate step, if desired. The fixation and washing time usually required for photographic materials is much reduced by the use of quick stabilization in both photostats and in the diffusion-transfer process described below.

*Dye Transfer and Diffusion Transfer.* Dye transfer is the basic principle of Eastman Kodak's Verifax process. It produces up to about seven positive copies from a temporary negative. The negative stock is translucent paper coated with a photographic emulsion with a dye-forming and hardening component. The coated side is placed in contact with the original and the back against a glass plate enclosing a bright light. The exposed negative is put through a developing bath where black dye is formed. It is hardened in the exposed areas and remains wet in the unexposed (image) areas. The negative is then pressed against plain paper onto which the wet-dye image is transferred in much the same way as a rubber-stamp image is made.

In diffusion transfer, negative stock coated with a silver halide emulsion is exposed with the original. The unexposed silver halides of a negative diffuse onto chemically treated positive paper when they are placed in contact in a developing bath. When removed and peeled apart, the room light exposes the silver halides on the positive stock to produce a black image.

**Whiteprint, or Diazo, Process.** This method, known commercially as Ozalid, is used in machines made by the Charles Bruning Co. The process produces positive copies directly, but it requires unbound originals, on translucent material. The original is placed face up on a piece of paper coated with diazonium compounds. The two sheets pass into the machine, and under a source of ultraviolet light. The ultraviolet, passing through the translucent original, destroys all the diazo compound except that which is shielded by dark areas on the original. The copy is then exposed to liquid or gaseous ammonia, which darkens the remaining diazo compound, producing a positive copy.

**Blueprint.** The blueprint process is used to reproduce architectural and engineering drawings, often on coated plastic or cloth instead of paper. A translucent original is required, and negative copies (white on blue) are standard. The coating on blueprint material contains iron compounds that react to light. Although both blueprint and whiteprint machines often require special translucent originals to be made, they are used to print few copies, and are considered copying, rather than duplicating equipment.

**Thermography.** This dry-copying process, introduced by the 3M Corporation as Thermofax, utilizes the action of heat on heat-sensitive chemicals. The original must be unbound, and its written portions must contain either carbon or a metallic compound, materials that transmit heat readily. The original is placed in contact with a sheet of coated paper and exposed to a heat source in the copier. The heat transmitted through the characters of the original causes the heat-sensitive substance to darken, forming a positive image on the copy.

**Xerography, or Electrostatic Copying.** Since 1960, xerography ("dry writing") has been the major copying process, supplanting thermography and diffusion transfer. Invented in 1938 by Chester F. Carlson, it was introduced commercially in 1951 by what is now Xerox Corporation.

The process utilizes the fact that in certain substances an electrostatic charge will be dissipated by light where it strikes, but will remain in unlit areas. Thus, when light is reflected from the document to be copied onto a charged surface coated with such a substance, a charged area corresponding to the dark, or written, parts of the original will remain.

In machines produced by Xerox, the charged image is formed on the surface of a metal drum coated with selenium. The image is made visible by the application of a plastic powder, called toner, that has been given the opposite electrical charge, and is thus attracted to the charged image on the drum. The toner image is then transferred to plain, uncoated paper by the attraction of another opposite charge placed behind the paper. The toner is fused onto the paper by heat to produce a permanent image. In electrostatic copiers made by other manufacturers, special paper coated with zinc oxide is used, and the charged image is created directly on the paper. Toner is then applied and fused into place.

Xerographic copying can be extremely fast, producing as many as 60 copies per minute. The process also allows the copying of bound originals, and there are machines capable of enlargements and reductions. See also XEROGRAPHY.

WILLIAM D. O'TOOLE, *Xerox Corporation*

**COPYRIGHT** is the exclusive right that protects an author, composer, or artist from having his work recorded, performed, displayed, translated, distributed, or reproduced by way of copies, phonorecords, or other versions (derivative works) except with his permission, subject to specified limitations. This intangible property right comes into existence automatically on creation of an original musical or dramatic composition; a novel, poem, or work of nonfiction; a painting; or a map—to name but a few of the intellectual productions that qualify for such legal protection.

## UNITED STATES COPYRIGHT LAW

Prior to Jan. 1, 1978—the effective date generally of the Copyright Act of 1976, a comprehensive revision of the U. S. copyright law—prepublication protection was usually referred to in the United States as a *common law copyright.* For this protection, no legal formalities had to be observed, so long as the work remained unpublished.

On the other hand, prior to Jan. 1, 1978, a *statutory copyright*—that is, a copyright under the U. S. Copyright Act of 1909 (which was superseded by the new law)—was obtained in either of two ways. One was by publication of the work with a proper notice of copyright, and the other was by registration of certain works (such as lectures, dramatic and musical compositions, motion pictures, and works of art) before publication. Upon such publication or registration, the common law copyright terminated. Thus the common law copyright in the United States was sometimes called "a right of first publication," and the question of whether a particular work had been published was often of considerable importance. Under the Copyright Act of 1976, this cumbersome and confusing dual system of protection was replaced by a single federal system of statutory protection for all copyrightable works, both published and unpublished.

**Subject Matter.** The works protected by copyright must be original (not copied) with the author and "fixed" (embodied) in a tangible medium of expression from which they can be perceived, reproduced, or otherwise communicated. Such works include literary, musical, and dramatic works; pantomines and choreographic works; pictorial, graphic, and sculptural works; motion pictures and other audiovisual works; and sound recordings.

Certain material is not copyrightable—for example, words, names, titles, and slogans. Ideas, procedures, processes, systems, principles, and discoveries, regardless of the form in which they are described, explained, or illustrated, are not subject to copyright, but the particular manner in which they are expressed or described may be protected.

**Deposit and Registration.** Within three months after publication in the United States of a work with notice of copyright, deposit must be made of two complete copies (and/or phonorecords) of the best edition, in the Copyright Office, Library of Congress, Washington, D. C., for use or disposition by the library. The register of copyrights may by regulation exempt categories of material from the deposit requirements or provide for alternate forms of deposit (for example, photographs) aimed at obtaining a satisfactory archival record, especially in the case of pictorial, graphic, and sculptural works. At any time after publication, the register may ask for such deposit, and failure to comply may result in penalties.

The owner of copyright in any work, or of any exclusive right in the work, may register the copyright claim by delivering to the Copyright Office the specified deposit, application, and fee. In the case of an unpublished work, a work first published outside the United States, or a contribution to a collective work, the deposit includes one complete copy or phonorecord of the unpublished, foreign-published, or collective work, and two in the case of other published works. Again, these requirements are subject to regulations by the register, who may ease the deposit requirements, including a single registration for a group of related works by the same individual author. The deposit for the Library of Congress may serve as the deposit for the copyright registration if the deposit is accompanied by the application and fee for the registration. Neither the deposit for the library's use nor the registration in the Copyright Office is a condition of copyright protection. However, the copyright registration is generally a prerequisite to commencement of an infringement action and for the award of statutory damages and attorney's fees.

**Subsisting Copyrights.** For statutory copyrights in existence on Jan. 1, 1978, the former two-term system of protection applies, except that the second term is extended from 28 years to 47 years. The duration of the initial term of 28 years continues unchanged, as does the necessity of filing a renewal application (plus a small fee) in the Copyright Office during the last (28th) year to obtain the second (and longer) term.

For statutory copyrights in their renewal term on Dec. 31, 1976, or for which timely renewal registration was subsequently made, their duration was automatically extended by the new law to 47 years, for a total term of protection of 75 years. The renewal application cannot be filed in advance, and late filings are not accepted. Failure to file the renewal application in time results in permanent lapse of the copyright.

If the author is alive during the 28th year, the right to renewal is vested in him or her. If, however, the work was published posthumously or was produced on a hire basis, then the proprietor during the 28th year is entitled to the renewal. If the author does not survive into the 28th year, and the work was not so published or produced, the author's widow (or widower) and the author's children can file for renewal. If no widow, widower, or children are living, the right then goes to the executor or administrator of the author's will, or, in the absence of a will, to the next of kin.

If during the original term of copyright the author had transferred rights for the renewal term, he or she will be bound by his transfer if he or she survives to file the renewal application. If the author does not survive, the other statutory beneficiaries noted above are entitled to the renewal copyright free of the rights previously granted by the author. That is, the author's assignees and licensees cannot use or otherwise exploit the work during the second term of copyright, unless, during the original copyright, a derivative work was created. For example, a motion picture based on an originally protected work can be distributed, exhibited, or televised in the United States during the new or extended copyright term.

Beginning Sept. 19, 1962, Congress periodically extended the term of protection in works that were nearing the end of the renewal term. Such copyrights, which would otherwise have expired after Sept. 19, 1962, and before Dec. 31, 1976, were extended through Dec. 31, 1976. Also, by virtue of the new act, such renewal copyrights were further extended from their "28 years plus" to 47 years. In addition, all copyright terms now run to the end of the calendar year.

**New Works.** Protection for a work created on or after Jan. 1, 1978, begins at the time of its creation and lasts for the author's life and 50 years after the author's death. If it is a joint work, the 50 years is measured from the death of the last survivor of the joint authors. For anonymous and pseudonymous works and works made for hire, the copyright endures for 75 years from first publication, or 100 years from creation, whichever expires first.

Copyright in works created but not published or copyrighted before Jan. 1, 1978, subsists from Jan. 1, 1978, and endures at least for the terms accorded new works. However, the copyright in such works shall not expire before Dec. 31, 2002, and if published before Dec. 31, 2002, shall not expire before Dec. 31, 2027.

**Termination of Transfers.** A transfer or license of copyright (or of a right under copyright) executed by the author of a work (excluding a work made for hire) on or after Jan. 1, 1978, other than by will, will be subject to termination under certain circumstances during a five-year period beginning 35 to 40 years from the date of execution.

Transfers executed before Jan. 1, 1978, by any of the persons designated to apply for renewal copyright may also be terminated under certain conditions during a period of five years beginning at the end of 56 years from the original copyright date, or beginning Jan. 1, 1978, whichever is later. In both cases, notice (in the form prescribed by the register) must be served not less than two or more than ten years before the selected termination date.

Transfers of copyright ownership must be in writing and signed by the owner of the rights conveyed in order to be valid, and must be recorded in the Copyright Office. Failure to record such a document within one month after its execution in the United States (or within two months abroad) will result in voiding it in favor of any subsequent transferee or mortgagee for a valuable consideration, without notice and taken in good faith, if the appropriate instrument (pertinent legal document) has been duly recorded first. A written nonexclusive license, on the other hand, whether recorded or not, prevails over a conflicting transfer of copyright ownership if the license was taken before the transfer or in good faith before recording of the transfer and without notice of it. It should be noted that purchase of any material object does not automatically convey any rights in the copyright. Nor does acquisition of a copyright include ownership of the material object, unless by specific agreement.

**Infringement of Copyright.** To constitute copyright infringement, three elements must be present. (1) There must be a substantial appropriation of protectible material. (2) The use of the material does not come within the privilege of "fair use" (defined below). And (3) the material is used in a medium reserved exclusively to the copyright proprietor.

In the case of recordings of musical compositions, the music copyright proprietor possesses the exclusive right of first recording. However, after he has acquiesced in the manufacture of records of the work, any other person may make similar use of the work on payment of a royalty of 2¾ cents per record or ½ cent per minute of playing time, whichever amount is larger.

**"Fair Use."** The appropriation of protectible material is measured by the criterion of "fair use." This means a taking that is substantial but is permitted by statute (and prior to the copyright law of 1976 was permitted by decisional law) because of overriding public policy. For example, a drama critic, television commentator, news reporter, teacher, or research scholar may freely reproduce portions of the subject under review to a greater extent (including multiple copies for classroom use) than can one whose use is of a commercial nature and may interfere with sales or other exploitation of the work by the proprietor.

An exact measuring rod does not exist for marking the borderline beyond which a taking is substantial or for delimiting fair use. Accordingly, a trade practice has developed whereby publishers request "permission" (nonexclusive license) from one another for the right to take extracts from copyrighted works. A license is a transfer by the copyright proprietor of less than his entire copyright. (A transfer of the entire copyright is an assignment.)

The statute of limitations contained in the copyright act must be scrupulously observed. No civil action or criminal proceedings can be maintained unless begun within three years after the claim accrued. The penal provisions of the act make willful infringement for profit punishable by imprisonment and/or a fine.

**Errors and Omissions.** Subject to certain safeguards for innocent infringers, and specified correctible action, copyright is no longer lost because of error in or omission of the copyright notice. The law describes the procedures whereby the errors and omissions may be corrected.

**Changes in the Electronic Era.** Public broadcasting, cable television systems (CATV), and photocopying are only three of the numerous extraordinary technological and commercial changes that have occurred since the 1909 revision of the copyright law. The 1976 law permits library and archival photocopying and distribution of single copies under limited circumstances. However, systematic library photocopying constitutes copyright infringement.

Public broadcasting of published nondramatic musical works and published pictorial, graphic, and sculptural works are subject to compulsory licensing if the parties do not reach agreement, with the terms and rates fixed by the presidentially appointed five-member Copyright Royalty Tribunal. Similarly, secondary transmissions by CATV are subject to compulsory license, but the royalty fee is fixed by the new act, and the tribunal distributes the fees less costs among the entitled copyright owners after determining the appropriate division.

After 69 years of exemption, public performances by juke boxes of nondramatic music are now under compulsory license, with a fixed fee of $8 per box, the net fees again to be distributed by the tribunal. As to the use of copyrighted works in computers, the new act does not alter the uncertainty of the pre-1976 law.

## INTERNATIONAL COPYRIGHT

Britain and all European countries maintain a single copyright system. Under the Bern Convention, to which virtually all European countries belong, the members accord protection to the unpublished works of the members' nationals and to works first (or simultaneously) published in one of the convention countries, even though the author is not a national of a convention country. No other formality need be observed as a condition of obtaining such copyrights. Practical problems frequently have arisen because first or simultaneous publication in a convention country is not always feasible.

**Universal Copyright Convention.** The eventual response was the Universal Copyright Convention (UCC) in 1955, to which the United States and the other major countries of the world (except mainland China) belong. The UCC requires that each signatory protect the unpublished works of other signatories' nationals (without formalities), their published works whether first published within or outside a UCC country, and any work first (or simultaneously) published in a UCC country irrespective of the author's nationality and residence.

Each UCC member country is allowed to impose formalities for works first published in its territory or created by one of its nationals. These include conditions for obtaining and maintaining copyright such as notice, deposit of copies, registration, fees, local manufacture, and publication. However, each member country must comply with the following rule as to works first published in another UCC country, the author of which is not one of the first country's nationals. It must regard all such formalities as satisfied if, beginning with first publication, all published copies bear the symbol © accompanied by the name of the copyright proprietor and the year of first publication, placed in such manner as to give reasonable notice of claim of copyright.

**U. S. Requirements.** The UCC form and position of notice satisfy the notice requirement of the U. S. Copyright Act, so that an American proprietor need affix to copies only a single notice such as "© 1978 Dr. Seuss" in such manner and location as shall give reasonable notice of the claim. The word "Copyright" or abbreviation "Copr." may be used in place of the symbol ©, and other minor variations are authorized.

In the case of a published sound recording, the form of notice would read "℗ 1978 Elektra." Here, too, a recognizable abbreviation or alternative designation may be used in place of the owner's name. The notice must be placed on the surface, label, or container of all publicly distributed phonorecords of the sound recording, in such manner and location as to give reasonable notice of the claim.

## PROTECTION IN OTHER COUNTRIES

Copyright protection in most countries outside the United States endures, generally speaking, for the life of the author and 50 years after his death. This is the minimum term under the Bern Convention, except for a shorter period of protection that may be given to cinematographic and photographic works and works of applied art. The minimum term of protection under UCC is the life of the author and 25 years after death, unless the member country does not so compute protection, in which event it is no less than 25 years from the date of first publication or registration, as the case may be. However, in regard to photographic works and works of applied art the minimum term of protection is ten years.

Under both conventions, the guiding principle is "national treatment." One who is entitled to convention protection does not obtain an international—or super—copyright. Rather, one secures a separate domestic copyright in each member country, a copyright that is no less favorable than the one each member gives its own authors, plus the specific minimum safeguards required by the respective conventions.

Some countries have extended their term of copyright under certain circumstances as a result of the interruptions caused by World Wars I and II, when normal exploitation of literary property could not be effected by author or proprietor. Moreover, some countries have extended their general copyright term to a period in excess of the life of the author and 50 years after his or her death. Thus one cannot rely blindly on the original "life-plus-50" Bern formula to determine the copyright/public domain status of works abroad, and each situation must be examined on its own facts. Incidentally, the Bern Convention recognizes the "moral right" of the author during his or her lifetime, even after a sale, to claim authorship credit and to object to action regarding the work that would be prejudicial to his or her reputation.

The U. S. Copyright Act of 1976 protects unpublished works without regard to the nationality or domicile of the author. Published works are protected if the author is a national or domiciliary of the United States or of a country with which the United States has treaty obligations (including the foreign sovereign authority), or is stateless; or the work is first published in the United States or a UCC country; or the work is covered by a presidential proclamation extending protection to works originating in a specified country that extends protection to U. S. works on substantially the same basis as to its own works.

**Canadian Copyright.** The Canadian copyright law does not require the observance of formalities as a condition of obtaining copyright. Unpublished works of U. S. subjects are protected, as are unpublished works of subjects of Britain and Bern Convention and UCC countries, and those of residents within the British monarch's dominions. Published works are protected if first published in such territories. The term of protection is, as a general rule, the life of the author and 50 years following his or her death. If, after the author's death, an attempt is made to withhold the work from the public, it may be subjected to compulsory license. In any event, 25 years after the author's death his or her works become subject to compulsory license. Also at the end of that time there is a reversion of the copyright to the author's estate, free of agreements made by the author during his or her lifetime.

## HISTORY OF COPYRIGHT LAW

**Origins in England.** The establishment by William Caxton of his press at Westminster, England, in 1476 marked the beginning of means for easily reproducing literary works and making them readily and widely available. The crown soon recognized the need to regulate the newly developing trade of printing and bookselling, which could spread new and perhaps "dangerous" political and religious ideas. Regulation (that is,

censorship) was accomplished in several ways, such as by royal restrictions of the right to print, by royal grants and patents of the exclusive right to print certain books, and by requiring the deposit of printed copies and the imprinting of the names of the author and printer in each copy. Also, the Stationers' Company, a trade association of printers and booksellers chartered by Queen Mary in 1557, maintained a register in which each member made an entry of the title of each book he purchased from an author or from another member. The stationers thus established a court for the determination of claims of priority and piracy (verbatim copying). However, by 1694 various means of regulation of the press had failed, including the Stationers' Company, and protection of literary property was in serious jeopardy.

Several years of uncontrolled literary piracy ensued. The passage in 1710 of the Statute of Anne marked the beginning of modern English copyright law. The statute provided protection against unauthorized printing, reprinting, or importing books for a limited term of years. However, so long as a work remained unpublished it did not come within the statute and, presumably, was covered by common law protection indefinitely. In the precedent-setting case of *Donaldson* v. *Becket* (1774) the House of Lords decided that protection for published works was to be found in the statute or not at all.

In the United States a somewhat similar question as to perpetual common law copyright arose in the classic case of *Wheaton* v. *Peters*, decided by the Supreme Court in 1834. The court held that copyright in the published work was solely a creature of statute, so that the proprietor thereof was required to comply with the statute or his work entered the "public domain—that is, became public property, which anyone could freely use, adapt, or exploit in its original or any form.

**Development in the United States.** Not until the adoption of the Constitution in 1789 was Congress vested (by Article I, section 8) with the power to protect literary property and inventions. Formerly, the separate states had enacted their own copyright statutes. The subject matter of literary protection under the new federal act of 1790 did not go beyond maps, charts, and books. Foreign authors were not eligible for protection until the passage of the Chace Act in 1891.

In the intervening century, Charles Dickens and other leading English authors had been freely pirated by U. S. publishers. Meanwhile, American authors complained bitterly that their own books were being ignored by many U. S. publishers in favor of royalty-free English works. There was strenuous petitioning over the years by such American literary giants as Twain, Longfellow, Holmes, Emerson, and Whittier. American authors were adversely affected by the unfair competition of the large and accessible number of English works in the U. S. "public domain." This, coupled with the creation in Europe of the Bern Union (which opened the door to European copyright for Americans) led to the Chace Act.

Between the passage of the Act of 1790 and the previous major revision in 1909, the protectible subject matter expanded considerably. Congress added prints (1802); musical compositions (1831); the right of public performance in dramatic compositions (1856), which had previously been protected only against printed copies;

photographs (1865); works of fine art, the right of translation, and the right to dramatize nondramatic literary works (1870); and the right to the performance in public of musical compositions (1897).

The 1909 act extended the control of the "proprietor" (the author, his assignees, or his heirs) to the right to make any other version of a literary work (for example, an abridgment) and the right to convert a drama into a nondramatic work. Proprietors of musical works were protected against unauthorized recordings.

Through codification and reenactment in 1947 as Title 17 of the U. S. code, the 1909 act added new protective categories of works (lectures, sermons, and addresses prepared for oral delivery; models or designs for works of art; reproductions of works of art; and drawings or plastic works of a scientific or technical character). In 1952 the copyright proprietor of a nondramatic literary work was given control over public renditions for profit and the making of transcriptions or records.

In 1971, Congress established a limited copyright in sound recordings that were first recorded and issued beginning Feb. 15, 1972, and before Jan. 1, 1975, for the purpose of protecting them against unauthorized duplication and piracy. In 1974, with general revision still mired in hearings, Congress eliminated the Jan. 1, 1975, cutoff date, thus making the new right a permanent part of the copyright law.

The long-awaited general revision of the copyright law enacted Oct. 19, 1976, radically altered the American copyright system. The federal statute preempted state common law copyright. It also adopted the "author's life-plus 50 years" term of protection for new works and existing unpublished works not previously copyrighted (with some exceptions and qualifications). It brought cable television, juke boxes, and public broadcasting use of certain copyrighted works within the new act but subject to new forms of compulsory licensing (under a Copyright Royalty Tribunal). Other provisions prohibited library photocopying except under specified conditions, instituted a new mechanism for terminating transfers of copyrights, phased out the "manufacturing clause" (which deals with books and periodicals by U. S. citizens and residents or in the English language), and liberalized the system of copyright notices that had for too long punished American creators instead of nurturing and protecting them.

A further revision in 1988 brought the U. S. law into compliance with the provisions of the Bern Convention, providing improved international protection for U.S. copyright holders. It eliminated the requirement of copyright notice for all U.S. and foreign works eligible for protection in the United States, and of registration for eligible foreign works.

STANLEY ROTHENBERG[*]
*Author of "Copyright and Public
Performance of Music"*

### Bibliography

Abrams, Howard B., *The Law of Copyright* (Boardman 1988).

Peters, Marybeth, *Copyright Procedures Handbook* (Boardman 1988).

Rothenberg, Stanley, *Copyright Law—Basic Materials* (Boardman 1956).

Rothenberg, Stanley, *Copyright and Public Performance of Music* (Nijhoff 1954).

Strong, William S., *The Copyright Book: A Practical Guide*, 2d ed. (MIT Press 1984).

**COQ D'OR,** kôk-dôr', an opera in three acts by Nikolai Rimsky-Korsakov, and a ballet based on the opera. The opera, the last of Rimsky-Korsakov's 14 operas, has a libretto by Vladimir Bielsky, from a story by Pushkin.

*Le Coq d'Or* was first presented in Moscow on Oct. 7, 1909. Censors refused at first to permit its performance because parts of it closely resembled the humiliating events of the Russo-Japanese War. The composer's family objected in 1914, when Diaghilev turned the opera into an opera-ballet, with singers in stage boxes and dancers on stage miming the roles. In 1937 the ballet became an independent work, and the opera resumed its original form. A famous part of the score is the queen's *Hymn to the Sun.*

WILLIAM ASHBROOK[*]
*Author of "Donizetti"*

**COQUELIN,** kô-klaṇ', **Constant** (1841–1909), French actor, who was the finest comedian of his day. He was called *aîné* (elder) to distinguish him from his younger brother Ernest, called Coquelin *cadet* (younger), who was also an actor. Although Coquelin brilliantly interpreted both classic and modern roles, he is best remembered as the creator of the title role in Rostand's *Cyrano de Bergerac.* His flexible voice, mobile face, large nose, and expressive eyes fitted him for comic parts in which he joined verve and spirit with technical perfection.

**Life.** Coquelin was born in Boulogne, France, on Jan. 23, 1841. He made his debut at the Comédie Française in 1860 in *Molière's Dépit amoureux,* and in 1864 he became a *sociétaire,* or member of the company. Soon he established an international reputation, performing in such roles as Figaro in Beaumarchais' *The Marriage of Figaro* and Mascarille in Molière's *Étourdi.*

Coquelin left the Comédie Française in 1886 to tour Europe and the United States. He returned to the company in 1890 but left it in 1892. After another American tour (1893–1894), he went back to Paris, where he acted at the Renaissance and Porte-St.-Martin theaters. In 1897 he and his brother took over the Porte-St.-Martin and presented *Cyrano,* which became one of the great hits of theater history. Coquelin toured the United States in 1900–1901 with Sarah Bernhardt, and then he acted in her theater in Paris. He died at Couilly-St.-Germain on Jan. 27, 1909.

EDITH MELCHER, *Author of
"The Life and Times of Henry Monnier"*

**Further Reading:** Salmon, Eric, ed., *Bernhardt and the Theater of Her Time* (Greenwood Press 1984).

**COQUILLA NUT,** kō-kē'yə, the hard nut of the coquilla palm (*Attalea funifera*), used as vegetable ivory, from which small articles can be carved. The nuts, from 3 to 4 inches (7.5 to 10 cm) long, are enclosed in fleshy fruits.

The coquilla palm, which occurs almost exclusively in the Brazilian state of Bahia, is also the source of Bahia piassava fibers, long wiry brown fibers that are stripped from the enlarged leafstalk bases. Because of their durability and resiliency when wet, the fibers are used in the manufacture of street-sweeping brooms, scrubbing brushes, and hawsers for ships.

LAWRENCE ERBE
*University of Southwestern Louisiana*

**COR ANGLAIS.** See ENGLISH HORN; OBOE.

**Star coral**

Brain coral (*foreground*) and sea whip (*background*)

**Staghorn coral**

CORALS are marine animals, usually living in shallow temperate or tropical waters. Some corals are solitary, but most live in colonies, sometimes forming huge coral reefs. Colony formations occur in a large variety of shapes.

**CORAL,** kôr'əl, is a small marine animal that has a stony skeleton and lives in colonies. The gradual accumulation of coral skeletons over a period of thousands of years results in the formation of coral reefs.

**The Coral Animal.** Coral animals, or polyps, are small coelenterates that resemble miniature sea anemones. They belong to the order Madreporaria in the class Anthozoa. Although some are solitary, the great majority live in colonies produced by budding (a form of asexual reproduction). Each individual, or unit, of the colony consists of the coral animal, or polyp, which is fastened permanently in a calcareous cup. The polyp has a columnar body topped by a flat disc bearing tentacles and the central mouth. The polyp can contract into the cup to some extent but cannot detach itself from it. The cup is secreted by the surface layer of the coral polyp and therefore lies entirely outside the polyp's tissues.

The cups of the members of the colony fuse and form a calcareous mass of various compact or branching shapes. This mass is enlarged by the continuous increase in the number of polyps through budding and by the continuous deposition of calcareous substance. The polyps remain alive only on the surface of the mass, but the calcareous depositions of their predecessors remain as permanent parts of the mass.

In this way a colony of a given species of coral may attain a width or height of several feet. The rate of growth varies from ¼ inch (0.64 cm) to several inches annually in different types of corals. The combined activity of many colonies of various species over the centuries build up a calcareous ridge or mound that may attain a depth of hundreds or even thousands of feet. Such masses are known as *coral reefs.*

**Occurrence and Types of Reefs.** In general, reef-building corals require warm waters and flourish only in tropical and subtropical areas, although there are some reefs at considerable depths off the west coast of Norway. Two areas where they abound are (1) the Indo-Pacific region from the east coast of Africa through the islands of the western Pacific to Hawaii and (2) the western Atlantic region from Bermuda to Brazil. There are no coral reefs on the west coast of Africa or of the Americas.

There are three types of coral reefs: fringing reefs, barrier reefs, and atolls. A *fringing reef* grows close to the shore. It consists of a reef front, or edge, where active coral growth is occurring, and the reef flat between the front and the shore, which is exposed by low tide and consists of coral mud and sand, dead coral, and debris of various kinds. A *barrier reef* has the same structure as a fringing reef but is much farther from land, and hence there is a wide lagoon between the reef flat and the shore. An *atoll* is a circular or horseshoe-shaped reef surrounding a lagoon. Reefs in general are not continuous walls of coral rock but are broken up into islands and minor reefs by passages.

The most famous reef is the Great Barrier Reef along the northeast coast of Australia. It is 1,250 miles (2,000 km) long and in some places over 100 miles (160 km) from shore.

**Formation of Reefs.** Since reef-building corals grow only in waters 150 feet (45 meters) deep or less, the great height that many reefs have attained over the centuries requires explanation. Coral polyps could not function 1,000 feet (300

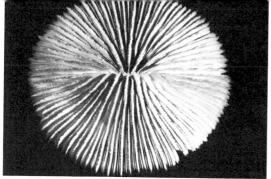

Mushroom coral

Lace coral

Rose coral

A soft coral

meters) below the surface of the sea to produce reefs there.

Three main theories have been advanced to explain reef formation. In Charles Darwin's *subsidence theory*, the reefs result from the subsidence (sinking) of sloping land as the coral grows. As the land subsides, a fringing reef becomes a barrier reef, leaving stretches of water between the present level of the land and the reef. An atoll is regarded as the fringing reef of an island that has sunk out of sight.

The second theory, the *submerged bank theory*, postulates that coral reefs grow on flat preexisting surfaces during or after the submergence of those surfaces. Reginald A. Daly's *glacial control theory* starts from the fact that the surface of the ocean was lowered during the glacial periods. Flat platforms were cut by wave action below the surface of the water and on the shores during this period. As the ice melted and the water rose, coral growths, which were established on these platforms as soon as temperatures became warm enough, kept pace with the rising ocean level.

All three theories admit submergence as a prime factor in establishing reefs of great depth. Darwin's subsidence theory, after undergoing some eclipse, has become the most favored explanation. Borings into reefs mostly support the subsidence theory, although some of them indicate that reefs may rest on a level, wave-cut platform as suggested by the Daly theory.

L. H. HYMAN
*Author of "The Invertebrates"*

**Bibliography**
Bemert, Gunnar, and Ormond, Rupert, *Red Sea Coral Reefs* (Methuen 1981).
Guilcher, Andre, *Coral Reef Geomorphology* (Wiley 1988).
Hyman, L. H., *The Invertebrates*, vol. 1 (McGraw 1940).
Jones, O. A., and Endean, R., eds., *Biology and Geology of Coral Reefs*, 4 vols. (Academic Press 1973–1977).
Kuhlman, D., *Living Coral Reefs of the World* (Arco 1985).
Romashko, Sandra D., *Living Coral and Other Inhabitants of the Reef*, 3d ed., (Windward 1985).
Voss, Gilbert L., *Coral Reefs of Florida* (Pineapple Press 1988).

**CORAL GABLES,** kor'əl gā'bəlz, a residential city in southeastern Florida, in Dade county. It is on the Atlantic coast, at the mouth of Biscayne Bay, just southwest of Miami.

Points of interest include the Fairchild Tropical Garden, a landscaped botanical garden of 85 acres (210 hectares), and the Tropical Park racetrack, just west of the city. Coral Gables is the seat of the University of Miami, a four-year coeducational institution. The Latin American corporate headquarters of several major oil and manufacturing firms are in the city. Incorporated in 1925, Coral Gables is governed by council and manager. Population: 42,249.

**CORAL REEFS.** See CORAL.

**CORAL SEA,** kôr'əl, an arm of the Pacific Ocean lying east of Queensland, Australia, and west of Vanuatu and New Caledonia. It extends from the Solomon Islands on the north to the Chesterfield Islands on the south. The sea's numerous coral reefs make it hazardous for ships.

During World War II the U.S. Navy scored a decisive victory over the Japanese in the Battle of the Coral Sea on May 7–8, 1942, thereby blocking Japan's advance toward Australia. See also WORLD WAR II—9. *War in the Southern and Southwestern Pacific.*

**CORAL SNAKE,** a brightly colored American venomous snake that is closely related to the cobra. Two species are found in the United States. The eastern coral snake (*Micrurus fulvius*) ranges from coastal North Carolina and Florida to Texas, while the Arizona coral snake (*Micruroides euryxanthus*) is found in the southwestern United States and adjacent Mexico.

Coral snakes have smooth shiny scales, and most are brightly patterned with alternating rings of red, yellow or white, and black. The two species found in the United States have black snouts and red rings bordered with yellow. Coral snakes feed on cold-blooded prey—fishes, lizards, and other snakes—which they kill with their highly toxic venom. They are secretive snakes and are not often seen in the daytime.

Since coral snakes are not aggressive, there are relatively few cases of snakebite due to them, and almost 50% of coral snakebite victims show no signs of venom poisoning, probably because the extremely short fangs, which are less than ¼-inch (6 mm) long, failed to penetrate the skin of the victim. However, of the 50% that show signs of poisoning, almost half die unless they receive prompt treatment with antivenin.

There are about 45 kinds of coral snakes in tropical and subtropical America. They are classified in three genera: *Leptomicrurus, Micrurus,* and *Micruroides* in the family Elapidae.

H. G. DOWLING
*American Museum of Natural History*

**CORAL TREE,** any of several tropical trees often grown for their scarlet pealike flowers. Coral trees belong to the genus *Erythrina* of the legume family (Leguminosae). Probably the most popular species is *E. indica*, which is native to India and Malaya. It ranges in height from 20 to 30 feet (6 to 9 meters) and has prickly stems. Its leaves are composed of three large leaflets, and its flowers are borne in dense clusters. They ripen into beanlike pods about a foot (30 cm) long.

A popular greenhouse species is *E. crista-galli*, which is native to Brazil and is often called the common coral tree. It grows from 6 to 8 feet (1.8 to 2.5 meters) tall and has spiny branchlets and leathery leaflets. In tropical countries the flowers of this species are sometimes cooked and eaten, and the bright red beans are made into decorative necklaces.

DONALD WYMAN
*Arnold Arboretum, Harvard University*

**CORALLINE,** kôr′ə-lin, a term referring to any substance resembling or composed of hardened calcium carbonate like that secreted by coral animals, such as brain corals, horn corals, and staghorn corals. The term "coralline" is also applied to numerous algae that secrete corallike calcium carbonate. For example, blue-green algae, along with coral-forming coelenterates, have contributed greatly to the formation of both ancient and modern ocean reefs. Also some red and green algae secrete calcium carbonate and are thus coralline.

DAVID A. OTTO
*Stephens College*

**CORAM, Thomas,** kô′rəm (1668–1751), English philanthropist. He was born in Lyme Regis, Dorset. He served as a seaman but rose to become a captain and a prosperous shipwright. Coram went to America in 1693 and engaged principally in

Western, or Arizona, coral snake.

boat-building at Taunton, Mass., until 1704.

After returning to England, Coram became appalled by the number of children he saw abandoned in London, many of them starving. He worked for 17 years to obtain a royal charter (1739) authorizing the establishment of a hospital for foundling infants. The first child was admitted in 1741.

Coram's devotion to the project won the interest of William Hogarth, who presented his fine portrait of Coram to the hospital, and of G. F. Handel, who gave recitals there. As Coram had spent nearly all his private means on philanthropic schemes, an annuity of £161 was raised for him in 1749 by subscription. He died in London on March 29, 1751.

**CORAOPOLIS,** kôr-ē-op′ə-lis, an industrial borough in southwestern Pennsylvania, in Allegheny county, 11 miles (18 km) northwest of Pittsburgh, on the Ohio River. It has oil refineries, iron and steel plants, and metal works. Coraopolis was settled about 1760. Population: 6,747.

**CORATO,** kō-rä′tō, a city and commune in Italy, in the Apulia region, located 25 miles (40 km) northwest of Bari. It is the market center for the products of the area (grapes, olives, almonds, cattle) and produces wine and olive oil. Ten miles (16 km) southwest of the city is the 13th-century Castel del Monte, built by Emperor Frederick II; it is one of the most beautiful of the remaining examples of medieval architecture in southern Italy. The castle is built in the shape of a vast octagon with eight hexagonal towers. Population: commune, 41,138 (1981 census).

**CORBEIL-ESSONNES,** kôr-bâ-ye-sôn′, a town in France, in the department of Essonne, at the junction of the Essonne and Seine rivers, 18 miles (29 km) south-southeast of Paris. Formed in 1951 by the amalgamation of the former communes of Corbeil and Essonnes, it is an important industrial center, producing electronic equipment, paper, cotton textiles, furniture, clocks, foundry products, chocolate, flour, and starch.

Both Corbeil and Essonnes have churches dating from the 12th century. Corbeil was the capital of a countship from the 10th century until 1108, when it was annexed to France. Population: 37,741 (1982 census).

**CORBET,** kôr′bət, **Richard** (1582–1635), English poet and bishop. His name is also spelled *Corbett.* He was born at Ewell, Surrey, the son of a gardener or nurseryman, and was educated at Pembroke and Christ Church colleges, Oxford (B. A., 1602; M. A., 1605). A close friend of Ben Jonson and other poets and dramatists, Corbet was a celebrated practical joker and wit, a lover of the theater, and a high-spirited bon vivant. He became dean of Christ Church College in 1620, bishop of Oxford in 1628, and bishop of Norwich in 1632. He owed his advancement in the church, at least to some extent, to the influence of his patron, the Duke of Buckingham. Corbet died at Norwich on July 28, 1635.

Corbet's poems include ballads, such as *The Fairies' Farewell* and *Journey to France,* as well as many rollicking, good-humored satires directed for the most part against the Puritans.

**CORBETT,** kôr′bət, **Harvey Wiley** (1893–1954), American architect, who helped to evolve the modern skyscraper style. He was born in San Francisco, Calif., on Jan. 8, 1893, and was educated at the University of California at Berkeley and the École des Beaux-Arts, Paris. The firm of Pell and Corbett built such traditional works as the classical civic center in Springfield, Mass., begun in 1911. Then, abandoning traditional idioms as other architects of the time were doing, Corbett became particularly fascinated with the skyscraper as it developed in New York City after the 1916 law requiring setbacks above a certain height.

The firm of Helmle and Corbett designed the Bush Terminal office building, Brooklyn, begun in 1918, which, despite its overt Gothicism, gives an impression of overall simplicity and verticality. The Roerich tower (1929), in Manhattan, is a subtle composition of brick in gradations of color and diminishing shapes. The firm of Corbett, Harrison, and MacMurray collaborated with other firms on the design of Rockefeller Center, built between 1932 and 1940. Corbett died in New York City on April 21, 1954.

WALTER KIDNEY, *"Progressive Architecture"*

**CORBETT** (kôr′bət), **James John** (1866–1933), American professional boxer, who held the heavyweight championship from 1892 to 1897. The first heavyweight to rely on boxing skill rather than on brute strength, he defeated John L. Sullivan for the title on Sept. 7, 1892.

Corbett was born in San Francisco on Sept. 1, 1866, and attended Sacred Heart College. While working as clerk in a bank, he joined the Olympic Club and at the age of 18 began to box as an amateur. He became a professional in 1886 and drew attention when he defeated heavyweight Joe Choynski in a 27-round bout near Benicia, Calif., on June 5, 1889. The following year he outpointed Jake Kilrain in 6 rounds, and on May 21, 1891, he battled the West Indian Peter Jackson to a 61-round draw.

"Gentleman Jim," so called because of his fine manners and clean living, fought Sullivan in New Orleans for a $25,000 purse and $20,000 stake. The match was the first heavyweight title bout fought with padded gloves and the first under the Marquis of Queensberry rules. Corbett used guile and finesse, avoiding Sullivan's rushes and scoring with counterpunches. He knocked out the champion in 21 rounds.

CULVER PICTURES, INC.

James J. Corbett

Corbett defended his title successfully against Charles Mitchell (England), Peter Courtney, and others, but on March 17, 1897, he was defeated at Carson City, Nev., when Robert Fitzsimmons of England knocked him out in the 14th round. Corbett made two attempts to regain the title but was defeated twice by James J. Jeffries (who had won the crown from Fitzsimmons), in 23 rounds on May 11, 1900, at Coney Island, N. Y., and in 10 rounds on Aug. 14, 1903, in San Francisco. Corbett fought a total of 33 bouts, winning 26.

Gentleman Jim appeared in plays, vaudeville, and motion pictures, and took part in radio programs. His autobiography *The Roar of the Crowd* was published in 1925. He died at his home in Bayside, N. Y., on Feb. 18, 1933. Corbett was elected to Boxing's Hall of Fame in 1954.

BILL BRADDOCK, *New York "Times"*

**CORBIÈRE,** kôr-byâr′, **Tristan** (1845–1875), French poet, whose personal, realistic works pointed toward the later symbolist and surrealist movements. Édouard Joachim Corbière, who later took the pseudonym Tristan, was born at Coat Congar, Brittany, on July 18, 1845, the son of a naval officer who wrote novels. Early illness forced him to spend his life at Roscoff, on the Breton coast, except for a trip to Palestine and Italy and a few years in Paris, where he led an exhausting life among bohemians. He died at Morlaix, Brittany, on March 1, 1875.

*Les amours jaunes* (1873), Corbière's collected poems, met with indifference until Paul Verlaine praised them in his *Les poètes maudits* (1884). In his engaging verses, written in familiar, fragmented language that is often slangy and purposely unbalanced, Corbière mocks poetic clichés, deflating both romantic rhetoric and Parnassian formalism. He writes of Brittany and the sea with an unconventional realism, and of Paris, art, and his own sentiments with humor and sarcasm.

EDWIN JAHIEL, *University of Illinois*

The Corcoran Gallery of Art: one of its galleries showing 19th-century American paintings.

**CORBIN, Margaret** (1751—?1800), American Revolutionary War heroine. Margaret Cochran was born in what is now Franklin county, Pa., on Nov. 12, 1751. After her father was killed and her mother taken prisoner by Native Americans in 1756, she was raised by an uncle. In 1772 she married John Corbin, who enlisted in the first company of the Pennsylvania Artillery Regiment early in the Revolution. Margaret was with him when he was killed during the defense of Fort Washington, on Nov. 16, 1776. She took his place at the cannon and was wounded in the arm. She became the only female member of the Invalid Regiment, stationed at West Point until disbanded in 1783, and the first woman to receive a pension from Congress.

Nothing is known with certainty of her later life. One account identifies as Margaret Corbin the "Captain Molly" living in Swimtown (Highland Falls), N.Y., who died around 1800. Other accounts hold that Corbin lived in Westmoreland county, Pa., until her death (on Jan. 16, 1800, in one version).

**CORBUSIER, Le.** See LE CORBUSIER.

**CORCORAN,** kôr′kə-rən, **Thomas Gardiner** (1900—1981), American lawyer who helped draft and maneuver through Congress many of the complex legislative bills of the New Deal. Born in Pawtucket, R.I., on Dec. 29, 1900, he received two degrees from Brown University and two from Harvard University (graduating first in his class) by the age of 25. After spending a year as secretary to Supreme Court Justice Oliver Wendell Holmes, Corcoran joined a New York City law firm.

On the recommendation of his former Harvard mentor, Felix Frankfurter, Corcoran went to Washington in 1932 to work for the Reconstruction Finance Corporation. Coming to the attention of Pres. Franklin D. Roosevelt, who dubbed him "Tommy the Cork," Corcoran teamed with Benjamin V. Cohen, another young lawyer, to draft such measures as the Securities Exchange Act (1934), the Public Utility Holding Company Act (1935), and the Fair Labor Standards Act (1938). With influence far beyond the minor positions that he held, Corcoran also helped write President Roosevelt's speeches and served as liaison to Congress. After 1941 Corcoran practiced law in Washington. He died there on Dec. 6, 1981.

KEITH W. OLSON
*University of Maryland*

**CORCORAN GALLERY OF ART,** kôr′kə-rən, in Washington, D.C., one of the oldest art galleries in the United States and a major center of American art. It was founded in 1869 by the American financier, philanthropist, and art collector William Wilson Corcoran (1798—1888), who dedicated the museum "to the encouragement of American genius." A highly regarded school of art is connected with the museum.

The Corcoran Gallery collection was at first housed in a building designed by James Renwick. In 1897 it was moved to a new, larger building designed by Ernest Flagg. Besides its galleries, the museum boasts the stunning 18th-century gilded French room, the Salon Doré.

Corcoran's own collection forms the nucleus of the museum's American art collection. This includes about 900 paintings, as well as sculpture, drawings, and prints dating from the early 18th through the 20th century. A bequest in 1926 by Sen. William A. Clark added Dutch, Flemish, French, Italian, and other works.

The Corcoran continues to organize the Biennial Exhibition of American Painting, an acclaimed series begun in 1907 (when it attracted works by Homer, Cassatt, Eakins, Sargent, Henri, and Marin, among others). To augment exhibitions, a wide range of educational programs is offered for all ages, and various musical programs, ranging from classical to jazz, are held for the public, often in the museum's 200-seat auditorium.

**CORD,** a measure of firewood. The standard cord is a stack of 4-foot (1.2-meter) pieces of wood, piled parallel, 4 feet high and 8 feet (2.4 meters) long. Such a pile contains 128 cubic feet (3.6 cubic meters), but air spaces between the pieces reduce the volume of solid wood to 60 to 100 cubic feet (1.7—2.8 cubic meters). The term *face cord* usually refers to a stack that is 4 feet high and 8 feet long, with all pieces of a specified length. A face cord of 16-inch (41-cm) pieces equals about one-third as much as a standard cord.

If a cord contains 80 cubic feet (2.2 cubic meters) of solid wood with a moisture content of 25%, then its available heat content would be about 24.4 million Btu for a fairly dense wood such as northern red oak or beech. This is equal to about 135 gallons (510 liters) of fuel oil, assuming that burning efficiency is 50% for wood and 65% for oil. A cord of spruce, which is much less dense, equals about 85 gallons (320 liters) of oil.

**CORDAGE,** kôrd′ij, a general term that includes string, twine, cord, rope and cable. Cordage can be made from vegetable or synthetic fibers. Therefore, wire rope and wire cable are not considered cordage. The term "line" is also used in certain applications, as in a clothesline or, collectively, in ship's lines. The term "hawser" is applied to marine mooring ropes, generally over 5 inches (12.5 cm) in circumference. Twine is usually under 3/32 inch (0.24 cm) in diameter, cord up to 3/16 inch (0.47 cm) in diameter, and rope is 3/16 inch (0.47 cm) in diameter and over. Netting, whether for tennis nets or fishing nets, is composed of twine that is constructed in a particular pattern of mesh by knotting.

Terms that are used in the specification of cordage include "breaking or tensile strength," which is the maximum force applied to a specimen in a tensile test carried to rupture; "elongation," the increase in length resulting from a load being applied (as in a tensile test); and "linear density," the weight or mass per unit of length measured under a tension defined by the standard for a particular type of rope.

The major factors in making twine, cord, rope, or netting are the selection of the fiber and the design and manufacture of the product. The user or manufacturer establishes the basic criteria of strength, weight, elongation, life factors, and application standards.

## 1. Cordage Fibers

The two basic classes of raw materials used in cordage are natural (or vegetable fibers) and synthetic fibers. Prior to World War II, natural fibers were used; but the invention of nylon, a long-chain synthetic polyamide, provided a stronger, more durable fiber. After the war the rope-making industry began to use nylon.

Vegetable fibers continue to be used, especially in smaller cordage, but synthetics have extensively replaced natural fiber rope.

### NATURAL FIBERS

They are classified as hard fibers and soft fibers. Hard fibers form the structural system of the plant leaf, and soft fibers are found in the inner bark (bast layer) of the plant stem.

**Abaca.** The principal hard fiber used in cordage is abaca, obtained from the tropical plant *Musa testilis*, a member of the banana family. Abaca is the strongest of the natural fibers. It is commonly known as Manila hemp, which is a misnomer since the hemp plant belongs to the soft fiber group. The Philippine Islands produced more than 90% of the world supply of this fiber prior to World War II, and the East Indies provided the balance. The Philippines remains the chief source for the United States of both the fiber and the rope made from it.

**Sisal and Henequen.** Sisal (*Agave sisalana*) and henequen (*A. fourcroydes*) are the other two major hard fibers. Henequen is sometimes called Mexican or Cuban sisal. The various sisals are usually identified by the country of origin. Tanzania, Kenya, Indonesia, Brazil, and Haiti are the major producers of sisal; Mexico is the major producer of henequen. Sisal and henequen are resistant to salt water and are used for rope, twine, sacking, and cable insulation.

**Jute.** Jute, a soft fiber, comes from the stalks of two closely related plants, *Corchorus capsularis* and *C. olitorius.* Pakistan and India produce 98% of the world's jute. Because it is cheap to produce, jute is the major soft cordage fiber. It is made into yarns, twines, and ropes, and is blended with hard fibers to produce stronger types of ropes.

**Hemp.** Hemp (*Cannabis sativa*), the second-leading soft fiber, was the most important cordage fiber in the world until the 19th century. At that time the invention of rope-making machinery and the introduction of abaca into the United States gradually gave the advantage to the hard fibers. Today, the Soviet Union and Italy are the leading producers of hemp. Other important hemp-producing countries are Yugoslavia, Hungary, Romania, and Poland. A small quantity is produced in the United States, principally in Kentucky and Wisconsin.

**Cotton.** Small cords sold in significant volume, such as clothesline, sash cord, and mason line, are made with cotton, a soft fiber that is sometimes blended with the synthetic fiber polyester. Most of the cotton used for cordage is produced in the United States.

### SYNTHETIC FIBERS

The loss during World War II of Far Eastern sources for natural fibers encouraged the development of synthetic fibers. High-tenacity nylon and polyester fibers are mostly produced in the United States, while polypropylene is available worldwide. All are petroleum based, so their cost is related to the price of oil. Owing to their higher strengths, improved durability, and more consistent properties, synthetic fiber ropes have taken over the great majority of applications in the industrialized world.

Synthetic fibers used in rope are the industrial or high-tenacity grades. They were developed first for use in tires and seat belts.

**Nylon.** The first synthetic fiber to be successfully used in cordage was nylon. This high-tenacity nylon originally had been developed for the tire industry. The fiber-forming substance of this manufactured fiber is a long-chain synthetic polyamide in which less than 85% of the amide linkages are attached directly to two aromatic rings. There were initial rope-making problems in twisting and forming the soft nylon yarns and strands. But stabilizing methods were developed, and nylon cordage became a viable product. The major attributes of nylon cordage are a high strength-to-weight ratio, excellent resistance to mildew, bacterial decay, aging, and abrasion, and elasticity under strain. High-tenacity nylon will stretch approximately 10% at working loads and return close to its original length after the load is removed, enabling a rope to provide energy absorption, which is important in many applications.

Basic three-strand nylon ropes had almost three times the strength, at the same weight, over manila (abaca), and so they began slowly to be preferred in spite of higher initial costs. Today, nylon cordage is generally considered the standard for general-purpose use, and its properties became the basis for comparing other synthetic ropes.

**Polyester.** Following nylon, high-tenacity polyester started to be used for cordage. The fiber-forming substance of this manufactured fiber is any long-chain synthetic polymer composed of at least 85% by weight of an ester of a substituted aromatic carboxylic acid. The major attributes of polyester are low stretch, no water absorption, good ultraviolet resistance, and ex-

Synthetic ropes with very high strength-to-weight ratios, almost no stretch, and excellent resistance to being cut are used to tow large ships.

cellent abrasion resistance, particularly when wet. The strength of polyester ropes initially was about 14% less than that of nylon, but improved grades of high-tenacity fibers now can make them nearly equal.

**Olefin.** The most popular synthetic fiber now used in rope is a member of the olefin family. This family comprises manufactured fibers in which the fiber-forming substance is any long-chain synthetic polymer composed of at least 85% by weight of ethylene, propylene, or other olefin units. Polypropylene is the fiber most commonly used. Its primary advantage is that it is lightweight (it will float) and of relatively low cost. Its major disadvantages are its low melting point and its decomposition under ultraviolet light. Three-strand polypropylene rope, for example, is about 55% stronger than the same size manila rope at one-third less weight, but it has 44% less strength than a nylon rope. Most companies manufacturing polypropylene cordage extrude their own fiber from resin pellets. Colors can easily be added and, in fact, are desirable as they reduce the decomposition caused by ultraviolet light.

**High Performance Fibers.** Some synthetic fibers used for cordage are identified as "high modulus." That is, they have extremely high strength-to-weight ratios, virtually no stretch, and excellent resistance to being cut. This makes it possible to produce synthetic ropes that can replace wire ropes with some additional advantages, such as lighter weight, easier handling, and less bulk. These same fibers are finding use as composites with other materials for bullet-proof clothing, very strong and lightweight boat hulls, military protective gear, and cut-proof gloves. For example, extended chain polyethylene is a high modulus fiber, which has ten times

the strength of steel for its weight, is light enough to float, and has a high degree of chemical resistance.

These fibers are considerably more expensive than nylon or polyester; but ropes made from them have replaced wire in such applications as guy wires, sailboat rigging, deep-sea and oceanographic moorings, lifelines on ships, and as strength members for electromechanical cables.

## 2. Manufacturing of Cordage

For cordage to be used effectively, it must be made with closely packed fiber structures that retain their dimensions and form over a reasonable service life. Compactness is attained by successive twisting operations: the fibers are compacted by being twisted into yarns, the yarns into strands or cords, and the strands into ropes that are either stranded or braided. The degree and effectiveness of compacting are determined by factors such as the amount of twist, the tension in the component units as they are being twisted together, and the compression and confinement induced by restrictions such as tubes and dies, applied to the component units of the rope or cord as the twist is being effected.

**Cords and Twines.** Cords and twines are of two general types: twisted or plied, and laid or cabled. The difference between these two types of cords or twines lies in the process of foreturn. This process is made up of two operations: twisting and laying. In twisting, a number of yarns are bunched and compacted into a bundle by twist; in laying, yarns, or twisted strands of fine yarns, are individually twisted while the group as a whole is being twisted, thus providing foreturn and a balanced twisted structure. Twisting may be considered a strand-forming operation, whereas laying is a dual twisting operation.

An operator checks the angle of strands of braided cover rope attached to upright bobbins.

**Stranded Rope.** In the construction of a multiyarn cordage structure, such as rope, compactness is achieved by strand-forming and rope-laying operations. The necessary compression for compactness is attained by pulling yarns through a compression tube, called the strand tube, ensuring at the same time that the yarns are properly arranged in order to obtain as even a distribution in the cross section of the strand as possible. As the strand is pulled through the compression tube, a twist is imparted to it. The machine forming the strand then winds the strand on a bobbin.

The laying process for a basic three-strand rope is one of twisting these strands together to form a rope. A rope laid (twisted) with three strands is designated a plain or hawser-laid rope. A rope of four strands is designated a shroud-laid rope. A rope laid with three or more ropes is designated a cable-laid rope. In all rope-laying operations, the ropes are twisted in reverse direction to the strands. Since the effect of twisting the compact rope structure is to untwist the strand structure because of the reverse twist, the rope-laying operation must provide not only a means for twisting the rope but also an additional means for restoring twist to the strands. The twisting of a stranded rope is called afterturn. The twisting by which turn is restored or retained in a stranded rope is called foreturn.

**Braided Rope.** In making braided rope the yarns or strands are crossed and recrossed either in the same direction or in opposite, maypole, directions, in a manner such that each yarn or strand passes alternately over and under one or more of the others. In braiding machines upright bobbins, placed on a flat plate, move in serpentine path around one another to achieve the interlacing. For small size cords or coverings where higher productive speeds are required,

the bobbins are arranged at a low angle to rotate in circular tracks, with half the bobbins in an inner track and the other half in an outer track. The yarns or strands from the outer-track bobbins cross the inner ones alternately over and under to achieve the interlacing effect, the inner-track bobbins moving in one direction and the outer-track bobbins in the opposite direction.

A carrier holds the bobbin of yarn or strand. Simultaneously with the motion of the carrier, a hauling capstan pulls the interlocked strands through a die and winds it on a reel. The tightness of the braid is determined by the hauling rate, the tension or twist in the respective yarns or strands, whether or not the braid is twisted around a core of yarns, and the extent of interlocking of respective yarns or strands. Extremes in compactness or tightness of braid can be attained for different uses.

The production of braided rope is determined by the number of picks per inch, which is the distance between intersecting strands. The distance, in turn, is controlled by the tension over the yarns or strands. This latter factor is a matter of major concern inasmuch as the swinging motion of the bobbins, bringing the strands closer or farther away from the forming die, will cause variable tension.

Solid braided rope is cylindrical, with each strand alternately passing under and over one or more of the other strands of the rope while all strands are rotating around the axis with the same direction of rotation. This is the basic construction that has been used for most clotheslines, sash cords, and small utility cords for about 100 years. Solid braids are normally made from cotton, synthetic, and blended fibers with a diameter of 3/32 inch (0.24 cm) to 1/2 inch (1.25 cm).

Single or hollow braided cords and ropes are cylindrical, with one strand (or group of strands) rotating in one direction about the axis and another rotating in the opposite direction, each passing under and over the other, similar to the way a maypole is wound. Plain braids have strands that go over and under, while twill braids have one strand going over two strands and under two strands, rotating in the opposite direction. A double-braided rope is constructed from an inner hollow braided core rope and an outer braided cover rope, engineered so they supplement each other in strength. Braided ropes can also be made flat, as in parachute cord. There are many variations to these basic constructions. Parallel fibers, electrical cables, or lead (for weighted commercial fishing nets) can be inserted into the hollow core of braided rope. Kernmantle rope, which has a very high tensile strength, is designed for mountain climbing and rescue work. Braided ropes are distinguished by their diamond pattern, are generally made from synthetic fibers, and can be made from 3/32 inch (0.24 cm) to 10 inches (25 cm) in diameter. Some braided ropes have a tensile strength in excess of 2,000,000 pounds (900,000 kg).

## 3. History of Cordage

Cordage is one of mankind's oldest tools and articles of manufacture. It has helped people obtain food, shelter, and clothing since prehistoric times. Primitive peoples twisted strips of hide, sinew, hair, vines, and plant fibers into rope long before they learned to spin or weave. Rope or cord bound ax head to handle, made snares, nets, and fishlines, and tied logs together to form a raft. Carrying cords made of flax have been found in the Neolithic lake dwellings of Switzerland. Pre-Columbian Indians of the Western Hemisphere swung crude vine rope bridges across canyons as the prototype of the modern suspension bridge.

History, tradition, and literature bear witness to the contribution of cordage to civilization. Rope was used in the construction of the Tower of Babel and the pyramids of ancient Egypt. During the Middle Ages, rope-rigged scaffolds were essential in the building of the great cathedrals, and rope was used for crude litters to transport the sick. Rope has been an essential shipboard tool since the sail was first used to harness the power of the wind. By means of it early Norsemen attached planks to the ribs of their ships and Asians bound the planks together.

In the Western Hemisphere, American Indians made rope from numerous animal and vegetable fibers—hair, skin, and dried sinew; wild cotton plants, yucca, dogbane, agave, elm, willow, and nettle. In colonial America, early settlers followed the examples set by the Indians, who used the wild hemp of New England for fishing nets and lines, and native flax and "silk grass" for rope and other types of cordage. Bounties were paid to encourage the production of hemp in the colonies, and Virginia colonists were pledged to cultivate silk grass before they shipped out of England.

Rope making was one of the earliest industries in America. Records indicate that rope was made in Boston by John Harrison in 1630, in a ropewalk that may have been simply an open area of ground. Ropewalks later developed into long, low buildings, sometimes 1,200 feet (360 meters) in length, in which the rope maker walked backward, paying out the fiber from a bundle around his waist and spinning it into yarn as he went. Henry Wadsworth Longfellow describes this method in his poem *The Ropewalk.*

The first machine for laying rope was invented in 1793 by Capt. Joseph Huddart, an Englishman, and in 1810 the machine methods used for spinning cotton were successfully adapted to hemp and flax by Philippe de Girard of France.

A number of basic patents on cordage machinery were issued to John Good of New York City, beginning in 1869. His patents included machines that combed and lapped fibers and spin rope yarns without cutting. In November 1885 he patented a method for making rope that was stronger than that produced by any other machine and made possible the use of cheaper fibers. By 1900, machines based on Good's patents were used in 75% of the world's cordage factories. In 1854, John Tolman of Boston invented a method of braiding small cordage using cotton, the principles of which are used today.

The cordage industry has expanded worldwide since the mid-19th century. This has been caused by industrial growth as well as commercial fishing and the offshore oil industry. Both of the latter are heavy users of ropes, cordage, and netting.

While the majority of cordage is produced and consumed in the United States, many other countries have the capability to service their own industries as well as those that are worldwide in nature, such as recreational boating, commercial marine, and oil. The emerging synthetic cordage producing countries outside the United States are Britain, West Germany, South Korea, Canada, Brazil, and Portugal. Brazil, Haiti, Tanzania, Portugal, Mexico, and the Philippines produce the majority of natural fiber cordage.

In keeping with its historic contribution to civilization, cordage continues to serve an increasing range of uses. This includes: baler and binder twins for farming; industrial slings; winch ropes and stringing lines for the utility industry; lassos for roping livestock; purse, seine, and lead lines for commercial fishing nets; ship tie-up lines and tow ropes; oceanographic mooring and sonic array tow lines; helicopter pendants; space tethers for astronauts; strength members for oil booms; extraction ropes for airborne missiles; oil-field mooring hawsers for oil tankers; and, with the new high-performance fibers, such articles as artificial ligaments, high-altitude balloon tethers, lifelines, subsea moorings, antenna tower guys, and no-stretch bowstrings for archery. Improvements in both fiber and rope-making technology will allow synthetics to replace wire in an increasing range of strength member requirements.

G. P. FOSTER
*Director, Cordage Institute*

**High-performance cordage is widely used on sailboats to control sail position and shape.**

CORDAGE INSTITUTE

CORDAITALES include a prehistoric tree of the genus Cordaites. The tree is shown here in reconstruction.

**CORDAITALES,** kôr-dā-ĭ-tā'lēz, a large order of extinct trees that were similar in many respects to modern conifers. They were generally large trees with extensive branching systems and large amounts of wood. Their leaves were simple (undivided) and sessile (not stalked), and their pollen-and-seed-bearing structures were borne on slender stems at the distal parts of the tree.

The cordaitaleans probably first appeared early in the Carboniferous period, about 400 million years ago, although it is possible that they may have evolved earlier. They reached their maximum development in the late Carboniferous and Permian periods, from about 300 million to 230 million years ago. The existence of cordaitaleans after the Permian—in the Mesozoic era—is open to question. Wood fragments and leaves bearing some resemblance to those of the cordaitaleans have been found in early Mesozoic rocks, but these specimens do not demonstrate conclusively that cordaitaleans were present in the Mesozoic era.

The Cordaitales are divided into three families: the Pityaceae, the Poroxylaceae, and the Cordaitaceae. The status of the first two families, however, is still uncertain. Trees of the family Pityaceae are known to have had a great deal of secondary wood. In the forms where foliage is known to have existed, the leaves were pointed. Although certain specimens of woody stems were once assigned to this family, they have since been found to be more fernlike in their mode of reproduction. The Poroxylaceae is a small family of trees of which only fossil stems have been found. Specimens of certain strap-shaped leaves are believed to have belonged to these trees, but they have never been found actually attached to the stems and may belong to plants of other groups.

The largest and best-known family is the Cordaitaceae. Trees of this group may have reached heights of 100 feet (30 meters), and they had trunks 3 feet (1 meter) in diameter near the base. Inside the stem was a core of pith tissue characterized by partitions of tissue separated by air spaces. The primary wood tissue was arranged in small bundles at the periphery of the pith, similar to the wood structure of modern conifers. Surrounding the primary wood was dense secondary wood tissue.

The leaves of the Cordaitaceae were generally strap-shaped, but some were almost grasslike, while others were more nearly spatula-shaped. They varied greatly in length among different species. The veins in the leaves were closely spaced and appear to be parallel but actually were branched, with branches running parallel to each other.

The fruiting structure, called a cordaianthus of the Cordaitaceae, was a small budlike body. These bodies were borne in two rows in the axils (leaf angles) of slender, pointed leaves. They bore helically arranged scales on a short stem. The end scales of some bore pollen sacs, while the end scales of others bore ovules. The seeds had two coats, a soft outer coat and a hard inner one. Some seeds apparently had winglike structures and were dispersed by the wind.

THEODORE DELEVORYAS
*Yale University*

**CORDAY,** kôr-dā', **Charlotte** (1768–1793), French revolutionist who murdered Jean Paul Marat. Marie Anne Charlotte Corday d'Armont was born in St.-Saturnin, Normandy, on July 27, 1768. She came from an impoverished noble family, and was a descendant of the great playwright Pierre Corneille.

She attended a convent school in Caen and led a sheltered life until 1793, when the leaders of the Girondist faction, moderate republicans under ban in Paris, arrived in Caen. Greatly influenced by them, she hoped to further their struggle against the radical Jacobins who were in power. Believing that Marat, who was the publisher of the journal *L'ami du peuple*, was a key man in the enemy camp, she went to Paris in order to kill him.

On July 13, 1793, she purchased a butcher's knife and tried to see Marat at his home in the Rue des Cordeliers, where he was living with his young wife and sister. Posing as a Jacobin sympathizer who wished to betray Girondist leaders, she was refused admittance, but she returned again in the evening. Once more Marat was protected, but overhearing her request, he ordered her admission. Because of a painful skin condition, he spent many hours in a warm bath. He received her, and they discussed the political situation. When he predicted that the municipal leaders of Normandy would soon be guillotined, she drew her knife and stabbed him to death. Arrested, she defended her action at her trial. She died bravely on the guillotine in Paris on July 17, 1793.

Corday had expected death and martyrdom; in order that her identity would be known she had pinned her baptismal certificate to her dress when she went to Marat's house, as well as a note explaining her motive. She apparently thought of herself as a savior of France, an 18th century Joan of Arc. But instead of helping the Girondist leaders, who probably did not know of her intention, her deed merely increased the severity of the Jacobin leadership's repressive policy.

RICHARD M. BRACE
*Oakland University*

**CORDELE,** kor-dēl', a city in south central Georgia, the seat of Crisp county, 58 miles (93 km) south of Macon. The city is a trade center for an agricultural and lumbering area raising peanuts, pecans, cotton, corn, and watermelons. Its industries are largely devoted to the processing of agricultural and forest products but include the manufacture of textiles, machinery, air conditioners, fertilizer, and soft drinks. Veterans' Memorial Park, a state park noted for year-round fishing, is about 8 miles (13 km) west on Lake Blackshear.

Cordele was founded and incorporated in 1888. It has a council-manager form of government. Population: 11,608.

**CORDELIERS CLUB,** kôr-də-lirz', a prominent political club during the French Revolution. Founded in 1790 as the Society of the Friends of the Rights of Man and Citizen, it derived its popular name from its original meeting place, a Cordelier (Franciscan) monastery. Among the leading members of the club were Georges Jacques Danton, Camille Desmoulins, Jacques Hébert, and Jean Paul Marat. With dues of approximately a penny a month, the Cordeliers generally attracted members from lower strata of society than the Jacobins, with whom they were frequently in conflict. The Cordeliers were tireless critics of every government in power: monarchist, Girondist, or Jacobin.

When Louis XVI failed in his attempt to flee France in June 1791, the club responded with a petition to the National Assembly calling for a plebiscite to decide the king's fate. They pressed hard for his dethronement. By 1793, advanced revolutionaries like Hébert and Jacques Roux were in charge of the club. These men favored the creation of a revolutionary army to pacify the country and to ensure the provisioning of Paris. Their stated tactics included direct action, terror, and mob rule.

The breakup of the club was closely tied to the defeat of the Hébertists by Robespierre and the Committee of Public Safety. The committee resisted the onslaught of Cordelier abuse and bided its time. When a proposed Cordelier insurrection failed to develop, the Revolutionary Tribunal sentenced the leaders of the club to death in March 1794. Shortly after, the doors of the Cordeliers Club were closed.

RICHARD M. BRACE
*Oakland University*

**CORDIERITE,** kôrd'ē-ər-īt, is a mineral silicate of magnesium and aluminum. It is also called *dichroite* and *iolite*. Cordierite crystals are transparent to translucent, have a glassy luster, and are various shades of violet-blue. The color usually changes from blue to gray when the crystals are turned in different directions. This effect is known as *dichroism*—hence the alternative name, dichroite. Sometimes a third color change is also seen in the mineral. Cordierite is named in honor of the French geologist Louis Cordier (1777–1861).

Transparent crystals of cordierite are sometimes used as gems, under the name *saphir d'eau*. Such gemstones come from Ceylon. Other notable localities of cordierite are in Germany, Finland, Norway, and the island of Madagascar. In the United States, crystals are found chiefly in Connecticut and New Hampshire.

Composition, $Mg_2Al_3(AlSi_5O_{18})$; hardness, 7–7.5; specific gravity, 2.6–2.7; crystal system, orthorhombic.

**CORDILLERA,** kôr-dil-yâr'ə, a rugged, lofty, elongated mountain range or a series of such ranges, usually parallel to each other. More specifically, the term denotes the various ranges of the Andes of South America, and less frequently any similar mountain range in the "world ridge," which rims the Pacific Ocean. In Colombia and Venezuela the cordilleras are named, according to position, Cordillera Occidental, Central, and Oriental. Various local names are in use in Ecuador, Peru, Bolivia, Chile, and Argentina.

The structure of mountains of this type is complex, usually the result of folding and faulting accompanied by volcanic activity. In South America the ranges are surmounted by numerous volcanic peaks. One of these, Argentina's Mt. Aconcagua, which is 22,834 feet (6,960 meters) high, is the highest point in the Western Hemisphere. A number of these volcanoes have been active in historic times. Aside from the volcanic peaks, the crests include many narrow ridges, some of which reach into the zone of permanent snow. Between the ranges there are numerous inhabited valleys, basins, and low plateaus with a wide range of elevations. See also ANDES.

SAMUEL N. DICKEN
*University of Oregon*

**CORDITE,** kôr'dīt, is a smokeless propellant for guns and rockets. Based on the discovery of ballistite by Alfred Nobel, cordite was developed by Sir Frederick Abel and James Dewar. It became the official British cannon propellant in 1895. Originally cordite contained 30% cellulose nitrate, 65% nitroglycerin, and 5% petroleum jelly; however, part of the nitroglycerin has since been replaced by dibutyl phthalate, dinitrotoluene, or nitroguanidine to reduce the rate of gun barrel erosion and to eliminate muzzle flash.

Preparation of cordite begins with the mixing of nitroglycerin and cellulose nitrate under water. The water is filtered off, and the cake is dried in warm air. For *solventless cordite*, the cake is passed between hot steel rolls until it forms a coherent sheet, which is then rolled up and placed in the heated cylinder of a hydraulic press. The propellant is extruded into cords (hence the name) at a pressure of about 5,000 pounds per square inch (350 kg per sq cm). The diameter of the cords may be as large as 5 inches (12.7 cm), for use in artillery rockets. The cross section of the cord may take the form of a cross or a slotted tube to provide the surface area desired. For *solvent cordite* the nitroglycerin–cellulose nitrate cake is mixed with nitroguanidine and minor ingredients in the presence of acetone, after which it is extruded into cords and dried for several days to remove the acetone.

HARRISON H. HOLMES
*E. I. du Pont de Nemours & Co.*

**CÓRDOBA,** kôr'thō-bä, **Francisco Hernández de** (died 1518), Spanish explorer, who led the expedition that first uncovered the Maya civilization of Yucatán. Little is known of him until he appeared in Cuba with a group that came up from Panama. In 1517 he and his party set out on a slave-hunting expedition that brought them to the coast of the Yucatán peninsula. They were the first Europeans to contact the Maya Indians and to see evidences of their advanced civilization. They sailed around the peninsula and down to the Gulf of Campeche before turning homeward. In brushes with the Indians some of the party were killed and almost all the rest wounded. They touched Florida before returning to Havana. Within a fortnight after their return, Córdoba died of his wounds on his estate at Espíritu Santo, in 1518. Córdoba's expedition brought back the information that led to the exploration of the Mexican coast by Juan de Grijalva in 1518 and the ultimate conquest of Mexico by Cortés (1519–1521).

JOHN FRANCIS BANNON
*St. Louis University*

**CÓRDOBA,** kôr′thō-vä, **Francisco Fernández de** (1475?–1526), Spanish explorer of Nicaragua. After Gil González Dávila began to explore Nicaragua in the 1520's, the governor of Panama, Pedrarias, sent Fernández de Córdoba in 1524 to win the province in the governor's name. Córdoba founded the short-lived town of Bruselas, on the Gulf of Nicoya, and then Granada and later León, both inland. He was the first white man to explore Lake Nicaragua and to find its outlet to the Caribbean, the Río San Juan.

Emboldened by the example of rebellious captains in Honduras, Córdoba planned to desert his superior and set himself up as master of Nicaragua. Apprised of the scheme, Pedrarias captured him and had him tried and executed.

JOHN FRANCIS BANNON
*St. Louis University*

**CÓRDOBA,** kôr′thō-vä, a city in central Argentina, is one of the country's largest industrial centers. It is the capital of Córdoba province, situated on the Río Primero, about 400 miles (644 km) northwest of Buenos Aires. It lies on the slopes of the scenic Sierra de Córdoba (known also as the Córdoba Hills), facing east toward the Pampa—at the heart of an important tourist and agricultural region. Córdoba has become Argentina's leading center of automotive production, with a growing subsidiary complex and many other industries. Dams on the Río Primero and other rivers have contributed to the development of the area, providing hydroelectric power, water for irrigated agriculture, and man-made lakes that have become tourist resorts.

Córdoba, founded in 1573, has preserved much of its Spanish colonial architecture, which gives it beauty and distinction. Its cultural resources include museums, an astronomical observatory, theaters, and educational institutions. The present National University of Córdoba, Argentina's oldest university, grew from a school founded in 1613 and was chartered as a university in 1622. It was the seat of rationalistic thought that helped bring on the independence movement from Spain. In 1918 it was the scene of student revolts that led to a continent-wide movement toward autonomy in university administration. Population: 1,200,000 (1999 est.).

LAURENCE R. BIRNS
*New School for Social Research*

**CÓRDOBA,** kôr′thō-vä, a city in Mexico, is in Veracruz state, 55 miles (90 km) southwest of the city of Veracruz. Situated in a fertile valley 3,000 feet (900 meters) above sea level, it markets and processes the region's coffee, tobacco, sugarcane, and tropical fruits. Córdoba was founded in 1618 and preserves fine examples of colonial architecture. Spain recognized the independence of Mexico in the Treaty of Córdoba, signed in 1821. Population: 130,695 (1990 census).

**CÓRDOBA,** kôr′thō-vä, is a city in southern Spain and the capital of Córdoba province. The city lies at the foot of the Sierra de Morena, on the north bank of the Guadalquivir River. In addition to marketing much of the surrounding province's agricultural products, Córdoba has factories producing electrical fittings, bronze, copper, and aluminum products, cement, chemicals, preserved fruits, and paper.

In the past the craftsmanship of Córdoba's artisans in leather, and in gold and silver filigree was highly esteemed. In the fields of science and letters Córdoba prides itself on such names as Seneca, Maimonides, Averroës, Juan de Mena, Luis de Góngora, and the Duke de Rivas.

**History of the City.** Córdoba, a Phoenician and later a Carthaginian town, became part of the wealthy Roman colony of Baetica in the 2d century B.C. The Visigoths invaded it in the 6th century A.D. and destroyed much that Rome had built. When the city was captured by the Muslims in 711, a new chapter began. In 756 Abdar-Rahman I proclaimed Córdoba independent of the authority of the caliphate of Damascus. While by no means peaceful, the following two centuries saw a flowering of commerce and culture in Moorish Spain. Abdar-Rahman III (reigned 912–961) assumed the title of caliph; during his reign the city was one of the world's most prestigious intellectual centers, with outstanding scholars in the fields of medicine, mathematics, botany, and other sciences. The luxurious palace of Medina-Zahra was built nearby.

The Muslim wars of the 11th century saw the destruction of Medina-Zahra and a weakening of the government of Moorish Spain. At the same time the Christian kingdoms in the north were beginning to gather momentum in the Reconquest of Spain. Ferdinand III of Castile took Córdoba in 1236 and imposed a new culture and language on the city, without, however, eradicating the glory of its Moorish past.

CÓRDOBA, Argentina, contains among its many colonial buildings a cathedral begun in the 17th century.

EWING GALLOWAY

CÓRDOBA, Spain, on the Guadalquivir River, has a restored Roman bridge still in use.

**Places of Interest.** The city's architecture reflects a variety of styles. The best-known building is the cathedral (Mezquita). Built as a mosque in the 8th century, it was enlarged during the caliphate. Modifications by the Christians in the Middle Ages included the construction of a series of small chapels along the walls, and, in the 16th century, the erection of an altar and choir in the center of the nave. Practically intact are the Patio de los Naranjos and the extensive nave, an area of unique beauty. The interior contains over 800 graceful columns, and in the subdued light the forest of columns appears to extend as far as the eye can see.

Near the cathedral, on the site of a Visigothic palace, is the Alcázar, the residence of the caliphs, enlarged by Alfonso XI in the 14th century. Near this spot is a Roman bridge, rebuilt by the Moors, which is guarded across the river by the Calahorra fortress. Portions of Roman and Arabic walls still stand. There is an archaeological museum and, in the fine arts museum, as in many churches and other buildings, there are a number of valuable paintings. In the hills near the city are a 15th century monastery with its outlying hermitages, and the ruins of Medina-Zahra.

**The Province.** The Sierra Morena mountains mark the northern frontier of Córdoba province; to the south, rolling hills rise to the slopes of the Sierra Nevada. The Guadalquivir River enters from the east and meanders across the province in a west southwest direction toward Seville and the Atlantic Ocean. From the north flow the Cuzma, the Guadiato, and the Bembezar, tributaries to the main river, and from the south the Guadajoz and the Genil, the latter forming part of the boundary between Córdoba and Seville to the south. Southwest winds are funneled into the province by the Guadalquivir valley, bringing more heat and moisture than the Mediterranean climate would normally afford.

The soil of the province is generally very fertile and rainfall, carefully distributed by small irrigation systems, is sufficient to place Córdoba among Spain's leading producers of wheat, barley, oats, corn, cotton, and olives. Flax grows well here under irrigation and grapes are widely cultivated. The region around Montilla, in the south, produces a good dry wine. Mineral and metal deposits have not been extensively exploited, but in the north, where lead and zinc are mined, Peñarroya has a zinc smelter with energy supplied by local coal deposits. Some copper is mined in Córdoba province, and traces of uranium have been found there. Population: city, 306,248 (1996 est.); province, 761,401 (1996 est.).

M. M. LASLEY, *University of Florida*

**CÓRDOBA, National University of,** the oldest institution of higher education in Argentina and one of the earliest in Latin America. It was founded by Bishop Fernando Trejo y Sanabría of Tucumán as El Nuevo Colegio Máximo, a school for Spaniards and Indians. King Philip III of Spain granted it a university charter in 1622. The name was changed to the Royal University of San Carlos y Nuestra Señora de Montserrat in 1800, and the present name was adopted when the university was nationalized in 1856. There are faculties of law and social sciences; medicine; exact, physical, and natural sciences; economics; philosophy and humanities; architecture and town planning; dentistry; and an institute of mathematics. Each faculty has a specialized library. A general library houses extensive source material on colonial history. Enrollment in the mid-1960's reached 47,000.

**CORDON BLEU,** kôr-dōn′ blû, a noted cooking school in Paris, France. The name derives from the blue ribbons or baldrics worn by members of the Order of the Holy Ghost, famous for its excellent dinners. Le Cordon Bleu was founded in 1895 by Marthe Distell to teach cooking to young ladies of wealthy French families. It became a leading school for professional and amateur cooks, drawing students from many countries.

Classes contain six to eight students. Regular attendance is required to earn one of the three diplomas granted by the school: le Certificat Elémentaire, le Diplôme de l'Année, or le Grand Diplôme. Examinations are both oral and practical. Private lessons, demonstrations without student participation, and one-month summer courses are also offered for those not seeking a diploma.

ESTHER B. ARESTY
*Author of "The Delectable Past"*

**CORDOVA.** See CÓRDOBA.

**CORDOVA,** kôr-dō′və, a port city in southeastern Alaska, situated at the east end of Prince William Sound, near the delta of the Copper River. It is 140 miles (225 km) southeast of Anchorage. The city is an important fishing community with a deep-water harbor and small-boat facilities. It has canneries and cold storage plants for salmon, halibut, crabs, clams, and shrimp. Other industries are lumbering and trapping.

Founded in 1908, Cordova was a boom town for 30 years when it served as the sea terminus of the Copper River and Northwestern Railroad, which was built to transport copper from the Copper River mines 120 miles (193 km) inland. The mine and railroad ceased operations in 1938. The city was severely damaged by the earthquake of March 1964. Cordova was incorporated in 1909 and is governed by a council and manager. Population: 2,454.

**CORDOVAN,** kôr′də-vən, is the name originally given to a soft fine goatskin leather first manufactured in large quantities in the Spanish city of Córdoba. Today the name is also used for a grain leather made from the best and strongest portions of a horsehide. The leather is used mostly for making heavy shoes and boots.

**CORDUROY,** kor′də-roi, is a cotton fabric made with one set of warp threads (the threads running lengthwise in the fabric) and two sets of filling threads (threads running crosswise). One set of filling threads interlaces with the warp to form a ground fabric; the other set "floats" over certain warp threads and interlaces with them only at certain intervals. These "floats" are later cut and brushed to form a pile. The name "corduroy" is derived from the French words *cord du roi* (meaning "king's cord"), although the fabric itself was developed in England.

The cords, or rows of cut pile tufts, are called *wales.* The depression between adjacent wales is called a *welt.* If there are 2 to 6 wales per inch, the fabric is known as a *wide wale corduroy.* This fabric is made into car coats and other outerwear garments. Corduroy with 6 to 10 wales per inch is called a *medium wale corduroy* and is made into slacks, shirts, and handbags. *Pinwale corduroy* has 10 to 18 wales per inch and is used for infants' wear and women's skirts.

ERNEST B. BERRY, *School of Textiles*
*North Carolina State University*

**CORE.** See CONGRESS OF RACIAL EQUALITY.

**CORELLI,** kō-rel′lē, **Arcangelo** (1653–1713), Italian composer and violinist, who created the first great works of the chamber music repertoire. He excelled in the baroque *sonata,* an early type of chamber music, and his forms and methods of composition were imitated in Europe through the middle of the 18th century. Corelli was also an outstanding composer of the baroque *concerto grosso,* a forerunner of the modern concerto, in which small groups of instruments were set off against a full orchestra. All his works are marked by concise, noble expression and refined, elevated style. In addition, Corelli was a violin virtuoso, whose advanced methods of bowing and other revolutionary techniques profoundly influenced the development of the art of violin playing.

Corelli was born at Fusignano, Italy, on Feb. 17, 1653. At the age of 13, he went to Bologna, where he studied violin, and in 1670 he entered the famed violin school there. By 1675, he was in Rome, which was his home for most of the remainder of his life.

Corelli's 12 church sonatas (Opus 1, 1681) made him famous. He obtained the patronage of powerful and cultured people, including Cardinal Panfili and Queen Christina of Sweden. Another patron Cardinal Pietro Ottoboni invited him to live in his palace, where Corelli gave weekly concerts that were among the outstanding musical events of the period.

Corelli continued to compose sonatas, all of which were well received, especially his solo violin sonatas (Opus 5, 1700). Toward the end of his life, Corelli began to write his *concerti grossi,* which with their fusion of the emerging orchestral concerto style and the older virtuoso solo and chamber style provided a fitting climax to his distinguished career. He died in Rome on Jan. 8, 1713.

FRANKLIN B. ZIMMERMAN
*Author of "Henry Purcell: His Life and Times"*

**CORELLI,** kō-rel′ē, **Marie** (1855–1924), pen name of Mary Mackay, English novelist. She was born in London, the daughter of Charles Mackay, the poet. She gave up a promising career as a pianist after a "psychic experience" convinced her in 1885 that she could write. Her novels—high in moral fervor and long on melodrama—such as *Barabbas: A Dream of the World's Tragedy* (1893) and *Sorrows of Satan* (1895), were enormously popular and made her a fortune, but they are little read today. In 1901, Miss Corelli settled in Stratford-on-Avon, where she fought encroaching modernization. She died in Stratford on April 21, 1924.

**COREOPSIS,** kôr-ē-op′sis, is a large genus of annual and perennial plants, many of which are cultivated for their solitary, yellow flower heads that blossom in the summer and fall. Each flower head consists of several petallike rays radiating from a central disk.

The best annual species for garden cultivation is *Coreopsis tinctoria,* known as the golden coreopsis. It grows up to 3 feet (1 meter) tall and its flower heads, which consist of yellow rays and a reddish-brown center, may be 2 inches (5 cm) across. A popular perennial species, *C. auriculata nana,* has all-yellow flower heads. It grows only about 8 inches (20 cm) tall and is often used as ground cover. Another popular perennial is *C. grandiflora,* which grows 1 to 2 feet (30 to 60 cm) tall. All species are easily grown from seed.

DONALD WYMAN
*The Arnold Arboretum, Harvard University*

**CORFAM,** kôr′fam, is a man-made material used mainly in shoes, but also used for luggage, briefcases, handbags, wallets, and belts. The material is tough, flexible, and water-repellent; it holds its shape well and requires little care.

Corfam is described as a "poromeric" material because it is *porous* and is made from *polymers.* The structure of the material is comparable to that of leather. In cross section, Corfam is found to be fibrous on its underside with an increasing density in the material towards the upper surface, which is smooth and tough.

The production of Corfam is very complex. Polyester fibers are arranged to form a web, which is then impregnated with a polymeric sub-

CORFU, the capital city of the island department of Corfu, is the island's major port.

stance that acts as a binder. A layer of urethane polymer is then deposited on the web. The material is then colored, finished, and embossed to achieve the desired appearance.

EDWIN C. WATSON
*E. I. du Pont de Nemours & Company, Inc.*

**CORFU,** kôr-foō′, is the second-largest of Greece's Ionian Islands. It is located off the western coast of Greece and has an area of 227 square miles (588 sq km). The northeastern part of Corfu (Greek *Kérkira*) is separated from the Albanian coast by the narrow Corfu Channel. Along with the neighboring islands of Paxos, Antipaxos, and other small islands, it forms the department of Corfu. Corfu is also the name of the island's chief city, which serves as the capital of the department and as the seat of the Greek Orthodox metropolitan of Corfu and Paxos. Among Corfiote products are olives, wine, and honey. Tourism has also become important to the island's economy.

**History.** The island of Corfu (ancient Corcyra) was colonized by Greeks from the city of Eretria early in the 8th century B.C. Around 733 B.C. it was taken by Corinth. In 435 B.C. the islanders defeated a Corinthian fleet in a battle near Actium. Two years later, with Athenian help, they repulsed another Corinthian naval attack. Falling under Roman control in 229 B.C., Corfu later became part of the Byzantine Empire. Christianity was introduced around 40 A.D. by St. Jason and St. Sosipater. During the 5th century Gaiseric and the Vandals sacked the island, and in the 6th century it was sacked again, by Totila and the Ostrogoths. The Norman Duke of Apulia, Robert Guiscard, took Corfu from the Byzantines twice for short periods in the 11th century. His nephew, Roger II of Sicily, sent a fleet which occupied the island in 1147, only to lose it back to the Byzantines in 1149. In 1185 the Normans held Corfu again for a short time. A Genoese pirate, Vetrano, seized it in 1199. Following the capture of Constantinople in 1204, during the Fourth Crusade, Corfu became Venetian, but around 1214 it was taken by the Greek despotate of Epirus. In 1259 Corfu, which had been conquered by Manfred of Sicily, was given to him as part of a dowry when he married a daughter of Michael II of Epirus. In 1267, Corfu became a possession of Manfred's successors, the Angevins of Naples and Sicily. Venice regained control of the island in 1386 and held it for 411 years.

*Venetian Rule.* The long Venetian domination of Corfu did not extinguish the basically Greek characteristics of the majority of the islanders; and the Greek Orthodox faith was allowed to function, although under restrictions. In 1456 the body of St. Spyridon was brought to Corfu from Constantinople, which had fallen to the Ottoman Turks. He became the island's patron saint.

Since the Venetians viewed Corfu as a vital link in their commercial empire, they fortified it strongly. The Ottoman Turks first attacked it in 1431. Subsequently, the most important Turkish attacks occurred in 1537, when the island was ravaged for 13 days, and in 1716, when a 48-day Turkish siege was repulsed. At the Battle of Lepanto in 1571, 1,500 Corfiotes fought with Venice and her allies against the Ottoman Empire.

*Modern Period.* The last years of Venetian domination were marked by such misgovernment that the islanders welcomed the French, who took Corfu in 1797. However, a joint Russian-Ottoman attack drove the French out in 1799; and in 1800 Corfu became part of the Septinsular Republic. France regained Corfu in 1807 and retained it until 1814. In 1815 it was included in the United States of the Ionian Islands, a British protectorate, and in 1864 Britain ceded Corfu and all the Ionian Islands to Greece. On July 20, 1917, representatives from Serbia, Croatia, Montenegro, and Slovenia met on Corfu and signed the Pact of Corfu, which proclaimed the establishment of a united South Slav (Yugoslav) state. Italy bombarded and occupied the island from Aug. 31 to Sept. 27, 1923. In April 1941 it was captured by the Germans and was not liberated until 1944.

Corfu has long been known as one of the most beautiful islands of Greece. The Empress Elizabeth of Austria, wife of Francis Joseph I, built the villa Achilleion there. After her death, the villa was purchased by the German emperor William II. He participated personally in archaeological excavations on the island. Greece's King George I established a royal residence at the Villa Mon Repos. There his grandson, Prince Philip of Greece, was born in 1921. He became the Duke of Edinburgh and husband of Britain's Queen Elizabeth II. The villa was later used as the summer residence of Greece's King Constantine II. Population: of the department, 105,043 (1991 census); of the island, 38,875 (1991 preliminary census).

GEORGE J. MARCOPOULOS
*Tufts University*

**CORI,** kôr′ē, **Carl Ferdinand** (1896–1984) and **Gerty Theresa Radnitz** (1896–1957), American biochemists, who as husband and wife became one of the 20th century's outstanding research teams. They discovered the chemical reactions by which glycogen (the form in which sugar is stored in the animal body) is changed into a form of glucose that can be used by cells for the production of energy. When they received the 1947 Nobel Prize for physiology (shared with the Argentine physiologist Bernardo A. Houssay), the Coris were jointly cited "for their discovery of the course of the catalytic conversion of glycogen."

**Contributions to Science.** During the 1920's the Coris began their studies of the metabolism of carbohydrates in animal cells and tissues. They isolated the compound glucose-1-phosphate as a metabolic intermediate. The discovery of this compound, subsequently known as "Cori ester," was an important step in their investigations. The Coris went on to describe the events that occur as glycogen is converted through glucose-1-phosphate as an intermediate to glucose (blood sugar) in the liver. The glucose is then transported by the blood to other tissues and organs where it is used as an energy source. They also showed that lactic acid, one of the substances formed from glucose in muscle cells, was carried by the blood back to the liver. In the liver, the lactic acid is either oxidized to form carbon dioxide and water or it is converted back to glycogen, the storage form of sugar. These events are now known as the "Cori cycle"; they are basic to an understanding of the life processes of higher animals.

In tracing the metabolic steps of sugar metabolism, the Coris found that each step is catalyzed by a specific protein known as an enzyme. The Coris and their associates purified and crystallized five of the enzymes involved in sugar metabolism, making it possible to study their specific catalytic functions. The enzyme studied in greatest detail by the Coris themselves was phosphorylase, which changes glycogen into glucose-1-phosphate. The Coris also demonstrated that some hormones could affect the various steps in the metabolism of sugar.

**Life.** Carl Cori was born in Prague, Bohemia, on Dec. 5, 1896, and Gerty Theresa Radnitz was born in Prague on Aug. 15, 1896. Both studied medicine at the German University of Prague, and as fellow students they published their first research paper together. They received their M.D. degrees in 1920 and were married that year. They then moved to Vienna, where Carl worked in the pharmacology department of the University of Graz and Gerty in the Children's Hospital of Vienna. They went to the United States in 1922 and became U. S. citizens in 1928.

From 1922 to 1931 both Carl and Gerty Cori worked at the State Institute for the Study of Malignant Diseases in Buffalo, N. Y. In 1931 they went to Washington University School of Medicine in St. Louis, Mo., where they both became professors of biological chemistry, and Carl became the head of the department.

The Coris wrote more than 200 scientific papers. They were elected to the National Academy of Sciences and received many awards in addition to the Nobel Prize. Gerty Cori died in St. Louis, Mo., on Oct. 26, 1957. Carl Cori died in Cambridge, Mass., on Oct. 19, 1984.

DAVID H. BROWN
*Washington University School of Medicine*

**CORIANDER,** kôr′ē-an-dər, a herbaceous annual of the parsley family, long cultivated for its tiny, aromatic, seedlike fruits that are used for seasoning various foods, including curry, pickles, and pastries. The fruits are also used as a flavoring in vermouth and certain medicines. The extract of the fruit is deemed a better flavoring than either the oil of coriander or the dried fruits.

The coriander (*Coriandrum sativum*), is native to the Mediterranean and Caucasus regions and is extensively cultivated in India, Asia Minor, Morocco, and parts of Europe. It is also grown in the United States, where the plant has escaped cultivation and now grows wild.

The smooth slender stems of the coriander range in height from 1 to 3 feet (30–90 cm). The leaves, which may be entire, compound, or finely divided, have an unpleasant odor when crushed, but the ripe fruits have a delicate fragrance.

LAWRENCE ERBE
*University of Southwestern Louisiana*

**CORINNA,** kō-rin′ə, was a lyric poet of ancient Greece. On the basis of anecdotes associating her with Pindar, she has traditionally been dated about 500 B.C. New papyri discovered in the 20th century suggest, but do not prove, that she lived as late as the 2d century B.C.

Living at Tanagra, near Thebes, in Boeotia, Corinna was one of the few Greek poets to use the Boeotian dialect. Her poems about Boeotian legends are in a style so simple that they could be of any period. Scholars believe that she composed some 50 books of epigrams and odes; even the few fragments that remain are well worth attention. In Greek tradition she appears as the rival or teacher of Pindar, over whom she is said to have won the laurel five times in public competition. Her victory was the result, according to one writer, of her physical charms; according to another, of the effect of her Boeotian dialect on the judges.

**CORINNE,** kô-rēn′, a novel by Mme. de Staël published in 1807. It is her foremost piece of fiction and had a strong influence on the romantic novel. *Corinne, ou L'Italie* was the result of the author's trip to Italy; descriptions of the Italian countryside and society are mixed into the narrative and reflect the moods of the characters.

Corinne, a beautiful Anglo-Italian poet who represents the best qualities of Italy, is Mme. de Staël herself. Believing that romantic love is its own justification, she leaves the confining society of England for a freer artistic life in Rome. When her lover, Lord Oswald Nevil, under family pressure marries her English half sister Lucille, Corinne dies of a broken heart.

**CORINTH,** kō-rint′, **Louis** (1858–1925), German painter, whose spontaneous style and brilliant use of impasto color made him a forerunner of expressionism. He was born in Tapiau, Prussia, on July 21, 1858. From 1890 to 1900 he exhibited in Munich with the Secessionists (q.v.). In 1900 he settled in Berlin.

Corinth's style underwent a profound change about 1911, when he suffered a severe stroke; his work showed more emotional power and artistic strength. Among his major paintings are *Ecce Homo* (1925; Basel Museum), a number of late self-portraits, and many brilliant views of the Walchensee in Bavaria. Corinth died in Zandvoort, Holland, on July 17, 1925.

THE RUINS OF CORINTH are dominated by the seven great columns of the Temple of Apollo that still stand.

FRITZ HENLE, FROM PHOTO RESEARCHERS

**CORINTH,** kor'inth, is a city in Greece, at the southwestern end of the Isthmus of Corinth. Corinth (Greek *Kórinthos*) is the capital of the *nomos* (department) of Corinthia (Korinthia). The chief crops of the region are grapes, tobacco, and olives. The modern city was founded on the coast in 1858, when an earthquake razed the old town of Corinth, situated 4 miles (6 km) to the southwest at the base of Acrocorinth, the citadel of the ancient city. A new village has since grown up at the old site.

**Characteristics of Ancient Corinth.** Corinth was one of the most powerful and prosperous cities of ancient Greece. Its early wealth was based on agriculture, but largely because of the city's location on the Isthmus of Corinth it soon became a major trading state. Corinth had ports both on the Gulf of Corinth and the Saronic Gulf, named Lechaeum and Cenchreae respectively. Corinth also controlled the paved roadway (*diolkos*) that was built across the isthmus in the 6th century B.C. and over which both cargo and ships could be hauled. This route was much preferred to the hazardous sea voyage around the southern tip of the Peloponnesus; Corinth thus became a main junction for trade between the eastern and western Mediterranean. The city's own commercial activities were extensive, especially in the West, where Corinth founded many colonies, including Syracuse and Corcyra (Corfu). The Isthmian sanctuary of Poseidon was governed by Corinth, and the Panhellenic festival celebrated there every two years added to the city's prestige. The reputation of Corinth as a city of pleasure was unrivaled in Greece. There was an ancient saying: "It is not given to every man to go to Corinth." The dominant position of Acrocorinth made Corinth one of the most important military properties in Greece. Philip V of Macedonia (reigned 221–179 B.C.) spoke of Corinth, along with Chalcis and Demetrias, as the "fetters of Greece."

Corinth is named in early myths as the realm of Sisyphus and the place where Bellerophon, aided by the goddess Athena, bridled the winged horse Pegasus. Corinth was also the setting for one of the great tragedies of Euripides, *Medea*.

**History.** Corinth was inhabited from the early Neolithic period, that is, from about 5,500 B.C., but little is known of the prehistoric site. The city was ruled by the Bacchiad kings during the 8th and 7th centuries B.C. During the time of the tyrants Cypselus and his son Periander (about 620–550 B.C.), Corinth began to lose its preeminence in trade to Athens; but with the advent of an oligarchic government in the middle of the 6th century B.C., the city embarked on a major building program, while continuing to manufacture and export terra-cottas, bronzes, and many other products. The Hellenic League, formed to repel Persian invaders, held its meetings (481–479 B.C.) at the Isthmian sanctuary, and from that time the sanctuary was the most important topographical symbol of Hellenic unity. It was there also that Philip II of Macedonia and his son Alexander revived the Hellenic League late in the 4th century B.C.

Corinth was an ally of Sparta during the Peloponnesian War 431–404 B.C.), but was Sparta's enemy during the Corinthian War (394–386 B.C.). Corinth was ruled by a succession of Macedonian commanders from 338 B.C. until the citadel was captured in a daring night raid by Aratus of Sicyon in 243 B.C.; Corinth then became a member of the Achaean League. The city changed hands several times in the next half century but became Achaean again in 196 B.C. After the Roman army of Lucius Mummius defeated the Achaean forces in 146 B.C., Corinth was largely destroyed.

Julius Caesar ordered the refounding of Corinth in 44 B.C., and the new city soon became as important as the Greek city had been. It was the capital of Achaea in 51 A.D. when the Apostle Paul was brought before the Roman governor, L. Junius Gallio, by the Jews of Corinth. The city was burned by Herulian invaders in 267, greatly damaged by an earthquake in 375, and, in 395, sacked by Alaric and his Goths. A series of devastating earthquakes and a plague nearly depopulated the city by the mid-6th century. Corinth was ruled in the succeeding centuries by Avars, Byzantines, Franks, Venetians, Knights of St. John, and Turks. Population: 28,903 (1991 census).

JAMES R. WISEMAN
*University of Texas*

**Further Reading:** Davidson, Gladys R., *The Minor Objects, Vol. XII* (Am. School of Classical Studies, Athens 1987); Salmon, J. B., *Wealthy Corinth: A History of the City to 338 B.C.* (Oxford 1984).

**CORINTH,** kôr'inth, a manufacturing city in northeastern Mississippi, near the Tennessee border. It is the seat of Alcorn county. The city is a shipping point in a cotton and livestock area. Its products include hydraulic motors, sawmill machinery, lumber, plastics, bricks, clothing, and electric organs. On Oct. 3–4, 1862, Union forces defeated Confederates there in an engagement of the Civil War. Government is by mayor and council. Population: 14,054.

**CORINTH, Gulf of,** kôr'inth, an inlet of the Mediterranean Sea in Greece. It was once known as the *Gulf of Lepanto.* About 80 miles (130 km) long, it extends from the Gulf of Patras to the Isthmus of Corinth and separates the Peloponnesus from central Greece.

**CORINTH, Isthmus of,** kôr'inth, a strip of land in Greece that connects the Peloponnesus with central Greece. Its width ranges from 3.5 to 8 miles (5.6 to 13 km).

In ancient times, ships were dragged across the isthmus. In 67 A. D. the Roman emperor Nero began a canal through it. A modern canal was built in 1881–1893, connecting the Gulf of Corinth with the Saronic Gulf, and shortening the voyage from the Adriatic Sea to Piraeus by some 200 miles (320 km). The site of the ancient Isthmian games is not far south of the canal.

**CORINTHIAN ORDER,** in classical architecture, one of three Greek styles (with Doric and Ionic) for a column and its segments. See CAPITAL; COLUMN.

**CORINTHIANS, Epistles of Paul to the,** kə-rin'-thē-ənz, the 7th and 8th books of the New Testament. They are letters written by St. Paul from Ephesus, and between them they give a vivid picture of the strengths and weaknesses of the early church and of Paul's sense of his mission and its accomplishments.

The significance of Corinth in the ancient world can scarcely be overestimated. It was one of the greatest cities of its time, with a population of 200,000 citizens and 500,000 slaves. The city lay on an isthmus between northern and southern Greece and served as a bridge for trade between the two sections of the country. Further, since Cape Maléa, at the southeastern tip of Greece, was so dangerous to circumnavigate, ships were dragged on rollers across the isthmus where the Corinth canal now is. A great part of east-west Mediterranean trade therefore passed through Corinth, and it had a cosmopolitan and varied citizenry.

Corinth was an extremely wealthy and wicked city. It was the center of a number of pagan cults, the most notable being that of Aphrodite, whose temple crested the hill behind the city. The temple had a thousand priestesses, who were sacred prostitutes. They came down to the city streets every evening to ply their trade.

**I Corinthians.** Paul's work in Corinth is described in Acts 18:1–18. After he had left Corinth and was working in Ephesus, news reached him that all was not well in Corinth. He therefore wrote the First Epistle to the Corinthians to deal with the problems there. Within the letter are moving accounts of the Last Supper, of the Resurrection and its effects, and of the proper relationship between men in everyday life.

The problems facing the church in Corinth were many. There were divisions within the church (I Corinthians 1:10–12), with members more concerned with arguing the claims of rival leaders than remembering Christ. There was intellectual pride (I Corinthians 1:25 to 2:16), as the Corinthians forgot the claims of Christ in their pride at their own cleverness. Immorality was blatant, so much so that a man was living with his own stepmother (I Corinthians 5:1). The Greek passion for litigation was everywhere in evidence. Members of the Christian church disputed with one another in the law courts instead of settling their differences in the fellowship of the church and the spirit of Christ (I Corinthians 6:1–8). Antinomianism was rife. Some Corinthians believed that because they lived under grace and not under law they had license to do as they liked (I Corinthians 6:12–20). Paul reminds them that the body is the temple of the Holy Spirit.

The Corinthians themselves raised questions about problems that troubled them; for example, the status of marriage (I Corinthians 7:1–39). Paul writes that he would prefer to see them remain unmarried so that they could concentrate on preparing for the coming of Christ. However, he allows marriage for those who do not have the self-discipline to live in single purity.

There was a question of Christian presence at the ritual of meat offerings to idols (I Corinthians 8 to 10). In the ancient world, if a man sacrificed to the gods in a temple, he received back some of the sacrificial meat and with it made a feast for his friends. The result was that most social occasions were held in pagan temples. The Corinthians wanted to know whether Christians could attend such parties. For Paul, such occasions were not for Christians.

There were questions about religious practices (I Corinthians 11–14). Originally, the Lord's Supper had been a common meal to which everyone contributed. It had since become a meal at which the rich refused to share with the poor, and true fellowship was destroyed. There was also disorder during the church services, with too many people seeking to speak at one time. The confusion was compounded because the Corinthians set a high value on speaking with tongues. Paul reminded them that they were all members of the body of Christ. As such, they should share equally in the Lord's Supper in the spirit of love. He also adjured them to keep order in their meetings and to speak only when moved to prophecy concerning the goodness of God and the betterment of the church.

The church's teaching on the resurrection of the dead was questioned by some Corinthians. To Paul, this was an essential part of Christian belief. He did not preach the immortality of the soul alone, but the resurrection of the whole man, body and soul. However, the risen body would not be in its present physical state but rather in a spiritual form resembling the transfigured body of the risen Christ. Thus he affirmed the preservation of the total man: that after death the personality would continue to exist, so that you will still be you and I will still be I (I Corinthians 15).

Finally, in I Corinthians 16, Paul pleads for a cause that is very dear to him: the collection of funds from his churches for the poor in Jerusalem. Such help and such a collection, he said, was a sign of the true unity of the church.

**II Corinthians.** The second letter, as we have it now, is probably actually two letters, arranged in the reverse order of that in which they were written. It is likely that Paul's first letter was not enough to ease the difficulties of the church in Corinth, and that he paid a visit to the city. However, it was a visit of such insult and insolence that it nearly broke his heart. On his return he wrote the sorrowful letter now contained in II Corinthians 10 to 13.

Paul's apostleship had been attacked; his message had been under fire; his appearance and his speech had been insulted; his very motives had been questioned. Against his will he set out to justify himself and his claims, and to insist that God had given him grace in which even his weakness had become strong.

This sad letter apparently had its effect. II Corinthians 1 to 9 was written after peace had been restored. Once again, in chapters 8 and 9, he presses the claims of the collection for Jerusalem. And in II Corinthians 2:5–11 we find Paul in the beauty of Christian forgiveness pleading for sympathy and understanding for the man who had been the cause of all his troubles.

I and II Corinthians are letters of problems, of troubles, of heartbreak, and of reconciliation. No other letters show so well what Paul was like as a man and as a pastor. No other letters show us so well what the early church was like. It has been said that they take the roof off and enable us to see into the life and the meetings of an early Christian congregation. See also PAUL, SAINT.

WILLIAM BARCLAY
*The University of Glasgow*

**CORINTO,** kō-rēn'tō, the chief port of Nicaragua, is on the Pacific Ocean, about 70 miles (110 km) northwest of Managua. It is situated in Chinandega department, on the southeast end of Aserradores Island, from which two bridges carry road and rail traffic to Managua and other Nicaraguan population centers. The port handles more than half of the country's trade tonnage, including exports of cotton, coffee, sugar, hides, frozen shrimp, and timber. There are several beach resorts nearby. Corinto was founded in 1840. Population: 24,250 (1985 est.).

**CORIOLANUS,** kôr-ē-ə-lā'nəs, **Gaius Marcius,** legendary Roman hero of the 5th century B.C. It is uncertain whether Coriolanus received his name because he captured the Volscian city of Corioli, as the tradition records, or because he was the eponymous founder or, perhaps, even a god of the city.

The story runs that he was a brave, proud Roman patrician opposed both to the popular tribunes of the people and to the distribution of grain to the starving masses. His hostility grew when he failed to be elected consul. When attacked and subsequently convicted by the tribunes for his opposition to their cause and also accused of aiming at tyranny, he fled Rome, taking refuge in the Volscian town of Antium, from which he led a Volscian army against Rome. The city was at the point of falling in 491 B.C., when the arrogant noble was turned back by the tears and prayers of his mother, Veturnia, and his wife, Volumnia. Coriolanus was then put to death by the Volsci.

RICHARD E. MITCHELL
*University of Illinois*

**CORIOLANUS,** kôr-ē-ə-lā'nəs, is the last of William Shakespeare's tragedies. It was probably written about 1608 but was not published until the folio of 1623, which gives the only authentic text. This text, however, is somewhat unsatisfactory, as it is marred by mislineation and misprints. The full stage directions suggest the author's hand. As with *Antony and Cleopatra,* which immediately preceded it, the source for *Coriolanus* is Thomas North's translation of Plutarch. Although both plays are on Roman subjects, they are strikingly different in material and treatment. Gone are the exotic sensuousness, the passionate love story, the highly imaginative and lyrical poetry of *Antony and Cleopatra;* in their place are found the sternness and turmoil of war and political conflict.

The center of interest is the soldier Caius Marcius Coriolanus—aggressive, unreflective, tactless, destroyed by convictions essentially antisocial, a rock of strength in himself but a rock which almost wrecks the ship of state. Shakespeare's adaptation emphasizes heredity and environment as explanations of Coriolanus' character, depicting him attractively in his relations with his family and his friend Menenius and showing his vigor and courage as a warrior for Rome. But his hotheadedness, his inflexible self-sufficiency, and his aristocratic distrust of the common people make him unsympathetic even before he turns to treason. So outspoken and uncompromising a nature is best reflected in a poetry which is vigorous and blunt rather than lilting or lifting.

Though Shakespeare's interest in the play was not primarily political, the play is a political one, since the downfall of Coriolanus is the result of his expression of political views. At the beginning he opposes the granting of tribunes to the plebeians, who are mutinous from hunger, both because their cowardice in war has not earned representation and because he fears their rising power. Welcoming the news that the Volscians are armed, he fights valiantly against them and their leader, Tullus Aufidius, at Corioli (for which he is given the title Coriolanus) and, returning to Rome for the third time crowned with the oaken garland, is named consul by the Senate. But the voices of the plebeians are also necessary for confirmation and are to be obtained by the personal appeal of the candidate in a gown of humility, a characteristic which Coriolanus distinctly lacks. His openness of character cannot mask his contempt, and his vituperative scorn, successfully evoked by the tribunes, leads from abuse to banishment as a traitor. He joins Aufidius in a new attack on Rome, from which he is diverted only by the pleas of his family. Aufidius, disappointed in the attainment of his object, now accuses him of betraying the Volscians, and a new outburst by Coriolanus before the people whose loved ones he had earlier slain culminates in his death.

Shakespeare gives Coriolanus as much human warmth as he can, shows clearly his virtues and defects, and accounts for his downfall wholly in terms of his own character. Coriolanus' mother, Volumnia, a Roman matron of heroic stature and stoic temperament; his quiet but gentle and loving wife, Virgilia; and the humorous, kindly Menenius are admirably drawn. Yet it must be perfectly clear that the play stands or falls on the character of Coriolanus, and though Shakespeare was interested in the mainsprings of human character rather than in political argument, Coriolanus is essentially unattractive. It is perhaps possible to admire his strength, his openness, even the firmness of his political idealism, but it is difficult, especially in the light of modern democratic institutions, to like him, and impossible to pity or love him.

ROBERT HAMILTON BALL
*Queens College of the City of New York*

**Further Reading:** Cahn, Victor L., *The Heroes of Shakespeare's Tragedies* (P. Lang 1988); Granville-Barker, Harley, *Prefaces to Shakespeare: Coriolanus* (David & Charles 1982); Holt, Leigh, and Hogg, James, *From Man to Dragon: A Study of Shakespeare's Coriolanus* (Longwood 1976); Mehl, Dieter, *Shakespeare's Tragedies: An Introduction* (Cambridge 1987); Poole, Adrian, *Coriolanus* (G. K. Hall 1988).

**CORIOLIS,** kô-ryô-lēs', **Gaspard Gustave de** (1792–1843), French mathematical physicist, who gave the first satisfactory explanation of the forces acting on a body moving in a rotating frame of reference. Coriolis wrote a number of papers on mechanics, including a brilliant analysis of the mechanics of billiards, and gave the first modern definitions of work and kinetic energy.

His most important work, *Sur les équations du mouvement relatif des systèmes de corps,* appeared in 1835. Coriolis saw that if an object is thrown vertically into the air, its distance from the center of the rotating earth is increased. To

**CORIOLIS FORCE**

ACTUAL                          APPARENT

An object moves from a rotating disk's center toward a fixed point beyond the disk. An observer at the center of the disk and unaware of its rotation supposes that a force being exerted on the object is curving its path.

fall back to its origin, it must travel through a greater arc than its point of origin travels through in the same time. Thus, the object must somehow be accelerated as it rises through this arc. Coriolis suggested that inertial forces, now named "Coriolis forces," must act on the object to accomplish this acceleration. Coriolis forces are of importance in meteorology and oceanography.

Coriolis was born in Paris on May 21, 1792. He studied at the École Polytechnique and the École des Ponts et Chaussées and taught at both schools. He died in Paris on Sept. 19, 1843.

L. PEARCE WILLIAMS, *Cornell University*

**CORIOLIS FORCE,** kôr-ē-ō′lis, an imaginary force that appears to be exerted at right angles to the path of an object moving with respect to a rotating frame of reference. For example, if a chalk is drawn in a straight path across a phonograph record as the record spins, a curved line is left on the record. If an observer could be stationed at the record's surface, it would appear to him as though a force were pushing the chalk sidewise. The Coriolis force is named for Gaspard Gustave de Coriolis, a 19th century French mathematician who first described the effect.

The same effect is observed when an object moves in relation to a 3-dimensional rotating frame of reference, such as the earth. The curved path that the object traces represents its tendency to follow its original direction in space—Newton's first law—at the same time that it is moving horizontally relative to the earth's surface, to which it is attracted by gravity. Winds and ocean currents are subjected to the Coriolis force; they tend to be deflected to the right of their path of motion in the Northern Hemisphere and to the left in the Southern.

Similarly, the path of a projectile exhibits the effect of the Coriolis force, as does the path of a satellite in orbit about the earth. The Coriolis force must be taken into account when plotting the course of a long-range projectile or an intercontinental missile.

JAMES E. MILLER, *New York University*

**CORK, Earls of.** See BOYLE (family).

**CORK,** the seat of county Cork, Ireland, is a manufacturing and commercial center and the main seaport on the south coast. It is 135 miles (216 km) southwest of Dublin. Once famous for cut glass and silverware, Cork is now noted for manufacture of tires, textiles, bacon, woolens, steel, and ships. It has a power station and an oil refinery in its fine harbor, which is a port of call for transatlantic shipping.

Most of the best architecture of Cork is of the 19th century, two fine examples being the courthouse and St. Patrick's Church. St. Anne's Church, Shandon, was built in the early 18th century and is famous for its Shandon Bells, which, like Blarney Castle (a few miles from the city), have made the name of Cork famous. The University College of Cork, a constituent of the National University of Ireland, dates from 1845. Cork has an opera house of modern design as well as schools of music and art. The 18th century painter James Barry and the 19th century sculptor John Hogan are the best known of a long line of artists linked with Cork.

Cork owes its origin to a small settlement that grew up around a monastery founded by St. Finbar early in the 7th century. Its name derives

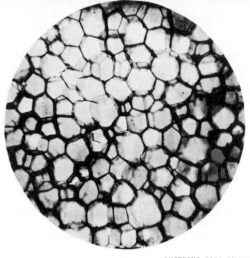

ARMSTRONG CORK COMPANY

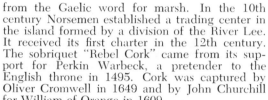

CORK is removed from the tree (right) in large sections. The enlargement (above) shows the structure of the air-filled cells that account for the lightness of cork.

EWING GALLOWAY

from the Gaelic word for marsh. In the 10th century Norsemen established a trading center in the island formed by a division of the River Lee. It received its first charter in the 12th century. The sobriquet "Rebel Cork" came from its support for Perkin Warbeck, a pretender to the English throne in 1495. Cork was captured by Oliver Cromwell in 1649 and by John Churchill for William of Orange in 1609.

Cork is Ireland's largest county and includes the beautiful, deeply indented southern coast. Bantry Bay at the county's western fringe is a magnificent natural harbor; Whiddy Island in the bay was under development in the late 1960s as the European terminal for the largest tankers afloat. East Cork is one of the most fertile areas in the country, producing large quantities of barley, oats, milk, and butter. Cork is a city and county borough. Population: city, 180,000 (1996 census); county, 283,116 (1991 census).

THOMAS FITZGERALD
*Department of Education, Dublin*

**CORK** is the outer bark of an oak tree (*Quercus suber*) that grows in commercial stands only around the Mediterranean Sea, particularly in Spain, Portugal, and North Africa. Although the area involved is only about the size of New Jersey, it provides almost the entire world supply of cork, and all attempts to establish cork forests elsewhere have been unsuccessful.

Unlike most oak trees, the cork oak is an evergreen. Its leaves resemble holly leaves but lack sharp points and are soft and velvety to the touch. Most fully grown cork trees range from 30 to 40 feet (9 to 12 meters) in height and have trunks 3 to 4 feet (0.9 to 1.2 meters) in diameter, but there are many old trees 50 feet (15 meters) or more in height and 5 feet (1.5 meters) in diameter at the base. On the average, a cork tree lives about 150 years, although there are some 200 years old.

Because bark helps to carry essential sap in a tree, most trees will die if their bark is removed. In the cork oak, however, the outer layer of bark, called the phellem, is only a protective covering, and it can be removed without injury. The bark grows in two layers. The inner bark is alive and acts as a base on which a new inner layer is added each year. As new inner layers

are added, the outermost layers cease to be a living part of the tree. They then serve merely as insulation to protect the tree against hot desert winds. This protective outer layer can be removed, in an operation known as *stripping*, without injuring the tree.

**Stripping and Processing.** It takes about 25 years for the first layer of bark to become thick enough to be stripped. Because of its uneven surface and grain, the first layer of bark stripping can be used only for products in which the cork is ground finely. The second stripping, made 8 or 9 years later, is of better quality, but it is not until the third stripping that a tree begins to yield the high-quality, even-grained cork needed for such solid cork products as bottle stoppers. The average productive life of a tree is 100 years, and once it matures it can be stripped every 8 or 9 years. The governments of most cork-producing countries have legislation protecting the cork supply.

A two-bladed hatchet ordinarily is used to remove the bark. Care must be taken not to injure the inner layer of bark; if this layer is damaged, no new cork will grow, and if the injury is severe, the tree may die. Two cuts are made around the trunk of the tree, one at ground level and one just below the main branches. Then two vertical cuts are made, and the bark is pried off with the wedge-shaped handles of the hatchets. Sometimes the larger branches are stripped in the same way, although cork from these is usually thin and of poor quality.

After the cork has been stripped, it is dried for a few days, weighed, and taken to a boiling station, which is usually located in the forest or in a nearby town. Boiling removes tannic acid and sap, increases the elasticity of the cork, and permits it to be flattened for shipping. It also loosens the rough outer layer, which is then scraped off. The flattened pieces of cork are taken to larger cities for manufacture into cork products or for shipment to manufacturers in other countries.

**Uses.** Because of its physical properties, which are based on its unique cellular construction, cork has many uses. In a piece of natural cork 1 cubic inch (16.4 cc) in size there are approximately 200 million cells about 1/1000 of an inch (0.025 mm) in diameter, each

**797**

Double-crested cormorant

separated from the next by a thin, threadlike, but remarkably strong membrane of resinous material, which acts as a binder. More than 50% of the volume of cork is accounted for by the air within these cells. The most important physical properties of cork are its buoyancy, light weight, compressibility, resilience, resistance to moisture and liquid penetration, high coefficient of friction, low thermal conductivity, ability to absorb vibration, and stability. It is these properties that make it useful and adaptable to so many products. Because of high costs, however, cork is being supplemented by newer, less expensive materials.

R. L. ACKLIN, *Armstrong Cork Company*

**CORLISS,** kôr′lis, **George Henry** (1817–1888), American inventor, known for the Corliss steam engine. He was born in Easton, N. Y., on June 2, 1817, and spent most of his life in Providence, R. I. In 1849 he invented a valve gear to regulate the amount of steam admitted to an engine cylinder in response to the load requirement. The Corliss valve-engine, which is still used, is sometimes called the most significant advance in steam power since the era of James Watt.

For the Centennial Exposition, held in Philadelphia in 1876, Corliss' company built a huge engine, billed as the "eighth wonder of the world." It had a flywheel 30 feet (9 meters) in diameter, and the engine weighed 700 tons (630 metric tons). Corliss died in Providence, R. I., on Feb. 21, 1888.

LEONARD M. FANNING
*Author of "Fathers of Industries"*

**CORM,** kôrm, a short, thick, erect underground stem of certain monocot plants, such as crocus and gladiolus. Corms, like bulbs, serve as food-storage organs and as sources of new vegetative growth. Unlike bulbs, which consist largely of specially thickened scale leaves, corms are composed primarily of stem tissue: the scale leaves are usually small and thin.

During growth, the corm sends down new roots, and its terminal ("center") bud develops into a flowering shoot. Its axillary, or side, buds commonly develop late in the season into little corms, called *cormels,* which may take several years to reach flowering size. Food material passed down from the mature plant is stored below ground in the base of the stem, which enlarges to form a new corm on top of the old, shriveled one. Corms of some plants remain covered with the dried remains of the leaves.

**CORMORANT,** kôr′mə-rənt, a family of 26 species of aquatic birds found in coastal and large inland waters throughout the world. In Peru, Chile, and South Africa, the excrement of cormorants is used as guano, a fertilizer rich in nitrogen and phosphates; and in the Orient, cormorants are used to catch fish.

Ducklike birds, cormorants may be from 19 to 40 inches (48 to 100 cm) long. They have long necks, slender, hooked bills, and long, stiff tails. Their plumage is usually blackish and often has a metallic sheen. Some cormorants have white underparts and brightly colored eyes, bills, and bare patches on the face, and some develop ornamental crests or patches of white when breeding. The sexes are almost identical.

Cormorants swim low in the water. They dive from the surface to pursue prey, but normally swallow it at the surface. They are voracious fish-eaters, but they may also eat some crustaceans, amphibians, and mollusks. Most hunt in shallow water, often remaining submerged for less than a minute, but some dive to depths of 120 feet (36 meters). Cormorants propel themselves under water mainly with their feet; all four of their toes are joined by webs and their legs, which are set far back on their bodies, are streamlined. Their plumage is not very water-repellent, and the birds return to land to dry and preen. Most cormorants are strong fliers, but the Galápagos cormorant cannot fly at all.

Nests built by cormorants are usually made of sticks and seaweed and are found on rocks, flat ground, or in trees. The female normally lays 2 to 4 pale blue or green eggs that have a chalky covering. The sexes share parental duties. Incubation takes from 3 to 5 weeks. The young, blind and naked when they are hatched, leave the nest after 5 to 8 weeks, but may be fed by their parents for many more weeks.

Cormorants make up the family Phalacrocoracidae in the order Pelecaniformes.

N. PHILIP ASHMOLE, *Yale University*

**CORN,** in medicine, an elevated painful thickening of the skin at an area subjected to sustained pressure or pinching, as on the small toe where a bony prominence or joint irregularity presses the skin against an ill-fitting shoe. The thickening appears cone-shaped in cross section with the point extending down toward the deeper skin tissues and bone. Usually, the corn is surrounded by considerable swelling and redness. In addition to the hard variety, there is a soft type of corn that occurs between the toes when there is overlapping and moisture.

The most urgent remedy for corns is the wearing of properly fitting shoes. Various plasters, pastes, and other preparations containing a 10–40% salicylic acid solution may be used to soften corns. Chronic cases sometimes require surgery to remove an underlying bony prominence.

SIDNEY HOFFMAN, M. D.
*St. John's Episcopal Hospital, Brooklyn, N. Y.*

# CORN

ORNAMENTAL CORN. Corn kernels vary in color from yellow to white to red, purple, brown, and variegated.

HYBRID CORN. Nearly all corn-growing acreage in the United States is planted with hybrid corn seed.

**CORN** is the most important cereal in the Western Hemisphere. In the United States the dollar value of the corn crop is equal to the combined value of wheat, oats, barley, rice, rye, and sorghum. On a world basis, corn is exceeded in value only by wheat and rice. Though corn ranks third among the world's cereals as a human food, in the United States it is used principally for livestock feed and industrial processing.

Corn (*Zea mays*) has many local and regional common names. "Corn" (originally "Indian corn") is the one commonly used in the United States and Canada, which grow about one-half of the world's total crop. In Britain, however, and continental Europe the term "corn" and its equivalents in other languages have been used for centuries to denote any of the small-seeded cereals such as barley, wheat, and rye. (Cereals are plants of the grass family grown primarily for their edible seed.) In Europe, Latin America, and many other parts of the world, "maize" and its cognates in other languages are the terms in common use for *Zea mays.*

Corn no longer exists in the wild state. Though there are a number of factors involved, a primary reason is that the corncob no longer releases the seed-containing kernels on its own, as presumably occurred in the wild ancestor. Men must remove and plant the kernels if the plant is to reproduce itself continually.

## THE PLANT

Corn is a coarse, annual plant of the grass family (Gramineae) that probably originated in tropical South America. It is the largest of the cereals, reaching 3 to 15 feet (1 to 4.5 meters) or more in height. The plant has a solid, jointed stem, or stalk, and large but narrow, wavy-margined leaves. Secondary stalks, called tillers, may be produced from the base of the plant. In addition to the usual fibrous root system of cereal plants, corn also produces *prop roots* from the lower joints, or nodes, of the stalk.

Corn is a monoecious plant; that is, each plant possesses both male and female flowers. Since the flowers are small and inconspicuous, they are referred to as *florets.* The male, or staminate, florets are borne in a cluster (botanically, a panicle), called the *tassel,* at the top of the stalk. The staminate florets produce the pollen necessary for fertilization. The female, or pistillate, florets are borne in a cluster (botanically, a spike), called a *cob,* which arises from a joint of the stalk. There are usually 1 to 3 cobs per stalk. The cob is covered with a protective husk of leaves, and after fertilization develops into an *ear* of corn.

Each mature female floret on the cob contains a seed-bearing organ, the pistil. The pistil consists of a rounded ovary, in which the seed actually develops, and a long, threadlike strand known as the *silk.* Botanically, the silk is the style (stalk) and stigma (pollen receptor) of the pistil, presumably mostly the latter since the silk is receptive to pollen grains along most of its length. The silks, which extend beyond the protective husk enclosing the cob in order to receive the pollen grains, are commonly 16 to 20 inches (40 to 50 cm) long.

**Reproduction.** Corn is wind pollinated; that is, the pollen from the staminate florets of the tassel is carried by the wind to the pistillate florets of the cob. Each pollen grain possesses a special nucleus that eventually divides to form two male nuclei, or sperm. When a pollen grain falls on a silk and germinates, it develops a long tube that passes down through the silk until it reaches and penetrates the embryo sac within the ovary. The embryo sac also contains special nuclei. One sperm fuses with the egg nucleus of the embryo sac to give rise to the embryo corn plant. The second sperm fuses with two other nuclei (the polar nuclei) to give rise to the *endosperm,* or starchy food-storage tissue of the seed.

The embryo, endosperm, and ovary wall then mature into a small, one-seeded fruit, commonly referred to as a kernel. A cob generally bears from 8 to 24 rows (actually 4 to 12 paired rows) of kernels. The kernel is a type of fruit known

SIX TYPES OF CORN (*left to right*): popcorn, sweet corn, flour corn, flint corn, dent corn, pod corn.

USDA

botanically as a caryopsis, in which the outer wall of the fruit (derived from the ovary wall) is fused to the seed coat of the enclosed seed. A corn kernel may be considered as consisting of an outer hull (about 6% of the kernel), the endosperm (about 83%), and the embryo (about 11%). The embryo with its large, flat, shield-shaped scutellum, or seed leaf (cotyledon), is known as the *germ*.

## TYPES OF CORN

The commonly recognized types of corn, distinguished largely by the type of endosperm and the shape of the grain, include dent, flint, flour, pop, sweet, pod, and waxy. At one time these types were given scientific names. But since the genus *Zea* is fully domesticated, and all of these types are cultivated forms that interbreed freely, there is little valid basis for taxonomic distinctions.

Each type may exist in a wide array of kernel colors, plant heights, ear sizes, and lengths of growing season. Kernel colors vary from yellow to white to red, purple, brown, and variegated. The majority of commercial corns are either yellow or white. Some tropical forms of corn may grow to more than 15 feet (4.5 meters), and require a full year from planting to maturity. At the other extreme, some varieties may grow no taller than 3 feet (1 meter) and mature in 70 days. Ear sizes may also vary from about 2 inches (5 cm) to 2 feet (60 cm).

Such differences in type have been stabilized by a combination of natural and artificial selection; each type is adapted to the climatic conditions under which it is commonly grown.

**Dent Corn.** If a typical dent kernel is viewed in cross section, the outer portion, which consists of hard endosperm, will appear horny and translucent. The central part of the kernel, which contains soft endosperm, will be lighter in color and somewhat floury in texture. This soft endosperm extends to the top of the kernel. During drying, shrinkage is greatest in the soft endosperm, causing the top of the kernel to become depressed, hence the name "dent." This is the important corn of commerce—it is used as feed for livestock and as a raw material for industrial processing and for the production of alcohol and other fermentation products.

**Flint Corn.** This type has a smooth kernel and either a complete absence of soft starch or a limited amount fully surrounded by hard endosperm. Flint corn tends to be quite resistant to

diseases causing ear rots and seedling blights. Flints are also more tolerant of low temperature during germination. For these reasons flint corns predominate near the extreme limits of corn production. However, flints also occur in tropical and semitropical areas where these temperature limitations do not prevail.

**Flour Corn.** This type resembles flint corn in kernel size and shape. Hard starch is essentially lacking, and the starch present has a chalky appearance and texture even when the kernel is fully mature and dried. These soft-kernel types are preferred by some Indian tribes where grinding is done by hand.

It has been demonstrated that some of the flour kernel types have an improved amino acid balance and are therefore better protein sources than the other kernel types. This improvement, however, is characteristic of only a few genetic types and does not extend to all flour corns.

**Popcorn.** Popcorn is grown to a very limited extent outside the United States. Its endosperm is mostly of the hard type. Two main forms are recognized: rice and pearl. The pearl types are similar to flint corn except for a much smaller kernel size. The rice types have a pointed kernel.

The popcorns are characterized by the ability to "pop," or explode, upon heating. The mechanism of popping is not fully understood. It is commonly assumed, however, that steam develops

A DRAWING OF RECONSTRUCTED WILD CORN. Wild corn is thought to have differed in several ways from modern corn. For example, wild corn had combination male and female flower clusters protected by only leafy husks. When the plant was mature, these husks opened to permit the dissemination of the wild corn seed. In modern corn, however, the separate female flower cluster is enclosed in husks that must be opened manually to free the seeds.

within the kernel upon heating, and when sufficient pressure develops, the kernel explodes. If corn contains too much or too little moisture, the kernel will fail to pop. When the moisture content is optimum, about 13% of the kernel by weight, popping expansion often exceeds 30 volumes, that is, 30 times the original size of the kernel.

**Sweet Corn.** The sweet, or sugary, characteristic of this corn is a simply inherited genetic trait. The enzymes necessary for the conversion of sugars to starch are absent or relatively inefficient, resulting in a soft, sugary endosperm.

Corn is eaten fresh in many parts of the world, but outside the United States relatively little of the corn so eaten is of the sweet type. The flint types predominate, although dents and flours may also be used. The American Indians ate green (immature) corn, but made no extensive use of sweet corn for this purpose.

**Pod Corn.** Pod corn is characterized by the tremendous size of the glumes (the modified leaves, or bracts, at the base of each floret-bearing branchlet), so that each individual kernel is completely surrounded and enclosed by a husk. It is a primitive type and of no commercial importance.

**Waxy Corn.** This form was introduced from China in 1907. The endosperm has a waxlike appearance, and consists entirely of amylopectin starch. It is used as a substitute for tapioca starch.

### DEVELOPMENT OF HYBRIDS

Many methods have been used to improve corn. Some form of selection has been practiced since man first began to domesticate primitive corn. Selection by man, accompanied by natural selection, must have involved the abilities both to survive under primitive conditions and to produce sufficient grain to justify seed gathering.

Extensive comparisons of hybrids were conducted in the period from 1877 to 1920. Crosses between dent varieties usually gave yield increases of 10% or less above that of the higher-yielding parent. Crosses between dent and flint or dent and flour varieties produced somewhat higher average yields, but such crosses did not meet with general favor and never became commercially important. It is now recognized that the failure to achieve substantial yield increases by this method was due to a lack of sufficient genetic diversity. All of the corn varieties grown within the United States possess some degree of genetic relationship. When crosses are made between types separated for long periods, either by distance (geographically) or by being grown under diverse environmental conditions (ecologically), yield increases ranging up to 50% have been obtained. Such hybrids are now being used commercially in some parts of the world.

By 1920 it was commonly assumed that neither mass selection (breeding to conform to an ideal type) nor varietal hybridization offered promise of further increases in corn yields. We now know this belief to be incorrect, but at that time the opinion was sufficiently general to give impetus to a new breeding method, the development of hybrids through the crossing of inbred lines.

**Inbreeding.** Many of the inbreeding hybridization programs were initiated in the 1920's. The first step in this process is the development of *inbred* lines. Corn is normally cross-pollinated, that is, pollen from one plant is carried to the female florets of another. The development of inbred lines requires self-fertilization: both the pollen and female florets are of a single plant. Self-fertilization is accomplished by covering the ear shoot before the silks emerge and, at the appropriate time, transferring pollen from the tassel to these protected silks. Such inbreeding reveals hidden defects; in the first generations, large differences are observed among the progenies, or descendants, of different plants, as well as among the progeny arising from a single plant. Progeny lacking in vigor or disease resistance or possessing other undesirable characteristics are discarded. Inbreeding of the superior plants among the better progenies is continued. After three to five generations of inbreeding, each of the lines retained becomes highly uniform, but large differences exist between one line and another.

USDA

CORN PLANTING by the wheel-track method consists of dropping the kernels in tracks made by the four small front wheels, and covering them with soil by the wheels at the rear.

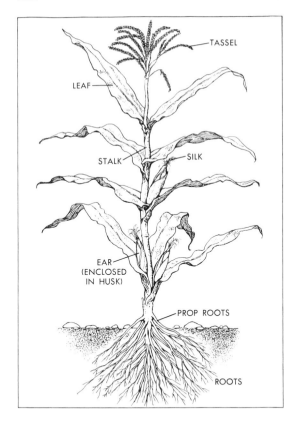

TASSEL

LEAF

STALK

SILK

EAR
(ENCLOSED
IN HUSK)

PROP ROOTS

ROOTS

sulting from the crossing of two inbred strains) is borne on a relatively low-yielding inbred parent. Double-cross seed (resulting from the crossing of two single-cross strains) is produced on a high-yielding single-cross parent.

Techniques have been developed that permit the prediction of double-cross yields. This is necessary because of the large number of items involved. Ten inbred lines can be combined to produce 45 single crosses and 630 double crosses. If the number of lines is increased to 50, the corresponding number of single and double crosses becomes 495 and 96,030, respectively. The predicted double crosses are evaluated under field conditions, and only the best are used commercially.

Selective elimination of inbred lines during inbreeding and subsequent testing is great. As an average, fewer than 5 out of 100,000 of the lines started survive to the stage of commercial use.

The first hybrids entering commercial use produced yields 25% to 30% greater than the previously grown open-pollinated varieties. Initially, the major emphasis was on yield improvement. As success was realized for this characteristic, increasing emphasis was given to insect and disease resistance.

**Acceptance of Hybrids.** In 1930, less than 0.1% of the corn acreage in the corn belt of the United States was planted to hybrid seed. Acceptance of the hybrids by farmers was relatively rapid, and by 1943 the entire corn acreage of Iowa was planted to hybrid seed. Outside the corn belt, adoption was less rapid, but by 1956 over 90% of the U. S. corn acreage was planted with hybrid seed.

## WHERE CORN IS RAISED

Although of tropical origin, corn is grown from latitude 58° N, in Canada and Siberia, to 42° S, in New Zealand. Within this broad belt corn is an important crop only where temperature and moisture conditions are favorable. Corn does poorly where the mean summer temperature is less than 66° F (19° C) and reaches its greatest concentration and productivity in the Northern Hemisphere where the daily temperatures in July average between 70° and 80° F (21°–27° C). In addition to suitable temperatures, adequate rainfall is also very important. Corn may be grown under semiarid conditions, but the highest yields are obtained in areas having 20 inches (500 mm) or more of rainfall per year, with an ample and well-distributed summer rainfall.

The largest area that best meets these requirements is the United States. There, favorable climate plus soils with good tilth (suitable clustering, or aggregation, of minute soil particles into tiny clumps) and a high native fertility combine to permit the most extensive corn production in the world. U. S. production reaches its highest concentration in the corn belt, which includes western Ohio, Indiana, Illinois, Iowa, and parts of Missouri, Kansas, Nebraska, South Dakota, and Minnesota. Iowa, which normally leads the states in production, produces more corn than any nation other than the United States itself.

In other areas of the Northern Hemisphere where both temperature and rainfall requirements are met, corn becomes of local importance. In Europe these areas include Portugal, part of Spain, southern France, Italy, and the Balkans, including Greece. In Asia, Turkey produces corn

**Topcrosses.** The appearance of an inbred line is an unsatisfactory guide to its performance in hybrid combinations. All lines, however, must possess sufficient general vigor to make their commercial use feasible. The next task is to evaluate the inbred lines in hybrid combinations. The *topcross* (inbred x open-pollinated variety) is often used for this preliminary evaluation. Large numbers of lines are involved in these field trials, which are replicated ("repeated") many times using many different plants. The average yield of all topcrosses may approximate the yield of the tester parent (the open-pollinated variety used in the cross), with some of them inferior and others superior to this general average. The inbred parents contributing to low yields are discarded, and further testing is limited to those inbred lines having the highest average yield in topcross hybrids.

**Single and Three-Way Crosses.** The next step in testing involves the production of *single crosses* or *three-way crosses*. In the production of single crosses, each parent is of a single inbred line: inbred A x inbred B; in three-way crosses, one parent is itself a single cross, while the other parent is of a single inbred line: (A x B) x C. Such hybrids are subjected to extensive testing under the cultural and management conditions typical of the area. Again, only those inbred parents that contribute to the highest field performance are retained.

**Double Crosses.** The hybrid seeds planted by most farmers are double crosses, which are produced by crossing two single-cross parents: (A x B) x (C x D). The reason for this preference is higher seed yield. Single-cross seed (re-

along the Black Sea and Mediterranean coasts. In the USSR, corn production reaches its greatest intensity in the region of the Black and Caspian seas. China produces a large amount of corn, with production centered in the eastern provinces. Corn is becoming increasingly important in the drier regions of Thailand, Indonesia, and the Philippines, where rice production has been limited. In the Southern Hemisphere, Argentina, Brazil, and the Republic of South Africa are the largest producers of corn.

World production of corn totals some 6.5 billion U. S. bushels (165.1 billion kg)—a U. S. bushel of corn is equivalent to 56 pounds or 25.4 kg. The leading producer is the United States, accounting for 50% of the total. Europe produces 13% and Asia 12%, both exclusive of Russia, which accounts for 5%. The balance of production is accounted for by South America, 9%; Africa, 7%; and North America, 4% excluding the United States.

## COMMERCIAL USES OF CORN

Corn ranks third among the world cereals as a human food. In the United States, however, it is used principally for livestock feed and industrial processing. Processing takes one of three forms: wet milling, dry milling, or fermentation.

Approximately 85% of the U. S. corn crop is fed to livestock. The grain is high in energy, low in crude fiber, and highly digestible. It is therefore very suitable for concentrated feeds. Protein percentage varies with variety and cultural and seasonal conditions, but normally ranges between 8.5% and 10.5%. Corn protein is deficient in two of the essential amino acids: lysine and tryptophan. These deficiencies require that protein supplements form part of the ration in any efficient feeding operation.

Genetic types that have a greatly improved amino acid balance have been found. Feeding trials with such types have given rates of gain (from corn alone) which are essentially equal to normal corn supplemented with soybean oil meal. These new types should have great value where corn forms a substantial part of the human diet.

In earlier years, yellow corn was found to be a better feed for swine than white corn. This difference was shown to be due to the presence of carotene pigment (which is a biological precursor of vitamin A) in yellow corn. However, vitamin A requirements can be met by the addition of synthetic materials or good quality alfalfa leaf meal or other green feed. With such supplements, white and yellow corn are equal in feeding value.

**Wet Milling.** Slightly more than 5% of the U. S. corn crop is used by the wet-milling industry. The primary products are starch and oil, both of which may be modified to suit a large number of industrial uses. Protein (gluten feed) and oil cake are important by-products that are used in livestock feeds.

Wet milling involves steeping, or soaking, followed by grinding to release the starch, then flotation and screening to remove the germ, hulls, and cellular debris. Steeping is done in large tanks of warm, dilute sulfurous acid solution. The purpose of the steep is to soften the kernel, to control microbial activity selectively, and to bleach the starch. After steeping, the corn is passed through a special grinding mill called a degerminator. The partially ground corn then passes through a germ separator. The germs,

after separation from the hulls and starchy endosperm, pass through a series of reels, or shakers, and are washed to remove as much of the adhering starch as possible. They then pass through special squeezers to remove excess water, and are finally dried before going to the oil expellers.

The incompletely ground endosperm material is subjected to further grinding and sieving to remove as much germ and fibrous material as possible. The slurry, or watery mixture, remaining after the final screening contains starch, protein, and water-soluble materials. The starch and protein are separated by continuous-flow centrifugal separators.

The purified starch may be modified by heat, acid, alkali, or enzymes to fill special industrial needs. The starch may be hydrolyzed to produce dextrose or corn syrup. Other modifications lead to thick- or thin-boiling starches and dextrins. The thin-boiling starches are used extensively in the textile industry for sizing (stiffening or glazing) yarn and finishing cloth. They are also used in the preparation of certain confections such as jelly beans and gumdrops. Dextrins are used in the production of many types of adhesives.

After the germ is dried, the oil may be removed by expeller (pressure) or solvent processes. The extracted oil is a mixture of glycerides (combinations of fatty acids and alcohol derived from glycerol alcohol). Several methods of refining are available. Each method yields a purified fraction and a soap stock, or "foots," fraction. The purified fraction may be used as a cooking or salad oil or for the production of mayonnaise or margarine. The soap stock fraction is saponified ("hydrolyzed") to produce various types of soap powders.

The gluten (a tough, elastic protein substance) fraction is recovered by settling or centrifugation, followed by a further reduction of moisture by special presses, and finally by drying. The dried product may be sold for livestock feed or subjected to further processing for the production of zein (a protein) and amino acids.

The steep water contains soluble carbohydrates, proteins, and minerals. These materials may be recovered by evaporation, added to the gluten and fiber fractions, and sold as feed. Large quantities of steep water are also used in the production of such antibiotics as penicillin.

**Dry Milling.** Dry milling represents the second-largest industrial use of corn and is a relatively simple process. It involves the physical separation of the hull from the endosperm and germ of the kernel, through successive grinding and sieving operations.

After cleaning, the corn is rapidly tempered, or treated, to increase its moisture content to about 20% by weight. This toughens the hull and permits a more complete separation of the hull from the endosperm. The corn is then ground in a Beal degerminator, which loosens the hull and germ with a minimum of grinding of the endosperm. The hull, also called the bran (see BRAN), and germ may then be separated by suction. Further separation is achieved by passing through a slotted cylinder called a hominy reel. The endosperm is separated into sizes by means of appropriate screens. The sizes of major interest are designated as hominy, grits, meal, and flour. The hominy fraction is cooked with malt and then flaked. The flaked material may be toasted to produce cornflakes or marketed untoasted as

MECHANICAL CORN PICKERS harvest the ripe ears of corn and leave the rest of the plant in the field.

GRANT HEILMAN, LITITZ, PA.

"brewers' flakes," "foundry flakes," or "paper-hangers' flakes." The untoasted flakes may be used as a carbohydrate source in fermentation or for the production of special types of paste. Grits and meal are used for human consumption. The flour is used as an ingredient in pancake mixes, as a filler or binder in meat products, or as a wheat flour substitute.

**Fermentation.** The fermentation industry uses starch and sugar as raw materials. Ethyl alcohol is the most important of the fermentation products. Other products include acetaldehyde, acetic acid, acetone, acetylmethylcarbinol, and butyl alcohol. Many of these products, in turn, may be used as substrates, or bases, for further fermentation products. Yeast and bacterial cultures are used for fermentation; the strain of the organism and the cultural conditions used determine the final product.

## CULTIVATION OF CORN

**Requirements—*Growing Season*.** Corn is a warm-weather crop, and its planting is commonly delayed until the average air temperature is 60° F (15.5° C) or higher. At lower temperatures both germination and growth are slowed, and susceptibility to seedling blights is increased. Corn can be safely planted about 10 to 14 days after the last killing frost. Delays beyond the optimum may lead to yield reductions of 2 or more bushels per acre (125 kg or more per hectare) for each week of delay.

**Crop Rotation.** Corn is generally grown in rotation, or alternation, with other crops. The type of rotation to be used is determined by the possibility of erosion; the fertility of the soil; requirements for weed, insect, and disease control; and, of course, the relative value of other crops adapted to the area. Corn, however, may be grown several years in succession on soils with low erosive potential where high levels of management can be maintained.

**Fertilizers.** In corn yielding 100 bushels per acre (6,300 kg per hectare), the harvested grain will remove about 90 pounds (40 kg) of nitrogen, 18 pounds (8 kg) of phosphorus, and 25 pounds (11 kg) of potash from the soil. The management system must provide for the replacement of these elements, as well as calcium, magnesium, and any necessary microelements, if high yields are to be maintained. Nitrogen may be supplied by crops of legumes (plants of the pea family that convert nitrogen in the air into organic nitrogen compounds) and green manure (plants grown to be plowed under), but these often fail to supply adequate amounts for the most profitable yields. At present price levels, nutrient requirements may be supplied most economically through the use of commercial fertilizers. The objective should be to replace the depleted elements and to maintain optimum conditions for growth throughout the entire rotation cycle.

**Water.** The corn crop uses large quantities of water, with the heaviest demand during the pollination and early grain-filling stages. The need for water often exceeds the amount falling as rain during the growing season. This deficit is overcome by moisture stored in the soil in the period between crops. It is for this reason that corn culture reaches its greatest intensity on deep, friable ("crumbly") soils having a large water-storage capacity. Some of the soils of the corn belt may store as much as 10 inches (25 cm) of available moisture in a 5-foot (1.5-meter) depth, or profile, of soil. Storage capacity in sandy soils is quite limited. Adequate fertilization increases the efficiency of water use.

**Tillage.** Corn planting may utilize conventional or minimum tillage operations. The conventional method involves discing or chopping, to permit ready incorporation of plant residues, followed by plowing. Either fall or spring plowing may be used, although fall plowing, where possible, is usually preferred. Shortly before planting, the field is again disced and harrowed to produce a firm, finely pulverized seedbed. A runner or disc-opener, which automatically drops, spaces, and covers the seed, is standard in the corn belt. This entire operation is relatively expensive, as it requires repeated trips over the field to complete the entire operation. These repeated trips also pack down the soil. As a result of the compaction involved, water infiltration may be reduced, with a corresponding increase in the possibility of runoff and erosion.

FIELD CHOPPERS chop ripe corn plants (ears, stalks, leaves) into silage for feed.

Several types of minimum, or reduced, tillage methods are available for planting. One of the simplest of these is wheel-track planting. In this, the field is plowed as in the conventional method. Then planting is done in tractor-wheel tracks or in the tracks of other wheels constructed for this purpose. A still simpler procedure is to attach a planter to the side of the plow, and plow and plant in one operation.

Any of these minimum tillage procedures will provide a space between rows that is uncompacted and will therefore permit rapid water penetration. The loose soil also retards the germination of weed seed. When seasonal conditions are unfavorable, stands, or the number of plants in a given area, may be lower for minimum tillage than for conventional planting methods. Where equal stands are obtained, however, yields under these contrasting systems are essentially similar.

The rate of planting (the number of plants for a given area) varies with soil type, fertility level, water supply, and speed of maturing of the variety grown. In dryer areas, planting rates may be half of those used where rainfall is adequate. Early maturing varieties should be planted at a higher rate than those utilizing the full growing season. The yield of grain per plant provides a rough index of the proper use of moisture and fertility. Average ear weights of about ½ pound (227 grams) indicate maximum efficiency in the use of moisture and fertility. Ear weights averaging more than ½ pound indicate that the stands are too thin.

**Weed Control.** Weed control is an important aspect of corn production. It may be accomplished by cultivation, by chemicals, or by a combination of these methods. Weeds that are particularly troublesome in corn include Johnson grass, quack grass, morning glory, cocklebur, crabgrass, foxtails, pigweeds, lamb's-quarters, and nut sedge.

Mechanical cultivation, to be effective, must be started when weeds are small. The most effective implements at this growth stage are the rotary hoe, the spike-tooth harrow, and the spring-tooth weeder. These stir the soil surface

and thus kill emerging weed seedlings. The best results are obtained when the ground is slightly crusted and the weeds are just beginning to emerge. Later cultivation or weeding is done with a shovel cultivator. Care must be taken to avoid deep or too close cultivation, or damage to the root system will result.

Selective herbicides are very important in weed control. The use of these chemicals has increased rapidly since 1948, with 25% of the U. S. corn acreage being treated in 1959, 39% in 1962, and 68% in 1965. Herbicides may be applied for control of weeds before planting, between planting and emergence of the corn, and after emergence of the corn.

**Diseases.** Corn is subject to many diseases. Some of these may cause heavy losses in local areas, but they are seldom devastating over large areas. Yield losses due to nutritional imbalance can readily be remedied by proper management practices. Parasitic diseases are less easily controlled.

Parasitic diseases may be caused by bacteria, fungi, or viruses. The more important groups of diseases are seedling blights, leaf blights, stalk rots, and ear rots. Certain fungi, particularly *Fusarium* and *Diplodia*, may be involved in each group. Seedling blights kill the young plant at the time of emergence from the soil or shortly afterward. These can be controlled by the selection of sound seed, by planting at the proper time, and by the nearly universal practice of treating the seed with an effective fungicide.

Many different organisms may cause leaf blights, but the most common are fungi species of the genus *Helminthosporium*. Under severe conditions, northern leaf blight (caused by *H. turcicum*) may greatly reduce yields by destroying leaf tissue. Lines and hybrids have been developed that possess a high degree of resistance to the leaf-blight diseases.

Bacterial stalk rots attack corn during the active growth stage. The incidence of disease is low and losses are usually minor. The fungal stalk rots are primarily diseases of senescence, or old age. Infection takes place at an early growth stage but the disease symptoms do not become apparent until the late filling stage of ear development. Ears from the infected stalks may be lightweight and chaffy. The greatest loss, however, comes from the breaking of the stalks, with an increase in harvest difficulties and losses.

The same group of fungi that causes stalk rots also causes ear rots, though the two classes of diseases arise from separate infections. The ear rots may cause severe reduction in kernel size and ear weight, with resulting reduction in both grain quality and yield. One of these fungi, *Gibberella*, though comparatively safe for cattle and sheep, is toxic to man and other nonruminant animals.

No effective control measures are known for stalk or ear rots, other than the development of resistant varieties.

For a long period, corn was relatively free from serious virus attacks. Since 1963, however, several virus diseases have been reported, each causing heavy yield losses. At least three different viruses are involved: corn stunt, maize dwarf mosaic, and wheat streak mosaic. Corn stunt has been found in most of the states in the southeastern section of the United States. Losses have been so severe that in areas like the Yazoo Delta of western Mississippi, corn has been almost completely replaced by other crops. Maize dwarf mosaic has been most severe in bottom lands of the Ohio and its tributaries. In 1964, losses in Ohio alone were estimated to exceed 5 million bushels (127 million kg). The casual viruses are quite different, but they produce essentially the same symptoms in infected plants. Wheat streak mosaic is widely distributed in Ohio, Indiana, and Michigan, and it probably will spread throughout the corn belt. The development of resistant types offers the most promise of effective control for each of these virus diseases.

**Insect Control.** A large number of insects feed on corn, but relatively few of these cause serious and widespread damage. Losses from insects such as seed corn maggots, wireworms, cutworms, and flea beetles, which attack corn in the germination or early seedling stage, may be minimized by providing conditions for rapid germination and growth. Insecticides may also be used where heavy infestations are expected. Rootworms are becoming increasingly difficult to control. Populations have developed resistance to the chlorinated hydrocarbon insecticides. Breeding for resistance appears to offer considerable promise.

Insects that feed on leaves and stalks, such as European cornborers, earworms, stalk borers, and army worms, may be controlled by insecticides, but proper timing of application is of great importance. Resistant corn types have been developed for some insects, and this approach appears to offer the most promise for effective control.

**Harvesting.** Corn may be harvested for fodder (coarse livestock feed), silage (cut and partially fermented livestock feed), or grain. The practice of cutting and shocking (stacking) corn for fodder has decreased markedly since 1915. Approximately 10% of the corn acreage in the United States is utilized for silage. This harvest practice is most common in the northern and northeastern states and makes the most efficient use of the corn crop. The "hard dough" stage (when the endosperm contents begin to assume a hard, doughy consistency) of grain develop-

ment is the preferred stage for harvesting for silage. Since stalks, leaves, and ears are ensiled, the crop has approximately one-third more feeding value for beef cattle than when only the grain is utilized. Harvesting is normally done with a field chopper, which cuts the standing stalks and chops them into sections ½ to 1½ inches (13 to 38 mm) long. Both pit-type and tower-type silos are used for the storage of corn.

Harvesting for grain has passed through successive stages. In earlier days, corn was cut and then shocked, and then the ears husked for storage after they were completely dry. A later method involved husking the corn from the standing stalks. Because of mold and other factors, it is unsafe to crib corn until the moisture content drops to 20 to 25%. The ears, therefore, were allowed to become partially dry on the stalks before being husked. After husking, the ears were stored in slatted cribs where they continued to dry throughout the winter. Labor requirements for field husking were materially less than for the earlier system. Harvesting from the standing stalks continued as the most common practice until the late 1930's.

With the advent of hybrids, with greater resistance to lodging (leaning or falling over), mechanical harvesting became practical. One- and two-row pickers came into general use. The one-row pickers were tractor-drawn or semi-mounted. The two-row pickers were tractor-mounted or self-propelled. By 1956, over 95% of the crop in the corn belt was harvested by mechanical pickers. Harvest losses are lowest when corn is picked as soon as it becomes ripe. But at this stage, moisture content is often too high for safe crib storage. Under such early-harvest conditions some form of artificial drying is required. Drying can be effected by unheated air blown through the stored corn.

The next development involved harvesting corn as shelled grain rather than as ear corn. Either picker-shellers or corn heads added to a grain combine are used. These machines gather the ears and shell the grain in one continuous operation. The corn combine system is the more general, and by 1966 approximately half of the Illinois corn acreage was harvested in this manner. Here also the grain is too wet for safe storage and must be sold immediately or dried artificially.

The cost of producing an acre of corn has decreased in proportion to the increased use of power machinery. In the days of single-row, horse-drawn implements, when harvesting was a hand operation, 30 or more man-hours were required to grow and harvest an acre of corn (75 or more man-hours per hectare of corn). With the implements and practices in current use, less than 4 man-hours per acre, or 10 man-hours per hectare, are required.

G. F. Sprague
*U. S. Department of Agriculture*

### DOMESTICATION OF CORN

Although corn has been grown in Europe, Asia, and Africa for several hundred years, there are no substantiated written, pictorial, linguistic, or archaeological records of the existence of corn outside the New World before 1492.

**The Indians' Corn.** The earliest recorded contact of Europeans with corn occurred on Nov. 5, 1492, when a Spanish scouting party returning from the interior of Cuba reported that a grain called *mahiz* tasted good and could be baked, dried, and made into flour. The 16th century explorations of the mainland found advanced Indian cultures growing corn from Canada to Chile; all of the principal kinds of corn that we recognize today—pop, sweet, flour, flint, and dent —were extensively cultivated on the American continents before the arrival of the Europeans.

In a comparison of 15th and 20th century corn, modern corn would show an increase in cob size and in the number and weight of seeds (kernels) per plant; however, in other details few differences would be noted. Improved cultural and fertilization practices and controlled hybridization have changed the corn of the Indians to today's high-yielding corn.

**Wild Corn.** To perpetuate domesticated corn, man must remove the seed from the ear, plant the seed, reduce competition between corn seedlings and other plants, and harvest the ears. Thus the reproduction, dissemination, and survival of domesticated corn are entirely dependent on man. The ancestral wild corn reproduced and disseminated its seed and survived without the intervention of man.

Evidence that wild corn existed in the New World long before man arrived on either continent has been found in a drill core brought up from more than 200 feet (60 meters) beneath Mexico City. This core contained fossil pollen estimated to be at least 80,000 years old. Some of the pollen grains were identified as those of corn by E. Barghoorn, a Harvard University paleobotanist, and this fossil pollen shows a remarkably close resemblance to modern corn pollen. Yet the ancient corn plants that produced the pollen of modern appearance could not also have produced ears of the type that characterize modern domesticated corn.

Tiny primitive corncobs have recently been discovered by R. S. MacNeish of the National Museum of Canada, in layers of refuse deposited by early inhabitants of caves in the Tehuacán Valley, Puebla, Mexico. The oldest corncob and corn plant fragments from the lowest level of refuse have been estimated by radiocarbon dating to be 7,200 years old, that is, to date from 5200 B.C. The composition of debris from the lowest level indicates that the earliest inhabitants of these caves existed by hunting and plant collecting rather than by practicing agriculture. Later inhabitants did engage in agriculture and domesticated wild corn, developing races of corn some of which are still grown in parts of Mexico today.

No intact corn plants have been uncovered in these Mexican caves, but a reconstruction of wild corn from the intact cobs, fragments of cobs, and other plant parts found in the caves has been made by P. C. Mangelsdorf, a Harvard University botanist. The corn was a tiny podpop type of low productivity. The cobs, less than an inch long, had an average of 55 small seeds, or kernels, arranged in pairs, usually in eight rows. The glumes (modified leaves) of the paired female spikelets were relatively long and soft and partially enclosed each kernel. The central axis of the cob, known as the rachis, was slender, soft, and relatively fragile. An unbranched spike of paired pollen-producing male spikelets projected from the apex of the small ear. These combination male and female inflorescences on the wild corn were protected by only two husks, which undoubtedly opened at maturity, permitting seed dispersal through breakage of the cob rachis by weather or animal damage.

In contrast with domesticated corn, which has large ears borne low on the stalk, the ears of the wild corn were probably borne high on short-stalked plants that lacked tillers (secondary stalks). This wild type was the only type of corn found in the preagricultural level. These archaeological remains of wild corn are very similar in appearance to the wild corn proposed by E. L. Sturtevant in the late 19th century and to the primitive corn genetically reconstructed by P. C. Mangelsdorf.

**Early Domestic Corn.** Remains of wild corn were present in the upper levels of the Tehuacán caves in decreasing amounts until 250 A.D. A change from wild toward modern corn was found in some cobs dating from 7,200 to 5,400 years ago (5200–3400 B.C.), and the rate of change increased during a period lasting from 5,400 to 4,300 years ago (3400–2300 B.C.). This change, most probably induced by man's reducing weed competition, consisted of increased cob and kernel size.

More striking alterations, evidenced in only a few cobs prior to 5,400 years ago (3400 B.C.), had completely replaced wild and early cultivated corn types by 2,100 to 1,300 years ago (200 B.C.–700 A.D.). These changes involved increased toughness of the rachis (central axis of the cob), the elimination of staminate spikes (male florets) from the apex of the cobs, and an increase in the length and number of protective husks for the ear as a whole. This corn was completely domesticated and could not have reproduced itself without man's assistance. These changes probably resulted from a combination of improved cultural practices, such as irrigation; gene mutations that resulted in a lowering of the position of the ear on the stalk and increased the number of ear husks; and random, uncontrolled hybridization of wild or early cultivated corn with closely related wild species of gama grass (*Tripsacum*) or teosinte (*Euchlaena*). Since no remains of these relatives of corn were found in the Tehuacán Valley, it has been assumed that this hybridization originally took place somewhere else.

Under domestication, the tiny-eared, small-seeded corn plant has evolved into the world's most productive cereal.

JOHN R. EDWARDSON
*University of Florida*

**Bibliography**

Cancian, Frank, *Change and Uncertainty in a Peasant Community: The Maya Corn Farmers of Zinacantan* (Stanford Univ. Press 1972).
Hallaur, Arnel R., and Miranda, J. B., Jr., *Quantitative Genetics in Maize Breeding*, rev. ed. (Iowa State Univ. Press 1988).
Hardeman, Nicholas P., *Shucks, Shocks and Hominy Blocks: Corn as a Way of Life in Pioneer America* (La. State Univ. Press 1981).
*Improvement and Production of Maize, Sorghum and Millet*, 2 vols. (Unipub 1980).
Inglett, George E., ed., *Maize: Recent Progress in Chemistry and Technology* (Academic Press 1982).
Jugenheimer, R. W., *Corn* (1976; reprint, Krieger 1986).
Kiesselbach, T. A., *The Structure and Reproduction of Corn* (Univ. of Neb. Press 1980).
McGee, Denis C., *Maize Diseases: A Reference Source for Seed Technologists* (Am. Phytopathological Soc. 1988).
*Small-Scale Maize Milling* (Unipub 1985).
Watson, S. A., and Ramstad, P. E., eds., *Corn: Chemistry and Technology* (Am. Assn. of Cereal Chemists 1987).
Woodier, Olwen, *Corn: Meals and More*, ed. by Jill Mason (Storey Comm. 1987).

**CORN BELT** is a common name for a section of the midwestern United States where corn is the traditional crop. It includes western Ohio, Indiana, Illinois, Iowa, and parts of Missouri, Kansas, Nebraska, South Dakota, and Minnesota. Each year these states, led by Iowa and Illinois, produce about 80% of the nation's corn crop.

Although called the corn belt, this section is a region of diversified farming. The commodities that account for the major share of cash receipts, however, usually are corn, soybeans, beef cattle, and hogs. Livestock tends to lead crops in value.

**CORN BORER,** any of several moth larvae that bore into corn plants. The most important is the European corn borer (*Ostrinia nubilalis*), which is considered to be the most destructive insect pest of corn—particularly sweet corn—in North America; it also attacks other vegetable and flower garden plants. Although native to Europe, it has become widely distributed in North America, especially in the corn belt.

The European corn borer develops from white, scalelike eggs laid on the undersides of corn leaves by the adult moth. The eggs hatch in about one week, and the larvae feed on the leaves first and then tunnel the stalks and ears of corn. The fully grown larva, which is flesh-colored and marked with brown dots, is nearly ¾ inch (1.9 cm) long. It passes the winter inside the roots or stem of the host plant and in the late spring changes to a pupa.

The adult moth emerges from the pupa in June. Male moths are slightly smaller and darker than the females, but both sexes are buff-colored with dark, wavy bands on the wings. The wingspread is about 1 inch (2.5 cm). One or two generations develop each summer.

Other corn borers found in North America are the southwestern corn borer (*Zeadiatraea grandiosella*), the southern cornstalk borer (*Diatraea crambidoides*), and the lesser cornstalk borer (*Elasmopalpus lignosellus*). All the corn borers belong to the family Pyralidae.

RALPH H. DAVIDSON
*Ohio State University*

**CORN COCKLE,** a common Eurasian weed that often grows in corn and wheat fields in the midwestern United States. The corn cockle is an annual, sometimes biennial, plant about 3 feet (1 meter) tall. It bears silky, grayish leaves and somewhat spotted, purplish flowers about an inch (2.5 cm) wide. The seeds of the plant are poisonous and must be sorted out from wheat grains that are to be used as poultry feed. The corn cockle, *Agrostemma githago*, belong to the pink family (Caryophyllaceae).

DONALD WYMAN
*The Arnold Arboretum, Harvard University*

**CORN CRAKE.** See RAILS.

**CORN EARWORM,** a destructive moth larva, nearly worldwide in distribution. It is also known as the *bollworm* or *tomato fruitworm*. One of the six most harmful insect pests of corn and cotton, it also attacks tomatoes, tobacco, beans, and other plants. The corn earworm is a particularly harmful pest because it may devour any part of the plants that it attacks.

The corn earworm develops from tiny eggs laid by the adult moth on the corn silk. The fully grown larva is about 1½ inches (3.8 cm) long and varies in color from green through shades of brown to almost black. Since the larvae are cannibalistic, usually only one or two worms are found in each corn ear.

The corn earworm pupates underground. The adult moth, which emerges from the pupa, is buff-colored with dark wing markings; its wingspread is 1½ inches (3.8 cm). The period of development from egg to adult is about 30 days at midsummer temperatures. There are usually two generations each year in the northern United States and as many as five or six generations in the South.

The corn earworm (*Heliothis zea*) is a member of the family Noctuidae.

RALPH H. DAVIDSON, *Ohio State University*

**CORN ISLANDS,** two small islands in the Caribbean Sea, 40 miles (65 km) from Nicaragua. Called in Spanish the Islas del Maíz, they are in the Nicaraguan department of Zelaya but were leased to the United States for 99 years under the Bryan-Chamorro Treaty (signed 1914, ratified 1916). This treaty was originated to safeguard the future of the proposed trans-Nicaraguan canal, which was never built. Termination of the treaty was ratified by the U.S. Senate in 1971. Great Corn, a vacation resort, and Little Corn have a combined area of 4.6 square miles (12 sq km). Coconuts are the islands' chief product.

**CORN LAWS,** statutory regulations in Britain designed to safeguard domestic food production, farmers' incomes, and agricultural rents.

**Origins.** English corn laws originated in the Middle Ages. As early as 1177, penalties were imposed on persons exporting grain ("corn" in English usage) without a license, and as early as 1463, imports of foreign grain were prohibited except when home prices exceeded 6 shillings 8 pence per "quarter" of eight bushels. Such medieval restrictions were local and temporary. The outlines of a general protective system took shape only in the 17th and 18th centuries, when Parliament, composed mainly of an estate-owning aristocracy and a country gentry, decreed corn bounties on British exports (1660, 1663, 1673, and 1689) and placed bans on imports (1757, 1759, and 1769).

As British population increased in the 18th century and new mercantile and industrial interests emerged, the system of regulation was subject both to criticism, notably from Adam Smith, and to amendment. In an attempt to reconcile interests, an important act of 1773 forbade exports except when wheat prices fell below 44s. per quarter and allowed imports when the price rose above 48s. Bitter disputes centered on a further act of 1791, which raised the latter price to 54s. By then it was apparent that despite improved methods of production, British farmers could not meet home demand. Sporadic food riots had reflected earlier discontent; now there was highly organized opposition, much of it influential.

**Urban Opposition.** High prices during the Napoleonic Wars improved the economic position of the landlord (through rents) and the farmer (through incomes), but at the expense of recurrent urban disturbances, particularly in the new industrial areas. When, therefore, in 1813 a parliamentary select committee demanded postwar agricultural protection, there were angry counterdemands for cheap food.

In the same year an enormous harvest was followed by an unprecedented fall in wheat prices, and in 1815—in the face of bitter protests from the cities—Parliament passed a new corn law fixing 80s. per quarter as the price above which imports were allowed in at a nominal duty. Despite the act—some said because of it—domestic prices fluctuated sharply, and neither landlords nor farmers were able to maintain their wartime prosperity between 1815 and 1822, when the 1815 act was amended.

Questions of corn prices obviously involved not only fiscal policy but currency and credit policy, and many farmers felt that restrictions on credit and high interest charges more than counterbalanced any benefits they derived from the 1815 act. Meanwhile, opposition to the whole policy of protection sharpened during the 1820's, when the views of David Ricardo and other classical political economists were widely diffused—often in popular terms and colored by bitter criticism of landlords.

Further amendment of the 1815 act followed in 1828, when a sliding scale of import duties based on home prices was introduced. Critics claimed as they had before that speculators benefited more than farmers, but for both economic and political reasons the issue ceased to raise as much controversy during the early 1830's as it had 10 years before.

**Repeal.** The controversy was revived in changed circumstances and with far-reaching ramifications in May 1839, when the Anti-Corn-Law League was founded in Manchester. The league immediately embarked on a well-organized crusade to repeal protection. The leaders of the league, notably Richard Cobden, believed that industrial depression, which had begun in 1836, could be overcome only by increasing exports of British manufactures and balancing trade by increasing corn imports. Repeal was made the touchstone of an industrial economy. The league insisted that landlords should lose their special social and political power and that farmers should behave like businessmen. At the same time it appealed to the working classes by offering cheap food.

The tactics of the league provoked substantial criticism, but Sir Robert Peel, who became Conservative prime minister in 1841, followed a policy of freeing trade that culminated logically in his government's repeal of the corn laws in 1846. Peel paid a high political price—a split in his party—but he was supported in the critical debates by many individuals, including some landlords and many businessmen who had no sympathy with the Anti-Corn-Law League. Peel, however, paid a generous tribute to Cobden, whose arguments based on economic change and social justice were the basis of the government's own.

Repeal came into full effect in 1849, not in time, however, to materially assist the Irish, who faced famine in 1846 and whose plight had moved Peel. A small remaining nominal duty on all corn imports was abolished in 1869. By that time Britain had adopted a full free-trade policy that continued until 1932. The corn laws were never reintroduced, even during the severe depression that followed the prosperity of the 1850's and 1860's.

ASA BRIGGS, *University of Sussex*
*Author of "The Age of Improvement"*

**CORN SALAD** is an annual herb, *Valerianella locusta*, var. *olitoria*, used as a potherb or in salads. It is also called lamb's lettuce or field salad. It grows about 1 foot (30.5 mm) high, its spoon-shaped leaves forming a rosette. It has light blue flowers. Since corn salad leaves have relatively little taste, they normally are mixed with more flavorsome greens in the preparation of salads.

**CORNEA,** kôr′nē-ə, a transparent structure that lies directly over the pupil of the eye. The cornea is part of the sclera, the outermost coat of the eyeball. Although the cornea has no blood vessels, it does contain many nerves and is extremely sensitive to touch. It is kept moist by the constant flow of tears and other secretions from glands in the eyelids. See also EYE—*Anatomy and Physiology* (Sclera and Cornea).

BERNARD KRONENBERG, M. D.
*New York Medical College*

**CORNEILLE,** kôr-nā′, **Pierre** (1606–1684), French dramatist, who was one of the great writers of the classical age. The founder of French tragedy, he is called the French Shakespeare. Corneille has been variously acclaimed as a moralist in the garb of a dramatist, as a "professor of energy" exalting man's power to impress his own will on his destiny, and as an idealist upholding heroism and the stern cult of duty against the claims of sentiment. His characters do indeed attempt to resolve their inner conflicts and transcend their lowest qualities.

But Corneille, having an extraordinary flair for the dramatic, is primarily a great inventor of plots, the most varied and inexhaustible plot maker that France has produced. He equaled the dramatic achievements of the ancient Greeks and the Elizabethans, and he has continued to captivate audiences through more than three centuries.

**Early Life.** Corneille was born in Rouen on June 6, 1606, into a family of lawyers and officials. He was educated by the Jesuits, who stressed Latin and theatrical performances. As a student Corneille was impressed by Seneca and the other Stoics and by the fiery Roman poet Lucan. He then read law, but he felt either too shy because of a stammer or too literary to enter practice. His characters, however, were to prove superb debaters and impeccable reasoners.

Corneille spent most of his life as a magistrate in Rouen with occasional trips to Paris. In his early 20's he composed a comedy, *Mélite* (1629–1630), which was well received in Paris. For the next few years he wrote comedies of love and intrigue, such as *La Veuve* (1634). Next to his rival Molière, Corneille was the finest comic writer of his day, and his most original comedy, *L'illusion comique* (1635), is still staged.

**Middle Years.** In the 1630's public taste was beginning to favor tragedy over comedy. Cardinal Richelieu wrote tragedies himself and encouraged other dramatists, including Corneille, to depict heroic characters acting under powerful emotions.

Corneille's *Le Cid,* a tragicomedy ending with the promise of eventual happiness, was produced in 1637. The play was based on an earlier Spanish drama about the medieval hero Rodrigo Díaz de Bivar (the Cid), and the French Rodrigue, like his prototype, is an impetuous warrior against the Moors. But he is more rational, more tender, and psychologically more refined. The

Pierre Corneille,
from a portrait by
Charles LeBrun

GIRAUDON

play centers on the conflict between honor and passion. Honor causes Rodrigue to kill the father of Chimène, the lady he loves, in a duel, and Chimène, although deeply attached to Rodrigue, feels bound by honor to demand his punishment. The struggle within the protagonists is complicated by the fact that the two opposing forces are inextricably intertwined. Honor is passionately cherished, and love is ennobled by the sense of honor. The play's poetry is fresh and ardent, its structure faultless. *Le Cid* scored a triumph with the public, although a cabal of jealous poets charged Corneille with violating the unities of time, space, and action—the Aristotelian principles of drama—which were part of the developing French classicism.

In 1640, Corneille repeated his success with two tragedies on Roman historical subjects—*Horace* and *Cinna. Polyeucte* (1642) was a bold attempt to produce a tragedy on a religious subject. In the play an Armenian nobleman suddenly embraces Christianity and becomes a fanatical hater of pagans. He prefers martyrdom to the society of his haughty Roman wife, who, however, follows him to conversion and death.

Unlike Shakespeare's tragedies with their multiplicity of characters and scenes, these three tragedies strictly regard the classical unities, concentrating the action in a few individuals in a limited time and space. The plays are considered the high point of Corneille's achievement, and *Polyeucte,* although coolly received in his time, is now hailed as his masterpiece.

**Later Years.** By the mid-1640's, Corneille had mastered his technique; his verse flowed forth with powerful effect on the stage. In his numerous late plays he attempted diverse subjects with varied and intricate plots, unlike his younger rival Racine, whose plots tended to repeat themselves. In 1644, Corneille produced *Rodogune,* a tragedy of violence. It is expertly constructed but has cascades of incidents and borders on melodrama. The female characters, determined and cruel, are the equals of Lady Macbeth. *Héraclius* (1646–1647), even more involved, displays Corneille's aversion to the extreme economy insisted on by the purer classicism of Racine.

Corneille, meanwhile, had not altogether forsaken comedy. *Le Menteur* (1643), adapted from a Spanish comedy of intrigue, displays a brilliant verve, and *Don Sanche d' Aragon* (1649), a curious heroic comedy, has stylistic brilliance.

When the play *Pertharite* (1651) failed to please audiences, Corneille stopped writing dramas for a while. In 1660 he published his reflections on the technique of tragedy, one of the important critical studies of the period. Later came more plays—*Attila* (1667), *Tite et Bérénice* (1670), and *Suréna* (1674)—but by this time Racine and others, more expert than Corneille at delineating love and writing less sculptural but more musical and tender verse, had captured the public fancy.

Corneille's last years were melancholy. Impoverished and out of favor, he withdrew from the theatrical world and wrote Christian verse. He died in Paris on Sept. 30, 1684.

HENRI PEYRE, *Yale University*

**Further Reading:** Barnwell, H. T., *The Tragic Drama of Corneille and Racine: An Old Parallel Revisited* (Oxford 1982); Greenberg, Mitchell, *Corneille, Classicism and the Ruses of Symmetry* (Cambridge 1986); Lodge, Lee D., *A Study in Corneille* (Gordon Press 1976).

**CORNEILLE,** kôr-nā′yə, **Thomas** (1625–1709), French dramatist. The younger brother of the playwright Pierre Corneille (q.v.), he had great facility in pleasing the average, often mediocre, taste of audiences. Although he enjoyed an extraordinary vogue in his lifetime, his plays are rarely presented today.

Thomas Corneille was born in Rouen, Normandy, on Aug. 20, 1625. He was educated by the Jesuits, excelled in Latin poetry, and read law. His early plays were comedies based on Spanish themes. Then, following popular tastes, he looked to the novel for intricate plots with exaggerated heroes. His *Timocrate* (1656), for example, based on a novel by La Calprenède, involves a masked warrior fighting in two opposing camps. The play was the greatest success of the century. *La mort de l'empereur Commode* (1658), dealing with the crimes and suicide of the Roman emperor, is more ambitious and better constructed. One of Corneille's best works is *Ariane* (1672), about Phèdre's daughter who was abandoned by Theseus. He also turned Molière's *Don Juan* into the popular verse play *Le festin de pierre* (1677). In 1685, Corneille became a member of the French Academy, for which he compiled two dictionaries. He died at Les Andelys, Eure, on Dec. 8, 1709.

HENRI PEYRE, *Yale University*

**CORNEJO,** kôr-ne′hō, **Mariano Harlan** (1870–1941), Peruvian diplomat and legal expert. He was born at Arequipa, Peru, on Oct. 29, 1870. He received a degree in jurisprudence at the University of Lima in 1889 and became a professor of law there in 1895. He was a member of the Chamber of Deputies from 1893 to 1903 and a senator from 1911 to 1920. A delegate to the constituent assembly of 1919–1920, he was the principal author of the Constitution of 1920.

As minister to Ecuador (1904), he negotiated the Cornejo-Valverde Treaty in an attempt to settle a long-standing boundary dispute. He later became minister to France (1920–1931). He also served on the Permanent Court of International Justice and drew up its code of criminal procedure. He died in Paris in 1941.

Cornejo was one of Peru's main contacts with European affairs. In the late 19th century he was one of a small group of intellectuals who advanced the view that nationalism should be directed toward encouraging educational reform, social progress, and the modern scientific spirit.

LAURENCE R. BIRNS
*The New School for Social Research, New York*

**CORNELIA,** kôr-nēl′yə, Roman matron of the 2d century B. C., whose name is synonymous with Roman matronal virtue because of her devotion to the care and education of her children. She was the daughter of Scipio Africanus and the wife of Tiberius Sempronius Gracchus, to whom she bore 12 children, boys and girls in alternating order. Widowed in 154 B. C., she saw to the education of her children and refused to marry even the king of Egypt.

Of her children, only three survived. These were Sempronia, who married Scipio Aemilianus, and two sons, Tiberius and Gaius Gracchus, both of whom lost their lives attempting to reform the state. Her declaration that she would rather be known as the mother of the Gracchi than as the daughter of Scipio Africanus is carved on the base of a statue. Both in the late Republic and in the Empire, she was remembered for her motherly concern, her own erudition, and her interest in Greek culture.

Another Cornelia, daughter of Metellus Scipio, married P. Crassus, the son of the triumvir Crassus, in 55 B. C. Upon his death she married the triumvir Pompey in 52 B.C.

RICHARD E. MITCHELL
*University of Illinois*

**CORNELIUS,** kôr-nēl′yəs, **Saint,** pope from 251 to 253. His election was delayed because of the persecution of Emperor Decius, during which time the Roman church was governed by a college of priests. During the persecution many Christians proved weak and broke away from the church. Soon after Cornelius' election, in March 251, he encountered opposition on the treatment of these apostates. Though he demanded penance from the backsliders, the rigorists denounced him, and their leader Novitian set himself up as an antipope. The intervention of St. Cyprian ended in Cornelius' victory and the excommunication of Novitian.

Peace, however, was short-lived. A plague caused the people once again to blame the Christians, and there was a new outbreak of persecution. But Cornelius' leadership prevented the many apostasies of the earlier persecution. Cornelius was exiled to Centum Cellae, where he was apparently martyred in 253. His feast, along with that of St. Cyprian, is celebrated on September 16.

JOSEPH S. BRUSHER, S. J.
*University of Santa Clara*

**CORNELIUS,** kôr-nēl′yəs, was a centurion of an Italian cohort, and the first Gentile to be baptized as a Christian without submitting to the ceremonial laws of the Jews. He is described in Acts 10 of the Bible as a well-respected adherent of the Mosaic religion, though not a full proselyte. A vision advised Cornelius to send for Peter, who also had had a vision telling him that he should consider no man impure, thus permitting the apostle to dine with Cornelius. Later, the Holy Spirit appeared before Peter, who baptized Cornelius. The protests of the Jewish Christians over his act led Peter to defend the baptism and meal at the Council of Jerusalem.

The incident emphasizes the efforts to bring Gentiles into the church without obliging them to be circumcised or to follow the dietary laws. It was used in addition to demonstrate that any man who feared God and did right was acceptable to Him.

**CORNELIUS,** kôr-nā′lē-o͞os, **Peter** (1824–1874), German composer of operas and songs. He was born on Dec. 24, 1824, in Mainz. He was briefly on the stage but soon shifted to music. After being music critic for two Berlin journals, he joined the circle around Liszt in Weimar devoted to encouraging new forms of music. His best-known work is the delicate, elegant comic opera *Der Barbier von Bagdad* (1858; based on *A Thousand and One Nights*), which sought to express these new forms. The opera, whose premiere was conducted by Liszt, was not fully appreciated until a revival in 1885.

Cornelius left Weimar for Vienna, where he became friendly with Wagner. A second opera, *Der Cid,* produced in Weimar in 1865, was successful. Cornelius then moved, with Wagner, to Munich and became a professor at the conservatory there. Much of his best music is in his songs, many written to his own poetry. The opera *Gunlöd* (based on the *Edda*) was unfinished at the time of his death in Mainz on Oct. 26, 1874.

**CORNELIUS,** kôr-nā′lē-o͞os, **Peter von** (1783–1867), German painter, who shared leadership of the Nazarene movement with Johann Overbeck. Cornelius' paintings are now generally considered cold, mechanical, and too dependent on 15th century models. Yet he had considerable influence on younger artists through his teaching, forceful personality, and organizational talents.

Cornelius was born in Düsseldorf, probably on Sept. 23, 1783. Because his father was director of the city's art gallery, Cornelius became familiar with art at an early age. In his youth he was swept away by the romantic passion for the Middle Ages, and his first important works were illustrations for the *Nibelungenlied* and for Goethe's *Faust.* When he showed his drawings to Goethe in 1811, the poet tactfully suggested that Cornelius go to Italy for further study.

Cornelius left that year for Rome, where he joined the circle of artists around Johann Overbeck known as the Brotherhood of St. Luke. These artists, now commonly called Nazarenes, lived in the abandoned monastery of Sant'Isidoro, where they attempted to revive the communal ideals of the Middle Ages, believing that great art depends on collective endeavor. One of Cornelius' characteristic paintings of this period, *The Wise and Foolish Virgins* (Kunstmuseum, Düsseldorf), reveals the reverence for Raphael common to all the Nazarenes.

In 1814, Cornelius hit upon the idea of reviving the moribund technique of fresco painting. Given a commission to decorate the walls of the Casa Bartholdy in Rome, Cornelius, Overbeck, Philipp Veit, Wilhelm Schadow, and Franz Catel painted a fresco cycle illustrating the story of Joseph. This work was much admired at the time and assured the fame of the group.

In 1819, Cornelius returned to Germany. He settled in Munich, where the patronage of King Ludwig I of Bavaria enabled him to embark on an ambitious series of religious and secular commissions. In 1841 he went to London to advise on the fresco decorations of the new Parliament building. During Cornelius' last years, which were spent at the Prussian court in Berlin, his increasingly rigid outlook cramped his artistic vision and powers. Cornelius died in Berlin on March 6, 1867.

WAYNE DYNES
*Vassar College*

**CORNELL, Alonzo Barton,** kôr-nel' (1832–1904), American businessman and public official. He was born in Ithaca, N.Y., on Jan. 22, 1832. A son of Ezra Cornell, he was a director of the Western Union Telegraph Company from 1868 to 1899. He served as chairman of the New York State Republican Committee (1870–1878); surveyor of customs, New York (1869–1873); and speaker of the New York Assembly (1873).

Cornell was appointed naval officer in the New York customhouse in 1877, before serving as governor of New York from 1880 to 1883. As governor he appointed competent staff, modernized the state finances, and vetoed extravagant legislation. He died in Ithaca on Oct. 15, 1904.

**CORNELL, Ezra,** kôr-nel' (1807–1874), American capitalist and philanthropist who helped develop a nationwide telegraph system in the United States and founded Cornell University in Ithaca, N.Y. He was born in Westchester Landing, N.Y., on Jan. 11, 1807, the eldest of 11 children of a Quaker potter. After a limited formal education he began to assist his father. Moving upstate, to De Ruyter, N.Y., he worked as a carpenter, mechanic, and millwright. In 1828 he settled in Ithaca. By 1830 he was manager of flour and plaster mills.

Cornell became active in Whig politics and speculated in real estate. When he lost his job in 1841, he leased a farm and experimented with crop and herd improvement. He soon became an agent for a local plow manufacturer. While selling in Maine, he met Francis O. J. Smith, who was part owner of Samuel F. B. Morse's patent for the telegraph. Cornell sketched a machine to lay wires underground, and Smith promptly hired him to direct construction in 1844 of the world's first telegraph line, from Washington, D.C., to Baltimore, Md.

Thenceforward, Cornell devoted himself to developing the use of the telegraph, which until the telephone was invented in 1876 was the only type of rapid communication. Beginning as construction foreman, he became president of his first telegraph company in 1847 and soon had lines from New York to Philadelphia and into the Middle West. When the Western Union Telegraph Company was formed, by merger, in 1855, Cornell became its chief stockholder, a position he held for 15 years.

After the merger, Cornell returned to Ithaca to devote himself to farming and public service. He was elected to the New York state assembly (1861–1863) and the state senate (1863–1867). An increasing fortune, eventually estimated at $4 million, enabled him to make philanthropic contributions, such as the gift to Tompkins county of the Cornell Public Library in Ithaca in 1863. His most important philanthropies were to Cornell University, a land-grant institution, which with the advice of Andrew Dickson White, a fellow state senator, he established in 1865 and generously endowed. Cornell died in Ithaca on Dec. 9, 1874.

HERBERT FINCH
*Cornell University*

**CORNELL, Joseph,** kôr-nel' (1903–1972), American artist who was internationally acclaimed for his innovative contributions to assemblage, collage, and films made between 1931 and 1972. He is best known for intimately scaled box constructions that helped to define assemblage—an ap-

proach to creating three-dimensional works of art from found materials—as a new territory for 20th-century artists as diverse as Louise Nevelson, Robert Rauschenberg, and Edward Kienholz.

Cornell was born on Dec. 24, 1903, in Nyack, N.Y. He attended Phillips Academy in Andover, Mass., as a science major between 1917 and 1921, after which he did not pursue higher formal education or art training. Between 1921 and 1931 he was a textile salesman in New York City. Christian Science, to which he converted around 1925, remained a lifelong influence. In 1929 Cornell moved with his mother and invalid brother to Flushing, Queens, N.Y., where he lived until his death, on Dec. 29, 1972.

In 1940 Cornell devoted himself to making art, after almost a decade of creative experimentation inspired by exploring New York City's cultural resources since moving to Queens in 1921. Most significant was his exposure to the surrealist painters and sculptors who had fled to the United States because of Europe's turbulent political atmosphere during the 1930s (he first displayed his work in a surrealist exhibition at the Julian Levy Gallery in 1932). The surrealists' emphasis on spontaneous creativity and the transformation of found objects accelerated Cornell's desire to make collages, small constructions, and films from the materials he had first collected in the 1920s as souvenirs of his interests in the arts, humanities, and sciences.

Averaging 14 by 9 by 5 inches (36 by 23 by 13 cm), Cornell's glass-paned box constructions resemble miniature theaters or shadow boxes that intermingle a sense of reality and poetry in their evocative union of form and content. From humble and unrelated materials such as clay pipes, watch springs, seashells, broken glass, stamps, and cutouts from publications and engravings, he created images and themes that addressed the passage of time, the perception of beauty and knowledge in the commonplace, and the cult of personality (a number of his constructions were homages to famous actresses and dancers whom he, a reclusive bachelor, admired from afar). Recurring in his collages and films, these concerns and his exploration of art as an act of selection and transformation account for the highly indi-

Joseph Cornell's *Soap Bubble Set* (1947–1948) evokes a miniature universe with a celestial theme. Like surrealist cabinets of curiosity, the artist's box constructions comprised mundane objects in arcane arrangements.

vidualistic yet broadly uplifting sensibility consistently attributed to his work.

LYNDA ROSCOE HARTIGAN
*Curator, National Museum of American Art*

### Bibliography

Ashton, Dore, *A Joseph Cornell Album* (1974; reprint, Da Capo 1989).

Caws, Mary Ann, ed., *Joseph Cornell's Theater of the Mind* (Thames & Hudson 1993).

McShine, Kynaston, ed., *Joseph Cornell* (1980; reprint, Mus. of Modern Art/te Neues 1990).

O'Doherty, Brian, "Joseph Cornell: Outsider on the Left," in *American Masters: The Voice and the Myth* (Random House 1973).

Tashjian, Dickran, *Joseph Cornell: Gifts of Desire* (Grassfield Press 1992).

**CORNELL, Katharine,** kôr-nel' (1893–1974), American actress, often called the "first lady of the theater." She was especially identified with the role of Elizabeth Barrett Browning in *The Barretts of Wimpole Street*, which she played more than 700 times.

Born of American parents in Berlin, Germany, on Feb. 16, 1893, Cornell grew up in Buffalo, N.Y., where her father managed a theater. She made her professional debut in 1917 with the Washington Square Players in New York City and achieved stardom in 1921 in *A Bill of Divorcement*. That same year she married Guthrie McClintic, who became her business partner and directed most of her later performances. In 1931 she formed her own production company for the presentation of *The Barretts of Wimpole Street*, and in 1933–1934 she took the play on one of the longest tours in American theatrical history, performing in some 75 cities. She died in Martha's Vineyard, Mass., on June 9, 1974.

Cornell also gave celebrated performances in *Will Shakespeare* (1923), *Candida* (1924 and frequent revivals), *Romeo and Juliet* (1934), *Saint Joan* (1936), *The Three Sisters* (1942), *The Constant Wife* (1951), and *Dear Liar* (1960). She wrote two autobiographical volumes, *I Wanted to Be an Actress* (1939) and *Curtain Going Up* (1943).

HOWARD SUBER
*University of California at Los Angeles*

**Bibliography:** Mosel, Tad, and Gertrude Macy, *Leading Lady: The World and Theatre of Katharine Cornell* (Little, Brown 1978); Pederson, Lucille M., *Katharine Cornell: A Bio-Bibliography* (Greenwood Press 1993).

**CORNELL UNIVERSITY,** in Ithaca, N.Y., a unique institution among American universities in that it is both an independent Ivy League institution of higher education and the land-grant university of the state of New York. It also includes the Medical College and the Graduate School of Medical Science, both located in New York City. It was founded in 1865 when Ezra Cornell and Andrew Dickson White, then both senators in the New York state legislature, decided to combine Cornell's land and resources with the proceeds from the sale of the public land awarded to New York state under the Morrill federal land-grant college act of 1862 to establish a university. White became the first president of the university, committed to Ezra Cornell's decision to "found an institution where any person can find instruction in any study."

Cornell University operates four state-supported colleges of the State University of New York (SUNY): the New York State College of Agriculture and Life Sciences, the New York State College of Human Ecology, the New York State School of Industrial and Labor Relations, and the New York State College of Veterinary Medicine. The privately endowed colleges consist of the College of Arts and Sciences; the College of Architecture, Art, and Planning; the College of Engineering; the School of Hotel Administration; the Law School; the Graduate School; the Samuel Curtis Johnson Graduate School of Management; the Medical College; and the Graduate School of Medical Science. Many interdisciplinary programs are offered as well.

**Research Centers.** When the faculty and graduate students from more than one school or college wish to work together in a continuing collaboration concentrated on a special subject, a center for this purpose is created within the university. The ten specialized centers in operation at Cornell reflect the diversity of subjects covered: the Materials Science Center, the Statistical Center, the Water Resources Center, the Center for Housing and Environmental Studies, the Center for International Studies, the Radiophysics and Space Research Center, the Center for Applied Mathematics, the Aviation Safety Center, the Center for Environmental Quality Management, and the Center for Research in Education. Cornell's Laboratory of Nuclear Studies operates a federally financed 10-billion electron volt synchrotron. The Center for International Studies coordinates the work of a series of special academic programs devoted to such foreign area studies as the Southeast Asia program, the China program, the Latin American program, the international agricultural development program, and the international population program.

**Facilities.** Cornell's activities are centered mainly in Ithaca, on a campus comprising more than 90 major buildings on several hundred acres of land. The university owns an aeronautical laboratory in Buffalo, N.Y. Cornell also operates the New York State Agricultural Experiment Station in Geneva, N.Y.; administers cooperative extension programs in every county of New York state; has research teams at work in a number of foreign countries, notably the Philippines, Peru, Colombia, and Liberia; and operates the huge, federally funded space radar telescope in Arecibo, Puerto Rico. Buildings of interest on the Ithaca campus include the Uris undergraduate library, with its 183-foot (56-meter) bell tower, a university landmark; the John M. Olin Library, completed in 1961; Willard Straight Hall, the student union; and the Statler Inn. Among more recent improvements are additions to the classroom and research building, the Hotel School, and the Space Science addition. There is also a new Performing Arts Center, Alumni Athletic Field House, and Biotechnology Research building.

The university's libraries house special collections on Dante, Petrarch, Pascal, Wordsworth, Kipling, Joyce, and Shaw. Other important library holdings include the Wason Collection on China and the Chinese, the Echols Collection on Southeast Asia, and the History of Science Collection. There are also units devoted to Americana (including regional history), Icelandic literature, China and Southeast Asia, abolition and slavery, superstition, and many other areas of interest. The Cornell University Press, which was founded in 1869, is one of the oldest university presses in the United States. It publishes more than 75 titles annually. Scholarly magazines issued from Cornell include the *Administrative Science Quarterly, Cornell Engineering Quarterly, Cornell Hotel and Restaurant Administration Quarterly, Cornell Plantations, Cornell Veterinary Quarterly, Diacritics, Graduate School of Nutrition News, Human Ecology, Industrial Labor Relations Review, Law Forum,* and *Philosphical Review.*

STEVEN MULLER*, *Cornell University*

**CORNER, George Washington** (1889–1981), American medical biologist who made several important contributions to the understanding of female sex hormones and the menstrual cycle and was the first to recover an egg from the oviduct of a primate. Corner was the first to prove that the corpus luteum (the small, yellowish mass of cells that forms in an egg follicle after an egg has been expelled from the ovary) causes the lining of the uterus to undergo changes necessary for the survival of an embryo. With the biochemist Willard Allen, Corner then prepared a partially purified corpus luteum extract that was responsible for changing the uterine lining. This extract was subsequently further purified by Allen, who isolated the hormone now known as progesterone.

Relating his findings about the corpus luteum to the menstrual cycle (a phenomenon occurring only in humans and other primates), Corner obtained the first reliable evidence that menstruation is not always associated with ovulation. Working with monkeys he found that the breakdown and sloughing off of the uterine lining in menstruation is directly related to the degeneration of the corpus luteum.

Corner was born in Baltimore, Md., on Dec. 12, 1889. He attended Johns Hopkins University, receiving his medical degree in 1913. He was an assistant professor of anatomy at the University of California at Berkeley from 1915 to 1919, then returned to Johns Hopkins as an associate professor. In 1923 he became a professor at the University of Rochester School of Medicine, but in 1940 he returned to Baltimore, where he directed the embryology department of Carnegie Institute until 1955. After 1963 he was executive officer, then editor, at the American Philosophical Society in Philadelphia. His books include *The Hormones in Human Reproduction* (1942), *Ourselves Unborn* (1944), and *Anatomist at Large* (1958). Corner died in Huntsville, Ala., on Sept. 28, 1981.

ALFRED NOVAK, *Stephens College*

**CORNER,** in business and finance, a situation in which the ownership of a product, commodity, or security becomes so concentrated that short sellers are unable to secure the goods in question except from one owner group. Corners have occurred most often on the stock exchanges or the commodity markets. Even on these markets, corners are now of historical interest only. The most recent attempt at a corner on the New York Stock Exchange occurred in 1923 and failed as the exchange suspended trading in the stock.

A corner develops with a sharp rise in the price of a stock, whether natural or manipulated. As the price rises, some speculators sell the stock short. That is, they sell stock that they do not own, at the current price, for future delivery, expecting a price decline. They hope to buy the stock for delivery later, at a lower price, thereby making a profit. Short sellers often borrow stock to make the initial delivery and then must make delivery to the lender on demand.

If there is only one source from which the stock can be bought in quantity to cover short-sale deliveries, the short sellers must settle with the controlling source at the source's price. At this point the short sellers are cornered. Such activity is possible on a major scale only on highly organized markets, such as the stock exchanges or commodity markets.

Corners have arisen both naturally and from manipulation. Natural corners occur when an owner has such a large amount of one stock that he or she can control the price. In a manipulated corner a group is formed deliberately to gain control of the "floating supply" of a stock—the shares actually available for trading purposes at any one time.

Stock exchanges and commodity markets have long viewed corner activity with disfavor. In the United States the Securities Exchange Act of 1934 gave the Securities and Exchange Commission authority over stock-exchange trading practices. Manipulative corners are expressly outlawed in the act, and even a natural—that is, unplanned—corner is subject to immediate investigation to determine whether criminal proceedings should be instituted.

WILLIAM N. KINNARD, JR.
*University of Connecticut*

**CORNER BROOK,** an industrial and commercial city on the west coast of Newfoundland, Canada, at the mouth of the Humber River. It is Newfoundland's second-largest city in population and economic importance after St. John's. Corner Brook is the site of one of the world's biggest newsprint mills; it also has a cement factory and a gypsum plant. The city has long been a center of the herring fisheries of the Bay of Islands area. The Humber River provides excellent salmon fishing.

Corner Brook was formed by the amalgamation of four towns—Corner Brook East, Corner Brook West, Curling, and Townsite—and was incorporated as a city on April 27, 1955. Population: 21,893.

ALLAN M. FRASER
*Provincial Archivist of Newfoundland*

**CORNET,** kôr-net', a valved brass instrument similar to and identical in range with the B-flat trumpet. It was developed in France in the 1820s by the addition of valves (pistons) to the small, coiled post horn (cornet). Hence its full name—*cornet-à-pistons.* It should not be confused with the earlier cornett, a rudimentary woodwind.

The cornet has a gently expanding bore and a cup-shaped mouthpiece slightly deeper than that of the trumpet. (Some players prefer to use a standard trumpet mouthpiece.) It is commonly constructed in the key of B flat; however, it may be

Cornet.

G. LEBLANC CORP.

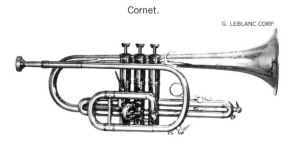

lowered to A by the addition of a length of tubing, or "shank." There is also an E-flat model used exclusively in wind bands.

The cornet earned its first popularity in dance bands, with the result that it was regarded as a vulgar instrument. Toward the end of the 19th century it briefly replaced the trumpet in many orchestras in England and the United States, but since then it has been used principally in brass and parade bands.

Rossini used the cornet in scoring *William Tell* (1829), and other opera composers—Meyerbeer, Bizet, and Gounod—followed his lead. Stravinsky assigned the cornet a rambunctious solo in the first version of *Petrouchka* (1911) but redesignated the part for trumpet in the revised score (1949).

SHIRLEY FLEMING
*Editor of "Musical America"*

**CORNFLOWER** is a name commonly applied to two unrelated plants. Probably the best-known species is *Centaurea cyanus*, which belongs to the composite family. Also known as *bachelor's button,* it is a very popular garden annual, ranging in height from 1 to 2 feet (30–60 cm) and bearing white, pink, or blue flower heads 1 to 2 inches (25 to 50 mm) wide. Native to southern Europe, this species grows best in full sunshine and is propagated by seed, either sown in the greenhouse and transplanted to pots or sown in the garden after the danger of frost is past.

The other cornflower, *Uvularia grandiflora,* is a hardy perennial wild flower of the lily family. It ranges from Quebec to Georgia and grows about 1½ feet (45 cm) tall. Its drooping, yellow, bell-shaped flowers are 1½ inches (37 mm) long and the alternate leaves are lanced-shaped. The rootstock of this species is thick and creeping, and propagation is best by a simple division of the roots in the early fall.

DONALD WYMAN
*The Arnold Arboretum, Harvard University*

**CORNFORD, Frances Crofts** (1886–1960), English poet. A granddaughter of Charles Darwin, she was born in Cambridge, England, on March 30, 1886. In 1909 she married Francis Macdonald Cornford, a fellow and lecturer of Trinity College, Cambridge. She died in Cambridge on Aug. 19, 1960.

Mrs. Cornford used traditional poetic techniques as well as traditional poetic themes. Her verse, from her first volume, *Poems* (1910), to her *Collected Poems* (1954), is quiet and grave—evocative of the countryside around Cambridge, the seasons, familiar friends, and homely events.

Mrs. Cornford's volumes include *Spring Morning* (1915), in which she emerged as a distinct poetic personality; *Different Days* (1928); and *Mountains and Molehills* (1935).

**CORNHILL MAGAZINE,** an English literary monthly, founded in 1860 by George M. Smith of Smith, Elder and Company. Its first editor was William Makepeace Thackeray. The periodical took its name from Cornhill Street, London, the location of its original office. The *Cornhill Magazine* published works by John Ruskin, George Eliot, Matthew Arnold, and Anthony Trollope, as well as Thackeray's last three novels, *Lovel the Widower, The Adventures of Philip,* and *Denis Duval.* The magazine's later editors included Sir Leslie Stephen, who was Thackeray's

RUSS KINNE, FROM PHOTO RESEARCHERS

Cornflowers

son-in-law and Virginia Woolf's father, and Sir John Murray, who also edited the *Quarterly Review.* The *Cornhill Magazine* ceased publication in 1939 because of paper shortages that developed in World War II.

**CORNICE,** kôr'nis, in classical architecture, the uppermost of the three horizontal bands that form an entablature supported by a row of stone columns. The term "cornice" is also used in a general sense for any similar feature at the top of a wall or above a door or window.

The classical cornice, corresponding to the eaves of a wooden roof, projects beyond the lower two parts of the entablature—the frieze and the architrave. Because a block of stone can overhang its support only slightly, the projection of a cornice is achieved gradually by building up a series of moldings, each overhanging the one below. The top molding is the *cyma,* of reversed curve profile, which may incorporate waterspouts. Below the cyma is the *corona,* or principal projecting molding, which forms a flat strip. Under the corona are minor bed moldings, which rest on forms that vary according to the different classical orders of Greek architecture. In the Doric order these forms, called *mutules,* are thin, closely spaced, sloping slabs decorated with *guttae,* or peglike pendants. They derive from the ends of wooden roofing planks and

CORNICE, in classical architecture, surmounts the frieze, forming the uppermost part of the entablature.

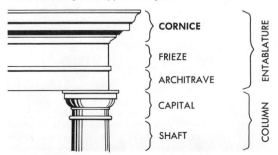

from wooden pegs used in earlier Greek buildings. In the Ionic order, the mutules and guttae are replaced by a dentil range, or row of plain, closely spaced blocks similar to teeth. In the Corinthian order, the dentil range becomes a series of larger, widely spaced blocks called *modillions*. See also GREEK ARCHITECTURE.

EVERARD M. UPJOHN, *Columbia University*

**CORNING, Erastus** (1794–1872), American merchant, manufacturer, financier, and politician, who played a significant role in the industrial and commercial development of New York state. A leading hardware merchant and iron manufacturer, he put his profits from these sources into land companies and railroads, promoting the formation of the New York Central Railroad and becoming its first president.

Corning was born in Norwich, Conn., on Dec. 14, 1794. Working for his uncle in a hardware store in Troy, N. Y., he gained the experience to establish his own business in Albany. His formation of the Corning Land Company in 1835 led to construction of a railroad into Pennsylvania and a canal from the Chemung River to the Erie Canal, as well as to the commercial and industrial growth of the community of Corning, N. Y. He served four terms as mayor of Albany and was a state senator from 1842 to 1846, a member of Congress for two terms, and a leading figure in the Democratic party. He died in Albany on April 9, 1872.

NORMAN A. MERCER, *Union College*

**CORNING** is a city in south central New York, in Steuben county, situated on the Chemung River, on the fringe of the Finger Lakes region. It is the home of the Corning Glass Works, a leading manufacturer of technical glass in both volume and diversification.

The Corning Glass Center, built in 1951 to celebrate the 100th anniversary of the glass works, is a unique tourist and educational attraction. On view is the original casting of the 200-inch (508-cm) reflector made at Corning in 1934 for the observatory on Mt. Palomar in California. The Museum of Glass displays glass from the world's great civilizations. Exhibits in the Hall of Science and Industry show the part played by glass in today's world, and the museum library contains a notable collection of printed works on glass. At the Steuben Glass factory visitors may watch craftsmen at work, hand forming and engraving Steuben crystal.

Corning was incorporated as a village in 1848 and named for Erastus Corning, a New York state financier. It was incorporated as a city in 1890 and has a mayor-council form of government. Population: 10,842.

NANCY J. PERRIN, *Corning Public Library*

**CORNISH LANGUAGE AND LITERATURE.** See CELTIC LANGUAGES; CELTIC LITERATURES.

**CORNPLANTER** (1746?–1836), American Indian chief of the Seneca, who figured prominently in United States-Indian relations, signing treaties and generally promoting peace. The son of a Dutch trader and a Seneca woman, he also was known as *John Abeel* (*O'Bail*).

Cornplanter claimed to have fought as a boy against Gen. Edward Braddock (July 1755) during the French and Indian War. In the American Revolution he opposed patriot Gen. John Sullivan's 1779 invasion of the Iroquois country. Thereafter he favored peace. In the treaties of Fort Stanwix (1784) and Fort Harmar (1789) he assented to unpopular land cessions, and his life was threatened. In 1791 he attempted to prevent the Western Indians from making war. The federal government awarded him an annuity and a land grant below the junction of the Connewango and Allegheny rivers. There he raised horses and cattle, and he permitted the establishment of a Quaker school. Though he became a Christian, he was disillusioned with the whites at the time of his death on Feb. 18, 1836.

DAVID H. CORKRAN, *Author of*
*"The Cherokee Frontier"; "The Creek Frontier"*

**CORNSTALK** (1720?–1777), American Indian warrior. A Shawnee chief, he warred against the white settlers during the colonial and Revolutionary periods, and his murder incited the Shawnee to further hostility.

Cornstalk led war parties against the Virginia frontier in 1759 and 1763. Thereafter he was friendly to the settlers until 1774, when the Shawnee, impelled by murders and encroachments by the whites, demanded war. On Oct. 10, 1774, he led his tribesmen in an all-day battle against the Virginians at Point Pleasant (now in West Virginia), but was defeated and he made peace with the British governor, Lord John Dunmore.

At the start of the American Revolution he tried to keep the Shawnee at peace, and when British intrigue was about to win them over, he went to Point Pleasant to warn the Virginia garrison. However, he was taken hostage and, when a white man was ambushed, frontiersmen murdered him and his son in November 1777.

DAVID H. CORKRAN, *Author of*
*"The Cherokee Frontier"; "The Creek Frontier"*

**CORNUS.** See DOGWOOD.

**CORNWALL** is a county in the extreme southwest of England, adjoining Devon on the east. It occupies a peninsula about 80 miles (130 km) long and 50 miles (80 km) wide at its base, fac-

CORNWALL has numerous harbors on its south coast. This one is at Fowey, a characteristic Cornish town.

NOEL HABGOOD, FROM PHOTO RESEARCHERS

ing the Atlantic Ocean on the north and west and the English Channel on the east and south. Its eastern boundary is marked by the Tamar River. The county includes the Isles of Scilly (see SCILLY ISLES) about 30 miles (50 km) southwest of Land's End, the tip of the peninsula.

Cornwall is known for its beautiful seashore scenery. Inland are windswept moors dotted with abandoned mine buildings, relics of the age when Cornish tin deposits were profitably worked. Bodmin, the county town, gives its name to the great Bodmin Moor, about 800 feet (245 meters) above the sea and rising in places to almost 1,400 feet (425 meters). Conical white "mountains," visible from a distance, are actually spoil from the china clay mines at St. Austell. More than 1 million tons of the clay are exported annually.

Because of its location, Cornwall has the mildest climate in Britain. Market gardens around Penzance, England's most westerly town, and in the Isles of Scilly specialize in early-season flowers and vegetables for English markets. Tresco Isle is noted for its subtropical plants and like other Isles of Scilly is popular with vacationers. St. Mary's is the largest island. On the Atlantic coast of Cornwall, artists tend to congregate in the neighborhood of St. Ives. Falmouth, Cornwall's ocean port, has a good deepwater anchorage and yards for ship repair.

There are many prehistoric remains in Cornwall, and as long ago as the first century B.C. Phoenicians, Greeks, and Romans mined its tin. Roman references to "Ictis" were probably to St. Michael's Mount, a tall granite island just east of Penzance. Cornwall was later occupied by the Celts. King Arthur is said to have held court at Tintagel Castle, on the north coast. Although Bodmin is the traditional county seat, Truro is Cornwall's administrative center. Cornwall is a duchy, and one of the titles of the eldest son of a British monarch is duke of Cornwall. Population: 479,600 (1994 est.).

GORDON STOKES*
*Author of "English Place-Names"*

**CORNWALL,** a city in eastern Ontario, Canada, on the St. Lawrence River, about 50 miles (80 km) southeast of Ottawa. It is the seat of the united counties of Stormont, Dundas, and Glengarry. Situated on the St. Lawrence Seaway and the Cornwall Canal, it is a port of entry. An international bridge connects it with the United States, 9 miles (14 km) east of Massena, N.Y.

Cornwall is an important industrial city, producing cotton and rayon textiles, paper and pulp, flour, machinery, foundry products, chemicals, bedding, and furniture. Building stone is quarried nearby. The city is the trading center for a mixed farming and dairying area.

It was founded in 1784 by United Empire Loyalists, who named it New Johnstown for Sir John Johnson, under whom they had served in the American Revolution. The name was changed in 1797 to Cornwall in honor of the duke of Cornwall, eldest son of George III of England. It was incorporated as a town in 1834 and became a city in 1945. The population was doubled in 1957 by the annexation of considerable land, including Cornwall Island in the St. Lawrence River. Population: 47,403.

**CORNWALL, Earls of.** See GAVESTON, PIERS; RICHARD, EARL OF CORNWALL.

NATIONAL PORTRAIT GALLERY, LONDON

Charles Cornwallis, the British general, in a portrait painted by Thomas Gainsborough in 1783.

**CORNWALLIS,** kôrn-wol'is, **Charles** (1738–1805), British general in the American Revolution and governor general of India. He was born in London on Dec. 31, 1738, the son of the 1st Earl Cornwallis. Educated at Eton and Clare College, Cambridge, he became an ensign in the 1st (Grenadier) Guards just before his 18th birthday. He attended the military academy at Turin, and while serving in Germany during the Seven Years' War rose to lieutenant colonel.

At his father's death in 1763 he became the 2d Earl Cornwallis. He took his seat in the House of Lords, where his abilities and connections led to appointments as aide-de-camp to the king, chief circuit court justice south of the Trent River, and joint vice-treasurer of Ireland.

**Career in North America.** Although opposed to the measures that provoked the American Revolution, he accepted as a duty a command in North America with the rank of major general. He aided the British victory at the Battle of Long Island on Aug. 27–28, 1776. Later that year he pursued Washington's army across New Jersey, halting at New Brunswick on orders from Gen. William Howe. Hurrying forward again after Washington's victory at Trenton on Dec. 26, 1776, Cornwallis failed to entrap the patriots and went into winter quarters. Cornwallis was largely responsible for the British victory at Brandywine, Pa., Sept. 11, 1777, and led British forces into Philadelphia on the 28th.

After a brief visit to England he returned as a lieutenant general, second in command to Sir Henry Clinton. He opposed the evacuation of Philadelphia but accompanied the British Army on its retreat to New York and repulsed the Americans under Gen. Charles Lee at the Battle of Monmouth on June 28, 1778. He again returned to England to attend his ill wife, who died in 1779, but rejoined Clinton in August 1779 and participated in the siege of Charleston, S.C. (April 1–May 12, 1780). When the city fell, Clinton returned to New York. Cornwallis took command of British forces in the South.

On Aug. 16, 1780, at Camden, S. C., Cornwallis routed the army of Gen. Horatio Gates. He boldly pursued the Americans, now commanded by Gen. Nathanael Greene, but Patriot victories at King's Mountain (Oct. 7, 1780) and Cowpens (Jan. 17, 1781) sapped his reserves so that he marched to the coast and entrenched at Yorktown, Va. Surrounded by a superior force of French and American troops, he surrendered on Oct. 19, 1781, virtually ending the war.

**Later Years.** In 1785, Cornwallis was envoy to the court of Frederick the Great of Prussia. From 1786 to 1793 he was governor-general of India, where he made reforms in the civil and military service and personally led the campaigns that won British victory in the Third Mysore War. For this he was created Marquess Cornwallis in 1792 and in 1793 was promoted to general. He was appointed to the cabinet in 1795, and as the only general was responsible for defense. As viceroy of Ireland in 1798 he defeated a rebellion abetted by French troops. As the British plenipotentiary, with Joseph Bonaparte he drew up the treaty for the Peace of Amiens (March 27, 1802). He returned to India as governor-general and died there at Ghazipur on Oct. 5, 1805.

PAUL C. BOWERS, JR.
*The Ohio State University*

**CORO,** kō′rō, is the capital of Falcón state in Venezuela. It is situated near the Caribbean Sea, at the base of the Paraguaná Peninsula, 160 miles (260 km) by road northeast of Maracaibo.

One of the oldest Spanish settlements in South America, Coro was founded in 1527 by Juan de Ampués. From 1529 to 1546 it was colonized by Germans for the banking house of Welser, which had been granted the area for economic development. Under the Welsers, Coro became a slave market, but it also served as a base for the exploration of western Venezuela, notably by Nikolaus Federmann (q.v.). In 1806 the patriot Francisco de Miranda and a few volunteers landed near Coro in premature attempt to liberate Venezuela from Spanish rule.

Venezuela's 20th-century oil prosperity bypassed Coro, although ports were developed and refineries built on the nearby Paraguana peninsula. Coro is chiefly a market town for a rather poor agricultural region whose chief export product is goatskins. Most of the area is too dry for farming. Population: 124,616 (1990 census).

**COROLLA** is the collective name for all the petals of a flower. See FLOWER–*Parts of Flowers.*

**COROMANDEL COAST,** kor-ō-man′dəl, the southeastern coast of India, extending about 450 miles (720 km) from the Cauvery River delta at Point Calimere north to the Kistna River delta. Coromandel is part of the Carnatic region. Its name is probably derived from "Cholamandala," meaning "region of the Chola kingdom" (10th–12th centuries). The coast's rough seas become especially violent during the winter monsoon season and are a major shipping hazard. Although the Kistna, Penner, Vellur, and Cauvery rivers flow across the coast into the Bay of Bengal, there are no good harbors. Madras, the most important port, has an artifical harbor that was constructed at great cost. Other ports are Negapatam and Pondicherry.

HARRY STEWARD, *University of Toronto*

**CORONA,** kə-rō′nə, a city located in southern California, in Riverside county, 40 miles (64 km) southeast of Los Angeles. The city is a packing and shipping center for citrus fruits grown in the area. Glass, ceramics, orchard equipment, and lemon by-products are made there. There is quarrying of clay, sand, and gravel nearby. Corona is governed by a city manager. Population: 124,966.

**CORONA,** kə-rō′nə, in astronomy, the tenuous outermost part of the sun's atmosphere. The corona has a pearly white color and can be observed only during a solar eclipse or by means of a coronagraph. See SUN–*Corona.*

**CORONA,** kə-rō′nə, in meteorology, a sequence of colored rings observed around the sun or moon when these bodies are viewed through thin clouds composed of water droplets. The colors range through the spectrum from a blue inner ring to a red outer ring. The corona is larger when the cloud droplets are smaller. The colors of the corona are produced by the bending of light rays around the edges of the tiny droplets, thus separating the light into the colors of the spectrum. By contrast, a *halo* is a ring around the sun or moon caused by the bending of light rays as they pass through clouds of ice crystals. The innermost, or blue ring, of a corona appears close to the edge of the sun or moon, whereas a halo is separated by an angle of either 22° or 46° from the sun or moon. A corona may be designated as *solar* or *lunar* according to whether it is associated with the sun or moon. On the other hand, to an astronomer the *solar corona* is the outer envelope of the sun, visible during a total eclipse or with an instrument called the *coronagraph.* It is not a phenomenon of the earth's atmosphere.

JAMES E. MILLER, *New York University*

**CORONA AUSTRALIS.** See CONSTELLATION.

**CORONA BOREALIS,** kə-rō′nə bō-rē-al′əs, a summer constellation of the Northern Hemisphere, lying between Boötes and Hercules. The name is Latin for Northern Crown—the crown given by the gods to Ariadne in Greek mythology. The constellation consists of a semicircle of stars, of which the brightest, Alphecca, has a magnitude of 2.22. The star T Coronae is a recurrent nova that increased hundreds of times in brightness in 1866 and again in 1946. See also CONSTELLATION.

**CORONA DISCHARGE,** kə-rō′nə, is a type of electrical conduction that occurs at or around the surface of a high-voltage terminal. Corona discharge happens as a result of ionization of the gas surrounding the terminal; the ionization of the gas is caused by the high voltage.

When the gas is air, the corona discharge appears as a blue glow that is accompanied by the pungent odor of ozone. Arc-over or sparking may occur over an ionized path if the voltage level is increased beyond the corona onset voltage.

The occurrence of corona discharge around a high-voltage transmission line adversely affects the insulators and thereby limits the maximum operating voltage. In research, corona discharges are produced to study the electrical breakdown of gases.

MARVIN BIERMAN, *RCA Institutes Inc.*

**CORONADO,** kō-rō-nä'thō, **Francisco Vásquez de** (1510–1554), Spanish conquistador, who was leader of the expedition that first explored what is now the Southwest of the United States.

Born in Salamanca, Spain, Coronado went to Mexico in 1535 with the first viceroy, Don Antonio de Mendoza. In New Spain he married Doña Beatriz de Estrada, the daughter of the late treasurer of the colony. Mendoza entrusted young Coronado with responsible assignments in and around the capital, and in 1538 named him governor of the frontier province of Nueva Galicia.

One of Coronado's first tasks as governor was to support the reconnaissance expedition of Fray Marcos de Niza to find the so-called Seven Golden Cities of Cíbola. De Niza returned with a glowing report of the cities, as seen from afar. Hopes of great riches soared in New Spain. Viceroy Mendoza planned to undertake the conquest, but he was unable to leave his post and named Coronado in his stead.

**The Great Expedition.** In February 1540 a colorful band—336 soldiers and several hundred Indian allies—left Compostela, capital of Nueva Galicia. At Culiacán, Coronado and a small party set off in advance of the main body of the army. The route led northward along the western slope of the Sierra Madre, through the gorge of the Río Sonora, and up the Valle de Sonora toward the future international boundary. From the upper Gila, Coronado's party trudged through the *despoblado* (wilderness), in eastern Arizona, and finally came to the first of the "cities of Cíbola," the Zuñi pueblo of Háwikuh. Its adobe houses were hardly golden.

From Cíbola, Coronado sent García López de Cárdenas northwest to investigate other rumors of rich towns. Cárdenas and his men found the Hopi towns and beyond them the Grand Canyon of the Colorado, but they uncovered no great riches. Coronado and the army had, meanwhile, pushed eastward to the upper Rio Grande valley. Again, disappointment met them among the Pueblo peoples.

During the winter, passed at Tiguex (now Bernalillo, N. Mex.), Indians from the east told of the land of Gran Quivira, fabulous and golden. In the spring of 1541, Coronado was off again, onto the Llano Estacado (Staked Plain), through the Texas and Oklahoma panhandles, into Kansas. He pushed beyond the Arkansas to the Smoky Hill River, in central Kansas, and then turned back. Quivira was even less attractive than Cíbola and the Pueblo country.

**Later Years.** In the late summer of 1542, Coronado made his sorry report to Mendoza: the north had little riches to offer. Coronado went to Guadalajara, now the capital, and resumed his governorship of Nueva Galicia. He continued in that post until he had to appear in Mexico City to answer charges resulting from the official check (*residencia*) made on him as governor and as leader of the Cíbola expedition. Early in 1545 he was cleared and restored to honor and positions of trust in the viceregal capital. Coronado died on Sept. 22, 1554, and was buried in the church of Santo Domingo, in Mexico City.

JOHN FRANCIS BANNON, *St. Louis University*

**Further Reading:** Day, A. Grove, *Coronado's Quest: Discovery of the American Southwest* (Mutual Pub. 1987); Everett, Dianna, *Coronado and the Myth of Quivira* (Panhandle-Plains Hist. Soc. 1986); Udall, Stewart L., *To the Inland Empire: Coronado and Our Spanish Legacy* (Doubleday 1987); Winship, George P., ed., *The Journey of Coronado: 1540–1542* (1922; reprint, AMS Press 1972).

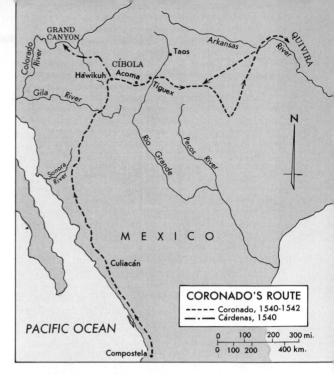

CORONADO'S ROUTE
----- Coronado, 1540-1542
—·— Cárdenas, 1540

**CORONADO,** kō-rō-nä'thō, **Juan Vásquez de** (1525?–1565), Spanish conquistador. A member of a distinguished family, he was born in Salamanca, Spain, and educated at the university there. In 1550 he went to Guatemala, and for the next 14 years he held administrative posts there and in San Salvador, Honduras, and Nicaragua. He founded Cartago in Costa Rica in 1563. Returning to Spain in 1564 he was appointed captain general of Costa Rica, and was also made governor of Nicaragua for a 3-year term. Coronado set sail from Spain at the head of a large party in 1565 but lost his life in a shipwreck in October.

**CORONADO,** kor-ə-nä'dō, a resort and residential city in southwestern California, in San Diego county. It is 2 miles (3 km) southwest of San Diego, on an island in San Diego Bay, which is connected with the mainland by a narrow strip of land. A U.S. Naval Air Station and a U.S. Naval Amphibious Base are there. Government is by city manager. Population: 24,100.

**CORONAGRAPH,** kə-rō'nə-graf, a telescope designed for observing the sun's outer atmosphere, or corona. The corona has about one millionth the brightness of the solar surface and is difficult to photograph because of the scattering of light by the earth's atmosphere; it can be observed only during solar eclipses or by means of a coronagraph. The first such device was built by the French astronomer Bernard Lyot in 1931. Many are now in operation, located at high-altitude sites to reduce the problem of light scattering.

A coronagraph requires very high-quality optical materials and careful construction. The objective forms an image of the sun at a point where an occulting disk can cover the disk of the sun; the image is then passed onto a photographic plate by a second lens. Several circular stops or light baffles are positioned near this lens to catch scattered or stray light.

LAURENCE W. FREDERICK, *University of Virginia*

**CORONARY ARTERY.** See HEART.

**CORONARY THROMBOSIS** is the formation of a blood clot in an artery supplying blood to the heart. Formation of the clot prevents blood, which contains oxygen and nutrients, from reaching that portion of the heart muscle normally supplied by the artery. Thus the tissue may die, and the heart may no longer be able to function properly, leading to the person's death. One who has suffered a coronary thrombosis is commonly said to have had a "heart attack." These episodes may also be called coronary occlusions or myocardial infarctions.

**Causes.** Coronary thrombosis is a leading cause of death, particularly among men. It may strike at almost any time of life, but it occurs most often in the third, fourth, or fifth decade. It is more common in people who are overweight, who have diabetes, or who have high blood pressure.

Blood clots are also likely to form in a coronary artery whose inner surface has been roughened by changes associated with atherosclerosis. Such roughened areas may serve as sites to which blood platelets readily adhere and ultimately initiate the clotting process. Unfortunately, the cause of atherosclerosis is not well understood. There appears to be an association between the amount of certain fatty substances, especially cholesterol, in the blood and the occurrence of atherosclerosis, and some physicians recommend diets that contain low amounts of these fatty substances in an attempt to prevent their patients from suffering potentially fatal heart attacks.

**Symptoms and Diagnosis.** Although an episode of coronary thrombosis may produce no symptoms at all, the victim usually feels a tight squeezing sensation in the chest, a sensation that may extend to the left arm, the neck, and sometimes the left ear. He may perspire profusely and feel a sense of impending doom. In contrast to attacks of angina, in which the pain lasts for only a few minutes, the pain of a coronary thrombosis may last for many hours. Sometimes, the attack is immediately fatal because the heart's normal rhythm is interrupted and the brain is deprived of blood. In other cases, the pain may gradually subside over a period of hours, after which the healing processes begin.

Physicians can confirm the occurrence of a coronary thrombosis through a variety of tests. Following an episode of coronary thrombosis, the patient's white blood cell count and his blood sedimentation rate may both increase. Fever may occur, and the physician, examining the chest with a stethoscope, can sometimes hear a rubbing sound as the damaged surface of the heart rubs against the sac (pericardium) in which it is enclosed. In addition, characteristic changes may be seen on an electrocardiogram.

**Treatment.** The treatment of a coronary thrombosis consists chiefly of maintaining the patient's circulation and preventing the blood clot from enlarging until the body's healing processes have been able to replace the damaged tissue with a firm scar. Such treatment may consist of administering oxygen, anticoagulants (substances that prevent the blood from clotting), and various drugs to maintain the patient's blood pressure if it should drop too low. A coronary thrombosis is serious, but many individuals recover fully and lead active normal lives.

ERNEST BEUTLER, M. D.
*City of Hope Medical Center, Duarte, Calif.*

**CORONATION,** the ceremony at which kings traditionally have received the crowns that are the insignia of their regal authority. In pre-Christian societies of Europe authority was usually conferred on rulers by ceremonial rites in which typically the man designated or elected as ruler was borne on the shoulders of the chief men of the tribe around the assembled people. After the man had been carried three times around the assembly, he was given the symbols of his military and political authority, a spear and a diadem of rich cloth that was wound around his head. When Europe was Christianized in the early Middle Ages, the religious service of benediction was added to the pagan ceremony. The Christian precedent for benediction came from the Old Testament, which told of kings such as Saul being anointed and crowned by prophets.

After the Christian ceremony was introduced, the king's anointing became the essential element of the coronation. By virtue of the unction received, the king became part priest and had the heavy responsibility of ruling over his people as a good Christian king. He became, as the Latin coronation texts state, a *mixta persona*, part priest and part layman.

The pure oil of the catechumen was used exclusively for anointing in all countries except France and England, where the chrism, a mixture of oil and balsam, was also used. After the king had been anointed with the holy oil of the catechumen, he was signed on the forehead with the chrism. Because of this special procedure, French and English kings were believed to possess special curative powers. Such powers, discharged by touch, were associated with English kings until the early 18th century.

**England.** The oldest known liturgy for a Christian coronation in Europe is an English one ascribed to Egbert, archbishop of York, in the middle of the 8th century. Egbert's ceremony was introduced during the performance of the Mass. After reading the Gospel, the priest officiating—customarily the archbishop of Canterbury—recited the prayers of benediction and then poured oil from a horn on the royal head while the anthem *Zadok the Priest* was sung. Then, while an intercessory benediction was recited, the assembled lords and bishops placed a scepter, or staff of authority, in the king's hands and a helmet on his head. After the assembly had hailed the king three times, he was enthroned and received the fealty of his new subjects. The ceremony terminated with the mass and special prayers.

A more elaborate ceremony that was used for the first time at the coronation of Edward II in 1307 became the basis of English practice until the Reformation in the 16th century. The oath sworn by the king in that ceremony acquired an essential role in the development of constitutional government, for the king vowed under oath to protect the church, to govern according to the established laws and customs of the realm, and to give good government to his subjects. Eventually it was argued that if a king broke this oath his subjects no longer owed allegiance to him and could depose him. Such arguments were employed to justify deposing Edward II in 1327 and Richard II in 1399.

When James I was crowned king of England in 1603, the coronation service was performed in English for the first time, and the Anglican Communion service was substituted for the Latin Mass. Although subsequent alterations were made,

THE CORONATION of Elizabeth II by the Archbishop of Canterbury in Westminster Abbey, London, June 2, 1953.

coronations of English rulers in the 20th century are basically the same as that introduced in 1307.

**France.** A late form of the Anglo-Saxon ceremony, in which the coronation preceded the Mass and the king received a ring and a crown, was introduced in France in the 10th century. Various archbishops and bishops crowned the French kings in the 10th and 11th centuries, but by the 12th century this had become the prerogative of the archbishop of Reims. After having anointed the king, he placed a crown on the king's head and presented to him the royal insignia of sword, scepter, and spurs. Thereafter, whenever the king held a solemn assembly of his nobles, the archbishop of Reims placed the crown on his head as a symbol of reaffirmation. The coronations of the Bourbon kings in the 17th and 18th centuries were fundamentally like those of the Capetian kings in the 10th through 13th centuries. When Napoleon I was crowned emperor in Paris, however, Pope Pius VII assisted and Napoleon himself placed the crown on his head.

**Holy Roman Empire.** Perhaps the most celebrated coronation in the history of western Europe occurred on Christmas Day, 800, in the Basilica of St. Peter's at Rome. On that day Pope Leo III crowned Charlemagne emperor of what came to be known as the Holy Roman Empire. After performing the Mass, Leo placed a crown on Charlemagne's head, and the assembled people shouted: "To Charles Augustus, crowned of God, great and pacific emperor of the Romans, life and victory!"

Customarily, the successors of Charlemagne—especially the German emperors, beginning with Otto the Great in 962—received the imperial crown from the pope in Rome. The last German emperor to be so crowned was Frederick III in 1440. Thereafter the coronation ceremony used by the German electors was employed for the coronation of the emperor. Usually it was held at Aachen, in the basilica constructed by Charlemagne. Two imperial electors, the archbishops of Trier and Mainz, presented the emperor-elect to the archbishop of Cologne, who conducted the coronation ceremony, anointed the emperor, and bestowed on him the insignia of imperial power. All three archbishops then placed the crown on his head. The ceremony ended with a Mass, in which the emperor took Communion. All the emperors crowned at Aachen were considered canons of the church.

**Other Countries.** Coronation ceremonies are still celebrated in Sweden, Norway, and the Netherlands. Denmark, Belgium, and Greece have abandoned theirs and the other countries of Europe no longer have monarchies.

Imperial Russia had the most magnificent and colorful coronations in eastern Europe, where the ceremony was endowed with much ritual and great religious significance. As early as the reign (1113–1125) of Vladimir the grand dukes of Russia were crowned king, but a definite ceremonial was not established until the reign (1462–1505) of Ivan III. Then and thereafter Russian coronations were held at the Church of the Assumption in the Kremlin at Moscow. The Russian Orthodox metropolitans of Moscow, Novgorod, Kiev, and St. Petersburg presided, but the metropolitan of Moscow recited the prayers and anointed the czar, who crowned himself.

The Russian imperial coronation was derived partly from the ceremony developed at Constantinople for the emperors of the Byzantine Empire. Because Byzantine imperial power was transmitted either by inheritance or by designation by predecessor, the coronation ceremony was not essential; it did not add to the power of the *basileus*. At the ceremony, which was held in the Church of Santa Sophia at Constantinople, the patriarch of Constantinople placed the crown on the emperor's head at the conclusion of religious rites. This act only symbolized divine approval. It did not imply control of the patriarch over the emperor.

BRYCE LYON, *Brown University*

**CORONATION GULF,** an arm of the Arctic Ocean, more than 100 miles (160 km) long and half as wide. Coronation Gulf is located in the Kitikmeot region of the territory of Nunavut in Canada and forms part of the passageway between the mainland and Victoria Island in the Arctic Archipelago. The gulf leads from Dolphin and Union Strait on the west to Dease Strait on the east and forms part of the Northwest Passage.

**CORONEL,** kō-rō-nel', a coal-mining center and seaport in Chile, 19 miles (30 km) by road and rail south of Concepción. Most of Chile's coal production comes from the area around the Gulf of Arauco, on which Coronel is situated. Part of the coal is used by the Huachipato steel center (one of South America's largest), near Concepción. Population: 74,090 (1992 preliminary census).

Early in World War I, on Nov. 1, 1914, a naval battle was fought in the Pacific off Coronel. Germany's Far East Squadron, under Vice Adm. Maximilian von Spee, defeated a British flotilla commanded by Rear Adm. Sir Christopher Cradock, who was killed in the action.

**CORONER,** kôr'ə-nər, a public officer whose primary function is to investigate suspicious or unnatural deaths in order to ascertain whether criminal behavior was the cause. Although not uniquely an Anglo-American institution, the office of coroner as it evolved in the United States can be traced to 12th century England. Originally the coroner exercised a judicial responsibility in criminal matters that usually took the form of an inquest—an investigative hearing where evidence was reviewed to determine if a prosecution should be initiated. However, with the passage of time, the functions of the coroner's office have become primarily medical, confined to a search for the cause and manner of death. The district attorney has gradually assumed the judicial role of deciding whether to prosecute; the police have taken over the responsibility for investigation.

The office of coroner, which is elective, does not in itself require medical training. By the late 1960's, the traditional role of coroner had been replaced in all but 14 states—either statewide or in some counties—by the medical examiner system, which appoints professionals with experience in forensic pathology. The duties of medical examiners consist primarily of making the medicolegal determination of cause and manner of death in any case not certified by a physician or in any attended by suspicious circumstances. In 1877, Massachusetts adopted the first medical examiner system in the United States, and New York City established one in 1918. Both were early models for other states and cities.

LINDA ALDEN RODGERS
*School of Law, Columbia University*

**CORONIUM,** kə-rōn'ē-əm, is a hypothetical chemical element that was once believed to exist in the sun. The evidence for its existence consisted of certain bright lines that appeared in the spectrum of the solar corona. These lines, first observed in 1869, were characteristic of no earthly element then known. Since the unknown lines were observed high above the surface of the sun, it was suggested that the supposed element was much lighter than hydrogen, the lightest element known on earth. Similar lines that were detected in the earth's aurorae were attributed to "geocoronium," another hypothetical element supposedly lighter than hydrogen.

The solution of this problem was not found until the 20th century. In 1941 the Swedish astronomer Bengt Edlén, working from experimental data, showed that iron atoms that had lost about a dozen electrons would produce the lines hitherto attributed to coronium. In order for iron to be so strongly ionized, however, temperatures of a million degrees or more are required. In the 1950's, X-rays originating in the sun were observed by means of instruments carried beyond the earth's shielding atmosphere by rockets. These observations demonstrated conclusively that the solar corona is indeed at such extreme temperatures. There remains no question that coronium as a separate element does not exist and that the "coronium" lines are produced by ordinary elements. Similarly, the lines formerly attributed to "geocoronium" are now known to be produced by atomic nitrogen that is emitting radiation in the earth's upper atmosphere.

ISAAC ASIMOV, *Boston University*